FROMMER'S

COMPREHENSIVE TRAVEL GUIDE

U.S.A. '91-'92

by Edouard De Blaye
Introduction by Susan Poole
Edited by Maxwell R.D. Vos

PRENTICE
HALL
PRESS

NEW YORK • LONDON • TORONTO • SYDNEY • TOKYO • SINGAPORE

A Disclaimer

Readers are advised that prices fluctuate in the course of time, and travel information changes under the impact of the varied and volatile factors that affect the travel industry. The author and publisher cannot be held responsible for the experiences of the reader while traveling. Readers are invited to write the publisher with ideas, comments, and suggestions for future editions.

Note: Eastern Airlines, listed throughout the book, is no longer in operation.

FROMMER BOOKS

Published by Prentice Hall Press
A Division of Simon & Schuster Inc.
15 Columbus Circle
New York, NY 10023

ISBN 0-13-333014-1
ISSN 0899-2797

Text design by Levavi & Levavi, Inc.

**PRENTICE
HALL
PRESS**

Manufactured in the United States of America

CONTENTS

Part Three   THE MIDWEST

Part Four   THE MOUNTAIN STATES

Part Five   THE SOUTHWEST

Maps

SYMBOLS AND ABBREVIATIONS

Abbreviations in Hotels, Restaurants, Sights, and Shopping

A/C	air-conditioned	M	moderate (price range)
adj.	adjoining	Mon-Fri	Monday through Friday
AE	American Express (credit card)	Mon-Sat	Monday through Saturday
B	budget (price range)	nr.	near
CB	Carte Blanche (credit card)	rest(s).	restaurants(s)
d.	double (room)	resv.	reservations
DC	Diners Club (credit card)	rm(s)	room(s)
dwntwn	downtown	s.	single (room)
E	expensive (price range)	s/d	single or double rooms
gar.	garage	svce	service
grdn(s)	garden(s)	w.	with
hols.	holidays	V	VISA (credit card)
hr.	hour, hours	VE	very expensive (price range)
hrdrsr	hairdresser		
I	inexpensive (price range)	vic.	vicinity
J&T	jacket and tie required	wknd(s)	weekend(s)
Jkt.	jacket required	ZIP	ZIP Code
MC	MasterCard (credit card)		
min.	minutes		

Abbreviations on the Road

Ave.	Avenue	NW	northwest
Blvd.	Boulevard	Pkwy.	Parkway
Dr.	Drive	Pl.	Place
E.	east	Rd.	Road
Expwy.	Expressway	r.t.	round-trip
Fwy.	Freeway	S.	south
Hwy.	Highway	SE	southeast
km	kilometers	SW	southwest
mi.	miles	Sq.	Square
N.	north	Tpke.	Turnpike
NE	northeast	W.	west

What the Symbols Mean

HOTELS

Modest but acceptable, with a good price-to-quality ratio.

A quality establishment, but with shortcomings in service or comfort.

Worth a detour.

Exceptional comfort or service, among the best in the U.S. Try to fit it into your trip.

One of the dozen best hotels in the country. Don't miss it.

RESTAURANTS

Modest but acceptable, with a good price-to-quality ratio.

A quality establishment, but with shortcomings in service or cuisine.

Worth a detour.

Exceptional standard in service or cuisine, among the best in the U.S. Try to fit it into your trip.

One of the dozen best restaurants in the country. Don't miss it.

BUILDINGS, MUSEUMS, OR NATURAL FEATURES

Interesting and worth a visit or at least a look.

Remarkable and should be seen.

A building, museum, or natural feature that should not be missed.

Unique of its kind, and worth a journey in itself.

CITIES OR AREAS

Interesting and worth a visit.

Remarkable and should be seen.

A city or area that should not be missed.

Exceptionally interesting, and worth a journey in itself.

OF SPECIAL INTEREST

Highly recommended as an unusual and worthwhile experience, of very special interest.

INTRODUCTION

□ □ □

Any traveler in the United States will find the very vastness of the country—some 3,628,062 sq. mi. (9,396,681 km²)—impressive, even a trifle intimidating. Within this huge area, the 50 states of the Union, including Alaska, separated from the contiguous 48 by about 500 mi. (305 km), and Hawaii, 2,500 mi. (1,525 km) offshore in the Pacific, offer the traveler a bewildering range of options: from the semitropical Everglades to San Francisco Bay, from the Native American reservations of Arizona to the fishing villages of New England, from the arid landscape of Nevada to the deep woods of Vermont, from the Great Plains of the Dakotas to the beaches of California, from the volcanoes of Hawaii to the glaciers of Alaska, from the deserts of New Mexico to the sprawling megalopolis of Boswash (the conurbation that stretches from Boston through New York, Philadelphia, and Baltimore to Washington along the northeastern corridor).

Choice of diversions is equally limitless. You can hunt big game or fish for salmon; run the Colorado River rapids on a rubber raft; follow the trail of the pioneers in a covered wagon; see the Indianapolis 500, the world's most dangerous automobile race; or watch a rocket launching from Cape Canaveral. You can explore America in an RV, a real home on wheels, or if you can afford it, spend a dream vacation at a super-luxury California spa/resort. You can discover the ski resorts of the Rockies or the Sierra Nevada, encounter the future at EPCOT and good ole Mickey at Walt Disney World, and wonder at some of the world's great natural marvels—from the Grand Canyon to Death Valley, from Niagara Falls to the geysers of Yellowstone National Park. And then of course there are America's wondrous cities—New York, Los Angeles, Chicago, San Francisco, Washington, New Orleans—all repositories of great art, culture, and architecture, providing some of the premier urban experiences of the world.

For Americans setting out to get to know their own country, the options may indeed seem endless—for the foreign visitor they can be overwhelming—so let's try to make some sense out of this welter of options.

WHERE & WHEN

For practical purposes the United States can be divided into eight great tourist regions.

THE NORTHEAST & MID-ATLANTIC: From the Canadian frontier to the Potomac and from the shores of Maine to Niagara Falls, its principal regions are New England, with its slightly old-fashioned charm, and Boswash, sheltering 50 million people along the Boston–Washington corridor. American History with a capital *H* is evident everywhere, from Philadelphia's Independence Park to Boston's Freedom Trail, from New York's Federal Hall to Washington's Capitol Hill. So, too, are the great names associated with science and learning: Yale, Harvard, Columbia, and Princeton. See the chapters on Boston, Cape Cod, New York, Niagara Falls, the Atlantic Coast, Philadelphia, Pittsburgh, Baltimore, and Washington.

Best Time to Visit: Cities in the spring and fall, beaches in summer. Fall foliage colors are at their peak in Vermont in late September, and move south to New York state by mid-October. Winter skiing begins in late November.

THE SOUTH: From Washington, D.C., along the Atlantic coast to Florida and west to Louisiana and Arkansas, this is the homeland of bourbon, of the great plantations of the legendary *Gone with the Wind* era. Traces of this Old South exist in the historic cities of Alexandria, Williamsburg, Charleston, and Savannah, and in the plantation country along the Mississippi River in Louisiana and Mississippi. This region has given birth to much that is original in American culture—jazz (from New Orleans), the blues (from Memphis), and country music (from Nashville). Today the romance of Rhett Butler's and Scarlett O'Hara's South has been replaced by the progressive New South represented by such cosmopolitan cities as Atlanta, New Orleans, and Miami. See the chapters on Charleston, Savannah, Atlanta, Nashville, Memphis, New Orleans, Florida's East Coast, Tampa/St. Petersburg, Orlando, and Miami/Miami Beach.

Best Time to Visit: Spring, fall, and winter; temperatures tend to be hot and humid with temperatures averaging 80°–90°F (26.6°–32.2°C) in Florida and along the Gulf Coast.

THE MIDWEST: From North Dakota to the Great Lakes and from Missouri to Kansas, this region is often called the Heartland of America, where the plains stretch to a vast horizon and where grain and cattle have been, and still are, king. Although few tourists go there, many of its cities—St. Louis, Kansas City, Minneapolis, and above all, Chicago—are well worth seeing. See the chapters on Detroit, Cleveland, Cincinnati, Chicago, Milwaukee, Minneapolis/St. Paul, Indianapolis, St. Louis, and Kansas City.

Best Time to Visit: Spring and fall; winters are harsh (20°F/−6.6°C, and lower in the northernmost states); scorching summer temperatures can rise above 100°F (38°C) on the plains.

THE MOUNTAIN STATES: Montana, Wyoming, Idaho, Colorado, and Utah—a spectacular scenic playground, this is one of the country's most beautiful and dramatic regions. Colorado and Utah with their dozens of national parks and awesome landscapes are worth a trip in themselves. City highlights also include Salt Lake City, the terminus of the great Mormon trek overland, and Denver, a thoroughly modern city that has not entirely shaken off its earlier heritage as a wild and wooly frontier town. Great summer hiking and winter skiing. See the chapters on Denver, the Rocky Mountains, Salt Lake City, Utah National Parks, Yellowstone National Park, and the Black Hills and Mount Rushmore.

Best Time to Visit: Year round. Summers are sunny and moderately hot, except in desert areas where the thermometer can register 110°F (44°C) plus. Spring and fall are temperate, although temperatures can drop mightily at night.

THE SOUTHWEST: From Texas to Arizona, including the adjoining states of New Mexico and Oklahoma, a land of tawny, rust-colored deserts and lunar landscapes, of splendid canyons and Native American reservations, it also boasts archeological remains from the dawn of civilization. Fascinating culturally and historically, especially for those in search of the Old West. See the chapters on Dallas/Fort Worth, Houston, Albuquerque, San Antonio, Santa Fe, Navajoland, the Grand Canyon, Phoenix, and Tucson.

Best Time to Visit: Fall, winter, and spring, before the temperatures rise.

THE NORTHWEST: The beautiful countrysides of Oregon and Washington—rugged coastline, mountain peaks, lakes, rivers, rich farmland, and burgeoning wine country—are attracting more visitors every year. Two major cities, Portland and Seattle, are also attracting more and more people to their livable cosmopolitan environments. See the chapters on Portland, Seattle, and the Pacific Coast.

Best Time to Visit: Summer and fall—least rainfall in July.

THE WEST: The Pacific Coast of California along with Nevada. California, America's experimental social laboratory, sets the pace for the rest of the country, exporting its technology, lifestyle, and social trends, fads, and fashions to the other 49 states. An eclectic mix of European, Asian, and Latin American cultures, movie stars and millionaires, computer age technology, alternative lifestyle devotees, natural wonders; and fine wineries. And then, of course, there's glitter gulch Las Vegas in nearby Nevada. See the chapters on Las Vegas, Death Valley, Reno, San Francisco, Sequoia National Park, Yosemite National Park, Los Angeles, San Diego, and the California Coast.

Best Time to Visit: Anytime except in the rainy early spring.

ALASKA & HAWAII: While not a region per se, the states of Alaska and Hawaii are major destinations for both Americans and foreign visitors. See the chapters on Anchorage and Alaska, and Honolulu and the Hawaiian Islands.

Best Time to Visit: Spring and summer for Alaska, year round for Hawaii.

Average Temperatures, in ° Fahrenheit, for Representative Cities

	Jan	Feb	Mar	Apr	May	June	July	Aug	Sept	Oct	Nov	Dec
Anchorage	23	25	28	35	46	57	62	58	48	39	33	28
Atlanta	44	47	52	62	70	76	80	82	71	62	52	44
Chicago	25	27	35	48	57	68	73	71	64	55	41	30
Dallas	44	48	55	64	73	80	86	86	77	66	55	48
Denver	30	32	37	48	58	66	73	71	62	51	39	32
Kansas City	30	33	44	55	66	73	80	78	69	59	44	33
Las Vegas	44	50	57	66	73	86	93	91	82	68	57	48
Los Angeles	55	55	57	59	62	66	68	69	68	62	51	55
Miami	68	68	71	73	77	80	82	82	80	78	71	69
Minneapolis	13	15	30	44	57	66	73	69	62	50	33	19
New York	30	30	39	48	60	69	77	75	66	55	44	33
San Francisco	50	51	53	55	55	59	59	60	62	60	57	51
Washington, D.C.	37	39	44	55	66	73	78	77	69	59	48	39

The daily newspaper *USA Today*, on sale in all large cities, carries a daily weather map, detailed and in color, as well as forecasts for the whole U.S. Its "weather hotline" (900/370-8728) tells you the temperatures and weather forecasts for about 490 cities in the U.S. and abroad.

SPECIAL VACATION IDEAS

NATIONAL PARKS & FORESTS: Scattered throughout the United States are 50 national parks—well over 30 million acres (12.15 million ha) of land that has been set aside for the specific preservation of the landscape and its wildlife. Among the most popular are: Acadia (Maine), Glacier (Montana), Grand Canyon (Arizona), Grand Teton (Wyoming), Great Smoky Mountain (Tennessee and North Carolina), Hawaii Volcanoes (Hawaii), Mammoth Cave (Kentucky), Mount Rainier (Washington), Olympic (Washington), Rocky Mountain

(Colorado), Sequoia/Kings Canyon (California), Shenandoah (Virginia), Yellowstone (Wyoming, Montana, and Idaho), Yosemite (California), and Zion (Utah).

Camping facilities, ranging from primitive campsites to rustic cabins, are usually open from late spring to early fall (year round at some parks). Rates are reasonable, and because of the parks' popularity, it's wise to reserve ahead.

For more information, refer to *The National Park Guide* by Michael Frome (Prentice Hall Press) or his *America's Favorite National Parks 1989* (Prentice Hall Press), or contact the **National Park Service,** U.S. Dept. of the Interior, P.O. Box 37127, Washington, DC 20013-7127 (202/343-4747).

The national forests are less well known and usually less crowded. For a complete list, contact the **National Forest Service,** U.S. Department of Agriculture, P.O. Box 96090, Washington, DC 20019-6090 (202/447-3957).

STATE PARKS: Most states also maintain state parks, often with some type of camping facilities. Again, at the more popular parks you'll need to reserve ahead —for example, in New York to camp on the Long Island shoreline at Hither Hills State Park in Montauk, you have to enter a lottery at the beginning of the year. Although this is unusual, reservations are wise to avoid disappointment.

For **information about state parks,** contact each state's tourism organization. See the Appendix.

THEME PARKS: Almost every state worth its name has a theme park of some sort. They run the gamut from Sea World to Opryland and include, of course, the stars, Walt Disney World and Disneyland. If you're planning a trip to either of the last two, pick up copies of *The Unofficial Guide to Disney World and EPCOT* by Bob Sehlinger and John Finley (Prentice Hall Press) and *The Unofficial Guide to Disneyland* by Bob Sehlinger (Prentice Hall Press). Both are vital planning aides.

Just for the record, here are the top-drawing amusement and theme parks: Walt Disney World Disney/MGM Studios, and EPCOT center (Lake Buena Vista, Fla.); Disneyland (Anaheim, Calif.); Universal Studios (Universal City, Calif.); Knott's Berry Farm (Buena Vista, Calif.); Busch Gardens (Tampa, Fla.; also in Williamsburg, Va.); Universal Studios Florida (Orlando, Fla.); Sea World of Florida (Orlando, Fla.; also in San Diego, Calif.; Aurora, Ohio; and San Antonio, Texas); Six Flags Great Adventure (Jackson, N.J.; also in Arlington, Texas; Atlanta, Ga.; St. Louis, Mo.; Gurnee, Ill.; and Valencia, Calif.); Cedar Point (Sandusky, Ohio); Kings Island (Cincinnati, Ohio); Opryland USA (Nashville, Tenn.); Marriott's Great America (Santa Clara, Calif.); AstroWorld (Houston, Texas); and Hersheypark, the granddaddy of them all (Hershey, Penna.).

For a list of amusement parks, contact the **International Association of Amusement Parks and Attractions,** 4230 King St., Alexandria, VA 22302 (703/671-5800).

AMERICA'S ZOOS: Scattered across the continent are more than 750 licensed zoos. Some, such as the Bronx Zoo in New York City and the San Diego Zoo, have gained an international reputation for their design, providing natural habitats for most species. Others, like the Gladys Porter Zoo in Brownsville, Texas, have as their primary goal the preservation of endangered species and often breed such animals in order to return them to the wild whenever possible.

For any lover of animals and devotee of zoos, the following (arranged by state) are all well worth a visit. Most have an admission fee, and almost all have a last admittance time no less than half an hour before the official closing time.

Arizona: Arizona-Sonora Desert Museum and Biological Park, 2021 N. Kinney Rd., Tucson (602/883-1380); Phoenix Zoo, 5810 E. Van Buren, Phoenix (602/273-1341).

California: San Diego Zoo, 2900 Zoo Dr., San Diego (619/231-6164); Los Angeles Zoo, 5333 Zoo Dr., Griffith Park, Los Angeles (213/666-4650).
District of Columbia: National Zoo, 3001 Connecticut Ave. NW, Washington (202/673-4800).
Florida: Miami Metrozoo, 12400 SW 152nd St., Miami (305/251-0400).
Georgia: Zoo Atlanta, 800 Cherokee Ave. SE, Atlanta (404/624-5678).
Louisiana: Audubon Zoo, 6500 Magazine St., New Orleans (504/861-2537).
Missouri: St. Louis Zoo, Forest Park, St. Louis (314/781-0900).
New York: Bronx Zoo, Bronx River Pkwy. at Fordham Rd., Bronx (212/367-1010); Central Park Zoo, Fifth Ave. and 64th St., New York (212/439-6500).
Texas: Gladys Porter Zoo, 500 Ringgold St., Brownsville (512/546-7187); Dallas Zoo, 621 Clarendon, Dallas (214/946-5154).
Washington: Woodland Park Zoo, 5500 Phinny Ave. N., Seattle (206/684-4800).
Wisconsin: Milwaukee County Zoo, 10001 W. Bluemound Rd., Milwaukee (414/771-3040).

ATTENDING A SPECIAL EVENT: Festivals abound throughout the United States with special events ranging from maple sugar festivals, cherry blossom festivals, winter carnivals, crafts fairs, ethnic celebrations, antiques fairs, flea markets—everything from Mardi Gras to Oktoberfest—as well as block-buster cultural events like the Spoleto Festival in Charleston or Tanglewood in Massachusetts. In each chapter you'll find major special events highlighted, but for a full list, contact any state's tourist organization (see the list in the Appendix). Inquire well in advance. Some events draw large audiences.

VISITING NATIONAL MONUMENTS: These are monuments that recall the great moments of American history—places like Gettysburg, Penna.; Custer Battlefield, Mont.; the Alamo, Texas; and Minute Man National Historical Park, Mass. For information, contact the **National Park Foundation,** 1850 K St. NW, Suite 210, Washington, DC 20006 (202/785-4500). A good resource is *The Complete Guide to America's National Parks* (Prentice Hall Press).

ACTIVE VACATIONS: For up-to-date information about specialty travel in general, obtain a copy of *Specialty Travel Index,* a bi-yearly magazine, either from your travel agent, your library, or by subscription from Specialty Travel Index, 305 San Anselmo Ave., Suite 217, San Anselmo, CA 94960 (415/459-4900). Cost is $8 for one year.
    Here's a very brief resource list to stimulate ideas:
    Ballooning: Contact the **Balloon Federation of America,** P.O. Box 400, Indianola, IA 50125 (515/961-8809).
    Bicycling: *Bicycle USA,* published nine times a year, puts out an issue called *Tourfinder,* which lists tour operators around the U.S. It's available to the public for $4. Contact Bicycle USA, 6707 Whitestone Rd., Suite 209, Baltimore, MD 21207 (301/944-3399).
    Birdwatching: Contact the **National Audubon Society** Headquarters, 950 Third Ave., New York, NY 10022 (212/832-3200).
    Camping and Hiking: Contact the **Sierra Club,** Outing Department, 730 Polk St., San Francisco, CA 94109 (416/776-2211).
    Skiing: The **U.S. Ski Association,** P.O. Box 100, Park City, UT 84060 (801/649-9090).
    Spelunking: The **National Speleological Society,** Cave Ave., Huntsville, AL 35810 (205/852-1300), can put you in touch with fellow enthusiasts.
    Tennis: Contact the **U.S. Tennis Association,** 1212 Ave. of the Americas, New York, NY 10036 (212/302-3322).
    Wilderness Trips: The major source is the **Sierra Club** (see address above),

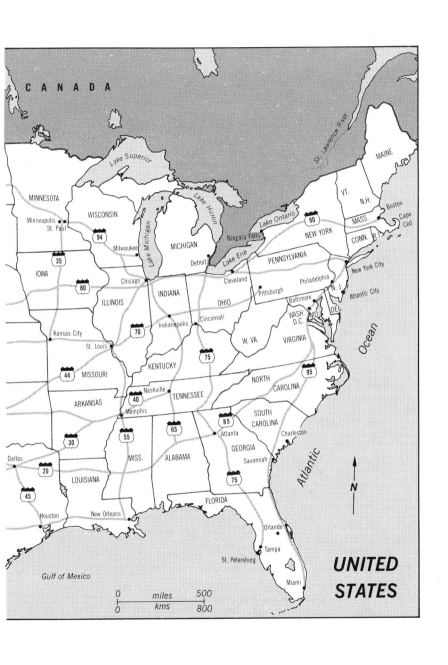

CANADA

MINNESOTA

Minneapolis
St. Paul

WISCONSIN

Lake Superior

Milwaukee

Lake Michigan

Lake Huron

MICHIGAN

Detroit

Lake Ontario

Niagara Falls

Lake Erie

MAINE

VT.

N.H.

MASS.

Boston

Cape
Cod

CONN.

R.I.

NEW YORK

90

PENNSYLVANIA

Cleveland

Pittsburgh

Philadelphia

N.J.

New York City

Atlantic City

94

35

IOWA

80

Chicago

ILLINOIS

INDIANA

OHIO

Cincinnati

W. VA.

VIRGINIA

Baltimore

WASH.
D.C.

MD.

DEL.

70

Indianapolis

Kansas City

St. Louis

44

MISSOURI

KENTUCKY

75

NORTH
CAROLINA

95

ARKANSAS

40

Nashville

TENNESSEE

Memphis

65

85

SOUTH
CAROLINA

Charleston

Atlanta

30

55

MISS.

ALABAMA

GEORGIA

Savannah

Ocean

Atlantic

Dallas

20

LOUISIANA

75

45

Houston

New Orleans

FLORIDA

Orlando

Tampa

N

Gulf of Mexico

St. Petersburg

Miami

UNITED
STATES

St. Lawrence River

0   miles   500
0   kms   800

which organizes wilderness treks to various forests and parks. Other organizations include: **Appalachian Mountain Club,** 5 Joy St., Boston, MA 02108 (617/523-0636), with single annual membership at $40 and family membership at $65; **American Wilderness Alliance,** 7500 E. Arapahoe Rd., Suite 355, Englewood, CO 80112 (303/771-0380); **American Forestry Association,** P.O. Box 2000, Washington, DC 20013 (202/667-3300; toll free 800/368-5748); **Nature Expeditions International,** P.O. Box 11496, Eugene, OR 97440 (503/484-6529); and **Yosemite Institute,** P.O. Box 487, Yosemite, CA 95389 (209/372-4441).

TRAVEL FOR PARTICULAR GROUPS

FOR STUDENTS: It's worth using your high school or college ID to obtain an International Student Identity Card, because although it's not as widely recognized in the U.S. as it is abroad, it still delivers some savings. Available from the **Council on International Educational Exchange (CIEE),** 205 E. 42nd St., New York, NY 10017 (212/661-1414), and 312 Sutter St., Room 407, San Francisco, CA 94108 (415/421-3473).

Student travel tour operators include: **Contiki Holidays,** 1432 E. Katella Ave., Anaheim, CA 92805 (toll free 800/626-0611), for ages 18 through 35; for ages 15 through 20, **Arista Student Travel Association, Inc.,** 11 E. 44th St., New York, NY 10017 (212/687-5121; toll free 800/847-4257).

FOR SINGLES: The only way to avoid the extra cost of the single supplement is to find someone to share those "doubles" rates. The following organizations specialize in matching up individuals for this purpose (most charge modest monthly or annual membership fees): **Travel Companion Exchange,** P.O. Box 833, Amityville, NY 11701 (516/454-0673 or 516/454-0880); and **Saga International Holidays,** 120 Boylston St., Boston, MA 02116 (toll free 800/343-0273), for ages 60 and over.

FOR FAMILIES: Careful planning makes all the difference between a successful enjoyable vacation and one that ends with exhausted, irritable parents and cranky kids. Here are just a few hints to help:

1. Get the kids involved. Let them, if they're old enough, write to the tourist offices for information and color brochures. Give them a map on which they can outline the route; let them help decide the itinerary.

2. Packing. Although your home may be toddler-proof, accommodations are not. Bring portable gates for stairways and other off-limits areas, and also some blank plugs to cover outlets.

3. En route. Carry a few simple games to relieve boredom in the car. A few snacks will also help and will save money. In some states it's mandatory for children under age 2 to have an infant's car seat; you may want to bring your own on a fly-drive trip. Check Amtrak for special family discounts; the airlines, too, have reduced air fares for those under 17; both let under-2s travel free.

4. Accommodations. Children under a certain age usually stay free in their parents' room. Look for establishments that have pools and other recreational facilities. Reserve equipment such as cribs and playpens in advance.

5. Resources. What to do with the kids this year: *Traveling with Children in the U.S.A.* by Leila Hadley (Morrow), *Travel with Children* by Maureen Wheeler (Lonely Planet), and *How to Take Trips with Your Kids* by Joan and Sanford Portnoy (Harvard Common Press).

Traveling by Train or Bus

On Amtrak, children under 2 travel free. Children 2 to 12 travel for half fare. Also don't forget to ask about special family fares and promotions, as well as package rates that include accommodations and a car.

On Greyhound, when accompanied by an adult, children under 5 travel free; children 5 to 11 pay half fare.

FOR THE DISABLED: Standards of accessibility vary so widely that planning is crucial. Here are a few helpful hints:

    1. Accessibility Information. Unfortunately there are few centralized sources. Two of the best are the **Travel Information Service,** Moss Rehabilitation Hospital, 1200 W. Tabor Rd., Philadelphia, PA 19141-3099 (215/456-9602), which charges nominally for mailing materials; and **The Itinerary,** P.O. Box 2012, Bayonne, NJ 07002 (201/858-3400), a bimonthly magazine for disabled travelers costing $10 per year.

    2. Golden Access Passport. This admits a disabled person and companion into a national park, forest, or wildlife refuge at no charge. At some sites a 50% discount on camping and other facilities is also given. For information, call the National Park Service (202/485-9666).

    3. Tour Packagers. There are many, but two that are recommended and have been in the business a long time are **Evergreen Travel Service/Wings on Wheels Tours,** 19505 44th Ave., West Lynnwood, WA 98036 (206/776-1184), which has tours everywhere, even to China and Thailand; and **Whole Person Tours,** P.O. Box 2012, Bayonne, NJ 07002 (201/858-3400).

    4. Book Resources. *Access to the World: A Travel Guide for the Handicapped* by Louise Weiss (H. Holt & Co.) and *Travel for the Disabled: A Handbook of Travel Resources & 400 Worldwide Access Guides* by Helen Hecker (Twin Peaks Press).

Traveling by Bus and Train

A companion can accompany a disabled person at no charge aboard Greyhound. This is available only to disabled people who have a letter from their doctor certifying that they are handicapped and who cannot negotiate the bus steps alone.

Amtrak has a standard handicapped person's fare of at least 25% off regular fare. Amtrak also provides wheelchair-accessible sleeping accommodations in both eastern and western trains. Although pets are not allowed, guide dogs are permissible and travel free of charge. Notify your reservation agent for the lowest fare and authorization for any special needs.

FOR SENIORS: For the fastest-growing travel group, there's a lot available:

    1. Discounts. To find them, there's one major resource: *The Discount Guide for Travelers Over Fifty-Five* by Caroline and Walter Weinz (E.P. Dutton). The only other way to find them is to ask for them everywhere—at cinemas, theaters, museums, hotels, restaurants, attractions, and on local transit.

    2. Information Sources. The **American Association of Retired Persons (AARP),** 1909 K St. NW, Washington, DC 20049 (202/872-4700); **Mature Outlook,** 6001 N. Clark St., Chicago, IL 60660 (toll free 800/336-6330); and the **National Council of Senior Citizens,** 925 15th St. NW, Washington, DC 20005 (202/347-8800).

    3. Tour and Other Specialists. Fascinating, reasonably priced learning vacations are offered by **Elderhostel, Inc.,** 80 Boylston St., Suite 400, Boston, MA 02116 (617/426-7788); the **AARP Travel Service,** 100 N. Sepulveda Blvd., El Segundo, CA 90245 (toll free 800/227-7737); **Saga International Holidays,** 120 Boylston St., Boston, MA 02116 (617/451-6808; toll free 800/343-0273); and **Grand Circle Travel, Inc.,** 347 Congress St., Boston, MA 02210 (617/350-7500). The last two concentrate on foreign destinations.

    4. Book Resources. *Travel Easy: The Practical Guide for People Over 50* by Rosalind Massow (AARP).

RECOMMENDED TOURING ITINERARIES: It is relatively easy to take in the sights of widely separated regions by flying to a major transportation hub and renting a car with unlimited mileage. Below you will find suggestions for touring itineraries lasting from 1 week to 1 month, covering the main tourist areas of the United States. Note that the cheapest available rates for rental cars and motor homes are currently offered in California (for the West Coast) and Florida (for the East Coast). For the Northeast, choose Boston over Washington as your home base, and avoid New York, which has the highest car-rental rates in the whole country.

For detailed descriptions of touring areas listed in the itineraries table, consult the chapters corresponding to the names marked with an asterisk (see the index).

Region	Cities or Tourist Areas	Length of Stay (in days)	Miles	Via Highway No.
		If you only have a week . . .		
Arizona	1. Phoenix*	2	—	
	2. Navajoland* & Monument Valley	2	395	I-17, U.S. 89, U.S. 160, U.S. 163
	3. Grand Canyon*	2	173	U.S. 160, U.S. 89, Ariz. 64
	4. return to Phoenix	1	218	U.S. 180, I-17
			786	
S. Dakota	1. Rapid City	1	—	
	2. Badlands Nat'l Park	2	70	I-90, S.Dak. 240
	3. Mt. Rushmore*	1	86	S. Dak. 44, U.S. 16
	4. Devil's Tower Nat'l Monument	1	153	U.S. 85, I-90, U.S. 14
	5. Spearfish	1	84	U.S. 14, I-90
	6. return to Rapid City	1	53	I-90
			446	
East Coast	1. Boston*	2	—	
	2. Cape Cod* & Martha's Vineyard or Nantucket	3	89	Mass. 3, U.S. 6
	3. Newport, R.I.	1	86	U.S. 6, R.I. 24, R.I. 138
	4. return to Boston	1	68	R.I. 138, R.I. 24, Mass. 24
			243	
East Coast	1. Boston*	2	—	
	2. Salem & Gloucester	2	37	Mass. 1A, Mass. 128
	3. Portland, Maine	1	91	Mass. 128, Mass. 133, Mass. 1A, I-95
	4. Portsmouth, N.H.	1	50	I-95
	5. return to Boston	1	55	I-95
			233	
East Coast	1. Washington*	3	—	
	2. Annapolis	1	28	U.S. 50
	3. Chincoteague	1	113	U.S. 50, U.S. 13, Va. 175
	4. Williamsburg	1	176	U.S. 13, I-64, Va. 31
	5. return to Washington	1	205	U.S. 60, I-64, I-95
			522	

Florida	1. Orlando*, and Disney World	3	—	
	2. West Palm Beach	1	161	Fla. Tpke.
	3. Fort Lauderdale	1	42	U.S. 1
	4. Miami*	2	25	U.S. 1
			228	

Great Lakes	1. Chicago*	2		
	2. Milwaukee*	1	87	I-94
	3. Sault Ste. Marie	1	398	U.S. 43, U.S. 41, U.S. 2, I-75
	4. Mackinaw City	1	56	I-75
	5. Holland	1	284	U.S. 31
	6. return to Chicago	1	140	U.S. 31, I-94
			965	

Rockies	1. Denver*	1	—	
	2. Colorado Springs	1	76	I-25
	3. Canon City	1	44	Colo. 115, U.S. 50
	4. Gunnison	1	121	U.S. 50
	5. Glenwood Springs	1	173	U.S. 50, Colo. 92, Colo. 133, Colo. 82
	6. Dillon	1	91	I-70
	7. return to Denver	1	76	I-70
			581	

Rockies	1. Denver*	1	—	
	2. Great Sand Dunes & Alamosa	1	239	I-25, U.S. 160
	3. Santa Fe*	2	140	U.S. 285
	4. Durango and Mesa Verde	2	215	U.S. 84, U.S. 160
	5. return to Denver	1	390	U.S. 160, I-25
			984	

West	1. Los Angeles*	2	—	
	2. Las Vegas*	2	272	I-15
	3. Palm Springs	1	309	I-15, I-10, Calif. 111
	4. San Diego*	2	133	Calif. 111, Calif. 74, Calif. 79, I-15
			714	

West	1. San Francisco*	2	—	
	2. Sacramento	1	86	I-80
	3. Reno	1	136	I-80
	4. Lake Tahoe*	2	56	U.S. 395, U.S. 50
	5. return to San Francisco	1	204	U.S. 50, I-80
			482	

If you have two weeks or more . . .

Florida & Georgia	1. Atlanta*	2	—	
	2. Savannah*	2	256	I-75, I-16
	3. St. Augustine	1	175	I-95, U.S. 1
	4. Orlando* & Disney World	3	200	I-95, I-4
	5. Palm Beach	1	146	I-95, U.S. 1
	6. Miami*	2	75	I-95, U.S. 1
	7. Sarasota	1	212	U.S. 41
	8. St. Petersburg*	1	51	U.S. 41, I-275
	9. Tallahassee	1	256	U.S. 19, U.S. 27
	10. return to Atlanta	1	268	U.S. 319, I-75
			1,628	

Region	Stop		Miles	Route
Florida & Louisiana	1. Atlanta*	2	—	
	2. Great Smoky Mountains	2	231	U.S. 19, U.S. 441
	3. Nashville*	2	225	U.S. 441, I-40
	4. Memphis*	2	200	I-40
	5. Vicksburg	1	231	I-55, I-20
	6. New Orleans*	4	250	U.S. 61, I-10
	7. Montgomery	1	312	I-10, I-65
	8. return to Atlanta	1	168	I-85
			1,617	
Arizona & The Grand Canyon	1. Phoenix*	3	—	
	2. Grand Canyon*	2	218	I-17, U.S. 180
	3. Las Vegas*	2	290	Ariz. 64, I-40, U.S. 93
	4. Zion National Park	2	162	I-15, Utah 9
	5. Monument Valley	2	256	Utah 9, U.S. 89, Ariz. 98, U.S. 160, U.S. 163
	6. Canyon de Chelly	2	112	U.S. 163, U.S. 160, U.S. 191
	7. Native American Pueblos	1	81	U.S. 191, Ariz. 264
	8. return to Phoenix	1	281	Ariz. 264, U.S. 89, I-17
			1,375	
California	1. Los Angeles*	3	—	
	2. Death Valley*	2	306	I-15, Calif. 127
	3. Sequoia Nat'l Park*	1	362	Calif. 190
	4. Yosemite Nat'l Park*	2	177	Calif. 190, Calif. 178, Calif. 65, Calif. 198
	5. San Francisco*	3	210	Calif. 198, Calif. 180, Calif. 41
	6. California Coast*	3	487	Calif. 120, I-205, I-580
	7. return to Los Angeles	1	126	U.S. 101, Calif. 1
			1,668	
California & Navajoland	1. Denver*	2	—	
	2. Mesa Verde Nat'l Park	2	416	I-25, U.S. 160
	3. Monument Valley	2	158	U.S. 160, U.S. 163
	4. Canyon de Chelly	2	112	U.S. 163, U.S. 160, U.S. 191
	5. Santa Fe*	3	287	U.S. 191, Ariz. 264, I-40, I-25
	6. Durango	1	215	U.S. 84, N. Mex. 96, N. Mex. 44, U.S. 550
	7. Colorado Springs	2	316	U.S. 160, I-25
	8. return to Denver	1	66	I-25
			1,573	
Colorado & Yellowstone	1. Denver*	2	—	
	2. Dinosaur Nat'l Park	1	303	I-70, Colo. 13, Colo. 64, U.S. 40
	3. Salt Lake City*	3	200	U.S. 40, I-80
	4. Jackson, Wyo.	1	301	I-15, U.S. 26
	5. Yellowstone Nat'l Park*	4	79	U.S. 89
	6. Casper	1	293	U.S. 20, Wyo. 120, U.S. 20

	7. Rocky Mountain Nat'l Park	2	275	I-25, U.S. 34
	8. return to Denver	1	70	U.S. 34, U.S. 36
			1,521	
Texas & Louisiana	1. Dallas*	3	—	
	2. Austin	1	192	I-35
	3. San Antonio*	2	80	I-35
	4. Houston*	3	196	I-10
	5. Baton Rouge	1	281	I-10
	6. New Orleans*	3	81	I-10
	7. Vicksburg	1	253	I-10, U.S. 61
	8. return to Dallas	1	362	I-20
			1,445	

If you have three weeks or more . . .

East Coast & the South	1. Boston*	2	—	
	2. New York*	2	212	I-95
	3. Philadelphia*	2	100	I-278, I-95
	4. Washington*	2	134	I-95
	5. Williamsburg	1	160	I-395, I-95, I-64
	6. Roanoke	1	221	I-64, I-81
	7. Great Smoky Mountains	1	303	I-81, U.S. 441
	8. Atlanta*	2	231	U.S. 441, U.S. 19
	9. Charleston*	2	306	I-20, U.S. 78, I-26
	10. Raleigh	1	261	U.S. 52, I-95, U.S. 70
	11. Virginia Beach	1	184	U.S. 64, I-95, U.S. 58
	12. Assateague Island	1	106	U.S. 60, U.S. 13, Va. 175
	13. Atlantic City	1	145 +Ferry	Va. 175, U.S. 13, U.S. 113, U.S. 9, Garden St. Pkway
	14. New York*	1	128	I-95, I-278
	15. return to Boston	1	212	I-95
			2,706	
California & Nevada	1. San Francisco*	4	—	
	2. Sacramento	1	93	I-80
	3. Reno*	2	137	U.S. 50, U.S. 395, I-80,
	4. Death Valley*	2	380	Nev. 50, U.S. 95, Nev. 267
	5. Zion Park & Bryce Canyon	3	381	Calif. 190, Calif. 127, Nev. 373, U.S. 95, I-15, Utah 9
	6. Grand Canyon	2	312	U.S. 89, Ariz. 64
	7. Las Vegas*	2	290	Ariz. 64, I-40, U.S. 93
	8. Los Angeles*	3	282	I-15, I-10
	9. return to San Francisco	2	487	Calif. 1, U.S. 101
			2,365	
California & Grand Canyon	1. Los Angeles*	3	—	
	2. San Diego*	2	125	Calif. 1, I-5
	3. Phoenix*	2	356	I-8, Ariz. 85
	4. Grand Canyon*	2	218	I-17, U.S. 180
	5. Las Vegas*	2	290	Ariz. 64, I-40, U.S. 93
	6. Death Valley*	2	143	U.S. 95, Nev. 373, Calif. 190

	7. Sequoia Nat'l Park*	1	362	Calif. 190, Calif. 178, Calif. 65, Calif. 198
	8. Yosemite Nat'l Park*	2	177	Calif. 180, Calif. 41
	9. San Francisco*	3	210	Calif. 120, I-205, I-580, I-80
	10. return to Los Angeles	2	487	U.S. 101, Calif. 1
			2,371	
Utah, Arizona, & Nevada	1. Las Vegas*	2	—	
	2. Zion Park & Bryce Canyon	3	243	I-15, Utah 9, U.S. 89, Utah 12
	3. Salt Lake City*	2	262	Utah 12, U.S. 89, I-15
	4. Canyonlands & Arches Park	3	243	I-15, U.S. 6, U.S. 191
	5. Mesa Verde Park	2	150	U.S. 191, U.S. 666, U.S. 160
	6. Monument Valley	2	158	U.S. 160, U.S. 163
	7. Canyon de Chelley	1	112	U.S. 163, U.S. 160, U.S. 191
	8. Indian Pueblos	1	81	U.S. 191, Ariz. 264
	9. Glen Canyon	2	141	Ariz. 264, U.S. 89
	10. Grand Canyon*	2	137	U.S. 89, Ariz. 64
	11. return to Las Vegas	1	290	Ariz. 64, I-40, U.S. 93
			1,840	

If you have a month or more . . .

Colorado, Yellowstone, the Pacific Northwest, & California	1. Denver*	3	—	
	2. Rocky Mountain Nat'l Park	1	70	U.S. 36, U.S. 34
	3. Casper	1	275	U.S. 34, I-25
	4. Yellowstone Nat'l Park*	3	293	U.S. 20, Wyo. 120, U.S. 20
	5. Butte	1	212	U.S. 89, I-90
	6. Spokane	1	315	I-90
	7. Seattle*	2	293	U.S. 2, Wash. 174, Wash. 155, U.S. 2, Wash. 522
	8. Pacific Coast*	2	468	Ferry + U.S. 101, U.S. 30
	9. Portland*	2	—	—
	10. Medford & Jacksonville	1	250	I-5
	11. Sacramento	2	341	I-5
	12. San Francisco*	3	93	I-80
	13. Yosemite Nat'l Park*	2	210	I-580, I-205, Calif. 120, Calif. 41
	14. Death Valley*	2	321	Calif. 41, Calif. 120, U.S. 395, Calif. 190
	15. Las Vegas*	1	143	Calif. 190, Nev. 373, U.S. 95
	16. Zion Park & Bryce Canyon	2	243	I-15, Utah 9, U.S. 89, Utah 12
	17. Grand Junction	1	337	Utah 12, U.S. 89, I-70
	18. return to Denver	1	259	I-70
			4,124	

BEFORE YOU LEAVE HOME

SOURCES OF INFORMATION: Begin planning as far in advance as possible, especially if you will travel during peak seasons. Every state has a central tourist information office and a series of regional offices; most cities also have convention and tourist bureaus; both will provide a lot of information. For a complete listing of state tourist organizations, see the Appendix; for city bureaus, see each city chapter under "Tourist Information."

You can also contact the **International Association of Convention and Visitors Bureaus,** P.O. Box 758, Champaign, IL 61824-0758 (217/359-8881).

USING A TRAVEL AGENT: To use a travel agent successfully you need to find a good one, and you need to know where you want to go and what you want to do, so that you're free to go over the details with the agent, modifying your plans to incorporate his or her professional advice. Ask for personal recommendations among your friends, or contact the **American Society of Travel Agents (ASTA),** 1101 King St., Alexandria, VA 22314 (703/739-2782), whose members have been in business a minimum of 3 years; or the **Institute of Certified Travel Agents,** 148 Linden St. (P.O. Box 56), Wellesley, MA 02181 (617/237-0280), whose certification means that the agent has taken an 18-month training course sponsored by the institute.

If your main interest is saving money on airfares, to really make good use of your travel agent, keep asking for the lowest fare and request the agent to check out the many ways that can be used to find the lowest price—flying to a destination in two or more segments to take advantage of discounts on particular highly competitive or infrequently flown routes, traveling on certain days of the week, etc. If the agent is not willing to do this, you need to find one who will, although you may be charged a modest additional fee for these services.

WHAT & HOW TO PACK: Just some brief hints:

1. Leave at home clothes that need to be ironed before each wearing, unless you're staying at a deluxe resort/hotel. Pack drip-dry coordinated separates so that you can vary your outfits easily.

2. Pack a pair of comfortable shoes.

3. Travel light, even if you're driving—lugging heavy bags in and out of the trunk is tedious. Two small, light bags are better than one heavy, large one.

4. If you're flying, pack one carry-on bag with toiletries and other necessities, in case checked luggage gets lost. Airlines are strictly enforcing the limit of two carry-on bags; both must fit under the seat (about 9 × 14 × 22 in.; 25 × 35 × 92cm) or in an overhead bin (10 × 14 × 36 in.; 23 × 35 × 56cm).

5. Pack an extra folding bag for shopping finds.

6. Make a list of all items to be packed a few weeks before you leave.

7. Take copies of any important documents and also record traveler's check numbers. Stow separately.

INSURANCE: If you're taking a prepaid package tour, cruise, or charter flight, you may want to take out a special traveler's insurance for a specific trip that covers baggage loss, cancellation/trip interruption, and medical emergencies. Always check the fine print for exclusions from coverage, limits, and restricted definitions of whatever sort. Be sure that the policy is adequate to cover nondiscounted airfares and unexpected hotel expenses, if you do have to interrupt your trip for any emergency reason. Such policies are obtainable from an insurance broker or travel agent. Whatever you do, before you leave home, check:

1. Your homeowner's insurance; if it doesn't cover off-premises theft and loss you may want to purchase a floater to protect you during your vacation.

2. Your health insurance, for any pre-treatment emergency requirements —hotline numbers, etc. Most standard health-insurance policies will cover you while on vacation.

3. Your auto insurance, for full coverage—accident insurance for medical expenses, injury to other passengers in your car, and loss of pay if you're injured; liability for injury you cause to another person or property; comprehensive and collision; and uninsured-motorist protection if you're involved in an accident with an uninsured driver of another car.

4. Your personal insurance, because if it does not cover you for injury or death when flying, you may want to amend your policy. Although your plane ticket price automatically includes airline-liability insurance, the limits are set by individual state laws and each claim is hard fought and consequently costly. Some credit-card companies automatically provide flight insurance if your ticket is charged to that account—American Express, for example.

A TRAVEL-PLANNING CHECKLIST: Here is a quick list of things to take care of in advance and at the very last minute:

In Advance

1. Leave with a friend or neighbor a house key, your auto-registration number, and a trip itinerary (including, if possible, names of specific accommodations where you will be staying).

2. Write or call state and local tourist boards along your route and at your destination for information on attractions, special events, and special weather conditions (remember the vagaries of weather when packing).

3. Have your car checked and serviced. Fluid levels and tire pressures should be up to capacity, oil and oil filter clean, and ignition system tuned.

4. Prepare an emergency road kit, including basic tools, flares, flashlight, a duplicate set of car keys (to be kept with you), and a first-aid kit; check the jack and spare tire.

5. Think about health needs (do you need a medical or dental checkup before you go?). Carry an adequate supply of any prescription drugs and medications you require, and take along a copy of important prescriptions, in case of loss. Have extras for other important personal items, such as a pair of glasses and contact lenses.

6. Store valuables at home in a safe place. You may want to rent a safe-deposit box for silverware and jewelry, or register major appliances (stereo, television) with the police (check your homeowner's insurance for theft coverage).

7. Check important documents and their expiration dates: driver's license, credit cards, auto-insurance policy, auto registration, auto club membership card.

8. Purchase traveler's checks and record the check numbers in two places, keeping both lists separate from the checks.

9. Install automatic timers on a few lights in your home, or arrange for a friend to turn various lights on and off during your absence.

10. Discontinue deliveries, such as mail and newspapers, or arrange for a friend to pick up such items. Have someone check periodically for unexpected deliveries, pamphlets, or circulars, which tend to pile up at the door, sending a clear message to thieves that no one is home.

11. Arrange for yardwork at regular times.

At Departure

1. Disconnect electrical appliances, lower the thermostat, and turn off gas jets, including the hot-water heater. Set automatic timers on lights.

2. Make sure all the important documents get packed. Those traveler's checks can't help you if you leave them in the desk drawer.

3. Make a final check of all doors and windows as you are leaving the house.

4. And finally, check your travel documents, making sure that the destinations printed on your airline tickets are correct. Also, if you're flying, reconfirm your flight (even though that's not required for domestic flights).

GETTING AROUND

BY CAR: Although it may not be the least expensive way to go unless you're traveling with family or friends (which lowers the per-person cost considerably), it's certainly the most flexible.

Driving Your Own Car

PRE-TRIP PREPARATIONS Inspect your car thoroughly before setting out on a long trip. The best time to do this is when the engine and tires are cool. Run through the following:

1. Check all lights—headlights, tail lights, parking lights, license-plate lights, and hazard lights. Test the brake lights, backup lights, and turn signals.

2. Make sure the horn, seatbelts, and windshield wipers are functioning properly.

3. Inspect the tires carefully and replace any tire that is cut, shows sidewall bulges, or has bald patches on its tread. Also replace any tire whose tread depth is worn to 1-16th in. (1mm) or less. Check for uneven wear. If there's any sign of this, take the car for wheel alignment. While the tires are cool, check the tire pressure and inflate to correct pressure. Don't forget to fill the spare.

4. With the engine off and the vehicle on a level surface, check all fluid levels: the oil level should be between "add" and "full" on the dipstick; top up the engine coolant (a 50/50 mixture of antifreeze and water) to the appropriate level, as marked on the plastic reservoir; check the power-steering and automatic-transmission fluid levels according to the instructions in the owner's manual. Fill the windshield washer bottle and test the system.

5. Check the battery. Make sure it's clean and dry. Top up the electrolyte (water) level, if necessary. It should be half an inch (about 1.25cm) above the vertical plates in the battery. Replace the battery if the case is cracked or leaking. Also replace any battery cables that have damaged strands. Clean corroded battery and cable connections, and tighten any loose cable clamps on the battery posts.

6. Inspect the drive belts and replace any that are cracked, frayed, glazed, or contaminated by grease or oil. Press the belt with your thumb midway between the pulleys. The belt needs tightening if it depresses more than half an inch (about 1.25cm).

7. Squeeze the radiator and heater hoses. If they feel brittle or spongy, replace them. With the engine running, check also for any leaks in the cooling system.

8. After inspection, road-test the car, checking to see if it pulls to the left or right on a straight road. If it does, it may need a front-end alignment. Also test the brakes. If the brake pedal feels spongy, have the brakes checked by a professional.

9. Before you leave, check that the following documents are still valid: vehicle registration, safety-inspection sticker, auto insurance, auto-club membership, and driver's license.

MAPS There are several good road atlases: *The Mobil Road Atlas & Trip Planning Guide* (Prentice Hall Press); *The Rand McNally Road Atlas & Vacation Guide* is also very popular. Many auto clubs also supply maps to members (see below).

PACING Don't drive more than 300–400 miles a day. Stop every 2 hr or so, and try to phone and make reservations for the night by midafternoon to avoid a wearying search at the end of an exhausting day's drive.

LEGAL ISSUES Watch the speed limit, which in most states is 55 m.p.h. The higher speed limit of 65 m.p.h. voted by Congress in 1987 is, for the time being, essentially restricted to the highways of some 20 states in the South, West, and Northwest, in particular, Arizona, Arkansas, California, Colorado, Missouri, Nevada,

New Mexico, North Dakota, Oklahoma, South Dakota, Texas, Utah, and Wyoming. But since voters in other states may approve the higher 65-m.p.h. speed limit, be sure to check roadside postings carefully every time you cross a state line.

Buckle up! Seatbelts for driver and front-seat passengers are mandatory in about half the states, most notably Connecticut, Illinois, Indiana, Iowa, Louisiana, Michigan, Mississippi, New Jersey, New Mexico, New York, Ohio, Oklahoma, and Utah. Seatbelts must be worn by all passengers in the District of Columbia, California, Massachusetts, and Washington. Note also that in all 50 states and in Washington, D.C., children under 4 must be in a child's seat or be buckled up.

AUTO CLUBS Join one of the auto clubs. They will supply maps, recommended routes, guidebooks, accident and bail-bond insurance, and, most important of all, emergency road service. The leader, with 850 offices and 28 million members, is the **American Automobile Association (AAA),** with national headquarters at 1000 AAA Dr., Heathrow, FL 32745 (407/444-7000). Check telephone book for local offices. Membership for both U.S. citizens and foreign visitors ranges from $17 to $56, depending on which particular local office you join. AAA also has a 24-hr. emergency toll-free number: 800/336-4357.

Other recommended auto clubs include the **Allstate Motor Club,** P.O. Box 3094, Arlington Heights, IL 60006 (toll free 800/323-6282); and the **Amoco Motor Club,** P.O. Box 9049, Des Moines, IA 50368 (toll free 800/334-3300).

A NOTE FOR FOREIGN VISITORS The AAA can provide you with a "Touring Permit" validating your driving license. Members of some foreign auto clubs that have reciprocal arrangements with AAA enjoy AAA's services at no charge.

Auto Rentals

To rent a car you need a major credit card or you'll have to leave a sizable cash deposit ($100 or more for each day). Minimum driver age is usually 21, and you'll need a valid driver's license.

SHOP AROUND Rates vary from company to company, from location to location (airport vs. downtown, Florida vs. New York City). In addition, companies offer unlimited-mileage options vs. per-mile charges and also special discounts on weekends, for example. So it pays to shop around. Use the major companies' toll-free 800 numbers to do this. Other variable costs to check include drop-off charges if you're picking up the car in one city and leaving it in another; the cost of daily collision damage and personal accident insurance. And always return your car with a full tank—the rental companies charge excessive prices for gasoline.

THE COMPANIES The majors are: **Hertz** (toll free 800/654-3131), **Avis** (toll free 800/331-1212), **National** (toll free 800/227-7368), **Budget** (toll free 800/527-0700), and **Dollar** (toll free 800/421-6868). Also check the smaller local companies and **Rent a Wreck** (toll free 800/535-1391), if there is one in a particular city.

BY RECREATIONAL VEHICLE (RV): Accommodating four to six people,
these vehicles are ideal for long family trips. Air-conditioned, and equipped with showers, refrigerators, and a full kitchen, they're also comfortable. Throughout the U.S., campsites have hookups for electricity, water, and sewage disposal.

Book Resources

The *RV Park and Campground Directories*—one national book and two smaller editions covering the eastern U.S. and Canada and the western U.S. and Canada (Prentice Hall Press)—contain thousands of listings in easy-to-read chart format that are cross-referenced to maps, as well as establishments that sell and service RVs. The AAA also publishes regional campground directories.

Renting an RV

Check the *Yellow Pages* under "Recreational Vehicles—Renting & Leasing." Major companies include **Cruise America** (toll free 800/327-7778), **U-Haul RV Rentals** (toll free 800/468-4285), and **Go Vacations, Inc.** (toll free 800/387-3998).

For information, contact the **Recreation Vehicle Dealer's Association,** 3251 Old Lee Hwy., Suite 500, Fairfax, VA 22030 (703/591-7130). The RVDA publishes *Rental Ventures,* a directory of rental agencies, for a small charge.

BY AIR: Since deregulation in 1987, shopping the airlines has become increasingly complex and travel by air increasingly irksome as airlines delay and often cancel flights without warning.

Shop Around

Use the toll-free lines to call all the airlines that go to your destination. Always ask the agent for the lowest fare as opposed to a particular fare, such as an APEX (an advance-purchase fare). This way you're asking them to search for the cheapest ticket to your destination. Once you've located it and made a reservation, still check a day or so before your departure to see if there has been a fare change since you booked—you'll be due a refund if it has decreased, but no extra charge if it has increased—because airlines, as the departure date draws nearer, will make more seats available for discounting if the flight is not being booked. That's why, for example, you can call on Wednesday, June 23, and be told that no discount seats are available, and then call on Thursday, June 24, and obtain a discount seat. So it really is worth calling almost daily up to the departure time to see if any discounts have opened up.

The Regular Fare Structure

At the top there's **first class.** You're paying for larger seats, more leg room, superior service and meals. In **business class,** the next step down, you get a little extra leg room and some extra little services, including free drinks. A **coach** or **economy** fare puts you in cramped seating, and ensures typical airline food and service.

For all three classes above you can book at the last moment, you incur no cancellation penalties, and your round-trip ticket will be good for a year, longer if you renew it.

Personal Rating of the Nine Major U.S. Airlines

Airline	Service	Punctuality
American United	Good	Good
Delta* Northwest	Good	Moderate
Pan Am** USAir Continental	Moderate	Moderate
TWA** Eastern**	Mediocre	Poor

*Acceptable food in flight
**Very poor food in flight

Discount Fares

Referred to variously as Excursion, Super Saver, or Advance Purchase (APEX), these offer savings as much as 35% to 45% of the regular fare—but they do have strings attached.

Usually they must be booked anywhere from 1 week to a month in advance; they carry penalties for changing either the date of departure or return, and also for cancellation.

To find these discount fares, check your local newspaper advertisements. Among them, sometimes you'll find promotions for specified destinations or for age groups such as senior citizens. Discounts can be quite substantial, 50% or more.

Other money-savers are: flying off-season (mid-Jan through Mar and Oct through mid-Dec, except Thanksgiving weekend); off-hour flights (10am–3pm and after-8pm departures); day-of-the-week reductions (usually Tuesday, Wednesday, Thursday, or Saturday when traffic is lightest); and routing with stops or connections ("direct" means stops but no change of plane; "nonstop" means exactly that).

Be aware, too, that you may be able to save a lot of money by splitting your trip into segments and taking advantage of particularly low fares on a given segment. For example, a travel agent looking for the lowest fare from Pittsburgh to Portland, Oregon, might see only an American Airlines fare of $505 each way, but if the agent "digs" he or she may find that you can fly from Pittsburgh to Denver and then from Denver to Portland for a total of only $320—a great savings. It's worth checking alternative routings either through an agent or by calling the airlines constantly and asking them, "Isn't there anything cheaper?"

Anyone requiring only a one-way fare should always look into the comparable price of a round-trip Super Saver or other discount ticket. Sometimes it's simply cheaper to take the round-trip ticket and throw away the return half (better yet, you can sell it to someone). Anomalies like this can always be found.

Airline Passes, Charters, and Tour Packages

Often airlines will offer special passes for particular groups—like senior citizens or youths. For example, in the past some major airlines have offered a pass to 62-year-olds-plus, good for 1 year's unlimited flying anywhere within their system.

Frequent-flyer plans can cut costs dramatically. Bonus points accumulate every time you fly, and recently the airlines have been offering triple-mileage bonuses. Estimates are that the public currently has billions of dollars' worth of free flying miles!

Often you can take advantage of an all-inclusive tour package which will deliver a very low airfare, and possibly some extra discounts on car rentals, accommodations, and sightseeing. These are most often offered in Florida and the Southwest. Remember that you don't have to use the whole package, but you may still save money by purchasing it and not using what you don't want.

Flying as an Air Courier

Although this fun, low-cost way of flying is more available for foreign travel, there are one or two companies that recruit people to fly as couriers carrying packages to domestic destinations. Anyone can become a courier. All you do is give up your baggage allowance, except for a carry-on. The courier company handles the check-in and pickup of packages at each airport. Special arrangements do have to be made to enable two people to fly, often on staggered flights. The savings, though, are remarkable.

One such company is **Now Voyager Freelance Courier,** 74 Varick St., Mezzanine B, New York, NY 10013 (212/431-1616), with domestic flights only to Los Angeles as we go to press (subject to change).

Notes and Special Air Fares for Foreign Visitors

There are about nine "major" airlines (although several are owned by the same corporate parent), a dozen somewhat smaller "nationals," and hundreds of local commuter carriers, offering day and night service at more than 1,000 airports. Taking the plane in the U.S.A. has become almost as simple as taking the subway or a cab. Some lines, like Trump's or Pan Am's New York–Washington and New York–Boston shuttles, require no reservations and fares are paid in flight to an attendant.

SPECIAL AIRFARES   Foreign visitors can take advantage of the special promotional airfares that have been discussed above, but from time to time they can also obtain special passes *before they leave home* that allow unlimited flying anywhere on the airline's network for a stated time period, usually 21 days, 1 month, 3 months, etc. These passes do usually carry restrictions—blackout days of the week; holidays, etc.; no backtracking; and so on. In the recent past none have been available, but it is well worth your while to check before leaving home for any that may have come on the market.

SMOKING   By federal law, since Feb 1990 smoking has been banned on all flights within the U.S. lasting 6 hr or less. On longer flights, only cigarettes may be smoked in designated sections of the aircraft.

Some Easy Flying Hints

Use the secondary airports if you can, like Midway instead of O'Hare in Chicago; Dulles instead of National in Washington, D.C.; Newark instead of LaGuardia or Kennedy in New York.

Allow plenty of time between connecting flights; unless you have to, don't book the last flight of the day since you'll be stuck overnight if you miss it or are bumped.

To protect themselves against people who reserve seats and don't show up, the airlines do overbook their planes. If everyone shows up, obviously something has to give and passengers do get "bumped." The airlines, however, must abide by certain rules in resolving the situation. If the airlines can arrange alternative flights that arrive within 1 hr of the originally scheduled flight, then it does not have to pay compensation of any sort. If the delay is longer, compensation is mandatory. Airlines usually offer ticket vouchers. If you are bumped, find out immediately what the airline will do to make your enforced delay more comfortable—meal vouchers, overnight accommodations, etc. Speak to a supervisor if a reservations clerk cannot give you a good answer. Also, if you have connecting flights, make sure that those airlines are informed.

For a booklet entitled *Fly Rights* that discusses passengers' rights, send $1 to the Consumer Information Center, Department 148V Pueblo, CO 81009 (719/948-3334).

If you have any complaints about the airlines—regarding lost baggage, bumping, or anything else—inform the Office of Community and Consumer Affairs, U.S. Department of Transportation, 400 7th St. SW, Room 10405, Washington DC 20590 (202/366-2220).

BY TRAIN

Although the savings over air travel can be negligible, going by train is a comfortable option if you have the time. It takes 49 hr by train from Chicago to San Francisco, 28 hr from New York to New Orleans, and 33 hr from Seattle to Los Angeles. On some routes—Washington to New York, for example—you're better off taking the Metroliner than the airplane. Total travel time by train will be about the same or less.

Amtrak services more than 500 cities, in all states except Maine, Oklahoma,

South Dakota, Hawaii, and Alaska. Facilities along the Boswash corridor and on long-distance lines west of the Mississippi are good, but a bit uneven elsewhere. Some of these trains boast panoramic cars from which you can admire the landscape—they include the *California Zephyr* (Chicago–San Francisco), the *Coast Starlight* (Seattle–Los Angeles), the *Southwest Chief* (Chicago–Los Angeles), the *Desert Wind* (Chicago–Salt Lake City–Los Angeles), the *Empire Builder* (Chicago–Seattle), and the *Sunset Limited* (New Orleans–Los Angeles). Long-distance trains have full dining and lounge cars; on others there's usually a snack bar and lounge.

Seat Types and Fares

Reclining day-coach seats are allocated on both a first-come, first-served basis and a reservation basis, depending on the train. The most economical for over-night is a reclining coach seat with a pull-up leg rest—pillows and blankets are provided as well.

Sleeping compartments vary between eastern and western trains. East of the Mississippi River, a single traveler can reserve a roomette, which consists of one lounge seat, which is stowed away when the bed is pulled down from the wall, a private toilet, and a closet. Or two travelers can reserve a bedroom with two lounge or bench seats, two berths, and toilet facilities. On trains running west of the Mississippi River, two options are available. There's an economy room, with two lounge seats by day and two berths by night; or a deluxe bed-room, with showers and private toilet facilities. The price of sleeping accommodations is added on to the coach fare and includes three meals daily in the dining car.

Railpasses and Special Fares

All Aboard America passes can be purchased in the U.S. and allow unlimited travel within one of Amtrak's regional divisions for 45 days, with two stop-overs allowed in addition to your final destination. One-region travel is currently priced at $189 for coach accommodations (they can be upgraded). A two-region ticket is $269, and a three-region (total country) ticket costs $309. Be sure to check regular fares to compare, since the savings on such a pass are proportionate to the distance traveled.

Amtrak also offers substantial discounts for families and the handicapped.

The Auto Train

Running between Lorton, Va. (just south of Washington, D.C.), and San-ford, Fla. (just north of Orlando), this nonstop train will transport you *and* your car. Coach accommodations, dinner with wine, and a Continental breakfast are provided. The Auto Train leaves daily at 3:30pm (at both ends) and takes approx-imately 18 hr. Sleeping accommodations are available for an extra charge. Off-peak fares in 1990 were $269 one way for an adult and a car, but they vary sub-stantially from season to season.

Amtrak Tours, Information, and Bookings

Get a copy of Amtrak's National Timetable from any Amtrak station, from ticket agents, or by contacting Amtrak, 60 Massachusetts Ave. NW, Washington, DC 20002 (toll free 800/USA-RAIL).

The reservations system is computerized; tickets can be purchased at sta-tions and sales offices, from travel agents, or aboard the train (for a small added fee). Some major stations now have self-service machines that dispense re-served tickets (you must have booked by telephone and have an assigned reserva-tion number).

Amtrak offers some 75 tour packages throughout the U.S. For information, pick up the booklet "Amtrak's America" at train stations or travel agencies, or call the toll-free number above and request a copy.

Notes for Foreign Visitors

Amtrak offers the **USA Railpass,** available only to non–U.S. citizens. This pass is unique in that it offers 45 days of travel with an *unlimited* number of stopovers, and is available for individual regions as well as for the entire country.

BY BUS: The least expensive way to travel, but often the most time-consuming (New York to Chicago takes 17 hr.). Greyhound, which acquired its only major rival, Trailways, in 1987, now reaches more than 8,000 cities and towns. Coaches are air-conditioned in summer (bring a sweater) and heated in winter, and long-distance buses have toilets. Rest and meal stops are made about every 4 hr.—best to bring your own snacks, though.

For longer trips, book an express or nonstop bus. Also, plan to arrive at your destination in daylight; some bus terminals are located in unsavory neighborhoods.

Always ask about promotional fares. For extensive travel, Greyhound's **Ameripass** is a real bargain, priced in 1990 at $189 for 7 days, $249 for 15 days, and $349 for 30 days, with optional extensions for $10 per day (do it before the pass expires). The Ameripass may be purchased at any Greyhound bus terminal.

No reservations are necessary, but you should arrive at least a half hour before departure time. Greyhound also offers reasonably priced package tours.

Note: Although plagued by persistent labor disputes in 1990, Greyhound is now operating at close to full capacity.

For Information

Contact the **Greyhound Bus Company,** NCNB Plaza, 901 Main St., Suite 2400, Dallas, TX 75202 (214/744-6500), or check the telephone directory for the local number.

Notes for Foreign Visitors

Greyhound's **International Ameripass** gives unlimited travel within the U.S. and Canada. For 7 days of travel, the cost is $140; for 15 days, $225; for 30 days, $280. The pass can be purchased in New York, San Francisco, and Los Angeles. It can also be purchased from International Greyhound in Europe. Designed mainly for students, the pass is basically available to any foreigner with a passport.

HITCHHIKING: Although hitching a ride is against the law in many states, people still do it. As a general rule it's forbidden on major highways and on limited-access roads (Interstates, freeways, expressways, and turnpikes).

The best way to find a ride is by contacting a ride-line group: Their telephone numbers can easily be obtained on any college campus, and the only cost is a few dollars' membership fee and a share of the gas costs.

Hitchhiking is either illegal or severely restricted in the following states: Alaska, Arizona, Arkansas, Colorado, Delaware, Georgia, Maryland, Michigan, Minnesota, Montana, New Jersey, North Dakota, South Carolina, Tennessee, Texas, and Utah.

GROUP TOURS/PACKAGES: These fly/drive, rail/drive, fully escorted, and various other types of tours save time and effort—and often money. Before booking though, you should:

1. Check to see if the tour operator is reliable. You can be pretty sure of this if the operator is a member of USTOA (United States Tour Operators Association), 211 E. 51st St., Suite 12B, New York, NY 10022 (212/944–5727), which requires for membership a minimum 3 years in business and hefty professional liability insurance. Also, check with your local Better Business Bureau.

2. Read the fine print. Make sure you know exactly what the overall price includes and what it doesn't; what the cancellation penalties are; and whether or not the company is free to cancel if not enough people sign up or to change the prices before departure.

DISCOUNT TRAVEL

The travel industry is so large and diverse that, like any other retail industry, there are an increasing number of professional discounters as well as newsletters and other information sources that clue you in on the latest travel discounts and bargains, from airfares to hotels and tour packages.

NEWSLETTERS: The following are reputable and useful:

Consumer Reports Travel Letter, Subscription Department, P.O. Box 53629, Boulder, CO 80322 (303/447-9330; toll free 800/525-0643): Particularly useful for airfare discounts. A monthly, the subscription is $37.

Travel Smart, 40 Beechdale Rd., Dobbs Ferry, NY 10522 (914/693-8300): One of the oldest in the business. Published 12 times a year, an introductory subscription is $37, with a $44 renewal rate.

LAST-MINUTE TRAVEL CLUBS & OTHER DISCOUNTERS: The first category purchases the excess inventory of travel suppliers and then sells it off at a discount to its membership. Members are given a toll-free hotline to call to obtain the latest offerings; occasionally, too, they receive newssheets detailing future offerings. Among such organizations are:

Discount Travel International, 114 Forrest Ave., Narberth, PA 19072 (215/668-7184; toll free 800/824-4000): Annual membership is $45.

Last Minute Travel Club, 132 Brookline Ave., Boston, MA 02215 (617/267-9800): Annual membership for one is $30; for two, $35.

Moment's Notice, 40 E. 49th St., New York, NY 10017 (212/486-0503): Annual fee is $45, which covers spouse, family, or other travel companions.

Stand Buys Ltd. and Travelers Advantage, CUC Travel Services, 40 Oak View Dr., Trumball, CT 06611 (toll free 800/848-8402): Annual fee is $49.

Worldwide Discount Travel Club, 1674 Meridian Ave., Miami Beach, FL 33139 (305/534-2082): Family membership is $50; individual membership, $35.

Encore Marketing International, 4501 Forbes Blvd., Lanham, MD 20706 (301/459-8020), operates three specialty discounting organizations: Short Notice (annual membership is $36) gives you access to last-minute discounts on tour packages and organized trips; Encore (annual membership is $48) provides additional free nights at hotels and discounts on car rentals and airfares; Villas of the World ($60 for one year) delivers 20%- to 25%-per-night discounts on villa, resort, and hotel accommodations.

Recently, several specialist airfare discounters have appeared. They only deal in air tickets and for a fixed fee they will sell you a discount ticket. They are able to do this because they rebate part of the standard agent's commission to you, the customer.

McTravel, 641 W. Lake St., Chicago, IL 60606 (312/876-1116; toll free 800/333-3335), is one of the better-known organizations in this area.

WHERE TO STAY

HOTELS & MOTELS: For the last word in decor and facilities like health clubs or spas, there are the major players like Hilton, Hyatt, Ritz Carlton, Sheraton, Westin. In big cities, especially New York, Washington, Los Angeles, and Chicago, expect to pay $200 and up a night. Elsewhere, expect to pay $70–$100 double in a two-star establishment, $100–$150 in three- and most four-stars, and $160 and up in a few deluxe, four-star hotels. (*Money-Saving Hint:* Always ask about weekend packages, corporate rates, and any other special promotions being offered.)

Below the leaders are a host of motel chains offering comfortable rooms with full facilities at moderate prices. Sure they're standardized, but at least you know what to expect. Among them are Best Western, Holiday Inn, Howard Johnson, La Quinta Motor Inns, Ramada Inns, Rodeway Inns, Travelodge, and Vagabond. Doubles range from $50 to $80. (*Money-Saving Hint:* Again, ask about weekend packages and other discount rates. Use their toll-free numbers listed in the Appendix.)

Even more standardized, often located on the outskirts of cities and with limited facilities (sometimes without a restaurant) are the budget motel chains. Color TV and telephone, though, tend to be standard. Look for Days Inns, Econo Lodges, Friendship Inns, Motel 6, Red Roof Inns, Holiday Inns' Hampton Inns, and Marriott's Fairfield Inns. Doubles range between $30 and $45.

INNS: Staying at a country inn is extremely popular across the whole country, although perhaps the greatest number of inns are in the Northeast, the South, and California. Many of these accommodations are historic homes that may have once served as stagecoach stops or even mansions for the wealthy. Usually they have a distinctive ambience, traditional antique or other noteworthy furnishings, and a personality that reflects the style and interests of the innkeepers. By definition, an inn should have a restaurant; otherwise, technically it's only a bed-and-breakfast establishment, but sometimes the definitions blur. Many inns often lack TV and room phone—the whole atmosphere is usually one of quiet relaxation. Inns and children do not usually mix—the kids find them boring—but the peace and quiet and personal charm of inns do appeal to most of us harried urban dwellers. The price tag can be high—from $80 and up, depending on the character and style of the particular inn.

How to Locate Them

Consult one of the many books available. In my opinion, the best among the many series is *Marilyn Wood's Wonderful Weekends* (Prentice Hall Press), which contains full descriptions of several hundred inns in the states surrounding New York City—Connecticut, Rhode Island, Massachusetts, Vermont, Pennsylvania, New York, New Jersey, and Delaware.

BED-&-BREAKFAST: These establishments are increasingly popular and also increasingly sophisticated. Some are beautifully renovated historic homes and breakfasts are lavish; others are simply homes and breakfast is taken with the family. Both types are very personal and a great way to meet the locals.

How to Locate Them

Check with local tourist offices for locations in a specific area, as well as local newspapers. Book resources include *Frommer's Bed & Breakfast North America* (Prentice Hall Press), which among other things lists all the bed-and-breakfast registries that you can contact to locate pre-inspected B&Bs. The *West Coast Bed & Breakfast Guide* and the *East Coast Bed & Breakfast Guide* (both Prentice Hall Press) describe and picture in four-color the prime B&B places.

YOUTH HOSTELS, Y's & UNIVERSITY ACCOMMODATIONS:

There are more than 230 youth hostels across the country that are open to members of any age. Annual membership is $10 for those age 17 and under, $25 for ages 18–55, and $15 for ages 55 and over. Nightly charges in rural hostels are in the $5–$10 range; in urban and resort areas, $10–$20. Sleeping accommodations are usually in small single-sex dorms, although some hostels have private and family accommodations. Cooking and laundry facilities are available.

For more information, contact **American Youth Hostels, Inc.,** National

Administrative Offices, P.O. Box 37613, Washington, DC 20013 (202/783-6161).

The 40 or so YMCA (Young Men's Christian Association) and YWCA (Young Women's Christian Association) hostels are clustered in the bigger cities, charging $15–$20 a night without bath or $30–$40 with bath (you'll pay a little more in the major cities). Generally they are pleasant and well equipped (pools, health clubs), with private rooms. Because of their popularity you should arrive early to secure a room.

The largest YMCA in New York City, **Sloane House,** 356 W. 34th St., New York, NY 10001 (212/760-5860), will make advance reservations for you at other Ys, and also offers discount vouchers good at 42 YM/YWCAs.

During the summer many campus accommodations are open to travelers. Accommodations are usually very comfortable and low priced. For more information, contact the **Council on International Educational Exchange (CIEE)**, Sloane House, 356 W. 34th St., New York, NY 10001 (212/695-0291), and ask for their publication *Where to Stay USA,* which is co-published with Prentice Hall Press and also available in bookstores.

CAMPING: There's an excellent network of 8,000 public and 8,000 private campgrounds across the U.S., many with sites fully equipped with water, electricity, sewer connections, barbecues, showers, general store, and often with a swimming pool and other recreational facilities. For a family tent site the fee is $15–$20 per night, $18–$30 for a motor home or cabin. Send $3 to **Kampgrounds of America (KOA),** P.O. Box 30162, Billings, MT 59114 (406/248-7444), for a list of some 650 KOA campgrounds.

Book Resources: *RV Park & Campground Directories* (Prentice Hall Press); *Camp USA* (Prentice Hall Press). The AAA also publishes regional campground directories.

TIPS ON HAPPY STAYS: Make reservations particularly in peak tourist seasons and in large cities where conventions and other special events may block out accommodations. Small inns and bed-and-breakfasts also require advance bookings, particularly on weekends.

If you expect to arrive late, ask for "guaranteed late arrival"—that way your room will be held. When you book, make sure you understand the rate categories: European Plan (EP) is room only; Continental Plan (CP), room and Continental breakfast; Modified American Plan (MAP), room, full breakfast, and dinner; American Plan (AP), room, breakfast, lunch, and dinner. Don't forget to include local and state taxes in the total price.

A NOTE ON TAXES In considering how much you want to pay for your accommodations, be sure to take into account the sales tax and/or occupancy tax levied by many states and localities throughout the country. These two taxes, taken together, could add almost 25% to the cost of your accommodations. (See the table of sample tax rates in the next chapter, "For the Foreign Visitor.")

FOOD & DRINK

The United States, this great melting pot of cultures, offers many cuisines to choose from: at one end of the spectrum are four-star restaurants serving "nouvelle cuisine"; at the other end, little Greek *tavernas,* Mexican *cantinas,* and Thai restaurants with unbeatable prices. From the authentic New York "deli" (sorely missed in other parts of the country) to Chinese restaurants better than any in Asia, the U.S. has them all.

CUISINE OF THE NORTHEAST: The whole Northeast, and especially New England, prominently features seafood, beginning with the typical Boston dish, *clam chowder,* a thick shellfish soup. Other respected specialties are *Boston baked beans* (salt pork, beans, onions, and molasses baked slowly in a clay crockpot), and *Yankee pot roast* (beef braised with onions, tomatoes, carrots, and celery). Cape Cod (*Chatham, Wellfleet, Cotuit*) and Long Island (*Blue Point*) are famous for their oysters. Chesapeake Bay, south of Baltimore, is well known for its blue crabs, scallops, and *Pocomoke* oysters. Chesapeake Bay crabs are the base for Maryland's great specialty, *crabcakes*, little crabmeat patties, breaded and sautéed.

The best *lobsters* come from Maine, the northernmost state of New England. They are the heart of a dish of Native American origin, the *clambake*, which involves digging a hole in the sand at the bottom of which raw fish, clams, and lobsters are laid on a bed of red-hot stones and allowed to cook under a tarpaulin or a layer of branches.

Besides its shellfish, Long Island, to the east of New York City, is famous for its *Long Island ducklings*. Vermont, near the Canadian border, is the birthplace of *cheddar cheese soup* and the principal producer of *maple syrup*, traditionally served with pancakes and waffles. New England offers two desserts drawn from the cookbooks of the earliest settlers: sweet *pumpkin pie*, and *Indian pudding*, made from cornmeal and molasses and generally topped with whipped cream, which is an old Boston tradition.

Other northeastern specialties include: *clam fritters* (Maine and Rhode Island); *codfish balls* (New England); *crab Imperial*, crabmeat baked in a white-wine sauce (from Maryland); *hoagie* or submarine, an enormous hero sandwich made with ham, salami, provolone, onions, tomatoes, lettuce, and fresh pepper, all doused in olive oil (a Philadelphia classic); *lobster pie*, a flaky pastry crust filled with lobster in white sauce (Maine); *Manhattan clam chowder*, a New York City variation on Boston clam chowder, with tomatoes, green pepper, carrots, and celery instead of milk and potatoes; *New England boiled dinner*, a local version of the classic French pot-au-feu; *New York cheesecake*, served plain or with pineapple or strawberry topping; *oyster pie*, a country pie from Pennsylvania filled with oysters and mushrooms in a light white sauce; *pepper pot*, a thick, highly seasoned tripe soup (from Pennsylvania); *Philadelphia cheese steak*, a sandwich made from thin slices of steak covered in fried onions and melted cheese; *red flannel hash*, made of corned beef, potatoes, and red beets cooked in a frying pan over a low flame, the New England treatment for leftovers; *shad roe*, rolled in bacon, broiled, and served on toast (a springtime specialty in Maryland); *shoofly pie*, a Pennsylvania-Dutch open tart with a filling of brown sugar and molasses; *snail salad*, cut into thin slices and served in a tart marinade (Rhode Island); *succotash*, a dish of Native American origin consisting of sweet-corn kernels and lima beans cooked in milk over a low flame (Massachusetts and Rhode Island).

CUISINE OF THE SOUTH: Although much more venturesome than that of New England, the cuisine of the South also draws heavily on the excellent seafood of the Atlantic and the Gulf of Mexico: oysters, scallops, *soft-shell crabs* (good with scallops), *stone crabs* (very hard-shelled crabs), shrimp, sea bass, swordfish, etc. Rice figures in many meat and fish dishes, notably *Hopping John* (rice, bacon, and red beans), *Limping Susan* (rice, bacon, and gumbo), or *dirty rice* (rice, vegetables, and chopped chicken liver).

But the two famous dishes of the region are still *southern fried chicken*, crisp on the outside and moist on the inside, and *Virginia ham* (the best comes from Smithfield, near Norfolk), which Queen Victoria consumed in such quantity that she ordered 20 a month. Smoked for 6 weeks over a hickory-wood fire, from which it derives its delicate amber color, it is served baked with honey, wine, apricots or pineapple—a real treat.

Another great regional dish is *spareribs*, related to *soul food*, which was the cuisine of the slave quarters in the plantations of the Old South. It was a simple but delicious style of cooking based on ingredients spurned by whites, such as pigs' trotters, tripe, or catfish stewed with bacon, and accompanied by such poor man's vegetables as turnips, dandelion greens, collards, and kale.

Spoon bread, the typical cornbread of the South, is served so soaked in molasses and butter that it can only be eaten with a spoon—hence the name.

Florida citrus fruits (oranges, lemons, limes, grapefruit) are not the least important of the South's dependable delicacies, witness such classics as *orange bread pudding, orange baked custard,* or the most famous of all, *key lime pie.* Another famous southern dessert, *pecan pie,* is very sweet and on the heavy side. Students of liquid refreshment should take care to try a *mint julep* on a hot summer's day: bourbon (or cognac), fresh mint, and sugar poured over crushed ice.

Other southern specialties include: *Brunswick stew,* of pork and vegetables, usually served with a barbecue (Georgia and Alabama); *burgoo,* originally a ragoût of game, now a lamb-and-vegetable stew (Kentucky); *Carpetbagger steak,* stuffed with oysters (a favorite in Georgia, and also found in Louisiana); *chess pie,* made of sugared cream in a chessboard pattern (Kentucky, Tennessee, Virginia); *cobbler,* a fruit pie with a thick crust (Kentucky, Tennessee); *conch chowder,* thick soup made with conch, salt pork, and tomatoes (Florida); *fried pie,* batter turnovers filled with fruit, usually apples or peaches (Arkansas, Louisiana); *greens,* turnip-tops, collards, or mustard greens cooked slowly with a ham bone, a traditional African American dish; *hominy grits,* thick corn gruel (Virginia); *hushpuppies,* fried balls of cornmeal; *peanut soup,* celery-and-carrot soup with peanut butter, sour cream, and chopped peanuts (Virginia and Georgia); *picadillo,* chopped pork, onion, and olives, highly spiced and served with rice and beans (of Cuban origin, now a Florida classic); and *red rice,* cooked with tomatoes and ham (very popular in Savannah).

CREOLE CUISINE:

Créole or Louisiana cooking is a very successful synthesis of several strains—French, Spanish, African, and Caribbean. The interaction produces deftly seasoned delicacies exemplified by the two best-known dishes: *gumbo,* a thick okra-and-vegetable soup to which may be added a choice of sausage, chicken, shrimp, crab, and fish, the whole seasoned with gumbo filé (powdered sassafras leaves); and *jambalaya,* a kind of New World paella made with rice, tomatoes, shrimp or crayfish, oysters, sausage, and chicken.

Also worth looking for are *shrimp remoulade* New Orleans style, *oysters Benedict* (fried oysters wrapped in bacon and covered with hollandaise sauce), *oysters Bienville* (baked, with mushrooms, shrimp, and white-wine sauce), *oysters Casino* (baked and served under a layer of bacon with cocktail sauce), *oysters Rockefeller* (baked with spinach, au gratin, and flavored with Pernod), the *crayfish* (or *crawfish*) which abound in Louisiana's "bayous," and two delicious fish from the Gulf of Mexico, *pompano,* usually served "en papillote" (cooked in paper), and *red snapper.* Rice, fish, and shellfish figure in many Créole main dishes.

Contrary to expectation, *pig's ears,* a New Orleans favorite, have nothing to do with pigs or ears; they are horns of batter filled with cream. Other desserts are the famous *bananas Foster* (caramelized bananas with a dash of rum served with vanilla ice cream), *sweet-potato pudding, beignets* (square sugar doughnuts) eaten with the traditional *café au lait* (made with chicory), as served in the morning at the Café du Monde in New Orleans, and *pain perdu,* an old French country recipe (stale bread soaked in milk, eggs, brandy, and lemon juice, and fried in butter). And don't miss paying your respects to *café brûlot* (black coffee with cognac flambé, lemon peel, cloves, cinnamon) and spices: "black as night, soft as love, and hot as hell," in the words of the poet.

Other Créole specialties include: *blackened redfish,* filets of red snapper broiled over a high flame till the outside is blackened, a very typical Cajun dish; *boudin,* pork-and-rice sausage, highly spiced (*boudin rouge* is seasoned blood-and-lard sausage); *Calas cakes,* little fried ricecakes flavored with cinnamon or orange-flower water (a standard New Orleans dessert); *crab Imperial, New Orleans style,* crabmeat, red pepper, and green onions, covered in a spicy mayonnaise and glazed in the oven (not to be confused with crab Imperial, Maryland style); *filet mignon debris,* a medium filet mignon covered in a rich brown sauce made with burgundy, cognac, and crisp little pieces of leftover roast beef, the debris of the name (a New Orleans specialty); *muffuletta,* the great Créole sandwich, served on a round roll and made with salami, mortadella, provolone, and ham, garnished with olives; *poor boy* (or *po' boy*), a New Orleans–style hero of roast beef, ham, or sausage.

MIDWESTERN CUISINE: This country of wide-open spaces and great herds of cattle is not distinguished for the originality of its cuisine, in spite of a flow of immigrants from Germany, Italy, and Scandinavia. The always-dependable dishes are *meat and potatoes* or *freshwater fish* from the region's lakes and rivers. The reputation of such restaurants as Morton's in Chicago, the Hereford House in Kansas City, and the Iowa Beef Steak House in Des Moines—to name only a few—rests on their red meats: *T-bone steak, sirloin* or *New York steak, rib-eye* or *Delmonico steak, porterhouse steak* or *chateaubriand, tournedos, filet mignon, top loin* or *shell steak*, etc., usually served with *french fries* or *baked potatoes*, of which the best are made from Idaho potatoes. (Idaho is "the Potato State.")

Other midwestern specialties are: *barbecued ribs*, spareribs brushed with barbecue sauce and cooked over an open fire of wood or charcoal till glazed (they have made the name of such restaurants as Carsons, in Skokie, Illinois); *deep-dish pizza*, which originated in Chicago, a pizza with a very thick, soft crust baked in a casserole; *five-way chili*, made with beans, spaghetti, chopped beef, onions, and cheese (comes from Cincinnati and should not be confused with Tex-Mex chili); *pan-fried chicken* (a specialty in Indiana, Missouri, and Ohio); *pasties* are turnovers filled with meat (Michigan); *sour-cream raisin pie*, a thick, creamy, raisin-filled cake covered in meringue (Indiana, Minnesota, and Wisconsin); persimmon pudding, made with the flavorful small native fruit (Indiana); and *toasted ravioli*, a specialty of St. Louis, is fried meat-filled ravioli.

SOUTHWESTERN CUISINE: Better known as Tex-Mex, this is essentially an adaptation of Mexican dishes (and particularly their explosive chili sauces) for the North American palate. Among the best-known dishes from this region north of the Rio Grande are *chili con carne* (chopped beef with red beans, minced onions, cumin or paprika, tomatoes, and chili); *tortillas* (flat cornmeal cakes used instead of bread); *frijoles refritos* (boiled beans mashed, seasoned with chili, and refried in a pan; traditional cowboy fare); *enchiladas* (tortillas stuffed with meat, beans, or cheese and baked in the oven); *tamales* (patties of chopped meat, cornmeal, and chili powder, steamed in a cornhusk); and *barbecue* (beef or pork brushed with a special spicy sauce and cooked over a wood or charcoal fire; usually eaten with corn on the cob). To wash it all down there's nothing better than a few generously proportioned *margaritas* (tequila and lime juice, served over crushed ice in a frosted glass whose rim has been dipped in salt).

Other southwestern specialties include: *carne adobada,* pork marinated in a chili sauce; *chicken-fried steak,* thin slices of steak floured and sautéed, a cowboy tradition; *chiles rellenos*, green peppers stuffed with meat or cheese, brushed with egg and fried; *hot links*, spicy Texan sausages broiled over a barbecue; *jerky*, air-dried beef (Oklahoma, Texas); *menudo*, tripe and cornmeal stew (New Mexico, Texas); *Rocky Mountain oysters*, fried bull's (although usually lamb's) testicles, a Colorado specialty; *sopaipilla*, fried honey-dipped bread served hot (Arizona, New Mexico).

WESTERN & NORTHWESTERN CUISINE: Geography and climate have endowed the Pacific coast, and particularly California, with an abundance of fine foodstuffs. *Dungeness crabs*, superb salmon (*chinook, king, coho, sockeye*), *Dolly Varden trout, Rex* and *Petrale* sole, halibut, tuna, anchovy, *geoduck clams* (great shellfish whose meat weighs up to 15 lb. (6.8 kg) served sliced and grilled as steak or chopped in tasty soup; a Washington state specialty), *razor clams*, turtles, oysters (*Olympia, Petit Points, Pigeon Points, Quilcene, Tamales Bay, Drakes Bay, Yakima Bay*, and others), and above all the delectable—but now strictly protected—*abalone* are its glories of seafood.

There are so many fruits and vegetables that it's hard to choose: *figs* in the San Joaquin Valley, *tomatoes* in the Sacramento Valley, *vineyards* in the Sonoma

30 □ FROMMER'S USA

and Napa Valleys, *avocados* in the San Diego Valley, *dates* in the Coachella Valley, *lettuce* and *melons* in Imperial Valley, are among the best in the country.

Two unexpected discoveries in the region: crusty, tasty, yeasty *sourdough bread* (the best is from San Francisco), and *chop suey,* a stew or stir-fry of meat, beansprouts, mushrooms, and celery, served with rice, country fare of the Chinese workers who helped to build the first California railroads. Failing chop suey, lovers of Chinese food can choose among thousands of Cantonese, Mandarin, Hunan, or Szechuan restaurants, most of them better than their counterparts in the Far East.

Other western specialties include: *artichoke soup* (from California); *barbecued salmon,* fresh marinated salmon cooked over hot coals or a wood fire (the great northwestern specialty); *Caesar salad,* romaine lettuce, chopped hard-boiled egg, toast croutons, anchovies, and Parmesan cheese; *cioppino,* seafood stew seasoned with spices, herbs, and fresh tomatoes; *crab (or shrimp) Louie,* salad made with lettuce, hard-boiled egg, crabmeat, and mayonnaise blended with chili sauce (found all along the Pacific coast); and *Hangtown Fry,* scrambled eggs with oysters (California, Washington).

FOR FURTHER READING

To attempt to present an overview of U.S. history, economics, politics, and culture in the space permitted in this introduction seems folly indeed. Instead, we have chosen to compile this selective booklist. Readers can pick and choose from the following titles in the areas that interest them, whether it be a history of the African Americans in America (*From Slavery to Freedom* by John Hope Franklin and Alfred Moss) or a recent novel about New York City in the '80s (*Bonfire of Vanities* by Tom Wolfe). Some titles, admittedly, may be difficult to find in bookshops, but all should be available in public libraries.

Economic, Political, and Social History

Acuno, Rodolfo. *Occupied America: A History of Chicanos* (2nd ed.).
Algren, Nelson. *Chicago: City on the Make.*
Bailyn, Bernard. *The Ideological Origins of the American Revolution.*
Beard, Charles M. *An Economic Interpretation of the Constitution of the United States.*
Becker, Carl L. *The Declaration of Independence: A Study of the History of Political Ideas.*
Birmingham, Stephen. *America's Secret Aristocracy.*
Boorstin, Daniel J. *The Exploring Spirit: America and the World, Then and Now.*
————. *The Americans* (3 vols.).
Brandon, William. *The Last American: The Indian in American Culture.*
Bridenbaugh, Carl, and Jessica Bridenbaugh. *Rebels and Gentlemen: Philadelphia in the Age of Franklin.*
Brown, Dee. *Bury My Heart at Wounded Knee: An Indian History of the American West.*
Burns, James MacGregor. *The Vineyard of Liberty.*
Cather, Willa. *My Antonia.*
Catton, Bruce, and the American Heritage Editors. *American Heritage Picture History of the Civil War.*
Chen, Jack. *The Chinese of America.*
Commager, Henry Steele, ed. *The American Destiny.*
Connell, Evan. *Son of Morning Star: Custer and the Little Big Horn.*
Cooke, Alistair. *The Americans: Fifty Talks on Our Life and Times.*
Dangerfield, George. *Awakening of American Nationalism, 1815–1828.*
De Voto, Bernard. *Course of Empire.*
Du Plessix Gray, Francine. *Hawaii, the Sugar-Coated Fortress.*
Edmonds, Walter D. *Drums Along the Mohawk.*
Fitzgerald, Frances. *Fire in the Lake: The Vietnamese and the Americans in Vietnam.*

Franklin, John Hope, and Alfred Moss. *From Slavery to Freedom: A History of Negro America.*
Galbraith, John Kenneth. *The Great Crash of 1929.*
Garreau, Joel. *The Nine Nations of North America.*
Genovese, Eugene D. *The Political Economy of Slavery: Studies in Economy and Society of the Slave South.*
Goldman, Eric. *Rendezvous with Destiny: A History of Modern American Reform.*
Goldman, Eric F. *The Crucial Decade and After: America, 1945–1960.*
Handlin, Oscar. *The Uprooted* (rev. ed.).
Hellman, Lillian. *Scoundrel Time.*
Hofstadter, Richard. *The Age of Reform: From Bryan to F.D.R.*
————. *The American Political Tradition and the Men Who Made It.*
Howe, Irving. *World of Our Fathers.*
Inge, M. Thomas, ed. *Handbook of American Popular Culture.*
Jordan, Winthrop D. *White over Black: American Attitudes Toward the Negro, 1550–1812.*
Lewis, David L. *When Harlem Was in Vogue.*
Lewis, Oscar. *La Vida: A Puerto Rican Family in the Culture of Poverty.*
Liebling, A. J. *Back Where I Come From.*
Marquis, Arnold. *Guide to America's Indians: Ceremonials, Reservations, and Museums.*
McPherson, James. *Battle Cry of Freedom.*
McPhee, John. *Coming into the Country.*
Mencken, H. L. *The American Language.*
Morison, Samuel Eliot. *The Growth of the American Republic.*
Parish, Peter J. *The American Civil War.*
Parrington, Vernon L. *Main Currents in American Thought.*
Rose, Al. *Storyville, New Orleans.*
Schlesinger, Arthur M., Jr. *The Age of Jackson.*
————. *The Rise of the City.*
Shannon, William V. *The American Irish.*
Terkel, Studs. *American Dreams: Lost and Found.*
————. *Division Street: America.*
————. *Hard Times: An Oral History of the Great Depression in America.*
Trudgill, Peter. *Coping with America* (2nd ed.).
Turner, Frederick J. *The Frontier in American History.*
Whitman, Walt. *Democratic Vistas and Other Papers.*
Williams, Juan. *Eyes on the Prize: America's Civil Rights Years, 1954–1965.*
Wilson, Edmund, and Joseph Mitchell. *Apologies to the Iroquois: With a Study of the Mohawks on High Street.*
Wilson, Robert A., and Bill Hosokawa. *East to America: A History of Japanese in the United States.*
Woodward, Bob, and Carl Bernstein. *All the President's Men.*
Woodward, C. Vann. *The Origins of the New South, 1877–1913.*
Zinn, Howard. *The Twentieth Century: A People's History.*

Art, Architecture, Photography, and Film
Adams, Ansel. *Classic Images.*
Agee, James. *Agee on Film.*
Baigell, Matthew. *Dictionary of American Art.*
Barnouw, Erik. *Tube of Plenty: The Evolution of American Television* (rev. ed.).
Everson, William. *American Silent Film.*
Goldberger, Paul. *The City Observed: New York. A Guide to the Architecture of Manhattan.*
Highwater, Jamake. *Song from the Earth: American Indian Painting.*
Jacobs, Jane. *The Death and Life of Great American Cities.*

Jacobs, Lewis. *The Rise of the American Film.*
Kael, Pauline. *Deeper into the Movies.*
Kidder-Smith, G. E. *The Architecture of the United States.*
Larkin, Oliver W. *Art and Life in America.*
Mumford, Lewis. *The Culture of Cities.*
Novotny, Ann. *Alice's World: The Life and Photography of an American Original: Alice Austin, 1866–1952.*
Rifkind, Carole. *A Field Guide to American Architecture.*
Rose, Barbara. *American Art Since 1900* (rev. and expanded ed.).
Sklar, Robert. *Movie-Made America: A Cultural History of American Movies.*
Steichen, Edward. *Steichen: A Life in Photography.*
Trachtenberg, Allan. *America and Lewis Hine.*

Fiction, Poetry, Theater, and Travel
Adams, Henry. *The Education of Henry Adams.*
Baldwin, James. *Go Tell It on the Mountain.*
Bellow, Saul. *The Adventures of Augie March.*
Brooks, Van Wyck. *The Flowering of New England, 1815–65.*
Chandler, Raymond. *The Raymond Chandler Omnibus.*
Cooper, James Fenimore. *The Last of the Mohicans.*
——————. *The Deerslayer.*
Crane, Stephen. *The Red Badge of Courage.*
Dickens, Charles. *American Notes.*
Dickinson, Emily. *Collected Poems of Emily Dickinson.*
Doctorow, E. L. *Ragtime.*
Dos Passos, John. *USA.*
Dreiser, Theodore. *Sister Carrie.*
Ehrlich, Eugene, and Gorton Carruth. *The Oxford Illustrated Literary Guide to the United States.*
Ellison, Ralph. *The Invisible Man.*
Faulkner, William. *The Sound and the Fury.*
——————. *Absalom! Absalom!.*
Fitzgerald, F. Scott. *The Great Gatsby.*
Garland, Hamlin. *Main Travelled Roads.*
Hammett, Dashiell. *The Maltese Falcon.*
Harte, Bret. *The Outcasts of Poker Flat.*
Hawthorne, Nathaniel. *The Scarlet Letter.*
Hecht, Ben. *The Collected Stories of Ben Hecht.*
Hemingway, Ernest. *In Our Time.*
Howells, William Dean. *The Rise of Silas Lapham.*
Irving, Washington. *Diedrich Knickerbocker's A History of New York.*
James, Henry. *The American Scene.*
——————. *The Bostonians.*
Kerouac, Jack. *On the Road.*
Kingston, Maxine Hong. *The Woman Warrior: Memories of a Girlhood Among Ghosts.*
La Farge, Oliver. *Laughing Boy.*
Lee, Harper. *To Kill a Mockingbird.*
London, Jack. *Call of the Wild.*
MacDonald, Ross. *The Underground Man.*
Mailer, Norman. *The Deer Park.*
McInerney, Jay. *Bright Lights, Big City.*
Melville, Herman. *Bartleby the Scrivener.*
Michener, James A. *Hawaii.*
Mitchell, Margaret. *Gone with the Wind.*
Moon, William Least Heat. *Blue Highways: A Journey into America.*
Morris, Jan. *Manhattan '45.*
Mukherjee, Bharati. *Darkness.*

Norris, Frank. *McTeague: A Story of San Francisco.*
Raban, Jonathan. *Old Glory: An American Voyage.*
Reeves, Richard. *American Journey: Traveling with Tocqueville in Search of Democracy in America.*
Roth, Philip. *Portnoy's Complaint.*
Runyon, Damon. *Guys and Dolls.*
Sinclair, Upton. *The Jungle.*
Steffens, Lincoln. *The Shame of Cities.*
Stein, Gertrude. *The Making of Americans.*
Steinbeck, John. *The Grapes of Wrath.*
————. *Travels with Charley in Search of America.*
Stevenson, Robert Louis. *Travels in Hawaii.*
Twain, Mark. *The Adventures of Huckleberry Finn.*
————. *Roughing It.*
Updike, John. *Rabbit Run.*
Walker, Alice. *The Color Purple.*
Warren, Robert Penn. *All the King's Men.*
West, Nathanael. *The Day of the Locust.*
Wharton, Edith. *The Age of Innocence.*
White, E. B. *Here Is New York.*
White, Edmund. *States of Desire: Travels in Gay America.*
Whitman, Walt. *Leaves of Grass.*
Wilder, Thornton. *Our Town.*
Williams, Tennessee. *Cat on a Hot Tin Roof.*
Wilson, Edmund. *Patriotic Gore: Studies in the Literature of the American Civil War.*
Wright, Richard. *Native Son.*

Biography
Amory, Cleveland. *The Proper Bostonians.*
Burns, James MacGregor. *Roosevelt: The Lion and the Fox.*
Flexner, James Thomas. *Washington: The Indispensable Man.*
Goodwin, Doris Kearns. *Lyndon Johnson and the American Dream.*
Hecht, Ben. *Child of the Century.*
Link, Arthur S. *Woodrow Wilson and the Progressive Era, 1910–1917.*
McCullough, David. *Mornings on Horseback.*
Miller, Merle. *Plain Speaking: An Oral Biography of Harry S Truman.*
Morris, Edmund. *The Rise of Theodore Roosevelt.*
Padover, Saul. *Jefferson.*
Sandburg, Carl. *Abraham Lincoln: The Prairie Years and the War Years.*
Schlesinger, Arthur M., Jr. *A Thousand Days.*
Van Doren, Carl C. *Benjamin Franklin.*
Vidal, Gore. *Lincoln.*

FOR THE
FOREIGN VISITOR

□ □ □

Although American fads and fashions have spread across Europe and other parts of the world so that America may seem like familiar territory before your arrival, there are still many peculiarities and uniquely American situations that any foreign visitor will encounter. This chapter is meant to clue you in on what they are. International visitors should also read the Introduction carefully.

PREPARING FOR YOUR TRIP

DOCUMENT REGULATIONS: Canadian citizens may enter the U.S. without visas; they need only proof of residence.

British, Dutch, French, German, Italian, Japanese, Swedish, and Swiss citizens traveling on valid national (or EC) passports do not need a visa for holiday or business travel in the U.S. of 90 days or less if they hold round-trip or return tickets and if they enter the U.S. on an airline or cruise line that participates in the no-visa travel program.

(Note that citizens of these visa-exempt countries who first enter the U.S. may then visit Mexico, Canada, Bermuda, and/or the Caribbean islands and then reenter the U.S., by any mode of transportation, without needing a visa. Further information is available from any U.S. embassy or consulate.)

Citizens of countries other than those above require:

□ a valid **passport,** with an expiration date at least 6 months later than the scheduled end of the visit to the U.S.; and

□ a **tourist visa,** available without charge from the nearest U.S. consulate; the traveler must submit a completed application form (either in person or by mail) with a passport photograph attached.

Usually you will be given your visa at once, or within 24 hr. at most; try to avoid the summer rush in June–Aug. If applying by mail, enclose a large stamped, self-addressed envelope, and expect an average wait of 2 weeks. Visa application forms are also available at airline offices or from leading travel agents as well as from U.S. consulates. The U.S. tourist visa (visa B-2) is theoretically valid for a year, and for any number of entries, but the U.S. consulate that gives you the tourist visa will determine the length of stay for a multiple- or single-entry visa. However, there is some latitude here, and if you are of good appearance and can give the address of a relative, friend, or business connection living in the U.S. (useful, too, for car rental, passage through Customs, etc.), you have an excellent chance of getting a longer permit if you want one.

MEDICAL REQUIREMENTS: No inoculations are needed to enter the U.S. unless you are coming from areas known to be suffering from epidemics, especially of cholera or yellow fever. Applicants for immigrants' visas (and only they) must undergo a screening test for AIDS under a law passed in 1987.

If you have a disease requiring treatment with medications containing controlled drugs, carry a valid, signed prescription from your physician to allay any suspicions that you are smuggling drugs. Ditto for syringes.

TRAVEL INSURANCE (BAGGAGE, HEALTH & LOSS): All such insurance is voluntary in the U.S.; however, given the very high cost of medical care, I cannot too strongly advise every traveler to arrange for appropriate coverage before setting out. There are specialized insurance companies that will, for a relatively low premium, cover:

□ loss or theft of your baggage;
□ trip-cancellation costs;
□ guarantee of bail in case you are sued;
□ sickness or injury costs (medical, surgical, and hospital);
□ costs of an accident, repatriation, or death.

Such packages (for example, "Europe Assistance" in Europe) are sold by automobile clubs at attractive rates, as well as by banks and travel agencies.

GETTING TO THE U.S.

Travelers from overseas can take advantage of the **APEX (Advance Purchase Excursion) fares** offered by all the major U.S. and European carriers. Aside from these, attractive values are offered by **Icelandair** on flights from Luxembourg to New York or Orlando; and by **Virgin Atlantic** from London to New York/Newark or Miami.

Some large airlines (for example, TWA, American, Northwest, United, and Delta) offer travelers on their transatlantic or transpacific flights special discount tickets under the name **Visit USA,** allowing travel between any U.S. destinations at minimum rates. They are not on sale in the U.S., and must therefore be purchased before you leave your foreign point of departure. This system is the best way of seeing the U.S. at low cost. You should obtain information well in advance from your travel agent or the office of the airline concerned, since the conditions attached to these discount tickets can be changed without advance notice.

GETTING AROUND

For information on transportation around the U.S., see the "Notes for Foreign Visitors" sections in the Introduction under the modes of transportation.

FAST FACTS FOR THE FOREIGN TRAVELER

ACCOMMODATIONS: See the Introduction.

AUTOMOBILE ORGANIZATIONS: See "Getting Around—By Car," in the Introduction.

BUSINESS HOURS: Public and private **offices** are usually open 9am–5pm Mon–Fri, except in Hawaii and parts of California (7:30 or 8am–4pm).

Banking hours are generally 9am–3pm Mon–Fri, but in some cases till 6pm on Fri, and sometimes also on Sat morning.

Post offices are open 8am–5:30 or 6pm Mon–Fri and 8am–noon on Sat.

Store hours are 9:30 or 10am–5:30 or 6pm Mon–Sat, though often till 9pm one or two evenings a week. Shopping centers, drugstores, and supermarkets are open 9am–9pm 6 days a week (7 days, and even in some cases 24 hr., in certain large cities).

Museum hours vary widely. The norm for big cities is 10am–5pm 6 days a week (closing day is usually Mon). Some art museums stay open till 9pm one or, rarely, two evenings a week.

CLIMATE: Any season is a good time for travel in the U.S.—provided you understand how to juggle climates and distances! Summer is hot and humid in the

East and the Southeast from New York to Louisiana. From Texas to California it can be scorching—95° F (35°C) in the shade is not unusual. On the other hand, it's a delightful time to visit the Northwest and the Rockies. Winter is severe across the North and a good deal of the Central Tier—the mercury often goes down to 10°–15°F(−12° to −9.5°C) in Chicago and Denver—but very agreeable in Florida and California. From coast to coast, the best seasons for travel are spring and (even more) fall, which can be very mild during the "Indian Summer." See the table of average temperatures for representative cities in the Introduction.

CURRENCY & EXCHANGE: The U.S. monetary system has a decimal base: one **dollar** ($1) = 100 **cents** (100¢).

The commonest **bills** (all green) are the $1 ("a buck"), $5, $10, and $20 denominations. There are also $2 (seldom encountered), $50, and $100 bills (the two latter are not welcome when paying for small purchases).

There are six denominations of **coins:** 1¢ (one cent, or "penny"); 5¢ (five cents, or "nickel"); 10¢ (ten cents, or "dime"); 25¢ (twenty-five cents, or "quarter"); 50¢ (fifty cents, or "half dollar"); and rare—and prized by collectors—the $1 piece (both the older, large silver dollars and the newer, small Susan B. Anthony coin).

Traveler's Checks and Credit Cards

Traveler's checks denominated in *dollars* are accepted without demur at most hotels, motels, restaurants, and large stores. But as any experienced traveler knows, the best place to change traveler's checks is at a bank.

However, the method of payment most widely used is the **credit card:** VISA (BarclayCard in Britain, Chargex in Canada), MasterCard (EuroCard in Europe, Access in Britain, Diamond in Japan, etc.), American Express, Diners Club, and Carte Blanche, in descending order of acceptance. You can save yourself trouble by using "plastic money," rather than cash or traveler's checks, in 95% of all hotels, motels, restaurants, and retail stores (except for those selling food or liquor). A credit card can serve as a deposit when renting a car, as proof of identity (often carrying more weight than a passport), or as a "cash card," enabling you to draw money from banks that accept them.

Note: The "foreign-exchange bureaus" so common in Europe are rare even at airports in the U.S., and nonexistent outside major cities. Try to avoid having to change foreign money, or traveler's checks denominated other than in U.S. dollars, at a small-town bank, or even a branch bank in a big city; in fact, leave any currency other than U.S. dollars at home—it may prove more nuisance to you than it's worth.

CUSTOMS & IMMIGRATION: Every adult visitor may bring in, free of duty: 1 liter of wine or hard liquor; 200 cigarettes or 100 cigars (but *no* cigars from Cuba) or 3 lb. (1.35kg) of smoking tobacco; $400 worth of gifts. These exemptions are offered to travelers who spend at least 72 hr. in the U.S. and who have not claimed them within the preceding 6 months. It is altogether forbidden to bring into the country foodstuffs (particularly cheese, fruit, cooked meats, and canned goods) and plants (vegetables, seeds, tropical plants, etc.). Foreign tourists may bring in or take out up to $10,000 in U.S. or foreign currency with no formalities; larger sums must be declared to Customs on entering or leaving.

The visitor arriving by air, no matter what the port of entry—New York, Boston, Miami, Honolulu, Los Angeles, or the rest—should cultivate patience and resignation before setting foot on U.S. soil. The U.S. Customs and Immigration Services are among the slowest and most suspicious on earth. On some days, especially summer weekends, you may wait to have your passport stamped at Miami or New York's John F. Kennedy Airport for nearly 2 hr., sometimes 3 hr. The situation is just as bad at other major international airports. Add the time it takes to clear Customs and you will see that you should make very generous allowance for delay in planning connections between international and domestic flights—an average of 2–3 hr. at least.

In contrast, for the traveler arriving by car or by rail from Canada, the border-crossing formalities have been streamlined to the vanishing point. And for the traveler by air from Canada, Bermuda, and some points in the Caribbean, you can go through Customs and Immigration at the point of *departure*, which is much quicker and less painful.

DRINKING LAWS: As with marriage and divorce, every state, and sometimes every county and community, has its own laws governing the sale of liquor. The only federal regulation (based on a judgment of the U.S. Supreme Court on June 23, 1987) restricts the consumption of liquor in public places anywhere in the country to persons aged 21 or over (states not respecting this rule may be penalized by a withdrawal of federal highway funds).

Hours of operation for liquor stores, as well as for bars and nightclubs, are strictly limited in certain states; in most, establishments selling liquor are closed Sun and public holidays. In Alabama, Maine, New Hampshire, Ohio, Oregon, Pennsylvania, Utah, and Vermont, liquor may be sold by the bottle only in state-owned outlets.

Not all restaurants are licensed to serve beer, wine, or hard liquor, though you may generally bring your drink with you. As far as possible, restaurants not having beverage licenses are noted as such in this book.

ELECTRIC CURRENT: U.S. wall outlets give power at 110–115 volts, 60 cycles, compared to 220 volts, 50 cycles, in most of Europe. Besides a 110-volt converter, small appliances of non-American manufacture, such as hairdryers or shavers, will require a plug adapter with two flat, parallel pins.

EMBASSIES & CONSULATES: All embassies are located in the national capital, Washington, D.C.; some consulates are located in major cities, and most nations have a mission to the United Nations in New York City.

Listed here are the embassies and consulates of the major English-speaking countries—Australia, Canada, Ireland, New Zealand, and the United Kingdom. If you are from another country, you can get the telephone number of your embassy by calling "information" in Washington, D.C. (202/555-1212).

Australia

EMBASSY 1601 Massachusetts Ave. NW, Washington, DC 20036 (202/797-3000).

CONSULATES Chicago—Quaker Tower, 321 N. Clark St., Suite 2930, IL 60610 (312/645-9440). **Honolulu**—1000 Bishop St., Penthouse, HI 96813 (808/524-5050). **Houston**—3 Post Oak Central A.H., 1990 Post Oak Rd., Suite 800, TX 77056 (713/629-9131 or 520-3179). **Los Angeles**—611 N. Larchmont Blvd., CA 90004 (213/469-4300). **New York**—International Building, 636 Fifth Ave., NY 10111 (212/245-4000). **San Francisco**—360 Post St., CA 94108 (415/362-6160).

Canada

EMBASSY 501 Pennsylvania Ave. NW, Washington, DC 20001 (202/682-1740).

CONSULATES Atlanta—One CNN Center, Suite 400 South Tower, GA 30303 (404/577-6810). **Boston**—3 Copley Pl., Suite 400, MA 02116 (617/536-

1731). **Buffalo**—One Marine Midland Center, Suite 3550, NY 14203 (716/825-1345). **Chicago**—310 S. Michigan Ave., Suite 1200, IL 60604 (312/427-1031). **Cleveland**—Illuminating Bldg., 55 Public Sq., OH 44113 (216/771-0150). **Dallas**—St. Paul Place, 750 N. St. Paul, Suite 1700, TX 75201 (214/922-9811). **Detroit**—660 Renaissance Center, Suite 1100, MI 48243 (313/567-2340). **Los Angeles**—300 S. Grand Ave., 10th Floor, CA 90071 (213/687-7432). **Minneapolis**—701 Fourth Ave. South, MN 55415 (612/333-4641). **New York**—1251 Ave. of the Americas, NY 10020 (212/586-2400). **San Francisco**—One Maritime Plaza, Golden Gateway Center, CA 94111 (415/981-8541). **Seattle**—412 Plaza 600, Sixth and Stewart, WA 98101 (206/443-1777).

Ireland

EMBASSY 2234 Massachusetts Ave. NW, Washington, DC 20008 (202/462-3939).

CONSULATES Boston—Chase Bldg., 535 Boylston St., MA 02116 (617/267-9330). **Chicago**—400 N. Michigan Ave., IL 60611 (312/337-1868). **New York**—515 Madison Ave., NY 10022 (212/319-2555). **San Francisco**—655 Montgomery St., Suite 930, CA 94111 (415/392-4214).

New Zealand

EMBASSY 37 Observatory Circle NW, Washington, DC 20008 (202/328-4800).

CONSULATES Los Angeles—Tishman Bldg., 10960 Wilshire Blvd., Suite 1530, Westwood, CA 90024 (213/477-8241).

United Kingdom

EMBASSY 3100 Massachusetts Ave. NW, Washington, DC 20008 (202/462-1340).

CONSULATES Atlanta—245 Peachtree Center Ave., Suite 912, GA 30303 (404/524-5856). **Chicago**—33 N. Dearborn St., IL 60602 (312/346-1810). **Houston**—601 Jefferson, Suite 2250, TX 77002 (713/659-6270). **Los Angeles**—3701 Wilshire Blvd., Suite 312, CA 90010 (213/385-7381). **New York**—845 Third Ave., NY 10022 (212/752-8400).

EMERGENCIES: In all major cities you can call the police, an ambulance, or the fire brigade through the single emergency telephone number **911.** Another useful way of reporting an emergency is to call the telephone-company operator by dialing **0** (zero, *not* the letter "O"). Outside major cities, call the county sheriff or the fire brigade at the number you will find in the local telephone book.

   If you encounter such travelers' problems as sickness, accident, or lost or stolen baggage, it will pay you to call **Travelers' Aid,** an organization which specializes in helping distressed travelers, whether American or foreign. Check the local telephone book for the nearest office, or dial 0 (zero) and ask the telephone operator.

HOLIDAYS: On the following legal national holidays, banks, government offices, post offices, and many stores, restaurants, and museums are closed:

January 1 (New Year's Day)
Third Monday in January (Martin Luther King Day)
Third Monday in February (Presidents Day, Washington's Birthday)
Last Monday in May (Memorial Day)
July 4 (Independence Day)
First Monday in September (Labor Day)
Second Monday in October (Columbus Day)
November 11 (Veteran's Day/Armistice Day)
Last Thursday in November (Thanksgiving Day)
December 25 (Christmas Day)

Also celebrated in some cities and states are the following:

February 12 (in the North) (Lincoln's Birthday)
March 17 (St. Patrick's Day)
April 19 (Patriot's Day)

In addition, many states and cities have their own special holidays.

Finally, the Tuesday following the first Monday in November is Election Day, and is a legal holiday in presidential-election years.

INFORMATION: See the opening of each chapter and the Appendix for a list of state tourism information offices.

LEGAL AID: The foreign tourist, unless positively identified as a member of the Mafia or of a drug ring, will probably never become involved with the American legal system. If you are pulled up for a minor infraction (for example, of the highway code, such as speeding), never attempt to pay the fine directly to a police officer; you may wind up arrested on the much more serious charge of attempted bribery. Pay fines by mail, or directly into the hands of the clerk of the court. If accused of a more serious offense, it is wise to say and do nothing before consulting a lawyer. Under U.S. law, an arrested person is allowed one telephone call to a party of his choice. Call your embassy or consulate.

MAIL: If you want your mail to follow you on your vacation, you need only fill out a change-of-address card at any post office. The post office will also hold your mail for up to 1 month. If you aren't sure of your address, your mail can be sent to you, in your name, **c/o General Delivery** at the main post office of the city or region where you expect to be. The addressee must pick it up in person, and produce proof of identity (driver's license, credit card, passport, etc.).

Generally to be found at intersections, mailboxes are blue with a red-and-white stripe, and carry the inscription "U.S. MAIL." If your mail is addressed to a U.S. destination, don't forget to add the five-figure postal code or ZIP (Zone Improvement Plan) Code, after the two-letter abbreviation of the state to which the mail is addressed (CA for California, MA for Massachusetts, NY for New York, and so on).

MEASUREMENTS: While most of the rest of the world is on the metric system, for nonscientific purposes the United States still adheres to its own units of measurement. See the Appendix for tables that will help you with conversions, for both standard metric measurements and clothing and shoe sizes.

MEDICAL EMERGENCIES: See "Emergencies," above.

NEWSPAPERS AND MAGAZINES: With a few exceptions, such as the *New York Times, USA Today,* the *Wall Street Journal,* and the *Christian Science Monitor,* daily newspapers in the U.S. are local, not national. Most large cities have at least two daily papers, of which the most important, after those mentioned above, are the *Washington Post*, the *Chicago Tribune*, and the *Los Angeles Times*. These papers are much larger than the great dailies of Europe or Australia; their Sunday editions can weigh 6–7 lb. (2.75–3.2 kg).

There are also innumerable newsweeklies like *Newsweek, Time, U.S. News & World Report*, and specialized periodicals, such as the monthly magazines each devoted to a single city—*New York* magazine (weekly), *Chicago* magazine, *Los Angeles* magazine, *The Washingtonian*—ideal starting points for your voyage of discovery into the city concerned.

The airmail editions of foreign newspapers and magazines are on sale only belatedly, and only at the airports and international bookstores in the largest U.S. cities.

POST: See "Mail."

RADIO & TELEVISION: Audiovisual media, with three coast-to-coast networks—ABC, CBS, and NBC—joined in recent years by the Public Broadcasting System (PBS) and the cable network CNN, play a major part in American life. In the big cities, televiewers have a choice of about a dozen channels (including the UHF channels), most of them transmitting 24 hr. a day, without counting the pay-TV channels showing recent movies or sports events. In smaller communities the choice may be limited to four TV channels (there are 1,200 in the entire country), and a half dozen local radio stations (there are 6,500 in all), each broadcasting a particular kind of music—classical, country, jazz, pop, gospel—punctuated by news broadcasts and frequent commercials.

SAFETY: In general, the U.S. is safer than most other countries, particularly in rural areas, but there are "danger zones" in the big cities, pinpointed in this guide, which should be approached only with extreme caution.

As a general rule, isolated areas such as gardens and parking lots should be avoided after dark. Elevators and public-transport systems in off-hours, particularly between 10pm and 6am, are also potential crime scenes. You should drive through decaying neighborhoods with your car doors locked and the windows closed. Never carry on your person valuables like jewelry or large sums of cash; traveler's checks are much safer.

TAXES: In the U.S. there is no VAT (Value-Added Tax), or other indirect tax at a national level. Every state, and each city in it, has the right to levy its own local tax on all purchases, including hotel and restaurant checks, airline tickets, etc. It is automatically added to the price of certain services such as public transportation, cab fares, phone calls, and gasoline. It varies from 4% to 10% depending on the state and city, so when you are making major purchases such as photographic equipment, clothing, or high-fidelity components, it can be a significant part of the cost.

Each locality also has the right to levy its own separate tax on hotel occupancy. Since this tax is in addition to any general sales tax, taken together these two taxes can add a considerable amount to the basic cost of your accommodations.

The table below shows the rate of sales tax and hotel tax for certain major cities:

City	Sales Tax	Hotel Tax
Atlanta	5.00%	6.00%
Boston	5.50%	5.50%

Chicago	8.00%	8.00%
Dallas	8.00%	8.00%
Denver	7.00%	11.00%
Los Angeles	7.00%	12.00%
Miami	5.00%	5.00%
New Orleans	9.00%	9.00%
New York	8.25%	13.25%
Philadelphia	6.00%	6.00%
San Francisco	6.50%	11.00%
Washington, D.C.	6.00%	8.00%

TELEPHONE, TELEGRAPH, TELEX: Pay phones are an integral part of the American landscape. You will find them everywhere: at street corners; in bars, restaurants, public buildings, stores, service stations; along highways; etc. Outside the metropolitan areas public telephones are more difficult to find. Stores and gas stations are your best bet.

Unlike the mail and the railroads, the telephone is not a public-service system. It is run by private corporations, which perhaps explains its high standard of service. Throughout the country it is almost completely automated, and local calls cost only 20¢–30¢.

For **long-distance or international calls,** stock up with a supply of quarters; the pay phone will instruct you when, and in what quantity, you should put them into the slot. For direct overseas calls, first dial 011, followed by the country code (Australia, 61; New Zealand, 64; United Kingdom, 44; and so on), and then by the city code and the number of the person you wish to call. For Canada and long-distance calls in the U.S., dial 1 followed by the area code and number you want.

Before calling from a hotel room, always ask the hotel phone operator if there are any telephone surcharges. These are best avoided by using a public phone, calling collect, or using a telephone charge card.

For **reversed-charge or collect calls,** and for **person-to-person calls,** dial 0 (zero, *not* the letter "O") followed by the area code and number you want; an operator will then come on the line, and you should specify that you are calling collect, or person-to-person, or both. If your operator-assisted call is international, ask for the overseas operator.

For local **directory assistance** ("information"), dial 411; for **long-distance information,** dial 1, then the appropriate area code and 555-1212.

Like the telephone system, **telegraph and telex** services are provided by private corporations like ITT, MCI, and above all, Western Union, the most important. You can bring your telegram in to the nearest Western Union office (there are hundreds across the country), or dictate it over the phone (a toll-free call, 800/325-6000). You can also telegraph money, or have it telegraphed to you, very quickly over the Western Union system.

TELEPHONE DIRECTORY: See "Yellow Pages," below.

TIME: The U.S. is divided into four **time zones** (six, if Alaska and Hawaii are included). From east to west, these are: eastern standard time (EST), central standard time (CST), mountain standard time (MST), Pacific standard time (PST),

Alaska standard time (AST), and Hawaii standard time (HST). Always keep changing time zones in mind if you are traveling (or even telephoning) long distances in the U.S. For example, noon in New York City (EST) is 11am in Chicago (CST), 10am in Denver (MST), 9am in Los Angeles (PST), 8am in Anchorage (AST), and 7am in Honolulu (HST).

Daylight saving time is in effect from the last Sun in April through the last Sat in Oct (actually, the change is made at 2am on Sun) except in Arizona, Hawaii, part of Indiana, and Puerto Rico. Daylight saving time moves the clock 1 hr. ahead of standard time.

TIPPING: This is part of the American way of life, on the principle that you must expect to pay for any service you get. Here are some rules of thumb:

Bartenders: 10%–15%.
Bellhops: at least 50¢ per piece; $2–$3 for a lot of baggage.
Cab drivers: 15% of the fare (20% in large cities).
Cafeterias, fast-food restaurants: no tip.
Chambermaids: $1 a day; more in big-city hotels.
Cinemas, movies, theaters: no tip.
Checkroom attendants (restaurants, theaters): 50¢ a garment; $1 in large cities.
Doormen (hotels or restaurants): not obligatory, but $1 at top hotels.
Gas-station attendants: no tip.
Hairdressers: 15%–20%.
Parking-lot attendant: 50¢ ($1 in hotels).
Redcaps (airport and railroad station): at least 50¢ per piece; $2–$3 for a lot of baggage.
Restaurants, nightclubs: 15%–20% of the check.
Sleeping-car porters: $2–$3 per night to your attendant.

TOILETS: Foreign visitors often complain that public toilets are hard to find in most U.S. cities. True, there are none on the streets, but the visitor can usually find one in a bar, restaurant, hotel, museum, department store, or service station —and it will probably be clean (although the last-mentioned sometimes leaves much to be desired). Note, however, a growing practice in some restaurants and bars of displaying a notice that "toilets are for the use of patrons only." You can ignore this sign, or better yet, avoid arguments by paying for a cup of coffee or soft drink which will qualify you as a patron. The cleanliness of toilets at railroad stations and bus depots may be more open to question, and some public places are equipped with pay toilets, which require you to insert one or two 10¢ coins (dimes) into a slot on the door before it will open.

YELLOW PAGES: There are two kinds of telephone directory available to you. The general directory is the so-called **White Pages,** in which private and business subscribers are listed in alphabetical order. The inside front cover lists the emergency number for police, fire, and ambulance, and other vital numbers (like the Coast Guard, poison-control center, crime-victims hotline, etc.). The first few pages are devoted to community service numbers, including a guide to long-distance and international calling, complete with country codes and area codes.

The second directory, printed on yellow paper (whence its name, *Yellow Pages*), lists all local services, businesses, and industries by type of activity, with an index at the back. The listings cover not only such obvious items as automobile repairs by make of car, or drugstores (pharmacies), often by geographical location, but also restaurants by type of cuisine and geographical location, bookstores by special subject and/or language, places of worship by religious denomination, and other information that the tourist might otherwise not readily find. The *Yellow Pages* also include city plans or detailed area maps, often showing postal ZIP Codes and public transportation routes.

PART ONE

THE NORTHEAST AND MID-ATLANTIC

CHAPTER 1

BOSTON

□ □ □

Cradle of American puritanism and the largest city in New England, Boston has played a starring role in U.S. history since the 17th century. In 1630 a group of 800 English colonists led by governor-to-be John Winthrop landed at **Charlestown,** on the north shore of the Charles River. During the following months the settlers acquired the south shore and moved there, on what is now **Beacon Hill.** They established a village of fishermen, craftsmen, and fur traders (commerce with the Native Americans flourished for a long time) known originally as **Tremont** because of its three hills. But the new arrivals, being loyal subjects of His Majesty, quickly renamed the town Boston, after their small Lincolnshire birthplace. Boston was the scene of the 1770 revolt against British rule (the Boston Massacre), which snowballed into the 1773 Boston Tea Party. And nearby **Lexington, Concord,** and **Bunker Hill** became the theater two years later for the first major battles against British colonialism. After its 1776 liberation by George Washington, Boston grew and prospered, quickly becoming the third-largest American city, with a population of 93,000 in 1840, 360,000 in 1890, and more than 500,000 in 1914. After World War I the city passed through almost four decades of eclipse, suffering economic setbacks and political and racial conflicts. The city lost a third of its inhabitants during this troubled time.

In the early 1960s, the capital of Massachusetts initiated an exemplary urban-renewal plan. Witness the **Government Center,** with its futurist architecture; the sweeping gray-green silhouette of the **John Hancock Tower,** designed by I.M. Pei (62 stories: 790 ft., 243m); as well as the new business district near the harbor. Boston's renaissance coincided, not accidentally, with the presidency of one of the city's most illustrious sons, John Fitzgerald Kennedy, the first Roman Catholic president in the country's history.

With the possible exception of New York, Boston has produced more noteworthy politicians, writers, and intellectuals than any other U.S. city: from Paul Revere to Ralph Waldo Emerson, from John Hancock to John Adams, from Benjamin Franklin to Samuel Morse (inventor of the telegraph), and from Edgar Allan Poe to architect Louis Sullivan and actor Jack Lemmon. Boston also prides itself on the first American newspaper, the *Boston Newsletter,* published by postmaster John Campbell from 1704 to 1776.

Taking pride, as it understandably does, in its glorious history, Boston is the most European of American cities. If you follow the red arrows of the **Freedom Trail** along the small, winding downtown streets, you will encounter all the landmarks of Boston life over 350 years: the venerable **Boston Common,** the country's first public park (1634); charming **Faneuil Hall,** known as "the cradle of American liberty"; the one-time British governor's mansion (**Old State House**); the elegant patrician homes of **Beacon Hill;** and the old red-brick houses of the **North End,** a once-seedy area now the heart of picturesque Little Italy, with Italian food stores, cafés, and restaurants. Some old Boston buildings, like the **Paul Revere House** (1677), are among the oldest still standing in the country. Important waves of immigrants (mostly Roman Catholic)—especially Irish, but also Italian, Polish, and more recently, Puerto Rican—have transformed this sanctuary of American puritanism into a vast, expanding industrial center (navy yards, electronics, machine tools, clothing), a port city, and a very active university town: one Bostonian in six is a student. Home of two of the world's most prestigious universities—**Harvard,** which recently celebrated its 350th anniversary, and the **Massachusetts Institute of Technology (M.I.T.)**—a world-renowned symphony orchestra, countless museums, libraries, and more, Boston is, not surprisingly, still referred to as "the Athens of North America." Since the 1988 opening of the unsightly **J. B. Hynes Veterans Memorial Convention Center,** Boston has joined the list of leading convention cities in the U.S., with 14,000 hotel rooms and nine million visitors a year.

BASIC FACTS: Capital of the state of Massachusetts. Area code: 617. Time zone: eastern. ZIP Code (of central post office): 02109. Founded: 1630. Approximate population: city, 580,000; metropolitan area, 4,100,000. Seventh-largest metropolitan area in the U.S.

CLIMATE: Except for a brief and sunny spring, Boston's climate is less than ideal. Summer is heavy with humidity (mean July temperature, 72°F, 22°C), and winter is freezing and snow-covered (mean Jan. temperature, 29°F, −2°C). Outside of spring, the best time to visit Boston is during the chilly but clear days of autumn.

DISTANCES: Chicago, 965 mi. (1,545km); Montréal, 318 mi. (508km); New York, 209 mi. (335km); Niagara Falls, 480 mi. (768km); Washington, 431 mi. (690km).

ARRIVAL & TRANSIT INFORMATION

AIRPORT: Logan International Airport (BOS): 3 mi. (5km) east. Information: toll free 800/235-6426. Ranks worst in on-time arrivals among major U.S. airports.

DOMESTIC AIRLINES: American (542-6700), Bar Harbor (262-3700), Continental (569-8400), Delta (567-4100), Eastern (262-3700), Midway (toll free 800/621-5700), Northwest (267-4885), Pan Am (toll free 800/221-1111), Trump Air (toll free 800/247-8786), TWA (367-2800), United (482-7900), and USAir (482-3160).

FOREIGN CARRIERS: Aer Lingus (toll free 800/223-6537), Air Canada (toll free 800/422-6232), British Airways (toll free 800/247-9297), Lufthansa (toll free 800/645-3880), and Swissair (423-7778).

CITY LINK: Cab fare to city center, about $10–$12; time, 20–25 min. Bus: Airways Transportation Co. (267-2981); leaves every 30 min.; serves major dwntwn hotels; fare, $5.50; time, 25–30 min. There is a not-too-convenient dwntwn connection by subway (MBTA Blue Line). Taxi Boat: Airport Water Shuttle (328-0600) motorboat service to two dwntwn quays, Long Wharf and Rowes Wharf; time, 7 min.; leaves every 15 min.; fare, $7. Helicopter: Hub Express (toll free 800/962-4744) runs a regular hourly schedule between the main terminal at Logan Airport and six heliports in the suburbs and in the downtown financial district; fare, $45–$55; time, 5–20 min. Unless you are planning some East Coast excursions, the proximity of the airport and the compact layout of dwntwn Boston may make car rental superfluous. There is also a good public transportation system which combines bus and subway (MBTA) (722-3200).

CAR RENTAL (at the airport unless otherwise indicated): Avis (424-0800), Budget (569-4000), Dollar (569-5300), Hertz (569-7272), National (569-

6700), Thrifty, 125 Bremen St., East Boston (569-6500). For dwntwn locations, consult the local phone directory.

LIMOUSINE SERVICES: Carey Limousine (623-8700), Cooper's Limousine (482-1000), Fifth Avenue Limousine (286-1590).

TAXIS: Taxis are hard to find and expensive. They may be hailed on the street, but priority response goes to waiting lines at the major hotels and phone orders. Major companies: Boston Cab (536-5010), Checker Cab (536-7000), Red Cab (734-5000), and Town Taxi (536-5000).

TRAIN: Amtrak, South Station, Atlantic Ave. and Summer St. (482-3660).

INTERCITY BUSES: Greyhound, 10 St. James Ave. (423-5810).

INFORMATION & TOURS

TOURIST INFORMATION: Greater Boston Convention & Tourist Bureau, Prudential Plaza, MA 02199 (617/536-4100).
   Visitor Information Center, Tremont St. at Boston Common (338-1976).
   Foreign Visitor Center, 15 State St. (242-5642).
   Recorded phone message giving an up-to-date listing of cultural events and shows: 617/267-6446.

GUIDED TOURS: Bay State Cruises (harbor cruise), 20 Long Wharf (617/723-7800): mid-May to late October. Also high-speed catamaran service to Martha's Vineyard (June–Sept).
   Boston by Foot (guided walking tours), 77 N. Washington St. (617/367-2345): daily, May–Oct.
   Clipper Cruise Lines (boat). (See "Guided Tours" in the chapter on Baltimore.)
   Gray Line Tours (bus), Statler Office Bldg., 275 Tremont St. (617/426-8805): guided tours of the city and environs.
   Old Town Trolley (bus), 329 W. 2nd St. (617/269-7010); 90-min. tours of historic Boston in a turn-of-the-century streetcar replica.

SIGHTS, ATTRACTIONS & ACTIVITIES

ADVENTURE TOURS: The New England Aquarium (Central Wharf) organizes daily **whale-watching boat trips** May–Oct. Cost, $22; resv. needed (973-5277).

ARCHITECTURAL HIGHLIGHTS: ⌂ **Government Center,** City Hall Plaza: Complex of ultramodern administrative buildings including **City Hall,** a commanding brick-and-concrete structure humorously nicknamed "the Aztec Tomb" by Bostonians, and the **J. F. Kennedy Federal Building,** designed by I. M. Pei. Worth a look.
   John Hancock Tower, Copley Square (247-1977): New England's tallest building, a striking 62-story skyscraper in steel and glass by I. M. Pei, 790 ft. (243m) tall. (See "Panoramas," below.) Open daily. Worth seeing.

DOWNTOWN BOSTON

🔭🔭 **Massachusetts Institute of Technology (M.I.T.),** Massachusetts Ave. at Memorial Dr., Cambridge: The country's (and
perhaps the world's) most prestigious university of science and technology,
M.I.T. is home to 9,000 students who make up a veritable breeding ground of
future academics and Nobel Prize winners (eight Nobel laureates currently teach
at M.I.T.). The many interesting buildings on the 127-acre campus include I. M.
Pei's **Green Building** (Pei was a student at M.I.T.) and the chapel designed by
Eero Saarinen. Open Mon.–Fri. **Information Center:** 77 Massachusetts Ave.
(253-4795). An absolute must-see.

🔭 **Prudential Tower,** 800 Boylston St. (236-3318): This modern, 752-ft (229m) skyscraper offers a very lovely panorama
from the **Skywalk** on the 50th floor (see "Panoramas," below). Open daily.

CHURCHES/SYNAGOGUES: ☼🔭 **King's Chapel,** Tremont St. and School

St. (227-2155): Boston's first Episcopalian church. The present building, on the
site of an Anglican chapel dating from 1686, was erected in 1754. A favorite of
British sovereigns, the church has received many royal gifts: the communion
plate is from George III, the pulpit from James II, and the red velvet cushions
from Queen Anne. See it. Open Tues.–Sun.

🔭🔭 **Old North Church,** 193 Salem St. (523-6676): One of the prettiest and the most history-laden of Boston's churches. The two
lanterns hanging in this church's bell tower on the night of April 18, 1775,
warned Bostonians of the British offensive against Concord and Lexington (an
episode immortalized in the words of Longfellow, "One if by land, two if by
sea"). Very beautiful interior decoration. Not to be missed. Open daily.

🔭 **Park Street Church,** 1 Park St. (523-3383): One of Boston's
most famous churches (1809) was a powder magazine during
the War of 1812. William Lloyd Garrison here delivered the first public speech
against slavery (1829), and the hymn "America" was first sung here (July 4,
1831). See it. Open daily.

🔭 **Trinity Church,** Copley Square (536-0944): Romanesque
Episcopalian church completed in 1877. Henry Hobson
Richardson's interesting architecture was inspired by Spain's Salamanca cathe-
dral. Sumptuous interior. Absolutely worth a look. Open daily.

HISTORIC BUILDINGS: 🔭 **U.S.S. *Constitution* & Museum,** Constitution

Rd., Charlestown (426-1812): The renowned frigate launched in 1797, unde-
feated in 42 engagements at sea, is nicknamed *Old Ironsides* and is the oldest
commissioned ship in the U.S. Navy. Don't miss it. Open daily.

🔭🔭 **Faneuil Hall,** Merchants Row (227-1638): Former indoor market (1742), beautifully restored. Scene of the first public meetings protesting British rule, thus the nickname "Cradle of Liberty." The place
offers many historic sights, including relics from the **Ancient & Honorable Artillery Company,** the country's oldest military school (1638). Attracts 10 million
visitors each year. Not to be missed. Open daily.

🔭 **Granary Burying Ground,** Tremont St. at Bromfield St.:
Boston's oldest cemetery (1660), with the graves of Samuel
Adams, John Hancock, Paul Revere, Benjamin Franklin's parents, and the five
casualties of the Boston Massacre (see "Monuments," below). Worth a visit.
Open daily.

🔭 **Harrison Gray Otis House,** 141 Cambridge St. (227-3956):
Beautiful Federal-style mansion designed in 1796 by Charles
Bulfinch. Currently headquarters for the Society for the Preservation of New England Antiquities. Six museum rooms have been restored to reflect the taste and
decoration of Boston during the 1800s. Worth a visit. Guided tours Tues.–Sat.

🔭🔭 **Harvard University,** around Harvard Square, Cambridge:
Temple of secular learning, Harvard (17,000 students) is the

country's oldest (1636) and most famous university. Attended by the cultural and political elite (from poet Henry Longfellow to Pres. John F. Kennedy), its ivy-covered buildings have become the symbol of the East Coast's Ivy League, whose members include Columbia, Harvard, Princeton, and Yale. Among the university's many interesting modern buildings are the **Graduate Center,** designed by Walter Gropius, and the **Carpenter Center,** conceived by Le Corbusier. Many remarkable museums, as well: the **Peabody Museum** (archeology and pre-Columbian art), the **Fogg Museum** (classic and modern paintings and sculptures, Chinese art), the group of four **University Museums of Natural History** (zoology, botany, mineralogy, etc.), and the **Arthur M. Sackler Museum,** opened in 1985, which features modern art and exhibitions of contemporary works. Tours Mon–Sat. **Information Center:** 1350 Massachusetts Ave. (495-1573). Don't miss it.

Old Corner Bookstore, School St. and Washington St. (523-6658): Once a library frequented by Henry Wadsworth Longfellow, Harriet Beecher Stowe, Nathaniel Hawthorne, and other celebrated writers, one of Boston's oldest buildings (1712) is today an interesting bookstore specializing in works on New England history. Open daily. See it.

Old State House, 206 Washington St. (720-3290): The former British governor's mansion dating from 1713, where the Declaration of Independence was read from the balcony, and where John Hancock was sworn in as Massachusetts's first governor (1789). Also Boston's city hall from 1830 to 1841, it now houses many historic relics and temporary exhibitions. Its elegant architecture is overborne by surrounding skyscrapers. An absolute must-see. Open daily.

Paul Revere's House, 19 North Square (523-2338): Boston's oldest (1677) house, carefully restored, contains period furniture and much personal memorabilia of the renowned Revolutionary War hero Paul Revere. Picturesque little square and surrounding area. Not to be missed. Open daily.

MARKETS: ※晶晶 **Quincy Market,** Merchants Row (227-1638): Picturesque indoor market in the heart of historic Boston comprising three spacious concourses dating from the 19th century. The city's hottest tourist attraction (12 million visitors each year) with boutiques, restaurants, terraced cafés, Sunday flea market. A tremendously colorful scene that shouldn't be missed. Open daily.

MONUMENTS: 晶 **Boston Massacre Site,** 30 State St.: A circle of stones marks the site of the "bloodbath of March 5, 1770," the historic episode during which British soldiers, stoned by the crowd, opened fire on the demonstrators and killed five people, including Crispus Attucks, the first black victim of the Revolutionary War.

Bunker Hill Monument, Monument Square, Charlestown (252-5641): This 214-ft. (67m) granite obelisk on the far side of the Charles River commemorates the Battle of Bunker Hill (June 17, 1775), the baptism by fire of the Minutemen facing British troops. Fine panorama of the city and the harbor from the top of the obelisk (294 steps; no elevator). Worth a look. Open daily.

Not far from the Bunker Hill Monument is the **State Prison of Charlestown,** where anarchists Nicola Sacco and Bartolomeo Vanzetti were executed on August 23, 1927, after a seven-year court battle that divided the nation.

MUSEUMS OF ART: 晶 **Institute of Contemporary Art,** 955 Boylston St. (266-5151): Has 20th-century art plus notable concerts, films, and temporary exhibitions. The building is a former police station. Worth a visit. Open Wed.–Sun.

※晶晶晶 **Isabella Stewart Gardner Museum,** 280 The Fenway (566-1401): Startling baroque "palazzo" with a wonderful colonnaded courtyard in the Venetian style. Remarkable collection of European masters, Italian primitive art, and Flemish tapestries. Among the most famous works: Fra Angelico's *The Assumption of the Virgin,* Vermeer's *The Concert,* Rembrandt's *Storm on the Sea of Galilee,* Tintoretto's *Woman in Black,* Titian's *The Rape of Europa,* Matisse's *Terrace in St. Tropez,* and Degas's *Madame Gaujelin.* Boston's loveliest museum. (Unfortunately some of these paintings were stolen in the March 1990 break-in and have not yet been recovered.) Free concerts Tues, Thurs, and Sun. Open Tues–Sun in summer; Wed–Sun the rest of the year. Not to be missed.

☀ 🔔🔔🔔 **Museum of Fine Arts,** 465 Huntington Ave. (267-9300): Hundreds of masterworks from Rembrandt to Morris Louis and from Monet to Gauguin (see especially his famous painting *Who are we? Where do we come from? Where are we going?*). Among its other notable works: a Greek head of Aphrodite from the 4th century B.C., Van der Weyden's *St. Luke Painting the Virgin,* El Greco's *Portrait of Brother Paravicino,* Renoir's *Dance at Bougival,* Cézanne's *Winding Road,* van Gogh's *House at Auvers,* and Jackson Pollock's *Number Ten.* Very fine collections of Asian and Egyptian art. The West Wing was designed by I. M. Pei. Don't miss it. Open Tues–Sun.

🔔 **Public Library,** 666 Boylston St. (536-5400): Rich public library (more than three million volumes). Italian Renaissance architecture by Charles McKim. Noteworthy bronze doors by Daniel Chester French and remarkable interior decoration. Open Mon–Sat.

MUSEUMS OF SCIENCE & HISTORY: 🔔 **Bell's Laboratory,** 185 Franklin St.: Interesting little telephone museum in the lobby of the New England Telephone Building. Includes notably an exact replica of Alexander Graham Bell's studio.

🔔 **Boston Tea Party Ship & Museum,** Congress St. Bridge (338-1773): The spot where the revolt against the British began (1773). Life-size replica of the British sailing ship *The Beaver,* whose cargo of 100,000 pounds of tea was dumped overboard by protesting Bostonians. Historic exhibition and, of course, tea is served. Not to be missed. Open daily.

🔔 **Bunker Hill Pavilion,** 55 Constitution Rd., Charlestown (241-7575): Neighbor of the frigate *Constitution* (see "Historic Buildings," above) and the Bunker Hill Monument (see "Monuments," above), this specially conceived hall offers a multimedia show that reproduces the Battle of Bunker Hill on 14 movie screens and seven soundtracks. Hear Israel Putnam's immortal words, "Don't fire until you see the whites of their eyes." Worth a look. Open daily.

🔔 **Christian Science Publishing House,** 1 Norway St. (450-2000): Inside is a concave glass terrestrial globe, 28 ft. (9m) in diameter, that is truly astonishing. Open daily. In the Administration Building next door is the headquarters of the Church of Christ, Scientist (300,000 members worldwide). See it.

🔔 **Computer Museum,** Museum Wharf, 300 Congress St. (423-6758): From the good old UNIVAC 1 of the 1950s to the massive AN/FSQ-7, the biggest computer in the world (175 tons), this museum offers a complete panorama of the history of data processing. Demonstrations of state-of-the-art technology. Marvelous. Open daily in summer; Tues.–Sun the rest of the year.

🔔🔔 **John F. Kennedy Library & Museum,** University of Massachusetts, Columbia Point Campus, 5 mi. (8km) SE on I-93 (929-4523): The life of the 35th president in movies, documents, and photographs in a very effective futurist setting designed by I. M. Pei. Very lovely view of the skyline and the ocean. Open daily.

🔔 **John F. Kennedy National Historic Site,** 83 Beals St., Brookline (566-7937): The birthplace of the president on the outskirts of Boston. JFK lived in the house from 1917 to 1921. Period furniture and Kennedy family memorabilia. Simple and moving. See it. Open daily.

Museum of Science & Hayden Planetarium, Science Park (589-0100): Large, ultramodern science museum devoted to technology and natural history, including a life-size dinosaur replica. The interesting medical section has a giant model of the human heart. Boasts the largest Omnimax 360° film screen in the world (73 ft. / 22m in diameter; 84 speakers). For science and astronomy buffs. Open Tues–Sun.

New England Aquarium, Central Wharf (742-8870): Huge, four-story glass aquarium with more than 7,000 fish and marine creatures of all kinds, from sea lions to sharks. Worth a visit. Open daily. (See also "Adventure Tours," above.)

Old South Meeting House, Washington St. and Milk St. (482-6439): Built in 1729 on the site of an earlier house of worship where Benjamin Franklin was baptized in 1706, this red-brick building, once a religious and public meeting center, is today home to the historical museum of the city. This was also the starting point of Bostonians (some disguised as Indians) who took part in the Boston Tea Party (see above). A definite must-see. Open Mon–Sat.

State House, Beacon St. (727-2121): The gold-domed Massachusetts legislative building, designed by Charles Bulfinch (1795). Its unique historical archives contain notably the passenger list of the *Mayflower* and the original Massachusetts Constitution of 1780, the country's first written constitution. Very lovely Hall of Flags. Not to be missed. Open daily.

PANORAMAS: Bunker Hill Monument (see "Monuments," above).

John Hancock Observatory, 200 Clarendon St. (247-1977): Splendid panorama of the city and harbor from the 60th floor of the John Hancock Tower. Absolutely worth a look. Open daily until 11pm.

Prudential Tower, 800 Boylston St. (236-3318): The observation platform on the 50th floor affords a 360° panorama of the city that is almost as impressive as the view from the John Hancock Observatory. Worth a look. Open daily until 11pm.

PARKS & GARDENS: Arnold Arboretum, Arborway, Jamaica Plain (524-1717): This very lovely 265-acre park was designed by Frederick Law Olmsted, the renowned landscape architect. It contains more than 6,000 kinds of trees and shrubs, and offers floral exhibits year round. 25 min. from dwntwn.

Boston Common, Tremont St., Park St., and Beacon St. (267-6446): The first of the country's large public parks (1634), it encompasses 48 acres of trees, lawns, and shrubberies in the heart of Boston. Once a training ground for the redcoats, it is much enjoyed by amblers and soapbox orators, but should be avoided after nightfall. The Bostonian gathering point for all great occasions, the Common was the site of Pope John Paul II's outdoor mass before 200,000 people (1979). The adjacent **Public Garden** has a lake for boating in summer and skating in winter.

Mount Auburn Cemetery, 580 Mt. Auburn St., Cambridge (547-7105): The country's oldest garden cemetery, this flower-filled park overlooking the Charles contains the graves of such notables as Henry Wadsworth Longfellow, Justice Oliver Wendell Holmes, and Mary Baker Eddy, founder of the Christian Science church. Worth a detour. Open daily.

PERFORMING ARTS: For a daily listing of all shows and cultural events, consult the entertainment pages of the daily papers *Boston Globe* (morning), *Boston Herald-American* (morning), and *Christian Science Monitor* (morning); the weekly *Boston Phoenix;* and the monthly magazine *Boston.* **Bostix,** a kiosk in Faneuil Hall Marketplace, Faneuil Hall Square (723-5181), sells half-price tickets for all shows on the day of performance. Cash only.

    Alley Theatre, 1253 Cambridge St., Cambridge (491-8166): Contemporary theater.

    Boston Center for the Arts, 539 Tremont St. (426-5000): Concerts, recitals, avant-garde theater, ballet. Year round.

    Boston University Theatre, 264 Huntington Ave. (266-3913): Modern and classical theater.

    Charles Playhouse Theatre, 106 Boylston St. (426-6912): Drama, comedy, modern theater.

    Hatch Shell, Esplanade, Memorial Dr. (727-9548): Open-air Boston Pops Orchestra concerts and Boston Ballet Company performances. Summer only.

    Loeb Drama Center, 64 Brattle St., Cambridge (547-8300): Home of the American Repertory Theater, offering classical and modern works.

    Next Move Theatre, 1 Boylston Pl. (423-5572): Experimental theater.

    Opera Company of Boston, 539 Washington St. (426-5300): Boston's new grand opera house, with artistic director Sarah Caldwell.

    Shubert Theatre, 265 Tremont St. (426-4520): Broadway shows (often previews). Year round.

    Symphony Hall, 301 Massachusetts Ave. (266-1492): Home of the celebrated Boston Symphony Orchestra, one of the country's "big six" orchestras (principal conductor: Seiji Ozawa); Sept–Apr. Also the home of the Boston Pops Orchestra (principal conductor: John Williams); May–July.

    Tower Auditorium, 621 Huntington Ave. (576-2737): Concerts, Off Broadway theater, ballet.

    Wang Center for the Performing Arts, 268 Tremont St. (482-9393): Home of the Boston Ballet Company.

    Wilbur Theatre, 246 Tremont St. (426-1988): Modern theater, Broadway shows. Year round.

SHOPPING: The Coop, 1 Federal St. at Harvard Square, Cambridge: The world's biggest student-oriented store: from textbooks to blue jeans, from posters to backpacks, and from records to the latest in microcomputers. A classic since 1882.

    Copley Place, 100 Huntington Ave.: Gigantic shopping center with a futurist look (interior gardens, huge waterfalls), plus dozens of luxury boutiques, from Neiman-Marcus to Gucci and Vuitton to Tiffany's. Spectacular.

    ☼ **Filene's,** 426 Washington St.: A real landmark. In the famous basement of this crowded store are Boston's best deals on cut-rate clothing—in a hurly-burly atmosphere. Many other interesting stores close by, along Washington St. and Summer St.

    Newbury Street: Boston's chic shopping street, with fashionable boutiques, art galleries, famous food stores. Worth a look.

    Tower Records, Massachusetts Ave. and Newbury St.: The biggest and most up-to-date record and video store in the world (more than 40,000 square ft., 3,730m²). Impressive. Close to Symphony Hall.

SPECIAL EVENTS: For the exact schedule of events below, consult the **Greater Boston Convention & Tourist Bureau** (see "Tourist Information," above).

    Patriots Day Celebration (mid-Apr): Parades, celebrations, and the Boston Marathon, a local tradition since 1896.

    Esplanade Concerts (first 2 weeks of July): Free open-air concerts by the world-famous Boston Pops Orchestra at the Hatch Memorial Shell (on the banks of the Charles River). Don't miss it.

    Harborfest (July): A celebration of Boston's history and harbor. Fireworks, concerts, regattas.

Charles River Regatta (last Sun in Oct): Boat races on the Charles, a classic of the Boston season.

Harvard-Yale Football Game (Nov): When the great rivals Harvard and Yale clash, the famous match-up guarantees excitement and a great atmosphere. The game is played in Cambridge and New Haven, alternating every year.

SPORTS: Boston has four professional teams:
Baseball (Apr–Oct): Red Sox, Fenway Park (267-8661).
Basketball (Oct to late Apr): Celtics, Boston Garden (523-6050).
Football (Sept–Dec): New England Patriots, Sullivan Stadium (543-7911).
Ice Hockey (Oct–Apr): Bruins, Boston Garden (227-3206).

Horse Racing
Suffolk Downs, on Mass. 1A, East Boston (567-3900), year round.

STROLLS: ☀️🏛 **Freedom Trail:** This red-arrow-marked circuit begins at Beacon St. and Park St. and winds for 2½ mi. (4km) through 16 colonial and Revolutionary-era sites. National Park Service rangers offer free 90-min. tours. Its **Visitor Center,** where a short film is shown, is at 15 State St. (223-0058). Don't miss it.

☀️🏛 **Beacon Hill,** around Mt. Vernon St.: Boston's aristocratic neighborhood, with old gas lamps, cobblestone streets, lovely private homes with elegant facades and carefully polished brass nameplates. A whiff of nostalgia. An absolute must-see (especially, gorgeous **Louisburg Square**).

🏛 **North End,** bordered by Commercial St. and John F. Fitzgerald Expwy.: Surrounded by warehouses and the docks of Boston's old harbor, this picturesque area composed of small, narrow streets with red-brick houses has become the local **Little Italy** over the years. Numerous agreeable restaurants, bars, and food stores contribute to a colorful atmosphere (especially during religious festivals). From Commercial St. or Atlantic Ave., you can enjoy an unobstructed view of the port and its maritime traffic.

THEME PARKS: See **Old Sturbridge Village,** in "Farther Afield," below.

WINTER SPORTS RESORTS: Boston Hills (26 mi. / 42km north on Mass. 28 and 125; 508/683-2733): Four lifts, open mid-Dec to mid-Mar.
Crotched Mountain (100 mi./160km NW on Mass. 2, Mass. 12, U.S. 202, and N.H. 47; 603/588-6345): Twelve lifts, open mid-Nov to Apr.
Temple Mountain (87 mi./139km NW on Mass. 2, Mass. 12, U.S. 202, and N.H. 101; 603/924-6949): Seven lifts, open Dec–Apr.
Wachusett Mountain (58 mi./93km NW on Mass. 2 and Mass. 140; 508/464-5101): Four lifts, open Dec–Mar.

ACCOMMODATIONS

A Note on Accommodations: Room rates in Boston are coded as follows: **VE,** Very Expensive ($140 and up); **E,** Expensive ($90–$140); **M,** Moderate ($60–$90); **I,** Inexpensive ($30–$60); **B,** Budget (up to $30). A listing of toll-free numbers is in the Appendix.

Personal Favorites (in order of preference)
♟♟♟♟♟ **Ritz Carlton Hotel** (dwntwn), 15 Arlington St., MA 02117 (617/536-5700; toll free 800/241-3333). 278 rms, A/C, color TV. AE, CB, DC, MC, V. Gar. $20, health club, sauna, two rests. (including the Ritz Carlton Dining Room), two bars, 24-hr. rm svce, hrdrsr, boutiques, concierge, free crib. *Note:* "The" grand palace of Boston since 1927 and one of

the 12 best hotels in the country, across from the Public Garden. Elegant, refined decor, irreproachable comfort w. period furniture and ultracorrect svce. Renowned bar and rests. (the Ritz Café is the "in" place for working breakfasts). VIP floor. Recently received a $25-million facelift. Free limousine service to and from the business district. VE

🍸🍷🍷🍷 **The Charles Hotel** (vic.), 1 Bennett St. (at Eliot St.), MA 02138 (617/864-1200; toll free 800/882-1818). 299 rms, A/C, color TV, in-rm movies. AE, CB, DC, MC, V. Valet gar. $20, pool, health club, sauna, two rests. (including Rarities), bar, 24-hr. rm svce, nightclub, boutiques, hrdrsr, concierge. *Note:* This relatively new luxury hotel in the European manner is very near the Harvard campus, and has become a favorite roost for passing VIPs from Jack Nicholson to corporate tycoons. The elegant red-brick building commands a view of the Charles River and the Boston skyline. Comfortable, agreeably furnished rms, exemplary svce, rest. of quality—and the best jazz joint in greater Boston. 15 min. from dwntwn. **VE**

☀🍷🍷🍷 **The Bostonian** (dwntwn), Faneuil Hall Marketplace, MA 02109 (617/523-3600; toll free, see Preferred). 155 rms. A/C, cable color TV. AE, CB, DC, MC, V. Valet gar. $18, rest. (the Seasons), bar, 24-hr. rm svce, free crib. *Note:* The hotel's modern red-brick architecture is perfectly integrated into the Old Boston setting. Inside is an elegant four-story glass atrium and cramped but comfortable rms with exposed beams and fireplaces (some w. balconies). Intimate, sophisticated atmosphere and impeccable svce, plus an excellent rest. (the Seasons). The best location in Boston, across from Faneuil Hall and Quincy Market. **VE**

☀🍷🍷🍷 **Omni Parker House** (dwntwn), 60 School St., MA 02107 (617/227-8600; toll free, see Omni). 540 rms. A/C, color TV in-rm movies. AE, CB, DC, MC, V. Gar. $18, health club, sauna, three rests. (including The Last Hurrah), coffeeshop, three bars, rm svce, disco, hrdrsr, boutiques, free crib. *Note:* In this venerable (dates from 1855), history-laden palace in the heart of Boston, Charles Dickens stayed, Ho Chi Minh was a bellboy, and the Kennedys are a familiar sight. Marble, woodwork, and Oriental rugs abound in the sumptuously renovated building. The rms are elegantly comfortable and the atmosphere calm and distinguished. Reception and svce of the highest quality. Good rests. A favorite of connoisseurs. **VE**

🍷🍷 **Howard Johnson Hotel** (dwntwn), 200 Stuart St., MA 02116 (617/482-1800; toll free, see Howard Johnson's). 352 rms, A/C, color TV, in-rm movies. AE, CB, DC, MC, V. Free parking, pool, sauna, rest. (57 Restaurant), bar, rm svce, disco, hrdrsr, free crib. *Note:* Rather ordinary modern architecture, but a very good location just off the Common. Functional rms w. balconies and a satisfactory rest. Fair svce. Business clientele. VIP suites on the 23rd floor. Movie theaters. **E–VE**

🍷🍷 **Boston Park Plaza Hotel** (dwntwn), 50 Park Plaza, MA 02117 (617/426-2000; toll free 800/225-2008). 976 rms, A/C, color TV, in-rm movies. AE, CB, DC, MC, V. Gar. $12, health club, rest. (Fox & Hounds), coffeeshop, bars, 24-hr. rm svce, hrdrsr, boutiques, free crib. *Note:* Massive, aging palace near the Common w. slightly faded interior decoration but comfortable rms. Svce so-so, and the group and convention clientele is somewhat obtrusive. Very good location. **E–VE**

🍷 **Chandler Inn** (nr. dwntwn), 26 Chandler St., MA 02116 (617/482-3450; toll free 800/842-3450). 56 rms, A/C, color TV. AE, CB, DC, MC, V. Parking $12, bar. *Note:* Small, modest, and inviting hotel, 5 min. from dwntwn. Free breakfast. Recently renovated. Very good value for those on a budget. **M**

🍷 **Quality Inn Tremont** (formerly the Bradford Hotel) (dwntwn), 275 Tremont St., MA 02116 (617/426-1400). 288 rms, A/C, color TV, in-rm movies. AE, CB, DC, MC, V. Parking $15, rest.

bar, rm svce, disco. *Note:* Oldish but well-maintained hotel in the theater district. Regular clientele. Recently renovated. A good overall value. **M–E**

Other Accommodations (from top bracket to budget)

Boston Harbor Hotel (dwntwn), 70 Rowes Wharf (on Atlantic Ave.), MA 02110 (617/439-7000; toll free 800/752-7577). 230 rms, A/C, color TV, in-rm movies. AE, CB, DC, MC, V. Valet gar. $20, pool, health club, sauna, rest. (Rowes Wharf), bar, 24-hr. rm svce, nightclub, boutiques, concierge, free crib. *Note:* This most distinctive and luxurious of Boston's dwntwn hotels, uncompromisingly postmodern in appearance, towers above the bustle of Boston Harbor from its 16 floors. Elegant decoration and furnishing; spacious, ultra-comfortable rms with minibars, remote-control TVs, and private balconies (the best overlooking the water). Svce of the highest order. Direct water-taxi link with airport (7 min.). Big-business clientele. **VE**

Four Seasons (dwntwn), 200 Boylston St., MA 02116 (617/338-4400; toll free, see Four Seasons). 288 rms, A/C, color TV, in-rm movies. AE, CB, DC, MC, V. Valet gar. $16, pool, health club, sauna, two rests. (including Aujourd'hui), two bars, 24-hr. rm svce, nightclub, concierge, free crib. *Note:* Opened in 1985, this elegant, modern 15-story hotel overlooking the Public Garden is a favorite of financial-industry executives. Spacious, comfortable rms w. minibars (the most pleasant have a view of the park). The decor complements the hotel's period furniture and unassuming modernism. Personalized svce of great distinction. Excellent nouvelle cuisine rest. One of Boston's finest. **VE**

Westin Hotel (nr. dwntwn), 10 Huntington Ave., MA 02117 (617/262-9600; toll free, see Westin). 800 rms, A/C, color TV, in-rm movies. AE, CB, DC, MC, V. Parking $15, pool, health club, sauna, three rests. (including Ten Huntington), coffee shop, three bars, 24-hr. rm svce, nightclub, boutiques, concierge, free crib. *Note:* New 36-story building which towers over Copley Place Shopping Center. Spectacular lobby w. waterfalls and interior gardens. Ultramodern comfort w. vast, well-equipped rms (those on the top floors have a very lovely view of the city). Efficient, diligent svce. Houses Boston's most expensive suite ($1,500 a night). Frequented by VIPs and businesspeople. Very good location. **VE**

Copley Plaza Hotel (dwntwn), 138 St. James Ave. (at Copley Square), MA 02116 (617/267-5300; toll free 800/826-7539). 393 rms, A/C, color TV, in-rm movies. AE, CB, DC, MC, V. Valet parking $20, two rests. (including Café Plaza), two bars, 24-hr. rm svce, boutiques, hrdrsr, concierge, free crib. *Note:* Along with the Ritz Carlton, this 1912 dowager can lay claim to the title of Queen Mother of Boston's hotels. Its 75th anniversary was celebrated with a comprehensive restoration designed to restore its former splendor. Svce and comfort above reproach; works of art and period furniture. Distinguished reception; excellently located nr. Prudential Center and the smart stores of Newbury St. Guests are mostly regulars. **VE**

Meridien (dwntwn), 250 Franklin St., MA 02110 (617/451-1900; toll free, see Meridien). 328 rms, A/C, color TV, in-rm movies. AE, CB, DC, MC, V. Gar. $15, pool, health club, sauna, two rests. (including Julien), two bars, disco, boutiques, concierge, crib $20. *Note:* Italian Renaissance–style palace dating from 1922 which once housed the Federal Reserve Bank. Luxurious, well-conceived rms w. minibars. Attentive reception and service with a touch of elegance à la française. Excellent nouvelle cuisine rest. (Julien) appreciated by businesspeople. Very central location. Business clientele. Recommended. **VE**

Royal Sonesta (vic.), 5 Cambridge Pkwy., Cambridge, MA 02142 (617/491-3600; toll free 800/766-3782). 397 rms. A/C, color TV, in-rm movies. AE, CB, DC, MC, V. Free parking, two pools, health club, three rests. (including the River Front), four bars, rm svce, night-club, hrdrsr, concierge, free crib. *Note:* Large postmodern convention hotel, recently enlarged. Irreproachable comfort and facilities. The interior is adorned w. numerous original works of contemporary art, from Roy Lichtenstein to Buckminster Fuller. Spacious rms with minibars. VIP floors. Excellent svce and a very lovely view of Boston from the opposite side of the Charles River. Business clientele. Convenient to M.I.T. An excellent location, 20 min. from dwntwn. **E−VE**

♀♀ **Holiday Inn Government Center** (dwntwn), 5 Blossom St.,
♀♀ MA 02114 (617/742-7630; toll free, see Holiday Inns). 300 rms, A/C, color TV, in-rm movies. AE, CB, DC, MC, V. Parking $7, pool, rest. (Lobster Trap), coffee shop, bar, rm svce, disco, boutiques, free crib. *Note:* Functional, modern 15-story tower à la Holiday Inn but more inviting than usual. Comfortable rms, group clientele. Quite close to the Charles and to City Hall. Interesting wknd packages. **E−VE**

♀♀ **Lenox Hotel** (dwntwn), 701 Boylston St. (at Exeter St.), MA
♀♀ 02116 (617/536-5300; toll free 800/225-7676). 222 rms, A/C, color TV, in-rm movies. AE, CB, DC, MC, V. Nearby valet parking $10, two rests. (including Lenox Pub & Grill), two bars, rm svce, hrdrsr. *Note:* Elegant luxury in a small turn-of-the-century hotel at the heart of Back Bay. Traditional comfort and furnishing; rms (some w. fireplaces) decorated in American Colonial or French Provincial. Thoughtful, friendly svce. Diamond Jim's is an agreeable piano bar. Good value overall. **E−VE**

♀♀ **Midtown Hotel** (nr. dwntwn), 220 Huntington Ave., MA
♀♀ 02115 (617/262-1000; toll free 800/343-1177). 160 rms, A/C, color TV. AE, CB, DC, MC, V. Free parking, pool, rest., bar, valet svce. *Note:* Relatively modern motel across from the Prudential Tower. Spacious, comfortable rms. The svce fluctuates. Interesting wknd packages. **M−E**

♀ **Eliot Hotel** (nr. dwntwn), 370 Commonwealth Ave., MA
♀ 02215 (617/267-1607). 100 rms, A/C, color TV. AE, CB, DC, MC, V. Parking, adjacent bar. *Note:* All the rms in this modern, tranquil hotel are mini-suites with or without kitchenettes. Interesting deals for longer stays. International clientele. A good value. 10 min. from dwntwn. **M**

♀ **Quality Inn Cambridge** (vic.), 1651 Massachusetts Ave.,
♀ Cambridge, MA 02138 (617/491-1000; toll free, see Quality Inns). 135 rms, A/C, color TV, in-rm movies. AE, CB, DC, MC, V. Free parking, pool, rest., bar, rm svce. *Note:* Classic modern-style motel w. pleasant reception and svce and comfortable rms. Close to Harvard. 20 min. from dwntwn. **M−E**

♀ **Susse Chalet** (vic.), 800 Morrissey Blvd., MA 02122 (617/
♀ 287-9100; toll free 800/258-1980). 177 rms, A/C, color TV. AE, MC, V. Free parking, pool, adjacent coffee shop, crib $3. *Note:* Relatively old but well-maintained motel 15 min. from dwntwn on the Southeast Expwy. Inviting rms. Close to the University of Massachusetts and the Kennedy Library. Ideal if you're driving through. Very good value. **I**

Airport Accommodations

♀♀ **Hilton Logan Airport** (vic.), 75 Service Rd., Logan Airport,
♀♀ MA 02128 (617/569-9300; toll free, see Hilton). 542 rms, A/C, color TV, in-rm movies. AE, CB, DC, MC, V. Free parking, pool, rest. (Appleton's), coffee shop, bar, rm svce, disco, free crib. *Note:* This entirely renovated convention hotel offers comfortable, well-soundproofed rms w. private balconies and cheerful svce. Business clientele. 25 min. from dwntwn. **E−VE**

YMCAs/Youth Hostels

Boston International Hostel (nr. dwntwn), 12 Hemenway St., MA 02115 (617/536-9455). 220 beds. Youth hostel, 10 min. from dwntwn. Coffee shop.

YMCA Boston (nr. dwntwn), 316 Huntington Ave., MA 02115 (617/536-7800). 300 rms, pool, health club, rest. Men and women.

RESTAURANTS

A Note on Restaurant Prices: Boston restaurant prices, per person, excluding drinks and service charges, are coded as follows: **VE,** Very Expensive ($60 and up); **E,** Expensive ($40–$60); **M,** Moderate ($25–$40), **I,** Inexpensive ($15 –$25); **B,** Budget (up to $15).

Personal Favorites (in order of preference)

Le Marquis de Lafayette (dwntwn), in the Lafayette Swissôtel, 1 Ave. de Lafayette (451-2600). A/C. Lunch Mon–Fri; dinner Mon–Sat; closed hols. AE, CB, DC, MC, V. J&T. Specialties: escalope of foie gras w. pineapple-ginger confit, Venison saddle w. black-pepper sauce, aiguillete of duck in maple syrup, filet of beef w. marrow, veal medallions w. mango and ginger, remarkable pastries. The menu changes regularly. Very fine wine list (with some finds at reasonable prices). *Note:* This relative newcomer to the Boston gastronomic scene won a place of honor in just a few months under the guidance of Louis Outhier, owner of the famous three-star Oasis restaurant in La Napoule (France). He skillfully modifies classic *grande cuisine* with nouvelle cuisine tendencies, and the results are brilliant. The decor is of a sober elegance w. beveled mirrors, period furniture, and crystal chandeliers. Ultracorrect but unsmiling svce. Resv. a must long in advance given the limited seating in the dining room (60 seats). One of the best on the East Coast. *French.* **E–VE**

L'Espalier (nr. dwntwn), 30 Gloucester St. (262-3023). A/C. Dinner only, Mon–Sat; closed hols. AE, CB, DC, MC, V. J&T. *Specialties:* shrimp and scallops w. vanilla and dry-sherry butter sauce, lobster-truffle ravioli, cassoulet, veal sautéed in honey and lemon, pigeon mousse in pastry shell, grilled bass w. soy-and-lemon sauce, filet of beef bordelaise w. green peppercorns, excellent desserts, and a rich wine list. The menu changes regularly. *Note:* The temple of Boston nouvelle cuisine since Dodin Bouffant moved to New York, it offers light, inspired cuisine from chef Frank McClelland. Pretty, antique decor in an elegant, Edwardian three-story house in the Back Bay section. Very lovely floral arrangements. Exemplary svce. Trendy clientele. Resv. a must. Valet parking $5. *French/Continental.* **E–VE**

Biba (dwntwn), 272 Boylston St. (426-7878). A/C. Lunch Mon–Fri; dinner Sun–Fri. AE, MC, V. Jkt. *Specialties:* ash-baked potato w. osetra caviar, lobster w. green-curry broth, calves' brains w. crisp-fried capers, roast suckling pig, walnut tart w. warm plums, mascarpone soufflé. Interesting, fairly priced wine list. *Note:* Recently opened by the very talented chef Lydia Shire (formerly of the Bostonian Hotel's Seasons), this distinguished rest. in the new Heritage Building across from the Public Garden has quickly become Boston's "in" place. The interior is rather startling Hollywood Mexican, the svce a touch lackadaisical. Highly recommended in spite of the incongruous setting; successful enough that resv. should be made some days ahead. *American.* **M–E**

Locke Ober Café (dwntwn), 3 Winter Place (542-1340). A/C. Lunch/dinner daily; closed hols. AE, CB, DC, MC, V. J&T. *Specialties:* lobster Savannah, duckling bigarade, sole bonne femme, oysters Rockefeller, filet Mirabeau, steak tartare, Nesselrode sundae, Indian pudding. *Note:* The most famous eating place in Boston. Since 1875 this venerable institution has retained its Victorian woodwork and its old-world club atmosphere. The only break with tradition: Women are now admitted to the mezzanine, or most elegant, dining room. Cuisine and svce exemplary on all counts. Resv. advised. A favorite of Boston society (especially the late President Kennedy). *Continental/American.* **I–M**

Anthony's Pier 4 (dwntwn), 140 Northern Ave. (423-6363). A/C. Lunch/dinner daily; closed Dec 25. AE, CB, DC, MC,

V. Jkt. *Specialties:* clam chowder, fish chowder, lobster, and remarkable seafood of all kinds, fresh and reasonably priced. Good wine list. *Note:* Criticized by purists for its "eating factory" appearance, Anthony's Pier 4 is, according to a *Boston Globe* poll, the favorite restaurant of Bostonians. Not surprisingly, it is often jampacked despite the imposing dimensions of the windowed dining rm. Generous portions, diligent svce, and an agreeable view of the harbor. Rather amusing marine bric-a-brac decor, very noisy atmosphere. No dinner resv., unfortunately. Valet parking. *Seafood.* **I–M**

☆ ♀ **Ye Olde Union Oyster House** (dwntwn), 41 Union St. (227-2750). A/C. Lunch/dinner daily; closed Thanksgiving, Dec 25. AE, CB, DC, MC, V. *Specialties:* clam chowder, oysters, coquilles St-Jacques, lobster, fish of the day. *Note:* Boston's oldest oyster bar (1826) in a more-than-three-centuries-old little one-story house is a tourist favorite. Superb raw bar on the mezzanine. Charming period decor. Cheerful svce. Resv. are useless. *Seafood.* **I**

♀ **Cactus Club** (nr. dwntwn), 939 Boylston St. (236-0200). A/C. Lunch/dinner daily; closed hols. AE, MC, V. *Specialties:* prairie oysters, cinnamon chorizo-stuffed empanadas, conch fritters, steak skewer w. grilled vegetables, grilled pork loin w. red beans and rice, grilled swordfish steak w. jalapeño butter, chicken breasts stuffed w. tomatillo salsa, capirotada (fruited bread pudding), piñon torte. *Note:* By far the best Tex-Mex food to be found in Boston; tasty dishes and outsize drinks (try the giant cactus bowl). Amusing decor with bare adobe walls, a buffalo head, Stetsons, Texas longhorns, saddles, spurs, and cactus all over. A relaxed, likable place with swift, deft svce, popular with the locals. *American.* **I**

Other Restaurants (from top bracket to budget)

♀♀♀ **Aujourd'hui** (dwntwn), in the Four Seasons (see "Accommodations," above) (338-4400). A/C. Breakfast/lunch/dinner daily. AE, CB, DC, MC, V. J&T. *Specialties:* blini of scallops w. caviar, seared tuna salad w. raspberry vinaigrette, rare breast of mallard w. sauce of port and peaches, rack of lamb à la Szechuan, fresh figs with ice cream and custard. The menu changes regularly. Remarkable wine list. *Note:* Superb, elegant rest. w. airy, inventive French cuisine from the wonderful Mark Baker. Opulent decor of somber woodwork, floral upholstery, and large bay windows overlooking the Public Garden. Ultra-polished svce. Big business clientele. One of Boston's most fashionable places. Resv. strongly advised. *French.* **M–E**

♀♀♀ **Jasper's** (dwntwn), 240 Commercial St. (523-1126). A/C. Dinner only, Mon–Sat; closed hols. AE, CB, DC, MC, V. Jkt. *Specialties:* lobster chowder w. corn fritters, pork rib eye w. clams and garlic sauce, grilled bluefish, rack of lamb with grilled leeks, breast of pigeon with oysters, caramelized rice pudding w. tangerine. The menu changes regularly. *Note:* Inventive, elegant American nouvelle cuisine from chef Jasper White, but the prices are painful. Pretty pastel decor w. elegant floral arrangements. Efficient if starchy svce. Trendy clientele. Quite close to the harbor. Resv. a must. Valet parking. *American.* **M–E**

♀♀♀ **Hamersley's Bistro** (dwntwn), 578 Tremont St. (267-6068). A/C. Dinner only, Mon–Sat; closed Dec 25. AE, MC, V. Jkt. *Specialties:* grilled wild mushrooms on toasted garlic country bread, boned leg of lamb stuffed w. kale, olives and roasted sweet peppers, roast chicken w. garlic and lemon, sautéed salmon w. raisins and leeks, chocolate and pecan terrine w. crème anglaise, souffléed lemon custard. Decently priced wine list. *Note:* Gordon Hamersley's country cooking is one of the gastronomic joys of Boston, and has been voted the best bistro cuisine in the city by the readers of *Boston* magazine. The white walls, open kitchen, paper napkins, and niggardly lighting don't add up to an attractive setting—but the friendly proprietress, the relaxed but efficient svce, and the young, fashionable crowd make this a place that no visitor to Boston should miss. Resv. a must. *American.* **M**

🍷🍷🍷 **Michela's** (vic.), 1 Athenaeum St., **Cambridge** (225-2121). 🍴🍴 A/C. Lunch Mon–Fri, dinner Mon–Sat; closed hols. AE, CB, DC, MC, V. Jkt. *Specialties:* zuppa di fagioli (white-bean soup), risotto of wild mushrooms, polenta soufflé w. puréed peas, pizza w. pancetta and artichokes, squid stuffed w. sausage and rosemary, roast filet of salmon marinated in fresh thyme and jalapeño, lamb stew w. olives, excellent homemade desserts. Good list of Italian and California wines. *Note:* Occupying the ground floor of an attractively redesigned printers'-ink plant, Michela's gives a new twist to Italian *nuova cucina.* Michela Larson gracefully interweaves the recipes of her native Italy with American, Portuguese, and—since the arrival of her new chef Terry Endow— even Californian traditions. Novel "patio" look with colored wall-paintings; noisy. The adjoining Michela's Café offers excellent value. Locally popular. *Italian/American.* **M**

🍷🍷 **Suntory** (dwntwn), 212 Stuart St. (338-2111). A/C. Lunch 🍴🍴 Mon–Sat; dinner daily. AE, CB, DC, MC, V. Jkt. *Specialties:* sushi, shabu-shabu, tempura, teppanyaki, yakitori. *Note:* Experts consider this the best Japanese rest. in Boston. It is one of a dozen luxury rests. around the world (including one in Chicago and one in Honolulu) owned by the renowned Japanese brewer Suntory. Sober, elegant Oriental decor. The customer has a choice between the sushi bar and the upstairs dining rms, specializing in different types of Japanese cuisine. An excellent locale. Resv. advised, given its success. *Japanese.* **I–M**

🍷🍷 **Casa Romero** (nr. dwntwn), 30 Gloucester St. (enter through the adjacent alley) (536-4341). A/C. Dinner only, daily; closed hols. AE, CB, DC, MC, V. Jkt. *Specialties:* higaditos, garlicky roast rack of lamb, grilled tuna steak w. roasted red peppers, chicken with coriander. *Note:* Very elaborate Mexican cuisine in a pretty hacienda setting w. tiles and dark wood. Elegantly romantic atmosphere and attentive svce. No resv. *Mexican.* **I**

🍷🍷 **Legal Seafoods** (dwntwn), 35 Columbus Ave. (426-4444). A/C. Lunch/dinner daily; closed Thanksgiving, Dec 25. AE, CB, DC, MC, V. *Specialties:* huge variety of seafood that is cooked, steamed, fried, or grilled to perfection; clam chowder, smoked hake pâté cioppino, mussels au gratin. *Note:* One of the country's best seafood restaurants in a vast, modern, and luminous setting of mirrors, polished brass, and a dining rm spread over several levels. Legal Seafoods is at once a rest. chain and a retail fish store, and the more than 30 tons of fresh seafood it sells each week are its best recommendation. No resv. Inevitable waits, sometimes lengthy ones. Erratic svce. Other locations: 43 Boylston St., Newton (277-7300); and Kendall Square, Cambridge (864-3400). Excellent value. *Seafood.* **B–I**

🍷 **Felicia's** (dwntwn), 145A Richmond St. (second floor) (523-9885). A/C. Dinner only, daily; closed Easter, Thanksgiving, Dec 25. AE, MC, V. Jkt. *Specialties:* fresh homemade pasta, shrimp Toscano, chicken w. verdicchio, seafood cannelloni, veal Margarita. *Note:* Wholly authentic Italian trattoria with charming period decor and diligent, courteous svce. Locally popular for more than 30 years. No resv., unfortunately. *Italian.* **I**

🍷 **Jimmy's Harborside** (nr. dwntwn), 242 Northern Ave., on the waterfront (423-1000). A/C. Lunch/dinner Mon–Sat; closed Dec 25. AE, CB, DC, MC, V. Jkt. *Specialties:* clam chowder, shrimp Charles, oysters Rockefeller, excellent seafood. Good American wine list. *Note:* The best clam chowder in all Boston. Remarkable seafood at reasonable prices and a very lovely view of the harbor (especially from the second floor). Locally very popular for more than a half century. Very efficient svce. One disappointment: Jimmy's closes relatively early (9:30pm). Resv. advised. Valet parking. *Seafood.* **I**

☼☽♀ **The Last Hurrah** (dwntwn), in the Omni Parker House (see ☽☼ Ⴤ "Accommodations," above) (227-8600). A/C. Lunch/ dinner daily (until midnight). AE, CB, DC, MC, V. Jkt. *Specialties:* Boston scrod (haddock), clam chowder, prime rib, daily specials. *Note:* A favorite hangout of Boston journalists and politicians in the basement of the venerable Parker House Hotel. Pleasant atmosphere, especially at lunch (the orchestra is a bit obtrusive in the evening). Pretty, retro decor w. a mahogany bar and Tiffany lamps. Resv. advised. *American.* I

Ⴤ **Imperial Teahouse** (dwntwn), 70 Beach St. (426-8439). A/C. Lunch/dinner daily (until 2am). AE, CB, DC, MC, V. *Specialties:* dim sum (at lunch), soup of eight delights, char siu ding, braised duck. *Note:* A highly commendable rest. in the heart of Boston's Chinatown. Vast and inviting, w. elegant Oriental decor and good svce. Resv. are possible but waits are inevitable on the wknd. *Chinese.* **B–I**

Ⴤ **No Name** (dwntwn), 15½ Fish Pier (338-7539). A/C. Ⴤ Lunch/dinner Mon–Sat (until 9:30pm). No credit cards. *Specialties:* clam chowder, grilled fish, fried clams. *Note:* On the pier itself, this seafood rest. w. rather spartan decor is one of the most popular in Boston. The seagulls and the ship horns add to the local color. The cuisine is as simple as the decor, but the seafood is the highest quality. Efficient svce and an excellent value. A Boston classic since 1917. *Seafood.* **B–I**

Cafeterias/Fast Food

☼☽ **Elsie's** (vic.), 71 Mt. Auburn St., Cambridge (354-8781). ☽☼ Lunch/dinner daily. No credit cards. *Note:* Entire generations of Harvard students have sung the praises (and continue to do so) of Elsie's huge sandwiches. A "must" for all (preferably famished) visitors.

Museum of Fine Arts Cafeteria (nr. dwntwn), 465 Huntington Ave. (267-9300). Lunch only, Tues–Sun. *Note:* Excellent cafeteria cuisine.

BARS & NIGHTCLUBS

☼☽ **Bull & Finch Pub** (dwntwn), Hampshire House, 84 Beacon St. ☽☼ (227-9600). Very lively pub (especially on weekends) and by far the most popular bar in Boston. Was the model for the television show "Cheers." Trendy restaurant on the second floor. Rather pleasant retro decor.

The Channel Club (nr. dwntwn), 25 Necco St. (451-1905). Hard rock, pop, and reggae in a dark, cavernous setting, beside the Fort Point Channel of the harbor. Locally popular. Nightly.

Citi (formerly Metro) (nr. dwntwn), 15 Landsdowne St., at Kenmore Square (262-2424). New wave, video-equipped disco; the "in" club.

Daisy Buchanan's (nr. dwntwn), 240A Newbury St. (247-8516). Relaxed, comfortable singles bar, frequented by local football and baseball stars.

Links (dwntwn), 120 Boylston St. (423-3832). Progressive dance music from swing to new wave. Casual dress. Open Thurs–Sun.

Nick's Comedy Stop (dwntwn), 100 Warrenton St. (482-0930). A very crowded comedy club in the heart of the theater district and a classic on the Boston scene for more than 30 years.

RegattaBar (vic.), in the Charles Hotel (see "Accommodations," above) (864-1200). Upscale jazz club near Harvard Square in Cambridge. All the big names from Paquito D'Rivera to Sonny Rollins to Tommy Flanagan. Call for performance dates and times. The best jazz music in the Boston area.

The Ritz Bar (dwntwn), in the Ritz Carlton Hotel (see "Accommodations," above) (536-5700). Open daily. Classy, very British bar. "High society" describes the decor, the svce, and the prices.

Ryles (vic.), Inman Square, Cambridge (876-9330). Live jazz, pop, and blues with the biggest stars. Locally popular.

Zanzibar (dwntwn), 1 Boylston Place (451-1955). Hot pop-music dance club with jungle motif decor. Open Wed–Sat.

NEARBY EXCURSIONS

CONCORD (20 mi./32km NW on Mass. 2): Known as "the cradle of the Republic," this charming historic New England town owes its name to the treaty, or concord, signed with the Native Americans soon after it was settled in 1635. A bloody confrontation at the North Bridge between British troops and the Minutemen on April 19, 1775, set the Revolutionary War in full motion. There are many historical landmark houses and museums here, including the **Old Manse,** Monument St. (open Thurs–Mon), **Orchard House,** 399 Lexington Rd. (open daily), **Concord Antiquarium Museum,** 200 Lexington Rd. (508/369-9609; open daily); and **Concord Art Association,** 37 Lexington Rd. (508/369-2578; open Tues–Sun). Many famous writers are buried in the **Sleepy Hollow Cemetery** on Bedford St., including Ralph Waldo Emerson and Nathaniel Hawthorne. Well worth the trip. Makes a good joint excursion with Lexington (see below).

GLOUCESTER (35 mi./56km NE on U.S. 1 and Mass. 128): Old fishing village with narrow, picturesque streets and very lovely beaches and cliffs nearby. Don't miss the **Hammond Castle Museum,** 80 Hesperus Ave. (508/283-2080; open daily). Built in the late 1920s by inventor John Hayes Hammond in the image of a medieval castle, the museum is dramatically situated on the Atlantic Ocean and houses its collection of Roman, medieval and Renaissance art as well as an 8,200-pipe organ.

LEXINGTON (12 mi./19km NW on Mass. 2): With Concord, another hallmark town of the Revolutionary War. There are a number of historic structures and relics here, including the **Hancock-Clarke House,** 36 Hancock St. (617/862-5598; open daily), where Paul Revere sounded warning for the Minutemen; **Buckman Tavern,** 1 Bedford St. (617/861-0928; open daily), on the site of the battle against the British (April 19, 1775); and **Munroe Tavern,** 1332 Massachusetts Ave. (617/862-1703; open daily), which served as a hospital for British troops. Worth a side trip.

LINCOLN (18 mi./29km NW on Mass. 2 and 126): See the **Gropius House,** 68 Baker Bridge Rd. (617/227-3956). The Walter Gropius family residence and the first of his designs realized in this country, this house's unadorned lines were considered avant-garde at the time of its construction (1937). Original Bauhaus furniture. Open Fri–Sun. A "must" for architecture lovers. A recommended joint excursion with Concord (see above).

MARBLEHEAD (17 mi./27km NE on Mass. 1A): On a large Massachusetts Bay promontory, this former fishing port was founded in 1629 by British sailors from Cornwall and has since become a well-known summer resort. Numerous interesting colonial houses. Don't miss the **town hall,** on Washington Square (617/631-0528; open daily), and its famous painting, *Spirit of '76.* Very popular boat races on summer wknds.

PLYMOUTH (39 mi./65km SE on Mass. 3): A name known to every American. The first permanent British colony of New England was founded on December 21, 1620, by the pilgrims of the *Mayflower.* (For more details, see the chapter on the Atlantic Coast.)

PORTSMOUTH (55 mi./88km NE on I-95): With its old waterfront neighborhood known as **Strawbery Banke,** this former New Hampshire capital of British colonial times offers one of the most handsome groups of historic buildings in the country. (For more details, see the chapter on the Atlantic Coast.)

ROCKPORT (38 mi./61km NE on U.S. 1, Mass. 128, and Mass. 127): Charming little port that has become a haven for artists. See especially the famous **Paper House,** 52 Pigeon Hill St. (508/546-2629; open daily July–Aug, rest of the year by appointment)—a baroque monument to the glory of the newspaper. A recommended combined excursion w. Gloucester (see above).

ROUTE 128 (at the I-95N and I-95S fork): Along 26 mi. (42km), this Boston beltway encompasses the largest complex of science and space research laboratories in the country. Some 700 firms, including all the giants of the electronics industry (General Electric, Honeywell, Raytheon, Wang, Digital, Geodyne, etc.), are represented, as well as NASA and U.S. Army research centers. Overall, some 50,000 scholars, engineers, and technicians make the famous Rte. 128 one of the most highly concentrated centers of brain power in the world. Also known as the "Silicon Valley of the East Coast."

SALEM (16 mi./26km NE on Mass. 1A): First capital of Massachusetts (1626–30) and scene of the infamous witch trials of 1692 (described in Arthur Miller's famous play *The Crucible*), which ended only after the hanging of 19 victims of religious fanaticism. Lovely old houses carefully preserved in the harbor area **(Maritime National Historic Site)** and around Chestnut St., notably. Many remarkable museums including the **House of the Seven Gables,** 54 Turner St. (open daily), dating from 1668, which inspired Nathaniel Hawthorne's famous novel; **Witch House,** 310½ Essex St. (open daily), where the "witches" were interrogated; the **Peabody Museum,** E. Indian Sq. (open daily), and its rich naval collections; and the **Witch Museum,** 19½ Washington Sq. (open daily), which offers a detailed re-creation of a witch trial. The **Information Center,** 178 Derby St. (617/744-4323), offers relatively complete brochures and written material. An excursion not to be missed.

SAUGUS (8 mi./13km NE on U.S. 1): Cradle of the American iron and steel industry, Saugus was the site of the continent's first foundry (1646). Don't miss the **Iron Works National Historic Site,** 224 Central St. (617/233-0050), a minutely detailed replica of the period's first smelting furnaces with forging demonstrations. Open daily, Apr–Oct. Worth the detour.

FARTHER AFIELD

CAPE COD (202 mi./323km r.t. on Mass. 3S and U.S. 6E): A virtual island, this sandy, 60-mile-long (97km) area is where the Pilgrims of the *Mayflower* landed in 1620. Charming old fishing villages and beautiful seascapes. The two neighboring islands—**Martha's Vineyard** and **Nantucket**—are favorite vacation spots of well-to-do New Yorkers and Bostonians, offering fishing, sailing, and a temperate summer climate. (For more details, see the chapter on Cape Cod.) An excursion not to be missed.

OLD STURBRIDGE VILLAGE (65 mi./104km SW on the Massachusetts Tpke., I-84, and U.S. 20) (508/347-3362): Faithful rendition of an 18th-century New England village, with more than 40 old houses, stalls, workshops, and people in period dress. Interesting slice of history. Also, a nearby car museum, the **Sturbridge Automuseum,** 2 mi. (4km) west on U.S. 20. Worth a visit. Open daily Apr–Oct, Tues–Sun the rest of the year.

Heading back to Boston, turn off at **Webster** (via Mass. 131 and 197), a small industrial town on the edge of the largest natural body of water in Massachusetts. Renamed **Lake Webster** for convenience sake, the lake's official name is actually **Lake Chargoggagoggmanchauggagoggchaubunagungamaug,** a term which, in the Nipmuc dialect, means "you fish on your side, I fish on my side, no one fishes in the middle." In addition to having the longest and most complicated name in U.S. geography, the lake is also a fishing paradise, with trout, perch, and pike. Worth going out of your way for.

Where to Stay En Route

IN STURBRIDGE The 🍴🍴 **Publick House Inn,** Mass. 131, Sturbridge, MA 01566 (508/347-3313). 17 rms. A charming little colonial inn dating from 1771 with a very satisfactory restaurant. **M**

☀ **THE BERKSHIRES** (336 mi./538km r.t. on I-90W and U.S. 20N to Pittsfield): With its undulating landscapes, dense forests, and dozens of lakes and charming old New England villages, the Berkshires region is a favorite vacation haven in all seasons: in winter for cross-country skiing; in summer for its music and theater festivals (the Tanglewood Music Festival, the Williamstown Theater Festival, and the Berkshire Theater Festival are among the most popular in the country); and from mid-Sept to late Oct, for the sumptuous colors of its autumn leaves.

Crossing through the Berkshires from the Vermont border to southern Connecticut, U.S. 7 allows a complete picture of the area and its most remarkable locales: **Lenox,** the picturesque town celebrated by Nathaniel Hawthorne (*Tanglewood Tales*), has been the backdrop each summer for half a century for the **Tanglewood Music Festival** (late June to late Aug) with the Boston Symphony Orchestra (for information, call 413/637-1940).

Pittsfield offers, among other attractions, the **Berkshire Museum,** 39 South St., with its collection of European paintings (Rubens, van Dyck, etc.); **Arrowhead,** 780 Holmes Rd., the residence-museum where Herman Melville wrote *Moby-Dick;* and the very lovely Shaker village of **Hancock** (5 mi./8km west on U.S. 20) (413/443-0188), a religious community founded in 1790 where some 20 period buildings still stand. A visit not to be missed.

Stockbridge, a magnificent little summer community that seems to come straight out of an old picture book, has attracted many artists (sculptor Daniel Chester French, painter Norman Rockwell, author Norman Mailer, etc.) and is home to the renowned **Berkshire Theater Festival** (late June to Sept; for information, call 413/298-5536). Two stops not to be missed: the **Norman Rockwell Museum,** on Main St., and the **studio of Daniel Chester French,** on Mass. 183.

Williamstown, another charming little village typical of the Berkshires with its old houses in pastel tones, has a very beautiful art museum with rich impressionist collections, the **Sterling and Francine Clark Institute,** 225 South St. Home of venerable **Williams College** (est. 1793) and of the **Williamstown Theater Festival** (late June to late Aug), which offers modern and classical theater with famous actors. An absolute must since 1954. (For information, call 413/597-3400.)

A visit to the Berkshires is not to be missed for all lovers of art and culture. For regional tourist information, contact the **Berkshire Hills Visitors Bureau,** Berkshire Commons South, Pittsfield, MA 01201 (413/443-9186).

Where to Stay En Route

IN LENOX ☀ 🍴🍴 **Apple Tree,** 224 West St., Lenox, MA 01240 (413/637-1477). 33 rms. Century-old inn amid lovely gardens. **M–E**

IN PITTSFIELD 🍴🍴 **Hilton Inn,** Berkshire Common and West St., Pittsfield, MA 01201 (413/499-2000). 175 rms. Modern comfort. **M**

♗ **Heart of the Berkshires,** 970 W. Housatonic, MA 01201
(413/443-1255). 16 rms. Small, functional motel. **I**

IN STOCKBRIDGE ☀ ♙♙♙ **Red Lion Inn,** Main St. at U.S. 7, Stockbridge, MA
01262 (413/298-5545). 100 rms. Charming inn dating from 1773. **I–E**

IN WILLIAMSTOWN ♙♙♙ **Orchards,** 222 Adams Rd., Williamstown, MA 01267
(413/458-9611). 49 rms. Elegant old-English–style inn. **E**

♗ **Berkshire Hills,** Cold Spring Rd. (U.S. 7S), MA 01267 (413/
458-3950). 21 rms. Small motel in the woods. **I–M**

🔭 **VERMONT & THE NEW HAMPSHIRE MOUN-
TAINS:** (568 mi./908km r.t. from Boston via I-93N, N.H.
106N, U.S. 3N, N.H. 25E, N.H. 16N, U.S. 302W, N.H. 10S, U.S. 4W, U.S. 7S,
Vt. 9E, N.H. 9E, N.H. 101E, U.S. 3S, Mass. 128W, and Mass. 2E): This trip,
requiring at least three or four days and taking you through some of the most
beautiful wooded country in the U.S., is suitable for all seasons: the long winter
snows, the lovely New England spring, the radiant summer, or the splendid autumn which sets the forests of New Hampshire's **White Mountains** and
Vermont's **Green Mountains** ablaze with color.

Leaving Boston northward along I-93, you soon come to your first stop,
Concord, the capital of New Hampshire. See the 1819 **Statehouse,** on Main St.
(603/271-2154; open Mon–Fri), with its hall of flags and its characteristic
dome. If you enjoy handcrafts you'll certainly want to visit the ⛪ **Concord Arts
and Crafts Center,** 36 N. Main St. (open Mon–Sat).

Farther north on N.H. 106 you'll come to ⛪ **Canterbury Shaker Village,** on
Shaker Rd. off N.H. 106 (603/783-9511), open Tues–Sat from mid-May
through Oct. Founded in 1792 and today one of the only two active Shaker villages remaining in the U.S., it can still show half a dozen of its original buildings
and a little museum illustrating the unusual Shaker life-style. Well worth the side
trip.

The next stop is ☀ **Laconia,** a popular summer resort in the heart of the
"lakes region" (one of the lakes is New Hampshire's largest, Lake Winni-
pesaukee). Continue north to ☀ **White Mountain National Forest,** a wooded
tract of 741,000 acres (300,000ha) whose highest peak, 🔭 **Mount Washington,**
rises to 6,288 ft. (1,917m). A road reached from **Glen House** on N.H. 16, and a
cog railway whose terminus is a little north of Crawford House on U.S. 302
(603/846-5404), will take you to the top of Mt. Washington from the end of
May till Oct, and give you a breathtaking view. Many winter-sports resorts and
spectacular gorges are nearby: **Crawford Notch, Dixville Notch, Franconia
Notch, Pinkham Notch,** etc.

A very lovely scenic drive, the ⛪ **Kancamagus Highway** (N.H. 112) crosses
the White Mountains from side to side. On your way, don't fail to visit the lovely
resort of ⛪ **Bretton Woods,** famous as the scene of a 1944 international monetary conference which fixed the price of gold at $35 per ounce and created the
International Bank for Reconstruction and Development (World Bank).

Regaining the right bank of the Connecticut River at **Woodsville,** your
route stays on it for about 50 mi. (80km) on beautiful, scenic N.H. 10, passing
the historic little town of ☀ **Hanover,** the home of famous Dartmouth College,
founded in 1796. ☀⛪ **Woodstock,** the next stop, with its charming old houses, is
one of Vermont's best-known ski resorts. Continuing toward the Green Mountains and **Sherburne Pass,** you'll come to **Rutland** and its renowned marble
quarries; at the ⛪ **Vermont Marble Exhibit,** 61 Main St. (802/459-3311), open
daily from late May through Oct, see how marble is quarried and then turned
into works of art.

Manchester, the next stop, has been a popular summer and winter resort for more than a century. The ☀⛰ **Equinox Skyline Drive,** a mountain road rising as high as 3,835 ft. (1,169m), will give you a magnificent view of the endless woodlands of the **Green Mountain National Forest;** it can be reached from U.S. 7, 6 mi (9km) south of Manchester. Road open May–Oct; difficult in rainy or foggy weather. Don't miss it. There's a very popular classical-music festival every summer at the **Southern Vermont Art Center,** West Rd.; call 802/362-1405 for programs and schedules.

The trip ends at ☀ **Bennington,** where in 1777, in one of the decisive engagements of the War of Independence, Ethan Allen's "Green Mountain Boys" held off the British under General Burgoyne. Lovely old Colonial houses at ⛰ **Old Bennington,** and a remarkable **city museum** on W. Main St. (802/447-1571; open daily Mar–Nov), with paintings by the American primitive, Grandma Moses. Don't miss it.

Finally, back to Boston across the Appalachian foothills, following various scenic highways: Vt. 9, N.H. 9, and N.H. 101. A spectacular excursion for lovers of unspoiled nature.

Where to Stay En Route

IN BENNINGTON, VT. 🍴 **Vermonter,** Vt. 9W, Bennington, VT 05201 (802/442-2529). 32 rms and cottages. Comfortable, well-run little motel on a lake with sand beach. Closed Mar–Apr. **I**

IN BRETTON WOODS, N.H. ☀ 🍴🍴 **Mount Washington,** U.S. 302, Bretton Woods, NH 03575 (603/278-1000). 216 rms. Charming old Edwardian-style hotel against a splendid mountain backdrop. **E–VE** (Modified American Plan)

IN CONWAY, N.H. ☀ 🍴🍴 **Merrill Farm,** N.H. 16, Conway, NH 03818 (603/447-3866). 43 rms. Picturesque riverside country inn whose oldest parts date from 1780. Open May–Oct. **M–E**

IN WOODSTOCK, VT. 🍴🍴🍴 **Woodstock Inn and Resort,** Village Green, Woodstock, VT 05091 (802/457-1100). 120 rms. Luxurious resort hotel with a clear view over the town. **VE**

☀🍴🍴 **Kedron Valley,** Vt. 106, South Woodstock, VT 05071 (802/457-1473). 29 rms. Charming old inn built in 1840 and prettily restored. Closed Apr. **M–E**

Where to Eat En Route

IN MENDON, VT. ☀🍷🍷 **Countryman's Pleasure,** Townline Rd. (802/773-7141). Dinner only, Tues–Sat. Poached salmon, rack of lamb. Century-old Colonial-style house; open-air dining in good weather. **I–M**

IN NORTH CONWAY, N.H. ☀🍷🍷 **Scottish Lion,** on U.S. 302 (603/356-6381). Lunch/dinner daily. 1872 country inn; Scottish-inspired food. **I**

CHAPTER 2

CAPE COD

□ □ □

With Martha's Vineyard and Nantucket♆

It was in **Provincetown** Bay, at the northern end of Cape Cod, that on November 19, 1620, the 101 Pilgrim Fathers disembarked from the *Mayflower* and set foot for the first time on American soil. The long, sandy promontory, for years a region of simple fishing villages, has undergone a profound change since the beginning of the 20th century: it is now one of the most sought-after and select resort areas in the country. The peninsula of Cape Cod, shaped strangely like a lobster's claw, is a 70-mile stretch of sand dunes, pine forests, immaculate beaches discreetly hidden from the highway, nature reserves such as the **Cape Cod National Seashore** and **Monomoy National Wildlife Refuge** (once a haunt of pirates), and spruce little towns of old houses and unobtrusive newer estates such as **Brewster, Chatham, Falmouth, Harwich, Orleans, Sandwich,** and **Yarmouth.**

Much of the political and financial establishment of New York and Boston, led by the Kennedy family, has taken to summering at the Cape or on one of the two delightful islands nearby, **Martha's Vineyard** and **Nantucket.** The price of this success is that the "sold out" notices go up all along the Cape seashore in July and August, particularly over weekends. The best times to go are spring and, even better, fall; the favorite amusements (besides idling or strolling on the 275 mi./440km of fine sand beaches), are sailing, surfing, and above all deep-sea fishing. There are more than a dozen species of big-game fish in these waters, including a highly prized variety of giant tuna.

BASIC FACTS: State of Massachusetts. Area code: 508. Time zone: eastern. First colonized: 1637 (Sandwich), 1639 (Hyannis-Yarmouth), 1642 (Martha's Vineyard). Approximate population: 175,000 year round; 500,000 in July–Aug.

CLIMATE: Although the city of Boston is quite close, Cape Cod enjoys a much less extreme climate due to the sea breezes in summer (mean temperature in July 71°F/22°C) and the Gulf Stream in winter (mean temperature in Jan 38°F/4°C). Spring and fall offer enjoyable temperatures and plenty of sunshine.

DISTANCES: Boston, 55 mi. (89km); New York, 270 mi. (432km).

ARRIVAL & TRANSIT INFORMATION

AIRPORTS: Hyannis-Barnstable Municipal Airport (HYA), 1 mi. (1.6km) north of Hyannis. Cab, $4. Information: 775-2020.

Martha's Vineyard Airport (MVY), 6 mi. (9.6km) west of Edgartown. Cab, $15. Information: 693-0550.
Nantucket Memorial Airport (ACK), 3 mi. (5km) south. Cab, $10. Information: 228-2765.

AIRLINES: Delta Connection (toll free 800/345-3400), Hyannis and Nantucket to Boston; Continental Express (toll free 800/525-0280), Hyannis, Martha's Vineyard, and Nantucket to Boston and New York.

BUS OR CAR RENTAL? Given the distances involved, the only ways of seeing Cape Cod are by bus or a rental car. Greyhound buses provide direct connections between Hyannis or Woods Hole (from which the ferry leaves for the islands) and Boston or New York. Bonanza Bus Lines offers several buses a day from Hyannis or Provincetown to the station in Providence, R.I., where connections can be made with Amtrak trains.

CAR RENTAL: Avis, Hyannis-Barnstable Airport (775-2888); Budget, on Mass. 132, Hyannis (775-3832); Hertz, Hyannis-Barnstable Airport (775-5825); National, on Mass. 132, Hyannis (771-4353); Thrifty, on Mass. 132, Hyannis (771-0450).

TRAIN: Nearest Amtrak station: 100 Gaspee St., Providence, R.I. (401/751-5416). From May to Sept there is regular svce (6 hr.) between New York and Hyannis; for information, call toll free 800/872-7245. Also between Boston (Braintree T Station) and Hyannis, May–Oct; for information, call 617/771-1145.

INTERCITY BUSES: Bonanza, 17 Elm St., Hyannis (775-5524); Boston (617/423-5810); Provincetown (487-9007); Woods Hole (548-5011).

FERRY: Boston–Nantucket or Provincetown, Bay State Spray Cruises (June–Sept). 3 hr. by catamaran. 20 Long Wharf, Boston (617/723-7800).
Falmouth–Martha's Vineyard, from the end of May to mid-Oct, on the *Island Queen* (548-4800).
Hyannis–Martha's Vineyard and Nantucket, Hyline (May–Dec), Pier 1, Ocean St. Dock (778-2600); Steamship Authority (in summer), Ocean St. Dock (771-4000).
Provincetown–Boston, Bay State Spray Cruises (June–Sept), Town Wharf (487-1741).
Woods Hole–Martha's Vineyard and Nantucket (year round), Steamship Authority (540-2022; toll free 800/352-7144).

INFORMATION & TOURS

TOURIST INFORMATION: Cape Cod Chamber of Commerce, U.S. 6 and Mass. 132, Hyannis, MA 02061 (508/362-3225); **Martha's Vineyard Chamber of Commerce,** Beach Rd., Vineyard Haven, MA 02568 (508/693-0085); **Nantucket Island Chamber of Commerce,** Main St., Nantucket, MA 02554 (508/228-1700); **Provincetown Chamber of Commerce,** 307 Commercial St., Provincetown, MA 02657 (508/487-3424).

GUIDED TOURS: Hyline, Pier 1, Ocean St. Dock, Hyannis (778-2600): Boat excursions, summer only.
Cape Cod & Hyannis Railroad, 252 Main St., Hyannis (771-1145): Entertaining round-trip between Hyannis and Woods Hole in a little steam train. Daily May–Oct.

Island Tours, Straight Wharf Boat Basin, Nantucket (228-0334): 75-min. bus tours of the island. Daily May–Oct.

Portuguese Princess, Town Wharf, Provincetown (487-2651): 3½hr. narrated whale-watch boat excursion. Daily Apr–Nov.

Whale Watcher cruises, P.O. Box 254, Barnstable Harbor (775-1622): Narrated 4-hr. whale-watching excursion. Twice daily from early Apr to late Oct. Resv. required.

CAPE COD NATIONAL SEASHORE (26 mi./41km NE
of Hyannis along U.S. 6): A 44,000-acre nature reserve along the shore, offering beautiful seascapes including dramatic white ocean beaches, dunes, woodlands, and marshes. Established in 1961 by President Kennedy to protect the less-developed areas of the Cape from commercialism, the area preserves notable examples of typical Cape Cod architecture. There are **Visitor Centers** at Provincetown and at Eastham (349-3785). Worth going out of your way for.

MARTHA'S VINEYARD & NANTUCKET (respectively
5 mi./8km and 30 mi./48km off Woods Hole): These islands, home to a very active whaling community in the 18th century, have now become fashionable summer resorts with a wealth of attractions for holidaymakers. They have many charming small villages with beautiful old houses, the climate is generally temperate, and there are ferries all year from Woods Hole. Martha's Vineyard is also a naturalist's paradise. Both are worth visiting. Off Martha's Vineyard lies the half-wild little island of **Chappaquiddick.**

MONOMOY NATIONAL WILDLIFE REFUGE (3 mi./
5km, off Chatham): Designated a wilderness area by the federal government in 1970, Monomoy Island attracts tens of thousands of migrating birds to its dunes (late May to Nov). Access by boat only from Chatham. For further information: Refuge manager, Morris Island, Chatham, MA 02633 (508/945-0594).

PROVINCETOWN (50 mi./80km NE of Hyannis along
U.S. 6): The first landfall for the Pilgrims (see the introduction to this chapter). A picturesque little port at the tip of Cape Cod, whose waters attracted at the turn of the century a large colony of Portuguese fishermen, still plying their trade today. Today the town is an artists' colony and hosts a large gay community. A 247-ft. (77m) granite tower with a splendid view over the Cape, and a little historical museum commemorate the landing of the Pilgrims. An absolute must-see.

YARMOUTH (4 mi./6km north of Hyannis by Willow Rd.):
One of the oldest (1639) villages on the Cape, with an authentic New England atmosphere. Not to be missed.

MUSEUMS: At Brewster, the **Drummer Boy Museum,** 2½ mi. (4km) west on Mass. 6A (896-3823), is housed in a converted windmill built in 1750; devoted to Revolutionary history. Worth the detour. Open daily from the end of May to the end of Oct only.

At Nantucket, the **Whaling Museum,** Broad St. (228-1736), depicts the life of the Nantucket whalers that inspired Herman Melville to write *Moby-Dick*. Fascinating. Open daily in summer, wknds the rest of the year.

At Provincetown, the **Historical Museum** and **Pilgrim Monument,** Mon-

CAPE COD

Atlantic Ocean

Cape Cod National Seashore

Provincetown Airport

Provincetown

Truro

Wellfleet

S. Wellfleet

Eastham

Orleans

Brewster

Cape Cod Bay

W. Barnstable

Barnstable

Yarmouth Port

Dennis

E. Dennis

S. Yarmouth

West Dennis

Dennis Port

E. Harwich

Harwich Port

Chatham

Monomoy National Wildlife Refuge

Monomoy Island

Nantucket Sound

To Nantucket Island

W. Yarmouth

Hyannis

Craigville

Centerville

Osterville

Mashpee

Sandwich

Sagamore

Bourne

Massachusetts Military Reservation

Waquoit

N. Falmouth

Pocasset

Falmouth

Woods Hole

To Martha's Vineyard

Buzzards Bay

New Bedford

Plymouth

6

6

3

25

195

28

N

kms. 10
miles 6

0
0

ument Hill (487-1310), give the history of the *Mayflower* and the Pilgrims. Open daily Apr–Nov.

At Sandwich, the **Glass Museum,** 129 Main Sq. (888-0251). Interesting museum of glassmaking with a collection of 3,000 exhibits; open daily in summer, wknds the rest of the year. The ⚐ **Heritage Plantation,** Grove St. and Pine St. (888-3300), is a small historical museum housed, as its name suggests, in a 19th-century plantation house. It has a fine collection of classic cars, including a fabulous 1931 Duesenberg that belonged to Gary Cooper. Don't miss it. Open daily from the end of May to the end of Oct; closed the rest of the year.

SPECIAL EVENTS: For the exact schedule of events below, consult the appropriate chamber of commerce (see above under "Information & Tours").

Daffodil Weekend (Nantucket; last wknd in Apr): Classic-car parade.

Academy Playhouse (Orleans; late June through Aug): Theater festival with comedy, drama, and musicals. For information, call 255-9929.

Blessing of the Fleet (Provincetown; late June): Lively and colorful.

Antiques Fair (Hyannis; July): More than 50 exhibitors.

Striped Bass & Bluefish Derby (Martha's Vineyard; mid-Sept to mid-Oct): Annual deep-sea fishing tournament which attracts some 2,000 skilled contestants.

ACCOMMODATIONS

A Note on Accommodations: Room rates on and around Cape Cod are coded as follows: **VE,** Very Expensive ($140 and up); **E,** Expensive ($90–$140); **M,** Moderate ($60–$90); **I,** Inexpensive ($30–$60); **B,** Budget (up to $30). A listing of toll-free numbers is in the Appendix.

Personal Favorites (in order of preference)

☼ ♟ ♟ ♟ **Jared Coffin House,** 29 Broad St., Nantucket, MA 02554 (508/228-2400). 58 rms, color TV (in most). AE, CB, DC, MC, V. Free parking, rest. (Jared's) bar, rm svce, free crib. *Note:* Old private house artistically restored, to which five adjoining buildings, dating from 1720 to 1870, have been added after an elegant job of renovation. Comfortable rms w. period furniture, each decorated in a different style. Romantic atmosphere, beautiful gardens, exemplary svce and reception. Very acceptable rest. Resv. required. Open year round. **M–E**

♟ ♟ ♟ **New Seabury Resort,** Redbrook Rd., New Seabury, MA 02649 (508/477-9111; toll free 800/752-9700). 368 rms (some w. kitchenettes), A/C, color TV, in-rm movies. AE, CB, DC, MC, V. Free parking, private beach, health club, sauna, two golf courses, 16 tennis courts, boating, rest., bar, rm svce, nightclub, free crib. *Note:* Resort complex offering both comfort and luxury, standing in its own 1,900+ acres, with 5 mi. (8km) of private beach. Individual villas or spacious rms w. patios. Efficient svce but so-so rest. Sailboats available to guests; very comprehensive sports facilities. Resv. advised, well in advance. Open year round. **E–VE**

☼ ♟ ♟ **Old Yarmouth Inn,** Mass. 6A, Yarmouth Port, MA 02675 (508/362-3191). 14 rms, color TV. AE, MC, V. Free parking, rest., bar. *Note:* Charming little inn housed in Cape Cod's oldest (1692) building. Huge, comfortable rms; excellent rest. serving traditional American food; svce a little inattentive. Resv. a must. Open Mar–Nov. **M–E**

☼ ♟ ♟ **Charlotte Inn,** 27 S. Summer St., Edgartown, Martha's Vineyard, MA 02539 (508/627-4751). 24 rms, color TV in some. AE, MC, V. Free parking, rest. (L'Etoile), antiques shop, free breakfast. *Note:* The best in Martha's Vineyard, with both style and refinement; five delightful houses from the 1820s lovingly restored. Rms elegant and comfortable, w. antique furniture and private patios. Well-regarded rest.; reception and svce w. a smile. A few steps from the harbor. **E-VE**

♀♀ **Coonamessett Inn,** Jones Rd. (at Gifford St.), Falmouth, MA
Ⅼ Ⅼ 02541 (508/548-2300). 22 rms, A/C, color TV. AE, CB, DC, MC, V. Free parking, rest., bar, free breakfast. *Note:* Typical small country farmhouse, Cape Cod style, in its own fine gardens beautifully situated at the edge of a lake. Interior arrangements at once lavish and cozy. Good rest. Open year round. **E,** but lower rates off-season.

♀ **Captain Gosnold Village,** 230 Gosnold St., Hyannis, MA
Ⅼ 02601 (508/775-9111). 54 rms and studios half w. kitchenettes, color TV, in-rm movies. AE, MC, V. Free parking, pool, gardens. *Note:* Likable motel near the beach, w. friendly reception and svce. Inviting rms w. refrigerators. Very pleasant gardens. Free airport limo. Ideal for families. Good value out of season. Open year round. **M**

♀ **Earl of Sandwich Motor Manor,** Old Kings Hwy. (Mass. 6A),
Ⅼ E. Sandwich, MA 02537 (508/888-1415). 24 rms, A/C, color TV. AE, CB, DC, MC, V. Free parking, nearby coffee shop, free breakfast, crib $5. *Note:* Comfortable little motel in vaguely Tudor style; friendly reception; good value; open year round. **I-M,** but lower rates off-season.

♀ **Americana Holiday,** 99 Main St., West Yarmouth, MA 02673
Ⅼ (508/775-5511). 154 rms, A/C, color TV, in-rm movies. MC, V. Free parking, three pools, sauna, health club, bicycles, putting green, nearby coffee shop, crib $5. *Note:* Classic motel style, modest but well maintained, w. utilitarian comforts. Family clientele. Good overall value. Open Mar–Nov. **I-M,** but lower rates off-season.

Other Accommodations (from top bracket to budget)

♀♀♀ **Nantucket Inn,** 27 Macy's Lane, Nantucket, MA 02554
Ⅼ Ⅼ Ⅼ (508/228-6900; toll free 800/343-7000). 100 rms, A/C, cable color TV. AE, CB, DC, MC, V. Free parking, two pools, two tennis courts, health club, rest. (Windsong), bar, rm svce, nightclub. *Note:* A newcomer to the ranks of the area's deluxe hotels. Modern architecture gives the effect of an island rising out of an attractive garden. All the rms are commodious and comfortable minisuites furnished in period style. Svce of the highest order. Caters to VIPs and conferences. Free bus service to the beach and dwntwn Nantucket; time, 5 min. A fine place; open year round. **E-VE,** but lower rates off-season.

♀♀♀ **Tara Hyannis Resort,** 35 Scudder Ave., Hyannis, MA 02601
Ⅼ Ⅼ Ⅼ (508/775-7775). 225 rms, A/C, cable color TV. AE, CB, DC, MC, V. Free parking, two pools, golf, tennis court, health club, saunas, rest. (Silver Shell), coffee shop, bar, rm svce, nightclub, hrdrsr, cinema, concierge, free crib. *Note:* A comfortable, luxurious modern hotel, 5 min. from the beach, surrounded by more than 50 acres of gardens. Very comprehensive sports facilities. Spacious rms w. patios or balconies. Good svce. Group clientele. Attractive vacation packages. Open year round. **E-VE,** but lower rates off-season.

♀♀ **Wychmere Harbor Club,** 23 Snow Inn Rd., Harwich Port,
Ⅼ Ⅼ MA 02646 (508/432-1000). 115 rms, color TV, in-rm movies. AE, MC, V. Free valet parking, pool, sauna, tennis court, putting green, boating, rest., bar, rm svce, disco, crib $10. *Note:* Elegant older hotel right on the harbor; peerless layout and amenities. Rms w. private balconies or patios, the nicest overlooking the water. Well-thought-of rest. w. open-air terrace in good weather. Thoughtful svce. Private beach and lovely garden open to guests. Open early May to Oct. **E-VE** (modified American Plan), but lower rates off-season.

☀♀♀ **Queen Anne Inn,** 70 Queen Anne Rd., Chatham, MA 02633
Ⅼ Ⅼ (508/945-0394). 30 rms, most A/C, color TV in public rms. AE, CB, DC, MC, V. Free parking, pool, boating, rest., bar, rm svce, free crib. *Note:* Gracious Victorian house very near the beach; enormous antique-furnished

rms (some with balconies and fireplaces), the best overlooking garden and bay. A warm welcome here; also admirable cooking. Observation trips by boat offered during whale migrations. This small hotel can be warmly recommended. Open year round. **E–VE**

🍸🍸 **Sheraton–Ocean Park Inn,** U.S. 6, Eastham, MA 02642 🛏🛏 (508/255-5000; toll free, see Sheraton). 107 rms, A/C, cable color TV. AE, CB, DC, MC, V. Free parking, two pools, tennis court, health club, sauna, rest., bar, rm svce, disco, crib $5. *Note:* Congenial hotel at the entrance to Cape Cod National Seashore. Comfortable rms, good sports facilities, efficient svce. Free bus to beach in season. Good value out of season. Interesting full American Plan rates. Open year round. **E,** but lower rates off-season.

🍸🍸 **Bradford Gardens,** 178 Bradford St., Provincetown, MA 🛏🛏 02657 (508/487-1616). 18 rms (doubles only, 10 w. kitchenettes), color TV. AE, MC, V. Free parking. *Note:* Two elegant cottages dating from 1820, w. comfortable rms, patios, and balconies. No bar, no rest., but coffee shop nearby. Open from Apr to the end of Nov. Near beach. **M–E,** but lower rates off-season.

☼🍸🍸 **Daggett House,** 59 N. Water St., Edgartown (Martha's Vine-🛏🛏 yard), MA 02539 (508/627-4600). 26 rms, cable color TV in lounge. MC, V. Free parking. *Note:* Inviting rms in a charming 17th-century house and two adjoining cottages; atmosphere very characteristic of New England. Beautiful gardens; no bar, no rest., but free breakfast. Private beach. Open year round. **M–E,** but lower rates off-season.

🍸 **Green Harbor,** Shore Rd., East Falmouth, MA 02536 (508/🛏 548-4747). 40 rms (doubles only, 17 w. kitchen), A/C, color TV. AE, CB, DC, MC, V. Free parking, pool, beach. Boats available to guests. *Note:* Small, quiet, comfortable motel ideal for families. No bar, no rest. Open year round. **M,** but lower rates off-season.

🍸 **Lewis Bay Motel,** 53 South St., Hyannisport, MA 02601 🛏 (508/775-6633). 63 rms (doubles only), A/C, color TV. AE, CB, DC, MC, V. Free parking, pool, rest., bar. *Note:* Typical motel nr. the terminal of the Nantucket ferry, looking out over the harbor and marina. Run-of-the-mill comfort, affable svce, good overall value. Open year round. **M,** but lower rates off-season.

🍸 **Cranberry Cottages,** Box 146, U.S. 6, Eastham, MA 02642 🛏 (508/255-0602). 14 cottages for two to four persons, 7 w. kitchen. Cable color TV. No credit cards. Free parking, crib $9. *Note:* Pleasing little Cape Cod cottages in a shady grove. No bar, no rest. Ideal for families; open year round. **I–M**

🍸 **Iyanough Hills Motor Lodge,** Iyanough Rd., Hyannis, MA 🛏 02601 (508/771-4804). 104 rms, A/C, cable color TV. AE, MC, V. Free parking, free breakfast, pool, sauna. Adjoining coffee shop, gardens. *Note:* Congenial, well-run motel 5 min. from Hyannis airport. Huge, comfortable rms, some w. kitchenettes. Good-natured svce. Attractive family packages. Very good overall value. Open year round. **I–M,** but lower rates off-season.

RESTAURANTS

A Note on Restaurant Prices: Cape Cod restaurant prices, per person, excluding drinks and service charges, are coded as follows: **VE,** Very Expensive ($60 and up); **E,** Expensive ($40–$60); **M,** Moderate ($25–$40) **I,** Inexpensive ($15–$25); **B,** Budget (up to $15).

Personal Favorites (in order of preference)

☼🍸🍸🍸 **Chillingsworth Restaurant,** 2449 Main St., Brewster (896-🍽🍽🍽 3460). A/C. Lunch Tues–Sat. year round; dinner Tues.–Sun.

late June to mid-Sept, wknds only in spring and fall; brunch Sun. AE, CB, DC, MC, V. Jkt. *Specialties:* magret de canard with figs, broiled shrimp in sauce chinois, escalope of salmon with asparagus, lobster w. basil and cognac cream, grilled pheasant w. raspberry sauce. Menu changes regularly. Rather sparse wine list. *Note:* French-inspired cuisine in an enchanting colonial house almost three centuries old amid wonderful gardens. Handsome Louis XV decor. Polished reception and svce. A truly remarkable place. Resv. a must. *French/Continental.* **M–E** (prix fixe)

🍷🍷🍷 **Chanticleer,** 9 New St., Siasconset (Nantucket Is.) (257-🍷🍷 6231). Lunch/dinner Thurs–Tues; closed Nov to early May. MC, V. Jkt. *Specialties:* scallops with truffles, bass with sorrel, quail w. brandy, roast rack of lamb w. herbs, fruit sherbets. Fine wine list. *Note:* An oasis for those who love to eat, wholly French and under the masterly direction of the admirable chef, J. Charles Berruet. Engaging, urbane decor and atmosphere; one of the best rests. on the island. Resv. advised. *French.* **M–E**

🍷🍷 **21 Federal,** 21 Federal St., Nantucket (228-2121). Lunch/🍷🍷 dinner daily; brunch Sun.; closed Wed off-season. AE, MC, V. *Specialties:* lobster ravioli w. chanterelles, sautéed Muscovy duck w. figs and port, catch of the day, luscious homemade desserts. *Note:* housed in a charming 1847 Greek Revival building and affiliated w. its famous namesake in Washington, D.C., 21 Federal offers innovative modern American food and efficient, friendly svce. A fine place. Resv. advisable. *American/Seafood.* **I–M**

🍷🍷 **L'Etoile,** in the Charlotte Inn (see "Accommodations," 🍷🍷 above), 27 S. Summer St., Edgartown, Martha's Vineyard (627-5187). Dinner daily; brunch Sun.; closed Jan to mid-Feb. AE, MC, V. Jkt. *Specialties:* lobster w. cognac and cream, rack of lamb w. red wine and garlic, sautéed scallops w. wild mushrooms, pheasant w. plums. Fine wine list. *Note:* This hotel rest., very busy during the season, is one of the most elegant and highly regarded on the island. Refined French-inspired cuisine with a menu that changes regularly. Attractive Victorian setting amid lovely gardens, irreproachable svce, resv. a must. *French/Continental.* **E** (prix fixe)

🍷🍷 **The Paddock,** W. Main St. at W. End Rotary, Hyannis (775-🍷🍷 7677). A/C. Lunch/dinner daily, mid-Apr to mid-Nov; closed the rest of the year. AE, CB, DC, MC, V. Jkt. *Specialties:* coq au vin, rack of lamb, roast duckling, lobster, scampi. *Note:* A fashionable place, done up in the purest Victorian idiom. Cuisine very worthy, but devoid of imagination. Open-air terrace for fine days. Excellent svce, resv. a must, valet parking. *Continental/Seafood.* **I–M**

☼🍷🍷 **Cap'n Linnell House,** Skaket Rd., Orleans (255-3400). Dinner daily, brunch Sun; closed Dec 25. AE, CB, DC, MC, V. *Specialties:* scallops, tournedos, chicken provençale, Mandarin duck. *Note:* Modest, inviting sea captain's home from the 1850s. Rather elaborate cooking. Open-air dining in summer; live jazz in season. Very popular locally, so resv. advised. *Continental/Seafood.* **I**

Other Restaurants (from top bracket to budget)

☼🍷🍷 **Jared's,** in the Jared Coffin House (see "Accommodations," above), 29 Broad St., Nantucket (228-2400). Breakfast/dinner daily. AE, CB, DC, MC, V. Jkt. *Specialties:* shrimp Victoria, lobster in court bouillon, sautéed scallops, quail, tournedos, fish of the day. *Note:* Elegant dining rm in a carefully restored 19th-century house. Romantic atmosphere w. classical background music. Patio open in summer. Resv. advised. *Continental/Seafood.* **M**

🍷🍷🍷 **Anthony's Cummaquid Inn,** 2 Main St. (Mass. 6A), Yar-🍷🍷 mouth Port (362-4501). A/C. Dinner daily; brunch Sun; closed Dec 25. AE, MC. Jkt. *Specialties:* fish and shellfish, aged beef. *Note:* Same management, excellent fare, and slightly touristy atmosphere as the well-known Anthony's Pier 4 in Boston—a top character reference! Elegant colonial decor and most engaging country ambience. Very good svce. One of the most sought-after places on the Cape, so resv. are advised. Valet parking. *Steak/Seafood.* **I–M**

☀☆♈♈♗ **Daniel Webster Inn,** 149 Main St., Sandwich (882-3622). A/C Breakfast/lunch/dinner daily. AE, CB, DC, MC, V. Jkt. *Specialties:* fish and shellfish of the day, veal Oscar, prime beef, sautéed scallops, roast duckling. Fine wine list. *Note:* Decent but unimaginative cooking. Magnificently reconstructed interior of an 18th-century tavern. Excellent svce. Very popular locally, so resv. are advised. Beautiful English-style gardens. *Steak/Seafood.* **I–M**

♈♈♗ **The Straight Wharf,** Straight Wharf, Nantucket (228-4499). Dinner only, Tues–Sun; closed from the end of Sept to mid-June. AE, DC, MC, V. *Specialties:* sautéed soft-shell crabs, catch of the day, sushi. The menu, built around fresh fish and garden produce, changes daily. *Note:* Noteworthy modern cuisine under the direction of Marian Morash, author of several bestselling cookbooks. Ultra-professional svce. Pretty seaside decor w. unobstructed view of the harbor. Open-air terrace for fine days. Resv. must be made well in advance. *Continental/Seafood.* **I–M**

♈ **Riverway Lobster House,** Mass. 28, Bass River Bridge, South ♗ Yarmouth (398-2172). A/C. Dinner daily; brunch Sun; closed Mon off-season, Dec. 25. AE, CB, DC, MC, V. *Specialties:* lobster, roast beef, souvlaki, fish of the day. *Note:* Appealing colonial atmosphere with big open fireplaces and exposed beams. Excellent fish and shellfish. Locally popular; excellent value. *American/Seafood.* **I–M**

☀♈♈♗ **Bishop Terrace,** 118 Main St., West Harwich (432-0253). A/C. Lunch/dinner daily; brunch Sun. MC, V. Jkt. *Specialties:* stuffed lobster, roast duckling, ribs of beef, swordfish steak. *Note:* Pleasant glassed-in terrace in an inviting 250-year-old colonial house. Classic, appetizing fare; friendly svce. Resv. advised. Valet parking. Dancing wknds. *Continental/Seafood.* **I**

♈♈♗ **Coonamessett Inn,** in the hotel of the same name (see "Accommodations," above), Jones Rd. at Gifford St., Falmouth (548-2300). A/C. Breakfast/lunch/dinner daily; brunch Sun. AE, CB, DC, MC, V. Jkt. *Specialties:* fresh lobster and fish of the day. *Note:* Impressive dining rm w. lake view and a cathedral ceiling. Built in 1796. Cooking and svce both urbane. Resv. advised; a fine place. Dancing in summer. Very good value. *Seafood.* **I**

♈ **Captain's Chair,** 166 Bay View St., Hyannis (775-5000). ♗ A/C. Lunch Mon–Fri; dinner nightly; closed Mon in winter, Thanksgiving, Dec 25. AE, CB, DC, MC, V. *Specialties:* fish of the day, sautéed scallops, roast beef, duck à l' orange. *Note:* Country setting with a fine view of the bay. Piano bar. Unfussy, unaffected cooking and svce. *Steak/Seafood.* **B–I**

♈ **Landfall,** 2 Luscombe Ave., Woods Hole (548-1758). Lunch/ ♗ dinner daily; closed from the end of Sept to mid-June. AE, CB, DC, MC, V. *Specialties:* sandwiches (at lunch), broiled swordfish, baked lobster, catch of the day. *Note:* This likable fish-and-seafood restaurant stands right on the docks and offers a very fine view of the harbor. Appropriate 100% maritime decor. Friendly svce, good value. *American.* **B–I**

☀♈ **Moors,** Beach Rd. and Bradford St., Provincetown (487- ♈♗ 0840). Lunch/dinner daily; closed Oct–Mar. AE, CB, DC, MC, V. *Specialties:* Portuguese dishes, caldeirada, broiled fish. *Note:* The setting is a very picturesque reconstruction of an old whaler's house. Tasty, unpretentious food, relaxed atmosphere. *Continental/Seafood.* **B–I**

♈ **Zachariah's,** Kelley St., Edgartown (Martha's Vineyard) (627- ♗ 4394). A/C. Breakfast/lunch/dinner Mon–Sat; brunch Sun. closed Dec 25. AE, DC, MC, V. *Specialties:* fish of the day, steak, some very acceptable French dishes. *Note:* Pleasant, friendly inn dating from 1742. Food worthy but no more than that; svce assiduous. A short distance from the Chappaquiddick ferry. *Continental/American/Seafood.* **B–I**

BARS & NIGHTCLUBS

Asa Bearse House, 415 Main St., Hyannis (771-4131). Sophisticated modern jazz. Open nightly, summer only.

Atlantic Connection, 126 Circuit Ave., Oak Bluffs, Martha's Vineyard (693-7129). The Vineyard club of choice. DJ dancing, jazz, big-name dance bands. Open Thurs–Sun, summer only.

Fiddlebee's, 72 North St., Hyannis (771-6032). Live classic rock music. Open nightly, summer only.

Muse, 44 Atlantic Ave., Nantucket (228-6873). Rock, reggae, and ska bands. Also DJ dancing. Open nightly, Mar 1 to late Dec.

Surf Club, 315A Commercial St., Provincetown (487-1367). The Provincetown jug band, now in its 23rd season. Pop and rock music live seven nights a week. Open summer only.

Woodshed, Mass. 6A, Brewster (896-7771). Boisterous summer club with live music in a rustic, informal setting. Open nightly, summer only.

NEARBY EXCURSIONS

NEWPORT (60 mi./96km SW of Sagamore Bridge via U.S. 6, Mass. 124, and R.I. 138): American yachting capital (see Chapter 5 on the Atlantic Coast).

PLYMOUTH (12 mi./19km NW of Sagamore Bridge on Mass. 3): Pretty little port which has come down in history because of its connection with the epic of the *Mayflower* (see Chapter 5 on the Atlantic Coast for details about the Plymouth Plantation reconstruction and the *Mayflower II*). Not to be missed.

CHAPTER 3

NEW YORK🔦🔦🔦🔦

□ □ □

New York has 120 or more skyscrapers, around whose feet swirl crowds of all nations, colors, and tongues. But it is not—repeat, not—America. New York is everything and the opposite of everything: a unique melting pot of races, cultures, and religions. Any adjective you can conceive can be applied to this symbol of the New World, visited each year by 19 million tourists (including 3½ million foreigners), all singing the same chorus: "I love New York!"

It was a little more than 4½ centuries ago, in 1524, that Giovanni da Verrazano, a Florentine navigator in the service of King François I of France, dropped anchor—the first European to do so—in the bay of what was to become the most exciting, the most electric, and the most neurotic city of our times, the city that the architect Le Corbusier described as "a magnificent catastrophe on an enormous scale." In 1609 a British navigator employed by the Dutch East India Company, Henry Hudson, sailed up the river that bears his name, as far as Albany, now the capital of New York State, 155 mi. (250km) north of the river's mouth, thereby giving the Dutch their claim to the region. And 17 years later, in 1626, Peter Minnewit (or Minuit, as it is more commonly spelled), the first governor-general of New Netherland, purchased the island of Manhattan, 12½ mi. (20km) long and 2½ mi. (4km) wide at its widest point, from the Algonquin Indians for the moderate amount of 60 florins ($24), paid in cloth, glass beads, and other trinkets. He had his 200 Batavian and Walloon colonists build the fort of Nieuw Amsterdam on the site of what is now **Wall Street.**

Over the next half century the British, asserting a prior claim based on the explorations of John Cabot in 1497–98, pushed steadily toward New Amsterdam from the north and northeast. By 1664 the town's position was so untenable that when a British fleet sailed into the bay, the Dutch governor, Peter Stuyvesant, surrendered without a fight. New Netherland was given by King Charles II of England to his brother, the Duke of York (later the ill-fated King James II), and divided into the twin colonies of New York, named in honor of its new patron, and New Jersey. It was briefly recaptured and held by the Dutch in 1673–74, but otherwise remained British until the Revolution.

When it was designated the first official capital of the young United States in 1784, the city already boasted 33,000 inhabitants, and it has never stopped growing. In 1898 the original city on Manhattan Island was swelled by the accession of four more boroughs, **Brooklyn, Queens, the Bronx,** and **Staten Island,** each with its own style, ethnic mix, and individual character. Indeed, few of the world's great cities present as wide a gamut of characteristics as New York.

Where can more striking contrasts be found than between the trendsetters haunting the fashionable stores on Madison Ave. or Fifth Ave. and the homeless who sleep curled in corners at nearby Grand Central Terminal? Or between the twin 1,350-ft. (412m), 110-story towers of the World Trade Center or the luxury apartment houses of the Upper East Side or Battery Park City, and the wretched slums of Harlem, of "Loisaida" (a phonetic rendering by Hispanics of "Lower East Side"), or Fort Apache, the most disreputable neighborhood in the Bronx? If temples of haute cuisine like Lutèce, the Quilted Giraffe, and Le Bernardin are called "restaurants" in New York, how can the greasy spoons of the Bowery or the South Bronx bear the same name? What can the trendy lovers of opera and classical music who flock to Lincoln Center and the gaudy crowds of Greenwich Village, Chinatown, or La Marqueta, the popular marketplace for Puerto Rican foods, have in common? There's no obvious link except that "the Big Apple" (New York's nickname, which came from New Orleans jazz musicians who during the 1920s saw New York as a succulent fruit to bite into) simply *is* all these things at once—a giant melting pot for more than 7 million human beings, of whom a quarter were born in foreign lands.

The mixture of races is reflected in a mixture of tongues, which has in turn engendered a flourishing foreign-language press. New York boasts no fewer than three daily papers in Chinese, along with others in Spanish, Italian, Polish, German, Korean, Greek, and Russian.

The sheer size of New York is at the root of most of its problems—pollution, unemployment, the crime rate, the traffic snarls, the homeless, the lack of coherent city planning—and sometimes even calls into question its ability to survive. The Big Apple nearly went broke in the 1970s. But although the city lost 400,000 jobs during those dark days, it experienced a kind of economic, architectural, and cultural renaissance in the 1980s. In a skyline which changes like a kaleidoscope, old surfaces of stone or brick gave way to arrogant facades of steel, glass, and concrete: New York, "the upright city," reached for the sky to express its superabundance of energy. The former massive exodus toward distant suburbs suddenly reversed itself, causing an unprecedented real-estate boom in Manhattan and restoring to the city its almost-forfeited title as the world's financial and cultural torchbearer. In the 1990s, trouble has again appeared; no doubt the next few years will see many changes.

Not content with being the country's literary and artistic capital, New York is also its greatest port, through which 30,000 ships pass every year; its biggest stock market (Wall Street handles more than 70% of all the country's financial transactions); its biggest convention city (almost 10,000 trade shows and conventions annually); the center for its communications and media businesses; its biggest industrial city; and—for good measure—the second-largest international airport in the world. Of the 500 largest corporations in America, 118 have their headquarters here; more than 1,800 foreign corporations, including at least 250 banks, maintain branches or representatives' offices here. The revenues of New York businesses, at some $350 billion annually, exceed the gross national product of such countries as Brazil and Canada, and represent one-tenth of the GNP of the United States.

Obviously the tourist can't hope to see all this in two or three days. You should set aside at least a week for any kind of worthwhile overview of the modern Babylon, this enormous, jovial city which boasts no fewer than 350 theaters, 500 art galleries, and nearly 150 museums devoted to every form of human self-expression, no matter how far-fetched. As the publicity leaflets of the New York Visitors Bureau proudly proclaim, "You name it, and New York has a museum for it."

The city's numberless shops, boutiques, and department stores, its thousands of restaurants, its bars, its jazz dives, and its nightclubs warrant a visit all by themselves. Not to mention the famous "sidewalks of New York," for this is a city where life is often to be seen out on the street—even when it takes the form of potholes and piles of garbage.

Here are some of the scenes that make Manhattan "the world's greatest show":

□ A walk up Avenue of the Americas (Sixth Ave.), through the high-rises of Rockefeller Center;
□ The sight of the Pan Am building astride Park Ave., the most affluent residential street in the city;
□ A bird's-eye view, from a helicopter, of Manhattan's more than 120 skyscrapers, of which a full third are of recent construction;

□ A ride around Central Park in a horse-drawn cab (for those who enjoy tourist picture postcards);
□ A trip on the Staten Island Ferry, which gives you, for 50¢, the best view of the city; for backdrop you'll have the Statue of Liberty, which celebrated its 100th birthday with appropriate festivities in 1986;
□ The modern-day bohemian picture of Washington Square, with its roller skaters, chess players, and buskers;
□ The very "in" art galleries and wild and crazy fashion boutiques of Soho;
□ The magic panorama of New York by night from the top of the Empire State Building;
□ The Visitors' Gallery at the New York Stock Exchange, with the crowd of shouting, gesticulating brokers below;
□ The faces of "intellectuals," straight out of a Woody Allen movie, to be seen thronging the counterculture shrines and avant-garde galleries of Soho and Tribeca;
□ The screaming neon signs and Asian-bazaar atmosphere of Times Square.

As the writer John Dos Passos used to say, "If you can be bored in New York, you're in sorry shape."

Manhattan is laid out in a grid system (dating from 1811), with streets running from east to west and numbered from 1 to 220, and avenues running from south to north and numbered from 1 to 12, with three of the most famous—Lexington, Park, and Madison—sandwiched between Third Ave. and Fifth Ave. Broadway is the only major deviation from the grid pattern: it slants across the city from west (in the north) to east (in the south). In Lower Manhattan, in Greenwich Village and below Houston (or "Zero") St., the oldest section of the city, most streets are named rather than numbered, and the grid system of midtown is practically nonexistent. Fifth Ave. is the boundary between the east and west sides, and all midtown and uptown street addresses are numbered according to their distance from it. For New Yorkers, "uptown" means north of where you are, "downtown" means south, and "crosstown" refers to anywhere east or west of your location: this is crucial when asking for directions.

Some 12,000 "Yellow Cabs," 4,000 buses, and 250 mi. (400km) of subway lines (carrying nearly four million riders every working day) serve Manhattan and the adjoining boroughs. Aside from a few notoriously tough neighborhoods such as the north end of Harlem between 125th St. and 155th St., New York is no more unsafe for tourists than any other great city. In spite of the persistent legend to the contrary, FBI figures rank New York ninth among U.S. cities in terms of homicides (25 a year per 100,000 inhabitants), far behind Washington, Miami, Atlanta, Detroit, or St. Louis. Sensible caution should still be exercised: Don't walk alone after dark in Central Park, in the East Village and the Lower East Side (below 14th St. between First Ave. and the East River), or around Times Square after midnight. And keep alert in the subway late at night.

There are about 15,000 restaurants, cafeterias, and fast-food outlets in New York, and 100,000 hotel rooms in all categories. But demand exceeds supply, so reserve your hotel room (unless you're in search of adventure, avoid New York hotels charging less than $60 a night). It's a good idea to make reservations, too, at any restaurant with two or more stars.

New York has dozens of tourist agencies that run conducted tours of the city; some of these are mentioned under "Guided Tours," below. But the fun way to see the Big Apple is to set out through its streets on foot, without any very precise destination in mind. It is by rubbing shoulders with the nine million people of all sorts and sizes who live here that you'll capture the real flavor of the city. Manhattan's big attraction is not the Statue of Liberty or even its incredible skyline, but the endless ebb and flow of the nameless multitudes in "the city that never sleeps."

You'd need a good-sized phone book to list all the famous people who were born in one or another of New York's five boroughs. President Theodore Roosevelt was born here; so were physicist J. Robert Oppenheimer, 19th-century railroad tycoon Cornelius Vanderbilt, and Jonas Salk, inventor of the polio vaccine. You can add publisher DeWitt Wallace, founder of *Reader's Digest;* playwrights Arthur Miller, Eugene O'Neill, and Neil Simon, and violinist Yehudi Menuhin. Then there's choreographer Jerome Robbins and composers George Gershwin and Aaron Copland, sculptor George Segal, designer Louis Comfort Tiffany, and singers Harry Belafonte and Barbra Streisand. How about movie directors Stanley Kubrick, Martin Scorsese, and Woody Allen; actresses Mae West, Lauren Bacall, Rita Hayworth, and Jane Fonda; actors Groucho Marx, Humphrey Bogart, Danny Kaye, Mickey Rooney, Burt Lancaster, Walter Matthau, Tony Perkins, Robert De Niro, Alan Alda, and Al Pacino? To say nothing of writers Washington Irving, Henry James, J. D. Salinger, Henry Miller, James Baldwin, Irwin Shaw, Robert Ludlum, Mario Puzo, James Michener, Harold Robbins, and Herman Wouk, and tennis player John McEnroe. Want more? Let's close with a list of famous jazzmen: Benny Carter, Sonny Rollins, Buddy Rich, Bud Powell, Artie Shaw, Fats Waller, and Gerry Mulligan.

BASIC FACTS: State of New York. Area codes: 212 (Manhattan, the Bronx), 718 (Queens, Brooklyn, Staten Island), 516 (Long Island). Time zone: eastern. Manhattan ZIP Codes: 10001–10040. Founded: 1615. Approximate population: city, 7,360,000; metropolitan area, 9,170,000. Largest city and largest metropolitan area in the U.S. The "New York / Northeastern New Jersey Standard Consolidated Area," lying in a 50-mi. (80km) radius around Manhattan and taking in parts of New Jersey and Connecticut, has a population of more than 18 million.

CLIMATE: Its climate is one of the principal drawbacks of New York. Aside from a few weeks of agreeable weather in spring (mid-Apr to mid-May) and fall (mid-Sept to mid-Oct) the rest of the year swings between sweating and shivering weather. Summer is usually hot and muggy, with an average temperature of 77°F (25°C) in July, but high humidity. Luckily, all public buildings, stores, hotels, and restaurants are heated and air-conditioned, but watch out for the rise—or fall—in temperature when you leave. Winter is often severe, with temperatures dropping to 10°F (−15°C), particularly when the icy winds out of the north whistle down the glass-and-steel canyons of Manhattan's avenues. There's no rainy season, but it rains intermittently year round (except in winter, when it snows) to make up for it. It's wise to bring raincoats and umbrellas in spring and fall.

DISTANCES: Boston, 209 mi. (335km); Chicago, 806 mi. (1,290km); Dallas, 1,550 mi. (2,480km); Denver, 1,768 mi. (2,830km); Detroit, 634 mi. (1,015km); Los Angeles, 2,790 mi. (4,465km); Miami, 1,309 mi. (2,095km); Montréal, 378 mi. (605km); New Orleans, 1,335 mi. (2,136km); Niagara Falls, 410 mi. (656km); Philadelphia, 100 mi. (160km); Washington, D.C., 234 mi. (375km).

ARRIVAL & TRANSIT INFORMATION

AIRPORTS: The three New York airports, served by 106 airlines, collectively handle the world's heaviest passenger traffic: nearly 80 million travelers a year.
   John F. Kennedy International Airport (JFK), in Queens, 15 mi. (24km) SE of Manhattan (718/656-4444).
   La Guardia Airport (LGA), in Queens, 8 mi. (13km) NE of Manhattan (718/656-4444).

Newark International Airport (EWR), in Newark, N.J., 16 mi. (25km) SW of Manhattan (201/961-2000).

U.S. AIRLINES: American (619-6991), America West (toll free 800/247-5962), Continental (319-9494), Delta (239-0700), Eastern (986-5000), Midway (toll free 800/621-5700), New York Helicopter (toll free 800/645-3494), Northwest (toll free 800/225-2525), Pan Am (687-2600), Trump Shuttle (toll free 800/247-8786), TWA (290-2121), United (867-3000), and USAir (736-3200).

FOREIGN CARRIERS: Aer Lingus (557-1110), Air Canada (869-1900), Air France (247-0100), British Airways (toll free 800/247-9297), El Al (768-9200), Icelandair (967-8888), Japan Air Lines (838-4400), KLM (759-3600), Lufthansa (718/895-1277), Sabena (936-7800), S.A.S. (718/657-7700), Swissair (718/995-8400), Varig (682-3100), and Virgin Atlantic (toll free 800/862-8621).

CITY LINK: There is comparatively easy access between all three of the metropolitan airports and Manhattan.

John F. Kennedy International

Cab fare to mid-Manhattan, about $30–$35; time, about 50 min., but 1 hr. or more at peak traffic periods. Traffic can be nightmarish at rush hours.

Bus: Carey Transportation (718/632-0500), departs every 30 min. for Grand Central Terminal (E. 42nd St. and Park Ave.) and the Port Authority Bus Terminal (W. 42nd St. and Eighth Ave.) with intermediate stops at selected midtown hotels. Fare, $9.50; time, 50 min. to 1 hr. and 15 min.

Helicopter: New York Helicopter (toll free 800/645-3494), departs approx. every 30 min., linking the Manhattan heliports at the World Trade Center and E. 34th St. to the TWA Terminal at JFK. Fare, $62; time, approximately 12 min.

La Guardia

Cab fare from La Guardia to midtown Manhattan, about $20–$22; time, about 30–40 min.

Bus: Carey Transportation (718/632-0500), departs every 20–30 min., serving Grand Central Terminal and the Port Authority Bus Terminal (W. 42nd St. and Eighth Ave.) with intermediate stops at selected hotels. Fare, $7.50; time, 35–45 min.

Water Taxi: Pan Am Water Shuttle (toll free 800/543-3779), between E. 34th St. in midtown or Pier 11 (South St. and Wall St.) in dwntwn Manhattan and the Pan Am Shuttle at the Marine Terminal, La Guardia Airport; leaves hourly Mon–Fri. Fare, $25 one way, $45 round trip; time, 40 min. (Wall St.), 30 min. (E. 34th St.).

Newark International

Cab fare from Newark to midtown Manhattan, about $40–$45; time, about 45 min.

Bus: NYC Minibus Service (201/961-2535), departs approx. every 35 min., serving the principal Manhattan hotels; fare, $14; time, 50 min.

New Jersey Transit (201/629-8767), departs every 30 min. for the Port Authority Bus Terminal (W. 42nd St. and Eighth Ave.); fare, $7; time, 30 min.

CAR RENTAL (all serving the three New York airports as well as operating out of the in-town locations listed): Avis, 10 Manhattan offices (toll free 800/331-1212); Budget, nine Manhattan offices (toll free 800/527-0700); Dollar, two Manhattan offices (toll free 800/421-6868); Hertz, 10 Manhattan offices (toll free 800/654-3131); National, nine Manhattan offices (toll free 800/227-7368); and Thrifty, two Manhattan offices (toll free 800/367-2277).

LIMOUSINE SERVICES: Allstar Limousine Service (718/784-7766), Carey Limousine (599-1122), Farrell's Limousine Service (988-4441), London Towncars (988-9700), and Scripps Edward Limousine (371-2460).

TAXIS: New York City has two kinds of taxis, both licensed and regulated by a city agency: metered cabs and unmetered ("gypsy") cabs. The tourist unfamiliar with New York is advised to stick to metered cabs where the fare is as shown on the meter. For trips to (or even more, back from) one of the outer boroughs (except the airports), a metered cab may be hard to find; in that case it may be advisable to telephone a local unmetered cab company or "car service," taking care to agree beforehand on the fare.

Easily recognized because they're painted yellow, metered cabs may be hailed on the street, or taken from the waiting lines outside the major hotels; some may also be called by phone: **Skyline** (718/482-8686) and **Two-Way Radio** (741-0070). Many of the drivers are recent immigrants, ill-acquainted with the topography of New York and even with the English language. A tip equivalent to 20% of the meter fare is expected.

PUBLIC TRANSPORTATION: Car-rental rates in New York are among the highest in the nation; parking lots and garages are crowded and very expensive; fines for illegal parking are hard to avoid. Taxis (abundant and fairly expensive), buses, and subways are the best means of getting around Manhattan. The subway is noisy, dirty, and aging, but it runs around the clock (late-evening and night trips should be avoided) and is much the quickest and cheapest way of traveling; the fare is $1.15 regardless of how far you ride. You'll need exact change or a token on New York City buses, where the fare is the same; tokens only (purchased when you enter the station) on the subway. Trains run either local or express, and provide very complete service in Manhattan and the outer boroughs. For information, call the New York Transit Authority (718/330-1234).

TRAIN: Amtrak has two major stations in Manhattan:
Grand Central Terminal, Park Ave. and E. 42nd St. (582-6875): Trains to Chicago, Niagara Falls, Montréal, and Toronto.
Pennsylvania Station, Eighth Ave. and W. 31st St. (582-6875): All other destinations. For reservations on the Metroliner (fast train to Philadelphia, Baltimore, and Washington) *only,* call (toll free 800/523-8720).
And there's also the **Rockefeller Center Ticket Office,** 12 W. 51st St. (582-6875).

INTERCITY BUSES: Greyhound, Port Authority Bus Terminal, Eighth Ave. and W. 42nd St. (971-6322 or 730-7460).

MANHATTAN AREAS & NEIGHBORHOODS

Manhattan—an Indian word meaning "the island of hills"—is a mosaic of neighborhoods, each of which is pretty much a separate village with its own distinct character. The island does indeed constitute a huge multiracial, socially diverse patchwork, with the boundaries between the patches sharply drawn.

Note: Given the size of Manhattan, the different hotels, restaurants, buildings, museums, etc., referred to below are classified by these areas or neighborhoods. From south to north, Manhattan's principal neighborhoods are:

LOWER MANHATTAN (WALL STREET & THE FINANCIAL DISTRICT): (around Wall St. and Broad St., from City Hall to the Battery): Here you'll find the banks, the financial institutions, and the New York Stock Ex-

change. Wall Street takes its name from the wooden palisade built in 1653 by Gov. Peter Stuyvesant to protect Nieuw Amsterdam against incursions by the English and the Indians. This district, whose narrow streets are fenced in by skyscrapers, is the historic heart of Manhattan. Like most business districts it's at its liveliest during office hours, but such major tourist attractions as the South Street Seaport, apartment complexes like Battery Park City, and the stores and restaurants that grow up around them keep the streets fairly busy in the evenings and on weekends too.

TRIBECA (below Canal St. to City Hall, and west of W. Broadway): An acronym of "*TRI*angle *BE*low *CA*nal St." This neighborhood, originally called "Lower Broadway," has succeeded Soho as the fashionable hangout for the city's intelligentsia. Real-estate speculation has reached fever pitch here; run-down warehouses and old abandoned workshops are slowly giving way to trendy boutiques and to lofts where big-name artists and actors make their homes.

CHINATOWN (around lower Mott St., Bayard St., and Pell St.): The first Chinese immigrant is said to have moved into a small, closetlike room here in 1865, and Chinatown grew up around him almost by accident. Today almost 150,000 people of Asian origin (mostly Chinese from Hong Kong or Taiwan) are crowded into this ever-expanding Far Eastern enclave, less colorful than San Francisco's Chinatown but nonetheless picturesque, with its lanterns, dragon carvings, pagoda-topped pay phones, and jumble of stores and restaurants.

LOWER EAST SIDE (from Canal St. north to E. Houston St. and from the Bowery east to the East River): An area that once housed thousands of newly arrived immigrants in cold-water tenements, it is slowly—very slowly—being rehabilitated into lower- and middle-income housing, but still provides the homes for many of the city's poorest residents. In one of its local areas, the **Bowery** (around the Bowery and Delancey St.), Peter Stuyvesant, last governor of Nieuw Amsterdam, built himself a farm outside the city wall; it was known as *de bouwerij*, which means "farm" in old Dutch. A century ago this was the theater and red-light district. Today it is a run-down neighborhood where bums, junkies, and winos congregate. Here you will also find Orchard St., famous for discount famous-name clothes.

LITTLE ITALY (around Mulberry St. south of E. Houston St.): Butted up against Chinatown (and today being progressively absorbed into it), this former stronghold of Neapolitan, Calabrian, and Sicilian immigrants has been all but forsaken by its original inhabitants. Of the 800,000 New Yorkers of Italian origin, only 5,000 to 10,000 still live in Little Italy. It has become an ethnic tourist attraction, featuring cafés, the aroma of espresso, statues of the Madonna, restaurants, and groceries tricked out in the Italian national colors, with religious processions that look as though they come straight out of the movie *The Godfather*.

SOHO (*SO*uth of *HO*uston St. between Sixth Ave. and Broadway, with W. Broadway as its main thoroughfare): Just 20 years ago this neighborhood of huge workshops and factories built in the mid-19th century was practically abandoned, in spite of the acknowledged splendor of its cast-iron facades. SoHo began its recovery in the early 1960s, when artists and intellectuals, driven out of Greenwich Village by spiraling rents, invaded the lofts of SoHo—which are now also priced at the top of the market.

NOHO (*NO*rth of *HO*uston St. between the Bowery and Broadway): At the beginning of the 19th century this was the "swell" neighborhood, where Cornelius Vanderbilt, the Croesus of the day, chose to live. Now it's full of young punk rockers, loft apartments, electronics and microcomputer stores, and the Public Theater—a doggedly trendy part of town.

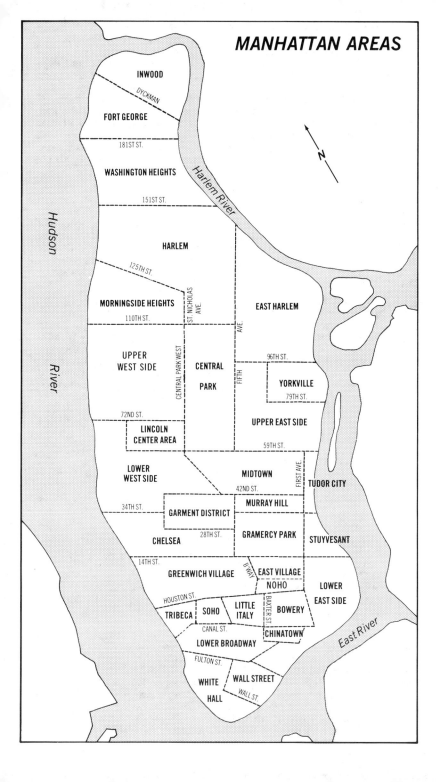

GREENWICH VILLAGE (around Washington Square at the lower end of Fifth Ave., from slightly below Houston St. north to W. 14th St. and from Broadway west to the Hudson River): It began as a real village of farmers, settled by the first English colonists out among the fields and the woods. New Yorkers still call it the Village, but by the 19th century it had already become an artists' and writers' colony and has numbered among its inhabitants Edgar Allan Poe, Henry James, and John Dos Passos. With its narrow streets, little brick houses, small shops, and taverns, the Village was long regarded as New York's literary and bohemian center. Now the upper middle class and the tourists have taken over, but the neighborhood is still picturesque. Stay away on summer weekends because of the crowds.

EAST VILLAGE (around Tompkins Square Park, from E. Houston St. north to E. 14th St. and from the Bowery east to the East River): This neighborhood, north of the Lower East Side, is where new cultural movements and schools of avant-garde art ("graffiti art," "real art," "street art") are born. The influx of young, creative people have made it one of the most lively, newsworthy parts of the city. Many art galleries. As you proceed farther east past First Ave. to Aves. A, B, C, and D, the area becomes progressively blighted and progressively dangerous, especially at night.

CHELSEA (around Chelsea Park at Eighth, Ninth, and Tenth Aves., from W. 14th St. to W. 30th St. and from Fifth Ave. to the Hudson River): Forty years ago this was largely a district of Hispanic immigrants, as witness the many Spanish-language store signs still to be seen on 14th Street. Now Chelsea has become typical of New York's "mixed bag" neighborhoods, where old New Yorkers live cheek by jowl with new arrivals, where run-down, grimy brick buildings and old, elegant brownstones stand shoulder to shoulder with modern high-rises. For some reason New York's best art and fashion photographers seem to live here.

GRAMERCY PARK (around Gramercy Park at Lexington Ave. and 20th St., from E. 14th St. to E. 30th St. and from Fifth Ave. east): Includes both the high-rise apartments of **Stuyvesant Town** (east of First Ave. between E. 14th St. and E. 19th Sts.) and the elegant little brownstones and town houses around Gramercy Park itself, as well as the office towers along lower Third Ave. and Park Ave. South and the huge hospitals between First Ave. and the East River in the E. 20s.

MIDTOWN (from 30th St. to 59th St., river to river): Takes in the whole center of Manhattan, south of Central Park. From the frantic bustle of the **Garment District** (Sixth Ave. and Seventh Ave. between 30th St. and 39th St.), where fabrics and ready-to-wear clothing are manufactured, to the permanent Big Top of **Broadway and the Theater District** (from Sixth Ave. to Eighth Ave. between W. 43rd and W. 53rd Sts.), the heart of America's show business, with more than 50 theaters and music halls and dozens of cinemas, their lights blazing through the crush of nighttime idlers (not a safe district after midnight); from the magical reflections off the glass facades of the **Rockefeller Center** high-rises to the porno movie houses and the drug and sex industry of **Times Square** (soon, it is hoped, to fall before a giant urban-renewal project), by way of the big new office buildings of **Murray Hill** (between Third Ave. and Madison Ave. south of E. 42nd St.) and the little island of tranquility of 1920s-style fantasy of **Tudor City** (around First Ave. between E. 38th St. and E. 44th St.), where a cluster of apartment houses, in an unusual neo-Tudor idiom, stands on a huge elevated platform overlooking the East River and the "glass palace" of the U.N. (many diplomats and U.N. officials live here)—midtown is a microcosm of the city itself.

UPPER WEST SIDE (from Central Park to the Hudson River between W. 60th St. and W. 125th St.): At the end of the 19th century this was an upscale "WASP" neighborhood, the chicest in Manhattan. At the end of the 1930s it started a long process of deterioration, which was only halted in the 1970s. Now it has become fashionable again, attracting a young, well-to-do, trendy crowd of actors, musicians, movie directors, bankers, and intellectuals who have made the area along Columbus Ave. from W. 65th St. to W. 95th St. into a sort of smart new version of Greenwich Village. It includes the huge **Lincoln Center** for the Performing Arts complex, and at its northern extremity, the Morningside Heights neighborhood with Columbia University and the Cathedral of St. John the Divine.

UPPER EAST SIDE (from Fifth Ave. to the East River between E. 59th St. and E. 96th St.): The gilt-edged ghetto of New York's upper classes, symbolized by the uniformed chauffeurs and their long limousines gliding silently down Park Ave., and by the luxurious apartment houses that run the length of East End Ave. The only lighter note to be found in this money-oriented universe is provided by the little restaurants and singles bars of First Ave. and Second Ave.

"EL BARRIO" (East Harlem around Lexington Ave. and Fifth Ave. between E. 105th St. and E. 125th St.): *Barrio* is the Spanish for "neighborhood," and this is the Puerto Rican neighborhood, its heart the renowned Marqueta, the colorful covered market with its swirling crowds and hundreds of stalls. It's a Hispanic enclave in the heart of Harlem.

HARLEM (between Central Park North, or 110th St., and 155th St.): Originally named Nieuw Haarlem after the town in the Netherlands, and founded as a community for Dutch settlers in 1658 by Gov. Peter Stuyvesant, Harlem was, in the latter part of the 19th century, one of the most elegant residential districts in Manhattan, as witness the imposing upper-class houses of Convent Ave., Sugar Hill, Mount Morris Park West, and Strivers' Row. The first African Americans arrived around 1910, and with the coming of the first jazz bands at the famous Cotton Club, the Savoy Ballroom, and the Apollo Theater, Harlem became for a while the center of New York's nightlife. Today its community of 300,000 African Americans makes it the symbol of Black America. However, the real-estate speculators are slowly moving in on behalf of their yuppie clients. Several museums and some distinguished turn-of-the-century architecture merit your attention, but stay away from the high-risk areas such as Lenox Ave. around W. 125th St. and Eighth Ave. around W. 116th St.

UPPER MANHATTAN (WASHINGTON HEIGHTS) (north of 155th St.): Most of this area is taken up by middle-class apartment buildings, but the George Washington Bridge and its bus station are at 177th St., and at the northern tip of Manhattan is Fort Tryon Park and the Cloisters.

INFORMATION & TOURS

Note: All telephone numbers are in the 212 area code, unless otherwise indicated.

TOURIST INFORMATION: The **New York Convention and Visitors Bureau** (midtown), 2 Columbus Circle, NY 10019 (397-8222).

Information Desk (midtown), in the lobby at 30 Rockefeller Plaza (806-7000). Multilingual hostesses; guided tours of Rockefeller Center.

GUIDED TOURS: **Adventures on a Shoestring** (walking tours) (midtown), 300 W. 53rd St. (265-2663): Conducted walking tours of Chinatown, Greenwich Village, and other picturesque neighborhoods. For lovers of the unexpected.
    American Sightseeing / Short Line Tours (bus) (midtown), 166 W. 46th St. (354-5122): Conducted tour of the city in glass-roofed sightseeing bus; shuttle connection with principal hotels.
    Circle Line (boat) (midtown), Pier 83, W. 43rd St. at the Hudson River (563-3200): Around Manhattan Island by boat; a spectacular three-hour ride. Daily, Apr to mid-Nov.
    Gray Line Tours (bus) (midtown), 900 Eighth Ave., at W. 54th St. (397-2600): Guided tours of the city and surroundings.
    Harlem Spirituals (bus) (midtown), (302-2594): Guided tours of Harlem, including its museums, ethnic restaurants, jazz clubs, and even gospel singing in a Baptist church (Sun only). Tours leave daily from the Short Line Tours Terminal, 166 W. 46th St. Resv. advised.
    Island Helicopters (helicopter) (midtown), E. 34th St. Heliport, at the East River (683-4575): Flights over Manhattan and the Statue of Liberty. Unforgettable. Fare: $30–$50, according to duration of flight.
    Manhattan Trolley (bus) (Lower Manhattan), 210 Front St. (677-7268): 90-min. shuttle tour across Lower Manhattan in a replica of a turn-of-the-century streetcar, making stops at South Street Seaport, Battery Park, the World Trade Center, Chinatown, Little Italy, etc. Pass gives riders unlimited boarding rights between 11am and 5pm Wed–Sun.
    New York Big Apple Tours (bus) (midtown), 22 W. 23rd St. (691-7866): Conducted tours of Manhattan with multilingual guides—French, German, Italian, Spanish, etc. For foreign visitors.

SIGHTS, ATTRACTIONS & ACTIVITIES

ARCHITECTURAL HIGHLIGHTS: 🏛 **The Beresford** (Upper West Side), 211 Central Park West at W. 81st St.: Luxury apartment building dating from 1929, designed by architect Emery Roth. With its ocher sandstone facade, rococo carvings, and three unusual towers, this designated historic landmark has been, and still is, home to many celebrities such as violinist Isaac Stern, tennis star John McEnroe, and TV newscaster Peter Jennings. Definitely worth a look.
    Dakota Apartments (Upper West Side), 1 W. 72nd St. at Central Park West: Perhaps the most prestigious address in New York. A strange blend of English Victorian and German neo-Gothic, this 1884 structure by Henry Hardenbergh was New York's first luxury apartment building. Among its present residents are Lauren Bacall; John Lennon, who also lived here, was assassinated outside the entrance, and the building was a setting for the movie *Rosemary's Baby*. A sight you shouldn't miss.
    Federal Reserve Bank (Lower Manhattan), 33 Liberty St. (720-6130): The world's largest hoard of gold—900,000 ingots worth $114 billion—slumbers in the armored vaults here, 80 ft. (24m) underground and protected by a steel door weighing 90 tons. Visits, by appointment only, Mon–Fri; no still or movie cameras permitted. For daydreaming.
    Jacob K. Javits Convention Center (midtown), Eleventh Ave. and W. 35th St. (216-2000): Designed by the great

SOHO, LITTLE ITALY, AND CHINATOWN AREA

BLEECKER STREET

WEST HOUSTON STREET

KING STREET

CHARLTON STREET

VANDAM STREET

SPRING STREET

SULLIVAN STREET

THOMPSON STREET

PRINCE STREET

SPRING STREET

MERCER STREET

CROSBY STREET

SOHO

BROADWAY

HUDSON STREET

VARICK STREET

AVENUE OF THE AMERICAS

WEST BROADWAY

WOOSTER STREET

GREENE STREET

BROOME STREET

HOWARD STREET

DESBROSSES STREET

CANAL STREET

VESTRY STREET

GREENWICH STREET

LAIGHT STREET

LISPENARD STREET

WALKER STREET

LAFAYETTE STREET

HUBERT STREET

BEACH STREET

N. MOORE STREET

WHITE STREET

FRANKLIN STREET

TRIBECA

To Brooklyn Battery Tunnel→

FRANKLIN STREET

LEONARD STREET

HARRISON STREET

JAY STREET

WORTH STREET

LOWER BROADWAY

I. M. Pei, this futuristic convention center, largest of its kind in the Western world, has an immense facade of glass made up of more than 16,000 individual panes, supported by a web of metal girders; the design was inspired by London's famous Crystal Palace, and will delight all lovers of contemporary architecture. Opened in April 1986 at a cost of more than $500 million. Positively worth seeing.

☼🔔🔔 **Lincoln Center for the Performing Arts** (Upper West Side), Broadway and W. 64th St. (877-1800): This renowned cultural center comprises five elegant, modernist theaters and concert halls arranged in a harmonious pattern around a central plaza. **Avery Fisher Hall** (1962), designed by Max Abramovitz, is the home of the New York Philharmonic; **Alice Tully Hall**, home of the Chamber Music Society, and the adjoining **Juilliard School of Music** are by Pietro Belluschi; Philip Johnson designed the **New York State Theater** (1964), which houses the New York City Ballet and the New York City Opera; the **Vivian Beaumont Theater** (1965) is the work of Eero Saarinen, while the **Metropolitan Opera House** (1966), home of the world-famous Metropolitan Opera (or "The Met"), with its Chagall murals, is from the hand of Wallace K. Harrison. The very lovely marble fountain in the central plaza, designed by Philip Johnson, is illuminated at night. This is a visit you should certainly make.

🔔 **Madison Square Garden Center** (midtown), 4 Pennsylvania Plaza, at Seventh Ave. and W. 32nd St. (563-8300): A 20,000-seat covered stadium (the Arena), which with its adjoining little brother, the Felt Forum, draws more than five million spectators a year to various events. For a century this hall and its predecessors has been the scene of the most important sporting events, shows, and political occasions in New York City. The present building dates from 1968. Penn Station (trains to Boston, Miami, New Orleans, and Washington) is on the levels below Madison Square Garden.

☼🔔 **New York Stock Exchange** (Lower Manhattan), 20 Broad St. (656-5167): The center of the U.S. financial community; gesticulating brokers and frantic agitation. Don't miss the show from the Visitors' Gallery.

🔔 **Radio City Music Hall** (midtown), Ave. of the Americas (Sixth Ave.) at W. 50th St. (757-3100): The largest movie theater in the world, with 6,000 seats and a stage 144 ft. (44m) across and 65 ft. (20m) deep. Splendid art deco lobby with giant chandeliers in crystal weighing two tons apiece. Home of the world-renowned precision-dancing Rockettes; draws more than eight million visitors a year. Guided tours daily (call 246-4600 for information). Don't miss it.

☼🔔 **United Nations** (midtown), First Ave. between E. 42nd St. and E. 48th St. (963-7713): Designed by Le Corbusier and Oscar Niemeyer, the 39-story, 1952 "glass palace" of the Secretariat towers over the East River. Guided tours daily; you should see it, preferably between early Sept and mid-Dec when the General Assembly is in session and the flags of the 159 member nations, ranked in alphabetical order, are flown in front of the complex.

Skyscrapers

☼🔔 **AT&T Building** (midtown), 550 Madison Ave. at E. 56th St.: Its salmon-colored granite facade, popular Renaissance-inspired arcade, and the pediment drawn from a Chippendale breakfront make this building by the well-known duo Philip Johnson and John Burgee one of the most innovative of postmodern high-rises. In the lobby is a deliberately old-fashioned statue of Mercury and an exhibition of AT&T's technological achievements. A must-see.

🔔 **Chase Manhattan Bank Building** (Lower Manhattan), 1 Chase Manhattan Plaza: 60 stories of steel and glass—one of the world's largest bank buildings (about 15,000 people work here), designed by

the firm of Skidmore, Owings & Merrill. The underground vault is protected by six armored doors weighing 45 tons each. There is a strange sculpture by Jean Dubuffet on the plaza. Worth a look.

☀️🔔🔔 **Chrysler Building** (midtown), 405 Lexington Ave. at E. 42nd St.: Art deco masterpiece designed by William Van Alen in 1930; 77 stories rising 1,048 ft. (319m), capped by a stainless-steel spire which looks like the jawbone of a swordfish. Superb lobby with remarkable wood inlays, African marble, and modernist wall paintings. You'll be able to admire the architecture while visiting **Con Edison's Conservation Center,** an interesting little energy exhibit on the ground floor. Nearly 9,000 people come to work here every day. Open Tues–Sat.

☀️🔔 **Citicorp Center** (midtown), Lexington Ave. and E. 54th St.: An unusual modern (1978) 79-story building designed by Hugh Stubbins, with a roofline angled to receive and store solar energy. It stands on four massive columns so tall that the second floor is 14 stories above ground. "The Market" is an enticing, very popular atrium-garden with cafés, restaurants, shops, bookstores, and even a church. Free concerts at lunchtime. Definitely worth visiting.

☀️🔔 **Empire State Building** (midtown), 34th St. and Fifth Ave.: Built in 1929–31 on the site of the original Waldorf Hotel, this world-famous skyscraper, designed by Shreve, Lamb and Harmon, was long the tallest building in the world (today it's third-tallest) and the quintessential symbol of New York. Its construction required 60,000 tons of steel; it is solid enough that when, on a foggy day in 1945, a B-25 bomber flew straight into the 79th floor—and 14 people were killed—the building sustained no damage whatsoever. The 102 floors are served by 73 elevators. For further details, see "Panoramas," below. Don't miss it.

🔔 **Equitable Building** (Lower Manhattan), 120 Broadway at Cedar St.: One of the earliest (1915) high-rises in the city; its monumental mass led to the adoption of the city's first zoning law in the following year. Should be seen.

🔔 **Equitable Center** (midtown), 787 Seventh Ave. at W. 52nd St.: Impressive brand-new high-rise by architect Edward Larrabee Barnes, proudly wearing its name in letters of gold across the front. Spectacular glass atrium with huge pop-art painting by Roy Lichtenstein, wall painting by Thomas Hart Benton, and other works of modern art from the collection of the Whitney Museum. At street level you'll also find two outstanding restaurants: Le Bernardin and Palio. Has brought new class and distinction to the Broadway area; not to be missed.

🔔 **Flatiron Building** (Gramercy Park), 175 Fifth Ave. at E. 23rd St.: The first true office skyscraper built in New York (1903). Its name derives from its 22-floor height and its dramatic triangular form. The architect was D. W. Burnham. Worth a look.

🔔 **Ford Foundation Building** (midtown), 320 E. 42nd St.: Beautiful 1967 glass-and-brick building by Kevin Roche and John Dinkeloo; headquarters of the Ford Foundation, which sponsors research in the physical and social sciences. A splendid tree-planted lobby serves as an indoor garden, the first of its kind in Manhattan. Worth a look.

☀️🔔🔔 **I.B.M. Building** (midtown), 590 Madison Ave. at E. 56th St.: Edward Larrabee Barnes designed this 40-floor tower of polished green granite and green glass; the head office of the giant international computer company is one of New York's loveliest modern skyscrapers. There's an unexpected tropical greenhouse with giant reeds and a Japanese garden on the ground floor. Interesting temporary art exhibitions. Don't fail to visit it.

🔔 **Lever House** (midtown), 390 Park Ave. at E. 54th St.: This elegant 24-story Skidmore, Owings & Merrill building, dating

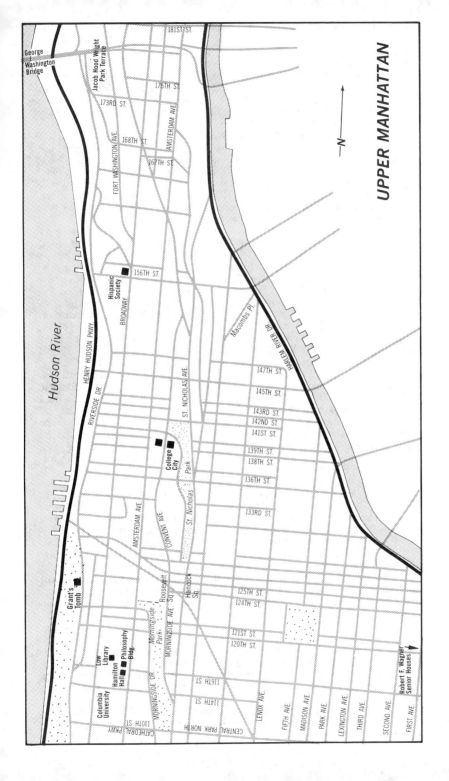

from 1952, is one of the earliest all-glass curtain-wall buildings. A classic of its kind, and worth seeing.

Marriott Marquis Hotel (midtown), 1535 Broadway at W. 45th St.: Impressive 52-story high-rise designed by John Portman; its looming mass dominates Times Square. It's one of the most comprehensive hotel facilities in the world; note the 46-floor glass-walled lobby, which absolutely must be seen.

J. P. Morgan & Co. Tower (Lower Manhattan), 60 Wall St.: This new giant by architect Kevin Roche rears its 47-story bulk of pure postmodernism far above its downtown neighbors; worth a look.

Pan Am Building (midtown), 200 Park Ave. at E. 45th St.: The masterpiece of the great Walter Gropius, completed in 1963. This elegant 59-story octagon, 810 ft. (247m) tall, atop Grand Central Terminal, is one of the world's biggest office buildings, housing 25,000 workers. The best view is the Park Ave. view. A sight not to be missed.

Park Avenue Tower (midtown), 65 E. 55th St.: One of Manhattan's most flamboyant buildings, with its astonishing marble and granite lobby, pyramidal cap, and ever-changing surface colors—pink to chestnut to metallic gray. It's half *Star Wars,* half art deco, and all the work of the prolific Chicago architect Helmut Jahn. Worth seeing.

Philip Morris Building (midtown), Park Ave. at E. 42nd St.: This ultramodern high-rise, headquarters of a cigarette conglomerate, is principally noteworthy for the annex of the **Whitney Museum** on its ground floor, with sculptures by Calder, Segal, Claes Oldenburg, Nevelson, etc., standing in an indoor garden open to the public. Should not be missed.

Rockefeller Center (midtown), between Fifth Ave. and Sixth Ave. from W. 48th St. to W. 52nd St.: A breathtaking forest of skyscrapers, 21 in all, built during the early 1930s in the heart of Manhattan. Among the best-known and most often visited are the 70-story **General Electric Building** (formerly the RCA Building), where NBC has its TV studios, with a restaurant (the **Rainbow Room**) on the 65th floor; **Radio City Music Hall** (see "Architectural Highlights," above); the 51-floor **McGraw-Hill Building;** the **Exxon Building** (54 floors); and the **Time-Life Building** (48 floors). Also terraced gardens, an open-air ice-skating rink (in winter), an underground shopping mall, restaurants, cafés, etc. In 1989 Japan's Mitsubishi Estates Co. acquired a controlling interest in Rockefeller Center for $846 million.

Seagram Building (midtown), 375 Park Ave. at E. 52nd St.: Lovely skyscraper of steel and bronze-tinted glass, a 1958 work of Ludwig Mies van der Rohe and the crowning achievement of the International School. The splendid interior decor was designed by Philip Johnson around works by Picasso, Chagall, Rodin, and others. An absolute must-see.

Trump Tower (midtown), 725 Fifth Ave. between 56th St. and 57th St.: This 68-story tower with a profusion of gilding and pink marble had cost a mere $150 million by the time it was completed in 1983. The six-floor lobby, with an unbelievable indoor waterfall 82 ft. (25m) high, is tenanted by some of the world's most upscale boutiques: Charles Jourdan, Cartier, Loewe, and the like. The quintessence of nouveau riche ostentation. It has to be seen.

Waldorf-Astoria Hotel (midtown), 301 Park Ave. at E. 50th St.: When it was opened in 1931, this imposing structure with its 47 floors and 1,900 rooms was described as "the largest and most luxurious hotel in the world." It has retained, through several facelifts, some vestiges of its original glory, such as its magnificent art deco lobby and its unique ballroom, the Starlight Roof, whose roof really does open to the stars. Worth seeing.

Woolworth Building (Lower Manhattan), 233 Broadway at Barclay St.: A curious Gothic Revival skyscraper originally described as a "cathedral of commerce." It was the world's tallest building from its construction in 1913 until the completion of the Chrysler Building in 1930. Rising 60 floors and 792 ft. (241m), it is the work of the great Cass Gilbert. Wonderful entrance hall with delightful stone gargoyle carvings and gold-leaf mosaics; the building's tower is modeled after the campanile of St. Mark's Basilica in Venice. Very much worth seeing.

World Financial Center (Lower Manhattan), bordered by West St., Vesey St., and Liberty St. and the Hudson River: Part of the Battery Park City complex (see "Strolls," below), architect Cesar Pelli's grouping of four austerely geometric futurist towers is one of the most ambitious developments Manhattan has seen in the past decade. The four innovative glass-and-granite towers are headquarters to such financial giants as American Express, Merrill Lynch, and Dow Jones. The magnificent **Winter Garden** is a giant glasshouse with palms and other tropical vegetation; there are also marble-floored plazas and terraces overlooking the river, as well as fashionable cafés and restaurants. Definitely worth a visit.

World Trade Center (Lower Manhattan), bordered by West St., Church St., Vesey St., and Liberty St.: Twin shimmering silver towers, designed by architects Minoru Yamasaki and Emery Roth, 110 floors high and rising 1,350 ft. (411m)—1,710 ft. (521m) with the TV antenna. These are the tallest buildings in New York and the second-tallest (after Chicago's Sears Tower) in the world. Opened in 1977, they took 15 years to build. Now 70,000 people work in them, and 80,000 tourists visit them, every day. If you want to know what New York looks like from a bird's-eye view, you really have no other place to go—you must come here. See "Panoramas," below.

BEACHES: Coney Island Beach, Surf Ave. between Ocean Pkwy. and W. 37th St., Brooklyn: The Konijn Eiland (Rabbit Island) of the original Dutch settlers has become New York's most popular beach; on some summer days more than a million people can be found on its 3.2 mi. (5km) of fine sand or in the nearby amusement park. (The boardwalk has become run-down; be careful there at night.) The best hot dogs in the city are to be had at **Nathan's Famous,** Surf Ave. and Stillwell Ave. The overall effect is kitsch, but amusing. Directly accessible by subway.

Jacob Riis Park, Beach 149th St. to Beach 169th St., Queens: A mile-long (1.6km) sandy beach with a huge parking lot; a spot particularly favored by gay nudists. Access is via the Marine Pkwy. Bridge, or by subway and bus.

Jones Beach State Park, Bay Pkwy. and Meadowbrook Pkwy., Long Island: Farthest from Manhattan, but also the nicest beach in the metropolitan area. It's a huge state park of 2,413 acres (977ha) along the ocean, with 6 mi. (10km) of splendid sand beach. Metro Apple Express buses (718/788-8000) depart for the beach from E. 56th St. and Second Ave. in Manhattan.

Manhattan Beach, Ocean Ave. between Oriental Blvd. and Mackenzie St., Brooklyn: The favorite beach of the city's young, it's relatively uncrowded though near Manhattan. Accessible by subway and bus.

Rockaway Beach, Beach 1st St. to Beach 149th St., Queens: Fine 10-mi. long (16km) beach on a narrow spit of land which closes off the southern end of Jamaica Bay. Direct subway access.

BROADCASTING & MOVIE STUDIOS: The principal New York TV studios allow public audiences to watch their shows being taped. In general, reservations must be made days or even weeks in advance, because of the limited number of seats. Some shows admit only spectators over 18, and none admit children under 6 months old. Write or call:

ABC Guest Relations, 38A W. 66th St., New York, NY 10023 (887-7777).
CBS Ticket Bureau, 51 W. 52nd St., New York, NY 10019 (975-4321).
NBC Ticket Bureau, 30 Rockefeller Plaza, New York, NY 10112 (664-4444). NBC also offers conducted tours of its studios Mon–Sat (644-7174).
    The **New York Convention and Visitors Bureau,** 2 Columbus Circle (397-8222), usually has some free same-day tickets for TV shows; out-of-town or foreign visitors are given priority.

CHURCHES/SYNAGOGUES: ⓐ **Church of the Ascension** (Greenwich Village), 36 Fifth Ave. at 10th St. (254-8620): Designed by Richard Upjohn; the first church (1841) built in New York in the Gothic Revival style then popular in England. Extensively restored in 1885–89 under the direction of Stanford White. Very fine mural of the Ascension, and stained-glass windows, by John La Farge. Carvings of angels by Louis Saint-Gaudens. Worth seeing. Open daily.

☀ⓐ **Cathedral of St. John the Divine** (Upper West Side), Amsterdam Ave. at W. 112th St. (316-7540): Largest Gothic cathedral in the world, 601 ft. (183m) long, 124 ft. (38m) wide, and capable of seating 10,000 people; the great rose (west) window is 40 ft. (12m) across. The work of Ralph Adams Cram, it was begun in 1892. The transept and twin towers were never completed, though work has been resumed on them in the last 10 years. Must be seen.

☀ⓐ **St. Patrick's Cathedral** (midtown), Fifth Ave. and 50th St. (753-2261): Roman Catholic cathedral, built in 1888. A fine, flamboyant example of Gothic by James Renwick, somewhat overshadowed by the surrounding high-rises despite its 330-ft. (100m) spires. Very rich interior. The seat of New York's Catholic archdiocese. Worth a visit. Open daily.

☀ⓐ **St. Paul's Chapel** (Lower Manhattan), Broadway and Fulton St. (602-0800): The oldest (1766) church in the city, designed by Thomas McBean; George Washington had his private pew in the north aisle, while Jefferson and Cornwallis were other famous parishioners. The elegant Georgian design is reminiscent of London's St. Martin-in-the-Fields. Should be seen. Open daily.

☀ⓐ **Temple Emanu-El** (Upper East Side), Fifth Ave. and 65th St. (744-1400): The largest synagogue in the country, with 2,500 seats, built in 1929 in majestic Romano-Byzantine style. Open daily.

☀ⓐ **Trinity Church** (Lower Manhattan), Broadway and Wall St. (602-0872): Dwarfed today by the surrounding skyscrapers of the financial district, the steeple of this church was, when it was built in 1846 on the site of two earlier churches, the tallest structure in New York. Its churchyard is the oldest in the city (1681); in it may be found the tombs of Robert Fulton, inventor of the steamboat, and Alexander Hamilton. A favorite place for lunchtime picnics among Wall Street workers. Undergoing renovation. Open daily.

HISTORIC BUILDINGS & STRUCTURES: ☀ⓐ **Brooklyn Bridge** (Lower Manhattan), between City Hall Park, Manhattan, and Cadman Plaza, Brooklyn: The first (1883) steel-cable suspension bridge in the world, designed by engineer Johann August Roebling. A triumph of technical skill with its two piers resting on hydraulic caissons, this magnificent structure also offers an impressive view of Manhattan, especially at night. A sight not to be missed.

ⓐ **Carnegie Hall** (midtown), 154 W. 57th St. at Seventh Ave. (247-7800): One of New York's two famous concert halls, the other being Avery Fisher Hall at Lincoln Center. The 1891 inaugural concert in this lovely 2,700-seat auditorium was conducted by Tchaikovsky himself. In 1986 it reopened after a $50-million renovation had restored all its former splendor, but some feel its outstanding acoustics have been somewhat compromised. For concert schedules, consult the entertainment pages of the daily papers.

ⓐ **City Hall** (Lower Manhattan), Broadway at Murray St. (566-8682): An elegant Renaissance-style 1811 building of marble and brown sandstone. Guided tours by appointment Mon–Fri. Should be seen.

Columbia University (Upper West Side), Broadway and W. 116th St. (280-2845): Founded in 1754 as King's College, this is one of the oldest and most respected of American universities—a member, along with Harvard, Yale, Princeton, and others, of the famous Ivy League. Its campus, attended by 19,000 students, has 60 buildings, of which the most interesting are Low Memorial Library, whose Palladian style is reminiscent of the Pantheon in Rome; University Hall; the Sherman Fairchild Center for the Life Sciences; and Butler Library, which contains five million books. Conducted tours of the campus Mon–Fri.

Dyckman House (Upper Manhattan), 4881 Broadway at 204th St. (304-9422): The only 18th-century Dutch Colonial house still standing in modern Manhattan. Built by William Dyckman in 1782, it is decorated and furnished in a style typical of the wealthy farmers of the period. Worth the side trip. Open Tues–Sun.

Ellis Island (Lower Manhattan), Upper Bay off Battery Park (269-5755): Reopened early in 1990 after six years (and more than $150 million) of rehabilitation work, this impressive cluster of brick and red sandstone buildings is mute witness to some of the most moving episodes in American history. From 1892 to 1954, 17 million immigrants from all parts of the world shuffled through these great echoing halls, now splendidly restored, before trying their luck on U.S. soil. Now a living Museum of Immigration (even the original graffiti have been scrupulously preserved on the walls of the Great Hall, the dormitories, and the baggage room), Ellis Island illustrates four centuries of immigration into the U.S. with original documents, maps, photographs, old passports, personal mementos, etc. Fascinating. Open daily; ferry from Battery Park.

Federal Hall National Memorial (Lower Manhattan), 26 Wall St. (264-8711): As steeped in history as any building in Manhattan. The first City Hall was built here in 1699; here the Stamp Act imposed by the British in 1765 was rejected by the colonists; here the British made their headquarters during the War of Independence; here George Washington delivered his inaugural address as first president of the U.S. in 1789; here the first Congress met in 1789–90. The present building, in the Doric style, dates from 1842. J. Q. A. Ward's statue of Washington dominates the facade. Don't miss it. Open Mon–Fri.

Gracie Mansion (Upper East Side), East End Ave. at E. 88th St. (570-4751): Pretty country house in the Federal style, built in 1799 by a wealthy merchant named Archibald Gracie; now the official residence of the mayor of New York. Visits by appointment Tues–Wed Apr–Nov.

Grand Central Terminal (midtown), E. 42nd St. and Lexington Ave. (935-3960): Busiest railroad station in the world. This magnificent example of the beaux arts style, dating from 1912, is a kind of underground cathedral, and is a designated historic landmark. The central hall has a lovely ceiling. The flood of humanity that descends on the station at rush hours (150,000 commuters daily) must be seen to be believed. Trains to Chicago, Montréal, Niagara Falls, etc. Guided tours on Wed.

Theodore Roosevelt Birthplace National Historic Shrine (Gramercy Park), 28 E. 20th St. (260-1616): Birthplace of the 26th president, the much-loved "Teddy" Roosevelt, with his furniture and personal memorabilia. He lived here from 1858 to 1872. The original house burned to the ground; the present replica dates from 1923. Regular classical concerts and temporary exhibitions. Open Tues–Sat.

Yeshiva University (Upper Manhattan), 500 W. 185th St. (960-5390): The oldest (1886) and largest (7,000 students) Jewish university in America. Interesting buildings both Oriental in feeling—with Byzantine domes, like Tanenbaum Hall—or modern like the Science Center; museum devoted to Jewish history, architecture, and art, with particularly interesting models of synagogues from the 3rd to the 19th century. Open Tues, Thur, and Sun during the academic year.

MARKETS: ⌂ **Antiques Fair & Flea Market** (midtown), Ave. of the Americas between W. 24th St. and W. 26th St. (718/965-1076): Picturesque open-air flea market held every Sat and Sun (weather permitting) for more than a dozen years. Opens 6am. You'll find everything from fine art and real collector's pieces to junk. Well worth a visit. Open year round.

⌂ **Canal West Flea Market** (SoHo) Canal St. at W. Broadway: Lively flea market with lots of bargains. Open Sat and Sun throughout the year from 7am on. Worth a look.

⌂ **Essex Street Market** (Lower East Side), Essex St. between Broome St. and Stanton St.: Built in 1938 by then-mayor Fiorello La Guardia, this enormous covered market, the city's largest, is worth visiting not only for its many stalls overflowing with all kinds of foodstuffs, but for the variety of languages you'll hear—Yiddish, Spanish, Greek, Italian, Polish, Vietnamese, and many more. Worth seeing. Open daily except Jewish holidays.

☼⌂ **Fulton Fish Market** (Lower Manhattan), at South St. and Fulton St.: Adjacent to the South Street Seaport Museum (see "Museums of Science and History," below), this fish market, in existence since 1869 though the present building dates only from 1907, is one of the most important on the East Coast. Atmosphere and local color guaranteed, from 3am on, seven days a week. Guided tours daily at dawn: Richard Lord's Tours (962-1608 for resv.).

☼⌂ **La Marqueta** (El Barrio), Park Ave. between E. 110th St. and E. 116th St.: Puerto Rican covered market displaying all the exotic fruit, vegetables, seeds, spices, smoked meats, and fish from that Caribbean island. One of the most colorful (and aromatic) places in New York.

⌂ **Paddy's Market** (midtown), Ninth Ave. between W. 37th St. and W. 42nd St.: Once the stronghold of Greek and Italian grocers and produce merchants, this has become a kind of U.N. of the food business, displaying products of all nations. Its annual International Food Festival takes place in May, and is much appreciated by New Yorkers.

MONUMENTS: ⌂ **General Grant National Memorial** (Upper West Side), Riverside Dr. and W. 122nd St. (666-1640): Tomb of Gen. Ulysses S. Grant, commander of the Union armies during the Civil War and 18th president of the U.S., and his wife. The marble and granite memorial is derivative of the mausoleum of Halicarnassus, one of the seven wonders of the ancient world, and is beautifully situated on a height overlooking the Hudson. The surrounding park should be avoided after dark. Open Wed–Sun.

☼⌂⌂ **Statue of Liberty National Monument,** Liberty Island, in New York Harbor (363-3200): Probably the most famous statue in the world. Affectionately known as "Miss Liberty," or "The Green Lady," this colossal work of French sculptor Frédéric-Auguste Bartholdi and French engineer Gustave Eiffel is 152 ft. (46m) tall (305 ft./93m including its base), and consists of 300 plates of copper fitted around a steel armature; the whole weighs 225 tons (200,000kg). A gift from the people of France to the people of the United States, since she was unveiled in 1886 *Liberty Enlightening the World* has become a symbol of the U.S., and once again opened to the public after a two-year rehabilitation project for the centennial in 1986. An elevator takes you to the statue's feet, and you then climb a spiral staircase of 168 steps to the top, where 40 people can enter the head (without crowding) and enjoy the magnificent view it affords of New York. There is an interesting little museum of immigration in the statue's base. A must for every visitor, but bear in mind that in summer, when 12,000 tourists make the trip every day, you may have to wait a couple of hours. Access by ferry from Battery Park at the southern tip of Manhattan (call 269-5755 for boat schedules). Open daily.

Washington Arch (Greenwich Village), Washington Sq. at the foot of Fifth Ave.: An 86-ft. (26m) triumphal arch by Stanford White, erected in 1892–95 to mark the centennial of George Washington's election to the presidency. The surrounding park is the heart of Greenwich Village. You should certainly see it.

MUSEUMS OF ART: **American Craft Museum** (midtown), 40 W. 53rd St. (956-6047): The youngest (1987) of the city's art museum is entirely devoted to handcrafts in wood, metal, fabric, ceramics, etc. There are hundreds of objects on display, from an art deco rocking chair to blown glass. This triumph of the unusual occupies the ground floor of a 30-story high-rise opposite the Museum of Modern Art (see below). Don't miss it. Open Tues–Sun.

Brooklyn Museum, 200 Eastern Pkwy. at Washington Ave., Brooklyn (718/638-5000): One of the country's most richly stocked and innovative museums, best known for its fine Egyptian collection and its primitive art, particularly from North America, Africa, and Polynesia; also offers interesting special exhibitions. Among the major works on display are *Palazzo Dogale in Venice* by Monet, *Mlle Fiocre* by Degas, *The Lady in Red* by Thomas Anshutz, and 12 bas-reliefs from the palace of the Assyrian king Assurbanipal at Nimrud. A new display area houses one of the world's largest collections of sculpture by Auguste Rodin. Not to be missed. Open Wed–Mon. Directly accessible by subway.

The Cloisters (Upper Manhattan), Fort Tryon Park at Fort Washington Ave. and 193rd St. (923-3700): Medieval French and Spanish cloisters acquired at the turn of the century by the millionaire art patron John D. Rockefeller, and transported stone by stone to the U.S. from the monasteries of St. Michael de Cuxa, Saint-Guilhem-le-Désert, and Bonnefont-en-Comminges, as well as others. Admirable collection of medieval art including the famous series of 15th-century "Unicorn Tapestries," and the almost equally famous Mérode Altarpiece painted around 1425. Lovely gardens overlooking the Hudson make up a magnificent whole which you mustn't miss. One of the most beautiful and least-known museums in the city. Open Tues–Sun.

Cooper-Hewitt Museum (Upper East Side), 2 E. 91st St. at Fifth Ave. (860-6868): In what was once the sumptuous private house of the Carnegie family, this museum, entirely devoted to the decorative arts, displays a rich collection of furniture, ceramics, old fabrics (including a silken bonnet and mittens from China that are more than 2,000 years old), wallpaper, bronzes, architectural drawings, etc., as well as interesting temporary exhibitions. Should be seen. Open Tues–Sun.

El Museo del Barrio (Upper East Side), 1230 Fifth Ave. at E. 104th St. (831-7272): Exhibitions of painting, sculpture, and photography by Latin American artists, in the heart of the Puerto Rican quarter ("El Barrio") of New York. Also public concerts, movies, plays, etc. Fascinating. Open Wed–Sun.

Forbes Collection (Greenwich Village), 62 Fifth Ave. at 12th St. (620-2389): A highly eclectic private museum belonging to the late publisher and businessman Malcolm Forbes. It includes the world's largest collection of Fabergé Easter eggs, some old paintings, 500 ship models, and an army of 12,000 lead toy soldiers. Unexpected. Open Tues, Wed, Fri, and Sat.

Frick Collection (Upper East Side), 1 E. 70th St. at Fifth Ave. (288-0700): European masters (Velázquez, Vermeer, Gainsborough, Boucher, Van Eyck, and many others of equal stature) and fine furniture displayed in a lovely little Renaissance-style palace designed by architect Thomas Hastings for the Pittsburgh steel magnate Henry Clay Frick. Delightful covered courtyard. Among the most famous paintings on exhibition: *Man in a Red Hat* by Titian, *Self-Portrait* by Rembrandt, *Portrait of Philip IV* by Veláz-quez, and Holbein the Younger portraits *Sir Thomas More* and *Thomas Crom-well*. Perhaps New York's most exquisite museum; not to be missed. Open Tues–Sun.

☀️♟♟♟ **Solomon R. Guggenheim Museum** (Upper East Side), 1071 Fifth Ave. at E. 89th St. (360-3500): One of the world's most beautiful and original museum buildings, truly a work of art in its own right, designed in 1959 by Frank Lloyd Wright, the greatest American architect, in the form of an inverted spiral supposedly inspired by the legendary Tower of Babel. Splendid collection of impressionist and modern painting and sculpture by Kan-dinsky, Paul Klee, Delaunay, Picasso, Rauschenberg—but also by Renoir, Cé-zanne, van Gogh, Manet, and the like. In all, some 5,000 paintings, sculptures, and drawings including such acknowledged masterpieces as Kandinsky's *Blue Mountain,* Picasso's *Moulin de la Galette,* Jackson Pollock's *Ocean Greyness,* Chagall's *Green Violinist,* and *The Watchmaker* by Paul Cézanne. You should plan not to leave New York without coming to the Guggenheim. Open Tues–Sun.

Note: The museum closed in May 1990 to restore the Frank Lloyd Wright landmark and to construct a 10-story tower with new galleries. The $40-million complete renovation is scheduled to be completed by the fall of 1991.

♟ **Hall of Chinese History** (Chinatown), 146 Bowery (941-7661): Priceless collection of Chinese art treasures spanning more than 4,000 years, including life-size terra-cotta warriors, military horses, and chariots of the Quin Dynasty. Chinese historical art objects of different dy-nasties. Open daily.

♟ **International Center of Photography** (Upper East Side), Fifth Ave. at E. 94th St. (860-1777): The only museum in New York entirely devoted to photography. Temporary exhibitions and a permanent collection by the greatest masters of the lens: Robert Capa, Henri Cartier-Bresson, Ernst Haas, David Seymour, Marc Riboud, Ken Heyman, Edward Weston, and Ansel Adams. A larger (and friendlier) annex to the museum was opened in September 1989 at 1133 Ave. of the Americas at W. 43rd St. (768-4680). Fascinating. Open Tues–Sun.

♟♟ **Isamu Noguchi Garden Museum,** 32-37 Vernon Blvd. at 33rd Rd., Long Island City, Queens (718/204-7088): Very beautiful museum and sculpture garden with more than 250 works by the fa-mous American sculptor Isamu Noguchi, who died in 1988; not to be missed. Open Wed and Sat Apr–Nov.

☀️♟♟♟♟ **Metropolitan Museum of Art** (Upper East Side), Fifth Ave. at 82nd St. (535-7710): Familiarly known to New Yorkers as "the Met," this cultural colossus is the world's largest art museum—more than three million objects are displayed in 236 galleries plus a very fine Rooftop Sculpture Garden with a clear view of the Manhattan skyline. The presentation is admira-ble: from Egyptian temples to Gauguin and from medieval art to Jackson Pol-lock, the Met offers you a complete panorama of mankind's artistic evolution over the last 5,000 years. You should take care to see the new Lila Acheson Wal-lace Wing, devoted to 20th-century art. Among the world-famous works of art you will see are Giovanni Pisano's *Head of King David*, the *Mezzetin* of Antoine Watteau, Rembrandt's *Aristotle Contemplating the Bust of Homer,* Vermeer's *Woman at a Window,* an *Annunciation* by Hans Memling and another by Botti-celli, a *Crucifixion* by Jan van Eyck, *The Harvest* by Pieter Breughel the Elder, Ingres's *Princesse de Broglie,* Gauguin's *Ia Orana Maria,* Picasso's *Portrait of Ger-trude Stein,* Georgia O'Keeffe's *Cow's Skull, Red, White, and Blue* and *Autumn Rhythm* by Jackson Pollock. Five million people visit the museum every year; you should allow at least two full days for it. It is in itself worth the trip to New York. Open Tues–Sun.

    Museum of Holography (SoHo), 11 Mercer St. (925-0526): The world's first museum devoted to holography, a process invented in 1949 in which the exposure of photographic film by laser light permits the development of three-dimensional images. Spectacular and surprising. Housed in a landmark cast-iron building. Open Tues–Sun.

    Museum of Modern Art (MOMA) (midtown), 11 W. 53rd St. (708-9480): From impressionism to cubism, from expressionism to abstract art, MOMA's collection of 100,000 priceless works covers the spectrum from Dali to Monet, from Bacon to Chagall, and from Andy Warhol to de Kooning and Mark Rothko. Recently modernized, and enlarged by the construction of an adjoining 52-story tower designed by Cesar Pelli with an enormous glassed-in atrium, MOMA also boasts a superb garden court with modern sculpture by Lipchitz, Rodin (*The Burghers of Calais*), Picasso, Nevelson, Henry Moore, Reginald Butler, and others. With its 5,000 visitors a day, this is one of the most popular museums in the country. Its most cherished canvas, Picasso's *Guernica*, was returned to Spain in 1981, but you can still admire the same artist's famous *Demoiselles d'Avignon,* along with such other masterpieces as van Gogh's *Starry Night,* Matisse's *The Dance,* Douanier Rousseau's *Sleeping Gypsy,* the waterlily triptych by Monet, Edward Hopper's *House by the Railroad,* and *Christina's World* by Andrew Wyeth. This museum alone could justify the trip to New York. Open Thur–Tues.

    Studio Museum in Harlem (Harlem), 144 W. 125th St. (864-4500): This little-known museum in the heart of Harlem has interesting temporary exhibitions of the work of black artists, both American and Third World. Worth the trip. Open Wed–Sun.

    Whitney Museum of American Art (Upper East Side), 945 Madison Ave. at E. 75th St. (570-3676): Founded in 1930 by sculptor Gertrude Vanderbilt Whitney, this remarkable museum displays the most representative works by contemporary American artists, from Georgia O'Keeffe and Louise Nevelson to Edward Hopper and George Segal. The odd granite-and-concrete building in the shape of a truncated Aztec pyramid dates from 1954, and is the work of Marcel Breuer. Major exhibits: *Circus* by Calder, *Early Sunday Morning* by Edward Hopper, *Dempsey and Firpo* by George Bellows, Charles Demuth's *My Egypt,* and Jackson Pollock's *Number 27.* Don't miss it. Open Tues–Sun. The museum has two annexes, one at street level in the Philip Morris Building, the other at street level in the Equitable Center (see "Skyscrapers," above).

MUSEUMS OF SCIENCE & HISTORY: American Museum of the Moving Image/AMMI 35th Ave. at 36th St., Queens (718/784-0077):

The nation's first public museum wholly devoted to chronicling the history of cinema, television, and video art. This $15-million shrine to the motion picture, inaugurated in September 1988, is part of the old Astoria Studios, once Paramount Pictures' production center for silent films. The 60,000-item collection includes vintage movie cameras and television sets, old posters, photographs, souvenirs, costumes of movie and TV stars, and three theaters where visitors can see films or TV serials rarely seen. A must for movie buffs. Open Tues–Sun.

    American Numismatic Society (Upper Manhattan), Audubon Terrace, Broadway at 155th St. (234-3130): The largest numismatic library in the world, and one of the greatest collections ever assembled of coins, medals, and decorations, including rare Chinese, Greek, and Roman gold coins. A collector's paradise. Open Tues–Sun.

    AT&T Infoquest (midtown), 550 Madison Ave. at E. 56th St. (605-5555): Four-level exhibition space devoted to communications and information technology. The visitor programs an "access card" with his or her first name, which is then displayed in lights on a "Gateway to the Information Age," and serves as a key to the 40 interactive exhibits. Fascinating. Open Tues–Sun.

Children's Museum of Manhattan (Upper West Side), 212 W. 83rd St. (721-1234): Opened in 1989, this technologically sophisticated four-story museum has about 60 exhibition areas, including a fully functioning TV studio, a 20-foot (6m) domed theater called the Brainatarium, and hands-on exhibits. A must for children and adults alike. Open Tues–Sun.

Fraunces Tavern Museum (Lower Manhattan), 54 Pearl St. (425-1778): This picturesque tavern in dull-brown brick is as faithful a replica as can be made of the original structure, dating from 1719, which was razed by two successive fires in 1837 and 1852; it belonged to Samuel Fraunces (the name is a corruption of "Français," French), a black man from the Antilles who became steward to George Washington. It was here that Washington gave a farewell banquet for his generals before temporarily leaving New York for Philadelphia in 1783. Museum, with historical collection, open Mon–Fri. On the ground floor there's a very acceptable restaurant with incomparable American Colonial atmosphere; breakfast/lunch/dinner Mon–Fri. Don't miss it.

Hayden Planetarium (Upper West Side), Central Park West at W. 81st St. (769-5000): This famous planetarium, and its comprehensive museum of the history of astronomy, form an integral part of the Museum of Natural History (see below). You'll be interested in a 30-ton meteorite found in Greenland in 1897, a reproduction of the solar system, and an exact representation of the moon's surface. For ardent amateur astronomers. Exciting. Open daily.

***Intrepid* Sea-Air-Space Museum** (midtown), Pier 86 at W. 46th St. (245-2533): The famous World War II and Vietnam War aircraft carrier, 890 ft. (270m) long, now converted into a floating museum with aircraft, helicopters, ballistic missiles, and space capsules. Interesting audiovisual show. Impressive. Open Wed–Sun.

Jewish Museum (Upper East Side), 1109 Fifth Ave. at E. 92nd St. (860-1888): Housed in the Warburg Mansion, a French Gothic Château-style building, the world's largest Jewish museum illustrates the history of Judaism by means of painting, sculpture, manuscripts, ceremonial objects, etc. Samuel Friedenberg numismatic collection. Take care to see the beautiful composition by sculptor George Segal, entitled *Holocaust*. In 1991 the museum will begin a $15-million expansion. Open Sun–Thurs.

Morris-Jumel Mansion (Upper Manhattan), W. 160th St. and Edgecombe Ave. (923-8008): With its four-column portico, this elegant 1765 Georgian mansion was Washington's headquarters before the battle of Harlem Heights in 1776. This is the only surviving pre-Revolutionary house in Manhattan. Very fine old furniture. For lovers of glimpses from the past. Open Tues–Sun.

Museum of the American Indian (Upper Manhattan), Audubon Terrace, Broadway at 155th St. (283-2420): The most comprehensive collection of Native American art in the country, with more than a million artifacts—of which, for reasons of space, only 10,000 can be exhibited at any one time. A remarkable panorama of Native American culture from North, Central, and South America. Among the curiosities are personal possessions of such famous chiefs as Geronimo, Sitting Bull, and Crazy Horse. Important groups of pre-Columbian art, of kachina dolls, and of Iroquois masks. Even though badly run-down, this museum should not be missed. The museum's collection will be transferred to the Smithsonian Institution in Washington, D.C., in 1992. Open Tues–Sun.

Museum of Broadcasting (midtown), 1 E. 53rd St. (752-7684): Enormous archive of tapes on which are stored the most important radio and TV broadcasts by the three networks—ABC, CBS, and NBC—from the 1920s to the present day; more than 25,000 programs, from which the visitor may select favorites for replay. For those who believe that the golden age of radio and TV is past. Open Tues–Sat.

Museum of the City of New York (Upper East Side), Fifth Ave. and E. 103rd St. (534-1672): New York history in models, dioramas, paintings, prints, toys, old furniture, etc., from the foundation of New Amsterdam in the 17th century. Multimedia show on "the Big Apple." Fascinating. Open Tues–Sun.

Museum of Natural History (Upper West Side), Central Park West at W. 79th St. (769-5100): Some 34 million objects enrich the collection of this, the largest natural-history museum in the world. Particularly important zoology and anthropology sections, with every animal in creation, including dinosaurs and a 98-ft. (30m) blue whale. Many dioramas showing the habitats of the people, and animals, of America, Asia, Africa, and the Pacific. Gallery of meteorites and minerals. Enormous collection of fossils. One of the world's largest assemblages of gemstones, including some unique and valuable specimens. Movies shown on the giant "Naturemax" screen. Dazzling new permanent-exhibition hall retracing the 12,000-year cultural history of the peoples of the Andean highlands and Amazon basin. Don't miss this one. Open daily.

New-York Historical Society (Upper West Side), 170 Central Park West at 77th St. (873-3400): An indispensable complement to the Museum of the City of New York (see above), with a very rich collection of American decorative art (Tiffany lamps, silverware, toys), and in particular 433 of the 435 famous original watercolors by John James Audubon of the *Birds of America*. History of transportation in New York. The library has more than four million manuscripts, prints, photos, engravings, and rare books relating to New York. Must certainly be seen. Open Tues–Sun.

New York Public Library (midtown), Fifth Ave. and 42nd St. (930-0730): Imposing Italian Renaissance structure, guarded by two enormous stone lions and housing the second-largest public library in the country, after the Library of Congress in Washington: 30 million works, paintings, posters, etc. Among the rarities: a letter from Christopher Columbus dated 1493, and a rough draft of the Declaration of Independence in the handwriting of Thomas Jefferson. Very interesting temporary exhibitions. Open Mon–Sat.

Pierpont Morgan Library (midtown), 29 E. 36th St. (685-0610): This magnificent library, assembled by financier and art patron J. Pierpont Morgan, specializes in valuable manuscripts and rare books. Since 1906 it has been housed in a sumptuous Renaissance palazzo by McKim, Mead & White, opened to the public in 1924. It has, among its other treasures, three Gutenberg Bibles, the 15th-century illuminated *Book of Hours* of Catherine of Cleves, 9th-century Coptic manuscripts, the oldest-known edition of Boccaccio's *Decameron* (1473), and autograph letters by Shakespeare, Byron, Shelley, Dickens, etc. Its temporary exhibitions are wonderful. The book lover's paradise. Open Tues–Sun.

Police Academy Museum (Gramercy Park), 235 E. 20th St. (477-9753): This fascinating museum, part of the New York City Police Academy, houses crime-fighting artifacts including Al Capone's machine gun, real contraband, counterfeit money, unusual weapons, badges, and uniforms dating from 1845 to the present day. Open Mon–Fri.

Queens Museum, Flushing Meadow–Corona Park, Grand Central Pkwy. and Roosevelt Ave., Queens (718/592-5555): Since 1972 this museum has occupied the former New York City building of the 1964 World's Fair. Halfway between Kennedy and La Guardia airports, it's worth a side trip because of its extraordinary 9,000-sq.-ft. scale model of New York. A sight not to be missed. Open Tues–Sun.

South Street Seaport Museum (Lower Manhattan), East River at the foot of Fulton St. (669-9400): The historic port

district of old New York converted into an open-air museum, with carefully restored 19th-century houses, pubs, restaurants, shops, a covered market, and
street musicians. Along its piers are moored old ships such as the very fine four-
master *Peking* (1911), the *Ambrose* lightship (1907), the three-master *Wavertree*
(1885), and the schooner *Lettie G. Howard* (1893). In addition, a maritime museum (207 Water St.) houses ship models, navigational instruments, tools, and
fish-market artifacts. The setting is admittedly touristy, but lively and colorful; it
could have come straight out of an old picture book. Stay away Thurs and Fri
evenings when the horde of Wall St. brokers comes out to play. Don't miss it.
Open daily.

NIGHTTIME ENTERTAINMENT: No city in the world offers a gamut of
nighttime diversions equal to New York's. Leaving aside its dozens of theaters,
concert halls, and opera houses, including the prestigious Met and Carnegie
Hall, the visitor may find it hard to choose among several hundred bars, discos,
comedy clubs, jazz dives, dance halls, and nightclubs—ranging from smart to
sleazy. When it comes, specifically, to nightclubs, bars, and discos, the problem is
to pick the "in" places; on the New York scene, discos, in particular, can be born,
flourish, and die in less than a year. Some safe bets will be found listed under
"Bars and Nightclubs," below.

For lovers of theater and musicals, no visit to New York can be complete
without at least one evening on Broadway, "the greatest show on earth." The
42 theaters around Times Square generally present high-grade entertainment,
from Shakespeare to Arthur Miller and from Neil Simon to the latest musicals.
Elsewhere in the city, more than 300 Off and Off Off Broadway houses are
home to avant-garde plays or comedy clubs which may become tomorrow's big
hits. Most of New York's theaters may be old and uncomfortable, but with 10
million playgoers a year the "Sold Out" signs are often up, so tickets should
be obtained well in advance. You can use a ticket broker, or charge tickets
on your credit card through Telecharge (239-6200) or Ticketron (246-0102).
TKTS, at Broadway and 47th St. (midtown) or the mezzanine of 2 World
Trade Center (Lower Manhattan), sells tickets at half price; the drawback is
that they are available only on the day of the performance and there are often
long waiting lines. Matinee tickets from noon on, and evening tickets from
3pm. Cash only. Open daily. Finally, in the big hotels, the concierge may be in-
duced by the suggestive rustle of $10 bills to unearth the ticket(s) that you have
been told are not to be had. For other information, see "Performing Arts,"
below.

OUTDOOR ART & PLAZAS: The streets and squares of New York boast
many important works of art, including an amusing 40-ft. (12m) fiberglass com-
position by Jean Dubuffet entitled *Group of Four Trees,* in the Chase Manhattan
Plaza in Lower Manhattan. In front of Lincoln Center (Upper West Side) are
Reclining Figure, a monumental bronze by British sculptor Henry Moore, and
The Ticket Window by Alexander Calder. Other noteworthy pieces include *The
Alamo,* an enormous cubic structure by Tony Rosenthal on Astor Pl. (NoHo);
Shadows and Flags, a group of seven abstracts in black-painted steel by Louise
Nevelson at Liberty St. and William St. (Lower Manhattan); *Red Cube,* a 24-ft.-
high (7m) steel sculpture balanced on point by Isamu Noguchi at 140 Broadway
(Lower Manhattan); *The Pathfinder Mural,* a spectacular six-story mural, two
years in the making, featuring such figures as Fidel Castro, Malcolm X, Nelson
Mandela, Mother Jones, and Lenin at West St. and Charles St. (Greenwich Vil-
lage); a strange mobile globe in bronze by the German Fritz Koenig in the World
Trade Center Plaza (Lower Manhattan); and a giant Jacques Lipchitz outside the
Law School at Columbia University, Broadway and 116th St. (Morningside
Heights). In a more classical vein are the monumental 45-ft. (14m) *Atlas Bearing*

the Heavens and the famous *Prometheus* by Paul Manship in gilt bronze dominating the lower plaza of Rockefeller Center (midtown).

PANORAMAS: ☀️🛆 **Brooklyn Bridge** (Lower Manhattan), between City Hall Park in Manhattan and Cadman Plaza, Brooklyn: The city's oldest (1883) suspension bridge; a beautiful piece of functional architecture in steel, whose pedestrian walkway affords a superb view of downtown Manhattan. A sight not to be missed.

☀️🛆🛆 **Brooklyn Heights Esplanade,** Columbia Heights between Remsen St. and Orange St., Brooklyn: Smart residential neighborhood on a hill overlooking the East River. Writer Truman Capote used to live here; Norman Mailer is a current resident. Splendid view of the skyline and the southern tip of Manhattan from the promenade that runs above the Brooklyn-Queens Expwy. You should definitely see it.

☀️🛆🛆🛆 **Empire State Building** (midtown), 34th St. and Fifth Ave. (736-3100): Probably the world's most famous skyscraper, particularly to *King Kong* fans. Its 102 stories and 223 ft. (68m) of TV transmitting antenna add up to a total height of 1,414 ft. (431m). There are two observation platforms, one in the open air on the 86th floor, the other closed and glassed in on the 102nd floor. On a clear day you can see more than 60 mi. (100km) over four states. New York's most astonishing view, especially by night, attracting two million visitors a year. Open daily till 11:30pm. Don't miss it. For more details, see "Architectural Highlights: Skyscrapers," above.

🛆 **Roosevelt Island Aerial Tramway** (Upper East Side), Second Ave. at E. 60th St. (832-4555): Running 200 ft. (60m) above the East River, parallel to the Queensboro Bridge, this cable car connecting Manhattan and Roosevelt Island gives you a fine view of the East Side skyline. Runs every 15 min., daily.

☀️🛆🛆 **Staten Island Ferry** (Lower Manhattan), Ferry Terminal, Peter Minuit Plaza (248-8097 or 718/727-2508): New York's most spectacular view for 50¢. The ferry links the southern tip of Manhattan to Staten Island, and passes near the Statue of Liberty. It runs daily around the clock, leaving every 15 min. in rush hours, once an hour late at night. The trip takes about 25 min. each way. An experience not to be passed up.

☀️🛆🛆 **Statue of Liberty,** Liberty Island, in New York Harbor (363-3200): Reached by an elevator and a spiral staircase (trying), and 12 stories high, the statue's head offers a splendid view of New York and the bay through the windows in the crown. Advisable only for those in good physical condition. Open daily; accessible by ferry from Battery Park (call 269-5755 for boat schedules).

☀️🛆🛆 **World Trade Center** (Lower Manhattan), at West St., Church St., Vesey St., and Liberty St. (466-7397): These twin towers, 1,350 ft. (411m) tall—1,710 ft. (521m) with the TV antenna—took the championship away from the Empire State Building, but were themselves defeated by the 1,454-ft. (443m) Sears Tower in Chicago. Unique panorama of New York from the Observation Deck on the 107th floor, or the open terrace on the 110th floor of the No. 2 tower. Open daily till 9:30pm. An absolute must for every visitor. For more information, see "Architectural Highlights: Skyscrapers," above.

PARKS & GARDENS: ☀️🛆 **Battery Park** (Lower Manhattan), Battery Pl. and State St.: Standing at the tip of Manhattan Island, with a magnificent view of New York Bay and the Statue of Liberty, this park marks the spot where Giovanni da Verrazano is supposed to have made his first landfall in 1524. The lowering bulk of **Castle Clinton,** a fort built in 1811 to defend the city against British warships, was an immigrant-processing center from 1855 to 1890. At the water's edge are the terminals for the Statue of Liberty, Ellis Island, and Staten Island ferries. For those who like to take souvenir photographs, a stroll around here is definitely indicated.

Bowling Green (Lower Manhattan), Battery Pl. and Broadway: According to legend, this is where Peter Minuit bought Manhattan from the Indians. There is still lawn bowling here as there was in Dutch Colonial days—the distant ancestor of present-day American 10-pin bowling. Should be seen.

Brooklyn Botanic Gardens, 1000 Washington Ave. off Eastern Pkwy., Brooklyn (718/622-4433): On a 50-acre (20.5ha) site tucked between Olmsted and Vaux's masterly **Prospect Park** and the Brooklyn Museum you'll find azaleas and rhododendrons, lilacs, wisteria, one of the country's most beautiful rose gardens, a Japanese water garden, an unspoiled tract of New York woodland, a lovely grove of cherry trees, and more. The greenhouses reopened in 1988 after a two-year expansion project; they house among other attractions an unequaled collection of bonsai (Japanese miniature trees). The gardens are scrupulously maintained—no graffiti or litter—and it's hard to believe you're in the city. Combine this with a visit to the adjoining Brooklyn Museum (see "Museums of Art," above) for a day's escape.

Central Park, between Fifth Ave. and Central Park West from 59th St. to 110th St.: This magnificent park, covering 840 acres (340ha) in the center of the city (twice the size of the principality of Monaco) is Manhattan's lung; it was designed by Frederick Law Olmsted and Calvert Vaux, fathers of American landscape architecture. Much frequented by New York joggers and cyclists. Pleasantly undulating, and stitched together by more than 30 mi. (50km) of surfaced roads, footpaths, and riding trails, it also has several lakes (on some of which boating is available), an herb garden, a small zoo with a special children's zoo, an ice-skating rink, a carousel, and other attractions. Many tourists take a daytime ride through the park in a horse-drawn carriage, but the park is less safe at night; avoid it after dark unless you are attending one of the many festivals and free concerts in summer. Should certainly be seen.

Fort Tryon Park (Upper Manhattan), between Riverside Dr. and Broadway from W. 192nd St. to Dyckman St.: A gift of the Rockefeller family to the city, this park occupies the site of the old Fort Washington, which played an important role during the War of Independence. There's a splendid view of the Hudson flowing below. Lovely terraced flower gardens. Don't miss it. In the middle of the park stands the Cloisters (see "Museums of Art," above). Strolls should not be taken after dark.

Gramercy Park, Lexington Ave. between E. 20th St. and E. 21st St.: In the middle of a square lined with fine century-old buildings stands this quiet, green oasis in mid-Manhattan, the last private square in New York. Only residents, and guests at the Gramercy Park Hotel on the square, have access to it. You should see it.

Inwood Hill Park (Upper Manhattan), bounded by the Hudson River and Harlem River, Dyckman St., and Payson Ave.: 434 acres (176ha) of hilly woods along the river, centuries-old trees, and lawns much appreciated by picnickers, at the northern tip of Manhattan. Here once stood the village of Shorakkopoch, consisting in part of cave dwellings belonging to the Algonquins who, in 1626, sold Manhattan Island to Peter Minuit for a mess of pottage.

New York Botanical Gardens, 200th St. and Southern Blvd., The Bronx (220-8700): This splendid 250-acre (102.5ha) tract of greenery has everything: the only first-growth timber still standing within the city limits; acres of tree-studded lawns; beautiful flowerbeds; the tremendous, recently renovated Enid Haupt Conservatory with its stunning seasonal flower shows; a rushing country stream, beside which stands an 18th-century snuff mill where you can have a snack. Less elegant and intimate than the Brooklyn gardens, but more spacious. Free, unless you bring your car (parking $4).

☼�⚱ **Washington Square** (Greenwich Village), Fifth Ave. at Waverly Pl.: A square whose triumphal arch (by Stanford White) is dedicated to George Washington, in the heart of Greenwich Village. Here was once the burial ground for African American slaves and executed criminals. Today jam sessions, roller skaters, artists, and sidewalk orators of every kind may be found here; a lively, colorful place, though overwhelmed by tourists. Unfortunately it has for several years been one of the city's top open-air drug markets. Nevertheless, don't fail to see it.

☼�⚱ **Woodlawn Cemetery,** Jerome Ave. at E. 233rd St., The Bronx (920-0500): Huge landscaped cemetery with 250,000 graves, some sumptuous crypts, and beautiful gardens, now a designated bird sanctuary. Among the illustrious dead here are writer Herman Melville (*Moby-Dick*), Duke Ellington, newspaperman and publisher Joseph Pulitzer (founder of the prizes that bear his name), 19th-century railroad magnate Jay Gould, five-and-dime king Frank W. Woolworth, and the great New York City mayor Fiorello La Guardia. Worth a visit. Open daily.

PERFORMING ARTS: For daily listings of the innumerable shows and cultural events in New York, consult the entertainment pages of the **daily papers** *New York Times* or *Daily News* (morning) and *New York Post* (morning and evening), as well as the weeklies *The Village Voice, New York* magazine, and *The New Yorker,* or call **New York City On Stage** (587-1111) for current theater schedules.

Alice Tully Hall (Upper West Side), Lincoln Center, 140 W. 65th St. (362-1911): Recitals, chamber concerts, movies.

American Place Theater (midtown), 111 W. 46th St. (247-0393): Off Broadway theater.

Apollo Theater (Harlem), 253 W. 125th St. (749-5838): Harlem's great popular theater, made famous by Duke Ellington, Count Basie, Billie Holliday, and others. The Wednesday Amateur Night, emceed by the ageless Ralph Cooper, provides a preview of the stars of the future, and the chance to be a part of the toughest, funniest audience in town. Go by cab and use caution in the neighborhood.

Astor Place (NoHo), 434 Lafayette St. (254-4370): Musicals, Off Broadway theater.

Avery Fisher Hall (Upper West Side), Lincoln Center, 140 W. 65th St. (874-2424): Home of the New York Philharmonic, one of the world's great orchestras (principal conductor, Zubin Mehta).

Booth Theatre (midtown), 222 W. 45th St. (239-6200): Contemporary theater.

Broadhurst Theater (midtown), 235 W. 44th St. (239-6200): Contemporary theater.

Broadway Theater (midtown), 1681 Broadway at W. 52nd St. (239-6200): Musicals.

Brooklyn Academy of Music, 30 Lafayette St., Brooklyn (718/636-4100): Concerts, contemporary theater, opera, ballet.

Brooklyn Center for the Performing Arts, Nostrand Ave. and Ave. H, Brooklyn (718/434-1900): Ballet, recitals.

Brooks Atkinson Theater (midtown), 256 W. 47th St. (719-4099): Contemporary theater.

Carnegie Hall (midtown), 154 W. 57th St. (247-7800): Concerts, recitals.

Cherry Lane Theater (Greenwich Village), 38 Commerce St. (989-2020): The oldest Off Broadway theater.

Circle in the Square (Greenwich Village), 159 Bleecker St. (254-6330): Musicals, Off Broadway theater.

Circle Repertory Company (Greenwich Village), Seventh Ave. at W. 4th St. (924-7100): Off Broadway theater.

City Center Theater (midtown), 131 W. 55th St. (246-8989): Ballet, modern dance.

Delacorte Theater (Upper West Side), W. 81st St. in Central Park (861-7277): Open-air theater; the New York Shakespeare Festival is staged here every summer.

Douglas Fairbanks Theater (midtown), 432 W. 42nd St. (239-4321): Musicals, recitals.

Edison Theater (midtown), 240 W. 47th St. (757-7164): Musicals.

Ethel Barrymore Theater (midtown), 243 W. 47th St. (239-6200): Contemporary theater.

Eugene O'Neill Theater (midtown), 230 W. 49th St. (246-0220): Contemporary theater.

Forty-Sixth Street Theater (midtown), 226 W. 46th St. (221-1211): Contemporary theater.

Gershwin Theater (midtown), 1633 Broadway at W. 51st St. (586-6510): Musicals.

Guggenheim Bandshell (Upper West Side), Lincoln Center, 140 W. 65th St. (887-1800): Open-air concerts.

Helen Hayes Theater (midtown), 240 W. 44th St. (944-9450): Contemporary theater.

Imperial Theater (midtown), 249 W. 45th St. (239-6200): Musicals.

Joyce Theater (Chelsea), 175 Eighth Ave. at W. 19th St. (242-0800): Modern dance.

The Kitchen (Chelsea), 512 W. 19th St. (255-5793): Experimental events.

La Mama Experimental Theater Club (East Village), 74 E. 4th St. (475-7710): Avant-garde theater.

Lamb's Theater (midtown), 130 W. 44th St. (997-1780): Contemporary theater.

Longacre Theater (midtown), 220 W. 48th St. (239-6200): Musicals.

Majestic Theater (midtown), 245 W. 44th St. (239-6200): Musicals.

Manhattan Theater Club (midtown) 131 W. 55th St. (645-5590): Off Broadway theater.

Marquis Theater (midtown) 1535 Broadway at 46th St. (246-0102): Musicals.

Martin Beck Theater (midtown), 302 W. 45th St. (246-6363): Musicals.

Merkin Concert Hall (Upper West Side), 129 W. 67th St. (362-8719): Concerts, recitals.

Metropolitan Opera House (Upper West Side), Lincoln Center, 140 W. 65th St. (362-6000): Home of the New York Metropolitan Opera (artistic director, James Levine).

Minskoff Theater (midtown), 200 W. 45th St. (869-0550): Musicals, revues.

Mitzi E. Newhouse Theater (Upper West Side), Lincoln Center, 140 W. 65th St. (239-6200): Concerts, recitals, musicals.

Neil Simon Theater (midtown), 250 W. 52nd St. (757-8646): Contemporary theater.

Nederlander Theater (midtown), 208 W. 41st St. (246-0102): Contemporary theater.

New York State Theater (Upper West Side), Lincoln Center, 140 W. 65th St. (870-5570): Home of the New York City Opera (director, Christopher Keene) and the New York City Ballet (director, Peter Martins).

Norman Thomas Theater (midtown), 111 E. 33rd St. (685-3233): Musicals.

Playwrights Horizon (midtown), 416 W. 42nd St. (564-1235): Off Broadway theater.

Plymouth Theater (midtown), 236 W. 45th St. (239-6200): Contemporary theater.

Promenade Theater (Upper West Side), 2162 Broadway at W. 76th St. (580-1313): Off Broadway theater.
Provincetown Playhouse (Greenwich Village), 133 MacDougal St. (477-5048): One of the best-known Off Broadway theaters.
Public Theater (NoHo), 425 Lafayette St. (598-7150): Very popular; Off Broadway and classical theater.
Roundabout Theater (Gramercy Park), 100 E. 17th St. (420-1883): Off Broadway theater.
St. James Theater (midtown), 246 W. 44th St. (398-0280): Musicals.
Second Avenue Theater (East Village), 189 Second Ave. at 12th St. (674-1460): Musicals.
Shubert Theater (midtown), 225 W. 44th St. (239-6200): Musicals.
Sullivan St. Playhouse (Greenwich Village), 181 Sullivan St. (674-3838): Off Broadway theater. The musical *The Fantasticks* has run here since 1960—a world record.
Theater Four (midtown), 424 W. 55th St. (246-8545): Contemporary theater.
Vivian Beaumont Theater (Upper West Side), Lincoln Center, 140 W. 65th St. (877-1800): Musicals, light opera.
Walter Kerr Theater (midtown), 219 W. 48th St. (582-4022): Musicals, modern theater.
Westside Arts Theater (midtown), 470 W. 43rd St. (541-8394): Contemporary theater.
Winter Garden Theater (midtown), 1634 Broadway at W. 51st St. (239-6200): Operetta, musicals.
WPA Theater (Chelsea), 519 W. 23rd St. (206-0523): Off Broadway theater.

SHOPPING: In spite of high state and local sales taxes (8.25%), New York maintains its reputation as the "shopping capital of the world" for at least three reasons: (1) the tremendous range of choice in a city with almost 200,000 shops, stores, and merchants of all kinds; (2) the generally attractive level of prices; (3) the clustering of certain kinds of stores in certain neighborhoods, making the shopper's task easier. Note, also, that if you have your purchases shipped to an address outside New York State, you should not be charged the 8.25% sales tax. If you can't find what you want through these listings, consult the *Yellow Pages*.

Shopping Areas
The concentrations of various kinds of retailers in New York is roughly as follows:
Antiques Dealers and Art Galleries: Second Ave. and Third Ave. between E. 47th St. and E. 57th St.; Madison Ave. between E. 57th St. and E. 80th St.; Greenwich Village; SoHo.
Cameras, Photography, Electronics: W. 32nd St. to W. 34th St. between Sixth Ave. and Seventh Ave.; Essex St. (Lower East Side); W. 45th St. to W. 47th St. between Fifth Ave. and Sixth Ave.
Cookware: The Bowery from Houston St. to E. 3rd St.
Fabrics: W. 35th St. to W. 41st St. between Fifth Ave. and Eighth Ave.; Broadway between Canal St. and 8th St.
Flowers: W. 28th St. and Sixth Ave.
Furs: W. 26th St. to W. 30th St. between Broadway and Sixth Ave.
Jewels and Diamonds: W. 47th St. between Fifth Ave. and Sixth Ave. ("Diamond Row"); Fifth Ave. between 42nd St. and 59th St.
Lamps and Lighting Fixtures: The Bowery between Delancey St. and Grand St.
TV/Stereo Equipment: Canal St.; W. 45th St.; Leonard St., Warren St., and Chambers St. between Broadway and Greenwich St. (Tribeca).

Some Recommended Establishments

ANTIQUES DEALERS **Manhattan Art and Antiques Center** (midtown), 1050 Second Ave. at E. 56th St., comprising more than 100 antiques dealers and art galleries on three levels; **Place des Antiquaires** (midtown), 125 E. 57th St., an elegant gallery-mall with 70 dealers in art and antiques.

BOOKS In addition to the independent bookstores, the nationwide chains are well represented: **Barnes and Noble** (Chelsea), 105 Fifth Ave. at 18th St.; **B. Dalton Booksellers** (midtown) 666 Fifth Ave.; **Doubleday** (midtown), 673 Fifth Ave. at 53rd St.; **Strand** (East Village), Broadway at 12th St., with two million secondhand books in carload lots.

DEPARTMENT STORES **Bergdorf Goodman** (midtown), 715 Fifth Ave. at 57th St.; **Bloomingdales** (midtown), 1000 Third Ave. at 59th St., New York chicest, to see and be seen; ☼ **Macy's** (midtown), W. 34th St. and Broadway, largest store in the world, with 400,000 items, 150,000 customers per day; **Saks Fifth Ave.** (midtown), 611 Fifth Ave. at 50th St., with very yuppie customers; **Lord & Taylor** (midtown), 424 Fifth Ave. at 34th St.

FOOD **Balducci's** (Greenwich Village), 424 Ave. of the Americas (Sixth Ave.) at W. 9th St.; **Dean & DeLuca** (SoHo), 121 Prince St.; **Fay and Allen's Foodworks** (Upper East Side), 1241 Third Ave. at E. 72nd St.; **Sherry-Lehmann** (Upper East Side), 679 Madison Ave. at E. 60th St., New York's most famous wine store; **Zabar's** (Upper West Side), Broadway at W. 80th St., the biggest food store in the country, offering an unbelievable range of choice, which is best visited like a museum.

GADGETS AND GIFTS **Hammacher Schlemmer** (midtown), 147 E. 57th St., with every kind of gift idea for the home, including the silliest (and the most expensive).

MICROCOMPUTERS AND VIDEO GAMES **Camera World** (Gramercy Park), Park Ave. S. at E. 28th St.; **Computer Factory** (Upper East Side), 485 Lexington Ave. at E. 72nd St.; **47th St. Photo** (midtown), 115 W. 45th St.

MILITARY SURPLUS, T-SHIRTS, LOW-PRICED CLOTHING **Canal Jean Co.** (SoHo), 504 Broadway at Spring St.; **Hudson's** (East Village), Third Ave. at E. 13th St.; **Unique Clothing Warehouse** (NoHo), 726 Broadway at Waverly Pl.; **Urban Outfitters** (NoHo), 628 Broadway between Houston St. and Bleecker St.

OUTLET AND THRIFT STORES **Century 21** (Lower Manhattan), 12 Cortland St. at Church St.; **Job Lot** (Lower Manhattan), 140 Church St. at Warren St.; **Romano** (midtown), Twelfth Ave. and W. 45th St.

PHOTOGRAPHIC EQUIPMENT **47th St. Photo** (midtown), 67 W. 47th St.; **Hirsch** (midtown), 699 Third Ave. at E. 44th St.; **Willoughby's** (midtown), 110 W. 32nd St.

POSTERS **L'Affiche Galerie** (SoHo), 145 Spring St., for modern art posters; **Jerry Ohlinger** (Greenwich Village), 242 W. 14th St., for movie posters; **The Old Print Shop** (Gramercy Park), 150 Lexington Ave. at E. 29th St., for old art posters; **Triton Gallery** (midtown), 323 W. 45th St., for theater posters.

RECORDS **Disc-O-Mat** (midtown), Lexington Ave. and E. 58th St.; **King Karol** (midtown), 1500 Broadway at W. 44th St.; **Sam Goody's** (midtown), 1290 Sixth Ave. at W. 53rd St.; **Tower Records** (NoHo), 692 Broadway at 4th St., with one of the country's largest selections, 400,000 records in all; **J & R Music World** (Lower Manhattan), 23 Park Row.

SPORTING GOODS **Herman's** (midtown), 135 W. 42nd St. or 845 Third Ave. at 51st St.; **Paragon** (Gramercy Park), 867 Broadway at E. 17th St.

STEREO AND ELECTRONIC EQUIPMENT **ABC Trading Co.** (SoHo), 31 Canal St.; **Grand Central Radio** (midtown), 155 E. 45th St., with equipment for European voltages; **Harvey Electronics** (midtown), 2 W. 45th St. at Fifth Ave., with equipment for any voltage you need; **Rabson's** (midtown), 119 W. 57th St., also with equipment for European and other foreign voltages; **Uncle Steve** (Chinatown), 343 Canal St., with unbeatable prices.

TOYS ☀ **F. A. O. Schwarz** (midtown), Fifth Ave. at 58th St., the world's biggest toyshop; **Macy's** (midtown), W. 34th St. and Broadway.

SPECIAL EVENTS: For the exact schedule of events below, consult the **New York Convention and Visitors Bureau** (see "Tourist Information" under "Information and Tours," above).

Chinese New Year (Jan–Feb): Ten days of gargantuan banquets, processions, fireworks, and the dragon parade through the streets of Chinatown. Colorful.

St. Patrick's Day Parade (Mar 17): On this feast day of the Irish, the sons and daughters of Erin parade up Fifth Ave. from 44th St. to 86th St. One of the most popular parades in the U.S. More than 150,000 revelers.

Easter Parade (Easter Sunday): Parade on Fifth Ave. near St. Patrick's Cathedral; more like a fashion show than a religious occasion.

Washington Square Art Show (last weekend in May/first in June; last weekend in Aug/first in Sept): Transforms the sidewalks of Washington Sq. and the surrounding streets into a huge open-air art gallery, where hundreds of artists and craftspeople exhibit their work.

Festa di San Antonio/Feast of St. Anthony of Padua (mid-June): An Italian street "festa" dedicated to the food of the motherland. In Little Italy—a spring must.

Lesbian and Gay Pride Day Parade (last Sunday in June): Since 1970, a yearly procession along Fifth Ave. of all New York's homosexual groups, with more than 100,000 marchers. Colorful.

JVC Jazz Festival (late June to early July): Two weeks of concerts and club appearances around the city, with the biggest names in jazz. For information, call 787-2020.

Shakespeare in the Park (June–Sept): Free open-air performances of Shakespeare's and other great plays at the Delacorte Theater in Central Park.

Harbor Festival (July 1–4): Naval review and parade of boats in the harbor.

San Paolino Festival (mid-July): Spectacular procession of the "Giglio," a four-story tower borne on men's backs through the streets of Williamsburg; the biggest Italian religious festival in Brooklyn.

Mostly Mozart Festival (mid-July to late Aug): Concerts in Avery Fisher Hall ranging from recitals and chamber music to choral and orchestral programs dedicated to the "divine Wolfgang" and his contemporaries.

Greenwich Village Jazz Festival (late Aug to early Sept): The leading jazz performers play for 10 days in a dozen clubs in the Village.

Caribbean Festival (Labor Day weekend): Starting on Thurs with nightly music performances representing different parts of the Caribbean—including reggae, steel band, and calypso—this colorful celebration culminates in an exuberant parade on the Mon of Labor Day. Spicy food, dancing in the streets—the closest thing to Mardi Gras in New York. Takes place on Eastern Pkwy. in Brooklyn.

San Gennaro Festival (10 days in Sept): The feast of the patron saint of Naples, and of New York's Little Italy. Pizza and chianti at every street corner in Little Italy. Plenty of atmosphere.

Columbus Day Parade (2nd Mon in Oct): Spectacular parade on Fifth Ave., commemorating the discovery of America by Christopher Columbus—the great Italian-American occasion. On the previous day there is an equally spectacular procession of the Latin American communities—the **Hispanic-American Day Parade.**

New York City Marathon (late Oct to early Nov): 20,000 marathoners compete along a course from the Staten Island end of the Verrazano-Narrows Bridge through Brooklyn, Queens, and the southern Bronx, and into Manhattan to the finish line in Central Park. One of the world's biggest marathons.

Macy's Thanksgiving Day Parade (fourth Thurs in Nov): The prettiest parade of the year, with tens of thousands of participants, bands, floats, and giant balloons in procession down Broadway. You might call it New York's Carnival. Don't miss it.

Times Square New Year's Eve (Dec 31): If you want to wish yourself a Happy New Year, you have to be in Times Sq. for the 12 strokes of midnight. A must for New Yorkers since 1904.

SPORTS: New York boasts eight major-league teams in four professional sports:
Baseball (Apr–Oct): Mets, Shea Stadium, Queens (718/507-6387); Yankees, Yankee Stadium, Bronx (293-6000).
Basketball (Oct–Apr): Knicks, Madison Square Garden, midtown (564-4400); New Jersey Nets, Byrne Meadowlands Arena, E. Rutherford, N.J. (201/935-3900).
Football (Sept–Dec): Giants, Giants Stadium, E. Rutherford, N.J. (201/935-8222); Jets, Giants Stadium, E. Rutherford, N.J. (201/421-6600).
Ice Hockey (Sept–Apr): Islanders, Nassau Coliseum, Hempstead, Long Island (516/794-4100); Rangers, Madison Square Garden, midtown (563-8300).

Horse Racing
Aqueduct Race Track, Rockaway Blvd., Ozone Park, Queens (718/641-4700), with racing Jan–May and Oct–Dec.
Belmont Park Race Track, Hempstead Tpke. at Plainfield Ave., Belmont, Long Island (718/641-4700), with racing May–July and Sept–Oct.
Meadowlands Racetrack, at the Meadowlands, E. Rutherford, N.J. (201/935-8500), with trotters Jan–Aug and thoroughbred racing Sept–Dec.
Yonkers Raceway, Central Ave. and Yonkers Ave., Yonkers (914/968-4200), with racing Mar to mid-Apr, June to mid-July, Sept–Oct, and Dec.

STROLLS: ⚓ **Battery Park City** (Lower Manhattan), along West St. between Battery Pl. and Chambers St.: New residential complex on land reclaimed from the Hudson at the southern tip of Manhattan. The fill was excavated from the site of the nearby World Trade Center. Pleasant walkway along the river, and a splendid tropical garden in an enormous glass-roofed atrium 128 ft. (40m) high (the Winter Garden at World Financial Center) with a stunning view of the Hudson River and several shops and cafés. A sight to be seen.

☀⚓ **Chinatown,** around lower Mott St., Bayard St., and Pell St.: Picturesque Chinese district next door to Little Italy. Countless stalls, groceries, restaurants, and stores with souvenirs (often made in Japan or Korea). Uncommonly gaudy and crowded, especially on Mott St., Chinatown's main drag. Interesting little museum of Chinese culture, religion, and art at 8 Mott St. (964-1542), open daily. A stroll you shouldn't miss.

☖ **Columbus Ave.** (Upper West Side), around Lincoln Center: Long overlooked by well-to-do New Yorkers, this neighborhood regained its lost youth a couple of decades ago, and now attracts yuppies, artists, and intellectuals. Many trendy boutiques, fashionable restaurants, outdoor cafés. The style is well-heeled intelligentsia crossed with screwy. Amusing.

☀☖ **Diamond Row** (midtown), W. 47th St. between Fifth Ave. and Sixth Ave.: The New York diamond-merchants' street, where a polyglot crowd of dealers haggles in all languages—from Flemish to Yiddish—over 80% of all the precious stones bought and sold in the U.S. Take a look at all the diamonds, rubies, and emeralds glittering in the display windows.

☖ **Fifth Ave.** (midtown), between E. 48th St. and E. 59th Sts.: The stores here are a *Who's Who* of international high fashion: Bergdorf Goodman, Cartier, Tiffany, Van Cleef & Arpels, Saks Fifth Avenue, Valentino, Gucci, Ted Lapidus. For well-lined bank accounts.

☀☖ **Greenwich Village,** around Washington Sq.: New York's traditional bohemian quarter, with old houses and narrow streets. Many inviting bars and little restaurants. Bookstores, art galleries, dress shops, antiques dealers, jazz clubs, and souvenir stores are all there to tempt the idler. The people are an amusing intellectual-hippy mix, but you'll find junkies here too. Although it appeals blatantly to the tourist trade, it's worth a visit.

☖ **Harlem,** between Central Park North (110th St.) and W. 155th St.: "The black capital of America," with several interesting museums, the Apollo Theater, and some lovely 19th-century houses, particularly along Striver's Row (139th St. between Seventh Ave. and Eighth Ave.), which are worth visiting. Don't walk alone after dark; the rate of deaths by violence is, according to police statistics, twice as high in Harlem as in the rest of Manhattan.

☖ **Little Italy,** around Mulberry St.: With its typically Italian grocery stores, cafés, bars, *trattorias,* and funeral parlors, this is a postcard Italy of chianti, pizza, and espresso—but it's being slowly swallowed by its neighbor, Chinatown. Guaranteed local color, especially on such saints' days as San Antonio (mid-June) or San Gennaro (mid-Sept). Worth the detour.

☖ **SoHo,** around W. Broadway south of Houston St.: The artists' quarter, with art galleries, far-out boutiques, and trendy restaurants. Many lofts—former commercial or light-industrial space converted into artists' studios or luxury apartments for yuppies. Lovely old cast-iron facades around Broome St. and Greene St.

☀☖ **Times Square and the Theater District** (midtown), Broadway between W. 42nd St. and W. 52nd St.: Dozens of theaters and movie houses with their neon signs flashing, but also porno houses and the headquarters of the retail drug traffic. Currently in the midst of a vast urban-renewal project. Fascinating—but imprudent alone after midnight.

THEME PARKS: ☀☖ **Coney Island Astroland Park,** W. 10th St. between Surf Ave. and the Boardwalk, Brooklyn (718/265-2100): The granddaddy of American amusement parks, born 1884. Numerous attractions, including the famous 60-year-old giant roller-coaster *Cyclone,* a spectacular Ferris wheel, and a Parachute Jump tower, all historical landmarks. Kitsch but picturesque. Overrun by New Yorkers on summer weekends. Open weekends only, Apr and May; daily, June to mid-Sept; weekends only to mid-Oct; closed the rest of the year. Reached directly by subway from Manhattan.

☖ **Six Flags Great Adventure,** in Jackson, N.J., 60 mi. (96km) SW on the N.J. Tpke., I-195E, and N.J. 537S (201/928-3500): Enormous 1,700-acre (688ha) theme park with more than 100 attractions—carousels and giant roller-coasters including the terrifying "Great American Scream Machine (173 ft./53m high; 68 m.p.h.), as well as a safari zoo with 2,000 wild animals which you can see from your car. Variety and other shows. Open daily, Apr–Sept; weekends only to late Oct; closed the rest of the year.

WINTER SPORTS RESORTS: Although most New York skiers prefer the slopes of the Adirondacks (see "Farther Afield," below), there are some very acceptable resorts nearer the city, notably the following in the Catskills:

Bellayre Mountain, 154 mi. (246km) NW on I-87N and N.Y. 28W (914/254-5600): 7 lifts. Open Dec–Mar. For snow conditions, call toll free 800/942-6904.

Holiday Mountain, 101 mi. (162km) NW along I-87N and N.Y. 17W (914/796-3161): 9 lifts. Open Dec–Mar.

Hunter Mountain Ski Bowl, 155 mi. (248km) NW on I-87N and N.Y. 23A West (518/263-4223): 16 lifts. Open Nov–Apr.

ZOOS: **Bronx Zoo,** Fordham Rd. and Bronx River Pkwy., Bronx (367-1010): One of the top 10 zoos in the U.S., with 3,600 creatures of 700 different species on 265 acres (107ha). Although the overall layout of a zoo dating from 1899 has to be somewhat antiquated, this one has some interesting reconstructions of natural habitats: "Wild Asia," "Jungle World," "World of Darkness" for nocturnal animals, etc. The "World of Birds" is a splendid collection of tropical birds. You can visit the zoo by monorail or by a miniature safari train. Reached by subway directly from Manhattan: East Side IRT (Green) Line no. 5 to E. Tremont Ave. Very well worth visiting. Open daily.

New York Aquarium, Boardwalk and W. 8th St., Coney Island, Brooklyn (718/265-3474): Very well-stocked aquarium where you can see 200 species of marine creatures, from the giant octopus to the shark and from the beluga whale to the electric eel. Shows by trained sea creatures. Reached by subway directly from Manhattan: IND (Orange) Lines F or D to W. 8th St. Worth the trip. Open daily.

Staten Island Zoo, Barrett Park, 614 Broadway, W. New Brighton, Staten Island (718/442-3100): Best known for its reptiles, this interesting little zoo exhibits animals as strange as they are rarely seen, including 32 varieties of rattlesnake (the world's largest collection), scorpions, alligators, crocodiles, and other reptiles and amphibians. Fascinating. Open daily.

ACCOMMODATIONS

A Note on Accommodations: Room rates in New York City are coded as follows: **VE,** Very Expensive ($140 and up); **E,** Expensive ($90–$140); **M,** Moderate ($60–$90); **I,** Inexpensive ($30–$60); **B,** Budget (up to $30). A listing of toll-free numbers is in the Appendix.

Personal Favorites (in order of preference)

Carlyle (Upper East Side), Madison Ave. at E. 76th St., NY 10021 (212/744-1600). 500 rms, A/C, color TV, in-rm movies. AE, CB, DC, MC, V. Gar. $30, health club, two rests. (including Carlyle Restaurant), bar, 24-hr. rm svce, nightclub, concierge. *Note:* Splendid and refined, w. rms for servants and luxury kennels, the Carlyle is the most elegant and chic hotel in New York, favored by the Kennedy family and former President Reagan, among others. Spacious and luxuriously inviting rms w. minibars and VCRs. Exemplary, personalized svce. Discreet, plush ambience. Perfection—at a price. Good rest., ideal for lunch. Very popular piano bar (Café Carlyle). 80% of the rms are rented by the year. Luxury, calm, and voluptuousness. Probably the best hotel in the U.S. **VE**

Sherry Netherland (Upper East Side), 781 Fifth Ave. (at 59th St.), NY 10022 (212/355-2800). 370 rms, A/C, color TV, in-rm movies. AE. Gar. $26, rest. (Quaglino's), bar, rm svce, nightclub, hrdrsr, crib $10. *Note:* Quiet and distinguished, with one of New York's best locations, facing Central Park and a stone's throw from the smart Fifth Ave. stores. The building is slightly kitsch Gothic Revival, but the rms and suites are very elegant, some w. balconies or terraces. Many clients rent by the year. Exceptionally polished svce; Italian rest. which doesn't deserve its high reputation. The only grand hotel in New York that accepts only one credit card. One of the dozen best hotels in the country; the movie stars' favorite. **VE**

Plaza Athénée (Upper East Side), 37 E. 64th St., NY 10021 (212/734-9100; toll free 800/255-3050). 199 rms. A/C, color TV, in-rm movies. AE, CB, DC, MC, V. Valet gar. $30, rest. (La Régence), bar, 24-hr. rm svce, free crib, concierge. *Note:* This newcomer on the New York hotel scene is an outpost of the luxurious and very exclusive Paris hotel of the same name. Same refined elegance, same intimate, protected atmosphere. Remarkably comfortable rms and suites w. Louis XVI furniture and refrigerators, some w. private terraces, solariums, and dining rms. Flawless personalized svce. Remarkable rest. w. sumptuous turn-of-the-century decor. Lots of class, but pricey; one duplex suite goes for $1,800 a night. Belongs to Britain's Trusthouse Forte hotel chain. Draws VIPs and leaders of the European financial community. Very near Central Park. **VE**

Holiday Inn Crowne Plaza (midtown), W. 49th St. and Broadway, NY 10019 (212/977-4000; toll free, see Holiday Inns). 770 rms, A/C, color TV, in-rm movies. AE, CB, DC, MC, V. Valet gar. $25, pool, health club, sauna, two rests. (including Broadway Grill), two bars, rm svce. *Note:* Futuristic 46-floor tower of crystal opened in 1989—a splendid piece of modern architecture from the drawing-board of Alan Lapidus. New York's handsomest new hotel, w. elegant, civilized interiors, spacious, well-laid-out rms, and exemplary standards of comfort. Good physical-fitness facilities for a New York City hotel; ultra-professional svce. Rms on the six highest floors, w. spectacular views, are reserved for VIPs. Conveniently located on Broadway at the heart of the theater district. Business and package-tour clientele. One of the great successes among Manhattan's hotels. **VE**

Waldorf-Astoria (midtown), 301 Park Ave. (at E. 49th St.), NY 10022 (212/355-3000; toll free, see Hilton). 1,752 rms, A/C, color TV, in-rm movies. AE, CB, DC, MC, V. Valet gar. $28, five rests. (including Bull & Bear), three bars, 24-hr. rm svce, nightclub, hrdrsr, boutiques, free crib, concierge. *Note:* A landmark since 1931; everybody of any importance on the planet has stayed in this immense rococo caravanserai. The art deco lobby is superb, and the Starlight Roof is the only ballroom in New York whose roof opens to the stars. The rms have been entirely redecorated and refurnished at a cost of $150 million. Very good rm svce; inadequate reception. Excellent location. A favorite w. foreigners, since the help speaks 37 languages. Luxurious VIP suites in the adjoining Waldorf Towers. Interesting wknd packages. President Bush occupies the Presidential Suite when he is in town. **VE**

Doral Tuscany Hotel (midtown), 120 E. 39th St., NY 10016 (212/686-1600; toll free 800/847-4078). 120 rms, A/C, color TV, in-rm movies. AE, CB, DC, MC, V. Gar. $22, rest., bar, rm svce, nightclub, free crib. *Note:* Remarkable reception and atmosphere in one of New York's best small hotels. Spacious, elegant rms w. refrigerators and VCRs. Faultless comfort; polished svce. Regular clientele. A favorite w. those in-the-know, half a block from Park Ave. Good rest. (Time and Again). Interesting wknd discounts. **VE**

Algonquin (midtown), 59 W. 44th St., NY 10036 (212/840-6800). 170 rms, A/C, color TV. AE, CB, DC, MC, V. Gar.

$18, rest., bar, rm svce, drugstore, crib $12. *Note:* Turn-of-the-century hotel popular w. distinguished writers and theater-goers, since it's a stone's throw from Broadway. Authentic 1900 decor. Reception and svce attentive. The rms are cozily old-fashioned. The Blue Bar is famous; the after-theater buffet is fashionable but so-so. There's a slight aura of the past, for those who hanker for the bohemian 1930s when Dorothy Parker, James Thurber, and others met at the "Algonquin Round Table." Sir John Gielgud and Lord Olivier have been among the hotel's patrons. Designated historic landmark. A comprehensive program of rehabilitation, currently under way, should eventually restore its pristine splendor. **VE**

Gramercy Park Hotel (Gramercy Park), 2 Lexington Ave. (at E. 21st St.), NY 10010 (212/475-4320; toll free 800/221-4083). 507 rms, A/C, color TV. AE, CB, DC, MC, V. Parking adj., rest., bar, rm svce. *Note:* Quiet, agreeable 1920s hotel far from Manhattan's bustle. Courteous reception and svce. Comfortably renovated. Regular clientele w. many Europeans. Relaxed, inviting atmosphere. The best rms overlook Gramercy Park. Very acceptable rest. A good place to stay. **E**

Best Western Milford Plaza (midtown), 270 W. 45th St., NY 10036 (212/869-3600; toll free, see Best Western). 1,310 rms, A/C, color TV, in-rm movies. AE, CB, DC, MC, V. Gar. $12, two rests. (including Mama Leone's), bar, rm svce, nightclub. *Note:* The old Royal Manhattan renovated and improved. Rms small and functional at best; most have refrigerators. Many package tours and airline crews come here from abroad. The only plus: accommodation and show-ticket packages at very attractive prices ("Show Time New York"). In the heart of the Broadway theater district—not a safe neighborhood after midnight. **M–E**

Pickwick Arms (midtown), 230 E. 51st St., NY 10022 (212/355-0300; toll free 800/742-5945). 400 rms, A/C, cable color TV. AE, CB, DC, MC, V. No private parking. Roof grdn, rest., coffee shop, bar, rm svce. *Note:* An excellent buy for the budget traveler, in the heart of the fashionable East Side. Scrupulously clean rms, recently renovated (some without private bath). Some studios w. kitchenette. Functional level of comfort; friendly, multilingual svce (many foreign guests). Resv. advisable well in advance. Conveniently located near the U.N. Very good overall value. **I–M**

Other Hotels (from top bracket to budget)

Marriott Marquis (midtown), 1535 Broadway (at W. 44th St.), NY 10036 (212/398-1900; toll free, see Marriott). 1,876 rms, color TV, in-rm movies. AE, CB, DC, MC, V. Valet gar. $28, health club, sauna, three rests. (including The View revolving rest. on the top floor), coffee shop, four bars, 24-hr. rm svce, theater, boutiques, concierge. *Note:* The most eye-catching luxury hotel in New York: an ultramodern 52-story high-rise by architect John Portman. The glass-walled lobby is 46 floors high, w. fountains, indoor grdns, and glass-walled elevators. Exceptionally spacious, comfortable rms, w. unobstructed views of Manhattan from the top two floors. Impersonal but efficient svce. As in all Marriotts, the rests. are mediocre. Overlooks Times Sq. and the theater district. Two VIP floors. Well-equipped business center. **VE**

Regency Hotel (Upper East Side), 540 Park Ave. (at E. 61st St.), NY 10021 (212/759-4100; toll free, see Loews). 350 rms, A/C, color TV, in-rm movies. AE, CB, DC, MC, V. Valet gar. $25, health club, sauna, rest. (540 Park), bar, 24-hr. rm svce, nightclub, hrdrsr, concierge, crib $10. *Note:* Favored by the financial upper crust for 25 years. All the charm of a European luxury hotel; elegant rms w. minibars and period furniture, some w. kitchenettes. Quiet, distinguished atmosphere. Excellent rm svce. The very good rest. is the ideal place for a working breakfast or lunch. Many rms rented by the year. Elegant and urbane. Recently underwent a $17-million facelift. **VE**

Drake Swissôtel (midtown), 440 Park Ave. (at E. 56th St.), NY 10022 (212/421-0900; toll free 800/372-5369). 640

rms, A/C, color TV, in-rm movies. AE, CB, DC, MC, V. Valet gar. $20, two rests. (including Lafayette), bar, 24-hr. rm svce, nightclub, free crib, concierge. *Note:* Since it was bought by Swiss interests this venerable, and indeed somewhat decrepit, pile has been restored to its former luster by a multi-million-dollar facelift. Its spacious peach-and-ivory rms w. marble bathrooms and refrigerators, exemplary svce, and excellent rest. (Lafayette) supervised by the great French chef Louis Outhier, combine to make it one of the best places to stay on Park Ave. Free morning limo to Wall St. Draws many business travelers from Europe. **VE**

♀♀♀ **Grand Hyatt New York** (midtown), Park Ave. at E. 42nd St., ໄ ໄ ໄ NY 10017 (212/883-1234; toll free, see Hyatt). 1,400 rms, A/C, color TV, in-rm movies. AE, CB, DC, MC, V. Valet gar. $25, two rests. (including Trumpet's), bars, 24-hr. rm svce, nightclub, boutiques, drugstore, free crib. *Note:* Ultramodern, w. a tinge of poetry, built by Donald Trump, New York's leading real-estate developer. The huge 34-story glass facade reflects the surrounding high-rises. Splendid four-story lobby adorned by a giant sculpture. Luxurious and comfortable rms, but often short on space. Efficient multilingual help; exemplary rm svce. Unhappily, no physical-fitness facilities in the hotel. Well-regarded rest. Interesting wknd discounts. Adjacent to Grand Central Terminal on the site of the old Commodore Hotel. VIP suites on the top two floors. **VE**

♀♀♀ **Helmsley Palace Hotel** (midtown), 455 Madison Ave. (at E. ໄ ໄ ໄ 49th St.), NY 10022 (212/888-7000; toll free 800/221-4982). 961 rms, A/C, color TV, in-rm movies. AE, CB, DC, MC, V. Gar. $38, two rests. (including the Trianon), two bars, 24-hr. rm svce, nightclub, hrdrsr, boutiques, free crib, concierge. *Note:* Extravagant grand hotel deluxe built at a cost of $100 million. The attempt to integrate the modern 51-story glass tower w. an 1882 Renaissance Revival house, the Villard Mansion, doesn't come off. The opulence is often strident but the comfort and rm svce are incomparable. Opposite St. Patrick's Cathedral. One triplex suite rents for $1,800 a night plus taxes and svce. Very successful since its 1980 opening. **VE**

♀♀♀ **Helmsley Park Lane** (midtown), 36 Central Park South, NY ໄ ໄ ໄ 10019 (212/371-4000; toll free 800/221-4982). 640 rms, A/C, color TV, in-rm movies. AE, CB, DC, MC, V. Gar. $32, rest., bar, 24-hr. rm svce, nightclub, hrdrsr, free crib. *Note:* 46 floors of glass and steel overlooking Central Park. Huge, very comfortable rms w. refrigerators, the best w. park views. Big business clientele. Rm svce on the surly side. The Park Room is a so-so rest. Multilingual help. **VE**

♀♀♀ **Hilton and Towers at Rockefeller Center** (midtown), 1335 ໄ ໄ ໄ Ave. of the Americas (at W. 54th St.), NY 10019 (212/586-7000; toll free, see Hilton). 2,117 rms, A/C, color TV, in-rm movies. AE, CB, DC, MC, V. Valet gar. $24, health club, rest. (Grill 53), coffee shop, three bars, 24-hr. rm svce, disco, hrdrsr, free crib. *Note:* Huge 46-floor tourist mill. Modern, functional rms, some very small. Public areas and rests. crowded and noisy. Svce often overburdened. The Hilton and Towers has been revamped to the tune of $80 million w. a three-level convention area connected to the hotel by a glass-enclosed bridge. Excellent location. Draws American and Japanese business travelers. Interesting wknd discounts. VIP suites in the Executive Tower from the 39th to the 44th floor. Business center. **VE**

♀♀♀ **Parker Meridien** (midtown), 118 W. 57th St., NY 10019 ໄ ໄ ໄ (212/245-5000; toll free, see Meridien). 697 rms, A/C, color TV, in-rm movies. AE, CB, DC, MC, V. Valet gar. $24, pool, health club, sauna, tennis court, squash, two rests., bar, 24-hr. rm svce, nightclub, concierge, free crib. *Note:* The first French-owned hotel in New York, belonging to the hotel chain of Air France. Unimaginative modern building, but elegant, refined interior w. many works of art. Rms on the diminutive side, w. minibars. Very complete fitness facilities. Hard-working rm svce. Good nouvelle cuisine rest. Business clientele. A favorite w. those in-the-know. Interesting wknd discounts. A stone's throw from Central Park. **VE**

🛏🛏🛏 **Morgan's** (midtown), 237 Madison Ave. (at E. 38th St.), NY 10016 (212/686-0300; toll free 800/334-3408). 154 rms, A/C, color TV, in-rm movies. AE, CB, DC, MC, V. Valet gar. $24, rest. (Pierpoint Restaurant), bar, 24-hr. rm svce. *Note:* Conceived by the promoters of the famous old Studio 54 and the Palladium, Steve Rubell and Ian Schrager, Morgan's is the most original, the most amusing, and the most "switched-on" luxury hotel in Manhattan. White, black, and gray decor w. hi-tech stainless-steel bathrooms by Andrée Putnam. Smallish rms w. *Star Wars* TV/stereo/hi-fi equipment. The help—young, smiling, and relaxed—wear uniforms designed by Calvin Klein and Giorgio Armani. Movie stars, leading dress designers, and trendy artists stay here (Cher, Margaux Hemingway, and Giorgio Armani are regulars). The "in" place. **VE**

🛏🛏🛏 **Parc Fifty One** (formerly the Grand Bay Hotel at Equitable Center; midtown), 152 W. 51st St., NY 10019 (212/765-1900; toll free 800/338-1338). 179 rms, A/C, color TV, in-rm movies. AE, CB, DC, MC, V. Valet gar. $25, two rests. (including Palio), bar, 24-hr svce, concierge on every floor. *Note:* New (1987) grand hotel in the great European luxury hotel tradition. The decoration and furnishings are sumptuous, w. Italian marble, Oriental rugs, crystal chandeliers, and an abundance of works of art. Remarkably spacious, comfortable rms w. minibars, two TV sets, and marble bathrooms. Ultra-polished svce. Excellent Italian rest. Free morning limo to Wall St. Big business clientele. Admirably located halfway between Rockefeller Center and the theater district, on the site of the old Taft Hotel. **VE**

🛏🛏🛏 **The Pierre** (Upper East Side), 2 E. 61st St. (at Fifth Ave.), NY 10021 (212/838-8000; toll free, see Four Seasons). 197 rms, A/C, color TV, in-rm movies. AE, CB, DC, MC, V. Gar. $24, rest. (Café Pierre), bar, rm svce, nightclub, hrdrsr, boutiques, free crib, concierge. *Note:* The Pierre long enjoyed a reputation as New York's best hotel, but doesn't deserve it today. Plush but depressing interior decoration; svce sometimes defective. Wonderfully situated opposite Central Park. So-so rest. Thronged w. aristocratic and/or wealthy Europeans. Along w. the Stanhope, one of New York's most expensive hotels. **VE**

🛏🛏🛏 **Rihga Royal Hotel** (midtown), 151 W. 54th St. (at Seventh Ave.), NY 10019 (212/307-5000; toll free 800/937-5454). 500 suites, A/C, color TV, in-rm movies. AE, CB, DC, MC, V. Gar. $25, pool, health club, rest. (Halcyon), bar, 24-hr. rm svce, concierge. *Note:* The 54-story Rihga Royal, which opened in May 1990 in the heart of the new West Side, is New York's tallest hotel. Every rm is a one- or two-bedroom luxury suite w. contemporary furnishings and marble bath. Each suite offers three phones (two lines each), a refrigerator and icemaker, two TVs, a VCR, and computer/fax outlets. Flawless, polished svce. Very complete amenities. Big business clientele. **VE**

🛏🛏🛏 **The Royalton** (midtown), 44 W. 44th St. (at Ave. of the Americas), NY 10036 (212/869-4400). 175 rms, A/C, color TV, in-rm movies. AE, CB, DC, MC, V. Valet gar. $26, rest. (44), bar, 24-hr. rm svce, concierge. *Note:* A 90-year-old Neo-Georgian limestone building turned into a haven for well-traveled sophisticates by superstar of French design Philippe Starck. Reopened in October 1988 after 18 months and more than $40-million renovation program. Spacious suitelike rms w. minimalist decor in beige shades, startling contemporary furniture and stainless-steel bathrooms (some rms w. working fireplaces). Spectacular columned lobby that stretches from W. 43rd St. to W. 44th St. Faultless svce. The 44 Restaurant is notable. Same management as the famed Morgan's (see above). **VE**

🛏🛏🛏 **The Stanhope** (Upper East Side), 995 Fifth Ave. (at 81st St.), NY 10028 (212/288-5800; toll free 800/828-1123). 132

rms (of which 106 are suites), A/C, color TV, in-rm movies. AE, CB, DC, MC, V. No private parking; rest. (Stanhope Dining Room), bar, rm svce, nightclub, free crib, concierge. *Note:* On elegant Fifth Ave. opposite the Metropolitan Museum of Art, this small, intimate, ultra-luxurious hotel was elegantly restored in the tradition of the grand hotels of Europe in 1986 at a cost of $26 million. Its discreet, refined decorative scheme weds Louis XVI furniture, Baccarat crystal chandeliers, impressionist paintings, cream-colored leather and silk. Free Chanel toiletries in every bathroom. Extremely polished svce. A sidewalk cafe fronting the hotel serves drinks and light meals during warm months. The rest. is of the highest order, but the prices are even higher than that. Among the most expensive hotels in town, where single rooms start at $275 a night and the most lavish suite reaches $4,000 a night. **VE**

    United Nations Plaza (midtown), 1 United Nations Plaza (at E. 44th St.), NY 10017 (212/355-3400; toll free, see Hyatt). 444 rms, A/C, color TV, in-rm movies. AE, CB, DC, MC, V. Valet gar. $26, pool, health club, sauna, tennis court, rest. (Ambassador Grill), bar, rm svce, free crib. *Note:* The hotel begins on the 28th floor of an ultramodern 40-story glass tower by architect Kevin Roche. Pool and tennis court in the sky. Comfortable, inviting rms w. refrigerators, all w. superb view of New York. Efficient svce. Overlooks the East River and the U.N. building. Good French rest. Clientele of diplomats and big-business travelers; free morning Wall St. limo. A favorite w. those in-the-know. **VE**

    Vista International New York (Lower Manhattan), 3 World Trade Center, NY 10048 (212/938-9100; toll free, see Hilton). 820 rms, A/C, color TV, in-rm movies. AE, CB, DC, MC, V. Gar. $20, pool, health club, sauna, tennis court, squash, two rests. (including the American Harvest), two bars, rm svce, concierge. *Note:* The only hotel of quality in the Wall St. district. Ultramodern and comfortable; very inviting rms w. minibars, some w. Statue of Liberty views. Comprehensive physical-fitness facilities. Business clientele. Good rest. specializing in modern American cuisine (The American Harvest). Not really suitable for tourists; the neighborhood is almost deserted at night. **VE**

    Novotel (midtown), 226 W. 52nd St. (at Broadway), NY 10019 (212/315-0100; toll free 800/221-3185). 470 rms, A/C, color TV, in-rm movies. AE, CB, DC, MC, V. Valet parking $17, rest. (Café Skylight), two bars, rm svce, nightclub, crib $20. *Note:* The second French hotel in New York, on the top 27 floors of an ungraceful new building a few blocks from Times Sq. Ultramodern furnishings; spacious, well-equipped rms; good rests.; inviting wine bar. Reception and svce in the French manner. Business clientele. Interesting wknd discounts. **VE**

    Sheraton Centre (formerly the Americana; midtown), 811 Seventh Ave. (at W. 52nd St.), NY 10019 (212/581-1000; toll free, see Sheraton). 1,818 rms, A/C, color TV, in-rm movies. AE, CB, DC, MC, V. Gar. $24, two rests. (including Rainier's), coffee shop, two bars, rm svce, disco, hrdrsr, drugstore, free crib. *Note:* Enormous 50-story concrete tower crowded w. groups and conventions. The top five floors have luxurious VIP suites. Functionally comfortable; svce sometimes defective. The favorite hotel of former President Carter. Recently renovated. Interesting wknd and vacation packages. Near the theater district. **VE**

    Days Inn New York (formerly the Holiday Inn Coliseum; midtown), 440 W. 57th St., NY 10019 (212/581-8100; toll free, see Days Inn). 603 rms, A/C, color TV, in-rm movies. AE, CB, DC, MC, V. Gar. $16, open-air pool (in summer), rest., bar, rm svce. *Note:* The most attractive things about this reasonably modern motel (consisting of an 18- and an 11-floor tower), are its location near Lincoln Center and its rooftop pool in summer. Functionally comfortable; svce undependable. Caters to groups and conventions (special rates). **E–VE**

♟♟ **Dorset** (midtown), 30 W. 54th St., NY 10019 (212/247-
♟♟ 7300; toll free 800/227-2348). 210 rms, A/C, color TV, in-
rm movies. AE, CB, DC, MC, V. Gar. $20, rest., coffee shop, bar, rm svce,
free crib. *Note:* Discreet, charming, polished small hotel a stone's throw from
the Museum of Modern Art and the smart Fifth Ave. stores. Inviting, comfortable rms, the best overlooking the interior court. Attentive service. Coffee
shop very popular w. TV and show-business people at lunchtime. A fine place.
E–VE

♟♟ **Mayflower** (Upper West Side), 15 Central Park West, NY
♟♟ 10023 (212/265-0060; toll free 800/223-4164). 377 rms,
A/C, color TV. AE, CB, DC, MC, V. Pay parking available; rest. (The Conservatory), bar, rm svce, free crib. *Note:* The favorite place to stay for theater-goers,
music lovers, and opera buffs; Lincoln Center is a few minutes' walk. Decor and
furnishings completely renovated; spacious, comfortable rms w. refrigerators
(ask for one overlooking Central Park). Cordial, efficient svce; pleasant but expensive rest. Interesting wknd discounts. Free shuttle to/from the Jacob K. Javits Convention Center. **E–VE**

♟♟ **New York Penta** (formerly the Statler Hilton; midtown), 401
♟♟ Seventh Ave. (at W. 33rd St.), NY 10001 (212/736-5000; toll
free 800/225-3456). 1,700 rms, A/C, color TV, in-rm movies. AE, CB, DC,
MC, V. Gar. $22, health club, sauna, squash, three rests. (including the Globe-
trotter), two bars, rm svce, nightclub, hrdrsr, boutiques, concierge, crib $20.
Note: Huge group-and-convention hotel across the street from Madison Square
Garden and five blocks from the Javits Convention Center. Recently renovated at
a cost of $35 million. Comfortable rms, some too small; svce sometimes over-
worked. Two VIP floors. **E–VE**

♟♟ **Ramada Inn** (midtown), 790 Eighth Ave. (at W. 49th St.), NY
♟♟ 10019 (212/581-7000; toll free, see Ramada Inns). 366 rms,
A/C, color TV, in-rm movies. AE, CB, DC, MC, V. Gar. $16, pool, rest., bar,
valet svce, free crib. *Note:* Typical convention and package-tour hotel. Rms quite
large and functionally comfortable. Reception and svce undependable. Well located near the theater district. Rooftop swimming pool (open in summer). **E–VE**

♟♟ **Roosevelt** (midtown), Madison Ave. at E. 45th St., NY 10017
♟♟ (212/661-9600; toll free 800/344-1212). 1,070 rms, A/C,
color TV, in-rm movies. AE, CB, DC, MC, V. Valet gar. $24, two rests. (includ-
ing Crawdaddy's), two bars, rm svce, concierge. *Note:* One of the best locations
in the city, in the heart of the midtown business district, opposite Grand Central
Terminal and three blocks from the airport limo for Kennedy and La Guardia
airports. Massive, unattractive building, but renovated, comfortable interior.
Good Créole rest. popular at lunchtime. Svce a little undependable. Business clientele. **E–VE**

♟♟ **Roger Smith Winthrop** (midtown), 501 Lexington Ave. (at E.
♟♟ 47th St.), NY 10017 (212/755-1400; toll free 800/445-
0277). 183 rms, A/C, color TV. AE, CB, DC, MC, V. Public parking adjacent;
rest. (Nibbles), bar, free crib. *Note:* Older, elegant small hotel in the heart of midtown. Spacious, comfortable rms done in pastel shades, all w. refrigerators and
some w. kitchenettes and fireplaces. Free breakfast on wknds. Good svce; central
location. Currently undergoing renovation. **E–VE**

♟ **Empire** (Upper West Side), W. 63rd St. and Broadway, NY
♟ 10023 (212/265-7400; toll free 800/223-9868). 500 rms,
A/C, cable color TV. AE, CB, DC, MC, V. Parking $16, rest., coffee shop, bar,
valet svce, free crib. *Note:* Pleasant, comfortable hotel a stone's throw from Lincoln Center. Has just undergone a major ($20-million) facelift. Very adequate
rest. (Empire Grill). A fine place; try to reserve well ahead. Special rates for foreign visitors. **E–VE**

♟♟ **Wyndham** (midtown), 42 W. 58th St., NY 10019 (212/753-
♟♟ 3500). 200 rms, A/C, cable color TV. AE, CB, DC, MC, V.

Parking lot adj. (fee), rest. (closed wknds), bar. *Note:* Charming, intimate hotel in the European manner, much frequented by literary and theatrical folk, with the "feel" of a venerable London club. Spacious, cozily comfortable rms and svce of the highest order (but no rm svce). One of the few remaining New York hotels w. elevator operators. Well located a block from Central Park and the smart stores on Fifth Ave. Make resv. well ahead. A fine place. **E**

Comfort Inn Murray Hill (midtown), 42 W. 35th St., NY 10001 (212/947-0200; toll free 800/228-5150). 118 rms, A/C, color TV, in-rm movies. AE, CB, DC, MC, V. No private parking; rest. (Myong Dong), bar, free crib. *Note:* Completely renovated at a cost of $4.5 million, this once run-down small hotel now offers you modern, comfortable, inviting rms. Friendly, efficient svce. Business clientele. Free breakfast. Acceptable Korean rest. A couple of blocks from the Garment District and the Empire State Building. **E**

Edison (midtown), 228 W. 47th St., NY 10036 (212/840-5000; toll free 800/223-1900). 1,000 rms, A/C, color TV. AE, CB, DC, MC, V. Gar. $15, rest., coffee shop, two bars, free crib. *Note:* Massive, antiquated 50-year-old hotel; deplorable svce but functionally comfortable. Recently renovated. Clientele largely of groups and Europeans. Smack in the middle of the theater district. Cafeteria (Polish Tea Room) much frequented by theater people. **E**

Salisbury (midtown), 123 W. 57th St., NY 10019 (212/246-1300; toll free 800/223-0680). 320 rms, A/C, color TV. AE, CB, DC, MC, V. No private parking; rest. (Terrace Café), rm svce, free crib. *Note:* Opposite Carnegie Hall, this charming, scrupulously clean old hotel is run by the Calvary Baptist Church; hence no alcoholic beverages are served in rest. Vast, comfortable rms, most w. refrigerators; friendly reception and svce. Caters mostly to musicians and theater-goers. Good value. **E**

Esplanade (Upper West Side), 305 West End Ave. (at W. 74th St.), NY 10023 (212/874-5000; toll free 800/367-1763). 200 rms, A/C, cable color TV. AE, CB, DC, MC, V. No private parking. *Note:* Charming, older hotel in the heart of the Upper West Side. Huge, agreeably decorated rms, some w. kitchenettes, the best w. views of Riverside Park and the Hudson River. Svce w. a smile. Interesting wknd discounts. Clientele of regulars. **M–E**

Gorham (midtown), 136 W. 55th St., NY 10019 (212/245-1800). 163 rms, A/C, color TV. AE, CB, DC, MC, V. Parking adj. $20; rest., bar, rm svce, crib $10, concierge. *Note:* One of the best of New York's charming small hotels. Spacious, comfortable rms w. kitchenettes and refrigerators. Pleasing reception and svce. Favored by Europeans. Good overall value. Ideal for families and budget travelers. **M–E**

Chatwal Inn (Gramercy Park), 429 Park Ave. South (at E. 29th St.), NY 10016 (212/532-4860; toll free 800/826-4667). 55 rms, A/C, cable color TV. AE, CB, DC, MC, V. Valet parking $20, rest., rm svce. *Note:* Built in the early 1980s, this modern hotel off the beaten tourist path is one of New York's best buys. Its reasonable rates and proximity to the Garment District attract textile and clothing executives. Inviting, comfortable suites and rms; good svce; free breakfast; good overall value. Interesting wknd discounts. **M–E**

Wellington (midtown), W. 55th St. and Seventh Ave., NY 10019 (212/247-3900; toll free 800/652-1212). 700 rms, A/C, color TV. AE, CB, DC, MC, V. Gar. $14, rest., coffee shop, bar, boutiques. *Note:* Slightly cramped rms, some w. kitchenettes, recently renovated. Very acceptable standard of comfort. Attracts musicians (Carnegie Hall is two blocks away) and groups. Good value overall. **M–E**

Wentworth (midtown), 59 W. 46th St., NY 10036 (212/719-2300; toll free 800/223-1900). 245 rms, A/C, color TV.

AE, CB, DC, MC, V. No private parking; rm svce. *Note:* Near as it is to the Garment District, this is a favorite hotel for out-of-town buyers. Aging and functionally comfortable, it offers good value. Clean, prettily decorated rms; efficient svce. **M–E**

Collingwood Hotel (midtown), 45 W. 35th St., NY 10001 (tel. 212/947-2500; toll free 800/641-2525). 250 rms, A/C, color TV. AE, CB, DC, MC, V. Parking lot adj. (fee). *Note:* Clean, comfortable hotel, ideal for budget travelers. Entirely redecorated; many rms w. kitchenette. Friendly reception; package-tour clientele. Near Macy's and the Empire State Building. **M**

Wales (Upper East Side), 1295 Madison Ave. (at E. 92nd St.), NY 10128 (212/876-6000). 70 rms, most w. A/C, cable color TV. AE, CB, DC, MC, V. No private parking; coffee shop (Sarabeth's Kitchen), rm svce. *Note:* Modest, well-run turn-of-the-century hotel. Rms a little confining, but inviting and scrupulously clean; most have kitchenettes, and some overlook Central Park. Pleasant coffee shop. A nice district, a 10-min. walk from the Metropolitan Museum of Art. Good value; regular clientele. **M–E**

Diplomat (midtown), 108 W. 43rd St., NY 10036 (212/921-5666). 75 rms. A/C. AE, MC, V. No private parking. *Note:* Small economy hotel very nr. Times Sq. and the theater district. Large, functionally comfortable rms, all air-conditioned and w. private bath. Many overseas guests. After-dark strolls in the neighborhood are not advised. Good overall value. **I–M**

Excelsior (Upper West Side), 45 W. 81st St., NY 10024 (212/362-9200; toll free 800/368-4575). 150 rms, A/C, color TV. AE, MC, V. Nearby parking, coffee shop, valet svce. *Note:* Older family-style hotel a block from Central Park and the Hayden Planetarium. Rms w. kitchenettes. Very acceptable comfort level. The rms on the uppermost floors have a fine view of the city. Pleasant and safe neighborhood; good value. **I–M**

Airport Accommodations

Holiday Inn JFK, 144-02 135th Ave., Jamaica (Queens), NY 11436 (718/659-0200; toll free, see Holiday Inns). 300 rms, A/C, color TV, in-rm movies. AE, CB, DC, MC, V. Free parking, pool, health club, sauna, rest. (Claudine's), bar, rm svce, nightclub, free crib. *Note:* New 12-story building; the first hotel built near JFK in 20 years. Comfort and facilities above the Holiday Inn average. Rms perfectly soundproofed, spacious, and well designed. Efficient svce. Free airport limo. Caters to groups and business travelers; ideal for a stopover between flights. **E–VE**

Days Hotel La Guardia (formerly the Holiday Inn), 100-15 Ditmars Blvd., East Elmhurst (Queens), NY 11369 (718/898-1225; toll free, see Days Inns). 224 rms, A/C, color TV, in-rm movies. AE, CB, DC, MC, V. Free parking, pool, rest., bar, rm svce, nightclub, free crib. *Note:* Typical airport motel 3 min. from La Guardia. Completely renovated rms w. refrigerators. Free airport limo. Efficient svce. **E–VE**

YMCA/Youth Hostels

International House (Upper West Side), 500 Riverside Dr. (at W. 122nd St.), NY 10027 (212/316-8400). 500 rms. Students' residence open from the end of May to the end of Aug. Good facilities.

McBurney YMCA (midtown), 206 W. 24th St., NY 10011 (212/741-9226). 270 rms. Men only. Limited standard of comfort. Health club.

New York International Youth Hostel (Upper West Side), 891 Amsterdam Ave. (at W. 103rd St.), NY 10025. 480-bed youth hostel opened 1989 in a historic-landmark building. Outdoor grdns. Coffee shop.

Sloane House YMCA (midtown), 356 W. 34th St., NY 10001 (212/760-

5850). 1,500 rms. The biggest YMCA in the U.S. Men, women, couples, and families w. children. Coffee shop, health club.

Vanderbilt YMCA (midtown), 224 E. 47th St., NY 10017 (212/755-2410). 435 rms. Men, women, and families. Good facilities (pool, health club), coffee shop. The most comfortable and inviting YMCA in New York. Down the road from the U.N.

West Side YMCA (Upper West Side), 5 W. 63rd St., NY 10023 (212/787-4400). 558 rms. Men, a limited number of women. Pool, health club, coffee shop. A stone's throw from Lincoln Center.

RESTAURANTS

A Note on Restaurant Prices: New York restaurant prices, per person, excluding drinks and service charges, are coded as follows: **VE,** Very Expensive ($60 and up); **E,** Expensive ($40–$60); **M,** Moderate ($25–$40) **I,** Inexpensive ($15–$25); **B,** Budget (up to $15).

Personal Favorites (in order of preference)

Lutèce (midtown), 249 E. 50th St. (752-2225). A/C. Lunch Tues–Fri, dinner Mon–Sat; closed Aug until Labor Day. AE, CB, DC, MC, V. J&T. *Specialties:* sweetbreads in white wine w. capers, scallops sautéed w. truffles, roast back of rabbit w. homemade noodles, filet of sturgeon w. Chambertin sauce and julienned celery root, filets de St. Pierre (John Dory) w. fresh mint, navarin of lobster w. Pernod, filet mignon in pastry shell, chicken w. tarragon, bitter-chocolate mousse, tarte tatin. Menu changes regularly. Very fine wine list, balanced and clear (there are 20,000 bottles in the cellar). *Note:* Classic French *grande cuisine* at its best; for a quarter of a century Lutèce has earned the title of New York's best rest. Under the direction of André Soltner, from Alsace, the menu is progressively enriched and refined. Pretty winter garden on the ground floor; elegant little rms, recently renovated, upstairs. Flawless reception and svce. Resv. a must, many days or even weeks ahead. Former President Reagan's special favorite is the filet of salmon w. mustard. One of the country's 12 finest rests. *French.* **M** (lunch), **VE** (dinner)

Le Bernardin (midtown), 155 W. 51st St. (489-1515). A/C. Lunch/dinner Mon–Sat; closed hols. AE, CB, DC, MC, V. J&T. *Specialties:* lobster vichyssoise, monkfish w. cabbage; cod salad w. juniper, basil, and truffle oil; scallop salad w. cream and juice of truffles; slice of salmon w. julienne of fennel; poached halibut w. warm herbed vinaigrette; filet of pompano w. parsley; carpaccio of tuna. Menu changed regularly. Good wine list at reasonable prices. *Note:* This remarkable, relatively young (1986) seafood rest., housed in the dazzling Equitable Center, quickly established itself in a place of honor on the New York gastronomic scene. The credit goes to its chef and owner, the talented Gilbert Le Coze, whose former rest. in Paris rated a coveted two stars from Michelin. The exceptional quality of the seafood, the short cooking times, and a particular talent for refined simplicity explain its unprecedented popularity (it almost requires a miracle to get a dinner resv.). Elegant London club interior w. Danish teak woodwork, bluish-gray tones, and rather hackneyed maritime paintings. Exemplary service supervised by the omnipresent Maguy Le Coze, Gilbert's sister. Resv. absolutely essential. One of the 12 best rests. in the country. *Seafood.* **M** (lunch), **VE** (dinner)

Chanterelle (Tribeca), 2 Harrison St. at Hudson St. (966-6960). A/C. Dinner only, Tues–Sat; closed hols. and July 1–15. AE, DC, MC, V. J&T. *Specialties:* grilled seafood sausage, crabmeat ravioli, rack of lamb w. thyme and mustard, Muscovy duck w. sherry vinegar and wild mushrooms, rhubarb tart w. scallops and shad roe, braised rabbit w. cream-and-herb sauce, red snapper w. red-wine butter sauce, poached pears in sauternes sabayon, orange-flavored chocolate torte. *Note:* In 1989 this rest., worthy of three stars in any French gastronomic guidebook, moved from its original cramped quarters in SoHo to a setting scarcely larger (15 tables) but agreeably renovated on the ground floor of the old Mercantile Exchange in the heart of Tribeca. Chef David Waltuck and his wife, Karen, continue to offer ambitious, inspired food, the quintessence of French nouvelle cuisine American style. Efficient but rather casual svce. You'll need to make your resv. days, or even weeks, ahead; a splendid place with prices to match. *French.* **E**

San Domenico (midtown), 240 Central Park South (265-5959). A/C. Lunch Mon–Sat, dinner daily; closed hols. and first 10 days of Jan. AE, DC, MC, V. J&T. *Specialties:* seafood ravioli, smoked goose ham w. julienned zucchini and parmesan cheese, Muscovy duck w. olives, red snapper filets in tomato-and-arugula dressing, roasted smoky veal chop in bacon-cream sauce, lobster fricassée w. artichokes, braised faraona (guinea hen) w. cabbage and porcini mushrooms, mascarpone torte w. espresso-coffee sauce. Menu changes regularly. Italian-California wine list. *Note:* This offspring of the famous Ristorante San Domenico in Imola, near Bologna, was opened in 1988 and has already challenged Palio (see below) for the title of New York's best Italian rest. The authenticity and elegance of its traditional Italian food is unrivaled; the decor is also authentic Italian, from the Florentine terra-cotta floor tiles to the painted stucco walls, decorated by craftsmen brought specially from Rome. Uncommonly efficient svce. Resv. a must, far ahead. This is one of the finest, but prices are sometimes painful. *Italian.* **E–VE**

Shun Lee Palace (midtown), 155 E. 55th St. (371-8844). A/C. Lunch/dinner daily; closed Thanksgiving. AE, CB, V. Jkt. *Specialties:* hot-and-sour soup, Szechuan lobster, smoked duckling w. scallion pancake, crispy whole sea bass w. Hunan sauce, chow fon beef, frogs' legs w. broccoli, jellyfish w. hot mustard and thousand-year-old eggs, carp w. ginger and shallots. So-so desserts. *Note:* Purists might find cause for regret in the slight over-Americanization of chef T. T. Wang's cuisine in this excellent Chinese rest., but the result is still delectable. There are Szechuan, Hunan, and Mandarin dishes, more elaborate at dinner than at lunch. Elegant, intimate Far Eastern setting; discreet but efficient svce. *Chinese.* **M**

Gotham Bar and Grill (Greenwich Village), 12 E. 12th St., nr. Fifth Ave. (620-4020). A/C. Lunch Mon–Fri, dinner nightly; closed hols. AE, CB, DC, MC, V. Jkt. *Specialties:* quail salad w. shiitake mushrooms, duck-breast carpaccio w. pesto, braised rabbit w. pancetta, black bass in port wine w. leeks, roast squab w. saffron, plum tart w. plum sherbet. The menu changes seasonally. Good wine list at fair prices. *Note:* A quintessential New York City rest. Bright and young French-trained chef Alfred Portale offers a vibrant and innovative cuisine of clear Mediterranean inspiration. Spacious and strikingly designed multilevel dining rm w. a pink marble bar. Attentive but not obtrusive svce. One of the best places in town for true food lovers. Resv. highly advised. *American.* **M–E**

Oyster Bar and Restaurant (midtown), in Grand Central Terminal at E. 42nd St. and Vanderbilt Ave. (490-6650). A/C. Lunch/dinner Mon–Fri; closed hols. AE, CB, DC, MC, V. Jkt. *Specialties:* every kind of oyster and clam on the half shell, broiled fish and shellfish, clam chowder, bouillabaisse, Florida stone crab (in season), pan-roasted shellfish, blanquette of Belons oysters w. leeks, cheesecake. Splendid list of California wines. *Note:* A vast, tile cavern on the lower level of Grand Central Terminal. Usually crowded and noisy, particularly at lunch, but still one of the best selections of fish and shellfish in the entire country, at prices that are reasonable given the quality of the food. Svce sometimes distracted. Resv. advised. A New York landmark since 1913. *Seafood.* **I–M**

Palm (midtown), 837 Second Ave. at E. 45th St. (687-2953). A/C. Lunch Mon–Fri, dinner Mon–Sat. (until midnight);

closed hols. AE, CB, DC, MC, V. Jkt. *Specialties:* shrimp sautéed w. herbs, clams Posillipo, steak tartare, steak, prime cuts, lamb chops, Maine lobster, cheesecake. *Note:* A living legend for six decades among those who like solid food. Superb steaks, enormous lobsters, and some passable Italian dishes. The portions are gargantuan. The caricatures on the walls are amusing, but the place is very noisy and resolutely macho, down to the sawdust on the floor. Svce efficient but disagreeable. The annex across the avenue (Palm Too) is less picturesque, but the meat is of the same high quality. Resv. accepted for lunch only. *Steak/Seafood.* **M–E**

  Hatsuhana (midtown), 17 E. 48th St. (355-3345). A/C. Lunch Mon–Fri, dinner Mon–Sat; closed hols. AE, CB, DC, MC, V. Jkt. *Specialties:* sea urchin, sushi, chawan mushi, sashimi, tempura. *Note:* Purists maintain that you will find here the widest choice of the best sushi in all New York. Modern, comfortably furnished setting w. dining rms on two levels, and sushi bars behind which the artist-chefs, past masters in the preparation and presentation of their 35 varieties of raw fish, go about their business. Generally crowded, especially at lunch. Svce overburdened. Many Japanese businessmen come here; resv. advised. Also at 237 Park Ave. (661-3400). *Japanese.* **M**

  Rosa Mexicano (midtown), 1063 First Ave. at E. 58th St. (753-7407). A/C. Lunch/dinner daily (till midnight), brunch Sun. AE, CB, DC, MC, V. *Specialties:* taquitos, guacamole, carnitas, chiles en mogada, snapper w. coriander, shell steak w. sautéed chilis poblanos, budín azteca. Excellent margaritas. *Note:* A worthy representative of Mexico, this likable, fashionable rest. will give you, as it were, a foretaste of exotic vacations. The food is completely authentic, the atmosphere congenial, the bar inviting though crowded, and the rustic decor executed in a beautiful shade of pink. Efficient, smiling svce. Resv. a must. A fine place. *Mexican.* **I–M**

  Broadway Grill (midtown), in the Holiday Inn Crowne Plaza (see "Accommodations," above) (315-6161). A/C. Lunch/dinner daily (till midnight). AE, CB, DC, MC, V. *Specialties:* fashionable pizzas (w. clams, grilled eggplant, duck confit, caramelized onion, etc.), calamari, veal chop, roast chicken w. new potatoes, steak, banana split. *Note:* Located on the second floor of the brand-new Crowne Plaza Hotel, this vast rest.-grill serves medium luxe cuisine at no-frills prices. The ideal spot for a meal before or after the theater (Broadway is around the corner). The svce is somewhat rushed but generally efficient. *American.* **I–M**

  Frank's (Greenwich Village), 431 W. 14th St. (243-1349). A/C. Breakfast/lunch/dinner Mon–Fri (from 2am to 10pm); dinner only, Sat (from 5 to 11pm). AE, CB, DC, MC, V. *Specialties:* tagliarini puttanesca (pasta w. capers, olives, and anchovies), tripe Florentine, rack of lamb, steak, roast beef, veal cutlets, broiled kidney. *Note:* A stone's throw from Gansevoort Market, headquarters of the city's wholesale meat business, this stronghold of meat eating makes a point of opening its doors at 2am to feed breakfast to the neighborhood butchers. Manly food, sturdy portions, and prime meat as you would expect, all at very attractive prices. The long mahogany bar, lazy ceiling fans, and sawdusted floor contribute to a friendly, unpretentious setting. Efficient svce. A very good place indeed; a Manhattan landmark since 1912. *Steak.* **I–M**

Other Restaurants (from top bracket to budget)

  Lafayette (midtown), in the Drake Swissôtel (see "Accommodations," above) (832-1565). A/C. Dinner only, Mon–Sat; closed hols. and July 20–Aug 20. AE, CB, DC, MC, V. J&T. *Specialties:* sea-urchin soufflé, frogs' legs and watercress ravioli, sea bass in pastry crust w. tarragon sauce, crayfish w. zucchini and tomatoes in basil and olive-oil dressing, roast guinea hen w. timbale of parsley and olive-oil sauce, Barbary duck w. sesame and mango crêpes, truffled lamb medallions w. purée of leeks, tournedos of whiting

w. fava beans and tomato oil, chocolate-mousse cake w. passion fruit, gratin of raspberries. Menu changes regularly. Great wine list. *Note:* This sumptuous palace-style rest., opened in 1986, is already recognized as one of the three or four best places to eat in New York. Delicate, airy creations, clearly Mediterranean inspired, from the master hand of Louis Outhier, former owner of the famous l'Oasis at la Napoule on the French Riviera. Spacious, discreetly elegant dining room in shades of beige and salmon-pink; polished, attentive svce. Resv. should be made no less than 5 or 6 days ahead. Big business clientele. *French.* **E–VE**

La Côte Basque (midtown), 5 E. 55th St. (688-6525). A/C. Lunch/dinner Mon–Sat; closed hols. and the month of July. AE, CB, DC, MC, V. J&T. *Specialties:* "swan" of pastry w. foie gras and truffles, sweetbreads au Madère, duck in peppered vinaigrette, roast lamb w. thyme, pomponettes of truffles, lobster ragoût w. morels, cassoulet toulousain (white beans baked w. lamb, sausage, and duck), frozen raspberry soufflé. Fine wine list at outrageous prices. *Note:* Founded 30 years ago as an affiliate of the legendary Pavillon, once New York's greatest French rest., La Côte Basque is now its worthy successor. Pretty, flowery decor w. wall painting of the port of St. Jean de Luz. Grand cuisine which contrives to be both traditional and light, from the hand of the excellent chef Jean-Jacques Rachou. Svce and presentation are flawless, but the place is a little noisy. Resv. must be made some days ahead. Very "in" clientele. *French.* **E–VE**

An American Place (midtown), 2 Park Ave. at E. 32nd St. (684-2122). A/C. Lunch Mon–Fri, dinner Mon–Sat; closed hols. AE, CB, DC, MC, V. J&T. *Specialties:* grilled-vegetable terrine w. baked goat cheese, terrine of smoked fish w. three caviars, sauteed lobster w. chives, charred Black Angus steak marinated in beer w. caramelized onions, roast salmon in cider vinegar, broiled chicken w. fettuccine and wild mushrooms, chocolate pudding, mile-high strawberry shortcake. Very fine list of American wines at reasonable prices. The menu changes regularly. *Note:* Modern American cuisine admirable in its elegance and simplicity. Chef Larry Forgione, a virtuoso of short cooking times and light sauces, uses American products exclusively (even the caviar). Fashionable art deco interior; svce usually faultless. Resv. a must. *American.* **E–VE**

Aureole (Upper East Side), 34 E. 61st St. (319-1660). A/C. Lunch/dinner Mon–Sat; closed hols. AE, CB, DC, MC, V. Jkt. *Specialties:* sea-scallop "sandwich," onion soup w. confit of duck, pan-seared tuna steak w. gingery leeks, tea-smoked squab w. balsamic vinegar sauce, grouper w. caviar butter, beef sirloin w. brandy sauce and potato cake, bittersweet-chocolate timbale, double lemon millefeuille. Good wine list, short but decently priced. *Note:* After several years of intensive experience at the well-known River Café, distinguished chef Charles Palmer opened this elegant spot in November 1988, and it's one of Manhattan's newer fashionable addresses. The cuisine is contemporary, subtle and wide-ranging; the two-level setting is luminously decorated in shades of cream. Efficient, friendly svce. Resv. a must, but not always honored. *American.* **E–VE**

Bouley (Tribeca), 165 Duane St. at Hudson St. (608-3852). A/C. Lunch Mon–Fri, dinner Mon–Sat; closed hols. AE, DC, MC, V. J&T. *Specialties:* duck liver with roasted onions and balsamic vinegar, sea scallops w. verjuice sauce and purée of celery root, roast squab w. sweet onions and red cabbage, leg of lamb w. kidney beans, langoustine tails w. red Sancerre sauce, roast chicken w. cèpes, pot-au-feu of pheasant w. foie gras, fig millefeuille w. coconut ice cream. Menu changes regularly. Long list of French wines at discouraging prices. *Note:* Young American chef David Bouley, who studied in Switzerland and France with such grand masters as Bocuse, Girardet, and Vergé, cooks with wonderful delicacy and balance, using the finest in local produce. Decorated like an inn in Provence, with lots of flowers. The svce is a trifle offhand; patrons are a Wall St. crowd at lunch and fashionable

New York at dinner. Resv. a must. *French.* **E–VE**

♟♟♟ **Quilted Giraffe** (midtown), 550 Madison Ave. at E. 55th St.
♟♟♟ (593-1221). A/C. Lunch Tues–Fri, dinner Mon–Sat; closed hols. and the month of July. AE. J&T. *Specialties:* "Beggar's Purses" (pancakes stuffed w. beluga caviar and crème fraîche, grilled salmon glazed w. spicy mustard, duck cutlet w. lime and ginger, rack of lamb w. Chinese mustard, ragoût of lobster and monkfish, poached salmon w. red pepper and dill. Remarkable desserts. Wine list a little disappointing and overpriced. *Note:* The unchallenged shrine of nouvelle cuisine in New York. Long cramped into three very small, slightly kitschy rooms, its huge new premises and their futurist decor of steel and marble are more in keeping w. the inventive contemporary cuisine. The proprietor, Barry Wine, used to be a lawyer; driven by a lust for perfection he has (almost unbelievably) taught himself to be a great chef. Ultra-professional svce. Fashionable and/or very-big-business clientele. Resv. a must, some days (or weeks) ahead. A very good place indeed. *French.* **E** (lunch), **VE** (dinner)

☼♟ **Tavern on the Green** (Upper West Side), Central Park West at
☼♟ W. 67th St. (873-3200). A/C. Lunch Mon–Fri, brunch Sat–Sun, dinner nightly (until 1am). AE, CB, DC, MC, V. *Specialties:* lobster bisque, smoked-duck-breast salad, cold veal w. lentils, chateaubriand, sautéed shrimp w. ginger, chocolate truffle cake. *Note:* The food is at best uneven, but it's worth visiting for the spectacular setting on the edge of Central Park—a veritable fairyland in winter when the snow is on the ground and a gala flower-filled bosky scene in summer. The dining rms are exuberantly decorated w. chandeliers, stained glass, etched and carved mirrors, and pastel plaster ceiling featuring fantastic animal and flower motifs. Go for cocktails or a snack. Sheer New York. *Continental.* **E**

♟♟♟ **Palio** (midtown), 151 W. 51st St. (245-4850). A/C. Lunch
♟♟♟ Mon–Fri, dinner Mon–Sat; closed hols. AE, CB, DC, MC, V. J&T. *Specialties:* carpaccio, risotto w. quails, ricotta croquettes w. truffled butter, steamed sea bass w. zucchini, gnocchi w. frogs' legs and garlic, squab w. sage, prosciutto-stuffed chicken breast w. green sauce, black polenta pudding. The menu changes daily. Fine list of Italian and California wines at sensible prices. *Note:* Chef Andreas Hellrigl, the presiding genius here, is one of the finest exponents of the Italian *nuova cucina,* and brought here from the well-reputed Hotel Villa Mozart in Merano (Italy) a light, delicate cuisine which will be a revelation to lovers of traditional Italian food. Wall paintings by Sandro Chia, superbly depicting the "Palio" race in Siena, lend warmth and color to the bar. The dining rm, upstairs, is elegant in a more discreet fashion. One of the best contemporary Italian rests. in the country. Resv. a must. Valet parking. *Italian.* **M–E**

♟♟♟ **Mitsukoshi** (midtown), 461 Park Ave. at E. 57th St. (935-
♟♟♟ 6444). A/C. Lunch/dinner Mon–Sat; closed hols. AE, CB, DC, MC, V. Jkt. *Specialties:* sushi, sashimi, sukiyaki, shabu-shabu, tempura, beef negimaki, broiled fish, kaiseki (formal Japanese dinner of seven or nine courses),

---

OTHER FROMMER TRAVEL GUIDES: Readers may be interested in Frommer guides that treat the Northeast and Mid-Atlantic area in detail: *Frommer's Mid-Atlantic States, Frommer's New England, Frommer's New York State, Frommer's New York on $60 a Day,* and *Frommer's Washington, D.C. & Historic Virginia on $40 a Day.* City guides for this area are *Frommer's Atlantic City & Cape May, Frommer's Boston, Frommer's New York, Frommer's Philadephia,* and *Frommer's Washington, D.C.*

Frommer travel guides are available in most bookstores, or can be ordered by mail from Frommer Books, Prentice Hall Press, 15 Columbus Circle, New York, N.Y. 10023. Turn to the last pages of this book for ordering information and to learn about the **Dollarwise Travel Club.**

ginger ice cream. *Note:* Of the many Japanese rests. in Manhattan, this offers the greatest luxury and refinement. For lovers of raw fish there is an immense choice of sushi; the prices are also on the raw side. You may eat either at a Western-style table or in the quieter, more elegant tatami rms. Service w. a smile from kimono'd waitresses—unfortunately, a little hectic during the lunch-hour rush. Much favored by New York's Japanese business community; resv. advised. *Japanese.* **M–E**

☼ ♈♈♈ **River Café,** 1 Water St., Brooklyn (718/522-5200). A/C. Lunch/dinner daily; closed Dec 25. AE, CB, DC, MC, V. Jkt./J&T. *Specialties:* sautéed oysters w. endives and artichokes, snails in puff pastry, Black Angus steak w. bourbon sauce, broiled pheasant w. risotto of wild mushrooms, lamb cutlets w. charlotte of eggplant, braised sea bass w. morel mushrooms and tomatoes, mignon of veal w. pears, chocolate terrine, raspberry cheesecake. Exceptional wine list, particularly the California section. Menu changes regularly. *Note:* By day, and even more by night, one of the most fabulous sights New York has to offer. From a charming barge moored below the Brooklyn Bridge, you can see at a glance the distant Statue of Liberty and the skyscrapers of dwntwn Manhattan. The rest. was once so-so; now it serves a sophisticated, contemporary American cuisine by chef David Burke, using only U.S. raw materials, including the caviar and the olive oil. Ultra-professional svce; resv. essential many days ahead. Ask for a table near the bay window or, in summer, on the terrace. A must for tourists, but also draws many bankers from nearby Wall St. at lunchtime. *American.* **M** (lunch), **E** (dinner)

♈♈ **Auntie Yuan** (Upper East Side), 1191A First Ave. at E. 65th St. (744-4040). A/C. Lunch/dinner daily (until midnight). AE, CB, DC, MC, V. Jkt. *Specialties:* barbecued quail w. garlic, Chinese noodles w. sesame sauce and shallots, duck salad, steamed salmon w. black beans, orange beef, Peking duck, chicken soong, mediocre desserts. *Note:* Unlike the general run of neon-and-Formica eating places in Chinatown, this is one of the most beautiful rests. in New York: black Chinese lacquer, elegant flower arrangements, indirect lighting, luxury tableware, and waiters in tuxedos. The Taiwanese nouvelle cuisine of chef David Keh and his team is above criticism; so is the svce, which is uncommon in a Far Eastern rest. A fine place. Resv. required. Valet parking. *Chinese.* **M–E**

♈ **Christ Cella** (midtown), 160 E. 46th St. (697-2479). A/C. Lunch Mon–Fri, dinner Mon–Sat; closed hols. AE, CB, DC, MC, V. J&T. *Specialties:* steak, lamb chops, veal cutlets, lobster, roast beef, catch of the day, Caesar salad, Napoleon. Rather skimpy wine list. *Note:* Since 1926, New York's only steakhouse that can challenge the famous Palm. The steaks and lobster here are almost as big, and the svce a touch friendlier. The waiters will tell you the daily specials. Atmosphere and clientele resolutely masculine. Resv. a must. *Steak/seafood.* **M–E**

☼ ♈♈ **Coach House** (Greenwich Village), 110 Waverly Pl. (777-0303). A/C. Dinner only, Tues–Sun; closed hols. and the month of Aug. AE, CB, DC, MC, V. J&T. *Specialties:* black-bean soup, fried oysters, crab cakes, Virginia ham, rack of lamb, roasted snapper w. dill sauce, steak au poivre, blueberry pie, chocolate cake. Good list of California wines. *Note:* The Coach House has for 40 years been a leading exponent of the American culinary tradition, and by now has achieved landmark status. Charming colonial-inn setting a stone's throw from Washington Sq. in the heart of Greenwich Village. Exceptionally attentive, courteous svce. If you want to rediscover the authentic flavor of traditional American food, you must pay your respects here. Resv. a must. *American.* **M–E**

♈ **Il Nido** (midtown), 251 E. 53rd St. (753-8450). A/C. Lunch/dinner Mon–Sat; closed hols. AE, CB, DC, MC, V. Jkt. *Specialties:* ravioli malfatti, carpaccio, risotto w. asparagus, fritto misto, veal cutlet milanese, porcini mushrooms w. truffles (in season), crostini di polenta, scampi w. capers, zuppa di pesce, zabaglione w. Cointreau and champagne, tíramisu. Fine wine list. *Note:* In the early '80s Il Nido was regarded as one of Manhattan's two or three best Italian rests.; what remains today is still very fine, though the Tuscan cuisine is unimaginative and a little too orthodox. Elegantly rustic farmhouse decor. Somewhat noisy atmosphere. Ultra-professional svce. Business clientele; resv. a must. *Italian.* **M–E**

Manhattan Ocean Club (midtown), 57 W. 58th St. (371-7777). A/C. Lunch Mon–Fri, dinner Mon–Sat; closed Thanksgiving, Dec 25. AE, CB, DC, MC, V. Jkt. *Specialties:* crab cakes, five oysters baked five ways (Pernod, pepper, curry, pesto, and oregano), tuna steak w. tomato and mint vinaigrette dressing, sautéed salmon w. cucumber, grilled grouper w. peppercorns and mustard seeds, sautéed bay scallops, roast mahimahi (dolphin) w. citrus butter, vitello tonnato, a wealth of tempting desserts. Well-thought-out wine list at reasonable prices. *Note:* With Picasso ceramics on the walls, Mediterranean-style pillars, diffused lighting, and a pastel color scheme, this rest. will make you dream of travel. Huge selection of absolutely fresh, beautifully prepared fish and seafood. Elegant atmosphere, polished svce. Resv. recommended; a fashionable spot. *Seafood.* **M–E**

Smith & Wollensky (midtown), 201 E. 49th St. at Third Ave. (753-1530). A/C. Lunch Mon–Fri, dinner nightly; closed Jan 1 and Dec 25. AE, CB, DC, MC, V. Jkt. *Specialties:* crabmeat cocktail, 16-oz. (455g) steak, T-bone, filet mignon au poivre, veal cutlet, 4- to 5-lb. (1.8–2.3kg) lobster, broiled fish of the day, chocolate-mousse cake. Exceptional wine list, one of the best in New York. *Note:* In a huge two-story turn-of-the-century building, this typical New York steakhouse serves man-sized portions of choice red meat to a following of devotees. Its wine list, especially the California cabernet sauvignons, is also praiseworthy. Warm, efficient svce; a fine place in spite of prices on the high side. Resv. recommended. *Steak/seafood.* **M–E**

Tribeca Grill (Tribeca), 375 Greenwich St. at Franklin St. (941-3900). A/C. Lunch Mon–Fri, dinner Mon–Sat. AE, DC, MC, V. *Specialties:* lobster consommé w. favas and scallops, tomato porridge w. sausage bread, squab w. endive and lentils vinaigrette, smoked barbecued duck w. cannelini beans, calves' liver steak on onion marmalade, catch of the day, glazed lemon tart on poppyseed crust. Excellent house wines. *Note:* The hottest hit of the 1990 season. Celebrity owned—besides the managing partner, Drew Nieporent, proprietor of the nearby three-star rest. Montrachet, the other investors are Robert De Niro, Bill Murray, Christopher Walken, Sean Penn, and Mikhail Baryshnikov—this old warehouse w. exposed brick walls and brightly painted heating pipes offers good American bistro fare in a comfortable space. Generally overcrowded and noisy. The place to see and be seen. Resv. a must. *American.* **M–E**

Arizona 206 (Upper East Side), 206 E. 60th St. (838-0440). A/C. Lunch Mon–Sat, dinner nightly; closed Dec 25. AE, CB, DC, MC, V. Jkt. *Specialties:* chili of game and black beans, barbecued foie gras w. cactus-pear salad, pistachio-coated rabbit w. mole poblano, lamb in salad w. artichokes and chayote, broiled rib-eye steak w. jalapeño sauce, barbecued quail w. polenta, white-chocolate ice cream. Short but pleasant list of California wines. *Note:* One of New York's most original American rests., no less for its southwestern decor, w. adobe walls, rough beamed ceiling, open hearth, and natural-wood tables than for the inventive fare of its young chef Marilyn Frobuccino, whose southwestern food is natural, simple, and remarkable. Warm, relaxed but sometimes noisy setting; svce w. a smile. Since the yuppies have taken enthusiastically to the place, resv. are a must. Don't miss it. *American.* **M**

Chin Chin (midtown), 216 E. 49th St. (888-4555). A/C. Lunch Mon–Fri, dinner nightly. AE, DC, MC, V. Jkt. *Specialties:* velvet corn soup, steamed pork dumplings w. fresh ginger, tea-smoked duck, cold sliced kidneys Taiwan style, clams w. black-bean sauce, lobster Cantonese, crispy sea bass w. spicy sauce, Szechuan prawns, homemade fresh fruit sherbets. *Note:* Named for its proprietors Jimmy and Wally Chin, this rest. also styles itself "Restaurant chinois," bearing witness to the Western influence evident in its kitchen. Traditional Chinese ditches w. a dash of nouvelle cuisine. Elegant modern Oriental setting (especially the downstairs rm w. its handsome Chinese ceramics); highly professional waiters in tuxedos. Popular, so book ahead. *Chinese.* **M**

Darbár (midtown), 44 W. 56th St. (432-7227). A/C. Lunch/dinner daily, buffet lunch Sat–Sun. AE, CB, DC, MC, V. Jkt. *Specialties:* samosas, chicken tandoori, crab Malabar, reshmi kebab (baked chicken en brochette), marinated lamb w. cardamom and cumin, ghosht vindaloo (ragoût of lamb), bayngan ghurta (broiled eggplant w. tomatoes, onions, and spices), kheer (rice pudding w. cardamom). *Note:* The most sought-after and elegant of New York's Indian rests., on two levels, w. a friendly bar on the ground floor, fabric-covered walls, and magnificent decorative objects in hammered copper. Darbár serves a refined version of Mogul (northern Indian) food; the seasonings are added w. a careful hand but some dishes, like the murgh tikka masala (spicy chicken in tomato-onion and butter sauce), are volcanic. Svce efficient but a little brusque. Resv. advised. *Indian.* **M**

Gage & Tollner, 372 Fulton St., Brooklyn (718/875-5181). A/C. Lunch Mon–Fri., dinner nightly; closed Sun (July–Aug) and hols. AE, CB, DC, MC, V. Jkt. *Specialties:* she-crab soup, seafood gumbo, pan-fried oysters, catch of the day, English mixed grill (mutton chops w. veal kidney and sausages), chicken cooked in parchment, pan-fried quail w. spoon bread, lamb chops, hazelnut cheesecake. Huge selection of beer. *Note:* A handsome haven of authentic American cooking since 1879; the wall-mounted gas jets (recently wired for electricity) and the paneling are of the period. So, it might seem, are the waiters, proudly wearing their long-service stripes on their sleeves. Absolutely fresh seafood and wonderful meat as well. A designated landmark. Worth the 30-min. drive across the East River. *American.* **M**

Harlequin (Greenwich Village), 569 Hudson St. at W. 11th St. (255-4950). A/C. Lunch/dinner daily, brunch Sun; closed hols and last two weeks in Aug. AE, CB, DC, MC, V. Jkt. *Specialties:* brandada de bacalão (purée of dried salt cod and potatoes), angulas (bean-sprout-sized white eels), zortziko de pescados (fish stew Basque style), paella, honeyed duck w. grapefruit sauce, merluza (hake) in garlic and white wine, marinated quail w. fresh figs. Very good list of reasonably priced Spanish wines. *Note:* In this city, where the authentic Spanish restaurants can be counted on the fingers of one hand, Harlequin has become a place of pilgrimage for lovers of Iberian cooking. Chef José Barcena adds an elegant touch of nouvelle cuisine to the classic dishes of his homeland (his paella is absolutely the best in New York), while his charming wife, Ileana, greets guests with a smile. The decor is contemporary, chilly but comfortable, in shades of gray. Courteous, efficient svce. Locally popular; resv. highly advisable. *Spanish.* **M**

John Clancy's Restaurant (Greenwich Village), 181 W. 10th St. at Seventh Ave. (242-7350). A/C. Dinner only, nightly; closed hols. AE, CB, DC, MC, V. Jkt. *Specialties:* oysters on the half shell, gravlax, lobster bisque, swordfish en brochette, barbecued jumbo shrimp, sautéed shad roe w. bacon, trout w. rosemary butter, broiled sea bass w. coriander, English trifle. Good wine list. *Note:* Serving exclusively seafood—broiled over mesquite, raw, baked, or steamed—this Greenwich Village rest. has a host of groupies. The food is as fresh as can be, and cooked to perfection. Elegant, intimate setting in tones of pearl and gray, occupying two floors of a charming century-old town house. Svce relatively efficient and relaxed. Resv. advised. *Seafood.* **M**

Odeon (Tribeca), 145 W. Broadway (233-0507). A/C. Lunch Mon–Fri, dinner nightly (until 2:30am), brunch Sun. AE, DC, MC, V. Jkt. *Specialties:* consommé of duck w. julienne of vegetables, fresh pasta w. broiled shrimp and chardonnay sauce, poached oysters, baked red snapper w. saffron, pan-fried steak, cassoulet of lamb and vegetables, herb-roasted chicken, calves' liver w. sherry-vinegar sauce, poached salmon w. green peppercorn sauce, chocolate terrine à l'orange, poached peaches w. Sauternes sabayon. Good wine list. *Note:* Successful American nouvelle cuisine in a rather chilly 1930s setting of subdued chromium and marble. Trendy clientele from punk to banker; congenial but noisy atmosphere, especially at night. Efficient, smiling long-aproned servers. A godsend if you're up late in Tribeca. Resv. advised. *French.* **M**

Periyali (Chelsea), 35 W. 20th St. at Fifth Ave. (463-7890). A/C. Lunch Mon–Fri, dinner Mon–Sat; closed hols. AE, MC, V. Jkt. *Specialties:* fried calamari, tiropita (cheese pie), herbed shish kebab, kouneli stifado (ragoût of rabbit), baked sea bass w. tomato and white-wine sauce, garides Periylai (grilled shrimp w. herbs and lemon), sautéed chicken livers w. lentils, moussaka, Greek pastry. Good selection of little-known Greek wines. *Note:* Generally held to be the best place in New York for those who like their Greek cooking contemporary and (surprise, surprise) amazingly light. Warm Mediterranean setting w. dark woodwork and whitewashed walls hung with antique pots and pans. Friendly, smiling svce. A fine place, locally very popular; resv. a must. *Greek.* **M**

Provence (Greenwich Village), 38 MacDougal St. (475-7500). A/C. Lunch/dinner Tues–Sun; closed hols. AE. *Specialties:* fish soup, Provençal onion-and-anchovy tart, rabbit pâté in aspic, skate w. caper sauce, roast lamb w. ratatouille, poached seafood in broth w. aioli, grilled rabbit (w. mustard, sage, and braised cabbage), cassoulet, crème brûlée. *Note:* A popular French bistro serving good, honest cuisine using fresh ingredients. Svce is gracious and the atmosphere comfortable. The garden w. fountain is especially appealing in summer. Extensive wine list. Reserve well ahead, especially for wknds. *French.* **M**

Windows on the World (the Restaurant) (Lower Manhattan), 1 World Trade Center (938-1111). A/C. Lunch Mon–Fri (private club; $8 entrance fee for nonmembers), dinner Mon–Sat, brunch and dinner Sun (till 7:30pm). AE, CB, DC, MC, V. J&T. *Specialties:* sautéed shrimp w. leeks and broccoli, asparagus vinaigrette, roast tenderloin of beef w. morel sauce, broiled salmon w. orange-and-chive sauce, scaloppine w. wild mushrooms, marinated pheasant w. wild thyme, rack of lamb, fricassée of lobster and scallops, good desserts including amaretto soufflé. *Note:* The highest skyscraper rest. in the world, 107 floors and 1,318 ft. (402m) above the sidewalk, could easily have turned into a tourist trap, w. a wonderful view of Manhattan on a clear day. As it turns out, the food is on a par w. the view (and what a view it is!), and the superb wine list boasts 800 labels fairly priced. The svce is amiable and efficient. Resv. must be made days, or weeks, in advance for 7–8:30pm dinner. Free parking under the tower. *Continental.* **M**

Peter Luger, 178 Broadway, Brooklyn (718/387-7400). A/C. Lunch/dinner daily. No credit cards. Jkt. *Specialties:* shrimp cocktail, steak, roast beef, creamed spinach, cheesecake, chocolate mousse. Rickety wine list. *Note:* Since 1887 this venerable, vaguely Germanic tavern has been serving the best T-bone and porterhouse steaks in the city on its scrubbed wooden tables. The svce is rough. You should eat here, though the surrounding streets are not inviting after dark. 30 min. from midtown. Resv. advised. *Steak.* **M**

Russian Tea Room (midtown), 150 W. 57th St. (265-0947). A/C. Lunch/dinner daily (till 12:30am). AE, CB, DC, MC, V. Jkt. *Specialties:* borscht, caviar w. blinis, zakuski, Kiev cutlet, lamb steak, Caucasian shashlik, pirozhki, broiled salmon w. lemon butter. The desserts and wine list are unworthy of a good rest. *Note:* The rest. is sandwiched between skyscrapers, the clientele is well-heeled, the decor is Christmas-tree primitive—and the place is crowded seven days a week. The Russian food is adequate, the prices high. You may see such stars of stage, screen, and concert hall as Woody Allen, Dustin Hoffman, and Isaac Stern. Svce so-so. A place to see and be seen. Resv. advised. Was a setting for the movie *Tootsie*. *East European*. **M**

Chikubu (midtown), 12 E. 44th St. (818-0715). A/C. Lunch Mon–Fri, dinner Mon–Sat; closed Jan 1. AE, DC. *Specialties:* sushi, sashimi, soba (noodles in soy sauce), yosenabe (fish-and-cabbage soup), tonkatsu (pan-fried pork chops), shioyaki (fish broiled whole), nabe (stews), kamemeshi (a Japanese risotto), pumpkin pudding. *Note:* With its contemporary decor in light wood and tones of pearl-gray, this rest. is a favorite of Manhattan's Japanese community, though so far it has largely escaped the attention of tourists. Chikubu's specialty is Kyoto cuisine, noted for its slow-cooked dishes and stews. Relatively quiet for a Japanese rest. An excellent place to eat; resv. advisable. *Japanese*. **I–M**

Nusantara (midtown), 219 E. 44th St. between Second Ave. and Third Ave. (983-1919). A/C. Lunch Mon–Fri, dinner Mon–Sat. AE. *Specialties:* nasi goreng (fried rice) w. saté (broiled meat or fish), rijstaffel (rice accompanied by 20 or so assorted side dishes), squid stuffed w. mousse of fish, broiled red snapper in chili sauce, lamb curry w. cumin, coconut tart, krakatau (flambéed pineapple). *Note:* Seekers after the exotic will not be disappointed by this new, luxurious Indonesian rest., whose cuisine is as original as its lovely decor w. woodwork, carved chairs, and a giant dragon's head at the entrance. Considerate, efficient svce. An excellent place to eat, particularly in the light of its moderate prices. Resv. advisable. *Indonesian*. **I–M**

Bridge Café (Lower Manhattan), 279 Water St. (227-3344). A/C. Lunch Mon–Fri, dinner nightly, brunch Sat–Sun. AE, DC. *Specialties:* soft-shell crab (in season), curried oysters vinaigrette, duck w. green peppercorns, sautéed salmon, chicken breast w. black beans and garlic, apple-and-walnut cake w. rum sauce. *Note:* This early 19th-century seamen's tavern, now a lunchtime meeting place for yuppies, is often graced by Edward I. Koch, the former mayor of New York, as well as a clutch of Wall St. bankers. The cuisine is uneven, w. good and bad appearing side by side. Pleasant atmosphere; good-mannered but muddle-headed svce. A fashionable place in the shadow of the Brooklyn Bridge. No resv., and sometimes a long wait. *American*. **I–M**

El Rincon de España (Greenwich Village), 226 Thompson St. (475-9891). A/C. Lunch/dinner daily; closed hols. AE, CB, DC, MC, V. *Specialties:* shrimp à la Carlos, grilled chorizo sausage, mariscada (ragoût of seafood), paella valenciana, cod Galician style, octopus w. tomato. Mediocre desserts. *Note:* Small, dark, and usually crowded, this typical tavern a few blocks from Washington Sq. serves as tasty Spanish food as you'll find. The servings are generous, the Rioja wine flows like water, and the svce is as relaxed as the jam-packed, noisy atmosphere. Inevitable background music provided by guitars. Resv. desirable. Other location: 82 Beaver St., Lower Manhattan (344-5228). *Spanish*. **I–M**

Gallagher's Steak House (midtown), 228 W. 52nd St. (245-5336). A/C. Lunch/dinner daily (until midnight). AE, CB, DC, MC, V. Jkt. *Specialties:* oysters on the half shell, steak, roast beef, lamb chops, steak-and-kidney pie, brains w. hazelnut butter, lobster, broiled catch of the day. Very good cheesecake. *Note:* Long considered one of New York's best steakhouses, the fabled Gallagher's has lost some of its luster in the course of half a century. Its meats, still displayed for your inspection in a large glass-walled aging box as you come in, are as good as ever, but there are weaknesses in the kitchen, and the svce is less professional than it used to be. Unchanged are the gallery of yellowing photos of entertainers and early sports greats on the walls, and the elderly barmen working behind the oval bar in the middle of the room. Resv. advised. *Steak*. **I–M**

La Gauloise (Greenwich Village), 502 Ave. of the Americas at W. 13th St. (691-1363). A/C. Lunch/dinner Tues–Sun, brunch Sat–Sun; closed hols. AE, MC, V. *Specialties:* salad of green beans and confit of duck, lamb chops w. sweet garlic, skate w. brown-butter sauce, rabbit w. tarragon and mustard, steak au poivre, blanquette of veal, paillard of salmon, roast chicken, crème brûlée w. ginger. Good wine list but overpriced. *Note:* Authentic re-creation of a Parisian brasserie 1920s style, complete w. art deco lamps, dark paneling, and lovely mirrors. Excellent bistro food, and at attractive prices. Svce a little out of control. Congenial, very Greenwich Village clientele and atmosphere. Very good value overall. Resv. advised. *French.* **I–M**

    Nanni (midtown), 146 E. 46th St. (697-4161). A/C. Lunch Mon–Fri, dinner Mon–Sat; closed hols. AE, CB, DC, MC, V. Jkt. *Specialties:* fettuccine alla Nanni, fresh homemade pasta, chicken ortolana, sea bass alla marecchiara, veal cutlet milanese, game (in season). *Note:* The best little *trattoria* in New York. Intimate setting pleasantly renovated; praiseworthy food at reasonable prices. Quick, efficient svce. Often noisy and crowded. A very good place. *Italian.* **I–M**

    The Nice Restaurant (Chinatown), 35 E. Broadway (406-9510). A/C. Lunch/dinner daily. AE. *Specialties:* spring rolls w. shrimp, chopped squab in lettuce leaf, fried prawns, roast suckling pig, lacquered duck, salted chicken, melon-and-coconut soup. *Note:* Huge (ask to be seated upstairs) and frantic though it is, this is one of Chinatown's best. Truly outstanding Cantonese food; unusually (for a Chinese rest.) efficient svce. The elaborate decor might be described as Hong Kong through the eyes of Hollywood. Popular enough that resv. are advised. *Chinese.* **I–M**

    Sabor (Greenwich Village), 20 Cornelia St. (243-9579). A/C. Dinner nightly; closed hols. AE, MC, V. *Specialties:* white-bean soup, shrimp in lime sauce, red snapper w. salsa verde, ropa vieja (shredded beef w. tomatoes and cinnamon), empanadas, pork filet w. pineapple, zarzuela of shellfish, fried plantains, key lime pie, coco quemado (baked coconut dessert). *Note:* A Greenwich Village landmark serving flavorful, highly spiced Cuban food. The decor is minimal—cream-washed exposed brick and wicker baskets. Diligent, efficient svce. Generally crowded; resv. advised. Good value on balance. *Latin American.* **I–M**

    Japonica (Greenwich Village), University Pl. at E. 12th St. (243-7752). A/C. Lunch/dinner daily. AE, CB, DC. *Specialties:* avocado Japonica, gyoza, kyoage, nabeyaki udon, negimaki, sushi, sashimi. *Note:* This small, pretty, unpretentious rest. is well known for the ultra-fresh quality of its sushi and sashimi. Svce is swift and courteous; the decor above the sushi bar changes to reflect the seasons. Expect to wait if you arrive after 7:30pm, particularly on wknds. *Japanese.* **I**

    Spring Street Natural (Soho), 62 Spring St. at Lafayette St. (966-0290). A/C. Lunch/dinner daily. AE, CB, DC, MC, V. *Specialties:* hummus, black-bean soup, shrimp tempura, baked bluefish (w. red onion, mushrooms, leeks, and sake), breast of chicken w. broccoli, melted Brie w. lemon butter, stir-fried vegetables w. brown sauce. Daily specials ensure freshness. Modest wine list. Good fish and salad dishes. *Note:* Large loft-style rest. w. polished-wood decor, plenty of greenery, and classical music in the background. Svce can be a little "relaxed." *Seafood/vegetarian.* **I**

    Sylvia's (Harlem), 328 Lenox Ave. at W. 126th St. (996-0660). A/C. Breakfast Mon–Sat, lunch/dinner daily, brunch w. music live on Sun. No credit cards. *Specialties:* typical southern food—smothered steak, stewed chicken w. dumplings, fried chicken, turnips and collard greens, barbecued spareribs, butter beans w. ham bone, sweet-potato pie. *Note:* Sylvia Woods's rest. in the heart of Harlem has been an institution for more than 20 years. The flavors and spices of her cuisine are as savory and colorful as the Deep South where she was born. The decor is unobtrusive and the neighborhood unattractive; you should come and go by cab. But the atmosphere is warm and the svce congenial. The clientele is made up mostly of regulars and local politicians, w. a sprinkling of celebrities and tourists who come, in increasing numbers, to discover Harlem and Sylvia's food. A fine place. *American.* ❙

    ♀ **Acme Bar & Grill** (NoHo), 9 Great Jones St. (420-1934). A/C. Lunch/dinner daily; closed Thanksgiving and Dec 25. No credit cards. *Specialties:* golden fried oysters, jambalaya, chicken fried steak, fish grilled over pecan wood, grilled chicken. *Note:* A no-frills, American-diner ambience at this big, bright, cheerful meeting place for neighborhood loft dwellers and newly arrived gentry in trendy NoHo. Renowned for its jukebox and the shelf of hot sauces that runs the length of the rest. From "Cajun Power Garlic Sauce" (Louisiana) to "Acme Almost Flammable Hot Sauce of Chile Habanero" (Mexico) or the fearsome "Pepper Creek Farms Jalapeño TNT" (Texas). No resv. accepted. *American/Cajun.* ❙

    ♀ **Cabana Carioca** (midtown), 123 W. 45th St. (581-8088). A/C. Lunch/dinner daily; closed hols. AE, CB, DC, MC, V. *Specialties:* caldo verde (vegetable soup), feijoada (the Brazilian national dish—stewed beef, sausage, and black beans), shrimps Paulista (cooked in white wine), mixed grill, broiled pork chops w. rice and black beans, steak. Excellent caipirinhas (a punch made w. lime juice and cachaça, a high-octane Brazilian spirit). *Note:* The unchallenged shrine of Brazilian cooking, Cabana Carioca is one of the most pleasing and authentic ethnic rests. in Manhattan. Its enormous helpings and diminutive prices keep the regulars coming back in crowds, and draw every Brazilian passing through town. Colorful tropical atmosphere and decor. Another location, half a block away, is Cabana Carioca II (midtown), 133 W. 45th St. (730-8375). Resv. advised. *Brazilian.* ❙

    ♀ **Cinco de Mayo** (SoHo), 349 W. Broadway (226-5255). A/C. Lunch/dinner daily. AE, DC, MC, V. *Specialties:* ceviche, camarones (sautéed shrimp in a mustard-and-jalapeño vinaigrette), enchiladas de mole poblano, pollo en salsa de cacahuate, flan de chocolate, batido de Kahlúa. *Note:* Practically the only Mexican rest. rated in the *New York Times* as coming close to authentic by a visiting Mexican food expert. Lively bar scene up front; less noisy in back. Attractive, not hokey decor. Menu w. rarely featured regional dishes. Punchy margaritas and a selection of tequilas to go along w. them. *Mexican.* ❙

    ♀ **Gaylord** (East Village), 87 First Ave. at E. 7th St. (529-7990). A/C. Lunch/dinner daily. AE, MC, V. *Specialties:* samosa, crab bhuna, tandoori chicken, beef Madras, vegetarian thali, nan stuffed w. minced lamb, cold chicken and cucumber in tamarind sauce. *Note:* Really good, nongreasy Indian food served in an elegant atmosphere. If you can't secure a table here, turn the corner and check into any one of the many Indian rests. that line E. 6th St. between First Ave. and Second Ave. Although Gaylord is somewhat pricier than most of these, it's worth it. Resv. recommended. *Indian.* ❙

    ♀ **Lou G. Siegel's** (midtown), 209 W. 38th St. (921-4433). A/C. Lunch Sun–Fri, dinner Sun–Thur; closed Jewish hols. AE, CB, DC, MC, V. *Specialties:* brisket, roast beef, broiled veal cutlets, gefilte fish, stuffed cabbage, goulash, chopped liver. *Note:* Authentic Jewish food since 1917: from pastrami to roast beef and from matzoh balls to pastry, everything is scrupulously kosher. At both lunch and dinner it's packed w. workers from the nearby Garment District. Friendly, efficient svce. Depressing decor. Styles itself "the world's most famous kosher rest." *Continental.* ❙

    ♀ **Bayamo** (NoHo), 704 Broadway near E. 4th St. (475-5151). A/C. Lunch/dinner daily; closed Thanksgiving and Dec 25. AE, CB, DC, MC, V. *Specialties:* ropa vieja (traditional Cuban beef stew), picadillo de camarones (spicy shrimp minced w. cheese, tortilla, and guacamole), chicken w. ginger, pan-fried lo mein noodles. *Note:* Named for a Cuban village where Chinese settlers had immigrated in the early 1900s, this busy two-level rest. is in the heart of the action along lower Broadway. The rm is dominated by a huge papier-mâché red pepper simulating the boats of the Chinese immigrants to Cuba, and the brilliant wall frescoes are interesting to contemplate while you sip one of the house special margaritas or Foster's beer. Curious combination of Chinese-Latino cuisine. Stick to the simpler dishes. Good for a snack or a full dinner. *Cuban/Chinese.* **B–I**

☼ ♀ **Hard Rock Café** (midtown), 221 W. 57th St. (459-9320).
☼ ♣ A/C. Lunch/dinner daily (till 3am). AE, MC, V. *Specialties:* pig sandwich (roast pork), hamburgers, salads, ice-cream sundaes. *Note:* A pretty faithful copy of London's famous establishment of the same name, this funky landmark of rock'n'roll serves excellent hamburgers and sandwiches, and praiseworthy desserts. Far-out decor w. a 45-ft. (14m) bar in the shape of a guitar, and the rear half of an elderly 1959 Cadillac Biarritz cemented into the facade. Very high-level sound system. Very popular w. the New York young; serves between 1,800 and 2,500 customers a day. No resv. Also a crowded rock joint. *American.* **B–I**

♀ **Abyssinia** (SoHo), 35 Grand St. (226-5959). A/C. Dinner
♣ nightly, brunch Sat–Sun. AE. *Specialties:* kitfo (raw chopped beef seasoned w. spiced butter and topped w. hot chili powder), ye'beg tibs (lamb w. tomato, onion fried w. rosemary, and black pepper), doro wot (chicken marinated in hot Berber sauce, served w. boiled egg), shuro (purée of chickpeas, tomatoes, onions, garlic, and other herbs), chocolate-chip cake, pear-and-almond tart. *Note:* A mecca for a young crowd who come here for the great-value cuisine eaten sans tableware, using the large, round bread as plate and scoop. You sit on traditional wooden stools at low, round, woven basket tables in two small rms decorated w. authentic Ethiopian artifacts too. Fun and different. Brief wine and beer selection. *Ethiopian.* **B**

☼ ♀ **Carnegie Delicatessen** (midtown), 854 Seventh Ave. at W.
☼ ♣ 55th St. (757-2245). A/C. Breakfast/lunch/dinner daily (till 4am). No credit cards. *Specialties:* chicken soup w. matzoh balls, corned beef, brisket, pastrami, roast beef, smoked herring and salmon, cheese blintzes, Jewish specialties. Excellent cheesecake. *Note:* Generally acknowledged to be New York's best deli, the place is overrun at lunchtime. Gigantic sandwiches, remarkable desserts. The ideal place to eat on the run, before or after a show. A lively local institution since 1935; part of Woody Allen's movie *Broadway Danny Rose* was shot here. No resv. Beer but no liquor. *American.* **B**

♀ **Grand Palace** (Chinatown), 94-98 Mott St. (219-3088).
♣ A/C. Lunch/dinner daily. AE. *Specialties:* shark's-fin soup, sliced pigeon and vegetable, fried crab w. ginger and onion, chicken in salt, Peking duck. *Note:* On wknds if you can push your way through the crowds outside, you'll discover a vast hall filled w. large, round tables all occupied by Chinese families and friends, dining on everything from cuttlefish and abalone to ducks' feet and frog—a veritable slice of Hong Kong/Canton life. *Chinese.* **B**

♀ **Siam Inn** (midtown), 916 Eighth Ave. between W. 54th St.
♣ and W. 55th St. (489-5237). A/C. Lunch Mon–Fri, dinner nightly. AE, CB, DC. *Specialties:* Tom Yum Koong soup, beef w. basil leaves and chili, broiled salmon w. green curry, masaman curry (w. jumbo shrimp, avocado, coconut milk, peanuts, spices, and chili), pad Thai. *Note:* Among the many Thai rests. that have opened recently in New York, this small, simply decorated place offers some of the most authentic cuisine. Svce is gracious. *Thai.* **B**

Other Well-Known Restaurants

Gloucester House (midtown), 37 E. 50th St. (755-7394). Lunch/dinner Mon–Sat. AE, DC, MC, V. J&T. Remarkably fresh seafood at enormously high prices against a backdrop of seafaring decor. **VE**

Le Cirque (Upper East Side), 58 E. 65th St. (794-9292). Lunch/dinner

Mon–Sat. AE, CB, DC. Trend-setting rest. whose patrons range from Richard Nixon and Fiat chairman Giovanni Agnelli to Liza Minelli and the Greek shipowner Livanos. Super-high prices. President Reagan has occasionally honored the place w. his presence. **VE**

Rainbow Room (midtown), 30 Rockefeller Plaza (632-5000). Dinner Tues–Sat, brunch Sat–Sun. AE. On the 65th floor of the General Electric Building (formerly the RCA Building), this dazzling recently remodeled art deco rest. is so New York City, it offers a splendid view of the lighted skyline and nostalgic dining and dancing. Prices are predictably steep. **VE**

Four Seasons (midtown), 99 E. 52nd St. (754-9494). Lunch/dinner Mon–Sat. AE, CB, DC, MC, V. The "Pool Room" w. its enormous skylight and marble pool is a triumph of elegant modern design. The wine list is exhaustive. A favorite of New York's publishing community in particular. Super-expensive. Designated an official New York City landmark in 1989. **E–VE**

Café des Artistes (Upper West Side), 1 W. 67th St. (877-3500). Lunch Mon–Fri, dinner nightly, brunch Sat–Sun. AE, DC, MC, V. Ultimately, the plush Central European atmosphere and the exquisite painted murals are what draw regulars to this festive rest. However, the food is not as consistently pleasing as the setting. **E**

Elaine's (Upper East Side), 1703 Second Ave. at E. 88th St. (534-8103). Dinner daily. AE, MC, V. The watering place for celebrities and show-business personalities. Elaine stands guard by the door; only regulars like Woody Allen, Willie Nelson, or Luciano Pavarotti are allowed in without argument. Go if you insist on seeing the famous feeding. **E**

"21" Club (midtown), 21 W. 52nd St. (582-7200). Lunch/dinner Mon–Sat. AE, CB, DC, MC, V. Movers and shakers make this their "club" for socializing and deal making. A famous old speakeasy, recently renovated for the '90s, it's a famed New York "power" spot. The food is only one of the issues—the "21" burger is $24. **E**

Cafeterias/Specialty Spots/Fast Food

☀ **Broadway Diner** (midtown), 1726 Broadway at W. 55th St. (765-0909). Breakfast/lunch/dinner daily (from 7am to 11pm). Corned-beef hash w. poached eggs, hamburgers, very good sandwiches, and broiled chicken in an *American Graffiti*-style luncheonette, all Formica, chromium, and stainless steel. For 1940s enthusiasts.

☀ **Exterminator Chili** (Lower Manhattan), 305 Church St. (219-3070). Breakfast/lunch/dinner daily. As the name implies, the house specialty is the excellent chili—75 varieties, from vegetarian to hot-as-Hades. Also laudable omelets, hamburgers, and hot dogs. Super-kitsch decor, Elvis Presley style; amusing clientele, half-bohemian, half-punk.

Hamburger Harry's (Lower Manhattan), 157 Chambers St. (267-4446). Lunch/dinner daily (till 11:30pm). Some 16 kinds of hamburgers (connoisseurs call them the best in New York) and champagne by the glass, a stone's throw from the World Trade Center. Other location: 145 W. 45th St., midtown (840-0566).

Katz's Delicatessen (Lower East Side), 205 E. Houston St. at Ludlow St. (254-2246). Breakfast/lunch/dinner daily. No credit cards. Cafeteria-style deli w. the authentic New York flavor. Gigantic sandwiches of brisket, corned beef, tongue, roast beef, etc.

☀ **Museum of Modern Art Garden Café** (midtown), 11 W. 53rd St. (708-9400). Lunch Thurs–Tues. The tourists' favorite: big bay windows w. unobstructed view of the Sculpture Garden. Crowded out at lunch. Praiseworthy food.

Nathan's Famous (midtown), 1482 Broadway at W. 43rd St. (382-0620). Open daily from 7am to 3am. New York's best hot dogs, excellent french fries and sandwiches, but so-so burgers. Three other locations in Manhattan and

Brooklyn, besides the famous original at Coney Island (see "Nearby Excursions," below).

☀ **Tap Room Manhattan Brewing Co.** (SoHo), 40-42 Thompson St. (219-9250). A/C. Open daily (until midnight). AE, MC, V. Large tavern dominated by the huge copper vats of the Manhattan Brewing Co. in the heart of Soho. Several house brews are on tap, accompanied by acceptable British-pub style food; buffet brunch on wknds.

Where to Eat What in New York

American: Acme Bar & Grill (p. 134), An American Place (p. 126), Arizona 206 (p. 129), Aureole (p. 126), Bridge Café (p. 132), Broadway Grill (p. 125), Carnegie Delicatessen (p. 135), Coach House (p. 128), Gage & Tollner (p. 130), Gotham Bar and Grill (p. 124), Hard Rock Café (p. 135), River Café (p. 128), Sylvia's (p. 133), Tribeca Grill (p. 129), "21" (p. 136)

Brazilian: Cabana Carioca (p. 134)

Chinese: Auntie Yuan (p. 128), Chin Chin (p. 129), Grand Palace (p. 135), The Nice Restaurant (p. 133), Shun Lee Palace (p. 124)

Continental: Café des Artistes (p. 136), Elaine's (p. 136), Lou G. Siegel's (p. 134), Rainbow Room (p. 136), Tavern on the Green (p. 127), Windows on the World Restaurant (p. 131)

Cuban-Chinese: Bayamo (p. 134)

East European: Russian Tea Room (p. 131)

Ethiopian: Abyssinia (p. 135)

Fast Food/Specialty Spots/Cafeterias: Broadway Diner (p. 136), Exterminator Chili (p. 136), Hamburger Harry's (p. 136), Katz's Delicatessen (p. 136), Museum of Modern Art Garden Café (p. 136), Nathan's Famous (p. 136), Tap Room Manhattan Brewing Co. (p. 137)

French: Bouley (p. 126), Le Cirque (p. 135), Chanterelle (p. 123), La Côte Basque (p. 126), Four Seasons (p. 136), La Gauloise (p. 132), Lafayette (p. 125), Lutèce (p. 123), Odeon (p. 130), Provence (p. 131), Quilted Giraffe (p. 127)

Greek: Periyali (p. 131)

Indian: Darbár (p. 130), Gaylord (p. 134)

Indonesian: Nusantara (p. 132)

Italian: Nanni (p. 133), Il Nido (p. 128), Palio (p. 127), San Domenico (p. 124)

Japanese: Chikubu (p. 132), Hatsuhana (p. 125), Japonica (p. 133), Mitsukoshi (p. 127)

Latin American: Sabor (p. 133)

Mexican: Cinco de Mayo (p. 134), Rosa Mexicano (p. 125)

Seafood: Le Bernardin (p. 123), John Clancy's Restaurant (p. 130), Gloucester House (p. 135), Manhattan Ocean Club (p. 129), Oyster Bar and Restaurant (p. 124), Spring Street Natural (p. 133)

Spanish: Harlequin (p. 130), El Rincon de España (p. 132)

Steak: Christ Cella (p. 128), Frank's (p. 125), Gallagher's Steak House (p. 132), Palm (p. 124), Peter Luger (p. 131), Smith & Wollensky (p. 129)

Thai: Siam Inn (p. 135)

Vegetarian: Spring Street Natural (p. 133)

BARS & NIGHTCLUBS

In a city with some 15,000 bars, discos, nightclubs, dance halls, strip joints, etc., it isn't easy to make a current list of the "in" places. Here are some dependable values, classified by type.

BARS/PUBS: The Ballroom (Chelsea), 253 W. 28th St. (244-3005). An unusual nightspot which contrives to be simultaneously a cabaret, comedy club, Off Off Broadway theater, commendable restaurant, and excellent "tapas" bar, serving the highly esteemed Spanish hors d'oeuvres. One of the most popular places in Chelsea. Karen Akers is one of the stars who appear here regularly. Open Tues–Sat.

Café Carlyle (Upper East Side), in the Hotel Carlyle (see "Accommodations," above) (744-1600). Preppy piano bar, enlivened for the last two decades by the talented Bobby Short. Also a restaurant. Open nightly.

Café Skylight (midtown), in the Novotel (see "Accommodations," above) (315-0100). On a terrace on the seventh floor of the Novotel, this wine bar has a panoramic view of Broadway and Times Sq. Large selection by the glass or the bottle. Excellent sandwiches, cheeses, and pâtés to accompany the wine. Spectacular view after dark. Open nightly till 1am.

Chumley's (Greenwich Village), 86 Bedford St. (675-4449). The entrance is unmarked—a reminder that this was originally a speakeasy. Sawdust on the floor, fire burning in winter. Bar area is small and decorated with book jackets, reminders of the original denizens. A Greenwich Village literary landmark. Good burgers. Open nightly until midnight.

Clarke's (midtown), 915 Third Ave. at E. 56th St. (759-1650). Only the uninitiated refer to this very lively bar by its full name, P.J. Clarke's. Rather hearty masculine atmosphere. So-so restaurant. Crowded at night. Open nightly till 4am.

Landmark Tavern (midtown), 626 Eleventh Ave. at W. 46th St. (757-8595). A/C. AE. Authentic Victorian-style bar built in 1868 w. tin ceiling, tile floor, and pot-belly stove. Good Irish-style food too, available at lunch and dinner. Open daily from noon to midnight.

Lion's Head Ltd. (Greenwich Village), 59 Christopher St. nr. Seventh Ave. (929-0670). Likeable, relaxed bar full of intellectual scribblers; very Greenwich Village. Also a restaurant. Open nightly until 4am.

McSorley's Old Ale House (East Village), 15 E. 7th St. (473-8800). Classic alehouse serving beer. Young, student crowd along w. locals from the Ukrainian neighborhood. Historic atmosphere—one of Brendan Behan's haunts. The corned-beef sandwiches are also famous. Open daily from 11am to 4am.

West End Gate (formerly West End Café; Upper West Side), 2911 Broadway at W. 114th St. (666-9160). A well-known student hangout across the street from Columbia University; a lively place with excellent jazz, long frequented by Jack Kerouac, Allen Ginsberg, and the first beatniks. 50 different kinds of beer. Recently renovated; now under the same management as the Village Gate. Open daily until 4am.

☼ **White Horse Tavern** (Greenwich Village), 560 Hudson St. (243-9260). One of Manhattan's oldest literary cafés (1880), once the favorite of Dylan Thomas and Norman Mailer. Gently bohemian clientele; excellent hamburgers. Open daily from noon to 3am.

COUNTRY & WESTERN MUSIC: Lone Star Road House (midtown), 240 W. 52nd St. (245-2950). Since its illustrious ancestor, the Lone Star Café, closed in 1989, this has become New York City's shrine to country music, attracting all the big stars. Pleasant bar; acceptable Tex-Mex rest. Open daily.

O'Lunney's (midtown), 915 Second Ave. at E. 49th St. (751-5470). Another place for country music lovers, *Urban Cowboy* style, with bluegrass as well on Sun. Also a passable restaurant. Open Mon–Sat.

DISCO/ROCK: ☼ Au Bar (midtown), 41 E. 58th St. (308-9455). Intimate, very upscale bar-restaurant modeled on a smart London club. Dance floor, elegant dining room, library(!), and smoking room. A world away from the ear-splitting modern disco. Thronged by well-brought-up yuppies. Open nightly.

B2/Be Square (formerly Area) (Tribeca), 157 Hudson St. (966-5881). Classical art deco disco for the Wall St. crowd (there is even an automatic teller machine, the first in a New York club). Open Wed–Sat.

China Club (Upper West Side), 2130 Broadway at W. 75th St. (877-1166).

One of the most amusing "in" discos in the city. The decor, Far Eastern crossed with art deco, is bizarre. Frequented by New York celebrities and entertainers. Open nightly.

El Morocco (midtown), 307 E. 54th St. (750-1500). The famous '30s nightspot restored to its original splendor, with big swing band, artificial palm trees, and zebra-skin upholstery. A triumph of kitsch, modestly self-styled "the world's most famous nightclub." Open nightly.

Limelight (Chelsea), 660 Ave. of the Americas at W. 20th St. (807-7850). This enormous disco, in an old Gothic church, seats 1,000 people on three floors. The bar is in the adjoining chapel. Very "in" atmosphere. Open nightly.

Mars (Greenwich Village) 28 Tenth Ave. at W. 13th St. (691-6262). One of the latest "hot spots" on New York's after-dark scene: from pop to reggae and from rock to new wave in an old warehouse bursting out with lasers and psychedelic strobes. Trendy. Open Tues–Sun.

M.K. (Chelsea), 204 Fifth Ave. at 27th St. (779-1340). Slightly pretentious nightclub where admission is rigorously selective. J&T a must. This is where you'll see everyone who's anyone in New York, as well as stars of stage and screen. Fashionable. Open nightly.

Nell's (Greenwich Village), 246 W. 14th St. (675-1567). Very trendy semi-private nightclub which draws New York's artistic and literary crowd. Sumptuously venerable Victorian decor; background music ranges from modern jazz to Dvorak. For with-it intellectuals. Open nightly.

✵ **Palladium** (East Village), 126 E. 14th St. (473-7171). World's biggest disco, 320,000 sq. ft. (30,000m²) on seven floors. The famous architect Arato Isozaki did the interior, where 3,500 people can be comfortable. Far out. Open Wed–Sat.

Red Zone (midtown), 440 W. 54th St. (582-2222). The main dance floor of this huge disco is surrounded by outsize movie screens. The new trendy place, with its own rest. Open Wed–Sat.

Ritz (midtown), 254 W. 54th St. (541-8900). Old movie house now a rendezvous for rockers. Ear-splitting audio. Lavish neo-deco decor. Very with-it atmosphere. Open nightly.

✵ **Roseland** (midtown), 239 W. 52nd St. (247-0200). Enormous 1930s dance hall, straight out of *They Shoot Horses, Don't They?* Super-kitsch in a very populist way; some evenings you can count 3,000 dancers. Guaranteed atmosphere; patriotic decor with huge star-spangled banner. A sight to be seen. Open Thurs–Sun.

S.O.B. (Sounds of Brazil) (Greenwich Village), 204 Varick St. at W. Houston St. (243-4940). Fashionable super-disco; Latin rhythms to an American beat. One of the "hottest" places in town. Open Tues–Sun.

Stringfellow's (Gramercy Park), 35 E. 21st St. (254-2444). Aggressively hi-tech disco, a triumph of multicolored neon. Waitresses in pink tutus. A fashionable place. Open Mon–Sat.

✵ **The Tunnel** (Chelsea), 220 Twelfth Ave. at W. 27th St. (244-6444). Giant disco (can hold up to 2,500) in an old dockside railroad terminal; the rails are still on the ground, and form an integral part of the decor. Off-the-wall rock ambience. Neighborhood unsafe at night; arrange for a cab. Open nightly.

COMEDY CLUBS: Caroline's (Lower Manhattan), Pier 17 at 89 South St. (233-4900). One of the most famous comedy clubs in the country, with Jay Leno, Billy Crystal, or Howie Mandel at the head of the bill. Preppy atmosphere and patrons. Open Tues–Sun.

Catch a Rising Star (Upper East Side), 1487 First Ave. at E. 77th St. (794-1906). As the name suggests, specializes in discovering new talent.

Chicago City Limits (Upper East Side), 351 E. 74th St. (772-8707). An old reliable of satire, political, and other. Open Wed–Sat.

Improvisation (The Original) (midtown), 358 W. 44th St. (765-8268).

The oldest (1963) of New York's comedy clubs, which has showcased such future superstars as Richard Pryor, Joe Piscopo, and Robin Williams. Casual ambience and decor with no affectations. Open nightly.

JAZZ: The magic **Jazzline** telephone number (718/465-7500) gives current programs for all the jazz clubs.

Blue Note (Greenwich Village), 131 W. 3rd St. (475-8592). The biggest stars of the day. Rest. as well. Open nightly.

Bottom Line (Greenwich Village), 15 W. 4th St. (228-7880). Jazz, rock, blues. Switched-on clientele. Resv. a must.

Bradley's (Greenwich Village), 70 University Pl. at W. 11th St. (228-6440). Very good modern jazz in an elegant dark-paneled setting. Also acceptable rest. Usually crowded; resv. a must. Open daily.

Carlos I (Greenwich Village), 432 Ave. of the Americas at W. 10th St. (982-3260). Rest.-jazz club featuring some solid performers. Agreeable decor; praiseworthy Caribbean cooking. Open nightly.

Fat Tuesday's (Gramercy Park), Third Ave. and E. 17th St. (533-7902). Modern and traditional jazz; rest. as well. Open nightly.

Indigo Blues (midtown), 221 W. 46th St. (221-0033). Excellent modern jazz from Ahmad Jamal to Billy Taylor. Also rest. Open daily.

Michael's Pub (midtown), 211 E. 55th St. (758-2272). New Orleans jazz; rest. Every now and then Woody Allen still turns up on a Mon evening to play clarinet. Open Mon–Sat.

Sweet Basil (Greenwich Village), 88 Seventh Ave. South (242-1785). Modern jazz; several stars appear regularly, including Art Blakey and the Jazz Messengers. Pretty rustic decor; likable atmosphere. Open nightly.

Village Gate (Greenwich Village), Bleecker St. and Thompson St. (475-5120). Very famous jazz club; Dizzy Gillespie comes here. Open nightly.

Village Vanguard (Greenwich Village), 178 Seventh Ave. (255-4037). The jazz shrine of New York City since 1935; probably the world's most famous jazz club. All the biggest names in jazz put in an appearance here. Generally crowded. Open nightly.

Zanzibar & Grill (midtown), 550 Third Ave. at E. 36th St. (779-0606). New jazz club and rest. w. live music daily. The setting is a kind of tropical art deco.

NEARBY EXCURSIONS

CONEY ISLAND (Surf Ave., Brooklyn): Beach somewhat run-down, crowded in summer (see "Beaches," above). Kitsch but entertaining amusement park (see "Theme Parks," above). Famous aquarium (see the New York Aquarium under "Zoos," above), and New York's best hot dogs at Nathan's Famous, Surf Ave. and Stillwell Ave. (718/946-2202). In a word, don't miss it, but avoid the summer weekend crush, and be alert at night.

STATEN ISLAND (10 mi./16km SW via the Brooklyn-Battery Tunnel, I-278, and the Verrazano-Narrows Bridge, or via ferry from Battery Park, in Lower Manhattan): Facing Manhattan across New York Bay, this small island, only 14 by 8 mi. (22 by 12km), still retains a rural touch with its many parks, old villages, and rolling hills that invite you to a stroll. You should certainly see **Richmondtown Restoration,** 441 Clarke Ave. at Arthur Kill Rd. (718/351-1617), a museum village with 30 or so carefully restored buildings from the 17th to 19th century, including the Voorlezer's House, the country's oldest surviving elementary school, built around 1690.

Not far away is the curious **Jacques Marchais Center of Tibetan Art,** 338 Lighthouse Ave. (718/987-3478), open Fri–Sat afternoons in Apr, Oct, and Nov; Wed–Sun afternoons May–Sept. This interesting museum of Buddhist art stands in its own fine Oriental garden.

The **Snug Harbor Cultural Center,** 1000 Richmond Terrace (718/448-2500), open daily, is a cultural and creative-arts center in what used to be a sailors' retirement home dating from the early 19th century. Interesting Greek Revival and Victorian buildings, art museum, fine sculpture garden, and 80-acre (39ha) park.

An oasis of peace and calm within New York's city limits, 30 min. from Manhattan by the Staten Island Ferry.

VERRAZANO-NARROWS BRIDGE (9 mi/15km SW via the Brooklyn-Battery Tunnel and I-278): The bridge connecting Brooklyn to Staten Island was designed by Othmar Ammann, an architect of Swiss origin. It's the world's third-longest suspension bridge, with a total length of 13,700 ft. (4,176m); the central span is 4,260 ft. (1,299m) long. The piers are 689 ft. (210m) high; there are two decks, each with six lanes. Opened in 1964, it cost $305 million. More than 50 million vehicles cross it every year. A truly riveting sight. **Fort Wadsworth,** at the Staten Island approach to the bridge, has a fine view of New York Bay.

FARTHER AFIELD

THE HUDSON VALLEY (229 mi./366km r.t. via U.S. 9N, N.Y. 9A, U.S. 9N, N.Y. 199W, N.Y. 28N/S and N.Y. 375N/S, I-87S, U.S. 9W, Palisades Interstate Pkwy., and the George Washington Bridge): A car trip along a very lovely valley, which reminds seasoned travelers of the Rhine. Next to Manhattan this may be richer in historical associations than any other part of New York State. Leave Manhattan on U.S. 9, the northward extension of Broadway, and begin the tour with a visit to **Philipse Manor Hall State Historic Park,** Warburton Ave. and Dock St., Yonkers (914/965-4027) (visit by appointment, Wed–Sun from the end of May to Nov). Built in 1682, this was the home of a family of noble loyalists from England. Superb Georgian-style interior decoration. Not far is the **Hudson River Museum,** 511 Warburton Ave. (914/963-4550), open Wed–Sun, where exhibits bearing on the art and history of the Hudson Valley are housed in an imposing 19th-century home.

Tarrytown, 11 mi. (17km) north, was founded in the 17th century by the Dutch, and made famous by Washington Irving, whose house, **Sunnyside,** W. Sunnyside Lane (914/631-8200), is open daily Apr–Nov, Wed–Sun rest of the year. Many other fine old homes have been restored at the expense of the Rockefeller family. They include **Lyndhurst,** 635 S. Broadway (914/631-0046), open Tues–Sun Apr–Oct (wknds only, the rest of the year), a splendid 1838 Gothic Revival estate overlooking the river; and **Philipsburg Manor,** on U.S. 9, Kingsland Point Park (914/631-7766), open daily, a beautiful 1683 manor house, still with its old mill, where a very popular classical-music festival is held every summer. Near here, see the old Dutch church built in 1685 and the charming little **Sleepy Hollow cemetery** (Broadway and Pierson), with the graves of Washington Irving, Andrew Carnegie, and William Rockefeller.

U.S. 9 continues northward through **Ossining,** with the famous **Sing Sing Federal Penitentiary** (no visitors), on its way to **Croton-on-Hudson** and the lovely **Van Cortlandt Manor,** Croton Point Ave. (914/631-8200), open daily, dating from the War of Independence and built on the old post road to Albany; fine 18th-century garden. Between Garrison and Cold Spring, on a height of land overlooking the river, see **Boscobel,** built in 1805 in the Federal style by wealthy landowner States Morris Dyckman, with its beautiful orangery.

North another 23 mi (36km) is **Poughkeepsie,** home of **Vassar College,** long the most famous women's college in the country, co-ed since 1969; its campus on Raymond Ave. is worth a look.

On to **Hyde Park,** birthplace of Franklin D. Roosevelt; visit the ☼ 🏛 **Roosevelt-Vanderbilt National Historic Sites,** on U.S. 9 (914/229-9115), open daily Apr–Oct, Thurs–Mon Nov–Mar. You'll see the house where the 32nd president was born; his tomb, and that of his wife, Eleanor, are in the rose garden. There's a museum, a library with Roosevelt's private papers, and the sumptuous mansion of the railroad magnate Frederick Vanderbilt, built in 1898 to the Beaux Arts design of McKim, Mead and White. Don't miss it.

A little off U.S. 9 at **Staatsburg, the** 🏛 **Mills Mansion Historic Site** (914/889-4100), a magnificent 65-room 1895 classical revival building by Stanford White, certainly deserves a visit. Elegant Louis XV and Louis XVI furniture. Open Wed–Sun Apr–Oct.

☼ 🏛 **Rhinebeck,** a little distance north, has two claims to fame: the oldest inn in the country (see the Beekman Arms, under "Where to Stay," below), and a wonderful collection of early aircraft at the **Old Rhinebeck Aerodrome,** Stone Church Rd. (914/758-8610). Weekend air shows mid-May to Oct; museum open daily mid-May to Oct. Then take the opposite bank of the Hudson River on to ☼ 🏛 **Woodstock,** at the foot of the Catskills. This agreeable little summer resort and artists' colony is famous for its chamber-music festival (started in 1916), and also as the scene (August 15–17, 1969) of the legendary rock festival, which was attended by almost half a million people, and which in a sense marked the end of the '60s. Should be seen.

Head back to Manhattan via ☼ **Kingston,** founded by the Dutch in 1652 and the first capital of New York State before it was burned by the British. Many interesting buildings including the 🏛 **Senate House Historic Site** of 1676 at 312 Fair St. (914/338-2786), open Wed–Sun. (wknds only, Jan–Mar).

George Washington made his headquarters in ☼ **Newburgh,** 34 mi. (55km) south, from Apr 1782 to Aug 1783 during the War of Independence, and it was from here that he made the official announcement of the end of hostilities. You may visit the site at 84 Liberty St. (914/562-1195), Wed–Sun Apr–Dec (wknds only, Jan–Mar). Also see the **New Windsor Cantonment Site,** Temple Hill Rd. (914/561-1765), open Wed–Sun from late Apr through Oct, the last encampment of the Continental Army. Interesting museum. Don't miss this page of history.

On your way to West Point, make a detour along N.Y. 32 to the ☼ **Storm King Art Center,** Old Pleasant Hill Rd. in Mountainville (914/534-3115), open Wed–Mon Apr–Nov, a fine museum of modern art in a superb 350-acre (142ha) park adorned with monumental sculpture by such artists as Isamu Noguchi, Alexander Calder, and Louise Nevelson. Don't miss it.

☼ 🏛 **West Point,** home of the U.S. Military Academy, founded in 1802, turns out 4,000 cadets a year. **Fort Putnam** (1779), dominating the campus, the **Cadet Chapel,** and the **West Point Museum** are all worth visiting. At the **Information Center,** at Thayer Gate (914/938-2638), you can obtain dates and times of parades in Apr–May and Sept–Oct. Don't miss it.

☼ **Bear Mountain State Park,** just south of West Point, is a lovely wooded park of some 5,000 acres (2,000ha) overlooking the Hudson. **Perkins Memorial Drive,** a scenic highway, will take you to the top of Bear Mountain and give you a splendid view across the valley. If you like flea markets you should stop at ☼ 🏛 **Nyack** (where painter Edward Hopper was born) to see its **Arts & Crafts & Antiques,** with almost 100 art galleries, handcraft shops, and antiques dealers (914/358-8443), open Tues–Sun.

Finally, back to Manhattan by the Palisades Interstate Pkwy. and the George Washington Bridge; allow 2 to 3 days for this exciting tour.

Where to Stay En Route

The following hotels, motels, and inns are recommended as suitable places for a stopover.

IN BEAR MOUNTAIN STATE PARK The 🛏 **Bear Mountain Inn,** U.S. 9W, Bear Mountain, NY 10911 (914/786-2731). 60 rms. Small rustic motel inside the park. **I–M**

HYDE PARK The 🛏 **Roosevelt Inn,** 38 Albany Post Rd., Hyde Park, NY 12538 (914/229-2443). 26 rms. Modest but very well-run motel w. modern comforts. Open Mar–Dec. **I**

LAKE MOHONK / NEW PALTZ The ☀ 🛏🛏🛏 **Mohonk Mountain House,** N.Y. 299, New Paltz, NY 12561 (914/255-1000; 212/233-2244 in New York City). 280 rms, some without bath. Flamboyant castle-hotel dating from 1879; the Victorian structure is a designated historic landmark. Resv. strongly advised at all times, and as far in advance as possible during the summer. **VE** (American Plan)

NEWBURGH The 🛏🛏 **Diplomat Motor Inn,** 845 Union Ave., Newburgh, NY 12550 (914/564-7550). 80 rms. Small, comfortable hotel overlooking Washington Lake. **I–M**

RHINEBECK The ☀ 🛏🛏 **Beekman Arms,** Beekman Sq., Rhinebeck, NY 12572 (914/876-7077). 48 rms. The oldest inn (1766) in the country; period decor and atmosphere but modern standards of comfort. **I–M**

WEST POINT The ☀ 🛏 **Hotel Thayer,** S. Entry (off N.Y. 218), U.S. Military Academy, West Point, NY 10996 (914/446-4731). 200 rms. Venerable old hotel on the academy campus looking out on the Hudson. **I–M**

Where to Eat En Route

The following restaurants and inns are suitable places for a meal, if you're following the above itinerary.

GARRISON The ☀ 🍽 **Bird and Bottle Inn,** Old Albany Post Rd. (914/424-3000). Lunch/dinner daily (closed Mon–Tues mid-Nov to Apr). Authentic Revolutionary-period tavern attractively restored. French-inspired cuisine of refinement. **M**

HYDE PARK The 🍽🍽🍽 **Escoffier Room,** on U.S. 9, 3 mi. (5km) north of town (914/471-6608). Lunch/dinner Tues–Sat. This is the dining rm of the Culinary Institute of America, where the country's future culinary greats are trained. Very carefully prepared French-inspired cuisine. Resv. a must. **M**

KINGSTON 🍽🍽 **Hillside Manor,** 240 Boulevard (914/331-4386). Lunch Mon–Fri, dinner nightly. Tasty Italian food; romantic country-inn decor w. wonderful views. **M**

POUGHKEEPSIE The ☀🍽🍽 **Treasure Chest,** 568 South Rd. (914/462-4545). Lunch Mon–Fri, dinner nightly. Charming inn in a 250-year-old building. Excellent Continental cooking. **I–M**

RHINEBECK The ☀🍽🍽 **Beekman Arms,** Beekman Sq. (914/876-7077). Lunch/dinner daily. This is the oldest inn (1766) in the country; period decor and atmosphere. Classic cuisine. **M–E**

STORMVILLE 🍽🍽🍽 **Harrald's,** N.Y. 52 (914/878-6595). Dinner only, Mon and Wed–Sat. One of the finest rests. on the East Coast; with refined Continental cuisine and exemplary svce. **E** (prix fixe)

🔭 **LONG ISLAND** (244 mi./390km r.t. by the Queens-Midtown Tunnel, Long Island Expwy., N.Y. 25A, N.Y. 106N,

N.Y. 25A West, N.Y. 25W, ferry from Greenport to Shelter Island, N.Y. 1145, N.Y. 27W, N.Y. 27E, Robert Moses Pkwy. South, Ocean Pkwy. West, Loop Pkwy., the beaches at Long Beach, Atlantic Beach, Rockaway Beach, Flatbush Ave., the Belt Pkwy., the Brooklyn-Queens Expwy., and the Brooklyn-Battery Tunnel): White-sand beaches, dozens of little museums, old homes that recall the island's past, and picturesque fishing harbors, all just 2 or 3 hours' drive from the center of New York. Long Island has always been the favorite country retreat of celebrities, including Pres. Theodore Roosevelt; Albert Einstein (who worked out his General Theory of Relativity between two sailing trips); painters Willem de Kooning and Jackson Pollock; sculptor Isamu Noguchi; writers James Fenimore Cooper, John Steinbeck, Saul Bellow, Truman Capote, Edward Albee, and Kurt Vonnegut; and many others.

Leaving Manhattan to the east via the Queens-Midtown Tunnel and the Long Island Expwy. (I-495), stop first at **Kings Point**, home of the ⚓ **U.S. Merchant Marine Academy** with its 1,000 students, at King's Point Rd. (516/773-5000), open daily; there are parades of the midshipmen Sat in spring and fall.

Another 15 mi. (24km) east is ☀ **Oyster Bay,** a busy pleasure-boat harbor at the head of a long, narrow bay. See the ⚓ **Raynham Hall Museum,** 20 W. Main St. (516/922-6808), open Tues–Sun. This old farmhouse, which was bought by Samuel Townsend in 1738, has been scrupulously restored; it played an important part in the War of Independence, particularly as the headquarters of the "Queens Rangers." ☀ ⚓ **Sagamore Hill Historic Site,** 304 Cove Neck Rd. (516/922-4447), open daily May–Sept (Tues–Sun Oct–Apr), was the Summer White House from 1901 to 1909, and the final home of Theodore Roosevelt, who died in 1919. Authentic furnishings and many personal memorabilia of "Teddy"; not to be missed. It's only a short distance to the ⚓ **Theodore Roosevelt Memorial Sanctuary,** E. Main St. at Cove Rd., open daily, tomb of the 26th president in an 11-acre (4ha) park which is also a sea-bird sanctuary (516/922-3200). Should be seen.

On to the interesting ⚓ **Whaling Museum,** commemorating a trade that once flourished on these shores, at **Cold Spring Harbor,** on Main St. (516/367-3418), open Tues–Sun. At nearby **Huntington,** lovers of poetry will be sure to pay their respects at the ⚓ **birthplace of Walt Whitman** at 246 Old Walt Whitman Rd. (516/427-5240), with a museum and library devoted to the famous poet, open Wed–Sun.

Continuing eastward, don't fail to visit ☀ ⚓⚓ **"Eagles Nest,"** Little Neck Rd. in **Centerport** (516/261-5656), open Tues–Sun, a lovely house belonging to the Vanderbilt family, which stands in a 43-acre (17ha) park looking out over **Northport Bay.** It is now the home of the **Vanderbilt Museum,** with its natural-history collection. N.Y. 25A now passes part of **Sunken Meadow State Park,** a well-laid-out recreation area with huge sand beach and golf course, on its way to ☀ **Stony Brook,** a delightful seaside village founded in 1655 by settlers from Boston, which seems to have changed very little since colonial times. Several old houses and a remarkable group of small museums of art and history, ⚓⚓ **The Museums at Stony Brook,** Main St. at N.Y. 25A (516/751-0066), open Wed–Sun. Don't miss them—particularly the unique collection of 250 horse-drawn vehicles, coaches, and carriages. The road now passes through **Port Jefferson,** terminal of the ferry for Bridgeport, Conn., and rejoins N.Y. 25, passing through **Riverhead** (interesting **Suffolk County Historical Museum,** 300 W. Main St., open Mon–Sat) on its way to **Greenport** and the ferry.

☀ ⚓ **Sag Harbor,** at the head of Gardiners Bay, was once one of the most important whaling ports in the world; it inspired James Fenimore Cooper to write several stories about sailors and the sea. Besides the little streets lined with charming small houses, you should see the **Custom House,** on Garden St., a late 18th-century building which also served as the post office, and the **Whaling and Historic Museum,** Garden St. and Main St. (516/725-0770), open daily mid-May to Sept.

At **East Hampton,** founded in 1648 and also once a prosperous whaling port, the fishermen have by now given way to artists and wealthy summer sojourners. In and around the town are many 19th-century windmills, including one at 14 James Lane (516/324-0713), open daily June–Oct and by appointment the rest of the year; this is the ⚓ **birthplace of John Howard Payne** (1791–1852), who wrote the words of "Home, Sweet Home." On to the east, and after a look at the **Town Marine Museum** in **Amagansett** on Bluff Rd. (516/267-6544), open Tues–Sun. in summer (by appointment the rest of the year), with its delightful ship models, you reach ❀ **Montauk,** at the eastern tip of the island, a busy and picturesque fishing port (swordfish, tuna). Its miles of deserted beach, and the facilities for leasing sailboats, make it a very appealing resort. From ⚓ **Montauk Point State Park,** with its 1795 lighthouse built on the orders of George Washington, you'll have a splendid view of the ocean. Don't miss it. The Okeanos Ocean Research Foundation offers **whale-watching cruises** daily May–Sept, from Viking Dock, Montauk (516/728-4522).

On your way back to the city along N.Y. 27W, stop at ⚓ **Southampton,** one of the island's two oldest towns (1640). With its many Colonial houses, it is today an elegant beach resort noted for its luxurious homes and fashionable shops. See the **Old Halsey Homestead** (1648), the oldest wooden house in all New York State, on S. Main St. (516/283-3527), open Tues–Sun. from mid-June to mid-Sept. Return to Manhattan via N.Y. 27W as far as **Bay Shore,** where the Robert Moses Pkwy. leads off on the left to the long beach at **Jones Beach State Park,** very popular with New Yorkers during the summer. In the last stage of the trip you follow a succession of coastal highways between **Long Beach** and **Brooklyn.** On the way, lovers of lonelier beaches can explore **Fire Island National Seashore,** a thin belt of pine-planted sand dunes 31 mi. (50km) long abounding in fish and wildlife; it can be reached at either end of the park by bridge, or by ferry from Sayville or Bay Shore.

A very full 2- to 3-day trip.

Where to Stay En Route

The following hotels, motels, and inns are recommended as suitable places for a stopover.

EAST HAMPTON   The ❀ 🍴🍴 **1770 House–Philip Taylor,** 143 Main St., East Hampton, NY 11937 (516/324-1770). 10 rms. Charming old inn dating from 1770, elegantly and comfortably furnished. **E–VE**

EAST NORWICH   🍴🍴 **Burt Bacharach's Inn,** jct. N.Y. 25A and N.Y. 106, East Norwich, NY 11732 (516/922-1500). 72 rms. Modern, very comfortable motel; acceptable rest. **E**

GREENPORT   The 🍴🍴 **Sound View Inn,** North Rd., Greenport, NY 11944 (516/477-1910). 70 rms. Comfortable motel w. private beach. **M–E**

MONTAUK   The 🍴🍴🍴 **Montauk Yacht Club and Inn,** Star Island, Montauk, NY 11954 (516/668-3100). 107 rms. One of the most comfortable hotel-marinas on the eastern seaboard. **VE**

SHELTER ISLAND   The 🍴🍴 **Pridwin,** Shore Rd., Shelter Island, NY 11964 (516/749-0476). 40 rms. Comfortable motel on its own beach. Open May–Oct. **M–E**

SOUTHAMPTON   The 🍴🍴 **Cold Spring Bay** on N.Y. 27, Southampton, NY 11968 (516/283-7600). 64 rms. Inviting motel on Peconic Bay. **M**
        🍴 **Shinnecock,** 240 Montauk Hwy., Southampton, NY 11968
        🔑 (516/283-2406). 30 rms. Functional motel a stone's throw from the beach. **M**

Where to Eat En Route

The following inns and restaurants are suitable places for a meal, if you're following the above itinerary.

BAYVILLE 🍴🍴 **Steve's Pier 1,** 33 Bayville Ave. (516/628-2153). Lunch/dinner daily. Continental rest. on Long Island Sound. Excellent value. **I**

COLD SPRING HARBOR The 🍴🍴 **Old Whaler,** 105 Harbor Rd. (516/367-3166). Lunch/dinner daily. Good, reasonably priced seafood rest. in a charming inn dating from 1680 with view of the harbor. **I**

EAST HAMPTON The 🍴🍴 **Maidstone Arms,** 207 Main St. (516/324-5006). Dinner Wed–Mon. Pleasant French country inn setting, praiseworthy Continental cuisine. **M**

EAST HILLS 🍴🍴🍴 **L'Endroit,** 290 Glen Cove Rd. (516/621-6630). Lunch/dinner Mon–Sat. Excellent contemporary French cuisine in a delightful rustic setting. **I–M**

MONTAUK The 🍴🍴 **Blue Marlin,** Edgemere St. and Flamingo St. (516/668-9880). Lunch/dinner Wed–Mon; closed Jan–Feb. Good seafood rest. in a pretty Early American setting. Good value. **I**

SHELTER ISLAND 🍴 **Clamdiggers,** 15 Grand Ave. at North Ferry (516/749-2005). Lunch/dinner Wed–Mon; closed Nov–May. Good fish rest. in an early 19th-century building. **B–I**

SOUTHAMPTON 🍴🍴 **Herb McCarthy's Bowden Square,** N. Sea Rd. (516/283-2800). Lunch/dinner daily. Tasty food with a slight Irish accent. Dinner on the terrace in summer. **M**

STONY BROOK The 🍴🍴🍴 **Three Village Inn,** 150 Main St. (516/751-0555). 1785 Colonial inn with very good country food. A great place. **M**

🔭🔭 **FINGER LAKES** (785 mi./1,256km r.t. via the George Washington Bridge, Palisades Interstate Pkwy., U.S. 6W, N.Y. 17N, I-81N, N.Y. 175W, U.S. 20W, N.Y. 89S, N.Y. 79W, N.Y. 14N, U.S. 20W, N.Y. 21S, N.Y. 53S, N.Y. 54S, N.Y. 17E, I-81S, I-84E, N.J. 23S, I-80N, I-95N, and the George Washington Bridge): With its 11 lakes extended like fingers (the Iroquois legend says that God wanted to leave his handprint on the most beautiful place in his creation), its famous vineyards with about 40 growers, its green hills, caves, gorges, and waterfalls, the Finger Lakes region draws more than half a million holidaymakers a year. As well as its beautiful landscapes, this quietly charming countryside offers a foothold in history, as the birthplace of some of the ideas and institutions that have helped to shape America: the abolition of slavery (Auburn), women's rights (Seneca Falls), and the Mormon church (Palmyra).

Head NE out of Manhattan by the George Washington Bridge, the Palisades Interstate Pkwy., and N.Y. 17 (also known as the Southern Tier Expwy.) on to I-81. Your first stop will be at ☀ **Syracuse,** capital of the lakes district, 270 mi. (430km) NE of New York, famed for its parks and its museums. Make a point of seeing the **Everson Museum of Art,** 401 Harrison St. (315/474-6064), open Tues–Sun, the first museum designed by I. M. Pei, with a fine collection of American painting and ceramics; the **Erie Canal Museum,** Erie Blvd. and Montgomery St. (315/471-0593), open Tues–Sun, with exhibits on the construction of the historic canal; and ⚓ **Onondaga Lake Park,** Onondaga Lake Pkwy. (315/451-7275), open daily May–Oct, where you'll find an interesting **Salt Museum** as well as a faithful reconstruction of **Fort Ste. Marie de Gannentaha,** the first camp set up here by the French in the 17th century.

After a stop at the delightful tourist town of **Skaneateles,** on the northern shore of the lake of the same name, go on to **Auburn** at the tip of **Owasco Lake,** a site settled by Native Americans since the 11th century. In the 19th century it had two famous residents: William H. Seward, the secretary of state who bought Alaska from the Russians for a trifling consideration (see "Introducing Alaska" in Chapter 57 on Anchorage), and Harriet Tubman, a former slave whose influence and determination were instrumental in bringing about abolition; she saved more than 300 black slaves in flight from their Southern masters through her network of secret helpers, the Underground Railroad. The ⚓ **Tubman House** at 180 South St. (315/253-2621), now a museum, may be visited by appointment only; don't miss it.

Some 16 miles (25km) farther west, ☀ **Seneca Falls** is a place of pilgrimage for American feminists; here, in 1848, was held the first Convention for Women's Rights. The ⚓ **National Women's Hall of Fame,** 76 Fall St. (315/568-2936), open Tues–Sun, commemorates two centuries of the struggle for equal rights, and pays tribute to such past leaders as Amelia Jenks Bloomer, Elizabeth Cady Stanton, Mary Cassatt, Abigail Adams, Helen Hayes, and Marian Anderson.

The route now runs along the left shore of **Cayuga Lake,** 40 mi. (64km) long, and after a stop to admire **Taughannock Falls,** higher than Niagara (215 ft/65m), you'll arrive in **Ithaca,** home of renowned ☀ **Cornell University** with 17,500 students. Visit the campus in its magnificent natural setting with two gorges formed by glacial runoff that cut through the campus and plummet about 100 ft. at their steepest point. The ⚓ **Herbert F. Johnson Museum,** Central Ave. (607/255-6464), open Tues–Sun, is an interesting art museum which you shouldn't miss. Another absolute must-see is the brand-new ⚓⚓ **Performing Arts Center** and its innovative architecture designed by James Stirling and Michael Wilford.

Going on to the west, you come next to ⚓⚓ **Watkins Glen,** at the southern tip of beautiful **Seneca Lake,** the deepest in the region (630 ft/192m). Best known for its race track and **racing-car museum,** at 110 N. Franklin St. (607/535-4202), open Thurs–Sun afternoon June–Aug (by appointment the rest of the year), the town is scored across by the impressive glens that give it its name. Don't fail to see it.

Now drive northward along the whole length of Seneca Lake as far as **Geneva;** if you enjoy fishing you'll want to know that summer visitors call it "the fisherman's paradise." ☀ **Canadaigua** is a little summer resort 17 mi. (27km) farther west at the tip of the lake of the same name; don't fail to stop at the **Sonnenberg Gardens,** a lovely 50-acre (20ha) landscaped park on N.Y. 21N, open daily May–Oct; also see the ⚓ **Granger Homestead,** 295 N. Main St. (716/394-1472), the splendidly restored 1816 house of Gideon Granger, postmaster general under Presidents Jefferson and Madison. Complete with period furniture and a collection of horse-drawn carriages.

History buffs are advised to turn aside to **Palmyra,** 16 mi. (25km) north, where in 1820 the prophet Joseph Smith had the vision of the angel Moroni that led him to found the Mormon religion. See his childhood home, now a museum, on Stafford Rd., open daily; also **Hill Cumorah,** the hill where the prophet is said to have found the golden pages of the Book of Mormon. Visitor Center on N.Y. 21 (315/597-5851), open daily.

Head on past Lake Canandaigua to ⚓⚓ **Hammondsport,** New York State's largest wine-growing center; the first vines were brought here from Germany and Switzerland in 1829. Many vineyards give conducted tours of their storehouses, among them **Bully Hill Vineyards,** Bully Hill Rd. via N.Y. 54A (607/868-3610), open Mon–Sat; and **Taylor Wineries,** on Pleasant Valley Rd. via N.Y. 54 (607/569-2111), open daily May–Oct (Mon–Sat the rest of the year), with the largest and finest cellars in the region. Two other places you won't want to miss here: the **Wine Museum of Greyton H. Taylor,** with everything about vines and wine, on G. H. Taylor Memorial Dr. via N.Y. 54A (607/868-4814), open daily May–Oct; and the **Glenn H. Curtiss Museum,** birthplace of one of the great early figures of aviation, now a historical museum, at Lake St. and Main St. (607/569-2160), open daily July–Sept (Mon–Sat in spring and fall, closed the rest of the year). Hammondsport shouldn't be bypassed.

Next stop is ⚲⚲ **Corning,** the world's glass capital, where the giant 200-in. (5m) mirror of the Mount Palomar telescope was cast. Don't miss the **Corning Glass Center,** Centerway (607/974-8271), open daily, with its fascinating museum containing a unique collection of 23,000 glass objects, some of them 3,500 years old. Also interesting is the ⚲ **Rockwell Museum,** Denison Pkwy. and Cedar St. (607/937-5386), specializing in western art with pictures by Remington, Russell, Bierstadt, etc., and also displaying the very fine glass collection of Baron Steuben. Open daily.

At the end of the tour lies ☀ **Elmira,** famous as Mark Twain's favorite vacation spot; the author of *Huckleberry Finn,* who came here regularly for 20 years, is buried in **Woodlawn Cemetery** on Walnut St. You should also see his ⚲ writing study on the campus of **Elmira College,** Park Pl. (607/734-3911), open by appointment only; a must.

Back to Manhattan by way of **Binghamton,** an industrial city at the confluence of the Chenango River and Susquehanna River; the **Roberson Center for the Arts and Sciences,** 30 Front St. (607/772-0660), open Tues–Sun, has interesting collections of art and historical material. Then through the foothills of the **Pocono Mountains.**

A trip of at least 4 to 5 days, ideal for nature lovers.

Where to Stay En Route

The following hotels, motels, and inns are recommended as suitable places for a stopover.

GENEVA ☀⚑⚑⚑ **Geneva on the Lake,** 1001 Lochland Rd., Geneva, NY 14456 (315/789-7190). 29 suites. Lovely old villa overlooking Lake Seneca; period furniture and romantic atmosphere. **VE**

☀⚑⚑ **Belhurst Castle,** Lochland Rd., Geneva, NY 14456 (315/781-0201). 12 rms. A small castle in the Romanesque style built on the shores of Lake Seneca in 1885 w. decor and furniture of the period. **M–E**

HIMROD The ⚑ **Rainbow Cove,** on N.Y. 14, Himrod, NY 14842 (607/243-7535). Inviting, likable small motel on Lake Seneca. Very good value. Closed Oct to mid-May. **I**

SKANEATELES The ☀⚑⚑ **Sherwood Inn,** 26 W. Genesee St., Skaneateles, NY 13152 (315/685-3405). 16 rms. Charming 1807 inn w. rest. on Lake Skaneateles. Good value. **I–M**

Where to Eat En Route

The restaurants and inns that follow are suitable places for a meal, if you're following the above itinerary.

ELMIRA HEIGHTS ☀⚑⚑⚑ **Pierce's 1894,** 228 Oakwood Ave. (607/734-2022). Dinner Tues–Sun, brunch Sun. Cuisine of a very high order in a lovely Victorian rest., run by the Pierce family since 1894. **I–M**

GENEVA The ☀ ♈♈ **Belhurst Castle,** on N.Y. 14 (315/781-0201). Impeccably prepared and served Continental cuisine in this small castle in the Romanesque style built on the shores of Lake Seneca in 1885 w. decor and furniture of the period; terrace on fine days. **I–M**

ITHACA ☀ ♈♈♈ **L'Auberge du Cochon Rouge,** 1152 Danby Rd. (607/273-3464). Dinner nightly, brunch Sun. Some of the best food in the region—magnificent, refined French cuisine. Elegant old farmhouse w. duck pond. **I–M**
♈♈ **Turback's,** 919 Elmira Rd. (607/272-6484). Dinner nightly, brunch Sun. Luxurious Victorian manor; very skilled Continental cuisine. **I**

SKANEATELES The ☀ ♈♈ **Sherwood Inn,** 26 W. Genesee St. (315/685-3405). Charming 1807 inn on Lake Skaneateles w. lake-view rest. and flawless traditional hotel cuisine. **I**

SYRACUSE ♈♈♈ **Pascale Wine Bar and Restaurant,** 304 Hawley Ave. (315/471-3040). Dinner only, Mon–Sat. Wonderful French food at painless prices, and an elegant Victorian setting, account for the success of this very good rest. **I–M**

TRUMANSBURG The ♈♈ **Taughannock Farms Inn,** on N.Y. 89 (607/387-7711). Dinner nightly, brunch Sun. In this old farmhouse overlooking Cayuga Lake and Taughannock Park, you'll be served excellent family cooking at reasonable prices. Very good value. **I–M**

🏛🏛🏛 **ADIRONDACK PARK** (806 mi./1,290km r.t. via the Saw Mill River Pkwy., Taconic State Pkwy., I-90W, U.S. 4N, N.Y. 29W, I-87N, N.Y. 9N, N.Y. 22N, N.Y. 86W, N.Y. 30S, N.Y. 8W, I-90E, N.Y. 28S, N.Y. 80E, I-90E, I-87S, Palisades Interstate Pkwy. South, and the George Washington Bridge): There are places steeped in history like Lake George, Saratoga, and Ticonderoga, but also, and just as important, there are 2,800 lakes, 1,200 mi. (1,920km) of rivers, thousands of miles of brooks and streams, 42 mountains more than 4,000 ft. (1,200m) high, deep forests, peaks crowned with snow in winter, dozens of campgrounds, 750 mi. (1,200km) of marked trails. Plus a **Visitor Center** situated on N.Y. 30 in Paul Smith's, N.Y., about 15 mi. (24km) north of Saranac Lake, open daily year round. The Adirondacks (from the Iroquois name for the Algonquin, "Ha-de-ron-dah," or "skin-eaters"), are a paradise for lovers of unspoiled nature.

Leaving Manhattan northward along the Henry Hudson, Saw Mill River, and Taconic State Pkwys., make your first stop 155 mi. (248km) from Manhattan at ☀ **Albany,** the capital of New York State. Visit the **State Capitol,** a fine 1898 French Renaissance-style building on State St. (518/474-2418), open daily, and the **State University** on its beautiful campus at Washington Ave. and Western Ave. (518/442-5571), open Mon–Fri. Also, take time to admire **Empire State Plaza,** one of the most successful complexes of modern architecture in the country, comprising a dozen striking structures devoted to administrative or cultural uses, including the **Performing Arts Center** (familiarly known as "the egg" on account of its shape), the 44-story **Corning Tower Building,** with an observation platform at the top, and the fascinating 🏛 **New York State Museum** (518/474-5877), open daily. There are a number of 🏛 architecturally interesting old buildings you should see, including the 1761 **Schuyler Mansion** at 32 Catherine St.; the 1798 **Ten Broeck Mansion,** 9 Ten Broeck St., open Wed–Sun; and **Historic Cherry Hill,** dating from 1787, at 523½ Pearl St., open Tues–Sun.

Then on to ☀ 🏛 **Saratoga National Historical Park,** where in engagements on September 19 and October 7, 1777, American forces under the command of Gen. Horatio Gates inflicted a decisive defeat on Gen. John Burgoyne's British army, as a result of which France decided to make common cause with the Americans. Visitor center-museum open daily (518/664-9821), and marked road around the battlefield. Don't miss it. Not far away is **Saratoga Springs,** whose renowned hot springs, two racecourses, and a polo ground attract every year a crown of race-goers—not to mention lovers of classical music and ballet: the ☀ **Saratoga Performing Arts Center,** S. Broadway (518/587-3330), is open July and Aug. Also see the very unusual ⚱ **Petrified Sea Gardens,** 3 mi. (5km) west on N.Y. 29 (518/584-2421), open daily late June through Aug, with its fossils of prehistoric plants.

Glens Falls, which owes its name to the falls on the Hudson south of the town, has a beautiful art museum, the **Hyde Collection** at 161 Warren St. (518/792-1761), open afternoons Tues–Sun, with many paintings by such masters as Rembrandt, Rubens, and Picasso. Between mid-July and Aug it is also the scene of the very popular ⚱ **Lake George Opera Festival** (for information, call 518/793-6641).

Continue on I-87N to ☀⚱ **Lake George,** a pretty little resort town at the southern end of the lake of the same name. **Fort William Henry Museum,** Canada St., open daily May–Oct, is an exact replica of a British fort built in 1755. The **Lake George Steamboat Co.,** Beach Rd. (518/668-5777), offers 1- to 4-hr. lake cruises, May–Oct.

Follow the lovely N.Y. 9N, which traces the shore of Lake George for almost 35 mi. (56km), to ☀🏛 **Ticonderoga,** another summer resort with historic interest. For almost two centuries it was the storm-center of countless battles and bloody engagements among Native Americans, French, British, Canadians, and Americans, witness the history of **Fort Ticonderoga,** built by the French in 1755 under the name of Fort Carillon and destroyed by the British in 1777, after it had been occupied by Ethan Allen and his Green Mountain Boys in the early morning of May 10, 1775. Now restored to its original condition and converted to a military museum, it should be visited by all history buffs; you'll find it on N.Y. 74 (518/585-2821), open daily mid-May to mid-Oct.

Next comes a 50-mi. (80km) scenic drive on N.Y. 9N and N.Y. 22N along the great and magnificent ☀ **Lake Champlain** as far as ☀⚱ **Ausable Chasm,** 200-ft. (60m) gorges carved by the Ausable River and spilling into Lake Champlain in a series of torrential falls, a sight to be seen. Continuing westward, you come upon some more spectacular gorges (like the **High Falls Gorge,** near **Wilmington,** on N.Y. 86), before you reach ☀🏛 **Lake Placid,** the famous resort town where the Winter Olympics have been held twice: in 1932 and 1980. With the 5,344-ft. (1,629m) crest of New York State's highest mountain, Mount Marcy, looming in the background, Lake Placid draws a full house of tourists in winter and summer alike.

Leaving Lake Placid, the route touches, like gems on a long necklace, the countless lakes and resort areas of the Adirondacks: **Saranac Lake, Tupper Lake, Long Lake, Blue Mountain Lake**—where you should be sure to visit the splendid ⚱ **Adirondack Museum,** devoted to the history of the region, on N.Y. 30 (518/352-7311), open daily mid-June to mid-Oct—before reaching ☀ 🏛 **Utica,** a small industrial city on the Mohawk River distinguished by possessing one of the finest art museums in the entire state, the **Munson-Williams-Proctor Institute,** 310 Genesee St. (315/797-0000), open Mon–Fri. Works of Picasso, Jackson Pollock, Kandinsky, Paul Klee, and Thomas Cole, and sculptures by Calder and Henry Moore among others. Don't miss it.

Last stop is ☀ 🏛 **Cooperstown,** on Otsego Lake, a town dear to all American sports fans because it was here, in 1839, that Gen. Abner Doubleday devised the game of baseball; that's why it is now the site of the ☀ **National Baseball Hall of Fame and Museum,** Main St. (607/547-9988), open daily, devoted to the history of the national sport and its greatest players—attendance topped 300,000 last year. Also see the **Farmer's Museum,** N.Y. 80N (607/547-2533), open daily May–Oct, illustrative of rural life in the 19th century; and **Fenimore House,** on N.Y. 80N (607/547-2533), open daily May–Oct, a lovely museum of American folklore dedicated to the writer James Fenimore Cooper, whose father founded the town in 1786. Don't miss it.

Then back to Manhattan on I-90 and I-87. This trip, to which you should devote 5 days at least, can easily be combined with the tour of the Hudson Valley, since both follow the same highways for part of their routes (see "Hudson Valley," above).

Where to Stay En Route

The following hotels, motels, and inns are recommended as suitable places for a stopover.

BLUE MOUNTAIN LAKE ⚑ **Hemlock Hall,** N.Y. 30, Blue Mountain Lake, NY 12812 (518/352-7706). 23 rms. Inviting little country motel on a lake. Closed Oct 15–May 15. **M–E**

BOLTON LANDING The ☼⚑⚑⚑ **Sagamore Omni Hotel,** N.Y. 9N, Bolton Landing, NY 12814 (518/644-9400; toll free, see Omni). 350 rms. Wonderful Victorian palace, built in 1883 and now a designated historic landmark. Wonderfully situated on Lake George. Elegant and distinguished. Open year round. **VE** (Modified American Plan)

COOPERSTOWN The ☼⚑⚑ **Otesaga Hotel,** Lake St., Cooperstown, NY 13326 (607/547-9331). 135 rms. Elegant, luxuriously furnished grand hotel in the Georgian style on Otsego Lake. Closed late Oct through Apr. **E–VE**
⚑ **Lake View Motel,** 6 mi. (10km) north on N.Y. 80, Cooperstown, NY 13326 (607/547-9740). 14 rms. Small, engaging hotel w. direct access to the lake. Closed Nov.–Apr. **I–M**

LAKE GEORGE ⚑⚑ **Dunham's Bay Lodge,** N.Y. 9N, Lake George, NY 12845 (518/656-9242). 44 rms. Modern, comfortable motel on Lake George. Closed Oct 15–May 15. **M–E**
⚑⚑ **Tahoe Beach Club,** N.Y. 9N, Lake George, NY 12845 (518/668-5711). 73 rms. Large, modern motel-marina on the lake. Closed from the end of Oct to mid-Apr. **I–M**

LAKE PLACID The ☼⚑⚑⚑ **Mirror Lake Inn,** 35 Mirror Lake Dr., Lake Placid, NY 12946 (518/523-2544). 100 rms. Luxury motel w. elegant Colonial interior on the lake. Rebuilt after a fire. Open year round. **M–E**
⚑ **Alpine Air Motel,** 99 Saranac Ave., Lake Placid, NY 12946 (518/523-9261). 24 rms. Small motel w. inviting cottages on a riverbank. **I**

LONG LAKE The ⚑ **Shamrock Motel,** N.Y. 30, Long Lake, NY 12847 (518/624-3861). 17 rms and cottages. Rustic but comfortable lakeside motel. Closed Oct–May. **I**

SARANAC LAKE The ☼⚑⚑ **Hotel Saranac,** 101 Main St., Saranac Lake, NY 12983 (518/891-2200). 92 rms. Venerable hotel built in the '20s, now run w. masterly touch by the pupils of the hotel school at Paul Smith's College. Open year round. **I–M**

SARATOGA SPRINGS The ☼⚑⚑ **Inn at Saratoga,** 231 Broadway, Saratoga Springs, NY 12866 (518/583-1890). 40 rms. Delightful late 19th-century inn, elegantly comfortable. Open year round. **M–E** (except Aug during race meet)
⚑ **Turf and Spa,** 140 Broadway, Saratoga Springs, NY 12866 (518/584-2550). 42 rms. Conventional but well-run motel. **I** (except Aug)–**M**

Where to Eat En Route

The following restaurants and inns are suitable places for a meal, if you're following the above itinerary.

ALBANY ※♈♈ **Jack's Oyster House,** 42 State St. (518/465-8854). Lunch/dinner daily. One of the city's oldest rests., passed from father to son since 1913. Excellent Continental food. **M**

GLENMONT The ♈♈ **Stone Ends Restaurant,** U.S. 9W (518/465-3178). Dinner only, Mon–Sat. Excellent contemporary American cuisine in a rustic mountain-chalet setting. **I–M**

LAKE GEORGE The ♈ **Trolley Steak and Seafood,** Canada St. (518/668-3165). Lunch/dinner daily; closed Nov to mid-May. Appealing steakhouse w. very attractive prices. Terrace in summer. **B–I**

LAKE PLACID The ♈ **Alpine Cellar,** Wilmington Rd. (518/523-2180). Dinner only, nightly; closed Apr to mid-May and Nov to mid-Dec. Bavarian setting and atmosphere. Very laudable German food. **I**

SARATOGA SPRINGS The ※♈♈ **Union Coach House,** 139 Union Ave. (518/584-6440). A coaching inn dating from 1872, as does the decor. Praiseworthy Continental cuisine. **M**

UTICA ♈♈ **The Metro,** 606 Huntington St. (315/733-4130). Lunch Mon–Fri, dinner Mon–Sat. Elegant rest. serving Continental cuisine, in a 1920s building which once housed a bank. **I**

CHAPTER 4

NIAGARA FALLS

□ □ □

Although of modest size (35 mi./55km long), the Niagara River ("thundering waters" in the Iroquois language) has the most famous, the most visited, and the most photographed falls in the world. Formed during the last glacial period 30,000–50,000 years ago, the falls, located midway between Lake Erie and Lake Ontario (which differ 324 ft./99m in water level), offer visitors a fabulous spectacle. Viewing the roaring waters of the **Horseshoe Falls** and the **American Falls** hurtling down from as high as 184 ft. (56m) is an awesome experience, especially from the Canadian side of the river—or better yet, on board the *Maid of the Mist* amid the swirling waters near the base of the falls.

Legend has it that the French explorer Jacques Cartier, in 1535, was the first "paleface" to be dazzled by the falls. Their "official discovery" 78 years later is credited to another Frenchman, Samuel de Champlain. Defining the border between New York State and the Canadian province of Ontario, the falls have become over the years one of the top tourist attractions in the United States (15 million visitors each year). Despite Oscar Wilde's celebrated witticism—"the wedding trip brings two disappointments, the second being Niagara Falls"—tens of thousands of newlyweds have made Niagara Falls the country's honeymoon capital since 1806. This pleasant tradition will no doubt endure for some time to come; while the falls recede about 11.8 inches (30cm) every year, it will take at least 125,000 years before they reach Lake Erie and totally disappear!

Although the falls were formally given parkland status by the state of New York in 1885, the chemical and metallurgical industries, heavy consumers of electricity (the power station built below the falls is one of the most powerful in the United States), pollute and disfigure the American side. Also distressing to the eye is the scene on the Canadian side of the falls, which has been gradually transformed into a giant amusement park of dismaying vulgarity. But in spite of these ecological affronts, the falls remain an incredible living spectacle, even in winter when the water is frozen. Maximum rate of flow is approximately 740,000 gallons (7,000 cubic meters) per second.

BASIC FACTS: State of New York. Area codes: U.S. side, 716; Canadian side, 416. ZIP Code: 14302. Time zone: eastern. First discovery by a European, 1535?/1613. Settled: 1806. Approximate population of Niagara Falls: American side, 72,000; Canadian side, 70,000.

CLIMATE: Summer temperatures are relatively high, averaging 77°F (25°C) in July and Aug, but much more tolerable and a lot less humid than in New York City. Spring and autumn, both quite brief, are sunny but chilly. Winters—from the end of Oct to the end of Apr—are glacial, to the point where the falls themselves are frozen.

DISTANCES: Boston, 480 mi. (768km); Cleveland, 200 mi (320km); Montréal, 421 mi. (674km); New York, 395 mi. (634km); Toronto, 145 mi. (232km); Washington, 425 mi. (680km).

ARRIVAL & TRANSIT INFORMATION

AIRPORT: Buffalo International Airport (BUF): 22 mi. (35km) SE. Information: 632-3115.

AIRLINES: American (856-7050), Continental (852-1233), Eastern (852-3170), Northwest (854-0903), United (856-2900), USAir (632-3000).

CITY LINK: The **cab** fare from Buffalo Airport to Niagara Falls is about $25–$30; time, 35–40 min. **Bus:** Niagara Scenic Lines (648-1500), departing every hour between 8:30am and 8:30pm, serves the major hotels of Niagara Falls; fare, $8 (American side) or $9 (Canadian side); time, 50–60 min.
 There is ample bus service in the Niagara Falls/border area (Metro Transit System: 855-7211); renting a car with unlimited mileage is thus not necessary unless you are planning an excursion to outlying places.

CAR RENTAL (at the Buffalo International Airport unless otherwise indicated): Avis (632-1808); Budget (632-4662); Dollar (631-9880); Hertz (632-4772); National (633-1000); Thrifty, 4646 Genesee St., Buffalo (634-5990).

LIMOUSINE SERVICES: Buffalo Limousine (835-4997), Carey Limousine (toll free 800/336-4646).

TAXIS: Although in theory you can hail a taxi on the street, the best way is to telephone **LaSalle Cab** (284-8833) or **United Cab** (285-9331).

TRAIN: Amtrak Station, Hyde Park Blvd. and Lockport Rd., Niagara Falls, N.Y. (285-4224). Area unsafe at night.

INTERCITY BUSES: Greyhound has bus stations on both sides of the border: **in the U.S.** at 343 4th St. at Wendell Way, Niagara Falls (716/282-1331); and **in Canada** at 6761 Oakes Dr., Niagara Falls (416/732-3501).

INFORMATION & TOURS

TOURIST INFORMATION: The **Niagara Falls Convention & Visitors Bureau,** (U.S.), 345 3rd St., Suite 101, Niagara Falls, NY 14303 (716/285-2400; toll free 800/338-7890).
 Niagara Falls Visitor & Convention Bureau (Canada), 4673 Ontario Ave., Suite 202, Niagara Falls, ON L2E 3R1 (416/356-6061).

GUIDED TOURS (AMERICAN SIDE): Gray Line Tours (bus) (716/694-3600): Guided tour of both sides of the falls and surrounding areas, serving major hotels.
 Maid of the Mist (boat), Prospect Tower (716/284-4233): Boat tour to the foot of the falls through clouds of foam and spray; passengers are furnished with rain slickers. This is an unforgettable experience, not to be missed. Daily May–Oct.
 Niagara Viewmobile, Prospect Point (716/282-0028): Tour by open-air shuttle system along the falls. Daily mid-May–mid-Oct.
 Rainbow Helicopter Tours (helicopter), 454 Main St. (716/284-2800): Tour of the falls by air, lasting 6–7 min.; $35. Impressive.

GUIDED TOURS (CANADIAN SIDE): Double Deck Tours (bus), 3957 Bossert Rd. (416/295-3051): Tour along the falls in an English double-decker bus. Pleasantly quaint.

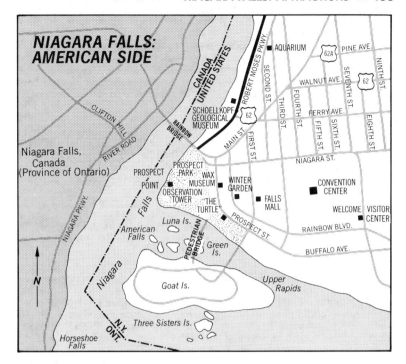

Gray Line Tours (bus), 6761 Oakes Dr. (416/354-4524).

Maid of the Mist (boat), Niagara River Pkwy. (416/358-5781): Boat tour to the foot of the falls through clouds of foam and spray; rain slickers furnished. An unforgettable experience, not to be missed. Daily May–Oct.

Niagara Helicopters (helicopter), 3731 Victoria Ave. (416/357-5672): Helicopter flights above the falls. Impressive. Year round.

SIGHTS, ATTRACTIONS & ACTIVITIES— AMERICAN SIDE

THE FALLS: ☼ ⚏ **American Falls,** between the east bank and Goat Island, 1,082 ft. (330m) wide, 184 ft. (56m) high. More headlong than the Canadian falls. Best viewing is in the morning from Prospect Point.

☼ ⚏ **Cave of the Winds,** at the foot of Goat Island (716/282-8979): Underground grotto at the foot of the American Falls. Spectacular observation point. Access is by elevator and then by tunnel. Wooden footbridges allow you to venture within a few feet of **Bridal Veil Fall** (slickers and rubber boots provided). Open daily, mid-May to mid-Oct. Don't miss this!

MUSEUMS: ⚏ **Aquarium of Niagara Falls,** 701 Whirlpool St. (716/285-3575): From piranhas and sharks to dolphins and electric eels, more than 2,000 marine animals from the world over can be seen here. The aquarium is of modern design and surrounded by beautiful gardens graced with outdoor sculpture. Worth seeing. Open daily.

⚏ **Native American Center for the Living Arts,** 25 Rainbow Mall (716/284-2427): Curiously designed in the shape of a tortoise's shell. Inside you'll find temporary art exhibitions, Native American crafts boutiques, a restaurant, etc. Worth a look. Open daily in summer, Tues–Sun the rest of the year.

☀ 🔔 **Schoellkopf Geological Museum,** Prospect Park (716/278-1780): Features the geological history of the falls. Interesting as much for its spiral design as for its collection of minerals tracing the evolution of the falls area over 500 million years. Lovely view of the Niagara River gorge. Altogether captivating. Open daily in summer, Wed–Sun the rest of the year.

PANORAMAS: ☀ 📷 **Goat Island,** in the Niagara River between the American and Canadian sides: Offers a striking view of the Horseshoe Falls from **Terrapin Point,** located at the extreme SW tip of the island. You'll enjoy an equally fantastic vista of the American falls, and especially the Bridal Veil Falls, from tiny **Luna Island,** reached by footbridge from the extreme NW point of Goat Island. Truly a must for every visitor.

☀ 🔭 **Prospect Point Observation Tower,** Prospect Park (716/278-1770): A 282-ft. (86m) tower with a long footbridge over the void offering a magnificent scenic view of the American Falls. The *Maid of the Mist* tour boat leaves from the foot of the tower; see "Guided Tours (American Side)," above. Absolutely must be seen. Open daily.

PARKS & GARDENS: ☀ 📷 **Goat Island,** in the Niagara River between the American and Canadian sides: Auto and footbridges permit access to this little island planted squarely in the middle of the roaring Niagara River. Visitors will enjoy both splendid viewing and the chance for a pleasant stroll among the island's trees and flowers. It was here, in times past, that local Native American tribes practiced human sacrifice and buried their chiefs. Not to be missed.

🔔 **Wintergarden,** Rainbow Blvd. (716/278-8196): Immense seven-story greenhouse of ultramodern design. More than 7,000 plants and tropical trees flourish within the futuristic decor created by overhead walkways, glass elevators, waterfalls, and lagoons. Very pleasant atmosphere. Open daily.

SPECIAL EVENTS: Intertribal Pow-Wow (mid-May): Festival of Native American art and culture with hundreds of participants from all the tribes of North America. Dances, singing, handcraft exhibitions, Native American food. This colorful event takes place at the Native American center for the Living Arts, American side. Call 716/284-2427 for information.

Artpark, 7 mi. (11km) north on Robert Moses Pkwy. (June–Sept): Modern-art festival displaying current, original works of art in a vast 200-acre (80ha) park setting. Jazz, dance, opera, theater. For information, call 716/754-9001.

Tuscarora Nation Picnic, 5 mi. (8km) NE on N.Y. 104. (mid-July): Annual fair of the Tuscarora Native American reservation. Shows, dances, craft exhibitions.

Festival of Lights (late Nov to early Jan): Animated displays, nightly entertainment and light shows, parades, fireworks. An annual salute to winter.

SIGHTS, ATTRACTIONS & ACTIVITIES—
CANADIAN SIDE

THE FALLS: ☀ 📷 **Horseshoe Falls,** between the west bank and Goat Island, 2,099 ft. (640m) across, 176 ft. (54m) high. The most spectacular falls; in sunny weather magnificent rainbows form above it, especially during the afternoon. Strikingly illuminated evenings by four-billion-candlepower floodlights. Can be viewed clearly from **Table Rock.**

MUSEUMS: ☼ ⚲ **Niagara Falls Museum,** 5651 River Rd. (416/356-2151): One of the oldest museums in North America (1827). Note especially the display tracing the history of daredevil attempts to survive a trip over the falls in an amazing variety of contraptions (small boats, barrels, inner tubes). It's also worth taking a look at the picturesque bric-a-brac of the other exhibits. Open daily in summer; weekends the rest of the year.

PANORAMAS: ⚲ **Niagara Spanish Aerocar,** Niagara River Pkwy., 3½ mi. (5km) north (416/354-5711): A sort of open cable car. Its 1,800-ft. (549m) route goes over the Niagara River rapids. Worth seeing. Open daily mid-April to mid-Oct.

⚲ **Minolta Tower,** 6732 Oakes Dr. (416/356-1501): A 325-ft. (99m) tower with a 360° panoramic view of the falls. Superb observation point. Open daily.

☼ ⚲⚲ **Skylon Tower,** 5200 Robinson St. (416/356-2651): Soaring to 518 ft. (158m), the tower offers unobstructed viewing and the most beautiful bird's-eye view of both the American and the Canadian falls. The revolving restaurant at the top of the tower is mediocre, but don't miss the views! Open daily.

☼ ⚲⚲⚲ **Table Rock,** Queen Victoria Park, Niagara River Pkwy. (416/358-3268): Awesome viewing from this observation platform located 25 ft. (8m) above the river's surface at the base of the Canadian falls. This is a sight not to be missed (slickers and rubber boots are furnished). Open daily.

PARKS & GARDENS: **Queen Victoria Park,** Niagara River Pkwy.: A lovely English garden with flower-planted slopes stretching along the Niagara River. Splendid panoramic view of the American and Horseshoe Falls. A must-see.

SHOPPING: **Maple Leaf Village,** 5685 Falls Ave. (416/374-4444): Both an amusement park and a giant shopping center. An additional feature is the 350-ft. (107m) Kodak observation tower. Shops, food stalls, restaurant. Open daily. **Skylon Centre,** 5200 Robinson St. (416/356-2651): Shops, restaurants, a museum of automatons, and the **Imax Theatre,** an astonishing pyramidal movie house with a giant screen six stories tall. Worth a look. A stone's throw from the falls. Open daily.

THEME PARKS: **Marineland,** 7657 Portage Rd., 1 mi. (1.6km) south of the falls (416/356-9565): Modern zoo with performing animal shows, from bears to killer whales. Amusement park with gigantic roller coaster. Open daily year round.

ACCOMMODATIONS

A Note on Accommodations: Room rates in Niagara Falls are coded as follows: **VE,** Very Expensive ($140 and up); **E,** Expensive ($90–$140); **M,** Moderate ($60–$90); **I,** Inexpensive ($30–$60); **B,** Budget (up to $30). A listing of toll-free numbers is in the Appendix.

Personal Favorites (in order of preference)

⚲⚲⚲ **Radisson Niagara** (dwntwn), Mall and 3rd St., Niagara Falls, NY 14303 (716/285-3361; toll free, see Radisson). 396 rms, A/C, color TV, in-rm movies. AE, CB, DC, MC, V. Gar. $2, pool, health club, sauna, rest., coffee shop, bars, rm svce, nightclub, free crib. *Note:* Modern, functional hotel in the heart of the dwntwn area. Very complete facilities; spacious rms, some w. refrigerators; very efficient svce, pleasant pool. Favored by groups and convention-goers (direct access to the Convention Center). A 5-min. walk from the falls. **E–VE,** but lower rates off-season.

₪ ₪ ₪ **Oakes Inn** (dwntwn), 6546 Buchanan Ave., Niagara Falls, ON
₪ ₪ ₪ L2G 3W2, Canada (416/358-5926). 167 rms, A/C, color
TV, in-rm movies. AE, CB, DC, MC, V. Free parking, two pools, sauna, health
club, miniature golf, rest., bar, rm svce, disco, crib $10. *Note:* Large 12-story
modern hotel overlooking Horseshoe Falls on one of the best sites in the entire
city. Observation deck on top. Large, comfortable rms (the best—especially on
the top three floors—look out on the falls). Cheerful reception and svce. A fine
place. **M–E,** but lower rates off-season.

₪ ₪ **Michael's Inn** (dwntwn), 5599 River Rd., Niagara Falls, ON
₪ ₪ L2E 3H3, Canada (416/354-2727). 130 rms, A/C, cable col-
or TV. AE, CB, DC, MC, V. Free parking, sauna, rest. (Embers Open Hearth),
bar, rm svce, crib $10. *Note:* One of the best locations in Niagara Falls. Many rms
have a view of the falls or of the Niagara River; some have refrigerators. Honeymoon Suite, rather kitsch w. heart-shaped tubs for two. Modern and comfortable. Courteous, pleasant reception. Good steakhouse. Across from the Rainbow
Bridge. **M–E,** but lower rates off-season.

₪ ₪ **Ramada Inn** (nr. dwntwn), 401 Buffalo Ave., Niagara Falls,
₪ ₪ NY 14303 (716/285-2541; toll free, see Ramada Inns). 195
rms, A/C, color TV, in-rm movies. AE, CB, DC, MC, V. Free parking, pool,
bike rental, rest. (Circle), bar, rm svce, disco, free crib. *Note:* A classic motel,
modern and comfortable, a few steps away from the Convention Center. The terrace overlooks the Niagara River. Spacious rms w. balconies. Very acceptable rest.
Frequented by groups and conventioneers. Good value. A 5-min. walk from the
falls. **M–E,** but lower rates off-season.

₪ ₪ **Days Inn** (dwntwn), 201 Rainbow Blvd., Niagara Falls, NY
₪ ₪ 14303 (716/285-9321; toll free, see Days Inn). 220 rms,
A/C, color TV. AE, CB, DC, MC, V. Free parking, rest., bar, rm svce, disco, crib
$3. *Note:* Antiquated but well-maintained hotel w. a view of the Niagara River
rapids. Spacious rms, some w. refrigerators. Friendly reception and service. Favored by groups and organized tours. Two minutes' walk from the base of the
falls. Good value overall. **M–E,** but lower rates off-season.

₪ **Cascade Inn** (dwntwn), 5305 Murray St., Niagara Falls, ON
₪ L2G 2J3, Canada (416/354-2796). 67 rms, A/C, color TV,
in-rm movies. AE, CB, DC, MC, V. Free parking, rest. (breakfast only), bar,
rm svce, free crib. *Note:* Pleasant little motel open year round, close to the
Skylon Tower. Comfortable and well maintained. Some rms have balconies and
a view of the falls. Three minutes by foot from the falls. **M,** but lower rates off-
season.

₪ **Budget Host Motel** (dwntwn), 219 4th St., Niagara Falls, NY
₪ 14303 (716/282-1734). 57 rms, A/C, color TV. AE, CB,
DC, MC, V. Free parking, 24-hr. coffee shop adj., valet svce, crib $4. *Note:* Small
modern motel very nr. the falls and the Convention Center. Huge, comfortable
rms; friendly reception and svce. Very good value. **I–M**

Other Accommodations (from top bracket to budget)

₪ ₪ ₪ **Clarion Old Stone Inn** (dwntwn), 5425 Robinson St., Niagara
₪ ₪ ₪ Falls, ON L2G 7L6, Canada (416/357-1234; toll free, see
Clarion). 114 rms, A/C, color TV, in-rm movies. AE, CB, DC, MC, V. Free
parking, two pools, sauna, rest. (Millery Room), coffee shop, bar, rm svce, crib
$10. *Note:* Elegant country-style motel at the foot of the Skylon Tower; entirely
redecorated and refurnished. Spacious, very comfortable rms w. private balconies or patios. Very good svce; acceptable rest. Five-min. walk from the falls.

₪ ₪ **Best Western Your Host** (nr. dwntwn), 5551 Murray Hill St.,
₪ ₪ Niagara Falls, ON L2G 2J4, Canada (416/356-0551; toll free,
see Best Western). 280 rms, A/C, color TV, in-rm movies. AE, CB, DC, MC, V.
Free parking, two pools, saunas, rest. (Coach Room), coffee shop, bar, rm svce,
free crib. *Note:* Huge functional six-story motel close to the falls. Comfortable
rms w. private balconies or patios and refrigerators (some rather cramped). Good

svce. Ideal for families. The Skylon Tower is close by. **E**, but lower rates off-season.

Holiday Inn Downtown (dwntwn), 114 Buffalo Ave., Niagara Falls, NY 14303 (716/285-2521; toll free, see Holiday Inns). 194 rms, A/C, color TV, in-rm movies. AE, CB, DC, MC, V. Free parking, pool, health club, sauna, holidome (indoor recreation center), rest, bar, rm svce, disco. *Note:* Typical Holiday Inn, 2-min. walk from the falls. Functional comfort. Good facilities. Clientele of groups and organized tours. Rates seem high for a plain motel. Excellent location for visiting the falls. **E**, but lower rates off-season.

Inn at the Falls (formerly the Radisson; dwntwn), 240 Rainbow Blvd., Niagara Falls, NY 14301 (716/282-1212). 217 rms, A/C, color TV, in-rm movies. AE, CB, DC, MC, V. Free parking, pool, rest. (Wintergarden), coffee shop, bar, rm svce, disco, hrdrsr, boutiques. *Note:* Big new motel adjacent to the Wintergarden. Welcoming, comfortable rooms. Very acceptable rest. Good svce. Frequented by business travelers and groups (very close to the Convention Center). 3 min. on foot to the falls. **M–E**, but lower rates off-season.

Quality Inn Rainbow Bridge (dwntwn), 443 Main St., Niagara Falls, NY 14301 (716/284-8801; toll free, see Quality Inns). 166 rms, A/C, color TV, in-rm movies. AE, CB, DC, MC, V. Free parking, pool, rest., bar, valet svce, disco, crib $8. *Note:* A comfortable motel, recently renovated. Middling rest. Clientele mainly groups and organized tours. 5-min. walk from the falls. Good value overall. Right in the middle of dwntwn. **M**, but lower rates off-season.

Ameri-Cana Motor Inn (nr. dwntwn), 8444 Lundy's Lane, Niagara Falls, ON L2H 1H4, Canada (416/356-8444; toll free 800/263-3508). 120 rms, A/C, color TV, in-rm movies. AE, MC, V. Free parking, pool, two tennis courts, rest. (V.I.P.), coffee shop, bar, rm svce, free crib. *Note:* Classic type of motel, but very well maintained and surrounded by 25 acres (10ha) of lawns and gardens. It's 15 min. by car to the falls; there's also free shuttle svce during the summer. Spacious, comfortable rms. The rest. is adequate. Ideal for families. Generally a group clientele. Good value. **I–M**, but lower rates off-season.

Lincoln Motor Inn (nr. dwntwn), 6417 Main St. (Portage Rd.), Niagara Falls, ON L2G 5Y3, Canada (416/356-1748). 60 rms, A/C, color TV, in-rm movies. AE, MC, V. Free parking, pool, rest. (Traveller's Delight), bar, crib $5. *Note:* Comfortable, well-kept little motel 5 min. by car from the falls. The rms are spacious; the rest. is adequate. Friendly reception. Good value. **I–M**, but lower rates off-season.

Hotels in the Vicinity

Holiday Inn Conference Center (vic.), 100 Whitehaven Rd. (at E. River), Grand Island, NY 14072 (716/773-1111; toll free, see Holiday Inns). 262 rms, A/C, color TV, in-rm movies. AE, CB, DC, MC, V. Free parking, two pools, health club, sauna, golf, two tennis courts, putting green, marina, fishing, cross-country skiing in winter, rest., coffee shop, bar, rm svce, disco, free crib. *Note:* Large, modern, comfortable six-story motel on the banks of the Niagara River. Ideal for physical-fitness buffs. Pleasant rms w. balconies (some w. refrigerators); good svce. Holiday Inn style, only better. Groups and conventioneers make up much of the clientele. It's 15-min. driving distance from the falls or from Buffalo Airport. **M–E**, but lower rates off-season.

YMCAs/Youth Hostels

Niagara Falls Frontier Hostel (nr. dwntwn), 1101 Ferry Ave. (at Memorial Pkwy.), Niagara Falls, NY 14301 (716/282-3700): Youth hostel with 44 beds. Close to the Falls.

Niagara Falls International Hostel (vic.), 4699 Zimmerman Ave., Niagara

Falls, ON L2E 3M7 Canada (416/357-0770). 38 beds. Comfortable Tudor-style building.

YMCA (nr. dwntwn), 1317 Portage Rd., Niagara Falls, NY 14301 (716/285-8491): Men only. 58 rms, gym, pool.

RESTAURANTS

A Note on Restaurant Prices: Niagara Falls restaurant prices, per person, excluding drinks and service charges, are coded as follows: **VE**, Very Expensive ($60 and up); **E**, Expensive ($40–$60); **M**, Moderate ($25–$40); **I**, Inexpensive ($15–$25); **B**, Budget (up to $15).

Personal Favorites (in order of preference)

Ports of Call (nr. dwntwn), 3004 Niagara Ave. at 30th St., Niagara Falls, NY (716/285-7787). A/C. Dinner only, nightly. AE, CB, DC, MC, V. Jkt. *Specialties:* steak, prime rib, fresh seafood. *Note:* One of the most popular rests. on the American side. Very pleasing antique decor, carefully prepared food, romantic, intimate atmosphere. Very good svce. Next door is the Bakery nightclub. Resv. advised. An 8-min. drive from dwntwn. *Steak/American.* **I–M**

Victoria Park (dwntwn), Niagara Pkwy., Queen Victoria Park, Niagara Falls, Ont. (416/356-2217). Lunch/dinner daily; closed mid-Oct to mid-May. AE, MC, V. *Specialties:* fresh salmon, roast beef, homemade pastry. *Note:* Venerable Victorian-style rest. w. open terrace facing the park and the falls. Pleasant gardens. Rather pretentious cuisine. Excellent svce. *Continental.* **I**

Donna Felicia (vic.), 490 Center St., Lewiston, N.Y. (716/754-7901). A/C. Dinner nightly; closed Mon Sept–May, Thanksgiving, Dec 25, and the first three weeks in Jan. AE, MC, V. Jkt. *Specialties:* fettuccine Alfredo, filet of sole Florentine, veal cutlet al Nero, manicotti del mare. Good desserts. *Note:* One of the best tables in the region, featuring solid Italian cooking and good homemade pasta. The sauces are a bit too rich. Pleasant rustic decor; good svce. A 10-min. drive from the falls. Resv. advised. *Italian.* **I–M**

The Happy Wanderer (dwntwn), 6405 Stanley St., Niagara Falls, Ont. (416/354-9825). A/C. Lunch/dinner daily; closed hols. AE, DC, MC, V. *Specialties:* wienerschnitzel, sauerbraten, rouladen, schweinebraten. *Note:* Typical Bavarian-style chalet 2 min. from the falls. Rather kitschy interior decor. A classic of its kind for over 20 years. The German cuisine is hearty and the servings generous. *German.* **I**

Embers Open Hearth (dwntwn), in Michael's Inn (see "Accommodations," above) (416/354-2727). A/C. Breakfast/lunch/dinner daily; closed Dec. 25. AE, CB, DC, MC, V. *Specialties:* steak, prime rib, roast chicken, roast piglet. *Note:* Excellent broiled meats and spitted fowl, prepared while you watch, are the main attractions of this rest. Highly regarded by Niagara Falls residents. Honest, unimaginative cuisine. Diligent svce, good value. *Steak/American.* **I**

Riverside Inn (vic.), 115 Water St., Lewiston, N.Y. (716/754-8206). A/C. Lunch Mon–Sat, dinner nightly. AE, MC, V. *Specialties:* Alaska king crab, roast beef, steak, catch of the day. *Note:* Charming rustic inn on the American side of the Niagara River. Conventional, no-frills cuisine. Good wine list. Popular locally. Resv. advised. *Steak/Seafood.* **I**

Other Restaurants (from top bracket to budget)

Clarkson House (vic.), 810 Center St., Lewiston, N.Y. (716/754-4544). A/C. Dinner only, Tues–Sun; closed Dec 25. AE, MC, V. Jkt. *Specialties:* char-broiled steak, lamb chops, Maine lobster, roast beef. Good homemade desserts. *Note:* Old inn dating from the 19th century and retaining the elegant decor of that era. The cooking, however, is uneven. Popular w. local residents. 10 min. from Niagara Falls. Resv. desirable. *Steak.* **I-M**

🍸🍴 **Red Coach Inn** (dwntwn), 2 Buffalo Ave., Niagara Falls, N.Y. (716/282-1459). A/C. Lunch/dinner daily; closed Dec 25. AE, MC, V. Jkt. *Specialties:* trout meunière, roast duck, roast beef, veal boursin, chicken alouette. Good wine list. *Note:* Very pleasant decor in the style of an old English inn. During the summer, diners on the outdoor terrace enjoy a view of the Niagara River rapids. The cooking is respectable, the svce efficient. Resv. recommended. Heavily patronized by tourists. *Continental/American.* **I**

🍷 **Queenston Heights** (vic.), 6 mi. (9.5km) north on Niagara Pkwy., Niagara Falls, Ont. (416/262-4274). A/C. AE, MC, V. Lunch/dinner daily, brunch Sun; closed Dec 25. *Specialties:* ribs, roast beef, roast pork, leg of lamb, quail, rabbit stew. *Note:* Lovely view of the Niagara River from the glassed-in terrace. Tudor decor, w. a pleasant patio for summer dining. The cooking is estimable and the svce friendly. A 10-min. drive from the falls. Resv. advised. *Continental.* **I**

🍷 **Suisha Gardens** (dwntwn), 5705 Falls Ave., Niagara Falls, Ont. (416/357-2660). A/C. Lunch daily during the summer, dinner nightly year round; closed Dec 25. AE, CB, DC, MC, V. Jkt. *Specialties:* tempura, sukiyaki, teriyaki. *Note:* Located on the second floor of the Maple Leaf Village Shopping Center, Suisha is the only Japanese restaurant in Niagara Falls worthy of the name. The cuisine is 100% authentic, although the decor is all-purpose Oriental. The cooks show off their dexterity w. the chopping knife right in front of your eyes. Resv. advised during the summer and on wknds. *Japanese.* **I**

🍷 **Alps** (nr. dwntwn), 1555 Military Rd., Niagara Falls, N.Y. (716/297-8990). A/C. Lunch/dinner Tues–Sun (until 2am). AE, CB, DC, MC, V. *Specialties:* roast beef, Greek dishes, lobster, baklava. *Note:* Some good Greek-inspired dishes in a rest. whose decor suggests a mountain chalet. The quality of the cooking doesn't seem to suffer much from this curious mix of styles. *American/Greek.* **B-I**

🍷 **Carlos O'Brians** (dwntwn), 5645 Victoria Ave., Niagara Falls, Ont. (416/357-1283). A/C. Lunch/dinner daily (until midnight); closed Mon Nov. to late March and Dec 25. AE, DC, MC, V. *Specialties:* steak, prime rib, catch of the day, shellfish. *Note:* Pleasant tavern w. inviting rustic decor. Good broiled prime cuts and fish dishes. Relaxed atmosphere, friendly svce. Popular w. the locals. Resv. suggested wknds. *Steak/Seafood.* **B-I**

Como Restaurant (nr. dwntwn), 2220 Pine Ave., Niagara Falls, N.Y. (716/285-9341). A/C. Lunch/dinner daily (until midnight); closed Dec 25. AE, MC, V. *Specialties:* homemade pasta, Italian dishes, steaks, sandwiches. *Note:* Both a deli and an Italian rest., this establishment run by the same family since 1927 has become a local institution. You'll enjoy good, honest Italian-American cooking in a pleasant, relaxed atmosphere. Excellent value. 8 min. from dwntwn. *Italian/American.* **B-I**

🍷 **John's Flaming Hearth** (nr. dwntwn), 1965 Military Rd., Niagara Falls, N.Y. (716/297-1414). A/C. Lunch/dinner daily. AE, DC, MC, V. *Specialties:* steak, surf and turf (steak and lobster), catch of the day, pumpkin ice-cream pie. *Note:* Enormous rest. 10 min. from the falls. A true local institution. The USSR's Premier Kosygin ate here during his visit to the States in 1967. Good value. Usually crowded and noisy. Pleasant atmosphere. *Steak/Seafood.* **B-I**

🍷 **Ye Olde Barn** (nr. dwntwn), 7280 Lundy's Lane, Niagara Falls, Ont. (416/356-7075). A/C. Breakfast/lunch/dinner daily; closed Dec 25 and Jan 1. AE, DC, MC, V. *Specialties:* barbecued ribs, catch of the day, roast chicken. *Note:* Excellent barbecued ribs in a setting resembling a rustic old barn, as the name suggests. Exposed beams enhance the comfortable, pleasing ambience. Each year the Barn serves over 60,000 lbs. (27,200kg) of barbecued spareribs. Very good svce. An excellent place. 10 min. from dwntwn. *American/Seafood.* **B–I**

In the Vicinity

⛅🍷 **Schimschack's** (vic.), 2943 Upper Mountain Rd., Sanborn, N.Y. (716/731-4111). A/C. Dinner nightly, brunch Sun; closed Mon–Tues Dec–Apr, also Dec 24–25. AE, CB, DC, MC, V. Jkt. *Specialties:* Florida stone crab (in season), charcoal-broiled baby back ribs, steak, catch of the day, peanut-butter pie. *Note:* Located on the heights overlooking Lake Ontario—on a clear day you can see Toronto—this rest. offers excellent country cooking. Colonial-style decor w. a terraced dining room. Legend holds that Marilyn Monroe first met Joe Di Maggio here during the filming of the movie *Niagara.* Good svce. Definitely worth the 20-min. drive from Niagara Falls (via N.Y. 104, N.Y. 31, and N.Y. 429). *Steak/Seafood.* **I–M**

NEARBY EXCURSIONS IN NEW YORK STATE

⛅ **OLD FORT NIAGARA** (14 mi./22km north on Robert Moses Pkwy.) (716/745-7611): French military fortress dating from 1726; its well-preserved fortifications tower above Lake Ontario. Occupies the site of an earlier fortress built in 1679. Numerous artillery pieces from bygone eras are on display in the fort **museum,** and in the summer there are military parades featuring soldiers in period uniforms. Fort Niagara played an important role in the War of 1812. Worth a side trip. Open daily year round.

GRAND ISLAND (6 mi./9km south on I-190): Very popular summer vacation spot. Numerous parks, campsites, and picnic areas dot this 7½- by 5½-mi. (12- by 9km) island located in the middle of the Niagara River upstream from the falls. Amusement park—**Fantasy Island,** 2400 Grand Island Blvd. (716/773-7591)—open daily in summer.

⛅ **NIAGARA POWER PROJECT** (5 mi./8km north via Lewiston Rd./N.Y. 104) (716/285-3211): Inaugurated in 1963, this is one of the most powerful hydroelectric power stations in the U.S.; with a continuous output of 2.5 million kilowatts per hour, it can more than meet all the electricity needs of a city the size of Chicago. There's an arresting panoramic view of the river gorge from the **observation platform,** and an interesting model of the power station in the **Visitor Center.** Don't miss seeing this. Open daily.

NEARBY EXCURSIONS IN CANADA

⛅ **FORT GEORGE** (14 mi./23km north on the Niagara River Pkwy.) (416/468-4257): Constructed in 1796, this imposing fortress, sheltered behind massive ramparts, was formerly the principal British stronghold along the Canadian frontier. Consists of 12 restored buildings. Particularly active during the War of 1812. Open daily mid-May through Oct; visit by appointment during the rest of the year. An absolute must-see.

⛅ **NIAGARA-ON-THE-LAKE** (14 mi./22km north on the Niagara River Pkwy.): Formerly the capital of Upper Canada, this picturesque town founded in 1776 is one of the region's main tourist attractions. Built on a lovely site along Lake Ontario, the town contains dozens of carefully restored old houses (the town was put to the torch in 1813 during the second British-American war). Charming Edwardian-vintage ambience.

The **Shaw Festival Theatre** is very popular in the summer. For information, call 416/468-2172.

Visit not to be missed.

Where to Stay & Eat

Two 19th-century inns are highly recommended:

☀ ♟♟ **Pillar & Post Inn,** King St. and John St., Niagara-on-the-Lake, ON L0S 1J0 (416/468-2123). 91 rms. Also a good rest. **M–E**

♟♟ **Prince of Wales,** 6 Picton St., Niagara-on-the-Lake, ON L0S 1J0 (416/468-3246): 104 rms. Also a very decent rest. **M–E**

⛦ **WHIRLPOOL RAPIDS** (2 mi./3.5km north on the Niagara River Pkwy.): Very lovely view of the Niagara River's rapids and whirlpools. Should be seen.

CHAPTER 5

THE ATLANTIC COAST

□ □ □

From the Canadian Border to New York City

The Atlantic seaboard, for a stretch of some 900 mi. (1,400km) between the border with the Canadian province of New Brunswick and New York City, is at once the historic cradle of the United States, the theater of its seafaring destiny, and an eye-opening testimony to its diverse countrysides and landscapes.

The rocky, jagged shores of **Maine;** the gentle, eye-pleasing sands of **Long Island Sound** or the dunes of **Cape Cod;** the little fishing ports and pleasure harbors of New England with their innumerable churches and old brick or pastel-washed frame houses, such as **Bar Harbor, Mystic, Gloucester,** and **New Bedford,** are a wonderful background to the giant megapolis of Boston and New York. The stark Canadian winters and blizzards of **Acadia National Park** will help take your mind off New York's hot, sticky summers. And the futurist high-rises of Boston and New York must share your attention with some of the oldest buildings in this country, some of them going back more than 300 years. For it was along this coast, which you can drive from end to end in a matter of hours, that America first saw the light. From **Plymouth,** where the Pilgrims landed, the earliest permanent settlements in the northern U.S. are strung out like beads on a necklace: **Hartford** (1623), **New York** (1626), **Salem** (1626), **Boston** (1630), **Cambridge** (1630), **Portland** (1631), **Newburyport** (1635), **Providence** (1636), **New Haven** (1638), **Hyannis** (1639), and so on. The Atlantic seaboard between New York and Boston is, to this day, that part of the country most thickly populated by immigrants from the Old World and their descendants.

Besides these cities and history-laden harbor towns, there is much to attract lovers of the seashore, from the endless beaches of Massachusetts to the dozens of islands, big and little, scattered along the coast—including **Monhegan Island,** offshore from Maine, where according to some historians the Viking Leif Ericson made landfall around the year 1000, almost 500 years before Christopher Columbus "discovered" America. Big-game fishermen can indulge their passion at **Martha's Vineyard, Marblehead,** and **Nantucket Island,** all three also fashionable resorts. Art enthusiasts will not fail to visit such museum towns as **Portsmouth** and above all **Newport,** with its dream mansions; Newport, long the scene of the America's Cup races, is also well known for its regattas (see Chapter 1 on Boston, Chapter 2 on Cape Cod, and Chapter 3 on New York).

BASIC FACTS: States of Maine, New Hampshire, Massachusetts, Rhode Island, Connecticut, and New York. Area codes: 207 (Maine), 603 (New Hampshire), 617 and 518 (Massachusetts), 401 (Rhode Island), 203 (Connecticut), and 212, 718, 914, and 516 (New York). Time zone: eastern. Distance as the crow flies from New York City to the Canadian border at Calais, Maine: 810 mi. (1,300km).

CLIMATE: With the cold Labrador Current washing its entire coastline, the climate of the New England littoral tends to extremes. Harsh and snowy—indeed, in the case of Maine or New Hampshire, downright icy—winters (Jan mean temperature, 21°F/−6°C) are followed by a short, temperate spring and a summer that is rarely too hot but often very humid, particularly in the coastal strip from New York City to Cape Cod (avg. temperature for July, 69°F/21°C). By far the best time to visit the Atlantic coast is the fall, with its crisp, dry days (about 59°F/15°C), to say nothing of the glorious coloring of the leaves during the "Indian summer." Except in late summer and fall you'll do well to bring your umbrella.

ARRIVAL & TRANSIT INFORMATION

AIRPORTS: The **Bangor** International Airport (BGR), 2 mi. (3.5km) NW.
Boston: Logan International Airport (BOS) (see Chapter 1 on Boston).
Hartford: Bradley International Airport (BDL), 11 mi. (17km) north.
New York: John F. Kennedy International Airport (JFK), La Guardia Airport (LGA), and Newark International Airport (EWR) (see Chapter 3 on New York).
Portland: International Jet Port (PWM), 2 mi. (3km) west.
Providence: T. F. Green State Airport (PVD), 7 mi. (11km) south.

U.S. & FOREIGN AIRLINES: Hartford (area code 203): Air Canada (toll free 800/422-6232), American (527-5141), Continental (549-3673), Delta (527-1811), Eastern (525-0141), TWA (563-9943), United (522-4131), and USAir (522-2161).
Providence (area code 401): American (272-1200), Continental (351-7020), Eastern (831-4460), United (831-6950), and USAir (274-5600).
Boston, Cape Cod, New York: See Chapters 1, 2, and 3.

BUS OR CAR RENTAL? The Greyhound Bus Company has excellent service along the entire coast from New York to the Canadian border. However, the innumerable opportunities for side trips in the area strongly suggest renting a car or mobile home with unlimited mileage. (But don't do it in New York, where the rates are among the highest in the country.)

CAR RENTAL: See Chapters 1, 2, and 3 on Boston, Cape Cod, and New York. For rentals elsewhere, consult the local telephone directory.

TRAIN: Amtrak has stations on Union Pl. in **Hartford,** Conn. (203/525-4580); Union Ave. in **New Haven,** Conn. (203/777-4002); and at 100 Gaspee St. in **Providence,** R.I. (401/751-5416).
For the terminal in **Boston,** see Chapter 1; for the terminals in **New York,** see Chapter 3.

INTERCITY BUSES: The **Greyhound Bus Co.** has terminals or stops at 158 Main St., **Bangor,** Me. (207/945-3000); 1 Union Pl., **Hartford,** Conn. (203/522-9267); 45 George St., **New Haven,** Conn. (203/772-2470); 950 Congress

THE ATLANTIC COAST

St., **Portland,** Me. (207/772-6587); and 9 Congress St., **Portsmouth,** N.H. (603/436-0163).

For the terminal in **Boston,** see Chapter 1; for the terminal in Cape Cod, see Chapter 2; for the terminal in **New York,** see Chapter 3.

INFORMATION, TOURS & ADVENTURES

TOURIST INFORMATION: You'll find a flood of tourist information available from both state-government and local sources. On the road, feel free to stop at the local chambers of commerce or convention and visitors bureaus for on-the-spot assistance and information.

State-Government Sources

Connecticut Department of Economic Development, 865 Brook St., Rocky Hill, CT 06067 (203/566-3948).

Maine Publicity Bureau, 97 Winthrop St., Hallowell, ME 04347 (207/289-2423).

Massachusetts Office of Travel & Tourism, 100 Cambridge St., Boston, MA 02202 (617/727-3203).

New Hampshire Hospitality Association, 15 Pleasant St. (P.O. Box 1175), Concord, NH 03301 (603/228-9585).

Rhode Island Tourist Promotion Division, 7 Jackson Walkway, Providence, RI 02903 (401/277-2601).

Local Sources

Augusta Office of Tourism, 189 State St., Augusta, ME 04333 (207/289-5710).

Bangor Chamber of Commerce, 519 Main St. (P.O. Box 1443), Bangor, ME 04401 (207/947-0307).

Bar Harbor Chamber of Commerce, 93 Cottage St. (P.O. Box 158), Bar Harbor, ME 04609 (207/288-5103).

New Bedford–Bristol County Development Council, 70 N. 2nd St. (P.O. Box BR-976), New Bedford, MA 02741 (508/997-1250).

New Haven Convention and Visitors Bureau, 900 Chapel St., New Haven, CT 06510 (203/787-8367).

Newport County Chamber of Commerce, 10 America's Cup Ave. South, Long Wharf Mall, Newport, RI 02840 (401/847-1600).

Portland Chamber of Commerce, 142 Free St., Portland, ME 04101 (207/772-2811).

Portsmouth Chamber of Commerce, P.O. Box 239, Portsmouth, NH 03801 (603/436-1118).

Providence Convention and Visitors Bureau, 30 Exchange Terrace, Providence, RI 02903 (401/274-1636).

GUIDED TOURS: In addition to the information below, see also Chapters 1 and 2 on Boston and Cape Cod. For all other locations, see the local *Yellow Pages* under "Sightseeing."

Newport, R.I.

Viking Tours (bus), 10 America's Cup Ave. (401/847-6921): Guided bus tour of the city and surroundings, year round. Serves the principal hotels.

Viking Queen (boat), Goat Island Marina, Washington St. (401/847-6921): 1-hr. trip on Newport Bay and Rhode Island Sound, allowing you a view from offshore of the mansions of bygone millionaires. Daily May to mid-Oct.

Portland, Me.

Casco Bay Lines (boat), Custom House Wharf, Commercial St. (207/774-7871): Scenic-cruises around Portland Harbor and lovely Casco Bay with its 136 islands. Daily year round.

Portsmouth, N.H.
Portsmouth Harbor Cruises (boat), 64 Ceres St., Old Harbor (603/436-8084): Boat trips in the harbor and to the Isles of Shoals. Daily June–Oct.

ADVENTURES: Here are special cruises/trips available along the Atlantic coast.

Brunswick, Me.
Unicorn Expeditions (boat), P.O. Box T, Brunswick, ME 04011 (207/725-2255): 1–6 days rafting down the upper Hudson in New York State or the Kennebec River and Penobscot River in Maine. 2 days, $180; 5 days, $450 approximately. Spectacular. Daily Apr–Oct.

Camden, Me.
Maine Windjammer Cruises (boat), P.O. Box 617, Camden, ME 04843 (207/236-2938): 3- to 6-day cruises along the Maine coast aboard an authentic schooner from the olden days; a whiff of adventure. About $450 for 6 days. May–Oct.
Schooners *Roseway* and *Adventure* (boat), P.O. Box 696, Camden, ME 04843 (207/236-4449): See "Maine Windjammer Cruises," above.
Schooner *Stephen Taber* (boat), 70 Elm St., Camden, ME 04843 (207/236-3520): See "Maine Windjammer Cruises," above.

Conway, N.H.
Saco Bound Northern Waters (boat), U.S. 302E, Center Conway, NH 03813 (603/447-2177): One to several days' descent by raft or kayak of the Kennebec River and Penobscot River. Spectacular. Daily Apr–Oct.

Portland, Me.
Balloon Sports (balloon), 146 Glenwood Ave., Portland, ME 04103 (207/772-4401): Dirigible trips over Casco Bay and the Portland area; $85 per person. An unforgettable sight. Daily year round.
New England Whitewater Center (boat), 10 Exchange St., Portland, ME 04101 (207/772-4480): Rafting down the Kennebec River, Dead River, and Penobscot River, with comfortable lodging at the Sugarloaf Inn at Sugarloaf Mountain. Also, in spring, descent of the Swift River in New Hampshire. Spectacular. Daily Apr–Oct.

Providence, R.I.
Stumpf Balloons (balloon), P.O. Box 1143, Providence, RI 02901 (401/253-0111): Balloon trips over Narragansett Bay and the Providence area; an unforgettable sight. Daily year round.

SPECIAL EVENTS: For exact dates of the events listed below, check with the state-government and local sources listed earlier in this chapter under "Tourist Information," as well as with those listed below:
Boothbay Harbor Chamber of Commerce, P.O. Box 356, Boothbay Harbor, ME 04538 (207/633-2353).
Bridgeport Chamber of Commerce, 180 Fairfield Ave. (P.O. Box 999), Bridgeport, CT 06601 (203/335-3800).
Newburyport Chamber of Commerce, 29 State St., Newburyport, MA 01950 (508/462-6680).
Ogunquit Chamber of Commerce, P.O. Box 2289, Ogunquit, ME 03907 (207/646-5533).
Plymouth Chamber of Commerce, 91 Samoset St., Plymouth, MA 02360 (508/746-3377).

Rockland Chamber of Commerce, P.O. Box 508, Rockland, ME 04841 (207/596-0376).

Augusta, Me.
Whatever Week (late June to early July): All kinds of boat races ("anything that floats") on the Kennebec River. Giant barbecue, parade, fireworks.

Bar Harbor, Me.
Art Exhibit (third wknds of July and Aug): Work by local artists.

Boothbay Harbor, Me.
Windjammer Cruises (mid-July): Review of old schooners in the bay; very picturesque.

Bridgeport, Conn.
Barnum Festival (late June to early July): Parades, concerts, and art exhibitions bearing on the history of the circus. The 10-day event includes a drum corps competition, circus, rodeo, etc.

Newburyport, Mass.
Yankee Homecoming (late July to early Aug): Boat races, parades, food festival.

New Haven, Conn.
Powder House Day (late Apr to early May): Pageant showing the capture of the arsenal during the Revolutionary War.

Newport, R.I.
Music Festival (2 weeks in mid-July): Chamber-music concerts in the mansions of 19th-century millionaires; call 401/846-1133 for information.
Jazz Festival (mid-Aug): With all the big stars. Fort Adams State Park.
Wooden Boat Show and Classic Yacht Regatta (mid-Aug): Annual yachting competition, very popular with sailboat buffs.

Ogunquit, Me.
Ogunquit Playhouse (late July to Labor Day): Plays of high quality and musicals; call 207/646-5511 for information.

Plymouth, Mass.
Thanksgiving Week (Nov): Commemorating the first celebration of Thanksgiving by the Pilgrim Fathers.

Portland, Me.
New Year's Eve Portland (Dec 31): Shows, parades, fireworks, concerts.

Portsmouth, N.H.
Jazz Festival (late June to early July): Jazz concerts on the historic Portsmouth waterfront; call 603/436-7678 for information.

Providence, R.I.
House and garden tours of privately owned Colonial, Federal, and Victorian homes. Costumed guides and candlelight tours, wknds June.

Rockland, Me.
Maine Lobster Festival (first wknd of Aug): 3 days of joyous gluttony devoted to that most illustrious denizen of Maine's waters—the lobster. Also wooden crate race in Penobscot Bay and parade.

A NORTH TO SOUTH ITINERARY
The section of this guide devoted to the Atlantic coast has been organized as an itinerary, starting at Calais, Me., and ending in New York City, a distance of almost 900 miles (1,440km). You may choose not to drive the whole distance; key towns such as Bangor, Portland, Boston, Portsmouth, Providence, Hartford, and New York are linked by air, bus, and train, while car rentals are available

everywhere. In that case, you may select from the following travel plan the parts that appeal to you most.

Distances Down the Atlantic Coast

From	To	Distance
Calais, Me.	Roosevelt/Campobello	53 mi. (84km)
Roosevelt/Campobello	Bar Harbor	110 mi. (176km)
Bar Harbor	Camden	78 mi. (125km)
Camden	Augusta	42 mi. (67km)
Augusta	Wiscasset	18 mi. (29km)
Wiscasset	Boothbay Harbor	12 mi. (19km)
Boothbay Harbor	Bath	22 mi. (36km)
Bath	Brunswick	10 mi. (16km)
Brunswick	Portland	26 mi. (44km)
Portland	Kennebunkport	30 mi. (45km)
Kennebunkport	Ogunquit	11 mi. (18km)
Ogunquit	York	7 mi. (11km)
York	Portsmouth, N.H.	6 mi. (10km)
Portsmouth, N.H.	Newburyport, Mass.	21 mi. (33km)
Newburyport, Mass.	Boston area (Gloucester, Marblehead, Rockport, Salem)	28–72 mi. (45–115km)
Boston area	Quincy	9 mi. (15km)
Quincy	Hull	15 mi. (24km)
Hull	Plymouth	32 mi. (51km)
Plymouth	Sagamore	18 mi. (29km)
Sagamore	New Bedford	30 mi. (48km)
New Bedford	Providence, R.I.	29 mi. (46km)
Providence, R.I.	Bristol	14 mi. (23km)
Bristol	Portsmouth	6 mi. (9km)
Portsmouth	Newport	10 mi. (16km)
Newport	Narragansett Pier	17 mi. (27km)
Narragansett Pier	Mystic, Conn.	30 mi. (48km)
Mystic, Conn.	Groton	6 mi. (10km)
Groton	New London	2 mi. (3km)
New London	Hartford	44 mi. (71km)
Hartford	New Haven	40 mi. (64km)
New Haven	Stratford	12 mi. (19km)
Stratford	Bridgeport	3 mi. (5km)
Bridgeport	Stamford	20 mi. (32km)
Stamford	Greenwich	7 mi. (11km)
Greenwich	Rye Brook, N.Y.	6 mi. (9km)
Rye Brook, N.Y.	New York City	22 mi. (36km)

A Note on Accommodation Rates: Room rates along the Atlantic Coast are coded as follows: **VE,** Very Expensive ($140 and up); **E,** Expensive ($90–$140); **M,** Moderate ($60–$90); **I,** Inexpensive ($30–$60); **B,** Budget (up to $30). A listing of toll-free numbers is in the Appendix.

A Note on Restaurant Prices: Atlantic Coast restaurant prices, per person, excluding drinks and service charges, are coded as follows: **VE,** Very Expensive ($60 and up); **E,** Expensive ($40–$60); **M,** Moderate ($25–$40); **I,** Inexpensive ($15–$25); **B,** Budget (up to $15).

CALAIS: Small market town on the Canadian border. Some 15 mi. (25km) south, a marker at the side of U.S. 1 marks the

45th parallel and tells you that you are precisely halfway between the Equator and the North Pole. Still on this stretch of U.S. 1, opposite Red Beach, the **St. Croix Island International Historic Site** marks the place of the first attempted European settlement on the Atlantic coast north of Florida, in 1604 by French explorer Samuel de Champlain and 78 of his companions. The park is not open to the public.

ROOSEVELT CAMPOBELLO INTERNATIONAL PARK (at Lubec): Campobello Island, at the mouth of the St. Croix River, is jointly owned by the U.S. and Canada, and marks the border between the two countries. It was here that Franklin D. Roosevelt had his summer home, where he contracted polio. The Visitor Center, with movies of the life and career of the 32nd president of the U.S., is on Me. 189 (506/752-2922), open daily from Memorial Day to the end of Oct. Should be seen.

BAR HARBOR: Charming old fishing village on **Mount Desert Island,** a site explored by the French at the beginning of the 17th century. Much favored by vacationers for the last 100 years because of the neighboring **Acadia National Park** (see below). The town, almost entirely rebuilt after a blaze in 1947, boasts dozens of hotels and restaurants in all price ranges. Boats may be hired for big-game fishing. A car-ferry, the *Bluenose,* connects Bar Harbor to Yarmouth, Nova Scotia, in Canada, in 6 hr. daily from mid-June through Sept: Ferry Terminal (207/288-3395). Don't fail to visit Bar Harbor.

Acadia National Park

Discovered in 1604 by French explorer Samuel de Champlain, and part of French Acadia until 1713, the site of Acadia National Park is a perfect representation on a small scale of all the natural beauties of the Maine seaboard. On its 64 sq. mi. (168km^2) of splendid landscapes, the only large national park in the Northeast finds room for jagged coastlines, pine forests, little fishing villages, deep blue lakes, steep cliffs, clear streams, storm-beaten granite islands, and mountains: **Cadillac Mountain,** at 1,530 ft (466m), is the highest on the Atlantic coast of the U.S.

The **Loop Road,** a 33-mi. (55km) scenic drive, takes you along the shore of the park's largest island, with fine views of its fjords (particularly **Somes Sound**) and its lakes; you should follow it in a clockwise direction, beginning from the **Visitors Center** at Hulls Cove on Me. 3, about 3 mi. (5km) NW of Bar Harbor. The **Abbe Museum of Indian Artifacts,** on Me. 3 at Sieur de Monts Springs (207/288-3519), open daily mid-May to mid-Oct, displays some interesting Native American material evidencing that Mount Desert Island has been inhabited since the Stone Age.

There is year-round ferry service between the mainland harbors and the little islands scattered offshore like **Isle-au-Haut, Little Cranberry Island,** and **Great Cranberry Island.** Many campsites, beaches with facilities, and 120 mi. (193km) of trails.

Opened in 1919, Acadia National Park is ranked second among national parks in the number of its visitors (4.5 million a year). For information, contact the Superintendent, Acadia National Park, P.O. Box 177, Bar Harbor, ME 04069 (207/288-3338). A nature lover's dream; don't miss it. Portions of the park are open year round. (For weather forecast, call 207/667-8910).

Where to Stay

Bayview Waterfront Resort, 111 Eden St., Bar Harbor, ME 04609 (207/288-5861). 38 rms, A/C, cable color TV. AE, CB, DC, MC, V. Free parking, pool, rest., bar, valet service, disco in season. *Note:* Elegant Georgian-style mansion standing in a fine garden. Spacious, tastefully decorated rms, period furniture, private patios, and open fireplaces. Excellent svce. Great charm and great quality. Open year round. **E–VE**

🔑🔑 **Atlantic Oakes,** Eden St. at Me. 3, Bar Harbor, ME 04609
(207/288-5802). 109 rms, cable color TV (no A/C). MC, V.
Free parking, pool, marina, five tennis courts, nearby coffee shop, free breakfast,
free crib. *Note:* Friendly, comfortable motel adjoining the *Bluenose* ferry terminal. Huge, inviting rms, all w. ocean view. Private marina; grdn. Affable reception. Open year round. **M–E,** but lower rates off-season.

🔑 **Testa's Hotel,** 53 Main St., Bar Harbor, ME 04609 (207/
288-3327). 16 rms, A/C, cable color TV. AE, CB, DC, MC,
V. On-street parking, rest., crib $8. *Note:* Modest but well-kept small hotel oppo-
site the beach. Reception w. a smile. Likable Italian rest. Very good value. Closed
mid-Oct to mid-June. I

Where to Eat

🍸🍸 **Bar Harbor Inn,** 7 Newport Dr. (207/288-3351). Breakfast/
lunch/dinner daily, brunch Sun; closed mid-Nov to Mar. AE,
MC, V. *Specialties:* stuffed mushrooms, broiled lobster, medallion of lamb in
marsala, catch of the day. Good wine list. *Note:* Charming 19th-century inn overlooking the bay. Conventional but elegant cooking; efficient svce. Distinguished
background music. A very good place; resv. advisable. *Continental/Seafood.* **I–M**

🍸 **Testa's,** in Testa's Hotel (see "Where to Stay," above) (207/
288-3327). A/C. Breakfast/lunch/dinner daily (till mid-
night); closed mid-Oct through June. AE, CB, DC, MC, V. *Specialties:* broiled or
steamed lobster, clams, steak, Italian dishes. *Note:* Modest, unpretentious little
trattoria serving excellent seafood and some decent Italian dishes. Run by the
same family for the last half century. Locally popular. Friendly svce; very good
value. *American/Italian.* **B–I**

IN NEARBY HANCOCK ☀🍸🍸 **Le Domaine,** U.S. 1, 18 mi. (30km) north of Bar
Harbor (207/422-3916). Dinner only, nightly; closed Nov–May. AE, MC, V.
Specialties: magret of duck w. cherries, rabbit w. prunes, catch of the day broiled
w. fennel, sautéed sweetbreads, calves' liver dijonnaise, émincé of beef w. aioli.
Note: The cooking of Nicole Purslow and the decor of this enchanting little
country inn w. its huge fireplace and open-hearth grill, smell sweetly of France.
All the vegetables and herbs come from her own garden. The breakfasts here are
memorable too. Applauded by tourists for more than four decades. Le Domaine
also offers seven very comfortable guest rms. *French.* **I–M**

IN NEARBY SEAL HARBOR 🍸 **Jordan Pond House,** Park Loop Rd., 2 mi. (3.2km)
north of Seal Harbor (207/276-3316). Lunch/dinner daily; closed Nov–May.
AE, DC, MC, V. Jkt. *Specialties:* steak, broiled lobster, broiled chicken, homemade ice cream. *Note:* Charming rest. in a little farmhouse, more than a century
old, on the grounds of Acadia National Park, which was generously donated to
the National Park Service in 1945 by John D. Rockefeller, Jr. Painstaking but
unimaginative cuisine; open-air dining on fine days. Good value. *American.* **B–I**

☀🔭 **CAMDEN:** In its splendid natural setting where the mountains plunge steeply into Penobscot Bay, with its mosaic of little
islands, this town is particularly lively in summer, with many productions at the
Camden Amphitheatre, on Atlantic Ave. (207/236-4404). From here many
sailboats offer 3- to 6-day cruises along the Maine coast (see "Adventures,"
above). You should stop here.

Where to Stay

🔑🔑 **High Tide,** Belfast Rd. at U.S. 1, Camden, ME 04843 (207/
236-3724). 26 rms and 3 cottages. No A/C; color TV. MC, V.
Free parking, beach, tennis court, adjoining golf course, nearby coffee shop, free
crib. *Note:* Charming old (1901) house on a private beach. Pleasant rms w. pri-

vate balconies; 7 acres (3ha) of lovely grdn overlooking Penobscot Bay. Serene, relaxing atmosphere; good value. Closed mid-Oct to early June. **I–M**

IN NEARBY LINCOLNVILLE ☙ **Mt. Battie,** U.S. 1, Lincolnville, ME 04849 (207/ 236-3870). 21 rms, A/C, color TV. AE, MC, V. Free parking, nearby coffee shop, free morning coffee. *Note:* Acceptable, small budget motel, functionally comfortable. Great ocean view. Good value. Closed late Oct to early May. **B–I**

IN NEARBY ROCKPORT ☙☙☙ **Samoset,** Warrenton St., Rockport, ME 04856 (207/594-2511). 150 rms, A/C, cable color TV. AE, CB, DC, MC, V. Free parking, two pools, health club, saunas, tennis court, golf course, marina, boats, rest. (Marcel's), bar, valet svce, disco, free crib, concierge. *Note:* Luxurious resort complex, modern and comfortable, overlooking Penobscot Bay. Spacious, comfortable rms w. private patios (most w. ocean view), in small buildings scattered around 230 acres (93ha) of green grdns and woods. Elegant rest.; attentive svce. A fine place. Interesting vacation packages. Open year round. **M–E,** but lower rates off-season.

IN NEARBY ROCKLAND ☙ **Navigator Motor Inn,** 520 Main St., Rockland, ME 04841 (207/594-2131). 62 rms, A/C, cable color TV. AE, MC, V. Free parking, rest., bar, rm svce. *Note:* Typical but inviting motel on the ocean, opposite the ferry terminal. Comfortable rms w. balconies and refrigerators, some w. kitchenettes. Efficient svce. Good overall value. **I–M,** but lower rates off-season.

Where to Eat

☼ ♈♈ **Aubergine,** 6 Belmont Ave. (207/236-6040). Dinner only, Tues–Sun; closed Nov to mid-May. AE, CB, DC, MC, V. Jkt. *Specialties:* terrine of duck, medaillons of lobster, classic French dishes. *Note:* Light, inspired French cuisine in a pretty Victorian setting w. period furniture. Romantic atmosphere; classical background music. Somewhat starchy svce. Resv. advised. *French.* **I–M**

IN NEARBY BELFAST ♈♈ **Penobscot Meadows Country Inn,** on U.S. 1 (207/ 338-5320). A/C. Dinner only, nightly; closed Tues–Wed mid-Sept to Memorial Day. *Specialties:* tomato soup w. cognac, shrimp w. ginger, chicken w. raspberries, lobster in pastry shell, catch of the day. *Note:* Pretty Victorian setting w. a clear view of Penobscot Bay and Blue Hill. Elegant ambience; very good svce; agreeable background music. Resv. advised. *American.* **I**

IN NEARBY LINCOLNVILLE ☼♈♈ **Lobster Pound,** on U.S. 1 (207/789-5550). A/C. Lunch/dinner daily; closed Nov–Apr. AE, CB, DC, MC, V. *Specialties:* lobster, catch of the day, roast turkey, steak, fried clams, good desserts. *Note:* As the name implies, the specialty is lobster, in a ragoût, broiled, or steamed; shellfish lovers can go to town here. Dining rm overlooking Penobscot Bay, or eat in the open on the wharf. Efficient, smiling svce; a local landmark for 30 years. *American.* **I–M**

IN NEARBY ROCKPORT ♈♈ **The Helm,** U.S. 1 (207/236-4337). A/C. Lunch/ dinner Tues–Sun; closed mid-Oct to early Apr. MC, V. *Specialties:* onion soup, steak au poivre, catch of the day, shellfish. *Note:* Locally popular little rest. serving good *cuisine bourgeoise* of French inspiration, and tasty homemade desserts. Friendly svce.; good value. *French/American.* **I**

IN NEARBY ROCKLAND ♈♈ **Marcel's,** in the Samoset (see "Where to Stay," above) (207/594-2511). A/C. Breakfast/lunch/dinner daily. AE, CB, DC, MC, V.

Jkt. Specialties: Maine lobster, highest-quality prime cuts and fish. *Note:* Elegant rest. w. view of Penobscot Bay and the ocean; classic grand-hotel food, impeccably prepared and served (by tuxedoed waiters). Pianist at dinner. Valet parking. Resv. advised. *Continental.* **I–M**

AUGUSTA: Maine's picturesque capital on the Kennebec River was founded in 1628 by settlers from Plymouth, Mass. Imposing **State House** (1832), on State St. and Capitol St. (207/289-2301), open Mon–Fri, by the celebrated Charles Bulfinch, who also designed the Massachusetts State House in Boston. Across the river, **Fort Western** was built in 1754 for protection against the Native Americans, and has been carefully restored. Should be seen.

WISCASSET: Tucked into the side of a hill at the mouth of the Sheepscot River, this enchanting little harbor, long the home of shipping tycoons and sea captains, is now an artists' and writers' colony. Louis-Philippe, king of France, landed here when he went into exile in the U.S. Charming early 19th-century houses along Main St. The **Musical Wonder House,** 16-18 High St. (207/882-7163), open daily June to mid-Oct, is an interesting museum of old music boxes and other automata. See also the picturesque **Lincoln County Museum and Old Jail,** built in 1811, the first penitentiary in the state, on Federal St. (207/882-6817), open daily July to Labor Day, by appointment the rest of the year. Should positively be seen.

BOOTHBAY HARBOR: With its old jetties and neat little houses, it gives you an engaging, representative picture of the seaports of Maine. A well-known regatta, Windjammer Days, is held in July. Should be seen.

Where to Stay

Linekin Bay, on Me. 27, Boothbay Harbor, ME 04538 (207/633-2494). 35 rms and 33 bungalows. No A/C; color TV in lounge. No credit cards. Free parking, pool, tennis court, marina, boats, fishing, waterskiing. *Note:* Rustic motel w. youthful, relaxed atmosphere reminiscent of a summer camp. Functionally comfortable (a little less in the bungalows). Wonderful for water-sports enthusiasts. Family clientele. Good value on balance. Closed mid-Sept to mid-June. **I–M** (American Plan)

IN NEARBY SOUTHPORT **Ocean Gate Motor Inn,** Me. 27, Southport, ME 04576 (207/633-3321). 55 rms, color TV; no A/C. AE, CB, DC, MC, V. Free parking, pool, tennis court, marina, boats, rest. (May–Oct), bar, valet svce, crib $5. *Note:* Inviting, comfortable motel on the ocean. Agreeable rms w. offshore or harbor view, some w. private porches; also cottages for two to six people. Reception and svce w. a smile. 85 acres (34ha) of pretty woods and grdns. A fine place. Closed Dec–May. **M–E,** but lower rates off-season.

Where to Eat

Brown Bros., Atlantic Ave. (207/633-5440). A/C. Breakfast/dinner daily; closed late Sept to mid-June. AE, CB, DC, MC, V. *Specialties:* lobster, catch of the day. *Note:* Picturesque rest. in an 18th-century salt shed overlooking the water; the menu emphasizes local seafood. In the hands of the same family for almost half a century. Relaxed atmosphere; good value. No lunch served. *Seafood.* **B–I**

BATH: Harbor town on the Kennebec River, with fine old houses and famous shipyards from which more than 4,000 vessels have been launched since the beginning of the 18th century. See the splendid **Maine Maritime Museum,** Washington St. (207/443-1316), open daily May–Oct; call ahead the rest of the year. Its exhibits cover three centuries of shipbuilding. Worth the side trip.

☀️⚱️ **BRUNSWICK:** This historic little port, dating from 1628, has wonderful old houses the whole length of Park Row and Federal St. Among them is the 1806 **Stowe House,** 63 Federal St. (207/725-5543), where Harriet Beecher Stowe wrote *Uncle Tom's Cabin;* the building is now a hotel and restaurant. See also **Bowdoin College,** founded in 1794, whose alumni include the writers Nathaniel Hawthorne and Henry Wadsworth Longfellow; the 14th president of the U.S., Franklin Pierce; and the first man to reach the North Pole, Adm. Robert Peary. The campus and its museums at Maine St. and College St., (207/725-3000), may be visited Tues–Sun year round. Must be seen.

☀️⚱️⚱️ **PORTLAND:** The most important fishing port north of Boston, on beautiful **Casco Bay,** whose 136 islands attract many summer vacationers. The **Portland Historic Trail** through the streets of the old port town takes you to several historic 18th-century homes, including **Tate House,** 1270 Westbrook St. (207/774-9781), open Tues–Sun mid-June to mid-Sept; and the **Wadsworth-Longfellow House,** birthplace of the poet, 487 Congress St. (207/772-1807), open Tues–Sat June to mid-Oct.

And don't overlook the **Portland Museum of Art,** 7 Congress Sq. (207/775-6148), open Tues–Sun, where you'll find choice works by such American artists as Andrew Wyeth, Winslow Homer, and John Marin.

Four mi. (6.5km) south on Me. 77, the **Portland Headlight** at Cape Elizabeth, dating from 1791 and built by order of George Washington, is the oldest lighthouse in the U.S. still in service. Worth seeing.

Don't miss trips on Casco Bay (see above under "Guided Tours"). A carferry, the *Scotia Prince,* links Portland to Yarmouth, Nova Scotia (Canada), in 11 hr., daily mid-May to Oct, from the International Terminal (207/775-5616).

Don't fail to visit Portland.

Where to Stay

🛏️🛏️ **Sonesta Hotel–Portland,** 157 High St., Portland, ME 04101 (207/775-5411; toll free 800/766-3782). 200 rms, A/C, cable color TV. AE, CB, DC, MC, V. Gar. $6, health club, sauna, two rests., two bars (including a rooftop lounge overlooking Casco Bay), rm svce, disco, free crib. *Note:* Portland's "grande dame," w. all New England charm. Comfortable rms, the best offering a beautiful view of Portland harbor. Flawless reception and svce. Centrally located in dwntwn Portland; free airport limo. **E–VE**

🛏️🛏️ **Ramada Inn,** 1230 Congress St., Portland, ME 04102 (207/774-5611). 149 rms, A/C, cable color TV. AE, CB, DC, MC, V. Free parking, pool, sauna, rest., bar, rm svce, disco, free crib. *Note:* Large, comfortable motel midway between the airport and dwntwn. Huge, functional rms; comprehensive facilities. Impersonal but efficient svce. Free limos to airport and dwntwn. Business clientele. Open year round. **M–E**

IN NEARBY PROUT'S NECK 🛏️🛏️🛏️ **Black Point Inn,** Me. 207, Prout's Neck, ME 04074 (207/883-4126). 81 rms, A/C, cable color TV. MC, V. Free parking, two pools, tennis court, putting green, sauna, private beach, boats, rest., bar, rm svce, nightclub, hrdrsr, free crib. *Note:* Handsome resort hotel in a lovely setting on the ocean. Spacious, comfortable rms; efficient svce. If you love calm and tranquility, this is the place for you. Closed Nov–May. **E–VE** (American Plan), but lower rates off-season.

Where to Eat

🍷🍷🍷 **Brattle Street,** 19 Brattle St. (207/772-4658). A/C. Dinner only, Mon–Sat; closed hols. AE, CB, DC, MC, V. Jkt. *Special-*

ties: roast lobster w. leeks, filet of salmon w. cucumbers and dill sauce, lamb ravioli w. rosemary and basil, duck w. lemon sauce and raspberries. *Note:* The excellent young chef, Dale Gussett, serves an ambitious, distinguished French nouvelle cuisine. The rest., one of Portland's most fashionable, occupies an elegantly restored old brick house in the historic district. Polished svce; successful enough that resv. are advisable. A fine place to eat. *French.* **M**

꙾᯾⍥⍨ **Boone's,** 6 Custom House Wharf (207/774-5725). A/C. Lunch/dinner daily; closed Thanksgiving and Dec 25. AE, CB, DC, MC, V. *Specialties:* clam chowder, fisherman's stew, clambake, enormous choice of seafood broiled, steamed, sautéed, or fried, but also some praiseworthy beef dishes and game in season. *Note:* The ads truthfully term it "A Waterfront Tradition Since 1898," while the building has been there since 1840. Superb, absolutely fresh lobster and catch of the day. Picturesque seafaring decor. Relaxed atmosphere; very good value. *Seafood.* **B–I**

꙾ **KENNEBUNKPORT:** Well-known beach resort with an interesting streetcar museum displaying 150 vehicles from all periods and places, from horse-drawn trams to cable cars: **Seashore Trolley Museum,** Log Cabin Rd. (207/967-2712), open daily, mid-June to early Sept; call ahead the rest of the year. Worth going out of your way for. President George Bush's summer home, an 11-acre (4.5ha) family compound known as **Walker's Point** on Ocean Ave., is built on a rocky promontory overlooking the Maine coast.

Where to Stay

꙾᯾⍥⍨ **The Colony Resort,** Ocean Ave. and Kings Rd., Kennebunkport, ME 04046 (207/967-3331). 139 rms, color TV; no A/C. AE, MC, V. Free parking, pool, tennis court, putting green, private beach, rest., bar, rm svce, disco, cinema, crib $5. *Note:* Charming old 1920s-style hotel w. direct access to beach. Lovely gardens. Elegant, comfortable rms; faultless svce. One of the best places to stay on the coast. Closed mid-Sept to mid-June. **E–VE** (American Plan)

꙾ **Nonantum Hotel,** Ocean Ave., Kennebunkport, ME 06046 (207/967-4050). 125 rms, some w. A/C, cable color TV. AE, MC, V. Free parking, pool, boats, rest., bar, valet svce. *Note:* Pleasant old hotel on the Kennebunk River. Accommodates part of the White House staff when President Bush is in town. Functional comfort; the best rms overlook the river. 5 min. on foot from beach. Good value overall. Closed Nov to mid-May. **E–VE** (Modified American Plan), but lower rates off-season.

꙾᯾ **OGUNQUIT:** The jagged, rocky shores of Maine here yield to sandy beaches; this is another delightful fishing port, as much for its setting as for the high quality of its lobsters. In summer, an important artists' colony exhibits in the Shore Rd. galleries. Beautiful fine-sand beach, 3 mi. (5km) long, ideal for surfing. Worth seeing.

Where to Stay

꙾ **Terrace by the Sea,** 11 Wharf Lane, Ogunquit, ME 03907 (207/646-3232). 60 rms, A/C, cable color TV. No credit cards. Free parking, pool, tennis court, beach, free breakfast. No bar, no rest. *Note:* Typical motel w. direct beach access. Comfortable rms w. balconies, patios, and refrigerators. Picnic tables. Efficient svce. Closed Dec–May. **M–E,** but lower rates off-season.

IN NEARBY MOODY ᯾᯾ **Ogunquit River Plantation,** U.S. 1, Moody, ME 03907 (207/646-9611). 80 rms, A/C, cable color TV. AE, MC, V. Free parking, pool, adj. coffee shop, free breakfast, free crib. *Note:* Modern, elegant motel on the

Ogunquit River. Spacious, comfortable rms w. balconies and refrigerators, all w. ocean or river view. Beach 5 min. by car (free jitney). Good svce. Very good value. Closed Nov–Apr. **I–M**

☀☼🏠 **YORK:** A picturesque anachronism, York could be taken for a small fragment of the Colonial period that has escaped the burden of the years. Many historic buildings, dating from 1720 to 1760, along York St. and Lindsay Rd.: the **Old Gaol,** whose cells were in use until the 1860s; the **Old School House** (1755); **Jefferd's Tavern** (1759); **First Parish Congregational Church** (1747); the **Elizabeth Perkins House** (1730); etc. All may be visited daily June–Sept.

Busy **York Harbor** provides the economic underpinnings for this little piece of a bygone era, with many charter companies offering trips on the ocean and deep-sea fishing parties. Must definitely be seen.

Where to Eat

🍷🍷 **Dockside Dining Room,** Harris Island Rd. (207/363-4800). A/C. Lunch/dinner Tues–Sun; closed mid-Oct through May. MC, V. *Specialties:* oven-baked sole stuffed w. lobster, roast duckling, steak teriyaki, broiled fish. *Note:* This light-filled rest. w. its huge picture windows stands right on York Harbor, overlooking the yacht basin. The food, though unimaginative, is pleasant and tasty. Good svce. *American.* **I**

☀☼🏠 **PORTSMOUTH:** Founded in 1630, the same year as Boston, the former capital of New Hampshire allows you to immerse yourself in 17th- and 18th-century America. In the Old Harbor neighborhood, **Strawbery Banke,** at Hancock St. and Marcy St. (603/433-1100), you can see three dozen craftsman's shops and old houses, built between 1695 and the end of the 19th century and carefully restored; open to visitors daily May–Oct; signposted pedestrian trail.

See also some fine upscale homes such as the **John Paul Jones House,** once the home of the famous naval commander, at 43 Middle St. (603/436-8420), open Mon–Sat mid-May to mid-Oct; the **John Langdon House,** which George Washington termed "the handsomest house in Portsmouth," 143 Pleasant St. (603/436-3205), open Wed–Sun June to mid-Oct; or the **Wentworth-Coolidge Mansion,** one of the oldest in the city (1695), on Little Harbor Rd. (603/436-6607), open daily mid-June to Labor Day.

Fort Constitution, on the site of a post built in 1632 which had its moment of glory during the War of Independence, is also worth a side trip; the present structure, imposing in granite, dates from 1808. Go 4 mi. (6.5km) east on N.H. 1B to New Castle (603/431-0113); open daily mid-June to mid-Sept; wknds only from mid-May to mid-June and mid-Sept to mid-Oct.

For history lovers, a visit to Portsmouth is a must.

Where to Stay

🛏🛏 **Holiday Inn,** 300 Woodbury Ave., Portsmouth, NH 03801 (603/431-8000; toll free, see Holiday Inns). 130 rms, A/C, color TV. AE, CB, DC, MC, V. Free parking, pool, health club, rest., bar, rm svce, disco, free crib. *Note:* A typical Holiday Inn, modern and comfortable, 5 min. from the Strawbery Banke historic district. Spacious rms; efficient svce; business clientele. Open year round. **M–E**

Where to Eat

☀🍷🍷 **Blue Strawbery,** 29 Ceres St. (603/431-6420). A/C. Dinner only, nightly; closed Mon–Tues Oct–May, and Dec 25. No credit cards. Jkt. *Specialties:* mussel soup, pork filet stuffed w. walnuts and cheese, broiled salmon w. squash and blueberries, striped bass w. scallops, cognac, and sour cream; menu changes regularly. Large wine list. *Note:* One of the best places to eat in New England, as chef Philip McGuire turns out sophisticated, contemporary American cuisine. Lovely old decor in a magnificently restored 1797 ship's chandlery. Ultra-polished svce. Much charm and distinction. Resv. a must. *American.* **M** (prix fixe)

NEWBURYPORT: The main thoroughfare of this harbor town with its three-centuries-old shipyards, **High Street** is a journey 200 years back through time. A living museum of American Federalist architecture, High St. displays rows of big, square, three-story houses, built around 1800 by rich shipowners or long-haul sea captains in an architectural idiom reminiscent of nearby Salem. Newburyport, at the mouth of the Merrimack River, is also renowned as the birthplace of the U.S. Coast Guard in 1790. Worth going out of your way for.

Where to Eat
IN NEARBY SALEM **Courtyard Café,** in the Salem Inn, 7 Summer St. (508/ 741-0680). A/C. Lunch/dinner daily. AE, CB, DC, MC, V. *Specialties:* stuffed lobster, sole meunière, mussel stew, broiled scrod, catch of the day. *Note:* This 1840s sea captain's house has been prettily converted into an inn, w. a charming patio where you can dine out on fine days. Excellent seafood. Svce w. a smile. *Seafood.* **I**

BOSTON, GLOUCESTER, MARBLEHEAD, ROCKPORT, SALEM:
See Chapter 1 on Boston.

QUINCY: An important industrial town founded in 1625, this Boston suburb is the home of the famous Adams family of statesmen and patriots, whose origin can be traced back to 1636 in the colony's earliest days. Among their number is John Adams, second president of the U.S., and his son, John Quincy Adams, sixth president. See the **John and John Quincy Adams Birthplaces,** two 17th-century saltbox houses at 133 and 141 Franklin St. (617/773-1177), open daily mid-Apr to mid-Nov; also the **Adams National Historic Site,** 135 Adams St. (same phone number and visiting days as the preceding), built in 1731, acquired by John Adams in 1787 and retained in the family until 1946, still with its original fixtures and furniture. The tombs of the two presidents are not far away, in the **United First Parish Church** (the only church in the country with crypts of *two* presidents), 1306 Hancock St. (617/773-1290), open Mon–Sat mid-May to Labor Day, by appointment the rest of the year. John Hancock, the first signer of the Declaration of Independence, was also a native of Quincy. Should be seen.

HULL: At the tip of **Nantasket Peninsula,** Hull boasts the oldest lighthouse in the country, the **Boston Light (Little Brewster Island).** The original, built in 1716, was destroyed 60 years later by the British when they were forced to evacuate Little Brewster Island; the present lighthouse, dating from 1783, is worth seeing.

PLYMOUTH: It was on these desolate, windswept shores that on December 21, 1620, after an Atlantic crossing that lasted 66 days, the *Mayflower* cast anchor in the lee of **Plymouth Rock,** with its passenger list of 101 men, women, and children known as the "Pilgrims." That first winter was terrible. Half the colonists perished, and were buried in secret, at night, on **Cole's Hill** so that the Wampanoag tribe should not be able to determine how few were the survivors. All the same, but for these Native Americans and their gifts of food, there might well have been no survivors.

Plymouth, affectionately referred to as "America's Hometown," was the first permanent British settlement north of Virginia, and to this day it looks like something from an old book of prints. The precious relics of the first settlers are carefully arranged in the **Pilgrim Hall Museum,** 75 Court St. (508/746-1620), open daily. There are many old houses around Water St. and Summer St., including the oldest in the city, the **Richard Sparrow House,** built in 1640 at 42 Summer St.

The *Mayflower II* is a full-size replica of its illustrious namesake, and like it, built in England. Having crossed the Atlantic in 1957, the *Mayflower II* is now at State Pier. The ship may be visited daily Apr–Nov.

See also on Water St. **Plymouth Rock** itself, now sheltered behind a Greek Revival columned portico in granite; this is the exact spot where the Pilgrims made their landfall. The Rock, which weighs about 6 tons (5,450kg), attracts a million tourists a year.

Three mi. (5km) south along Mass. 3A, the museum-village of **Plimoth Plantation** is a faithful reconstruction of the life of the original colonists in the 1620s, with costumed extras and a facsimile of a Wampanoag tribal encampment. It attracts more than 400,000 visitors each year. Find it on Mass. 3A (508/746-1622), open daily Apr–Nov.

Plymouth is an absolute must.

Where to Stay

🍊🍊🍊 **Sheraton Plymouth at Village Landing,** 180 Water St., Plymouth, MA 02360 (508/747-4900; toll free, see Sheraton). 175 rms, A/C, cable color TV. AE, CB, DC, MC, V. Free parking, pool, health club, sauna, rest., bar, rm svce, nightclub, concierge, crib $10. *Note:* Big vacation motel on the Plymouth waterfront. Spacious, very comfortable rms, some w. balconies, the best overlooking the ocean. Acceptable rest. Good svce. A stone's throw from Plymouth's principal tourist attractions. Open year round. **M–E**

🍊 **Cold Spring,** 188 Court St., Plymouth, MA 02360 (508/746-2222). 31 rms, A/C, color TV. AE, MC, V. Free parking, nearby coffee shop, free breakfast, crib $5. *Note:* Smart little motel in a typical New England building; functionally comfortable. Friendly reception. Good value. Closed Dec to mid-Mar. **I**

SAGAMORE:
The access port for **Cape Cod,** at the junction of U.S. 6 and Mass. 3. There are charming old fishing towns and splendid seascapes the whole 60-mi. (100km) length of Cape Cod, while the nearby islands of **Martha's Vineyard** and **Nantucket** are the favorite country retreat for well-off Bostonians and New Yorkers. Fishing, sailing, and a temperate climate in summer. For more details on the peninsula, see Chapter 2 on Cape Cod.

☼🔔 NEW BEDFORD:
Although by now partly given over to textile production, New Bedford has retained intact its seafaring traditions and its very large fishing fleet. The port, which is home to some 10,000 sailors, including a Portuguese colony that goes back almost to the town's foundation in 1640, was the world's largest whaling port in the 19th century, and inspired Herman Melville to write *Moby-Dick.* Readers of that great work will find fascinating new viewpoints opened to them, probably more than at any of the region's other museums devoted to man and the sea, at the superb **New Bedford Whaling Museum,** 18 Johnny Cake Hill (508/997-0046), open daily. Be sure also to see the lovely old houses of the **County Street Historic District,** which once belonged to wealthy merchants and whaler captains. Well worth the side trip.

Car-ferry service in summer between New Bedford and the island of Martha's Vineyard: **Cape Island Express Lines,** 1494 E. Rodney French Blvd. (508/997-1688), daily mid-May to Sept.

☼🔔 PROVIDENCE:
Sheltered at the head of the enormous **Narragansett Bay,** the capital of Rhode Island was christened "[Divine] Providence" by its founder, Roger Williams, a religious leader of Brit-

ish origin who in 1636 took refuge here from the dogmatic intolerance of the Salem puritans. The rich historical inheritance of this liberal, hard-working, business-oriented city is reflected in its ✻ **old neighborhoods,** of which Kennedy Plaza and Benefit St. are the finest examples.

Built at the beginning of the 20th century, the **Rhode Island State House,** on Smith St. (401/277-2311), open daily, with its imposing dome of white Georgia marble, fittingly sets off the downtown office high-rises. In it you may see the charter originally granted by King Charles II in 1663 to the new Rhode Island colony. Dating from 1762, the **Old State House,** 150 Benefit St. (401/277-2678), open Mon–Fri, is still dear to Rhode Islanders because it was here that the Declaration of Independence was originally signed on May 4, 1776— two full months before it was ratified by the original 13 colonies in Philadelphia.

The splendid Georgian **John Brown House** (1786), 52 Power St. (401/331-8575), open Tues–Sun, was described by John Quincy Adams as "the most magnificent mansion in the continent," and very definitely deserves a visit. Nearby, see the ✻ **First Baptist Church in America, 75** N. Main St. (401/751-2266), open daily, the oldest Baptist church in the country, founded by Roger Williams in 1638; the present building, a very fine work by architect Joseph Brown, dates from 1775.

While you're here, in the adjoining suburb of **Pawtucket** you should see the extremely interesting ✻ **Slater Mill Historic Site** (1793), often termed "the cradle of American industry." Its mill and its antique machines give you a vivid picture of America at the beginning of the Industrial Revolution in the very early 19th century. See it at Roosevelt Ave. and Main St. (401/725-8638), open daily from Memorial Day to Labor Day, wknds only the rest of the year.

Where to Eat

🍷🍷 **Al Forno,** 7 Steeple St. (401/273-9760). A/C. Dinner only, Tues–Sat; closed hols. AE, MC, V. *Specialties:* baked clams w. tomato sauce, fresh homemade pasta and pizza, hot sausage roasted w. vegetables, sautéed squid, filet of pork à l'orange, grilled tuna vinaigrette. *Note:* The gloomy exterior of this tiny rest. is discouraging, but the light, inventive cuisine of George Germond and his wife, Johanne, are worth going out of your way for. One negative: Al Forno accepts no reservations, so—small as it is (seating only 32), and successful as it is—you may have a long wait. *American/Italian.* I

🏛 **BRISTOL:** A busy port in the 19th century (in 1800–10 it was fourth in importance in the nation), Bristol can show you a rich gamut of Colonial houses, particularly along **Hope Street,** as well as some charming small museums. Among the latter, on Tower Rd., 1 mi. (1.6km) east along Metacom Ave. (401/253-2707), you'll find the **Haffenreffer Museum of Anthropology,** open Tues–Sun June–Aug, wknds only the rest of the year. It has a remarkable collection in the areas of Inuit, Native American, and Polynesian culture.

☀🏛 **PORTSMOUTH:** The **Green Animals Topiary Gardens** on R.I. 114 (401/847-1000), open daily May–Sept (wknds only in Oct; closed the rest of the year), is one of the most original examples of the landscape gardener's art on the eastern seaboard. You'll see dozens of shrubs and bushes trimmed into the shape of giant animals: elephant, lion, giraffe, antelope, etc. Very beautiful rose garden. Well worth the side trip.

Where to Eat

☀🍷🍷🍷 **Sea Fare Inn** (formerly Le Rochambeau), 3352 E. Main Rd. at R.I. 138 (401/683-0577). A/C. Lunch Tues–Fri, dinner Tues–Sun; closed mid-Feb to mid-Mar. AE, MC, V. J&T. *Specialties:* remarkable seafood prepared in an infinite variety of ways. Also choice beef and fowl. Menu changes daily. *Note:* Everything you could ask from a luxury inn. This rest., in an enormous 19th-century English-style manor house with crystal chandeliers, six open fireplaces, and nine dining rooms, is one of the most elegant in New England. Chef George Karousos turns out refined cuisine and light-as-air sauces. Svce exemplary in all respects. A fine place. *Continental/Seafood.* I–M

NEWPORT: America's yachting capital; in the bay off this famous Rhode Island resort the America's Cup races were held every four years for more than a century (1870–1983). It was this engaging little city, steeped in history, that in 1657 welcomed the first Quaker settlers from Europe and only a year later the first 15 Jewish families (from Holland) to come to the New World.

In the latter part of the 19th century Newport became the favorite summer home of New York millionaires such as the Astors, Belmonts, Vanderbilts, Stuyvesants, and McAllisters. It still preserves from its glory days some splendid residences, worthy of Scott Fitzgerald's *The Great Gatsby:* **Marble House,** on Bellevue Ave., modeled after Versailles, and **The Breakers,** a 70-room palace on Ochre Point Ave., both belonging to the Vanderbilt family; **Rosecliff,** with its huge ballroom, on Bellevue Ave.; and again on Bellevue Ave. such fantasy estates as the Victorian **Château-Sur-Mer, The Elms** (a copy of the old château at Asnières near Paris), the Louis XIII–style **Belcourt Castle,** and so on. All these houses are open daily Apr–Oct; call 401/847-1000 for information.

Among the town's other notable buildings are **Hammersmith Farm** on Ocean Dr., where John and Jackie Kennedy were married; the **Redwood Library,** at 50 Bellevue Ave. (401/847-0292), open daily, believed to be the oldest library in the U.S. still in operation (1748); and the **Touro Synagogue,** 85 Touro St. (401/847-4794), open Sun–Fri late June to Labor Day (Sun only, the rest of the year), an architectural treasure which, dating from 1763, is the oldest synagogue in the continental U.S.

Tennis fans won't want to miss the remarkable museum at the **International Tennis Hall of Fame,** Newport Casino, 194 Bellevue Ave. (401/849-3990), open daily June–Apr (closed in May), entirely devoted to the glories of that great game.

The world-famous **Jazz Festival** has returned to Newport after many years in eclipse, and again draws crowds in Aug of each year, as does the chamber-music festival in mid-July.

Newport alone is enough to justify your journey to the Atlantic seaboard.

Where to Stay

Sheraton River House Inn, Goat Island (causeway from Washington St.), Newport, RI 02840 (401/849-2600; toll free, see Sheraton). 253 rms, A/C, color TV. AE, CB, DC, MC, V. Free parking, two pools, health club, tennis court, marina, rest., coffee shop, bars, rm svce, disco, hrdrsr, free crib. *Note:* Luxurious convention hotel on a little island in dwntwn Newport, w. its own marina and heliport. Spacious, well-laid-out rms w. private balconies or patios. Very good svce. VIP floor. Caters to big-business people and well-heeled vacationers. Open year round. **E–VE**

Treadway Resort and Marina, 49 America's Cup Ave., Newport, RI 02840 (401/847-9000; toll free, see Treadway Inns). 133 rms, A/C, color TV. AE, CB, DC, MC, V. Free parking, pool, sauna, rest., bar, rm svce, free crib. *Note:* Very comfortable hotel-marina overlooking the harbor and the bay w. spectacular views. Huge, inviting rms w. balconies. Flawless svce. Excellent dwntwn location a stone's throw from Newport's main tourist attractions. Open year round. **M–E**

Where to Eat

White Horse Tavern, Marlborough St. and Farewell Sts. (402/849-3600). A/C. Lunch/dinner daily, brunch Sun; closed Jan 1 and Dec 25. AE, CB, DC, MC, V. Jkt. *Specialties:* rack of lamb, beef Wellington, ratatouille w. five kinds of mushrooms, roast duck, steak Diane.

Good wine list. *Note:* Gracious Colonial inn in one of the oldest (1673) buildings in New England. Slightly affected Continental cuisine; svce of a very high order. Resv. advised. *Continental.* **I–M**

NARRAGANSETT PIER: Among New England's most magnificent beaches. You should try to see the **Point Judith Lighthouse** at the south entrance to Narragansett Bay in heavy weather, when the enormous waves breaking over the rocky promontory offer mute testimony of past shipwrecks.

BLOCK ISLAND: Sighted in 1524 by Verrazano, the discoverer of New York, this picturesque little island, 12 miles (19km) out to sea from **Point Judith,** temperate in summer and winter alike, was a pirate stronghold as late as 1815. A treeless moor with many little ponds, a sanctuary for seabirds, and a paradise for fishermen (tuna, swordfish, sea bass, etc.), the island has some fine cliffs at **Mohegan Bluffs,** and strange black-sand beaches.

A favorite vacation resort in summer, it is reached by the **ferries** of the Interstate Navigation Co. from New London, Conn. (daily mid-June to Labor Day), from Providence and Newport, R.I. (daily late June to Labor Day), and from Point Judith, R.I. (daily year round). For information, call 203/442-9553 in Connecticut, 401/789-3502 in Rhode Island.

MYSTIC: This old whaling port, founded in 1654 and built athwart the Mystic River, has the country's finest maritime museum, **Mystic Seaport.** This is a fascinating reconstruction of a 19th-century seaport, with old houses, crafts workshops, sailing boats anchored at the docks, and staff in period costume. Allow at least 3 to 4 hr. for your visit. On Conn. 27 (203/572-0711), open daily year round. Don't miss it.

Where to Stay

Inn at Mystic, U.S. 1 and Conn. 27, Mystic, CT 06355 (203/536-9604). 67 rms, A/C, cable color TV. AE, MC, V. Free parking, pool, tennis court, boats, rest. (Flood Tide), bar, rm svce, crib $10. *Note:* Comfortable motel near Mystic Seaport and its living museum. Inviting rms w. fireplaces and whirlpool baths, some w. private balconies or patios. Very good svce; agreeable setting a quarter mile from the ocean. Open year round. **E,** but lower rates off-season.

Days Inn, 26 Michelle Lane, Mystic, CT 06355 (203/572-0574; toll free, see Days Inn). 122 rms, A/C, cable color TV. AE, CB, DC, MC, V. Free parking, pool, coffee shop, valet svce, free crib. *Note:* Typical modern motel near Mystic Seaport. Functionally comfortable rms; reception and svce w. a smile. Good value overall. Open year round. **I–M**

Where to Eat

Flood Tide, in the Inn at Mystic (see "Where to Stay," above) (203/536-8140). A/C. Breakfast/lunch/dinner daily; closed Dec 24–25. AE, MC, V. *Specialties:* duck w. peaches, Maine lobster, roast rack of lamb, jumbo shrimp stuffed w. crab and garnished w. bacon, beef Wellington, Caesar salad. *Note:* On a hill overlooking Mystic Harbor, this quiet, comfortable hotel rest. serves carefully prepared classic food. Attentive, polished svce. Resv. highly advisable. *Continental/American.* **I–M**

GROTON: Important naval base where the first diesel-powered submarine was built in 1912, and the first nuclear-powered submarine, U.S.S. *Nautilus,* in 1975. The *Nautilus* is now a floating museum, at Crystal Lake Rd. at Conn. 12 (203/449-3174), open Tues–Sun; closed June, Sept, and Dec.

NEW LONDON: Old seaport at the mouth of the Thames River (whence its name), since 1876 home of the **U.S.**

Coast Guard Academy, on I-95, exit 83 (203/444-8270). The Visitor Center and museum are open daily May–Oct, Mon–Fri the rest of the year; cadet parades on Fri in spring and fall.

Opposite the base, the **Lyman Allyn Museum**, 625 Williams St. (203/443-2545), open Tues–Sun, is rich in classical art and antiquities, 18th- and 19th-century American furniture, and enchanting old dolls and dollhouses. Downtown, on Huntington St., see **Whale Oil Row** with its early 19th-century classical revival shipowners' homes.

Ferry connection with Orient Point, at the NE tip of Long Island, N.Y.: 2 Ferry St. (203/443-5281), daily year round.

Where to Eat

IN NEARBY ESSEX ☼☏ **Griswold Inn**, Main St. (203/767-1812). A/C. Lunch/dinner daily; closed Dec 24–25. AE, DC, MC, V. *Specialties:* filet of beef w. fried oysters and sauce béarnaise, roast beef, broiled haddock, seafood of the day, meat pie, homemade sausages. *Note:* Founded in 1776, this delightful inn w. its historic decor is well worth a visit, as much for the inimitable atmosphere as for the quality of its praiseworthy, flavorful food. Superb old bar. Youthful, smiling svce. Resv. advised. A fine place. *American.* **I**

☼ **HARTFORD:** The world's insurance capital, where no fewer than 35 corporate headquarters buildings reach proudly for the sky, Hartford, founded by Dutch settlers in 1623, presents a happy mix of old and modern architecture. With their futuristic towers and their dozens of stores, boutiques, and restaurants, **Constitution Plaza** and the **Civic Center**, both in the heart of downtown, are among the most remarkable achievements of urban renewal in the country.

Lovers of the grand antique would sooner visit the 1796 **Old State House**, by Charles Bulfinch, where there is a fine portrait of George Washington by Gilbert Stuart. It's at 800 Main St. (203/522-6766), open daily. Or there's the 1782 **Butler-McCook Homestead**, with its ornate interior, at 396 Main St. (203/522-1806), open Tues–Thurs and Sun, mid-May to mid-Oct.

Book-lovers will want to see the charming 1870s home where Mark Twain wrote part of *Huckleberry Finn* and *Tom Sawyer* (and the adjoining cottage, once the home of Harriet Beecher Stowe, who wrote *Uncle Tom's Cabin*): **Nook Farm**, Farmington Ave. and Forest St. (203/525-9317), open daily June–Aug; Tues–Sun the rest of the year.

Another absolute must is the ☼ ▲▲ **Wadsworth Atheneum**, 600 Main St. (203/247-9111), open Tues–Sun, one of the oldest and richest art museums in America, with several hundred major works by artists both European (Caravaggio, Zurbarán, Rembrandt, Goya, Picasso, Monet, Gauguin) and American (Church, Sargent, Whistler, Wyeth, Calder).

Hartford prides itself on possessing the oldest continuously published daily paper in the country, the *Hartford Courant*, which was founded in 1764 and became a daily in 1837. Hartford is the birthplace of Noah Webster, author of the first American dictionary (1828). Hartford is also the heart of the firearms industry in the United States. Along the Connecticut River Valley (nicknamed "Gun Valley"), where the modern system of manufacturing firearms was invented in the 1800s, are such famous gun companies as Colt Industries, Remington, Smith & Wesson, and Winchester.

Where to Stay

♙♙♙ **Sheraton Hotel**, 315 Trumbull St., CT 06103 (203/728-5151; toll free, see Sheraton). 400 rms, A/C, color TV, in-rm movies. AE, CB, DC, MC, V. Gar. $9, pool, health club, sauna, rest., bar, 24-hr rm svce, disco, free crib. *Note:* Modern 22-floor hotel adjacent to Civic Center Plaza and its shops. Elegant furnishings; comfortable and well-equipped rms.

Good physical-fitness facilities. Efficient svce; acceptable rest. Business clientele. Located right in middle of dwntwn. Open year round. **E–VE**

♀ **Ramada Inn–Capitol Hill,** 440 Asylum St., Hartford, CT 06103 (203/246-6591; toll free, see Ramada Inns). 96 rms, A/C, color TV. AE, CB, DC, MC, V. Free parking, rest., bar, valet svce. *Note:* Elderly hotel recently renovated; functionally comfortable. Undependable svce. Very centrally located. Good value. Open year round. **M**

Where to Eat

♈♈♈ **L'Americain,** 2 Hartford Sq. W. (203/522-6500). A/C. Lunch Mon–Fri, dinner Mon–Sat; closed hols. AE, MC, V. Jkt. *Specialties:* oyster-and-mushroom ravioli, lobster-stuffed vine leaves, roast saddle of rabbit w. honey, broiled blackfish w. corn kernels, fruit Charlotte. *Note:* Local business people enjoy lunching at this elegant rest., discreetly decorated in shades of peach w. original paintings and antique chandeliers. The cuisine of chef Chris Pardue is remarkable for its imagination and refinement, and the svce. is ultra-professional. A splendid place right in the business district. Resv. a must. *American.* **I–M**

NEW HAVEN: Although only 75 mi. (120km) from New York, New Haven is a typical New England port, on whose stones 350 years of history (it was founded in 1638) have left their mark.

As Harvard has done for Cambridge, so rival 🔭 **Yale University** has raised New Haven to a place of eminence in science and learning. Founded in 1701 at **Brandford** and moved to New Haven in 1716, the university owes its name to a bygone patron of letters, Elihu Yale. On the old campus with its charming ivied buildings, mostly English Gothic Revival or Romanesque, see the **Peabody Museum of Natural History,** with its spectacular collection of prehistoric animals, at 170 Whitney Ave. (203/432-5050), open daily. Be sure to glance at the splendid **Art and Architecture Building,** York St. and Chapel St., a ground-breaking 1963 masterpiece from the drawing board of architect Carl Rudolph. The **Sterling Memorial and Beinecke Libraries,** Wall St. and High St. (203/432-2977), open daily, house between them more than three million works, including such rarities as a Gutenberg Bible, the Yale archives, and an unparalleled collection of playing cards. Louis I. Kahn's 1976 **Center for British Art and Studies,** 1080 Chapel St. (203/432-2800), open Tues–Sun, houses the most important public collection outside Great Britain of that country's art, including works by Hogarth, Constable, Turner, and many others. You should take a **guided tour of the campus,** given daily; apply to the University Information Office, Phelps Gateway, 344 College St. (203/432-2300).

On **The Green,** a 16-acre (6ha) park contemporary with the city, see 🏛 **three lovely churches** of Georgian design from 1813–14. Al Capp, the creator of "Li'l Abner," was born in New Haven.

Where to Stay

♀♀ **Park Plaza and Conference Center,** 155 Temple St., New Haven, CT 06510 (203/772-1700). 300 rms, A/C, color TV. AE, CB, DC, MC, V. Gar. $2, pool, rest. (Top of the Park), bar, rm svce, disco, crib $10. *Note:* Modern 19-story building overlooking dwntwn and the Yale campus; rest. w. panorama on top floor. Spacious, comfortable rms. Good svce on balance. Business clientele; open year round. **M–E**

Where to Eat

♈♈ **Robert Henry's,** 1032 Chapel St. (203/789-1010). A/C. Lunch Mon–Fri, dinner Mon–Sat; closed hols. AE, CB, DC, MC, V. Jkt. *Specialties:* artichoke hearts braised w. basil, lobster w. hazelnut butter, lamb on a skewer w. goat's-cheese ravioli, confit of duck w. apples, tuna tartare, broiled duck w. wild rice, good homemade desserts. *Note:* One of the handsomest rests. in New England, in the former Union League Club of New Haven, w. its high ceilings, marble columns, and elaborate Oriental decor. Light, imaginative American cuisine; very good svce. Locally popular; resv. advised. A stone's throw from the Yale campus. *American.* **I–M**

♈ **Delmonaco's,** 232 Wooster St. (203/865-1109). A/C. ♈ Lunch Sun–Mon and Wed–Fri, dinner Wed–Mon; closed hols. AE, CB, DC, MC, V. *Specialties:* spaghetti alla carbonara, fresh homemade pasta, sautéed scallops, veal cutlet milanese. *Note:* Large, noisy *trattoria* serving straightforward, tasty Italian food. Likable atmosphere; very efficient svce. Good value. *Italian.* **I**

🜨 **STRATFORD:** In 1955 Stratford acknowledged the destiny inseparable from its name and paid tribute to William Shakespeare with the **American Festival Theatre,** an annual summer festival. This is one of the most important classical-theater festivals in the country. For programs and schedules, contact 1850 Elm St., Stratford, CT 06497 (203/375-5000). Worth the detour.

BRIDGEPORT: An important industrial town on Long Island Sound, which is best known as the longtime winter home of the famous Barnum Circus, "The Greatest Show on Earth." Its principal attraction, a 28-inch (70cm) dwarf known as "General Tom Thumb," was himself a Bridgeport native; his tomb, with life-size effigy, is in Mountain Grove Cemetery, North Ave. and Dewey St. See the 🜨 **Barnum Museum,** reopened in 1989 following a $7.5-million renovation, 961 Main St. (203/384-5381), open Tues–Sun, with many personal memorabilia of the circus's founder, P. T. Barnum, who served for a time as mayor of Bridgeport, and of Gen. Tom Thumb. There is a **Barnum Festival,** with parades, concerts, and exhibitions of circus art, every year in late June or early July.

Daily year-round **car-ferry service** between Bridgeport and Port Jefferson, Long Island, N.Y., from Union Sq. Dock (203/367-8571).

🜨 **STAMFORD:** Both a residential suburb of New York and— by latest count—home to 24 of the Fortune 500 largest corporations, Stamford also has many scientific laboratories and research centers.

See the astonishing 1958 **First Presbyterian Church** by Wallace Harrison in the shape of a giant fish; 1101 Bedford Ave. (203/324-9522), open daily.

Where to Eat

IN NEARBY WESTPORT ♈ **Panda Pavilion,** 1300 Post Rd. E. (203/255-3988). A/C. Lunch/dinner daily. AE, MC, V. *Specialties:* spareribs w. sesame seeds, Hunan chicken w. honeyed walnuts, duck w. ginger and bamboo shoots, sesame beef, eggplant w. shrimp. *Note:* The food is absolutely authentic Chinese, though the setting—a maze of little rooms with wall paintings of romping pandas—is not. Pleasant, quick svce. Very good value. *Chinese.* **B–I**

☼ **GREENWICH:** A smart suburb for well-to-do New Yorkers, ☼ with a very New England vintage charm. Among its most remarkable and historic buildings are the 1685 **Bush-Holley House,** 39 Strickland Rd. (203/869-6899), open Tues–Fri, housing many works of art and pieces of antique furniture; and the 1690 **Putnam Cottage,** where Gen. Israel Putnam, a Revolutionary hero, was detained by, and escaped from, the British in 1779; it's at 243 E. Putnam Ave. (203/869-9697), open Mon, Wed, and Fri, or by appointment. Worth seeing.

Where to Eat

☼ ♈♈♈ **Bertrand,** 253 Greenwich Ave. (203/661-4459). A/C. ☼ ⚬⚬⚬ Lunch Mon–Fri, dinner Mon–Sat; closed hols. AE, MC, V.

Jkt. *Specialties:* seafood in puff pastry w. leeks and basil, salmon marinated w. aniseed, confit of duck w. chanterelle mushrooms, red snapper braised in white wine, sautéed breast of chicken w. cream of basil, very good desserts. Large wine list. *Note:* Chef Christian Bertrand was once the associate of André Soltner at New York's Lutèce (see Chapter 3 on New York). That tells you all you need to know about the quality and delicacy of the food. The decor, running to Roman arches, vaulted ceilings, and a glassed lobby, is on the elaborate side. Polished svce; resv. a must. Has quickly established itself as one of the best rests. in the New York area. *French.* **M–E**

RYE BROOK: This out-of-the-way little town north of White Plains, on the New York/Connecticut state border, reached by the Merritt Pkwy. and Conn. 15 from Greenwich, is the home of one of the most unexpected of America's museums: the **Museum of Cartoon Art,** entirely devoted to the characters of comic strips and cartoon movies. Has more than 60,000 pieces of original "cartoon art" from 1870 to the present day, and hundreds of cartoon movies, the oldest dating from 1899. The museum is housed in an 1876 medieval fortress which is itself a kind of museum piece, being the first American house built using poured concrete reinforced with iron beams. Everyone who enjoys the comics will want to visit it, on Comly Ave. (914/939-0234), open Tues–Fri and Sun.

NEW YORK: See Chapter 3 on New York City.

CHAPTER 6

PHILADELPHIA🕯🕯

□ □ □

With Atlantic City and the Pennsylvania Dutch Country

There is no properly brought-up U.S. citizen who doesn't know that Philadelphia is "the cradle of our nation." Here the Declaration of Independence was drawn up and adopted; here the Constitution, the cornerstone of the American government, was approved; here George Washington presided, for the eight years 1790–97, over the destiny of the new nation. Philadelphia can also claim the country's first bank, its first daily newspaper, its first hospital, its first stock exchange, its first zoo, its first mint, and its first school for African American children.

In the 18th century London was the only English-speaking city in the world larger than Philadelphia, and from so illustrious a past the American city has retained a sense of history, and a love of old buildings. Not far from the spot on the Delaware River where Englishman William Penn (who gave his name to the state of Pennsylvania) led the first Quaker settlers ashore in 1682 may still be found some of the country's best-known public buildings: **Independence Hall** with its famous **Liberty Bell; Congress Hall,** the **Old City Hall;** the **Jacob Graff House,** where Thomas Jefferson drafted the Declaration of Independence; **Carpenters' Hall,** where the first Continental Congress was held; **Franklin Court,** where stood the home of Benjamin Franklin, one of Philadelphia's most illustrious citizens; the house of **Betsy Ross,** who sewed together the first American flag. For the bicentennials of the Declaration of Independence (1976) and the Constitution (1987), much restoration and rehabilitation was done in **Independence National Park,** known as "America's most historic square mile."

Some of the nearby side streets with their pretty little red-brick houses, such as **Elfreth's Alley,** the oldest street in the U.S., are strangely reminiscent of 18th-century London. Art galleries, antiques shops, and above all, restaurants elbow each other in these little streets near Independence Mall. Philadelphia, which once had little enough to offer the gourmet, has become a place of pilgrimage; in the last dozen years more than 300 new restaurants, some of the highest order, have opened their doors here.

Lovers of the picturesque will make a point of visiting **Little Italy,** the domain of *Rocky,* of little family-owned *trattorie,* and open-air markets. To the north of the city, **Germantown,** founded by Mennonite settlers in the 17th century, is another interesting ethnic enclave; around Germantown Ave., a Native American trail in pre-Colonial days, there are many very lovely old homes.

Philadelphia (in classical Greek, "the city of brotherly love") is a thriving center of industry and commerce, with strong representation in health care, publishing, pharmaceuticals, petrochemicals, and electronics. Handling more than 40 million tons (18.1 million kg) of cargo annually, it's also one of the world's largest river ports. In spite of uncertainties in municipal politics, dozens of corporations have moved their head offices here, attracted by Philadelphia's strategic position halfway between New York and Washington, its abundant labor supply, its rich cultural life—and a booming real-estate market. U.S. 202, on the city's northern periphery, fills the role of the local Silicon Valley, as does the more famous "Route 128" in Boston.

"Philly," as its citizens affectionately call it, takes pride in a long-standing tradition of intellectual and artistic activity: it boasts no fewer than 1,400 churches, synagogues, and other places of worship; 90 museums; eight universities, including the renowned **University of Pennsylvania** and **Temple University;** and a world-famous symphony orchestra. In spite of its size, it is still a city on a human scale, watched over by the statue of William Penn, perched 548 ft. (167m) in the air atop the astonishing City Hall.

According to FBI figures, Philadelphia's crime rate (22.3 homicides per 100,000 inhabitants) is one of the lowest for any major U.S. city. But the 1985 bombing by the police of a house inhabited by members of the African American cult Move, which killed 11 people and incinerated 60 adjacent rowhouses has not yet been forgotten.

Famous children of "Philly" include movie directors Sidney Lumet and Arthur Penn; painter Thomas Eakins, painter-photographer Man Ray; sculptor Alexander Calder; the late Princess Grace of Monaco (Grace Kelly); comedians W. C. Fields and Bill Cosby; actor Richard Gere; contralto Marian Anderson, singer Patti LaBelle; jazzmen Rex Stewart, Benny Golson, Stam Getz, and Sam Wooding; and anthropologist Margaret Mead.

BASIC FACTS: State of Pennsylvania. Area code: 215. Time zone: eastern. ZIP Code: 19014. Founded: 1682. Approximate population: city, 1,680,000; metropolitan area, 5,780,000. Fifth-largest metropolitan area in the country.

CLIMATE: Spring and fall, usually sunny and cool, are the best times for a visit, but the climate of the Atlantic seaboard is unpredictable at best, so bring an umbrella and a raincoat. Winter is cold, though the temperature rarely drops below 23°F (−5°C), and the Jan average is 35°F (2°C). The weather is hot and sticky from June to Sept, with July averaging 78°F (25°C).

DISTANCES: Baltimore, 94 mi. (150km); Niagara Falls, 385 mi. (623km); New York, 100 mi. (160km); Pittsburgh, 308 mi. (498km); Washington, 134 mi. (215km).

ARRIVAL & TRANSIT INFORMATION

AIRPORT: Philadelphia International Airport (PHL), 7 mi. (11km) SW, is a very up-to-date terminal. Call 215/492-3181 for information.

U.S. AIRLINES: American (365-4000), Continental (592-8005), Delta (928-1700), Eastern (923-3500), Midway (toll free 800/621-5700), Northwest (toll free 800/225-2525), TWA (923-2000), United (568-2800), and USAir (563-8055).

FOREIGN AIRLINES: British Airways (toll free 800/247-9297) and Lufthansa (toll free 800/645-3880).

CITY LINK: The **cab** fare from the airport to dwntwn is about $18; time, about 20–30 min. Express train from the airport to dwntwn, the **SEPTA Airport Line,** leaves every 30 min.; serves the 30th St., 16th St., and Market St. East stations dwntwn; fare, $4; time, 25 min.

Taxis are expensive and reliable, but the **public transportation** system (bus, subway, and streetcar) is efficient and cheap (though to be avoided at night). For information, call SEPTA (574-7800). Subway fare: $1.50.

The dwntwn area is small enough that you shouldn't need to rent a car, unless you're planning trips to Atlantic City or Pennsylvania Dutch Country.

CAR RENTAL (at the airport unless otherwise indicated): Avis (492-0900); Budget (492-5500); Dollar (365-1605); Hertz (492-7205); National (492-2751); and Thrifty, 70th St. and Holstein Ave. (365-3900). For dwntwn locations, consult the local telephone directory.

LIMOUSINE SERVICES: Carey Limousine (492-8402), Dav-El Limousines (334-7900), and Royal Limo & Coach (toll free 800/248-7557).

TAXIS: Abundant during daylight hours; may be hailed in the street, or taken from the waiting lines at the major hotels or the downtown cab stands. After 5pm it's better to phone: **Quaker City Cab** (728-8000), **United Cab Assoc.** (625-9170), or **Yellow Cab** (922-8400).

TRAIN: Amtrak Station, 30th and Market Sts. (824-1600). There's a ticket office at 4 Penn Center (824-1600); for information and reservations for the Metroliner, call 824-4224.

INTERCITY BUSES: Greyhound, 1001 Filbert St. (931-4014).

INFORMATION & TOURS

TOURIST INFORMATION: The **Philadelphia Convention and Visitors Bureau,** 1515 Market St., Suite 2020, PA 19102 (636-3300).

International Visitors Center, 34th St. and Civic Center Blvd. (823-7261), has multilingual personnel.

Visitors Center, 16th St. and John F. Kennedy Blvd. (636-1666), open daily year round.

GUIDED TOURS: Audio Walk and Tour, Norman Rockwell Museum, 601 Walnut St. (925-1234): Rent a "Walkman" with prerecorded cassettes and visit the Historic District on foot. Open daily year round.

Centipede Tours, 1315 Walnut St. (735-3123): A 90-min. walk through the Historic District with Colonial-costumed guides. Original and instructive. Mid-May to mid-Oct on Wed, Fri, and Sat in good weather. Resv. advised.

Fairmount Park Trolley (bus) 16th St. and John F. Kennedy Blvd. (879-4044): Trip around Fairmount Park and its museums in a replica of a turn-of-the-century trolley; get on and off as often as you like. Also a 2-hr. guided tour across the city. Daily Apr–Nov.

Gray Line Tours (bus), 1525 John F. Kennedy Blvd. (569-3666): Guided tours of the city year round; serves the major hotels.

Philadelphia Carriage Co. (carriage), 500 N. 13th St. (922-6840): Carriage trip around the city center, leaving from the Carriage Stand in front of the Liberty Bell Pavilion. Daily Feb–Dec, weather permitting.

Philadelphia Tours (bus): A 2-hr. conducted tour in a London double-decker bus; leaves 16th St. and John F. Kennedy Blvd. at 10am Tues–Sat (271-2999).

R. & S. Harbor Tours (boat), Penn's Landing, Delaware Ave. and Lombard

St. (928-0972): Guided tour of the harbor and trip on the Delaware River. Daily mid-Apr to Oct.

SIGHTS, ATTRACTIONS & ACTIVITIES

ARCHITECTURAL HIGHLIGHTS: ⚓ **Boat House Row,** Kelly Dr., in Fairmount Park: Picturesque Victorian boathouses along the Schuylkill River, used by the many local rowing clubs. Afternoon regattas throughout the summer (for information on times, call 686-2176). Should be seen.

City Hall, Broad St. and Market St. (567-4476); John McArthur designed this flamboyant 1894 building in French-Renaissance style. The 548-ft. (167m) tower is crowned by a bronze statue of William Penn. With 750 rooms, it's the biggest City Hall in the country, and took 20 years to build. Open daily; guided tours Mon–Fri by appointment. Don't miss it.

One Liberty Place, 1 Liberty Pl.: Very fine 61-story skyscraper, whose conical crest recalls New York's famous Chrysler Building, was designed by Chicago architect Helmut Jahn and opened in 1987. At 816 ft. (248m), or 955 ft. (290m) with its needle, it was the first building to violate the hallowed limit of 548 ft. (167m)—the height of William Penn's hat on the City Hall statue—above which no building in Philadelphia had previously been allowed to rise. Nearby false-twin tower, **Two Liberty Place,** completed in 1990, at 58 stories stands slightly shorter than its predecessor. Should be seen.

U.S. Mint, 5th St. and Arch St. (597-7350): The world's largest, producing 25,000 coins a minute. Visitors' gallery and display of old coins and medals in the Rittenhouse Room. Interesting. Open daily in summer, Mon–Fri the rest of the year.

CHURCHES/SYNAGOGUES: **Christ Church,** 2nd St. between Market St. and Arch St. (922-1695): A handsome 1754 Colonial church, once attended by George Washington, Benjamin Franklin, and other historic figures. In the churchyard and the neighboring cemetery at 5th St. and Arch St. are buried seven signers of the Declaration of Independence, including Franklin. Should be seen. Open daily.

Gloria Dei Church, Delaware and Washington Sts. (389-1513): The oldest place of worship in Pennsylvania (1700). Called "Old Swedes' Church" because many of the first Scandinavian settlers worshiped here. Worth a visit. Open daily.

Old St. Mary's Church, 252 S. 4th St., between Locust St. and Spruce St. (923-7930): Built in 1763 as the city's original Roman Catholic cathedral. The tomb of Commodore John Barry, "Father of the U.S. Navy," is behind the church. Open daily.

St. George's United Methodist Church, 235 N. 4th St. (925-7788): The oldest (1769) Methodist church in the country; the first African American Methodist minister was ordained here in 1799. An interesting Colonial building; see the chalice that belonged to John Wesley, the English theologian who founded the Methodist church. Worth a visit. Open daily.

HISTORIC BUILDINGS: The largest group of historic buildings are in Independence National Historic Park, but others are scattered around town.

Independence National Historical Park

Called "America's most historic square mile." For information on all the buildings listed below, phone 597-8974. Park **Visitor Center:** 3rd St. and Chestnut St.

Carpenters' Hall, 320 Chestnut St. (925-0167): The 1770 Hall of the Carpenters' Guild; the First Continental Congress met here in 1774. Museum. Open Tues–Sat. Should be seen.

☀☖ **City Tavern,** 2nd St. and Walnut St. (923-6059): A careful reconstruction of a famous Revolutionary tavern, once described by Pres. John Adams as "the most elegant tavern in America." Here, two centuries ago, the Founding Fathers dined while framing the Constitution. Today it has become an appealing (and successful) restaurant with lunch/dinner daily.

☀☖☖ **Congress Hall,** 6th St. and Chestnut St.: Adjoining Independence Hall, this 1789 building housed the meetings of the first Congress of the United States from 1790 to 1800, while the Capitol in Washington was under construction. The reelection of George Washington to the presidency in 1793, and the election of John Adams in 1797, took place here. You can see the chambers of the House of Representatives (first floor) and the Senate (second floor). Don't miss it. Open daily.

☖ **First Bank of the U.S.,** 3rd St. between Walnut St. and Chestnut St.: The oldest American bank, founded in 1791 by Alexander Hamilton. Closed to visitors.

☀☖ **Franklin Court,** Market St. between 3rd St. and 4th St.: Group of old buildings conceived and designed by Benjamin Franklin. His house, where he died in 1790, was destroyed by fire in 1812. An underground museum is devoted to this genial inventor and statesman. A visit you should make. Open daily.

☀☖☖☖ **Independence Hall,** Chestnut St. between 5th St. and 6th St. (627-1776): With its rounded bell tower, four-faced clock, and elegant Georgian facade in ocher brick, Independence Hall is one of the most historically meaningful public buildings in the U.S. The Declaration of Independence was signed here on July 4, 1776, and the Constitution was adopted here in 1787. In the former assembly hall, now renovated, you can see several pieces of historic furniture, including Washington's armchair. Independence Hall, open daily, is worth the trip all by itself.

☀☖ **Jacob Graff House,** 701 Market St. at 7th St.: A 1975 reconstruction of the house where Thomas Jefferson was living in 1776 while he worked on the text of the Declaration of Independence. The two rooms he occupied have been carefully re-created. A short film is shown on this historic episode. A must. Open daily.

☀☖☖ **Liberty Bell Pavilion,** Independence Mall between Market St. and Chestnut St.: The bell here, which once was perched on the tower of Independence Hall, was the first to be rung after the first public reading of the Declaration of Independence on July 8, 1776. Bearing on its side the engraved inscription (Leviticus 10:25) "Proclaim liberty throughout all the land unto all the inhabitants thereof," the bell was cracked in 1835 and has not sounded since 1846. This symbol of Liberty is now housed in a glass structure built in 1976 in the center of the mall. A must—on no account to be missed—for every visitor to Philadelphia.

☀☖ **Old City Hall,** 5th St. and Chestnut St.: In spite of its name this building was never City Hall; it was the first seat of the U.S. Supreme Court from 1791 to 1800. Museum devoted to life in 18th-century Philadelphia. Interesting. Open daily.

☀☖ **Todd House,** 4th St. and Walnut St.: Handsome middle-class home dating from 1785, where Dolley Payne Todd lived before she married Pres. James Madison and became first lady. Interesting reconstruction of life in a middle-class Quaker family of the period. Open daily.

Historic Buildings Outside the Park

☀☖ **"A Man Full of Trouble" Tavern,** 127-129 Spruce St. (922-1759): Picturesque tavern built in 1759 and splendidly re-

PHILADELPHIA
CENTER CITY

stored to its original condition. Furniture and handcrafts of the 17th and 18th centuries. By appointment only; should be seen.

Betsy Ross House, 239 Arch St. (627-5343): Pretty little Colonial house which once belonged to the seamstress Betsy Ross, and where (so the story goes), at the request of George Washington, she sewed the first American flag ("Old Glory," with, at that time, only 13 stars). Don't miss it. Open daily.

Edgar Allan Poe National Historic Site, 532 N. 7th St., at Spring Garden St. (597-8780): Home of Edgar Allan Poe in 1843–44, where he wrote some of his most famous poems and stories, particularly *The Raven* and *The Gold Bug*. This is the illustrious author's only national memorial. A must for all book lovers. Open daily.

Penn's Landing, Delaware Ave. and Chestnut St. (923-8181): Maritime museum, marina, and cultural center, this huge recreation complex on the banks of the Delaware River stands where the first Quaker settlers, led by William Penn, are believed to have landed. The floating museum comprises half a dozen big sailing ships and old vessels including the U.S.S. *Olympia*, Admiral Dewey's flagship during the Spanish-American War of 1898, and the *Mosholu*, one of the biggest four-masters in the world. Should be visited. Open daily.

MARKETS: ☀🔔 **Italian Market,** along 9th St. between Christian St. and Federal St.: Open-air market in the heart of Little Italy; used as background in the movie *Rocky*. Colorful. Tues–Sat.

Reading Terminal Market, 12th St. and Arch St. (922-2317): A real institution since 1893, with every kind of food known to land or sea piled in picturesque disorder on dozens of stalls. A wonderful place for a quick snack, where you can sample some of the local specialties such as cheese-steak sandwiches, snapper soup, and the famous Bassett's ice cream. A sight that should be seen. Open Mon–Sat.

MONUMENTS: 🔔 **Bolt of Lightning,** Franklin Sq. near the Benjamin Franklin Bridge: A 102-ft.-tall (33m) stainless-steel sculpture designed as a memorial to Benjamin Franklin by celebrated American-Japanese sculptor Isamu Noguchi (1984). Worth a glance.

Tomb of the Revolutionary War's Unknown Soldier, Washington Sq. at Walnut St. and 6th St.: In the west sector of huge Washington Sq., this tomb of an unknown soldier from the War of Independence is watched over by a life-size statue of George Washington. Also buried here are hundreds of other Revolutionary combatants, as well as civilian victims of yellow-fever epidemics.

MUSEUMS OF ART: 🔔 **Athenaeum of Philadelphia,** 219 S. 6th St. (925-2688): Paintings, sculpture, and Empire furniture which once belonged to Joseph Bonaparte, brother of Napoleon. Library devoted to the architecture and decorative arts of the 19th century—the building itself is a fine 1847 example of Victorian architecture. Should be seen. Open Mon–Fri.

Barnes Foundation, 300 N. Latch's Lane in Merion, 7 mi. (12km) NW on I-76 and City Ave. (667-0290): One of the world's most extraordinary private collections, comprising a full 1,000 paintings, mostly impressionist and modern, including 150 Renoirs and 60 Cézannes. They include Renoir's *Women Bathing in the Forest* and *Woman Reading,* Cézanne's *Card Players,* Seurat's *Three Sitters,* and Picasso's *Comedians.* Unfortunately it admits no more than 200 visitors on Fri and Sat, and only 100 on Sun. Closed in July and Aug. Reservations an absolute must—but in spite of the inconveniences, don't fail to see it.

Norman Rockwell Museum, 601 Walnut St. (922-4345): Works on display from the 60-year career of this famous painter and illustrator include drawings, paintings, posters, lithographs, etc., with a faithful reconstruction of his studio. Should be seen. Open daily.

☼☖☖ **Pennsylvania Academy of the Fine Arts,** Broad St. and Cherry St. (972-7600): Founded in 1805 and now installed in an elegant Victorian building, this is the oldest academy of fine arts in the country. The museum has a fine collection of American painting from the 18th century to the present day, with works by Charles Willson Peale, Benjamin West, Thomas Eakins, Thomas Sully, etc. Should be seen. Open Tues–Sun.

☼☖☖☖ **Philadelphia Museum of Arts,** 26th St. and Benjamin Franklin Pkwy. (763-8100): Rising majestically at the end of Ben Franklin Pkwy., this is one of the greatest, as well as one of the largest, art museums in America, housing nearly 500,000 paintings, sculptures, drawings, watercolors, prints, and other works of art. Imposing Greco-Roman building whose monumental staircase figured in the movie *Rocky*. Superb collections of medieval art, Oriental art, and European painting (particularly works by Marcel Duchamp). Among the most famous works on display: *Christ on the Cross and the Virgin and St. John* by Rogier van der Weyden, Giovanni di Paolo's *Miracle of St. Nicolas of Tolentino,* Charles Willson Peale's *The Staircase Group,* Marcel Duchamp's *Nude Descending a Staircase,* van Gogh's *Sunflowers,* Cézanne's *The Large Bathers,* Fernand Léger's *The City, Woman and Child Driving* by Mary Cassatt, and *Three Musicians* by Picasso. An absolute must for art lovers. Open Tues–Sun.

☼☖ **Rodin Museum,** 22nd St. and Benjamin Franklin Pkwy. (763-8100): The largest collection of Rodin sculptures, drawings, and watercolors outside France, including versions of *The Thinker, The Gates of Hell,* and *The Burghers of Calais.* Should be seen. Open Tues–Sun.

☖ **Rosenbach Museum,** 2010 Delancey Pl. at 20th St. (732-1600): Interesting period furniture, silverware, porcelains, art objects, rare books, and valuable manuscripts. Also temporary exhibitions. Should be seen. Open Tues–Sun; closed in Aug.

MUSEUMS OF SCIENCE & HISTORY: ☼☖ **Academy of Natural Sciences Museum,** 19th St. and Benjamin Franklin Pkwy. (299-1020): Many prehistoric animals, including a dozen dinosaurs; a panorama of the animal kingdom throughout the world, in facsimiles of its natural habitats; Egyptian mummies; an enormous selection of precious stones and minerals. A must-see. Open daily.

☖ **Afro-American Historical and Cultural Museum,** 7th St. and Arch St. (574-0380): The first American museum entirely devoted to African American art and culture in Africa and the U.S.; also a history of racial discrimination. A must-see. Open Tues–Sun.

☖ **Army-Navy Museum,** Chestnut St. between 3rd St. and 4th St. (597-8974): In a building **(Pemberton House)** that is a facsimile of the home of a wealthy Quaker merchant of the Colonial period, this museum recapitulates the history of the U.S. Army and Navy during the War of Independence. Interesting. Open daily.

☖ **Civil War Library and Museum,** 1805 Pine St. (735-8196): With 12,000 different books and documents, this is one of the richest Civil War libraries in the country. Unique collection of period weapons, uniforms, flags, and other memorabilia. A must for all history buffs. Open Mon–Fri; wknds by appointment only.

☖ **Fireman's Hall Museum,** 149 N. 2nd St. (923-1438): Unique collection of material relating to firefighting in the 18th and 19th centuries, the largest of its kind in the country. Housed in an 1876 fire station. Should be seen. Tues–Sat.

☼☖☖ **Franklin Institute Science Museum,** 20th St. and Benjamin Franklin Pkwy. (448-1200): One of the country's most complete and up-to-date science museums. Everything on nuclear fission and fusion, computers, astronomy, space flight, and aviation. A giant human heart 20 ft. (6m) high demonstrates the circulation of the blood. The **Futures Center,** a $72-million wing opened in May 1990, takes visitors on a thoughtful journey into the near and distant future through technology exhibits, including experimental high-speed trains, robotized lunar mining and other chores, and undersea gardening. Also home of the highly regarded **Fels Planetarium.** Fine view of the city. Not to be missed. Open daily.

      Historical Society of Pennsylvania, 1300 Locust St. (732-6201): Interesting small history museum with some important Colonial objects, from William Penn's furniture to Martha Washington's cookbook. Worth seeing. Open Tues–Sat.

      Marine Corps Memorial Museum, Chestnut St. between 3rd St. and 4th St. (597-8974): On the site of **New Hall,** built in 1791 by the Carpenters' Guild, this relatively new museum commemorates the birth and early days of the U.S. Marine Corps. For military-history enthusiasts. Open daily.

      Mummers Museum, 2nd St. and Washington Ave. (336-3050): The "Mummers" parade—8 hr. of spectacle and music along Broad St. on Jan 1 (see "Special Events," below). The museum has memorabilia, costumes, videotapes, and sound recordings of past parades. Free concerts Tues evenings May–Oct. Must be seen. Open Tues–Sun.

      National Museum of American Jewish History, 55 N. 5th St. (923-3811): Bears witness to the contributions that America's Jewish communities have made to the arts, the sciences, and society since 1654. Memorabilia of famous Philadelphians, including Haym Salomon, the financier of the War of Independence. There is a synagogue attached to the museum. Open Sun–Thurs.

      Perelman Antique Toy Museum, 270 S. 2nd St. (922-1070): Charming museum of old toys—dolls, animals, piggy banks, mechanical toys, etc.—in the 1758 Abercrombie House. More than 4,000 exhibits in all, some of great value. Worth seeing. Open daily.

      Philadelphia Maritime Museum, 321 Chestnut St. (925-5439): Smallish but well-laid-out maritime museum with many ship models, treasures recovered from shipwrecks, and an exhibition on underwater exploration. Should be seen. Open daily.

      Please Touch Museum, 210 N. 21st St. (963-0666): Unusual museum for children under 7. In an inviting, colorful setting, the young visitors are encouraged to participate directly in educational experiences relating to art, technology, and natural science. Fascinating for young and old alike. Open Tues–Sun.

      Port of History Museum, Penn's Landing, Delaware Ave. and Walnut St. (925-3804): Temporary exhibitions of visual art, photography, design, etc.; also concerts, shows, dance, and a multimedia spectacle entitled *Philadelphia: Visions & Realities*. Should be seen. Open Wed–Sun.

      University Museum, 33rd St. and Spruce St. (898-4000): One of the finest museums of archeology and anthropology in the world. From Egyptian mummies to Inuit and Polynesian art, and from African masks to Roman, Chinese, and Mayan antiquities, you will find here a complete panorama of the ancient cultures of five continents. Not to be missed. Open Tues–Sun (but closed Sun in summer).

OUTDOOR ART & PLAZAS: More than 200 modern sculptures embellish the greensward and avenues of **Fairmount Park.** Notable among them are the *Swann Memorial Fountain* by Alexander Calder (a native Philadelphian), *Washington Monument* by Rudolf Siemering, *Cowboy* by Frederic Remington, *Spirit of*

Enterprise by Jacques Lipchitz, *Playing Angels* by Carl Milles, and *Stone Age in America* by John Boyle.

Other remarkable modern sculptures are Claes Oldenburg's giant *Clothespin* in chromed steel, 45 ft. (13m) high, standing like a challenge in front of **City Hall** at 15th St. and Market St. and *Bolt of Lightning* by Isamu Noguchi (see "Monuments," above).

PANORAMAS: ⚓ **City Hall,** Broad St. and Market St. (686-1776): Fine view of dwntwn Philadelphia and the Delaware Valley from the top of the Observation Tower at 548 ft. (167m). Reopened in 1989 following renovation.

PARKS & GARDENS: ☼⚓ **Fairmount Park,** NW of the city on both sides of the Schuylkill River: 8,900 acres (3,600ha) of woods, lawns, and lovely gardens, designed by the famous landscape architect Frederick Law Olmsted, one of the two creators of Central Park in New York. The "lung" of Philadelphia, with more than 100 mi. (160km) of paths for cycling and jogging. Many carefully restored Colonial houses, including the Georgian **Mount Pleasant Mansion** (1761) and the 1798 **Strawberry Mansion,** a blend of the Federal and Greek Revival styles. Open-air symphony concerts in summer at **Robin Hood Dell.** Highly regarded zoo (see below). Well worth a visit. For information, call 686-2176.

☼⚓ **Independence Mall,** bounded by 5th St. and 6th St. between Race St. and Walnut St.: Shady, flower-planted promenade with lawns and fountains, in the heart of historic Philadelphia. The glass pavilion housing the Liberty Bell stands in the middle of the mall. Shouldn't be missed.

⚓ **Laurel Hill Cemetery,** Randolph Dr.: Adjoining Fairmount Park and overlooking the Schuylkill River, this landscaped cemetery offers an unbelievably rich selection of funerary art, from Victorian crypts with marble angels and lions, to a replica of the Egyptian temple of Philae and giant obelisks in the style of the Washington Monument. The bronze statue of a goddess by Alexander Calder should also be seen. Worth a look. Open daily.

⚓ **Pennsylvania Horticultural Society,** 325 Walnut St. (625-8250): The oldest horticultural society in the country, founded in 1765. Its garden contains flowers, plants, and shrubs typical of that period. Worth seeing. Open Mon–Fri Mar–Sept.

PERFORMING ARTS: For a daily listing of all shows and cultural events, consult the entertainment pages of the daily papers *Philadelphia Inquirer* (morning) and *Philadelphia Daily News* (evening), and of the monthly *Philadelphia* magazine. **Tix Stop,** a discount ticket booth in the Philadelphia Visitors Center, 16th St. and John F. Kennedy Blvd. (564-4414), sells half-price tickets for all shows on the day of performance, Tues–Sat; cash only.

☼ **Academy of Music,** Broad St. and Locust St. (893-1930): A fine classical revival building dating from 1847; home of the Philadelphia Orchestra (principal conductor, Ricardo Muti), of the Opera Company of Philadelphia (director, Margaret Ann Everitt), and of the Pennsylvania Ballet (artistic director, Robert Weiss). Also big-name recitals.

Annenberg Center, University of Pennsylvania, 3680 Walnut St. (898-6791): Modern and classical theater, children's theater, musicals. Home of the Philadelphia Drama Guild.

Forrest Theater, 1114 Walnut St. (923-1515): Broadway and Off Broadway hits, musicals.

Mann Music Center, George's Hill, W. Fairmount Park (567-0707): Concerts by the Philadelphia Orchestra, June–Aug. Big-name recitals.

Plays and Players Theatre, 1714 Delancey St. (440-8282): Modern and classical theater; home of the Philadelphia Company.

Robin Hood Dell East, 33rd St. and Dauphin St., Fairmount Park (477-8810): Pop, jazz, gospel music concerts (summer only).

Schubert Theater, Broad St. and Locust St. (732-5446): Ballet performances by the Pennsylvania Ballet and other companies, opera, comedy.
Society Hill Playhouse, 507 S. 8th St. (923-0210): Modern theater, Off Broadway shows.
The Spectrum, Broad St. and Pattison Ave. (389-5000): Concerts by leading pop and rock stars.
☼ **Walnut Street Theater,** 9th St. and Walnut St. (574-3550): One of the oldest theaters (1809) in the country. Comedy, drama, experimental theater, modern dance. Home of the Pennsylvania Opera Theater (artistic director, Barbara Silverstein).

SHOPPING: ⌂ **Antique Row,** Pine St. from 9th St. to 12th St.: Philadelphia's haven for antiques buffs. The three-block area comprises dozens of stores and curio shops appealing to collectors.
The Bourse, 5th St. between Market St. and Chestnut St. (625-9393): More than 50 boutiques, shops, and restaurants in a handsomely restored Victorian-style building, once the home of the Philadelphia Stock Exchange. Opposite the Liberty Bell Pavilion. Open daily.
The Gallery, 9th St. and Market St. (925-7162): The biggest shopping center in the city, with 250 stores, boutiques, and restaurants under one roof, with indoor gardens, fountains, and glass-walled elevators. Spectacular. Open daily.
☼ **Jewelers' Row,** 7th St. and Sansom St.: The diamond and jewelry district, with more than 300 stores—Philadelphia's answer to New York's W. 47th St. A sight not to be missed.
John Wanamaker, 13th St. and Market St. (422-2000): The most famous department store in Philadelphia, truly a city within the city, with a splendid nine-story rococo-columned main hall, post office, and free organ recitals at 11:15am and 5:15pm. Open daily.
New Market, 2nd St. between Pine St. and Lombard St. (627-7500): Modern all-glass shopping center, with indoor gardens and waterfalls, contrasting sharply with the surrounding red-brick structures; 50 boutiques and restaurants. Open daily.

SPECIAL EVENTS: For the exact schedule of events listed below, consult the **Philadelphia Convention and Visitors Bureau** (see "Tourist Information," above).
☼ **Mummers Parade** (Jan 1): Big costumed parade, with bands and floats, down Broad St.; 8 hr. of colorful carnival. 20,000 marchers in ornate costumes. A solidly entrenched tradition since 1901; don't miss it.
☼ **Devon Horse Show** (9 days in late May to early June), 22 mi. (35km) NW on U.S. 30 in Devon: One of the biggest horse shows in the country, with more than 1,200 horses competing. Harness races. Spectacular. For information on schedules, call 964-0550.
Elfreth's Alley Fête Day (first wknd in June): Tour of the charming old houses on Elfreth's Alley (see "Strolls," below), with colonially costumed guides. Don't miss it.
Mellon Jazz Festival (late June): More than 40 concerts, many of them free. Features the greatest soloists.
Freedom Week (late June to July 4): A week of festivities celebrating Independence, with processions, fireworks, fountain festival, nighttime Mummers Parade. Shouldn't be missed.
Thanksgiving Day Parade (Thanksgiving Day): Parade of giant floats through the dwntwn streets.
Army-Navy Football Game (last Sat in Nov or first Sat in Dec): A football classic, held at Veterans Stadium.

SPORTS: Philadelphia has four professional teams:
Baseball (Apr–Oct): Phillies, Veterans Stadium (463-1000).
Basketball (Oct–Apr): 76ers, Spectrum Sports Arena (339-7676).
Football (Aug–Dec): Eagles, Veterans Stadium (463-5500).
Ice Hockey (Oct–Apr): Flyers, Spectrum Sports Arena (465-4500).

Horse Racing

Garden State Park, N.J. 70 in Cherry Hill (609/488-8400): Thorough-bred racing from mid-Feb to mid-June; harness, Aug–Dec.
Philadelphia Park, Street Rd., Bensalem (639-9000): Flat racing June–Feb.

STROLLS: ▲ **Chinatown,** bounded by Franklin Sq. and 11th St. from Arch St. to Vine St.: With more than 15,000 people, this is one of the most important Chinese districts in America's great cities. There are no fewer than 80 restaurants and an interesting cultural center at 125 N. 10th St. (923-6767), with visits by appointment. Worth the side trip.

Elfreth's Alley, north of Arch St. between Front St. and 2nd St. Narrow cobbled lane dating from the late 1690s; probably the oldest street in the country. Still has around 30 original craftsmen's and sailors' houses, the oldest from 1728. There's a museum, with period furnishing and equipment, in **Elfreth's House,** no. 126 (574-0560), open daily. Not to be missed.

Head House Square, 2nd St. and Pine St.: Head House is an old hall built in 1775, surrounded by old buildings, boutiques, art galleries, restaurants, and the New Market Shopping Center (see "Shopping," above). Concerts in summer. Very lively atmosphere.

Rittenhouse Square, 18th St. and Walnut St.: One of the city's most elegant residential neighborhoods, a mixture of up-scale 19th-century houses and luxurious modern apartment buildings, with a shady square in the middle where in spring and summer there are flower shows, concerts, and art exhibitions. Worth a look.

Society Hill Area, bounded by Front St., Walnut St., 7th St., and Lombard St.: So called after the Free Society of Traders founded by William Penn. Many celebrated figures of the Revolutionary period once lived here. Their houses, now scrupulously restored, add to the charm of the neighborhood, which with its tree-lined streets and little red-brick houses is straight out of the 18th century. Don't miss it.

South Philly, bounded by Front St. and 20th St., Washington Ave. and South St.: Colorful working-class neighborhood which became widely known through the movie *Rocky*. There are many cafés and family *trattorie* around the **Italian Market,** making this local **Little Italy** a must for visitors; don't miss it.

THEME PARKS: ▲ **Sesame Place,** 100 Sesame Rd. in Langhorne, 22 mi. (35km) NE on I-95 (757-1100): Amusement park for small children, based on the TV program "Sesame Street" and its characters. More than 100 games and other attractions. The kingdom of the moppets. Open daily May to early Sept, wknds only, Labor Day to mid-Oct; closed the rest of the year.

Six Flags Great Adventure, at Jackson, N.J., 56 mi. (90km) NE via I-95, Pennsylvania Tpke. Connection, New Jersey Tpke. north, I-195E, and N.J. 537S (201/928-3500): Huge 1,700-acre (688ha) theme park, with a hundred attractions including carousels, one of the world's fastest roller coasters (68 m.p.h.), and a drive-through safari-zoo with 2,000 wild animals (you stay in your car). Shows and vaudeville. Open daily Apr–Sept, wknds only to late Oct; closed the rest of the year.

WINTER SPORTS RESORTS: ⛷ **Doe Mountain,** near Hereford, 58 mi. (92km) along U.S. 76W, U.S. 422W, and Penna. 100N (682-7109): Seven lifts; open Dec to mid-Mar.

⛷ **Spring Mountain Ski Area,** near Limerick, 36 mi. (57km) via U.S. 76W, U.S. 422W, and Penna. 29N (287-7900): Six lifts; open mid-Dec to mid-Mar.

ZOOS: ☀⛲ **Zoological Garden,** Fairmount Park, 34th St. and Girard Ave. (387-6400): Opened in 1874, this is the oldest zoo in the U.S. More than 1,600 animals; important collections of reptiles and primates. Children's zoo. Monorail tour. Worth a visit. Open daily.

ACCOMMODATIONS

A Note on Accommodations: Room rates in Philadelphia are coded as follows: **VE,** Very Expensive ($140 and up); **E,** Expensive ($90–$140); **M,** Moderate ($60–$90); **I,** Inexpensive ($30–$60); **B,** Budget (up to $30). A listing of toll-free numbers is in the Appendix.

Personal Favorites (in order of preference)

♟♟♟♟ **Four Seasons** (dwntwn), 1 Logan Sq., PA 19103 (215/963-1500; toll free, see Four Seasons). 371 rms, A/C, color TV, in-rm movies. AE, CB, DC, MC, V. Valet gar. $14, pool, health club, sauna, two rests. (including the Fountain), bar, 24-hr. rm svce, concierge. *Note:* The most distinguished place to stay in Philadelphia; eight-floor modern building adj. an office high-rise from which it is separated by a lovely landscaped courtyard and grdn w. fountains. Spacious, ultra-comfortable rms decorated in Federal style, w. minibars (some w. balconies). Excellent svce. Sophisticated rest. Very well located a stone's throw from the museum district. Big business clientele. Interesting wknd discounts. **VE**

☀♟♟♟♟ **Hotel Atop the Bellevue** (dwntwn), 1415 Chancellor Court (at Broad St. and Walnut St.), PA 19102 (215/893-1776; toll free, see Preferred). 173 rms, A/C, color TV, in-rm movies. AE, CB, DC, MC, V. Valet gar. $12, pool, health club, sauna, squash courts, jogging track, massage, two rests. (including Founders), coffee shop, bar, 24-hr. rm svce, boutiques, concierge. *Note:* Occupying the top seven floors of the venerable Bellevue Building, a designated turn-of-the-century landmark, this super-deluxe hotel reopened in 1989 after 18 months (and $100 million) of renovation. The luxury and refinement are European in flavor; spacious rms w. every imaginable convenience (VCRs, minibars, marble bathrooms w. TV and telephone). Period furnishings. Magnificent seven-story atrium–winter garden. Absolutely first-class physical-fitness facilities; personalized svce; rest. open to hotel guests only. Quality with elegance; VIP clientele. **VE**

♟♟♟ **Rittenhouse Hotel** (dwntwn), 210 W. Rittenhouse Sq., PA 19103 (215/564-9000; toll free, see Preferred). 98 rms, A/C, color TV, in-rm movies. AE, MC, V. Valet gar. $12, pool, health club, sauna, rest. (Two Ten), bar, 24-hr. rm svce, concierge. *Note:* Brand-new elegant 33-floor high-rise w. elegant faceted exterior overlooking Rittenhouse Sq., Philadelphia's poshest residential address. The hotel has the 11 lower floors; the rest of the building offers luxury apartments. Exceptionally spacious, inviting rms and suites, unusually well equipped (three telephones, two TVs, VCR). Excellent physical-fitness facilities. Polished, efficient svce. A favorite of those in-the-know. **VE**

♟♟ **Radisson Suites Hotel** (dwntwn), Benjamin Franklin Pkwy. at 18th St., PA 19103 (215/963-2222; toll free, see Radisson). 285 suites, A/C, color TV, in-rm movies. AE, CB, DC, MC, V. Gar. $10, rest. (Palace Café), bar, rm svce, free crib, concierge. *Note:* Large 28-floor cylindrical tower, a block or two from Logan Circle and the museum district. Has only suites, spacious, w. terraces and refrigerators. Ideal for long stays and/or business travelers (fully equipped Business Center). No physical-fitness facilities. Caters mostly to groups and conventions. **E–VE**

♀♀ **Comfort Inn Penn's Landing** (dwntwn), 100 N. Delaware Ave., PA 19107 (215/627-7900; toll free 800/228-5150). 185 rms, A/C, color TV, in-rm movies, AE, CB, DC, MC, V. Free parking, rest. adj., bar, rm svce, free breakfast. *Note:* New 10-story motel on the banks of the Delaware River. Functional, comfortable rms overlooking river or city. Friendly reception and svce. Ideal for visiting Independence Mall and its historic monuments. Very good overall value. **M**

♀ **Super 6–Cherry Hill** (formerly the Tudor Inn; vic.), N.J. 70W, Cherry Hill, NJ 08002 (609/234-0700). 120 rms, A/C, color TV, in-rm movies. AE, CB, DC, MC, V. Free parking, pool, health club, sauna, rest., bar, rm svce, crib $2. *Note:* Comfortable, well-equipped motel across the road from the Garden State Racetrack, 15 min. by car from dwntwn Philadelphia by the Benjamin Franklin Bridge. Spacious rms, most w. refrigerators. Ideal if you're driving. Good value. **I–M**

Other Accommodations (from top bracket to budget)

♀♀♀ **Sheraton Society Hill** (dwntwn), 1 Dock St., PA 19106 (215/238-6000; toll free, see Sheraton). 365 rms, A/C, color TV, in-rm movies. AE, CB, DC, MC, V. Valet gar. $12, pool, health club, sauna, rest. (Americus), bar, 24-hr. rm svce, nightclub, boutiques, free crib, concierge. *Note:* Very new hotel in an original version of the red-brick idiom, in the heart of the Society Hill historic district. Ultramodern furnishings and facilities. Spectacular four-story glass-walled lobby. Huge, very comfortable rms w. refrigerators. Efficient svce. Courtesy limo to business district. Perfect for visiting Independence Mall. Interesting wknd discounts. **VE**

♀♀♀ **Wyndham Franklin Plaza** (dwntwn), 2 Franklin Plaza, PA 19103 (215/448-2000; toll free 800/822-4200). 761 rms, A/C, color TV, in-rm movies. AE, CB, DC, MC, V. Valet gar. $14, pool, health club, tennis court, sauna, two rests. (including the Terrace), coffee shop, two bars, rm svce, nightclub, hrdrsr, drugstore, free crib. *Note:* Large, ultramodern convention hotel w. 26 floors, Philadelphia's biggest. Functional, comfortable rms w. refrigerators; impersonal but efficient svce; very good physical-fitness facilities. Caters mostly to groups and business travelers. Halfway between City Hall and the museum district. **VE**

♀♀♀ **The Hershey** (dwntwn), Broad St. and Locust St., PA 19107 (215/893-1600; toll free 800/533-3131). 428 rms, A/C, color TV, in-rm movies. AE, CB, DC, MC, V. Valet gar. $13, pool, health club, sauna, squash courts, rest. (Café Académie), two bars, rm svce, disco, concierge, crib $10. *Note:* Ultramodern 25-story tower in the heart of dwntwn. Inviting, spacious, very comfortable rms, some w. refrigerator. Spectacular four-floor atrium. Excellent svce; mediocre rest.; VIP floor. Since the financial district is right next door many business travelers stay here. **E–VE**, but lower rates off-season.

☼♀♀♀ **The Warwick** (dwntwn), 17th St. and Locust St., PA 19103 (215/735-6000; toll free 800/523-4210). 180 rms, A/C, color TV, in-rm movies. AE, CB, DC, MC, V. Valet gar. $12, rest. (1701 Café), bar, rm svce, disco, hrdrsr, drugstore, free crib, concierge. *Note:* Elegant, intimate little hotel dating from the '20s. Lobby sumptuously decorated w. rare rugs and period pieces. Spacious, inviting rms, some w. kitchenettes. Polished svce. Conveniently located very near Rittenhouse Sq. and the business district. Clientele of wealthy businessmen. Has both charm and distinction; offers interesting wknd discounts. **E–VE**

♀♀♀ **Penn Tower Hotel** (formerly the Hilton; nr. dwntwn), Civic Center Blvd. at 34th St., PA 19104 (215/387-8333; toll free 800/356-7366). 225 rms, A/C, color TV, in-rm movies. AE, CB, DC, MC, V.

Gar. $10, pool, health club, rest., bar, rm svce. *Note:* Large, very modern hotel on the University of Pennsylvania campus, w. completely renovated interior. Inviting, comfortable atmosphere; efficient svce. VIP floor. With the Civic Center and the Convention Hall nearby, attracts mostly groups and conventions. **M–E**

Holiday Inn Independence Mall (dwntwn), 4th St. and Arch St., PA 19106 (215/923-8660; toll free, see Holiday Inns). 364 rms, A/C, color TV, in-rm movies. AE, CB, DC, MC, V. Gar. $8, rooftop pool, rest. (Benjamin's), coffee shop, bar, rm svce, disco, free crib. *Note:* Large, comfortable, very well-run motel; rms and facilities recently modernized. Pool open in summer only. One of the best locations for visiting the Historic District. Group and tourist clientele. A better class of Holiday Inn. **M–E**

Quality Inn Downtown Suites (dwntwn), 1010 Race St., PA 19016 (215/922-1730; toll free, see Quality Inns). 96 suites, A/C, color TV. AE, CB, DC, MC, V. Free gar., health club, sauna, rest. (Silver Palace), bar, rm svce. *Note:* Unusual all-suites hotel in the heart of Chinatown, in a building which used to be a rocking-chair factory—Victorian rococo, now pleasingly restored. Spacious, comfortable suites w. kitchenettes; good svce. Well situated, near City Hall and the picturesque Reading Terminal Market. Group clientele. **M–E**

Quality Inn Center City (formerly the Franklin Motor Inn; nr. dwntwn), 501 N. 22nd St., PA 19130 (215/568-8300; toll free, see Quality Inns). 280 rms, A/C, color TV, in-rm movies. AE, CB, DC, MC, V. Free parking, pool, rest., coffee shop, bar, rm svce. *Note:* Recently renovated motel in the museum district. Comfortable rms, though some are on the small side; good svce. Good value on balance. Group clientele. 10 min. from dwntwn. **M**

Days Inn–Roosevelt (nr. dwntwn), 4200 Roosevelt Blvd. at U.S. 1, PA 19124 (215/289-9200; toll free, see Days Inns). 115 rms, A/C, color TV, in-rm movies. AE, MC, V. Free parking, rest., bar. *Note:* Motel north of the city. Functionally comfortable; acceptable rest. Great if you're driving; 15 min. from dwntwn. **I**

Roosevelt Motor Inn (vic.), 7600 Roosevelt Blvd., PA 19152 (215/338-7600). 101 rms, A/C, color TV. AE, MC, V. Free parking, rest., bar. *Note:* Typical, well-run motel w. acceptable comforts and facilities. Ideal if you're driving; 25 min. from dwntwn. **I**

St. Charles Hotel (dwntwn), 1935 Arch St., PA 19103 (215/567-5651). 70 rms, A/C, color TV. AE, MC, V. No private parking, bar, or rest. *Note:* Small hotel, aging but clean, near Logan Circle and the museum district. Decent levels of comfort; friendly reception. Some rms w. shared baths. Caters mostly to students; great for the budget traveler. **I**

Airport Accommodations

Holiday Inn–Airport (vic.), 45 Industrial Hwy., in Essington, PA 19029 (215/521-2400; toll free, see Holiday Inns). 306 rms, A/C, color TV, in-rm movies. AE, CB, DC, MC, V. Free parking, pool, rest., coffee shop, bar, rm svce, disco, free crib. *Note:* Large modern six-story motel in true Holiday Inn style, 5 min. from the airport. Comfortable, well-soundproofed rms; free airport limo. Business clientele. **M–E**

YMCAs/Youth Hostels

Chamounix Mansion (nr. dwntwn), Chamounix Dr., Fairmount Park (215/878-3676). Inviting youth hostel in a renovated 19th-century farmhouse. Dormitories (50 beds). Closed at Christmas.

International House (nr. dwntwn), 3701 Chestnut St. (215/387-5125). If you're on a tight budget, this is the best place in town (though reserved for students only). Nr. U. of Pennsylvania; acceptable rest.

RESTAURANTS

A Note on Restaurant Prices: Philadelphia restaurant prices, per person, excluding drinks and service charges, are coded as follows: **VE**, Very Expensive ($60 and up); **E**, Expensive ($40–$60); **M**, Moderate ($25–$40); **I**, Inexpensive ($15–$25); **B**, Budget (up to $15).

Personal Favorites (in order of preference)

Le Bec Fin (dwntwn), 1523 Walnut St. (567-1000). A/C. Lunch Mon–Fri, dinner Mon–Sat (two sittings, at 6 and 9pm); closed hols. and mid-Aug to early Sept. AE, CB, DC, MC, V. J&T. *Specialties:* scallops sautéed w. sugar peas; squab w. cream sauce, thyme, and garlic; medaillons of veal w. morel mushrooms; oysters in millefeuille pastry shell; veal kidneys moutardier; civet of lobster. Remarkable desserts; large wine list. Menu changed seasonally. *Note:* Along with New York's Lutèce and Washington's Jean Louis, Le Bec Fin is one of the most honorable exponents of French haute cuisine in the country. Chef George Perrier, from Lyons, works wonders at his stoves; his dishes and sauces are marvels of delicacy and balance. Elegant, flower-bedecked setting w. only 14 tables, so that resv. must be made at least 8 days ahead for weeknights, and weeks ahead for Fri and Sat evenings. Full of big-business people and celebrities passing through. Flawless svce. One of the 12 best rests. in the country. *French.* **M** (lunch), **VE** (dinner)

The Fountain (dwntwn), in the Four Seasons (see "Accommodations," above) (963-1500). A/C. Breakfast/lunch/dinner daily. AE, CB, DC, MC, V. Jkt. *Specialties:* linguine w. shrimp and cream of saffron, cold tomato soup w. coriander, red snapper w. three caviars, salmon in puff pastry, roast pheasant w. cabbage and walnuts, sautéed veal cutlet w. turnips, chocolate ramekin. Very fine wine list, particularly strong on half bottles; low-calorie menu available. *Note:* This relatively new (1983) luxury-hotel rest. has quickly become recognized as offering some of the best food in Philadelphia. Luxurious, expensive decor featuring wood paneling, Italian marble floors covered in Oriental rugs, and magnificent flower arrangements. Unimpeded view of Logan Sq. and the fountain for which the rest. is named. Modern cuisine in every way remarkable. Ultra-polished svce. The fashionable place for entertaining. Resv. a must. *Continental.* **M–E**

Susanna Foo (dwntwn), 1512 Walnut St. (545-2666). A/C. Lunch/dinner Mon–Sat; closed hols. and 2 weeks in Aug. AE, MC, V. J&T. *Specialties:* smoked-duck salad w. endive and mango, curried-chicken dumplings w. grilled eggplant salad, salmon w. lemon-grass, sweetbreads w. Kung Pao sauce, sautéed quail w. shiitake and ginger, fried honey banana w. almond and warm coconut sauce. Menu changes regularly. Good list of French and California wines. *Note:* The most interesting Far Eastern rest. in greater Philadelphia. Chef Susanna Foo, who arrived here from her native China in 1979, serves up a wholly original merger of different traditions and tastes: Chinese, French, Mexican, and Californian. Rather chilly modern decor; courteous and attentive svce. You shouldn't miss this great dining experience. Resv. strongly advised. *Chinese.* **I–M**

The Garden (dwntwn), 1617 Spruce St. (546-4455). A/C. Lunch Mon–Fri, dinner Mon–Sat; closed hols. AE, CB, DC, MC, V. Jkt. *Specialties:* carpaccio, pasta primavera, oysters on the half shell, mussels and clams w. chives, roast chicken w. cognac, aged prime beef, broiled breaded Dover sole, raspberry and chocolate cake. Rather skimpy wine list. *Note:* With its open-air garden, yellow umbrellas, and centuries-old trees surrounded by old Georgian houses, this dwntwn rest. offers you the loveliest setting you could ask for on a fine day. The five indoor dining rms are no less delightful. Excellent, unaffected bistro food; the meat is especially noteworthy. Friendly, smiling svce. Locally popular; resv. advised. *Continental/American.* **M**

Il Gallo Nero (dwntwn), 254 S. 15th St. (546-8065). A/C. Lunch Tues–Fri, dinner Tues–Sat; closed hols. and July. AE,

CB, DC, MC, V. J&T. *Specialties:* fresh homemade pasta (w. truffles in season), paglia e fieno, sautéed porcini mushrooms, risotto, ossobuco, northern Italian dishes. Menu changes seasonally. Fine list of Italian wines. Low-calorie menu available. *Note:* Housed in a two-centuries-old building which was once a music conservatory, this rest., somewhat overdecorated in the rococo idiom, offers light food in the Tuscan tradition. Diligent svce. The favorite rest. of Luciano Pavarotti as well as other musical celebrities. Resv. advised. *Italian.* **M**

♀ **The Commissary** (dwntwn), 1710 Sansom St. (569-2240). ♿ A/C. Breakfast Mon–Fri, lunch/dinner daily. AE, CB, DC, MC, V. *Specialties:* homemade soups and salads, fresh pasta, daily specials, excellent desserts. Menu changes daily. *Note:* Steve Poses, who owns this attractive place (ground-floor cafeteria and second-floor rest.), used to be a student of urban planning; here he has studied to ennoble the fast-food business. The setting is at once modern and comfortable, the regional American cuisine often original and well prepared, the atmosphere gently bohemian, the svce. efficient but relaxed. A fine place. *American.* **B–I**

☀♀ **The City Tavern** (dwntwn), 2nd St. and Walnut St. (923-6059). A/C. Lunch/dinner daily; closed Jan 1, Dec 25. AE, MC, V. Jkt. *Specialties:* salmagundi salad, chicken w. cider, roast beef, catch of the day, Indian pudding. *Note:* This famous Revolutionary War tavern, rebuilt in 1974, perfectly recaptures the feeling of the 1770s, when John Adams described it as "the most elegant tavern in America." Period-costumed waitresses and a harpist at dinner. Unpretentious, praiseworthy food based on old recipes. Resv. advised. A must for history buffs. *American.* **I–M**

♀ **Ragozzino's** (dwntwn), 737 S. 10th St. (923-2927). A/C. ♿ Lunch/dinner Mon–Sat. (until 2am). No credit cards. *Specialties:* hoagies (Philadelphia-style giant sandwiches). *Note:* The hoagie is a real Philadelphia institution: an enormous hero on a loaf sliced down the middle, w. ham, salami, provolone, onions, lettuce, tomato, and green pepper, the whole doused with olive oil. Dainty eaters stay away. Philadelphia's biggest, tastiest hoagies are to be had at Ragozzino's, a stone's throw from the Italian Market. *American.* **B**

Other Restaurants (from top bracket to budget)

♀♀♀ **Ciboulette** (dwntwn), 1312 Spruce St. (790-1210). A/C. Lunch/dinner Mon–Sat. AE. J&T. *Specialties:* warm eggplant terrine, sautéed foie gras on a bed of vegetables and shallots, roast duckling w. honey-and-ginger glaze, salmon w. lentils and burgundy sauce, roast saddle of lamb w. zucchini tart and goat cheese, terrine of bitter chocolate covered w. pear coulis, crème brûlée. Rather wimpy wine list. *Note:* The Provençal-inspired French cooking of young chefs Bruce Lim and Francesco Martorella is wonderfully elegant and balanced. The decor is resolutely austere in tones of beige; the svce, highly professional. The five-dish tasting menu is a bargain at $55. At a rest. so successful, and so small (40 seats), resv. are a must—but so is the rest. itself for all lovers of good food. *French.* **M** (**E** for tasting menu).

♀♀ **A Propos** (dwntwn), 211 S. Broad St. (546-4424). A/C. ♿ Breakfast/lunch/dinner daily; closed July 4. AE, CB, DC, MC, V. *Specialties:* fresh homemade pasta, a variety of pizzas, mesquite-broiled meat, fish, and chicken. The desserts, particularly the chocolate cake, are excellent. *Note:* Chef Aliza Green's California cuisine is as up-to-date as the decor, with its pretty winter-garden terrace and its friendly bar. Youthful, hip clientele. A fashionable place; often noisy. *American.* **I–M**

♀♀ **Bookbinder's Seafood House** (dwntwn), 215 S. 15th St. ♿ (545-1137). A/C. Lunch Mon–Fri, dinner nightly; closed Sun July–Aug, Thanksgiving, Dec 25. AE, CB, DC, MC, V. J&T. *Specialties:* oysters on the half shell, snapper (snapping turtle) soup, mussels in red sauce, Florida stone crabs in season, crab Imperial, fried squid, lobster Coleman, filet of flounder stuffed w. crabmeat. Weak on wines and desserts. *Note:* "Booky's," as Philadelphians call it, has been a landmark for half a century (by the way, don't confuse it with its near namesake, Old Original Bookbinders, a typical tourist rest. in the heart of the Historic District), and has belonged to four generations of the Bookbinder family. Dependable but unimaginative food; traditional seafaring decor w. the inevitable fishing trophies stuffed and mounted on the walls. Popular for business lunches; often crowded and noisy. Svce on the curt side. Resv. advised. *Seafood.* **I–M**

Fish Market (dwntwn), 18th St. and Sansom St. (567-3559). A/C. Lunch Mon–Fri, dinner nightly; closed hols. AE, CB, DC, MC, V. Jkt. *Specialties:* crabmeat quiche, sole Oscar, bouillabaisse, catch of the day, shellfish. *Note:* The Fish Market, which started life as no more than a retail fishmonger's, over the years has become one of the best fish rests. in Philadelphia. The fish and shellfish are absolutely fresh, but sometimes overcooked. Preppy atmosphere. Always crowded at lunchtime; resv. advised. *Seafood.* **I–M**

Friday, Saturday, Sunday (nr. dwntwn), 261 S. 21st St. (546-4232). A/C. Lunch Mon–Fri, dinner nightly. AE, DC, MC, V. *Specialties:* wild-mushroom soup, smoked bluefish w. horseradish cream, poached salmon w. sorrel, curried duck, rack of lamb, Cornish hen Normandie stuffed w. apples and walnuts. *Note:* Elegant, romantic little bistro w. a truly Parisian flavor. The daily menu, scrawled on a chalkboard, is resolutely nouvelle cuisine. Trendy clientele; friendly, hard-working svce; a very good place. *Continental.* **I–M**

Siva's (dwntwn), 34 S. Front St. (925-2700). A/C. Lunch Tues–Fri, dinner Tues–Sun. AE, CB, DC, MC, V. Jkt. *Specialties:* pakora (buns stuffed w. spiced meat or fish), chicken tandoori, bivyarri (ragoût of mutton, chicken, and rice), Indian-style fish. *Note:* One of the best and most authentic Indian rests. on the East Coast. Pretty Oriental decor with bronze-inlaid teak doors, Indian fabrics, ocher-and-gold color scheme, and cane chairs. Excellent northern Indian food; diligent svce. Resv. advised. A Philadelphia classic. *Indian.* **I–M**

Asakura at Tokyo Center (dwntwn), 1207 Race St. (988-0274). A/C. Lunch Mon–Fri, dinner nightly. AE, MC, V. *Specialties:* sushi, tempura, sashimi, teriyaki, sukiyaki. *Note:* Chinatown's only Japanese restaurant. Chefs from Tokyo offer a wide variety of Japanese dishes from simple vegetable tempura to esoteric sushi. Dining is Western style at tables or Japanese style in the tatami room. Live jazz Fri–Sat. Resv. advised. *Japanese.* **I**

Marabella's (dwntwn), 1420 Locust St. (545-1845). A/C. Lunch/dinner daily; closed hols. AE, MC, V. Jkt. *Specialties:* fresh homemade pasta, gourmet pizzas, catch of the day, broiled chicken and veal chops, chocolate and raspberry cake. *Note:* This new-age trattoria is warm and colorful; its fresh homemade pastas (particularly the outstanding tortellini with goat cheese) are excellent, as are the attractively priced broiled (over mesquite) specialties. The decor is bold and brassy, and the place is usually noisy, but the svce is quick and efficient. Locally very popular; resv. recommended. *Italian.* **I**

Sansom Street Oyster House (dwntwn), 1516 Sansom St. (567-7683). A/C. Lunch/dinner Mon–Sat; closed hols. AE, CB, DC, MC, V. *Specialties:* oysters and clams, broiled fish of the day, crab Imperial. *Note:* Likable seafood bistro where the decor is unpretentious but the seafood is remarkably fresh. Locally popular; often noisy. Setting recently refurbished. No resv., so sometimes a long wait. Excellent value. *Seafood.* **B–I**

Famous 4th St. Delicatessen (dwntwn), 4th St. and Bainbridge St. (922-3274). A/C. Breakfast/lunch/dinner daily (7am–6pm, to 4pm Sun); closed Jewish hols. No credit cards. *Specialties:* corned-beef sandwiches, pastrami, kugel, whitefish, lox, chocolate-chip cookies, milkshakes. *Note:* This New York–style deli is a favorite of those in-the-know. The decor and svce are without pretension or affectation, boasting collections of old telephones and old milk cartons. Generous servings; very popular locally. Has been in the same family for 60 years. *American.* **B**

☼🍷 **Jim's Steaks** (dwntwn), 400 South St. at 4th St. (928-1911). A/C. Lunch/dinner daily (till 1am). No credit cards. *Specialties:* cheese steak, hoagies. *Note:* Undisputed master of these two local specialties. Hoagies are giant hero sandwiches of ham, provolone, and salami; cheese steaks are thin slices of steak broiled w. onion, green pepper, tomato sauce, and cheese, all served on a crusty loaf of Italian bread. Both are real Philadelphia institutions. You can eat them here in a superb art deco setting—black-and-white tiles and sparkling chrome. Generally crowded at lunch. *American.* **I**

☼🍷 **Melrose Diner** (nr. dwntwn), 1501 Snyder Ave. at Broad St. (467-6644). A/C. Breakfast/lunch/dinner around the clock daily. No credit cards. *Specialties:* chicken soup, scrapple (leftover pork, sliced and fried up w. buckwheat meal or cornmeal), hamburgers, pork chops, apple pie. *Note:* A South Philly favorite for more than half a century. Praiseworthy plain food served w. a smile in generous portions. Crowded at all hours of day and night. A real landmark. *American.* **I**

🍷 **H. A. Winston & Co.** (dwntwn), 1500 Locust St. at 15th St. (546-7232). A/C. Lunch/dinner daily (until midnight). AE, MC, V. *Specialties:* onion soup, sandwiches, salads, hamburgers, broiled chicken, catch of the day. *Note:* In the opinion of experts, the best burgers in Philadelphia, in more than 25 varieties: from hamburger à la Russe w. caviar and sour cream to hamburger Hawaiian w. pineapple and coconut. Agreeable decor. Locally popular. *American.* **I**

In the Vicinity

☼🍷🍷🍷 **Joe's,** 450 S. 7th St. at Laurel St., in Reading, 60 mi. (96km) NW on I-76 and U.S. 422 (373-6794). A/C. Dinner only, Tues–Sat; closed hols. AE, CB, DC, MC, V. Jkt. *Specialties:* wild-mushroom soup, mushrooms in pastry shell, morels Marie stuffed w. mousse of pheasant, shiitake w. pepper and burgundy sauce, duck in sauce bourguignonne w. fresh mushrooms, squab stuffed w. mushrooms. Good homemade desserts. *Note:* One of Pennsylvania's best, and certainly one of its most original, rests. Owner Jack Czarnecki, an expert who picks his own wild mushrooms in the surrounding woodlands, knows them all and blends their different flavors to perfection; his food is delicate and inspired. The rest., which has been in the Czarnecki family since 1916, is well worth the 1¼-hr. trip from Philadelphia by car. Resv. a must. *Continental.* **M**

Cafeterias/Fast Food

Eden (nr. dwntwn), 3701 Chestnut St., in International House (387-2471). Lunch/dinner daily. MC, V. *Specialties:* broiled chicken, fresh pasta, catch of the day, vegetarian and nouvelle cuisine daily specials. *Note:* Remarkable cafeteria food at modest prices. Same management as the Commissary (see above). Patronized by students. On fine days you can eat in the open air. Other locations: 1527 Chestnut St. (972-0400) and 3701 Chestnut St. (387-2471). **I**

BARS & NIGHTCLUBS

A Propos (dwntwn), 211 S. Broad St. (546-4424). Very "with-it" singles bar full of local yuppies. Also very acceptable rest. (see "Restaurants," above). Open daily.

Borgia Café (dwntwn), 408 S. 2nd St. (923-6660). Excellent modern jazz —the purist's choice—in a smoke-filled room.

Comedy Works (dwntwn), 126 Chestnut St. (922-5997). Famous comedy club above the Middle East Restaurant. A landmark on the Philadelphia scene.

Downey's (dwntwn), 526 Front St. at South St. (625-9500). Irish pub favored by local sports figures; dance floor. Also praiseworthy rest. Usually crowded. Open nightly.

Flanigan's (dwntwn), 532 2nd St. (928-9898). The fashionable rock joint; elegant. Open Tues–Sat.

Funny Bone (dwntwn), 221 South St. (440-9670). One of the local high places of improvisation, featuring the biggest stars in that sky.

Magnolia (dwntwn), 1603 Latimer St. (546-4180). This popular bar draws a business-suited crowd of singles. Live music Mon–Sat. Good Créole-Cajun eatery adjacent (1602 Locust St.).

Polo Bay (dwntwn), in the Warwick (see "Accommodations," above) (546-8800). The favorite nightclub of Philadelphia's yuppies. Caribbean ambience. Open nightly.

P.T.'s (dwntwn), 6 S. Front St. (922-5676). Singles bar, jazz, disco, back-gammon. Relaxed, comfortable atmosphere. Open nightly.

Revival (dwntwn), 22 S. 3rd St. (627-4825). The 20s–30s age bracket piles into the two large rooms for contemporary dance music, videos, and perfor-mance art. Open Wed–Sun.

Spectacles (dwntwn), in the Sheraton Society Hill (see "Accommoda-tions," above) (238-6000). Philadelphia's "in" disco. Very preppy. Spectacular contemporary decor.

NEARBY EXCURSIONS

CAMDEN (1 mi./2km east by the Benjamin Franklin Bridge): This little New Jersey city, founded in 1681 and now an industrial suburb of Philadelphia, boasts the 🏛 **house of Walt Whitman**, singer of the "American Dream," where he spent the last 8 years of his life, at 330 Mickle St. (609/964-5383), open Wed–Sun. You'll find the original furniture, books, and personal memorabilia of the "Good Gray Poet." His tomb is in Harleigh Cemetery, Heddon Ave. and Vesper Blvd.

Camden is also the home of Campbell Soup, and has an unusual museum devoted to old soup tureens in silver, faïence, and porcelain: the 🏛 **Campbell Museum,** Campbell Pl. (609/342-6440), open Mon–Fri.

DOYLESTOWN (28 mi./44km north on Penna. 611): Cap-ital of picturesque Bucks County, country retreat of many art-ists, writers, and theatrical people. Be sure to see the 🏛 **home of Pearl Buck**, the novelist and Nobel laureate, at 520 Dublin Rd., Hilltown Township (249-0100), open Mon–Fri, plus Sun May–Sept; closed mid-Jan to Mar. It was here that she wrote her most famous novel, *The Good Earth,* which won the Pulitzer Prize in 1932.

While you're here, don't miss the cavernous 🏛 **Mercer Museum** and its fa-mous collection of old Americana at Pine St. and E. Ashland St. (345-0210), open daily Mar–Dec.

You can conveniently combine this trip with visits to **New Hope** and **Wash-ington Crossing Historical Park** (see below).

GERMANTOWN (7 mi./11km north on Broad St. and Germantown Ave.): Settled toward the end of the 17th century by Mennonite immigrants from the Rhineland in Germany, this old village, now a residential neighborhood, has dozens of old houses that are designated historic monuments. Its main thoroughfare, **Germantown Avenue,** is an old Native American trail which is itself a "National Historic Landmark."

Among the most interesting buildings (all open to the public Tues–Sun Apr–Dec) are: **Cliveden,** a 1767 Georgian house at 6401 Germantown Ave.; George Washington's summer residence at 5442 Germantown Ave., the 1773

Deshler-Morris House; the **Germantown Historical Society Complex,** comprising several museums in houses built between 1745 and 1798, at 5214 Germantown Ave. (844-0514); the 1744 **Grumblethorpe House,** at 5267 Germantown Ave.; **Stenton,** at 18th St. and Windrim Ave., constructed in 1730, which was Washington's headquarters during the Battle of Germantown; **Upsala,** 6430 Germantown Ave., a 1798 gem of Federal architecture; and the town's oldest house, the 1690 **Wyck** at 6026 Germantown Ave. Don't miss this visit.

☀🏛️ **LONGWOOD GARDENS** (at Kennett Sq., 31 mi./49km SW on I-95S, U.S. 322N, and U.S. 1S): Magnificent 350-acre (140ha) park, once the property of Pierre S. DuPont, where something is in bloom almost any time of year; there are tropical greenhouses, lush Italian gardens, an arboretum, an orchid house, and pools covered with giant water lilies. Concerts and shows in summer. Open daily; call 388-6741 for information. Well worth the trip.

On the way see ☀ **Brandywine Battlefield,** on U.S. 1 at Chadds Ford (459-3342), where the colonists sustained a defeat at the hands of the British in 1777. Visitor Center; Washington's and Lafayette's headquarters. Open Tues–Sun.

Another place you shouldn't miss is the ☀🏛️ **Brandywine River Museum,** on U.S. 1 at Chadds Ford (388-7601), open daily, housed in a century-old mill. Contains Andrew Wyeth's private collection of his own works; those of his father, the famous illustrator N. C. Wyeth; and paintings by his father's teacher, Howard Pyle, and many other American artists.

☀🏛️ **NEW HOPE** (46 mi./73km NE on I-95N and Penna. 32): Charming 300-year-old village on the banks of the Delaware River, which has long proved irresistible to artists and writers. Many old houses, boutiques, art galleries, and inns. Apr–Nov you can take a picturesque trip in a **mule-drawn barge** along the Old Delaware Canal; apply on New St. (609/862-2842).

On the way, be sure to visit ☀ **Washington Crossing State Park,** on either side of the Delaware River at the exact spot where Washington and 2,400 of his men crossed it in a snowstorm on the night of December 25, 1776, on his way to capture the town of Trenton by surprise. This brilliant feat of arms, reenacted every year on Dec 25 by costumed extras, was one of the turning points of the War of Independence. Memorials; museum on Penna. 32 (493-4076). Open daily; don't miss it.

☀🏛️ **OLD FORT MIFFLIN** (Fort Mifflin Rd., 8 mi./12km SW along Broad St. and Penna. 291) (365-9781): Sometimes called "the Alamo of the War of Independence"; scene of a fierce engagement against the British in the fall of 1777. Rebuilt in 1798. Open wknds only, Mar–Nov. Military parades in period uniform on Sun in summer. Should be seen.

☀🏛️ **POTTSTOWN** (36 mi./57km NW on I-76 and U.S. 422): Here, in 1714, ironmaster John Potts opened Pennsylvania's first industrial foundry. His family home, **Pottsgrove Mansion,** a very fine 1752 example of Colonial architecture on W. King St. (326-4014), is open to visitors Tues–Sun.

Some 13 mi. (20km) SW along Penna. 724 and 345, look in on the ☀🏛️ **Hopewell Furnace National Historic Site** (582-8773), a museum-village clustered around an old foundry which was active between 1770 and 1883, and has been restored in the style of the period 1820–40. Interesting museum; demonstrations of blacksmithing in summer. Don't miss this page from American history. Open daily.

☀ **PRINCETON** (41 mi./65km NE on I-95 and U.S. 206): Gracious little university town, steeped in history, which was briefly (June–Nov 1783) the capital of the United States. While in session at Princeton, the Congress learned of the signing of the peace treaty ending the Revolutionary War in Sept 1783; from here, too, Washington delivered his famous "Farewell Orders to the Armies."

With its 6,000 students and Anglo-English charm, Ivy League ☼🏛 **Princeton University,** founded in 1746, is one of the most socially exclusive as well as one of the most distinguished universities on the eastern seaboard. Its faculty has included eight Nobel Prize winners (one of them Albert Einstein, who died here in 1955). Interesting tour of the campus, open daily (609/452-3603), with its collection of modern sculptures by Calder, Picasso, Moore, Noguchi, Lipchitz, and others. See, too, the **Woodrow Wilson School of Public and International Affairs,** designed by Minoru Yamasaki, architect of New York's World Trade Center, and **Nassau Hall,** built in 1756, where the Second Continental Congress met in 1783. The **University Art Museum** (undergoing renovation) has works by such painters as Raphael, Cranach, van Dyke, Rubens, and Monet. Don't miss it.

You can visit Princeton along with **New Hope** and **Washington Crossing State Park** (see above).

☼🏛 **VALLEY FORGE NATIONAL HISTORICAL PARK** (N. Gulph Rd. and Penna. 23, 20 mi./33km NW on I-76) (783-7700): George Washington's camp from Dec 1777 to June 1778, one of the darkest periods of the Revolutionary War. Some 3,000 soldiers died here of cold, hunger, or disease during that terrible winter. Washington's headquarters, a commemorative chapel, and a museum are open daily; guided tours from the Visitor Center, mid-Apr to Oct. Lovely countryside all around; don't miss it.

☼🏛 **WINTERTHUR MUSEUM & GARDENS** (36 mi./57km SW on I-95 and Del. 52) (302/654-1548): Once the 200-bedroom home of chemical tycoon Henry F. DuPont. Sumptuous collection of decorative art and American furniture from the 17th to the 19th century. Resv. a must for conducted tours of the principal collections. Magnificent 200-acre (80ha) English-style park. Open Tues–Sun. Well worth going out of your way for.

Combine it with a visit to **Longwood Gardens** and the **Brandywine Museum and Battlefield** (see above).

ATLANTIC CITY & CAPE MAY

☼🏛 **ATLANTIC CITY** (215 mi./344km r.t. via N.J. 42S, the Atlantic City Expwy. east, N.J. 585S, the Garden State Pkwy. north, Atlantic City Expwy. west, and N.J. 42N): The trip begins at Atlantic City, Philadelphia's seaside entertainment extension. This seaside resort, flashy and kitsch, was founded as recently as 1852; after the introduction of legalized gaming it was considered Las Vegas's poor relation, but has become the new mecca for American gamblers. In 1976, when the New Jersey legislature legalized roulette wheels and slot machines, Atlantic City awoke from a 25-year sleep; it now accommodates 32 million visitors every year, who leave behind them about $3 billion. Its location—only 3 hr. from New York and 1½ hr. from Philadelphia, by car—has contributed greatly to its prosperity. Two other points of civic pride: the game of *Monopoly* was inspired by Atlantic City street names, and every year since 1921 Miss America has been crowned here.

The city's enormous **Convention Hall** is another curiosity in itself; it seats 41,000 people and has the largest organ in the world, with 32,000 pipes and 1,477 registers. A still-bigger convention center is under construction nearby, to be opened in 1991.

Along the 5-mi. (8km) **Boardwalk** beside the ocean—the East Coast's an-

swer to the Las Vegas Strip—and at the bay side are the flashy, luxurious casinos, which draw their flocks of conventioneers and package tourists. In obvious contrast to these luxury casinos are the surrounding wooden shacks, abandoned flophouses, and debris-strewn lots. Atlantic City has more than 18,000 slot machines, but no movie theaters and only one supermarket.
Well worth a visit.

Tourist Information

Atlantic City Convention & Visitors Bureau, 2314 Pacific Ave., Atlantic City, NJ 08401 (609/348-7100; toll free 800/262-7395).

Transportation

Greyhound (bus), 2101 Arctic Ave. (609/345-6617): Service to/from New York, Philadelphia, and Washington.

New Jersey Transit (bus), Arctic Ave. and Arkansas Ave. (609/344-8181): Service to/from Cape May, New York, and Philadelphia.

USAir Express (airplane), Municipal Airport (toll free 800/428-4322): Flights to/from Cape May, Baltimore, Philadelphia, and Washington.

Trump Air (helicopter), Steel Pier Heliport (609/344-0833): Flights to/from New York City (Manhattan).

Amtrak (train): Kirkman Blvd. at the foot of the Atlantic City Expwy. (toll free 800/872-7245): Service to/from Philadelphia (five round-trips daily; time, 1 hr.), Washington (one round-trip daily; time, 3 hr.), and New York (one round-trip daily; time, 2 hr. 20 min.).

Guided Tours & Excursions

Gray Line Tours (bus), 9 N. Arkansas Ave. (609/344-0965).

Where to Stay

♟♟♟ **Trump Taj Mahal Hotel & Casino,** 26 S. Pennsylvania Ave. (at the Boardwalk), Atlantic City, NJ 08401 (609/348-2000; toll free 800/225-7777). 1,250 rms (including 400 luxury suites), A/C, color TV, in-rm movies. AE, CB, DC, MC, V. Valet gar. $10, pool, health club, sauna, beach, 12 rests. (including Sinbad's) and coffee shops (some open around the clock), 24-hr. bars, rm svce, nightclub, casino, shows, boutiques. *Note:* The latest (Apr 1990) and most extravagant resort of Atlantic City. Pseudo-Indian palace built at a cost of $1.2 billion, this kitchy, 42-story giant complete w. minarets, onion-shaped cupolas, cascading fountains, hanging gardens, and bejeweled 8-ft.-high (2.2m) elephants, has a casino the size of four football fields w. more than 3,000 slot machines and 167 gaming tables. The rms and suites (one of them, the Alexander the Great penthouse suite, costs a mere $10,000 a night) offer incomparable comfort and amenities. Highly professional svce but so-so rests. Direct beach access. Group and convention clientele. Worth a glance by itself. **VE**

♟♟♟ **Caesars Hotel Casino,** 2100 Pacific Ave., Atlantic City, NJ 08401 (609/348-4411; toll free 800/257-8555). 646 rms, A/C, color TV, in-rm movies. AE, CB, DC, MC, V. Valet gar. $10, two pools, health club, sauna, three tennis courts, beach, seven rests. (including Le Posh), two 24-hr. coffee shops, 24-hr. bars, rm svce, casino, shows, boutiques. *Note:* This cream of the local hotel crop has undergone a much-needed facelift; the exterior is strident and unconvincing, but the rms are inviting and comfortable. Same management as the famous Caesars Palace establishments at Las Vegas and Lake Tahoe. Rest. (Le Posh) in the highest deluxe category; efficient svce. Direct beach access. The casino does the biggest business in Atlantic City. **E–VE,** but lower rates off-season.

♟♟♟ **Harrah's Marina Hotel Casino,** 1725 Brigantine Blvd., Atlantic City, NJ 08401 (609/441-5000; toll free 800/524-1351). 758 rms, A/C, color TV, in-rm movies. AE, CB, DC, MC, V. Valet gar. $10, pool, health club, sauna, three tennis courts, marina, four rests. (including the Meadows), two 24-hr. coffee shops, 24-hr. bars, rm svce, nightclub, casino, shows, hrdrsr, boutiques, free crib. *Note:* The best place to stay in Atlantic City, away from the hubbub of the Boardwalk. Large, ultramodern marina-hotel whose 18 floors overlook the yacht basin and Absecon Bay: a facsimile of the giant Las Vegas casino-hotels with the waterway thrown in. Spacious, very comfortable rms; efficient reception and svce; very complete facilities. Group and convention clientele. **E–VE,** but lower rates off-season.

Tropworld Casino Resort (formerly the Tropicana), Iowa Ave. and the Boardwalk, Atlantic City, NJ 08401 (609/340-4000). 1,014 rms, A/C, cable color TV. AE, CB, DC, MC, V. Valet gar. $10, two pools, health club, sauna, two tennis courts, beach, miniature golf, five rests., two 24-hr. coffee shops, 10 24-hr. bars, rm svce, nightclub, casino, Luna Park, boutiques. *Note:* Large casino-hotel on the beach, aimed at the family market (very well-equipped amusement park with roller-coasters, Ferris wheel, dodge-'em cars, clowns, and magicians). Completely renovated interior; very comfortable rms, ultra-professional svce. Two blocks from Convention Center. Package-tour and convention clientele. **E–VE,** but lower rates off-season.

Showboat Hotel Casino, 801 Boardwalk, Atlantic City, NJ 08401 (609/343-4000; toll free 800/621-0200). 516 rms, A/C, cable color TV. AE, CB, DC, MC, V. Valet gar. $10, pool, beach, bowling, 11 rests., coffee shops, and bars (some 24-hr.), rm svce, nightclub, casino, shows, free crib. *Note:* New casino hotel, rather curiously designed with a cut-off corner facade, and direct access to beach. Other than the inevitable casino w. dozens of tables and hundreds of slot machines, the main attraction of the hotel is its 60-lane bowling alley. Flawless comfort and facilities; spacious rms (many w. ocean view); good svce. Group and convention clientele. **E–VE,** but lower rates off-season.

The Admiral's Quarters, 655 Absecon Blvd., Atlantic City, NJ 08401 (609/344-2201; toll free 800/833-3242). 74 mini-suites, A/C, cable color TV. AE, MC, V. Parking, pool, no bar, no rest., free breakfast. *Note:* Small, quiet, comfortable hotel 5 min. from the Boardwalk and 10 min. from the airport. Offers only mini-suites w. refrigerators, kitchenettes, and private balconies. Direct shuttle to beach and casinos. Business clientele. **M–E,** but lower rates off-season.

Comfort Inn West, Black Horse Pike at Dover Pl., West Atlantic City, NJ 08232 (609/645-1818; toll free 800/228-5150). 198 rms, A/C, color TV, in-rm movies. AE, CB, DC, MC, V. Free parking, pool, coffee shop, free crib. *Note:* Inviting, modern motel near the municipal airport. Very comfortable rms; reception and svce w. a smile. Shuttle bus to casino district. Group clientele. **M,** but lower rates off-season.

Continental Motel, 137 S. Illinois Ave., Atlantic City, NJ 08404 (609/345-5141). 60 rms, A/C, color TV. AE, MC, V. Free parking, pool, bar. *Note:* Aging small motel a block or two from the Boardwalk and the casinos. Decently comfortable; ideal for budget travelers. **I–M,** but lower rates off-season.

Fiesta Motel, Tennessee Ave. and Pacific Ave., Atlantic City, NJ 08401 (609/344-4193; toll free 800/341-2279). 72 rms, A/C, cable color TV. AE, DC, MC, V. Free parking, pool, coffee shop, rm svce. *Note:* Modest but well-run motel very nr. the Boardwalk, w. completely renovated decor and facilities. Friendly reception. Good overall value. **I–M,** but lower rates off-season.

Where to Eat

Knife & Fork Inn, Albany Ave. and Atlantic Ave. (344-1133). A/C. Dinner only, nightly; closed Sun Oct to late Mar, Dec 25, Yom Kippur. AE. Jkt. *Specialties:* mussels marinière, shellfish, lobster Thermidor, bouillabaisse, crab Newburg, catch of the day; also some meat dishes. *Note:* The best seafood rest., and quite simply the best rest., in the culinary wasteland called Atlantic City. The crabs and scallops are particularly worthwhile. Plush-type decor; uncommonly efficient svce. Resv. strongly advised. A local landmark since 1912. *Seafood.* **M**

🍷🍷 **Dock's Oyster House,** 2405 Atlantic Ave. (345-0092). A/C. Dinner only, Tues–Sun; closed Thanksgiving, Dec–Feb. AE, MC, V. *Specialties:* linguine w. clams, oyster stew, lobster broiled or stuffed w. crabmeat, catch of the day, steak, cheese pie. *Note:* Dock's Oyster House, in the hands of the Dougherty family for four generations, is the oldest (1897) seafood rest. in Atlantic City, notwithstanding its vaguely Scandinavian-contemporary decor. Its success is due to absolutely fresh fish and shellfish. Friendly, relaxed svce; resv. advised. *Steak/Seafood.* **I–M**

🍷🍷 **Peking Duck House,** 2801 Atlantic Ave. at Iowa Ave. (344-9090). A/C. Lunch/dinner daily. AE, CB, DC, MC, V. *Specialties:* shrimp lo-mein, shark's-fin soup, Peking duck, chicken w. lotus flour, beef w. tiger-lily flowers, fried ice cream flambé. *Note:* Chinese food at a high level, inventive and refined, from the skillets of the very talented Kenny Poo from Hong Kong. The decor, on the contrary, featuring beige-toned walls and subdued lighting, is not in the least Oriental. The Peking duck is remarkable. A very good place. Resv. advised, particularly on wknds. *Chinese.* **I–M**

🍷 **Angelo's Fairmount Tavern,** 2300 Fairmount Ave. (344-2439). A/C. Lunch/dinner daily. No credit cards. *Specialties:* fresh homemade soup and pasta, classical Italian dishes, Sicilian specialties. Everyone takes a caffè espresso. *Note:* This former speakeasy, frequented by local politicians and newspaper people, serves the kind of good, tasty food you'd expect from a typical Italian *trattoria.* The menu changes regularly at the whim of owner Angelo "The Meatball" Mancuso. Excellent value. No resv. *Italian/American.* **I**

🌞🍷 **Smithville Inn,** on U.S. 9 at Smithville, 10 mi. (16km) north via U.S. 30 and U.S. 9 (652-7777). A/C. Lunch/dinner daily; closed Dec 25. AE, CB, DC, MC, V. *Specialties:* chicken pot pie, stuffed pork chops, roast duck. *Note:* Picturesque Colonial-style inn in "The Historic Towne of Smithville," a careful replica of an 18th-century village. The food is acceptable but unimaginative. Much favored by tourists; resv. advised in summer. *American.* **I**

🌞🍷 **White House Sub Shop,** 2301 Arctic Ave. at Mississippi Ave. (345-8599). A/C. Lunch/dinner daily (till midnight). No credit cards. *Specialties:* submarines, cheese steaks. *Note:* The unchallenged champion of the "submarine" sandwich, the local equivalent of the Philadelphian "hoagie" or the New York "hero": an Italian roll stuffed with salami, ham, turkey, prosciutto, provolone, lettuce, tomatoes, onions, green peppers, etc. The rest. proudly claims (and has signed photos on the wall to prove it) such famous patrons as Jerry Lewis, Frank Sinatra, Ray Charles, and Joan Rivers. The decor is pure art deco kitsch. A local landmark since 1946. *American.* **B**

SOUTH FROM ATLANTIC CITY: The trip continues along N.J. 585, a scenic route which follows the shoreline for almost 40 mi. (65km), and offers some fine ocean views. At **Margate,** immediately south of Atlantic City, see the amazing 🐘 **Lucy,** a six-story building shaped like an elephant, constructed in 1881; you reach the beast's "stomach" by climbing spiral staircases in its legs. Worth seeing; open daily Jul–Aug, wknds only in spring and fall; closed the rest of the year. The next stop, 10 mi. (16km) farther south, is **Ocean City,** a beach resort whose resolutely sober family atmosphere is a striking contrast to Atlantic City; the town is "dry," and attracts a number of religious conventions every year.

🌞🏛 **CAPE MAY:** Farther along N.J. 585 you come to Cape May, the oldest seaside resort (1631) in the country; its famous visitors have included Presidents Lincoln and Grant, Horace Greeley, and the department-store magnate John Wanamaker. Its Victorian elegance, and its hundreds of pretty old pastel-washed houses with their white porches and lacy carpenter's-Gothic fretwork, seem to have come straight out of a 19th-century picture postcard. The whole town is a designated National Historic Landmark. On its magnificent beach, 4 mi. (7km) long, you can pick up the so-called Cape May diamonds—pebbles of quartz polished by the action of the waves. You can tour the center of the town in a horse-drawn carriage, or in an imitation 19th-century streetcar, leaving from Beach Dr. at Gurney St. (609/884-5404). Paul Volcker, long head of the Federal Reserve Board, comes from Cape May. You shouldn't miss it.

Return back to Philadelphia by the Garden State Parkway and Atlantic City Expwy. An interesting, varied itinerary taking 2–3 days.

Where to Stay

The Chalfonte, 310 Howard St., Cape May, NJ 08204 (609/884-8409). 103 rms. Picturesque old hotel (1876) in the purest gingerbread tradition. Closed Nov–Apr. **M–E**

The Mainstay Inn & Cottage, 635 Columbia Ave., Cape May, NJ 08204 (609/884-8690). 13 rms (9 w. private bath), all no-smoking. Charming Victorian structure dating from 1872. At one time a men's gambling club. Minimum stay in summer is 3 days. Distinction and style. Closed Dec–Mar. **M–E**

The Queen Victoria, 102 Ocean St., Cape May, NJ 08204 (609/884-8702). 13 antiques-filled rms (7 w. private bath). Elegantly furnished Victorian villa. Minimum stay on wknds is 2–4 days. Open year round. **M–E**

Where to Eat

Lobster House, Fisherman's Wharf (609/884-8296). Lunch/dinner daily. Excellent seafood rest. on the harbor; very popular locally. **B–I**

Watson's Merion Inn, 106 Decatur St. (609/884-8363). Dinner only, nightly; closed Nov–Mar. Good regional American food in an authentic 1885 Victorian setting. **I–M**

GETTYSBURG & PENNSYLVANIA DUTCH COUNTRY

PENNSYLVANIA DUTCH COUNTRY: (274 mi./441km r.t. via I-76W, U.S. 222S, U.S. 322W, U.S. 15S, U.S. 30E, U.S. 202N, and I-76E): After visiting **Valley Forge National Historical Park,** site of one of the darker pages of American military history (see "Nearby Excursions," above), you can drive on through Pennsylvania Dutch Country.

Begin your tour at **Ephrata Cloister,** a rural religious community at 632 W. Main St., Ephrata, 6 mi. (9km) south of the Pennsylvania Tpke. and I-76 on U.S. 222S and U.S. 322W (717/733-6600). Founded in 1732 by Conrad Beissel, a Baptist pastor from Germany, this contemplative community of country folk observed an ascetic rule of life: unmarried people of opposite sexes were segregated, wooden benches and headrests were used instead of beds, and so on. It continued its archaic life-style until 1934. You can still visit a dozen buildings from the period 1735–50; open daily. Should not be missed.

This stop is a good introduction to a more detailed inspection of Pennsylvania Dutch Country, a region whose people are among the most unusual—and least known—in America. They are often, and wrongly, taken for people of Dutch descent; in fact their ancestors were German ("Deutsch") settlers who came here in the 17th century from the Rhineland and the Palatinate, whose original customs have been preserved almost intact. These austere, devout, hard-working country folk are divided into three main religious denominations:

Amish, Moravian, and Mennonite. They agree, however, in rejecting almost everything that smacks of modernity, whether vaccination, chemical fertilizers, automobiles, radios, or quite simply electricity, which the more pious among them regard as an invention of the devil. The "Plain People," as they are called, use only buggies for conveyance and only kerosene lamps for light; they speak the same Low German as their ancestors and wear the same dark-hued, archaic dress vividly portrayed in the movie *Witness*. Some 15,000–20,000 Amish in Pennsylvania Dutch Country live in closed communities observing to the letter the teachings of the Bible. But these Americans from an earlier epoch are progressively disappearing. (There are also Amish communities of some hundreds of souls in Ohio, Indiana, Texas, and Canada. As for the Mennonites, who unlike the Amish have come to terms with some manifestations of progress, such as electricity, there are believed to be some 200,000 of them in the U.S. and Canada.)

For an unforgettable experience, you should visit the ☀☖ **Amish farms and markets around Lancaster, York, Intercourse, Strasburg, and Bird-in-Hand.** Note, however, that for religious reasons the Amish reject any depiction of the human form, and thus forbid the use of still or movie cameras.

Paradoxically, a mere 40 mi. (64km) from this region so firmly rooted in the past you will find the famous nuclear power plant at **Three Mile Island,** where in 1979 the beginning of a meltdown threw the whole of Pennsylvania into a panic. Three Mile Island has played a leading part in alerting mankind to the dangers of nuclear energy.

Some useful addresses for visitors to Pennsylvania Dutch Country:

INFORMATION   The **Mennonite Tourist Information Center,** 2209 Millstream Rd., Lancaster, PA 17601 (717/299-0954): Organizes guided tours and house visits with Mennonite families; open Mon–Sat.

Other very active information centers are the **Pennsylvania Dutch Visitors Bureau,** 501 Greenfield Rd., Lancaster, PA 17601 (717/299-8901); and **People's Place,** Main St., Intercourse, PA 17534 (717/768-7171), with an Amish museum, movies, and a library; open Mon–Sat.

☖ FARM VISITS   The **Amish Homestead,** 3 mi. (5km) east of Lancaster on Penna. 462 (717/392-0832), open daily; also **Amish Farm and House,** 5 mi. (8km) east of Lancaster on U.S. 30 (717/394-6185), open daily.

☖ MARKET VISITS   The **Central Market,** Pennsylvania Sq., Lancaster, held on Tues, Fri, and Sat; **Meadowbrook Market,** 5 mi. (8km) east of Lancaster at Leola, on Penna. 23, held on Fri and Sat; **Farmer's Market,** 6 mi. (10km) east of Lancaster at Bird-in-Hand on Penna. 340, held on Wed, Fri, and Sat; and the **Farmer's Market,** Market St. and Penn St. in York, held on Tues, Fri, and Sat.

SIGHTS   The ☖ **Landis Valley Museum,** 2451 Kissel Hill Rd., Lancaster, 2 mi. (4km) north on Penna. 272 (717/569-0401): 250,000 authentically old exhibits, from Conestoga wagons to spinning wheels. Interesting. Open Tues–Sun.

☖ **Strasburg Railroad,** 8 mi. (12km) SE of Lancaster via U.S. 30 and Penna. 896 (717/687-7522): Trip on a steam train through Amish country. Also a spectacular railroad museum. Open daily May–Oct; wknds only, Mar–Apr and Nov.

☖ Hershey

After a long look at Lancaster and the surrounding countryside, you go on to Hershey. Known as "the chocolate capital of the world," this smiling little town of 13,000 people, perpetually pervaded by the aroma of chocolate, is the home of the world's largest chocolate factory. Milton S. Hershey, founder of the Hershey Corporation in 1903, also gave his name to the town. At **Hershey's Chocolate World,** Hersheypark Dr. (open daily), you can see the entire production cycle from the planting of a cocoa tree down to the finished chocolate bar. See also the very interesting **Hershey Museum of American Life,** with scenes from the life and history of the Pennsylvania Dutch and their Native American predecessors.

Hersheypark, on Hersheypark Dr. (717/534-3900), is a big amusement park with dozens of carousels, roller coasters and other attractions; open daily mid-May to Sept; closed the rest of the year. There's a large rose garden, where tulips and chrysanthemums are also grown in season, at **Hershey Gardens,** Hotel Rd., open daily mid-Apr to Oct. Must definitely be seen.

After another 50 mi. (80km) of driving south, you arrive at—

Where to Stay En Route

IN HERSHEY   The ⚑⚑⚑ **Hershey Lodge,** Chocolate Ave. at University Dr., Hershey, PA 17033 (717/533-3311). 460 rms. Large, modern motel w. adj. tennis courts and golf course. **E**

IN LANCASTER   The ⚑⚑⚑ **Willow Valley Resort,** 2416 Willow St. Pike (at U.S. 222), Lancaster, PA 17602 (717/464-2711). Luxurious motel in the heart of the country; does a heavy convention business. **M–E**

IN MOUNT JOY   The ☀ ⚑⚑ **Cameron Estates Inn,** Donegal Springs Rd., Mount Joy, PA 17552 (717/653-1773). 18 rms. Elegant 19th-century manor house surrounded by a beautiful garden. **M–E**

IN STRASBURG   The ⚑⚑ **Historic Strasburg Inn,** Penna. 896, Strasburg, PA 17579 (717/687-7691). 103 rms. Charming Colonial-style inn. **M–E**

Where to Eat En Route

IN BIRD-IN-HAND   The ♟ **Plain and Fancy Farm Restaurant,** on Penna. 340 (717/768-8281). Breakfast/lunch/dinner (till 8pm) Mon–Sat. Tasty family cooking in an authentic Amish farm. **B**

IN MOUNT JOY   ☀♟♟ **Groff's Farm,** 650 Pinkerton Rd. (717/653-2048). Lunch/dinner (till 7:30pm) Tues–Sat. Typical, rather elaborate Pennsylvania Dutch cooking, in a pleasantly restored 1756 building. Resv. advised, particularly at dinner. **I–M**

☀🔭 **GETTYSBURG NATIONAL MILITARY PARK:** The **Visitor Center** is on Penna. 134 (717/334-1124), open daily. Here, on July 1–3, 1863, was fought the bloodiest battle of the Civil War. The Confederate troops of Gen. Robert E. Lee sustained 28,000 casualties, and the Union forces under Gen. George Meade, 23,000. It was this welter of kindred blood that moved Lincoln to compose the famous *Gettysburg Address,* appealing for peace and reconciliation between North and South.

To visit the battlefield thoroughly you must make a circuit of more than 35 mi. (56km). There are hundreds of commemorative objects, including 400 cannon and more than 1,600 monuments, engraved tablets, and markers. The **Battlefield Tower** observation tower is 305 ft. (92m) high, and nearby is a cyclorama with movies depicting the course of the battle. Don't miss this visit.

Not far from the battlefield is the ☀☖ **Eisenhower National Historic Site,** reached only by bus from the Visitor Center (717/334-1124). No more than 1,100 people may be admitted on any day; open daily Apr–Oct, Wed–Sun the rest of the year. Many personal items associated with "Ike" and his wife, Mamie. Must certainly be seen.

Then back to Philadelphia via York and Lancaster, so that if need be you can catch anything you missed earlier in Pennsylvania Dutch Country. Fascinating three- to four-day trip; a must for all lovers of history—or of the unusual.

Where to Stay

🛏🛏 **Quality Inn Gettysburg Motor Lodge,** 380 Steinwehr Ave., Gettysburg, PA 17325 (717/334-1103). 89 rms. Comfortable, inviting motel next to the Battlefield Visitor Center. Recently renovated. **I–M**

CHAPTER 7

PITTSBURGH°

□ □ □

Long known as "Smoky City," this once gloomy and polluted industrial center has been transformed in less than two decades into a modern, sparkling metropolis. The glass-and-steel high-rises of "Steel City"—another of Pittsburgh's nicknames—its luxury hotels, and its ultramodern office buildings now reach skyward around the "Golden Triangle," once a slum, now the heart of the business district.

Steel (almost 25% of U.S. output), glass, nuclear engineering (the first American nuclear power plant was built near Pittsburgh), aluminum, data processing, chemicals, robotics, and pharmaceuticals all contribute to the wealth of this dedicated, hard-working city—to say nothing of its busy river port, which handles more than 60 million tons (54.5 billion kg) of freight a year. For more than a century Pittsburgh was synonymous with steel and coal, and so renowned for its ugliness that after World War II, when the great architect Frank Lloyd Wright was asked how to go about modernizing the city, he replied that it would make more sense to tear it down and start over. Fortunately this pessimism was ignored when a gigantic urban-renewal plan was put into effect toward the end of the 1960s; it has already borne much fruit, and is still being carried forward through such reconstruction projects as **Renaissance II** (total cost, $6 billion) and the **Pittsburgh Technology Center,** now under construction on the site of an old steel mill on the banks of the Monongahela River.

The first settlement was French: Fort Duquesne, built in 1754 at the confluence of the Monongahela River, Allegheny River, and Ohio River. The British captured it in 1758 and renamed it in honor of their prime minister, William Pitt the Elder; later the fort passed its name on to the city. Pittsburgh was the arsenal of the Union during the War Between the States; three-quarters of a century later it played the same role during World War II. Today "Renaissance City" is the third-largest corporate headquarters after New York and Chicago, home base for 13 Fortune 500 U.S. industries, among which are Alcoa, Heinz Foods, Rockwell International, USX Corporation (formerly U.S. Steel), and Westinghouse. From the summit of **Mount Washington,** reached by cable car, the visitor can again enjoy the view of the city and the three rivers that run through it, now that stringently enforced antipollution laws have almost abolished the obscuring smog once spewed forth by its factories.

Thanks to the lavish donations of such local captains of industry and finance as Carnegie, Frick, and Mellon, Pittsburgh boasts some of the country's wealthiest and most beautiful museums, including the famous **Carnegie Institute,** a justly renowned symphony orchestra, and no fewer than seven universities and colleges of great quality such as Carnegie-Mellon University (6,000 students) and the University of Pittsburgh (35,000 students).

Famous people born in Pittsburgh include painter Andy Warhol; choreographer Martha Graham; dancer Gene Kelly; jazz musicians Art Blakey, Billy Eckstine, Roy Eldridge, Errol Garner, Earl Hines, Ahmad Jamal, and Kenny Clarke; conductor Billy May; and Stephen Foster, composer of "Swannee River," "My Old Kentucky Home," and other treasures of American folk song.

BASIC FACTS: State of Pennsylvania. Area code: 412. Time zone: eastern. ZIP Code: 15230. Founded: 1758. Approximate population: city, 420,000; metropolitan area, 2,280,000. 19th-largest U.S. metropolitan area.

CLIMATE: With 200 days of rain a year, bring your umbrella in any season. Winter is moderately cold (Jan mean, 31°F/−1°C). In summer the thermometer rarely goes above 77°F (25°C); the July mean is 75°F (24°C). Spring and autumn are brisk.

DISTANCES: Buffalo, 219 mi. (350km); Cincinnati, 290 mi. (465km); Cleveland, 129 mi. (206km); New York, 368 mi. (590km); Philadelphia, 308 mi. (498km); Washington, 247 mi. (396km).

ARRIVAL & TRANSIT INFORMATION

AIRPORT: Greater Pittsburgh International Airport, 17 mi. (27km) west. Call 778-2525 for information.

DOMESTIC AIRLINES: American (771-4437), Continental (391-6910), Delta (566-2100), Northwest (toll free 800/225-2525), Pan Am (toll free 800/221-1111), TWA (391-3600), United (288-9900), and USAir (922-7500).

FOREIGN CARRIERS: British Airways (toll free 800/247-9297) and Canadian International (391-6351).

CITY LINK: The **cab** fare from the airport to downtown is about $28; time, 35 min. Bus: **Airlines Transportation Co.** (471-8900), leaves about every 30 min., serving principal downtown hotels; fare, $8; time, about 40–50 min.
  The **bus, streetcar, and subway public transportation** provided by Port Authority Transit/PAT (231-5707) is relatively efficient.
  The downtown area isn't big enough to require renting a car.

CAR RENTAL (at the airport unless otherwise indicated): Avis (262-5160); Budget (262-1500); Dollar (262-1300); Hertz (262-1705); National (262-2312); Thrifty, 1432 Beers School Rd. (264-1775). For dwntwn locations, consult the local telephone book.

LIMOUSINE SERVICES: Carey Limousine (731-8671), Limo Center (923-1650), and Riemer's Limousine (661-6054).

TAXIS: Cabs are few and dear. Theoretically they can be hailed on the street, but it's better to phone, at least 15–30 min. ahead of time: **Colonial Cab** (833-3300), **People's Cab** (681-3131), or **Yellow Cab** (665-8100).

TRAIN: Amtrak Station, Liberty Ave. and Grant St. (621-4850).

INTERCITY BUSES: Greyhound, 11th St. and Liberty Ave. (392-6527).

RIVER CRUISES: 3- to 10-day cruises on the Mississippi River and Ohio River aboard the *Delta Queen* or the *Mississippi Queen,* sternwheelers dating from the 1920s. Luxurious kitsch. See Chapter 15 on New Orleans.

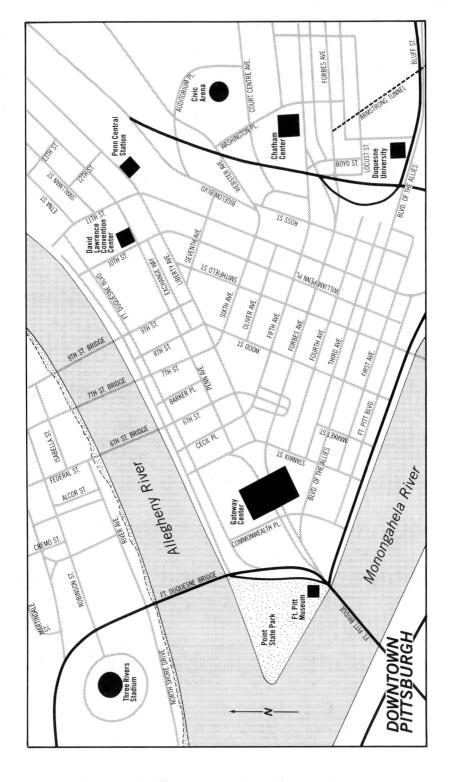

DOWNTOWN PITTSBURGH

N

Monongahela River

Allegheny River

Three Rivers Stadium

NORTH SHORE DRIVE

MARTINDALE ST.

ROBINSON ST.

RIVER AVE.

CREMO ST.

ALCOR ST.

FEDERAL ST.

ISABELLA ST.

9TH ST. BRIDGE

7TH ST. BRIDGE

6TH ST. BRIDGE

FT. DUQUESNE BRIDGE

Point State Park

Ft. Pitt Museum

FT. PITT BRIDGE

Gateway Center

COMMONWEALTH PL.

STANWIX ST.

BLVD. OF THE ALLIES

MARKET ST.

FT. PITT BLVD.

FIRST AVE.

THIRD AVE.

FOURTH AVE.

FORBES AVE.

FIFTH AVE.

WOOD ST.

OLIVER AVE.

SIXTH AVE.

SMITHFIELD ST.

SEVENTH AVE.

LIBERTY AVE.

EXCHANGE WAY

CECIL PL.

6TH ST.

BARKER PL.

PENN AVE.

7TH ST.

8TH ST.

9TH ST.

FT. DUQUESNE BLVD.

10TH ST.

11TH ST.

David Lawrence Convention Center

ETNA ST.

SMALLMAN ST.

12TH ST.

13TH ST.

Penn Central Station

WILLIAM PENN PL.

ROSS ST.

BIGELOW BLVD.

WEBSTER AVE.

WASHINGTON PL.

AUDITORIUM PL.

Civic Arena

COURT CENTRE AVE.

Chatham Center

BOYD ST.

LOCUST ST.

Duquesne University

ARMSTRONG TUNNEL

BLUFF ST.

FORBES AVE.

BLVD. OF THE ALLIES

INFORMATION & TOURS

TOURIST INFORMATION: The **Greater Pittsburgh Convention and Visitors Bureau,** 4 Gateway Center, PA 15222 (412/281-7711; toll free 800/821-1888).

Visitor Information Center, 18 Gateway Towers at Liberty Ave. (412/281-9222).

For a **telephone recording** with an up-to-date listing of cultural events and shows, call 412/391-6840.

GUIDED TOURS: The **Gateway Clipper Fleet** (boat), Monongahela Wharf, Station Sq. Dock (355-7980): Paddlewheeler trips on the three rivers; Apr–Nov.

Gray Line Tours (bus) (761-7000): Guided tours of the city and surroundings; serves principal downtown hotels. Apr–Oct.

SIGHTS, ATTRACTIONS & ACTIVITIES

ARCHITECTURAL HIGHLIGHTS: ☼🏛 **Alcoa Building,** 425 Sixth Ave.: The 30-story aluminum-clad building is 410 ft. (125m) high and of revolutionary design; it was one of the first skyscrapers in the world with an aluminum frame. Worth a look, but not open to visitors.

☼🏛 **Cathedral of Learning,** University of Pittsburgh campus, Fifth Ave. and Bigelow Blvd. (624-6000): The only university skyscraper in the country, 520 ft. (160m) high, with 42 floors. The Gothic Revival design, now redolent of kitsch, dates from 1935. The 21 lecture rooms grouped around the entrance hall are each decorated in a different idiom: Byzantine, Roman, Renaissance, Tudor, Empire, and so on. Observation platform on the 36th floor. Guided tours. Open daily; should be seen.

☼🏛 **Civic Arena,** Washington Pl. at Centre Ave. and Bedford Ave. (642-2062): Huge 20,000-seat arena with a roof that opens. The shiny stainless-steel dome, three times larger than that of St. Peter's in Rome, can be folded back in 2½ minutes. Concerts, sports events, and conventions. Worth a look.

🏛 **CNG Tower,** Liberty Ave. and 7th St.: A 30-story postmodern tower in brown-and-buff granite, capped with a steel arch of unusual design. A 1987 work of architects Bob Evans and William Pedersen. Worth seeing.

🏛 **Heinz Hall,** 600 Penn Ave. (392-4800): A beautiful rococo 1920s movie house converted into a concert hall and now home to the famous Pittsburgh Symphony. Guided tours by appointment; should be seen.

☼🏛🏛 **P.P.G. Industries,** 1 PPG Pl. at 4th St. and Market St. (434-3832): Symbol of the new Pittsburgh designed by the well-known architectural team of Philip Johnson and John Burgee: a group of six ultramodern Neo-Gothic buildings, with facades all in glass, grouped around a huge plaza with a winter garden, shops, restaurants, and stores. The 40-story central tower, PPG Tower, stands 635 ft. (193m) high; its pinnacled silhouette recalls the Houses of Parliament in London. Open-air concerts on the plaza in summer. Very much worth seeing.

🏛 **Stephen Collins Foster Memorial Hall,** University of Pittsburgh campus, Forbes Ave. at Bigelow Blvd. (624-4100): Imposing monument commemorating Pittsburgh's native son Stephen Collins Foster, who wrote many well-loved songs. Library with personal memorabilia of the composer, and an auditorium where the Three Rivers Shakespeare Festival is held every year, as well as many concerts. For lovers of music history. Open Mon–Fri.

🏛 **University of Pittsburgh,** Fifth Ave. and Bigelow Blvd. (624-4148). One of the oldest (1787) and most famous of American universities, with 35,000 students. Of the 60 or so buildings scattered across its 132-acre (53ha) campus, several are worth going to see: the **Cathedral of Learning**, the **Heinz Chapel**, and the **Stephen Collins Foster Memorial**, in particular. Campus open daily.

CHURCHES/SYNAGOGUES: ☼⚑ **Heinz Chapel**, University of Pittsburgh campus, S. Bellefield Ave. (624-4157): Modern building in the French Gothic Revival style, with a series of splendid stained-glass windows, each 73 ft. (22m) high. Definitely worth seeing; open Sun–Fri.

⚑ **St. Paul's Cathedral**, Fifth Ave. and Craig (621-4951): Imposing Gothic landmark with its twin towers and world-famous Beckerath organ. Open daily. Tours by appointment.

HISTORIC BUILDINGS: ☼⚑ **Allegheny County Courthouse**, Grant St. and Fifth Ave.: Remarkable Romanesque Revival building by Henry Hobson Richardson dating from 1888; one of the finest courthouses in the U.S. A sight not to be missed; open Mon–Fri.

☼⚑ **Fort Pitt Blockhouse**, Point State Park (471-1764): Last vestige of the original fort built by the British in 1764 on the remains of Fort Duquesne; it saw some vigorous action during the French and Indian War. Worth a visit; open Wed–Sun.

MARKETS: ⚑ **Market Square**, Market Pl.: Picturesque shopping area in the heart of downtown Pittsburgh with gardens, benches, and friendly pigeons; many bars, restaurants, and pubs in the vicinity. Very lively.

MONUMENTS: ☼⚑ **Point State Park Fountain**, Point State Park: Monumental fountain at the tip of Point State Park at the confluence of the Allegheny River and Monongahela River. The computer-controlled fountain, fed by an underground spring, issues in colorful plumes of water rising to 150 ft. (45m); Easter to mid-Nov. A spectacular sight.

MUSEUMS OF ART: ☼⚑⚑ **Carnegie Institute Museum of Art**, 4400 Forbes Ave. (622-3131): Lovely museum with an important collection of impressionists and post-impressionists (Sarah Scaife Gallery) alongside classical paintings and sculptures and antique furniture. Among its best-known works: *Virgin and Child with Angel* by Francesco Francia, *Toilette of Venus* by Simon Vouet, *Reefs near Dieppe* by Monet, *The Something-or-Other Circus* by Jean Dewasne, and George Segal's amazing *Tightrope Walker*. Should be visited; open Tues–Sun.

☼⚑⚑ **Frick Art Museum**, 7227 Reynolds St. (371-0600): European old masters (Tintoretto, Rubens, Fragonard, Boucher, and others) in an elegant Renaissance-style mansion once the home of the coal-and-steel magnate Henry Clay Frick; also many pieces of furniture that belonged to Marie Antoinette. Must certainly be seen; Tues–Sun.

MUSEUMS OF SCIENCE & HISTORY: ⚑ **Allegheny Observatory**, Perrysville Ave., Riverview Park (321-2400): One of the best-known observatories in the U.S., boasting a 30-in. (75cm) telescope. Open to budding astronomers in Wed–Fri evenings Apr–Oct. Resv. a must.

⚑ **Bessemer Court**, Station Sq. (471-5808): Open-air museum displaying a giant 10-ton (9,100kg) Bessemer converter (for converting pig iron into steel), the symbol of Pittsburgh's industrial might. Also antique cars, old railway carriages, and other relics of the golden age of transportation. Worth seeing; open Tues–Sun.

☼⚑ **Buhl Science Center**, Allegheny Sq. (321-4300): Modern, well-designed science museum; temporary exhibitions on different aspects of science, particularly astronomy and computers. Also well-equipped planetarium, laser show, and model railroad much appreciated by the younger set (Nov–Feb). Worth a visit; open daily.

☼☆🏛🏛 **Carnegie Institute Museum of Natural History,** 4400 Forbes Ave. (622-3313): Best known for its hall of dinosaurs, this very handsome natural history museum also has fine displays of minerals, precious stones, and zoology, as well as a fascinating exhibition devoted to the Arctic world. Not to be missed. Open Tues–Sun.

☼☆🏛 **Fort Pitt Museum,** 101 Commonwealth Pl., Point State Park (281-9284): Interesting military museum on the French and Indian War. This facsimile of a fort occupies the site of the original (1764) Fort Pitt. Military parades in period uniform Sun afternoons in summer. Worth a visit; open Tues–Sun.

🏛 **Historical Society of Western Pennsylvania,** 4338 Bigelow Blvd. (681-5533): A journey back into 19th-century Pennsylvania, through collections of old furniture, unusual glass bottles, paintings, documents, and other historical items. For lovers of bygone days. Tues–Sat.

🏛 **Soldiers and Sailors Memorial Hall and Museum,** Fifth Ave. and Bigelow Blvd. (621-4253): Weapons, uniforms, military mementoes, and flags from the country's wars. Should be seen; open daily.

PANORAMAS: ☼☆🏛🏛 **Mount Washington:** There are two cable cars to the top of Mount Washington: the **Monongahela Incline** from W. Carson St. nr. Station Sq. (231-5707) and the **Duquesne Incline** from W. Carson St. near Fort Pitt Bridge (381-1665). Fine view of the city and the Golden Triangle with its three rivers; shouldn't be missed.

🏛 **U.S.X. Tower,** 600 Grant St. (471-4100): Fine view of the city from the Top of the Triangle restaurant on the 62nd floor (admission fee). So-so food but congenial bar. Open Mon–Sat.

PARKS & GARDENS: ☼☆🏛 **Conservatory-Aviary,** Ridge Ave. and Arch St. (323-7234): Wonderful collection of the world's birds, more than 220 species in all, in reconstructions of their natural habitats. A sight to be seen. Open daily.

🏛 **Phipps Conservatory,** Schenley Park, Schenley Dr. (622-6914): Lovely tropical greenhouses and flower shows; splendid cactus and orchid gardens. Don't miss it; open daily.

☼☆🏛🏛 **Point State Park,** at the west end of Fort Duquesne Blvd. and Fort Pitt Blvd.: A 36-acre (15ha) park on the site of the first settlement, at the confluence of the Monongahela River and Allegheny River; panoramic view of the city and Mount Washington. Monumental fountain and traces of old Fort Pitt. Must be seen.

🏛 **Schenley Park,** Schenley Dr.: A stone's throw from the University of Pittsburgh, this 456-acre (185ha) park is popular at all times of year; there are several picnic areas, a public golf course, a small lake, several miles of trails, and a skating rink. Cross-country skiing in winter.

PERFORMING ARTS: For daily listings of all shows and cultural events, consult the entertainment pages of the daily papers *Pittsburgh Post-Gazette* (morning) and *Pittsburgh Press* (evening), as well as the monthly *Pittsburgh* magazine. **Tix,** a discount ticket booth in Oliver Plaza, U.S.X. Tower (642-2787) sells half-price tickets for all shows on the day of performance, Mon–Sat; cash only.

Benedum Theater for the Performing Arts, 719 Liberty Ave. (456-2600): The old Stanley Theater, entirely renovated in 1987. Home of the Pittsburgh Opera (director, Tito Capobianco), the Civic Light Opera, and the Pittsburgh Ballet Theater. Also Broadway hits.

Fulton Theater, 101 6th St. (471-9700): Classical concerts and recitals.
Heinz Hall, 600 Penn Ave. (281-5000): Home of the Pittsburgh Symphony, under principal conductor Lorin Maazel (Sept–May). Concerts and recitals by distinguished soloists. Broadway hits.
Kresge Theater, Carnegie-Mellon University campus, Schenley Park (578-2407): Contemporary theater, musicals.
New City Theatre, Bouquet St. and Sennott St. (624-5041): Modern American theater; home of the City Theatre Company (Oct–Apr).
Pittsburgh Playhouse Theater Center, 222 Craft Ave. (621-4445): Contemporary and classic theater; children's shows.
Pittsburgh Public Theater, Allegheny Sq. (321-9800): Comedy, drama; the best of Pittsburgh's many theaters.
Stephen C. Foster Memorial Theater, U. of Pittsburgh campus, Forbes Ave. and Bigelow Blvd. (624-4100): Contemporary and classic theater, concerts; the Three Rivers Shakespeare Festival takes place here every year.
Syria Mosque, Bigelow Blvd. (621-8700): Former home of the Pittsburgh Symphony; contemporary theater, concerts.

SPECIAL EVENTS: For the exact schedule of events below, consult the **Greater Pittsburgh Convention and Visitors Bureau** (see "Tourist Information," above).
Folk Festival (end of May): The food, dance, music, and crafts of the many countries that have contributed to the great ethnic melting pot of Pittsburgh: Ireland, Scotland, Germany, Czechoslovakia, Hungary, Russia, and many more. Held at the David L. Lawrence Convention Center.
Three Rivers Shakespeare Festival (late May to mid-Aug): Presents three new plays every year at the Stephen C. Foster Memorial Theater.
Three Rivers Art Festival (3 weeks in June): Open-air art exhibitions, public concerts, movie festival, plays, etc.
Shadyside Art Festival (early Aug): Draws artists, craftspeople, and spectators from the whole region.
Three Rivers Regatta (first wknd in Aug): Very popular boat races (Formula I and rowing).
Jazz Festival (early Sept): With the biggest names.

SPORTS: Pittsburgh has professional teams in three major sports:
Baseball (Apr–Oct): Pirates, Three Rivers Stadium (323-5000).
Football (Aug–Dec): Steelers, Three Rivers Stadium (323-1200).
Ice Hockey (Oct–Apr): Penguins, Civic Arena (642-1800).

Horse Racing
The Meadows, **Meadowlands,** at Exit 8 from I-79 (563-1224), year round.

STROLLS: ⚓ **Bank Center Mall,** Fourth Ave. and Wood St. (288-9553): Turn-of-the-century houses, charmingly restored, in what was once the heart of Pittsburgh's downtown business district. Fashion shops, stores, movie houses, restaurants. A pleasant place.
☼⚓ **Station Square,** on the south bank of the Monongahela River at the foot of the Smithfield St. Bridge (261-9911): Terminal of the Pittsburgh & Lake Erie Railroad, no longer in use, now the favorite place for strolling, window-shopping, and distractions. Dozens of stalls, bars, and restaurants; lively and colorful day and night.

THEME PARKS: ⚓ **Kennywood Park,** 4800 Kennywood Blvd., in West Mifflin, 8 mi/12km SE along Penna. 837 (461-0500): Typical theme park with many attractions and five different roller coasters. Open Tues–Sun mid-May to Sept.

WINTER SPORTS RESORTS: ⚲ **Boyce Park Ski Area,** 18 mi. (28km) east via I-376 and Penna. 286 (733-4665): Four lifts; open Dec–Feb.

ZOOS: ⚲ **Pittsburgh Zoo,** Highland Ave., Highland Park (665-3640): More than 2,000 animals in reconstructions of their natural habitats, and a very modern aquarium, in a 65-acre (26ha) park. Worth a visit; open daily.

ACCOMMODATIONS

A Note on Accommodations: Room rates in Pittsburgh are coded as follows: **VE,** Very Expensive ($140 and up); **E,** Expensive ($90–$140); **M,** Moderate ($60–$90); **I,** Inexpensive ($30–$60); **B,** Budget (up to $30). A listing of toll-free numbers is in the Appendix.

Personal Favorites (in order of preference)

🛏🛏🛏 **Vista Pittsburgh Hotel** (dwntwn), 1000 Penn Ave., PA 15222 (412/281-3700; toll free, see Hilton). 614 rms, A/C, color TV, in-rm movies. AE, CB, DC, MC, V. Valet parking $8, pool, health club, sauna, two rests. (including American Harvest), coffee shop, bar, 24-hr. rm svce, disco, boutiques, free dwntwn limo, free crib. *Note:* Newest of the big dwntwn hotels; large, massive 26-story tower across from the David L. Lawrence Convention Center w. direct access to it by an enclosed walkway. Ultra-comfortable facilities and furnishings; spacious, inviting rms w. minibars; efficient svce. Good rest. serving American food; three VIP floors; business and convention clientele. Very well located. **E–VE**

🛏🛏🛏 **Hyatt Pittsburgh** (dwntwn), 112 Washington Pl. at Chatham Center, PA 15219 (412/471-1234; toll free, see Hyatt). 400 rms, A/C, color TV, in-rm movies. AE, CB, DC, MC, V. Valet gar. $8, pool, health club, sauna, rest. (Hugo's Rotisserie), coffee shop, bars, rm svce, disco, free crib. *Note:* Occupies the top 11 floors of a modern, architecturally unattractive, 20-story office building. The hotel is very comfortable and well equipped, but rms are on the small side. Diligent svce; praiseworthy rest.; VIP suites on the top floor. Business clientele; in the heart of the business district. **E–VE**

🛏🛏 **Sheraton Hotel at Station Square** (nr. dwntwn), 7 Station Sq. Dr., PA 15219 (412/261-2000; toll free, see Sheraton). 293 rms, A/C, in-rm movies. AE, CB, DC, MC, V. Free parking, pool, sauna, rest. (River's Edge), coffee shop, bar, rm svce, disco, boutiques, free crib. *Note:* Very modern 15-story hotel across the Monongahela River. Impeccable comfort and facilities; futurist seven-story lobby; spacious rms, the best overlooking the river and city. Reasonably efficient svce. In the center of Station Sq. w. its dozens of trendy shops and rests. Group and convention clientele. **E–VE**

☼🛏🛏 **The Priory** (nr. dwntwn), 614 Pressley St., PA 15212 (412/231-3338; toll free 800/533-4667). 24 rms, A/C, cable color TV. AE, CB, DC, MC, V. Free parking; no bar or rest., but free breakfast and cocktails. *Note:* Delightful small hotel, charming in a European way, on the quiet North Side across the Allegheny River; the turn-of-the-century structure was originally a Benedictine priory, whence the name. Comfortable, elegant rms; inviting flower-planted patio w. fountain. Polished reception and svce. About as far as you can get from the typical mass-market convention hotel, 5 min. from dwntwn. A very good place to stay. **M–E**

🛏 **Envoy Inn Pittsburgh West** (vic.), 100 Kisow Dr., PA 15205 (412/922-0120; toll free 800/227-7378). 118 rms, A/C, color TV, in-rm movies. AE, CB, DC, MC, V. Free parking, adj. rest. *Note:* Economical, very acceptable motel; clean, inviting rms. 20 min. from dwntwn via I-279W, I-79N, and Penna. 60; 10 min. from airport; ideal if you're driving. Free morning coffee; good value. **B–I**

🛏 **Motel 6 Pittsburgh** (nr. dwntwn), 211 Beecham Dr., PA 15205 (412/922-9400). 125 rms, A/C, color TV, in-rm movies. AE, DC, MC, V. Free parking. *Note:* New motel offering unbeatable value 15 min. from dwntwn and 10 min. from the airport. Serviceable comfort; ideal for the budget traveler. **B**

Other Accommodations (from top bracket to budget)

🛎🛎🛎 **Hilton Pittsburgh and Towers** (dwntwn), Commonwealth Pl. in Gateway Center, PA 15222 (412/391-4600; toll free, see Hilton). 718 rms, A/C, color TV, in-rm movies. AE, CB, DC, MC, V. Valet gar. $8, health club, sauna, two rests. (including Sterling's), two bars, rm svce, nightclub, hrdrsr, drugstore, free crib, concierge. *Note:* Recently renovated massive modern building w. the best view in Pittsburgh, from the point where the three rivers come together; ask for a room overlooking Point State Park. Comfortable but rather cramped rms; VIP suites on three top floors; efficient svce. Business and convention clientele. **E–VE**

☀🛎🛎🛎 **Westin William Penn** (dwntwn), 530 William Penn Pl., PA 15219 (412/281-7100; toll free, see Westin). 595 rms, A/C, color TV, in-rm movies. AE, CB, DC, MC, V. Gar. $8, two rests. (including the Terrace Room), bar, rm svce, nightclub, free crib, free Continental breakfast, concierge. *Note:* Since 1906 many distinguished American personalities, including presidents, have seen the crystal chandeliers, the gilt, and the wood paneling in this revered local institution. The plush Edwardian decor is currently undergoing renovation. Huge, luxuriously comfortable rms; very good svce; big business and VIP clientele. The building is a designated historic landmark. **E–VE**

🛎🛎🛎 **Marriott Greentree** (nr. dwntwn), 101 Marriott Dr., PA 15205 (412/922-8400; toll free, see Marriott). 480 rms, A/C, color TV, in-rm movies. AE, CB, DC, MC, V. Free parking, three pools, health club, sauna, two tennis courts, rest. (Ashley's), coffee shop, two bars, rm svce, disco, hrdrsr, free airport limo, free crib. *Note:* Large, modern, functional convention hotel 10 min. from dwntwn on I-279. Spacious, well-soundproofed rms (many w. minibars). Agreeable decor and setting. Rest. satisfactory but no more; efficient svce. Group and business clientele. 15 min. from airport. **E**

🛎🛎 **Ramada Suites Hotel** (formerly the Bigelow Hotel; dwntwn), 1 Bigelow Sq., PA 15219 (412/281-5800; toll free, see Ramada Inns). 341 suites, A/C, cable color TV. AE, CB, DC, MC, V. Valet parking $4, health club, sauna, squash courts, rest. (Ruddy Duck), bar, rm svce. *Note:* Modern suites-only hotel; comfortable, spacious accommodations w. kitchenette and refrigerator; convenient location at the heart of the business district. Good svce; well-equipped business center; acceptable rest. Business clientele. Good value. **M–E**

🛎🛎 **Best Western–Parkway Center Inn** (nr. dwntwn), 875 Greentree Rd., PA 15220 (412/922-7070; toll free, see Best Western). 151 rms, A/C, color TV, in-rm movies. AE, CB, DC, MC, V. Free parking, pool, health club, sauna, rest., bar, rm svce, hrdrsr, free airport limo, free breakfast (Mon–Fri), free crib. *Note:* Excellently run motel; agreeable rms, some w. kitchenettes and refrigerators. For a motel, very comprehensive facilities. 10 min. from dwntwn on I-279 and 15 min. from the airport; ideal if you're driving. **M**

🛎🛎 **Holiday Inn–Allegheny Valley** (vic.), 180 Gamma Dr., PA 15238 (412/963-0600; toll free, see Holiday Inns). 184 rms, A/C, color TV, in-rm movies. AE, CB, DC, MC, V. Free parking, pool, coffee shop, bar, rm svce, free crib. *Note:* Typical functional motel, 20 min. from dwntwn on Penna. 28. Spacious rms (some w. refrigerators). The Holiday Inn style. Group clientele. Ideal if you're driving. **M**

🛎🛎 **Howard Johnson Lodge–South** (vic.), 5300 Clairton Blvd., PA 15236 (412/884-6000; toll free, see Howard Johnson's). 94 rms, A/C, color TV. AE, CB, DC, MC, V. Free parking, pool, adj. coffee shop and bar, rm svce, free breakfast, free crib. *Note:* Older but comfortable motel nr. Allegheny County Airport. Spacious, inviting rms; cheerful svce; good value. 15 min. from dwntwn on Penna. 51; ideal if you're driving. **I–M**

    Redwood Inn (vic.), 2898 Banksville Rd., PA 15216 (412/ 343-3000). 95 rms, A/C, color TV, in-rm movies. AE, CB, DC, MC, V. Free parking, pool, coffee shop, bar, rm svce, disco, free crib. *Note:* Conventional motel but w. huge, comfortable rms and friendly reception and svce. Very good overall value. 10 min. from dwntwn on I-279 and U.S. 19; ideal if you have a car. **I–M**

    Knights Inn–Pittsburgh (vic.), 4800 Steubenville Pike, PA 15205 (412/922-6900). 110 rms, A/C, color TV, in-rm movies. AE, CB, DC, MC, V. Free parking, pool, adj. 24-hr. coffee shop, crib $3. *Note:* Good value 15 min. from dwntwn on Penna. 60. Very acceptable standards of comfort; some rms w. kitchenettes and refrigerators. Worthwhile reductions for long-term stays. Ideal if you're driving. **I**

Airport Accommodations

    Ramada Inn Airport (vic.), 1412 Beers School Rd., Coraopolis, PA 15108 (412/264-8950; toll free, see Ramada Inns). 135 rms, A/C, color TV, in-rm movies. AE, CB, DC, MC, V. Free parking, pool, rest. (Myron's), bar, rm svce, disco, free crib. *Note:* Inviting, comfortable six-floor motel a quarter mile (400m) from the airport (free shuttle). Spacious, well-soundproofed rms; efficient svce. Business clientele. Perfect for a stopover between flights. **M**

YMCA/Youth Hostels

    Point Park College Youth Hostel (dwntwn), 201 Wood St., PA 15222 (412/392-3824 or 391-4100). 100 beds. Coffee shop. Youth hostel open year round. Very central.

RESTAURANTS

A Note on Restaurant Prices: Pittsburgh restaurant prices, per person, excluding drinks and service charges, are coded as follows: **VE,** Very Expensive ($60 and up); **E,** Expensive ($40–$60); **M,** Moderate ($25–$40); **I,** Inexpensive ($15–$25); **B,** Budget (up to $15).

Personal Favorites (in order of preference)

    The Colony (vic.), Greentree Rd. and Cochran Rd. (561-2060). A/C. Dinner only, Mon–Sat; closed hols. AE, CB, DC, MC, V. Jkt. *Specialties:* lump crabmeat, scampi in garlic sauce, charcoal-broiled steak, filet mignon, veal chop, broiled swordfish. Good desserts; rather weak wine list. *Note:* Fine example of a rest. seriously devoted to American food. The menu is limited to a dozen (remarkable) meat and (impeccably fresh) fish dishes. The decor and atmosphere are those of a luxurious country club, w. an open brick grill in the center of the rm; the svce is in all respects flawless. Business and local VIP clientele. A Pittsburgh landmark since 1960; resv. advisable during the week, indispensable on wknds. Valet parking. 20 min. from dwntwn. *Steak/American.* **M–E**

    Grand Concourse (nr. dwntwn), 1 Station Sq. (261-1717). A/C. Lunch Mon–Fri, dinner nightly, brunch Sun; closed Thanksgiving, Dec 25. AE, CB, DC, MC, V. *Specialties:* oysters on the half shell, Charley's chowder, linguini primavera, catch of the day, New York strip steak, paella, rack of lamb. *Note:* One of the most unusual rest. settings in the country, in a turn-of-the-century railroad station. The enormous rest., in its wonderful rococo space with soaring vaults and stained-glass windows, specializes in the freshest possible seafood. Lively, congenial atmosphere; ask to be seated in the River Room, at a table w. a river view. Efficient, diligent svce. Locally popular, and a must for the visitor. In spite of its size, you'd be well advised to reserve ahead. *Seafood/American.* **I–M**

Arthur's (dwntwn), 209 Fourth Ave. at PPG Pl. (566-1735). A/C. Lunch Mon–Fri, dinner Mon–Sat; closed hols. AE, CB, DC, MC, V. Jkt. *Specialties:* German beer soup, seafood fettuccine Alfredo, vitello liberatore (stuffed w. scallops and mozzarella), beef Wellington, heritage pie (amaretto pastry). *Note:* In the Burke Landmark Building (1836, one of the oldest in dwntwn Pittsburgh), this charming, rather Victorian little rest. comprises four intimate dining rms each w. an open fireplace. Conventional Continental cuisine w. an Italian flavor; elegant svce; romantic atmosphere, particularly at dinner. The bar has an impressive choice of 275 kinds of single-malt scotch. Resv. suggested. *Continental/Italian.* **M–E**

Brady St. Bridge Café (nr. dwntwn), 2228 E. Carson St. (448-1818). A/C. Lunch Mon–Fri, dinner daily. AE, MC, V. *Specialties:* gourmet pizzaelles (small pizzas topped w. basil, w. artichoke, w. Cajun-style eel, etc.), fettuccine San Marco (w. seafood), broiled chicken w. sorrel, salmon w. grapefruit butter, meat and fish broiled over wood fire. Desserts on the weak side. *Note:* Opened not long ago, this charming South Side bistro offers light, modern California-style cuisine. Rather fussy Victorian setting w. old paneling, mirrors, ill-assorted knickknacks and a profusion of greenery. Friendly svce; relaxed atmosphere. Locally popular; resv. suggested at dinner. *American.* **I**

Klein's (dwntwn), 330 Fourth Ave. (232-3311). A/C. Lunch Mon–Fri, dinner Mon–Sat; closed hols. AE, DC, MC, V. *Specialties:* crab Imperial, blackened redfish, clambake, bouillabaisse, broiled fish, Maine lobster. *Note:* Since it opened in 1900, this has been the favored resort of local seafood lovers. Everything's absolutely fresh and reasonably priced, though sometimes a little overcooked. Charmingly old-fashioned seafaring decor contemporary w. the establishment; diligent svce in a relaxed atmosphere. A real local landmark in the heart of dwntwn. Resv. advised. A very good place. *Seafood.* **I–M**

Café del Sol (nr. dwntwn), 2104 Murray Ave. (422-1303). A/C. Lunch/dinner daily, brunch Sat–Sun. AE. *Specialties:* tapas, enchiladas, huevos rancheros, steak criollo, Mexican fried chicken in mole sauce, paella, flan. No liquor. *Note:* This tiny (12-table) Spanish-Hispanic rest. serves tasty, authentic food at very attractive prices; local color is enhanced by wall paintings. Crowded since its opening, with long waiting lines on the sidewalk on wknds. Careful svce; resv. advisable. Latin-American music Fri–Sat evenings. *Spanish/Latin American.* **B–I**

Other Restaurants (from top bracket to budget)

Carlton Restaurant (dwntwn), 1 Mellon Bank Center at Grant St. (391-4099). A/C. Lunch Mon–Fri, dinner Mon–Sat; closed hols. AE, CB, DC, MC, V. Jkt. *Specialties:* Charcoal-grilled prime meats and fresh seafood, lamb chops, prime rib, roasted quail, Cajun dishes, own pastries. *Note:* A favorite with businesspeople. Voted best steaks in Pittsburgh by readers of *Pittsburgh* magazine. Tables are somewhat close together and the place can get noisy. Service attentive and discreet. Always crowded. Resv. strongly suggested. *American/Continental.* **M–E**

The Common Plea (dwntwn), 308 Ross St. (281-5140). A/C. Lunch Mon–Fri, dinner nightly; closed hols. and Sun mid-May to mid-Sept. AE, CB, DC, MC, V. Jkt. *Specialties:* scallops and shrimp Norfolk, bouillabaisse, roulade of veal w. crabmeat, broiled seafood platter, good homemade desserts. Menu changes regularly. *Note:* For more than 15 years this little rest., a stone's throw from the City Council Building and the Court House, has been the lunchtime favorite of local politicians and lawyers. The food is generally excellent, and emphasizes seafood. Heavy wood tables and rococo decor. Very good svce; resv. advised, a must at lunch. Ask to be seated upstairs. *Continental.* **I–M**

Le Pommier (nr. dwntwn), 2104 E. Carson St. (431-1901). A/C. Dinner only, Tues–Sat. AE, MC, V. Jkt. *Specialties:* salmon cooked in foil, sweetbread salad, braised duck w. red-wine sauce, breast of chicken stuffed w. goat cheese, chocolate mousse and Grand Marnier cake. Menu changes regularly. *Note:* Remarkable food, inspired by modern French originals, in a prettily converted shop more than a century old. Elegant countrified decor w. unadorned brick walls and candle-lit tables; attentive, efficient svce; an excellent place to eat. Resv. a must; 15 min. from dwntwn. *French/American.* **I–M**

♈♈ **Louis Tambellini's** (nr. dwntwn), 860 Saw Mill Run Blvd.
♈♈ (481-1118). A/C. Lunch/dinner Mon–Sat (until midnight); closed hols. AE, MC, V. Jkt. *Specialties:* homemade pasta and gnocchi, baked scampi, shrimp Louie, linguini w. mussels, redfish Cajun style, poached salmon w. vegetables, rack of lamb, Italian dishes, caffe espresso. *Note:* In spite of its strong Italian overtones, the cuisine of the Tambellini family gives precedence to seafood—broiled, poached, or baked. Remarkable fish and shellfish. Very elegant modern decor; diligent, unfussy svce. Big enough that resv. are not needed. Valet parking; 15 min. from dwntwn. *Italian/Seafood.* **I–M**

♈♈ **Chinese on Carson** (nr. dwntwn), 1506 Carson St. (431-1717). A/C. Lunch Mon–Sat, dinner daily; closed hols. AE, DC, MC, V. *Specialties:* lobster egg rolls, chicken Kung Pao, Peking duck, ching chioa beef, long-life noodles (w. seafood), braised duck w. crabmeat and scallops. *Note:* Connoisseurs judge this luxurious venture by Richard Lee (also owner of the Oriental Balcony and Mr. Lee's North Garden) to be by a wide margin the finest Far Eastern rest. in Pittsburgh—one of the few major U.S. cities without a Chinatown. Impeccable Cantonese and Szechuan cooking in an attractive lavender-toned Oriental setting. Resv. strongly advised. *Chinese.* **I**

☀♈ **Froggy's** (dwntwn), 100 Market St. at First Ave. (471-3764).
☀♈ A/C. Lunch Mon–Fri, dinner Mon–Sat; closed hols. AE, DC, MC, V. *Specialties:* sandwiches, salads, hamburgers, steaks. *Note:* In the Firstside, the old warehouse district along the Monongahela, this granddaddy of local singles bars is alleged to serve the best drinks in all of dwntwn, as well as excellent steaks and hamburgers. Draws journalists and sports fans, particularly when there's a game at the nearby Three Rivers Stadium. A likable, relaxed place. Resv. suggested. *American.* **B–I**

☀♈ **Max's Allegheny Tavern** (nr. dwntwn), 537 Suismon St. at
☀♈ Middle St. (231-1899). A/C. Lunch/dinner Mon–Sat, brunch Sun. AE, CB, DC, MC, V. *Specialties:* sauerbraten, würst platte (sausage plate), wienerschnitzel, weisswurst, apfelstrudel. Draft beer. *Note:* This picturesque turn-of-the-century tavern is one of the oldest on the Northside, a neighborhood across the Allegheny. Authentically German food and atmosphere at very attractive prices. Pretty turn-of-the-century-type decor with Tiffany-style lamps, ceiling fans, tile floors, and superb bar in massive walnut. Noisy but congenial; locally popular. Resv. for parties of five or more only, so you'll have to wait. *German.* **B–I**

♈ **Tequila Junction** (nr. dwntwn), The Shops at Station Sq. (261-3265). A/C. Lunch/dinner daily. AE, CB, DC, MC, V. *Specialties:* crabmeat enchiladas, chimichangas, tamales, burritos. *Note:* Charming Mexican-inn decor in brick and adobe; good, unpretentious food; svce more friendly than efficient. Locally popular; no resv. *Mexican.* **B–I**

Restaurants in the Vicinity

♈♈ **Hyeholde** (vic.), 190 Hyeholde Dr., Coraopolis (264-3116).
♈♈ A/C. Lunch Mon–Fri, dinner Mon–Sat; closed hols. AE, CB, DC, MC, V. Jkt. *Specialties:* sherry bisque, rack of lamb persillade, apple-stuffed breast of chicken w. sauce velouté, baked Virginia spots (a local fish; in season), squab w. champagne, filet mignon, Hyeholde trifle. Very fine wine list. *Note:* Very nr. the airport, this unexpected English Tudor manor house, w. exposed beams, open fireplaces, and wall hangings, serves very commendable classic

grande cuisine—and charges prices to match. Dinner by candlelight and romantic atmosphere. Pretty grdns; attentive svce; resv. advised. Valet parking. *Continental.* **M–E**

Cafeteria/Fast Food

Applebee's (dwntwn), 411 Smithfield St. (261-2277). Lunch/dinner Mon–Sat. No credit cards. Excellent sandwiches, salads, roast beef, cookies, and home-baked pies; perfect for a meal on the run. An old standby of its kind. Other location: 214 Fifth Ave. (566-2441).

Original Hot Dogs Shop (nr. dwntwn), 3901 Forbes Ave. (621-7388). Lunch/dinner daily (till 4:30am); no credit cards. The "Big O," as the students at the nearby University of Pittsburgh fondly call it, is generally held to serve the best hot dogs in town.

BARS & NIGHTCLUBS

Cardillo's Club Café (dwntwn), 56-58 S. 12th St. (381-3777). Thought to host the best modern jazz in town. Open nightly.

Chauncey's (nr. dwntwn), Station Sq. (232-0601). Favored by the local yuppics; has an acceptable rest. A preppy place. Open daily.

Froggy's (dwntwn), 100 Market St. (471-3764). The granddaddy of local singles bars; excellent drinks in a warm atmosphere; also a rest. serving laudable meat dishes (see "Restaurants," above). Open Mon–Sat.

Gandy Dancer Saloon (nr. dwntwn), 1 Station Sq. (261-1717). Congenial piano bar adjoining the Grand Concourse (see "Restaurants," above). Live music; oyster bar. Open nightly.

Graffiti (nr. dwntwn), 4615 Baum Blvd. (682-4210). This nightclub presents a wide-ranging variety of music: jazz, folk, rock, classical. Youthful clientele and atmosphere. Open Tues–Sat.

Hemingway's (nr. dwntwn), 3911 Forbes Ave. in Oakland (621-4100). One of the best-known jazz spots in town. Open nightly.

Shadyside Balcony (nr. dwntwn), 5520 Walnut St. (687-0110). Live modern jazz; praiseworthy rest. Locally popular. Open daily.

Tramp's (dwntwn), 212 Blvd. of the Allies (261-1990). Another very popular singles bar in what used to be a flourishing brothel. Also rest. Amusing ambience. Open Mon–Sat.

NEARBY EXCURSIONS

AMBRIDGE (18 mi./28km NW on Penna. 65): **Old Economy Village** is the former community of the Utopian Christian "Harmony Society," founded around 1825 by a pastor of German origin, George Rapp. Many buildings of the period: communal kitchens, festival hall, workshops, church, granary, cellar, etc., with their original furniture. The community, which practiced celibacy and community property, survived until its dissolution in 1905. A fascinating visit. Open Tues–Sun.

FALLINGWATER (at Mill Run, 70 mi./112km SE via Penna. 51S, U.S. 40E, and Penna. 381N) (329-8501): With its terraces cantilevered out over Bear Run, this "house over the waterfall," dating from 1936, is one of the most celebrated achievements of Frank Lloyd Wright, the man who can almost be said to have invented the contemporary private house. Open Tues–Sun mid-Apr to mid-Nov, wknds only in winter; resv. advised. Well worth the detour; best combined with a visit to Fort Necessity (see below).

FORT NECESSITY NATIONAL BATTLEFIELD (58 mi./93km SE via Penna. 51S and U.S. 40E) (329-5512): Site of the first major battle fought by George Washington, at the time a colonel in the British army, against the French and their Indian allies on July 3, 1754. The engagement, which resulted in a British defeat, marked the official beginning of the French and Indian War. Replica of the fort originally built by Washington, museum, early 19th-century tavern. Open daily; best visited in combination with Fallingwater (see above).

HARTWOOD ACRES (215 Saxonburg Blvd., 12 mi./ 19km north via Penna. 8 and Saxonburg Blvd.) (767-9200): Faithful reproduction of a great English country house, with Gothic Tudor buildings, antique furniture, formal gardens, stud farm, etc. Worth going out of your way for. Open Tues–Sun.

PRABHUPADA'S PALACE OF GOLD (near Wheeling, W. Va., 72 mi./115km SW via I-79S, I-70W, W. Va. 88, U.S. 250S, and Limestone Hill Rd.) (304/843-1600): Sumptuous palace in the Indian style built by Hare Krishna devotees as a sanctuary dedicated to their spiritual director Srila Prabhupada. More than 8,000 sq. ft. (740m^2) of 22-karat gold leaf was used in its construction, as well as 52 different kinds of marble, carved teakwood furniture, and crystal chandeliers imported from Austria. Fine gardens with rose gardens, fountains, and original sculptures. Very good rest. (Nathaji's). Definitely worth visiting; open daily.

PITHOLE CITY (102 mi./163km north via I-79, U.S. 62E, and Penna. 227N) (814/589-7912): The drilling, on August 27, 1859, of the first U.S. oil well on the banks of Oil Creek, 4 mi. (6km) west, made the fortune of Pithole—for a short while. In 5 months of the year 1865 its population rose from 15 to 10,000, but in 1867 its prosperity vanished as abruptly as it had come. The first boom town created by "black gold" is now totally abandoned, and only a few vestiges remain of its extraordinary past. Visitor Center open Tues–Sun, Memorial Day to Labor Day. Should be seen.

TOUR-ED MINE (Red Belt West at Tarentum, 20 mi./32km NW on Penna. 28) (224-4720): Former underground coal mine, first worked in the 1780s. Visit to the original plant and buildings. Interesting mining museum. Open daily May to Labor Day.

CHAPTER 8

BALTIMORE

□ □ □

Hub of the 17th-century tobacco trade, Baltimore, like Boston and New York, is one of the continent's oldest metropolises. It is also one of the birthplaces of religious tolerance in America: the Royal Charter of 1649 expressly granted freedom of worship to the colony of Maryland, created 17 years earlier by a decree of King Charles I. Tucked away at the head of the huge Chesapeake Bay (187 mi./300km long), Baltimore, named in honor of the first British "proprietor" of the colony, Cecilius Calvert, 2nd Baron Baltimore, has always been a bustling commercial crossroads between the East Coast and the South. Point of origin of the country's first railroad line (1827)—the legendary Baltimore & Ohio— Maryland's biggest city is still the principal Atlantic outlet for midwestern grain and Appalachian coal.

Port city and home to industry and business, Baltimore is also a bastion of culture: some of the people associated with the city are Edgar Allan Poe, who died here in 1849 in still-mysterious circumstances; Francis Scott Key, who wrote "The Star-Spangled Banner" here (1814); critic Henry L. Mencken (1880–1956); author Leon Uris, born here in 1924; and John Dos Passos, who died here in 1970. Baltimore is famous for its five universities, an internationally known **symphony orchestra,** and an architectural heritage too often ignored by tourists. The city is an attractive blend of tradition and vitality: the glass-and-steel skyscrapers of **Charles Center** and the patrician homes of **Mount Vernon Place** rubbing shoulders with the picturesque rowhouses, the shot-and-a-beer joints and cobblestone alleyways of **Fell's Point** and **Otterbein Homesteading;** the imposing Victorian architecture of **City Hall;** the delicate grace of the **Walters Art Gallery;** and the United States' oldest Catholic cathedral, the **Basilica of the Assumption** (1821), miraculously spared by the 1904 fire that destroyed much of the historic section. **Fort McHenry,** built in 1794–1805 with star-shaped fortifications characteristic of the period, and tenaciously held against the British during the War of 1812, attracts close to a million visitors each year. The new port area, the **Inner Harbor,** is one of the finest examples of urban renewal in the United States, with many lively and colorful boutiques, stores, and crowded seafood restaurants (Chesapeake Bay blue crabs and oysters are justly famous). This area alone is worth the trip to Baltimore. Other areas worth a look are the old ethnic neighborhoods: **Little Italy** (around High St. and Pratt St., Central Ave. and Eastern Ave.); **Greektown** (Eastern Ave. from no. 3500 to no. 4800); **Little Lithuania** (Hollins St. and Carrollton St.); the Polish and Ukrainian neighborhoods of **Highlandtown** (around Patterson Park); and the old Jewish quarter, nicknamed **Corned Beef Row** because of a multitude of deli restaurants (Lombard St. around Lloyd St. and Central Ave.).

Some of Baltimore's famous sons and residents are: Billie Holiday, the great blues singer; drummer Chick Webb; jazz musician Eubie Blake; Wallis Warfield Simpson, who married Edward VIII of England (1937) and became the Duchess of Windsor; composer Philip Glass; and the legendary Babe Ruth, known to baseball fans as the "Sultan of Swat."

BASIC FACTS: State of Maryland. Area code: 301. Time zone: eastern. ZIP Code (of central post office): 21233. Settled: 1661. Founded: 1729. Approximate population: city, 760,000; metropolitan area, 2,340,000. 18th-largest U.S. metropolitan area.

CLIMATE: As in all the Northeast Corridor cities, the winter is cold (mean Jan temperature, 37°F/3°C), but with less snow than in Boston or New York. Summer is hot and humid with sudden downpours due to the proximity of Chesapeake Bay (mean July temperature, 79°F/26°C). Autumn is rainy, and an umbrella is a must in Sept–Oct. The best season to visit Baltimore is spring which, although windy, is almost always pleasant.

DISTANCES: New York, 200 mi. (320km); Philadelphia, 93 mi. (150km); Pittsburgh, 218 mi. (350km); Washington, 40 mi. (65km).

ARRIVAL & TRANSIT INFORMATION
AIRPORT: Baltimore-Washington International Airport (BWI): 10 mi. (16km) south of Baltimore, 32 mi. (51km) north of Washington. Call 859-7100 for information.

U.S. AIRLINES: American (850-5800), Delta (768-9000), Eastern (768-3100), Northwest (821-0994), TWA (338-1156), United (850-4557), and USAir (727-0825).

FOREIGN CARRIERS: Icelandair (toll free 800/223-5500) and KLM (toll free 800/777-5553).

CITY LINK: Cab fare to city center about $15; time, 20 min. Cab fare to dwntwn Washington from BWI, $36–$40; time, 45 min. Bus: **Airport Connection** (859-3000); leaves every 30 min.; stops at the major dwntwn hotels; fare, $7; time, 25 min. Also stops at 16th St. NW and K St. in dwntwn Washington: fare, $10; time, 50 min.; leaves every 45 min. The proximity of the airport and the compact layout of downtown Baltimore may make car rental superfluous. Good public transportation system by subway and bus (MTA: 539-5000), or streetcar replica (Balto Trolley Works: 396-4259).

CAR RENTAL (at the airport unless otherwise indicated): Avis (859-1680); Budget (859-0850); Dollar (684-2020); Hertz (859-3600); National (859-8860); Thrifty, 15 Hammonds Ferry Rd., Glen Burnie (768-4900). For dwntwn locations, consult the local telephone book.

LIMOUSINE SERVICES: Carey Limousine (233-7400); Chesapeake Limousine (366-3000).

TAXIS: Taxis can be hailed on the street or summoned by telephone. The major companies are **Diamond Cab** (947-3333), **Sun Cab** (235-0300), and **Yellow Cab** (685-1212). Baltimore cab fares are among the lowest in the nation.

TRAIN: Amtrak, Pennsylvania Station, 1515 N. Charles St. (539-2112).

INTERCITY BUSES: Greyhound, 210 W. Fayette St. (752-1393).

INFORMATION & TOURS

TOURIST INFORMATION: The **Baltimore Area Convention & Visitors Association,** 1 E. Pratt St. (plaza level), MD 21202 (301/659-7300).

Visitor Center, in the Robbins Building, Pratt St. and Howard St. (301/837-4636).

For a **recorded telephone message** giving an up-to-date listing of cultural events and shows, call 301/837-4636.

GUIDED TOURS: About Town Tours (bus) (301/592-7770): Guided tour of the city. Leaves from major hotels.

Baltimore Patriot (boat), Inner Harbor (685-4288). Harbor cruise, mid-Apr to mid-Oct.

Clipper Cruise Line (boat): Information: 7711 Bonhomme Ave., St. Louis, MO 63105 (toll free 800/325-0010). Has 7-, 10-, and 14-day luxury yacht cruises (100 berths) along the Atlantic coast from Boston or Baltimore to Fort Lauderdale and the Virgin Islands.

Inner Harbor Tours (boat), Inner Harbor's Finger Pier (752-1515): Narrated cruises to Fort McHenry. Leaves Inner Harbor every half hour 11am–5:30pm.

Insomniac Tours (bus), 3414 Philips Dr. (301/653-2998): An original and highly successful idea, this guided tour of Baltimore for night owls leaves at 1:30am and returns at dawn, with dinner included. Resv. a must.

Lady Baltimore (boat), W. Bulkhead at Light St. (301/727-3113): Cruises along Chesapeake Bay to Annapolis (end of May to Sept).

SIGHTS, ATTRACTIONS & ACTIVITIES

ARCHITECTURAL HIGHLIGHTS: ※🏛 **Charles Center,** bounded by Charles St., Baltimore St., and Liberty St.: New business district begun in the early 1960s. Among the 15 commercial and residential skyscrapers are the very handsome **One Charles Center,** 24 floors of bronze-colored glass, by Mies van der Rohe; and the 13,000-seat **Civic Center.** Fountains and modern sculptures (see "Outdoor Art and Plazas," below). Worth a glance.

🏛 **Social Security Headquarters,** 6401 Security Blvd.: Here 240 million Social Security files are available for reference in these immense archives, housed in the country's largest administrative building after the Pentagon. Computer enthusiasts will want to visit the impressive complex. Worth a look. Open Mon–Fri.

🏛 **World Trade Center,** Pratt St. at Inner Harbor (837-4515): I. M. Pei's innovative pentagonal 30-story building. The observation platform on the 27th floor offers an unobstructed view of the city and the port (see "Panoramas," below).

CHURCHES/SYNAGOGUES: ※🏛 **Basilica of the Assumption,** Cathedral St. and Mulberry St. (727-2564): Be sure to see the United States' oldest Catholic cathedral (1821) with its interesting classical revival architecture. Visits by appointment.

HISTORIC BUILDINGS: 🏛 **Asbury House,** 10 E. Mt. Vernon Pl. (685-5290): Luxurious private residence dating from the 1850s, with decorative balconies and wrought-iron fences. Very lovely interior decor with a startling three-story spiral staircase. See it. Open Mon–Fri.

🏛 **City Hall,** 100 N. Holiday St. (396-4550): Baltimore's City Hall is one of the finest examples of Victorian architecture in the United States (1875) and was entirely restored in 1975. Imposing dome, 252 ft. (77m) high. Visits by appointment Mon–Sat.

※🏛 **Edgar Allan Poe House,** 203 N. Amity St. (837-3262): The last residence of the famous writer who died in 1849 in still-mysterious circumstances. Open Wed–Sat. His grave is close by, at **Westminster Presbyterian Church Yard,** Fayette St. and Greene St. (328-7228). A group of admirers leads a graveside ceremony each Oct 7 at midnight to commemorate the anniversary of his death. Worth making the trip.

Fort McHenry National Monument and Historic Shrine, at the east end of Fort Ave. (962-4299): Splendidly restored early 19th-century fortress at the entrance to the harbor. When, on the morning of September 14, 1814, from the English warship on which he was held prisoner, Francis Scott Key, a lawyer and sometime poet, saw the tattered flag still streaming above the fort after a night of intense bombardment, he was inspired to write the words to what has become the national anthem. Fort McHenry is one of five public buildings authorized to fly the flag year round. You will also find a museum, a very fine panorama, and military parades in summer; the fort attracts more than 800,000 visitors each year. Not to be missed. Open daily.

Johns Hopkins University, Charles St. and 34th St. (338-8000): Founded in 1876 through the generosity of Johns Hopkins, a wealthy local businessman, this is one of the country's most respected universities (3,000 students) and a highly prestigious medical center. The campus has many Georgian-style buildings such as **Gilman Hall,** the elegant **Homewood House,** the interesting **Archeological Museum** (Egyptian and Roman antiquities; open Mon–Fri), and the very original **Bufano Sculpture Garden,** with amusing topiary sculptures by Italian artist Beniamino Bufano. See it. Open daily.

Shot Tower, Fayette St. and Front St. (396-5894): From the top of this slim, 227-ft. (70m) brick tower which dates from 1828, molten lead was poured into a vat of water below to make cannon balls. Open daily.

Star-Spangled Banner Flag House, 844 E. Pratt St. (837-1793): Picturesque small house dating from 1773 and home to an interesting collection of Revolutionary War relics. Here Mary Pickersgill and her teenage daughter, sewed the flag that inspired Francis Scott Key's poem which became the national anthem; at the time it had 15 stars and 15 stripes. (They were paid $405.90 for parts and labor.) The flag on display is a replica; the original is in the National Museum of American History in Washington. Period souvenirs and documents. Open daily (Mon–Sat in winter).

U.S. Frigate *Constellation*, Pier 1, Pratt St., Inner Harbor (539-1797): The oldest U.S. warship (1797) still afloat. Laid up in 1945 after 148 years of continuous faithful service, she is now a floating museum. Not to be missed. Open daily.

MARKETS: **Lexington Market,** Lexington St. and Eutaw St. (685-6170): One of the United States' oldest indoor markets (1782). Destroyed by fire in 1949, it was reconstructed in its original form in 1952 and houses more than 160 different food businesses. The city's gastronomic pride, with its extremely colorful decor. Not to be missed. Open Mon–Sat.

MONUMENTS: **Washington Monument,** Charles St. and Monument St. (396-7939): The oldest monument dedicated to our first president (1842). This massive white column offers a very fine view of the city from 172 ft. (54m) up (no elevator). Open Fri–Tues. See it.

MUSEUMS OF ART: **Museum of Art,** N. Charles St. and 31st St. (396-7100): This interesting museum is just 20 min. from dwntwn and houses many beautiful paintings and sculptures. Among the most famous are Titian's *Man with a Fur*; Rembrandt's *Portrait of Titus*; Renoir's *The Washerwomen*; 43 Matisses, including *Blue Nude* and *Seated Odalisque*; and 16 Picassos, including *Portrait of Allan Stein*. Not to be missed. Open Tues–Sun.

Peabody Institute, E. Mt. Vernon Pl. (659-8100): Home of a renowned music conservatory, it offers free concerts Wed at

noon. Open Mon–Fri. With a six-story atrium, interior balconies, and forged-iron pillars, the library (300,000 volumes) is worth a visit for its design alone.

☀☆♈♈ **Walters Art Gallery,** 600 N. Charles St. (547-9000): Archeology, old masters, jewelery, weapons from antiquity to modern times, and a very rich collection of Armenian manuscripts in the elegant Italian Renaissance–style home of philanthropist William T. Walters, and in the new wing opened in 1974. One of the country's best art museums. Some of its most famous exhibits including Giovanni di Paolo's *Carrying of the Cross*, Raphael's *Madonna of the Candelabra*, Orcagna's *Crucifixion*, Corot's *Very Early Spring*, and Manet's *At the Café-Concert*. Reopened in 1989 after radical renovation. A definite must-see. Open daily.

MUSEUMS OF SCIENCE & HISTORY: ♈♈♈ **Babe Ruth Museum,** 216
Emory St. (727-1539): The house in which the most famous baseball player of all time was born (1895) is now a museum devoted to the man known as the "Sultan of Swat." Open daily.

♈♈ **B & O Railroad Museum,** Mount Clare Station, Pratt St. and Poppleton St. (237-2387): The world's biggest collection of old locomotives in a Baltimore & Ohio Railroad station that is the oldest in the United States (1830). A visit not to be missed. Open Wed–Sun. (In this same station, in 1844 Samuel Morse inaugurated the telegraph system that bears his name, transmitting from Washington the famous message: "What hath God wrought.")

♈ **H. L. Mencken House,** 1524 Hollins St. (396-7997): Home for more than 68 years of the celebrated journalist, author, and critic Henry Louis Mencken, the "Sage of Baltimore," this stately 19th-century rowhouse is fully restored with Mencken's original furniture and many of his personal belongings. Interesting. Open Wed–Sun.

♈ **Maryland Science Center,** 601 Light St. (685-2370): Unusual assembly of octagonal structures housing an ultra-sophisticated planetarium **(Davis Planetarium)** which reproduces a space voyage as well as various exhibits on the evolution of science and a giant model of a human cell. Fascinating. Open Tue–Sun.

☀♈♈ **National Aquarium,** Pier 3, Pratt St., Inner Harbor (576-3810): One of the East Coast's most modern and spectacular aquariums. Futurist architecture in the form of a glass pyramid. 8,000 specimens of 600 different species. Also, a shark tank and facsimiles of natural habitats. A new pavilion, opened in May 1990, includes a 1.2-million-gallon (4.5-million-liter) pool with bottlenose dolphins and beluga whales, a 1,300-seat amphitheater, and a 40-ft. (12m) model of a humpback whale suspended in the pavilion's three-story atrium. Attracts more than 1½ million visitors each year. An absolute must-see. Open daily.

♈ **Peale Museum,** 225 Holliday St. (396-1149): One of the United States' oldest museums (1814). Once the City Hall, it covers the history of Baltimore from the earliest settlement to the present. Interesting. Open Tues–Sun.

OUTDOOR ART & PLAZAS: **Charles Center,** bounded by Baltimore St., Charles St., and Liberty St.: This ultramodern architectural ensemble boasts numerous fountains, esplanades (among them, **Center Plaza**, which recalls Siena's famous piazza del Campo), and sculpture (notably a 32-ft./10m bronze flame by Francesco Somaini). Open-air concerts in summer.

PANORAMAS: **Federal Hill Park:** See "Parks and Gardens," below.
♈♈ **Top of the World,** Pratt St. at Inner Harbor (837-4515): Observation platform on the 27th floor of the **World Trade Cen-**

ter (see "Architectural Highlights," above). The best panoramic view of the city and the harbor. Open daily.
Washington Monument: See "Monuments," above.

PARKS & GARDENS: ☖ **Cylburn Arboretum,** 4915 Greenspring Ave. (369-0180): 168-acre (70ha) landscaped park, 20 min. from dwntwn via the Jones Falls Expwy. A favorite of nature lovers, with its numerous trails and its countless varieties of plants. Open daily. The botanical museum **(Cylburn Mansion)** is open Mon–Fri.
 ☖ **Druid Hill Park,** Druid Park Lake Dr.: Dating from the 1850s, this lovely urban park is home to a very substantial zoo (more than 1,000 animals), flower displays **(Conservatory),** lakes, groves, playing fields, and picnic grounds, all 10 min. from dwntwn via Jones Falls Expwy.
Federal Hill Park, Warren Ave. and Battery Ave.: Gardens at the southern end of the Inner Harbor affording a very fine view of the city and the harbor.

PERFORMING ARTS: For daily listings of all shows and cultural events, consult the entertainment pages of the daily papers: *Baltimore Sun* (morning) and *Baltimore Evening Sun* (evening); and of the monthly magazine *Baltimore.*
Arena Players, 801 McCulloh St. (728-6500): Modern theater, drama, comedy.
Center Stage, 700 N. Calvert St. (332-0033): Classical and modern theater.
Lyric Opera House, 1404 Maryland Ave. (685-5086): Baltimore Opera Company in residence, Feb–June. Director, Michael Harrison.
Meyerhoff Symphony Hall, 1212 Cathedral St. (783-8000): Home of the Baltimore Symphony Orchestra; principal conductor, David Zinman. Oct–May.
Morris A. Mechanic Theatre, Hopkins Pl. (625-1400): Broadway hits.
Peabody Institute and Conservatory of Music, 1 E. Mt. Vernon Pl. (659-8165): Very popular chamber-music recitals.
Pier 6 Concert Pavilion, Pier 6, Inner Harbor (727-5580): Big-name concerts and shows, June–Sept.
Theatre Project, 45 W. Preston St. (752-8558): Experimental theater.
Vagabond Players, 806 S. Broadway (563-9135): One of the oldest "little theaters" in the United States. Drama, comedy, modern theater, Broadway shows.

SHOPPING: **Harborplace,** Light St. and Pratt St. (332-4191): Some 150 food stores, stalls, fashionable boutiques, and restaurants (including Jean Claude's Caf and Phillips) in two huge glass pavilions on the basin of the Inner Harbor. Lively, picturesque ambience. Open daily.

SPECIAL EVENTS: For the exact schedule of the events below, consult the **Baltimore Area Convention & Visitors Association** (see "Tourist Information," above).
Preakness Festival Week (mid-May): Public concerts, exhibits, ballooning exhibitions, and shows the entire week preceding the Preakness Stakes, a famous horse race since 1873 and one of the three events that make up thoroughbred racing's Triple Crown.
Pier 6 Concerts (June–Sept): Open-air concerts on the water's edge. Jazz, classical, variety. Locally very popular.
Showcase of Nations Festival (every wknd, June–Sept): Festival dedicated to the folk music, crafts, and foods of the different ethnic groups living in Baltimore.
I Am an American Day (early Sept): The United States' biggest patriotic

parade, with more than 10,000 flags and 25 marching bands. A truly spectacular tradition for more than 50 years. Patterson Park.

City Fair (mid-Sept): Open-air shows, parades, food festival. Inner Harbor.

New Year's Eve Extravaganza (Dec 31): Concerts, fireworks, parades. Inner Harbor.

SPORTS: Baltimore has two professional teams:

Baseball (Apr–Oct): Orioles, Memorial Stadium (481-6000).

Ice Hockey (Oct–Apr): Skipjacks, Baltimore Arena (347-2010).

Horse Racing

Laurel Race Track, U.S. 1, in Laurel (725-0400), thoroughbred racing Sept–Dec; **Pimlico Race Course,** 5201 Park Heights Ave. (542-9400), racing year round.

STROLLS: ☼⚓ **Fells Point,** Broadway south of Eastern Ave.: These once-seedy, run-down docks are today undergoing complete renovation, a unique group of more than 300 rowhouses, 2½ centuries old, lining narrow, picturesque cobblestone alleyways. With many restaurants and pubs, the area is lively and bustling after dark.

🔔🔔 **Inner Harbor,** Pratt St. and Calvert St.: The old harbor, now undergoing renovation, is lively and colorful with boutiques, restaurants, yacht marinas, ultramodern aquarium, and museums. It's worth coming to Baltimore just to see it.

☼🔔🔔 **Mount Vernon Place,** Charles St. and Monument St.: A very handsome ensemble of opulent 19th-century patrician homes, including **Asbury House** (see "Historic Buildings," above), bordered by public gardens. Museums, elegant boutiques. The ideal place for a stroll, it should positively not be missed.

⚓ **Otterbein Homesteading,** around Sharp St., Conway St., and Hanover St.: A group of houses dating from 1780–1800, originally inhabited by German immigrants, still with original gas lamps and cobblestones. Present-day residents were able to buy the houses for a symbolic $1 each, on condition that they would renovate them at their own expense and preserve their original character. See especially the **Old Otterbein United Methodist Church,** at Sharp St. and Conway St., Baltimore's oldest church in continuous use (1786). Worth a look.

ACCOMMODATIONS

A Note on Accommodations: Room rates in Baltimore are coded as follows: **VE,** Very Expensive ($140 and up); **E,** Expensive ($90–$140); **M,** Moderate ($60–$90); **I,** Inexpensive ($30–$60); **B,** Budget (up to $30). A listing of toll-free numbers is in the Appendix.

Personal Favorites (in order of preference)

☼🏛🏛🏛 **Peabody Court** (dwntwn), 612 Cathedral St., MD 21201 (301/727-7101; toll free 800/345-3457). 104 rms, A/C, color TV, in-rm movies. AE, CB, DC, MC, V. Valet gar. $6, two rests. (including The Conservatory), bar, 24-hr. rm svce, concierge, free crib. *Note:* "The" grand hotel of Baltimore, facing the very aristocratic Mount Vernon Sq. Rather massive 1930s building, but w. an interior decor that is both intimate and elegant. Very comfortable rms w. Empire-style furniture, marble bathrooms, and minibars. Service and reception are of rare quality, and the rest. (The Conservatory) is truly remarkable. VIP and big-business clientele; the favorite hotel of connoisseurs. Just off the business district. **E–VE**

🏛🏛🏛 **Hyatt Regency** (dwntwn), 300 Light St., MD 21202 (301/528-1234; toll free, see Hyatt). 490 rms, A/C, color TV, in-rm movies. AE, CB, DC, MC, V. Valet gar. $6, pool, tennis, health club, sauna, two rests. (the Trellis Garden is one), coffee shop, two bars, rm svce, nightclub, hrdrsr, free crib. *Note:* One of Baltimore's newest luxury hotels, in an ultra-modern all-glass building. Its unique location—next to dwntwn on the edge of the Inner Harbor—offers direct access to the Convention Center. Large, very comfortable rms—the best have a view of the port. Very complete facilities. Efficient svce. Big-business clientele. Interesting wknd packages. VIP floor. **VE**

☀☊☊☊ **Clarion Inn Harrison's Pier 5** (dwntwn), 711 Eastern Ave., MD 21202 (301/783-5553; toll free, see Clarion). 71 rms, A/C, color TV, in-rm movies. AE, CB, DC, MC, V. Parking $8, pool, health club, sauna, rest. (Eastern Shore), bar, rm svce, concierge. *Note:* Innovative modern building w. enormous glassed-in atrium and rest. overlooking the harbor. Opened in May 1989, the hotel boasts every modern comfort and facility. Spacious rms w. balconies (the best overlooking the water); efficient, courteous svce. Adjoins the National Aquarium, and neighbors the Convention Center, whence a largely business clientele. The best location in Baltimore, at the tip of Pier 5; atmosphere and setting offer the kind of change which is really as good as a rest. **E–VE**

☊☊ **Admiral Fell Inn** (nr. dwntwn), 888 S. Broadway, MD 21231 (301/522-7377). 40 rms, A/C, color TV. AE, MC, V. Free parking, rest., bar, rm svce, free breakfast, concierge. *Note:* Charming little hotel in the heart of the picturesque Fells Point section (see "Strolls," above). Was once a vinegar factory and long a sailor's lodging house. It offers luxury without ostentation in spacious, comfortable rms w. canopy beds, private patios, and ultra-professional svce. Very creditable rest. An excellent location, 8 min. from dwntwn. Free Inner Harbor shuttle. **E–VE**

☊ **Comfort Inn** (dwntwn), 24 W. Franklin St., MD 21201 (301/576-8400; toll free 800/228-5150). 194 rms, A/C, color TV, in-rm movies. AE, CB, DC, MC, V. Parking $5, coffee shop, bar, rm svce, free crib. *Note:* Modern, comfortable motel just off the business district. Spacious rms. Business clientele. Good value. No-smoking rms. **M**

Other Accommodations (from top bracket to budget)

☊☊☊☊ **Stouffer Harborplace** (dwntwn), 202 E. Pratt St., MD 21202 (301/547-1200; toll free, see Stouffer). 622 rms, A/C, color TV, in-rm movies. AE, CB, DC, MC, V. Valet parking $9, pool, health club, sauna, rest. (Windows), two bars, 24-hr. rm svce, nightclub, boutiques, concierge. *Note:* Big brand-new convention hotel, facing the Inner Harbor as its name implies. The modern design is pleasing, but for a greenish facade in doubtful taste. Comfortable, very well equipped rms w. minibar, computer–phone hook-ups, and bathroom phone. The rest. has a fine view over the harbor. Two blocks from the Convention Center; business clientele; VIP floor. Interesting wknd packages. **E–VE**, but lower rates off-season.

☊☊☊ **Harbor Court** (dwntwn), 550 Light St., MD 21202 (301/234-0550; toll free, see Preferred). 204 rms, A/C, color TV, in-rm movies. AE, CB, DC, MC, V. Gar. $9, pool, tennis, squash, health club, sauna, rest., bar, rm svce, nightclub, hrdrsr, concierge, free crib. *Note:* New hotel of pleasant modern architecture, on the waterfront of the Inner Harbor. Rms are ultra-comfortable and well-equipped mini-suites (the best have a view of the port). Attentive, personalized svce and a very adequate rest. (Hampton's). An excellent location, 5 min. from dwntwn. First-grade sports facilities. **E–VE**

☊☊☊ **Sheraton Inner Harbor** (dwntwn), 300 S. Charles St., MD 21201 (301/962-8300; toll free, see Sheraton). 334 rms, A/C, color TV, in-rm movies. AE, CB, DC, MC, V. Gar. $8, pool, health club, sauna, two rests., two bars, 24-hr. rm svce, disco, free crib. *Note:* 15-story hotel of rather characterless modern architecture. Spacious, comfortable rms w. minibars and good sports facilities. Svce sometimes overburdened. Group and convention clientele. Very convenient to the Inner Harbor and the business district, w. direct access to the Convention Center. No-smoking rms. **E–VE**

Holiday Inn Inner Harbor (dwntwn), 301 W. Lombard St., MD 21201 (301/685-3500; toll free, see Holiday Inns). 370 rms, A/C, color TV, in-rm movies. AE, CB, DC, MC, V. Parking $4, pool, health club, sauna, rest., bar, rm svce, free crib. *Note:* Classic Holiday Inn style, with functional comfort and less-than-perfect svce. Group and convention clientele. Across from the Civic Center. Interesting wknd packages. **M–E**

Belvedere (nr. dwntwn), 1 E. Chase St., MD 21202 (301/332-1000; toll free 800/692-2700). 180 rms, A/C, color TV. AE, CB, DC, MC, V. Gar. $4, pool, health club, two rests., two bars, rm svce, nightclub, hrdrsr, boutiques, free crib. *Note:* A classic hotel, elderly but comfortable, 10 min. from the business district. Spacious, pleasing rms (some are a bit dated) and a good rest. (John Eager Howard Room). Svce varies. Group clientele. Interesting wknd packages. **M–E**

Days Inn Inner Harbor (dwntwn), 100 Hopkins Pl., MD 21201 (301/576-1000; toll free, see Days Inns). 250 rms, A/C, color TV, in-rm movies. AE, CB, DC, MC, V. Parking $4, pool, coffee shop, bar, rm svce, concierge, free crib. *Note:* Modern, nine-story motel in the middle of dwntwn. Functional comfort and facilities. Well-conceived, spacious rms (some w. minibar) and relatively friendly reception. Business clientele. **M**

Best Western Hallmark (formerly the Howard House; dwntwn), 8 N. Howard St., MD 21201 (301/539-1188; toll free, see Best Western). 93 rms, A/C, color TV. AE, CB, DC, MC, V. Parking $6, rest. (Gallery), bar, free crib. *Note:* Small and aging, but well placed in the heart of the business district; welcoming and intimate. Entirely modernized rms. A very good value. Regular clientele. **M**

Howard Johnson's (vic.), 5701 Baltimore National Pike, Catonsville, MD 21228 (301/747-8900; toll free, see Howard Johnson's). 147 rms, A/C, color TV, in-rm movies. AE, CB, DC, MC, V. Free parking, pool, coffee shop, valet svce, free breakfast Mon–Fri, free crib. *Note:* Classic motel w. direct access to the Baltimore Beltway, exit 15. Modern comfort. Some rms have balconies. Ideal if you're driving—25 min. from dwntwn. Good value. **I–M**

Schaefer Hotel (formerly the Abbey Hotel; nr. dwntwn), 723 St. Paul St., Madison, MD 21202 (301/332-0405). 35 rms, A/C, color TV. AE, MC, V. Parking $4, adjacent coffee shop, free coffee. *Note:* Small, antiquated hotel but nicely located quite close to Mount Vernon Pl. Rather cramped but pleasant rms (some have no bathroom). Cheerful service. Good value. **I**

Airport Accommodations

Guest Quarters Airport (vic.), 1300 Concourse Dr., Linthicum, MD 21090 (301/850-0747; toll free 800/424-2900). 251 suites, A/C, color TV, in-rm movies. AE, CB, DC, MC, V. Free parking, pool, health club, sauna, rest., bar, rm svce, nightclub, free crib. *Note:* Modern, functional airport hotel 5 min. from the terminal; suites only, spacious and well laid-out, w. refrigerator; some w. microwave. Elegant atrium; very good svce. The perfect place for a rest between flights. **E–VE**

YMCA/Youth Hostels

Baltimore Hostel (youth hostel, dwntwn), 17 W. Mulberry St., MD 21201 (301/576-8880). 40 beds.

RESTAURANTS

A Note on Restaurant Prices: Baltimore restaurant prices, per person, excluding drinks and service charges, are coded as follows: **VE,** Very Expensive

($60 and up); **E,** Expensive ($40–$60); **M,** Moderate ($25–$40); **I,** Inexpensive ($15–$25); **B,** Budget (up to $15).

Personal Favorites (in order of preference)

☼♀♀♀ **The Conservatory** (dwntwn), in the Peabody Court (see "Accommodations") (727-7101). A/C. Dinner only, Tues–Sun. AE, CB, DC, MC, V. J&T. *Specialties:* goat cheese in pastry shell w. Devonshire sauce, Virginia squab w. poached quail eggs, lobster with vanilla sauce, chocolate-mousse cake w. raspberries. The menu changes regularly. Fine wine list but astronomical prices. *Note:* The view of Baltimore from the top floor of the Peabody Court Hotel is splendid, as are the cuisine and the setting. Enchanting if rather extravagant art deco conservatory decor, and an atmosphere as romantic as your heart could desire. Ultra-refined svce. By far, Baltimore's most chic and expensive rest. *French.* **E**

♀♀ **Café des Artistes** (nr. dwntwn), 1501 Sulgrave Ave. (664-2200). A/C. Lunch Mon–Fri, dinner daily. AE, CB, DC, MC, V. Jkt. *Specialties:* duck pâté, scallops w. red grapes, red snapper in puff pastry, steak, roast rack of lamb, Dover sole au gratin. The menu changes regularly. Well-stocked wine list. *Note:* Formerly located near the Morris Mechanic Theater, this fashionable bistro offers very pleasing French-inspired cuisine in a new intimate setting. The paintings and prints on display are themselves worth a visit. Irreproachable svce. Locally very popular. Resv. highly advised. 25 min. from dwntwn on the Jones Falls Expwy. Free valet parking. *French.* **M**

♀♀ **Brass Elephant** (nr. dwntwn), 924 N. Charles St. (547-8480). A/C. Lunch Mon–Fri, dinner daily; closed hols. AE, CB, DC, MC, V. J&T. *Specialties:* fresh homemade pasta, northern Italian cuisine (the menu changes regularly). Very good desserts. Extensive wine list. *Note:* In an elegant Victorian residence that once belonged to a rich 19th-century businessman, this rest. of great quality is a favorite of local society people. Light, inspired Italian cuisine. Very effective decor of woodwork, marble, and crystal. Excellent svce. The only good Italian rest. outside of Baltimore's Little Italy. *Italian.* **M**

♀♀ **The Chart House** (dwntwn), 601 E. Pratt St. (539-6616). A/C. Lunch (self-service buffet)/dinner daily. MC, V. *Specialties:* crab soup, oysters Rockefeller or Casino, crabcakes, clam chowder, spiced shrimp, broiled scallops, baked stuffed flounder, broiled catch of the day. *Note:* This locally popular seafood rest., in a converted old warehouse w. a glass skylight and enormous exposed beams, has an unobstructed view of the National Aquarium and is linked to it by a walkway. First-class fish and shellfish at reasonable prices; well-mannered, efficient svce. Excellent value. *Seafood.* **I**

☼♀ **Louie's Bookstore Café** (dwntwn), 518 N. Charles St. (962-1224). A/C. Lunch/dinner (till 2am) daily; closed hols. MC, V. *Specialties:* soft-shelled crabs, crab chowder, crabcakes, broiled catch of the day, good homemade desserts. *Note:* Artsy blend of seafood bistro and bookstore (enter through the bookstore—the rest. is in back), w. chamber music in the background. Excellent, very inexpensive fish and shellfish; agreeably bohemian atmosphere. Locally popular. *Seafood.* **B–I**

☼♀ **John W. Faidley Seafood** (dwntwn), Lexington market, 400 W. Lexington St. (727-4898). Lunch only, Mon–Sat. No credit cards. *Specialties:* fresh Maryland oysters and crabs, clams, crabcakes. *Note:* Superb seafood bar in the picturesque enclosed Lexington Market. Baltimore's most authentic bistro, serving seafood that couldn't be fresher. Pleasant ambience. No resv. Open for lunch only. A local favorite for close to a century. *Seafood.* **B–I**

Other Restaurants (from top bracket to budget)

♀♀♀ **Danny's** (nr. dwntwn), 1201 N. Charles St. (539-1393). A/C. Lunch Mon–Fri, dinner Mon–Sat; closed the last 2 weeks of July. AE, CB, DC, MC, V. Jkt. *Specialties:* crab imperial, beef Wellington, steak Diane, fresh salmon, Maine lobster, very good desserts. *Note:* A good trendy rest. w. faux Louis XV decor. The prices are somewhat excessive, the svce lackadaisical — nevertheless, a Baltimore classic for more than a quarter century. *Continental.* **M–E**

Tio Pepe (dwntwn), 10 E. Franklin St. (539-4675). A/C. Lunch Mon–Fri, dinner daily; closed hols. AE, MC, V. J&T. *Specialties:* gazpacho, gambas al ajillo, paella valenciana, roast suckling pig, roast baby pheasant w. grape sauce, rack of lamb Segovia style, brazo gitano. Excellent house sangria and a good Spanish wine list. *Note:* One of the most famous rests. of Baltimore. Remarkable variations on Iberian cuisine in a sober but elegant Castilian cave setting. Impeccable svce. Resv. a must. *Spanish.* **M**

Haussner's (nr. dwntwn), 3244 Eastern Ave. at Clinton St. (327-8365). A/C. Lunch/dinner Tues–Sat; closed Dec 25. AE, CB, DC, MC, V. J&T. *Specialties:* sauerbraten, wienerschnitzel, hasenpfeffer, fish of the day. Very good desserts (try the strawberry pie). More than 100 dishes to choose from. German beer on tap. *Note:* Rather amusing kitsch decor w. an abundance of paintings and busts of Roman emperors in the best firehouse style. Rest. established in 1926. Locally very popular. Good svce. No resv. *German/American.* **I–M**

Sabatino's (nr. dwntwn), 901 Fawn St., Little Italy (727-9414). A/C. Lunch/dinner daily (until 3am); closed Thanksgiving, Dec 25. Jkt. AE, MC, V. *Specialties:* fresh homemade pasta, shrimp napoletana, veal marsala. *Note:* A favorite of Baltimore's Italian community, serving serious, unpretentious cuisine in generous portions. Diligent svce and a pleasant ambience. Open very late. *Italian.* **I**

Olde Obrycki's Crab House (nr. dwntwn), 1729 E. Pratt St. (732-6399). A/C. Lunch Tues–Fri, dinner Tues–Sun; closed Nov–Mar. AE, CB, DC, MC, V. *Specialties:* crab soup, fried clams, blue crabs, crabcakes, seafood, fish of the day. *Note:* One of the best spots in Baltimore for sampling the famous Maryland crabs and washing them down with draft beer (the rest. is only open during crab season, Apr–Nov). Charming, colonial decor and a pleasant, if noisy, ambience. The adj. annex is rather claustrophobic. An excellent spot. Rest. established in 1865. *Seafood.* **I**

Uncle Lee's (nr. dwntwn), 3317 Greenmount Ave. (366-3333). A/C. Lunch/dinner daily. AE, CB, DC, MC, V. *Specialties:* bird's-nest soup, mu shu pork, spicy orange beef, lobster Cantonese. *Note:* One of the few acceptable Chinese rests. in Baltimore. Typical modern Oriental decor. Efficient if less-than-cheerful svce. 25 min. from dwntwn. Other location (the cuisine is rather less satisfying): 44 South St. (727-6666). *Chinese.* **I**

Bertha's (nr. dwntwn), 734 S. Broadway (327-5795). A/C. Lunch/dinner daily (bar open until 2am). AE, CB, DC, MC, V. *Specialties:* mussels marinière, fish of the day, omelets, steaks, daily pasta specials. *Note:* A truer-than-life old English pub in the picturesque Fells Point section. Daily specials are written on a blackboard. Honest, unpretentious cuisine. Diligent svce. English-style tea in the afternoon (resv. necessary). Locally very popular. *Continental/American.* **B–I**

Ikaros (nr. dwntwn), 4805 Eastern Ave. (633-9825). A/C. Lunch/dinner Wed–Mon; closed Thanksgiving, Dec 25. AE, CB, DC, MC, V. *Specialties:* stuffed grape leaves, lemon soup, calamari, moussaka kapama (lamb and tomatoes), spanakotiropita (cheese-and-spinach pie), catch of the day, baklava. *Note:* The oldest and the best Greek rest. in the city. The decor is nothing special, but the cuisine is 100% authentic. Locally very popular. Inevitable waits on wknds. Resv. advised. *Greek.* **B–I**

Cafeteria/Fast Food

Woman's Industrial Exchange (dwntwn), 333 N. Charles St. (685-4388). Breakfast/lunch only, Mon–Fri. No credit cards.

Specialties: crabcakes, chicken croquettes, sandwiches, salads, dishes of the day, homemade pies, floating island. *Note:* A real local institution, nearly a century old. *Cuisine bourgeoise,* not of the lightest, served in 1920s cafeteria-style decor that is nicely old-fashioned. Motherly svce. Locally very popular.

BARS & NIGHTCLUBS

Balls (dwntwn), 200 W. Pratt St. (659-5844). A sports bar on three levels featuring Top 40 tunes. Casual. Open nightly.

The Cat's Eye (nr. dwntwn), Thames St. (276-9085). Popular Irish bar of the Fell's Point district, bedecked w. harpoons and oars. Features traditional music or rock 'n' roll nightly.

Hammerjacks (nr. dwntwn), 1101 S. Howard St. (752-3302). High-energy rock in a spacious multilevel setting. Young crowd. Open nightly.

Max's (dwntwn), 735 S. Broadway (675-6297). Live rock and reggae bands. Mixed crowd. Open nightly.

Thirteenth Floor Lounge, in the Belvedere (see "Accommodations," above) (547-8220). A fashionable piano-bar on the 13th floor of the hotel with a relaxed atmosphere and a lovely view. Open nightly.

NEARBY EXCURSIONS

ELLICOTT CITY (11 mi./18km west on Md. 144): Former iron-working center, founded in 1774 on the banks of the Patapsco River. It was also the temporary terminus of the United States' first railroad, the Baltimore & Ohio (interesting museum in the old station, which dates from 1830). The city has conserved a good number of its early 19th-century stone and log houses on the hills overlooking the river and an interesting Historic District downtown. Well worth going out of your way. Visitor Information: 3430 Court House Dr. (301/992-2027).

ANNAPOLIS (28 mi./45km south on Md. 2): Charming colonial town more than 300 years old. Capital of Maryland and home of the U.S. Naval Academy (interesting naval museum). Very picturesque port quarter with beautiful old houses. See Chapter 9 on Washington.

CARROLL COUNTY FARM MUSEUM (in Westminster, 28 mi./45km NW on Md. 140) (301/848-7775): Large agricultural estate dating from 1852, transformed into a living museum of the 19th century, with a Victorian-style dwelling house, forge, stables, craft shops, etc. Interesting slice of history. Open Tues–Sun in summer, wknds only spring and autumn; closed the rest of the year. Worth the trip.

FARTHER AFIELD

GETTYSBURG (110 mi./180km r.t. on Md. 140N, Md. 97N, and return): The Civil War's bloodiest battlefield. See Chapter 6 on Philadelphia.

PENNSYLVANIA DUTCH COUNTRY (130 mi./210km r.t. on I-83N/S): Here, the 17th century has left a clear imprint in modern America. See Chapter 6 on Philadelphia.

CHESAPEAKE BAY & WYE MILLS (165 mi./264km r.t. on Md. 2S, U.S. 50E, and Md. 33W): See **Wye Mills,** a picturesque little village that has kept its authentic 18th-century look; **Easton,** famous for its antique shops; **St. Michaels,** with its marvelous maritime museum **(Chesapeake Bay Museum);** and the gorgeous **St. Mary's Square,** with its old houses. Return via **Oxford,** capital of pleasure boating and point of origin for the 300-year-old Oxford–Bellevue ferry, oldest in the country. A very pleasant trip. See also Chapter 9 on Washington.

Where to Stay En Route

IN OXFORD   ♟♟**Robert Morris Inn,** on Md. 333, Oxford, MD 21654 (301/226-5111). 28 rms. Charming little colonial-style inn with a view of the water. Good rest. **I–M**

IN EASTON   ♟♟**Tidewater Inn,** Dover St. and Harrison St., Easton, MD 21601 (301/822-1300). 120 rms. Elegant 200-year-old, historic landmarked building. Rest. renowned for its seafood. **I–M**

ATLANTIC BEACHES (274 mi./438km) r.t. on Md. 2S, U.S. 50E, Md. 528N, Del. 1N, U.S. 9S, Del. 18W, Del. 404W, U.S. 50W, and Md. 2N): Lots of beaches and fashionable seaside resorts between **Ocean City** (to the south) and **Rehoboth Beach** (to the north). See Chapter 9 on Washington. On the way, you can see **Annapolis** (see above).

WASHINGTON, D.C.♚♚♚

□ □ □

The federal capital, that "city of heroes and monuments," the first city ever planned for a specific purpose, was brought into being by George Washington through an act of political will—and through the visionary genius of Maj. Pierre-Charles l'Enfant. This French architect, who served as a volunteer during the War of Independence, drew up an urban plan of majestic simplicity for a concentric city pierced by wide avenues—a plan that imparts to the city its ordered charm, at once graceful and austere. Even so, the capital of the young Republic almost failed to survive its rough handling in 1814 by the British, who sacked it and burned its principal buildings.

Here and there along the great green carpet of the **Mall** stand some of the most historic (and most visited) landmarks in the country. America's most famous address is 1600 Pennsylvania Avenue, better known as **The White House,** official residence of America's presidents since John Adams in 1800. Not far away, on a little hill, the imposing **Capitol** with its majestic dome, modeled on that of St. Peter's in Rome, dominates the city's skyline, as the architectural embodiment of American democracy properly should. A mile and a half to the west, interrupting the otherwise unbroken prospect down the Mall and across the **Potomac River** to **Arlington Cemetery,** the giant obelisk of the **Washington Monument** leaps skyward to honor the Father of his Country.

City of government offices and museums, embassies, gardens, and statues. City of officials, reporters, and diplomats (some 20,000 in all, from heads of mission to clerical staff). City of monuments ranging from the extraordinary (the **Lincoln Memorial,** the **Jefferson Memorial,** the **National Gallery of Art East Wing**) to the downright disgraceful (the **Pentagon,** the **J. Edgar Hoover Building**). City of learning, with its five universities and 20 colleges—and strategic heart of the formidable power of the U.S.A. Washington is all these things and more, an elegant, cosmopolitan city like none other in the world.

Nevertheless, unlike their fellow Americans, the inhabitants of Washington are not fully enfranchised. The Founding Fathers, apparently concerned that the local population might loom too large in the eyes of the legislature, constitutionally denied it the right to vote. In 1961 the Congress finally acknowledged the anachronism and gave Washingtonians a vote in presidential elections. Since 1975 they have also been allowed to elect their own mayor—but they still have no vote in Congress.

Sadly, this great city has one of the highest unemployment rates in the country. Side by side with the army of white-collar workers who cluster around the centers of power is an economically distressed population (among those under 21, the unemployment rate is 36%) with a high incidence of drug addiction. As a direct consequence of this, FBI statistics credit the nation's capital with a crime rate three times the national average (72 murders per 100,000 inhabitants)—something of a paradox for a city that is the seat of the Supreme Court, and thus of the Law.

But even so, Washington—with its classical revival buildings, its cluster of museums (including the renowned **Smithsonian Institution** and the **National Gallery of Art**) unmatched anywhere in the world, its wide tree-lined avenues, its reflecting pools fringed with Japanese cherries (try to be there when they're in flower, in late Mar or early Apr), and its appealing and historic **Georgetown** district—lacks nothing that the visitor could ask for. Some 19 million pilgrim-tourists, including a million foreigners, visit the capital every year, making travel and tourism the second-largest industry in the city. (However, tourism is down by 17% since 1988 because of a soft economy and the image of violence of the nation's capital.)

Long considered a cultural desert, with the construction in 1971 of the **John F. Kennedy Center,** Washington acquired a world-class artistic and theatrical complex. Nevertheless, it remains after dark one of the dullest, starchiest places in the country. The only interest offered by Washington's nightlife is the extraordinary profusion of restaurants—French, Caribbean, Ethiopian, Créole, Thai, Arabic, Japanese, Spanish, Italian, Chinese, East European, Vietnamese, Latin American, you name it—which have made the city a sort of gastronomic Tower of Babel.

Washington's famous children include Duke Ellington and his son, Mercer Ellington; the late FBI director J. Edgar Hoover; the late Secretary of State John Foster Dulles; playwright Edward Albee; author Frank Slaughter; comedian and actress Goldie Hawn; actor William Hurt; and singer-dancer Chita Rivera.

A Note on Orientation: The spider-web layout of Washington is divided into four geographic quadrants with the Capitol as their center: Northwest (NW), Northeast (NE), Southwest (SW), and Southeast (SE). Streets running north and south are designated by numbers; those running east and west, by letters of the alphabet. The grid system of numbered and lettered streets is slashed diagonally by wide avenues bearing the names of states of the Union: Massachusetts, Wisconsin, Pennsylvania, Connecticut, etc.

A Note on Telephone Area Codes: Unless otherwise indicated all phone numbers in this chapter are in area code 202.

BASIC FACTS: District of Columbia. Area codes: 202 (District of Columbia), 301 (Maryland), 703 (Virginia). Time zone: eastern. ZIP Code (of the central post office): 20013. Founded: 1790. Approximate population: city, 610,000; metropolitan area, 3,650,000. 10th-largest metropolitan area in the country.

CLIMATE: The last word you would think of to describe the Washington climate is "agreeable." It's a hot, sticky steambath in summer (July average temperature, 79°F/26°C), cold and very humid in winter with snowfalls and icy roads (Jan average, 37°F/3°C). That leaves spring and fall, usually sunny and pleasant (especially May and Oct), as the best times of year to visit Washington.

DISTANCES: Atlanta, 608 mi. (975km); Baltimore, 40 mi. (65km); Chicago, 668 mi. (1,070km); New York, 234 mi. (375km); Niagara Falls, 425 mi. (680km); Philadelphia, 134 mi. (215km); Pittsburgh, 247 mi. (395km); Savannah, 633 mi. (1,012km).

ARRIVAL & TRANSIT INFORMATION

AIRPORTS: The **Baltimore-Washington International Airport** (BWI), 32 mi. (51km) NE, for medium- and long-haul flights. Hard to reach from dwntwn Washington; for information, call 301/859-7100.

    Dulles International Airport (IAD), 26 mi. (42km) west, for medium- and long-haul flights; for information, call 703/471-7838.

Washington National Airport (DCA), 4 mi. (7km) south, for medium-haul flights; for information, call 703/685-8000.

U.S. AIRLINES (area code 202 unless otherwise indicated): American (393-2345), Continental (478-9700), Delta (301/468-2282), Eastern (393-4000), Midway (toll free 800/621-5700), Northwest (737-7333), Pan Am (845-8000), Trump Air (toll free 800/247-8786), TWA (737-7400), United (742-4600), and USAir (783-4500).

FOREIGN CARRIERS: Air France (toll free 800/237-2747), All Nippon Airways (toll free 800/235-9262), British Airways (toll free 800/247-9297), Lufthansa (toll free 800/645-3880).

CITY LINK: The **cab** fare from Baltimore-Washington Airport to dwntwn is about $40–$45; time, 55 min. Cab fare from Dulles International to dwntwn, about $35–$40; time, 45 min. (60 min. or more during rush hours). Cab fare from National Airport to dwntwn, about $10–$14; time, 15–20 min.
   Bus: The **Washington Flyer** (703/685-1400); serves the Air Terminal at 1517 K St. NW and the major dwntwn hotels; leaves National Airport every 20 min. (fare, $5; time, 25 min.); leaves Dulles International every 30 min. (fare, $12; time, 45–60 min.). The Washington Flyer also connects National Airport and Dulles International, leaving every 30 or 60 min.; fare, $10; time, 45 min. The **Airport Connection** (301/859-3000) connects Baltimore-Washington Airport and the Air Terminal at 1517 K St. NW, leaving every 45 min.; fare, $12; time, about 60–70 min.
   A **subway** (Metrorail Blue and Yellow Lines) connects National Airport to dwntwn Washington, leaving every 10 min.; fare, $1.05; time, 18 min.
   Public transportation by bus and subway (ultramodern and comfortable) covers the city effectively, but is complicated for visitors; for information on **Metrobus and Metrorail,** call 202/637-7000. With 11,000 cabs on the street there is no shortage, but not all of them are trustworthy.
   The city is not so large that you'll need to rent a car, unless you plan to drive out into the country or along the eastern seaboard; rental rates with unlimited mileage are noticeably lower than in New York.

CAR RENTAL (area code for both airports is 703): Avis, Dulles Airport (661-8874), National Airport (739-4810); Budget, Dulles Airport (437-9373), National Airport (920-3360); Dollar, Dulles Airport (661-6780), National Airport (553-0775); Hertz, Dulles Airport (471-6020), National Airport (979-6300); National, Dulles Airport (471-5278), National Airport (783-1590); Thrifty, Dulles Airport (471-4544), National Airport (548-1600).
   For dwntwn locations, consult the local telephone book.

LIMOUSINE SERVICES: Carey Limousine (202/892-2000), Dav El Limousine (toll free 800/922-0343), Dial-A-Limousine (301/983-9557), Scripps Edward Limousine (toll free 800/223-6710).

TAXIS: Washington cabs are not metered; they charge according to the number of "zones" they must pass through between starting point and destination (there should be a legible city map, with the zones marked, in the passenger compartment). Fares tend to be lower than in many U.S. cities. Drivers can pick up additional passengers as long as they're going the same way; each passenger or party may be charged a separate fare. Many of the drivers are recent immigrants, only superficially acquainted with the English language (and the city).
   Cabs may be hailed on the street, taken from the waiting lines outside major

hotels, or called by phone. The principal companies are (all area code 202): **Capitol Cab** (546-2400), **Diamond Cab** (387-6200), **Liberty Cab** (636-1600), **Red Top Cab** (522-3333), and **Yellow Cab** (544-1212).

TRAIN: The Amtrak terminal is at Union Station, 50 Massachusetts Ave. NE (202/484-7540); the city ticket office, 1721 K St. NW (202/484-7540). For reservations and information for the Metroliner, call 202/484-5580.

INTERCITY BUSES: Greyhound, 1005 1st St. at L St. NE (202/565-2662).

INFORMATION & TOURS

TOURIST INFORMATION: The **Washington Convention and Visitors Association,** 1212 New York Ave. NW, DC 20005 (202/789-7000).
    International Visitors Information Service, 733 15th St. NW, DC 20005 (202/783-6540): Orientation for visitors from abroad.
    Visitor Information Center, 1455 Pennsylvania Ave. NW (202/789-7000). Open 9am–5pm Mon–Sat.
    A **recorded message** giving a list of current shows and cultural events may be reached at 202/737-8866.

GUIDED TOURS: **Canal Cruisers** (boat), Georgetown Canal between 30th St. and Thomas Jefferson St. NW (202/472-4376): Trips in a mule-drawn barge along the C.&O. Canal, Wed–Sun mid-Apr through Sept. A picturesque rustic treat that lasts 90 min.
    Gray Line Tours (bus) (301/386-8300): Guided tours of the city and surroundings, serving major hotels.
    Helicopter Sightseeing Tour (helicopter), National Airport, Commuter General Aviation Terminal (703/892-2650): Helicopter flight over the capital; spectacular.
    Old Town Trolley Tours (bus): 2-hr. shuttle tour across the city in a replica of a turn-of-the-century streetcar. A ticket gives unlimited boarding rights. The best sightseeing tours in town. Daily year round, serving major hotels. Fare: $8. For information, call 202/269-3020.
    Tourmobile Sightseeing (bus): A very practical shuttle system which allows you to visit Washington's principal monuments, with a couple of dozen stops along the route. Get off and on again as often as you like. Runs daily year round. Fare is $7, payable on the bus. Also serves Arlington National Cemetery and Mount Vernon. For information, call 202/554-7950.
    Washington Boat Lines (boat), 6th St. and Water St. SW (202/554-8000): Mini-cruises along the Potomac as far as Mount Vernon; daily Apr–Oct.
    The Washington Post, 1150 15th St. NW (202/334-7969): Guided tour around one of the largest daily papers in the country—the paper that blew the whistle on Watergate. Fascinating. By appointment only, Mon and Thurs. Children must be at least age 11.

SIGHTS, ATTRACTIONS & ACTIVITIES

ADVENTURE TOURS: **Adventures Aloft** (balloon), 1938 Lewis Ave., Rockville, Md. (301/881-6262): Balloon rides over the Washington countryside from any of several different launch sites in Maryland or Virginia. Spectacular. Year round.
    Balloons Unlimited (balloon): 115 Pleasant St., Vienna, Va. (703/281-2300): Balloon rides over the Washington countryside from any of several different launch sites in Virginia. Fare: $90 per person. Spectacular. Year round.
    Blue Ridge Outfitters (boat), W.Va. 340, Harpers Ferry, W.Va. (304/

725-3444): White-water raft trips down the rapids of the Shenandoah River or the gorges of the Potomac. Daily Apr–Oct. Canoe rentals.

ARCHITECTURAL HIGHLIGHTS: ☼⚖ **Bureau of Engraving and Printing,** 14th St. and C St. SW (447-0193): Tens of billions of dollars in banknotes, Treasury notes, and stamps are printed here every year. From glassed-in galleries you can watch banknotes being printed and packaged (about $50 million are produced daily). Coins are struck at Philadelphia, Denver, and San Francisco. Not surprisingly, very strict security is imposed here; photography is forbidden. Open Mon–Fri. An encouragement to daydreams.

☼⚖ **Canadian Embassy,** 501 Pennsylvania Ave. NW (682-1740): Opened in 1989, this magnificent building, one of the very few original modern constructions in Washington, is open to the public for scheduled tours Mon, Wed, Fri, and Sat. The embassy is located across from the National Gallery of Art. Worth a visit.

⚖ **FBI Headquarters–J. Edgar Hoover Building,** E St. between 9th St. and 10th St. NW (324-3447): Headquarters of the war on crime—and one of the ugliest buildings in Washington. Conducted tours Mon–Fri. Marksmanship demonstrations by G-men. Memorabilia of crime in the 1920s and '30s, and an armory with 5,000 weapons on display. For lovers of detective fiction.

☼⚖ **John F. Kennedy Center for the Performing Arts,** New Hampshire Ave. and F St. NW (254-3600): Huge cultural complex on the banks of the Potomac, opened in 1971; opera house, theater, cinema, concert hall, and art gallery. The very successful modern design is the work of architect Edward Durrell Stone. The heart of Washington's cultural (and social) life, drawing four million visitors a year. Open daily. Must definitely be seen.

⚖ **Old Executive Office Building,** Pennsylvania Ave. and 17th St. NW (395-5895): Adjoining the White House, this interesting example of French classical revival architecture dating from 1871–88 originally housed the Departments of State, the Navy, and War. It now accommodates the vice-president of the U.S. and members of the White House staff. Open Sat by appointment.

☼⚖ **Old Post Office,** Pennsylvania Ave. and 12th St. NW (289-4224): Imposing Victorian building designed by Daniel Burnham and dating from 1899, surmounted by a Big Ben–style tower 315 ft. (96m) high with an observation deck. Once the central post office, it now houses government offices as well as many boutiques and restaurants under an enormous glass roof, The Pavilion. An appealing place which should definitely be seen. Open daily.

⚖ **Panamerican Union Building,** 17th St. and Constitution Ave. NW (458-3000): A strange compromise between Spanish Colonial and French Renaissance idioms, this graceful 1910 building, designed by Paul Cret and Albert Kelsey, is the headquarters of the Organization of American States (OAS). Lovely interior courtyard; Aztec garden; interesting museum of modern Latin American art adjoining. Should be seen. Open Mon–Fri.

☼⚖ **Pentagon Building,** bounded by Jefferson Davis Hwy., Washington Blvd., and Shirley Hwy., Arlington, Va. (703/695-1776): The heart and head of U.S. defense, with five floors on a groundplan of 32 acres (13ha), 17.5 mi. (28km) of corridors, 32,000 employees, and a parking lot for 10,000 cars. Constructed in 1941–43, it's still the biggest office building in the world. Imposing, but without architectural distinction. Guided tours Mon–Fri. Best ways to get there: Bus 16 from dwntwn Washington or the Blue or Yellow subway line. Worth a look.

☼ **Supreme Court Building,** Maryland Ave. and 1st St. NE (479-3000): Cass Gilbert's fine exercise in the classical revival style

DOWNTOWN WASHINGTON, D.C.

RHODE ISLAND AVE.

O ST.

N ST.

M ST.

9TH ST.

11TH ST.

8TH ST.

7TH ST.

L ST.

NEW YORK AVE.

K ST.

NEW JERSEY AVE.

1ST ST.

1ST ST.

N. CAPITOL ST.

anklin Park

Washington Convention Center

MASSACHUSETTS AVE.

6TH ST.

5TH ST.

H ST.

City Post Office

N

13TH ST.

10TH ST.

G ST.

2ND ST.

Union Station

F ST.

E ST.

J. Edgar Hoover Bldg.

D ST.

D. ST.

PENNSYLVANIA AVE.

C STREET

LOUISIANA AVE.

DELAWARE AVE.

Senate Office Bldg.

Internal Revenue

Justice Dept.

CONSTITUTION AVE.

MARYLAND AVE.

Museum of African Art

useum of American History

Natural History Museum

National Gallery

Reflecting Pool

Supreme Court

MADISON DR.

E. CAPITOL ST.

The Mall

Hirshhorn Museum

National Air and Space Museum

4TH ST.

3RD ST.

JEFFERSON DR.

U.S. Capitol

Folger Library

Smithsonian

Freer Gallery

Sackler Gallery

INDEPENDENCE AVE.

MARYLAND AVE.

Botanic Garden

Library of Congress

VIRGINIA AVE.

195

12TH ST.

395

S. CAPITOL ST.

NEW JERSEY AVE.

G ST.

Washington Channel

I ST.

OHIO DR.

DELAWARE AVE.

K ST.

L ST.

M ST.

dates from 1935. The white Vermont marble and Corinthian columns are reminiscent of the days of ancient Greece. Majestic interior decoration. When the Court is in session the public is admitted to hearing cases (Mon, Tues, and Wed, Oct–Apr). Guided tours Mon–Fri when the court is not in session. An absolute must.

Union Station, 40 Massachusetts Ave. NE (298-1908): In sheer size, this marble-and-granite 1907 railroad station is the largest in the country; its majestic design was inspired by the Baths of Diocletian in Rome. Reopened in the fall of 1988 after decades of neglect and decay. Daniel H. Burnham's building, splendidly restored at a cost of $140 million, now houses around 100 boutiques, stores, restaurants, and movie houses on three levels, as well as the station itself. Lively, colorful atmosphere, particularly at lunchtime.

Voice of America, 330 Independence Ave. SW (485-6231): Transmits around the clock to five continents in 42 languages. Guided tours Mon–Fri (resv. advised). For radio hams.

Watergate Complex, New Hampshire Ave. and Virginia Ave. NW: Luxury complex beside the Potomac; scene of the political scandal that cost Richard M. Nixon the presidency in 1974. Smart shops, restaurants, luxury hotel. The elegant architecture is worth a look.

CHURCHES/SYNAGOGUES: 🔔 Franciscan Monastery, 1400 Quincy St.
NE (526-6800): This Romanesque monastery with its graceful cloister, standing in its own beautiful garden, houses the curious "Holy Land of America"—a faithful facsimile of some of the most sacred places in the Holy Land such as the crib at Bethlehem, the Garden of Gethsemane, and so on, as well as of the Roman catacombs and the grotto at Lourdes. Tours conducted daily by the friars.

Islamic Center, 2251 Massachusetts Ave. NW (332-8343): America's largest mosque, and largest Islamic cultural center, built with funds contributed by all the Muslim countries that have diplomatic relations with the U.S. The center, an elegant building with fine surface carving and a 160-ft. (48m) minaret, oriented toward Mecca, is open to visitors every day except during the Fri prayers. Should be seen.

National Shrine of the Immaculate Conception, 620 Michigan Ave. NE (526-8300): The largest Roman Catholic church in the U.S., on the campus of Catholic University; its Romanesque-Byzantine nave is 459 ft. (140m) long and surmounted by a 331-ft. (101m) bell tower. The huge dome is blue, with touches of gold. Organ and carillon concerts on Sun. Worth seeing.

St. John's Episcopal Church, 16th St. and H St. NW (347-8766): On Lafayette Sq. across from the White House, St. John's Episcopal Church was built in 1816 to the design of Benjamin H. Latrobe, the city's first public architect. It has become known as "the Church of the Presidents," because more than a dozen have worshipped there, beginning with James Madison in the year after the church was built. Since then, Pew 54 has traditionally been reserved for the president of the U.S. Unquestionably worth a visit. Open daily.

St. Matthew's Cathedral, 1725 Rhode Island Ave. NW (347-3215): Familiar to many Americans as the scene of funeral services for Pres. John F. Kennedy on November 25, 1963. The cathedral is located a few blocks from the White House. Worth seeing.

Scottish Rite Supreme Council, 1733 16th St. NW (232-3579): Dating from 1915, this former Masonic temple designed by J. Russell Pope is modeled on the famous tomb of King Mausolus of Halicarnassus, one of the seven wonders of antiquity. Its interior, embellished with purple ceilings, polished black marble columns and doors, and light fixtures in bronze, is sumptuous. Open daily by appointment; shouldn't be missed.

☼ **Washington National Cathedral,** Wisconsin Ave. and Massachusetts Ave. NW (537-6200): Very fine cathedral in the Gothic Revival style, Episcopalian but open to all denominations; one of the largest in the country. The interior, particularly the stained glass, is sumptuous. Designed by British architect George Bodley, the cathedral was finally completed in Sept 1990, 83 years from the day when Pres. Theodore Roosevelt presided at the laying of the cornerstone. It stands atop Mount St. Alban, the capital's highest hill (419 ft./128m). Within is the tomb of Pres. Woodrow Wilson. Library of rare books. Should definitely be visited.

🔔 **Washington Temple,** 9900 Stoneybrook Dr., Kensington, Md., at Beltway Exit 33 (301/587-0144): One of 40 Mormon temples around the world built on the model of the temple at Salt Lake City, to an unusual design executed in 1976. Non-Mormons may not enter the temple, but the Visitor Center is open daily. Particularly impressive when floodlit after dark.

HISTORIC BUILDINGS: ☼🔔 **Blair House,** 1651-1653 Pennsylvania Ave. NW: Blair House and the adjoining **Blair-Lee House,** opposite the White House, have since 1942 served as the official residence of foreign heads of state when visiting the U.S. The two buildings, which have been extensively restored, are not open to the public. The 1824 Blair House has played an important part in American history. It was here, on April 18, 1861, that President Lincoln offered the command of the Union army to Gen. Robert E. Lee; Lee refused, and later became commander-in-chief of the Confederacy. President Truman lived at Blair House from 1948 to 1952 while the White House was being restored.

☼🔔🔔 **The Capitol,** 1st St. between Constitution Ave. and Independence Ave. (224-3121): This imposing structure, home of the 435-member House of Representatives and the 100-member Senate, is capped by a dome 258 ft. (79m) high designed by Charles Bulfinch after the dome of St. Peter's in Rome. A 19-ft. (6m) bronze statue of *Liberty,* by Thomas Crawford, crowns the whole. Originally erected in 1793–1812, burned by the British in 1814, and built anew in 1816–29, the building has been enlarged several times, most recently in 1962. Very rich interior decoration with colossal statues and wall paintings, especially in the main **Rotunda,** from which 40-min. conducted tours leave, allowing access to the Visitors' Galleries of the House and the Senate. The **Senate Dining Room,** renowned for its bean soup, is also open to the public. See also, beneath the Rotunda, the crypt originally intended for the tomb of George Washington; here is the catafalque used for the funerary vigil of Abraham Lincoln, and of the unknown soldiers of World War II and the Korean War. From the west front you have a fine view along the Mall to the Washington Monument and the Lincoln Memorial in the distance. Don't miss the Capitol; it's worth the trip to Washington all by itself. Guided tours daily, every 15 min.; call 225-6827 for information.

🔔 **Christian Heurich Mansion,** 1307 New Hampshire Ave. NW (785-2068): Home of the Columbia Historical Society, this luxurious 1892 private house, built of brown sandstone in the Renaissance Revival style, boasts no fewer than 43 rooms. Very fine Victorian furniture; library devoted to the history of the capital. Should be seen. Open Wed–Sat.

☼🔔 **Decatur House,** 748 Jackson Pl. NW (842-0920): This red-brick town house a stone's throw from the White House, and rich in historical associations, was built in 1818 by Benjamin H. Latrobe for Commodore Stephen Decatur, hero of the war against the Barbary pirates. It has been home to a succession of distinguished men, including one future president (Martin Van Buren), three secretaries of state, and several other prominent politicians. For almost a century and a half it was a center of Washington social life. Splendid period furniture and decoration. Worth a visit. Open Tues–Sun.

☼🔔 **Dumbarton Oaks,** 1703 32nd St. NW (338-8278): Elegant small early 19th-century manor house in the heart of historic

Georgetown. Since 1940 the house and its lovely landscaped gardens have belonged to Harvard University. It has important collections of Byzantine and pre-Columbian art, and a library of 80,000 books on art. The new wing of the museum was designed in 1963 by Philip Johnson. In 1944 a conference of the four Great Powers (the U.S., Great Britain, China, and the Soviet Union) on international security was held here; this conference worked out the framework for the U.N. Don't fail to visit. Open Tues–Sun. Gardens are open daily.

Ford's Theater, 511 10th St. NW (426-6924): Here Abraham Lincoln was assassinated, on April 14, 1865, by John Wilkes Booth during the performance of a play. The oldest theater in Washington still in use. There is a small Lincoln museum in the basement. An absolute must. Open daily.

Georgetown University, 37th St. and O St. NW (687-3634): Founded in 1789 and still run by the Society of Jesus (the Jesuit order), this is the oldest Roman Catholic university in the U.S.; it has 12,000 students. On a bluff overlooking the Potomac, the campus has a number of interesting buildings in the Gothic style, including the Healy Building, which houses the administrative offices and Information Center. Worth a look. Open daily.

Library of Congress, 10 1st St. SE (287-5458): The world's largest library, in an impressive Italian Renaissance granite building modeled on the Opéra in Paris. The interior is sumptuously decorated. The catalog lists 85 million books and other items in 470 languages, from a Gutenberg Bible to the original draft of the Declaration of Independence, not to mention Pierre-Charles l'Enfant's preliminary plan of Washington. Built around the 6,847 volumes from Thomas Jefferson's personal collection, which he sold to Congress for $23,950 after the original Library had been burned by the British in 1814, the Library of Congress today possesses more than 20 million books; it is a depository library, and since 1870 has received two free copies of every book published in the United States. Don't fail to see the Library, and particularly the marble staircase of the Grand Hall and the dome of the main Reading Room. Open Mon–Sat.

Octagon House, 1799 New York Ave. at 18th St. NW (638-3105): Unusual octagonal structure dating from 1798, which served as a temporary home for President Madison after the British burned the White House in 1814; now the headquarters of the American Institute of Architects. Temporary exhibitions; interesting period furniture. Open Tues–Sun.

Old Stone House, 3051 M St. NW (426-6851): Believed to be the oldest surviving building in Washington from the pre-Revolutionary period (about 1765). The charming little two-story house with massive stone walls located in the heart of Georgetown was both a private home and a place of business. Magnificently restored in the original manner and decor of the 18th century. Worth a visit. Open Wed–Sun.

Petersen House, 516 10th St. NW (426-6830): The house where President Lincoln was taken after Booth's fatal shot at Ford's Theater across the street (see above); he died here the next morning, April 15, 1865, at 7:22am. Memorabilia of the affair that horrified America. Open daily.

Tudor Place, 1644 31st St. NW (965-0400): Opulent 1810 mansion in the heart of charming old Georgetown; the Greek Revival building designed by William Thornton is one of the finest in Washington. Built for Martha Parke Custis Peter, granddaughter-in-law of George Washington, Tudor Place remained in the hands of the Peter family for eight generations, until 1983. Splendid period furniture and decor. May be seen Tues–Sat by appointment only. Should not be missed.

The White House, 1600 Pennsylvania Ave. NE (456-7041): The most famous building in the U.S., home to every American president since John Adams in 1800. Designed by architect James Hoban following the style of the Irish mansion of the Duke of Leinster, the White House owes its name to the whitewash with which its blackened frontage was hastily covered after the British burned it in 1814. Rebuilt in 1817, the original structure has been often enlarged and altered, particularly by the 1824 addition of a graceful elliptical portico along the side of the house facing the Mall. More than a million and a half visitors pass through the White House each year; tickets are free, and may be obtained from the kiosk in the Ellipse in front of the south front, but only five reception rooms, of the total of 32 rooms in the Executive Mansion, are open to the public; there is no admission either to the president's private quarters on the second floor, or to his office and the offices of his staff in the West Wing. On a busy day, particularly in summer, you may have to wait as long as 2 hr. for your guided tour, but they are given from 10am until noon Tues–Sat; closed Jan 1 and Dec 25. Visitors' entrance is the east gate on E. Executive Ave. If you write sufficiently far ahead to your (or a friendly) senator or congressperson, you may be able to obtain a ticket for a "personalized" VIP visit to the White House, which will allow you to avoid the long waiting lines in summer. You should specify a choice of dates. Requests, in writing, should be addressed to a senator at the United States Senate, Washington, DC 20510, or a congressperson at the United States House of Representatives, Washington, DC 20515. In any case, be sure to see the White House.

Woodrow Wilson House, 2340 S St. NW (387-4062): Home of former President Wilson from the end of his second term until his death in 1924, then of his widow until she died in 1961, this elegant red-brick Georgian-style town house is now a museum. Many personal memorabilia of the 28th president; reconstructs the atmosphere and the way of life of the upper middle class in the '20s. Should be seen. Open Tues–Sat Mar–Dec, wknds only in Feb; closed Jan.

MARKETS: Eastern Market, 7th St. and North Carolina Ave. SE (546-9135): The last of the many European-style covered markets once to be found in Washington, dating from 1873. Dozens of open stalls selling meat, poultry, vegetables, fish, cheese, etc. Lively and colorful; open Tues–Sat. Worth a look, especially Sat morning when strolling musicians add to the local color. Don't fail to breakfast or lunch at the **Market Lunch,** open 7:30am–2:30pm Tues–Sat; it's at 225 7th St. at C St. SE (547-8444).

MONUMENTS: Arlington National Cemetery, opposite Memorial Bridge, Arlington, Va. (703/692-0931): Overlooking the Potomac, this largest and most famous of America's national cemeteries shelters 213,000 of the dead, both illustrious like Presidents William Howard Taft and John F. Kennedy (before whose tomb burns an eternal flame), Adm. Richard Byrd, Sen. Robert F. Kennedy, Gen. George Marshall, and Pierre-Charles l'Enfant, or nameless, like the Unknown Soldier, whose tomb commemorates the dead of the two World Wars and the Korean and Vietnam Wars. A guard of honor of the Third Infantry ("The Old Guard") watches over the tomb 24 hr. a day; the changing of the guard, every half hr. during daylight, daily year round, is a spectacular sight. Lovely countryside, and a unique view of Washington from **Arlington House** (see "Panoramas," below). Every year more than four million people visit Arlington; bus trips daily, though the vehicles are not allowed to enter the cemetery itself. Don't miss it.

Jefferson Memorial, Tidal Basin, Potomac Park SW (426-6841): A graceful circular building by John Russell Pope (1943) in white marble, surrounded by an Ionic colonnade reminiscent of the Pantheon in Rome. Commemorates the author of the Declaration of Independence and third president of the U.S. A masterpiece of classical architecture which you have to see (try to be there in early Apr when the Japanese cherries are in bloom). Open daily.

☼☆☆ **Lincoln Memorial,** 23rd St. south of Constitution Ave. NW (426-6841): Washington's finest monument, the work of Henry Bacon (1922). Majestic white marble building inspired by the Parthenon in Athens, and setting off the Capitol at the other end of the Mall. A colossal statue of Lincoln by Daniel Chester French looks down on the visiting throngs. The memorial's 36 Doric columns correspond to the states of the Union at the time of Lincoln's death. Engraved on the walls of the two side rooms are the salient sentences from his second Inaugural Address and his famous Gettysburg Address of 1863. Open daily; don't miss it. Particularly impressive at sunset and when floodlit after dark.

☼☆ **Theodore Roosevelt Memorial,** north end of Theodore Roosevelt Island, reached by footbridge from George Washington Memorial Pkwy. (285-2601): Erected in 1965 in memory of the 26th president of the U.S., this austere monument in its wooded setting is an allusion to Theodore Roosevelt's interest in nature conservation; the island is itself a wildlife reserve. Worth a look. Open daily.

☼☆ **U.S. Marine Corps War Memorial,** Arlington Blvd., Arlington, Va. (703/433-4173): Impressive group in bronze, 64 ft. (23m) high, by Felix de Weldon. Inspired by Joe Rosenthal's photograph of marines raising Old Glory on the island of Iwo Jima in 1945. Fine view over Washington. Military parades on Tues at 7pm June–Aug. Must be seen.

☼☆ **Vietnam Veterans Memorial,** Constitution Ave. at 21st St. NW (426-6700): A 492-ft.-long (150m) monument of polished black granite in the shape of a large letter "V," bearing the names of some 58,000 GIs reported dead or missing during the Vietnam War. The design, by Maya Ying Lin, then a 21-year old architecture student at Yale, is both tragic and moving in its simplicity. It was unveiled in 1982. The memorial is the most popular monument in Washington and one of its most powerful sights, attracting 12,000–15,000 visitors daily.

☼☆☆ **Washington Monument,** the Mall near 15th St. NW (426-6839): A 555-ft. (169m) obelisk in white Maryland marble designed by architect Robert Mills in 1885, in memory of the first president (see "Panoramas," below).

MUSEUMS OF ART: ☼☆ Corcoran Gallery of Art, 17th St. and New York Ave. NW (638-3211): The most important collection of American art after New York's Metropolitan Museum, with works by many artists including Mary Cassatt, Childe Hassam, John Singleton Copley, and Rembrandt Peale; also paintings by such European masters as Rembrandt, Corot, Daumier, and Degas from the Clark Collection. Highly regarded school of fine arts. Very popular temporary exhibitions. Must positively be seen. Open Tues–Sun.

☆ **Fondo del Sol Art Center,** 2112 R St. NW (483-2777): Unusual museum conceived as a way of presenting and promoting the work of contemporary Caribbean and Latin American artists and artisans. Also has a fine collection of pre-Columbian art and of *santos* (religious statues carved in wood). Interesting temporary exhibitions. Worth a look. Open daily.

☼☆ **Museum of Modern Art of Latin America,** 201 18th St. at Constitution Ave. NW (458-6016): Part of the Panamerican Union Building (see "Architectural Highlights," above), this enchanting little museum displays a remarkable range of works by contemporary Caribbean and Latin American painters and sculptors; the exhibits are changed every 6 months. Lovely Aztec garden with giant statue of the god Xochipilli, the "Flower Prince." Should be seen. Open Tues–Sat.

☼☆☆ **National Gallery of Art,** Constitution Ave. between 3rd St. and 7th St. NW (737-4215): The cultural jewel of Washington, in a handsome 1941 classical revival setting by John Russell Pope. Along with New York's Metropolitan, this is one of the outstanding museums in the country, and the world. Fabulous collection of paintings from Leonardo da Vinci (his only canvas in the U.S.) to Kandinsky, from Botticelli to Salvador Dalí. The new (east) wing of the museum, designed by I. M. Pei and linked to the main building by an underground passage, is a masterpiece of modern architecture (1978) and houses contemporary works of art by Robert Motherwell, Picasso, Henry Moore, Alexander Calder, and others. Among the gallery's most famous works are Fra Angelico's *Adoration of the Magi*, Titian's *Portrait of Doge Andrea Gritti*, El Greco's *St. Martin and the Beggar*, Rogier van der Weyden's *Portrait of a Woman*, Vermeer's *Woman Weighing Pearls*, a *Self-Portrait* by Rembrandt, *Family of Acrobats* by Picasso, and *Box in a Bag* by Marcel Duchamp. The eight million visitors who come here every year are the largest number for any art gallery in the world; allow at least one full day. Top-class temporary exhibitions (O'Keeffe, Gauguin, etc.). Excellent cafeteria. The National Gallery justifies a trip to Washington all by itself.

National Museum of Women in the Arts, New York Ave. and 13th St. NW (783-5000): Founded as recently as 1987, this museum is entirely devoted to women artists. There are some 500 paintings, sculptures, and ceramics, from the Renaissance (Lavinia Fontana) through the impressionists (Mary Cassatt) to the moderns (Georgie O'Keeffe, Helen Frankenthaler, and so on). The impressive Renaissance Revival building dates from 1908 and was originally intended as a Masonic temple with a superb Grand Hall. Should be seen; open Tues–Sun.

Phillips Collection, 1600 21st St. NW (387-2151): The country's oldest (1921) museum of modern art, with very fine European impressionists (Monet, Renoir, Cézanne, van Gogh) and American abstractionists (Mark Rothko, Hans Hofmann, Jackson Pollock) in the Phillips family's elegant mansion. A new $8-million annex was opened to the public in 1989. An absolute must. Open Tues–Sun.

The Smithsonian Institution

The world's largest complex of museums and research centers for the arts, science, and history. Created in 1846, the foundation has 5,000 members and its establishments are visited by 25 million people annually. They include:

Freer Gallery, 12th St. and Jefferson Dr. SW (357-2104): Wonderful collection of Far Eastern art (Chinese bronzes, Hindu sculptures, Japanese screens), and some important American paintings by James McNeill Whistler, John Singer Sargent, Winslow Homer, and others, in an elegant "palazzo" in the Florentine tradition. Whistler's *Peacock Room* is worth a visit all to itself. Presently undergoing renovations.

Hirshhorn Museum, Independence Ave. and 8th St. SW (357-3235): Wonderful modern sculptures and paintings, from Rodin and Miró to Dalí and Henry Moore, in a futurist circular museum designed by Gordon Bunshaft in 1974 and irreverently nicknamed "the doughnut." More than 4,000 paintings and 2,000 sculptures collected over a half century by Joseph H. Hirshhorn, a financier of Latvian origin, and donated by him to the Smithsonian in 1966. Among the most famous works on exhibition: Rodin's *Burghers of Calais,* Snelson's *Needle Tower,* Oldenburg's *Geometric Mouse,* Henry Moore's *Seated Woman,* Brancusi's *Sleeping Muse,* Jackson Pollock's *Aquatic Silhouette,* and *Heads of Jeanette* by Matisse. Not to be missed. Open daily.

National Museum of African Art, 950 Independence Ave. SW (357-4600): This wonderful underground museum designed by Junzo Yoshimura, along with the adjoining Sackler Gallery (see below), cost $73 million and opened in 1987. It houses the nation's largest collection of African art comprising some 6,000 objects in all, from Angolan ceremonial masks by way of Benin metal sculptures and wood figures from Zaire to copper vessels from the Lower Niger. Unusual and fascinating; don't miss it. Open daily.

☀☒ **National Museum of American Art,** 8th St. and G St. NW (357-3111): Paintings, sculptures, and graphics by American artists from Colonial times to the present day, including works by Sargent, Homer, Wyeth, Prendergast, Whistler, and George Catlin, the greatest painter of Native Americans. Must be seen. In the south wing of the building is the ☒ **National Portrait Gallery,** 8th St. and F St. NW (357-2627), with busts and portraits of famous figures in American history, including Gilbert Stuart's well-known *George Washington* and a portrait of Mary Cassatt by Degas. Should be seen. Open daily.

☒ **Renwick Gallery,** 1611 Pennsylvania Ave. NW (357-3111): Interesting museum of decorative art, with posters, drawings, etc. The fine flower of popular artistic expression. Unusual temporary exhibitions. Worth a visit. Open daily.

☀☒ **Arthur M. Sackler Gallery,** 1050 Independence Ave. SW (357-2104): Another very fine underground museum opened in 1987, adjoining the National Museum of African Art, a flawless achievement aesthetically and architecturally. More than 1,000 objects are displayed here from China, Southeast Asia, India, and the Middle East; the Chinese jades and Persian manuscripts are particularly beautiful. A must-see. Open daily.

MUSEUMS OF SCIENCE & HISTORY: ☀☒ Anderson House Museum,
2118 Massachusetts Ave. NW (785-2040): Home of the respected Society of the Cincinnati, a patriotic organization founded in 1783, this luxurious Beaux Arts mansion from 1906 displays a rich collection of historical items bearing on the War of Independence. Portraits, books, period weapons. Many antique art objects. For history buffs. Open Tues–Sat.

☒ **B'nai B'rith Klutznick Museum,** 1640 Rhode Island Ave. NW (857-6583): Jewish religious and folk art; history of Judaism in the U.S. (note a letter from George Washington to the Jewish community of Newport, R.I.) and of the Jewish contribution to the American trade union movement. Interesting. Open Sun–Fri; closed Jewish hols.

☒ **Children's Museum,** 800 3rd St. NE (543-8600): Kids are allowed—even encouraged—to play with the grown-up stuff, including the computers. Well worth visiting. Open daily.

☀☒ **Daughters of the American Revolution/DAR Museum,** 1776 D St. NW (628-1776): A complex of turn-of-the-century buildings occupied by the DAR, a patriotic organization now numbering some 200,000 members, which was founded in 1890 for descendants of those who fought in the War of Independence. Includes a museum of decorative art with 33 "State Rooms" decorated in the style of the Revolutionary period; one of the country's most important genealogical libraries, tracing the family trees of the earliest immigrants and their descendants; and **Constitution Hall,** a 3,800-seat auditorium. A must for history buffs. Open daily.

☀☒ **Folger Shakespeare Library,** 201 E. Capitol St. SE (544-7077): The world's largest collection of Shakespeariana, with 180,000 works; also possesses an Elizabethan-style theater (performances Oct–July) and a scaled-down replica of London's famous Globe Theatre. Open daily Apr–Aug, Mon–Sat the rest of the year.

☀☒ **Frederick Douglass Memorial Home,** 1411 W St. SE (426-5960): The founder of the Black Liberation movement in America, the African American activist Frederick Douglass, who was himself born a slave, lived here from 1877 until his death in 1895. Famous orator, journalist, lawyer, and for a time, U.S. Ambassador to Haiti, he is looked on as the father of the civil rights movement—a forerunner of Martin Luther King, Jr.

Interesting personal museum and well-stocked library. Open daily; should be seen.

☀️☖ **Marine Corps Museum,** Bldg. 58, Washington Navy Yard, M St. and 9th St. SE (433-3534): 200 years of the United States Marine Corps' history, illustrated by its weapons, its uniforms, and other soldierly souvenirs, arranged in chronological order from the foundation of this elite unit in 1775. The museum is hard to reach without a car. Open daily.

☖ **Martin Luther King Library,** 901 G St. NW (727-1111): In this austerely beautiful black building by Mies van der Rohe is a library devoted to the winner of the Nobel Peace Prize, with many works relating to the struggle for civil rights. Also books, movies, and photographs on the history of the city of Washington, and the archives of the now-defunct daily *Washington Star.*

☀️☖☖ **National Archives,** Constitution Ave. between 7th St. and 9th St. NW (523-3183): Imposing Greek Revival building designed by John Russell Pope, containing the country's most prized historical documents, from the originals of the Constitution, the Bill of Rights, and the Declaration of Independence, to the 1783 Treaty of Paris bearing the signature of Benjamin Franklin and the seal of King George III of England, the 1945 instruments of surrender of Germany and Japan, and the notorious Watergate tapes. Among innumerable other documents and curiosities is the photo album of Hitler's mistress, Eva Braun. Fascinating; must certainly be seen. Open daily.

☀️☖☖ **National Building Museum,** 4th St. and F St. NW (272-2448): This building, perhaps the most unusual in Washington, originally built to house the proliferating offices of the Civil War veterans' pension administration, now displays temporary exhibitions. Splendid interior hall with 75-ft. (22m) Corinthian columns. A positive must-see. Open daily.

☖ **National Geographic Society,** 17th St. and M St. NW (857-7588): Home of the world-famous *National Geographic* magazine. In Explorers Hall you'll find brilliantly conceived exhibitions devoted to the exploration of land, sea, and outer space, and a terrestrial globe 11 ft. (3m) in diameter. Should be seen. Open daily.

☀️☖ **National Library of Medicine,** 8600 Rockville Pike, Bethesda, Md. (301/496-6308): The world's largest medical library in an ultramodern building belonging to the National Institutes of Health, with four million books, professional periodicals, manuscripts, and other works in 70 languages, accumulated in the course of 150 years. Visitor Center and guided tours. If you're a disciple of Hippocrates, this is for you. Open Mon–Fri.

☖ **National Rifle Association Firearms Museum,** 1600 Rhode Island Ave. NW (828-6194): More than 1,500 firearms, from 15th-century arquebuses to the latest in sub-machine guns; one of the largest in the world, as you would expect from an association numbering three million enthusiasts. Open daily.

☖ **Naval Observatory,** 34th St. and Massachusetts Ave. NW (653-1507): Standing amid spacious gardens adjoining the official home of the vice-president of the U.S., this observatory administered by the U.S. Navy is responsible for determining standard American time. Interesting astronomical museum (admission at 2pm Mon–Fri). Every Mon when the moon is full, budding astronomers may scan the heavens through a 26-in. (65cm) telescope.

☀️☖ **Navy Museum,** Bldg. 76, Washington Navy Yard, 9th St. and M St. SE (433-2651): From the mizzenmast of the famed frigate *Constitution* to a replica of the command station of a submarine, complete with periscope, and including a destroyer moored in front of the museum and open to visitors, you will find here a complete history of the U.S. Navy, from the engagements of the War of Independence to the age of nuclear missiles. Fascinating. Museum hard to reach except by car. Open daily.

The Smithsonian Institution

As well as the various art museums listed above, the Smithsonian Institution also comprises:

Anacostia Museum, 1901 Fort Pl. SE (357-2700): In a largely African American neighborhood in the south of Washington, this museum reopened in 1987 at a new location. It presents temporary exhibitions dealing with the role of minorities, ethnic and other, in American society. Should be seen. Open daily.

National Air and Space Museum, Independence Ave. and 7th St. SW (357-1400): Possibly the most remarkable aeronautical museum in the world, designed by Gyo Obata and opened in 1976. Here, under an enormous vaulted roof, are displayed the most memorable machines in the history of flying and space exploration: the *Kitty Hawk Flyer,* the Wright Brothers' first plane; the *Spirit of St. Louis,* first aircraft to be flown solo across the Atlantic (in 1927); the *Bell X-1,* the first aircraft to exceed the speed of sound; the fastest aircraft in the world, the *X-15,* which has reached Mach 6; a copy of *Sputnik 1,* the Soviet satellite which was the first to be placed in orbit around the earth; the *Apollo 11* module, which made the first lunar landing in 1969. There are extraordinary audiovisual shows and an ultramodern planetarium **(Albert Einstein Spacearium).** The most visited museum in the world—10 million people come here every year. Very good new restaurant (the Wright Place) and cafeteria (Flight Line). An absolute must. Open daily.

National Museum of American History, Constitution Ave. and 14th St. NW (357-1481): Immense museum of science and technology. On the ground floor is a 280-ton (255,000kg) locomotive which had to be moved into place before the museum was built! Comprehensive collection of historic objects, from George Washington's false teeth and the ceremonial dresses of First Ladies to "Old Glory," the original star-spangled banner which inspired Francis Scott Key to write the words of the national anthem, and from Alexander Graham Bell's first telephone to a wooden gunboat that lay for 200 years beneath the waters of Lake Champlain. Not to be missed. Open daily.

National Museum of Natural History, Constitution Ave. and 10th St. NW (357-2700): A comprehensive Museum of Man. A spectacular 92-ft. (28m) blue whale; the largest stuffed elephant in the world, weighing 8 tons (7,275kg); a life-size diplodocus. Anthropological material from the Western Hemisphere, Africa, and Asia. Extensive collection of minerals including the world-famous Hope Diamond of 44 carats. Archeology, biology, fascinating insect "zoo" (the children's favorite), etc. An absolute must. Open daily.

PANORAMAS: **Arlington House/Custis-Lee Mansion,** Arlington National Cemetery, Arlington, Va. (703/557-0613): On a hill above Arlington National Cemetery (see "Monuments," above), this very fine Greek Revival house, once the home of Gen. Robert E. Lee, the Confederate commander-in-chief during the Civil War, has a splendid view of the Potomac River and downtown Washington. Lee abandoned Arlington House in 1861, at the beginning of the war, and never set foot there again. Overlooks the tomb of Pres. John F. Kennedy. Don't miss the view. Open daily.

Bell Tower of the Old Post Office, 1100 Pennsylvania Ave. at 12th St. NW (523-5691): This 315-ft. (96m) Gothic Revival clock tower crowns the former central post office and has a spectacular view of downtown Washington. Elevator. Open daily 10am–6:45pm (to 9pm June–Sept). Worth a look.

Washington Monument, The Mall, nr. 15th St. NW (426-6839): A 555-ft. (169m) white marble obelisk dedicated to the first president of the U.S. A masterpiece of simple grandeur, this monument, which has become the city's symbol, was unveiled in 1885 and opened to the public 3 years later. From an observation platform 502 ft. (153m) up, there is a truly spectacular panoramic view; on a clear day you can see the Blue Ridge Mountains 50 mi. (80km) away. Elevator. Since more than two million tourists come here every year, you may have a long wait in line, particularly in summer. Open daily 8am–midnight in summer; 9am–5pm the rest of the year. Don't miss it.

Washington National Cathedral, Wisconsin Ave. and Massachusetts Ave. NW (537-6200): The Pilgrim Observation Gallery at the top of the cathedral's tower, 300 ft. (91m) above the ground, has a fine view of the northern part of the city as far as the banks of the Potomac. Worth seeing. Open daily 10am–3pm.

PARKS & GARDENS: For information about National Park Service monuments and parks in the Washington, D.C., area, call 619-7222. For a recorded message listing daily activities in the parks, call 619-7275.

Botanic Garden Conservatory, Maryland Ave. between 1st St. and 2nd St. SW (225-8333): A tropical jungle under glass, an incredible display of orchids, and some beautiful gardens at the foot of the Capitol: a botanic cross-section of all five continents. Worth seeing. Open daily.

Kenilworth Aquatic Gardens, Kenilworth Ave. and Douglas St. NE (426-6905): On the bank of the Anacostia River, a wonderful aquatic garden with lotus, water hyacinth, bamboo, and water lilies by the thousand (flowering spectacularly June–Aug). Worth seeing. Open daily.

Lafayette Square, Pennsylvania Ave., between Jackson Pl. and Madison Pl. NW: This charming tree-shaded little square in front of the main facade of the White House is a godsend to footsore tourists (and demonstrators who want to express dissatisfaction outside the White House railings). Besides an equestrian statue (1853) of Andrew Jackson, seventh president, the square is embellished with statues of four foreign-born heroes of the War of Independence: the German Friedrich Wilhelm von Steuben, the Pole Tadeusz Kosciuszko, and two Frenchmen, the Comte de Rochambeau and the Marquis de Lafayette. On the north side of the square is St. John's Episcopal Church, attended by many presidents of the U.S. In the corner of the square, Blair House, at 1651 Pennsylvania Ave. NW, is the official residence of foreign heads of state visiting Washington (not open to the public). If you want to take souvenir snapshots in front of the White House, this is the place to do it.

The Mall, between the Capitol and the Potomac River. This broad green carpet runs through the center of Washington on either side of the 655-yard (600m) **Reflecting Pool.** On the **Ellipse,** a great oval of lawn behind the White House, stands the Zero Milestone, placed there in 1923 to mark the zero mile of the great U.S. highways. One of the loveliest views in Washington, and a squirrels' paradise.

Meridian Hill Park, 16th St. between Euclid St. and Florida Ave. NW (426-6851): Hidden from public view behind high walls, this 12-acre (5ha) terraced park, though little known to Washingtonians, is perhaps the most beautiful landscaped complex in the capital. Completed in 1936, the park, sometimes known as **Malcolm X Park,** comprises a garden in the French style with clumps of trees, stone benches, and a statue of Joan of Arc on horseback, as well as a baroque Italian garden with a magnificent 13-step waterfall reminiscent of the famous fountains of the Villa d'Este near Rome. A sight you shouldn't miss, but the neighborhood is unsafe after nightfall. Open daily.

National Arboretum, 3501 New York Ave. NE (475-4815): Floral displays throughout the year, particularly impressive in spring when the azaleas are in flower. Pretty Japanese garden and delightful collection of bonsai (dwarf trees). On the banks of the Anacostia River. Worth a detour. Open daily.

Potomac Park, along Ohio Dr. SW (485-9666): Extensive tree-lined walk along the Potomac and Washington Chan-

nel on either side of the Jefferson Memorial. The beautiful cherry trees given by
the Japanese government in 1912 are in flower in late Mar and early Apr around
the Tidal Basin and East Potomac Park. Two golf courses; fishing; skating in winter; boat rental. A lovely sight in season. Much favored by joggers. Open daily.

🔔 **Rock Creek Park,** along Rock Creek Pkwy. and Beach Dr. NW
(426-6829): 1,754 acres (710ha) of winding, rolling parkland
on either side of Rock Creek, a tributary of the Potomac. Golf, tennis, horseback
riding, open-air concerts in summer in the **Carter Barron Amphitheater.** A joggers' favorite, but don't go there after dark.

☼🔔 **Roosevelt Island,** Potomac River, reached by a footbridge
from the George Washington Pkwy. at Arlington, Va. (285-
2601): Unspoiled nature 10 min. from downtown, with a memorial dedicated
to Pres. Theodore Roosevelt. Open from sunrise to sunset daily. Worth the
trip.

PERFORMING ARTS: For a daily listing of all shows and cultural events, consult the entertainment pages of the daily papers *Washington Post* (morning) and
Washington Times (morning), and of the monthly magazine *The Washingtonian.*
Ticket Place, 12th and F St. Plaza NW (842-5387): Sells tickets at half price for
all same-day performances: shows, ballet, concerts, plays, etc. Open Tues–Sat
11am–7pm. Cash only.
American Film Institute, Kennedy Center, New Hampshire Ave. NW at
Rock Creek Pkwy. (785-4600): The depository library of the American cinema,
with all the great classics.
American Playwrights, 1742 Church St. NW (232-1122): Modern theater, comedy, drama.
Arena Stage, 6th St. and Maine Ave. SW (488-3300): Three contiguous
theaters; musicals, contemporary and classical theater.
Carter Barron Amphitheater, Rock Creek Park, 4850 Colorado Ave. NW
(829-3200): Open-air concerts in a 4,000-seat auditorium in the woods; folk,
pop, and jazz. Mid-June to Aug.
D.C. Space, 7th St. and E St. NW (347-1445): Popular comedy club in the
spirit of "Saturday Night Live."
Folger Theater, 301 E. Capitol St. SE (546-4000): Classical (Shakespeare)
and modern theater.
Ford's Theater, 511 10th St. NW (347-4833): The theater where Abraham
Lincoln was assassinated, now a designated historic monument with the original
decor restored. Musicals, modern theater.
John F. Kennedy Center for the Performing Arts, New Hampshire Ave.
NW at Rock Creek Pkwy. (467-4600): Major, ultramodern entertainment com-
plex with five different halls and auditoriums: the **Concert Hall,** home of the Na-
tional Symphony (principal conductor, Mstislav Rostropovich), concerts and
recitals of classical music; the **Eisenhower Theater,** modern and classic plays and
Broadway hits; the **Opera House,** home of the Washington Opera (director Mar-
tin Feinstein); ballet; the **Terrace Theater,** chamber music; **Theater Lab,** Off
Broadway and experimental theater.
Lisner Auditorium, George Washington University, 21st St. and H St. NW
(994-6800): Opera, classical concerts, jazz; recitals.
National Theater, 1321 Pennsylvania Ave. NW (628-6161): Musicals,
Broadway hits.
Source Theater, 1835 14th St. NW (462-1073): Modern and experimen-
tal theater.
Trinity Theater, 36th St. and O St. NW (965-4680): Musicals, Off Broad-
way plays.
Washington National Cathedral, Wisconsin Ave. and Massachusetts Ave.
NW (537-6247): Concerts of sacred music, recitals, organ recitals.
Wolf Trap Farm Park for the Performing Arts, 1624 Trap Rd. at Va. 676,

Vienna, Va. (703/255-1868): Big open-air auditorium used in summer for shows and concerts—jazz, classical, pop, opera, folk, ballet. Enormously popular. June–Sept. For details, see "Special Events," below.

SHOPPING: Georgetown (see "Strolls," below) has innumerable boutiques and fashion shops. In the **Watergate** building, **Les Champs** is a shopping arcade with some 30 luxury boutiques and shops (Guy Laroche, Gucci, Yves St. Laurent, etc.).

The Shops (1331 Pennsylvania Ave. NW), **International Square** (1850 K St. NW), **The Pavilion at the Old Post Office** (1100 Pennsylvania Ave. NW), and **Esplanade Mall** (1990 K St. NW) are four ultramodern downtown shopping malls, each with dozens of trendy boutiques and shops as well as plenty of bars and restaurants.

Another successfully designed, modern-style shopping center is **Georgetown Park Mall**, 3222 M St. NW, with a round 100 establishments doing business in a pretty Victorian-rococo setting.

The traditional department stores have for the most part fled to the huge shopping plazas on the outskirts of the city, the smartest and most accessible of which is **Mazza Gallerie** at 5300 Wisconsin Ave. NW, in Chevy Chase, Md.; there's a subway stop right outside.

Highly recommended for the transient visitor are the gift shops of the various **museums on the Mall** and the **Indian Craft Shop** in the Dept. of Interior Bldg., 1800 C St. NW; their gifts are original and usually affordable as well.

If food is important to you, visit **Sutton Place Gourmet**, 3201 New Mexico Ave. NW, or better still, at 10323 Old Georgetown Rd. in Bethesda, Md., Washington's answer to Zabar's in New York or Fauchon's in Paris.

SPECIAL EVENTS: For the exact schedule of events below, consult the **Washington Convention and Visitors Association** (see "Tourist Information," above).

Cherry Blossom Festival (late Mar to early Apr): Parade with floats, marathon, fireworks, famous lantern-lighting ceremony, and concerts, when the Japanese cherries are in flower.

Flying Circus (May–Oct): Displays of aerobatics in old propeller-driven craft of the barnstorming era, every Sunday at 2pm. Picturesque and entertaining. You'll find it at the end of a 40-min. drive from downtown Washington along I-66W, U.S. 211W, and U.S. 17S, on U.S. 17 at Bealeton, Va. (703/439-8661). If you're nostalgic about goggles and leather helmets, this is for you.

Friday Evening Parade (mid-May to mid-Sept): Unusually spectacular; the marines on parade Fri at 8:45pm, U.S. Marines Barracks, 8th St. and I St. SE. You have to reserve several days ahead (433-6060).

Sunset Salute (late May to late Aug): The Marine Corps Silent Drill Platoon, the Marine Band and Drum and Bugle Corps offer a Sunset Salute to their slain fellows at the foot of the Iwo Jima Memorial in Arlington, starting at 7:30pm every Tues.

Memorial Day Ceremony (Memorial Day): The president lays a wreath at the tomb of the Unknown Soldier in Arlington National Cemetery. In the evening, the National Symphony gives an open-air concert on the lawn in front of the Capitol.

Kemper Open PGA Golf Tournament (May): Great annual tournament on the Avenel Golf Course.

Kool Jazz Festival (early June): The world's biggest names in jazz come to the Kennedy Center for 48 hrs.

Hispanic Festival (late June): The city's largest community-run festival. Features parades, ethnic foods, plays, music. More than 350,000 revellers. On the Mall.

Outdoor Concerts on the Mall (June–Aug): Places and times vary from day to day; consult the newspapers or call 426-4011.

July 4th Celebration (July 4): Concerts and fireworks on the Mall.

Wolf Trap Festival (June–Sept): Open-air concerts of classical music, jazz, ballet, opera, etc.; draws 600,000 spectators yearly. At Wolf Trap Farm, Vienna, Va. (703/255-1868 or 202/432-0200), 14 mi. (22km) west on George Washington Memorial Pkwy., I-495S, and Dulles Airport Rd.

Adams-Morgan Day Festival (Sept): A truly international celebration with ethnic food, music, crafts, and wares representing more than 50 countries. The city's biggest block party. At 18th St. and Columbia Rd. NW.

SPORTS: Washington has three professional teams:

Basketball (Oct–Apr): Bullets, Capital Center, Landover, Md. (301/350-3400).

Football (Aug–Dec): Redskins, RFK Stadium (546-2222).

Ice Hockey (Oct–Apr): Capitals, Capital Center, Landover, Md. (301/350-3400).

Horse Racing

Laurel Race Track, Baltimore-Washington Pkwy. exit to Md. 198, 18 mi. (28km) NW in Laurel, Md. (301/725-0400), for thoroughbred racing, Sept–Feb.

Rosecroft Raceway, 6336 Rosecroft Dr., 8 mi. (13km) SE, in Oxon Hill, Md. (301/567-4000), has harness racing Jan–May and Oct–Dec.

STROLLS: ⚓ **Adams Morgan,** bounded by Columbia Rd., Florida Ave., and 18th St. NW: A sort of local melting pot, it remains lively and bustling until 2am, unlike the rest of Washington. The neighborhood restaurants reflect the cosmopolitan crowd: Ethiopian, Créole, Chinese, Japanese, French, Mexican, Caribbean, Brazilian, and more. Worth a visit.

⚓ **Potomac Banks** (see the Potomac Park and Roosevelt Island entries under "Parks and Gardens," above): Very pleasant in fine weather.

⚓ **Embassy Row,** Massachusetts Ave. between Sheridan Circle and Observatory Circle NW: The world's largest diplomatic quarter, with some 80 embassies, consulates, and legations in a span of less than a mile (1.6km). You should see this national display of national flags and coats-of-arms.

☀⚓ **Georgetown,** around Wisconsin Ave. and M St. NW: In Colonial days, Georgetown was a leading port for the export of tobacco; today it's a charming residential district. While some of its former elitist glitter has worn off, it's still — with its old houses, little narrow streets, boutiques, nightclubs, and variety of restaurants — both the Greenwich Village and the SoHo of the nation's capital. But avoid Georgetown on weekend nights because heavy-drinking crowds often become rowdy and abusive. You should make a point of seeing the **Old Stone House** at 3051 M St. NW, the city's oldest house (1765), and **Dumbarton Oaks,** 1703 32nd St. NW, with its fine collections of Byzantine and pre-Columbian art. You might like to do as many tourists do every summer — take a barge ride on the **C. & O. Canal.** The house where John F. Kennedy lived before his election to the presidency is at 3307 N St. NW; no visitors. **Washington Harbor,** 3030 K St. NW, is a vast terraced esplanade on the Potomac — an imaginative piece of postmodern design by Arthur Cotton Moore. And there are many more things to see; don't miss this stroll.

THEME PARKS: ☀⚓ **Kings Dominion,** I-95 and Va. 30 at Doswell, Va., 78 mi. (124km) SW on I-95 (804/876-5000): Comprehensive theme park on 800 acres (324ha), with a picturesque reconstruction of Old Europe, including a miniature Eiffel Tower. There are 44 rides, featuring four roller coasters (including Shock Wave) and a Log Flume. Big-name shows; safari zoo. Open daily June to Labor Day, wknds only from late Mar to June and Labor Day to early Oct; closed the rest of the year.

Wild World, 13710 Central Ave. at Md. 214, in Mitchellville, Md., 15 mi. (24km) east on E. Capitol St. and Central Ave. (301/249-1500): Giant roller coaster (Wild One); inner-tube ride; million-gallon (3.8-million-liter) wave pool for surfers, the biggest of its kind in the world; and dozens of other family attractions. 20 min. from downtown Washington. Open daily, early May through Sept.

WINTER SPORTS RESORTS: Blue Knob, nr. Bedford, Pa., 150 mi.
(240km) NW on I-270N and I-70N, Pennsylvania Tpke. west, U.S. 200N, and Penna. 869W (814/239-5111): 6 lifts.

Canaan Valley, nr. Davis, W. Va., 180 mi. (288km) west on I-66W, Va. 55W, and W.Va. 32N (304/866-4121): 4 lifts; one of the best resorts in the region.

Massanutten, nr. Elkton, Va., 125 mi. (200km) SW on I-66W, I-81S, U.S. 33E, and Va. 644N (703/289-9441): 5 lifts.

Ski Liberty, nr. Gettysburg, Pa., 65 mi. (104km) NW on I-270N, U.S. 15N, Md. 140W, Penna. 16W, and Penna. 116E (717/642-8282): 5 lifts.

Ski Roundtop, nr. York, Pa., 121 mi. (194km) north on I-95N, I-695W, I-83N, Penna. 382W, and Penna. 177N (717/432-9631): 10 lifts.

Wintergreen, nr. Greenfield, Va., 168 mi. (268km) SW on I-66W, U.S. 29S, I-64W, Va. 6E, and Va. 151S (804/325-2200): 5 lifts.

ZOOS: National Zoological Park, 3001 Connecticut Ave. NW (673-4717): One of the finest and best-known zoos in the country; almost 3,000 animals representing 600 species, some of them very rare, such as the Indian white tiger, one of the few pairs of Komodo dragons in the western hemisphere, and pandas donated by the People's Republic of China, in facsimiles of their natural environment. Belongs to the Smithsonian Institution. A must-see. Open daily.

ACCOMMODATIONS

A Note on Accommodations: Room rates in Washington are coded as follows: **VE,** Very Expensive ($140 and up); **E,** Expensive ($90–$140); **M,** Moderate ($60–$90); **I,** Inexpensive ($30–$60); **B,** Budget (up to $30). A listing of toll-free numbers is in the Appendix.

Although Washington has some 35,000 hotel rooms, it can be difficult to make a reservation at certain peak periods. **Washington D.C. Accommodations,** 1534 U St. NW, DC 20009 (toll free 800/554-2220), and **Capital Reservations,** 1201 K St. NW, DC 20005 (202/842-4187), offer a free hotel-reservation service.

Personal Favorites (in order of preference)

Four Seasons (nr. dwntwn), 2800 Pennsylvania Ave. NW, DC 20007 (202/342-0444; toll free, see Four Seasons). 198 rms, A/C, color TV, in-rm movies. AE, CB, DC, MC, V. Valet parking $12, rest. (Aux Beaux Champs), coffee shop, bar, 24-hr. rm svce, free crib, concierge. *Note:* The luxury hotel w. the highest occupancy rate in Washington. Its ocher brick intended to harmonize w. Georgetown's old houses. Elegantly comfortable; refined interior; polished, personalized svce. Spacious rms w. period furniture, some w. balconies, the best overlooking Rock Creek Park. Excellent rest. Free limo to dwntwn. The VIP's favorite. **VE**

Sheraton Carlton (dwntwn), 923 16th St. NW, DC 20006 (202/638-2626; toll free, see Sheraton). 200 rms, A/C, color TV, in-rm movies. AE, CB, DC, MC, V. Valet parking $12, health club, rest.

(Allegro), bar, 24-hr. rm svce, hrdrsr, concierge, crib $25. *Note:* The great lady among Washington hotels since 1926; reopened in Oct 1988 after 10 months (and $16 million) of renovation, this Italian-Renaissance palace has recaptured its original luster. Only two blocks from the White House, the Sheraton Carlton has accommodated many presidents of the U.S. Unusually spacious rms, mahogany-furnished, w. marble bathrooms, refrigerators, and three phones apiece. Personalized svce. Admirable but very expensive Italian rest. Excellent location; attracts many VIPs and foreign dignitaries. **VE**

🛏🛏🛏 **Madison** (dwntwn), 15th St. and M St. NW, DC 20005 (202/862-1600; toll free 800/424-8577). 353 rms, A/C, color TV, in-rm movies. AE, CB, DC, MC, V. Gar. $10, two rests. (including the Montpelier Room), two bars, rm svce, crib $25, concierge. *Note:* Ungraceful modern building elegantly and tastefully decorated within, w. period furniture, master paintings, and rich Oriental rugs. Big businesspeople, foreign dignitaries, prominent politicians, and entertainers (including Henry Kissinger, Frank Sinatra, Bob Hope, and David Rockefeller) have been coming here for a quarter of a century. Spacious, comfortable rms w. minibars. Thoroughly professional staff; overpriced, pretentious rest. Opposite the *Washington Post* building. Boasts one of Washington's most expensive suites, at $2,500 a night, plus tax. **VE**

🛏🛏🛏 **Watergate Hotel** (nr. dwntwn), 2650 Virginia Ave. NW, DC 20037 (202/965-2300; toll free 800/225-5843). 238 rms, A/C, color TV, in-rm movies. AE, CB, DC, MC, V. Valet gar. $12, pool, health club, sauna, rest., coffee shop, bars, rm svce, hrdrsr, boutiques, concierge, free crib. *Note:* Relatively modern luxury hotel of original design, part of the celebrated Watergate development on the Potomac, a stone's throw from the Kennedy Center. Inviting, comfortable rms, the best w. river view; elegant decor w. Far Eastern works of art. Remarkable rest. (Jean Louis); flawless svce. Attracts many well-heeled foreigners. 10 min. from dwntwn. **VE**

🛏🛏🛏 **Hilton-Capitol** (nr. dwntwn), 1001 16th St. NW, DC 20036 (202/393-1000; toll free, see Hilton). 549 rms, A/C, color TV, in-rm movies. AE, CB, DC, MC, V. Gar. $8, health club, sauna, two rests. (including Trader Vic's), coffee shop, bar, 24-hr. rm svce, nightclub, hrdrsr, boutiques, concierge, free crib. *Note:* After many years of neglect and decay, this wonderfully located convention hotel, in the heart of the business district and only three blocks from the White House, recently underwent a $55-million facelift. Rms are now larger, redecorated, and w. minibars; facilities have been completely renovated. Four VIP floors w. their own elevator and concierge. New, fully equipped business center. Svce (at last) efficient and hustling. The airport buses have their terminal here. Business and convention clientele. **VE**

🛏🛏 **Embassy Row** (nr. dwntwn), 2015 Massachusetts Ave. NW, DC 20036 (202/265-1600; toll free 800/424-2400). 196 rms, A/C, color TV, in-rm movies. AE, CB, DC, MC, V. Valet gar. $10, pool, rest. (Lucie), bar, 24-hr. rm svce, concierge, free breakfast. *Note:* Elegant little hotel in the heart of the embassy district. Built in 1970 and entirely renovated in 1984. Comfortable rms and suites, w. minibars. Foreign and diplomatic clientele. The help speaks a number of languages but the svce is undependable. Acceptable rest. Interesting wknd discounts. **VE**

🛏🛏 **Channel Inn** (nr. dwntwn), 650 Water St. SW, DC 20024 (202/554-2400; toll free 800/368-5668). 100 rms, A/C, color TV. AE, CB, DC, MC, V. Free parking, pool, rest, coffee shop, bar, rm svce, disco, free crib. *Note:* Agreeable motel right on the water; comfortable, more-than-usually spacious rms w. balconies, the best overlooking Washington Channel and the marina. Efficient svce. 5 min. from the Mall and its museums. Tourist clientele. Good value on balance. Interesting wknd discounts. **M–E**

🛏🛏 **Howard Johnson at Kennedy Center** (nr. dwntwn), 2601 Virginia Ave. NW, DC 20037 (202/965-2700; toll free, see

Howard Johnson's). 192 rms, A/C, color TV. AE, CB, DC, MC, V. Free gar., rooftop pool, rest., bar, free crib. *Note:* Traditional eight-floor motel a block or two from the Kennedy Center, opposite the Watergate complex and 10 min. from dwntwn. Functionally comfortable rms w. refrigerators, some w. balconies. Efficient reception and svce. Favored by show-business people. Good overall value. **M**

Normandy Inn (nr. dwntwn), 2118 Wyoming Ave. NW, DC 20008 (202/483-1350; toll free 800/424-3729). 74 rms, A/C, color TV, in-rm movies. AE, CB, DC, MC, V. Gar. $6, rm svce. *Note:* Charming hotel, aging but very well maintained, in the heart of the embassy district, 10 min. from dwntwn. Functionally comfortable. Friendly reception and svce. Regular clientele; good value. **M**

Braxton Hotel (dwntwn), 1440 Rhode Island Ave. NW, DC 20037 (202/232-7800). 62 rms, A/C, color TV, in-rm movies. AE, MC, V. On-street parking; no bar or rest. *Note:* Small dwntwn budget hotel, offering a respectable level of comfort and a warm welcome. Ideal for shoestring travelers. **I**

Other Accommodations (from top bracket to budget)

Grand Hotel (nr. dwntwn), 2350 M St. NW, DC 20037 (202/429-0100; toll free 800/848-0016). 265 rms, A/C, color TV, in-rm movies. AE, CB, DC, MC, V. Valet gar. $12, pool, health club, rest. (the Promenade), piano bar, 24-hr. rm svce, concierge, free crib. *Note:* Opened in 1985 as the Regent, this is one of the most elegant of Washington's new grand hotels. Subdued, distinguished postmodern design capped w. a copper dome. A profusion of marble and paneling, especially in the lobby. Comfortable, inviting rms, although a bit cramped, but immense Italian marble bathrooms. Extremely distinguished svce; rest. of a high order. Clientele of wealthy businessmen—the hotel is located right in the West End business district. **VE**

Willard Inter-Continental (dwntwn), 1401 Pennsylvania Ave. NW, DC 20004 (202/628-9100; toll free, see Inter-Continental). 365 rms, A/C, color TV, in-rm movies. AE, CB, DC, MC, V. Valet parking $15, rest. (Willard Room), coffee shop, bar, 24-hr. rm svce, boutiques, concierge, free crib. *Note:* This venerable Beaux Arts building dates from 1901, is a designated historic monument, and has long been known as "the hotel of presidents." Long allowed to deteriorate, and indeed threatened with demolition, a $75-million restoration program completed in 1986 has restored all its old splendor as well as its sumptuous interior. All the world's greats have stayed here, from Mark Twain to Richard Nixon. The standard rms are somewhat cramped; the suites and studios, on the contrary, are unusually elegant and comfortable. The lobby promenade known as Peacock Alley was, at the turn of the century, a favorite meeting place for politicians and the representatives of special-interest groups—whence the term "lobbyist." Highly regarded but overpriced rest. The Round Robin Bar is famous. Svce of the highest order. Boasts one of Washington's most expensive suites—$2,500 a night, plus tax. One of the great names among American hotels. **VE**

Grand Hyatt (dwntwn), 1000 H St. NW, DC 20001 (202/582-1234; toll free, see Hyatt). 907 rms, A/C, color TV, in-rm movies. AE, CB, DC, MC, V. Valet parking $12, two rests., two bars, 24-hr. rm svce, disco, drugstore, concierge, free crib. *Note:* Big new brick, stone, and concrete cube, well-located across from the Convention Center, but completely lacking in architectural originality. Its 12-story lobby w. skylight, giant waterfall, pool, and indoor grdns is, on the other hand, an altogether praiseworthy piece of design. Huge, well-designed rms; unexpectedly efficient svce given the sheer size of the place. VIP floor; group and convention clientele. **VE**

Hay-Adams Hotel (dwntwn), 1 Lafayette Sq. NW, DC 20006 (202/638-6600; toll free, see Preferred). 138 rms, A/C, color TV, in-rm movies. AE, CB, DC, MC, V. Valet gar. $12, two rests. (including the John Hay Room), coffee shop, bar, 24-hr. rm svce, concierge. *Note:* The best location in town, right across from the White House. Charming old hotel in the European fashion, a favorite of visiting foreign statesmen and dignitaries for more than half a century. Spacious, elegant rms w. balconies and minibars, some w. fireplaces, the best looking out on Lafayette Sq. Period furniture. Excellent svce, discreet and attentive. Good rests. Quality and style. **VE**

♬♬♬ **Hilton Washington and Towers** (nr. dwntwn), 1919 Connecticut Ave. NW, DC 20009 (202/483-3000; toll free, see Hilton). 1,150 rms, A/C, color TV, in-rm movies. AE, CB, DC, MC, V. Valet gar. $7, pool, tennis courts, health club, sauna, two rests., coffee shop, two bars, rm svce, disco, drugstore, free crib. *Note:* Massive white tourist barracks in the shape of two arcs of a circle, standing in 6 acres (2ha) of grdn. Up-to-date comfort. Spacious rms w. refrigerators, some w. balconies. Very complete facilities; rather distracted svce and average rests. Crowded year round by groups and conventions. Two top floors reserved for VIPs (Hilton Towers). It was in front of this hotel that an attempt was made to assassinate President Reagan on March 30, 1981. 10 min. from dwntwn. **VE**

☼♬♬♬ **Jefferson Hotel** (dwntwn), 1200 16th St. NW (at M St.), DC 20036 (202/347-2200; toll free 800/368-5966). 107 rms, A/C, color TV, in-rm movies. AE, CB, DC, MC, V. Valet parking $15, two rests. (including the Hunt Club), bar, 24-hr. rm svce, concierge, free crib. *Note:* Charming little '20s hotel, tastefully renovated. Each spacious, comfortable rm is decorated in a different style; most have four-poster beds. Flawless personalized svce. The Hunt Club is one of Washington's fashionable rests. Distinction and elegance nr. the embassy district and four blocks from the White House. The politicians' favorite. **VE**

♬♬♬ **J. W. Marriott** (dwntwn), 1331 Pennsylvania Ave. NW, DC 20004 (202/393-2000; toll free, see Marriott). 774 rms, A/C, color TV, in-rm movies. AE, CB, DC, MC, V. Valet parking $12, pool, health club, sauna, two rests. (including Celadon), coffee shop, bars, 24-hr. rm svce, nightclub, hrdrsr, boutiques, concierge, free crib. *Note:* The flagship hotel of the Marriott chain, an ultramodern palace whose design earns no plaudits, strategically placed a stone's throw from the Mall and the White House. Luckily, the interior decoration and equipment are more successful. Enormous, boastful lobby w. marble floors and huge crystal chandeliers; spacious, well-designed rms; efficient though impersonal svce. As in all Marriotts, so-so rests. Business and convention clientele. VIP floor ("Marquis Floor"); direct access to "The Shops" at National Place, a shopping mall with 110 shops and 20 rests. The movie *Broadcast News* was in part shot here. **VE**

♬♬♬ **Ritz-Carlton** (formerly the Fairfax; nr. dwntwn), 2100 Massachusetts Ave. NW, DC 20008 (202/293-2100; toll free 800/424-8008). 220 rms, A/C, color TV, in-rm movies. AE, CB, DC, MC, V. Valet parking $10, rest. (Jockey Club), bar, 24-hr. rm svce, nightclub, concierge, crib $20. *Note:* This elegant, classy old hotel in the heart of the embassy district has undergone a much-needed facelift, and is now smart and distinguished, achieving a harmonious combination of elegance and comfort. There are, however, still shortcomings in maintenance and svce. Spacious rms w. minibars; good hotel rest. (a favorite of President Kennedy and Nancy Reagan). Big business and diplomatic clientele. A Washington landmark for half a century. **VE**

♬♬♬ **Washington Court** (formerly the Sheraton Grand; dwntwn), 525 New Jersey Ave. NW, DC 20001 (202/628-2100; toll free 800/321-3010). 243 rms, A/C, color TV, in-rm movies. AE, CB, DC, MC, V. Valet parking $10, rest. (Krupin's Signature Room), coffee shop, bar, 24-hr. rm svce, concierge, free dwntwn limo, free crib. *Note:* The newest of Capitol Hill's luxury hotels: an elegant, modern 15-story building w. a vast pink-marble lobby, waterfall, and indoor grdn in what is quickly becoming the conventional manner. Comfortable rms w. refrigerators. Very acceptable rest. serving American cuisine. Efficient svce. Business clientele. A block or two from the Capitol and Union Station. **VE**

Loews L'Enfant Plaza (nr. dwntwn), 480 L'Enfant Plaza SW, DC 20024 (202/484-1000; toll free, see Loews). 372 rms, A/C, color TV, in-rm movies. AE, CB, DC, MC, V. Valet parking $7, pool, two rests., bar, rm svce, disco, boutiques, concierge, free crib. *Note:* Successful essay in futurist architecture, occupying the top four floors of an ultramodern office complex w. underground shopping mall and direct subway access. Luxurious, comfortable rms w. minibars, most w. balconies. Inviting open-air pool on the 12th floor. Very good svce. A few blocks from the Mall and its museums. Business and group clientele. A good place to stay. **E–VE**

One Washington Circle (dwntwn), 1 Washington Circle NW, DC 20037 (202/872-1680; toll free 800/468-3532). 152 suites, A/C, color TV, in-rm movies. AE, CB, DC, MC, V. Valet parking $9, pool, rest., bar, rm svce, nightclub, concierge, free breakfast. *Note:* Modern, very comfortable hotel halfway between the White House and Georgetown. Suites only, spacious and w. kitchenettes and refrigerators (most w. balconies). Elegantly decorated and furnished. Irreproachable svce. Business clientele. Inviting little grdn. An excellent place to stay. **E–VE**

Vista International (dwntwn), 1400 M St. NW, DC 20005 (202/429-1700; toll free, see Hilton). 398 rms, A/C, color TV, in-rm movies. AE, CB, DC, MC, V. Valet parking $10, health club, sauna, two rests. (including American Harvest), three bars, 24-hr. rm svce, nightclub, concierge, free crib. *Note:* Inviting luxury hotel on the edge of the business district. Fine 14-story glass atrium with café and winter grdn. Very comfortable, well-equipped rms, the best looking out on the atrium. Good rest. serving modern American cuisine. Ultra-professional svce. Group and business clientele; two VIP floors. A very good place to stay. **E–VE**

Holiday Inn Capitol (dwntwn), 550 C St. SW, DC 20024 (202/479-4000; toll free, see Holiday Inns). 529 rms, A/C, color TV, in-rm movies. AE, CB, DC, MC, V. Parking $6, pool, rest. (Smithson's), bar, rm svce, nightclub, hrdrsr, boutiques, free crib. *Note:* Huge modern nine-floor motel a stone's throw from the Mall and the Capitol. A typical Holiday Inn, w. comfortable rms, efficient reception and svce. Group and convention clientele; interesting wknd discounts. Ideal base for visits to the Mall museums. **E–VE**

Washington Hotel (dwntwn), 515 15th St. (at Pennsylvania Ave.), NW DC 20004 (202/638-5900; toll free 800/424-9540). 350 rms, A/C, color TV, in-rm movies. AE, CB, DC, MC, V. Gar. $8, rest. (Two Continents), bar, rm svce, free crib. *Note:* Massive, aging luxury hotel now entirely renovated. Very well located 3 min. from the White House and 5 min. from the Mall and its museums. Spacious, comfortable rms; efficient svce. The top-floor bar has one of the finest views of the city. Interesting wknd discounts. A Washington landmark since 1918. **E–VE**

Quality Hotel–Capitol Hill (dwntwn), 415 New Jersey Ave. NW, DC 20001 (202/638-1616; toll free, see Quality Inns). 340 rms, A/C, color TV, in-rm movies. AE, CB, DC, MC, V. Free parking, pool, rest. (Coach and Parlor), bar, rm svce. *Note:* Comfortable 10-floor motel 5 min. from the Capitol and Union Station. Functional rms; efficient reception and svce; so-so rest. Caters to groups and conventions. Rooftop pool open in summer w. view of the city. **E**, but lower rates off-season.

Comfort Inn (dwntwn), 500 H St. NW, DC 20001 (202/289-5959; toll free 800/228-5150). 197 rms, A/C, color TV, in-rm movies. AE, CB, DC, MC, V. Parking $8, health club, sauna, rest., bar, valet svce, free crib. *Note:* New hotel very nr. the Convention Center. Comfortable, well-designed rms; efficient reception and svce. Business and group clientele. Interesting wknd discounts. **M–E**

Days Inn Connecticut Ave. (formerly the Best Western; nr. dwntwn), 4400 Connecticut Ave. NW, DC 20008 (202/244-5600; toll free, see Days Inns). 155 rms, A/C, color TV, in-rm movies. AE, CB, DC, MC, V. Free parking, pool, adj. rest., free breakfast. *Note:* Relatively elderly but comfortable motel, recently renovated. Spacious rms; smiling reception. Interesting family rates. Good value overall. 7 min. from dwntwn by subway. **M–E**

Hotel Bellevue (dwntwn), 15 E St. NW, DC 20001 (202/638-0900). 140 rms, A/C, color TV. AE, DC, MC, V. Free parking, rest. (Tiber Creek), bar, rm svce. *Note:* One of Washington's oldest hotels, but comfort and facilities are maintained at a very acceptable level. Entirely renovated rms, some w. refrigerators; inviting rest. and pub. Friendly svce. A stone's throw from the Capitol and Union Station. Good overall value; interesting wknd discounts. **M–E**

Tabard Inn (dwntwn), 1739 N St. NW, DC 20036 (202/785-1277). 42 rms, A/C, color TV, in-rm movies. MC, V. Street parking, rest., bar. *Note:* Charming little hotel, elderly and a touch bohemian (built in 1860, it's the oldest in Washington). Comfortable Victorian-style rms, some without private bathrooms. Four floors, no elevator. Clientele of artists and intellectuals, creating a very European atmosphere. Pleasant rest. and bar. 5 min. from the White House. Worthwhile wknd discounts. **M–E**

Harrington Hotel (dwntwn), 11th St. and E St. NW, DC 20004 (202/628-8410; toll free 800/424-8532). 308 rms, A/C, color TV. AE, CB, DC, MC, V. Free parking, coffee shop (Kitcheteria), bar. *Note:* Elderly but acceptable grand hotel in a fast-improving neighborhood nr. the Mall and the White House, a few blocks from Pennsylvania Ave. Very commendable standard of comfort. Group clientele. Very good value. **I–M**

Windsor Park (nr. dwntwn), 2116 Kalorama Rd. NW, DC 20008 (201/483-7700). 43 rms; A/C, color TV. MC, V. On-street parking. *Note:* A good deal for the budget traveler in the Embassy Row area. Spare, clean rms, all w. private bath and small refrirator. Short walk to zoo and metro. Very good value. **I**

Airport Accommodations

Ramada Renaissance Dulles Airport (vic.), 13869 Park Center Rd., Herndon, VA 22071 (703/478-2900; toll free, see Ramada Inns). 301 rms, A/C, cable color TV. AE, CB, DC, MC, V. Free valet parking, two pools, tennis court, health club, sauna, rest., coffee shop, bars, 24-hr. rm svce, disco, hrdrsr, free crib. *Note:* Luxurious, modern airport hotel 2 min. from the terminal (free shuttle). Spacious, well-equipped rms w. refrigerators. Comprehensive facilities. Efficient reception and svce. Ideal for a stopover between flights. Business clientele; two VIP floors. 40 min. from dwntwn. **E–VE**

Stouffer Concourse (vic.), 2399 Jefferson Davis Hwy., Arlington, VA 22202 (703/979-6800; toll free, see Stouffer). 388 rms, A/C, color TV, in-rm movies. AE, CB, DC, MC, V. Free parking, pool, health club, sauna, two rests. (including Ondine), two bars, 24-hr. rm svce, nightclub, concierge, free crib. *Note:* Uninspired modern 12-floor tower overwhelmed in a sea of glass and concrete by the office buildings of Crystal City. Fortunately the interior is more attractive, w. spacious, very comfortable rms. Efficient multilingual svce. Group and business clientele; two VIP floors; free shuttle to the National Airport terminal 5 min. away; 15 min. from dwntwn. **E–VE**

🏠 **Econo Lodge Arlington** (vic.), 2485 S. Glebe Rd., Arlington,
VA 22206 (703/979-4100; toll free 800/446-6900). 163
rms, A/C, color TV, in-rm movies. AE, MC, V. Free parking, pool, rest., bar,
valet svce, free crib. *Note:* Typical suburban motel 5 min. from National Airport.
Rms very large; functional comforts; reception w. a smile. Free shuttle to National Airport, the Pentagon, and nearby subway station. Good value overall. Group
clientele. **I–M**

YMCAs/Youth Hostels
International Guest House (nr. dwntwn), 1441 Kennedy St. NW, DC
20011 (202/726-5808). Priority given to visitors from abroad. Operated by the
Mennonite church, w. the lowest rates in Washington. Very acceptable comfort.
International Hostel (dwntwn), 1009 11th St. NW, DC 20001 (202/737-2333). 250 rms. Youth hostel open to members and nonmembers. Very central.

RESTAURANTS
A Note on Restaurant Prices: Washington restaurant prices, per person,
excluding drinks and service charges, are coded as follows: **VE**, Very Expensive
($60 and up); **E**, Expensive ($40–$60); **M**, Moderate ($25–$40); **I**, Inexpensive
($15–$25); **B**, Budget (up to $15).

Personal Favorites (in order of preference)
🍷🍷🍷🍷 **Jean Louis** (nr. dwntwn), in the Watergate Hotel (see "Accommodations," above) (298-4488). A/C. Dinner only,
Mon–Sat. AE, CB, DC, MC, V. J&T. *Specialties:* ragoût of cèpes (mushrooms),
pigeon-and-hare pâté blanquette of fish w. fresh mint, magret of duck w. honey
and dates, venison w. artichokes and basil in Chartreuse sauce, oyster fritters w.
truffle butter, fresh foie gras w. peaches, saddle of rabbit w. wild mushrooms. Remarkable desserts. Well-stocked but overpriced wine list. The menu is changed
periodically. *Note:* French-style nouvelle cuisine triumphant, under the command of one of the great chefs of his generation, the young Jean Louis Palladin,
whose prestigious La Table des Cordeliers in Le Gers, France, rated two stars in
Michelin. Sauces light as air, refined but simple preparation, the choicest (American) raw materials, perfect cooking, and elegant preparation combine to make his
cuisine a genuine masterpiece. Recently renovated decor in pastel tones, but surroundings somewhat claustrophobic. Service exemplary in all respects. Since
there are only 42 seats, you should reserve a number of days ahead. President
Reagan had his 70th birthday dinner here. One of the dozen best rests. in the
country, but prices to match. *French.* **VE**

🍷🍷🍷 **Twenty-one Federal** (dwntwn), 1736 L St. NW (331-9771).
A/C. Lunch Mon–Fri, dinner Mon–Sat; closed hols. AE,
MC, V. Jkt. *Specialties:* wild-mushroom ravioli, herb-crusted sole w. tomatoes
and chive butter, roast loin of pork w. chiles, black beans and corn pudding, carpaccio of swordfish, grilled oysters w. pancetta, fish chowder, mixed grill of
quail, duck sausage and sweetbreads, "palette" of chocolate desserts. Fairly
priced. *Note:* Named after its Nantucket forebear, this newcomer deserves its early success. The cuisine of chef and part-owner Bob Kinkead is modern American
cooking at its best. Luxurious decor w. exotic blond woods and a marble mosaic
floor. Frequented by journalists, lobbyists, lawyers, and politicians (Edward
Kennedy, John Chancellor, and Art Buchwald are regulars). Service is attentive
yet unobtrusive. Good wine list. Getting a table is a problem; book *at least* a day
or two ahead. *American.* **M–E**

☀🍷🍷🍷 **Occidental** (dwntwn), 1475 Pennsylvania Ave. NW (783-1475). A/C. Lunch/dinner daily (until 11:30pm); closed
hols. AE, CB, DC, MC, V. Jkt. *Specialties:* ravioli stuffed w. lump crab, grilled
Cornish hen w. chili butter, hamburgers, steak, pepper salmon, pheasant w. wild
mushrooms, rack of lamb w. garlic and cream, médaillon of beef w. shallots,

bread pudding in bourbon sauce, squash ice cream. Fine list of American wines. *Note:* Once known as "the restaurant where statesmen dine," as witness the 2,500-odd photographs of leading politicians on the walls, this turn-of-the-century rest., now splendidly restored, is a true Washington classic. In the Grill, on the ground floor, the food is agreeably bistro style; upstairs in the Restaurant it's a more sophisticated American nouvelle cuisine. Efficient, smiling svce. Resv. a must. An excellent place a stone's throw from the White House. *American.* **M** (Grill), **E** (Restaurant)

☆☆ **Primi Piatti** (dwntwn), 2013 I St. NW (223-3600). A/C. Lunch Mon–Fri, dinner Mon–Sat; closed hols. AE, CB, DC, MC, V. *Specialties:* mixed antipasti, inventive pizzas cooked over a wood fire, fresh homemade pasta, fritto misto, cacciuco di carne (meat stew), fish, chicken and meat broiled with polenta, chocolate terrine with strawberry coulis. Good list of Italian wines. *Note:* Here you will find no sophisticated fare or trendy sauces; the emphasis is rather on basic Italian dishes such as mixed hors d'oeuvres, various kinds of homemade pasta, broiled foods, and pizza, all of them nonetheless pleasing and tasty. Hence the name of this huge, modern, likable *trattoria* in the heart of dwntwn. Noisy, relaxed atmosphere; yuppie patrons; fashionable place. Resv. not honored so you'll have to wait, especially at lunchtime. *Italian.* **I–M**

☆☆ **Szechuan Restaurant** (dwntwn), 615 I St. NW, Chinatown (393-0130). A/C. Lunch/dinner daily. AE, MC, V. *Specialties:* hot-and-sour soup, duck smoked over tea leaves, fish rolls, shrimp Szechuan, sesame chicken, pork tripe w. chili and black mushrooms, sweet-hot crispy beef, Mongolian pork, lamb in garlic sauce. Dim sum at Sat and Sun lunch. *Note:* By general consent Washington's best Chinese rest., serving excellent Hunan and Szechuan food. Very popular with residents who frequent Chinatown, especially on wknds. Modernized, light-filled decor; service surly but efficient. Very good value; resv. advised. *Chinese.* **I**

☀☆☆ **Old Ebbitt Grill** (dwntwn), 675 15th St. NW (347-4800). A/C. Breakfast/lunch/dinner daily (until 1am). AE, DC, MC, V. *Specialties:* spaghetti w. four cheeses, cannelloni w. spinach, crabcake, hamburgers, baked scrod, broiled fish of the day, calves' liver w. onions, roast pork w. applesauce, chicken pot pie. Good homemade desserts. *Note:* Founded in 1856, the Old Ebbitt Grill is Washington's oldest saloon, though the present building, once a vaudeville theater, dates only from the turn of the century. The menu includes all the great American classics and some specialties as well. Pretty Victorian setting w. marble floors, Persian rugs, oak beams, and gas lamps; fine bar. Locally popular. Resv. a must. Favored by White House staffers at lunchtime. Same management as Clyde's (see below). *American.* **I–M**

☆☆ **Crisfield** (vic.), 8012 Georgia Ave., Silver Spring, Md. (301/589-1306). A/C. Lunch/dinner Tues–Sun; closed Dec 25 and the last week in Aug. No credit cards. *Specialties:* clam chowder, oysters on the half shell, crabcake, crab Imperial, catch of the day sautéed or stuffed with crabmeat. *Note:* Seafood rest. w. no mannerisms or affectations; the decor is period Formica, but the seafood is absolutely fresh and cooked to perfection. You can eat standing at the counter. Quick, efficient svce. Very popular locally; unfortunately no resv., so you'll have to wait. 25 min. from dwntwn. *Seafood.* **I–M**

☆ **Le Caprice** (nr. dwntwn), 2348 Wisconsin Ave. NW (337-3394). A/C. Lunch Tues–Fri, dinner Tues–Sun. AE, MC, V. *Specialties:* Provençal salad w. marinated goat cheese and artichoke, oysters and crab in puff pastry, salmon and trout w. champagne-cream sauce, duck breast w. potato croquettes and creamed mushrooms, beef à la ficelle, triple-chocolate terrine. The menu changes regularly. *Note:* Charming little French bistro offering ambitious fare at reasonable prices. Tiny and intimate decor w. outdoor dining in good weather. Svce young and congenial. Resv. suggested. Good value. *French.* **M**

♀ **El Caribe** (nr. dwntwn), 3288 M St. NW, Georgetown (338-
♈ 3121). A/C. Lunch/dinner daily; closed hols. AE, CB, DC,
MC, V. *Specialties:* empanadas, shrimp w. garlic, paella, zarzuela of seafood, roast
pork w. bananas, arroz con pollo, beef tongue w. tomato, squid stuffed w. ham,
South American dishes. *Note:* A real Georgetown "find": traditional Spanish
dishes and some very successful Latin American specialties. The setting is that of
a typical Spanish home w. its whitewashed walls and visible beams. Efficient svce;
very good value; resv. advised. *Latin American/Spanish.* **I–M**

♀ **Sushi Ko** (nr. dwntwn), 2309 Wisconsin Ave. NW, George-
♈ town (333-4187). A/C. Lunch Tues–Fri, dinner Tues–Sun.
AE, MC, V. *Specialties:* sushi, miso soup, shrimp tempura, teriyaki, yakitori.
Note: Many of the patrons of this small, unimaginatively decorated Japanese bistro come from the nearby Japanese Embassy; in spite of the downbeat setting it's
the best sushi bar in Washington; opened in 1979. Poker-faced svce; resv. advised. *Japanese.* **I**

Other Restaurants (from top bracket to budget)

♈♈♈ **Le Lion d'Or** (dwntwn), 1150 Connecticut Ave. NW, w. en-
♈♈♈ trance on 18th St. (296-7972). A/C. Lunch Mon–Fri, dinner
Mon–Sat; closed hols. AE, CB, DC, MC, V. J&T. *Specialties:* hot rabbit pâté,
sautéed morels w. fresh pasta (in season), ravioli of foie gras, soufflé of lobster,
civet of duck w. red wine, roast filet of lamb w. herbs, salmon in pastry shell,
game (in season), sweetbreads w. shallots. Very good desserts and soufflés; large
wine list at reasonable prices. Menu changes regularly. *Note:* The owner, Jean
Pierre Goyenvalle, is one of the most talented French chefs now working in the
U.S.; his splendid, very elaborate cuisine is a happy marriage of the traditional w.
nouvelle tendencies (such as shorter cooking times). The decor is elegantly old-
fashioned; the svce is courteous and polished. Can be noisy. Resv. a must, since
this is the favorite rest. of local VIPs. One of the best places to eat on the East
Coast. Free parking at dinner. *French.* **E–VE**

♈♈♈ **Morton's** (nr. dwntwn), 3251 Prospect St. NW, Georgetown
♈♈♈ (342-6258). A/C. Dinner only, nightly; closed hols. AE, CB,
DC, MC, V. Jkt. *Specialties:* wonderful aged beef, veal or lamb chops, catch of the
day, Maine lobster, so-so desserts. *Note:* This pillar of the local dining scene has
been acclaimed for a decade as Washington's best steakhouse. Steak, porterhouse,
and ribs of beef that are quite exceptional, but also fine fish and gigantic lobsters,
broiled to perfection. Comfortable, elegant London club-style interior, w. an interesting collection of paintings by LeRoy Neiman. Excellent svce, quick and efficient. No resv. after 7pm. Same management as the well-known Morton's in
Chicago. Rather noisy; a favorite w. local politicians and lobbyists. *Steak/
Seafood.* **E**

♈♈♈ **Vincenzo** (dwntwn), 1606 20th St. NW (667-0047). A/C.
♈♈♈ Lunch Mon–Fri, dinner Mon–Sat; closed hols. AE, CB, DC,
MC, V. Jkt. *Specialties:* linguine w. clams, fritto misto di mare (seafood mixed
grill), fresh homemade pasta w. crab, tripe Florentine style, rabbit chasseur (w.
white wine, mushrooms, and shallots), seafood stew, catch of the day. Desserts
and wine list both underwhelming. *Note:* The talented Vince MacDonald, who
long restricted himself to seafood, has now broadened his menu to include classic dishes from Tuscany—with no less happy results. The decor, involving whitewashed walls and tiled floor, is on the austere side, but the svce is ultra-
professional; business clientele and many regulars. The best place in Washington
for modern Italian cuisine; resv. a must. *Italian/Seafood.* **E**

♈♈♈ **McPherson Grill** (dwntwn), 950 15th St. NW (638-0950).
♈♈♈ A/C. Lunch Mon–Fri, dinner Mon–Sat. AE, CB, DC, MC,
V. Jkt. *Specialties:* oyster cream stew, corn-tortilla napoleon of cured salmon w.
chive cream, pork chop w. smoky tomato relish, round-bone lamb steak w. oregano, crumbled goat cheese and black olives, swordfish steak w. butter sauce of

green onions and dill, chicken w. cumin and ancho chiles, anise-crust lemon-meringue pie. Fine, moderately priced list of California wines. *Note:* A rest. for elegant, sophisticated modern American food in an attractive black-and-white deco setting. The cuisine is light and on a consistently high level of inspiration; svce is attentive and distinguished. A good place, very near the White House. Resv. a must at lunch and advisable at dinner owing to the press of well-behaved yuppies. Same management as Occidental (see above). *American.* **M**

🍷🍷 **Galileo** (dwntwn), 1110 21st St. NW (293-7191). A/C. Lunch Mon–Fri, dinner Mon–Sat; closed hols. AE, CB, DC, MC, V. *Specialties:* olive focaccia, fettuccine w. pistachio and Gorgonzola cheese, risotto w. lobster and tomato sauce, ravioli, bollito misto (beef stew), grilled sweetbreads w. pancetta and wild mushrooms, veal chop w. rosemary, filets of venison w. green-peppercorn sauce and polenta, grilled grouper w. herbs and timbale of endive, braised beef w. Barolo sauce. Undistinguished desserts. Menu changes daily. Reasonable wine list. *Note:* Washington's best Italian *nuova cucina;* young chef Roberto Donna is a maestro of airy sauces and innovative taste combinations. Has moved recently to more spacious, less noisy quarters; svce usually efficient but can lapse into chaos. Resv. must be made one or more days ahead, since this place is favored by those in-the-know. Same management as Primi Piatti (see above). Valet parking. *Italian.* **M**

🍷🍷🍷 **Germaine's** (nr. dwntwn), 2400 Wisconsin Ave. NW (965-1185). A/C. Lunch Mon–Fri, dinner nightly; closed Jan 1, Dec 25. AE, CB, DC, MC, V. Jkt. *Specialties:* Vietnamese spring rolls, Korean kimchi, Thai beef w. basil, Indonesian sate, Japanese chicken teriyaki, Peking duck. Good wine list. *Note:* Germaine Swanson, the very talented Vietnamese who created this enormously popular rest., offers you a tasty cross-section of Far Eastern cuisines: Vietnamese, Korean, Chinese, Japanese, Thai, and more. Some of her dishes, like her "pine cone fish," or the scallop salad w. pine nuts, have already become classics. Light-filled, elegant setting w. a huge skylight. Flawless svce. An excellent place to eat. Resv. advised. *Far Eastern.* **M**

🍷🍷 **Joe and Mo's** (dwntwn), 1211 Connecticut Ave. NW (659-1211). A/C. Breakfast/lunch Mon–Fri, dinner Mon–Sat; closed hols. AE, CB, DC, MC, V. Jkt. *Specialties:* crabcakes, steak, veal chops, roast beef, filet mignon, rack of lamb, broiled catch of the day. *Note:* A Washington landmark beloved of businesspeople, reporters, and politicians, especially for the excellent breakfast and at lunchtime. Top-quality meat and fish; the roast beef is the best in town. Classic steakhouse decor and atmosphere; courteous, efficient svce. Resv. advised at lunch. Valet parking. *Steak.* **M**

🍷🍷 **Tony & Joe's Seafood Place** (nr. dwntwn), 3000 K St. NW, Georgetown (944-4545). A/C. Lunch/dinner daily. AE, CB, DC, MC, V. Jkt. *Specialties:* oysters on the half shell or baked, linguine w. clam sauce, barbecued shrimp Cajun style, seafood stew, clams Casino, crab Imperial, grilled salmon steak w. basil butter, broiled or fried catch of the day, chocolate pudding. Limited but reasonably priced wine list. *Note:* Though shellfish-rich Chesapeake Bay is so nr., you can count on the fingers of one hand the seafood rests. in Washington that deserve to be so styled; Tony & Joe's, in the ornate Washington Harbor complex, is one of them. The rest. is new, w. enormous picture windows and a view across the Potomac; its seafood is absolutely fresh, skillfully but simply prepared. Very good svce. Resv. strongly advised; a fine place. *Seafood.* **M**

🍷 **Bombay Palace** (dwntwn), 1835 K St. NW (331-0111). A/C. Lunch/dinner daily. AE, CB, DC, MC, V. *Specialties:* samosas, chicken tikka, tandoori prawns, chicken tandoori, curries, ghosh vindaloo (lamb stew). So-so desserts and wine list. *Note:* Elegance prevails; the blue-green walls are liberally hung with artworks, the lighting is indirect, the seats luxurious. The refined cuisine of this first-class Indian rest. is no less elegant, and will particularly delight those who prefer their exoticism subdued to the American taste. Remarkably attentive svce; business crowd at lunch, tourists at dinner. Resv. advisable; a fine place to eat. *Indian.* **I–M**

Café Berlin (dwntwn), 322 Massachusetts Ave. NE (543-7656). A/C. Lunch Mon–Fri, dinner daily, brunch Sun; closed hols. AE, CB, DC, MC, V. *Specialties:* asparagus vinaigrette w. Westphalian ham, pickled herring, goulash, roast smoked pork, wienerschnitzel, sauerbraten, Black Forest cake, apfel strudel. Short but honorable wine list. *Note:* This relative newcomer, an inviting café w. open terrace in fine weather, quickly established itself (admittedly against very limited competition) as Washington's best German rest. The wienerschnitzel alone is enough to justify a visit. Friendly, hard-working svce; attracts many politicians from nearby Capitol Hill. No resv. accepted for the terrace. *German.* **I–M**

La Colline (dwntwn), 400 N. Capitol St. NW (737-0400). A/C. Breakfast/lunch Mon–Fri, dinner Mon–Sat; closed hols. AE, CB, DC, MC, V. Jkt. *Specialties:* smoked salmon house style, fresh foie gras, gratin of crayfish, salmon w. beurre blanc and baby turnips, braised sweetbreads w. zucchini, parsleyed ham, bouillabaisse, breast of duck w. blackcurrant; skip desserts. Good wine list at reasonable prices. *Note:* The likable, bearded, 40-ish chef Robert Greault has worked a miracle: he serves excellent, elegant, varied bistro food at half the prices charged by other French rests. of the same caliber. Huge, modern, comfortable dining rm; ultra-professional svce, but a bit overtaxed. Very popular w. the locals, so resv. advised. At the foot of Capitol Hill near Union Station. *French.* **I–M**

Nora (nr. dwntwn), 2132 Florida Ave. NW (462-5143). A/C. Dinner only, Mon–Sat; closed hols. MC, V. *Specialties:* gravlax (pickled salmon w. dill), roast sweet peppers w. goat cheese, grilled pork chop w. tarragon, soft-shelled crabs w. basil, roast chicken w. mustard-cream sauce, smoked trout w. horseradish sauce. Very good homemade desserts. Menu changes regularly. Good wine list at reasonable prices. *Note:* Charming little bistro serving American nouvelle cuisine; only the highest-grade meat, poultry, and fish and the freshest of farm vegetables are used, and these are simply but skillfully prepared. Cool, pleasant rustic setting w. antique furniture and quilts worthy of a museum of American folk art. Ultra-professional svce. Locally popular; you must make resv. A good place to go. *American.* **I–M**

Bacchus (dwntwn), 1827 Jefferson Pl. NW (785-0734). A/C. Lunch Mon–Fri, dinner Mon–Sat; closed hols. AE, MC, V. *Specialties:* mezze (hors d'oeuvres), bel lahm (lamb stew w. yogurt), stuffed eggplant w. pomegranate sauce, chicken or lamb or fish kebab, chicken rice pilaf, kafta mechwi (broiled chopped beef w. pine-nut rice), malfouf mahchi (cabbage stuffed w. meat), Oriental pastry. Modest wine list. *Note:* The best place in Washington for authentic Lebanese and Middle Eastern cuisine. Conventional modern setting; considerate svce. Resv. advised. Excellent value; another branch is at 7945 Norfolk Ave., Bethesda, Md. (301/657-1722). *Middle Eastern.* **I**

China Inn (dwntwn), 631 H St. NW, Chinatown (842-0909). A/C. Lunch/dinner daily (until 3am). AE, MC, V. *Specialties:* spiced shrimps, clams w. black-bean sauce, Cantonese roast duck, "fish dipped in boiling water w. spices," roast pork Chow Mai Fun, lemon chicken, steamed sea bass w. ginger. So-so desserts. *Note:* A Chinatown classic for more than half a century, serving good Cantonese food at prices very easy on the wallet. Recently modernized and enlarged. Friendly svce (unusual for a Chinese rest.). Locally popular; very good value. *Chinese.* **I**

Enriqueta's (nr. dwntwn), 2811 M St. NW, Georgetown (338-7772). A/C. Lunch Mon–Fri, dinner nightly; closed hols. AE, CB, DC, MC, V. *Specialties:* tacos, enchiladas verdes, tamales, mussels w. chili, stuffed green pepper, mole poblano (turkey in chocolate sauce), shrimp w. coriander, chicken w. tomatillo sauce, cremitas. *Note:* Enriqueta's dishes have the true Mexican flavor; the setting, too, is as lively, noisy, and colorfully decorated as you could hope for south of the Rio Grande. Diligent svce. Resv. are advised; dinner only. *Mexican.* I

♀ **Meskerem** (dwntwn), 2434 18th St. NW (462-4100). A/C.
🍷 Lunch Wed and Sat–Sun, dinner daily (until midnight). AE, CB, DC, MC, V. *Specialties:* kebabs, sambusas, shrimp wat (stew), kifto (highly seasoned steak tartare), tibbs (beef or lamb sautéed w. onion and sweet pepper), vegetarian dishes. Ho-hum desserts; skimpy wine list. *Note:* Delicious stews wrapped in spicy, flavorful pancakes (injera) and eaten without knives or forks are the staple at this unusual and exotic Ethiopian rest. Beef, lamb, or chicken stews —highly seasoned (wats) or somewhat less explosive (alechas)—should be washed down w. pitchers of beer. The setting, in contrast to Washington's other Ethiopian rests., is elegant and almost luxurious, particularly on the third (top) floor with its stained-glass skylight. Uncommonly courteous svce. Locally popular; resv. advisable. *Ethiopian.* I

♀ **The American Café** (dwntwn), 227 Massachusetts Ave. NE
🍷 (547-8500). A/C. Lunch/dinner daily (till 1am). AE, MC, V. *Specialties:* excellent sandwiches and homemade soups, pizza, quiches, salads, sesame pasta, tarragon chicken, food broiled over mesquite wood, chili, daily specials. *Note:* In this modern, agreeable setting you'll enjoy a late supper or a lunch on the run. Interesting specialty salads. Young, trendy clientele. A stone's throw from the Capitol and Union Station. Relaxed svce. Very good value. Other locations: 1211 Wisconsin Ave. NW (337-3606) and 1300 F St. NW (737-5153). *American.* I

♀ **Clyde's** (nr. dwntwn), 3236 M St. NW (333-9180). A/C.
🍷 Lunch/dinner daily (until 1am), brunch Sat–Sun. AE, CB, DC, MC, V. *Specialties:* sandwiches, hamburgers, omelets, steak tartare, specialty salads, broiled foods, barbecued spareribs. *Note:* Once favored by Washington's gilded youth, this likable New York–style saloon still has a devoted following, especially among visitors. Good hamburgers (except when they're overcooked). Lovely greenhouse setting in the back dining room. Often crowded and noisy; relaxed atmosphere; svce disorganized but good-humored. A landmark in Washington for more than 20 years. *American.* **B–I**

Restaurants in the Vicinity

☼🍷♀♀♀ **L'Auberge Chez François** (vic.), 332 Springvale Rd. (Va.
🍾🍾🍾 674), Great Falls, Va. (703/759-3800). A/C. Dinner only, Tues–Sun; closed hols. AE, MC, V. Jkt. *Specialties:* quiche, salmon soufflé, Alsatian choucroute, sautéed kidneys, filet of lamb w. tarragon, red snapper in pastry shell, truffled sweetbreads, duckling bigarade, navarin of seafood, coq au riesling. Very good homemade ice cream and tarts. Fine list of Alsatian wines. Menu changes regularly. *Note:* The food and the atmosphere are those of a deluxe inn in France. Some country dishes (tripe, homemade pâté de campagne), and some more sophisticated (salmon soufflé). Charming rustic decor w. open-air dining in summer; irreproachable svce; resv. a must. 35 min. from dwntwn. A fine place. *French.* **M–E**

☼🍷♀ **Evans Farm Inn** (vic.), 1696 Chain Bridge Rd. (Va. 123),
🍾 McLean, Va. (703/356-8000). A/C. Lunch/dinner daily; closed Dec 25. AE, CB, DC, MC, V. *Specialties:* roast beef, barbecued chicken, Smithfield ham, barbecued spareribs, roast duckling, catch of the day. *Note:* Charming Colonial-style inn 30 min. by car from Washington. The dining rms overlook the grdn and herb grdn where the farm's vegetables and herbs are grown (ask to be seated in the dining rm nr. the entrance, w. its big stone hearth). Open-

air meals in summer. Country food harking back to traditional Virginia recipes; family clientele. Usually crowded on wknds. Waiters in 18th-century costume. *American.* I–M

Cafeterias/Specialty Spots

☀ **Au Pied de Cochon** (nr. dwntwn), 1335 Wisconsin Ave. NW, Georgetown (333-5440). A/C. Breakfast/lunch/dinner daily (open around the clock). AE, MC, V. *Specialties:* omelets, rillettes, cold cuts, onion soup, quiches, pig's trotters, shallot steak, beef bourguignon, coq au vin, etc. *Note:* Picturesque French bistro w. a terrace, in the heart of Georgetown. Svce on the brusque side, but an entertaining place. Sturdy portions. Usually crowded; good value.

National Gallery Terrace Café (dwntwn), Constitution Ave. and 4th St. NW (347-9401). A/C. Lunch only, daily (till 4:30pm). No credit cards. *Specialties:* sandwiches, soup, quiches. *Note:* Ultramodern, inviting museum cafeteria overlooking the east wing atrium; very acceptable food.

Sholl's Colonial Cafeteria (dwntwn), 1990 K St. NW in Esplanade Mall (296-3065). A/C. Lunch/dinner Mon–Sat (until 8pm); closed Jan 1, Dec 25. No credit cards. *Specialties:* calves' liver w. onions, spaghetti, roast chicken, daily specials, homemade pastry. *Note:* A popular cafeteria, much appreciated by Washingtonians. Offers excellent value; usually crowded at lunch. No alcoholic beverages. A Washington landmark since 1928.

Where to Eat What in Washington

American: The American Café (p. 276), Clyde's (p. 276), Evans Farm Inn (p. 276), McPherson Grill (p. 273), Nora (p. 275), Occidental (p. 271), Old Ebbitt Grill (p. 272), Twenty-one Federal (p. 271)

Cafeterias/Specialty Spots: Au Pied de Cochon (p. 277), National Gallery Terrace Café (p. 277), Sholl's Colonial Cafeteria (p. 277)

Chinese: China Inn (p. 275), Szechuan Restaurant (p. 272)

Ethiopian: Meskerem (p. 276)

French: L'Auberge Chez François (p. 276), Le Caprice (p. 272), La Colline (p. 275), Jean Louis (p. 271), Le Lion d'Or (p. 273)

German: Café Berlin (p. 275)

Indian: Bombay Palace (p. 275)

Italian: Galileo (p. 274), Primi Piatti (p. 272), Vincenzo (p. 273)

Japanese: Sushi Ko (p. 273)

Latin American: El Caribe (p. 273)

Mexican: Enriqueta's (p. 276)

Middle Eastern: Bacchus (p. 275), Dar Es Salam (p. 274)

Asian: Germaine's (p. 274)

Seafood: Crisfield (p. 272), Tony & Joe's Seafood Place (p. 274)

Steak: Joe and Mo's (p. 274), Morton's (p. 273)

BARS & NIGHTCLUBS

Bayou (nr. dwntwn), 3135 K St. at Wisconsin Ave. NW, Georgetown (333-2897): Live rock and New Wave; youthful, relaxed ambience. Open nightly.

The Birchmere (vic.), 3901 Mt. Vernon Ave., Alexandria, Va. (703/549-5919): One of the best clubs in the country for folk and bluegrass; the biggest names appear here. Open Tues–Sat.

Blues Alley (nr. dwntwn), on the alley behind 1073 Wisconsin Ave. NW, Georgetown (337-4141). The oldest jazz club in Washington, and still the best. All the big names from Dizzy Gillespie to Chick Corea and McCoy Tyner. Also acceptable Créole rest. Open nightly; two or three shows an evening.

Brickskeller (nr. dwntwn), 1523 22nd St. NW (293-1885). Very popular bar serving 500 varieties of domestic and imported beer; also rest. (so-so). Usually crowded. Open nightly until 2am.

Chelsea's (nr. dwntwn), 1055 Thomas Jefferson St. NW, Georgetown (298-8222). Fashionable disco with live music, Latin rhythms. Open Tues–Sun.

Comedy Café (dwntwn), 1520 K St. NW (638-5653). Oldest and best-known comedy club in Washington, presenting all the big names and young local talent as well. Open Thurs–Sat; resv. advised.

Fifth Column (dwntwn), 915 F St. NW (393-3632): Luxurious disco in a former branch bank. Marble dance floor, video music, and spectacular laser shows. Also acceptable rest. and art gallery. Clientele on the smart side. Open Tues–Sat.

Hard Rock Café (dwntwn), 999 E St. NW (737-7625). Local offspring of the famed London rock joint. The main downstairs bar is shaped like a gigantic piano. Congenial but very noisy atmosphere. Also rest. Directly across the street from FBI headquarters.

Kilimanjaro (dwntwn), 1724 California St. NW (328-3838). Washington's hottest "world music" club, in the Adams Morgan area, with live African, reggae, and calypso music. One of the few clubs in town popular with both Caucasians and African Americans. Open nightly.

The Ritz (dwntwn), 919 E St. NW (638-2582). New multiplex nightclub in dwntwn Washington, with five music spots on three floors. Very "in" atmosphere. Worth a detour. Open Wed–Sat.

F. Scott's (nr. dwntwn), 1232 36th St. NW, Georgetown (342-0009). Well-known, congenial bar frequented by students from nearby Georgetown U. and intellectuals. Pretty art nouveau decor. Also undistinguished rest. Open nightly.

Tracks (nr. dwntwn), 1111 1st St. SE (488-3320). The fashionable gay club, drawing a very mixed crowd. Disco w. live music. Lots of action. Open nightly (until 6am Fri–Sat).

NEARBY EXCURSIONS

ALEXANDRIA, VA. (7 mi./11km south on George Washington Memorial Pkwy. and Washington St.; area code 703): Founded in the mid-18th century by Scottish merchants, this appealing little Colonial town on the Potomac has not kept pace with its mighty neighbor, Washington. With its cobbled streets, traditional streetlamps, and enchanting old houses, ※�&& **Old Town Alexandria,** around King St. and Fairfax St., looks like a print from an old British book. No visit to Washington is complete without a pilgrimage to Mount Vernon (see below) and the other historic spots in Alexandria which are associated with the life of George Washington: **Gadsby's Tavern,** 134 N. Royal St. (838-4242), open Tues–Sun; **Carlyle House,** 121 N. Fairfax St. (549-2997), open Tues–Sun; the **Stabler-Leadbeater Apothecary Shop,** 105 S. Fairfax St. (836-3713), open Mon–Sat; the **Lee-Fendall House,** 614 Oronoco St. (548-1789), open Tues–Sun; **Old Presbyterian Meeting House,** with the tomb of the Unknown Soldier of the War of Independence, 321 S. Fairfax St. (549-6670), open Mon–Sat; and **Christ Church,** 118 N. Washington St. (549-1450), open daily.

For other historic buildings in Alexandria, inquire at the **Alexandria Tourist Council,** itself quartered in the oldest house in town, **Ramsay House** (ca. 1724), 221 King St. (838-4200), open daily. Also see **Robert E. Lee's boyhood home,** 607 Oronoco St. (548-8454), open daily.

See also the ※�& **George Washington Masonic National Memorial,** an unusual Masonic temple with a 333-ft. (102m) tower copied from the famous Pharos (lighthouse) of Alexandria, one of the seven wonders of antiquity, with an observation platform at the top. The memorial displays a large collection of

Washington artifacts, including the family Bible and the clock that was stopped at the time of Washington's death. It's at Shooter's Hill, W. King St. and Russell Rd. (683-2007), open daily, and well worth the side trip. If you like handcrafts shops you should stop at the **Torpedo Factory Arts Center**, 105 N. Union St. (703/838-4565). Now a complex for more than 200 professional artists—painters, potters, weavers, sculptors, jewelers, and stained-glass artists—this factory was a munitions-manufacturing center during both World Wars. Open daily.

Where to Eat

La Bergerie, 218 N. Lee St. (683-1007). Lunch/dinner Mon–Sat. AE, CB, DC, MC, V. Excellent Basque food in a charming antique setting. **I–M**

Taverna Cretekou, 818 King St. (548-8688). Lunch/dinner Tues–Sun. AE, CB, DC, MC, V. The best Greek rest. in the Washington, D.C., area. **I–M**

ANNAPOLIS, MD. (31 mi./50km east on U.S. 50; area code 301): Briefly the capital of the U.S. (Congress met here from November 26, 1783, to August 13, 1784), and capital of Maryland since 1695, this lovely 300-year-old harbor town is best known today as the home of the U.S. Naval Academy. It offers a wide range of diversions to the visitor.

You can **cruise the harbor** and the Severn River aboard the *Harbor Queen*, boarding at City Dock at the foot of Main St. (268-7600), daily from Memorial Day to Labor Day.

You can visit the **State House** (1772–79), the oldest legislative building still in use in the country, at State Circle (974-3400), open daily. Here, in 1783, George Washington laid down his office as commander-in-chief of the Continental Army. Here, too, in 1784, the Treaty of Paris, which had been signed at Versailles the previous year, was ratified, ending the War of Independence.

Stroll among the beautifully restored old houses of Cornhill St., Maryland Ave., and Prince George St.: the **Hammond-Harwood House, Chase Lloyd House, William Paca House,** and so on.

Watch a noon parade of uniformed midshipmen, admire the model sailing ships at the maritime museum, or meditate before the ※ **tomb of John Paul Jones** in the chapel of the **U.S. Naval Academy** at the foot of King George St. (263-6933). There are conducted tours daily Mar–Thanksgiving; more than a million visitors come here annually. Rediscover the 18th century in an old tavern near the docks.

For further information, contact the **State House Visitor Center,** State Circle (974-3400), open daily. Don't fail to visit Annapolis.

Where to Eat

Harbor House, 97 Prince George St. (268-4118). Lunch/dinner daily. AE, MC, V. Successful conversion of an old warehouse looking out over the harbor, w. terrace for fine days. Very good fish and seafood. **I**

Treaty of Paris (Maryland Inn), Church Circle at Main St. (263-2641). Lunch/dinner daily. AE, CB, DC, MC, V. Historic (1776) inn serving excellent traditional food. **I**

DULLES INTERNATIONAL AIRPORT (in Chantilly, Va., 26 mi./42km west via the George Washington Memorial Pkwy., I-495, and Dulles Airport Rd.) (703/471-7838): Lovers of architecture will appreciate the pure lines of the terminal designed in 1962 by the great Finnish-American architect Eero Saarinen. This was the first U.S. airport specifically intended for the jet age, and its roof, in-curved like a hammock and secured by cables, has served as a model for many other buildings around the world. The airport is named after John Foster Dulles, President Eisenhower's much-traveled secretary of state. Worth seeing.

Not far from Saarinen's building, on the road leading to the airport, take a look at the astonishing inverted pyramid, in three-colored glass, of the 🔺🔺 **Center for Innovative Technology,** designed by the well-known Miami team of Bernardo Fort-Brescia and Laurinda Spear. The CIT tower is beyond a doubt the most original contemporary building in Washington—a city not greatly endowed with innovative architecture.

☀🔔🔔 **FREDERICKSBURG, VA.** (50 mi./80km south on I-95; area code 703): Halfway between Washington and Richmond, the capital of Virginia, this charming vestige of the past occupies a proud place in American history. Capt. John Smith, founder of Jamestown, the first permanent British settlement on the continent, visited the site in 1608. George Washington spent his childhood here, James Madison practiced law here before going on to become the fifth president of the U.S., and some of the bloodiest battles of the Civil War were fought here, as the town changed hands seven times between 1862 and 1864.

Houses that have seen the passage of one or two centuries line Charles St. and Caroline St. in the heart of the historic district. Among them are: the **Rising Sun Tavern,** 1306 Caroline St. (371-1494), open daily, which was built in 1760 by George Washington's youngest brother, Charles; the **Mary Washington House,** 1200 Charles St. (373-1569), open daily, which George Washington presented to his mother in 1772 and where she lived until her death; the **James Monroe Museum,** 908 Charles St. (373-8426), open daily, where the future president lived; the **Hugh Mercer Apothecary Shop,** 1020 Caroline St. (371-3486), open daily, with its authentic 18th-century interior; and **Kenmore,** 1201 Washington Ave. (373-3381), open daily, one of Virginia's loveliest historic homes, built in 1752 by Col. Fielding Lewis, George Washington's brother-in-law.

Don't fail to visit Fredericksburg.

☀🔔🔔 **MOUNT VERNON** (15 mi./25km south on the George Washington Memorial Pkwy. and Mount Vernon Memorial Hwy.) (703/780-2000): This splendid Colonial mansion following a design by Washington overlooks the Potomac, and is where George Washington died on December 14, 1799. The main building, with its white, colonnaded Georgian facade turned to the river, was begun in 1754 on land that had been in the family since 1674. Washington lived here as a planter with his wife, the former Martha Custis, for 15 years, from 1759 until 1775 when he became commander-in-chief of the Continental Army. Returning in 1783, he continued to enlarge the house and its gardens. After 8 years as president he retired here finally in 1797 and remained until his death 2 years later. After the death of Martha in 1802, Mount Vernon remained in the Washington family until 1858, when it was purchased, along with 198 acres (80ha), by the Mount Vernon Ladies Association, carefully restored, and operated as a national memorial.

In part built by Washington himself, the main block has 19 rooms, of which the most interesting are the president's library and the room where he died. Very beautiful original furniture. A feature of the main reception room is the key to the Bastille, a gift from Lafayette. A little apart are the kitchen, the workers' and slaves' quarters, and the Washington family vault with the caskets of George and Martha Washington.

Drawing a million people a year, this is one of the most-visited places in the U.S.; long waiting lines on weekends and in summer. The access road is a scenic highway along the river. Open daily; don't miss it.

🔔 **NASA–GODDARD SPACE FLIGHT CENTER & MUSEUM** (Baltimore Pkwy., Exit 22, Greenbelt, Md.)

WASHINGTON, D.C.,
AND ENVIRONS

(301/286-8101): The whole gamut of NASA rockets, satellites, and space capsules. Temporary exhibitions illustrating the history of NASA, and movies on the conquest of space. In addition to displaying real rockets, the center launches model rockets at 1:30pm on the first and third Sun of the month. Fascinating. 25 min. from dwntwn along New York Ave., U.S. 50E, and Baltimore Pkwy. North. Open Wed–Sun.

☼🕶🔭 NATIONAL AIR & SPACE MUSEUM–PAUL E. GARBER FACILITY (Old Silver Hill Rd., Suitland, Md.):

The restoration workshop and annex of the famous museum in dwntwn Washington. A hundred craft, old (the 1914 Blériot Type XI) and new (the cruise missile) are displayed side by side with machines in process of restoration like the *Enola Gay,* from which the atom bomb was dropped on Hiroshima.

An absolute must for aviation buffs, 30 min. from dwntwn along Independence Ave., Pennsylvania Ave. SE, and Old Silver Hill Rd. Guided tours by appointment only; resv. should be made at least 2 weeks ahead with the Tour Scheduler at the dwntwn museum (202/357-1400).

☼🔭 WOODLAWN PLANTATION (18 mi./29km south via

George Washington Memorial Pkwy. and Mount Vernon Memorial Hwy.) (703/780-4000): Splendid home adjoining Mount Vernon, built between 1800 and 1805 by William Thornton, one of the architects of the Capitol, on land given by George Washington to his adopted daughter as a wedding present. The mansion is a typical Virginia plantation house.

Also on the grounds is the **Pope-Leighey House,** designed by the great Frank Lloyd Wright; this cypress wood, brick, and glass structure was originally erected at Falls Church, Va., in 1940 and was moved to its present location in 1964. It's well worth going out of your way to visit these two very dissimilar houses.

Woodlawn Plantation is open daily; Pope-Leighey House, daily Mar–Dec, and wknds only Jan–Feb.

FARTHER AFIELD

☼🕶🔭 SHENANDOAH NATIONAL PARK: (76 mi./122km

west on I-66 to Front Royal at the north entrance to the park): This magnificent wooded park covering 300 sq. mi. (777km²) is 80 mi. (129km) long but only 2–13 mi. (3–21km) wide; encompassing the crests of the **Blue Ridge Mountains,** it is traversed from end to end by one of the most spectacular scenic highways in the country, ☼ **Skyline Drive.** The Blue Ridge Mountains, the easternmost ridge of the Appalachians, owe their name to the veil of bluish mist that usually clings to most of the peaks. Shenandoah Park (it means "daughter of the stars" in the local Native American tongue), which averages about 2,000 ft. (610m) above sea level, is almost entirely covered with a thick forest of conifers, oaks, and birches, which shelter a numerous and varied wildlife including brown bears, deer, foxes, lynx, and more than 200 species of birds. Along the Skyline Drive more than 75 overlooks have been constructed, allowing you views all the way west to the Shenandoah Valley or east to the Piedmont plateau.

Skyline Drive is continued to the south by an equally spectacular mountain road, the **Blue Ridge Parkway,** which is the best route to **Great Smoky Mountains National Park,** 750 mi. (1,200km) to the south (see Chapter 13 on Nashville).

Shenandoah Park and the neighboring **George Washington Forest** are at their best in spring, and even more at the peak of the fall foliage display. They also boast some of the finest caves on the East Coast: **Skyline Caverns,** near Front Royal; ☀ **Luray Caverns** and **Endless Caverns,** near Luray; and **Grand Caverns,** near Grottoes.

☀ **Natural bridge,** south of Lexington, is also worth a detour. A limestone arch 215 ft. (66m) high and 65 million years old, it has been termed "one of the Seven Wonders of the New World."

The park is open year round. For information, contact the Superintendent, Rte. 4, Box 348, Luray, VA 22835 (703/999-2229). A must for nature lovers.

Some 25 mi. (40km) east of Shenandoah Park, don't fail to visit ☀ 🔔🔔 **Monticello,** on Va. 53 near Charlottesville (804/295-8181). The luxurious estate of Thomas Jefferson, third president of the U.S., is one of the finest surviving examples of 18th-century American architecture, spectacularly situated on a height of land. Designed and built by Jefferson over a period of 40 years. Period furniture and decoration. The tomb of Thomas Jefferson is in the nearby family graveyard. Open daily; don't miss it.

Where to Stay and Eat En Route

IN CHARLOTTESVILLE ☀ 🍴🍴🍴 **Boar's Head Inn,** Ivy Rd. (U.S. 250), Charlottesville, VA 22905 (804/296-2181). 175 rms. Delightful country inn built around an 1834 grain-mill. Remarkable comfort and facilities. **M–E**

IN NEW MARKET 🍴 **Shenvalee,** U.S. 11, New Market, VA 22844 (703/740-3181), half a mile south of town. 42 rms. Inviting, comfortable motel on 200 acres (80ha) of park and grdn. Tennis and golf. Excellent value. **I–M**

IN WASHINGTON, VA. ☀🍴🍴🍴🍴 **Inn at Little Washington,** Middle St. and Main St., Washington, VA 22747 (703/675-3800). Dinner only, Wed–Mon. Modern, delicate, inventive cuisine and svce of the highest order in a plush English-inn setting. Some of the best food in the entire region, as well as 10 luxuriously comfortable rms. Resv. a must, well in advance. **E–VE**

🔔🔔 **EASTERN SHORE** (395 mi./632km) r.t. via U.S. 50E, U.S. 113S, U.S. 13S, Va. 175E and 175W, U.S. 13N, and U.S. 50W—about 500 mi./800km if you go and return via the Chesapeake Bay Bridge-Tunnel): Leaving Washington on New York Ave. and U.S. 50 (John Hansen Hwy.), you'll soon come to your first stop, **Annapolis** (see "Nearby Excursions," above). The road then follows the shoreline of the **Chesapeake Bay,** a great arm of the sea 185 mi. (300km) long and parallel to the Atlantic Ocean, famous for its seafood. After passing through 🔔 **Wye Mills,** a picturesque little village whose authentic 18th-century character has been preserved, you come to **Easton,** capital of the Eastern Shore and an antique-lover's paradise. There are many old houses to see, as well as the superb Courthouse Sq. The Third Haven Friends Meeting House, 405 S. Washington St. (301/822-0293), open daily, was built by Quaker settlers in 1682 and is one of the oldest religious buildings in the country.

Before continuing toward Cambridge and Ocean City, go out of your way to the charming little fishing port of ☀🔔 **St. Michaels,** where you'll find the fascinating 🔔 **Chesapeake Bay Maritime Museum** on Waterside (301/745-2916), open daily Apr–Dec (wknds only the rest of the year), as well as the enchanting St. Mary's Sq. with its old houses.

Another worthwhile side trip is to **Oxford,** a pleasure-sailing center and terminus of the oldest ferry in the U.S., the **Oxford–Bellevue Ferry,** which has been in operation for three centuries.

Southwest of **Cambridge,** another little Colonial port, take Md. 16 as far as 🔔 **Church Creek,** where you will come upon Old Trinity Church (1675), one of the oldest in the country. Back on U.S. 50, when you're 5 mi. (8km) west of Mardela Springs, look out for the **Mason-Dixon Line Marker,** the first stone placed in 1763 on the historic line marking the traditional boundary between the northern and southern U.S. (The Mason-Dixon Line owes its name to Charles Mason and Jeremiah Dixon, two British surveyors who in 1763 were instructed to determine the boundaries of the land given 130 years earlier by the Crown to Cecilius Calvert, Second Baron Baltimore, and to William Penn. Following the line of latitude 39 degrees 42 minutes 26.3 seconds from the sea to the Alleghenies, the Mason-Dixon Line forever divides the Yankee North from the Dixie South.)

Then on to ⚓ **Ocean City,** Maryland's only Atlantic coast resort, with a beautiful fine-sand beach 3 mi. (5km) long, and dozens of hotels and motels in all price ranges—but also huge crowds in summer.

Your last stop will be at ⚓⚓ **Assateague Island National Seashore,** a long chain of sand dunes alternating with marshes and pinewoods which are home to myriads of birds and to many wild ponies, said to be descended from those brought here by the first Spanish explorers in their galleons. On the last Wed–Fri of July the ponies are swum across the arm of the sea that separates **Assateague Island** from **Chincoteague Island** to be sold at auction; in the week before this yearly ritual of "pony penning," the whole region devotes itself to carnival—and pony races. A visit to this nature reserve, famous also for its oysters and shellfish, is worth the trip all by itself. For information, contact the Superintendent, Assateague Island National Seashore, Rte. 2, Box 294, Berlin, MD 21811 (301/ 641-1441), or the Refuge Manager, Chincoteague National Wildlife Refuge, P.O. Box 62, Chincoteague, VA 23336 (804/336-6122).

You can return to Washington either the same way you came, along U.S. 13 and U.S. 50, or by going farther south to the very spectacular 17-mi. (28km) **Chesapeake Bay Bridge-Tunnel** and then jogging back north along I-64 and I-95. This will enable you to visit Wiliamsburg, Yorktown, and Richmond (see below). Allow at least 3–4 days for this very comprehensive trip, which you shouldn't miss.

Where to Stay En Route

IN EASTON, MD. ☼ ⚑⚑ **Tidewater Inn,** Dover St. and Harrison St., Easton, MD 21601 (301/822-1300). 120 rms. Elegant two-century-old building, now a designated historic monument. Rest. highly regarded for its seafood. **M–E**

IN OXFORD, MD. ⚑⚑ **Robert Morris Inn,** Md. 333, Oxford, MD 21654 (301/ 226-5111). 33 rms. Closed Feb. Charming little Colonial-style inn overlooking the water. Praiseworthy rest. **I–M**

IN OCEAN CITY, MD. ⚑⚑⚑ **Sheraton Fontainebleau Inn,** 10100 Ocean Hwy., Ocean City, MD 21842 (301/524-3535; toll free, see Sheraton). 250 rms. Big, ultramodern 16-story tower on the beach. **E–VE**

⚑⚑ **Plim Plaza Hotel,** Boardwalk and 2nd St., Ocean City, MD 21842 (301/289-6181). 181 rms. Standard motel. **M–E**

IN CHINCOTEAGUE, VA. ☼ ⚑⚑ **Driftwood,** Beach Rd. at Assateague Bridge, Chincoteague, VA 23336 (804/336-6557). 52 rms. Congenial little motel at the entrance to the park. For lovers of the sea. **I–M**

⚑⚑ **The Refuge,** one block west of Assateague Bridge, Chincoteague, VA 23336 (804/336-5511). 68 rms. Inviting motel with view of the wildlife refuge. **I–M**

Where to Eat En Route

IN ST. MICHAELS, MD. ♀ **The Harbor,** St. Michaels, Md. (301/745-9001). Lunch/dinner Tues–Sat. This restaurant's reputation is founded on its blue crabs and other Chesapeake Bay seafood. **I**

IN OXFORD, MD. ♀ **The Masthead Club,** Mill St. at the Strand (301/226-5303). Dinner nightly, brunch Sat–Sun. Excellent local seafood. I

☼☌ **GETTYSBURG & PENNSYLVANIA DUTCH COUNTRY** (265 mi./424km r.t. via I-270N, U.S. 15N, U.S. 30E

and 30W, I-83S, and I-95S): The greatest and most glorious battlefield of the Civil War, and in Amish country, a 17th-century survival (for details, see Chapter 6 on Philadelphia). On the way, stop in **Catoctin Mountain Park** on Md. 77 west of Thurmont. In this lovely rolling, wooded landscape is hidden **Camp David,** country retreat of the presidents and scene of many famous diplomatic meetings, among others that of Sept 1978, at which Anwar El Sadat and Menachem Begin negotiated a peace treaty between Egypt and Israel. No visitors. A 2-day trip interesting on account of its variety. (For recommended accommodations and restaurants, see Chapter 6 on Philadelphia.)

Washingtonians will find a foretaste of Amish country at the **Dutch Country Farmers Market** in Burtonsville, Md., at the intersection of U.S. 29 and Md. 198 (301/421-4046). A score of stands kept by Amish countryfolk wearing traditional garments and head coverings sell farm products from vegetables to meat and from cheese to home-baked pastry—all guaranteed to contain no chemical additives or pesticides. Locally popular; open Fri–Sat. 30 min from dwntwn Washington.

☌ **POTOMAC VALLEY** (165 mi./264km r.t. via the George Washington Memorial Pkwy., River Rd. West, Whites Ferry,

U.S. 15S, Va. 7W, Va. 9W, Va. 671N, Md. 65N, Md. 34E, Alt. U.S. 40E, and I-270S): Picturesque drive running for much of its length along the Potomac River. It begins with a visit to the ☼☌ **Chesapeake & Ohio Canal National Historical Park and Great Falls.** Begun in 1828, the canal was intended to link Georgetown, now a suburb of Washington, with the Ohio Valley, but work was abandoned in the 1870s because of competition from the railroads. There survives to this day, on the stretch near the Great Falls of the Potomac, an entire system of bridges and locks, now surrounded by a pretty wooded park which is maintained jointly by the states of Maryland and Virginia. Interesting little museum; open daily (301/739-4200).

Cross the Potomac at **Whites Ferry** (toll ferryboat) and continue to ☌ **Leesburg,** a charming little Colonial town founded in 1758 and in great part restored to its original appearance. Be sure to see the **Loudoun County Historical Museum** at 16 W. Loudoun St. (703/777-7427), open daily. Today Leesburg is an important thoroughbred center.

Now on to ☼☌ **Harpers Ferry,** proudly standing at the confluence of the Shenandoah River and Potomac River. In this Civil War landmark town, the old U.S. Army arsenal has been completely restored; there are also many historic houses in the Old Town. It is best known as the scene of John Brown's rebellion against slavery in 1859, which later became a symbol to the northern states. It ended in his execution by hanging at **Charles Town,** 8 mi. (13km) south, where the ambience of the 18th century has also been scrupulously preserved. Don't fail to visit John Brown's Fort, rebuilt on the exact site of the drama, on Old Arsenal Sq., open daily.

Continuing northward, you'll come to ☼☌ **Antietam National Battlefield Site and Cemetery,** where the defeat of the Confederate troops of General Lee ended the South's first invasion of the North. This, September 17, 1862, was the single bloodiest day of the entire Civil War, with 23,000 killed and wounded in a matter of a few hours. The battlefield may be visited. Visitor Center and museum on Md. 65 (301/432-5124), open daily.

The last stop is at ☼ **Frederick,** a place of strategic importance during the Civil War and an architectural trove of ante-bellum mansions and museums around Market St. and Patrick St. Be sure to see the **Francis Scott Key Museum,**

123 S. Bentz St. (301/663-8703), open by appointment only, birthplace of the author of the words of the national anthem. His tomb, marked by the U.S. flag, may be seen at Mount Olivet Cemetery at the south end of Market St., open daily. Then back to Washington on I-270. A 1-day trip particularly worthwhile in warm weather.

Where to Eat En Route

IN LEESBURG ※🍴 **Green Tree,** 15 S. King St. (703/777-7246). Lunch/dinner daily; authentic 18th-century recipes in a very lovely antique setting. An unusual experience. I

🔭 WILLIAMSBURG & COLONIAL VIRGINIA (320 mi./
512km r.t. via I-95S and I-64E, and the reverse route returning): Your first stop will be at ※🔭 **Richmond,** capital of Virginia since 1780 and capital of the Confederacy from 1861 to 1865. Founded in 1607 as a trading post for the first settlers and the local Native American tribes, Richmond soon flourished thanks to its tobacco business; on the eve of the Civil War it had some 40 curing plants.

While skyscrapers and modern buildings now cluster along the banks of the James River, bearing witness to the economic and industrial vigor of present-day Richmond, the older neighborhoods of the center city are still a living museum of Virginia's great Colonial epoch. The warehouses of **Shockoe Slip,** at Main St., Canal St., and Cary St., the oldest part of the city, are now home to artists, boutiques, and fashionable restaurants. The respectable middle classes live in the **Fan District,** in the shade of the trees in **Monroe Park. Church Hill** is the district around the wooden church of the Revolutionary patriots, **St. John's Church,** at 25th St. and Broad St. (804/648-5015), open daily; here Patrick Henry made his immortal pronouncement: "As for me, give me Liberty, or give me Death." Somehow the neighborhood has preserved a subtle aura of the 19th century. A more solemn note is struck by ※ **Monument Avenue,** Richmond's processional boulevard, lined with trees, mansions, and monuments in honor of its most illustrious citizens, particularly Jefferson Davis and Gen. Robert E. Lee.

Try not to miss the **State Capitol** (1788), on Capitol Sq. (804/786-4344), open daily, whose design closely follows that of the Maison Carrée in Nîmes; also the three-story neoclassical ※ **White House of the Confederacy** and the adjoining museum, rich in historical material, at 1201 E. Clay St. (804/649-1861), open daily; here Jefferson Davis made his home during the Civil War.

You should see the lovely 🔭 **Virginia Museum of Fine Arts,** at Boulevard and Grove Ave. (804/367-0844), open Tues–Sun, with fine art nouveau and art deco material, jewelry by Fabergé, and paintings by great European masters.

Driving east from Richmond you will come next to ※🔭 **Williamsburg,** capital of Virginia from 1698 to 1780, and the most famous museum town in the U.S., looking just as it did in the 18th century. Thanks to funding from John D. Rockefeller, Jr., Williamsburg was able to launch, in 1926, a gigantic salvage operation involving almost 150 old buildings. The many craftsmen's workshops, booths, taverns, and displays with people in 18th-century attire attract more than a million visitors to Williamsburg every year. The evidences of the past lie all around you here: the 1705 **State Capitol** (east end of Duke of Gloucester St.); the (British) **Governor's Palace and Gardens** (on Palace Green); the **Raleigh Tavern** (Duke of Gloucester St.), frequented by Jefferson, Henry, and other Revolutionary leaders; and the old **Public Gaol** (Nicholson St.), completed in 1704, where debtors, criminals, and pirates were imprisoned. Most of these historic buildings are open to visitors daily throughout the year. The **Visitor Center,** on Colonial Pkwy. at Va. 132 (804/229-1000), provides useful information, leaflets, and museum tickets, and will make hotel reservations for you.

Williamsburg is worth the trip all by itself, but there are three places nearby that justify a detour. ※ **Jamestown,** 9 mi. (14km) SW on Colonial Pkwy., was the first permanent British settlement in North America (1607), and has many historic buildings including the 1639 ⚓ **Old Church Tower.** Visitor Center (804/229-1733) open daily.

☼⚓ **Yorktown,** 13 mi. (20km) SE on Colonial Pkwy., was the scene of the last engagement of the War of Independence, where the American and French troops of Washington and Rochambeau, on October 19, 1781, accepted the surrender of General Cornwallis, putting an end to British rule over the Thirteen Colonies. The battlefield may be visited; Visitor Center (804/898-3400) open daily.

Finally, ☼⚓ **Busch Gardens – The Old Country,** 3 mi. (5km) east on U.S. 60 (804/253-3350), is a 360-acre (121ha) theme park with quaint European villages; open daily mid-May to Labor Day, wknds only in spring and fall; closed the rest of the year. Topped two million guests last year.

On your way back to Washington along I-64W and I-95N, be sure to see **Fredericksburg** and **Alexandria** (see "Nearby Excursions," above). This is a trip that will appeal to lovers of History with a capital H; allow at least 3 days. Don't miss it.

Where to Stay En Route

IN RICHMOND ☼ 🛎🛎🛎🛎 **Sheraton Jefferson Hotel,** Franklin St. and Adams St., Richmond, VA 23220 (804/788-8000). 276 rms. One of the finest old hotels (1895) in the country. Sumptuous interior superbly restored; the Rotunda and its grand staircase are worth a visit in themselves. **E–VE**

🛎🛎 **Days Inn Marketplace,** 612 E. Marshall St., Richmond, VA 23240 (804/649-2378). 140 rms. Elderly but comfortable hotel nr. the State Capitol. **I–M**

IN WILLIAMSBURG ☼ 🛎🛎🛎🛎 **Williamsburg Inn,** Francis St., Williamsburg, VA 23185 (804/229-1000). 102 rms. Elegant Colonial building in the heart of the Historic District, with remarkably good facilities and standards of comfort. Regency decor and furnishings. **VE**

🛎🛎🛎 **Royce Hotel,** 415 Richmond Rd., Williamsburg, VA 23185 (804/229-4020). 313 rms. Modern, very comfortable hotel whose appearance and decor harmonize wonderfully with the Historic District a block or two away. **E–VE**

🛎🛎 **Best Western Patrick Henry Inn,** York St. and Page St., Williamsburg, VA 23185 (804/229-9540). 301 rms. Inviting, friendly motel a 2 min. walk from the State Capitol. Very good value. **I–M**

🛎 **Days Inn Downtown,** 902 Richmond Rd., Williamsburg, VA 23185 (804/229-5060). 100 rms. Small, conventional, but well-run motel near the center of town. Very good value. **I–M**

Where to Eat En Route

IN RICHMOND ☼🍴 **Tobacco Company,** 1201 E. Cary St. (804/782-9431). Lunch/dinner daily. A rest. very popular w. the locals, in a former 19th-century tobacco warehouse. Excellent conventional cooking. **I–M**

IN WILLIAMSBURG ☼🍴 **Trellis,** Duke of Gloucester St., Merchants Sq. (804/229-8610). Lunch/dinner daily, brunch Sun. Imaginative, delicate American nouvelle cuisine from the hand of the talented chef Marcel Desaulniers; some of the best food in Virginia at extremely reasonable prices. Inviting shady terrace. A fine place. **I–M**

☼🍴 **King's Arms Tavern,** Duke of Gloucester St. (804/229-2141). Lunch/dinner daily. Authentic 18th-century tavern with its original Colonial decor attractively restored. Traditional American food. **I**

PART TWO

THE SOUTH

CHAPTER 10

CHARLESTON♟♟

□ □ □

Called "The Holy City" because of its many churches and dozens of bell towers, Charleston—formerly spelled "Charles Towne," for King Charles II—is one of the most gracious cities in the United States, and one of the most popular among tourists. Under British rule Charleston was the largest Atlantic port south of Philadelphia, enjoying a strategic position at the junction of the Ashley River and Cooper River. Elegant and cosmopolitan, Charleston attracted a large Huguenot (French Protestant) colony in the 18th century (until 1928 there were still religious services conducted in French), as well as strong currents of Irish, German, Scottish, and even West Indian immigration.

Charleston surrendered to General Sherman in Feb 1865 after a 2-year siege. Despite the wounds of war, a terrible earthquake in 1886, and many devastating fires and hurricanes—among which was the terrifying hurricane Hugo in Sept 1989, one of the 10 worst hurricanes to reach the U.S. mainland in this century (24 people dead and $3.5 billion in property damage in the Carolinas)—this charming, aristocratic city of the Old South, bypassed by time, has conserved a number of interesting traces of the past: **Fort Sumter,** whence came the spark that ignited the Civil War; the **Dock Street Theatre,** the country's oldest (1736); **Cabbage Row,** immortalized as "Catfish Row" in the opera *Porgy and Bess;* the **Charleston Museum,** founded in 1773 (the country's first); the venerable houses of **Old Charleston,** with their Doric columns and wrought-iron balconies; and dozens of plantations with lush tropical gardens. Each spring since 1977 Charleston has played host to the American version of Italy's famous **Spoleto Festival,** offering ballet, theater, and classical and contemporary music to enthusiasts from all over the country.

Center of the rice and indigo trades in Colonial times, then a prosperous slave market before the Civil War, Charleston is presently an active port at the heart of a highly mechanized agricultural region, with a booming tourist trade (more than two million visitors each year), but a hotel capacity that is still relatively limited. Charleston is 14th on the list of the 20 American cities experiencing the most rapid economic growth.

BASIC FACTS: State of South Carolina. Area code: 803. Time zone: eastern. ZIP Code: 29401. Founded: 1670. Approximate population: city, 69,000; metropolitan area, 480,000.

CLIMATE: Almost any season is a good one to discover Charleston. Winter is generally mild (average Jan temperature, 50°F/10°C) and summer hot (average July temperature, 80°F/27°C), although raincoats and umbrellas are in order because of tropical storms. Spring (gardens bloom in Mar and Apr) and autumn, Oct and Nov especially, are the ideal seasons to visit this popular tourist destination.

DISTANCES: Atlanta, 289 mi. (462km); Miami, 455 mi. (728km); Savannah, 106 mi. (170km); Washington, 527 mi. (844km).

ARRIVAL & TRANSIT INFORMATION

AIRPORT: International Airport (CHS): 12 mi. (20km) NW. Information: 767-1100. New contemporary terminal.

AIRLINES: American (722-7108); Delta (577-3230); Eastern (723-7851); United (747-0591), and USAir (723-6107).

CITY LINK: Cab fare to city center, about $16; time, about 20 min. Bus: **Airport Limousine** (767-7111); fare, $8; time, about 30 min. Although cab fares are reasonable, renting a car with unlimited mileage is advisable for visiting the numerous parks and plantations surrounding the city. Rather inadequate public transportation (bus) system (SCE&G), but fast, convenient dwntwn shuttle service; Call 722-2226 for information.

CAR RENTAL (at the airport unless otherwise indicated): Avis (767-7030); Budget (554-8070); Hertz (767-7047); National (767-3078); Thrifty, 3565 W. Montague (552-7531). For dwntwn locations, consult the local telephone book.

LIMOUSINE SERVICES: Dav El Limousines (toll free 800/922-0343), Parker Limousine Service (723-7601).

TAXIS: Taxis cannot be hailed on the street but must be summoned by phone: **Yellow Cab** (577-6565). Rates rather low.

TRAIN: Amtrak, 4565 Gaynor Ave. (toll free 800/872-7245).

INTERCITY BUSES: Greyhound, 89 Society St. (722-1115).

INFORMATION & TOURS

TOURIST INFORMATION: Charleston Convention & Visitors Bureau, P.O. Box 975, SC 29402 (803/723-7641). **Historic Charleston Foundation,** 51 Meeting St., SC 29401 (803/722-3405).
   Visitor Information Center, Arch Building, 85 Calhoun St., SC 29402 (803/722-8338). Offers the best printed material.

GUIDED TOURS: American Sightseeing (bus), 28½ Alexander St. (767-7115). Guided tour of the city and environs; serves the major hotels.
   Charleston Carriage Co. (city tour in horse-drawn carriage), 96 N. Market St. (577-0042). Daily year round. Resv. suggested.
   Gray Line Tours (bus) (722-4444). Guided tour of the city and environs. Leaves from major dwntwn hotels.
   Gray Line Water Tours (harbor cruise), Municipal Marina, Lockwood Blvd. (722-1112). Offers a view of the U.S. Navy's famous Polaris submarines. Daily year round.
   Fort Sumter Tour, Municipal Marina, Lockwood Blvd. (722-2628). Worth going out of your way for. Daily except Dec 25.

SIGHTS, ATTRACTIONS & ACTIVITIES

ARCHITECTURAL HIGHLIGHTS: ⚓ **The Citadel,** Moultrie St. and Elmwood Ave. (792-5006): Also known as "the West Point of the South," this celebrated military academy, founded in 1842 (1,900 students), occupies the site of an early 19th-century fort built to quell slave revolts. Commanding fortress-style architecture with battlements and turrets, a military museum, and archives of

Gen. Mark Clark, World War II hero. Cadet parades on Fri at 3:30pm. Worth a look. Open daily.

☼⚓ **U.S.S. Yorktown,** Patriots Point, left bank of the Cooper River (884-2727): This World War II aircraft carrier, which has been transformed into a floating museum with planes, helicopters, and weapons, also affords a very lovely view of the city, the harbor, and Fort Sumter. Anchored not far from here is the **Savannah,** the first nuclear-powered freighter, and other U.S. Navy ships. Worth the trip. Open daily.

BEACHES: ⚓ Bulls Island, 3 mi. (5km) off the South Carolina coast: Long

stretches of underdeveloped beach and hiking trails. Access by ferry: Capt. John Pryor, 1222 Calais Dr., Mount Pleasant (803/884-0448).

CHURCHES/SYNAGOGUES: ⚓ Huguenot Church, 110 Church St. (722-

4385): Consecrated in 1687, rebuilt in 1796 and again in 1845 after two fires, this is the only church in the country that has retained the Calvinist liturgy of the Huguenots. Until 1928 services were conducted in French. Worth a look. Open daily.

☼⚓ **Kahal Kadosh Beth Elohim,** 90 Hasell St. (723-1090): The country's second-oldest synagogue, founded in 1749 (the oldest is in Newport, R.I.). The present building, which dates from 1840, is considered one of the most beautiful examples of the Greek Revival style in the country. Open Mon–Fri. Worth a glance.

⚓ **St. Michael's Church,** Meeting St. and Broad St. (723-0603): With its 186-ft.-tall (57m) bell tower, this unusual church is Charleston's oldest (1761) and was attended by George Washington. Its distinctive portico was painted black in the Revolution to spoil the aim of gunners. The organ dates from 1768. Worth a look. Open daily.

☼⚓ **St. Philip's Church,** 142 Church St. (722-7734): On this site the first Anglican church south of Virginia was built in 1670, the year Charleston was founded. The present building dates from 1838; its soaring steeple was an aiming point for Northern gunners during the Civil War. Was severely damaged by hurricane Hugo in 1989. The adjacent cemetery is the resting place of many notables, including Edward Rutledge, one of the signers of the Declaration of Independence. See it. Open daily.

HISTORIC BUILDINGS: ☼⚓ Dock Street Theatre, Church St. and Queen St.

(723-5648): This hall opened in 1936 on the site of the country's oldest theater (1736). The architecture, inspired by the Georgian theaters of the 19th century, includes a carefully restored section of the former Planter's Hotel (1809). Open Mon–Fri in summer, Mon–Sat the rest of the year. See it.

⚓ **Fort Moultrie,** W. Middle St., Sullivan's Island (883-3123): Col. William Moultrie dealt the English one of their first and gravest defeats of the Revolutionary War here in 1776. The present fort, rebuilt in 1809, served as a prison, in the last year of his life, for the captured Osceola, who led the revolt of the Seminoles in Florida, the bloodiest of the Native American Wars. Across the channel from Fort Sumter. See it. Open daily.

⚓⚓ **Fort Sumter,** Fort Sumter Island (883-3123): One of the hallowed places of American history. Built on an artificial island in the middle of Charleston's harbor, Fort Sumter was the target both of the South's surprise attack that touched off the Civil War (4:30am, April 12, 1861), and of a bloody northern siege 1863–65. Can be reached only by boat from the Municipal Marina (see "Guided Tours," above). Interesting military museum and a very lovely view of the old city's skyline. A visit not to be missed. Open daily.

☼⚓⚓ **Old Charleston,** around Meeting St., George St., and Church St.: Very lovely vignette of the past—pastel houses with

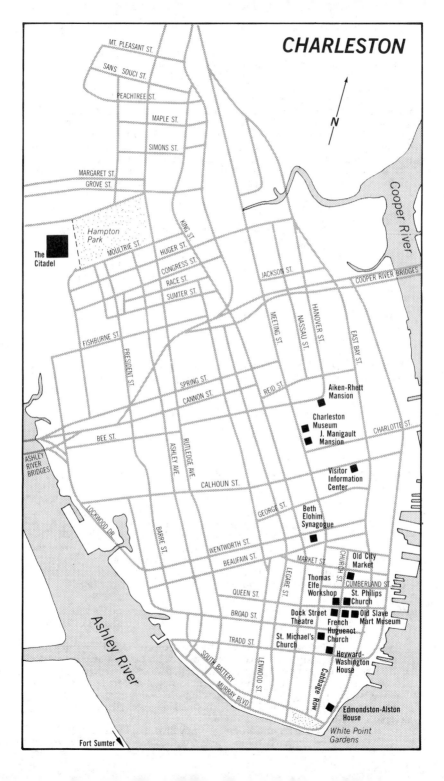

wrought-iron railings and small, narrow cobbled streets. There are many historic homes to see, such as the **Nathaniel Russell House,** 51 Meeting St., a fine example of the Adam style with its splendid staircase (1808); the imposing Greek Revival **Edmondston-Alston House,** 21 E. Battery St., built in 1828 by a wealthy merchant on a choice piece of land with a stunning view of Charleston harbor; the **Heyward-Washington House,** 87 Church St., once home to George Washington (1772); the **Joseph Manigault House,** 350 Meeting St., another magnificent example of the Adam style (1803); the **Thomas Elfe Workshop,** 54 Queen St., former studio of the famous cabinetmaker Thomas Elfe (1760); and the **Calhoun Mansion,** 16 Meeting St., noted for its sumptuous Victorian interiors (1870). All these buildings are open daily to visitors. With more than 2,000 landmarked 18th- and 19th-century buildings, Old Charleston constitutes one of the nation's most spectacular collections of historic architecture. For detailed information, consult the **Visitor Information Center,** 85 Calhoun St. (722-8338). A visit not to be missed.

Provost Dungeon, 122 E. Bay St. (792-5020): The **Old Exchange Building** (1771), originally used as a customshouse, was a small British fort where American patriots were imprisoned during the Revolutionary War (Provost Dungeon). Interesting exhibition dedicated to this period, plus films about Charleston's artistic heritage. Open Tues–Sun. See it.

MARKETS: ✳️⚓ **City Market,** Meeting St. and Market St.: A mixture of flea market and yard sale with merchandise of all kinds. Lively and colorful, it has been the center of local commerce for two centuries.

MUSEUMS OF ART: ✳️⚓ **City Hall Art Gallery,** 80 Broad St. (577-6970): A very fine collection of famous portraits, including John Trumbull's rendering of George Washington, in an interesting 1801 building. It originally served as the regional office of the Bank of the United States. See it. Open Mon–Fri.

Gibbes Art Gallery, 135 Meeting St. (722-2706): An interesting collection of 18th- and 19th-century American paintings, miniatures, and Japanese prints. Temporary exhibitions, as well. See it. Open daily.

MUSEUMS OF SCIENCE & HISTORY: ⚓ **Charleston Museum,** 360 Meeting St. (722 2996): The country's oldest museum (1773), in a modern, well-designed building since 1980. Natural history, anthropology, fine arts, relics of colonial times. Contains notably the life-size replica of the first submarine used during the Civil War, the *Hunley.* An absolute must-see. Open daily.

Old Powder Magazine, 79 Cumberland St. (722-3767): This former Revolutionary War gun-powder factory was part of the original city fortifications and is Charleston's oldest public building (1713). Today it houses a history museum run by the National Society of Colonial Dames of America. Worth a look. Open Mon–Fri.

PARKS & GARDENS: ⚓ **Hampton Park,** Rutledge Ave. and Cleveland St.: A splendid array of blooming camellias and azaleas in spring and roses in summer. Open daily.

Palmetto Islands County Park, east on U.S. 17N, half a mile (.8km) past Snee Farm, then left on Long Point Rd.: Special features of this park in a tropical setting include a spacious open meadow, heavily wooded areas, a 2-acre (1ha) pond, and a mile-long canoe trail. Marsh boardwalks as well as jogging, hiking, and bicycle paths wind throughout the park. Public fishing and boating docks border Boone Hall Creek. Pedal boat, canoes, and bicycle rental. Open daily year round.

White Point Gardens, Murray Blvd. and E. Battery St.: A lovely flowered promenade at the junction of the Ashley

River and Cooper River which offers a spectacular view of the city, the harbor, and Fort Sumter. A scene not to be missed. Open daily.

PERFORMING ARTS: For daily listings of all shows and cultural events, consult the entertainment pages of the daily papers *Charleston News & Courier* (morning) and *Charleston Evening Post* (evening).

Dock Street Theatre, Church St. and Queen St. (723-5648): Classical and modern theater, from Shakespeare to Broadway, Oct–May.

Gaillard Municipal Auditorium, 77 Calhoun St. (577-4500): Concerts, ballet, recitals. Home of the Charleston Civic Ballet, Charleston Symphony Orchestra, and Charleston Opera Company.

Spoleto Festival/USA, Middleton House Plantation (722-2764): 17-day celebration of the arts, from classical music to theater and from jazz to opera and dance. The nation's most famous and most comprehensive festival. Late May to early June.

SHOPPING: Charleston Place, 130 Market St.: Three dozen luxury boutiques—from Gucci to Ralph Lauren and from Laura Ashley to Godiva chocolates—brought together in a very effective faux antique decor. Right in the center of Charleston. A must for all visitors. Open daily.

SPECIAL EVENTS: For the exact schedule of events below, consult the **Visitor Information Center** (see "Tourist Information," above).

Festival of Houses (mid-Mar to mid-Apr): The most beautiful old homes, specially opened to the public. Try to time your visit for it. For information, call 723-1623.

Spoleto Festival/USA (late May to early June): American version of the famous Italian "Festival of Two Worlds" founded by Gian Carlo Menotti. Classical music, ballet, jazz, opera, theater, art exhibitions, and more. Not to be missed. For information, contact P.O. Box 157, Charleston, SC 29402 (803/722-2764); the box office is at 14 George St.

House & Garden Tours (mid-Oct): Nocturnal, candlelit walks through the city's gardens and loveliest historic homes. Spectacular. For information, call 722-4630.

International Film Festival (late Oct to early Nov): Annually presents more than 500 works of filmmakers worldwide, plus film symposia.

STROLLS: ⌂ **Cabbage Row,** 89-91 Church St.: The picturesque cluster of old rowhouses that inspired George Gershwin's setting for *Porgy and Bess* (called "Catfish Row" in the opera). An absolute must-see.

🔍🔍 **Old Charleston:** See "Historic Buildings," above.

ACCOMMODATIONS

A Note on Accommodations: Room rates in Charleston are coded as follows: **VE,** Very Expensive ($140 and up); **E,** Expensive ($90–$140); **M,** Moderate ($60–$90); **I,** Inexpensive ($30–$60); **B,** Budget (up to $30). A listing of toll-free numbers is in the Appendix.

Personal Favorites (in order of preference)

☀♟♟♟♟ **Planters Inn** (dwntwn), 112 N. Market St., SC 29401 (803/722-2345; toll free 800/845-7082). 45 rms, A/C, color TV. AE, CB, DC, MC, V. No private parking; rest. (Robert's), bar, 24-hr. rm svce, concierge, free crib. *Note:* Charming little luxury hotel that has become a favorite of connoisseurs. Elegant, carefully restored 19th-century building. Spacious rms w. antique furniture (some have fireplaces). Personalized service in an elegant, cushy atmosphere. Excellent rest. (Charleston's best). Class and style. **M–E**

♟♟♟ **Omni at Charleston Place** (dwntwn), 130 Market St., SC ♟♟♟ 29401 (803/722-4900; toll free, see Omni). 450 rms, A/C, color TV, in-rm movies. AE, CB, DC, MC, V. Gar. $6, pool, health club, sauna, two rests. (including Shaftesbury's), two bars, 24-hr. rm svce, disco, boutiques, hrdrsr, concierge, free crib. *Note:* Classy new hotel inaugurated in 1986, w. architecture that blends with the Old Charleston setting. Elegant, refined decor and vast, well-conceived rms w. stylish furniture. Impeccable svce and reception. VIP and big-business clientele. At the very heart of historic Charleston, w. direct access to Charleston Place Mall and its luxury boutiques. An excellent location. **E–VE**

☀♟♟♟ **Lodge Alley Inn** (dwntwn), 195 E. Bay St., SC 29401 (803/722-1611; toll free 800/845-1004). 98 rms, A/C, color TV. AE, MC, V. Valet parking $6, rest., bar, rm svce, nightclub (in season), free crib. *Note:* Elegant hotel in a prettily renovated 1773 mansion. Comfortable, tastefully decorated rms and suites w. period furniture, refrigerator, and balcony (some w. kitchenette and fireplace). Distinguished reception and svce. Rest. of quality (French Quarter). Attractive location in the heart of the historic district. **E,** but lower rates off-season.

♟♟ **Heart of Charleston** (nr. dwntwn), 200 Meeting St., SC 29401 (803/723-3451; toll free 800/845-2504). 118 rms, A/C, color TV. AE, CB, DC, MC, V. Free parking, pool, rest., bar, valet svce. *Note:* This comfortable, well-maintained motel w. excellent svce is a very good value. A few minutes' walk from Charleston's principal tourist attractions. **I–M**

☀♟ **Two Meeting Street Inn** (formerly Carr's Guest House; nr. dwntwn), 2 Meeting St., SC 29401 (803/723-7322). 8 rms, A/C; no TV, no single rms, no credit cards. Parking, bar. *Note:* The charm of an old family-run European pension in a small, late 19th-century villa. Spacious, inviting rms (some without private bathroom). View of the bay. Good value overall. Resv. a must. **I–M**

♟ **Days Inn Historic District** (dwntwn), 155 Meeting St., SC 29401 (803/722-8411; toll free; see Days Inns). 124 rms, A/C, cable color TV. AE, DC, MC, V. Free parking, pool, coffee shop (no alcohol), free crib. *Note:* Classic motel particularly well situated for a visit to Old Charleston. Comfortable rms. Good value. **I**

Other Accommodations (from top bracket to budget)

♟♟♟ **Holiday Inn Mills House** (formerly the Hyatt House; dwntwn), 115 Meeting St., SC 29401 (803/577-2400; toll free, see Holiday Inns). 210 rms, A/C, color TV, in-rm movies. AE, CB, DC, MC, V. Gar. $7, pool, rest. (Barbadoes Room), bar, rm svce, concierge, free crib. *Note:* Comfort and svce above the norm for a Holiday Inn. Elegant decor, stylish furniture, and a deftly reconstructed colonial atmosphere. In the heart of Old Charleston. **E,** but lower rates off-season.

♟♟♟ **Sheraton Charleston Hotel** (nr. dwntwn), 170 Lockwood Dr., SC 29403 (803/723-3000; toll free, see Sheraton). 338 rms, A/C, color TV, in-rm movies. AE, CB, DC, MC, V. Free parking, pool, four tennis courts, rest., coffee shop, bar, rm svce, disco, free crib. *Note:* One of the most recent additions to the local hotel scene, w. spacious, very comfortable rms w. balconies (the best have a view of the Ashley River) and good svce. Very complete facilities. Adequate rest. (Charleston Terrace). 3 min. from the center of historic Charleston (free shuttle bus). **M–E**

☀♟♟ **Indigo Inn** (dwntwn), 1 Maiden Lane, SC 29401 (803/577-5900; toll free 800/845-7639). 40 rms, A/C, color TV. AE, MC, V. Parking, adj. coffee shop, rm svce. *Note:* An artistically renovated, early 19th-century warehouse, this small, luxurious hotel offers elegant, tastefully decorated, stylishly furnished rms. Delightful private patio. Excellent svce. Just off the City Market in the very heart of Charleston. **M–E**

※ ♀ ♀ **Vendue Inn** (dwntwn), 19 Vendue Range, SC 29401 (803/ 577-7970; toll free 800/845-7900). 26 rms, A/C, color TV. AE, MC, V. Free parking, bicycles, rest. (Morton's), rm svce, free breakfast. *Note:* Charming little luxury hotel in a lovely three-story residence dating from 1824. Period decor as romantic as can be. Exceptionally polished reception and svce. Well-regarded rest. A very classy place. **M–E**

♀ ♀ **Holiday Inn Riverview** (nr. dwntwn), 301 Savannah Hwy., SC 29407 (803/556-7100; toll free, see Holiday Inns). 178 rms, A/C, cable color TV. AE, CB, DC, MC, V. Free parking, pool, rest., bar, rm svce, disco, free crib. *Note:* This 14-story tower w. a view of the Ashley River offers functional, balconied rms and a scenic rest.-bar at the top. Holiday Inn style. Good value. 10 min. from dwntwn. **M,** but lower rates off-season.

♀ **Best Western Dorchester Motor Lodge** (vic.), 3668 Dorchester Ave. (at I-26), SC 29405 (803/747-0961; toll free, see Best Western). 200 rms, A/C, color TV, in-rm movies. AE, CB, DC, MC, V. Free parking, pool, rest., bar, rm svce, nightclub. *Note:* Typical but comfortable motel in the northern end of Charleston. Cheerful reception. Its location, just 10 min. from dwntwn on I-26, makes it ideal if you're driving. **I**

♀ **Lord Ashley** (nr. dwntwn), 1501 Savannah Hwy., SC 29407 (803/766-1611). 48 rms, A/C, cable color TV. AE, DC, MC, V. Free parking, pool, adj. coffee shop, crib $2. *Note:* Small, modest, but well-maintained motel, 10 min. from dwntwn on U.S. 17. Functional comfort and a good value. **I**

♀ **Motel 6 South** (vic.), 2058 Savannah Hwy., SC 29407 (803/ 556-5144). 111 rms, A/C, color TV, free in-rm movies. AE, DC, MC, V. Free parking, pool, free crib. *Note:* Ultra-economical, modern, and functional motel that is an excellent value and ideal if you're driving—15 min. from dwntwn (at the intersection of S.C. 7 and U.S. 17). **B**

Accommodations in the Vicinity

※ ♀ ♀ ♀ **Kiawah Island Inn & Villas** (vic.), Kiawah Island (P.O. Box 12910), SC 29412 (803/768-2121; toll free 800/845-2471). 150 rms, A/C, cable color TV. AE, DC, MC, V. Free parking, four pools, tennis, two golf courses, health club, two rests. (including Jasmine Porch), bar, rm svce, disco, crib $5. *Note:* Luxurious vacation complex that is ideal for water sports offering a 9½-mi. (15km) private beach, boat rentals, and waterskiing. Comfortable rms w. balconies and patios. Also available are 350 cottages and villas w. kitchenettes. Svce leaves a bit to be desired. Interesting wknd packages. 20 mi. (32km) south of Charleston on U.S. 17, S.C. 171, and S.C. 700. **E–VE,** but lower rates off-season.

Airport Accommodations

♀ ♀ **La Quinta** (vic.), 2499 La Quinta Lane, SC 29418 (803/797-8181; toll free, see La Quinta). 122 rms, A/C, color TV, in-rm movies. AE, CB, DC, MC, V. Free parking, pool, rest., rm svce, free morning coffee, free crib. *Note:* New motel 5 min. from the airport. Comfortable, spacious rms plus cheerful reception and svce make this a very good value. 20 min. from dwntwn. **I**

RESTAURANTS

A Note on Restaurant Prices: Charleston restaurant prices, per person, excluding drinks and service charges, are coded as follows: **VE,** Very Expensive ($60 and up); **E,** Expensive ($40–$60); **M,** Moderate ($25–$40); **I,** Inexpensive ($15–$25); **B,** Budget (up to $15).

Personal Favorites (in order of preference)

♀♀♀ **Robert's** (dwntwn), in the Planters Inn (see "Accommodations," above) (577-7565). A/C. Dinner only, Mon–Sat (svce

until 8pm). AE, MC, V. Jkt. *Specialties:* seafood mousse w. lobster bisque, chateaubriand béarnaise or périgourdine, duckling orientale, excellent desserts.
Menu changed regularly. *Note:* A Charleston classic in a new setting elegantly
renovated. A remarkable experience despite chef Robert Dickson's passion for *bel
canto.* The menu always includes six different dishes or entrées. Good svce; resv. a
must. *Continental/French.* **E** (prix fixe)

    The Colony House (dwntwn), 35 Prioleau St. (723-3424).
A/C. Lunch Mon–Sat; dinner nightly; closed hols. AE, MC,
V. *Specialties:* she-crab soup, crab gratinée, baked pompano, catch of the day,
steak, game (in season). *Note:* The best broiled and baked fish in Charleston in a
150-year-old, pleasantly laid-out dock warehouse. The same establishment as the
Wine Cellar (see below), but less chic. Resv. advised. Locally popular. Free parking. *Seafood/American.* **I–M**

    Marianne's (dwntwn), 235 Meeting St. (722-7196). A/C.
Dinner only, nightly (until 1am); closed Jan 1, Thanksgiving,
Dec 25. AE, MC, V. Jkt. *Specialties:* house pâtés, rack of lamb, baron of beef,
paupiettes of red snapper, excellent homemade pastries. The menu changes regu-
larly. *Note:* French bistro-style cuisine and decor. Good wine list. Friendly svce.
Resv. advised. *French.* **I–M**

    Poogan's Porch (dwntwn), 72 Queen St. (577-2337). A/C.
Lunch/dinner daily. AE, MC, V. *Specialties:* she-crab soup,
gumbo, Cajun shrimp, broiled steak or catch of the day, peanut-butter pie. *Note:*
The new fashionable place, in a lovely old house in the historic district. Food of
Créole antecedents, elegantly prepared and served. Rather noisy; excellent svce.
A very good place to eat—and a popular one, so make resv. (ask for a table on the
veranda). *American.* **I**

    A. W. Shuck's (dwntwn), 35 Market St. (723-1151). A/C.
Lunch/dinner daily; closed hols. AE, DC, MC, V. *Specialties:*
oysters, clams, scampi, fish of the day, stuffed shrimp, seafood casserole. *Note:*
Seafood bistro which serves first-rate fish year round. Generous portions at the
bar. Pleasant ambience. Resv. not necessary. *Seafood.* **I**

Other Restaurants (from top bracket to budget)
    The Wine Cellar (dwntwn), 35 Prioleau St. (723-9463). A/C.
Dinner only, nightly; closed Sun in winter, Jan 1, Dec 25. AE,
MC, V. Jkt. *Specialties:* parsleyed rack of lamb, pompano sautéed with almonds,
red snapper in chablis, tournedos, duckling à l'orange. The menu changes
regularly. Fine wine list. *Note:* Modern, carefully prepared French-American
cuisine served in an elegantly rehabilitated old storeroom. A favorite of the local smart set. Resv. a must. Very good svce. Parking. *French/American.* **M** (prix
fixe)

    Jilich's on East Bay (dwntwn), 188 E. Bay St. (577-4342).
A/C. Lunch Mon–Fri; dinner Mon–Sat. AE, CB, DC, MC,
V. Jkt. *Specialties:* blue-crab soup w. sherry, barbecued shrimp w. grits, good seafood, praline cheesecake w. pecan sauce. *Note:* This relative newcomer to the local
gastronomic scene offers typical Carolina Low Country cuisine. Pretty, rustic decor of exposed brick walls and beams under an elegant skylight. An "in" spot
with an ambience that is both romantic and relaxed. Good svce. Resv. advised.
American. **I–M**

    East Bay Trading Co. (dwntwn), East Bay St. and Queen St.
(722-0722). A/C. Lunch Mon–Fri; dinner nightly; closed
Sun in winter, hols. AE, DC, MC, V. *Specialties:* beef Wellington, roast lamb,
prime rib, catch of the day, good homemade desserts. *Note:* In an old harbor
warehouse w. picturesque, if overelaborate, decor, this pleasant rest. offers excellent European-inspired cuisine. Cheerful svce. Locally popular. Resv. advised.
Continental/American. **I**

    82 Queen (dwntwn), 82 Queen St. (723-7591). A/C.
Lunch/dinner daily; closed Thanksgiving, Dec 25. AE, MC,

V. Jkt. *Specialties:* fish of the day, regional dishes. The menu changes regularly. *Note:* An "in" place in a charming early 19th-century residence. Carefully prepared cuisine centering on seafood. First-rate svce. Locally very popular. Resv. highly recommended. The adjacent Wine Bar is the ideal spot for a before- or after-dinner drink. *Seafood.* I

☼♈ **Ferante's** (dwntwn), 32 N. Market St. (723-3614). A/C. Dinner only, nightly; closed hols. AE, CB, DC, MC, V. Jkt. *Specialties:* fresh pasta, scaloppine al marsala, fish of the day, roast duck, lamb cacciatore. *Note:* Pleasant rest. w. Italian-inspired cuisine in an old fishermen's chapel complete w. stained glass and frescoes. Irreproachably fresh seafood and very creditable meat dishes. Svce varies. Resv. advised. *Italian/Seafood.* I

♈ **Charleston Ice House** (dwntwn), 188 Meeting St. (723-6123). A/C. Breakfast/lunch/dinner daily (until midnight); closed Thanksgiving, Dec 25. AE, MC, V. *Specialties:* fish of the day, Greek dishes, sandwiches, excellent desserts. *Note:* Picturesque, lively atmosphere in the heart of the Old City Market. Honest, unpretentious cuisine. Excellent value. Locally popular. *Greek/American.* B–I

♈ **Marina Variety Store** (nr. dwntwn), Municipal Marina, Lockwood Blvd. (723-6325). A/C. Breakfast/lunch/dinner daily. No credit cards. *Specialties:* clam chowder, fish of the day, Kentucky-style fried chicken, hamburgers. *Note:* Generally jam-packed at lunchtime, this bistro on the banks of the Ashley River offers decent cuisine at very reasonable prices. Efficient svce. Pleasant view of the yacht basin. Locally very popular. *Seafood/American.* B

Cafeterias/Specialty Spots

Gaulart & Maliclet (dwntwn), 98 Broad St. (577-9797). Breakfast/lunch/dinner daily. AE, MC, V. *Specialties:* gazpacho, homemade soups, pâtés, sandwiches, and daily specials that can be eaten at the counter. Fine wine list. *Note:* Small, pleasant bistro especially popular among lawyers and bankers at lunch hour. An excellent spot.

Reuben's Downtown Delicatessen (dwntwn), 251 Meeting St. (722-6883). Lunch daily, dinner Mon–Sat (until 9pm). No credit cards. *Specialties:* New York–style deli offering hearty sandwiches, homemade soups, and salads. *Note:* Usually packed with locals. Located in old building (1880s). No resv.

BARS & NIGHTCLUBS

A. W. Shuck's (dwntwn), 35 Market St. (723-1151). Inviting oyster bar (see "Restaurants," above). Open Mon–Sat.

Café 99 (dwntwn), 99 S. Meeting St. (577-4499). Singles bar locally popular. Live music nightly.

Myskyn's Tavern (dwntwn), 83 Market St. (577-5595). Congenial pub and rest. with live jazz. Open Mon–Sat.

Watercolors (dwntwn), in the Omni Hotel, 130 Market St. (722-4900). The area's classiest disco attracts a young professional crowd.

NEARBY EXCURSIONS

☼🏛 **BOONE HALL PLANTATION** (8 mi./13km NE on U.S. 17) (803/884-4371): Former cotton plantation dating from 1681. Only the slave quarters and the outbuildings are original. The classic Georgian-style house is 50 years old and served as the setting for *Gone With the Wind.* Very lovely avenue of century-old oaks. Worth a visit. Open daily.

☼🏛 **CHARLES TOWNE LANDING** (1500 Old Towne Rd.; 803/556-4450): This colonial village, rebuilt at the spot where the English landed in 1670, faithfully reconstructs the life and atmosphere of the first British colonists. The grounds include 660 acres (267ha) of parks, plantations, and gardens, plus a replica of the 17th-century merchant ship *Adventure*. Not to be missed. Open daily.

☀☖ **CYPRESS GARDENS** (23 mi./37km north on U.S. 52) (803/553-0515): Superb camellia and azalea gardens and giant cypresses amid pools, once a part of the Dean Hall Plantation (1725). Boat rides. Not to be missed. Open daily.

☖ **FRANCIS MARION NATIONAL FOREST** (18 mi./ 29km NE on U.S. 17 or S.C. 41): Dotted with lakes and swamps, this 250,000+-acre (100,000+ha) forest contains subtropical vegetation and many remains of Native American and colonial plantings. Camping, boating, fishing, hunting, and a hiker's paradise. For information, contact District Ranger, Rte. 3, Box 630, Moncks Corner, SC 29461 (803/887-3311).

☀☖☖ **MAGNOLIA PLANTATION** (10 mi./16km NW on S.C. 61) (803/571-1266): One of the country's most beautiful gardens, it dates from the late 1670s and boasts 900 varieties of camellias (some more than two centuries old), 250 varieties of azaleas and magnolias, and a majestic avenue of moss-covered, century-old oaks.

On the way, visit **Drayton Hall,** 2 mi. (3km) north on S.C. 61 (803/766-0188), one of the oldest plantations of the Southeast (1738), inhabited until 1974 by seven successive generations of the Drayton family. Beautiful Palladian architecture. An absolute must-see. Open daily.

☀☖ **MIDDLETON PLACE GARDENS** (14 mi./22km NW on S.C. 61) (803/556-6020): The oldest and one of the most beautiful landscaped gardens in the country, with cypress groves and thousands of azaleas (1741). The flower beds and plantations were severely damaged by hurricane Hugo in 1989. The gardens and the Tudor-style wing, miraculously spared by Civil War battles, house the Spoleto Festival/USA each year (see "Special Events," above). Not to be missed. Open daily.

☖ **OLD DORCHESTER STATE PARK** (20 mi./32km NW on S.C. 642) (803/873-1740): Archeological reserve close to the source of the Ashley River on the site of a village founded by Massachusetts colonists (1696). The British occupied it during the Revolutionary War and then razed it in 1781. Traces of Fort Dorchester and the church remain. Archeological digs in process. Interesting museum. Worth going out of your way for. Open daily.

FARTHER AFIELD

ATLANTIC ISLANDS (318 mi./509km r.t. on U.S. 17S, S.C. 700, S.C. 174, U.S. 21, S.C. 281, S.C. 170, U.S. 278, and U.S. 17N): Vacation excursion for 3 or more days for lovers of beaches, water sports, and semitropical wildlife more or less untamed. The suggested circuit includes visits (in the following order) to:

☀☖ **Kiawah Island:** 9,600 acres (4,000ha) of lush, subtropical vegetation plus 10 mi. (16km) of superb beaches, woods, and ponds haunted by alligators, deer, sea turtles, and 140 different species of birds. Accessible by road. The **Kiawah Island Resort,** a very comfortable three-star hotel, organizes island tours by Jeep and by boat (803/768-2121; see "Accommodations in the Vicinity," above). Visit not to be missed.

☖ **Edisto Island:** The best public beach in South Carolina (**Edisto Beach State Park**)—1.8 mi. (3km) of immaculate sand and a real treasure trove for seashell collectors.

☖ **Hunting Island:** 4,800 acres (2,000ha) of semi-wild nature, deserted beaches, subtropical forests, and swamps. Campgrounds and hiking trails. Island accessible by U.S. 21. Park open year round.

🛎 **Parris Island:** Settled in 1562 by the French Huguenot Jean Ribaut (there is a monument to him here), Parris Island is today home to a well-known U.S. Marines training camp. Military museum, War Memorial Building (803/525-3650). Open daily.

☀🛎🛎 **Hilton Head Island:** The largest island on the Atlantic coast between New Jersey and Florida, a fashionable summer getaway since the early 1960s, offers 12 mi. (19km) of beach, 18 golf courses, more than 200 tennis courts, and six marinas, plus a marvelous climate year round and an unpolluted sea. A vacation paradise. There are a dozen luxury hotels and motels, including the 🛎🛎🛎🛎 **Inter-Continental,** 135 S. Port Royal Dr., Hilton Head, SC 29928 (803/681-4000), 415 rms, **E–VE;** and the 🛎🛎 **Sea Crest Motel,** Avocet St., Hilton Head, SC 29928 (803/785-2121), 90 rms, **M–E.** Hilton Head is accessible by U.S. 278. Well worth going out of your way.

On the trip back to Charleston, see ☀🛎🛎 **Beaufort:** Built on the island of Port Royal, this pretty little town of 8,600 with charming old houses was home to the first Protestant colony in America (1562), the French Huguenots. Numerous antebellum structures, including St. Helena Episcopal Church (1724), the Arsenal (1795), and the John Mark Verdier House Museum (1790). Visitor Center, 910 Bay St. (803/524-3163). Not to be missed.

CHAPTER 11

SAVANNAH ⚕⚕

□ □ □

Once a major cotton- and tobacco-trading center, today the headquarters of the paper industry, Savannah, like its neighbor and rival, Charleston, is a living page from the history books. It is also one of the most beautiful cities in the U.S. The 13th—and last—of the colonies founded by the British on American shores, Savannah was conceived in 1733 as the continent's first "modern" city. Its founder, Gen. James Oglethorpe, an ecologist ahead of his time, created a checkerboarded urban plan of harmonious alternation between gardens, houses, and squares—green oases planted with mossy oaks, pines, and azaleas. Its cover of trees gives Savannah some shelter from the heat of a climate that can be truly oppressive in summer.

Since no house here is like its neighbor, the city displays the whole gamut of southern architectural styles—more than Atlanta, Charleston, or New Orleans, Savannah is *the* city of the Deep South. The colonnaded verandas, ornate facades, and flowered gardens along **Bull Street,** the wrought-iron balconies and pastel-washed houses with their stoops on **Abercorn Street,** come together in a living picture of peaceful, romantic charm straight out of *Gone With the Wind.*

The urban-restoration project in the **Savannah Historic District,** begun more than three decades ago, has been energetically implemented. But though Savannah boasts a complex of old buildings unequalled in America, it is no drowsy, languishing museum city. Miraculously spared during the Civil War by General Sherman because its inhabitants gave him a kindly reception at the end of his famous "March to the Sea" in 1864, Savannah is today a city on the move; you have only to walk along the docks on the **Savannah River,** or around the new **City Market** or **Riverfront Plaza,** the old cotton-mill district, to satisfy yourself of that.

Actor Stacy Keach, poet Conrad Aiken, and songwriter Johnny Mercer were born in Savannah.

BASIC FACTS: State of Georgia. Area code: 912. Time zone: eastern. ZIP Code (of the central post office): 31402. Founded: 1733. Approximate population: 142,000.

CLIMATE: A winter almost as mild as Florida's (Jan average, 52°F/11°C) is succeeded by an early, riotous spring (don't miss the azaleas in bloom in mid-Apr). After the hot, sticky summer (81°F/27°C average in July) comes the sunny fall, both typically subtropical with sudden late-afternoon downpours from mid-June to Sept. Every season has something to offer to the visitor.

DISTANCES: Atlanta, 251 mi. (401km); Charleston, 106 mi. (170km); Miami, 496 mi. (794km); Orlando, 292 mi. (467km); Washington, 633 mi. (1,012km).

ARRIVAL & TRANSIT INFORMATION

AIRPORT: Savannah International Airport (Travis Field) (SAV), 8 mi. (13km) NW; for information, call 964-0528.

AIRLINES: American (233-9988), Delta (234-1221), Eastern (236-4411), United (toll free 800/241-6522).

CITY LINK: The **cab** fare from the airport to dwntwn is about $14–$16; time, about 20 min. Bus: **McCall's Limos** (966-5364) serves major dwntwn hotels; leaves according to published schedule; fare, $8; time, 25 min.

Since the airport is close in and the city compact, you won't need to rent a car unless you plan excursions into the country around.

Cabs are relatively inexpensive, and public (bus) transportation by **Chatham Area Transit/CAT** (233-5767) is reasonably efficient.

CAR RENTAL (at the airport unless otherwise indicated): Avis (964-1781); Budget (964-9186); Hertz (964-1220); National (964-1771); Thrifty, 1714 Dean Forest Rd. (964-2341). For dwntwn locations, consult the local telephone directory.

LIMOUSINE SERVICES: Dav El Limousine (toll free 800/922-0343), McCall's Limos (966-5364).

TAXIS: Cabs may be hailed on the street, taken from the waiting lines outside the major hotels, or—most conveniently—called by phone: **Adam Cab** (927-7466) or **Yellow Cab** (236-1133).

TRAIN: Amtrak Station, 2611 Seaboard Coast Line Dr. (toll free 800/872-7245).

INTERCITY BUSES: Greyhound, 610 W. Oglethorpe Ave. (232-2135).

INFORMATION & TOURS

TOURIST INFORMATION: The **Savannah Convention and Visitors Bureau,** 222 W. Oglethorpe Ave., GA 31499 (912/944-0456; toll free 800/444-2427).

Savannah Visitors Center, 301 W. Broad St. (912/944-0456), open daily.

For a **recorded message** giving a current list of shows and cultural events, call 233-2787.

GUIDED TOURS: Cap'n Sam's Cruises (boat), River St. and Bull St. (234-7248): Cruises in the harbor and on the Savannah River, daily year round.

Carriage Tours (horse-drawn carriage), Madison Sq. (236-6756): Around Savannah in a horse-drawn carriage; unusual and pleasing. Daily, weather permitting.

Gray Line Tours (bus), 215 W. Boundary St. (236-9604): 2-hr. guided tour of the Historic District, serving major hotels and the Visitors Center.

Helen Salter's Savannah Scenic Tours (bus), 1113 Winston Ave. (355-4296): Conducted tours of the city and surroundings; serves leading dwntwn hotels.

Historic Savannah Foundation Tours (bus), 41 W. Broad St. (234-8687): Guided tours of Savannah's rich architectural heritage.

Savannah Sun Cruise (boat): 1-day mini-cruise along the Georgia coast on the S.S. *Savannah Sun;* lunch and dinner-dance. Leaves from Sheraton Savannah Resort Dock, 612 Wilmington Island Rd. (897-3310; toll free 800/331-0354).

SIGHTS, ATTRACTIONS & ACTIVITIES

ARCHITECTURAL HIGHLIGHTS: ⚷ **City Hall,** Bull St. and W. Bay St. (233-9321): Fine turn-of-the-century classical revival building capped by a gilded copper dome. Note the two British cannon in bronze, captured at the Battle of Yorktown and given to the city of Savannah by George Washington in 1791. Open Mon–Fri.

⚷ **U.S. Customs House,** Bull St. and E. Bay St. (944-4253); Erected in 1850 on the site where the city's founder, Englishman James Oglethorpe, built his first home in 1733. The capitals of its imposing granite columns are carved into the shape of tobacco leaves, as a tribute to this important local source of wealth.

BEACHES: ⚷ **Savannah Beach,** 18 mi. (28km) east on U.S. 80: Lovely fine-sand beach, some 6 mi. (9.5km) long, on **Tybee Island.** Historic lighthouse (1736) and interesting museum. Many hotels, motels, and restaurants; try the **Sands Motel,** Ocean Front at 14th St. (912/786-4596), 30 rms. The beaches are very popular in the warm weather.

CHURCHES/SYNAGOGUES: ⚷ **Christ Episcopal Church,** Johnson Sq. between E. St. Julian St. and E. Congress St. (232-4131): The first church in the colony (1733); among its famous rectors were John Wesley and George Whitefield, founders of the Methodist church. The present church with its immaculate white columns, dating from 1838, is the third to occupy the site. Should be seen. Open Tues–Fri.

⚷ **Congregation Mikve Israel,** 20 E. Gordon St. (233-1547): The only Gothic Revival synagogue in the country, built in 1878 for a congregation of German and Portuguese Jews which was founded in 1733. Museum with many ancient manuscripts, historical documents, letters from Presidents Washington, Jefferson, and Madison, etc. Guided tours Mon–Fri. Should be seen.

☀⚷ **First African Baptist Church,** 23 Montgomery St. (233-6597): Home of the oldest African American congregation in the country, founded in 1777 at Brampton Plantation. The present church dates from 1861. Should be seen; open daily.

☀⚷ **Independent Presbyterian Church,** Bull St. and W. Oglethorpe Ave. (236-3346): Founded in 1755 by members of the Church of Scotland; the design recalls the famous London church St. Martin-in-the-Fields on Trafalgar Sq. Georgian interior. Should be seen; open Mon–Fri.

HISTORIC BUILDINGS: ⚷ **King-Tisdell Cottage,** 514 E. Huntington St. (234-8000): Charming 1896 cottage with intricate gingerbread ornamentation. Dedicated to preserving the African American history and culture of Savannah and the Sea Islands, the exhibit rooms contain art objects, documents, and furniture typical of the turn-of-the-century black middle class. Open daily; worth a visit.

☀⚷⚷ **Savannah's Historic District,** a 2.2-sq.-mi. (5.9km²) area bounded by the Savannah River, Gaston St., and E. and W. Broad Sts.: More than 1,000 19th-century buildings scrupulously restored—the country's largest group of historic houses. Among the most interesting and elegant are:

The **Andrew Low House,** 329 Abercorn St. (233-6854), open Fri–Wed, a charming home dating from 1848. Among its illustrious guests are numbered Gen. Robert E. Lee and British writer William Makepeace Thackeray. Belonged at one time to Juliette Gordon Low, who founded the Girl Scouts in 1912.

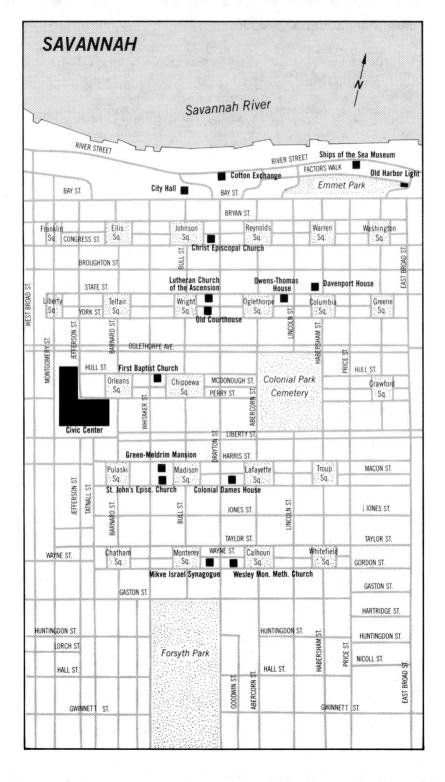

SAVANNAH

N

Savannah River

RIVER STREET

RIVER STREET

Ships of the Sea Museum

FACTORS WALK

Cotton Exchange

Old Harbor Light

BAY ST.

City Hall

BAY ST.

Emmet Park

BRYAN ST.

Franklin Sq.

CONGRESS ST.

Ellis Sq.

Johnson Sq.

Reynolds Sq.

Warren Sq.

Washington Sq.

Christ Episcopal Church

BROUGHTON ST.

EAST BROAD ST.

WEST BROAD ST.

STATE ST.

BULL ST.

Lutheran Church of the Ascension

Owens-Thomas House

Davenport House

Liberty Sq.

Telfair Sq.

YORK ST.

Wright Sq.

Oglethorpe Sq.

Columbia Sq.

Greene Sq.

Old Courthouse

MONTGOMERY ST.

JEFFERSON ST.

BARNARD ST.

OGLETHORPE AVE.

LINCOLN ST.

HABERSHAM ST.

PRICE ST.

HULL ST.

First Baptist Church

HULL ST.

Orleans Sq.

WHITAKER ST.

Chippewa Sq.

McDONOUGH ST.

PERRY ST.

Colonial Park Cemetery

Crawford Sq.

ABERCORN ST.

Civic Center

LIBERTY ST.

DRAYTON ST.

HARRIS ST.

Green-Meldrim Mansion

Pulaski Sq.

Madison Sq.

Lafayette Sq.

Troup Sq.

MACON ST.

JEFFERSON ST.

TATNALL ST.

BARNARD ST.

St. John's Episc. Church

Colonial Dames House

BULL ST.

JONES ST.

LINCOLN ST.

JONES ST.

TAYLOR ST.

TAYLOR ST.

WAYNE ST.

Chatham Sq.

Monterey Sq.

WAYNE ST.

Calhoun Sq.

Whitefield Sq.

GORDON ST.

Mikve Israel Synagogue

Wesley Mon. Meth. Church

GASTON ST.

GASTON ST.

HARTRIDGE ST.

HUNTINGDON ST.

HUNTINGDON ST.

HUNTINGDON ST.

LORCH ST.

Forsyth Park

HABERSHAM ST.

PRICE ST.

NICOLL ST.

HALL ST.

HALL ST.

GOODWIN ST.

ABERCORN ST.

EAST BROAD ST.

GWINNETT ST.

GWINNETT ST.

Davenport House, 324 E. State St. (236-8097), open daily, is a fine example of the Georgian "Federal" style dating from 1820, with superb old furniture and original elliptical staircase.

The **Green-Meldrim House,** Madison Sq. (233-3845), open Mon–Sat, an interesting Gothic Revival building with a characteristic wrought-iron portico, was General Sherman's headquarters at the end of the Civil War.

The **Juliette Gordon Low Birthplace,** Oglethorpe Ave. and Bull St. (233-4501), open Thurs–Tues, is an elegant 1821 house in Regency style, birthplace of the woman who founded the Girl Scouts.

The **Owens-Thomas House,** 124 Abercorn St. (233-9743), open daily (closed in Sept), is one of the loveliest examples of the Regency idiom in the U.S., built in 1816 to the design of the British architect William Jay. Lafayette stayed here.

The **William Scarbrough House,** 41 W. Broad St. (233-7703), open Mon–Fri, another remarkable example of the Regency style, dates from 1819. It's the home of the Historic Savannah Foundation, with a museum devoted to the process of rehabilitating old houses.

Don't fail to visit the Historic District.

MARKETS: ☼⚓ City Market, W. St. Julian between Montgomery St. and

Barnard St.: Opened in 1986 on the site of the first City Market, which dates back more than a century and a half, this new commercial center boasts hundreds of food, fashion, and handcraft shops, a flea market, and a dozen art galleries, as well as inviting bars and taverns in little Colonial-style brick buildings. Open daily; don't miss it. (The destruction of the original City Market in the 1950s, to make room for a sleazy parking lot, touched off a flood of indignant local patriotism and the creation of the Historic Savannah Foundation, which now protects the city's architectural heritage.)

MUSEUMS OF ART: ☼⚓ Telfair Mansion and Art Museum, 121 Barnard

St. (232-1177): Fine old porcelain, silverware, and traditional 18th- and 19th-century painting and sculpture from Europe and America, displayed in an elegant upper-class mansion in the Regency style, the work of William Jay. Be sure to see the splendid Octagon Room. This was the residence of the British governor from 1760 until the end of the War of Independence. Open Tues–Sun; not to be missed.

MUSEUMS OF SCIENCE & HISTORY: ☼⚓ Great Savannah Exposition,

303 W. Broad St. (238-1779): Temporary exhibitions and remarkable audiovisual shows illustrating the history of Savannah and the state of Georgia, in a 19th-century locomotive barn cunningly restored. In the **Spirit of the South Theater,** Disney-invented theatronic figures explain the city's 1733 beginnings. Open daily; not to be missed.

⚓ **Savannah Science Museum,** 4405 Paulsen St. (355-6705): Botany, zoology (interesting collection of reptiles and amphibians), aquarium. Exhibitions on medicine and physics. Well-designed planetarium. Should be seen; open Tues–Sun.

⚓ **Ships of the Sea Museum,** 503 E. River St. (232-1511): Interesting maritime museum on the banks of the Savannah River, with many ship models, old figureheads, and a fine scrimshaw collection. Reconstructions of a ship's carpenter's shop and a chandlery. Worth a visit. Open daily.

PANORAMAS: ⚓ Talmadge Memorial Bridge, north of W. Boundary St.:

From this bridge across the Savannah River you'll get a very good view of the city and of Riverfront Plaza along a line from north to south. Worth a look.

PARKS & GARDENS: ☼⚓ **Bonaventure Cemetery,** Bonaventure Rd., 10 min. east of dwntwn along the Wilmington River: Beautiful scenery. Hurricane-scrubbed boulders rear up from the damp earth and live oaks grieve in veils of Spanish moss. Look for the graves of composer Johnny Mercer and poet Conrad Aiken. Open daily; worth the detour.

☼⚓⚓ **City's Squares,** along Abercorn St., Barnard St., Bull St., Habersham St., and Houston St.: Wonderful public gardens, planted with azaleas, palm trees, pines, and moss oaks, in the heart of the Historic District. The finest are those along Bull St.: **Chippewa Square, Johnson Square, Madison Square, Monterey Square,** and **Wright Square.** A sight to be seen.

⚓ **Colonial Park Cemetery,** E. Oglethorpe Ave. and Abercorn St.: Dating from 1750, this was for many years the only public burial ground in the colony. Contains the graves of many founders of Georgia and of Button Gwinnett, one of the signers of the Declaration of Independence. It has been a city park since 1896. The old tombstone inscriptions are well worth a glance.

⚓ **Forsyth Park,** Gaston St. and Bull St.: With its great fountain, reminiscent of the one in Paris's place de la Concorde, and its Confederate Monument, this is the largest public park in Savannah. Try to see it, particularly in spring when the azaleas are in bloom.

☼⚓ **Trustee's Garden Site,** E. Broad St. at E. Bryan St.: Originally the site of a botanic garden planted in 1733 by the first English settlers on the model of the Chelsea Gardens in London, with a view to raising medicinal plants, vines, and mulberry trees for silkworms. The first peaches planted here are the origin of Georgia's renowned peach crop. In 1762 a fort was built here; it was captured in 1782 by Gen. "Mad Anthony" Wayne during the war against the British. Today you'll find here several elegantly restored 19th-century houses, as well as the **Pirate's House,** a sailors' tavern reminiscent of that described by Robert Louis Stevenson in *Treasure Island* (see "Restaurants," below). Should be seen.

PERFORMING ARTS: For a daily listing of all shows and cultural events, consult the entertainment pages of the daily papers *Savannah Morning News* (morning) and *Savannah Evening Press* (evening).

City Lights Theater Company, 15 W. York Lane (234-9860): Every year hosts the famous Savannah Playwright's Festival (Feb–Mar).

Savannah Civic Center, Montgomery St. at Liberty St. (236-4275): This auditorium is the home of the Savannah Symphony Orchestra; also ballet, Broadway hits, musicals.

Savannah Theater, Chippewa Sq. (233-7764): One of the oldest theaters in the country. Drama, comedy, contemporary theater.

SPECIAL EVENTS: For the exact schedule of events below, consult the **Savannah Visitors Center** (see "Tourist Information," above).

Georgia Week (Feb): Parades, concerts, exhibitions; a colorful commemoration of the founding of Georgia.

St. Patrick's Day (mid-Mar): One of the biggest popular parades on the East Coast, drawing more than 250,000 participants every year. Second only to New York's.

Savannah Tour of Homes and Gardens (late Mar to early Apr): Guided tours, by daylight or by candlelight, of some 30 historic private houses and their gardens. Sponsored by Christ Episcopal Church and the Historic Savannah Foundation. For information, call 234-8054.

Night in Old Savannah (third wknd in Apr): Folklore and food festival; jazz concerts.

Christmas in Savannah (Dec): A month of festivities in the Historic District, with parades, concerts, house tours, cultural events, etc.

SPORTS: Savannah has a minor-league team in **baseball** (Apr–Oct), the Savannah Cardinals (farm team of the St. Louis Cardinals), Grayson Stadium (391-9150).

Deep-Sea Fishing
The Georgia coast rivals that of Florida in its abundance of fish, and attracts many sport-fishermen in season. Some recommended charter-boat operators are **Bottom Line Charters,** 1412-B Walthour Rd. (897-6503); *Neva Miss* **Charters,** 2 Cedar Point (897-2706); and **Salt Water Charters,** 111 Wickersham Dr. (598-1814).

STROLLS: ※⚖ **Bull Street,** between Bay St. and Forsyth Park: Savannah's elegant main street, with many old houses, historic churches, and superb flower-planted squares. A walk you should take.

⚖ **Factors Walk,** between Bull St. and E. Broad St.: Running between old buildings formerly used in the cotton business, these narrow cobbled ramps, reached by a network of wrought-iron footbridges, have retained all the flavor of the 19th century. Their cobblestones were once ballast in ships coming here from Europe. There, cotton merchants, called factors in the early 1800s, inspected bales of Sea Island fibers before closing a deal. A sight not to be missed.

※⚖ **Waterfront Area,** around John P. Rousakis Riverfront Plaza: Old brick warehouses along the Savannah River, now converted into boutiques, restaurants, pubs, art galleries, nightclubs. Lively and colorful by day and night alike. At sunrise and sunset the view from the quays is magnificent. One of the finest examples of urban renovation in the U.S.; don't miss it.

ACCOMMODATIONS
A Note on Accommodations: Room rates in Savannah are coded as follows: **VE,** Very Expensive ($140 and up); **E,** Expensive ($90–$140); **M,** Moderate ($60–$90); **I,** Inexpensive ($30–$60); **B,** Budget (up to $30). A listing of toll-free numbers is in the Appendix.

Personal Favorites (in order of preference)
※ 🍷🍷🍷 **The Mulberry** (dwntwn), 601 E. Bay St., GA 31401 (912/238-1200; toll free 800/554-5544). 125 rms, A/C, color TV, in-rm movies. AE, DC, MC, V. Free parking, pool, rest. (Christopher's), bar, 24-hr. rm svce, free crib. *Note:* Small, gracious, unusually designed luxury hotel. The main building began life as a livery stable in the 1860s, was converted into a Coca-Cola bottling plant, and has now been tastefully restored, w. an elegant classical revival decor. Period furniture, many art objects; pretty interior grdn. Spacious rms, some w. minibars; impeccable svce; very good hotel rest. Distinction and charm in the heart of Old Savannah. **E,** but lower rates off-season.

※ 🍷🍷🍷 **Foley House Inn** (dwntwn), 14 W. Hull St., GA 31401 (912/232-6622; toll free 800/647-3708). 20 rms, A/C, color TV, in-rm movies. AE, MC, V. Street parking, hot tub, valet svce, free breakfast, free crib. *Note:* Charming, luxuriously restored 19th-century mansion looking out on Chippewa Sq. in the heart of the Historic District. Original Victorian setting and period furniture. Each rm is decorated in its own style, most having private patios, Jacuzzis, VCR's, and fireplaces. Ultra-polished reception and svce. Since there is no elevator, avoid the rms on the third and fourth floors. For those who love glimpses of the past. Resv. advisable, a good while ahead. **E–VE,** but lower rates off-season.

🍷🍷🍷 **Hilton–De Soto** (dwntwn), Liberty St. and Bull St., GA 31402 (912/232-9000; toll free, see Hilton). 250 rms, A/C, color TV, in-rm movies. AE, CB, DC, MC, V. Free parking, pool, bicycles for rent, rest. (Pavilion), coffee shop, bar, 24-hr. rm svce, nightclub, free airport limo, free crib. *Note:* The most famous hotel in Savannah, on the site of the old, and now legendary, De Soto Hotel. The modern building agrees well enough w. its surroundings. Comfortable rms, some w. private balconies or patios. Attentive svce. A favorite w. those in-the-know. Very centrally located. **M–E**

Ballastone Inn (dwntwn), 14 E. Oglethorpe Ave, GA 31401 (912/236-1484). 18 rms, A/C, color TV, in-rm movies. AE, MC, V. Street parking, café nearby, 24-hr. rm svce, concierge, free Continental breakfast. *Note:* Charming guesthouse built in 1835. Period furnishings and gracious svce including turn-down w. brandy and pralines. Courtyard grdn w. fountain. **E–VE**

Ramada Inn Civic Center (dwntwn), 201 W. Oglethorpe Ave., GA 31401 (912/651-6556; toll free, see Ramada Inns). 202 rms, A/C, cable color TV. AE, CB, DC, MC, V. Free parking, pool, sundeck, rest. (Juliette's), bar, rm svce, hrdrsr, free crib. *Note:* Modern, comfortable motel in brick w. wrought-iron balconies. Rather huge rms. Friendly reception and svce, very acceptable rest. Good value in the heart of the Historic District. **I–M**

Travelodge (dwntwn), 512 W. Oglethorpe Ave., GA 31401 (912/233-9251; toll free, see Travelodge). 56 rms, A/C, color TV. AE, CB, DC, MC, V. Free parking, adj. pool and rest., free coffee. *Note:* Typical small motel very nr. the Visitor Center and the Historic District. Functionally comfortable rms, efficient reception and svce. Good value; ideal for the budget traveler. **I**

Other Accommodations (from top bracket to budget)

Hyatt Regency (dwntwn), 2 W. Bay St., GA 31401 (912/238-1234; toll free, see Hyatt). 346 rms, A/C, color TV, in-rm movies. AE, CB, DC, MC, V. Valet gar. $6, pool, health club, bike rental, marina, rest. (Windows), coffee shop, bar, rm svce, disco, boutiques, concierge. *Note:* The giant among local hotels. Modern, uninspired high-rise, but spacious, very comfortable rms w. balconies, the best overlooking the Savannah River. Moorings, for a fee. Efficient svce; business and group clientele. Very well located on the river, a couple of blocks from City Hall. Recently renovated. **E–VE**

Planters Inn (formerly the Royal Colony; dwntwn), 29 Abercorn St., GA 31401 (912/232-5678; toll free 800/554-1187). 57 rms, A/C, cable color TV. AE, CB, DC, MC, V. Valet gar. $6, bar, rm svce, concierge, free breakfast, free crib. *Note:* Urbane, intimate small hotel looking onto Reynolds Sq. in the center of the Historic District. Elegant, comfortable layouts w. four-poster beds, period furniture, and private balconies. Exceptionally attentive svce. An excellent place to stay. **M–E**

Magnolia Place Inn (dwntwn), 503 Whitaker St., GA 31401 (912/236-7674; toll free 800/238-7674). 13 rms, A/C, color TV, in-rm movies. AE, MC, V. Limited-parking lot, valet svce, concierge, free Continental breakfast. *Note:* Artfully restored Victorian mansion built in 1878 w. landscaped courtyard. Overlooks Forsyth Park. Antique-filled rms w. private patios or balconies (some w. Jacuzzi). Cheerful reception and svce. **M–E**

17 Hundred 90 Inn (dwntwn), 307 E. President St., GA 31401 (912/236-7122). 14 rms, A/C, color TV, in-rm movies. AE, CB, DC, MC, V. Street parking, rest., bar, valet svce, free breakfast, crib $6. *Note:* Delightful old Colonial home dating, as the name indicates, from 1790. Each rm is decorated in different fashion, but all in the Georgian style of the last century. Oversize beds and antique furniture. Personalized reception and svce. Acceptable rest. One of the most charming places to stay in Savannah. **M–E**

Days Inn Historic District (dwntwn), 201 W. Bay St., GA 31401 (912/236-4440; toll free, see Days Inns). 252 rms,

A/C, color TV, in-rm movies. AE, DC, MC, V. Free parking, pool, 24-hr. rest., valet svce, free crib. *Note:* Modern motel in the heart of Savannah; the dark-red brick facade melds perfectly w. its Historic District setting. Spacious, comfortable rms, some w. kitchenettes, the best overlooking the Savannah River. Efficient svce. Group clientele. Good value. **I–M**

    Best Western Riverfront Inn (dwntwn), 412 W. Bay St., GA 31401 (912/233-1011; toll free, see Best Western). 142 rms, A/C, color TV, in-rm movies. AE, CB, DC, MC, V. Free parking, pool, rest. (Bottle Works), bar, free crib. *Note:* Conventional but well-run motel standing, as its name implies, almost on the bank of the Savannah River and very nr. the Historic District. Huge, comfortable, recently renovated rms, friendly reception and svce. Ideal if you're driving. Excellent value. **I–M**, but lower rates off-season.

    La Quinta (nr. dwntwn), 6805 Abercorn St., GA 31405 (912/355-3004; toll free, see La Quinta). 154 rms, A/C, color TV, in-rm movies. AE, DC, MC, V. Free parking, pool, rest., free breakfast, free crib. *Note:* Warm, inviting motel nr. Oglethorpe Mall w. its dozens of shops, stores, and rests. Comfortable, well-designed rms. Business clientele. 8 min. from dwntwn. Good value. **I**

In the Vicinity

    Sheraton Savannah Resort and Country Club (vic.), 612 Wilmington Island Rd., GA 31410 (912/897-1612; toll free, see Sheraton). 202 rms (in the hotel) or cottages, A/C, color TV, in-rm movies. AE, CB, DC, MC, V. Free parking, pool, sauna, health club, golf course, putting green, five tennis courts, horseback riding, private beach, boats, fishing, water sports, two rests., two bars, rm svce, disco, free crib. *Note:* Very lovely resort hotel on the Wilmington River less than 15 min. by car from Savannah, completely renovated and tastefully decorated. Comfortable cottages and villas clustering around a charming old 1920s hotel. Acceptable rests.; attentive svce. Ideal for open-air sports, w. one of the finest golf courses in the country. The American Plan is very good value. Interesting wknd discounts. **E** (hotel) **and VE** (cottages), but lower rates Nov–Mar.

RESTAURANTS

    A Note on Restaurant Prices: Savannah restaurant prices, per person, excluding drinks and service charges, are coded as follows: **VE,** Very Expensive ($60 and up); **E,** Expensive ($40–$60); **M,** Moderate ($25–$40); **I,** Inexpensive ($15–$25); **B,** Budget (up to $15).

Personal Favorites (in order of preference)

    Elizabeth on 37th (nr. dwntwn), 105 E. 37th St. (236-5547). A/C. Dinner only, Mon–Sat; closed hols and Aug. AE, MC, V. Jkt. *Specialties:* wild-mushroom pies, rack of lamb w. pistachios, spiced southern quail, shrimp Savannah, sea bass filets w. vegetables wrapped in parchment, oysters and country ham w. leeks in cream sauce, green onion pancake; superb desserts. Good wine list at reasonable prices. *Note:* Since it opened in 1981 Savannah's top-rated rest. has won plaudits from all the food critics. Imagination, lightness, and top-quality materials (especially seafood) are the three golden rules of Elizabeth Terry, the extraordinary self-taught chef. Her husband, Michael, a former Atlanta lawyer and a wine lover, makes a wonderful sommelier. The rest. occupies a beautifully restored old house just south of Forsyth Park. Praiseworthy svce. A wonderful place to eat, 10 min. from dwntwn. Resv. a must. *American.* **M**

    Pirate's House (dwntwn), 20 E. Broad St. (233-5757). A/C. Lunch/dinner daily, brunch Sun. AE, CB, DC, MC, V. Jkt. *Specialties:* seafood bisque, "shrab" (combination of shrimp and crabmeat), gumbo, oysters Savannah, jambalaya, seafood w. red rice, flounder Florentine, roast duckling, catch of the day, steak; 40-item dessert menu. *Note:* This huge, picturesque museum-tavern, 2½ centuries old, houses one of Georgia's best rests., serving many regional specialties such as "red rice" Savannah style (w. tomatoes and spices). Legend has it that Captain Flint, of Stevenson's classic adventure story *Treasure Island*, drew his last breath here. Amusing maritime decor; splendid bar. An experience not to be missed—but take care not to lose yourself; the place boasts no fewer than 23 rooms, each decorated differently! Resv. advised. *Seafood/American.* I–M

�w♐ **Johnny Harris** (nr. dwntwn), 1651 E. Victory Dr. (354-
♐♐ 7810). A/C. Lunch/dinner Mon–Sat; closed Jan 1, Dec 25.
AE, CB, DC, MC, V. Jkt. (J&T on Fri–Sat evenings.) *Specialties:* crabmeat au gratin, steak, barbecued pork, southern fried chicken, prime rib, catch of the day. *Note:* A three-generation-old institution for lovers of good, solid food. The beef and the barbecued spareribs, served w. fresh vegetables (something uncommon enough to deserve mention), are highly recommended. Diligent svce. Uninspiring rustic decor. A 10-min. drive from dwntwn. Locally very popular; resv. recommended. *American.* I

♐♐ **The Boar's Head** (dwntwn), 1 N. Lincoln St. at River St. (232-
3196). A/C. Lunch/dinner daily; closed hols. AE, MC, V.
Specialties: oysters on the half shell, steak, lobster and catch of the day broiled over a wood fire, veal Florentine. *Note:* Prime fresh seafood and fine red meat broiled over a wood fire are the strong suits of this rustic-seeming rest. overlooking the Savannah River. Bare brick and wood paneling appeal to the tourist trade, but create a congenial atmosphere. Friendly, hard-working svce. Resv. advised. Very good value. *Steak/Seafood.* I

♐ **Mrs. Wilke's Boarding House** (dwntwn), basement of 107 W.
♐ Jones St. (232-5997). A/C. Breakfast/lunch Mon–Fri. No
credit cards. *Specialties:* barbecued spareribs, southern fried chicken, collard greens, ham and gravy, swordfish steak, homemade cakes, banana pudding. *Note:* Colorful boarding house, serving authentic regional food—all you can eat—in a somewhat minimal setting. Visitors and businesspeople sit side by side, family style. The best value in Savannah. No resv. Locally popular. *American.* B

Other Restaurants (from top bracket to budget)

♐♐♐ **45 South** (nr. dwntwn), 20 E. Broad St. (233-1881). A/C.
♐♐♐ Lunch Mon–Fri, dinner Mon–Sat; closed hols. AE, DC, MC,
V. Jkt. *Specialties:* mussels and artichokes w. ginger, roulade of salmon w. leeks, snapper filet w. julienne of vegetables, peppered breast of duck w. polenta and spinach, strawberry puff pastry. *Note:* Inspired, delicate American nouvelle cuisine, particularly noteworthy for its light-as-air sauces. Hasn't lost its appeal—on the contrary—since moving to its new address; very good svce. Over the past couple of years has established a strong local following; resv. advised. *American.* I–M

☼♐♐ **Olde Pinke House** (dwntwn), 23 Abercorn St. (232-4286).
♐♐♐ A/C. Lunch Mon–Sat, dinner nightly; closed Dec 25. AE,
MC, V. Jkt. (tie suggested). *Specialties:* seafood crêpes, turtle-bean soup, baby flounder stuffed w. crab, shrimp Créole, chateaubriand, chicken Cordon Bleu. *Note:* A designated historic monument, this attractive pink mansion (whence the name) serves excellent traditional European food and some local dishes as well. Charming 18th-century decor, w. waitresses in period dress. Resv. recommended. Congenial tavern (Planters Tavern) in the cellar. *Seafood/Continental.* I–M

♐♐ **River's End** (vic.), 3122 River Rd., in Thunderbolt (354-
♐♐ 2973). A/C. Dinner only, Mon–Sat; closed hols. AE, CB,
DC, MC, V. Jkt. *Specialties:* scampi, catch of the day, sautéed flounder w. grape sauce, steak, Maine lobsters, homemade pies. *Note:* Elegant, polished cuisine whose billing—"direct from fishing boat to cooking stove"—is fully justified.

Fine view of the Intracoastal Waterway and the fleet of shrimp boats (customers can moor their own boats in front of the rest.). Preppy crowd; resv. advised. *Seafood.* **I–M**

☖ **Garibaldi's Café** (dwntwn), 315 W. Congress St. (232-7118). ☖ A/C. Dinner only, nightly; closed Thanksgiving and Dec 25. AE, MC, V. *Specialties:* fresh homemade pasta, northern Italian dishes, broiled duck, catch of the day. *Note:* Charming *trattoria* in a converted 1870s firehouse in the heart of the Historic District. Praiseworthy Italian food; excellent espresso; youthful, trendy atmosphere; resv. advised. *Italian.* **I**

☼☖ **Crystal Beer Parlor** (dwntwn), 301 W. Jones St., at Jefferson St. (232/1153). A/C. Lunch/dinner Mon–Sat. AE, MC, V. *Specialties:* hamburgers, fried chicken, crab stew, gumbo, fried-oyster sandwich. *Note:* Congenial, very popular pub w. pleasantly faded decor—yellowed photos on the walls, ceiling fans, worn wood floor. Excellent draft beer and overstuffed sandwiches. A Savannah landmark since 1933. Relaxed atmosphere; no resv. *American.* **B–I**

☼☖ **Wall's Bar-B-Que** (dwntwn), 515 E. York St. (232-9745). Lunch/dinner Thurs–Sat. No credit cards. *Specialties:* sandwiches, southern fried chicken, deviled crabcakes, barbecued spareribs. *Note:* This modest, almost grungy place on an unpaved alley between Houston St. and Price St. is credited by the experts w. the best barbecued ribs and crabcakes in town. The experience should not be missed, in spite of the depressing atmosphere and setting. No resv. *American.* **B**

Cafeterias/Fast Food

Morrisson's (dwntwn), Bull St. and Bryan St. (232-5264). Lunch/dinner daily (till 8:30pm). MC, V. Roast beef, daily specials, salads, sandwiches. Good cafeteria food in an old Savannah setting. Locally popular. Other location: 7804 Abercorn St. at Oglethorpe Mall (352-3521).

BARS & NIGHTCLUBS

Comedy House (nr. dwntwn), 317 Eisenhower Dr. (356-1045). Typical comedy club presenting comedians from across the U.S. Shows Tues–Sat.

Emma's (dwntwn), Riverfront Plaza (232-1223). Cozy, friendly piano bar. Emma Kelly, billed as the woman of 6,000 songs, plays her piano every night. You name it, she plays it. One of the oldest Savannah traditions.

Mikki's Piano Jazz Lounge (dwntwn), 219 W. St. Julian St. at City Market (233-3015). Savannah's best jazz lounge with live music nightly.

Spanky's (dwntwn), 317 E. River St. (236-3009). Congenial saloon on the banks of the Savannah River; an amusing contrast between the historic setting and the youthful atmosphere. Pizzas and sandwiches. Locally popular. Open nightly.

Sweet Georgia Brown's (dwntwn), 312 W. St. Julian St. (232-7464). Piano bar New Orleans style. Savannah's answer to Pat O'Brien's. Congenial atmosphere. Open Mon–Sat.

NEARBY EXCURSIONS

☼☖ **FORT JACKSON** (3 mi./5km east via President St. and Woodcock Dr.) (232-3945): Situated on the banks of the Savannah River and surrounded by moats, this is one of the oldest (1809) forts in Georgia to survive intact. Its moments of glory were in the War of 1812 and the War Between the States. Now it houses many 19th-century military accessories and devices illustrating the history of its construction and its battles. Interesting. Open Tues–Sun Mar–Nov, wknds only the rest of the year.

☼☖ **FORT McALLISTER HISTORIC PARK** (25 mi/40km south on U.S. 17 and Ga. 144) (727-2339): Carefully restored Civil War fort, originally built by the Confederates for the defense of Savannah. Its capture by Union forces on December 13, 1864, spelled the downfall of the city and marked the end of Sherman's "March to the Sea." Military museum. Open Tues–Sun; worth the side trip.

FORT PULASKI NATIONAL MONUMENT (15 mi./
24km east on U.S. 80) (786-5787): One of the largest and best-known defense works on the eastern seaboard, named after the Revolutionary War hero who was killed at the Battle of Savannah in 1779. Witnessed fierce artillery exchanges between North and South during the Civil War. Completely restored before World War II. Museum. Open daily; well worth the detour.

HILTON HEAD ISLAND (38 mi./60km NW on U.S. Alt.
17, S.C. 170, S.C. 46, and U.S. 278): Discovered by the Spaniards in 1526, this inviting island has become one of the most sought-after summer resorts in the country, by virtue of its superb beaches, piney woods, and old plantation houses. Dozens of hotels, motels, vacation cottages, art galleries, and elegant boutiques; 200 tennis courts, 18 golf courses, six marinas, etc. Worth the detour. For details, see Chapter 10 on Charleston.

FARTHER AFIELD

CUMBERLAND ISLAND NATIONAL SEASHORE
(145 mi./232km SW on I-95, Ga. 40, and a ferry): Along the entire Atlantic coast, this is the island most nearly in an unspoiled, natural state. Long uninhabited, this island 16 mi. (26km) long by 1½–3 mi. (2–5km) wide, covered in moss oaks and dwarf palmettos, with its marshes and empty beaches, teems with ibis, duck, alligators, and wild ponies. Reached by boat from **St. Mary's,** daily in summer, Thurs–Mon Sept–June; resv. necessary (for information, call 912/882-4335). Limited number of camping sites available. The tiny (nine-rm) ※ ⌂ **Greyfield Inn,** P.O. Drawer B, Fernandina Beach, FL 32034 (904/261-6408), occupies an old Colonial-style villa built by millionaire Thomas Carnegie, who once owned the island (rates: **E**). A memorable experience for lovers of nature-in-the-raw. Should be combined with the trip to **Golden Isles** (see below).

OKEFENOKEE NATIONAL WILDLIFE REFUGE (122
mi./195km SW on U.S. 17, Ga. 196, U.S. 82, and U.S. 1): The largest wetlands park in the country after Florida's Everglades, with an area of 700 sq. mi. (2,080km²). Enormous variety of flora and fauna: black bear, deer, lynx, alligators, water birds, etc. Canoe trips through the swamp. No overnight facilities. Park open daily year round. For information, ask the refuge manager, Rte. 2, Folkston, GA 31537 (912/496-3331). Well worth the detour; combine it with the excursion to **Golden Isles** (see below).

GOLDEN ISLES (about 180 mi./288km) r.t. via I-95S and
U.S. 17N): According to legend, the isles owe their name to the many hoards of treasure buried in their sands by the famous pirate Edward Teach, better known as Blackbeard. Another version attributes it to the wonderfully warm and sunny climate of the Georgia coast. Either way, you'll find some of the lushest, most gracious islands on the Atlantic coast. The Golden Isles offer a whole gamut of vacation activities: fishing, golf, sailing, horseback riding, etc. Don't miss them.

First you come to **Jekyll Island,** the smallest but also the most chic of the Golden Isles, originally named Île de la Somme by the French Huguenots who landed here in 1562; the last shipload of African slaves to enter the U.S. was unloaded here in 1858. Jekyll became an exclusive winter resort for titans in American industry and finance from 1885 to the end of World War II: Rockefeller, Gould, J. P. Morgan, Vanderbilt, Joseph Pulitzer, and Goodyear were among those who built sumptuous villas here, which are now open to visitors, daily year round.

On **St. Simons Island,** where until the Civil War there were rich plantations, the English General Oglethorpe, the founder of Savannah, built Fort Frederica, now **Fort Frederica National Monument** (638-3639), in 1736. Burned down in 1758, the fort and the little town it protected were abandoned. Open daily. Wonderful beaches lined with forests of oak, pine, and palm trees.

Sea Island boasts many beautiful seaside homes as well as dozens of ocean-front hotels and motels. ♜ ♜ ♜ ♜ **The Cloister,** 100 First St., Sea Island, GA. 31561 (912/3611; toll free 800/732-4752), is one of the grandest grand hotels on the Georgia coast. Luxurious accommodations (764 rms or cottages. Rates: **VE**).

CHAPTER 12

ATLANTA ♀

□ □ □

Atlanta, known and loved by generations of movie-goers through *Gone With the Wind*, was the paragon of southern cities at the time of the Civil War: brilliant, lavish, and cultured. After one of the most ferocious battles of that war —117 days of siege by General Sherman (1864)—90% of the city lay in ruins. The only traces that remain from this tragic period are the recently restored **Underground Atlanta** and its famous **Zero Mile Post** marking the terminus of the first Western & Atlantic Railroad line (1837). Not far from here is **Peachtree Street,** dear to the heart of Scarlett O'Hara and today Atlanta's most elegant and lively downtown thoroughfare. Founded as Terminus in 1837 and incorporated as Marthasville in 1843, the city received its present name in 1845, perhaps reflecting a feminine form of Atlantic in the railroad's name.

Like a phoenix, Atlanta rose from the ashes of the Civil War to become the economic and cultural capital of the Deep South. Today it is a modern, ever-expanding metropolis, and ranks ninth among the American cities in terms of economic growth rate. Testifying to Atlanta's extraordinary financial and industrial vitality are more than 1,800 factories (automobile, aviation, chemical, paper, steel, food), the CNN television empire, 130 banks, and dozens of multinational corporations (including Georgia Pacific, Nabisco, and especially Coca-Cola, maker of the universally famous beverage, which Doc Pemberton invented here in 1886).

A veritable turntable for road, rail, and air transportation, Atlanta possesses one of the busiest airports in the world, Hartsfield International Airport. Georgia's capital also boasts some of the most spectacular modern structures in the U.S., including the country's tallest hotel (the **Westin Peachtree Plaza,** an immense glass-and-steel, 73-story tower), the **IBM Building** by Philip Johnson and John Burgee, and the new **Carter Presidential Center,** both library and international conference center.

In 1973 Atlanta became the third major American city to elect a black mayor (after Cleveland and Los Angeles). Atlanta was the birthplace of Nobel Peace Prize winner Martin Luther King, Jr.—don't miss the **Martin Luther King, Jr., Historic District** in the heart of downtown; its children also include historian Daniel Boorstin, novelist Margaret Mitchell, cable TV magnate Ted Turner, and the architect who revolutionized contemporary hotel construction, John Portman.

BASIC FACTS: Capital of the state of Georgia. Area code: 404. Time zone: eastern. ZIP Code (of central post office): 30301. Founded: 1837. Approximate population: city, 430,000; metropolitan area, 2,680,000. 13th-largest metropolitan area in the country.

CLIMATE: Spring is rather brief but pleasant, especially May. Summer is hot and sticky (mean July temperature, 80°F/27°C, but with 70% humidity). Winter is relatively mild but rainy (mean Jan temperature, 45°F/5°C). The best season to visit Atlanta is autumn; Sept, Oct, and Nov are the sunniest months.

DISTANCES: Miami, 659 mi. (1,055km); Nashville, 242 mi. (387km); New Orleans, 481 mi. (770km); Savannah, 251 mi. (401km); Washington, 608 mi. (975km).

ARRIVAL & TRANSIT INFORMATION

AIRPORT: Hartsfield Atlanta International Airport (ATL): 9 mi. (14km) SW. Its new terminal is the largest in the world. It is, with 48 million passengers each year, the world's second busiest airport. Information: 530-6600.

DOMESTIC AIRLINES: American (521-2655), Continental (436-3300), Delta (765-5000), Eastern (435-1111), Northwest (577-3271), TWA (522-5738), United (394-2234), and USAir (toll free 800/428-4322).

FOREIGN CARRIERS: British Airways (toll free 800/247-9297), Japan Air Lines (toll free 800/525-3663), Lufthansa (toll free 800/645-3880), Sabena (toll free 800/645-3790).

CITY LINK: Cab fare to city center, about $18; time, 30 min. Bus: **Atlanta Airport Shuttle** (toll free 800/438-0038); leaves every 20 min.; serves major dwntwn hotels; fare, $9; time, 40 min. Direct **subway (MARTA)** connection to dwntwn; leaves every 20 min.; fare, $1. The proximity of the airport and the compactness of dwntwn Atlanta may mean that you don't need to rent a car. Atlanta also has an efficient public transportation system (bus, subway), currently being expanded (MARTA) (522-4711).

CAR RENTAL (at the airport unless otherwise indicated): Avis (530-2700); Budget (530-3000); Dollar (766-0244); Hertz (530-2900); National (530-2800); Thrifty, 3114 Sylvan Rd. SW (761-5286). For dwntwn locations, consult the phone directory.

LIMOUSINE SERVICES: Carey Limousine (681-3366), Dav El Limousine (toll free 800/922-0343), Sun Belt Limo (toll free 800/438-0038).

TAXIS: Expensive and undependable, taxis may not be hailed on the street but must be summoned by phone. The best are **Checker Cab** (351-1111), **London** (688-5658), and **Yellow Cab** (521-0200).

TRAIN: Amtrak, Peachtree Station, 1688 Peachtree St. NW (872-9815).

INTERCITY BUSES: Greyhound, 81 International Blvd. (522-6300).

INFORMATION & TOURS

TOURIST INFORMATION: Convention & Visitors Bureau, 233 Peachtree St. NE, Suite 200, GA 30342 (404/521-6600).
Visitor Information Center, Peachtree Center Mall (404/521-6633). For a **recorded message** giving a list of current shows and cultural events, call 404/329-4500.

GUIDED TOURS: Atlanta Preservation Center Tours, 84 Peachtree St. NW (522-4345): Walking tours of Atlanta downtown offered daily Apr–Oct.

Gray Line Tours (bus) (767-0594): Guided tour of the city and environs, serving principal dwntwn hotels.

SIGHTS, ATTRACTIONS & ACTIVITIES

ARCHITECTURAL HIGHLIGHTS: ☼⚒ **Federal Reserve Bank,** 104 Marietta St. NW (521-8747): Imposing Greek Revival building on the site of the Jacobs Pharmacy where, in May 1886, John Pemberton created the famous Coca-Cola formula. Today it houses immense, rigorously guarded workshops where many millions of banknotes are printed each day. Interesting currency museum. Open Mon–Fri by appointment only.

☼⚒⚓⚓ **IBM Building,** 1207 W. Peachtree St. NW (877-6800): Atlanta's most dramatic building (1987). Beautiful postmodern skyscraper, crowned by a 100-ft. (30m) copper pyramid topped by a lantern. Philip Johnson/John Burgee designed, 50 stories and 825-ft. (251m) high, the building detailing is "American Gothic" and inspired by the famous Tribune Tower in Chicago. Worth a look.

☼⚒⚓⚓ **Peachtree Center,** bounded by Baker St., Ellis St., Williams St., and Courtland St. NE: Futurist complex of office skyscrapers, an ultramodern 73-story hotel, and a giant shopping mall with luxury boutiques, restaurants, bars, and interior gardens linked by walkways and footbridges. One of the country's most spectacular architectural assemblies. An absolute must-see.

BROADCASTING & MOVIE STUDIOS: ⚒ **CNN** (formerly Omni) **Center,** Marietta St. and Techwood Dr. NW (659-0000): One of dwntwn Atlanta's most recent additions. Its ultramodern, sometimes assertive buildings include the **Cable News Network** studios, office buildings, restaurants, movie theaters, hotels, and sports and convention centers. 45-min. guided tour around the studios, editorial offices, and technical equipment of CNN leaves daily every hour on the hour from 10am; call 827-2400 for information. Worth a look.

HISTORIC BUILDINGS & STRUCTURES: ⚒ **A. G. Rhodes Memorial Hall,** 1516 Peachtree St. NW (881-9980): Victorian Romanesque Revival building built in 1903 in the style of a Bavarian castle. Headquarters of the Georgia Trust for Historic Preservation. Interesting changing exhibits. Tours Mon–Fri. Worth a visit.

☼⚒ **Alonzo F. Herndon House,** 587 University Pl. NW (581-9813): Born a slave, Alonzo F. Herndon rose to become the city's wealthiest black citizen as founder of Atlanta Life Insurance Co. The luxurious 15-room mansion he built in 1910 offers a glimpse of a remarkable life. Original furniture and turn-of-the-century memorabilia. Tours Tues–Sat. Should be seen.

☼⚒ **Fox Theatre,** 660 Peachtree St. NE (892-5685): Once a Masonic temple dating from 1929 with an onion dome and minarets, and then a movie theater with rather dizzying Hollywood-Moorish architecture, the Fox, a historical landmark, is now a 4,500-seat concert hall. An absolute must-see. Guided tours by appointment.

⚒ **Georgia State Capitol,** Capitol Sq. (656-2846): Georgia's legislative building, dating from 1889, is a replica of the Washington Capitol. The 237-ft. (72m) dome is covered with gold leaf from the Dahlonega mines north of Atlanta. The complex includes a very lovely Hall of Flags and an interesting museum of science and industry. Open Mon–Fri.

⚒ **Oakland Cemetery,** 248 Oakland Ave. SE at Memorial Dr. (577-8163): Landscaped, 84-acre (34ha) cemetery with tens of thousands of graves, the oldest dating back to the Civil War. The site also has many grand mausoleums in the Victorian style, including that of Margaret Mitchell Marsh, author of *Gone With the Wind*. Visitor Center open daily.

☼Å **Underground Atlanta,** Alabama St. and Central Ave. (523-2311): Beneath the modern city, a labyrinth of cobblestone streets and houses spared by the fire of 1864. This area was used as a hospital during the Battle of Atlanta. Under the Central Ave. bridge stands the **Zero Mile Post,** marking the point where the Western & Atlantic Railroad line, and the city, began. Reopened in 1989 following a $142-million expansion and renovation, this festive "town center," as much above ground as below the 19th-century viaducts, bustles with restaurants and nightclubs, upscale boutiques, crafts shops, old-fashioned pushcart vendors, and impromptu street performances. A visit you shouldn't miss. Open daily.

Å **Wren's Nest,** 1050 Gordon St. NW (753-8535): Home of Joel Chandler Harris, who created the Uncle Remus stories and characters: Br'er Rabbit, Br'er Fox, and others. Contains original furnishings, personal papers, and first editions of his works. Open Tues–Sun. Worth seeing.

MARKETS: ☼Å **Atlanta State Farmers' Market,** in Forest Park, 10 mi. (16km) south on I-75 (366-6910): The largest open-air market in the Southeast (144 acres/60ha). Hundreds of farmers display their produce every day, 24 hrs. a day. Worth a look.

MUSUEMS OF ART: Å **Emory University Museum of Art and Archeology,** Emory University Campus, Decatur Rd. and Oxford Rd. NE (727-7522): This small but well-rounded fine-arts museum contains a collection of Greek and Roman antiquities as well as prints and drawings from the Renaissance to the present (including works by Dalí, Kandinsky, and Matisse). Open Tues–Sat. Worth a visit.

☼ÅÅÅ **High Museum of Art,** 1280 Peachtree St. NE (892-4444): Rich collection of European paintings and sculptures, especially from the Renaissance. Richard Meier designed the ultramodern setting of pure geometric forms, and won the Pritzker Prize (in comparable terms, the Nobel Prize of architecture) for the beauty and originality of his work. The museum is part of the vast **Robert W. Woodruff Arts Center,** built in 1968 in memory of the 122 members of the Atlanta Arts Association who died in an air disaster in Paris (1962). (The French government gave Rodin's *L'Ombre* to the association.) Among the museum's most famous works: Bellini's *Virgin and Child,* Veronese's *Rest on the Flight into Egypt,* Annibale Carracci's *Crucifixion,* and many Picasso etchings. The Robert Woodruff Arts Center also includes a concert hall **(Symphony Hall),** home of the Atlanta Symphony Orchestra; two theaters (including the **Alliance Theater);** and the **Atlanta College of Art.** A visit not to be missed. Open Tues–Sun.

MUSEUMS OF SCIENCE & HISTORY: Å **Atlanta Historical Society,** 3101 Andrews Dr. NW (261-1837): Interesting architectural models of Georgian houses, à la *Gone With the Wind.* You can see everything from an 1840s plantation farm **(Tullie Smith House)** to aristocratic Palladian homes **(Swan House)** and slave quarters **(Coach House).** Very lovely old furniture. Not to be missed. Open daily.

Å **Atlanta Public Library,** Peachtree St. and Forsyth St. (688-4034): The Margaret Mitchell Room displays personal items that belonged to Margaret Mitchell, the typewriter on which she wrote *Gone With the Wind,* and other memorabilia. A must for *GWTW* buffs. Open daily.

Å **Carter Presidential Center,** 1 Copenhill Ave. NE (331-3942): Built on the wooded hill where, according to legend, General Sherman watched Atlanta burn, this group of ultramodern circular buildings includes an international conference center, a museum, and a library with 27 million written and on-film documents concerning the 39th president of the United States. It contains, notably, a faithful replica of the White House's Oval Office. More than 600,000 visitors each year. The complex includes a very beautiful Japanese garden and a lovely view of the Atlanta skyline. Worth the trip. Open daily.

    🔔 **Cyclorama,** in Grant Park, Cherokee Ave. and Georgia Ave. SE (624-1071): This huge fresco of the Battle of Atlanta is the largest circular wall mural in the world (390 by 48 ft./22 by 15m). Painted in 1885–86 by a group of 12 Polish and German artists, it has recently been restored. Sound-and-light show. An absolute must-see. Open daily.

    🔔 **Fernbank Science Center,** 156 Heaton Park Dr. NE, in Decatur (378-4311): In the middle of a 62-acre (26ha) park, the center includes an observatory and one of the country's largest planetariums. For astronomy buffs. Open daily.

    🔔🔔 **Martin Luther King, Jr., Historic District,** 407 Auburn Ave. NE (331-3919): The life of the Nobel Peace Prize winner, assassinated in a Memphis hotel in 1968, is retraced in the **King Library and Archives.** His grave is in the middle of an ornamental lake behind the **Ebenezer Baptist Church,** where Martin Luther King, Jr., pursued his pastoral mission from 1960 until his death. In front of the grave burns an eternal flame illuminating the simple words "Free at last." The **King Birthplace** is close by at 501 Auburn Ave. There's an **Information Center** at 413 Auburn Ave. A moving visit. Open daily.

    🔔 **Toy Museum of Atlanta,** 2800 Peachtree Rd. NE (266-8697): Very handsome toy museum displaying priceless 19th-century specimens. More than 100,000 items, some of which are incredibly rare. An absolute must-see. Open daily.

    🔔 **The World of Coca-Cola Pavilion,** Martin Luther King, Jr., Dr., at Central Ave. (676-5151): Unusual museum which explores the more than 100-year-old history of the famous soft drink. Inaugurated in Aug 1990, the three-story pavilion contains more than 1,000 Coke-related artifacts and memorabilia, including a replica of a 1930s soda fountain, a hi-tech "bottling fantasy," and a 4,500-sq.-ft. (410m²) company store. Adjacent to the Underground Atlanta complex. Entertaining. Open daily.

PANORAMAS: The ☀️🔔🔔 **Sun Dial** bar and revolving restaurant, on the 73rd floor of the Westin Peachtree Hotel (589-7500): Offers the most spectacular view of Atlanta (admission fee); on a clear day you can see more than 25 mi. (40km).

PARKS & GARDENS: 🔔 **Grant Park,** Cherokee Ave. SE: Vast landscaped park housing a very modern zoo and Civil War fortifications **(Fort Walker),** in addition to the Cyclorama (see "Museums of Science and History," above). Worth a visit.

    🔔 **Piedmont Park,** Piedmont Ave. at 14th St. NE: This very fine park with lake and swimming area accommodates the annual **Arts Festival** (see "Special Events," below).

    Woodruff Park, Peachtree St. and Pryor St. at Auburn Ave.: Gift of the Coca-Cola magnate Robert W. Woodruff, this spot in the heart of Atlanta is very popular with lunch-hour picnickers.

    Think twice before taking a nighttime stroll in any of Atlanta's parks. The city has seen a rising crime rate for the last few years, according to FBI statistics.

PERFORMING ARTS: For a daily listing of all shows and cultural events, consult the entertainment pages of the daily papers *Atlanta Journal* (morning) and *Atlanta Constitution* (evening), as well as the monthly magazine *Atlanta.*

    Academy Theater, 173 14th St. NE (892-0880): Modern comedies and experimental theater.

    Atlanta Civic Center, 395 Piedmont Ave. NE (523-6275): Concerts, recitals. Home of the Atlanta Ballet. Hosts each May a series of performances by New York's Metropolitan Opera.

Chastain Memorial Park, between Powers Ferry Rd. and Lake Forrest Dr.: Open-air concerts by the Atlanta Symphony Orchestra, June–Aug.

Fox Theatre, 660 Peachtree St. NE (892-5685): Ballet, concerts, musicals, and a summer film festival. Home of the Theater of the Stars (Broadway shows). Year round.

Peachtree Playhouse, Peachtree St. and 13th St. (237-8829): Classical theater and performances by the Ruth Mitchell Dance Company.

Symphony Hall, 1280 Peachtree St. NE (892-2414): Home of the Atlanta Symphony Orchestra (principal conductor, Yoel Levi), Sept–May.

Robert W. Woodruff Arts Center, 1280 Peachtree St. NE (892-2414): Home of the Alliance Theater (classical theater, comedy, drama) and of the Atlanta Children's Theater.

SHOPPING: Lennox Square/Phipps Plaza, Peachtree Rd. and Lenox Rd., Buckhead: One of the country's largest and most trafficked shopping areas. A tourist attraction and shoppers' paradise with specialty shops galore and top-name department stores (Macy's, Saks, Gucci, Tiffany, etc.).

SPECIAL EVENTS: For the exact schedule of events below, consult the **Atlanta Convention & Visitors Bureau** (see "Tourist Information," above).

Dogwood Festival (Apr): Concerts, parades, shows, hot-air balloon rides, tours of old houses. International Flower show to celebrate spring.

Atlanta Hunt and Steeplechase (first Sat in Apr): "The" outdoor social event of the spring. An afternoon of glorious food, fashion, drink, and incidentally, a horse race.

Chattahoochee River Ramblin' Raft Race (third wknd in May): This spectacular, crazy raft race along the rapids of the Chattahoochee River attracts 300,000 participants.

Atlanta Jazz Series (late June): Concerts with the biggest stars.

Georgia Pacific Atlanta Golf Classic (third week in June): PGA tour event. Atlanta Country Club, Paper Mill Rd., Marietta.

Arts Festival (Sept): Concerts, ballets, art exhibitions in Piedmont Park; the festival attracts 2,000,000 spectators each year.

SPORTS: Atlanta has three professional teams:

Baseball (Apr–Oct): Braves, Atlanta Stadium (522-7630).

Basketball (Oct–Apr): Hawks, Omni Coliseum (681-3605).

Football (Sept–Dec): Falcons, Atlanta Stadium (325-2667).

STROLLS: ⚲ **West Paces Ferry Road,** between Peachtree Rd. and Northside Pkwy.: One of the most beautiful residential districts in the Southeast. Plenty of winding driveways leading to hidden estates, including the white-columned Governor's Mansion, 391 W. Paces Ferry Rd. (261-1776); tours Tues–Thurs. Should not be missed.

THEME PARKS: ⚲ **Six Flags over Georgia,** 7561 Six Flags Rd. (12 mi./19km west on I-20) (739-3400): This giant theme park dedicated to the history of Georgia boasts more than 100 attractions, including a triple-loop roller coaster (the Mind Bender). Worth the detour. Open daily June–Sept, wknds only in spring and autumn; closed the rest of the year. The park attracts more than two million visitors a year.

⚲⚲ **Stone Mountain,** 16 mi (26km) NE on U.S. 78 (498-5600): Large, 3,200-acre (1,295ha) theme park including a Civil War memorial, an authentic 19th-century plantation, a car museum, a cable car, a paddle-boat lake ride, and an Old West–style steam engine. In addition, there's the impressive, 825-ft.-high (250m) granite monolith (the largest in the world) with giant sculptures resembling those of Mount Rushmore. The 165- by 72-ft. (55- by 24m) bas-relief represents three southern heroes: Confederate Pres. Jefferson Davis, Gen. Robert E. Lee, and Gen. "Stonewall" Jackson. Not to be missed. Open daily year round.

ACCOMMODATIONS

A Note on Accommodations: Room rates in Atlanta are coded as follows: **VE,** Very Expensive ($140 and up); **E,** Expensive ($90–$140); **M,** Moderate ($60–$90); **I,** Inexpensive ($30–$60); **B,** Budget (up to $30). A listing of toll free numbers is in the Appendix.

Personal Favorites (in order of preference)

Ritz-Carlton Buckhead (nr. dwntwn), 3434 Peachtree Rd. NE, GA 30326 (404/237-2700; toll free 800/241-3333). 550 rms, A/C, color TV, in-rm movies. AE, CB, DC, MC, V. Valet parking $8, pool, health club, sauna, two rests. (including The Dining Room), coffee shop, two bars, 24-hr. rm svce, disco, boutiques, concierge, free crib. *Note:* In the heart of the new business and entertainment district of Buckhead, this modern, 22-story structure is one of the most recent additions to the local luxury-hotel scene. Its decor and amenities are in the grand tradition, and its svce impeccable. The period-furnished rms are spacious and elegant, and colored in pastel tones, with in-rm safes and bathroom phones. The hotel also boasts an excellent rest. (Atlanta's best), and adjacent luxury shopping areas. Two VIP floors. Big-business clientele. Interesting wknd packages. Highly recommended. **VE**

Westin Peachtree Plaza (dwntwn), 210 Peachtree St. (at International Blvd.), GA 30343 (404/659-1400; toll free, see Westin). 1,080 rms, A/C, color TV, in-rm movies. AE, CB, DC, MC. Valet gar. $9, pool, health club, four rests. (including the Sun Dial), five bars, 24-hr. rm svce, nightclub, boutiques, hrdrsr, free crib. *Note:* This futurist, glass-and-steel tower by John Portman is the world's tallest hotel—73 stories high—w. waterfalls and interior gardens on eight floors. It offers total comfort, despite rather cramped rms, and efficient svce, despite the hotel's immense size. One of the country's most spectacular buildings, and the most eye-catching spot in Atlanta. Good rest. (the Southern Café). Business and group clientele. No-smoking floors. Recently underwent a $30-million renovation. **VE**

Omni Hotel at CNN Center (formerly Omni International; dwntwn), 100 CNN Center, GA 30335 (404/659-0000; toll free, see Omni). 471 rms, A/C, color TV, in-rm movies. AE, CB, DC, MC, V. Valet gar. $8, pool, health club, skating rink, squash, two rests. (including Bugatti's), coffee shop, three bars, 24-hr. rm svce, disco, hrdrsr, drugstore, free crib. *Note:* Rather chilling sci-fi decor w. 15-story lobby and glass elevators. Rms are comfortable, w. balconies and minibars, and the svce is efficient. In the heart of the business district, the hotel is directly connected to the Georgia World Congress Center. Fairly obtrusive group and business clientele. VIP floor. **VE**

Best Western American (dwntwn), 160 Spring St., GA 30303 (404/688-8600; toll free, see Best Western). 325 rms, A/C, cable color TV. AE, CB, DC, MC, V. Gar. $4, pool, rest. (Gatsby's), bar, rm svce, disco, hrdrsr, free crib. *Note:* Modern, comfortable, eight-story motel. Rms have patios or balconies. The svce is good, as is the value. Business clientele. Next to the Georgia World Congress Center. VIP floor. **M–E**

Comfort Inn (formerly the Ibis Hotel; nr. dwntwn), 101 International Blvd., GA 30303 (404/524-5555; toll free 800/535-0707). 260 rms, A/C, cable color TV, in-rm movies. AE, CB, DC, MC, V. Gar. $3, pool, rest., bar, free crib. *Note:* Ultramodern motel next to the Georgia World Congress Center. Inviting interior decor and comfortable, well-conceived rms. Cheerful reception and a very adequate rest. w. buffet. Excellent value. Business clientele. **M**

♀ **Days Inn Downtown** (dwntwn), 300 Spring St. NE, GA
🏠 30303 (404/523-1144; toll free, see Days Inns). 260 rms,
A/C, color TV, in-rm movies. AE, CB, DC, MC, V. Free parking, pool, coffee
shop, bar, rm svce, free crib. *Note:* Modern, comfortable motel, quite centrally
located. Very agreeable rms plus efficient reception and svce. Convention and
group clientele. Good value. **M**

♀ **Holiday Inn I-85** (nr. dwntwn), 1944 Piedmont Circle, GA
🏠 30324 (404/875-3571; toll free, see Holiday Inns). 251 rms,
A/C, color TV, in-rm movies. AE, CB, DC, MC, V. Free parking, pool, rest.,
bar, rm svce, free crib. *Note:* Functional Holiday Inn–style comfort 20 min. from
dwntwn on I-85. Spacious rms, some with balconies. Fair svce and reception.
Ideal if you're driving. **I–M**

Other Accommodations (from top bracket to budget)

♀♀♀♀ **Marriott Marquis** (dwntwn), 265 Peachtree Center Ave., GA
🏠🏠🏠🏠 30303 (404/521-0000; toll free, see Marriott). 1,675 rms,
A/C, color TV, in-rm movies. AE, CB, DC, MC, V. Valet gar. $9, pool, tennis,
health club, sauna, four rests. (including Pompano's), coffee shop, four bars, rm
svce, disco, boutiques, hrdrsr, crib $5. *Note:* This new hotel is one of the most
spectacular and tallest in the South—50 stories of glass and concrete in the heart
of Atlanta, designed by John Portman. The 520-ft.-high (160m) atrium houses
interior grdns and glass elevators. Spacious, ultra-comfortable rms and very complete amenities. Six VIP floors. Efficient svce, but very average rest. (like all
Marriotts). Interesting wknd packages. **VE**

♀♀♀♀ **Swissotel-Atlanta** (nr. dwntwn), 3391 Peachtree Rd. NE (at
🏠🏠🏠🏠 Lenox Sq.), GA 30326 (404/365-0065; toll free 800/637-
9477). 375 rms, A/C, color TV, in-rm movies. AE, CB, DC, MC, V. Valet gar.
$10, pool, health club, sauna, squash courts, rest., two bars, 24-hr. rm svce,
nightclub, concierge. *Note:* Brand-new super-luxury hotel in the heart of
Buckhead, the city's shopping mecca. Opened in January 1991, this soaring, elegant 28-story tower houses unrivaled comfort and facilities. Spacious, well-laid-
out rms; very fine hotel rest. Svce worthy of the Swiss tradition. Very comprehensive physical-fitness facilities. A fine place to stay. **VE**

♀♀♀ **Hilton & Towers** (dwntwn), 255 Courtland St. NE (at Harris
🏠🏠🏠 St.), GA 30084 (404/659-2000; toll free, see Hilton). 1,220
rms, A/C, color TV, in-rm movies. AE, CB, DC, MC, V. Valet parking $8, pool,
health club, four tennis courts, sauna, four rests. (including Nikolai's Roof), 24-
hr. coffee shop, three bars, rm svce, disco, boutiques, hrdrsr, free crib. *Note:*
Immense, 30-story tourist barracks completely taken over by group and convention clientele. All the usual Hilton comfort, but the svce is a little overburdened. Spacious, well-furnished rms. Five-story atrium with glass elevators.
Very good luxury rest. and good recreational facilities. Three VIP floors. In
the heart of dwntwn Atlanta. Interesting wknd packages. **E–VE**

☼♀♀♀ **Hyatt Regency** (dwntwn), 265 Peachtree St. NE, GA 30303
🏠🏠🏠 (404/577-1234; toll free, see Hyatt). 1,285 rms, A/C, color
TV, in-rm movies. AE, CB, DC, MC, V. Valet gar. $7, pool, health club, three
rests., bars, rm svce, disco, hrdrsr, free crib. *Note:* A hotel classic dating from
1967, w. a 23-story atrium, interior grdns, and glass elevators. Vast rms w. balconies offer lavish comfort. The svce is rather uncertain but the panoramic view of
Atlanta from the revolving rest. at the top, Polaris, is spectacular. No-smoking
rms. The first of the grand hotels designed by John Portman. Two VIP floors.
Group clientele. Recently renovated. **E–VE**

♀♀ **Days Hotel–Atlanta at Lenox** (nr. dwntwn), 3377 Peachtree
🏠🏠 Rd. NE, GA 30326 (404/264-1111; toll free, see Days Inns),
300 rms, A/C, color TV, in-rm movies. AE, CB, DC, MC, V. Free valet parking,
health club, sauna, rest. (Brentwood Café), bar, rm svce, free crib. *Note:* Flagship
of the big Atlanta-based hotel chain. Modern, functional 11-story tower in the
heart of Buckhead. Comfortable, inviting rms; good svce. Free shuttle to any

point within 3 mi. (5km). Right next to the subway (8 min. from dwntwn). Business clientele. Good value. **M–E**

 Lanier Plaza Hotel (nr. dwntwn), 418 Armour Dr. NE, GA 30324 (404/873-4661; toll free 800/554-8444). 344 rms, A/C, color TV, in-rm movies. AE, CB, DC, MC, V. Free parking, pool, rest., coffee shop, bar, rm svce, nightclub, hrdrsr, concierge, free crib. *Note:* Undistinguished but inviting hotel away from the bustling city center. Comfortable rms w. balcony and refrigerator; ultra-professional svce. Business clientele. 8 min. from dwntwn. **M–E**

 Pierremont Plaza (dwntwn), 590 W. Peachtree St. NW, GA 30308 (404/881-6000; toll free 800/531-6660). 505 rms, A/C, color TV, in-rm movies. AE, CB, DC, MC, V. Gar. $6, pool, rest., bar, rm svce, disco, hrdrsr, free crib. *Note:* Modern, serviceable hotel close to the business district. The rms are spacious and comfortable (some w. refrigerators); the svce leaves a bit to be desired. Business clientele. A good value overall. **M–E**

 Terrace Garden Inn (vic.), 3405 Lenox Rd., GA 30326 (404/261-9250; toll free 800/241-8260). 372 rms, A/C, cable color TV. AE, CB, DC, MC, V. Free indoor parking, two pools, tennis, squash, health club, sauna, rest. (Garden Tree), coffee shop, bar, rm svce, disco, hrdrsr, free crib. *Note:* Very comfortable luxury motel w. lovely gardens and spacious, balconied rms. Good svce. An excellent location, 20 min. from dwntwn on I-85. Ideal for the car traveler. Good recreational facilities. Business clientele. **M–E**

 La Quinta–Piedmont (formerly the Stafford Inn; nr. dwntwn), 2115 Piedmont Rd. NE, GA 30376 (404/876-4365; toll free, see La Quinta). 194 rms, cable color TV. AE, CB, DC, MC, V. Free parking, pool, rest., bar, free crib. *Note:* Inviting up-to-date motel halfway between dwntwn and the new Buckhead business district. Comfortable; friendly, smiling reception. Good value. 10 min. from dwntwn. **I–M**

 Travelodge Central (dwntwn), 311 Courtland St. NE, GA 30303 (404/659-4545; toll free, see Travelodge). 70 rms, A/C, cable color TV. AE, CB, DC, MC, V. Free parking, pool, adjacent 24-hr. coffee shop, rm svce, free crib. *Note:* Small, three-story motel in the heart of dwntwn. Slightly threadbare decor and comfort, but very adequate rms (some w. balconies). Overall good value. **I–M**

 Motel 6 West (vic.), 4100 Wendell Dr. SW, GA 30336 (404/696-0757). 175 rms, A/C, color TV, free in-rm movies. AE, DC, MC, V. Free parking, pool, free crib. *Note:* Modern comfort at ultra-economical prices. Located 25 min. from dwntwn and 6 min. from the Six Flags Over Georgia theme park. One of the best values in the area. Ideal for the motorist. **B**

Airport Accommodations

 Hyatt Atlanta Airport (formerly the Holiday Inn Crowne Plaza; vic.), 1900 Sullivan Rd., College Park, GA 30337 (404/991-1234; toll free, see Hyatt). 399 rms, A/C, color TV, in-rm movies. AE, CB, DC, MC, V. Free parking, two pools, health club, rest., bar, rm svce, crib $10 *Note:* Modern, comfortable, 12-story hotel affording direct access to the Convention Center (nr. the airport). Spacious, well-soundproofed rms and efficient svce. VIP floor. Group and business clientele. Free airport shuttle. Has undergone a $5-million remodeling and renovation. **E**

RESTAURANTS

A Note on Restaurant Prices: Atlanta restaurant prices, per person, excluding drinks and service charges, are coded as follows: **VE,** Very Expensive ($60 and up); **E,** Expensive ($40–$60); **M,** Moderate ($25–$40); **I,** Inexpensive ($15–$25); **B,** Budget (up to $15).

Personal Favorites (in order of preference)

🍸🍸🍸🍸 **The Dining Room** (nr. dwntwn), in the Ritz-Carlton Buckhead (see "Accommodations," above) (237-2700). A/C. Lunch Mon–Fri, dinner Mon–Sat; closed hols. AE, CB, DC, MC, V. J&T. *Specialties:* cream of coriander with lobster, marinated tuna in ginger cream; soft-shell crab w. avocado purée, tomatoes, and olives; rack of lamb with sweet-pepper sauce; strudel of crayfish; poppyseed-and-raspberry parfait. The menu changes daily. Splendid wine list w. great vintages sold by the glass (cruvinet). *Note:* Once the owner of the renowned Boheneck restaurant in the Black Forest of Germany (two stars in Michelin), the very talented chef Guenter Seeger has made this classic, elegant palace rest. into one of the finest in the South. Inspired nouvelle cuisine happily unites innovation w. a meticulous attention to detail. Vast marble-and-mahogany dining room w. stylish furniture and hunting pictures. Exemplary white-gloved svce. One of the dozen best rests. in the country. Resv. a must. Valet parking. 15 min. from dwntwn. *French/Continental.* **E–VE**

🍸🍸🍸 **Pano's & Paul's** (nr. dwntwn), 1232 W. Paces Ferry Rd. (261-3662). A/C. Dinner only, Mon–Sat; closed hols. AE, CB, DC, MC, V. J&T. *Specialties:* crabcakes, red snapper w. hazelnut butter, quail w. wild mushrooms, roast veal chop w. basil butter, crème brûlée, Mississippi mud pie. Very fine wine list. *Note:* One of the best rests. in Atlanta. Classic, French-inspired cuisine impeccably presented. Ideally romantic Victorian decor. Distinguished music in the background. Discreet but ultra-professional svce. Trendy clientele. Resv. recommended. 25 min. from dwntwn on I-75 and Northside Pkwy. *Continental.* **M–E**

🍸🍸 **Coach and Six** (nr. dwntwn), 1776 Peachtree Rd. NW (872-6666). A/C. Lunch/dinner daily; closed hols. AE, CB, DC, MC, V. Jkt. *Specialties:* black-bean soup, Florida stone crabs, lobster, fish of the day. Meat in all forms—steak, roast beef, lamb chops—has brought fame to this rest. Chocolate-mousse pie. *Note:* A veritable local institution w. opulent, elegant old English club decor. The ambience is pleasant, if often overcrowded and noisy. Resv. advisable (but rarely honored, unfortunately). Diligent svce. A favorite spot among Atlanta carnivores for more than 20 years. Valet parking. *American.* **I–M**

🍸🍸 **Bone's** (nr. dwntwn), 3130 Piedmont Rd. NE (237-2663). A/C. Lunch Mon–Sat, dinner nightly; closed hols. AE, CB, DC, MC, V. Jkt. *Specialties:* excellent meats, Maine lobster, fish of the day. Average desserts and wine list. *Note:* A local red-meat shrine, this New York–style steakhouse is famous for the high quality of its meat (corn-fed Iowa cattle) and for its generous servings. Rather brusque but efficient svce. Amusing caricatures on the walls as well as old photographs of Atlanta. Business clientele. The tab can climb quickly if you choose lobster over T-bone steak. Resv. advised. Valet parking. *Steakhouse.* **I–M**

🍸🍸 **La Grotta** (nr. dwntwn), 2637 Peachtree Rd. NE (231-1368). A/C. Dinner only, Tues–Sat; closed hols. AE, CB, DC, MC, V. J&T. *Specialties:* tortellini verdi, carpaccio, scaloppine al pesto, vitello tonnato. Very good list of Italian wines at reasonable prices. *Note:* Authentic Italian cuisine—especially the remarkable fresh pasta—in a pretty, rustic setting w. terraced grdn offering open-air dining in nice weather. Very good svce. Resv. advised. Valet parking. 20 min. from dwntwn. *Italian.* **I–M**

🍸 **Aunt Fanny's Cabin** (vic.), 2155 Campbell Rd., in Smyrna (404/436-5218). A/C. Lunch Mon–Fri, dinner nightly, brunch Sun; closed 5 days at Christmas. AE, CB, DC, MC, V. *Specialties:* Virginia ham, rainbow trout, fried chicken, steak, traditional southern dishes. *Note:* Occupies former slave quarters more than a century old. Picturesque decor, friendly reception, and pleasant music. No resv. Valet parking. 30 min. from dwntwn on I-75N. A "must" for all Atlanta visitors. *American.* **B–I**

🍸 **Mary Mac's Tea Room** (nr. dwntwn), 224 Ponce de Leon Ave. NE (876-6604). A/C. Lunch/dinner Mon–Fri (until

8pm); closed hols. No credit cards. *Specialties:* fried chicken, southern-style shrimp, peanut-butter pie. *Note:* Only the name suggests a tea room. Rustic, flavorful southern cooking in a relaxed, if generally noisy and overcrowded, atmosphere. An excellent spot w. unbeatable prices. Nr. Georgia Tech. Inevitable waits (sometimes fairly long). *American.* **B**

Other Restaurants (from top bracket to budget)

�w♡♡ **103 West** (nr. dwntwn), 103 W. Paces Ferry Rd. (233-5993). ♨♨ A/C. Dinner only, Mon–Sat. AE, CB, DC, MC, V. Jkt. *Specialties:* lump-crabmeat cakes, profiteroles filled w. foie gras, veal chop w. morels, pot-au-feu w. tarragon-scented chicken, broiled noisettes of lamb w. pommes soufflées, roast breast of duck, crème brûlée. Menu changes regularly. The wine list has earned an Award of Excellence from the respected *Wine Spectator,* but the prices are exorbitant. *Note:* Despite its appallingly kitsch decor—fake-marble columns, Aubusson tapestries, trompe-l'oeil wall paintings—crowds have flocked to this successful new venture by the inventive Pano Karatassos, who already owns Pano's & Paul's, Cappriccio Ristorante, and the Fish Market. Impeccably prepared and served international high-style food, w. prices to match. Resv. a must. *French/American.* **M–E**

♡♡♡ **Capriccio Ristorante** (nr. dwntwn), 3018 Maple Dr. NE ♨♨ (237-0347), A/C. Dinner only, Mon–Sat; closed hols. AE, CB, DC, MC, V. Jkt. *Specialties:* capriccio spaghettini w. lobster, agnololotti w. crabmeat, black and white fettuccine, veal piccata al limone, roast rack of lamb w. rosemary and grilled polenta, tartufo al cioccolato. Splendid list of Italian wines. *Note:* The best northern Italian rest. in Atlanta. As w. the other ventures of the duo who launched Pano's & Paul's and 103 West (see above), the decor is ostentatiously rococo. Svce is of the best; a very good place to eat, in the center of Buckhead. Resv. a must. Valet parking; 20 min. from dwntwn. *Italian.* **M**

♡♡♡ **City Grill** (dwntwn), 50 Hurt Plaza (524-2489). A/C. Lunch ♨♨ Mon–Fri, dinner nightly. AE, CB, DC, MC, V. Jkt. *Specialties:* oysters Casino, trout almondine, filet mignon, prime rib on the bone, salmon tartare, grilled catch of the day, baked Alaska. *Note:* Housed in the old Federal Reserve Bank of Atlanta building, this rest. has a devoted local following for its sound, satisfying American food, attracting diners who are tired of the excesses and inventions of nouvelle cuisine. Excellent svce; striking setting. Business clientele; resv. strongly advised. A fine place in the heart of dwntwn. *American.* **M**

♡♡♡ **Hedgerose Heights Inn** (nr. dwntwn), 490 E. Paces Ferry Rd. ♨♨ NE (233-7673). A/C. Dinner only, Tues–Sat; closed hols. AE, CB, DC, MC, V. Jkt. *Specialties:* pirozki w. béarnaise sauce, roast breast of pheasant w. Swiss chard, venison medallions w. wild mushrooms and cream sauce, beef Taras Bulba (carpaccio). Very good homemade desserts; great list of California wines. *Note:* A charming old house, sympathetically decorated in shades of peach w. an abundance of flowers. Swiss chef Heinz Schwab presides over an elegant, refined kitchen. Intimate atmosphere; very popular, so resv. highly advisable. *Continental.* **M**

♡♡ **Fish Market** (nr. dwntwn), 3393 Peachtree Rd. NE (262- ♨♨ 3165). A/C. Lunch/dinner Mon–Sat; closed hols. AE, CB, DC, MC, V. Jkt. *Specialties:* lobster tails in mustard sauce, seafood pastas, sautéed Dover sole, Florida stone crabs, fish of the day, chocolate-pecan cake. Fine wine list. *Note:* Elegant rest. w. Mediterranean decor offering Atlanta's largest choice of seafood. Everything is truly fresh, and grilled, fried, or poached to perfection. Excellent svce. Dinner resv. necessary. Locally very popular. Valet parking. *Seafood.* **I–M**

☼♡♡ **Sun Dial** (dwntwn), 73rd floor of the Westin Peachtree Plaza ♨♨ (see "Accommodations," above) (589-7506). A/C. Lunch/ dinner daily, brunch Sun. AE, CB, DC, MC, V. Jkt. *Specialties:* shrimp provençal, peanut soup, meat broiled over a wood fire, catch of the day. *Note:* One of the highest revolving rests. in the world. Creditable cuisine at best, but an exceptional view of Atlanta and its skyscrapers. Resv. necessary. A "must" for tourists. Very good value at lunch. *Steakhouse.* I–M

    Trotter's (nr. dwntwn), 3215 Peachtree Rd. NE (237-5988). A/C. Lunch Mon–Fri, dinner nightly, brunch Sun; closed hols. AE, CB, DC, MC, V. *Specialties:* fish and prime beef broiled over a wood fire, fresh homemade pasta. The menu changes regularly. *Note:* Susan De Rose and Richard Lewis are masters of modern American cuisine and of natural foods (they grow their own herbs). The result is always original and innovative. Pure art deco, 1920s ambience, w. equestrian motifs on the wall. Rather uncertain svce. A fashionable place. Valet parking. *American.* I–M

    Bamboo Luau (nr. dwntwn), 2263 Cheshire Bridge Rd. (636-9131). A/C. Lunch/dinner daily (till 3am). MC, V. *Specialties:* dim sum, Singapore noodles, chicken in black-bean sauce, fish and shellfish Cantonese style. *Note:* One of Atlanta's very few authentic Chinese rests. (incongruously serving Polynesian drinks). Elegant Far Eastern decor; efficient svce. A favorite with those in-the-know. *Chinese.* I

    Nakato (nr. dwntwn), 1893 Piedmont Rd. NE (873-6582). A/C. Dinner only, nightly; closed Jan 1, Dec 25. AE, CB, DC, MC, V. *Specialties:* sushi, sukiyaki, sashimi, teppanyaki, tempura. *Note:* Truly authentic Japanese cuisine. Very handsome Oriental decor w. separate dining rms. Efficient, if slightly abrupt, svce. Locally popular. Resv. advised on wknds. *Japanese.* I

    Pittypat's Porch (dwntwn), 25 International Blvd. (Peachtree Center) (525-8228). A/C. Dinner only, nightly; closed hols. AE, CB, DC, MC, V. *Specialties:* roast pheasant, stuffed quail, barbecued meat, bison steak, catch of the day, southern dishes. *Note:* Has a *Gone With the Wind* atmosphere and decor w. friendly svce and an agreeable bar; appeals greatly to tourists. Amusing collection of rocking chairs. *American.* I

    Indigo (nr. dwntwn), 1397 N. Highland Ave. NE (876-0676). A/C. Dinner only, Tues–Sun; closed hols. AE, MC, V. *Specialties:* conch chowder, broiled catch of the day, Caribbean dishes, key lime pie. *Note:* The best local source for the sunny, savory food of the Caribbean. Decorated like a fisherman's cottage in the South Seas, w. an open kitchen and a view of the chefs bustling around the stove. Relaxed atmosphere and svce. Locally popular; unfortunately no resv. accepted. *Caribbean.* I

    Sierra Grill (nr. dwntwn), 1529 Piedmont Rd. (873-5360). A/C. Lunch Mon–Fri, dinner Mon–Sat; closed hols. AE, MC, V. *Specialties:* spicy oysters w. spinach, smoked chicken fajitas, grilled rainbow trout wrapped in cornhusks, chile relleño, southwestern specialties. *Note:* Nice little Santa Fe–style rest. w. imitation adobe walls. The food will make you think you're in New Mexico; the svce is friendly and smiling. Excellent value. *American.* I

    The Varsity (nr. dwntwn), 61 North Ave. (881-1706). Lunch/dinner daily (until 12:30am). No credit cards. *Specialties:* hamburgers, chili dogs, sandwiches, orange freezes, apple pie. *Note:* By general consensus, the best hamburgers in Atlanta for close to 50 years. Also prides itself on being the largest drive-in rest. in the world, w. two floors for parking. Every day it serves 15,000 hot dogs, 10,000 burgers, 2,500 lbs. (1,135kg) of fries, a ton (910kg) of onion rings, and 300 gal. (1,135l) of homemade chili sauce to top it all. An absolute must-see. Right next to Georgia Tech. An authentic local institution. *American.* B

Cafeteria/Fast Food

    David Bros. Cafeteria (vic.), State Farmers' Market, Forest Park (404/366-7414). Breakfast/lunch/dinner daily (until 8:30pm). *Specialties:* roast beef, fried chicken, hamburgers, fried fish, excellent vegetables, pastries. *Note:* This excellent, lively, locally popular spot is in the heart of the Farmers' Market, 20 min. from dwntwn on I-75.

BARS & NIGHTCLUBS

Atlanta Nights (dwntwn), 505 Peachtree St. NE (892-4998). Since its opening in 1986, this disco has become a favorite "meet place" for upscale Atlantans. Studio 54, southern style. Open Tues–Sun.

Blues Harbor (dwntwn), 155 Kenny's Alley (524-3001): Chicago-style blues and jump-swing live. The cover varies with the act. Open Wed–Sat.

Club Rio (dwntwn), 195 Luckie St. (525-7467): Giant nightspot dwntwn with six bars and dance floors. Two years after Rob Lowe put Club Rio on the map, this former film warehouse is still one of the reigning fashion dens. Open nightly.

☼ **Dante's Down the Hatch** (dwntwn), Lower Alabama St. and Pryor St., in Underground Atlanta (577-1800). Jazz and folk music in an old galleon setting that is both picturesque and pleasant. Supper served until midnight. Open nightly.

Elan (vic.), Park Place, 4505 Ashford-Dunwoody Rd. (393-1333). Deluxe singles bar/disco. Trendy clientele. A rest. as well (mediocre). Locally very popular. 20 min. from dwntwn. Open Mon–Sat.

Hemingway's (vic.), 3910 N. Druid Hills Rd. (325-3094). Live country-rock music in a spirited ambience. Guaranteed cowboy atmosphere. Open nightly.

Limelight (nr. dwntwn), 3330 Piedmont Rd. NE (231-3520). The biggest disco in the South. Spectacular. Open nightly.

Manuel's Tavern (nr. dwntwn), 602 N. Highland Ave. (525-3449). Pleasant and very popular singles bar with English pub decor and a clientele of journalists and politicians. A classic of its kind for 20 years.

Walter Mitty's Jazz Café (nr. dwntwn), 816 N. Highland Ave. NE (876-7115). Excellent modern jazz.

Waverly Hotel (nr. dwntwn), 2450 Galleria Pkwy. (953-4500). Very crowded tea dances every Fri evening with orchestras à la Glenn Miller and Woody Herman. Attracts hundreds of devotees each wknd.

NEARBY EXCURSIONS

☼🛍 **CALLAWAY GARDENS** (86 mi./138km SW on I-85S and U.S. 27S in Pine Mountain): One of the most beautiful botanic gardens in the country, with 2,400 acres (1,000ha) of splendid gardens and woods, 13 lakes (fishing, boating, waterskiing), four golf courses, and more than 12½ mi. (20km) of hiking trails. Attracting many thousands of visitors annually, it is well worth the 90-min. car ride from Atlanta. Open Mar to late Sept.

In **Warm Springs,** 15 mi. (24km) farther west, visit the ⚱ **Little White House,** summer home of Pres. Franklin D. Roosevelt, where he died on April 12, 1945. Worth the trip.

Where to Stay En Route

IN PINE MOUNTAIN 🏨 **Callaway Gardens Hotel,** Hwy 27, Pine Mountain, GA 31822-2000 (404/663-2281; toll free 800/282-8181). 355 rms. Four-star hotel, w. three 18-hole and one 9-hole golf courses. **E–VE**

☼⚱ **KENNESAW MOUNTAIN NATIONAL BATTLE-FIELD PARK** (Old U.S. 41 and Stilesboro Rd. in Marietta, 25 mi./40km NW on I-75N) (404/427-4686): Listed as one of the 10 most visited national parks in the U.S., Kennesaw Mountain commemorates a decisive battle of the Civil War (1864). Museum with slide presentation of the battle, hiking trails of original earthworks. Open daily year round.

Also in the vicinity, ⚓ **Big Shanty Museum,** 2829 Cherokee St., Kennesaw (404/427-2117), houses *The General,* one of two vintage locomotives that were the subject of a famous Civil War spy chase re-created in the Walt Disney movie *The Great Locomotive Chase.* Worth a visit. Open daily.

⚓ **LAKE LANNIER ISLANDS** (42 mi./68km NW on I-85N and U.S. 985 in Buford) (404/945-6701): 1,200-acre (485ha) pine-forested resort surrounding a vast man-made lake with facilities for camping, swimming, sailing, picnicking, tennis, and horseback riding. Open year round.

Accommodations vary from houseboats to the plush 𝕾𝕾𝕾𝕾 **Stouffer Pineisle Resort,** G. 347, Buford, GA 30518 (404/945-8921); 250 rms with an 18-hole golf course (rates: **E–VE**).

🔭 **MADISON** (60 mi./96km east on I-20E and U.S. 129N): This truly antebellum southern town just 1 hr. from Atlanta contains Civil War–period houses so beautiful that General Sherman refused to burn them on his devastating march to the sea. Over half of the well-preserved antebellum and Victorian houses are shown during home tours in May and Dec (call 404/342-4454 for information). Has been used from time to time as the setting for movies and TV shows. Worth going out of your way for.

⚓ **ROSWELL** (25 mi./40km north on U.S. 19N): Founded in 1830, this quaint little community in the North Atlanta area features many pre–Civil War houses. Group tours can be arranged through the **Roswell Historical Society,** 98 Bulloch Ave. (404/992-1665). Clustered around Roswell Sq. are a number of boutiques, craft and clothing shops, and restaurants. Worth a visit.

CHAPTER 13

NASHVILLE 🔥

□ □ □

And the Great Smoky Mountains

The mecca of country music, deftly portrayed by director Robert Altman in his movie *Nashville,* is today a mixture of southern conservatism and razzle-dazzle prosperity—show business, publishing, banking, insurance, etc. It was founded in 1779 as Fort Nashborough by a group of North Carolina pioneers under the leadership of James Robertson. The little fort of rough-hewn logs named after Revolutionary War hero Gen. Francis Nash may still be seen, scrupulously restored, on the west bank of the Cumberland River.

From its past as a city of the Old South, the capital of Tennessee has retained its gracious, spacious upper-class homes and magnificent gardens, its taste for religion (707 churches), a fondness for education (the city boasts no fewer than 16 colleges and universities) and some venerable traditions. From the explosion of the popularity of country music that began in the 1950s, Nashville derives a multitude of record shops, souvenir stores, and huge billboards; a network of urban highways; the nouveaux riches palaces of the country-music stars, with their year-round congregation of busloads of worshipful fans; and endless suburbs punctuated with screaming neon signs, hamburger joints, and used-car lots. The recording industry contributes to the wealth of "Music City USA" at the rate of $600 million a year. Here, where the famous "Nashville Sound" was born, a hundred recording studios turn out, in good years and bad alike, more than half the country's pop music.

It should, then, come as no surprise that the city's most famous monument is not the life-size replica of the **Parthenon** (whence the name "Athens of the South," bestowed on the city by its inhabitants), not the beautiful **Cheekwood Botanical Garden,** not even the elegant **Hermitage,** where Pres. Andrew Jackson ended his days—but rather that shrine for all lovers of country music, the **Grand Ole Opry.** Into this huge modern auditorium, designed to serve also as a recording studio, thousands of enthusiastic spectators squeeze every weekend to witness the videotaping of TV shows whose popularity, now a full 50 years old, shows no signs of abating. Dreamed up by radio pioneer George D. Hay, the "Grand Ole Opry" (the local pronunciation of "Grand Old Opera") came into the world in Nov 1925 over the airwaves of a little local radio station, 650 WSM; before long it was to be relayed across the country over the NBC network. It was, and remains, the principal instrument of the triumph of country music, and thus of Nashville's prosperity.

From Nashville you can easily reach several interesting tourist destinations: Chattanooga and the Tennessee Valley, the Great Smoky Mountains, and Mammoth Cave National Park, among others. "Music City USA" ranks 15th among U.S. cities in terms of its economic growth rate.

Singer Rita Coolidge was born in Nashville.

BASIC FACTS: Capital of the State of Tennessee. Area code: 615. Time zone: central. ZIP Code: 37202. Founded in: 1779. Approximate population: city, 490,000; metropolitan area, 960,000. Rank among U.S. cities: 22nd.

CLIMATE: The summer in Nashville is a little less humid than in Memphis, but just as hot, averaging 80°F (27°C) in July. From Mar through July the humidity is accentuated by storms, which are sometimes violent. The winters are moderately cold, with Jan temperatures averaging 38°F (3°C). The fall, when the weather is cool but fair, is the best time to visit Tennessee.

DISTANCES: Atlanta, 242 mi. (387km); Cincinnati, 269 mi. (430km); Memphis, 210 mi. (336km); St. Louis, 328 mi. (525km).

ARRIVAL & TRANSIT INFORMATION

AIRPORT: The new Nashville Metropolitan Airport (BNA) is 6 mi. (10km) SE. Information: 275-1675.

AIRLINES: American (244-5500), Delta (244-9860), Eastern (244-3780), Northwest (242-8381), Pan Am (toll free 800/221-1111), Southwest (255-1221), TWA (244-9010), United (toll free 800/241-6522), and USAir (256-1944).

CITY LINK: The **cab** fare to city center is about $13–$15; time, 15–20 min. (30 min. during rush hours). Bus: **Airport Shuttle Service** (275-2555), serving principal hotels; fare, $8; time, 25 min. Also **city bus (MTA)** leaving from Fourth Ave. North and The Arcade: fare, 90¢; time, 30 min.
   Public transportation is by bus, provided by the Metropolitan Transit Authority/MTA (242-4433); it's inefficient, but unless you plan on excursions out of town (recommended), or a visit to the Grand Old Opry, the city is small enough that you may not need to rent a car.

CAR RENTAL (at the airport unless otherwise noted): Avis (361-1212); Budget (366-0800); Dollar (366-0449); Hertz (361-3131); National (361-7467); Thrifty, 1315 Vultee Blvd. (361-6050).

LIMOUSINE SERVICE: Carey Limousine (889-5304), Dav El Limousines (toll free 800/922-0343), Imperial Limousines (361-3055).

TAXIS: In theory cabs may be hailed on the street, but it's difficult to find one cruising. It's best to telephone: **Checker** (254-5031), **Nashville Cab** (274-7070), **Yellow Cab** (256-0101).

INTERCITY BUSES: Greyhound, 200 Eighth Ave. S. (255-1691).

MISSISSIPPI CRUISES: 3- to 10-day cruises aboard the 1920s paddle-wheelers *Delta Queen* or *Mississippi Queen*. Luxurious kitsch. See Chapter 15 on New Orleans.

INFORMATION & TOURS

TOURIST INFORMATION: The **Nashville Chamber of Commerce– Visitors Division,** 161 Fourth Ave. N., TN 37219 (615/259-4700).

Tourist Information Center, Exit 85 from I-65 at J. Robertson Pkwy. (615/242-5606). Open daily.

GUIDED TOURS: Belle Carol Riverboat Co. (boat), First Ave. N. and Broadway or McGavock Pike Dock (244-3430): Trips on the Cumberland River aboard the heroic-age paddlewheelers *Music City Queen* and *Captain Ann*. Mar–Dec.

General Jackson (boat), 2812 Opryland Dr. (889-6611): 3-hr. musical mini-cruises and dinner cruises aboard the giant (1,200-passenger) paddlewheeler *General Jackson*. Year round.

Gray Line Tours (bus), 314 Hermitage Ave. (244-7330): Guided tour of city and surroundings; serves principal hotels.

Grand Ole Opry Tours (bus), 2810 Opryland Dr. (889-9490): Guided tour of the Grand Ole Opry, the city's principal attractions, and the homes of country-music stars.

SIGHTS, ATTRACTIONS & ACTIVITIES

ARCHITECTURAL HIGHLIGHTS: ▲ **The Parthenon,** Centennial Park West End and 25th Ave. N. (259-6358): A surprising life-size replica, in marble and reinforced concrete, of the famous Athenian temple of Pericles' time. This version, dating from 1931, houses temporary cultural exhibitions and a giant replica of Phidias's statue of the goddess Athena that once adorned the Parthenon in Athens. It shouldn't be missed. Open Tues–Sun.

Ryman Auditorium, 116 Fifth Ave. N. (254-1445): This former church in red brick is considered the *real* "Mecca of Country Music" by purists; it was here that the Grand Ole Opry made its home from 1943 until the present auditorium was opened in 1974. Once celebrated for its acoustics, the Ryman Auditorium used to host a very different kind of performer: Sarah Bernhardt, Enrico Caruso, and the like. Today it is a gallery of country-star souvenirs. An absolute must for fans. Open daily.

BROADCASTING STUDIOS: ▲▲▲ **Grand Ole Opry House,** 2804 Opryland Dr., 10 mi. (16km) NE via I-40 and Briley Pkwy. (889-3060): The largest (4,400 seats) recording studio in the world, where the biggest stars of country music perform every Fri and Sat evening (two shows), with additional Tues, Thurs, Sat, and Sun matinee performances in summer. Tickets may be purchased only at the box office, or by mail from 2802 Opryland Dr., TN 37214; in summer, resv. must be made many weeks ahead. Visitors can also view shows being taped for cable TV by the Nashville Network Mon–Fri evenings; for information, call TNN Viewer Services (883-7000). This is a visit you shouldn't miss.

Recording Studios of America, 1510 Division St. (254-1282): For a mere $10 you can have yourself recorded here with a "canned" accompaniment; a godsend for aspiring singers. Open Mon–Sat.

Studio B, Country Music Hall of Fame, 4 Music Sq. E. (256-1639): The historic RCA studio where the likes of Elvis Presley, Chet Atkins, Charley Pride, and Eddy Arnold recorded some of their biggest hits. You can visit it along with the Country Music Hall of Fame (see "Museums of Science and History," below). Don't miss it. Open daily.

CHURCHES/SYNAGOGUES: ▲ **Presbyterian Church,** Church St. and Fifth Ave. N. (254-7584): Remarkable example of the Egyptian Revival architecture so much in vogue at the end of the 19th century; it was used as a hospital for Union casualties during the Civil War. Worth seeing. Open Mon–Fri.

    Upper Room Chapel, 1908 Grand Ave. (340-7207): This Georgian-style chapel holds, among its other treasures, a giant reproduction in polychromed wood of Leonardo da Vinci's *Last Supper.* Religious-art kitsch of the highest order. Open Mon–Sat.

HISTORIC BUILDINGS: **Belle Meade Mansion,** Harding Rd. and Leake Ave., 7 mi. (12km) SW on West End Ave. (356-0501): With its elegant portico and enormous state room, this very lovely 1854 plantation house dubbed "Queen of Tennessee Plantations," was once the home of one of the country's most renowned stud farms (it produced Iroquois, the first American horse to win the English Derby, in 1881). Fine collection of old carriages. A definite must-see. Open daily.

    Belmont Mansion, 1900 Belmont Blvd. at Acklen Ave. (269-9537): This luxurious 1850s Palladian home was a center of Nashville social life for more than half a century, and has now been magnificently restored to all its former grandeur. On the campus of Belmont College. Positively must be seen. Open Tues–Sat.

    Fisk University, 17th Ave. N. and Jackson St. (329-8543): In the heart of Nashville's historic district, this university, founded in 1866, possesses some interesting old buildings, including **Jubilee Hall** and the **Carl Van Vechten Art Gallery.** Worth a look.

    Fort Nashborough, 170 First Ave. N. at Church St. (255-8192): Built on the site of the first white settlement in 1779, this rugged log replica of an 18th-century fort, surrounded by its stockade, admirably reconstructs the daily life of the pioneers, with walk-ons in period clothing. Don't fail to visit it. Open Tues–Sat.

    The Hermitage, 4580 Rachel's Lane, in Hermitage, 12 mi. (19km) NE via I-40 and Old Hickory Blvd. (889-2941): Andrew Jackson's country house, built in 1819 and enlarged in 1834 after a fire, is one of the finest classical revival buildings in the Deep South. Superb original furniture. The tombs of the seventh president and his wife, Rachel, stand amid lovely gardens. Don't miss it. Open daily.

    State Capitol, Sixth Ave. and Charlotte Ave. (741-2692): Built on a hill overlooking the city, this classic of the Greek Revival style is the work of architect William Strickland, who in 1859 was buried within its walls. On the main lawn is the tomb of James Polk, 11th president of the U.S., and statues of local heroes including Pres. Andrew Jackson and Sgt. Alvin York, the most decorated U.S. soldier of World War I. Open daily. Should be seen.

    Travellers' Rest, 636 Farrell Pkwy., 6 mi. (9km) south on U.S. 31 (832-2962): Plantation house with its original two-story-porch architecture, dating from the early 1800s, standing among groves of giant magnolias and maples. Often visited by Andrew Jackson, Lafayette, and other notables. Worth a visit. Open daily.

MUSEUMS OF ART: **Cheekwood Fine Arts Center,** Forrest Park Dr., 7 mi. (11km) SW via U.S. 70S and Tenn. 100 (352-5310): 18th-century English furniture; 19th-century European and American paintings. Temporary exhibitions. Imposing 1932 building in the Georgian style surrounded by an outstandingly lovely botanic garden, with orchids, camellias, rose gardens, Japanese garden, etc. You should certainly go. Open Tues–Sun.

    Van Vechten Gallery, 17th Ave. N. and Jackson St. (329-8543): This very lovely modern-art museum on the campus of Fisk University has more than 100 works by 20th-century American artists, donated by painter Georgia O'Keeffe after the death of her husband, photographer Alfred Stieglitz. Well worth seeing. Open Tues–Sun.

NASHVILLE

N

Museum of Tobacco Art & Industry

JAMES ROBERTSON PKWY

GAY ST.

GAY ST.

2ND AVE

To Opryland, Grand
Ole Opry

JAMES ROBERTSON PKWY

WOODLAND ST.

Cumberland River

Bicentennial Park

1ST AVE

5TH AVE

Cordell Hull Bldg.

Municipal Auditorium

State Capitol

State Office Bldgs.

CHARLOTTE AVE.

DEADERICK ST.

State Library

Ft. Nashborough

State Supreme Court

Performing Arts Center

CHURCH ST.

War Memorial Aud.

Life & Casualty Tower

Belle Carol
Riverboat Co.

2ND AVE

UNION ST.

Public Library

GAY ST.

CHARLOTTE AVE.

6TH AVE

7TH AVE

COMMERCE ST.

Ryman Auditorium

10TH AVE

CHURCH ST.

BROADWAY

4TH AVE

3RD AVE

12TH AVE

13TH AVE

14TH AVE

CHURCH ST.

GRUNDY ST.

11TH AVE

McGAVOCK ST.

DEMONBREUN ST.

5TH AVE

To Tenn. Fairgrounds

FRANKLIN ST.

15TH AVE

Union Station

Bus Terminal

BROADWAY

CLARK

SHIRLEY ST.

PEABODY ST.

McGAVOCK ST.

40

LEA AVE

LAFAYETTE ST.

DEMONBREUN ST.

Music Square Park

LAUREL ST.

PINE ST.

GLEAVES ST.

7TH AVE

FOGG ST.

EWING ST.

Academy Theater

ASH ST.

MUSIC SQ. W

Country Music Wax Museum
Country Music Hall of Fame

DIVISION ST.

8TH AVE

MUSIC SQ. E.

SIGLER ST.

Toney Rose Park

ALLISON ST.

Music
Row

MUSIC CIRCLE

HAWKINS ST.

VILLA ST.

15TH AVE

HAWKINS ST.

OVERTON ST.

SOUTH ST.

Cumberland Museum
& Science Center

Fort Negley
Park

65

MUSEUMS OF SCIENCE & HISTORY: ※å Country Music Hall of Fame and Museum, 4 Music Sq. E. (256-1639): Innumerable memorabilia of all the idols of country music: Chet Atkins's first guitar, the car used by Burt Reynolds in the movie *Smokey and the Bandit*, Dolly Parton's show dresses, Elvis Presley's massive gold Cadillac. Enthralling; an absolute must for all fans. You will also visit the legendary **RCA Studio B** (see "Broadcasting and Movie Studios," above). Don't miss this one.

å **Country Music Wax Museum,** 118 16th Ave. S. (256-2490): A pantheon in wax: 60 or so of country music's greatest stars in their authentic stage costumes and their original musical instruments. Upstairs is a private collection of Waylon Jennings memorabilia. Very touristy, but a must for all country-music fans. Souvenir shop and restaurant adjoining. Open daily.

å **Cumberland Science Museum,** 800 Ridley Blvd. (259-6099): Interesting material on zoology and Native American history; also a very up-to-date planetarium. Open Tues–Sun.

※å **George Jones' Car Collectors' Hall of Fame,** 1534 Demonbreun St. (255-6804): Very fine collection of antique cars, most of which belonged to country music or rock stars like Elvis Presley, Roy Orbison, Webb Pierce, and Bobby Goldsboro. Worth seeing. Open daily.

※å **Museum of Tobacco Art and History,** 800 Harrison St. at Eighth Ave. N. (242-9218): Traces the history of tobacco from its origins among the earliest Native Americans. Fine collection of old pipes, snuffboxes, and tobacco jars. Curious and interesting. Open Tues–Sat.

å **State Museum,** James K. Polk Bldg., 505 Deaderick St. (741-2692): Colorful presentation of Tennessee history from the Stone Age to the War Between the States, illustrated by a display of more than 5,000 old objects. Worth visiting. Open daily.

NIGHTTIME ENTERTAINMENT: The capital of country music has, as you might expect, one of the country's heaviest concentrations of nightclubs, bars, and dance halls to the square mile. Certain tourist traps should be given a wide berth: they're to be found on Printer's Alley and Broadway, the two "hot" streets in the entertainment district. Besides the Grand Ole Opry and the clubs listed further on in this chapter, don't miss a trip to the **Ernest Tubb Midnight Jamboree,** 2414 Music Valley Dr. (889-2474). It's a sort of country-music jam session which meets every Sat in a well-known record store at midnight, after the show at the nearby Grand Ole Opry. Public admitted free. Very popular locally.

PARKS & GARDENS: å Opryland Hotel Conservatory, 2800 Opryland Dr. (889-1000): The 10,000 trees and tropical plants arrayed here in a six-story-high greenhouse make this wonderful winter garden, with its streams, waterfalls, and statues, a must for all who visit Opryland, whether or not they stay at the hotel. Should be seen. Open daily; 10 min. from dwntwn.

※åå **Tennessee Botanical Gardens–Cheekwood,** Forrest Park Dr. (352-5310): Beautiful 30-acre (12ha) botanic garden surrounding the Cheekwood Fine Arts Center (see "Museums of Art," above). Besides greenhouses with a simulated tropical forest and numberless varieties of camellias and orchids, the garden boasts several lovely specialty gardens: rose garden, Japanese garden, wildflower garden, herb garden. Don't fail to visit. Open Tues–Sun.

PERFORMING ARTS: For current listings of shows and cultural events, consult the entertainment pages of the two daily papers, *The Tennessean* (morning) and *The Nashville Banner* (evening), as well as the monthly *Nashville*.

Centennial Park, W. End Ave. and 25th Ave. (259-6399): Open-air concerts by the Nashville Symphony, every wknd June–Aug. Also folk and country-music concerts.

Grand Ole Opry, 2804 Opryland Dr., 10 mi. (16km) NE via I-40 and Briley Pkwy. (889-3060): The shrine of country music. Shows and live concerts every Fri and Sat evening year round; matinees Tues, Thurs, Sat, and Sun in summer. You must reserve—as far ahead as possible.

Municipal Auditorium, 417 Fourth Ave. N. (259-6461): Hosts political meetings, conventions, and live concerts.

Music Village USA, Music Village Blvd. in Hendersonville, 20 mi. (32km) NE via I-65, Two Mile Pkwy., and U.S. 31E (822-1800): Shows and live concerts by the biggest stars in country music. Concerts Mon–Sat May–Aug, wknds only Sept–Oct; closed the rest of the year.

Nashville Academy Theater, 724 Second Ave. S. (254-9103): Specializes in classical theater and children's shows.

Opryland, 2802 Opryland Dr., 10 mi. (16km) NE via I-40 and Briley Pkwy. (889-6700): Live TV shows, live pop, jazz, blues, country, gospel, or rock 'n' roll concerts, Broadway-style revues. Adjoining are the Grand Ole Opry and a giant amusement park. Open daily Memorial Day to Labor Day, wknds only in spring and fall; closed the rest of the year.

Tennessee Performing Arts Center, 505 Deaderick St. (741-7975): Ultra-modern complex of three adjoining auditoriums: **Andrew Jackson Hall,** offer-ing concerts (home of the Nashville Symphony, under principal conductor Kenneth Schermerhorn) Sept–May; the **James K. Polk Theater,** for drama, com-edy, operetta, chamber-music recitals (home of the Tennessee Repertory Thea-ter); and the **Andrew Johnson Theater,** a theater-in-the-round for modern and avant-garde material (Sept–May; also big-name shows).

War Memorial Auditorium, Memorial Sq., Seventh Ave., and Union St. (741-2148): Pop and classical concerts.

SHOPPING: The Arcade, between Fourth Ave. and Fifth Ave. N.: Picturesque turn-of-the-century shopping arcade under an elegant glass roof. Dozens of un-usual shops and stalls in the heart of dwntwn.

Fountain Square, Metrocenter Blvd. and I-265: The newest and most col-orful of the local shopping centers. Boutiques, stores, cafés, restaurants, cinemas, and open-air concerts on the shores of a charming little lake 5 min. from dwntwn.

Record Stores

Many specialized stores around Music Row, including **Conway's Twitty,** 1530 Demonbreun; **Country Music Factory Outlet,** 319 11th Ave. S.; **Ernest Tubb,** 417 Broadway; **The Great Escape,** 1925 Broadway—offering a huge se-lection of country-music records at bargain prices; also **Sam Goody's,** Fountain Sq.

Western Wear

Lovers of cowboy boots and western clothing will find an unequalled selec-tion in the innumerable outlets for this kind of merchandise that abound in Nashville. Some of these are: **Alamo of Nashville,** 324 Broadway; **Boot Coun-try,** 2412 Music Valley Dr.; **Loretta Lynn's Western Wear Stores,** 120 16th Ave.; and **Genesco Manufacturing Outlets,** 511 Main St. (discount clothing and boots).

SPECIAL EVENTS: For exact dates, consult the **Nashville Chamber of Com-merce** (see "Tourist Information," above).

Tennessee Crafts Fair (May): A handcrafts fair which draws more than 150 of the state's best-known craftspeople; very popular locally.

International Country Music Fan Fair (mid-June): Country music's great annual festival, which attracts more than 200,000 fans every year. Don't miss it.

Longhorn Rodeo Series (every wknd July–Sept): One of the most famous professional rodeos east of the Mississippi; local color guaranteed.

National Quartet Convention (Sept–Oct): Very popular gospel-music festival.

SPORTS: Nashville has no major-league teams, but has a minor-league team in—**Baseball** (Apr–Oct): Sounds, Greer Stadium (242-4371).

THEME PARKS: ☼▲▲ **Opryland USA,** 2802 Opryland Dr., 10 mi. (16km) NE via I-40 and Briley Pkwy. (889-6700): Adjoining the legendary Grand Ole Opry, this huge, inventive amusement park features popular music of all kinds—country, jazz, blues, folk, rock, musical comedy, etc.—but also offers dozens of carousels, roller coasters, bars, restaurants, boutiques, and even a mini-zoo for children. Don't miss it. Open daily Memorial Day to Labor Day, wknds only in spring and fall; closed the rest of the year.

ACCOMMODATIONS

A Note on Accommodations: Room rates in Nashville are coded as follows: **VE,** Very Expensive ($140 and up); **E,** Expensive ($90–$140); **M,** Moderate ($60–$90); **I,** Inexpensive ($30–$60); **B,** Budget (up to $30). A listing of toll free numbers is in the Appendix.

Personal Favorites (in order of preference)

☼♀♀♀ **The Hermitage** (dwntwn), 231 Sixth Ave. N., TN 37219 (615/244-3121; toll free 800/251-1908). 112 suites, A/C, color TV, in-rm movies. AE, CB, DC, MC, V. Valet parking $5, rest. (Hermitage Dining Room), two bars, rm svce, nightclub, boutiques, concierge, free breakfast. *Note:* Elegant small turn-of-the-century hotel of Beaux Arts classic design, splendidly restored; one- and two-bedroom suites, luxuriously decorated, w. minibars and antique furniture. Faultless svce. Good rest. Free breakfast served on a pretty porch. Elegant and charming; the favorite hotel of those in-the-know, in the heart of dwntwn. **E–VE**

☼♀♀♀ **Union Station Hotel** (dwntwn), 1001 Broadway, TN 37206 (615/726-1001). 128 rms, A/C, color TV, in-rm movies. AE, CB, DC, MC, V. Valet parking $5, three rests. (including Arthur's), bar, 24-hr. rm svce, nightclub, concierge, free crib. *Note:* The most innovative of the local luxury hotels. Opened in 1987, this elegant, comfortable establishment occupies seven floors of the old Union Station, an imposing turn-of-the-century structure in Railroad Gothic crowned by a tall Big Ben–style tower. Beautifully restored decor w. mosaic floors, stained-glass windows, and hand-carved wood paneling. Very spacious, well-equipped rms; excellent svce. Halfway between dwntwn and Music Row; a fashionable place to stay. Free airport shuttle. **E**

♀♀♀ **Maxwell House Clarion** (nr. dwntwn), 2025 Metro Center Blvd., TN 37228 (615/259-4343; toll free, see Clarion). 290 rms, A/C, color TV, in-rm movies. AE, CB, DC, MC, V. Free parking, pool, two tennis courts, health club, two rests. (including Crown Court), coffee shop, bar, rm svce, disco, free crib. *Note:* Modern, elegant hotel 8 min. from dwntwn, close to Fountain Sq. Shopping Mall; spacious, comfortable rms, recently renovated (some w. refrigerators). Attentive svce; very acceptable rest. VIP floor. Business clientele; a good place to stay. Free airport shuttle. **M–E**

♀♀ **Ramada Inn–Downtown** (dwntwn), 840 James Robertson Pkwy., TN 37203 (615/244-6130; toll free, see Ramada). 180 rms, A/C, color TV, in-rm movies. AE, CB, DC, MC, V. Free parking, pool, rest., bar, rm svce, nightclub, free crib. *Note:* Recently renovated five-floor motel very conveniently situated nr. the Capitol and the business district. Large, comfortable rms; efficient svce (for a convention and package-tour hotel); free airport shuttle. Good value overall. **I–M**

♀ **La Quinta** (nr. dwntwn), 2001 Metro Center Blvd., TN 37228 (615/259-2130; toll free, see La Quinta). 121 rms,

A/C, color TV, in-rm movies. AE, CB, DC, MC, V. Free parking, pool, 24-hr. coffee shop adj., valet svce, free crib. *Note:* Rustic, but functional and comfortable, motel; friendly reception and svce. Very good value. 8 min. from dwntwn. **I**

Motel 3 (dwntwn), 800 James Robertson Pkwy., TN 37203 (615/244-2630). 83 rms, A/C, cable color TV. AE, CB, DC, MC, V. *Note:* Small four-story hotel at the foot of the State Capitol; modest but well run. Friendly reception. Some rms w. balconies. Good value. **I**

Other Hotels (from top bracket to budget)

Opryland Hotel (vic.), 2800 Opryland Dr., TN 37214 (615/889-1000). 1,892 rms, A/C, color TV, AE, CB, DC, MC, V. Valet parking $6, pool, six tennis courts, four rests. (including the Old Hickory Room), coffee shop, four bars, 24-hr. rm svce, disco, shows, hrdrsr, boutiques, free crib. *Note:* Enormous vacation complex oriented to mass tourism; ideal for visiting Opryland and the Grand Ole Opry, which it adjoins. Flashy Deep South interior. Spacious, comfortable rms, the best overlooking a lovely indoor botanic grdn ("The Conservatory"); also indoor lagoon w. waterfalls and streams; mediocre rests. Obtrusive package-tour and convention clientele. Rates tend toward the exorbitant. 20 min. from dwntwn. **VE,** but lower rates off-season.

Stouffer Hotel (dwntwn), 611 Commerce St., TN 37203 (615/255-8400; toll free, see Stouffer). 673 rms, A/C, color TV, in-rm movies. AE, CB, DC, MC, V. Valet parking $7, pool, health club, sauna, rest., coffee shop, bar, 24-hr rm svce, nightclub, boutiques, concierge, free crib. *Note:* Elegant, ultramodern tower whose 27 stories dominate the Convention Center—an excellent location in the heart of dwntwn. Huge, very comfortable rms; efficient svce; business and convention clientele. Two top floors reserved for VIPs. Direct access to the brand-new Nashville Convention Center. **E–VE**

Hyatt Regency (dwntwn), 623 Union St., TN 37219 (615/259-1234; toll free, see Hyatt). 478 rms, A/C, color TV, in-rm movies. AE, CB, DC, MC, V. Gar. $4, two rests. (including the revolving Polaris on the 28th floor), two bars, rm svce, disco, concierge, free crib. *Note:* A hefty cube of concrete directly across from the State Capitol, w. a spectacular 28-story glass atrium. Very comfortable rms of agreeably contemporary design; efficient but impersonal svce. Mediocre rests. Large package-tour and convention business (the Convention Center is only two blocks away). Excellent dwntwn location. **E**

Doubletree Hotel (formerly the Radisson; dwntwn), 2 Commerce Pl., TN 37219 (615/244-8200; toll free 800/528-0444). 337 rms, A/C, color TV, in-rm movies. AE, CB, DC, MC, V. Valet gar. $5, pool, health club, sauna, two rests. (including the Hunt Room), two bars, rm svce, disco, boutiques, free crib. *Note:* This modern building makes no appeal to the eye, but the rms and interior decoration are elegant and comfortable. Right in the heart of dwntwn Nashville. Efficient svce. The 12th (top) floor is reserved for VIPs. Business clientele. Interesting wknd packages. **M–E**

Holiday Inn Vanderbilt (nr. dwntwn), 2613 W. End Ave., TN 37203 (615/327-4707; toll free, see Holiday Inns). 300 rms, A/C, color TV, in-rm movies. AE, CB, DC, MC, V. Free parking, pool, rest. (Commodore), bar, rm svce, disco, free crib. *Note:* Modern 14-floor building very nr. Vanderbilt University. Functionally comfortable in the Holiday Inn manner. Good value. 5 min. from dwntwn. **I–M**

Quality Inn Hall of Fame (nr. dwntwn), 1407 Division St., TN 37203 (615/242-1631; toll free, see Quality Inns). 103 rms, A/C, color TV, in-rm movies. AE, CB, DC, MC, V. Free parking, pool, rest., bar, rm svce, disco, free crib. *Note:* Recently renovated motel, well placed for a visit to the Country Music Hall of Fame and the attractions of Music Row. Comfortable rms; smiling reception. Family and group clientele. Free airport shuttle (until 7pm). **I–M**

🛏 **Days Inn Central** (dwntwn), 211 N. 1st St., TN 37213 (615/243-1551; toll free, see Days Inns). 180 rms, A/C, color TV, in-rm movies. AE, DC, MC, V. Free parking, pool, health club, coffee shop, bar, free crib. *Note:* Modern nine-story motel 5 min. from the Capitol and the business district. Serviceably comfortable; friendly reception. Good value; excellent if you're driving since it can be reached from I-24/I-65 via Exit 85. **I**, but lower rates off-season.

🛏 **Motel 6** (vic.), 311 W. Trinity Lane, TN 37207 (615/227-9696). 126 rms, A/C, color TV, free in-rm movies. AE, DC, MC, V. Free parking, pool, nearby coffee shop. *Note:* Economy-style but engaging motel 10 min. from dwntwn and 15 min. from the Grand Ole Opry. Up-to-date amenities. Unbeatable value; perfect for the budget traveler. **B**

Airport Accommodations

🛏🛏🛏 **Sheraton Music City** (vic.), 777 McGavock Pike, TN 37214 (615/885-2200; toll free, see Sheraton). 412 rms, A/C, color TV, in-rm movies. AE, CB, DC, MC, V. Free parking, two pools, health club, sauna, two tennis courts, rest. (Belair), bar, 24-hr. rm svce, disco, concierge. *Note:* Crowning a hilltop from which it overlooks its 23 acres (9ha) of park and landscaped grdns, this very handsome convention hotel draws a large business clientele. Elegant, sumptuous decor; very comfortable rms w. private balcony and refrigerator. Friendly svce and reception. Good rest. serving American cuisine. Free shuttle to the airport terminal 5 min. away; 10 min. from Opryland, 20 min. from dwntwn. **M–E**

🛏 **Courtyard by Marriott** (vic.), 2508 Elm Hill Pike, TN 37214 (615/883-9500; toll free 800/321-2211). 145 rms, A/C, color TV, in-rm movies. AE, DC, MC, V. Free parking, pool, health club, rest., bar, valet svce. *Note:* Newly built traditional motel w. huge, inviting rms and efficient svce. 5 min. from the airport (free shuttle); great for a stopover between flights. **M**, but lower rates on wknds.

RESTAURANTS

A Note on Restaurant Prices: Nashville restaurant prices, per person, excluding drinks and service charges, are coded as follows: **VE**, Very Expensive ($60 and up); **E**, Expensive ($40–$60); **M**, Moderate ($25–$40); **I**, Inexpensive ($15–$25); **B**, Budget (up to $15).

Personal Favorites (in order of preference)

🍷🍷🍷 **Julian's** (nr. dwntwn), 2412 W. End Ave. (327-2412). A/C. Dinner only, Mon–Sat; closed hols. and 2 weeks in July. AE, CB, DC, MC, V. Jkt. *Specialties:* duck à l'orange, salmon Florentine in pastry shell, roast quail w. peaches, rack of lamb, veal chop w. morels, game (in season), fruit soufflés, good desserts. Fine wine list. *Note:* Gracious and elegant, Nashville's best rest. has chosen as its home a charming old house w. columns in the best Deep South style. The cuisine is flawlessly classic, the svce exemplary. Only 55 people can be seated here, so resv. are strongly advised. *French.* **M–E**

🍷🍷🍷 **Mario's** (nr. dwntwn), 2005 Broadway (327-3232). A/C. Dinner only, Mon–Sat; closed hols. AE, CB, DC, MC, V. Jkt. *Specialties:* fresh homemade pasta, zuppa di pesce, osso buco, veal marsala, roast duck, broiled fish. Excellent wine list (over 10,000 bottles). *Note:* The jovial Mario Ferrari serves excellent northern Italian food at relatively reasonable prices in his locally popular rest. The svce has too much to do and the place is often noisy. Favored by local celebrities. Resv. strongly advised. *Italian.* **I–M**

🍷🍷 **Maude's Courtyard** (nr. dwntwn), 1911 Broadway (320-0543). A/C. Lunch Mon–Fri, dinner Mon–Sat, jazz brunch

Sun; closed Jan 1, Dec 25. AE, CB, DC, MC, V. *Specialties:* stuffed tomatoes, rack of lamb, broiled red meats, catch of the day, roast chicken. *Note:* Charming old southern-style house attractively restored, w. inner courtyard for al fresco dining. Good, tasty food at reasonable prices; crowded w. Music Row executives at lunchtime. Resv. advisable; an excellent place to eat. *Continental.* I

♀ **Dynasty** (nr. dwntwn), 3415 W. End Ave. (269-0188). A/C. Lunch/dinner daily; closed Thanksgiving. AE, MC, V. *Specialties:* Peking duck, Mongolian beef, sweet-and-sour fish. *Note:* The best Chinese rest. in Nashville, serving elegant, authentic food. All-purpose Far Eastern decor; diligent svce; very good value. Resv. advised. *Chinese.* B–I

�️♀ **Elliston Place Soda Shop** (nr. dwntwn), 2111 Elliston Pl. (327-1090). A/C. Breakfast/lunch/dinner Mon–Sat (until 9pm). No credit cards. *Specialties:* fried chicken, country ham, hamburgers, spaghetti Créole, roast beef au jus, roast turkey, excellent fresh vegetables, banana split. *Note:* An early (1939) precursor of today's fast-food establishments, and a monument of local gastronomy. Nothing in the decor or the atmosphere has changed since it opened, nor has the dependable, tasty family-style cooking. The place is as clean as ever; the waitresses are as motherly as ever; even the original soda fountain is still in action. Most of the patrons are students from nearby Vanderbilt U. A very good place to eat. *American.* B

Other Restaurants (from top bracket to budget)

♀♀♀ **Arthur's** (dwntwn), in the Union Station Hotel (see "Accommodation," above) (255-1494). A/C. Lunch/dinner Mon–Sat; closed hols. AE, CB, DC, MC, V. J&T. *Specialties:* veal normande, beef Wellington, Dover sole meunière, flaming desserts; the menu changes regularly. Good wine list. *Note:* The classical French-inspired haute cuisine and the elegantly luxurious setting have made this rest. a favorite w. notables, whether local or visiting. The svce is a touch pretentious. Resv. necessary. *Continental.* E (prix fixe)

♀♀ **Sperry's** (vic.), 5109 Harding Rd. (353-0809). A/C. Dinner only, nightly; closed hols. AE, CB, DC, MC, V. Jkt. *Specialties:* snails, stuffed mushrooms, Alaska crabmeat, fine broiled meat and fish, banana Foster. *Note:* A small, quite intimate rest. nr. the Belle Meade Mansion, done up as an English pub in the Tudor style. Warm, candlelit atmosphere. The cuisine, though unimaginative, is polished. Good svce. Resv. not accepted. Free parking. 20 min. from dwntwn. *Steak/seafood.* I–M

�️♀♀ **Stock-Yard** (dwntwn), 901 Second Ave. (255-6464). A/C. Lunch Mon–Fri, dinner Mon–Sat; closed hols. AE, CB, DC, MC, V. *Specialties:* all kinds of charcoal-grilled steak, pork and lamb chops, broiled chicken. Good desserts. *Note:* Located as its name suggests in the old slaughterhouses dwntwn, this picturesque place serves the best broiled steak in Nashville. Country music and dancing every evening in the adj. Bullpen Lounge. Locally popular; free parking. *Steak.* I–M

♀ **Jimmy Kelly's** (nr. dwntwn), 217 Louise Ave. (329-4349). Dinner only, Mon–Sat. (till midnight). AE, DC, MC, V. *Specialties:* steak, Virginia ham, fried chicken, catch of the day. *Note:* A Nashville landmark for more than half a century, across from the Vanderbilt U. campus. Pleasing Victorian decor, relaxed atmosphere. Very good steaks and authentic southern food. A fine place. Resv. suggested. *American.* I

♀♀ **Crawdaddy's** (nr. dwntwn), 14 Oldham St., on the river (255-5434). A/C. Lunch Mon–Fri, dinner nightly, brunch Sun. AE, CB, DC, MC, V. *Specialties:* gumbo, fish Créole style, Cajun dishes, steaks. *Note:* No unworthy representative, this, of New Orleans cooking, in a charming (but hard-to-find) Victorian setting beside the Cumberland River. Open deck for outdoor dining. Very good svce, inviting bars. Also dancing. Resv. suggested. *American.* B–I

☕ **Los Cuñados** (nr. dwntwn), 1910 Belcourt Ave., Hillsboro
🍴 Village Mall (383-8920). A/C. Lunch/dinner Mon–Sat. AE,
MC, V. *Specialties:* tacos, enchiladas, tamales, chiles rellenos, steak ranchero, fish
Veracruzana. *Note:* Nashville's most legitimate Mexican rest., where all the
south-of-the-border classics are flawlessly prepared and served. Warm decor and
atmosphere; hard-working svce. Locally popular; resv. advisable. *Mexican.* **B–I**

☼☕ **Satsuma Tea Room** (dwntwn), 417 Union St. (256-5211).
🌣🍴 A/C. Lunch only, Mon–Fri. No credit cards. *Specialties:*
homemade soups and salads, turkey à la king, filet of sole amandine, pork chop w.
mashed potato, vegetable luncheon (tomato, zucchini, and leaf vegetables w.
fresh pasta), crème caramel, lemon cake, excellent homemade ice cream. Menu
changes daily. *Note:* This is the southern home-cooking of your dreams. The Satsuma Tea Room is a local institution, taken over every noon hour by hordes of
regulars (ask to be seated upstairs, where the noise level is lower). Good plain
decor and svce; no resv. A very fine place. *American.* **B**

Cafeterias/Fast Food

☼☼ **Loveless Motel & Restaurant** (vic.), on Tenn. 100 at Rte. 5,
🌣 15 mi. (24km) SW (646-9700). Breakfast/lunch/dinner
Tues–Sun (till 9pm). Well worth the 20-min. drive from dwntwn. Despite its
dingy appearance, this motel serves some of the best country cooking in all Tennessee. Remarkable hickory-smoked country ham and fried chicken; excellent
homemade biscuits and jam. Friendly waitresses. No alcoholic beverages; no
credit cards. In view of its popularity, you should make resv.

Morrison's (nr. dwntwn), 1000 Two Mile Pkwy. at Rivergate Mall (859-
1359). A/C. Lunch/dinner daily (till 8pm). MC, V. Cafeteria-buffet offering
very good value. Roast beef, and desserts worth your attention.

BARS & NIGHTCLUBS

The capital of country music offers its visitors numberless nightclubs, bars,
strip joints, dance halls, and dives where jazz, folk, or country music may be
heard. There are, however, tourist traps to be avoided on Printers Alley and
Broadway. The list given below includes the best places for lovers of authentic
folk and country music.

Bluebird Café (vic.), 4104 Hillsboro Rd. (383-1461). Live country, folk,
and jazz; highly recommended. Also a rest. Open nightly. 20 min. from
dwntwn.

Bluegrass Inn (nr. dwntwn), 1914 Broadway (329-1112). For lovers of real
bluegrass; nr. the Vanderbilt campus. Open Wed–Sat.

Boots Randolph's (dwntwn), 209 Printers Alley (256-5500). The well-
known sax player (and owner) Boots Randolph puts on an excellent performance, but the atmosphere is touristy. Also a so-so rest. Open Mon–Sat.

Bullpen Lounge (dwntwn), 901 Second Ave. (255-6464). Pleasing bar-
disco downstairs in the Stock-Yard rest. (see above). Open Mon–Sat.

Captain's Table (dwntwn), 313 Church St. (251-9535) Las Vegas–style
shows; also a mediocre rest. Open nightly.

Exit/In (nr. dwntwn), 2208 Elliston Pl. (321-4400). One of the best
country-music joints; Robert Altman filmed *Nashville* here. Also a fair-to-
middling rest. Open nightly.

Monroe's Bluegrass Country (vic.), 2620 Music Valley Dr. (885-0777).
Real bluegrass music by one of its great stars, Bill Monroe. Across from the Opryland Hotel. Open daily.

Station Inn (dwntwn), 402 12th Ave. (255-3307). Shrine of local bluegrass
and "newgrass." Open Tues–Sun.

Western Room (dwntwn), 210 Printers Alley (256-9339). This club showcases new country-music talent. Open Mon–Sat.

Wrangler (vic.), 1204 Murfreesboro Rd. (361-4440). Locally popular disco offering country and western. Nice atmosphere. Nr. the airport and 20 min. from dwntwn. Open nightly.

Zanies Comedy Showplace (nr. dwntwn), 2025 Eighth Ave. S. (269-0221). Very popular comedy club with a star-studded schedule. Also mediocre rest. Open Tues–Sun.

NEARBY EXCURSIONS

CHEATHAM LAKE (30 mi./48km NW on Tenn. 12): Large body of water formed by a dam and locks on the Cumberland River. Water sports, fishing, camping; wildlife reserve. Fine scenic drive along the Cumberland River. Worth the side trip.

CUMBERLAND CAVERNS PARK (80 mi./128km SE on I-24 and U.S. 70) (668-4396): Impressive patchwork of underground caves, once a saltpeter mine. It includes some of the largest and most impressive caverns in the country, particularly the "Hall of the Mountain King," 600 ft. (183m) wide and 140 ft. (43m) high. The temperature in the caves stays around 56°F (13°C) winter and summer alike. Conducted 90-min. tour daily, June to the end of Aug, wknds only in spring and fall; by appointment Nov–Apr. Worth going out of your way for.

FARTHER AFIELD

CHATTANOOGA & THE TENNESSEE VALLEY (515 mi./824km r.t. via I-24S, U.S. 231S, Tenn. 82S, Tenn. 50E, U.S. 64E, I-24S, U.S. 72W, U.S. Alt. 72W, U.S. 45N, Tenn. 22N, U.S. 64E, U.S. 43N, and U.S. 31N): The trip begins with a visit to the famous **Jack Daniel's Distillery** at Lynchburg, the country's oldest (1866) registered whisky distillery. The rule here is "look but don't taste"—Lynchburg is in a "dry" county! Open daily; resv. advised (759-4221).

Next stop is **Chattanooga,** a thriving commercial town on the banks of the Tennessee River. Near here, in 1863, was fought one of the decisive engagements of the War Between the States, "the battle above the clouds" on 2,225-ft. (678m) **Lookout Mountain,** which dominates the town and offers a fine view over four states. The amazing incline railroad, which rises at an angle of 72°, has its lower terminus at 3917 St. Elmo Ave. (841-4224); operates daily year round. Fine railroad museum, the **Tennessee Valley Railroad Museum,** at 4119 Cromwell Rd. (894-8028); open daily June to the end of Aug, wknds Mar–May and Sept–Nov.

Nine miles (14km) south of Chattanooga, see **Chickamauga and Chattanooga National Military Park,** Georgia, the country's most visited battlefield. Here, on September 19–20 and November 23–25, 1863, Confederates under Gen. Braxton Bragg and Union troops under Gen. George H. Thomas fought two bloody battles, ending in a Northern victory which left 34,000 dead and wounded on both sides. You can drive around the battlefield on a 3-mi. (5km) signposted road. Visitor Center open daily; worth the detour.

Then on to the **NASA Space and Rocket Center,** on Governors Dr. in **Huntsville,** Alabama (205/837-3400), with the world's largest space museum. Life-size replica of a lunar crater, simulated test flights into space, simulated launching ramp, museum of rockets and lunar modules, astronaut training center, etc. Fascinating; mustn't be missed. Open daily.

Before ending this trip with a tour of the battlefield of **Shiloh** (see Chapter 14 on Memphis), be sure to turn aside to Florence for a glimpse of the huge **Wilson Dam,** one of the largest in the world, and its giant lock on the Tennessee River. Visitor Center open daily.

This is a very full 3- to 4-day trip.

Where to Stay En Route

IN CHATTANOOGA ⛄⛄⛄ **Holiday Inn–Chattanooga Choo-Choo,** 1400 N. Market St., Chattanooga, TN 37402 (615/266-5000; toll free, see Holiday Inns). 327 rms. Built, as you might expect, in the old railroad terminal; original decor. **M**

IN HUNTSVILLE ⛄⛄ **Holiday Inn Space Center,** 3810 University Dr., Huntsville, AL 35816 (205/837-7171). 181 rms. Typical modern Holiday Inn 3 min. from the Space Center. **I–M**

⛄ **Comfort Inn,** 3788 University Dr., Huntsville, AL 35816 (205/533-3291). 66 rms. Conventional small, well-run hotel 3 min. from the Space Center. **I**

IN FLORENCE ⛄ **Regency Inn,** 1241 Florence Blvd., Florence, AL 35630 (205/764-5421). 84 rms. Comfortable, inviting motel. **I**

GREAT SMOKY MOUNTAINS NATIONAL PARK & SURROUNDINGS

(605 mi./968km r.t. along I-40E, Tenn. 441S, U.S. 23N, and I-40W): This vacation trip for nature lovers begins, ironically enough, with a visit to "Atom City"—**Oak Ridge,** where the bomb dropped on Hiroshima was manufactured. Visit the ΔΔ **American Museum of Science and Energy,** largest of its kind in the world, at 300 S. Tulane Ave. (576-3200), open daily. Several atomic facilities are open to the public; for a complete list, check with the Oak Ridge Convention and Visitors Bureau, 300 S. Tulane Ave. (482-7821).

Your second stop will be at ΔΔ **Great Smoky Mountain National Park,** which draws more visitors (more than 10 million a year) than any other in the country. Within its limited compass—50 mi. (80km) long and 15–19 mi. (25–30km) wide—it contains all the glories of the Appalachians, the oldest mountain range in North America, with more than 20 peaks rising above 6,560 ft. (2,000m), as well as 812 mi. (1,300km) of hiking trails. Its deep forests, home to black bear, deer, and other wildlife, are often wreathed in the mist and tattered clouds that give it its name.

Once the unapproachable realm of the Cherokee Nation, Great Smoky Mountains park now offers the tourist some magnificent landscapes (particularly from June to mid-July when the rhododendrons are in bloom), and some spectacular scenic drives. Park open daily year round (some park roads may be temporarily closed in winter). You should come to Nashville if only to see it. For information, contact the Superintendent, Great Smoky Mountain National Park, Gatlinburg, TN 37738 (615/436-1200).

At the edge of the park, Δ **Gatlinburg,** a popular tourist resort, and its next-door neighbor **Pigeon Forge,** where the singer Dolly Parton operates her theme park **Dollywood,** Dollywood Lane (428-9400), open daily May–Oct, both have many hotels and restaurants. Spectacular ☼Δ **aerial tramway** and sightseeing chair lift to the top of **Mount Harrison** at 3,500 ft. (1,065m): 1001 Parkway, Gatlinburg (436-5423), open daily year round. The view from the summit includes Gatlinburg, Pigeon Forge, and the Great Smoky Mountains National Park.

A fitting close to this trip is a visit to the picturesque little hot-springs town of **Asheville,** North Carolina, nestling in the woods east of the park. Birthplace of writer Thomas Wolfe, Asheville boasts some noteworthy buildings including ☼ΔΔ **Biltmore House,** once the summer home of millionaire George W. Vanderbilt. Built by architect Richard Hunt, this imposing château in French Renaissance style is said to be the world's largest private house, with 255 rooms, of which barely a quarter are open to the public. The garden was designed by Frederick Law Olmsted, who designed New York's Central Park. You'll find it on U.S.

25 (704/255-1700). Open daily; don't miss it. A popular festival of music and Appalachian folk dancing is held here every Aug.

You should certainly make this 4- to 5-day trip; it can be combined with the foregoing itineraries into a feature-packed tour lasting 10 days to 2 weeks.

Where to Stay En Route

IN GATLINBURG 🔑🔑🔑 **Park Vista Hotel,** Airport Rd., Gatlinburg, TN 37738 (615/436-9211). 315 rms in an 18-story tower w. a scenic view of the mountains. Ultramodern comfort. **M–E**

🔑🔑 **River Terrace,** River Rd., Gatlinburg, TN 37738 (615/436-5161). 206 rms. Comfortable, well-equipped motel. **M**

🔑 **Johnson's Inn,** Baskins Creek Rd., Gatlinburg, TN 37738 (615/436-4881). 78 rms. Inviting small motel located on the bank of a stream. Closed Dec–Apr. **I**

IN GREAT SMOKY MOUNTAINS NATIONAL PARK 🔑 **Wonderland Club Hotel,** P.R. 2, Gatlinburg, TN 37738 (615/436-5490). 27 rms. The only hotel inside the park. Rustic atmosphere. Open May–late Oct. **M**

IN ASHEVILLE ☀ 🔑🔑🔑🔑 **Grove Park Inn,** 290 Macon Ave., Asheville, NC 28804 (704/252-2711). 509 rms. Turn-of-the-century palace built of granite boulders dug from its Blue Ridge Mountain site. Patronized by all the world's notables. Urbane and elegant. **E–VE**

☀🔭🔭 **Pisgah View Ranch,** N.C. 151S, Candler, NC 28715 (704/667-9100). 50 rms. A country inn lost in the forest 13 mi. (20km) from Asheville. Highly recommended. Open May–Oct. **I–M**

☀☀☀🔭 **MAMMOTH CAVE NATIONAL PARK & KENTUCKY COUNTRY** (520 mi./832km r.t. via I-65N, Ky. 70, Ky. 84E, Ky. 61N, U.S. 31W, 31N, and 31S, Blue Grass Pkwy. N, U.S. 68S, U.S. 150N, Blue Grass Pkwy. S, and I-65S): Discovered in 1799 by a bear hunter, the 🔭🔭 **Mammoth Caves** deserve their name: they are the longest system of underground caves in the world, but only 300 mi. (483km) has been explored so far. They are interspersed with caverns, deep sink-holes, and spectacular underground lakes and rivers. Some chambers are 196 ft. (60m) high. Guided tours (tiring) daily year round. Wear sturdy shoes and warm clothes. Call 502/758-2328 for information on schedules. The recommended approach is via Ky. 70. Don't miss it.

Continue to ☀🔭 **Abraham Lincoln's Birthplace,** a stately marble-and-granite memorial, erected in 1911 by public subscription of more than 100,000 anonymous contributors. Inside is the log cabin where the 16th president was born on February 12, 1809. The museum should not be missed. Open daily year round; for information, call 502/358-3874.

Go a little out of your way to see the legendary ☀ **Fort Knox,** on U.S. 31W (502/624-3351), site of the **United States Bullion Depository,** the country's second-largest gold reserve. The treasure is kept in a two-level steel, granite, and concrete cave, proof against bombs and sealed by an armored door weighing 28 tons (25,500kg). Unhappily it's closed to visitors, but on its grounds you may visit the 🔭 **Patton Museum** (502/624-3812), with its rich collection of tanks and other weapons of war; open daily year round.

On the way to **Lexington** and the famous **Kentucky Horse Park** (see Chapter 22 on Cincinnati), don't miss **Bardstown,** where you can make a sentimental pilgrimage to ☀ **"My Old Kentucky Home"** on U.S. 150 (502/348-3502), open daily year round; this lovely 18th-century Colonial house inspired Stephen Foster to write his immortal ballad. See also the **Oscar Getz Museum of Whisky,** 5th St. at Xavier Dr. (502/348-2999), open daily, which traces the history of that popular beverage, and 🔭 **St. Joseph's Cathedral,** 310 W. Stephen Foster

Ave. (502/348-3126), open daily; built in 1816, this was the first Roman Catholic cathedral west of the Alleghenies. It has a number of paintings presented by King Louis-Philippe of France during his exile.

The last stage of the journey takes you to ☼ **Harrodsburg,** the first settlement in Kentucky (1774). ⚱ **Old Fort Harrod,** on U.S. 68 (606/734-3314), open daily year round, is an exact replica of the original fort; don't miss it. Two other nearby attractions are: the ☼ **Shaker Village at Pleasant Hill,** 3500 Lexington Rd. (606/734-5411), open daily year round, a museum village once inhabited by the Shakers and boasting no fewer than 30 of the original 19th-century buildings; and the ⚱ **Perryville Battlefield,** on U.S. 68 (606/332-8631), open daily Apr–Oct, where there is a museum with a diorama of the battle, one of the bloodiest of the War Between the States.

This itinerary is interesting for its variety, and for its beautiful landscapes.

Where to Stay En Route

IN MAMMOTH CAVE NATIONAL PARK 🍴 **Mammoth Cave,** 3 mi. (5km) inside the park on Ky. 70 Park Rd., Mammoth Cave Nat'l. Park, KY 42259 (502/758-2225). 58 rms. Typical functional motel near the entrance to the caves. **I**

IN BARDSTOWN 🍴 **Parkview,** 418 E. Stephen Foster Ave., Bardstown, KY 40004 (502/348-5983). 32 rms. Small, inviting motel opposite "My Old Kentucky Home." **I**

IN LEXINGTON 🍴🍴 **Master Hosts–Campbell House Inn,** 1375 Harrodsburg Rd., Lexington, KY 40504 (606/255-4281). 300 rms. Luxurious, comfortable motel with golf course. **I–M**

IN HARRODSBURG ☼ 🍴🍴 **Inn at Pleasant Hill,** 3500 Lexington Rd., Harrodsburg, KY 40330 (606/734-5411). 72 rms. Comfortable rms built into the original structure of a 19th-century Shaker village. Picturesque old-fashioned charm. Good rest. **I–M**

CHAPTER 14

MEMPHIS

□ □ □

It was in 1541, near the site of modern Memphis, that Hernando de Soto, the first Spanish explorer of the interior, crossed the wide and muddy Mississippi River. His feat was replicated 132 years later by the French explorers Marquette and Joliet; they in turn were followed by Robert Cavelier de LaSalle, who during his 1682 voyage down the Mississippi to the Gulf of Mexico proclaimed French sovereignty over the region.

Memphis occupies a strategic position at a point where the Mississippi bends to welcome the Wolf River. Dominating the Mississippi from a commanding height, much as the ancient Memphis of the Pharaohs towered above the Nile, the city served briefly during the Civil War years as the capital of the Confederacy. This status ended abruptly in 1862, when Memphis was taken by Northern troops in a bloody naval battle in which some 30 ships were engaged.

Memphis owes its prosperity primarily to cotton—often referred to as "white gold"—for which it has long been the major market in the world. Soybeans and hardwood also play important roles in its economy. Its port activity (12 million tons/10.9 billion kg shipped annually) and its dense railroad network have made Memphis one of the busiest shipping centers in the South. The city has mushroomed, growing 28% in population between 1960 and 1980. Fond of calling itself the "Home of the Blues," Memphis has come to be a comfortable blend of highways and skyscrapers with traces of a more gracious past such as **Overton Square** and **Beale Street,** picturesque examples of successful renovation in the old city. It was on Beale Street, close by the banks of the Mississippi, that the legendary composer W. C. Handy wrote "Memphis Blues" and "St. Louis Blues," two great classics of traditional jazz. In later years Memphis became the adopted home of Elvis Presley; although the singer died in 1977, idolatrous fans by the tens of thousands still flock to visit his grave and the gardens of **Graceland,** the Presley mansion.

Memphis is the proud birthplace (in 1952) of the first Holiday Inn, now part of one of the largest hotel empires in the world, whose headquarters are still in the city, as are those of Federal Express and more than 800 other enterprises, concentrated for the most part in the port area of **Presidents Island.** Also acclaimed as the pork barbecue capital of the world, with nearly 100 barbecue restaurants, in four recent national polls, Memphis was voted the cleanest, most orderly, and most peaceful city in the United States. It was, however, in a Memphis motel that civil rights leader and Nobel Peace Prize winner Martin Luther King, Jr., was assassinated (April 4, 1968). Among Memphis's celebrated sons and daughters are actor/comedian George Hamilton, actress Cybill Shepherd, and singers Aretha Franklin and Alberta Hunter.

BASIC FACTS: State of Tennessee. Area code: 901. Time zone: central. ZIP Code: 31801. Founded in 1819. Approximate population: city, 640,000, metropolitan area, 980,000. Ranked 15th in size among the nation's cities and 41st among its metropolitan areas.

CLIMATE: The dominant presence of the Mississippi River guarantees humidity year round, even in winter when the temperature hovers around freezing. In

July and Aug the city resembles a giant sauna, with temperatures around 82° – 86° F (28° –30° C). Spring, and especially autumn, are the only two seasons recommended for your visit.

DISTANCES: Atlanta, 365 mi. (585km); Chicago, 531 mi. (850km); Dallas, 450 mi. (720km); Nashville, 210 mi. (336km); New Orleans, 390 mi. (625km); St. Louis, 284 mi. (455km).

ARRIVAL & TRANSIT INFORMATION

AIRPORT: Memphis International Airport (MEM), 10 mi. (6km) SE.

AIRLINES: American (526-8861), Delta (761-5441), Northwest (525-7681), TWA (toll free 800/221-2000), United (522-9222), and USAir (526-0661).

CITY LINK: The **cab** fare from the airport to downtown is about $14; time, 25 min. Bus: **Yellow Cab** (577-7777) leaves every half hour and serves the principal downtown hotels; fare, $6; time, 30 min.
The city itself is not so large that renting a car is essential, but be warned that **public transportation (bus)** is inadequate; for information, call MATA (274-6282).

CAR RENTAL (at the airport unless otherwise noted): Avis (345-2847); Budget (767-1000); Dollar, 2031 E. Brooks Rd. (345-3890); Hertz (345-5680); National (345-0070); Thrifty, 2230 E. Brooks Rd. (345-0170). Consult the local telephone directory for downtown rental locations.

LIMOUSINE SERVICES: Dav-El Limousines (toll free 800/922-0343), Memphis Executive Limousine Service (396-7733).

TAXIS: Taxis may not be hailed in the street but can be summoned by telephone; try **United Cab** (525-0521) or **Yellow Cab** (577-7777).

TRAIN: Amtrak Station, 545 S. Main St. (526-0052; toll free 800/872-7245). Unsafe area at night.

INTERCITY BUSES: Greyhound, 203 Union Ave. (523-9253). Unsafe area at night.

MISSISSIPPI CRUISES: 3- to 10-day cruises are available on the *Delta Queen* or the *Mississippi Queen,* paddlewheelers dating from the 1920s. Luxurious kitsch. See Chapter 15 on New Orleans.

INFORMATION & TOURS

TOURIST INFORMATION: The **Memphis Convention and Visitors Bureau,** 50 N. Front St., Suite 450, TN 38103 (901/576-8181).
Visitor Information Center, 207 Beale St., TN 38103 (901/526-4880).

GUIDED TOURS: Carriage Tours of Memphis, 422 S. Main St. (527-7542): Offers horse-drawn carriage tours of Old Memphis; daily year round; weather permitting.

CENTRAL MEMPHIS

Mississippi River

Mud Island

N

Monorail and Walkway to Mud Island

Wolf River

Memphis Queen Dock

RIVERSIDE DR.

Jefferson Davis Park

Confederate Park

PROMENADE ST.

FRONT ST.

CENTER LANE

MAIN ST.

Mid-America Mall

2ND ST.

3RD ST.

Court Square

City Hall

Convention Center

NOVEMBER 6 ST.

Brinkley Park

MARKET AVE.

Civic Center

POPLAR AVE.

Magevney House

JEFFERSON AVE.

COURT AVE.

MADISON AVE.

4TH ST.

MONROE AVE.

ADAMS AVE.

LAUDERDALE ST.

WINCHESTER AVE.

DANNY THOMAS BLVD.

ALABAMA AVE.

HIGH ST.

EXCHANGE AVE.

Mallory-Neely House

To Overton Park & Brooks Art Museum

Morris Park

Fontaine House

VICTORIAN VILLAGE

ORLEANS ST.

To Pink Palace Museum

Forrest Park

MOSBY AVE.

ROBESON AVE.

LANE AVE.

Winchester North Park

MANASSAS ST.

Bus Terminal

GAYOSO AVE.

Peabody Hotel

W.C. Handy Park

Cotton Exchange

MCCALL AVE.

BEALE ST.

Orpheum Theatre

To Graceland

Gray Line Tours (bus), 2050 Elvis Presley Blvd. (942-4662): Guided bus tours of the city; serves the principal hotels.

Mata-Showboat (bus): 70-min. shuttle tour through the city's 20 major attractions aboard a replica of an old Mississippi River showboat. Pass ($2) gives riders unlimited boarding rights. The showboat runs 7 days a week year round. Call 274-6282 for schedule information.

Memphis Queen Line (boat), Monroe Ave. at Riverside Dr. (527-5694): Offers boat tours on board the *Memphis Queen*, daily Mar–Dec.

SIGHTS, ATTRACTIONS & ACTIVITIES

ARCHITECTURAL HIGHLIGHTS: ⚱ **Civic Center,** Front St. and 3rd St. between Exchange Ave. and Adams Ave.: A costly (over $60-million) modern architectural complex containing most of the city and Shelby County office buildings (Federal Building, City Hall). There's also the Vincent de Frank Music Hall, home of the Memphis Symphony Orchestra, and the immense Cook Convention Center used year round as a convention and exposition site. Worth a look.

⚱ **Cotton Exchange Building,** Front St. and Union Ave. (525-3361): Skyscraper home of the nation's—and the world's—most important cotton exchange. Nearly half the U.S. cotton crop is traded here. Visits arranged by appointment only, Mon–Fri.

HISTORIC BUILDINGS: ⚱ **Court Square,** Court St. between 2nd St. and Mid America Mall: Heart of Memphis's urban life for more than a century, this pretty little square with its refreshing oases of green is surrounded by some of the oldest and most interesting buildings in the city; the **Porter Building,** the **Tennessee Club Building,** and the **Lincoln American Tower** are especially noteworthy. Definitely not to be overlooked.

☀⚱ **Graceland,** 3717 Elvis Presley Blvd. (332-3322): For 20 years the home of Elvis Presley until his death on August 16, 1977, at the age of 42. The "King's" mansion features a lovely columned portico. The graves of Elvis and his parents are in the nearby garden of meditation. Every year 650,000 tourists visit the museum, where an almost infinite number of Presley souvenirs are on display. Tours of Presley's automobile collection, his personal touring bus, and the *Lisa Marie*, his private Convair jet are also available. The whole is a triumph of artistic kitsch (note especially the cast-iron entrance gate). Open daily Mar–Oct. and every day but Tues during the rest of the year. This is a must-see, whether or not you are an Elvis fan.

⚱ **Lorraine Motel,** 406 Mulberry St. (521-1560): Site of the assassination of Dr. Martin Luther King, Jr., on April 4, 1968, the motel is now a memorial to the former civil rights leader and winner of the Nobel Peace Prize. Undergoing renovation. Will become America's first National Civil Rights Center, with exhibits, audiovisual and sound-and-light displays. Scheduled for completion in 1991.

☀⚱ **Orpheum Theater,** 89 Beale St. (525-3000): A former movie house and vaudeville theater built in 1928. Superb rococo decor, wonderfully restored, complete with large crystal chandeliers and a mighty Wurlitzer. These days, the theater hosts musical comedies and various other theatrical events.

⚱ **Sun Recording Studio,** 706 Union Ave. (521-0664): Back in the 1950s singer Elvis Presley cut his first record in this studio. Johnny Cash, Jerry Lee Lewis, Roy Orbison, and other famous pop stars also recorded here. The studio is now owned by Elvis Presley Enterprises. Of interest to rock fans. Open daily year round. Recordings are made every evening from 6pm until midnight.

Victorian Village (see "Strolls," below).

⚱ **W. C. Handy's Home,** 352 Beale St. (527-2583): The home where W. C. Handy, "Father of the Blues," wrote his most famous music. Located on historic Beale St. Collection of Handy memorabilia on display. Worth a visit. Open daily.

INDUSTRIAL TOURS: Coors Brewing Co., 5151 E. Raines Rd. (797-2200): Tour of the Brewery and free beer-tasting. Pleasant Visitors Center shaped like an old Mississippi paddlewheeler. Open Mon–Fri year round.

Federal Express, Memphis Airport (395-3460): Each weeknight visitors can watch "the sort." More than a million packages, disgorged from the planes landing each minute, are tracked, stacked, and routed from the company's tower. Tours of the facility start at 11:15pm and 12:30am Mon–Fri nights. Resv. necessary at least a week ahead. Spectacular.

Stroh Brewing Co., 5151 E. Raines Rd. (797-2200): Tour of the brewery and free beer-tasting. Open Mon–Fri year round. Pleasant Visitors Center shaped like an old Mississippi paddlewheeler.

MONUMENTS: ⚓ **Memphis Belle,** Mud Island, access by monorail from Front St. (576-7230): On display is a World War II B-17 bomber, the first to finish 25 missions in the European theater before returning to the States. Was immortalized in David Putnam's movie, *Memphis Belle.*

MUSEUMS OF ART: ⚓ **Dixon Gallery and Gardens,** 4339 Park Ave. (761-5250): Formerly an elegant upper-class home, now a museum housing the works of French and American impressionist painters, English portraits, and historic furniture and porcelain. Surrounded by 7 acres (2.8ha) of very lovely landscaped gardens featuring outdoor sculpture and generous plantings of azaleas and camellias. Open Tues–Sun.

☼⚓ **Memphis Brooks Museum of Art,** Overton Park at Poplar Ave. (722-3500): Known especially for its prestigious Samuel H. Kress Collection of valuable Italian Renaissance paintings, this lovely museum also has interesting contemporary American art, and European painting and sculpture from the 17th through the 19th century. Free Sun concerts; also films on the history of art. Don't miss it. Open Tues–Sun.

☼⚓ **National Ornamental Metal Museum,** 347 W. California Ave. (774-6380): A museum of decorative arts devoted entirely to the use of metal in art and architecture. The only museum of its kind in the United States. Demonstrations of iron-working at the forge. Worth a look. Open Tues–Sun.

⚓ **University Gallery,** Norriswood Ave. (678-2224): Interesting collections of African and Egyptian art. Located on the campus of Memphis State University. Open Tues–Sun.

MUSEUMS OF SCIENCE & HISTORY: ⚓ **Memphis Pink Palace Museum,** 3050 Central Ave. (454-5600): A venerable museum of local history and natural history in a beautiful building made of pink marble from Georgia (hence its name). Displays of zoological and geological interest; history of the Civil War; collection of African hunting trophies. Also a planetarium. Worth seeing. Open Tues–Sun.

☼⚓ **Mississippi River Museum,** Mud Island (576-7230): Features an astonishing giant model of the Mississippi River which reproduces, exactly to scale, the final 1,000 miles (1,600km) of the river's course to the Gulf of Mexico. This is a spectacular display, not to be missed. Open daily Apr–Nov.

NIGHTTIME ENTERTAINMENT: ☼⚓ **Beale Street,** between Riverside Dr. and Hernando St.: The city's principal thoroughfare (Main St.) in the early

1800s became known, a century later, as the "cradle of the Blues." Today, Beale Street is the heart of the old town's pleasure district and its ebullient nightlife. Teems with bars, restaurants, nightclubs, movie houses, and theaters. A visit to the street is imperative (see "Strolls," below).

    Overton Square, Madison Ave. and Cooper St.: The only place in Memphis that can challenge Beale Street in terms of swinging nightlife. Restaurants, bars, shows. (See "Strolls," below.)

PARKS & GARDENS: Dixon Gallery Gardens (see "Museums of Art," above).

    Jefferson Davis Park, Riverside Blvd. at Jefferson Ave.: A pleasant little city park offering a lovely view of the Mississippi and the **Mud Island** amusement park. Faces **Confederate Park,** one of the battlefields of the Civil War. There are fortifications dating from the war, and also a statue of Jefferson Davis, president of the Confederacy, who lived in Memphis after the war.

    Memphis Botanic Garden, 750 Cherry Rd., Audubon Park (685-1566): This 87-acre (35ha) landscape contains 12 different kinds of gardens, from a rose garden to tropical plants and a Japanese garden. Spectacular. Open daily.

PERFORMING ARTS: For current listings of shows and cultural events, consult the entertainment pages of the daily papers, *Memphis Commercial Appeal* (morning) and the monthly *Memphis.*

    Circuit Playhouse, 1705 Poplar Ave. (726-5521): Contemporary theater, comedies, and musicals. Sept–June.

    Dixon Meyers Hall, Cook Convention Center, 255 N. Main St. (523-7645): Big live concerts.

    Gaslight Dinner Theater, 1110 Brooks Rd. E. (396-7474): Broadway shows. Dinner theater.

    Mid-South Coliseum, Fairgrounds at E. Parkway South and Southern Ave. (274-7400): Live rock and country music concerts.

    Memphis Opera, Memphis State University Campus (678-3021): Home of the city's opera company, directed by Robert Driver. Oct–Feb.

    Orpheum Theater, 89 Beale St. (525-3000): Comedies, plays, musicals, opera, ballet. A very lovely art deco vaudeville palace built in 1928, elegantly restored. Open all year.

    Playhouse-on-the-Square, 51 S. Cooper St., at Overton Sq. (726-4656): The only professional repertory theater in the city. Broadway hits, contemporary theater. Year round.

    Memphis Theater, 630 Perkins Rd. Ext. (682-8323): Contemporary and classical theater. Sept–June.

    Vincent de Frank Music Hall, Cook Convention Center, 255 Main St. (454-2043): Home of the Memphis Symphony Orchestra, under principal conductor Alan Balter. Sept–May.

SPECIAL EVENTS: For exact dates, consult the **Memphis Visitor Information Center** (see "Tourist Information," above).

    Memphis in May International Festival (May to early June): A month-long celebration honors the culture, art, and music of a different country each year. Also world championship barbecue cooking contest.

    Great River Carnival (June): Parades, dances, concerts, regattas. Very colorful.

    Elvis Presley International Tribute Week (Aug): A week-long celebration of the myth and music of Elvis Presley.

    Memphis Music Festival (Sept): Jazz, blues, rock, and country music is performed in legendary Beale Street's many bars and restaurants.

Mid-South Fair (late Sept to early Oct): Renowned agricultural and commercial fair. Features the largest rodeo east of the Mississippi.

Liberty Bowl Football Classic (Dec): One of the big events of the college football season.

SPORTS: Memphis has a minor-league team in—**Baseball** (Apr–Oct): Chicks, Tim McCarver Stadium (272-1687).

STROLLS: ☼⚓ **Beale Street,** between Riverside Dr. and Hernando St.: The "cradle of the Blues." Made world-famous by W. C. Handy, composer of "Memphis Blues" and "St. Louis Blues," who lived on Beale St. in the early 20th century. At Beale St. and 3rd St. you'll find **W. C. Handy Park** and the monument memorializing the composer. A monument to the late "King" of Rock is located nearby in **Elvis Presley Plaza.** This colorful section of the city bustles with activity generated by its old honky-tonks, bars, and pawnshops turned into new nightspots, restaurants, boutiques, and theaters. Must not be missed. (See also "Nighttime Entertainment," above.)

⚓ **Mid America Mall,** between the Civic Center and Beale St.: Flanked by stores and skyscrapers, this street in the heart of the business district is reserved for pedestrian traffic. There are gardens and examples of modern sculpture. Very lively by day, often deserted at night. Worth a look.

☼⚓ **Overton Square,** Madison Ave. and Cooper St.: Charming section of the old town, cleverly restored. You'll find old-time stores, outdoor cafés, restaurants. One of the bastions of Memphis nightlife. Absolutely deserves a visit. (See also "Nighttime Entertainment," above.)

☼⚓⚓ **Victorian Village,** in the vicinity of 600 Adams Ave.: Delicious 19th-century architectural relic from the days when cotton was still "white gold," and Memphis its capital. The Village contains 20 or so remarkable old buildings, most now classified as historic monuments. Among the more noteworthy are the **Woodruf-Fontaine House,** 680 Adams Ave. (526-1469), open daily, a perfect example of the Second Empire style dating from 1870; **Magevney House,** 198 Adams Ave. (526-4464), open Tues–Sat, the oldest building in Memphis, built in 1831 for Irish immigrant Eugene Magevney as recompense for his services as the city's first schoolteacher; and the **Mallory-Neely House,** 652 Adams Ave. (523-1484), open daily, an elegant Victorian residence in the Italian style, dating from 1852. All these buildings have been painstakingly restored with period furniture and decor. A visit to the Victorian Village is a must for those who enjoy beautiful architecture.

THEME PARKS: ⚓ **Adventure River Water Park,** I-40 NW and Whitten Rd. (382-9283): Huge 25-acre (10ha) park featuring aquatic attractions such as an oversize pool with waves for surf-lovers, giant slides, and swimming pools for children. Open every day from June to the end of Aug, wknds only in May and Sept; closed the rest of the year.

⚓ **Libertyland,** Fairgrounds at Central Ave. and East Pkwy. (274-1776): This unusual amusement park salutes our nation's past from the colonial period to the 1900s. Open daily mid-June to mid-Aug, wknds only Apr to mid-June and mid-Aug to late Sept; closed the rest of the year.

☼⚓⚓ **Mud Island,** 125 N. Front St. (576-7241): On this island in the middle of the Mississippi are 50 acres (21ha) of gardens, exhibitions, and an immense museum devoted to "Ol' Man River." (See the **Mississippi River Museum** in "Museums of Science and History," above.) Accessible by monorail from Front St. With its numerous restaurants, bars, shops, shows, and exhibitions, the island is a lively place, especially in the evening. Open daily Apr–Thanksgiving; hours vary.

ZOOS: ⚄ **Memphis Zoo and Aquarium,** 2000 Galloway, in Overton Park (726-4775): Features more than 2,000 animals from 400 species. Giant aquarium. Outstanding tropical bird house, spectacular reptile facilities, and natural African settings for larger beasts. Open daily year round.

ACCOMMODATIONS

A Note on Accommodations: Room rates in Memphis are coded as follows: **VE,** Very Expensive ($140 and up); **E,** Expensive ($90–$140); **M,** Moderate ($60–$90); **I,** Inexpensive ($30–$60); **B,** Budget (up to $30). A listing of toll free numbers is in the Appendix.

Personal Favorites (in order of preference)

☼♟♟♟♟ **The Peabody** (dwntwn), 149 Union Ave., TN 38103 (901/529-4000; toll free, see Preferred). 452 rms, A/C, color TV, in-rm movies. AE, CB, DC, MC, V. Valet parking $8, pool, sauna, health club, three rests. (including Chez Philippe), three bars, 24-hr. rm svce, disco, hrdrsr, shops, concierge, free crib. *Note:* Fabulous luxury hotel dating from 1869, rebuilt in 1925 and recently restored to its former splendor. Elegant and comfortable. Resplendent entrance hall in Renaissance style w. colonnades and a marble fountain where ducks (symbol of the Peabody) swim and preen themselves. Exemplary svce. One of the best in the Deep South. A designated historic monument. **E–VE**

♟♟♟ **Radisson** (dwntwn), 185 Union Ave., TN 38103 (901/528-1800; toll free, see Radisson). 283 rms, A/C, color TV, in-rm movies. AE, CB, DC, MC, V. Parking $4, pool, sauna, bar, rest. (The Veranda), rm svce, disco, crib $10, free breakfast. *Note:* Architecturally, a very pleasing blend of an ultramodern 11-story building w. a lovely old facade of the original historic building. Spectacular six-story lobby w. waterfalls and a winter garden. Comfortable, spacious rms; attentive svce. Good rest. offering Créole cuisine. Big business clientele because of the proximity of the financial district. Free airport transportation. An excellent place to stay. **M–E**

♟♟ **Ramada Inn Convention Center** (nr. dwntwn), 160 Union Ave., TN 38103 (901/525-5491; toll free, see Ramada). 180 rms, A/C, color TV, in-rm movies. AE, CB, DC, MC, V. Free parking, pool, rest. (Seasons), bar, rm svce, free crib. *Note:* Located in the heart of Memphis, this large modern motel is quite comfortable but without any distinctive appeal. Most of the guests are businesspeople, for whom a special VIP floor is reserved. Spacious rms. **M–E**

♟♟ **Holiday Inn Overton Square** (nr. dwntwn), 1837 Union Ave., TN 38104 (901/278-4100; toll free, see Holiday Inns). 143 rms, A/C, color TV, in-rm movies. AE, CB, DC, MC, V. Free parking, pool, rest. (Bluff City Diner), bar, room svce, free crib. *Note:* Modern eight-story motel nr. Overton Sq. and its nightlife. Functional comfort in typical Holiday Inn style. Good value. **I–M**

♟ **Best Western Riverbluff Inn** (nr. dwntwn), 340 W. Illinois Ave., TN 38106 (901/948-9005; toll free, see Best Western). 99 rms, A/C, color TV, in-rm movies. AE, CB, DC, MC, V. Free parking, pool, rest. (Riverview), bar, valet svce, free crib. *Note:* Pleasant little motel a minute away from the banks of the Mississippi. The rms are spacious and comfortable; some have refrigerators. Friendly reception and svce. Good value. Lovely view of the Memphis skyline. **I–M**

♟ **Hampton Inn–Medical Center** (nr. dwntwn), 1180 Union Ave., TN 38104 (901/276-1175; toll free 800/426-7866). 126 rms, A/C, color TV, in-rm movies. AE, DC, MC, V. Free parking, pool, café nearby, free Continental breakfast, free crib. *Note:* Well-run, comfortable motel 5 min. from dwntwn. Inviting, functional rms, congenial svce. Good overall value. **I**

Other Hotels (from top bracket to budget)

French Quarter Inn (nr. dwntwn), 2144 Madison Ave., TN 38103 (901/728-4000; toll free 800/843-0353). 106 suites, A/C, color TV, in-rm movies. AE, CB, DC, MC, V. Free parking, health club, rest. (Café Toulouse), bar, 24-hr. rm svce. *Note:* Small luxury hotel w. suites only, spacious and comfortable, w. minibars; some have private balconies. The rest. offers very acceptable Créole cooking. Personalized svce. Close by is Overton Sq. w. its shops and nightlife. Free airport transportation. Favored by those in-the-know. **E**

Holiday Inn Crowne Plaza (dwntwn), 250 N. Main St., TN 38104 (901/527-7300; toll free, see Holiday Inns). 406 rms, A/C, color TV, in-rm movies. AE, CB, DC, MC, V. Valet parking $5, pool, sauna, health club, two rests. (including Chervil's), coffee shop, two bars, rm svce, nightclub, shops, free crib. *Note:* The flagship hotel of the Memphis-based Holiday Inn Corporation. Centrally located 18-story tower w. a view of the Mississippi. Beautiful contemporary design. Nothing is wanting in comfort and facilities. Spacious rms w. balconies; most have refrigerators as well. Efficient svce; good rest. Caters to businesspeople and groups; VIP floor. Direct access to Convention Center. Free airport transportation. **E**

Omni Memphis (formerly the Hyatt Regency; vic.), 939 Ridge Lake Blvd., TN 38119 (901/684-6664; toll free, see Omni). 380 rms, A/C, color TV, in-rm movies. AE, CB, DC, MC, V. Free parking, pool, rest. (Sawyers), bar, rm svce, nightclub, free crib. *Note:* A 28-story circular tower made of glass and designed by architect John Portman; locals call it "the glass silo." The decor is futuristic and rather chilly. Comfort and facilities are impeccable. Inviting rms w. minibars. Good svce, so-so rest. Caters to businesspeople and groups. 20 min. from dwntwn, 10 min. from the airport (free shuttle). **E**

Brownstone Hotel (dwntwn), 300 N. 2nd St., TN 38105 (901/525-2511). 243 rms, A/C, color TV, in-rm movies. AE, CB, DC, MC, V. Free parking, pool, rest., bar, rm svce, free crib. *Note:* Another favorite of business travelers, a few steps from the Convention Center. Comfortable and functional; recently renovated. Reception and svce no more than adequate. VIP floor. **M–E**

Days Inn Downtown (formerly the Benchmark; dwntwn), 164 Union Ave., TN 38103 (901/527-4100; toll free, see Days Inns). 106 rms, A/C, color TV, in-rm movies. AE, MC, V. Free parking, rest. (Rivers), bar, rm svce, free crib. *Note:* Friendly, relatively modern hotel in the heart of the dwntwn area across from the Peabody Hotel. Spacious rms, cheerful svce. Newly renovated. An excellent value. **I–M**

Coach House (nr. dwntwn), 1262 Union Ave., TN 38104 (901/725-1900; toll free 800/962-5005). 178 rms, A/C, color TV, in-rm movies. AE, DC, MC, V. Free parking, pool, rest., bar, free crib. *Note:* Well-run, congenial motel, recently renovated. Functionally comfortable rms, friendly reception and svce. Very good value; 6 min. from dwntwn. **I**

La Quinta Medical Center (nr. dwntwn), 42 S. Camilla St., TN 38104 (901/526-1050; toll free, see La Quinta). 130 rms, A/C, color TV, in-rm movies. AE, CB, DC, MC, V. Free parking, pool, adj. 24-hr. coffee shop, valet svce, free crib. *Note:* This is the classic modern motel, comfortable and functional. Spacious rms, efficient svce. Ideal for those traveling by car. 8 min. from dwntwn. **I**

Airport Accommodations

Sheraton Airport Inn (vic.), 2411 Winchester Rd., TN 38105 (901/332-2730; toll free, see Sheraton). 212 rms, A/C, color TV, in-rm movies. AE, CB, DC, MC, V. Free parking, pool, two tennis courts, rest., bar, rm svce, nightclub, free breakfast, free crib. *Note:* Conventional airport motel 2 min. (by 24-hr. free shuttle) from the terminal. Comfortable, well-soundproofed rms, efficient svce. Business clientele. Interesting wknd packages. 8 min. by car from Graceland. **M**

RESTAURANTS

A Note on Restaurant Prices: Memphis restaurant prices, per person, excluding drinks and service charges, are coded as follows: **VE,** Very Expensive ($60 and up); **E,** Expensive ($40–$60); **M,** Moderate ($25–$40); **I,** Inexpensive ($15–$25); **B,** Budget (up to $15).

Personal Favorites (in order of preference)

♟♟♟ **Chez Philippe** (dwntwn), in the Peabody Hotel (see "Accommodations," above) (529-4188). A/C. Dinner only, Mon–Sat. AE, CB, DC, MC, V. Jkt. *Specialties:* warm salad of lobster prepared w. truffle butter, lamb tenderloin w. garlic cake, crab mousse w. mustard sauce, Dover sole, medaillons of venison w. Pommard. Excellent wine list. *Note:* Dubbed "nouvelle Delta" cuisine, the cooking of Chez Philippe's young chef José Gutierrez is a miracle of creativity and balance. The rest.'s luxurious decor w. its painted trompe-l'oeil murals, crystal chandeliers, and sumptuous tableware is a feast for the eye. Svce is highly polished, and the total effect is close to perfection. This is the most prestigious rest. in Memphis, as your check will demonstrate. Resv. a must. Free valet parking. *French.* **E**

☼♟♟ **Rendezvous** (dwntwn), 52 S. 2nd St. (General Washburn Alley) (523-2746). A/C. Dinner only, Tues–Sat (until midnight); closed also 2 weeks in late July and 2 weeks in late Dec. AE, CB, DC, MC, V. *Specialties:* fantastic barbecued pork ribs. Beer but no wine. *Note:* Picturesque basement rest. which puts you in mind of a country general store; "decorated" with a profusion of posters, furnishings, and souvenirs of the Old South. The atmosphere is relaxed and the svce diligent. An excellent bet, right in the heart of Memphis. A local institution since 1948, thanks to the Vergos family. *American.* **I**

♟♟ **Folk's Folly** (vic.), 551 S. Mendenhall Rd. (767-8200). A/C. Dinner only, nightly; closed hols. AE, CB, DC, MC, V. Jkt. *Specialties:* broiled prime beef, Créole-style vegetables. *Note:* The biggest and the best steaks in Memphis. Pleasant decor and atmosphere. Very popular w. locals. Resv. advised. 25 min. by car from dwntwn. *Steak.* **I–M**

☼♟ **Leonard's** (nr. dwntwn), 1140 S. Bellevue Blvd. (948-1581) A/C. Lunch only, Mon–Sat (until 5pm); closed hols. MC, V. *Specialties:* barbecued pork ribs and shoulders, lemon ice-box pie. *Note:* A Memphis tradition since 1932. Every day hordes of hungry patrons gather to devour mountains of superb barbecued pork ribs. The decor is rustic and unpretentious. No resv. An experience not to be missed. Three other locations in Memphis (open for lunch and dinner): consult the city telephone directory. *American.* **B–I**

☼♟ **John Will's Barbecue Pit** (nr. dwntwn), 2450 Central Ave. (274-8000). A/C. Lunch/dinner daily. AE, MC, V. *Specialties:* beef and pork ribs, pork shoulder, beef brisket and sausage barbecued, pork and beef sandwich plates, apple cobbler. *Note:* Significantly named by the readership of *Memphis* magazine the best of the city's 100 or so barbecue rests., Will's has been consistently packed since it opened in 1983, and on Sat evening the wait can be tedious. Modern setting w. natural-wood paneling, inevitably adorned w. photographs of prize hogs and cattle. A fine place with attractive prices. No resv. *American.* **B–I**

Other Restaurants (from top bracket to budget)

♟♟♟ **Justine's** (nr. dwntwn), 919 Coward Pl. (527-9973). A/C. Dinner only, Mon–Sat (until midnight); closed hols. AE, CB, DC, MC, V. J&T. *Specialties:* vichyssoise, crabmeat Justine, pompano Claudet, tournedos béarnaise, trout Marguéry, rum-cream pie. *Note:* Superb classic French cuisine, elegant antebellum decor (the building dates from 1843), surrounded by beautiful grdns. Patrons can dine outdoors in good weather. One of the best rests. in the Deep South. Irreproachable svce. Resv. are indispensable. Valet parking. *French.* **M–E**

🍷🍷🍷 **Hemmings** (vic.), 7615 W. Farmington Blvd. (757-8323). A/C. Lunch/dinner daily (until midnight). AE, CB, DC, MC, V. Jkt. *Specialties:* steamed mussels in tomato-cilantro cream, roast quail on grilled corn relish w. black-bean sauce, grilled yellowfin tuna w. tomatoes and lime butter, crabcake w. salmon caviar and chardonnay butter, chocolate ravioli, Jack Daniel's pecan pie w. crème fraîche. Good wine list. *Note:* Brainchild of Paul Westphal, formerly manager of the well-known Peabody Hotel, this newcomer on the Memphis gastronomic scene is the only possible challenger to Chez Philippe (see above) for the title of the city's finest rest. Airy, imaginative California-style dishes are served in an elegant setting w. huge picture windows and high ceilings. Flawless svce; resv. a must. 25 min. from dwntwn in the residential neighborhood of Germantown. *American.* **M**

🍷🍷 **Dux** (dwntwn), in the Peabody Hotel (see "Accommodations," above) (529-4199). A/C. Breakfast/lunch/dinner daily. AE, CB, DC, MC, V. Jkt. *Specialties:* smoked catfish w. coriander, mussel-and-clam stew, filet of pork in mustard, scallops of veal sautéed in cream, catch of the day, and prime beef broiled over a mesquite-wood fire. Delicious desserts. The menu changes frequently. *Note:* A rest. of palatial elegance and cooking of the first order. Lovely rococo decor, exemplary svce. Very "in" for business lunches. Dux's success makes resv. advisable. *Ameican/Seafood.* **I–M**

🍷🍷 **Jim's Place East** (vic.), 5560 Shelby Oaks Dr. (388-7200). A/C. Lunch Mon–Fri, dinner Mon–Sat; closed hols. AE, MC, V. Jkt. *Specialties:* steak or catch of the day broiled over a wood fire, along w. some good Greek dishes. *Note:* A Memphis standby serving southern food w. a faint Greek accent. Comfortable, inviting country-club atmosphere, friendly svce; locally very popular, so make resv. 25 min. from dwntwn via I-40 (take the Sycamore View Rd. exit). *American/Greek.* **I–M**

🍷🍷 **King Cotton Café** (dwntwn), 50 N. Front St. (576-8150). A/C. Lunch Mon–Fri, dinner Mon and Thurs–Sat; closed hols. AE, DC, MC, V. *Specialties:* lamb chops, steak, broiled catch of the day, Créole dishes. Good homemade desserts. *Note:* On the mezzanine of the Morgan Keegan Tower in the heart of the cotton-trading district (whence its name), this charming bistro serves tasty and often imaginative "Delta" food. An agreeable atmosphere, w. pleasant background music at dinner. Courteous svce. Resv. advised; free parking at dinner. *American.* **I–M**

🍷🍷 **Grisanti's** (vic.), 1489 Airways Blvd. (458-2648). A/C. Lunch Mon–Fri, dinner Mon–Sat; closed hols. AE, CB, DC, MC, V. Jkt. *Specialties:* fresh homemade pasta, cannelloni alla Gusi, veal cutlets milanese, steaks. Good wine list. *Note:* A Memphis favorite since 1909. The best local Italian rest. Resv. advised. Big John Grisanti, the owner, is a legendary local institution. Casual atmosphere. Valet parking. *Italian.* **I**

🍷 **Captain Bilbo's** (dwntwn), 263 Wagner Pl. (526-1966). A/C. Dinner only, nightly. AE, MC, V. *Specialties:* Maine lobsters, fish and oysters from the Gulf of Mexico, shrimp seven ways, gumbo, prime cuts. *Note:* Pleasant seafood rest. located in an old warehouse overlooking the Mississippi. Appropriate nautical decor. Relaxed atmosphere. Friendly bar w. live music every evening. Valet parking. *Seafood.* **I**

🍷 **Molly's La Casita** (nr. dwntwn), 2006 Madison Ave. (726-1873). A/C. Lunch/dinner daily. AE, CB, DC, MC, V. *Specialties:* tacos al carbon, burritos, chiles rellenos, enchiladas, tamales verdes. *Note:* One of the best places in town for aficionados of authentic Mexican cuisine. Pleasant atmosphere, typical but pretty decor. Very popular locally. Other location: 4972 Park Ave. (685-1616). *Mexican.* **B–I**

☼♀ **Buntyn** (nr. dwntwn), 3070 Southern Ave. (458-8776). A/C. Lunch/dinner Mon–Fri. (until 8pm). No credit cards. *Specialties:* fried chicken, meatloaf, fried catfish, Waldorf salad, special house-style vegetables, banana pudding, cobblers. *Note:* In spite of its unappealing neon and Formica decor, this immensely popular rest. has continued to attract faithful followers for over 40 years. Its southern-style fried chicken and platters of house-style vegetables are themselves worth a visit. No resv. accepted. *American.* **B**

Cafeterias/Specialty Spots
Little Tea Shop (dwntwn), 69 Monroe Ave. (525-6000). Lunch only, Mon–Fri. No credit cards. *Specialties:* fried steak, turnip greens w. baked ham, chicken pan pie, pork chop w. broccoli puffs, collard greens, banana cream pie. *Note:* First-rate southern-style home-cooking in a friendly atmosphere. One of Memphis's oldest rests. (since 1918).

BARS & NIGHTCLUBS
Alfred's (dwntwn), 197 Beale St. (525-3711). Popular downtown rock-and-roll spot. Nightly.

Friday's (nr. dwntwn), 2115 Madison Ave. (278-4026). Bar-disco. Nice atmosphere. Open nightly until 1am. Attractive Victorian-kitsch decor. Also very acceptable rest.

Mallards (dwntwn), in the Peabody Hotel (see "Accommodations," above) (529-4140). Very popular bar. Live jazz. Also a laudable rest. Open nightly.

Rum Boogie Café (dwntwn), 182 Beale St. (528-0150). Very popular jazz-rest. club. Open nightly.

Sir-Lafs-A-Lot (nr. dwntwn), 535 S. Highland St. (324-5653). Locally popular comedy club. Shows Wed–Sun. Also rest. Resv. recommended.

NEARBY EXCURSIONS

☼🔔🔔 **CHUCALISSA INDIAN VILLAGE** (1987 Indian Village Rd., 10 mi./16km SW on U.S. 61) (785-3160): Native American village dating from approximately A.D. 900 and mysteriously abandoned six centuries later (Chucalissa means "Abandoned house"). Numerous dwellings have been re-created based on the findings of ongoing archeological excavations; interesting museum of Choctaw arts and crafts. Well worth the trip. Open Tues–Sun.

FARTHER AFIELD

☼🔔 **SHILOH NATIONAL MILITARY PARK** (230 mi./ 368km r.t. via U.S. 64 E. and Tenn. 22S and return): Site of the first major land battle of the Civil War, April 6–7, 1862. Northern troops under Gen. Ulysses S. Grant won out after confused and unusually bloody combat— 24,000 men were reported dead, wounded, or missing. Films are shown at the military museum, and visitors can take a self-guided 10-mi. (16km) automobile tour of the battlefield. The surrounding countryside is lovely; of particular interest are the numerous tumuli from the pre-Columbian era. For history buffs. The Visitor Center is open daily (901/689-5275).

☼🔔🔔 **HOT SPRINGS NATIONAL PARK** (396 mi./634km r.t. on I-40W, I-30W, and U.S. 70W and return): One of the most famous and popular in the United States. Well before Spanish explorer Hernando de Soto "discovered" the springs in 1541, Native Americans recognized their healing powers and revered the place as holy. Proclaimed a federal reservation in 1832 by the U.S. Congress and promoted in 1921 to the status of a national park, the springs and the picturesque charm of their locale annually attract hundreds of thousands of visitors seeking treatment for rheumatic and nervous conditions. Every day about a million gallons (4 million liters) of water gush forth, at a temperature of 143°F (62°C), from the 47 separate hot springs within the park. The surrounding countryside with its lakes and wooded mountains is very lovely. The Visitor Center at Reserve Ave. and Central Ave. is open daily (toll free 800/272-2081). Definitely worth the trip.

Where to Stay Near the Park

Arlington Resort, P.O. Box 5652, Central Ave. at Fountain St., Hot Springs, AR 71901 (501/623-7771; toll free 800/643-1502). 490 rms. A luxury hotel dating from the '20s, pleasingly renovated. **I–M**

Buena Vista, Buena Vista Dr. (Rte. 3, Box 175), Hot Springs, AR 71913 (501/525-1321; toll free 800/255-9030), 4 mi. (6.5km) south on Ark. 7S. 40 rms w. kitchenettes. Very pleasant cottages on the shores of Lake Hamilton. **I–M**

Where to Eat

Hamilton House, 130 Van Lyell Dr. (501/525-2727), 6 mi. (10km) south on Ark. 7S. Dinner only, Mon–Sat. Elegant antique decor, on the shores of Lake Hamilton. *Continental.* **I–M**

NASHVILLE (420 mi./672km r.t. on I-40E and return): The capital of Country Music. Worth a visit. For details, see Chapter 13 on Nashville. Might well be combined with a visit to Shiloh National Military Park (see above).

NEW ORLEANS

□ □ □

And the Mississippi Delta

Birthplace of Louis Armstrong and Sidney Bechet, this most French of U.S. cities was founded in 1718 by Jean Baptiste Le Moyne, sieur de Bienville, governor of Louisiana. Named in honor of Philippe, Duke of Orléans, Regent of France at the time, the city nowadays presents a fascinating fusion of races and cultures.

By turns French, Spanish, then French again, and finally sold to the U.S. in 1803 by Napoléon I under the terms of the Louisiana Purchase, the city has harmoniously blended its "Créole" inheritance from the first French and Spanish settlers with the "Cajun" influence of Acadian refugees from Canada in 1755, and has subsequently added dashes of Italian, Caribbean, German, Irish, and African American. As a result, what was 250 years ago a village of trappers and gold prospectors is now a cosmopolitan city that has retained its liking for the open sea (its port is second in the U.S. only to New York City's) and for good food (New Orleans, New York, and San Francisco are the country's gastronomic capitals), as well as an inimitably attractive life-style. Beloved by European tourists, the "Gateway of the Mississippi" can claim, among its other distinctions, to have invented jazz. (Originally spelled "jass," the word had an indelicate significance in Créole, having to do with sexual intercourse; later it came to denote a kind of African dance.) As for its famous **Mardi Gras,** a festival of 19th-century origin lasting several weeks, its only rival anywhere in the world is the Carnival in Rio. Tourism, with six million visitors a year, is already established as the most important source of revenue, ousting both the oil industry (which has been in deep depression since the early '80s) and port traffic. In 1988 a Rand-McNally poll showed that New Orleans was among the most popular destinations in the country for vacationers.

With its colorful streets, balustraded old houses, flower-filled courtyards, and wrought-iron balconies, the **French Quarter (Vieux Carré,** literally "Old Square") is an architectural unity of a kind rare in North America. The strolling visitor will chance, unexpectedly but delightfully, on Mississippi docks that haven't changed since the days of the showboats; on the friendly crowds of **Jackson Square,** historic heart of the French Quarter, with its painters and street musicians; on 150-year-old bars still haunted by the memory of pirate Jean Lafitte; on the authentic tradition of Dixieland in venerable **Preservation Hall;** on the impressive 1795 **Cabildo,** once the Spanish governor's palace, now a museum; on the slightly motheaten strip joints of Bourbon St., New Orleans's hot strip. To say nothing of those landmarks of local gastronomy, like Antoine's or Galatoire's, where the finest traditions of Créole cooking are still very much alive: oysters Rockefeller (baked and seasoned with Pernod), gumbo (a thick soup of shrimp, shellfish, crabmeat, and rice), jambalaya (an exotic melange of rice, tomatoes, shrimps, oysters, and sausages or chicken), shrimp with sauce remoulade, bananas Foster (in liqueur, with ice cream), or pompano (a basslike fish) en papillote, to name but a few.

Not far from the French Quarter, the delightful **Garden District**, with its old houses and aura of aristocracy, rubs shoulders with the new city created by black gold, with its inescapable high-rises including the prestigious 53-story **Place St. Charles Building** and the colossal **Superdome**, which with its 90,000 seats is the world's largest indoor stadium. This huge 27-story concrete cathedral of football is entirely air-conditioned. Lovers of the picturesque will not feel that it compensates them for the disappearance of the fabled **Storyville**, a district of saloons, gaming houses, and brothels around Basin St., which was demolished in 1917 at the request of the military, who wished to protect soldiers on leave from its temptations; its destruction was a heavy loss for "The Big Easy," as jazz musicians have nicknamed the city.

The lower Mississippi Valley, and its immense delta opening onto the Gulf of Mexico, represents one of New Orleans's principal tourist attractions. Its lush vegetation of live oaks draped in Spanish moss, of creepers and water lilies; its endless network of bayous (creeks); its elegant 19th-century plantations— these make up the "Cajun country," where live 300,000 descendants of the French-speaking Acadians. There are no terms too strong for recommending a visit to this fascinating, little-known region.

Writer Truman Capote and actress Dorothy Lamour were born here; among the great musicians who first saw daylight in "the cradle of jazz" are Red Allen, Barney Bigard, Lee Collins, Fats Domino, Baby and Johnny Dodds, Bunk Johnson, Nick Larocca, Albert Nicholas, Jelly Roll Morton—and of course, Louis Armstrong and Sidney Bechet.

FBI statistics put New Orleans near the top of the list of U.S. cities in terms of crime. It pays to be careful if you're walking alone, after dark, outside the central streets of the French Quarter. Badly lit streets should always be avoided at night, especially in the area of the Bienville Housing Project, north of the French Quarter. Be sure to take taxis where advised to do so.

BASIC FACTS: State of Louisiana. Area code: 504. Time zone: central. ZIP Code: 70140. Founded in: 1718. Approximate population: city 540,000; metropolitan area, 1,340,000. Rank among U.S. metropolitan areas: 29th.

CLIMATE: From its proximity to the Gulf of Mexico, New Orleans derives a subtropical climate. The best time for a visit is between Oct and Mar, since the winters are unusually mild (Jan average, 53°F/12°C), as is the autumn, with temperatures usually above 68°F (20°C) in Oct. Summer is disagreeably hot and sticky (July average, 82°F/28°C). Between Mar and Sept don't forget your raincoat and umbrella; it rains copiously and almost daily. The average annual rainfall of 60.88 in. (1,522mm) is one of the highest in the country.

DISTANCES: Atlanta, 481 mi. (770km); Dallas, 493 mi. (790km); Houston, 356 mi. (570km); Memphis, 390 mi. (625km); Tampa, 633 mi. (1,012km).

ARRIVAL & TRANSIT INFORMATION

AIRPORT: New Orleans International Airport (MSY), 12 mi. (19km) NW. Information: 464-0831.

AIRLINES: American (523-2188), Continental (581-2965), Delta (529-2431), Northwest (525-0423), Southwest (523-5683), TWA (529-2585), United (toll free 800/241-6522), and USAir (toll free 800/428-4322).

CITY LINK: The **cab** fare to city center is about $20; time, about 25–30 min. Bus: **Airport/Rhodes Transportation** (469-4555), leaves every 30 min., serving principal downtown hotels; fare, $8; time, 45 min.

The public transportation system by bus and streetcar is efficient and cheap; particularly useful are the **Central Business District Shuttle** and the **Vieux Carré Shuttle,** which operate only on working days. For information, call the Regional Transit Authority (569-2700).

If your visit is to be confined to the French Quarter and the Central Business District, you won't need to rent a car; on the other hand, if you follow my emphatic advice and travel to the "bayou" and plantation country, to Lake Pontchartrain, or to the shores of the Gulf of Mexico, you will.

CAR RENTAL (at the airport unless otherwise noted): Avis (464-9511); Budget (464-0311); Dollar (468-3643); Hertz (468-3695); National (466-4335); Thrifty, 1415 Airline Hwy., in Kenner (467-8796). For dwntwn locations, consult the local telephone directory.

LIMOUSINE SERVICES: Cappel Limo Service (288-4696), Carey Limousines (523-5466), Dav El Limousines (toll free 800/922-0343).

TAXIS: Taxis may be hailed on the street, taken from the waiting lines in front of the major hotels, or summoned by telephone. Cabs are numerous and their fares are relatively low within the city limits. Recommended companies: **Checker-Yellow Cabs** (525-3311), **Liberty Bell Cabs** (822-5974), and **United Cabs** (522-9771).

TRAIN: Amtrak, Union Station, 1001 Loyola Ave. (528-1610; toll free 800/872-7245).

INTERCITY BUSES: Greyhound, 1001 Loyola Ave. (525-9371).

MISSISSIPPI CRUISES: 3- to 10-day cruises on the Mississippi River, Ohio River, and Cumberland River aboard the *Delta Queen* or the *Mississippi Queen,* paddle-steamers built in the 1920s. Luxurious kitsch. For information, contact the **Delta Queen Steamboat Co.,** 30 Robin St. Wharf, New Orleans, LA 70130 (504/586-0631; toll free 800/543-1949).

INFORMATION & TOURS

TOURIST INFORMATION: The **Greater New Orleans Tourist and Convention Commission,** 1520 Sugar Bowl Dr., LA 70112 (504/566-5011). For events information, call 504/566-5047.

Jean Lafitte National Historical Park Visitor Center, French Market, 916 N. Peters St. (504/589-2636): Organizes a series of different daily walking tours of the French Quarter. Art exhibitions, concerts, audiovisual shows, etc.

Welcome Visitor Center, 529 St. Ann St. (504/568-5661): Also information on Louisiana and the Cajun country.

GUIDED TOURS: The **Canal Street Ferry** (boat), at the foot of Canal St.: Free Mississippi crossing; fine view of river and city. Last ferry leaves from the Canal St. terminal at 10:45pm.

Cajun Queen Cruises (boat), Poydras St. Wharf at Riverwalk (504/529-

4567 or 524-0814): 4½-hr. trips through the Louisiana bayous which Jean La-
fitte and his fabled buccaneers used as hideouts for themselves and their plunder.
 Cotton Blossom Zoo Cruise (boat), Canal St. Dock (504/586-8777): A
1-hr. trip along the Mississippi from the Canal St. Dock to the Audubon Park and
Zoological Garden. Three round-trips daily throughout the year.
 Créole Queen Cruises (boat), Poydras St. Wharf (529-4567): Trips along
the Mississippi to the battlefield of Chalmette; nightly jazz dinners aboard the
Créole Queen, newest of the Mississippi paddlewheelers. Daily.
 Gay '90s Carriages (carriage), 1824 N. Rampart St. (943-8820): Carriage
tour of the French Quarter leaving from Jackson St. Picturesque. Daily year
round, weather permitting.
 Gray Line Tours (bus), Jackson Brewery at Toulouse St. (587-0861):
Guided tours of city and surroundings; serves principal dwntwn hotels.
 New Orleans Steamboat Co. (boat), Toulouse St. Wharf at Jackson Sq.
(586-8777): Mississippi and bayou trips aboard the paddlewheeler *Natchez* or
Jean Lafitte; dinners with dancing aboard the riverboat *President,* the largest
floating dance hall on the river. Daily.
 Southern Seaplane (seaplane), 1 Coquille Dr., Belle Chasse (394-5633):
Discover the city, Lake Pontchartrain, and the bayous as seen from above. Spectacular.
 Saint Charles Avenue Streetcar (streetcar), Canal St. and Carondelet St.:
Follows the route of Tennessee Williams' famous *Streetcar Named Desire;* you
can visit the charming Garden District with its lovely old houses. Opened in
1835, this 13-mi.-long (21km) streetcar line is one of the oldest in the world. It's
wiser not to ride it at night. Fare: 60¢ (exact change required). Has recently undergone a $47-million renovation. For information, call 569-2600.

SIGHTS, ATTRACTIONS & ACTIVITIES

ADVENTURES: Honey Island Swamp Tours (boat), Indian Village Rd.; in
Slidell, 24 mi. (38km) NE on I-10 (641-1769): 2-hr. guided tour into the heart
of one of the country's wildest, remotest wetlands. Fascinating.

ARCHITECTURAL HIGHLIGHTS: ⌂ **Civic Center,** bounded by La Salle St.
and Poydras St. and Loyola Ave. and Tulane Ave.: Heart of the **Central Business
District,** with interesting high-rise buildings. The imposing 11-story **City Hall**
faces the **State Office Building,** the **State Supreme Court Building,** and the
New Orleans Public Library. Worth a look.
 ⌂ **Loyola University,** 6363 St. Charles Ave. (865-3240): This
highly regarded Catholic university dates from 1912, and has
some fine Tudor Gothic buildings. Campus visits by appointment.
 ⌖⌂ **Superdome,** Sugar Bowl Dr. (587-3810): Largest enclosed
stadium in the world, with 90,000 seats; air-conditioned
throughout. Scene every year of the famous Sugar Bowl. The dome is 262 ft.
(80m) high and 678 ft. (207m) across. Absolutely riveting. Tours daily.
 ⌖⌂ **World Trade Center,** 2 Canal St. (525-2185): A 33-story high-
rise overlooking the harbor, with the offices of many international corporations as well as foreign consulates. The observation platform on
the 31st floor and the revolving bar on the 33rd floor have a wonderful view of
the French Quarter and the river. A definite must-see.

CHURCHES/SYNAGOGUES: ⌂ **Old Ursuline Convent,** Chartres St. and
Ursuline St. (592-2001): This Ursuline convent, dating from 1745, once housed
an orphanage as well as the city's first school for African American children. Today it is the presbytery and record house of the adjoining Italian church of St.

Mary's. It has been recently restored. Worth seeing; open to visitors Wed afternoon only.

St. Louis Cathedral, Jackson Sq. (525-9585): Built in 1794 on the site of two earlier churches, both destroyed, this is one of the oldest Catholic cathedrals in the country. A fine classical building in the French style. Open daily.

HISTORIC BUILDINGS: **Beauregard-Keyes House,** 1113 Chartres (523-7257): Beautiful Greek Revival house built around 1826, now a designated historic monument. After the War Between the States it was the home of Confederate Gen. Pierre G. T. Beauregard, and later of novelist Frances Parkinson Keyes. Elegant patio and garden; period furniture. Don't miss it. Open Mon–Sat.

Cabildo, 709 Chartres St., at Jackson Sq. (568-6968): Built in 1795 as the Spanish Governor's Palace. The sale of Louisiana to the U.S. by Napoléon I (the Louisiana Purchase) was ratified here in 1803. Undergoing restoration after a fire which damaged much of the building. It's scheduled to reopen in 1992.

Gallier House, 1118-1132 Royal St. (523-6722): Luxurious private house built in 1857 by architect James Gallier, with one of New Orleans's finest Victorian interiors. Open Mon–Sat; don't miss it.

Hermann-Grima Historic House, 820 St. Louis St. (525-5661): Plush home typical of New Orleans's "golden age" (1830–60), with flower-planted patios, kitchens (demonstrations of Créole cooking in summer), slave quarters, and stables. Very fine old furniture; a beautiful vignette from the past. Open Mon–Sat.

Longue Vue House and Gardens, 7 Bamboo Rd. (488-5488): Faithful 1942 replica of a great 19th-century Louisiana plantation, with lovely furniture of the period. 8 acres (3.2ha) of magnificent garden, inspired in part by the famous Generalife at Granada in Spain. Worth seeing. Open Tues–Sun.

Madame John's Legacy, 632 Dumaine St. (568-6968): One of the oldest houses in New Orleans; erected in 1727 and rebuilt after a fire in 1788, it was completely restored in 1981. Interesting collection of Louisianan folk art. Open Tues–Sun.

Napoléon House, 500 Chartres St. (524-9752): Intended for Napoléon I by the mayor of New Orleans, Nicholas Girod, who had dreams of rescuing the fallen emperor from his imprisonment on St. Helena. Picturesque café on the ground floor. Worth seeing.

Old Absinthe House, 240 Bourbon St. (523-3181): The oldest and most famous bar in the Vieux Carré; here Gen. (later Pres.) Andrew Jackson and pirate Jean Lafitte drew up their plan for the Battle of New Orleans against the invading British. Don't miss it. (See "Bars and Nightclubs," below.)

Pitot House, 1440 Moss St. (482-0282): On the bank of Bayou St. John, this old plantation house once belonged to James Pitot, first elected mayor of New Orleans; dating from 1799, it is one of the last remaining examples of the Antillean style. Worth seeing. Wed–Sat.

Pontalba Apartments, Jackson Sq.: Built in 1846–49 by Baroness Pontalba, daughter of the last Spanish governor, these were the first apartments constructed in the U.S., in a lovely southern idiom with characteristic grace notes in wrought iron. Writer William Faulkner was among the illustrious tenants. **"The 1850s House,"** 523 St. Ann St. (568-6968), with original furniture and decoration of the period, may be visited Wed–Sun. Another unusual museum is the **Pontalba Historical Puppetorium,** 514 St. Peter St. (522-0344), where the deeds-at-arms of pirate Jean Lafitte, and other pages from the city's history, are portrayed by means of animated puppets. Don't miss it. Open Tues–Sun.

☀ ♨ ♨ **The Presbytère,** 751 Chartres St. at Jackson Sq. (568-6968): Abutting on St. Louis Cathedral, this 1791 building, in the same style as but older than the Cabildo, housed the Supreme Court under Spanish colonial administration. Holds part of the collection of the **Louisiana State Museum,** including many articles and costumes relating to Mardi Gras, as well as fine ceramics in the Newcomb style and engravings of birds by naturalist John James Audubon. Open Tues–Sun. Should not be missed.

☀ ♨ **Preservation Hall,** 726 St. Peter St. (522-2238 or 523-8939): Grandfather of jazz halls, dating from 1846. The decor is on its last legs but the ambience is incomparable. Open nightly; don't miss it.

♨ **U.S. Customs House,** Decatur St. and Canal St. (589-2976): Imposing edifice strangely blending the Greek Revival and Egyptian Revival styles, built between 1849 and 1881. The famous marble lobby and scrupulously restored interior decoration should definitely be seen. Open Mon–Fri.

MARKETS: ☀ ♨♨ **French Market,** bounded by N. Peters St., Decatur St., St. Ann St., and Barracks St. (522-2624): A covered market dating from 1836 (the oldest portions from 1791) built on the site of an old Native American market. One of the most interesting sights of the French Quarter, with its picturesque displays of fruit and vegetables, its flea market, trinket merchants, strolling musicians, and terrace cafés, of which the legendary **Café du Monde** is open day and night. Amusing and colorful.

MONUMENTS: ♨ **Andrew Jackson Statue,** Jackson Sq.: This equestrian statue of Gen. Andrew Jackson, who defeated the British here in 1815, is the work of sculptor Clark Mills. It sits in the middle of the old "Place d'Armes" (Parade Ground), renamed Jackson Sq. when the city's best-known statue was placed here in 1856. Should be seen.

♨ **Streetcar Named Desire,** Esplanade Ave., in front of the Old U.S. Mint: This streetcar, which once ran along Royal St. and St. Charles Ave., was made famous in Tennessee Williams's play *A Streetcar Named Desire.* The car displayed here dates from 1906. Worth a look.

MUSEUMS OF ART: ♨ **Contemporary Arts Center,** 900 Camp St. (523-1216): Large cultural complex comprising two auditoriums and three art galleries, in a renovated former warehouse. Interesting temporary exhibitions, music recitals, shows, etc. Should be seen. Tues–Sun.

☀ ♨ ♨ **New Orleans Museum of Art/NOMA,** Lelong Dr., City Park (488-2631): Fine Greek Revival building, inside which you'll find a remarkable microcosm of the history of art, from the primitive cultures of Asia, Africa, and the pre-Columbian Americas right down to cubism, via the great masters of the Renaissance (Samuel Kress Endowment) and a fabulous collection of Fabergé eggs. Among the best known of the works on display are Veronese's *Holy Conversation, Country House* by Monet, *Portrait of Estelle Musson* by Degas, and Max Ernst's *Everyone Here Speaks Latin.* A wealth of American art: Georgia O'Keeffe, Andy Warhol, Jacques Lipchitz, etc. Ceramic miniatures. Not to be missed; open Tues–Sun.

MUSEUMS OF SCIENCE & HISTORY: ☀ ♨ **Chalmette National Historical Park,** on Bernard Hwy. in Arabi, 6 mi. (10km) east along St. Claude Ave. (589-4430): The spot where Gen. Andrew Jackson won his victory in 1815 in the last great battle of the War of 1812 against the British. Military museum and 98-ft. (30m) memorial obelisk on the bank of the Mississippi. In the great National Cemetery adjoining lie 12,000 Union soldiers who fell during the Civil War. For history buffs. Open daily.

☼🔔 **Confederate Museum,** 929 Camp St. (523-4522): The oldest Civil War museum in Louisiana, with a memorial to Jefferson Davis, president of the Confederacy. Interesting. Open Mon–Sat.

☼🔔 **Historic New Orleans Collection,** 533 Royal St. (523-4662): The history of Louisiana and New Orleans narrated by means of an interesting collection of maps, pictures, photographs, and historic documents displayed in two lovely old houses, **Merieult House** (1792) and the **Williams Residence** (about 1880). Temporary exhibitions. A positive must-see. Open Tues–Sat.

🔔 **Louisiana Science Center,** Julia St. Wharf at Riverwalk (529-3622): Museum of science and astronomy opened in 1987. Visitors are invited to perform numerous scientific experiments, may program a computer, share in the sensations of an astronaut in space, or watch movies projected onto the giant screen of the IMAX Theater. Fascinating. Open daily.

☼🔔🔔 **Louisiana State Museum,** in several different buildings (568-6968): Priceless historical collections going back to French and Spanish colonial times, housed in the **Cabildo** (closed for restoration), **The Presbytère, Madame John's Legacy, "The 1850s House"** (see above), or the **Old U.S. Mint** (see below). For details, see the individual museums.

☼🔔 **Old Pharmacy Museum,** 514 Chartres St. (524-9077): An apothecary's store dating from 1823, "La Pharmacie Française," founded by Louis Dufilho, America's first licensed pharmacist. Very picturesque. Open Tues–Sun.

☼🔔🔔 **Old U.S. Mint,** 400 Esplanade Ave. (568-8213): This fascinating museum, opened in 1982, is housed in an Ionic temple which was once a mint. Displays souvenirs of the early jazz age (instruments that belonged to Louis Armstrong, Bix Beiderbecke, and the Original Dixieland Jazz Band are of special interest), and traces the evolution of the art form from its Afro-American origins to the present day. A must for all jazz fans. Also a museum of Carnival which you shouldn't miss. Open Wed–Sun. Part of the Louisiana State Museum.

🔔 **Voodoo Museum,** 724 Dumaine St. (523-7685): Interesting small museum devoted to the cult of Voodoo, which commanded a large following among 19th-century slaves, and its high priestess, the famous Marie Laveau. Occult displays and artifacts. The museum also presents ritual shows and offers walking tours. Open daily.

NIGHTTIME ENTERTAINMENT: The city that, at the beginning of the 20th century gave birth to jazz, still proudly upholds its musical heritage, particularly in the Vieux Carré. After nightfall the quiet, slightly countrified streets of the **French Quarter** come briskly back to life. A throng of idlers moves along the brilliantly lit streets, some of which are closed to wheeled traffic, and which teem with bars, jazz clubs, and other more or less wholesome pleasure resorts. Typical is the famous **Bourbon Street:** you mustn't leave New Orleans without seeing it. For details, see "Bars and Nightclubs," below.

OUTDOOR ART & PLAZAS: 🔔 **K & B Plaza,** Lee Circle on St. Charles Ave. (586-1234): Very fine collection of more than 50 modern sculptures in stainless steel, bronze, granite, aluminum, and other materials by U.S. and foreign artists. The outdoor exhibits may be seen daily; those in the hall, only Mon–Fri. A sight not to be missed.

PANORAMAS: 🔔 **Greater New Orleans Bridge,** Pontchartrain Expwy.: Spanning the river from New Orleans to Algiers, this great work of art, constructed in 1958, is the second-largest metallic nonsuspension bridge in the country; looking north from it you have a nice view of the harbor and the Vieux Carré.

☼🔔 **World Trade Center,** 2 Canal St. (525-2185): Observation platform on the 31st floor **(Viewpoint)** and revolving bar on the 33rd floor **(Top of the Mart)** reached by outside glass-walled elevator. Fine view over the city, the Mississippi, and the harbor. Open daily till 1am.

PARKS & GARDENS: ⚓ **Audubon Park and Zoological Garden,** St. Charles Ave. opposite Tulane University (861-2537): Beautiful 400-acre (162ha) park ringed with century-old oak trees, on the site of an old sugar plantation on the banks of the Mississippi. Well-known zoo with over 1,200 animals in reproductions of their natural habitats; lagoons, golf courses; picnic areas.

☼⚓ **City Park,** City Park Ave. at Marconi Dr. (north of the city, almost at the edge of the great Lake Pontchartrain): In a bygone age this was where duelists liked to settle their disputes, and on some Sundays a dozen duels were fought on the favorite ground of **Dueling Oaks.** Fine rose gardens, four public golf courses, many lagoons and lakes for canoeing. The park is almost 2½ mi. (4km) long, and in the southern part is located the **New Orleans Museum of Art** (see above). You shouldn't fail to visit it.

⚓ **Greenwood Cemetery and Metairie Cemetery,** Metairie Rd. and City Park Ave.: Famous for their sumptuous tombs, particularly those of Gen. Stonewall Jackson and of Josie Arlington, a well-known madam who died in 1914—all standing amid magnolias and tropical trees. Should be seen, but don't go there alone—the above-ground tombs offer hiding places for muggers. Open daily.

⚓ **Longue Vue Gardens,** 7 Bamboo Rd. (488-5488): Faithful reproduction of the famous Generalife Gardens at Granada (see "Historic Buildings," above). Worth a look. Open Tues–Sun.

⚓ **Louis Armstrong Park,** bounded by N. Rampart St., St. Peter St., St. Philip St. and N. Villere St.: Originally known as Congo Sq. and later renamed after the city's most famous jazz musician, this was once a meeting place for African American slaves who came here on Sun to dance, sing spirituals, and generally let off steam. Tradition has it that jazz was born here—where today, appropriately, stand the **Municipal Auditorium** and the **Theater for the Performing Arts.** Should be seen.

⚓ **St. Louis Cemetery No. 1,** 400 Basin St.: One of the oldest cemeteries (1788) in the country. Among its splendid mausoleums, raised well above the ground because of the high water table, are those of the chessmaster Paul Morphy and the voodoo queen Marie Laveau. Part of the movie *Easy Rider* was shot here. Don't fail to visit it—but don't venture alone into this unsafe neighborhood. Open daily.

PERFORMING ARTS: For current listings of shows and cultural events, consult the entertainment pages of the daily *Times-Picayune/States-Item* (morning and evening), and the monthly *New Orleans* magazine.

Contemporary Arts Center, 900 Camp St. (523-1216): Concerts, ballet, modern and avant-garde theater.

Municipal Auditorium, 1201 St. Peter St. (525-7677): Concerts, opera, touring companies, ballet, etc. Year round.

New Orleans Center For Creative Arts/NOCCA, 6048 Perrier St. (899-0055): Concerts.

Orpheum Theater, 129 University Pl. (525-0500): Home of the New Orleans Symphony, under principal conductor Maxim Shostakovich (Sept–May).

Petit Théâtre du Vieux Carré/The Little Theater, 616 St. Peter St. (522-2081): The city's oldest theater (1797), with a magnificent antique interior. Drama, comedy, classical theater.

Saenger Performing Arts Center, 143 N. Rampart St. (524-2490): A 1920s movie house, an extravagant essay in the Renaissance style, now beautifully restored. Broadway hits, concerts.

Theater of the Performing Arts, 801 N. Rampart (525-1018): Home of the New Orleans City Ballet and the New Orleans Opera House Association. Also theater in the round.

Tulane University–Dixon Hall, Audubon Pl. (865-5269): Concerts, recitals, ballet.

SHOPPING: Canal Place, 365 Canal St. (525-0175): The city's most upscale shopping center, with about 50 fashion boutiques and exclusive stores such as Gucci, Bally, Saks Fifth Avenue, and Brooks Brothers. Open daily.

Jackson Brewery, Decatur St. and St. Peter St. (529-1211): A 19th-century brewery transformed into a picturesque food bazaar, with more than 60 cafés, restaurants, and stores selling food and amusing gifts. Lively, likable atmosphere. Open daily.

Magazine Street, between Canal St. and Napoleon Ave.: Charming 19th-century commercial thoroughfare with many antique shops; should be seen.

Riverwalk, Riverside between Canal St. and Poydras St. (522-1555): The newest of the great downtown shopping centers, on the site of the 1984 World's Fair along the Mississippi. Nearly 200 fashion boutiques, elegant stores, cafés, and restaurants. Has drawn crowds ever since its 1987 opening.

Royal Street, between Iberville St. and Dumaine St.: These seven blocks of Royal St. in the French Quarter are chockablock with antiques. Probably concentrate more quality antique jewelry and furnishings than any comparably sized area in the U.S. Becomes a pedestrian mall during shopping hours.

SPECIAL EVENTS: For exact dates, consult the **Greater New Orleans Tourist and Convention Commission** (see "Tourist Information," above).

Sugar Bowl (Jan 1): 3 days of popular celebration before the Sugar Bowl football game.

Mardi Gras (Feb–Mar): The only carnival of its kind in the world, and for 150 years New Orleans's most popular annual event. It celebrates Mardi Gras (literally "Fat Tuesday," but more commonly known in English as "Shrove Tuesday"), the eve of Ash Wednesday, the first day of Lent. Carnival was raised to its present level of splendor in 1857 by a secret society known as "The Mystic Krewe of Comus," and although often threatened with prohibition because of the fistfights and public disorders it occasioned, has survived in the teeth of all opposition thanks to the goodwill of 60 or so colorful associations, the "Krewes." It is these Krewes that sweep through the streets on the day of the great final parade, with their gaudy banners and frenzied bands going on before them, each following a different route. The Rex Parade, led by the King ("Rex") and followed by the mostly white Krewes, goes down St. Charles Ave. to Canal St., where the mayor of New Orleans is waiting to drink a toast with the Rex to the glory of the city. The Zulu Parade, with its "Zulu King," and the Indian Parade, both made up of African American Krewes, twist and turn through the downtown streets and the suburbs, never mixing with the parade of the Rex and his subjects, the Mystic Krewe of Comus, Knights of Momus, Krewe of Proteus, Krewe of Bacchus, Knights of Hermes, Krewe of Babylon, and the rest. But in any of the parades the costumes, masks, and floats will be magnificent, the Krewes setting no limit to their imagination and sense of humor. The Carnival season really begins in early Jan with an unbroken series of masked balls, parades, and torchlit processions, culminating on Shrove Tuesday in the country's greatest popular celebration. It's worth going to New Orleans just to see it.

USF & G Classic (late Mar): Prestigious PGA tournament with the world's best professional golfers. At English Turn.

French Quarter Festival (Apr): Free open-air concerts, dancing in the streets, boat races on the Mississippi; the Vieux Carré's own festival.

Spring Fiesta (4 days long, 1 week after Easter): Costume parades, public balls, art exhibitions. The city's oldest houses and the plantations in the vicinity are open to the public especially for the festival.

New Orleans Jazz and Heritage Festival (Jazzfest) (late Apr to early May): One of the most famous of all jazz festivals, drawing the greatest performers throughout the city; also rock, gospel, rhythm and blues, country and western, blues, Cajun, folk, Latin American, and African concerts. Riverboat concerts. Draws about 350,000 listeners. The great annual music festival.

Food Festival (late June to early July): Well-known gastronomic festival, a must for all lovers of Créole and Cajun food.

SPORTS: New Orleans boasts a professional football team:
Football (Aug–Dec): Saints, Superdome (522-2600).

Horseracing

The Fairgrounds, 1751 Gentilly Blvd. (944-5515); racing Wed–Sun Apr–Nov. One of the oldest tracks (1872) in the country.
Jefferson Downs Racetrack, 1300 Sunset Blvd., in Kenner (466-8521). On the shore of Lake Pontchartrain. Racing Apr–Nov.

STROLLS: ☼🔔 **Bourbon Street,** between Canal St. and Ursulines Ave.: On these 10 blocks, New Orleans has turned sin into a pedestrian mall, with innumerable bars, nightclubs, jazz dives, strip joints, and (sometimes slightly sordid) peep shows. Noisy and colorful by night, silent and depressing by day. This is the place Pigalle or Barbary Coast of the Old South; you should take a look.

☼ **Garden District,** around St. Charles Ave. between Jackson Ave. and Louisiana Ave.: 19th-century upper-class homes standing in delightful gardens; don't miss this page from the past. Take the picturesque St. Charles Ave. streetcar (it used to be the streetcar named Desire) from Canal St.—but don't come here after dark.

☼🔔🔔 **Jackson Square,** bounded by Decatur St., Chartres St., St. Peter St., and St. Ann St.: The oldest public garden in New Orleans, and its historic center; in French Colonial times it was called "The Parade Ground." On it stand some of the city's most notable buildings: the Cabildo, St. Louis Cathedral, the Pontalba Apartments, the old Jackson Brewery, and others, overlooking the equestrian statue of the seventh president of the U.S., which reigns unchallenged over the square. Lively, appealing atmosphere thanks to the crowds of strollers, painters, and street musicians; don't miss it.

🔔 **Moon Walk,** along the quays across Jackson Sq.: Elevated walkway along the bank of the Mississippi, with a scenic view of the heart of the French Quarter and the shipping on Ol' Man River. Owes its name not to its suitability for moonlight walks, but to a former mayor of the city, Moon Landrieu. A sight to be seen.

🔔 **Pirate's Alley,** between Chartres St. and Royal St.: Once a place of assembly for pirates and smugglers, this narrow alleyway in the shadow of the cathedral now belongs to painters and artists. Worth a look.

☼🔔🔔 **Royal Street,** between Esplanade Ave. and Canal St.: The Vieux Carré's smart street; almost every building on it is worth your attention: the **Gallier House** (no. 118), **Miro House** (no. 529), **Merieult House** (no. 533), **Court of Two Sisters** (no. 613), **Maison Le Monnier** (no. 640). Many boutiques, art galleries, antiques shops, restaurants, etc. The first Carnival ball was held at no. 127 in 1857, thus inaugurating the Mardi Gras festival. A walk not to be missed.

ZOOS: 🔔🔔 **Aquarium of the Americas,** Canal St. (861–2537): Opened in Sept. 1990, this hi-tech structure features more than 7,500 specimens and 60 exhibits ranging from the Mississippi Delta to the Amazon rain forest. Open daily.

☼🐚🐚 **Audubon Zoo,** Audubon Park, St. Charles Ave. (861-2537): One of the 10 best in the U.S., with more than 1,500 creatures displayed in reconstructions of their natural habitats, including very rare white tigers and white alligators. Also a fine collection of Australian fauna. Open daily.

ACCOMMODATIONS

A Note on Accommodations: Room rates in New Orleans are coded as follows: **VE,** Very Expensive ($140 and up); **E,** Expensive ($90–$140); **M,** Moderate ($60–$90); **I,** Inexpensive ($30–$60); **B,** Budget (up to $30). A listing of toll free numbers is in the Appendix.

Note: Hotel rates take a sharp upturn during the Sugar Bowl Game weekend and Mardi Gras; you can generally only book for 3 or more nights at these times, and you should make reservations as far ahead as possible.

Personal Favorites (in order of preference)

☀🐚🐚🐚🐚 **Omni Royal Orleans** (dwntwn), 621 St. Louis St., LA 70140 (504/529-5333; toll free, see Omni). 350 rms, A/C, color TV, in-rm movies. AE, CB, DC, MC, V. Valet parking $8, pool, health club, sauna, four rests. (including the Rib Room), three bars, 24-hr. rm svce, nightclub, hrdrsr, concierge, free crib. *Note:* Splendidly situated on the site of the old St. Louis Exchange Hotel in the heart of the Vieux Carré, a stone's throw from Antoine's, Brennan's, and other landmarks of local gastronomy, as well as from the antiques shops of Royal St. Luxuriously elegant 1920s-style decor and atmosphere, w. Italian marble lobby, lavish flower arrangements, and crystal chandeliers. Rms very comfortable, though a little on the small side. Excellent svce; good rests.; fabulous rooftop pool. The favorite hotel of those in-the-know. **E–VE**

🐚🐚🐚🐚 **Windsor Court** (dwntwn), 300 Gravier St., LA 70140 (504/523-6000; toll free 800/223-6800). 324 rms and suites, A/C, color TV, in-rm movies. AE, CB, DC, MC, V. Valet gar. $8, pool, health club, two rests. (including the Grill Room), two bars, 24-hr. rm svce, nightclub, concierge, free crib. *Note:* Luxurious, ultramodern palace very nr. the French Quarter, its facade elegantly clad in pink granite, w. balconies and bay windows. Well-bred interior decoration w. fine collection of old English pictures. Ultracomfortable rms and suites with minibars (some w. kitchenettes) and marble bathrooms; the ultimate luxury is an underwater stereo system in the pool! Excellent luxury hotel rest.; thoughtful, polished svce; fashionable clientele. An establishment of the highest class. **VE**

☀🐚🐚🐚 **Pontchartrain Hotel** (nr. dwntwn), 2031 St. Charles Ave., LA 70140 (504/524-0581; toll free 800/777-1700). 100 rms, A/C, cable color TV. AE, CB, DC, MC, V. Free valet parking, rest. (Caribbean Room), coffee shop, bar, 24-hr. rm svce, nightclub, concierge, free crib. *Note:* A little removed from the Vieux Carré and its nightlife, this *grande dame* of local hotels has been in the hands of its founding family, the Aschaffenburgs, for three generations. Its small size, and the high quality of its svce, make it a haven of peace, much frequented by VIPs and visiting celebrities. Elegant rms w. minibars and period furniture; rest. of high quality which appeals to businesspeople for breakfast or lunch. 10 min. from dwntwn. **E–VE**

☀🐚🐚 **Soniat House** (dwntwn), 1133 Chartres St., LA 70116 (504/522-0570; toll free 800/544-8808). 23 rms, A/C, color TV. AE, MC, V. Valet parking $10, bar, limited-menu rm svce, concierge, free breakfast, crib $25. *Note:* Very lovely old 1830s dwelling house w. carriage entrance and majestic staircase. The rms or suites are huge and tastefully decorated, w. beds of hand-carved wood and period furniture. Inviting patio w. fountain and tropical plants. Personalized reception and svce. An excellent place to stay, partaking fully of the charm of the Vieux Carré. **E–VE**

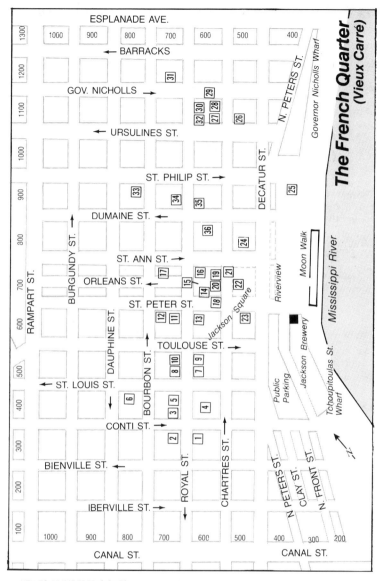

The French Quarter (Vieux Carré)

ESPLANADE AVE.

1300 · 1000 · 900 · 800 · 700 · 600 · 500 · 400

← BARRACKS

GOV. NICHOLLS →

← URSULINES ST.

ST. PHILIP ST. →

DUMAINE ST. ←

ST. ANN ST. →

ORLEANS ST. ←

ST. PETER ST. →

TOULOUSE ST. →

← ST. LOUIS ST.

CONTI ST. →

BIENVILLE ST. ←

IBERVILLE ST. →

CANAL ST. · CANAL ST.

RAMPART ST. · BURGUNDY ST. · DAUPHINE ST. · BOURBON ST. · ROYAL ST. · CHARTRES ST. · DECATUR ST.

N. PETERS ST. · CLAY ST. · N. FRONT ST.

Governor Nicholls Wharf · Moon Walk · Riverview · Mississippi River · Jackson Square · Jackson Brewery · Public Parking · Tchoupitoulas St. Wharf

KEY TO NUMBERED SIGHTS

1. Old Bank of Louisiana
2. Old Bank of the U.S.
3. Old La. State Bank
4. Court House
5. Casa Faurie
6. The Hermann House
7. Maison Seignouret
8. Merieult House
9. Casa de Comercio
10. Court of Two Lions
11. LeMonnier House
12. Maison de Fléchier
13. Maison LeMonnier
14. Spanish Arsenal
15. LaBranche House
16. St. Anthony's Garden
17. Salle d'Orléans
18. Père Antoine's Alley
19. The Presbytère
20. St. Louis Cathedral
21. The Cabildo
22. Pirate Alley
23. Pontalba Buildings
24. 1850 House
25. Court of the Two Sisters
26. Old Ursulines Convent
27. Beauregard House
28. Soniat House
29. Clay House
30. LaLaurie House
31. Thierry House
32. The Gallier House
33. Lafitte's Blacksmith Shop
34. cornstalk fence
35. Miltenberger House
36. "Madame John's Legacy"

Maison Dupuy (dwntwn), 1001 Toulouse St., LA 70112 (504/586-8000; toll free 800/535-9177). 196 rms, A/C, cable color TV. AE, CB, DC, MC, V. Valet gar. $8, pool, health club, rest. (Le Bon Créole), bar, rm svce, free crib. *Note:* A large hotel, modern and elegant, on the edge of the French Quarter, built around a delightful flower-planted patio w. a fountain and a heated pool. Very successful imitation-antique decor. Huge, comfortable rms w. balconies, the best overlooking the patio. Efficient svce; acceptable rest. Good value; recommended. **E**

Le Richelieu (dwntwn), 1234 Chartres St., LA 70116 (504/529-2492; toll free 800/535-9653). 88 rms, A/C, cable color TV. AE, CB, DC, MC, V. Free parking, pool, rest., bar, rm svce, concierge, free crib. *Note:* One of the best values in the French Quarter, the Richelieu what used to be a luxurious private house belonging to an old macaroni factory. Like most hotels in the Vieux Carré it is built around an inviting interior courtyard, w. big, welcoming rms tastefully decorated, and all the engaging charm of the slightly outdated. Friendly reception and svce. **M–E**

Château Motor Hotel (dwntwn), 1001 Chartres St., LA 70116 (504/524-9636). 40 rms, A/C, color TV. AE, CB, DC, MC, V. Free garage, pool, coffee shop, bar, rm svce. *Note:* With its red-brick walls, its shutters, its cast-iron balconies, and its creeper-covered facade, this winsome little hotel in the heart of the Vieux Carré offers excellent value. Largish, comfortable rms, the best overlooking the courtyard with its banana palms, azaleas, and fountain. Pleasing terrace for coffee. A good place to stay. **I–M**

La Salle Hotel (dwntwn), 1113 Canal St., LA 70112 (504/523-5831; toll free 800/521-9450). 60 rms, A/C, color TV. AE, CB, DC, MC, V. Parking (charge) next door, rm svce (breakfast only). *Note:* Small economy hotel, now 60 years old, on the edge of the French Quarter. A commendable standard of comfort is maintained, though some rms lack private baths. Friendly reception; youthful clientele. Ideal for budget travelers. Unsafe area at night. **I–M**

Other Hotels (from top bracket to budget)

Westin Canal Palace (dwntwn), 100 Rue Iberville, LA 70130 (504/566-7006; toll free, see Westin). 438 rms, A/C, color TV, in-rm movies. AE, CB, DC, MC, V. Valet gar. $9, pool, three rests. (including Le Jardin), two bars, 24-hr. rm svce, nightclub, hrdrsr, boutiques, concierge, free crib. *Note:* One of the newest luxury hotels in the city, overlooking the Mississippi and the elegant Canal Place Shopping Center from the eminence of its 29 stories. Exceptionally huge, comfortable rms, w. marble bathrooms, minibars, and clear views over the river or the French Quarter. Ultra-professional svce. Very well situated a stone's throw from the Vieux Carré and the World Trade Center. Business clientele. **VE**

Fairmont (formerly the Roosevelt; dwntwn), University Pl., LA 70140 (504/529-7111; toll free, see Fairmont). 730 rms, A/C, color TV, in-rm movies. AE, CB, DC, MC, V. Valet parking $8, pool, two tennis courts, two rests. (including Sazerac), 24-hr. coffee shop, 24-hr. bars, rm svce, disco, hrdrsr, drugstore, concierge, free crib. *Note:* An elderly luxury hotel of Victorian elegance, a few steps from the Vieux Carré and on the edge of the Central Business District. Ultra-comfortable, lavishly decorated rms, though some are on the cramped side. Exemplary svce. Very commendable luxury rest. Big business clientele. A landmark among local hotels. Recently renovated. **E–VE**

Hilton Riverside and Towers (dwntwn), 2 Poydras St., LA 70140 (504/561-0500; toll free, see Hilton). 1,600 rms, A/C, color TV, in-rm movies. AE, CB, DC, MC, V. Valet parking $10, two pools, health club, sauna, 11 tennis courts, squash, three rests. (including Winston's), two coffee shops, four bars, 24-hr. rm svce, disco, hrdrsr, concierge, free crib. *Note:* Enormous tourist barracks on the river, its massive silhouette by no means improving the view from Riverwalk. All rms overlook the city, the harbor, or both. Irreproachably comfortable; efficient svce; mediocre rests. Well-regarded jazz club (Pete Fountain's Night Club). The top three floors are reserved for VIPs; on one is a Presidential Suite at $1,300 a night. Group and convention clientele of an obtrusive kind; the Convention Center and the French Quarter are nearby. **E–VE**

Inter-Continental (dwntwn), 444 St. Charles Ave., LA 70130 (504/525-5566; toll free, see Inter-Continental). 497 rms, A/C, color TV, in-rm movies. AE, CB, DC, MC, V. Valet parking $8, pool, two rests. (including Les Continents), two bars, 24-hr. rm svce, nightclub, boutiques, concierges. *Note:* Ultramodern luxury hotel in the heart of the Central Business District and 5 min. from the French Quarter, of ungraceful exterior but elegant and urbane within, boasting many contemporary sculptures and other works of art. Spacious and remarkably comfortable rms w. minibars, some w. balconies. Very complete facilities; flawless svce; rest. of quality. Big business clientele. Interesting wknd discounts. **E–VE**

Maison de Ville (dwntwn), 727 Toulouse St., LA 70130 (504/561-5858; toll free 800/345-3457). 23 rms, suites, or cottages, A/C, cable color TV. AE, DC, MC, V. Valet parking $12, pool, rest. (Bistro at Maison de Ville), bar, rm svce, concierge. *Note:* The most luxurious and exclusive small hotel in the French Quarter, its main building dates from the mid-19th century, while the adjoining cottages (200-year-old former slave quarters) bear the name of naturalist John James Audubon, who once lived there. The whole has been lavishly and effectively restored, w. period furniture. Shady patios and inviting pool. Reception and svce of the highest order. Excellent rest. The favorite of those in-the-know. **E–VE**

Monteleone Hotel (dwntwn), 214 Royal St., LA 70140 (504/523-3341; toll free 800/535-9595). 600 rms, A/C, cable-color TV. AE, CB, DC, MC, V. Valet parking $6, pool, putting green, two rests. (including Le Café), coffee shop, four bars (one revolving), rm svce, nightclub, hrdrsr, boutiques, free crib. *Note:* Inviting older hotel at the entrance to the Vieux Carré. The package-tour and convention guests make a lot of noise, but the comfort and svce are flawless. Acceptable rest.; very agreeable nightclub and terrace w. pool on the top floor. A New Orleans landmark for the past century. **E–VE**

Radisson Suite Hotel (formerly the Sugar House Park; dwntwn), 315 Julia St., LA 70130 (504/525-1993; toll free, see Radisson). 251 suites, A/C, color TV, in-rm movies. AE, CB, DC, MC, V. Parking $6, pool, rest. (Sugar House), bar, rm svce, jazz club, concierge, free crib. *Note:* Typical hotel for the business traveler, very nr. the Convention Center. Spacious, inviting suites w. private balconies or patios and refrigerators. Spectacular six-story glass-walled lobby. Business and convention clientele. Good value. Recently redecorated and refurnished. **E–VE**

Avenue Plaza Hotel (nr. dwntwn), 2111 St. Charles Ave., LA 70130 (504/566-1212; toll free 800/535-9575). 200 rms. A/C, color TV, in-rm movies. AE, CB, DC, MC, V. Parking $4, pool, sauna, health club, rest., bar, hrdrsr. *Note:* In the Garden District 10 min. from dwntwn by the St. Charles Ave. streetcar, this hotel offers good athletic facilities and inviting rms w. kitchenettes and refrigerators. Good value overall. The perfect place for viewing the Mardi Gras procession as it passes. **M–E**

Holiday Inn French Quarter (dwntwn), 124 Royal St., LA 70130 (504/529-7211; toll free, see Holiday Inns). 252 rms, A/C, color TV, in-rm movies. AE, CB, DC, MC, V. Free parking, pool, rest. (Jambo's), bar, free crib. *Note:* The functional Holiday Inn style at the entrance to the Vieux Carré. Comfortable rms. The rest. makes a praiseworthy effort. Package-tour and group clientele. Good value, considering the location. **M–E**

Provincial (dwntwn), 1024 Chartres St., LA 70116 (504/ 581-4995; toll free 800/535-7922). 97 rms, A/C, color TV, in-rm movies. AE, CB, DC, MC, V. Free parking, pool, rest. (Honfleur), rm svce, free crib. *Note:* Delightful older hotel, as quiet and discreet as its name implies, in the Vieux Carré very nr. the French Market. Inviting, comfortable rms w. period furnishings and private balconies. Pretty inner courtyards. The clients are mostly regulars, because they know this is a good place to stay. **M–E**

The Columns (nr. dwntwn), 3811 St. Charles Ave., LA 70115 (504/899-9308). 17 rms, A/C. AE, DC, MC, V. Valet parking $6, rest., bar, rm svce. *Note:* A prosperous Victorian's elegant home built in 1833 and now a designated historic monument. Enormous rms furnished in period, but some lacking private baths. The movies *Tightrope* and *Pretty Baby* were shot here. Romantic ambience; reception and svce of the friendliest. In the heart of the Garden District, 15 min. from dwntwn by the St. Charles Ave. streetcar. **I–M**

Days Inn Canal Street (nr. dwntwn), 1630 Canal St., LA 70112 (504/586-0110; toll free, see Days Inns). 216 rms, A/C, color TV, in-rm movies. AE, CB, DC, MC, V. Free parking, pool, rest., bar, free crib. *Note:* Typical functional motel, recently renovated; 5 min. by car from the Superdome or the French Quarter. Comfortable rms, some w. balconies; efficient reception and svce. Good value overall. **I–M**

Quality Inn Midtown (nr. dwntwn), 3900 Tulane Ave., LA 70119 (504/486-5541; toll free, see Quality Inns). 100 rms, A/C, color TV, in-rm movies. AE, CB, DC, MC, V. Free parking, pool, rest., bar, rm svce, disco, crib $3. *Note:* Comfortable, attractive motel a little away from the center. Spacious rms w. balconies. Friendly reception and svce. Great if you're driving; easily accessible from the Pontchartrain Expwy. Free shuttle to Amtrak and Greyhound stations. Good value 10 min. from dwntwn. **I–M**

Best Western Patio Motel (nr. dwntwn), 2820 Tulane Ave., LA 70119 (504/822-0200; toll free, see Best Western). 76 rms, A/C, color TV, in-rm movies. AE, DC, MC, V. Free parking, two pools, adj. coffee shop and bar. *Note:* Congenial small motel 8 min. from dwntwn. Serviceably comfortable rms, the best overlooking the patio w. a pool. Smiling reception and svce. Free shuttle connection w. Amtrak station and bus terminal. Good value. **I–M**

French Quarter Maisonnettes (dwntwn), 1130 Chartres St., LA 70116 (504/524-9918). 7 rms, A/C, black-and-white TV. No credit cards. Parking $6, nearby coffee shop. *Note:* Gracious little Vieux Carré home built in 1825. The rms, each w. kitchenette and tastefully decorated, open on a pretty shaded courtyard. Reception w. a smile. Excellent value. You'll need to book a number of weeks ahead. Closed in July. A very good place. **I–M**

La Quinta Gretna (nr. dwntwn), 50 Terry Pkwy., in Gretna, LA 70056 (504/368-5600; toll free, see La Quinta). 154 rms, A/C, color TV, in-rm movies. AE, CB, DC, MC, V. Free parking, pool, adj. 24-hr coffee shop, valet service, free crib. *Note:* Excellent value 10 min. from dwntwn across the Mississippi. Modern comforts; reception and svce w. a smile. Ideal if you're driving. **I**

St. Charles Inn (nr. dwntwn), 3636 St. Charles Ave., LA 70115 (504/899-8888). 40 rms, A/C, color TV. AE, CB, DC, MC, V. Parking $5, rest., bar, free breakfast. *Note:* Well-run small budget motel 10 min. from dwntwn on the St. Charles Ave. streetcar. Pleasantly decorated rms; friendly reception. Excellent value. **I**

Airport Accommodations

Hilton Airport Hotel & Conference Center (vic.), 901 Airline Hwy., in Kenner, LA 70062 (504/469-5000; toll free, see Hilton). 324 rms, A/C, color TV, in-rm movies. AE, CB, DC, MC, V. Free parking, pool, two tennis courts, putting green, health club, rest. (Café LaSalle), bar, rm svce, nightclub, free airport limo. *Note:* Brand-new luxury hotel right across from the airport. Spacious, well-soundproofed rms overlooking pool or garden. Efficient svce. Business clientele. VIP floor. Great if you're stopping over between flights. 25 min. from dwntwn. **E**

YMCA/Youth Hostels
Marquette House International Hostel (nr. dwntwn), 2253 Carondelet St. (504/523-3014). 100 beds. Youth hostel in an antebellum house nr. the Garden District.
YMCA International Center (nr. dwntwn), 936 St. Charles Ave. (504/568-9622). 139 rms. Pool, health club, rest. Men and women.

RESTAURANTS
A Note on Restaurant Prices: New Orleans restaurant prices, per person, excluding drinks and service charges, are coded as follows: **VE,** Very Expensive ($60 and up); **E,** Expensive ($40–$60); **M,** Moderate ($25–$40); **I,** Inexpensive ($15–$25); **B,** Budget (up to $15).
A Note on New Orleans Food: For more than 150 years New Orleans rightly prided itself on its gastronomic skills. During this period, half a dozen great restaurants have in turn enjoyed their days of glory: Antoine's, which created Créole cuisine in the 19th century; Galatoire's, at the beginning of the 20th century; Arnaud's, in the 1920s and '30s; Brennan's, in the years following World War II; Le Ruth's, Mosca's, and Commander's Palace, for the past 15 years. These seven "greats" have had their ups and downs over the years, but they are still counted among the best restaurants in the city.
The two great cuisines of New Orleans, ranked by many among the country's greatest gastronomic resources, are "Créole" (the more delicate) and "Cajun" (the earthier). They have one thing in common: both, in the words of Paul Prudhomme, the truculent figure who is the best-known chef in New Orleans today, are "Louisiana-born with French roots." But if Créole and Cajun food still acknowledge a predominantly French inheritance, they also pay tribute to other cuisines which immigration has brought to the city: Spanish, African, Italian, Caribbean, Native American. However—still quoting Prudhomme—the most compelling influence on Créole cuisine was undoubtedly that of the cooks who had charge of the kitchens in Louisiana plantation homes.

Personal Favorites (in order of preference)
Commander's Palace (nr. dwntwn), 1403 Washington Ave. (889-8221) A/C. Lunch/dinner daily, brunch Sat–Sun; closed Shrove Tuesday, Dec 24–25. AE, CB, DC, MC, V. Jkt. (J&T at dinner). *Specialties:* turtle soup; smoked turkey hash w. poached eggs and sage hollandaise; catfish w. greens, Créole sauce, and hush puppies; oysters Trufant; roast quail w. shrimp; filet mignon Debris; pompano en papillote; chocolate-fudge Sheba w. crème anglaise. Fine wine list. *Note:* In the heart of the charming old Garden District, a stately Victorian house accommodates New Orleans's most elegant rest., belonging to the senior branch of the well-known Brennan family. While the cuisine has its passing moments of weakness, there are some dishes, such as the veal Marcelle or the filet mignon Debris, which belong in anyone's anthology of great food. Exquisite flower-planted courtyard in summer; Dixieland at brunch (very crowded) Sat–Sun. Courteous and efficient svce; resv. a must. 10 min. from dwntwn; valet parking. One of the dozen best rests. in the country. *Créole.* **M–E**
Le Ruth's (vic.), 636 Franklin St., in Gretna (362-4914). A/C. Dinner only, Tues–Sat; closed hols, Shrove Tuesday, and the month of July. AE, MC, V. J&T. *Specialties:* oyster-and-artichoke soup, crabmeat St. Francis, roast duck w. oysters, lake trout Oliva, roast rack of lamb w. fried

parsley, veal Marie. Superb sherbet and homemade ice cream, almond tart. Louisiana's finest wine list, backed by a 25,000-bottle cellar. *Note:* This obscure neighborhood on the other side of the river has little to recommend it; nor does the appearance of the rest. itself, apart from a few fine paintings. But the food is among the best to be found. Their light sauces—unusual in New Orleans—and their talent for innovation make of Larry and Lee Le Ruth, the sons of founder Warren Le Ruth, the Bocuse brothers of the region. Flawless svce. You'll need to make resv., and do it some days ahead. Well worth the 15-min. drive from the Vieux Carré. *Créole.* **M–E**

Emeril's (vic.), 800 Tchoupitoulas St. (528-9393). A/C. Lunch Mon–Fri, dinner Mon–Sat; closed hols. AE, CB, DC, MC, V. Jkt. *Specialties:* wild-mushroom tart, roast quail Milton, rack of lamb w. mustard crust, pan-roasted salmon w. fresh herbs and wilted greens, Créole cream cheesecake. The menu changes regularly. Small but adequate wine list. *Note:* Former chef of the Commander's Palace, Emeril Lagasse is the hottest young chef in town. His adventurous and delicate fare must be defined as Créole/Southwestern/New American, or "Haute Créole" as dubbed by some food critics. Carved out of a former factory in the warehouse district, the rest. is decorated in a modernistic style w. brick walls, high ceilings, and exposed pipes. Friendly but professional svce. The best new rest. in New Orleans (opened in Mar 1990). Resv. a must. *American.* **M–E**

Galatoire's (dwntwn), 209 Bourbon St. (525-2021). A/C. Lunch/dinner Tues–Sun; closed Shrove Tuesday and hols. No credit cards. J&T (at dinner). *Specialties:* shrimp remoulade, eggs Sardou, crabmeat ravigote, trout Marguéry, sweetbreads financière, chicken Clemenceau, seafood-stuffed eggplant, oysters Bienville. *Note:* Another landmark since the beginning of the 20th century; the attractive 1900 decor, w. its mirrors and ceiling fans, is guaranteed authentic. Only Ruth's and the Commander's Palace can rival the food, and the svce is exemplary. This is a noisy place, and—another black mark—Galatoire's accepts no resv., inexcusable in a rest. of this quality. The wine list is poor. New Orleans's quintessential bistro. *Créole.* **I–M**

Henri (dwntwn), in Le Meridien Hotel, 1614 Caral St. (525-6500). A/C, Lunch Mon–Fri, dinner Mon–Sat; closed July 4. AE, CB, DC, MC, V. J&T. *Specialties:* salmon soufflé, braised filet of venison w. spaetzle noodles and wild mushrooms, warm duckling salad w. cabbage and ravioli of foie gras, beef tournedos w. caramelized shallots and red-wine sauce, poached cherries in cabernet sauvignon w. cinnamon ice cream. Menu changes regularly; fine wine list. *Note:* The kitchens of this deluxe hotel rest. are supervised by Marc Haeberlin, chef of the famous Auberge de l'Ill in Alsace, which is one of France's finest three-star rests. Enough said. Elegant, intimate dining on two levels; polished, efficient svce. Business crowd at lunchtime. Resv. strongly advised. An excellent advertisement for French nouvelle cuisine. *French.* **I** (lunch), **E–VE** (dinner).

Mr. B's (dwntwn), 201 Royal St. (523-2078). A/C. Lunch/dinner daily, jazz brunch Sun; closed Shrove Tuesday, Dec 25. AE, CB, DC, MC, V. Jkt. *Specialties:* oysters Madras; gumbo; jambalaya; pasta; fish, andouille (spicy smoked pork sausage), and meat broiled over hickory-wood fire; veal sauté w. fettuccine Alfredo; bread pudding. Good list of California wines. *Note:* The fresh homemade pasta and the Créole-style broiled dishes are the house specialties of this congenial place, developed by the Brennan family who also own the prestigious Commander's Palace. Decor and atmosphere are reminiscent of a London club, and this is a favorite luncheon spot for business-people. Its popularity makes resv. advisable. *Créole.* **I–M**

Ruth's Chris Steak House (nr. dwntwn), 711 N. Broad Ave. (486-0810). A/C. Lunch/dinner daily; closed hols. AE, CB, DC, MC, V. Jkt. *Specialties:* the finest of red meats, mediocre desserts. *Note:* For decades the favorite spot of New Orleans meat-eaters. Remarkable meats (especially the Porterhouse steak for two), and an inimitable butter sauce. Attentive svce. Clientele of businesspeople and leading figures in local sports or politics. The neighborhood is unattractive after dark; take a cab. Open till 11:30pm. Other locations: 3633 Veterans Memorial Blvd., Metairie (888-3600). *Steak.* **M**

☆☆ **Bon Ton Café** (dwntwn), 401 Magazine St. (524-3386). A/C.
Lunch/dinner Mon–Fri; closed hols. AE, MC, V. Jkt. *Specialties:* turtle soup, crayfish étouffée, jambalaya, crabmeat au gratin, fried catfish, redfish Bon Ton, bread pudding with whisky. *Note:* This old rest., a New Orleans classic for three decades, w. its countrified atmosphere and charming checked red gingham tablecloths, serves some of the most authentic Cajun food going. Generally crowded and noisy at lunch, quieter in the evening. Very near the Vieux Carré. Resv. a must. *Cajun.* **I**

☆ **Chez Hélène** (nr. dwntwn), 1540 N. Robertson St. (947-1206). A/C. Lunch daily, dinner Tues–Sun. No credit cards. *Specialties:* oysters Rockefeller, gumbo, "dirty rice" (rice w. chopped chicken livers), trout Marguéry, fried chicken Créole, red beans and sausages, stuffed pepper, bread pudding with whisky. *Note:* By general consent the city's best value for lovers of real Créole cooking. The excellent chef Austin Leslie, nephew of the foundress, draws on old family recipes. Chez Hélène, with its nonexistent decor, democratic atmosphere, and soul-music jukebox, was the model for the TV series "Frank's Place." Svce very slow; neighborhood unsafe after dark—take a cab. *Créole.* **B–I**

☆ **Felix's** (dwntwn), 739 Iberville St. (522-4440). A/C.
Lunch/dinner daily (till midnight); closed hols. AE, MC, V. *Specialties:* oysters Rockefeller, steak, gumbo, fish of the day. *Note:* Oyster bar and rest. which is crowded midday and evening by hungry customers. Regulars usually sit at the counter to avoid the long wait for a table. Absolutely fresh oysters on the half shell and seafood, very attractively priced. Noisy, genial atmosphere. No resv. *Seafood.* **B–I**

Other Restaurants (from top bracket to budget)

☆☆☆ **Crozier's** (vic.), 3126 W. Esplanade Ave., Metairie (833-8108). A/C. Lunch Tues–Fri, dinner Tues–Sat; closed hols. AE, CB, DC, MC, V. Jkt. *Specialties:* pâté of duck, coq au vin, tournedos Gérard (w. foie gras), trout w. fennel, steak au poivre, sweetbreads meunière. Weakish wine list. *Note:* Lyon native Gérard Crozier's food is—most unusually for New Orleans—100% French, without any Créole tinge. Charming reception and intimate quarters in the suburb of Metairie, almost on the shores of Lake Pontchartrain. Efficient svce; resv. a must. Very well worth the 20-min. drive from the French Quarter. *French.* **M–E**

☆☆ **Isadora** (nr. dwntwn), 1100 Poydras St. (585-7787). A/C. Lunch Mon–Fri, dinner Mon–Sat; closed hols. AE, MC, V. Jkt. *Specialties:* saffron-scented ragoût of seafood and lobster, crayfish ravioli w. scallops and tarragon sauce, grilled lamb chops w. shrimp and pistou seasoning, basil-scented red snapper and crabmeat w. lemon-cognac sauce, sautéed sweetbreads w. poached quail eggs, excellent homemade desserts. *Note:* This rest., serving a very innovative nouvelle cuisine Créole style, came to be regarded as one of the finest in New Orleans within a matter of months of opening in 1988. Art deco–inspired setting w. etched glass and white papier-mâché palm trees. Svce on the abrupt side; at so popular a place, across from the Superdome, resv. are a must. *Créole.* **M–E**

☆☆☆ **Christian's** (nr. dwntwn), 3835 Iberville St. (482-4924). A/C. Dinner only, Mon–Fri; closed Thanksgiving, Dec 25. AE, CB, DC, MC, V. Jkt. (tie preferred but not obligatory). *Specialties:* oysters Roland, smoked soft-shell crabs, shrimp remoulade, redfish filet w. green-peppercorn sauce, veal Christian, sautéed chicken w. blackberry vinegar, Créole-style bouillabaisse, good homemade sherbets, chocolate mousse. *Note:* Christian

Ansel, a legitimate successor to the Galatoire dynasty, has housed his rest. in a pastel-washed old chapel, where he serves excellent French-inspired Créole food. Original settling, flawless svce; a very good place to eat. Resv. advised. 15 min. from dwntwn. *Créole.* **M**

♈♈♈ **Versailles** (nr. dwntwn), 2100 St. Charles Ave. (524-2535). A/C. Dinner only, Mon–Sat; closed Shrove Tuesday and 1 week in July. AE, CB, DC, MC, V. Jkt. *Specialties:* snails in pastry shell, crabmeat Florentine, Madras shrimp curry, bouillabaisse, duck w. port wine, trout sautéed w. capers and artichokes, veal escalope Fleury, filet mignon Helder, orange mousse. Good wine list (especially the German section). *Note:* Like a great wine, this rest. belonging to Günter Preuss continues to improve w. the years. Classic French-Créole food flawlessly prepared and served. Elegant paneling-and-mirror decor. Very popular locally, so resv. highly advisable. Valet parking. 10 min. from dwntwn. *Créole/French.* **M–E**

☼♈♈ **Antoine's** (dwntwn), 713 St. Louis St. (581-4422). A/C. Lunch/dinner Mon–Sat; closed Shrove Tuesday and hols. AE, CB, DC, MC, V. Jkt. *Specialties:* oysters Rockefeller, oysters Foch, pompano en papillote, étouffée of crayfish, filet of beef Robespierre, tournedos marchand de vin, chicken Rochambeau, souffléed potatoes, baked Alaska. Vast wine list backed by 35,000 bottles in the cellar. *Note:* The oldest rest. in the Vieux Carré is by now a sort of living legend. It was here that, in the 19th century, Antoine Alciatore created some of the most renowned Créole dishes, such as oysters Rockefeller and pompano en papillote. The decor has not changed since it was new (in 1840), and the present proprietor, Bernard Guste, is a fifth-generation descendant of the legendary Antoine. The waiters, some of whom have worked here for more than three decades, can be abrupt and the food is somewhat dated. But in spite of its slightly touristy atmosphere this is still one of the three or four best places to eat in the city. Ask to be seated in the big dining rm at the back, w. its dark paneling. Resv. strongly advised. *Créole.* **M**

♈♈ **Bistro at Maison de Ville** (dwntwn), in the Maison de Ville (see "Accommodations," above) (528-9206). A/C. Lunch/ dinner Mon–Sat. AE, DC, MC, V. Jkt. *Specialties:* tapenade w. eggplant, caviar, grilled shrimp w. coriander, cod cakes w. tomato purée, confit of duck salad, soft-shell crabs w. mustard Créole style, sweetbreads w. lemon butter and capers, salad of smoked roast quail on spinach, lemon tart, gratin of fruit. *Note:* Charming, romantic little hotel rest. w. dark paneling, intimate bar, and red upholstery. The cuisine is a happy marriage of classical Créole tradition w. contemporary French ideas. Since the rest. seats only 40, resv. are a must. *Créole/French.* **M**

♈♈ **Brennan's** (dwntwn), 417 Royal St. (525-9711). A/C. Lunch/dinner daily; closed Dec 25. AE, MC, V. Jkt. (at dinner). *Specialties:* eggs Sardou, crabmeat béarnaise, oyster soup, filet Stanley, redfish w. crabmeat and red-wine sauce, chicken Pontalba, shrimp Clemenceau, bananas Foster. Superb wine list, especially the bordeaux. *Note:* Brennan's is the most widely known rest. in New Orleans—and also one of the most delightful. Standing in the heart of the Vieux Carré, it achieved its greatest triumphs in the 1940s. Since 1973, when the family split into two rival branches (the senior branch now presides over Commander's Palace and Mr. B's), the food has gone noticeably downhill. Now little more than a conventional tourist rest., Brennan's nonetheless retains the unique appeal of its courtyard, shaded by banana palms. Its famous breakfasts are much better than the lunches or dinners. The svce is confused and uninterested. Resv. recommended, but not always honored. *Créole.* **M–E**

♈♈ **Alex Patout's Louisiana Restaurant** (dwntwn), 211 Royal St. (525-7788). A/C. Lunch Mon–Fri, dinner nightly. AE, CB, DC, MC, V. Jkt. *Specialties:* chicken and sausage gumbo, tournedos à la Alex (w. crayfish-cream sauce and fried eggplant), lady fish (broiled redfish topped w. shrimp and crabmeat), duck w. oyster dressing, sautéed lumb crabmeat, grilled speckled trout wrapped in bacon, pecan pie. *Note:* Longtime chef-owner of the famous Patout's restaurant in New Iberia, La., transferred in 1988 to the heart of the French Quarter, Alex Patout blends his Cajun cooking heritage w. Créole touches from his new surroundings. The result is "Haute Louisiana" cuisine at its best. Elegant atmosphere. Excellent svce. A local favorite. Resv. strongly suggested. *Cajun/Créole.* **M**

K. Paul's Louisiana Kitchen (dwntwn), 416 Chartres St. (942-7500). A/C. Dinner only, Mon–Fri; closed hols. AE. *Specialties:* Cajun popcorn (fried crayfish), jambalaya, shrimp Bayou Tèche, duckling à l'étouffée, blackened redfish, sweet-potato/pecan pie. Menu changes regularly. *Note:* This bistro began the revolution in local gastronomy. The chef, Paul Prudhomme, is a man of weight, both literally and figuratively, who came here from the Commander's Palace; he is the moving cause of the fashion for Louisiana food throughout the U.S. The food here is authentically Cajun, and the ambience relaxed, casual, and fun-loving, w. Formica decor and paper napkins. The svce does not aim to please. Always crowded, w. unavoidable waiting lines (no resv. accepted). Food quality uneven due to repeated absences of chef Prudhomme. *Cajun.* **I–M**

Mike Anderson's (dwntwn), 215 Bourbon St. (524-3884). A/C. Lunch/dinner daily; closed hols. AE, MC, V. *Specialties:* gumbo, crayfish bisque, ragoût of shrimp, catch of the day Créole style, crabmeat au gratin, steak. *Note:* Next door to the famous Galatoire's, Mike Anderson's is a godsend for those who are tired of the latter's long waiting lines. While it doesn't pretend to rival Galatoire's perfection, Mike Anderson's Créole dishes and Louisiana-style fish are definitely praiseworthy. Pleasant nautical decor w. huge aquariums. Diligent svce. *Seafood/Créole.* **I–M**

Pascal's Manale (nr. dwntwn), 1838 Napoleon Ave. (895-4887). A/C. Lunch Mon–Fri, dinner nightly; closed Dec 25. AE, CB, DC, MC, V. *Specialties:* barbecued shrimp, crabmeat Rockefeller, gumbo, spaghetti Collins, veal au marsala, snapper Catherine (w. hollandaise sauce). Skimpy wine list. *Note:* Another old (1913) landmark of local good food, which harmoniously blends the Créole influence into a basically Italian repertory. What matters here is the food, not the setting or the svce. Generally crowded and noisy; resv. rarely honored, so long waits are inevitable, especially at wknds. Not a good neighborhood at night; take a cab. *Créole/Italian.* **I–M**

Acme Oyster House (dwntwn), 724 Iberville St. (522-5973). A/C. Lunch/dinner Mon–Sat; closed hols. AE, MC, V. *Specialties:* oysters, "poor boys" (Créole sandwiches), fried catfish, gumbo, oyster loaf. Draft beer. *Note:* The most representative of the Vieux Carré's oyster bars; the belons, Blue Points, Whitstables, Plaquemines, and so forth are fresh from the sea, and opened under your very eyes. Connoisseurs eat them standing, leaning an elbow on the old counter, and wash them down w. a draft beer. Relaxed atmosphere, full of local color. *Seafood/Créole.* **B–I**

Eddie's (nr. dwntwn), 2119 Law St. (945-2207). A/C. Lunch/dinner Mon–Sat (until midnight); closed hols. AE, MC, V. *Specialties:* seafood gumbo, pork chop stuffed w. oysters, Créole fried chicken, red beans and rice w. sausage, bread pudding w. whisky. *Note:* This little rest., tucked away in a nondescript building in the African American district of Gentilly is not easy to find, but it offers Créole food as authentic and tasty as you could ever hope for. Unpretentious decor but friendly reception and svce. One of the best underground-gourmet places in New Orleans. 10 min. from dwntwn. (take a cab). *Créole.* **B–I**

Gumbo Shop (nr. dwntwn), 630 St. Peter St. (525-1486). A/C. Lunch/dinner daily; closed hols. AE, CB, DC, MC, V. *Specialties:* crayfish bisque, seafood gumbo, red beans w. rice, shrimp remoulade, sandwiches, good homemade ice cream (try the praline sundae). *Note:* Delightful little Créole bistro serving some of the best seafood gumbo in town. The fresh-fruit daiquiris are outstanding, too. Relaxed, inviting atmosphere, a hop, skip, and jump from Jackson Sq. in the heart of the Old Quarter. Lots of tourists. *Créole.* **B**

Mandina's (nr. dwntwn), 3800 Canal St. (482-9179). A/C. Lunch/dinner daily. No credit cards. *Specialties:* poor boy sandwiches, shrimp remoulade, spaghetti w. meatballs, gumbo, jambalaya, fried soft-shell crabs, Dobergé cake. *Note:* The king of the "poor boy" (a roast beef or sausage sandwich), also serving other commendable Créole dishes. Crowded at lunchtime, this likable neighborhood rest. nonetheless represents one of the best values in the entire city. The atmosphere and the svce are unaffected and unconstrained. *Créole.* **B**

Mother's (dwntwn), 401 Poydras St. (523-9656). A/C. Breakfast/lunch/dinner daily; closed hols. No credit cards. *Specialties:* Ferdi (a roast-beef and ham "poor boy" sandwich with "débris" sauce), crayfish étouffée, red beans and rice w. sausage, sandwiches, seafood gumbo, sweet-potato pie. Beer on draft. *Note:* For almost half a century this has been a local landmark for its wonderful "poor boys" and tasty Créole food. Distinctive bistro atmosphere, often w. long waiting lines at lunch. The servings (particularly the "poor boys") are generous. A fine place right in the business district. *Créole.* **B**

Restaurants in the Vicinity

La Provence (vic.), on U.S. 190 in Lacombe (626-7662). A/C. Lunch Wed–Fri, dinner Wed–Sun; closed Dec 25 and the month of Sept. AE, MC, V. Jkt. *Specialties:* salmon mousse, quail gumbo, sweetbreads w. crayfish sauce, duck w. Madagascar green peppercorns, steak au poivre Robert Aymes, rack of lamb w. herbs from Provence. Handsome wine list at decent prices. *Note:* In spite of his name, Chris Kerageorgiou is from France, and what's more, from Provence. His remarkable and wholly French cuisine can accommodate itself to influences of Greek and Créole origin. Agreeable country setting; romantic atmosphere and dedicated svce. Successful enough that you'll need resv. 40 min. from dwntwn. along the spectacular Pontchartrain Causeway. A fine place. *French.* **M**

Mosca's (vic.), 4137 U.S. 90W in Waggaman, 5 mi. (8km) west of the Huey Long Bridge (436-9942). A/C. Dinner only, Tues–Sat; closed hols. No credit cards. *Specialties:* baked oysters Mosca, marinated crabmeat salad, spaghetti bordelaise, shrimp à l'Italienne, chicken cacciatore, game (in season). Unimpressive wine list. *Note:* The most original Italian rest. in Louisiana. The unpretentious white building, w. its rather shabby decor, is a full 20 min. by car from dwntwn and hard to find after nightfall. But the marriage of Italian and Créole cuisines achieved by the Mosca family reaches a perfection unequalled anywhere else, particularly in the fresh homemade pastas. The servings are generous, the svce efficient and casual. Often crowded and noisy, so resv. are definitely advised (but none are accepted on Sat). *Créole/Italian.* **I–M**

Cafeterias/Fast Food/Specialty Spots

Café du Monde (dwntwn), 800 Decatur St., at St. Anne St. (581-2914). Old café inside the French Market, open round the clock 7 days a week, and immensely popular. The beignets (French doughnuts) are renowned. There's an inviting terrace. A New Orleans classic since the 1860s. No credit cards.

Camellia Grill (nr. dwntwn), 626 S. Carrolton Ave. (866-9573). Breakfast/lunch/dinner daily (till 1am). No credit cards. Noteworthy for all kinds of omelets (try the cheese or the chili). Also very good sandwiches, cheeseburgers, and homemade pastries; the pecan pie is not to be missed. Engaging atmosphere, locally popular far into the night. Take the St. Charles Ave. streetcar to Carrollton Ave., a 25-min. ride.

Central Grocery (dwntwn), 923 Decatur St. (523-1620). Authentic turn-of-the-century grocery carrying foods of all nations. It prides itself on having originated the famous "muffuletta sandwich"—ham, mozzarella, salami, provolone, and mortadella on a hard roll. Local color (and aroma) guaranteed. Open 8am–5pm daily. No credit cards.

BARS & NIGHTCLUBS

Blue Room (dwntwn), in the Fairmont Hotel (see "Accommodations," above) (529-4744). Very preppy nightclub; dancing over dinner to a big band. Big-name stars. Open daily.

City Lights (nr. dwntwn), 310 Howard Ave. at St. Peter St. (568-1700). The fashionable disco joint in the old warehouse district. Elegantly modern setting; trendy crowd. Valet parking. Open Tues–Sat.

Denim n' Diamonds (nr. dwntwn), 1 Galleria Rd., Metairie (836-5055). The fashionable country-and-western club; wear jeans and boots! Open Wed-Sat.

Flagons (nr. dwntwn), 3222 Magazine St. (895-6471). Popular wine bar and early 1900s-style bistro. A favorite of the young professional crowd, on the edge of the Garden District. Open nightly.

Lulu White's Mahogany Hall (dwntwn), 309 Bourbon St. (525-5595). New Orleans jazz by the well-known Dukes of Dixieland. Decor reminiscent of an old speakeasy of the 1920s. Open nightly.

Maple Leaf Bar (vic.), 8316 Oak St. (866-9359). The local shrine of Cajun music, rhythm and blues. Generally crowded, especially when Beausoleil, the top group in the Cajun music hit parade, plays for its multitude of fans. Exciting ambience. Open nightly.

Muddy Waters (dwntwn), 8301 Oak Ave. (866-7174). Excellent live rock in a relaxed, youthful atmosphere; open daily.

Napoleon House (dwntwn), 500 Chartres St. (524-9752). Comfortable, intimate bar serving very good cocktails and fast meals (muffuletta sandwiches). The period decor is of guaranteed authenticity (see "Historic Buildings," above).

Old Absinthe Bar (dwntwn), 400 Bourbon St. (525-8108). In the 1920s it was a speakeasy; now it's an excellent club offering modern jazz, rhythm and blues; the biggest stars appear here regularly. Very popular locally. Open nightly.

Old Absinthe House (dwntwn), 240 Bourbon St. (523-3181). The oldest (1806) and best-known bar in the Vieux Carré, its walls papered with thousands of visiting cards from patrons around the world. Always crowded, but don't fail to pay your respects (see "Historic Buildings," above). Open nightly.

Parade (dwntwn), 801 Bourbon St. (529-2107). Gay disco bar, open around the clock.

Pat O'Brien's (dwntwn), 718 St. Peter St. (525-4823). The piano bar is noisy, but there's a pretty, shaded courtyard. The cocktails are good (try the aptly named "Hurricane"). Open nightly till 4am. The busiest bar in the French Quarter.

Pete Fountain's (nr. dwntwn), in the Hilton Hotel (see "Accommodations," above) (523-4374). New Orleans jazz by the renowned clarinettist Pete Fountain. Open Tues–Sat.

Preservation Hall (dwntwn), 726 St. Peter St. (523-8939). The principal shrine of New Orleans jazz. No refreshments. Concerts nightly. See "Historic Buildings," above.

Snug Harbor (dwntwn), 626 Frenchmen St. (949-0696). Very good modern-jazz club just outside the French Quarter. Also rest. Open nightly.

Storyville Jazz Hall (dwntwn), 1104 Decatur St. (525-8199). A sort of friendlier, more comfortable Preservation Hall, with authentic New Orleans jazz, but also blues and rock. Open Mon–Sat.

Tipitina's (nr. dwntwn), 501 Napoleon Ave. (897-3943). Disco, jazz, Cajun music; very far from smart, but definitely amusing. Very popular locally. 15 min. from dwntwn. Open nightly. Also rest.

Tyler's Beer Garden (nr. dwntwn), 5234 Magazine St. (891-4989). Locally popular oyster bar open late; also contemporary live jazz and rock Thurs–Sat. 15 min. from dwntwn. Open nightly.

NEARBY EXCURSIONS

☀☖ **LAKE PONTCHARTRAIN** (north of the city, reached via Pontchartrain Expwy. and West End Blvd. or by Elysian Fields Ave.): A saltwater lake 40 by 25 mi. (64 by 40km) in extent, and nowhere more than 20 ft. (6m) deep. Ideal for fishing, water sports, and swimming, with many inviting beaches. Scenic drive along Lake Shore Dr. and Hayne Blvd. And don't miss the ☀☖☖ **Lake Pontchartrain Causeway,** a spectacular over-water toll road opened in 1969, whose two separate but parallel highways run 24 mi. (39km) from one shore of the lake to the other. This is the longest highway bridge in the world, and a riveting sight.

FARTHER AFIELD

☖☖ **CAJUN COUNTRY** (420 mi./672km r.t. via U.S. 90W, U.S. 167N, U.S. 190E, La. 1S, and U.S. 90E): After two centuries, the Cajun country still has some 400,000 French-speaking inhabitants, descendants of the Acadian colonists expelled from Canada by the British in 1755. (The word "Cajun" was originally written "Acadian," and referred to the people of the former French territories in Canada; local pronunciation modified it first to "Cadian," then to "Cagian," and finally to the present "Cajun.")

You begin your tour at **Houma,** capital of Terrebonne Parish (a parish is the Louisiana equivalent of a county), an old fishing port specializing in shellfish and dubbed "the Venice of America." Visit the ☖ **Southdown Plantation,** a hybrid of Greek Revival and Victorian traditions built in the latter part of the 19th century and now a museum of Cajun history; it's on La. 311W (504/851-0154), and open daily. Then on to **Morgan City,** an important shrimping harbor, and headquarters for offshore oil exploration. Here you should see the **Swamp Gardens,** a strange marshy botanic garden with foot trails (Heritage Park). On your way to **New Iberia,** founded as its name indicates during the Spanish supremacy in Louisiana, don't fail to stop off at ☀☖☖ **Oaklawn Manor Plantation** in Franklin, a sumptuous 1830s dwelling in lovely gardens on Bayou Tèche; you'll find it on U.S. 90 (318/828-0434); open daily. There are several other attractions worth stopping for at New Iberia: the pretty Bouligny Plaza at the town's center; **Shadows-on-the-Tèche,** 317 E. Main St. (504/369-6446), open daily, a fine 1834 classical revival plantation house; **Avery Island,** birthplace of Tabasco, a big salty island where you should look for ☀☖☖ **Jungle Gardens,** a riot of azaleas, camellias, and tropical plants as well as a wildlife refuge for migratory birds, on La. 329; open daily. Another extraordinary garden nearby is **Live Oak Gardens** on La. 14 in Jefferson Island, open daily; the moss-overgrown trees for which it is named are more than a century old.

Your next stop will be at ☀ **St. Martinville,** the most French of Cajun towns, renowned for its "butcher's festival" the Sun before Mardi Gras. Founded in 1760 by those Acadian immigrants whose tribulations inspired Longfellow to write his *Evangeline,* this charming little town straight out of old France was once known as "little Paris" because of its splendidly worldly way of life. There is a fine ☖ **Church of St. Martin of Tours** at 103 Main St., with memorabilia of Louis XVI and Marie Antoinette.

Nine miles (14km) north is ☀ **Lafayette,** capital of the new Acadia, a busy commercial center almost half of whose inhabitants are French-speaking. Visit the **Lafayette Museum** at 1122 Lafayette St. (318/234-2208), open Tues–Sun, in what used to be the home of Alexandre Mouton, the first governor of Louisiana (1836); also the interesting **Acadian Village** on U.S. 167 (318/981-2364), open daily, with its scrupulously restored 19th-century buildings. A local festival you should try to catch is the ⚖⚖ **Acadian Festival** in mid-Sept: 2 days of music and culinary delights. For further information, contact the LaFayette Convention & Visitors Commission, 16th St. at Evangeline Thrwy. (318/232-3808).

Now you proceed to ⚖ **Opelousas**, another center of the Acadian influence in Louisiana, with its charming antebellum houses and its museum dedicated to Jim Bowie, a hero of the Battle of the Alamo, who lived for a time in this area: **Jim Bowie Museum,** U.S. 190W and Academy St., open Mon–Fri.

On your way back to New Orleans, don't fail to visit **Baton Rouge,** the state capital (see "Plantation Country," below), making a detour to take in ☼⚖⚖ **Madewood Plantation House** on La. 308 near Napoleonville, an 1846 plantation which is one of the best preserved in the entire South (504/524-1988), open daily.

Allow 4–5 days for this trip, which will give you a good idea of this little "France in the Southland," little known but extremely picturesque. If you'd like to learn more about the defense of the French language in Cajun country, and cultural activities in the area, contact **Codofil,** 217 W. Main St., Lafayette, LA 70501 (318/265-5810).

Where to Stay En Route

IN LAFAYETTE 🍸🍸**Acadiana,** 1801 W. Pinhook Rd., Lafayette, LA 70508 (318/233-8120). 300 rms. Modern, friendly hotel. **I–M**

🍸🍸 **Lafayette Hilton and Towers,** 1521 Pinhook Rd., Lafayette, LA 70508 (318/235-6111). 328 rms. Big, modern 15-story glass tower. **M–E**

🍸 **La Quinta Motor Inn,** 2100 NE Evangeline Thrwy., Lafayette, LA 70501 (318/233-5610). 139 rms. Conventional but comfortable motel. **I**

🍸 **Motel 6,** 2724 NE Evangeline Thrwy., La Fayette, LA 70501 (318/233-2055). 101 rms. Brand-new budget motel. **B**

IN NEW IBERIA ☼ 🍸🍸**Mintemere Plantation,** 1400 E. Main St., New Iberia, LA 70560 (318/364-6210). 5 rms w. a charm all their own, in an authentic 19th-century plantation house. No credit cards. **E**

🍸🍸 **Holiday Inn,** 2801 Center St., New Iberia, LA 70560 (318/367-1201). 180 rms. A Holiday Inn modern style. **I**

🍸 **Best Western,** 2700 Center St., New Iberia, LA 70501 (318/364-3030). 103 rms. Well-run classical motel. **I**

Where to Eat En Route

IN BREAUX BRIDGE 🍽🍽 **Mulate's,** 325 Mills Ave. (La. 94) (318/332-4648). Breakfast/lunch/dinner daily. AE, MC, V. Excellent Cajun food. Dancing. Truly a local institution. **B–I**

IN HENDERSON 🍽🍽**Robin's,** La. 352 (318/228-7594). Lunch/dinner daily. AE, CB, DC, MC, V. One of the best places to eat in Cajun country. **B–I**

IN LAFAYETTE 🍽🍽 **Café Vermilionville,** 1304 Pinhook Rd. (318/237-0100). Lunch Mon–Fri, dinner nightly, jazz brunch Sun. AE, MC, V. The oldest (1800) rest. in Lafayette, w. excellent Cajun food. **B–I**

🍽🍽 **Don's Seafood,** 301 E. Vermilion St. (318/235-3551). Lunch/dinner daily. AE, CB, DC, MC, V. Very good Cajun-style fish and broiled steak. **B–I**

🍽 **Randol's,** 2320 Kaliste Saloom Rd. (318/981-7080). Lunch/dinner daily. MC, V. The place is famous for crab. **B–I**

GULF COAST, FROM NEW ORLEANS TO MOBILE, ALABAMA

(330 mi./528km r.t. via I-10E, Miss. 607S, U.S. 90E, Miss. 163S, Miss. 188N, and I-10W): Fine shorescapes and historic seafaring towns make this trip a natural extension of your visit to New Orleans.

You begin with a dive into the future at the ※ **J. C. Stennis National Space Technology Laboratories** (601/688-2370), NASA's second-largest research center, where all space-vehicle engines are tested. It's near Pearlington at Exit 2 from I-10; open daily. Then take a scenic ocean drive along I-90 through the beach resorts of **Bay St. Louis, Pass Christian,** and **Long Beach,** with their luxurious seaside homes once thronged by rich southern families, and on to **Gulfport** and its celebrated **Marine Life Aquarium,** in the Small Craft Harbor (601/863-0651), open daily.

Don't miss the excursion to ※ **Gulf Islands National Seashore** and a visit to ※ **Old Fort Massachusetts,** an imposing defense work constructed 1859–66. It was on these islands, the cradle of French-speaking civilization in the southern U.S. from 1699 to 1753, that in 1721 there disembarked 80 "casket girls," who came from France with their dowries and their trousseaux to ensure that Louisiana should not remain unpopulated. Fort Massachusetts was used for a while as a prisoner-of-war camp for Confederate soldiers during the War Between the States. You reach it from Gulfport on the *Pan American Clipper*, Small Craft Harbor (601/684-1014); it's open daily from mid-May through Aug.

Drive on to the lovely ▲ **home of Jefferson Davis,** president of the Confederacy, on W. Beach Blvd. in Beauvoir (601/388-1313), now a museum, open daily. Nearby, at ▲ **Biloxi,** a very busy shrimp-and-oyster port founded by the French in 1699, there are many lovely old houses standing in stunning tropical gardens. The town also has beaches so magnificent that in summer it becomes a much-sought-after resort.

Farther east, at ▲ **Pascagoula** with its "singing river" (the Pascagoula River gives off a strange sound, something like a swarm of bees, particularly on summer and fall evenings), visit the Old Spanish Fort (1718), which in spite of its name was built by the French, and is splendidly preserved; it's at 4602 Fort St. (601/769-1505), and is open Fri–Wed.

At the end of your journey you'll have time for a detailed inspection of ※▲▲ **Mobile,** with its old neighborhoods full of fine colonial houses in the French style, and gardens where the azaleas bloom Feb–Apr; look for these around Church St., de Tonti Sq., and Old Dauphinway. See Fort Condé, built by the French in 1724, at 150 S. Royal St., open daily; the Cathedral of the Immaculate Conception at Dauphin St. at Clairborne St., an imposing Greek Revival basilica dating from 1835, open daily; Oakleigh, a magnificent antebellum mansion which derives its name from the centuries-old oaks in its very lovely gardens, 350 Oakleigh Pl. at Savannah St. (205/432-1281), open daily; and the majestic battleship ※ **U.S.S. Alabama,** covered with glory from World War II and the Korean War, which lies at anchor opposite the harbor, on Battleship Pkwy. via the George C. Wallace Tunnels (205/433-2703), open daily. For further information, contact the **Mobile Convention & Visitors Bureau,** 63 S. Royal St. (205/433-5100).

On the way back to New Orleans, make a detour via ※ **Bellingrath Gardens and Home,** 20 mi. (32km) south of Mobile, to see its sumptuous gardens planted with hundreds of different varieties of flowers, including 250,000 azaleas, some of which were brought from France in 1754; it's on Bellingrath Hwy. at Mon Louis (205/973-2217), open daily. Near ▲ **Dauphin Island,** a well-known resort town, on August 5, 1864, was fought the sea battle that led to the blockade of Mobile Bay by a Union fleet under the command of Adm. David G. Farragut. Visit Fort Gaines, captured by Union troops on August 23, 1864. Wonderful fine-sand beaches and a bird sanctuary.

This is a very full 4- to 5-day trip.

Where to Stay En Route

IN BILOXI ♟♟ **Royal d'Iberville,** 1980 W. Beach Blvd., Biloxi, MS 39531 (601/ 388-6610). 264 rms. Comfortable luxury hotel on the ocean. **M–E**

IN MOBILE ♟♟♟ **Stouffer Riverview Plaza,** 64 Water St., Mobile, AL 36602 (205/438-4000). 375 rms. Ultramodern 28-floor tower. **M–E**

♒♟♟ **Malaga Inn,** 359 Church St., Mobile, AL 36602 (205/438-4701). 40 rms. Charming 1862 home designated as a historic monument. **I–M**

Where to Eat En Route

IN BILOXI ♒♟♟ **Mary Mahoney's Old French House,** Rue Magnolia and Rue Water (601/374-0163). Lunch/dinner Mon–Sat. Créole and Cajun specialties in a charming upper-class home dating from 1737. **B–I**

PLANTATION COUNTRY (285 mi./456km r.t. via U.S. 90W, La. 18W, La. 1N, U.S. 61N, La. 66N, La. 10E, La. 68S, U.S. 61S, La. 30S, La. 75E, La. 44S, U.S. 61S, and La. 48S): Settled from the beginning of the 18th century by planters, wealthy Créole gentry of French or Spanish origin who exported to Europe the cotton, tobacco, rice, and indigo raised by armies of slaves, the lower Mississippi Valley still displays its garland of luxurious plantations as silent witness of an urbane, elegant past. Your 3-day journey through some of the finest plantations in Louisiana begins with a visit to ♒♒♒ **Oak Alley Plantation,** on La. 18 at Vacherie (504/523-4351), open daily. Built in 1839 by a rich French sugar planter, Jacques Telesphore Roman, it has been called "the queen of Louisiana plantations" because of its elegant Doric design and the extraordinary span of 300-year-old oak trees that overshadow its main driveway.

Then on to ♒♒♒ **Nottoway Plantation,** on La. 1 at White Castle (504/ 525-2730), open daily. With 64 rooms, this is the largest plantation home in the Southland, built in a gracious blend of Italianate and Greek Revival styles, with a double staircase in the hallway, an impressive ballroom, and a columned front (c. 1859).

As you pass, admire the **Plaquemine Locks** on Main St. at Plaquemine, huge locks built at the beginning of the 20th century with a lookout tower rising above the Mississippi (504/687-8159), open Wed–Sun. La. 1 takes you on to ♒ **Baton Rouge,** the capital of Louisiana. Take a look at "Catfish Town," a huge, picturesque covered market in what were once warehouses along the Mississippi, now with dozens of shops and restaurants; it's on Government St. on the River Front (504/346-8888), open daily. You should also see the ♒ **State Capitol,** dominated by its massive 450-ft. (135m) tower built in 1932 with stone and marble from many countries; from its summit there is an all-around view of the city. It's at Riverside Mall and Spanish Town Rd. (504/342-7317), open daily. Two museums you must certainly see are the ♒ **Louisiana Arts and Science Center,** occupying a splendid old railroad station no longer in use, at 100 S. River Rd. (504/344-9463), open Tues–Sun; and the ♒ **Louisiana State University Rural Life Museum,** where you'll find a score of buildings and craftsmen's workshops from the 19th century, at 6200 Burden Lane at the junction of I-10 (504/ 765-2437), open Mon–Fri.

Drive on to ♒♒ **Port Hudson Battlefield,** on U.S. 61, 14 mi. (22km) north of Baton Rouge, scene of the longest (and one of the bloodiest) sieges of the Civil War, where 6,800 Confederate troops held off 30,000–40,000 Union soldiers from May 23 to July 9, 1863. Observation towers, museum (504/654-3775). Open daily.

A little farther north, stop at ☀ **St. Francisville,** with its charming old houses dating from the day when this little town, built on a ridge overlooking the river, was an important staging point for traffic traveling the Mississippi between New Orleans and Natchez. In the countryside around are many very beautiful plantations, including the 1830 ☀🏠 **Greenwood Plantation,** regarded as the most perfect example of the southern colonial style of architecture; many movies have been made here. It's on Highland Rd. (504/655-4475), open daily. Also 🏠 **Myrtles Plantation,** dubbed "America's Most Haunted House," with its fine wrought-iron balustrade running the whole length of the veranda, on U.S. 61 (504/635-6277), open daily; ☀🏠 **Rosedown Plantation,** built in 1835, one of Louisiana's most sumptuous antebellum homes, standing in superb formal gardens in the French style, on La. 10 (504/635-3332), open daily; and 🏠 **Asphodel Plantation,** built 1820–33, the setting for the Paul Newman/Joanne Woodward movie *The Long Hot Summer,* on La. 68 (504/654-6868), open Mon–Fri.

After returning to Baton Rouge, your route follows the curves of the Mississippi and brings your journey to a close with visits to five of Louisiana's most famous plantations. These are, in order:

☀🏠 **Ashland–Belle Hélène,** which, standing behind its majestic two-story colonnade, perpetuates the lordly, romantic classicism of the Old South; on La. 75 between Geismar and Darrow (504/473-1328), open daily.

☀🏠 **Houmas House Plantation,** on La. 942 at Burnside (504/473-7841), open daily, a sugar plantation built in 1840 in splendid Greek Revival style, with beautiful antique furniture.

🏠 **Tezcuco Plantation,** on La. 44 in Darrow (504/562-3929), open daily, a lovely building with wrought-iron-trimmed galleries, ornate friezes, and medallions, now designated as a historic monument.

☀🏠 **San Francisco Plantation,** La. 44 at Garyville (504/535-2341), open daily, an elegant 1856 Gothic Revival plantation house with a magnificent grand staircase and ornate interior decoration.

Finally we come to ☀🏠 **Destrehan Plantation,** on La. 48 at Destrehan (504/764-9315), open daily, the oldest intact plantation in the Mississippi Delta.

This itinerary is expressly designed for those who love vivid glimpses of the past; don't miss it.

Where to Stay En Route

IN BATON ROUGE 🍷🍷🍷 **Embassy Suites,** 4914 Constitution Ave., Baton Rouge, LA 70808 (504/924-6566). 224 suites. Very modern suites-only hotel. **M–E**

☀🍷🍷 **Mt. Hope Plantation,** 8151 Highland Rd., Baton Rouge, LA 70802 (504/766-8600). 10 rms. Authentic Old South–style plantation house built in 1817. **M**

IN JACKSON ☀🍷🍷 **Asphodel Plantation,** La. 68, Jackson, LA 70748 (504/654-6868). 18 rms. A luxurious 1830s antebellum home. **M–E**

🍷 **Glencoe,** La. 68, Jackson, LA 70748 (504/629-5387). 8 rms. Fine example of late Victorian Gothic. **M–E**

IN ST. FRANCISVILLE ☀🍷🍷 **Cottage Plantation,** U.S. 61, St. Francisville, LA 70775 (504/635-3674). 12 rms. Typical Louisiana plantation house dating from 1795. **M**

🍷 **St. Francisville Inn,** 118 N. Commerce St., St. Francisville, LA 70775 (504/635-6502). 8 rms. Big Victorian home in a very handsome park. **M**

IN WHITE CASTLE ☀🍷🍷 **Nottoway Plantation,** La. 1, White Castle, LA 70788 (504/545-2730). 12 rms. Louisiana's largest plantation house, and one of its most beautiful. Also very good rest. **E**

Where to Eat En Route

IN BATON ROUGE ☨☨☨ **Chalet Brandt,** 7655 Old Hammond Hwy. (504/927-6040). Dinner only, Tues–Sat. The fish soup and the veal w. chanterelle and morel mushrooms are among the successful achievements of this excellent Continental/Créole rest. and its Swiss chef-owner Charles Brandt. Pretty interior. **I–M**

IN BURNSIDE ☨ **The Cabin,** La. 44 and La. 22 (504/473-3007). Lunch daily, dinner Thurs–Sat. Excellent fish and Créole dishes in former slave quarters a century and a half old. **I**

IN DONALDSONVILLE ☀☨ **Lafitte's Landing,** Sunshine Bridge Service Rd. (504/473-1232). Lunch daily, dinner Tues–Sun. Remarkable Créole and Cajun food by chef John Folse. The building on the bank of the Mississippi, dating from 1797, may once have belonged to pirate Jean Lafitte. **I**

CHAPTER 16

FLORIDA'S EAST COAST ♙♙

□ □ □

Florida's Atlantic coast, where swimsuits and suntan oil hold undisputed sway, unrolls its hundreds of miles of white sand beaches and coconut trees from **Amelia Island** on the Georgia border in the north to **Miami** in the south. It has remarkably comprehensive facilities to offer vacationers, often at very attractive prices—as witness the arrival every year of some 25 million U.S. tourists (mostly from the big cities of the Northeast), more than a million Canadians, and some hundreds of thousands of visitors from Europe and Latin America. In reality, the great beach resorts of **Daytona Beach** (famous for its auto races), the elegant and upscale **Palm Beach,** the more easy-going **Fort Lauderdale** and **Pompano Beach, Boca Raton,** and **Miami** (see Chapter 19 on Miami) form a single agglomeration of hotels—one of the largest in the world.

But Florida (discovered by Juan Ponce de León on Easter Sunday 1513, it owes its name to this accident of the calendar—the Spanish for "Easter Sunday" is *Pascua Florida*) is more than a string of immaculate beaches, wild mangrove swamps, or a network of fish-filled lakes and rivers. It boasts some of America's most popular tourist attractions. **St. Augustine,** the oldest city in the United States, was founded by the Spanish conquistador Don Pedro Menéndez de Avilés in 1565—just 19 years after Sir Walter Raleigh's short-lived attempt to settle Roanoke Island, "the lost colony," and 55 years before the British colonists disembarked from the *Mayflower* at Plymouth. **Marineland** is the oldest marine zoo in the world and one of the most popular. The **Kennedy Space Center,** headquarters of the astronauts, has been internationally famous since the moon landing and the first shuttle launches. **Lake Okeechobee,** one of the largest freshwater lakes in the country (30 by 40 mi./60 by 48km), is a paradise for bass and catfish fishermen. **Daytona Beach** is a popular resort, invaded every year by tens of thousands of car-racing enthusiasts come to watch the Daytona 24 Hours, the Daytona 500, and other famous races.

Finally, less than 2 hr. by car from the Atlantic coast, three of the world's greatest theme parks await the tourist: the Magic Kingdom of **Walt Disney World;** its twin attraction, **Epcot,** the amazing 21st-century amusement park whose 18-story steel-and-concrete sphere has become the new symbol of the state of Florida; and the brand-new **Disney–MGM Studios,** a movie theme park which blends filmmaking with backstage studio tours and ride-through, walk-through attractions. And let's not forget **Sea World,** an enormous marine zoo where sharks, killer whales, and dolphins frolic in the public gaze (see Chapter 18 on Orlando).

BASIC FACTS: State of Florida. Area codes: 904 (St. Augustine and Daytona Beach); 305 or 407 (all others). Time zone: eastern. Founded in: 1565 (St. Augustine), 1567 (first Spanish garrison at Miami). Distance from Amelia Island to Miami Beach: approx. 400 mi. (640km).

CLIMATE: Florida is well known for its sunshine. Winter is the ideal time for a visit—also the most crowded and expensive. The sun shines continually and the mercury swings between 60° and 68°F (16° and 20°C)—perfect for walking, even if too cool for swimming. Summer is hot and humid, with short but frequent tropical downpours, not to speak of prowling hurricanes. Spring and autumn are consistently sunny and pleasant, justifying the legend on Florida auto registration plates which reads "The Sunshine State."

ARRIVAL & TRANSIT INFORMATION

AIRPORTS: There are seven major airports that act as gateways to the Florida east coast:
   Daytona Beach Regional Airport (DAB), 5 mi. (8km) west of Daytona.
   Fort Lauderdale–Hollywood International Airport (FLL), 6 mi. (9.5km) south of Fort Lauderdale.
   Jacksonville International Airport (JAX), 15 mi. (24km) north of Jacksonville.
   Melbourne Regional Airport (MLB), 1 mi. (2km) NW of Melbourne.
   Miami International Airport (MIA) (see Chapter 19 on Miami).
   Orlando International Airport (MCO) (see Chapter 18 on Orlando).
   West Palm Beach International Airport (PBI), 3 mi. (5km) west of West Palm Beach.

AIRLINES: **Fort Lauderdale**—American (467-3040), Continental (525-4126), Delta (763-2211), Eastern (463-1515), Northwest (525-7204), TWA (522-1100), United (525-7321), and USAir (toll free 800/428-4322).
   Jacksonville—American (354-2593), Continental (354-3452), Delta (398-3011), Eastern (355-7392), TWA (toll free 800/221-2000), United (toll free 800/241-6522), and USAir (toll free 800/428-4322).
   Miami—See Chapter 19 on Miami.
   Orlando—See Chapter 18 on Orlando.

CAR RENTAL: To cover this large area adequately you will need a car, and besides, rental rates are comparatively reasonable. In addition to the many car-rental agencies in **Miami** and **Orlando** (see those chapters for details), rentals are available at the following gateway cities (at airport locations unless otherwise noted):
   Fort Lauderdale—Avis (359-3250); Budget, 1501 N. Federal Hwy. (921-8585); Dollar (525-2604); Econo Car, 2125 S. Federal Hwy. (763-7369); Hertz (525-5281); National (525-3634).
   Jacksonville—Avis (741-2327); Budget (741-3555); Hertz (741-2151); National (741-7581); Thrifty (741-3366).

TRAIN: In addition to the Amtrak stations in Miami and Orlando (see those chapters for details), there are stations/stops along the Florida east coast at 200 W. 21st Terrace, Fort Lauderdale (toll free 800/872-7245); 3570 Clifford Lane, Jacksonville (904/768-1553); and Tamarind Ave. and Datura St., West Palm Beach (toll free 800/872-7245).

INTERCITY BUSES: In addition to the Greyhound offices in Miami and Orlando (see those chapters for details), there are Florida east coast offices at 138 S. Ridgewood Ave., Daytona Beach (904/255-7076); 513 N.E. 3rd St., Fort Lauderdale (305/764-6551); 10 N. Pearl St., Jacksonville (904/356-1841); 100 Malaga St. at King St., Saint Augustine (904/829-6401); and 100 1st St., West Palm Beach (407/833-8534).

INFORMATION, TOURS & SPECIAL EVENTS

TOURIST INFORMATION: For general information on the region, write or call the **Florida Division of Tourism,** 126 Van Buren St., Tallahassee, FL 32301 (904/487-1462). For more specific information, when in the area, contact:

Boca Raton Chamber of Commerce, 1800 N. Dixie Hwy., Baca Raton, FL 33432 (407/395-4433).

Cocoa Beach Tourism & Convention Council, 400 Fortenberry Rd., Cocoa Beach, FL 32952 (407/452-4390).

Daytona Beach Chamber of Commerce, P.O. Box 2775, Daytona Beach, FL 32015 (904/255-0415).

Fort Lauderdale Convention & Visitors Bureau, 500 E. Broward Blvd., Suite 104, Fort Lauderdale, FL 33394 (305/765-4466).

Grant (see the Melbourne Chamber of Commerce).

Hallandale Chamber of Commerce, P.O. Box 249, Hallandale, FL 33009 (305/454-0541).

Jacksonville Convention & Visitors Bureau, 6 E. Bay St., Suite 200, Jacksonville, FL 32202 (904/353-9736).

Jensen Beach Chamber of Commerce, 1910 Jensen Beach Blvd., Jensen Beach, FL 33457 (407/334-3444).

Kissimmee Convention & Visitors Bureau, 1925 E. Irlo Bronson Memorial Hwy. (P.O. Box 2007), Kissimmee, FL 32742 (407/847-5000).

Melbourne Chamber of Commerce, 1005 E. Strawbridge Ave., Melbourne, FL 32901 (407/724-5400).

Miami Department of Tourism & Conventions (see Chapter 19 on Miami).

Orlando Area Chamber of Commerce (see Chapter 18 on Orlando).

Palm Beach Chamber of Commerce, 45 Coconut Row, Palm Beach, FL 33480 (407/655-3282).

Pompano Beach Chamber of Commerce, 2200 E. Atlantic Blvd., Pompano Beach, FL 33062 (305/941-2940).

St. Augustine Chamber of Commerce, 52 Castillo Dr., St. Augustine, FL 32084 (904/829-5681).

Titusville Chamber of Commerce, 2000 S. Washington St., Titusville, FL 32780 (407/267-3036).

West Palm Beach Chamber of Commerce, 501 N. Flagler Dr., West Palm Beach, FL 33401 (407/833-3711).

GUIDED TOURS: For the Miami and Orlando areas, see the chapters on those cities. In other localities on the Florida east coast, consult the local *Yellow Pages* under "Sightseeing."

SPECIAL EVENTS: For exact dates of the events listed below, check with the chambers of commerce and visitors bureaus listed above under "Tourist Information."

Boca Raton
High Goal Polo (Jan–Apr): A popular polo championship event.

Cocoa Beach
National Surfing Tourneys (Easter and Labor Day).

Daytona Beach
Auto Races: Daytona 24 Hours (early Feb); Daytona 500 (mid-Feb), the nation's big stock-car race.
AMA Motorcycle Races (early Mar).

Stock-car Races: Like the Firecracker 400 (July 4).
Florida International Festival (late July): orchestral and chamber concerts, recitals.

Fort Lauderdale
Winterfest and Boat Parade (Dec): 3 weeks of cultural, artistic, and sporting events culminating in a spectacular parade on the water.

Grant
Seafood Festival (Feb): A gigantic fish, shellfish, and seafood blowout, attracting 50,000 participants to a glutton's festival that lasts 48 hrs.

Hallandale
Seminole Indian Tribal Fair (early Feb): A Native American cultural event in which every tribe in North America participates. Dance displays, handcraft exhibition, ethnic cooking. For information, call 305/583-7112.

Jacksonville
Florida National Jazz Festival (Oct): One of the country's best-known modern-jazz events.

Jensen Beach
Turtle Watch (June–July, every evening): Visitors may see enormous (220–440 lbs./100–200kg and up) sea turtles crossing the sand to lay their eggs at the water's edge.

Kissimmee
Silver Spurs Rodeo (third wknd in Feb, wknd of July 4): For lovers of the real Old West.
Florida State Air Fair (end of Oct to the beginning of Nov): Complete with parachute jumps, aerobatics, etc.

Melbourne Beach
Turtle Crawl (June–Aug): Thousands of newly hatched baby turtles struggling to reach the sea. Spectacular.

Pompano Beach
Boat Parade (July 4 and mid-Dec): The boats are decorated and illuminated.

St. Augustine
Cross & Sword (Mon–Sat mid-June to Sept): A musical celebration of the founding of the city.
Days in Spain (mid-Aug): Processions, shows, and fiesta in honor of the first Spanish conquistadors.

Titusville
Valiant Air Command Air Show (early Mar): The world's greatest air show, featuring exclusively World War II combat planes. Aerobatics, ground displays, etc.

West Palm Beach
Silver Sailfish Derby (mid-Jan to early Feb): Big-game fishing championship events.

SPORTS: The east coast of Florida plays host to five major-league **baseball** teams at their spring training camps (Feb–Mar):
Atlanta Braves, Municipal Stadium, West Palm Beach (407/683-6100).
Los Angeles Dodgers, Holman Stadium, Vero Beach (407/569-4900).

Montréal Expos, Municipal Stadium, West Palm Beach (407/689-9121).
New York Mets, St. Lucie County Sports Complex, Port St. Lucie (407/879-7378).
New York Yankees, Fort Lauderdale Stadium, Fort Lauderdale (305/776-1921).

DEEP-SEA FISHING: Almost three million visitors go deep-sea fishing in Florida every year, from Fernandina Beach to Key West on the Atlantic coast (sea bream, mackerel, barracuda, swordfish), and from Naples to Pensacola along the Gulf of Mexico (blue marlin, tarpon). Rates for fully equipped big-game fishing boats are around $350 for a half day (6 hr.) or $450 for a full day (10 hr.). Some recommendations:
Jacksonville: Ray Barnes (904/744-4771).
Fort Pierce: Ken Moore (407/461-4790).
Fort Lauderdale: Ray McCleary (305/463-1357).

A NORTH TO SOUTH ITINERARY

The section of this guide devoted to the east coast of Florida has been organized as an itinerary, starting at Amelia Island and ending in Miami Beach, a distance of almost 400 miles (640km). You may choose not to drive the whole distance; key towns such as Jacksonville, Daytona, Orlando, Palm Beach, Fort Lauderdale, and Miami are linked by air, bus, and train, and car rentals are available everywhere (at some of the lowest rates in the country, particularly off-season). In that case, you can select from the following travel plan the parts that appeal to you most!

Distances Down the Florida East Coast

From	To	Distance
Amelia Island	Fort Caroline	30 mi. (48km)
Fort Caroline	Jacksonville	14 mi. (22km)
Jacksonville	St. Augustine	40 mi. (64km)
St. Augustine	Fort Matanzas	15 mi. (24km)
Fort Matanzas	Marineland of Florida	5 mi. (7km)
Marineland of Florida	Daytona Beach	32 mi. (51km)
Daytona Beach	Kennedy Space Center	52 mi. (83km)
Kennedy Space Center	Orlando	46 mi. (75km)
Orlando	Sea World	13 mi. (21km)
Sea World	Walt Disney World	7 mi. (11km)
Epcot	Cypress Gardens	34 mi. (54km)
Cypress Gardens	Cocoa Beach	97 mi. (155km)
Cocoa Beach	Patrick AFB	5 mi. (8km)
Patrick AFB	Vero Beach	48 mi. (74km)
Vero Beach	Fort Pierce	14 mi. (22km)
Fort Pierce	Jensen Beach	19 mi. (31km)
Jensen Beach	Lake Okeechobee	39 mi. (62km)
Lake Okeechobee	Jupiter Beach	33 mi. (52km)
Jupiter Beach	Palm Beach	18 mi. (28km)
Palm Beach	Boca Raton	28 mi. (45km)
Boca Raton	Pompano Beach	8 mi. (12km)
Pompano Beach	Fort Lauderdale	7 mi. (11km)
Fort Lauderdale	Hollywood	8 mi. (12km)
Hollywood	Miami Beach	17 mi. (26km)

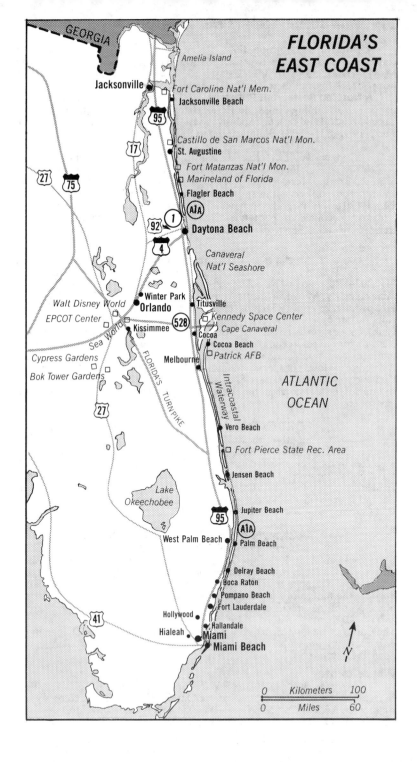

A Note on Accommodations: Room rates along the Florida Coast are coded as follows: **VE,** Very Expensive ($140 and up); **E,** Expensive ($90–$140); **M,** Moderate ($60–$90); **I,** Inexpensive ($30–$60); **B,** Budget (up to $30). A listing of toll free numbers is in the Appendix.

A Note on Restaurant Prices: Along the Florida Coast restaurant prices, per person, excluding drinks and service charges, are coded as follows: **VE,** Very Expensive ($60 and up); **E,** Expensive ($40–$60); **M,** Moderate ($25–$40); **I,** Inexpensive ($15–$25); **B,** Budget (up to $15).

AMELIA ISLAND: By turns French (a group of Huguenots, or French Protestants, led by Jean Ribaut landed here in 1562), Spanish, British, Mexican, and American—and often a stronghold for pirates and other adventurers—this small island is not on the beaten track, but it offers 14 mi. (20km) of magnificent beaches, and is a fisherman's dream. For further information, contact the **Fernandina Beach Chamber of Commerce,** 102 Centre St., Fernandina Beach, FL 32032 (904/261-3248).

Where to Stay

Amelia Island Plantation, 3000 First Coast Hwy. (on Fla. A1A, 6 mi./10km south of Fernandina Beach), Amelia Island, FL 32034 (904/261-6161; toll free 800/874-6878). 625 rms or studios. A/C, cable color TV. Mini-apartments for two to eight people. AE, CB, DC, MC, V. Free parking, 23 pools, 25 tennis courts, three golf courses, putting green, health club, private beach, horseback riding, fishing, bicycles, sauna, rest. (Dune Side Club), coffee shop, bars, rm svce, disco, hrdrsr, beauty parlor, grocery, crib $10. *Note:* Luxurious resort complex in a rustic setting on the ocean, with 4 mi. (6km) of magnificent beaches and more than 1,300 acres (526ha) of dunes and woods. A paradise for lovers of sports and fresh air. Spacious rms or mini-apartments w. kitchenettes and private patios. Reception and svce on the impersonal side—but still one of the best hotels in the Southeast. Interesting vacation packages. **E–VE** (apartments), but lower rates off-season.

FORT CAROLINE: Fort Caroline was erected in 1564 at the mouth of the St. John's River by a party of 300 French colonists under the leadership of René de Laudonnière. A few months later the fort was taken by the Spaniards and its entire garrison (except for 70 women and children) put to the sword. In 1568 the French launched a reprisal raid against the Spaniards and burned the fort to the ground. It was partially rebuilt by the British, and achieved its moment of glory during the Civil War. It's located at 12713 Fort Caroline Rd., Jacksonville (904/641-7155); open daily.

JACKSONVILLE: With its 650,000 inhabitants and cluster of ultramodern skyscrapers along the banks of the St. John's River, Jacksonville is one of the Southeast's busiest ports, handling large shipments of automobiles from Japan and Korea. Very busy airport. In terms of economic growth it ranks 16th among major American cities. The **Mayport Naval Base,** at the mouth of the river, is one of the navy's most important, and the home port of the aircraft carriers U.S.S. *Forrestal* and U.S.S. *Saratoga.* With an area of 840 sq. mi. (2,180km²), Jacksonville is the largest city in area in the U.S. The **Cummer Gallery of Art,** 829 Riverside Ave. (904/356-6857), is an interesting art museum with a collection of 700 pieces of Meissen (Dresden) china; open Tues–Sun.

Where to Stay

Omni Hotel, 245 Water St., Jacksonville, FL 32202 (904/ 355-6664; toll free, see Omni). 354 rms, A/C, color TV, in-rm movies. AE, CB, DC, MC, V. Valet parking $6, pool, health club, two rests., bars, 24-hr. rm svce, disco, boutiques, concierge, free crib. *Note:* Latest of the area's luxury palaces—six stories of austerely postmodern glass and steel at the edge of the St. John's River. Forms part of the new Enterprise Center, a huge complex of office buildings, stores, and rests. Spacious, well-equipped rms w. refrigerators; elegant interior, ultra-professional svce. Strategically located in the heart of dwntwn Jacksonville. Business clientele. Two VIP floors. **E–VE**

Jacksonville Hotel (formerly the Hilton), 565 S. Main St., Jacksonville, FL 32207 (904/398-8800). 292 rms, A/C, color TV, AE, DC, MC, V. Free gar., pool, rest. (Wharf), coffee shop, bar, rm svce, disco, hrdrsr, boutiques, free crib. *Note:* Modern 10-story grand hotel on the bank of the St. John's River. Comfortable rms w. private balconies, the best overlooking the river. Efficient reception and svce. Well located. Group and business clientele. Interesting vacation packages. **E**

Best Western Inn I-95 South, 5221 University Blvd. W., Jacksonville, FL 32216 (904/737-1690; toll free, see Best Western). 187 rms, A/C, color TV, in-rm movies. AE, CB, DC, MC, V. Free parking, pool, tennis court, rest., bar, valet svce, free crib. *Note:* Typical up-to-date motel 10 min. from dwntwn along I-95. Comfortable, homelike rms, friendly svce, inviting garden. Ideal if you're driving. **I**

Motel 6, 6107 Youngerman Circle, Jacksonville, FL 32244 (904/777-6100). 126 rms, A/C, color TV, free in-rm movies. DC, MC, V. Free parking, pool, free crib. *Note:* Ideal for motorists; a good value. **B**

IN NEARBY JACKSONVILLE BEACH **Holiday Inn,** 1617 N. 1st St., Jacksonville Beach, FL 32250 (904/249-9071; toll free, see Holiday Inns). 150 rms, A/C, color TV, in-rm movies. AE, CB, DC, MC, V. Free parking, pool, sauna, health club, two tennis courts, rest. (Kelly's), bar, rm svce, disco, crib $5. *Note:* Standard vacation hotel w. direct access to beach. Functional rms w. balconies and refrigerators; impersonal reception and svce. Typical Holiday Inn style. Tourist clientele. **M–E**

Where to Eat

Crawdaddy's, 1643 Prudential Dr. (904/396-3546). A/C. Lunch Mon–Sat, dinner nightly, brunch Sun. AE, CB, DC, MC, V. *Specialties:* chicken Cajun, jambalaya, seafood gumbo. *Note:* This fisherman's-hut setting will fulfill your wildest dreams of the exotic; the New Orleans cooking is excellent, and the svce attentive. There's dancing too, and the place has a big local following, so resv. are advisable. *Créole.* **I**

Wharf, in the Jacksonville Hotel (see "Where to Stay," above) (904/398-5235). A/C. Breakfast/Lunch/dinner daily. AE, DC, MC, V. Jkt. *Specialties:* shrimp Wellington, roast beef, fish of the day. *Note:* Very creditable hotel rest. w. excellent seafood. Basic maritime decor; efficient svce. Resv. advised. *Continental/Seafood.* **I**

Patti's, 7300 Beach Blvd. (904/725-1662). A/C. Dinner only, nightly; closed Thanksgiving, Dec 25. AE, DC, MC, V. *Specialties:* fresh homemade pasta, lasagne, chicken parmigiana. *Note:* Completely authentic little *trattoria;* food ditto, if a little unimaginative. Locally popular. *Italian.* **I**

ST. AUGUSTINE: The oldest city in the U.S., founded in 1565 by Don Pedro Menéndez de Avilés, this bastion of Spanish colonialism retains a few interesting monuments (scrupulously restored) from its troubled past.

The Sights

Castillo de San Marcos National Monument, Castillo Dr. and Menendez Ave. (904/829-6506): Impressive fortress built in 1672—the oldest masonry fortification in the country—which commands Matanzas Bay. Its 13-ft.-thick (4m) walls make it a weighty symbol of the Spanish military presence in Florida. Splendidly restored. Open daily. Don't miss it.

Casa del Hidalgo, St. George St. and Hypolita St. (904/829-6460): Preserves for us the atmosphere of 17th-century St. Augustine. Open Mon–Fri.

Fountain of Youth, 155 Magnolia Ave. and William St. (904/829-3168): Supposed site of the "Fountain of Youth" discovered by the sailors of Ponce de León in 1513, when they first landed in Florida—making it the first place in North America on which Western Europeans set foot. Native American cemetery and planetarium nearby.

Lightner Museum, Cordova St. and King St. (904/824-2874): Occupying the 300 rooms of the former Alcazar Hotel built in 1888, this museum, bequest of a wealthy Chicago publisher, displays a collection of 19th-century art objects. Open daily.

Oldest House, 14 St. Francis St.: The oldest house (1703) still standing in the city. Open daily.

Oldest Store Museum, 4 Artillery Lane: Amusing 19th-century bazaar, with more than 100,000 period objects on display. Open daily.

Nombre de Dios Mission, San Marco Ave.: Site of the country's oldest mission, where the first mass was celebrated in 1565; its huge stainless-steel cross, the highest in the U.S., rises 192 ft. (60m).

Zorayda Castle, 83 King St. (904/824-3097): A replica, constructed in 1833, of the Alhambra of Granada in Spain. Open daily.

And, especially, don't forget **San Augustin Antiguo** (Old St. Augustine), around St. George St., with its picturesque cobbled alleyways and balconied houses made of the local building material, "coquina," a conglomerate of seashells and sand.

A visit to this city is a must. The **Visitor Information Center** is at 10 Castillo Dr. (904/824-3334).

Where to Stay

Ponce de Leon Resort, 4000 Ponce de Leon Blvd. (U.S. 1), St. Augustine, FL 32085 (904/824-2821; toll free 800/824-2821). 200 rms, A/C, cable color TV. AE, CB, DC, MC, V. Free parking, pool, six tennis courts, golf course, rest., bar, rm svce, nightclub, free airport limo, free crib. *Note:* Excellent value 5 min. by car from the beach or the Old City. Enormous, attractive rms w. balconies. Svce efficient and w. a smile. Interesting American Plan and vacation packages. The golfer's or tennis-player's dream. **M–E**

Comfort Inn, 1111 Ponce de Leon Blvd., St. Augustine, FL 32084 (904/824-5554; toll free 800/228-5150). 84 rms, A/C, color TV, in-rm movies. AE, CB, DC, MC, V. Free parking, pool, free crib. *Note:* A new motel near St. Augustine's Old City. Comfort and facilities up to snuff; cordial reception and svce. Very good value. **I–M,** but lower rates off-season.

Monterey, 16 Avenida Menendez, St. Augustine, FL 32084 (904/824-4482). 59 rms, A/C, cable color TV. AE, CB, DC, MC, V. Free parking, pool, adj. coffee shop, valet service, free airport limo, crib $5. *Note:* Modest but well-run little motel opposite the Castillo San Marcos. The best rms overlook the bay. Interesting vacation packages. **I,** but lower rates off season.

Where to Eat

Raintree, 102 San Marco Ave. (904/824-7211). A/C. Lunch Mon–Fri, dinner daily; closed Dec 25. AE, CB, DC, MC, V. *Specialties:* broiled fresh tuna w. mango butter, scampi Raintree, steak au poivre, broiled Maine lobster, catch of the day. Good homemade desserts (try the lime cheesecake). *Note:* St. Augustine's best rest., in a charming old Victorian-style house, offering simple but tasty food prepared with the finest ingredients. On fine days it's pleasant to eat out in the grdn. Flawless svce, elegant atmosphere; resv. advisable. *Continental.* **I–M**

☆ **Columbia,** 98 St. George St. (904/824-3341). A/C. Lunch/ dinner daily; brunch Sun. AE, CB, DC, MC, V. *Specialties:* black-bean soup, paella, red snapper Alicante. *Note:* Charming early 20th-century *meson* in the Castilian style; Spanish- and Cuban-inspired food at very refreshing prices. Agreeable background music, friendly svce. In the heart of St. Augustine's historic quarter. A local favorite since 1905. *Spanish/Latin American.* **B–I**

🔔 **FORT MATANZAS:** The Spanish name means "Fort of the Massacres," and on the site of this fortified bastion built in 1740 (restored in 1924), more than 250 French Huguenots were indeed massacred by the Spaniards in 1565. Reached by boat from the Visitor Center; open daily. For information, call 904/471-0116. Worth a look.

🔔 **MARINELAND OF FLORIDA** (on Fla. A1A) (904/471-1111): The world's oldest marine zoo, opened in 1938, where hundreds of sharks, barracuda, porpoises, dolphins, moray eels, and the like may be watched through portholes in two enormous pools. Florida's other great sea zoo, Sea World at Orlando (see below), is more up-to-date and definitely more spectacular. Nevertheless, this one is worth going out of your way for. Open daily.

🔔 **DAYTONA BEACH:** A very popular beach resort (particularly among surfers), with 23 mi. (38km) of sand along which cars may drive freely (though slowly) at low tide; there are also dune buggies for hire.

The town is also famous for its auto and stock-car races: the Daytona Sunbank 24 Hours and Daytona 500 in Feb, the Firecracker 400 on July 4, etc. The 🔔 **Daytona International Speedway,** 1801 Speedway Blvd. (904/254-6767), where these events are held, can accommodate 125,000 spectators, and has parking for 35,000 cars! Open to visitors year round.

You should also see the 🔔 **Museum of Arts & Sciences,** 1040 Museum Blvd. (904/255-0285), where a fine collection of Latin American and Caribbean art is displayed in a building of ultramodern design. Open Tues–Sat.

And take in the 🔔 **Ponce de Leon Inlet Lighthouse,** south of the town. Dating from 1884, the 175-ft. (53m) tower has been converted into an original kind of maritime museum (904/761-1821); open daily. Well worth the side trip.

Where to Stay

☆☆☆ **Hilton Daytona,** 2637 S. Atlantic Ave., Daytona Beach, FL 32018 (904/767-7350; toll free, see Hilton). 215 rms, A/C, color TV, in-rm movies. AE, CB, DC, MC, V. Free parking, two pools, two tennis courts, health club, sauna, putting green, boats, rest. (The Roof), coffee shop, bars, rm svce, disco, free crib. *Note:* Rather ponderous modernist structure, but very spacious, comfortable rms w. refrigerators and their own balconies. Every facility of a great resort hotel. Efficient svce. Caters to groups and conventions. There is a laudable rest. on the top floor. **E–VE,** but lower rates off-season.

☆☆ **Holiday Inn Surfside,** 2700 N. Atlantic Ave., Daytona Beach, FL 32018 (904/672-3770; toll free, see Holiday Inns). 383 rms, A/C, color TV, in-rm movies. Free parking, two pools, rest., bar, rm svce, disco, free crib. *Note:* Modern 12-story tower on the beach; the Holiday Inn style at its friendliest and most comfortable. Group clientele. Interesting vacation packages. **M–E,** but lower rates off-season.

☆ **Days Inn Oceanfront Central,** 1909 S. Atlantic Ave., Daytona Beach, FL 32018 (904/255-4492; toll free, see Days Inns). 196 rms, A/C, color TV, in-rm movies. AE, DC, MC, V. Free parking, pool, rest., bar, free crib. *Note:* Comfortable, unpretentious family motel directly on the beach. Rms w. private patios, the best overlooking the ocean. No alcoholic beverages in the rest. **I–M,** but lower rates off-season.

YMCA/YOUTH HOSTEL The **Daytona Beach International Hostel,** 140 S. Atlantic Ave., Daytona Beach (904/258-6937). Comfortable youth hostel (100 beds), almost on the beach.

Where to Eat

Aunt Catfish's, 4009 Halifax Dr. at the west end of Port Orange Bridge (904/767-4768). A/C. Lunch/dinner daily, brunch Sun; closed Thanksgiving, Dec 25. AE, CB, DC, MC, V. *Specialties:* shellfish, catch of the day, steak, roast beef au jus, good homemade desserts. *Note:* Extra-fresh seafood and honest red meat at reasonable prices. Conventional seafaring decor; relaxed atmosphere. Locally popular. *Steak/Seafood.* **B–I**

CAFETERIA/FAST FOOD Morrison's, 200 N. Ridgewood (904/258-6396). Lunch/dinner daily (till 8:30pm). MC, V. *Specialties:* fried shrimp, fish of the day, roast beef. *Note:* Honest cafeteria food.

KENNEDY SPACE CENTER: Originally known as Cape Canaveral, the **John F. Kennedy Space Center** is America's largest interplanetary target range. Since the first rocket (a converted German V2) was launched in 1950, and including the most recent space shuttles, more than 2,300 devices have been launched into space from this NASA facility, which employs more than 25,000 technicians on its narrow seaside peninsula. It was from here that, on July 16, 1969, *Apollo XI* carried Neil Armstrong, Michael Collins, and Edward Aldrin on their historic mission—Armstrong and Aldrin were the first men to set foot on the moon.

Double-decker buses take guided tours to the giant hangar where space shuttles and space vehicles are assembled; this **Vehicle Assembly Building,** 512 ft. (160m) high, is the largest of its kind in the world. Other highlights of the tour are the astronaut training center and several launching zones. There is a well-stocked space museum (**Spaceport USA**) and a cinema with a five-story screen (IMAX theater) where films of space shuttle launches are shown.

Open daily except Dec 25 and certain launch days. For information on timetables, call 407/452-2121. Don't miss this one. Inside Florida there is a toll-free number (800/432-2153) which will give you advance information on launchings.

Where to Stay in the Area

Hilton, 1550 N. Atlantic Ave., in Cocoa Beach, FL 32931 (407/799-0003; toll free, see Hilton). 300 rms, cable color TV. AE, CB, DC, MC, V. Free valet parking, pool, boats, rest., bar, rm svce, disco, free crib. *Note:* Ultramodern six-story hotel on the ocean, w. huge, comfortable rms. VIP floor. Efficient svce. 15 min. by road from Kennedy Space Center. Caters mostly to tourists. **M–E**

Holiday Inn, 260 E. Merritt Island Causeway, in Merritt Island, FL 32952 (407/452-7711; toll free, see Holiday Inns). 128 rms, A/C, cable color TV, in-rm movies. AE, CB, DC, MC, V. Free parking, pool, tennis court, rest. (C. W. Dandy's), bar, rm svce, nightclub, free crib. *Note:* Modern, functional Holiday Inn–style motel on the banks of the Indian River; ideal for visitors to Cape Kennedy, which is 15 min. by car. **I–M,** but lower rates off-season.

Travelodge Apollo, 3810 S. Washington Ave. (U.S. A1A), in Titusville, FL 32780 (407/267-9111; toll free, see Travelodge). 112 rms, A/C, cable color TV. AE, CB, DC, MC, V. Free parking, pool, rest., bar, valet svce, crib $5. *Note:* On the Indian River only 15 min. by car from Cape Kennedy; offers very acceptable standards of comfort, a cordial reception, and a good view over the center's firing ranges. Very good value overall. **I**

Motel 6, 3701 N. Atlantic Ave., in Cocoa Beach, FL 32931 (407/783-3103). 104 rms, A/C, color TV, in-rm movies. AE, DC, MC, V. Free parking, pool, free crib. *Note:* Unsurpassed value a quarter of an hour from Cape Kennedy; ideal for motorists. Facing beach; no rest. or bar. **B**

IN NEARBY MELBOURNE (25 mi./40km south). **Radisson Suite Hotel Oceanside,** 3101 N. Fla. A1A, Indialantic, FL 32903 (407/773-9260; toll free, see Radisson). 166 suites, A/C, color TV. AE, CB, DC, MC, V. Free parking, pool, health club, sauna, rest., bar, rm svce. *Note:* Luxury hotel of original postmodern design at the water's edge. Spacious and remarkably comfortable suites w. their own balconies overlooking the ocean. New facilities; excellent svce; 30 min. by car from Kennedy Space Center. Very acceptable rest. Clientele of well-to-do vacationers. **E–VE,** but lower rates off-season.

Days Inn, 4455 New Haven Ave., Melbourne, FL 32904 (407/724-5840; toll free, see Days Inns). 235 rms, A/C, color TV. AE, DC, MC, V. Free parking, pool, tennis court, 24-hr. coffee shop, free crib. *Note:* A great place at very reasonable prices. Inviting rms w. balconies; grdn w. small artificial lake. 45 min. by car from the Kennedy Space Center. Very good value. No alcoholic beverages permitted in rest. **I,** but lower rates off-season.

Where to Eat in the Area

Bernard's Surf, 2 S. Atlantic Ave., Cocoa Beach (407/783-2401). A/C. Lunch Mon–Sat; dinner nightly; closed Dec 25. AE, DC, MC, V. *Specialties:* red snapper, stuffed avocado, steak, shrimp Louie, catch of the day. *Note:* A very large menu and a softly romantic atmosphere of an evening are the two main attractions of this rest.; the food is commendable but unimaginative. Resv. advised. *Steak/Seafood.* **B–I**

Lobster Shanty, 2000 S. Orlando, Cocoa Beach (407/783-1350). A/C. Lunch/dinner daily; closed Thanksgiving, Dec 25. *Specialties:* rock shrimp, scallops, sea trout, red snapper, grilled catch of the day. *Note:* Very good fish rest. right on the dock, often packed at peak hr. so resv. a must. Attractive paneled decor highlighted by aquariums. Painstaking svce. A fine place, 25 min. by road from Kennedy Space Center. *Seafood.* **B–I**

IN NEARBY MELBOURNE BEACH **Nick's Steakhouse,** 903 Oak St. on Fla. A1A (407/723-6659). A/C. Dinner only, daily. AE, CB, DC, MC, V. *Specialties:* clams and oysters on the half shell, crab, pompano en papillote, swordfish steak, roast beef, steak Delmonico broiled over a wood fire. Praiseworthy wine list. *Note:* Conventional, unpretentious, congenial steakhouse. Excellent broiled dishes; intimate atmosphere; good svce. Resv. advisable. *Steak/Seafood.* **I**

ORLANDO (46 mi./74km west of the Kennedy Space Center): The tourist capital of Florida, with a thronged airport and a multitude of hotels, motels, and restaurants. Very near Walt Disney World and other major attractions. For detailed tourist information, see Chapter 18 on Orlando.

SEA WORLD (61 mi./95km SW of the Kennedy Space Center): Enormous, ultramodern sea zoo. Shark aquarium with glass tunnel for sightseeing; trained orcas (killer whales) and dolphins, sea lions, giant turtles, etc. Waterskiing displays. A spectacle that beggars description—and attracts almost three million tourists yearly. Well worth going out of your way for. Open daily. For detailed tourist information, see Chapter 18 on Orlando.

WALT DISNEY WORLD (71 mi./115km SW of the Kennedy Space Center): The largest, and most famous, theme park in the world, visited by more than 300 million people since it opened in 1971. With an area of 28,000 acres (11,335ha)—twice the size of Manhattan Island—this is an amusement park on a planetary scale. It's open every day, 12 months a year. If there were nothing else to see in Florida, you should go just for this. For detailed tourist information, see Chapter 18 on Orlando.

EPCOT (71 mi./115km SW of the Kennedy Space Center): This other child of the Walt Disney family, opened in 1982, is a 21st-century theme park with many of the attractions of a World's Fair. Designed to accommodate 25 million visitors a year, it cost $1 billion to build—2½ times more than Walt Disney World and four times more than Disneyland. Connected by monorail to Walt Disney World, this futuristic amusement park, overshadowed by its 18-story steel-and-concrete sphere, is also worth the trip to Florida all by itself. For detailed tourist information, see Chapter 18 on Orlando.

DISNEY-MGM STUDIOS (71 mi./115km SW of the Kennedy Space Center): This newest (1989) member of the Walt Disney family offers you a guided tour through the studios, where you will be shown workshops, sets, and all kinds of special effects, including earthquakes and tidal waves. You can also watch work in progress on movies, TV series, and cartoons. Fascinating. For detailed tourist information, see Chapter 18 on Orlando. Don't miss it.

TYPHOON LAGOON (71 mi./115km SW of the Kennedy Space Center): Disney's new water park for the wet set! You can snorkel among thousands of tropical fish, plummet down eight different flumes to the 2½-acre (1ha) pool, and ride the waves (up to 7 ft./2m high) produced by a giant surf-making machine. For detailed tourist information, see Chapter 18 on Orlando.

CYPRESS GARDENS (101 mi./164km SW of the Kennedy Space Center): For more than a quarter of a century these magnificent tropical gardens on the shores of Lake Eloise have been one of Florida's principal tourist attractions. Underwater displays; waterskiing ballets in wonderful Esther Williams–style kitsch. Definitely worth the side trip. Open daily. For detailed tourist information, see Chapter 18 on Orlando.

COCOA BEACH: Several miles of fine beaches, celebrated for the beauty of their sunsets. A great place for surfing, big-game fishing—or picnicking while you watch the launches from the nearby Kennedy Space Center.

PATRICK AIR FORCE BASE: Examples of most of the types of spacecraft launched from the Kennedy Space Center are on exhibition in front of the base's Technical Laboratory, reached on Fla. A1A. Impressive. Open daily.

VERO BEACH: Enormous, uncrowded beach, much appreciated by those in-the-know. The charming little town is liberally adorned with flowerbeds.

Where to Stay

Holiday Inn Oceanside, 3384 Ocean Dr., Vero Beach, FL 32963 (407/231-2300; toll free, see Holiday Inns). 104 rms,

A/C, cable color TV. AE, CB, DC, MC, V. Free parking, pool, rest., bar, rm svce, nightclub, free crib. *Note:* Holiday Inn style right on the beach. Serviceably comfortable; rms w. balconies overlooking the ocean. Good value in summer. **M–E,** but lower rates off-season.

Where to Eat

♀ **The Patio,** 1103 Miracle Mile (Fla. 60) (407/567-7215).
⚒ A/C. Lunch/dinner daily (open till 1am), brunch Sun. AE, MC, V. *Specialties:* crab au gratin, scampi, chicken Kiev, filet mignon. *Note:* Some of the Continental dishes are successful. The decor, as the name suggests, is Spanish inspired, and the two together make for an agreeable stop. *Continental.* **B–I**

⚓ **FORT PIERCE:** Between the ocean and the Indian River lies a 332-acre (135ha) nature reserve, open to the public. There are 21 mi. (30km) of beaches, surfing, swimming, saltwater fishing, and freshwater fishing in the St. Lucie River. The **St. Lucie County Museum,** at 414 Seaway Dr. (407/464-6635), is interesting; it has a reproduction of a Seminole village. Open Mon–Sat year round.

⚓ **JENSEN BEACH:** Once the pineapple capital of Florida, this popular beach resort now specializes in big-game and freshwater fishing. Every evening during June and July, huge sea turtles up to 500 lbs. (227kg) crawl onto the beaches of **Hutchinson Island** to lay their eggs. Tourists and residents come at night with flashlights to watch the sight.

Where to Stay

♔♔ **Sheraton Beach,** 10978 S. Ocean Dr., Hutchinson Island, FL 34957 (407/229-1000; toll free, see Sheraton). 100 rms, color TV, in-rm movies. AE, CB, DC, MC, V. Free parking, pool, beach, rest., bar, rm svce, nightclub, concierge, free crib. *Note:* Modern 8-story building on the beach w. exterior glass elevtr. Comfortable rms (some w. balconies). Rooftop rest. w. spectacular ocean view. Good value overall. **M-E,** but lower rates off-season.

Where to Eat

♀ **Conchy Joe's Seafood,** 3945 NE Indian River Rd. (407/
⚒ 334-1130). A/C. Lunch/dinner daily; closed Thanksgiving, Dec. 25. AE, MC, V. *Specialties:* local seafood, conch fritters, steak. *Note:* Very popular water-view rest. built by the Seminoles. Unpretentious nautical setting w. outdoor dining and some open fire cooking. *Seafood.* **B–I**

☼⚓ **LAKE OKEECHOBEE** (38 mi./62km SW of Jensen Beach on Fla. 76): The largest freshwater lake in Florida, with an area of 730 sq. mi. (1,890km²). A fisherman's heaven, with perch, bream, and largemouth bass, of which 1,500 tons (1.36 million kg) are caught annually. You'll find a choice of boat rentals, motels, and campsites at **Belle Glade** and **Okeechobee.**

⚓ **JUPITER BEACH:** Several very beautiful nature reserves dedicated to birds and marine animals (**Joseph Verner Reed Wilderness Sanctuary, Hobe Sound National Wildlife Refuge,** etc.), some of which can be reached only by boat, are well worth visiting. Also the usual beach diversions. Very nearby, **Jonathan Dickinson State Park** marks the spot where the *Reformation,* carrying a group of Quaker settlers, was shipwrecked in 1696;

the survivors, captured by Seminoles, succeeded in making their way back to St. Augustine, 225 mi. (360km) to the north, on foot. Perched on a bluff overlooking Jupiter Inlet, the **Jupiter Lighthouse,** first lighted in 1860, still guides ships approaching the Florida Coast. Museum (407/747-6639) open Sun only.

Where to Stay

♀♀♀ **Jupiter Bay Resort,** 350 S. U.S. 1 FL 33477 (407/744-0210). 150 apts. and villas, A/C, color TV, rm service. This is a luxurious resort hotel with comfortable studios and apartments in individual houses and small, two- and three-story buildings, surrounded by scenic gardens. The rooms have patios or private balconies, and the service is first rate. Convenient restaurant.

Where to Eat

♀ **Harpoon Louie's,** 1065 Fla. A1A (407/744-1300). A/C. Breakfast/lunch/dinner daily; closed Thanksgiving, Dec 25. AE, MC, V. *Specialties:* catch of the day, broiled meats. *Note:* Agreeable little rest. at the water's edge, overlooking the Jupiter Lighthouse. Simple but good food; svce w. a smile; locally popular. *American/Seafood.* **B–I**

PALM BEACH (& WEST PALM BEACH): This beach resort is celebrated for its royal palms, its high fashion, and its social exclusiveness; in the eyes of rich Florida vacationers it easily outshines Miami Beach. Worth Ave. and Royal Poinciana Plaza are lined with luxury boutiques. With no fewer than nine polo grounds, the town is considered the world capital for this sport—but with 110 championship courses, it is no less a paradise for golfers.

It still boasts many magnificent mansions built by 19th-century giants of finance, including that of Henry Flagler, co-founder of Standard Oil and builder of Florida's first trunk railroad between Daytona Beach and Key West: his 🏛 **Whitehall,** a marble palace dating from 1901 with 55 opulently decorated rooms, must certainly be seen. It's at Coconut Row at Whitehall Way (407/655-2833), and is open Tues–Sun.

Another remarkable museum, housed in an intelligently redesigned movie house, is the 🏛 **Lannan Museum,** at 601 Lake Ave., in Lake Worth (407/582-0006). It displays one of the country's richest private collections of modern art, including paintings and sculpture by Julian Schnabel, Morris Louis, Sandro Chia, and others. The overall effect is exceptionally striking. Open Tues–Sat.

At West Palm Beach, don't miss the 🏛 **Union Congregational Church,** at 2727 Georgia Ave. (407/832-0581), with its enormous (75- by 27-ft./23- by 8-m) stained-glass window, assembled like a mosaic from 10,000 pieces of colored glass. Designed by Conrad Pick.

Going west 18 mi. (28km) along U.S. 98, you will come to 🏛 **Lion Country Safari,** on Southern Blvd. W. (407/793-1084). This modern wild-animal park covers 640 acres (260ha), and has more than 1,000 wild animals roaming free. It's open daily; visits by car only.

Where to Stay

♀♀♀♀♀ **The Breakers,** S. County Rd., Palm Beach, FL 33480 (407/655-6611; toll free, see Preferred). 528 rms, A/C, cable color TV. Modified American Plan in winter. AE, CB, DC, MC, V. Free parking (valet parking $6), pool, 19 tennis courts, two golf courses, beach, sauna, masseur, two rests. (including the Florentine Room), bars, rm svce, nightclub, hrdrsr, cinema, boutiques, concierge. *Note:* A jewel among U.S. hotels since 1926. Imposing Italianate palace w. white marble colonnades, Flemish tapestries, and crystal chandeliers. Roomy, comfortable (though slightly somber) rms w. minibars, superb English-style grdns, and direct access to beach. Reception and svce of the highest quality (in season, the hotel has about 1,100 on staff). The Florentine Room is an excellent rest. Comprehensive sports facilities. Interesting wknd packages. Very upscale clientele. One of the 12 best hotels in the country. **VE,** but lower rates off-season.

P.G.A. Sheraton Resort, 400 Ave. of the Champions, Palm Beach Gardens, FL 33410 (407/627-2000; toll free, see Sheraton). 333 mini-suites, A/C, cable color TV. AE, CB, DC, MC, V. Free valet parking, three pools, 19 tennis courts, five golf courses, private beach, boats, bicycling, health club, sauna, squash, croquet, putting green, three rests. (including Explorers), three bars, rm svce, nightclub, hrdsr, concierge, crib $15. *Note:* Paradise for tennis players and golfers at the edge of a large lake, set in 2,360 acres (955ha) of park and grdn. Modern and very comfortable. Spacious mini-suites w. refrigerators and private balconies; also fully equipped villas. Attentive svce. 15 min. from the sea by car. Trendy group clientele. **E–VE,** but lower rates off-season.

Best Western Palm Beach Lakes Inn (formerly the Ramada Inn), 1800 Palm Beach Lakes Blvd., West Palm Beach, FL 33401 (407/683-8810; toll free, see Best Western). 200 rms, A/C, color TV. AE, CB, DC, MC, V. Free parking, pool, tennis court, golf course, nearby coffee shop, valet svce, free crib. *Note:* Relatively modern, functional motel w. large rms and refrigerators. Group clientele. Good overall value. **I–M,** but lower rates off-season.

Days Inn, 2300 W. 45th St., West Palm Beach, FL 33407 (407/689-0450; toll free, see Days Inns). 238 rms, A/C, color TV, in-rm movies. AE, CB, DC, MC, V. Free parking, pool, putting green, coffee shop, free airport limo, free crib. *Note:* Representative motel, 10 min. from dwntwn Palm Beach. Comfortable rms, quite friendly reception and svce. Rms for nonsmokers. Good value. **I–M,** but lower rates off-season.

Where to Eat

Café l'Europe, 150 Worth Ave., on the Esplanade (407/655-4020). A/C. Lunch/dinner Mon–Sat; closed hols. AE, CB, DC, MC, V. J&T (at dinner). *Specialties:* scallops St-Jacques au Noilly, mignonette of beef w. peppercorns, capon breast sautéed w. leeks and chanterelles, poached salmon w. dill sauce and salmon caviar, roast lamb en croûte, very good desserts; remarkable wine list. *Note:* One of Florida's smartest rests. in an ideally romantic setting of paneling, mirrors, and brasswork. Refined and elegant cuisine; svce (in tuxedos) impeccable. Pleasant classical background music. On its way to becoming one of the greatest rests. on the East Coast. Resv. necessary. *Continental.* **M–E**

Charley's Crab, 456 S. Ocean Blvd. (407/659-1500). A/C. Lunch/dinner daily, brunch Sun. AE, CB, DC, MC, V. Jkt. *Specialties:* Mediterranean fish chowder; mussels diablo (w. jalapeño peppers); pasta primavera; catch of the day broiled, poached, sautéed, or Cajun style; red snapper Veracruz style; pompano en papillote; luscious homemade desserts. Excellent wine list. *Note:* Florida branch of Detroit's famous Joe Muer's Seafood; no lover of fish or shellfish should miss it. Absolutely fresh produce cooked to perfection; beautifully situated looking out on the ocean, but unimaginatively decorated. Attentive, courteous svce. Reserve ahead, especially at dinner. Valet parking. *Seafood.* **I–M**

Testa's Restaurant, 221 Royal Poinciana Way (407/832-0992). A/C. Breakfast/lunch/dinner daily (until 1am); closed Dec 1–May 15. AE, CB, DC, MC, V. *Specialties:* stone crabs (in season), steak, seafood, Italian dishes, strawberry pie. *Note:* Family owned since 1921, Testa's has become a landmark. Basically Italian, the cuisine does well also w. native seafoods. Beautiful glass-roofed tropical grdn patio or sidewalk café. Good svce. Resv. advised. *Italian/Seafood.* **B–I**

IN NEARBY BOYNTON BEACH (12 mi./19km south) **Bernard's,** 1730 N. Federal Hwy. (U.S. 1) (407/737-2236). A/C. Dinner only, nightly; closed Dec

25 and Mon May–Oct. AE, CB, DC, MC, V. Jkt. (at dinner). *Specialties:* Bahamian chowder, chicken New Orleans, steak au poivre, poached salmon w. dill, filet of grouper, gâteau nougatine. *Note:* The elegant setting—a Spanish-style home from the 1920s—and the delicacy of the cooking make this one of the most sought-after rests. in the area. Lovely tropical grdn, illuminated in the evening. Ultra-professional svce; valet parking. Resv. advised. *Continental/American.* **I–M**

         DELRAY BEACH: A popular resort community as well as a commercial flower-growing center, Delray Beach boasts one of the state's most beautiful and unusual museums, the **Morikani Museum of Japanese Art,** 4000 Morikani Park Rd. (407/495-0233), open Tues–Sun. Standing in a 56-acre (23ha) park complete with lakes, waterfalls, Japanese gardens, and a bonsai collection, the enchanting museum offers a comprehensive overview of Japanese culture and folk art, from dolls to painting and traditional furniture. As is the Japanese custom, you must take your shoes off before going in. Don't miss it.

Where to Eat

         Roberto, 640 E. Atlantic Ave. (407/278-8351). A/C. Dinner only, Tues–Sun; closed hols. AE, MC, V. Jkt. *Specialties:* duck w. cassis, veal cutlet w. madeira. Menu changes regularly. Fine Italian wines. *Note:* Chef Roberto Tempo, a master of the Chaîne des Rôtisseurs, dishes up excellent classic cuisine in this gracious Louis XV–style setting. Impeccable svce; resv. indispensable. Prix fixe. *Continental.* **M**

         BOCA RATON: Charming, and rapidly growing, beachfront city. Seat of **Florida Atlantic University,** with 10,000 students, and the research laboratories of IBM. The **Boca Raton Hotel & Club** (see "Where to Stay," below), a magnificent 1930s luxury hotel, is worth the side trip by itself.

Where to Stay

         Boca Raton Hotel & Club, 501 E. Camino Real, Boca Raton, FL 33432 (407/395-3000; toll free 800/223-6800). 988 rms, A/C, color TV, in-rm movies. Modified American Plan. AE, CB, DC, MC, V. Valet parking $5, four pools, 22 tennis courts, golf course, putting green, marina, boats, waterskiing, health club, sauna, seven rests., eight bars, rm svce, disco, hrdrsr, boutiques, cinema, crib $7. Free jitney to the beach. *Note:* A Spanish baroque luxury hotel from the 1930s is here surprisingly wedded to a modern 27-floor tower overlooking Lake Boca Raton. The best rms (those in the older section) look out on 540 acres (220ha) of lush tropical grdns; the tower rms, w. balconies, face the lake. Exemplary svce, but the group clientele is often quite obtrusive. Remarkable sports facilities and interesting golf/tennis packages. VIP floor. One of the great hotels of the East Coast. **VE,** but lower rates off-season.

         Best Western University Inn, 2700 N. U.S. 1, Boca Raton, FL 33431 (407/395-5225; toll free, see Best Western). 90 rms, A/C, cable color TV. AE, CB, DC, MC, V. Free parking, pool, tennis court, coffee shop, bar valet svce, free breakfast, free crib. *Note:* A classic small motel, a few steps from the campus of Florida Atlantic University and IBM's Research Laboratory. Huge, comfortable rms; agreeable svce. Good value off-season. **M,** but lower rates off-season.

IN NEARBY DEERFIELD BEACH (2 mi./3.2km south)

         La Quinta, 351 W. Hillsboro Blvd., Deerfield Beach, FL 33441 (305/421-1004). 130 rms, A/C, color TV, in-rm movies. AE, CB, DC, MC, V. Free parking, pool, rest. adj., free crib. *Note:* Brandnew motel nr. the Deerfield Beach Country Club, pleasantly designed in Spanish Colonial style. Comfortable, well-laid-out rms, svce w. a smile. 5 min. from the beach; good value. If you're driving, there is direct access to I-95. **I–M**

Where to Eat

♟♟♟ **La Vieille Maison,** 770 E. Palmetto Park Rd. (407/391-6701). A/C. Dinner only, nightly (two sittings, at 6:30 and 9:30pm); closed hols. AE, CB, DC, MC, V. Jkt. *Specialties:* terrine of trout w. truffles, shrimp in Pernod, pompano w. pecans, quail w. grapes, sweetbreads sautéed w. morels, duckling w. turnips, tarte tatin, lemon soufflé pancake. Superb wine list. *Note:* Almost perfect classic haute cuisine by young and talented chef Yves Labbé. Sumptuous Mediterranean-style 1920s villa w. a patio; very beautiful cut flowers and antique furniture. Refined atmosphere. Valet parking. Resv. required. Prix fixe. *French/Continental.* **E**

♟♟ **Maxaluna,** Crocker Center, 21150 Military Trail (407/391-7177). A/C. Lunch Mon–Fri, dinner daily; closed Thanksgiving, Dec 25. AE, CB, DC, MC, V. *Specialties:* linguine w. steamed clams, spinach fettuccine w. squab breast and wild mushrooms, stuffed veal chop, prawns wrapped in zucchini sliced broiled pompano, roast squab w. pine nuts, yellowfin tuna w. caramelized onions, "chocolate fog." Fine, reasonably priced wine list. *Note:* Maxaluna, which likes to describe itself as a "Tuscan rôtisserie," is one of the most interesting new rests. in Florida, serving light, imaginative California-Italian food and using only the finest local produce (particularly seafood). Pretty contemporary decor, ingeniously combining bare brick, waxed paneling, and stainless steel, but rather noisy. Hard-working svce. Yuppy clientele. Resv. highly advisable. Same ownership as Max's Place in North Dade (see Chapter 19 on Miami). *Italian/American.* **I–M**

♟ **Fuji,** Del Mar Shopping Village, Palmetto Park Rd. (407/392-8778). A/C. Lunch Mon–Sat, dinner nightly. AE, CB, DC, MC, V. *Specialties:* sushi, sashimi, shabu-shabu, tempura. *Note:* One of the few authentic Japanese rests. on the Florida coast. You may choose between Western-style seating and tatami mats. Everything is as fresh as can be. Interesting modern decor w. flags and banners hanging from the ceiling. Efficient svce. *Japanese.* **B–I**

POMPANO BEACH: Perhaps because of its 7 mi. (11km) of beach, this resort has for some time been experiencing the fastest growth in tourism on Florida's Gold Coast. At the **Goodyear Blimp Visitor Center,** 1500 NE Fifth Ave. (305/946-8300), you may pay your respects close up to the famous Goodyear blimp, which is based here every year Nov–May. Open daily.

Where to Stay

♟♟♟ **Palm Aire Resort & Spa,** 2501 Palm Aire Dr., Pompano Beach, FL 33069 (305/972-3300; toll free 800/327-4960). 195 rms, A/C, color TV, in-rm movies. AE, CB, DC, MC, V. Free parking, six pools, four golf courses, 37 tennis courts, squash, health club, sauna, private beach, water sports, three rests., bars, rm svce, disco, hrdrsr, concierge, crib free. *Note:* Luxurious, comfortable convention hotel standing in 1,800 acres (730ha) of parkland and blooming grdns right on the beach; commodious rms w. private patios (some w. kitchenettes). Hot springs. Family and Modified American Plan (MAP) packages worth looking into. Very good svce and some of the most comprehensive sports facilities in Florida. A wonderful place for lovers of sports and stressed businesspeople. **E–VE,** but lower rates off-season.

♟ **Motel 6,** 1201 N.W. 31st Ave., Pompano Beach, FL 33069 (305/977-8011). 127 rms, A/C, color TV, free in-rm movies. AE, DC, MC, V. Free parking, pool, free crib. *Note:* Up-to-date comfort at a modest price, 20 min. from dwntwn. One of the best values in the region. Ideal if you're driving. **B**

Where to Eat

♟ **Harris Imperial House,** 50 N. Ocean Blvd. (305/941-2200). A/C. Lunch Mon–Fri, dinner nightly. AE, CB, DC, MC, V.

Specialties: Cantonese dishes, sesame chicken, steak, South Seas Supreme. *Note:* The run-of-the-mill Far Eastern decor may lead you to expect a ho-hum Chinese rest.—but the cooking is an unusual harmony of good old American steak w. Cantonese dishes and the delicacies of Polynesia. The result may disconcert you —but the buffet is a good value. Valet parking. Locally popular, so resv. advisable. *Chinese/American.* I

FORT LAUDERDALE: Nicknamed "The Venice of America" because of its 165 mi. (266km) of canals and the 35,000 boats moored there year round, Fort Lauderdale is indeed a tourist attraction of Venetian caliber. Its 5 mi. (11km) of beaches, hundreds of hotels, motels, and rooming houses with a total of 25,000 rooms, 2,500 restaurants of all kinds and in all price ranges, the fashionable boutiques of Las Olas Blvd., one of the world's biggest pleasure-boat harbors (the Bahia Mar Yacht Basin, to which every pleasure sailor would like to make a pilgrimage)—all these attractions have made this busy, friendly city one of the leading tourist resorts in Florida. It doesn't hurt, either, that with 3,000 hr. of sunshine annually, Fort Lauderdale holds the U.S. record.

For boat trips around the canals and the Intracoastal Waterway, try **Jungle Queen Cruises,** Bahia Mar Yacht Basin, Fla. A1A (305/462-5596), which offers them daily year round.

You should also see **Butterfly World,** 3600 W. Sample Rd., Coconut Creek (305/977-4400). This new theme park opened in 1988 contains thousands of live butterflies from around the world on its 3 acres (1ha) of tropical gardens and its rain forest area with waterfalls. Open daily. Don't miss it.

Don't miss the splendid, new **Museum of Art,** a masterpiece from the hand of architect Edward Larrabee Barnes, at 1 E. Las Olas Blvd. (305/525-5500), open Tues–Sun; or **Ocean World,** 1701 SE 17th St. Causeway (305/525-6611), the classic marine zoo in Florida. Dozens of sea creatures, from sharks to dolphins, from sea lions to giant turtles—some of them trained to do the most wonderful tricks. Open daily.

Where to Stay

Sheraton Bonaventure Resort & Spa, 250 Racquet Club Rd., Fort Lauderdale, FL 33326 (305/389-3300; toll free, see Sheraton). 493 rms, A/C, color TV, in-rm movies. AE, CB, DC, MC, V. Valet parking $6, five pools, two golf courses, 23 tennis courts, health club, horseback riding, six rests. (including Renaissance), coffee shop, bars, rm svce, nightclub, hrdrsr, boutiques, concierge, free crib. *Note:* One of the best-known luxury hotels on the east coast of Florida. Its superb tropical setting, hot springs, and unrivaled sports facilities have made it a favorite of VIPs. Lavish decor and ultra-comfortable layout. Excellent svce. If you're a physical-fitness buff, this is the place for you. **E–VE,** but lower rates off-season.

Pier 66 Hotel & Marina, 2301 S.E. 17th St. Causeway, Fort Lauderdale, FL 33316 (305/525-6666; toll free, see Preferred). 388 rms, A/C, cable color TV. AE, CB, DC, MC, V. Valet parking $5, two pools, two tennis courts, health club, sauna, marina, boats, four rests., four bars (one a revolving bar on the top floor), 24-hr. rm svce, disco, hrdrsr, free jitney to beach, free crib. *Note:* This is Fort Lauderdale's most famous building, a great white 17-story tower overlooking the Intracoastal Waterway, topped by a revolving bar in the shape of a flying saucer; it recently underwent a $21-million facelift. Capacious rms w. refrigerators, most w. balconies or patios, and a view of the ocean or the marina. Outside glass elevator. Group clientele; efficient svce. Windows on the Green is a good rest. Very comprehensive sports facilities. All in all, a very good place to stay. **E–VE,** but lower rates off-season.

Holiday Inn–Fort Lauderdale Beach, 999 N. Atlantic Blvd., Fort Lauderdale, FL 33304 (305/563-5961; toll free, see

Holiday Inns). 240 rms, A/C, color TV, in-rm movies. AE, CB, DC, MC, V. Valet parking $2, pool, rest., bar, rm svce, free crib. *Note:* A great, modern 12-story pile, Holiday Inn style, right on the ocean and very near the famous Galeria Mall w. its 150 stores and boutiques. Most rms (some w. balconies, all w. refrigerators) overlook the beach. Svce on the impersonal side. **M–E,** but lower rates off-season.

⚲ **Beach Plaza Hotel,** 625 N. Atlantic Blvd., Fort Lauderdale, FL 33304 (305/566-7631; toll free 800/451-4711). 43 rms, A/C, color TV, in-rm movies. AE, DC, MC, V. Free parking, pool, adj. 24-hr. coffee shop, free crib. *Note:* Charming little motel right on the beach. Comfortable rms w. private patio or balcony and refrigerator, the best overlooking the pool-grdn. Friendly svce; interesting vacation packages. Good value overall. **I–M,** but lower rates off-season.

⚲ **Merrimac,** 551 N. Atlantic Blvd., Fort Lauderdale, FL 33304 (305/564-2345). 37 apartments, A/C, color TV. AE, CB, DC, MC, V. Free parking, pool, nearby coffee shop. *Note:* Modest but well-maintained cluster of mini-apartments (most w. kitchenettes), w. balconies and ocean view; ideal for families. Direct access to the beach. **I–M,** but lower rates off-season.

⚲ **Motel 6,** 1801 Fla. 84, Fort Lauderdale, FL 33315 (305/760-7999). 108 rms, A/C, color TV. DC, MC, V. Free parking, pool, free crib. *Note:* Good value at an unbeatable price. **B**

IN NEARBY DANIA (5 mi./8km south) ⚲ **Motel 6,** 825 E. Dania Beach Blvd. (at NE Seventh Ave.), Dania, FL 33004 (305/921-5505). 163 rms, A/C, color TV. AE, DC, MC, V. Free parking, pool, free crib. *Note:* Ideal for motorists. **B**

YMCA/YOUTH HOSTEL **Sol Y Mar/AYH,** 2839 Vistamar St., Fort Lauderdale, FL 33304 (305/566-1023). Youth hostel w. 36 beds, nr. the beach.

Where to Eat

☼⚲♉♉♉ **Casa Vecchia,** 209 N. Birch Rd. (305/463-7575). A/C. Dinner only, nightly; closed Memorial Day, July 4, Labor Day. AE, CB, DC, MC, V. Jkt. *Specialties:* cima alla genovese, fresh homemade pasta, osso buco, red snapper Livorno style, trout primavera. Also cannoli, fruit sherbets. The Italian wine list has more show than substance. *Note:* This 1930s mansion, set in beautiful grdns, once belonged to the Pond (cosmetics) family, and boasts period furniture, art objects, and much greenery. The northern Italian cuisine is as elegant as the interior; the svce is on the same level. View of the grdns and the Intracoastal Waterway w. the passing vessels. One of the best places to eat on the Florida east coast, w. the same management as La Vieille Maison in Boca Raton (see above). Resv. a must. Valet parking. *Italian.* **E**

♉♉♉ **Down Under,** 3000 E. Oakland Park Blvd. (305/563-4123). A/C. Lunch Mon–Fri; dinner nightly; closed hols. AE, CB, DC, MC, V. Jkt. *Specialties:* duck confit, frogs' legs salad, chicken Madagascar, red snapper Louisiana style, oysters Créole, trout Imperial, Indian veal curry. Great Californian and French wine list. *Note:* From the amusing Victorian-rococo interior you will have a fine view of the Intracoastal Waterway and its traffic. Innovative, delicate French-inspired food w. a touch of the exotic. Fine list of California wines. Sometimes very noisy. Same management as La Vieille Maison in Boca Raton and Casa Vecchia (see above). Valet parking. Resv. advised. One of Florida's great rests. *French/Continental.* **I–M**

☼⚲♉♉ **Mai Kai,** 3599 N. Federal Hwy. (305/563-3272). A/C. Dinner only, nightly (served till midnight); closed hols. AE, CB, DC, MC, V. Jkt. *Specialties:* shrimp Szechuan, lemon chicken, Peking duck, steamed trout, roast pigeon, lobster Tahiti. *Note:* The Mai Kai offers you an original selection of food, w. Cantonese and Szechuan dishes predominating, but also including excellent steaks and fabulous Polynesian cocktails (try the "Mystery Drink"). No one could ask for a more exotic decor than this Hollywood-style corner of the South Seas w. its pool, waterfall, and Siamese temple. Impeccable svce. Very popular locally, so don't forget to reserve ahead. Polynesian floor show. Valet parking. A classic of its kind since the 1950s. *Chinese/Polynesian.* **I–M**

🍸 **La Reserve,** 2115 NE 32nd Ave. at Oakland Park Blvd. Bridge 🍷 (305/563-6644). A/C. Dinner only, nightly; closed hols. AE, CB, DC, MC, V. Jkt. *Specialties:* shrimp niçoise, vegetable pâté, beef sirloin in St. Amour wine sauce, lobster au gratin, pan-seared veal chop w. wild mushrooms, duckling w. cherries, salmon w. mustard sauce, fruit soufflés. *Note:* The excellent food and the view out over the Intracoastal Waterway are trump cards for this delightful, typically French rest. Elegant decor w. lots of flowers, romantic atmosphere, and dinner by candlelight. The adj. rest.-annex, Ginger, serves praiseworthy bistro food in less formal surroundings. Resv. strongly advised. *French.* **I–M**

🍸 **Paesano,** 1301 Las Olas Blvd. (305/467-3266). A/C. Lunch 🍷 Mon–Fri, dinner nightly; closed Thanksgiving. AE, MC, V. *Specialties:* Fresh homemade pasta, saltimbocca, crostata di vitello, snapper Adriatico. Rather skimpy wine list. *Note:* You'll think you're in a Roman *trattoria,* and you'll find some of the best Italian food in the region at enticingly low prices. Very popular locally, and deservedly so. Resv. suggested. *Italian.* **I**

🍸 **Nathan's Famous,** 1930 E. Sunrise Blvd. (305/763-4934). A/C. Lunch/dinner daily (11am–11pm). No credit cards. *Specialties:* stuffed clams, pastrami, corned beef, hot dogs, very good homemade french fries. *Note:* The delicatessen sandwiches and daily specials here are praiseworthy, but no match for those at Miami Beach's Wolfie's Rascal House. But the place (a branch of the well-known Nathan's of New York) is very popular, especially at lunchtime. *American.* **B**

IN NEARBY PORT EVERGLADES 🍸 **Burt & Jack's,** Berth 23 (305/522-5225). A/C. Dinner only, nightly; closed Dec 25. AE, CB, DC, MC, V. Jkt. *Specialties:* red meats, broiled fish. *Note:* An old Spanish mission on the ocean, surrounded on three sides by water; one of the owners is actor Burt Reynolds. Wonderful broiled dishes; huge fireplaces; romantic decor w. many art objects. Resv. a must. *Steak/Seafood.* **I–M**

CAFETERIA/FAST FOOD Morrison's, 1700 N. U.S. 1 (305/565-3242). Lunch/dinner daily (till 8pm). MC, V. Roast beef, fish of the day. Locally popular.

🏛 **HOLLYWOOD:** Founded in the 1920s by a California realestate promoter (whence the name), this beach resort has always been a great commercial success. With more than 20 public courses, it is the golfer's favorite beach. Don't fail to visit **Six Flags Atlantis,** 2700 Stirling Rd. (305/926-1000), one of the world's largest water-sports parks, with 80 attractions on some of 65 acres (26ha). Open daily June–Sept, wknds only Oct–Dec. See, too, the **Seminole Indian Reservation** at 3551 N. State Rd. 7 (305/583-7112), one of the last inhabited Native American villages in Florida. Handcrafts, mini-zoo, bingo hall for 1,400 people at 4150 N. Fla. 7 (305/961-4519). Open daily.

Where to Stay

💰💰💰 **Diplomat Resort & Country Club,** 3515 S. Ocean Dr., Hollywood, FL 33022 (305/457-8111; toll free 800/327-1212). 1,160 rms, A/C, color TV, in-rm movies. AE, CB, DC, MC, V. Valet gar. $7, pool, golf, 19 tennis courts, health club, boats, three rests. (including the Celebrity Room), five bars, rm svce, disco, hrdrsr, boutiques, free crib. *Note:* Enormous 15-floor tourist complex w. direct access to the beach. Exemplary comfort and layout; spacious rms w. refrigerators and private patios or balconies (some have kitchenettes). Excellent sports facilities. Svce not always dependable; group and convention clientele somewhat obtrusive. **E–VE,** but lower rates off-season.

MIAMI BEACH: "The Pearl of Florida"! See Chapter 19 on Miami.

CHAPTER 17

TAMPA AND ST. PETERSBURG

□ □ □

This urban agglomeration of about two million people, Florida's largest after Miami, comprises two distinct cities located along the same bay. One, **St. Petersburg,** is an outward-looking vacation community. The more businesslike **Tampa,** with its glittering skyscrapers, and flourishing industries, prides itself on being the site (in 1539) of the first Spanish encampment on U.S. soil. It was from this base camp, at the mouth of the Little Manatee River, just south of Tampa, that Hernándo de Soto and his 600 companions set out on their expedition across the southeastern U.S. in an extraordinary odyssey that took them 4,800 mi. (7,700km), from Florida to Texas and Mississippi. Tampa also boasts one of the highest growth rates in the country: 53% in the last decade.

But it is not the tourist industry, buoyant though it may be, that has brought all this prosperity to Tampa. A youthful population, including many workers who moved here from the North and a large concentration of refugees from Cuba (Tampa's **Ybor City** district is a kind of Little Havana), has contributed much. St. Petersburg, on the other hand, along with such neighboring resort towns as **Clearwater, Madeira Beach, Indian Shores,** and **Treasure Island,** is best known for its immense beaches and the beauty of its offshore islands, which draw more than a million visitors a year. Tampa, a modern, dynamic port city, puts its major industries on parade along the bay: phosphates, uranium processing, breweries, tobacco. With so large a Cuban population, Tampa could scarcely escape becoming the cigar capital of the U.S.: it turns out more than three million of them every day.

Besides the splendid deep-water bay, Tampa and St. Petersburg have two principal tourist attractions: the numberless excursions that can be made from here either into central Florida (**Walt Disney World, EPCOT, Disney–MGM Studios, Cypress Gardens, Sea World,** etc.) or along the shores of the Gulf of Mexico (Sarasota, Sanibel and Captiva Islands, etc.). Some 5.7 million tourists spent time in the Tampa Bay area last year according to a recent survey.

BASIC FACTS: State of Florida. Area code: 813. ZIP Codes (of the central post offices): 33733 (St. Petersburg), 33602 (Tampa). Founded: 1876 (St. Petersburg), 1823 (Tampa). Approximate population: city, 250,000 (St. Petersburg), 340,000 (Tampa); metropolitan area, 1,980,000. 20th-largest metropolitan area in the country.

CLIMATE: St. Petersburg earns its nickname of "Sunshine City"; the sun shines almost all the time, and the Tampa Bay area has one of the most agreeable climates in the U.S. Almost never does the mercury dip below 59°F (15°C) even in the depth of winter; the Jan mean temperature is 61°F (16°C). In summer, the July mean is 82°F (28°C), and the high rarely exceeds 86°F (30°C). To put it succinctly: it's always spring here, and you'll have a pleasant stay any time of year.

DISTANCES: Atlanta, 455 mi. (728km); Miami, 268 mi. (428km); New Orleans, 633 mi. (1,012km); Orlando, 83 mi. (132km).

ARRIVAL & TRANSIT INFORMATION

AIRPORTS: The **St. Petersburg–Clearwater International Airport** (PIE), 9 mi. (14km) north of St. Petersburg, 17 mi. (27km) SW of Tampa. For information, call 813/535-7600.
    Tampa International Airport (TPA), 16 mi. (26km) NE of St. Petersburg, 5 mi. (8km) NW of Tampa. An airport of revolutionary design, one of the most modern in the country. For information, call 813/276-3400.

U.S. AIRLINES (the Tampa phone number is given first; the St. Petersburg number, if any, follows): American (221-5831), Continental (874-7151; 894-5588), Delta (286-1800; 894-1861), Eastern (877-8811; 896-7631), Midway (toll free 800/621-5700), Northwest (885-7811; 896-3131), Pan Am (229-0951; 822-4261), TWA (229-7961; 898-3131), United (223-1751), and USAir (toll free 800/428-4322).

FOREIGN CARRIERS: Air Canada (toll free 800/422-6232) and British Airways (toll free 800/247-9297).

CITY LINK: From the two airports to the two cities there is a variety of transportation available.
    To Downtown St. Petersburg: The **cab** fare from St. Petersburg–Clearwater Airport is $12; time, 20 min. From Tampa Airport: fare, about $22; time, about 40 min. Bus between Tampa Airport and St. Petersburg: **The Limo** (822-3333), serving principal hotels. Fare to St. Petersburg, $10; to St. Petersburg Beach, $12; time, about 40 min. to 1 hr.
    To Downtown Tampa: The **cab** fare from Tampa Airport is about $14; time, about 15 min. Bus between Tampa Airport and downtown Tampa: **Central Florida Limo Service** (276-3730), serving principal hotels; fare, $9; time, 20 min. **City bus:** Line 30 serves downtown Tampa; fare, 60¢.
    Public transportation (bus) is inefficient: in Tampa, HART (254-4278); in St. Petersburg, PSTA (530-9911).
    Given the many interesting destinations for excursions around the area, and the very low rates prevailing in Florida, it makes a lot of sense to rent a car with unlimited mileage.

CAR RENTAL (at Tampa International Airport unless otherwise indicated): Avis (276-3500); Budget (877-6051); Dollar (883-3640); Hertz (883-3350); National (883-3783); Thrifty, 1208 N. Ward St. (877-7583). For downtown locations in Tampa and St. Petersburg, consult the appropriate local telephone directory.

LIMOUSINE SERVICES: Carey Limousine (538-4800 in St. Petersburg, 228-7927 in Tampa) and Esquire Limo Service (725-1777 in St. Petersburg, 725-1777 in Tampa).

TAXIS: In theory cabs may not be hailed on the street, but may be taken from the waiting lines outside the major hotels, or more conveniently, summoned by phone. Recommended companies **in St. Petersburg** are Blue Star Cab (327-4104) and Yellow Cab (821-7777); **in Tampa,** United Cab (253-2424) and Yellow Cab (253-0121). Cab fares are on the high side.

TRAIN: Amtrak has stations at 3601 31st St. N. in St. Petersburg (522-9475) and at Nebraska Ave. and Twiggs St. in Tampa (229-2473).

INTERCITY BUSES: Greyhound has terminals at 180 9th St. in St. Petersburg (895-4455) and 610 E. Polk St. in Tampa (229-2174).

INFORMATION & TOURS

TOURIST INFORMATION: The **St. Petersburg Chamber of Commerce,** 100 Second Ave. N., St. Petersburg, FL 33731 (813/821-4069).

Suncoast Welcome Center, junction of Fla. 688 and I-275, St. Petersburg (813/576-1449).

Tampa Chamber of Commerce, 801 E. John F. Kennedy Blvd., Tampa, FL 33601 (813/228-7777).

Tampa/Hillsborough Convention and Visitors Association, 100 S. Ashley Dr., Suite 850, Tampa, FL 33601 (813/223-1111; toll free 800/448-2672).

GUIDED TOURS: Both St. Petersburg and Tampa have several options for guided tours.

St. Petersburg

Belle of St. Petersburg (boat), 401 Second Ave. NE (823-1665 or 823-8171): 2-hr. cruises on Tampa Bay. Also dinner-dances. Year round.

Gray Line Tours (bus), 921 3rd St. S. (822-3577): Guided bus tours of the city and surroundings, year round.

Trolley tours (bus): 2-hr. guided tour of St. Petersburg and St. Petersburg Beach, in a bus cunningly disguised as an old-time streetcar. You may dismount and reboard as often as you like along the route. Daily year round; call 596-9776 for information.

Tampa

Around the Town Tours (bus), 14009 N. Dale Mabry Hwy. (961-4120): Guided bus tours of the city and surroundings; year round.

Gray Line Tours (bus) (273-0845): Guided bus tours of the city and surroundings, serving principal hotels; year round.

Sea Escape Cruises (boat), Port of Tampa (toll free 800/432-0900): 1-day mini-cruise on the Gulf of Mexico; on board are restaurants, bars, pool, and casino. Fare is $79 per person including buffet. Daily year round.

TAMPA

SIGHTS, ATTRACTIONS & ACTIVITIES

ARCHITECTURAL HIGHLIGHTS: ☀️⚓ **Performing Arts Center,** 1010 N. MacInnes Pl. (222-1010): Opened in 1987 at a cost of $55 million, this ultramodern performing-arts complex comprises three adjacent auditoriums: **Festival Hall,** with 2,400 seats, home of the Florida Symphony Orchestra and the Tampa Ballet; the 900-seat **Playhouse;** and the 300-seat **Robert and Lorena Jaeb Theater.** Beautifully sited on the Hillsborough River. Worth seeing. Guided tours by appointment (222-1000).

⚓ **University of Tampa,** 401 John F. Kennedy Blvd. at the Hillsborough River (253-3333): The main building of this university, founded in the 1930s, used to be the Tampa Bay Hotel, a turn-of-the-century palace whose Hispano-Moorish architecture and 13 minarets are imitative of the

TAMPA

N

To Silver Springs

FLETCHER AVE.

BR 41

Univ. of So. Florida

Mus. of Science & Industry ■

582

FOWLER AVE.

FLORIDA AVE.

NEBRASKA AVE.

Busch Gardens

583

■ Tampa Bay Downs

BUSCH BLVD. ■

580

Temple Terrace

Tampa Dog Track

580

Lowry Park

Hillsborough River

56TH ST.

4

HILLSBOROUGH AVE.

Tampa

HIGHLAND AVE.

45

BUFFALO AVE.

301

Tampa Int'l Airport

92

ARMENIA AVE.

Ybor City St. Mus.

569

BROADWAY

Univ. of Tampa ■

275

60

ADAMO DR.

60

JFK BLVD.

BR 41

22ND ST. CAUSEWAY

HOWARD FRANKLIN BRIDGE

WEST SHORE BLVD.

D. MABRY HWY.

TAMPA SOUTH CROSS TOWN EXPWY.

BAYSHORE BLVD.

David Island

Peter O. Knight Airport

CAUSEWAY BLVD.

BAYSHORE RD.

78TH ST.

Old Tampa Bay

618

GANDY BLVD.

GANDY BRIDGE

Jai Alai Fronton

573

MACDILL AVE.

Hillsborough Bay

41

INTER BAY BLVD.

MacDill AFB

BAYSHORE RD.

St. Petersburg

Tampa Bay

Alhambra in Granada (Spain). The **Henry B. Plant Museum,** a triumph of rococo styling, is worth a visit all to itself. Open Tues–Sat.

BEACHES: ⚓ **Davis Municipal Beach,** Courtney Campbell Pkwy.: Huge, very popular beach near the airport; noisy.
 There are dozens of miles of beaches less than an hour's drive away, at **Bradenton Beach, Clearwater Beach, Crystal Beach, Sarasota,** etc.

INDUSTRIAL TOURS: The **Stroh's Brewing Co.,** 11111 N. 30th St. (971-7071): Brewery tour and free tasting, Mon–Fri. Call for times.
 Villazon and Co., 304 N. Armenia Ave. (879-2291): One of Florida's best-known cigar factories; visits Mon–Fri. Call for times.

MUSEUMS OF ART: ⚓ **Tampa Museum of Art,** 601 Doyle Carlton Dr. (223-8130): Greek, Roman, and Egyptian antiquities; paintings by European masters and moderns. Interesting temporary exhibitions. Imposing Greek Revival architecture. Should be seen. Open Tues–Sun.

MUSEUMS OF SCIENCE & HISTORY: ⚓ **Museum of Science and Industry,** 4801 E. Fowler Ave. (985-5531): One of the country's few open-air museums. Many displays and demonstrations relating to the environment, agriculture, geology, electricity, etc. Simulation of a hurricane; observation of sunspots with the aid of a heliostat. Don't fail to visit. Open daily.

PARKS & GARDENS: ⚓ **Lowry Park,** North Blvd. and W. Sligh Ave. (223-8230): 105-acre (42ha) park with recently opened zoo where animals roam freely in specially designed habitats. Also Fairyland, a children's theme park built around characters from Mother Goose. Open daily.

PERFORMING ARTS: For a daily listing of all shows and cultural events, consult the entertainment pages of the daily paper *Tampa Tribune* (morning).
 Falk Theater, University of Tampa campus, 401 W. John F. Kennedy Blvd. (251-0254): Ballet, recitals.
 McKay Auditorium, U. of Tampa campus, W. John F. Kennedy Blvd. at the Hillsborough River (253-3333): Concerts, operettas. Home of the Spanish Lyric Theater.
 Tampa Bay Performing Arts Center, 1010 N. MacInnes Pl. (222-1045): Ultramodern complex comprising three adjoining performance halls. Concerts, ballet, opera, classic and contemporary theater, Broadway shows. Home of the Florida Symphony Orchestra, the Tampa Ballet (season Oct–Mar), and the Tampa Oratorio Society.
 Tampa Theater, 711 N. Franklin St. (223-8286): A 1926 movie theater, plushly decorated in the rococo style. Concerts, contemporary theater, movies.

SHOPPING: The **Market on Harbour Island,** 601 S. Harbour Island Blvd. (223-9898): Ultramodern shopping mall which combines the atmosphere of a European open-air market, with cobbled streets, fountains, plazas, arcades, and an enormous carousel. More than 50 varied boutiques and stores as well as a score of restaurants, bars, and cafés. Lovely view of the waterfront. Connected to Tampa City by monorail. Very spectacular.
 ☼ **Ybor Square,** 13th St. and Eighth Ave. (247-4497): Complex of boutiques and stores in a 19th-century cigar factory, now a designated historic monument. Imaginative decor; worth seeing.

SPECIAL EVENTS: For the exact schedule of events below, consult the **Tampa/Hillsborough Convention and Visitors Association** (see "Tourist Information," above).

Florida State Fair (Feb): Very popular agricultural and business fair, with cattle show, handcraft market, flower shows (especially orchids), rodeos, pop concerts. At the Fairgrounds, I-4 and U.S. 301.

GTE Suncoast Classic (mid-Feb): Brings the top stars of the PGA Tour to Tampa Palms Golf & Country Club.

Gasparilla Pirate Invasion (Feb): Boat parade, carnival, folklore parades; colorful. Commemorates the taking of Tampa by pirate José Gaspar.

Spring Arts and Crafts Fiesta (Mar): Festival of South American art and folklore. Balls. Held in Ybor City.

SPORTS: Tampa boasts professional teams in two sports (one for spring training only):

Baseball (spring training, Feb–Mar): Cincinnati Reds, Reds Spring Training Field, Plant City (752-7337); Pittsburgh Pirates, McKechnie Field, Bradenton (748-4610).

Football (Aug–Dec): Buccaneers, Tampa Stadium (879-2827).

Horse Racing
Tampa Bay Downs, Race Track Rd., Oldsmar (855-4401), 11 mi. (17km) NW of Tampa on Fla. 580. Thoroughbred racing Tues–Sat Dec–Apr.

Jai Alai
Tampa Fronton, S. Dale Mabry Hwy. and Gandy Blvd. (831-1411), 5 mi. (8km) SW of Tampa on I-275. Matches daily except Thurs and Sun, Jan–June.

STROLLS: ☼🏛 **Waterfront,** Harbor St., Shrimp Docks, and 13th St.: The port district, always busy with the unloading of cargoes—fish, bananas, tropical fruit, or whatever. You'll have a good view of the impressive trawler fleet from the 22nd St. Causeway. A must.

☼🏛 **Ybor City,** bounded by Columbus Dr., Fifth Ave., 22nd St., and Nebraska Ave.: A Cuban enclave in the heart of Tampa, complete with cigar factories, shops, and typical restaurants. The first Cuban immigrants to settle here were the cigar-manufacturing workers brought from Key West by Vicente Martinez Ybor in 1886. The scent of tobacco (no longer imported from Cuba, but from Puerto Rico, Honduras, and the Dominican Republic) perfumes a warm, colorful atmosphere embracing the descendents of Cuban and other Spanish-speaking immigrants, and many Italians as well. The **Ybor City State Museum,** 1818 Ninth Ave. (247-6323), traces the history of Cuban cigar manufacturing from its inception in the mid-19th century to the current industry in Florida. Open Tues–Sat. Lively and picturesque, especially at night, Ybor City is not to be missed.

THEME PARKS NEARBY: 🏛 **Adventure Island,** 4545 Bougainvillea Ave. (971-7978): A 19-acre (7ha) park entirely devoted to the pursuit of surfing, diving, and swimming. You can splash in an enormous pool with artificial waves and waterfalls, or float down the artificial rapids. Entertaining. Open daily in summer, weekends only in spring and fall; closed in winter. Adjacent to Busch Gardens.

☼🏛🏛 **Busch Gardens–"The Dark Continent,"** 3000 Busch Blvd. (971-8282): One of the most famous theme parks in Florida, with a vast zoo (3,500 animals), trained animal shows, and reconstructed African villages. Gigantic, thrilling roller coaster; rides by monorail, boat, or miniature train. Broadway-style shows. Tour of the Anheuser-Busch brewery. Not to be missed. Open daily year round. Admission is $24.

☼🏛🏛 **Silver Springs,** 95 mi (152km) NE of Tampa on I-75N and Fla. 40E (904/236-2121): The springs of the Silver River, the largest of which attains a record flow rate of half a billion gallons (2 billion liters) a day, form a magnificent lake of remarkably clear water, where many TV movies and documentaries have been made. Glass-bottom-boat rides over the 100,000-

year-old underwater grottoes—a truly spectacular sight. Impressive reptile zoo. The park attracts more than 1.5 million visitors a year; don't miss it. Open daily year round.

ACCOMMODATIONS

A Note on Accommodations: Room rates in Tampa are coded as follows: **VE,** Very Expensive ($140 and up); **E,** Expensive ($90–$140); **M,** Moderate ($60–$90); **I,** Inexpensive ($30–$60); **B,** Budget (up to $30). A listing of toll free numbers is in the Appendix.

Personal Favorites (in order of preference)

☀ ⓛ ⓛ ⓛ ⓛ **Saddlebrook** (vic.), 100 Saddlebrook Way, Wesley Chapel, FL 34249 (813/973-1111; toll free 800/237-7519). 500 suites, A/C, color TV, in-rm movies. AE, CB, DC, MC, V. Valet parking $6, pool, two golf courses, putting green, 37 tennis courts, sauna, health club, bike rentals, fishing, three rests. (including the Cypress Room), bar, rm svce, disco, hrdrsr. *Note:* If you enjoy golf or tennis you'll be in paradise here, 30 min. north of Tampa on I-75 (take Exit 58). Luxurious vacation village standing amid 480 acres (194ha) of gardens, wooded hills, and lakes. Spacious, comfortable suites w. private balconies and refrigerators, many w. kitchenettes. Very acceptable rests. Extravagant outsize pool; as for the golf courses, they were laid out by Arnold Palmer himself. For exhausted businesspeople and lovers of outdoor sports. Worthwhile vacation discounts. One of the best places to stay in Florida. **VE,** but lower rates off-season.

ⓛ ⓛ ⓛ **Wyndham Harbour Island Hotel** (nr. dwntwn), 725 S. Harbour Island Blvd., Harbour Island, FL 33602 (813/229-5000; toll free 800/822-4200). 300 rms, A/C, color TV, in-rm movies. AE, CB, DC, MC, V. Valet gar. $6, pool, health club, 15 tennis courts, marina, boats, bike rentals, two rests. (including Harbour View), bar, rm svce, nightclub, boutiques, concierge, free breakfast, free crib. *Note:* Beautiful grand hotel on the water, w. splendid view of the bay and the Tampa skyline. Luxurious, comfortable rms w. refrigerators and period furniture. Discreet, attentive svce; excellent rest. Adjoining the Market in Harbour Island w. its dozens of shops and rests. Business clientele. 5 min. from dwntwn by Franklin St. Bridge, or 90 seconds by people mover. **E**

ⓛ ⓛ ⓛ **Guest Quarters** (nr. dwntwn), 555 N. West Shore Blvd., FL 33609 (813/875-1555; toll free 800/424-2900). 221 suites. A/C, color TV, in-rm movies, AE, CB, DC, MC, V. Valet gar. $3, pool, health club, sauna, rest. (Bay Café), bar, 24-hr. rm svce, library, concierge, free buffet breakfast, free crib. *Note:* Hulking white 16-story tower of conventional design, offering only spacious, very well equipped suites w. kitchenette, minibar, and two remote-control TVs. All have private balcony. Ultra-professional reception and svce. Free shuttle bus to airport (5 min.). Large business clientele; 10 min. from dwntwn. Good value. **E–VE**

ⓛ ⓛ ⓛ **Radisson Bay Harbor Inn** (nr. dwntwn), 7700 Courtney Campbell Causeway, FL 33607 (813/889-8900; toll free, see Radisson). 260 rms, A/C, color TV, in-rm movies. AE, CB, DC, MC, V. Free parking, pool, two tennis courts, boats, windsurfing, rest. (Yankee Trader), bar, rm svce, disco, hrdrsr, free crib. *Note:* Big six-story hotel on the bay w. private beach. Faultless comfort; very complete facilities; attentive svce. Pretty tropical decor. Business and vacation clientele. Good value. 15 min. from dwntwn, 5 min. from the airport (free shuttle). **E**

ⓛ ⓛ **Holiday Inn Downtown** (dwntwn), 111 W. Fortune St., FL 33602 (813/223-1351; toll free, see Holiday Inns). 313 rms, A/C, color TV, in-rm movies. AE, CB, DC, MC, V. Free parking, pool, health club, rest., bar, rm svce, nightclub, free crib. *Note:* Modern 14-story building adjoining the Performing Arts Center; comfort and facilities above the Holiday Inn average. Spacious rms, some w. minibars. VIP floor. Well located in dwntwn Tampa, and a favorite w. business travelers. Very good value; free airport limo. **I–M**

♀ **Best Western Safari Inn** (nr. dwntwn), 4139 Busch Blvd., FL
🛏 33617 (813/988-9191; toll free, see Best Western). 99 rms, A/C, color TV, in-rm movies. AE, CB, DC, MC, V. Free parking, pool, sauna, rest., bar, valet svce, free crib. *Note:* The perfect base for a visit to nearby Busch Gardens (free shuttle). Comfortable rms w. patio or balcony, some w. refrigerator. Cordial reception; family clientele. Good value. **I–M**

♀ **Motel 6** (nr. dwntwn), 333 E. Fowler Ave., FL 33612 (813/
🛏 932-4948). 150 rms, A/C, color TV, in-rm movies. AE, MC, V. Free parking, pool. *Note:* Unbeatable value right nr. the famous Busch Gardens. Modern and comfortable; 15 min. from dwntwn by I-275. Ideal for motorists and family parties. **B–I**

Other Accommodations (from top bracket to budget)

♀♀♀ **Sheraton Grand Hotel** (nr. dwntwn), 4860 W. John F. Ken-
🛏🛏🛏 nedy Blvd., FL 33609 (813/286-4400; toll free, see Shera-ton). 325 rms, A/C, color TV, in-rm movies. AE, CB, DC, MC, V. Valet gar. $6, pool, two rests. (including J. Fitzgerald's), bar, 24-hr. rm svce, nightclub, boutiques, free breakfast, free airport limo, free crib, concierge. *Note:* Eleven floors of spectacular glass-and-steel futurist design; beautiful glass-walled lobby w. indoor grdn. Elegant, refined decor; spacious, ultra-comfortable rms w. refrigerators. Rest. of a high order; personalized svce. Two VIP floors. A favorite place w. big-businesspeople; 10 min. from dwntwn and 5 min. from the airport. **E–VE**

♀♀♀ **Hyatt Regency** (dwntwn), 2 Tampa City Center, FL 33602
🛏🛏🛏 (813/225-1234; toll free, see Hyatt). 517 rms, A/C, color TV, in-rm movies. Valet gar. $6, pool, sauna, health club, two rests., coffee shop, bars, 24-hr. rm svce, nightclub, concierge, crib $10. *Note:* Rather massive tower a stone's throw from the Hillsborough River; spectacular lobby w. two-story waterfall and grdns. Ultramodern comfort and facilities; well-designed, spacious rms; efficient svce. Centrally located in the heart of the business district; attracts business travelers and groups. Two VIP floors. The largest of the dwntwn hotels. Interesting wknd discounts. Recently renovated. **E**

♀♀ **Days Inn Downtown** (formerly the Sheraton; dwntwn), 515
🛏🛏 E. Cass St., FL 33602 (813/229-6431; toll free, see Days Inns). 180 rms, A/C, color TV, in-rm movies. AE, CB, DC, MC, V. Free gar., pool, rest., bar, valet svce, crib $5. *Note:* Typical motel in dwntwn Tampa; spacious, comfortable rms; entirely redecorated. Business clientele. Efficient svce; very good value; next to the Convention Center. **I–M**

♀ **Tahitian Inn** (nr dwntwn), 601 S. Dale Mabry Hwy., FL
🛏 33609 (813/877-6721; toll free 800/541-2255). 80 rms, A/C, color TV, in-rm movies. AE, DC, MC, V. Free parking, pool, coffee shop (breakfast and lunch only), rm svce, free crib. *Note:* Very acceptable small motel; relatively spacious, comfortable rms; friendly svce. Good value. 10 min. from dwntwn and 8 min. from the airport. **I–M**

Airport Accommodations

♀♀♀ **Marriott Airport** (vic.), International Airport, Tampa, FL
🛏🛏🛏 33607 (813/879-5151; toll free, see Marriott). 300 rms, A/C, color TV, in-rm movies. AE, CB, DC, MC, V. Valet parking $6, pool, health club, sauna, two rests. (including C.K.'s), bar, rm svce, nightclub, free crib. *Note:* Modern hotel in the airport terminal. Agreeable, well-soundproofed rms; very complete facilities; efficient svce. C.K.'s, a revolving rest. at the top, is praiseworthy. VIP floor. Business clientele; ideal for a stopover between flights. **E–VE**

RESTAURANTS

A Note on Restaurant Prices: Tampa restaurant prices, per person, excluding drinks and service charges, are coded as follows: **VE**, Very Expensive ($60 and up); **E**, Expensive ($40–$60); **M**, Moderate ($25–$40); **I**, Inexpensive ($15–$25); **B**, Budget (up to $15).

Personal Favorites (in order of preference)

Bern's Steak House (nr. dwntwn), 1208 S. Howard Ave. (251-2421). A/C. Dinner only, nightly; closed Dec 25. AE, CB, DC, MC, V. Jkt. *Specialties:* onion soup, red meats, lamb chops, sautéed chicken w. sesame, "wild fried steak," homemade pastry and sherbet. The enormous wine list weighs 7 lbs. (3kg) and offers no fewer than 7,000 different labels. *Note:* Bern's likes to call itself "The World's Best and Most Famous Steak House," but joking apart, the charcoal-broiled steaks are truly remarkable, the vegetables are organically grown—and the prices are highly seasoned. To choose the degree of aging, weight, and cooking time for your steak, you almost need a slide rule. Gaudy opulent decor and a rather high noise level, Gigantic wine cellar (500,000 bottles). Excellent svce. Resv. strongly advised; valet parking. *Steak/American.* **M–E**

Columbia (dwntwn), 2117 E. Seventh Ave. (248-4961). A/C. Lunch/dinner daily. AE, CB, DC, MC, V. *Specialties:* white-bean soup, red snapper Alicante, filet mignon criolla, chicken valenciana, paella. *Note:* Huge Spanish baroque-style house in the heart of Ybor City, Tampa's Cuban district. Lovely decor of *azulejos* (blue tiles) and houseplants. Tasty, Spanish-inspired food; flamenco music and show every evening except Sun. Diligent svce; a Tampa landmark since 1905. Resolutely tourist atmosphere; resv. advised. Valet parking. Other location; The Market on Harbour Island (229-2992). *Spanish/Latin American.* **I–M**

Café de Paris (nr. dwntwn), 4430 W. John F. Kennedy Blvd. (287-8422). A/C. Lunch Mon–Fri, dinner Mon–Sat; closed Jan 1, Dec 25. AE, CB, DC, MC, V. Jkt. *Specialties:* chateaubriand bouquetière, shrimp Monte Carlo, bouillabaisse. *Note:* Somewhat pretentious cuisine in a deluxe bistro setting. The sauces could, w. advantage, be lighter, but the food is faultlessly prepared and presented. Courteous svce; good wine list at reasonable prices. Resv. necessary. *French.* **I–M**

Spanish Park (dwntwn), 3517 E. Seventh Ave., Ybor City (248-6138). A/C. Lunch Mon–Fri, dinner Mon–Sat; closed hols. AE, CB, DC, MC, V. *Specialties:* shrimp Valdez, Spanish-style bean soup, paella, piccadillo w. plantains, broiled pompano, chicken w. yellow rice (prepared w. chablis), swordfish steak, flan, rice pudding. Splendid homemade sangría. *Note:* The most popular and dependable of Tampa's countless Spanish-Cuban rests., serving absolutely authentic food. Pretty Spanish-colonial setting w. colonnaded patio and Moorish tiled roof; uncommonly efficient svce. Strongly recommended; resv. advised; excellent value. *Spanish/Latin American.* **B–I**

Other Restaurants (from top bracket to budget)

Harbour View Room (dwntwn), in the Wyndham Harbour Island Hotel (see "Accommodations," above) (229-5001). A/C. Breakfast/lunch/dinner daily, brunch Sun. AE, CB, DC, MC, V. Jkt. *Specialties:* fresh pasta w. shrimp, lobster w. pink-champagne sabayon, poached sea bass w. lettuce and stone crabs, grilled gingered swordfish, savarin of grouper w. mussel ragoût, fine desserts. Good wine list. *Note:* This is nouvelle cuisine Florida style, delicate and imaginative, served in a gracious contemporary setting. As its name implies, this luxurious hotel rest. offers wraparound harbor and marina views, and svce as polished as it comes. At lunchtime there's a crowd of businessmen. Resv. strongly advised. Valet parking. *American/Seafood.* **I–M**

Lauro Ristorante (dwntwn), Ashley Tower, 100 S. Ashley St. (884-4366) A/C. Lunch Mon–Fri, dinner nightly; closed Sun in summer, Jan 1, Dec 25. AE, CB, DC, MC, V. Jkt. *Specialties:* oysters au gratin, mushrooms stuffed w. snails and Gorgonzola cheese, agnolotti, linguine w. seafood, sautéed trout in lemon butter, grouper alla Livornese, sole Cleopatra (w. mushrooms and artichokes), quail w. porcini mushrooms, rack of lamb w. mustard, creamed sweetbreads, delicious desserts. Good list of Italian wines. *Note:* This upper-crust rest., occupying the street floor of an elegant office tower, serves airy, delicate Italian food from the hand of its excellent chef Lauro Medaglia. Subdued but luxurious rose-and-gray setting; svce flawless if a little highfalutin'. Tampa's latest "in" place; you must book ahead for dinner. Valet parking. *Italian.* **I–M**

☼ ♈♲ **Tobacco Company Restaurant** (nr. dwntwn), 4115 E. Busch Blvd. (985-8200). A/C. Lunch Mon–Fri, dinner nightly (until 2am), brunch Sun; closed Jan 1, Dec 25. AE, DC, MC, V. *Specialties:* beef Bourbon w. mushroom sauce, poached salmon hollandaise, broiled steak or fish, prime ribs. Remarkable wine list at bargain prices. *Note:* The enchanting Victorian decor w. genuine Tiffany windows, art objects, and the old cigar-rolling machines from which the rest. takes its name, are worth a visit all by themselves; so are the tropical grdns w. their peacocks and other exotic birds. Elegant, polished cuisine makes this incontestably Tampa's most original rest. Very good svce; resv. advised. Adjacent to Busch Gardens. Dancing nightly. *Steak/Seafood.* **I–M**

♈ **Café Pepe** (nr. dwntwn), 2006 W. John F. Kennedy Blvd. (253-6501). A/C. Lunch/dinner Mon–Sat. AE, DC, MC, V. *Specialties:* paella, shrimp suprema, Cuban rice and black beans, chicken w. rice, coconut sherbet. *Note:* With its whitewashed walls, flagons of sangría, and noisy, colorful atmosphere, Café Pepe is a little bit of Old Castile transplanted to Tampa. Locally very popular; resv. advised. *Spanish/Latin American.* **I**

Cafeterias/Fast Food

☼ **Silver Ring Café** (dwntwn), 1831 E. Seventh Ave. (248-2549). Breakfast/lunch only, Mon–Sat; closed July. The unchallenged king of the "Cuban sandwich" (ham, salami, pork, Swiss cheese on a toasted bun). A real local landmark.

BARS & NIGHTCLUBS

Baja Beach Club (dwntwn) 901 N. Franklin St., Tampa (224-9685): The hottest nightclub dwntwn. Features dancing to top-40 music played by a disc jockey. Fashionably casual atmosphere.

Ocean Club (nr. dwntwn), 4811 W. Cypress Ave., Tampa (875-6458). Singles bar-disco very popular with the youthful upper crust of the area. Good atmosphere.

Selena's (nr. dwntwn), 1623 Snow Ave., Tampa (251-2116). The fashionable Cajun rock and jazz joint, with live music; also very acceptable restaurant. Very popular with the locals. Open nightly.

Tobacco Company (nr. dwntwn), 4115 E. Busch Blvd. The tropical ambience of this bar-disco is a triumph. Also commendable rest. (see above). Open daily.

ST. PETERSBURG

SIGHTS, ATTRACTIONS & ACTIVITIES

ARCHITECTURAL HIGHLIGHTS: ⚓ **Municipal Marina,** 300 Second Ave. SE (893-7329): Lovely pleasure-boat basin on Tampa Bay, with 610 moorings. Worth a look.

☼⚓ **Pier Place,** 800 Second Ave. NE (894-6767): Curious five-story inverted pyramid of a building, overlooking the port's

2,400-ft. (730m) jetty. Many boutiques and restaurants. Fine view of the bay from the top-floor Observation Deck. A sight to be seen. Open daily.

☼⚲ **Stetson University College of Law,** 15th Ave. at 61st St. (345-1300): Fine exercise in Spanish-colonial architecture set among beautiful courtyards and tropical gardens; one of the loveliest campuses in the country. Definitely worth seeing.

☼⚲ **Sunshine Skyway Bridge** on I-275 linking St. Petersburg and Bradenton: Double road bridge, 12 mi. (19km) long, consisting of one highway on piles dating from 1954, and an ultramodern structure opened in 1987 whose twin 426-ft. (130m) towers dominate the entrance to Tampa Bay. This is one of the most spectacular pieces of engineering in the U.S.; from it there's a wonderful view of the bay and the Gulf of Mexico, but don't try it if you suffer from dizzy spells. The approach works best from the south.

BEACHES: ⚲ **Bay Beach,** N. Shore Dr. and 13th Ave. NE: Fine beach on Tampa Bay.

⚲ **Municipal Beach,** Gulf Blvd. at Treasure Island: The most popular of the public beaches, directly on the ocean; huge and well maintained.

⚲ **North Shore Beach,** N. Shore Dr. and Eighth Ave.: Popular beach on the bay; many sports facilities.

☼⚲ **Pass-a-Grille Beach,** Gulf Way from 1st Ave. to 22nd Ave., St. Petersburg Beach: The most beautiful, and one of the least crowded, beaches in St. Petersburg.

⚲ **Spa Beach,** Second Ave. NE, The Pier: Most accessible of the St. Petersburg beaches, and often crowded. Many boutiques and restaurants nearby.

MUSEUMS OF ART: ⚲ **Museum of Fine Arts,** 255 Beach Dr. NE (896-2667): Small but comprehensive museum of painting, sculpture, and decorative arts, from Far Eastern and Pre-Columbian art to contemporary American painters and photographers. Should be seen. Open Tues–Sun.

☼⚲⚲ **Salvador Dalí Museum,** 1000 3rd St. S. (823-3767): The Reynolds Morse Collection makes this one of the world's largest museums entirely devoted to Salvador Dalí. Comprises 93 oils, including *The Discovery of America by Christopher Columbus* and *The Hallucinogenic Toreador;* 200 original watercolors and drawings; and hundreds of sketches, lithographs, sculptures, and pop-art works by the famous surrealist painter. Initially opened in Cleveland, Ohio, the museum was moved to St. Petersburg in 1982 in a brand-new state-of-the-art museum complex. Don't miss it. Open Tues–Sun.

MUSEUMS OF SCIENCE & HISTORY: ☼⚲ **Haas Museum Complex,** 3511 Second Ave. S. (327-1437): Complex of old houses converted into a museum of life in 19th-century Florida. Reconstruction of a blacksmith's forge, hairdresser's salon, dentist's office, etc. Fine collection of shells and minerals. Notice the huge banyan tree, its trunk 62 ft. (19m) in diameter, in front of the blacksmith's forge. Instructive and amusing. Open Thurs–Sun.

☼⚲⚲ **Science Center of Pinellas County,** 7701 22nd Ave. N. (384-0027): Very educational science museum; visitors are asked to take part in all kinds of experiments in computer technology, botany, and natural science. Very modern planetarium. Fascinating for children and adults alike. Open Mon–Fri.

PARKS & GARDENS: ☼⚲ **Fort De Soto Park,** Pinellas Bayway at Fla. 679 (462-3347): Covering five little islands at the entrance to Tampa Bay, this 880-acre (356ha) park looking out on the ocean has facilities for every kind of water

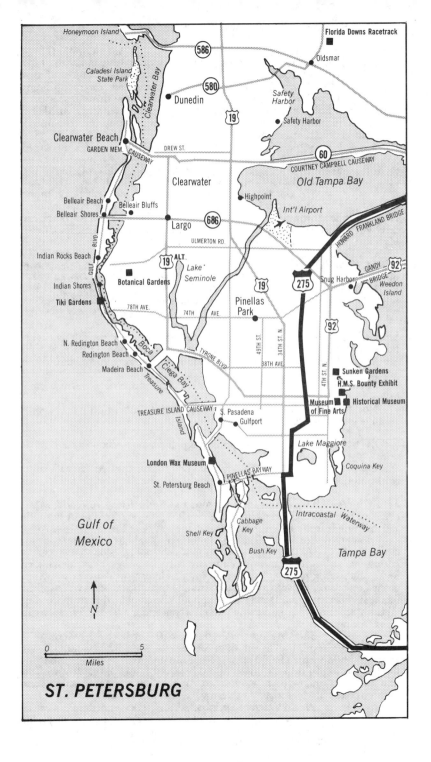

Honeymoon Island

Florida Downs Racetrack

586

Oldsmar

Caladesi Island
State Park

580

Safety
Harbor

Dunedin

19

Safety Harbor

Clearwater Beach

GARDEN MEM. CAUSEWAY   DREW ST.

60

COURTNEY CAMPBELL CAUSEWAY

Old Tampa Bay

Clearwater

Highpoint

Int'l Airport

Belleair Beach

Belleair Bluffs

Belleair Shores

Largo

686

ULMERTON RD.

HOWARD FRANKLAND BRIDGE

Indian Rocks Beach

19 ALT.

GANDY

92

Lake
Seminole

BRIDGE

Botanical Gardens

19

275

Snug Harbor

Weedon
Island

Indian Shores

Tiki Gardens

78TH AVE.

74TH   AVE.

Pinellas
Park

92

N. Redington Beach

Redington Beach

TYRONE BLVD.

49TH ST.

34TH ST. N

Madeira Beach

38TH AVE.

4TH ST. N

Sunken Gardens

H.M.S. Bounty Exhibit

TREASURE ISLAND CAUSEWAY

S. Pasadena

Gulfport

Museum
of Fine Arts

Historical Museum

Lake Maggiore

London Wax Museum

PINELLAS BAYWAY

Coquina Key

St. Petersburg Beach

Intracoastal   Waterway

Gulf of
Mexico

Cabbage
Key

Shell Key

Bush Key

Tampa Bay

275

N

0   5

Miles

275

ST. PETERSBURG

sport as well as for camping. Fort dating from the Spanish-American War (1898). Access by a long highway toll bridge. Worth seeing; open daily sunrise to sunset.

Suncoast Seabird Sanctuary, 18328 Gulf Blvd., Indian Shores (391-6211): Refuge for wounded seabirds: pelicans, herons, egrets, and ospreys. In all, representatives of more than 40 species, in huge open-air holding cages, from which they will be released when cured. The largest veterinary hospital of its kind in the U.S. Guided tours daily; a must for animal lovers and camera buffs.

Sunken Gardens, 1825 4th St. N. (896-3186): A kind of tropical paradise, with more than 7,000 species of plants and flowers from around the world, inhabited by parrots, monkeys, and exotic birds. A St. Petersburg landmark for half a century; must definitely be seen. Open daily.

Tiki Gardens, Fla. 699 at 196th Ave. and Gulf Blvd., Indian Shores (595-2567): Picturesque reconstruction of a Polynesian village, a stone's throw from the sea. Splendid mangroves and lovely tropical gardens with Polynesian temples and statues. Unusual boutiques. A must for lovers of picture postcards from faraway places. Open daily.

PERFORMING ARTS: For a daily listing of all shows and cultural events, consult the entertainment pages of the morning paper, *St. Petersburg Times.*

Bayfront Center Theater, 400 1st St. S. (893-7211): Concerts, recitals, ballet. Home of the Florida West Coast Symphony (season Sept–May), the St. Petersburg Opera Company, and the St. Petersburg Concert Ballet.

SPECIAL EVENTS: For the exact schedule of events below, consult the **St. Petersburg Chamber of Commerce** (see "Tourist Information," above).

International Folk Fair (Feb): Folk festival honoring the diverse ethnic groups that make up the population of St. Petersburg.

Festival of States (late Mar to Apr): Art exhibitions, processions, fireworks, balls.

Florida Tournament of Bands (Dec): Brings together in competition the best high-school bands in the state.

SPORTS: St. Petersburg hosts spring training for one major-league baseball team:

Baseball (mid-Mar to mid-Apr): St. Louis Cardinals, Al Lang Stadium (822-3384).

THEME PARKS NEARBY: **Homosassa Springs Nature World,** 77 mi. (123km) north of St. Petersburg on U.S. 19N (904/628-2311): A beautiful aquatic garden around the springs that are the source of the Homosassa River. They flow at a rate of 100,000 gal. (378,000 liters) a minute; the water is crystal clear, and at 72°F (22°C). For some reason which zoologists don't understand, saltwater as well as freshwater fish are attracted to the springs. Boat rides; underwater observation gallery. This is the only theme park in the country with a group of manatees in captivity, not to mention hippopotamuses as well as alligators and other saurians. Don't miss it. Should be combined with the visit to Weeki Wachee Springs (see below) and Tarpon Springs (see "Nearby Excursions," below).

Sarasota Jungle Gardens, 3701 Bayshore Rd., Sarasota, 38 mi. (60km) south of St. Petersburg on I-275S and U.S. 41S (355-5305): More than 5,000 plant species, and hundreds of exotic birds flying free in a spectacular tropical jungle. Also very lovely landscaped gardens with flamingos, swans, and peacocks. A must-see; combine it with visits to Sarasota and De Soto National Memorial (see "Nearby Excursions," below).

Weeki Wachee Springs, 57 mi. (91km) north of St. Petersburg on U.S. 19N (904/596-2062): Aquatic displays and Esther Williams–style water nymphs make this one of Florida's most popular attractions. You'll find the world's only theater 16 ft. (4m) below the surface of the water, from which you can watch in comfort through huge walls of glass, 2⅞ in. (4cm) thick, while the nymphs go through their revolutions—an amazing sight. Boat rides on the Weeki Wachee River. Very lovely orchid gardens. Don't miss it; open daily year round.

ACCOMMODATIONS

A Note on Accommodations: Room rates in St. Petersburg are coded as follows: **VE**, Very Expensive ($140 and up); **E**, Expensive ($90–$140); **M**, Moderate ($60–$90); **I**, Inexpensive ($30–$60); **B**, Budget (up to $30). A listing of toll free numbers is in the Appendix.

Personal Favorites (in order of preference)

Don Cesar Beach Resort (vic.), 3400 Gulf Blvd., St. Petersburg Beach, FL 33706 (813/360-1881; toll free 800/247-9810). 276 rms, A/C, color TV. AE, CB, DC, MC, V. Free parking, pool, health club, sauna, two tennis courts, boating, fishing, waterskiing, private beach, bicycles, three rests. (including King Charles), three bars, 24-hr. rm svce, nightclub, hrdrsr, boutiques, art gallery, concierge, free crib. *Note:* A 1930s luxury hotel—the light-hearted Spanish baroque building is painted a lovely pink, whence the hotel's nickname, "The Pink Lady." The best rooms, overlooking the Gulf of Mexico, are splendid, but those overlooking the parking lot are much less so. Excellent svce and very good rest. Clientele of upscale groups and trendy vacationers. Beautiful landscaped grdns; direct beach access. A landmark among Florida hotels. **VE**, but lower rates off-season.

The Heritage (dwntwn), 234 Third Ave. N., St. Petersburg, FL 33701 (813/822-4814). 80 rms, A/C, color TV. AE, CB, DC, MC, V. Valet parking $6, pool, rest., bar, rm svce, concierge. *Note:* Gracious small hotel from the 1920s, agreeably restored to its pristine elegance, w. a charming atrium–winter grdn. Very comfortable period-furnished rms, attentive svce, very centrally located. A favorite of those in-the-know. **M–E**, but lower rates off-season.

Days Inn Marina (formerly the Sheraton; nr. dwntwn), 6800 34th St., St. Petersburg, FL 33711 (813/867-1151; toll free, see Days Inns). 158 rms, A/C, color TV, in-rm movies. AE, CB, DC, MC, V. Free parking, two pools, five tennis courts, marina, boating, sailboat instruction, private beach, fishing, rest., bar, rm svce, nightclub, free crib. *Note:* Elderly but congenial motel on the bay. The redecorated rms are spacious and comfortable; some have kitchenettes and refrigerators, and all have private balconies or patios. Also 10 rustic bungalows. Efficient svce; pretty tropical grdns. The ideal vacation motel. Near the Sunshine Skyway, 10 min. from dwntwn. **M–E**, but lower rates off-season.

Trails End (vic.), 11500 Gulf Blvd., Treasure Island, FL 33706 (813/360-5541). 54 rms, A/C, color TV. AE, CB, DC, MC, V. Free parking, pool, beach, adj. rest. and bar, valet svce, free crib. *Note:* Small, undistinguished, but inviting motel w. direct beach access. Relatively large rms (two-thirds of them w. kitchenette), the best overlooking pool and grdn. Interesting vacation packages. Good overall value. **I–M**, but lower rates off-season.

Ponce de Leon (dwntwn), 95 Central Ave. (at Beach Dr.), St. Petersburg, FL 33731 (813/894-7971). 100 rms. A/C, color TV. AE, MC, V. Street parking, coffee shop, bar. *Note:* Aging but well-run hotel w. commendable sandards of comfort and svce, in dwntwn St. Petersburg a stone's throw from the yacht basin. Unbeatable value. The coffee shop (Corner Café) is very acceptable. **B–I**.

Other Accommodations (from top bracket to budget)

Adam's Mark Caribbean Gulf Resort (vic.), 430 S. Gulfview Blvd., South Clearwater Beach, FL 34630 (813/443-5714; toll free 800/444-2326). 206 rms, A/C, color TV, in-rm movies. AE, CB, DC, MC, V. Free gar., pool, beach, water sports, rest. (Jack's Place), coffee shop, bar, rm svce, disco, free crib. *Note:* Modern, comfortable resort hotel looking out on the ocean; spacious, inviting rms w. private patio or balcony and panoramic view. Friendly, efficient svce, mediocre rest., package-tour and convention clientele. 30 min. from dwntwn. St. Petersburg, 25 min. from Tampa Airport. **E–VE,** but lower rates off-season.

Hilton and Towers (dwntwn), 333 1st St., St. Petersburg, FL 33701 (813/894-5000; toll free, see Hilton). 333 rms, A/C, color TV, in-rm movies. AE, CB, DC, MC, V. Free valet parking, pool, sauna, rest., bars, rm svce, disco, concierge, free crib. *Note:* Large modern 15-story building in dwntwn St. Petersburg, facing bay and yacht basin. Spacious, comfortable rms w. offshore view, some w. refrigerators. Efficient svce. Two VIP floors. Group clientele. **M–E,** but lower rates off-season.

Alden (vic.), 5900 Gulf Blvd., St. Petersburg Beach, FL 33706 (813/360-7081; toll free 800/237-2530). 140 mini-suites and studios, A/C, color TV, in-rm movies. AE, CB, DC, MC, V. Free parking, two pools, boating, windsurfing, adj. 24-hr. coffee shop, valet svce. *Note:* Modern, comfortable motel on the beach. One- to three-rm suites w. private balconies or patios and kitchenettes. Agreeable grdns, ideal for vacationers w. children. Good value on balance. Friendly reception. 20 min. from dwntwn St. Petersburg. **M–E,** but lower rates off-season.

Dolphin Beach Resort (vic.), 4900 Gulf Blvd., St. Petersburg Beach, FL 33706. (813/360-7011; toll free 800/237-8916). 174 rms, A/C, color TV, in-rm movies. AE, CB, DC, MC, V. Free parking, pool, boating, waterskiing, rest., bar, rm svce, disco, free crib. *Note:* Attractive vacation motel on the beach; rms w. balconies and gulf view, half w. kitchenettes. Comprehensive facilities. Perfect for sailors. Good value; 20 min. from dwntwn St. Petersburg. **M–E,** but lower rates off-season.

La Quinta (formerly Las Casas; nr. dwntwn), 4999 U.S. 19N, St. Petersburg, FL 33714 (813/527-8421; toll free see La Quinta). 120 rms, A/C, color TV, in-rm movies. AE, CB, DC, MC, V. Free parking, pool, health club, adj. 24-hr. rest., bar, valet svce, free breakfast. *Note:* Charming Castilian-style hacienda in a splendid tropical grdn w. fountain, palm trees, and gardenia bushes. Inviting, comfortable rms; excellent svce. Very good value; a fine place to stay. 10 min. from dwntwn. **I–M**

Friendship Inn (formerly Quality Inn; nr. dwntwn), 2260 54th Ave., St. Petersburg, FL 33714 (813/521-3511; toll free, see Friendship Inns). 116 rms, A/C, color TV, in-rm movies. AE, CB, DC, MC, V. Free parking, pool, sauna, health club, rest., valet svce, bar, crib $10. *Note:* Relatively new, comfortable five-floor motel, recently renovated. Functional rms and facilities; reception w. a smile. Good overall value. 15 min. from dwntwn w. direct access to I-275, an ideal place to stay if you're driving. **I–M**

Beach Park Motor Inn (dwntwn), 300 Beach Dr. NE, St. Petersburg, FL 33701 (813/898-6325). 26 rms, color TV. AE, MC, V. Free parking, adjacent to public beach, nearby coffee shop, free crib. *Note:* Small, modern, functional economy motel. Inviting rms w. refrigerator (some w. kitchenette). Well located overlooking Tampa Bay and City Park, and a hop, skip, and a jump from the Pier with its cluster of shops and rests. Friendly svce; good value; interesting vacation packages. **I,** but lower rates off-season.

RESTAURANTS

A Note on Restaurant Prices: St. Petersburg restaurant prices, per person, excluding drinks and service charges, are coded as follows: **VE,** Very Expensive ($60 and up): **E,** Expensive ($40–$60); **M,** Moderate ($25–$40); **I,** Inexpensive ($15–$25); **B,** Budget (up to $15).

Personal Favorites (in order of preference)

King Charles (vic.), in the Don Cesar Beach Resort (see "Accommodations," above) (360-1881). A/C. Dinner only, nightly, brunch Sun. AE, CB, DC, MC, V. Jkt. *Specialties:* chicken Florentine, veal Oscar, roast beef au jus, médaillons of lobster en bellevue (cold in jelly), game (in season), catch of the day, good desserts. *Note:* Luxurious grand-hotel rest. w. a view out over the Gulf of Mexico, serving distinguished classic food. Very preppy atmosphere. First-class svce; agreeable background music. Resv. a must. *Continental.* **M–E**

☆☆ **Pepin's** (nr. dwntwn), 4125 4th St. (821-3773). A/C. Lunch Tues–Fri, dinner Tues–Sun; closed hols. AE, MC, V. *Specialties:* salad Sevillana, shrimp w. almonds, chicken w. yellow rice, red snapper béchamel, baked pompano, steak. *Note:* Congenial Spanish-style tavern serving excellent fish and choice red meats. Friendly, efficient svce; locally very popular (especially for business lunches), so resv. strongly advised. A fine place to eat. Other location: 19519 Gulf Blvd., Indian Shores (596-9100). *Spanish/Latin American.* **I–M**

☆☆ **Peter's Place** (dwntwn), 208 Beach Dr. NE (822-8436). A/C. Lunch/dinner Tues–Sat; closed for lunch May–Oct. AE, MC, V. Jkt. *Specialties:* seafood crêpes, duck w. peaches, lobster Thermidor, filet Cordon Bleu, mousse w. liqueur. Menu changes regularly. *Note:* A stone's throw from the city's pleasure-boat marina, this intimate, plush rest. is a favorite w. local society. The sauces are a little heavy but the food is a pleasure to eat. Polished svce. Resv. necessary. *Continental.* **I–M**

☼☆ **Siple's Garden Seat** (vic.), 1234 Druid Rd., Clearwater (442-9681). A/C. Lunch/dinner daily, in season; dinner only, nightly, off-season. AE, CB, DC, MC, V. *Specialties:* clam chowder, roast duckling, baked shrimp, steak, roast beef, catch of the day, macadamia-nut pie. Skimpy wine list. *Note:* Since 1920 this inviting family home w. its country-club charm has been delighting lovers of wholesome, tasty food. Beautiful gardens and an unobstructed view of Clearwater Harbor, w. impressive sunsets. Friendly, efficient svce. A fine place. Resv. advised. *Continental/Seafood.* **B–I**

Other Restaurants (from top bracket to budget)

☆☆ **Bradford's Coach House** (dwntwn), 1900 4th St. N. (822-7982). A/C. Lunch/dinner Tues–Sun; closed May–Sept. AE, MC, V. *Specialties:* shellfish, steak, roast beef, grilled catch of the day. *Note:* Very popular steakhouse across from the Sunken Gardens serving very good red meat and remarkably fresh seafood. Efficient svce; congenial English-pub atmosphere. *Steak/Seafood.* **I**

☼☆☆ **Heilman's Beachcomber** (vic.), 447 Mandalay Ave., Clearwater Beach (442-4144). A/C. Lunch/dinner daily (until midnight). AE, DC, MC, V. *Specialties:* stone crab (in season), shrimp Rockefeller, calves' liver w. onions, roast lamb, steak, fried chicken, broiled fish of the day (snapper, grouper, swordfish, etc.), good homemade desserts. *Note:* The classic all-American rest., straight out of the 1940s w. decor, food, and waiters to match. Generous servings. Locally popular since 1948; a very fine place to eat, right on the beach. Resv. advised. *Steak/Seafood.* **I**

☆ **Arigato** (vic.), 3600 66th St. N., St. Petersburg (343-5200). A/C. Dinner only, nightly; closed hols. AE, CB, DC, MC, V. *Specialties:* sashimi, teriyaki, sukiyaki, teppanyaki. *Note:* Japanese steakhouse in the classical tradition, voted by readers of the St. Petersburg *Times* the best Far Eastern rest. in the area. The flashing knife-work of the Japanese chefs is worthwhile entertainment in itself. Lots of lanterns, Japanese pictures and shoji screens (translucent sliding partitions). Resv. advised. Very good value. 25 min. from dwntwn. Other location: 1500 U.S. 19, North Clearwater (799-0202). *Japanese.* **B–I**

☆ **The Kingfish** (vic.), 12789 Kingfish Dr., Treasure Island (360-0881). A/C. Lunch/dinner daily; closed Thanksgiving, Dec 25. MC, V. *Specialties:* catch of the day, broiled or baked shellfish at bargain prices. *Note:* Traditional oyster bar and seafood rest. Looking out over the Treasure Island yacht basin. Absolutely fresh seafood. Unpretentious nautical setting. Locally popular; very good value. *Seafood.* **B–I**

☀☽♆ **Scandia** (vic.), 19829 Gulf Blvd., Indian Shores (595-4928). A/C. Lunch/dinner daily. AE, MC, V. *Specialties:* kolde bord (hors d'oeuvres), frikadeller (meat balls), roast loin of pork w. braised red cabbage, remarkable homemade desserts and pastries. *Note:* Nice little inn, convincingly traditional-Danish in decor and otherwise, w. small, intimate dining rms. The tasty food will convince you you're in Denmark—particularly the house-specialty desserts. Smiling svce. Locally very popular, so resv. advisable. Very good value. 30 min. from dwntwn St. Petersburg. *Scandinavian.* **B–I**

Cafeterias/Fast Food

Buba's Munch Bar (vic.), 436 75th Ave., St. Petersburg Beach (360-1069). An enormous selection of hoagies, Cuban, Italian, and other sandwiches, pizzas and mixed salads. Great for a meal on the wing. Open Mon–Sat 10am–4pm. Very convenient to the St. Petersburg Beach Causeway.

BARS & NIGHTCLUBS

Le Bistro (vic.), in the Don Cesar Beach Resort (see "Accommodations," above, St. Petersburg Beach) (360-1881). Snug, intimate bar with a view of the Gulf of Mexico; preppy clientele. Disco. Open nightly.

Gallery Lounge (vic.), 7500 Blind Pass Rd., St. Petersburg Beach (360-0549). Fashionable disco with live music as well. Open daily.

O'Durkin's (vic.), 6990 Seminole Blvd., Seminole (391-7855). Live "classic" rock in exciting surroundings; also good rest. Open Mon–Sat.

Le Pompano (vic.), 19325 Gulf Blvd., Indian Shores (596-0333). Congenial disco with live music. Also very praiseworthy French rest. Fine location on the water. Open nightly.

NEARBY EXCURSIONS

🔔 **DE SOTO NATIONAL MEMORIAL** (on Fla. 64 in Bradenton, 30 mi./48km south of St. Petersburg along I-275 and U.S. 41) (792-0458): Museum of the Spanish Conquest built at the mouth of Tampa Bay, where Hernándo de Soto first dropped anchor on May 30, 1539. Recaptures the 4,000-mi. (6,400km), 4-year expedition of the famous conquistador and his 600 companions to explore the Southeast, from Florida to Mississippi. His party included Francisca Hintestrosa, wife of one of his soldiers, who is thought to be the first woman colonist in United States. Their journey is retraced in detail by a movie shown at the Visitor Center. Small military museum. Well worth the side trip. Open daily.

☀♟♟ **SARASOTA** (39 mi./62km south of St. Petersburg via I-275 and U.S. 41): Sarasota is the birthplace of American golf (the first course in the country was laid out here in 1886 by Scotsman John Hamilton Gillespie), but it has been better known as the world capital of the circus since 1927, when "the King of the Circus," John Ringling himself, chose the town as the winter quarters of the Ringling Bros. & Barnum and Bailey Circus. Today it's the home of the great **Ringling Museum of Art** complex on U.S. 41 (355-5101), comprising four architecturally remarkable buildings. First is John Ringling's own home, **Ca' d' Zan,** a lavish replica of a 32-room Venetian Gothic palace complete with antique furniture and a 4,000-pipe organ. Then comes the superb art gallery with its collection of European masters: El Greco, Frans Hals, Rembrandt, Gainsborough, Poussin, and above all, Rubens. A new wing, recently built, displays contemporary works of art and revolving exhibitions. The **Asolo Museum Theater** is an authentic 18th-century Italian baroque theater, taken down and transported stone by stone to Florida in 1949 from the castle of Asolo, near Venice. Finally, there are a richly stocked **circus museum,** illustrating circus history from Roman times on, and some splendid grdns. Don't miss it; open daily year round.

In early June of every year since 1964 Sarasota has played host to the **Music Festival of Florida,** with its well-attended classical symphony concerts and chamber-music recitals. For information, call 407/953-4252.

TARPON SPRINGS (35 mi./56km north of St. Petersburg on U.S. 19N): Picturesque little sponge-fishing port with an important Greek community. Pretty view of the docks from Dodecanese Blvd. Fine Greek Orthodox **Cathedral of St. Nicholas,** built in 1943 in the Neo-Byzantine style, at 36 N. Pinellas Ave. (937-3540), open daily. Boat rides from the waterfront to the sponge-fishing grounds and demonstrations of sponge fishing. And don't fail to see the **Spongeorama** at Sponge Docks (942-3771), open daily, a museum entirely devoted to this unusual industry. You shouldn't miss Tarpon Springs.

Where to Eat

Louis Pappas, Riverside, 10 W. Dodecanese Blvd. (937-5101). Lunch/dinner daily. AE, DC, MC, V. Local color guaranteed. *Greek.* **B–I**

FARTHER AFIELD

WALT DISNEY WORLD & CENTRAL FLORIDA (160 mi./256km r.t. via I-4E, U.S. 17S, U.S. 27S, and Fla. 60W): A very crowded itinerary taking you to the fabulous 🏰🏰🏰 **Disney World,** 🏰🏰🏰 **EPCOT,** 🏰🏰🏰 **Disney–MGM Studios,** 🏰🏰 **Sea World,** 🏰 **Wet' n Wild,** and 🏰🏰 **Cypress Gardens** (for these six theme parks, among the most famous in the country, see Chapter 18 on Orlando). On the way you'll see 🏰 **Bok Tower Gardens** at Lake Wales on U.S. 27A (676-1408), a bird sanctuary surrounded by splendid landscaped gardens. Unusual carillon concerts, with 53 bells weighing from 17 lb. (7kg) to 11 tons (10,000kg), daily at 3pm. Also *Mystery of the Passion,* with 250 performers, on Tues, Thurs, Sat, and Sun from mid-Feb to mid-Apr. Don't miss this trip; for hotels, motels, and restaurants, see Chapter 18 on Orlando.

EVERGLADES NATIONAL PARK (313 mi./500km SE of Tampa on I-75S, U.S. 41E, U.S. 1S, and Fla. 997S): The only subtropical national park in the U.S. Its flora and fauna are of exceptional richness. For details, see Chapter 19 on Miami.

GULF OF MEXICO (256 mi./409km r.t. from St. Petersburg via I-275S and U.S. 41S, returning on I-75N and U.S. 41N): Dozens of superb, uncrowded beaches: **Longboat Key, Lido Key, Siesta Key,** and **Venice** near Sarasota; **Fort Myers Beach, La Costa,** and **Sanibel** (the best beach in Florida for finding seashells) **and Captiva Islands** near Fort Myers. On the way visit the **De Soto National Memorial** and the Ringling museums at Sarasota (see "Nearby Excursions," above). At **Fort Myers,** see the 🏰 **Thomas Edison Winter Home,** 2350 McGregor Blvd. (334-3614), where the famous inventor spent his winters for almost half a century. Open daily.

For boat rides on the rivers and swamps of Florida, **Everglades Jungle Cruise,** City Yacht Basin, Fort Myers (334-7474), daily year round.

This 1- or 2-day trip is perfect for nature lovers.

CHAPTER 18

ORLANDO ♟♟

□ □ □

With Walt Disney World, EPCOT, and Central Florida

"The City Beautiful," as Orlando residents like to call their town, had modest beginnings as a simple military encampment during the war against the Seminole tribe (1835–42). Today its purpose and chief claim to fame are to host the millions of American and foreign tourists who have made this central Florida area an enormous year-round vacation spot. **Walt Disney World, Cape Kennedy, Sea World, Daytona Beach, Cypress Gardens, St. Augustine, EPCOT, Silver Springs** . . . all are less than 2 hr. by car from the Orlando airport, an ultramodern facility amply served by regular and charter flights coming from the northern states, Europe, and Canada.

An important distribution center for citrus fruits and other Florida fruits and vegetables, this modern, dynamic commercial metropolis, whose population has more than doubled since the Cape Canaveral Space Center (now the **Kennedy Space Center**) was created in 1950, has one of the largest concentrations of hotel accommodations in America (75,000 rooms), more than Los Angeles or Chicago. Orlando's economy is the second fastest growing among major U.S. cities. This garden city, studded with parks and lagoons, is a winter resort favored by many northern residents, and a favorite honeymoon destination for young newlyweds. In addition, the surrounding countryside with its dozens of lakes makes the area a summer paradise for campers and caravaners.

Instead of impressive historical monuments, Orlando and its region offer some of the most famous tourist attractions in the world, beginning with Walt Disney World and its sister facility, the sprawling futuristic EPCOT (25 million visitors annually), the **Disney–MGM Studios,** the brand-new **Universal Studios,** and the fabulous Cypress Gardens featuring Esther Williams–style water ballet. In a more traditional vein but also worth visiting is the residential suburb of **Winter Park,** just north of Orlando, with its lovely European-style homes, music and art festivals, and canals reminiscent of Venice.

As a finishing touch, the inauguration in 1983 of the immense **Orange County Convention Center** has made the city one of the most important convention cities in the country.

BASIC FACTS: State of Florida. Area codes: 407 (Orlando/Walt Disney World); 813 or 904 (other zones). ZIP Code: 32802 (city of Orlando).

Founded: 1837. Approximate population: city, 130,000; metropolitan area, 960,000.

CLIMATE: As in all of Florida, winters in Orlando are mild and sunny (mean Jan temperature, 62°F/17°C). The summer is oppressive, with frequent showers, but somewhat less humid than at the Florida shore (average temperature in July is 82°F/28°C). With the thermometer hovering around 71°–77°F (22°–25°C), spring and fall are uniformly pleasant.

DISTANCES: Atlanta, 436 mi. (698km); Miami, 236 mi. (378km); New Orleans, 644 mi. (1,030km); New York, 1,160 mi. (1,856km); Savannah, 292 mi. (467km); Washington, 925 mi. (1,480km).

ARRIVAL & TRANSIT INFORMATION

AIRPORT: Orlando International Airport (MCO): 8 mi. (13km) SE. For information, call 407/826-2414. The fastest-growing major airport in the country (17.5 million passengers last year).

U.S. AIRLINES (Orlando telephone numbers unless otherwise indicated): American (896-2334), Continental (295-6000), Delta (849-6400), Eastern (843-7280), Midway (toll free 800/621-5700), Northwest (351-3190), Pan Am (422-0701), TWA (351-3855), United (toll free 800/241-6522), and USAir (toll free 800/428-4322).

FOREIGN CARRIERS: British Airways (toll free 800/247-9297), K.L.M. (toll free 800/777-5553), and Icelandair (toll free 800/223-5500).

CITY LINK: The **cab** fare from the airport to dwntwn Orlando is about $18; from the airport to Lake Buena Vista hotels, about $22; from the airport to Walt Disney World, about $35. Bus: **Mears Motor Shuttle** (407/423-5566); serves major hotels in Orlando and the area; fare, $8–$15, according to destination.

Although Orlando and all central Florida are amply served by regular long-distance and excursion bus lines, you should seriously consider renting a car with unlimited mileage for trips to Walt Disney World and other area attractions. Car-rental rates in Florida are among the most reasonable in the entire U.S., while municipal public bus service is woefully lacking; for bus information, call Tri-County Transit (407/841-8240).

CAR RENTAL (at the Orlando International Airport unless otherwise indicated): Avis (851-7600); Budget (850-6700); Dollar (851-0677); Hertz (859-8400); National (855-4170); Thrifty, 7201 McCoy Rd. (859-6990). For dwntwn locations, consult the local telephone directory.

LIMOUSINE SERVICES: American Limousine (859-2250), Carey Limousine (855-0442), Dav El Limousines (toll free 800/922-0343).

TAXIS: Cabs can be hailed on the street or from waiting lines at designated taxi stations; you can also phone for taxi service, in which case try **City Cab** (422-4561) or **Yellow Cab** (699-9999).

TRAIN: Amtrak Station, 1400 Sligh Blvd. (843-7611; toll free 800/424-1111).

INTERCITY BUSES: Greyhound, 300 W. Amelia St. (407/843-0344).

INFORMATION & TOURS

TOURIST INFORMATION: The **Orlando Chamber of Commerce,** 75 E. Ivanhoe Blvd. (P.O. Box 1234), FL 32802 (407/425-1234).

Orlando/Orange County Convention & Visitors Bureau, 7208 Sand Lake Rd., Fl 32819 (407/363-5800).

Orlando Tourist Information Center, 8445 International Dr., Suite 152, FL 32819 (407/363-5871). Open daily year round.

GUIDED TOURS: American Sightseeing Tours (bus), 9526 Boyce Ave., Orlando (407/859-2250): Guided tour of tourist attractions in the area, serving major hotels.

Falcon Helicopter Service (helicopter), 8990 International Dr., Orlando (407/352-1753): Helicopter flights over Walt Disney World and Central Florida area. Spectacular. Daily.

Gray Line Tours (bus) 4950 L. B. McLeod Rd., Orlando (407/422-0744): Guided tour of area attractions, serving major hotels.

Scenic Boat Tours (boat), 312 Morse Blvd. at Lake Osceola, Winter Park (407/644-4056): Guided tour by boat on Winter Park's lagoons and canals. Daily.

SIGHTS, ATTRACTIONS & ACTIVITIES

ADVENTURE TOURS: Rosie O'Grady's Flying Circus (balloon tours/ ballooning), Church St. Station, Orlando (407/422-2434): Dawn departure on clear days. The tour lasts 4 hr. and costs $140 per person, champagne brunch included. Spectacular.

MUSEUMS OF ART: ⚓ **Charles Hosmer Morse Museum of American Art,** 133 E. Welbourne Ave., Winter Park (407/644-3686): Very lovely art deco collection including lamps, blown glass, chandeliers, and stained-glass windows by Louis Comfort Tiffany. Also old ceramics, paintings, and furniture. Open Tues–Sun.

⚓ **Orlando Museum of Art,** 2416 N. Mills Ave., Orlando (407/896-4231): Pre-Columbian and primitive African art; also 20th-century American painting and sculpture. Interesting temporary exhibits. Worth a look. Open Tues–Sun.

MUSEUMS OF SCIENCE & HISTORY: ⚓ **Orange County Historical Museum,** 812 E. Rollins St., Orlando (407/898-8320): Traces the history of the settlement of Florida. From a re-created 19th-century saloon and grocery store to examples of Indian crafts. Worth a look. Open Tues–Sun.

☼⚓ **Orlando Science Center,** 810 E. Rollins St., Orlando (407/896-7151): Comprehensive museum of science and technology. Be sure to see the exhibit devoted to space travel, including the model of a lunar space colony. Ultramodern planetarium. Open daily.

⚓ **Tupperware Exhibit and Museum,** U.S. 17/92/441, 5 mi. (8km) south of the Florida Tpke., Kissimmee (407/847-3111): Narrated tour of the company headquarters illustrating the design, manufacturing, and distribution of Tupperware products. A museum gallery houses a collection of historic food containers from Egyptian artifacts (4000 B.C.), to Ming Dynasty porcelain to Tiffany bowls of opalescent glass. Interesting. Open Mon–Fri.

ORLANDO
AND VICINITY

PARKS & GARDENS: ⚐ **Bok Tower Singing Gardens,** at Lake Wales, 61 mi. (97km) SW on I-4 and U.S. 27 (813/676-1408): 128-acre (52ha) botanical gardens with a bird sanctuary **(Mountain Lake Sanctuary)** and dominated by a 205-ft. (62m) bell tower, whose 53 bells weigh from 17 lbs. (7kg) to 11 tons (10,000kg). Marvelous carillon concerts daily at 3pm. In the nearby **Lake Wales Amphitheater,** on U.S. 27A (813/676-1495), visitors can enjoy performances of the Passion Play with 250 participants (Tues, Thurs, Sat, and Sun mid-Feb to mid-Apr). Spectacular. (The same troupe presents the Passion Play at Spearfish, June–Aug; see Chapter 34 on Mount Rushmore.)

⚐ **Eola Park,** Central Blvd., Orlando: Charming little public park located in the middle of the downtown area on the shore of Lake Eola. Flowerbeds; fountains illuminated after dark. Particularly dazzling when the azaleas are in flower, Feb–Mar.

⚐ **Leu Gardens,** 1730 N. Forest Ave., Orlando (407/849-2620): Lovely tropical gardens in the center of Orlando. 56 acres (22ha) of camellias, orchids, roses, and azaleas. Not to be missed.

⚐ **Loch Haven Park,** Princeton Blvd. and Mills Ave., Orlando: City park that is the site of the principal museums in Orlando: the Orlando Museum of Art, the Orange County Historical Museum, and the Orlando Science Center (see "Museums of Art" and "Museums of Science and History," above).

PERFORMING ARTS: For a daily listing of all shows and cultural events, consult the entertainment pages of the daily paper *Orlando Sentinel* (morning and evening) and *Orlando* magazine.

Annie Russell Theater, Rollins College Campus, Park Ave. and Holt Ave., Winter Park (407/646-2501): Modern theater, musical comedies. Year round.

Bob Carr Performing Arts Center, 401 W. Livingston Ave., Orlando (407/849-2020): Ballet, theater, concerts. Home of the Florida Symphony Orchestra (principal conductor, Kenneth Jean); season Sept–May.

Central Florida Civic Theatre, 1010 E. Princeton, Orlando (407/896-7365): Classical and contemporary theater, musical comedies. Year round.

Tupperware Auditorium, U.S. 441S, Orlando (407/847-3111): Concerts, recitals, big-name entertainers.

SHOPPING: Flea World, U.S. 17/92 in Sanford (14 mi./22.5km NE) (407/645-1792): The largest flea market in the world. More than 1,500 booths and mountains of varied merchandise. Open Fri–Sun 8am–5pm. Worth the trip.

SPECIAL EVENTS: For the exact schedule of events below, consult the **Orlando Convention and Visitors Bureau** (see "Tourist Information," above).

Scottish Highland Games (end of Jan): Festival of dance, music, and athletic events in the grand Scottish tradition (407/422-8226).

Central Florida Fair (Feb–Mar): Horse shows, entertainment, parades.

Bach Festival (end of Feb): Concerts of classical music in Winter Park.

Autumn Art Festival (Sept): Art exhibits, concerts; Winter Park.

Florida State Air Fair (end of Oct): Festival of parachuting and aerobatics at Kissimmee. Many aircraft on display. Spectacular.

Citrus Sports Holiday (Dec): 3 weeks of sports and competitions culminating in the Citrus Bowl football game on Jan 1.

Christmas Parade (Christmastime): All the famous Walt Disney characters parade daily down Walt Disney World's "Main Street USA."

SPORTS: Orlando has one professional team, and four major-league teams have spring training facilities here:

Baseball (Spring training Feb–Mar): Boston Red Sox, Chain O' Lakes Park, Winter Haven (813/293-3900); Houston Astros, Osceola Stadium, Kissimmee (407/839-3900); Kansas City Royals, Boardwalk Stadium, Haines City (toll free 800/525-8233); Minnesota Twins, Tinker Field, Orlando (407/849-6346).

Baseball (June–Sept): Orlando Twins, Tinker Field, Orlando (407/849-6346).

Horse Racing
Ben White Raceway, 1905 Lee Rd., Orlando (407/293-8721), Mon–Sat Oct–May. Harness racing.

Jai Alai
Orlando Jai Alai Fronton, N. Fern Park, U.S. 17/92 (407/339-6221), Mon–Sat Sept–Dec.

STROLLS: ☼🏛 **Church Street Station,** 129 W. Church St., Orlando (407/4222434): Quaint shops, saloons, restaurants, and nightclubs in a pleasing old-fashioned setting in the heart of Orlando's historical center. Picturesque and lively, especially in the evening. Open daily.

☼🏛 **Winter Park,** 4 mi. (6.4km) north off Orange Ave.: Once the winter home of wealthy northeasterners, Winter Park has retained a small-town atmosphere with its graceful estates along Lake Virginia Park Ave. A four-block shopping district lined with palm trees, has boutiques, specialty stores, and cafés across from Central Park. Worth a detour.

THEME PARKS NEARBY: ☼🏛🏛 **Cypress Gardens,** at Winter Haven, 55 mi. (89km) SW by I-4, U.S. 27, and Fla. 540 (813/324-2111): For a good half century these fabulous tropical gardens on the shores of Lake Eloise have been among Florida's principal tourist attractions. There are tours via electric boat of flowers and foliage from five continents (more than 8,000 species from 70 countries). Exotic birds swoop and chatter in the immense aviary. Exhibitions of synchronized waterskiing, Esther Williams style, are given four times a day year round. One million people come here every year. Mustn't be missed.

☼🏛 **Silver Springs,** near Ocala, 86 mi. (138km) NW by the Florida Tpke., U.S. 27, Fla. 35, and Fla. 40 (904/236-2121): Every year 1.5 million people visit the springs that feed the Silver River and the superb lake whose incredibly clear waters frequently attract moviemakers shooting underwater sequences. The springs produce 500 million gal. (2,000 million liters) of water per day. Tours in glass-bottom boats reveal underwater grottos more than 100,000 years old. Truly spectacular. Also a very beautiful park with deer, and a famous vivarium (Reptile Institute). Very much worth the detour. Open daily.

☼🏛🏛 **Universal Studios Florida,** 10 mi (16km) SW, at the intersection of I-4 and the Florida Tpke. (407/363-8000): Florida's most recent theme park opened its doors in May 1990 at a cost of $600 million. A must for movie buffs, this working motion-picture and television-studio complex—direct rival of Disney–MGM Studios—features thrill rides based on such motion pictures as *King Kong, Jaws, E.T.,* and *Back to the Future.* Among other attractions is the Screen Test Theater where audience volunteers receive costumes, scripts, and a chance to perform in scenes to be edited into TV productions; a walk-through backlot with set locations ranging from a New England village to a San Francisco street to New York City's Upper East Side; and more than 40 restaurants and shops, including Mel's Diner from *American Graffiti.* A 1-day ticket is $29 for adults, $24 for children 3 to 11. Mustn't be missed. Open daily.

☼ 🏛🏛🏛 **Walt Disney World,** 22 mi. (35km) SW on I-4 at Lake Buena
☼ 🏛🏛🏛 Vista (407/824-4321): The largest and most famous amusement park in the world, rising miraculously from Florida swampland. Opened to
the public in 1971—5 years after the death of its creator, Walt Disney—the park
has already been visited by more than 300 million people. Park employees number over 32,000. Conceived along the lines of its older sister park, Disneyland
(see Chapter 54 on Los Angeles), Walt Disney World—an amusement park taking the whole planet for its theme—stretches over 28,000 acres (twice the size of
Manhattan); its parking facilities can accommodate 30,000 cars. In effect, Walt
Disney World contains four distinct amusement parks linked by road and monorail: Disney–MGM Studios, Typhoon Lagoon, the Magic Kingdom, and
EPCOT.

The Magic Kingdom: Computer-controlled with chronometric precision,
spectacular rides such as Cinderella's Castle, Mission to Mars, Twenty Thousand
Leagues under the Sea, and Pirates of the Caribbean dazzle young and old alike.
For convenience, the park is organized as six miniature villages, each with its own
style: **Adventureland,** with its boat tour through the jungle; **Fantasyland,** inhabited by the loveable Disney characters; **Frontierland,** in traditional Far West
style; **Liberty Square,** with its gallery of 41 U.S. presidents and a house haunted
by 999 ghosts; **Main Street USA,** in the style of a turn-of-the-century small town;
and **Tomorrowland,** with a space adventure theme.

EPCOT: This theme park of the 21st century, with overtones of a World's
Fair, opened its doors in Oct 1982. Drawing up to 25 million visitors each year,
EPCOT (acronym for "Experimental Prototype Community of Tomorrow")
has only a tenuous thematic link with the fictional world of Mickey Mouse or
Donald Duck. Several theme pavilions (Earth, Energy, Transportation, etc.),
sponsored by such industrial giants as Exxon, IBM, General Motors, Kodak, and
Bell Telephone, adjoin a "window on the world" where scrupulously re-created
Japanese temples jostle the Eiffel Tower, Québec's Château Frontenac, St. Mark's
Square in Venice, a Bavarian village, Mayan pyramids, a London street, Beijing's
Temple of Heaven, etc. The whole ensemble is dominated by a giant 18-story
sphere made of reinforced concrete and steel, reminiscent of a huge golf ball,
which has become EPCOT's symbol. And there's the largest aquarium in the
world, Living Seas, and its 7,500 sea creatures which visitors can observe from an
underwater train moving through glass tunnels at the bottom of the gigantic 6-
million-gallon (22.6-million-liter) aquarium basin. The futuristic EPCOT,
whose construction consumed 5 years and $1 billion (twice the cost of Walt Dis-
ney World and four times that of Disneyland), has turned out the favorite among
the Disney parks.

Disney–MGM Studios: This $500-million theme park, opened in 1989 at a
site just south of EPCOT, is a dazzling 135-acre (54ha) high-tech playground
that blends film making with backstage studio tours and ride-through attractions. Movie and TV productions are shot on its three sprawling film studios and
backlot street scenes, while in the animation building, Disney cartoonists churn
out shorts for theatrical release. Housed in a copy of Hollywood Boulevard
Mann's Chinese Theater, the **Great Movie Ride,** one of its focal points, trans-
ports visitors through classic films such as *The Wizard of Oz, Raiders of the Lost
Ark, Alien,* and *Singin' in the Rain.* **Superstar Television** allows audience volunteers to join the actors in famous television scenes as well as other simulation exhibits. Another highlight is **Catastrophe Canyon,** where large-scale special
effects such as earthquakes and floods are created and cleaned up every 3.5 minutes. Disney–MGM Studios hopes to attract three to five million visitors a year.

Typhoon Lagoon: Disney's new water park for the wet set. Guests are able
to snorkel among thousands of tropical fish, plummet down eight different
flumes to the 2½-acre (1ha) pool and ride the waves, up to 7 ft. (2m), artificially
produced by a giant surf-making machine.

In addition to these innumerable attractions, Walt Disney World offers visitors an immense 7,500-acre (3,000ha) forest reserve of cypress, pine, and laurel trees, two artificial lakes with 4.5 mi. (7km) of sandy beaches, three golf courses, fully equipped camping facilities, and every imaginable sport, including tennis, swimming, waterskiing, sailing, fishing, horseback riding, etc.

There are a dozen or so hotels ideally located for Walt Disney World visitors, among which are the astounding **Contemporary Resort** (served by monorail), the new **Caribbean Beach Resort, Grand Floridian Beach Resort, Disney's Village Resort, Walt Disney World Dolphin and Swan Resorts,** and the more intimate, highly successful **Polynesian Resort.**

Open daily all year, Walt Disney World is in itself worth the trip to Florida. Plan to spend at least 2 or 3 full days here, and avoid weekends and holidays. Admission fees: $31 per day for adults, $100 for 4 days. There's a 20% reduction for children aged 3 to 9 years. Albeit fatiguing, this is an experience that should not be missed by children, or by adults who don't want to grow up. Call 407/824-4321 for price and schedule information.

Wet 'N Wild, in Orlando, 6 mi. (10km) SW on I-4, Exit 435S (407/351-3200): Aquatic fun park with some outstanding attractions: a giant six-story slide, a white-water course, a giant water roller coaster, and a lagoon with enormous artificial waves for would-be surfers. Spectacular. Open daily mid-Feb to mid-Nov.

ZOOS: **Gatorland Zoo,** at Kissimmee, 7 mi. (11km) south on U.S. 17 (407/855-5496): Florida's largest alligator farm featuring 6,000 alligators, crocodiles, and giant turtles, as well as pink flamingos and zebras, in a 35-acre (14ha) tropical park. Tour by miniature train. Open daily year round.

Reptile World Serpentarium, 5705 E. Irlo Bronson Memorial Hwy., St. Cloud (20 mi./35km south on U.S. 92 and U.S. 192) (407/892-6905): More than 1,500 snakes and other reptiles, including some of the world's most dangerous specimens. Snake venom is collected here for distribution, and visitors have several chances a day to witness the "milking" of cobras, rattlesnakes, and other venomous creatures. If you like horror stories, you'll love this! Open Tues–Sun; closed Sept. Should be seen.

Sea World of Florida, 7007 Sea World Dr., Orlando (407/351-3600): One of the largest marine zoos in the world, surrounded by 150 acres (61ha) of gardens. On display are a giant shark aquarium with walk-through glass tunnel, a killer whale, sea lions, sea turtles, and trained dolphins performing on cue. Splendid view from the top of the 450-ft. (140m) revolving tower. There are also waterski shows, a Polynesian show, and a buffet luau every evening. Sea World has almost three million visitors annually. Open daily year round. An absolute must-see.

ACCOMMODATIONS

A Note on Accommodations: Room rates in Orlando are coded as follows: **VE,** Very Expensive ($140 and up); **E,** Expensive ($90–$140); **M,** Moderate ($60–$90); **I,** Inexpensive ($30–$60); **B,** Budget (up to $30). A listing of toll free numbers is in the Appendix. *Note:* The toll free 24-hr. reservations number for all hotels in the greater Orlando area is 800/522-7666.

Personal Favorites (in order of preference)

Hyatt Regency Grand Cypress, 1 Grand Cypress Blvd., Orlando, FL 32819 (407/239-1234; toll free, see Hyatt). 750 rms, A/C, color TV, in-rm movies. AE, CB, DC, MC, V. Valet parking $6, pool, 12 tennis courts, two golf courses, private beach, marina, health club, sauna, boating, three rests. (including La Coquina), four bars, 24-hr. rm svce, disco, boutiques, concierge, free crib. *Note:* One of the most spectacular hotels in the U.S., built around a superb lagoon–swimming pool (the largest in the world) w. waterfalls and a giant slide. There's a magnificent 18-story atrium w. extensive plantings of flowers, waterfalls, and glass-walled elevators. Spacious rms w. private patios or balconies. Ultramodern comfort. The decor is elegant, w. master paintings and other works of art. Efficient svce. 1,500 acres (600ha) of grdns and groves; private lake with sandy beach. Home of the famous Jack Nicklaus Academy of Golf. 10 min. from dwntwn, 10 min. from Walt Disney World. The new paragon of Florida luxury hotelkeeping. Two VIP floors. **VE,** but lower rates off-season.

Walt Disney World Swan, 1200 Epcot Resort Blvd., Lake Buena Vista, FL 32830 (407/934-3000; toll free, see Westin). 758 rms, A/C, color TV, in-rm movies. AE, CB, DC, MC, V. Valet parking $6, pool, tennis court, health club, sauna, two rests., coffee shop, bar, 24-hr. rm svce, nightclub, concierge, free crib. *Note:* A brand-new and spectacular achievement of architect Michael Graves; the building, washed in hot pastel tones, has a gigantic sculpture of a swan brooding over each of its four wings (whence the name). Spacious, ultra-comfortable rms; very elegant interiors. Enormous heated lagoon-pool. Flawless reception and svce. Connected to EPCOT Center by tram, and by ferryboat to Disney–MGM Studios. **VE**

Disney's Polynesian Resort, Lake Buena Vista, FL 32830 (407/824-2000; resv. 407/934-7639). 855 rms, A/C, cable color TV. AE, MC. Free parking, pool, two golf courses, tennis court, health club, private beach, waterskiing, fishing, boating, rest. (Papeete Bay Verandah), coffee shop, bar, rm svce, nightclub, hrdrsr, boutiques, free crib. *Note:* Fragrance of the Southern Seas 3 min. by monorail from Walt Disney World. Lovely Polynesian-style pavilions on the shores of a lagoon. Rms are cramped but pleasant and the svce somewhat weak, but on balance the experience is positive. Pretty indoor gardens; good Polynesian rest. Three VIP floors. Clientele is mostly families. One of the best places to stay around Walt Disney World. **VE,** but lower rates off-season.

Gold Key Inn, 7100 S. Orange Blossom Trail, Orlando FL 32809 (407/855-0050; toll free 800/327-0304). 210 rms, A/C, color TV, in-rm movies. AE, CB, DC, MC, V. Free parking, pool, tennis court, sauna, putting green, rest. (Piccadilly), bar, rm svce, disco, free crib. *Note:* One of the best values in the Orlando area. Comfortable, well-equipped motel. The spacious rms have balconies; some have refrigerators. Reception is cheerful and pleasant. Good rest. Ideal for families. 10 min. by car from the airport (free shuttle bus), and from Sea World, 20 min. from Walt Disney World. A fine place to stay. **M–E**

Disney's Caribbean Beach Resort, Lake Buena Vista, FL 32830 (407/934-3400; for resv. 407/934-7639). 2,112 rms, A/C, cable color TV. AE, MC, V. Free parking, eight pools, private beach, marina, boating, coffee shops, bars, boutiques, free crib. *Note:* The perfect base for taking in EPCOT Center, Disney–MGM Studios, and Typhoon Lagoon, this brand-new hotel complex south of the park also offers the lowest rates ($70–$95 a rm). Colorfully decorated in a style w. Caribbean overtones, the new hotel comprises dozens of small two-story buildings grouped around a 42-acre (17ha) man-made lake whose shores have been turned into a tropical grdn. Inviting, well-designed rms, pleasant lakeside strolls, amusing bazaar with many cafés and all kinds of fast food. Good value. **M–E,** but lower rates off-season.

Chalet Suzanne, U.S. 27, Lake Wales, FL 33859 (813/676-6011). 30 rms, A/C, cable color TV. AE, CB, DC, MC, V. Free parking, pool, fishing, boating, rest., bar, crib $10. *Note:* Charming lakeside inn, seemingly right out of a Hans Christian Andersen fairy tale. The decor leans rather heavily toward bric-a-brack, but the rms are comfortable and inviting. Very good rest.; excellent svce. 10 min. by car from Cypress Gardens and Bok Tower Gardens. Private airfield. A very good place to stay. **M–E**

Days Inn–Universal Studios East, 5827 Caravan Court, Orlando, FL 32819 (407/351-3800; toll free, see Days Inns).

261 rms, A/C, color TV, in-rm movies. AE, MC, V. Free parking, pool, 24-hr. rest., free crib. *Note:* Large, standard-style motel. Functional comfort 12 min. by car from Walt Disney World. Totally renovated in 1988. Good value. **I–M**

Motel 6, 5731 W. Irlo Bronson Hwy. (U.S. 192), Kissimmee, FL 32741 (407/396-6333). 347 rms, A/C, color TV, in-rm movies. AE, DC, MC, V. Free parking, pool, free crib. *Note:* New budget motel 5 min. by car from Walt Disney World. Ideal for families. One of the best values in the entire Orlando area. **B–I**

Other Accommodations (from top bracket to budget)

Disney's Contemporary Resort, Lake Buena Vista, FL 32830 (407/824-1000; for resv. 407/934-7639). 1,052 rms, A/C, cable color TV. AE, MC, V. Free valet parking, two pools, health club, sauna, tennis courts, beach, waterskiing, three rests. (including Top of the World), coffee shop, bars, rm svce, disco, hrdrsr, boutiques, free crib. *Note:* Original, modern design. This enormous white truncated pyramid, 15 stories high, envelopes the monorail beam, which links it directly to Walt Disney World. Spacious, comfortable rms, all w. balconies or patios, overlooking the surrounding lagoons. The lobby is worth the visit all by itself. Svce is a bit vague but courteous. The rest. at the top is good and offers a panoramic view. VIP floor. Among the most spectacular accommodations in the Disney empire. Resv. far in advance are a must. **VE,** but lower rates off-season.

Grenelefe Golf and Tennis Resort, 3200 Fla. 546, Winter Haven, FL 33844 (813/422-7511). 950 rms, A/C, cable color TV, in-rm movies. AE, CB, DC, MC, V. Free parking, five pools, private beach, three golf courses, 20 tennis courts, waterskiing, marina, sauna, horseback riding, three rests. (including Grene Heron), three bars, disco, rm svce, movie theater, free crib. *Note:* Huge, luxurious vacation complex w. a lovely tropical lagoon. Comfortable rms w. balconies in two-story bungalows (most w. kitchenette) on the shores of Lake Marion. Svce beyond reproach. Exceptional sports facilities. 8 min. by car from Cypress Gardens, 35 min. from Walt Disney World. **E–VE,** but lower rates off-season.

Radisson Plaza Hotel, 60 Ivanhoe Blvd., Orlando, FL 32804 (407/425-4455; toll free, see Radisson). 324 rms, A/C, color TV, in-rm movies. AE, CB, DC, MC, V. Free parking, pool, two tennis courts, sauna, health club, two rests. (including Thorndikes), two bars, 24-hr. rm svce, disco, concierge. *Note:* Large 15-story modern hotel located in the heart of dwntwn. Functional but elegant design. Rms are vast and well laid out, w. minibars. Faultless facilities and comfort; very good svce. Rests. are average. Business travelers and convention-goers are the staple clientele. Two VIP floors. Free airport shuttle. **E–VE**

Sheraton Orlando North Hotel and Towers, Maitland Blvd. and I-4, Orlando, FL 32853 (407/660-9000; toll free, see Sheraton). 400 rms, A/C, color TV, in-rm movies. AE, CB, DC, MC, V. Valet parking $6, pool, tennis court, sauna, health club, two rests., two bars, rm svce, nightclub, hrdrsr, boutiques, concierge, free crib. *Note:* Ultramodern hotel w. an immense glass lobby housing a winter grdn. Very comfortable, elegant rms w. balconies and refrigerators. Comprehensive facilities; attentive svce; rests. no more than adequate. Business and group clientele. VIP floor. 15 min. from Orlando's business section. **E–VE**

Marriott Orlando, 8001 International Dr., Orlando, FL 32809 (407/351-2420; toll free, see Marriott). 1,076 rms, A/C, color TV, in-rm movies. AE, CB, DC, MC, V. Free parking, three pools, four tennis courts, three rests. (including Grove Restaurant), bars, rm svce, disco, free crib. *Note:* Enormous tourist complex composed of two-story cottages surrounded by grdns and exotic lagoons. Spacious, comfortable rms, some w. kitchenettes and refrigerators. Ultra-professional svce and reception. Rests. are so-so.

Frequented by convention and other groups. Good value. 10 min. from Walt Disney World, 15 min. from dwntwn. **E**

🛏🛏 **Ramada Florida Center,** 7400 International Dr., Orlando, FL 32809 (407/351-4600; toll free, see Ramada). 400 rms, A/C, color TV, in-rm movies. AE, CB, DC, MC, V. Free parking, two pools, two rests., bar, rm svce, disco, (in season), free crib. *Note:* Large, relatively modern hotel 15 min. by car from Walt Disney World. Comfortable, inviting rms, some w. refrigerators, the best overlooking the outdoor pool. Good svce. Free airport shuttle. Good value. Ideal for families. **M–E**

🛏🛏 **Sheraton Lakeside Inn,** 7711 W. Irlo Bronson Memorial Hwy. (U.S. 192), Kissimmee, FL 32741 (407/828-8250; toll free, see Sheraton). 650 rms, A/C, color TV, in-rm movies. AE, CB, DC, MC, V. Free parking, two pools, four tennis courts, pedalboats, miniature golf, three rests., coffee shop, bars, rm svce, nightclub, free crib. *Note:* Large, comfortable, recently modernized motel. Large, inviting rms. Pleasant setting on a lagoon. Good svce overall. 10 min. from Walt Disney World. **M–E,** but lower rates off-season.

🛏🛏 **Delta Courts of Flags** (formerly the Ramada), 5715 Major Blvd., Orlando, FL 32819 (407/351-3340; toll free 800/877-1133). 824 rms, A/C, color TV, in-rm movies. AE, CB, DC, MC, V. Free parking, three pools, two tennis courts, sauna, two rests., two bars, rm svce, disco, hrdrsr, free crib. *Note:* Large vacation and conference motel located halfway between dwntwn Orlando and Walt Disney World. The spacious rms w. balconies (some w. refrigerators) are in small four-story buildings surrounded by grdns. Reasonably complete facilities. Frequented by families and groups. Good value. 10 min. from dwntwn, 15 min. from Walt Disney World. **M**

🛏🛏 **Days Inn South of Magic Kingdom,** intersection of I-4 and U.S. 27, Lake Buena Vista, FL 32830 (813/424-2596; toll free, see Days Inns). 121 rms, A/C, color TV, in-rm movies. AE, CB, DC, MC, V. Free parking, pool, adj. rest., valet svce, free crib. *Note:* Comfortable, appealing rms, the best directly overlooking the pool and grdn. Svce and reception w. a smile. If you're driving, you'll find direct access to I-4 at Exit 23. 10 min. from Walt Disney World, 20 min. from Cypress Gardens. Good value. **I–M,** but lower rates off-season.

🛏🛏 **Holiday Inn Orlando West,** Fla. 50W at the Florida Tpke., Ocoee, FL 32761 (407/656-5050; toll free, see Holiday Inns). 170 rms, A/C, color TV, in-rm movies. AE, CB, DC, MC, V. Free parking, pool, rest. (C.W. Dandy's), bar, rm svce, hrdrsr, free crib. *Note:* Typical Holiday Inn, w. pool and enticing grdns, comfortable rms, acceptable rest., friendly reception and svce. Good value overall, and away from the hurly-burly of holiday trippers. 20 min. from Walt Disney World, 20 min. from the airport. **I–M**

🛏🛏 **Quality Inn Resort,** 5905 International Dr., Orlando, FL 32819 (407/351-2100; toll free, see Quality Inns). 300 rms, A/C, color TV, in-rm movies. AE, CB, DC, MC, V. Free parking, pool, sauna, rest., bar, rm svce, disco, hrdrsr, crib $4. *Note:* Large, round modern 21-story tower. Inviting rms. Functional facilities and comfort level; efficient svce. Very good value. 20 min. from Walt Disney World, 10 min. from dwntwn. **I–M,** but lower rates off-season.

🛏🛏 **USA Inn,** 2639 Garfield Dr., Cypress Gardens, FL 33884 (813/324-5950; toll free 800/237-8040). 158 rms, A/C, cable color TV. AE, CB, DC, MC, V. Free parking, pool, rests., bar, rm svce, crib $5. *Note:* Standard but comfortable motel. Functional rms w. balconies. Adequate rest. Good value. Efficient svce. 5 min. by car from Cypress Gardens, 40 min. from Walt Disney World. **I–M,** but lower rates off-season.

🛏 **Budget Host Driftwood,** 970 Cypress Gardens Blvd., Winter Haven, FL 33880 (813/294-4229; toll free 800/283-4678). 22 rms, A/C, cable color TV. AE, CB, DC, MC, V. Free parking, pool, rest., crib $4. *Note:* Standard small motel 5 min. from Cypress Gardens. Comfortable rms, some w. kitchenette and refrigerator. Friendly reception and svce. 30 min. from Disney World. **I,** but lower rates off-season.

♀ **King's Motel,** 4836 W. Irlo Bronson Hwy. (US 192),
⌂ Kissimmee, FL 32741 (407/396-4762; toll free 800/327-9071). 98 rms, A/C, cable color TV. AE, MC, V. Free parking, pool, boating, fishing, nearby rest. *Note:* Modern, well-maintained motel on attractive Lake Cecil. Comfortable, appealing rms, some w. kitchenette. Friendly, smiling svce. 10 min. from Walt Disney World and Sea World. Good value. **I,** but lower rates off-season.

♀ **Orlando Motor Lodge,** 1825 N. Mills Ave., Orlando, FL
⌂ 32803 (407/896-4111). 68 rms, A/C, color TV, in-rm movies. AE, DC, MC, V. Free parking, pool, fishing, coffee shop. *Note:* Modest but very acceptable motel on Lake Rowena (boats available). Rms w. balconies, some w. kitchenettes. Good value. 30 min. drive to Walt Disney World. **I,** but lower rates off-season.

♀ **Motel 6 West,** 7455 W. Irlo Bronson Hwy., Kissimmee, FL
⌂ 32741 (407/396-6422). 148 rms, A/C, color TV, in-rm movies. AE, DC, MC, V. Free parking, pool. *Note:* New motel w. unbeatable rates. Functional comfort. 5 min. from Walt Disney World and EPCOT. Excellent value. Ideal for budget travelers. **B–I**

Airport Accommodations

♀♀♀ **Marriott Orlando Airport,** 7499 Augusta National Dr., Or-
⌂ ⌂ lando, FL 32822 (407/851-9000; toll free, see Marriott). 484 rms, A/C, cable color TV, in-rm movies. AE, CB, DC, MC, V. Free parking, pool, tennis court, health club, sauna, two rests. (including Courtney's), two bars, rm svce, free crib. *Note:* Large airport hotel, modern and comfortable. Rms are soundproof and very large. Reasonably complete facilities; efficient svce. Middling rests. VIP floor. Business clientele. 10 min. from dwntwn, 20 min. from Walt Disney World. Free airport shuttle. **M–E**

♀♀ **La Quinta Inn Florida Mall,** 8601 S. Orange Blossom Trail, Or-
⌂ ⌂ lando, FL 32809 (407/859-4100; toll free, see La Quinta). 131 rms, A/C, color TV, in-rm movies. AE, CB, DC, MC, V. Free parking, pool, adj. 24-hr. coffee shop, valet svce, free crib. *Note:* Inviting motel 10 min. from the airport and 20 min. from Walt Disney World. Very large, comfortable rms. Good value. Airport shuttle svce. **I–M**

YMCA/Youth Hostels

Orlando International Hostel, 227 N. Eola Dr., Orlando 32801 (407/843-8888). Appealing youth hostel on Lake Eola.

RESTAURANTS

A Note on Restaurant Prices: Orlando restaurant prices, per person, excluding drinks and service charges, are coded as follows: **VE,** Very Expensive ($60 and up); **E,** Expensive ($40–$60); **M,** Moderate ($25–$40); **I,** Inexpensive ($15–$25); **B,** Budget (up to $15).

Personal Favorites (in order of preference)

♀♀♀ **La Coquina,** in Hyatt Regency Grand Cypress (see
⌂⌂⌂ "Accomodations" above) (407/293-1234). A/C. Lunch/dinner daily; brunch Sun. AE, DC, MC, V. Jkt. *Specialties:* Shrimp and salmon sausage w. papaya coulis, crab-stuffed ravioli, venison and quail en croûte w. peppercorns, mahimahi en papillote. Fine wine list. *Note:* Impressive two-story glass-walled rest. w. food ranging from fine to exceptional. Overlooks a lake w. inlet harboring a flock of flamingos. Elegant leafy decor w. palm trees and other greenery. Flawless svce. Resv. highly advised. Orlando's finest address. *French/American.* **M–E**

ΨΨΨ **Maison et Jardin,** 430 S. Wymore Rd., Altamonte Springs
ααα (407/862-4410). A/C. Lunch Mon–Fri, dinner nightly;
brunch Sun; closed hols. AE, CB, DC, MC, V. Jkt. *Specialties:* rack of lamb diable, scampi Costa Brava, veal Oscar, chateaubriand bouquetière, sweetbreads
bonne femme, bouillabaisse. Fine wine list (over 400 selections). *Note:* Framed
by trees and shrubberies of jasmine and azalea, this lovely arcaded Mediterranean-style villa boasts one of the most flower-filled settings in Florida. Antique furniture and Oriental rugs contribute to the opulent decor. Excellent classic French cuisine, though a tad pretentious. Svce excellent. Resv. advised. 45 min. from Walt Disney World. *French/Continental.*
I–M

☼ ΨΨΨ **Chalet Suzanne,** U.S. 27N, Lake Wales (813/676-6011).
ααα A/C. Breakfast/lunch/dinner daily; closed Mon May–Nov.
AE, CB, DC, MC, V. Jkt. *Specialties:* romaine soup, lobster Newburg, curried
shrimp, chicken Suzanne, lamb chops English style, rum cake, crêpes Suzettes.
Note: One of the best rests. in Florida, in the middle of an orange grove. Picturesquely miscellaneous decor. The cuisine in general and the sauces in particular
are meticulously worked out. Even the soups merit an award of excellence; some
of them accompanied the *Apollo* astronauts to the moon. Cheerful, conscientious
svce. Resv. advised. An excellent establishment which has already celebrated its
50th anniversary. *Continental.* **M–E**

ΨΨ **Chatham's Place,** 7575 Dr. Phillips Blvd., Orlando (407/
αα 345-2992). A/C. Lunch Mon–Fri, dinner Tues–Sat. MC, V.
Specialties: snails w. angel-hair pasta, rack of lamb w. rosemary, grilled yellowfin
tuna w. grilled-pineapple salsa, catch of the day, bananas Foster, Black Velvet
cake. Wine and beer but no hard liquor. *Note:* If you love fish—grilled, steamed,
or sautéed—this is some of Orlando's best. The seafood is impeccably fresh, the
surroundings attractive and comfortable, the svce friendly and efficient. Note
that there is no smoking anywhere in the rest. A very good place; resv. advisable.
American. **I–M**

ΨΨ **Barney's Steak House,** 1615 E. Colonial Dr., Orlando (407/
αα 896-6864). A/C. Dinner only, nightly; closed Thanksgiving,
Dec 25. AE, CB, DC, MC, V. *Specialties:* broiled meats and fish, ribs of beef, giant
salad bar. *Note:* The favorite steakhouse of Orlando residents, according to an
Orlando Sentinel poll. Top cuts of meat, cooked to perfection. Modern decor,
pleasant background music. Relaxed atmosphere, very good svce. No resv., unfortunately. *Steak.* **B–I**

Ψ **Maison des Crêpes,** 348 N. Park Ave., Winter Park (407/
α 647-4469). A/C. Lunch/dinner Mon–Sat; closed hols. and
early July. AE, CB, DC, MC, V. *Specialties:* pancakes (30 varieties), soups, fish of
the day, filet Royal. *Note:* As the name indicates, pancakes of various types are the
house specialty here, but the fish of the day and the chef's soups are equally worth
recommending. Rustic, flowery setting. 40 min. from Walt Disney World.
French/Seafood. **B–I**

Other Restaurants (from top bracket to budget)

☼ ΨΨΨ **Empress Room,** aboard the *Empress Lilly* riverboat, Disney
ααα World Village, Lake Buena Vista (407/828-3900). A/C. Dinner only, nightly. AE, MC, V. J&T. *Specialties:* oyster soup w. spinach, artichoke
bottoms w. salmon mousse, Dover sole w. wild mushrooms, chicken in cider,
wild boar w. blueberries, soufflé Grand Marnier, cloche au chocolat. Very fine
wine list. *Note:* This life-size replica of a paddlewheeler is a fixture in the Disney
empire. The dining room's Louis XV decor and the formal svce are impressive.
The cuisine is rather pretentious, but dishes such as the sole stuffed w. salmon
mousse are truly inspired. Be prepared for a hefty bill. Resv. indispensable (the
rest. seats only 60). *Continental.* **M–E**

♚♚♚ **Le Cordon Bleu,** 537 W. Fairbanks Ave., Winter Park (407/
♚♚♚ 647-7575). A/C. Lunch/dinner Mon–Sat; closed hols. AE,
CB, DC, MC, V. Jkt. *Specialties:* shellfish au gratin, red snapper Imperiale, bouillabaisse, filet mignon w. vodka sauce, smoked duck w. French brie, rack of lamb,
lobster w. hazelnut butter. Excellent wine list. *Note:* Chef George Vogelbacher is
Swiss, but his cooking is firmly in the French tradition. Prepared w. a daring and
imaginative touch, his classic dishes are well-nigh irresistible. Decor suggests an
elegant, vaguely Victorian bistro. Polished svce. 45 min. from Walt Disney
World. *French/Continental.* **M–E**

♚♚ **Freddie's Steak House,** U.S. 17, Fern Park, (407/339-3265).
♚♚ A/C. Dinner nightly, brunch Sun; closed Dec 25, Jan 1.
AE, CB, DC, MC, V. Jkt. *Specialties:* beef ribs, roast duck, fish of the day (pompano, grouper). *Note:* For over 40 years the name "Freddie's" has been synonymous w. superb broiled meats and fish. Ambience is that of a rather intimate
English club. Excellent svce. A fine place to eat; resv. advised. 30 min.
from Walt Disney World. Popular with the locals. Valet parking. *Steak/Sea-
food.* **I–M**

♚♚ **Top of the World,** in Disney's Contemporary Resort (see "Ac-
♚♚ commodations," above) (407/824-3950). A/C. Breakfast/
lunch/dinner daily; brunch Sun. AE, MC. Jkt. *Specialties:* roast duck Curaçao,
veal cutlets Romanoff, broiled red snapper. Good desserts. *Note:* Located on the
15th and top floor of the astonishing Contemporary Resort, this rest. enjoys an
incomparable view. Ultramodern setting and decor. The cooking is traditional
European and somewhat lacking in imagination. Worthwhile for its unrestricted
view of the Magic Kingdom. There's also dancing and Broadway shows. Resv. a
must, several days in advance. Valet parking. *Continental.* **I–M (E** for Broadway
shows)

♚♚ **Christy's Sundown,** Ave. K and 3rd St. S. (U.S. 17), Winter
♚♚ Haven (813/293-0069). A/C. Lunch/dinner Mon–Sat;
closed hols. AE, MC, V. *Specialties:* broiled red snapper, lobster, steak, shish kebab, Greek-style chicken. *Note:* Rest. in rustic Mediterranean decor, very popular
w. vacationers in the Cypress Gardens and surrounding areas. Solid, carefully
prepared cuisine. Good desserts. Svce is rather dour but efficient. Resv. advised.
40 min. from Walt Disney World. Dancing. *Steak/Continental.* **I**

♚♚ **Disney Village Club,** 2200 Club Lake Dr., Lake Buena Vista
♚♚ (407/828-3830). A/C. Lunch/dinner daily, brunch Sun.
AE, MC, V. Jkt. (evenings). *Specialties:* onion soup au gratin, eggs Florentine,
chateaubriand, steak Diane, gold brick sundae. *Note:* Elegant country-club atmosphere. The cooking is French-inspired and reasonably priced. Intimate, inviting setting, cheerful svce. Resv. a must. 15 min. from Walt Disney World.
Valet parking. Excellent value. *French/Continental.* **I**

☼♚♚ **Lili Marlene's Aviators Pub,** 129 Church St., Orlando (407/
☼♚♚ 422-2434). A/C. Lunch/dinner daily (until midnight). AE,
CB, DC, MC, V. *Specialties:* roast beef, steak aviateur, veal Cordon Bleu, catch of
the day. *Note:* Located in the heart of Church Street Station with its yesteryear
shops and turn-of-the-century saloon, this pleasant, amusing pub offers a number of serviceable, adequately prepared dishes. Especially lively in the evening. 25
min. from Walt Disney World. *Steak/Continental.* **I**

☼♚♚ **Papeete Bay Verandah,** in Disney's Polynesian Village Resort
☼♚♚ (see "Accommodations," above) (407/824-1391). A/C.
Breakfast/lunch/dinner daily, brunch Sun. AE, MC. *Specialties:* chicken Pago
Pago, beef Bora Bora, pork ribs Fiji, ribs of beef, broiled lobster. *Note:* The Tahitian setting is one of the most successful of the Walt Disney World creations. The
decor and the savory Polynesian cooking together provide a truly exotic dining experience. Breakfast and lunch buffets are less convincing. Lovely view
of the lagoon. Evenings, there's a Polynesian show. Dinner resv. advised. *Polynesian.* **I**

♀ **Ran-Getsu of Tokyo,** 8400 International Dr., Orlando (407/
♀ 345-0044). A/C. Dinner only, daily. AE, CB, DC, MC, V.
Specialties: sushi, sukiyaki, shabu-shabu, tempura, yosenabe. *Note:* The largest
Japanese rest. in the U.S., with the longest sushi bar in Florida. The chefs, trained
in the mother house in Tokyo, practice their demonic skills before your eyes.
Open, comfortable dining areas on two levels. Locally very popular; resv. advised. *Japanese.* **I**

♀ **Sea World Polynesian Luau,** 7007 Sea World Dr., Orlando
♀ (407/363-2195). A/C. Dinner only, one sitting at 6:45pm.
AE, MC, V. *Specialties:* Kalúa pig (roast suckling pig), lomi-lomi salmon (prepared w. tomatoes and onions), corn on the cob, roast chicken, coconut cake,
Hawaiian desserts. *Note:* Open-air buffet dinner in the great tradition of the Hawaiian luau. Meat, fish, and chicken are cooked in *imus*—ovens dug into the
ground and lined w. blocks of lava. Unusual and flavorful food accompanied by
colorful Hawaiian music and dance. If you enjoy the exotic, try this. Resv. required. *Polynesian.* **I**

♀ **Townsend's Fish House & Tavern,** 35 W. Michigan, Orlando
♀ (407/422-5560). A/C. Lunch Mon–Fri, dinner daily. AE,
DC, MC, V. *Specialties:* raw oysters, Cajun alligator tail, Captain Bligh plate (lobster, scallops, shrimp, mahi-mahi), grilled Norwegian salmon, stone crabs in season, key lime pie, Mississippi mud pie. *Note:* Excellent values and impeccably
fresh seafood make Townsend's a favorite rest. among residents. Agreeable, relaxed atmosphere w. very popular predinner "happy hour" and live music Wed–
Sat evenings. Marble bars and lots of brightwork; efficient though somewhat flus-
tered svce. *Seafood.* **I**

♀ **Linda's La Cantina,** 4721 E. Colonial Dr., Orlando (407/
♀ 894-4491). A/C. Dinner only, Tues–Sat; closed late July to
mid-Aug, Thanksgiving, Dec 25. AE, MC, V. *Specialties:* lasagne, veal parmigiana, Italian dishes, broiled steak. *Note:* Classic steakhouse w. nondescript decor
offering decent Italian cooking and choice meats at very affordable prices. Popular w. the locals for over 40 years. No resv. accepted; be prepared to wait. 25 min.
from Walt Disney World. *Italian/Steak.* **B–I**

☼ ♀ **Steerman's Quarters,** aboard the *Empress Lilly* riverboat, Dis-
♀ ney World Village, Lake Buena Vista (407/828-3900). A/C.
Breakfast/lunch/dinner daily. AE, MC, V. *Specialties:* steak, meats, sandwiches,
salads. *Note:* Located on the lower deck of this make-believe Mississippi paddlewheeler, Steerman's serves very good broiled meats such as Texas-style T-bone
steak. Children love breakfasting w. the familiar Disney characters (resv. a must).
Pleasant, relaxed atmosphere. 15 min. from Walt Disney World. *American.* **B–I**

♀ **Ronnie's,** 2702 E. Colonial Dr., Orlando (407/894-2943).
♀ A/C. Breakfast/lunch/dinner daily (7am–11pm). No credit
cards. *Specialties:* Jewish deli delights, corned beef, pastrami, homemade desserts
(excellent cheesecake). *Note:* New York–style delicatessen, w. gigantic sandwiches and waistline-destroying desserts. Often crowded at lunch. 25 min. from
Walt Disney World. *American.* **B**

Cafeterias/Fast Food

Morrison's, 1840 E. Colonial Dr., Orlando (407/896-2091). Open daily
(until 8:30pm). MC, V. *Specialties:* roast beef, sandwiches, soups, salads, homemade pastry. *Note:* Cafeteria cooking, honest and well prepared. Other locations:
140 Winter Haven Mall, Winter Haven (813/293-1003), and 700 N. Orlando
Ave., Winter Park (407/644-7853).

BARS & NIGHTCLUBS

Bonkerz, 4315 N. Orange Blossom Trail, Winter Park (407/298-2665).
The best comedy club in the area, featuring the very top comedians.

Cheek to Cheek, 8391 N. Orlando Ave., Winter Park (407/644-2060). Open Tues–Sat. Preppy-style dancing to live music from the 1940s. Very decent Italian restaurant (Villa Nova).

J.J. Whispers, 904 Lee Rd., Orlando (407/629-4779). Disco music, live orchestras, five dance floors. A hot spot for several years. Also rest. Open nightly.

Park Avenue Club, 4315 N. Orange Blossom Trail, Orlando (407/295-3750). "In" disco with a youthful clientele. Generally crowded weekends.

Phineas Phogg's Balloon Works, Church St. Station, 129 W. Church St., Orlando (407/422-2434). Locally popular disco. Amusing ambience. Open nightly.

Rosie O'Grady's Goodtime Emporium, Church St. Station, 129 W. Church St., Orlando (407/422-2434). Dixieland jazz in turn-of-the-century saloon setting. Very touristy atmosphere. Open nightly.

Sullivan's Trailway Lounge, 1108 S. Orange Blossom Trail, Orlando (407/843-2934). Trendy western club, featuring country music stars.

Village Lounge, Walt Disney World Village, Lake Buena Vista (407/828-3830). Live modern jazz. Also a decent rest.

NEARBY EXCURSIONS

KENNEDY SPACE CENTER/SPACEPORT USA (46 mi./75km east on Fla. 50) (407/452-2121; toll free 800/432-2153): The primary American space-vehicle launch site. Since 1950 more than 2,200 spacecraft, including the famous shuttle, have been launched from this narrow finger of land at the tip of Cape Canaveral. Participants on the 2-hr. guided bus tour visit the rocket- and shuttle-assembly areas, the astronaut training center, and the various launch sites. Interesting space museum. Open daily; closed Dec 25. Should not be missed. Call the toll-free number for information on scheduled launchings. (For information on nearby hotels and restaurants, see Chapter 16 on Florida's East Coast.)

DAYTONA BEACH (55 mi./89km NE on I-4): Immense beach, 25 mi. (40km) long, accessible by car and dune buggy. Famous also for automobile racing (the Daytona Sunbank 24 and Daytona 500 in Feb, the Daytona 400 in July, etc.). Definitely worth a detour. (See Chapter 16 on Florida's East Coast.)

ST. AUGUSTINE (115 mi./185km NE on I-4 and I-95): The oldest city in the U.S., founded in 1565 by Don Pedro Menendez de Áviles. Charming Spanish colonial city, cleverly restored (Castillo de San Marcos, Mission Nombre de Dios, Zorayda Castle, etc.). A visit here can readily be combined with a trip to Daytona Beach. (See chapter 16 on Florida's East Coast.)

FARTHER AFIELD

THE ATLANTIC COAST FROM CAPE CANAVERAL TO MIAMI (390 mi./625km r.t. on Fla. A1A, U.S. 1, and I-95): Very satisfying vacation tour for devotees of sea and shore. Can also include visits to the Kennedy Space Center, Palm Beach, Fort Lauderdale, and Miami. See Chapter 16 on Florida's East Coast and Chapter 19 on Miami.

TAMPA/ST. PETERSBURG & THE GULF OF MEXICO (166 mi./265km r.t. on I-4): Many inviting beaches along the Gulf of Mexico: Treasure Island, St. Petersburg Beach, Longboat Key, Venice. Can also include the cities of Sarasota, Tarpon Springs, etc. See Chapter 17 on Tampa/St. Petersburg.

MIAMI AND
MIAMI BEACH 📯

□ □ □

With the Everglades and Key West

Originally known as Fort Dallas, a small military post established in 1835 at the mouth of the Miami River, the youngest of America's great cities officially saw the light in 1870 as a simple post office and trading post. It didn't begin to grow until 1896, when Henry M. Flagler, an enterprising railroad tycoon, decided to extend the East Coast Railroad south from Palm Beach and to build the Royal Palm Hotel at Miami. Today the city (whose name, from the Seminole *Mayami,* means a broad stretch of water) has become synonymous with vacations and lavish hotels, but it has higher aspirations.

First of all this enormous, complex metropolis, growing demographically at an explosive rate (35% in 10 years), would like to outgrow its reputation, disseminated by the TV series "Miami Vice," as a drug dealers' paradise and a racial melting-pot where Cubans, Haitians, Jamaicans, Salvadorans, and other Hispanics engage in confrontation with whites and African Americans rather than assimilation. It is indeed the case that in this tropical, cosmopolitan version of New York City, which in a comparatively few years has become the main financial clearinghouse for trade between the U.S. and Latin America, these different ethnic groups live beside one another or even on top of one another.

There are vacationers drawn to the beaches of **Miami Beach, Key Biscayne,** and **Surfside,** or to a dream cruise in the Caribbean (Miami is the world's cruiseship capital). There are millionaires who, finding **Coconut Grove** and **Coral Gables** no longer exclusive enough for their tastes, are withdrawing from Miami in favor of **Palm Beach** and **Naples.** There are retirees from New York and Chicago who have come to live out their lives in the Florida sun. There are businesspeople and bankers of all nationalities—at last count there were more than 250 banks in Miami, 76 of them foreign. There are well-heeled South Americans doing their shopping in the smart stores of **Bal Harbor** and the **Miracle Mile.** There are big-game fishermen and boating buffs who can indulge their passion here—43,000 pleasure boats claim Miami or Miami Beach as their port of registration, from little outboards to 120-ft. (40m) yachts; as to the fishing, biologists can point to no fewer than 600 species in the waters of southern Florida. There are Latin American exiles, anti-Castro Cubans for the most part, who have come to try their luck in the U.S., making Miami the largest bilingual city in the country. Store signs on the picturesque **Calle Ocho** (8th St.), the Main Street of **Little Havana,** bear witness to this in a kind of American-flavored Spanish: "perros calientes," for example, for "hot dogs." In 1960 the "Port of the Americas," as Miami has been termed, was still 75% Anglo; today, only 45%. The mayor of the city, Xavier Suarez, was born in Cuba.

The kindly climate brings down every year to Miami and other resort cities as far as **Fort Lauderdale** or even **Boca Raton** (see Chapter 16 on Florida's East Coast) hordes of shivering citizens nicknamed "snowbirds," in flight from the snows and blizzards of the North. Even the hot, humid summer weather has its devotees thanks to lower off-season prices. In all, almost 12 million visitors annually descend on the 650 hotels and motels and the 4,500 restaurants, cafeterias, and snack bars of Miami and Miami Beach, making mass tourism the leading local industry (for the state of Florida as a whole it brings in $10 billion a year). The second industry is still the trade in early fruits and vegetables and in citrus crops, of which Florida is the country's largest producer. The third is believed to be the drug trade—over the past decade Miami, with Los Angeles, has become the main market and principal drug clearinghouse in North America. In the light of this fact, it will not surprise you to learn that, according to FBI figures, Miami is one of the country's most dangerous cities. Once night has fallen in the downtown business district of Miami, only the rash go out alone on foot.

With its innumerable theme parks and its many theaters and museums, the superb, ultramodern **Metro-Dade Cultural Center,** its symphony orchestra, and its internationally famous Miami City ballet, the Floridian metropolis is in no sense a cultural desert. As well as its own attractions, Miami offers the visitor a whole range of interesting excursions: for example, to the famous **Everglades National Park** with its unending subtropical marshlands. Not to forget the **Florida Keys,** a chain of 43 small coral islands protruding like a huge comma into the Gulf of Mexico as far as **Key West,** barely 90 miles (144km) from the coast of Cuba. Once the lair of pirates and smugglers, the Keys are today a paradise for deep-sea fishermen, and a sort of tourist annex of Miami.

Actor Sidney Poitier is perhaps the best known of Miami's famous children.

BASIC FACTS: State of Florida. Area code: 305. Time zone: eastern. ZIP Codes: 33101 (Miami), 33139 (Miami Beach). Founded: 1870. Approximate population: city, 530,000; metropolitan area, about 2,950,000 (of whom 1,250,000 are Hispanics). 11th in size of U.S. metropolitan areas.

CLIMATE: There is no need to dwell on Miami's benign winters, averaging 69°F (20°C) Dec–Feb; it is this that draws the crowds of lucky vacationers. With its heavy heat (average in July, 82°F/28°C), summer is much less pleasant. For the rest of the year the thermometer rarely goes above 77°F (25°C), ideal for ocean bathing or just doing nothing. But watch out for tropical hurricanes in the fall.

DISTANCES: Atlanta, 659 mi. (1,055km); Key West, 161 mi. (258km); New Orleans, 856 mi. (1,370km); Orlando, 240 mi. (385km); Savannah, 496 mi. (794km); Washington, D.C., 1,075 mi. (1,720km).

ARRIVAL & TRANSIT INFORMATION

Note: In view of the sheer size of the Miami metropolitan area, which includes 27 different communities and stretches 40 mi. (64km) from north to south, the different places, museums, and monuments referred to below are identified according to district: Miami, Miami Beach, Coral Gables, etc.

AIRPORT: Miami International Airport (MIA), 7 mi. (11km) NW, 9th busiest U.S. airport, with 25 million passengers each year. There'll be a long wait at Arrivals on international flights. Call 871-7021 for information.

U.S. AIRLINES: American (358-6800), Continental (871-1400), Delta (448-7000), Eastern (873-3000), Midway (toll free 800/621-5700), Northwest (377-0311), Pan Am (874-5000), TWA (371-7471), and United (377-3461).

FOREIGN CARRIERS: Air Canada (toll free 800/422-6232) and British Airways (toll free 800/247-9297).

CITY LINK: The **cab** fare to city center is about $14; time, 20 min. Cab fare to Miami Beach, Coral Gables, or Key Biscayne is $16–$20, according to destination.

Airport bus: **Super Shuttle** (871-2000) provides door-to-door service to any Miami or Miami Beach destination; operates at 15-min. intervals, 24-hr. daily (resv. a must when you're traveling *to* the airport); fare, $7–$18, according to destination; time, 30–45 min., according to destination.

Municipal bus: **METROBUS** (638-6700), Lines 3 and 20 to dwntwn; fare, $1; time, 45–50 min.

Cabs are costly because of the distances involved. Public bus transportation is complex and unsafe; the elevated rail system (**METRORAIL** and **METROMOVER**) is modern but still incomplete. The sensible solution is to rent a car with unlimited mileage; Florida rates are very low, and you may be able to leave the car in another city, such as Orlando, Fort Lauderdale, or Tampa, without surcharge.

CAR RENTAL (at Miami International Airport unless otherwise noted): Avis (526-3000); Budget (871-3053); Dollar (887-6000); Hertz (871-0300); National (526-5200); Thrifty, 2701 W. LeJeune Rd. (871-2277). For dwntwn locations, consult the city telephone directory.

LIMOUSINE SERVICES: American Limo Service (688-7700), Carey Limousine (764-0615), Executive Limo (947-6144).

TAXIS: In theory cabs may be hailed on the street; in practice it's advisable to take them at the stands outside the major hotels, or simply to phone. The principal cab companies are **Central Cab** (532-5555), **Metro Taxi** (888-8888), and **Yellow Cab** (444-4444).

TRAIN: Amtrak station, 8303 NW 37th Ave., Miami (835-1221).

INTERCITY BUSES: Greyhound, 99 NE 4th St., Miami (374-7222), and 7101 Harding Ave., Miami Beach (538-0381).

INFORMATION & TOURS

TOURIST INFORMATION: The **Greater Miami Convention and Visitors Bureau,** 701 Brickell Ave., Suite 2700, Miami, FL 33131 (305/539-3000; toll free 800/283-2707).

Miami Beach Visitor and Convention Authority, 555 17th St., Miami Beach, FL 33139 (305/673-7050): Information on Miami Beach.

GUIDED TOURS: American Sightseeing (bus), 11077 NW 36th Ave., Miami (688-7700): Guided tour of the city and surroundings; serves the principal hotels.

Gray Line Tours (bus), 1642 NE 21st Terrace, Miami (325-1000): Guided tour of the city and surroundings; serves the principal hotels.

Dade Helicopter, 950 McArthur Causeway, Miami (374-3737): Impressive. Daily year-round service.

Island Queen (boat), Miamarina, 400 SE Second Ave., Miami (379-5119): Trips on the bay; daily year-round service.

Nikko Gold Coast Cruises (boat), Haulover Park Marina, 10800 Collins

Ave., Miami Beach (945-5461): Trips to Biscayne Bay and the Florida Canal; daily year-round service.

Old Town Trolley (bus), Bayside Marketplace (374-8687): 2-hr. guided tour of Miami's principal attractions in a replica of an old-time trolley. You may get off and on as often as you please along the route. Daily year round.

Sea Escape (shipboard cruise), 1080 Port Blvd., Port of Miami, Miami (379-0000): 1-day mini-cruise to the Bahamas and back, with excursions on shore. Leaves at 8:30am, returns at midnight. On board are rests., bars, pool, casino. Fare is $99 per person, including meals. Daily year round.

SIGHTS, ATTRACTIONS & ACTIVITIES

ADVENTURES: Wilderness Experiences, Inc. (Jeep and boat), Loop and Dill Rd., in Big Cypress National Preserve (813/695-3143): Airboat trip lasting 1 or more days across the swamps of Big Cypress National Preserve, north of Everglades National Park (see "National Parks Nearby," below). This 100-mi. (160km) tour will reveal to you the fauna and flora unique to the Everglades. Year round, by resv. only. Don't miss it. For more information, write P.O. Box 653954, Miami, FL 33265.

Windjammer Cruises (boat), P.O. Box 120, Miami Beach, FL 33119 (305/534-7447; toll free 800/327-2600): 6-, 13-, and 19-day cruises through the Antilles and the islands of the Caribbean, aboard wonderful old-time sailing ships. Reckon on $700 for 6 days. A real change.

ARCHITECTURAL HIGHLIGHTS: ※🏛️ **Art Deco District,** around Collins Ave. between 6th St. and 23rd St., and Ocean Dr. between 9th St. and 15th St., Miami Beach: More than 800 fine 1920s and 1930s buildings in pastel hues; the fine flower of art deco. The whole neighborhood is undergoing extensive rehabilitation. Guided walking tours available; call 672-2014 for information. A sight not to be missed.

⠀⠀⠀⠀※🏛️ **Atlantis Condominium,** 2025 Brickell Ave., Miami (285-1269): This ultramodern azure-blue building with its giant skylight open to the heavens, by the celebrated architectural team of Bernardo Fort-Brescia and Laurinda Spear, is one of the symbols of the New Miami and has appeared in stock footage for the TV series "Miami Vice." Not to be missed.

⠀⠀⠀⠀🏛️ **Bacardi Buildings,** 2100 Biscayne Blvd., Miami: Modern structures with mosaic murals that recall the famous facade of the University of Mexico in Mexico City. Worth a look.

⠀⠀⠀⠀🏛️ **Coral Castle,** 28655 U.S. 1 at SW 286th St., Homestead (248-6344): An extravaganza in the style of a fortified castle, carved from blocks of coral by a solitary craftsman from 1925 to 1940. Stone furniture; 9-ton (8,200kg) swinging rock gate. Fantastic. Open daily.

⠀⠀⠀⠀※🏛️ **Metro Dade Cultural Center,** 101 W. Flagler St., Miami (372-7666): Ultramodern complex, very Mediterranean in flavor, designed by the architect Philip Johnson. Around a large plaza stand several remarkable buildings: the **Center for the Fine Arts** (see below), the **Historical Museum of Southern Florida** (see below), and the **Miami Public Library,** with 1.5 million volumes. The artistic and cultural heart of Miami; don't fail to see it.

⠀⠀⠀⠀※🏛️ **Miamarina,** Bayshore Dr., Bay Front Park, Miami (579-6955): Well-known, crowded boat basin for pleasure craft, with more than 200 berths. Boats may be rented for deep-sea fishing or boat trips on Biscayne Bay. A spectacular sight.

⠀⠀⠀⠀※🏛️ **Miami Beach Hotel Row,** Collins Ave. and Indian Creek between 21st St. and 71st St. Miami Beach: Grand hotels and other sumptuous buildings huddled on the narrow strip of land between the ocean and Indian Creek Canal. A remarkable sight.

⠀⠀⠀⠀🏛️ **Miami Herald Building,** 1 NE Herald Plaza, Miami (376-2909): A superbly successful piece of modern architectural design; one of the loveliest buildings of its kind. Guided tour of the newspaper on Mon, Wed, Fri; resv. required.

※☆ **Port of Miami,** Port Blvd., Miami: The busiest passenger ship terminal in the United States. Many liners, including the huge *Norway* (formerly the *France*), have their home port here; more than 3 million passengers pass through yearly. Note to photographers: The liners usually sail Fri–Mon toward the end of the afternoon.

High-Rise Buildings

※☆ **Centrust Tower,** 101 E. Flagler St., Miami (376-5780): Giant 35-story building, 562 ft. (175m) high, looking like a pop-art wedding cake, by the distinguished architect I. M. Pei. Miami's finest skyscraper; must certainly be seen.

☆ **Southeast Financial Center,** 1 SE Financial Center, Miami (670-4833): Florida's tallest high-rise at 764 ft. (238m), 55 floors. Worth a look.

BEACHES: ※☆☆ **Bill Baggs Cape Florida State Park,** at the southern end of Crandon Blvd., Key Biscayne: The local favorite. Pretty natural setting; picnic zones. Crowded on weekends.

☆ **Haulover Beach,** 16 mi. (25km) on Fla. 1A, North Miami Beach: Much favored by families; good for surfing and fishing.

☆☆ **Miami Beach,** along Collins Ave.: The private beaches of the great hotels, side by side with several public beaches. The beach has recently been widened for a stretch of many miles. Access via 21st St., 35th St., 46th St., 53rd St., 64th St., and 73rd St.

☆ **South Beach,** 5th St. and Ocean Dr., Miami Beach: For surfers. Trendy bistros.

Surfside, Collins Ave. from 88th St. to 96th St., North Miami: As its name implies, a great beach for surfers.

☆☆ **Venetian Pool,** 2701 De Soto Blvd., Coral Gables: Wonderful Venetian-style lagoon in the heart of town.

☆☆ **Virginia Beach,** 6 mi. (9km) SE along Rickenbacker Causeway, Virginia Key (next to Planet Ocean and Miami Seaquarium): Ideal for scuba-diving.

CHURCHES/SYNAGOGUES: ☆ **King Solomon Temple,** 910 Lincoln Rd., Miami Beach (534-9776): Built in 1976 exactly according to the plan of King Solomon's temple in Jerusalem as described in the Old Testament. Worth seeing.

※☆☆ **Spanish Monastery of St. Bernard,** 16711 W. Dixie Hwy., North Miami Beach (11 mi./18km north) (945-1462): Cloister of the monastery of St. Bernard of Clairvaux, built in 1141 at Segovia in Spain. It was bought and transported, stone by stone, to the U.S. by press baron William Randolph Hearst, and re-erected on its present site in 1952. It houses a number of medieval works of art. Now the property of the Episcopal church. Lovely gardens; well worth going out of your way for.

HISTORIC BUILDINGS: ☆ **The Barnacle State Historic Site,** 3485 Main Hwy., Coconut Grove (448-9445): One of the most beautiful examples of the local Caribbean-style architecture of the last century. Owned originally by Commodore Ralph Munroe, this luxurious private home, dating from the 1880s, was built in the midst of tropical gardens that are alone worth the visit. A lovely breath of the past. Open Wed–Sun.

※☆☆ **Villa Vizcaya,** 3251 S. Miami Ave., Miami (579-2813): Former residence of International Harvester magnate James

Deering dating from 1912. This Venetian-style 72-room palace, which stands at the shore of the Atlantic, has fine collections of European art—paintings, furniture, sculpture, and antique rugs—in styles ranging from Renaissance to baroque, rococo, etc. The villa, which served as the meeting place in Sept 1987 for Pope John Paul II and President Reagan, is surrounded by 9.6 acres (4ha) of superb gardens. Don't miss it. Open daily.

MONUMENTS: ⛲ **Kennedy Memorial Torch of Friendship,** Bayfront Park, Biscayne Blvd. at NE 5th St., Miami: Fountain crowned by a "torch of friendship" with its eternal flame, and a plaque to the memory of the assassinated president. The torch symbolizes friendship among all the nations of the Western Hemisphere.

⛲ **Pepper Fountain,** Bayfront Park, Biscayne Blvd. and NE 5th St., Miami: A spectacular fountain honoring the late Claude Pepper, who represented Florida in Congress for almost 60 years. Designed by California sculptor Isamu Noguchi, its jets and lights are computer controlled. Definitely worth seeing.

MUSEUMS OF ART: ☼⛲ **Bass Museum,** 2121 Park Ave., Miami Beach (673-7530): Recently reopened after major alterations, this very comprehensive art museum has a rich collection of European old masters (notably Rubens's *Holy Family*) and moderns, impressionists, and contemporary American painters, as well as a gallery of Far Eastern art. Definitely worth a visit. Open Tues–Sun.

⛲ **Center for the Fine Arts,** 101 W. Flagler St., Metro-Dade Cultural Center, Miami (375-1700): Interesting modern works and temporary exhibitions in a very beautiful, austere building by Philip Johnson. Worth visiting. Open Tues–Sun.

⛲ **Cuban Museum of Arts,** 1300 SW 12th Ave., Miami (858-8006): The whole museum is devoted to the cultural heritage of Miami's important Cuban community. Temporary exhibitions. Should be seen. Open Tues–Sun.

⛲ **Lowe Art Museum,** 1301 Stanford Dr., Coral Gables (284-3535): Standing on the University of Miami campus, this ambitious art museum houses part of the famous Samuel H. Kress Collection of Renaissance and baroque art, the Alfred I. Barton Collection of primitive art, the Virgil Barker Collection of American art, and interesting temporary exhibitions. Worth the side trip. Open Tues–Sun.

☼⛲ **Metropolitan Museum and Art Center,** 1212 Anastasia Ave., Coral Gables (442-1448): Eclectic art museum in the old Biltmore Country Club; houses important collections of modern painting and sculpture (including Jacques Lipchitz's lovely sculpture *Our Tree of Life*), and of Pre-Columbian and African art, as well as a "costume museum" with more than 5,000 antique garments. Definitely worth a visit. Open Tues–Sun.

Villa Vizcaya: See "Historic Buildings," above.

MUSEUMS OF SCIENCE & HISTORY: ⛲ **Gold Coast Railroad and Museum,** 12400 SW 152nd St. at Coral Reef Dr., South Dade (253-0063): Railroad museum with more than 200 steam locomotives and passenger cars, including the legendary *Ferdinand Magellan* armored car which Presidents Franklin D. Roosevelt, Harry S Truman, Dwight D. Eisenhower, and Ronald Reagan used as a "rolling White House." Also a 24-mi. (33km) circuit by steam train. Open daily; it can conveniently be visited in conjunction with the nearby Metrozoo.

⛲ **Historical Museum of Southern Florida,** 101 W. Flagler St. in the Metro-Dade Cultural Center, Miami (375-1492): Fascinating historical museum that traces the evolution of southern Florida and the Caribbean from the Stone Age to modern times. Native American art; treasures salvaged by divers from shipwrecks. A must-see. Open daily.

🏛 **Miami Youth Museum,** 5701 Sunset Dr., Bakery Center, South Miami (661-2787): This is definitely a teaching museum; young (and not-so-young) visitors are encouraged to touch and handle all the objects on display. Also mounts very interesting temporary exhibitions. Open Tues–Sun.

🌞🏛🏛 **Museum of Science and Space Transit Planetarium,** 3280 S. Miami Ave., Miami (854-4247): Impressive museum of anthropology, devoted to the fauna and flora of Florida as well as biology and the development of modern science (chemistry, physics, energy sources). Also a giant planetarium with movies of journeys into space. Fascinating. Open daily.

🏛 **Weeks Air Museum,** Tamiami Airport, 14710 SW 128th Ave., South Dade (233-5197): Museum devoted to the preservation and restoration of aircraft from before World War II. More than 30 machines are on display, some of them very rare. For admirers of the intrepid birdmen. Open Tues–Sun.

PANORAMAS: The most spectacular view of Miami and its skyscrapers may be obtained for a comparatively modest fare from a 🌞 **helicopter** (see "Guided Tours," above).

PARKS & GARDENS: 🌞🏛 **Bayfront Park of the Americas,** from NE 5th St. to SE 2nd St. between Biscayne Blvd. and Biscayne Bay, Miami: Lovely waterfront city park with a clear view of the city and the port. Contains several noteworthy monuments, including the **Kennedy Memorial Torch of Friendship** and the new Pepper Fountain designed by sculptor Isamu Noguchi (see "Monuments," above). Don't miss seeing it.

🏛 **Bill Baggs Cape Florida State Park,** south end of Crandon Blvd., Key Biscayne (361-5811): 400 acres (162ha) of mangroves, woods, and inviting beaches 20 min. by car from Miami. You can see the oldest lighthouse in Florida, where there was a bitter battle with the Seminole tribe in 1836. Should be seen.

🏛🏛 **Fairchild Tropical Gardens,** 10901 Old Cutler Rd., Coral Gables (667-1651): One of the country's largest (83 acres/33.6ha) botanic grdns. Extraordinarily beautiful jungle and tropical grdns with more than 5,000 different varieties of exotic plants; you see all this from a mini-train. A must-see. Open daily.

🏛 **Japanese Garden,** Watson Park, McArthur Causeway, Miami (285-1027): Lovely little Japanese grdn with pagoda, tea house, statues, lake, and waterfalls; romantically exotic. Open daily.

🏛 **Lummus Park,** 404 NW North River Dr. and NW 3rd St. Miami: On the banks of the Miami River, this park is now the site of the **Fort Dallas** camp, built in 1835 at the mouth of the river and once under the command of William Tecumseh Sherman. Abandoned in 1838, this unique example of pioneer architecture was later moved to its present location. Worth seeing. Open daily.

🌞🏛🏛 **Venetian Pool,** 2701 De Soto Blvd., Coral Gables (442-6483): Lovely Italian grdn with palm trees, waterfalls, and porticos. The wonderful swimming-pool lagoon, in the pit of an old coral-limestone quarry, is enough to justify the trip. Has recently undergone a $2.3 million restoration. Open daily.

PERFORMING ARTS: For current listings of shows and cultural events, consult the entertainment pages of the two daily papers, *Miami Herald* and *Diario de las Americas* (morning), as well as the monthly *Miami/South Florida* magazine.

Coconut Grove Playhouse, 3500 Main Hwy., Coconut Grove (442-

2662): Modern and classical theater; home of the Players State Theater Company (season Oct–May).

Colony Theater, 1040 Lincoln Rd., Miami Beach (532-4880): Modern and avant-garde theater; performances by the Miami City Ballet (director: Edward Villella).

Dade County Auditorium, 2901 W. Flagler St., Miami (547-5414): Ballet, opera, concerts. Home of the Greater Miami Opera (director: Robert Hever).

Gusman Center for the Performing Arts, 174 E. Flagler St., Miami (358-3338): Classical concerts, musical comedy, performances by the Miami City Ballet. Home of the New World Symphony Orchestra (director: Michael Tilson Thomas). Former movie theater with flamboyant art deco architecture.

Jackie Gleason Theater of the Performing Arts (TOPA), 1700 Washington Ave., Miami Beach (673-7300): Symphony concerts, recitals by leading artists, Broadway hits. Undergoing renovation.

Miami Marine Stadium, 3601 Rickenbacker Causeway, Key Biscayne (361-6730): Nautical stadium with 6,500 seats; open-air concerts by the Summer Pops Orchestra. Aquatic shows. Open July–Aug.

Ring Theater, University of Miami, 1380 Miller Dr., Coral Gables (284-3355): Modern theater, drama, comedy; performs six plays a year.

Ruth Foreman Theater, 11300 NE Second Ave., North Miami Beach (895-7469): Contemporary theater.

SHOPPING: Bal Harbor Shops, 9700 Collins Ave., Bal Harbor (866-0311): Dozens of luxury boutiques and stores from Saint Laurent and Gucci to Cartier and Neiman-Marcus.

Bayside Marketplace, 401 Biscayne Blvd., Miami (577-3344): Shopping center inaugurated in 1987 running alongside Bayfront Park and its marina. The two great pavilions house 165 unusual boutiques, cafés, and restaurants. Very lively atmosphere.

Lincoln Road Mall, Lincoln Rd. between Alton Rd. and Washington Ave., Miami Beach (531-8881): More than 175 very reasonably priced boutiques, stores, and art galleries along a pedestrian mall lined with plantings and fountains.

Mayfair Mall, Grand Ave. and Mary St., Coconut Grove (448-1700): One of the country's most elegant shopping centers; spectacular architecture with tropical gardens, waterfalls, and lagoons; fashion boutiques (Balmain, Charles Jourdan), antique dealers, restaurants, nightclubs, etc.

Miracle Mile, SW 22nd St. between Douglas Rd. and Le Jeune Rd., Coral Gables: The Miami area's most popular shopping street, drawing a very cosmopolitan crowd.

Omni Shopping Mall, 1601 Biscayne Blvd., Miami (374-6664): 160 fashion boutiques and stores of all kinds, six movie houses, and 13 restaurants in a slightly chilly glass-and-steel setting.

SPECIAL EVENTS: For exact dates, consult the **Greater Miami Convention and Visitors Bureau** and the **Miami Beach Visitor and Convention Authority** (see "Tourist Information," above).

Orange Bowl Festival (Jan 1): 8 days of festivities and parades culminating in the Orange Bowl football game.

Coconut Grove Arts Festival (Feb): Hundreds of artists exhibit their work in the streets of Coconut Grove; there's also a food festival. Draws more than half a million visitors every year.

Miami Beach Festival of the Arts (Feb): Concerts, art exhibitions, theater; a very popular festival.

International Boat Show (late Feb): One of the biggest of its kind, at the Miami Beach Convention Center.

Grand Prix of Miami (late Feb or early Mar): Formula 1 Grand Prix held in the streets of downtown Miami. Spectacular.

Calle Ocho Festival/Carnaval Miami (Mar): 9 days of dancing, parades, and celebration along the famous Calle Ocho in Little Havana. The biggest Hispanic festival in the U.S., drawing more than a million revelers.

Miami Unlimited Hydroplane Regatta (early June): Some of the world's fastest and most powerful boats compete in these outboard races on Biscayne Bay, starting from the Marine Stadium.

Festival of the Americas (late Oct): All Miami's Hispanic communities, headed by the Cubans, meet in Tropical Park for this colorful, exuberant folklore festival.

SPORTS: Miami hosts a major-league baseball team for spring training (plus a farm team), and boasts professional basketball and football franchises, three thoroughbred racetracks, and a major sport uniquely its own—jai alai.

Baseball: Baltimore Orioles (Mar–Apr), Miami Stadium (635-4395); and Miami Marlins (Apr–Aug), Orange Bowl Stadium (579-6971).

Basketball: Heat (Oct–Apr), Miami Arena (577-4328).

Football (Sept–Dec): Dolphins, Joe Robbie Stadium (576-1000).

Horse Racing

Calder Race Course, 21001 NW 27th Ave., North Dade (625-1311), with racing mid-Nov–mid-Jan.

Gulfstream Park, U.S. 1, Hallandale (944-1242), open Mon–Sat Jan–Apr.

Hialeah Park Race Course, E. 4th Ave. at 22nd St., Hialeah (885-8000), with races three days a week, Nov–May.

Jai Alai

Jai Alai Fronton, 3500 NW 37th Ave., Miami (633-6400), has games nightly Mon–Sat late Dec to mid-Sept.

Deep-sea Fishing

Lovers of sports fishing may have trouble deciding among the dozens of boat-rental facilities in Miami and Miami Beach. Rates for fully equipped deep-sea fishing boats are around $350 for a half day of 6 hr., or $550 for a full day of 10 hr. For a list of rentals, contact:

Crandon Park Marina, 4000 Crandon Blvd., Key Biscayne (361-1281).

Dinner Key Marina, 3400 Pan American Dr., Coconut Grove (579-6980).

Haulover Beach Park Marina, 10800 Collins Ave., Sunny Isles (947-3525).

Miamarina, Bayshore Dr., Bay Front Park, Miami (579-6955).

STROLLS: ☼⛵ **Coconut Grove,** around S. Bayshore Dr. and SW 27th Ave.: The "Greenwich Village" of Miami, parts of which date back to 1870, owes its name to its many coconut palms. Many artists live here; there are also smart stores. A lively neighborhood by day or night; you should see it.

⛵ **Coral Gables,** around Coral Way and LeJeune Rd.: Elegant residential district with parks, Venetian-style canals, and broad, shady avenues. Beautiful homes in Neo-Moorish and Mediterranean idioms. A well-known university. You should take a look.

⛵ **Key Biscayne,** around Crandon Blvd.: Luxury hotels, dream homes, and beautiful Crandon Park with its immense beaches combine to make this island, linked to Miami by a spectacular toll road, one of the favorite retreats of the famous, including ex-President Richard Nixon.

☼⛵ **Little Havana,** SW 8th St. (the famous "Calle Ocho") between SW 12th Ave. and 37th Ave.: Havana in the U.S., with Cuban restaurants, fruit stalls, craftshops (including some where cigars are still handmade after the Cuban manner), and Spanish signs. Lots of local color; don't miss a stroll here, especially in the evening. For information, call 324-8127.

☀☖☖ **Miami Beach,** around Collins Ave.: Once a marshy, impenetrable, mosquito-ridden mangrove swamp, this narrow 8-mi. (13km) peninsula has become synonymous with vacationing and with flashy luxury. Each year more than eight million tourists come here, summer and winter, to stay in the thousands of hotels, motels, rental apartments, and second homes. Principal attractions are the beaches, recently enlarged and renovated at a cost of $60 million, and the magnificent Art Deco District (see "Architectural Highlights," above). Linked to Miami by five causeways crossing Biscayne Bay. Don't miss it.

THEME PARKS: ☖ **Everglades Holiday Park,** 21940 Griffin Rd. and U.S. 27, Fort Lauderdale (434-8111): Airboat trip through the swamps of the Everglades among the alligators and other wildlife. Organized camping, fishing, and hunting. Well worth the 40 min. by car from Miami. Open daily year round.

☀☖☖ **Fruit and Spice Park,** 24801 SW 187th St. at Coconut Palm Dr., Homestead (247-5727): A botanical garden unique of its kind in the U.S. In a 20-acre (8ha) garden, 200 species of trees and 500 different kinds of shrubs and plants offer a representative selection of the world's exotic fruits and spices, from the black sapodilla to the rosy papaya, the Brazilian jaboticaba, 40 kinds of mango, and 60 kinds of banana. Amazing. Conducted tours. At a giftshop in the park you can choose from a huge assortment of exotic fruits fresh, dried or preserved. Well worth the side trip. Open daily. 40 min. from dwntwn along U.S. 1S.

☖ **Monkey Jungle,** 14805 SW 216th St., South Dade (235-1611): Hundreds of primates, from baboons to gorillas, roaming free in a reproduction of an Amazon Basin forest. It's the visitors who are caged, on roads protected by chain-link fences. Worth a visit. Open daily. 30 min. from dwntwn on U.S. 1S.

☀☖☖ **Orchid Jungle,** 26715 SW 157th Ave., Homestead (247-4824): World's largest open-air orchid garden, with several thousand varieties on display. Trips through the jungle. Spectacular. Open daily. 40 min. from dwntwn on U.S. 1S.

☖ **Parrot Jungle,** 11000 SW 57th Ave., South Miami (666-7834): Many species of parrots, pelicans, marabou storks, and pink flamingos in a lush tropical garden. Shows by trained birds at set times. Open daily. 20 min. from dwntwn on U.S. 1S.

☀☖☖ **Planet Ocean,** 3979 Rickenbacker Causeway, Virginia Key (361-5786): More than 100 attractions devoted to the sea and our dependence on it. From scuba-diving to a simulated hurricane by way of an "authentic" iceberg. Instructive, but also fascinating. Open daily. 5 min. from dwntwn.

☀☖ **Seaquarium,** 4400 Rickenbacker Causeway, Virginia Key (361-5705): One of the world's biggest marine zoos, with 12,000 fish and sea creatures. Home of the celebrated dolphin Flipper and the killer whale Lolita. Don't miss the fine tropical aquarium. Monorail tour. Opposite Planet Ocean (see above). Open daily. 5 min. from dwntwn.

☖ **Six Flags Atlantis,** 2700 Stirling Rd., Hollywood (926-1000): Huge water-sports park with more than 80 different attractions. Giant pool with artificial waves for lovers of surfing; waterskiing shows; super-slides, etc. Open daily June–Sept, wknds only, Apr–May and Oct–Dec. 25 min. from dwntwn on I-95.

ZOOS: ☀☖☖ **Metrozoo,** 12400 SW 152nd St. at Coral Reef Dr., South Dade (251-0400): Big zoo of ultramodern design; the animals are semi-free with no bars or cages, on 280 acres (113ha) of gardens and wilderness, reminiscent of the natural habitats of the 100 or so species on display, including the very rare white tigers from Bengal and Australian koalas. You go around on a monorail. Wonderful and fascinating; not to be missed. Open daily.

ACCOMMODATIONS

A Note on Accommodations: Room rates in Miami/Miami Beach are coded as follows: **VE,** Very Expensive ($140 and up); **E,** Expensive ($90–$140); **M,** Moderate ($60–$90); **I,** Inexpensive ($30–$60); **B,** Budget (up to $30). A listing of toll free numbers is in the Appendix.

Note: Many hotels in Miami and Miami Beach require a checkout notice of 24 or 48 hr. Ask about the checkout policy when you register.

Personal Favorites (in order of preference)

The Alexander, 5225 Collins Ave., Miami Beach, FL 33140 (305/865-6500; toll free 800/327-6121). 210 suites, A/C, color TV, in-rm movies. AE, CB, DC, MC, V. Valet gar. $8, pool, marina, boating, two rests. (including Dominique's), bars, rm svce, nightclub, concierge, free crib. *Note:* Miami Beach's super-luxury hotel, standing in a lovely tropical grdn adorned w. lagoon/swimming pools. High-toned and exclusive. Imposing lobby; spacious, elegant suites w. period furniture, each w. kitchenette, refrigerator, and private patio or balcony offering a splendid prospect of the ocean or Indian Creek. Personalized svce. Direct access to beach. VIP clientele; discreet, distinguished atmosphere. One of the 12 best hotels in the United States, and rates accordingly. **VE**

Grand Bay, 2669 S. Bayshore Dr., Coconut Grove, FL 33133 (305/858-9600; toll free 800/221-2340). 180 suites and mini-suites, A/C, color TV, in-rm movies. AE, CB, DC, MC, V. Valet gar. $8, pool, health club, sauna, two rests. (including the Grand Café), bar, 24-hr. rm svce, disco (Régine's), hrdrsr, concierge, crib $15. *Note:* With its modern truncated-pyramid design and unobstructed view over Biscayne Bay, this luxurious hotel, opened in 1984, has quickly become *the* place to stay in Miami. Elegant, very comfortable suites w. private balconies; the decor is a harmonious blend of modern art, crystal chandeliers, Oriental rugs, and period furniture. Remarkable svce. Good luxury hotel rest. In front of the hotel stands a fine modern sculpture by Alexander Liberman called *Windward.* The Grand Bay belongs to the Italian hotel chain Ciga. 10 min. from dwntwn. **VE,** but lower rates off-season.

Mayfair House, 3000 Florida Ave., Coconut Grove, FL 33133 (305/441-0000; toll free 800/345-3457). 181 rms, A/C, color TV, in-rm movies. AE, CB, DC, MC, V. Valet parking $10, roof pool, two rests. (including the Mayfair Grill), bars, 24-hr. rm svce, disco, hrdrsr, boutiques, concierge, free crib. *Note:* An integral part of the super-smart, super-snob Mayfair Mall, w. its dozens of luxury shops, this charming little European-style hotel combines comfort and elegance. Tastefully decorated, w. interior courts and fountains; spacious rms w. private balcony and refrigerator. Personalized svce. Free limousine svce (reserve ahead). An urbane, stylish place favored by those in-the-know. **VE,** but lower rates off-season.

Inter-Continental, 100 Chopin Plaza, Miami, FL 33131 (305/577-1000; toll free, see Inter-Continental). 646 rms, A/C, color TV, in-rm movies. AE, CB, DC, MC, V. Valet gar. $10, pool, health club, two tennis courts, squash, three rests. (including the Pavillon Grill), coffee shop, two bars, 24-hr. rm svce, nightclub, concierge, free crib. *Note:* A big, massive, ultramodern 34-floor tower, groaning under its burden of marble, Flemish tapestries, and other ornaments in flamboyant style. Spacious, very comfortable rms w. refrigerators; very complete facilities; first-grade svce; first-class rest. Spectacular five-story lobby with a 70-ton (63,600kg) monumental sculpture by Henry Moore. Surrounded by dwntwn's office high-rises; the business traveler's favorite. **E–VE**

☀☿♀♀ **Hotel Place St. Michel,** 162 Alcazar Ave., Coral Gables, FL 33134 (305/444-1666; toll free 800/533-4667). 28 rms, A/C, color TV, in-rm movies. AE, CB, DC, MC, V. Free parking, rest. (Restaurant St. Michel), piano bar, rm svce, concierge, free breakfast, free crib. *Note:* Delightful small hotel of great charm, built in the 1920s and elegantly restored. Every rm is individually decorated w. period furniture and old paintings. Excellent French rest. Polished reception and svce; everything in the old European style. The favorite of those in-the-know, who keep coming back. 10 min. from dwntwn. **M–E**

♀♀ **Miami Lakes Inn,** Main St., Miami Lakes, FL 33014 (305/821-1150; toll free 800/245-2537). 305 rms, A/C, color TV, in-rm movies. AE, CB, DC, MC, V. Free valet parking, two pools, nine tennis courts, squash courts, two golf courses, health club, sauna, putting green, two rests. (including Legends), coffee shop, two bars, rm svce, disco, boutiques, crib $10. *Note:* The resort hotel par excellence, far from the crowds of Miami and Miami Beach, in an elegant country club–like building surrounded by gardens. Spacious, inviting rms w. private balconies or patios; some w. refrigerators. Comprehensive sports facilities. Service w. a smile and aiming to please. Wknd discounts. Good value. 15 min. from airport, 40 min. from dwntwn. **E,** but lower rates off-season.

♀ **Century,** 140 Ocean Dr., Miami Beach, FL 33139 (305/674-8855). 24 rms, A/C, color TV. AE, MC, V. Street parking, rest. nearby, valet svce. *Note:* Alluring little art deco hotel recently renovated. Situated on the quiet, southerly stretch of Ocean Dr. Low-key charm from the roses in the bedroom to the morning coffee, imported from Balducci's and drunk on a sunny veranda. Amicable svce. A popular spot w. artists and photographers from Europe and the United States. **M**

♀ **Mardi Gras,** 3400 Biscayne Blvd., Miami, FL 33137 (305/573-7700). 50 rms, A/C, color TV, in-rm movies. AE, CB, DC, MC, V. Free parking, pool, rest., bar, valet svce. *Note:* A modest but well-run small motel 5 min. from dwntwn. Some rms w. kitchenettes. Functionally comfortable; friendly reception. Good value. **I,** but lower rates off-season.

Other Accommodations (from top bracket to budget)

♀♀♀♀ **The Colonnade Hotel,** Ponce de Leon at Miracle Mile, Coral Gables, FL 33134 (305/441-2600; toll free, *see* Preferred). 157 rms, A/C, color TV, in-room movies. AE, CB, DC, MC, V. Valet parking $8, pool, health club, sauna, two rests. (including the Aragon Cafe), bars, 24-hr. rm svce, nightclub, concierge, crib $15. *Note:* New luxury hotel located atop a 15-story office building in the fashionable Coral Gables district. Elegant European decor w. mahogany furnishings. Spacious, comfortable rms w. minibars (some w. balconies). Personalized svce. Excellent rest. A favorite w. those in the know. **VE,** but lower rates off-season.

♀♀♀♀ **Doral Ocean Beach Resort,** 4833 Collins Ave., Miami Beach, FL 33140 (305/532-3600; toll free 800/327-6334). 420 rms, A/C, color TV, in-rm movies. AE, CB, DC, MC, V. Valet gar. $8, pool, two tennis courts, health club, sauna, beach, boating, panoramic rest. (Roof Garden, on top floor), coffee shop, bar, 24-hr. rm svce, nightclub, drugstore, boutiques, free crib. *Note:* Built of tinted glass, at the same time modern and baroque, the Doral Ocean Beach is one of Miami's most luxurious hotels, its spacious, comfortable rms offering a very fine view of the ocean or of Indian Creek. Direct access to the beach. Excellent svce. Free limo connection with the five golf courses of the Doral Resort Country Club. 15 min. from dwntwn. Interesting vacation packages. **VE,** but lower rates off-season.

ℙℙℙ **Doubletree Hotel** (formerly the Coconut Grove), 2649 S. Bayshore Dr., Coconut Grove, FL 33133 (305/858-2500; toll free 800/528-0444). 190 rms, A/C, color TV, in-rm movies. AE, CB, DC, MC, V. Valet parking $7, pool, two tennis courts, sauna, fishing, boating, two rests. (including the Café Brasserie), two bars, rm svce, disco, free crib. *Note:* Refined and distinguished—particularly the recently renovated interior. Spacious rms, most w. balcony and ocean view, some w. kitchenettes. Exemplary svce. Pleasant all-around view (but uneven food) in the top-floor rest. Opposite Coconut Grove Convention Center and Dinner Key Marina. 15 min. from dwntwn. **E–VE**

ℙℙℙ **Fontainebleau Hilton,** 4441 Collins Ave., Miami Beach, FL 33140 (305/538-2000; toll free, see Hilton). 1,204 rms, A/C, color TV, in-rm movies. AE, CB, DC, MC, V. Valet gar. $9, two pools, health club, sauna, seven tennis courts, boating, beach, bicycles, three rests. (including the Dining Galleries), two coffee shops, four bars, rm svce, disco, hrdrsr, drugstore, concierge, boutiques, free crib. *Note:* The mammoth of local hotels. Since 1954 this giant vacation complex, whose extravagant architecture is signed by Morris Lapidus, now entirely renovated, has been Miami Beach's best-known address. Spacious, comfortable rms w. balconies (some w. refrigerators). The overburdened svce at times leaves something to be desired. The lagoon/swimming pool w. waterfalls and the tropical garden justify a visit in themselves. Direct beach access. Group and convention clientele. 20 min. from dwntwn. **E–VE,** but lower rates off-season.

ℙℙℙ **Hyatt Regency,** 400 SE Second Ave., Miami, FL 33131 (305/358-1234; toll free, see Hyatt). 615 rms, A/C, color TV, in-rm movies. AE, CB, DC, MC, V. Valet parking $9, pool, two rests. (including the Esplanade), coffee shop, bars, 24-hr. rm svce, nightclub, free crib. *Note:* Big 24-story tower on the bank of the Miami River; modern design w. spectacular glass-walled lobby. Ultra-comfortable rms w. balconies. Very comprehensive facilities. Opposite the Convention Center in the heart of dwntwn, the hotel draws business and convention travelers. Two top floors reserved for VIPs. **E–VE,** but lower rates off-season.

ℙℙℙ **Marriott Hotel & Marina–Biscayne Bay,** 1633 N. Bayshore Dr., Miami, FL 33132 (305/374-3900; toll free, see Marriott). 757 rms, A/C, color TV, in-rm movies. AE, CB, DC, MC, V. Valet parking $9, two pools, boating, marina, two rests. (including Véronique's), two bars, rm svce, hrdrsr, boutiques. *Note:* Big convention motel whose twin 31-story towers rise straight from the water's edge; marina for 180 boats. Spacious rms w. balcony and bay view. Every possible comfort; praiseworthy rest. serving Continental cuisine. In spite of all those floors, the svce is efficient—but physical-fitness facilities are deficient. Direct access to the Plaza Venetia and Omni shopping malls via glassed-in skywalk. Group clientele. **E–VE,** but lower rates off-season.

ℙℙℙ **Omni International Hotel,** 1601 Biscayne Blvd., Miami, FL 33132 (305/374-0000; toll free, see Omni). 535 rms, A/C, color TV, in-rm movies. AE, CB, DC, MC, V. Valet gar. $9, pool, two rests. (including the Fish Market), coffee shop, two bars, rm svce, nightclub, boutiques, free crib. *Note:* Truly a city within a city, this 30-story glass-and-concrete tower forms part of the immense Omni/Plaza Venetia Shopping Mall, w. its 160 stores and boutiques, six cinemas, and 13 rests. The interior is done in a rather chilly hi-tech, but the rms are very comfortable, the best overlooking Biscayne Bay. Efficient svce. Bar w. seafood rest. Insufficient sports facilities. Three VIP floors. The favorite of visiting Latin American businessmen. **E–VE,** but lower rates off-season.

ℙℙℙ **Sheraton–Bal Harbor** (formerly the Americana), 9701 Collins Ave., Bal Harbour, FL 33154 (305/865-7511; toll free, see Sheraton). 675 rms, A/C, color TV, in-rm movies. AE, CB, DC, MC, V. Valet parking $8, two pools, two tennis courts, health club, sauna, boating, two rests. (including The Twenties), 24-hr. coffee shop, bars, rm svce, nightclub (in season), drugstore, boutiques, free crib. *Note:* All the comfort you might expect from a modern, well-equipped luxury hotel; spacious rms w. minibars, most w. balconies too. Direct beach access; fine tropical grdn on the ocean. Efficient svce. Attracts groups and conventions. Good value off-season. 25 min. from dwntwn. **E–VE,** but lower rates off-season.

Sheraton–Brickell Point, 495 Brickell Ave., Miami, FL 33131 (305/373-6000; toll free, see Sheraton). 598 rms, A/C, color TV, in-rm movies. AE, CB, DC, MC, V. Valet parking $8, pool, two rests., bars, rm svce, nightclub, crib $10. *Note:* Ultramodern 18-story tower overhanging Biscayne Bay. Comfortable rms w. a view. Rather comprehensive facilities. Lovely tropical decor w. a flower-planted terrace. Acceptable rest. overlooking the bay. Well situated very nr. the financial district. **E,** but lower rates off-season.

Singapore, 9601 Collins Ave., Bal Harbour, FL 33154 (305/865-9931; toll free 800/327-4911). 238 rms, A/C, color TV. AE, CB, DC, MC, V. Free parking, pool, putting green, rest., coffee shop, two bars, rm svce, disco, free crib. *Note:* Comfortable motel w. direct access to the beach; many rms have kitchenettes and private balconies. Friendly reception and svce. Good value. 25 min. from dwntwn. **M–E,** but lower rates off-season.

Dupont Plaza, 300 Biscayne Blvd., Miami, FL 33131 (305/358-2541; toll free 800/327-3480). 290 rms, A/C, color TV. AE, CB, DC, MC, V. Valet gar. $6, two pools, marina, rest., bar, rm svce, hrdrsr, free crib. *Note:* Modern, functional hotel right on Biscayne Bay; the best rms have a fine view. Svce not always dependable. Group and convention clientele. In the heart of dwntwn Miami. Good value. **I–M,** but lower rates off-season.

PLM Marina Park Hotel, 340 Biscayne Blvd., Miami, FL 33132 (305/371-4400; toll free 800/223-9862). 194 rms, A/C, color TV, in-rm movies. AE, CB, DC, MC, V. Free parking, coffee shop, bar, rm svce. *Note:* Comfortable, completely renovated hotel at the edge of Bay Front Park and Biscayne Bay. Huge, inviting rms, some w. refrigerators, the best overlooking the harbor and the bay. Courteous svce. Clientele of groups and package tours. Good value. Next to the Bayside Marketplace. **I–M,** but lower rates off-season.

Days Inn Medical Center, 1050 NW 14th St., Miami, FL 33136 (305/324-0200; toll free, see Days Inns). 214 rms, A/C, color TV, in-rm movies. AE, CB, DC, MC, V. Free parking, pool, 24-hr. coffee shop. *Note:* Typical functional motel 5 min. by car from dwntwn and nr. the Civic Center. Spacious, inviting rms. Good value. Ideal if you're driving. **I–M,** but lower rates off-season.

Monaco Resort, 17501 Collins Ave., Sunny Isles, FL 33160 (305/932-2100). 110 rms, A/C, color TV, in-rm movies. AE, CB, DC, MC, V. Free parking, pool, health club, sauna, coffee shop (breakfast/lunch), bar, rm svce, free crib. *Note:* Aging but comfortable motel right on the ocean; pleasing, well-laid-out rms w. refrigerator (some w. kitchenette). Direct beach access. Grdn w. picnic tables and barbecues. Friendly svce; good value; 35 min. from dwntwn. **I–M,** but lower rates off-season.

Crossway Airport Inn, 1850 NW Le Jeune Rd., Miami, FL 33126 (305/871-4350). 216 rms, A/C, color TV, in-rm movies. AE, CB, DC, MC, V. Free parking, pool, rest., bar, valet svce, nightclub, crib $4. *Note:* Conventional, unpretentious motel of vaguely Spanish appearance; some rms spacious, others less so, but all comfortable in a utilitarian way. Acceptable reception and svce. Public golf course adj. Good value overall; 5 min. from the airport, 15 min. from dwntwn. **I,** but lower rates off-season.

Ocean Roc, 19505 Collins Ave, Sunny Isles, FL 33160 (305/931-7600). 95 rms, A/C, color TV, in-rm movies. AE, CB,

DC, MC, V. Free parking, pool, coffee shop, rm svce. *Note:* Elderly but very well run small hotel on the beach; nice rms w. balconies and refrigerators (some w. kitchenettes), the best overlooking the ocean. Friendly reception. In summer, one of Miami Beach's best bargains. 35 min. from dwntwn. **I,** but lower rates off-season.

     Royalton Hotel, 131 SE 1st St., Miami, FL 33132 (305/374-7451). 130 rms, A/C. AE, CB, DC, MC, V. Parking (for a fee) adj., coffee shop, bar. *Note:* Older hotel w. small but functional rms in the middle of the dwntwn Cuban district. While reception and comfort are not of the best, the prices can't be beat. **I,** but lower rates off-season.

     Bel Aire Hotel, 6515 Collins Ave., Miami Beach, FL 33141 (305/866-6511). 111 rms, color TV. AE, CB, DC, MC, V. Free parking, pool, coffee shop, bar, valet svce. *Note:* Small vacation hotel, economical but well run, ideal for restricted budgets. Quiet family atmosphere. 20 min. from dwntwn, and a few steps from a public beach. Very good value. **I,** but lower rates off-season.

Airport Accommodations

     Hilton Miami Airport and Marina, 5101 Blue Lagoon Dr., Miami, FL 33126 (305/262-1000; toll free, see Hilton). 500 rms, A/C, color TV, in-rm movies. AE, CB, DC, MC, V. Free valet parking, pool, three tennis courts, health club, sauna, marina, boating, three rests. (including the Cove), bars, 24-hr. rm svce, disco, free airport and dwntwn limos, concierge, free crib. *Note:* Immaculate 14-story tower on a peninsula in the middle of a lagoon; first-grade comfort and facilities. Elegant, spacious rms w. private balconies or patios. VIP suites on the three top floors. Efficient svce. Business and convention clientele. **E–VE,** but lower rates off-season.

YMCA/Youth Hostel

     Youth Hostel/AYH, 1438 Washington Ave., Miami Beach, FL 33139 (305/534-2988). Very central. 120 beds. Two blocks from a public beach.

RESTAURANTS

     A Note on Restaurant Prices: Miami restaurant prices, per person, excluding drinks and service charges, are coded as follows: **VE,** Very Expensive ($60 and up); **E,** Expensive ($40–$60); **M,** Moderate ($25–$40); **I,** Inexpensive ($15–$25); **B,** Budget (up to $15).

Personal Favorites (in order of preference)

     Café Chauveron, 9561 E. Bay Harbor Dr., Bay Harbor Island (866-8779). A/C. Lunch daily (Nov–Apr), dinner nightly; closed end of July to early Oct. AE, CB, DC, MC, V. Jkt. (tie advised). *Specialties:* seafood in scallop shell w. champagne sauce, bouillabaisse marseillaise, rack of lamb w. spring vegetables, Dover sole bonne femme. The desserts, particularly the soufflés, are very good; the wine list is large but the prices exorbitant. *Note:* One of the most distinguished and luxurious rests. on the eastern seaboard. After the death of the founder, Roger Chauveron, in 1983, his son André took it firmly in hand, and it remains the unchallenged temple of classic French cuisine in Miami. Flowery, elegant interior w. a view of the bay, but on the noisy side. Exemplary reception and svce. Resv., far in advance, a must. Valet parking; private dock for boats. 25 min. from dwntwn. *French.* **E–VE**

     Pavillon Grill, in the Inter-Continental Hotel (see "Accommodations," above), Miami (372-4494). A/C. Dinner only, Mon–Sat; closed Thanksgiving, Dec 25. AE, CB, DC, MC, V. J&T. *Specialties:* frogs' legs cakes w. vermouth mayonaise, marinated lamb w. fresh pasta, ragoût of lobster broiled over mesquite, filet of beef w. papaya and lime, scallops w. asparagus. Long list of California wines. *Note:* Columns of green Italian marble, mahogany panels, and English leather make up the decor of this remarkable luxury hotel rest. Delicate, refined modern cuisine—but with prices to match. Svce of the highest order. Resv. a must—this place is in fashion. Valet parking. *American/ French*. **E**

  Joe's Stone Crab, 227 Biscayne St., Miami Beach (673-0365). A/C. Lunch Tues–Sat, dinner nightly; closed May 15–Oct 15. AE, CB, DC, MC, V. Jkt. *Specialties:* oysters on the half or fried; everything that swims in the Atlantic or any other ocean, broiled or poached; extraordinary stone crabs w. mustard sauce; key lime pie. *Note:* A Miami landmark since 1913; its black-and-yellow stone crabs are famous coast to coast. Their high season runs Oct–Feb; their claws are removed and they're thrown back into the sea, where the claws grow again. The rest. is often noisy and crowded. Excellent svce; unfortunately no resv., so waits (sometimes rather long) are inevitable. Valet parking. *Seafood*. **M**

  Restaurant St. Michel, in the Hotel Place St. Michel (see "Accommodations," above), Coral Gables (446-6572). A/C. Breakfast Mon–Fri, lunch/dinner daily. AE, CB, DC, MC, V. Jkt. *Specialties:* pancake w. lobster and wild mushrooms, rack of lamb bouquetière, poached salmon w. champagne sauce and sorrel, duckling w. blackcurrants and pears. Very good desserts, but a rather lightweight wine list. *Note:* On the ground floor of the charming little Hotel Place St. Michel, this intimate rest. is a triumph of art deco elegance. Sophisticated modern cuisine of French derivation. Svce exemplary in all respects. Favorite lunchtime rest. for businesspeople. Resv. advised; a fine place. *French/Continental*. **I–M**

  Max's Place, 2286 NE 123rd St., North Dade (893-6888). A/C. Lunch Mon–Fri, dinner nightly. AE, CB, DC, MC, V. *Specialties:* clams w. mushrooms, oyster pancakes, gourmet pizza done over a wood fire, polenta w. cream of Gorgonzola cheese and basil, fresh homemade pasta, roast duck marinated w. ginger and soy sauce, roast salmon w. balsamic vinegar and honey, yellowtail w. pistachios, hot apple tart w. caramel. Skimpy wine list. *Note:* Florida version of the California-type rest. nowadays so much in vogue from New York to Los Angeles. Generally inventive cuisine; some simple dishes broiled over mesquite. Has drawn crowds (mostly "with-it" young people) ever since it opened. Resv. advised. Well worth the 25-min. drive (via Biscayne Blvd.) from dwntwn. Same owner as Maxaluna in Boca Raton (see Chapter 16 on the Florida East Coast). *American*. **I–M**

  Le Festival, 2120 Salzedo St., Coral Gables (442-8545). A/C. Lunch Mon–Fri, dinner Mon–Sat; closed hols, and Sept–Oct. AE, MC, V. Jkt. *Specialties:* salmon mousse, cheese soufflé, chicken normande, duck à l'orange, snapper Dugléré, tarte tatin. *Note:* Small French bistro of the refined and elegant sort; chef Jacques Baudeau offers a flawless cuisine. Attentive svce. Well-chosen wine list. A fine place. *French*. **I–M**

  Las Tapas, 401 Biscayne Blvd., Bayside Marketplace, Miami (372-2737). A/C. Lunch/dinner daily. AE, MC, V. *Specialties:* more than 50 different kinds of *tapas,* from serrano ham to calf tripe, fried squid, garlicky mushrooms, octopus w. olive oil and paprika, eel w. green sauce, and chorizo sausage to pork shank w. mustard—and so on, and on. *Note:* As the name suggests, *tapas,* the tasty hot or cold hors d'oeuvres of Spain are the house specialty, and draw enthusiastic crowds of devotees. Attractive decor w. big picture windows and an inviting bar. Deft, smiling svce. Very popular locally; a fine place. *Spanish*. **I**

  La Esquina de Tejas, 101 SW 12th Ave., Miami (545-5341). A/C. Breakfast/lunch/dinner daily (till midnight). No credit cards. *Specialties:* fish soup, chicken w. rice, picadillo, pig's-trotter stew, roast pork w. rice and black beans, flan, Cuban coffee. *Note:* One of the small, traditional Cuban rests. of which there are so many in Little Havana, offering absolutely authentic food at very attractive prices. This one has some claim to celebrity in that President Reagan stopped here once on a visit to Miami and tried the chicken w. rice, w. side orders of black beans and fried plantain. Guaranteed atmosphere and local color. No resv. *Latin American.* **B**

Other Restaurants (from top bracket to budget)

♆♆♆ **Vinton's,** in the La Palma Hotel, 116 Alhambra Circle, Coral Gables (445-2511). A/C. Lunch Mon–Fri, dinner Mon–Sat; closed hols. AE, CB, DC, MC, V. Jkt. *Specialties:* boudín of shrimp and scallops, ragoût of sweetbreads w. oysters, bouillabaisse, salmon w. sorrel, duck w. raspberries. Fine wine list, but no hard liquor. *Note:* One of the best prestige rests. in Miami. The food and the svce, both exemplary, run like a Swiss watch thanks to Hans Eichman. The decor is elegant and the atmosphere romantic (every lady is offered a flower, and a cushion for her feet). Resv. advised. Outdoor dining Nov–May. *French/Continental.* **M–E**

♆♆♆ **Chef Allen's,** 19088 NE 29th Ave., North Miami Beach (935-2900). A/C. Dinner only, nightly. AE, MC, V. Jkt. *Specialties:* hot baked brie w. glazed pears, spinach-and-Gorgonzola ravioli w. jumbo shrimp Fra Diavolo, homemade pasta, broiled fresh fish and beef, dessert soufflés. Menu changes daily. *Note:* The newest of Miami's fashionable rests., its innovative, imaginative cuisine from the hand of the talented Allen Susser, a rising star among younger American chefs. Elegant modern setting w. kitchen visible to diners in its enclosure of glass. Friendly, attentive svce; successful enough that you should reserve several days ahead. *American.* **M**

♆♆♆ **The Forge,** 432 Arthur Godfrey Rd., Miami Beach (538-8533). A/C. Dinner only, nightly (until 2am); closed hols. AE, CB, DC, MC, V. Jkt. *Specialties:* shrimp Merlin, steak Java, chicken w. walnuts, snapper Singapore, veal w. morel mushrooms. Wonderful desserts. Very fine wine list w. more than 3,000 labels. *Note:* Luxury rest. (w. disco) in an excessive art nouveau decor, w. molded ceilings, crystal chandeliers, much stained glass, and enough paintings and sculptures to turn many a museum green w. envy. Polished svce; fashionable diners; noisy atmosphere. Resv. advised. Valet parking. *Continental.* **M**

♆♆ **Christy's,** 3101 Ponce de Leon Blvd., Coral Gables (446-1400). A/C. Lunch Mon–Fri, dinner nightly; closed Labor Day. AE, CB, DC, MC, V. Jkt. *Specialties:* steak, roast beef, filet mignon, fish of the day, lobster, lamb chops, Caesar salad. Slightly meager wine list. *Note:* First-rate meat and fish, in an urbane British-club setting, w. leather seats, bronze candlesticks, and velvet curtains. Very elegant atmosphere; faultless svce. Business clientele. The fashionable place for meat eaters. Resv. a must. *Steak/Seafood.* **M**

♆♆ **The Depot,** 5830 S. Dixie Hwy., South Miami (665-6261). A/C. Dinner only, nightly (until 2am). AE, CB, DC, MC, V. Jkt. *Specialties:* ribs of beef, steak, Maine lobster, rack of lamb printanier, sautéed crabmeat. *Note:* The best red-meat rest. in Miami, w. excellent seafood as well. Original railroad decor w. displays of model trains. A nice place. Diligent svce. Popular locally; resv. advisable. Valet parking. 20 min. from dwntwn. *Steak/Seafood.* **I–M**

♆♆ **Gatti's,** 1427 West Ave., Miami Beach (673-1717). A/C. Dinner only, Tues–Sun; closed July–Oct. AE, CB, DC, MC, V. Jkt. *Specialties:* excellent homemade fresh pasta, angel hair primavera, veal scaloppine alla Gatti, stone crabs, pompano amandine, osso buco, fish of the day. *Note:* A Miami classic since 1925, always in the hands of the Gatti family. Setting and food have much to recommend them, but the svce is inattentive unless you're a regular. Resv. advised. Valet parking. *Italian.* **I–M**

♆♆ **Rusty Pelican,** 3201 Rickenbacker Causeway, Key Biscayne (361-3818). A/C. Lunch/dinner daily, brunch Sun. AE, CB, DC, MC, V. *Specialties:* mushrooms stuffed w. snails, pompano sauté amandine, broiled catch of the day, Polynesian dishes, chocolate-and-orange soufflé, banana pudding. Limited but honestly priced wine list. *Note:* The Rusty Pelican's main claim to fame is its location, w. unimpeded views of Biscayne Bay and the dwntwn skyscrapers, especially impressive at sunset. The food served in the attractive seafaring setting can best be described as commonplace. Efficient svce; lots of tourists. It's best to reserve ahead and ask for a window table. Valet parking. *Seafood.* **I–M**

🍷🍽 **Centro Vasco (Juanito's),** 2235 SW 8th St., Miami (643-9606). A/C. Lunch/dinner daily (until midnight). AE, CB, DC, MC, V. *Specialties:* zarzuela de mariscos, snapper in salsa verde, chicken Basque style, paella, filet Madrilène. So-so desserts. *Note:* Specializing in Basque food, this is one of Little Havana's most popular rests. The sangría is mixed, as it should be, at your table. The Spanish-tavern decor is agreeable, and the svce attentive. Resv. advised. Crowded bar serving excellent daiquiris. Valet parking. *Spanish.* **I**

🍷🍽 **Malaga,** 740 SW 8th St., Miami (858-4224). A/C. Lunch/dinner daily. AE, CB, DC, MC, V. *Specialties:* black-bean soup, carne asada mechada (pot-au-feu), picadillo, hamhocks w. rice, pompano or red snapper w. sauce Créole, arroz con pollo, paella, rice pudding. *Note:* Malaga is an exception to the Miami rule that Cuban rests. have depressing interiors; w. its charming shady patio and domestic Castilian decor, it almost qualifies as a luxury rest. Tasty food served in huge portions; svce with a smile. Very popular locally, so resv. advised. Flamenco shows at dinner. *Latin American.* **I**

🍷 **Joe's Seafood Restaurant,** 400 NW North River Dr, Miami (374-5637). A/C. Lunch/dinner daily; closed Dec 25. AE, CB, DC, MC, V. Jkt. *Specialties:* ceviche, fried oysters, fish and shellfish of the day. *Note:* Admirable seafood rest on the bank of the Miami River; remarkably fresh seafood served in a marine-crossed-w.-rustic setting. Terrace for lunch or dinner outdoors in fine weather. Inconsistent svce. Well located in the heart of Miami. Very popular locally. *Seafood.* **I**

🍷 **Canton Too,** 2614 Ponce de Leon Blvd., Coral Gables (448-3736). A/C. Lunch Mon–Sat, dinner daily. AE, MC, V. *Specialties:* honeyed chicken, Cantonese specialties. *Note:* Aficionados call this the best Chinese rest. in Miami, a city where Far Eastern food worthy of the name is not easily found. The decor deserves no merit awards, but the food is absolutely authentic and the svce hard-working. Popular w. residents; resv. advisable at dinner. *Chinese.* **B–I**

🍷 **La Tasca,** 2741 W. Flagler St., Miami (642-3762). A/C. Lunch/dinner daily. AE, CB, DC, MC, V. *Specialties:* white-bean soup, roast chicken Cuban style, shrimp enchilada, red snapper w. salsa verde, paella, diplomat pudding. *Note:* Likable little outpost of Cuba a short distance from Little Havana; old-style decor and svce. Clientele of regulars; a favorite with those in-the-know. *Latin American/Spanish.* **B–I**

☀🍷 **Versailles,** 3555 SW 8th St., Miami (444-0240). A/C. Lunch/dinner daily (until 2am). AE, CB, DC, MC, V. *Specialties:* Cuban sandwiches, homemade soups, rice w. black beans, chicken w. rice, picadillo, Palomilla steak, cheesecake. *Note:* One of the most authentic Cuban rests. on the famous Calle Ocho, the main drag of Little Havana. Straightforward, savory food. In spite of the mirrored ceilings, the name Versailles is not reflected in the decor. Usually crowded and noisy, but a pleasant place. No resv. *Latin American.* **B–I**

☀🍷 **Wolfie's Rascal House,** 17190 Collins Ave., Sunny Isles (947-4581). A/C. Breakfast/lunch/dinner daily (until 2am). No credit cards. *Kosher specialties:* soup, corned beef, pastrami, brisket; excellent (and enormously popular) deli items, homemade pastries. *Note:* Ideal for breakfast or a late supper. At lunch customers come in droves. 35 min. from dwntwn. Other location: Wolfie's, 2038 Collins Ave. at 21st St., Miami Beach (538-6626); open 24 hr. *American.* **B**

Cafeteria/Fast Food

☼ **Latin American Cafeteria,** 2940 Coral Way, Coral Gables (226-2393). Typical cafeteria, open around the clock and serving enormous sandwiches and tasty, unpretentious Cuban food (fried pork w. rice and beans, pan-fried steak, etc.). 1950s-style decor. Open daily. No credit cards. Four other locations in Miami (see the local telephone book).

BARS & NIGHTCLUBS

The **Jazz Hotline** (382-3938) will give you details of current programming by local jazz clubs.

The great **hotels** of Miami and Miami Beach (Fontainebleau, Omni, Doral Ocean Beach, Hyatt, Sheraton–Bal Harbour, Doubletree Hotel, etc.) all have bars and discothèques. Other good places include:

Biscayne Baby, 3336 Virginia St., Coconut Grove (445-3751). Favorite of the trendy young; for lovers of rock 'n' roll.

Casanova's, 740 E. 9th St., Hialeah (883-8706). A shrine of salsa and disco. Trendy atmosphere and patrons.

Club Nu, 245 22nd St. at Collins Ave., Miami Beach (672-0068). Fashionable New York–style rock club; youthful, trendy clientele.

Cye's Rivergate, 444 Brickell Ave., Miami (358-9100). Fashionable singles bar and rest. under a handsome skylight; open nightly. Also a disco; open Wed–Sat.

Les Violins, 1751 Biscayne Blvd., Miami (371-8668). Fashionable nightclub which puts on some far-out Latin American floor shows. Also a so-so rest.

Monty Trainer's, 2560 S. Bayshore Dr., Coconut Grove (858-1431). Amusing open-air bar-rest. serving very acceptable seafood. Live jazz and reggae; dancing. Youthful, congenial atmosphere. Open nightly.

Tobacco Road, 626 S. Miami Ave., Miami (374-1198). Miami's oldest bar, where the blues play until 5 in the morning and where it never, never seems late.

Village Inn, 3131 Commodore Pl., Coconut Grove (445-8721). Fashionable jazz club, with a rest., in the artists' neighborhood of Coconut Grove.

Woody's on the Beach, 455 Ocean Dr. at 4th St., Miami Beach (538-5401). A popular local rock club, owned by musician Ron Wood of the Rolling Stones. Open nightly.

NEARBY EXCURSIONS

🔔 **MICCOSUKEE INDIAN VILLAGE** (27 mi./43km west on U.S. 41) (223-8380): Authentic Native American village of the Miccosukee tribe. Handcraft exhibitions, alligator wrestling, airboat trips into the swamps, restaurant with authentic Indian food. Open daily. Every year an 🔔 **exhibition of Native American art and dance** is held here (late Dec to early Jan), with representatives from more than 40 tribes. Worth going out of your way for, especially if you can combine it with the **Shark Valley Tram Tours** (see "Everglades National Park," below).

NATIONAL PARKS NEARBY

🔔 **BISCAYNE NATIONAL PARK** (30 mi./48km SW on U.S. 1, on the Florida Tpke. at N. Canal Dr., in Homestead): The latest of Florida's national parks, Biscayne, standing on the shore, comprises mostly a considerable stretch of water with a string of inhabited islands and some coral reefs teeming with fish (180,000 acres/73,000ha). A paradise for scubadiving, underwater fishing (snapper, mackerel, dorado), and birdwatching (blue herons, egrets, pelicans). Campsites, accessible only by boat. For information, contact P.O. Box 1369, Homestead, FL 33030 (305/247-7275). For lovers of nature in the raw.

EVERGLADES NATIONAL PARK (45 mi./72km SW on U.S. 1 and Fla. 27): Opened in 1947, this is the country's only tropical national park. Alligators, barracudas, sea turtles, pumas, lynxes, pelicans, egrets, pink flamingos, migratory birds, and at least a thousand varieties of fish abound in this enormous (2,100-sq.-mi./5,440km²) stretch of marshes, cypress stands, and mangrove swamps which the Seminoles knew by the beautiful name of Pay-Hay-Okee ("River of Grass"). A 50-mi. (80km) asphalt road, the **Flamingo Road,** makes its way through the park; there are many observation platforms and elevated walkways from which you can admire the landscape. From May to Nov visits are rendered unpleasant by clouds of mosquitos and other bloodthirsty insects, to say nothing of persistent rain during the summer; nevertheless, the rich wildlife and exotic vegetation are certainly worth seeing. **Visitor Center** at Flamingo.

It was in the Everglades that the local Native Americans made their last stand in the terrible Seminole Wars of 1835–42. After 2,000 warriors had successfully held off 20,000 soldiers for 3 years, they were wiped out or deported to Oklahoma. Although defeated, the Seminoles never signed a peace treaty with the U.S. government, and are thus—theoretically—still in a state of war. For further information, contact the Superintendent, Everglades National Park, P.O. Box 279, Homestead, FL 33030 (305/247-6211).

Guided Tours

Backcountry Cruises (boat) and **Wilderness Tram Tours** (bus) (305/243-2241) leave from Flamingo Area at the south of the park. Resv. advised.

Everglades Boat Tours (boat) (813/695-2591) leave from Park Docks in Everglades City, at the NW corner of the park.

Shark Valley Tram Tours (bus) (305/221-8455) leave from the Shark Valley parking facility on U.S. 41 north of the park. You'll encounter abundant wildlife, especially in winter. Resv. a must.

Where to Stay in the National Park

Flamingo Lodge, at the end of Fla. 27, Everglades National Park, FL 33030 (305/253-2241). 102 rms and 16 bungalows; also houseboats for rent. AE, CB, DC, MC, V. Relatively modern and comfortable. **M**

Everglades Rod & Gun Club, P.O. Box G, Everglades City, FL 33929 (813/695-2101). 20 rms. No credit cards. Comfortable in a rustic way. **I**

JOHN PENNEKAMP CORAL REEF PARK (60 mi./96km SW on U.S. 1, in Key Largo): The country's first underwater national park, dating from 1960, is 21.5 mi. (34km) long by 6.5 mi. (10km) wide; the water is nowhere deeper than 45 ft. (15m). There is a superb display of sea flora and fauna, with more than 650 varieties of tropical fish as well as many shipwrecks. Wonderful for scuba-divers; also trips in glass-bottom boats. Spectacular. Open daily year round; for information, phone 305/451-1202.

Where to Stay in the Park

Jules' Undersea Lodge, P.O. Box 3330, Key Largo, FL 33037 (305/451-2353). The only hotel of its kind in the world, with two fully equipped suites (bunks, kitchenette, closed-circuit TV) in a steel capsule anchored 30 ft. (10m) below the surface. Patrons can reach it only by diving and passing through an airlock. Unobstructed view of the underwater life through huge portholes. Rates: $300 per person per day, including meals and unlimited diving. Resv. required, a long time ahead.

FARTHER AFIELD

FLORIDA EAST COAST (640 mi./1,024km r.t. to St. Augustine on U.S. 1N, returning on I-95S): The great vacation artery of the Southeast. At least a week's trip with optional extensions to Orlando

and Walt Disney World. For details, see Chapter 16 on Florida's East Coast and Chapter 18 on Orlando.

☀ 🔭 KEY WEST & THE KEYS HIGHWAY (330 mi./528km

on U.S. 1, r.t.): Nicknamed Cayo Hueso (Bone Island) by the Spaniards and later anglicized as Key West, this old pirates' lair is the southern-most city in the continental U.S. Literary and bohemian, the picturesque town of Key West, now a little more than a century and a half old, is an important naval base, a fashionable vacation resort—it was for a while President Truman's sum-mer residence—and the favored retreat of such writers as playwright Tennessee Williams, poet Robert Frost, and novelists John Dos Passos and James Herlihy (*Midnight Cowboy*). Ernest Hemingway lived here and wrote some of his most successful works, including *The Snows of Kilimanjaro* and *For Whom the Bell Tolls*. His house, at 907 Whitehead St. (294-1575), is open daily to visitors, and shouldn't be missed. Another well-known resident was naturalist John James Audubon, whose former house at 205 Whitehead St. is today a small 🏛 **museum** (294-2116) devoted to the works of the distinguished artist-ornithologist; open daily. The **Key West Lighthouse Museum,** 938 Whitehead St. (294-0012), open daily, displays some interesting military memorabilia, including a minia-ture Japanese submarine captured at Pearl Harbor. Splendid view from the top. The famous 🏛 **Key West Aquarium,** Wall St. and Whitehead St. (296-2051), open daily, has a comprehensive collection of the rich marine life of the Gulf of Mexico and the Atlantic Ocean, from the brightly tinted creatures of the tropical reefs to sharks. A must-see. Pleasant strolls along the 🏛 **streets of old Key West,** particularly Duval St.

The ☀ **Overseas Highway,** by which Key West is reached, is built for the most part on a causeway over the water; the route involves a total of 40 bridges. There are spectacular seascapes, particularly from 🔭 **Seven Mile Bridge** between Marathon and Key West.

A very worthwhile excursion is to the impressive **Fort Jefferson National Monument** on the Dry Tortugas, 70 mi. (112km) offshore from Key West. The fort, nicknamed "the Gibraltar of the Gulf," was used as a prison at the end of the Civil War; Dr. Samuel Mudd, who gave medical assistance to John Wilkes Booth, the assassin of Abraham Lincoln, was among those detained there. It can be reached by seaplane from Stock Island in 40 min. on Key West Seaplanes Service (294-6978); or from the Key West airport on Air-Sea Key West (296-5511).

Key West is also one of the country's greatest centers for **big-game fishing.** Lovers of the sport will find dozens of places to rent boats. Prices are markedly lower than in Miami; a half-day charter averages $150–$200, and a full day runs $250–$300. Some recommended captains include Admiral Busby & Sons (294-0011), Dick Stammers (296-7550), and Yankee Fleet (294-7009).

Allow at least 3–4 days for this fascinating trip; it can conveniently be com-bined with a visit to Everglades National Park (see above).

Where to Stay in Key West

🛏🛏🛏 **Marriott's Casa Marina,** 1500 Reynolds St., Key West, FL 33040 (305/296-3535). 310 rms. AE, CB, DC, MC, V. *Note:* Facing the ocean; luxurious hotel of the 1920s. **VE**

☀🛏🛏 **Pier House,** 1 Duval St., Key West, FL 33040 (305/294-9541). 120 rms. AE, MC, V. *Note:* In the center of town; com-fortable in a baroque way. **E–VE,** but lower rates off-season.

🛏 **Santa Maria,** 1401 Simonton St., Key West, FL 33040 (305/296-5678). 51 rms. AE, CB, DC, MC, V. *Note:* Rather mod-ern, comfortable hotel with a commendable rest. **M–E,** but lower rates off-season.

🛏 **South Beach Motel,** 508 South St., Key West, FL 33040 (305/296-5611). 47 rms. AE, MC, V. Congenial hotel on the water; functional rms w. view. **M–E,** but lower rates off-season.

THE FLORIDA KEYS

GULF OF MEXICO

Florida

Florida Bay

ATLANTIC OCEAN

John Pennekamp Coral Reef State Park

Key Largo

Key Largo

Tavernier Key

Plantation Key

Windley Key

Theatre of the Sea

Upper Matecumbe Key

Islamorada

Fiesta Key

Craig

Layton

Long Key

Conch Key

Duck Key

Honda Key

Grassy Key

Flipper's Sea School

Vaca Key

Key Colony Beach

Crawl Key

Marathon

Boot Key

Pigeon Key

Sunshine Key

Bahia Honda Key

Spanish Harbor

No Name Key

Big Pine

White Heron Nat'l Wildlife Refuge

Ramrod Key

Big Pine Key

Little Torch Key

Cudjoe Key

Summerland Key

Sugarloaf Key

Lower Sugarloaf Key

Saddle Bunch Keys

Big Coppitt Key

Content Keys

Snipe Keys

Boca Chica Keys

Stock Island

Key West

(At Key West)
Aquarium
Audubon House
Marine Memorial
Martello Towers
Conch Train

Marquesas Keys

OVERSEAS HIGHWAY

WATERWAY

INTRACOASTAL

N

Where to Eat in Key West

A & B Lobster House, 700 Front St. (294-2536). Dinner only, Mon–Sat. AE, CB, DC, MC, V. Broiled fish and shellfish; harbor view. **I–M**

Very near here, stop off for a drink at **Sloppy Joe's,** Greene St. and Duval St. (294-5717), Hemingway's favorite bar.

🍷🍷 **Louie's Backyard,** 700 Waddell Ave. (294-1061). Lunch/ dinner daily. AE, CB, DC, MC, V. The fashionable place for eating at the water's edge; nouvelle cuisine seafood, served outside in fine weather. **I–M**

Kyushu, 921 Truman Ave. (294-2995). Lunch/dinner daily. AE, MC, V. Very commendable Japanese food; pretty setting, locally popular. **B–I**

🔆🍷 **Half Shell Fish Market,** 231 Margaret St., Land's End Village (294-5028). Good seafood rest. w. very attractive prices; noisy and colorful. No credit cards. **B–I**

OTHER FROMER TRAVEL GUIDES: Readers may be interested in Frommer guides that treat the Southeast area in greater detail: *Frommer's Southern Atlantic States* and *Frommer's Washington, D.C. and Historic Virginia on $40 a Day.* City guides for this area are: *Frommer's Atlanta, Frommer's Miami, Frommer's New Orleans, Frommer's Orlando,* and *Frommer's Washington, D.C.*

Frommer travel guides are available in most bookstores, or can be ordered by mail from Frommer Books, Prentice Hall Press, 15 Columbis Circle, New York, N.Y. 10023. Turn to the last pages of this book to learn about the **Dollarwise Travel Club,** and for ordering information.

PART THREE

THE MIDWEST

CHAPTER 20

DETROIT ⚜

□ □ □

"The automobile capital of the world," Detroit is America's most important industrial city after Chicago, accounting for 70% of domestic automobile production and more than half the country's output of weaponry (during World War II the city was known as "the arsenal of the democracies"). It would be more poetic to speak of it as the capital of soul music, the place where Diana Ross and Stevie Wonder began their careers.

The city's site, on a strait (in French, a *détroit,* hence the name) linking Lake Huron and Lake Erie, was first explored by the French in 1610. The city itself was founded 91 years later by an enterprising fur trader, Antoine de la Mothe Cadillac (whose name became world-famous a couple of centuries later when it was attached to a luxury automobile). This garrison town, originally called Fort Pontchartrain, was captured by the British in 1760 and renamed Detroit. The British successfully fended off attacks by a consolidated group of Native Americans led by the Ottawa chief Pontiac (another name destined for a famous automobile), but lost the city with the rest of the Northwest Territory to the Americans in the Revolutionary War. The British stirred up the local tribes to attack the Americans in hopes of regaining the city, but Gen. ("Mad") Anthony Wayne defeated them decisively at the Battle of Fallen Timbers (1794). The opening of steam navigation on the Great Lakes in 1818 touched off Detroit's rocket-trip to prosperity, and when Henry Ford's first mass-produced automobile rolled off the production line in 1901 the rest became inevitable. The city's population rose from 20,000 in 1850 to 280,000 in 1900, 950,000 in 1920, and (suburbs included) over 4.5 million today.

Home to the three giants of the auto industry—General Motors, Ford, and Chrysler—Detroit is also the nation's largest used-car market, as witness the hundreds of billboards cheek by jowl along **Livernois Avenue,** an important petrochemical and space-industry complex. In addition it's the fifth-ranking freshwater port in the U.S., which can accommodate seagoing vessels of up to 25,000 tons coming through the St. Lawrence Seaway. In spite of all these advantages, "the city that put the world on wheels" bore the brunt of the world economic slump, with 150,000 layoffs between 1970 and 1988. The unemployment rate is one of the highest in the country, with peaks of 30% (and up to 60% among young African American workers). The crime rate has followed a similar curve; according to the FBI, Detroit is one of the nation's more violent cities (60 murders per 100,000 people), well ahead of Miami, New York, or Chicago.

After the race riots of July 1967, which left 43 dead and 2,000 wounded, the face of "Motown," as Detroit is often called, changed radically; an exodus caused the population of the city proper to fall by more than 800,000. Stores, hotels, restaurants, offices, and movie houses have forsaken "downtown" for outlying residential suburbs, leaving behind them a kind of no-man's-land, dark tumbledown ghettos, and urban throughways subject to asphyxiating pollution during rush hours. But since 1975 a successful program of urban renewal, pivoting on the **Civic Center,** has spread to the banks of the Detroit River facing the Canadian border. The heart of the program is the **Renaissance Center,** or RenCen, an impressive $750-million architectural complex comprising six glass-clad futurist structures—four of them 39 floors high and two of them 21 stories—and the enormous 73-floor Westin Hotel tower, designed by celebrated architect John Portman and opened in 1977. Another architectural landmark is the new **Millender Center,** a huge modern cluster of offices, a hotel, stores, and restaurants linked to the RenCen by the **Skywalk,** a glassed-in overpass.

Famous children of Detroit include the father of the modern automobile industry, Henry Ford, born in the nearby town (now suburb) of Dearborn; director Francis Ford Coppola; actor George Peppard; comedian and star of "Magnum P.I.," Tom Selleck; legendary heavyweight champion Joe Louis; singing star Diana Ross; actresses Gilda Radner and Lily Tomlin; rock musician Alice Cooper; and aviator Charles Lindbergh.

BASIC FACTS: State of Michigan. Area code: 313. Time zone: eastern. ZIP Code: 48226. Founded in: 1701. Approximate population: city, 1,030,000; metropolitan area, 4,640,000. Sixth-largest metropolitan area in the U.S.

CLIMATE: Because of its unique geographical location, Detroit labors under a humid climate and extremes of temperature—chilling in winter (average Jan temperature: 26°F/−3°C), warm and sticky in summer (average July temperature: 73°F/23°C). Spring is rainy and uncomfortably cool. Only the fall, particularly Oct, offers attractive weather for the tourist.

DISTANCES: Chicago, 268 mi. (430km); Cincinnati, 259 mi. (415km); New York, 634 mi. (1,015km); Niagara Falls, 392 mi. (628km); Washington, 506 mi. (810km).

ARRIVAL & TRANSIT INFORMATION

AIRPORTS: Detroit City Airport (DET), 5 mi. (8km) NE. Call 267-6400 for information.
     Detroit Metropolitan Airport (DTW), 21 mi. (34km) SW. Call 924-3550 for information.

U.S. AIRLINES: American (965-1000), Continental (963-4600), Delta (355-3200), Eastern (965-8200), Midway (toll free 800/621-5700), Northwest (962-2002), Pan Am (toll free 800/221-1111), TWA (962-8650), United (336-9000), and USAir (963-8340).

FOREIGN CARRIERS: Air Canada (833-3200), British Airways (toll free 800/247-9297), and Sabena (toll free 800/645-3790).

CITY LINK: Cab fare from Detroit Metropolitan Airport to city center is about $28, and time, about 30–40 min.; from Detroit City Airport, about $14, and time, about 15 min. Bus: **Commuter Transportation** (941-3252), serving principal dwntwn hotels and the Renaissance Center, departs Detroit Metropolitan Airport every 30 min. for the 45-min. trip for a fare of $11; departs Detroit City Airport every 45 min. for the 15-min. trip for $6.
     Inadequate public bus transportation system (Department of Transportation; 933-1300), but spectacular automated "People Mover" operating through the entire dwntwn district. Since the metropolitan area is large and the Metropolitan Airport a long way out, it's a good idea to rent a car with unlimited mileage, unless you plan to stay in the heart of dwntwn.

CAR RENTAL (at the airports unless otherwise indicated): Avis (942-3450); Budget (326-6880); Dollar (942-1900); Hertz (729-5200); National (941-

7000); Thrifty, 29111 Wick Rd., Romulus (946-7830). For dwntwn locations, consult the local phone directory.

LIMOUSINE SERVICES: Carey Limousine (885-2600), Michigan Limo Service (546-6112).

TAXIS: An abundance of cabs at reasonable rates. You can hail them on the street, take them from the waiting lines outside the big hotels, or summon them by phone. The leading companies are **Checker** (963-7000), **Radio Cab** (491-2600), and **Unity Cab** (834-3300).

TRAIN: Amtrak Station, 2601 Rose St. at Vernor Hwy. (963-7396). Area unsafe at night.

INTERCITY BUSES: Greyhound, 130 E. Congress St. at Randolph St. (961-8562).

INFORMATION & TOURS

TOURIST INFORMATION: The **Detroit Convention & Visitors Bureau,** 100 Renaissance Center (Suite 1950), MI 48243 (313/259-4333).
    Department of Public Information, 608 City-County Bldg., 2 Woodward Ave., MI 48226 (313/224-3755).
    Detroit Visitor Information Center, 2 E. Jefferson Ave., MI 48226 (313/567-1170).

GUIDED TOURS: Boblo Steamers (boat excursions, May–Sept), at the foot of Clark Ave. (313/843-8800).
    Gray Line Tours (bus), Cobo Hall (Civic Center) and principal hotels (313/833-7692). Guided tours of the city.

SIGHTS, ATTRACTIONS & ACTIVITIES

ARCHITECTURAL HIGHLIGHTS: ☼⚓ **Civic Center,** Woodward Ave. and Jefferson Ave. (224-1010): Ultramodern architectural complex on the banks of the Detroit River in the heart of dwntwn. Its constituent parts include the 20-story white marble tower of the **City-County Building,** protected by *The Spirit of Detroit,* Marshall Fredericks's massive bronze statue; **Cobo Hall,** one of the country's largest convention and exhibition halls, with 11,000 seats and roof parking for 1,700 vehicles; **Hart Plaza,** a wide esplanade near the spot where Cadillac and his French companions first came ashore in 1701, in the center of which is **Dodge Fountain,** a strange metallic construction with computer-controlled water jets and lights, designed by Isamo Noguchi; **Orchestra Hall,** home of the Detroit Symphony Orchestra; **Joe Louis Arena,** an indoor stadium with 15,000 seats; **Mariner's Church,** the city's oldest (1848), with a modern belfry and carillon, which was moved 780 ft. (244m) to its present site when the Civic Center was built; **Michigan Consolidated Gas Co. Building,** a 40-story glass skyscraper designed by Minoru Yamasaki. Don't miss this impressive sight.

    ☼⚓ **Detroit People Mover,** 150 Michigan Ave. (224-2160): Elevated, automated rail system which encircles Detroit's central business district. The 3-mi.-long (5km) concrete ribbon, with 13 artfully decorated stations, links the Renaissance Center, Cobo Hall, Greektown, and the major attractions downtown for just 50¢. Worth a ride for the view.

    ⚓ **Millender Center,** Randolph St. and Jefferson Ave. (222-1500): Latest of the new downtown architectural complexes, with office buildings, luxury hotel, stores, and restaurants, all linked by a glass Skywalk to the impressive Renaissance Center across Jefferson Ave. Worth a look.

Renaissance Center, Jefferson Ave. at Randolph St. (568-5600): A spectacular grove of seven skyscrapers, ranging from 20 to 73 floors in height, at the edge of the Detroit River. The exceptional modern design bears the stamp of John Portman. Giant hotel, stores, restaurants, indoor gardens; symbol of the new Detroit. A sight not to be missed. (Call 591-3611 for tours.)

Wayne State University, 5050 Cass Ave. (577-2424): Founded in 1868, the university is highly regarded for its medical school—one of the finest in the country—and its architecturally distinguished campus, whose 100 buildings house 30,000 students. Among the most noteworthy: **McGregor Memorial Center,** the **College of Education Building,** and the **De Roy Auditorium,** all by Minoru Yamasaki, architect of New York's World Trade Center. Campus open to visitors Mon–Sat.

HISTORIC BUILDINGS: **Fisher Building,** 3011 W. Grand Blvd. (874-4444): A 28-story masterpiece of 1930s art deco by Albert Kahn, with restaurants, boutiques, theaters, and art galleries. Sumptuous interior. Well worth going out of your way for.

Fox Theater, 2211 Woodward Ave. (567-6000): One of the country's largest (5,000 seats) and gaudiest remaining movie palaces (built 1928). Restored in 1988 to its pre-Depression glory as part of a $35-million renovation of downtown Detroit. Looks like the Buddhist temples that inspired it, with its 10-ft. (3m) Chinese dragons and 2-ton (1,800kg) chandelier. A must-see.

Orchestra Hall, 3700 Parsons at Woodward Ave. (883-3700): A 2,000-seat concert hall dating from 1920, "an acoustic miracle" according to the great cellist Pablo Casals. Recently renovated, it is again the home of the Detroit Symphony Orchestra.

MARKETS: **Eastern Market,** Russell St. at Fisher Fwy. (833-1560): Picturesque European-style open-air market dating from 1892. Worth a look. Open mornings only, Mon–Sat.

MUSEUMS OF ART: **Detroit Institute of Arts (DIA),** 5200 Woodward Ave. (833-7900): One of the country's finest, with great masters of European painting, Far Eastern art, superb murals by the Mexican Diego Rivera (*Detroit Industry*), and a fine collection of medieval armor. Among the most famous exhibits: Caravaggio's *Conversion of Mary Magdalene,* Titian's *Man with a Flute,* van Eyck's *St. Jerome,* Pieter Breughel the Elder's *A Village Wedding,* Frans Hals's *Portrait of Hendrick Swalmius,* Cézanne's *Mme Cézanne,* and a self-portrait by Gauguin. There are also works by contemporary American painters including Stuart Davis, Mark Rothko, Andy Warhol, and Charles Demuth. Not to be missed. Open Tues–Sun.

MUSEUMS OF SCIENCE & HISTORY: **Children's Museum,** 67 E. Kirby Ave. (494-1210): A fascinating place for children and adults alike, with collections relating to the history of Native Americans and exhibits on different cultures (African, Inuit, etc.). Fauna and flora of Michigan; planetarium next door. Amazing sculpture in the shape of a horse, made entirely of automobile bumpers (and what could be more appropriate to Detroit?). Open Mon–Sat.

Detroit Science Center, 5020 John R St. (577-8400): This museum houses a wide-ranging cross section of pushbutton exhibits on diverse scientific subjects; the visitor is invited to participate in hands-on fashion. Spherical cinema with 360° projection of science films. Interesting to visit. Open Tues–Sun.

☼🔔 **Historical Museum,** 5401 Woodward Ave. (833-1805): Reconstructs the appearance and atmosphere of mid-19th-century Detroit: cobbled streets, stores, restored domestic interiors, models, and temporary exhibitions. For those who love glimpses of the past. Open Wed–Sun.

☼🔔 **Motown Records Museum,** 2468 W. Grand Blvd. (875-2264): Not far from the Wayne State campus, this unpretentious little museum is devoted to the performers who made their name on the Motown record label. See the rough-and-ready sound studio where the Jackson Five, Smokey Robinson, and other Diana Ross discoveries made their first recordings. Open to the public Fri only; also Mon–Thurs by appointment. A must for soul-music fans.

🔔 **Public Library,** 5201 Woodward Ave. (833-1000): There are 2.5 million books housed in this 1921 Italian Renaissance building made of Vermont marble and decorated with enormous frescoes. They include very rare old volumes as well as many works on the history of the auto industry and of the trade union movement. Open Mon–Sat.

OUTDOOR ART & PLAZAS: Other than the above-mentioned *Spirit of Detroit* by Marshall Fredericks and Dodge Fountain (see "Architectural Highlights," above), the visitor to the Civic Center may take pleasure in Giacomo Manzù's beautiful *Passo di Danza;* the *Joe Louis Monument,* a gigantic black arm with clenched fist hanging from cables by sculptor Robert Graham; and Isamo Noguchi's spiraled *Pylon.* On Cass St. in front of the Michigan Bell Telephone Bldg., you should take a look at a stabile by Alexander Calder known as *Young Lady and Her Suite.*

PANORAMAS: ☼🔔 **The Summit** is a bar and restaurant on the 73rd floor of the Westin Hotel in Renaissance Center (568-8600). You have to pay for the view —but it's the most spectacular in Detroit.

PARKS & GARDENS: 🔔 **Belle Isle,** MacArthur Bridge (267-7115): On a 3-mi.-long (5km) island in the Detroit River stands this 1,000-acre (400ha) park: swimming, public golf course, jogging, aquarium, naval museum, mini-zoo. Free concerts in summer. Fine view of the city's skyline. Worth a look.

🔔 **Grosse Pointe Shore,** Lake Shore Dr.: An elegant residential neighborhood, with woods and lovely gardens, along Lake St. Clair; it boasts many affluent private houses. You should take a stroll there.

PERFORMING ARTS: For current listings of shows and cultural events, consult the entertainment pages of the two daily papers, *Detroit Free Press* (morning) and *Detroit News* (morning and evening); also the monthly magazines *Detroit Monthly* and *Metropolitan Detroit.*

Art Institute Auditorium, 5200 Woodward Ave. (833-7900): Concerts.

Attic Theater, 3031 W. Grand Blvd. (875-8284): Drama and comedy.

Fisher Theater, Second Ave. at Grand Blvd. (872-1000): Broadway hits. Year round.

Fox Theater, 2211 Woodward Ave. (567-6000): Top-notch variety, drama, comedy, and musical events.

Hilberry Theater, 4743 Cass Ave. (577-2972): Classical theater.

Music Hall Center for the Performing Arts, 350 Madison Ave. (963-7680): Dance, concerts.

Orchestra Hall, 3700 Parsons at Woodward Ave. (833-3700): Home of the Detroit Symphony (music director: Neeme Jarvi). Classical and jazz concerts.

Theater Company–University of Detroit, 4001 W. McNichols Rd. (927-1130): Drama and comedy; Sept–May.

SPECIAL EVENTS: For exact dates, consult the **Detroit Convention & Visitors Bureau** (see "Tourist Information," above).
Auto Show (Jan): Very popular auto exposition.
International Grand Prix (end of June): A spectacular Formula 1 Grand Prix race, run in downtown Detroit.
International Freedom Festival (late June to early July): Celebrates U.S.-Canadian friendship with parades, shows, food festivals, concerts, and fireworks on either side of the international border.
Meadow Brook Music Festival (late June to Aug): In Rochester, Minn. Open-air concerts of classical music, pop, and jazz.
Montreux-Detroit Jazz Festival (late Aug to early Sept): The biggest stars in the jazz firmament; draws big crowds from the area.

SPORTS: Detroit boasts four professional teams:
Baseball (Apr–Oct): Tigers, Tiger Stadium (962-4000).
Basketball (Oct–May): Pistons, Palace, in Auburn Hills (313/377-0100).
Football (Sept–Jan): Lions, Pontiac Silverdome (the world's largest inflatable dome), in Pontiac (313/335-4151).
Ice Hockey (Oct–May): Red Wings, Joe Louis Arena (567-7333).

Horse Racing
Hazel Park Race Track (harness racing), 1650 E. 10 Mile Rd., in Hazel Park (313/398-1000), has racing Apr to mid-Oct.
Ladbroke-DRC, 28001 Schoolcraft Rd., in Livonia (313/525-7300). Racing Apr–Nov.
Northville Downs (harness racing), 301 S. Center St., in Northville (313/349-1000). Racing Jan–Apr. and Oct–Dec.

STROLLS: ⚑ **Greektown,** Monroe St. at Beaubien St.: The heart of Detroit's important Greek community; picturesque atmosphere with lively covered market (Trappers Alley), boutiques, and restaurants.

THEME PARK: ⚑ **Boblo Island:** On an island in Canadian territory, which can be reached only by two venerable cruise vessels dating from the early 1900s (the *Columbia* and the *Sainte Claire*), stands this big theme park with its giant roller coaster and 314-ft. (96m) observation tower, with more than 75 attractions; pretty walk along the riverbank. The dock for Boblo Steamers is at the foot of Clark Ave. (843-8800). Open daily late May to Sept 1.

TROLLEY: ⚑ **Washington Blvd. Trolley Car:** A picturesque old streetcar line whose ramshackle trams were once the pride of Lisbon, Portugal. It runs from the RenCen to Grand Circus Park, and boasts the world's last remaining open double-decker (933-1300).

WINTER SPORTS RESORTS: ⚑ **Alpine Valley,** 6775 E. Highland Rd., in White Lake Township (44 mi./70km NW on I-75 and Mich. 59W) (313/887-2180): 10 lifts. Operates Nov–Mar.

ZOOS: ⚑ **Royal Oak Zoo,** Woodward Ave. and 10 Mile Rd. (10 mi./16km north) (398-0900): One of the best known in the U.S., with 400 species living in careful reconstructions of their natural habitat. The reptiles, penguins, and marine mammals are of particular interest. Miniature-railroad tour. Should be seen. Open daily.

ACCOMMODATIONS
See the listing of toll-free numbers in the Appendix.
A Note on Accommodations: Room rates in Detroit are coded as follows:

VE, Very Expensive ($140 and up); **E,** Expensive ($90–$140); **M,** Moderate ($60–$90); **I,** Inexpensive ($30–$60); **B,** Budget (up to $30). A listing of toll free numbers is in the Appendix.

Personal Favorites (in order of preference)

♘♘♘♘ **River Place Inn** (nr. dwntwn), 1000 Stroh River Pl., MI 48207 (313/259-2500; toll free, see Preferred). 109 rms, A/C, color TV, in-rm movies. AE, CB, DC, MC, V. Free valet parking, pool, tennis court, squash, health club, sauna, bicycling, croquet, rest. (River Room), bar, 24-hr. rm svce, concierge. *Note:* Standing on the Detroit River, this brand-new ultra-luxurious hotel commands a sweeping view of the downtown high-rises and the Canadian shore. The handsome turn-of-the-century brick building w. its pinnacle roof has been marvelously restored. Unrivalled comfort and amenities; spacious rms w. period furniture, minibar, multiple telephones, and private safe. Attentive, personalized svce; acceptable rest.; comprehensive physical-fitness facilities; well-equipped business center. Interesting wknd discounts. By far the best hotel in Detroit; 5 min. from dwntwn. **VE**

♘♘♘ **Radisson Pontchartrain Hotel** (dwntwn), 2 Washington Blvd., MI 48226 (313/965-0200; toll free, see Radison). 420 rms, A/C, color TV, in-rm movies. AE, CB, DC, MC, V. Valet parking $6, pool, health club, sauna, two rests. (including Elaine's), two bars, 24-hr. rm svce, nightclub, jazz (Fri in summer), concierge, free breakfast, free crib. *Note:* A modern and comfortable 23-story hotel built on the site of old Fort Pontchartrain. Elegant, well-designed rms, the best looking out over the Detroit River. Very good svce, acceptable rest. The business traveler's favorite. Central location opposite Cobo Hall. No-smoking rms. Interesting wknd packages. Recently underwent a $15-million facelift. **E–VE**

※♘♘♘ **Dearborn Inn Marriott** (vic.), 20301 Oakwood Blvd., in Dearborn, MI 48124 (313/271-2700; toll free, see Marriott). 179 rms and cottages, A/C, color TV. AE, CB, DC, MC, V. Free parking, pool, two tennis courts, health club, two rests. (including the Early American Room), bar, rm svce, nightclub, free crib. *Note:* Built in 1931 by Henry Ford I, this big Georgian manor house sits in an enormous grdn halfway between the airport and dwntwn, and very nr. the Ford Museum. Friendly colonial-style rms, as well as very comfortable individual cottages. Attentive reception and svce. Recently renovated and full of charm; ideal if you're driving. **M–E**

♘♘ **Radisson St. Regis** (nr. dwntwn), 3071 W. Grand Blvd., MI 48202 (313/873-3000; toll free, see Radisson). 224 rms, A/C, color TV, in-rm movies. AE, CB, DC, MC, V. Free valet parking, rest. (Restaurant St. Regis), bar, rm svce, entertainment. *Note:* Charming older hotel, opposite the General Motors headquarters building, w. huge, inviting rms, polished svce, and an acceptable rest. Guests are mostly businesspeople and regulars. Recently renovated. 10 min. from dwntwn. **E–VE**

♘ **Days Inn Downtown** (dwntwn), 231 Michigan Ave., MI 48226 (313/965-4646; toll free, see Days Inns). 287 rms, A/C, color TV, in-rm movies. AE, CB, DC, MC, V. Indoor parking $3, pool, health club, rest., bar, free crib. *Note:* Large modern concrete block very nr. the Civic Center and Cobo Hall; rather large functional rms (some no-smoking). Business clientele. Rates on the high side for a motel. **M–E**

♘ **Balmar Motel** (nr. dwntwn), 3250 E. Jefferson Ave., MI 48207 (313/568-2000). 60 rms, A/C, color TV, in-rm movies. AE, DC, MC, V. Free parking, pool, rest. adjacent, private grdn, free crib. *Note:* Modest but well-run small motel 15 min. from dwntwn; friendly reception and svce. Good value. **I**

Other Accommodations (from top bracket to budget)

♘♘♘ **Hyatt Regency Dearborn** (vic.), Michigan Ave. at Fairlane Town Center, in Dearborn, MI 48126 (313/593-1234; toll free, see Hyatt). 768 rms, A/C, color TV, in-rm movies. AE, CB, DC, MC, V. Free parking (valet parking $8), pool, health club, sauna, three rests. (including La Rotisserie), coffee shop, three bars, rm svce, disco, free crib. *Note:* Ultramodern steel-and-glass edifice. w. a spectacular 16-story lobby and glass elevator shafts. Revolving bar on top floor. All the usual Hyatt comfort, very good svce, spacious rms. Business clientele. Very near Ford's manufacturing headquarters, 20 min. from dwntwn, 5 min. from the airport—and has its own helicopter pad! Monorail link to a nearby shopping center. VIP floor. **E–VE**

Omni International (dwntwn), 333 E. Jefferson, MI 48226 (313/222-7700; toll free, see Omni). 254 rms, A/C, color TV, in-rm movies. AE, CB, DC, MC, V. Valet indoor parking $9, pool, two tennis courts, sauna, squash, rest. (333 East), coffee shop, bar, rm svce, hrdrsr, boutiques, concierge, free crib. *Note:* New 20-story hotel in the recently constructed Millender Center; an elegant modern building w. commodious, comfortable rms (most w. balconies). Very comprehensive sports facilities. Efficient svce; group and business clientele. A good place to stay in the heart of dwntwn. Connected to RenCen by the Skywalk. **E–VE**

Westin Hotel (dwntwn), Renaissance Center, MI 48243 (313/568-8000; toll free, see Westin). 1,404 rms, A/C, color TV, in-rm movies. AE, CB, DC, MC, V. Gar. $9, pool, health club, sauna, two rests. (one of which, The Summit, is a revolving rest. on the top floor), coffee shop, four bars, 24-hr. rm svce, nightclub, hrdrsr, boutiques, free crib. *Note:* Futuristic 73-story cylindrical tower which bears the clear imprint of the famous architect John Portman. Eight-story-high lobby, w. indoor grdns and fountains. All rms are cramped but comfortable, and enjoy a panorama of the city or the Detroit River. La Fontaine is an acceptable rest. Efficient svce. Convention or business clientele. Has its own heliport. Detroit's most dazzling address. **E–VE**

Embassy Suites Hotel (vic.), 28100 Franklin Rd., in Southfield, MI 48034 (313/350-2000; toll free 800/362-2779). 240 suites, A/C, color TV, in-rm movies. AE, CB, DC, MC, V. Free parking, pool, health club, sauna, whirlpool, rest. (Jacques Demers' Restaurant), bar, rm svce, disco, free full breakfast and evening cocktails, free crib. *Note:* Luxury all-suites hotel located 30 min. from Detroit Metro Airport and 20 min. from dwntwn. Large, comfortable two-rm suites, each w. refrigerator, three telephones, and two color TVs. Spectacular nine-story landscaped atrium. Flawless svce. **E–VE**

Holiday Inn Dearborn (vic.), 22900 Michigan Ave., in Dearborn, MI 48124 (313/278-4800; toll free, see Holiday Inns). 333 rms, A/C, color TV, in-rm movies. AE, CB, DC, MC, V. Free parking, three pools, sauna, two rests. (including Chambertin), bar, rm svce, nightclub, free crib. *Note:* Archetypal Holiday Inn on the banks of the Rouge River; comfortable balconied rms, some w. kitchenettes. Very creditable rest. Good value. Near the Ford Museum; 20 min. from dwntwn. **M**

Shorecrest Motor Inn (dwntwn), 1316 E. Jefferson Ave., MI 48207 (313/568-3000; toll free 800/992-9616). 54 rms, A/C, color TV, in-rm movies. AE, CB, DC, MC, V. Free parking; rest. (The Clique), rm svce, free crib. *Note:* Aging but decent, comfortable motel; utilitarian rms w. refrigerators. Next to Renaissance Center. Good value. **I–M**

International Plaza Inn (dwntwn), 111 E. Larned, MI 48216 (313/363-1771; toll free 800/346-0540). 30 rms, A/C, cable color TV. AE, MC, V. Free parking; no bar or rest., but 24-hr. rm svce w. meals (including free breakfast) served in the rms. *Note:* The best place in dwntwn Detroit is this unassuming but well-run motel across from Renaissance Center. Inviting rms, some w. kitchenette and minibar. Svce and reception w. a smile. Very good value. **I**

Red Roof Inn (vic.), 26300 Dequindre Dr. (at I-696), in Warren, MI 48091 (313/573-4300; toll free 800/848-7878).

137 rms, A/C, color TV, in-rm movies. AE, CB, DC, MC, V. Free parking, nearby coffee shop, free crib. *Note:* Modest small motel w. little to recommend it but its low rates. Functional comfort but nothing more. Free morning coffee. 20 min. from dwntwn. Ideal if you're driving (direct access to highways). **I**

Travelodge Dearborn (vic.), 23730 Michigan Ave., in Dearborn, MI 48124 (313/565-7250; toll free, see Travelodge). 78 rms, A/C, color TV, in-rm movies. AE, CB, DC, MC, V. Free parking, pool, coffee shop, free crib. *Note:* Typical well-run motel; comfortable rms, some w. balconies. Free morning coffee. 5 min. from the Ford Museum and Greenfield Village, 20 min. from dwntwn. Good value. **I**

Airport Accommodations

Hilton Inn Airport (vic.), 31500 Wick Rd., in Romulus, MI 48174 (313/292-3400; toll free, see Hilton). 272 rms, A/C, color TV, in-rm movies. AE, CB, DC, MC, V. Free parking, pool, two tennis courts, health club, sauna, rest., bar, rm svce, nightclub, free crib. *Note:* The usual airport motel, recently renovated. Attractive decor; well-soundproofed, sizable rms; efficient svce. Business clientele. Free airport limo. **E**

YMCA/Youth Hostel

YMCA (dwntwn), 2020 Witherell St., MI 48226 (313/962-6126). Men only; also functions as a youth hostel. 220 rms, pool, sauna, health club. Unsafe area, especially at night.

RESTAURANTS

A Note on Restaurant Prices: Detroit restaurant prices, per person, excluding drinks and service charges, are coded as follows: **VE,** Very Expensive ($60 and up); **E,** Expensive ($40–$60); **M,** Moderate ($25–$40); **I,** Inexpensive ($15–$25); **B,** Budget (up to $15).

Personal Favorites (in order of preference)

Rattlesnake (dwntwn), 300 River Pl. (567-4400). A/C. Lunch Mon–Fri, dinner daily; closed Jan 1, Memorial Day, Labor Day, Dec 25. AE, MC, V. Jkt. *Specialties:* scallop-and-crayfish timbale w. basil and shallots, soft-shell crabs tempura style w. ginger-pepper butter, roast rack of lamb w. artichokes and peppers, grilled swordfish w. Szechuan peppercorns, three-flavor polenta, white-chocolate ravioli. Fine list of wines at reasonable prices. *Note:* The young, talented chef Jimmy Schmidt (former co-owner of Denver's well-known Rattlesnake Club), has taken less than a year to establish his new rest. as the finest in Detroit. The discreet decor admirably sets off the elegant, imaginative food. Smiling, congenial svce. Resv. strongly advised at this fashionable spot. *American.* **M–E**

The Whitney (nr. dwntwn), 4421 Woodward Ave. at Canfield Ave. (832-5701). A/C. Lunch Mon–Fri, dinner Mon–Sat, brunch Sun; closed hols. AE, MC, V. Jkt. *Specialties:* sautéed foie gras, roast rack of lamb w. rosemary, grilled Maine lobster, game and venison (in season), raspberry mousse and chocolate taco. Menu changes regularly. Long wine list. *Note:* "Hollywood magnificence" would be the best thumbnail description of this opulent setting: a luxurious Victorian mansion filled to bursting w. Flemish tapestries, precious crystal, marble, old paneling, and Tiffany stained-glass windows. Chef Baldwin's kitchen dishes up a pretty blend of elegance and simplicity. Polished, attentive svce; distinctive background music. Resv. required. Valet parking. In spite of the unattractive neighborhood, an excellent place to eat. *American.* **M–I**

Joe Muer's Seafood (nr. dwntwn), 2000 Gratiot Ave. (567-1088). A/C. Lunch Mon–Fri, dinner Mon–Sat; closed hols.

AE, DC, MC, V. J&T. *Specialties:* top-quality fish and shellfish; good list of California wines. *Note:* A local institution since 1929. This immense rest., w. its comfortable wood-paneled and exposed-brick rooms, is host every day to crowds of fish- and seafood-lovers, who are attracted by one of the broadest selections in the country. Two black marks: svce rather perfunctory; resv. not accepted. Private valet parking. 15 min. from dwntwn. *Seafood.* **M−E**

　　🍸🍸 **Van Dyke Place** (nr. dwntwn), 649 Van Dyke St. (821-2620).
　　♿🍸 A/C. Dinner only, Mon–Sat; closed hols. AE, MC, V. J&T.
Specialties: boudin of pheasant and duckling, assorted domestic caviars, paupiettes of braised veal, rack of lamb, abalone steak. Menu changes regularly. Very fine wine list. *Note:* Super-chic rest. housed in the mansion of a 19th-century captain of industry, elegantly decorated in Louis XVI style w. crystal chandeliers, gilt-framed pictures, and period furniture. The cuisine, while praiseworthy, doesn't quite measure up to the decor. Svce is attentive. Resv., in advance, a must. 10 min. from dwntwn. *French/Continental.* **M−E**

　　🔆🍸🍸 **Pontchartrain Wine Cellars** (dwntwn), 234 W. Larned St.
　　🔆♿🍸 (963-1785). A/C. Lunch Mon–Fri, dinner Mon–Sat; closed hols. and early Aug. AE, CB, DC, MC, V. Jkt. *Specialties:* escargots bourguignons, gazpacho, escalope sauce Diable, leg of lamb w. ratatouille, veal Cordon Bleu, braised sweetbreads, fish of the day, pear Hélène. As you would expect from the rest.'s name, an excellent wine list, reasonably priced; try a "cold duck" cocktail, made from champagne and burgundy. *Note:* Very successful French-inspired food, served in the romantic atmosphere of an old Paris bistro. Svce efficient but on the abrupt side. An outstanding rest. of its kind since 1935. Resv. advised; valet parking. *Continental.* **I−M**

　　🔆🍸 **Jacoby's** (dwntwn), 624 Brush St. (962-7067). A/C. Lunch
　　🔆 daily, dinner Mon–Sat. AE, DC, MC, V. *Specialties:* schnitzel, sauerbraten, bratwurst, lake perch, sandwiches, German beer on draft. *Note:* The lawyers' and politicians' favorite since 1904. Looks and feels like a picturesque old brewhouse. Solid, honest food somewhat lacking in imagination. Svce w. a smile. Next to RenCen. *German/American.* **B−I**

Other Restaurants (from top bracket to budget)

　　🍸🍸🍸 **Les Auteurs** (vic.), 222 Sherman Dr., Royal Oak (544-2887).
　　♿🍸🍸 A/C. Lunch Mon–Sat, dinner nightly; closed hols. AE, DC, MC, V. Jkt. *Specialties:* wild-mushroom pizza, black-bean cake w. smoked chicken, tomato salsa and sour cream, southwestern chili, grilled salmon on a bed of baby corn w. mustard sauce, lamb shank w. saffron rice, white- and dark-chocolate "linguine" w. chocolate sauce. Menu changes regularly. *Note:* Despite its location in an outer suburb of Detroit, this elegant bistro has become a smash hit since its opening in May 1988, principally because of the light, imaginative cuisine of chef Keith Famie, a disciple of Girardet and Bocuse. The long, overly narrow dining rm is decorated w. menus and photographs of celebrity chefs from around the world. Friendly, attentive svce; well worth the 25-min. drive from dwntwn along I-75N and W. 11 Mile Rd. Resv. required. *American.* **M**

　　🍸🍸🍸 **Opus One** (dwntwn), 565 E. Larned St. (961-7766). A/C.
　　♿🍸🍸 Lunch Mon–Fri, dinner Mon–Sat; closed hols. AE, CB, DC, MC, V. Jkt. *Specialties:* crayfish bisque, veal w. shrimp, seafood en croûte, very good beef, bass w. champagne sauce, roast duck w. young vegetables, apple tart w. cinnamon ice cream. Wonderful wine list appropriately including the famous California wine Opus One, from which the rest. takes its name. *Note:* A successful newcomer on the local scene; light, imaginative modern food served in a pretty turn-of-the-century setting. Uncommonly efficient svce; resv. a must. *French/American.* **I−M**

　　🍸🍸 **London Chop House** (dwntwn), 155 W. Congress St. (962-
　　♿🍸 0777). A/C. Lunch/dinner Mon–Sat. (till 2am); closed hols.

DETROIT

N

Fisher Building

LODGE FRWY.

WOODWARD AVE.

Art Institute Auditorium

Detroit Institute of Arts

Detroit Science Center

Wayne State University

Historical Museum

Public Library

KIRBY AVE.

Orchestra Hall

PARSONS

GRAND BLVD.

BRUSH

WARREN AVE.

PIQUETTE AVE.

W. GRAND BLVD.

EDSEL FORD FRWY.

MT. ELLIOTT AVE.

ELMWOOD AVE.

KIRBY AVE.

FREDERICK

FOREST AVE.

CANFIELD AVE.

WILLIS AVE.

ELMWOOD AVE.

GRATIOT AVE.

VERNOR HWY.

CHENE ST.

ST. AUBIN AVE.

MACK AVE.

WILKINS ST.

Eastern Market

RUSSELL ST.

RIVARD

CHRYSLER FRWY.

ERSKINE ST.

CANFIELD AVE.

GRAND RIVER AVE.

94

75

3

10

AE, CB, DC, MC, V. J&T. *Specialties:* fettuccine w. seafood and artichokes, lake perch, oysters au champagne, broiled venison cutlets w. cherries, rack of lamb w. mustard sauce, sautéed sturgeon w. salsa butter, pheasant w. wild mushrooms, veal Oscar, frozen hazelnut soufflé. Excellent wine list w. more than 300 varieties. Menu changes regularly. *Note:* A local institution for more than half a century; everyone who's anyone in Detroit (including the Ford family), has eaten, eats, or will eat in this noisy, comfortable cellar decorated British style, despite a noticeable drop in quality in the last 2–3 years. Resv. advised. Valet parking. *American/Continental.* **E–VE**

🍷🍷 **Carl's Chop House** (nr. dwntwn), 3020 Grand River Ave.
🍷🍷 (833-0700). A/C. Lunch/dinner daily (until 1am); closed Memorial Day, Dec 25. AE, CB, DC, MC, V. *Specialties:* the city's best prime ribs, steaks and lamb chops for more than half a century; also excellent pickled herring. *Note:* All the warmth of an Amtrak waiting room and a strictly flea-market decor, but efficient svce. Not far from Tiger Stadium, Carl's attracts many fans on game days. A good place. Resv. advised. Valet parking. *Steak/Seafood.* **I–M**

🍷🍷 **Money Tree** (dwntwn), 333 W. Fort St. at Washington Blvd.
🍷🍷 (961-2445). A/C. Breakfast/lunch Mon–Fri, dinner Mon–Sat; closed hols. AE, CB, DC, MC, V. Jkt. *Specialties:* quiches, crêpes, and salads at lunch; catch of the day and more substantial dishes (rack of lamb w. mint, roast chicken w. ginger, roast veal w. basil, cassoulet, shrimp pêcheur) at dinner. Very good desserts. *Note:* A likable, friendly café-restaurant in a modern setting; cuisine often inventive, svce relaxed and cheerful. Open-air terrace in summer. Agreeable background music. *Continental.* **I–M**

🍷 **Chung's** (nr. dwntwn), 3177 Cass Ave. (831-1100). A/C.
🍷 Lunch/dinner daily. AE, DC. *Specialties:* shrimp in lobster purée, steak "Kew," wor hip harr, Cantonese specialties. *Note:* The best rest. in Detroit's Chinatown; wilted Far Eastern decor but many Chinese customers—always a good sign. *Chinese.* **I**

🍷 **New Hellas** (dwntwn), 583 Monroe St. (961-5544). A/C.
🍷 Lunch/dinner daily (until 2am). AE, MC, V. *Specialties:* moussaka, broiled lamb, squid, shish kebab, spanakopita (spinach-and-cheese pie), baklava. *Note:* An absolutely authentic Greek rest. in the heart of Greektown. Generally noisy and crowded. Open very late. No resv., so inevitable waits (usually). *Greek.* **B–I**

🍷 **Sheik Restaurant** (dwntwn), 316 E. Lafayette St. (964-8441).
🍷 A/C. Lunch Tues–Fri, dinner Tues–Sun; closed hols. MC, V. *Specialties:* tabouleh, hummus, shish kebab, more than 20 different lamb dishes; rice pudding. *Note:* This rest. has been a family business since it opened in 1923; recently redecorated, it offers authentic Lebanese cooking at attractive prices. Friendly reception and svce, pleasant atmosphere. Very popular locally; excellent value. *Middle Eastern.* **B–I**

Restaurants In the Vicinity

🍷🍷 **La Cuisine** (vic.), 417 Pelissier St., in Windsor, Canada (519/
🍷🍷 253-6432). A/C. Lunch/dinner Tues–Sat. AE, DC, MC, V. Jkt. *Specialties:* boeuf gros sel, kidneys w. three mustards, bouillabaisse. Good desserts. *Note:* A real French rest., well worth the jaunt into Canada (10 min. by car through the Windsor Tunnel; non–U.S. citizens should bring their passports). Congenial bistro atmosphere. Wine but no hard liquor. Resv. advised for dinner. *French.* **I–M**

Cafeterias/Specialty Spots

American Coney Island (dwntwn), 114 W. LaFayette St. (961-7758). A/C. Breakfast/lunch/dinner daily (open around the clock). No credit cards. By general consent the best hot dogs in town. Locally popular since 1914.

BARS & NIGHTCLUBS

Baker's Keyboard Lounge (vic.), 20510 Livernois (864-1201). One of the world's oldest and best-known jazz clubs, where you can hear all the stars. Open Tues–Sun. 20 min. from dwntwn.

Galligan's (dwntwn), 519 E. Jefferson Ave. (963-2098). Detroit's most popular Irish pub. Plenty of action. Bar food. Noisy and likable. Open Mon–Sat.

Lindell AC (nr. dwntwn), 1310 Cass Ave. (964-1122). Popular, fun singles bar, much frequented by sports fans. Open daily.

Soup Kitchen (dwntwn), 1585 Franklin St. (259-2643). Blues and jazz in a nice saloon setting; also a decent rest. Open daily.

St. Andrews Hall (dwntwn), 431 E. Congress (961-8137). Enormous three-level disco in a deconsecrated church two blocks from RenCen. Locally very popular; open daily.

Watt's Mosambique (vic.), 8406 Fenkell (864-0240). Good African American jazz in an outlying district, 25 min. from dwntwn.

NEARBY EXCURSIONS

ANN ARBOR (46 mi./74km west on I-94): University town with a happy, youthful personality; seat of the **University of Michigan,** S. State St. and S. University Ave. (313/763-4636). One of the largest (35,000 students) and oldest (1817) universities in the Midwest, which moved here in 1837, 20 years after its founding in Detroit. Many buildings in the Gothic style; libraries; museums of art, archeology, and natural history. Also home to the **Gerald R. Ford Presidential Library,** 1000 Beal Ave. (313/668-2218), housing the personal archives of the 38th president. Campus open to visitors Mon–Fri; worth the trip.

CRANBROOK (500 Lone Pine Rd. in Bloomfield Hills, 25 mi./40km NW via Woodward Ave. and Mich. 1) (313/645-3134): Internationally famous educational and cultural center on a 288-acre (92ha) estate endowed early in this century by George G. Booth, publisher of the *Detroit News,* and his wife, Ellen. It includes among its facilities an academy of fine arts, a scientific institute with an observatory and planetarium, the very lovely neo-Gothic Christ Church, and an impressive 1908 manor house (Cranbrook House) in the Tudor style designed by Albert Kahn (visits Sun July–Aug; the rest of the year by appointment; 313/645-3149), all standing amid beautiful landscaped gardens with groves and fountains. Open daily (gardens, May–Oct only). Don't miss it.

FAIR LANE MANSION (Evergreen Rd., University of Michigan–Dearborn Campus, in Dearborn) (313/593-5590): Sumptuous private home built in 1915 for $2 million by Henry Ford; this pseudo-Scottish castle in rough stone boasts no fewer than 56 rooms and a garage for 12 cars! Open daily May–Sept, Sun only the rest of the year. Well worth the detour.

HENRY FORD MUSEUM & GREENFIELD VILLAGE (23 Oakwood Blvd. in Dearborn, 10 mi./16km west via Michigan Ave. and U.S. 12) (313/271-1620): Established in 1929 by Henry Ford, who was born here in 1863, the **Henry Ford Museum** is intended as a tribute to the dynamic qualities of the American people. It presents a complete panorama of the country's development from the days of the pioneers. To see it in detail requires at least 2 days. Very rich collection of art and handcrafts; impressive aircraft and automobile museum, including the first car built by Henry Ford, a great 600-ton (545,000kg) Allegheny locomotive, and the Fokker aircraft in which Admiral Byrd first flew over the North Pole in 1926.

The adjacent **Greenfield Village** comprises 100 or so 17th-, 18th-, and 19th-century buildings drawn from all parts of the country and restored with scrupulous care. Among them are Henry Ford's birthplace, Edison's laboratory, and the courthouse in which Abraham Lincoln appeared as an attorney—a slice of living history that you shouldn't miss. It draws more than 1 ½ million visitors a year. Open daily.

HISTORIC FORT WAYNE (6325 W. Jefferson Ave., 5 mi./ 8km south of Detroit via Jefferson Ave.) (313/297-9360): Fort built in the period before the Civil War and in a fine state of preservation, with tunnels, a blockhouse, and its powder kegs. Interesting museum of military and Native American history. Open Wed–Sun May–Oct.

MEADOW BROOK (Adams Rd. in Rochester, 25 mi./ 40km north on I-75) (313/370-3140): This enormous Tudor-style manor house on the campus of Oakland University was built in 1926 by the widow of automobile tycoon John Dodge, and contains around 100 richly furnished and decorated rooms. Open daily in summer, Sun only the rest of the year. Accommodates a famous (notorious?) music festival each summer.

POINT PELEE NATIONAL PARK (32 mi./51km SE via the Detroit-Windsor Tunnel and Ontario Rte. 3): This Canadian nature reserve of a little more than 2,400 acres (972ha) is a paradise for wildlife enthusiasts; its expanse of marsh and woodland, standing on two of the great migratory routes between Canada and South America, is host to more than 340 different species of birds. Many trails and waterfront paths. Visitor Center. Camping not permitted. The perfect place for dedicated birdwatchers. Open daily, early Apr to Sept. For information, phone 519/322-2365. (Non–U.S. citizens should bring their passports.)

WINDSOR (Canada): Cosmopolitan city of 200,000 across the Detroit River, reached by bridge or tunnel. Numerous parks, boutiques, restaurants. Spectacular view of the Detroit skyline, particularly after dark. (Non–U.S. citizens should bring their passports.)

CHAPTER 21

CLEVELAND [⚱]

□ □ □

This, now the second-largest, city in Ohio (after Columbus) was founded on Lake Erie at the mouth of the **Cuyahoga River** by Gen. Moses Cleaveland. The spelling was later modified by the editor of a local newspaper who found the name too long for his taste. Sprawling over more than 50 mi. (80km), Cleveland's metropolitan area is a riveting microcosm of America's industrial evolution over the last century. Interminable gray, polluted suburbs—home to steel mills, oil refineries, automobile factories, plus electronics and machine-tool plants—lie cheek by jowl with a few luxurious residential areas **(Shaker Heights, Beachwood)** around a downtown which now consists of no more than a couple of dozen blocks of houses surrounding the **Mall** and the completely renovated **Public Square.** The city's tallest building, the 52-story **Terminal Tower,** and the **B.P. America/Standard Oil tower** (45 stories) dominate the square. The seventh most populous city in the country in 1950, Cleveland lost nearly a quarter of its population in the 1970s as a result of upheavals in the oil and steel industries; in 1978 Cleveland even became the first major city since the Depression era to go into default. Twelve years later the city is in the midst of a building boom— **Tower City Center, Nautica Complex** at the Flats, **North Coast Harbor**—sleek new skyscrapers rise among neoclassic and Gothic structures downtown. The first ground has also been broken for the **Rock-and-Roll Hall of Fame,** a $50-million flashy glass-and-metal museum designed by architect I. M. Pei, scheduled to open in 1992. But despite newfound economy activity, the unemployment rate is still well above 10%, and more than a third of Cleveland's inhabitants live below the poverty line.

Among its other claims to fame, Cleveland can boast the first modern striptease, in the person of an obscure tapdancer named Carrie Findel. Tired of the audience's boos, she declared one night, "I've a surprise for you. Each week, I'll take off one more part of my costume." The show lasted 52 weeks.

Two other truly American legends are associated with Cleveland: Superman, the famous comic-strip hero, who made his first appearance in 1934; and John Davison Rockefeller, the incarnation of capitalism triumphant, who, beginning in 1870, laid the foundations of the immense Standard Oil empire. Cleveland is also headquarters for 35 of the most important U.S. industrial corporations. Medicine is another flourishing aspect of the local economy. Besides schools and research institutes of renown like **Case Western Reserve University** and the **Cleveland State University Hospitals,** the city also has the **Cleveland Clinic,** known worldwide for the organ transplants and cardiac surgery performed here.

Ohio's industrial capital is a veritable mosaic of nationalities, with the second-largest concentration of Hungarians after Budapest, as well as Italian, Irish, Polish, German, Chinese, Greek, Serb, Czech, and Ukrainian communities —overall, a good 60 or so different nationalities are represented. With such a mix of ethnic groups, it's no wonder that Cleveland was the first major U.S. metropolis (1967) to elect an African American mayor, Carl B. Stokes. Cleveland is also rich in first-rate cultural and theatrical institutions: its symphony orchestra is internationally renowned, and its **Museum of Art** is one of the best in the country.

Among Cleveland's famous natives are actors Paul Newman, Burgess Meredith, and Dorothy Dandridge; TV personality Phil Donahue; and composer and band leader Henry Mancini.

BASIC FACTS: State of Ohio. Area code: 216. Time zone: eastern. ZIP Code: 44101. Founded: 1796. Approximate population: city, 520,000; metropolitan area, 2,750,000. 11th-largest metropolitan area in the United States.

CLIMATE: As in all the Great Lakes region, winter is very cold and snowy (average Jan temperature: 27°F/3°C) and summer hot and humid (average July temperature: 70°F/22°C). Spring is normally very brief, and autumn mild and sunny; these are the two ideal seasons for visiting Cleveland.

DISTANCES: Chicago, 343 mi. (549km); Cincinnati, 247 mi. (395km); Detroit, 170 mi. (272km); New York, 485 mi. (776km); Washington, 350 mi. (560km).

ARRIVAL & TRANSIT INFORMATION

AIRPORTS: Burke Lakefront Airport (BKL): 1 mi. (2km) north. Delta Connection only. Information: 781-6411.
Cleveland Hopkins International Airport (CLE): 10 mi. (16km) SW. Information: 265-6000.

U.S. AIRLINES: American (881-4341), Continental (771-8419), Delta (781-8800), Eastern (861-7300), Midway (toll free 800/621-5700), Northwest (267-0515), Pan Am (toll free 800/221-1111), TWA (781-2700), United (356-1311), and USAir (696-8050).

FOREIGN CARRIERS: Air Canada (toll free 800/422-6232).

CITY LINK: Cab fare to city center from Hopkins International, about $16–$18; time, 25–30 min. (up to 45 min. during rush hr.). An airport–city center **train** leaves every 20 min. from the R.T.A. Terminal, Public Sq.; fare, $1; time, 25 min. Bus: **Hopkins Airport Limousine** (267-8282): leaves every 30 min.; serves major dwntwn hotels; fare, $6; time, 35–40 min. Unless your touring will be limited to the dwntwn area, you may wish to rent a car to cope with the sprawling metropolitan area and the difficulty of getting a taxi in the suburbs (the wait sometimes approaches an hour). A rather efficient public transportation system (bus and train); for R.T.A. information, call 621-9500.

CAR RENTAL (at Hopkins International Airport unless otherwise indicated): Avis (265-3700); Budget (433-4433); Dollar (267-3133); Hertz (267-8900); National (267-0060); Thrifty, 16079 Brookpark Rd. (267-6811). For dwntwn agencies, consult the phone directory.

LIMOUSINE SERVICES: American Limousines Service (221-9330), Elegant Limousine Service (582-1555).

TAXIS: The fares are relatively reasonable. Taxis may be hailed on the street dwntwn, but it's advisable to phone for them: **Americab** (881-1111) or **Yellow Cab** (623-1500).

TRAIN: Amtrak, Lakefront Station, 200 E. Cleveland Memorial Shoreway Dr. (861-0105).

DOWNTOWN CLEVELAND

← N→

Lake Erie

Port of Cleveland

Burke Lakefront Airport

Cleveland Stadium

Amtrak Station

City Hall

The Mall

Public Library

St. John's Cathedral

Erieview Tower

Bus Station

Cleveland State University

Trinity Cathedral

Terminal Tower

Public Square

Cuyahoga River

MEMORIAL SHOREWAY

ERIESIDE AVE.

N. MARGINAL RD.

S. MARGINAL RD.

DAVENPORT AVE.

LAKESIDE AVE.

HAMILTON AVE.

ST. CLAIR AVE.

ROCKWELL AVE.

SUPERIOR AVE.

PAYNE AVE.

EUCLID AVE.

CHESTER AVE.

PROSPECT AVE.

HURON RD.

CANAL RD.

SUPERIOR AVE.

FRONT AVE.

SUMMIT AVE.

CARNEGIE AVE.

CEDAR AVE.

CENTRAL AVE.

CHARITY AVE.

PERKINS AVE.

PROSPECT AVE.

36 ST.
35 ST.
32 ST.
30 ST.
26 ST.
23 ST.
21 ST.
19 ST.
18 ST.
17 ST.
14 ST.
12 ST.
14 ST.
11 ST.
10 ST.
9 ST.
9 ST.
6 ST.
3 ST.

90

6

INTERCITY BUSES: Greyhound, 1465 Chester Ave. (781-0520).

INFORMATION & TOURS

TOURIST INFORMATION: The **Cleveland Convention & Visitors Bureau,** 3100 Terminal Tower, Tower City, OH 44113 (216/621-4110; toll free 800/ 321-1001).
   Recorded telephone message giving an up-to-date listing of cultural events and shows: 216/621-8860.

GUIDED TOURS: Goodtime Cruises (boat): Lake Erie and Cuyahoga River cruises. Depart from the E. 9th St. Pier (216/861-5110), daily May–Sept.
   Trolley Tours (bus), W. 9th St. at St. Claire Ave. (216/771-4484). Narrated 2-hr. tour aboard a fleet of replica trolley cars. Daily Apr–Nov. Resv. requested.

SIGHTS, ATTRACTIONS & ACTIVITIES

ARCHITECTURAL HIGHLIGHTS: ❀⚖ **B.P. America Headquarters,** 200 Public Sq. (586-8831): One of the newer additions to the downtown skyline (1986), this $250-million megalith rears its 45 glass-and-concrete stories from the dead center of Public Sq. Lovely eight-story glass atrium with indoor gardens, fountains, and restaurants. Worth a look. Open Mon–Sat.
   ⚖ **City Hall,** Lakeside Ave. and E. 6th St. (664-2000): Cleveland's city hall, overlooking Lake Erie. Be sure to see the famous Archibald Willard painting, *Spirit of '76,* in the rotunda. Open Mon–Fri.
   ⚖ **Cleveland Clinic,** 9500 Euclid Ave. (444-2200): Second-largest private hospital in the country after the Mayo Clinic in Rochester, Minn. Employs 8,900 doctors, researchers, and staff. A pioneer in cardiac surgery since 1967, the clinic performs more than 3,000 open-heart operations each year. The world-renowned Cleveland Clinic has treated the likes of ex-King Khaled of Arabia, King Hussein of Jordan, and the former president of Brazil, General Figueiredo. The most recent addition to the complex is the Cesar Pelli–designed clinic building, an enormous white-granite ziggurat.
   ⚖ **Federal Reserve Bank,** 1455 E. 6th St. (579-2000): Built with pink Sienna marble in 1923, this bank features the world's largest vault door and a spectacular interior lobby. Worth a glance. Open Mon–Fri.
   ⚖ **Playhouse Square,** Euclid Ave. between E. 13th St. and E. 17th St.: Symbol of Cleveland's cultural renaissance, this urban-renewal project cost $20 million and endowed the city with one of the largest performance and concert hall complexes in the country. The three theaters and the cabaret, elegantly restored, present theatrical performances, ballet, opera, and classical and pop concerts. Open daily. For information on current performances, call 241-6000. Absolutely worth going out of your way for.
   ⚖ **Public Square,** Ontario St. and Superior Ave.: The heart of the business district, where all the major dwntwn thoroughfares converge: Euclid Ave., Ontario St., and Superior Ave. Towering above the square are the city's tallest building, the **Terminal Tower** (52 stories), and the B.P. America skyscraper (45 stories). Quite lively by day, but not very engaging after dark. Imposing memorial: **Soldiers and Sailors Monument.** The appealing public park is adorned with statues.

MARKETS: ❀⚖ **West Side Market,** Lorain Ave. at W. 25th St. (664-3386): Picturesque old European-style covered market with more than 100 food stalls of-

UNIVERSITY CIRCLE
AND CLEVELAND HEIGHTS AREA

CLEVELAND
HEIGHTS

To Shaker Heights
Thistledown Racetrack →

COVENTRY RD.

MAYFIELD AVE.

OVERLOOK RD.

DERBYSHIRE RD.

EUCLID HEIGHTS BLVD.

EDGEHILL RD.

KENILWORTH RD.

DERBYSHIRE RD.

OVERLOOK RD.

MURRY HILL RD.

Garfield Tomb

City Line

Lakeview
Cemetery

Forest Hills
Park

123 ST.

120 ST.

MAYFIELD AVE.

EUCLID AVE.

Case Western
Reserve University

ADELBERT RD.

CEDAR AVE.

Institute of Music

Western Reserve Hist. Soc.

Institute
of Art

Severance Hall

EAST BLVD.

Museum of
Natural History

EAST BLVD.

Museum of Art

EAST BLVD.

To Rockefeller Park

Wade Park

105 ST.

107 ST.

105 ST.

CARNEGIE AVE.

100 ST.

HOUGH AVE.

97 ST.

95 ST.

CHESTER AVE.

101 ST.

Health Education Museum

EUCLID AVE.

Cleveland Clinic

To Cleveland Hopkins
Int'l Airport

93 ST.

90 ST.

88 ST.

← N

fering products from all over the world. A colorful Cleveland classic dating from 1912. Open Mon, Wed, Fri, and Sat.

MUSEUMS OF ART: ☀︎𐂷 Museum of Art, 11150 East Blvd. at University Circle (421-7340): One of the top American art museums. From "The Treasure of the Guelphs" to Rauschenberg, the museum houses a sumptuous panorama of Oriental, European, and American art. Some of the best-known works: El Greco's *Christ on the Cross,* Velázquez's *The Clown Calabazas,* Rembrandt's *The Jewish Student,* Cézanne's *Mont Sainte-Victoire,* and two famous Picassos, *Life* and *Harlequin with Violin.* The handsome, marble Greek Revival building faces the **Cultural Gardens** and its sculptures. Itself worth a trip to Cleveland. Open Tues–Sun.

MUSEUMS OF SCIENCE & HISTORY: 𐂷 Dunham Tavern Museum, 6709 Euclid Ave. (431-1060): Former coaching inn (1824) along the Buffalo–Detroit route, now a historical museum with interesting temporary exhibitions. Open Wed and Sat only.

☀︎𐂷 **Health Education Museum,** 8911 Euclid Ave. (231-5010): The oldest (and one of the best) medical museums in the country, with an astonishing giant electronic brain and Juno, the transparent Plexiglass woman. In all, more than 150 giant anatomical models. Marvelous. Open daily.

𐂷 **Howard Dittrick Museum of Medical History,** 11000 Euclid Ave. (368-3648): A natural complement to the Health Education Museum, this museum documents a complete panorama of the evolution of medicine, surgery, and pharmacology through a collection of more than 10,000 old and new medical objects. A must for all disciples of Hippocrates. On the third floor of the Allen Library. Open Mon–Sat.

𐂷 **Museum of Natural History,** Wade Oval Dr. at University Circle (231-4600): Very interesting museum displaying rich collections covering animals (dinosaurs, mammoths, giant insects), prehistoric times (including the three-million-year-old "Lucy" skeleton), Native American culture, geology, and more. An absolute must. Open daily.

𐂷 **NASA Lewis Research Center,** 21000 Brookpark Rd. (433-2001): This NASA research center adjacent to Hopkins International Airport offers guided tours of research laboratories with, notably, a supersonic wind tunnel plus an exhibition and films on space exploration. Open daily.

𐂷 **Ralph Mueller Planetarium,** Wade Oval Dr. at University Circle (231-4600): The renowned observatory and planetarium are an integral part of the Museum of Natural History (see above). Astronomy shows and other presentations. Open daily June–Aug, wknds only the rest of the year.

𐂷 **Shaker Historical Museum,** 16740 S. Park Blvd., Shaker Heights (921-1201): This tiny museum houses furniture, clothing, and artifacts of Cleveland's 19th-century Shaker sect. Interesting. Open Tues–Fri and Sun.

☀︎𐂷 **Western Reserve Historical Society Museum,** 10825 East Blvd. at University Circle (721-5722): Magnificently reconstructed U.S. history from independence to the present, including Shaker crafts and old costumes unique to the United States. Contains one of the world's largest genealogical collections. Also houses a vast automotive and aeronautical museum with more than 200 old models. Absolutely worth a visit. Open Tues–Sun.

NIGHTLIFE: The Flats, Old River Rd. between Front Ave. and Center St.: Once known strictly for heavy industry, this area around the mouth of the Cuyahoga River is the place to be after dark in Cleveland. Here, 20 or so restaurants and nightclubs are crammed into a couple of blocks, running the gamut from

punk-rock joints to big-band dance spots. Many have large terraces overlooking the river for outdoor dining during the summer and river-view dining in winter. Has become the favorite haunt of swinging singles.

PANORAMAS: ⚓ **Terminal Tower,** Public Sq. (621-7981): 52-story tower (761 ft./238m) with an observation platform on the 42nd floor. The best view of Cleveland and Lake Erie. Open wknds only.

PARKS & GARDENS: ⚓ **Brookside Park,** Denison Ave. and Fulton Pkwy.: Joggers will enjoy these 153 acres (64ha) of gardens, which encompass the **Cleveland Metroparks Zoo,** one of the most highly rated zoos in the country (more than 3,000 animals). Open daily.

☀⚓ **Lake View Cemetery,** 12316 Euclid Ave. (421-2665): Splendid landscaped cemetery that overlooks Lake Erie, as the name indicates. Among noteworthy graves here are those of James Garfield, 20th president of the United States, whose enormous mausoleum affords a spectacular view of the city, and John D. Rockefeller, founder of the famous dynasty. See it. Open daily.

⚓ **North Coast Harbor,** E. 9th St. and Lake Erie: This multi-million-dollar harbor, completed in 1989, is the latest addition to the 13-mile (21km) Lakefront State Park system lining Lake Erie's southern shore. On top of the harbor promenade and park areas, new developments—including a maritime museum, historic shipyard, aquarium, and shops—are planned. A sight to be seen.

⚓ **Rockefeller Park,** along Liberty Blvd.: A calm, green oasis between Lake Erie and Case Western Reserve University. The park's 296 acres (120ha) offer very fine Japanese gardens, greenhouses, and the **Cultural Gardens,** adorned with sculptures and architectural designs from 24 different countries. Worth a look.

PERFORMING ARTS: For daily listings of all shows and cultural events, consult the entertainment pages of the daily paper *Cleveland Plain Dealer* and the monthly *Cleveland* and *Northern Ohio Live* magazines.

Cleveland Play House, 8500 Euclid Ave. (795-7000): The oldest regional repertory theater in the nation. Classical and contemporary theater.

The Front Row Theatre, 6199 Wilson Mills Rd., Highland Heights (449-5000): Big-name stars.

Hanna Theater, 2067 E. 14th St. (621-5000): Musicals.

Karamu House & Theatre, 2355 E. 89th St. (795-7070): Experimental theater, concerts, and ballet. The first professional African American theater established outside New York.

Lakewood Little Theater, 17801 Detroit Ave., Lakewood (521-2540): Home of the Kenneth C. Beck Center for Cultural Arts. Sept–June.

Playhouse Square Center, 1501 Euclid Ave. (241-6000): These three contiguous halls—the **Ohio Theater,** the **State Theater,** and the **Palace Theater**—offer classical and modern theater, concerts, ballet, and opera, as well as the **Great Lakes Theatre Festival** (see "Special Events," below).

Severance Hall, 11001 Euclid Ave. at East Blvd. (231-1111): This pseudo Greek temple is the home of the Cleveland Symphony Orchestra, one of the country's "big six" orchestras, under principal conductor Christoph von Dohnányi; season Sept–May. The orchestra can be heard June–Sept at the superb outdoor **Blossom Music Center,** 1145 W. Steels Corners Rd., Cuyahoga Falls (231-7300).

SHOPPING: ⚓ **The Arcade,** 401 Euclid Ave. (621-8500): One of the oldest enclosed shopping centers in the world (1890), this five-level, glass-skylighted, art nouveau wonder features 80 bars, boutiques, and restaurants. Free concerts at noon. Don't miss a visit. Open Mon–Sat.

The Galleria at Erieview, E. 9th St. and St. Clair Ave. (861-4343): New $43-million glitzy, glass-roofed shopping-and-dining showplace opened in the fall of 1987. Nearly 60 nationally known specialty stores, from Laura Ashley to Eddie Bauer and Ann Taylor. Open daily.

SPECIAL EVENTS: For the exact schedule of events below, consult the **Cleveland Convention & Visitors Bureau** (see "Tourist Information," above).

Jazz Festival (June): With the biggest stars.

Great Lakes Theatre Festival (late June to Oct): One of the Midwest's best theater festivals.

All Nations Festival (June): Ethnic folk groups from all over the United States.

Riverfest (late July): Procession of decorated boats on the Cuyahoga River, waterskiing displays, free open-air concerts, food festival. Draws a crowd of more than half a million.

National Air Show (Labor Day wknd): An exhibition of all types of planes and flight demonstrations over Lake Erie. A classic since 1929.

SPORTS: Cleveland boasts three professional teams:

Baseball (Apr–Oct): Indians, Cleveland Stadium (861-1200).

Basketball (Oct to late Apr): Cavaliers, Coliseum, in Richfield (659-9100).

Football (Sept–Dec): Browns, Cleveland Stadium (696-5555).

Horse Racing

Northfield Park Raceway, 10705 Northfield Rd., Northfield (467-4101): Harness races year round.

STROLLS: ⚓ **Coventry Road,** enter from Chester Ave: The local Greenwich Village, with fashionable boutiques and numerous restaurants. Don't miss the annual festival here in July. Worth the trip.

⚓ **Historic Warehouse District,** W. 3rd St. to W. 10th St. between Superior Ave. and Front St. (344-3937): The city's former warehouse and garment district downtown features a cluster of newly restored 19th-century buildings, boutiques, restaurants, and antiques galleries. A walk not to be missed.

⚓ **Little Italy,** around Mayfield Rd. and Murray Hill Rd.: This traditional Italian neighborhood has become home to artists' studios, fine-arts galleries, restaurants, cafés, and bakeries. Check out the Murray Hill Market, 2181 Murray Hill Rd. (791-9679), for crafts, and the 2026 Galleries Building, 2026 Murray Hill Rd. (421-9000), a school-turned-gallery space. Worth a look.

⚓ **Ohio City,** around Lorain Ave. and W. 25th St.: Cleveland's old middle-class neighborhood, with fine Victorian houses, many antiques shops, and restaurants.

☀⚓ **Shaker Heights,** around N. Park Blvd. and Eaton Rd.: One of the country's plushest residential areas, with splendid, tree-shaded Tudor and Georgian turn-of-the-century homes. Take a look.

THEME PARKS: ☀⚓ **Cedar Point Amusement Park,** near Sandusky (50 mi./ 80km west on U.S. 90/250) (419/626-0830): On Lake Erie, this huge amusement park offers among its 55 attractions nine roller coasters, including the world's highest (201 ft./61m) and fastest (70 m.p.h./113kmph), the Magnum XL-200, plus a zoo, aquarium, beach, restaurants, and marina. Open daily mid-May to the end of Sept.

On the way back, see the ⚓ **Birthplace-Museum of Thomas Edison,** 9

Edison Dr., in Milan (17 mi./27km farther south) (419/499-2135): Residence-turned-museum in memory of the great inventor. Open Tues–Sun Feb–Nov.

   ⚓ **Geauga Lake Park,** Ohio 43 near Aurora (26 mi./42km SE) (562-7131): 280-acre (113ha) amusement park featuring a wave pool, water slides, 85 rides, and four roller coasters including the Raging Wolf Bobs, a wooden coaster covering 25 acres (10ha) and offering a 2-min. ride. Spectacular. Open daily Memorial Day to Labor Day, wkends only in May.

   ⚓ **Sea World,** 11000 Sea World Dr., in Aurora (23 mi./37km SE on Ohio 43) (216/562-8101): An enormous marine-life zoo in the middle of an 80-acre (32ha) park, with sea lions, elephant seals, dolphins, and killer whales. Spectacular animal shows. Open daily May–Oct.

WINTER SPORTS RESORTS: ⚓ **Alpine Valley,** 10620 Mayfield Rd., in Chesterland (30 mi./48km east on U.S. 322): Five chair lifts. For information, call 216/285-2211.

ACCOMMODATIONS

   A Note on Accommodations: Room rates in Cleveland are coded as follows: **VE,** Very Expensive ($140 and up); **E,** Expensive ($90–$140); **M,** Moderate ($60–$90); **I,** Inexpensive ($30–$60); **B,** Budget (up to $30). A listing of toll free numbers is in the Appendix.

Personal Favorites (in order of preference)

   ♟♟♟ **Ritz Carlton** (dwntwn), Tower City Center, W. 3rd St., OH 44113 (216/736-7171; toll free, see Ritz Carlton). 207 rms, A/C, color TV, in-rm movies. AE, CB, DC, MC, V. Gar. $6, pool, health club, rest. (The Grill), coffee shop, bar, 24-hr. rm svce, nightclub, concierge. *Note:* This brand-new palace hotel, occupying the top nine floors of an ultramodern office building towering over the Cuyahoga River, is the most luxurious and comfortable hotel in a city somewhat deficient in this respect. Remarkably comfortable rms w. marble bathrooms and minibars; personalized svce; very acceptable rest. Conveniently located in the heart of the business district. VIP floor; big-business clientele. **VE**

   ♟♟ **The Clinic Center Hotel** (nr. dwntwn), 2065 E. 96th St., OH 44106 (216/791-1900; toll free 800/321-7100). 348 rms, A/C, color TV, in-rm movies. AE, CB, DC, MC, V. Free valet parking, pool, rest. (Classics), coffee shop, bar, 24-hr. rm svce, concierge, free crib. *Note:* This modern hotel is 10 min. from dwntwn and a few steps from the Cleveland Clinic. It offers spacious, inviting rms and a very satisfactory Olde English tavern–style rest. Especially attentive svce. **E**

   ♟♟ **Sheraton City Center** (formerly the Bond Court; dwntwn), 777 St. Clair Ave., OH 44114 (216/771-7600; toll free, see Sheraton). 480 rms, A/C, color TV, in-rm movies. AE, CB, DC, MC, V. Gar. $5, rest., coffee shop, two bars, rm svce, free crib. *Note:* Relatively modern, 22-story tower offering comfortable rms (the best have a view of Lake Erie) and good svce. Business clientele. Adjacent to the Convention Center in the heart of the business district. Three VIP floors. No-smoking rms. Recently renovated. **E**

   ☼♟♟ **Glidden House** (nr. dwntwn), 1901 Ford Dr., OH 44106 (216/231-8900). 60 rms, A/C, cable color TV. AE, CB, DC, MC, V. Free parking; no bar or rest.; valet svce, free buffet breakfast, free crib. *Note:* Once the private house of the famous Glidden paint-making family, this vaguely French-Gothic turn-of-the-century mansion was made over into a comfortable inn in 1989. Eight inviting suites and 52 rms in a new wing. Soothing, discreet atmosphere, but svce still a trifle undependable. Conveniently located in the heart of the University Circle district, 10 min. from dwntwn. **M–E**

♀♀ **Budget Inns of America** (formerly Howard Johnson's; vic.),
14043 Brookpark Rd., OH 44142 (216/267-2350). 115 rms,
A/C, cable color TV. AE, CB, DC, MC, V. Free parking, coffee shop, bar, rm
svce, free crib. *Note:* A very good value, this relatively modern motel is quite convenient to the international airport and offers vast rms w. private patios or balconies and efficient, if hardly cheerful, svce. 8 min. from the airport and 20 min.
from dwntwn. Ideal for the motorist. **I**

Other Accommodations (from top bracket to budget)

♀♀♀ **Radisson Plaza Hotel** (dwntwn), 1701 E. 12th St., OH 44114
(216/523-8000; toll free, see Radisson). 252 suites, A/C, color TV, in-rm movies. AE, CB, DC, MC, V. Gar. $5, pool, health club, two tennis
courts, sauna, rest., bar, rm svce, free breakfast, free crib. *Note:* Opened in July
1990 as a component of the new Reserve Square Center, a 23-floor complex occupying an entire dwntwn block, this hotel comprises spacious, well-designed
suites, each w. microwave oven, refrigerator, and marble bathroom. Impeccable
comfort, ultra-professional svce. With its very central location it attracts mainly
business travelers, and has a VIP floor. **E–VE**

☼♀♀♀ **Stouffer Tower City Plaza** (dwntwn), 24 Public Sq., OH
44113 (216/696-5600; toll free, see Stouffers). 500 rms,
A/C, color TV, in-rm movies. AE, CB, DC, MC, V. Gar. $6, pool, health club,
two rests. (including the French Connection), coffee shop, two bars, rm svce,
nightclub, concierge, free crib. *Note:* Located in the heart of Cleveland, this old
luxury hotel has undergone a $24-million renovation. It offers generally comfortable, spacious rms (some are entirely renovated, others merely adequate) w.
private patios; impersonal reception and svce; well-regarded rest.; superb art deco
pool and a spectacular 10-story atrium. Group and convention clientele; three
VIP floors. **E–VE**

♀♀ **Holiday Inn Lakeside** (dwntwn), 1111 Lakeside Ave. (at E.
12th St.), OH 44114 (216/241-5100; toll free, see Holiday
Inns). 370 rms, A/C, color TV, in-rm movies. AE, CB, DC, MC, V. Free parking, pool, health club, sauna, rest., coffee shop, bar, 24-hr. rm svce, nightclub,
free crib. *Note:* Modern 18-story building w. an unobstructed view of the city
and of Lake Erie. Very satisfying comfort, Holiday Inn style. Groups and business clientele. Three VIP floors. Two blocks from the Convention Center. **M–E**

♀♀ **Quality Hotel Beachwood** (formerly the Beachwood Inn;
vic.), 26300 Chagrin Blvd., Beachwood, OH 44122 (216/
831-5150; toll free, see Quality Inns). 199 rms, A/C, color TV, in-rm movies.
AE, CB, DC, MC, V. Free parking, pool, health club, rest., bar, rm svce, disco,
free crib. *Note:* Appealing, comfortable hotel on the outskirts of the smart residential suburb of Shaker Heights. Good facilities; pleasant, recently renovated
rms; efficient svce. Located nr. a number of corporate head offices, it attracts business travelers and (since it offers direct access to the highway system) those traveling by car. 25 min. from dwntwn. **M–E**

♀♀ **Lakefront Plaza** (nr. dwntwn), 5700 S. Marginal Rd., OH
44103 (216/432-2220). 200 rms. A/C, color TV, in-rm
movies. AE, CB, DC, MC, V. Free parking, pool, sauna, tennis, rest., bar, valet
svce. *Note:* Modern and inviting motel 5 min. from dwntwn. Functional, comfortable rms (most with view of Lake Erie). Good svce. Rest. poor. Business clientele. Overall good value. **I–M**

♀ **Travelodge Beachwood** (vic.), 3795 Orange Pl., Beachwood,
OH 44122 (216/831-7200; toll free, see Travelodge). 128
rms, A/C, color TV, in-rm movies. AE, CB, DC, MC, V. Free parking, adjacent
coffee shop, free breakfast, free crib. *Note:* A convenient, well-kept motel not far
from chic Shaker Heights. 25 min. from dwntwn. Ideal for motorists. **I**

♀ **Motel 6** (vic.), 7219 Eagle Rd., Middleburg Heights, OH
44130 (216/234-0990). 95 rms, A/C, color TV, in-rm mov-

ies. AE, DC, MC, V. Free parking. *Note:* Small economy motel 5 min. by car from Hopkins International Airport. Unpretentious but up-to-date; friendly reception. Ideal if you're on a budget. **B**

Airport Accommodations

♀♀ **Sheraton Hopkins Airport** (vic.), 5300 Riverside Dr., OH 44135 (216/267-1500; toll free, see Sheraton). 416 rms, A/C, color TV, in-rm movies. AE, CB, DC, MC, V. Free parking, pool, health club, sauna, rest. (Port Brittany), coffee shop, bar, rm svce, nightclub, concierge, free crib. *Note:* A grand hotel w. immediate access to the airport terminal. Spacious, comfortable rms w. private patios or balconies. The facilities are very complete, the svce efficient. Free airport shuttle. Very adequate rest. Business clientele. VIP floor. **E–VE**

♀ **Holiday Inn Cleveland Airport** (vic.), 4181 W. 150th St., OH 44135 (216/252-7700; toll free, see Holiday Inns). 144 rms, A/C, color TV. AE, CB, DC, MC, V. Free parking, pool, rest., bar, valet svce, free crib. *Note:* Classic but comfortable five-story motel w. relatively spacious rms and agreeable reception and svce. 5 min. from the airport (free shuttle) and 20 min. from dwntwn. A good overall value. **I–M**

RESTAURANTS

A Note on Restaurant Prices: Cleveland restaurant prices, per person, excluding drinks and service charges, are coded as follows: **VE**, Very Expensive ($60 and up); **E**, Expensive ($40–$60); **M**, Moderate ($25–$40); **I**, Inexpensive ($15–$25); **B**, Budget (up to $15).

Personal Favorites (in order of preference)

♀♀♀ **Z Contemporary Cuisine** (nr. dwntwn), 20600 Chagrin Blvd., Shaker Heights (991-1580). A/C. Dinner only, Mon–Sat. AE, MC, V. Jkt. *Specialties:* veal medallions w. caramelized soy sauce, risotto w. porcini mushrooms in madeira sauce, salmon w. golden caviar and lobster roe. Rich desserts. The menu changes weekly. Remarkable wine list reasonably priced. *Note:* Critics may dislike the minimalist white decor, highlighted by abstract art, of this stark dining rm on the ground floor of a high-rise office building designed by Walter Gropius. But the menu of chef and owner, Zachary Bruell, adds a welcome sophistication to the locally standard upscale cuisine. The menu includes a variety of grilled entrées, all in California styling. The service is reliable and gracious. Resv. essential. *American.* **M–E**

♀♀♀ **Ristorante Giovanni** (vic.), 25550 Chagrin Blvd., Beachwood (831-8625). A/C. Lunch Mon–Fri, dinner Mon–Sat; closed hols. AE, CB, DC, MC, V. Jkt. *Specialties:* figs and prosciutto; fresh homemade pasta; linguine w. clam sauce; veal chop milanese; swordfish sautéed w. pine nuts, mussels, and white wine; sweetbreads alla Toscana. Fine list of Italian and California wines. *Note:* Nobody would dispute that this is the best of Cleveland's many Italian rests.; the totally authentic menu emphasizes seafood. Elegant setting; flawless svce. At a place so successful resv. are a must. *Italian.* **I–M**

♀♀ **That Place on Bellflower** (nr. dwntwn), 11401 Bellflower Rd. (231-4469). A/C. Lunch Mon–Sat, dinner nightly; closed hols. AE, DC, MC, V. Jkt. *Specialties:* turbot St-Germain, roast duck, veal Oscar, Renaissance salmon, scallops remoulade, good desserts. Fine wine list. *Note:* Eclectic, French-inspired cuisine (as its fleur-de-lys, or bellflower, requires) in a former coaching inn that has been elegantly restored. The menu changes periodically. Very good svce. Open-air dinner in summer. Romantic atmosphere. Resv. advised. *French/Continental.* **I–M**

♀♀ **Shujiro** (vic.), 2206 Lee Rd., Cleveland Heights (321-0210). A/C. Lunch Mon–Fri, dinner nightly; closed hols. MC, V. *Specialties:* sashimi, tempura, sushi, fried soft-shell crabs, grilled eel kabayaki.

Note: The best local representative of Japanese cuisine, and one of Cleveland's most highly regarded spots. Modern decor of exposed woodwork and a dining rm where one can eat Western-style or on tatami mats. Chef Hiroshi Tsuji blends Japanese simplicity and classicism w. French and Chinese influences. The kimono-clad servers are exceptionally attentive. Resv. advised. 20 min. from dwntwn. *Japanese.* **I**

Great Lakes Brewing Co. (nr. dwntwn), 2516 Market St. (771-4404). A/C. Lunch/dinner Mon–Sat (until midnight). AE, DC, MC, V. *Specialties:* homemade soup, salads, sandwiches, meat and cheese pies, daily specials, draft beer. *Note:* Ohio's first (and so far only) microbrewery, occupying a 19th-century warehouse, serves both its widely respected draft beers—Heismann (light) and Elliott's Amber (dark)—in this English-style pub. Good sandwiches and daily specials in a congenial setting which allows for open-air meals during the summer. Patrons are a mixed bag from yuppies to blue-collar workers. Resv. accepted but often unnecessary. *American.* **B–I**

The Mad Greek (nr. dwntwn), 2466 Fairmount Blvd., Cleveland Heights (421-3333). A/C. Lunch Mon–Sat, dinner nightly (until midnight); closed hols. AE, DC, MC, V. *Specialties:* moussaka, stuffed grape leaves, mezedakia, pita, kebabs, and everything in between—the food and Greek wine here are truly authentic. Limited but interesting wine list. *Note:* An enjoyable ambience in a rustic patio setting enveloped by whitewashed walls and a profusion of greenery. It offers agreeable Greek cuisine at low prices as well as some very good Indian dishes: tikka chicken, curries (the owner is Indian and his wife Greek). Friendly, cheerful svce. Locally popular. *Greek.* **B–I**

Other Restaurants (from top bracket to budget)

French Connection (dwntwn), in the Stouffer Tower City Plaza (see "Accommodations," above) (696-5600). A/C. Lunch/dinner daily, brunch Sun; closed hols. AE, CB, DC, MC, V. J&T. *Specialties:* lobster bisque, sweetbread ravioli w. saffron, poached salmon w. vermouth, rack of lamb in pastry shell, roast veal w. grapefruit, suprême of lobster and poultry in pistou dressing, remarkable desserts. Fine list of French and California wines at sometimes excessive prices. *Note:* Far and away the most elegant and most luxurious rest. in Cleveland, the French Connection has been called one of the 10 most romantic rests. in the country in a *USA Today* poll: paintings by the masters, period furniture, pastel tones, and windows that give a view of Public Sq. Irreproachable luxury-hotel cuisine and first-rate svce. Resv. a must. *French.* **M–E**

Sammy's (dwntwn), 1400 W. 10th St. (523-5560). A/C. Lunch/dinner Mon–Sat; closed hols. AE, CB, DC, MC, V. J&T. *Specialties:* sautéed sweetbreads w. pecans and madeira, pork medallion w. red cabbage, marinated mushrooms stuffed w. scallops, grilled tuna w. warm tomato vinaigrette. The menu changes regularly. Remarkable desserts (particularly the boule de neige). Outstanding wine list. *Note:* In an old warehouse on the Cuyahoga River, this fashionable rest. offers elegant, inventive cuisine and modern decor of exposed brick and large bay windows w. a view of the river. The svce is exemplary, the ambience rather noisy, and the clientele hip. Resv. a must, given its success. Valet parking. *American/Continental.* **M**

Burgess Grand Café (dwntwn), 1406 W. 6th St. (574-2232). A/C. Breakfast Mon–Fri, lunch/dinner daily, brunch Sun. AE, MC, V. Jkt. (J&T Sat evening). *Specialties:* black pasta w. calamari and marinara sauce, poached eggs w. chicken livers and madeira sauce, sautéed sweetbreads w. Pommery mustard sauce, grilled chicken w. sun-dried tomatoes, good homemade desserts. Interesting list of wines at reasonable prices. *Note:* Engaging café from a bygone era, housed in an elegantly renovated older building in the warehouse district. Imaginative, often inspired cuisine, generous helpings, excellent svce. Also live jazz Wed, Fri, and Sat. A splendid place, popular enough that you should reserve ahead. In the heart of dwntwn. *American.* **I–M**

Guarino's (nr. dwntwn), 12309 Mayfield Rd. (231-3100). A/C. Lunch/dinner Mon–Sat; closed hols. AE, CB, DC, MC, V. Jkt. *Specialties:* fettuccine Alfredo, cannelloni, snails marinara, veal marsala, very good grilled fish. Good list of Italian wines. *Note:* Since 1918 this *trattoria* in the heart of Little Italy has been a local institution. A favorite of musicians and fans of the Cleveland Symphony Orchestra (Severance Hall is nearby), the rest. offers al fresco dining in the patio in summer. Prompt, friendly svce. 10 min. from dwntwn. *Italian.* **I**

Pearl of the Orient (nr. dwntwn), 20121 Van Aken Blvd., Shaker Heights (751-8181). A/C. Lunch Mon–Fri, dinner nightly; closed Thanksgiving, Dec 25. AE, CB, DC, MC, V. *Specialties:* mu shu pork, hot-and-sour soup, Mongolian duck, steamed fish, beef Szechuan. *Note:* Entirely authentic Chinese cuisine in a rather cold modern decor w. Far Eastern artwork. Attentive svce. Locally popular. Resv. advised. 15 min. from dwntwn. *Chinese.* **I**

James Tavern (vic.), 28699 Chagrin Blvd., Woodmere Village (464-4660). A/C. Lunch/dinner daily, brunch Sun. AE, CB, DC, MC, V. *Specialties:* roast beef, roast pork Savannah, chicken parmesan, veal madeira, fish of the day. *Note:* Warm, pleasant atmosphere of an old colonial tavern w. large fireplaces and old furniture. The very reasonably priced food is more substantial than refined. Friendly, efficient svce; hearty portions. Locally popular. Resv. advised. 25 min. from dwntwn. *American.* **B–I**

Balaton (vic.), 12523 Buckeye Rd. (921-9691). A/C. Lunch/dinner Tues–Sat (until 9pm). No credit cards. *Specialties:* goulash, paprika chicken, wienerschnitzel, stuffed cabbage, palacsinta, dobos torte. Hungarian wine and beer, but no hard liquor. *Note:* Exceptionally tasty Hungarian and German cuisine served in a Formica-and-paper-napkins setting. More than generous portions at very modest prices. A favorite rest. of Cleveland's large Hungarian community. *Continental/German.* **B–I**

Hofbrau Haus (nr. dwntwn), 1400 E. 55th St. (881-7773). A/C. Lunch Mon–Fri, dinner nightly. AE, DC, MC, V. *Specialties:* bratwurst, wienerschnitzel, pork hocks. Good wine list. *Note:* The best German rest. in all of Cleveland. Authentic Germanic cuisine and ambience in a fairly noisy atmosphere, w. dancing on wknds. Offers buffet or à la carte dishes. Locally popular. Resv. advised. *German.* **B–I**

Miller's Dining Room (nr. dwntwn), 16707 Detroit Ave., Lakewood (221-5811). A/C. Lunch/dinner daily (until 8pm); closed Memorial Day, July 4, Labor Day. No credit cards. *Specialties:* chicken à la king, veal chop Créole, roast pork, braised leg of lamb, excellent homemade tarts and desserts. *Note:* The most authentic home-cooking in Cleveland at prices you won't believe. The decor is 1930s-retro, and the servers seem to be of that era as well. Generous portions and a relaxed atmosphere. A remarkable value. Regular clientele. An address to remember. 10 min. from dwntwn. **B–I**

Cafeterias/Fast Food/Specialty Spots

Corky & Lenny's (vic.), 13937 Cedar Rd., South Euclid (321-3310). Breakfast/lunch/dinner daily (until midnight). No credit cards. *Specialties:* superb sandwiches, homemade soup, smoked fish, and salads. *Note:* There is no decor to speak of in this very popular, rather noisy local hangout. 20 min. from dwntwn. Other location: 27091 Chagrin Blvd. (U.S. 422) in Woodmere (464-3838). Open Tues–Sun.

Shorty's Delux Diner (dwntwn), 1540 Columbus Rd. (621-5321): Amusing replica of a 1950s diner, including gum-snapping waitresses and authentic Seeburg jukeboxes full of oldies. Good hamburgers, sandwiches, and malts. No credit cards. Lunch and dinner daily, *American Graffiti* revisited.

BARS & NIGHTCLUBS

Aquilon (dwntwn), 1575 Merwin Ave. (781-1575). A well-established club located on the fourth floor of an old warehouse. Features dancing in a stylish decor and a great view of the Cuyahoga River. Open Wed–Sun.

Club Coconuts (dwntwn), 1148 Main Ave. (579-9960). The hot new dance club—$4-million, high-tech computer-operated light and sound effects, and a 400-person dance floor. Open nightly.

Club Isabella (nr. dwntwn), 2025 Abington Rd. (229-1177). Open daily. Very popular nightclub a few steps from the university. The decor is a pleasing blend of art deco and contemporary styles. Excellent live jazz. Rather chic atmosphere.

Euclid Tavern (nr. dwntwn), 11629 Euclid Ave. (229-7788). This neighborhood-style bar in the University Circle area is the place to go for serious rock and blues. Open nightly.

Improv Comedy Club (dwntwn), 2000 Sycamore St. (696-4677). Located in the renovated Powerhouse, this new comedy club features top comedians on national tours. Also rest. Resv. recommended. Open nightly.

Peabody's Café (nr. dwntwn), 2140 S. Taylor Rd., Cleveland Heights (321-4072). Folk music and blues live Tues–Sat. 20 min. from dwntwn.

The Theatrical Grille (dwntwn), 711 Vincent Ave. (241-6166). Open Mon–Sat. Singles bar, shows, live jazz.

NEARBY EXCURSIONS

CANTON (55 mi./88km south on I-77): Home of former President William McKinley (the 25th president is entombed at 7th St. NW), this major industrial center on the edge of "Steel Valley" houses the ✳🔔 **Pro Football Hall of Fame,** 2121 George Halas Dr. NW (456-8207). There, the gridiron devotee can trace history of the national sport, from early pro teams like the Canton Bulldogs (led by the legendary Jim Thorpe) to the current Super Bowl champs. Under the football-shaped dome, a 350-seat theater runs a different action movie every hour highlighting great teams and great games. Museum store. Well worth the detour. Open daily.

On your way back, don't miss a visit to the ✳🔔 **Stan Hywet Hall and Gardens** in **Akron,** "the rubber capital of the world." Listed in the National Register of Historic Places, this 65-room manor house built in 1911–15 by Frank A. Sciberling, founder of the Goodyear Rubber Co., is considered one of the finest examples of Tudor Revival architecture in the United States. Many antiques and art treasures dating from the 14th century. Magnificent grdns with flower displays in spring and fall. Should be seen. Open Tues–Sun.

CUYAHOGA VALLEY RAILROAD (departure from 6311 Granger, at the intersection of Ohio 17 and 21 in Independence, south of Cleveland): An amusing, pleasing trip in a little steam-engine train along the picturesque Cuyahoga Valley to **Hale Farm** (see below) and **Akron** (see above). Runs wknds only, mid-June to mid-Oct. For information, call 216/657-2000.

HALE FARM & WESTERN RESERVE VILLAGE (in Bath, 24 mi./38km south on I-77, Bath Rd. exit) (216/575-9137): Small, carefully restored pioneer town from the early 19th century offers pottery making and other period craft demonstrations. Well worth the trip. Open Tues–Sun May–Oct and in Dec.

KELLEYS ISLAND (50 mi./80km west on U.S. 6, then by ferry): This charming little vacation island on Lake Erie gets very crowded in summer. Fishing, sailing, camping, beaches, etc. Accessible by ferry from Sandusky (runs daily Apr–Nov; call 419/626-5557 for schedule information). Worth a visit. This makes a good joint excursion with Cedar Point (see "Theme Parks," above).

KIRTLAND (22 mi./35km NE on I-90): Site of the oldest Mormon temple in the country (1836), Kirtland was the place where the westward-bound Mormons made their first stop (see Chapter 31 on Salt Lake City). The temple, at 9020 Chillicothe Rd. in Kirtland Village, is open daily. Worth a look.

CHAPTER 22

CINCINNATI ⚲

□ □ □

Following the Roman example, Cincinnati is built around the terraced slopes of seven hills, on the northern bank of the Ohio River where it borders Kentucky and Indiana. Founded in 1788 as Losantiville, it was renamed Cincinnati in 1790 by Gov. Arthur St. Clair in honor of the Order of Cincinnati, a brotherhood founded in 1783 by Revolutionary War army officers who admired the famous Roman hero Lucius Quinctius Cincinnatus.

A Native American way-station before the region was settled, Cincinnati became an important hub of rail, river, and road communication in the 19th century. Despite seven cholera epidemics in less than a century and many catastrophic floods and disastrous harvests, tens of thousands of German and Irish immigrants, as well as a host of notable visitors—Charles Dickens, Harriet Beecher Stowe, John Audubon, Henry Clay, and John Quincy Adams—have helped to make Cincinnati the third-largest city in Ohio and the "queen city of the West," in the words of the poet Longfellow.

The home of many large multinational corporations, including Procter & Gamble, Cincinnati is today one of the most dynamic commercial and industrial urban centers in the Midwest. The friendliness of its inhabitants and their taste for good food, music, and the arts make it one of the five or six most pleasant U.S. cities in which to live, according to polls. Once described by Winston Churchill as the most beautiful city of the American heartland, Cincinnati boasts a symphony orchestra of acknowledged reputation and two well-respected universities, but few praiseworthy monuments. In contrast to many other midwestern cities, Cincinnati has made it a point of honor to preserve the original character of the downtown district and the **Riverfront** area along the Ohio, investing many millions of dollars in architectural renovation and in the construction of a vast, enclosed pedestrian walkway network, the **Skywalk System,** which connects old buildings with new downtown skyscrapers.

On a more prosaic note, Cincinnati was known as "Porkopolis" and the "pork capital of the U.S.A." because of its important meatpacking industry. It now prefers to proclaim itself "the world capital of baseball," having produced the country's first professional baseball team, the Red Stockings in 1869, now called the Red Sox. Food-lovers won't want to miss another local specialty, the famous five-way chili, pride of Cincinnati since 1922: spaghetti smothered in ground beef, onions, beans, and cheese.

Some native children of Cincinnati are William Howard Taft, 27th U.S. president; actors Tyrone Power and Doris Day; ballerina Suzanne Farrell; orchestra conductor James Levine; and director/producer Steven Spielberg.

BASIC FACTS: State of Ohio. Area code: 513. Time zone: eastern. ZIP Code: 45202. Settled: 1788. Approximate population: city, 360,000; metropolitan area, 1,750,000. 22nd-largest metropolitan area in the country.

CLIMATE: A raincoat and umbrella are *de rigueur* in any season in Cincinnati. Winter is cold (around 32°F/0°C, in Jan) and damp; summer is hot and sticky (average July temperature: 76° F/24° C). Spring and autumn are the less soggy seasons and the most pleasant for visitors.

DISTANCES: Chicago, 290 mi. (465km); Cleveland, 247 mi. (395km); Detroit, 259 mi. (415km); Nashville, 269 mi. (430km); Philadelphia, 565 mi. (905km).

ARRIVAL & TRANSIT INFORMATION

AIRPORT: Greater Cincinnati International Airport (CVG): 13 mi. (21km) SW. Information: 606/283-3151.

AIRLINES: American (621-6200), Continental (381-8020), Delta (721-7000), Northwest (toll free 800/225-2525), TWA (381-1600), United (721-3303), and USAir (621-9220).

CITY LINK: Cab fare to city center, about $22; time, around 25 min. Bus: **Jetport Express** (606/283-3702); leaves about every 30 min.; serves principal dwntwn hotels; fare, $8; time, about 35 min. Because corporate offices are dispersed throughout the Cincinnati suburbs, businesspeople may want to rent a car, but because of the compact layout of the city itself, tourists can easily do without. Good public transportation system (bus), Queen City Metro (621-4455).

CAR RENTAL (at the airport unless otherwise indicated): Avis (606/283-3764); Budget (606/283-3131); Dollar (606/283-3571); Hertz (606/283-3535); National (606/283-3655); Thrifty, 596 Petersburg Rd., Hebron (606/689-5200). For dwntwn locations, consult the phone directory.

LIMOUSINE SERVICES: Carey Limousine (531-7321), Dav El Limousines (toll free 800/922-0343).

TAXIS: Taxis may not be hailed on the street but can be gotten by waiting on line in front of the major hotels or can be summoned by phone: **Yellow Cab** (241-2100).

TRAIN: Amtrak station, 1901 River Rd. (579-8506).

INTERCITY BUSES: Greyhound, 1005 Gilbert Ave. (352-6000).

INFORMATION & TOURS

TOURIST INFORMATION: The **Cincinnati Convention & Visitors Bureau,** 300 W. 6th St., OH 45202 (513/621-2142).
   For a **recorded announcement** with an up-to-date listing of cultural events and shows, call 513/421-4636.

GUIDED TOURS: B.B. Riverboats (boat), at the end of Greenup St., Covington, Ky. (across the river by suspension bridge) (606/261-8500): Ohio River cruises, year round.
   Gray Line (bus), 122A W. 5th St. (513/241-8000): Guided tours of the city.

STERNWHEELER RIVER CRUISES: 3- and 10-day cruises along the Mississippi and Ohio Rivers on the *Delta Queen* or the *Mississippi Queen* paddle-steamers dating from the 1920s. Luxurious kitsch. (See Chapter 15 on New Orleans.)

SIGHTS, ATTRACTIONS & ACTIVITIES

ADVENTURES: Balloons Unlimited (balloon), 508 Greenup St., Covington, Ky. (across the river by suspension bridge) (606/581-6966): Hot-air balloon flights over the Cincinnati countryside. Daily departures (weather permitting) from the northern Kentucky riverfront. Transportation to the launch site available. Resv. needed. Spectacular.

ARCHITECTURAL HIGHLIGHTS: 🛢 City Hall, 801 Plum St. at 8th St. (352-3000): Imposing Romanesque city hall in pink granite. Its large marble staircase, stained-glass windows, and ceiling decoration are worth a look. Open Mon–Fri.

🛢 **Hamilton County Courthouse,** 1000 Main St. (632-8331): One of the largest law libraries in the country housed in a fine example of Ionic-style architecture. Open Mon–Fri.

🛢 **Procter & Gamble Headquarters,** Procter & Gamble Plaza: Twin 24-story postmodernist towers designed by the renowned architecture firm of Kohn, Pedersen, Fox (1985). Dominates two-block-long stretches of beautiful gardens. No visits allowed. Worth a glance.

🛢 **Riverfront Stadium,** 201 E. Pete Roseway (352-6333): The local shrine for baseball and football fans (60,000 seats). Superb location on the Ohio River. Open Apr–Jan.

🔆🛢 **Union Terminal,** 1301 Western Ave. (421-5650): No longer in use, this splendid art deco train station by Roland Wank (1931) has some very lovely wall mosaics and a huge rotunda. Currently undergoing reconstruction, the terminal will house the Museum of Natural History and the Cincinnati Historical Society beginning in 1991.

CHURCHES/SYNAGOGUES: 🔆🛢 Basilica of the Assumption, Madison Ave. and 12th St., Covington, Ky. (606/431-2060): A kind of small-scale pastiche of Notre-Dame in Paris (or the nearby Cathedral of St. Denis), with flying buttresses and gargoyles in the purest French Gothic style. Dating from 1901, this basilica has one of the largest stained-glass windows in the world. On the other side of the Ohio River. Open daily.

🔆🛢 **Isaac M. Wise Temple,** 8th St. and Plum St. (793-2556): Built in 1865, this synagogue, in startling Byzantine-Moorish style topped with two minarets, is named for the founder of the Hebrew Union College (see "Historic Buildings," below). Visits by appointment. Don't miss it.

🔆🛢 **St. Peter in Chains Cathedral,** 8th St. and Plum St. (421-5354): Seat of the archdiocese of Cincinnati, this 1845 cathedral, renovated in the late 1950s, has interesting Greek Revival architecture and a portico supported by 12 Corinthian columns. Striking interior decor and a gold crucifix by the famous Renaissance sculptor Benvenuto Cellini. An absolute must-see. Open daily.

HISTORIC BUILDINGS: 🛢 Hebrew Union College, 3101 Clifton Ave. (221-1875): The oldest rabbinical school in the country (1875). Historical library and an interesting museum of archeology and religious art. Open Sun–Fri.

🔆🛢 **Music Hall,** 1241 Elm St. (621-1919): One of the most famous concert halls in the country, renowned for its exceptional acoustics, it is home to the Cincinnati Symphony Orchestra and the May Festival. Rich interior decoration and very lovely Victorian architecture from 1878.

⚓ **Showboat *Majestic*,** Public Landing on the Ohio River at the foot of Broadway: The last floating theater in the country, this authentic showboat is a historic landmark. For information on current shows, call 241-6550; Apr–Oct.

⚓ **Suspension Bridge,** joining Cincinnati and Covington, Ky., across the Ohio River: Designed by John Roebling, this work of art was, at the time of its construction (opened 1876), the longest suspension bridge in the world. It also served as the model for the famous Brooklyn Bridge in New York, opened 16 years later. Presents a pretty view of the Cincinnati skyline.

⚓ **William H. Taft National Historic Site,** 2038 Auburn Ave. (684-3262): Birthplace of the 27th president, this elegantly restored building dates from 1840. Open daily.

MARKETS: ⚓ **Findlay Market,** Race St. and Elder St.: Picturesque open-air market dating from 1852. A bastion of local gastronomy. Open Wed–Thurs and Sat.

MONUMENTS: ⚓ **Tyler Davidson Fountain,** Fountain Sq.: This bronze fountain was cast in Munich in 1871 and is now the city's emblem. Especially worth a look at night when it's illuminated.

MUSEUMS OF ART: ☼⚓ **Art Museum,** Art Museum Dr. in Eden Park (721-5204): Greek Revival building dating from 1887 housing very rich collections of European paintings, especially impressionists and abstract painters. Among the best-known works: El Greco's *Christ on the Cross,* Gainsborough's *Portrait of Mrs. Thicknesse,* Cézanne's *Blue Still Life,* Gris's *Violin and Score,* Sargent's *Italian Girl,* Matisse's *The Gray Hat,* and Chagall's *The Red Chicken.* Large collection of Persian and medieval art as well. An absolute must-see. Open Tues– Sun.

⚓ **Contemporary Arts Center,** 115 E. 5th St. (721-0390): On the second floor of the **Mercantile Center Building** with its very lovely arcade, this wonderful museum offers temporary exhibitions and events dedicated to modern art in every form, especially works by regional artists. Open Tues–Sun.

⚓ **Taft Museum,** 316 Pike St. (241-0343): European masters (Turner, Goya, Rembrandt, van Dyck, Corot) and Chinese and Limoges porcelain in a beautiful Federal-style upper-class residence, dating from 1820, once owned by President Taft's half-brother. See it. Open daily.

MUSEUMS OF SCIENCE & HISTORY: ⚓ **Cincinnati Fire Museum,** 315 W. Court St. (621-5553): Portrays the history of firefighting since 1808. "Hands-on" displays, firefighting artifacts. Housed in a restored firehouse (1907). Interesting. Open Tues–Sun.

☼⚓ **Museum of Natural History,** 1720 Gilbert Ave. (621-3889): Remarkable reproductions of Native American dwellings and an astonishing artificial cavern with waterfalls. Exhibits of local fauna and flora as well as a planetarium. One of the best natural history museums in the country. Don't miss it. Open Tues–Sun. The museum will move to Union Terminal (see "Architectural Highlights," above) in 1991.

⚓ **Stowe House,** 2950 Gilbert Ave. (632-5120): Harriet Beecher Stowe, author of *Uncle Tom's Cabin,* lived here while she was doing the documentary research for her famous novel. Interesting exhibition of African American history. Open Tues–Thurs.

CINCINNATI

to Stowe House

BOAL ST.
MILTON ST.
YOUNG ST.
HIGHLAND AVE
LIBERTY HILL
READING RD
ELSINORE PL.
PENDLETON ST
GILBERT AVE
71
N

Museum of
Natural History

Art
Museum

Eden
Park

Playhouse
in the Park

ELSINORE AVE
IDA ST.
WAREHAM DR.
VAN METER ST.
MONASTERY ST.
ST. GREGORY ST.
PAVILLION ST.
OREGON ST.
BAUM ST.
KILGOUR ST.
HILL ST.
CARNEY ST.
HATCH ST.
PARADROME ST.
PARKSIDE PL.

EGGLESTON AVE
CULVERT ST.
71
SENTINEL ST.
COLUMBIA VIADUCT
EASTERN AVE

Riverview
Park

Taft
Museum
BUTLER ST.
PIKE ST.
Lytle
Park

PETE ROSE WAY
FRONT ST.

Riverfront
Coliseum

OHIO RIVER

☼🔔 **Vent Haven Museum,** 33 W. Maple Ave., Fort Mitchell, Ky. (606/341-0461): Marvelous museum entirely dedicated to the arts of puppetry and ventriloquism. Nearly 600 marionettes on display and a very rich specialized library. Unusual and wonderful. Visit by appointment Mon–Fri May–Sept.

PANORAMAS: 🔔 **Carew Tower Observatory,** 5th St. and Vine St. (381-3448): Fine panorama of the city from the top of this 48-story (560-ft./175m) art deco tower, Cincinnati's tallest building. Open Mon–Sat May–Aug, Tues–Sat the rest of the year.

🔔 **Skywalk System,** 16 blocks around the Convention Center and Fountain Sq.: Network of elevated enclosed walkways connecting major dwntwn hotels, buildings, and stores. Affords fine views of the skyline.

PARKS & GARDENS: 🔔 **Ault Park,** east end of Observatory Ave.: Very handsome park offering a panorama along the Ohio River and the city. Worth going out of your way for.

☼🔔 **Eden Park,** Eden Park Dr. (352-4086): 180 acres (73ha) of park, floral exhibitions, and specialized botanic gardens with one of the largest tropical greenhouses in the world, the **Krohn Conservatory** (352-4086), plus museums, overlooking the Ohio. Absolutely worth a visit.

🔔 **Fountain Square,** on 5th St. between Walnut St. and Vine St.: A bucolic oasis in the heart of the city with agreeable gardens and monumental fountain (see "Monuments," above). A popular spot for a stroll in good weather (especially at lunch hour).

🔔 **Mount Airy Forest and Arboretum,** 5080 Colerain Ave. (541-8176): The verdant getaway of Cincinnati. Close to 1,440 acres (583ha) of forest and meadowland less than 9 mi. (15km) from dwntwn, with picnic grounds and hiking trails.

PERFORMING ARTS: For daily listings of all shows and cultural events, consult the entertainment pages of the daily papers *Cincinnati Enquirer* (morning) and *Cincinnati Post* (evening), and the monthly *Cincinnati* magazine.

Music Hall, 1241 Elm St. (621-1919): Home of the Cincinnati Opera, with director James de Blasis (Feb–July); the Cincinnati Symphony Orchestra, with principal conductor Jesús López Cobos (Sept–May); and the Cincinnati Ballet Company, with artistic director Ivan Nagy (Sept–May). Also houses the famous May Festival (see "Special Events," below).

Playhouse in the Park, 962 Mt. Adams Circle (421-3888): Modern theater in winter and musical comedies in summer.

Riverbend Music Center, 6295 Kellogg Ave. (232-6220): Concerts by the Cincinnati Symphony, big-name shows including stars of jazz, rock, and pop. May–Sept.

Showboat *Majestic,* Public Landing, foot of Broadway (241-6550): Contemporary theater in spring, summer, and fall.

Taft Theatre, 5th St. and Sycamore St. (721-0411): Road shows, Broadway musicals.

SPECIAL EVENTS: For the exact schedule of events below, consult the **Cincinnati Convention & Visitors Bureau** (see "Tourist Information," above).

May Festival (May): The oldest annual choral and operatic festival in the country (established 1873) features some of the world's finest soloists.

Riverfront Stadium Festival (late July): One of the most famous and most attended jazz, rock, soul, and rhythm-and-blues festivals in the country. For information, call 871-3900. At Riverfront Stadium.

ATP Tournament (mid-Aug): Professional tennis tournament held annually at the Jack Nicklaus Sports Center.

Riverfest (Labor Day wknd): 48 hr. of festivities based on themes from Cincinnati's historical heritage. Spectacular fireworks, Ohio River cruises, sports events. Draws 750,000 people every year.

Oktoberfest (last week of Sept): The local version of the renowned Munich beer festival with food, music, games, and ongoing entertainment in the six-block area surrounding Fountain Sq. Cheerful and colorful. 500,000 celebrants.

International Folk Festival (3 days in mid-Nov): Folk groups from more than 30 countries participate in this very lively festival dedicated to the food, arts, and crafts of different countries.

SPORTS: Cincinnati has two professional teams:

Baseball (Apr–Oct): Reds, Riverfront Stadium (421-4510).

Football (Sept–Jan): Bengals, Riverfront Stadium (621-3550).

Horse Racing

River Downs Racetrack, 6301 Kellogg Ave. (10 mi./16km east on U.S. 52) (232-8000). Thoroughbred racing Wed–Mon. Apr–Sept.

Turfway Park Race Course, 7500 Turfway Pike, Florence, Ky. (10 mi./16km SW on I-75) (606/371-0200). Thoroughbred racing Wed–Sun Sept–Apr.

STROLLS: ⚱ **Dayton Street,** between Baymiller St. and Linn St.: This was once known as "Millionaires' Street" because of its magnificent Italianate mansions built 1860–90 by Cincinnati's richest families. One of these luxurious residences is now the **John Hauck House Museum,** 812 Dayton St. (721-3570), open to the public Thurs–Fri and Sun. Well worth the trip.

☀⚱ **Main Strasse,** 6th St. and Philadelphia St., Covington, Ky. (606/491-0458): Dozens of different boutiques and stalls constitute this very lively shopping district, once inhabited exclusively by German immigrants. Overlooking it all is a pretty belfry 105 ft. (33m) high with a 43-bell carillon which plays at scheduled hours.

☀⚱ **Mount Adams,** Eden Park Dr.: The Greenwich Village or the Montmartre of Cincinnati, with narrow streets, museums, art galleries, boutiques, and numerous restaurants in a bohemian-chic setting. This historic area presents a spectacular view of the Ohio River Valley, downtown Cincinnati, and Northern Kentucky. A visit not to be missed.

⚱ **Public Landing,** along the Ohio River at the end of Broadway: The exact point where Benjamin Stites, a Revolutionary War veteran, and 25 of his friends landed and founded Cincinnati on December 28, 1788. Today it is the site for a nice stroll along the river's edge to view the large cruise ships moored on the Ohio. A lovely scene.

THEME PARKS: ⚱ **The Beach,** 2590 Waterpark Dr., Mason (26 mi./42km NE on I-75) (398-7946): One of the top five water parks in the country, off I-71 across from Kings Island (see below). 25,000-sq. ft. (2,300m²) wavepool with waterslides, innertube rides, sand beach, liquid fireworks, etc. Picnic area, restaurants. Open daily Memorial Day–Labor Day.

⚱ **Kings Island,** Kings Mill Rd., Kings Island (26 mi./42km NE on I-71) (398-5600): Ultramodern amusement park on 1,600 acres (650ha). Some 40 attractions, five thrill rides (including the terrifying "Beast" roller coaster and two log flumes), mini-zoo, reconstructions of old villages, and a miniature Eiffel Tower. Open daily Memorial Day–Labor Day, wknds only in spring and autumn. 25 min. from dwntwn.

Sports fans shouldn't miss the **Jack Nicklaus Sports Center** (398-5200), next door to Kings Island, with two superb golf courses designed and built by Jack Nicklaus himself, and an 8,500-seat tennis stadium, plus the ⚱**College Foot-**

ball Hall of Fame (398-5410), dedicated to great moments in college football. Films, exhibitions. Open daily Apr–Dec, wknds only the rest of the year. A must for sports-lovers.

ZOOS: 🐾 **Cincinnati Zoo,** 3400 Vine St. (281-4701): One of the top 10, and the second oldest, of U.S. zoos. Houses 6,000 animals of 800 species in a variety of realistic habitats, including a feline collection unmatched in the world. Note particularly the white tigers and an impressive band of gorillas. Attracts a million visitors a year. An absolute must-see. Open daily.

ACCOMMODATIONS

A Note on Accommodations: Room rates in Cincinnati are coded as follows: **VE,** Very Expensive ($140 and up); **E,** Expensive ($90–$140); **M,** Moderate ($60–$90); **I,** Inexpensive ($30–$60); **B,** Budget (up to $30). A listing of toll free numbers is in the Appendix.

Personal Favorites (in order of preference)

🏨🏨🏨 **Westin** (dwntwn), Fountain Sq., OH 45202 (513/621-7700; toll free, see Westin). 450 rms, A/C, color TV, in-rm movies. AE, CB, DC, MC, V. Valet gar. $7, pool, health club, sauna, two rests. (including Delmonico's), two bars, 24-hr. rm svce, nightclub, drugstore, boutiques, free crib. *Note:* The paragon of luxury hotels in Cincinnati. Ultramodern, comfortable 17-story building of rather cold concrete-and-glass design, but the rms are spacious and have minibars. Good svce and an excellent rest. In the heart of the business district, affording direct access to the Convention Center via the Skywalk. No-smoking floors. **VE**

☀️🏨🏨🏨 **Cincinnatian Hotel** (dwntwn), 601 Vine St., OH 45202 (513/381-3000; toll free, see Preferred). 147 rms, A/C, color TV, in-rm movies. AE, CB, DC, MC, V. Valet gar. $12, rest. (The Palace), bar, 24-hr. rm svce, nightclub, concierge, free crib. *Note:* This Victorian palace w. a mansard roof is a historical landmark. Built in 1882, it reopened its doors in 1987 after a $23-million refurbishing that restored its old-world charm and former splendor. Spectacular eight-story atrium w. a large marble staircase. Exceptionally vast and comfortable rms w. period furniture and pastel walls, some w. private balconies overlooking the atrium. Impeccable, personalized svce and a first-rate rest. Another fine address in the heart of Cincinnati. **VE**

🏨🏨🏨 **Hilton Terrace** (dwntwn), 15 W. 6th St., OH 45202 (513/381-4000; toll free, see Hilton). 339 rms, A/C, color TV, in-rm movies. AE, CB, DC, MC, V. Valet parking $6, health club, sauna, two rests. (including Gourmet), three bars, rm svce, entertainment, hrdrsr, drugstore, free crib. *Note:* For long the best hotel in Cincinnati, this elegant building was designed by Louis Skidmore. Business clientele. Comfortable rms recently renovated (some w. refrigerators) and very good svce. In the heart of dwntwn. **E–VE**

🏨🏨 **Quality Hotel Riverview** (nr. dwntwn), 666 W. 5th St., Covington, KY 41011 (606/491-1200; toll free, see Quality Inns). 236 rms, A/C, color TV, in-rm movies. AE, CB, DC, MC, V. Free parking, pool, tennis, health club, sauna, revolving rest. on the top floor (Riverview Room), coffee shop, two bars, rm svce, nightclub, hrdrsr, free crib. *Note:* Modern round 18-story tower w. comfortable, spacious rms. Offers a fine panorama of dwntwn Cincinnati from the other side of the Ohio (ask for a room with a river view). Business clientele. Very good value. A favorite of connoisseurs. Free Cincinnati and airport shuttles. **M**

🏨 **Best Western Mariemont Inn** (nr. dwntwn), 6880 Wooster Pike, OH 45277 (513/271-2100; toll free, see Best Western). 60 rms, A/C, cable color TV. AE, CB, DC, MC, V. Free parking, rest. (National Exemplar), bar, valet svce, free crib. *Note:* Quaint little inn built in 1926 w. English manor charm, a few steps from Ault Park. Inviting atmosphere, comfortable rms, and friendly, cheerful svce. Adequate rest. and a very good overall value. 10 min. from dwntwn on Columbia Pkwy. (U.S. 50E). An ideal spot for motorists. ∎

Travelodge Newport (nr. dwntwn), 222 York St., Newport, KY 41071 (606/291-4434; toll free, see Travelodge). 104 rms, A/C, cable color TV. AE, DC, MC, V. Free parking, pool, nearby rest., free breakfast, free crib. *Note:* Well-run economy motel 5 min. from dwntwn Cincinnati across the Ohio River. Utilitarian comforts; some rms w. kitchenette. Good value, particularly for the budget traveler. ∎

Other Accommodations (from top bracket to budget)

Hyatt Regency (dwntwn), 151 W. 5th St., OH 45202 (513/579-1234; toll free, see Hyatt). 485 rms, A/C, color TV, in-rm movies. AE, CB, DC, MC, V. Valet parking $10, pool, health club, sauna, two rests. (including Champs), bar, rm svce, disco, boutiques, concierge, free crib. *Note:* Opened in 1984, this large, modern 22-story building has a spectacular, three-story lobby; its facilities and comfort are unparalleled. Vast, well-laid-out rms and ultra-professional svce. VIP floor. Mediocre rests. Business and group clientele. Faces the Convention Center. Direct access to Skywalk. **E–VE**

Omni Netherland Plaza (dwntwn), 35 W. 5th St., OH 45202 (513/421-9100; toll free, see Omni). 621 rms, A/C, color TV. AE, CB, DC, MC, V. Valet gar. $9, three rests. (including Orchids), bars, rm svce, nightclub, hrdrsr, boutiques, concierge. *Note:* Lovely 1920s palace magnificently renovated in 1983 to the tune of $25 million. The splendid art deco lobby is a historical landmark. Spacious, very comfortable rms and efficient, attentive svce. Very central location, steps away from the Convention Center. Excellent rest. Big business clientele. Direct access to the Skywalk. **E–VE**

Clarion Cincinnati (formerly Stouffer's; dwntwn), 141 W. 6th St., OH 45202 (513/352-2100; toll free, see Clarion). 900 rms, A/C, color TV, in-rm movies. AE, CB, DC, MC, V. Valet gar. $9, pool, health club, sauna, squash, two rests. (including Top of the Crown), bars, rm svce, nightclub, hrdrsr, boutiques, concierge, free crib. *Note:* Relatively modern hotel in two adj. towers of 21 and 32 stories. Comfortable rms but rather mediocre svce and rests. Very centrally located. Group clientele (the hotel is directly across from the Convention Center). Four VIP floors. Currently undergoing renovation. **M–E**

Vernon Manor (nr. dwntwn), 400 Oak St., OH 45219 (513/281-3300; toll free 800/543-3999). 166 rms, A/C, color TV. AE, CB, DC, MC, V. Free valet parking, rest. (The Forum), coffee shop, bar, rm svce, nightclub, hrdrsr, free crib. *Note:* An old Cincinnati classic tastefully renovated. Spacious rms w. elegant decor (a third w. kitchenettes) and excellent svce. Quiet surroundings. VCR rentals. Regular clientele. 5 min. from dwntwn. **M–E**

Imperial House West (nr. dwntwn), 5510 Rybolt Rd., OH 45248 (513/574-6000; toll free 800/543-3018). 200 rms, A/C, color TV, in-rm movies. AE, CB, DC, MC, V. Free parking, pool, health club, sauna, rest. (Dante's), bar, rm svce, disco, free crib. *Note:* Comfortable, well-designed five-story motel w. spacious, inviting rms, some w. kitchenette and refrigerator. Friendly reception and svce. Business and package-tour clientele. Very good value. 20 min. from dwntwn along I-74. ∎

Days Inn Downtown (nr. dwntwn), 2880 Central Pkwy, OH 45225 (513/599-0400; toll free, see Days Inns). 103 rms, A/C, cable color TV. AE, DC, MC, V. Free parking, pool; no bar or rest.; crib $5. *Note:* Unassuming little motel nr. the university, completely renovated in 1988. Good overall value; 5 min. from dwntwn. ∎

Accommodations in the Vicinity

Carrousel Inn (formerly Best Western; nr. dwntwn), 8001 Reading Rd., OH 45237 (513/821-5110; toll free 800/543-4970). 286 rms, A/C, color TV, in-rm movies. AE, DC, MC, V. Free parking, three pools, health club, two tennis courts, sauna, miniature golf, two rests. (including Robert's), bar, rm svce, nightclub, free crib. *Note:* Very comfortable country club–style motel on almost 15 acres (6ha) of lovely grdns. Spacious rms w. private balconies or patios (some w. kitchenettes). Comprehensive recreational facilities, efficient svce, and a good rest. (Robert's). Group and convention clientele. Excellent value, 15 min. from dwntwn. **I–M**

Airport Accommodations

☀�♔♔ **Cincinnati Drawbridge Motor Inn** (vic.), I-75 at Buttermilk Pike, Fort Mitchell, KY 41017 (606/341-2800; toll free 800/354-9794). 505 rms, A/C, color TV, in-rm movies. AE, CB, DC, MC, V. Free parking, three pools, two tennis courts, health club, sauna, two rests. (including Gatehouse Tavern), 24-hr. coffeeshop, two bars, rm svce, disco, free crib. *Note:* Vast motel with Tudor decor. Very appealing rms w. balconies, good recreational facilities, and agreeable reception and svce. Business clientele. Excellent value. Very adequate rest. (Gatehouse Tavern). VIP floor. Bavarian brewery adjacent. 8 min. from the airport (free shuttle); 10 min. from dwntwn. **I–M**

YMCA/Youth Hostels

Cincinnati Youth Hostel (nr. dwntwn), 2200 Maplewood Ave., OH 45219 (651-2329). Dormitories, 8 min. from dwntwn.

RESTAURANTS

A Note on Restaurant Prices: Cincinnati restaurant prices, per person, excluding drinks and service charges, are coded as follows: **VE,** Very Expensive ($60 and up); **E,** Expensive ($40–$60); **M,** Moderate ($25–$40); **I,** Inexpensive ($15–$25); **B,** Budget (up to $15).

Personal Favorites (in order of preference)

♔♔♔♔ **Maisonette** (dwntwn), 114 E. 6th St. (721-2260). A/C. Lunch Mon–Fri, dinner Mon–Sat; closed hols. and early July. AE, CB, DC, MC, V. J&T. *Specialties:* braised duck in beaujolais, sautéed escalopes of foie gras w. apples, sole stuffed w. scallops, salmon tartare w. caviar, rack of lamb w. morels, filet of brill in pastry shell, white-chocolate mousse w. chocolate sauce. Low-fat and low-salt entrées. Long list of French and California wines. *Note:* One of the 12 best rests. in the country. The svce is as polished as it is attentive; the rosetoned decor is luxurious without being ostentatious; and the classic cuisine is altogether remarkable. Resv. a must well in advance. Itself worth the trip to Cincinnati. Valet parking in the evening. A local institution for more than 30 years. *French.* **M–E**

♔♔♔ **Pigall's** (dwntwn), 127 W. 4th St. (721-1345). A/C. Lunch Mon–Fri, dinner Mon–Sat; closed hols. and early Aug. AE, CB, DC, MC, V. J&T. *Specialties:* scallops provençal, noisette of veal w. lobster, Dover sole w. basil, duck w. cabernet sauvignon, roast partridge périgourdine (sauce w. truffles), soufflé Grand Marnier. A splendid wine list. *Note:* Another renowned Cincinnati table since 1956. Irreproachable French cuisine in the grand manner. Elegant decor w. crystal chandeliers and smoked mirrors. Svce somewhat unreliable. Resv. a must. *French.* **M**

♔♔ **Chester's Road House** (vic.), 9678 Montgomery Rd. (793-8700). A/C. Lunch Mon–Sat, dinner nightly, brunch Sun; closed Thanksgiving, Dec 24–25, Jan 1. AE, CB, DC, MC, V. Jkt. *Specialties:* rack of lamb, ribs of beef, trout meunière, liqueured cappuccino. Good wine list. *Note:* The bucolic, less refined version of the same owner's Maisonette in a converted 1900 farmhouse. Simple but tasty cuisine in a pretty, rustic setting w. abundant greenery. A local favorite. An excellent locale. No resv. on Sat. 25 min. from dwntwn. *Continental/American.* **I–M**

☀�Ｙ♔ **Lenhardt's** (nr. dwntwn), 151 W. McMillan (281-3600). A/C. Lunch/dinner Tues–Sun; closed first 15 days of Aug, Christmas hols. AE, CB, DC, MC, V. *Specialties:* wienerschnitzel, sauerbraten, jägerschnitzel, Kassler riffehen, chicken paprikash, goulash, Viennese pastries.

Fine list of German wines. *Note:* One of the best German rests. in all Ohio, in the former residence of a wealthy 19th-century brewer a stone's throw from the university. Diligent svce. Resv. advised for evenings and wknds. A classic of its kind for more than 80 years. Very popular locally. Very good value. 10 min. from dwntwn. *German.* I

Other Restaurants (from top bracket to budget)

The Phoenix (dwntwn), 812 Race St. at 9th St. (721-2255). A/C. Lunch Tues–Sat, dinner Mon–Fri; closed hols. AE, CB, DC, MC, V. J&T. *Specialties:* Ohio quail stuffed w. smoked duck and walnut dressing, langoustines and smoked scallops in phyllo pastry, lamb chop in tomato-rosemary beurre blanc w. shoestring sweet potatoes, salmon in champagne-cream sauce w. leeks, bananas Foster, cheesecake. Choice wine list. *Note:* As though a phoenix were rising from its own ashes, this luxury rest. was opened in 1988 in the former premises of a men's club, luxuriously renovated at a cost of $5 million. Imaginative, airy American cuisine w. a faint southwestern accent, served in an elegant Victorian setting w. period paneling and stained glass. Smart, opulent surroundings, flawless svce. A good place to eat; be sure to reserve ahead. *American.* **M–I** Valet parking.

Charley's Oyster Bar & Grill (vic.), 9769 Montgomery Rd. (891-7000). A/C. Dinner only, nightly; closed Jan 1, Thanksgiving, Dec 25. AE, CB, DC, MC, V. Jkt. *Specialties:* clam bake, paella, fish of the day, shellfish. *Note:* The best seafood rest. in Cincinnati (but also very decent steak, veal, and lamb), highly laudable despite often-faltering svce. The marine decor is somewhat incongruous in this 1850s manor house. Resv. advised. Valet parking. 25 min. from dwntwn. *Seafood.* **I–M**

The Precinct (nr. dwntwn), 311 Delta Ave. at Columbia Pkwy. (321-5454). A/C. Dinner only, nightly; closed hols. AE, CB, DC, MC, V. Jkt. *Specialties:* broiled steak, steak au poivre, roast beef, steak Remington (w. sautéed green peppers and mushrooms), lobster, catch of the day. The slender wine list nonetheless offers some interesting selections. *Note:* The very best beef in Cincinnati (so say devotees), aged and broiled over a wood fire according to the best principles, from the modest 8-oz. (226gm) filet mignon to the gigantic 22-oz. (622gm) Porterhouse. The setting is a former police precinct looking like a little red-brick castle. Lots of noise from the disco on the second floor; hard-working svce. A businessman's favorite, so resv. advised. 10 min. from dwntwn. *Steak/Seafood.* **I–M**

China Gourmet (nr. dwntwn), 3340 Erie Ave., East Hyde Park Mall (871-6612). A/C. Lunch/dinner Mon–Sat; closed hols. AE, CB, DC, MC, V. *Specialties:* Chinatown shrimp, Cantonese lobster, Szechuan kung po, pike w. ginger. *Note:* Excellent Chinese cuisine—mostly Cantonese but Hunan and Szechuan dishes are served as well. Modern jungle-style Oriental decor. Friendly ambience. Locally popular. 15 min. from dwntwn. *Chinese.* I

The Diner on Sycamore (dwntwn), 1230 Sycamore St. (721-1212). A/C. Lunch/dinner daily (until midnight); closed Dec 25. AE, MC, V. *Specialties:* nachos, hamburgers, broiled fish sandwiches, milkshakes. *Note:* A real 1950s diner complete w. stainless steel, aggressively pink tiles, and Formica counter—straight out of a painting by Edward Hopper. Unexceptional food, decent hamburgers in an entertainingly funky setting. Great for an after-show meal. *American.* **B–I**

Grammer's (dwntwn), 1440 Walnut St. (721-6570). A/C. Lunch/dinner Mon–Sat; closed hols. AE, CB, DC, MC, V. *Specialties:* sauerbraten, wienerschnitzel, fleisch teller (assorted meats), strudel, Black Forest cake. *Note:* Recently restored to its old splendor, this bastion of German cuisine established in 1872 offers solid meals for big appetites. The svce, unfortunately, does not approach the stature of the setting or the cuisine. Open until 1am Fri–Sat. Resv. advised on wknds. An excellent value. *German/American.* I

☼⊻♈ **Mike Fink's Restaurant** (nr. dwntwn), at the end of Greenup St. on the Ohio River, Covington, Ky. (606/261-4212). A/C. Lunch/dinner daily (until midnight); closed Dec 25. AE, CB, DC, MC, V. *Specialties:* raw seafood bar; fried catfish; grilled halibut; filet of sole topped w. shrimp, crabmeat, and scallops; fish of the day. *Note:* Very popular seafood rest. in an old riverboat from the good ol' days. Fine, authentic cuisine and a pleasant ambience. Lovely view of Cincinnati from the other side of the river, especially after dark. Resv. advised. *Seafood.* I

Restaurants in the Vicinity

☼⊻♈♈ **Golden Lamb** (vic.), 27 S. Broadway, Lebanon (932-5065). A/C. Lunch/dinner daily, brunch Sun; closed Dec 25. AE, CB, DC, MC, V. Jkt. *Specialties:* roast leg of spring lamb, duck à l'orange, filet of pork w. sage, Shaker sugar pie. Somewhat pedestrian wine list. *Note:* This charming inn, once a stagecoach rest stop, dates from 1803 and has played host to 10 presidents and countless celebrities. The cuisine is as simple and flavorful as the day it opened. Lovely antique decor. Pleasant ambience and svce. Well worth the 50-min. car ride from Cincinnati. Resv. advised. Also 18 spare, basic rms. *American.* B–I

Cafeterias / Specialty Spots

Camp Washington Chili Inc. (nr. dwntwn), Colerain Ave. and Hopple St. (541-0061). In business since 1946, C.W. is considered by purists the best of the countless chili places in Cincinnati. Formica decor but friendly reception and svce. Nr. the university. Unlike many chili chain rests. this one never multiplied. There is only one Camp Washington. Open 24 hr. Mon–Sat and 10am–6pm Sun. No credit cards.

Izzy's (dwntwn), 819 Elm St. (721-4241). The best-known deli in Cincinnati since 1901. Overstuffed kosher sandwiches w. potato pancakes, homemade soup, corned beef, legendary Reubens; the desserts could endanger your figure. Breakfast/lunch Mon–Sat (until 5pm). Other location: 610 Main St. (241-6246); breakfast/lunch/dinner Mon–Sat (until 9pm). No credit cards.

Skyline Chili (dwntwn), 643 Vine St. (241-2020). Lunch/dinner Mon–Sat (until 7pm). No credit cards. A must for all visitors. Chili—as the name indicates—is the big house specialty, and it is served in many variations. More than 40 other branches in Cincinnati and the suburbs (consult the phone directory). A Cincinnati institution since 1949.

BARS & NIGHTCLUBS

Arnold's Bar & Grill (dwntwn), 210 E. 8th St. (421-6234). The oldest (1861) tavern in Cincinnati, with live traditional jazz, ragtime, and swing. Acceptable sandwiches and snacks. Locally popular; mixed crowd of yuppies and students. Open Mon–Sat.

The Blind Lemon (dwntwn), 936 Hatch St. (241-3885). Open nightly. Intimate and much-frequented singles bar with live jazz, folk, and blues music nightly. One of the best spots in Mt. Adams, the heart of Cincinnati nightlife.

Conservatory (nr. dwntwn), 640 W. 3rd St., Covington, Ky. (on the other side of the river) (606/491-6400). Open Mon–Sat. Jkt. A fashionable disco with a sophisticated ambience. A fair rest. as well.

Flanagan's Landing (dwntwn), 212 W. Pete Rose Way (421-4055). Engaging Irish pub very nr. Riverside Stadium. Noisy and crowded, especially when the Bengals or the Reds are playing. Pleasant open-air beer garden on fine days. Open daily.

Oldenberg Brewery (vic.), I-75 at Buttermilk Pike (606/341-2800). Larger-than-life Bavarian-style beer garden; nothing is missing, from the enormous 650-person dining room and dance floor to the blaring of the obligatory brass band. The beer (brewed in a real brewery next door) and the music flow like water. A jumping joint. 15 min. from dwntwn, 10 min. from the airport. Open Mon–Sat.

The Precinct (nr. dwntwn), 311 Delta Ave. (321-5454). Open daily. A very popular rest./bar/disco in a former police station. Youthful, relaxed ambience. Very decent steakhouse 10 min. from dwntwn (see "Restaurants," above).

Rookwood Pottery (nr. dwntwn), 1077 Celestial St. (721-5456). Open daily. This pleasant bar/disco in the quaint original kilns of an old pottery factory at the top of Mt. Adams is very popular with the locals. Also an average rest.

NEARBY EXCURSIONS

DAYTON (60 mi./80km NE on I-75): See the aviation museum at the **Wright-Patterson Air Force Base,** on Ohio 444 (513/255-3284), the largest museum of military aviation in the world: more than 200 machines on display, from the Wright Brothers' glider to the huge B-52 bomber and space rockets. An absolute must-see. Open daily. The graves of Orville and Wilbur Wright are in neighboring **Woodland Cemetery,** at the east end of Woodland Ave.

FORT ANCIENT STATE MEMORIAL (nr. Lebanon, 36 mi./58km NE on I-71 and Ohio 350E) (513/932-4421): Surprising fortified city constructed between 400 B.C. and A.D. 600 by Hopewell Indians (a tribe of the Mound Builders culture who lived at the beginning of our era in Ohio and Wisconsin and about whom historians know almost nothing). The still-visible earthen walls rise to 22 ft. (7m) in some places. Many burial mounds and other relics. Interesting archeological museum. Definitely worth the trip. Open Wed–Sun Apr–Sept, wknds only in Oct.

KENTUCKY HORSE PARK (in Lexington, 72 mi./115km south on I-75 and Iron Works Pike) (606/233-4303): In the heart of Bluegrass Land and its famous stud farms, this 960-acre (365ha) equestrian museum attracts hundreds of thousands of visitors devoted to the cult of the thoroughbred. Visits to the stable (more than 600 stalls) and training field. Museum dedicated to horse-racing greats. Seasonal parade of stallions and a number of races Apr–Oct. A must for all admirers of "man's most noble conquest." Open daily Apr–Oct, Wed–Sun the rest of the year.

MOUND CITY GROUP NATIONAL MONUMENT (in Chillicothe, 95 mi./152km NE on U.S. 50E and Ohio 104N) (614/774-1125): 23 burial mounds of the Hopewell Indians (500 B.C. to A.D. 600). The densest concentration of prehistoric monuments of this kind in the country. Exhibition of religious relics. Worth the trip. Open daily.

Not far from here is the **Sugarloaf Mountain Amphitheater** (enter on U.S. 23N and Ohio 159), offering an interesting theatrical presentation of the heroic life and the death of Tecumseh, leader of the Shawnee tribe and last Native American warrior leader to resist the advance of the "palefaces" east of the Mississippi (1813). Open Mon–Sat until 8:30pm mid-June to early Sept. For information, call 614/775-4100.

SERPENT MOUND STATE MEMORIAL (75 mi./120km east on Ohio 32E, 41N, and 73W) (513/587-2796): Native American totem 1,302 ft. (407-m) long in the form of a stylized serpent, made of stone and yellow clay between 800 B.C. and A.D. 1400. The largest mound of this type in the U.S. If the grass were clipped around the monument, this unusual work would look even more impressive. Well worth going out of your way for, nevertheless. Open Wed–Sun Apr–Oct. A good joint excursion with Mound City Group National Monument (see above) and with ▵ **Fort Hill State Memorial** (15 mi./24km NE of Serpent Mound State Memorial on Ohio 73S and 41N), former fortified camp of the Hopewell people built at the top of a hill. Museum of archeological finds. Open Wed–Sun Apr–Oct.

▵ **SHARON WOODS VILLAGE** (14 mi./22km NE on U.S. 42) (563-9484): A very realistic portrayal of small-town life in Ohio in the mid-19th century. The authentic old houses were transported to Sharon Woods from their original locations. An absolute must-see. Open Wed–Sun May–Nov.

CHAPTER 23

CHICAGO 🍦🍦🍦

□ □ □

An immense metropolis, with suburbs extending more than 62 miles (100km) along the southwest bank of Lake Michigan, Chicago was the second-largest city in the U.S. until 1984, when it was ousted by Los Angeles. Two French explorers helped found Chicago, a name deriving from the Native American word *checagou* (wild onion), a plant that once grew abundantly on the banks of the Chicago River. The Jesuit Fr. Jacques Marquette and the trapper Louis Joliet were the first Europeans to visit the site, in 1673. Jean Baptiste Point du Sable, an African American businessman from Santo Domingo, in 1796 created the first fur-trading post on the banks of Lake Michigan, a Native American name meaning "Great Lake." (This founding father is himself a symbol of the ethnic mix that has given the city its uniquely cosmopolitan character: his father was a Frenchman from Québec, his mother was a black slave from Santo Domingo, and his wife was a Potawatomi.) In 1803 a military encampment named Fort Dearborn was built at the mouth of the Checagou River. Its garrison was massacred by local Native American tribes 9 years later and the fort was abandoned until 1816. With the mass settlement of homesteaders from the east around 1833, this crossroads city between the Great Lakes and the plains of the Midwest entered a period of prodigious economic growth. Even the virtual destruction of the city by fire in 1871, when it had 300,000 inhabitants, could not check its burgeoning vigor. In 1900 its population had risen to 1.7 million and surpassed 3.5 million in 1960. Though its numbers have since fallen to just under 3,000,000 inhabitants, the third American city after New York and Los Angeles remains the capital of the American heartland.

A city of drive and superlatives—"the city that works," according to its late mayor, Richard J. Daley—Chicago claims the busiest airport in the world (**O'Hare International Airport,** with close to 58 million passengers per year), the largest railroad station, the largest inland port, the tallest skyscraper in the world (the **Sears Tower,** 110 stories and 1,454 ft./443m, 90 ft./30m higher than New York's World Trade Center), the tallest church (the Chicago Temple, 568 ft./173m), the largest water-treatment plant in the world, the world's largest commercial building (**Merchandise Mart,**) the world's most important grain exchange, and the largest convention center in the world (**McCormick Place**).

Chicago is the world capital of grain, chewing gum, agricultural machinery, mail order, frivolous magazines (the *Playboy* empire started here), electrical equipment, meat packing, the telephone, and the hamburger (the first McDonald's opened in 1955 in Des Plaines, near O'Hare Airport, and today enjoys the status of a relic). The second financial and industrial center of the U.S. after New York, Chicago also prides itself on possessing the world's first skyscraper, the **Manhattan Building** (1884), designed by William Le Baron Jenney. Today, three of the five tallest buildings in the world are in Chicago.

The merest glance at Chicago's impressive skyline will disclose a greater wealth of architectural theory and practice than you are likely to find in any other U.S. city. By the end of the last century, architects of the famous "Chicago School" (such as William Le Baron Jenney, Daniel Burnham, Dankmar Adler, and Louis Sullivan) had realized some of the masterpieces that anticipated by 20–

30 years the birth of art deco in Europe: **Burnham's** with its 16 stories, at the time the tallest office building in the world; the **Auditorium Building;** the **Carson, Pirie, Scott & Co.** and **Marshall Field** department stores; and **The Rookery,** the world's oldest steel-frame skyscraper (1886), just to cite a few. Frank Lloyd Wright, Sullivan's favorite pupil and the greatest American architect of all time, created in the 1890s his revolutionary "Prairie Style" for individual houses, with low, uncluttered lines married harmoniously to the surrounding foliage and gardens. In the suburb of **Oak Park** you can admire a series of such houses, which, though constructed 90 years ago, still appear remarkably modern. With Wright's example to follow, a succession of architects both American (Root, Holabird and Roche, Raymond Hood, James Gamble Rogers) and foreign (the Germans Ludwig Mies van der Rohe and Walter Gropius, one-time members of the Bauhaus, and Finland's Eero Saarinen) has over the past century made Chicago into a shining light of urban architecture. Witness such classic structures as the **Chicago Tribune Tower,** the **Wrigley Building,** and especially Mies van der Rohe's **Lake Shore Drive Apartment Towers,** where in 1948 the "curtain wall" technique was first used in the United States. There is also Skidmore, Owings and Merrill's superb **John Hancock Center** (affectionately nicknamed "Big John" by Chicagoans) and Helmut Jahn's audacious **State of Illinois Center,** opened in 1986.

Many of us know Chicago as the brutal, opportunistic city seen in classic screen portrayals of the St. Valentine's Day Massacre, Al Capone, Dillinger, and Prohibition. The reality is far more complex: this city is home to one of the most extraordinary ethnic mixtures on the planet. Poles (with 800,000 people of Polish extraction, Chicago is the largest Polish city in the world after Warsaw), Greeks, Italians, Slavs, African Americans, Chinese, Mexicans, Irish, Swedes, Puerto Ricans, and Germans all have their neighborhoods, their life-styles, their folklore, their museums, and their cuisine (the city has more than 5,000 restaurants of all kinds). Almost a third of current Chicagoans were born outside the United States, and a remarkable racial mix (42% white, 40% African American, 14% Hispanic, 4% Asian) has enhanced the Homeric political contests that have become traditional at municipal elections.

A sprawling city full of contrasts—the chic galleries and stores of the **Magnificent Mile;** the African American areas of the **South Side, Cabrini-Green,** and **Bronzeville;** the frenetic activity of the **Loop,** the financial district constrained within the clangorous tracks of the Elevated; the luxury homes along **North Lake Shore Drive,** the chic restaurants and boutiques of **Printer's Row** and **River North**—Chicago has some of the most fascinating museums, public gardens (574 in all), and urban landscapes in America. Its seven universities include the **University of Illinois, Loyola** (Catholic), and the **University of Chicago,** where in 1942 Enrico Fermi achieved the world's first controlled atomic chain reaction. These plus the nuclear research center, **Argonne National Laboratory** in Darien, are among the most prestigious breeding-grounds for American Nobel Prize winners (53 to date). Chicago is the birthplace of Walt Disney, Jason Robards, Kim Novak, John Dos Passos, Edgar Rice Burroughs (the creator of Tarzan), and Ernest Hemingway (born, as was Burroughs, in the suburb of Oak Park), and is today one of the three great American art capitals (with New York and Los Angeles), offering a wealth of opportunity to lovers of theater, opera, jazz, and other cultural events. The **Chicago Symphony Orchestra,** directed by such legendary figures as Fritz Reiner and Georg Solti, is considered by experts one of the two or three best instrumental ensembles in the world. A jazz capital since the 1920s and undisputed bastion of the blues, Chicago has also given birth to talents as varied as Benny Goodman, Gene Krupa, Mezz Mezzrow, Bud Freeman, Jo Jones, Lennie Tristano, Muggsy Spanier, and Herbie Hancock. Finally, you may be surprised to learn that, according to the FBI, Chicago's crime rate is 15th among American cities.

BASIC FACTS: State of Illinois. Area codes: 312 (dwntwn and O'Hare Airport), 708 (suburbs). Time zone: central. ZIP Code: 60607. Settled: 1803. Approximate population: city, 2,980,000; metropolitan area, 8,300,000. Third-largest American city.

CLIMATE: The climate is very rigorous, with glacial winters (sometimes −22°F/−30°C) and lots of snow; spring and autumn are brief. Chicago owes its "Windy City" nickname to the terrible blizzards that blow in from northern Canada across the flat expanse of the Great Lakes. Summer, sometimes quite hot (average temperature: 78°F/26°C) but always breezy, is by far the best season to visit Chicago.

DISTANCES: Detroit, 268 mi. (430km); Indianapolis, 181 mi. (290km); Milwaukee, 87 mi. (139km); Minneapolis, 406 mi. (650km); New York, 806 mi. (1,290km); St. Louis, 290 mi. (465km); Washington, 668 mi. (1,070km).

ARRIVAL & TRANSIT INFORMATION

AIRPORTS: Two major airports: **Midway Airport** (MDW), 11 mi. (17km) SW, with aging facilities. Information: 767-0500.
    O'Hare International Airport (ORD), 18 mi. (29km) NW, the busiest airport in the world (close to 58 million passengers per year), with a takeoff or landing every 20 seconds and served by 50 airlines. Information: 686-2200.

U.S. AIRLINES: American (372-8000), Continental (686-6500), Delta (346-5300), Eastern (467-2900), Midway (767-3400), Pan Am (toll free 800/221-1111), TWA (558-7000), United (569-3000), and USAir (726-1201).

FOREIGN CARRIERS: Air Canada (527-3900), Air France (toll free 800/237-2747), British Airways (786-1340), KLM (861-9300), Lufthansa (686-5800), Sabena (toll free 800/645-3790), and Swiss Air (630-5800).

CITY LINK: Cab fare to city center **from O'Hare,** about $25–$28; time, about 45 min. Bus: Continental Air Transport (454-7800); leaves every 20 min.; stops at the major dwntwn hotels; time, about 50 min.; fare, $9.
    Cab fare to city center **from Midway,** about $15; time, about 20 min. Bus: Continental Air Transport (454-7800); leaves every 30 min.; time, about 35 min.; fare, $7.
    Between high cab fares and O'Hare's distance from downtown, renting a car may be advisable if you're planning a prolonged stay. Chicago has a very efficient public transportation system (subway and bus), including notably an express subway connection between the Loop and O'Hare (CTA). Fare, $1.25; time, about 35 min. (call 836-7000 for information). CTA station is located under Terminal 4.

CAR RENTAL (at O'Hare International Airport unless otherwise indicated): Avis (694-5600); Budget (reservations 708/968-6661); Dollar (671-5100); Hertz (686-7272); National (694-4640); Thrifty, 3901 Mannheim Rd., Schiller Park (708/298-3383). For downtown agencies, consult the local telephone book.

LIMOUSINE SERVICES: Carey Limousines (663-1220), Dav El Limousine (toll free 800/922-0343), Lake Shore Limousine (334-2343).

TAXIS: Cabs may be hailed on the street, gotten in waiting lines at the entrances to the major hotels, or summoned by phone. The major cab companies are:

American United (248-7600), **Flash Cab** (561-1444), and **Yellow Cab** (829-4222). Cabs are still relatively inexpensive in spite of a recent fare increase.

TRAIN: Amtrak, Union Station, 225 S. Canal St. (558-1075); ticket office, 203 N. LaSalle St. (558-1075).

INTERCITY BUSES: Greyhound, 630 W. Harrison St. (781-2900).

INFORMATION & TOURS

TOURIST INFORMATION: Chicago Convention and Tourism Bureau, McCormick Place-on-the-Lake, IL 60616 (312/567-8500). Open Mon–Fri.
   Information Bureau (with multilingual hostesses), Water Tower, Chicago Ave. and Michigan Ave. (312/280-5740). Open daily.
   Illinois Travel Information Center, 310 S. Michigan Ave. (312/793-2094). Open Mon–Fri. Tourist information on the state of Illinois.
   Recorded telephone announcement giving an up-to-date listing of cultural events (312/346-3278) and shows (312/977-1755).

GUIDED TOURS: American Sightseeing (bus), 530 S. Michigan Ave. (427-3100): Guided tour of the city. Serves major hotels.
   Archi Center, 330 S. Dearborn St. (Monadnock Building) (922-3431): Wonderful walking and bus tours around the major architectural achievements of Chicago and its suburbs. Also, photo exhibits, lectures, a well-stocked library, etc. Open daily.
   Chicago Motor Coach Co. (bus), 750 S. Clinton (922-8919): Narrated 1-, 2-, and 3-hr. tours of the Loop, Lakefront, Grant Park, West and North Sides aboard double-decker bus, London style. Departures every 15 min. from Sears Tower. Courtesy hotel pickup available. Daily.
   CTA Culture Bus (bus), Art Institute, Michigan Ave. and Adams St.: Stops at Chicago's major monuments and museums. You may get on and off as many times as you please. Runs Sun and hols. Apr–Sept. For information, call 836-7000.
   Gray Line Tours (bus), 33 E. Monroe St. (346-9506): Guided tours of the city.
   Mercury Skyline Cruiseline (boat), Wacker Dr. and Michigan Ave. (332-1353): Lake and Chicago River rides May–Sept.
   Oak Park Tour Center (walking tours), 158 N. Forest Ave. and Lake St., Oak Park (312/848-1500): Guided tours of this residential area, cradle of the "Prairie House" style created by Frank Lloyd Wright. Visitor center open daily Mar–Nov.
   Untouchable Tours (bus) (881-1195): Chicago's only bus tour of gangland sites, from Al Capone's headquarters to the site of the St. Valentine's Day Massacre. The driver and tour guide dress as gangsters, pack plastic pistols in shoulder holsters, and spice up the commentary with hoodlum argot and their own sound effects. Highly unusual. Departs from Michigan Ave. and Pearson, Wed and Fri–Sun.

SIGHTS, ATTRACTIONS & ACTIVITIES

ARCHITECTURAL HIGHLIGHTS: ⚓ **Board of Trade,** 141 W. Jackson Blvd. (435-3590): The most important commodity exchange in the world, a huge art deco building with 44 stories (588 ft./184m high) crowned by a giant statue of Ceres, goddess of the harvest. Visitors gallery is on the fifth floor. A sight not to be missed. Open Mon–Fri.
   ☼⚓ **Chicago Mercantile Exchange,** 30 S. Wacker Dr. (930-8249): The world's second-largest grain exchange, as well as one of the

most important international currency-futures markets, housed in twin modern towers on the Chicago River. The Visitors' Gallery, open Mon–Fri, offers a spectacular view of the frantic activity on the Exchange floor.

City Hall, 121 N. La Salle St. (744-4000): Chicago's city hall and county administration building. Imposing neoclassical structure which dates from 1910. Admission by invitation only, Mon–Fri. See it.

Federal Center, Adams St. and Dearborn St.: Courthouse with two Mies van der Rohe towers, 387 and 560 ft. (121m and 175m) high, it also houses various federal agencies. Imposing Calder sculpture in front of the south tower. Worth a glance.

Illinois Institute of Technology, 3300 S. Federal St. (567-3025): Technical university (6,000 students) whose campus, remarkable for the purity and simplicity of its lines, was designed by Mies van der Rohe (see especially Crown Hall). Campus tours Sat Sept–May: Perlstein Hall, 10 W. 33rd St. For architecture buffs.

Merchandise Mart, Wells St. and Kinzie St.: The largest commercial building in the world, it was erected in 1928 and has more than 900 furniture showrooms. An astonishing sight to see. Guided tours Tues and Thurs Mar–Dec. (call 661-1440 for resv.).

Richard J. Daley Center, Richard Daley Plaza (443-7980): Elegant, modern skyscraper in bronze and steel tones (648 ft./198m, 31 stories) named for the former mayor of Chicago, it houses the city's administrative services. Be sure to see this building with its giant abstract sculptures by Picasso (48 ft./15m tall) and Miró (34 ft./11m tall) on the main esplanade.

State of Illinois Center, 100 W. Randolph St. at La Salle St. (814-6660): Be sure to see this, the most surprising and innovative building in all Chicago. A 1985 "hi-tech" masterpiece, this hemispherical tower of blue and pink tinted glass is built around a gigantic windowed atrium 17 stories tall. This building by German-born architect Helmut Jahn houses administrative offices of the State of Illinois. Unusual fiberglass sculpture by Jean Dubuffet, *Monument with Standing Animal,* in front of the building.

United States Post Office, 433 W. Van Buren St. (765-3009): The largest post office in the world, it handles more than 40 million letters and 500,000 parcels each day. Interesting tours Mon–Fri Jan–Nov; you must make resv. several days in advance.

University of Chicago, 5801 S. Ellis Ave. (702-1234): Founded in 1890 by John D. Rockefeller, it is one of the most respected of American universities (8,000 students). There are a number of interesting buildings here by Frank Lloyd Wright, Mies van der Rohe, and Eero Saarinen, among others. On **Stagg Field** (S. Ellis Ave. between E. 56th St. and E. 57th St.) a bronze composition by British sculptor Henry Moore marks the exact spot where on December 2, 1942, history's first controlled nuclear chain reaction was set off by a team of researchers under the direction of Enrico Fermi, Italian Nobel Prize winner for physics. Not far from there is the **Oriental Institute** (1155 E. 58th St.) offering very rich collections of Assyrian and Egyptian art (open Tues–Sun), and the Neo-Gothic **Rockefeller Memorial Chapel** (1156 E. 59th St.) with its 72-bell carillon (1910). Guided tour of the campus Mon–Fri at 10am (call 702-8374 for information). Worth the trip.

University of Illinois, Circle Campus, Dan Ryan Expwy. and Eisenhower Expwy. (996-5000): The most modern university in the United States (1965). Note the futurist architecture, especially the administration building with its 28 stories which get larger toward the top. On the campus is **Hull House** (800 S. Halsted), pioneering center for social work founded in 1889 by Jane Addams, Nobel Peace Prize winner. Interesting tours Mon–Fri (and Sun in summer); call 996-7780 for information.

☼�⚲ **Water Tower Place,** 845 N. Michigan Ave. (440-3165): The most luxurious and spectacular shopping center in the United States (see "Shopping," below). The **Water Tower,** in the form of a medieval fortress, is one of the few buildings spared by the great fire of 1871. It houses the local tourism office. A must-see.

Skyscrapers

⚲ **Amoco Building,** 200 E. Randolph Dr.: The second-tallest skyscraper in Chicago and the fourth tallest in the world, 1,107 ft./80 stories (346m) high. Dating from 1973, its facade, initially covered in marble, has been replaced by sturdier granite. No guided tours. Interesting Harry Bertoia "sonic" sculpture on the ornamental pool in front of the tower (see "Outdoor Art and Plazas," below).

☼�⚲ **Chicago Tribune Tower,** 435 N. Michigan Ave. (222-3993): Raymond Hood's amazing octagonal Neo-Gothic skyscraper, 36 stories high, dating from 1925. Home of the *Chicago Tribune,* the city's largest newspaper. Tours Mon–Sat; resv. necessary.

⚲ **First National Bank Building,** 1 First National Plaza at Monroe St. and Dearborn St.: Built in 1969 by architects Murphy, Perkins and Will, it is the tallest bank in the world (60 stories) and should be seen. Guided tours Tues–Thurs; call 732-6037 for resv.

☼�⚲⚲ **John Hancock Center,** 875 N. Michigan Ave. (751-3681): Superb derrick-shaped skyscraper with a facade of smoked glass and black and bronze aluminum, 1,127 ft./100 stories (343m) high. The sixth-tallest skyscraper in the world, it combines shops, offices, and apartments in one building. This work by Skidmore, Owings and Merrill is topped with two gigantic telecommunication antennas 336 ft. (100m) tall. Since its construction in 1969, it has become the symbol of Chicago. The observation platform on the 94th floor should not be missed (see "Panoramas," below).

☼�⚲⚲ **Marina City,** 300 N. State St.: The twin 60-story cylindrical towers by architect Bertrand Goldberg date from 1964. The first floors constitute a parking garage with a spiral ramp. These, the most famous (and most photographed) apartment buildings in the United States dominate the Chicago River. Private marina. Should be seen.

⚲⚲ **Sears Tower,** 233 S. Wacker Dr. (875-9696): The tallest skyscraper in the world, 1,454 ft. (443m) and 110 stories. 17,000 employees work in this huge, vertical ant's nest serviced by 102 elevators. Designed by the same team of architects that did the John Hancock Center, it is the property of Sears Roebuck & Co. Opened in 1974, its construction took 4 years. The installation of two TV antennas brought the tower to a total height of 1,706 ft. (520m). The lobby has a giant Calder mobile called *Universe.* (For more details, see "Panoramas," below.) Not to be missed.

⚲ **333 West Wacker Dr.:** This very handsome 36-story glass tower, its frontage delicately curved to follow the bank of the Chicago River, is by New York architect William Pedersen; it won an award from the American Institute of Architects in 1984. Worth seeing.

☼�⚲ **Wrigley Building,** 400 N. Michigan Ave. (558-8080): One of the most famous monuments in Chicago and the headquarters of the Wrigley's chewing gum empire, this architecturally startling 35-story skyscraper (complete with Renaissance campanile) dates from 1924. The four huge clocks at the top of the tower are each two stories tall. Beautifully illuminated in the evening. A definite must-see.

BEACHES: ⚲ **North Ave. Beach** and ⚲ **Oak St. Beach** are the most popular Chicago beaches, just north of the city. The pollution level of Lake Michigan stays relatively low thanks to seven giant water-purification plants.

CHURCHES/SYNAGOGUES: ⌂ **Chicago Temple,** also known as the **First United Methodist Church,** 77 W. Washington St. (236-4548): Built in 1924, the tallest church in the world—568 ft. (173m) including the cross on top of the Gothic tower—offers the interesting "Open-Air Chapel" on its roof. Worth a look. Open daily.

HISTORIC BUILDINGS: ☼⌂ **Auditorium Building,** 430 S. Michigan Ave. (922-4046): Built in 1887–89 by Louis Sullivan and Dankmar Adler, it is one of the masterpieces of the Chicago School. Extraordinary interior decor. Both concert hall and headquarters of **Roosevelt University** (6,500 students). A must-see.

☼⌂ **Manhattan Building,** 431 S. Dearborn St.: The first real skyscraper in history (1884) though a mere eight stories, this William Le Baron Jenney building anticipated modern construction techniques. Worth a look.

⌂ **Monadnock Building,** 53 W. Jackson Blvd. (922-1890): When completed in 1893, this was the tallest office skyscraper in the world; designed by Burnham and Root. For art history lovers.

⌂ **Orchestra Hall,** 220 S. Michigan Ave. (435-8111): Dating from 1904, this acoustically perfect auditorium is home to the renowned Chicago Symphony Orchestra, whose music director for many years was Sir Georg Solti. The building figures on the national inventory of historic landmarks. Tours by appointment.

☼⌂ **Robie House,** 5757 S. Woodlawn Ave. (702-8374): On the University of Chicago campus (see above), this brick building dating from 1909 is the forerunner of Frank Lloyd Wright's "Prairie House" style. Today it is home to the Institute of International Affairs. Open Mon–Sat. A definite must-see.

⌂ **The Rookery,** 209 S. La Salle St.: The oldest steel-frame skyscraper in the world (1886); by Burnham and Root. The white-and-gold hall of this historic landmark was redesigned by Frank Lloyd Wright at the turn of the century. Worth a look.

MONUMENTS: ⌂ **Buckingham Fountain,** Grant Park at the end of Congress St.: A colossal public fountain in pink Georgia marble, with a jet rising to more than 131 ft. (41m). Dramatic illuminations and enchanting water shows in the evenings, May–Sept. Worth a look. (See also "Outdoor Art and Plazas," below.)

MUSEUMS OF ART: ☼⌂⌂ **Art Institute,** Michigan Ave. and Adams St. (443-3600): Elegant Italian Renaissance–style palazzo, constructed for the World's Fair of 1893 and splendidly renovated. More than a thousand paintings by European and American masters, from Rembrandt to Matisse and from Ben Shahn to Mark Rothko. Among the most famous: Caravaggio's *Resurrection,* El Greco's *Assumption of the Virgin,* Delacroix's *Lion Hunt,* Seurat's *Sunday Afternoon on the Isle of Grande-Jatte,* van Gogh's *Vincent's Room in Arles,* Picasso's *The Old Guitarist,* Juan Gris's *Cubist Portrait of Picasso,* Reginald Marsh's *Tattoo* and *Haircut,* Edward Hopper's *Nighthawks,* and Grant Wood's *American Gothic.* Also, wonderful stained glass by Chagall, and fine collections of Chinese sculpture and preColumbian art. Plays host to many prestigious traveling exhibitions. One of the most beautiful art museums in the United States and in the world, with a pleasant cafeteria and open-air restaurant in summer. The Art Institute alone is worth the trip to Chicago. Open daily.

☼⌂⌂ **Chicago Cultural Center,** 78 E. Washington St. (346-3278): In the former **Public Library,** this sumptuous, Renaissance-style building from the end of the 19th century houses distinguished temporary

DOWNTOWN CHICAGO

Navy Pier

Chicago Harbor

N. LAKE SHORE DR.

Oak St. Beach

John Hancock Center

Water Tower Place

E. GRAND AVE.

Chicago Tribune Tower

E. WACKER DR.

Standard Oil Building

Art Institute

Chicago Cultural Center

E. MONROE DR.

Buckingham Fountain

N. MICHIGAN AVE.

International Museum of Surgical Sciences

E. ONTARIO ST.

E. OHIO ST.

Richard J. Daley Center

First National City Bank Building

Orchestra Hall

N. STATE ST.

Newberry Library

N. CLARK ST.

State of Illinois Center

E. JACKSON BLVD.

Marina City

City Hall

E. RANDOLPH ST.

E. ADAMS ST.

N. LA SALLE ST.

Chicago Historical Society

Merchandise Mart

Chicago River

W. WACKER DR.

E. WASHINGTON

Board of Trade

Federal Center

Sears Tower

CONGRESS ST.

E. NORTH AVE.

N. ORLEANS ST.

E. CHICAGO AVE.

W. ONTARIO ST.

W. OHIO ST.

to Polish Museum

LARRABEE ST.

DAN RYAN EXPWY.

N. MILWAUKEE AVE.

KENNEDY EXPWY.

W. CHICAGO AVE.

W. GRAND AVE.

W. OGDEN AVE.

N. ELIZABETH ST.

W. RANDOLPH ST.

W. WASHINGTON ST.

W. MADISON ST.

W. MONROE DR.

W. JACKSON BLVD.

W. ADAMS ST.

EISENHOWER EXPWY.

290

W. NORTH AVE.

exhibitions. The interior is richly adorned with Carrara marble, mosaics, and Tiffany-style windows. Should be seen. Open Mon–Sat.

⚱ **Du Sable Museum of African-American History,** 740 E. 56th Pl. (947-0600): Very rich, interesting collections of African and African American art. Symbolically bears the name of a founder of Chicago, a black businessman from Santo Domingo (see the introduction to this chapter). Open Sun–Fri.

⚱ **Mexican Fine Arts Center,** 1852 W. 19th St. (738-1503): The city's newest ethnic museum. Art exhibits and performances from Mexico and Mexican artists in the United States. The only museum of its kind in the Midwest. Worth a visit. Open Tues–Sun.

☼⚱ **Museum of Contemporary Art,** 237 E. Ontario St. (280-2660): A truly marvelous little museum founded in 1967 housing modern and avant-garde art in all forms: painting, sculpture, poetry, film, music, dance, video, photography. Temporary exhibitions. Open Tues–Sun. Not to be missed.

⚱ **Newberry Library,** 60 W. Walton St. (943-9090): Dating from 1887 and boasting more than 1.4 million volumes as well as several million manuscripts, this library is famous for its works on the Renaissance, Native Americans, and music history. Open Tues–Sat.

☼⚱⚱ **Terra Museum of American Art,** Erie St. at N. Michigan Ave. (664-3939): Rather small in size but big in content, the Terra Museum, which opened in 1987, is the newest museum of American art in the United States. A strange blend of modern architectural idioms (large bay windows, white marble from Vermont) adapted to older structures. 800 major works of classical and contemporary American artists: Bingham, Cassatt, Demuth, Homer, Hopper, Morse, Peale, Prendergast, Sargent, Sheeler, Whistler, Wyeth, etc. A must for all art-lovers. Right in the middle of the Magnificent Mile. Open daily.

MUSEUMS OF SCIENCE & HISTORY: ☼⚱ Academy of Sciences, 2001 N. Clark St. (549-0606): Museum wholly devoted to the natural history and ecology of the Great Lakes region, notably a reconstruction of a 350-million-year-old forest with wildlife displays, as well as a "walk-through" cave and canyon. A definite must-see. Open daily.

☼⚱⚱ **Adler Planetarium,** 1300 S. Lake Shore Dr. (322-0300): This world-renowned institution covers the history of astronomy from the ancients to our time. Space shows and telescope observation in summer. Exhibits on space explorations (*Voyager* and *Apollo II* flights). Fine art deco architecture. Not to be missed. Open daily.

⚱ **Balzekas Museum,** 6500 S. Pulaski Rd. (582-6500): Permanent exhibits of antique weapons, armor, dolls, fine and folk art, rare maps and prints spanning more than 1,000 years of Lithuanian history. Interesting. Open daily.

⚱ **Chicago Fire Academy,** 558 W. De Koven St. (744-6691): The famous fire-brigade school built on the site of Patrick O'Leary's stable, where legend puts the origin of the fire that totally ravaged Chicago on October 8, 1871, and left more than 90,000 people homeless. Tours of the training center Mon–Fri. Resv. necessary. See it.

⚱ **Chicago Historical Society,** Clark St. at North Blvd. (642-4600): A wonderful museum dedicated to American history —the Civil War and the life of Abraham Lincoln in particular—as well as to the evolution of Chicago from its founding to the present. Temporary exhibitions, demonstrations of old trades. Fully renovated in 1988. Not to be missed. Open daily.

⚱⚱ **Field Museum of Natural History,** Roosevelt Rd. at Lake Shore Dr. (922-9410): One of largest museums of natural history and ethnology in the world, with 200,000 exhibits ranging from reproductions of plants around the world to Egyptian tombs and meteorites. Section devoted to the history of Native Americans not to be missed. Open daily. A definite must-see.

International Museum of Surgical Sciences, 1524 N. Lake Shore Dr. (642-3555): This interesting museum of surgery from prehistoric times to the present includes displays of ancient instruments and of an apothecary's shop from the 19th century. Open Tues–Sun.

Museum of Science and Industry, E. 57th St. and S. Lake Shore Dr. (684-1414): Science and industry from cavedwelling days to the present, including a 15-ft.-tall (5m) working model of a human heart. Authentic German U-boat from World War II. Old locomotives, cars, planes by the dozen, plus a re-creation of a working coal mine and an entirely mechanized midwestern farm. There are a number of robots which can be operated by visitors, plus a wing devoted to space research (**Crown Space Center**) with a 360° film-projection system, OMNIMAX. Four million visitors per year. The handsomest museum in Chicago. Open daily and not to be missed.

Oriental Institute Museum, 1155 E. 58th St. (702-9520): Established in 1894 as part of the University of Chicago, this museum of the ancient Near East displays artifacts of architecture, art, religion, and everyday life of ancient Egypt, Assyria, Mesopotamia, Persia, Syria, and Palestine. Among the important objects on view, a monumental statue of Tutankhamen, a 40-ton winged Assyrian bull, and a fragment of the Dead Sea Scrolls. Not to be missed. Open Tues–Sun.

The Peace Museum, 430 W. Erie St. (440-1860): The first and only museum of its kind in the nation dedicated solely to the role of arts, sciences, labor, minorities . . . on issues of war and peace. Recent shows have included exhibits of art by South African artists, the life and times of Martin Luther King, Jr., and the Vietnam Veterans Memorial. Interesting. Open daily.

Polish Museum, 984 N. Milwaukee Ave. (384-3352): The second-largest Polish city in the world after Warsaw by right should and does have a museum devoted to Poland, its art, its culture, its folklore —and the Polish contribution to American history (among others, Gen. Tadeusz Kosciuszko, hero of the Revolutionary War, and musician and statesman Ignace Jan Paderewski). Open daily.

Scholl Museum of Folk Culture, 909 W. Armitage Ave. (525-7793): One of the newest museums of Chicago. Offers all aspects of folk culture from exhibits to concerts and demonstrations, and a wonderful collection of folk art and music from around the world. Fascinating. Open Tues–Thurs and Sat.

Shedd Aquarium, 1200 S. Lake Shore Dr. (939-2438): The largest aquarium in the world—more than 8,000 fish and marine animals from the dolphin to the piranha—with its own artificial coral reef. The 460,000 gals. (1.75 million liters) of seawater required for the tanks is hauled by truck and rail from the Atlantic. Since 1929 this has been a must-see for every visitor. A $43-million addition completed in mid-1990 gives midwesterners the experience of walking along an ocean coastline and shows off cold-water mammals rarely seen outside major aquariums on either coast.

Spertus Museum of Judaica, 618 S. Michigan Ave. (922-9012): Rich collection of Jewish manuscripts, craft tools, and religious objects. Paintings, sculptures, temporary exhibitions. Open Sun–Fri.

NIGHTLIFE: **Rush St.,** between Chicago Ave. and Division St.: The mecca of Chicago nightowls, full of bars, nightclubs, discos, jazz clubs. Guaranteed atmosphere. (Chicago has some of the most active nightlife of any city in the United States.)

OUTDOOR ART & PLAZAS: In addition to the previously mentioned giant sculptures by Picasso, Miró, and Dubuffet (see "Architectural Highlights," above), Chicago's streets and plazas offer numerous noteworthy works of art: a 3,000-sq.-ft. (280m²) Chagall mosaic, *The Four Seasons* (First National Plaza); *Batcolumn,* a kind of giant steel baseball bat 100 ft. (31m) tall by Claes Oldenburg (600 W. Madison); a 53-ft.-high (16m) Calder sculpture, *Flamingo,* which weighs 50 tons (45,500kg; Federal Center Plaza); a giant bronze sundial by Henry Moore in front of the entrance to the Adler Planetarium (1300 S. Lake Shore Dr.); and a startling "sonic" sculpture by Harry Bertoia that sits above an ornamental pool in front of the Amoco Building (200 E. Randolph Dr.).

PANORAMAS: ※△△ **John Hancock Center Observatory,** 875 N. Michigan Ave. (751-3681): At 1,127 ft. (343m), the sixth-tallest skyscraper in the world. The observation platform located on the 94th floor offers a unique, impressive view of the city and lake in clear weather. Platform open daily 9am–midnight.

△ **Navy Pier,** at the end of E. Grand Ave.: This mile-long jetty extending into Lake Michigan dates from the beginning of the century and was once a berth for ocean-going vessels. It is a great place for strolling with its public benches, lawns, and turn-of-the-century gas lamps. Its unobstructed view of the Chicago skyline is not to be missed.

※△△ **Sears Tower Skydeck,** 233 S. Wacker Dr. (875-9696): The tallest skyscraper in the world at 1,454 ft. (443m) and equipped with the fastest elevator in the world (1,753 ft./548m per min.: it takes exactly 70 seconds to reach the 103rd floor), it is the head office of Sears Roebuck & Co. Its asymmetrical cubist structure was designed to offer maximum structural resistance to Chicago's windy weather. Observation platform on the 103rd floor open daily 9am–midnight. In clear weather, you can see for 37 mi. (60km). What a sight! Lovely giant Calder mobile, *Universe,* in the lobby. Not to be missed.

PARKS & GARDENS: △△ **Garfield Park,** 300 N. Central Park Blvd. (533-1281): Splendid tropical greenhouses (the largest in the world) with palm trees, luxurious vegetation, 400 kinds of cactus, ornamental lakes, and water lilies. Beautiful floral exhibitions. Quite spectacular. Open daily.

△ **Graceland Cemetery,** 4001 N. Clark St. (525-1105): A lovely landscaped cemetery among hills and ornamental ponds. Sumptuous mausoleums housing the mortal remains of rich Chicago families, bankers, industrial magnates, as well as famous architects Louis Sullivan and Daniel Burnham, the founders of the Chicago School. It also offers an unimpeded view of Lake Michigan and the city. Open daily.

△ **Grant Park,** along Lake Michigan between E. Randolph Dr. and McCormick Pl. (294-2493): An enormous public park in the middle of the city with numerous museums and a fine view of the lake and the skyscrapers. See it.

※△ **Lincoln Park,** along Lake Shore Dr. between La Salle Dr. and Hollywood Ave.: A sprawling park and lovely botanical garden extending close to 5 mi. (8km) along the shore of Lake Michigan, it is home to the famous zoo (one of the oldest in the United States) plus public beaches and marinas. A nice perspective on the city from a distance. During the tense days of the anti–Vietnam War demonstrations in 1968, it was the meeting spot of the "Yippies" (Youth International Party). Worth the walk.

(Just off Lincoln Park, in a garage that once stood at 2122 N. Clark St., the famous Saint Valentine's Day Massacre occurred on February 14, 1929: seven gangsters were gunned down on the orders of Al Capone. He died in Miami in 1947, after spending 8 years in Alcatraz. He is buried in lot 48 of Chicago's Mount Olivet Cemetery.)

PERFORMING ARTS: For a listing of all shows and cultural events, consult the entertainment pages of the daily papers, the *Chicago Sun Times* (morning) and the *Chicago Tribune* (morning), of the weekly *The Reader,* and the monthly magazine *Chicago.* Or call 977-1755 for a recorded announcement of current cultural offerings. **Hot Tix,** a booth at 24 S. State St., sells half-price tickets for all shows on the day of the performance. Major credit cards accepted. Open Mon–Sat.

Apollo Theater Center, 2540 N. Lincoln Ave. (935-6100): Drama, comedy.

Arie Crown, McCormick Pl. (791-6000): Modern theater.

Auditorium Theatre, 50 E. Congress Pkwy. (922-2110): Concerts, recitals, ballet performances. Open year round.

Blackstone Theatre, 60 E. Balbo Ave. (341-6813): Broadway hits.

Body Politic Theatre, 2261 N. Lincoln Ave. (871-3000): Contemporary theater.

Chicago Theatre, 175 N. State St. (431-2356): Big-name concerts, Broadway hits.

Civic Opera House, 20 N. Wacker Dr. (372-7800): Home of the Chicago Opera Theatre and of the Lyric Opera of Chicago. Open Feb–June.

Goodman Theatre, 200 S. Columbus Dr. (443-3800): The oldest theater in Chicago, offering everything from Shakespeare to contemporary theater.

Orchestra Hall, 220 S. Michigan Ave. (435-6666): Home of the Chicago Civic Orchestra and of the Chicago Symphony Orchestra, one of the five best orchestras in the world (music director, Sir Georg Solti; music director designate, Daniel Barenboim). Open Sept–May.

Petrillo Music Shell, Columbus Dr. and Jackson Blvd., in Grant Park (294-2420): Free outdoor concerts, late June to Aug.

Royal George Theatre, 1641 N. Halsted St. (988-9000): Broadway hits, modern theater.

Shubert Theatre, 22 W. Monroe St. (977-1700): Broadway hits and shows with big-name stars.

Steppenwolf Theatre, 2851 N. Halsted St. (472-4141): Drama, classical theater. One of the best theater buildings of the Chicago School.

Victory Gardens Theatre, 2257 N. Lincoln Ave. (871-3000): Specializing in plays by local playwrights.

SHOPPING: ☀ **Marshall Field & Co.,** 111 N. State St.: The most beautiful and most famous department store in Chicago. This almost 100-year-old classic of the consumer society has a superb Tiffany-windowed dome comprising 1.6 million pieces of colored glass. Wonderful ice-cream sundaes for lovers of giant desserts can be found on the third floor (in the Crystal Palace).

☀ **Carson, Pirie, Scott & Co.,** 1 S. State St.: Another venerable representative of the local breed of department stores and a sample of Chicago School architecture from the end of the 19th century, designed by Louis Sullivan. Splendid rococo entrance hall of ornamental cast metal. See it.

☀ **"Magnificent Mile,"** N. Michigan Ave. between Illinois St. and Oak St.: Chicago's swankiest thoroughfare, with fashion boutiques, art galleries, and such tony stores as Gucci, Burberry's, Saks Fifth Avenue, Neiman Marcus, Charles Jourdan, Louis Vuitton, Chanel, Armani, Bally, and more. This is the local counterpart of New York's Fifth Avenue or Rodeo Drive in Beverly Hills. Definitely worth seeing.

State Street, between Wacker Dr. and Congress Pkwy.: The main pedestrian and commercial street at the heart of the Loop. Boutiques and department stores by the dozen offer many a bargain.

☀ **Water Tower Place,** 845 N. Michigan Ave.: The country's first "vertical" shopping center covering 2,140,000 sq. ft.

(200,000m²), with more than 125 stores, boutiques, 11 restaurants, and seven movie theaters. The shopping area is on the first eight floors of this 74-story tower which houses the Ritz Carlton Hotel. Luxurious, very stylish interior with fountains, gardens, and glass elevators.

SPECIAL EVENTS: For the exact schedule of events below, consult the **Chicago Convention & Tourism Bureau** (see "Tourist Information," above).

Chicago Auto Show (late Feb): The most popular auto show in the United States, with an attendance of nearly a million people.

St. Patrick's Day Parade (Mar 17): Pompoms, marching bands, and drum majorettes.

Ravinia Festival (June–Sept): One of the most popular music festivals in the United States, with open-air symphonic concerts, ballet, jazz, and folk music. Highland Park. Call 728-4642 for information.

Grant Park Concerts (late June to Aug): Free open-air classical concerts, plus a very famous blues festival. For information, call 819-0614.

Taste of Chicago (July/Aug, date varies): The world's largest culinary festival: 3,000,000 participants. All kinds of food are available for a whole week in Grant Park.

Chicago Sailboat Race (July): Boat races on Lake Michigan.

Venetian Night Festival (mid-Aug): Shows and concerts on the lakeshore.

Jazz Festival (Sept): With the greats—the world's largest free jazz festival.

International Film Festival (2 weeks in late Oct or early Nov): A tribute to foreign cinema.

SPORTS: Chicago has five professional teams:

Baseball (Apr–Oct): Cubs, Wrigley Field (404-2827); White Sox, Comiskey Park (924-1000).

Basketball (Oct–Apr): Bulls, Chicago Stadium (943-5800).

Football (Sept–Dec): Bears, Soldier Field/Grant Park (663-5408).

Ice Hockey (Sept–Apr): Black Hawks, Chicago Stadium (733-5300).

Horse Racing

Arlington International Racecourse, Euclid and Wilke, in Arlington Heights (708/255-4300): Dubbed the "Taj Mahal" of horse racing, this $200-million structure opened in 1989 features sky boxes, marble stairways, and 15 restaurants. Racing daily June–Sept.

Balmoral Park, Dixie Hwy. and Elmscourt Lane, in Crete (312/568-5700).

Hawthorne Park, 3501 S. Laramie Ave., in Cicero (708/652-9400).

Maywood Park, 8600 W. North Ave., in Maywood (708/343-4800): Racing daily.

Sportsman's Park, 3301 S. Laramie Ave., in Cicero (708/652-2812): Racing Mar–Dec.

STROLLS: ⚲ **Chinatown,** around S. Wentworth Ave. and W. Cermak Rd.: Picturesque Chinese quarter with numerous characteristic stores, restaurants, and guaranteed local color. See especially the ornamental gate built in 1975 at S. Wentworth Ave. at W. Cermak Rd., **City Hall,** the Buddhist temple, and the **Ling Long Museum.**

Gold Coast, Lake Shore Dr. between North Ave. and E. Ontario St.: The spectacular, luxurious face that Chicago presents to Lake Michigan, where skyscrapers abut opulent 19th-century palaces and estates.

River North, north of the river and west of Michigan Ave.: Chicago's latest "in" neighborhood replete with trendy rests., galleries, and boutiques. Chicago's answer to SoHo.

The Loop, west of Michigan Ave. around State St. and Madison St.: Chicago's business district, complete with department stores, hotels, and restaurants, surrounded by the famous, clanking elevated train (the "El"). The heart of the Loop—the intersection of State St. and Madison St.—is nicknamed "the busiest corner in the world." City streets are oriented from this intersection: north-south in relation to Madison, east-west in relation to State. Animated and colorful by day, to be avoided at night if you're on foot. Absolutely worth a look.

Magnificent Mile, N. Michigan Ave. from the Chicago River to E. Oak St.: Lined with chic stores (see "Shopping," above), hotels, boutiques, art galleries, and prestigious buildings, it is one of the most elegant—and snooty—thoroughfares in the United States. Go out of your way to see it.

Old Town, around N. Wells St. and Division St.: The "Latin Quarter" or the "Greenwich Village" of Chicago, with its brick houses from the 19th century plus restaurants, nightclubs, antiques stores, and fashionable boutiques. Very lively by night.

Prairie Ave. Historic District, Prairie Ave. around 18th St. and Cullerton St.: The 19th-century millionaire's neighborhood, currently undergoing renovation. Sumptuous private houses, cobblestone streets, gas lamps. Many old buildings should be seen: **Glessner House,** 1800 S. Prairie Ave., by Henry Hobson Richardson (1886), today houses the Chicago Architecture Foundation which organizes guided tours (Tues–Sun; call 326-1393 for information) of Chicago's architectural masterpieces; **Kimball House,** 1801 S. Prairie Ave., dates from 1890; **Coleman House,** 1811 S. Prairie Ave., from 1886; **Keith House,** 1900 S. Prairie Ave., from 1871. Neighboring **Clark House** is the oldest house in Chicago (1837). Not to be missed.

THEME PARKS: Six Flags Great America, in Gurnee, 40 mi. (65km) north on I-94 (708/249-1776): Enormous (200-acre/80ha) amusement park offering hundreds of attractions, with a giant roller coaster. Facsimiles of pioneer villages plus shows and special events. Open daily from the end of May to early Sept, wknds only in spring and autumn; closed the rest of the year.

WINTER SPORTS RESORTS: Holiday Park Ski Area (42 mi./68km NW on U.S. 12) (708/546-8222): 5 ski lifts. Open Dec–Mar.

Pines Ski Area (64 mi./102km SE on I-90 and Ind. 49) (219/462-4179): 5 lifts. Open Dec–Mar.

Ski Valley (66 mi./106km SE on I-90, U.S. 421, and Ind. 2) (219/326-0123): 6 lifts. Open Dec–Mar.

Wilmont Ski Area (54 mi./87km NW on U.S. 12, Ill. 59 and 83, and WI Country C) (414/862-2301): 14 lifts. Open Nov–Mar.

ZOOS: Brookfield Zoo, entrances at 31st St. and First Ave. (15 mi./24km SW on W. Cermak Rd., and 22nd St. and First Ave. (708/242-2630): One of the top 10 zoos in the United States (192 acres/80ha). Natural habitats from the Sahara Desert to tropical forests and from South America to the Pacific Islands. Mini-train tour (Mar–Nov). Definitely worth going out of your way to see. Open daily year round.

ACCOMMODATIONS

A Note on Accommodations: Room rates in Chicago are coded as follows: **VE,** Very Expensive ($140 and up); **E,** Expensive ($90–$140); **M,** Moderate ($60–$90); **I,** Inexpensive ($30–$60); **B,** Budget (up to $30). A listing of toll free numbers is in the Appendix.

Note: Despite its 55,000 available rooms, and an ambitious hotel-construction program going back to 1979, Chicago and the metropolitan area suffer from a chronic shortage of hotel space. It is advisable, therefore, to make reservations as far in advance as possible.

Personal Favorites (in order of preference)

The Drake (nr. dwntwn), 140 E. Walton Pl., IL 60611 (312/787-2200; toll free, see Hilton). 535 rms, A/C, color TV, in-rm movies. AE, CB, DC, MC, V. Valet gar. $18, two rests. (including the Cape Cod Room), coffee shop, two bars, 24-hr. rm svce, hrdrsr, boutiques, drugstore, concierge, free crib. *Note:* A flawless palace in the shadow of the John Hancock Center. Here, all is tranquility, luxury, and pleasure. Spacious rms (the best have a view of the lake) and an elegant, refined interior w. an imposing marble lobby, grand staircase, and ultra-fashionable tea rm. The pleasing svce and reception includes attention to such details as turning the mattress every evening. Its class and style make this the best hotel in Chicago and one of the 12 best in the United States; its Cape Cod Room is also one of the city's finest rests. A business clientele and traveling VIPs enjoy its exceptional location, facing Lake Michigan and a few steps from the Magnificent Mile (see "Strolls," above). VIP floor. One of the gems of the Vista International group. Interesting wknd packages. The Drake recently underwent renovation down to the last detail. The best address in Chicago since 1920. **VE**

Four Seasons (nr. dwntwn), 120 E. Delaware Pl., IL 60611 (312/280-8800; toll free, see Four Seasons). 343 rms, A/C, color TV, in-rm movies. AE, CB, DC, MC, V. Valet gar. $18, pool, health club, sauna, rest. (Seasons), bar, 24-hr rm svce, boutiques, concierge, free crib. *Note:* Opened in 1989, the Four Seasons is the newest of Chicago's luxury palace hotels, occupying 16 floors of a flamboyant 66-floor Neo-Gothic high-rise right on the Magnificent Mile. Spacious, elegant rms w. fine view of lake or city; unmatched comfort and facilities; absolutely top-flight svce. Direct access to the Avenue Atrium, a vertical shopping mall with dozens of boutiques and smart shops. A prestige address. **VE**

Mayfair Regent (formerly the Lake Shore Drive Hotel; nr. dwntwn), 181 E. Lake Shore Dr., IL 60611 (312/787-8500; toll free 800/545-4000). 204 rms, A/C, color TV, in-rm movies. AE, CB, DC, MC, V. Valet gar. $12, two rests. (including Ciel Bleu), coffee shop, bar, 24-hr. rm svce, hrdrsr, concierge, free crib. *Note:* Venerable but now entirely renovated palace from the turn of the century, whose slightly dated decor houses smart comfort in the European tradition. Spacious rooms with minibars and marble bathrooms. Attentive svce which anticipates your wants. Fine rests., plus a much-frequented tea rm. Beautiful view of the lake and the city. Part of the Hong Kong "Regent" chain of hotels. Interesting wknd packages. One of Chicago's most fashionable hotels. **VE**

Swissotel Chicago (nr. dwntwn), 323 E. Wacker Dr., IL 60601 (312/565-0565; toll free 800/654-7263). 645 rms, A/C, color TV, in-rm movies. AE, CB, DC, MC, V. Garage $14, pool, health club, sauna, two rests. (including Le Prince), coffee shop, bar, 24-hr. rm svce, concierge. *Note:* This shimmering triangular building, its 45 floors looking out over Lake Michigan, was opened in 1988—the first hotel built in the U.S. by Swissotel, a subsidiary of Swissair. Very comfortable rms, each w. minibar and two phone lines. Unusually thoughtful facilities for the business traveler, including a TV studio! Svce in the best tradition of Swiss hotels; high-class rest. A favorite w. those in-the-know. **VE**

Raphael (nr. dwntwn), 201 E. Delaware Pl., IL 60611 (312/943-5000; toll free 800/821-5343). 175 rms, A/C, color TV. AE, CB, DC, MC, V. Valet gar. $18, rest., bar, 24-hr. rm svce, nightclub, free crib. *Note:* Small, calm, elegant hotel very close to the Magnificent Mile. Large, comfortable rms w. minibars offer lovely views of the Gold Coast. Polished svce. Interesting wknd packages. A favorite of connoisseurs. **E–VE**

🏨🏨 **Days Inn Lake Shore Drive** (nr. dwntwn), 644 N. Lake Shore Dr., IL 60611 (312/943-9200; toll free, see Days Inns). 580 rms, A/C, color TV, in-rm movies. AE, CB, DC, MC, V. Parking $8, pool, rest., coffee shop, bar, rm svce, free crib. *Note:* The biggest attraction of this modern 33-story tower is its location directly on the shore of Lake Michigan, affording a splendid view of the lake and the city. A good idea if you're driving, because of the reduced-rate parking. Revolving rest. at the top. Less-than-ideal svce. Favored by rather obtrusive groups. A good overall value. **M–E**

🏨🏨 **Best Western Inn of Chicago** (formerly the St. Clair Hotel; nr. dwntwn), 162 E. Ohio St., IL 60611 (312/787-3100; toll free, see Best Western). 357 rms, A/C, color TV, in-rm movies. AE, CB, DC, MC, V. Parking $10, 24-hr. coffee shop, bar, rm svce. *Note:* Old luxury hotel entirely modernized w. marble lobby and very comfortable rms. Good svce and a very central location close to the Magnificent Mile. A favorite of businesspeople. Interesting wknd packages. **M–E**

🏨 **Comfort Inn** (nr. dwntwn), 601 W. Diversey Pkwy., IL 60614 (312/348-2810; toll free 800/228-5150). 73 rms, A/C, color TV. AE, CB, DC, MC, V. Street parking; no bar or rest., but free breakfast. *Note:* Small, modern, and comfortable motel very nr. the Lincoln Park Zoo w. spacious rms and friendly, pleasant reception. Good value. **I–M**

Other Accommodations (from top bracket to budget)

🏨🏨🏨🏨 **Nikko Hotel** (nr. dwntwn), 320 N. Dearborn St., IL 60610 (312/744-1900; toll free 800/645-5687). 425 rms, A/C, color TV, in-rm movies. AE, CB, DC, MC, V. Valet gar. $18, health club, two rests. (including Les Célébrités), coffee shop, bars, 24-hr. rm svce, nightclub, concierge, free crib. *Note:* Big, modern 20-floor tower situated alongside the Chicago River, and affording great daytime and romantic nighttime views of both the river and the Loop. Spacious, comfortable Western-style rms w. marble bathroom and minibar, or Japanese rms with tatami mats. Uncommonly effective soundproofing; efficient, smiling svce. Delightful Japanese grdn, and the well-regarded Japanese rest. (Benkay) looks out on the river. American and Japanese business clientele. Three floors ("Nikko floors") reserved for VIPs. **VE**

🏨🏨🏨 **Park Hyatt** (nr. dwntwn), on Water Tower Sq. at 800 N. Michigan Ave., IL 60611 (312/280-2222; toll free, see Hyatt). 255 rms, A/C, color TV, in-rm movies, AE, CB, DC, MC, V. Valet gar. $15, pool, sauna, two rests. (including La Tour), bar, 24-hr. rm svce, nightclub. *Note:* This extremely exclusive hotel—the most expensive in Chicago w. one suite priced at $2,500 a night—accommodates neither groups nor conventions. It offers luxurious, elegant rms w. minibars, exemplary svce, a decent rest., and a pleasant tea rm. A favorite hotel of big business. Interesting wknd packages. Faces the Water Tower in the midst of the Magnificent Mile. **VE**

🏨🏨🏨 **Tremont** (nr. dwntwn), 100 E. Chestnut, IL 60611 (312/751-1900; toll free 800/223-5560). 127 rms, A/C, color TV, in-rm movies. AE, CB, DC, MC, V. Valet gar. $18, health club, rest. (Cricket's), coffee shop, bar, 24-hr. rm svce, nightclub, concierge, free crib. *Note:* A hotel known for its excellence for more than half a century. Period furnishings and chandeliers; spacious, comfortable rms. Very British in style; notably good svce. The highly praised rest. is a facsimile of New York's 21 Club. Clientele of well-heeled regulars. **VE**

🏨🏨🏨 **Chicago Hilton & Towers** (formerly the Conrad Hilton; dwntwn), 720 S. Michigan Ave., IL 60605 (312/922-4400; toll free, see Hilton). 1,610 rms, A/C, color TV, in-rm movies. AE, CB, DC, MC, V. Gar. $10, pool, health club, sauna, three rests. (including Buckingham's), 24-hr. coffee shop, three bars, rm svce, disco, hrdrsr, boutiques, concierge, free crib. *Note:* Sturdy pioneer of the production-line hotel, restored to all its original splendor at a cost of $180 million. Heavy, forbidding architecture but a luxurious interior, especially the great lobby w. its imposing staircase and the Versailles-style ballroom. Spacious, comfortable rms, the most pleasant of which have a view of Grant Park. Slightly overburdened svce. Convention and other groups. Three VIP floors and the most expensive suite in Chicago, at $4,000 a night. Good rest. w. modern American cuisine (Buckingham's). Well-equipped business center. Fine location next to the Loop. **E–VE**

Hyatt Regency (nr. dwntwn), 151 E. Wacker Dr., IL 60601 (312/565-1234; toll free, see Hyatt). 2,020 rms, A/C, color TV, in-rm movies. AE, CB, DC, MC, V. V. Gar. $12, health club, sauna, four rests. (including Stetson's), 24-hr. coffee shop, four bars, 24-hr. rm svce, nightclub, hrdrsr, boutiques, free crib. *Note:* Luxurious and comfortable rms in two adj. towers of 34 and 36 stories, of modern design. The spectacular glass atrium w. pool and interior grdns on four floors is worth a look. Efficient, if impersonal, svce. One of the best locations in Chicago, on the Chicago River. Business clientele. Four floors, reserved for VIPs. Interesting wknd packages. Recently renovated decor. **E–VE**

Knickerbocker (nr. dwntwn), 163 E. Walton Pl., IL 60611 (312/751-8100; toll free 800/621-8140). 256 rms, A/C, color TV, in-rm movies. AE, CB, DC, MC, V. Valet gar. $18, rest. (Prince of Wales), coffee shop, bar, rm svce, nightclub, concierge, free crib. *Note:* A landmark among Chicago's hotels since 1927, entirely renovated in 1983. Exceptionally spacious rms, half w. two bathrooms. The lobby, public rms, and rest. have been restored to their original splendor. Very good svce. Well located halfway between the lake and the Magnificent Mile. **E–VE**

Omni Ambassador East (nr. dwntwn), 1301 N. State Pkwy., IL 60610 (312/787-7200; toll free, see Omni). 274 rms, A/C, color TV, in-rm movies. AE, CB, DC, MC, V. Gar. $16, rest. (The Pump Room), bar, 24-hr. rm svce, disco, hrdrsr, boutiques, concierge, free crib. *Note:* Old-world charm, elegance, and comfort in a historic landmark building. Frequented by celebrities since 1926 (Humphrey Bogart and Lauren Bacall spent their honeymoon here). Very fine svce. Mediocre and overpriced rest. Total absence of exercise facilities. Recently renovated. Very close to Old Town and its nightlife. **E–VE**

Palmer House Hilton (dwntwn), 17 E. Monroe St., IL 60690 (312/726-7500; toll free, see Hilton). 1,720 rms, A/C, color TV, in-rm movies. AE, CB, DC, MC, V. Gar. $10, pool, health club, sauna, five rests. (including the Empire Room), three bars, rm svce (until midnight), nightclub, hrdrsr, drugstore, boutiques, concierge, free crib. *Note:* More than a century old, making it a survivor from an earlier age of Chicago hotels. Carefully restored decor and recently modernized facilities, but antiquated ambience and only moderate comfort. Less-than-agreeable svce. Conventions and other large groups. In the heart of the Loop. Two VIP floors. Interesting wknd packages. **E–VE**

Claridge Hotel (formerly the Tuscany; nr. dwntwn), 1244 N. Dearborn St., IL 60610 (312/787-4980). 175 rms, A/C, color TV, in-rm movies. AE, CB, DC, MC, V. Valet gar. $14, rest., coffee shop, bar, rm svce, free breakfast and daily paper, free crib. *Note:* Engaging older hotel, entirely renovated. Comfortable, intimate setting; inviting, well-laid-out rms w. minibar; efficient svce. A good value overall; many guests are regulars. Very nr. the Old Town and the Magnificent Mile. **E**

Holiday Inn Mart Plaza (nr. dwntwn), 350 N. Orleans St., IL 60654 (312/836-5000; toll free, see Holiday Inns). 525 rms, A/C, color TV, in-rm movies. AE, CB, DC, MC, V. Parking $9, pool, health club, rest., bar, rm svce, disco, hrdrsr, boutiques, free crib. *Note:* This modern and comfortable convention hotel occupies the top eight floors of the Apparel

Center Building and faces the Merchandise Mart. Comfort and amenities above the norm for a Holiday Inn. Excellent location quite close to the Loop. Business clientele. Very nice view of the city from most rms. Unsafe neighborhood at night; take a cab. **E**

�077 **Allerton Hotel** (nr. dwntwn), 701 N. Michigan Ave., IL 60611 (312/440-1500; toll free 800/621-8311). 450 rms, A/C, color TV. AE, CB, DC, MC, V. Adjacent valet parking lot, rest. (L'Escargot), bar, rm svce, hrdrsr. *Note:* A veteran of the 1920s in the heart of the Magnificent Mile, w. renovated rms and amenities. Still has lots of charm, even if the svce doesn't always measure up. Highly recommendable rest. Interesting wknd packages. Overall, a good value. **M–E**

�077 **Hilton Hyde Park** (nr. dwntwn), 4900 S. Lake Shore Dr., IL (312/288-5800; toll free, see Hilton). 300 rms, A/C, color TV, in-rm movies. AE, CB, DC, MC, V. Free parking, pool, rest., coffee shop, bar, rm svce, free crib. free shuttle to and from dwntwn. *Note:* Relatively modern and functional motel 10 min. from the Loop. Friendly reception and svce. Ideal for drivers. **M–E**

�077 **Bismarck Hotel** (dwntwn), 171 W. Randolph St., IL 60601 (312/236-0123; toll free 800/643-1500). 515 rms, A/C, color TV. AE, CB, DC, MC, V. Valet parking $10, two rests. (including the Walnut Room), bar, rm svce, nightclub, hrdrsr, free crib. *Note:* Located right in the heart of the Loop, this Chicago classic still retains much of its beauty. Entirely renovated decor and rm amenities. The svce leaves something to be desired but the rest. is still a favorite of local politicians. Rather obtrusive convention and other groups. Neighborhood unsafe at night; take a taxi. **M–E**

�077 **Blackstone** (dwntwn), 636 S. Michigan Ave., IL 60605 (312/427-4300). 307 rms, A/C, color TV. AE, CB, DC, MC, V. Valet parking $10, rest., bar, rm svce, nightclub, free crib. *Note:* A turn-of-the-century hotel facing Grant Park and Buckingham Fountain. Comfortable, but could use a facelift. Mediocre svce. Interesting family rates. Historic landmark. **M–E**

�077 **Essex Inn** (nr. dwntwn), 800 S. Michigan Ave., IL 60605 (312/939-2800; toll free 800/621-6909). 255 rms, A/C, color TV, in-rm movies. AE, CB, DC, MC, V. Valet parking $6, pool, sauna, rest., bar, rm svce, free crib, free shuttle to and from the Loop. *Note:* Pleasant, recently restored hotel nr. dwntwn. Comfortable rms w. minibars. Efficient svce. Good value. Ideal location for museum visits. **M–E**

�077 **Quality Inn Downtown** (formerly the Holiday Inn; nr. dwntwn), 1 Mid City Pl., IL 60606 (312/829-5000; toll free, see Quality Inns). 405 rms, A/C, color TV, in-rm movies. AE, CB, DC, MC, V. Free parking, pool, rest., bar, rm svce, nightclub. *Note:* Modern 17-story motel nr. Union Station. Comfortable rms w. balconies. Uneven svce. Direct access to the highway network makes it an ideal location if you're driving. Interesting wknd packages. **M–E**

�077 **Avenue Motel** (nr. dwntwn), 1154 S. Michigan Ave., IL 60605 (312/427-8200; toll free 800/621-6909). 78 rms, A/C, color TV. AE, CB, DC, MC, V. Free parking, pool, coffee shop, bar, rm svce, free shuttle to and from dwntwn. *Note:* Conventional but well-maintained motel located close to the Field Museum. Overall, a good value. **I–M**

�077 **Ohio House** (nr. dwntwn), 600 N. La Salle St., IL 60610 (312/943-6000). 50 rms, A/C, color TV. AE, MC, V. Free parking, adj. coffee shop, free shuttle to and from the Loop. *Note:* Small, convenient motel close to the Merchandise Mart. No-frills comfort and a good value for those on a budget. Neighborhood unsafe at night; take a taxi. **I–M**

�077 **Rodeway Inn** (formerly the Ramada Inn; nr. dwntwn), 506 W. Harrison St., IL 60607 (312/427-6969; toll free, see Rodeway Inns). 154 rms, A/C, color TV, in-rm movies. AE, CB, DC, MC, V. Free valet parking, pool, rest., bar, rm svce. *Note:* Typical motel offering modern comfort, quite close to the University of Illinois campus. Business clientele. Good value. Direct access to the highway network makes it an ideal location if you're driving. **I–M**

 Travelodge Downtown (dwntwn), 1240 S. Michigan Ave., IL 60605 (312/427-4111; toll free, see Travelodge). 50 rms, A/C, color TV. AE, CB, DC, MC, V. Parking, rest. and bars nearby, free crib. *Note:* No-frills motel close to Soldier Field that offers clean, well-maintained rms at reasonable prices. Efficient reception and svce. Overall, a good value. **I–M**

Airport Accommodations
 Hilton O'Hare (vic., 40 min. from dwntwn), O'Hare International Airport (P.O. Box 66414), IL 60666 (312/686-8000; toll free, see Hilton). 886 rms, A/C, color TV, in-rm movies. AE, CB, DC, MC, V. Valet gar. $6, two rests., coffee shop, bars, rm svce, nightclub, free crib. *Note:* Relatively modern hotel located within the airport itself. Moving walkway to and from the terminal. Enormous soundproof rms. Often overcrowded. So-so rests. and svce. Business and group clientele. **E–VE**

 Holiday Inn Midway (vic., 15 min. from dwntwn), 7353 S. Cicero Ave., IL 60629 (312/581-5300; toll free, see Holiday Inns). 161 rms, A/C, cable color TV. AE, CB, DC, MC, V. Free parking, pool, rest., bar, rm svce, disco, free crib, free shuttle to and from Midway Airport. *Note:* Classic airport motel in the Holiday Inn style, offering no-frills comfort and facilities. **M**

YMCAs/Youth Hostels
 International House–AYH (nr. dwntwn), 1414 E. 59th St., IL 60637 (312/753-2270). Youth hostel. 200 rms. Generally packed during the school year; easier to get into in the summer. **B**

 YMCA (nr. dwntwn), 30 W. Chicago Ave., IL 60610 (312/944-6211). 500 rms, pool, health club. For men and women. **B**

RESTAURANTS
 A Note on Restaurant Prices: Chicago restaurant prices, per person, excluding drinks and service charges, are coded as follows: **VE,** Very Expensive ($60 and up); **E,** Expensive ($40–$60); **M,** Moderate ($25–$40); **I,** Inexpensive ($15–$25); **B,** Budget (up to $15).

Personal Favorites (in order of preference)
 Everest Room (dwntwn), 440 S. La Salle St. (663-8920). A/C. Lunch Mon–Fri, dinner Tues–Sat; closed hols. AE, DC, MC, V. *Specialties:* green-almond soup w. beluga caviar, lobster lasagne, pastry bag of shrimp w. leek and wild mushrooms, filet of halibut in potato crust, venison w. tiny dumplings, seafood sausage, shrimp and salmon on marinated cabbage, sautéed raspberries in Alsatian raspberry liqueur, chocolate fantasy. Broad and intelligently chosen wine list. *Note:* As the name implies, the Everest Room commands a breathtaking view of the city from the 40th floor of the Midwest Stock Exchange skyscraper. The fancy and delicate cuisine of Alsatian master chef Jean Joho is up to the setting. Two-level art deco dining rm w. crystal chandeliers, marble stairs, and expanses of mirrors. Efficient and knowledgeable svce. Resv. mandatory. One of the dozen best rests. in the country. *French.* **E–VE**

 Yoshi's Café (nr. dwntwn), 3257 N. Halsted St. (248-6160). A/C. Dinner Tues–Sun, brunch Sun. AE, MC, V. Jkt. *Specialties:* poached seafood sausage; salad of foie gras; veal medallion in caramelized ginger; mixed grill of tuna, salmon, and bass w. three sauces; roulade of lamb and artichokes. The menu changes regularly. Remarkable desserts (notably the green-tea ice cream). *Note:* Japanese variations on the nouvelle cuisine theme by a culinary virtuoso, Yoshi Katsumura. Inventive, refined cuisine at relatively modest prices. Charming modern-art decor. Resv. necessary, given the limited seating (48 places) and the success of this fashionable bistro. *Continental.* **M**

♈♈♈ **Spiaggia** (nr. dwntwn), 980 N. Michigan Ave. (280-2750). ☺☺☺ A/C. Lunch Mon–Sat, dinner nightly; closed hols. AE, CB, DC, MC, V. Jkt. *Specialties:* pizza w. duck sausage and sage, farfalle rosse con verdure (butterfly pasta w. tomatoes and green vegetables), eggplant risotto, carpaccio, lobster-filled black pasta triangles w. roast red-pepper cream, vitello tonnato, calves' liver veneziana, veal chop w. sage, zabaglione. Fine Italian wine list. *Note:* Located in the mezzanine of the sparkling One Magnificent Mile Building and offering an unobstructed view of Lake Michigan through its immense bay windows, Spiaggia has rapidly become the best Italian rest. in Chicago. Northern Italian cuisine, modern and sophisticated in its preparation. The svce is very able and the postmodern decor a model of elegance. Resv. necessary. *Italian.* **M–E**

♈♈♈ **Carlos'** (vic.) 429 Temple Ave., Highland Park (708/432-☺☺☺ 0770). A/C. Dinner only, closed Tues, holidays. AE, CB, DC, MC, V. Jkt. *Specialties:* Scallops and asparagus in pastry shells, ravioli of squab meat w. mild garlic sauce, salmon w. herb butter and ratatouille salsa, roasted pheasant w. fresh herbs, white and dark chocolate cake w. coconut and almond paste filling. The wine list is vast and costly. *Note:* Carlos and Deborah Nieto's restaurant is as gracious and welcoming as ever. Small, changing menu of nouvelle cuisine dishes and elaborate desserts. Book ahead, since there are only 60 seats—ask for an upstairs table. Svce prompt and efficient Resv. recommended. *French.* **M–E**

♈♈ **Gordon** (nr. dwntwn), 500 N. Clark St. (467-9780). A/C. ☺☺ Lunch Mon–Fri, dinner nightly, brunch Sun. AE, CB, DC, MC, V. Jkt. *Specialties:* black-bean soup, beignets of artichoke béarnaise, lamb cutlet w. honey and cumin, seafood stew, médaillon of pork w. dates, roast turbot w. thyme, duckling in pastry shell, tournedos w. garlic, salmon w. Chinese mustard, swordfish w. shiitake mushrooms. *Note:* The menu changes daily. Scrumptious desserts. Remarkable fish, light sauces prepared w. style and imagination. Brilliant and original new decor. Fashionable clientele. Resv. necessary. Excellent location despite a less-than-attractive neighborhood. *American/ Seafood.* **M**

♈♈ **Printer's Row** (dwntwn), 550 S. Dearborn St. (461-0780). ☺☺ A/C. Lunch Mon–Fri, dinner Mon–Sat; closed hols. AE, CB, DC, MC, V. Jkt. *Specialties:* fresh pasta w. rosemary and wild mushrooms, pheasant galantine w. pine nuts and chutney, rack of lamb w. pepper-and-cream sauce, smoked chicken w. curried mayonnaise, venison sausage w. cabbage and endive, ragoût of sweetbread w. sorrel. Limited desserts and wine list. The menu changes regularly. *Note:* Modern, imaginative American cuisine w. an occasional sublime touch from the very talented young chef, Michael Foley. Warm decor of pale paneling and claret tones in a former print shop. Efficient svce. One of Chicago's trendiest spots. Resv. advised. *American.* **I–M**

♈♈ **House of Hunan** (nr. dwntwn), 535 N. Michigan Ave. (329-☺☺ 9494). A/C. Lunch/dinner daily; closed Thanksgiving. AE, CB, DC, MC, V. Jkt. *Specialties:* hot-and-sour soup, mandarin lamb, soong chicken, five-color scallop roll, steamed pike, spicy Hunan beef, lobster Cantonese w. ginger, sweet-and-sour pork. Characterless desserts. *Note:* Enormous menu w. more than 100 dishes, from the spiciest to the mildest, harmoniously uniting recipes from China's four great culinary regions: Hunan, Szechuan, Canton, and Peking. The result is almost always remarkable. Very elaborate old-style decor. Svce is attentive and efficient—a distinction for a Chinese rest. *Chinese.* **I–M**

☼♈♈ **Berghoff** (dwntwn), 17 W. Adams St. (427-3170). A/C. ☺☺ Lunch/dinner Mon–Sat (until 9:30pm); closed hols. AE, MC, V. *Specialties:* Bismarck herring, wienerschnitzel, ragoût à la Deutsch, Kassler rippchen (smoked pork), sauerbraten, roast goose, whitefish, lavish desserts. Draft beer from Munich plus a good wine list. *Note:* A Chicago classic since 1898, when it opened as a simple saloon. Authentic German paneling, decor, and cuisine offering efficient svce and generous portions. Often packed and noisy. Resv. for parties of six or more. Friendly bar. Excellent value. *German.* **I**

♀ **L'Escargot** (nr. dwntwn), in the Allerton Hotel (see "Accommodations") (337-1717). A/C. Breakfast/lunch/dinner daily, brunch Sun; closed hols. AE, CB, DC, MC, V. Jkt. *Specialties:* sausage in pastry shells, Burgundy snails, rack of lamb in pastry shell, cassoulet toulousain, duckling à l'orange, rabbit w. tarragon, kidneys in mustard, mushroom-stuffed trout. Good house desserts. Fine wine list at reasonable prices. *Note:* Charming little French bistro located on the ground floor of the Hotel Allerton. Very fine cuisine bourgeoise and friendly svce. Locally popular. Resv. advised. Good value. Other location: 2925 N. Halsted St. (535-5522). *French.* **I–M**

☀♀ **Carson's, The Place for Ribs** (nr. dwntwn), 612 N. Wells St. (280-9200). A/C. Lunch/dinner daily (until midnight). AE, CB, DC, MC, V. *Specialties:* spareribs, New York sirloin steak, barbecued chicken, potatoes au gratin, ice-cream sundaes. *Note:* A true local institution, which expert opinion credits w. the Midwest's best ribs. The barbecued pork in its sweet but pungent sauce literally melts in the mouth. Also excellent beef. Generous servings in a comfortable, masculine setting; good svce; no resv., so you may have a long wait. Other location: 8617 Niles Center Rd., Skokie (708/675-6800). *American.* **B–I**

Other Restaurants (from top bracket to budget)

♀♀♀♀ **Le Français** (vic.), 269 S. Milwaukee Ave., in Wheeling (30 min. NW on I-94 and Ill. 68W) (708/541-7470). A/C. Lunch Tues–Fri, dinner Mon–Sat; closed hols. AE, CB, DC, MC, V. J&T. *Specialties:* duck consommé; carpaccio of tuna w. quail eggs; sweetbread ravioli w. sorrel sauce; aiguillette of duck rouennaise; stuffed sole Jean Banchet; catch of the day, broiled, poached, or sautéed and served w. spring vegetables; baked sweetbreads w. endive. Outstanding sherbets and desserts. Menu changes daily; magnificent wine list. *Note:* Opened in 1972 by Jean Banchet, the finest French chef in the land, this delightful country inn in a secluded suburb of Chicago passed in 1989 into the hands of two talented young chefs, Roland and Mary Beth Liccioni. Their culinary skills create a miraculous balance between traditional French and modern American cuisine. The setting is sumptuous but rather noisy. Reception and svce of the finest. Make resv. well ahead —the rest. only seats 90. Dinner seatings at 6pm and 9pm. Valet parking; 45 min. from dwntwn. *French/American.* **E–VE**

♀♀♀ **Ambria** (nr. dwntwn), 2300 N. Lincoln Park W. (472-5959). A/C. Dinner only, Mon–Sat; closed hols. AE, DC, MC, V. Jkt. *Specialties:* lobster gazpacho w. basil, foie gras sauté vinaigrette, salmon tartare w. caviar, pistachio sweetbreads, gâteau d'escargots in beurre blanc, turbot in Oriental sauce, sautéed duck w. wild rice, hare filet w. pears. Apple and crème-caramel cake. *Note:* A must for all lovers of remarkable eating experiences. The "tasting/sampling" menu (must be ordered 24 hr. in advance) is a festival of modern culinary elegance, signed by Gabino Satelino, the excellent Basque chef. Rather depressing paneled decor, insufficiently relieved by touches of art nouveau. Diligent if sometimes disorganized svce. Resv. should be made several days in advance. Valet parking ($4). *French.* **E** (prix fixe).

♀♀♀ **Charlie Trotter's** (nr. dwntwn), 816 W. Armitage Ave. (248-6228). A/C. Dinner only, Tues–Sat; closed hols. AE, CB, DC, MC, V. Jkt. *Specialties:* foie gras and mango ravioli, soft-shell crabs w. curry cream, roast saddle of lamb w. turnips and foie gras, sweetbreads w. pancetta and coriander butter, venison médaillons w. hazelnut flan and truffled mascarpone, banana-and-chocolate mousse, sauterne and olive-oil cake. Judiciously selected wine list at decent prices. *Note:* This newcomer is challenging Carlos' for the title of "most innovative and imaginative" modern-cuisine rest. in town. Delicate, elegant dishes from the hands of Charles Trotter, who came down w. a serious attack of "nouvelle cuisine-itis" after taking his degree in political science at U. of Wisconsin. The rest. is in an agreeably restored turn-of-the-century house; reception and svce are of the finest. Since this is an "in" place, make resv. several days ahead. Valet parking $4. *American.* **M–E**

☀☽♈♈♈ **Cricket's** (nr. dwntwn), in the Tremont Hotel (see "Accommodations," above) (280-2100). Breakfast/lunch/dinner daily, New Orleans–style brunch Sat–Sun. AE, CB, DC, MC, V. J&T. *Specialties:* crème Senegalese, oysters Rockefeller, scallops basquaise, sweetbreads financières, roast quail, grilled salmon, minced chicken mornay, kidney dijonnaise, rice pudding. Fine expensive wine list. *Note:* Warm, clublike ambience and serious, irreproachable cuisine. Funny, eclectic decor including sports team pennants and airplane models recalling the 21 Club in New York. Exceptionally attentive, polished svce. The favorite rest. of the tycoons. Resv. essential. Valet parking ($5). *Continental.* **M–E**

♈♈♈ **Nick's Fishmarket** (nr. dwntwn), 1 First National Plaza, Dearborn St. and Monroe St. (621-0200). A/C. Lunch/dinner Mon–Sat; closed hols. AE, CB, DC, MC, V. Jkt. *Specialties:* sautéed squid in oregano, ungaretti stew (seafood stew), fresh salmon, abalone, ricci, mahi-mahi (dolphin à la Hawaiian), soft-shell crab meunière, sautéed scallops, all kinds of wonderful fish and shellfish. Well-stocked wine cellar (but high prices). *Note:* Excellent seafood rest. in an elegant, intimate setting, complete w. private booths. Sister rest. of the famous Nick's Fishmarket in Honolulu. Impeccable svce. Resv. advised. Valet parking ($4). *Seafood.* **M–E**

♈♈ **Morton's** (nr. dwntwn), 1050 N. State St. (266-4820). A/C. Dinner only, Mon–Sat; closed hols. AE, CB, DC, MC, V. Jkt. *Specialties:* shellfish, remarkable red meats, veal chops Sicilian, broiled Maine lobster, fish of the day, soufflé Grand Marnier. Well-stocked wine cellar (especially California wines), but indecent prices. *Note:* Famous steakhouse serving the highest-quality meats at commensurate prices. Pleasant English pub decor, but rather noisy ambience. Impeccable svce. No resv., unfortunately, which often means substantial waits, especially on wknds. Other location: 1876 1st St., in Highland Park (432-3484). *Steak.* **M–E**

☀♈♈ **Eli's, The Place for Steak** (nr. dwntwn), 215 E. Chicago Ave. (642-1393). A/C. Lunch Mon–Fri, dinner nightly; closed hols. and mid-Dec to Jan. AE, CB, DC, MC, V. Jkt. *Specialties:* very fine meats (as the name indicates), calves' liver w. onions, and the best cheesecake in Chicago. *Note:* A favorite of local journalists and politicians as well as visiting celebrities. Rather busy decor, agreeable ambience, highest-quality svce. Resv. advised. Very popular piano bar. Valet parking ($3). *Steak.* **I–M**

☀♈♈ **Shaw's Crab House** (nr. dwntwn), 21 E. Hubbard St. (527-2722). A/C. Lunch Mon–Fri, dinner nightly; closed Thanksgiving, Dec 25. AE, CB, DC, MC, V. *Specialties:* stone crabs and soft-shell crabs (in season), crabcakes, Dungeness crabmeat, frogs' legs provençal, garlic chicken, broiled fish, pecan pie, crème brûlée. Skimpy but fairly priced wine list. *Note:* Enormously popular seafood rest. in a redecorated former newspaper warehouse. Mildly nostalgic setting and atmosphere right out of the 1930s. The impeccably fresh fish and seafood are attractively priced, the svce efficient, the value very good. *Seafood.* **I–M**

♈♈ **La Strada** (dwntwn), 155 N. Michigan Ave. (565-2200). A/C. Lunch Mon–Fri, dinner Mon–Sat; closed hols. AE, CB, DC, MC, V. J&T. *Specialties:* zuppa pavese, posillipo mussels, carpaccio, excellent homemade pasta, calves' liver veneziana, risotto milanese, veal forestiera, involtini di melanzane. Remarkable Italian wine list. *Note:* Very good northern Italian cuisine and one of the richest, most abundant selections of Italian wines in the United States. Opulent decor under an elegant skylight roof. Svce a bit overzealous. Resv. advised. *Italian.* **I–M**

Café Ba-Ba-Reeba (nr. dwntwn), 2024 N. Halsted St. (935-5000). A/C. Dinner only, nightly; closed hols. AE, CB, DC, MC, V. *Specialties:* tapas (Spanish hot and cold hors d'oeuvres), paella, swordfish steak w. olives, broiled calamari w. lemon and garlic, lamb sausage w. grapes and pine nuts, chicken grilled w. honey and cumin. Huge selection of sherries. *Note:* Chalk up another triumph for Rich Melman, owner of the successful Lettuce Entertain You restaurant chain. The best tapas in Chicago, and very praiseworthy Spanish regional cooking. As noisy and relaxed as a typical rest. in Madrid, w. an inviting outdoor patio for fine days. Helpful, smiling svce. Very popular locally; an excellent place. *Spanish.* I

Casbah (nr. dwntwn), 514 W. Diversey Pkwy. (935-7570). A/C. Dinner only, nightly; closed hols. AE, CB, DC, MC, V. Jkt. *Specialties:* stuffed grape leaves, couscous, shish kebab, trout broiled w. herbs, veal w. olives, kibbeh, Armenian dishes, baklava. *Note:* This warm, distinguished Middle Eastern rest. has become a local favorite over the years. The decor is right out of a Chicago version of *1,001 Nights,* music and ambience included. Attentive svce. Resv. advised. Excellent value. *Middle Eastern.* I

Emperor's Choice (nr. dwntwn), 2238 S. Wentworth Ave. (225-8800). A/C. Dinner nightly (until 1am), brunch Sat–Sun. AE, MC, V. *Specialties:* steamed oysters w. ginger and coriander, fried shrimp w. sweet peppers, kwo teh, Peking duck, mu-shu pork, sole w. black beans and coriander, inconsequential desserts. *Note:* The best place in Chicago's small Chinatown, serving authentic and often imaginative Hong Kong food. The friendly waiters seem to speak little English. The tiny dining rm is hung w. portraits of Chinese emperors. Resv. advisable; very good value. *Chinese/Seafood.* I

Frontera Grill (nr. dwntwn), 445 N. Clark St. (661-1434). A/C. Lunch/dinner Tues–Sat. AE, CB, DC, MC, V. Jkt. *Specialties:* shrimp-stuffed avocados w. garlic and lime, tacos al carbón, grilled guinea hen w. garlic, ceviche, stuffed green peppers with chili-and-tomato sauce, roast turkey w. red mole, grilled lamb chop, fried plantains w. whipped cream. *Note:* The young and talented Rick Bayless is an American chef who is crazy about Mexican food, having lived and traveled south of the Rio Grande for many years. His rather elaborate cuisine is totally authentic and delicious. The decor is pleasantly rustic and the svce friendly. Has enjoyed much success since its 1987 opening. No resv. taken. Expect a long wait after 7pm. *Mexican.* I

Hatsuhana (nr. dwntwn), 160 E. Ontario St. (280-8287). A/C. Lunch Mon–Fri, dinner Mon–Sat; closed hols. AE, CB, DC, MC, V. Jkt. *Specialties:* sushi, sashimi, tempura, teriyaki. *Note:* Excellent authentic Japanese rest. in a modern, immaculate setting. Svce sometimes disorganized. American and Japanese business clientele. The dexterity w. which the chefs handle their knives is a sight in itself. *Japanese.* I

Yugo Inn (nr. dwntwn), 2824 N. Ashland Ave. (348-6444). A/C. Dinner only, Mon–Sat. No credit cards. *Specialties:* ajvar, pjeskavica (Serbian hamburgers), moussaka, muckalica, grilled fish. *Note:* From moussaka to goulash, all the authentic flavors of the Balkans. Very good value. Resv. advised. *Balkan.* I

Chestnut Street Grill (nr. dwntwn), Water Tower Pl., 845 N. Michigan Ave. (280-2720). A/C. Lunch/dinner daily; closed Thanksgiving, Dec 25. AE, CB, DC, MC, V. *Specialties:* fried calamari, mussels broiled or marinières, clambake, fish, broiled fish and meats, so-so desserts. The homemade tartar sauce is splendid, and the selection of California wines good. *Note:* On the mezzanine of the sparkling Water Tower Place Shopping Mall, this rest. offers excellent broiled (over oak or hickory) foods in an attractive turn-of-the-century setting. The service is overburdened but generally efficient. On the noisy side; ask for a table at the far end of the room. Resv. advised but not essential. A favored place. *Seafood/Steak.* B–I

Greek Islands (nr. dwntwn), 200 S. Halsted St. (782-9855). A/C. Lunch/dinner daily (until midnight); closed Thanksgiving, Dec 25. AE, CB, DC, MC, V. *Specialties:* pastitsio, gyros, moussaka, souvlaki, braised lamb, excellent grilled fish, baklava. *Note:* The best Greek rest., and one of the largest, in Chicago, a city full of Greeks. A modern setting and excellent, authentic cuisine at very good prices. Greek hospitality and a friendly, if noisy, ambience. Free valet parking. *Greek.* **B–I**

♆ **R. J. Grunt's** (nr. dwntwn), 2056 Lincoln Park West (929-5363). A/C. Lunch/dinner daily, brunch Sun; closed Thanksgiving, Dec 25. AE, CB, DC, MC, V. *Specialties:* hamburgers, roast beef, chili, barbecued fish, steak teriyaki, giant sandwiches. *Note:* Progenitor of a whole family of typically American rests., the "Lettuce Entertain You" chain, which boasts honest cuisine, reasonable prices, and an amusing atmosphere that is both "hip" and relaxed. Friendly, cheerful svce. Nice view of Lincoln Park. No resv. *American.* **B–I**

☼♆ **Ed Debevic's** (nr. dwntwn), 640 N. Wells St. (664-1707). A/C. Lunch/dinner daily (until midnight); closed Thanksgiving, Dec 25. No credit cards. *Specialties:* chili, hamburgers, fried chicken, meatloaf, chocolate milkshakes. *Note:* An amusing replica of a 1950s-style diner that seems to have come right out of *American Graffiti.* Even the background music is from that era. If there is nothing unforgettable about the food, the atmosphere is fun, the prices more than modest, and the crowd particularly diverse. Relaxed svce. Another success from the "Lettuce Entertain You" restaurant chain. No resv. *American.* **B**

☼♆ **Pizzeria Uno** (nr. dwntwn), 29 E. Ohio St. (321-1000). A/C. Lunch Tues–Sun, dinner nightly (until midnight); closed Thanksgiving, Dec 25. AE, CB, DC, MC, V. *Specialties:* Chicago-style pizza (thick yet light crust), salads, sandwiches, homemade soup (excellent minestrone). *Note:* The best pizza in Chicago and perhaps in America. Noisy atmosphere. Walls decorated w. amusing graffiti. Generous portions (a "medium" pizza is plenty for two). Efficient svce. A local favorite since 1943. Other location: Pizzeria Due, 619 N. Wabash Ave. (943-2400). *Italian.* **B**

Restaurants in the Vicinity

♆♆♆ **Le Français** (see "Other Restaurants," above).

☼♆♆♆ **The Cottage** (vic.), 525 Torrence Ave., in Calumet City (708/891-3900). A/C. Lunch Tues–Fri, dinner Tues–Sat; closed hols. MC, V. Jkt. *Specialties:* duck ravioli, grilled lamb sausage w. roast peppers, steak Madagascar, "Cottage" pork chop, salmon in pastry shell, roast duckling w. raspberries, remarkable homemade desserts. The menu changes with the seasons. Weakish wine list. *Note:* Delightful little old-world inn that has become a shrine for fine-cuisine lovers. Chef Carolyn Buster deftly blends French, Austrian, and Californian influences in her quest for perfection. Rustic-opulent ambience. Very good svce. Worth the 30-min. car ride from dwntwn on I-94S and Sibley Blvd. Free parking. Resv. advised. *Continental/French.* **I–M**

Cafeterias/Specialty Spots

D. B. Kaplan's (nr. dwntwn), Water Tower Pl. (7th floor) 845 N. Michigan Ave. (280-2700). Lunch/dinner daily (until 10pm). No credit cards. *Specialties:* salads, omelets, and giant sandwiches (more than 160 different kinds). *Note:* The best deli in Chicago. Ideal for a light meal before or after a show. **B**

Hemingway's House (nr. dwntwn), 1825 N. Lincoln (943-1825). Lunch/dinner daily (to midnight). AE, MC, V. *Specialties:* 190 kinds of sandwiches, quiches, fresh pastas. *Note:* Pleasant ambience. **B**

Mr. Beef (nr. dwntwn), 666 N. Orleans St. (337-8500). Lunch only, Mon–Fri. No credit cards. *Specialties:* remarkable Italian beef sandwiches (roast beef and roast peppers)—a Chicago specialty. *Note:* The rather depressing decor does not seem to discourage the clientele. **B**

Mrs. Levy's Delicatessen (dwntwn), in the Sears Tower (ground floor),

2335 Wacker Dr. (933-0220). Breakfast/lunch/dinner daily. No credit cards. *Specialties:* cabbage soup, Jewish dishes, corned beef, excellent sandwiches and homemade apple pie. *Note:* A very popular bistro at lunchtime. **B**

Where to Eat What in Chicago

American: Carsons, The Place for Ribs (p. 536), Charlie Trotter's (p. 537), Ed Debevic's (p. 539), Gordon (p. 535), Printer's Row (p. 535), R. J. Grunt's (p. 539)

Balkan: Yugo Inn (p. 538)

Cafeterias/Specialty Spots: D. B. Kaplan's (p. 539), Hemingway's House (p. 539), Mr. Beef (p. 539), Mrs. Levy's Delicatessen (p. 539)

Chinese: Emperor's Choice (p. 538), House of Hunan (p. 535)

Continental: The Cottage (p. 539), Cricket's (p. 537), Yoshi's Café (p. 534)

French: Ambria (p. 536), L'Escargot (p. 536), Everest Room (p. 534), Le Français (p. 536), Carlos' (p. 535)

German: Berghoff (p. 536)

Greek: Greek Islands (p. 539)

Italian: Pizzeria Uno (p. 539), Spiaggia (p. 535), La Strada (p. 537)

Japanese: Hatsuhana (p. 538)

Mexican: Frontera Gill (p. 538)

Middle Eastern: Casbah (p. 538)

Seafood: Chestnut Street Grill (p. 538), Nick's Fishmarket (p. 537), Shaw's Crab House (p. 537), Gordon (p. 535)

Spanish: Café Ba-Ba-Reeba (p. 538)

Steak: Eli's, The Place for Steak (p. 537), Morton's (p. 537)

BARS & NIGHTCLUBS

As in New York, there is a magic telephone number in Chicago—**Jazz Institute Hot Line** (427-3300)—with a daily listing of all jazz club programs.

Andy's (nr. dwntwn), 11 E. Hubbard St. (642-6805): The best jazz club in Chicago, according to the experts. Lively, 1920s-style ambience. Rest. as well (jkt. required). Open daily.

B.L.U.E.S. (nr. dwntwn), 2519 N. Halsted St. (528-1012): A great blues place in a great blues city.

Butch McGuire's (nr. dwntwn), 20 W. Division St. (337-9080). Chicago's most famous singles bar. A relaxed, pleasant atmosphere. Original decor. A quite good rest., too. A must for all visitors. Open daily.

Buddy Guy's Legends (dwntwn), 754 S. Wabash St. (427-0333). A down-home comfortable haunt behind the Hilton Hotel owned by blues guitarist Buddy Guy. Blues, rock, and R&B live, nightly.

Checkerboard Lounge (nr. dwntwn), 423 E. 43rd St. (624-3240). Another famous locale for lovers of authentic blues. Rough neighborhood at night—take a cab.

Chicago Improv (nr. dwntwn), 504 N. Wells St. (782-6387). Brand-new comedy club similar in atmosphere to Improvisations in New York and Los Angeles. Wanna-Be Comics mix with visiting celebs and top-name acts. Open nightly.

Excalibur (formerly the Limelight; nr. dwntwn), Dearborn St. and Ontario St. (266-1944). Enormous discothèque with multilevel dance floors, game rooms, bars, and restaurant in a Romanesque castlelike building. Open nightly.

Joe Segal's Jazz Showcase (dwntwn), in the Blackstone Hotel, 636 S. Michigan Ave. (427-4300). Renowned jazz club offering everything from bebop to avant-garde jazz. Open Tues–Sun.

John Barleycorn Memorial Pub (nr. dwntwn), 658 W. Belden Ave. (348-8899). Very popular, intimate pub with classical background music and silent movies. Open daily.

Kingston Mines (nr. dwntwn), 2458 N. Halsted St. (477-4646). Jazz and blues in the heart of the North Side, a fashionable upper-class neighborhood. Locally popular. Open nightly.

Old Town School of Folk Music (nr. dwntwn), 909 W. Armitage Ave. (525-7793). A temple of Chicago folk music, as the name indicates.

Park West (nr. dwntwn), 322 W. Armitage Ave. (266-6262). Big pop and jazz stars performing two shows a night. Rather snobby ambience.

☼ **Second City Theater** (nr. dwntwn), 1616 N. Wells St. (337-3992). A stronghold of improvisation, where comedians like Mike Nichols, Elaine May, John Candy, Dan Ackroyd, John Belushi, and a good many of the "Saturday Night Live" troupe were discovered.

NEARBY EXCURSIONS

BATAVIA (36 mi./56km west on Eisenhower Expwy. and East-West Tollway): Built on 6,800 acres (2,700ha) where peaceful herds of bison graze, the **Fermilab Particle Accelerator,** Kirk Rd. at Pine St., is the largest synchrotron particle accelerator in the world. Its annular tunnel, 4 mi. (6.4km) in circumference, accelerates atomic particles to nearly the speed of light. The Visitors Center is located in **Wilson Hall,** a 16-story building in the center of the synchrotron. Guided tours are given Mon–Fri by appointment only (708/840-3351). A must for physics buffs.

ELMHURST (17 mi./27km west on I-90): The **Lizzadro Museum of Lapidary Art,** 220 Cottage Hill Ave. in Wilder Park (312/833-1616), offers one of the world's largest collections of minerals and worked precious stones, notable jade figurines from the Far East. Open Tues–Sun.

EVANSTON (12 mi./19km north on Lake Shore Dr. and U.S. 41): Site of **Northwestern University** (10,000 students), this pretty residential area on the banks of Lake Michigan houses the headquarters of Rotary International and the United Methodist Church. On the university campus, be sure to see the **Dearborn Observatory** (2131 Sheridan Rd.), the **Shakespeare Garden,** and the **Pick-Staiger Concert Hall.**

North of the campus is the **Grosse Point lighthouse,** Sheridan Rd. and Central St., erected after a shipwreck on Lake Michigan off Evanston took 300 lives (tours of the lighthouse Sat–Sun in summer).

☼ **OAK PARK** (9 mi./14km west on the Eisenhower Expwy.): The suburban cradle of the famous "Prairie School" which greatly influenced American architecture from the beginning of the century. There are at least a score of interesting buildings to see here, work of the famous Frank Lloyd Wright (see "Guided Tours," above). Among the most noteworthy are **Wright's house-studio,** at Forest Ave. and Chicago Ave. (open daily year round), in which he lived for more than 20 years; the **Harry Adams House,** 710 Augusta St. (dates from 1913); the **Unity Temple,** 875 Lake St. (dates from 1906); and the **River Forest Tennis Club,** 615 Lathrop Ave. There's a **Visitors Center** at 158 N. Forest Ave. (848-1500), open daily Mar–Nov. Definitely worth the trip.

Authors Ernest Hemingway and Edgar Rice Burroughs, the prolific creator of Tarzan (27 volumes from 1912 to 1964), also hail from Oak Park.

PULLMAN COMMUNITY (I-94 between 104th St. and 115th St.): This model company town, built in 1880 by railroad magnate George Pullman for his employees, is an interesting sample of American social history. The **Visitors Center** is at 614 E. 113th St. (312/785-8181).

☼☖ **WILMETTE** (16 mi./26km north on Lake Shore Dr. and U.S. 41): Luxurious suburb on the shores of Lake Michigan complete with a fine sand beach. The startling **Baha'i House of Worship,** Sheridan Rd. and Linden Ave. (708/256-4400), religious center for the Baha'i faith, should definitely be seen. Founded in Iran in the last century, the faith has been flourishing in the United States for some 50 years. Innovative nine-sided design surrounded by nine gardens overlooking Lake Michigan. Open daily. Worth the trip.

FARTHER AFIELD

☼☖ **INDIANA DUNES NATIONAL LAKESHORE** (92 mi./ 148km r.t. on I-90E and U.S. 12E, returning the same way): A captivating landscape composed of giant sand dunes—some as high as 192 ft. (60m)—of pine forests, of immense beaches with room for many thousands of bathers, and of marshes along the shores of Lake Michigan. Unique fauna and flora (notably carnivorous plants, cacti, oaks, and sumacs) flourish on the 14,227 acres (5,760ha) of the park, giving the whole an appearance of tropical vegetation in summer, the best season for a visit. There are also dozens of miles of rambling trails, picnic areas, and fully equipped campsites for nature-lovers. (Four-wheel-drive vehicles and dune buggies are prohibited.) **Visitor Center** at the intersection of Kenil Rd. and U.S. 12. Definitely worth the trip. For further information, contact Superintendent, 1100 N. Mineral Springs Rd., Porter, IN 46304 (219/926-7561).

☖ **LAKE COUNTRY** (124 mi./199km r.t. on I-90N, U.S. 12N, Ill. 120E, and U.S. 14S): A string of rural lakes (**Long Lake, Fox Lake, Pistakee Lake, Grass Lake, Chain O'Lakes State Park**), this favorite fine-weather rural retreat for Chicagoans is a paradise for fishing, sailing, and strolling.

On the way back, go out of your way to pass through **Woodstock,** a peaceful little town of Victorian charm where Orson Welles spent his childhood and made his earliest appearances as a Shakespearean actor in the **Opera House,** 121 Van Buren St. See also the **Old Courthouse Inn & Jail,** 101 N. Johnston St.; **Town Square;** etc.

☼☖☖ **GALENA & THE BANKS OF THE MISSISSIPPI** (406 mi./650km west, r.t. on I-90N, U.S. 20W, Ill. 84S, and I-80 and I-55E): The charming little town of **Galena,** on the banks of the river of the same name, is a former mining town that made its fortune in the last century from lead. A visit here is a pleasant voyage back into history: 85% of its buildings are designated as landmarks, like the **Ulysses S. Grant Home,** 500 Bouthillier St. (815/777-0248), open daily, the former home of the 18th U.S. president. Photographers, and lovers of old buildings, will find here a wonderful glimpse of the past.

This 2- or 3-day trip leads next along the banks of the Mississippi (a beautiful scenic route) to **Rock Island,** former capital of the Saul and Fox tribes under Chief Black Hawk. The army defeated them in a decisive battle in 1832. **Black Hawk State Park,** with an observation tower overlooking the valley, as well as a Native American museum, commemorates the event. For information, call 309/788-9536. Also see the **Arsenal,** the **John M. Browning Museum** with a rich collection of arms (open Wed–Sun), and the reconstruction of old ☖ **Fort Armstrong.** Return to Chicago on I-80 and I-55, an ideal route for history lovers.

Where to Stay En Route

IN GALENA   ☼ ♉ ♉ **DeSoto House,** 230 S. Main St., IL 61036 (815/777-0090). 55 rms. A more-than-100-year-old hotel, nicely restored. **M–E**

IN ROCK ISLAND   ♉ ♉ **Sheraton,** 17th St. at Third Ave., IL 61201 (309/794-1212). 177 rms. Modern and comfortable. **I–M**

CHAPTER 24

MILWAUKEE

□ □ □

From its Germanic antecedents the world's brewing capital has inherited a taste for order, work, classical music (its symphony orchestra is justly renowned), and solid food. A city in transition, from a quiet, conservative factory town to a lively, cosmopolitan metropolis, the new Milwaukee is known for its clean streets, relatively low crime rate, and minimal traffic congestion. In a strategic position on Lake Michigan at the confluence of three rivers—the Milwaukee, the Menominee, and the Kinnickinnic—the site of the city, whose original Native American name, Millioki, signifies "gathering-place by the waters," was visited in 1674 by French missionary Jacques Marquette and trapper Louis Joliet. The present economic capital of Wisconsin was founded in 1818 as a trading post by French fur trader Salomon Juneau; it attained stature as a major city in 1889, when the first modern brewery was opened.

Today Milwaukee produces more beer than any other city in the world, and two of the country's largest breweries, Pabst and Miller (both of German origin) have their headquarters here. Other well-known names in the roster of local industry include Harley-Davidson motorcycles, Allis-Chalmers heavy equipment, and Evinrude outboard motors; these and others have contributed to the economic growth of "the machine-shop of America," as Milwaukee has been called, taking advantage of the city's access to the ocean via the Great Lakes and the St. Lawrence Seaway.

"The German Athens"—another of Milwaukee's sobriquets—an austere but by no means a charmless city, with its churches, its mixture of historic and ultramodern buildings, its museum, and its lovely lakeside promenade, is known for its *gemütlichkeit,* a warm combination of hospitality and joie de vivre. Moreover, Milwaukee plays host every year to a well known beer festival, the Oktoberfest, reminiscent of the Munich event of the same name.

It is German immigration that has left the clearest stamp on Milwaukee, from the impressive **City Hall** to the **Pabst Theater,** not to mention the many cafés and "bier gartens," but the influence of other immigrant strains—Irish, Greek, and above all Polish—is also clearly evident. Witness America's first Polish cathedral, **St. Josaphat's Basilica,** built at the beginning of the 20th century, and the **Annunciation Greek Orthodox Church,** last major work of the great architect Frank Lloyd Wright.

Born here were entertainer Liberace, clarinetist Woody Herman, actors Spencer Tracy and Gene Wilder, and singer Al Jarreau.

BASIC FACTS: State of Wisconsin. Area code: 414. Time zone: central. ZIP Code: 53201. Founded in: 1818. Approximate population: city, 600,000; metropolitan area, 1,600,000. Ranks 23rd in size among U.S. metropolitan areas.

CLIMATE: Summer and fall are the best seasons for visiting Milwaukee. Temperatures are generally pleasant, though there can be sudden changes; mean temperature in July is 71°F (22°C). Winter is glacial and very windy; the mercury stays well under freezing, with a Jan average temperature of 22°F (−6°C). Spring is brief and brisk (41°–50°F/5°–10°C).

DISTANCES: Chicago, 87 mi. (139km); Duluth, 424 mi. (678km); Minneapolis, 365 mi. (584km); Omaha, 495 mi. (792km); St. Louis, 376 mi. (602km).

ARRIVAL & TRANSIT INFORMATION

AIRPORT: General Mitchell International Airport (MKE), 6 mi. (10km) south. Information: 747-5300.

AIRLINES: American (344-6700), Continental (342-3099), Eastern (344-7910), Midwest (747-4646), Northwest (272-8920), TWA (933-8292), United (273-8400), and USAir (toll free 800/428-4322).

CITY LINK: The **cab** fare to city center is about $16; time, 20–25 min. Bus: **A.A.A. Airport Shuttle** (272-1955) leaves every 30 min., serving principal dwntwn and outlying hotels; fare, $6.50–$10 according to destination; time, about 35 min.

Since the airport is near the city, which is not large, it may be unnecessary to rent a car unless you intend to take trips outside the city. Good public transportation system (bus): **Milwaukee County Transit System** (344-6711 for information).

CAR RENTAL (at the airport unless otherwise indicated): Avis (744-2266); Budget (481-2409); Dollar (747-0066); Hertz (747-5200); National (483-9800); Thrifty, 4747 S. Howell Ave. (747-1410). For dwntwn locations, consult the local telephone directory.

LIMOUSINE SERVICES: Carey Limousine (271-5466), Dav El Limousines (toll free 800/922-0343).

TAXIS: Cabs may not be hailed on the street; they must be taken from the waiting lines outside the major hotels or summoned by phone. Principal companies are **City Veterans Taxicab** (933-2266) and **Yellow Cab** (271-1800).

TRAIN: Amtrak Station, 433 W. St. Paul Ave. (933-3081).

INTERCITY BUSES: Greyhound, 606 N. 7th St. (272-8900).

INFORMATION & TOURS

TOURIST INFORMATION: The **Milwaukee Convention & Visitors Bureau,** 756 N. Milwaukee St., WI 53202 (414/273-3950; toll free 800/231-0903).

For a **recorded message** giving a list of current shows and cultural events, call 799-1177.

GUIDED TOURS: Edelweiss Boat Tours (boat), 1110 Old World 3rd St. Dock (272-3625): Lunch, brunch, and dinner cruises May–Oct along the Milwaukee River and into Lake Michigan, aboard the *Edelweiss* or the *Edelweiss II.*

Gray Line Tours (bus), 1200 W. Wells (276-9588): Guided tours of city and surroundings.

Iroquois Boat Line Tours (boat), Clybourn St. Bridge Dock (332-4194): Trips on Lake Michigan and the Milwaukee River (late June to Sept 1).

Milwaukee County Transit System (bus), 1492 N. 17th St. (344-6711): Conducted tours of city and surroundings (June 1 to Sept 1).

SIGHTS, ATTRACTIONS & ACTIVITIES

ARCHITECTURAL HIGHLIGHTS: ⌂ **Civic Center Plaza,** between N. 7th St. and N. 9th St., north of W. Wells St.: Wide esplanade with fountain, statuary, and monumental bell tower, bordered by the **County Courthouse,** Police Headquarters, the huge **Convention Center (MECCA),** and the **Public Museum.** The heart of the city's government; worth a look.

⌂ **McKinley Marina,** 1750 N. Lincoln Memorial Dr. (273-5224): Lovely pleasure harbor with 650 moorings on Lake Michigan. Along the breakwaters, devotees of rod and reel pursue their favorite quarry—Coho salmon, trout, and lake perch. Boats may be rented May–Oct. Must be seen.

⌂ **Milwaukee Center,** E. Wells St. and Water St.: This ultramodern $100-million complex, symbol of the new Milwaukee, stands across from City Hall and comprises a 28-floor office tower, the brand-new Wyndham Hotel, two theaters, many stores and boutiques, etc.

⌖⌂ **Oriental Theater,** 2230 N. Farwell Ave. (276-8711): Built in 1927 and recently restored to all its old splendor, the Oriental is worth seeing just for its remarkable East Indian–style decor complete with onion-shaped domes and terra-cotta lions. Movie buffs flock to the foreign and hard-to-find films shown at this landmark movie theater. Open daily.

⌖⌂ **Performing Arts Center/PAC,** 929 N. Water St. (273-7206): This modern (1969), austerely geometric complex comprises four theaters and concert halls as well as an open-air auditorium. Home of the world-famous Milwaukee Symphony Orchestra, the First Stage Milwaukee Theater, the Pennsylvania-Milwaukee Ballet, and the Florentine Opera Company. Pretty gardens on the Milwaukee River. Visits by appointment only. Worth going out of your way for.

⌂ **Skywalk System,** connecting 10 city blocks around MECCA and the Grand Avenue Mall: Following in the footsteps of the Twin Cities and Cincinnati, Milwaukee has become the third midwestern metropolis to treat itself to a "skywalk," the network of glassed-in, air-conditioned pedestrian walkways that links major downtown buildings. This one, especially the stretch overlooking the river, offers some fine views.

⌖⌂ **War Memorial Complex,** 750 N. Lincoln Memorial Dr. (273-5533): This modern building by the great architect Eero Saarinen, splendidly situated on the shore of Lake Michigan, commemorates the dead of all wars. It houses the **Milwaukee Art Museum** (see "Museums of Art," below), and offers a fine view of lake and city. Don't miss it.

BEACHES: ⌂ **Bradford Beach,** 2400 N. Lincoln Memorial Dr. at E. Bradford Ave. (961-9799): The best of the seven public beaches along the lakefront. Even in summer Lake Michigan's water temperature doesn't get much above the low 60s; for dedicated swimmers only.

CHURCHES/SYNAGOGUES: ⌖⌂ **Annunciation Greek Orthodox Church,** 9400 W. Congress St. (461-9400): Last major work of Frank Lloyd Wright; the imaginative Byzantine structure is crowned by a magnificent blue dome in the shape of a flying saucer. Visit by appointment only, Mon–Fri. An absolute mustsee.

⌂ **Central United Methodist Church,** 639 N. 25th St. (344-1600): A triumph of contemporary energy-saving design. Built partially underground, this unusual church, whose roof is also its garden, has a large bell tower which captures and stores solar energy. Worth seeing.

St. Joan of Arc Chapel, 601 N. 14th St. (224-6873): Authentic medieval French chapel from the 15th century, transported and reerected in 1965, stone by stone, on the campus of **Marquette University** (see "Historic Buildings," below). According to legend, Joan of Arc prayed here before going to the stake. Remarkable example of Gothic architecture, not to be missed. Open daily.

St. Josaphat's Basilica, 2336 S. 6th St. (645-5623): This is the oldest Polish basilica in North America, built at the turn of the century by Slavic immigrants with material salvaged from the demolition of the Federal Building in Chicago. Its majestic dome is reminiscent of St. Peter's in Rome; ornate interior with many pictures and relics of Polish saints. Worth a visit. Open daily.

HISTORIC BUILDINGS: **Capt. Frederick Pabst Mansion,** 2000 W. Wisconsin Ave. (931-0808): Luxurious 37-room home of 19th-century brewer Frederick Pabst (1893); splendid upper-middle-class interior from the turn of the century with period furniture and decoration scrupulously restored. Worth a visit. Open daily Mar–Dec, wknds only the rest of the year.

City Hall, 200 E. Wells St. (278-2221): Impressive in the purest Flemish Renaissance style, with monumental eight-story lobby surrounded by wrought-iron balconies, and a 393-ft. (122m) belfry. Worth visiting. Open Mon–Fri.

Grain Exchange Room, 225 E. Michigan Ave. (272-6230): Situated in the Mackie Building, the beautiful Grain Exchange Room, whose gold-leaf trim and giant wall murals have been renovated to their 1879 Victorian Renaissance splendor, depicts the growth and development of Milwaukee during the Gilded Age. Worth a look. Visits by appointment only, Mon–Fri.

Kilbourntown House, 4400 W. Estabrook St., Estabrook Park (5 mi./8km north on I-43) (273-8288): Beautiful Greek Revival house from 1844 with an interesting collection of furniture and art objects from the second half of the 19th century. Worth the side trip. Open Tues, Thurs, Sat, and Sun June–Sept.

Marquette University, Wisconsin Ave. between N. 11th St. and 17th St. (288-7250): Well-known university (13,000 students) founded in 1881; the campus has many interesting buildings, including the **Joan of Arc Chapel** (see above), the **Marquette Hall Carillon,** which with 48 bells of different sizes is one of the largest in the country (frequent recitals), and the **Haggerty Museum of Art,** with a permanent collection of 5,000 works of art, open daily. Worth a visit.

Pabst Theater, 144 E. Wells St. (278-3663): Famous for its acoustics and its richly baroque interior, this fine theater, built in 1895, has been restored to all its original splendor. Classical concerts, chamber-music recitals, and theatrical entertainment. Worth seeing.

INDUSTRIAL TOURS: Your visit to Milwaukee wouldn't be complete without a visit to the breweries on which its fame and fortune are founded.

Miller, 4251 W. State St. (931-2337): Second-largest brewery in the world. Visits to the plant and museum, with free beer tasting, Mon–Sat mid-May to mid-Sept, Tues–Sat the rest of the year.

Pabst, 915 W. Juneau Ave. (223-3709): One of the city's oldest; plant tours and tasting Mon–Sat June to the end of Aug, Mon–Fri the rest of the year.

Sprecher, 730 W. Oregon St. (272-2337): This little batch brewery, special-

DOWNTOWN
MILWAUKEE

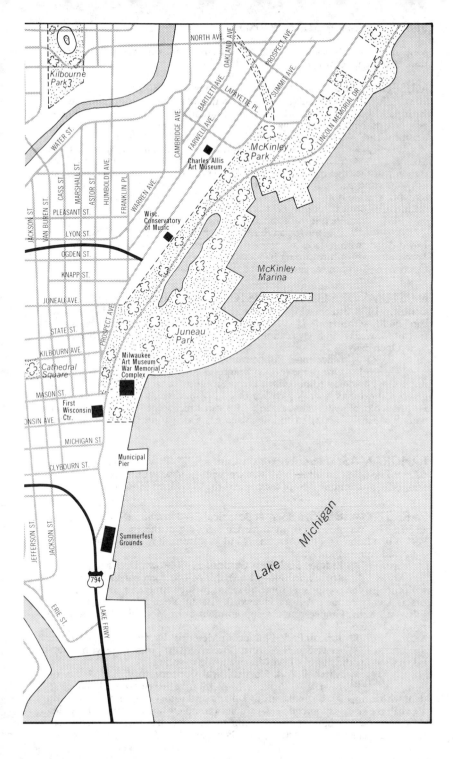

izing in premium beers, was the first to be licensed following the end of Prohibition. Visit by appointment.

MUSEUMS OF ART: ⌂ Charles Allis Art Museum, 1801 N. Prospect Ave. at
1630 E. Royall Pl. (278-8295): Huge collection of Asian art from China, Korea, Japan, and Persia, as well as French and contemporary American paintings—property of the late "king of farm machinery," Charles Allis—housed in a very beautiful Tudor-style home built in 1909. See it. Open Wed–Sun.

      🔔🔔 **Milwaukee Art Museum,** 750 N. Lincoln Memorial Dr. (271-9508): This very modern building by Eero Saarinen standing at the edge of Lake Michigan houses old masters, German expressionists, American painters (particularly of the "Ashcan School"), and interesting temporary exhibitions. Also has one of the world's largest collections of Haitian primitive paintings. Recently enlarged. Shouldn't be missed. Open Tues–Sun.

      🔔 **Villa Terrace,** 2220 N. Terrace Ave. (271-3656): Charming villa in the Italian Renaissance style designed in 1923 by architect David Adler, with terraces and gardens overlooking Lake Michigan. Sculpture, 18th-century furniture, Shaker handcrafts, old porcelain. Definitely a must-see. Open Wed–Sun June to late Aug; Wed, Sat, and Sun the rest of the year.

MUSEUMS OF SCIENCE & HISTORY: ⌂ Milwaukee County Historical
Center, 910 N. 3rd St. at Père Marquette Park (273-8288): Housed in a former bank building from around 1910, this interesting little museum retraces the history of Milwaukee in lively fashion. Old workshops, exhibitions, etc. Should be seen. Open daily.

      🔅🔔🔔 **Milwaukee Public Museum,** 800 W. Wells St. (278-2702): One of the country's largest natural-history museums. Besides important zoological (dinosaurs in a reconstruction of their natural habitat) and geological exhibits, there's a replica of Old Milwaukee, a European village, a Hopi pueblo, a New Delhi bazaar, a Mexican street scene, etc. Also a "wizard wing," which will appeal to budding scientists. Fascinating; don't miss it. Open daily.

PANORAMAS: ⌂ First Wisconsin Center, 777 E. Wisconsin Ave. (765-
4321): The tallest building in Milwaukee, with an observation deck on the 41st floor offering a unique view of the city and the lake. Open Mon–Fri.

PARKS & GARDENS: ⌂ Boerner Botanical Gardens, 5879 S. 92nd St. (425-
1130): This very lovely botanical garden standing in the enormous **Whitnall Park** is best known for its rose gardens and its seasonal flower exhibitions. Open daily mid-Apr to mid-Oct.

      🔔 **Bradley Sculpture Garden,** 2145 Brown Deer Rd. (10 mi./ 16km north along I-43) (271-9508): Very handsome modern-sculpture garden comprising some 60 works by such American and foreign artists as Henry Moore, Barbara Hepworth, Isamu Noguchi, Martha Pan, and Ellsworth Kelly. Guided tours by appointment only, Mon–Fri. For hours and resv., call 276-6840. Well worth going out of your way for.

      🔔 **Juneau Park,** N. Lincoln Memorial Dr. from Wisconsin Ave. to McKinley Marina: Lovely verdant promenade with beautiful views along the shore of Lake Michigan. Worth seeing.

      🔅🔔🔔 **Mitchell Park Horticultural Conservatory,** 524 S. Layton Blvd. at W. Pierce St. (649-9800): This remarkable botanic garden, whose three glass cupolas are as tall as a seven-story building and cover an area half the size of a football field, exhibits a complete range of tropical and desert vegetation which, given the local climate, is somewhat unexpected. Spectacular flowers in Aug. An absolute must. Open daily.

⚓ **Père Marquette Park,** Old World 3rd St. between W. State St. and W. Kilbourn Ave.: This little triangular garden, in the heart of downtown on the bank of the Milwaukee River, marks the spot where French Jesuit Fr. Jacques Marquette and trapper Louis Joliet are supposed to have first come ashore in 1674. Should be seen.

⚓ **Schlitz Audubon Center,** 1111 E. Brown Deer Rd. (352-2880): 185 acres (75ha) of wild, wooded park on Lake Michigan, host to foxes, deer, and many other wild animals. Open Tues–Sun.

PERFORMING ARTS: For current listings of shows and cultural events, consult the entertainment pages of the two daily papers, *Milwaukee Journal* (evening) and *Milwaukee Sentinel* (morning), as well as the monthly *Milwaukee* magazine.

Dance Factory, 710 W. Virginia St. (643-7677): Performances of classical and modern ballet.

Emil Blatz Temple of Music, Washington Park, U.S. 41 and Washington Blvd. (278-4389): Open-air concerts of classical and pop music: "Music Under the Stars" (July–Aug).

Helfaer Theater, on the campus of Marquette University, 13th St. and Clyborn St. (224-7504): Modern and classical theater; concerts.

Melody Top Theater, 7201 W. Good Hope Rd. (353-7700): Musical comedies, Broadway hits. Tues–Sun early June to mid-Sept.

Milwaukee Repertory Theater, 108 E. Wells St. (224-9490): Traditional and contemporary theater in a new performing-arts complex with three adjacent auditoriums: the Mainstage Theater, the Stienke Theater, and the Stackner Cabaret. Open Sept–July.

Pabst Theater, 144 E. Wells St. (278-3663): Musical comedy, concerts, and contemporary theater in a lovely turn-of-the-century baroque setting, superbly restored.

Performing Arts Center/PAC, 929 N. Water St. (273-7206): This ultramodern group of buildings houses the Milwaukee Symphony Orchestra, under principal conductor Zdenek Macal (Sept–June); the Pennsylvania-Milwaukee Ballet (Sept–May); the First Stage Milwaukee Theater (a children's theater); and the Florentine Opera Company and Bel Canto Chorus, under music director John Gage (Nov–May).

Riverside Theater, 116 W. Wisconsin Ave. (271-2000): Broadway hits, touring companies, big-star shows.

Skylight Comic Opera, 813 N. Jefferson St. (271-8815): Operettas, musical comedies.

UWM Fine Arts Theater, 2200 E. Kenwood Blvd. (229-4308): Concerts of classical music and jazz.

SHOPPING: Grand Avenue Mall, W. Wisconsin Ave. and 3rd St. (224-0384): Enormous shopping mall on three levels, radiating out from a spectacular glassed-in rotunda. More than 180 stores, boutiques, restaurants, and cafés of all kinds. The heart of Milwaukee shopping. Directly connected to the Skywalk System. Open daily.

☼ **Old World Third Street,** 3rd St. between W. Wells St. and W. Highland Ave.: Well-known food shops such as Usinger's Famous Sausage, the Spice House, and Wisconsin Cheese Mart, Inc., restaurants, antique shops. A lively, colorful neighborhood, reminiscent of an old European city. Most shops open Mon–Sat.

☼ **W.K. Walthers, Inc.,** N. 60th St. and Florist Ave. (527-0770): The world's largest store entirely devoted to model-railroad equipment; a 50-year-old tradition. A must for all buffs. Open Mon–Fri year round.

SPECIAL EVENTS: For exact dates on the events listed below, consult the **Milwaukee Convention & Visitors Bureau** (see "Tourist Information," above).

Lakefront Festival of the Arts (June): Open-air concerts, art and craft exhibitions.

Summerfest (late June to early July): Top-name entertainers perform on 10 separate stages along Milwaukee's lakefront. Ethnic and American foods festival, sports events, circus, boating displays on the lake. Colorful and crowded.

Great Circus Parade (mid-July): The big annual circus festival, with a very spectacular street parade; it draws more than 800,000 spectators.

Wisconsin State Fair (10 days in Aug): Very popular agricultural fair, also with big-name shows, auto races, fireworks, etc.

Greater Milwaukee Open Golf Tournament (early Sept): Annual PGA tournament with top touring golf pros at the beautiful Tuckaway Country Club in Franklin.

Oktoberfest (Sept–Oct): Oceans of beer and music, tons of food; lots of warmth. The country's biggest beer festival.

Holiday Folk Fair (Nov): Folklore shows, food festival, and arts from around the world.

SPORTS: Milwaukee boasts professional teams in four major spectator sports:

Baseball (Apr–Oct): Brewers, County Stadium (933-1818).
Basketball (Oct–Apr): Bucks, Bradley Center (272-0500).
Football (Sept–Dec): Green Bay Packers, County Stadium (342-2717).
Ice Hockey (Sept–Apr): Admirals, Bradley Center (272-0500).

STROLLS: ☼⚱ **Lakefront,** along Lincoln Memorial Dr.: One of the country's finest urban landscapes; beautiful gardens and opulent private homes along Lake Michigan. Definitely worth seeing.

☼⚱ **Old World Third Street,** 3rd St. between W. Wells St. and W. Highland Ave.: The shopping district of Old Milwaukee (see "Shopping," above). A stroll that shouldn't be missed.

THEME PARKS: ☼⚱ **Old World Wisconsin,** Wisc. 59 in Eagle (35 mi./ 56km SW) (594-2116): Picturesque museum-village, comprising 50 or so 19th-century buildings, scrupulously restored, with authentic furniture and equipment, and walk-ons in period dress. A pleasant glimpse of the past. Open daily May–Oct. Well worth the side trip.

⚱ **Six Flags Great America,** on Grand Ave. in Gurnee, Ill. (32 mi./51km south on I-94) (708/249-1776): 200-acre (81 ha) theme park with giant roller coaster, waterfalls with giant slides, and more than 100 other attractions. Facsimile of a pioneer village. Shows. Open daily in summer, wknds only in spring and fall; closed the rest of the year.

WINTER SPORTS RESORTS: ⚱ **Alpine Valley,** 36 mi. (57km) SW on Wisc. 15 and County D Rd. (642-7374): 15 lifts. Dec to mid-Mar.

⚱ **Little Switzerland,** 30 mi. (48 km) NW on U.S. 41 and Wisc. AA Rd. (644-5020): 8 lifts. Nov–Mar.

ZOOS: ⚱ **Milwaukee County Zoo,** 10001 W. Bluemound Rd. (7 mi./11km west on U.S. 18) (771-3040): One of the best-designed and most comprehensive zoos in the country, with more than 3,000 animals from giant gorillas to white tigers. See it from the mini-train. Open daily year round. 10 min. from dwntwn.

ACCOMMODATIONS

A Note on Accommodations: Room rates in Milwaukee are coded as follows: **VE,** Very Expensive ($140 and up); **E,** Expensive ($90–$140); **M,** Moderate

($60–$90); **I,** Inexpensive ($30–$60); **B,** Budget (up to $30). A listing of toll free numbers is in the Appendix.

Personal Favorites (in order of preference)

☀♀♀♀ **Pfister Hotel** (dwntwn), 424 E. Wisconsin Ave., WI 53202 (414/273-8222; toll free, see Preferred). 306 rms, A/C, color TV, in-rm movies. AE, CB, DC, MC, V. Valet parking $4, pool, health club, sauna, rest. (The English Room), coffee shop, two bars, 24-hr. rm svce, disco, hrdrsr, concierge, free child's cot. *Note:* Much admired by Enrico Caruso, this luxury hotel from the 1890s was recently expanded w. the addition of an ultramodern tower. Elegant decor w. many works of art. The rms in the old building, w. lake views, are charming; the rms in the tower, they are simply functional. Polished svce; very good rest.; the "grande dame" of local hotels. **E–VE**

♀♀♀ **Hyatt Regency** (dwntwn), 333 W. Kilbourn Ave., WI 53203 (414/276-1234; toll free, see Hyatt). 484 rms, A/C, color TV, in-rm movies. AE, CB, DC, MC, V. Gar. $6, two rests. (one revolving on the top floor), coffee shop, two bars, 24-hr. rm svce, nightclub, concierge. *Note:* Huge ultramodern glass-and-concrete cube w. spectacular 18-story lobby and glass-walled elevators. Typical Hyatt comfort, but svce leaves a little to be desired. Group and convention clientele; direct access to the Skywalk System. VIP floor. "333" is a commendable rest. Has recently completed a $4-million renovation program. **E–VE**

♀♀ **Marc Plaza** (dwntwn), 509 W. Wisconsin Ave., WI 53203 (414/271-7250; toll free 800/558-7708). 500 rms, A/C, color TV, in-rm movies. AE, CB, DC, MC, V. Parking $3, pool, health club, sauna, two rests. (including Le Bistro), coffee shop, bar, rm svce, nightclub, hrdrsr, boutiques, free crib. *Note:* The largest and one of the oldest of the hotels in Milwaukee, several times renovated and now w. heated indoor pool and sauna. A favorite of business travelers; a VIP section is reserved for them on the 20th–24th floors. Very central. Excellent svce. Same management as the Pfister Hotel. No-smoking floors. **M–E**

♀♀ **Park East Hotel** (dwntwn), 916 E. State St., WI 53202 (414/276-8800). 160 rms, A/C, color TV, in-rm movies. AE, CB, DC, MC, V. Free parking, health club, rest. (Park Room), bar, rm svce. *Note:* A modern, functionally designed building within a stone's throw of the lake. Spacious, comfortable rms, some w. lake views. Friendly reception. Very good value. **I–M**

☀♀ **Knickerbocker** (dwntwn), 1028 E. Juneau Ave., WI 53202 (414/271-9890). 300 rms, A/C, color TV. AE, MC, V. Parking adj. rest. (Sally's Steak House), coffee shop, bar. *Note:* Elderly but well-maintained hotel; also apartments by the week or month. A very acceptable standard of comfort. Some rms have a view of nearby Lake Michigan. The Steak House is very popular. An old Milwaukee landmark. **I**

Other Hotels (from top bracket to budget)

♀♀♀ **Wyndham Milwaukee Center** (dwntwn), 139 E. Kilbourn Ave., WI 53202 (414/276-8686; toll free 800/822-4200). 221 rms, A/C, color TV, in-rm movies. AE, CB, DC, MC, V. Gar. $7, health club, sauna, rest. (Kilbourn Café), two bars, rm svce, disco, boutiques, free crib. *Note:* Part of the brand-new Milwaukee Center complex, this elegant hotel became the VIP's favorite almost as soon as it opened in July 1988. Mahogany paneling, velvet, and a profusion of artworks combine to make the setting both intimate and elegant. Spacious, very comfortable rms; impeccable svce; acceptable rest. Right in the theater district and across from City Hall. **E–VE**

♀♀ **Hilton Inn Milwaukee River** (nr. dwntwn), 4700 N. Port Washington Rd., Glendale, WI 53212 (414/962-6040; toll free, see Hilton). 164 rms, A/C, color TV, in-rm movies. AE, CB, DC, MC, V. Free parking, pool, health club, rest. (Anchorage), bar, rm svce. *Note:* Typical modern luxury motel on the bank of the Milwaukee River. Very good seafood rest. Efficient svce. Comfortable rms, the best w. views across the river. 10 min. from dwntwn. **M-E**

📞 **Astor Hotel** (dwntwn), 924 E. Juneau Ave., WI 53202 (414/ 271-4220; toll free 800/558-0200). 96 rms, A/C, color TV, in-rm movies. AE, CB, DC, MC, V. Parking $4, rest., bar, valet svce, free breakfast, free crib. *Note:* Venerable but charming hotel in a quiet residential neighborhood nr. the lake. Friendly reception and svce. Many antiques and period reproductions. Some rooms w. kitchenettes. Satisfactory rest. (Nantucket Shores). Good value overall. 5 min. from dwntwn (free shuttle). **M**

📞📞 **Howard Johnson Plaza Hotel** (formerly the Admiral Inn; dwntwn), 611 W. Wisconsin Ave., WI 53203 (414/273-2950; toll free, see Howard Johnson's). 248 rms, A/C, color TV, in-rm movies. AE, CB, DC, MC, V. Free valet parking, pool, rest., bar, rm svce, free crib. *Note:* Functional 10-story motel adj. the Convention Center (MECCA). Modern comforts; huge well-designed rms; efficient svce. Group and convention clientele. **I-M**

📞📞 **Ramada Inn Downtown** (dwntwn), 633 W. Michigan Ave., WI 53203 (414/272-8410; toll free, see Ramada). 152 rms, A/C, color TV, in-rm movies. AE, CB, DC, MC, V. Free parking, pool, rest., bar, rm svce, free child's cot. *Note:* Conventional motel nr. the business district; spacious, comfortable rms, some w. refrigerators. Good svce. Business clientele. Good value. **I-M**

📞 **Continental Motor Inn** (nr. dwntwn), 3001 W. Wisconsin Ave., WI 53208 (414/344-7500). 54 rms, A/C, color TV, in-rm movies. AE, CB, DC, MC, V. Free parking, rest. *Note:* Well-run small motel nr. the County Stadium. Functionally comfortable; friendly reception; very good value. 10 min. from dwntwn. **I**

📞 **Hotel Wisconsin** (dwntwn), 720 N. 3rd St., WI 53203 (414/ 271-4900). 250 rms, A/C, color TV. AE, MC, V. Free parking, rest., bar. *Note:* Elderly hotel a little worn at the edges but clean and well kept. Comfortable though by no means luxurious rms; deficient reception and svce. Very centrally located a block from Grand Avenue Mall. Good value for the budget traveler. **I**

In the Vicinity

☼📞📞📞📞 **The American Club** (vic.), Highland Dr., Kohler, WI 53044 (414/457-8000; toll free 800/458-2562), 50 mi. (80km) north on I-43 and Wisc. 23. 162 rms, A/C, color TV, in-rm movies. AE, CB, DC, MC, V. Free gar., pool, health club, 12 tennis courts, beach, sauna, canoes, cross-country skiing in season, bicycles, trap shooting, carriage rides, two rests. (including Immigrant and Winery), coffee shop, bar, 24-hr. rm svce, disco, concierge, free crib. *Note:* Splendid British-style country inn standing in a beautiful private park, an authentic wildlife reserve. Spacious, lavishly comfortable rms in two small three-story buildings which are designated historic monuments. Impeccable reception and svce. Very good sports facilities; rests. of real quality. A haven of peace and elegance 1 hr. from Milwaukee. **E-VE**

Airport Accommodations

📞📞 **The Grand Hotel** (formerly the Red Carpet Hotel; vic.) 4747 S. Howell Ave., WI 53207 (414/481-8000; toll free 800/ 558-3862). 510 rms, A/C, color TV, in-rm movies. AE, CB, DC, MC, V. Free parking, two pools, health club, sauna, eight tennis courts, squash, bowling alley, two rests. (including Harold's), bars, rm svce, nightclub, hrdrsr, cinema, free airport limo, free crib. *Note:* Huge, massive modern six-floor motel opposite the airport. Comfortable, well-soundproofed rms, all recently remodeled. Comprehensive sports facilities. Business clientele. Good value. 20 min. from dwntwn. **M-E**

℗ **Motel 6** (vic.), 5037 S. Howell Ave., WI 53207 (414/482-
⌂ 4414). 119 rms, A/C, color TV, in-rm movies. AE, DC, MC,
V. Free parking, pool, free crib. *Note:* Unbeatable value, across from the airport
and 20 min. from dwntwn. Ideal if you're passing through by car, w. immediate
access to I-94. Resv. suggested. **B–I**

YMCA/Youth Hostels

Red Barn Hostel (vic.), 6750 Loomis Rd. (414/529-3299). 36 beds.
Country youth hostel open May–Oct; 12 mi. (19km) from dwntwn.

RESTAURANTS

A Note on Restaurant Prices: Milwaukee restaurant prices, per person, excluding drinks and service charges, are coded as follows: **VE**, Very Expensive
($60 and up); **E**, Expensive ($40–$60); **M**, Moderate ($25–$40); **I**, Inexpensive
($15–$25); **B**, Budget (up to $15).

Personal Favorites (in order of preference)

※🍸🍸🍸 **Karl Ratzsch's** (dwntwn), 320 E. Mason St. (276-2720).
A/C. Lunch Tues–Sun, dinner nightly; closed hols. AE, CB,
DC, MC, V. Jkt. *Specialties:* rouladen, planked whitefish, sauerbraten, wienerschnitzel, hamhock w. sauerkraut, duckling w. red cabbage, Dover sole, schaum
torte. Superb 25-page list of German wines at reasonable prices. *Note:* A landmark of local gastronomy; the best German rest. in Milwaukee. Atmosphere and
decor haven't changed since 1903; even the classical-music trio at dinner is in
period. Antique paneling, hand-painted murals, and chandeliers. Exemplary
svce. Resv. advisable at the end of the week. Still in the hands of the Ratzsch family, as it has been since it opened. *German/Continental.* **I–M**

🍸🍸🍸 **John Byron's** (dwntwn), First Wisconsin Center, 777 E.
Michigan Ave. (291-5220). A/C. Lunch Mon–Fri, dinner
Mon–Sat; closed hols. AE, CB, DC, MC, V. Jkt. *Specialties:* rack of lamb,
poached sole w. salmon mousse, grilled marinated breast of duck, catch of the
day, pheasant w. morel mushrooms. Menu changes regularly. Very fine wine list
at astonishingly reasonable prices. *Note:* On the galleria level of Milwaukee's tallest high-rise, the First Wisconsin Center, this very fine rest. features the inventive
cuisine of its excellent chef, Sanford d'Amato. Friendly, comfortable setting w.
fine view of the port of Milwaukee. Svce of the best; live classical music in the
background at dinner. No pipes or cigars. A favorite for business lunches; be sure
to reserve ahead. *Continental.* **I–M**

※🍸🍸 **John Ernst** (dwntwn), 600 E. Ogden Ave. (273-1878). A/C.
Lunch/dinner Tues–Sun. AE, CB, DC, MC, V. Jkt. *Specialties:* sauerbraten w. potato pancakes, Kassler rippchen, wienerschnitzel,
jägerschnitzel, goulash, fish of the day. *Note:* A beautiful scene from 19th-century
Germany, favored by local socialites since 1878. Authentic Bavarian decor w.
huge open fireplace. Assiduous svce. Resv. advised at end of week. Milwaukee's
oldest rest. *German.* **I–M**

🍸🍸 **Armadillo Grill** (dwntwn), 1235 N. Van Buren Ave. (291-
9933). A/C. Lunch Mon–Fri, dinner nightly. AE, MC, V.
Specialties: fajitas, lamb enchiladas, chicken stuffed w. yellow cornmeal, ham and
goat cheese, black-bean chili, wood-roasted chicken, broiled steak and fish. Long
list of California wines and excellent homemade margaritas. *Note:* Flavorful, sunlit dishes from the Southwest. Excellent broiled foods (mesquite-wood fire).
Classic Santa Fe–style decor and a relaxed atmosphere. Live jazz at dinner Wed–
Sat; popular w. residents. *American.* **I**

🍸 **Toy's Chinatown** (dwntwn), 830 N. 3rd St. (271-5166).
A/C. Lunch/dinner daily; closed hols. AE, DC, MC, V. Jkt.
Specialties: Cantonese food: chow mein, sweet-and-sour shrimp, spareribs. *Note:*
The food, and the elaborate Far Eastern decor, have made this one of

Milwaukee's favorite Chinese rests. for three generations. Svce on the abrupt side. Very good value. Opposite the Hyatt Regency Hotel. *Chinese.* **I**

♀ **Jake's Delicatessen** (nr. dwntwn), 1634 W. North Ave. (562-
🍸 1272). A/C. Lunch/dinner daily. No credit cards. *Specialties:* corned beef, short ribs, giant sausage, pastrami, kosher specialties. *Note:* Likable New York–style deli w. wonderful sandwiches to go. Often crowded at noontime. Resv. advised. *American.* **B–I**

Other Restaurants (from top bracket to budget)

♀♀♀ **Grenadiers** (dwntwn), 747 N. Broadway (276-0747). A/C.
Lunch Mon–Fri, dinner Mon–Sat; closed hols. AE, CB, DC, MC, V. J&T. *Specialties:* chicken w. morels, Calcutta lamb curry, breast of veal w. raspberries, fish of the day, Dover sole in champagne sauce, scrumptious desserts. The menu changes regularly; the wine list is good. *Note:* The young German chef, Knut Apitz, is indubitably producing some of the most inventive, delicate food around. Elegant Empire-style classical decor and a delightful glassed-in Garden Room. Very polished svce. One of the best places to eat in Milwaukee, in the heart of dwntwn. Valet parking; resv. necessary. *Continental.* **I–M**

♀♀ **Alioto's** (vic.), 3041 N. Mayfair Rd., in Wauwatosa (476-
6900). A/C. Lunch/dinner Mon–Sat. AE, CB, DC, MC, V. Jkt. *Specialties:* breaded steak Sicilian style, prime rib, roast duck, traditional Italian dishes. *Note:* A very popular place w. lovers of prime beef and/or Italian cooking—even though the unmemorable decor reminds you of a railroad station waiting rm. Good svce. 20 min. from dwntwn. A landmark since 1923. *Italian/Steak.* **I**

♀♀ **Boulevard Inn** (nr. dwntwn), 4300 W. Lloyd St. (445-4221).
A/C. Lunch/dinner daily, brunch Sun; closed hols. AE, CB, DC, MC, V. Jkt. *Specialties:* sauerbraten, sweetbreads w. shallots and champagne, New York steak, sautéed scallops, duckling w. red cabbage, fish of the day, cheesecake. *Note:* All the great standbys of German and Continental cuisine, admirably prepared and served, in a pleasant country-inn setting but w. a pervasive musical background. 15 min. from dwntwn. Locally popular; resv. advised. *German/Continental.* **I**

☼♀♀ **Jack Pandl's Whitefish Bay Inn** (vic.), 1319 E. Henry Clay St.
(964-3800). A/C. Lunch/dinner Mon–Sat; closed hols. AE, CB, DC, MC, V. *Specialties:* fish from Lake Michigan, German dishes, roast duck, schaum torte. *Note:* A favorite of Milwaukee's German colony since 1915. Excellent broiled whitefish. Comfortable atmosphere; fine old decor. Efficient svce; generous servings. German beer on draft. Resv. advised. 20 min. from dwntwn. *German/Seafood.* **I**

♀♀ **Maniaci's Café Siciliano** (nr. dwntwn), 6904 N. Santa Monica
Blvd. (352-5757). A/C. Dinner only, Mon–Sat; closed hols. AE, CB, DC, MC, V. *Specialties:* fresh homemade pasta, chicken cacciatore, piccata of whitefish, shrimp Michelle, veal Grand Prix, cannoli. *Note:* A more authentic Italian *trattoria* you couldn't find in Italy; the food is from the southern part of the country, absolutely authentic and very reasonably priced. Reception and svce w. a smile. Romantic Italian courtyard w. white stucco walls and tile floor. Well worth the 20-min. trip from dwntwn by car. Resv. advised. *Italian.* **I**

♀ **Jake's** (vic.), 6030 W. North Ave., in Wauwatosa (771-0550).
🍸 A/C. Dinner only, nightly; closed Thanksgiving, Dec 24–25. AE, DC, MC, V. Jkt. *Specialties:* steak au poivre, filet of beef, scallops, fish of the day. Good wine list. *Note:* Superb meats broiled to perfection. Agreeable decor; friendly svce. No resv. 15 min. from dwntwn. Other location: 21445 W. Capitol Dr., in Brookfield (781-7995), w. dinner nightly. *Steak.* **I**

☼♀ **Sally's Steak House,** in the Knickerbocker Hotel (see "Ac-
commodations," above) (272-5363). A/C. Lunch Mon–Fri, dinner Mon–Sat; closed hols. AE, CB, DC, MC, V. *Specialties:* clam chowder,

chicken Vesuvio, spiedini, steak Sicilian, duck stuffed w. chestnuts, very fine broiled meats. *Note:* Because of its substantial servings and generous drinks, this cozy, English country-style rest. is a favorite of sports stars passing through town, and of actor Paul Newman, among other celebrities. Relaxed ambience and svce.; a fine place to eat. Locally popular for 25 years. Resv. advised. *Steak/Italian.* I

☞ **Dos Bandidos** (nr. dwntwn), 5932 N. Green Bay Ave. (228-1911). A/C. Lunch Mon–Fri, dinner nightly; closed hols. AE, MC, V. *Specialties:* tacos, fajitas, spinach and crabmeat enchiladas, chiles relleños, steak ranchero, excellent margaritas. *Note:* Typical Mexican cantina w. an abundance of greenery and an inviting open patio. The food is absolutely authentic and far above average. No resv. 15 min. from dwntwn by I-43 and Silver Spring Dr. *Mexican.* B–I

☞ **Old Town** (nr. dwntwn), 522 W. Lincoln Ave. (672-0206). A/C. Lunch Tues–Fri, dinner Tues–Sun. AE, MC, V. Jkt. *Specialties:* böreck, moussaka, baked lamb, paprika chicken, roast duckling, homemade pies and strudels. *Note:* One of Milwaukee's favorite ethnic rests. Spicy but well-prepared Balkan food in a pretty setting. Hearty portions. Efficient svce. Noisy background music. Resv. advised at the end of the week. 15 min. from dwntwn. *Continental.* B–I

Cafeterias/Fast Food/Specialty Spots
Water Street Brewery (dwntwn), 1101 N. Water St. (272-1195). Open daily until 2am. AE, MC, V. Engaging old-time brewery serving a wide choice of its own beers, as well as national and imported labels. Hors d'oeuvres, lavish sandwiches and daily specials are also available.

Watts Tea Shop (dwntwn), 761 N. Jefferson St. (276-6352). AE, MC, V. A century-old Milwaukee tradition; excellent daily specials, sandwiches, and house salads. Lunch only, Mon–Sat. B

BARS & NIGHTCLUBS
Bermudas (dwntwn), 500 N. Water St. at Clyburn (765-0891). Trendy disco frequented by a college crowd; a jumping joint. Open Tues–Sat.
Bombay Bicycle Club (dwntwn), in the Marc Plaza (see "Accommodations," above) (271-7250). Excellent piano-bar; live jazz. Open Mon–Sat.
The Brown Bottle (nr. dwntwn), 221 W. Galena Court (271-4444). A very Germanic rathskeller housed in the one-time Schlitz brewery; more than 140 different labels of beer from five continents. Also acceptable rest. Open Mon–Sat.
John Hawk's Pub (dwntwn), 607 N. Broadway at E. Michigan Ave. (272-3199). Model British pub with 40 different brands of beer; a nice place. Live jazz Fri–Sat; open daily.
La Playa (dwntwn), in the Pfister Hotel (see "Accommodations," above) (273-8222). Tropical-style nightclub with large live orchestra. Superb view from the 23rd floor of the Pfister Hotel. Trendy crowd. Open Mon–Sat.
Major Goolsby's (dwntwn), 340 W. Kilbourn Ave. at N. 4th St. (271-3414). This popular bar across from the MECCA Arena attracts mostly local sports stars and their fans. Sports memorabilia abounds on every wall. Good burgers. Open nightly.
Park Avenue (dwntwn), 500 N. Water St. (765-0891). Disco; big-star shows. Youthful atmosphere; locally popular. Open Tues–Sat.
Safe House (dwntwn), 779 N. Front St. (271-2007). An amusing rest. and nightclub in the James Bond tradition. *Note:* Only an ordinary brass plaque labeled "International Exports Ltd." marks the entrance. The fashionable spot. Open nightly.

NEARBY EXCURSIONS

BROOKS STEVENS AUTOMOTIVE MUSEUM (10325 N. Port Washington, in Mequon, 10 mi./16km north on I-43N) (241-4185): Amazing collection of racing cars and production-line models from 1905 to the present day. One of the country's finest auto museums; a must for car buffs. Open daily.

LIZARD MOUND STATE PARK (County A Rd. at West Bend, 38 mi./60km NW on U.S. 45N and Wisc. 144) (338-4445): Comprises 30 or so mounds of earth in the shape of beasts, birds, or geometric forms, the work of Native Americans dating from A.D. 500–1000. Well worth the side trip. Open daily.

OSHKOSH (83 mi./132km NW on U.S. 41N): On the banks of big Lake Winnebago, this friendly town of 50,000 people plays host for a week every year (late July to early Aug) to the world's largest air show, the E.A.A. International Fly-in Convention, which attracts more than 300,000 spectators and participants. Thousands of early aircraft, from Mustangs to Spitfires and B-26s to World War I biplanes. Aerial acrobatics festival; flight demonstrations. For prop-plane enthusiasts. Interesting aeronautical museum, the **E.E.A. Air Museum,** 3000 Poberezny Rd. (426-4800), open daily. Don't miss this one. It should be combined with the excursion to Lizard Mound State Park (see above).

RACINE (29 mi./46km SE on I-94S and Wisc. 20E): This pleasant little industrial town on Lake Michigan, most of whose inhabitants are of Danish descent, is the home of Johnson's Wax. The company's head office, built in 1939–50 to the design of the great architect Frank Lloyd Wright, is an outright masterpiece of the modernist style. Guided tour of the buildings at 14th St. and Franklin St. Tues–Fri; resv. (631-2154) a must. Don't miss it.

FARTHER AFIELD

SPRING GREEN & WISCONSIN DELLS (315 mi/ 504km r. t. via I-94N, U.S. 12S, Wisc. 60W, U.S. 14E, and I-94S): 3- to 4-day trip beginning with a visit to **Wisconsin Dells,** where the Wisconsin River has cut beautiful, wild gorges that can be reached only by boat. Guided sightseeing tours daily mid-Apr to late Oct, 11 Broadway (608/254-8555). There is a Winnebago tribal village, Wisc. 13 and River Rd. (608/254-2268), with a museum; tribal dances daily in summer. Many other tourist attractions. Well worth the trip.

Then on to ☼ **Baraboo,** 12 mi. (19km) south of Wisconsin Dells, with the interesting **Circus World Museum** at 426 Water St. (608/356-0800), open daily mid-May to Sept, once the winter quarters of the famous Ringling Bros. circus. Parades, shows, menagerie, and more than 150 circus caravans of all ages; don't miss it. Also a very fine railroad museum at **North Freedom,** 8 mi. (12km) west on Wisc. 136 and County PF (608/522-4261), open daily mid-May to Sept, with a trip in a turn-of-the-century steam train. Amusing.

The next stop is at ☼ **Spring Green,** the town where the well-known architect Frank Lloyd Wright grew up, and where he built one of his houses, **Taliesin East,** 4 mi. (6km) south on Wisc. 23 (608/588-2511). Open daily mid-May to mid-Oct; an absolute must-see. Another sight that shouldn't be missed is the extraordinary **"House on the Rock,"** by architect Alexander J. Jordan, hanging 450 ft. (137m) above the Wisconsin River, with its waterfalls, pools, and trees integrated spectacularly into the design of the building. It stands 9 mi. (14km) south on Wisc. 23. Open daily from Apr 1 to Oct 31 (608/935-3639). Many other attractions nearby, including the world's largest carousel. A fascinating expedition, which shouldn't be missed.

Where to Stay in Wisconsin Dells

Shamrock Motel, 1321 Wisconsin Dells Pkwy., Wisconsin Dells, WI 53965 (608/254-8054). 62 rms. An inviting motel standing in its own grdns. Open mid-May to the end of Oct. **I–M**

Tiki Motel, 1370 E. Hiawatha Dr., Wisconsin Dells, WI 53965 (608/253-4741). 32 rms. Small, congenial hotel on a lake. Open early May to mid-Oct. **I–M**

Where to Stay in Spring Green

The Prairie House, at the intersection of U.S. 14 and Wisc. 23, Spring Green, WI 53588 (608/588-2088). 51 rms. Classic but well-run motel open year round. **I**

Where to Eat in Spring Green

Spring Green Restaurant, on Wisc. 23 (608/588-2571). Lunch/dinner daily. AE, MC, V. Very commendable American food served in the world's only Frank Lloyd Wright–designed rest. **B–I**

CHAPTER 25

MINNEAPOLIS AND ST. PAUL

□ □ □

Lying on opposite sides of the Mississippi River, the Twin Cities complement each other harmoniously, while each retains its own distinct style and character. Minneapolis is dynamic, active, and mostly Scandinavian and Lutheran. St. Paul, the state capital, is more traditional; its people are mostly Irish or German, and Catholic. Minneapolis has its modern high-rises, its network of Skyways, its bustling nightlife, and the **Minnehaha Falls** of which Longfellow sang. St. Paul has fine classical buildings such as the **State Capitol,** designed by Cass Gilbert, the imposing **City Hall,** and **St. Paul's Cathedral,** one of the country's largest. Minneapolis is politically progressive and tolerant; Hubert Humphrey, the populist leader who was once vice-president of the U.S., was for many years first mayor of the city and then a senator from Minnesota. St. Paul may be more starchy and conservative, but the liberal Democrat Eugene McCarthy began his career here as a teacher at St. Thomas College. St. Paul is also the birthplace of F. Scott Fitzgerald, the chronicler of the "lost generation." Minneapolis, more prosaically, can lay claim to Charles M. Schulz, the creator of *Peanuts;* the late oil tycoon J. Paul Getty; movie director George Roy Hill; and rock singer Prince.

The site of the Twin Cities was explored in 1680 by the French missionary Fr. Louis Hennepin; their present prosperity began with the construction of the first flour mills in the 1850s. Successive waves of immigration—German, Irish, Polish, and above all, Scandinavian—did the rest. Minneapolis stands where the grain-growing prairies of the Dakotas and Minnesota (a name derived from two Sioux words: *minne,* meaning "water," and *sota,* meaning "sky-colored") meet the waters of the Mississippi River where they are still—but only just—navigable; today it is still one of the country's principal agricultural markets. Along with St. Paul, it has also become the home of important electronic, chemical, forest-product, and food companies such as Honeywell, Control Data, General Mills, Pillsbury, and 3M Corporation; the hub for Northwest Airlines as well as one of the country's capitals of rock music. Following on Prince's reputation, practitioners of the "Minneapolis sound," an aggressive style of rhythm and blues, have gained international acclaim. While the winters are very harsh, Minneapolis and St. Paul rank among the greenest cities in the country, with 936 lakes and 513 parks or public gardens between them.

The Twin Cities pride themselves on being the intellectual capital of the Midwest, with the University of Minnesota, well-known symphony and chamber orchestras, an opera, many museums of high quality, and the famous **Guthrie Theater.** They are also the heart of a fabulous vacationland of deep forests, swift-running rivers teeming with fish, and numberless lakes, including **Lake Superior,** at 32,480 sq. mi. (84,130km²) the world's largest body of fresh water. Such a wealth of tourist attractions has earned for Minneapolis/St. Paul the title of "Gateway of the Land of 10,000 Lakes," and for Minnesota the reputation of a hikers' and campers' paradise, at least during the summer months.

Last but not least, the Twin Cities represent in one sense a haven of peace and safety; by comparison with other great metropolitan areas their crime rate is among the lowest in the country (one-half Seattle's, one-sixth New York's).

BASIC FACTS: State of Minnesota (St. Paul is the state capital). Area code: 612. Time zone: central. ZIP Codes: 55401 (Minneapolis); 55101 (St. Paul). Founded: 1840 (St. Paul); 1847 (Minneapolis). Approximate population: Minneapolis, 350,000; St. Paul, 260,000; metropolitan area, 2,260,000. Rank among U.S. metropolitan areas: 15th.

CLIMATE: With temperatures in July averaging 77°F (22°C), the summer is the only good time for a visit. The first snows of fall appear in mid-Oct. As to the winters, the only adjective that does them justice is "polar." Jan temperatures average 13°F (−10°C), with the mercury sometimes plunging to −22°F to −38°F (−30°C to −40°C), and demonstrating the value of the cities' "Skyways"—two networks of glassed-in, heated pedestrian walkways which link together the principal buildings of downtown Minneapolis and downtown St. Paul, respectively.

DISTANCES: Chicago, 406 mi. (650km); Kansas City, 443 mi. (710km); Milwaukee, 365 mi. (584km); Rapid City, 633 mi. (1,012km); St. Louis, 567 mi. (908km); Winnipeg, 460 mi. (736km).

ARRIVAL & TRANSIT INFORMATION

AIRPORT: Minneapolis/St. Paul International Airport (MSP), 10 mi. (16km) SE of Minneapolis, 9 mi. (15km) SW of St. Paul. Call 726-5555 for information.

U.S. AIRLINES: American (332-4168), America West (toll free 800/247-5692), Continental (332-1471), Delta (339-7477), Midway (toll free 800/621-5700), Northwest (726-1234), TWA (333-6543), United (339-3671), and USAir (338-5841).

FOREIGN CARRIERS: Air Canada (toll free 800/422-6232) and Canadian International (toll free 800/426-7000).

CITY LINK: The **cab** fare to dwntwn Minneapolis is about $18–$20 for the 35-min. trip; to dwntwn St. Paul, about $15 for the 40-min. trip. Bus: to Minneapolis, **MSP Airport Express** (726-6400), and to St. Paul, **St. Paul Airport Limousine** (726-5479); each departs every 30 min. serving principal dwntwn hotels, at a fare of $8 for the 45-min. trip.

Unless you intend to confine yourself to the two dwntwn districts with their covered walkways, the size of the metropolitan area and its profusion of green space make it advisable to rent a car with unlimited mileage.

The **public bus system, MTC** (827-7733), is trustworthy and practical for trips around dwntwn or between the Twin Cities.

CAR RENTAL (at the airport unless otherwise indicated): Avis (726-5220); Budget (727-2000); Dollar, in the Sheraton Airport Hotel (854-9001); Hertz (726-1600); National (726-5600); and Thrifty, 2801 E. 78th St., Bloomington (854-8080). For dwntwn locations, consult the local telephone directory.

LIMOUSINE SERVICES: Carey Limousine (824-7665), Dav El Limousines (toll free 800/922-0343), Twin Star Limousine (toll free 800/999-8333).

TAXIS: Cabs may be hailed on the street or taken from the waiting lines outside the big hotels, but are best summoned by phone. Recommended companies: **in**

Minneapolis, Blue & White (333-3331), and Yellow Cab (824-4444); **in St. Paul,** Town Taxi (331-8294) and Yellow Cab (222-4433).

TRAIN: Amtrak, Midway Station, 730 Transfer Rd., St. Paul. (339-2382).

INTERCITY BUSES: Greyhound, at 29 N. 9th St., Minneapolis (371-3311), and 25 W. 9th St., St. Paul (222-0509).

MISSISSIPPI CRUISES: 3- to 10-day cruises aboard the *Delta Queen* or the *Mississippi Queen,* paddlewheel steamers built in the 1920s. Luxurious kitsch. See Chapter 15 on New Orleans for details.

MINNEAPOLIS

INFORMATION & TOURS

TOURIST INFORMATION: The **Minneapolis Convention and Visitor Commission,** 1219 Marquette Ave., MN 55403 (612/348-4313; toll free 800/445-7412).
   The Connection: For information on current shows and cultural events in the Twin Cities, call 922-9000.

GUIDED TOURS: Gray Line Tours (bus), 835 Decatur Ave. N., Minneapolis (591-9199): Conducted tours of the city and surroundings. Also serves St. Paul. Open Mon–Sat Apr–Sept, Sat only the rest of the year.

SIGHTS, ATTRACTIONS & ACTIVITIES

ADVENTURES: Stillwater Balloons, 14399 60th St. N., Stillwater (439-1800): Spectacular dirigible-balloon trips over the picturesque St. Croix Valley. Operate daily, weather permitting.

ARCHITECTURAL HIGHLIGHTS: ☀⚱ **Guthrie Theater,** 725 Vineland Pl. (377-2224): This hall of ultramodern design is home to one of the country's best-known theatrical companies, founded in 1963 by the late Sir Tyrone Guthrie. The 1,400-seat hall occupies a 200° arc of a circle around an open stage. Year-round concerts and plays; don't miss these shows.
   ⚱ **Hennepin County Government Center,** Third Ave. S. and 5th St. (348-5596): Twin towers of pink granite, each 339 ft. (106m) high, rise on either side of a huge lobby lit by picture windows, designed by architect John Carl Warnecke. This is the seat of the county government; worth a look.
   ⚱ **Hubert H. Humphrey Metrodome,** 900 S. 5th St. (332-0386): Impressive air-conditioned stadium with 60,000 seats, under a plastic dome; the Minnesota Twins and Minnesota Vikings make their headquarters here. Open Mon–Fri.
   ☀⚱ **IDS Tower,** 80 S. 8th St. (372-3131): At 57 floors, 775 ft. (236m), this flat-topped multifaceted glass tower is one of the tallest high-rises in the Midwest, designed by architects Philip Johnson and John Burgee. You should take a look.
   ⚱ **Minneapolis Grain Exchange,** 400 S. 4th St. (338-6212): The world's second-largest grain exchange, noisy and frenetic. The Visitors' Gallery may be visited by appointment only. Open daily.

Norwest Center, Marquette Ave. at S. 7th St. (344-1200): Brand-new (1989) 57-story building of yellowish-tan stone and glass that evokes the skyscrapers of the 1930s, the General Electric (formerly RCA) Building at Rockefeller Center in New York in particular. This Cesar Pelli–designed tower joins its next-door neighbor, the IDS Center, to give Minneapolis a truly notable skyline. Well worth a look.

Orchestra Hall, 1111 Nicolet Ave. (371-5656): Home of the world-famous Minnesota Orchestra (formerly the Minneapolis Symphony Orchestra). The austere building has some of the finest acoustics ever achieved. See "Performing Arts," below.

Skyway, around Marquette Ave. and Nicollet Mall: Ingenious system of heated walkways and footbridges connecting downtown's principal hotels, stores, and office buildings. This network—the world's largest—connects some 25 blocks downtown. Very useful in winter, when temperatures drop to −6° F to −22° F (−20° C to −30°C). You should certainly take a walk here.

Upper Lock, Portland Ave. (333-5336): This giant lock, with a rise and fall of 49 ft. (15m), marks the upper limit of the navigable waters of the Mississippi. An observation platform is open daily Apr 1–Oct 31. Spectacular.

CHURCHES/SYNAGOGUES: **Basilica of St. Mary,** Hennepin Ave. and 16th St. (333-1381): Renaissance-style building inspired by the basilica of St. John Lateran in Rome. Open daily; worth a look.

HISTORIC BUILDINGS: **City Hall,** 5th St. and Third Ave. S. (348-2491): The imposing 1891 City Hall, with its Big Ben clock tower, is a surprising contrast to its next-door neighbor, the ultramodern Hennepin County Government Center. Here you will find the *The Father of Waters,* the largest statue ever carved from a single block of Italian Carrara marble. Definitely should be seen. Open Mon–Fri.

University of Minnesota, Washington Ave. on either side of the Mississippi River (624-6504): One of the Midwest's oldest (1851) and most important universities, with 58,000 students. On its campus, one of the largest in the country, are two museums worth seeing: the **Bell Museum of Natural History,** open Tues–Sun, and the **University Art Gallery,** open daily.

MUSEUMS OF ART: **Minneapolis Institute of Arts,** 2400 Third Ave. S. (870-3131): This very lovely museum of classical design is home to more than 70,000 art objects of all periods and places. Rich collection of great European masters from El Greco to Matisse; also Egyptian and Far Eastern art. Temporary exhibitions. Among the best-known works on display are *Temptation of Christ* by Titian, *Portrait of Cardinal Borghese* by Pietro da Cortona, Rembrandt's *Lucretia,* and van Gogh's *Olive Grove,* as well as *Composition in Red* by Piet Mondrian, *White Feathers* by Matisse, and *Flayed Steer* by Chaim Soutine. Excellent cafeteria. An absolute must. Open Tues–Sun.

Minneapolis Sculpture Garden, Vineland Pl. (375-7577): Opened in Sept 1988 across from the Walker Art Center, this sculpture garden, designed by architect Edward Larrabee Barnes, has become one of the country's most important sites of its kind. Many of the 40 works displayed have been commissioned for this specific site, notably Claes Oldenburg's spectacular 52-ft.-long (15m) fountain called *Spoonbridge and Cherry* and a Frank Gehry sculpture of a 22-ft.-high (6m) glass fish. Other works by Roy Lichtenstein, Henry Moore, Siah Armajani, Jacques Lipchitz, Richard Serra, Isamu Noguchi. . . . Open daily. Not to be missed.

Walker Art Center, Vineland Pl. (375-7600): Contemporary art of all kinds—painting, sculpture, photography—as well as concerts, movies, and temporary exhibitions, in an interesting modern building whose new wing was designed by the distinguished Japanese architect Kenze Tangé. Twentieth-century American art is particularly well represented, with works by Edward Hopper, Roy Lichtenstein, Andy Warhol, Robert Rauschenberg, Barnet Newman, Louise Nevelson, George Segal, and others. Fascinating; shouldn't be missed. Open Tues–Sun. Pleasant cafeteria.

MUSEUMS OF SCIENCE & HISTORY: ⚱ American Swedish Institute,
2600 Park Ave. S. (871-4907): This museum of Swedish art and folk tradition is housed in an amusing turn-of-the-century Roman Revival mansion. Also temporary exhibitions devoted to Swedish-American culture. Open Tues–Sun.

⚱ **Hennepin County Historical Society Museum,** 2303 Third Ave. S. (870-1329): Illustrates in lively fashion the history of the settlement of Minnesota from pioneer days to the turn of the century, with old workshops and reconstructions of domestic interiors. An absolute must. Open Tues–Sun.

⚱ **Minneapolis Planetarium,** Public Library, 300 Nicollet Mall (372-6644): Relatively small but well-designed planetarium, with a dome 40 ft. (12.5m) high. For star-gazers. Open daily in summer; on Thurs, Sat, and Sun the rest of the year.

PANORAMAS: ⚱ Foshay Tower, 821 Marquette Ave. (341-2522): First local
skyscraper, built in 1929. Has a museum and observation deck on the 32nd floor with a 360° panorama of the city. Worth a look. Open daily Apr–Oct.

PARKS & GARDENS: ✳⚱ Minnehaha Park, Minnehaha Pkwy. and
Hiawatha Ave. S. (348-8942): This magnificent park on the banks of the Mississippi, famous for its 54-ft. (17m) waterfall, was immortalized by Longfellow in *The Song of Hiawatha,* where he writes of its "laughing waters." Worth going out of your way for.

⚱ **Wirth Park,** Wayzata Blvd. and Wirth Pkwy.: Starting point of a panoramic drive through parks (**Eloise Butler Wild Flower Gardens**) and past lakes (**Lake Calhoun, Lake Harriet, Lake Hiawatha**) along the Minnehaha Pkwy.

PERFORMING ARTS: For current listings of shows and cultural events, con-
sult the entertainment pages of the daily *Minneapolis Star & Tribune* (morning) and the monthly *Minneapolis–St. Paul.* **Tickets to Go,** a discount-ticket booth in the IDS Crystal Court (333-6841), sells half-price tickets for all shows on the day of performance. Cash only. Open Tues–Sat.

Dudley Riggs Theater, 2605 Hennepin Ave. (332-6620): Comedies, modern theater.

Guthrie Theater, 725 Vineland Pl. (377-2224): Classical and contemporary theater; one of the country's finest stock companies. Performances Tues–Sun May–Feb. Also concerts.

Hennepin Center for the Arts, 6th St. and Hennepin Ave. (332-4478): Home of the Minnesota Dance Theater, Feb–May.

Met Center, 7901 Cedar Ave. S., in South Bloomington (853-9333): Big-name shows, musical comedies, circus shows.

Orchestra Hall, 1111 Nicollet Ave. (371-5656): Recitals, classical concerts. Home of the Minnesota Orchestra (principal conductor: Edo de Waart). Oct–Apr.

Showboat, University of Minnesota campus (625-4001): Melodrama, comedy, operetta on board an authentic "showboat" moored on the Mississippi in front of the university campus. June–Aug.

SHOPPING: **Cobblestone Antiques,** 210 Third Ave. N. (338-2258): Antiques emporium in the warehouse district that houses some 60 dealers. A must-see for antique buffs.
The Conservatory, 800 Nicollet Mall: Downtown's newest shopping complex. Beautiful pink marble structure featuring 50 upscale shops, from Ann Taylor to F.A.O. Schwarz.
Nicollet Mall, on Nicollet Ave. between Washington Ave. and Grant St.: One of the country's best-known pedestrian malls; 12 blocks of stores, boutiques, and restaurants in the heart of downtown. Pleasant promenade lined with trees and fountains. Worth a visit.
Warehouse District, bounded by First Ave. and Third Ave. N.,. and 2nd St. and 6th St. N.: Art galleries, antiques shops, boutiques, restaurants, and funky bars in beautifully renovated turn-of-the-century buildings. A Minneapolis landmark.

SPECIAL EVENTS: For exact dates, consult the **Minneapolis Convention and Visitors Commission** (see "Tourist Information," above).
Midsummer (10 days in June): International biennial music festival held in the Hyland Lake Park Reserve in Bloomington. A joyous celebration of music for every taste—pop, classical, jazz, folk, etc.
Aquatennial Festival (late July): Colorful celebration of the many lakes and rivers of the Twin Cities. Parades on the Mississippi, boat races, sporting events, giant torchlight procession, open-air shows.
Sommerfest (end of July to Aug): Much appreciated by music-lovers. Series of theme concerts by the Minnesota Orchestra, shows, opera.
Renaissance Festival (wknds mid-Aug to late Sept): Re-creation of a 16th-century English village complete with foods, crafts, jugglers, magicians, and music. Takes place in nearby Shakopee; call 445-7361 for more information.

SPORTS: Minneapolis is home to three major-league professional teams and a minor-league basketball team:
Baseball (Apr–Oct): Twins, Hubert Humphrey Metrodome (375-7444).
Basketball (Oct–Apr): Timberwolves, Timberwolves Arena (337-3865).
Football (Sept–Dec): Vikings, Hubert Humphrey Metrodome (333-8828).
Ice Hockey (Sept–Apr): North Stars, Metro Center (853-9300).

Horse Racing
Canterbury Downs, Minn. 101 and County Rd. 83 in Shakopee (445-7223), 20 mi. (32km) SW on I-35W and Minn. 13 and Minn. 101. Racing Apr–Nov.

STROLLS: **Nicollet Mall** (see "Shopping," above).
St. Anthony Falls, Main St. SE and Central Ave.: These 45-ft. (15m) falls mark the upper limit of navigation on the Mississippi. Spectacular walk along the dam and the locks. There are many cafés, stores, and restaurants on the riverbanks (River Place, St. Anthony Main, etc.).

THEME PARKS: **Murphy's Landing,** 2187 E. Minn. 101, in Shakopee, 22 mi. (35km) SW of Minneapolis on I-35W and Minn. 13 and Minn. 101 (445-6900): Replica of an 1850s pioneer village with church, school, blacksmith, grocer's, etc. Extras in period costume; craft demonstrations. The old buildings, all authentic, were moved here from their original sites elsewhere in Minnesota. Well worth the side trip. Open Tues–Sun May to late Oct, and in Dec.
Valleyfair Amusement Park, Minn. 101 in Shakopee, 20 mi. (32km) SW of Minneapolis on I-35W and Minn. 13 and Minn. 101 (445-6500): Unusual amusement park laid out in turn-of-the-

century style. Old carousels, old vehicles, streetcars. Also rafting down the river and giant roller coaster. Can conveniently be visited along with Murphy's Landing, above.

WINTER SPORTS RESORTS: ⚲ **Afton Alps Ski Area,** 19 mi. (30km) SE of St. Paul on U.S. 61 and Minn. 20 (436-5245): 20 ski lifts; open Nov–Mar.

⚲ **Birch Park Ski Area,** 20 mi. (32km) NE of St. Paul on Minn. 5 and Wisc. 64 (439-2428): 11 ski lifts; open Nov–Mar.

⚲ **Buck Hill,** 18 mi. (29km) south of Minneapolis on I-35W (435-7174): 7 ski lifts; open Nov–Mar.

⚲ **Hyland Hills,** 15 mi. (24km) SW of Minneapolis on I-35W and 494 (835-4604): 7 ski lifts; open Nov–Mar.

ZOOS: ☀⚲⚲ **Minnesota Zoo,** 20 mi. (32km) via Cedar Ave. and Minn. 77 to Apple Valley (432-9000): Highly regarded ultramodern zoo covering 495 acres (200ha). From the monorail which takes you around, you can see more than 450 species in their natural habitats. Worth going out of your way for. Open daily year round.

ACCOMMODATIONS

A Note on Accommodations: Room rates in Minneapolis are coded as follows: **VE,** Very Expensive ($140 and up); **E,** Expensive ($90–$140); **M,** Moderate ($60–$90); **I,** Inexpensive ($30–$60); **B,** Budget (up to $30). A listing of toll free numbers is in the Appendix.

Personal Favorites (in order of preference)

🏯🏯🏯🏯 **The Whitney** (dwntwn), 150 Portland Ave., MN 55401 (612/339-9300; toll free 800/345-3457). 97 rms, A/C, cable color TV. AE, CB, DC, MC, V. Free valet parking, rest. (Whitney Grille), piano bar, 24-hr. rm svce, concierge, free crib. *Note:* Overlooking the Mississippi and the St. Anthony Falls, this charming small hotel, luxuriously renovated, has quickly gained acceptance as the best place to stay in Minneapolis. Huge, comfortable, high-ceilinged rms w. mahogany furniture and refrigerator (the best looking out on the river); first-class rest.; flawless svce. Boasts the most expensive ($1,600 a night) suite in town. VIP and celebrity guest list including Prince, Bruce Willis, and Michael Jackson. Free limo to dwntwn. **VE**

🏯🏯🏯 **Radisson Plaza** (dwntwn), 35 S. 7th St., MN 55402 (612/339-4900; toll free, see Radisson). 355 rms, A/C, color TV, in-rm movies. AE, CB, DC, MC, V. Parking $6, health club, sauna, two rests. (including Festival), coffee shop, two bars, rm svce, nightclub, boutiques, free crib. *Note:* A new tall tower of blue glass in the purest postmodern style, w. an impressive 18-story glass lobby. Huge, luxuriously comfortable rms; attentive, personal svce. Three VIP floors. Well-outfitted health club on the 17th floor. Direct access to the Skyway. Business clientele; this is now *the* place to stay in dwntwn Minneapolis (Soviet leader Mikhail Gorbachev stopped here during his visit to the U.S. in June 1990). **E–VE**

🏯🏯 **Hotel Luxeford** (dwntwn), 1101 La Salle Ave., MN 55403 (612/332-6800; toll free 800/662-3232). 230 suites, A/C, color TV, in-rm movies. AE, CB, DC, MC, V. Parking $6, health club, sauna, rest., bar, rm svce, free breakfast, free crib. *Note:* Nothing but suites, comfortable and spacious, w. kitchenettes and refrigerators; this new 12-story hotel is a favorite w. many business travelers. Very centrally located. Flawless reception and svce. A fine place to stay. **E**

🏯🏯 **Holiday Inn Metrodome** (formerly the Radisson Inn; dwntwn), 1500 Washington Ave. S., MN 55454 (612/333-4646; toll free, see Holiday Inns). 265 rms, A/C, color TV, in-rm movies. AE, CB, DC, MC, V. Parking $6, pool, health club, sauna, rest., coffee shop, bar, rm svce, free crib. *Note:* Very handsome, comfortable modern hotel right across from the Metrodome and the university campus. Spacious, inviting rms; facilities and svce above the Holiday Inn norm. Good value overall. **M–E**

🛎🛎 **Best Western Regency Plaza** (dwntwn), 41 N. 10th St., MN 55403 (612/339-9311; toll free, see Best Western). 192 rms, A/C, color TV, in-rm movies. AE, CB, DC, MC, V. Free parking, pool, rest. (Harrigan's), coffee shop, piano bar, rm svce, free crib. *Note:* Relatively modern but very comfortable hotel almost at the center of town, next to the Greyhound bus terminal. Large, well-designed rms; decor and facilities recently renovated. Friendly reception and svce. Business clientele. Very good value. **I–M**

🛎 **Econo Lodge** (formerly the Imperial Inn; nr. dwntwn), 2500 University Ave. SE, MN 55414 (612/331-6000; toll free 800/446-6900). 80 rms, A/C, color TV. AE, CB, DC, MC, V. Free parking, pool, adj. 24-hr coffee shop, free breakfast, free crib. *Note:* Functional, well-kept motel nr. the university; inviting rms, some w. kitchenettes. Good value; 8 min. from dwntwn. **I**

Other Accommodations (from top bracket to budget)

🛎🛎🛎 **Hyatt Regency Hotel** (dwntwn), 1300 Nicollet Mall, MN 55403 (612/370-1234; toll free, see Hyatt). 534 rms, A/C, color TV, in-rm movies. AE, CB, DC, MC, V. Parking $7, pool, health club, four tennis courts, squash, two rests. (including the Willows), two bars, 24-hr rm svce, nightclub, hrdrsr, boutiques, concierge, free crib. *Note:* An imposing white 20-story mammoth, a 5-min. walk from the Convention Center. All the comfort and facilities you'd expect of a Hyatt. Fine interior lobby with fountain. VIP floor, no-smoking floor. Ultraprofessional svce. Group and convention clientele somewhat intrusive. **E–VE**

🛎🛎🛎 **Marquette Hotel** (dwntwn), 710 Marquette Ave., MN 55402 (612/332-2351; toll free, see Hilton). 280 rms, A/C, color TV, in-rm movies. AE, CB, DC, MC, V. Gar. $12, rest. (Windows on Minnesota), coffee shop, bar, rm svce, drugstore, hrdrsr, concierge, free crib. *Note:* This elegant, modern hotel, much favored by business travelers and former President Ford, occupies 19 of the 57 floors of the immense IDS Tower. Remarkably spacious, inviting rms; exemplary comfort and facilities. Very good svce. Access via Skyway to principal dwntwn buildings. Two VIP floors. Windows on Minnesota is a highly regarded rest. w. a panoramic view at the top of the IDS Tower. A good place to stay. **E–VE**

🛎🛎🛎 **Marriott City Center** (formerly the Amfac; dwntwn), 30 S. 7th St., MN 55402 (612/349-4000; toll free, see Marriott). 582 rms, A/C, color TV, in-rm movies. AE, CB, DC, MC, V. Valet parking $13, sauna, two rests. (including the Fifth Season), coffee shop, two bars, rm svce, hrdrsr, drugstore, boutiques, free crib. *Note:* Here are 32 stories of glass and steel in the heart of dwntwn Minneapolis. Spacious, extremely comfortable rms (23 at the top of the tower are duplex rms), all w. spectacular view. Efficient svce. Two VIP floors. Very good luxury rest. Big business clientele. Direct access to Skyway. **E–VE**

🛎🛎 **Holiday Inn Downtown** (dwntwn), 1313 Nicollet Mall, MN 55403 (612/332-0371; toll free, see Holiday Inns). 324 rms, A/C, color TV, in-rm movies. AE, CB, DC, MC, V. Parking $5, pool, sauna, rest., coffee shop, bar, free crib. *Note:* Typical Holiday Inn right in dwntwn Minneapolis. Functional comfort; acceptable rest. Rather intrusive group and convention clientele. Interesting wknd packages. Very nr. the Convention Center. **M–E**

🛎🛎 **Burnsville Fantasuite Hotel** (vic.), 250 N. River Ridge Circle, Burnsville, MN 55337 (612/890-9550; toll free 800/666-

DOWNTOWN MINNEAPOLIS

15TH AVENUE NE

MAIN STREET SE

BROADWAY ST NE

3RD AVENUE N

15TH AVENUE NE

2ND STREET N

4TH STREET S

5TH STREET S

OLSON MEMORIAL HWY

2ND STREET S

1ST AVENUE N

2ND AVENUE

Riverplace

St. Anthony Main

Mississippi

St. Anthony Falls

Post Office

Minneapolis Public Library

City Center

6TH STREET SE

CENTRAL AVENUE

1ST AVENUE S

1ST STREET S

2ND STREET S

Chamber of Commerce

Bus Depot

Tourist Information Desk

5TH STREET SE

PORTLAND AVENUE

WASHINGTON AVENUE S

CHICAGO AVENUE

Hubert H. Humphrey Metrodome

MARQUETTE AVENUE

9TH STREET S

4TH AVENUE S

5TH AVENUE S

6TH STREET S

7TH STREET S

8TH STREET S

11TH AVENUE S

Orchestra Hall

2ND AVENUE S

3RD AVENUE S

10TH STREET S

11TH STREET S

NICOLLET MALL

12TH STREET S

HENNEPIN AVENUE

Loring Park

Guthrie Theatre

Walker Art Center

14TH STREET S

PARK AVENUE

19TH STREET

22ND STREET

Minneapolis Institute of Arts

American Swedish Institute

7829). 98 rms, A/C, color TV, in-rm movies. AE, MC, V. Free parking, pool, health club, rest., bar, valet svce. *Note:* Guests at this unusual motel, 20 min. from dwntwn and 10 min. from the airport, have a choice: on the one hand, standard, reasonably priced rms; on the other, some 20 suites decorated in a Disneyland-fantasy style and ranging from an Arctic igloo with bearskin on the ceiling via Pharaoh's tomb to the "Moby Dick" suite enclosed in an artificial whale. Kitsch at its purest. For the most popular suites, resv. should be made well ahead. An amusing alternative for the overworked business traveler. **I** (rooms); **E–VE** (suites).

    Days Inn–University (formerly the Cricket Inn; nr. dwntwn), 2407 University Ave. SE, MN 55119 (612/623-3999; toll free, see Days Inn). 130 rms, A/C, cable color TV. AE, CB, DC, MC, V. Free parking, nearby coffee shop, free breakfast, free crib. *Note:* Functional six-floor motel nr. the U. of Minnesota campus. Huge, comfortable rms, some w. refrigerators. Good value. 8 min. from dwntwn. **I**

    Fair Oaks (nr. dwntwn), 2335 Third Ave. S., MN 55404 (612/871-2000). 97 rms, A/C, color TV, in-rm movies. AE, CB, DC, MC, V. Free parking, rest. *Note:* Small, unpretentious, but acceptable hotel only 5 min. from dwntwn. Functional comfort; friendly reception. Ideal for budget travelers. **I**

RESTAURANTS

    A Note on Restaurant Prices: Minneapolis restaurant prices, per person, excluding drinks and service charges, are coded as follows: **VE**, Very Expensive ($60 and up); **E**, Expensive ($40–$60); **M**, Moderate ($25–$40); **I**, Inexpensive ($15–$25); **B**, Budget (up to $15).

Personal Favorites (in order of preference)

    510 Restaurant (nr. dwntwn), 510 Groveland Ave. (874-6440). A/C. Lunch Mon–Fri, dinner Mon–Sat; closed hols. AE, CB, DC, MC, V. Jkt. *Specialties:* terrine of seafood, filet of pork w. fig coulis, salmon or bass w. beurre blanc and Pernod, rack of lamb w. zucchini custard, breast of chicken broiled w. cucumbers and crème fraîche, fruit or Grand Marnier soufflé. Excellent list of French and California wines. *Note:* For those who enjoy classical French cooking in the grand manner, this is the best place to eat in the Twin Cities. The luxurious gray-and-ivory decorative scheme is complemented by thick carpets, crystal chandeliers, and Chippendale furniture. Efficient, competent svce. Much in favor with local society and visiting celebrities. Resv. indispensable. Valet parking. *French.* **M–E**

    Goodfellow's (dwntwn), at the Conservatory, 800 Nicollet Mall (332-4800). A/C. Lunch/dinner Mon–Sat; closed hols. AE, MC, V. Jkt. *Specialties:* chilled red gazpacho, wild-rice fritters w. Créole rémoulade, pheasant breast w. game sausage and Bing cherry sauce, ragoût of hickory-cured shrimp and veal sweetbreads w. pear onion and tarragon, sautéed walleye pike w. horseradish cream and tomato-basil sauce, frozen Macadamia-nut bombe w. raspberry sauce. Menu changes daily. Remarkable wine list, one of the finest in the Midwest. *Note:* A brainchild of the inventive team of John Dayton and Stephan Pyles, proprietors of the well-known Routh Street Café and Baby Routh in Dallas, Goodfellows and its younger sibling Tejas (see below) have since 1988 brought Minneapolis a new style of American cuisine: light, imaginative, and exciting. Spacious, elegant peach-colored space w. modern art on the walls. Excellent svce; resv. a must. Don't miss this gastronomic experience. *American.* **M–E**

    New French Café (dwntwn), 128 N. 4th St. (338-3790). A/C. Breakfast/lunch/dinner daily, brunch Sat–Sun; closed hols. AE, CB, DC, MC, V. *Specialties:* homemade terrines and pâtés, lamb chops w. green peppercorns, filet of salmon w. white wine and cream of shallots, rack of lamb w. zinfandel, poached halibut w. vermouth and lime, Queen of Sheba (blackberry-and-cream cake), mango sherbet. The menu changes regularly. *Note:* Worthy representative of French-Californian nouvelle cuisine, and serving food that is usually inventive and elegant. The smooth white decor, under the high ceiling of this renovated warehouse, gives a rather chilly effect. Very popular breakfast; the patrons, mostly trendy, are artists and yuppies. Resv. strongly advised. *French/American.* **M**

♀♀ **Murray's** (dwntwn), 26 S. 6th St. (339-0909). A/C. Lunch
🍴 Mon–Sat, dinner nightly. AE, CB, DC, MC, V. *Specialties:* barbecued shrimp, all kinds of meat including an excellent "Butter Knife Steak," catch of the day. *Note:* The steak lover's favorite for more than 40 years. Antiquated decor in dull beige tones and rather intrusive background music at dinner, but the meat is remarkable. Assiduous svce. A local institution. *Steak.* **I–M**

♀ **Black Forest Inn** (nr. dwntwn), 1 E. 26th St. (872-0812).
🍴 A/C. Lunch/dinner daily (till 1am); closed hols. AE, CB, DC, MC, V. *Specialties:* sauerbraten, wienerschnitzel, bratwurst, smoked pork chops w. sauerkraut, hot apfelstrudel, German beer. *Note:* A true-to-life German inn; inviting arbored patio w. pretty fountain for fine days. The clientele of artists and students (the College of Art and Design is a nr. neighbor) makes for a generally colorful, noisy atmosphere. Very efficient svce. Locally popular for two decades. *German.* **B–I**

♀ **Tejas** (dwntwn), in the Conservatory, 800 Nicollet Mall (375-
🍴 0800). A/C. Lunch/dinner daily. AE, MC, V. *Specialties:* duck empanada w. black-bean sauce and green-chile salsa, tortilla soup w. smoked tomatoes, chicken and avocado, poblano pepper stuffed w. roast pork and apricot, smoked shrimp enchilada, venison chile w. black beans and goat cheese. *Note:* This relative newcomer on the gastronomic scene offers innovative southwestern cuisine supervised by famous chef and co-owner Stephan Pyles (Routh Street Café in Dallas, Texas). At $10 or so, the dinner entrées are a real bargain. In the basement of the new Conservatory Shopping Mall. Casual, elegant surroundings. Arrive early or late or expect to wait. *American.* **B–I**

♀♀♀ **Whitney Grille** (dwntwn), in the Whitney Hotel (see "Accom-
🍴 modations," above) (339-9300). A/C. Breakfast/lunch/ dinner daily; brunch Sat–Sun. AE, CB, DC, MC, V. Jkt. *Specialties:* grilled duck w. Minnesota wild rice, rack of lamb, catch of the day, game (in season), chocolate-mocha pie. Fine wine list. *Note:* This is a fitting rest. for a great luxury hotel; the faultless food is European-inspired. Diligent, polished svce; much favored by the business crowd. Resv. strongly advised. *American/Continental.* **M**

☼♀♀♀ **Jax Café** (nr. dwntwn), 1928 University Ave. NE (789-7297).
🍴 A/C. Lunch/dinner daily, brunch Sun; closed hols., Christmas Eve. AE, CB, DC, MC, V. Jkt. *Specialties:* steak, prime ribs, rainbow trout, baked salmon, chicken Kiev, duckling, tournedos béarnaise. *Note:* Trout lovers can catch their own here, in a specially designed pool complete with rustic brook and mill wheel. Excellent *cuisine bourgeoise* in a charming dining rm built out over the grdn. Very popular locally, especially for business luncheons, for the last half century. Resv. suggested. 10 min. from dwntwn. *Steak/Seafood.* **I–M**

♀♀ **D'Amico Cucina** (dwntwn), Butler Sq., 100 N. 6th St. (338-
🍴 2401). A/C. Dinner nightly. AE, MC, V. *Specialties:* sautéed polenta squares w. porcini sauce, tagliatelle w. truffle butter, pan-fried pork chops w. garlicky white-bean timbale, tuna carpaccio, snapper wrapped in eggplant, sautéed lamb w. garlicky mashed potatoes, cannoli w. mascarpone cheese and vanilla. Interesting but pricey list of Italian wines. *Note:* Opened as recently as Sept 1987, this modern, sophisticated *trattoria* w. its exposed beams and marble floors has quickly established itself as the finest Italian rest. in the Twin Cities (which are not overendowed in this respect!). Sunlit, imaginative food from Larry D'Amico and Greg Westcott, served in an agreeably relaxed setting. Locally very popular; resv. a must. Valet parking. *Italian.* **I–M**

♀ **Faegre's** (dwntwn), 430 First Ave. N. (332-3515). A/C. ♣ Lunch Mon–Fri, dinner nightly, brunch Sun. AE, CB, DC, MC, V. *Specialties:* Caesar salad, Brazilian black-bean soup, fish stew w. saffron, fritto misto w. herbs and tomatoes, halibut w. olive oil and oregano, gâteau marjolaine. *Note:* One of the most popular dwntwn rests. among local yuppies. The modern decor emphasizes high glass walls and a sidewalk café which is very pleasant in fine weather. Innovative and often original American nouvelle cuisine. Also a crowded singles bar. *American.* **I**

♀♀ **Fuji Ya** (dwntwn), 420 S. 1st St. (339-2226). A/C. Lunch/ ♣♣ dinner Mon–Sat; closed hols. AE, CB, DC, MC, V. Jkt. *Specialties:* sushi, teppanyaki, teriyaki, tempura, sukiyaki. *Note:* Charming Japanese rest. w. a modern, light-filled decor. The dexterity w. which the chefs handle their chopping knives is equalled only by their speed. Ask to be seated in the Teppanyaki Room on the ground floor. Fine view of the Mississippi and its locks. A very good place to eat; resv. advised. *Japanese.* **I**

♀ **Nankin Café** (dwntwn), 2 S. 7th St. (333-3303). A/C. ♣ Lunch/dinner daily; closed hols. AE, CB, DC, MC, V. *Specialties:* chow mein, chop suey, Cantonese and Szechuan dishes. *Note:* This venerable (1919) local institution boasts one of the country's largest menus, w. over 100 Chinese dishes, not to mention some traditional American offerings. Modern Far Eastern decor. Excellent value. *Chinese/American.* **B–I**

☼♀ **Nye's Polonaise Room** (nr. dwntwn), 112 Hennepin Ave. ♣ (379-2021). A/C. Lunch/dinner daily (till midnight). AE, DC, MC, V. *Specialties:* pirogies, borscht, hamhock w. sauerkraut, T-bone steak, bigosz, spareribs. *Note:* Gigantic servings of hearty Polish-American food, w. waltzes and polkas in the background. Strong on atmosphere and local color. Moderate eaters don't belong here. Dinner-dances on wknds. Excellent value. *East European/American.* **B–I**

♀ **Pracna on Main** (nr. dwntwn), 117 Main St. (379-3200). ♣ A/C. Lunch/dinner daily. AE, CB, DC, MC, V. *Specialties:* sandwiches, homemade soups, barbecued spareribs, steak, daily specials. *Note:* A likable imitation of an old-time saloon on the banks of the Mississippi. Simple but very acceptable food. Open-air terrace for fine weather. Youthful, relaxed atmosphere. Locally popular. *American.* **B–I**

Cafeteria/Fast Food

Ediner (nr. dwntwn), 3001 Hennepin Ave. (822-6011). Open daily. No credit cards. Cafeteria amusingly decorated in pastel shades, 1950s style. Hamburgers, daily specials. Good cafeteria food. **B**

BARS & NIGHTCLUBS

Jazzline (633-0329) gives detailed information on current programming at Twin Cities jazz clubs.

Brave New Workshop (nr. dwntwn), 2605 Hennepin Ave. (332-6620): Highly regarded comedy club where all the stars, as well as local artists, come out to shine.

Fine Line Music Café (dwntwn), 318 First Ave. N. (338-8100): Excellent live blues and jazz in a sophisticated setting.

First Ave. and 7th St. Entry (dwntwn), 701 First Ave. N. (338-8388). Rock and funky jazz in the converted former Greyhound bus depot; lots of warmth. Setting for Twin Cities rock singer Prince's movie *Purple Rain.*

Loon Café (dwntwn), 500 First Ave. N. (332-8342). One of the best known of the dwntwn singles bars; also so-so rest. Attracts well-dressed yuppies. Open nightly.

New French Bar (dwntwn), 128 N. 4th St. (338-3790). Very "in" singles bar frequented by artists and foundation people. Open nightly.

Rupert's (nr. dwntwn), 5410 Wayzata Blvd. (544-4993). Much frequented disco with live jazz or swing and a big 1940s-style orchestra. Open Tues–Sat.

ST. PAUL

INFORMATION & TOURS

TOURIST INFORMATION: The **St. Paul Convention and Visitors Bureau,** 600 NCL Tower, 445 Minnesota St., MN 55101 (612/297-6985; toll free 800/627-6101).
The Connection: For information on current shows and cultural events in the Twin Cities, call 922-9000.

GUIDED TOURS: Gray Line Tours (bus): See "Minneapolis, Guided Tours," above.
Padelford Packet Boat Co. (boat), Harriet Island Park, St. Paul (227-1100): 2-hr. mini-cruises on the Mississippi aboard three elderly paddlewheelers, the *Jonathan Padelford,* the *Anson Northrup,* and the *Josiah Snelling.* Early May to late Sept.

SIGHTS, ATTRACTIONS & ACTIVITIES

ADVENTURES: Inner Tube Rides, intersection of Wisc. 35 and Wisc. 64 at Somerset, Wisc., 27 mi. (43km) NE of St. Paul on Minn. 5 and Wisc. 64 (715/247-3728): Shooting the rapids of the Apple River on inflated inner tubes. Time: 45 min. to 3 hr., according to distance. The favorite local sport; entertaining and low risk. Open daily mid-May to mid-Sept.

ARCHITECTURAL HIGHLIGHTS: ☀☖ **Ordway Music Theater,** 345 Washington St. (224-4222): Opened in 1985, this splendid auditorium with its glass-and-brick, accordion-fronted facade is now the home of the famous St. Paul Chamber Orchestra and the Minnesota Opera; many other concerts are also given here. A definite must-see.
☖ **Minnesota World Trade Center,** 30 E. 7th St. between Wabasha St. and Cedar St. (297-1580): Completed in 1987, this 40-story building is St. Paul's tallest and the hub of international business in the region. Its retail area, with dozens of shops, eateries, and restaurants, has brought additional vigor to the dwntwn revival. Worth a look.
☖ **Skyway,** around 6th St. and Cedar St.: Same network of heated walkways as in Minneapolis, connecting the main dwntwn buildings and department stores. Should be seen.

CHURCHES/SYNAGOGUES: ☖ **Old Muskego Church,** on the campus of Luther Theological Seminary, 2481 Como Ave. (641-3456): The first (1844) church in the country built by Norse immigrants; moved to its present site in 1904. Worth seeing.
☀☖ **Cathedral of St. Paul,** 239 Selby Ave. (228-1766): Built in 1915, this is a reasonably exact replica of St. Peter's in Rome, with its dome 175 ft. (53m) high, its great west rose window, and its massive granite-and-travertine construction. Open daily; don't miss it.

HISTORIC BUILDINGS: ☖ **Alexander Ramsey House,** 265 S. Exchange St., at Walnut St. (296-8681): Fine Victorian house which was the home of the first governor of the Minnesota Territory (1872). Period furniture and decoration. Should be seen. Open Tues–Sun Apr–Dec.

☼▨♨ **City Hall and Court House,** 15 W. Kellogg Blvd., at Wabasha St. (298-4012): This 1932 building displays 19 floors of marble and rare woods from around the world. Impressive 60-ton statue, 44 ft. (13m) high, in white onyx by the Swedish sculptor Carl Milles, of *The Indian God of Peace*. Shouldn't be missed. Open Mon–Fri.

☼♨♨ **Fort Snelling,** Minn. 5 and Post Rd., 6 mi. (10km) SW on Minn. 5 (726-1171): Former stone fortress from the 1820s, scrupulously restored; attained its greatest importance in the wars against the Sioux and Chippewa. Picturesque site where the Mississippi River and Minnesota River meet. Has retained all the flavor of the adventurous 19th-century frontier. Military parades in period uniform, daily May–Oct. Don't miss it.

☼♨♨ **Landmark Center,** 75 W. 5th St. (292-3225): This fine 1892 example of the Roman Revival style, once known as the Old Federal Courts Building, is capped by a tall belfry reminiscent of Trinity Church in Boston. Today it's an active cultural center with an auditorium, exhibition galleries, and the **Schubert Piano Museum.** Open daily; don't miss it.

☼♨♨ **State Capitol,** Aurora Ave. between Cedar Park and Park Ave. (296-2881): The Minnesota legislature building, designed by the great Cass Gilbert, has one of the world's largest self-supporting domes, inspired by the work of Michelangelo in Rome. No fewer than 21 kinds of marble and 25 different types of stone are employed in this important building, whose foundation stone was laid in 1896. Open daily.

MUSEUMS OF ART: ⌂ Minnesota Museum of Art, 305 St. Peter St. (292-4355): This modest museum, settled here in its new permanent home since 1989, has an interesting collection of American art from the end of the 19th century to the present day, as well as African and Asian art. Open Tues–Sun.

MUSEUMS OF SCIENCE & HISTORY: ⌂ Children's Museum, 1217 Bandana Blvd. N. (644-5305): Although this is a teaching museum, it's very popular with children. Among other attractions it has careful replicas of a TV studio, a grocery store, and a doctor's office, as well as computers and dozens of machines of all kinds which visitors can operate themselves. Open daily in summer, Tues–Sun the rest of the year.

♨ **Gibbs Farm Museum,** 2097 W. Larpenteur Ave. (646-8629): Authentic 1850s farm, showing daily life of 19th-century country people. For lovers of living history; should be seen. Open May–Oct Sun and Tues–Fri.

☼♨♨ **Science Museum of Minnesota,** 30 E. 10th St. (221-9454): Group of ultramodern buildings housing interesting natural-science collections in paleontology, biology, anthropology, geology, etc., as well as an auditorium and an innovative cinema with a giant hemispherical screen, the **William L. McKnight 3M Omnitheater.** Very dramatic. Open daily in summer, Tues–Sun the rest of the year.

PARKS & GARDENS: ♨ Cherokee Park, Cherokee Blvd. and Ohio St.: Lovely view from the heights of the park overlooking the Mississippi. Worth seeing.

♨ **Como Park,** Lexington Pkwy. and W. Como Ave. (292-7400): A 445-acre (180ha) park 15 mi. (24km) by car from dwntwn. Flower shows, zoo, 70-acre (28ha) lake.

♨ **Indian Mounds Park,** Earl St. and Mounds Blvd.: Funerary mounds of Sioux chiefs on the banks of the Mississippi. Should be seen.

♨ **Phalen Park,** Arcade St. and Larpenteur Ave.: Huge public garden around a lake, which draws many visitors winter and summer alike. Golf course.

PERFORMING ARTS: For current listings of shows and cultural events, consult the entertainment pages of the daily paper, the *St. Paul Pioneer Press-Dispatch* (morning and evening), as well as the monthly *Minneapolis-St. Paul* magazine. **Tickets to Go,** a discount-ticket booth in Town Square (333-6841), sells half-price tickets for all shows on the day of performance. Cash only; open Tues–Sat.

Actors Theatre, 28 W. Seventh Pl. (227-0050): Resident company. Comedy, drama, contemporary and classic plays.

Civic Center, 143 W. 4th St. (224-7403): Live pop and rock concerts.

Ordway Music Theater, 345 Washington St. (224-4222): Opera, recitals, pop and classical concerts, dance. Home of the St. Paul Chamber Orchestra—the only full-time chamber orchestra in the U.S.—(principal conductor: Hugh Wolff); and of the Minnesota Opera (director: Kevin Smith). Lovely modern building.

O'Shaughnessy Auditorium, 2004 Randolph Ave. (690-6000): Classical concerts, opera.

World Theater, 10 E. Exchange St. (298-1300): Fine old theater beautifully restored. Shows and concerts. This was long the setting for the taping of the popular radio program "Prairie Home Companion." Now, "Good Evening," the radio show that succeeded "Prairie Home Companion," is broadcast live from this theater each Sat night to more than 160 Public Radio stations across the country.

SHOPPING: St. Paul Center, 7th St. and Cedar St.: Located at the World Trade Plaza, this elegant shopping mall includes the 100 shops, eateries, and restaurants of Town Court and Town Square (see below), as well as Dayton's and Carson Pirie Scott department stores. Open 7 days a week.

Town Square, 7th St. and Minnesota St.: More than 70 boutiques, stores, and cafés around a huge indoor public garden where waterfalls, pools, and tropical plants combine to create a beautiful setting. Spectacular.

SPECIAL EVENTS: For exact dates, consult the **St. Paul Convention and Visitors Bureau** (see "Tourist Information," above).

Winter Carnival (late Jan to early Feb): Processions, ice-carving contests, sporting events (marathon), professional car racing (on ice), parades through the city. Very popular since its inception in 1885; draws hundreds of thousands of outdoors enthusiasts every year.

Minnesota State Fair (late Aug to early Sept): This very popular fair-exhibition draws more than a million visitors yearly. Horse shows. Plenty of atmosphere.

SPORTS: Same as Minneapolis (see above).

STROLLS: ☀⚑ **Summit Avenue,** around Lexington Ave.: Smart, elegant main drag with opulent churches and upper-class homes from the second half of the 19th century. These include the **James J. Hill House,** 240 Summit Ave. (297-2555), open Wed–Thurs and Sat, built by the railroad magnate in 1891; the house of author **F. Scott Fitzgerald** at 599 Summit Terrace (no visitors); the very lovely 1862 **Burbank-Livington-Griggs House** at 432 Summit Ave. (no visitors); and the **Governor's Mansion** at 1006 Summit Ave. (297-2161), with visits by appointment on the third Sat of each month.

ACCOMMODATIONS

A Note on Accommodations: Room rates in St. Paul are coded as follows: **VE,** Very Expensive ($140 and up); **E,** Expensive ($90–$140); **M,** Moderate ($60–$90); **I,** Inexpensive ($30–$60); **B,** Budget (up to $30). A listing of toll free numbers is in the Appendix.

Hotels (from top bracket to budget)

☀ ♨♨♨ **St. Paul Hotel** (dwntwn), 350 Market St., MN 55102 (612/ 292-9292; toll free 800/457-9292). 254 rms, A/C, color TV, in-rm movies. AE, CB, DC, MC, V. Gar. $8, rest. (L'Etoile), coffee shop, bar, rm svce, nightclub, concierge, free crib. *Note:* Venerable turn-of-the-century luxury hotel in the European style, decor and facilities elegantly renovated. Quality and style; large, luxuriously comfortable rms; flawless svce. Excellent French rest. Centrally located with direct Skyway access; favored by those in-the-know. **E–VE**

♨♨♨ **Radisson Hotel St. Paul** (dwntwn), 11 E. Kellogg Blvd., MN 55101 (612/292-1900; toll free, see Radisson). 475 rms, A/C, color TV, in-rm movies. AE, CB, DC, MC, V. Gar. $6, pool, health club, two rests. (including Le Carrousel), coffee shop, two bars, rm svce, disco, hrdrsr, free crib. *Note:* Modern luxury hotel of conventional type intended for groups and conventions. Comfortable rms, the best overlooking the attractive winter grdn/pool. Revolving rest. on the 22nd floor w. a clear view of the city and the Mississippi River. Efficient svce, VIP svce. In the heart of dwntwn, w. direct access to Skywalk. Completed an $8-million renovation in 1989. **E**

♨♨ **Embassy Suites Downtown** (dwntwn), 175 E. 10 St., MN 55101 (612/224-5400; toll free 800/362-2779). 210 suites. A/C, color TV, in-rm movies. AE, CB, DC, MC, V. Parking $5, pool, sauna, rest. (Woolley's), bar, rm svce, free breakfast, free crib. *Note:* Upscale modern hotel built around a glassed-in eight-story atrium w. winter grdns, waterfalls, fountains—and ducks! Suites only: spacious and comfortable, w. kitchenette and refrigerator. Efficient svce; very central. Business clientele. **M–E**

♨♨ **Holiday Inn–St. Paul Center** (dwntwn), 411 Minnesota St., MN 55101 (612/291-8800; toll free, see Holiday Inns). 241 rms, A/C, color TV, in-rm movies. AE, CB, DC, MC, V. Parking $5, pool, rest. (La Rôtisserie), coffee shop, bar, rm svce, piano bar, boutiques, free crib. *Note:* Rather futurist architecture in the heart of dwntwn St. Paul; 14-story glassed-in lobby w. indoor fountains and grdns. Comfort and facilities above the Holiday Inn standard; efficient svce. Direct access to Town Square Shopping Mall and the Skyway network. Business and group clientele. Interesting wknd discounts. **M**

♨ **Civic Center Inn** (dwntwn), 175 W. 7th St., MN 55102 (612/292-8929). 203 rms. A/C, color TV, in-rm movies. AE, CB, DC, MC, V. Free parking, 24-hr. coffee shop, bar, rm svce, free crib. *Note:* Huge high-rise motel standing (as you would expect from its name) across from the Civic Center in the heart of dwntwn. Functionally comfortable; efficient svce. Group and convention traffic. Good value on balance. **I–M**

♨ **Travelodge St. Paul** (nr. dwntwn), 149 E. University Ave., MN 55101 (612/227-8801; toll free, see Travelodge). 50 rms, A/C, color TV, in-rm movies. AE, CB, DC, MC, V. Free parking, nearby rest., free crib. *Note:* Small, modest, unpretentious motel very nr. the State Capitol. Spacious rms w. balconies; functionally comfortable. Free morning coffee. Ideal for budget travelers. **I**

Airport Accommodations

♨♨♨ **Hotel Sofitel** (vic.), 5601 W. 78th St., in Bloomington, MN 55435 (612/835-1900; toll free, see Resinter). 288 rms, A/C, color TV, in-rm movies. AE, CB, DC, MC, V. Free valet parking, pool, health club, sauna, two rests. (including Le Café Royal), coffee shop, bar, rm svce, nightclub, concierge, free crib. *Note:* This modern hotel, part of the French-owned Sofitel chain, strongly upholds the gastronomic standards of its native country w. three good rests. and cafés, one of which (La Terrasse) is open late. Pleasant six-story lobby-grdn. Very comfortable rms; smiling reception. Business clientele. 15 min. from dwntwn. Minneapolis, 10 min. from the airport. Interesting wknd discounts. **E–VE**

DOWNTOWN ST. PAUL

1. Minnesota Office of Tourism
2. Ordway Music Hall
3. Civic Center
4. St. Paul Public Library
5. State Capitol
6. St. Paul Cathedral
7. Minnesota Museum of Art
8. Minnesota State Fairgrounds
9. Minnesota World Trade Center
10. Science Museum of Minnesota
11. 3M William L. McKnight Omnitheatre
12. Union Depot Place

YMCA/Youth Hostel

Cæcilian Hall (vic.), 2004 Randolph Ave., MN 55104 (612/690-6604). 103 beds. Youth hostel on the campus of St. Catherine's College, halfway between Minneapolis and St. Paul. Open June to late Aug.

RESTAURANTS

A Note on Restaurant Prices: St. Paul restaurant prices, per person, excluding drinks and service charges, are coded as follows: **VE,** Very Expensive ($60 and up); **E,** Expensive ($40–$60); **M,** Moderate ($25–$40); **I,** Inexpensive ($15–$25); **B,** Budget (up to $15).

Restaurants (from top bracket to budget)

Blue Horse (nr. dwntwn), 1355 University Ave. (645-8101). A/C. Lunch Mon–Fri, dinner Mon–Sat; closed hols. AE, CB, DC, MC, V. J&T (at dinner). *Specialties:* fettuccine Alfredo, steak Diane, Dungeness crab w. sauce Poulette, veal Cordon Bleu, roast duckling, broiled walleye pike. Imposing list of California and imported wines. *Note:* For more than 25 years the most fashionable and distinguished rest. in the Twin Cities. Elegant but intimate setting. Fish and seafood dishes can be highly recommended. Very polished svce. Resv. a must 20 min. from Minneapolis. Valet parking. *Continental.* **M**

Forepaugh's (dwntwn), 276 S. Exchange St. (224-5606). A/C. Lunch Mon–Fri, dinner nightly, brunch Sun. AE, MC, V. Jkt. *Specialties:* sautéed scampi, scallops in beurre blanc, veal Calvados, tournedos béarnaise, stuffed capon. Very good desserts; large wine list. *Note:* Successful union of classical and modern French cuisine under the skilled hand of chef Bernard Lagarde, in a big, elegant Victorian house (1870), tastefully restored. Svce of the highest order; romantic atmosphere; very popular locally. Resv. a must. valet parking. *French.* **I–M**

Lexington (nr. dwntwn), 1096 Grand Ave. (228-5878). A/C. Lunch/dinner Mon–Sat (until midnight); closed Dec 24–25. No credit cards. Jkt. *Specialties:* steak, prime rib, fresh salmon, roast pheasant, catch of the day. *Note:* This well-established family rest. has enjoyed a solid reputation since 1934. The cooking is professional, but unimaginative despite the 35 dishes on the menu. The cocktails are generously poured. Very popular locally; rcsv. advised. 8 min. from dwntwn. *Steak/Seafood.* **I–M**

Gallivan's (dwntwn), 354 Wabasha St. (227-6688). A/C. Lunch/dinner Mon–Sat; closed hols. AE, MC, V. *Specialties:* broiled pike, steak, roast beef, fresh seafood. *Note:* Irish-style pub, usually noisy and crowded. A local institution, particularly favored by newspaper people and politicians. The food is simple but very acceptable. Also a piano bar w. dancing; an entertaining place. *American.* **I**

Leeann Chin's (dwntwn), 214 E. 4th St. (224-8814). A/C. Lunch daily, dinner Mon–Sat; closed hols. AE, MC, V. *Specialties:* fun ki soup, cream-cheese wontons, lemon chicken, sweet-and-sour pork, beef Szechuan, Cantonese shrimp, almond-cookie ice cream. *Note:* This enormous Far Eastern rest. occupies the former Union Pacific Railroad station. The Cantonese and Szechuan buffet at lunch and dinner is the real thing. Elegantly decorated in pink and beige w. many Chinese vases, jades, and ivory carvings. Efficient svce; locally popular so resv. advised. Valet parking evenings. Other location: 900 Second Ave., Minneapolis (338-3488). *Chinese.* **B–I**

Venetian Inn (nr. dwntwn), 2814 Rice St. at Little Canada (484-7215). A/C. Lunch/dinner Mon–Sat; closed hols. AE, CB, DC, MC, V. *Specialties:* fresh homemade pasta, lasagne, barbecued spareribs, steak, catch of the day. *Note:* The food is mostly Italian but the prime beef is also excellent and very reasonably priced. In the hands of the Vitale family for more than half a century. Friendly, smiling svce. Locally popular; this place can be confidently recommended. Resv. advised. 15 min. from dwntwn. *Italian.* **B–I**

☕ **Mickey's Diner** (dwntwn), 36 W. 7th St. (222-5633). A/C. Lunch/dinner daily 24 hr. No credit cards. *Specialties:* buckwheat pancakes, homemade soups, sandwiches, hamburgers, fried liver and onions, steak, baked pinto beans, broiled chicken, milkshakes, good desserts. *Note:* Wonderful diner of the traditional kind, gleaming w. chrome and Formica; built in 1937, this is a designated historic structure. Food and prices have changed little in half a century. If you enjoyed *American Graffiti,* you'll love this one. No resv. *American.* **B**

Cafeteria/Fast Food

Café Latte (nr. dwntwn), 850 Grand Ave. (224-5687). Open daily. AE. Interesting soups and daily specials as well as excellent desserts, in a modern neon-and-chrome setting. Very popular locally. **B**

BARS & NIGHTCLUBS

Jazzline (633-0329) gives detailed information on current programming in the Twin Cities jazz clubs.

Dixie (nr. dwntwn), 695 Grand Ave. (222-7345). Fashionable bar; trendy patrons.

Gallivan's (dwntwn), 354 Wabasha St. (227-6688). Friendly, jam-packed piano bar with dancing. Also a rest. (see above). Open Mon–Sat.

St. Paul's Heartthrob Café and Nightclub (dwntwn), 30 E. 8th St. (224-2783). Noisy, throbbing roller disco; the setting is from the '50s but the crowd is much younger. Also a rest.

NEARBY EXCURSIONS

🏛 **ROCHESTER** (88 mi./140km SE on U.S. 52): One of the capital cities of U.S. medicine. With its 800 doctors and hundreds of researchers and technicians, the **Mayo Clinic,** founded in 1898 by Dr. William Worrall Mayo and his sons, William James and Charles Horace, is world-renowned, particularly in the field of cardiac surgery. The research laboratories and diagnostic center, 200 1st St. SW (507/284-2511), are open to visitors Mon–Fri. Also the lavish home of the Mayo family, **Mayowood** (507/282-9447), conducted tour by appointment daily except Mon and Fri. (Tours leave from the corner of County Road 122 and Salem Road SW.) Well worth the side trip.

Where to Stay in Rochester

👑👑👑 **Radisson Hotel Centerplace,** 150 S. Broadway, Rochester, MN 55904 (507/281-8000; toll free, see Radisson). 213 rms. Ultramodern grand hotel w. private entrance to the Mayo Clinic. **E**

☀️🏛🏛 **ST. CROIX VALLEY** (32 mi./51km NE on I-35W and Minn. 36): Wonderful panoramic drive on Minn. 95 from **Stillwater** to **Taylors Falls,** 30 mi. (48km) north, along "America's River Rhine," as the St. Croix River has been called.

From **Somerset,** on the right bank of the St. Croix, you can go down the Apple River on an inner tube (see St. Paul "Adventures," above). Don't miss it.

Where to Stay En Route

IN STILLWATER ☀️🏛🏛🏛 **Lowell Inn,** 102 N. 2nd St., Stillwater, MN 55082 (612/439-1100). 21 (very comfortable) rms. AE, CB, DC, MC, V. The elegant colonial setting is more than a century old; the rest. is excellent. Boat trips are available on the St. Croix River. **M-E**

FARTHER AFIELD

GRAND PORTAGE NATIONAL MONUMENT (318 mi./508km NE of Minneapolis via I-35 and U.S. 61): Owes its name to the "portage road" along Lake Superior, where the first French trappers, at the end of the 17th century, carried their canoes on their backs. The original 9-mi. (15km) Native American trail is still there, but muddy and mosquito-infested. At Grand Portage, terminus of the ferry for Isle Royale National Park (see below), which operates from mid-June to the beginning of Sept (call 218/728-1237 for information), the 1788 fur-trading post has been partially reconstructed to its original form and is worth a visit (open daily, mid-May to mid-Oct). U.S. 61 offers you a panoramic drive along Lake Superior.

ISLE ROYALE NATIONAL PARK (343 mi./548km NE of Minneapolis via I-35 and U.S. 61 and ferry from Grand Portage): America's most unspoiled national park. This magnificent island, 45 by 8 mi. (72 by 13km) in size, was so named by French trappers; it's a kind of open-air zoo, with dozens of animal species from the red fox to the elk and from the wolf to the fish-eagle. The only ways you can get around are by outboard boat (you can hire one there), by canoe, or on foot since no vehicles are allowed on the island. There are 155 mi. (250km) of footpaths through the beautiful, unspoiled landscape, but beware of fog and mosquitos in summer.

Isle Royale is also the scene of many 19th-century shipwrecks, and has been designated a **national underwater museum,** with scuba-diving facilities and guided tours of underwater attractions provided by the National Park Service. Note that scuba-diving should be attempted only by experts because of the low water temperature in Lake Superior (60°F/16°C).

The park is open May–Oct. For lovers of nature and/or fishing, a visit (and a stay) here should on no account be missed. For further information, contact the Superintendent, Isle Royale National Park, 87 N. Ripley St., Houghton, MI 49931 (906/482-0984).

Where to Stay in the Park

There are 30 or so camping areas. In addition, ※ **Rock Harbor Lodge,** on the east end of the island, has 60 comfortable rooms and 20 bungalows for rent June–Sept, but reservations must be made very far ahead. In summer apply to National Park Concessions, P.O. Box 405, Houghton, MI 49931 (906/337-4993); off-season, National Park Concessions, Mammoth Cave, KY 42259 (502/773-2191).

VOYAGEURS NATIONAL PARK (294 mi./470km north of Minneapolis via I-35 and U.S. 53): Another miraculously preserved wildlife sanctuary, covering 217,000 scenic acres (88,000ha) of lakes, islands, forests, and watercourses on the Canadian border, with a hundred camping areas but no hotels. Wear warm clothes, even in summer; not for nothing is the nearest city, **International Falls,** known as "America's Icebox," routinely reporting winter temperatures of −30° to −40°F (−34° to −40°C). A fisherman's paradise, with boats available for rent on the spot. For information, contact the Superintendent, Voyageurs National Park, P.O. Box 50, International Falls, MN 56649 (218/283-9821).

LAKE DISTRICT & SUPERIOR NATIONAL FOREST (845 mi./1,352km r. t. via U.S. 10N, Minn. 27E, U.S. 169N,

Minn. 18W, Minn. 371N, U.S. 2E, U.S. 169N, Minn. 1E, U.S. 61N, U.S. 615, and I-35S): An enthralling trip for devotees of nature in the raw, through the myriad lakes and endless forests of northern Minnesota.

The trip begins along a smooth-flowing stretch of the Mississippi, taking you to the 🏠 **boyhood home of Charles A. Lindbergh,** the first man to make a nonstop solo flight across the Atlantic, with many personal mementoes of the famous flyer. At Lindbergh Dr. at Little Falls (612/632-3154), it is open daily May to mid-Sept, by appointment the rest of the year.

Then on along **Mille Lacs Lake** and **Leech Lake,** which between them boast 750 mi. (1,200km) of shoreline (there are dozens of friendly inns and motels around 🏠🏠 **Brainerd, Walker,** and **Grand Rapids,** birthplace of actress and singer Judy Garland). Next, drive to 🏠🏠 **Chippewa National Forest,** 3,400 sq. mi. (880,000ha) of dense standing timber with 2,000 lakes of all sizes—a paradise for hunters, fishermen, and canoeists. Superior National Forest is one of the last places in the country where wolves may be found in the wild.

On your way, stop at 🏠 **Hibbing,** "the iron-ore capital of the world," with the world's largest open-pit iron-ore mine, the Hull-Rust Mine, on Third Ave. (218/262-4900). You can inspect the enormous hole, 3 mi. (5km) long and 535 ft. (163m) deep, from an observation platform open daily mid-May to mid-Sept. More than a billion tons of material have been removed from the mine since it opened in 1918. Well worth seeing. Hibbing has two famous children of whom it is equally proud: the Greyhound Bus Company and singer Bob Dylan.

Just 45 mi. (72km) NE of Hibbing is another well-known mine, the ☀🏠 **Soudan Iron Mine,** on Minn. 169 in Soudan (218/753-2245). This, the first underground mine in Minnesota, which closed down in 1962 after 80 years of commercial production, is well worth going out of your way for. Make a point of going the 2,400 ft. (730m) under the surface (in 3 min.) to the now-disused workings, which you can tour in a little electric train; remember to dress for the 52°F (11°C) temperature down there. Fascinating. Open daily Memorial Day–Labor Day.

The excursion ends with a visit to **Grand Portage National Monument** and **Isle Royale National Park** (see above).

On the way back, **Duluth,** a busy commercial port with its astonishing Aerial Lift Bridge, is a stop you shouldn't fail to make.

You should allow at least a week for this spectacular drive—but you're not advised to make it in any season except summer!

Where to Stay En Route

As noted above, there are dozens of friendly inns and motels around Brainerd, Walker, and Grand Rapids.

IN DULUTH 🍴🍴🍴 **Fitger's Inn,** 600 E. Superior St., Duluth, MN 55802 (218/722-8826). This converted brewery now boasts 48 rms, most overlooking Lake Michigan. **M–E**

🍴🍴 **Best Western Edgewater East,** 2330 London Rd., Duluth, MN 55812 (218/728-3601). 120 rms. A functionally comfortable roadside motel. **I–M**

Where to Eat En Route

As noted above, there are dozens of friendly inns around Brainerd, Walker, and Grand Rapids.

IN DULUTH 🍴 **Grandma's Saloon and Deli,** 522 Lake Ave. S., near the lift bridge (218/727-4192). Lunch/dinner daily. Honest, down-home food in a quaint early-1900s building. **B–I**

CHAPTER 26

INDIANAPOLIS

□ □ □

Today a flourishing metropolitan area of more than 1,000,000 inhabitants, Indianapolis was not initially a pioneer encampment like so many other midwestern cities. Its site was determined by simple logic, rather than by some caprice of history or nature: Indianapolis is at the dead center of Indiana. The city's layout was inspired by that of Washington, D.C., and follows a rigorous geometry. Wide diagonal avenues converge on **Monument Circle** like the spokes of a wheel, and a right-angled grid of streets connects the city's principal monuments: the imposing **State Capitol,** the **World War Memorial Hall,** the **Soldiers and Sailors Monument,** the **Scottish Rite Cathedral,** and the national headquarters of the **American Legion.**

Indianapolis was long considered provincial, politically conservative (the John Birch Society originated here), and boring (it was once known as "Naptown"). But over the last dozen years the capital of Indiana has come to be perceived as a modern, lively, and safe city (the crime rate is one of the lowest in the country). Witness the renovation around picturesque **City Market and Union Station,** the construction of the **Hoosier Dome Complex** (an impressive enclosed stadium that seats 63,000), the brand-new $64-million zoo, and the new **Eiteljorg Museum,** a remarkable museum of Western art that opened in June 1989, as well as the scheduled completion of the splendid **White River State Park.**

Neither Robert Cavelier, sieur de La Salle, the Frenchman who explored Indiana along the St. Joseph River (1679), nor Gen. William Henry Harrison, who defeated the great Shawnee chief Tecumseh in the battle of Tippecanoe (1811), could have dreamed that Indiana's capital would one day be famous for the world's oldest auto race (since 1911), held on Memorial Day weekend, the thrilling and perilous "Indianapolis 500." At the heart of the famed corn belt, Indianapolis is one of the largest grain and cattle markets in the country. It is also the headquarters of the giant pharmaceutical company Eli Lilly (29,000 employees) and a mecca for amateur sports, as well as one of the most important hubs of rail and road communication in North America, where no fewer than four major Interstate highways converge. The state of Indiana is rightly called "the crossroads of America."

Some of the city's notable native children are guitarist Wes Montgomery, author Kurt Vonnegut, Jr., comedian and talk-show host David Letterman, the late actor Steve McQueen, and the famous bandit John Dillinger.

BASIC FACTS: Capital of Indiana. Area code: 317. Time zone: eastern. ZIP Code: 46204. Founded: 1820. Approximate population: city, 725,000; metropolitan area, 1,250,000. 13th-largest city in the U.S.; 31st-largest metropolitan area in the U.S.

CLIMATE: Indianapolis weather is typical of the midwestern Great Plains: radiant springs; oppressive, humid summers (mean July temperature 76°F/24°C); mild, pleasant autumns; and rather harsh winters (mean Jan temperature 28°F/−2°C). Spring is the ideal season to visit the area.

DISTANCES: Chicago, 181 mi. (290km); Cincinnati, 106 mi. (170km); Nashville, 297 mi. (446km); St. Louis, 235 mi. (376km).

ARRIVAL & TRANSIT INFORMATION

AIRPORT Indianapolis International Airport (IND): 7 mi (11km) SW. For information, call 248-9594.

AIRLINES: American (262-1054), Continental (635-0290), Delta (634-3200), Eastern (639-6611), Northwest (631-0377), TWA (635-4381), United (638-6363), USAir (248-1211).

CITY LINK: The **cab** fare from the airport to dwntwn is about $12–$14; time, about 15 min. Bus: **Airport Limo Shuttle Express** (247-7301), serving major dwntwn hotels, leaves every 20 min.; fare, $5; time, about 20 min. Unless you intend to make excursions outside the city, the relatively small dwntwn area makes renting a car unnecessary. The **public bus** transportation system is good, and runs around the clock on some routes. **Metro Trolleys,** a shuttle service using minibuses got up like old streetcars, runs dwntwn Mon–Sat on north-south and east-west routes. For information, call **Metro Transit** (635-3344).

CAR RENTAL (at Indianapolis International Airport unless otherwise indicated): Avis (244-3307); Budget (248-1100); Dollar (241-8206); Hertz (243-9321); National (243-1159); and Thrifty, 5860 Fortune Circle W. (242-2282). For dwntwn locations, consult the local telephone directory.

LIMOUSINE SERVICES: Carey Limousine (247-7307), VIP Limousine Service (635-2308).

TAXIS: Taxis are few and relatively expensive; they may be found outside the major hotels or simply summoned by phone: **Hoosier Cab** (243-8800), **Metro Taxi** (643-1112), or **Yellow Cab** (673-5421).

TRAIN: Amtrak station, 350 S. Illinois St. (632-1905).

INTERCITY BUSES: Greyhound, 127 N. Capitol Ave. (635-4501).

INFORMATION & TOURS

TOURIST INFORMATION: The **Indianapolis City Center,** Pan American Plaza, 201 S. Capitol Ave., IN 46225 (317/237-5200; toll free 800/323-4639). Well-qualified facility for public information.

For a **telephone recording** with an up-to-date listing of cultural events and shows, call 317/237-5210.

GUIDED TOURS: Gray Line Tours (bus), 9102 N. Meridian St. (317/573-0699). Guided tours of the city, serving the major hotels.

SIGHTS, ATTRACTIONS & ACTIVITIES

ARCHITECTURAL HIGHLIGHTS: ☀️⚓ **Hoosier Dome,** 100 S. Capitol Ave. (262-3452): This 63,000-seat stadium with a 19-story-high fiberglass roof opened in 1984 and is one of the largest in the country. Built at a cost of $65 million, it can accommodate conventions, auto shows, and trade fairs, as well as the Colts' home football games. The stadium is part of the enormous **Indiana Convention Center** (632-4321), with five exposition halls, two large ballrooms, and 55 meeting rooms. Impressive. Guided tours daily.

    Indiana University–Purdue University at Indianapolis (IUPUI), W. Michigan St. (274-2134): These two universities, with 23,000 students in all, were merged in 1969 into the present first-rate educational complex. With six hospitals and 90 clinics, faculties, and specialty schools, the **University Medical Center** enjoys a worldwide reputation in the areas of cancer, heart surgery, and organ transplants. IUPUI is also famous for its high-caliber sports teams. Interesting modern architecture. Campus visits Mon–Fri.

    Indianapolis Motor Speedway, 4790 W. 16th St. (241-2500): Some 6 mi. (9km) NW, this is the most celebrated auto raceway in the world. Nearly 400,000 spectators come here each May for the spectacular and sometimes deadly "Indy 500," staged on the 2.5-mi. (4km) oval course. Arie Luyendyk holds the track speed record set in 1990—an average of 185.984 m.p.h. (297.574km/h). Interesting racing museum, **Indy Hall of Fame Museum.** Guided tour of the raceway (sorry—the bus goes no faster than 37 m.p.h./60km/h). Open daily. For speed demons. (Seats for the Indianapolis 500 range from $18 to $90 and are scooped up weeks and months in advance. For reservations, call 317/248-6700, or write: P.O. Box 24152, Speedway, IN 46224.)

    Madame Walker Urban Life Center and Theatre, 617 Indiana Ave. (635-6915): Built in the late '20s as a tribute to Madame C. J. Walker, the country's first African American female self-made millionaire, this legendary theater with stunning African and Egyptian decor reopened in Oct 1988 after a $3.2-million renovation. Hosts a variety of arts and cultural events including a week-long African American film festival in late Oct. Its splendid interior is worth a visit by itself. Tours by appointment Mon–Sat.

CHURCHES/SYNAGOGUES: **Carmelite Monastery,** 2500 Cold Spring Rd. (925-5654): The chapel, entranceway, and gardens of this medieval castlelike monastery are open to the public. Worth a look. Open daily.

    Scottish Rite Cathedral, 650 N. Meridian St. (635-2301): This stunning Gothic-Tudor–style cathedral dates from 1929, and has a 212-ft. (65m) tower with a 54-bell carillon. The baroque interior, wood carvings, and two organs with 5,500 pipes are an absolute must-see. Open Mon–Fri.

HISTORIC BUILDINGS: **Benjamin Harrison Memorial Home,** 1230 N. Delaware St. (631-1898): The former residence of the 23rd president houses interesting furniture, paintings, and period decoration (dates from 1874). See it. Open daily.

    State Capitol, between Washington St. and Ohio St. and Capitol Ave. and Senate Ave. (232-8687): The home of the state legislature is a Corinthian-style building from 1888, constructed of Indiana limestone and topped with a large brass dome. Worth a look. Visit by appointment Mon–Fri.

    Union Station, 39 Jackson Pl. (635-7955): A perfect example of urban renewal, this once-abandoned station dating from 1888 is now a vast shopping area with more than 70 stores and boutiques, 40 restaurants, three movie theaters, five nightclubs, and a hotel with unusual decor. Very lively ambience. Since reopening in 1986, it has attracted more than 25 million visitors. Don't miss it. Open daily.

MARKETS: **City Market,** 222 E. Market St. (634-9266): Picturesque enclosed market dating from 1886 in an original cast-iron structure. Dozens of

food stalls, boutiques, little restaurants. Lively and colorful. Open Mon–Sat. See it.

MONUMENTS: ☼⌂ **Soldiers and Sailors Monument,** Monument Circle (633-1794): This imposing monument rising 278 ft. (87m) in the heart of the city was erected in memory of those who died in the Revolutionary War. There is elevator access to the observation platform at the top. Not to be missed. Open daily.

⌂ **World War Memorial,** 431 N. Meridian St. (635-1964): Monument and commemorative exhibition room dedicated to the dead of the two World Wars, Korea, and Vietnam. Interesting military museum as well as gardens. Worth a visit. Open daily. In the northeast corner of the square is a four-story building that is the **American Legion national headquarters.**

MUSEUMS OF ART: ☼⌂⌂ **Eiteljorg Museum of American Indian and Western Art,** 500 W. Washington St., White River State Park (636-9378): This magnificent museum houses, in its single $14-million building opened in June 1989, one of the country's most beautiful collections of Native American and Western art, including works by Frederic Remington and Georgia O'Keeffe. In all there are 240 paintings, 150 bronzes, and more than a thousand examples of old Native American handcrafts such as wickerwork, pottery, and masks. Don't miss it. Open daily July–Aug, Tues–Sun the rest of the year.

⌂ **Morris-Butler House Museum,** 1204 N. Park Ave. (636-5409): Interesting museum of Victorian decorative arts (the Helena Rubinstein collection) in a building that dates from 1862. Worth a visit. Open Tues–Sun.

☼⌂⌂ **Museum of Art,** 1200 W. 38th St. (923-1331): On a hill overlooking the White River, this remarkable art museum comprises three theme pavilions: Clowes Pavilion, medieval and Renaissance art; Krannert Pavilion, Oriental and primitive art; Lily Pavilion of Decorative Arts, European and American paintings (including Turner watercolors, works by El Greco, Claude Lorrain, Rembrandt, van Dyck). Pretty gardens with modern sculptures, including Robert Indiana's pop masterpiece, *LOVE.* Not to be missed. Open Tues–Sun.

MUSEUMS OF SCIENCE & HISTORY: ⌂⌂ **Children's Museum,** 3000 N. Meridian St. (924-5431): This very instructional children's museum is the world's largest. It presents very lifelike collections and displays from the earliest times (an Indiana cave, a giant dinosaur, an Egyptian tomb complete with mummies) through the present (a huge miniature railroad network, computers, brand-new planetarium, etc.). Wonderful for children of all ages. Open daily in summer, Tues–Sun the rest of the year.

⌂ **Indiana State Museum,** 202 N. Alabama St. (232-1637): This interesting museum, in the former city hall, documents the natural and cultural history of Indiana, especially since the pioneer era. Giant Foucault pendulum in the entranceway. Open daily.

⌂ **James Whitcomb Riley Home,** 528 Lockerbie St. (631-5885): Very lovely Victorian house dating from 1872, between 1892 and 1916 the home of James Whitcomb Riley, the "Hoosier poet." Period decor and layout. See it. Open Tues–Sun.

⌂ **National Track and Field Hall of Fame,** 200 S. Capitol Ave. (261-0483): Located in the Hoosier Dome, this museum honors American track and field greats like Jim Thorpe and Bruce Jenner. The history of track and field since 1904 is chronicled through the display of photos, uniforms, trophies, and early track equipment. Interesting. Open daily.

DOWNTOWN INDIANAPOLIS

N

Military Park

TOLEDO ST.

BLACKFORD ST.

State Office Bldgs.

State Capitol

Bus Terminal

WASHINGTON ST.

SENATE AVE.

CAPITOL AVE.

OHIO ST.

Christ Church

Soldier & Sailors Monument

Indiana Nat'l Bank Tower

Market Square Center

Market Square Arena

Market Square

MARKET ST.

COURT ST.

WABASH ST.

MIAMI ST.

NEW YORK ST.

Convention Center

Merchants Plaza

MARYLAND ST.

CHESAPEAKE ST.

MCCREA ST.

SCIOTO ST.

DELAWARE ST.

NEW JERSEY ST.

LOUISIANA ST.

COLLEGE AVE.

FLETCHER AVE.

Union Station

MERIDIAN ST.

ILLINOIS ST.

SOUTH ST.

EMPIRE ST.

MISSOURI ST.

HENRY ST.

GEORGIA ST.

PEARL ST.

To Indianapolis Int'l Airport

65 70

PANORAMAS: 🛆 **Crown Hill Cemetery,** 3402 Boulevard Pl. (925-8231): This vast landscaped cemetery—one of the largest in the country—is the burial place of poet James Whitcomb Riley (his grave offers an unimpeded view of the city), President Benjamin Harrison, and the notorious John Dillinger. The monumental entranceway to the cemetery is itself worth a trip.

🛆 **The Teller's Cage,** 1 Indiana Sq. (266-5211): The best view of the city (admission fee) from the 35th floor of the Indiana National Bank Tower. Choose the bar over the restaurant. Open Mon–Fri.

PARKS & GARDENS: 🛆 **Eagle Creek Park,** 7840 W. 56th St., west of I-465 (924-9151): This much-frequented and largely unspoiled (deer running wild) setting of 4,400 acres (1,780ha) lies on the western edge of the city. It offers golf courses, canoeing, and walking areas for summer; cross-country skiing in winter.

🛆 **Riverside Regional Park,** 2420 E. Riverside Dr.: Smaller than Eagle Creek Park, with "only" 902 acres (365ha), Riverside Park, steps away from downtown, is divided lengthwise by the White River. Golf courses, pool, and an inviting picnic area.

PERFORMING ARTS: For daily listings of all shows and cultural events, consult the entertainment pages of the daily papers *Indianapolis News* (evening) and *Indianapolis Star* (morning).

Beef 'n Boards, 9301 Michigan Rd. NW (872-9664): Dinner theater offering Broadway shows and recitals with big-name stars.

Circle Theater, 45 Monument Circle (639-4300): Home of the Indianapolis Symphony Orchestra (principal conductor: Raymond Leppard); performances Oct–May. Offers many other musical shows as well.

Clowes Memorial Hall, 4600 Sunset Ave. (283-9696): Home of the Indianapolis Ballet and the Indianapolis Opera; season Oct–Apr.

Hilton U. Brown Theatre, 304 W. 49th St. (926-1581): Open-air concerts and musical comedies in July and Aug.

Indiana Repertory Theatre, 140 W. Washington St. (635-5252): Classical and modern theater; performances Oct–Apr.

Indianapolis Civic Theater, 1200 W. 38th St. (923-4597): One of the oldest theater troupes in the country, performing drama and comedy.

SHOPPING: **City Market** (see "Markets," above).

Shadeland Antique Mall, 344 N. Shadeland Ave.: Well-known, and enormous, flea market—mecca for antiques buffs. Nearly a hundred dealers and stalls selling antiques and works of art.

Union Station (see "Historic Buildings," above).

SPECIAL EVENTS: For the exact schedule of the events below, consult the **Indianapolis City Center** (see "Tourist Information," above).

500 Festival (May): Unquestionably *the* big event of the year, the 500 Festival is a month-long city celebration—parades, costume balls, mini-marathon—that leads up to the Indy 500 car race on Memorial Day wknd, one of the world's most prestigious sports events.

Indiana Black Expo (July): The nation's largest exposition of its kind. A 3-day event highlighting African American achievements in culture, art, and commerce. The expo's picnic provides ethnic food and live entertainment.

GTE/U.S. Men's Open (early Aug): World-class players compete in a week-long event held in a modern 10,000-seat tennis stadium.

Indiana State Fair (Aug.): One of the largest and most colorful agricultural fairs in the country, with horse racing, cattle shows, and more.

Indiana Speed Week (a week in early Sept): The spectacular U.S. championship of drag racing at Indianapolis Raceway Park. For velocity lovers.

SPORTS: Indianapolis has four professional teams:
Baseball (Apr–Sept): Indians, Bush Stadium (632-5371).
Basketball (Oct–Apr): Pacers, Market Sq. Arena (263-2100).
Football (Sept–Dec): Colts, Hoosier Dome (297-7000).
Ice Hockey (Oct–Apr): Ice, State Fairgrounds Coliseum (924-1234).

STROLLS: ⚜ **Lockerbie Square,** bounded by N. York St., College St., Michigan St., and East St.: Narrow, cobblestone streets, brick sidewalks, and pretty, brightly colored 19th-century houses make this a fine area for a stroll.

WINTER SPORTS RESORTS: ⚜ **Nashville Alps Ski World Resort,** 59 mi. (94km) south on Ind. 37 and Ind. 46 (812/988-6638): Five chair lifts. Open mid-Dec to early Mar.

ZOO: ☀⚜ **Indianapolis Zoo,** 1200 W. Washington St. (638-8072): New $64-million, 64-acre (26ha) facility, very complete and well conceived with 2,000 animals roaming simulated environments. The nation's first major zoo in decades to be built from the ground up. Rare birds and the world's largest totally enclosed Whale and Dolphin Pavilion. Miniature train rides. See it. Open daily.

ACCOMMODATIONS

A Note on Accommodations: Room rates in Indianapolis are coded as follows: **VE,** Very Expensive ($140 and up); **E,** Expensive ($90–$140); **M,** Moderate ($60–$90); **I,** Inexpensive ($30–$60); **B,** Budget (up to $30). A listing of toll free numbers is in the Appendix. *Note:* Indianapolis hotels charge higher prices during the Indy 500 season (last Sun in May), at which time a 3-night minimum stay is also in effect.

Personal Favorites (in order of preference)

👑👑👑 **Westin** (dwntwn), 50 S. Capitol Ave., IN 46204 (317/262-8100; toll free, see Westin). 570 rms, A/C, color TV, in-rm movies. AE, CB, DC, MC, V. Valet parking $6, pool, health club, two rests. (including Graffitis), coffee shop, bars, 24-hr rm svce, nightclub, concierge, free crib. *Note:* Since opening in Jan 1989 this has supplanted the Hyatt Regency as Indianapolis's most luxurious hotel. A successful venture in postmodern architecture w. a gigantic 15-floor atrium; elegant decor and furnishings. Spacious, well-designed rms, some reserved for nonsmokers. Very good svce. Very well located across from the Capitol and the Convention Center, which can be reached directly by Skywalk. VIP floor; big business clientele. In both size and comfort the city's foremost hotel. **E–VE**

☀👑👑👑 **Canterbury** (dwntwn), 123 S. Illinois St., IN 46225 (317/634-3000; toll free, see Preferred). 99 rms, A/C, color TV, in-rm movies. AE, CB, DC, MC, V. Valet gar. $8, rest. (Beaulieu), piano bar, rm svce, concierge, crib $15. *Note:* This small, elegant European-style luxury hotel has been sumptuously renovated, 1920s style. Very comfortable rms, w. Chippendale furniture and refrigerators, though some are somewhat cramped. Intimate atmosphere; ultra-correct svce; first-rate rest. Complimentary breakfast and limousine transportation dwntwn. A favorite of connoisseurs, in the heart of the city. **VE**

☀👑👑 **Holiday Inn Union Station** (dwntwn), 123 W. Louisiana St., IN 46225 (317/631-2221; toll free, see Holiday Inns). 276 rms, color TV, in-rm movies. AE, CB, DC, MC, V. Free parking, pool, sauna, health club, rest. (Louisiana Street), bar, rm svce, nightclub, boutiques, concierge, free airport shuttle, free crib. *Note:* The most innovative hotel in town stands in the enormous urban-renewal project around the former train station, amid dozens of bars, rests., and fashionable boutiques. Very lively ambience. The customer may choose between classic, comfortable hotel rms and the luxurious

Pullman cars of yesteryear. Good overall svce. A delightful experiment by the Holiday Inns chain. Group and convention clientele. **E–VE**

☀️🔑 **Indianapolis Motor Speedway Motel** (vic.), 4400 W. 16th St., IN 46222 (317/241-2500). 106 rms, A/C, color TV, in-rm movies. AE, DC, MC, V. Free parking, pool, golf, coffee shop, bar, rm svce, Indianapolis 500 museum, crib $6. *Note:* Pleasant motel on the grounds of the famous auto raceway. Modern comfort. No resv. during Indy 500 time in May. Very good value. **I**

🔑 **Days Inn East** (nr. dwntwn), 7314 E. 21st St., IN 46219 (317/359-5500; toll free, see Days Inn). 120 rms, A/C, color TV, in-rm movies. AE, DC, MC, V. Free parking, pool, adjacent 24-hr. coffee shop, free crib. *Note:* Conventional motel nr. the new industrial area on the city's eastern periphery and convenient to the beltway (I-465). Functional comfort. Ideal for the motorist. 10 min. from dwntwn. Good value. **B–I**

Other Accommodations (from top bracket to budget)

🔑🔑🔑 **Hyatt Regency** (dwntwn), 1 S. Capitol Ave., IN 46204 (317/632-1234; toll free, see Hyatt). 496 rms, A/C, color TV, in-rm movies. AE, CB, DC, MC, V. Valet gar. $6, five rests. and bars (including a revolving bar at the top), rm svce, hrdrsr, drugstore, free crib. *Note:* An ultra-luxurious hotel, modern and comfortable. The red-brick construction is rather massive but the 20-story glass-walled atrium is spectacular. Across from the Capitol and the Convention Center. Rather unreliable svce. Very acceptable rest. (Eagle's Nest). VIP floor. No physical fitness facilities. One among the favorites of businesspeople. **E–VE**

🔑🔑🔑 **Marriott** (nr. dwntwn), 7202 E. 21st St., IN 46219 (317/352-1231; toll free, see Marriott). 250 rms, A/C, color TV, in-rm movies. AE, CB, DC, MC, V. Free parking, pool, health club, sauna, putting green, rest. (Durbin Junction), bar, rm svce, nightclub, free crib. *Note:* This large, modern motel on the eastern periphery of Indianapolis is close to the new industrial area. Unusual architecture. Comfortable, spacious rms and efficient svce. Group and business clientele. VIP floor. Interesting wknd packages. 10 min. from dwntwn on I-70. **E**

🔑🔑🔑 **Hilton** (dwntwn), Ohio St. and Meridian St., IN 46206 (317/635-2000; toll free, see Hilton). 371 rms, A/C, color TV, in-rm movies. AE, CB, DC, MC, V. Parking $4, pool, two rests. (including Seasons), coffee shop, two bars, rm svce, nightclub, free breakfast, free crib. *Note:* Relatively modern glass-and-concrete luxury hotel in the heart of dwntwn. The glass-walled elevator affords an unobstructed view of the city. Spacious, comfortable rms and good svce. Business clientele. Just off Monument Circle. **M–E**

🔑🔑 **Riverpointe Suites Hotel** (nr. dwntwn), 1150 N. White River Pkwy., IN 46222 (317/638-9866). 140 suites, A/C, cable color TV, AE, MC, V. Free parking pool, two tennis courts, health club, sauna, rooftop sundeck, rest. (Westbank), bar, valet svce. *Note:* An ideal place for longer stays. The hotel offers spacious, well-equipped suites w. kitchenettes, an inviting, comfortable layout, and a very good location on the White River, 5 min. from dwntwn. Agreeable reception and svce. Good value. **M**

🔑🔑 **Ramada Inn Downtown** (dwntwn), 501 W. Washington St., IN 46204 (317/635-4443; toll free, see Ramada Inns). 232 rms, A/C, color TV, in-rm movies. AE, CB, DC, MC, V. Free parking, pool, health club, rest. (T.G.I. Friday's), bar, rm svce, crib $6. *Note:* Chain motel w. no exceptional attraction or advantage apart from its very central location. Modern comfort. Standard rms w. balconies and refrigerators. Completed a multi-million-dollar renovation in 1989. **I–M**

🔑 **La Quinta East** (nr. dwntwn), 7304 E. 21st St., IN 46219 (317/359-1021; toll free, see La Quinta). 122 rms, A/C, color TV, in-rm movies. AE, CB, DC, MC, V. Free parking, pool, adjacent 24-hr.

coffee shop, valet svce, free crib. *Note:* This classic highway motel is modern and comfortable and 10 min. from dwntwn on I-70. Spacious, inviting rms (some no-smoking). Cheerful svce. Good value. **I**

Red Roof Inn South (nr. dwntwn), S. Emerson Ave. at I-465, IN 46203 (317/788-9551; toll free 800/848-7878). 106 rms, A/C, color TV, in-rm movies. AE, DC, MC, V. Free parking, adjacent coffee shop, free crib. *Note:* This modest, unassuming little motel on the southeastern edge of the city offers functional comfort and is ideal for the motorist passing through (direct access to the city beltway, I-465). Good overall value. **B–I**

Motel 6 (nr. dwntwn), 2851 Shadeland Ave., IN 46219 (317/546-5864). 154 rms, A/C, color TV, free in-rm movies. AE, DC, MC, V. Free parking, pool, free crib. *Note:* An unbeatable value, 10 min. from dwntwn. Functional comfort. Ideal for the motorist. **B**

Airport Accommodations

Holiday Inn Airport (vic.), 2501 S. High School Rd., IN 46241 (317/244-6861; toll free, see Holiday Inn). 274 rms, A/C, color TV, in-rm movies. AE, CB, DC, MC, V. Free parking, pool, sauna, health club, rest. (Chanteclair), coffee shop, bar, rm svce, disco, free airport shuttle, free crib. *Note:* This typical Holiday Inn may not have a great deal of personality but it does have, strangely enough, one of the best rests. in town. Comfortable rms w. balconies. Efficient svce. **M–E**

RESTAURANTS

A Note on Restaurant Prices: Indianapolis restaurant prices, per person, excluding drinks and service charges, are coded as follows: **VE**, Very Expensive ($60 and up); **E**, Expensive ($40–$60); **M**, Moderate ($25–$40); **I**, Inexpensive ($15–$25); **B**, Budget (up to $15).

Personal Favorites (in order of preference)

Fletcher's American Grill & Café (dwntwn), 107 S. Pennsylvania St. (632-2500). A/C. Lunch Mon–Fri, dinner Mon–Sat; closed hols. AE, CB, DC, MC, V. Jkt. *Specialties:* seafood sausage in a cream sauce w. angel-hair spinach pasta and snails, blackened red snapper in lime marinade, Moulard duck breast w. poached apples in Calvados brown sauce, stuffed lamb medallions, Harlequin soufflé. *Note:* Light, imaginative dishes from the master hand of chef-proprietor Fletcher Boyd. The ground-floor dining room (The Grill) offers meat, chicken, and mesquite-broiled fish in a relaxed atmosphere, while the second-floor The Café serves a more elaborate American nouvelle cuisine in an elegant pastel-hued setting. Very good svce; resv. strongly advised. Free parking. *American.* **M–I**

Peter's (dwntwn), 936 Virginia Ave. (637-9333). A/C. Dinner only, nightly; closed hols. and the first week in July. AE, CB, DC, MC, V. Jkt. *Specialties:* cold chicken salad w. peanut-butter sauce and crisp julienne of vegetables, gourmet pizzas, fried walleye pike w. feta cheese and lemon, rabbit tenderloin grilled w. rosemary and red-pepper sauce, beef Angus steak. Menu changes regularly. Good wine list. *Note:* Small, intimate rest. seating only 52, its chaste white walls enlivened by modern paintings. Delicate and often innovative midwestern food. Resv. essential; a highly recommended spot. *American.* **I–M**

Jonathan's Restaurant and Pub (vic.), 96th St. and Keystone Crossing (844-1155). A/C. Lunch/dinner daily, brunch Sat–Sun; closed hols. AE, DC, MC, V. Jkt. *Specialties:* very fine red meat and fish broiled over a wood fire, spareribs, veal Oscar, roast pork loin. *Note:* A delightful British-style inn on the northern edge of Indianapolis. Well worth the 25 min. by car from dwntwn. Diligent svce. An excellent locale. Resv. advised. Pub open until 2am. *Steak/Seafood.* **I–M**

T.G.I. Friday's (dwntwn), in the Ramada Inn Downtown (see "Accommodations," above) (685-8443). A/C. Breakfast/

lunch/dinner daily (until 1am). AE, MC, V. *Specialties:* steak hamburgers, Mexican dishes, homemade soup. *Note:* An amusing bistro frequented by a young local crowd. Generous servings; pleasant ambience and decor; very crowded bar. 25 min. from dwntwn. *American/Mexican.* **B–I**

⚓ **Dodd's Town House** (nr. dwntwn), 5694 N. Meridian St. (257-1872). A/C. Dinner only, Tues–Sun. AE, MC, V. *Specialties:* steak, fried chicken, grilled fish of the day, wonderful homemade cakes and pies. No alcoholic beverages. *Note:* The most popular rest. in town for more than a quarter century. The decor may be as modest as the prices, but Betty Dodd's cooking is very tasty and the portions copious. Efficient svce. Clientele of regulars. Resv. recommended. *American.* **B**

Other Restaurants (from top bracket to budget)

🍸🍸🍸 **Chanteclair** (vic), in the Holiday Inn Airport (see "Accommodations," above) (243-1040). A/C. Dinner only, Mon–Sat; closed hols. AE, CB, DC, MC, V. Jkt. *Specialties:* rack of lamb, veal medallions with chanterelle mushrooms, pheasant Souvaroff, sweetbreads madeira, tournedos Rossini. Very good wine list. *Note:* A first-rate rest. in a Holiday Inn may be surprising, but it's for real. Aside from some heavy sauces and uncertain svce, this is one of the best places to eat in Indianapolis. Elegant ambience. Resv. a must. *French/Continental.* **M**

🍸🍸 **King Cole** (dwntwn), 7 N. Meridian St. (638-5588). A/C. Lunch Mon–Fri, dinner Mon–Sat; closed hols. AE, CB, DC, MC, V. Jkt. *Specialties:* roast duckling, baked clams, rack of lamb, pompano en papillote, fish of the day, lemon soufflé. Good wine list. *Note:* A favorite of local businesspeople for more than 50 years. Rich, cozy atmosphere w. old paintings, woodwork, and sumptuous table linens. Irreproachable cuisine and svce. Resv. highly recommended. *Continental.* **I–M**

☼🍸🍸 **St. Elmo Steak House** (dwntwn), 127 S. Illinois St. (635-0636). A/C. Dinner only, nightly; closed hols. and the first 15 days of July. AE, DC, MC, V. Jkt. *Specialties:* aged prime cuts, lamb chops, lobster, seafood. *Note:* A local institution since 1902 and "the" steakhouse par excellence. Pleasant old-fashioned decor. Excellent svce. Resv. advised. Generous cocktails. Free parking. *Steak/Seafood.* **I–M**

🍸🍸 **Iron Skillet** (nr. dwntwn), 2489 W. 30th St. (923-6353). A/C. Dinner Wed–Sun, brunch Sun; closed Dec 24–25. AE, CB, DC, MC, V. *Specialties:* fried chicken, steak, oven-baked pike. *Note:* In a 19th-century building, this pleasant rest. on the edge of a golf course presents the daily menu on a blackboard and offers honest, tasty regional fare. Attentive, friendly svce. Locally very popular. Resv. recommended. Free parking. *American.* **B–I**

🍸 **Hollyhock Hill** (vic.), 8110 N. College Ave. (251-2294). A/C. Dinner Tues–Sun (until 8pm), brunch Sun; closed Labor Day, Dec. 24–25. AE, MC, V. *Specialties:* southern fried chicken, steak, broiled fish of the day. *Note:* Pleasant family rest. w. rather kitsch grdn decor. Traditional, no-frills cuisine at very modest prices. Hefty portions. Locally popular. 25 min. from dwntwn. *American.* **B–I**

🍸 **Shapiro's Delicatessen** (dwntwn), 808 S. Meridian St. (631-4041). A/C. Breakfast/lunch/dinner daily. No credit cards. *Specialties:* giant sandwiches, pastrami, corned beef, stuffed cabbage, brisket, chopped liver, cheesecake. *Note:* The experts agree that this is the best deli around; it's been a classic since 1905. Usually packed at lunchtime (inevitable waits). Other location: 2370 W. 86th St. (872-7255). *American.* **B**

Restaurants in the Vicinity

🍸🍸 **The Glass Chimney** (vic.), 12901 N. Meridian St., Carmel (844-0921). A/C. Dinner only, Mon–Sat; closed hols. AE, MC, V. J&T. *Specialties:* lobster bisque w. cognac, pheasant chasseur, wild boar and game (in season), duckling bigarade, rack of lamb, veal kidneys w. mustard sauce, Coho salmon. *Note:* A few remarkable dishes but also some weaknesses in the cooking and svce; the place could do better. Charming old decor and a pleasant patio-grdn. Resv. advised. Locally popular. 35 min. from dwntwn. *Continental.* I–M

Cafeterias/Fast Food
L. S. Ayres Tea Room (dwntwn), 1 W. Washington St. (262-2658). Lunch only, Mon–Sat. No credit cards. *Note:* Cafeteria in the department store of the same name. Dependable soups and daily specials. Good svce.
Laughner's Cafeteria (nr. dwntwn), 4030 S. East St. (787-3745). Lunch/dinner daily (until 8pm). *Specialties:* fried chicken, roast beef, fish of the day, homemade desserts. *Note:* Very popular cafeteria with charming nostalgic decor. Many more locations (check the local phone book).

BARS & NIGHTCLUBS
Crackers Comedy Club (vic.), 8702 Keystone Crossing (846-2500). Much-frequented comedy club with big-name stars. Open Wed–Sat. Resv. advised.
Ike & Jonesy's (dwntwn), 17 W. Jackson Pl. (632-4553). A disco with a big local following, for fans of the "golden oldies" of the '50s and '60s. Open Mon–Sat.
Quincy's (vic.) in the Adam's Mark Hotel, 2544 Executive Dr. (248-2481). "In" disco with an elegant atmosphere. Open Mon–Sat.
Rick's Café (dwntwn), Union Station, Track Side (634-6666). The decor comes straight from the movie *Casablanca*. Bastion of "Naptown sound."
Safari Bar and Restaurant (nr. dwntwn), 5910 E. 82nd St. (842-2968). The biggest hits from the Top 40 in an amusing tropical setting with a marble dance floor. Favored by local yuppies.
T.G.I. Friday's (dwntwn), in the Ramada Inn Downtown (see "Accommodations," above) (685-8443). Hip bar and disco (see also "Restaurants," above). Open nightly.

NEARBY EXCURSIONS

COLUMBUS (40 mi./64km south on I-65): In the late 1930s this obscure prairie town launched an energetic construction program of buildings both public and private, commissioned from world-famous architects like Eliel and Eero Saarinen, Cesar Pelli, Kevin Roche, Richard Meier, I. M. Pei, and Harry Weese, and enriched with works by artists of the caliber of sculptor Henry Moore. To date some 50 outstanding examples have been completed. Guided tours from the Visitors Center, 506 5th St. (812/372-1954). Open daily Apr–Oct, Mon–Sat the rest of the year. An absolute must.

CONNER PRAIRIE PIONEER SETTLEMENT (13400 Allisonville Rd., Noblesville; 18 mi./28km NE on Ind. 19) (776-6000): This authentic village-museum dating from the 19th century faithfully reproduces pioneer life between 1820 and 1840 with the help of 36 minutely restored old buildings, including the blacksmith's forge and the cobbler's workshop, as well as a plush, patrician residence in the Federal style. Handcraft demonstrations offered in period costume. For history lovers. Open Tues–Sun Apr to late Nov.

MOUNDS STATE PARK (in Anderson, 48 mi./76km NE on I-69 and Ind. 32) (642-6627): A number of prehistoric tumuli including an earthwork 9 ft. (2.7m) tall and 1,280 ft. (400m) in circumference, built by Native American civilizations which remain an enigma to archeologists. Handsome, 247-acre (100ha) park with campgrounds and picnic areas. Worth going out of your way for. Open daily.

☼☖ **NASHVILLE** (43 mi./68km south on Ind. 135): This charming authentic pioneer town is now a haven for artists with numerous antique shops, art galleries, etc. A noteworthy point of interest, the ☖ **John Dillinger Historical Museum,** at 104 S. Van Buren St. (812/988-7172), traces the career of the well-known gangster. Housed in a rambling Victorian mansion, the museum has wax effigies of historical figures from both sides of the law, including J. Edgar Hoover, Melvin Purvis, and Baby Face Nelson, as well as Dillinger himself. There are also displays of Dillinger-related artifacts, among them the pants he wore when he was gunned down by FBI agents in 1934, and his lucky rabbit's foot. Open daily Mar–Nov.

A few miles south, see the **Brown County State Park:** 15,500 acres (6,275ha) of wooded hills with splendid, glowing bronze tones in autumn; and enormous **Lake Monroe,** both of which offer ideal excursion destinations for nature lovers. (A good joint excursion with a visit to Columbus; see above).

☖ **ZIONSVILLE** (12 mi./19km north on U.S. 421): Charming little 19th-century town on the outskirts of Indianapolis with many elegant boutiques and an interesting pioneer museum, the **Patrick Henry Sullivan Museum,** 225 W. Hawthorne St. (873-4900). Open Tues–Sat.

CHAPTER 27

ST. LOUIS ♔

□ □ □

Founded in 1764 by Pierre Laclède, a French fur trader and devotee of the sainted King Louis IX of France, then sold to the U.S. in 1803 by Napoleon as part of the Louisiana Purchase, the "Gateway to the West" stands at the confluence of the Illinois River with two greater rivers, the Mississippi and the Missouri. A crossroads for rail, road, and river traffic, its strategic position inevitably made it the starting point for the Westward Expansion in the 19th century. It was from St. Louis that Meriwether Lewis and William Clark started out on their famous expedition, 7,689 mi. (12,302km) to the shores of Oregon and back again in 1804–06. It was from St. Louis, too, that the covered wagons of the pioneers, the heavily laden Conestogas or "prairie schooners," lumbered off on their mission to open up the Middle West to the Pacific.

Once the city of jazz, of former African American slaves, and of great paddlewheelers stemming the current of "Ol' Man River," St. Louis has also been, for a century or more, a thriving industrial center, the home of Monsanto, McDonnell Douglas, General Dynamics, Ralston Purina, and more. Second only to Detroit as a producer of automobiles in the U.S., the "Gateway to the West" prides itself most of all on its leading part in the history of flight. It was the *Spirit of St. Louis* in which Charles Lindbergh made the first solo flight across the Atlantic from west to east in 1927; its progeny descendants include the F-4 *Phantom*, F-15 *Eagle*, F-16 *Fighting Falcon*, and F-18 *Hornet* warplanes, as well as the first *Mercury* and *Gemini* spacecraft.

As a legacy of the heavy inflow of German and Italian immigrants at the turn of the century, St. Louis still possesses the world's largest brewery (Anheuser-Busch) and the best Italian restaurants between New York and the West Coast. Two great culinary inventions, which have attained the status of national icons, first saw the light of day here at the Louisiana Purchase Exposition (St. Louis World's Fair) of 1904: the hot dog and the ice-cream cone. But the finest contemporary symbol of this midwestern city, with its touch of southern charm, is the **Gateway Arch.** The shining 630-ft. (192m) archway of stainless steel, designed by Finnish-American architect Eero Saarinen, rises beside the Mississippi River. Dedicated to the memory of those durable pioneers who won the West, this gigantic double-downstroke has attracted two million visitors a year since it was unveiled in 1965.

Long considered the archetypical provincial town, graceless and boring, in the 1980s St. Louis underwent an artistic, architectural, and cultural boom—witness the success of the St. Louis Symphony, which has become one of the best orchestras in the country. In the past decade the city has undertaken a tremendous program of urban renewal, but rather than mar the glorious view through the Gateway Arch with a jumble of high-rises, St. Louis made an inspired choice: it would make an old city over into a new one. Among the triumphs of renovation are **Compton Heights, Washington Heights (Benton Park),** and mainly **Laclede's Landing,** on the river, with its narrow cobblestone streets, cast-iron lamp standards, and dozens of boutiques, bars, and restaurants. Another resounding success is the former **Union Station,** now a shopping mall delightfully disguised as a medieval castle.

On the darker side, St. Louis has a crime rate which makes solitary walks at night inadvisable.

Famous St. Louis natives include poet and critic T. S. Eliot; actresses Virginia Mayo, Betty Grable, Shelley Winters, and Marsha Mason; actors Vincent Price and Kevin Kline; and singer Josephine Baker.

BASIC FACTS: State of Missouri. Area code: 314. Time zone: central. ZIP Code: 63166. Founded: 1764. Approximate population: city, 420,000; metropolitan area, 2,520,000. 13th-largest metropolitan area in the U.S.

CLIMATE: Unavoidably, given the proximity of the Father of Waters, the climate is disagreeably hot and sticky from June to Sept, with a July mean temperature of 81°F (27°C). Winter is harsh (Jan mean, 33°F/1°C), but snowfall is light. The spring is unusually rainy and windy, with tornados occurring in May and early June. There remains only the fall, by far the best season for a visit with its cool, sunny days.

DISTANCES: Chicago, 290 mi. (465km); Indianapolis, 235 mi. (376km); Kansas City, 259 mi. (415km); Memphis, 284 mi. (455km); Nashville, 328 mi. (525km).

ARRIVAL & TRANSIT INFORMATION

AIRPORT: Lambert–St. Louis International Airport (STL), 10 mi. (16km) NW. For information, call 314/426-8000.

AIRLINES: American (231-9505), Continental (241-7205), Delta (421-2600), Eastern (621-8900), Northwest (toll free 800/225-2525), Southwest (421-1221), TWA (291-7500), United (454-0088), and USAir (421-1018).

CITY LINK: The **cab** fare from the airport to downtown is about $18–$20; time, about 35 min. (1 hr. during rush hr.). Bus: **Airport Limo Svce** (429-4940), serving major dwntwn hotels, leaves every 20 min.; fare, $6; time, about 40–50 min. **City bus:** Bi-State has an express service between the airport and dwntwn, leaving every 40 min.; price, 75¢; time, 1 hr.

The size of the metropolitan area, and its distance from the airport, may make it advisable to rent a car unless you intend to confine yourself to seeing downtown St. Louis. The **public transportation system** (bus) is quite extensive but slow: for information, call Bi-State Transit System (231-2345).

CAR RENTAL (at Lambert International Airport unless otherwise indicated): Avis (426-7766); Budget (731-6000); Dollar (423-4004); Hertz (426-7555); National (426-6272); and Thrifty, 4140 Cypress Rd., St. Ann (423-3737). For dwntwn locations, consult the local telephone directory.

LIMOUSINE SERVICES: Carey Limousine (946-4114), Dav-El Limousines (toll free 800/922-0343), and Show Me Limo Service (522-0888).

TAXIS: Cabs may, at your pleasure, be hailed on the street, taken from the waiting lines in front of the major hotels, or summoned by phone. Recommended companies: **Allen Cab** (241-7722), **Laclede Cab** (652-3456), and **Yellow Cab** (361-2345).

TRAIN: Amtrak, 550 S. 16th St. (241-8806).

INTERCITY BUSES: Greyhound, 809 N. Broadway (231-7800).

MISSISSIPPI RIVER CRUISES: Sternwheeler river cruises, 3–10 days on the Mississippi aboard the *Delta Queen* or the *Mississippi Queen,* 1920s paddle-wheelers. Luxurious kitsch. See Chapter 15 on New Orleans for details.

INFORMATION & TOURS

TOURIST INFORMATION: The **St. Louis Convention and Visitors Commission,** 10 S. Broadway, Suite 300, MO 63102 (314/421-1023; toll free 800/325-7962).
    Visitors Center, 445 N. Memorial Dr. (314/241-1764).
    For a **telephone recording** with an up-to-date listing of cultural events and shows, call 421-2100.

GUIDED TOURS: Fostaire Helicopter Ride (helicopter), 400 N. L. K. Sullivan Blvd. (421-5440): Helicopter flights over the city; year round, weather permitting.
    Gray Line Tours (bus) (618/241-1224): Conducted tours of the city and surroundings; serves principal downtown and midtown hotels. Daily Apr–Oct.
    River Excursions (boat), St. Louis Levee, beneath the Gateway Arch (621-4040): 1-hr. trips on the Mississippi aboard the paddlesteamer *Huck Finn, Tom Sawyer,* or *Becky Thatcher,* replicas of 19th-century steamboats. Daily Apr–Nov.
    Riverboat *President* (boat), St. Louis Levee, beneath the Gateway Arch (621-4040): 3-hr. mini-cruises aboard the largest river excursion boat in the U.S. Dance cruises in the evening. Daily June–Sept.
    St. Louis Carriage Co. (carriage) (621-3334): Rides in a horse-drawn carriage, serving downtown and the Riverfront. Year round, weather permitting. Reservations a must.
    St. Louis Tram Tours (bus), 516 Cerre St. (241-1400): 2-hr. conducted tour across the city, in a replica of a turn-of-the-century open streetcar. Serves major hotels. Daily.

SIGHTS, ATTRACTIONS & ACTIVITIES

ARCHITECTURAL HIGHLIGHTS: Busch Stadium, Walnut St., Broadway, Spruce St., and 7th St. (241-3900): Ultramodern circular stadium, seating 53,000, where Cardinals fans congregate for home games. Also home of the St. Louis Sports Hall of Fame (see "Museums of Science and History," below). Conducted tours of the stadium daily June–Aug, except on days of games. Should be seen.
    City Hall, Memorial Plaza (622-4000): Huge building in the Renaissance style, an exact copy of the Hôtel de Ville in Paris. It is worth a look.
    Fabulous Fox Theater, 527 N. Grand Blvd. (534-1678): Originally considered to be one of the two or three finest movie theaters in the country, this 1929 architectural gem has been restored to all the fabulous rococo glory that its name implies. Now houses all kinds of performing arts: pop concerts, big-star shows, musicals, etc. Guided tours by appointment Tues, Thurs, and Sat at 10:30am. An absolute must.
    Metropolitan Square Building, Broadway at Olive St. (436-7400): The city's first real skyscraper. This modern 42-story

building stands only 618 ft. (188m) because a strict city ordinance bans new buildings towering over the 630-ft. (192m) Gateway Arch. Worth a look.

Powell Symphony Hall, 718 N. Grand Blvd. (533-2500): This old (1925) movie theater also has a sumptuous kitsch ivory-and-gold interior. Splendidly renovated in 1967, it has since then been home to the St. Louis Symphony Orchestra. Well worth a look.

Union Station, 1820 Market St. (421-6655): St. Louis's old central station, dating from 1894 and once the largest in the world, architecturally a strange amalgam of railroad station and medieval fortress. Now houses a luxury hotel plus dozens of boutiques, stores, and restaurants. This gloriously successful urban-renewal project cost $135 million. Happy, relaxed atmosphere; definitely deserves a visit. Open daily.

CHURCHES/SYNAGOGUES: Christ Church Cathedral, 1210 Locust St. (231-3454): A perfect example of English Gothic, with its carved marble altar and Tiffany stained-glass windows, this beautiful place of worship was erected 1867–1911 on the site of the first Episcopalian parish (1819) built west of the Mississippi. Well worth a visit; open Sun–Fri.

Old Cathedral, 209 Walnut St. (231-3250): Erected in 1831 on the site of the first Roman Catholic church in St. Louis (1770), and given the status of a basilica by Pope John XXIII (its official title is Basilica of St. Louis King of France), it was also designated a national monument by Pres. John F. Kennedy shortly before his death. Religious museum in the crypt, open daily. The oldest Roman Catholic cathedral west of the Mississippi; definitely worth visiting.

St. Louis Cathedral, 4431 Lindell Blvd. at Newstead Ave. (533-2824): This imposing Roman-Byzantine building, the city's "new" Roman Catholic cathedral, dates from 1907; it boasts a giant dome and a nave almost entirely clad in beautiful mosaics. The whole interior is richly decorated. Don't miss it. Open daily.

HISTORIC BUILDINGS: Campbell House, 1508 Locust St. (421-0325): Museum-home of Robert Campbell, a rich fur trader in the latter part of the 19th century. Visitors can immerse themselves in the history of the local upper middle class. Original furniture, decorations, and clothing. Interesting. Open Tues–Sun Mar–Dec, by appointment in Jan–Feb.

Chatillon–de Menil Mansion, 3352 De Menil Pl. (771-5828): This handsome 1848 Greek Revival house at the top of Arsenal Hill was long used as a landmark by Mississippi riverboats. Fine antique furniture. Open Tues–Sat; don't miss it. Also a laudable restaurant (lunch only).

Eads Bridge, foot of Washington Ave.: The work of architect James Eads, this was the first bridge (1874) on the central stretch of the Mississippi to span the entire river from side to side. It was also the first to be built with two decks and steel arches. Worth a look.

Goldenrod *Showboat*, Riverfront, 700 N. L. K. Sullivan Blvd. (621-3311): Authentic 1909 showboat, one of the last still in existence. Presents melodramas, comedies, variety. Dinner-theater. Each year, too, the National Classic Jazz and Ragtime Festival (see "Special Events," below) takes place here. A must for those who crave local color. Open Tues–Sun.

Old Courthouse, 11 N. 14th St. at Market St. (425-4465): This imposing building, with its 173-ft.-high (53m) dome of cast iron decorated with interesting historical frescoes, was completed in 1859. Here, from 1846 to 1857, was tried the famous case of Dred Scott, the first African American man to contend that slavery could not be enforced outside the

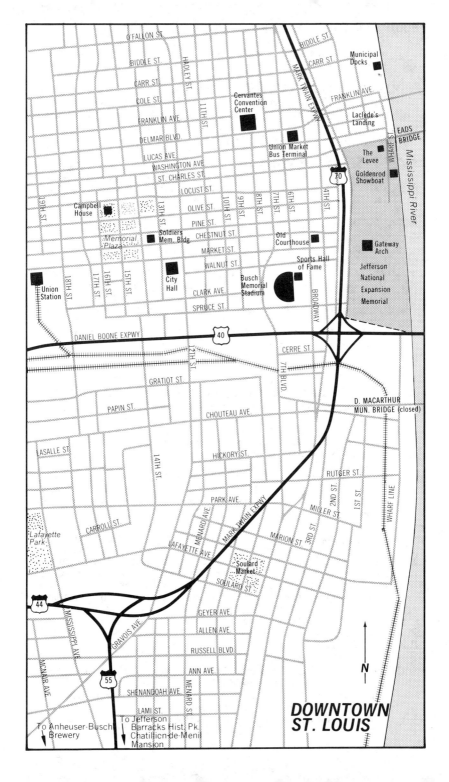

DOWNTOWN
ST. LOUIS

states where it was legal. Many memorabilia of this historic case. Well worth a visit; open daily.

INDUSTRIAL TOURS: ☀ **Anheuser-Busch Brewery,** 13th St. and Lynch St. (577-2626): The largest brewery in the world, whose two major brands, Budweiser and Michelob, sell at the rate of more than five million bottles and cans daily. Free tasting. Don't miss the stables of the famous Clydesdale draft horses, the symbol of Anheuser-Busch. Open Mon–Sat.

MARKETS: ⚖ **Soulard Market,** 7th St. and Lafayette Ave. (622-4180): From meat to vegetables and from homemade preserves to live animals, all the produce of the soil is found in this colorful covered market. A St. Louis landmark since 1847. Open Wed–Sat.

MONUMENTS: ☀⚖⚖ **Gateway Arch,** 2nd St. at the foot of Chestnut St. (425-4465): Colossal arch of stainless steel, 630 ft. (192m) high, designed by the famous Finnish-American architect Eero Saarinen. Completed in 1965, it symbolizes the Winning of the West by the 19th-century pioneers. An elevator composed of small capsules moving at an oblique angle takes you to the top, where the view is splendid. At the base is the interesting Museum of Westward Expansion (see "Museums of Science and History," below). The tallest and most imaginative memorial in the country; worth the trip to St. Louis all by itself. Open daily.

☀⚖ **Wedding of the Waters,** Aloe Plaza at Market St.: Monumental fountain comprising 14 figures in bronze, which symbolizes the confluence of the Mississippi and the Missouri, by Swedish sculptor Carl Milles. Worth seeing.

MUSEUMS OF ART: ☀⚖ **Cupples Art Gallery,** 3673 W. Pine Blvd. (658-3025): This curious 1890s mansion in the Roman style stands on the campus of St. Louis University; its facade is abundantly ornamented with sculpture, while its 32 rooms are luxuriously decorated with wood paneling, Tiffany windows, and wrought iron. Houses a fine collection of modern engravings by Miró, Kandinsky, Chagall, Braque, and others, as well as interesting temporary exhibitions. Open Sun–Fri; should positively be seen.

⚖ **Dog Museum,** 1721 S. Mason Rd. (821-3647): Housed in the historic Jarville House, this museum, which moved from New York City in 1987, presents an extraordinary array of items depicting the dog throughout history. Also a reference library. A must for animal lovers. Open daily.

☀⚖⚖ **St. Louis Art Museum,** Forest Park, Art Hill (721-0067): Housed in Cass Gilbert's Fine Arts Palace, designed for the 1904 World's Fair, this great museum has recently been enlarged and houses a remarkable collection of art from prehistoric times to the present day. It's particularly strong in European and American painting and sculpture; also Chinese bronzes and African and pre-Columbian art. Among its best-known treasures: Hans Holbein's *Lady Guldeford,* Titian's *Ecce Homo,* Jordaens's *Suffer the Little Children to Come Unto Me,* Matisse's *Bathers with a Tortoise,* Maurice Prendergast's *Seashore,* John McCrady's *Swing Low, Sweet Chariot,* and Mark Rothko's *Red, Orange, Orange on Red.* Don't miss it. Open Tues–Sun.

MUSEUMS OF SCIENCE & HISTORY: ⚖ **Eugene Field House and Toy Museum,** 634 S. Broadway (421-4689): Birthplace of the Eugene Field, with many exhibits associated with the author of *Little Boy Blue.* Interesting collection of old toys and dolls. Worth a look; open Tues–Sun.

⚖ **Magic House Children's Museum,** 516 S. Kirkwood Rd., Kirkwood, 8 mi. (12km) west on U.S. 44 (822-8900): A museum of the extraordinary intended specifically for children. Dozens of attractions including microcomputer games, an electrostatic generator that will literally make your hair stand on end, a three-story-high giant slide, a maze, and so on. An absolute must for kids. Open Tues–Sun. 15 min. from downtown.

    McDonnell Douglas Prologue Room, McDonnell Blvd. and Airport Rd. (232-5421): Small aeronautical and space museum in the company's head-office building. Many preliminary designs, photographs, and scale models of planes and rockets illustrating the company's achievements since it was founded in 1920. Be sure to see the facsimiles of the *Mercury* and *Gemini* space capsules. For aviation buffs. Open Tues–Sun June–Aug; 30 min. from downtown.

    Missouri Historical Society, Forest Park, Lindell Blvd. and De Baliviere Ave. (361-1424): Much material on the history of St. Louis, Missouri, and the West: weapons, clothing, models of boats, posters, etc. One section is devoted to the 1904 World's Fair. The Lindbergh Room displays material relating to the 1927 transatlantic flight of the *Spirit of St. Louis.* Fascinating. Open Tues–Sun.

    Museum of Westward Expansion, at the base of Gateway Arch, 2nd St. at the foot of Chestnut St. (425-4465): Remarkable audiovisual display tracing the history of the settlement of the West, and of the construction of the arch. Dioramas, historical films, etc. Don't miss it. Open daily.

    National Bowling Hall of Fame and Museum, 111 Stadium Plaza (231-6340): traces the history of bowling from Ancient Egypt to the present day. Exhibits associated with the great names in bowling. Should be seen; open daily.

    National Museum of Transport, 3015 Barrett Station Rd., Barretts, 16 mi. (25km) SW on I-44W and I-270N (965-7988): From mule-drawn streetcars to electric locomotives, two centuries of transportation in the U.S. Hundreds of antique locomotives, railroad cars, buses, trucks, streetcars, horse-drawn vehicles, etc. Well worth the trip. Open daily. 25 min. from downtown.

    St. Louis Science Center, Forest Park, 5100 Clayton Ave. (289-4400): Huge educational complex comprising the **Mc-Donnell Planetarium** with its ultramodern equipment (laserium, Star Theater, etc.), the **Medical Museum,** and the **Museum of Science and Natural History.** Among them they offer a complete panorama of the natural sciences and the evolution of man, from a life-size dinosaur to a simulated earthquake. Fascinating; don't miss it. Open daily.

    St. Louis Sports Hall of Fame, Busch Stadium, 100 Stadium Plaza (421-3263): A must for all fans, particularly lovers of football and baseball. Many sports memorabilia, trophies, World Series movies, etc. A must-see; open daily year round.

PANORAMAS: **Gateway Arch,** 2nd St. at the foot of Chestnut St. (425-4465): From the top of Eero Saarinen's 630-ft. (192m) stainless-steel arch there's a spectacular view of the city and the Mississippi River. On a clear day you can see 30 mi. (48km) in all directions. Access to the Observation Room is by an unusual elevator whose passenger capsules move on an inclined plane (see also "Monuments," above). A sight to be seen. Open daily.

PARKS & GARDENS: **Forest Park,** bounded by Lindell Blvd., Skinker Blvd., Kingshighway Blvd., and Oakland Ave. (535-5050): 1,293 acres (482ha) of gardens, lakes, and groves less than 15 min. from dwntwn; the 1904 World's Fair was held here. Many museums and a well-known zoo; skating rink; two public golf courses. Worth a visit; open daily.

    Grant's Farm, 10501 Gravois Rd., in Grantwood Village (843-1700): Deer and buffalo roam free on 281 acres (114ha) of park and woodland belonging to the Anheuser-Busch brewery. See the log cabin where, in 1856, lived Ulysses S. Grant, who went on to become Northern commander-in-chief during the Civil War and 18th president of the U.S.; plus the stables of the famous Clydesdales and a very fine collection of horse-drawn vehicles. A mini-train takes you around the exhibits. Open Tues–Sun June–Aug, Thurs–Sun in spring and fall; closed the rest of the year. 25 min. from downtown on Mo. 30SW.

☼♨♨ **Laumeier Sculpture Park,** Geyer Rd. and Rott Rd. (821-1209): One of the country's finest modern-sculpture gardens, with works of such American and foreign artists as Donald Judd, Dennis Oppenheim, Michael Steiner, Giacomo Manzù, David von Schlegell, Lynn Chadwick, Jackie Ferrara, Ernest Trova, etc. Be sure to see *The Way,* a monumental sculpture by Jack Zehrt. Also a gallery offering contemporary art exhibitions, plus a museum shop. An absolute must. Park open daily; gallery Wed–Sun. 20 min from downtown on I-44.

♨ **Lone Elk Park,** Mo. 141 and N. Outer Rd. (889-3192): Small wildland park with free-roaming animals—bison, Barbados sheep, elk, deer, etc., which you can see from your car along a scenic drive. Walking trails and picnic area. Well worth the trip. 25 min. from downtown on I-44W. Open daily.

☼♨♨ **Missouri Botanical Garden,** 4344 Shaw Blvd. (577-5100): Named Shaw Garden after the businessman and amateur botanist who laid it out in 1859, this magnificent 79-acre (32ha) botanic garden has a superb rose garden, waterfalls, a "scented garden" for the blind, and Seiwa En, the largest Japanese garden in North America. Tropical domed greenhouse, more than a century old, the Climatron. You tour the garden in a mini-train. Don't miss it; open daily.

PERFORMING ARTS: For daily listings of all shows and cultural events, consult the entertainment pages of the daily *St. Louis Post-Dispatch* (morning), the weekly *Riverfront Times,* and the monthly *St. Louis* magazine.

American Theater, 416 N. 9th St. (231-7000): The biggest Broadway hits. The building dates from 1917.

Black Repertory Company, 2240 St. Louis Ave. (231-3706): Contemporary theater, dance performances. At the 23rd St. Theatre.

CASA/Conservatory and School for the Arts, 560 Trinity Ave. at Delmar (863-3033): Concerts, classical-music recitals, opera.

Edison Theater, Forsyth Blvd. and Hoyt Dr. (889-6543): Contemporary and avant-garde theater; ballet performances by the St. Louis Dancers. On the campus of Washington University.

Fabulous Fox Theater, 527 N. Grand Blvd. (534-1111): Pop concerts, big-name shows, musicals, etc. Wonderful rococo interior. Sept–May.

Goldenrod **Showboat,** Riverfront, 700 N. L. K. Sullivan Blvd. (621-3311): Melodrama, comedy, variety; dinner-theater. Also the location of the annual National Classic Jazz and Ragtime Festival. It's an authentic 1909 showboat.

Loretto–Hilton Center, 130 Edgar Rd. (968-4925): Classical and contemporary theater; home of the Repertory Theater of St. Louis and the Opera Theater of St. Louis. Sept–Apr.

Municipal Theater/MUNY, Forest Park (361-1900): 12,000-seat open-air amphitheater presenting musicals, ballet, operettas, Broadway hits. Mid-June to Aug.

Powell Symphony Hall, 718 N. Grand Blvd. (534-1700): Classical concerts and recitals in a richly decorated auditorium. Home of the renowned St. Louis Symphony, founded in 1880, the second oldest in the country (principal conductor: Leonard Slatkin). Mid-May to mid-Sept.

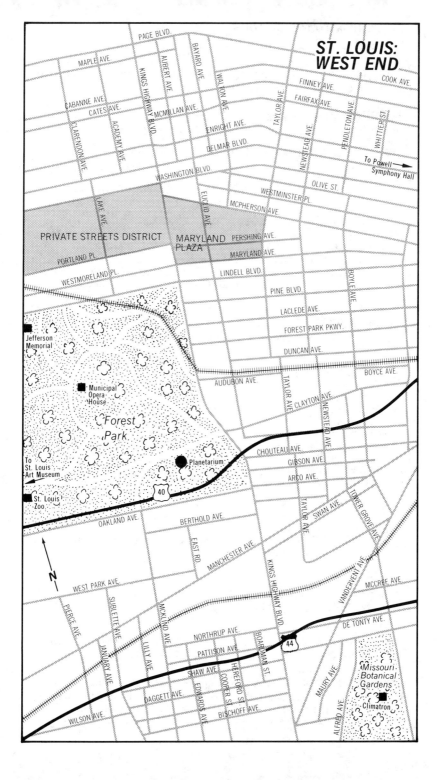

Theater Project Company, 4219 Laclede St. (531-1301): Off Broadway shows.

Westport Playhouse, 600 West Port Pl. (275-8787): St. Louis's only theater-in-the-round. Contemporary theater, big-name shows, musicals.

SHOPPING: **Maryland Plaza,** between Kingshighway Blvd. and Euclid Ave.: Dozens of luxury stores, bars, restaurants, and unusual boutiques: style and quality both.

Plaza Frontenac, Clayton Rd. at Lindbergh Blvd. (432-5800): Two floors of department stores (Saks Fifth Avenue, Neiman-Marcus), boutiques, and trendy restaurants in an ultramodern setting.

☼ **St. Louis Centre,** bounded by Washington Ave. and 6th St., 7th St., and Locust St. (231-5913): One of the largest urban shopping malls in the country. Opened in 1985, this enormous four-floor complex stretches across two full blocks in the heart of downtown, with more than 200 stores, shops, and restaurants.

Union Station, 1820 Market St. (421-6655): The old St. Louis Central Railroad Station, built at the turn of the century and now converted, at a cost of $135 million, into a vast shopping mall with more than 120 boutiques, stores, restaurants, and cafés, as well as fountains, a lagoon, and a luxury hotel.

SPECIAL EVENTS: For the exact schedule of events below, consult the **St. Louis Convention and Visitors Commission** (see "Tourist Information," above).

International Festival (last wknd in May): International food festival, dancing, folklore displays, and exhibitions of foreign handcrafts. Lively and colorful. Forest Park.

National Classic Jazz and Ragtime Festival (mid-June): Annual festival of New Orleans jazz and ragtime aboard the *Goldenrod* Showboat; a classic in the field since 1964. For information, call 621-3311.

Veiled Prophet Fair (4 days around July 4): St. Louis's great popular festivity. Parades, fireworks, open-air concerts, marathon, art exhibitions, etc. Draws hundreds of thousands of participants. Riverfront.

Strassenfest (late July to early Aug): The festival of the local German community; music, overeating, and beer flowing—in a manner of speaking—like water.

Jour de Fête à Ste. Geneviève (second wknd in Aug): Parades, art exhibitions, old-house tours (see "Nearby Excursions," below). For information, call 883-5750.

Forest Park Balloon Race (Sept): Annual hot-air-balloon race, drawing contestants from all over the country. Forest Park.

SPORTS: St. Louis has two professional teams:
Baseball (Apr–Oct): Cardinals, Busch Memorial Stadium (421-3060).
Ice Hockey (Oct–Apr): Blues, Arena (781-5300).

Horse Racing
Fairmount Park, U.S. 40 at Collinsville, Ill. (618/345-4300): Thoroughbred-racing Mar–Nov; harness racing Nov–Mar.

STROLLS: ⚓ **The Hill,** around S. Kingshighway Blvd. and Shaw Blvd: The local "Little Italy," with food stores and *trattorie* more Italian than Rome; even the fire hydrants are painted in the Italian national colors. Lively and colorful.

☼⚓ **Laclede's Landing,** Riverfront north of Eads Bridge: The heart of historic St. Louis, come to life right out of the 1870s, bears witness to the city's prosperity right after the War Between the States. Cobbled alleys, cast-iron lamps, old shops, boutiques, nightclubs, and restaurants. A picturesque environment at the river's edge; you shouldn't miss this stroll.

☀☖☖ **The Levee,** N. L. K. Sullivan Blvd., between the Poplar St. Bridge and Eads Bridge: Beside this quay on the Mississippi are moored a number of craft: *Goldenrod* Showboat, a paddlewheeler from 1909 now converted into a floating theater (see "Historic Buildings," above); U.S.S. *Inaugural*, a World War II minesweeper, now a naval museum; and the river cruisers now used for short trips on the Mississippi, *Huck Finn, President, Tom Sawyer,* and *Becky Thatcher.* Should be seen.

THEME PARKS: ☖ **Six Flags over Mid-America,** Allentown Rd., in Eureka, 30 mi. (48km) SW on I-44 (938-4800): Enormous theme park with a round 100 carousels, roller coasters, and other attractions, including a huge Ferris wheel known as "Colossus." Open daily from the end of May to Aug, wknds only in spring and fall; closed the rest of the year.

ZOOS: ☀☖ **St. Louis Zoological Park,** Forest Park (781-0900): One of the top 10 zoos in the country, with 2,800 animals in reconstructions of their natural habitat; be sure to see "Big Cat Country," where lions, tigers, and other big cats live in semi-freedom. Impressive "Jungle of the Apes," with gorillas, chimpanzees, and orangutans. Worth visiting in its mini-train. Open daily.

ACCOMMODATIONS

A Note on Accommodations: Room rates in St. Louis are coded as follows: **VE,** Very Expensive ($140 and up); **E,** Expensive ($90–$140); **M,** Moderate ($60–$90); **I,** Inexpensive ($30–$60); **B,** Budget (up to $30). A listing of toll free numbers is in the Appendix.

Personal Favorites (in order of preference)

♟♟♟ **Adam's Mark** (dwntwn), 4th St. and Chestnut St., MO 63102 (314/241-7400; toll free 800/444-2326). 910 rms, A/C, color TV, in-rm movies. AE, CB, DC, MC, V. Valet gar. $8, two pools, health club, sauna, racquetball, rest. (Faust's), coffee shop, three bars, 24-hr. rm svce, disco, hrdrsr, boutiques, concierge, free crib. *Note:* The best location in St. Louis, at the foot of the Gateway Arch. Ultramodern 18-story building w. unobstructed view of city, arch, or river. Richly decorated interior w. Flemish tapestries, Italian marble, French crystal chandeliers, two Ludovico De Luigi bronze horses in the lobby. Very spacious, comfortable rms, some w. refrigerators. Flawless reception and svce. Two VIP floors; big business clientele; in the heart of dwntwn. **E–VE**

☀♟♟♟ **Hyatt Regency at Union Station** (formerly the Omni International; dwntwn), 1 Union Station, MO 63103 (314/231-1234; toll free, see Hyatt). 542 rms, A/C, color TV in-rm movies. AE, CB, DC, MC, V. Valet parking $10, rest., coffee shop, bar, 24-hr. rm svce, nightclub, boutiques, free crib. *Note:* This new gem of the local hotel scene occupies a whole lavishly restored wing of the former Union Station, and boasts high vaulting, marble floors, stained glass, and magnificent turn-of-the-century decor (see "Architectural Highlights," above). Huge, elegant rms; ultramodern comfort; excellent svce. Direct access to Union Station Shopping Mall w. its 120 boutiques, cafés, and rests. An unusual, unusually successful, hotel w. a unique atmosphere. Three VIP floors. **E–VE**

☀♟♟♟ **Hotel Majestic** (dwntwn), 1019 Pine St., MO 63101 (314/436-2355; toll free 800/451-2355). 95 mini-suites, A/C, cable color TV. AE, CB, DC, MC, V. Valet gar. $8, rest. (Richard Perry's), bar, 24-hr. rm svce, concierge, free crib. *Note:* Elegant small European-style hotel in an old dwntwn building luxuriously rehabilitated. Classy interior w. marble floors and Oriental rugs. All rms are spacious, comfortable mini-suites w. period furniture. Personalized reception and svce. Very good rest. (American cuisine). VIP and big business clientele. Style and distinction. **E–VE**

♀♀ **Radisson Hotel Clayton** (formerly the Clayton Inn; nr. dwntwn), 7750 Carondelet Ave., Clayton, MO 63105 (314/726-5400; toll free, see Radisson). 212 rms, A/C, color TV, in-rm movies. AE, CB, DC, MC, V. Free valet gar., two pools, health club, sauna, two rests., bar, rm svce, nightclub, hrdrsr, free breakfast, free crib. *Note:* Modern hotel in a new residential neighborhood on the west edge of the city. Spacious contemporary rms w. minibars. Good physical-fitness facilities; diligent svce; acceptable rests. (the Café Clayton also offers a fine view of the city). Business and group clientele. Airport shuttle. 15 min. from dwntwn by car. **M–E**

♀♀ **Days Inn at the Arch** (formerly the Hilton Bel Air; dwntwn), 333 Washington Ave., MO 63102 (314/621-7900; toll free, see Days Inns). 182 rms, A/C, color TV, in-rm movies. AE, CB, DC, MC, V. Parking $5, pool, sauna, rest., bar, valet svce, free crib. *Note:* Large, modern 17-story tower halfway between the Gateway Arch and the Cervantes Convention Center. Functional but inviting. Spacious rms w. balconies, the best looking out on the arch. Business clientele. Good value on balance. **M–E**

♀ **Forest Park Hotel** (nr. dwntwn), 4910 W. Pine Blvd., MO 63108 (314/361-3500; toll free 800/622-4910). 200 rms, A/C, color TV, in-rm movies. AE, CB, DC, MC, V. Free parking, pool, 24-hr. coffee shop, bar, rm svce, nightclub, free crib. *Note:* Aging but spick-and-span hotel agreeably modernized. Rms a little cramped but comfortable. Friendly reception and svce. Very near Forest Park, 15 min. from dwntwn. Very good value; regular clientele. **I–M**

Other Accommodations (from top bracket to budget)

♀♀♀♀ **Mayfair Hotel** (dwntwn), St. Charles St. at 8th St., MO 63101 (314/421-2500; toll free, see Preferred). 169 suites. A/C, color TV, in-rm movies. AE, CB, DC, MC, V. Gar. $8, pool, health club, two rests. (including the Mayfair Room), bar, rm svce, concierge. *Note:* Originally built in 1925, this luxurious small hotel in the European manner reopened in July 1990 after a complete renovation which has magnificently restored its pristine appearance. Suites only, spacious and sinfully comfortable, w. minibar. Polished, considerate svce; rests. of high quality. VIP clients. Very well located near the Cervantes Convention Center. The new *grande dame* of St. Louis's hotels. **E–VE**

♀♀♀ **Marriott's Pavilion** (dwntwn), 1 Broadway, MO 63102 (314/421-1776; toll free, see Marriott). 672 rms, A/C, color TV, in-rm movies. AE, CB, DC, MC, V. Gar. $8, pool, sauna, health club, two rests. (including J. W. Carver's), bars, rm svce, hrdrsr, concierge, free breakfast, free crib. *Note:* A successful union of the former Spanish pavilion (whence the hotel's name) from the 1964 New York World's Fair, now the hotel lobby, with two modern, functional 25-story towers overlooking Busch Stadium. Comfortable, well-designed rms w. minibars, the best looking out on Gateway Arch. Efficient svce. Group and convention clientele. Very complete facilities. On the noisy side when there's a game at Busch Stadium, but excellent location in the heart of dwntwn. **E–VE**

♀♀ **Embassy Suites** (dwntwn), 901 N. 1st St., MO 63102 (314/241-4200; toll free 800/362-2779). 300 suites, A/C, color TV, in-rm movies. AE, CB, DC, MC, V. Parking $6, pool, health club, sauna, rest. (Joe B's), bar, rm svce, disco, free breakfast, free crib. *Note:* Modern hotel for the business traveler; suites only, spacious and comfortable w. balconies, minibars, and refrigerators. Spectacular eight-floor-high lobby w. interior grdn. Right in the Laclede's Landing neighborhood, w. its rests., boutiques, and lively nightlife. Free shuttle thru business district. **E**

♀♀ **Clarion Hotel** (formerly Stouffer's; dwntwn), 200 S. 4th St., MO 63102 (314/241-9500; toll free, see Clarion). 853 rms,

A/C, color TV, in-rm movies. AE, CB, DC, MC, V. Gar. $8, two pools, health club, sauna, rest. (Top of the Riverfront), coffee shop, bars, rm svce, hrdrsr, concierge, free crib. *Note:* Modern 28-floor circular towers on the Mississippi. Spacious, agreeable rms, some w. refrigerators. Svce functional, but no more. Acceptable revolving rest. on top floor; unobstructed view of Gateway Arch (ask for a rm overlooking the river). Rather obtrusive group and convention clientele. Three VIP floors. Recently redecorated and refurnished. **M–E**

🍷🍷 **Holiday Inn Riverfront** (dwntwn), 200 N. 4th St., MO 63102
(314/621-8200; toll free, see Holiday Inns). 458 rms, A/C, color TV, in-rm movies. AE, CB, DC, MC, V. Free gar., pool, sauna, rest., coffee shop, bar, rm svce, nightclub, free breakfast. *Note:* Huge 30-story tower looking out on the Mississippi. Holiday Inn style, completely modernized. The better rms, w. balconies (a third w. kitchenettes), overlook the river and the Gateway Arch. Efficient svce. Excellent location; business clientele. **M–E**

🍷🍷 **Drury Inn** (dwntwn), Union Station, 201 S. 20th St., MO 63103 (314/231-3900; toll free 800/325-8300). 180 rms, A/C, color TV, in-rm movies. AE, CB, DC, MC, V. Free parking, pool, rest., bar, valet svce, free crib. *Note:* Unusual red-brick structure adj. Union Station—a skillfully renovated turn-of-the-century YMCA! Captivating interior as well; very comfortable rms, some w. refrigerator. Good svce; good value overall. Business clientele. **M–E**

🍷 **Motel 6 Northeast** (vic.), 1405 Dunn Rd., MO 63138 (314/869-9400). 81 rms, A/C, color TV, in-rm movies. AE, DC, MC, V. Free parking, pool. *Note:* Unbeatable value if you're traveling by car, 20 min. from dwntwn via I-70 and Mo. 367. Functionally comfortable. **B–I**

🍷 **Thrifty Inn** (dwntwn), 1100 N. 3rd St., MO 63102 (314/421-6556; toll free 800/325-8300). 48 rms, A/C, color TV. AE, CB, DC, MC, V. Street parking, no bar or rest. *Note:* Brand-new small motel a hop, skip, and a jump from the nightlife of bohemian Laclede's Landing. Comfortable, functional rms; friendly reception. Very good value 5 min. from the Convention Center. **B**

Airport Accommodations

🍷🍷🍷 **Oakland Park Inn** (vic.), 4505 Woodson Rd., MO 63134 (314/427-4700; toll free 800/426-4700). 155 rms. A/C, cable color TV. AE, DC, MC, V. Free parking, pool, health club, sauna, rest. (Oak Room), bar, rm svce. *Note:* Luxurious, cozy airport hotel, recently enlarged. Spacious, very comfortable rms; flawless svce; very acceptable rest. 5 min. from airport (free shuttle). Business clientele. **M–E**

YMCA/Youth Hostel

Huckleberry Finn (nr. dwntwn), 1904 S. 12th St., MO 63104 (314/241-0076). 40 beds. Typical youth hostel. Set-up somewhat seedy.

RESTAURANTS

A Note on Restaurant Prices: St. Louis restaurant prices, per person, excluding drinks and service charges, are coded as follows: **VE**, Very Expensive ($60 and up); **E**, Expensive ($40–$60); **M**, Moderate ($25–$40) **I**, Inexpensive ($15–$25); **B**, Budget (up to $15).

Personal Favorites (in order of preference)

🍸🍸🍸🍸 **Tony's** (dwntwn), 826 N. Broadway (231-7007). A/C. Dinner only, Mon–Sat; closed hols. and the first week in July. AE, CB, DC, MC, V. J&T. *Specialties:* fresh homemade pasta (tagliatelle marinara, cavatelli e broccoli), lobster albanello, veal piemontese, fish of the day, first-class red meats, zabaglione. Superb desserts. Menu changes regularly. Very fine list of European and American wines. *Note:* Since 1949 Vincent Bommarito has presided, diplomatically but firmly, over this shrine of Italian-American gastronomy. The antique decor w. numerous artworks and subdued lighting make for a romantic atmosphere. Reception and svce of the highest order. Resv. advisable. One of the best Italian rests. in the U.S. Prices to match. Valet parking. *Italian/ Continental.* **M–E**

☙☙☙ **Fio's La Fourchette** (nr. dwntwn), 1153 St. Louis Galleria, Brentwood Blvd. and Clayton Rd. (863-6866). A/C. Dinner only, Tues–Sat; closed hols. AE, MC, V. Jkt. *Specialties:* mousse of veal and Brie cheese in pastry shell, broiled sweetbreads w. leeks, roast duck w. fennel and rosemary, médaillons of veal w. mushroom-and-brandy cream, seafood (flown in daily), very good homemade desserts (particularly the soufflé praline). Menu changes regularly. *Note:* With its modern, light-filled decor, luxuriant plants, and pastel-colored walls, this charming rest., hidden away in an outlying shopping center, quickly established itself as the best local exponent of French nouvelle cuisine. Every dish bears witness to the imaginative elegance and refinement of the very talented young Swiss chef Fio Antognini, while the prices are surprisingly moderate. Very good svce. An excellent place to eat; resv. strongly advised. 25 min. from dwntwn. *French.* **M**

☙☙☙ **Richard Perry** (dwntwn), in the Hotel Majestic (see "Accommodations," above) (771-4100). A/C. Breakfast/lunch/ dinner daily, brunch Sun. AE, CB, DC, MC, V. Jkt. *Specialties:* grilled rabbit sausage w. honey-mustard sauce, sea scallops w. citrus-butter sauce, chicken hash over basil-tinged waffles, lamb cutlet w. red-currant sauce, lobster w. fresh pasta, roast duck w. dates, sole stuffed w. lobster mousse in green sauce, roast pork w. cassis, savory desserts. Very good list of American wines. *Note:* The rest.'s last move and redecoration mellowed the atmosphere, but didn't change the excellence of Richard Perry's food, inspired by old American regional recipes. Diligent svce. Locally popular, so resv. advised. Valet parking evenings. *American.* **I–M**

☙☙ **Al Baker's** (nr. dwntwn), 8101 Clayton Rd. (863-8878). A/C. Dinner only, Mon–Sat; closed hols. and 2 weeks in July. AE, CB, DC, MC, V. Jkt. *Specialties:* fresh homemade pasta, steamed mussels, hobo steak w. mustard sauce, lamb Monastiraki, beef w. marsala, sautéed yellowtail w. red-wine vinegar and shallots, veal Oscar New Orleans style, fish of the day. The best wine list in St. Louis. *Note:* Somewhat overornate decor w. a profusion of art objects, old paintings, tapestries, and period furniture, but the predominantly Italian food is elegant and relatively light. Remarkable svce. A St. Louis landmark; resv. advised. 25 min. from dwntwn. Valet parking. *Italian/ Continental.* **M**

☼☙☙ **Busch's Grove** (nr. dwntwn), 9160 Clayton Rd. (993-0011). A/C. Lunch/dinner Tues–Sat. MC, V. *Specialties:* toasted ravioli (a St. Louis specialty), "Russ's salad," calves' liver w. onions, prime rib, barbecued ribs, steak, fish of the day, peanut-butter cream pie. *Note:* A local tradition for almost a century; if you can eat only one meal in St. Louis, eat it here— particularly in fine weather, when the regulars crowd into the grdn w. its romantic arbors. The food is as serious, and flawless, as the svce. A very fine place. 20 min. from dwntwn. *American.* **I–M**

☙ **Café Zoe** (dwntwn), 1923 Park Ave. (241-9122). A/C. Lunch Mon–Sat, dinner Fri–Sat only. AE, MC, V. *Specialties:* duck salad w. grapes, sandwiches, shrimp w. pesto sauce, broiled chicken w. rosemary, Thai marinated beef, very good desserts. Menu changes regularly. *Note:* Crowded daily at lunch by white-collar workers, Zoe's is the fashionable place for a quick meal. Imaginative dishes w. a touch of American nouvelle cuisine (particularly the specialty salads and the broiled foods) at very attractive prices. Relaxed atmosphere. Resv. advised for dinner. *American.* **B–I**

Other Restaurants (from top bracket to budget)

☙☙☙☙ **Anthony's** (dwntwn), Equitable Bldg., 10 S. Broadway (231-2434). A/C. Lunch Mon–Fri, dinner Mon–Sat; closed hols.

AE, CB, DC, MC, V. J&T. *Specialties:* duck w. sauce bigarade, scallops poached in white wine, roast rack of lamb, scampi w. mustard, sweetbreads and chanterelle mushrooms in dill sauce, veal Francesca. Very good wine list. *Note:* Smoked mirrors and polished steel make for a rather chilly, impersonal setting, but the cuisine of Tony Bommarito (brother of Vince, the owner of Tony's) will quickly warm you up again. Some sophisticated dishes of French-Italian inspiration. Ultra-professional svce. Valet parking. Resv. strongly advised. *Continental.* **M–E**

🍸🍸🍸 **Giovanni's** (nr. dwntwn), 5201 Shaw Ave. (772-5985). A/C. Dinner only, Mon–Sat; closed hols. and the first week of July. AE, DC, MC, V. J&T. *Specialties:* "presidential bow tie" (smoked salmon pasta as served to President Reagan at his inaugural banquet), peppardelle con porcini, osso buco, saltimbocca alla Giovanni, seafood ravioli, chicken florentina, broiled scampi. Very good desserts; large wine list. *Note:* All the gastronomic classics of northern Italy in an elegant peach-colored setting w. old paintings and crystal chandeliers. Warm, intimate atmosphere. Excellent svce. One of St. Louis's great rests.; resv. necessary. Valet parking. 10 min. from dwntwn. *Italian.* **M**

🍸🍸 **Cardwell's** (nr. dwntwn), 8100 Maryland Ave. (726-5055). A/C. Lunch Mon–Sat, dinner nightly. AE, CB, DC, MC, V. Jkt. *Specialties:* grilled scallops w. spicy Thai peanut sauce; scallopine of fresh venison w. wild tart cherry and red wine sauce; sautéed catfish w. roasted pecans, fresh fennel, and bacon; broiled pompano filet w. lime butter and papaya jelly; first-class grilled meats cooked over a pecan-wood fire; remarkable soufflés. Good wine list. Menu changes regularly. *Note:* St. Louis's most imaginative rest. serving American nouvelle cuisine. The young chef, Bill Cardwell, whose creative talents are becoming more and more evident, never ceases to surprise and to charm. Decor of dark woods, open kitchen, and noisy atmosphere. Svce a trifle helter-skelter. Resv. advised. Valet parking. *American.* **M**

🍸🍸 **Chez Louis** (nr. dwntwn), in the Seven Gables Inn, 26 N. Meramec Ave., Clayton (863-8400). A/C. Lunch Mon–Fri, dinner Mon–Sat; closed hols. AE, DC, MC, V. *Specialties:* salad of smoked duck and endive, scallops w. lobster sauce, sea bass w. clams, fresh tuna béarnaise, lamb cutlets provençal. Very good desserts; splendid wine list w. more than 100 labels. *Note:* Elegant little French bistro serving chef Bernard Douteau's light, imaginative cuisine. Cozy 1900s inn decor w. a handsome collection of posters and artworks. Impeccable svce; successful enough for you to need resv. Valet parking. 20 min. from dwntwn on the Daniel Boone Expwy. and Clayton Rd. *French.* **M**

🍸🍸 **Ruth's Chris Steak House** (dwntwn), 101 S. 11th St. (241-7711). A/C. Lunch Mon–Fri, dinner nightly; closed hols. AE, CB, DC, MC, V. *Specialties:* absolutely prime meats (try the porterhouse steak for two), Maine lobster, lamb chops, broiled chicken, eight kinds of potato. Ho-hum desserts. *Note:* This well-known chain of rests., headquartered in New Orleans, styles itself "the home of serious steaks," and deserves the title. Corn-fed beef, richly marbled and broiled to a turn. Typical steakhouse setting, conventional but comfortable; efficient svce; business clientele. The best place for meat in St. Louis. Resv. advised. *Steak.* **M**

☼🍸🍸 **Kemoll's** (dwntwn), Broadway at Olive St. (534-2705). A/C. Dinner nightly; closed hols. AE, DC, MC, V. *Specialties:* fried artichokes, fettuccine verdi, paglia e fieno, cannelloni, shrimp in mustard sauce, chicken Conti, saltimbocca alla romana. *Note:* Huge, popular Italian rest. serving excellent fresh homemade pasta and Italian regional specialties. Moved into the new Metropolitan Sq. Building in 1989. Pleasant, noisy atmosphere; lots of regular patrons. Friendly svce; resv. advised. Run by the Kemoll family since 1927. *Italian.* **I–M**

🍸 **House of Jamaica** (nr. dwntwn), 6235 Delmar Blvd., University City (725-4308). A/C. Lunch/dinner Mon–Sat; closed hols. AE, DC, MC, V. *Specialties:* Codfish fritters, curried goat, jerked beef stew, escovitched or broiled fish, jerk chicken w. marinade, beef soup. *Note:* Classic Jamaican cooking in an appropriately exotic setting. The food is flavorful, but some of the sauces are explosive. Very slow svce; excellent value, and popular with the locals, especially students at nearby Washington University. 25 min. from dwntwn. *Jamaican.* **B–I**

> **La Sala** (dwntwn), 513 Olive St. (231-5620). A/C. Lunch/dinner Mon–Sat (until 11pm); closed hols. AE, CB, DC, MC, V. *Specialties:* tacos, chiles rellenos, botana mexicana, enchiladas. Good margaritas. *Note:* Very popular Mexican rest. a stone's throw from Busch Stadium. Agreeable folk-type setting; good, unpretentious food. Crowded on days of games and evenings after shows. The buffet at lunch is good value. Pleasant background music. No resv. *Mexican.* **B–I**

> **Yen Ching** (nr. dwntwn), 1012 S. Brentwood Blvd. (721-7507). A/C. Lunch Mon–Fri, dinner nightly. AE, MC, V. *Specialties:* sizzling-rice soup, Szechuan chicken, princess prawns, spicy crispy beef, sweet-and-sour fish, Mongolian beef, Peking and Szechuan dishes. *Note:* One of the few acceptable Far Eastern rests. in St. Louis. The food is authentic and tasty, the decor totally uninteresting, and the svce. friendly. Locally very popular; resv. advised. *Chinese.* **B–I**

Cafeterias/Fast Food

Culpeppers (nr. dwntwn), 300 N. Euclid Ave. (361-2828). Lunch/dinner daily (until midnight). AE, MC, V. Remarkably good homemade soups (onion, vegetable, chicken, gazpacho, etc.) and substantial sandwiches have made the reputation of this nice, noisy bar.

Miss Hulling's (dwntwn), 11th St. and Locust St. (436-0840). Open Mon–Sat (from morning till 8pm). AE, DC, MC, V. Very respectable cafeteria food in a pleasant garden setting. A St. Louis tradition for 60 years. Other location: 725 Olive St. (436-0404), same hrs.

O'Connell's Pub (nr. dwntwn), 4652 Shaw Ave. at Kingshighway Blvd. (773-6600). Lunch/dinner Mon–Sat (until midnight). MC, V. By general consent the best hamburgers in town. Also excellent roast-beef sandwiches and several kinds of beer. Typical Irish-pub atmosphere.

BARS & NIGHTCLUBS

Funny Bone Comedy Club (dwntwn), 940 W. Port Plaza (469-6692). National and local headliners for a modest price and a two-drink minimum.

Goldenrod Showboat (dwntwn), Riverfront, 700 N. L. K. Sullivan Blvd. (621-3311). Bar, jazz, variety, melodrama on an old Mississippi sidewheeler. Amusing. Open Tues–Sun.

Houlihan's (dwntwn), 147 St. Louis Union Station (436-0844). Popular, inviting singles bar with an acceptable rest. Open nightly.

Mississippi Nights (dwntwn), 914 N. 1st St. (421-3853). Fashionable nightclub in the heart of Laclede's Landing. Live music nightly.

Muddy Water Saloon (dwntwn), 724 N. 1st St. (421-5335). The best modern jazz club in town. Live music on wknds. Trendy clientele. Open nightly.

64 West (nr. dwntwn), 5130 Oakland Ave. (535-6455). $5-hi-tech nightclub and café featuring a spectacular laser light show and a 16-video-monitor matrix wall. Popular with yuppies. Open nightly.

Whitey Herzog's (dwntwn), Power House Bldg., Union Station (621-5900). Nightclub named for the longtime St. Louis Cardinals baseball manager. Complete music library from big band to the latest video hits. Also a rest. Open nightly.

NEARBY EXCURSIONS

BONNE TERRE (62 mi./99km SW via I-55 and U.S. 67): In this small town, where mining was actively pursued from

1870 to 1962, there still remain enormous excavations under its streets which are open to visitors; inquire at Park St. and Allen St. (358-2148); open daily year round. Don't fail to see the amazing **Billion Gallon Underground Lake,** with its 17 mi. (27km) of navigable channels, visited every year by more than 7,000 scuba-divers. North of the town, **Washington State Park,** on Mo. 47 (586-2995), open daily year round, possesses hundreds of Native American petroglyphs. Worth seeing. Combine this with the trip to Sainte Geneviève (see below).

Where to Stay

☼⚐⚐ **Mansion Hill Country Inn,** Mansion Hill Dr., Bonne Terre, MO 63628 (358-5311). 10 rms. Charming, elegantly restored Victorian home. Closed Sun–Mon. **M**

☼ **CAHOKIA MOUNDS STATE HISTORIC SITE** (in Collinsville, Ill., 9 mi./15km east via I-70) (618/346-5160): One of the richest archeological sites in the country—a primitive community extending over 885 acres (380ha), inhabited between 700 and 1400 A.D. and with a population in the tens of thousands. There remain today only two score huge earthen mounds, of the 100 or so originally built, whose size and shape are reminiscent of Mayan pyramids. Particularly impressive is **Monks Mound,** a huge terraced earthwork rising 98 ft. (30m), which owes its name to the Trappist monastery built at its foot in 1809. Interesting archeological museum. Well worth the side trip. Open daily.

☼ **FORT KASKASKIA STATE HISTORIC SITE** (in Ellis Grove, Ill., 52 mi./83km SE over the Poplar Street Bridge along Ill. 3) (618/589-3741): Built by the French in 1736, and destroyed by them in 1763 to prevent its passing into the hands of the British under the terms of the Treaty of Paris, this fort, of which only traces remain today, occupied a strategic position in a bend of the Mississippi. The nearby **Pierre Menard Mansion,** built in 1802 in the style of a Louisiana plantation house, at the foot of a bluff overlooking the river, is worth a visit. Nicknamed the "Mount Vernon of the West" on account of its elegant design, and today superbly restored, the house was visited by Lafayette in 1824. Well worth the side trip. Open daily year round. Combine this with the visit to Cahokia Mounds State Historic Site (above).

☼ **HANNIBAL** (108 mi./172km NW via I-70 and Mo. 79): Little Mississippi River port where Samuel Langhorne Clemens, better known as Mark Twain, passed much of his youth. Now entirely devoted to the cult of the famous author of *Tom Sawyer* and *Huckleberry Finn,* the city abounds in all kinds of museums. Make a point of seeing the ⚐ **Mark Twain Museum,** with numerous family souvenirs, in the house where he spent his childhood at 208 Hill St. (221-9010), open daily. Also the ⚐ **Mark Twain Cave,** 2 mi. (3km) south on Mo. 79 (221-1656), open daily Apr–Oct, which gave him the idea for *The Adventures of Tom Sawyer.*

Mississippi trips aboard the paddlesteamer *Mark Twain,* Center St. Dock (221-3222), daily May–Oct.

Well worth the detour.

☼ **JEFFERSON BARRACKS HISTORICAL PARK** (Broadway at Kingston Rd., 10 mi./16km south on I-55) (544-5714): Military barracks built in 1826; many of the original buildings have been restored. Interesting military museum. The future Gens. Robert E. Lee and Ulysses S. Grant served here as young officers. Should be seen. Open Wed–Sun.

☼ **MERAMEC CAVERNS** (at Stanton, 65 mi./104km SW on I-44) (468-3166): Vast limestone caves on five levels, used to store gunpowder during the Civil War, and as a hiding place by Jesse James and his gang in the 1870s. The temperature remains constant at 60°F (16°C). Open daily Mar–Dec. A definite must-see.

☼ ♟♟ **SAINTE GENEVIEVE** (64 mi./102km south on I-55 and U.S. 61): One of the oldest (1720) French settlements in the Midwest. The town, which once rivaled St. Louis, still has 40 or so buildings dating from the late 18th and early 19th centuries, giving it something of the flavor of Old France. Among them are the 1770 **Bolduc House** at 123 S. Main St., the 1770 **Amoureaux House** on St. Mary's Rd., the 1790 **Green Tree Inn** at 224 St. Mary's Rd., the 1785 **Guibourd-Valle House** at 1 N. 4th St., and the 1818 **Felix Valle Home** at 198 Merchant St. They are all open daily Apr–Nov. Interesting **historical museum** at Merchant St. and Dubourg Sq. (883-3461), open daily year round.

Very popular festival in Aug (see "Special Events," above). The **Tourist Information Office** is at 66 S. Main St., Sainte Geneviève, MO 63670 (314/883-7097).

Don't miss Sainte Geneviève.

Where to Stay

☼ **St. Gemme Beauvais Inn,** 78 N. Main St., Sainte Geneviève, MO 63670 (314/883-5744). 12 rms, 7 with bath. Elegant 1847 mansion. **I–M**

☼ **Sainte Geneviève,** Main St. and Merchant St., Sainte Geneviève, MO 63670 (314/883-3562). 14 rms. Charming little late 19th-century inn. **I**

OTHER FROMMER TRAVEL GUIDES: Frommer city guides that treat several midwestern cities and their environs in greater deatil are: *Frommer's Chicago, Frommer's Minneapolis & St. Paul,* and *Frommer's St. Louis & Kansas City.*

Frommer travel guides are available in most bookstores, or can be ordered by mail from Frommer Books, Prentice Hall Press, 15 Columbus Circle, New York, N. Y. 10023. Turn to the last pages of this book to learn about Frommer's **Dollarwise Travel Club,** and for ordering information.

CHAPTER 28

KANSAS CITY⚜

□ □ □

Famous for its slaughterhouses (the country's largest) and the size of its steaks, Kansas City, which has been called "the heart of America," is yet much more than the simple "cow town" it was known as in the days of the Old West. First explored by French trappers, the region around Kansas City is unquestionably one of the richest agricultural areas of America, as well as the world's second-largest cattle market. Its strategic position midway between Chicago and the Rockies made it an obligatory stagecoach stop on both of the two great westward routes of the 19th century: the Sante Fe Trail to Albuquerque and the Mexican frontier, and the Oregon Trail to Portland and the Pacific Northwest. From its double historic role, as a center of communications and cattle raising, Kansas City has retained a tradition of hospitality, some first-class hotels, and some of the nation's finest steakhouses, beginning with the renowned Golden Ox in the very precincts of the famous **Stockyards.**

The city's political past is murky; under the Pendergast brothers, corruption and influence-peddling were elevated to a system of government. In the 1920s Kansas City boasted almost 300 speakeasies, brothels, gaming houses, and jazz clubs. Between the two World Wars these dozens of nightclubs, some respectable and some less so, along Vine St. and 18th St. in a district then known as "Little New York," produced musicians of the caliber of "Fats" Waller, Count Basie, Lester Young, and Charlie Parker, making Kansas City one of the great capitals of jazz. Missouri's second city still hosts, every September, a very popular jazz festival. Other remembrances of things past are the picturesque neighborhoods of **Westport Square** and the **City Market,** an open-air market more than a century and a half old, not far from the Missouri River. Kansas City is noted, too, as America's greeting-card and writing-paper capital, since it is headquarters of the vast Hallmark operation.

The broad avenues with their dozens of statues and fountains (many of European origin), the friendliness of the citizens and their taste for good, solid food, and the beauty of the surrounding countryside, particularly the **Lake of the Ozarks,** make Kansas City an attractive and often-overlooked destination, as well as a thriving metropolis. As early as 1946, French biographer and novelist André Maurois wrote in his *Journal de voyages,* "who in Europe, or even in America, knows that Kansas City is one of the loveliest cities on earth?"

In 1989 *Fortune* magazine named Kansas City one of the three best metropolitan areas in the U.S. for business (after Dallas – Fort Worth and Atlanta).

Famous people born in Kansas City include the jazz musicians Charlie Parker and Ben Webster, movie director Robert Altman, and actor Ed Asner. Neighboring **Independence** is the birthplace of movie star Ginger Rogers, but is perhaps best known as the beloved hometown of Pres. Harry S Truman.

BASIC FACTS: State of Missouri; its twin city is Kansas City, Kansas, across the state border. Area code: 816. Time zone: central. ZIP Code: 64108. Founded: 1821. Approximate population: city, 440,000; metropolitan area, 1,560,000. Ranks 24th in size among U.S. metropolitan areas.

CLIMATE: The climate of the Midwest plains is the most pleasant in the spring, apart from frequent showers, and in the fall, which is the ideal season for a visit. Summer is hot and humid, with average temperatures in July of 82°F (28°C). Winter is very harsh and often below freezing, especially in Jan with a mean temperature of 30°F (−1°C). *Warning:* There are often tornadoes in late spring.

DISTANCES: Chicago, 500 mi. (800km); Dallas, 490 mi. (785km); Denver, 600 mi. (960km); Memphis, 450 mi. (720km); Minneapolis, 443 mi. (710km); St. Louis, 259 mi. (415km).

ARRIVAL & TRANSIT INFORMATION

AIRPORT: Mid-Continent International Airport (MCI), 18 mi. (29km) NW, one of the most up-to-date in the country. For information, call 243-5200.

AIRLINES: Air Midwest (toll free 800/835-2953), American (221-7767), America West (471-7141), Continental (471-3700), Delta (471-1828), Eastern (toll free 800/327-8376), Midway (toll free 800/621-5700), Northwest (474-1104), Southwest (474-1221), TWA (842-4000), United (471-6060), and USAir (toll free 800/428-4322).

CITY LINK: The **cab** fare to city center is about $25–$30; time, 30–40 min. Bus: **KCI Airport Express** (243-5950), serving the principal hotels, leaves every 30 min.; fare, about $10–$15; time, 45 min.

Since the dwntwn district is compact, you may not need to rent a car, unless you intend to make the (very worthwhile) excursions available in the area. Public transportation (bus) is relatively efficient; call the Area Transit Authority **(The Metro)** (221-0660) for information. Bright-red open-air **trolleys** run a continuous circuit through Kansas City dwntwn, Westport, Crown Center, and Country Club Plaza with several stops along the route, 7 days a week Mar–Dec; fare, $3 with three reboarding passes; call 221-3399 for information.

CAR RENTAL (at Kansas City International Airport unless otherwise indicated): Avis (243-5760); Budget (243-5757); Dollar (243-5600); Hertz (243-5765); National (243-5770); Thrifty, 11530 NW Prairie View Rd. (464-5670). For dwntwn locations, consult the local telephone directory.

LIMOUSINE SERVICES: Carey Limousine (587-4077), Mid-America Limousine (346-4848).

TAXIS: Cabs may not be hailed on the street, but they can be taken at the stands in front of the major hotels, or summoned by telephone: **Economy Cabs** (621-3436) or **Yellow Cab** (471-5000).

Warning: Cabs in Kansas City operate on a deregulated meter system and each cab company is free to set its own rates. Consequently, fares can vary widely.

TRAIN: Amtrak station, 2200 Main St. (421-4725).

INTERCITY BUSES: Greyhound, 1101 Troost Ave. (221-2835).

INFORMATION & TOURS

TOURIST INFORMATION: The **Kansas City Convention and Visitors Bureau,** City Center Sq. Building (Suite 2550), 1100 Main St., MO 64105 (816/221-5242; toll free 800/767-7700).

For a **tape-recorded list of current cultural events and shows,** call 816/ 474-9600.

GUIDED TOURS: Kansas City Sightseeing (bus) (833-4083): Guided tours of the city, serving principal dwntwn hotels.
  Missouri River Excursions (boat), Westport Landing, at the foot of Grand Ave. (913/281-5300): Trips along the Missouri on board the *Missouri River Queen.* Daily Mar–Oct.

SIGHTS, ATTRACTIONS & ACTIVITIES

ARCHITECTURAL HIGHLIGHTS: 🏛 **Board of Trade,** 4800 Main St. (753-7500): World's largest winter-wheat market. From the visitors' gallery on the third floor you can watch the frenzied brokers. Should be seen. Open Mon–Fri.
  🏛 **City Hall,** 414 E. 12th St. (274-2605): A building from the early '30s in the purest art deco style. From the 30th floor there's a fine view of the city (see "Panoramas," below).
  🏛 **Crown Center,** Pershing St. and Grand Ave. (274-8444): Ultramodern commercial and office complex built on a rise overlooking the city at a cost of $300 million. Includes two luxury hotels; some 60 stores and boutiques; 18 restaurants; six movie houses; a theater, the **Hallmark Visitors Center,** focusing on the history of the greeting card industry; and a huge plaza with free concerts in summer and ice skating in winter. Lively, animated scene; you should see it. Open daily.
  🏛 **Livestock Exchange and Stockyards,** Genessee St. and 17th St. (842-6800): Well-known slaughterhouses and the country's most important livestock exchange. Auctions Tues, Wed, Thurs morning (visitors allowed). Guaranteed local color; don't miss it.

MARKETS: ☀🏛 **City Market,** Walnut St. and 3rd St. (842-1271): Picturesque open-air market in existence for more than a century and a half. Dozens of stalls and food stands. Justifies Kansas City's reputation for good food. Open Mon–Sat.

MONUMENTS: 🏛 **Liberty Memorial,** 100 W. 26th St. (221-1918): This 217-ft. (66m) tower (elevator) offers a very fine view of the city. Museum dedicated to those who fought in World War I. A must-see. Open Tues–Sun.

MUSEUMS OF ART: 🏛 **T. H. Benton Home,** 3216 Belleview Ave. (931-5722): Victorian house and studio which the famous regionalist painter Thomas Hart Benton (nicknamed "the Michelangelo of Neosho, Mo.") occupied from 1937 until his death in 1975. Those who admire his work should not fail to visit it. Open daily.
  🏛🏛 **Henry Moore Sculpture Garden,** 4525 Oak St. (561-4000): Installed in 17 acres (6.9ha) in front of the Nelson Atkins Museum of Art (see below), this new sculpture garden opened on June 4, 1989. Contains the most extensive collection of Henry Moore's bronzes outside England. 12 larger-than-life works in a landscaped setting. Not to be missed. Open daily.
  ☀🏛🏛 **Nelson-Atkins Museum,** 4525 Oak St. (561-4000): Art from ancient civilizations (Sumerian, Greek, and Egyptian). Many paintings by European masters from Titian to van Gogh. Remarkable collection of Far Eastern (particularly Chinese) art. Among the best-known works on display are Caravaggio's *St. John the Baptist,* a *Virgin and Child* by Petrus Christus,

Nicolas Poussin's *Triumph of Bacchus,* and Thomas Hart Benton's *Persephone.* An absolute must. Unusually good museum cafeteria. Open Tues–Sun.

MUSEUMS OF SCIENCE & HISTORY: ⚱ Kansas City Museum, 3218
Gladstone Blvd. (483-8300): Interesting museum of anthropology, housed in the sumptuous 72-room mansion of a 19th-century millionaire. Many Native American art objects. Plays up the importance of Kansas City in the westward expansion. Also a planetarium. Open Tues–Sun.

> ⚱ **Linda Hall Library,** Rockhill Rd. on the University of Missouri campus (363-4600): Once the country's richest libraries, entirely given over to science and technology, with works from as early as the 17th century. Interesting. Open Mon–Sat.

> ☼⚱ **Toy & Miniature Museum,** 5235 Oak St. (333-2055): In a very beautiful, and carefully restored, 1911 building, this fascinating museum displays splendid collections of old toys, miniatures, and dollhouses. You have to see it. Open Wed–Sun.

PANORAMAS: ⚱ City Hall, 414 E. 12th St. (274-2605): Observation platform on the 30th floor; worth seeing. Open Mon–Fri.

PARKS & GARDENS: ⚱ Barney Allis Plaza, 12th St. between Central Ave.
and Wyandotte Ave.: Municipal park in the heart of dwntwn, opened in 1986, which has become very popular in fine weather for its shaded benches, hot-dog vendors, and enormous fountain (illuminated at night).

> ⚱ **Penn Valley Park,** 31st St. and Main St.: On the site of a former slum area once known as "Vinegar Hill," this beautiful 176-acre (71ha) landscaped park designed by the architect George Kessler offers scenic footpaths among lawns and trees, as well as a small artificial lake.

> ⚱ **Swope Park,** Meyer Blvd. and Swope Pkwy.: A very large (1,730 acres/700ha) park at the southern edge of the city. Golf, tennis, boating, and a distinguished zoo (see "Zoos," below). Open daily.

PERFORMING ARTS: For current listings of shows and cultural events, consult the entertainment pages of the daily *Kansas City Star* (morning).
American Heartland Theatre, Crown Center, 2450 Grand Ave. (842-9999): New professional theater company performing well-known Broadway plays and musicals.

Coterie Theater, Crown Center, 2400 Pershing St. (474-6552): Children's shows; very popular locally. Season is Feb to mid-Dec.

Folly Theater, 12th St. and Central Ave. (842-5500): Modern drama and comedy; concerts. Designated historic monument.

Lyric Theater, 1029 Central Ave. (471-7344): Home of the Kansas City Symphony Orchestra (principal conductor: William McGlaughlin), with performances Nov–May; and of the Lyric Opera, Apr and mid-Sept to mid-Oct.

Midland Center for the Performing Arts, 1228 Main St. (421-7500): Home of the Theater League. Broadway hits and theater tours.

Missouri Repertory Theater, 4949 Cherry St. (276-2700): Classical and modern theater on the U. of Missouri campus, with seasons July–Sept and Jan–Apr.

Municipal Auditorium, 1310 Wyandotte St. (421-8000): Musicals, concerts. Striking example of art deco design.

Starlight Theater, in Swope Park, 63rd St. and Swope Pkwy. (333-9481): Open-air concerts and big-star shows, May–Sept. A summer-season classic for the last 30 years.

State Ballet of Missouri, 706 W. 42nd St. (931-2232): One of the best ballet companies in the Midwest. Performances Oct–Mar.

SHOPPING: The **AT&T Town Pavilion,** 1111 Main St. (472-9600): In the heart of the Petticoat Lane business district, this huge recent complex occupies three of the 38 floors of the new AT&T tower. Comprises more than 70 boutiques, stores, and restaurants.

Country Club Plaza, 47th St. and Main St. (753-0100): Locally known as "The Plaza," this is the country's oldest (1922) shopping center, a monument to the consumer society. More than 160 boutiques, stores, restaurants, and nightclubs in a very successful Spanish-Moorish setting with fountains, statues, murals, and tree-lined walks. Well worth seeing.

Crown Center, 2400 Pershing Rd. (274-8444): Luxurious avant-garde shopping center with 60 or so boutiques and stores (see "Architectural Highlights," above).

SPECIAL EVENTS: For exact dates, consult the **Kansas City Convention and Visitors Bureau** (see "Tourist Information," above).

Kansas City Rodeo (late June to early July): For rodeo fans.

Jazz Festival (early Sept): Very popular, featuring the biggest names in jazz.

American Royal Livestock, Horse Show, and Rodeo (Nov): A triumph of the cowboy idiom; one of the most renowned festivals in the Midwest, and a classic of its kind since 1899.

SPORTS: Kansas City has professional teams in two major sports:

Baseball (Apr–Oct): Royals, Harry S Truman Sports Complex (921-8000).

Football (Sept–Dec): Chiefs, Harry S Truman Sports Complex (924-9400).

STROLLS: ⚲ **Antiques and Art Center,** 45th St. and State Line: A score of antiques shops and art galleries in the heart of one of Kansas City's oldest districts; well worth looking over.

⚲ **Westport Square,** Broadway at Westport Rd. (931-3440): This charming old district has managed to retain the full flavor of the past. Old shops, nicely restored 19th-century buildings, and inviting restaurants. One of the centers of the city's nightlife. Worth a look.

THEME PARKS: ⚲ **Benjamin Ranch on the Santa Fe Trail,** I-435S and E. 87th St. (761-5055): Facsimile of an Old West town, with riding, shows, rodeos in summer, and cowboy food. A pleasant place. Open daily.

⚲ **Oceans of Fun,** 12 mi. (19km) NE along I-435 to Exit 54 (459-9283): Enormous lagoon-pool holding a million gallons (3.7 million liters) of water, with giant slides, artificial surf, and dozens of aquatic attractions. Adjoins the Worlds of Fun complex (see below). Open daily Memorial Day–Labor Day.

⚲ **Worlds of Fun,** 10 mi. (16km) NE along I-435 to Exit 54 (454-4545): A 163-acre (66ha) amusement park with more than 100 different attractions, including a thrilling giant roller coaster, the Timber Wolf. Shows, public concerts. Open daily May–Sept, wknds only in spring and fall; closed the rest of the year.

ZOOS: ⚲ **Kansas City Zoo,** Swope Park, I-435 and Gregory Blvd. (333-7405): Fine collection of animals, many of which live in native habitats—African veldt, tropical habitat, ape house, and waterfowl exhibit. Narrow-gauge railroad rides. Open daily.

ACCOMMODATIONS

A Note on Accommodations: Room rates in Kansas City are coded as follows: **VE,** Very Expensive ($140 and up); **E,** Expensive ($90–$140); **M,** Moderate ($60–$90); **I,** Inexpensive ($30–$60); **B,** Budget (up to $30). A listing of toll free numbers is in the Appendix.

Personal Favorites (in order of preference)

♀♀♀ **Allis Plaza Hotel** (formerly the Vista International; dwntwn), 200 W. 12th St., MO 64105 (816/421-6800; toll free, see Preferred). 572 rms, A/C, color TV, in-rm movies. AE, CB, DC, MC, V. Valet gar. $8, pool, tennis courts, health club, sauna, two rests. (including Harvest), bars, rm svce, disco, boutiques, concierge, free crib. *Note:* An ungraceful ultra-modern 22-story tower—but w. lavish interior and furnishings, and a spectacular indoor waterfall. Spacious, very comfortable rms, some w. refrigerators. Two VIP floors and one no-smoking floor. Efficient reception and svce. Conveniently located across the street from the Convention Center. Business and convention clientele.**E–VE**

♀♀♀ **Hyatt Regency** (nr. dwntwn), 2345 McGee St., MO 64108 (816/421-1234; toll free, see Hyatt). 732 rms, A/C, color TV, in-rm movies. AE, CB, DC, MC, V. Valet gar. $8, two pools, health club, sauna, two tennis courts, two rests. (including Peppercorn Duck Club), coffee shop, three bars (Skies is a revolving bar on the top floor), rm svce, concierge, free crib. *Note:* A 40-story building, more imposing than elegant, this crown jewel among the city's deluxe hotels possesses, like most of the new Hyatts, a spectacular glass-walled foyer six floors high. Spacious, comfortable rms w. refrigerators. Efficient svce. Entirely renovated after the 1981 collapse of two skywalks in the lobby left 111 dead. Group and convention clientele. Two VIP floors; no-smoking rms. **E–VE**

♀♀♀ **Adam's Mark** (nr. dwntwn), 9103 E. 39th St., MO 64133 (816/737-0200; toll free 800/444-2326). 372 rms, A/C, color TV, in-rm movies. AE, CB, DC, MC, V. Free parking, two pools, health club, sauna, two tennis courts, rest. (Remington's), coffee shop, two bars, rm svce, nightclub, free crib. *Note:* Adjacent to the Harry S Truman Sports Complex, this modern luxury hotel is typical of its genre, and draws large number of groups and conventions. Huge well-laid-out rms; very good svce. Remington's is a well-regarded steakhouse. 15 min. from dwntwn on I-70. **M–E**

♀♀ **Radisson Suite Hotel** (formerly the Radisson Muehlbach; dwntwn), 106 W. 12th St. (at Baltimore Ave.), MO 64105 (816/221-7000; toll free, see Radisson). 214 rms, A/C, color TV, in-rm movies. AE, CB, DC, MC, V. Free valet parking, health club, two rests. (including Walt Bodine's Steakhouse), coffee shop, bar, rm svce, nightclub, free crib. *Note:* Long considered the city's smartest and most elegant hostelry, the Radisson has welcomed every president of the U.S. from Theodore Roosevelt on. Now restored to its pristine magnificence, it offers suites only, spacious and very comfortable, w. a desk, two phones, computer hookup, and minibar. Efficient, careful svce; acceptable rests.; fully equipped business center. Conveniently located in the heart of the business district. Business and VIP clientele. **M–E**

☼♀♀ **Raphael** (nr. dwntwn), 325 Ward Pkwy., Country Club Plaza, MO 64112 (816/756-3800; toll free 800/821-5343). 124 rms, A/C, color TV, in-rm movies. AE, CB, DC, MC, V. Free valet gar., rest. (Raphael), bar, rm svce, free breakfast, free crib. *Note:* This is a small, elegant hotel in the European tradition, worlds away from the crowds of organized groups and conventions. Spacious rms w. minibars; discreet svce which anticipates your needs. A good place to stay. Interesting wknd discounts. 15 min. from dwntwn. **E**

♀ **Rodeway Inn Downtown** (dwntwn), 6th St. and Main St., MO 64106 (816/842-6090; toll free, see Rodeway Inns). 240 rms, A/C, color TV. AE, CB, DC, MC, V. Free parking, pool, 24-hr. coffee shop, bar, rm svce, hrdrsr. *Note:* Conventional (but well-run) motel a few steps from the business district. Functional layout; rms w. balconies (some w. refrigerators). Friendly reception and svce. Very good value. Repeat clientele. **I–M**

♀ **Budgetel Inn** (nr. dwntwn), 2214 Taney St., North Kansas
🛏 City, MO 64116 (816/221-1200; toll free 800/428-3438).
100 rms, A/C, cable color TV. AE, CB, DC, MC, V. Free parking, adj. coffee shop, valet svce. *Note:* Modest, unpretentious motel on the north bank of the river. Functionally comfortable; free morning coffee. Good value overall. 6 min. from dwntwn.

Other Accommodations (from top bracket to budget)

♀♀♀ **Ritz Carlton** (formerly the Alameda Plaza; nr. dwntwn),
🛏🛏🛏 Wornall Rd. at Ward Pkwy., MO 64112 (816/756-1500; toll free 800/241-3333). 374 rms, A/C, color TV, in-rm movies. AE, CB, DC, MC, V. Free gar., pool, tennis court, health club, sauna, two rests., two bars, 24-hr. rm svce, disco, drugstore, concierge, free crib. *Note:* Luxurious modern hotel w. an elegant and unusual Spanish interior. Comfortable rms w. minibars and private balconies. Excellent svce. Very good rest. w. panoramic view and glass-walled elevator. Inviting grdns w. waterfalls and statuary. Elegance w. quality. Served as headquarters for Ronald Reagan during the 1976 Republican National Convention. 15 min. from dwntwn. **E–VE**

♀♀♀ **Westin Crown Center** (nr. dwntwn), 1 Pershing Rd., MO
🛏🛏🛏 64108 (816/474-4400; toll free, see Westin). 724 rms, A/C, color TV, in-rm movies. AE, CB, DC, MC, V. Valet gar. $6, pool, health club, sauna, putting green, two tennis courts, two rests. (including Trader Vic's), coffee shop, three bars, 24-hr. rm svce, nightclub, hrdrsr, boutiques, cinemas, free crib. *Note:* Regarded simply as architecture the massive building doesn't quite come off, but the elegant interior boasts tropical grdns and a five-story waterfall. Comfortable rms w. balconies; friendly reception, good svce. No-smoking floor. Favored by business travelers. Interesting wknd discounts. 8 min. from dwntwn, adj. the Crown Center w. its dozens of stores and boutiques. **E–VE**

♀♀ **Americana on Convention Square** (formerly the Quality Inn;
🛏🛏 nr. dwntwn), 1301 Wyandotte St., MO 64105 (816/221-8800), 486 rms, A/C, color TV, in-rm movies. AE, CB, DC, MC, V. Gar. $6, pool, rest., coffee shop, bar, rm svce. *Note:* Large (28-floor) modern motel opposite the Convention Center. Spacious, comfortable rms, but inefficient svce. Rather obtrusive group and convention clientele. Nevertheless, a good overall value. **M**

♀♀ **Holiday Inn Downtown** (vic.), 424 Minnesota Ave., Kansas
🛏🛏 City, KS 66101 (913/342-6919; toll free, see Holiday Inns).
200 rms, A/C, color TV, in-rm movies. AE, CB, DC, MC, V. Free parking, pool, coffee shop, rm svce, free crib. *Note:* A typical Holiday Inn, barely 8 min. from dwntwn across the Kansas border. Comfortably functional, w. good-humored reception. Very good value; ideal if you're driving. **I–M**

♀♀ **Howard Johnson's Central** (dwntwn), 610 Washington St.,
🛏🛏 MO 64105 (816/421-1800; toll free, see Howard Johnson's).
185 rms, A/C, color TV, in-rm movies. AE, CB, DC, MC, V. Free parking, pool, rest., bar, rm svce, entertainment, free crib. *Note:* Conventional seven-story motel, recently renovated and comfortably up-to-date. Well located very near the Convention Center. Favored by business travelers; good value. **I–M**

♀ **Best Western Inn Central** (vic.), 501 Southwest Blvd. (at 7th
🛏 St.), Kansas City, KS 66103 (913/677-3060; toll free, see Best Western). 115 rms, A/C, color TV, in-rm movies. AE, CB, DC, MC, V. Free parking, pool, coffee shop, bar, valet svce, free crib. *Note:* Inviting and comfortable small motel just across the Kansas border 10 min. from dwntwn. Excellent reception; very good value. **I**

♀ **Travelodge Midtown** (nr. dwntwn), 3240 Broadway, MO
🛏 64111 (816/531-9250; toll free, see Travelodge). 52 rms,

KANSAS CITY AREA

A/C, color TV. AE, CB, DC, MC, V. Free parking, adj. coffee shop, free crib. *Note:* Low-priced but comfortable motel 5 min. from Crown Center and 10 min. from dwntwn. Free morning coffee. Good overall value. **I**

Motel 6 North (vic.), 8230 N.W. Prairie View Rd., MO 64152 (816/741-6400). 85 rms, A/C, color TV, free in-rm movies. AE, DC, MC, V. Free parking, pool, free crib. *Note:* Unbeatable value 20 min. from dwntwn along U.S. 169. No bar or rest. Ideal for motorists. **B–I**

Airport Accommodations

Hilton Airport Plaza Inn (vic.), 112th St. NW and I-29, MO 64195 (816/891-8900; toll free, see Hilton). 350 rms, A/C, color TV, in-rm movies. AE, CB, DC, MC, V. Free parking, two pools, health club, sauna, two tennis courts, two rests. (including Kona Kai), three bars, rm svce, nightclub, free airport limo, free crib. *Note:* Modern, comfortable motel 3 min. from the airport. Good sports facilities; good svce. Spacious, well-soundproofed rms, some w. refrigerators. Ideal for a stopover between flights. **M–E**

RESTAURANTS

A Note on Restaurant Prices: Kansas City restaurant prices, per person, excluding drinks and service charges, are coded as follows: **VE,** Very Expensive ($60 and up); **E,** Expensive ($40–$60); **M,** Moderate ($25–$40); **I,** Inexpensive ($15–$25); **B,** Budget (up to $15).

Personal Favorites (in order of preference)

The American Restaurant (nr. dwntwn), 25th St. and Grand Ave. (471-8050). A/C. Dinner only, Mon–Sat; closed hols. AE, CB, DC, MC, V. Jkt. *Specialties:* sautéed shrimp in fennel butter, rack of lamb w. green vegetables and hazelnuts, pheasant w. juniperberries, Montana elk steak w. blueberries, salmon poached in cream, carpetbagger (oyster-stuffed) steak. Delicious desserts, particularly the chocolate-whisky cake. Fine list of California wines. *Note:* Delicate, inventive food; along w. the rustic Golden Ox, this is the place to go in Kansas City. This multilevel rest. atop the Crown Center, elegantly decorated w. mirrors and paneling, affords a clear view over the city. Innovative cuisine, w. pride of place given to local produce. Exemplary svce. Resv. a must; valet parking. *American/Continental.* **M–E**

Bristol Bar and Grill (nr. dwntwn), 4740 Jefferson St. (756-0606). A/C. Lunch Mon–Fri, dinner nightly, brunch Sun; closed Dec 25. AE, CB, DC, MC, V. Jkt. *Specialties:* clam chowder, gumbo, scampi sauté; extensive choice of absolutely fresh fish and shellfish, broiled, poached, or baked. Menu changes daily. Fine wine list. *Note:* One of the best fish rests. in all the Midwest; superb seafood flown in daily. Elegant Victorian decor; in the farthest room, a lovely Tiffany-style window. Exemplary svce. The bar is the favorite watering hole for the local yuppies; live jazz. Resv. a must. *Seafood.* **M**

Golden Ox (nr. dwntwn), 1600 Genessee St. (842-2866). A/C. Lunch Mon–Fri, dinner nightly; closed Dec 24–25. AE, CB, DC, MC, V. *Specialties:* wonderful broiled red meats. *Note:* A landmark of local cuisine, in the precincts of the Kansas City stockyards, 15 min. from dwntwn. Even the somber, unoriginal western decor can't detract from the exceptional quality of the meats or the perfection w. which they are prepared (the chefs do their work around enormous broilers in the middle of the dining room, under the eyes of the diners). Diligent svce. If you love to eat meat, this place belongs in your address book; it's the best steakhouse in Kansas City. Resv. advised. *Steak.* **I**

Savoy Grill (dwntwn), 9th and Central (842-3890). A/C. Lunch Mon–Sat, dinner nightly. AE, CB, DC, MC, V. Jkt.

Specialties: world-famous Kansas City steaks, fresh fish, oysters on the half shell, shrimp de Jonghe, Maine lobster, gumbo, T-bone steak. *Note:* A Kansas City landmark since 1903; urbane old London club atmosphere, w. period service and decor guaranteed. Resv. advised. *Steak/Seafood.* **I–M**

🍸 **Arthur Bryant's Barbecue** (nr. dwntwn), 1727 Brooklyn
🍸 Ave. (231-1123). A/C. Lunch/dinner daily; closed Thanksgiving, Dec 25. No credit cards. *Specialties:* barbecued short ribs and beef brisket, smoked ham, sandwiches. *Note:* Both the neighborhood and the decor could reasonably be described as shabby-looking, but lovers of barbecue will find it here in generous portions, of remarkable quality, w. subtly spiced sauces and lots of local color, neon-and-Formica style. The clientele is numerous, and comes back often. No resv. *American.* **B**

🍸 **Stroud's** (vic.), 1015 E. 85th St. (333-2132). A/C. Lunch Fri–
🍸 Sun, dinner nightly; closed Thanksgiving, Dec 24–25. AE, MC, V. *Specialties:* fried chicken, fried catfish, chicken-fried steak. *Note:* This unassuming, discreetly decorated old roadhouse is a shrine to fried chicken Kansas style, and draws a crowd of regulars every day. Atmosphere relaxed and noisy; sometimes you'll have a long wait at the bar. Other location: 5410 NE Oak Ridge Rd. (454-9600). *American.* **B–I**

Other Restaurants (from top bracket to budget)

🍸🍸🍸 **La Méditerranée** (nr. dwntwn), 4742 Pennsylvania Ave.
🍸🍸🍸 (561-2916). A/C. Lunch/dinner Mon–Sat; closed hols. AE, CB, DC, MC, V. J&T. *Specialties:* bouillabaisse (must be ordered in advance), lobster w. truffle sauce, sole belle meunière, lamb w. purée of mushrooms, salmon w. morel sauce, tournedos Gilbert, amaretto soufflé. Magnificent wine list. *Note:* Even if the sauces are a little rich, chef Gérard Jahier's French food is excellent, as is the svce; the rest, has been agreeably redecorated. Free parking; resv. a must. *French/seafood.* **M**

🍸🍸 **Café Allegro** (nr. dwntwn), 1815 W. 39th St. (561-3663).
🍸🍸 A/C. Lunch Mon–Fri, dinner Mon–Sat; closed hols. AE, CB, DC, MC, V. Jkt. *Specialties:* homemade fresh pasta, veal loin stuffed w. wild mushrooms, peppered filet mignon w. Maytag bleu-cheese sauce, breast of chicken Mougin, baked halibut in phyllo pastry. Good, reasonably priced wine list w. cruvinet storage for wines to be served by the glass. *Note:* Charming bistro serving an eclectic modern cuisine which changes w. the seasons; the general appearance is that of a French country inn. Ultra-professional svce. Very popular locally, so resv. a must at lunch as well as dinner. *American.* **I–M**

🍸🍸 **Hereford House** (dwntwn), 2 E. 20th St. (842-1080). A/C.
🍸🍸 Lunch Mon–Fri, dinner nightly; closed hols. AE, CB, DC, MC, V. Jkt. *Specialties:* the finest meats perfectly broiled over an open fire; also excellent hamburgers. *Note:* One of the steakhouses that endear Kansas City to meatlovers. Typical western decor; casual atmosphere; resv. advised. A very fine place to eat. *Steak.* **I–M**

🍸 **Jess & Jim's Steak House** (vic.), 517 E. 135th St. at Locust St.,
🍸 Martin City (942-9909). A/C. Lunch/dinner daily; closed Thanksgiving, Dec 25. AE, MC, V. *Specialties:* excellent prime cuts at extremely reasonable prices. *Note:* Everything here, from the 8-oz. (200g) filet mignon to the 30-oz. (750g) porterhouse, including the baked potatoes that come with them, is enormous. Small appetites should stay away. The decor adds little to the value and no resv. are accepted, but the 45-min. trip from dwntwn is well worthwhile. Other location: Jess & Jim's Annex, 13035 Holmes Rd. (942-7454). *Steak.* **I**

🍸 **Houlihan's Old Place** (nr. dwntwn), 4743 Pennsylvania Ave.
🍸 (561-3141) A/C. Lunch/dinner daily; closed Dec 25. AE, CB, DC, MC, V. *Specialties:* onion soup, omelets, quiche, steak, hamburgers, salads. *Note:* Relaxed and friendly; the ideal place for a quick meal in an entertaining

turn-of-the-century setting. Friendly svce. Open late (until 11pm or midnight). Trendy clientele; resv. advised. *American.* **B–I**

♟ **Italian Gardens** (dwntwn), 1110 Baltimore Ave. (221-9311).
 ☖ A/C. Lunch/dinner Mon–Sat; closed hols. AE, CB, DC, MC, V. *Specialties:* cannelloni, lasagne, fettuccine Lipari, calves' liver alla Veneziana, veal scaloppine w. lemon sauce, steak. *Note:* Nice, unassuming small family rest. Diligent svce. Popular in the community for more than 60 years especially for lunch. The only attempt at interior decoration is provided by photos of show-business stars. *Italian/American.* **B–I**

♟ **Prospect of Westport** (nr. dwntwn), 4109 Pennsylvania Ave.
 ☖ (753-2227). A/C. Breakfast/lunch/dinner daily (until midnight), brunch Sun; closed hols. AE, CB, DC, MC, V. *Specialties:* fresh homemade pasta, fish, and daily specials, apple pie; menu changes regularly. *Note:* Enchanting modern decor of exuberant greenery beneath a high skylight. Delicate, imaginative cooking; svce w. a smile. Inviting open patio for fine days. One of Kansas City's fashionable spots; resv. advised. *American/Continental.* **B–I**

In the Vicinity

☀♟ **Stephenson's Apple Farm** (vic.), 16401 E. U.S. 40 at Lee's
 ☖ Summit Rd. (375-5400). A/C. Lunch/dinner daily, brunch Sun; closed Dec 24–25. AE, CB, DC, MC, V. *Specialties:* meat, ham, and chicken smoked over a wood fire, steaks, homemade pies, apple fritters, cider. *Note:* Picturesque country inn occupying an old farmhouse 25 min. from dwntwn. Pleasant countrified setting; very crowded, so resv. advised at this successful rest. *American.* **B–I**

Cafeteria/Fast Food/Specialty Spots

Gates & Sons (nr. dwntwn), 4707 Paseo at Swope Pkwy. (921-0409): A solid contender w. Arthur Bryant's for the title of best barbecued food in Kansas City. Short ribs of beef, smoked ham, sliced beef, barbecued beans—all excellent. There are five other Gates & Sons places in town (consult the city telephone directory). Open daily for lunch and dinner.

Winstead's (nr. dwntwn), 101 Brush Creek Blvd. (753-2244). Drive-in and eat-in hamburger emporium. The hamburgers are made from fresh ground meat. Terrific ice cream and giant sundaes. Seven locations, including the original one at Brush Creek Blvd.

BARS & NIGHTCLUBS

As you would expect from the former jazz capital of the world, Kansas City, too, has a magic phone number—the **Jazz Hotline** (931-2888)—which will give you the programs at all the city's jazz concerts and jazz clubs.

Blayneys (nr. dwntwn), 415 Westport Rd. (561-3747). Hosts live bands playing reggae, rock, or jazz in a small basement. Open Mon–Sat.

City Light (nr. dwntwn), 7425 Broadway (444-6969). Jazz live Mon–Sat. Dependable and cozy.

Grand Emporium (nr. dwntwn), 3832 Main St. (531-1504). Rock, blues, and reggae bands weekdays, jazz bands Fri–Sat. Also a rest. Casual atmosphere. Open Mon–Sat.

Houlihan's Old Place (nr. dwntwn), 4743 Pennsylvania Ave. (561-3141). Deservedly popular singles bar, adjoining the very acceptable rest. of the same name (see above). Open nightly.

Lone Star (nr. dwntwn), 4117 Mill St. (561-1881). Features the best in regional and national rock and roll acts. Open Mon–Sat.

Milton's Tap Room (nr. dwntwn), 805 W. 39th St. (753-9476). One of the best (and oldest) jazz clubs in K.C. Once sponsored Count Basie, Charlie Parker, and other jazz greats. Live music Wed–Sat.

Stanford's Comedy House (nr. dwntwn), 504 Westport Rd. (753-5653).

Kansas City's original comedy shop. Amateur night Tues, national headliners Wed–Sun. Also a very acceptable rest.

NEARBY EXCURSIONS

🏛 **FORT OSAGE** (21 mi/34km east on U.S. 24 and Sibley Rd., Sibley) (881-4431): The first fort built (1808) west of the Mississippi by the famous expedition of Lewis and Clark (see the Fort Clatsop National Memorial in Chapter 46 on the Pacific Coast), now carefully restored. Officers' cantonments, barracks for other ranks, museum, and trading post all look as though they had been lifted bodily from a period western. It's a good idea to combine this trip with a visit to Independence (see below). Open wknds only from mid-Nov to mid-Apr, daily the rest of the year.

☀🏛 **INDEPENDENCE** (7 mi/12km east via Independence Ave.): Starting point of the Santa Fe Trail and Oregon Trail, and once the provisional capital of the Mormons.
The **Harry S Truman Library and Museum,** U.S. 24 at Delaware St. (833-1400), open daily, contains among other memorabilia an exact facsimile of the Oval Office at the White House. Also, don't miss the 🏛 **Harry S Truman National Historic Site,** 219 N. Delaware St. (254-9929), a fine example of Victorian architecture where President Truman lived for more than half a century. Original furniture; open daily in summer, Tues–Sun the balance of the year.
On the way, stop at the **Mormon Visitors Center,** 937 W. Walnut St., which offers a complete history of the Church of Jesus Christ of the Latter-Day Saints. Close by, the **World Headquarters Auditorium,** 1001 W. Walnut St., has one of the largest church organs in the U.S.: 6,300 pipes (daily recitals in summer).
Also take a look at the very picturesque 🏛 **1859 Marshal's Home and Jail Museum** at 217 N. Main St. (252-1892), a genuine 19th-century prison and sheriff's office scrupulously restored. Open daily in summer, Tues–Sat the rest of the year. Well worth a visit.

🏛 **KANSAS CITY, KANSAS** (5 mi/8km west on U.S. 24): The twin city across the Kansas River. There is a group of 400 interesting **Native American tombs** in Huron Park, at Center City Plaza between 6th and 7th.
The **Agricultural Hall of Fame,** 630 N. 126th St. (913/721-1075), offers a fascinating course in the development of midwestern farming by means of extensive collections of old agricultural equipment and period buildings. Open daily Apr–Nov; should be seen.

☀🏛 **LIBERTY** (15 mi/24km NE on I-35 and Mo. 152): Visit the **Jesse James Bank Museum,** Old Town Sq. (781-4458), where in 1866 Jesse James, the legendary bandit of the Old West, committed the first bank holdup in the country's history. Open Mon–Sat.
See also the **Historic Liberty Jail,** 216 N. Main St. (781-3188), open daily, where Joseph Smith, founder of the Mormons, was imprisoned with a number of his followers, and where he was vouchsafed many revelations about Mormon doctrine. Worth the side trip.

🏛 **OLD SHAWNEE TOWN** (in Shawnee, Kans., 18 mi/29km SW along I-35 and Johnson Dr.) (913/268-8772 for information): Detailed reconstruction of a pioneer village in the period 1850–1900, with a dozen original buildings including the school and the jail, plus a score of facsimiles of structures from the time of the westward expansion. Picturesque and amusing; worth going out of your way for. Open Tues–Sun.

※☼♨ **ST. JOSEPH** (50 mi/80km north on I-29): Founded in 1826 by a French fur trader, Joseph Robidoux, this little market town, birthplace of the great saxophonist Coleman Hawkins and TV newscaster Walter Cronkite, still offers a whiff of adventure. It was the terminus of the Pony Express, which from Apr 1860 to Oct 1861 was the only link between Missouri and California thanks to its dauntless riders (the record time to Sacramento was 7 days, 17 hrs.).

The riders of the Pony Express, the most famous being the young Buffalo Bill, were, according to a contemporary newspaper advertisement, "young, slim, energetic and under 18. They must be consummate horsemen, ready to risk their lives every day. Orphans preferred. Pay: $25 a week." Every rider covered about 90 mi (145 km), with three changes of mount, before being relieved by another. Time allowed for change of mount: 2 min.—and the fastest did it in 15 seconds. At the time it cost $5 (later reduced to $1) to send a half-ounce letter from Missouri to California. A mere 4 days after the opening of the first transcontinental telegraph line on Oct 24, 1861, the Pony Express went out of business.

St. Joseph still displays some intersting links with the past: see the **Pony Express Stables Museum,** the company's birthplace, at 914 Penn St. (279-5059), open daily Apr–Sept only; the **Patee House Museum,** 12th St. and Penn St. (232-8206), open daily in summer, wknds only in spring and fall; and the **St. Joseph Museum,** 11th St. and Charles St. (237-8471), with many memorabilia of the westward expansion, open year round.

Finally, visit the **Jesse James House,** 12th St. and Penn St. (232-8206), where the famous outlaw was killed in 1882 by a member of his own band for a $10,000 reward. Open Mon–Sat Mar–Nov.

On the way, visit the little pioneer city of ※♨ **Weston,** on the banks of the Mississippi, with its dozens of interesting old houses. Particularly interesting is the **McCormick Distilling Co.,** 1 mi. (1.6km) SE on County Rd. JJ, one of the oldest (1856) distilleries in the U.S.; call 386-2276 for visiting hours.

FARTHER AFIELD

※♨♨ **LAKE OF THE OZARKS** (100 mi./160km SE on U.S. 71 and Mo. 7): This superb artificial body of water, more than 93 mi. (150km) long and surrounded by dense woods of oak and sassafras, was created in 1931 by the construction of the Bagnell Dam on the Osage River. Famous for its waterskiing, sailing, and fishing, this hilly region is attractive for the friendliness of its inhabitants, and for its wide range of all-season diversions: woodland walks in spring, water sports (more than 1,150 mi/1,840km of waterfront) in summer, cross-country skiing and skating in winter, and in fall the dazzling sight of the turning leaves. Lake excursions on the paddlewheel steamer *Tom Sawyer* from Bagnell Dam, near Lake Ozark (314/365-3300), daily Apr–Oct. Worth a protracted visit. There are hotels, motels, and restaurants at Camdenton, Clinton, Lake Ozark, and Osage Beach; three recommended hotels are:

Where to Stay En Route

※♨♨♨ **Marriott's Tan-Tar-A Resort,** State Rd. KK, Osage Beach, MO 65065 (314/348-3131). Luxurious resort complex right on the lake. 1,000 rms. Private marina. **E–VE**

♨♨♨ **Lodge of the Four Seasons,** Bus. U.S. 54, Lake Ozark, MO 65049 (314/365-3000). 313 rms. Elegant Spanish-style hotel standing amid 200 acres (80ha) of woods and grdns. Private marina. **E–VE**

♨♨ **Breckenridge on the Lake,** Lake Rd. 54–30 A., Osage Beach, MO 65065 (314/348-2293). 335 rms. Comfortable, friendly motel on the lake. **I–M**

PART FOUR

THE MOUNTAIN STATES

CHAPTER 29

DENVER☸

□ □ □

Midway between the Pacific coast and Missouri, Denver lies at the foot of the Rockies against the magnificent natural backdrop of the mountains. The "mile-high city"—to use the name conferred on it by its inhabitants—was dear to the heart of Buffalo Bill, whose grave overlooks the city from atop **Lookout Mountain.** More recently, Jack Kerouac eulogized it in his famous novel and bible of the beat generation, *On the Road.* A former gold and silver prospectors' camp, Denver served as a bridgehead for the westward expansion. Signs of the city's heroic past can be seen in structures like the **Capitol** dome, 243 ft. (76m) high, covered in pure gold leaf from Colorado mines. The neoclassical architecture of the imposing Capitol forms a striking contrast with the ultra-futurist **Denver Art Museum,** on the other side of the **Civic Center** and its gardens. Not far from here, the picturesque **Larimer Square** marks the heart of historic Old Denver with art galleries, cafés, restaurants, and 19th-century gas lamps.

Like all the mushrooming cities of the West, the capital of Colorado experienced an economic boom after World War II. Specializing in growth industries such as oil and mineral exploration, aeronautics, defense, graphics, and electronics, it is one of the energy capitals of the country with its oil, gas, coal, uranium, solar energy, and synthetic fuels. Not surprisingly, Denver, like Dallas and Houston, was severely affected by the oil crisis of the 1980s, and also by the recent events in the Mideast.

The proximity of the Rockies has also made Denver "queen city of the Plains," and one of the great capitals of American tourism. Less than 2 or 3 hr. away by car are the famous resorts at **Aspen, Vail, Copper Mountain,** and **Winter Park,** all filled with visitors both summer and winter. A veritable turntable between the East and the West, **Stapleton International Airport** is the fifth-busiest airport in the country.

An effective mix of modern skyscrapers, wide tree-lined thoroughfares, and wealthy suburbs, Denver, Colorado's capital, and its satellite, **Boulder,** located less than half an hour by car from downtown Denver, have more than 200 public parks and gardens between them. The one drawback is that the walls of the Rockies form an impassable barrier for automobile emissions and industrial fumes, smothering Denver each winter in a thick cloud of atmospheric pollution whenever the winds blow westward or a temperature inversion occurs. Famous children of Denver include actor Douglas Fairbanks and band leader Paul Whiteman.

BASIC FACTS: Capital of Colorado. Area code: 303. Time zone: mountain. ZIP Code: 80201. Settled: 1858. Approximate population: city, 490,000; metropolitan area, 1,910,000. 21st-largest metropolitan area in the U.S.

CLIMATE: With close to 300 clear days per year, Denver is one of the sunniest cities in the country. The high altitude and the brisk, dry air make summer very agreeable (average temperature: 68°F/20°C). In spring and autumn the air gets chilly even when the sun is shining. Winter brings blizzards from the Rockies and the temperature plunges to 5°F (−15°C), which can make outings dangerous (not to mention the frequent smog from mid-Nov to mid-Jan).

DISTANCES: Albuquerque, 421 mi. (675km); Kansas City, 600 mi. (960km); Los Angeles, 1,059 mi. (1,695km); Salt Lake City, 506 mi. (810km); Yellowstone, 638 mi. (1,022km).

ARRIVAL & TRANSIT INFORMATION

AIRPORT: Stapleton International Airport (DEN): 7 mi. (11km) NE. Fifthbusiest airport in the U.S. with 33 million passengers per year. For information, call 398-3844.

AIRLINES: American (595-9304), Aspen (398-4141), Continental (398-3000), Delta (696-1322), Eastern (623-4800), Northwest (825-6116), TWA (629-7878), United (398-4141), and USAir (toll free 800/428-4322).

CITY LINK: The **cab** fare to city center is about $10–$12; time, 20 min. Bus: **Airporter** (321-3222); leaves approximately every 30 min.; fare, $5. Many local bus lines (32, 38, and 52) which also serve the airport; fare, 70¢. Relatively efficient public transportation system (bus; R.T.D.) w. a free **shuttle** in the downtown area (16th St. Mall Shuttle) (722-1411). The proximity of the Rocky Mountains and the numerous excursion possibilities make it advisable to rent a car w. unlimited mileage.

CAR RENTAL (at Stapleton International Airport unless otherwise indicated): Avis (398-3725); Budget (341-2277); Dollar (398-2323); Hertz (355-2244); National (321-7990); Thrifty, 4000 Quebec St. (388-4634). For downtown locations, consult the telephone directory.

LIMOUSINE SERVICES: Carey Limousine (toll free 800/336-4646), Dav El Limousines (toll free 800/922-0343).

TAXIS: Taxis are few and may not be hailed on the street. There are taxi stations in front of all the major hotels, at the bus station, and at the Amtrak station. They may also be summoned by phone. One of the least expensive cities in the country for cab riders. Major companies: **Metro Cab** (333-3333), **Yellow Cab** (777-7777), and **Zone Cab** (861-2323).

TRAIN: Amtrak, Union Station, 17th St. and Wynkoop St. (893-3911 or 534-2812).

INTERCITY BUSES: Greyhound, 1055 19th St. (292-0652).

INFORMATION & TOURS

TOURIST INFORMATION: The **Denver Convention & Visitors Bureau,** 225 W. Colfax Ave., CO 80202 (303/892-1112 or 303/892-1505).

GUIDED TOURS: Gray Line Tours (bus) (303/289-2841). Guided tours of the city and around the Rockies. Serves principal hotels.

Historic Denver Tours (walking tours), 1330 17th St. (534-1858): 2-hr. guided walking tour of the historic center of Denver. Resv. necessary.

SIGHTS, ATTRACTIONS & ACTIVITIES

ADVENTURES: Colorado Adventure (boat), 43000 E. Eighth Ave. (333-7245): Rafting on the Colorado River and Green River (summer).
Timberline Bicycle Tours (bicycle), 3261 S. Oneida Way, CO 80244 (759-3804): Leisurely excursions of a week or more into the Colorado Rockies, the Grand Canyon, the national parks of Utah and Wyoming, etc. Board and lodging provided.
For a list of other commercial operators, see Chapter 30 on the Rocky Mountains.

ARCHITECTURAL HIGHLIGHTS: ※⚱ **Boettcher Concert Hall,** 13th St. and Curtis St. (592-7777): Home of the Denver Symphony Orchestra, this building has remarkable architecture and acoustics: the orchestra is positioned in the center of the hall, totally surrounded by the audience.
⚱ **Denver Center for the Performing Arts,** 14th St. and Champa St. (893-4000): Artistic and cultural heart of Denver, this ultramodern architectural complex includes notably six theaters **(Helen Bonfils Theater Complex),** a movie theater for art and experimental film, the Boettcher Concert Hall (see above), and a large shopping arcade under an 80-ft.-high (24m) skylight. A sight not to be missed. Open daily.
⚱ **Public Library,** 1357 Broadway (571-2000): The largest library in the Mountain States, w. 1.5 million volumes including an unrivaled collection of books, photographs, and documents on the history of the Old West. Open daily.

HISTORIC BUILDINGS: ⚱ **Daniels & Fisher Tower,** Arapahoe St. and 16th St. Mall: This 328-ft. (100m) brick tower was inspired by the renowned campanile of the piazza San Marco in Venice. At the time of its construction (1910) it was the tallest building in Denver. Not open to the public, unfortunately.
※⚱ **Molly Brown House,** 1340 Pennsylvania St. (832-4092): Nouveau-riche Victorian house that belonged to Molly Brown, wife of a gold-mining magnate and famous as "Unsinkable Molly" because she survived the sinking of the *Titanic* in 1912. Lovely old furniture and interesting collections of clothing, tapestries, and turn-of-the-century memorabilia. An absolute must-see. Open daily in summer, Tues–Sun off-season.
⚱ **State Capitol,** E. Colfax Ave. at Sherman St. (866-2604): The seat of the state legislature, a formidable granite structure 243 ft. (76m) tall modeled on the Washington Capitol. The dome is covered in pure gold leaf from Colorado mines. Superb panorama from the gallery at the top (elevator and rather steep stairs). Open Mon–Fri.
※⚱ **U.S. Mint,** 320 W. Colfax Ave. (844-3582): In business since 1862; turns out some 20 million coins each day. One of the three gold reserves in the country (Fort Knox and West Point, N.Y., are the other two), w. heaps of ingots high enough to set you dreaming. No picture-taking allowed. Open Mon–Fri.

INDUSTRIAL TOURS: Coors Brewery, 13th St. and Ford St., in Golden (277-2337), 15 mi. (24km) west on W. Colfax Ave. and U.S. 40: Tour of the brewery and beer tasting. Open Mon–Sat. year round.

MUSEUMS OF ART: ※⚱⚱ **Denver Art Museum,** 100 W. 14th Ave. (575-2793): One of the best collections of Native American and pre-Columbian art, including a unique group of reredos and sculpted religious figures (santos). Among its major works: Van der Weyden's *Portrait of Isabella of Portugal,*

Arcimboldo's *Summer,* and Monet's *Waterloo Bridge,* as well as remarkable Oriental art. Surprising architecture in the form of a modern fortified castle covered in shining ceramic, by Gio Ponti and James Sudler. Open Tues–Sun.

Museum of Western Art, 1727 Tremont Pl. at 17th St. (296-1880): In the venerable **Old Navarre Building** (1880), which has successively housed a girls' school, restaurants, and a brothel, this wonderful art museum dedicated solely to the heroic age of the Far West offers works by Frederic Remington, Charles Russell, Georgia O'Keeffe, and Albert Bierstadt, notably. Open Tues–Sat.

MUSEUMS OF SCIENCE & HISTORY: Colorado History Museum,
1300 Broadway (866-3682): For western history lovers, this museum retraces the life of the early pioneers and the Native Americans. Superb Anasazi pottery and interesting temporary exhibitions. Open daily.

Forney Transportation Museum, 1416 Platte St. (469-2635): One of the most important transportation museums in the country, w. more than 300 cars, various vehicles, and old locomotives, some of which are unique in the world. Open daily.

Museum of Natural History, City Park, 2001 Colorado Blvd. (370-6363): Very complete museum w. many dioramas of natural habitats, displaying the wildlife of five continents and prehistoric ways of life in America and Europe. Also includes a hall of dinosaurs, the ultramodern Gates planetarium, and a projection room with a four-story screen **(Phipps Imax Theater).** Open daily.

PANORAMAS: State Capitol, E. Colfax Ave. at Sherman St. (866-2604):
Spectacular panorama of the city and the mountains from the visitors' gallery at the top. Open Mon–Fri.

PARKS & GARDENS: Cheesman Park, Franklin St. and E. Eighth Ave.:
Vast grass-covered park w. a botanic grdn and tropical greenhouses (see below). Superb view of the Rockies from Cheesman Memorial.

City Park, between 17th Ave. and 26th Ave., York St., and Colorado Blvd.: Splendid 600-acre (243ha) park in the center of town w a golf course, many lakes and fountains, and a renowned zoo. Open daily.

Denver Botanic Gardens, 1005 York St. (331-4000): Incredibly beautiful floral park that includes a rose grdn, tropical greenhouses displaying more than 850 kinds of plants, a gorgeous Japanese grdn, and an unusual alpine grdn w. its own chalet. Part of Cheesman Park (see above). Open daily.

PERFORMING ARTS: For daily listings of all shows and cultural events, consult the entertainment pages of the daily papers *Denver Post* (morning) and *Rocky Mountain News* (morning), and the monthly magazines *Colorado* and *Denver.* **Ticket Bus,** a discount-ticket booth on the 16th St. Mall at Curtis St., sells half-price tickets for all shows on the day of performance only. Accepts MC, V. Open Mon–Sat.

Arvada Center for the Arts & Humanities, 6901 Wadsworth Blvd. (422-8050): Concerts, drama, comedy. Year round.

Auditorium Theater, 14th St. and Curtis St. (573-7151): Broadway hits. Year round.

Boettcher Concert Hall, 14th St. and Curtis St. (592-7777): Home of the Denver Symphony Orchestra, w. principal conductor Philippe Entremont. Sept–June.

Elitch Gardens Theater, 38th St. and Tennyson St. (458-8801): One of the country's oldest theaters. Mid-June to late Aug.

Fiddler's Green Amphitheater, 6350 S. Greenwood Pl. (741-5000): Big-name shows. Summer only.

Helen Bonfils Theater, 14th St. and Curtis St. (893-4100): Home of the Denver Center Theater Company. Classical theater.

Heritage Square Opera House, Colo. 40 and Colo. 93 in Golden (279-2789): Melodrama, dinner-theater. Year round.

Paramount Theater, 1621 Glenarm Pl. (469-5234): Shows, concerts, debates.

Red Rocks Amphitheater, Red Rocks Park, Colo. 26 (575-2637): Rock and pop open-air concerts. Summer only.

SHOPPING: Gart Brothers, Tenth Ave. and Broadway: The biggest sporting-goods store in the world. Unbelievable.

Kohleberg's, 1720 Champa St.: The best place in Denver for authentic Native American crafts.

Miller Stockman, 1555 Lawrence St.: From Stetson hats to cowboy boots and saddles, one of the best-stocked stores in the West. Seven other Miller Stockman stores throughout Denver.

SPECIAL EVENTS: For the exact schedule of events below, consult the **Denver Convention & Visitors Bureau** (see "Tourist Information," above).

Colorado Indian Market (mid-Jan): Craft exhibits, Native American dances, and traditional cuisines of more than 90 tribes. A wonderfully colorful spectacle.

National Western Stock Show & Rodeo (10 days in mid-Jan): The largest livestock fair and the biggest rodeo in the country. Celebrates the Old West w. special exhibits and events. Cowboy gear is *de rigueur.* This classic has been around since 1906 and should not be missed.

Red Rocks Park Summer Concerts (throughout the summer): Classical concerts, ballets, musical comedies in an open-air amphitheater that seats 10,000. The amphitheater is in the middle of a very handsome rocky arena 15 mi. (24km) SW of Denver.

Colorado Shakespeare Festival (July–Aug): Mary Rippon Outdoor Theater (University of Colorado at Boulder) presents three Shakespeare works each summer.

SPORTS: There are two major-league professional teams, and a minor-league farm team, in the Denver area:

Baseball (Apr–Oct): Zephyrs (Triple-A farm team of the Milwaukee Brewers), Mile High Stadium (433-8645).

Basketball (Oct to late Apr): Nuggets, McNichols Sports Arena (893-3865).

Football (Sept–Dec): Broncos, Mile High Stadium (433-7466).

STROLLS: △ **The Financial District,** 17th St. between Broadway and Arapahoe: Known as "Wall Street West," this financial district brings together some of the most spectacular skyscrapers in the Mountain States, including the **Anaconda Tower,** 40 stories of smoked glass; the **First National Bank Building;** and the 30-story **Security Life Building.** For modern-architecture lovers.

Larimer Square, Larimer St. between 14th St. and 15th St. (534-2367): The heart of Old Denver, with art galleries, cafés, boutiques, and restaurants, is especially lively by night. Charming turn-of-the-century Victorian town houses and gas lamps. Quite touristy but pleasant.

Sakura Square, 19th St. and Lawrence St.: A little piece of Japan in the middle of Colorado, "Cherry Blossom" Sq. has Japanese restaurants, boutiques, grdns, and a Buddhist temple. A welcome change of scenery.

DOWNTOWN DENVER

N

Union Station

WYNKOOP ST.

WAZEE ST.

BLAKE ST.

MARKET ST.

Larimer Sq.

LARIMER ST.

LAWRENCE ST.

Sakura Sq.

CENTER FOR THE PERFORMING ARTS

To Mile High Stadium

Univ. of Colo. /Denver

D & F Tower

ARAPAHOE ST.

Bus Terminal

H.G. Bonfils Theater

Prudential Plaza

CURTIS ST.

Boetcher Hall

City Audit.

CHAMPA ST.

STOUT ST.

COLFAX AVE.

MARIPOSA ST.

LIPAN ST.

KLAMATH ST.

SANTA FE

BR 70

SPEER BLVD.

12TH ST.

13TH ST.

14TH ST.

15TH ST.

16TH ST.

17TH ST.

18TH ST.

19TH ST.

CALIFORNIA ST.

WELTON ST.

First Nat'l. Bank of Denver

To Stapleton Int'l. Airport

GLENARM PL.

Old Navarre Bldg.

20TH AVE.

To Denver Zoo

TREMONT PL.

Security Life Bldg.

19TH AVE.

To Museum of Natural History

INCA ST.

GALAPAGO ST.

SPEER BLVD.

FOX ST.

ELATI ST.

DELAWARE ST.

CHEROKEE ST.

COURT PL.

Brown Palace

Cherry Creek

U.S. Mint

287

CHEYENNE PL.

18TH AVE.

17TH AVE.

13TH AVE.

Civic Center

LINCOLN ST.

BROADWAY

16TH AVE.

BANNOCK ST.

Denver Art Mus.

State Capitol

COLFAX AVE.

Sunken Gardens

ACOMA ST.

12TH AVE.

Colorado Heritage Ctr.

SHERMAN ST.

GRANT ST.

LOGAN ST.

14TH AVE.

SPEER BLVD.

11TH AVE.

BROADWAY

10TH AVE.

PENNSYLVANIA ST.

Molly Brown House

PEARL ST.

WASHINGTON ST.

40

9TH AVE.

8TH AVE.

CLARKSON ST.

OGDEN ST.

EMERSON ST.

7TH AVE.

To Botanic Gardens

🔔 **16th Street Mall,** 16th St. between Market St. and Cleveland Pl.: The business heart of Denver, w. dozens of specialized boutiques and department stores, numerous bars, restaurants, theaters. A free shuttle bus runs along the mall. Fountains and public benches, as well as street musicians, mimes, and jugglers, make this tree-lined pedestrian street an agreeable place for a stroll.

THEME PARKS: 🔔 **Elitch Gardens,** 4620 W. 38th Ave. at Tennyson St. (455-4771): Very complete theme park w. a giant roller coaster amid 28 acres (11.3ha) of very lovely grdns. Also offers open-air concerts. Open wknds only in May, daily June–Sept.; closed the rest of the year.

WINTER SPORTS RESORTS: With dozens of winter sports resorts, the Colorado Rockies are a skier's paradise. The most popular are:

🔔🔔🔔 **Aspen Mountain and Aspen Highlands,** 202 mi. (323km) SW on I-70 and Colo. 82 (303/925-1220): 19 lifts. This is the luxury resort of the Rockies.

🔔 **Breckenridge,** 92 mi. (147km) west on I-70 and Colo. 9 (303/453-2368): 15 lifts.

🔔 **Copper Mountain,** 86 mi. (137km) west on I-70 (303/968-2882): 20 lifts.

🔔 **Keystone Resort Ski Area,** 78 mi. (124km) west on I-70 (303/534-7712): 19 lifts.

🔔🔔 **Snowmass,** 199 mi. (313km) west on I-70 and Colo. 82 (303/923-2010): 16 lifts.

🔔🔔 **Steamboat Springs,** 177 mi. (283km) NW on I-70 and U.S. 40 (303/879-6111): 20 lifts.

☀🔔🔔 **Telluride,** plane from Denver to Durango, then 123 mi. (196km) north of Durango on U.S. 550, Colo. 62, and Colo. 145 (303/728-3856): 12 lifts.

🔔🔔🔔 **Vail,** 105 mi. (168km) west on I-70 (303/476-5601; toll free 800/525-3875): 22 lifts. The poshest of the Colorado resorts.

🔔🔔 **Winter Park,** 71 mi. (113km) NW on I-70 and U.S. 40 (303/726-5514): 18 lifts.

ACCOMMODATIONS

A Note on Accommodations: Room rates in Denver are coded as follows: **VE,** Very Expensive ($140 and up); **E,** Expensive ($90–$140); **M,** Moderate ($60–$90); **I,** Inexpensive ($30–$60); **B,** Budget (up to $30). A listing of toll free numbers is in the Appendix.

Personal Favorites (in order of preference)

🎗🎗🎗 **Hyatt Regency** (formerly the Fairmont; dwntwn), 1750 Welton St., CO 80202 (303/295-1234; toll free, see Hyatt). 540 rms, A/C, color TV, in-rm movies. AE, CB, DC, MC, V. Gar. $8, pool, tennis, two rests. (including the Marquis Room), coffee shop, two bars, 24-hr. rm svce, nightclub, concierge, free crib. *Note:* This elegant glass-and-steel tower (26 floors) is the last word in hotel comfort. Spacious, luxuriously arranged rms, each in its own style (most have refrigerators). Excellent svce and a very good French rest. VIP and big business clientele. The best spot in Denver. **E–VE**

🎗🎗🎗 **Burnsley Hotel** (dwntwn), 1000 Grant St., CO 80203 (303/830-1000; toll free 800/345-3457). 82 suites, A/C, cable color TV. AE, CB, DC, MC, V. Free parking, pool, rest. (The Burnsley), bar, rm svce, nightclub, 24-hr. concierge. *Note:* Small, intimate hotel composed exclusively of suites. Luxurious, ultra-comfortable facilities including vast bedrooms w. period furniture, refrigerators, private balconies, and a lovely view of the Rockies in the distance. Personalized svce, a very good rest., and renowned jazz club. A favorite of connoisseurs. **E–VE**

☼�꩜꩜ **Oxford Alexis** (dwntwn), 1600 17th St., CO 80202 (303/628-5400; toll free 800/228-5838). 80 rms, A/C, color TV. AE, CB, DC, MC, V. Valet gar. $8, health club, sauna, rest. (Oxford Club), bar, 24-hr. rm svce, concierge, free crib. *Note:* Denver's first luxury hotel (built a century ago in 1891) is a delightful little place that has been redone as good as new. The atmosphere is elegant and discreet, the rms comfortable and tastefully decorated, the rm svce excellent. Good rest. and a splendid art deco bar. Clientele of regulars. **E**

꩜꩜ **Best Western Landmark Inn** (nr. dwntwn), 455 S. Colorado Blvd. CO 80222 (303/388-5561; toll free, see Best Western). 279 rms, A/C, color TV, in-rm movies. AE, CB, DC, MC, V. Free parking, pool, sauna, rest. bar, rm svce, nightclub, free crib. *Note:* Modern motel specializing in business and convention clientele. w. big, comfortable rms, efficient reception and svce. In the heart of Denver's nightlife. 10 min. from dwntwn. **I–M**

꩜꩜ **Holiday Inn Sports Center** (nr. dwntwn), 1975 Bryant St. (at 19th Ave.), CO 80204 (303/433-8331; toll free, see Holiday Inns). 168 rms, A/C, color TV, in-rm movies. AE, CB, DC, MC, V. Free parking, pool, health club, rest. (Fans), bar, rm svce, free crib. *Note:* Large, round 13-story tower a few steps from Mile High Stadium offering the functional style and comfort of a Holiday Inn. Group and convention clientele. 5 min. from dwntwn. Lovely view of the skyline and the mountains from the rest. at the top. A very good value. Free airport shuttle. **I–M**

꩜ **La Quinta Central** (nr. dwntwn), 3500 Fox St., CO 80216 (303/458-1222; toll free, see La Quinta). 106 rms, A/C, color TV, in-rm movies. AE, CB, DC, MC, V. Free parking, pool, adj. 24-hr. coffee shop, bar, valet svce, free crib. *Note:* Modern, comfortable motel 6 min. from dwntwn w. spacious rms and efficient reception and svce. Good value. **I**

꩜ **Motel 6 East** (nr. dwntwn), 12020 E. 39th Ave., CO 80239 (303/371-1980). 137 rms, A/C, color TV, free in-rm movies. AE, DC, MC, V. Free parking, pool, free crib. *Note:* An unbeatable value in modern comfort quite close to the airport. Ideal for the motorist (direct access to the highways). **B**

꩜ **Regal Inn West** (nr. dwntwn), 3050 W. 49th Ave., CO 80221 (303/455-8888; toll free 800/851-8888). 196 rms, A/C, color TV. AE, CB, DC, MC, V. Free parking, pool, adj. 24-hr. coffee shop, free crib. *Note:* A classic motel 12 min. from dwntwn affording functional comfort. Ideal for the motorist. A good overall value. Free morning coffee. **B–I**

Other Accommodations (From top bracket to budget)

☼�꩜꩜꩜ **Brown Palace Hotel** (dwntwn), 321 17th St., CO 80202 (303/297-3111; toll free, see Preferred). 230 rms, A/C, cable color TV. AE, CB, DC, MC, V. Valet gar. $8, three rests. (including the Palace Arms), two bars, 24-hr. rm svce, entertainment, hrdrsr, concierge, free crib. *Note:* The grande dame of Denver hotels has been frequented by every American president since Theodore Roosevelt. A slightly incongruous modern tower overhangs the triangular building (1890). Elegant, eight-story atrium w. interior balconies, and fairly spacious, entirely renovated rms enhance the hotel's urbane character. Personalized svce and a reputable rest. Interesting wknd packages. **E–VE**

꩜꩜꩜ **Westin Tabor Center** (dwntwn), 1672 Lawrence St., CO 80202 (303/572-9100; toll free, see Westin). 420 rms, A/C, color TV, in-rm movies. AE, CB, DC, MC, V. Gar. $10, pool, health club, sauna, squash, two rests. (including Augusta), coffee shop, bar, piano bar, 24-hr. rm svce, boutiques, free crib. *Note:* This large 19-story building w. rather ungraceful modern architecture offers direct access to the 16th Street Mall and its dozens of boutiques and stores. Luxurious, comfortable rms w. minibars (some w. balconies) and very complete facilities. Very good svce and an exclusive, grand-hotel rest. Business clientele (the financial district is nearby). Has the most expensive suite in Denver ($1,000 a night). **E–VE**

ㄒㄒㄒ **Marriott City Center** (dwntwn), 1701 California St., CO ㄴㄴㄴ 80202 (303/297-1300; toll free, see Marriott). 610 rms, A/C, color TV, in-rm movies. AE, CB, DC, MC, V. Valet gar. $6, pool, health club, sauna, two rests. (including Marjolaine's), coffee shop, three bars, rm svce, boutiques, nightclub, concierge, free crib. *Note:* On the first 20 floors of the Arco Tower (42 floors). Spacious rms w. refrigerators. Ultramodern architecture, irreproachable comfort and facilities, unreliable svce. Two VIP floors. Business clientele. A very good location at the heart of the business district. **M–E**

☼ ㄒㄒ **Queen Anne Inn** (dwntwn), 2147 Tremont Pl., CO 80205 ㄴㄴ (303/296-6666). 10 rms, A/C; no TV or phone in rms. AE, MC, V. Free parking; no bar or rest., but free breakfast. *Note:* A happily restored gem of Victorian architecture, this little villa stands in the heart of the historic Clements District, 5 min. from dwntwn. Elegant, comfortable rms overlooking city or grdn; many collectibles and period furniture. You must reserve well ahead; if you're allergic to the conveyor-belt style of big hotel, this is for you. **M–E**

ㄒㄒ **Radisson** (formerly the Hilton; dwntwn), 1550 Court Pl., CO ㄴㄴ 80202 (303/893-3333; toll free, see Radisson). 750 rms, A/C, color TV, in-rm movies. AE, CB, DC, MC, V. Gar. $6, pool, health club, sauna, two rests. (including Windows), coffee shop, bars, rm svce, nightclub, hrdrsr, boutiques, free crib. *Note:* This massive building is something of a tourist barracks. Entirely renovated facilities afford functional comfort and decor. Relatively efficient svce. VIP floor. Very central location, close to the 16th St. Mall. Skating rink open in winter. Group and convention clientele. **M–E**

ㄒ **Writers' Manor Hotel** (nr. dwntwn), 1730 S. Colorado Blvd., ㄴㄴ CO 80222 (303/756-8877; toll free 800/525-8072). 325 rms, A/C, color TV, in-rm movies. AE, CB, DC, MC, V. Free parking, two pools, tennis, squash, health club, sauna, rest. (Churchill's), coffee shop, bar, rm svce, nightclub, free crib. *Note:* Attractive, comfortable motel 15 min. from dwntwn. Inviting rms w. private patios or balconies, some w. minibars. Good svce and a very adequate rest. Group and convention clientele. A very good value. **I–M**

ㄒ **Econo-Lodge Denver** (nr. dwntwn), 4760 E. Evans Ave., CO ㄴ 80222 (303/757-7601; toll free 800/446-6900). 78 rms, A/C, cable color TV. AE, CB, DC, MC, V. Free parking, pool, health club, rest., bar, crib $5. *Note:* Small, appealing motel 15 min. from dwntwn. Depressing surroundings, just off I-25, but a good overall value. Ideal for the motorist. No-smoking rms. **I**

ㄒ **Motel 6 West** (nr. dwntwn), 480 Wadsworth Blvd., CO ㄴ 80226 (303/232-4924). 120 rms, A/C, color TV, free in-rm movies. AE, DC, MC, V. Free parking, pool, free crib. *Note:* An unbeatable value in functional comfort that is ideal for the motorist, 15 min. from dwntwn. **B**

Airport Accommodations

☼ ㄒㄒㄒ **Stouffer Concourse** (nr. dwntwn), 3801 Quebec St., CO ㄴㄴㄴ 80207 (303/399-7500; toll free, see Stouffer). 400 rms, A/C, color TV, in-rm movies. AE, CB, DC, MC, V. Indoor valet parking $5, two pools, health club, sauna, rest., bars, 24-hr. rm svce, nightclub, concierge, crib $10. *Note:* Remarkable futurist architecture in the shape of a trapezoid. All the comfort and luxury of a first-rate hotel in a splendid 12-story glass atrium. Vast, well-conceived rms w. refrigerators and private balconies (the best have a view of the mountains). Extremely well soundproofed. Very efficient svce and a mediocre rest., as in all Stouffers. Free airport shuttle. Three top floors are reserved for VIPs. One of the country's most spectacular hotels. 20 min. from dwntwn. **E–VE**

ㄒㄒ **Stapleton Plaza Hotel & Athletic Center** (nr. dwntwn), 3333 ㄴㄴ Quebec St., CO 80207 (303/321-3500; toll free 800/525-1315). 300 rms, A/C, color TV, in-rm movies. AE, CB, DC, MC, V. Free parking, pool, health club, sauna, squash, rest. (Antares), two bars, 24-hr. rm svce, hrdrsr, boutiques, free crib. *Note:* Modern motel w. futurist decor and a spectacular 10-story atrium w. glass elevators. Comfortable rms w. interior balconies and minibars. Good recreational facilities. Business clientele. Efficient svce. Free airport shuttle. **M–E**

YMCA/Youth Hostels

Denver Youth Hostel (nr. dwntwn), 630 E. 16th Ave., CO 80203 (303/ 832-9996). Dormitories. Clean and inviting.

YMCA (dwntwn), 25 E. 16th Ave., CO 80202 (303/861-8300). 60 rms. Men and women. Pool, health club.

RESTAURANTS

A Note on Restaurant Prices: Denver restaurant prices, per person, excluding drinks and service charges, are coded as follows: **VE,** Very Expensive ($60 and up); **E,** Expensive ($40–$60); **M,** Moderate ($25–$40); **I,** Inexpensive ($15–$25); **B,** Budget (up to $15).

Personal Favorites (in order of preference)

Adirondacks (formerly the Rattlesnake Club; nr. dwntwn), 901 Larimer St. (Tivoli Center) (573-8900). A/C. Lunch/ dinner daily, brunch Sun. AE, CB, DC, MC, V. Jkt. *Specialties:* smoked trout w. sour cream and blinis, Maine crab w. chives and mustard seed, roast duck w. shallots and grilled pear, roast veal w. vinegar and green peppercorns, ice cream w. white chocolate and passion fruit. The menu changes regularly. Superb wine list. *Note:* The most celebrated rest. in the Rockies is the creation of the renowned young American chef Michael McCarty (of Michael's rest. in Santa Monica). This splendid rest. w. original decor—coffee-brewing kettles, tones of pink, with abstract paintings and a glass elevator shaft—occupies three levels of the former Tivoli brewery, now entirely remodeled. First-rate svce. VIP and gourmand clientele. Resv. are an absolute must, well in advance, except for the ground-floor Grill. One of the country's finest rests. *American.* **M–E**

Café Giovanni (dwntwn), 1515 Market St. (825-6555). A/C. Lunch Mon–Fri, dinner Mon–Sat; closed hols. AE, CB, DC, MC, V. Jkt. *Specialties:* fresh homemade pasta, chicken primavera, poached sweetbreads w. port, saltimbocca w. three cheeses, roast duckling, fish of the day, very good soufflés. The menu changes regularly. Rather weak wine list. *Note:* The Leone brothers, young and talented owners of this excellent rest., have transformed an old, decrepit downtown warehouse into an inviting, comfortable refuge where European-inspired cuisine (French and Italian, notably) reigns supreme. Flowery, elegant Victorian decor and first-rate svce. Resv. a must. One of Denver's best. *Continental/Italian.* **I–M**

Cliff Young's (dwntwn), 700 E. 17th Ave. (831-8900). A/C. Lunch Mon–Fri, dinner Mon–Sat. AE, CB, DC, MC, V. Jkt. *Specialties:* rack of lamb encrusted in herbs, halibut in fruit sauce, grilled salmon in lemon-dill butter, roast quail w. foie gras and wild rice. Baked goods made fresh daily. Extensive wine list. *Note:* Most innovative address of Restaurant Row (17th Ave.), this elegant small rest. serves creative American cuisine w. southwestern flair. The menu is varied, its presentation unsurpassed. Attentive svce; pleasant background music; resv. essential. *American.* **I–M**

The Broker (dwntwn), 821 17th Ave. (292-5065). A/C. Lunch Mon–Fri, dinner nightly; closed Dec 25. AE, CB, DC, MC, V. Jkt. *Specialties:* Broker-style shrimp, roast beef au jus, beef Wellington, chicken Cordon Bleu, poor choice of desserts. *Note:* The rest. has retained the original decor of this former bank vault, and as is only fitting, the place is very popular among businesspeople. An excellent locale. Resv. advised. Other locations: 1444 S. Havana St. (750-4060); I-70 and Peoria St. (371-6420). Valet parking Mon–Sat. *American/Continental.* **I–M**

Juanita's Uptown (nr. dwntwn), 1700 Vine St. (333-9595). A/C. Lunch Mon–Fri, dinner nightly. AE, MC, V. *Specialties:*

burritos, shrimp enchiladas, tacos, Tequila-cured salmon snapper Vera Cruz, chicken mole, flan. *Note:* The nicest of Denver's innumerable Mexican rests. The jukebox, Formica, and neon decor looks like a set out of *American Graffiti,* but the food is for real and the prices attractive. Youthful, relaxed ambience where double-breasted suits and jeans coexist comfortably. Very popular locally; resv. advisable. Other location: 1043 Pearl St., Boulder (449-5273). *Mexican.* **B–I**

🍷 **Michael's Trattoria** (nr. dwntwn), 1525 Blake St. (623-7648). 🍴 A/C. Lunch Mon–Fri, dinner Mon–Sat. AE, MC, V. *Specialties:* fresh homemade pasta, fettuccine Alfredo, cutlet milanese, veal marsala, chicken Abruzzi. Good list of Italian wines. *Note:* This locally popular rest. offers pleasant decor and ambience in a former butcher's shop that has been completely renovated. Generous portions and honest cuisine. *Italian.* **I**

Other Restaurants (from top bracket to budget)

🍷🍷🍷 **The Augusta** (dwntwn), in the Westin Tabor Center (see "Accommodations," above) (572-9100). A/C. Lunch Tues–Fri, dinner Tues–Sat. AE, CB, DC, MC, V. Jkt. *Specialties:* crépinette (sausage) of venison in dark-ale sauce, smoked Colorado trout in sour-cream dill, southern mixed grill, New York steak w. Maui onion confit, roast duck in apricot-brandy sauce, Coho salmon w. basil-tomato hollandaise, Provimi veal ribeye w. leek and pine nuts, chocolate-praline cheesecake. Short but excellent wine list. *Note:* The deluxe rest. of your dreams. With its huge picture windows looking out over the skyline, and its sleek black walls, Augusta is a model of contemporary elegance and provides an appropriate background for the subtle, delicate dishes of youthful chef Serge Delage. Polished, attentive svce; resv. highly recommended. A splendid place. *American.* **M–E**

🍷🍷 **Strings** (nr. dwntwn), 1700 Humboldt (831-7310). A/C. 🍴🍴 Lunch Mon–Sat, dinner nightly. MC, V. Jkt. *Specialties:* grilled eggplant w. mozzarella, mixed salads, fresh homemade pasta, grilled swordfish w. cabbage and peppercorns, garlic chicken in tomatillo sauce, remarkable desserts. *Note:* Excellent variations on the California cuisine moderne theme by Noel Cunningham. Hi-tech ocean-liner decor w. an open grill and a pleasant patio for al fresco meals. Friendly, cheerful svce. Hip clientele. Resv. a must in light of its success. *American.* **I–M**

🍷🍷 **Cactus Kelly** (dwntwn), International Collection, 601 S. 🍴🍴 Broadway (693-9026). A/C. Lunch/dinner Mon–Sat. AE, DC, MC, V. *Specialties:* black-bean nachos, cactus cocoon (fried avocado stuffed w. pork chili), ragoût of seafood, roast chicken w. lime juice and jalapeño dressing, chicken-fried steak w. potato purée, grilled snapper filet w. papaya sauce. *Note:* Fashionable rest. in the deluxe International Collection Shopping Mall w. such neighbors as Yves Saint-Laurent and Krizia, offering a modern, sunlit cuisine redolent of Mexican, Spanish, and Latin American influences. Chic Santa Fe–style setting. Attentive, smiling svce. Resv. strongly advised. *American.* **I–M**

🍷🍷 **Tante Louise** (nr. dwntwn), 4900 E. Colfax Ave. (355-4488). 🍴🍴 A/C. Lunch Mon–Fri, dinner Mon–Sat; closed hols. AE, CB, DC, MC, V. Jkt. *Specialties:* veal w. mustard, grilled filet of lamb, Peking duck, sweetbreads w. madeira. The menu changes regularly. Fine wine list. *Note:* This turn-of-the-century–style inn is elegant and intimate and offers lovingly prepared, delicate, imaginative cuisine. Agreeable svce. Distinguished musical background. Resv. advised. An excellent spot. 10 min. from dwntwn. *Continental.* **I–M**

☼🍷🍷 **Buckhorn Exchange** (nr. dwntwn), 1000 Osage St. (534- 🍴🍴 9505). A/C. Lunch/dinner daily; closed hols. AE, CB, DC, MC, V. *Specialties:* navy-bean soup, all kinds of meat cuts, T-bone steak, Rocky Mountain oysters, moose and bison steak, venison (in season) roast quail, homemade apple pie. *Note:* Patronized by Buffalo Bill in his day, the oldest rest. in Denver (1893) proudly displays the "No. 1" on its liquor license. First-rate prime cuts generously served. Authentic western decor including a vast collection of guns and hunting trophies. Absolutely worth a visit. Locally very popular. Resv. advised. *Steak.* **I**

☼♀♀ **Café Promenade** (dwntwn), 1424 Larimer St. (893-2692). ⚘🍴 A/C. Breakfast/lunch/dinner Mon–Sat; closed hols. AE, CB, DC, MC, V. Jkt. *Specialties:* from fresh pasta to pastries, everything here is homemade. Veal is the great specialty of the house. Remarkable desserts. Good wine list. *Note:* Gracious old-world–style tavern in the heart of Larimer Sq. offering delicate French-Italian–inspired cuisine. The agreeable patio is open in good weather. Courteous, cheerful svce. Pleasant classical background music in the evening. A fine place for business lunches. Resv. advised. *Continental.* **I**

☼♀ **Baby Doe's Matchless Mine** (nr. dwntwn), 2520 W. 23rd ⚘ Ave. (433-3386). A/C. Lunch Sun–Fri, dinner nightly; closed Dec 25. AE, CB, DC, MC, V. *Specialties:* bison steak, beef chops, chicken w. Calvados, duck à l'orange, catch of the day. *Note:* Reproduces the atmosphere of a famous Leadville (Colorado) gold mine from the 1880s. Amusing bric-a-brac decor. Very estimable, if not terribly original, cuisine. Rather touristy ambience. Dancing nightly as well. *Steak/American.* **I**

♀ **Gasho** (dwntwn), 1627 Curtis St. (892-5625). A/C. Lunch Mon–Sat, dinner nightly. AE, CB, DC, MC, V. *Specialties:* hibachi steak, teriyaki, sashimi, sukiyaki. *Note:* Denver's best Japanese rest. offers classic knife-wielding performances by the cooks under the admiring gaze of the customers. Lovely decor taken from a 300-year-old Japanese farm. Business clientele. Locally popular. Other location: 5071 S. Syracuse St. (773-3277). *Japanese.* **B–I**

☼♀ **Casa Bonita** (vic.), 6715 W. Colfax Ave., Lakewood (232-⚘ 5115). A/C. Lunch/dinner daily; closed hols. AE, MC, V. *Specialties:* enchiladas, tacos, chili con queso, tamales. *Note:* Huge rest. (seating for 1,100) that is so wild, it's cool. Classic Mexican dishes served in a vibrant, carnival atmosphere: palm trees, a 30-ft. (10m) waterfall, mariachi music, staged shootouts, and puppet shows. Locally popular. *Mexican.* **B**

♀ **Daddy Bruce's Bar-B-Que** (nr. dwntwn), 1629 E. Bruce Ran-⚘ dolph Ave. (295-9115). A/C. Lunch Tues–Sat, dinner Tues–Sun (until midnight). No credit cards. *Specialties:* spareribs, chicken, barbecued pork and beef, smoked turkey, sweet-potato pie. *Note:* A real institution; Denver's temple of soul food. The neighborhood is less than inviting and the decor is neo-Formica, but the barbecue is remarkable. A must for those in search of local color. No resv. *American.* **B**

Cafeteria/Fast Food

Furr's (nr. dwntwn), 4900 Kipling (423-4602). Open daily (until 8pm). Honest, well-prepared cafeteria food, particularly the roast beef. No credit cards.

BARS & NIGHTCLUBS

Bay Wolf (nr. dwntwn), 231 Milwaukee St. (388-9221). Open Mon–Sat. Fashionable singles bar and rest. Excellent live jazz.

Corner Room (dwntwn), in the Oxford Alexis Hotel, 1600 17th St. (628-5400). Open Mon–Sat. Inviting, pleasant art deco bar with an elegant atmosphere and piano jazz.

☼ **El Chapultepec** (dwntwn), 1962 Market St. (295-9126). ⚘ Since 1980, the best modern jazz in town. A Mexican rest. as well (praiseworthy). Open nightly.

Neo (nr. dwntwn), 350 S. Birch St., Glendale (320-0117). Open nightly. The "in" disco with rather flashy decor and a funky ambience.

Thrills (nr. dwntwn), 320 S. Birch St., Glendale (333-8555). Locally popular, very funky rock joint with a rest. (undistinguished). Open daily.

The Wharf (nr. dwntwn), 2430 S. Havana St. (671-5111). Live rock and jazz. Open Mon–Sat.

NEARBY EXCURSIONS

☼☆ **BOULDER** (30 mi./48km NW on U.S. 36): This residential extension of Denver is built in the foothills of the Rockies and has a young, upwardly mobile population keen on sports and the environment. Boulder is home to the **University of Colorado** (22,000 students), which includes a world-renowned medical school and many leading scientific institutes, among them the laboratories of the National Bureau of Standards and the National Center for Atmospheric Research, housed in a futurist building by I. M. Pei at 1850 Table Mesa Dr. (497-8720), open daily.

An interesting pioneer museum is the **Boulder Historical Museum**, 1206 Euclid Ave. (449-3464), open Tues–Sat. Don't miss a glance at the charming **Downtown Mall,** Pearl St. between 11th St. and 15th St., with its pedestrians-only street, boutiques, restaurants, and old town houses. Well worth going out of your way for. (For accommodations and restaurants, see Chapter 30 on the Rockies.)

☼☆ **BUFFALO BILL GRAVE** (in Lookout Mountain Park, 18 mi./28km west on I-70 and U.S. 6) (526-0747): A magnificent view over the city from the mountaintop where lies the tomb of the famous scout. Small museum dedicated to his adventurous career. Well worth the trip. Open daily in summer, Tues–Sun the rest of the year. On the way, visit the **Colorado Railroad Museum** in Golden (see below).

☼☆ **CENTRAL CITY** (34 mi./54km west on I-70 and Colo. 279): Spectacular little mining town from the days of the Gold Rush. The abundance of gold mined here earned it the nickname "the richest square mile on earth." Counting as many as 5,000 inhabitants in the 1870s, the town has barely 350 today. A walking tour of the town is fun but tiring (it was built on the side of a mountain at 8,496 ft./2,590m; start at the top and work downward). See the very handsome **Opera House** from 1878, Eureka St. (571-4435), open June–Aug. The **Central Gold Mine,** 126 Spring St. (582-5574), is open daily May–Sept. The **Gold Coin Saloon** on Main St. has been in operation since 1878. The **Teller House,** Eureka St. (582-3200), is a charming little Victorian hotel built in 1872 with a famous bar. There is also a picturesque narrow-gauge railroad. Well worth going out of your way for.

☆ **COMANCHE CROSSING MUSEUM** (in Strasburg, 30 mi./48km east on I-70) (622-4668): Open-air museum devoted to the builders of the 19th-century transcontinental railroad. Original buildings and historic memorabilia of all kinds. Open daily June–Aug only.

☼☆ **GOLDEN** (15 mi./24km west on W. Colfax Ave. and U.S. 40): The Colorado capital from 1862 to 1867. See the **Colorado Railroad Museum,** 17155 W. 44th Ave. (279-4591), with its interesting collection of old locomotives, one of the most important in the nation. Open daily. A recommended joint excursion with the nearby **Buffalo Bill Grave** (see above).

☆ **IDAHO SPRINGS** (34 mi./54km west on I-70): Old gold diggers' town in the midst of a still very active mining zone, now producing uranium, molybdenum, zinc, lead, tungsten. Today it is also a renowned tourist attraction with radioactive hot springs. The longest mine tunnel in the world (5 mi./7km) once joined Idaho Springs and Central City. Part of the tunnel still exists but is not open to the public. See the **Argo Gold Mill,** 23rd Ave. and Riverside Dr. (567-2421), a gold mine dating from 1913, open daily June–Sept. Well worth going out of your way for. A recommended joint excursion with **Central City** (see above) and **Mount Evans Scenic Road** (see "Farther Afield," below).

    🔔 **RED ROCKS PARK** (12 mi./19km SW on W. Colfax Ave. and Colo. 26) (575-2637): A natural, 10,000-seat amphitheater carved out in the middle of reddish rocks more than 300 ft. (100m) high. Offers a spectacular view of the city plus public concerts, big-name performances, and open-air shows in summer. It is also the stage for an open-air Mass on Easter Sunday attended by thousands (Easter sunrise service).

NATIONAL PARKS NEARBY: 🔔🔔 **Rocky Mountain National Park,** 70 mi. (112km) NW on U.S. 36 and 34. The most mountainous national park in America boasts 113 peaks of more than 10,000 ft. (3,050m), including **Longs Peak** (14,255 ft./4,345m). Torrents, glaciers, eternal snows, fish-filled lakes, very dense forests, and more than 300 mi. (480km) of hiking trails. Unspoiled nature and a paradise for mountain climbing, camping, and fishing. **Trail Ridge Road** crosses right through the park and offers splendid panoramas, as well as spectacular views of the mountain peaks. The road is closed mid-Oct. to mid-June. There are numerous hotels and motels open year round in **Estes Park, Grand Lake,** and **Granby.** The **Moraine Park Visitor Center and Museum** is 1 mi. (2km) from the east entrance of the park on U.S. 36 (open daily June–Sept). Note that part of U.S. 34, between Deer Ridge and Timber Creek, is closed in winter. For information, contact the Superintendent, Estes Park, CO 80517-8397 (303/586-2371). An excursion not to be missed. (For accommodations, see Chapter 30 on the Rockies.)

FARTHER AFIELD

    🔔🔔 **MOUNT EVANS SCENIC ROAD** (120 mi./190km r.t. on I-70W, Colo. 103, and Colo. 5): The highest asphalt road in the country, peaking at 14,260 ft. (4,346m). Fabulous landscapes can be seen all along the road, which is open in summer only (check in Idaho City before departure). A real trial for people and vehicles, but well worth the 5-hr. r.t. (not recommended to people with a heart condition or susceptible to vertigo). On the way, visit **Georgetown** and **Central City** (see "Nearby Excursions," above), two picturesque mining towns from the days of the Gold Rush.

    ☼🔔🔔 **COLORADO SPRINGS** (134 mi./214km r.t. on I-25S): Quaint garden city at 6,000 ft. (1,800m) frequented year round by tourists and vacationers. Home of the Air Force Academy, NORAD (headquarters for U.S. air defense) and the various computer manufacturers; the U.S. Olympic Training Complex represents the city's third major activity, after defense and data processing: sport. The U.S. Olympic Committee has settled in neighboring Colorado Springs, cheek-by-jowl with a couple of dozen sports organizations. These are the city's major tourist attractions.

    The 🔔 **U.S. Air Force Academy** lies 10 mi. (16km) north of the city at Exit 156B from I-25 (719/472-2555); its Visitor Center, with a small museum and movie shows, is open year round. On the very handsome campus, don't miss the 17-spired Cadet Chapel, a major landmark of futurist architecture.

    Its nerve center protected by the rocky shield of Cheyenne Mountain, SW of the city, ☼🔔🔔 **NORAD,** offers guided tours of its underground installations Mon, Thurs, and Sat; applications must be made 6 months ahead, in writing, giving the intended visitors' names, Social Security numbers, date of visit, and home telephone. Children under 2 years old are not admitted. Write: HQ AF Space COM/PAC, Attn. Tour Program, Peterson AFB, CO 80914-5001. NORAD's Command Center was faithfully reproduced in the movie *War Games.*

    A guided tour of the ☼🔔🔔 **U.S. Olympic Training Complex,** 1750 E. Boulder St. at Union Blvd. (719/578-4644), allows sports fans to watch their favorite athletes in training for boxing, track, basketball, gymnastics, or the like. Open daily; shouldn't be missed.

Lovers of the Old West must also take in the ⚐ **Pro Rodeo Hall of Champions,** 101 Pro Rodeo Dr. at Exit 147 from I-25 (719/593-8847), with its museum of the American cowboy, rodeo trophies, and western memorabilia. Open daily in summer, Tues–Sun the rest of the year. Along the same lines try to see ☼⚐ **Pike's Peak Ghost Town,** 400 S. 21st St. at U.S. 24 (719/634-0696), open daily mid-May to mid-Oct. This is a real 19th-century pioneer settlement with a strong far western flavor, complete with saloon, prison, hotel, smithy, drugstore, and so on, all certified authentic and of the period.

Numerous and very pretty excursions in the area, including:

Broadmoor-Cheyenne Mountain Hwy. (access by S. Nevada Ave.): A superb panoramic route and "shrine of the sun" dedicated to the famous humorous Will Rogers.

Garden of the Gods (access by U.S. 24 and 30th St. NW): Splendid reddish sandstone monoliths, particularly spectacular at sunrise and sunset.

Manitou Springs: A charming mountain spa at 515 Ruxton Ave. in Manitou Springs (719/685-5401) is the terminus of the **Cog Railway,** picturesque route leading to Pike's Peak (daily May–Oct). The **Scenic Incline Railway,** 518 Ruxton Ave. (719/685-9086), is a cable car that goes to the summit of Mount Manitou, offering an impressive view (daily May–Sept).

Pikes Peak (14,110 ft./4,301m): Accessible only in summer by a steep toll road or by the Cog Railway (see above). An excursion not to be missed.

Seven Falls (access by Cheyenne Blvd.): A very beautiful rocky canyon with waterfalls which are illuminated at dusk. Open daily year round. A wonderfully spectacular drive. (For accommodations, see Chapter 30 on the Rockies.)

A visit to Colorado Springs should not be missed.

☼⚐ **CHEYENNE** (200 mi./320km r.t. on I-25): Founded in the 19th century by the army in an effort to protect Union Pacific Railroad builders against Sioux attacks, the capital of Wyoming has retained its frontier-town flavor. Witness the **State Museum and Art Gallery,** Central Ave. and 24th St. (307/777-7024), open daily in summer, Mon–Sat the rest of the year; the **Frontier Days Old West Museum,** Carey Ave. (307/778-7290), open daily in summer, Tues–Sun the rest of the year; and the superb wall murals of the **State Capitol,** Capitol Ave., open Mon–Fri. Annually since 1897, Cheyenne, named for the Native American tribe, has sponsored the **Cheyenne Frontier Days,** the most fabulous rodeo festival in the country, the world's biggest outdoor rodeo celebration, the "Daddy of 'Em All," with 1,100 entrants and 400,000 cowboy fans. Late July; for information, call 307/778-7200. Itself worth the trip.

Where to Stay in Cheyenne

🛏 **Best Western Hitching Post Inn,** 1700 W. Lincolnway, Cheyenne, WY 82001 (307/638-3301). 210 rms. First-rate comfort. **I–M**

🛏 **La Quinta Inn,** 2410 W. Lincolnway, Cheyenne, WY 82001 (307/632-7117). 108 rms. Modern comfort. **I**

🛏 **Motel 6,** 1735 Westland Rd., Cheyenne, WY 82001 (307/635-6806). 108 rms. A very good, economical value. **B**

CHAPTER 30

THE ROCKY MOUNTAINS🍦🍦🍦

□ □ □

Comprising several parallel mountain chains, the Rocky Mountains form an impressive system more than 1,875 mi. (3,000km) long, extending from New Mexico to Canada. This granite barrier of almost Himalayan proportions, with 53 peaks reaching more than 14,000 ft. (4,260m), marks the Continental Divide: east of the Rockies, the Missouri and its tributaries flow toward the Gulf of Mexico; to the west, the Colorado ("mother of all rivers" in the evocative phrase of writer James Michener) and its tributaries flow toward the Pacific. The central section of the Rocky Mountain chain, its peaks sculpted into fantastic shapes by erosion, makes Colorado one of the most beautiful states in America.

Some 70 million years old, the Rockies long remained uninhabited—the earliest traces of Native American settlement go back barely 2,000 years. It is as though the reverential awe that the sight of these wild, magnificent mountains must have inspired kept the local tribes away. Although the first white settlers arrived only in 1820, the westward expansion of the succeeding decades made the Rockies an obligatory way station for the famed riders of the Pony Express (8 days from Kansas to California) and for the heavy stagecoaches of the Wells Fargo and Overland companies. The gold rush of 1859–60 caused a further influx of settlers into the mountains.

Today the Colorado Rockies have become one of the nation's great tourist attractions, favored equally by sun worshippers and skiers, with **Aspen, Vail, Steamboat Springs, Keystone, Telluride, Snowmass,** and **Copper Mountain** ranking among the most popular winter sports centers in the U.S. With Denver as their point of departure, motorists may enjoy numerous 2- to 10-day touring itineraries, allowing them to discover such gorgeous landscapes as the peaks and alpine lakes of **Rocky Mountain National Park** to the north, the wild gorges of the **Colorado National Monument** to the east, the desert solitude of the **Great Sand Dunes** and the fabulous Native American archeological sites of **Mesa Verde National Park** to the south. Dozens of **ghost towns** from the gold-rush days, such as Georgetown, Central City, or Cripple Creek, as well as roads affording breathtaking panoramic views, such as those that wind up **Pikes Peak** and **Mount Evans** (at 14,260 ft./4,346m, the highest road in the U.S.), further enhance the unique appeal of the Colorado Rockies. All in all, this is a region not to be missed, as much for the incomparable beauty of its landscapes as for its aura of adventure (see also Chapter 29 on Denver).

BASIC FACTS: State of Colorado. Area code: 303 or 719. Time zone: mountain. Population of Colorado: approx. 2.9 million.

CLIMATE: Very cold and snowy in winter (30°F/−1°C, on average), wonderfully sunny but cool in summer (70°F/21°C, on average), the climate of the Colorado Rockies is a delight for tourists. Spring (47°F/8°C, on average) and above all autumn (51°F/11°C, on average) are the ideal seasons for avoiding the crowds of summer vacationers and winter sports enthusiasts. Sweaters and sunglasses are advisable in all seasons.

ARRIVAL & TRANSIT INFORMATION

NEAREST AIRPORT: Denver Stapleton International Airport (DEN), 65 mi. (105km) SE of Rocky Mountain National Park; for information, call 303/398-3844.

Other airports giving access to the region are at Aspen, Colorado Springs, Durango, Grand Junction, Gunnison, Steamboat Springs, Telluride, and Vail.

AIRLINES: See Chapter 29 on Denver. **Aspen Airways/United Express** (toll free 800/241-6522) and **Rocky Mountain Airways/Continental Express** (toll free 800/525-0280) serve the main regional airports, with departures from Denver.

BUS OR CAR RENTAL? Numerous bus companies, including Greyhound, link Denver with most of the cities in the Rockies. But considering the distances involved and the range of possible touring routes, a rental car with unlimited mileage is strongly recommended.

CAR RENTAL: See Chapter 29 on Denver. For all other cities, consult the local telephone directory.

LIMOUSINE SERVICES: See Chapter 29 on Denver. For all other cities, consult the local telephone directory.

TRAIN: Amtrak (toll free 800/872-7245) has stations at 413 7th St., **Glenwood Springs;** Agate Ave., **Granby;** 2nd St. and Pitkin St., **Grand Junction;** and 420 Railroad Ave. at Fraser, **Winter Park.**

INTERCITY BUSES: Several companies offer service from Denver: **Airport Transportation Service** (303/476-7576), to Aspen, Beaver Creek, and Vail; **American Limo Service** (303/398-2518), to Boulder and Vail; **Aspen Limousine** (303/925-2400), to Aspen, Snowmass, and Vail; **Greyhound** (see Chapter 29 on Denver); **Resort Express** (toll free 800/334-7433), to Breckenridge, Copper Mountain, and Keystone; **Rocky Mountain Coach Lines** (303/293-2871), to Granby, Winter Park, and Steamboat Springs; **The Skiers' Connection** (toll free 800/824-1104), to Beaver Creek, Breckenridge, Copper Mountain, Keystone, and Vail; and **Steamboat Express Bus** (toll free 800/332-3204), to Steamboat Springs.

INFORMATION & TOURS

TOURIST INFORMATION: The **Colorado Tourism Board,** 1625 Broadway, Suite 1700, Denver, CO 80202 (303/592-5410; toll free 800/433-2656): Information on the entire Colorado Rockies region.

Other sources of local information include:
Aspen Resort Association, 303 Main St., Aspen, CO 81611 (303/925-1940).

Boulder Chamber of Commerce, 2440 Pearl St., Boulder, CO 80306 (303/442-1044).

Colorado Springs Convention and Visitors Bureau, 104 S. Cascade, Colorado Springs, CO 80902 (719/635-7506).

Denver (see Chapter 29 on Denver).

Durango Chamber Resort Association, 111 S. Camino del Rio, Durango, CO 81302 (303/247-0312).

Estes Park Chamber of Commerce, 500 Big Thompson Ave., Estes Park, CO 80517 (303/586-4431; toll free 800/443-7837).

Grand Junction Convention and Visitors Bureau, 360 Grand Ave., Grand Junction, CO 81501 (303/242-3214).

Gunnison Chamber of Commerce, 500 E. Tomichi Ave., Gunnison, CO 81230 (303/641-1501).

Leadville Chamber of Commerce, 809 Harrison Ave., Leadville, CO 80461 (719/486-3900).

Rocky Mountain National Park: Contact the Superintendent, Rocky Mountain National Park, Estes Park, CO 80517 (303/586-2371).

Salida Chamber of Commerce, 406 W. Rainbow Blvd., Salida, CO 81201 (719/539-2068).

Steamboat Springs Chamber Resort Association, 2305 Mt. Werner Circle (P.O. Box 774408), Steamboat Springs, CO 80477 (303/879-0880).

Telluride Chamber Resort Association, P.O. Box 653, Telluride, CO 81435 (303/728-3041).

Vail Resort Association, 241 E. Meadow Dr., Vail, CO 81657 (303/476-1000).

GUIDED TOURS: Gray Line Tours (bus): Tours of 1 day or longer through the Colorado Rockies (see Chapter 29 on Denver). For all other cities, consult the local telephone directory.

SIGHTS, ATTRACTIONS & ACTIVITIES

ADVENTURES: Adrift Adventures (boat), 1816 Orchard Pl., Fort Collins, CO 80521 (303/493-4005; toll free 800/824-0150): 1- to 5-day trips, by raft or rowboat, down the Green River, Dolores River, Colorado River, Arkansas River, and/or Yampa River (May–Sept.).

Adventure Bound (boat), 2392 H Rd., Grand Junction, CO 81505 (303/241-5633): 1- to 5-day rafting trips down the Colorado River, Green River, and Yampa River (May–Sept).

Blazing Paddles (boat), Mill St. and Hyman St., Aspen River, CO 81611 (303/925-5651): Half-day to 4-day rafting trips down the Roaring Fork River, Arkansas River, and Colorado River (May–Sept).

Brown's Rafting (boat), Brown's Fort, on U.S. 50, 7 mi. (11km) west of Cañon City, CO 81212 (719/275-7238): Half- or full-day rafting trips through the canyon of the Arkansas River (May to mid-Oct.).

Colorado Wagon Train (covered wagons), P.O. Box 73, Crawford, CO 81415 (303/921-3660): 6-night trips are offered weekly in summer. Vacationers sleep in tents, in a wagon, or under the stars. The cost is $530 a person; children under 14, $300. Meals included.

Four Corners Rafting (boat), P.O. Box 1032, Buena Vista, CO 81211 (719/395-8949; toll free 800/332-7238): Half-day to 3-day raft trips on the Arkansas River, Gunnison River, or Dolores River (May–Sept).

Ghost Town Scenic Jeep Tour (all-terrain vehicles), 11150 U.S. 50, Salida, CO 81201 (719/539-2144; toll free 800/332-9100): Jeep tours through the many ghost towns of the region.

River Rats, Inc. (boat), P.O. Box 3231, Aspen, CO 81611 (303/925-7648): Rafting trips down the Roaring Fork River, Arkansas River, Colorado River, Dolores River, and Green River (mid-May to mid-Sept).

River Runners Ltd. (boat), 11150 U.S. 50, Salida, CO 81201 (719/539-2144; toll free 800/332-9100 in state; 800/525-2081 out of state): Half- to 3-day rafting trips down the Arkansas River (mid-May to mid-Sept).

San Juan Scenic Jeep Tours (all-terrain vehicles), 480 Main St., Ouray, CO 81427 (303/325-4444): Jeep tours in the mountains, with visits to abandoned mines, ghost towns, etc. Also jeep rentals. (June–Oct.).

Snowmass Whitewater (boat), 50 Village Sq., Snowmass Village, CO 81615 (303/923-4544): Half- to 4-day rafting trips down the Arkansas River, Colorado River, and Roaring Fork River (May–Sept).

ATTRACTIONS: ⚓ **Estes Park Aerial Tramway,** 420 Riverside Dr., Estes Park, 65 mi. (105km) NW of Denver on U.S. 36 (303/586-3675): Cable car to the summit of Prospect Mountain (8,896 ft./2,712m). Spectacular view. Bar with picnic area at the summit. Open daily, mid-May to mid-Sept.

Georgetown Loop Railroad, in Georgetown, 57 mi. (91km) west of Denver on I-70 to Exit 226 or 228 (303/670-1686): Over a 7-mi. (11km), 1-hr. route, this picturesque narrow-gauge railway makes three complete loops as it runs over four dizzyingly high bridges, culminating at 638 ft. (270m) above the Georgetown Valley. In operation from 1884 to 1939, the "Loop" was put back into service in 1973. The views are spectacular. Six round-trips daily from the end of May to early Sept.

Mount Manitou Incline, 518 Ruxton Ave., Manitou Springs, 68 mi. (108km) south of Denver on I-25 and U.S. 24 (719/685-9086): Funicular railway to the summit of Mount Manitou (8,856 ft./2,700m). Impressive. Open daily May–Sept.

Pikes Peak Cog Railway, 515 Ruxton Ave., Manitou Springs, 68 mi. (108km) south of Denver on I-25 and U.S. 24 (719/685-5401): One of the highest cog railways in the world (14,110 ft./4,301m). Tremendous view, not to be missed. Open May–Oct 30; round trip takes 3 hr. Pikes Peak owes its name to Lt. Zebulon Pike, the first American to explore the Rockies, in 1806, on orders from Pres. Thomas Jefferson.

Royal Gorge, 11 mi. (19km) west of Cañon City on U.S. 50: Magnificent landscape of gorges along the Arkansas River. The suspension bridge over the canyon is the world's highest (1,053 ft./321m above the river). The funicular railway that goes to the bottom is the steepest in the world (slope: 45°). A cable car offers a superb view of the gorges. You may combine all three.

The Silverton, Durango, 38 mi. (60km) east of Mesa Verde National Park on U.S. 160, and 379 mi. (606km) SW of Denver on I-25 and U.S. 160 (303/247-2733): In operation since 1882, the Silverton is the last regularly scheduled narrow-gauge railroad in the U.S. Four 7-hr. round trips between Durango and Silverton (90 mi./140km) daily May–Oct. Splendid scenery along the Animas Canyon. Recommended for Old West train buffs. Adults pay $38; children, $16. Reservations essential.

CITIES, SIGHTS & EXCURSIONS: ☀⚓ **Aspen,** 202 mi. (323km) SW of Denver on I-70 and Colo. 82: Once a very active mining town, today one of the most elegant resorts in the Rockies (it was Robert Kennedy's favorite). Superb powder skiing. Four mountains all over 13,120 ft. (4,000m) high. Exceptionally comfortable and pleasant. Very popular summer festival of classical music. The largest single mountain resort in North America. Well worth the trip.

Beaver Creek, 10 mi. (16km) west of Vail on I-70 and U.S. 24: Colorado's most luxurious winter resort. With its immaculate slopes, it could be mistaken for a '50s postcard of a Swiss or Tyrolean village. A real haven of peace and solitude compared to the crowds and commotion of its famous neighbor, Vail. The favorite resort of movie stars and former Pres. Gerald Ford.

Black Canyon of the Gunnison National Monument, 70 mi. (112km) west of Gunnison on U.S. 50: Gorges 2,600 ft. (800m) deep cut into the granite. Magnificent landscapes, wild and beautiful. Mule rides available. Access to the gorges is controlled. Open year round. Worth a side trip. Gunnison is one of the nation's coldest cities in winter. For further information, contact the Superintendent, 2233 E. Main St. (P.O. Box 1648), Montrose, CO 81402 (303/249-7036).

Boulder, 30 mi. (48km) NW of Denver on U.S. 36: A residential community in the mountains near Denver. Famous for its university and scientific research institutes (meteorology, etc.). Interesting museum of the pioneers (see Chapter 29 on Denver, "Nearby Excursions").

Cañon City, 115 mi. (184km) SW of Denver on I-25, Colo. 155, and U.S. 50W: Hemmed in by a close ring of mountains, this picturesque little town settled during the early gold-mining days has always attracted filmmakers, earning the nickname "Colorado's Hollywood." Tom Mix, cowboy star of numerous silent films, made his camera debut here in 1910. The surrounding countryside has been the locale for many films (*Cat Ballou* and *True Grit* are just two examples), as well as several TV series. Cañon City is also the ideal departure point for rafting trips down the canyon of the Arkansas River.

Colorado Springs, 67 mi. (107km) south of Denver on I-25: There is a very nice touring route about 62 mi. (100km) long around Colorado Springs, passing by **Cheyenne Mountain Highway** (superb views from the road and a "Shrine of the Sun" dedicated to the famous cowboy humorist Will Rogers); the **Garden of the Gods** (amazing reddish rock formations, especially impressive at sunrise or sunset); **Manitou Springs,** a beautiful mountain hot spring, and nearby, the **Manitou Cliff Dwellings Museum** on U.S. 24 Bypass (719/685-5242), open daily May–Oct, devoted to ancient Native American cave dwellings; **Pikes Peak** (14,110 ft./4,301m), with its dizzingly steep toll road; and finally **Seven Falls,** a lovely rocky canyon whose waterfalls are illuminated by the setting sun. For more details on these and other attractions (NORAD, the U.S. Air Force Academy, the U.S. Olympic Training Complex, etc.), see Chapter 29 on Denver.

Glenwood Springs, 202 mi. (270km) SW of Denver on I-70: A vacation resort renowned for its hot thermal pools. Open-air bathing summer and winter. Rafting trips on the Colorado River and Roaring Fork River. The famous gunman "Doc" Holliday died here in 1887; his tombstone bears the simple epitaph, "He Died in His Bed" (of tuberculosis, actually, at age 35). A must.

Grand Lake, 115 mi. (184km) NW of Denver on I-70 and U.S. 40: One of the highest yachting harbors in the world (8,380 ft./2,554m). Many other lakes nearby. Splendid alpine scenery.

Grand Mesa National Forest, 52 mi. (83km) east of Grand Junction on I-70 and Colo. 65: An abundance of lakes and forests—a paradise for campers, and for fishing and hunting enthusiasts, at an average altitude of 9,840 ft. (3,000m).

Idaho Springs, 38 mi. (60km) west of Denver on I-70: Renowned hot-springs resort in the middle of an area rich in minerals. The history of the gold rush is told at the **Argo Gold Mill,** 2350 Riverside Dr. (303/567-2421), open daily May to early Sept. Many excursions in the vicinity, such as Mount Evans, Central City, Georgetown (see Chapter 29 on Denver).

Redstone, 29 mi. (45km) south of Glenwood Springs via Colo. 82 and Colo. 133: Old mining town, built from scratch by 19th-century magnate John Cleveland Osgood to house his coal miners. Splendidly restored, colorfully painted Victorian buildings. A mile from the town is Cleveholm, an imposing 42-room manor house where Osgood himself lived; its interior decoration and fittings are of unequaled luxury. Visits by appointment Mon–Fri (303/963-3408).

Steamboat Springs, 177 mi. (283km) NW of Denver on I-70 and U.S.: Very popular hot springs and winter-sports resort (nicknamed "Ski Town U.S.A."). **Tread of Pioneer Museum,** 5th St. and Oak St. (303/879-2214), open daily, late May to mid-Sept. Worth a side trip.

Telluride, 123 mi. (196km) north of Durango on U.S. 550, Colo. 62, and Colo. 145: Dominated by the sharp peaks and ridges of the San Juan Mountains, this picturesque little mining town, just over a century old, has scarcely aged since the gold-rush days. Its Main Street, which could come straight out of an old Western, is a designated historic monument. Spared so far from the tourist invasion, Telluride offers superb ski slopes in winter and exciting music and film festivals every summer.

☼ ♨♨♨ **Vail,** 105 mi. (168km) west of Denver on I-70: The best-known winter sports resort of the Rockies. Fabulous slopes, and a well-deserved reputation for fine accommodations and dining. Favorite vacation spot of the rich and famous.

PANORAMAS: ♨**Glenwood Canyon,** 15 mi. (24km) east of Glenwood
Springs on I-70: Very beautiful landscape of gorges along the Colorado River. Worth seeing.

☼ ♨ **Gold Camp Road,** 5 mi. (8km) west of Colorado Springs on Cheyenne Blvd.: A tortuous 35-mi. (56km) unpaved road following the track of an abandoned gold-rush railroad. Visit the ghost towns of **Goldfield** and **Cripple Creek** en route. Splendid views. Road open late May to Sept 30. Superb.

☼ ♨ **Independence Passroad,** 24 mi. (38km) SE of Aspen on Colo. 82: Fabulous landscapes high in the mountains, but a difficult road. Summit (12,095 ft./3,686m) closed in winter.

☼ ♨ **Million Dollar Highway,** 23 mi. (36km) along U.S. 550 from Ouray to Silverton: So named because of the large quantity of gold-bearing ore in the land over which it was built, this road offers some of the most beautiful scenery in the whole of Colorado. A must-see.

☼ ♨♨ **Mount Evans,** 64 mi. (102km) west of Denver on I-70, Colo. 103, and Colo. 5: The highest road in the U.S. climbs up this mountain, reaching 14,260 ft. (4,346m). A tough ride for both car and driver, but fabulous views. Road open in summer only.

♨ **Mount Pisgah Scenic Drive,** 1 mi. (2km) NW of Cripple Creek on Teller County Rd. 1: Scenic toll highway climbing to the 10,400-ft. (3,170m) peak of Mount Pisgah. Magnificent view of the Continental Divide and Pikes Peak. Open Memorial Day–Oct.

☼ ♨♨ **Phantom Canyon,** 35 mi. (56km) NE of Cañon City: One of the most spectacular panoramic routes in the U.S., w. 25 mi. (40km) of unpaved road between Cañon City and Cripple Creek. Wild and imposing. Road open only May to late Oct. Not recommended for mobile homes.

☼ ♨♨♨ **Pikes Peak,** 7 mi. (11km) west of Manitou Springs on U.S. 24 and Pikes Peak Road: The most famous mountain road in the U.S., with 18 mi. (28km) of sharp bends and steep climbs ending at 14,110 ft. (4,301m). In clear weather you can see Kansas, 165 mi. (264km) east. It was the splendor of this scenery that inspired Katherine Lee Bates to write "America the Beautiful" in 1893. Toll road open May to mid-Oct. Enough in itself to make your trip to the Rockies worthwhile.

♨ **Skyline Drive,** 4 mi. (6km) west of Cañon City on U.S. 50: This 3-mi.-long (5km) scenic drive offers a superb view of Cañon City 800 ft. (244m) below, and the surrounding mountains. Closed in bad weather.

♨♨ **Trail Ridge Road,** 70 mi. (112km) NW of Denver on U.S. 36: Following an old trail used by the Ute and Arapaho peoples, this section of U.S. 34 between Estes Park and Grand Lake peaks at over 12,168 ft. (3,710m)—a 4-mi. (6km) stretch of the road is above 11,808 ft. (3,600m). Fantastic views of the mountains and the midwestern prairies in the distance. Open early June to mid-Oct.

SPECIAL EVENTS: For detailed information on the festivals listed below,
consult the chambers of commerce and visitors' bureaus listed under "Tourist Information," above.

Aspen
Music Festival and School (June–Aug.): A renowned festival of classical music and a much-sought-after music school, one of the best in the U.S. A must for music lovers since 1949.

Boulder
Colorado Shakespeare Festival (July–Aug): Outdoor performances. Very popular locally.

Cripple Creek
Cripple Creek Western Theater (mid-June to mid-Sept): Home of Colorado's oldest and most famous melodrama company, the theater in the Imperial Hotel, 123 N. 3rd St. (719/689-2922), is the place to go to watch the hero (hurray!) triumph over the villain (hiss!).

Durango
Fiesta Days (end of July): Rodeo, parades, horse races, square dances. Lively and colorful.

Estes Park
Scottish-Irish Highland Festival (Sept): A week-long competition in bagpipe music, Irish music, Scottish and Irish dancing, and Celtic games. Gathering of clans from throughout the nation.

Leadville
Boom Days (last wknd in Aug): Reconstructs the saga of the gold rush. Local color guaranteed.

Manitou Springs
Pikes Peak Marathon (Aug): A 28-mi. (45km) foot race up Pikes Peak. One of the most demanding sports events in the world.

Salida
Arkansas River Boat Race (end of June): International kayak race, 26 mi. (42km) long, on the tumultuous waters of the Arkansas River. Spectacular.

Telluride
Summer Festival: A series of festivals beginning with bluegrass (June), followed by jazz (mid-July) and dance (late July), and ending with chamber music (early Aug).

WINTER SPORTS RESORTS: With dozens of winter sports resorts, the Colorado Rockies are a skier's paradise. The most popular resorts are:

Aspen and Aspen Highlands, 42 mi. (67km) south of Glenwood Springs on Colo. 82 (303/925-1220 for Aspen; 303/925-5300 for Aspen Highlands): 19 lifts. Open Nov to mid-Apr.

Beaver Creek, 10 mi. (16km) west of Vail on I-70 and U.S. 24 (303/476-4888): 10 lifts. Open mid-Nov to mid-Apr.

Breckenridge, 92 mi. (147km) west of Denver on I-70 and Colo. 9 (303/453-2368): 15 lifts. Open mid-Nov to mid-Apr.

Copper Mountain, 86 mi. (137km) west of Denver on I-70 and Colo. 9 (303/968-2882): 20 lifts. Open Nov–Apr.

Crested Butte, 30 mi. (48km) north of Gunnison on Colo. 135 (303/349-2333): 12 lifts. Open from the end of Nov until early Apr.

Keystone, 78 mi. (124km) west of Denver on I-70 (303/534-7712): 18 lifts. Open Nov–June.

Purgatory, 25 mi. (40km) north of Durango on U.S. 550 (303/247-9000): 9 lifts. Open from the end of Nov until mid-Apr.

    Snowmass, 30 mi. (48km) south of Glenwood Springs on Colo. 82 (303/925-1221): 14 lifts. Open Nov–Apr.

    Steamboat Springs, 177 mi. (283km) NW of Denver on I-70, Colo. 90, and U.S. 40 (303/879-6111): 19 lifts. Open Nov to mid-Apr.

    Telluride, 105 mi. (168km) north of Durango on I-70 (303/728-3856): 12 lifts. Open from the end Nov to Apr.

    Vail, 105 mi. (168km) from Denver on I-70 (303/476-5601): 16 lifts. Open Nov to mid-Apr.

    Winter Park, 71 mi. (113km) NW of Denver on I-70 and U.S. 40 (303/726-5514): 17 lifts. Open mid-Nov to Apr.

GHOST & MINING TOWNS: The gold rush of 1859–60 and the rich deposits of other minerals in the Rockies (silver, uranium, coal, tin, molybdenum) gave birth to dozens of mining camps, most of which have since become ghost towns. Some, such as St. Elmo, are completely abandoned today, while others, such as Leadville, still survive, though the luster of yesteryear has long since faded.

    Ashcroft, 15 mi. (24km) south of Aspen on Ashcroft Rd.: A well-preserved ghost town. Many of the buildings date from the 1880s.

    Central City, 44 mi. (70km) west of Denver on I-70, Colo. 119, and Colo. 279: Site of the first discovery of gold in 1859. Spectacular mountainside location. Many museums, hotels, and gold mines. A well-known opera house. (For more details, see "Nearby Excursions" in Chapter 29 on Denver.)

    Creede, 22 mi. (35km) NW of South Fork on Colo. 149: Frequented in its heyday by such legendary figures as Butch Cassidy and Calamity Jane, this mining town hemmed in on all sides by the mountains is today half-deserted.

    Cripple Creek, 40 mi. (64km) west of Colorado Springs on Gold Camp Rd.: Nicknamed "the $300-million cow pasture." Its mines have yielded more than $500 million worth of gold and silver. In 1900 it boasted as many as 500 mines and a population of 25,000 (barely 600 today). Sumptuous 1890s bordello, the **Old Homestead,** 353 E. Myers Ave.; open daily, late May to Oct. Museum and visit to an underground gold mine at the **Mollie Kathleen Gold Mine** on Colo. 67, open daily late May to Oct. In passing, look over the famous ghost towns of **Goldfield** and **Victor.** The road can be treacherous in bad weather.

    Fairplay, 85 mi. (136km) SW of Denver on U.S. 285: More than 30 carefully restored buildings from the gold-rush era. The **South Park City Museum,** 4th St. and Front St. (719/836-2387), open daily mid-May to mid-Oct, is worth looking over.

    Georgetown, 57 mi. (91km) west of Denver on I-70: One of the most famous mining towns in Colorado. Many museums and buildings classified as historic monuments, including the legendary **Hotel de Paris,** 409 Sixth Ave., open daily, built in 1875 by Frenchman Louis Dupuy. Equally interesting is the **Georgetown Loop Railroad,** a spectacular train ride (see "Attractions," above).

    Leadville, 103 mi. (164km) SW of Denver on I-70 and Colo. 91: Boasting up to 40,000 inhabitants in its glory days, this picturesque town perched at 10,150 ft. (3,100m)—which makes it the highest town in the U.S.—today has a mere 3,800 (most of them employees of the Climax mine, from which 90% of the world's production of molybdenum is extracted). It was in one of "Cloud City's" (a nickname given to Leadville) saloons in the 1880s that the famous sign "Don't shoot the pianist. He's doing his best." first appeared. Many museums and original buildings, among them the **Tabor Opera House,** at 308 Harrison Ave. (719/486-1147), open Sun–Fri from the

THE ROCKY MOUNTAINS

287

Roosevelt

Nat'l Forest

Ft. Collins

Steamboat Springs

Rocky Mtn.

34

Grand Lake

Nat'l

Estes

Routt

Arapaho

Park

25

Nat'l Forest

Nat'l Forest

Granby

Longmont

40

Boulder

Denver

Winter Park

Central City

85

ROCKY

Idaho Springs

White River

70

Georgetown

Beaver Creek

Grand Junction

Vail

6

Keystone

MOUNTAINS

Glenwood Springs

Nat'l Forest

Copper Mountain

Breckenridge

Colorado Springs

Climax

Pike

Snowmass

Buttermilk

Aspen

Mt. Elbert

Leadville

Nat'l Forest

Snowmass

Aspen

Fairplay

24

Ashcroft

Florissant

Crested Butte

Fossil Beds

Manitou Springs

Buena Vista

Nat'l Mon.

Pikes Peak

St. Elmo

San

Cripple Creek

Gunnison

Isabel

Salida

Nat'l

Canon City

For.

285

N

Durango

0   miles   25

0   kms   40

end of May to Oct, and the **Healy House,** built in 1878, 912 Harrison Ave., open daily June–Aug. A must-see. **Mount Elbert,** Colorado's highest summit, 14,433 ft. (4,400m) is 12 miles (18km) south via U.S. 24.

    St. Elmo, 58 mi. (92km) south of Leadville on U.S. 24 and Colo. 162: A spectacular, authentic ghost town from the gold-rush era, today completely abandoned. *Caution:* The last part of the road to the town is unpaved and passable only in dry weather.

NATIONAL PARKS NEARBY: **Colorado National Monument,** 4 mi.

(6km) west of Grand Junction on Colo. 340 (303/858-3617): Enormous red sandstone monoliths and deep gorges make for a sort of Monument Valley in miniature. Rim Rock Drive, a 22-mi. (35km) scenic drive, crosses the park. Open daily year round.

    Florissant Fossil Beds National Monument, 34 mi. (54km) west of Colorado Springs on U.S. 24 (719/748-3253): About 35 million years ago volcanic lava flows fossilized all the life forms in this prehistoric lake. Exceptionally fine examples of fossilized animals and plants are displayed in the visitor center. Open daily year round.

    Great Sand Dunes National Monument, 234 mi. (374km) south of Denver on I-25, U.S. 160, and Colo. 150 (719/378-2312): Stunning sand dunes, some 700 ft (210 m) or more high, in a mountain setting. Spectacular at sunrise and sunset. Park open daily year round. For more information, contact the Superintendent, Great Sand Dunes National Monument, Mosca, CO 81146; or call the number above.

    Mesa Verde National Park, 430 mi. (688km) SW of Denver on I-25 and U.S. 160: The most impressive Native American historic monument in the U.S. (see Chapter 39 on Santa Fe). Worth the trip all by itself. En route, visit Colorado Springs, the Great Sand Dunes National Monument, and The Silverton (see above).

    Rocky Mountain National Park, 70 mi. (112km) NW of Denver on U.S. 36 and U.S. 34 (303/586-2371): The most mountainous of all American wilderness parks, w. 113 peaks over 10,000 ft. (3,050m) high, including Longs Peak (14,255 ft./4,345m). Rushing rivers, glaciers, snows that never melt, lakes teeming w. fish, dense forests (deer, moose, big-horn sheep, etc.), and over 300 mi. (480km) of hiking trails. Untouched wilderness. A paradise for climbers, campers, fishing enthusiasts, the park is visited by 2.5 million nature lovers annually. The **Trail Ridge Road** (U.S. 34), which follows the route of an ancient Native American trail, cuts right through the park and offers splendid views, as well as spectacular glimpses of the mountaintops (closed mid-Oct to mid-June between Deer Ridge and Timber Creek). Many hotels and motels are open year round in Estes Park, Grand Lake, and Granby (see "Accommodations," below). **Moraine Park Visitor Center** and museum are located 1 mi. (1.6km) from the east entrance to the park on U.S. 36 (open daily June–Sept). For more information, contact the Superintendent, Rocky Mountain National Park, Estes Park, CO 80517-8397. For road and snow conditions in winter, call 303/586-4000.

ACCOMMODATIONS

A Note on Accommodations: Room rates in the Colorado Rockies are coded as follows: **VE,** Very Expensive ($140 and up); **E,** Expensive ($90–$140); **M,** Moderate ($60–$90); **I,** Inexpensive ($30–$60); **B,** Budget (up to $30). A listing of toll free numbers is in the Appendix.

Personal Favorites (by city)

ASPEN   **Hotel Jerome,** 330 E. Main St., Aspen, CO 81611 (303/920-1000; toll free 800/331-7213). 94 rms, A/C, color TV, in-rm movies. AE, CB, DC, MC, V. Free valet parking, pool, health club, sauna, two rests. (including

Silver Queen), bar, rm svce, concierge. *Note:* One of the oldest hotels in the Rockies (1889), and a designated historic monument. Exquisitely restored to its original elegance in 1985. Period furniture, many art objects. Spacious rms, tastefully decorated (all w. refrigerators and phones in the bathrooms). Considerate and polished svce. A great deal of distinction and charm, and you pay accordingly. Resv. essential well in advance. **VE,** but lower rates off-season.

Inn at Aspen, 38750 Colo. 82, Aspen, CO 81611 (303/925-1500; toll free 800/952-1515). 124 studios. A/C, cable color TV. AE, DC, MC, V. Free parking, pool, health club, sauna, skiing, rest., bar, rm svce, concierge. *Note:* Comfortable, inviting motel w. studios only, each having kitchenette, refrigerator, and private balcony or patio. Ideal for long vacations. Pleasant setting at the foot of the slopes; friendly ambience and reception. Good value overall. but lower rates off-season. **E–VE**

Grand Aspen, 515 S. Galena St., Aspen, CO 81612 (303/925-1150; toll free 800/242-7736). 175 rms, no A/C; cable color TV. AE, CB, DC, MC, V. Free parking, pool, rest., two bars, rm svce. *Note:* The biggest hotel in this resort town, right in the heart of Aspen. Pretty view of the mountains. Comfortable and well run. Caters to families and groups. Favored by those in-the-know. Recently renovated. **E–VE,** but lower rates off-season.

Limelite Lodge, 228 E. Cooper Ave., Aspen, CO 81611 (303/925-3025). 63 rms, no A/C; color TV, in-rm movies. AE, CB, DC, MC, V. Free parking, two pools, sauna, nearby coffee shop, free breakfast. *Note:* Charming little mountainside hotel nr. Wagner Park. Spacious, comfortable rms w. refrigerators. Family atmosphere. Enticing ski packages. **M–E,** but lower rates off-season.

BASALT **Best Western Aspenalt,** Colo. 82, Basalt, CO 81621 (303/927-3191; toll free, see Best Western). 36 rms, no A/C; color TV, in-rm movies. AE, CB, DC, MC, V. Free parking, fishing, adj. coffee shop–bar, free breakfast. *Note:* Stylish little motel in a pleasant setting on the banks of the Frying Pan River. Comfortable rms (some w. river view). Friendly reception. Good value. 20 min. from Aspen's ski slopes. **M,** but lower rates off-season.

BEAVER CREEK **Charter at Beaver Creek,** 120 Offerson Rd., Avon, CO 81620 (303/949-6660; toll free 800/824-3064). 59 rms in the hotel, 156 condos and apts., A/C, color TV. AE, CB, DC, MC, V. Free parking, two pools, health club, sauna, tennis court and golf course nearby, skiing, snowmobiles, rest., bar, rm svce, concierge, free crib. *Note:* Luxurious vacation complex of original alpine-village-style design, in a splendid setting. Ultramodern equipment. Spacious, comfortable rms w. refrigerators. Fully equipped condos and apts. w. kitchenettes and fireplaces. Excellent svce. Affluent tourist clientele. Free airport shuttle. **E–VE,** but lower rates off-season.

BOULDER **Boulderado Hotel,** 2115 13th St., Boulder, CO 80302 (303/442-4344; toll free 800/433-4344). 103 rms, A/C, color TV, in-rm movies. AE, CB, DC, MC, V. Free valet parking, three rests. (including Winston's Seafood Grille), three bars, rm svce, nightclub, free crib. *Note:* Beautiful turn-of-the-century Victorian palace. Sumptuous rococo decor w. an abundance of marble and paneling. Comfortable rms w. balconies, some w. refrigerators. Polished svce. A wonderful place to stay, in a central dwntwn location. Adequate rest. Good value. **M–E**

Best Western Golden Buff, 1725 28th St., Boulder, CO 80302 (303/442-7450; toll free, see Best Western). 112 rms, A/C, color TV, in-rms movies. AE, CB, DC, MC, V. Free parking, pool, sauna, health club, putting green, coffee shop, crib $5. *Note:* Comfortable modern motel w. views of the mountains. Spacious rms w. refrigerators, some w. kitchenettes. Good svce. **I–M**

BRECKENRIDGE 🏨 **Hilton Lodge,** 550 Village Rd., Breckenridge, CO 80424 (303/453-4500; toll free, see Hilton). 208 rms, no A/C; color TV, in-rm movies. AE, CB, DC, MC, V. Free indoor parking, pool, health club, sauna, rest., coffee shop, bar, nightclub (in winter only). *Note:* Charming mountain hotel, modern and comfortable. Ski slopes a stone's throw away. Huge inviting rms w. private balconies or patios and refrigerators. Good svce. Caters to groups. Interesting vacation packages. Very good value out of season. **M–E,** but lower rates off-season.

CAÑON CITY 🏨 **Cañon Inn** (formerly the Quality Inn), 3075 U.S. 50E, Cañon City, CO 81212 (719/275-8676). 104 rms, A/C, cable color TV. AE, CB, DC, MC, V. Free parking, pool, thermal springs, putting green, rest., bar, rm svce, free crib. *Note:* Functional modern motel surrounded by grdns. Spacious comfortable rms. Hot springs. Free airport shuttle. Good value. **I–M,** but lower rates off-season.

COLORADO SPRINGS ☀️🏨 **Broadmoor,** Lake Circle at Lake Ave., Colorado Springs, CO 80906 (719/634-7711; toll free 800/634-7711). 560 rms, A/C, color TV. AE, DC, MC, V. Gar. $6, three pools, three golf courses, 16 tennis courts, squash, health club, sauna, putting green, skiing, trapshooting, skating, boats, nine rests. (including the Penrose Room) and bars, rm svce, disco, movie theater, concierge, free crib. *Note:* Superb 1920s-style grand hotel built like a castle amid 3,000 acres (1,210ha) of park and private grdns. Luxurious, urbane interior; elegant, comfortable rms w. balconies (some w. kitchenettes or refrigerators). Exemplary svce. Ideal for devotees of every sport imaginable. One of the best hotels in the U.S. Caters to conventions and wealthy holiday-makers. At the foot of Cheyenne Mountain. **VE,** but lower rates off-season.

☀️🏨 **Antlers Doubletree Hotel,** 4 S. Cascade Ave. (at Pikes Peak), Colorado Springs, CO 80903 (719/473-5600; toll free 800/528-0444). 275 rms. A/C, color TV, in-rm movies. AE, CB, DC, MC, V. Valet parking $3, pool, rest. (London Grill), coffee shop, bar, rm svce, disco, concierge, free crib. *Note:* More than a century old, this charming, elegant hotel boasts a magnificent view of the town and the surrounding mountains. The interior and the fittings have been tastefully restored. Spacious, very comfortable rms; friendly, attentive svce; rest. of quality. Conveniently located in the heart of the dwntwn district. Free shuttles to airport and to Broadmoor Hotel and golf courses. A very good place to stay. **M–E,** but lower rates off-season.

🏨 **Raintree Inn Downtown,** 314 W. Bijou St., Colorado Springs, CO 80905 (719/471-8680). 206 rms, A/C, color TV, in-rm movies. AE, CB, DC, MC, V. Free parking, pool, rest, bar, rm svce, nightclub, free breakfast, free crib. *Note:* Pleasant motel surrounded by lovely grdns a stone's throw from dwntwn. Comfortable rms w. private balconies or patios. Efficient svce. Good value. **I–M,** but lower rates off-season.

🏨 **Motel 6,** 3228 N. Chestnut St., Colorado Springs, CO 80907 (719/520-5400). 84 rms, A/C, color TV, in-rm movies. AE, DC, MC, V. Free parking, pool. *Note:* Modest but comfortable little motel 5 min. from dwntwn. Rms w. fine mountain views. One of the best values in the area. **B**

DILLON 🏨 **Best Western Lake Dillon Lodge,** 1202 Summit Blvd., Frisco, CO 80443 (303/668-5094; toll free, see Best Western). 127 rms, A/C, color TV, in-rm movies. AE, CB, DC, MC, V. Free parking, pool, boating, fishing, rest., bar, valet svce, free crib. *Note:* Comfortable motel w. a view over the lake and the surrounding mountains. Modern decor and rather comprehensive amenities. Very good svce. Free transport to nearby ski resorts (in winter). Excellent value. **I–M,** but lower rates off-season.

DURANGO ☀🏨 **Tamarron Resort,** 18 mi. (28km) north on U.S. 550, Durango, CO 81302 (303/259-2000; toll free 800/525-5420). 350 rms and condos, A/C, cable color TV. AE, CB, DC, MC, V. Free parking, pool, health club, saunas, three tennis courts, golf, putting green, skiing, skating rink, snowmobiles, horseback riding, two rests., bars, rm svce, disco, hardrsr, concierge, free crib. *Note:* One of the most beautiful resort hotels in the U.S., in the heart of the San Juan National Forest. Spacious, extremely comfortable rms w. balconies and refrigerators. Condos w. fully equipped kitchenettes (some w. two bedrooms). Very efficient, friendly svce. Superb location. Hotel organizes rafting trips on the river and Jeep tours. Hunting and fishing guides available. Paradise for lovers of sports and the outdoors. A great place to stay. **E−VE,** but lower rates off-season.

☀🏨 **General Palmer House,** 567 Main Ave., Durango, CO 81301 (303/247-4747; toll free 800/523-3358). 39 rms, A/C, cable color TV. AE, CB, DC, MC, V. Nearby bar and rest., valet svce., free crib. *Note:* Elegant Victorian building dating from the 1890s, marvelously restored. Comfortable rms furnished w. antiques. Library. Friendly svce and reception. Minutes away from the Silverton train stations. **I−M,** but lower rates off-season.

☀🏨 **Strater,** 699 Main Ave., Durango, CO 81301 (303/247-4431). 93 rms, A/C, cable color TV. AE, CB, DC, MC, V. Free valet parking, rest. (Henry's), saloon, valet svce, boutiques. *Note:* Small rococo-style hotel built in the 1900s. Enormous rms, comfortable though not elegant. Woeful svce and reception, which denies the Strater a better rating. The Old West–style saloon (Diamond Belle), w. a ragtime pianist and costumed waitresses, deserves a visit all by itself, however. Entertaining parody-melodramas performed in summer in the adj. Diamond Circle Theater. (Mon–Sat June–Sept). A fine spot for lovers of the Old West. **I−M,** but lower rates off-season.

ESTES PARK ☀🏨 **Stanley Hotel,** 333 Wonderview Ave., Estes Park, CO 80517 (303/586-3371; toll free 800/762-5437). 100 rms, no A/C, cable color TV. AE, MC, V. Free parking, pool, tennis, rest., bar, rm svce, disco, crib $10. *Note:* Venerable, elegantly designed turn-of-the-century hotel situated at the east entrance to Rocky Mountain National Park; inspiration for Steven King's thriller *The Shining,* later a movie w. Jack Nicholson. Very spacious rms, pleasantly decorated. Spectacular setting at the foot of the mountains. Friendly svce. Many cultural activities (concerts, theater, exhibitions, etc.). A fine place to stay. **M−É,** but lower rates off-season.

☀🏨 **Longs Peak Inn and Guest Ranch,** Longs Peak Rte. 3A, Estes Park, CO 80517 (303/586-2110). 36 cottages and chalets, no A/C; TV in lounge. MC, V. Free parking, pool, horseback riding, fishing, rest., bar, movie theater, crib $5. *Note:* Friendly vacation ranch w. lovely view of the mountains. Relaxed atmosphere. Ideal for lovers of the wide-open spaces. Adequate rest. Near Rocky Mountain National Park. Open June to mid-Sept. **E−VE** (Modified American Plan).

🏨 **Alpine Trail Ridge Inn** (formerly the Friendship Inn), 927 Moraine Ave., Estes Park, CO 80517 (303/586-4585). 48 rms; no A/C; cable color TV. AE, CB, DC, MC, V. Free parking, pool, rest., bar, rm svce, crib $3. *Note:* Friendly small motel w. a superb view of the mountains. Comfortable rms, some w. balconies and refrigerators. Friendly, cheerful reception. Good value. Open early May to mid-Oct. **I−M,** but lower rates off-season.

GLENWOOD SPRINGS 🏨 **Hot Springs Lodge,** 415 6th St., Glenwood Springs, CO 81601 (303/945-6571). 107 rms, A/C, cable color TV. AE, CB, DC, MC, V. Free parking, pool, health club, sauna, miniature golf, rest., bar. *Note:* Congenial modern hotel for those who come to take the waters. Comfortable rms (some w. refrigerators). Excellent location on the banks of the Colorado River and just moments from the hot springs. Has one of the largest naturally heated pools in the world. Good value. **I−M,** but lower rates off-season.

GRANBY ☀️🏨 **C Lazy U Ranch,** Colo. 125, Granby, CO 80446 (303/887-3344). 6 rms in the inn, 33 one- to five-rm bungalows; no A/C; color TV in bar. No credit cards. Free parking, pool, two tennis courts, health club, horseback riding, skiing, skating rink, fishing, hunting, skeet range, rest., bar, open-air barbecue-buffets, valet svce, disco. *Note:* Authentic western ranch some 8,200 ft. (2,500m) up on the shores of a mountain lake. Heaven for riding enthusiasts in summer and cross-country skiers in winter. The bungalow rms are prettily decorated, pleasant, and comfortable. Robust and abundant food. Friendly reception and atmosphere. The best vacation spot in the Colorado Rockies. Rodeos in summer. Closed late Sept to early Dec and in Apr and May. $850 and up per week in summer (American Plan); $150 and up per day in winter (American Plan).

☀️🏨🏨 **Clarion Colorado Ranch,** Colo. 125, Granby, CO 80446 (303/887-3306; toll free, see Clarion). 60 rms; no A/C; color TV, in-rm movies. AE, CB, DC, MC, V. Free parking, pool, two tennis courts, health club, sauna, horseback riding, skiing, skating, snowmobile, boating, fishing, bowling alley, trap shooting, rest., bar, rm svce, free crib. *Note:* Luxurious vacation ranch hidden away in the Arapaho National Forest. Comprehensive recreational facilities. Very comfortable rms and suites; highly acceptable rest. Efficient svce w. a smile. The hotel boasts its own landing strip as well as 36 acres (14ha) of lake, teeming w. fish. Hunting guides available. Nature-lovers who prefer not to forgo every modern convenience will find this the resort of their dreams. **VE**

GRAND JUNCTION 🏨 **Hilton Inn,** 743 Horizon Dr., Grand Junction, CO 81506 (303/241-8888; toll free, see Hilton). 264 rms, A/C, color TV, in rm-movies. AE, CB, DC, MC, V. Free parking, pool, health club, three tennis courts, rest. (Jockey Club), bar, rm svce, disco, free crib. *Note:* Vast eight-story motel of rather gloomy design; spacious, comfortable rms. Efficient svce and reception. Adequate rest. Free airport shuttle. VIP floor. A highly recommended stopover. **M–E,** but lower rates off-season.

🍴 **Motel 6,** 776 Horizon Dr., Grand Junction, CO 81501 (303/243-2628). 100 rms, A/C, color TV, in-rm movies. AE, DC, MC, V. Free parking, pool. *Note:* The best deal in town if you're passing through by car. Serviceable amenities at unbeatable prices. Airport nearby. **B**

GRAND LAKE 🍴 **Western Riviera,** 419 Garmet St., Grand Lake, CO 80447 (303/627-3580). 17 rms; no A/C; cable color TV. MC, V. Free parking, snowmobiles, coffee shop next door, free crib. *Note:* Charming little motel by the lake. Warm, comfortable rms. Beautiful natural surroundings. Closed Apr to mid-May and mid-Oct to mid-Dec. **I,** but lower rates off-season.

GUNNISON 🍴 **Friendship Inn Colorado West,** 400 E. Tomichi Ave., Gunnison, CO 81230 (303/641-1288; toll free, see Friendship Inns). 50 rms, A/C, color TV, in-rm movies. AE, CB, DC, MC, V. Free parking, pool, coffee shop next door, crib $2. *Note:* Pleasant, well-run little motel. Spacious rms. Friendly reception. Free airport shuttle. Good value. **I,** but lower rates off-season.

KEYSTONE 🏨 **Keystone Resort,** 22010 U.S. 6, Keystone, CO 80435 (303/468-2316; toll free 800/222-0188). 152 rms, 775 condos and apts.; no A/C; color TV, in-rm movies. AE, CB, DC, MC, V. Free parking, 10 pools, golf, putting green, 14 tennis courts, sauna, skiing, boating, horseback riding, four rests. (including the Garden Room), two coffee shops, bars, rm svce, disco, boutiques, concierge, crib $3. *Note:* Huge ultramodern vacation complex on the banks of Lake Keystone in the heart of the Arapaho National Forest. Comfortable rms w. private balconies or patios. One- to four-bedroom condos and apts. Very good sports facilities. Splendid panoramic views over lake and mountains. Caters to conventions and groups. Rather average svce. Ordinary rests. Organizes rafting trips and Jeep tours. Attractive family and vacation packages. **E–VE,** but lower rates off-season.

LEADVILLE 🍷 **Best Western Silver King Motor Inn,** 2020 N. Poplar St., Leadville, CO 80461 (303/486-2610; toll free, see Best Western). 56 rms; no A/C; color TV, in-rm movies. AE, CB, DC, MC, V. Free parking, skiing, sauna, rest., bar, disco, crib $5. *Note:* Modern motel-chalet in the heart of this legendary gold-rush town. Spacious rms w. balconies. Decent rest. Friendly reception. Attractive vacation packages. (Take note of Leadville's high altitude—10,150 ft./ 3,100m—and its possible effects on your physical condition.) **I–M,** but lower rates off-season.

SNOWMASS VILLAGE 🍷🍷 **Snowmass Club,** 239 Snowmass Club Circle, Snowmass Village, CO 81615 (303/932-5600; toll free 800/525-0710). 76 rms in the hotel, 62 separate villas. A/C, color TV, in-rm movies. AE, CB, DC, MC, V. Free parking, two pools, health club, sauna, 13 tennis courts, golf, squash, putting green, skiing, snowmobiles, rest. (Four Corners), bar, rm svce, nightclub, concierge. *Note:* Paradise for sporting enthusiasts. Refined, elegant setting of modern design. Large rms, nicely decorated, w. private balconies or patios and refrigerators (some w. kitchenettes). Luxurious two- and three-bedroom villas. Worthwhile rest. Excellent svce. Free airport connection w. Aspen. Caters to wealthy holiday makers. Closed mid-Apr to May and mid-Oct to Nov. **E–VE,** but lower rates off-season.

STEAMBOAT SPRINGS 🍷🍷 **Sheraton Steamboat Resort,** 2200 Village Inn Court, Steamboat Springs, CO 80477 (303/879-2220; toll free, see Sheraton). 440 rms, A/C, color TV, in-rm movies. AE, CB, DC, MC, V. Free parking, two pools, four tennis courts, golf course, sauna, skiing, snowmobiles, rest., coffee shop, bars, rm svce, disco, boutiques, concierge. *Note:* A vacation complex at the foot of Mount Werner, comprising a modern hotel and eight stories of comfortable condos w. kitchenettes. Ideal for families. Good vacation and ski packages; good value overall. Closed mid-Apr to May and the end of Sept to mid-Nov. Free airport shuttle. **M–E,** but lower rates off-season.

    🍷 **Inn at Steamboat** (formerly the Quality Inn Subalpine), 3070 Columbine Dr., Steamboat Springs, CO 80477 (303/879-2600; toll free 800/432-2628). 31 rms; no A/C; color TV, in-rm movies. AE, CB, DC, MC, V. Free parking, pool, sauna, miniature golf, coffee shop (breakfast only in summer), free crib. *Note:* Quiet, friendly motel. Spacious rms w. balconies. Appealing winter sports packages. Good value. **M–E,** but lower rates off-season.

TELLURIDE 🍷 **Best Western Tomboy Inn,** 619 Columbia St., Telluride, CO 81435 (303/728-3871; toll free, see Best Western). 49 rms; no A/C; cable color TV. AE, CB, DC, MC, V. Free parking, sauna, skiing, nearby coffee shop, crib $4. *Note:* Comfortable, very well run small hotel. Spacious, inviting rms w. refrigerator, some w. kitchenette, most w. balcony and fireplace. Svce w. a smile. Good value. **I–M,** but lower rates off-season.

VAIL ☀🍷🍷 **Marriott's Mark Resort,** 715 W. Lions Head Circle, Vail, CO 81657 (303/476-4444; toll free, see Marriott). 350 rms, some w. A/C, color TV, in-rm movies. AE, CB, DC, MC, V. Free indoor parking, two pools, saunas, health club, four tennis courts, skiing, two rests. (including Windows), coffee shop, two bars, rm svce, disco, concierge, free crib. *Note:* Old luxury hotel, entirely renovated. Elegant, comfortable rms w. balconies, some w. kitchenettes. Thoughtful svce. Decent rest. The largest and best hotel in the resort, two steps from the slopes. Caters to groups and conventions. Free airport shuttle. **VE,** but lower rates off-season.

    🍷🍷🍷 **Westin Hotel,** 1300 Westhaven Dr., Vail, CO 81657 (303/ 476-7111; toll free, see Westin). 323 rms; no A/C; color TV, in-rm movies. AE, CB, DC, MC, V. Valet parking $5, pool, four tennis courts, health club, sauna, squash, outdoor thermal spa, rest. (Alfredo's), coffee shop, bars, 24-hr. rm svce, boutiques, concierge, free crib. *Note:* Very beautiful, new alpine-style hotel. Elegant atmosphere. Spacious, comfortable rms w. minibars and private patios. Excellent svce. Decent rest. Nestled on the banks of Gore Creek. One of the best hotels in the Rockies. Free airport shuttle. The plushest place in town. **VE,** but lower rates off-season.

The Lodge at Vail, 174 E. Gore Creek Dr., Vail, CO 81657 (303/476-5011; toll free 800/237-1236). 175 rms; no A/C; color TV, in-rm movies. AE, CB, DC, MC, V. Free valet parking, pool, sauna, skiing, two rests. (including the Wildflower Inn), bar, rm svce, night club, boutiques. *Note:* Huge mountain hotel, quaint and charming. Many rms w. balconies and kitchenettes. Good communal facilities. Outstanding rest. Good svce. Caters to groups. **VE,** but lower rates off-season.

Sitzmark Lodge, 183 Gore Creek Dr., Vail, CO 81657 (303/476-5001). 35 rms; no A/C; color TV, in-rm movies. AE, MC, V. Free parking, pool, sauna, skiing, rest. (Left Bank), bar, valet svce, crib $4. *Note:* Delightful mountain chalet in the heart of Vail Village. Lovely mountain view. Huge, comfortable rms w. balcony and refrigerator, some w. fireplace. The very acceptable rest. is unfortunately closed in fall and spring. Winning reception and svce in a friendly, inviting atmosphere. Very good value; you should reserve well ahead. **M–E**

Comfort Inn Vail, 0161 W. Beaver Creek Blvd., Avon, CO 81620 (303/949-5511; toll free 800/228-5150). 147 rms, A/C, color TV, in-rm movies. AE, CB, DC, MC, V. Free parking, pool, bicycles, coffee shop nearby, free breakfast. *Note:* Modern motel in the classic style. Pleasant, comfortable rms, some w. refrigerators. Friendly svce. 15 min. from dwntwn. Good value. **M–E,** but lower rates off-season.

WINTER PARK **Iron Horse Resort,** 257 Winter Park Dr., Winter Park, CO 80482 (303/726-8851; toll free 800/621-8190). 118 studios; no A/C; cable color TV. AE, DC, MC, V. Free parking, pool, health club, sauna, skiing, squash, rest., bar, valet svce. *Note:* A mountain resort for either winter or summer sports. Comfortable studios w. kitchenette, refrigerator, fireplace, and balcony. Efficient svce; family atmosphere. Good value. **E,** but lower rates off-season.

YMCAs/Youth Hostels

COLORADO SPRINGS **Garden of the Gods,** 3704 W. Colorado Ave., Colorado Springs, CO 80904 (719/475-9450). 48 beds. Youth hostel. Open mid-Apr to mid-Oct.

ESTES PARK **H-Bar-G Ranch,** 3500 H-Bar-G Rd., Estes Park, CO 80517 (303/586-3688). 130 beds. Youth hostel. Open late May to early Sept.

GRAND LAKE **Shadowcliff Youth Hostel,** Tunnel Rd., Grand Lake, CO 80447 (303/627-9966). 32 beds. Youth hostel. Open June–Sept.

TELLURIDE **Oak Street Inn,** 134 N. Oak St., Telluride, CO 81435 (303/728-3383). 83 beds. Youth hostel. Open year round.

WINTER PARK **Winter Park Hostel,** U.S. 40 at Vasquez Rd., Winter Park, CO 80482 (303/726-5356). 28 beds. Youth hostel. Open year round.

RESTAURANTS

A Note on Restaurant Prices: Colorado Rockies restaurant prices, per person, excluding drinks and service charges, are coded as follows: **VE,** Very Expensive ($60 and up); **E**, Expensive ($40–$60); **M**, Moderate ($25–$40); **I**, Inexpensive ($15–$25); **B**, Budget (up to $15).

Personal Favorites (by city)

ASPEN 🍷🍷🍷 **Gordon's**, 205 Mill St. (303/925-7474). A/C. Dinner nightly; closed mid-Apr to June and mid-Sept to mid-Nov. AE, CB, DC, MC, V. *Specialties:* chiles rellenos w. goat cheese; squid salad; potato pancakes w. golden caviar; free-range chicken w. sun-dried tomatoes and herbs; shrimp à la jamaïcaine w. black-bean sauce; grilled fresh tuna w. cheddar, tomatoes, and basil. Excellent desserts. *Note:* By far the best in town. Seductive, eclectic cuisine from the very talented Rebecca and Gordon Naccarato, formerly of Michael's in Santa Monica —quite a reference. Modern art adorns the walls. Friendly, obliging svce. Resv. highly recommended. An excellent place to dine. *American.* **M–E**

🍷🍷 **Wienerstube**, 633 E. Hyman (303/925-3357). A/C. Breakfast/lunch/dinner Tues–Sun; closed Jan 1, Dec 25. AE, DC, MC, V. *Specialties:* broiled bratwurst, sauerbraten, wienerschnitzel, veal Stroganoff; desserts on the weighty side. *Note:* Charming, locally popular Austrian-style inn where both food and atmosphere are thoroughly true to the original. Delightful patio-terrace for fine days. Friendly, smiling svce. Resv. advisable. *German/Continental.* **I–M**

🍷🍷 **Ute City Banque**, 501 E. Hyman St. (303/925-4373). A/C. Lunch/dinner daily; closed Apr to mid-May. AE, DC, MC, V. *Specialties:* duck à l'orange, rack of lamb provençal, crab Diablo. *Note:* The bank decor, vault included, is authentic and dates from 1885. Impeccable cooking, but lacks great imagination. Nice atmosphere. Good svce. Resv. recommended at dinner. *Continental.* **I–M**

🍷 **La Cocina**, 308 E. Hopkins (303/925-9714). No A/C. Dinner nightly; closed Nov–May. *Specialties:* Tacos, enchiladas, steak. *Note:* Small Mexican-style rest., modest and unpretentious. Popular locally. *Mexican/American.* **B**

BEAVER CREEK ✳🍷🍷 **Mirabelle**, 55 Village Rd. (303/949-7728). A/C. Dinner Tues–Sun; closed May and mid-Oct to mid-Nov. AE, MC, V. Jkt. *Specialties:* pâté de campagne, mousseline of fish in beurre blanc, poached salmon w. mussels and scallops, grilled lamb cutlet w. hollandaise sauce, lobster w. tarragon. Exceptional desserts. Fine wine list. *Note:* Light, inventive cooking by the very talented chef, Pierre Luc. Charming, old-fashioned, rustic decor (the building dates from 1898, which makes it one of the oldest ranches in the Vail area). Discreet, attentive svce. An outstanding rest. Many VIPs and wealthy people on vacation among the customers. Resv. highly recommended. *French.* **M–E**

BOULDER 🍷🍷 **Flagstaff House**, Flagstaff Rd. (303/442-4640). A/C. Dinner only, nightly; closed Jan 1, Dec 24–25. AE, CB, DC, MC, V. Jkt. *Specialties:* oysters Rockefeller, angel-hair pasta w. prosciutto and wild mushrooms, crab Lausanne, elk steak, Colorado beef, roast quail. Very good wine list (16,000-bottle cellar). *Note:* An elegant rest. w. a spectacular view of the mountains through huge bay windows. Romantic atmosphere. Terrace open in summer. Attentive svce. Some of the best fare in the region. Resv. recommended. *Continental.* **M**

🍷🍷 **John's**, 2338 Pearl St. (303/444-5232). A/C. Dinner only, nightly; closed hols. AE, CB, DC, MC, V. Jkt. *Specialties:* scallops sautéed w. capers and lemon, boneless chicken in mustard sauce, salmon à la bretonne, veal chop w. green pepper. Rather scanty wine list. *Note:* Pleasant little Provençal-style inn w. a fireplace and old-fashioned decor. Very successful French-style cooking. Friendly, efficient svce. Resv. recommended. *French/Continental.* **I–M**

BRECKENRIDGE � **Briar Rose,** 109 E. Lincoln St. (303/453-9948). No A/C. Dinner only, nightly; closed the first 2 weeks of June. AE, DC, MC, V. *Specialties:* game, roast beef, quail, Alaska king crab. Good, homemade desserts. *Note:* Authentic 19th-century guesthouse. Charming old-fashioned decor. The game dishes (in season) are all to be recommended. Excellent svce. *Continental/ American.* **I–M**

CENTRAL CITY ☀♈♈ **Black Forest Inn,** Colo. 279 at Black Hawk (303/279-2333). A/C. Lunch/dinner daily. No credit cards. *Specialties:* game (in season), roast pheasant, wild duck, elk steak. *Note:* One of the most famous rests. in the Rockies. The accent is definitely on wild game. Many German dishes too. Highly colorful German music and decor. Outdoor dining in good weather. Popular locally. Very good value. *German/American.* **I**

COLORADO SPRINGS ☀♈♈♈ **London Grill,** in the Antlers Doubletree Hotel (see "Accommodations," above) (719/473-5500). A/C. Lunch/dinner daily. AE, CB, DC, MC, V. Jkt. *Specialties:* scampi Thermidor, veal médaillons w. tarragon, sautéed Colorado trout, roast pheasant. Very respectable wine list. *Note:* This rest. of quality is in the venerable, elegant, century-old Antlers Doubletree Hotel. The French-inspired food is flawlessly prepared and served; the Victorian setting is of the period. Svce perhaps a touch pompous. Elegant background music. Resv. strongly advised; valet parking. *French/Continental.* **I–M**

♈♈ **Edelweiss,** 34 E. Ramona Ave. (719/633-2220). A/C. Lunch Mon–Fri, dinner nightly; closed Dec 24. AE, CB, DC, MC, V. *Specialties:* wienerschnitzel, sauerbraten, veal Oscar. *Note:* Traditional Bavarian-chalet decor and praiseworthy German food. Dinner outdoors in summer. Efficient svce. Popular locally. Resv. recommended. *German/Continental.* **I**

♈♈ **La Petite Maison,** 1015 W. Colorado Ave. (719/632-4887). A/C. Lunch Tues–Fri, dinner Tues–Sat; closed July 4, Dec 25. AE, DC, MC, V. *Specialties:* Anaheim chile stuffed w. goat cheese on black-bean purée, sautéed veal w. Amontillado sherry and fresh herbs, white-chocolate and almond tart w. apricot sauce. Menu changes regularly. *Note:* A charming little rest. house in a nicely renovated former private residence. Honest, tasty food. Friendly reception and svce. Very good value. Resv. recommended. 5 min. from dwntwn. *French/American.* **B–I**

CRIPPLE CREEK ☀♈ **Imperial Dining Room,** 123 N. 3rd St. (303/689-2922). No A/C. Breakfast/lunch/dinner daily; closed mid-Oct to mid-May. AE, DC, MC, V. *Specialties:* steak, baron of beef, gourmet buffet. *Note:* Magnificent Victorian dining rm in the Imperial Hotel, a registered historic monument dating from the gold-rush era of the last century. The decor alone makes a visit worthwhile. The food is worthy, but nothing more. Dinner-theater Tues–Sun, for which resv. highly advisable. *American.* **B–I**

DURANGO ☀♈♈ **Palace Grill,** 1 Depot Pl. (303/247-2018). A/C. Breakfast (summer only)/lunch/dinner daily; closed Thanksgiving, Dec 25. AE, DC, MC, V. *Specialties:* honey duck, sautéed trout Palace, mesquite-grilled steak, house salads and desserts. Good list of Californian wines. *Note:* One of the most agreeable and picturesque rests. in southern Colorado. Authentic Victorian decor w. Tiffany lamps and copper objets d'art (the building itself dates from 1881). Patio dining in summer. Excellent traditional American cooking. Relaxed atmosphere and svce. Very popular locally. Very good value. Resv. highly advisable in summer. Located near the famous Silverton Railroad terminal. *American.* **B–I**

☀♈ **Henry's,** Strater, in the Strater Hotel (see "Accommodations," above) (303/247-4431). A/C. Breakfast/lunch/dinner daily. AE, CB, DC, MC, V. *Specialties:* scampi, fresh salmon, roast beef, red meats. *Note:* Housed in the Strater Hotel, a picturesque Victorian building. Classic hotel cuisine. Rather inefficient svce. Pretty, old-fashioned decor. *Continental/ American.* **B–I**

ESTES PARK ♈♈ **Old Plantation,** 128 E. Elkhorn Ave. (303/586-2800). A/C. Lunch/dinner daily; closed Oct–May. AE, CB, DC, MC, V. *Specialties:* rainbow trout, roast duck, pot-au-feu, sautéed veal. *Note:* Old western-style rather original decor w. local artists' works. Generally pleasant rustic cuisine. Efficient svce. A classic since 1931. Resv. recommended. *American.* **B–I**

♈♈ **La Chaumière,** 12 mi. (19km) south on U.S. 36 in Pinewood Springs (303/823-6521). A/C. Dinner only, Wed–Sun; closed Feb. AE, MC, V. *Specialties:* veal sweetbreads, roast duck, fish of the day, veal cutlet à la normande, rack of lamb, filet mignon. Menu changes regularly. *Note:* Lovely chalet dining rm w. a central hearth. Very pleasant French-style cooking. Fixed-price menu. Unrestricted view of the mountains. Friendly svce. Excellent value. Resv. recommended. *French/Continental.* **I–M** (prix fixe).

♈ **La Casa,** 222 E. Elkhorn Ave. (303/586-2807). A/C. Lunch/dinner daily; closed Thanksgiving, Dec 25. AE, CB, DC, MC, V. *Specialties:* roast beef, tacos, enchiladas, tamales, Cajun dishes, excellent house margaritas. *Note:* This otherwise typical Mexican rest. also serves some fine Cajun dishes. Patio-terrace overlooking the Big Thomson River. Noisy but agreeable. Resv. advisable at dinner. *Mexican/American.* **I**

GEORGETOWN ☼♈ **The Ram,** 606 6th St. (303/569-3263). A/C. Lunch/dinner daily. AE, MC, V. *Specialties:* roast beef, steaks, good desserts. Good wine list. *Note:* Located in the heart of Georgetown, an old gold-rush town, this 19th-century saloon offers very good red-meat dishes at reasonable prices. Popular locally. *Steak.* **B–I**

GRAND JUNCTION ♈♈ **Far East,** 1530 North Ave. (303/242-8131). A/C. Lunch/dinner daily; closed hols. AE, CB, DC, MC, V. *Specialties:* Cantonese and Mandarin dishes, beef teriyaki, broiled steak. Also American selections. *Note:* One of the few "exotic" rests. in the Rockies. The Chinese-Polynesian decor is a success, as is the food. Popular locally. *Chinese/American.* **B–I**

LEADVILLE ♈ **Silver King,** in the Best Western Silver King Motor Inn (see "Accommodations," above) (303/486-2610). No A/C. Breakfast/lunch/dinner daily; closed Nov–Jan. AE, CB, DC, MC, V. *Specialties:* steak, mountain lake trout. *Note:* A modest, unpretentious motel rest. Good red meats and broiled dishes; friendly svce. Dancing in summer. *Steak/American.* **B–I**

LONGMONT ☼♈♈♈ **Sebanton,** 424 Main St. (303/776-3686). A/C. Lunch Tues–Fri, dinner Tues–Sat; closed hols. and Aug–Sept. AE, CB, DC, MC, V. Jkt. *Specialties:* escargots bourguignons, French onion soup, oysters in mousseline sauce, Lyonnaise sausage, duck à l'orange, fish of the day. Noteworthy desserts. *Note:* One of the best rests. in the Rockies. The fixed-price dinner (starting at $16) is a real bargain. Chef John Bomba's cooking is worth a special trip, and the svce is beyond reproach. Typical French-bistro decor w. checkered tablecloths. Rather noisy atmosphere. The menu changes regularly. Resv. highly recommended, given the rest.'s popularity. Halfway between Denver and Rocky Mountain National Park. *French/Continental.* **I**

LYONS ♈♈ **Black Bear Inn,** 42 Main St. (303/823-6812). A/C. Lunch/dinner Tues–Sun; closed hols. and mid-Jan to mid-Feb. AE, CB, DC, MC, V. Jkt. *Specialties:* chateaubriand, veal casserole, fish of the day, apple strudel. *Note:* Elegant alpine-style inn w. a big fireplace and hunting trophies. Classical European cooking, w. delicacy. Diligent svce. Resv. recommended. A recommended stop midway between Denver and Rocky Mountain National Park. *Continental.* **I–M**

MANITOU SPRINGS ❋♟ **Stagecoach Inn,** 702 Manitou Ave. (719/685-9335). A/C. Lunch/dinner daily. AE, DC, MC, V. *Specialties:* broiled red meats, fish of the day, homemade pastries and preserves. *Note:* A pleasant rest. housed in a former coaching inn of the 1880s. Authentic period decor, in a rustic style w. big fireplaces. Honest, tasty cooking. A fine place. Resv. recommended. *American.* **B–I**

STEAMBOAT SPRINGS ♟♟♟ **Hazie's,** at the top of Thunderhead Mountain (303/879-6111). A/C. Lunch/dinner daily. AE, MC, V. *Specialties:* fried oysters w. avocado sauce, sour cream and salmon roe, Florida snapper w. pistachio butter, chicken w. shrimp in lemon-ginger cream, venison sausage, fresh papaya granité. Good wine list. *Note:* Hazie's offers you not only an incomparable view of the Rockies from its huge picture windows but—uncommon for a rest. in the "splendid view" category—praiseworthy food from the hand of chef Richard Billingham. Lunch is light, dinner more elaborate. Relaxed but efficient svce. The rest. is reached by cable car, and is well worth the trip—it's one of the best places to eat in the Rockies. Reserve ahead. *American.* **I–M**

♟ **Pine Grove,** U.S. 40 (303/879-1190). A/C. Dinner only, nightly; closed Thanksgiving. AE, DC, MC, V. *Specialties:* roast beef, broiled trout, barbecued pork chops, fish of the day, game in season. *Note:* Pleasant ranch-style decor in a converted turn-of-the-century barn, w. open hearth and antique furniture. Honest, tasty cooking. Friendly svce. *American.* **I**

VAIL ♟♟♟ **Wildflower Inn,** in The Lodge at Vail (see "Accommodations," above) (303/476-5011). No A/C. Dinner only, Tues–Sun. AE, CB, DC, MC, V. Jkt. *Specialties:* celeriac tart, fresh pasta w. herbs and pine nuts, confit of poultry w. radicchio, filet of lamb w. green peppercorns, lamb cutlet w. vermouth sauce, braised breast of pheasant, hot plum tart. Very good wine list. Menu changes regularly. *Note:* The dining rm at The Lodge at Vail is a model of elegance and good taste w. its abundant flower decoration and its pastel tones (it won a Design of the Year Award). The cuisine, of French inspiration, is equally elegant. The svce is laudable and the whole amply deserves its three glasses. By far the best in Vail. The menu changes regularly. *Continental.* **M–E**

♟♟ **Alpen Rose Tea Room,** 100 E. Meadow Dr. (303/476-3194). No A/C. Breakfast/lunch/dinner Tues–Sun (until 2am); closed Memorial Day, late Apr through June, and mid-Oct to mid-Nov. AE, MC, V. *Specialties:* hausplatte, chicken Cordon Bleu, Mozart schnitte, roulade of beef w. red wine sauce. *Note:* This bakery-rest. is especially good at breakfast for its hot chocolate and cakes. More substantial fare at lunch, w. a strong emphasis on German dishes. Splendid view, and open-air terraces in fine weather. Popular locally. Resv. advised. *German/Continental.* **I**

♟♟ **Left Bank,** in the Sitzmark Lodge (see "Accommodations," above) (303/476-3696). No A/C. Dinner only, Thurs–Tues; closed mid-Apr to mid-June, Oct–Nov, and Dec 25. *Specialties:* onion soup, scallops w. cucumbers, braised veal sweetbreads, Colorado trout. Good homemade desserts. Extensive wine list. *Note:* Pleasant mountain-chalet atmosphere, and cooking to match. Popular locally. Resv. recommended. *French/Continental.* **I–M**

♟ **Cyrano's,** 298 Hanson Ranch Rd. (303/476-5551). No A/C. Breakfast/lunch/dinner daily; closed hols. AE, MC, V. *Specialties:* sandwiches, omelets, pepper steak, tournedos, abalone, chicken Oscar. *Note:* Congenial small rest. Very acceptable food at reasonable prices. Very popular bar next door. Dancing in season. Outdoor terrace in good weather. Other location: Cyrano's Too, Lions Head Circle (303/476-1441). Renowned mainly for its desserts and its impressive wine list (225 labels). *American/Steak.* **B–I**

CHAPTER 31

SALT LAKE CITY

□ □ □

The capital of Utah and the holy city of the Church of Jesus Christ of the Latter-Day Saints, more commonly known as the Mormon church, is situated about 15 miles (24km) south of the **Great Salt Lake,** for which it is named. The distant, usually snow-covered peaks of the **Wasatch Range,** more than 9,840 ft. (3,000m) high, enhance the beauty of the setting. In 1825 an adventurous fur trader named Jim Bridger discovered the Great Salt Lake, the largest body of water in the entire western United States. Some 22 years later, in July 1847, the Mormon preacher Brigham Young and 150 of his followers, fleeing religious persecution and open hostility in various East Coast and midwestern cities, founded Salt Lake City after a 1½-year forced march westward. Legend holds that Brigham Young, on seeing the Great Salt Lake and the site of the new Zion, exclaimed, "This is the place!" Today an imposing monument marks the spot where Young first came upon this superb view. Baptized "Deseret" ("honeybee" in Mormon nomenclature), the early encampment soon became Great Salt Lake City, then was simply called Salt Lake City, once Utah was admitted to the Union in 1896.

An industrious and prosperous city (electronics, missiles, food processing, medicine, chemicals), the Mormon capital is today a modern metropolis, clean and inviting, carved out of the surrounding desert. Only the Mormons' extraordinary spirit of sacrifice and devotion to work can explain this astonishing transformation in less than a century and a half.

An ideal point of departure for magnificent trips to such national parks as **Zion, Bryce Canyon, Grand Teton, Yellowstone,** and **Canyonlands**—not to mention numerous nearby winter vacation spots—Salt Lake City boasts two monuments directly inspired by the Mormon religion: the **Temple,** a massive granite edifice in the Gothic Revival style (only Mormons are admitted), and the **Tabernacle,** shaped like an immense inverted ship's hull, which has become one of the world's most famous concert halls. The imposing **State Capitol,** built on a hill overlooking the town, is also a symbol of the city. In deference to the Mormon way of life, many Salt Lake City restaurants do not serve any alcoholic beverages, but diners can bring their own (purchased from state package stores). It's best to confirm this arrangement by an advance phone call to the restaurant of your choice. Among Salt Lake City's native children are actresses Maude Adams and Loretta Young.

THE MORMONS: Founded in 1830 in New York State by the visionary Joseph Smith, the Church of Jesus Christ of the Latter-Day Saints (LDS), the church's formal name, imposes a strict behavior code. Mormons, who comprise 70% of Utah's population, eschew drugs, tobacco, alcohol, tea, coffee, and even Coca-Cola. They practice tithing, returning to their rich and powerful church approximately 10% of their personal income.

Young Mormons of both sexes dedicate 2 years of their lives to missionary work; they may be sent at their own expense anywhere in the world to proselytize. There are 7.2 million Mormons today throughout the world, two-thirds of them in the United States. Their 40 or so temples are all modeled on the one in Salt Lake City. The Mormon practice of polygamy, which caused much of the anti-

Mormon persecution during the last century (the church's founder, Joseph Smith, was lynched in 1844) and long delayed Utah's admission to the Union, was officially abolished in 1890. Highly moral, the Mormons are known for their religious zeal, their political conservatism, and their strong family ties.

BASIC FACTS: Capital of the State of Utah. Area code: 801. Time zone: mountain. ZIP Code: 84101. Founded: 1847. Approximate population: city, 168,000; metropolitan area, 1,100,000. 37th-largest metropolitan area in the country.

CLIMATE: With its magnificently sunny days and its colorful foliage, autumn is the ideal season for a visit to Salt Lake City and its nearby woodlands. Summers are quite hot but dry (average July temperature, 78°F/26°C). Spring brings a disconcerting alternation of sun and sudden showers (sometimes with snow). Winter is pure pleasure for ski buffs, with the thermometer hovering consistently around 32°F (0°C) Nov–Feb.

DISTANCES: Denver, 506 mi. (810km); Las Vegas, 439 mi. (702km); Portland, 768 mi. (1,230km); San Francisco, 750 mi. (1,200km); Yellowstone, 325 mi. (520km).

ARRIVAL & TRANSIT INFORMATION

AIRPORT: Salt Lake City International Airport (SLC), 3 mi. (5km) west. For information, call 575-2400.

AIRLINES: America West (328-0121), American (521-6131), Continental (359-9800), Delta (532-7123), Northwest (toll free 800/225-2525), Pan Am (toll free 800/221-1111), TWA (539-1111), and United (328-8011).

CITY LINK: The **cab** fare from Salt Lake City Airport to dwntwn Salt Lake City is about $12; time, 15 min. **Bus:** The major hotels have their own free limousine service; time, about 20 min. **City bus (UTA** line 50): Serves the dwntwn area; leaves every hour; fare, 50¢; time, 20 min.
    Unless you plan on excursions, the size of the city makes car rental unnecessary. The public bus transportation system is not extensive (Utah Transit Authority, 801/287-4636).

CAR RENTAL (at Salt Lake City Airport unless otherwise indicated): Avis (539-1117); Budget (363-1500); Dollar (596-2580); Hertz (539-2683); National (539-0200); and Thrifty, 1255 W. North Temple St. (595-6677). For dwntwn locations, consult the local telephone directory.

LIMOUSINE SERVICES: Bonneville Limo (364-6520) and Dav-El Limousines (toll free 800/922-0343).

TAXIS: You'll find taxis in waiting lines at the major hotels; they cannot be hailed on the street. Your best bet is to phone **City Cab** (363-5014) or **Yellow Cab** (521-2100).

TRAIN: Amtrak station, 320 S. Rio Grande (364-8562; toll free 800/872-7245).

INTERCITY BUSES: Greyhound, 160 W. South Temple St. (355-9579).

INFORMATION & TOURS

TOURIST INFORMATION: The **Salt Lake City Convention and Visitors Bureau,** 180 S. West Temple St., UT 84101 (801/521-2868): Open Mon–Fri.
    Utah Travel Council, Council Hall, Capitol Hill, UT 84114 (801/538-1030): Information on Utah's national parks and tourist attractions. The office is open daily in the summer, Mon–Fri. the rest of the year.
    Visitor Information Center, Temple Square at S. Temple St. (801/240-2534): Information about the Mormon church. Open daily.

GUIDED TOURS: Gray Line Tours (bus), 553 W. 100 South (521-7060): Guided tours of the city and its outskirts, serving the major hotels.
    Old Salty Tours (bus), leaves from the Water Tower at Trolley Sq. (801/359-8677): Tour of the city in an open mini-train (summer only).
    Western Leisure (bus), 1172 E. Brickyard Rd. (467-6100): Week-long tours to filming locations of well-known movies such as *Butch Cassidy and the Sundance Kid, Jeremiah Johnson,* etc. A must for movie buffs. Reservations essential.

SIGHTS, ATTRACTIONS & ACTIVITIES

ADVENTURES: Adrift Adventures (boat), P.O. Box 81032, UT 84108 (485-5978; toll free 800/874-4483): Down the Colorado River and Green River in rubber rafts or rowboats. 1- to 7-day trips (early Apr through Oct).
    Colorado River and Trail Expeditions (boat), 5058 S. 300 West (261-1789): Raft trips on the Colorado, Green, San Juan, or Dolores River (May–Sept).
    Holiday River Expeditions (boat), 544 E. 3900 South (266-2087; toll free 800/624-6323): Raft trips on the Colorado River, Green River, and San Juan River (May–Sept).
    Moki Mac River Expeditions (boat), 1821 E. Ft. Union Blvd. (943-6707): Raft trips on the Colorado River and Green River, lasting 1–14 days (May–Sept).
    Western River Expeditions (boat), 7258 Racquet Club Dr. (942-6669; toll free 800/453-7450): Raft trips on the Green and Colorado Rivers (May–Sept).
    For other raft trips, see "Adventures" in Chapter 32 on Utah National Parks.

ARCHITECTURAL HIGHLIGHTS: ⚓ **City and County Building,** Washington Sq. (535-7611): Built in 1894 along the lines of the Mansion House in London, this vast Romanesque edifice in dark sandstone served for 19 years as the State Capitol. Today it houses the city hall and the county's administrative offices. The building is set in a very lovely grdn w. 45 varieties of trees from around the world. Open Mon–Fri.
    ☀⚓ **LDS Church Office Building,** 50 E. North Temple St. (240-2331): The old Ionic-style building, inaugurated in 1917 (LDS Church Administration Bldg.), contains the offices of the president and the 12 "apostles" of the Mormon church. The new 30-story building, constructed in 1972, houses the largest genealogical library in the world. Tens of millions of computerized microfiches are said to make possible the reconstruction of genealogical trees for all U.S. citizens and many Europeans. Visitors can use the library Mon–Sat. (Duplicate microfilm is stored in an underground vault dug out of a mountain in Little Cottonwood Canyon, 17 mi./28km south of Salt Lake City.) An observation platform on the 26th floor offers a fine view of the city. Open Mon–Sat.

    Salt Palace Center, bounded by W. Temple St., 200 West St., S. Temple St., and 2 South St. (521-6060): Enormous arts complex and convention center covering two dwntwn blocks. Contains, among other facilities, the 200,000-sq.-ft. (18,000m²) **Salt Palace,** which hosts many expositions, conventions, and sporting events (28,000 seats); the **Salt Palace Arena** (concerts, rodeos, shows of many kinds); the **Capitol Theatre** (see below); and the **Art Gallery** (art exhibitions). The cultural heart of Salt Lake City.

    State Capitol, N. State St. and Capitol Hill (538-3000): One of the most imposing edifices of its type in the U.S. (1916). Inspired by the Capitol in Washington, D.C., its 285-ft. (87m) copper dome dominates the city. Constructed from Georgia marble and Utah State granite, the building houses the State Senate and House of Representatives as well as Utah's Supreme Court. Very rich interior decoration (note especially the **Gold Room**). From Capitol Hill you'll have a grand view of the city and distant mountains. Open Mon–Fri all year, daily in summer.

    Symphony Hall, 123 W. South Temple St. (533-6407): Spectacular modern building with an unusual chamfered design and an immense glass facade. The hall is well known for its fine acoustics, and is the home of the Utah Symphony Orchestra. Part of the Salt Palace Center Complex. Open Mon–Fri in summer, Tues and Thurs the rest of the year.

CHURCHES/SYNAGOGUES: ※ **Cathedral of the Madeleine,** 331 E. South Temple St. (328-8941): Topped by two 220-ft. (67m) towers, this Spanish Gothic-style cathedral dating from 1909 features a richly decorated interior: varieties of Tennessee marble, Venetian mosaics, stained-glass windows from Germany, carved oak statues, etc. Open daily.

    Mormon Temple: See Temple Square under "Historic Buildings," below.

HISTORIC BUILDINGS: ※ Beehive House, 67 E. South Temple St. (240-2671): Former residence of Brigham Young, founder of the city and the second president of the Mormon church. Built in 1854, the house was the official residence of Mormon presidents until 1918. On its small tower is the figure of a beehive—betokening the zeal of the Mormons—which is also incorporated in the Utah State Seal. Interesting period furniture. Not to be missed. Open daily. (**Lion House,** next door, dating from 1856, was Brigham Young's office until his death in 1877, and also the scene of family gatherings for Young's 19 wives and 56 children. Closed to the public.)

    Council Hall, State St. and 300 North St., Capitol Hill (538-1030): The former city hall and seat of government for the Territory of Utah (1866). Initially erected at 1 E. South St., the hall was moved, stone by stone, to its present location and rebuilt in 1962. Today it houses the Utah Travel Council and its Visitor Information Center (see "Tourist Information," above). Open daily in summer, Mon–Fri the rest of the year.

    Deseret Pioneer Village, 2601 Sunnyside Ave. (533-5881): Museum village re-creating the life of the valley's early Mormon pioneers, circa 1850–70. Some of the buildings are facsimiles, while others are the authentic original buildings, moved to their present place. Among them is **Brigham Young's country home,** painstakingly restored (**Brigham Young's Forest Farmhouse**). An interesting slice of history. Nearby you'll find the "This Is the Place" Monument (see "Monuments," below).

    Fort Douglas, Wasatch Dr. (524-4154): Constructed in 1862 by order of President Lincoln to protect transcontinental telegraph installations from tribal attacks, the fort has preserved several imposing buildings and fortifications of reddish sandstone. An interesting museum traces Utah's military history after the arrival of the Mormons. Open Tues–Sat.

    Governor's Mansion, 603 E. South Temple St. (538-1005): Built in 1902 by Thomas Kearns, a wealthy mine owner and

Utah senator, this luxurious residence with its rich interior (Italian marble, Russian mahogany) today serves as the residence of Utah's governor. Open Tues and Thurs afternoons, May–Dec, by appointment only the rest of the year.

🔔 **Hotel Utah, S.** Temple St. and Main St. (531-1000): After 76 years of welcoming famous visitors, this legendary palace of Italian Renaissance design, a designated historic monument, closed its doors in 1987. It has since reopened as an office building and meeting place for the Mormon church (to which it belongs), thus closing a chapter in Salt Lake City history. No visitors.

🌤🔔🔔 **Temple Square,** bounded by N. Temple St., S. Temple St., W. Temple St. and Main St. (240-2534): The historic heart and holy place of Joseph Smith's church. Enclosed within a 13-ft. (4m) wall of unbaked brick, the square contains those buildings that most symbolize the Mormon religion. First and foremost is the **Temple,** an imposing granite edifice in Mormon style, inaugurated in 1893 after 40 years in construction. At each of its two extremities are three pointed towers; the tallest, part of the main facade, measures 209 ft. (64m) in height and is crowned by Cyrus D. Dallin's gold statue of the angel Moroni. Reserved for baptism and marriage celebrations, sermons, and ordinations, the richly decorated Temple is off-limits to non-Mormons. The second noteworthy building, the **Tabernacle,** a vast 6,500-seat concert hall dating from 1867, has a wooden roof shaped like a turtle's carapace. Its exceptional acoustics are demonstrated daily via recitals on the 12,000-pipe organ. Recital times are noon Mon–Fri and 4pm Sat–Sun. Concerts of the famous Mormon Tabernacle Choir are held Thurs at 8pm and Sun at 9:30am. The brand-new **Museum of Church History and Art** (45 N. West Temple St.) chronicles the history of Mormonism from 1830 to the present. Contains fine art sculptures and paintings and religious artifacts from all over the world. Interesting; open daily. The last of the major buildings, the **Assembly Hall** (1882), can accommodate as many as 3,000 people for religious observances, concerts, meetings, funerals, etc. Concerts Mon–Sat in summer, Fri–Sat the rest of the year. There are also **visitor centers** with information on Mormon history and religion. Nearly four million visitors come to Temple Sq. each year.

MONUMENTS: 🔔 **Brigham Young Monument,** S. Temple St. and Main St.: Bronze statue of Salt Lake City's founder; note the figures of a Native American and a trapper at the base of the pedestal (1897). On the monument's north side is a plaque bearing the names of those Mormon pioneers who arrived with Brigham Young on July 24, 1847.

🌤🔔 **Eagle Gate,** S. Temple St. and State St.: Originally constructed in 1859 to mark the entrance to Brigham Young's private property, this monumental sculpture, composed of the emblems of the United States (the eagle) and the State of Utah (the beehive) supported by four massive arches, overlooks one of the city's principal intersections.

🔔 **Grave of Brigham Young,** First Ave. between State St. and A St.: Tomb of the Mormon leader, three of his wives, and several of their children, in a modest grdn surrounded by a wrought-iron railing. Lovely view of the city.

🔔 **Seagull Monument,** Temple Sq.: The figure of a seagull perches atop this bronze column (1913) in commemoration of the sea birds that in 1848 miraculously intervened to eat the grasshoppers threatening the harvest of the first settlers.

🌤🔔 **"This Is the Place" Monument,** Sunnyside Ave. at the entrance to Emigration Canyon: Erected in 1947 for the centennial celebration of the founding of Salt Lake City, the monument, designed by Brigham Young's grandson, Mahonry Young, marks the place from which the Mormon leader first discerned the site of the future capital of Utah (July 24, 1847). Lovely view of the valley. Visitor center open daily.

MUSEUMS OF ART: ⚱ **Salt Lake Art Center,** 20 S. West Temple St. (328-4201): Temporary art exhibitions (paintings, photos, crafts). Sculpture garden. Numerous concerts, ballet, conferences, films on art, etc. Part of the huge Salt Palace Center cultural complex (see "Architectural Highlights," above). Open daily.

   ⚱ **Utah Museum of Fine Arts,** University of Utah campus, 300 S. University St. (581-7332): Installed in the new building of the Art and Architecture Center, this relatively small but well-rounded museum offers a complete overview of the history of art, from Egyptian antiquities to contemporary American painting. Also a lovely collection of Louis XIV furniture and 17th-century tapestries.

MUSEUMS OF SCIENCE & HISTORY: ☀⚱ **Hansen Planetarium,** 15 S. State St. (538-2098): Well-known planetarium housed in a former turn-of-the-century public library building. A spectacular **Star Chamber** takes visitors on a vicarious tour of the planets. Space museum and specialty library. A must for astronomy buffs. Open daily.

   ☀⚱ **Pioneer Memorial Museum,** 300 N. Main St. (533-5759): Interesting museum focused on the Mormon era, just a few steps from the State Capitol. Created in 1950, the museum contains numerous and often-touching souvenirs from the time of the early Mormon pioneers (dolls, clothing, manuscripts, furniture, etc.). In the **Carriage House** next door, be sure to see the wagon used by Brigham Young in his 1847 trek to Salt Lake City. Open daily Jun–Aug, Mon–Sat the rest of the year.

   ⚱ **Utah Museum of Natural History,** University of Utah campus, Wasatch Dr. (581-6927): Rich geological, paleontological, and zoological collections. Outstanding display of five almost-complete dinosaur skeletons uncovered in earlier Utah excavations. Remarkable Hall of Minerals. Open daily.

PANORAMAS: ☀⚱ **LDS Church Office Bldg.,** 50 E. North Temple St. (240-2331): The observation deck on the 26th floor offers (free) the best view of the city and surrounding mountains. Open Mon–Sat.

PARKS & GARDENS: ⚱ **Jordan Park,** 1060 S. 9th West St.: Located on the shores of the Jordan River, this park and the adjacent **International Peace Gardens** features flowers and statues from 22 countries. Also a picnic area and a public swimming pool. Open daily May–Sept; closed the rest of the year.

   ☀⚱ **Liberty Park,** 1000 South St. and 600 East St. (972-7800): Very lovely 100-acre (41ha) park close to the center of the city. Notable features include a vast pond (boat rides), a children's amusement park, and the **Tracy Aviary.** Open daily.

   ⚱ **State Arboretum,** University of Utah campus (581-5322): Spread over the university campus are more than 7,000 trees from 350 different species.

PERFORMING ARTS: For a daily listing of all shows and cultural events, consult the entertainment pages of the daily papers the *Salt Lake City Tribune* (morning) and the *Desert News* (evening), and of the monthly magazine *Utah Holiday.*

   Capitol Theatre, 50 W. 200 South St. (538-2253): Built in 1913, this very lovely rococo theater, sumptuously renovated, offers ballet, opera, top entertainers, and Broadway shows. Home of the Utah Opera Company (directed by Glade Peterson), the Ballet West, and the Repertory Dance Theatre.

   Mormon Tabernacle, Temple Sq. (240-2205): Daily organ recitals (free), concerts of sacred music, and performances by the Mormon Tabernacle Choir Thurs and Sun (see "Historic Buildings," above).

Pioneer Memorial Theatre, 300 South St. and University St. (581-6961): Classic and contemporary theater, musical comedies (Sept–May). On the Utah State University campus.

Promised Valley Playhouse, 132 S. State St. (364-5677): Elegantly restored building dating from the end of the 19th century. Contemporary theater, drama, musical productions (Sept–May). Musical comedy with the Mormon epic as theme, Tues–Sat all summer (free tickets at the Temple Sq. Visitor Center).

Salt Lake Acting Co., 168 W. 500 North (363-0525): Drama, comedy, contemporary theater.

Special Events Center, Hempstead Rd., Utah State University campus (581-6641): Circular dome-covered arena seating 15,000. Hosts the "Runnin' Utes" basketball team, also concerts and performances of top entertainers.

Symphony Hall, Salt Palace Center, 123 W. South Temple St. (533-6407): Very beautiful architecture and peerless acoustics. Concerts, classical-music recitals. Home of the Utah Symphony Orchestra (principal conductor: Joseph Silverstein).

SHOPPING: ※ **Trolley Square,** bounded by 5th South St. and 6th South St. and 6th East St. and 7th East St. (521-9877): Former turn-of-the-century trolley depot, intelligently transformed into a business and entertainment center with 100 or so shops, booths, restaurants, and movie theaters. Strolling musicians and sidewalk artists. Lively, colorful atmosphere, lovely Victorian decor. Definitely deserves a visit. Open daily.

※ **ZCMI,** Main St. and S. Temple St. (321-8745): Founded by Brigham Young himself in 1868, the Zion's Cooperative Mercantile Institution (ZCMI) is the oldest department store in the United States. Its ornamental cast-iron facade is a designated historic monument. Next door is the **ZCMI Center,** an enormous four-story modern shopping mall containing many shops, specialty stores, and restaurants.

SPECIAL EVENTS: For the exact schedule of events below, consult the **Salt Lake City Convention and Visitors Bureau** (see "Tourist Information," above).

Utah Arts Festival (end of June): Art exhibits, shows, concerts, international food festival, etc.

Pioneer Day (July 24): Commemorates the founding of Salt Lake City by the first Mormons. Parades, rodeo. Very colorful spectacle.

Promised Valley (July–Aug): Musical show portraying the saga of Brigham Young and the early pioneers. Promised Valley Playhouse.

Utah State Fair (11 days in mid-Sept): The biggest fair in the state of Utah.

SPORTS: Salt Lake City has three professional teams:

Baseball (mid-June to Sept): Trappers, Derks Field (484-9900); minor-league team.

Basketball (Oct–Apr): Utah Jazz, Salt Palace (355-5151).

Ice Hockey (Oct–Apr): Golden Eagles, Salt Palace (521-6120).

STROLLS: ⌂ **Arrow Press Square,** West Temple St. across from Salt Palace Center: The old printers' and bookbinders' quarter, with beautifully restored early 19th-century buildings, boutiques, and trendy restaurants.

※⌂ **South Temple Street,** between Temple Sq. and 7th East St.: The most fashionable and historic street in Salt Lake City, featuring the elegant residences of 19th-century silver and copper magnates. Among these is the **Kearns Mansion** (see the Governor's Mansion under "Historic Buildings," above). Note also the **Cathedral of the Madeleine** (see "Churches/Synagogues," above) and the **Masonic Temple,** 650 E. South Temple St.

※⌂ **Trolley Square:** See "Shopping," above.

THEME PARKS: ☀☖ **Lagoon Amusement Park and Pioneer Village,** in Farmington, 17 mi. (27 km) north on I-15 (801/451-0101): Large amusement park with cleverly re-created 19th-century pioneer village. Stagecoach rides, vast lagoon/swimming pool. Rodeos in the summer, also musical shows. Truly worth the trip. Open daily Memorial Day–Labor Day, wknds only mid-Apr to Memorial Day and Labor Day to mid-Oct.

    ☖ **Raging Waters,** 1700 W. 1200 West (973-4020): Aquatic amusement park with at least a dozen pools, with 17 giant water slides, waterfalls, artificial surf, etc. Open daily May–Sept.

WINTER SPORTS RESORTS: ☖☖ **Alta,** 28 mi. (45km) SE on Utah 152 and Utah 210 (801/742-3333): 10 lifts. Open mid-Nov to mid-Apr.

    ☖☖ **Brighton Bowl,** 31 mi. (49km) SE on Utah 152 (801/943-8309): 5 lifts. Open mid-Nov to May.

    ☖ **Deer Valley,** 30 mi. (48km) SE on I-80 and Utah 224 (801/649-1000): 8 lifts. Open early Dec to mid-Apr.

    ☖ **Park City,** 27 mi. (43km) east on I-80 (801/649-8111): 14 lifts. Open mid-Nov. to the end of Apr.

    ☖ **Park West,** 26 mi. (41km) east on I-80 and Utah 224 (801/649-5400): 7 lifts. Open Nov to early April.

    ☀☖☖ **Snowbird,** 29 mi. (46km) SE on U.S. 83, Colo. 209, and Colo. 210 (801/742-2222): Cable car and 7 lifts. Open mid-Nov to June.

    ☖ **Solitude Ski Resort,** 23 mi. (36km) SE on Utah 152 (801/534-1400): 5 lifts. Open from the end of Nov through Apr.

    ☀☖☖ **Sundance Resort,** 63 mi. (100km) SE on I-15, Utah 52, U.S. 189, and Utah 92 (801/225-4107): 4 lifts. Managed by actor Robert Redford, who lives here. Far from the crowds and commotion of the typical ski resort.

ACCOMMODATIONS

    A Note on Accommodations: Room rates in Salt Lake City are coded as follows: **VE,** Very Expensive ($140 and up); **E,** Expensive ($90–$140); **M,** Moderate ($60–$90); **I,** Inexpensive ($30–$60); **B,** Budget (up to $30). A listing of toll free numbers is in the Appendix.

Personal Favorites (in order of preference)

    ☖☖☖ **Red Lion Salt Lake** (formerly the Sheraton; dwntwn), 255 S. West Temple St., UT 84101 (801/328-2000; toll free, see Red Lion Inns). 496 rms, A/C, color TV, in-rm movies. AE, CB, DC, MC, V. Free parking, pool, health club, sauna, rest. (Maxi's), coffee shop, bar, rm svce, nightclub, concierge, free crib. *Note:* Large, very modern 18-story hotel next to the huge Triad Center architectural complex. Peerless comfort and facilities. Spacious, inviting rms, some w. refrigerators. Very good svce, acceptable rest. Frequented by businesspeople and convention-goers (the Salt Palace is close by). Two VIP floors. Free airport shuttle. **E**

    ☖☖☖ **Marriott Hotel** (dwntwn), 75 S. West Temple St., UT 84101 (801/531-0800; toll free, see Marriott). 516 rms, A/C, color TV, in-rm movies. AE, CB, DC, MC, V. Parking $4, pool, health club, two tennis courts, squash, sauna, two rests. (including L'Abeille), two bars, rm svce, nightclub, boutiques, free crib. *Note:* Modern 15-story tower across from the Salt Palace Convention Center. Facilities and comfort are beyond reproach. Spacious rms w. balconies; attentive reception and svce. Rests. are so-so, as elsewhere in the Marriott chain. Business and group clientele. Interesting wknd packages. Free airport shuttle. Direct access to the adj. shopping center. VIP floor. The best location in Salt Lake City. **M–E**

    ☀☖☖ **Brigham Street Inn** (nr. dwntwn), 1135 E. South Temple, UT 84102 (801/364-4461). 9 rms, A/C, color TV. AE, MC, V. Free parking, valet svce, free breakfast, free crib. *Note:* Small luxury hotel, inti-

CENTRAL SALT LAKE CITY

mate and refined, in a charming Victorian residence dating from 1898 (no elevator). Rms are elegantly fitted out, each in its own style (some have fireplaces). Stylish reception and svce. Charm and distinction; 10 min. from dwntwn. **M–E**

 Howard Johnson Hotel (dwntwn), 122 W. South Temple, UT 84101 (801/521-0130; toll free, see Howard Johnson). 224 rms, A/C, color TV, in-rm movies. AE, CB, DC, MC, V. Free parking, pool, health club, rest. (J.B.'s), rm svce, hrdrsr, free crib. *Note:* Enormous 13-story motel in the center of dwntwn. Comfort up to contemporary standards, and a complete range of facilities. Inviting rms (some w. refrigerator); efficient svce. Free airport shuttle. Good value in a fine location across from the Salt Palace and Temple Sq. **I–M**

 Travelodge Downtown (dwntwn), 524 S. West Temple, UT 84101 (801/531-7100; toll free, see Travelodge). 60 rms, A/C, color TV, in-rm movies. AE, CB, DC, MC, V. Free parking; pool and rest. adj. *Note:* Small, unassuming but well-run motel w. functional comforts and a friendly reception. Centrally located three blocks from the Salt Palace. Good value. **I**

Other Accommodations (from top bracket to budget)

 Hilton Salt Lake (nr. dwntwn), 150 W. 500 South St., UT 84101 (801/532-3344; toll free, see Hilton). 351 rms, A/C, color TV, in-rm movies. AE, CB, DC, MC, V. Free parking, pool, sauna, two rests. (including Towne Hall), coffee shop, bar, rm svce, disco, hrdrsr, free crib. *Note:* Large, modern, functional hotel. Rms are comfortable and spacious and have balconies and refrigerators. Svce somewhat lacking. A favorite of business travelers. Good rests. Two VIP floors. 5 min. from dwntwn. **M–E**

 Little America (nr. dwntwn), 500 S. Main St., UT 84101 (801/363-6781; toll free 800/453-9450). 850 rms, A/C, color TV, in-rm movies. AE, CB, DC, MC, V. Free parking, two pools, health club, sauna, two rests. (including Little America), coffee shop, bar, rm svce, nightclub, hrdrsr, shops, free crib. *Note:* A 17-story hotel, modern and comfortable, surrounded by lovely grdns. Spacious rms, some w. refrigerators. Comprehensive facilities. Efficient reception and svce. Good value. Frequented by convention-goers and other groups. Free airport shuttle. 5 min. from Temple Sq. and the Convention Center. **M–E**

 Peery (dwntwn), 110 W. 300 South, UT 84101 (801/521-4300; toll free 800/331-0073). 77 rms, A/C, color TV, in-rm movies. AE, CB, DC, MC, V. Free parking, health club, sauna, two rests., bar, rm svce, free breakfast, free crib. *Note:* Constructed in 1910, this elegant small hotel, a designated historic monument, was completely renovated in 1985. Rms are huge and very comfortable. Svce is personalized. Free airport shuttle. Only a stone's throw from the Convention Center. A favorite of those in-the-know. **I–M** single, **M–E** (double).

 Tri-Arc Hotel (formerly the Travelodge Tri-Arc; nr. dwntwn), 161 W. 600 South St., UT 84101 (801/521-7373). 375 rms, A/C, cable color TV. AE, CB, DC, MC, V. Free parking, pool, sauna, tennis, rest. (13th Floor Supper Club), coffee shop, bar, rm svce, disco, hrdrsr, boutiques, free crib. *Note:* Modern 13-story building in the form of a triple arc. Completely renovated rms and facilities, all w. balconies and refrigerators. Offers a lovely view of the mountains. Efficient svce. Group clientele. Good value. 5 min. from dwntwn. **I–M**

 Shilo Inn (formerly the International Dunes; dwntwn), 206 S. West Temple St., UT 84101 (801/521-9500; toll free 800/222-2244). 200 rms, A/C, color TV, in-rm movies. AE, CB, DC, MC, V. Free parking, pool, sauna, rest., bar, rm svce, night club, shops, free breakfast, free crib. *Note:* Large hotel, comfortable and functional, in the center of town. Pleasant rms. w. balconies and minibars. Good value. Great location across from the Salt Palace. Free airport shuttle. **I–M**

♀ **Royal Executive Inn** (dwntwn), 121 N. 300 West St., UT
ᒻ 84103 (801/521-3450). 94 rms, A/C, color TV, in-rm movies. AE, CB, DC, MC, V. Free parking, pool, coffee shop next door, rm svce, free breakfast, crib $1. *Note:* Modest, unpretentious motel in the heart of dwntwn. Good reception, very decent comfort. Free airport shuttle. Good value. **I**

♀ **Motel 6** (nr. dwntwn), 176 W. 600 South St., UT 84101
ᒻ (801/531-1252). 110 rms, A/C, color TV, free in-rm movies. AE, DC, MC, V. Free parking, pool. *Note:* Small, super-economical but well-maintained motel, very nr. the center of town. An excellent value. Ideal for motorists. **B–I**

Airport Accommodations

♀♀ **Comfort Inn Airport** (formerly the Wynfield Inn; nr.
ᒻᒻ dwntwn), 200 N. Admiral Byrd Rd., UT 84116 (801/537-7444; toll free 800/228-5150). 160 rms, A/C, color TV, in-rm movies. AE, CB, DC, MC, V. Free parking, pool, rest., bar, rm svce, free crib. *Note:* Up-to-date, comfortable motel less than 5 min. from the airport (free shuttle). Spacious, inviting rms w. balcony and some w. refrigerator. Wholly professional svce; business clientele. Excellent for a stopover between flights. 12 min. from dwntwn. **I–M**

YMCA/Youth Hostels

Avenues Youth Hostel (dwntwn), 107 F St. (801/363-8137). 30 beds. Comfortable youth hostel eight blocks from Temple Sq. Open year round.

RESTAURANTS

A Note on Restaurant Prices: Salt Lake City restaurant prices, per person, excluding drinks and service charges, are coded as follows: **VE**, Very Expensive ($60 and up); **E**, Expensive ($40–$60); **M**, Moderate ($25–$40); **I**, Inexpensive ($15–$25); **B**, Budget (up to $15).

A Note on Utah's Liquor Laws: Liquor may be purchased in state-owned liquor stores, open every day except Sun; 3.2% beer may be purchased 7 days a week in most grocery stores. Many fine restaurants have liquor licenses. Patrons may purchase mini-bottles and mix their own drinks with setups provided by the restaurant. Most restaurants will also provide setups for "brown bag" liquor taken by the customer to the restaurant or lounge. Private clubs also offer "over-the-bar" drinks; visitors may purchase a 2-week membership to most private clubs in Utah for $5. Minimum drinking age is 21.

Personal Favorites (in order of preference)

☀♀♀♀ **La Caille at Quail Run** (vic.), 9565 S. Wasatch Blvd., in Sandy
(942-1751). A/C. Dinner nightly, brunch Sun; closed hols. AE, CB, DC, MC, V. Jkt. *Specialties:* oysters on the half shell, veal au citron, rack of lamb, duckling w. fruit, lobster in red butter. Basque cooking on Sun. Wine and liquor available. *Note:* This elegant Louis XVI–style manor about 12 mi. (20km) south of Salt Lake City is the site of one of the best rests. (if not the best) in Utah. The French-inspired cooking is of the first order, and the svce is courteous and distinguished. Lovely grdns. Resv. are a must. Valet parking. 25 min. from dwntwn. *Continental/French.* **I–M**

♀♀ **La Fleur de Lys** (dwntwn), 165 S. West Temple St. (359-
ᒻᒻ 5753). A/C. Dinner only, Mon–Sat; closed hols. AE, CB, DC, MC, V. Jkt. *Specialties:* pheasant chasseur, roast duckling à l'orange, soufflés. Good desserts. Wine and liquor. *Note:* Classic French cuisine impeccably prepared and served. Elegant decor and pleasant background music create a romantic atmosphere on picturesque Arrow Press Sq. Excellent svce; popular locally. Resv. advised. *French.* **I–M**

♀♀ **Bird's Café** (vic.), 1355 E. 2100 South St. (466-1051). A/C.
ᒻᒻ Lunch Mon–Fri, dinner nightly, brunch Sun; closed hols. AE, CB, DC, MC, V. *Specialties:* linguine w. shellfish in cream sauce, scallops au grat-

in, broiled lamb chops, poached fresh salmon w. pesto, pepper steak. The menu changes daily. Wine and liquor. *Note:* The modern, California-inspired cooking of chef Dennis Bird has made this rest. a Salt Lake City favorite. The daily specials, written on a blackboard, vary according to season and availability of ingredients. Dark paneling enhances the warm, intimate atmosphere. Svce is attentive. Dinner resv. indispensable. Outdoor dining, weather permitting. *American.* I

    ♟ **Robintino's** (nr. dwntwn), 120 N. 900 West (596-2626). A/C. Lunch Mon–Sat, dinner nightly; closed Easter, Thanksgiving, Dec 25. AE, DC, MC, V. *Specialties:* pizza, ravioli, fresh pasta, steaks, Italian dishes. Beer and wine. *Note:* Small, modest, unpretentious *trattoria.* Very decent homemade pasta. Popular w. the locals. *Italian/steak.* B–I

    ♟ **Mikado** (dwntwn), 67 W. 100 South (328-0929). A/C. Dinner only, Mon–Sat; closed hols. AE, CB, DC, MC, V. *Specialties:* sushi, sukiyaki, shrimp tempura, chicken teriyaki, shabu shabu. Wine and liquor. *Note:* The only genuine Japanese rest. in Salt Lake City. Smiling, discreet svce (in kimono). Western- and tatami-style dining rms. Popular locally. Resv. advised. *Japanese.* I

Other Restaurants (from top bracket to budget)

    ♟♟ **Le Parisien** (dwntwn), 417 S. 300 East St. (364-5223). A/C. Lunch Mon–Sat, dinner daily; closed hols. AE, DC, MC, V. *Specialties:* quiche Lorraine, lasagne, Dover sole meunière, rack of lamb, Italian dishes, catch of the day. Wine (a good list) and liquor available. *Note:* Charming country-style bistro serving excellent home-style food of both French and Italian antecedents. Open-air dining in fine weather. Efficient svce; resv. advisable but not essential. Convenient dwntwn location. *French/Italian.* I–M

    ♟♟ **Market Street Broiler** (nr. dwntwn), 260 S. 1300 East (583-8808). A/C. Breakfast/lunch Mon–Fri, dinner daily. AE, MC, V. *Specialties:* clam chowder, sautéed scallops, red snapper w. citrus, poached salmon, broiled catch of the day, steak, roast chicken, lamb chops. Good homemade desserts. Wine and liquor available. *Note:* Agreeable grill rm in contemporary style, housed in a former fire station. Sister rest. of the Market Street Grill (see below). First-class fish and seafood flown in daily; svce flawless in all particulars. A fine place. No resv. 15 min. from dwntwn. *American/Seafood.* I–M

    ♟♟ **Market Street Grill** (dwntwn), 54 Post Office Pl. (322-4668). A/C. Breakfast/lunch Mon–Sat, dinner nightly, brunch Sun; closed hols. AE, MC, V. *Specialties:* excellent meats and seafood cooked over a mesquite fire, roast chicken, lamb chops, prime rib. Good desserts. Wine and liquor. *Note:* Old-time steakhouse, very popular locally, in a building dating from the early 1900s. The ambience is pleasant, the svce rapid and efficient. Just a few steps from Temple Sq. Very good value. No resv. *American/Steak.* I

    ♟♟ **Ristorante Della Fontana** (dwntwn), 336 S. 4th East St. (328-4243). A/C. Lunch/dinner Mon–Sat; closed Memorial Day, July 4, Dec 25. AE, DC, MC, V. Jkt. *Specialties:* lasagne, homemade pasta, Italian dishes. Wine and liquor. *Note:* Multicolored stained-glass windows and an indoor waterfall give this rest., converted from an old church, one of the most original settings ever. Very decent Italian cuisine, very good svce. Popular locally; resv. advised. *Italian.* I

    ☼♟ **Lamb's Restaurant** (dwntwn), 169 S. Main St. (364-7166). A/C. Breakfast/lunch/dinner Mon–Sat; closed hols. AE, CB, DC, MC, V. *Specialties:* omelets, excellent homemade soups, fried trout, broiled snapper, corned beef and cabbage, braised lamb shank, rice pudding. Beer and wine. *Note:* The oldest rest. in Utah (1919). Local businesspeople prefer it for working breakfasts and lunches. Honest, serious family cooking. The pleasantly dated decor is charming and helps create a peaceful atmosphere. Excellent svce. This is a true Salt Lake City landmark. No resv. Very good value. *American,* B–I

    ♟ **The Old Salt City Jail** (nr. dwntwn), 460 S. 10th East St. (355-2422). A/C. Lunch/dinner daily; closed July 4, July 24, Dec

25. AE, DC, MC, V. *Specialties:* roast beef, steaks, barbecued meats, catch of the day. Beer and wine. *Note:* As its name indicates, this rest. is in a converted 19th-century jail. The quality of the meats is excellent, and the decor is amusing even if not authentic. The atmosphere and svce are congenial. Good value. *American/ steak.* **B–I**

      Rio Grande Café (dwntwn), 270 S. Rio Grande (364-3302). A/C. Lunch Mon–Sat, dinner nightly; closed hols. AE, CB, DC, MC, V. *Specialties:* tacos, enchiladas, chalupas, chimichangas. Wine and liquor. *Note:* The most authentic of the local Mexican rests. in both cooking and decor. Some of the sauces are dynamite. Very popular for lunch. Located in the former Denver & Rio Grande train station. No. resv. *Mexican.* **B–I**

Cafeterias/Fast Food
      Marianne's Delicatessen (dwntwn), 149 W. 200 South (364-0513). Open 11am–3pm Tues–Sat. AE, MC, V. Excellent sandwiches, many German specialties (rouladen, sauerbraten, and bratwurst), good daily specials, and memorable desserts explain this deli's popularity among the locals. No resv.

BARS & NIGHTCLUBS
      Barb Wire (dwntwn), 348 W. 500 South St. (362-2870). A great place for aficionados of traditional country and western. Open Tues–Sat.

      Bourbon Street (dwntwn), 78 W. 400 South St. (521-0589). Fashionable singles bar, popular locally. There's an entrance fee. Open Mon–Sat.

      D. B. Cooper's (dwntwn), 19 E. 200 South St. (532-2948). Very popular disco. One of the oldest private clubs in Salt Lake City. Open Mon–Sat.

      Zephyr (dwntwn), 79 W. 300 South St. (355-9913). Live rock and jazz. Open nightly.

NEARBY EXCURSIONS

BINGHAM CANYON COPPER MINE (27 mi./43km SW on I-15 and Utah 48): The largest open-pit copper mine in the world, owned by the Kennecott Co. The crater (2½ mi./4km in diameter, 3,148 ft./960m in depth) is the largest man-made excavation in the world. Five billion tons of rock and minerals have been mined since 1904. An impressive sight. Observation platform. Open daily May–Sept.

BONNEVILLE SALT FLAT (125 mi./200km west on I-80): An immense desert of salt 200 mi. (322km) long, as hard as cement. Used as an automobile test track since 1911. In 1970 the rocket vehicle *Blue Flame* set a then world speed record of 622.4 m.p.h. (1,001.4km/h). Present record: 633.6 m.p.h. (1,019.7km/h) attained by *Thrust 2*, driven by Richard Noble on Nevada's Black Rock Desert track on October 3, 1983. Races are held each year at the end of Sept, attracting a large crowd of fans.

GREAT SALT LAKE (31 mi/49km NW on I-15): At 72 mi. (115km) long and 30 mi. (48km) wide, but with a maximum depth of barely 28 ft. (8.5m), Great Salt Lake, the remains of Lake Bonneville, a prehistoric sea 13 times greater in size, is the largest natural body of water in the western United States. With ongoing evaporation, the salt content of the lake now averages 25% (seven times that of the oceans); this makes it unlivable for any form of animal life except shrimp. The lake's surface area continues to shrink: from 2,393 sq. mi. (6,200km²) in 1873 to 1,437 sq. mi. (3,724km²) today. The salt content is so high that even nonswimmers float with ease. (It's wise to protect your eyes from the salty water.) Because of repeated flooding, **Antelope Island** and **Saltair Beach,** formerly very popular, are no longer accessible.

⚒ TIMPANOGOS CAVE NATIONAL MONUMENT (36
mi./58km SE via I-15 and Utah 92) (801/756-5238): Underground limestone caves at a constant temperature of 43°F (6°C). Splendid multicolored crystalline formations. Visiting the caves can be rather trying. Open daily, spring through fall; closed in winter.

☀⚒⚒ SNOWBIRD SKI & SUMMER RESORT (29 mi./46km
SE along State St. and 9400 South St.) (742-2222): A 125-passenger aerial tramway links the floor of Little Cottonwood Canyon, 2,900 ft. (880m) above sea level, to the crest of Hidden Peak, 11,000 ft. (3,353m) in elevation. Unobstructed panorama of the Uinta Mountains and the Great Salt Lake Valley. The tramway operates daily year round except in May and late-Oct to late-Nov. A marvelous sight.

☀⚒ WASATCH-CACHE NATIONAL FOREST: 1,235,000
acres (500,000ha) of forests, lakes, canyons, and mountains to the north, east, and southeast of Salt Lake City. Includes several ski areas, among them Alta, Park West, and Snowbird (see "Winter Sports Resorts," above). The U.S. Ski Team has set up its year-round training site in the Wasatch Mountains. There are numerous camping and picnic areas. Hunting and fishing too. For **information,** contact the Supervisor, 8226 Federal Bldg., 125 S. State St., Salt Lake City, UT 84138 (801/524-5030). Nature unspoiled.

☀⚒ WHEELER HISTORIC FARM (6351 S. 900 East, 21 mi./
33km SE on I-15, Exit I-215) (801/264-2241): Authentic farm from the end of the 19th century, magnificently restored. Re-creates to perfection the 1890s life-style of the Mormon farmers. Costumed guides conduct the tour; if they wish, visitors can help milk cows, gather eggs, or feed and water the farm animals. An original, historical slice-of-life. Open daily.

FARTHER AFIELD

☀⚒⚒ NORTH OF GREAT SALT LAKE (209 mi./334km r.t. via
I-15N, Utah 83, and I-15S): Visit **Bear River Migratory Bird Refuge** near **Brigham City,** the largest migratory bird preserve in the U.S. Photo safaris encouraged. Open daily. Continue on to ⚒ **Golden Spike National Historic Site,** the place where, in 1869, the Central Pacific Railroad line coming from the west met the Union Pacific line from the east, creating the first transcontinental railroad. The anniversary of this event is celebrated each year on May 10 at 12:47pm, the exact day and hour of the original event. There's also a museum (801/471-2209) with exhibits and movies, open daily.

On your return, stop at the **Lagoon Amusement Park** (see "Theme Parks," above).

☀⚒⚒ SOUTH OF GREAT SALT LAKE (155 mi./248km r.t. via
I-15S, Utah 48, Utah 68, Utah 73, Utah 36, and I-80E): Visit **Bingham Canyon Copper Mine** (see "Nearby Excursions," above), then the **Stagecoach Inn,** former relay station of the legendary Overland Stage Coach Company and the Pony Express. Go on to **Camp Floyd** (801/768-8932), formerly the largest military outpost in the United States during the wars against the local native tribes. Its visitor center is open daily mid-March to mid-Nov. Next stop, **Ophir,** a famous ghost town of early pioneer days. Finally, of course, there is the **Great Salt Lake** itself (see "Nearby Excursions," above). A spectacular circuit.

For complete information on the three following parks, see Chapter 32 on Utah National Parks.

CANYONLANDS (248 mi./396km SE via I-15, U.S. 6, U.S. 191, and Utah 313): Magnificent ocher-colored rocky cliffs tower over the Colorado River. Along the way, visit 🔯 **Arches National Park,** where amid the reddish desert you'll find superb peaks and arches carved by erosion. An absolute must-see.

DINOSAUR NATIONAL MONUMENT (200 mi./ 320km east via I-80 and U.S. 40): The quarries bear many footprints of prehistoric animals. The visitor center displays a remarkable fossil collection. Open daily.

On the way, visit 🔯 **Flaming Gorge** and its exquisite scenery along the Green River, once the hideout of Butch Cassidy and the Sundance Kid.

GLEN CANYON (319 mi./510km south on I-15 and Utah 28, U.S. 89, Utah 24, and Utah 95): Multicolored cliffs bathed by the blue waters of **Lake Powell.**

En route, be sure to see the unspoiled natural beauty of 🔯 **Capitol Reef National Park,** with its impressive but hard-to-reach canyons.

🔯 **Natural Bridges National Monument,** 45 mi. (72km) south of Glen Canyon, features gigantic rocky arches carved out by erosion.

PIONEER TRAIL (90 mi./144km r.t. via I-15N, U.S. 89, I-84E, Utah 66, Utah 65, and Emigration Canyon Rd.): You'll go through **Farmington, Uintah, Weber Canyon, Morgan, East Canyon Lake, and Emigration Canyon.** A good third of this trip through gorgeous mountain scenery follows the old trail made by 19th-century Mormon pioneers.

UINTA NATIONAL FOREST (138 mi./220km r.t. via I-15S, Utah 92, U.S. 189, Utah 52, and I-15N): You'll visit **Timpanogos Cave National Monument** (see "Nearby Excursions," above) aboard a quaint little steam-powered train, the *Heber Creeper,* which leaves daily, mid-May to mid-Oct, from 6th West and Center St. in **Heber City** (801/654-2900).

There are splendid views along **Deer Creek Lake** and the gorges of the **Provo River,** one of the most beautiful spots in the Uinta forest. Don't fail to admire the waterfalls at **Bridal Veil Falls;** there's a funicular railway (801/225-4461) on U.S. 189 between **Wildwood** and **Olmstead,** open daily Apr–Nov.

To return to Salt Lake City, take I-15N. A trip packed with things to see.

YELLOWSTONE & GRAND TETON (325 mi./520km north via I-15, U.S. 26, and U.S. 89): The crown jewels among America's national parks (see Chapter 33 on Yellowstone), enough to justify the whole trip west.

On your way, I suggest stopping by the 🔯 **Craters of the Moon National Monument** to see the astonishing lunar landscapes sculpted by volcanic eruptions. Closed in winter. For information, contact P.O. Box 29, Arco, ID 83213 (208/527-3257).

ZION NATIONAL PARK (305 mi./488km SW via I-15, Utah 17, and Utah 9): The only canyon in the United States whose floor is accessible by automobile. Lovely landscapes, not to be missed. See Chapter 32 on Utah National Parks.

En route, visit 🔯 **Cedar Breaks** and its rocky plateaus pocked with strikingly colored amphitheater-shaped depressions. Be sure also to see 🔯 **Bryce Canyon** with its breathtaking gorges and ravines, almost as awesome as those of the Grand Canyon.

CHAPTER 32

UTAH NATIONAL PARKS 🔥🔥

□ □ □

With its 10 great national parks for a population of less than 1.5 million inhabitants, the Mormon State is incontestably the most richly endowed from the point of view of the tourist or the ecologist. Mostly lying in the southern part of the state, these 10 national parks or monuments boast some of the most breathtaking scenery in America. This is particularly true of **Zion National Park,** the only canyon in the country that can be entirely explored by car or on foot. Its many-colored gorges, several hundred feet high, bridling the headlong course of the Virgin River, are a sight not easily forgotten. Nearby **Bryce Canyon National Park** has, according to geologists, some of the most astonishing rock formations in the country, as well as a view almost as enthralling as the Grand Canyon of the Colorado. **Arches National Park** displays ranks of wonderful arches and windows carved by erosion out of the rusty rock of the desert. Its neighbor **Canyonlands National Park** is equally spectacular, with its great ocher-colored cliffs of rock looming above the serpentine curves of the Colorado River, an unforgettable sight at sunrise or sunset. More difficult of access, the wild canyons and rocky spurs of **Capitol Reef National Park** along the Fremont River are a perfect example of nature in the raw. Utah's other great national parks—**Natural Bridges National Monument, Glen Canyon National Recreation Area, Cedar Breaks, Dinosaur National Monument,** and **Rainbow Bridge** (one of the world's largest natural arches, 275 ft./85m across)—rank, each in its degree, among the natural wonders of the United States. Allow at least 1 week to 10 days just for the highlights.

BASIC FACTS: State of Utah. Area code: 801. Time zone: mountain. Founded: Zion, 1909; Bryce Canyon, 1923; Arches National Park, 1929; Capitol Reef, 1937. Approximate combined area of the parks: 3,196 sq. mi. (8,280km²).

CLIMATE: Utah's climate is like its scenery: beautiful but rugged. Summers are very hot, and winters icy. While in summer the mercury can climb to 95°F (35°C) by day, it can skid precipitously below 68°F (20°C) at night. There are frequent violent storms from July to Sept; watch out, because the heavy rains can convert an unsurfaced road into a mudslide. The best times to escape both climatic extremes and crowds of tourists are May–June and Sept–Oct. In any case, bring woolens for evening wear.

ARRIVAL & TRANSIT INFORMATION

NEAREST AIRPORTS: See Chapter 47 on Las Vegas or Chapter 31 on Salt Lake City.

AIRLINES: See Chapter 47 on Las Vegas and Chapter 31 on Salt Lake City.

BUS OR CAR RENTAL? Greyhound buses (for information, call toll free 800/528-6055) serve many communities near Utah's national parks, but offer no direct access to them. Given the distances and the number of places you may wish to visit, it makes sense to rent a car with unlimited mileage. Rates in Nevada (Las Vegas) are more favorable than in Utah (Salt Lake City).

CAR RENTALS: See Chapter 47 on Las Vegas and Chapter 31 on Salt Lake City.

TRAIN: For Amtrak, see Chapter 47 on Las Vegas and Chapter 31 on Salt Lake City. The nearest station to Arches and Canyonlands National Parks: Thompson D.R.G.&W. Station (toll free 800/872-7245). Nearest station to Bryce Canyon and Zion National Parks: Milford Amtrak Station, East St. and South St. (toll free 800/872-7245).

INTERCITY BUSES: The nearest long-distance Greyhound terminals are in Las Vegas (see Chapter 47) and Salt Lake City (see Chapter 31). The nearest local Greyhound stations are at 1355 S. Main St. in Cedar City (586-9465) and 525 E. Main St. in Green River (564-3421).

INFORMATION & ADVENTURE TOURS

TOURIST INFORMATION: The **Utah Travel Council,** Council Hall, Capitol Hill, Salt Lake City, UT 84114 (801/538-1030). Information on Utah's national parks and other great tourist attractions. For snow conditions, call 801/521-8102.

Visitor Centers
There are visitor centers in all the major parks:
Arches National Park, at the park entrance (801/259-8161).
Bryce Canyon National Park, 4 mi. (6km) from Bryce Canyon Airport (801/834-5322).
Canyonlands National Park, at Island in the Sky Point (801/259-7164).
Capitol Reef National Park, 6 mi. (9km) from the western entrance (801/564-3633).
Cedar Breaks National Monument, open from the end of May to mid-Sept only (801/586-9451).
Dinosaur National Monument, at the park entrance on the Colorado side and 7 mi. (11km) north of Jensen on the Utah side (303/374-2216).
Glen Canyon National Recreation Area, Glen Canyon Bridge at Page (602/645-2471).
Natural Bridges National Monument, at the park entrance (801/259-5174).
Zion National Park, at the south entrance (801/772-3256).

ADVENTURE TOURS: Adrift Adventures (Jeep and boat), 378 N. Main St., Moab (259-8594; toll free 800/874-4483): 1- to 7-day trips by raft or rowboat down the Colorado or Green River, operated early Apr to late Oct; also Jeep trips (Apr–Oct) in Canyonlands National Park.
Adventure River Expeditions (boat), 245 N. Broadway, Green River (801/564-3648): Rafting down the Colorado River, Green River, San Juan River, and Dolores River. May–Sept.
Bryce Zion Trail Rides, Inc. (horseback): Rides on horseback or muleback in Bryce Canyon or Zion National Park; daily Apr–Sept. For information, call 801/834-5361 (for Bryce Canyon) or 801/772-3967 (for Zion).
Cedar City Air Service (airplane), Municipal Airport, Cedar City (801/

586-3881): Unforgettable flights over Cedar Breaks, Bryce Canyon, and Zion National Parks.

Del Webb Tours (boat), Wahweap Lodge, Page (toll free 800/528-6154): Boat cruises on Lake Powell and trips to Rainbow Bridge.

Don Hatch River Expeditions (boat), 411 E. 2nd North (P.O. Box 1150), Vernal, UT 84078 (801/789-4316; toll free 800/342-8243): 1- to 5-day air-rafting trips on the Green River and the Yampa River in Dinosaur National Park; May–Sept.

Lake Powell Air Service (airplane), Municipal Airport, Page (602/645-2494): Unforgettable flights, lasting 30 min. to 2½ hrs., over Lake Powell, Rainbow Bridge, Monument Valley, Bryce Canyon, etc.

Lin Ottinger's Scenic Tours (all-terrain vehicles), 137 N. Main St., Moab (801/259-7312): 1-day trips in Arches and Canyonlands National Parks; Apr–Nov.

North American's Adventures (boat), 534 N. Main St., Moab (801/259-5865): Down the Green River and Colorado River by air raft or jetboat; Apr–Oct. Jeep trips in winter.

Red Tail Aviation (airplane), Canyonlands Field, on U.S. 191, 18 mi. (28km) north of Moab (801/259-7421): Spectacular flights over Arches and Canyonlands National Parks, Lake Powell, or Monument Valley.

Tag-A-Long Tours (boat), 452 N. Main St., Moab (toll free 800/453-3292): Boat trips down the Green River and Colorado River and around Canyonlands National Park; Apr–Oct.

MUSEUMS: Anasazi State Park Museum, Utah 12, Boulder (335-7306): Archeologists' dig on the site of a 100-room Native American dwelling dating from about A.D. 1050. A life-size replica of a six-room Anasazi dwelling reconstructs the life of its inhabitants eight or nine centuries back. At the nearby museum are exhibited many of the objects unearthed in the dig. Fascinating. Open daily.

Hollywood Stuntmen's Hall of Fame, 11 E. 100 North St., Moab (259-6100): Houses an extensive collection of movie and stunt-oriented memorabilia, including costumes, weapons, action photographs, as well as a theater where movie stunt footage is shown and live performances are held. Unusual. Open Tues–Sun Mar–Oct.

Iron Mission State Historical Museum, 585 N. Main St., Cedar City (586-9290): Site of the first iron foundry west of the Mississippi (1851). Contains an interesting array of wagons, stagecoaches, and other horse-drawn vehicles from Utah pioneer days. Also displayed are numerous Native American artifacts. Open daily.

Moab Museum, 118 E. Center St., Moab (259-9430): Has displays of prehistoric Native American artifacts and exhibits on geology, mineralogy, and pioneer history of southeastern Utah. Open daily.

Utah Field House of Natural History Museum, 235 E. Main St., Vernal (789-3799): Here, 14 life-size artificial dinosaurs welcome the visitor to this handsome grdn with its waterfall, artificial lake, and marshy area reproducing their natural habitat. The adjoining museum has a number of (genuine) fossils including an articulated dinosaur skeleton, as well as mineral and archeological collections. Open daily.

NATIONAL PARKS & MONUMENTS

ARCHES NATIONAL PARK (236 mi./378km SE of Salt Lake City via I-15, U.S. 6, and U.S. 191): Dozens of stone arches and superb red sandstone spurs, carved over 150 million years by erosion, water, wind, sun, and frost in a dun-colored rocky wasteland. Among them are **Landscape Arch,** biggest natural arch in the world (288 ft./88m across); **Park Avenue,** a spectacular rocky corridor between high vertical walls reminiscent of the famous street in New York; the sculptural group called the **Three Gossips;**

the huge, precariously poised **Balanced Rock;** the unbelievably elegant **Delicate Arch,** spanning the sheer gorge of the Colorado, which can be reached by a footpath; and the fantastically shaped arches of the beautiful **Devil's Garden.**

There are 21 mi. (34km) of surfaced roads and scores of miles of additional tracks for all-terrain vehicles, along which you can explore this open-air museum of natural architecture. The park is open year round, but beware extremes of temperature, winter and summer both. There are 53 authorized campsites.

For **information,** contact the Superintendent, Arches National Park, 125 W. 200 South, Moab, UT 84532 (801/259-8161 or 259-7164).

BRYCE CANYON NATIONAL PARK (241 mi./385km

NE of Las Vegas via I-15, Utah 9, U.S. 89, and Utah 12): One of the most beautiful national parks in America; its huge rock formations are almost as astonishing as those of the Grand Canyon of Colorado. Lying along the east side of the **Paunsaugunt Plateau** ("Country of the Beavers," in the local tribal tongue), a limestone mesa 8,200 ft. (2,500m) above sea level which, geologically speaking, is the bed of a 60-million-year-old sea, Bryce Canyon displays fairyland scenery of glittering rocks, cliff faces sculpted into gigantic organ pipes, and a dozen stepped amphitheaters in striking colors varying from yellow through orange to deep red (the famous **Pink Cliffs**). The scenic 17-mi. (27km) **Rim Drive,** as well as a number of hiking trails leading to the bottom of the canyon, will take you to dozens of rock formations with strange shapes and poetic names—Cathedral, Queen's Castle, Wall of Windows, Mormon Temple, Tower Bridge, The Alligator—which have won for the park the nickname "Silent City." Particularly in summer you'll also see plentiful and varied wildlife: cougars, gray foxes, coyote, mule deer, prairie dogs, chipmunks, and more than 160 species of birds. There are unforgettable views from **Sunset Point, Inspiration Point,** and **Bryce Point.** Rim Drive is partly closed in winter. Camping permitted (218 sites).

For **information,** contact the Superintendent, Bryce Canyon National Park, Bryce Canyon, UT 84717 (801/834-5322).

CANYONLANDS NATIONAL PARK (248 mi./396km

SE of Salt Lake City via I-15, U.S. 6, U.S. 191, and Utah 313): Huge, ocher-orange-colored rocky cliffs frowning down on the sinuous windings of the Green River and Colorado River, a fantasy world when seen at sunrise or sunset. Fabulous views from **Dead Horse Point, Grand View Point, and Needles Overlook.** Canyonlands National Park is a rocky maze cut out by 300 million years of erosion. The Colorado River, swollen with the waters of its Green River tributary, turns into a runaway bulldozer as it charges through **Cataract Canyon,** cutting gorges deep into the rock and carving out arches, columns, and needles which stand several hundred feet above the floor of the valley.

The park has only 25 mi. (40km) of surfaced roads, in the **Island in the Sky** sector; the rest, in the **Needles** and **Maze** sectors, can be reached only by Jeep, on foot, or on horseback. Many hiking trails; 80 authorized tentsites. Park open year round.

For **information,** contact the Superintendent, Canyonlands National Park, 125 W. 2nd St., Moab, UT 84532 (801/259-7164).

CAPITOL REEF NATIONAL PARK (209 mi./334km SE

of Salt Lake City via I-15, Utah 28, U.S. 89, and Utah 24): Wild canyons, beetling cliffs, and rounded rocky domes reminiscent of the Capitol in Washington, whence the name. The interior of the park is difficult of access (the famous bandit Butch Cassidy once took refuge here). Along this enormous mountain wall runs a spectacular unsurfaced scenic highway, the **Scenic Drive,** following the rim of a 25-mi. (40km) chain of gorges channeled by the Fremont River. Many rock paintings bear witness to Native American cultures from the

9th to the 13th century. The north of the park, reachable only by Jeep, displays the most beautiful rock formations, particularly **Cathedral Valley.** Authorized camping (40 sites). Park open year round.

For **information,** contact the Superintendent, Capitol Reef National Park, Torrey, UT 84775 (801/564-3633).

⚲ CEDAR BREAKS NATIONAL MONUMENT (215 mi./

344km NE of Las Vegas via I-15, Utah 14, and Utah 148): An enormous natural amphitheater created by erosion in the **Markagunt Plateau,** which rises to 9,840 ft. (3,000m). Natural rock carvings in beautiful hues of red, orange, violet, and yellow make a vivid contrast with the deep greens of the conifers of Dixie National Forest and the alpine meadows on the mountain peaks, covered with wildflowers from mid-June to mid-Aug. Scenic drive (Rim Drive), 6 mi. (11km) long. Camping permitted. Park open mid-May to mid-Oct.

For **information,** contact the Superintendent, Cedar Breaks National Monument, P.O. Box 749, Cedar City, UT 84720 (801/586-9548); an absolute must-see.

ᨒᨒ DINOSAUR NATIONAL MONUMENT (200 mi./

320km east of Salt Lake City along I-80 and U.S. 40): Quarries with many vestiges of prehistoric animals. The **Dinosaur Quarry Visitor Center** has remarkable animal fossils, including an extremely rare 140-million-year-old stegosaurus. Excavations in progress.

The Colorado sector of the park, an area of rugged desert and canyons sometimes as much as 2,625 ft. (800m) deep, offers unobstructed views of the Green River and Yampa River running below; access via U.S. 40, 2 mi. (3km) east of Dinosaur, Colorado, and a 32-mi. (51km) unsurfaced road (Harpers Corner Rd.). Camping permitted. Visitor center and excavation area open year round; rest of the park closed mid-Nov to mid-Apr as dictated by snowfall.

For **information,** contact the Superintendent, Dinosaur National Monument, Harpers Corner Rd. and U.S. 40 (P.O. Box 210), Dinosaur, CO 81610 (303/374-2216).

On your way, take a side trip through the ⚲ **Flaming Gorge National Recreation Area,** 55 mi. (88km) NW of Dinosaur National Monument via U.S. 40 and U.S. 191, a huge recreation area brought into existence by the 502-ft.-high (153m) Flaming Gorge Dam on the Green River. The artificial lake, 91 mi. (146km) long, offers fishing, sailing, water sports, and marinas. Lovely scenery. For information, contact the Ranger District Office, P.O. Box 157, Dutch John, UT 84046 (801/885-3315).

It was in **Brown's Hole,** an inaccessible valley downstream from the dam and almost on the Colorado border, that Butch Cassidy, the Sundance Kid, and their "Wild Bunch" used to take refuge after their raids.

☼ᨒᨒ GLEN CANYON NATIONAL RECREATION AREA

(286 mi./457km NE of Las Vegas via I-15, Utah 9, and U.S. 89): The park covers about a million acres (more than 4,000km²), off the beaten tourist track. Its multicolored cliffs are washed by the blue waters of **Lake Powell,** 196 mi. (315km) long and with 1,900 mi. (3,058km) of desert shoreline, the second-largest artificial lake (after Lake Mead) in the country. All water sports and wonderful fishing for perch, rainbow trout, moonfish, etc. Superb sunsets. A paradise for hikers and campers. Boat trips from Page to **Rainbow Bridge,** one of the biggest natural rock arches in the world, 278 ft. (85m) across by 290 ft. (88m) high; no nature lover should fail to see it. Camping permitted. Park open year round.

For **information,** contact the Superintendent, Glen Canyon National Recreation Area, P.O. Box 1507, Page, AZ 86040 (602/645-2471). (Also see Chapter 40 on Navajoland.)

NATURAL BRIDGES NATIONAL MONUMENT (350
mi./560km SE of Salt Lake City via I-15, Utah 28, U.S. 89,
Utah 24, and Utah 95): In the comparatively small compass of 7,770 acres
(3,150 ha), this very beautiful, wild, colorful park, inaugurated in 1908, offers
the visitor three great rock arches carved by two tributaries of the Colorado: **Kachina Bridge** (206 ft./63m across), **Owachomo Bridge** (180 ft./55m across),
and **Sipapu Bridge** (258 ft./82m across). The site, once settled by the legendary
Anasazi peoples, has more than 200 interesting architectural ruins, easily reached
by the visitor. **Bridge View Drive** is a splendid 8-mi. (13km) scenic route winding across the canyons from the visitor center. Park open year round, but be careful in bad weather since the area is subject to violent storms.

For **information,** contact the Superintendent, Natural Bridges National
Monument, P.O. Box 1, Lake Powell, UT 84533 (801/259-5174). The monument is administered from Canyonlands National Park (see above).

ZION NATIONAL PARK (169 mi./270km NE of Las
Vegas along I-15 and Utah 9): For 225 million years the head-
long Virgin River and its tributaries have carved their courses into the sandstone,
limestone, and schists of the mighty **Markagunt Plateau,** creating an extraordinary trangle of precipitous gorges as deep as 2,950 ft. (900m). The river's erosion
has produced a landscape of pillars, domes, and rock needles assuming the shapes
of cathedrals, statues, and monuments—all under a play of colors which vary,
according to the time of day and season of the year, from grayish-white through
orange and bright red to the deepest violet. **Zion Canyon,** largest of these gorges,
splashed with pink, red, and white, follows the windings of the Virgin River
North Fork, and is fringed with woods of poplar, oak, and maple. **Zion Canyon
Scenic Drive,** 7 mi. (10km) long, offers views of some of the most spectacular
peaks—**The Sentinel** (7,157 ft./2,181m), **Mountain of the Sun** (6,723 ft./
2,049m), **Lady Mountain** (6,940 ft./2,115m), **The Great White Throne**
(6,744 ft./2,056m)—on its way to the end of the gorge and the **Temple of
Sinawava,** a natural amphitheater which is at the same time a lush oasis.

Along the many hiking trails you will encounter some surprises. One of the
most popular leads from the Temple of Sinawava to **The Narrows,** an amazing
rocky defile through a canyon whose walls seem almost to touch overhead, and to
Weeping Rock Trail, where the spring welling out from the cliff face appears to be
weeping (whence the name). For the more adventurous, there's the **Hidden Canyon Trail** leading to the almost inaccessible canyon, **Zion Shangri La.**

The **Mukuntuweap Valley** (the Native American name for Zion Canyon),
has been inhabited by several Native American cultures, particularly the Anasazi,
Pueblo, and Paiute, since about the 6th century A.D. The present names, often
biblical in origin, were bestowed by the Mormon missionaries who explored the
area from 1861 on. The only canyon in the country that can be seen by car "from
the inside," Zion National Park is open year round, and is visited by 1.8 million
people annually. Camping permitted (376 sites).

For **information,** contact the Superintendent, Zion National Park,
Springdale, UT 84767 (801/772-3256).

SUGGESTED TOURING ITINERARIES

EAST UTAH PARKS (707 mi./1,131km r.t. from/to Salt
Lake City via I-15S, U.S. 6, U.S. 191, Utah 95, Utah 24, U.S.
89, Utah 28, and I-15N): Comprehensive itinerary taking in Arches National
Park, Canyonlands National Park, Natural Bridges National Monument, Glen
Canyon National Recreation Area, and Capitol Reef National Park (for details on
all these, see above).

SOUTH UTAH PARKS (712 mi./1,139km r.t. from/to
Las Vegas via I-15N, Utah 14, Utah 148, Utah 14, U.S. 89,

UTAH: NATIONAL PARKS AND MONUMENTS

N

COLORADO

WYOMING

Flaming Gorge Nat'l Rec. Area

Vernal

191

UINTA MTS.
Ashley Nat'l Forest

Green River

123 East Carbon

Price

Price River

Wellington

6

Manti-la Sal

WASATCH RANGE

Logan

91

Brigham City

Ogden

Clearfield

Salt Lake City

Kearns

Great Salt Lake

Orem
Provo

Springville

Uinta Nat'l Forest

15

6

Eureka

36

Tooele

Wasatch Nat'l Forest

GREAT SALT LAKE DESERT

IDAHO

84

NEVADA

Utah 12, U.S. 89, Utah 9, and I-15S): One of the most beautiful trips the U.S. can offer, allowing you to see Cedar Breaks National Monument, Bryce Canyon National Park, Glen Canyon National Recreation Area, and Zion National Park (for details on all these, see above).

ACCOMMODATIONS & RESTAURANTS

A Note on Accommodations: Room rates in the Utah National Parks Area are coded as follows: **VE,** Very Expensive ($140 and up); **E,** Expensive ($90–$140); **M,** Moderate ($60–$90); **I,** Inexpensive ($30–$60); **B,** Budget (up to $30). A listing of toll free numbers is in the Appendix.

A Note on Restaurant Prices: The Utah National Parks Area restaurant prices, per person, excluding drinks and service charges, are coded as follows: **VE,** Very Expensive ($60 and up); **E,** Expensive ($40–60); **M,** Moderate ($25–$40); **I,** Inexpensive ($15–$25); **B,** Budget (up to $15).

PERSONAL FAVORITES: The following hotels and restaurants are grouped by location near or in individual parks.

Arches National Park and Canyonlands National Park

Best Western Green Well, 105 S. Main St., Moab, UT 84532 (801/259-6151; toll free, see Best Western). 71 rms, A/C, color TV, in rm-movies. AE, CB, DC, MC, V. Free parking, pool, rest. (beer served), coffeeshop, crib $4. *Note:* Typical functional motel; huge, comfortable rms; friendly reception. In the center of town. **I–M,** but lower rates off-season.

Travelodge Moab, 550 S. Main St., Moab, UT 84532 (801/259-6171; toll free, see Travelodge). 56 rms, A/C, color TV, in-rm movies. AE, CB, DC, MC, V. Free parking, pool, rest., free crib. *Note:* Relatively old, but well-kept motel. Large rms. Friendly reception. Attractive family packages. **I,** but lower rates off-season.

Apache Motel, 166 S. 4th St., Moab, UT 84532 (801/259-5727). 33 rms, A/C, color TV, in-rm movies. AE, CB, DC, MC, V. Free parking, pool, free morning coffee. *Note:* A small, inexpensive motel. Attentive svce. Some rms w. kitchenettes. Organizes river-rafting trips. Good value. **I,** but lower rates off-season.

Grand Old Ranch House, 1266 U.S. 191 N, Moab, UT (259-5753). A/C. Dinner only, nightly. AE, CB, DC, MC, V. *Note:* The decor is a melange of Old West and Victorian styles (the building dates from 1896). Friendly, efficient svce. Good, German-inspired cuisine. Wine, beer, and liquor. A fine place. *Continental/American.* **I–M**

Bryce Canyon National Park

Best Western Ruby's Inn, Utah 63 (1 mi. north of the park entrance), UT 84764 (801/834-5341; toll free, see Best Western). 166 rms, A/C, color TV, in-rm movies. AE, CB, DC, MC, V. Free parking, pool, skiing and snowmobiles in winter, rodeos in summer, riding, rest., bar, boutiques, free crib. *Note:* A vast, efficient, modern hotel w. a small private lake. Comfortable rms w. balconies and fireplaces (some w. kitchenettes). Very good location (5 min. from the park by car). Friendly reception and svce. Organizes helicopter tours of Bryce Canyon. An excellent place to stay. **M**

Pink Cliffs Bryce Village, at the intersection of Utah 12 and Utah 22 (2 mi./3km north of the park entrance), Bryce Canyon National Park, UT 84717 (801/834-5303). 54 rms, A/C, color TV. MC, V. Free parking, pool, rest., bar, crib $4. *Note:* Country motel 5 min. by car from the park. Big, comfortable rms; friendly reception and svce. Free airport shuttle. Good value. Open Apr–Oct. **I,** but lower rates off-season.

Bryce Canyon Pines, Utah 12 (6 mi./10km from the NW park entrance) Bryce, UT 84759 (801/834-5336). 50 rms, most w. A/C, color TV. DC, MC, V. Free parking, pool, horseback riding, rest.

(beer served), crib $3. *Note:* Small, inviting motel w. huge, prettily decorated rms, some w. fireplaces. Free airport shuttle. Horseback excursions into the canyon in summer. Good value. **I,** but lower rates Nov–June.

☀☂ **Bryce Canyon Lodge,** Utah 12, Bryce Canyon National Park, UT 84717 (801/834-5361). 110 rms (cottages), a third w. A/C. AE, CB, DC, MC, V. Free parking, pool, horseback riding, rest., coffee shop, grocery store, crib $4. *Note:* Wonderful location in the heart of the park. Some rms modern and comfortable, others aging a little. Acceptable rest. Open mid-May to Oct; closed the rest of the year. Horseback or muleback trips into the canyon. For reservations, contact T. W. Services, 451 N. Main St. (P.O. Box 400), Cedar City, UT 84720 (801/586-7686). **I–M**

Capitol Reef National Park

☂ **Capitol Reef Inn,** 300 W. Main St., Torrey, UT 84775 (801/ 425-3271). 7 rms, A/C, color TV. MC, V. Free parking, coffee shop. *Note:* Tiny, well-maintained, serviceable hotel. Friendly reception. Open Mar to late-Nov. **B–I**

Cedar Breaks National Monument

☂☂ **Best Western El Rey Inn,** 80 S. Main St., Cedar City, UT 84720 (801/586-6518; toll free, see Best Western); 26 mi. (41km) from the park entrance. 75 rms, A/C, color TV, in-rm movies. AE, CB, DC, MC, V. Free parking, pool, sauna, rest. (beer served), rm svce, crib $4. *Note:* Comfortable, functional rms. Reception w. a smile; acceptable rest. (Sullivan's). Free airport shuttle. **I,** but lower rates off-season.

☂☂ **Brian Head Royale Inn,** 100 Hunter Ridge Dr., Brian Head, UT 84719 (801/677-2800); 10 mi. (16km) north of the park entrance on Utah 143. 93 rms. A/C, color TV, in-rm movies. AE, CB, DC, MC, V. Free parking, sauna, health club, skiing in winter, coffee shop. *Note:* Engaging little resort motel 9,800 ft. (2,900m) above sea level in the heart of Dixie National Forest. Comfortable, inviting rms w. refrigerator. Friendly reception and svce. Free shuttle connection w. Cedar City airport. **I**

Dinosaur National Monument

☂☂ **Weston Plaza** (formerly the Sheraton Inn), 1684 W. U.S. 40, Vernal, UT 84078 (801/789-9550), 19 mi. (30km) west of the park entrance. 102 rms, A/C, color TV, in-rm movies. AE, CB, DC, MC, V. Free parking, pool, putting green, rest., bar, valet svce, disco, free breakfast, free crib. *Note:* Modern, comfortable motel; spacious rms; efficient reception and svce. The best place to stay in the region. **I–M**

☂ **Weston Lamplighter Inn,** 120 E. Main St., Vernal, UT 84078 (801/789-0312), 19 mi. (30km) west of the park entrance. 200 rms, A/C, color TV, in-rm movies. AE, CB, DC, MC, V. Free parking, pool, coffee shop, valet svce, crib $5. *Note:* Inviting, well-run small motel; functionally comfortable. Good value. **I–M,** but lower rates off-season.

Glen Canyon & Rainbow Bridge

☂☂ **Wahweap Lodge and Marina,** on U.S. 89, Page, AZ 86040 (602/645-2433; toll free 800/528-6154), 5 mi. (8km) NW of Glen Canyon Bridge. 267 rms, A/C, color TV, in-rm movies. AE, CB, DC, MC, V. Free parking, pool, tennis court, beach, boating, fishing, rest., coffee shop, bar, rm svce, disco, crib $5. *Note:* Modern building, splendidly located on Lake Powell. Spacious, comfortable rms w. balconies or patios, some w. refrigerators. Reception and svce on the chilly side. Free airport shuttle. One- or several-day excursions arranged on Lake Powell and to Rainbow Bridge. Resv. advised, well ahead. **M,** but lower rates off-season.

☂☂ **Holiday Inn Page,** 287 N. Lake Powell Blvd., Page, AZ 86040 (602/645-8851; toll free, see Holiday Inns), 1 mi. (2km) from Glen Canyon Bridge. 129 rms, A/C, color TV, in-rm movies. AE, CB, DC, MC, V. Free parking, pool, rest., bar, rm svce, hrdrsr, free crib. *Note:* Typical

Holiday Inn; huge, comfortable rms w. balconies or patios, the best overlooking Lake Powell. Good svce. Free airport shuttle. **M,** but lower rates off-season.

　　🍷 **Lake Powell Motel,** on U.S. 89, Page, AZ 86040 (602/645-
　　🛏 2477; toll free 800/528-6154), 5 mi. (8km) northwest of Glen Canyon Bridge. 24 rms, A/C, color TV. AE, CB, DC, MC, V. Free parking, free morning coffee, crib $5. *Note:* Modest, unpretentious little motel w. a fine view of Glen Canyon and Lake Powell. Boats for rent; free airport shuttle. Same management as the Wahweap Lodge and Marina. **I,** but lower rates off-season.

　　🍸 **Glen Canyon Steak House,** 201 N. Lake Powell Blvd., Page,
　　🍴 (602/645-3363). A/C. Lunch/dinner daily. MC, V. *Note:* Classic western steakhouse. Bar; dancing. *Steak.* **I**

Natural Bridges National Monument

　　🍷 **Best Western Gateway,** 88 E. Center St., Blanding, UT
　　🛏 84511 (801/678-2278; toll free, see Best Western), 46 mi. (74km) east of the park entrance. 57 rms, A/C, color TV, in-rm movies. AE, CB, DC, MC, V. Free parking, pool, nearby coffee shop. *Note:* Comfortable, very well run small motel 45-min. drive from Natural Bridges National Monument. Spacious rms; friendly reception. Free airport shuttle. A very good address. **I**

　　🍷 **San Juan Inn,** on U.S. 163 at the San Juan River, Mexican Hat,
　　🛏 UT 84531 (801/683-2220). 22 rms, A/C, color TV. AE, MC, V. Free parking, coffee shop (beer served), crib $4. *Note:* Modest but serviceable motel on the San Juan River, 15-min. drive from Monument Valley and 45 min. from Natural Bridges National Monument. Good value on balance. Arranges rafting trips down the river and conducted tours of Monument Valley. **I**

Zion National Park

　　☼🛏 **Best Western Driftwood Lodge,** on Utah 9, Springdale, UT
　　　 84767 (801/772-3262; toll free, see Best Western), 2 mi. (3.5km) south of the park entrance. 25 rms, A/C, color TV. AE, CB, DC, MC, V. Free parking, pool, rest. (beer and wine served), rm svce, crib $2. *Note:* Charming little motel surrounded by grdns and trees. Comfortable rms w. balconies, overlooking the park; friendly reception and svce. Very acceptable rest. An excellent place to stay. **I–M,** but lower rates off-season.

　　☼🍷 **Zion Lodge,** Scenic Dr., Zion National Park, UT 84767 (801/
　　　 772-3213). 121 rms, A/C. AE, CB, DC, MC, V. Free parking, rest. (beer served), coffee shop, crib $4. *Note:* The only motel inside the park itself, in a superb natural setting. Friendly reception and svce; rustic comforts. Horseback excursions and conducted bus tours through the canyon arranged. For resv., contact T.W. Services, 451 N. Main St. (P.O. Box 400), Cedar City, UT 84720 (801/586-7686). Open Apr–Nov. **I–M**

　　🍷 **Bumbleberry Inn,** 897 Zion Park Blvd. (Utah 9), Springdale,
　　🛏 UT 84767 (801/772-3224), 1 mi. (1.6km) south of the park entrance. 24 rms, A/C, color TV. CB, DC, MC, V. Free parking, pool, rest. *Note:* Well-run, functional small motel. Spacious rms, some w. balconies. Inviting grdn. Good value. **I,** but lower rates off-season.

　　🍷 **Zion Park Hotel,** Utah 9, Springdale, UT 84767 (801/772-
　　🛏 3902), 1 mi. (1.6km) south of the park entrance. 19 rms, A/C, color TV, in-rm movies. AE, MC, V. Free parking, pool, adjacent coffee shop. *Note:* Unpretentious motel offering decent standards of comfort; caters mostly to families. **I,** but lower rates off-season.

CHAPTER 33

YELLOWSTONE NATIONAL PARK 🔥🔥🔥🔥

□ □ □

And Grand Teton National Park

A masterpiece of unspoiled nature, **Yellowstone National Park** is the most beautiful in the U.S., and probably in the world; nowhere else on the surface of the planet will you find such an astonishing variety of scenery gathered together in one place. With its boiling geysers, hot springs, steep canyons, mud volcanoes, frozen lakes, deep pine forests, dizzying waterfalls, and fossilized trees, Yellowstone is a glorious, untamed cross section of the North American continent—and one which, geologists tell us, has been three billion years in the making.

The wildlife is the entire animal kingdom in a nutshell: bison, elk, deer, pronghorn, black bear, grizzly, wild sheep, coyote, cougar, beaver, muskrat, and countless species of birds and fish. The whole great volcanic plateau, 60 mi. (100km) long and 56 mi. (90km) wide, lying some 7,870 ft. (2,400m) above sea level, is stitched together by 250 mi. (400km) of impeccably surfaced roads and more than 1,000 mi. (1,600km) of marked trails. The park is open, weather permitting, from May 1 to Oct 31, but its northern and northeastern entrances remain open year round (for snowmobiles only in winter). In all, almost 2½ million people every summer, and almost 100,000 every winter, visit the park, its six hotels and 12 campgrounds. Needless to say, reservations are a must for the peak months of July and Aug.

The uncanny alliance of the two normally hostile elements of fire and water constitute Yellowstone's principal tourist attractions. The park possesses no fewer than 10,000 hot springs and almost 200 geysers bubbling up from the bowels of the earth. To the amazement of many visitors, some geysers like the famous **Old Faithful** spew their columns of steam and boiling water dozens of feet into the air with clockwork regularity; others lie dormant for weeks, or years, before bursting forth again. All around lies an ominous landscape of evil-smelling fumaroles, multicolored pools, and boiling cauldrons of bubbling, sulfurous mud. Yet only a few miles away, the golden splendor of the **Grand Canyon of the Yellowstone** with its falls higher than Niagara's, or the azure depths of **Yellowstone Lake,** the largest mountain lake in the country at an elevation of 7,731 ft. (2,357m), await to take your mind off the nightmare spectacle of **Mud Volcano** or **Dragon Mouth.** The catastrophic 1988 fires consumed 780,000 of the 2.2 million acres of the park (315,800ha of the park's 890,000ha). The recovery process has added a new dimension to this wonder of nature, larger than the state of Rhode Island—fire-blackened trees now stand in fields of lush grass, shrubs, and wildflowers. Yellowstone Park's major attractions, including the Grand Canyon of the Yellowstone River, were unaffected by the fires of '88; most of the fire damage was in the park's backcountry areas.

Yellowstone is too large, and too varied, for a quick visit; many of its slopes are still untrodden, and can be reached only on foot or horseback.

Grand Teton National Park, only one-seventh the size of Yellowstone and more mountainous in its contours, is open year round. Its impressive mountain range numbers 31 peaks rising above 10,825 ft. (3,300m); the highest, **Grand Teton** itself, soars to 13,770 ft. (4,197m). This is a "young" granite range, little more than 10 million years old. It owes its name to the romantic imagination of 19th-century French-Canadian trappers, who saw in these sparkling, pointed snow-capped peaks rising above the valley of **Jackson Hole,** some fancied likeness to a woman's breast. More than 187 mi. (300km) of marked trails offer an unlimited choice of hiking or skiing excursions, according to the season. With the torrential **Snake River,** deep forests, lakes full of fish, and inaccessible mountain peaks, Grand Teton National Park encompasses some of the most beautiful natural landscapes in the U.S.

Wildlife Warning! While Yellowstone is a paradise for campers and mobile-home owners, camping is subject to very strict rules enforced by watchful rangers. As in all national parks, camping in the wild is strictly forbidden. There are also some simple precautions that must be taken regarding animals. Living free as they do, with no reason to fear human beings, animals will allow themselves to be photographed from quite close, especially around dawn and sunset. However, prudence is mandatory if you come suddenly face to face with a bear (there are about 500 black and grizzly bears inside the park), an elk (about 30,000), or a buffalo (about 2,500). Never feed or hold food within reach of an animal.

BASIC FACTS: State of Wyoming (with slight enroachments into the neighboring states of Idaho and Montana). Area code: 307. Time zone: mountain. ZIP Codes: Yellowstone, 82190; Grand Teton, 83013. Inaugurated: 1872 (Yellowstone is the oldest nature reserve in the world); 1929 (Grand Teton). Area: Yellowstone, 3,472 sq. mi. (8,993km^2); Grand Teton, 486 sq. mi. (1,260km^2).

CLIMATE: At these altitudes, winter is long and icy at Yellowstone and Grand Teton; mean temperatures are 5°F (−15°C). Heavy snowfalls, sometimes 16 ft. (5m) or more, make it very difficult to get around, even by snowmobile, from late Oct through Apr. Summer is short, sunny, and cool; everyone wears a sweater in the evening. You should take a raincoat or poncho too, because of occasional heavy rain in the afternoon. Fall is the perfect time for the color photographer. Whatever the season, don't try a swim in the lakes; even in summer the water temperature never goes above 40°F (5°C), and if you were to fall in you wouldn't survive as long as half an hour.

DISTANCES: Denver, 638 mi. (1,022km); Mount Rushmore, 549 mi. (875km); Salt Lake City, 325 mi. (520km); Seattle, 762 mi. (1,219km).

ARRIVAL & TRANSIT INFORMATION

NEAREST AIRPORTS: Bozeman Gallatin Field (BZN), 131 mi. (210km) NW of Yellowstone National Park; open year round.

Jackson Hole (JAC), 13 mi. (21km) south of Grand Teton National Park and 79 mi. (128km) south of Yellowstone National Park; open year round.

West Yellowstone (WYS), 30 mi. (48km) west of Yellowstone National Park; open in summer only.

AIRLINES: Several airlines fly into the area's three airports:
At **Bozeman Gallatin Field:** Continental (406/586-4749); Delta (toll free 800/221-1212), and Northwest (toll free 800/225-2525).
At **Jackson Hole:** American (toll free 800/433-7300), Continental (307/

733-9701), Delta (toll free 800/221-1212), and United Express (toll free 800/241-6522).

At West Yellowstone: Delta Connection (toll free 800/453-9417), in summer only.

BUS OR CAR RENTAL? Greyhound serves neither Yellowstone nor Grand Teton National Park.

The **Yellowstone National Park Co.** (307/344-7901) provides a shuttle bus from **Bozeman** (two departures daily), **Jackson** (two departures daily), and **West Yellowstone** (five departures daily) during the summer. The same company operates bus tours inside Yellowstone Park.

Given the distances, it makes sense to rent a car, but rates are relatively high and the choice of models is restricted.

CAR RENTAL: Rental cars are available at all three area airports.

At Bozeman Gallatin Field: Avis (406/388-6414), Budget (406/388-4091), Hertz (406/388-6939), and National (406/388-6694).

At Jackson Hole: Avis (307/733-3422), Budget (307/733-2206), Dollar (307/733-0355), Hertz (307/733-2272), and National (307/733-4132).

At West Yellowstone Airport (summer only): Avis (406/646-7635), Budget (406/646-7882), Hertz (406/646-7753), and National (406/646-7670).

TRAIN: The nearest Amtrak station is 135 mi. (215km) SW of Grand Teton National Park at 300 S. Harrison Ave., Pocatello, Idaho (toll free 800/872-7245).

INTERCITY BUSES: Greyhound has stations at 625 N. 7th St., Bozeman (406/587-3110), open year round; and at 127 Yellowstone Ave., West Yellowstone (406/646-7666), open in summer only.

INFORMATION & TOURS

TOURIST INFORMATION: The **Cody County Chamber of Commerce,** 836 Sheridan Ave. (P.O. Box 2777), Cody, WY 82414 (307/587-2297).

Grand Teton National Park: Superintendent, P.O. Drawer 170, Moose, WY 83012 (307/733-2880). There are visitors centers at Colter Bay, Jenny Lake, and Moose.

Jackson Hole Area Chamber of Commerce, 532 N. Cache St. (P.O. Box E-MTG), Jackson, WY 83001 (307/733-3316).

Yellowstone National Park: Superintendent, P.O. Box 168, Mammoth Hot Springs, WY 82190 (307/344-7381). There are visitors centers at Canyon Village, Fishing Bridge, Grant Village, Mammoth Hot Springs, Norris, and Old Faithful.

GUIDED TOURS: Gray Line Tours (bus): Conducted bus tours of Grand Teton and Yellowstone National Parks. Serves principal hotels in Jackson from 140 N. Cache St. (307/733-4325) and West Yellowstone (406/646-9374).

TW Services, Inc. (bus/snowmobile) (307/344-7901): All-season tourist excursions in Yellowstone National Park; serves the park's principal hotels at Canyon Village, Fishing Bridge, Mammoth Hot Springs, and Old Faithful.

SIGHTS, ATTRACTIONS & ACTIVITIES

ADVENTURES: Backcountry Bicycle Tours (bicycle), P.O. Box 4029, Bozeman, MT 59772 (406/586-3556): 6-day bicycle tours of Yellowstone National Park. $700 per head, including lodging in hotels, all meals, and van support. June–Sept.

Exum School of Mountaineering (climbing), P.O. Box 56, Moose, WY 83012 (307/733-2297): 2-day climbs, with guides, in Grand Teton National Park (summer only). Also climbing school.

L.D. Frome Wagons West (covered wagons), Afton, WY 83110 (307/886-5240; toll free 800/433-1595): Back to the days of the pioneers with 2-, 4-, or 6-day covered-wagon trips. Serves the principal Jackson hotels; resv. a must. Mon–Sat late May to early Sept. Spectacular.

Jackson Hole Climbing School (climbing), 165 N. Glenwood (P.O. Box 547), Teton Village, WY 83205 (307/733-4979): Climbing school and guided climbs in summer. For the dedicated.

Lewis & Clark Expeditions (boat), 86 E. Broadway, Jackson, WY 83001 (307/733-3127): White-water float trips down the Grand Canyon of Snake River, a 3- to 6-hr. trip. June to mid-Sept. Amusing.

National Park Float Trips (boat), P.O. Box 120, Moose, WY 83012 (307/733-5500): Boat or raft trips in Grand Teton National Park; bus connection from Jackson. Late May to mid-Sept.

Rocky Mountain Mushers Adventures (dog sledding), Jackson (307/733-7388): Full-day, half-day, or moonlight sled-dog trips in Grand Teton National Park and scenic Jackson Hole. Transportation to the point of departure is provided. Resv. required. Dec to mid-Apr.

Teton Country Prairie Schooner Holiday (covered wagons), Bar-T-Five Ranch, P.O. Box 2140, Jackson, WY 83001 (307/733-5386): 4-day covered-wagon trip between Yellowstone National Park and Grand Teton National Park; a guaranteed whiff of adventure. $400 per head, including meals. Mid-June to Aug.

Wild West Jeep Tours (four-wheel-drive), P.O. Box 7506, Jackson, WY 83001 (307/733-9036): Half-day tours of the Grand Tetons and other areas. Daily June–Sept.

Wyoming River Trips (boat), 1701 Sheridan Ave., Cody, WY 82414 (307/587-6661): Float trips through Red Rock Shoshone Canyon; spectacular. June to mid-Sept.

GRAND TETON NATIONAL PARK: The entrance is 13 mi. (21km) north of Jackson via U.S. 89.

Jackson Hole, 8 mi. (13km) north from Jackson on U.S. 89: A huge basin ("hole" was the vernacular term for basin, or valley, among the *coureurs de bois*) of glacial origin, 50 mi. (80km) long and 14 mi. (23km) wide at its widest, traversed by the turbulent **Snake River** and dotted by clear lakes teeming with fish: **Jackson Lake, Jenny Lake, Phelps Lake, Emma Matilda Lake,** etc. This high alpine valley, moist and fertile, with an abundance of elk, deer, buffalo, white pelicans, duck, and wild geese, has some magnificent views across to the granite crests of the **Grand Teton Range,** a sight you shouldn't miss. Many **campsites,** particularly at Colter Bay, Jenny Lake, Lizard Creek, Gros Ventre, and Signal Mountain. **Boat rental** at Jackson and Jenny Lakes. The **John D. Rockefeller Parkway** (U.S. 89), crossing the park from north to south, is usable year round. For information on road conditions, weather, and park activities, call (307)733-2220.

Rendezvous Peak, 12 mi. (19km) NW of Jackson via Wyo. 22 and Wyo. 390: Cable car from **Teton Village** to the top of Rendezvous Peak, 10,450 ft. (3,185m) high. Wonderful view of Jackson Hole Valley and the Grand Tetons. Late May to late Sept. For information, call (307)733-2291.

Scenic Drives

Bridger-Teton National Forest, 56 mi. (89km) between Dubois and Moran Junction along U.S. 26: Splendid forest scenery; worth going out of your way for.

John D. Rockefeller Parkway, 58 mi. (92km) between Jackson and Yellowstone National Park along U.S. 89: Follows the Snake River and the shore of Jackson Lake through very fine mountain scenery. Spectacular.

Signal Mountain Rd., 13 mi. (20km) NE of Moose Junction via Teton Park Rd.: Scenic drive 5 mi. (8km) long; from the top you'll have an unequalled view of Jackson Lake and the surrounding peaks.

YELLOWSTONE NATIONAL PARK: The main entrance is 59 mi. (95km) north of Jackson via U.S. 89; east entrance, 53 mi. (85km) west of Cody via U.S. 20; north entrance, 85 mi. (136km) SE of Bozeman via I-90 and U.S. 89.

Gibbon Falls, 29 mi. (47km) south of Mammoth Hot Springs on Grand Loop Rd.: Broad falls, with a drop of 84 ft. (26m) along the river of the same name.

Grand Canyon of the Yellowstone, 37 mi. (60km) SE of Mammoth Hot Springs on Grand Loop Rd.: The most glorious scenery in the park. Two dizzying falls, the 308-ft. (94m) **Lower Falls** (1½ times the height of Niagara) and the 109-ft. (33m) **Upper Falls.** Wild gorges, up to 1,200 ft. (366m) deep in places, with a perpetual play of yellow-to-orange color over their walls (whence the name of the Yellowstone River). A scenic drive links the main observation points, of which those at **Inspiration Point** and **Artist Point** are the most interesting.

Obsidian Cliff, 15 mi. (24km) south of Mammoth Hot Springs on Grand Loop Rd.: A great cliff, 246 ft. (75m) high and 885 ft. (270m) wide composed of volcanic glass (obsidian), from which the Native Americans used to quarry material for their arrowheads.

Shoshone Lake, 8 mi. (13km) east of Old Faithful on Grand Loop Rd., then 2½ mi. (4km) south by footpath: Beautiful wild isolated lake, reachable only on foot or on horseback. For lovers of unspoiled nature.

Tower Falls, 21 mi. (33km) east of Mammoth Hot Springs on Grand Loop Rd.: Spectacular 132-ft. (40m) falls on the Yellowstone River; its name comes from its rock formations in the shape of towers or broken columns.

Virginia Cascades, 24 mi. (38km) SE of Mammoth Hot Springs on Grand Loop Rd.: Beautiful waterfalls and rapids in the depths of the forest; one-way scenic drive.

Yellowstone Lake, 22 mi. (36km) north of the southern entrance to the park on U.S. 89: The highest (7,731 ft./2,357m), and, with its azure-blue waters, perhaps the most beautiful mountain lake in the U.S. It covers 138 sq. mi. (360km²) and is 308 ft. (94m) deep at its deepest. The water is icy-cold even in summer. View clear over to the distant **Absaroka Range,** with a dozen peaks rising above 9,840 ft. (3,000m). Boat trips from **Bridge Bay Marina** and **Grant Village Marina.**

Geysers and Thermal Springs

Yellowstone National Park has almost 200 geysers, more than any other place in the world except Iceland and New Zealand, and some 10,000 hot springs. Among the most impressive are:

Artist Paint Pots, between Norris Junction and Madison Junction along Grand Loop Rd.: A little footpath leads from Gibbon Meadows to these multicolored hot springs.

Beryl Spring, between Norris Junction and Madison Junction along Grand Loop Rd.: One of the most beautiful springs in the park.

Lower Geyser Basin, between Madison Junction and Old Faithful along Grand Loop Rd.: Comprises 25 geysers and 700 hot springs, among them **Fountain Paint Pot,** a flamboyant yellow-and-red cauldron, and two reliable geysers: **Great Fountain Geyser** erupts every 6–10 hr. to a height of 98–196 ft. (30–60m), and **White Dome Geyser** erupts every 17–90 min. to a height of 19–29 ft. (6–9m), with a fine concretion dome. An absolute must-see.

☀️🏛 **Mammoth Hot Springs,** 5 mi. (8km) south of the northern entrance to the park on U.S. 89: Fantastic limestone terraces formed from suspended material deposited by some 60 hot springs issuing at temperatures of 64°–165°F (18°–74°C). The steps, in a variety of shades of white, bright yellow, ocher, and green, have been built up since prehistoric times to heights of as much as 196 ft. (60m) in places. A wonder of natural beauty. Scenic drive to the top.

☀️🏛 **Midway Geyser Basin,** between Madison Junction and Old Faithful along Grand Loop Rd.: Famous for its colorful hot springs, particularly the **Excelsior Geyser,** a deep-blue lake 393 ft. (120m) long on the site of a huge geyser which has been dormant since 1888, and the **Grand Prismatic Spring,** a great smoking pool whose waters refract all the colors of the rainbow (elevated observation road).

🏛 **Monument Geyser,** between Norris Junction and Madison Junction along Grand Loop Rd.: Along a little footpath from the bridge across the Gibbon River, you'll have a 2-hr. walk to this continually active geyser with a throw of 5–10 ft. (1.5–3m).

☀️🏛 **Mud Volcano and Black Dragon's Cauldron,** between Yellowstone Lake and Canyon Village along Grand Loop Dr.: Huge witches' cauldron, grumbling and boiling, whose super-heated mud wells up and bursts in great evil-smelling bubbles. A fascinating sight.

☀️🏛 **Norris Geyser Basin,** 1 mi. (2km) west of Norris Junction along Grand Loop Dr.: Has some of the park's most spectacular hot springs, including the lovely emerald-colored **Emerald Springs** and the astonishing rainbow-colored **Porcelain Basin** (elevated observation road), as well as such impressive geysers as **Constant Geyser** (erupts several times an hour to a height of 30–40 ft./9–12m), and **Steamboat Geyser,** the highest in the park, with a throw of 20–380 ft. (6–116m) every 30–60 sec. Visitor center at **Norris.**

☀️🏛 **Old Faithful,** in front of the Old Faithful Inn at Old Faithful: The park's most famous, and most photographed, attraction. For more than a century Old Faithful has erupted with clockwork regularity for 2–5 min., to a mean height of 130 ft. (40m), once an hour. Since 1986, however, it has shown signs of flagging, and now erupts only every 78 min., more or less. A boon to devotees of souvenir snapshots.

🏛 **Sulphur Cauldron,** between Yellowstone Lake and Canyon Village along Grand Loop Rd.: Boiling springs emitting sulfurous steam along the steep banks of the Yellowstone River.

☀️🏛 **Upper Geyser Basin,** between Madison Junction and Old Faithful along Grand Loop Rd.: Nearly 70 geysers clustered around Old Faithful; among the most spectacular are **Castle Geyser** (every 3–10 hr.; 65–100 ft./20–30m), **Daisy Geyser** (irregular; 75 ft./23m), **Grand Geyser** (every 18–90 hr.; 200 ft./60m), and **River Side Geyser** (every 6–9 hr.; 75 ft./23m). Across Grand Loop Rd. in **Black Sand Basin** are countless petrified trees and a splendid emerald-green hot spring, **Emerald Pool,** issuing at 158°F (70°C). The most impressive group of geological phenomena in the park.

🏛 **West Thumb Geyser Basin,** on the western shore of Yellowstone Lake by Grand Loop Rd.: Miniature geysers and an array of hot springs beside the lake; beautiful scenery. A must-see.

Scenic Drives

☀️🏛 **Buffalo Bill Highway,** 80 mi. (128km) between Fishing Bridge, Yellowstone Lake, and Cody along U.S. 20: A 2-hr.

drive of rare scenic splendor passing **Shoshone Canyon, Sylvan Pass,** and the **Absaroka Mountains.** Wonderful view of **Yellowstone Lake** from **Lake Butte** (8,344 ft./2,544m).

☼⚑⚑ **Canyon Rim Scenic Road,** 1 mi. (1.6km) east or 2½ mi. (4km) south of Canyon Village on Grand Loop Rd.: A scenic drive of some 5 mi. (8km), partly on a one-way highway, along both rims of the Grand Canyon of the Yellowstone. Wonderful views of gorges and falls from **Inspiration Point, Lookout Point, Artist Point,** and **Grandview Point.**

☼⚑⚑ **Grand Loop Road,** 22 mi. (35km) north of the southern entrance to the park: Yellowstone Park's busiest road, a 142-mi. (227km) "figure 8," linking all the park's scenic sights and tourist attractions.

☼⚑⚑ **Mount Washburn Trail,** 10 mi. (17km) NE of Canyon Village along Grand Loop Rd.: If you make an 8-mi. (13km) hike to the 10,243-ft. (3,122m) top of **Mount Washburn** (6½-hr. r.t.), you'll find the most beautiful view in the entire park, from the distant **Grand Tetons** to **Jackson Lake.** Only for seasoned walkers.

SPECIAL EVENTS: For the exact schedule of events below, consult the **Cody County Chamber of Commerce** and **Jackson Hole Area Chamber of Commerce** (see "Tourist Information," above).

Cody
Frontier Festival (mid-June): Music, dancing, craft shows, open-air meals, horse shows, games . . . the Old West come to life again.

Plains Indian Powwow (late June): Festival of traditional Native American music and dance; many tribes from the U.S. and Canada take part. Colorful.

Jackson
All-American Cutter Race (late Jan): Dog-sled championship.

"The Shootout" (Memorial Day–Labor Day): Amusing parody of a western melodrama performed every evening in the Town Sq.

Jackson Hole Rodeo (June–Aug): Real cowboy atmosphere; nightly except Sun and Tues. For information, call 307/733-2808.

Jackson Hole Fall Arts Festival (3 weeks from mid-Sept to early Oct): Art shows, performances, dance, theater, film festival, etc.

Teton Village
Grand Teton Music Festival (July–Aug): Symphony concerts, chamber music, classical recitals—more than 35 different programs. At Teton Village, a very popular festival; for information, call 307/733-3155.

WINTER SPORTS RESORTS: ⚑⚑ **Alta-Grand Targhee Resort,** 42 mi. (67km) NW of Jackson via Wyo. 22, Idaho 31, and Idaho 33 (307/353-2304): Three lifts; open mid-Nov to mid-Apr.

⚑ **Old Faithful,** 30 mi. (48km) SE of West Yellowstone via U.S. 20 and Grand Loop Rd. (307/344-7381): No lifts; cross-country skiing only. Open mid-Dec to mid-Mar.

⚑ **Snow King Mountain,** 0.6 mi. (1km) south of Jackson on U.S. 26 (307/733-5200): 3 lifts. Open Dec–Apr.

⚑⚑ **Teton Village,** 13 mi. (20km) NW of Jackson via Wyo. 22 and Wyo. 390 (703/733-2292): One cable car, eight lifts. Also cross-country skiing, climbing. Open Dec to mid-Apr.

ACCOMMODATIONS
A Note on Accommodations: Room rates in the Yellowstone National Park Area are coded as follows: **VE,** Very Expensive ($140 and up); **E,** Expensive ($90–$140); **M,** Moderate ($60–$90); **I,** Inexpensive ($30–$60); **B,** Budget (up to $30). A listing of toll free numbers is in the Appendix.

YELLOWSTONE NATIONAL PARK

N

miles 0   10
kms 0   16

Sleeping Giant Rec. Area
Eagle Creek Rec. Area
Three Mile
To Cody
Sleeping Giant Winter Sports Area
Pahaska Rec. Area
East Entrance

SHOSHONE NAT'L FOREST

Absaroka Range

MONUMENT CREEK TRAIL

SOUTH BOUNDARY TRAIL

THOROFARE TRAIL

Yellowstone Lake

TRAIL CREEK TRAIL

BRIDGER-TETON NAT'L FOREST

Continental Divide

HEART LAKE TRAIL

Heart Lake

Big Game Ridge

Red Mtns.

Grant Village

West Thumb

GRAND LOOP ROAD

Old Faithful Geyser
Old Faithful
Lone Star Geyser

Shoshone Lake

Lewis Lake
Lewis Lake Campground

Pitchstone Plateau

JOHN D. ROCKEFELLER JR. MEM. PRWY

South Entrance
Snake River Campground
Flagg Ranch Village

Jackson Lake
To Jackson

GRAND TETON NAT'L PARK

SOUTH BOUNDARY TRAIL

Cave Falls Rec. Area

MONTANA
IDAHO

WEST BOUNDARY TRAIL

TARGHEE NAT'L FOREST

Personal Favorites Inside the Parks (in order of preference)

GRAND TETON   For reservations for the three hotels listed, contact **Grand Teton Lodge Co.,** P.O. Box 250, Moran, WY 83013 (307/543-2855).

☼♥♥ 🛏⅃ **Jackson Lake Lodge,** U.S. 89, Moran, WY 83013 (307/543-2855). 385 rms (42 in hotel, others in cottages), A/C. AE, MC, V. Free parking, pool, horseback riding, fishing, bicycles, rest. (Mural Room), coffee shop, bar, rm svce (until 10pm), nightclub, hrdrsr, airport shuttle, boutiques, free crib. *Note:* Large, modern, comfortable chalet-hotel overlooking Jackson Lake. The best rms (w. patios or balconies) are in the main building; the cottages are more rustic. Magnificent view of the Grand Tetons; beautiful glass-walled dining rm overlooking the lake. Very acceptable food and svce. Organizes downstream rafting trips. The best place to stay in Grand Teton National Park; hosted the American-Soviet discussions between James Baker and Edward Shevardnadze in Sept 1989. Open June to mid-Sept only. **M–E**

☼♥♥ 🛏⅃ **Jenny Lake Lodge,** Jenny Lake Rd., Moran, WY 83013 (307/733-4647). 30 bungalows; no A/C. AE, MC, V. Free parking, fishing, horseback riding, bicycles, rest., airport shuttle, free crib. *Note:* Log-cabin bungalows in the woods, w. private patios. Rustic comfort; for nature lovers. Has the best rest. in the park (resv. a must). Cheerful reception. Open June to mid-Sept. **VE** (Modified American Plan).

♥ 🛏 **Colter Bay Village,** U.S. 89, Moran, WY 83013 (307/543-2855). 209 rms in bungalows; no A/C. AE, MC, V. Free parking, fishing, marina, horseback riding, rest., coffee shop, bar, boutiques, free crib. *Note:* Bungalows among pine trees on Jackson Lake; pleasing rustic decor. Very good value. Open May–Sept. **I–M**

YELLOWSTONE   For reservations for the six hotels listed, contact **TW Recreational Services,** Yellowstone National Park, WY 82190 (307/344-7311). Unless otherwise indicated none of the hotels listed below is air-conditioned.

☼♥ 🛏 **Old Faithful Inn,** Grand Loop Rd., Yellowstone National Park, WY 82190 (307/344-7311). 320 rms (only half w. baths). AE, MC, V. Free parking, coffee shop, bar, nightclub, free crib. *Note:* A 1902 hotel in a diverting baroque-chalet style; wonderful entrance lobby, all in wood and four stories high. Rms are spacious but stark (ask for one overlooking the Old Faithful geyser). The plumbing could use some improvements, as could the food and the reception. The place is pleasant on balance, however—and its situation is like no other in the world. Open May to mid-Oct only; the neighboring **Old Faithful Snow Lodge** (65 rms) is open Dec–Mar. **I–M**

☼♥ 🛏 **Lake Yellowstone Hotel,** Grand Loop Rd., Yellowstone National Park, WY 82190 (307/344-7311). 292 rms (only 50% w. bath). AE, MC, V. Free parking, fishing, boating, rest., bar, hrdrsr., free crib. *Note:* Aging but still-elegant hotel beautifully situated on the shores of Yellowstone Lake. Huge, relatively comfortable rms (ask for a lake view); agreeable glass-walled dining rm; food and svce acceptable but no better. Open from the end of May through Sept. Also 110 bungalows offering rudimentary comforts. **M**

♥ 🛏 **Canyon Village Lodge & Cabins,** Grand Loop Rd., Yellowstone National Park, WY 82190 (703/344-7311). 588 rms (chalets). AE, MC, V. Free parking, horseback riding, rest., coffee shop, bar, hrdrsr, boutiques, free crib. *Note:* Rustic group of comfortable little cottages. Mediocre food, as everywhere in the park. Open June–Aug. **I–M**

♥ 🛏 **Grant Village,** on U.S. 89, Yellowstone National Park, WY 82190 (307/344-7311), 2 mi. (3.25km) south of Grand Loop Rd. 296 rms. AE, DC, MC, V. Free parking, coffee shop, bar. *Note:* The newest (1984) and most up-to-date motel in the park, on Yellowstone Lake. Functionally comfortable. Open June–Sept. **I**

Mammoth Hot Springs Hotel & Cabins, Grand Loop Rd. and U.S. 89, Yellowstone National Park, WY 82190 (307/344-7311). 94 rms (two-thirds w. bath) and 132 bungalows (half w. bath). AE, MC, V. Free parking, adj. coffee shop, bar, free crib. *Note:* Run-down old hotel 5 mi. (8km) south of the northern park entrance. Ask for a bungalow overlooking the petrified hot springs. Dour reception; resolutely mediocre coffee shop. Closed Apr and Oct–Nov; open all the rest of the year. **I**

Roosevelt Lodge & Cabins, Grand Loop Rd. at Tower Junction, Yellowstone National Park, WY 82190 (307/344-7311). 80 rms and cottages (a third w. bath). AE, MC, V. Free parking, horseback riding, coffee shop. *Note:* The most primitive, but also the most inviting, of the park's motels; it stands on a favorite campsite of Pres. Theodore Roosevelt, whence its name. Rather austere but pleasantly homelike log cabins in the woods. Stagecoach rides and evening steak cookouts cowboy style. For western fans. Open June to mid-Sept. **B–I**

Personal Favorites Outside the Parks (in order of preference)

Hatchet Motel, on U.S. 26, Moran, WY 83013 (307/543-2413), 8 mi. (13km) east of Moran Junction. 23 rms. No A/C. MC, V. Free parking, coffee shop. *Note:* Rustic elegance: a log-cabin chalet w. a view clear out over the mountains. Snugly comfortable rms; friendly reception w. a smile. Offers raft trips downriver. Good value. **I**

Jackson Hole Racquet Club, Star Route 3647, Jackson, WY 83001 (307/733-3990; toll free 800/443-8616). 120 suites and apts., cable color TV. AE, MC, V. Free parking, two pools, tennis court, squash, health club, sauna, skiing, rest., bar, grocery store, free crib. *Note:* The most luxurious resort hotel in the area. Elegantly countrified decor. Spacious, comfortable suites w. kitchenettes, refrigerators, fireplaces, and balconies or private patios; also two- or three-bedroom apartments. Flawless reception and svce; clientele of groups and racquets buffs. Open year round; reserve a long time ahead. Free shuttle to ski slopes. **E–VE,** but lower rates off-season.

Alpenhof Lodge, on Wyo. 390, Teton Village, WY 83025 (307/733-3242). 40 rms, cable color TV. AE, CB, DC, MC, V. Free parking, pool, sauna, skiing, horseback riding, rest. (Alpenhof), rm svce, crib $6. *Note:* Charming little alpine chalet; inviting rms, most w. balconies. Attentive svce; excellent rest. (one of the best in the area). Ideal for winter sports or for visiting Grand Teton Park. A fine place to stay. Owner Dietrich Oberreit and his family run it in the best tradition of Tyrolean innkeeping. Closed mid-Apr to mid-May and Oct–Nov. **M–E**

Snow King Resort, 400 E. Snow King Dr. (U.S. 89), Jackson, WY 83001 (307/733-5200; toll free 800/522-5464). 204 rms, A/C, cable color TV. AE, CB, DC, MC, V. Free parking, pool sauna, skiing, rest., coffee shop, bar, rm svce, disco, hrdrsr. *Note:* Large, modern, comfortable hotel at the base of the Snow King slopes. Huge, inviting rms, some w. balcony and views of the mountains. Ideal for winter sports. Good svce; acceptable rest. (Rafferty's); free airport shuttle. Open year round; group and convention clientele. **E,** but lower rates off-season.

Shoshone Lodge, U.S. 20 (P.O. Box 790WT), Cody, WY 82414 (307/587-4044), 4 mi. (6km) east of the eastern entrance to Yellowstone National Park. 16 cottages (3 w. kitchenettes). MC, V. Free parking, fishing, skiing, horseback riding, coffee shop, crib $2. *Note:* Small, inviting rustic motel on Grinnell Creek. Comfortable, individual log cabins. The kind of relaxed western atmosphere you associate w. campfires and square dances. The perfect place for nature lovers; run by the same family for three generations. Free airport shuttle; excellent value. Closed Nov–May. **I**

Wort Hotel, 50 N. Glenwood, Jackson, WY 83001 (307/733-2190; toll free 800/322-2727). 45 rms, A/C, color TV, in-rm movies. AE, CB, DC, MC, V. Free parking, nearby pool and tennis court (free shuttle), rest. (Goldpiece Dining Rm), bar, rm svce, disco. *Note:* A hotel straight out of a western movie, w. Old West atmosphere, fieldstone lobby fireplaces, and mounted animal heads. Huge, very comfortable rms; efficient, attentive svce; acceptable rest. The Silver Dollar Bar is very popular w. the locals. Free airport shuttle. **E,** but lower rates off-season.

Signal Mountain Lodge, Interpark Rd. (U.S. 89), Moran, WY 83013 (307/543-2831). 78 rms. AE, MC, V. Free parking, marina w. boating, bicycles, rest. (Aspen's), bar, grocery store, free crib. *Note:* Comfortable motel on Jackson Lake w. unimpeded view of the Grand Tetons; friendly reception and svce. Pleasant rms w. private patios or balconies (some w. kitchenettes and refrigerators). Many open-air activities available: fishing, swimming, boating, downstream rafting. Campsites adj. Open mid-May to mid-Oct. Very good value. **I–M,** but lower rates off-season.

Big Western Pine, 234 Firehole Ave. (U.S. 191), West Yellowstone, MT 59758 (406/646-7622). 44 rms, color TV, in-rm movies. AE, CB, DC, MC, V. Free parking, pool, sauna, snowmobiling, rest. (Rustler's Roost), bar. *Note:* Classic, well-run motel. Agreeable reception; acceptable rest. Located 600 yards (550m) from the western entrance to Yellowstone National Park. Free airport shuttle. Open year round; good value. **I,** but lower rates off-season.

Motel 6, 1370 W. Broadway, Jackson, WY 83001 (307/733-1620). 155 rms, A/C, color TV, free in-rm movies. AE, DC, MC, V. Free parking, pool, nearby rest. *Note:* Unbeatable value for visitors to Grand Teton National Park. Functionally comfortable; friendly reception. Open year round. **I**

Guest Ranches

Guest ranches are legion around Grand Teton and Yellowstone National Parks. Some of them make their livelihood from the tourist business, organizing horseback riding, Jeep excursions, and rafting, hunting, or fishing parties. Others are authentic cattle ranches, where (paying) guests can follow the life-style of the last cowboys. Most of these ranches offer American Plan rates which include lodging, full board, and all the horseback riding you can handle. Since this kind of open-air vacation is becoming more and more popular, you should reserve a good way ahead. None of the ranches listed below is air-conditioned. Some recommended establishments:

Bitterroot Ranch, P.O. Box 1042, Dubois, WY 82513 (307/455-2778; toll free 800/545-0019), 76 mi. (122km) SE of Moran Junction via U.S. 26 and East Fork Rd. 10 bungalows w. bath (caters to 25 guests). Free parking, pool, horseback riding, fishing, rest. *Note:* A genuine stock ranch along the Shoshone National Forest. Rustic bungalows nr. a trout river; organizes horseback rides; relaxed, inviting atmosphere. Very decent food. **E** (American Plan).

Crossed Sabres Ranch, P.O. Box WTC, Wapiti, WY 82450 (307/587-3750), 9 mi. (14km) east of the eastern entrance to Yellowstone National Park on U.S. 20. 18 bungalows w. bath (accommodating 50 guests); 1-week minimum stay. Free parking, horseback riding, fishing, rest., bar, square dancing, free crib. *Note:* The oldest guest ranch in Wyoming (1898; the main building dates from 1906). Comfortable log cabins in the woods. Smiling reception, family atmosphere. A wealth of open-air activities (rafting, cookouts, fishing, rodeos, horseback trips from one to several days). Closed Oct–Jun. **E** (American Plan).

Lost Creek Ranch, P.O. Box 95, Moose, WY 83012 (307/733-3435), 20 mi. (32km) north of Jackson along U.S. 26 and an unnumbered gravel-surfaced road 8 mi. (13km) north of Moose. 10 cottages w. private bath (accommodating 40–60 guests); 1-week minimum stay. Free parking, heated pool, tennis court, horseback riding, fishing, skeet shooting, trap range, rest., bar, nightclub, free crib. *Note:* The most luxurious, and most expensive, guest ranch in the entire valley, running about $2,500 per person per week.

Very comfortable countrified cottages w. private veranda, refrigerator, and fireplace. Spectacular view of the Grand Tetons. Comprehensive fitness facilities. Efficient svce and reception. Rafting and horseback trips through the Grand Tetons are available. Clientele of yuppies looking for the Old West. Closed Oct–May. **VE** (American Plan).

Moose Head Ranch, on U.S. 89 (P.O. Box 214), Moose, WY 83012 (307/877-3141), 26 mi. (42km) north of Jackson. 14 bungalows. Free parking, horseback riding, fishing, rest., free crib. *Note:* Functionally comfortable bungalows w. verandas and fireplaces. Organizes mountain trips and rafting. For open-air lovers. Private lake on 123 acres (50ha) of woodland and pasture. Closed Oct to mid-June. **E** (American Plan).

Red Rock Ranch, U.S. 89 and Gros Ventre River Rd. (P.O. Box 38), Kelly, WY 83011, (307/733-6288), 30 mi. (48km) NE of Jackson. 15 cottages (caters to 30 guests); 1-week minimum stay. Free parking, heated pool, sauna, horseback riding, fishing, rest. *Note:* A real working stock-rearing ranch on the banks of Crystal Creek, whose very comfortable cottages stand in deep woods. Certified western atmosphere. Guests may join in the fall stock roundups. Closed mid-Oct to June. **E** (American Plan).

R Lazy S Ranch, P.O. Box 308, Teton Village, WY 83025 (307/733-2655), 13 mi. (20km) NW of Jackson along Wyo. 22 and Wyo. 390. 14 bungalows w. bath (accommodating 45). 1-week minimum stay. Free parking, horseback riding, fishing, cookouts, evening programs. *Note:* Comfortable ranch at the foot of the Grand Tetons looking out across the mountains. Inviting log cabins, some w. living rm and fireplace. A nice place, w. tasty home-cooking, run since 1948 by the McConaghy family. Closed Oct to mid-June. **E** (American Plan).

Triangle X Ranch, P.O. Box 120, Moose, WY 83012 (307/733-5500 or 307/733-2183), 26 mi. (41km) north of Jackson on U.S. 26. 23 bungalows w. shower (accommodating 60); 1-week minimum stay. Free parking, horseback riding, skiing, snowmobiling, fishing, square dancing, free crib. *Note:* One of the best places to stay in the Tetons if you enjoy horseback riding and a Western flavor. This is a real breeding ranch on 1,200 acres (480ha) of woodland and meadow. Countrified comfort; spectacular views. Rafting and horseback trips offered in summer, big-game hunting parties in fall. Closed Apr and Nov–Dec. **E** (American Plan).

YMCA/Youth Hostels

Teton Village Hostel, McCollister Dr., Teton Village, WY 83025 (307/733-3415). 240 beds. Comfortable youth hostel, open also to nonmembers both summer and winter. Nr. the snowfields. Resv. essential long in advance.

RESTAURANTS

A Note on Restaurant Prices: The Yellowstone National Park Area restaurant prices, per person, excluding drinks and service charges, are coded as follows: **VE**, Very Expensive ($60 and up); **E**, Expensive ($40–$60); **M**, Moderate ($25–$40); **I**, Inexpensive ($15–$25); **B**, Budget (up to $15).

Personal Favorites (in order of preference)

Strutting Grouse, Jackson Hole Golf and Tennis Estates, 7 mi. (11km) north of Jackson Hole on U.S. 89 (733-7788). A/C. Lunch/dinner Tues–Sun; closed Oct to mid-May. AE, MC, V. Jkt. *Specialties:* snails Florentine, poached salmon steak, veal w. lemon and mushrooms, remarkable chocolate mousse. *Note:* The view of the Grand Tetons is so spectacularly beautiful that there's a danger of overlooking the really excellent European-inspired food at this elegant country club. Modern decor w. beautiful handwoven tapestries. Excellent svce. Resv. strongly advised, especially at dinner. A very good place. *Continental.* **I–M**

Jenny Lake Lodge, in the Jenny Lake Lodge (see "Accommodations," above) (733-4647). No A/C. Breakfast/lunch/

dinner daily. Closed mid-Sept to early June. AE, MC, V. *Specialties:* poached salmon w. capers in hollandaise sauce, roast leg of lamb boulangère, broiled rainbow trout, steak Delmonico w. bordelaise sauce. Menu changes regularly. Very fine wine list. *Note:* Excellent food in an unassuming log-cabin setting. Relaxed, cheerful atmosphere. Small enough that resv. are a must. A very good place to eat. *American/Continental.* **I–M**

Cadillac Grille, 55 N. Cache St., Jackson (733-3279). A/C. Lunch/dinner daily. AE, MC, V. *Specialties:* mixed salads, Cajun dishes, tuna or swordfish grilled over mesquite, tournedos w. Roquefort cheese, medallions of elk Cumberland, excellent desserts. Menu changes regularly. *Note:* The contemporary California cuisine of this engaging rest. perfectly matches its art deco pink-and-turquoise decorative scheme. Pleasant terrace in fine weather. Painstaking svce in a rather elegant setting. Locally popular; resv. a must. *American.* **I**

Aspens, in the Signal Mountain Lodge (see "Accommodations," above), in Moran (543-2831). No A/C. Breakfast/lunch/dinner daily; closed mid-Oct to mid-May. AE, MC, V. *Specialties:* prime rib, sautéed trout, steak, burgers, catch of the day. *Note:* Honest, unimaginative home-cooking served in large portions against an unforgettable backdrop of Jackson Lake and the Grand Tetons. Deft svce w. a smile; relaxed atmosphere; good value on balance. *American.* **B–I**

Vista Grande, Teton Village Rd., 7½ mi. (12km) NW of Jackson via Wyo. 22 and Teton Village Rd. (733-6964). A/C. Dinner only, nightly; closed Nov. MC, V. *Specialties:* chimichangas, fajitas, enchiladas, tacos al carbon. Excellent margaritas. *Note:* The Mexican food is as authentic and colorful as the decor, w. a fine view of the mountains thrown in. Cheerful svce. Locally popular, so resv. advised. Very good value. *Mexican.* **B–I**

NEARBY EXCURSIONS

CODY (80 mi./128km east of Fishing Bridge on Yellowstone Lake on U.S. 20): Founded in 1901 by the legendary "Buffalo Bill" (William Cody was his real name), and birthplace of the famous abstract painter Jackson Pollock, this picturesque pioneer settlement has retained its authentic far western flavor. Saloons, western boutiques, rodeos nightly June–Aug (587-5155 for information).

The **Buffalo Bill Historical Center,** dedicated to the famous scout and buffalo-hunter, is at 720 Sheridan Ave. (307/587-4771), open daily May–Sept, Tues–Sun Mar–Apr and Oct–Dec; closed Jan–Feb. Under one roof it houses four different collections, which make it one of the richest museums in the country on the Far West and its period. There are the **Buffalo Bill Museum** (personal memorabilia of William Cody); the **Winchester Arms Museum** (more than 5,000 firearms, including many specimens from the days of the Winning of the West); the **Whitney Gallery of Western Art** (fine paintings and sculptures by Bierstadt, Catlin, Miller, Moran, Remington, Russell, Wyeth, etc.), and the **Plains Indian Museum,** with an interesting collection of Indian ethnology: weapons, clothing, handcrafts, etc.

Nearby are the **Old Trail Town** and the **Museum of the Old West,** 1 mi. (1.6km) west on Yellowstone Hwy. (587-5302), open daily mid-May to late Sept, with authentic turn-of-the-century houses, which once stood beside the old stagecoach trail, now re-erected on the original site of Cody; these, too, are worth the detour. Among the buildings in this open-air museum which re-create the authentic flavor of a frontier town are the inevitable saloon, the general store, school, forge, and so on.

Lovers of the colossal won't overlook Gertrude Vanderbilt Whitney's **Buffalo Bill Monument,** at the west end of Sheridan Ave., believed to be the world's largest equestrian statue in bronze.

Where to Stay in Cody

Holiday Inn, 1701 Sheridan Ave., Cody, WY 82414 (307/ 587-5555). 184 rms. Very comfortable. **M**

The Irma Hotel, 1192 Sheridan Ave., Cody, WY 82414 (307/ 587-4221). 37 rms. Built (and named) by Buffalo Bill in 1902 for his daughter, Irma, and still has its period furniture and decor. A must for lovers of the Old West. **I**

Where to Eat in Cody

Irma Grill, 1192 Sheridan Ave. (587-4221). Breakfast/lunch/ dinner daily. In Buffalo Bill's old hotel (see above), a superb rm of the period. *American.* **B–I**

JACKSON (57 mi./92km south of the southern entrance to Yellowstone National Park): The ultimate cowboy town; relaxed, comfortable atmosphere. Many western boutiques. Don't miss the ☼ **"Million Dollar Cowboy Bar,"** 25 N. Cache St. (733-2207); the bar itself is 87 ft. (25m) long, and the stools are shaped like western saddles. A must-see.

Dirty Jack's Wild West Theater and Opera House, 140 N. Cache St. (733-4775), presents western-style musicals in an idiom much appreciated by fans, nightly June–Sept.

GHOST TOWNS: **Virginia City,** 85 mi. (136km) NW of West Yellowstone via U.S. 191, U.S. 287, and Mont. 287: One of the most picturesque and best-preserved ghost towns in the Northwest. Founded in 1863 by prospectors, this former capital of the Montana territory, along with its sister town of **Nevada City,** once boasted 10,000 inhabitants—today, barely 200 remain. There are many original buildings scrupulously restored: workshops, schools, brewery (Gilbert Brewery), Wells Fargo Express office, general store, offices of the *Montana Post* newspaper, opera house, Chinatown, and so on. So authentic is the setting that many westerns have been filmed here, notably *Little Big Man* and *The Missouri Breaks.* Interesting historical museum (Wallace St. in Virginia City) and railroad museum (Nevada City depot). Both recommended accommodations (below) date from gold-rush days.

The ghost towns of Virginia City and Nevada City, connected by a narrow-gauge railroad, are open to visitors June–Aug. Don't miss them; they're worth the side trip.

For **information,** contact Historic Virginia City, P.O. Box 338, Virginia City, MT 59755 (406/843-5377).

Where to Stay in Virginia City

Fairweather Inn, on Mont. 287, Virginia City, MT 59755 (406/843-5377). 15 rms (6 w. bath). MC, V. Adj. coffee shop. Closed Sept.–June. **I**

Nevada City Hotel, on Mont. 287, Virginia City, MT 59755 (406/843-5487). 15 rms, 12 bungalows. MC, V. Gold-rush camp atmosphere. Closed Sept.–June. **I**

CHAPTER 34

THE BLACK HILLS AND MOUNT RUSHMORE♛♛

□ □ □

Several of the country's most renowned tourist attractions lie within a 2-hr. drive of **Rapid City,** the second-largest town in South Dakota. The **Black Hills,** a huge, wooded outcrop of rock 93 mi. (150km) long by 62 mi. (100km) wide and rising in places to 6,400 ft. (2,000m), frown across the great cereal-growing plains of the Dakotas (a Sioux word meaning "alliance of friends"). The Black Hills, rich in seams of ore, were the scene in 1874 of the country's penultimate gold rush, before that of Alaska's Klondike. Several ghost towns or almost-deserted mining camps remain to bear witness to those wild times, when fame alighted on adventurers like Wild Bill Hickok, Calamity Jane, and Preacher Smith, all three of whom lie buried in the Mount Moriah Cemetery at **Deadwood.** Southeast of the Black Hills, **Wind Cave National Park** has underground limestone caverns considered among the finest in the world.

Some 60 mi. (100km) to the east, the glorious national park of the **Badlands** rears its contorted sandstone cliffs, whose savage beauty brings to mind the Grand Canyon of the Colorado; the colorful gorges are best seen at sunrise or sunset.

Finally, **Mount Rushmore National Memorial,** visited every year by more than 2½ million tourists, is one of the most extraordinary monuments in America. Here the features of Presidents George Washington, Thomas Jefferson, Abraham Lincoln, and Theodore Roosevelt, each some 60 ft. (20m) high, have been carved from the living rock. These colossal portraits, the work of visionary artist Gutzon Borglum (and after his death, his son, Lincoln) required 14 years (1927–41) of stubborn effort, and the removal of 450,000 tons of rock. After darkness falls, the sight of these enormous granite faces illuminated by floodlights is enthralling indeed. Not far from Mount Rushmore another solitary sculptor, Borglum's pupil, Korczak Ziolkowski, began work in 1948, with explosives, pneumatic drills, and bulldozers, on another huge mountainside statue: an equestrian figure, 564 ft. (172m) high and 640 ft. (195m) long of the renowned Sioux chief Crazy Horse, who defeated Lt.-Col. George A. Custer at the battle of the Little Big Horn. Here, too, the sculptor's work was continued after his death (in 1982) by his sons. When finished, sometime around the year 2000, the **Crazy Horse Memorial** will be by far the largest statue in the world.

BASIC FACTS: State of South Dakota. Area code: 605. Time zone: mountain. Zip Code: 57751.

CLIMATE: Summer, with mean July temperatures of 74°F (23°C) and occasional peaks of 95°F(35°C), or autumn, still sunny but cooler, are the best times to visit the Black Hills. Winter, too, has its own savage beauty, though the mercury rarely climbs above 14°F (−10°C) and the snow falls abundantly.

DISTANCES: Chicago, 896 mi. (1,434km); Denver, 375 mi. (600km); Minneapolis, 635 mi. (1,045km); Salt Lake City, 680 mi. (1,088km); Yellowstone, 549 mi. (878km).

ARRIVAL & TRANSIT INFORMATION

NEAREST AIRPORT: Rapid City Regional Airport (RAP), 9 mi. (15km) SE of the town. For information, call 394-4195.

AIRLINES: Continental (342-6707), Delta (toll free 800/221-1212), Northwest (toll free 800/225-2525), and United (toll free 800/241-6522).

CITY LINK: An airport bus, **Airport Limo** (343-5358), serves the principal Rapid City hotels: fare, $8; time, 20 min.

CAR RENTAL (at the airport unless otherwise noted): Avis (393-0740); Budget (393-0488); Dollar, 410 N. Campbell, Rapid City (342-7071); Hertz (393-0160); National (393-2664); Thrifty, 510 N. Campbell, Rapid City (393-0663).
  Car-rental rates are high, and the choice of models is limited—but even so, you can't do better than rent a car with unlimited mileage, given the distances to be covered and the many interesting places to see.

INTERCITY BUSES: Jack Rabbit Lines and Arrow Stage Lines, 333 6th St., Rapid City (348-3300). Both honor the Greyhound Ameripass.

INFORMATION & TOURS

TOURIST INFORMATION: The **Black Hills, Badlands, and Lakes Association,** 900 Jackson Blvd., Rapid City, SD 57702 (605/341-1462).
  Rapid City Visitors and Conventions Bureau, 444 Mt. Rushmore Rd., Rapid City, SD 57709 (605/343-1744).
  Custer County Chamber of Commerce, 447 Crook St., Custer, SD 57730 (605/673-2244).
  Deadwood–Lead Chamber of Commerce, 735 Historic Main St., Deadwood, SD 57732 (605/578-1876).
  Mount Rushmore National Memorial Visitor Center, U.S. 16A, Keystone, SD 57751 (605/574-2523).

GUIDED TOURS: **Alkali Ike Tours** (bus), P.O. Box 594, Deadwood, SD 57732 (605/578-3583 in summer, 605/278-2510 off-season): Guided tours of Deadwood and surrounding country.
  Golden Circle Tours (bus), 40 N. 5th St., Custer (605/673-4349): 80-mi. (130km) minibus tour of Custer, Mount Rushmore, and the Black Hills. Daily May–Sept.
  Gray Line Tours (bus), 1600 E. St. Patrick St., Rapid City (605/342-4461): Guided tours around the whole region; serves principal Rapid City hotels.
  Jeep to the Buffalo (Jeep), State Game Lodge, U.S. 16A, Custer (605/255-4541): Jeep trips through the buffalo herds of Custer State Park—for wildlife photographers.
  Rushmore Helicopters (helicopter), Keystone Helipad, Keystone (605/666-4461): Trips lasting 4–20 min. over Mount Rushmore and the Black Hills. Spectacular. Mid-May to mid-Sept.

Stagecoach West (bus), P.O. Box 264, Rapid City, SD 57709 (605/343-3113): A 9-hr. guided tour of the whole region; serves principal Rapid City hotels. Daily June–Sept.

THE MAJOR SIGHTS & ATTRACTIONS

BADLANDS NATIONAL PARK (83 mi./132km east of Rapid City on I-90 and S.D. 240): Spectacular canyons carved by erosion in the multicolored hills of clay and sandstone—a spectacle whose singular beauty has fascinated travelers through the ages. Several herds of buffalo roam free here. Badlands National Park was set up in 1939. **Visitor Center** open daily year round at Cedar Pass, east of the park. For information, call 605/433-5361.

BLACK HILLS (10 mi./16km west of Rapid City on U.S. 16): Glorious wooded mountains overlooking the vast Dakota plains, whose mineral wealth touched off a gold rush in 1874; several ghost towns still stand as witness. Once this land was held sacred by the Dakota.

CRAZY HORSE MEMORIAL (41 mi./65km SW of Rapid City on U.S. 16) (605/673-4681): The world's largest statue, 640 by 564 ft. (195 by 172m), is being created here. The work, begun in 1948, has already required the removal of eight million tons of rock—18 times more than at Mount Rushmore. Boston sculptor Korczak Ziolkowski, a pupil of Borglum's who at one time worked with him on the nearby Mount Rushmore Memorial, conceived and began this gigantic equestrian figure, carved with bulldozers and explosives from the granite of Thunderhead Mountain. The memorial pays tribute to the pride and greatness of Native Americans, in the person of the famous Crazy Horse, chief of the Oglala Sioux, and one of those who defeated Lt.-Col. George Armstrong Custer at the battle of the Little Big Horn. A model in the Visitor Center will give you an idea of the size and shape envisaged for the finished work: the horse's head will be as high as a 22-story building. After the sculptor died in Oct 1982, his wife, Ruth, and his 10 sons took over the work and expect to complete it around the end of the century. An impressive sight; open daily year round.

MOUNT RUSHMORE NATIONAL MEMORIAL (24 mi./38km SW of Rapid City on U.S. 16) (605/574-2523): Unique colossal sculptures, twice as big as the Sphinx in Egypt, cut into a granite cliff 6,000 ft. (1,830m) high. One of the most extraordinary memorials that history can record, the work of a single man (though completed by the hand of his son), John Gutzon de La Mothe Borglum, a sculptor of Danish descent from Idaho. Begun in 1927 when the sculptor was well over 50, these four gigantic portraits, each about 60 ft. (20m) high and carved from the rock with explosives and pneumatic drills, were not completed until Oct 1941, some months after his death. They symbolize the contribution made to U.S. history by four great presidents: George Washington, the struggle for independence; Thomas Jefferson, the foundation of a democratic state; Abraham Lincoln, the equality of all citizens and the preservation of the Union; Theodore Roosevelt, the influence of America on the world and the conservation of natural resources. Among others, Alfred Hitchcock's famous movie *North by Northwest* was shot here. Almost 2½ million people come here every year; the spectacular (in the most literal sense) sight is enough to make the trip worthwhile. Open daily year round.

WIND CAVE NATIONAL PARK (nr. Hot Springs, 53 mi./84km south of Rapid City on U.S. 16) (605/745-4600): One of the country's most beautiful natural caverns, lying at a depth of 196–328

THE BLACK HILLS AREA

N

WYOMING
SOUTH DAKOTA

Spearfish

Cheyenne
Crossing

Terry
Peak

Lead

Deadwood

ALT 14

Sturgis

Bethlehem
Cave

Wonderland
Cave

Old Fort Meade
Cav. Mus.

Black Hills
Nat'l Forest

385

Hill
City

Diamond
Crystal Cave

Sioux Indian
Mus.

Sitting Bull
Caverns

244

Crazy Horse
Mon.

Custer

Jewel Cave
Nat'l Mon.

16

89

Mt. Rushmore
Nat'l Memorial

87

ALT
16

Custer
St. Park

Wind Cave
Nat'l Park

Hot
Springs

Rockerville

36

79

Hermosa

40

Black
Hawk

Rapid
City

Mus. of
Geology

S.D. Air &
Space Museum

Bear
Country
USA

Chapel in
the Hills

14

44

240

Wall

90

377

Badlands
Nat'l Park

Pine Ridge
Reservation

To Wounded
Knee

34

85

ft. (60–100m) beneath the slopes of the Black Hills. There is a pedestrian walkway running 1.2–8 mi. (2–12km) through the colorful chambers of the cavern. Wear warm clothing and sturdy shoes—and don't try the walk unless you're in good shape physically. Discovered in 1881, the Wind Cave owes its name to the violent winds that blow between the cavern and the outer world according to changes in atmospheric pressure. Open for (exhausting) visits daily year round.

OTHER SIGHTS, ATTRACTIONS & ACTIVITIES

MUSEUMS OF SCIENCE & HISTORY: ☖ **Dahl Fine Arts Center,** 713 7th St., Rapid City (394-4101): Rotating exhibits of local and Native American art. Also houses an enormous 200-ft. (60m) circular mural by Bernard Thomas, depicting 200 years of American history. Open daily.

☖ **Museum of Geology,** 500 E. St. Joseph St., Rapid City (394-2467): A rich collection of animal fossils (dinosaurs, *Tyrannosaurus*) and minerals; gold nuggets. A must-see. Open daily June–Sept, Mon–Sat the rest of the year.

☖ **Rushmore-Borglum Story and Gallery,** Main St., Keystone (666-4449): An entire museum devoted to the sculptor of Mount Rushmore and his work. Photographs, paintings, models; history of the work. Interesting. Open daily May–Oct.

☖ **Sioux Indian Museum,** 515 West Blvd., Rapid City (348-0577): One of the country's finest Native American museums. Interesting old utensils, Sioux handcrafts. The adjoining **Minnilusa Pioneer Museum** is devoted to the period of the westward expansion. Must be seen. Open daily June–Sept, Tues–Sun the rest of the year.

☖ **South Dakota Air & Space Museum,** at Ellsworth Air Force Base, 11 mi. (17km) east of Rapid City off I-90 at Exit 66 (385-5188): Military museum whose special distinction is a score of different aircraft from the old reliable DC-3 to the giant B-52. Open daily year round. Also guided tours of the base, daily mid-May to mid-Sept.

SPECIAL EVENTS: **Black Hills Roundup** at Belle Fourche (July 4 wknd): One of the best-known rodeos in the Midwest; not to be missed.

Central States Fair at Rapid City (Aug.): Agricultural fair, rodeo, Native American dances, auto races, parades. Colorful.

Days of '76 at Deadwood (first wknd in Aug): Big historical parade in honor of the gold-rush days; rodeo; lively and colorful.

Black Hills Motorcycle Classic at Sturgis (first week in Aug): Each Aug over 100,000 "bikers" and spectators celebrate this week-long, internationally famous motorcycle-racing extravaganza.

Fall Festival at Custer (second wknd in Sept): Horse shows, giant barbecue, shows, concerts; very popular locally.

WINTER SPORTS RESORTS: ☖ **Deer Mountain,** at Lead, 49 mi. (78km) NW of Rapid City on I-90 and U.S. Alt 14 (584-3230): 5 lifts. Open Nov–Mar.

Terry Peak, at Lead, 49 mi. (78km) NW of Rapid City on I-90 and U.S. Alt 14 (584-2165): 5 lifts. Open Nov–Mar.

ACCOMMODATIONS IN THE AREA

A Note on Accommodations: Room rates in the Black Hills Region are coded as follows: **VE,** Very Expensive ($140 and up); **E,** Expensive ($90–$140); **M,** Moderate ($60–$90); **I,** Inexpensive ($30–$60); **B,** Budget (up to $30). A listing of toll free numbers is in the Appendix.

Personal Favorites (in order of preference)

☖☖ **Hilton Inn,** 445 Mt. Rushmore (at Main St.), Rapid City, SD 57701 (605/348-8300; toll free, see Hilton). 177 rms, A/C, color TV, in-rm movies. AE, CB, DC, MC, V. Free parking, pool, health club, rest. (Sylvan Room), coffee shop, bar, rm svce, boutiques, free crib. *Note:* Modern grand hotel in the center of Rapid City. Comfortable, spacious rms, most w. views of the Black Hills. Efficient svce; acceptable rest. The best place to stay in town. Open year round. **M,** but lower rates off-season.

State Game Lodge, on U.S. 16A, Custer, SD 57730 (605/255-4541; toll free 800/658-3530). 46 rms; no A/C; color TV in public area. AE, MC, V. Free parking, fishing, horseback riding, rest. (Pheasant Dining Rm), bar. *Note:* Elegant 1920s country hotel in the heart of Custer State Park; Presidents Calvin Coolidge (1927) and Dwight Eisenhower (1953) took a summer vacation here. Comfortable rms or bungalows w. kitchenette; very satisfactory rest.; friendly svce. Jeep trips arranged to the park's herds of buffalo. A fine place for nature lovers. Closed Nov–Apr. **I–M**

Bavarian Inn, U.S. 16, Custer, SD 57730 (605/673-2802). 52 rms, A/C, color TV, in-rm movies. AE, CB, DC, MC, V. Free parking, pool, sauna, tennis court, rest., bar, free crib. *Note:* An agreeable small motel w. distinction. Friendly reception; comfortable rms w. private balconies; very commendable food. Nr. the Crazy Horse Memorial. One of the best places to stay in the region. Open year round. **I–M,** but lower rates off-season.

Alex Johnson, 523 6th St., Rapid City, SD 57701 (605/342-1210; toll free 800/888-2539). 120 rms, A/C, color TV, in-rm movies. AE, DC, MC, V. Free valet parking, sauna, rest., bar, rm svce, nightclub, crib $5. *Note:* Charming old hotel, recently restored, in the center of Rapid City. Comfortable rms, some w. refrigerators. The Landmark Restaurant is acceptable. Svce not always dependable. Open year round. Listed on the National Register of Historic Places (1928). Sister hotel of the State Game Lodge in Custer (see above). **M,** but lower rates off-season.

Golden Hills Inn, 900 Miners Ave., Lead, SD 57754 (605/584-1800; toll free 800/658-5555). 100 rms, A/C, color TV, in-rm movies. AE, CB, DC, MC, V. Free parking, pool, health club, squash, skiing and snowmobiling in winter, rest. (Mountain Rose), bar, rm svce, disco. *Note:* Large, inviting, up-to-date convention hotel opened in June 1989. Spacious, comfortable rms; very fine physical-fitness facilities; efficient svce. Free shuttle link w. the casinos in Deadwood. Package-tour and business clientele. **M,** but lower rates off-season.

Franklin Hotel, 700 Main St., Deadwood, SD 57732 (605/578-2241). 54 rms, cable color TV, AE, CB, DC, MC, V. Paid parking, rest. (1903 Dining Rm), bar. *Note:* One of the oldest hotels (1903) in the Black Hills region. Elegant old decor, prettily restored. Nice rms, but avoid the annex on the other side of the street. An engaging breath of the past. Acceptable rest. Open year round. **I,** but lower rates off-season.

Best Western Town and Country, 2505 Mt. Rushmore Rd., Rapid City, SD 57701 (605/343-5383; toll free, see Best Western). 100 rms, A/C, color TV, in-rm movies. AE, CB, DC, MC, V. Free parking, two pools, rest., bar, crib $4. *Note:* Comfortable, well-run motel on the road to Mount Rushmore. Friendly reception. Most rms have private balconies or patios. Open year round. **I–M,** but lower rates off-season.

Cedar Pass Lodge, U.S. 16, Cedar Pass, SD 57750 (605/433-5460). 24 bungalows, A/C. AE, CB, DC, MC, V. Free parking, rest. *Note:* Spruce rustic cabins inside Badlands National Park, managed by the Oglala Sioux tribe. For lovers of unspoiled nature. Beautiful view. Open May 1–Oct 15. **B–I**

Powder House Lodge, U.S. 16, Keystone, SD 57751 (605/666-4646). 26 rms. AE, MC, V. Free parking, rest., bar. *Note:* Comfortable cottages in the woods, 4 mi. (6km) from Mount Rushmore. Friendly reception and svce. Very acceptable rest. Open May to the end of Sept. Good value. **I**

Sylvan Lake Resort, S.D. 89, Custer State Park, SD 57730 (605/574-2561). 65 rms and bungalows. AE, MC, V. Free parking, fishing, beach, boats, rest., coffee shop, bar. *Note:* There are 29 rms in the motel and 36 bungalows, some rms w. balconies on the lake. Rustic comfort; country atmosphere. Rates somewhat overpriced. Closed Oct–May. **M–E**

♀ **Rushmore View Motor Lodge,** U.S. 16A, Keystone, SD
🛏 57751 (605/666-4466). 31 rms, A/C, color TV, in-rm movies. AE, CB, DC, MC, V. Free parking, rest., bar, child's cot $4. *Note:* Conventional small motel w. a view of Mount Rushmore. The Copper Rm is an acceptable rest. Good value on balance. Closed mid-Oct to May. **I–M,** but lower rates off-season.

♀ **Best Western Four Presidents,** U.S. 16A, Keystone, SD
🛏 57751 (605/666-4472; toll free, see Best Western). 30 rms, A/C, color TV. AE, CB, DC, MC, V. Free parking, adj. coffee shop, child's cot $3. *Note:* Conventional small motel 3 mi. (5km) from Mount Rushmore. Functionally comfortable. Closed Dec to the end of Mar. **I–M,** but lower rates off-season.

♀ **Best Western Plains Motel,** 712 Glenn St., Wall, SD 57790
🛏 (605/279-2145; toll free, see Best Western). 74 rms, A/C, color TV, in-rm movies. AE, CB, DC, MC, V. Free parking, pool, coffee shop, child's cot $3. *Note:* Typical but appealing small motel at the entrance to Badlands National Park. Comfortable rms. Closed Dec–Mar. **I–M,** but lower rates off-season.

♀ **Super 8 Motel,** 201 Main St., Hill City, SD 57745 (605/574-
🛏 4141; toll free 800/843-1991). 34 rms, A/C, color TV, in-rm movies. MC, V. Free parking, nearby coffee shop, free crib. *Note:* Modern, comfortable small motel. Spacious rms; friendly reception. Near the depot for the "1880 Train" (see the Hill City excursion, below). Open year round. **I**

♀ **Motel 6,** 620 E. Latrobe St., Rapid City, SD 57701 (605/
🛏 343-3687). 150 rms. A/C, color TV, free in-rm movies. AE, DC, MC, V. Free parking, pool. *Note:* Economy motel north of town w. direct access to I-90 at Exit 59. Serviceable and well run; great if you're driving. **B–I,** but lower rates off-season.

YMCA/Youth Hostels

YMCA, 815 Kansas City St., Rapid City, SD 57701 (605/342-8538). Men and women; also youth hostel. 12 cots. Open in summer only. Pool.

RESTAURANTS IN THE AREA

A Note on Restaurant Prices: Black Hills Region restaurant prices, per person, excluding drinks and service charges, are coded as follows: **VE,** Very Expensive ($60 and up); **E,** Expensive ($40–$60); **M,** Moderate ($25–$40); **I,** Inexpensive ($15–$25); **B,** Budget (up to $15).

Personal Favorites (in order of preference)

🍸 **Bavarian Inn** (see the Bavarian Inn in "Accommodations in the
🍸 Area," above), in Custer (673-4412). A/C. Breakfast/lunch/ dinner daily; closed Thanksgiving, Dec. 25. MC, V. *Specialties:* veal Cordon Bleu, wienerschnitzel, rouladen, walleye pike, spätzle, apfel strudel. *Note:* Classic German setting and food; likable atmosphere. Dancing in season. Resv. advised. *German/American.* **I–M**

🍸 **The Sluice,** Heritage Dr., in Spearfish (642-5500). A/C.
🍸 Lunch/dinner Tues–Sun; closed hols. AE, MC, V. *Specialties:* truite amandine, prime rib, "miner's stew," buffalo steak, homemade desserts. *Note:* Popular w. tourists and locals alike for its turn-of-the-century mining-camp decor. The menu, running to an unexpected 30 pages, adds to its appeal. Very estimable food, pleasant svce. A very good place. *American.* **B–I**

🍸 **Powder House Lodge** (see the Powder House Lodge in "Accommodations in the Area," above), in Keystone (666-4646).
Breakfast/lunch/dinner daily; closed Oct to late May. AE, MC, V. *Specialties:*

buffalo steak, prime rib, broiled chicken, catch of the day, a variety of salads. *Note:* A rustic dining rm in the heart of the woods. Very praiseworthy food. Good value. *American.* **B–I**

Pheasant Dining Room, in the State Game Lodge (see "Accommodations in the Area," above), in Custer (255-4541). A/C. Breakfast/lunch/dinner daily; closed Nov–Apr. AE, MC, V. *Specialties:* buffalo steak, prime rib, broiled trout, roast pheasant, good homemade desserts. *Note:* Huge western-style dining rm more than half a century old; flavorful country cooking flawlessly prepared and served. Relaxed atmosphere. Locally popular; resv. advised. *Steak/American.* **B–I**

Ruby House, U.S. 16A, in Keystone (666-4404). A/C. Lunch/dinner daily; closed from the end of Oct to mid-Apr. AE, CB, DC, MC, V. *Specialties:* meats broiled over wood fire, Italian dishes. *Note:* Picturesque Far West–style saloon rest., the dining rm attractively decorated as a turn-of-the-century bawdy house. Attentive svce, laudable food. Worth a visit. *Steak.* **I**

Landmark Restaurant, in the Alex Johnson Hotel (see "Accommodations in the Area," above), in Rapid City (342-1210). A/C. Breakfast/lunch/dinner daily; closed Dec 24–25. AE, CB, DC, MC, V. *Specialties:* steak, prime rib, roast pheasant, fish of the day. *Note:* Hotel dining rm somewhat in need of redecoration, but serving good meats. The svce could use some attention. *Steak.* **I**

1903 Dining Room, in the Franklin Hotel (see "Accommodations in the Area," above), in Deadwood (578-2241). A/C. Breakfast/lunch/dinner daily; closed Dec 25. AE, DC, MC, V. *Specialties:* hamburger, steak, fish of the day. *Note:* The Victorian dining rm of the venerable Franklin Hotel dates, as its name suggests, from the turn of the century; so do the decor and atmosphere. The food, though acceptable, is unimaginative, the svce efficient. Resv. suggested in tourist season. Pleasant patio dining in summer. *American.* **B–I**

Flying T Chuckwagon Suppers, on U.S. 16, 6 mi. (10km) south of Rapid City (342-1905). No A/C. Dinner only, daily (one sitting only, at 7:30pm sharp); closed mid-Sept through May. MC, V. *Specialties:* barbecued beef, baked potatoes, beans, biscuits. Beer, but no wine or liquor. *Note:* Real cowboy chuckwagon suppers served as they used to be in tin plates and cups; live country and western music. An old barn and pioneers' covered wagons add to the local color. Resv. advisable; very popular w. the tourist trade. *American.* **B**

Copper Room, in the Rushmore View Motor Lodge (see "Accommodations in the Area," above), in Keystone (666-4466). A/C. Breakfast/lunch/dinner daily; closed Nov–May. AE, CB, DC, MC, V. *Specialties:* steak, broiled trout, salads. *Note:* Tiny motel dining rm in neon and Formica; modest, unpretentious food. *American.* **B–I**

Chute Rooster, U.S. 385, in Hill City (574-2122). Lunch/dinner daily; closed Mon–Tues in winter, Memorial Day, Dec 24–25. MC, V. *Specialties:* steak, prime rib, barbecued meats, catch of the day, beef stew. *Note:* A 19th-century barn turned into a western-style rest. Plentiful portions of solid food. Far West atmosphere, w. square dances in summer. Locally popular. *American.* **B–I**

Buffalo Room, on S.D. 244, Keystone (574-2515). A/C. Breakfast/lunch/dinner daily (till 8pm); closed from the end of Sept to the end of May. AE, MC, V. *Specialties:* fried chicken, prime rib, good desserts. *Note:* A rustic cafeteria, w. its western decor and fine art by South Dakota artists; magnificent bay window overlooking Mount Rushmore and its sculptures. Very acceptable food; swift, efficient svce. *American.* **B**

Wall Drug Store, 1 Main St., Wall (279-2175). A/C. Breakfast/lunch/dinner daily (till 10pm in summer, 8pm in spring and fall, 5pm in winter); closed Sun (in winter) and hols. AE, MC, V.

Specialties: steak, fried chicken, soups, sandwiches. *Note:* Self-service cafeteria in the middle of a huge, jumbled country store reminiscent of gold-rush days. The sight is worth your time—the food, less so. Picturesque. *American.* **B**

NEARBY EXCURSIONS

BEAR COUNTRY USA (8 mi./12km south of Rapid City on U.S. 16) (343-2290): Wildlife reserve with bears, wolves, cougar, buffalo, elk, and other animals roaming free; you stay in your car. Guaranteed excitement. Open daily May to mid-Oct.

CHAPEL IN THE HILLS (5 mi./8km west of Rapid City on S.D. 44 and Chapel Lane) (342-8281): Exact replica of the famous 12th-century "Borgund Stavkirke" in Laerdal, Norway; a magnificent building in carved wood. Open daily May–Oct, by request the rest of the year.

DEADWOOD (40 mi./64km NW of Rapid City on I-90 and U.S. Alt. 14): Picturesque gold-prospectors' town, still haunted by the redoubtable shades of such as Wild Bill Hickok, Calamity Jane, Preacher Smith, and Potato Creek Johnny. Its gold-rush population of 25,000 has fallen to barely 2,000 today, but its **Main Street** is on the National Register of Historic Monuments. Visit the famous **Saloon #10,** where Wild Bill Hickok was killed, at 657 Main St. (578-3346); open daily. At the **Old Town Hall,** on Lee St. (578-3583), you can see an amusing skit on his murderer's trial, Mon–Sat June–Aug. Other popular attractions: a gold mine, the **Broken Boot Mine,** on U.S. Alt. 14 (578-9997), open daily mid-May to mid-Oct; and the **Mount Moriah Cemetery,** with tombs of famous Wild West characters, at **Boot Hill,** open daily.

A new gaming law, enacted in Apr 1989, has made Deadwood the only city in the state with gambling since the practice was outlawed in the 1960s. In the saloons of the town that Wild Bill Hickok helped put on the map, only games allowed today are at poker and blackjack tables and in slot machines; the maximum bet is $5.

DEVILS TOWER NATIONAL MONUMENT (86 mi./140km NW of Rapid City via I-90 and Wyo. 24): Enormous (1,280-ft./390m) tower of streaked basalt, like the trunk of a giant tree, towering over the lovely Fourche River which washes its feet. The colors of this impressive volcanic bastion, which has inspired many legends and was used by Steven Spielberg as a setting for *Close Encounters of the Third Kind,* change with the time of day. Some thousand brave souls climb it every year. A truly riveting sight. Site of the nation's first National Monument, dedicated by Pres. Theodore Roosevelt in 1906. Visitor Center open daily May–Oct. For information, contact the Superintendent, P.O. Box 8, Devils Tower, WY 82714 (307/467-5370).

HILL CITY (28 mi./44km SW of Rapid City on U.S. 16): This charming little mountain village at the foot of **Harney Peak,** South Dakota's highest at 7,242 ft. (2,207m), boasts one of the Black Hills' best tourist draws: the **1880 Train.** Here you can travel to Keystone and back, a 2-hr. round-trip, aboard an authentic steam train, Far Western style—a picturesque journey through lovely countryside. Open daily mid-June to the end of Aug. For information, call 574-2222; resv. advised.

HOT SPRINGS (74 mi./118km SW of Rapid City on U.S. 16 and U.S. 385): Highly regarded thermal springs, with the world's largest indoor pool of naturally heated water, the **Evans Plunge,** 1145 N. River St. (745-5165). Open daily year round.

Don't fail to visit the ☀ **Mammoth Site,** on U.S. 18 bypass (745-6017), a huge 26,000-year-old mammoth graveyard under active excavation by paleontologists; it's believed to have a larger store of bones of this type than any other de-posit in the Western Hemisphere. A fascinating place to visit. Open daily Apr–Oct, by appointment the rest of the year.

JEWEL CAVE NATIONAL MONUMENT (59 mi./ 94km SW of Rapid City on U.S. 16) (673-2288): One of the most beautiful caverns in the country; superb formations of crystalline calcite produce unique visual effects. You should be in good physical condition, wearing warm clothes and sturdy walking shoes—it's a tiring visit. Open daily May–Oct.

LEAD (49 mi./78km NW of Rapid City via I-90 and U.S. Alt. 114): Clinging to its mountainside, this old pioneer village, now a very popular winter-sports resort, boasts the country's largest gold mine. Opened in 1876 and still in production, the **Homestake Gold Mine,** Main St. and Mill St. (584-3110), is also the country's deepest at 8,000 ft. (2,440m); it takes 45 min. just to ride to the bottom in the elevator cage, and the temperature when you get there can be as high as 132°F (56°C). The surface installations of the mine are open to visitors Mon–Fri. May–Oct.

From the nearby 7,076-ft. (2,157m) **Terry Peak,** accessible either by road or by chair lift (584-2165),there is a clear view of the Black Hills and the neighboring states of Wyoming, Montana, North Dakota, and Nebraska.

SPEARFISH (47 mi./75km NW of Rapid City on I-90): Famous for its trout hatcheries, Spearfish has also presented, June–Aug of every year since 1939, the **Black Hills Passion Play,** with 250 characters; it may be seen every Tues, Thurs, and Sun evening at 400 St. Joe St. (642-2646).

The **Matthews Opera House,** 614 Main St. (642-2626), a fine baroque structure from 1906, stages amusing melodramas from the gold-rush era on Mon, Wed, and Fri June–Aug; a must-see.

STURGIS (29 mi./46km NW of Rapid City on I-90): The **Old Fort Meade Cavalry Museum,** 1 mi. (2km) east on S.D. 34 (347-9822), may be visited daily from mid-May to the end of Sept. It was here that the 140 survivors of Lt.-Col. George Armstrong Custer's Seventh Cavalry regiment took refuge after their unit had been cut to pieces by 4,000 Sioux and Cheyenne under Sitting Bull and Crazy Horse at the battle of the Little Big Horn, on June 25, 1876. The museum has many memorabilia from those historic times; all western-history buffs should see it. It was at Fort Meade that "The Star-Spangled Banner" was first played in 1892 at official functions, a custom that led to its becoming the national anthem in 1931.

WALL (54 mi./86km SE of Rapid City on I-90): Gateway to **Badlands National Park** (see above), this tiny town founded in 1907 as a station on the Chicago & Northwestern Railroad is the home of the unusual and well-known **Wall Drug Store.** The legend is that Wall Drug Store began booming in the 1930s, when the owners posted signs on the highway advertising free ice water. From a little storefront pharmacy, Wall Drug has grown into a sprawling museum of Americana that doubles as a souvenir shop and restaurant. Western art decorates the wall, buffalo burgers are a specialty, and ice water is still free. Roadside signs won't let you miss the place, on U.S. 14 and I-90 (279-2175). Open daily Apr–Dec, Mon–Sat the rest of the year.

WOUNDED KNEE (89 mi./142km SE of Rapid City via S.D. 44 and Indian Rd. 27): Here, on December 29, 1890, the U.S. Army finally broke the resistance of the Sioux, killing 256 unarmed Native Americans including women and children. Some commentators have discerned in this sorry episode a sort of revenge exacted for Little Big Horn (see "Sturgis," above). Wounded Knee was also the scene of a symbolic Native American revolt

in 1973. Monument marks the place of the massacre. For western-history fans. The visit can conveniently be combined with the trip to Badlands National Park (see "The Major Sights and Attractions," above).

GHOST TOWNS: ⚒ **Rockerville,** 12 mi. (19km) SW of Rapid City on U.S. 16 (342-0200): An authentic 1878 prospectors' village with old workshops, restaurant, saloon, and theater all carefully restored. Guaranteed local color. Open daily mid-May to Oct.

⚒ **CUSTER STATE PARK** (42 mi./67km SW of Rapid City on U.S. 16): Some 73,000 acres (180,000ha) of dense forests, lakes, and unspoiled natural beauty, with one of the country's largest buffalo herds as well as many deer, elk, mountain goats, and other creatures. The **Needles Highway Scenic Drive** (closed in winter) is a 14-mi. (22km) panoramic road well worth the detour. The park is open all year.

PART FIVE

THE SOUTHWEST

CHAPTER 35

DALLAS AND
FORT WORTH *

□ □ □

A city for the 21st century, "Big D" to its admirers, Dallas somehow captures the myth of modern America. Its futurist buildings and grand hotels worthy of Ancient Egypt rival in their brashness the New York and Chicago skylines: witness **City Hall**, with its unadorned, geometric lines; the **Dallas Theater Center;** the startling **Allied Bank Tower,** with its beveled architecture; the immense blue-tinted facade of the **Hyatt Regency Hotel;** and next door, the **Reunion Tower** and its geodesic dome, resembling an enormous crown when illuminated at night. With a more diversified economy than its great rival Houston (oil, textiles, aeronautics, banking, insurance, publishing, chemicals, electronics), Dallas continues to sustain an enviable economic growth rate, despite the depression that has gripped Texas since the early '80s. It is a town of pioneers, founded less than 150 years ago by John Neely Bryan, a Tennessee lawyer who came seeking trade with the Caddo and Cherokee tribes. Named after then–Vice-President George Mifflin Dallas, the city entered its great boom period after World War II. Known as "the New York of the South," Texas's largest city is also one of the country's three great fashion capitals; its designer houses and shops are particularly famous for their luxury and elegance. In addition, Dallas has more retail shopping space per capita than any other U.S. city. While it has been disparagingly identified with the unscrupulous "J.R." in its namesake TV series, Dallas rightly prides itself on its millionaire district—**Highland Park**—more like a city within a city, with private police, exclusive schools and clubs, dream houses, and its very own moral code. It is an indicator of its wealth that, outside Saudi Arabia, Dallas boasts more Cadillacs per capita than any other city in the world.

Dallas first built its fortune on cotton, then oil in the 1930s, and continues to be one of the country's most artistically and culturally active cities despite the current economic slump. This is in keeping with the spiritual tradition of the city's early settlers, a group of 200 Utopian scientists, painters, writers, and naturalists from France, Switzerland, and Belgium who came here in the 1850s. The Dallas of today boasts a nationally famous orchestra and opera—the **Dallas Symphony Orchestra** and the **Dallas Opera**—and one of the most prestigious schools in the South, **Southern Methodist University** (9,000 students). The recently opened **Museum of Art,** furthermore, is a remarkable achievement, and modern architecture rises proudly over the city, with works by I. M. Pei, Richard Keating, Frank Lloyd Wright, Philip Johnson, Martin Growald, and Edward Larrabee Barnes gracing the urban landscape.

Although the police force is regarded as quick on the draw, the Dallas–Fort Worth metropolitan area ranks fifth among the most dangerous cities in the country. John F. Kennedy was assassinated here on November 22, 1963, from the **Texas School Book Depository,** an undistinguished yellow-brick building now partly transformed into a museum, which continues to draw tens of thousands of the 35th president's admirers each year.

With more than 40,000 hotel rooms in town, 20% of them built in the last 10 years, there's rarely a problem finding somewhere to stay.

BASIC FACTS: State of Texas. Area codes: 214 (Dallas), 817 (Fort Worth). Time Zone: Central. ZIP Codes: 75221 (Dallas), 76101 (Fort Worth). Founded: 1841 (Dallas), 1849 (Fort Worth). Approximate population: city 990,000 (Dallas), 430,000 (Fort Worth); metropolitan area (Dallas and Fort Worth), 3,700,000. Eighth-largest metropolitan area in the country.

CLIMATE: The Dallas climate fits the popular image of Texas: harsh and extreme. Brutal downpours punctuate the exceptionally hot, even torrid, summer (mean July temperature: 86°F/30°C, with peaks of 104°F/40°C and higher), but air conditioning reigns supreme. Winter is generally mild but punctuated by unpredictable temperature plunges (sometimes from 60°F/15°C to freezing in 24 hrs.). Spring and autumn are interspersed with often-violent thunderstorms and rather spectacular dust storms.

DISTANCES: Albuquerque, 637 mi. (1,020km); Houston, 243 mi. (390km); Memphis, 450 mi. (720km); New Orleans, 493 mi. (790km); San Antonio, 270 mi. (432km).

ARRIVAL & TRANSIT INFORMATION

AIRPORTS: The **Dallas–Fort Worth International Airport** (DFW) is 13 mi. (21km) west of Dallas, 17 mi. (28km) east of Fort Worth. Ultramodern in conception, the Dallas–Fort Worth airport is the world's largest in surface area (16,800 acres/6,800ha)—as big as Manhattan. Fourth-busiest airport in the world with 42 million passengers a year. For information, call 214/574-6720.

Dallas's **Love Field** (DAL) is 7 mi. (12km) north, for commuter flights. For information, call 214/352-2663.

U.S. AIRLINES (Dallas telephone numbers unless otherwise indicated): American (214/267-1151 in Dallas, 817/267-1151 in Fort Worth), Continental (214/263-0523 in Dallas, 817/268-2300 in Fort Worth), Delta (214/630-3200 in Dallas, 817/336-8341 in Fort Worth), Midway (toll free 800/621-5700), Northwest (214/988-0405), Pan Am (toll free 800/221-1111), Southwest (214/640-1221 in Dallas, 817/640-1221 in Fort Worth), TWA (214/741-6741), and United (214/988-1004).

FOREIGN CARRIERS: Air Canada (toll free 800/422-6232), Air New Zealand (toll free 800/262-1234), British Airways (toll free 800/247-9297), and Lufthansa (toll free 800/645-3880).

CITY LINK: Cab fare **from Dallas–Fort Worth Airport to downtown Dallas,** about $25; time, 40 min. Bus for the same route: Super-Shuttle (817/329-2000); provides door-to-door service to any Dallas destination; leaves every 30 min.; fare, $8; time, about 45 min.

Cab fare from Dallas–Fort Worth Airport **to downtown Fort Worth,** about $24; time, 40 min. Bus for the same route: Airporter Bus Service (817/334-0092); runs on the half hour from the Airporter Terminal at 1000 Weatherford St. and dwntwn Fort Worth hotels to DFW Airport; fare, $7. Super-Shuttle (817/329-2000); provides door-to-door service to any Fort Worth destination, leaving every hour; fare, $8; time, about 40 min.

Service is by Super-Shuttle **from Love Field:** fare to dwntwn Dallas, $5; cab fare, $12.

The **bus system** is thoroughly deficient (in Dallas, DART, 214/979-1111; in Fort Worth, CITRAN, 817/870-6200), the taxis few and expensive. This plus the enormous size of the metropolitan area makes renting a car with unlimited mileage a good idea. The new **McKinney Avenue trolley** (214/220-0610) runs a 2.8-mi. (4.5km) route through dwntwn, the Arts District, and the McKinney Strip (McKinney Ave.); fare, 50¢.

CAR RENTAL (at Dallas–Fort Worth Airport unless otherwise indicated): Avis (214/574-4100); Budget (214/871-9500); Dollar, 4125 W. Airport Fwy. (214/256-4576); Hertz (214/453-0370); National (214/574-3400); Thrifty, 7700 Estero Blvd., Irving (214/929-1320).

LIMOUSINE SERVICES: Carey Limousine (214/484-4774), Scripps Edward Limousine (toll free 800/223-6710), and USA Limousine (214/680-2414).

TAXIS: You'll find taxis in waiting lines at the major hotels; they may not be hailed on the street. The best arrangement, however, is to phone: **Republic Taxi** (214/631-5544 in Dallas) or **Yellow Cab** (214/426-6262 in Dallas, 817/335-3333 in Fort Worth).

TRAIN: Amtrak has stations **in Dallas** (Union Station) at 400 S. Houston St. (214/653-1101) and **in Fort Worth** at 1501 Jones St. (817/332-2931).

INTERCITY BUSES: Greyhound, 205 S. Lamar St., Dallas (214/655-7084), or 901 Commerce St., Fort Worth (817/332-4564).

DALLAS

INFORMATION & TOURS

TOURIST INFORMATION: The **Dallas Convention & Visitors Bureau,** 1201 Elm St., TX 75270 (214/746-6677).

There is also an **information office** open daily at Union Station, 400 S. Houston St. (214/954-1111).

GUIDED TOURS: Gray Line Tours Dallas (bus) (214/824-2424): Guided tour of the city, serving major hotels.

SIGHTS, ATTRACTIONS & ACTIVITIES

ARCHITECTURAL HIGHLIGHTS: ⚜⚜ **City Hall,** Municipal Plaza (670-5680): Impressive, futurist building in the shape of an inverted pyramid, a work of I. M. Pei. There is a lovely Henry Moore sculpture on the entrance plaza. Open Mon–Fri.

⚜ **Dallas Market Center,** 2100 Stemmons Fwy. (655-6100): This group of ultramodern buildings (**Apparelmart, Dallas Trade Mart, Decorative Center District, Infomart, World Trade Center,** etc.) makes up the world's biggest wholesale market. Interesting modern sculptures dot the surrounding grdns (**Sculpture Garden).** Guided tours by appointment.

⚜ **Dallas Theater Center,** 3636 Turtle Creek Blvd. (526-8857): Two 460-seat halls and one of the country's most important theatrical companies. Daring cantilevered architecture by Frank Lloyd Wright. An absolute must-see.

DOWNTOWN DALLAS

☀☖ꔛ **First Interstate Bank Tower,** Fountain Pl.: Designed by Henry Cobb, a pupil of I. M. Pei, this huge, beveled-glass prism stands 60 stories high and commands the 200 fountains and the cypresses of Fountain Place, a recently opened business center in downtown's north end.

☀☖ **Infomart,** 1950 Stemmons Fwy. (746-3500): This modern replica by Martin Growald of London's famous 1851 Crystal Palace houses the country's most important permanent marketing exhibition for the data-processing industry. Part of the Dallas Market Center complex.

ꔛꔛ **Morton H. Meyerson Symphony Center,** 2301 Flora St. (692-0203): Only concert hall designed by I. M. Pei, this shoebox-shaped limestone building with audacious glass curves, soaring lobbies, and unusually high ceilings was inaugurated in Sept 1989 at a cost of $106 million. Dubbed "The Mort" by local residents, the 2,066-seat hall is acoustically perfect. A huge canopy of wood and onyx above the stage moves up and down to adjust the sound to the performers.

☀☖ **Southfork Ranch,** Parker Rd. at FM 2551, in Plano (214/442-6536): The Ewing family ranch in the renowned "Dallas" TV series has become a fashionable tourist attraction. Guided tours of the ranch during shooting breaks. Three million people have visited Southfork Ranch since the program premiered in 1978. 45 min. from dwntwn on I-75, Tex. 44, and FM 2551. Open daily.

☀☖ꔛ **Texas Commerce Tower,** 2200 Ross Ave. (922-2300): The most spectacular building in Dallas. Designed by Richard Keating, of Skidmore, Owings & Merrill, this 55-story skyscraper of glass and granite is among the most compelling towers to rise in this decade in the U.S. Crowned by a great arch bringing the building to a dramatic conclusion, the Texas Commerce Tower presents a vast "sky window"—75 ft. (22m) high, 27 ft. (8.25m) wide—that slices out the center of the 41st through the 49th floors. An absolute must-see.

☖ **Texas Stadium,** Tex. 183 at Loop 12, in Irving (214/438-7676): One of the country's football shrines (holds 65,000) and home to the famous Cowboys. Guided tours daily Apr–Oct.

HISTORIC BUILDINGS: ☖ **Hall of State,** in State Fair Park, Parry Ave. and Second Ave. (421-5136): A handsome art deco ensemble of huge wall murals, temporary exhibitions on the history of Texas, and memorabilia of famous Texas heroes. For those who enjoy the gigantic. Open daily.

☖ **John Neely Bryan Cabin,** Main St., Elm St., and Market St.: Log cabin built in 1841 by the city's founder, it was later used as a post office and then a courthouse. Standing in a stark downtown plaza, the cabin is supposed to mark the spot where the city was founded. It's not open to the public, but have a look at it anyway.

☖ **Southern Methodist University,** Hillcrest Ave. at University Park (692-2000): Founded in 1915, this is one of the Southwest's most famous universities (9,000 students). On the 164-acre (66ha) campus there are nearly 100 Georgian-style buildings, plus the **Owen Arts Center** (see "Museums of Art," below).

☖ **J.F.K Historical Exhibit,** 411 Elm St. (653-6666): According to the official version, Lee Harvey Oswald shot President Kennedy from the Texas School Book Depository Building, now the Dallas County Administration Building. The most photographed building in Dallas. The sixth floor of the old schoolbook building has been transformed into a $3.5-million exhibit pertinently named "The Sixth Floor" and featuring films, 400 photographs, artifacts, and interpretive displays on the cultural context of John F. Kennedy's death. The window area from which Oswald allegedly fired the fatal shots has been re-created as it was that day, but it is behind a wall of glass. Visitors can look out through immediately adjacent windows with almost the same view of the motorcade route and Dealy Plaza. Fascinating. Open daily.

MARKETS: ⚖ **Farmers Produce Market,** 1010 S. Pearl Expwy. (748-2082): Located in the southeast corner of downtown Dallas, the striped sheds of the Dallas Farmers' Market offers all the season's fresh fruits, vegetables, flowers, and plants from the surrounding area. Open sunrise to sunset 7 days a week. Noisy and colorful.

MONUMENTS: ☀⚖ **John F. Kennedy Memorial,** J.F.K. (formerly Dealy) Plaza, at Main St., Commerce St., and Market St.: Granite cenotaph by Philip Johnson, sober and austere, near the place where President Kennedy was assassinated. Kind of an open-air cube with 30-ft.-high (9m) walls.

MUSEUMS OF ART: ☀⚖⚖⚖ **Dallas Museum of Art,** 1717 N. Harwood St. (922-0220): The most recent (1984) of the large Texas museums houses pre-Columbian art, great European masters (Cézanne, Gauguin, Monet, Pissarro, van Gogh), modern American painting (notably Jackson Pollock), as well as rich collections of African art. Don't miss the extraordinary giant sculpture by Claes Oldenburg, *Stake Hitch.* All this is housed in a splendid modern building by Edward Larrabee Barnes. Lovely grdns with waterfalls, shaded groves, and an uninterrupted view of the Dallas skyline. An absolute must-see. Open Tues–Sun.

⚖ **Owen Arts Center,** Hillcrest Ave. (692-2614): This huge arts complex on the Southern Methodist University campus includes the **Bob Hope Theatre** (built with a donation from the famous comedian, but Shakespeare is the playwright of choice here); the **Meadows Museum,** dedicated to classical Spanish painting and also offering temporary exhibitions; and a very fine modern-sculpture grdn. An absolute must-see. Open Tues–Sun.

MUSEUMS OF SCIENCE & HISTORY: ⚖ **Age of Steam Railroad Museum,** 7226 Wentwood Dr., Fair Park (239-1676): Superb collection of old steam locomotives. Open Thurs–Sun, daily during the State Fair.

⚖ **Biblical Arts Center,** 7500 Park Lane (691-4661): A surprising spectacle which includes a 124- by 20-ft. (38- by 6m) painting of the miracle of Pentecost with a sound-and-light show plus a replica of Christ's tomb. Open Tues–Sun.

⚖ **Dallas Museum of Natural History,** Second Ave. and Grand Ave., Fair Park (421-2169): This neoclassical building is a museum of southwestern and Texas natural history. More than 50 facsimiles of natural habitats plus rich zoological and botanical collections, including a 90-million-year-old fossil fish. An absolute must-see. Open daily.

⚖ **Kennedy Historical Exhibit,** "The Sixth Floor": In the Texas School Book Depository (see "Historic Buildings," above).

☀⚖ **Old City Park,** Gano St. and Harwood St. (421-5141): Authentic 19th-century Texas town restored in minutest detail, with a train station, booths, church, bank, school, etc. There are 40-some original buildings in all, from all over Texas. Open Tues–Sun.

⚖ **The Science Place,** First Ave. and Martin Luther King, Jr., Blvd., Fair Park (428-8351): Remarkably conceived exhibits on science, energy, and ecology. History of anatomy depicted on transparent human bodies; a planetarium too. Open daily.

OUTDOOR ART & PLAZAS: Apart from the **Sculpture Garden** in the middle of Dallas Market Center (see "Architectural Highlights," above), **City Hall** offers two interesting modern sculptures: Henry Moore's *The Dallas Piece,* three bronze blocks weighing 13 tons; and two "floating" sculptures by Marta Pan on an ornamental lake.

PANORAMAS: ⚖⚖ **Reunion Tower,** 300 Reunion Blvd. (741-3663): This 50-story tower capped with a geodesic dome where computer-operated lights dance at night is the new symbol of Dallas. Observation deck at the top. Open daily until midnight.

PARKS & GARDENS: ⚿ Civic Garden Center, First Ave. and Martin Luther King, Jr., Blvd., in State Fair Park: Lovely botanic garden with rose grdns and a tropical hothouse. Open daily.

⚿ **Dallas Aquarium,** First Ave. and Martin Luther King, Jr., Blvd., in State Fair Park (670-8441): This modest-sized (and hence, perhaps, un-Texan) aquarium is one of the most modern and complete in the Southwest, with 350 species of fish, reptiles, and amphibians. Open daily.

⚿ **L. B. Houston Park,** Wildwood Dr.: Kind of miniature nature reservation (20 min. from dwntwn on the Stemmons Fwy.) with gray fox, wild rabbit, beaver, raccoon, and first-growth timber from a vast forest that was almost completely cleared at the turn of the century. One of the few green areas in Dallas.

☀⚿ **State Fair Park,** Parry Ave. and Second Ave. (565-9931): Immense, 240-acre (97ha) fairground with fountains, ponds, floral exhibitions, an aquarium, and numerous museums (see above), as well as the famous **Cotton Bowl Stadium,** where the Cotton Bowl is played each Jan 1. In Oct it is the site of the **Texas State Fair,** which attracts three million visitors annually.

⚿ **Thanks-Giving Square,** bounded by Bryan St., Ervay St., and Pacific Ave.: A green oasis built below street level in the heart of the city with an unusual spiral chapel and meditation grdn designed by Philip Johnson, a striking contrast to neighboring skyscrapers.

PERFORMING ARTS: For a daily listing of all shows and cultural events, consult the entertainment pages of the daily papers *Dallas Morning News* (morning) and *Dallas Times Herald* (evening), and of the monthly magazine *D*.

Bob Hope Theatre, Owen Arts Center, Hillcrest Ave. (692-2573): Modern and classical theater on the Southern Methodist University campus.

Dallas Repertory Theatre, 1030 N. Park Center (369-8966): Classical theater, drama, comedy.

Dallas Theater Center, 3636 Turtle Creek Blvd. (526-8857): From Shakespeare to contemporary theater, Sept–May. Daring Frank Lloyd Wright architecture.

Majestic Theatre, 1925 Elm St. (880-0137): Theater, recitals, and a variety of performances in a splendid, recently restored building.

Morton H. Meyerson Symphony Center, 2301 Flora St. (692-0203): The Dallas Symphony Orchestra, with music director Eduardo Mata, in its new and spectacular home (Sept–May). Also big-name recitals of both classic and pop music.

Music Hall, First Ave. and Parry Ave., in State Fair Park (565-1116): Home of the Dallas Opera (director: Nicola Rescigno) (Nov–Dec) and the Dallas Ballet. Also offers Broadway hits (June–Aug).

New Arts Theatre, 301 N. Market St. at Ross (761-9064): Contemporary theater.

Theatre Three, 2800 Routh St. (871-3300): Drama, comedy.

RODEOS: ⚿ Kow Bell Indoor Rodeo, U.S. 287 in Mansfield (15 mi./24km SW on I-20 and Tex. 157) (817/477-3092): The only rodeo in the country open year round, with events each Fri at 8:30pm (plus Sat at 8pm June to late Aug). In an authentic breeding ranch that offers horseback riding daily. Don't miss it.

⚿⚿ **Mesquite Rodeo,** I-635 at Military Pkwy. in Mesquite (13 mi./21km west on Tex. 352) (214/285-8777): Rodeos 8:30pm Fri–Sat Apr–Sept. Experts consider this the most demanding, most violent rodeo challenge in all Texas. Guaranteed local color. 15 min. from dwntwn.

SHOPPING: **The Galleria,** L.B.J. Fwy. and Dallas Pkwy.: A monument of modern shopping that has been often copied, never matched. More than 200 luxury boutiques (Cartier, Tiffany, Charles Jourdan, etc.), stores, theaters, restaurants, and even a skating rink, all in air-conditioned comfort (*de rigueur* in Texas) under an enormous glass dome. Not to be missed. 15 min. from dwntwn.
   Luskey's, Forest Lane and Webb Chapel Rd.: Texas riding boots and all the necessary equipment for a real (or pretend) cowboy.
   Neiman-Marcus, Main St. and Ervay St.: The most chic, most expensive department store in the country. You can find anything at Neiman-Marcus, even the most imagination-defying gift ideas. Those with thin billfolds are advised to stay away.
   Resistol Hat Shop, 1505 Main St.: One of the largest assortments of cowboy hats in all Texas (no small claim, that).
   Wild Bill's, 1616A Commerce St.: The "Official Dallas Western Store" where you can get Wrangler jeans, cowboy boots, and Stetson hats. Across from Neiman-Marcus.

SPECIAL EVENTS: For the exact schedule of events below, consult the **Dallas Convention & Visitors Bureau** (see "Tourist Information," above).
   Cotton Bowl Festival (Jan 1): 8 days of festivities culminating in the famous football game. A classic since 1956.
   Texas State Fair (Oct): Shows, rodeos, sporting and special events—this animated fair attracts three million visitors each year. An absolute must-see.
   Texas–O.U. Weekend (Oct): Spectacular annual confrontation between the University of Texas and Oklahoma University football teams. An autumn ritual for the last 60 years.

SPORTS: Dallas has three professional teams:
   Baseball (Apr–Oct): Texas Rangers, Arlington Stadium (817/273-5222).
   Basketball (Oct–Apr): Dallas Mavericks, Reunion Arena (214/658-7068).
   Football (Sept–Dec): Dallas Cowboys, Texas Stadium (214/556-2500).

THEME PARKS: ⚐ **International Wildlife Park,** I-30 at Wild Life Pkwy., Grand Prairie (214/263-2201): Drive your car through this vast zoo-safari and see wild animals (including African wildlife) in their natural habitat. Open daily year round.
   ☼⚐ **Six Flags Over Texas,** I-30 and Tex. 360, Arlington (817/640-8900): Huge, "Texas style" amusement park (192 acres/78ha) with more than 100 different attractions including a giant roller coaster. Events, performances, etc. Open daily from the end of May to early Sept, wknds only in spring and autumn; closed the rest of the year.

ZOOS: The ⚐ **Dallas Zoo,** 621 E. Clarendon Dr. (946-5154): One of the most comprehensive zoos in the United States, with 2,000 animals on 48 acres (19.5ha). Open daily.

ACCOMMODATIONS
   A Note on Accommodations: Room rates in Dallas are coded as follows: **VE,** Very Expensive ($140 and up); **E,** Expensive ($90–$140); **M,** Moderate ($60–$90); **I,** Inexpensive ($30–$60); **B,** Budget (up to $30). A listing of toll free numbers is in the Appendix.

Personal Favorites (in order of preference)
   ☼ ♦♦♦♦ **The Mansion on Turtle Creek** (nr. dwntwn), 2821 Turtle Creek Blvd., TX 75219 (214/559-2100; toll free, see Preferred). 145 rms, A/C, cable color TV. AE, CB, DC, MC, V. Valet parking $9, pool, rest. (Mansion on Turtle Creek Restaurant), coffee shop, bar, 24-hr. rm

svce, nightclub, concierge, free crib. *Note:* Elegant Moorish-style manor house dating from the 1920s built on the grounds of a former oilman's 5-acre (2ha) terraced estate. Lovely period furniture w. pastel decor and flowers everywhere. Ultra-comfortable rms w. balconies or private patios. Correct, attentive svce. First-rate rest. A big favorite of businesspeople and celebrities. One of the great achievements of modern American hoteldom, owned by the wealthy Hunt family of Texas. **VE**

Hyatt Regency (dwntwn), 300 Reunion Blvd., TX 75207 (214/651-1234; toll free, see Hyatt). 940 rms, A/C, color TV, in-rm movies. AE, CB, DC, MC, V. Valet gar. $8, pool, two tennis courts, health club, sauna, two rests. (including Fausto's), coffee shop, three bars, 24-hr. rm svce, disco, free crib. *Note:* This illustrious grand hotel displays a 27-story, blue-tinted glass facade that reflects neighboring skyscrapers. Waterfall and interior grdns in the 19-story lobby. Unparalleled facilities and comfort plus an extraordinary view from the revolving rest. at the top (Antares), although the cuisine is mediocre. Very efficient svce. Quite close to the business district. Interesting wknd packages. VIP floor. Has undergone a $25-million facelift. **VE**

Plaza of the Americas (dwntwn), 650 N. Pearl Blvd., TX 75201 (214/979-9000; toll free 800/225-5843). 442 rms, A/C, color TV, in-rm movies. AE, CB, DC, MC, V. Valet gar. $10, health club, sauna, three rests. (including Café Royal), two bars, 24-hr. rm svce, nightclub, hrdrsr, boutiques, concierge, free crib. *Note:* Some of the most spectacular luxury-hotel architecture in Texas, w. an immense 15-story plant-filled atrium w. glass elevators overlooking a skating rink. Vast, luxurious rms w. balconies and modern, elegant decor. Very good svce and a renowned rest. Big business clientele. Part of the British group Trusthouse Forte, which owns the Travelodge chain. Very central location. **VE**

Stouffer (nr. dwntwn), 2222 Stemmons Frwy., TX 75207 (214/631-2222; toll free, see Stouffer). 542 rms, A/C, color TV, in-rm movies. AE, CB, DC, MC, V. Free parking, pool, health club, sauna, rest. (Bay Tree), coffee shop, two bars, rm svce, nightclub, free crib. *Note:* Right in the famous Dallas Market Center, this huge elliptical 30-story tower of pink granite makes up in originality for what it lacks in elegance. Up-to-the-minute comfort and facilities; spacious, well-planned rms. Many works of art and enormous three-story-high light fixture in lobby. Efficient reception and svce. Business clientele. Well located 5 min. from dwntwn and 20 min. from Dallas–Fort Worth Airport. Worthwhile wknd packages. **E–VE**

Stoneleigh Hotel (nr. dwntwn), 2927 Maple Ave., Tx 75201 (214/871-7111; toll free 800/447-9559). 155 rms, A/C, color TV. AE, CB, DC, MC, V. Free parking, pool, tennis, rest. (Ewald's), 24 hr. rm svce, concierge, free crib. *Note:* Oldish but comfortable hotel surrounded by ten acres of gardens, close to dwntwn. A favorite of show-business people. Spacious rms, some w. kitchenettes. Attentive svce. Good value overall. **E**

Best Western Market Center (nr. dwntwn), 2023 Market Center Blvd., TX 75207 (214/741-5041; toll free, see Best Western). 96 rms, A/C, color TV, in-rm movies. AE, CB, DC, MC, V. Free parking, pool, rest., two bars, crib $4. *Note:* Conventional but comfortable motel quite close to the Market Center. Direct access to the highway network. Good-natured reception and svce. This very good value is ideal for the car traveler—8 min. from dwntwn and 10 min. from Love Field. **I**

Days Inn Texas Stadium (vic.), 2200 E. Airport Fwy., TX 75062 (214/438-6666; toll free, see Days Inns). 178 rms, A/C, color TV, free in-rm movies. AE, CB, DC, MC, V. Free parking, pool, 24-hr. coffee shop adj., valet svce, free crib. *Note:* Typical highway motel across from Texas Stadium. Rms have refrigerators. Serviceable comforts; ideal if you're driving through. 15 min. from dwntwn. **I**

Motel 6 North (nr. dwntwn), 2753 Forest Lane, TX 75234 (214/620-2828). 100 rms, A/C, color TV, free in-rm movies.

AE, DC, MC, V. Parking, pool, free crib. *Note:* Modern, ultra-economical motel located 15 min. from dwntwn and 5 min. from the Galleria Shopping Mall. One of the best values in the area. Easy access to the highways makes it ideal for the car traveler. **B**

Other Accommodations (from top bracket to budget)

Fairmont (dwntwn), 1717 N. Akard St., TX 75201 (214/720-2020; toll free, see Fairmont). 600 rms, A/C, color TV, in-rm movies. AE, CB, DC, MC, V. Valet gar. $9, pool, health club, two rests. (including the Pyramid Room), 24-hr. coffee shop, bars, 24-hr. rm svce, disco, hrdrsr, boutiques, free crib. *Note:* "The" chic palace of Dallas (the most expensive suite costs more than $1,500 a night). Two modern towers w. elegant, luxurious interior decoration and spacious, very comfortable rms. Svce is of the highest caliber in an opulent, tasteful atmosphere. Excellent rest. Wealthy Texan and big business clientele. No-smoking floor. In the heart of dwntwn. Recently renovated. **VE**

The Adolphus (dwntwn), 1321 Commerce St., TX 75202 (214/742-8200; toll free 800/221-9083). 430 rms, A/C, cable color TV. AE, CB, DC, MC, V. Valet parking $9, health club, sauna, three rests. (including the French Rm), bar, piano bar, 24-hr. rm svce, hrdrsr, boutiques, concierge, free crib. *Note:* A venerable palace, engagingly sumptuous, built in 1912 by beer magnate Adolphus Busch, and a historical landmark for its original rococo architecture. Inside are very lovely 17th-century Flemish tapestries and spacious, elegant rms w. Chippendale furniture and minibars (some have a private patio). Good svce and a very good rest. (The French Rm). This celebrated locale in the heart of dwntwn Dallas hosts luminaries from all over the world. Has undergone $60 million worth of renovation. A favorite of connoisseurs. **VE**

Crescent Court Hotel (nr. dwntwn), 400 Crescent Court, TX 75201 (214/871-3200; toll free, see Preferred). 218 rms, A/C, cable color TV. AE, CB, DC, MC, V. Valet gar. $9, pool, health club, sauna, rest. (Beau Nash), coffee shop, bar, 24-hr. rm svce, disco, boutiques, concierge, free crib. *Note:* This new palace hotel designed by Philip Johnson is part Versailles, part Walt Disney World. But if the exterior provokes a bit of a giggle, the interior decoration is a masterpiece of classic elegance, w. numerous works of art and stylish furnishings. Vast, luxurious rms w. marble bathrooms, and each suite decorated in a different style. Exemplary svce and a rest. that is full of businesspeople at lunchtime. Free shuttle to and from dwntwn. An integral part of the vast Crescent Court commercial and office complex. **VE**

Loews Anatole (nr. dwntwn), 2201 Stemmons Fwy., TX 75207 (214/748-1200; toll free, see Loews). 1,600 rms, A/C, color TV, in-rm movies. AE, CB, DC, MC, V. Valet parking $6, three pools, six tennis courts, putting green, health club, sauna, eight rests. (including The Plum Blossom), 24-hr. coffee shop, eight bars, disco, rm svce, hrdrsr, boutiques, concierge. *Note:* A veritable city-within-a-city, the Anatole is the largest hotel in Dallas. The ultramodern interior (the exterior of this 27-floor reddish monolith is somewhat reminiscent of a prison) includes a superb 14-story grdn-lobby and very comfortable rms. Specializing in groups and convention clientele, this enormous futurist hotel is also a favorite of businesspeople. Good svce and very complete recreational facilities w. a hot spring. Three VIP floors. 7 acres (3ha) of grdns w. ponds, fountains, and groves, all facing the Dallas Market Center. Interesting wknd deals. **E–VE**

Westin Galleria (vic.), 13340 Dallas Pkwy., TX 75240 (214/934-9494; toll free, see Westin). 440 rms, A/C, cable color TV. AE, CB, DC, MC, V. Valet parking $6, pool, health club, sauna, two rests. (including the Huntington Grill), coffee shop, bar, 24-hr. rm svce, nightclub, hrdrsr, boutiques, free crib. *Note:* Modern, 21-story grand hotel in the famous Galleria Mall Shopping Center and its 200 stores and shops. The architecture lacks imagination, but the comfort and facilities are remarkable. All rms have balconies and refrigerators. Very efficient svce. Business and group clientele. No-smoking floors. 20 min. from dwntwn. **E–VE**

Sheraton Dallas (dwntwn), 400 N. Olive St., TX 75201 (214/922-8000; toll free, see Sheraton). 498 rms, A/C, color TV, in-rm movies. AE, CB, DC, MC, V. Valet gar. $12, health club, two rests., coffee shop, two bars, 24-hr. rm svce, nightclub, boutiques. *Note:* Modern, 30-story tower w. four VIP floors. Spacious, comfortable rms and relatively efficient svce. Entirely renovated decor and facilities. Obtrusive group clientele. No recreational facilities. In the heart of Dallas. **E–VE**

Omni Melrose (nr. dwntwn), 3015 Oak Lawn, TX 75219 (214/521-5151; toll free, see Omni). 185 rms, A/C, color TV, in-rm movies. AE, CB, DC, MC, V. Free parking, rest. (Landmark Café), bar, rm svce, disco, library, concierge, free crib. *Note:* Charming 1920s hotel, entirely renovated to the tune of $12 million. Elegant art deco decor; rms on the small side, but comfortable (some w. refrigerators). Attentive svce. Business clientele. VIP floor. Offering a free shuttle to and from Love Field, it is also close to the Dallas Theater Center. **E**

Summit Hotel (vic.), 2645 LBJ Fwy., TX 75234 (214/243-3363; toll free 800/226-3555), at Josey Lake. 376 rms, A/C, color TV, in-rm movies. AE, CB, DC, MC, V. Free parking, pool, sauna, rest. (Gabriel's), coffee shop, bar, rm svce, disco, hrdrsr, boutiques, concierges, free crib. *Note:* Large convention and package-tour motel on the northern outskirts of Dallas, housed in a drably functional modern building. Inviting, comfortable rms w. balcony (some w. refrigerator). Flawless svce. 15 min. from Dallas–Fort Worth Airport and 20 min. from Dallas's Love Field (free shuttle service to both). Interesting wknd packages. Good value. **M–E**

Aristocrat Clarion (dwntwn), 1933 Main St., TX 75201 (214/741-7700; toll free 800/252-7466). 172 suites, A/C, cable color TV. AE, CB, DC, MC, V. Free parking, rest., bar, rm svce, free breakfast, free crib. *Note:* A venerable Conrad Hilton palace built in 1925, now a historical landmark. It was carefully restored in 1985 in all its antique splendor. Offers only spacious, comfortable mini-suites (w. refrigerators). Attentive, personalized svce. A good overall value in the heart of the business district. Very adequate rest. **M–E**

Holiday Inn Downtown (dwntwn), 1015 Elm St., TX 75202 (214/748-9951; toll free, see Holiday Inns). 306 rms, A/C, color TV, in-rm movies. AE, CB, DC, MC, V. Parking $7, pool, rest., bar, rm svce, free crib. *Note:* Functional Holiday Inn accommodations in a modern 19-story tower in the heart of Dallas. Rather spacious rms w. balconies and very mediocre svce. Business and group clientele. Close to the Medical Center. **M–E**

Quality Inn Market Center (nr. dwntwn), 2015 N. Market Center Blvd., TX 75207 (214/741-7481; toll free, see Quality Inns). 280 rms, A/C, color TV, in-rm movies. AE, CB, DC, MC, V. Free parking, pool, health club, rest., coffee shop, bar, rm svce, free crib. *Note:* Modern 11-story motel offering easy access to Market Center, comfortable rms w. balconies or private patios, and friendly reception and svce. Business clientele. VIP floor. Very good value. 8 min. from dwntwn and 10 min. from Love Field (free shuttle). **I–M**

Non-Smokers Inn (nr. dwntwn), 9229 Carpenter Frwy., TX 75247 (214/631-6633; toll free 800/253-7377). 135 rms, A/C, cable color TV. AE, MC, V. Free parking, pool, sauna, health club, cafe adj., valet svce, crib $4. *Note:* Well-maintained motel 15 min. from dwntwn on Carpenter Frwy (Tx 183). Totally non-smoking. Inviting rms; some w. refrigerators. Close to the Texas Stadium. Very good value. **I**

Park Cities Inn (nr. dwntwn), 6101 Hillcrest Ave., TX 75205 (214/521-0330). 53 rms, A/C, color TV, in-rm movies. AE,

CB, DC, MC, V. Free parking, nearby coffee shop, free breakfast, free crib. *Note:* Small, modest motel across from Southern Methodist University. Satisfactory comfort and facilities. Some rms w. refrigerators. 10 min. from dwntwn. **I–M**

♀ **La Quinta Inn–Central** (nr. dwntwn), 4440 N. Central Expwy., TX 75206 (214/821-4220; toll free, see La Quinta). 101 rms, A/C, color TV, in-rm movies. AE, CB, DC, MC, V. Free parking, adjacent 24-hr. coffee shop, free crib. *Note:* A good value, 15 min. from dwntwn and close to Love Field. Spacious, comfortable (but rather dark) rms w. balconies; friendly reception and svce. Ideal for the car traveler. **I**

Accommodations in the Vicinity

♀♀♀♀ **Marriott Mandalay** (formerly Four Seasons; vic.), 221 E. Las Colinas Blvd., Irving, TX 75039 (214/556-0800; toll free, see Marriott). 424 rms, A/C, color TV, in-rm movies. AE, CB, DC, MC, V. Free valet parking, pool, tennis, health club, sauna, two rests. (including Enjolie), coffee shop, three bars, nightclub, rm svce, free crib. *Note:* An impressive 27-story white tower on the lake at Las Colinas, an enormous apartment complex known as Little Venice because of its canals and water taxis. Ultramodern facilities and comfort. Luxurious rms w. balconies and a spectacular view (the best overlook the lake). Efficient svce and a first-rate rest. Group and wealthy conventioneer clientele. Two VIP floors. 10 min. from dwntwn and 10 min. from Dallas–Fort Worth Airport. **E–VE**

Airport Accommodations

♀♀♀ **Hyatt Regency Airport** (formerly the Amfac; vic.), Dallas–Fort Worth Airport, TX 75261 (214/453-1234; toll free, see Hyatt). 1,388 rms, A/C, color TV, in-rm movies. AE, CB, DC, MC, V. Free parking, pool, eight tennis courts, two golf courses, putting green, health club, sauna, four rests., 24-hr. coffee shop, three bars, rm svce, disco, boutiques, free 24-hr. airport shuttle. *Note:* This ultramodern hotel in the midst of the airport itself is the largest airport hotel in the world. Irreproachable comfort and efficient svce. Well-soundproofed rms, most w. refrigerators. Rather intrusive business, group, and convention clientele. Interesting wknd packages. Good recreational equipment. Two VIP floors. Recently totally renovated. **E–VE**

♀ **La Quinta Inn DFW–Airport East** (vic.), 4105 W. Airport Fwy., Irving, TX 75062 (214/252-6546; toll free, see La Quinta). 168 rms, A/C, color TV, in-rm movies. AE, CB, DC, MC, V. Parking, pool, adj. 24-hr. coffee shop, free crib. *Note:* Modern, functional motel w. huge, comfortable rms and efficient svce. A very good value, 5 min. from the Dallas–Fort Worth Airport (free shuttle). **I**

RESTAURANTS

A Note on Restaurant Prices: Dallas restaurant prices, per person, excluding drinks and service charges, are coded as follows: **VE,** Very Expensive ($60 and up); **E,** Expensive ($40–$60); **M,** Moderate ($25–$40); **I,** Inexpensive ($15–$25); **B,** Budget (up to $15).

Personal Favorites (in order of preference)

♀♀♀♀♀ **Routh Street Café** (nr. dwntwn), 3005 Routh St. at Cedar Springs Rd. (871-7161). A/C. Dinner only, Tues–Sat; closed Sun, Mon, hols. AE, CB, DC, MC, V. Jkt. *Specialties:* The American nouvelle cuisine menu changes daily but may include Texas venison w. cranberry-chipotle sauce; grilled loin of lamb w. garlic custard, pasilla chiles, and Mexican oregano; blue-cornmeal catfish w. smoked bell-pepper sauce and jicoma-melon relish; chocolate-nut cake w. tropical fruit. A fine list of American wines at reasonable prices. *Note:* The young chef, Stephan Pyles, is one of the most gifted cooks of his generation; his cuisine, based on regional food and wood-fire cooking, is a marvel of balance and invention. Luxurious art deco decor in shades of peach-pink and gray. Ultra-professional svce. One of the 12 best rests. in the country, and a favorite of local yuppies. Resv. a must. *American*. **E** (prix fixe).

♆♆♆♆ **The French Room** (dwntwn), in the Adolphus (see "Accommodations," above) (742-8200). A/C. Dinner only, Mon–Sat. AE, CB, DC, MC, V. J&T. *Specialties:* red snapper w. watercress sauce, Dover sole w. cucumber and caviar, smoked-salmon salad, goose liver in aspic and brioche, veal medallion w. chives, stuffed breast of capon, sherbet plate, and praline mousse. The menu changes regularly. *Note:* Has stripped the "Dallas's most ostentatious and most romantic dining rm" title from the Fairmont Hotel's Pyramid Rm. The cuisine—a remarkable updating of classic French recipes—is supervised by Jean Banchet, longtime owner of the illustrious Le Français rest. in Wheeling, Ill. Opulent baroque decor w. crystal chandeliers, cherubim on the ceiling, and Louis XVI furniture. The svce is of rare distinction. Resv. a definite must. Valet parking. *French*. **E**

♆♆ **Actuelle** (nr. dwntwn), 2800 Routh St. in the Quadrangle (855-0440). A/C. Lunch Mon–Fri, dinner Mon–Sat; closed hols. AE, MC, V. Jkt. *Specialties:* breast of pheasant w. wild-mushroom strudel, grilled Angus tenderloin w. Madras curry sauce, mahi-mahi w. macadamia-nut butter. The menu changes seasonally. Interesting wine list. *Note:* The quiet, dignified modern setting of this new entrant for top culinary honors makes it a good choice for an important business dinner. The cuisine of European-trained chef Victor Gielisse has a Continental flavor while still emphasizing regional ingredients. Warm and attentive svce. Resv. strongly recommended; book at least a day or two ahead. *American*. **E**

♆♆ **Café Pacific** (nr. dwntwn), 24 Highland Park Village, Preston Rd. and Mockingbird Lane (526-1170). A/C. Lunch/dinner daily; closed hols. AE, DC, MC, V. Jkt. *Specialties:* clam chowder, fried clams, fresh grilled salmon, sautéed seafood, catch of the day. Complete wine list at appropriate prices. *Note:* Irreproachably fresh seafood makes this elegant rest. a favorite of connoisseurs. Modern, inviting decor of woodwork, polished brass, mirrors, and a wealth of plants. Attentive svce. Resv. advised, but the waits are sometimes long. An excellent place. *Seafood/American*. **I–M**

♆♆ **Mario's** (nr. dwntwn), 135 Turtle Creek Village Shopping Center, Oaklawn Ave. at Blackburn (521-1135). A/C. Dinner only, nightly; closed hols. AE, CB, DC, MC, V. Jkt. *Specialties:* fresh homemade pasta (including spinach lasagne, fettuccine), scaloppine al marsala, fish of the day, meats. Rather short wine list. *Note:* A fashionable, Italian-inspired rest. that also offers very fine red meat (a Texas necessity). Elegant ambience, and decor that includes a magnificent collection of Chinese porcelain and Venetian crystal. Exemplary svce. Resv. necessary. Valet parking. *Italian/Continental*. **I–M**

☼♆ **Mario's Chiquita** (nr. dwntwn), 4514 Travis St. (521-0721). A/C. Lunch/dinner Mon–Sat; closed Jan 1, Thanksgiving, Dec 25. AE, MC, V. *Specialties:* tacos al carbon, chile relleño, carne asada, mole poblano. *Note:* The most authentic of the countless Mexican rests. in Dallas, w. a pleasant atmosphere and vibrant, colorful decor. Efficient svce. Locally very popular. No resv. Other location: 221 W. Parker Rd., Plano (423-2977). *Mexican*. **B–I**

☼♆ **Sonny Bryan's** (nr. dwntwn), 2202 Inwood Rd. (357-7120). A/C. Breakfast/lunch daily (until 5pm). No credit cards. *Specialties:* barbecue, ham, pork chops, and beef. Beer but no wine. *Note:* A contender, w. Dickey's Barbecue (see below), for the "Best Barbecue in Dallas" award. Cooked over hickory-wood fires and smothered in an inimitable sauce, Sonny's barbecue has inspired a cult following. Shabby decor and nonexistent svce. Close to the Medical Center. An authentic local legend for nearly 30 years. No resv. *American*. **B**

♆ **Dickey's Barbecue** (nr. dwntwn), 4610 N. Central Expwy. (822-0240). A/C. Lunch/dinner Mon–Sat. No credit cards. *Specialties:* pork chops, barbecued beef, and sausage. *Note:* This local institution offers one of the finest opportunities to sample truly authentic Texas cuisine at ludicrously low prices. No-frills decor and svce. Consult the phone directory for other locations around Dallas. *American.* **B**

Other Restaurants (from top bracket to budget)

☀☆☼ 🍷🍷🍷 **Mansion on Turtle Creek** (nr. dwntwn), in the Mansion on Turtle Creek (see "Accommodations," above) (526-2121). A/C. Lunch/dinner daily, brunch Sat–Sun; closed Dec 25. AE, CB, DC, MC, V. J&T. *Specialties:* barbecued oyster salad, Texas lentil and lamb-sausage soup, sirloin steak w. pesto and smoked bacon, lobster tails, crème brûlée. The menu changes regularly. Extensive wine list. *Note:* Chef Dean Fearing's ultra-sophisticated cuisine combines French culinary finesse w. lively Tex-Mex flavors. Super-chic, Hispanic-Texan decor. Very correct svce. A favorite of local celebrities and high-rolling businesspeople. Resv. advised. Valet parking. *American/ Continental.* **M–E**

🍷🍷🍷 **The Riviera** (nr. dwntwn), 7709 Inwood Rd. (351-0094). A/C. Dinner only, daily; closed hols. AE, CB, DC, MC, V. J&T. *Specialties:* snails and tortellini w. spinach, fettuccine w. smoked chicken and wild mushrooms, blue-crab ravioli, rosemary-stuffed quail w. Gorgonzola-cheese polenta, grilled steak w. herbs Provençal, veal chop w. mustard, sole meunière, lemon tart, orange crème brûlée. Good wine list, mostly Californian. *Note:* Lori and David Holben, two young chefs who came here from the Café Royal in the Plaza of the Americas Hotel, deftly apply a blend of French and Italian techniques to upscale Texas produce—particularly fresh vegetables, game and fish. Pretty, flower-filled country-Provençal decor appropriate to the name; warm, attentive svce. Locally very popular; resv. a must. Valet parking. *Italian/ Continental.* **M–E**

🍷🍷🍷 **The Plum Blossom** (nr. dwntwn), in the Loews Anatole (see "Accommodations," above) (748-1200). A/C. Dinner only, Mon–Sat. AE, CB, DC, MC, V. Jkt. *Specialties:* lobster and shrimp Ying Yang, Mongolian pot-au-feu, Peking duck, coquille St-Jacques w. oyster sauce, fried ice cream. *Note:* Chinese cuisine that is as remarkable as the decor—a 6-ft.-high (5.5m) bronze Buddha sits regally amid the diners. Very good svce. Resv. a must. An experience that should not be missed. Valet parking. *Chinese.* **M**

🍷🍷 **Baby Routh** (nr. dwntwn), 2708 Routh St. (871-2345). A/C. Lunch/dinner daily, brunch Sun; closed hols. AE, CB, DC, MC, V. *Specialties:* black-bean and goat-cheese crêpes, smoked corn chowder w. green-vegetable cream, barbecue, fried chicken w. honey and spices, banana-rum cake, crème brûlée w. pumpkin and ginger. *Note:* The more rustic, less snobby offshoot of the famous Routh Street Café (see above) offers inventive modern cuisine from the talented Amy Ferguson. Spotlessly white, elegant decor w. a lovely patio. An "in" place. Resv. advised. *American.* **I–M**

☀☆ 🍷🍷 **Dakota's** (dwntwn), 600 N. Akard St. (740-4001). A/C. Lunch Mon–Fri, dinner nightly, brunch Sun; closed hols. AE, CB, DC, MC, V. *Specialties:* homemade pasta, blackened red snapper, mesquite-grilled steaks, game dishes. *Note:* With its marble walls, its cascading waterfall, and its elegant patio, all below ground level, this rest. draws Dallas's own VIPs as well as visiting celebrities. Good selection of grills, mainly steaks, chops, and seafood. Service is first-rate. Resv. advised. Valet parking. *American.* **I–M**

🍷🍷 **Newport's** (dwntwn), 703 McKinney (954-0509). A/C. Lunch Mon–Fri, dinner nightly, brunch Sun; closed hols. AE, MC, V. *Specialties:* raw oysters, ceviche, mesquite-grilled seafood, fresh salmon and swordfish, toothsome cheesecake. *Note:* Another well-established favorite for business lunches and dinners. Located in a converted turn-of-the-century brewery, Newport's is one of the neatest rustic rests. in town. The atmosphere is relaxing, the fish superb. Pleasant svce. Resv. recommended. *Seafood.* **I–M**

🍷🍷 **Royal Tokyo** (vic.), 7525 Greenville Ave. (368-3304). A/C. Lunch Mon–Fri, dinner nightly, brunch Sun; closed hols. AE,

CB, DC, MC, V. Jkt. *Specialties:* sushi, tempura, sukiyaki, teppanyaki, shabu shabu. *Note:* The experts agree that this is the best Japanese rest. in Dallas. Elegant Japanese decor w. a lovely water grdn. Very good svce. An excellent locale, 20 min. from dwntwn. Valet parking. *Japanese.* **I–M**

🍷🍷 **Raphael's** (nr. dwntwn), 3701 McKinney Ave. (521-9640). A/C. Lunch/dinner Mon–Sat; closed hols. and two weeks in June. AE, CB, DC, MC, V. *Specialties:* chile relleño, chicken mole, enchiladas, tamales, fajitas. *Note:* An old Dallas classic, w. vaguely Aztec decor and a warm, "ranchera" atmosphere. Very popular among local fans of authentic Mexican cuisine. Other location: 6718 Greenville Ave. (692-8431). *Mexican.* **B–I**

🍷 **S. & D. Oyster Company** (nr. dwntwn), 2701 McKinney Ave. (880-0111). A/C. Lunch/dinner Mon–Sat. AE, MC, V. *Specialties:* gumbo, oysters, Mexican Gulf shrimp, fish of the day. *Note:* Irreproachably fresh seafood served in a usually packed house, w. very effective New Orleans decor and a noisy, friendly ambience. No resv. unfortunately. *Seafood.* **B–I**

☼🍷 **Frank Tolbert Texas Chili Parlor** (nr. dwntwn), 4544 McKinney Ave. (953-1353). A/C. Lunch/dinner daily (until 2am). AE, CB, DC, MC, V. *Specialties:* "donkey tails" (hot-dog tortillas), chili con carne. *Note:* The state's most celebrated chili parlor, a must for all visitors. Relaxed atmosphere. In case you're allergic to chili, try the Sonofabitch Stew, perfectly adequate sustenance despite the name. *American.* **B**

☼🍷 **La Cave** (nr. dwntwn), 2019 N. Lamar St. (979-9463). A/C. Lunch/dinner Mon–Sat. AE, MC, V. *Specialties:* homemade pasta and soups, delicatessen meats, cheeses. *Note:* Congenial wine bistro w. very modest prices and an intimate atmosphere where French songs are *de rigueur.* An ideal spot for a quick bite to eat. Stampeded by the white-collar crowd at noon. *French.* **B**

Restaurants in the Vicinity

☼🍷🍷 **Clark's Outpost Barbecue Restaurant** (vic.), U.S. 377 at Gene Autry Dr., Tioga (817/437-2414). A/C. Lunch/dinner Wed–Sun. AE, MC, V. *Specialties:* calf fries; chili; fried zucchini w. horseradish; smoked sausage w. barbecue sauce; chicken-fried steak; barbecued spareribs, beef, ham, and turkey; homemade apple pie. *Note:* Way out in the country a full hour's drive north of Dallas, this tiny (nine tables) rest. of undistinguished but authentic appearance will serve you the best barbecues anywhere in Texas, lovingly prepared by Warren Clark. Ranchers flock here from all the surrounding country; in the parking lot their Jeeps and four-by-fours stand shoulder-to-shoulder with the Mercedeses and Rolls-Royces of the wealthy burghers from Dallas. The atmosphere is "capital R" Relaxed, and the place is so popular that you should certainly reserve ahead. A classic of its kind for more than 15 years; don't miss it. To get there, take I-35 north from Dallas, then the 288 loop as far as U.S. 380, east to U.S. 377, and then north again. *American.* **B–I**

Cafeterias/Fast Food

Luby's (vic.), 10425 N. Central Expwy. at Meadow Central Mall (361-9024). A/C. Lunch/dinner daily (until 8pm). No credit cards. Respectable fast-food cuisine, 20 min. from dwntwn. Other location: 5954 Alpha Rd. (233-3275).

Highland Park (nr. dwntwn), 4619 Cole St. (526-3801). A/C. Lunch/dinner Mon–Sat (until 8pm). No credit cards. Excellent cafeteria w. low prices. Other location: 5100 Beltline Rd. (934-8025).

BARS & NIGHTCLUBS

Andrew's (nr. dwntwn), 3301 McKinney Ave. (220-0566). Open daily. The "in" bar with a hip, youthful ambience; also a fair rest.

Belle Starr (nr. dwntwn), 7724 N. Central Expwy. (750-4787). Open daily. A saloon of typically Texan atmosphere w. dancing and the requisite country music.

Club Dada (nr. dwntwn), 2720 Elm St. (744-3232). Jazz, rockabilly, and New Wave in the heart of the artists' quarter of Deep Ellum in East Dallas. Draws a young crowd that would be at home in New York's SoHo.

Hard Rock Café (nr. dwntwn), 2601 McKinney Ave. (827-8282). A replica of the rock clubs operating under the same name in New York, Los Angeles, San Francisco, etc. Youthful crowd; noisy, laid-back atmosphere. Open daily.

☼ **Longhorn Ballroom** (nr. dwntwn), 216 Corinth (428-3128). Open Wed–Sat. A country-music paradise for 20 years.

R'N'R USA (formerly Confetti; nr. dwntwn), 5201 Matilda (369-6969). Open daily. A disco filled with locals.

Starck (nr. dwntwn), 703 McKinney Ave. (720-0130). Refined decor by the French founder Philippe Starck and a trendy ambience. The most elegant disco in Dallas. Open Thurs–Sun.

Video Bar (nr. dwntwn), 2812 Elm St. (939-9113). A favorite of video-music fans.

FORT WORTH

Once a true cowboy town on the Trinity River, Fort Worth was known in the 19th century as "the town where the West begins," where the huge herds of Texas cattle were watered on the way to railhead in Kansas. Established in 1849 to defend the pioneers against the Comanches, this former garrison town attracted some of the most famous and formidable characters of the West, from Doc Holliday to Wyatt Earp, as well as Butch Cassidy and the Sundance Kid. Inseparable neighbors, Dallas and Fort Worth constitute a gigantic metroplex almost 50 mi. (80km) long, crisscrossed with four-lane highways and nicknamed "Silicon Prairie" because of the area's high concentration of leading electronics companies. Despite its boots and Stetsons, the most Texan of Texas cities makes good use of its aeronautical, oil, and computer resources. Fort Worth nevertheless remains one of the biggest livestock (see the famous **Stockyards**) and grain markets in the country. Its famous rodeos continue to draw huge crowds, as do the very popular **Amon Carter Museum,** dedicated to the era of the Far West, and the splendid and futurist **Kimbell Art Museum.** The infamous "J.R." of "Dallas," Larry Hagman, is a famous celebrated son of Fort Worth.

Note: The area code for Fort Worth is 817.

INFORMATION & TOURS

TOURIST INFORMATION: The **Fort Worth Convention & Visitors Bureau,** 100 E. 15th St., TX 76102 (817/336-8791).

Visitor Information Center, 123 E. Exchange St. (817/624-4741).

GUIDED TOURS: Gray Line Tours Fort Worth (bus) (817/429-7563): Guided tour of the city, serving major hotels.

SIGHTS, ATTRACTIONS & ACTIVITIES

ARCHITECTURAL HIGHLIGHTS: ☼⚱ **Water Gardens,** Houston St. and 14th St. (870-7000): Superb landscape grdns in the middle of the city with concrete terraces, plantings, and futurist waterfalls. The water flows at a rate of 19,000 gallons (72,000l) per min. Designed by Philip Johnson; dates from 1974. An absolute must-see.

⚱ **Will Rogers Memorial Center,** 3400 W. Lancaster St. (870-8150): Dedicated to the famous cinema cowboy and humorist, this vast exhibition center includes the **Memorial Coliseum** and the **Will Rogers Auditorium,** where the big concerts, rodeos, auto shows, and other Fort Worth events take place, as well as several major museums of Fort Worth (see the Amon Carter Museum, Kimbell Art Museum, and Museum of Science & History, below).

HISTORIC BUILDINGS: ⚓ **Log Cabin Village,** 2100 Log Cabin Village Lane (926-5881): A group of authentic pioneer homes dating from the mid-19th century. For lovers of western history. Open daily.

☀⚓ **The Stockyards National Historic District,** Exchange Ave. and W. Main St. (626-3761): Fort Worth's original claim to fame. Retains some of the flavor of the old cattle drives and contains a variety of shops, art galleries, saloons, western boutiques, and restaurants. The atmosphere is amusing although rather touristy. Not to be missed, particularly on weekends.

☀⚓ **Sundance Square,** bounded by Commerce St., Houston St., 2nd St., and 3rd St.: The historic heart of Fort Worth, with old houses, brick sidewalks, and period gas lamps. Lots of restaurants, boutiques, and art galleries as well. Good for a stroll.

⚓ **Thistle Hill,** 1509 Pennsylvania, at Summit (336-1212): The last of the luxurious manors (1903) belonging to the surpassingly rich "cattle barons" of the 19th century. Magnificently restored in all its Texan opulence. Worth a look. Open Sun–Fri.

MUSEUMS OF ART: ☀⚓⚓ **Amon Carter Museum of Western Art,** 3501 Camp Bowie Blvd. (738-1933): American painting and sculpture, with special attention to western lore (notably, paintings by Frederic Remington and Charles Russell). The marvelous triangular Philip Johnson building, dedicated to the founder of the *Fort Worth Star-Telegram,* Amon Carter, also houses works by such contemporary artists as Georgia O'Keeffe, Ben Shahn, Grant Wood, and Stuart Davis. An absolute must-see. Open Tues–Sun.

⚓ **Fort Worth Museum of Modern Art,** 1309 Montgomery St., at Camp Bowie Blvd. (738-9215): Interesting temporary and permanent exhibits of 20th-century art including works by Pablo Picasso, Jackson Pollock, Mark Rothko, Clyfford Still, Frank Stella, and Andy Warhol. Among the best known of the works on display are *Manhattan II* by Lyonel Feininger, Ellsworth Kelly's *Curved Red on Blue,* Roy Lichtenstein's *Atom Burst,* and *En haut, à gauche* by Vassily Kandinsky. Tues–Sun.

☀⚓⚓⚓ **Kimbell Art Museum,** 3333 Camp Bowie Blvd. (332-8451): A Louis Kahn masterpiece from 1973, this building houses all forms of art from prehistoric times to Picasso and includes one of the finest private collections of European masters in the country. Among its most famous holdings: Giovanni Bellini's *Christ in Benediction,* Caravaggio's *The Cheaters,* Goya's *Matador Pedro Romero,* Rembrandt's *Portrait of a Young Jew,* and Picasso's *Man with a Pipe.* Open Tues–Sun. The patio restaurant is agreeable in good weather.

⚓ **Sid Richardson Collection of Western Art,** 309 Main St. (332-6554): Very fine collection of "western art" formed by the late oil tycoon Sid Richardson. The two most famous artists of this 19th-century romantic movement—Frederic Remington and Charles M. Russell—are represented by some 50 paintings. An absolute must for devotees of the Old West. Open Tues–Sun.

MUSEUMS OF SCIENCE & HISTORY: ⚓ **Museum of Science & History,** 1501 Montgomery St. (732-1631): A very educational museum of humankind w. a section on medical sciences and on anthropology, as well as a hemispherical dome for 70-mm film among the most modern in the world **(Omni Theater).** See it. Open daily.

PARKS & GARDENS: ⚓ **Botanic Gardens,** 3200 Botanic Garden Dr. (870-7686): Very lovely botanic grdn displaying more than 2,000 plant varieties as

well as an enchanting Japanese grdn with authentically Japanese tea houses. Open Tues–Sun.

PERFORMING ARTS: For a daily listing of all shows and cultural events, consult the entertainment pages of the daily papers *Fort Worth News Tribune* (morning) and *Fort Worth Star Telegram* (morning and evening), and of the monthly magazines *Fort Worth* and *Texas Monthly.*

Casa Mañana, 3101 W. Lancaster Ave. (332-9319): Broadway hits, concerts, modern theater. Texas's most famous theater-in-the-round.

Circle Theater, 3460 Bluebonnet Circle (921-3040): Drama, comedy.

Hip Pocket Theatre, 1620 Las Vegas Trail N. (246-1269): Open-air theater.

Tarrant County Convention Center Theatre, 1111 Houston St. (332-9222): Home of the Fort Worth Opera, the Fort Worth Ballet, and the Fort Worth Symphony Orchestra (principal conductor: John Giordano) (Sept–May).

Will Rogers Auditorium, 3301 W. Lancaster Ave. (332-0909): Concerts, recitals, shows with top stars.

William Edrington Scott Theater, 3505 W. Lancaster Ave. (738-6509): Modern and classic theater.

RODEOS: ♠ **Cowtown Coliseum,** 123 E. Exchange Ave., at the Stockyards (625-1025): Rodeos 8pm Sat Mar to late May and Sept to mid-Nov, in a spirited atmosphere. Don't miss it.

SHOPPING: Justin Boot Co., 717 W. Vickery: Factory outlet with prices 30%–50% below list. A good bet.

N. L. Leddy's Boots & Saddles, 2455 N. Main St.: Custom boots. Among the best.

SPECIAL EVENTS: For the exact schedule of events below, consult the **Fort Worth Convention & Visitors Bureau** (see "Tourist Information," above).

Fat Stock Show & Rodeo (late Jan–Feb): One of the country's best-known rodeos, for fans of real flesh-and-blood cowboys. A nearly 100-year-old tradition.

Chisholm Trail Roundup (second wknd in June): Lively and colorful cowboy parades, square dances, and barbecues.

Shakespeare in the Park (June): Open-air, free performances in Trinity Park, West Fort Worth.

Pioneer Days Celebration (late Sept): A lively celebration of the cult of the cowboy with carnivals, parades, and public dances.

THEME PARKS: See "Theme Parks" in Dallas, above.

ZOOS: ♠ **Zoological Park,** 2727 Zoological Park Dr., Forest Park (817/870-7065): Modern, very well-conceived zoo in a wooded setting. More than 800 animal species; of particular interest, a spectacular seal pond and one of the world's richest collections of reptiles and amphibians (in the Herpetarium). Open daily.

ACCOMMODATIONS

A Note on Accommodations: Room rates in Fort Worth are coded as follows: **VE,** Very Expensive ($140 and up); **E,** Expensive ($90–$140); **M,** Moderate ($60–$90); **I,** Inexpensive ($30–$60); **B,** Budget (up to $30). A listing of toll free numbers is in the Appendix.

Personal Favorites (from top bracket to budget)

♛♛♛♛ **Worthington** (formerly the Americana; dwntwn), 200 Main St., TX 76102 (817/870-1000; toll free 800/433-5677). 510 rms, A/C, color TV, in-rm movies. AE, CB, DC, MC, V. Valet parking $6, pool, health club, sauna, ice rink, two tennis courts, two rests. (including Reflections), coffee shop, bars, 24-hr rm svce, disco, boutiques, concierge, crib free. *Note:* The most recent, and most luxurious, of the local palaces, this architecturally startling hotel looks like a truncated pyramid. Spacious, ultra-comfortable rms w. balconies, some w. refrigerators. Elegant contemporary decor, very complete facilities, a good American-cuisine rest. (Reflections), and excellent svce. Big business clientele. In the heart of Fort Worth just off Sundance Sq. **E–VE**

Hyatt Regency (formerly the Texas Hotel; dwntwn), 815 Main St., TX 76102 (817/870-1234; toll free, see Hyatt). 515 rms, A/C, color TV, in-rm movies. AE, CB, DC, MC, V. Valet gar. $8, pool, health club, sauna, two rests. (including the Crystal Cactus Rm), two bars, rm svce, free crib. *Note:* Massive 1940s-style palace in the heart of dwntwn. The hotel in which President Kennedy spent the night before he was assassinated in Dallas. Luxurious, comfortable layout w. spacious, well-conceived rms and a six-story atrium w. a waterfall and ornamental pools. Impeccable svce and fair rests. A favorite among businesspeople. Interesting wknd packages. **E–VE**

Stockyards Hotel (nr. dwntwn), 109 E. Exchange Ave., TX 76106 (817/625-6427; toll free 800/423-8471). 52 rms, A/C, color TV. AE, CB, DC, MC, V. Valet parking $5, rest., bar, valet svce, nightclub, free crib. *Note:* The city's oldest (1902) hotel, carefully renovated. Comfortable, congenial Old West ambience and decor. Decent rest. and excellent svce. Local color seekers will enjoy the location, in the heart of the slaughterhouse district w. its rests. and nightlife. **E**

Green Oaks Inn (vic.), 6901 West Fwy., TX 76116 (817/738-7311; toll free 800/433-2174). 282 rms, A/C, color TV, in-rm movies. AE, CB, DC, MC, V. Free parking, two pools, two tennis courts, golf, health club, sauna, rest., bars, rm svce, disco, free crib. *Note:* Agreeable, Tudor-style motel amid 10 acres (4ha) of park and grdns. Spacious, comfortable rms and pleasant reception and svce. A good value and a favorite of connoisseurs, 15 min. from dwntwn. **M**

Plaza Hotel & Conference Center (nr. dwntwn), 2000 Beach St., TX 76103 (817/534-4801; toll free 800/223-2441). 300 rms, A/C, color TV, in-rm movies. AE, CB, DC, MC, V. Free parking, two pools, tennis court, health club, rest., bar, rm svce, free crib. *Note:* Spacious, comfortable hotel, recently renovated, about 3 mi. (5km) from dwntwn Fort Worth. Huge, inviting rms; acceptable rest.; ultra-professional svce; fully equipped business center. Very good value. **I–M**

Quality Inn South (nr. dwntwn), 4201 South Fwy., TX 76115 (817/923-8281; toll free, see Quality Inns). 98 rms, A/C, color TV, in-rm movies. AE, CB, DC, MC, V. Free parking, pool, coffee shop (breakfast and lunch only), bar, rm svce, free crib. *Note:* Small, appealing, and functional motel w. comfortable rms and affable reception and svce. A very good value that is ideal for the car traveler, 10 min. from dwntwn. **I**

Motel 6 North (nr. dwntwn), 3271 I-35W, TX 76106 (817/625-4359). 106 rms, A/C, color TV, free in-rm movies. AE, DC, MC, V. Free parking, pool, free crib. *Note:* An unbeatable value 10 min. from dwntwn, offering functional comfort and a warm welcome. **B**

RESTAURANTS

A Note on Restaurant Prices: Fort Worth restaurant prices, per person, excluding drinks and service charges, are coded as follows: **VE**, Very Expensive ($60 and up); **E**, Expensive ($40–$60); **M**, Moderate ($25–$40); **I**, Inexpensive ($15–$25); **B**, Budget (up to $15).

Personal Favorites (from top bracket to budget)

Michael's (nr. dwntwn), 3851 Camp Bowie Blvd. (377-8021). A/C. Lunch Tues–Fri, dinner Tues–Sat; closed hols. AE, CB, DC, MC, V. J&T. *Specialties:* venison pâté, sweetbread salad w. apples, oyster stew, rack of lamb, fish of the day, seasonal game. A good list of French and

California wines. *Note:* Fort Worth's best French rest. offers classic cuisine but w. light sauces from chef Michel Baudouin. The menu changes daily according to what's fresh at the market. The prix-fixe menu (five courses) is particularly fine. Charming Victorian decor and excellent svce. Resv. a must. *French.* **I–M**

☀☕🍷 **Cattlemen's** (nr. dwntwn), 2458 N. Main St. (Stockyards) (624-3945). A/C. Lunch Mon–Fri, dinner nightly; closed hols. AE, CB, DC, MC, V. Jkt. *Specialties:* grilled steak, barbecued beef, calf fries. *Note:* The most famous steakhouse in Texas. A stronghold of red meat in an appropriately western setting. Very relaxed atmosphere. Locally popular for 40 years. No resv., hence, inevitable waits. *Steak.* **I**

☕🍷 **Juanita's** (dwntwn), 115 W. 2nd St. (335-1777). A/C. Lunch/dinner daily (until 1am); closed Dec 25. AE, MC, V. *Specialties:* nachos, fajitas, broiled chicken w. chili butter, braised quail w. tequila, flan. *Note:* The most attractive of the town's innumerable Tex-Mex eating places. The slightly fussy food is more Mex than Tex. The setting is delightfully period, and on fine days you can eat outdoors. Svce w. a smile. Resv. advisable. Valet parking. The "in" place on Sundance Sq. *Mexican.* **I–M**

☀☕🍷 **Winfield's 08** (dwntwn), 301 Main St. (870-1908). A/C. Lunch Mon–Fri, dinner Mon–Sat; closed hols. AE, CB, DC, MC, V. *Specialties:* wonderful hickory-broiled meat and fish. *Note:* A charming little American rest. in a turn-of-the-century house on Sundance Sq. w. stained glass in the windows and Victorian decor. Attentive, efficient svce. Resv. advisable. Valet parking. A very good place. *American.* **B–I**

☀🍷 **Edelweiss** (nr. dwntwn), 3801-A Southwest Blvd. (738-5934). A/C. Dinner only, Tues–Sat; closed hols. *Specialties:* sauerbraten, wienerschnitzel, duck w. red cabbage, pork hocks. *Note:* Totally authentic German brasserie w. very adequate, if unimaginative, cuisine. Rather noisy ambience w. the requisite Bavarian orchestra. Efficient svce. Locally popular. No resv. *German.* **B–I**

☀🍸 **Joe T. Garcia's** (nr. dwntwn), 2201 N. Commerce St. (626-4356). A/C. Lunch Mon–Fri, dinner nightly; closed hols. No credit cards. *Specialties:* nachos, chile relleño, tacos, enchiladas, quesadillas, chimichangas, excellent margaritas. *Note:* A Tex-Mex family favorite for more than half a century, w. an agreeable patio and guaranteed local color. No resv. Locally very popular. Inevitable waits on the wknds. *American/Mexican.* **B–I**

🍸 **Szechuan** (nr. dwntwn), 5712 Locke Ave. at Camp Bowie Blvd. (738-7300). A/C. Lunch Mon–Sat, dinner nightly. AE, MC, V. *Specialties:* Szechuan chicken, Peking duck, sweet-and-sour shrimp. *Note:* The only Chinese rest. in Fort Worth that is worthy of the title, w. an extensive menu and generous portions. Classic Oriental decor and pleasant svce. *Chinese.* **B–I**

Cafeterias/Fast Food

Colonial (nr. dwntwn), 1700 Rogers Rd. (335-9372). A/C. Lunch/dinner daily (until 8pm). No credit cards. Very adequate cafeteria food at modest prices. Close to the university.

☀ **Paris Coffee Shop** (nr. dwntwn), 704 W. Magnolia St. (335-2041). Breakfast/lunch Mon–Sat. No credit cards. A local institution. Whether you're a cowboy, a trucker, a Texas millionaire, or a society lady, sooner or later you'll come to the Paris Coffee Shop. Very good chicken-fried steak, enchiladas, and chili.

BARS & NIGHTCLUBS

Billy Bob's Texas (nr. dwntwn), 2520 Rodeo Plaza (624-7117). Claims to be the world's largest honkytonk. Located a stone's throw away from the Stockyards' Cowtown Coliseum. Open for music and dancing wknds only.

Caravan of Dreams (dwntwn), 312 Houston St. (877-3000). Fashionable nightclub w. excellent jazz and live blues.

Cowboy Cantina (nr. dwntwn), 124 W. Exchange Ave. (625-6622). Texas-style ballroom with country music live. Perpetually crowded and noisy. Genuine local color.

Stagecoach Ballroom (nr. dwntwn), 2516 E. Belknap (831-2261). Huge, locally popular western dance hall with a guaranteed cowboy atmosphere.

☼ **The White Elephant Saloon** (nr. dwntwn), 106 E. Exchange
Ave. (624-1887). Open daily. Country-and-western music just around the corner from the famous slaughterhouses; a classic for more than a century, with relaxed decor and ambience, plus decent barbecue.

NEARBY EXCURSIONS

☼ **GRANBURY** (38 mi./60km SW of Fort Worth on U.S.
377): Charming little Texas town that has conserved and restored many of its buildings from the days of the great westward migration. Start with the picturesque **Opera House,** dating from 1886 and reopened to the public in 1975 after 50 years of slumber. Performances Thurs–Sun Mar–Dec. For information, call 817/573-9191. Not to be missed.

On the way, see the ▲ **Pate Museum of Transportation,** U.S. 377 between Fort Worth and Cresson (14 mi./22km south of Fort Worth) (871/332-1161): Small transportation museum, from the double-decker bus to the DC-3 and from the minesweeper to the venerable Model T. Rather jumbled but amusing. Open Tues–Sun.

Where to Eat in Granbury

🍷 **The Cuckoo's Nest,** 110 E. Pearl St. (817/573-9722): Original decor in a remodeled 19th-century theater. Lunch/dinner Tues–Sun. **B–I**

🍷 **Nutt House,** Town Sq. (817/573-9362): Delightful Victorian decor from the 1890s. Lunch only, Tues–Sun. The Nutt House also has a dozen rms to rent, with old-fashioned but comfortable furniture. **I**

☼ **WAXAHACHIE** (30 mi./48km south of Dallas on I-35E):
Called "Gingerbread City," Waxahachie boasts nearly 200 gingerbread-style and Victorian buildings, all historical landmarks and magnificently restored. Many movies were shot here, including *Tender Mercies* and *Place in the Sun.* Waxahachie has been selected to be home to the future giant atom smasher—the Super-Conducting Super-Collider, a ring 53 mi. (85km) in circumference—to become operational in 1997. Worth going out of your way for.

CHAPTER 36

HOUSTON

□ □ □

Where 150 years ago there was nothing but a muddy, mosquito-infested tent town, there stands today the Sunbelt's greatest city. Houston, once the capital of the Republic of Texas, owes its name to the first elected president of that short-lived nation—Sam Houston. One of the first Spanish explorers of the North American continent, Alvar Nuñez Cabeza de Vaca, remarked as early as 1528 on Houston's strategic position on the shore of Buffalo Bayou, and "The Bayou City," as Houston is sometimes called, is now the country's fourth-largest port (after New York, New Orleans, and Valdez). Its access to the sea is via the Ship Channel, a canal 50 mi. (80km) long, 400 ft. (122m) wide, and 40 ft. (12m) deep, passable by the largest deep-water vessels and each year carrying more than 70 million tons of goods.

Like its neighbor and rival, Dallas, Houston is a boom town—a mushrooming city with congested freeways and a spectacular skyline where more than 200 giant corporations have chosen to build their headquarters. Houston continued to flourish into the early 1980s, with annual economic and population growth averaging 15%. After the devastating oil bust of the mid-1980s and the slump in farm-product prices, the local economy (refining, petrochemicals, steel-making, electronic components, cotton, rice, etc.) is showing signs of recovery—almost 80% of the 220,000 lost jobs have been regained.

Houston negatives include: no coherent city planning, almost nonexistent public transportation, snarled auto traffic, a disturbing pollution level, a rising crime rate, and a police force generally regarded as quick on the draw.

World capital of the oil industry, Houston is also a city of science, culture, and sport. The **Lyndon B. Johnson Space Center,** headquarters for America's conquest of space, guided the first steps on the moon as well as every space flight launched from the Kennedy Space Center or California. The first word spoken by the first man to set foot on the moon, on July 20, 1969, was "Houston." The **Texas Medical Center,** the world's largest hospital complex with its 6,000 beds, two million patients a year, and 52,000 doctors, nurses, and employees, is known internationally for heart surgery and cancer research. Houston's six universities, its opera, and its symphony orchestra enjoy—and deserve—a high reputation. The **Astrodome,** an amazing covered stadium with 66,000 seats, 18 stories high, and air-conditioned throughout, is one of the most striking examples of contemporary American architecture.

Typically Texan, Houston is on the way to becoming a great cosmopolitan city as well; more than 52 consulates and 64 foreign banks have offices here.

Houston is the birthplace of singer Kenny Rogers, actors Dennis and Randy Quaid, actress Shelley Duval, cardiac-transplant pioneer Prof. Denton Cooley, and the late billionaire businessman and movie producer Howard Hughes.

BASIC FACTS: State of Texas. Area code: 713. Time zone: central. ZIP Code: 77052. Founded: 1836. Approximate population: city, 1,690,000; metropolitan area, 3,300,000. Fourth-largest city and ninth-largest metropolitan area in the country.

CLIMATE: Due to the proximity of the Gulf of Mexico, Houston's winters are agreeably mild (average 51°F/11°C in Jan), while spring and fall are relatively hot. In summer the temperature is high (average 86°F/30°C in July) and so is the humidity, but since everything is fiercely air-conditioned, you may need something warm to wear in hotels, restaurants, and office buildings. There are tornadoes, often violent, in the fall.

DISTANCES: Dallas, 243 mi. (390km); Mexican border, 360 mi. (576km); New Orleans, 356 mi. (570km); San Antonio, 197 mi. (315km).

ARRIVAL & TRANSIT INFORMATION

AIRPORTS: The **Houston Intercontinental Airport** (IAH), 20 mi. (32km) north, handles 14.5 million passengers a year. For information, call 230-3000.
   W. P. Hobby Airport (commuter flights) (HOU), 10 mi. (16km) SE, has 7.5 million passengers a year. For information, call 643-4597.

U.S. AIRLINES: American (650-1116), Continental (821-2100), Delta (448-3000), Eastern (443-4900), Northwest (868-9988), Pan Am (447-0088), Southwest (237-1221), TWA (222-7273), United (650-1055), and USAir (toll free 800/428-4322).

FOREIGN CARRIERS: Air Canada (toll free 800/422-6232), Air France (toll free 800/237-2747), British Airways (toll free 800/247-9297), and KLM (658-1781).

CITY LINK: Cab fare **from Houston Intercontinental Airport to city center,** is about $26; time, about 40 min. Bus: Airport Express (523-8888), every 20 min.; makes five stops dwntwn; fare, $8; time, about 60 min.
   Cab fare **from Hobby Airport to city center,** is about $15; time, 25 min. Hobby Airport Limo (644-8359) connects Hobby Airport to the city center; fare, $5; time, about 30–40 min.
   This is one of the country's most sprawling cities, and cab fares are high, so renting a car is probably the best solution, although for this, too, rates are among the highest in the country. Public (bus) transportation is almost nonexistent, but there is rather efficient minibus service downtown (Metropolitan Transit Authority/MTA; call 739-4000 for information).

CAR RENTAL (all at Houston Intercontinental Airport): Avis (443-5800); Budget (449-0145); Dollar (449-0161); Hertz (443-0800); National (443-8850); and Thrifty, 15845 John F. Kennedy Blvd. (442-5000). For dwntwn offices, consult the local telephone directory.

LIMOUSINE SERVICES: Carey Limousine Service (367-4759), River Oaks Limousine (880-5466), and Scripps Edward Limo (toll free 800/223-6710).

TAXIS: Theoretically cabs can't be hailed on the street, but it's easy to find one outside any of the large hotels, or to call one by phone: **Fiesta Cab** (225-2666), **United Cab** (699-0000), or **Yellow Cab** (236-1111).

TRAIN: Amtrak station, 902 Washington Ave. (224-1577; toll free 800/872-7245).

INTERCITY BUSES: Greyhound, 2121 S. Main St. (222-1161). Area unsafe.

INFORMATION & TOURS

TOURIST INFORMATION: The **Houston Chamber of Commerce,** 1100 Milam St., TX 77002 (713/658-2401).
   The **Houston Convention and Visitors Bureau,** 3300 Main St., TX 77002 (713/523-5050; toll free 800/231-7799).

GUIDED TOURS: Gray Line Tours (bus), 602 Sampson St. (223-8800): Guided tours of the city with departures from principal dwntwn hotels.

SIGHTS, ATTRACTIONS & ACTIVITIES

ARCHITECTURAL HIGHLIGHTS: ※△ **Astrodome,** Kirby Dr. and Loop 610 (799-9500): Second-largest (in height) covered stadium in the world, after that in New Orleans, with 66,000 seats. The plastic roof rises 18 stories. Used not only for sports events but also for concerts, exhibitions, and political meetings. Impressive; the most-visited building in Texas. Guided tours daily.
   ※△ **George R. Brown Convention Center,** 1001 Convention Center Blvd. (853-8000): Spanking-new convention center opened in Nov 1987. The brightly colored steamboat-shaped building has overtones of Paris's Centre Pompidou; its unbuttressed dome spans six city blocks and can accommodate a crowd of 35,000.
   ※△△ **Houston Civic Center,** I-45 at Milam St., between Texas Ave. and Dallas Ave.: A huge quadrilateral of ultramodern high-rises and municipal buildings in the heart of Houston, featuring the **Sam Houston Coliseum;** the **George R. Brown Convention Center** (see above); **Tranquility Park,** on 32 levels with its oversize fountain (see below); **City Hall;** the **Public Library,** with an amusing sculpture (*Geometric Mouse*) by Claes Oldenburg; and an auditorium, **Jesse H. Jones Hall** (see below). Very eye-catching.
   △ **Jesse H. Jones Hall for the Performing Arts,** 615 Louisiana St. (222-1103): A concert hall with remarkable acoustics, home of the Houston Symphony Orchestra. A daring design by the architect Caudill Rowlett Scott, with movable ceiling, which can be arranged to seat 1,800–3,000 people.
   ※△△ **Nina Vance Alley Theatre,** 615 Texas Ave., at Louisiana St. (228-8421): This futurist structure, comprising two auditoriums divided by a party wall, is one of Houston's most innovative buildings—a sort of 21st-century fortress designed by Ulrich Fransen.
   ※△△ **Pennzoil Towers,** Pennzoil Place: Twin towers shaped like oblique prisms, with slanted roofs, interior gardens at ground level, and a gigantic glass curtain wall rising 36 floors; a spectacular achievement of architects Philip Johnson and John Burgee (1976).
   △ **Republic Bank Bldg.,** Republic Bank Center: A strange 56-story postmodern skyscraper with a Neo-Gothic gabled roof suggesting the banking houses of early Antwerp, another exciting building by the Johnson-Burgee team. The 105-ft.-high (35m) entrance hall is reminiscent of Piranesi's drawings of the palaces of ancient Rome.
   △ **Texas Commerce Tower,** Texas Ave. at Travis St.: Fine modern building, five-sided and 75 floors high—the highest in Texas.

Texas Medical Center, bounded by Fannin St., Outer Belt, and Holcombe Blvd. (797-0100): Huge hospital complex covering 600 acres (243ha), considered the most up-to-date in the world. Its 14 hospitals and nine medical facilities attract researchers, students, and patients from all over the world. An acknowledged leader in cardiology, cancer care, rehabilitation, biomathematics, and space medicine. See, among others, the brand-new and spectacular St. Luke's Medical Tower by architect Cesar Pelli. The Visitor Information Center (790-1136) arranges individual or guided-tour visits Mon–Fri.

CHURCHES/SYNAGOGUES: **Christ Church Cathedral,** 1117 Texas Ave. (222-2593): The oldest church in Texas, dating from 1839 and rebuilt in 1893; interesting Neo-Gothic building with Tiffany windows. You should see it. Open daily.

Rothko Chapel, 3900 Yupon St., at Sul Ross (524-9839): This octagonal chapel in an out-of-the-way district was designed by Philip Johnson in austere reinforced concrete. It houses 14 dark, brooding paintings created by Mark Rothko in 1965 and 1966. Barnett Newman's very beautiful *Broken Obelisk,* a sculpture dedicated to Martin Luther King, Jr., sits in a reflection pool in front of the chapel. Don't miss this wonderful setting for meditation and contemplation. Open daily.

HISTORIC BUILDINGS: **Rice University,** 6100 S. Main St. (527-4929): Small in size with only 3,500 students, but greatly renowned for its faculties of science and engineering, this university founded in 1912 boasts dozens of very beautiful neoclassical and Mediterranean-style buildings, including **Lovett Hall,** the **Sewall Art Gallery,** and the ultramodern and original **Herring Hall** by architect Cesar Pelli.

MUSEUMS OF ART: **Bayou Bend Collection,** 1 Westcott St. (529-8773): Beautiful collection of American furniture from the 17th through the 19th century, housed in 28 rooms of the vast Renaissance-style home of Ima Hogg, daughter of a former governor of Texas. Can be seen Tues–Sat. by appointment; closed Aug.

Contemporary Arts Museum, 5216 Montrose Blvd. (526-3129): This strange silvered-aluminum parallelogram presents movies and temporary exhibitions of modern art and industrial design. Focuses on post-1945 American art. Open Tues–Sun.

Cullen Sculpture Garden, 1001 Bissonnet (526-1361): This outdoor extension of the Museum of Fine Arts, designed by Isamu Noguchi, contains selected pieces from the museum permanent collection, traveling exhibitions, and loans, positioned on landscaped levels with corresponding backdrops. On display are works by Bourdelle, Maillol, Matisse, Giacometti, Alexander Calder (*Crab*), Frank Stella (*Decanter*), and others.

Menil Collection, 1515 Sul Ross (525-9400): The personal collection of Dominique de Menil, which drew large crowds when it was exhibited a few years ago at the Petit Palais in Paris, is now housed in a building worthy of it. It comprises more than 10,000 works of art covering 5,000 years of history, from Etruscan and Anatolian sculpture to the works of such avant-garde painters as Pollock, Rothko, Rauschenberg, and Warhol, and surrealists like de Chirico and Magritte. The remarkable, light-filled modern building was designed by Renzo Piano, the architect of many distinguished buildings, including Paris's famous Centre Pompidou. This is among the world's most highly regarded private museums. Open Tues–Sun.

Museum of Fine Arts, 1001 Bissonnet (526-1361): A mixture of neoclassical and modern architecture (the interior of one of its modern wings, designed by Mies van der Rohe, presents an unusual theme of broken concrete shafts), this wonderful museum houses a splendid collection of European masters and well-known American painters (particularly Frederic Remington) and is rich in Native American pottery and pre-Columbian art. Some of the remarkable works on display are Fra Angelico's *Temptation of St. Anthony,* a *Virgin and Child* by Rogier van der Weyden, *Waterlilies* by Claude Monet, and van Gogh's *The Rocks.* Open Tues–Sun.

MUSEUMS OF SCIENCE & HISTORY: ※🔍 Museum of Natural Science, 1 Hermann Circle, Dr. Hermann Park (526-4273): From the diplodocus to the space rocket and from oil wells to artificial earthquakes, this is one of the biggest and best natural-science museums in the country. Here, too, are the **Hall of Medical Science,** with its giant models of the human body, and the **Burke Baker Planetarium,** where visitors can follow the transit of comets and the motion of the planets against the star-studded dome. Open daily.

PANORAMAS: The finest 🔍 overall view of this city of skyscrapers is to be had at ground level from the **Buffalo Bayou Sesquicentennial Park** (see below).
🔔 **Transco Tower,** 2800 Post Oak Blvd. (439-2000): From the 51st floor of this brand-new skyscraper next to the Galleria Center you can have a wonderful view of the skyline. Lovely fountain with a waterfall at the foot of the tower. Open Mon–Fri.

PARKS & GARDENS: 🔔 Allen's Landing, Main St. and Commerce St.: A tiny park overshadowed by skyscrapers, on the spot where the city's founders (two New York promoters named Augustus and John Allen) first moored their boat in 1836. For a long time this was Houston's commercial harbor. Particularly fine view.
🔔 **Buffalo Bayou Sesquicentennial Park,** Smith St. and Texas Ave.: Brand-new $5-million downtown park on the banks of the historic bayou where the city was founded in 1836. Features an overlook and water cascades with stairs. Offers a stunning view of the skyscrapers downtown.
🔔 **Memorial Park,** Woodway and Loop 610 (861-3765): A 155-acre (63ha) public park near downtown Houston. Paths for strollers; botanic garden. Houston's "lung."
🔔 **Sam Houston Historical Park,** 1100 Bagby St. (956-0480): Seven historic buildings (from a village church to a Texas-style plantation house) and stores dating from the 19th century, meticulously restored. Interesting journey into the past of the city and its inhabitants. Open daily.
※🔔 **Tranquility Park,** bounded by Rusk St., Bagby St., Smith St., and Walker St.: This very unusual park in the heart of downtown commemorates the historic *Apollo 11* mission of 1969—first landing by a manned space vehicle on the moon, in the Sea of Tranquility. The park has a 32-level fountain covering two city blocks, and five rocket-shaped towers. At every entrance, bronze tablets commemorate the Apollo mission in 15 languages. A must-see.

PERFORMING ARTS: For current listings of shows and cultural events, consult the entertainment pages of the two daily papers, *Houston Post* (morning) and *Houston Chronicle* (morning and evening), and the *Texas Monthly* magazine.
Showtix, a discount ticket booth in Tranquility Park, downtown, 400 Rusk at Smith (227-9292), sells half-price tickets for all shows on the day of performance, cash only. Open Tues–Sat.
Alley Theatre, 615 Texas Ave. (228-8421): One of the country's most renowned stock companies; from classical to experimental theater. Performances Tues–Sun Oct–May.

DOWNTOWN HOUSTON

0 Yards 200
0 Meters 200

RUIZ

FRANKLIN

CONGRESS
PRESTON
PRAIRIE
TEXAS
CAPITOL
RUSK
WALKER
McKINNEY
LAMAR
DALLAS
POLK
CLAY
BELL
LEELAND
PEASE
JEFFERSON
CALHOUN
GRAY

EASTEX FREEWAY
NORTH FREEWAY
SAN JACINTO

BAGBY BRAZOS SMITH LOUISIANA MILAM TRAVIS MAIN FANNIN CAROLINE AUSTIN LA BRANCH CRAWFORD JACKSON CHENEVERT HAMILTON

Sam Houston Park

KEY TO NUMBERED SIGHTS

1. Alley Theater
2. City Hall
3. Sam Houston Park
4. Sam Houston Coliseum
5. Pillot House
6. The Long Row
7. Old Cotton Exchange
8. Tranquility Park
9. Convention and Visitors Center
10. Amtrak Station
11. Greyhound Terminal
12. Music Hall
13. Trailways Terminal
14. Albert Thomas Space Hall of Fame
15. Jones Hall for Performing Arts
16. Pennzoil Towers
17. Old Market Square Park

Comedy Workshop, 2105 San Felipe (524-7333): Modern theater.

Jesse H. Jones Hall for the Performing Arts, 615 Louisiana St. (224-4240): Home of the Houston Symphony Orchestra (principal conductor: Christoph Eschenbach). Season Sept–May and July.

Miller Outdoor Theater, 100 Concert, Dr. Hermann Park (520-3290): Free open-air performances in summer. Shakespeare Festival, Houston Symphony Orchestra concerts, musical comedies, opera, pop concerts, etc.

Music Hall, 810 Bagby St. (222-1103): Home of the Theater Under the Stars (musical comedy, Broadway hits). Season Feb–May and Oct–Dec.

Stages Repertory Theatre, 3201 Allen Pkwy. (527-8243): Modern and experimental theater. One of the best repertory companies in the Southwest.

Tower Theater, 1201 Westheimer Rd. (529-5966): Drama, comedy, contemporary theater.

Wortham Theater Center, 501 Texas Ave. (237-1439): Lyric theater opened in 1987. Home of the Houston Grand Opera (under director David Gockley), which performs Sept–Mar; also of the Houston Ballet, the only permanent dance company in the South.

RODEOS: **Round Up Coliseum,** on Tex. 1093, in Simonton, 35 mi. (56km) west along Westheimer Rd. (346-1534): Rodeo, western dancing, barbecue dinner every Sat from 6pm on. Open year round except Sept. Guaranteed local color. 45 min. from dwntwn.

SHOPPING: ☀**Galeria Mall,** 5015 Westheimer Rd. (622-0663): Houston's ultimate shopping extravaganza, with more than 250 luxury boutiques from Neiman-Marcus to Tiffany's, restaurants, stores, bars, and even a public ice-skating rink, all air-conditioned under an enormous dome. Gigantism Texas style, elegant and spectacular.

Just Boots, 11385 Eastex Fwy. (442-2617): The place to go for cowboy boots—a large range at substantial savings. Various other locations.

Stelzig's, 3123 Oak Post Blvd. (629-7779): Western wear at its best. Has everything from elaborate saddles to steer-skull string ties. Various other locations.

SPECIAL EVENTS: For exact dates, consult the **Houston Convention and Visitors Bureau** (see "Tourist Information," above).

Houston Rodeo and Livestock Show (late Feb to early Mar): Rodeos, concerts, parades; one of the world's largest, with 25,000 entries and a million visitors yearly; guaranteed western atmosphere. Shouldn't be missed.

Houston Festival (late Mar to Apr): Dance, theater, art exhibitions, concerts.

Westheimer Art Show (Apr and Oct): Art exhibitions, public concerts on the "Strip." Worth seeing (see "Strolls," below).

Offshore Technology Conference (late Apr to early May): The world's biggest annual petroleum-industry exhibition.

SPORTS: Houston boasts professional teams in three major sports:

Baseball (Apr–Oct): Astros, the Astrodome (799-9500).

Basketball (Dec–Apr): Rockets, the Summit (627-0600).

Football (Sept–Dec): Oilers, the Astrodome (797-1000).

STROLLS: ⚓ **Old Market Square,** bounded by Congress, Milam, Preston, and Travis: Boutiques, pubs, and saloons in the style of the Old West's frontier days, all in attractively restored 19th-century row houses.

☀⚓ **River Oaks,** River Oaks Blvd. between Westheimer Rd. and the River Oaks Country Club: Dream homes and sumptuous oil barons' mansions. Worth a look.

꿎꙼ The **"Strip,"** Westheimer Rd. from about no. 100 to no. 1600: Terraced cafés, exotic restaurants, art galleries, antique shops, bookstores, nightclubs, flea market. Houston's liveliest district. Art festivals in Apr and Oct.

THEME PARKS: ꙼ **AstroWorld,** S. Loop 610 at Kirby Dr. (799-1234): Enormous (75-acre/30ha) amusement park with more than 100 attractions including the giant "Texas Cyclone" roller coaster. Shows; concerts. Open daily June–Sept, wknds only in spring and fall; closed the rest of the year.

꙼ **WaterWorld,** Kirby Dr. and S. Loop 610 (799-1234): Very popular aquatic amusement park adjoining AstroWorld. Enormous pool with artificial waves for surfers; giant slides; lagoon swimming pool with waterfalls. Spectacular. Open daily June–Aug, wknds only in May and Sept; closed the rest of the year.

ZOOS: ꙼ **Zoological Gardens,** Zoo Circle Dr. in Hermann Park (523-3211): Very fine zoo, known for its tropical jungle and its gorillas. The vampire bats eat lunch every day at 2:30pm. Huge aquarium.

ACCOMMODATIONS

A Note on Accommodations: Room rates in Houston are coded as follows: **VE,** Very Expensive ($140 and up); **E,** Expensive ($90–$140); **M,** Moderate ($60–$90); **I,** Inexpensive ($30–$60); **B,** Budget (up to $30). A listing of toll free numbers is in the Appendix.

Personal Favorites (in order of preference)

꘎꘎꘎꘎ **Ritz Carlton** (formerly the Remington; nr. dwntwn), 1919 Briar Oaks Lane, TX 77027 (713/840-7600; toll free 800/ 241-3333). 248 rms, A/C, color TV, in-rm movies. AE, CB, DC, MC, V. Valet parking $9, pool, three rests. (including the Conservatory and the Garden Rm), bar, nightclub, 24-hr. rm svce, concierge, free crib. *Note:* The most elegant, and one of the newest, of Houston's luxury hotels, in the smart River Oaks section near Memorial Park. A beautiful melding of American efficiency and European charm. Furnishings include many works of art and old pictures. Spacious, very comfortable rms; personalized reception and svce. Rest. of great quality. Discreet and stylish atmosphere. Rich business clientele. Boasts the city's most expensive suite at $1,500 a night. 20 min. from dwntwn. **VE**

꘎꘎꘎꘎ **Hyatt Regency Downtown** (dwntwn), 1200 Louisiana St., TX 77002 (713/654-1234; toll free, see Hyatt). 958 rms, A/C, color TV, in-rm movies. AE, CB, DC, MC, V. Valet gar. $9, pool, three rests. (including Hugo's Window Box), revolving rest.-bar (Spindletop) on the 33rd floor, entertainment, rm svce, free crib. *Note:* Typical Hyatt "smack in the eye" design; 30-floor foyer w. balconies, indoor grdns, and glass-caged elevators. Well-designed, friendly rms; irreproachable svce. Big business clientele. In the heart of Houston next to the Convention Center. VIP floor. Linked by "Skywalk" and air-conditioned tunnel to other dwntwn buildings. **E–VE**

꘎꘎꘎ **Lancaster Hotel** (dwntwn), 701 Texas Ave., TX 77002 (713/ 228-9500; toll free 800/345-3457). 93 rms, A/C, color TV. AE, CB, DC, MC, V. Valet parking $10, health club, rest. (Lancaster Grille), bar, rm svce, concierge, free crib. *Note:* A luxurious little 1920s palace built in 1926 and completely refurbished in 1982. Somewhat cramped but welcoming rms furnished w. antiques. Very British atmosphere. Professional and good-natured staff. The rest. is a favorite w. audiences from the Jesse H. Jones Concert Hall and the Alley Theater, right across from the hotel. Charm and quality. Limousine svce to dwntwn. **E–VE**

꘎꘎꘎ **Houstonian Hotel & Conference Center** (nr. dwntwn), 111 N. Post Oak Lane, TX 77024 (713/680-2826; toll free 800/ 231-2759). 297 rms, A/C, color TV, in-rm movies. AE, CB, DC, MC, V. Free gar. (valet parking $8), two pools, health club, five tennis courts, squash, sauna, bicycles, coffee shop, bar, rm svce, disco, boutiques, concierge, free crib. *Note:* Inviting modern hotel in a very handsome wooded setting across from Memorial Park. Best known as the legal Texas residence of President Bush, who stays here when in Houston. Comfortable, spacious rms w. refrigerator. Has one of the swankiest (and best-equipped) health clubs in town; hotel guests have full use of the health-spa facilities. Excellent svce; VIP floor ("Presidential Wing"). 5 min. from Galleria Center, 20 min. from dwntwn. A very good place to stay. **E–VE**

Allen Park Inn (nr. dwntwn), 2121 Allen Pkwy., TX 77019 (713/521-9321; toll free 800/231-6310). 250 rms, A/C, color TV, in-rm movies. AE, CB, DC, MC, V. Free parking, pool, health club, sauna, bicycling, 24-hr. coffee shop (Nashville Rm), bar, 24-hr. rm svce, hrdrsr, free crib. *Note:* Friendly, modern hotel of traditional type, nr. dwntwn. Spacious, comfortable rms w. balconies. Reception w. a smile. Very laudable rest. Caters largely to repeat customers; good value. 8 min. from dwntwn. **M**

Days Inn Downtown (dwntwn), 801 Calhoun St., TX 77002 (713/659-2222; toll free, see Days Inns). 600 rms, A/C, color TV. AE, CB, DC, MC, V. Free parking, pool, sauna, two rests., two bars, rm svce, disco, crib $10. *Note:* Huge, modern, well-laid-out 30-story hotel, very near the Exxon Building. Functionally comfortable; relatively efficient svce; business and group clientele. Interesting wknd discounts. **M**

La Quinta Inn–Greenway Plaza (nr. dwntwn), 4015 Southwest Frwy., TX 77027 (713/623-4750; toll free, see La Quinta). 128 rms, A/C, cable color TV. AE, CB, DC, MC, V. Free parking, pool, coffee shop, rm svce, free crib. *Note:* Modern, comfortable motel 20 min. from dwntwn. Friendly reception. Ideal if you're driving. Like all La Quinta motels, a good value. **I**

Rodeway Inn–Memorial Park (nr. dwntwn), 5820 Katy Frwy., TX 77007 (713/869-9211; toll free, see Rodeway Inns). 108 rms, A/C, color TV, in-rm movies. AE, DC, MC, V. Free parking, pool, coffee shop adj. *Note:* Well-run conventional motel very nr. Memorial Park; serviceable comforts, friendly reception and svce. Fine if you're driving; good value. 8 min. from dwntwn. **I**

Other Accommodations (from top bracket to budget)

La Colombe d'Or Inn (nr. dwntwn), 3410 Montrose Blvd., TX 77006 (713/524-7999). 6 suites, A/C, color TV. AE, CB, DC, MC, V. Free parking, rest. (La Colombe d'Or), bar, rm svce, concierge, free breakfast. *Note:* Houston's most luxuriously extravagant place to stay, this 1923 mansion, once the home of Humble Oil (now Exxon) chairman Walter Fondren, has been transformed into a compact mini-palace w. a mere six suites, each having its own huge bedroom, living rm, and dining rm, and all decorated w. objets d'art and antique furniture. The svce is polished to a high gloss. The name is that of a famous hotel at St-Paul-de-Vence on France's Côte d'Azur. Resv. must be made far in advance. Member of the prestigious Relais et Châteaux luxury chain. **VE**

J. W. Marriott (formerly the Inter-Continental; nr. dwntwn), 5150 Westheimer Rd., TX 77056 (713/961-1500; toll free, see Marriott). 518 rms, A/C, color TV, in-rm movies. AE, CB, DC, MC, V. Free parking, pool, tennis court, health club, sauna, squash, two rests. (including Les Continents), three bars, 24-hr. rm svce, disco, boutiques, concierge, free crib. *Note:* Ultramodern 23-story luxury hotel opposite the celebrated Galeria Mall shopping center, offering remarkably high standards of layout and comfort. Spacious rms; luxurious foyer featuring works by contemporary Texas artists. Comprehensive sports facilities; impeccable svce; prosperous business clientele. 20 min. from dwntwn. **E–VE**

ₜₜₜ Four Seasons Inn on the Park (nr. dwntwn), 4 Riverway, TX 77056 (713/871-8181; toll free, see Four Seasons). 383 rms, A/C, color TV, in-rm movies. AE, CB, DC, MC, V. Free parking (valet parking $5), two pools, health club, four tennis courts, sauna, bicycling, two rests., bar, 24-hr. rm svce, disco, concierge, free crib. *Note:* A modern hotel of real quality in Houston's most elegant neighborhood; lavishly comfortable rms w. balconies and views of Memorial Park (the best ones), but the older standard rms are small. Comprehensive facilities; La Reserve is an excellent rest. Personalized svce; caters to top businesspeople and rich Texans. No-smoking floor. Inviting grdn w. sculptures, fountains, a waterfall, and a little lake w. black swans. **E–VE**

ₜₜₜ The Wyndham Warwick (nr. dwntwn), 5701 S. Main St., TX 77251 (713/526-1991; toll free 800/822-4200). 298 rms, A/C, color TV, in-rm movies. AE, CB, DC, MC, V. Valet gar. $4, pool, sauna, health club, two rests. (including the Hunt Rm), bar, 24-hr. rm svce, disco, hrdrsr, boutiques. *Note:* Venerable 1920s luxury hotel in the European tradition, slightly disfigured by a new wing. A wealth of marbles, Aubusson tapestry, and wood paneling. Large, comfortable rms, some w. two bathrooms. Exemplary svce; view of Hermann Park. A place of elegance and charm; the favorite of politicians and visiting celebrities. **E–VE**

ₜₜₜ Doubletree–Allen Center (dwntwn), 400 Dallas St. (at Bagby), TX 77002 (713/759-0202; toll free 800/528-0444). 355 rms, A/C, color TV, in-rm movies. AE, CB, DC, MC, V. Valet gar. $8; two rests. (including Newport), bar, rm svce, nightclub, concierge, free crib. *Note:* This modern 20-floor tower of original design stands right in the Civic Center, one of the best locations in Houston. Comfortable, elegantly decorated rms; courteous, efficient svce. Very acceptable rests. Business clientele. Five blocks from the George R. Brown Convention Center. Interesting wknd packages. **VE**

ₜₜ Medical Center Hilton (nr. dwntwn), 6633 Travis St., TX 77030 (713/524-6633; toll free, see Hilton). 185 suites, cable color TV. AE, CB, DC, MC, V. Indoor parking $5, pool, health club, sauna, rest., bar, piano bar, rm svce, free crib. *Note:* Very comfortable hotel offering only mini-suites, very well laid out, w. refrigerators. Near Hermann Park and the museum district. Courteous reception and svce. Business clientele. Good overall value. **E**

ₜₜₜ Hilton Nassau Bay (vic.), 3000 NASA Rd. One, Clear Lake City, TX 77058 (713/339-9300; toll free, see Hilton). 244 rms, A/C, color TV, in-rm movies. AE, CB, DC, MC, V. Free parking, pool, fishing, water sports, marina, bicycling, rest. (Marina Bar & Grill), bar, rm svce, disco, boutiques, drugstore, free limo to Hobby Airport, crib $10. *Note:* This 14-floor hotel-marina on Clear Lake is ideal for visiting NASA's Lyndon B. Johnson Space Center. Comfortable, ultramodern facilities; spacious rms. w. balconies and lake view; efficient svce. Very good value; a fine place to stay, 35 min. from dwntwn. **M–E**

ₜₜ Ramada–Galleria West (nr. dwntwn), 7787 Katy Fwy., TX 77024 (713/682-1611; toll free, see Ramada). 287 rms, A/C, color TV, in-rm movies. AE, CB, DC, MC, V. Free parking, pool, rest., coffee shop, bar, rm svce, disco, free breakfast, crib $10. *Note:* Comfortable, up-to-date 11-story motel at the western exit from the city on I-10. Comfortable and functional. Friendly rms w. balconies. Ideal if you're driving. Good value. Interesting wknd packages. **I–M**

ₜ Best Western–Greenspoint Inn (nr. dwntwn), 11211 North Fwy., TX 77037 (713/447-6311; toll free, see Best Western). 144 rms, A/C, cable color TV. AE, CB, DC, MC, V. Free parking, pool, rest., bar, crib $10. *Note:* Typical motel at the northern exit from Houston on I-45. Functional comfort; cheerful svce. Ideal if you're traveling by car. 20 min. from dwntwn, 10 min. from Houston Intercontinental Airport (free airport limo.) Good value. **I**

Days Inn Wayside (nr. dwntwn), 2200 S. Wayside Dr., TX 77023 (713/928-2800; toll free, see Days Inn). 100 rms, A/C, cable color TV. AE, DC, MC, V. Free parking, pool, rest. (no alcoholic beverages), free breakfast, free crib. *Note:* Comfortable, functional hotel, halfway between Hobby Airport and dwntwn; 15 min. from dwntwn. Good value. **I**

Motel 6 (nr. dwntwn), 9638 Plainfield Rd., TX 77036 (713/778-0008). 205 rms, A/C, color TV, free in-rm movies. AE, DC, MC, V. Free parking, pool. *Note:* Modern, appealing motel w. very low rates. Close to Houston Baptist University; 25 min. from dwntwn by car via the Southwest Pkwy. Ideal if you're driving. One of the best values in the area. **B**

Airport Accommodations

Marriott Houston Airport Hotel (vic.), 18700 John F. Kennedy Blvd., TX 77032 (713/443-2310; toll free, see Marriott). 569 rms, A/C, color TV, in-rm movies. AE, CB, DC, MC, V. Free parking, pool, health club, sauna, two rests. (one, C.K.'s, on the top floor, revolves), two bars, disco, 24-hr. rm svce, hrdrsr, boutiques, free crib. *Note:* The architecture of this hotel, the only one in the airport complex, is original; the rms are comfortable and well soundproofed, w. refrigerators (some have private patios). Efficient svce; average rests. Business clientele. Free subway train to the terminal. Two VIP floors. Interesting wknd packages. **E**

Quality Inn–Hobby Airport (vic.), 1505 College Ave., TX 77587 (713/946-5900; toll free, see Quality Inns). 124 rms, A/C, color TV, in-rm movies. AE, CB, DC, MC, V. Free parking, pool, rest., bar, valet svce. *Note:* Relatively up-to-date and comfortable airport motel. Friendly reception and svce. Good value subject to one important reservation: no free airport shuttle. 5 min. from the terminal. **I**

YMCA/Youth Hostels

Perry House Hostel of the AYH (nr. dwntwn), 5302 Crawford St., TX 77004 (713/523-1009). 30 beds. Nr. the museums.

YMCA (dwntwn), 1600 Louisiana St., TX 77002 (713/659-8501). Men only. 147 rms, rest.

RESTAURANTS

A Note on Restaurant Prices: Houston restaurant prices, per person, excluding drinks and service charges, are coded as follows: **VE,** Very Expensive ($60 and up); **E,** Expensive ($40–$60); **M,** Moderate ($25–$40); **I,** Inexpensive ($15–$25); **B,** Budget (up to $15).

Personal Favorites (in order of preference)

Tony's (nr. dwntwn), 1801 Post Oak Blvd. (622-6778). A/C. Lunch Mon–Fri, dinner Mon–Sat; closed hols. AE, CB, DC, MC, V. J&T. *Specialties:* crab gazpacho, linguine pescatore, scallops Maxine, red snapper Hemingway, cappellini and lobster al bianco, piccata of veal w. truffles and wild mushrooms, fruit soufflés. *Note:* Remarkable French-inspired cuisine, deftly and delicately prepared. Exemplary svce from waiters in tuxedos; plush, flowery setting worthy of the rest.'s reputation. One of the South's finest wine cellars, w. 140,000 bottles. Resv. a must; the city's top power rest. for 20 years. Valet parking; 20 min. from dwntwn. *Continental.* **E**

De Ville (dwntwn), in the Four Seasons Hotel, 1300 Lamar Ave. (650-1300, ext. 4184). A/C. Breakfast/lunch/dinner daily. AE, CB, DC, MC, V. Jkt. *Specialties:* oyster bisque, snapper soup w. mushrooms, smoked salmon w. braised fennel, lamb nachos, goat-cheese soufflés. Very nice wine list. *Note:* The archetype of a luxury rest. Innovative, refined cooking. Art deco w. mahogany paneling, crystal, and Murano chandeliers reminiscent of the Edwardian era. Efficient svce; caters to senior executives and local VIPs. Resv. strongly advised. *French/American.* **M–E**

     Café Annie (nr. dwntwn), 1728 Post Oak Blvd. (840-8111). A/C. Lunch Tues–Fri, dinner Tues–Sat; closed hols. AE, CB, DC, MC, V. Jkt. *Specialties:* swordfish steak w. chipotle salsa, grilled sea scallops w. roasted tomato sauce and garlic cream, roast pheasant w. a pumpkin-seed crust, grilled quail and potato taco, lamb cutlets w. stewed onions, broiled sweetbreads w. ginger and mint. Very good wine list, fairly priced. *Note:* Few young Texan chefs of Robert Del Grande's generation offer so inventive and sophisticated a cuisine, in particular his remarkably light sauces. Has moved recently to much larger and more elegant quarters. Very good svce; resv. indispensable. Valet parking. *American.* **M–E**

     Uncle Tai's Hunan Yuan (nr. dwntwn), 1980 Post Oak Blvd. (960-8000). A/C. Lunch/dinner daily; closed Thanksgiving, Dec 25. AE, CB, DC, MC, V. Jkt. *Specialties:* three-color lobster, minced shrimp in garlic sauce, Hunan chicken, pork w. cashew nuts, diced boneless pigeon, smoked duck, sesame banana fritters. *Note:* This used to be one of the best rests. in New York; since moving bag and baggage to Houston in 1979, it has become the best Chinese rest. in the Southwest. Modern, elegant decor, but a little cold. Impeccable svce; 25 min. from dwntwn. Resv. advised. An experience you shouldn't miss. *Chinese.* **I–M**

     Churrascos (vic.), 9788 Bissonnet (541-2100). A/C. Lunch Mon–Fri, dinner nightly. AE, MC, V. *Specialties:* arepa (cheese tortilla), calamares relleños (stuffed squid), cerdo (broiled pork filet), meat and vegetable empanada, corvina (South American fish), churrasco (broiled beef) w. chimichurri sauce. Good list of wines at reasonable prices. *Note:* Since it was opened in 1988 by two self-taught brothers from Nicaragua (one has a doctorate in medicine and the other in economics) this rest. has been consistently crowded. In a city full to overflowing w. Mexican rests., the food at Churrascos comes as an agreeable surprise. Colorful, comfortable setting; friendly svce. 25 min. out along the Southwest Fwy. Resv. advisable. *Latin American.* **I–M**

     Ninfa's (nr. dwntwn), 2704 Navigation (228-1175). A/C. Lunch/dinner daily; closed July 4, Thanksgiving, Dec 25. AE, CB, DC, MC, V. *Specialties:* tacos al carbon, flautas, carnitas, chalupas, chilpanzingas, queso a la parrilla, sopaipillas. *Note:* The most popular of the (numberless) Mexican rests. in Houston; a local institution, usually crowded and noisy, w. no interior decoration. No resv. are accepted over the wknd, and a wait is unavoidable. Other locations: 6154 Westheimer Rd. (781-2740), 9333 Katy Fwy. (932-8760), and 8507 Gulf Fwy. (943-3183); plus five more around town. *Mexican.* **B–I**

     Chili's (vic.), 5930 Richmond (780-1654). A/C. Lunch/ dinner daily. MC, V. *Specialties:* chili, hamburgers. *Note:* As the name implies, the house chili here (chopped beef, spiced according to a secret Texan recipe) deserves your whole attention, and you shouldn't miss the experience. Popular country-style atmosphere. For several other locations in Houston, consult the local telephone directory. *American.* **B**

     Goode Company Barbecue (nr. dwntwn), 5109 Kirby Dr. (522-2530). A/C. Lunch/dinner daily. No credit cards. *Specialties:* barbecued beef, ham, and pork; chicken, sausages, and duck grilled over mesquite. *Note:* A real local landmark. Wonderful barbecued meats attractively priced: from $3 for a sandwich to $10 for a full meal w. three kinds of meat and two vegetables. Amusing funky decor and Texas atmosphere, right down to the picnic tables. Rather obtrusive background country music. Generally crowded; an experience you shouldn't miss. *American.* **B**

Other Restaurants (from top bracket to budget)

     La Reserve (nr. dwntwn), in the Four Seasons Inn on the Park (see "Accommodations," above) (871-8177). A/C. Lunch Mon–Fri, dinner Mon–Sat. AE, CB, DC, MC, V. Jkt. (J&T at dinner). *Special-*

ties: pheasant mousse w. myrtle vinegar, partridge terrine w. foie gras, lamb en croûte w. truffle butter, sautéed snails w. noodles and pesto, ragoût of lobster, remarkable desserts. Also, low-calorie diet menu. The menu changes weekly. *Note:* As in all the luxury rests. of the Four Seasons chain, you may choose between classic, elegantly prepared haute cuisine or a low-calorie menu limited in sodium and cholesterol. In either case, the food attains perfection. Beautiful flower arrangements in a luxurious setting; impeccable svce. Everything in the grand style—including prices. The realm of expense-account dining. *French/ Continental.* **M–E**

Charley's 517 (dwntwn), 517 Louisiana St. (224-4438). A/C. Lunch/dinner Mon–Sat; closed hols. AE, CB, DC, MC, V. Jkt. *Specialties:* Grilled gulf oysters w. pasta, quail stuffed w. boudin, wild boar grilled over mesquite wood, roast swordfish w. wild mushrooms, veal scaloppine w. sautéed apples in Calvados sauce. Menu changes regularly. Splendid wine list backed by more than 30,000 bottles in the cellar. *Note:* One of Houston's three or four best rests. The always inspired and often innovative cuisine of chef Clive Berkman features game and local produce. Elegant decor w. stained glass and a profusion of flowers. Business clientele at lunch, theater-goers at dinner—the rest. is across from Jesse H. Jones Hall and the Alley Theater. Resv. a must. Valet parking. *American/Continental.* **M–E**

Rotisserie for Beef and Bird (vic.), 2200 Wilcrest Dr. (977-9524). A/C. Lunch Mon–Fri, dinner Mon–Sat; closed hols. AE, MC, V. Jkt. *Specialties:* cream of pheasant soup, sautéed quail, grilled lobster, roast goose, pheasant and game, aged prime steak and venison, snapper sautéed in brown butter, very good homemade desserts. Fine wine list. *Note:* Lovers of unexpected delicacies will find here, year round, Asian venison, antelope, or Russian wild boar, but the more conventional dishes of game, venison, or ordinary red meat are equally recommended. The ovens and broilers are in full view of the patrons, enhancing the elegant country-club layout. Very good svce; yuppie clientele. *American/Steak.* **M**

Brennan's (nr. dwntwn), 3300 Smith St. (522-9711). A/C. Lunch/dinner daily, jazz brunch Sat–Sun; closed Dec 25. AE, CB, DC, MC, V. Jkt. *Specialties:* turtle soup, shrimp rémoulade, oysters Bienville, veal cutlet Tchoupitoulas, fresh duck liver w. sherry dressing, sautéed redfish w. crabmeat, bread pudding, bananas Foster. Good wine list. *Note:* Affiliated w. the famous Commander's Palace in New Orleans. Excellent Créole cuisine; pleasant setting in an old brick house w. a shady patio. Efficient svce; valet parking. Locally popular, especially for brunch, so resv. advised. *Créole.* **I–M**

Ruth's Chris Steak House (nr. dwntwn), 6213 Richmond Ave. (789-2333). A/C. Lunch Sun–Fri, dinner nightly; closed hols. *Specialties:* excellent broiled red meats, roast of beef, fried shrimp. Fine list of California wines. *Note:* As the name implies, the specialty here is steak, more steak, and steak again: from filet mignon to giant T-bone and from porterhouse to rib-eye. Affiliated w. New Orleans's famous restaurant of the same name. A few posters and other oil-company advertising constitute the entire scheme of decoration. Friendly, smiling svce; highly favored by local meat eaters; resv. advised. *Steak.* **I–M**

Cadillac Bar (nr. dwntwn), 1802 Shepherd Dr. at Katy Fwy. (862-2020). A/C. Lunch/dinner daily; closed Thanksgiving, Dec 25. AE, CB, DC, MC, V. *Specialties:* fajitas, garrito, cabrito grilled over a mesquite-wood fire, barbecues, roast quail, chorizo and melted cheese. *Note:* Authentic northern Mexican cooking, tasty and highly spiced. Guaranteed local color from the shoeshine boy through the guitar player. Locally popular; resv. advised. *Mexican.* **B–I**

Ouisie's Table (nr. dwntwn), 1708 Sunset Blvd. (528-2264). A/C. Lunch/dinner Tues–Sat; closed hols. AE, CB, DC, MC, V. *Specialties:* fresh homemade pasta, black-bean soup, vegetable lasagne, curries, trout Provençal w. zucchini, strudel. *Note:* Elouise Cooper, an excellent self-taught chef, serves imaginative food at very beguiling prices in a relaxed atmosphere and comfortable setting. Artists, yuppies, and professors flock to this rest. which is a hop, skip, and a jump from the museum district and nr. Rice University. Locally popular; resv. advised. *American.* **B–I**

♀ **Tony Mandola's Blue Oyster Bar** (nr. dwntwn), 1608 N.
🍸 Shepherd (864-0915). A/C. Lunch/dinner Mon–Sat. No credit cards. *Specialties:* gulf oysters, gumbo, red beans and rice, crayfish à l'étouffée, spaghetti w. shrimp and crab. *Note:* Wonderful Créole bistro whose flavorful, colorful food is worthy of the finest rests. in New Orleans. No pretensions to elegance, but friendly svce. Very popular locally; no resv.; 20 min. from dwntwn. Other location: 8105 Gulf Fwy. (640-1117). *Créole/Seafood.* **B–I**

☀️♀ **Captain Benny's Half Shell** (nr. dwntwn), 7409 S. Main (795-
☀️🍸 9051). A/C. Lunch/dinner Mon–Sat. No credit cards. *Specialties:* oysters and shrimp from the gulf, stuffed crab, crayfish in season, fried catfish, gumbo. *Note:* Absolutely fresh seafood efficiently served—and the prices are a pleasant surprise. A favorite of connoisseurs and usually packed, so you'll have to wait. Unusual nautical decor. One of the best places to eat in Houston; for other locations, consult the city telephone directory. *Seafood.* **B**

♀ **Otto's Barbecue** (nr. dwntwn), 5502 Memorial Dr. (864-
🍸 2573). A/C. Lunch/dinner Mon–Sat; closed hols. No credit cards. *Specialties:* barbecued brisket, ham, and sausages; hamburgers. *Note:* Generally agreed to offer Houston's best barbecued beef; Otto serves more than 1,400 lb. (600kg) daily—a reference in itself! Hamburger reigns supreme at the burger bar nr. the entrance. Unpretentious western setting and svce. Locally very popular since 1950. The favorite of President Bush. *American.* **B**

A Restaurant in the Vicinity

☀️♀♀ **Frank's Café** (vic.), 603 E. U.S. 90, 37 mi. (60km) east of
☀️🍸🍸 Houston in Dayton (409/258-2598). A/C. Lunch/dinner daily. AE, MC, V. *Specialties:* oysters, crabs, shrimp, and red snapper from the gulf; fried catfish; filet mignon; club steak; ribs of beef Delmonico; homemade pies. *Note:* One of the most famous roadhouses in Texas, on the old U.S. 90 from Houston to New Orleans. Remarkably fresh seafood; superb meats stored in a glass-enclosed aging refrigerator w. steaks on view, from which you can make your own choice—and all this at very reasonable prices. Cheerful, friendly svce. Frequented by people in-the-know since 1948 and well worth the 45-min. drive from the city. Resv. suggested. *American/Steak.* **I**

Cafeterias/Fast Food

Butera's (nr. dwntwn), 4621 Montrose Blvd. (523-0722). Lunch/dinner daily. AE, CB, DC, MC, V. Fine cafeteria-style deli on the grounds of the Chelsea Market. Generous sandwiches, flavorful salads.

Luby's (nr. dwntwn), 5215 Buffalo Speedway (664-4852). Open till 8pm daily. *Specialties:* Mexican dishes, fish of the day, steak, roast beef. *Note:* Decent food at very decent prices. There are 20 other locations in Houston; consult the city telephone directory.

BARS & NIGHTCLUBS

Al Mark's Melody Lane Ballroom (nr. dwntwn), 3027 Crossview (785-5301). Giant dance hall with live music; very popular locally, so local color guaranteed. 25 min. from dwntwn.

The Ale House (nr. dwntwn), 2425 W. Alabama at Kirby (521-2333). More than 100 different beers are on offer at this well-patronized bar; disco with New wave music upstairs. Open daily.

Cody's (nr. dwntwn), 3400 Montrose Blvd. (522-9747). A singles bar that is much frequented by yuppies after the day's toil; also very acceptable rest. and live jazz. Beautiful view of the city.

Comedy Workshop (nr. dwntwn), 2105 San Felipe St. (524-7333). Comedy club, very popular locally.

☼ **The Great Caruso** (vic.), 10001 Westheimer Rd. at Briar Park (780-4900). Original rest.-nightclub for lovers of opera and bel canto; even the waiters contribute to the illusion. Wonderful 1900s rococo opera-house decor. An entertaining place, well worth the 30-min. drive from dwntwn. Very acceptable food. Valet parking. Open nightly.

In Cahoots (vic.), 2626 Tanglewide Lane (784-8026). Where the country-and-western scene has shifted since Gilley's, of *Urban Cowboy* fame, closed last year. Open nightly.

Rockefeller's (nr. dwntwn), 3620 Washington Ave. (861-9365). Modern jazz, live, in a relaxed atmosphere. Open Mon–Sat.

Studebaker's (nr. dwntwn), 2630 Augusta Dr. (738-4142). Fashionable disco drawing a younger, "in" crowd. Near Galleria Center.

NEARBY EXCURSIONS

⚓ **PORT OF HOUSTON** (5 mi./8km east along Clinton Dr.): You'll get a fine view of the port, which handles more than 6,000 vessels a year, from the observation platform at Wharf No. 9; open daily. Free boat tours of the harbor Tues–Wed and Fri–Sun year round except for the month of Sept (225-4044 for resv.). Worth seeing.

⚓ **SAN JACINTO BATTLEGROUND** (21 mi./34km SE on I-45S, I-610N, Tex. 225, and Tex. 134) (479-2421): Battlefield on which Gen. Sam Houston's Texas volunteers won a decisive engagement against the Mexican dictator Santa Anna, only 2 months after the latter's victory at the Alamo (see Chapter 37 on San Antonio). A gigantic memorial column (elevator), capped with the Lone Star of Texas, was erected in 1939; at 570 ft. (174m), it's the tallest monument in the world, 15 ft. (5m) higher than the Washington Monument. Made of concrete clad in polished limestone, it weighs a total of 32,000 tons. Nearby is the battleship *Texas,* veteran of two World Wars, which served as General Eisenhower's headquarters during the Normandy landings of 1944. At the foot of the monument is a Museum of the History of Texas. Open daily in summer, Tues–Sun the rest of the year.

☼⚓ **LYNDON B. JOHNSON SPACE CENTER** (25 mi./40km SE along I-45 and NASA Rd. 1 in Clear Lake City) (483-4321): The nerve center of NASA, from which guidance has been provided for all manned space flights since 1962 (including the *Gemini, Apollo,* and *Mercury* missions and the space-shuttle flights), with live TV coverage for viewers around the world. There are 40,000 technicians on the payroll. The wonderful **Space Museum** has several models of spacecraft, including the gigantic *Saturn V,* genuine moon rocks, and a replica of the lunar landing module *Apollo 17,* which holds the record for the longest human stay: 75 hr. Guided tours of the **Control Center** and the astronaut training areas. Movies on various space missions. As exciting as the Kennedy Space Center. Open daily.

☼⚓ **GALVESTON** (51 mi./82km south on I-45): This beach resort and busy port was almost totally destroyed in 1900 by a tidal wave which left 6,000 dead. There are many fine upper-class 19th-century homes along the Strand, between 20th St. and 25th St., and on Broadway, among them the **Bishop's Palace,** 1402 Broadway, open daily, and **Ashton Villa,** 2328 Broadway, open daily, which belongs to former Texas Gov. Ross Sterling. Very popular beaches. A must-see. **Railroad Museum** in the Santa Fe Union station, 123 Rosenberg (409/765-5700): the largest collection of restored railroad equipment in the Southwest. On-the-way stop for a visit to the LBJ Space Center (see above).

Where to Stay in Galveston

☼♀♀ **Tremont House,** 2300 Ship's Mechanic Row, Galveston, TX
77550 (409/763-0300). 108 rms. AE, CB, DC, MC, V. *Note:*
An elegantly renovated 1880s hotel retaining its gracious Victorian atmosphere.
M–E

HUNTSVILLE (71 mi./113km north on I-45): Native city of
Texas's founder and first elected president, Sam Houston. His
birthplace, home, and tomb at 1836 Sam Houston Ave. (409/295-7824) may
be seen Tues–Sun.

NATIONAL PARKS NEARBY

☼ **PADRE ISLAND NATIONAL SEASHORE** (236 mi./
378km SW on U.S. 59, U.S. 77 and 37, and Tex. 358): A 113-
mi.-long (182km) peninsula with an average width of 3 mi. (5km). Almost entirely uninhabited, this long sweep of sand, with dunes rising to 45 ft. (15m) in
places, has once again become a paradise for campers (fully equipped camping
grounds), fishermen, and sailors after sustaining severe damage from a disastrous
oil slick in 1979. The spine of the peninsula, less contaminated by civilization,
has been made into a nature reserve for some 350 species of birds. The park is
connected to Corpus Christi by the John F. Kennedy Causeway and to Port Isabel by the South Padre Causeway. For lovers of unspoiled nature. For **information,** contact the Superintendent, Padre Island National Seashore, 9405 S. Padre
Island Dr., Corpus Christi, TX 78418 (512/937-2621).

On the way, stop off at the **King Ranch,** on Tex. 141 at Kingsville (37 mi./
59km SW of Corpus Christi via Tex. 44 and U.S. 77). Symbolic of Texan wealth
and power, this ranch of about 820,000 acres (332,000ha), the size of the state of
Rhode Island, is the largest privately held agricultural property in the world.
Founded in 1853 by Richard King, an enterprising sea captain, the property is
still owned by descendants of the King family. A 12-mi. (19km) road tour (impassable in bad weather) will allow you to gain a good impression of life on the
ranch. Open daily; for information, call 512/592-8516. A must for lovers of
wide-open spaces.

Where to Stay

There are hotels, motels, and restaurants at Corpus Christi (north of Padre
Island) and at Port Isabel, to the south, almost at the Mexican border.

♀♀♀ **Radisson South Padre Resort,** 500 Padre Blvd. at the Causeway, South Padre Island, TX 78597 (512/761-6511; toll free,
see Radisson). 275 rms and 120 suites. Large modern hotel on the ocean. **E–VE**

♀♀ **Best Western Sandy Shores,** 3200 Surfside, Corpus Christi,
TX 78403 (512/883-7456; toll free, see Best Western). 254
rms. Comfortable, functional motel right on the beach. **I–M**

♀ **White Sands,** on Tex. 100, Port Isabel, TX 78578 (512/943-
2414). 30 units. Small and modest but well-run motel w. a
private marina. **I**

CHAPTER 37

SAN ANTONIO

□ □ □

The first of America's great cities to elect a mayor of Mexican origin (Henry Cisneros in 1981), San Antonio is a living symbol of the Hispanic influence north of the Rio Grande; every year it attracts 10 million visitors.

Founded in 1718 as the Spanish military outpost of San Antonio de Bexar, with an accompanying Franciscan mission of San Antonio de Valero (both on the site of what is now the fort of the **Alamo**), the city was the capital of the Spanish province of Texas when, a century later, Mexico achieved independence. It shortened its name, changing its flag and its allegiance. But the restless settlers of Texas soon achieved confrontation with the Mexican authorities. On February 23, 1836, the redoubtable Gen. Antonio López de Santa Anna, at the head of 5,000 Mexican soldiers, arrived to lay siege to the fort and mission of the Alamo, in the heart of San Antonio. After 13 days of furious fighting, the assault was mounted on Mar 6. The Mexicans lost 1,600 men in the battle, but they took the town and killed every last man of the heroic garrison: 187 American and foreign volunteers, including Col. William Travis and the two legendary scouts Davy Crockett and Jim Bowie. "Remember the Alamo" became the Texans' battle cry, until their final victory over the Mexicans a month later at San Jacinto (see Chapter 36 on Houston). The famous Rough Riders, those volunteers who won so much renown in Cuba during the Spanish-American War, came into being in San Antonio in 1898. Among the recruiters of this army of firebrands was the future president Theodore Roosevelt, who signed up many of his Rough Riders at the bar of the famous **Menger Hotel,** still one of the city's greatest tourist attractions.

San Antonio has preserved many interesting architectural relics of its eventful past, perhaps the most important being the church of the Alamo, at once museum and historic shrine; a half dozen Franciscan missions, including the superb **San José Mission;** and the **Spanish Governor's Palace.** If you take into account the picturesque Mexican district with its colorful market, the **Mercado;** the German enclave of the **King William District** with its opulent 1870s homes; the **Paseo del Rio,** a pretty flower-planted promenade along the river with water buses, restaurants, cafés, and shops; or the charming **Villita,** a little bit of 18th-century Spain in the heart of the city, you'll see that San Antonio is unquestionably the most firmly rooted in history of all the great cities of Texas, though one of the most vigorous as well, with its food, garment, cement, and above all aircraft-maintenance industries (the huge **Kelly Air Force Base** is nicknamed "The Home of the Air Force," and the adjoining **Lackland Air Force Base** is the country's largest air force training base). San Antonio's growth rate ranks sixth among the country's major cities.

Famous San Antonians include Conrad Hilton, founder of the hotel chain that bears his name, and actresses Carol Burnett and Joan Crawford.

BASIC FACTS: State of Texas. Area code: 512. Time zone: central. ZIP Code: 78205. Founded: 1718. Approximate population: city, 975,000; metropolitan area, 1,320,000. The nation's 10th-largest city, 31st-largest metropolitan area.

CLIMATE: Renowned for its year-round sunshine, San Antonio proudly proclaims itself "The City Where Sunshine Spends the Winter"; if you love fine weather, this is the place for you. While winter is pleasantly mild (rarely below 51°F/10°C in Jan), summer is on the sultry side (July average, 84°F/29°C), only partly relieved by the occasional tropical storm coming up from the Gulf of Mexico.

DISTANCES: Albuquerque, 861 mi. (1,378km); Dallas, 270 mi. (432km); Houston, 197 mi. (315km); Mexican border, 157 mi. (252km); New Orleans, 548 mi. (877km); Tucson, 883 mi. (1,412km).

ARRIVAL & TRANSIT INFORMATION

AIRPORT: San Antonio International Airport (SAT), 8 mi. (12km) north. For further information, call 821-3411.

AIRLINES: American (222-0121), Continental (828-8381), Delta (222-2354), Southwest (696-1221), TWA (226-0626), United (223-2525), and USAir (toll free 800/428-4322).

CITY LINK: The **cab** fare from the airport to downtown is about $12–$14; time, 15 min. Bus: **Supervan** (344-7433), leaves every 20 min.; serves major dwntwn hotels; fare, $6; time, about 20 min.

Good public transportation system by bus and streetcar: Metropolitan Transit System (227-2020). Cabs are quite numerous and affordable. Unless you intend to visit the Franciscan missions around the city, you won't need to rent a car.

CAR RENTAL (at the airport unless otherwise indicated): Avis (826-6332); Budget (824-0737); Dollar (826-0363); Hertz (826-0651); National (824-1841); and Thrifty, 330 NE Loop 410 (341-4677). For dwntwn locations, consult the local telephone directory.

LIMOUSINE SERVICES: Carey Limousine (448-3492) and Don's Limousine (923-7556).

TAXIS: Theoretically, cabs can be hailed on the street, but it's more usual to take one from the waiting lines outside the major hotels, or from one of the stands along Paseo del Rio—or to phone. Major companies: **Checker Cab** (222-2151), **United Cab** (733-0852), and **Yellow Cab** (226-4242). There are also **taxi-boats** operating along Paseo del Rio (222-1701).

TRAIN: Amtrak station, 1174 E. Commerce St. (223-3226; toll free 800/872-7245).

INTERCITY BUSES: Greyhound, 500 N. St. Mary's St. (227-8351).

INFORMATION & TOURS

TOURIST INFORMATION: The **San Antonio Convention and Visitors Bureau,** 121 Alamo Pl. (P.O. Box 2277), TX 78298 (512/270-8700; toll free 800/447-3372).
    San Antonio Conservation Society, 107 King William St. (512/224-6163): Information on the King William Historic District.
    Visitor Information Center, 317 Alamo Pl. (512/270-8748).

GUIDED TOURS: B. & T. **Fuller Bus Tours** (bus), 129 E. Summit St. (734-8706): Guided tours in London-style double-decker bus; serves principal hotels.
    Gray Line Tours (bus), 800 W. Myrtle St. (227-5371): Guided tours of the city and surroundings; serves principal hotels.

River Boat Tours (boat), 430 E. Commerce St. (227-1701): Barge trips along Paseo del Rio (seven landing stages); also dinner cruises. Daily year round.

San Antonio City Tours (bus), Alamo Pl. (680-8724): 2-hr. guided tours of the missions around the city.

SIGHTS, ATTRACTIONS & ACTIVITIES

ARCHITECTURAL HIGHLIGHTS: ☼🔔 **Arneson River Theater,** 503 Villita St. (299-8610): Open-air theater of original design: the river flows between the spectators and the stage. Should be seen, preferably during a performance.

🔔 **HemisFair Plaza,** bounded by Commerce St., Market St., Durango St., and Alamo St. (299-8570): A huge esplanade, once the site of the HemisFair '68 World's Fair. There's an ultramodern **Convention Center** whose frontage displays a giant mosaic by the Mexican artist Juan O'Gorman, and several other interesting buildings: the **Tower of the Americas,** the city's tallest high-rise (see "Panoramas," below), the **Theater for the Performing Arts,** the **Mexican Cultural Institute** (see "Museums of Art," below), and the **Institute of Texan Cultures** (see "Museums of Science and History," below). Open daily.

CHURCHES/SYNAGOGUES: ☼🔔🔔 **San Antonio Missions National Historical Park:** Four Franciscan missions built between 1720 and 1731, and offering an interesting glimpse of Spanish Colonial culture in the 18th century. For information, call 229-6000. The 🔔🔔 **Mission San José de Aguayo,** 6539 San José Dr., 5 mi. (9km) south on Roosevelt Ave. (922-2731), is the most elegantly beautiful of all; superb chapel with richly carved sacristy window, and Native American encampment. Open daily. 🔔 **Mission San Francisco de la Espada,** 10040 Espada Rd., 6 mi. (10km) south on Roosevelt Ave. (627-2021), has been completely restored; note also, halfway between Mission San José and Mission San Juan Capistrano, the Espada Dam and aqueduct built by the friars (1731–45) to supply the missions. Open daily. 🔔 **Mission San Juan Capistrano,** 9101 Graf Rd., 6 mi. (10km) south on Roosevelt Ave. (229-5734), is very near San Francisco de la Espada; the well-preserved church is still in use. Open daily. 🔔🔔 **Mission de la Purísima Concepción de Acuña,** 807 Mission Rd. via Roosevelt Ave. (229-5732), is near downtown; it's the oldest unrestored Spanish mission in the country, and one of the best preserved. The chapel's wall paintings, and its acoustics, are famous. Open daily.

🔔 **San Fernando Cathedral,** 114 Military Plaza (227-1297): Fine example of 19th-century (1873) Gothic, on the site of an earlier (1758) church built by settlers from the Canary Islands. The remains of the defenders of the Alamo are supposed to have been buried in its foundations. A must-see; open daily.

HISTORIC BUILDINGS: ☼🔔🔔 **The Alamo,** Alamo Plaza (225-1391): Makes every Texan heart beat faster. Of the fort of the Alamo (the Spanish word for "poplar"), dating from 1744 and once so gallantly defended by Davy Crockett, Jim Bowie, Colonel Travis, and their 186 comrades-in-arms, there remain only the chapel, now a memorial of the battle, and the "Long Barrack," once the Franciscan convent of San Antonio de Valero, where the last defenders were killed on March 6, 1836. Today it houses a museum of Texas history. Open daily.

☼🔔 **Cos House,** 416 La Villita (299-8610): The most famous building in the La Villita Historic District. It was here that Gen. Perfecto de Cos, on December 10, 1835 (3 months before the siege of the Alamo), signed the instrument whereby the Mexicans surrendered the town to the patriots of Texas. Open daily.

☼🔔 **Menger Hotel,** 204 Alamo Plaza (223-4361): A local landmark since 1859. Historical figures of the caliber of Gens. Robert E. Lee and Ulysses S. Grant, not to mention Sam Houston, a founding father

DOWNTOWN SAN ANTONIO

KEY TO NUMBERED SIGHTS
1. The Alamo
2. La Villita
3. Market Square
4. Fiesta Plaza
5. Tower of the Americas
6. The Institute of Texan Cultures
7. San Antonio Museum of Transportation
8. Main Plaza
9. Military Plaza
10. King William Historical Area
11. The Heart of Texas
12. San Fernando Cathedral
13. Spanish Governor's Palace
14. Southwest Craft Center
15. Travis Park
16. Convention and Visitors Bureau

of the state of Texas, have frequented the place. At the bar here, in 1898, Theodore Roosevelt, the future president, recruited volunteers for his famous Rough Riders to serve in the Spanish-American War.

Navarro House State Historic Site, 228 S. Laredo St. (226-4801): Interesting buildings of adobe (native-style unbaked bricks made in this instance of *caliche,* a mixture of gravel, clay, and limestone) and whitewashed stone, and blending a number of unrelated architectural styles: Spanish Colonial, German, French, Victorian. Built in the 1850s, these three houses, still w. their original furniture and decoration, were the home of José Antonio Navarro, a rich Texan rancher and politician, born at San Antonio in 1795. Definitely worth a visit; open Tues–Sat.

Spanish Governor's Palace, 105 Military Plaza (224-0601): Official residence of the Spanish governors, built in 1749—witness the date and the coats-of-arms of the Habsburgs and of King Philip V engraved on the keystone. A fine colonial building w. 2-ft.-thick (61cm) walls and carved doors, still w. its original furniture; the only one of its kind surviving in Texas. Open daily.

Steves Homestead, 509 King William St. (225-5924): This fine Gothic Revival home on the banks of the San Antonio River dates from 1876; it is a mute witness to the wealth and urbanity of the German merchants who in the 19th century lived in the King William Historic District (see "Strolls," below). Splendid old furniture; huge landscaped grdn w. an indoor pool (River Haus). Open daily.

INDUSTRIAL TOURS: **Lone Star Brewing Co.–Buckhorn Hall of Horns,** 600 Lone Star Blvd. (226-8301 weekdays, 226-8303 weekends): This unusual museum, inside the brewery, displays an astonishing variety of 3,500 hunting trophies from around the world—polar bears to African antelope—as well as the Hall of Fins (marine life) and the Hall of Feathers (mounted birds). Reconstruction of the 1887 Buckhorn Saloon; free beer tasting. The adjoining **Hall of Texas History** has exhibits dealing with the history of the state from the time of the first Spanish explorers. Open daily.

MARKETS: **Market Square,** bounded by Dolorosa St., San Saba St., W. Commerce St., and Santa Rosa St. (299-8600): The local retailing center for more than a century, it includes the **Farmers' Market,** dealing in fruit and vegetables; the Mexican market **El Mercado,** where you may haggle in a colorful, authentically Mexican environment; and the **Centro de Artes del Mercado,** an arts-and-crafts market in a restored 1922 building. All are open daily year round; some businesses are open around the clock. Very lively.

MUSEUMS OF ART: **Marion Koogler McNay Art Museum,** 6000 N. New Braunfels Ave. at U.S. 81 (824-5368): Some old master paintings, but mostly moderns (Picasso, Chagall, Cézanne, Gauguin, van Gogh), pre-Columbian art, and 19th- and 20th-century bronzes, in a lovely Mediterranean-style villa overlooking San Antonio. Also temporary exhibitions. A must-see; open Tues–Sun.

Mexican Cultural Institute, HemisFair Plaza (227-0123): Mexican art, crafts, and archeology; revolving exhibits of work by contemporary Mexican artists. Interesting museum administered by the National University of Mexico; open Tues–Sun.

San Antonio Museum of Art, 200 W. Jones Ave. (226-5544): This new museum, housed in the former Lone Star Brewery (an 1880s building, magnificently restored and converted to its new use with interior overhead walkways and glass-walled elevators), is a complete success both artistically and architecturally. The important Robert W. Kinn and Nelson A. Rockefeller collections of pre-Columbian and Mexican art are on display here, as are Roman antiquities, Far Eastern and Spanish Colonial art, and 20th-century American painting and photography. Lovely modern-sculpture grdn. All this in an inviting setting on the banks of the San Antonio River. Open daily.

MUSEUMS OF SCIENCE & HISTORY: The **Buckhorn Hall of Horns and Hall of Texas History** (see the Lone Star Brewing Co. under "Industrial Tours," above).

Fort Sam Houston Museum, on I-35 at New Braunfels Ave., Bldg. 123 (221-4886): Headquarters of the Fifth U.S. Army, Fort Sam Houston is one of the oldest (1879) and most famous military posts in the southern U.S. It was here that the Apache chief Geronimo was imprisoned; here, too, U.S. military aviation was born in 1910. The museum contains thousands of objects from the 19th century (uniforms, weapons, documents, etc.). For military history buffs. Open Wed–Sun.

Hertzberg Circus Collection, 210 W. Market St. (299-7810): More than 20,000 items illustrating the history of the circus: posters, photographs, models of the Big Top, miniature circuses, souvenirs of Tom Thumb and the legendary Phineas T. Barnum. One of the most important collections of its kind in the world. Open daily May–Oct, Mon–Sat the rest of the year.

Institute of Texan Cultures, HemisFair Plaza (226-7651): An entity of the University of Texas, this museum illustrates in lively visual fashion the historical and cultural contributions made by various nations and ethnic groups to the foundation and expansion of Texas. Spectacular. Open Tues–Sun.

Texas Ranger Museum Memorial Hall, 3805 Broadway (824-2537): The history of the legendary Texas Rangers from their foundation in 1828 onward, illustrated by hundreds of drawings, photographs, old weapons, saddles, badges, souvenirs of pioneer days, etc. Interesting. Open Tues–Sun May–Aug, Wed–Sun the rest of the year.

Witte Museum, 3801 Broadway at Tuleta St. (226-5544): Fine museum of history, anthropology, and natural science entirely devoted to Texas. From dinosaurs and prehistoric Native American artifacts to houses of 19th-century pioneers, brought from different places across the state and rebuilt here. Open daily.

PANORAMAS: **Tower of the Americas,** HemisFair Plaza (229-8615): Soaring concrete tower 750 ft. (229m) high including its crowning TV antenna, the tallest building in the city. The observation platform 622 ft. (189m) up offers a unique view, for a radius of 100 mi. (160km) in fine weather. Revolving restaurant (mediocre) at the top. Open daily till 11pm.

PARKS & GARDENS: **Brackenridge Park,** N. Broadway, 2 mi. (3.5km) north of the city (732-8481): Lovely park on 340 acres (138ha) of rolling country a 5-min. drive from downtown. Celebrated zoo; miniature train and cable-car rides. Water grdns in the pit of an abandoned quarry (**Sunken Oriental Gardens**). **Texas Ranger Memorial Hall** and **Witte Museum** (see above). Many picnic areas. Worth a visit.

San Antonio Botanical Gardens, 555 Funston Pl. at N. New Braunfels Ave. (821-5115): On a height of land above the city (fine view from the Gazebo Observatory), this 33-acre (13ha) botanic grdn includes a lovely rose grdn, a little lake, a sunken courtyard surrounded by abstract glass structures designed by Argentine architect Emilio Ambasz (the **Lucile Halsell Conservatory**), a grdn for the blind labeled in Braille (the **Touch-and-Smell Garden**), and an enormous sampling of the flora of Texas. Open Tues–Sun.

PERFORMING ARTS: For daily listings of all shows and cultural events, consult the entertainment pages of the daily papers *San Antonio Express-News* (morning and evening) and *San Antonio Light* (morning and evening), and of the magazine *San Antonio Monthly.*

Alamo City Theater, 339 W. Josephine St. (299-8610): Contemporary theater, comedy, drama.

Arneson River Theater, 503 Villita St. (299-8610): A theater of unprecedented design—the spectators are on one bank of Paseo del Rio while the stage and the actors are on the other. Open-air music and theater (June–Aug).

Convention Center Arena, 210 E. Market St. (299-8500): Pop, rock, and jazz concerts.

Joe and Harry Freeman Coliseum, 3201 E. Houston St. (224-6080): Country-and-western concerts.

Laurie Auditorium, 715 Stadium Dr. (736-8117): Chamber music, classical recitals.

Majestic Performing Arts Center, 212 E. Houston St. (226-2626): Visiting Broadway shows, touring companies. Beautiful 1920s interior splendidly restored. Home of the San Antonio Symphony (principal conductor: Zdenek Macal) (Dec–Mar).

San Antonio Little Theater, 800 W. Ashby (733-7258): Shows, contemporary theater (Sept–May). Home of the San Antonio Little Theater.

Theater for the Performing Arts, Market St. and Bowie (299-8529): Concerts, ballet, opera. Home of the San Antonio Ballet (Oct–Dec).

SHOPPING: El Mercado/Mexican Market, W. Commerce St. and Santa Rosa St. (299-8600): Bargains for collectors of folk art: pottery, piñatas (ornamental pots filled with candies), handcrafts, silver jewelry, typical Mexican foodstuffs. Lively and colorful. Open daily.

Rivercenter Shopping Mall, 849 E. Commerce St. (225-1000): A classy, glassy, 10-acre (4ha), three-story dining, shopping, and entertainment complex on Paseo del Rio, opened in 1988 at a total cost of $200 million, with 135 shops, stores, and restaurants. With its little bridges across the river, all-glass facades, and mariachi band, Rivercenter is an astonishing blend of Mexico, America, and Venice.

Tienda Guadalupe, 1001 S. Alamo St. (226-5873): Genuine folk art and crafts.

SPECIAL EVENTS: For the exact schedule of events listed below, consult the **San Antonio Convention and Visitors Bureau** (see "Tourist Information," above).

Livestock Exposition and Rodeo (Feb): Popular stock fair and rodeo.

Fiesta San Antonio (mid-Apr): Parades, battle of flowers, processions on the river. One of Texas's most colorful festivals since 1891.

Cinco de Mayo (May 5): When the city celebrates Mexico's national holiday.

San Antonio Festival (June): International arts festival offering classical concerts, opera, ballet, theater, jazz, pop, rock, chamber music, etc.

Fiesta Noche del Rio (June–Aug): Open-air theater at Arneson River Theater.

Texas Folklife Festival (early Aug): Some 6,000 representatives from more than 30 ethnic groups who settled and built Texas join to share their traditions, crafts, skills, music, folk dances, and authentic cuisine.

Las Posadas (mid-Dec): Nighttime processions along Paseo del Rio; a tradition for more than 250 years.

SPORTS: San Antonio has two minor-league professional teams:
Baseball (Apr–Aug): Dodgers, Keefe Stadium (434-9311).
Basketball (Oct–Mar): Spurs, Hemisfair Arena (224-9578).

STROLLS: ☼⚐ **El Mercado/Mexican Market,** W. Commerce St. and Santa Rosa St.: The heart of the Mexican quarter; food stalls, craft shops. Lively and colorful; open daily (see "Shopping," above).

☼⚐ **King William Historic District,** around King William St. and S. St. Mary's St.: The 19th-century German district, now a residential neighborhood. King William St. (so named in honor of William I of Germany) is the main drag, lined with fine homes dating from 1870–90. Among them, no. 107, built in 1873, now houses the **San Antonio Conservatory Society** (free descriptive leaflets on the King William Historic District). Don't miss the **Steves Homestead** (see "Historic Buildings," above) at no. 509.

☼⚐ **Paseo del Rio,** along the San Antonio River: Pretty riverwalk, shaded with palm trees and cypresses, along the San Antonio River. Lined with cafés, restaurants, hotels, shops, and art galleries. The river (which meanders for 2½ mi./4km through downtown), its narrow bridges, and its water buses have won for San Antonio the nickname "Venice of the West."

☼⚐ **La Villita,** S. Presa St., Alamo St., and Nueva St. (299-8610): A corner of 18th-century Spain in the middle of San Antonio. The old adobe houses, deftly restored, now shelter galleries and craft shops surrounded by flower-planted patios, bougainvilleas, and banana palms. Don't overlook **Cos House,** where in 1835 was signed the first Mexican surrender to the Texans (see "Historic Buildings," above).

THEME PARKS: ☼⚐ **Sea World of Texas,** 10500 Sea World Dr. (523-3600): The world's largest marine-life theme park, with dozens of attractions on its 250 acres (101ha): "Shamu" the killer whale, sea lions, walrus, trained-dolphin shows, waterski ballets. Ultramodern facilities opened in 1988. Attracted more than three million visitors last year.

⚐ **Water Park USA,** I-35 at Coliseum Rd. (227-1100): A surfers' and divers' kingdom; pool with giant water slides and artificial waves. Fine-sand beach; picnic area. Open daily June–Sept.

ACCOMMODATIONS

A Note on Accommodations: Room rates in San Antonio are coded as follows: **VE,** Very Expensive ($140 and up); **E,** Expensive ($90–$140); **M,** Moderate ($60–$90); **I,** Inexpensive ($30–$60); **B,** Budget (up to $30). A listing of toll free numbers is in the Appendix.

Personal Favorites (in order of preference)

☼⚐⚐⚐⚐ **St. Anthony Hotel** (dwntwn), 300 E. Travis St., TX 78205 (512/227-4392; toll free 800/338-1338). 360 rms, A/C, color TV, in-rm movies. AE, CB, DC, MC, V. Valet gar. $8, pool, health club, two rests. (including the Brasserie), bars, 24-hr. rm svce, disco, concierge, free crib. *Note:* A major San Antonio landmark since 1909. Elegant and urbane, w. Oriental rugs and a profusion of marble and crystal. Spacious, completely renovated rms, some w. refrigerators. Period furnishings. Personalized svce. The best rms overlook Travis Park. Big business clientele; the best place to stay in the city. Good rest. serving American cuisine. **E–VE**

☼⚐⚐⚐ **La Mansión del Rio** (dwntwn), 112 College St., TX 78205 (512/225-2581; toll free, see Preferred). 337 rms, A/C, color TV, in-rm movies. AE, CB, DC, MC, V. Valet gar. $6, pool, rest. (Las Canarias), coffee shop, bar, 24-hr rm svce, nightclub, concierge, free crib. *Note:* Opened in

762 □ THE SOUTHWEST: SAN ANTONIO

1968, the Spanish Colonial hotel includes a part of the old building of St. Mary's University, skillfully restored. Pretty courtyard w. pool and bougainvilleas. Inviting but slightly constricting rms w. balconies and minibars. Efficient svce; elegant but expensive rest. Ask for a rm overlooking Paseo del Rio. Business and group clientele. Excellent location. **E–VE**

Marriott Rivercenter (dwntwn), 101 Bowie St., TX 78205 (512/223-1000; toll free, see Marriott). 1,004 rms, A/C, color TV, in-rm movies. AE, CB, DC, MC, V. Gar. $6, pool, health club, sauna, two rests., bars, 24-hr. rm svce, nightclub, concierge, free crib. *Note:* This giant among local hotels looks down from its 38-story glass-and-concrete tower over Hemisfair Plaza and the Alamo; the effect of this unabashed postmodernity, in so historic a place, is almost ludicrous. Huge, inviting, marvelously comfortable rms; ultra-professional svce. Direct access to Rivercenter Shopping Mall w. its dozens of shops, boutiques, and rests. Business and convention clientele (the hotel is right across from the Convention Center). Two VIP floors. **E–VE**

Menger Hotel (dwntwn), 204 Alamo Plaza, TX 78205 (512/223-4361; toll free 800/345-9258). 350 rms, A/C, color TV, in-rm movies. AE, CB, DC, MC, V. Valet gar. $4, pool, rest., bar, rm svce, drugstore, free crib. *Note:* An old hotel (1859) fraught w. history (see "Historic Buildings," above, for some of its illustrious guests). Has retained all its period flavor. Comfort and renovated facilities, but the svce leaves something to be desired. Pleasant indoor grdn; very famous bar (Roosevelt Bar). Unusually good location across from the Alamo. Good value. **M–E**

Travelodge on the River (dwntwn), 100 Villita St., TX 78205 (512/226-2271; toll free, see Travelodge). 132 rms, A/C, color TV, in-rm movies. AE, CB, DC, MC, V. Parking $4, pool, rest., bar, rm svce, nightclub. *Note:* Newish motel overlooking the San Antonio River. Comfortable rms w. private balconies; charming Spanish-style interior. Efficient svce; good value. Free airport limo. **I–M**, but lower rates off-season.

Rodeway Inn Downtown (dwntwn), 900 N. Main Ave., TX 78204 (512/223-2951; toll free, see Rodeway Inns). 128 rms, A/C, color TV, in-rm movies. AE, CB, DC, MC, V. Free parking, pool, rest. adj., free crib. *Note:* Conventional but well-run motel 5 min. by car from Paseo del Rio and the Alamo compound. Functional comforts. Svce a little flaky. Good overall value; fine if you're on a budget. **I**

Other Accommodations (from top bracket to budget)

Plaza San Antonio (formerly the Four Seasons; dwntwn), 555 S. Alamo St., TX 78205 (512/229-1000; toll free 800/421-1172). 252 rms, A/C, color TV, in-rm movies. AE, CB, DC, MC, V. Valet parking $7, pool, two tennis courts, health club, sauna, two rests. (including the Anaqua Rm), bars, 24-hr. rm svce, nightclub, concierge, free crib. *Note:* Very lovely modern hotel a stone's throw from La Villita and the Convention Center. Elegant and comfortable w. exotic touches. Luxurious rms w. private balconies overlooking a beautiful tropical grdn. Very good svce; excellent rest. Upscale business clientele. A very fine place. **E–VE**

Fairmount Hotel (dwntwn), 401 S. Alamo St., TX 78205 (512/224-8800; toll free 800/345-3457). 37 rms and suites, A/C, color TV, in-rm movies. AE, CB, DC, MC, V. Valet parking $8, rest. (Polo's), bar, 24-hr. rm svce, nightclub, concierge, free crib. *Note:* This luxurious three-story Victorian-style home, built in 1906, was transported some 550 yards (500m) to its present location on a wheeled platform—a world's record in all respects. Refined interior w. old paneling and Italian marble; the suites, the most luxurious and best equipped of any San Antonio hotel, have three phones, four-poster beds, VCR, and built-in stereo. Polished svce; rest. of a high order. The favorite of those in-the-know. Opposite the Convention Center. **E–VE**

Hyatt Regency (dwntwn), 123 Losoya St., TX 78205 (512/222-1234; toll free, see Hyatt). 632 rms, A/C, color TV, in-rm movies. AE, CB, DC, MC, V. Valet parking $8, pool, two rests. (including La Puerta), coffee shop, bars, rm svce, disco, boutiques, concierge. *Note:* Futuristic 16-story building w. indoor grdns, waterfalls, and spectacular glass lobby. Ultra-comfortable rms w. private balconies, the best overlooking the San Antonio River. Very good svce. Group and business clientele; VIP floor; interesting wknd discounts. Very near the Alamo and the Convention Center. **E–VE**

Sheraton Gunter (dwntwn), 205 E. Houston St., TX 78205 (512/227-3241; toll free, see Sheraton). 325 rms, A/C, color TV, in-rm movies. AE, CB, DC, MC, V. Valet gar. $5, pool, health club, rest. (Café Suisse), coffee shop, bar, rm svce, nightclub, hrdrsr, concierge, free crib. *Note:* This venerable institution dates from 1909, but furnishings and facilities have been completely renovated. Vast, inviting rms, some w. refrigerators; svce w. a smile. Wonderful location very nr. Paseo del Rio and the Alamo. Group and convention clientele. A San Antonio landmark. **E**

Crockett Hotel (dwntwn), 320 Bonham St., TX 78205 (512/225-6500; toll free 800/292-1050). 202 rms, A/C, color TV, in-rm movies. AE, CB, DC, MC, V. Valet parking $6, pool, rest. (Lela B's), coffee shop, bar, rm svce, free crib. *Note:* Reopened in 1983 after a rejuvenation costing over $15 million, this elderly grand hotel from the 1910s has recaptured all the elegance and charm of its distinguished past. Many works of art and period furniture. Rms a little cramped but comfortable and pleasantly decorated. Very good svce; charming patio–coffee shop. VIP floor. Wonderfully located across from the Alamo. **M–E**

La Quinta Convention Center (dwntwn), 1001 E. Commerce St., TX 78205 (512/222-9181; toll free, see La Quinta). 140 rms, A/C, color TV, in-rm movies. AE, CB, DC, MC, V. Free parking, pool, rest. nearby, valet svce, free crib. *Note:* Comfortable, serviceable motel a block or two from the Convention Center. Cheerful reception and svce; good value. Group and convention clientele. **M**

Holiday Inn Downtown (nr. dwntwn), 318 W. Durango St., TX 78207 (512/225-3211; toll free, see Holiday Inns). 317 rms, A/C, color TV, in-rm movies. AE, CB, DC, MC, V. Free parking, pool, rest., bar, rm svce. *Note:* A typical Holiday Inn a 5-min. drive from the Alamo and the Convention Center. Functional rms w. balconies; efficient svce; recently renovated. Interesting wknd discounts. Good value on balance. **I–M**

Days Inn Northeast (nr. dwntwn), 3443 N. Pan Am Expwy., TX 78219 (512/225-4521; toll free, see Days Inns). 122 rms, A/C, color TV, in-rm movies. AE, DC, MC, V. Free parking, pool, coffee shop. *Note:* Motel in the traditional manner, across from Water Park USA and 5 min. from dwntwn along I-35. Serviceably comfortable rms; friendly reception and svce. Good overall value; w. direct access to the freeways, it's particularly so if you're driving. **I**

Motel 6 East (nr. dwntwn), 138 NW White Rd., TX 78219 (512/333-1850). 100 rms, A/C, color TV, free in-rm movies. AE, DC, MC, V. Free parking, pool. *Note:* Unbeatable value 10 min. from dwntwn. Comfortable, serviceable rms. Direct access to the San Antonio bypass motorway. Ideal if you're driving through. **B**

Airport Accommodations

La Quinta Airport East (vic.), 333 NE Loop I-410, TX 78216 (512/828-0781; toll free, see La Quinta). 198 rms, A/C, color TV, in-rm movies. AE, CB, DC, MC, V. Free parking, pool, rest., bar, rm svce. *Note:* Modern, comfortable motel; free airport limo. Also great if you're driving. **I**

YMCA/Youth Hostels

Bullis House Inn International Hostel (nr. dwntwn), 621 Pierce St., TX 78208 (512/223-9426). 60 beds. Comfortable youth hostel in a fine old house. Open year round.

RESTAURANTS

A Note on Restaurant Prices: San Antonio restaurant prices, per person, excluding drinks and service charges, are coded as follows: **VE,** Very Expensive ($60 and up); **E,** Expensive ($40–$60); **M,** Moderate ($25–$40); **I,** Inexpensive ($15–$25); **B,** Budget (up to $15).

Personal Favorites (in order of preference)

Anaqua Room (dwntwn), in the Plaza San Antonio (see "Accommodations," above) (229-1000). A/C. Breakfast/lunch/dinner daily, brunch Sun. AE, CB, DC, MC, V. Jkt. *Specialties:* lobster ravioli, roast rack of lamb w. herbs, Dover sole meunière, médaillons of venison w. tomatoes, very good desserts. Menu changed regularly. Fine wine list. *Note:* The luxury-hotel rest. at its best; classic grand cuisine, of French inspiration, superbly prepared and served. Elegant, intimate decor and a prospect of grdns, patios, and fountains. Open-air dining on fine days. Exemplary svce; resv. a must. Big business clientele. *Continental/French.* **M–E**

P.J.'s (dwntwn), 700 N. St. Mary's St. (225-8400). A/C. Lunch/dinner daily; closed Dec 25. AE, CB, DC, MC, V. Jkt. *Specialties:* eye of lamb w. rosemary sauce, pinoch (seafood platter), steak California, fresh broiled salmon, mille-feuilles. Menu changes regularly. Very fine wine list. *Note:* Overlooking Riverwalk, P.J.'s is the favorite spot for a business lunch or dinner. Light, delicate food; ultra-polished svce (in tuxedo). Adj. disco. The fashionable place; resv. advised. *French/American.* **I–M**

Fig Tree (dwntwn), 515 Villita St. (224-1976). A/C. Dinner only, nightly; closed Thanksgiving, Dec 24–25. AE, CB, DC, MC, V. Jkt. *Specialties:* rack of lamb, duck à l'orange, coulibiac of salmon, catch of the day, game (in season). *Note:* In a charming 19th-century adobe house on Paseo del Rio, this romantic luxury rest. serves food as perfect as the setting. Svce of the highest order; charming little covered patio. Resv. advised. Valet parking. *French/Continental.* **M–E** (prix fixe).

Arthur's (nr. dwntwn), 4001 Broadway (826-3200). A/C. Dinner only, nightly. AE, DC, MC, V. *Specialties:* shrimp Martinique, seafood sausage w. saffron butter, lamb chop w. red-onion sauce, carpetbagger steak (stuffed w. fried oysters), médaillon of wild boar w. juniper-and-mustard sauce, exotic fruit pies. *Note:* The picture windows have an unobstructed view of Brackenridge Park. The quality of the materials (asparagus from France, fish delivered daily by air from both coasts) is matched only by the excellence of the cuisine. Elegant atmosphere; faultless svce. Yuppie clientele; live jazz at the bar. Resv. advised. 10 min. from dwntwn; valet parking. *American/Continental.* **I–M**

Casa Rio (dwntwn), 430 E. Commerce St. on Riverwalk (225-6718). A/C. Lunch/dinner daily; closed Sun Sept–Apr, hols. AE, CB, DC, MC, V. *Specialties:* carne asada, tacos, enchiladas, steak ranchero, chile relleño, menudo (tripe). *Note:* The almost aggressively tourist decor and atmosphere should not spoil your pleasure in the very acceptable Mexican food at extremely reasonable prices. Pleasant terrace along Paseo del Rio. Svce friendly enough, but short on efficiency. Riverboat dinners organized for groups of eight or more; mariachi music at dinner. Picturesque. Resv. advisable. *Mexican.* **B–I**

Earl Abel's (nr. dwntwn), 4200 Broadway (822-3358). A/C. Breakfast/lunch/dinner daily (around the clock); closed Dec 25. AE, MC, V. *Specialties:* fried chicken, hamburgers, T-bone steak, fried catfish, broiled trout, pecan pie. *Note:* For more than half a century this worthy exponent of large-scale food svce (more than a million meals a year) has been a family favorite. Decent, unpretentious food in generous portions; rather gloomy decor. Svce generally rushed. No resv.; 10 min. from dwntwn. *American/Steak.* **B–I**

Other Restaurants (from top bracket to budget)

Chez Ardid (nr. dwntwn), 1919 San Pedro Ave. (732-3203). A/C. Lunch Mon–Fri, dinner Mon–Sat; closed Jan 1, Dec

25. AE, MC, V. Jkt. *Specialties:* seafood sausage, hot crabmeat Ardid, escalope of veal normande, tournedos périgourdine, rack of lamb w. herbs, mussels in cream sauce, red snapper w. truffles and pistachios, floating island dessert. Good wine list. *Note:* San Antonio's worthy exponent of true French cuisine. Intimate atmosphere in a 19th-century mansion. Flawless svce; resv. recommended. 15 min. from dwntwn, 10 min. from airport. A very fine place. Valet parking. *French.* **M–E**

Crumpet's (nr. dwntwn), 5800 Broadway (821-5454). A/C. Lunch/dinner daily; closed Jan 1, Dec 25. AE, MC, V. Jkt. *Specialties:* fettuccine w. scallops, beef tenderloin w. green-peppercorn sauce, loin of veal w. morels, veal piccata w. lemon sauce, scrumptious homemade desserts. Unpretentious wine list. *Note:* The flawless European-derived food, the elegant setting, and the classical music in the background make this one of the best places to eat in town, much favored by the local Establishment. Warm and attentive svce. Resv. strongly advised. *Continental.* **I–M**

Boudro's (dwntwn), 421 E. Commerce St. (224-8484). A/C. Lunch/dinner daily. AE, MC, V. *Specialties:* gumbo (duck and sausage), redfish meunière w. pecans, blackened prime rib w. aromatic herb butter, bread pudding w. whisky sauce. *Note:* This charming rest. on Paseo del Rio, w. its massive stone walls, serves the best Créole food (and quite simply, some of the best food) in San Antonio. Pleasant little shady patio. Good svce; very relaxed atmosphere. Resv. strongly advised. *Créole.* **I–M**

Grey Moss Inn (vic.), 19010 Scenic Loop Dr. (Tex. 16) (695-8301). A/C. Dinner only, nightly; closed hols. AE, CB, DC, MC, V. *Specialties:* squash au gratin, steak and chicken broiled over a wood fire, pecan pie. *Note:* Some 20 mi. (32km) northwest of San Antonio, this rustic cottage surrounded by trees serves excellent, wholesome, tasty Texas food. Open-air dining in summer. Good svce; resv. advised. *American/Steak.* **I–M**

Paesano's (nr. dwntwn), 1715 McCullough Ave. (226-9541). A/C. Lunch Tues–Fri, dinner Tues–Sun; closed hols. AE, MC, V. *Specialties:* shrimp Paesano, steak pizzaiola, filet of red snapper w. mushrooms, scaloppine Francesca, spumone. *Note:* Charming small *trattoria*, intimate and inviting. Genuine Italian cuisine; good svce. Popular among local politicians and sports fans; resv. advised. *Italian.* **I**

The Barn Door (vic.), 8400 N. New Braunfels Ave. (824-0116). A/C. Lunch Mon–Fri, dinner Mon–Sat; closed hols. AE, MC, V. *Specialties:* fine prime cuts broiled over a wood fire. *Note:* Very popular steakhouse nr. the airport and 20 min. from dwntwn. Choice meats broiled to perfection, at very sensible prices. Engaging western decor. Very good value; given its popularity, resv. advised. *Steak.* **I**

La Fogata (nr. dwntwn), 2427 Vance Jackson Rd. (340-1337). A/C. Breakfast/lunch/dinner Tues–Sun; closed Jan 1, Dec 25. AE, CB, DC, MC, V. *Specialties:* tacos al carbón, enchiladas verdes, chimichangas, fajitas. All food is charcoal-broiled. *Note:* In spite (or perhaps because) of its spare, unassuming setting, La Fogata is held by purists to be the best of San Antonio's countless Mexican rests.; it's worth visiting the city just to try the homemade tortillas! Pleasant patio dining. Generous helpings; marvelously obliging and engaging svce. A favorite of those in-the-know. 15 min. from dwntwn. No resv. *Mexican.* **B–I**

Hunan River Garden (dwntwn), 506 Riverwalk (222-0808). A/C. Lunch/dinner daily. AE, MC, V. *Specialties:* classic Hunan and Szechuan dishes; highly seasoned sauces. *Note:* San Antonio's most picturesque Chinese rest., and its best, right on Paseo del Rio. Generous portions; efficient svce; often crowded. Excellent value. *Chinese.* **B–I**

Mi Tierra (dwntwn), 218 Produce Row (225-1262). A/C. Breakfast/lunch/dinner daily (around the clock). AE, MC, V. *Specialties:* baked cabrito (kid), fajitas, steak ranchero, enchiladas, menudo (tripe). *Note:* Popular and colorful, this Mexican rest. across from the famous

Mercado is a favorite w. the local Mexican community as well as local gringos or tourists. Although open around the clock, it's usually full. Christmas-tree-like decorations. Mariachi band evenings. No resv. An excellent place to eat. *Mexican.* **B**

Cafeterias/Fast Food
☼ **Mario's** (dwntwn), 325 S. Pecos St. (223-9602). A local shrine for Tex-Mex food. Excellent homemade soups and classic Mexican dishes. Open daily around the clock. Very popular locally, especially in the small hours. A stone's throw from the Mercado.

BARS & NIGHTCLUBS
Arthur's (nr. dwntwn), 4001 Broadway (826-3200). Excellent modern jazz Mon–Sat. Relaxed atmosphere. Also a very decent rest. (see above). 10 min. from dwntwn.

Farmer's Daughter (vic.), 542 NW White Rd. (333-7391). Big, colorful western-style dance hall, open Wed–Sun. 15 min. from dwntwn.

Jim Cullum's Landing, in the Hyatt Regency (see "Accommodations," above) (223-7266). Live New Orleans jazz Tues–Sat. Locally popular.

Mendiola's Ballroom (vic.), 16490 U.S. 81S (622-9204). The most picturesque, and popular, Mexican dance hall for miles around; local color guaranteed. Open Thurs–Sun.

P.J.'s (dwntwn), 700 N. St. Mary's St. (225-8400). Fashionable disco; also a very popular rest. (see above). On Paseo del Rio; open Mon–Sat.

NEARBY EXCURSIONS

☼🏛 **AQUARENA SPRINGS** (32 mi./51km NE on I-35) (396-8900): The springs of the San Marcos River, with splendid aquatic grdns; the crystal-clear water gives you a wonderful view of the rich vegetation and underwater life. Glass-bottom-boat rides; underwater shows in summer. Open daily year round.

☼🏛 **AUSTIN** (78 mi./124km NE on I-35): Founded as Waterloo in 1839 and later renamed in honor of Stephen F. Austin, one of the founders of Texas, the state capital is built on hills rising above the Colorado River (not to be confused with the river of the same name in the state of Colorado). **Old Pecan St.** is a charming historic district, with old houses, shops, and restaurants (6th St.). The imposing **State Capitol** in pink granite, north end of Congress Ave. (512/463-0063), is open daily. The **Lyndon B. Johnson Library and Museum,** on the University of Texas campus (512/482-5137), open daily, honors the 36th president of the U.S. The **French Legation Museum,** at 802 San Marcos St. (512/472-8180), open Tues–Sun, is the only foreign mission to the U.S. ever built outside Washington, D.C. (in 1840, when Texas was still an independent republic). The capital of Texas has also become the capital of "New Country Music" in the style of Willie Nelson and Waylon Jennings. Note the unusual downtown street-lighting system intended to produce "artificial moonlight."

🏛 **CASCADE CAVERNS PARK** (16 mi./26km NW on I-10) (755-9285): Very fine limestone caves with illuminated 88-ft. (27m) waterfall. Many marine fossils in the walls. Guided tours. Open daily.

☼🏛 **NATURAL BRIDGE CAVERNS** (17 mi./27km NE via I-35 and FM 3009) (651-6101): Immense underground caves once inhabited by primitive peoples; among the finest in Texas. Many chambers with strange shapes and evocative names: "Sherwood Forest," with its columns shaped like totem poles; "The Castle of the White Giants," with its 40-ft.-high (12m) "King's Throne," etc. The temperature inside the caves varies little, year round, from 70°F (21°C). Guided tours lasting about an hour. Open daily.

FARTHER AFIELD

BIG BEND NATIONAL PARK (394 mi./630km west via U.S. 90 and U.S. 385): One of the wildest and most beautiful of America's national parks. Impressive canyons along the Rio Grande, the river marking the Mexican border, whose right-angled "Big Bend" S of the **Chisos Mountains** gives the park its name. The rocky walls rise perpendicularly from the river to heights of 1,300 ft. (400m) at places such as **Santa Elena Canyon, Mariscal Canyon,** and **Boquillas Canyon.** The steep crests, once a refuge of the Comanche peoples, with their forests of oak, pine, and juniper and their great variety of wildlife (deer, coyote, peccary, mountain lion, and 400 species of birds), lie next to the Chihuahuan Desert, bristling with giant cactus and home to snakes, kangaroo rats, and roadrunners. There are also many dinosaur fossils in the park.

At its western edge are the ghost town of **Terlingua** and the little frontier town of **Lajitas,** whose Main Street comes straight out of a John Ford movie.

For air-rafting down the Rio Grande, contact **Big Bend River Tours,** P.O. Box 317, Lajitas, TX 79852 (915/424-3219); **Far Flung Adventures,** P.O. Box 31, Terlingua, TX 79852 (915/371-2489); or **Outback Expeditions,** P.O. Box 229, Terlingua, TX 79852 (915/371-2490; toll free 800/545-4240).

Warning! There are no gas stations between the Marathon on U.S. 90 and the park headquarters at **Chisos Basin,** 68 mi. (110km) to the south.

Don't fail to visit Big Bend National Park; for **information,** contact the Superintendent, Big Bend National Park, TX 79834 (915/477-2251).

Sights En Route

On the way, don't fail to see **Alamo Village** at **Brackettville,** 122 mi. (195km) west on U.S. 90 (512/563-2580), a faithful reconstruction of San Antonio in the 1830s, built in 1959 for the shooting of John Wayne's famous movie *The Alamo.* From a classic saloon to an attack on a stagecoach, complete with enough musketry to make you laugh, every horse-opera cliché gets its turn. Native American museum. Open daily year round; amusing.

Also see the **Judge Roy Bean Courtroom** at **Langtry,** 213 mi. (340km) west on U.S. 90 (915/291-3340). The legendary Roy Bean was, at the time of the Wild West, in his own person "the law west of Pecos." He did justice, after his fashion, in his saloon-court, "The Jersey Lily" (named, like the town, after Lillie Langtry, "The Jersey Lily," a famous British beauty of the day), now a designated historic monument. A picturesque page of living history. Open daily.

Where to Stay En Route

IN THE PARK   The ⚑ **Chisos Mountain Lodge,** Chisos Basin, Big Bend National Park, TX 79834 (915/477-2291). 34 rms and bungalows. Rustic comforts; cafeteria. **I**

AT LAJITAS   The ⚑ **Badlands Hotel** and **Cavalry Post Hotel,** Star Rte. 70, Box 400, Lajitas, TX 79852 (915/424-3471). 81 rms. Picturesque replicas of original Far West hotels. **I-M**

HILL COUNTRY & LYNDON B. JOHNSON RANCH

(328 mi./525km r.t. via I-10W, Texas 46W, Texas 16N, Texas 27N, Texas 41W, I-10E, Texas 16N, U.S. 290E, and I-35S): You come first to **Boerne,** founded by German settlers in 1849; its old stone houses with narrow windows and gabled roofs still bear witness to their Germanic origins. Note the Kendall Inn, an old coaching inn built in 1859.

You now take Texas 46 to ☀⚓ **Bandera,** a picturesque little western town nicknamed "the cowboy capital of the world" (rodeos and open-air festivals). Interesting **Frontier Times Museum,** 506 13th St. (512/796-3864), open daily.

Near **Mountain Home,** 60 mi. (96km) north, visit the ☀⚓ **Y.O. Ranch,** on Texas 41W (512/640-3222), one of the largest stock ranches in Texas (100 sq. mi./259km²). As well as a herd of more than 1,000 longhorns, the ranch has antelope, zebra, ostrich, and giraffe roaming free. Photo safaris arranged daily.

On to ☀⚓ **Fredericksburg,** the main destination of German immigrants to Texas in the 1850s, which has retained many of its original buildings and an unusual "Old European" flavor. Be sure to see the **Vereins Kirche,** a replica of the first church built in 1847, on Market Sq., open Mon–Fri, and the **Admiral Nimitz State Historical Park** at 340 E. Main St. (512/997-4379), open daily, a monument to the hero of World War II in the Pacific, who was a native of the town.

Continuing eastward, you come to **Lyndon B. Johnson State Historical Park,** 15 mi. (24km) west of Johnson City on U.S. 290, dedicated to the 36th president of the U.S.; free bus connection from the visitor center (512/644-2252), open daily, to the ☀ **LBJ Ranch House** and his birthplace; his tomb is in the family cemetery. Many memorabilia of the man who succeeded John F. Kennedy in the White House. At ⚓ **Johnson City** you can visit the Victorian **Boyhood Home,** one block south of Main St. (512/868-7128), open daily, where Lyndon B. Johnson lived from 1913 to 1934; don't miss it.

Now on to ☀⚓ **Austin,** capital of the state of Texas (see "Nearby Excursions," above).

Return to San Antonio via ☀⚓ **New Braunfels,** an engaging little German town founded in the 19th century by 5,000 German immigrants whose descendants have preserved unspoiled many of their inherited traditions: there's a very popular Wurstfest or sausage festival lasting for 10 days at the beginning of Nov. On the way, stop to admire ☀⚓ **Aquarena Springs** near **San Marcos** (see "Nearby Excursions," above).

Your last stop on the return leg should be at ☀⚓ **Natural Bridge Caverns** (see "Nearby Excursions," above).

This picturesque trip, with lots to see, should take you 3–4 days.

Where to Stay En Route

IN AUSTIN The 🏨🏨🏨 **Driskill Hotel,** 604 Brazos St., Austin, TX 78701 (512/474-5911). 175 rms. Luxury hotel of great quality dating from 1886. **M–E**
         🍸 **Best Western Capitol,** 300 E. 11th St., Austin, TX 78701 (512/476-7151). 145 rms. Typical motel, one block to state capitol. Recently renovated. **I–M**

IN FREDERICKSBURG The 🍸 **Ad Dietzel Motel,** on U.S. 87, Fredericksburg, TX 78624 (512/997-3330), (1 mi./1.6km west of town). 20 rms. A small and modest but very well run motel. **I**

IN KERRVILLE The 🏨🏨 **Best Western Inn of the Hills,** 1001 Junction Hwy., Kerrville, TX 78028 (512/895-5000). 217 rms. Large, modern, comfortable resort motel. **I–M**

☀⚓ **PADRE ISLAND NATIONAL SEASHORE** (165 mi./264km SE via I-37 and Texas 358): Wildlife sanctuary for sea creatures and birds on a deserted sandspit 113 mi. (182km) long; see Chapter 36 on Houston.

CHAPTER 38

ALBUQUERQUE††

□ □ □

And the Rio Grande Valley

Standing 5,300 ft. (1,600m) above sea level, in a ring of desolate mountains which define the valley of the **Rio Grande,** Albuquerque was founded in 1706 by Don Francisco Cuervo y Valdés, then governor of New Mexico. Named in honor of the Duke of Alburquerque (the first "r" has dropped out over the years), viceroy of New Spain, the city retains few traces of the colonial period. Only the **Old Town** with its fine **Plaza** bears witness to the past ascendancy of Spain, and here the atmosphere is distinctly touristy. Not far away are the ranks of impersonal office buildings and inevitable neon signs of the modern city.

Albuquerque was a staging-post on the Spanish colonial "Camino Real" between Mexico City and Santa Fe and, during the frontier days of the Far West, on the Santa Fe Trail. When the first transcontinental railroads were built in the last century, it was an important stop on the Santa Fe Railroad. Today it is the largest city in New Mexico, and its population, which quintupled between 1950 and 1980, is still growing. The city's industries—lasers, data processing, pharmaceuticals, solar energy, and nuclear weapons—face resolutely toward the future. In terms of industry and commerce Albuquerque ranks 12th among the 20 fastest-growing cities in the country. **Sandia Laboratories,** where in the years after 1942 the famous Manhattan Project resulted in history's first atomic bomb, employs 6,000 researchers and technicians and still dominates the city's industry. Noted for a very dry climate and an unusually cloudless sky (sunshine for 76% of the year), Albuquerque has become the world capital for ballooning, with a spectacular rally every Oct. The city is also an ideal point of departure for numerous excursions: toward **Santa Fe** (see Chapter 39); the cable car to the magnificent views at **Sandia Peak** (10,378 ft./3,163m); and the **Rio Grande Valley** (White Sands Desert, Valley of Fires, Mescalero Indian Reserve). Then there are the Native American **pueblos** of the fabled kingdom of Cibola, such as **Acoma** and **Zuñi,** and the **El Morro National Monument.**

Famous people born in Albuquerque include jazzman John Lewis of Modern Jazz Quartet fame.

BASIC FACTS: State of New Mexico. Area code: 505. Time zone: mountain. ZIP Code: 87101. Founded: 1706. Approximate population: city, 398,000; metropolitan area, 510,000. 40th-largest metropolitan area in the country.

CLIMATE: Perpetual sunshine and low humidity make the climate of Albuquerque special. In summer the thermometer can run quickly up to 95°F (35°C) or higher. In winter, brisk but sunny weather and plentiful snowfall above 8,000 ft. permit skiing on nearby Sandia Peak. Spring and, even better, fall are the ideal seasons for a trip.

DISTANCES: Dallas, 637 mi. (1,020km); Denver, 421 mi. (675km); El Paso, 267 mi. (427km); Kansas City, 790 mi. (1,265km); Phoenix, 453 mi. (725km); Salt Lake City, 609 mi. (975km); Santa Fe, 61 mi. (98km).

ARRIVAL & TRANSIT INFORMATION

AIRPORT: Albuquerque International Airport (ABQ), 5 mi. (8km) SE. For information, call 842-4366.

AIRLINES: America West (247-0737), American (toll free 800/433-7300), Continental (842-8220), Delta (243-2794), Southwest (831-1221), TWA (842-4010), United (toll free 800/241-6522), and USAir (toll free 800/428-4322).

CITY LINK: The **cab** fare to city center is about $10; time, 15 min. **City bus:** SUNTRAN (no. 50) until 7pm; fare, 60¢; time, 25 min. **Airport bus** to downtown Santa Fe (seven times a day): Shuttlejack (243-3244); fare, $18; time, 1 hr. 10 min.
   Since public transportation within the city by SUNTRAN bus is not very efficient (call 843-9200 for information), and excursions around the city are many and fascinating, it is highly advisable to rent a car with unlimited mileage.

CAR RENTAL (at the airport unless otherwise indicated): Avis (842-4080); Budget (247-3442); Dollar (842-4224); Hertz (842-4235); National (842-4222); Thrifty, 2039 Yale Blvd. SE (842-8733). For dwntwn locations, consult the phone directory.

LIMOUSINE SERVICES: Dav El Limo (toll free 800/922-0343).

TAXIS: Cabs must be summoned by phone; they may not be hailed on the street. Try **Albuquerque Cab** (883-4888) or **Yellow Cab** (247-8888).

TRAIN: Amtrak station, 314 1st St. SW (242-7816).

INTERCITY BUSES: Greyhound, 300 2nd St. SW (243-4435).

INFORMATION & TOURS

TOURIST INFORMATION: The **Albuquerque Convention and Visitors Bureau,** 625 Silver Ave. SW, Suite 210, NM 87125 (505/243-3696).

GUIDED TOURS: Albuquerque Trolley (bus) (242-1407): Guided tour of the city on a replica of an old-time streetcar. Serves principal hotels.
   Gray Line Tours (bus) (265-8311): Guided tours of city and surroundings. Depart from Sheraton Old Town Inn, 800 Rio Grande Blvd.

SIGHTS, ATTRACTIONS & ACTIVITIES

ADVENTURES: Balloon Rides (ballooning), 4740 Pan American Fwy. (884-1742): Champagne balloon flights, weddings. Year round. Groups from two to eight. Resv. recommended.

Wolf Whitewater River Co. (boat), P.O. Box 665, Sandia Park, NM 87407 (505/281-5042): Rafting down the Rio Grande rapids. May–Sept.
World Balloon Corp. (ballooning), 4800 Eubank Blvd. NE (293-6800): Leaves at dawn only when skies are clear. Best time of year: autumn or winter. About $100 per hour of flying time.

CHURCHES/SYNAGOGUES: ※☖ Church of San Felipe de Neri, on Old

Town Plaza: The most representative building from the Spanish period. Built in 1793 on the site of a church of 1706 destroyed in 1790, this colonial-style church and the adjacent convent are still in use for religious purposes. See the spiral staircase in the choir, wrapped around the trunk of a spruce. Open daily.

HISTORIC BUILDINGS: ※☖ University of New Mexico, E. Central Ave. and

University Blvd. (277-4001): One of the oldest (1889) and most respected universities in the Southwest (24,000 students). Remarkable example of Pueblo Native American architecture, standing amid 672 acres (280ha) of grdns. Several museums (see below). Visitors Bureau in the Fine Arts Center.

MUSEUMS OF ART: ☖ Albuquerque Museum, 2000 Mountain Rd. NW

(242-4600): Interesting exhibits on the history of New Mexico; exhibitions of contemporary work by local artists. Features the largest collection of Spanish Colonial artifacts in the U.S. Open Tues–Sun.

☖ **Fine Arts Center,** Central Ave. and Cornell Ave. (277-4001): Large cultural complex including a fine-arts museum (**Art Museum**) mainly used for temporary exhibitions, the **Fine Arts Library,** and several theaters and concert halls (**Keller Hall, Rodey Theatre, Popejoy Hall,** etc.). On the university campus; worth a visit. Open Tues–Sun.

※☖☖ **Indian Pueblo Cultural Center,** 2401 12th St. NW (843-7270): This cultural institute, operated by the Association of the 19 Pueblos of New Mexico, offers a complete overview of Native American art and customs. Original design derived from the architecture of Pueblo Bonito (see "Farther Afield," below). Traditional dances performed on weekends in summer. Craft shop. Authentic Native American restaurant. Guided tours of the pueblos. Open daily.

MUSEUMS OF SCIENCE & HISTORY: ※☖☖ Maxwell Museum of An-

thropology, Grand Ave. NE and University Blvd. (277-4404): One of the finest museums in the country devoted to the culture of the Native American. Everything about the "civilization of the Pueblos," particularly the mysterious Anasazi. Very fine Mimbres pottery. Equally rich in prehistoric material. On the university campus. Open daily.
Museum of Geology and Meteoritics, 200 Yale Blvd. (277-4204): Unique collection of more than 200 meteorites from around the world. For students of astronomy. On the university campus. Open Mon–Fri.

※☖☖ **Museum of Natural History,** 1801 Mountain Rd. NW (841-8837): The first such museum to be opened in the U.S. in 50 years. This hi-tech masterpiece, opened in 1986, offers a fascinating panorama of the land of the Rio Grande Valley, its plants and its animals, from prehistoric reptiles to a startling model of a volcano in eruption. An absolute must. Open daily.

☖ **National Atomic Museum,** Kirtland Air Force Base, Bldg. 20358, on Wyoming Blvd., 7 mi. (11km) from downtown (844-8443): Unusual museum devoted to nuclear weapons, with movies showing their effects, from the first A-bomb to the Minuteman missile. Pacifists should stay away. Open daily.

    🔔 **Rio Grande Nature Center,** 2901 Candelaria Rd. NW (344-7240): Standing on the east bank of the Rio Grande amid 7.2 acres (3ha) of park and woods, this all-glass structure houses rich collections of local geology, zoology, and history. Open daily.

PANORAMAS: ☀ **Sandia Crest,** 36 mi./58km NE along I-40E and N.M. 14, N.M. 165, and N.M. 536: Wonderful scenic drive (highest in the Southwest) through dense forests of oak, spruce, Ponderosa pine, and other conifers up to Sandia Crest (10,678 ft./3,255m) at the top of the Sandia Mountains. You can see 100 mi. (160km) in every direction, including the foothills of the Rockies and the valley of the Rio Grande. Highway open year round; Sandia Crest House, a restaurant with a panoramic view (243-0605), open daily.

    ☀ **Sandia Peak,** Tramway Blvd. (5 mi./8km NE along I-25): With its summit 10,378 ft. (3,163m) above sea level, the impressive Sandia Peak towers over Albuquerque and the Rio Grande Valley. On clear days (as they usually are) you can see the foothills of the Colorado Rockies 125 mi. (200km) to the north, and as far as the Mexican border 187 mi. (300km) south. Access by the longest cable car in the country (it rises 3,728 ft./1,165m over a journey of 2.5 mi./4km). For information on timetables, call 298-8518. The High Finance restaurant offers a panoramic view.

PARKS & GARDENS: ☀🔔 **Indian Petroglyph State Park,** 6900 Unser Blvd., 9 mi. (14km) west on I-40 (897-8819): Some 15,000 petroglyphs (figures carved from rock)—in this case, from lava by the ancestors of the Pueblo tribes between A.D. 1100 and 1600. Open daily.

PERFORMING ARTS: For current listings of shows and cultural events, consult the entertainment pages of the two daily papers, *Albuquerque Journal* (morning) and *Albuquerque Tribune* (evening), and the monthly *Albuquerque* magazine.

    Albuquerque Little Theatre, 244 San Pasquale SW (242-4750): Broadway hits, star-studded shows. Sept–June.

    Keller Hall, U. of N.M. campus (277-4402): Concerts and recitals.

    Ki Mo Theatre, 423 Central Ave. NW (848-1374): Home of the Albuquerque Opera Theater (Sept–May) and the New Mexico Repertory Theater (drama, comedy, classic theater).

    Popejoy Hall, U. of N.M. campus (277-3121): Home of the Albuquerque Civic Light Opera (musical comedy, operetta) and of the New Mexico Symphony Orchestra (music director: Neal Stulberg). Sept–May. For information, call 842-8565. Also concerts, classic and modern dance theater.

    Rodey Theatre, U. of N.M. campus (277-4402): Modern theater.

    The Vortex Theatre, 2004 W. Central Ave. (247-8600): Modern and classical theater; also experimental productions.

SPECIAL EVENTS: For exact dates, consult the **Albuquerque Convention & Visitors Bureau** (see "Tourist Information," above).

    Gathering of Nations Powwow (mid-Apr): The largest and most spectacular of the 300 powwows held across the country each year. 30,000 Native Americans from all over North America, among which more than 1,300 dancers and singers competing in traditional costumes and styles. University Arena.

    Old Town Fiesta (June): Concerts, art exhibitions, parades.

    New Mexico State Fair (Sept): Rodeo, horse races, country-music concerts. Local color guaranteed!

    International Balloon Fiesta (early Oct): World's greatest dirigible-balloon rally, attracting more than 500 participants from the U.S. and abroad. Features mass ascensions at sunrise. A splendid spectacle. For information, call 821-1000.

Fiesta Encantada (Dec): Public concerts, folklore festivals, exhibitions; the Old Town is beautifully lit with candles.

SPORTS: Albuquerque is home to a minor-league professional team:
Baseball: (Apr–Sept): Albuquerque Dukes (Triple-A farm team of the L.A. Dodgers), Albuquerque Sports Stadium (243-1791).

Horse Racing
The Downs, State Fairgrounds, 201 California St. (265-0943): Thoroughbred and quarter-horse racing Wed and Fri–Sun Jan–June.

STROLLS: ⚘🏛 **Old Town,** around Old Town Plaza: The heart of historic Albuquerque, with its beautiful tree-shaded Plaza, brick sidewalks, and bandstand. Several old buildings in Spanish Colonial idiom including above-mentioned Church of San Felipe de Neri. More than 150 boutiques, art galleries, souvenir shops, and restaurants. It flaunts its pitch for the tourist trade, but it's certainly picturesque. For information, call 842-9100.

WINTER SPORTS RESORTS: 🏛 **Sandia Peak Ski Area** (30 mi./48km NE on I-40, N.M. 14, and N.M. 536): 5 ski lifts. Operates Dec to mid-Apr. Can also be reached by cable car from Tramway Rd. north of Albuquerque. For information on snow conditions, call 296-9585.

ZOOS: 🏛 **Rio Grande Zoo,** 903 10th St. SW (843-7413): More than 1,200 animals of all kinds in beautifully designed "natural" habitats, including a rain forest; picnic area and swimming pools nearby. Open daily.

ACCOMMODATIONS

A Note on Accommodations: Room rates in Albuquerque are coded as follows: **VE,** Very Expensive ($140 and up); **E,** Expensive ($90–$140); **M,** Moderate ($60–$90); **I,** Inexpensive ($30–$60); **B,** Budget (up to $30). A listing of toll free numbers is in the Appendix.

Personal Favorites (in order of preference)

🏨🏨🏨 **Hyatt Regency** (dwntwn), 330 Tijeras NW, NM 87102 (505/842-1234; toll free, see Hyatt). 396 rms, A/C, color TV, in-rm movies. AE, CB, DC, MC, V. Valet gar. $8, pool, health club, saunas, rest. (McGrath's), bar, rm svce, nightclub, boutiques, free crib. *Note:* The newest (Aug 1990) and most luxurious hotel in town. Built beneath an unmistakable red pyramid cap, the 20-story neoclassic building provides panoramic views of the mountains and the city. Spectacular atrium graced by 28-ft. (8.5m) palm trees. Spacious, elegant rms w. two telephones and computer access. Very efficient svce. In the heart of dwntwn business and government districts. **E–VE**

🏨🏨🏨 **Sheraton Old Town Inn** (dwntwn), 800 Rio Grande Blvd., NM 87104 (505/843-6300; toll free, see Sheraton). 190 rms, A/C, color TV, in-rm movies. AE, CB, DC, MC, V. Free parking, pool, sauna, rest. (Customs House), coffee shop, bar, rm svce, disco, hrdrsr, boutiques, free airport limo, free crib. *Note:* The best address in Albuquerque, right near Old Town Plaza. Dramatic modern architecture. Spacious and comfortable rms, some w. terraces and minibars. Svce and welcome impeccable. Decor warm and colorful. Rest. very acceptable. Caters mostly to tourists. Recently renovated. **M–E**

☀️🏨🏨 **Clarion Carriage House** (formerly La Posada; dwntwn), 125 2nd St. NW, NM 87102 (505/242-9090; toll free, see

Clarion). 109 rms, A/C, color TV, in-rm movies. AE, CB, DC, MC, V. Free valet parking, rest. (Eulalia), coffee shop, bar, rm svce, nightclub, hrdrsr, crib $5. *Note:* Charming old hotel from the late '30s. A recent facelift has retained its appealing period flavor—a pretty fountain in the lobby, heavy overhanging eaves, and murals. Rms are more comfortable than elegant. Rest. of very respectable quality. Welcome and service w. a smile. Very well located, not 5 min. from the Plaza. Good quality-to-price ratio. An excellent place to stay. Free airport shuttle. **M–E**

🏨🏨 **Barcelona Court** (nr. dwntwn), 900 Louisiana Ave. NE, NM 87110 (505/255-5566). 164 suites w. kitchenettes, A/C, color TV, in-rm movies. AE, CB, DC, MC, V. Free parking, two pools, sauna. Coffee shop next door, rm svce, free airport limo, free breakfast, free crib. *Note:* This motel, 6 min. from the airport, has only spacious and welcoming suites, w. kitchenettes and refrigerators. Private balconies or patios. Decor is elegant and airy. Attentive svce. Business clientele, since the new business district is a few steps away. **M–E**

🏨 **El Centro Plaza** (formerly the Quality Inn; dwntwn), 717 Central Ave. NW, NM 87102 (505/247-1501). 144 rms, A/C, color TV, in-rm movies. AE, CB, DC, MC, V. Free parking, pool, rest., bar, valet svce, free airport limo, free crib. *Note:* Functional six-floor motel, completely modernized. Rms are attractive; the best have a park view. Agreeable svce, very good price-to-quality ratio. 3 min. from Old Town by car. **I**

🏨 **Motel 6 Midtown** (nr. dwntwn), 1701 University Blvd., NM 87102 (505/843-9228). 118 rms, A/C, color TV, free in-rm movies. AE, DC, MC, V. Free parking, nearby coffee shop, free crib. *Note:* This motel, 5 min. from the city center, offers an unbeatable price-to-quality ratio. Down-to-earth comfort. Ideal for motorists. Nr. the university campus. **B**

Other Accommodations (from top bracket to budget)

🏨🏨🏨 **Hilton Inn** (nr. dwntwn), 1901 University Blvd. NE, NM 87102 (505/884-2500; toll free, see Hilton). 428 rms, A/C, color TV, in-rm movies. AE, CB, DC, MC, V. Free parking, two pools, two tennis courts, skating rink (Nov–Mar), sauna, rest. (The Rancher's Club), coffee shop, bar, rm svce, disco, concierge, free airport limo, free crib. *Note:* Grand hotel, large and comfortable, w. 12 floors, largest in Albuquerque. Efficient svce and welcome. Spacious rms w. refrigerators (some w. balconies). Rest. renowned for its grill. Good recreational facilities. 5 min. from dwntwn by car. Guests mostly groups and conventions. Worthwhile wknd discounts. Two floors reserved for VIPs. **M–E**

🏨🏨 **Doubletree** (formerly the Regent; dwntwn), 201 Marquette Ave. NW (at 2nd St.), NM 87102 (505/247-3344; toll free 800/528-0444). 300 rms, A/C, color TV, in-rm movies. AE, CB, DC, MC, V. Free valet parking, rest. (Mayfair), coffee shop, bar, rm svce, nightclub, free airport limo, free crib. *Note:* Massive 15-story tower w. roof-grdn overlooking the Convention Center. Utilitarian comfort and svce. Recently underwent major modernization. Very centrally located. Caters mostly to groups and conventions. **M–E**

🏨🏨 **Holiday Inn Midtown** (nr. dwntwn), 2020 Menaul Blvd. NE, NM 87107 (505/884-2511; toll free, see Holiday Inns). 366 rms, A/C, color TV, in-rm movies. AE, CB, DC, MC, V. Free parking, pool, health club, sauna, rest., bar, rm svce, disco, free airport limo, free crib. *Note:* A typical Holiday Inn, 5 min. by car from dwntwn. Comfortable rms w. balconies. Svce and welcome impersonal. Good overall price-to-quality ratio. **M**

🏨 **La Quinta North** (nr. dwntwn), 5241 San Antonio Dr. NE, NM 87109 (505/821-9000; toll free, see La Quinta). 130 rms, A/C, color TV, in-rm movies. AE, CB, DC, MC, V. Free parking, pool, 24-hr. coffee shop, valet svce, free crib. *Note:* Comfortable, enticing country-style

motel w. unusually large and well-designed rms. Friendly reception and svce. If you're driving through this should suit you fine, w. its direct access to I-25. 8 min. from dwntwn. **I–M**

 De Anza Motor Lodge (nr. dwntwn), 4301 Central Ave. NE, NM 87108 (505/255-1654). 84 rms, A/C, color TV. AE, CB, DC, MC, V. Free parking, pool, coffee shop, crib $4. *Note:* Small, unassuming but very well run motel w. an engaging Native American layout. Serviceably comfortable rms; smiling reception. Great if you're on a budget. 5 min. from dwntwn. Very good value. **B–I**

An Airport Hotel

 Amfac Hotel (nr. dwntwn), 2910 Yale Blvd. SE, NM 87106 (505/843-7000; toll free, see Amfac Hotels). 269 rms, A/C, color TV, in-rm movies. AE, CB, DC, MC, V. Free parking, pool, two tennis courts, rest. ("Lil's"), coffee shop, bar, rm svce, drugstore, free airport shuttle, free crib. *Note:* Large, modern hotel 3 min. from the terminal. Ultra-professional svce; huge, comfortable rms w. balcony (some w. refrigerator). Fine for a stopover between planes. 12 min. from dwntwn. **M–E**

YMCA/Youth Hostels

Albuquerque International Youth Hostel (dwntwn), 1012 Central Ave. W., NM 87102 (505/243-6101). Youth hostel w. 12 rms, very centrally located.

RESTAURANTS

A Note on Restaurant Prices: Albuquerque restaurant prices, per person, excluding drinks and service charges, are coded as follows: **VE,** Very Expensive ($60 and up); **E,** Expensive ($40–$60); **M,** Moderate ($25–$40); **I,** Inexpensive ($15–$25); **B,** Budget (up to $15).

Personal Favorites (in order of preference)

 Al Monte's (nr. dwntwn), 1306 Rio Grande Blvd. NW (243-3709). A/C. Lunch Mon–Fri, dinner Mon–Sat; closed hols. AE, DC, MC, V. Jkt. *Specialties:* homemade pasta, veal Oscar, grilled squab, sole meunière, deviled crab, catch of the day. Good wine list. *Note:* Lavish but conventional decor. Continental-inspired classic cuisine, irreproachably prepared. Attentive svce. Inviting bar and open fireplaces; open-air dining in good weather. Resv. advised. The local favorite. *Continental.* **I–M**

 Stephens (dwntwn), 1311 Tijeras NW (842-1773). A/C. Lunch/dinner daily, brunch Sun. AE, MC, V. Jkt. *Specialties:* chicken w. tequila-and-lime sauce, rack of lamb, catch of the day, broiled prime beef cuts. *Note:* One of Albuquerque's most elegant rests., Stephens serves excellent contemporary American food drawing heavily on local produce and recipes. Efficient svce; locally very popular, so resv. strongly advised. *American.* **I–M**

 El Pinto (nr. dwntwn), 10500 4th St. NW (898-1771). A/C. Lunch/dinner Tues–Sun; closed hols. AE, MC, V. *Specialties:* guacamole, chile con carne, enchiladas, sopaipillas. *Note:* Memorable southwestern cooking in a hacienda setting. The inviting, tree-shaded courtyard w. its fountain is one of Albuquerque's pleasantest spots. Friendly, ultra-professional svce. Very popular w. locals, so resv. advised. Highly recommended. *Mexican/American.* **B–I**

 M. & J. Sanitary Tortilla Factory (dwntwn), 403 2nd St. SW (242-4890). A/C. Breakfast/lunch (till 4pm) Mon–Sat; closed hols. No credit cards. *Specialties:* burritos de carne adovada, tacos, menudos, enchiladas. *Note:* Considered by purists one of the most authentic Mexican rests. in the area. Decor Formica and neon style; continuous Mexican music; relaxed atmosphere. Locally popular; excellent price-to-quality ratio. No resv. *Mexican.* **B**

Other Restaurants (from top bracket to budget)

 Scalo (nr. dwntwn), Nob Hill Center, 3500 Central Ave. SE (255-8781). A/C. Lunch Mon–Fri, dinner Mon–Sat. AE,

MC, V. Jkt. *Specialties:* fresh homemade pasta, lamb chops w. roast garlic and chive sauce, broiled fish, northern Italian dishes. Good wine list. *Note:* The best place in town to eat Italian. Airy, admirable, wholly authentic food (don't miss the homemade pasta). Warm, friendly decor w. open kitchen and open-air dining in good weather. Ultra-professional svce. Resv. advised. *Italian.* **I–M**

☀☟☟ **Casa Vieja** (vic.), Corrales Rd. in Corrales (via Rio Grande Blvd. and N.M. 46N) (505/898-7489). A/C. Dinner only, Tues–Sun; closed Jan 1, Thanksgiving, Dec 25. AE, CB, DC, MC, V. Jkt. *Specialties:* osso buco w. risotto alla milanese, homemade pasta, veal scaloppine, saltimbocca, veal marsala, lime pie. *Note:* Charming adobe hacienda, more than a century and a half old, 12 mi. (19km) north of Albuquerque. Nice colonial decor w. open fires. Italian-leaning cuisine of excellent quality; rather restricted wine list. Efficient svce.; resv. advised. 25 min. from dwntwn. *Italian/Continental.* **I–M**

☀☟☟ **The Cooperage** (nr. dwntwn), 7220 Lomas Blvd. NE (255-1657). A/C. Lunch/dinner daily; closed Dec 25. AE, CB, DC, MC, V. *Specialties:* roast beef, barbecues, grilled fish and shellfish, chicken Kiev. *Note:* Unusual building in the shape of a giant vat, but comfortable inside. Excellent meats and seafood. Intimate atmosphere, open late (till 11pm); dancing Wed–Sat. 10 min. from dwntwn. Other location: 10200 Corrales NW (898-5555). *Steak/American.* **I**

☀☟☟ **Maria Teresa** (dwntwn), 618 Rio Grande Blvd. NW (242-3900). A/C. Lunch/dinner daily; closed Thanksgiving, Dec 25. AE, CB, DC, MC, V. Jkt. *Specialties:* steak, lobster, quail, truite amandine. Good wine list. *Note:* Beautiful hacienda (1840) standing in its own grdns, and designated as a historic monument. Very convincing decor. Meticulous presentation; svce on the slow side. Resv. advised. A few steps from Old Town Plaza. *Continental.* **I–M**

☟☟ **New Chinatown** (nr. dwntwn), 5001 Central Ave. NE (265-8859). A/C. Lunch/dinner daily; closed Thanksgiving, Dec 25. AE, CB, DC, MC, V. *Specialties:* Cantonese-Szechuan. *Note:* The best Chinese rest. in Albuquerque. Modern Oriental decor; good food and exotic drinks. Svce leaves something to be desired. Very good price-to-quality ratio at the buffet lunch. 10 min. from dwntwn. *Chinese.* **B–I**

☟ **La Hacienda** (dwntwn), 302 San Felipe NW (243-3131). A/C. Lunch/dinner daily; closed Jan 1, Thanksgiving, Dec 25. CB, DC, MC, V. *Specialties:* enchiladas, burritos, sopaipillas. *Note:* Pleasing, original Mexican-hacienda interior, w. three great trees at the center of the dining rm, but resolutely tourist atmosphere. Mexican-American cuisine no better than acceptable. Svce and welcome so-so. High noise level, agreeable music. Right on Old Town Plaza. Resv. advised. *Mexican.* **B–I**

Cafeterias/Fast Food

Duran Central Pharmacy (dwntwn), 1815 Central Ave. NW (247-4141). Breakfast/lunch 9am–6:30pm. No credit cards. Excellent southwestern food such as chili con carne, green chili, carne adovada, enchiladas, burritos, served in a genuine old-time drugstore setting. Very popular locally. Very near the Old Town.

Furr's (nr. dwntwn), 2272 Wyoming Blvd. NE (298-6886). Lunch/dinner daily (until 8pm). *Specialties:* roast beef, daily specials, sandwiches, baked fish. *Note:* Pleasant surroundings and atmosphere. Well regarded locally. Other locations: 6100 Central Ave. SE (265-1022) and 109 Montgomery Plaza NE (881-3373).

BARS & NIGHTCLUBS

Caravan East (nr. dwntwn), 7605 Central Ave. NE (265-7877). The local shrine of country music; a jumping joint. Open daily.

The Cooperage (nr. downtown), 7220 Lomas Blvd. NE (255-1657). Live jazz; dancing Wed-Sat. Also an acceptable rest.

Cowboy's (nr. dwntwn), 3301 Juan Tabo Blvd. NE (296-1959). Warranted real country music in a very cowboy setting.

Nicoles Lounge (nr. dwntwn), 2101 Louisiana Blvd. NE (881-6800). Fashionable disco; smart atmosphere. Also very acceptable rest. Open daily.

NEARBY EXCURSIONS

CIBOLA NATIONAL FOREST: 1,536,000 forested acres (640,000ha) surrounding Albuquerque, Mountainair, Grants, and Magdalena. Roads offering fine views, camping, hunting, fishing, skiing in midwinter, etc. For information: 10308 Candelaria Rd. NE, Albuquerque, NM 87112 (505/275-5207).

CORONADO STATE PARK & MONUMENT (22 mi./ 35km north via I-25 and N.M. 44N) (867-5351): Kuava ruins, Native American pueblo dating from A.D. 1300. The Spanish conquistador Francisco Vásquez de Coronado pitched his camp here during his fruitless search for a mythical Eldorado known to historians under the name of "the seven golden cities of Cibola." Interesting Native American museum. Visit to a restored *kiva* (place of worship). Definitely worth seeing. Open daily.

NATIVE AMERICAN PUEBLOS: There are 19 pueblos (villages) inhabited by 40,000 Native Americans as well as another dozen abandoned or in ruins, in central New Mexico, all antedating the arrival of the Spanish colonists about 3½ centuries ago. The Anasazi peoples, close relatives of the Aztecs and great builders, built these too, between A.D. 700 and 1100. **Bandelier National Monument** (see "Nearby Excursions" in Chapter 39 on Santa Fe), and especially **Chaco Canyon** (see "Farther Afield" in Chapter 39 on Santa Fe), both now in ruins, are among the most important archeological monuments of Native American culture. The Pueblo or Zuñi peoples who live there today are the descendants of the legendary Anasazi. The most isolated of minorities, the Pueblo or Zuñi tribes of New Mexico, and their Hopi cousins in Arizona, have always been settlers, as distinct from such nomadic peoples as the Apaches and Navajos, who formed a large majority of the Native American population in the Southwest.

Half a dozen of their pueblos near Albuquerque are open to tourists between sunrise and sunset, generally for a fee of around $3–$4 per car. The best time for a visit is during the yearly festival or on days of religious ceremony; calendar from Albuquerque Convention & Visitors Bureau, 625 Silver Ave. SW, Suite 210 (505/243-3696). *Note:* For religious reasons, some villages do not allow cameras (movie, still, or video) or tape recorders. In others, photographers must pay a fee of $3–$6.

The most picturesque of these pueblos are:

Acoma Pueblo, 65 mi. (104km) west by I-40W and N.M. 23 (505/252-1139): The oldest continuously inhabited site in the U.S., believed to have been settled around A.D. 600. Perched 6,400 ft. (1,955m) up on a rocky mesa, "Sky City," as historians have dubbed it, is by far the loveliest Native American pueblo in the country, and the least corrupted by Western civilization. Fine Spanish mission of San Esteban Rey (1629). Photography permitted; fee, $3.

Isleta Pueblo, 14 mi. (22km) south on U.S. 85 (505/869-3111): Busy handcraft center. The original church of 1620 was destroyed during the Indian Rebellion of 1680 and rebuilt 13 years later. No photographs.

Jémez Pueblo, 48 mi. (76km) north by I-25, N.M. 44, and N.M. 4: Renowned for its embroidery and basket-making; no photographs. Not far away, at Jémez Springs, is a beautiful Spanish mission dating from 1621.

    Zía Pueblo, 34 mi. (54km) north by I-25 and N.M. 44 (505/ 867-3304): Another pueblo well known for its pottery. Spanish mission dating from 1692. No photographs.

    Zuñi Pueblo, 179 mi. (286km) west via I-40, N.M. 32, and N.M. 53 (505/782-4481): One of the "seven golden cities of Cibola." The Zuñi, a separate branch of the Pueblo people, are excellent potters and jewelers. Photography permitted; fee $3. Late Nov or early Dec is the season of the Zuñi "shalako" (council of the gods), the most beautiful, and spectacular, Native American ceremony in the U.S. By all means go—but movie/still cameras are not allowed during "shalako."

GHOST TOWNS: In New Mexico there are a round dozen old mining towns dating from last century's gold and silver rushes; some of them are now completely abandoned. Examples are **White Oaks** (15 mi./24km NE of Valley of Fires State Park along U.S. 54 and N.M. 349) and ⚑ **Shakespeare** (46 mi./73km SW of Silver City by N.M. 90 and U.S. 70), where most of the ornate exteriors are still standing.

    Others are still more or less intact, but drained of their former vitality: **Chloride** (38 mi./60km NW of Truth or Consequences along I-25, N.M. 142, and N.M. 52), and **Hillsboro, Kingston,** and **Piños Altos** (see "Farther Afield," below).

    Among ghost towns closer to Albuquerque, the most picturesque are ⚑ **Cerrillos** (48 mi./76km NE via I-40 and N.M. 14) and ⚑ **Madrid** (45 mi./72km NE via I-40 and N.M. 14); for these two villages, see Chapter 39 on Santa Fe.

FARTHER AFIELD

    SANDIA LOOP DRIVE (80 mi./128km r.t. via I-40E, N.M. 14N, N.M. 536W, N.M. 165W, and I-25S): A panoramic route leading to the peak of **Sandia Crest** (10,678 ft./3,260m). Wonderful view over the Rio Grande Valley and surrounding countryside. The **Sandia Peak Ski Area** can also be reached by cable car (see "Panoramas," above). An unpaved portion of N.M. 165 is open to regular traffic May 15–Oct 15 only.

    SANTA FE & THE NATIVE AMERICAN PUEBLOS (240 mi./384km r.t. via I-25N, N.M. 44N and 4E, U.S. 285S, and I-25S): Exhilarating 2-day drive (longer if a visit is made to **Coronado State Park;** see "Nearby Excursions," above). The route continues through two typical Native American villages (see "Nearby Excursions," above), **Zía Pueblo** and **Jémez Pueblo,** best known for pottery and basketwork, respectively. Stop for a look at ⚑ **Valle Grande,** ranked by geologists as the world's largest volcanic crater (area, 175 sq. mi./453km²; mean depth, 486 ft./152m). Then on to the beautiful **Bandelier National Monument** (see "Nearby Excursions" in Chapter 39 on Santa Fe); **Los Alamos,** the historic birthplace of the atom bomb; and the pueblo of **San Ildefonso** with its beautiful plaza (see "Native American Pueblos," in Chapter 39 on Sante Fe), before reaching the capital of New Mexico with its monuments and its museums (for places to stay, see Chapter 39 on Santa Fe). Return to Albuquerque by I-25S. Set aside at least 48 hrs. for the trip, which mustn't be missed.

    SKY CITY & CHACO CANYON (473 mi./758km r.t. via I-25N, N.M. 44N and 57S; I-40W; N.M. 32S, 53W, and 53E; I-40E; N.M. 38S and 23N; and I-40E): A full 3- or 4-day trip for devotees of archeology and Native American culture, it takes you first to **Coronado State Park** (see "Nearby Excursions," above), then on to the astonishing ⚑ **Chaco Culture National Historical Park,** an archeological gem from our Amerindian past. Deserted by the Anasazi peoples around the end of the 13th century, this cluster of 75 ruined pueblos, one of which, Pueblo Bonito, boasted in its glory days no fewer than 800 rooms and 37 *kivas* (places of worship), well deserves a special trip. *Warning:* The road to Chaco Canyon is unsurfaced; dry weather only. A visitor center is located 2 mi. (3km) from the south entrance on N.M. 57; open daily (988-6727).

The third stage of the journey leads you to **Gallup,** "the Indian capital of the world." Every Aug some 50 tribes from all over the U.S. and Canada meet for the ⚥ **Intertribal Indian Ceremonial,** a very lively 4-day festival with dances, parades, rodeos, and handcraft displays. Don't miss it. Then on to **Zuñi Pueblo,** home of the famous "shalako" ritual (see "Native American Pueblos," above), and ⚥ **El Morro National Monument,** a shaft of rock 211 ft. (64km) high with many Native American rock carvings as well as inscriptions by Spanish conquistadors and early settlers in the Old West—an interesting sight. Visitor center open daily (783-4226).

The trip ends with a leisurely visit to the beautiful **Acoma Pueblo,** or "Sky City" (see "Native American Pueblos," above), before returning to Albuquerque via I-40E. This exciting trip is strongly recommended; it can be prolonged to take in **Mesa Verde National Park,** an important center of Native American culture (see Chapter 39 on Santa Fe), **Monument Valley,** or **Canyon de Chelly** (see Chapter 40 on Navajoland).

Where to Stay En Route

IN GALLUP   Three motels are recommended:

ₚ **Best Western–The Inn,** 3009 W. U.S. 66, Gallup, NM 87301 (505/722-2221). 124 rms. **I–M**

ₚ **Motel 6,** 3306 W. U.S. 66, Gallup, NM 87301 (505/863-4492). 80 rms. **B**

ₚ **Travelodge,** 1709 W. U.S. 66, Gallup, NM 87301 (505/863-9301). 50 rms. **I**

WHITE SANDS & THE RIO GRANDE VALLEY (582 mi./932km r.t. via I-25S, U.S. 82E, N.M. 24N, U.S. 70E, U.S. 380W, and I-25N):

After driving along the Rio Grande Valley for almost 225 mi. (360km), you'll come to ⚥⚥ **White Sands National Monument,** an extraordinary desert of gypsum whose dazzling-white sand dunes, as much as 45 ft. (15m) high, create an ever-changing landscape of otherworldly beauty. For information, contact the Superintendent, White Sands National Monument, P.O. Box 458, Alamogordo, NM 88311 (505/437-1058). Also not to be missed: the ⚥⚥ **Alamogordo Space Center** on U.S. 54N (505/437-2840; toll free 800/545-4021). The Space Center Museum, an all-glass cube overlooking the White Sands Proving Ground, has a fine collection of U.S. and Soviet satellites and space capsules, moon rocks, models of old and new rockets, etc., as well as a very up-to-date planetarium. Open daily.

Then on to ⚥ **Cloudcroft,** an agreeable little winter-sports resort with a flourishing artists' colony and the highest golf course (8,700 ft./2,650m above sea level) in the U.S. If you can, go on to visit **Mescalero,** capital of the lovely Apache reservation of the same name; museum, exhibition of Native American handcrafts.

The fourth stage takes you to **Ruidoso,** a ski resort in the middle of a forest, and to **Lincoln,** famous in the days of the Old West and now a museum town. The legendary Pat Garrett, the man who killed Billy the Kid, was long its sheriff. Billy the Kid is buried at **Fort Sumner,** also famous during the winning of the West, about 125 mi. (200km) north. Be sure to see the museum and the ⚥ **old courthouse** on U.S. 380 at Lincoln (505/653-4025).

Finish the journey by crossing the ⚥⚥ **Valley of Fires,** a desert of gray-and-black lava from an old volcano. At ⚥ **Trinity Site** near Alamogordo, 30 mi. (50km) west, on July 16, 1945, the first atomic bomb was tested as a trial run for

Hiroshima and Nagasaki. Area open to the public the first Sat of Apr and Oct. For information, call 505/437-6120. This beautiful 3- or 4-day trip can be combined with the visit to the 𝔸 **Gila Cliff Dwellings** (see below).

Where to Stay En Route

IN CLOUDCROFT 🏨 **The Lodge,** U.S. 82, Cloudcroft, NM 88317 (505/682-2566). 50 rms. Designated historic building. **M–E**

IN MESCALERO ☀ 🏨 **Inn of the Mountain Gods,** Carrizo Canyon, Mescalero, NM 88340 (505/257-5141). 250 rms. This luxurious resort complex, w. its private golf course, tennis courts, and lake, is on the Apache reservation of Mescalero. Spectacular. **M–E**

IN RUIDOSO 🏨 **Best Western Swiss Chalet Inn,** on N.M. 37, Ruidoso, NM 88345 (505/258-3333). 82 rms. **M**

🏨 **Super 8,** 100 Cliff Dr. (U.S. 70), Ruidoso, NM 88345 (505/378-8180). 63 rms. **I**

☀🏛 **GILA CLIFF DWELLINGS & SILVER CITY** (635 mi./ 1,016km r.t. via I-25S; N.M. 90W, 35N, 15N, 15S; U.S. 180N; N.M. 12N; U.S. 60E; and I-25N): A journey of 3–4 days across the vast **Gila National Forest,** beginning with a visit to **Isleta Pueblo** and its lovely church built in 1693 (see "Native American Pueblos," above). At **Socorro,** 50 mi. (80km) farther south, you can admire the fine fortified mission of 𝔸 **San Miguel,** 403 Camino Real (open Mon–Fri), built in 1615. Then on to 𝔸 **Truth or Consequences** and its hot springs, and to **Hillsboro** and 𝔸 **Kingston,** almost-deserted ghost towns from gold-rush days. Kingston once had 22 saloons for its 1,800 inhabitants. Go on to see the 𝔸 **Gila Cliff Dwellings National Monument,** N.M. 15 (536-9461), in 𝔸 **Gila National Forest;** for information, contact Ranger District, 2610 N. Silver St., Silver City, NM 88061 (505/388-8201).

Then drive to the old stagecoach stop of 𝔸 **Silver City,** once thronged with gold and silver miners, scene of the early exploits of the famous outlaw Butch Cassidy. As you pass it, stop for a look at 𝔸 **Piños Altos,** a picturesque ghost town built by gold miners in the 19th century, and often under attack by the Apaches under Cochise and Geronimo. Its most famous inhabitant was Judge Roy Bean, known as the "hanging judge."

On the road back to Albuquerque, make a detour through **Mogollon** (74 mi./118km north of Silver City via U.S. 80 and N.M. 78), another famous ghost town from the 19th century. One last sight you shouldn't miss, to your left as you follow U.S. 60E 14 mi. (22km) beyond Datil, is the forest of antenna dishes that make up the ☀🏛 **Very Large Array Telescope,** the largest radiotelescope in the world with 27 giant parabolic dishes each weighing more than 200 tons. Visitor center open daily. For information, call 505/772-4255.

Where to Stay En Route

IN SILVER CITY 🏨 **Drifter Motel,** 711 Silver Heights Blvd., Silver City, NM 88061 (505/538-2916). 69 rms. **I**

🏨 **Holiday Motor Hotel,** U.S. 180 E, Silver City, NM 88061 (505/538-3711). 80 rms. **I**

CHAPTER 39

SANTA FE

□ □ □

And the Pueblos

A state capital of truly human dimension, "La Villa Real de la Santa Fe de San Francisco" (the Royal City of the Holy Faith of St. Francis), now called simply Santa Fe, is the offspring of an unusual amalgam of Native American, Hispanic, and Anglo-Saxon traditions. Instead of urban motorways or great avenues intersecting at right angles, you'll find shady streets, most of them narrow and winding. Neon signs are banned from downtown. No glass or concrete skyscrapers; just low-rise ocher or beige houses of adobe (sun-dried brick), typically in traditional Native American design. The lovely **Plaza,** standing at the historic heart of the city, where the legendary **Santa Fe Trail** ends; the 1610 **Mission de San Miguel,** one of the oldest churches in the country; the **Palace of the Governors,** also dating from 1610; even the modern **State Capitol,** whose massive rounded shape recalls the old *kivas* (Native American places of worship)—all evoke a sense of the past. And the city's museums house many treasures from the Native American civilizations. Indeed, Santa Fe is the only state capital in the country that won't permit commercial jets to land at its airport, lest its authenticity be impaired!

Vigilantly protecting its colonial heritage, more than 3½ centuries old (the city was founded in 1609—11 years before the Pilgrims landed at Plymouth—by Don Pedro de Peralta, governor of the Spanish province of New Mexico), this oldest of the country's state capitals has never lacked for painters, sculptors, musicians, and writers. From D. H. Lawrence to Max Weber and Georgia O'Keeffe, from Ezra Pound to Aaron Copland, they came, attracted by the region's unique charm, the extraordinary luminosity of its skies, the majestic backdrop of the **Sierra Sangre de Cristo,** the southernmost spur of the Rocky Mountains. About 5,000 artists today live in Santa Fe.

Apart from the picturesque and colorful beauty of its own narrow streets and flower-filled patios, Santa Fe is the ideal starting point for many fascinating excursions to **Mesa Verde National Park** or to the surrounding **Hopi pueblos.** Some of these "pueblos" (villages) are already tainted by the "civilization" of electrical appliances and mass tourism. Others, such as **Taos Pueblo, San Ildefonso,** and **Santo Domingo,** have at least preserved their original appearance, if not their authentic character.

Note that, at an elevation of 7,000 ft. (2,134m), Santa Fe may give you a problem for your first few days, until you're accustomed to the altitude.

BASIC FACTS: Capital of the State of New Mexico. Area code: 505. Time zone: mountain. ZIP Code: 87501. Founded: 1609. Approximate population, 60,000; metropolitan area, 90,000.

CLIMATE: With more than 300 days of sunshine annually, you could say that the sun is a year-round fixture in Santa Fe but, thanks to the altitude, it's never unpleasantly hot; the July average temperature is 71° F (22° C). The evenings are cool even in summer. There is heavy snow in winter, for the delectation of skiers, on the slopes of the Sierra Sangre de Cristo; Jan average temperature, 35° F (2° C). In a word, it's always a good time of year to visit Santa Fe.

DISTANCES: Albuquerque, 61 mi. (98km); Denver, 386 mi. (618km); El Paso, 266 mi. (425km); Grand Canyon National Park, 465 mi. (744km); Phoenix, 521 mi. (834km); Salt Lake City, 610 mi. (976km).

ARRIVAL & TRANSIT INFORMATION

NEAREST MAJOR AIRPORT: Albuquerque International Airport (ABQ), 61 mi. (98km) SW (505/842-4366).

AIRLINES (at the Albuquerque airport): America West (247-0737), American (242-9464), Delta (243-2794), Southwest (831-1221), TWA (842-4010), and United (242-1411).

CITY LINK: Daily flights on **Mesa Airlines** operate up to seven times a day between Albuquerque International Airport and Santa Fe Municipal Airport; flight time, 25 min. For information and reservations, call toll free 800/637-2247.
   From Albuquerque International Airport, a minibus operated by Shuttlejack (505/982-4311) runs eight times a day to/from the principal Santa Fe hotels; fare, $15; time, about 75 min. Resv. advised.
   However, given the distance from Albuquerque to Santa Fe and the countless tempting excursions in the surrounding countryside, it makes a lot of sense to rent a car with unlimited mileage. Moreover, aside from the **Santa Fe Chile Line Trolley,** covered open-air buses that travel two routes (989-8595), there is no real public transportation system in Santa Fe and cabs are hard to come by.

CAR RENTAL (at Albuquerque International Airport unless otherwise indicated; if a second telephone number is given, it's for *free pickup at your place of residence in Santa Fe*): Avis (842-4080; 982-4361); Budget (247-3442; 984-8028); Dollar (842-4224); Hertz (842-4235; 982-1844); National (842-4222; 983-2232); and Thrifty, 2039 Yale Blvd. SE (842-8733; 984-1961).

LIMOUSINE SERVICES: Elegante Limo Service (473-1115).

TAXIS: Cabs may not be hailed on the street but may be summoned by phone. Recommended company: **Capital City Cab** (988-1211).

TRAIN: The nearest Amtrak station is on N.M. 41 at Lamy, 19 mi. (30km) south on U.S. 285 (toll free 800/872-7245).
   A shuttle runs daily between downtown Santa Fe and the station; contact Lamy Shuttle Service, 1476 Miracerros Loop N. (982-8829). Resv. advised.

INTERCITY BUSES: Greyhound, 858 St. Michaels Dr. (471-0008).

INFORMATION & TOURS

TOURIST INFORMATION: The **Santa Fe Chamber of Commerce,** 329 Montezuma St., NM 87501 (505/983-7317).

Santa Fe Convention and Visitors Bureau, Sweeney Center, 200 W. Marcy St. (P.O. Box 909), NM 87504 (505/984-6760; toll free 800/777-2489).
New Mexico State Tourism & Travel Division, J. M. Montoya Bldg., 1100 St. Francis Dr., NM 87503 (505/827-0291; toll free 800/545-2040 outside New Mexico): Information on all New Mexico's treasures of tourism.
Northern Indian Pueblos Council, P.O. Box 969, San Juan Pueblo, NM 87566 (505/852-4265). Information on the eight principal Native American pueblos around Santa Fe, activity schedule, etc.

GUIDED TOURS: Gray Line Tours (bus), 220 N. Guadalupe St. (471-9200 or 983-9491): Guided bus tours of the city and environs. Serves the main hotels.
Santa Fe Detours, in the La Fonda Hotel, 100 E. San Francisco St. (983-6565): 2-hr. walking tours of Santa Fe. Daily.

SIGHTS, ATTRACTIONS & ACTIVITIES

ADVENTURES: New Wave Rafting Co. (boat), 107 Washington Ave. (505/984-1444): White-water rafting down the Rio Grande, Rio Chama, and Arkansas River; half-day ($40), 1-day ($60–$70), and 2-day ($160–$200) trips. Summer only.
Rio Bravo River Tours (boat), 1412 Cerrillos Rd. (505/988-1153; toll free 800/451-0708): Rafting down the Rio Grande and White Rock Canyon; summer only.
Rio Grande Rapid Transit (boat), P.O. Box A, Pilar, NM 87571 (505/758-9700): Rafting down the Rio Grande and Rio Chama; summer only.
Southwest Safaris (airplane), P.O. Box 945, Santa Fe, NM 87504 (toll free 800/842-4246): 1-day trips by plane to Grand Canyon National Park, Mesa Verde, Canyon de Chelly, Monument Valley, and Carlsbad Caverns. Spectacular. Departures year round from Santa Fe Municipal Airport.

ARCHITECTURAL HIGHLIGHTS: ☼🔔 **La Fonda,** 100 E. San Francisco St. (982-5511): One of the most history-laden hotels in the U.S., going back to the opening of the Santa Fe Trail in the 1870s. A favorite stopping place for trappers, pioneers, and early traders. Billy the Kid was a dishwasher here at the beginning of his career of adventure. Long known as "The Inn at the End of the Trail," and often rebuilt (the last time was in 1919), La Fonda (literally "The Inn") is still one of the best hotels in the city. Worth seeing.
☼🔔 **Santa Fe Opera,** on U.S. 84, 7 mi. (11km) north (982-3851): Splendid conch-shaped open-air auditorium built on a mesa at the foot of the Jemez Mountains; a very successful piece of modern design. Every summer it hosts a highly regarded opera festival (see "Special Events," below). Open afternoons Mon–Sat during the opera season (June–Aug); it's advisable to make reservations. Worth going out of your way for.
🔔 **State Capitol,** Old Santa Fe Trail and Paseo de Peralta (984-9589): One of the newest (1966) state capitols in the country; an unusual circular building reminiscent of a traditional Native American *kiva* (place of worship). The New Mexico legislature meets here. Open Mon–Fri.

CHURCHES/SYNAGOGUES: 🔔 **Cathedral of St. Francis of Assisi,** Cathedral Plaza (982-5619): Built between 1869 and 1884 by Archbishop Jean Baptiste Lamy on the site of an older church destroyed by natives in 1680, said to be the country's oldest Marian shrine. Its *La Conquistadora,* brought here by the Spaniards in 1692, is the oldest statue of the Virgin still in existence in the U.S. A classic piece of architecture in the French Romanesque Revival style. Open daily.

Cristo Rey Church, Canyon Rd. and Camino Cabra: The largest Native American–style church in the country; its adobe walls are 7 ft. (2m) thick. Valuable stone reredos (altar screens) dating from 1760. Open daily.

Loreto Chapel, 219 Old Santa Fe Trail (984-7971): Gothic Revival chapel modeled on the Sainte-Chapelle in Paris, with an amazing spiral staircase, "The Famous Staircase," the work of an unknown cabinetmaker in 1878. Its 33 treads rise to a height of 22 ft. (7m), and are held together without nails or any visible support. Loreto Chapel is sometimes called Our Lady of Light Chapel. Open daily.

Mission of San Miguel, 401 Old Santa Fe Trail, at E. De Vargas St. (983-3974): This, the oldest church in the country still used for worship, was originally built around 1610 for residents of the Barrio. Its often-restored walls of thick adobe hide a wonderful interior, with the famous San José Bell which was cast in 1356 in Spain, a superb reredos (1798), and several old paintings. Open daily.

Santuário de Guadalupe, 100 Guadalupe St. (988-2027): One of the oldest shrines of the Virgin in the country, dating from about 1776–95. Dedicated to Our Lady of Guadalupe, the patron saint of Mexico, it houses some interesting handcrafts and religious art from the Spanish Colonial period. Open Mon–Sat.

Scottish Rite Temple, Washington Ave.: Enormous Masonic temple whose baroque design harks back to the Alhambra in Granada. No visitors.

HISTORIC BUILDINGS: **Oldest House,** 215 E. De Vargas St.: Believed to be the oldest building in the country still in use, this Native American house built of clay and straw was part of the original pueblo that stood on the site of Santa Fe in the 13th century. A fine example of early domestic adobe construction, the building has been converted into a souvenir shop. A stone's throw from the Mission of San Miguel. Open daily.

Palace of the Governors, The Plaza (827-6460): Both palace and fortress, this massive, elegant building has been the home, successively, of Spanish, Mexican, and U.S. governors; it is the oldest (1610) public building in continuous use in the U.S. Constructed of mud and partly destroyed in the Indian Rebellion of 1680, the original building with its patios, storehouses, and outbuildings has been restored many times. The author Lew Wallace, at the time governor of New Mexico, used his idle moments here to write the major part of his famous novel *Ben Hur* in 1880. Interesting museum, Native American craft shop, and impromptu market under the Portal, a long covered porch. Don't miss it; open daily Mar–Dec, Tues–Sun the rest of the year.

MUSEUMS OF ART & HISTORY: **Institute of American Indian Arts Museum,** 1369 Cerrillos Rd. (988-6281): A comprehensive panorama of modern Native American (including Inuit) arts and handcrafts: sculpture, pottery, textiles, jewelry, painting, etc. Fascinating. Temporary exhibitions. An absolute must. Open daily.

Laboratory of Anthropology/Museum of Indian Arts and Culture, 708-710 Camino Lejo (827-8941): Rich collection of Native American (particularly Navajo and Pueblo) art, from pottery to kachina dolls. Excellent specialized library. A must-see; open daily Mar–Dec, Tues–Sun the rest of the year.

Museum of Fine Arts, 107 W. Palace Ave. at Lincoln (827-4455): More than 8,000 works of southwestern artists from 1898 to the present, including several works by Georgia O'Keeffe. Handsome traditional adobe building dating from the turn of the century. Open daily Mar–Dec, Tues–Sun the rest of the year.

    Museum of International Folk Art, 706 Camino Lejo (827-8350): One of the best American museums of popular art and tradition, displaying dolls, masks, toys, religious objects, clothing—more than 125,000 different objects. Open daily Mar–Dec, Tues–Sun the rest of the year.

    Museum of New Mexico System (827-6463): Important grouping of four museums of art and culture, it comprises the **Museum of Fine Arts,** the **Palace of the Governors,** the **Museum of International Folk Art,** and the **Museum of Indian Arts and Culture** (see above); a fifth, the **Laboratory of Anthropology,** is open only to scholars and researchers.

    Wheelwright Museum, 704 Camino Lejo (982-4636): All kinds of Native American art—jewelry, pottery, textiles, and wickerwork. The design of this 1937 museum is based on traditional Navajo hogans or earthen huts. Interesting Native American craft shop. Open daily May–Sept, Tues–Sun the rest of the year.

PANORAMAS: **Cross of the Martyrs** is a great white cross on the crest of a hill with a fine view over the city. Erected in 1920, the monument commemorates the Franciscans who were killed in the Indian Rebellion of 1680. A brick walkway leading here from the intersection of Paseo de Peralta and Otero St. was opened in 1986.

PARKS & GARDENS: **River Park,** along the Santa Fe River between Old Santa Fe Trail and Don Gaspar Ave.: Pretty flower-planted, tree-shaded walk along the Santa Fe River (which is usually dry as a bone), marking the boundary of the Analco barrio ("the other side of the river" in the local tribal language), the old (11th- to 15th-century) Native American pueblo before the arrival of the Spanish settlers.

PERFORMING ARTS: For daily listings of all shows and cultural events, consult the entertainment pages of the daily papers, the *Albuquerque Journal* (morning) and *The New Mexican* (morning), particularly the latter's Friday supplement, *Pasatiempo,* or the "Day by Day" column of the weekly *Santa Fe Reporter.*

    Center for Contemporary Arts, 291 E. Barcelona Rd. (982-1338): Ballet, poetry recitals, big-name shows, theater.

    Greer Garson Theater, College of Santa Fe campus, St. Michael's Dr. (473-6511): Contemporary and classic theater.

    Lensic Theater, 211 W. San Francisco (982-0301): Home of the Santa Fe Orchestra (music director: William Kirschke). Bach and Mozart festivals in alternate years. Sept–May.

    New Mexico Repertory Theater, 1050 Old Pecos Trail (983-2382): Drama, comedy, contemporary theater.

    Paolo Soleri Outdoor Amphitheatre, Santa Fe's Indian School campus (988-6291): Big-name shows, rock concerts (summer only).

    St. Francis Auditorium, 107 W. Palace Ave. (983-2075): Home of the renowned Santa Fe Chamber Music Festival (July–Aug). Classical concerts, recitals.

    Santa Fe Actor's Theater, 430 W. Manhattan Ave. at Guadalupe (982-8309): Standard and contemporary theater, year round.

    Santa Fe Opera, on U.S. 84, 7 mi. (11km) north (982-3855): Open-air opera; cycle of five operas every summer (June–Aug). Nationally acclaimed.

SHOPPING: Deriving most of its income from tourism, Santa Fe abounds in Native American crafts shops, art galleries (almost 200), and all kinds of stalls that put unseemly prices on their goods and generate an unpleasantly rapacious atmosphere. If you're a dedicated window-shopper, in addition to the Plaza and its surroundings you may want to see:

    Canyon Road (see "Strolls," below).

SANTA FE

Cristo Ray Church

Museum of International Folk Art
Wheelright Museum

Smith Park

GONZALES RD.

PALACE AVE.
ALAMEDA
CANYON RD.

GARCIA ST.

OLD SANTA FE TRAIL

OLD PECOS TRAIL

Palace of Governors
St. Francis Cathedral
The Plaza
City Hall
Post Office
Sweeney Convention Center
Fine Arts Museum

Oldest House

State Capitol

PERALTA

BARCELONA RD.

CORDOVA RD.

DON GASPAR AVE.

GALISTEO ST.

WATER ST.

SANDOVAL

PASEO DE

PASEO DE PERALTA

CAMINO DEL CAMPO

HICKOX ST.

← To Taos

ALAMEDA

Santa Fe R.

AGUA FRIA

CERRILLOS RD.

Albuquerque

Museum American Indian Arts

84 85

285

85

← N

Guadelupe Street: The new "in" address for shopping.

Santa Fe Village, 227 Don Gaspar St.: Two dozen shops and art galleries in a fake pueblo setting very near the Plaza.

Sena Plaza and Prince Plaza, 115 E. Palace Ave.: Some 40 luxury shops and restaurants around pretty patios in two elegant 19th-century mansions.

Among the shops offering authentic Native American art objects and handcrafts (and not Taiwanese, Mexican, or Filipino knockoffs): **Packard's Indian Trading Co.** (61 Old Santa Fe Trail), **Bellas Artes Gallery** (301 García St.), and the museum shops at the Palace of the Governors and the Wheelwright Museum (see above).

SPECIAL EVENTS: For the exact schedule of events below, consult the **Santa Fe Chamber of Commerce** (see "Tourist Information," above).

Santa Fe Rodeo (mid-July): The great event for cowboys and rodeo lovers.

Spanish Market (last wknd of July): Exhibition of Hispanic crafts under the arcades of the Palace of the Governors.

Fiesta at Santo Domingo Pueblo (late July to early Aug): The best-known and most colorful Native American fiesta in the Rio Grande Valley.

Santa Fe Chamber Music Festival (6 weeks in July and Aug): One of the best classical-music festivals in the country; for information and reservations, call 983-2075.

Santa Fe Opera (July–Aug): Summer mecca for opera amateurs in an open-air auditorium in the sierra. Few big names, but a nursery for young talent with a large, faithful audience of opera lovers. Resv. a must, well ahead (call 982-3855).

Taos Summer Music Festival (mid-June to Aug): Very popular chamber-music festival (776-2388).

Indian Market (mid-Aug): One of the biggest Native American markets in the country; tribes from every quarter of the compass come to display their arts and crafts on the Plaza. Folk dances. 100,000 visitors each year.

Santa Fe Fiesta (3 days in mid-Sept): Parades, processions, dancing; celebrated every year since 1712 to commemorate the reconquest of the town by the Spaniards after the Indian Rebellion of 1680. The fiesta begins with the ritual burning of Zozobra, a 40-ft. (12m) papier-mâché effigy. One of the most famous popular festivals in the U.S.

Sundown Dance at Taos Pueblo (late Sept): Colorful festival.

Christmas Eve Celebrations in Santa Fe (Dec 24): Lights, dancing, processions.

Dates of other **Native American festivals** may be obtained from the Santa Fe Convention and Visitors Bureau, 200 W. Marcy St. (984-6760).

SPORTS: Horse Racing (Wed and wknds, early May to Labor Day): **The Downs,** 5 mi. (8km) south on I-25 (471-3311). Thoroughbred racing.

STROLLS: ☼☖ **Canyon Road:** The old road to Pecos in the days of the Santa Fe Trail, now an arts-and-crafts street. More than 50 galleries, shops, and restaurants. Other studios and shops on nearby **Camino del Monte Sol.** Commercial but picturesque atmosphere.

☼☖☖ **The Plaza:** The historic heart of Santa Fe, a fine, lively, colorful sight with its grdns, its 1862 commemorative obelisk, its old houses, and its Native American market set up every morning in the arcades of the Palace of the Governors. In the SE corner, a plaque marks the end of the fabled Santa Fe Trail, linking Independence, Mo., with the Rio Grande Valley. It was opened in 1822 by William Becknell, a particularly enterprising Kansas City businessman.

WINTER SPORTS RESORTS: ☖ **Santa Fe Basin,** 17 mi. (27km) NE on N.M. 475 (982-4429): 7 lifts; open Nov–Apr.

☖ **Sipapu Ski Area,** 60 mi. (96km) NE via U.S. 84, N.M. 503,

N.M. 76, and N.M. 518 (505/587-2240): 3 lifts; open Dec–Mar.
☀️♨♨ **Taos Ski Valley,** 89 mi. (142km) NE via U.S. 84, N.M. 68, U.S. 64, and N.M. 150 (505/776-2291): 9 lifts; open Nov–Apr.
For a recording giving **snow conditions** at different resorts, call 984-0606.

ACCOMMODATIONS

A Note on Accommodations: Room rates in Santa Fe are coded as follows: **VE,** Very Expensive ($140 and up); **E,** Expensive ($90–$140); **M,** Moderate ($60–$90); **I,** Inexpensive ($30–$60); **B,** Budget (up to $30). A listing of toll free numbers is in the Appendix.

Personal Favorites (in order of preference)

☀️♋♋♋ **The Bishop's Lodge** (vic.), Bishop's Lodge Rd. (3 mi./5km north on N.M. 22), NM 87501 (505/983-6377). 65 rms, A/C, color TV. No credit cards. Free parking, pool, sauna, four tennis courts, trap shooting, boating, fishing, horseback riding, rest. (Bishop's Lodge Restaurant), bar, rm svce, nightclub, cinema (in summer), crib $10. *Note:* Luxurious vacation ranch on the outskirts of Santa Fe. Very comfortable rms w. private patios, some w. fireplaces; very complete facilities. Superb setting and surroundings on 1,000 acres (400ha) at the foot of the Sangre de Cristo Mountains. Attentive svce; rest. of quality. Once the home of Archbishop Jean Lamy, on whom Willa Cather based her famous novel *Death Comes for the Archbishop.* Closed early Jan. through the end of Mar. A classic of Santa Fe since 1918. 5 min. from dwntwn. **E–VE** (Modified American Plan June–Aug).

♋♋♋ **Clarion Eldorado Hotel** (dwntwn), 309 W. San Francisco St., NM 87501 (505/988-4455; toll free, see Clarion). 218 rms, A/C, color TV, in-rm movies. AE, CB, DC, MC, V. Valet gar. $6, pool, saunas, rest. (The Old House), coffee shop, bar, rm svce, nightclub, boutiques, concierge. *Note:* The most elegant and one of the newest (1986) of the dwntwn hotels. A very successful design, deftly combining the imperatives of modern hostelry with the traditional esthetics of Santa Fe: adobe walls, exposed beams, and colorful decor w. Native American motifs. Luxurious, well-designed rms w. private balconies or patios and minibars (some w. fireplaces). Rooftop pool w. views clear across the city. Exemplary svce; very acceptable rest. Well-heeled tourist clientele. A stone's throw from the Plaza; an excellent place to stay. **E–VE,** but lower rates off-season.

☀️♋♋ **La Fonda** (dwntwn), 100 E. San Francisco St., NM 87501 (505/982-5511; toll free 800/523-5002). 160 rms, A/C, color TV, in-rm movies. AE, CB, DC, MC, V. Free parking, pool, rest. (La Plazuela), bars, rm svce, nightclub, art gallery, free crib. *Note:* Charming old Spanish Colonial–style hotel right on the Plaza. A genuine local institution (see "Architectural Highlights," above); the present building dates from 1919. Fine accommodations w. comfortable, tastefully decorated rms, some w. balconies and fireplaces. Pretty covered patio; acceptable rest.; pleasant rooftop bar; romantic atmosphere. Very good value in spite of the utterly inefficient svce. The best location in Santa Fe. **E,** but lower rates off-season.

☀️♋♋ **La Posada de Santa Fe** (dwntwn), 330 E. Palace Ave., NM 87501 (505/986-0000; toll free 800/727-5276). 116 rms; no A/C; color TV, in-rm movies. AE, CB, DC, MC, V. Free parking, pool, rest. (Staab House), bar, rm svce, hrdrsr, free crib. *Note:* Very pretty little older hotel in a lovely grdn; elegant Spanish Colonial decor. Huge, comfortable rms (some w. kitchenette and fireplace) and adobe casitas w. private patios. A stone's throw from the Plaza and the Palace of the Governors. Diligent svce; good rest. located in a luxury old 19th-century house. One of the best values in town. **M–E,** but lower rates off-season.

♋♋ **El Rey Inn** (nr. dwntwn), 1862 Cerrillos Rd., NM 87504 (505/982-1931). 56 rms, A/C, color TV. AE, DC, MC, V.

Free parking, pool, adj. coffee shop, free breakfast, free crib. *Note:* Engaging, well-run small motel in a verdant oasis 8 min. from dwntwn. Inviting rms w. exposed beams, some w. kitchenettes, refrigerators, and fireplaces. Attractive grdn w. fountain. Good value. **I–M**

Other Accommodations (from top bracket to budget)

Best Western Inn at Loreto (dwntwn), 211 Old Santa Fe Trail, NM 87501 (505/988-5531; toll free, see Best Western). 139rms, A/C, cable color TV, AE, CB, DC, MC, V. Free parking, pool, rest., coffee shop, bar, rm svce, disco, hrdrsr, drugstore, free crib. *Note:* A good piece of modern architecture in the Native American style, well adapted to its surroundings. Comfortable, congenial hotel a block or two from the Plaza; functional rms w. private balconies or patios. Very good reception; impeccable svce. Group and business clientele. **E,** but lower rates off-season.

St. Francis (formerly the De Vargas Hotel; dwntwn), 210 Don Gaspar Ave., NM 87501 (505/983-5700; toll free 800/666-5700). 82 rms, A/C, cable color TV. AE, MC, V. Free parking, rest. (Francisco's), bar, rm svce, concierge, crib $10. *Note:* This elegant little survivor from the '20s has preserved all its intimate, romantic flavor. Beautifully redecorated and reequipped at a cost of $6 million, it boasts comfortable rms w. refrigerator, period furniture, and original paintings. Thoughtful, personalized svce; admirable rest. Afternoon tea served daily in lobby. Excellent value only two blocks from the Plaza; the favorite of those in-the-know. **M–E**

Hilton of Santa Fe (dwntwn), 100 Sandoval St., NM 87501 (505/988-2811; toll free, see Hilton). 150 rms, A/C, color TV, in-rm movies. AE, CB, DC, MC, V. Free parking, pool, rest. (Chamisa), coffee shop, bar, rm svce, nightclub, free crib. *Note:* Relatively modern motel whose adobe design fits reasonably well into the colonial setting around it; 2-min. walk from the Plaza. Comfortable, well-equipped rms; efficient svce; so-so rest. Group and convention clientele. **M–E,** but lower rates off-season.

Garrett's Friendship Desert Inn (dwntwn), 311 Old Santa Fe Trail, NM 87501 (505/982-1851; toll free, see Friendship Inns). 82 rms, A/C, cable color TV. AE, MC, V. Free parking, pool, rest. (La Ristra Restaurante y Cantina), bar, valet svce, free crib. *Note:* Classic motel a few blocks from dwntwn. Very convincing colonial decor; vast, comfortable rms; attentive svce. A fine place to stay. **M,** but lower rates off-season.

Budget Inn (nr. dwntwn), 725 Cerrillos Rd., NM 87501 (505/982-5952; toll free 800/288-7600). 160 rms; no A/C; cable color TV. MC, V. Free parking, pool, rest., crib $10. *Note:* Functional but definitely comfortable motel 5 min. from the Plaza. Spacious rms; efficient reception and svce. Good value on balance. Group and package-tour clientele. **I–M**

Motel 6 (nr. dwntwn), 3007 Cerrillos Rd., NM 87501 (505/473-1380). 104 rms, A/C, color TV, free in-rm movies. AE, DC, MC, V. Free parking, pool. *Note:* Unbeatable value 8 min. from dwntwn in a rather depressing neighborhood. Inviting, functional rms; adjacent 24-hr. coffee shop. Perfect if you're driving. **B–I**

Accommodations in the Vicinity

Rancho Encantado (vic.), N.M. 4 (P.O. Box 57C), Tesuque, NM 87501 (505/982-3537), 8 mi. (13.5km) north on U.S. 285. 58 rms (7 in the hotel, 51 in cottages or mini-apts.), A/C, color TV (in apts.). AE, CB, DC, MC, V. Free parking, two pools, tennis court, horseback riding, bar, rm svce, crib $15. *Note:* Luxurious resort complex nestled in the mountains north of Santa Fe, on the edge of the Tesuque Reservation. Comfortable cottages and apartments in a beautiful grdn. Private patios. Valuable Native American furnishings and artifacts. Upscale clientele. Renowned rest. (Rancho Encantado Dining Rm). Library. Very good svce. Resv. should be made a number of weeks ahead, given the limited number of rms. One of the most famous hotels in the country; its guestbook has been signed by John Wayne, Maria Callas, Henry Fonda, and Gregory Peck. 15 min. from dwntwn. Open year round. **VE,** but lower rates off-season.

YMCA/Youth Hostels

Santa Fe International Hostel (nr. dwntwn), 1412 Cerrillos Rd., NM 87501 (505/988-1153). Dormitories; rms for couples and families. Open year round.

RESTAURANTS

A Note on Restaurant Prices: Santa Fe restaurant prices, per person, excluding drinks and service charges, are coded as follows: **VE,** Very Expensive ($60 and up); **E,** Expensive ($40–$60); **M,** Moderate ($25–$40); **I,** Inexpensive ($15–$25); **B,** Budget (up to $15).

Personal Favorites (in order of preference)

🍸🍸🍸 **Coyote Café** (dwntwn), 132 W. Water St. (983-1615). A/C. Lunch/dinner daily; closed Dec. 25. MC, V. *Specialties:* enchiladas w. green-chile sauce, grilled double pork chop w. chili-peanut sauce, cream of cilantro soup w. mussels and calamari, fried green chiles empanadas, pan-seared Pacific salmon w. avocado crema, marinated chicken on red chard and black-bean salsa. Menu changes regularly. *Note:* Mark Miller, former chef at Berkeley's famous Fourth Street Grill, is an anthropologist by training and draws inspiration from his travels through Mexico and the southwestern U.S. The result is a contemporary "ethnic" cuisine, rich in color and taste, which has been attracting an ever-growing number of devotees since the rest. opened in 1986. The rest., in what was once the Greyhound bus terminal, has high ceilings, bare walls enlivened by modern paintings, papier-mâché sculptures, and rustic tapestries which just accentuate the austerity of the decor. Friendly, smiling svce; successful enough that resv. are strongly advised. You'll have a memorable meal here. *American.* **I–M**

🍸🍸 **Santacafe** (dwntwn), 231 Washington Ave. (984-1788). A/C. Lunch Mon–Fri, dinner nightly. MC, V. *Specialties:* smoked-pheasant spring rolls w. four-chile sauce, manicotti of carne adobada, cassoulet, red-chile ravioli w. duck, grilled filet mignon w. roasted garlic and serrano-chile butter, stuffed chile, bread pudding w. honeyed whipped cream, espresso cheesecake. Menu changed regularly. *Note:* Coyote Café's only challenger for the Santa Fe rest. title. Airy, imaginative dishes from the hand of accomplished chef Michael Fennelly. The adobe Padre Gallegos House, where the rest. is housed, is a two-century-old designated historic monument. Outdoor courtyard dining in good weather. Flawless svce; resv. a must; a first-rate place. *American/Mexican.* **I–M**

🍸🍸 **Pink Adobe** (dwntwn), 406 Old Santa Fe Trail (983-7712). A/C. Lunch Mon–Fri, dinner nightly; closed Jan 1, Labor Day, Thanksgiving, Dec 25. AE, CB, DC, MC, V. *Specialties:* shrimp Créole, tournedos w. bordelaise sauce, steak Dunigan (w. green chile), pork Napoleon w. madeira sauce, Mexican dishes. Fine wine list. *Note:* One of the prettiest and most popular rests. in Santa Fe, in a three-century-old building. Charming setting in a number of small rms, w. a profusion of greenery and an open patio in summer. The food is very good on the whole, but New Mexican dishes are only average. Diligent svce. Often crowded and noisy; resv. a must. A Santa Fe classic. *Continental/Mexican.* **I–M**

🍸🍸 **La Tertulia** (dwntwn), 416 Agua Fria St. (988-2769). A/C. Lunch/dinner Tues–Sun; closed hols. and first week of Dec. AE, MC, V. Jkt. *Specialties:* steak verde, carne adobada, chile relleño, chalupas, Mexican dishes. *Note:* This elegant rest. in a converted 19th-century convent serves excellent Mexican-inspired food. Nice colonial Spanish art collection. Pleasant open courtyard. Exemplary svce; locally popular; resv. advised. *American/Mexican.* **I**

☼♀ **Maria's New Mexican Kitchen** (nr. dwntwn), 565 W. Cordova Rd. (983-7929). A/C. Lunch/dinner daily. MC, V. *Spe-
cialties:* fajitas, enchiladas, tamales, alas picosas de pollo (spicy chicken wings),
natillas. Excellent margaritas and a wide choice of beers. *Note:* Engaging, typically Mexican cantina, which the experts credit w. the best fajitas in Santa Fe. Its
blue-corn enchiladas and its chili salsa are also worth the trip. Old adobe setting
w. open fireplaces. Relaxed atmosphere and svce; a local favorite for more than 40
years. *Mexican.* **B**

Other Restaurants (from top bracket to budget)

♀♀♀ **Compound** (nr. dwntwn), 653 Canyon Rd. (982-4353).
A/C. Lunch/dinner Tues–Sun; closed hols. and Jan. AE.
J&T. *Specialties:* tomato bisque, tournedos w. green peppercorns and bordelaise
sauce, fresh foie gras w. braised endive, chocolate-walnut torte w. raspberry
sauce. *Note:* A happy marriage of Spanish Colonial setting and modern atmosphere 5 min. from the Plaza. Elegantly intimate decor; polished French-inspired
cuisine. Pretty, open patio; a little stuffy svce in white gloves. Resv. advised. The
chicest place in Santa Fe, and the only one to require a necktie. *Continental.* **M**

♀ **The Steaksmith at El Gancho** (nr. dwntwn), Old Las Vegas
Hwy. (988-3333). A/C. Dinner only, Wed–Mon; closed
hols. AE, MC, V. *Specialties:* steak, roast beef, broiled catch of the day, good
homemade desserts. *Note:* Generally crowded, this congenial, rustic steakhouse
serves excellent beef cuts and remarkably fresh fish at very sensible prices. Relaxed atmosphere; locally popular. A fine place, 8 min. from dwntwn. *Steak/
Seafood.* **I**

♀♀ **Francisco's** (dwntwn), in the St. Francis Hotel (see "Accommodations," above) (683-5700). A/C. Breakfast/lunch/
dinner daily, brunch Sun. MC, V. *Specialties:* fettuccine w. breast of chicken and
red chile, fresh salmon sautéed w. homemade pasta, northern Italian dishes, excellent homemade desserts. Fine wine list. *Note:* Elegant hotel rest., a little anach-
ronistic but still romantic. Open-air dining in fine weather. Italian and regional
strains blend successfully in the food. Svce a little pompous. Resv. advisable for
dinner. *Italian/American.* **B–I**

☼♀♀ **La Casa Sena** (dwntwn), 20 Sena Plaza, 125 E. Palace Ave.
(988-9232). A/C. Breakfast/lunch/dinner daily (until mid-
night); closed Dec 25. AE, CB, DC, MC, V. *Specialties:* black-bean soup, Black
Angus steak w. green-chile sauce, trout baked in clay. *Note:* Excellent southwestern food in a charming adobe *mesón* dating from the 1860s in Old Santa Fe. It's
near enough to the Plaza to attract a big tourist business, while the singing waiters at the bar provide unusual local color. A nice place. *Continental/Mexican.* **B–I**

♀ **Shohko Café** (dwntwn), 321 Johnson St. at Guadalupe St.
(983-7288). A/C. Lunch Mon–Fri, dinner nightly; closed
hols. AE, MC, V. *Specialties:* Imperial rolls, tempura, sushi, teriyaki, sukiyaki.
Note: This little Chinese-Japanese rest. behind the Hilton Hotel serves the best
Far Eastern food in town. Simple and unpretentious. Resv. advised. *Chinese/
Japanese.* **B–I**

☼♀♀ **Staab House** (dwntwn), in La Posada (see "Accommodations," above) (983-6351). A/C. Breakfast/lunch/dinner
daily. AE, CB, DC, MC, V. Jkt. *Specialties:* fajitas del norte, excellent broiled fish
and meat. Good wine list. *Note:* Staab House, occupying a historic home dating
from 1882, is one of the prettiest rests. in Santa Fe. Fine Victorian decor w. many
Native American and Spanish handcrafts. Classic hotel food impeccably prepared
and served; open-air eating on fine days. Excellent value. *Continental/American.*
B–I

☼♀ **The Shed** (dwntwn), 113½ E. Palace Ave. (982-9030). A/C.
Lunch only, Mon–Sat; closed hols. No credit cards. *Specialties:*
enchiladas, burritos, hamburgers, posolé, tacos, good homemade desserts (mo-
cha cake). *Note:* Delightful little rest. in the shadow of the cathedral, open for

lunch only. Excellent Mexican-inspired food in a very picturesque colonial setting w. colorful murals (the building dates from 1692). Pleasant open courtyard. Locally popular. Wine and beer. Unfortunately, no resv. *American/Mexican.* **B**

Cafeterias/Fast Food

Furr's (nr. dwntwn), Coronado Center, 522 W. Cordova Rd. (982-3816). Lunch/dinner daily (until 8pm). No credit cards. Praiseworthy cafeteria food at very low prices: chicken-fried steak, baked fish, etc.

   Swiss Bakery (dwntwn), 320 Guadalupe St. (988-3737). Open daily 7am– 6pm. As you would expect from the name, the house specialties are croissants and pastry—but the pizzas, quiches, sandwiches, and soups of the day are fine too. Agreeable open-air patio.

BARS & NIGHTCLUBS

   Bull Ring Lounge (dwntwn), 414 Old Santa Fe Trail (983-3328). Congenial bar, disco. Also honorable rest. Open nightly.

   Club West (nr. dwntwn), 213 W. Alameda St. (982-0099). Live rock; *the* fashionable club.

NEARBY EXCURSIONS

   BANDELIER NATIONAL MONUMENT (45 mi./72km NW via U.S. 84 and N.M. 4) (672-3861): Ruins of Native American cave dwellings and cliff houses dating from the 13th century, in a lovely wild setting on Frijoles Canyon ("Canyon of Beans"). The monument is named after Swiss ethnologist and writer Adolph Bandelier, who explored the area thoroughly in the 1880s. Along 70 mi. (113km) of footpaths you, too, can explore the caves and ruins of the different pueblos in the park. Among them are **Tyuonyi,** a three-story circular ruin which once had 400 rooms and three *kivas* (places of worship); **Long House,** which had more 300 rooms; and the **Ceremonial Cave** *kiva,* in a cave 150 ft. (46m) above the valley floor which can be reached only by ladders. Visitor center with archeological museum. Open daily; quite a tiring visit. Combine it if possible with a trip to Los Alamos (see below).

   CORONADO STATE PARK & MONUMENT (45 mi./ 72km south via I-25 and N.M. 44N) (867-5351): Ruins of a Kuava pueblo going back to A.D. 1300. The Spanish conquistador Francisco Vásquez de Coronado camped here in 1540 during his fruitless search for the mythical Eldorado known to historians as "the seven gold cities of Cibola." Interesting Native American museum. Visit to a restored *kiva.* Open daily.

   LOS ALAMOS (40 mi./65km NW on U.S. 84 and N.M. 4): Once the secret city of atomic research ("Atomic City"), this is where Robert Oppenheimer and his team devised the first A-bomb in 1942–43 as part of the so-called Manhattan Project. The **Bradbury Science Museum** on Diamond Dr. (667-4444), open daily, is an interesting museum of nuclear science and nuclear energy, with full-size models of "Little Boy" and "Fat Man," respectively the Hiroshima and Nagasaki bombs.

   On the way, visit **San Ildefonso** (see "The Pueblos," below) and **Puye Cliff Ruins** on N.M. 5 (753-7326), with a number of prehistoric dwellings and the ruins of a very large pueblo seven to eight centuries old. Guided tours daily.

   OLD CIENEGA VILLAGE MUSEUM (15 mi./24km SW on U.S. 85): Authentic museum-village tucked into the mountainside, depicting the life of the Spanish settlers between 1660 and the 19th century. Interesting; visits Mon–Fri Apr–Oct by appointment. Folklore festivals some weekends. For schedules, call 471-2261.

☼🏛 **PECOS NATIONAL MONUMENT** (25 mi./40km SE on I-25) (757-6032): Remains of a 14th-century pueblo which once had some 2,500 inhabitants; two magnificent *kivas* have been completely restored. The principal dwelling house was five stories high. Nearby are ruins of the first Spanish mission built in New Mexico (1542), destroyed during the Indian Rebellion of 1680. Church rebuilt in 1701 and finally abandoned at the end of the 18th century. Open daily.

☼🏛🏛 **TAOS** (70 mi./112km NE via U.S. 285 and N.M. 68): Picturesque little Spanish-Mexican-American community nestled in the foothills of the Sierra Sangre de Cristo ("Christ's Blood Mountains"), so called by the Spaniards because at twilight in winter the snow appears to take on a purplish cast. An artists' colony for more than a century, Taos now deploys dozens of art galleries and an unfortunate abundance of souvenir shops, but its museums and its pretty **Plaza** are enough to justify the trip. Among the more interesting museums: the **Ernest L. Blumenschein Home,** with its many works by local painters, at 13 Ledoux St., open daily; and the **Bent House Museum,** 18 Bent St., open daily Mar–Dec, residence of the first American governor of New Mexico, Charles Bent, who was killed and scalped there by native tribes in 1847. You should also see the house, and tomb, of the famous frontiersman Kit Carson, nicknamed "The Crack Shot of the West," who lived here for 24 years, at the **Kit Carson Home,** E. Kit Carson Rd. (758-4741), open daily; the beautiful Spanish mission of **San Francisco de Asis,** rebuilt in 1772, at Rancho de Taos, 4 mi. (6.5km) south on N.M. 68 (758-2754), open daily; the **D. H. Lawrence Ranch,** 18 mi. (29km) north on N.M. 3 (776-2245), open daily, where the British novelist who wrote *Lady Chatterley's Lover* is buried; and the great 🏛🏛 **Rio Grande Bridge** looking down on the river from its height of 650 ft. (198m), 10 mi. (16km) NW on U.S. 64.

You'll find it a good idea to combine this with a trip to **Taos Pueblo** (see "The Pueblos," below).

On your way back to Santa Fe, take the "High Road to Taos" along N.M. 3 and N.M. 76, dotted with delightful little Spanish Colonial villages like **Chimayo** (beautiful old church with a legend of healing powers, weavers' workshops), **Truchas** (where the movie *The Milagro Beanfield War* was shot), and **Cordova.** A trip full of worthwhile sights.

Where to Eat En Route

IN TAOS ☼🍷 **Apple Tree at Taos,** 123 Bent St. (758-1900). Breakfast/lunch/dinner daily. Attractive adobe house w. shady patio; the food is typically southwestern. *Mexican/American.* **B–I**

🍷 **Ogelvie's,** The Plaza (758-8866). Lunch/dinner daily. *Mexican/American.* **B–I**

IN CHIMAYO The 🍷🍷 **Rancho de Chimayo,** on N.M. 520 (984-2100). Lunch/dinner daily in summer, Tues–Sun the rest of the year; closed Jan. One of the best regional rests. in the state. Don't miss it. *Mexican.* **B–I**

IN TRUCHAS 🍷 **Truchas Mountain Café,** N.M. 76 (689-2444). Breakfast/lunch/dinner daily. Family-run café offering good Mexican-style dishes. Every meal comes w. homemade tortillas or remarkable sopaipillas. *Mexican/American.* **B–I**

GHOST TOWNS: 🏛 **Cerrillos,** 28 mi. (44km) SW via I-25 and N.M. 14: This old prospectors' town had 2,500 inhabitants, eight hotels, and 20 saloons in the 1880s; today its population is barely 200, but it still has many vestiges of its golden age. Sometimes used as a film set. Must be seen.

🏛 **Madrid,** 30 mi. (48km) SW via I-25 and N.M. 14: Once an important coal-mining center, now down to 200 inhabitants.

Interesting mining museum and dozens of abandoned houses. Open-air jazz and bluegrass concerts in summer. For information, call 473-0743. An absolute must-see.

THE PUEBLOS

There are more than a dozen still-inhabited Native American pueblos (the Spanish word for villages) within a 125-mi. (200km) radius of Santa Fe, almost all going back beyond the arrival of the colonizing Spaniards 3½ centuries ago. Heirs of the famous Anasazi people of the Middle Ages, the Pueblo peoples fall into four major families: the Hopi (see Chapter 40 on Navajoland), the Zuñi and the Acoma in west-central New Mexico, and the Rio Grande tribes, who live around the valley of the same name. Their numbers, perhaps 20,000 when the Spaniards came, declined to 5,000–6,000 in the 19th century, but have now reached almost 40,000.

The pueblos of the Rio Grande peoples may be visited between sunrise and sunset on payment of a fee of $3–$4 per vehicle; try to make your visit coincide with the annual festival or a religious ceremony (Jan 1, 22, 23; Feb 2; Easter; May 3; June 13, 24; Aug 10; Sept 29, 30; Nov 12; Dec 12, 25, 31). *Warning:* You must not photograph the village or its people unless authorized to do so (usually for a fee) by the chief of the pueblo. Discreet and respectful behavior is appropriate at all times.

The **Santa Fe Convention and Visitors Bureau,** 200 W. Marcy St. (984-6760), will give you the dates of festivities; information may also be obtained from the **Eight Northern Pueblos Council,** P.O. Box 969, San Juan Pueblo, NM 87566 (852-4265). The most picturesque pueblos are:

Acoma Pueblo, 127 mi. (204km) SW via I-25S, I-40W, and N.M. 23 (252-1139): The oldest community in the U.S., believed to have been first settled around A.D. 600. Perched 6,560 ft. (2,000m) up on a rocky mesa, "Sky City," as the historians have dubbed it, is by far the country's most beautiful pueblo, and the least tainted by Western "civilization." Spanish Mission of San Estebán Rey (1629). A visit you shouldn't miss. Photography permitted for a $3 fee.

Cochití Pueblo, 30 mi. (48km) SW via U.S. 85S and U.S. 22N (465-2244): Antedates the Spaniards; a center for the crafting of silver-and-precious-stone jewelry, ceramics, and drums, on the banks of the Rio Grande. No photographs.

Jémez Pueblo, 75 mi. (120km) south via I-25S, N.M. 44N, and N.M. 4N (834-7359): Famous for its embroidery, weaving, and wickerwork. No photographs. Not far away, at **Jemez Springs,** is a pretty Spanish Franciscan mission dating from 1621, near a prehistoric village.

San Ildefonso Pueblo, 28 mi. (44km) NW via U.S. 84 and N.M. 4 (455-2273): Lovely plaza with open-air market; best known for its Native American pottery and ceramics. One of the best-known Rio Grande pueblos. Photography permitted ($3).

San Juan Pueblo, 28 mi. (44km) north on U.S. 285 (852-4400): Chosen by the Spaniards as the site of their first capital in 1598. The great rebellion of 1680 originated in San Juan; it culminated with the taking of Santa Fe and the massacre of all the Spanish garrisons. It took the forces of Don Diego de Vargas 12 years to put the rebellion down. There's a restaurant with typical Native American food. Photography permitted ($3).

Santa Clara Pueblo, 27 mi. (43km) NW on U.S. 84 (753-7326): A typical example of pueblo architecture; fine pottery. Photography permitted ($3).

Santo Domingo Pueblo, 32 mi. (51km) SW via U.S. 85 and N.M. 22 (465-2214): The most authentic and traditional of the pueblos; turquoise jewelry and blankets. No photographs.

Taos Pueblo, 72 mi. (115km) NE via U.S. 285 and N.M. 68 (758-9593): The cultural capital of the Pueblo Nation, with the 13,000-ft. (3,970m) peaks of the Sangre de Cristo as a distant backdrop. It retains the traditional 13th-century ground-plan of terraces in dark-yellow or brown adobe, with construction on four or five levels linked by rudimentary flights of steps. Ruins of Mission San Gerónimo (1598) are adjacent to the central plaza. A firmly tourist atmosphere but a splendid setting. Photography permitted ($5).

☀️⚓ **Tesuque Pueblo,** 8 mi. (13km) NW on U.S. 285 (983-2667): The site has been continuously inhabited since about A.D. 1250. A mission, now ruined, was built here at the beginning of the 18th century. Crafts (pottery, jewelry, embroidery) and remarkable dancing at different times of year. Photography permitted ($3).

☀️⚓ **Zía Pueblo,** 65 mi. (104km) SW via I-25S and N.M. 44N (867-3304): Also famous for its pottery. Fine natural site. Spanish Mission of Nuestra Señora de la Asunción (1692). No photographs.

For more details on this and other New Mexico pueblos, see Chapter 38 on Albuquerque.

FARTHER AFIELD

☀️⚓⚓ **CUMBRES & TOLTEC SCENIC RAILROAD** (220 mi./ 352km r.t. on U.S. 84N and 84S): One of the highest and most spectacular railroads in the country, crossing the Cumbre Pass at an altitude of 9,860 ft. (3,006m). The little Far Western train makes a 64-mi. (102km) trip to link **Chama,** N.M., and **Antonito,** Colo., through splendid mountain and forest scenery and along wild gorges. Time: 7 hr. r.t.; operates daily mid-June to mid-Oct. Round-trip fare: $42 for adults, $20 for children. Resv. a must, obtainable from P.O. Box 789, Chama, NM 87520 (756-2151). A must for steam-train buffs; can be combined with a visit to Taos (see "Nearby Excursions," above).

☀️⚓⚓⚓ **MESA VERDE NATIONAL PARK** (580 mi./930km r.t. via U.S. 84N, N.M. 96E, N.M. 44W, U.S. 550N, U.S. 160W, and the reverse route to return): America's greatest monument from its Native American civilizations (8th through 13th centuries). Dozens of multilevel houses, towers, terraces, streets miraculously clinging to the cliff face, in a glorious setting of desert canyons. Every year 600,000 visitors confront the astonishing sight of these ghost villages, silent now for centuries. The sudden disappearance of their inhabitants, the Anasazi peoples, six centuries ago is still a riddle to historians: Was it an epidemic? a persistent drought? an invasion by wandering tribes? a slow leaching-out of the soil? A visit to these cliffs and their ruins, of which the most impressive are **Cliff Palace** (217 rooms and *kivas*) and **Spruce Tree House** (114 rooms, 8 *kivas*), is permitted only when accompanied by a ranger; it calls for stout shoes and good physical condition. Remarkable **Native American museum** near the visitor center, open daily. Unique view of the states of Colorado, Utah, Arizona, and New Mexico from **Park Point Fire Lookout** at 8,572 ft. (2,613m), halfway between the park entrance and the visitor center. Park open to vehicles daily year round.

For **information,** contact the Superintendent, P.O. Box 8, Mesa Verde National Park, CO 81330 (303/529-4465).

Along the way, visit the ☀️⚓⚓**Chaco Culture National Historical Park,** with ruins of 16 Anasazi pueblos abandoned around the end of the 13th century, another Amerindian gem. Some of these pueblos, like Pueblo Bonito, have no fewer than 800 rooms and 37 *kivas*. Unsurfaced access road, passable only in dry weather. Visitor center 2 mi. (3.2km) from the southern entrance on N.M. 57 (988-6716), open daily.

It's also well worth making the side trip to ⚓ **Aztec Ruins National Monument,** at Aztec (334-6174), one of the best-preserved primitive pueblos in the Southwest. Large 13th-century *kiva*, splendidly restored. Open daily.

And don't miss taking a ride on the ⚓⚓ **Silverton,** a little Far Western train dating from 1882 which takes 7 hr. to cover the 50 mi. (80km) from **Durango** to **Silverton,** and the return leg, through glorious mountain scenery; one of the most popular tourist attractions in the West. Operates daily mid-May to mid-Oct. For resv. (a must), contact the railroad at 479 Main Ave., Durango, CO 81301 (303/247-2733). Round-trip fare: $32 for adults, $16 for children.

This 580-mi. (930km) round-trip from Santa Fe and back again is enough in itself to warrant visiting the city.

Where to Stay En Route

IN THE PARK 🍴 **Far View,** P.O. Box 277, Mancos, CO 81328 (303/529-4421). 150 rms w. mountain views. A comfortable motel inside the park. Open from the end of Apr to the end of Oct. **I–M**

IN CORTEZ The 🍴 **Anasazi,** 666 S. Broadway, Cortez, CO 81321 (303/565-3773). 87 rms. Open year round. **I–M**

🍴 **Best Western Sands,** 1000 E. Main St., Cortez, CO 81321 (303/565-3761). 81 rms. Open year round. **I**

IN DURANGO The ☀ 🍴 **Strater Hotel,** 699 Main Ave., Durango, CO 81301 (303/247-4431). 94 rms. **I–M**

☀🛎 **General Palmer House,** 567 Main Ave., Durango, CO 81301 (303/247-4747). 39 rms. **I–M**

☀🛎 **NAVAJOLAND** (about 560 mi./900km r.t. via I-25S, I-40W, N.M. 264W, Ariz. 264W, and the reverse on the return trip): Spectacular scenery **(Monument Valley, Canyon de Chelly),** and the largest reservation in the U.S. See Chapter 40 on Navajoland.

On the way, visit the picturesque **Zuñi and Acoma Pueblos** (see Chapter 38 on Albuquerque). A spectacular itinerary; don't miss it.

NAVAJOLAND♛

□ □ □

With Monument Valley and Canyon de Chelly

Covering an area larger than Massachusetts, New Hampshire, and Vermont combined, the territory of Navajoland offers its visitors some of the most fantastic natural wonders of the North American continent: A spectacularly scenic expanse of red, pink, orange, and khaki-brown desert, pueblos perched on arid plateaus (the mesas), and the immense **Lake Powell.** Ironically nicknamed "The 51st State," Navajoland, or Navajo Country, is indeed the largest Native American reserve in the U.S. The land takes up much of northeastern Arizona and spills over into Utah and New Mexico. The Navajo, whose numbers at the end of the Indian Wars in 1864 had been reduced to a mere 8,000 by the depredations of Kit Carson and his soldiery, now administer the territory themselves from their capital at **Window Rock,** 112 mi. (180km) west of Albuquerque.

Nearly half the tribespeople on the reservation live below the official poverty line, and about a third are out of work. The enormous mineral wealth underlying Navajo territory, estimated at 2.5 million tons of coal, 80 million tons of uranium ore, 100 million barrels of oil, and 26 billion cubic yards of natural gas, have been leased to corporations by the auction method, and now bring in only $50 million a year in royalties to the Navajo.

The Navajo are generally tolerant of the tourists who visit them, but they impose some rules which must be respected. Native Americans and their homes may not be photographed without advance permission. Some sacred areas or monuments—for example, the Navajo Fortress in the Canyon de Chelly—are forbidden except to Native Americans. Additional information may be obtained on the spot.

The best known of the wonders of Navajoland is **Monument Valley,** not far from the Utah border; the setting of countless Hollywood Westerns (such as *Stagecoach*), its twisted canyons and pillars of red rock 980 ft. (300m) high (called the "cathedrals of the desert") have been seen by millions of Americans in TV commercials featuring a car perched atop an impossibly steep spire of rock. A tour of Monument Valley by car takes 2–3 hr. in dry weather and is an unforgettable experience. In winter you'll need a Jeep (see "Guided Tours," below).

The **Canyon de Chelly** (pronounced "de Shay"), 93 mi. (150km) to the south, is another fascinating place that can be reached by car, but explored only in an all-terrain vehicle (see "Guided Tours," below); its Native American settlements, dating from the 4th century, are worth the visit by themselves.

The **Navajo National Monument,** not far from Monument Valley, can be reached only on horseback or on foot; it has well-preserved ruins of 13th-century Native American pueblos. Nearer the center of Navajoland are the mesas inhab-

KEY TO NUMBERED SIGHTS:

1. Canyon de Chelly National Monument
2. Glen Canyon National Rec. Area
3. Grand Canyon National Park
4. Hopi Mesas/Reservation
5. Hubbell Trading Post
6. John Wesley Powell Memorial Museum
7. Mesa Verde National Park
8. Monument Valley
9. Navajo National Monument
10. Navajo Reservation
11. Navajo Tribal Museum
12. Petrified Forest National Park
13. Wupatki National Monument

ited by the Hopi, traditional enemies of the Navajo, which frown down on the Arizona desert from a height of many hundred feet. The Hopi are skilled craftspeople, producing silver jewelry, pottery, Kachina dolls, and beautiful basketwork.

As in all the country's tribal reservations, the sale of beer or liquor is forbidden in Navajoland.

A BRIEF HISTORY OF THE NATIVE AMERICANS OF NAVAJO- LAND: When Christopher Columbus first set foot on American soil, he thought he had arrived at the Indies; under this misapprehension, he dubbed the natives "Indians." The peoples thus misnamed had always comprised two mutually hostile groups: the settler tribes and the nomadic tribes. The **Navajo** (Navajo, or Navaho, comes from a Native American word meaning "people of the soil") are settlers; a warrior people, they came down from the northwest of Canada around the end of the 15th century and overran the lands hitherto occupied by the Hopi and Pueblo in northern Arizona. Under the influence of the Spanish colonists, this nomadic hunting tribe—whose physical appearance is captured in a Navajo poem: "My skin as brown as the face of Mother Earth, my hair as black as the sky of night"—became, over the years, a people of shepherds and grazers, and learned from the Pueblo peoples their techniques of cultivation, weaving, and sandpainting. The Navajo, who in 1864 had been almost exterminated by the famous scout Kit Carson and his white volunteers, are now America's largest Native American tribe. The census figures show 1,450,000 Native Americans belonging to 570 different tribes across the country; 200,000 of these are Navajo.

The Navajo speak an extraordinarily complex language belonging to the Athapaskan linguistic family, which also includes the Apaches of New Mexico and southern Arizona. A strongly spiritual people with a rich religious heritage and mystical bonds to their land and animals, the Navajo live in modest villages of traditional "hogans"—windowless wooden homes and huts of earth and clay supported by logs, with a door that must always face east. More open to outsiders than the Pueblo or the Hopi, the Navajo generally allow strangers to be present at the sacred rites and colorful religious ceremonies.

The **Hopi** (which means "peaceable people" in the native tongue) and their **Pueblo** neighbors belong to the great Shoshone family, which includes the Comanche, Ute, and Paiute tribes as well as others, all distant cousins of the Aztecs of Mexico. The Hopi are direct descendants of the Anasazi ("the Old Ones"), a race of remarkable builders, as witnessed in the ruins of Mesa Verde and Chaco Canyon. Driven from their villages, probably during the 15th century, by drought and famine, the Hopi, who today number around 6,000, were thrown back onto the mesas by the conquering thrust of the Navajo. Like their blood-brothers the Pueblo of New Mexico, the Hopi are a sedentary tribe, given to farming and stock breeding. For more than 1,000 years they have cultivated strains of corn that can survive in arid country, and a number of indigenous plants and vegetables, such as beans, pumpkin, tobacco, squash, potatoes, and tomatoes. In their isolated villages of stone-and-mortar houses, which cling like eagles' aeries to the high plateaus of the mesas, the Hopi practice the talent inherited from their Anasazi ancestors for the working of silver and for basket weaving (the Anasazi are known to archeologists as the "Basket Maker Pueblo"). They have also kept alive a religious tradition of ritual dances to invoke rain and avert bad luck: fire dances, eagle dances, serpent dances, and the like.

Their elaborate mythology is visibly manifested in the Kachina masks, which embody the spirits of ancestors, animals, or plants. Kachina dolls, much prized by visitors for their startling forms and colors, are a sort of miniature pantheon of the Hopi deities. Unlike the Navajo, the Hopi are intensely suspicious of strangers, and try to keep outsiders away from their religious ceremonies. Even to visit a Hopi village you must have advance authorization, which may be obtained from the Hopi Cultural Center at Second Mesa. For the schedule of Navajo and Hopi festivals, see "Special Events," below.

Those interested in the way of life, arts, and history of Native Americans should contact the **Bureau of Indian Affairs,** Office of Public Information, 18th St. and C St. NW, Washington, DC 20240 (202/343-1000).

BASIC FACTS: States of Arizona, New Mexico, and Utah. Area code: 602. Time zone: mountain. Approximate area: 25,100 sq. mi. (65,000km²). Reserve founded in: 1868. Nonmigrant tribal population: 200,000 Navajo and 6,000 Hopi.

CLIMATE: As in all semi-desert regions, summer (the season that draws most tourists) can be burning hot (95° –104° F / 35° –40° C) by day, but is much cooler at night. In spring and fall you'll need a sweater even in the daytime. Aug and Sept are the rainy season. In winter, the first snow falls on the mesas in Nov, and the mercury sometimes drops to 13° F (−10° C).

ARRIVAL & TRANSIT INFORMATION

NEAREST AIRPORTS: The **Albuquerque International Airport** (ABQ), 112 mi. (180km) east of Window Rock.
Flagstaff Pulliam Field (FLG), 180 mi. (290km) SW of Monument Valley.
Phoenix Sky Harbor International (PHX), 210 mi. (340km) SW of the mesas.

AIRLINES AT ALBUQUERQUE (area code 505): American (242-9464), America West (247-0737), Delta (243-2794), Southwest (831-1221), TWA (842-4010), and United (242-1411).

BUS OR CAR RENTAL? Given the distances to be covered, the sensible thing is to rent a car with unlimited mileage. There is no intercity bus service to Navajoland.

CAR RENTAL AT ALBUQUERQUE (area code 505; at the Albuquerque International Airport unless otherwise noted): Avis (842-4080); Budget (247-3442); Dollar (842-4224); Hertz (842-4235); National (842-4222); Thrifty, 2033 Yale Blvd. (842-8733). See also Chapter 41 on the Grand Canyon and Chapter 42 on Phoenix.

NEAREST TRAIN STATIONS: Amtrak has stations at 201 E. U.S. 66, in **Gallup,** New Mexico (toll free 800/872-7245), and E. 2nd St., in **Winslow,** Arizona (toll free 800/872-7245).

NEAREST BUS STATIONS: Greyhound has terminals at 300 2nd St. SW, **Albuquerque,** New Mexico (505/243-4435); 399 S. Malpais Lane, **Flagstaff,** Arizona (602/774-4573); and 105 S. Dean St., **Gallup,** New Mexico (505/863-3761).

INFORMATION & TOURS

TOURIST INFORMATION: Canyon de Chelly National Monument: Superintendent, P.O. Box 588, Chinle, AZ 86503 (602/674-5436). Visitor center.
Hopi Reservation: Cultural Center, P.O. Box 123, Kykotsmovi, AZ 86039 (602/734-2401); Tribal Office (602/734-2441, ext. 360).
Hubbell Trading Post: Ariz. 264 (P.O. Box 150), Ganado, AZ 86505 (602/755-3475). Visitor center.
NACA (Native Americans for Community Action): 2717 N. Steves Blvd., Suite 11, Flagstaff, AZ 86004 (602/526-2968). Information on cultural activities, art festivals, and powwows scheduled for the Hopi, Navajo, and Apache reservations in Arizona.

Navajo Indian Reservation: P.O. Box 308, Window Rock, AZ 86515 (602/871-6436). Visitor center.

There are other visitor centers at **Monument Valley** and **Navajo National Monument.**

GUIDED TOURS: You can visit the major sights of Navajoland on guided tours by car, bus, and airplane.

All-Terrain-Vehicle Excursions in Monument Valley
Goulding's Lodge Valley Tour, U.S. 163, Gouldings (801/727-3231). Full- and half-day trips. Daily Mar–Nov.
Monument Valley Tours, U.S. 163, Kayenta (602/697-3463). Full- and half-day trips. Daily year round.

All-Terrain-Vehicle Excursions in Canyon de Chelly
Thunderbird Lodge Tours, Chinle (602/674-5841). Full- and half-day trips. Daily May–Oct.

Bus Trips to the Hopi and Navajo Reservations
Nava-Hopi Tours (Gray Line), 401 Malpais Lane, Flagstaff (602/774-5003). Daily year round.

Flights Over Navajoland and Lake Powell
Lake Powell Air Service, Page Airport (602/645-2494).
Monument Valley Flying Service, Chinle (602/674-5657).

ADVENTURES: Ara Leisure Services (boat), Dept. 2916, N. 35th Ave., Suite 8, Phoenix, AZ 85017 (602/278-8888; toll free 800/528-6154). Cruises of 3 days and up on Lake Powell aboard fully equipped rented houseboats—a sort of floating motor home for 6–10 people, which will take you everywhere in the lake and into its dozens of splendid desert canyons. Rates begin at $1,200 a week in summer, $840 in spring or fall, and $690 in winter; 3- and 4-day rentals also available. You should reserve very far in advance. Don't miss this one.

MONUMENTS & SIGHTS IN NAVAJOLAND

CANYON DE CHELLY NATIONAL MONUMENT

(225 mi./360km NW of Albuquerque along I-40, U.S. 666, Ariz. 264, and U.S. 191): Spectacular landscapes which can be seen only from a Jeep (Apr–Oct). Native American cave dwellings from the 4th to the 14th century, including the **White House, Mummy Cave,** and **Antelope House.** In 1864 in this savagely beautiful canyon there took place one of the last engagements between the troops of Kit Carson and the native tribespeople who had taken refuge at the top of the **Navajo Fortress,** a huge rocky spur which is now sacred ground, forbidden to strangers. This is one of the few canyons in the country whose interior can be explored from an all-terrain vehicle. As well as the **Canyon de Chelly** itself, with its steep red sandstone walls, and **Spider Rock,** the 800-ft. (262m) needle of rock which is its most remarkable feature, the monument also includes the lateral canyons, **Canyon del Muerto** ("Dead Man's Canyon"), **Black Rock Canyon,** and **Monument Canyon.** At the visitor center, open year round, there is an interesting small archeological museum. Don't miss this trip.

For **information,** contact the Superintendent, Canyon de Chelly National Monument, P.O. Box 588, Chinle, AZ 86503 (602/674-5436). (See, also, the Thunderbird Lodge, in "Motels and Restaurants," below.)

GLEN CANYON & LAKE POWELL (122 mi./195km

west of Monument Valley along U.S. 163, U.S. 160, and Ariz. 98): **Lake Powell,** 196 mi. (315km) long with 1,900 mi. (3,058km) of shoreline, was created in 1963 by the construction of the **Page Dam** on the Colorado River; it has turned the **Glen Canyon National Recreation Area** into a tourist mecca for lovers of water sports, with its beautiful landscapes where the red-brown-ocher cliffs are mirrored in the clear blue lake, and its wonderful fishing for oversize trout, carp, and pike. Glen Canyon is no less rich in its variety of land animals: Rocky Mountain sheep, deer, coyote, puma, and even the occasional, extremely rare, golden eagle. At **Page** you can hire a comfortable houseboat to visit Lake Powell (see "Adventures," above).

For **information,** contact the Superintendent, Glen Canyon National Recreation Area, P.O. Box 1507, Page, AZ 86040 (602/645-2471).

HOPI MESAS (134 mi./214km NE of Flagstaff along U.S. 89, U.S. 160, and Ariz. 264): Primitive Native American villages, some as much as eight centuries old, clinging like eagles' nests to the rocky plateaus (mesas). Spectacular views. Authorization for visits must be obtained from the Hopi Cultural Center at Kykotsmovi (see "Tourist Information," above).

MONUMENT VALLEY (170 mi./272km NE of Flagstaff along U.S. 89, U.S. 160, and Ariz. 264): This is the country's best-known picture postcard, in glorious Technicolor: one of the most amazing landscapes in creation, more than 25 million years old. The "desert cathedrals," the red sandstone monoliths almost 2,000 ft. (more than 600m) high, with their evocative names—Camel Butte, Sentinel Mesa, Three Sisters, Big Chief, Elephant Butte—have provided the backdrop for countless westerns like *Stagecoach, Fort Apache, My Darling Clementine, The Searchers,* and *Billy the Kid,* as well as for Walt Disney's famous *The Living Desert.*

The recent history of Monument Valley is closely linked with that of Harry Goulding, an enterprising businessman who in 1923 opened a trading post and coaching inn on the site of the motel that now bears his name (see "Motels and Restaurants," below). It was Goulding who, in 1938, persuaded John Ford to shoot his first major western, *Stagecoach,* in this magnificent natural setting, thus making Monument Valley a symbol of the Wild West in dozens of movies still to come.

Private cars are admitted during the summer for the 14-mi. (23km) circuit, beginning at the visitor center; off-season, Jeeps only. For **information,** contact Park Headquarters, Monument Valley Navajo Tribal Park, P.O. Box 93, UT 84536 (801/727-3287).

NAVAJO NATIONAL MONUMENT (135 mi./216km NE of Flagstaff on U.S. 89 and U.S. 160): Very well-preserved 13th-century Native American cave dwellings, reachable on foot or horseback only. The most beautiful of the ruins, "Keet Seel," is 8 mi. (12km) from the visitor center. For **information,** contact Navajo National Monument, HC 71, Box 3, Tonalea, AZ 86044-9704 (602/672-2366).

MONUMENTS & SCENERY OUTSIDE THE NAVAJO RESERVE

GRAND CANYON OF THE COLORADO (181 mi./288km SW of Monument Valley via U.S. 163, U.S. 160, U.S. 89, and Ariz. 64): See Chapter 41 on the Grand Canyon.

MESA VERDE NATIONAL PARK (159 mi./254km NE of Monument Valley via U.S. 163 and U.S. 160): See Chapter 39 on Santa Fe.

METEOR CRATER (46 mi./74km east of Flagstaff on I-40): Some 22,000 years ago a two-million-ton meteorite crashed to earth here at a record speed of 33,000 m.p.h. (52,800 km/h), forming the world's largest nonvolcanic crater, 4,160 ft. (1.2km) across (3 mi./4.8km in circumference) and 544 ft. (170m) deep. It was used by NASA to train astronauts before their moon shots. Impressive. Open daily.

PETRIFIED FOREST NATIONAL PARK (102 mi./ 163km SW of Canyon de Chelly on U.S. 191 and I-40): This petrified forest, the largest in the world, is 200 million years old. Countless animals and plants have been fossilized by the lakebed sediments or by volcanic ash. It's best to enter from the south at **Rainbow Forest,** with its interesting museum illustrating the petrification of wood. Visitor center open daily. The **Painted Desert,** north of the visitor center, displays a blinding pattern of shimmering colors —blues, reds, and tawnies—particularly at sunrise and sunset. Scenic drive. *Warning:* It is strictly prohibited to take petrified woods or fossils as souvenirs.

For **information,** contact the Superintendent, Petrified Forest National Park, AZ 86028 (602/524-6228).

RAINBOW BRIDGE (reached by boat from Page, on Lake Powell): One of the largest natural spans in the world, 278 ft. (85m) across and 290 ft. (88m) high. It was a filming location for *2001: A Space Odyssey.*

SUNSET CRATER NATIONAL MONUMENT (17 mi./ 27km NE of Flagstaff on U.S. 89): Crater of a volcano that has been dormant for nine centuries; spectacular formations of reddish-orange lava. Open daily. For information, call 602/527-7042.

WUPATKI NATIONAL MONUMENT (35 mi./56km north of Flagstaff on U.S. 89): Ruins of a Native American village which was inhabited around A.D. 1100; the largest dwelling had some 100 bedrooms. Archeological museum. Open daily. For information, call 602/527-7040.

OTHER SIGHTS, ATTRACTIONS & ACTIVITIES

MUSEUMS: Hubbell Trading Post National Historic Site, 42 mi. (67km) south of Canyon de Chelly on Ariz. 264 at Ganado (602/755-3475): Picturesque trading post opened in 1876 by John Lorenzo Hubbell, an idealistic businessman who became a friend and protector to the Navajo. The present structure, with its unusual layout, dates from 1885; it houses an interesting ethnological collection, and is still a trading post for the local tribespeople. Open daily year round.

John Wesley Powell Memorial Museum, 6 N. Lake Powell Blvd. in Page, 130 mi. (208km) north of Flagstaff (602/645-9496): This little-known small museum pays tribute to the intrepid 19th-century geologist John Wesley Powell, the first to shoot the Grand Canyon rapids in a canoe. Fascinating. Also an astonishing collection of fluorescent minerals. Days and times of opening depend on the time of year.

Navajo Tribal Museum, 159 mi. (254km) NW of Albuquerque at the junction of Ariz. 264 and Indian Rte. 12, at Window Rock (602/871-6673): Remarkable Navajo jewelry, pottery, wickerwork, and weaving. Library, temporary exhibitions. Open daily in summer, Mon–Fri the rest of the year.

SPECIAL EVENTS: *Warning:* The Hopi people limit the number of visitors to what are regarded as sacred religious events. Cameras (still, movie, and video) and tape recorders are not permitted at any Hopi or Navajo festivals.

Hopi Festivals

For information and exact dates, call the **Hopi Cultural Center** (602/734-2401) or the **Hopi Tribal Office** (602/734-2441, ext. 360).

Niman or summer solstice festival (about June 21).

Hopi Home Dances (late July).

Snake or **Flute Dance** (Aug): Tourists allowed, but subject to restrictions.

Basket Dance (end of Oct to early Nov).

Soyal or winter solstice festival (about Dec 31).

Navajo Festivals

For information and exact dates, call the **Navajo Reservation** (602/871-6436).

All Indian Days (early July): Powwow and rodeo at Window Rock.

Squaw Dances (throughout the summer).

Navajo Nation Fair (early Sept): One of the most important Native American occasions in the country; dancing, horse racing, rodeo, art exhibition. At Window Rock.

Northern Navajo Fair (Oct): More than 2,000 Native Americans from various southwestern tribes attend this giant powwow at Shiprock.

Western Navajo Fair (mid-Oct): Parades, rodeos, handcrafts show, dance festival. At Tuba City.

Yei-bi-chi, or **Navajo Fire Dance** (throughout the winter).

Intertribal Festivals

Annual Gallup Indian Ceremonial (4 days in mid-Aug): Brings together representatives of a dozen tribes from all over the country for a festival of traditional dance like the Gaan Dance of the Apache, the Basket and Butterfly Dances of the Hopi, the Ribbon Dance of the Navajo, and so on. A great spectacle. For information: P.O. Box 1, Church Rock, NM 87311 (505/863-3896; toll free 800/233-4528).

MOTELS & RESTAURANTS

A Note on Accommodations and Restaurants: Room rates in Navajoland are coded as follows: **VE,** Very Expensive ($140 and up); **E,** Expensive ($90–$140); **M,** Moderate ($60–$90); **I,** Inexpensive ($30–$60); **B,** Budget (up to $30). A listing of toll free numbers is in the Appendix. Restaurant prices, per person, excluding drinks and service charges, are coded as follows: **VE,** Very Expensive ($60 and up); **E,** Expensive ($40–$60); **M,** Moderate ($25–$40); **I,** Inexpensive ($15–$25); **B,** Budget (up to $15).

Personal Favorites (in order of preference)

IN MONUMENT VALLEY 🏨 **Goulding's Monument Valley Lodge,** 2 mi. (3.2km) west of U.S. 163, Monument Valley, UT 84536 (801/727-3231). 62 rms, A/C, color TV, in-rm movies (John Wayne classics). AE, MC, V. Resv. required. Free parking, coffee shop. *Note:* Rustic motel at the foot of a towering cliff, this famous landmark was specially built for the filming of John Wayne's *She Wore a Yellow Ribbon.* Decently comfortable and w. an unforgettable view. Functional rms w. patios or balconies; Boy Scout summer-camp atmosphere. If the reception and svce were friendlier, it would be a good place to stay. The coffee shop is only just acceptable—but it's the only one within 19 mi. (30km). No alcoholic beverages. An ideal starting point for Jeep trips across Monument Valley ($36 for a full day). Don't miss stopping here. Hotel open year round; coffee shop closed Nov–Mar 15. **M,** but lower rates off-season.

🏨 **Holiday Inn,** Junction of U.S. 160 and U.S. 163, Kayenta, AZ 86033 (602/697-3221; toll free, see Holiday Inns). 100 rms, A/C, color TV. AE, CB, DC, MC, V. Free parking, pool, rest., rm svce, crib $6. *Note:* Typical motel, in the middle of the desert. Functionally comfortable. Open

year round. 30 min. by road from Monument Valley (conducted tours by Jeep).
I–M, but lower rates off-season.

    Wetherill Inn, U.S. 163, Kayenta, AZ 86033 (602/697-3231). 54 rms, cable color TV. AE, MC, V. Free parking, adj. coffee shop, free crib. *Note:* Rustic motel w. no air conditioning; limited comforts. Open year round. Organizes Jeep tours of Monument Valley. **M,** but lower rates Nov–Apr.

    Recapture Lodge, U.S. 191, Bluff, UT 84512 (801/672-2281). 21 rms, color TV. AE, MC, V. Free parking, pool, adj. coffee shop, free crib. *Note:* Pioneer-house-style rustic motel w. no air conditioning, but friendly reception and atmosphere; some rms have kitchenettes and refrigerators. Starting point for guided tours of the desert and rafting down the Colorado River. Also accommodations for groups and families. Open year round. 45 min. by car from Monument Valley. **B–I**

    San Juan Inn, U.S. 163, Mexican Hat, UT 84531 (801/683-2220). 22 rms, A/C, color TV. AE, MC, V. Free parking, coffee shop, crib $4. *Note:* Small, unpretentious hotel; limited comforts. Along the San Juan River. Organizes excursions to Monument Valley and rafting down the San Juan River. 15 min. by car from Monument Valley. **I**

IN CANYON DE CHELLY ☀ **Thunderbird Lodge,** 3 mi. (5km) SE of U.S. 191, Chinle, AZ 86503 (602/674-5841). 72 rms, A/C, cable color TV. AE, MC, V. Free parking, coffee shop, crib $2. *Note:* Rustic but comfortable hotel at the entrance to Canyon de Chelly. Reception w. a smile. Very acceptable coffee shop open until 8:30pm. No alcoholic beverages. Organizes Jeep trips into the canyons; fare, $15–$30 according to duration. Resv. advisable in summer. Don't miss staying here; it's an excellent value. Open year round. **I–M,** but lower rates off-season.

    Canyon de Chelly Motel, Navajo Rte. 7 (nr. U.S. 191), Chinle, AZ 86503 (602/674-5875). 51 rms, A/C, cable color TV, in-rm movies. AE, DC, MC, V. Free parking, free child's cot. *Note:* Typical motel nr. the canyon entrance; adj. coffee shop open 7am–8pm. Designed and furnished in the Navajo style. Open year round. **I–M,** but lower rates off-season.

ON THE HOPI RESERVATION ☀ **Hopi Cultural Center,** Ariz. 264 at Piñon Rd., Second Mesa, AZ 86043 (602/734-2401). 33 rms, A/C, cable color TV. MC, V. Free parking, rest. *Note:* Motel of unusual Pueblo design, functionally comfortable. Very acceptable rest. serving Hopi or American food, open till 8pm (to 10pm in summer). No alcoholic beverages. Among the typical Hopi dishes are nok qui ve (stew of hominy and mutton) and ba duf su ki (stew of pinto beans and hominy). Adj. museum and craft shop. Don't miss staying here, but you'll need to reserve way ahead. **I**

ON THE NAVAJO RESERVATION. Navajo Nation Inn, Ariz. 264, Window Rock, AZ 86515 (602/871-4108). 52 rms, A/C, color TV. AE, MC, V. Free parking, rest. *Note:* Typical small motel next to the Navajo Museum. Rest. open till 9pm. No alcoholic beverages. **I**

IN RAINBOW BRIDGE The **Wahweap Lodge and Marina** and **Holiday Inn Page** (see Chapter 32 on Utah National Parks).

CHAPTER 41

GRAND CANYON NATIONAL PARK🔥🔥🔥🔥

□ □ □

Discovered in 1540 by the Spaniard Garcia Lopez de Cárdenas, a member of Vásquez de Coronado's famous gold-seeking expedition, the Grand Canyon is one of the seven natural wonders of the world. It has taken more than 16 million years for the surging current of the Colorado River to carve its way down through the gray-white limestone, red sandstone, and green clay schist of the Kaibab Plateau; wind, heat, snow, and frost have done the rest. A true force of nature, the Colorado River in flood can run 224 ft. (70m) deep and 288 ft. (90m) wide. The river's intense yellow-brown color comes from the huge quantities of silt and alluvium that are continuously carried along. The gorges reach a height of 5,120 ft. (1,600m) in some places, and comprise an open book of terrestrial evolution: from the hard pre-Cambrian rocks (2 *billion* years old, the oldest on the planet), to the soft, fossil-rich tertiary rocks. Separated by 18 mi. (30km) at their widest points, the canyon's two rims offer extraordinary vistas over the 277-mi. (445km) stretch of canyon, and are accessible by car as well as on foot. The glorious views, notably at sunrise and sunset, make this masterpiece of creation one of the most astounding natural settings in the United States, and an ideal place for watching the wildlife, which includes 250 species of birds, 70 of mammals, 27 of reptiles, and 5 of amphibians.

The Grand Canyon of the Colorado (situated in Arizona, despite its name) became a national park in 1919. The **South Rim**—the more accessible—is open year round; the **North Rim** is open in summer only. Near **Grand Canyon Village,** the two rims are connected by a steep footpath of 21 mi. (34km); the road distance is closer to 218 mi. (350km).

Given the profusion of summer tourists and the relatively limited accommodations of the park, it is strongly advised that reservations be made weeks—if not months—in advance. This is true also for those who plan to go rafting down the Colorado or descend into the canyon on mule-back (see "Adventure Tours," below). About four million people visit the Grand Canyon each year.

BASIC FACTS: State of Arizona. Area code: 602. Time zone: mountain. ZIP Codes: 86023 (South Rim), 86052 (North Rim). First discovered by Europeans: 1540. Park dimensions: 1,875 sq. mi. (4,856km²). A national park since 1919.

CLIMATE: In summer, the tourist season par excellence, the high country of Arizona is very hot. Brief but violent downpours are a feature of virtually every July and Aug noontime. *Warning:* If the ground-level temperature is 95°–104°F (35°–40°C), it can easily reach 122°F (50°C) in the depths of the canyon. Winter is bitterly cold, with regular snowfalls which create a new and splendid landscape. The two ideal seasons for a visit to the Grand Canyon are autumn and especially spring, when the wildflowers are in bloom.

DISTANCES (from Grand Canyon Village): Albuquerque, 404 mi. (647km); Las Vegas, 291 mi. (465km); Los Angeles, 533 mi. (852km); Phoenix, 218 mi. (350km); Salt Lake City, 518 mi. (828km); San Francisco, 819 mi. (1,310km).

ARRIVAL & TRANSIT INFORMATION

NEAREST AIRPORTS: There is one local airport, and two others nearby.

SOUTH RIM   **Grand Canyon Airport** (GCN): 6 mi. (10km) south. Daily connections with Las Vegas and Phoenix.
Flagstaff Pulliam Field (FLG): 80 mi. (129km) SE. Daily connections with Phoenix.

NORTH RIM   **Page Municipal Airport** (PGA): 120 mi. (198km) NE. Daily connections with Las Vegas and Salt Lake City.

AIRLINES: At **Grand Canyon Airport:** Air Nevada (638-2441), America West (toll free 800/247-5692), and Scenic Airlines (toll free 800/634-6801).
In **Flagstaff:** America West (525-1346) and Sky West Airlines (toll free 800/453-9417).

CAR RENTAL (at Pulliam Airport in Flagstaff unless indicated): Avis (774-8421); Budget (779-0306); Dollar, Grand Canyon Airport, Grand Canyon (638-2625); Hertz (774-4452); National, 2320 Lucky Lane, Flagstaff (779-1975); and Thrifty, 500 S. Milton Rd., Flagstaff (779-0000).

BUS OR CAR RENTAL? Given the distances and the advantageous rental fees in Arizona as well as in neighboring California, renting a car with unlimited mileage is particularly recommended. Hitchhiking is prohibited inside Grand Canyon National Park.

TRAIN: The closest Amtrak station is at 1 E. Santa Fe Ave., Flagstaff (774-8679; toll free 800/872-7245).

INTERCITY BUSES: Greyhound buses are not permitted in Grand Canyon National Park. The closest Greyhound station is at 399 S. Malpais Lane, Flagstaff (774-4573). Connections between Flagstaff and the Grand Canyon via **Gray Line/Nava-Hopi** (774-5003).

SEEING THE GRAND CANYON

TOURIST INFORMATION: Write or phone the **Arizona Office of Tourism,** 1100 W. Washington St., Phoenix, AZ 85007 (602/542-8687); **Kaibab National Forest,** N. Kaibab Ranger District, P.O. Box 248, Fredonia, AZ 86022 (602/643-7395); or Superintendent, P.O. Box 129, **Grand Canyon National Park,** AZ 86023 (602/638-7888).
On site, go to the **Visitor Center,** Grand Canyon Village (eastern area). Open daily.
For a **recorded telephone message** with weather conditions, tourist ad-

vice, and road conditions 24 hr. a day, call 602/638-2245. For the **Visitor Activities Line,** call 602/638-9304 for a 24-hr. recording.

GUIDED TOURS: Bus Tours: Grand Canyon National Park Lodges, Grand Canyon Village (638-2631).
    Grand Canyon Railway (train) (toll free 800/843-8724): After a gap of 21 years steam trains run again along the 64-mi. (103km) route from Williams to the South Rim of the Grand Canyon, daily Apr–Nov; Time, 2 hr. 15 min. each way; fares, $38 round-trip for adults, $21 for children 12 and under. Spectacular.
    Plane rides over the Grand Canyon: Grand Canyon Airlines, Grand Canyon Airport (10 mi./16km south) (638-2407). Impressive.
    Helicopter rides over the Grand Canyon: Grand Canyon Helicopters, Tusayan Heliport (8 mi./13km south) (638-2419). Unforgettable.

ADVENTURE TOURS: Rafting down the Colorado (3–18 days): 22 authorized operators. For locations and rates, contact River Unit, Grand Canyon National Park, AZ 86023 (602/638-2401). Reservations must be made weeks (or months) in advance.
    Walking excursions between the two rims (Kaibab Trail and Bright Angel Trail): 12 hr. minimum (it takes 3–4 hr. to hike to the bottom on the popular Bright Angel Trail and twice as long to trek back up to the rim). This trek is physically trying, even for seasoned hikers, especially in summer when the temperature can reach 122°F (50°C) at the bottom of the canyon. Be sure to bring reserves of water and food, and do not stray from the trails under any circumstances. For information, call 638-2474 Mon–Fri.
    Mule-back excursions between the two rims (resv. mandatory): Grand Canyon National Park Lodges, Grand Canyon Village (638-2401). People weighing more than 200 lb. (91kg), pregnant women, children under age 12, and those susceptible to vertigo are prohibited. In winter the descent ends at Phantom Ranch (5-hr. trip). Guided mule trips cost from $70 per person; reserve 6 months ahead.

SIGHTS, ATTRACTIONS & ACTIVITIES

SOUTH RIM: ☼⚲ **West Rim Drive,** 18 mi. (13km) west of Grand Canyon Village: Splendid views over the canyon at **Maricopa Point, Hopi Point, Mohave Point, Pima Point** (the most beautiful view of the South Rim), and **Hermit's Rest,** a large, rustic building which dates from 1914. Private cars are prohibited on this road between May and mid-Sept. (there is a free shuttle bus).
    ☼⚲⚲⚲ **East Rim Drive,** 23 mi. (37km) east of Grand Canyon Village: Comprises, with West Rim Dr., one of the most beautiful spectacles in creation. Superb panoramas of the canyon at **Yavapai Point** (with an interesting museum), **Yaki Point, Grandview Point** (one of the loveliest views of the canyon), **Moran Point, Tusayan Ruins** (with an interesting museum), and **Desert View.** Enjoy an incomparable view of the **Painted Desert** and the neighboring forest from atop the restored **Indian Watchtower.** Private cars are permitted on this road year round.

NORTH RIM (open summer only): ⚲ **Bright Angel Point:** This spot offers a wonderful view of the canyon and is the point of departure for trips to the bottom of the gorge and toward the South Rim.
    ☼⚲⚲⚲ **Cape Royal:** At an elevation of 8,576 ft. (2,614m), this is the most magnificent view of the canyon and the Painted Desert. On the way, don't miss the view from Point Imperial, the highest point of either rim (8,803 ft/2,683m).
    ☼⚲⚲ **Point Sublime:** Worthy of its name, this point is reachable only in dry weather via a 17-mi. (27km) unpaved road.

※☆🔭🔭 **EXCURSIONS BETWEEN THE TWO RIMS** (218 mi./ 350km via Ariz. 64E, U.S. 89N, Alt. U.S. 89W, and Ariz. 67S): Besides the rigorous Kaibab Trail and Bright Angel Trail, mentioned previously (see "Adventure Tours," above), there is a magnificent car route along the South Rim—the barren reaches of **Echo Cliffs** and **Vermilion Cliffs** and the dense conifer forest of the **Kaibab Plateau.** On the way you'll get a unique perspective on the Colorado River from **Navajo Bridge,** one of the most spectacular spots in Arizona, which overlooks the riverbed from a height of more than 467 ft. (140m). This is a 2-day trip, with recommended lodging at the Grand Canyon Lodge or the Kaibab Lodge (see "Accommodations and Restaurants, North Rim," below).

MUSEUMS: 🏛 **Tusayan Ruins,** 20 mi. (32km) west of Grand Canyon Village: Traces of an Anasazi community from the 12th century and an archeological museum. Open daily.

🔔 **Yavapai Museum,** Grand Canyon Village: An interesting geological history of the Grand Canyon. Open daily.

OTHER ATTRACTIONS: **Grand Canyon Imax Theater,** Ariz. 64 and U.S. 180 at the south entrance to the park (638-2203): Discover the "hidden secrets" of the Grand Canyon on this original Imax motion picture shown on a seven-story-high, 82-in.-wide (2m) screen in 34 min. Spectacular.

WINTER SPORTS RESORTS: 🏛 **Fairfield Snow Bowl,** 73 mi. (117km) SE of the Grand Canyon on U.S. 180: Cross-country and downhill (2,300-ft./ 690m slope) skiing. Eight chair lifts. Open mid-Nov to mid-Apr. For information, call 779-6126 (or 779-4577 for snow conditions).

ACCOMMODATIONS & RESTAURANTS

A Note on Accommodations and Restaurants: Room rates in the Grand Canyon area are coded as follows: **VE,** Very Expensive ($140 and up); **E,** Expensive ($90–$140); **M,** Moderate ($60–$90); **I,** Inexpensive ($30–$60); **B,** Budget (up to $30). A listing of toll free numbers is in the Appendix. Restaurant prices, per person, excluding drinks and service charges, are coded as follows: **VE,** Very Expensive ($60 and up); **E,** Expensive ($40–$60); **M,** Moderate ($25–$40); **I,** Inexpensive ($15–$25); **B,** Budget (up to $15).

Reservations Inside the National Park

The National Park Service has contracted out all the food and lodging places inside Grand Canyon National Park to concessionaires, one for the North Rim and another for the South Rim. For reservations anywhere inside the park, contact the concessionaires directly:

South Rim: Contact Grand Canyon National Park Lodges, P.O. Box 699, Grand Canyon, AZ 86203 (602/638-2401).

North Rim: Contact T. W. Services, 451 N. Main St. (P.O. Box 400), Cedar City, UT 84720 (801/586-7686).

Inside the Park (South Rim)

Note: In general, in all food and lodging places on the South Rim, the service is not up to par, the reception is barely civil, with unprofessional personnel who are perpetually snowed under, waits at the restaurants (where the cuisine is mediocre and expensive) can be 2 hr. long and reservations are not always honored.

※☆📞 **El Tovar Hotel,** Village Loop Dr., AZ 86203 (602/638-2631). 76 rms, A/C, cable color TV. AE, CB, DC, MC, V. Free parking, rest., bar, rm svce, night club, boutique, free airport shuttle, free crib. *Note:* Exceptional location on the edge of the canyon. The rustic 1905 architecture—squared-off tree trunks and boulders—may lack sophistication,

GRAND CANYON

Kilometers 30
Miles 20
0

← N →

UTAH
ARIZONA

NEVADA

Lake Powell
GLEN CANYON NAT'L REC. AREA
Dam
Page
Navajo Bridge
Marble Canyon

KAIBAB INDIAN RESERVATION

KAIBAB NAT'L FOREST

GRAND CANYON NAT'L PARK

NORTH RIM
Phantom Ranch
Grand Canyon Village
Hermits Rest
Colorado River

HAVASUPAI INDIAN RESERVATION

Supai
Hualapai Hilltop

HUALAPAI INDIAN RESERVATION

LAKE MEAD NAT'L REC. AREA

Pierce Ferry
Temple Bar

LAKE MEAD NAT'L REC. AREA
Lake Mead

North Las Vegas
Las Vegas
Hoover Dam
Boulder City

LAKE MEAD NAT'L REC. AREA

Colorado River

NEVADA

Davis Dam

Searchlight

CALIF.

Tuba City
160
Little Colorado River Gorge
Cameron
River
Colorado

Little
Desert View
Tusayan Ruin/Museum
Grand View
Watchtower

KAIBAB NAT'L FOREST

64

Grand Canyon Caverns
Seligman
40

Peach Springs

66

Kingman

93

67

Wupatki Nat'l Monument
Sunset Crater Nat'l Monument
Lowell Observatory
Flagstaff
Fairfield Snow Bowl

KAIBAB NAT'L FOREST

Williams

95

67

89
89
89
67
15

but it has a certain charm. Functional rm comfort (some rms are cramped); there are a few suites w. balconies and a splendid view of the Grand Canyon. **E**

Maswik Deluxe, U.S. 180W, AZ 86023 (602/638-2631). 160 rms, A/C, cable color TV. AE, DC, MC, V. Free parking, coffee shop, bar, free crib. *Note:* The latest addition to Grand Canyon motels offers functional rms, some w. private balconies. **M**

Kachina Lodge, Village Loop Dr., AZ 86023 (602/638-2631). 48 rms, cable color TV. AE, CB, DC, MC, V. Free parking, check-in at the El Tovar Hotel, adj. coffee shop, free crib. *Note:* Relatively modern motel w. functional rms, the best of which afford a view of the canyon. **M–E**

Thunderbird Lodge, Village Loop Dr., AZ 86023 (602/638-2631). 55 rms, cable color TV. AE, CB, DC, MC, V. Free parking, check-in at the Bright Angel Lodge, adj. coffee shop, free crib. *Note:* Relatively modern motel that adjoins the Bright Angel Lodge. Functional rms, the best of which afford a view of the canyon. **M–E**

Bright Angel Lodge, W. Rim Dr., AZ 86023 (602/638-2631). 37 rms (15 w. bath), 50 bungalows, cable color TV. AE, CB, DC, MC, V. Free parking, coffee shop, bar, night club, hrdrsr, organized raft trips down the Colorado and mule-back excursions down into the canyon, free crib. *Note:* Old, rustic building surrounded by bungalows. Average comfort. A few rms w. views of the canyon. **I–M**

Yavapai Lodge, Mather Center, AZ 86023 (602/638-2631). 351 rms, cable color TV. AE, CB, DC, MC, V. Free parking, coffee shop, bar, disco, grocery store, free crib. *Note:* Functional motel in a pine grove across from the Visitors Center. **M**

Maswik Lodge, U.S. 180W, AZ 86023 (602/638-2631). 90 rms, 38 bungalows. AE, CB, DC, MC, V. Free parking, coffee shop, bar. *Note:* A tree-shaded rustic motel and individual bungalows. Rudimentary comfort. Closed Nov–Apr. **I**

Phantom Ranch, at the bottom of the canyon (Grand Canyon Village, AZ 86023) (602/638-2631). 40 beds in the dormitory and 10 bunk-bedded cabins. AE, CB, DC, MC, V. Pool, fishing, coffee shop. *Note:* The Grand Canyon's most spectacular and most authentic hotel. At the foot of the gorge, accessible only on foot or mule-back (at least a 5-hr. trip). Interesting mule-rental/lodging/meals package. Resv. necessary 6 months in advance for summer visits, as authorized descents into the canyon are limited to 90 people per day. Adventure accessible to everyone. **B–I**

Inside the Park (North Rim)

Grand Canyon Lodge, Bright Angel Point, AZ 86052 (602/638-2611; reservations through T. W. Services). 40 rms and 160 individual cottages. A/C. AE, CB, DC, MC, V. Free parking, rest., coffee shop, bar, movie theater, crib $5. *Note:* The relatively modern, functional motel and the rustic cottages for two to five people (the "western cabins" are the best choice) afford a magnificent view of the canyon. Adequate rest. Organizes raft trips down the Colorado and mule-back trips along the rim. Closed Oct–May. **I–M**

Outside the Park (South Rim)

Best Western Grand Canyon Squire Inn, Ariz. 64, AZ 86023 (602/638-2681; toll free, see Best Western), 2 mi. (3km) south of the park entrance. 150 rms, A/C, cable color TV. AE, CB, DC, MC, V. Free parking, pool, hot tub, tennis, health club, bowling, sauna, rest., coffee shop, bar, crib available. *Note:* This modern motel w. its excellent facilities is the most appealing and comfortable in the entire Grand Canyon area. Rustic, Native American–style decor. No-smoking rms. A 15-min. car ride from Grand Canyon Village. **M,** but lower rates off-season.

♀ **Moqui Lodge,** Ariz. 64, AZ 86023 (602/638-2424), at the
park entrance. 135 rms, cable color TV. AE, CB, DC, MC, V.
Free parking, tennis, horseback riding, coffee shop, bar. *Note:* This convenient
and basic motel offers reasonable comfort in 10 min. from the canyon. Closed
Jan–Feb. **I–M,** but lower rates off-season.

♀ **Quality Inn Red Feather Lodge,** Ariz. 64, AZ 86023 (602/
638-2673; toll free, see Quality Inns), 1 mi. (1.6km) south of
the park entrance. 185 rms, A/C, color TV, in-rm movies. AE, DC, MC, V. Free
parking, pool, coffee shop, bar, rm svce, free shuttle to/from the airport. *Note:*
Modern, comfortable motel w. spacious, balconied rms and cheerful reception.
10 min. from Grand Canyon Village. **M,** but lower rates off-season.

Outside the Park (North Rim)

♀ **Kaibab Lodge,** Ariz. 67, AZ 86022 (602/638-2389; toll free
800/525-0924). 24 bungalows. MC, V. Free parking, pool,
horseback riding, coffee shop. *Note:* Small, pleasant motel away from the Grand
Canyon crowds, 30 min. north of the North Rim. Ideal for the motorist. Fine
location in the heart of Kaibab National Forest. Excellent value. Open mid-May
to mid-Oct only. **I–M**

♀ **Jacob Lake Inn,** intersection of Alt. U.S. 89 and Ariz. 67, AZ
86051 (602/643-7232). 36 rms. AE, CB, DC, MC, V. Free
parking, tennis, coffee shop, grocery store. *Note:* Rustic motel in Kaibab National
Forest, 44 mi. (70km) north of the North Rim. Modest but functional comfort.
Motel units and cabins. **I**

YMCAs/Youth Hostels

American Youth Hostel, 76 Tonto St., Grand Canyon (South Rim), AZ
86023 (602/638-9018). Resv. recommended at least 2 days in advance.

Weatherford Hostel, 23 N. Leroux St., Flagstaff, AZ 86001 (602/774-
2731). 60 beds. Individual rms or dormitory accommodations in a beautiful
almost-100-year-old hotel w. coffee shop. Close to the train station.

An alternative solution is **Motel 6** (nr. dwntwn), 2010 E. Butler Ave., Flagstaff, AZ 86001 (602/774-1801). 150 rms. Pool. AE, DC, MC, V. **B–I**

Backpacking Campgrounds and Campsites

Permits are required for overnight hikes (but not for day hikes) in the national park. Permits are issued for three campgrounds, including Bright Angel at
the bottom of the canyon near Phantom Ranch, and for 10 campsites, including
Hermit Rapids at the end of Hermit Trail. For reservations, **Backcountry Reservations Office,** P.O. Box 129, Grand Canyon, AZ 86023. Hikers may also appear in person at a reservation office (on both rims) on the day of their hike.
Names will be placed on a waiting list for cancellations. For information only,
call 602/638-2472; reservations are not accepted by phone.

NEARBY EXCURSIONS

HAVASUPAI RESERVATION (62 mi./100km along unpaved road from Ariz. 66 after Grand Canyon Caverns, plus 8
mi./13km on foot or horseback to the bottom of Grand Canyon): This primitive
Native American reservation with its 300 inhabitants is completely cut off from
the rest of the world. Camping is $10 per day per person, and there is an inexpen-
sive 24-rm bungalow, **Havasupai Lodge;** add a $12 registration fee, but resv. are
a must. Accommodations are available through Havasupai Tourist Enterprise,
Supai, AZ 86435 (602/448-2121). **Grand Canyon Helicopters** (638-2419)
provides exclusive air service to the remote Havasupai Village from Grand Canyon Village. The ultimate change of scene.

LAKE POWELL (138 mi./220km NE on Ariz. 64W and
U.S. 89N): Water sports and magnificent landscapes, including

the celebrated **Rainbow Bridge,** the largest natural arch in the world (span of 272 ft./85m). An absolute must. For more details, see Chapter 32 on Utah National Parks.

NATIONAL PARKS NEARBY: 👓 **Bryce Canyon National Park,** 285 mi. (456km) north via Ariz. 64W, U.S. 89N, Alt. U.S. 89, and Utah 9W: See Chapter 32 on Utah National Parks.

👓 **Glen Canyon National Recreation Area,** 138 mi. (220km) NE via Ariz. 64W and U.S. 89N: See Chapter 32 on Utah National Parks.

👓 **Zion National Park,** 253 mi. (405km) NW via Ariz. 64W, U.S. 89N, Alt. U.S. 89, and Utah 12: See Chapter 32 on Utah National Parks.

FARTHER AFIELD

🔆👓 **HOPI & NAVAJO PUEBLOS** (280 mi./450km r.t. from the Grand Canyon on Ariz. 64E, U.S. 89N, U.S. 160N, Ariz. 264E): See Chapter 40 on Navajoland.

FLAGSTAFF & VICINITY (395 mi./632km r.t. on Ariz. 64S, U.S. 180W, I-17S, U.S. 89N, and Ariz. 64N): You'll need at least 2 days to enjoy the wonderful variety this trip offers, including the interesting sights below. **Sedona** is a suggested stopover town (for more details, see "Farther Afield" in Chapter 42 on Phoenix). You won't want to pass up this opportunity.

🔆👓 **Lowell Observatory,** Mars Hill Rd., Flagstaff (602/774-2096): The country's oldest observatory (1894), where the planet Pluto was discovered in 1930. Guided tours Tues–Sat. at 1:30pm. For astronomy lovers.

🔆👓 **Meteor Crater,** 46 mi. (74km) east of Flagstaff: A meteor hit the earth 22,000 years ago on this site at a speed of 33,000 m.p.h. (52,800km/h) and left the world's best-preserved crater—4,160 ft. (1.2km) in diameter 3 mi. (4.8km) in circumference, and 557 ft. (170m) deep. NASA uses it for astronaut training. Impressive. For information, call 602/774-8350.

🔆👓 **Montezuma Castle National Monument,** 50 mi. (80km) south of Flagstaff: Extraordinary, five-tier cave dwelling perched 64 ft. (20m) above the ground in a cliff shelter. Built by the Sinagua tribes in the 13th century, it is in remarkable condition. Open daily. Not to be missed. For information, call 602/567-3322.

🔆👓 **Oak Creek Canyon,** 15 mi. (24km) south of Flagstaff: Splendid rocky gorge landscapes that are almost as spectacular as the Grand Canyon; they've been used as the setting for many a western film. On the way, see **Sedona,** a picturesque little pioneer town that is today dedicated to modern painting and Native American crafts.

👓 **Sunset Crater National Monument,** 17 mi. (27km) north of Flagstaff: Volcanic crater that has been dormant for nine centuries. Spectacular red-orange lava formations. Worth a look. Open daily. For information, call 602/527-7042.

👓 **Wupatki National Monument,** 35 mi. (56km) north of Flagstaff: Ruins of a Sinagua village from circa A.D. 1100. The main dwelling contains around 100 rooms. Archeological museum. Open daily. For information, call 602/527-7040.

LAS VEGAS (611 mi./978km r.t. from the Grand Canyon on Ariz. 64S, U.S. 40W, U.S. 93, U.S. 95N): The world capital of gambling, in the heart of the desert (see Chapter 47 on Las Vegas). On the way, see:

🔔 **Grand Canyon Caverns,** 124 mi. (198km) SW of the Grand Canyon on Ariz. 64S, U.S. 40W, and Ariz. 66 (602/422-3223): Spectacular caverns 210 ft. (64m) underground (access by elevator) with a ¾-mi. (1km) trail. Open year round. Interior temperature is 56°F (13°C).

🔔🔔 **Oatman,** 193 mi. (308km) SW of the Grand Canyon on Ariz. 64S, U.S. 40W, and old U.S. 66 SW of Kingman. Superb, remarkably preserved ghost town from the days of the gold rush. It had as many as 10,000 inhabitants around 1910; it has barely 100 today. Regularly used as the backdrop of western movies. For information, call 602/768-3424.

☀🔔🔔 **Lake Mead and Hoover Dam,** 259 mi. (415km) west of the Grand Canyon on Ariz. 64S, U.S. 40W, and U.S. 93N: See Chapter 47 on Las Vegas.

CHAPTER 42

PHOENIX

□ □ □

Standing foursquare in the center of the **Valley of the Sun,** Arizona's capital, from the air, looks like a verdant oasis in the midst of a sandy, mountainous desert. The Hohokam, a people who mysteriously disappeared without a trace around the year A.D. 1400, appear to have devised a sophisticated irrigation system for the area, but around the turn of our century more up-to-date methods were initiated, and now Phoenix is the center of a green belt with market gardens, fields of cotton and alfalfa, citrus and olive groves, and even date palms. The city owes its name, too, to its Native American antecedents. As with the mythical bird reborn from its own ashes, the inhabitants of Phoenix have given new life to an arid plain that had been long left empty to the scorching sun.

Less than a century old, Phoenix is a successful blend of the romantic West and 20th-century America vigor. A perfect base for excursions to such vacation wonderlands as the Grand Canyon of the Colorado, Navajoland, Tucson and southern Arizona, or the Apache Trail (in the 19th century the region witnessed savage battles with the Apache under Cochise and Geronimo), Phoenix itself has become one of the principal tourist attractions of the West, especially in winter. Witness its 25,000 hotel rooms, its 80 golf courses, the **Heard Museum,** finest Native American museum in the country, and its dozen luxury grand hotels, including the famous **Arizona Biltmore** designed by the great Frank Lloyd Wright. With 300 days of sunshine a year and low humidity, **Sun City,** as Phoenix calls itself, is also a dream come true for tens of thousands of well-to-do retirees.

Covering an enormous area 25 mi. (40km) long by 40 mi. (65km) wide with its low ranch or Spanish Colonial houses, and lacking any conspicuous buildings (or even a downtown, properly so called), Phoenix may be showing us the shape of cities to come—a sort of Los Angeles in the desert, with a dizzying rate of population growth. Between 1950 and 1987 the number of people living in the city and its inner suburbs (the super-smart **Scottsdale** and **Paradise Valley,** and the less exclusive **Glendale, Mesa,** and **Tempe**) rose from 200,000 to 1,960,000—more than 800% in less than a third of a century. It comes as no surprise, then, that Phoenix enjoys the third-fastest economic growth rate among America's major cities, right behind Austin and Orlando.

Besides its many high-tech industries, such as electronics, telecommunications, and aerospace, Phoenix is headquarters of financial-services giant Greyhound, and of two of the largest hotel chains, Ramada Inns and Best Western.

BASIC FACTS: Capital of the state of Arizona. Area code: 602. Time zone: mountain. ZIP Code: 85026. Founded: 1864. Approximate population: city, 980,000; metropolitan area, 2,190,000. 20th-largest metropolitan area in the U.S.

CLIMATE: With one of the largest amounts of sunshine (86% sunny days) in the U.S., the inhabitants of Phoenix are the spoiled children of nature. Winter is brilliantly sunny by day (Jan average, 54°F/12°C) and cool at night. In summer the thermometer can easily rise above 95°F (35°C), but the dry desert air and the omnipresent air conditioning make the heat easy to take. Spring and fall are very pleasant, especially Apr and Oct. The rainy season is July–Aug, with only an occasional downpour in winter.

DISTANCES: Albuquerque, 453 mi. (725km); Denver, 805 mi. (1,288km); Grand Canyon National Park, 218 mi. (350km); Las Vegas, 285 mi. (456km); Los Angeles, 390 mi. (625km); Mexican border, 183 mi. (293km); Salt Lake City, 650 mi. (1,040km); San Diego, 355 mi. (568km); Tucson, 118 mi. (189km).

ARRIVAL & TRANSIT INFORMATION

AIRPORT: Phoenix Sky Harbor International (PHX), 4 mi. (6.5km) SE (273-3300).

AIRLINES: Alaska (921-3100), America West (894-0737), American (258-6300), Continental (258-8911), Delta (258-5930), Midway (toll free 800/621-5700), Northwest (273-7325), Southwest (273-1221), TWA (252-7711), United (273-3131), and USAir (258-7355).

CITY LINK: The **cab** fare from the airport to downtown is $10–$14 (rates vary widely among different cab companies, so inquire in advance); time, 10–15 min. Bus: **Supershuttle** (244-9000); serves any address in Phoenix or the metropolitan area on request; fare, $5–$12; time, 15–20 min. **Municipal buses:** The no. 2 line links the airport to dwntwn; leaves every 30 min.; fare, 75¢. Cab fares are very high, and the public bus transportation theoretically provided by **Phoenix Transit Systems/PTS** (253-5000) is almost useless in practice.

Given the size of the metropolitan area and the numerous excursion destinations around about, it makes a great deal of sense to rent a car with unlimited mileage, particularly at the low rates prevailing in Arizona.

CAR RENTAL (at the airport unless otherwise noted): Avis (273-3222); Budget (267-4000); Dollar (275-7588); General Rent-A-Car, 2800 E. Van Buren St. (273-0991); Hertz (267-8822); National (275-4771); and Thrifty, 4114 E. Washington St. (244-0311). For dwntwn locations, consult the local telephone directory.

LIMOUSINE SERVICES: Arizona Limousines/Dav El (267-7097), Carey Limousine (996-1955), and Luxury Limousines (948-3058).

TAXIS: Taxis cannot be hailed on the street. Your best bet is to call **Ace Taxi** (254-1999), **Checker Cab** (257-1818), or **Yellow Cab** (252-5252). Be sure to negotiate the fare in advance.

TRAIN: Amtrak, Union Station, 401 W. Harrison St. (253-0121; toll free 800/872-7245).

INTERCITY BUSES: Greyhound, 525 E. Washington St. (248-4050).

INFORMATION & TOURS

TOURIST INFORMATION: The **Arizona Office of Tourism,** 1100 W. Washington St., Phoenix, AZ 85007 (602/542-8687). Information covering the whole state of Arizona. Open Mon–Fri.
Phoenix and Valley of the Sun Convention and Visitors Bureau, 505 N.

2nd St., Suite 300, Phoenix, AZ 85004 (602/254-6500; toll free 800/528-0483).

For a **telephone recording** with an up-to-date list of cultural events and shows, call 602/252-5588.

GUIDED TOURS: Arizona Air (airplane), 15000 N. Airport Dr., Scottsdale (991-8252): 1-day air trips over the Grand Canyon, Monument Valley, Oak Creek Canyon, etc.; not to be missed.

Gray Line (bus), 1350 N. 22nd Ave., Phoenix (254-4550): Guided tours of Phoenix and surroundings; serves principal hotels.

Sky Cab (airplane), 14605 N. Airport Dr., Scottsdale (998-1778): Half- and full-day flights over the Grand Canyon, Lake Powell, Monument Valley, Canyon de Chelly, etc. Spectacular.

SIGHTS, ATTRACTIONS & ACTIVITIES

ADVENTURES: Arizona Awareness, 2422 N. 72nd Pl., Scottsdale (947-7852): Excursions on horseback, foot, or by Jeep through Arizona's mountains and deserts.

Arizona Balloon Company (balloon), 3935 W. Alice, Phoenix (483-8080): Spectacular balloon overflights of Phoenix and environs. Daily.

Arizona River Runners (boat), P.O. Box 47788, Phoenix (867-4866): Rafting down the Colorado River through the Grand Canyon; 3-, 6-, and 8-day round-trips.

Salt River Canyon Raft Trips (boat), 2242 W. Main St., Mesa (968-1552): Rafting near Phoenix; 1-day or longer trips.

Unicorn Balloon Company (balloon), 15001 N. 74th St., Scottsdale (991-3666): Dawn or afternoon balloon rides over Phoenix and the area; spectacular.

Wild West Jeep Tours, Inc. (Jeep), 7924 E. Chaparral Rd., Suite 104, Scottsdale (941-8355): 1-day excursions into the mountain and desert country around Phoenix.

ARCHITECTURAL HIGHLIGHTS: ☼🔔 **Arizona State University's Fine Arts Center,** the campus of Arizona State University, Tempe (965-2787): Spectacular grayish-purple stucco structure looking like a futuristic version of a Mayan sculpture. Designed by Antoine Predock, this sprawling architectural complex full of balconies, steps, loges, and arcades contains the A.S.U. Art Museum (see below), a 500-seat theater, a dance laboratory, and rehearsal halls.

☼🔔 **Gammage Center for the Performing Arts,** the campus of Arizona State University, Apache Blvd. at Mill Ave., Tempe (965-3434): The last major work of Frank Lloyd Wright, opened in 1964 after his death. The huge auditorium, a great architect's celebration of the curved line, has astonishing acoustics. Open Tues, Thurs, and Sat; must certainly be seen.

🔔 **Mystery Castle,** 7 mi. (11km) south on Central Ave. at 800 E. Mineral Rd., Phoenix (268-1581): A huge, bizarre sort of house at the foot of South Mountain Park, built by hand between 1927 and 1945 by the solitary eccentric Boyce Luther Gulley from a wide assortment of unusual salvage materials. It boasts no fewer than 18 rooms and 13 fireplaces, not to mention a chapel and a strange cantilevered staircase. Open Tues–Sun Oct 1–July 4.

🔔 **State Capitol,** W. Washington St. and 17th Ave., Phoenix (255-4581): The home of the Arizona legislature is an imposing turn-of-the-century structure in limestone and Arizona granite, capped with a copper-plated dome. Interesting museum of western history, open Mon–Fri. The beautiful grdns display a comprehensive selection of the local flora.

☼🔔 **Symphony Hall,** Civic Plaza, 2nd St. and Monroe St., Phoenix (264-4754): Ultramodern auditorium where the Phoenix Symphony makes its home, across from the famous **Convention Center.** The

GREATER PHOENIX

To Scottsdale

N

Desert Botanical Gardens

Zoo

Stadium

Hall of Fame

Pueblo Grande Ruins

HOHOKAM EXPWY.

State University

44TH ST.

THOMAS RD.

INDIAN SCHOOL RD.

32ND ST.

VAN BUREN ST.

Dog Track

Sky Harbor Int. Airport

MC DOWELL RD.

24TH ST.

WASHINGTON ST.

16TH ST.

CAMELBACK RD.

Indian School

CENTRAL AVE.

7TH ST.

BUCKEYE RD.

17

Civic Center

City Hall

7TH AVE.

College

State Coliseum & Fairgrounds

19TH AVE.

State Capitol

MARICOPA FRWY.

17

Metro Center

BLACK CANYON FRWY.

huge central court, embellished with fountains and statues, lies above an underground parking lot with more than 1,000 spaces.

CHURCHES/SYNAGOGUES: ⚱ **Mormon Temple,** 14 mi. (22km) east on U.S. 60 at 525 E. Main St., Mesa (964-7164): Mormon Temple of unusual design in a lovely grdn. Non-Mormons not admitted to the temple, but visitor center open daily, with audiovisual program on the history of the Mormon religion.

⚱ **St. Francis Xavier Church,** 4715 N. Central Ave., Phoenix (279-9547): Beautiful Jesuit church dating from 1959. On the facade, the statues of the Jesuit Fr. Eusebio Kino, the great missionary to Arizona, and of the famous Franciscan Fr. Junipero Serra, who evangelized California, stand on either side of St. Francis Xavier, one of the most illustrious members of the Society of Jesus. Inside, splendid stained-glass windows by Gabriel Loire. Open daily.

MUSEUMS OF ART: ☼⚱ **A.S.U. Art Museum,** on the campus of Arizona State University, Tempe (965-2787): Historical survey of American painting and sculpture, Native American and Latin American art, plus a comprehensive print collection. American crockery and contemporary ceramics. Spectacular architecture. Open Sun–Fri.

☼⚱ **Phoenix Art Museum,** 1625 N. Central Ave., Phoenix (257-1222): This interesting, relatively young (1969) museum displays 18th- to 20th-century French painting (Boucher, Greuze, Courbet, Fantin-Latour, Watteau, Dufy, Picasso), Oriental miniatures, and a fine collection of western art including works by Frederic Remington, Robert Henri, Charles Marion Russell, and the like. An absolute must. Open Tues–Sun.

MUSEUMS OF SCIENCE & HISTORY: ⚱ **Arizona Historical Society Museum,** 1242 N. Central Ave., Phoenix (255-4470): History of the settlement of Arizona illustrated by many objects dating from the time Phoenix was founded to the 1920s, in a building (the Ellis-Shackelford House) that itself dates from 1917. Reconstructions of a 19th-century drugstore and general store. For "Winning of the West" buffs. Open Tues–Sat.

⚱ **Arizona Mineral Museum,** Arizona State Fairgrounds, 19th Ave. and McDowell Rd., Phoenix (255-3791): From gold nuggets to copper ore, by way of precious stones and slices of petrified wood, a complete selection of the geological riches of Arizona. Interesting. Mon–Sat.

☼⚱ **Arizona Museum,** 1002 W. Van Buren St., Phoenix (253-2734): 2,000 years of Arizona history from prehistoric times through the civilization of the Hohokam peoples and the first European settlements to the present day. Fascinating. Open Wed–Sun.

⚱ **Bayless Country Store Museum,** 118 W. Indian School Rd., Phoenix (241-1368): Faithfully reconstructed "country store" which could have come straight out of a western: grocery, pharmacy, and hardware store all at the same time. Even the newspapers on display and the advertising posters are of the period. Picturesque. Open Tues–Sun.

⚱ **Center for Meteorite Studies,** Arizona State University campus, University Dr., Tempe (965-3576): Distinguished center for meteorite studies, with one of the world's largest collections (1,400 items) of extraterrestrial objects. For ardent astronomers. Open Mon–Sat.

⚱ **Hall of Flame Museum,** 6101 E. Van Buren St., Phoenix (275-3473): A large museum entirely devoted to fire-fighting paraphernalia. Interesting collection of old fire engines, the oldest going back to 1725. Amusing. Open Mon–Fri.

☼⚱⚱⚱ **Heard Museum,** 22 E. Monte Vista Rd., Phoenix (252-8840): The finest and one of the largest museums of anthropology and primitive art in the U.S., housed in an elegant Spanish Mission–style building.

Although it has some African, Asian, and Oceanic pieces of quality, the museum has specialized since its foundation in 1929 in the Amerindian cultures, particularly those of the Southwest, and especially the Hohokam, Mogollon, Anasazi, and Pueblo. Fine hall of prehistoric arts and a splendid group of Kachina dolls given by former Sen. Barry Goldwater; also exhibitions of contemporary Native American art. Spanish Colonial room evidencing the Spanish cultural influence on the southwestern U.S. and Mexico. Open daily.

Pueblo Grande Museum, 4619 E. Washington St., Phoenix (275-3452): Site of excavations that have unearthed a Native American village more than 2,000 years old. An observation platform allows you to follow the diggings under way, particularly on irrigation canals cut between the 6th and 8th centuries A.D. Remarkable archeological museum. Pueblo Grande was inhabited between 300 B.C. and A.D. 1450 by the mysterious Hohokam people. Open daily.

PANORAMAS: **Golden Eagle,** 201 N. Central Ave., Phoenix (257-7700): Restaurant on the 37th floor of the Valley National Bank Building with the best view of the city and the mountains (admission fee). The food is unimpressive but the bar is congenial. Open Mon–Sat. (till midnight).

South Mountain Park, 10919 S. Central Ave., Phoenix (262-6111): Fine view of the city and the Valley of the Sun from **Dobbins Lookout** at 2,330 ft. (710m).

PARKS & GARDENS: **Desert Botanical Gardens,** 1201 N. Galvin Pkwy. at Papago Park, Phoenix (941-1225): All kinds of desert vegetation, including 1,400 different species of cactus, growing in a beautiful 150-acre (60ha) mountainside park. An energetic 45-min. walk, but well worth it. Spectacular cactus exhibition in Mar. Open daily.

Encanto Park, N. 15th Ave. and W. Encanto Blvd., Phoenix: Golf, tennis, and canoeing in the heart of town; the inviting lake is a wildlife reserve for waterfowl.

South Mountain Park, 10919 S. Central Ave., Phoenix (262-6111): Large mountainous park covering 16,000 acres (6,475ha), with scenic drives, unspoiled canyons, weird rock formations, and dozens of miles of hiking trails—nature in the raw, 15 min. from downtown. Fine view of the city and valley; you should go there.

Squaw Peak Recreation Area, 2701 E. Squaw Peak Dr., Phoenix (262-6696): Northeast of town in the foothills of the Phoenix Mountains, this steeply contoured park has a 1.2-mi. (2km) trail with a panoramic view of the city.

PERFORMING ARTS: For daily listings of all shows and cultural events, consult the entertainment pages of the daily papers *Arizona Republic* (morning) and *Phoenix Gazette* (evening), as well as of the monthly *Phoenix* magazine.

Celebrity Theater, 440 N. 32nd St., Phoenix (224-0404): Comedy, drama, concerts, Broadway hits.

Gammage Center for the Performing Arts, on the campus of Arizona State University, Apache Blvd. at Mill Ave., Tempe (965-3434): Contemporary theater, ballet, classical concerts in a Frank Lloyd Wright auditorium (see "Architectural Highlights," above).

Herberger Theater Center, 222 E. Monroe St., Phoenix (252-8497): Brand-new cultural complex with two adjoining theaters. There are more than 600 performances (Broadway shows, contemporary theater) a year.

Kerr Cultural Center, 6110 W. Scottsdale Rd., Scottsdale (965-1020): Concerts of classical music, recitals, stage plays.

Phoenix Little Theater, Civic Center, 25 E. Coronado Rd., Phoenix (254-2151): Contemporary theater (highly eclectic programs).

Scottsdale Center for the Arts, 7383 Scottsdale Mall, Scottsdale (994-

2301): Contemporary and classic theater, dance, chamber music, concerts. Home of the Arizona Theatre Company. Annual Shakespeare Festival.

Sundome Theater for the Performing Arts, 19403 R. H. Johnson Blvd., Sun City West (584-3118): Big-name recitals.

Symphony Hall, Civic Center Plaza, 2nd St. and Monroe St. (264-4754): Ultramodern home of the Phoenix Symphony (principal conductor: James Sedares) and the Arizona Opera Company.

Veterans Memorial Coliseum, 1826 W. McDowell Rd., Phoenix (258-6711): Rock concerts; leading pop stars.

SHOPPING: The **Biltmore Fashion Park,** 2470 E. Camelback Rd., Phoenix (955-8400): 50 luxury stores and restaurants, including Saks Fifth Avenue, Gucci, and Ralph Lauren, in an ultramodern setting. High fashion.

The Borgata, 6166 N. Scottsdale Rd., Scottsdale (998-1822): One of the most imaginative, luxurious shopping centers in the U.S., its architecture modeled on that of a medieval Italian village (whence the name). Some 50 stores and shops of surpassing elegance. Definitely worth seeing.

Fifth Avenue Shops, 7120 Fifth Ave., Scottsdale (949-7997): 150 shops, art galleries, luxury ready-to-wear, and restaurants. Very elegant atmosphere.

Metrocenter, 9617 Metro Pkwy., West Phoenix (997-2641): Giant shopping center of strictly utilitarian appearance, with five department stores, more than 200 shops, 17 movie houses, and 47 restaurants, cafeterias, and snack bars. If you enjoy the colossal, this is for you.

Native American Art

For lovers of authentic Native American art, visit the **Heard Museum Shop,** 22 E. Monte Vista Rd., Phoenix; **Godber's,** Metrocenter, 9653A Metro Pkwy. W., and **McGee's Indian Den,** 7239 First Ave., Scottsdale.

SPECIAL EVENTS: For the exact schedule of events below, consult the **Phoenix and Valley of the Sun Convention and Visitors Bureau** (see "Tourist Information," above).

Fiesta Bowl Classic (Jan 1): 3 days of festivities, parades, and concerts, culminating in the renowned Fiesta Bowl football game.

Arizona National Livestock Show (Jan): Popular cattle show; guaranteed local color.

Phoenix Open Golf Tournament (Jan): The world's greatest players compete at the Tournament Players Club, Scottsdale.

World's Championship JCs Rodeo of Rodeos (mid-Mar): Rodeo championships, horseback parades; everyone's a cowboy on this day.

Indian Fair (Mar): Exhibitions of Native American crafts; traditional dances; food festival. At the Heard Museum; don't miss it.

International Grand Prix (June): A race through the downtown streets for the Formula One Grand Prize; spectacular.

Wrangler Jeans Rodeo Showdown (Oct): One of the Southwest's largest, complete with country-and-western concerts.

Arizona State Fair (late Oct to early Nov): One of the Southwest's biggest fair-exhibitions; cattle show, public concerts, games, etc. Plenty of atmosphere.

Thunderbird Balloon Race (Nov): Air-balloon races drawing competitors from around the world.

SPORTS: The Phoenix area is home to one major-league and two minor-league professional teams:

Baseball (Apr–Aug): Firebirds, Municipal Stadium, Phoenix (275-0500); minor league.

In addition, four major-league baseball teams have their spring-training camps in the Phoenix area (Feb–Mar): the Chicago Cubs, Ho Ho Kam Park, Mesa (964-4467); the Oakland Athletics, Phoenix Stadium, Phoenix (366-

3269): the San Francisco Giants, Scottsdale Stadium, Scottsdale (994-5123); and the Seattle Mariners, Tempe Diablo Stadium, Tempe (438-8900).

Basketball (Oct–May): Suns, Veterans Memorial Coliseum, Phoenix (263-7867).

Football (Sept–Dec): Cardinals, Sun Devil Stadium, Tempe (967-1010).

Dog Racing
Greyhound Park, 3801 E. Washington St., Phoenix (273-7181): Tues–Sun year round.

Horse Racing
Turf Paradise, 1501 W. Bell Rd., Phoenix (942-1101): Oct to mid-May.

Tubing
Arizona's most popular summer sport: floating down the rapids of the Salt River or the Verde River on well-inflated inner tubes; helmets must be worn because of the rocks. Spectacular and not really risky. More than 20,000 enthusiasts meet every weekend (mid-Apr to mid-Oct) at **Salt River Recreation, Inc.**, 33 mi. (54km) east via U.S. 60 (Apache Blvd.) and Bush Hwy.; for information, call 984-3305.

STROLLS: ☼☖ **Heritage Square**, E. Monroe St. and 7th St., Phoenix (262-5071): A group of perfectly restored 19th-century houses, including the very typical **Rosson House**, open Wed–Sun, once the luxurious home of Dr. Roland Rosson who was mayor around 1895; and the **Silva House Museum**, open Tues–Sun. The historic heart of Phoenix; shops and restaurants. Worth seeing.

☼☖ **Scottsdale**, around Scottsdale Rd. and Osborn Rd., Scottsdale: The smart suburb of Phoenix, with luxury hotels, fashionable restaurants, elegant shops, art galleries (around Fifth Ave. and Main St.), and the amazing **Borgata** at 6166 N. Scottsdale Rd. (see "Shopping," above), the last word in shopping centers.

THEME PARKS: ☼☖ **Big Surf**, 1500 N. Hayden Rd., Tempe (947-7873): 5-ft. (2m) artificial waves for surfers, in a huge lagoon-pool. Spectacular; open Tues–Sun Mar–Sept.

☼☖ **Rawhide**, 23023 N. Scottsdale Rd., Scottsdale (563-5111): Reconstruction of a Far West village; shops, restaurants, rodeos, stagecoach rides, mock-gunfire. Entertaining; if you love western movies, this is for you. Open daily from 5pm.

ZOOS: ☖ **Phoenix Zoo**, 5810 Van Buren St., Papago Park, Phoenix (273-7771): Modern, comprehensive zoo with some 1,200 animals in reconstructions of their natural habitats, including a herd of very rare Arabian oryx. Pretty scenery; mini-train for visitors. A positive must-see; open daily.

ACCOMMODATIONS
A Note on Accommodations: Room rates in Phoenix are coded as follows: **VE**, Very Expensive ($140 and up); **E**, Expensive ($90–$140); **M**, Moderate ($60–$90); **I**, Inexpensive ($30–$60); **B**, Budget (up to $30). A listing of toll free numbers is in the Appendix.

Personal Favorites (in order of preference)
☼☖☖☖☖☖ **Arizona Biltmore** (nr. dwntwn), 24th St. and Missouri St., Phoenix, AZ 85016 (602/955-6600; toll free, see Westin). 502 rms, A/C, color TV, in-rm movies. AE, CB, DC, MC, V. Free parking, three pools, health club, sauna, two golf courses, 18 tennis courts, putting green, bicycles, two rests. (including L'Orangerie), two bars, open-air buffet, rm svce, disco, boutiques, hrdrsr, concierge, free crib. *Note:* This luxurious grand hotel designed by Frank Lloyd Wright in a blend of art deco and traditional regional styles has been one of the glories of American hotelkeeping for more than half a

century. Long favored by Hollywood stars and famous politicians, the Biltmore is among the dozen finest hotels in the country. Its superb grdns blazing w. flowers and planted w. palm trees and cactus, pools, tennis courts, and two golf courses are all a fitting complement to the spacious, elegant rms (some w. private balconies or patios), faultless svce, and excellent food. VIP and big business clientele. Rates are more affordable in summer. 15 min. from dwntwn. A memorable place to stay. **VE,** but lower rates off-season.

☀☀ **The Pointe at Squaw Peak** (vic.), 7677 N. 16th St., Phoenix, AZ 85020 (602/997-2626; toll free 800/528-0428). 576 suites and villas, A/C, color TV, in-rm movies. AE, CB, DC, MC, V. Free parking, seven pools, health club, sauna, eight tennis courts, squash, putting green, four rests. (including Beside the Pointe), two bars, rm svce, disco, cinema (on wknds), hrdrsr, concierge, crib $10. *Note:* Luxury hotel-village in a lovely natural setting. The Spanish Colonial design, w. shaded patios and fountains, comes off beautifully. Spacious suites or individual cottages w. minibars and private balconies. Unusually high level of comfort and physical-fitness facilities. Praiseworthy panoramic rest. Very good svce. Tourist and convention clientele. A hotel of great quality surrounded by 280 acres (113ha) of unspoiled land and beautiful grdns. 20 min. from dwntwn. **VE,** but lower rates off-season.

☀☀ **Clarion Inn at McCormick Ranch** (vic.), 7401 N. Scottsdale Rd., Scottsdale, AZ 85253 (602/948-5050; toll free, see Clarion). 125 rms and 51 villas, A/C, color TV, in-rm movies. AE, CB, DC, MC, V. Free parking, pool, sauna, two golf courses, four tennis courts, horseback riding, boats, windsurfing, rest. (Piñon Grill), bar, rm svce, disco, concierge, crib $10. *Note:* Luxury motel on Camelback Lake. Very comfortable rms or individual villas w. private balconies and refrigerators. Decorated Castilian style. Splendid mountain view; attentive svce; comprehensive physical-fitness facilities and many outdoor activities, including hikes into the surrounding desert. Regular clientele. Very interesting summer discounts; a fine place to stay. **VE,** but lower rates off-season.

Hyatt Regency (dwntwn), 122 N. 2nd St., Phoenix, AZ 85004 (602/252-1234; toll free, see Hyatt). 711 rms, A/C, color TV, in-rm movies. AE, CB, DC, MC, V. Valet gar. $7, pool, health club, two rests. (one revolving, on the top floor), bar, rm svce, nightclub, boutiques, concierge, free crib. *Note:* Modern, imposing 24-story glass-and-concrete building in the heart of Phoenix. Inviting, well-designed rms, some w. balconies; so-so rest. (Compass). Business and group clientele. Efficient svce; all the Hyatt comfort and glitter; excellent location a stone's throw from the Convention Center. Good value on balance. **E–VE,** but lower rates off-season.

Sunburst Resort Hotel (vic.), 4925 N. Scottsdale Rd., Scottsdale, AZ 85251 (602/945-7666; toll free 800/854-2608). 212 rms, A/C, color TV, in-rm movies. AE, CB, DC, MC, V. Free parking, pool, eight tennis courts, putting green, rest. (Desert Rose), bar, rm svce, disco, concierge, crib $5. *Note:* Inviting, comfortable vacation complex in a huge grdn. Rustic colonial decor. Spacious rms w. refrigerators and private balconies or patios. Attentive svce. 5 min. from the luxury Fifth Ave. stores. Group and convention clientele. Good overall value. **E,** but lower rates off-season.

Fountain Suite Hotel (vic.), 2577 W. Greenway Rd., Phoenix, AZ 85023 (602/375-1777; toll free 800/527-7715). 316 rms, A/C, color TV, in-rm movies. AE, CB, DC, MC, V. Free parking, pool, health club, sauna, two tennis courts, squash, putting green, rest. (Hemingway's), bar, rm svce, disco, concierge. *Note:* Modern, very attractive hotel in the heart of "High Tech Corridor" (Black Canyon Fwy.). Spectacular lobby w. elegant colonnade, fountains, and octagonal vault. Spacious suites w. minibar, TV w. remote control, and electronic door locks. Efficient svce; very comprehensive facilities. Business clientele. 20 min. from dwntwn along I-17. Good value. **E,** but lower rates off-season.

Quality Inn Desert Sky (nr. dwntwn), 3541 E. Van Buren St., Phoenix, AZ 85008 (602/273-7121; toll free, see Quality

Inns). 90 rms, A/C, color TV, in-rm movies. AE, CB, DC, MC, V. Free parking, pool, rest., bar, rm svce, free crib. *Note:* Comfortable, well-run small motel very nr. the airport; inviting grdn and pool. Friendly svce; very good overall value. Package-tour and group clientele. 5 min. from dwntwn. **I,** but lower rates off-season.

Motel 6 Central (nr. dwntwn), 2323 E. Van Buren St., Phoenix, AZ 85006 (602/267-7511). 245 rms, A/C, color TV, in-rm movies. AE, DC, MC, V. Free parking, pool, rest. *Note:* Unbeatable value halfway between dwntwn and the airport. Functionally comfortable rms; excellent location 5 min. from dwntwn. Ideal if you're driving. **B**

Other Accommodations (from top bracket to budget)

Hyatt Regency Scottsdale at Gainey Ranch (vic.), 7500 E. Doubletree Ranch Rd., Scottsdale, AZ 85258 (602/991-3388; toll free, see Hyatt). 475 rms or suites and 13 individual villas, A/C, color TV, in-rm movies. AE, CB, DC, MC, V. Free valet parking, 10 pools, health club, sauna, two golf courses, nine tennis courts, putting green, boating, bicycling, two rests. (including the Golden Swan), coffee shop, three bars, 24-hr. rm svce, nightclub, concierge, free crib. *Note:* New ultra-luxurious resort complex on a little lake w. private beach, three-story water slide, and Venetian gondolas. Elegant Mediterranean-style buildings and spectacular lobby w. three-story-high modern sculpture. Spacious suites w. minibars and private balconies; individual villas w. two or four bedrooms. Very comprehensive sports facilities; excellent svce. 640 acres (256ha) of lawns and lush tropical grdns w. dozens of fountains, waterfalls, and 300 palm trees. Tourist and big business clientele. **VE,** but lower rates off-season.

Marriott's Camelback Inn (vic.), 5402 E. Lincoln Dr., Scottsdale, AZ 85252 (602/948-1700; toll free, see Marriott). 423 rms, A/C, color TV, in-rm movies. AE, CB, DC, MC, V. Free parking, three pools, health club, health spa, three golf courses, 10 tennis courts, horseback riding, putting green, three rests. (including Chaparral), three bars, 24-hr. rm svce, nightclub, hrdrsr, concierge, free crib. *Note:* A vacationers' paradise: little two-story cottages scattered through 125 acres (50ha) of splendid grdns w. the mountains as a backdrop. Almost as luxurious as the Arizona Biltmore, but less smart and—even more important—less stuffy. Spacious rms w. minibars and private patios or balconies (some w. kitchenettes and fireplaces); polished svce; food as indifferent as all Marriotts. Worthwhile vacation packages. Comprehensive physical-fitness facilities. Clientele of rich tourists. A real oasis in the desert, 20 min. from dwntwn. **VE,** but lower rates off-season.

The Wigwam (vic.), Indian School Rd. and Litchfield Rd., Litchfield Park, AZ 85340 (602/935-3811; toll free, see Preferred). 266 rms, A/C, color TV, in-rm movies. AE, CB, DC, MC, V. Free parking, pool, health club, saunas, three golf courses, eight tennis courts, horseback riding, trapshooting, three rests. (including the Terrace Dining Rm), bar, rm svce, disco, free crib. *Note:* Superb country club in a class w. the Arizona Biltmore, occupying 75 acres (30ha) of very lovely grdns in the middle of the desert. Inviting, comfortable rms w. refrigerators and private patios, some w. fireplaces, in little adobe-style cottages. Efficient svce. Group and convention clientele. Interesting golf and tennis packages. Resv. essential, very far ahead. Recently underwent an $18-million renovation. **VE** (American Plan), but lower rates off-season.

Doubletree Suites Gateway Center (nr. dwntwn), 320 N. 44th at Van Buren, Phoenix, AZ 85008 (602/225-0500; toll free 800/528-0444). 242 suites, A/C, color TV, in-rm movies. AE, CB, DC, MC, V. Free parking, pool, sauna, two tennis courts, rest. (Toffer's), bar, rm svce, nightclub, free breakfast, free crib. *Note:* New six-floor hotel very nr. the airport; suites only, huge and comfortable, w. kitchenettes and refrigerators. Central area w. glass-walled elevators. Cheerful reception and svce. Business clientele. 10 min. from dwntwn. **E,** but lower rates off-season.

♀♀♀ **Executive Park Hotel** (nr. dwntwn), 1100 N. Central Ave.,
Phoenix, AZ 85004 (602/252-2100; toll free 800/872-3932). 105 rms, A/C, color TV, in-rm movies. AE, CB, DC, MC, V. Free valet parking, pool, sauna, rest. (Scruples), bar, 24-hr. rm svce, concierge, free limo to dwntwn, free crib. *Note:* Ideal for the business traveler, in the heart of dwntwn Phoenix. A very successful venture in modern architecture, w. glassed-in exterior elevators. Huge, inviting rms w. refrigerator and private balcony (some w. panoramic view of the mountains). Highly professional svce; VIP floor. **E,** but lower rates off-season.

♀♀♀ **Sheraton Phoenix Hotel** (formerly the Hilton Adams)
(dwntwn), 111 N. Central Ave. (at Adams St.), Phoenix, AZ 85001 (602/257-1525; toll free, see Sheraton). 534 rms, A/C, color TV, in-rm movies. AE, CB, DC, MC, V. Parking $6, pool, health club, sauna, rest. (Sandpainter), coffee shop, bar, rm svce, nightclub, hrdrsr, free crib. *Note:* Modern, clean-lined 19-story tower in the heart of dwntwn, a stone's throw from the Convention Center; light, spacious rms w. refrigerators, some w. private patios. Faultless standards of comfort; good svce. Group and business clientele. **E,** but lower rates off-season.

♀♀ **Ramada Valley Ho Resort** (vic.), 6850 Main St., Scottsdale,
AZ 85251 (602/945-6321; toll free, see Ramada Inns). 289 rms, A/C, color TV, in-rm movies. AE, CB, DC, MC, V. Free parking, three pools, three tennis courts, putting green, rest. (Summerfield's), bar, rm svce, nightclub, hrdrsr, free crib. *Note:* Large, pleasant, comfortable motel nr. the smart Fifth Ave. stores in a huge tropical grdn. Comfortable, spacious rms w. private patios or balconies and refrigerators. Efficient svce; good value off-season. Group and convention clientele. 15 min. from dwntwn. **E,** but lower rates off-season.

♀♀ **Best Western Grace Inn at Ahwatukee** (nr. dwntwn), 10831
S. 51st St., Phoenix, AZ 85044 (602/893-3000; toll free, see Best Western). 160 rms, A/C, color TV, in-rm movies. AE, CB, DC, MC, V. Free parking, pool, health club, sauna, tennis court, rest. (Matthew's), bar, rm svce, disco, hrdrsr, free crib. *Note:* Admirable hotel in an elegant modern building near South Mountain Park. Faultless comfort and facilities; spacious rms w. refrigerator and private balcony. With direct access to I-10, it's very convenient if you're driving. VIP floor. 10 min. from the airport (free shuttle) and from the Arizona State U. campus. **M–E,** but lower rates off-season.

♀♀ **Holiday Inn Financial Center** (nr. dwntwn), 3600 N. Second
Ave., Phoenix, AZ 85013 (602/248-0222; toll free, see Holiday Inns). 290 rms, A/C, color TV, in-rm movies. AE, CB, DC, MC, V. Free parking, two pools, rest. (C. W. Dandy's), bar, rm svce, nightclub, free crib. *Note:* Modern 10-floor motel adj. Park Central Mall w. its 75 shops and rests. Typical Holiday Inn style; acceptable rest.; impersonal svce. Business clientele (the financial district is a block or two away). Free airport limo. **M–E,** but lower rates off-season.

♀ **Warren House East** (nr. dwntwn), 2911 E. Indian School
Rd., Phoenix, AZ 85016 (602/956-1345; toll free 800/331-7700). 64 rms, A/C, cable color TV. AE, MC, V. Free parking, pool, tennis court, adj. coffee shop, free crib. *Note:* Inviting, serviceable motel w. low rates. Comfortable rms, most w. kitchenettes and refrigerators. Friendly reception and svce. Very good value; 8 min. from dwntwn. **I**

♀ **Desert Rose** (nr. dwntwn), 3424 E. Van Buren St., Phoenix,
AZ 85008 (602/275-4421). 56 rms, A/C, color TV. AE, CB, DC, MC, V. Free parking, pool, coffee shop, rm svce, crib $4. *Note:* One of the best buys in Phoenix, 5 min. from dwntwn. Comfortable rms w. refrigerators and private balconies. Free airport limo. Ideal if you're driving. **B–I,** but lower rates off-season.

Airport Accommodations

🍷🍷 **Fiesta Inn** (nr. dwntwn), 2100 S. Priest Dr., Tempe, AZ 85282 (602/967-1441; toll free 800/528-6481). 270 rms, A/C, color TV, in-rm movies. AE, CB, DC, MC, V. Free parking, pool, health club, sauna, three tennis courts, putting green, rest., bar, rm svce, disco, concierge, free crib. *Note:* The ideal motel for a stopover between flights. Spacious, comfortable rms w. refrigerators. Good physical-fitness facilities; good rest. (The Other Place); excellent svce. Pretty, countrified decor w. original works of art. 8 min. from airport (free shuttle). Good value. **M–E,** but lower rates off-season.

Accommodations in the Vicinity

☼🍷🍷🍷 **The Boulders Resort and Club** (vic.), 34631 N. Tom Darlington Rd., Carefree, AZ 85377 (602/488-9009; toll free 800/233-7637). 120 casitas, A/C, color TV, in-rm movies. AE, CB, DC, MC, V. Free parking, two pools, health club, sauna, two golf courses, six tennis courts, putting green, horseback riding, three rests. (including Latilla Dining Rm), bar, rm svce, disco, crib $3. *Note:* One of the most imaginative hotel buildings in the West. Built in the open desert at the foot of a huge rockfall, the adobe-style casitas (individual villas) blend into the dun-and-ocher landscape behind them. Spacious rms decorated w. Native American motifs, all w. refrigerators, fireplaces, and private patios. Exemplary svce; rest. of quality. Jeep trips organized into the desert. Clientele of well-heeled tourists; this is the perfect vacationers' grand hotel. Closed mid-June to early Sept. 40 min. from dwntwn by Scottsdale Rd. **VE** (Modified American Plan), but lower rates off-season.

Guest Ranch

☼🍷🍷🍷 **Rancho de los Caballeros** (vic.), Vulture Mine Rd. (at U.S. 60), Wickenburg, AZ 85358 (602/684-5484). 73 rms, A/C, rental color TV. No credit cards. Free parking, pool, golf course, four tennis courts, horseback riding, trapshooting, rest., bar. *Note:* At once a luxury hotel and a true stock ranch w. cattle and real cowboys. Rustic but comfortable ambience. More than 20,000 acres (8,000ha) of desert lie open to riders, in groups or alone. Friendly reception and svce. Interesting American Plan packages. Open Oct 1 to mid-May. Resv. must be made very far in advance at this successful place. 1-hr. drive from Phoenix by U.S. 89N. A highly recommended spot. **E–VE** (American Plan), but lower rates off-season.

YMCA/Youth Hostels

Valley of the Sun International Hostel (nr. dwntwn), 1026 N. 9th St., Phoenix, AZ 85006 (602/262-9439). 40 beds. Conventional youth hostel, 5 min. from dwntwn.

YMCA–Phoenix (dwntwn), 350 N. First Ave., Phoenix, AZ 85003 (602/253-6181). Men and women. Pool, coffee shop, health club. Very central location.

RESTAURANTS

A Note on Restaurant Prices: Phoenix restaurant prices, per person, excluding drinks and service charges, are coded as follows: **VE,** Very Expensive ($60 and up); **E,** Expensive ($40–$60); **M,** Moderate ($25–$40); **I,** Inexpensive ($15–$25); **B,** Budget (up to $15).

Personal Favorites (in order of preference)

🍷🍷🍷 **Vincent Guerithault on Camelback** (nr. dwntwn), 3930 E. Camelback Rd., Phoenix (224-0225). A/C. Lunch Mon–Fri, dinner Mon–Sat; closed hols. AE, DC, MC, V. Jkt. *Specialties:* broiled oysters w. pimento, lobster baked w. Pernod w. ratatouille of young vegetables, salmon w. tomatillo-cream sauce, duck tamale w. green chiles and raisins, roast quail w. spicy jicama, fresh berries crème brûlée served in a sweet taco shell, lemon pie, sherbet. Splendid wine list. *Note:* Unquestionably the finest food in Phoenix and the surrounding area. The young, talented Vincent Guerithault, who learned his trade in France at the prestigious Oustau de Baumanière at Les Baux de Provence, serves a felicitous mix of recipes culled from his native France combined w. the ingredients and style of the American Southwest: Mexican ingredients and mesquite broiling. Also offers low-calorie dishes. Warm, rustic decor, w. exposed beams, furniture of country charm, and flowers everywhere. Excellent svce; atmosphere at once elegant and relaxing. Resv. a must. A very fine place. Valet parking. *French/American.* **M–E**

L'Orangerie (vic.), in the Arizona Biltmore (see "Accommodations," above), Phoenix (954-2507). A/C. Lunch/dinner daily. AE, CB, DC, MC, V. J&T. *Specialties:* crayfish salad, shrimp w. orange and pistachio, veal Leonardo, lamb w. mint and spinach, duckling w. raspberry sauce, pepper steak Mandalay, game (in season). Good desserts. Remarkable wine list (380 labels). *Note:* The luxury-hotel rest. at its splendid best, crystal chandeliers and all. Classic cuisine in the grand style, rather pompous (salmon Wellington, sauteed chicken w. madeira). Very polished svce in a setting from the hand of Frank Lloyd Wright. Agreeable background music. Resv. advised. *Continental.* **E**

The Other Place (vic.), 7101 E. Lincoln Dr., Paradise Valley (948-7910). A/C. Lunch Mon–Fri, dinner nightly. AE, CB, DC, MC, V. *Specialties:* gazpacho; southern fried chicken w. chorizo, cilantro, and pine nuts; steak; roast beef; catch of the day; carrot cake. *Note:* One of the prettiest Mexican hacienda settings in the city; good, varied, tasty food. Rather noisy background music. Locally popular; no resv. Other locations: 1666 S. Dobson Rd., Mesa (831-8877); 2100 S. Priest Dr. at the Fiesta Inn, Tempe (967-8721). *American/Mexican.* **I–M**

Jean Claude's Petit Café (vic.), 7340 E. Shoeman Lane, Scottsdale (947-5288). A/C. Lunch Mon–Fri, dinner Mon–Sat; closed hols. AE, CB, DC, MC, V. Jkt. *Specialties:* roast duckling w. peaches, broiled salmon w. tarragon sauce, chocolate soufflé. Menu changes regularly. Wine list limited but well balanced. *Note:* If you love modern, imaginative French cuisine, the excellent chef Jean Claude Poncet has made this the place for you. Charming Parisian-bistro decor; cheerful svce; congenial, romantic atmosphere. Resv. strongly advised. *French.* **I–M**

The Stockyards (nr. dwntwn), 5001 E. Washington St., Phoenix (273-7378). A/C. Lunch Mon–Fri, dinner nightly; closed Dec 25 and Sun June–Oct. AE, DC, MC, V. *Specialties:* oysters on the half shell, "Rocky Mountain oysters," excellent meats of all kinds, steak, T-bone, prime ribs. Unimpressive desserts and wine list. *Note:* For almost 50 years this steakhouse has been serving prime beef cuts, broiled to perfection, at reasonable prices. Wonderful turn-of-the-century-style decor. The bar is worth a visit all by itself. Efficient svce. Other location: 5010 E. Shea Blvd., Scottsdale (998-1141). *Steak.* **I**

Shogun (vic), 12615 N. Tatum Blvd., Scottsdale (953-3264). A/C. Lunch Mon–Fri, dinner nightly; closed hols. AE, MC, V. *Specialties:* sushi, tempura, sukiyaki, karage chicken. *Note:* The best Japanese rest. in the valley. Modern and elegant interior. Terrific sushi bar w. its two skilled craftsmen carving raw fish. Portions tend to be small, Japanese style. Outstanding service. Resv. suggested. *Japanese.* **I**

Caf Casino (nr. dwntwn), 1312 N. Scottsdale Rd., Scottsdale (947-1987). A/C. Breakfast/lunch/dinner daily; closed Dec 25. MC, V. *Specialties:* quiche Lorraine, boeuf bourguignon, daily specials. *Note:* French-style cafeteria w. a sidewalk-café atmosphere, substantial, praiseworthy French-inspired food. Excellent homemade pastry; very good svce; remarkable value. Wine and beer only. Other location: 4842 N. 24th St. at Camelback Rd., Phoenix (955-3430). *French/Continental.* **B**

Garcia's Del Este Restaurant (vic.), 7633 E. Indian School Rd., Scottsdale (945-1647). A/C. Lunch/dinner daily; closed

Easter, Thanksgiving, Dec 25. AE, MC, V. *Specialties:* soup w. meatballs, pollo fundido, chimichangas, quesadillas, fajitas. Excellent margaritas. *Note:* One of the lowest-priced and most authentic Mexican rests. in the region. Colorful setting and atmosphere; mariachi band evenings. Pleasant patio dining at lunch. Friendly, relaxed svce. No resv.; locally popular; generally crowded. Other locations: 3301 W. Peoria Ave., Phoenix (866-1850); 1604 E. Southern Ave., Tempe (820-0400). *Mexican/American.* **B-I**

Other Restaurants (from top bracket to budget)

Etienne's Different Pointe of View (nr. dwntwn), The Pointe at Tapatio Cliffs Hotel, 11111 N. 7th St., Phoenix (866-7500). A/C. Dinner nightly, brunch Sun; closed Sun June–Aug. AE, CB, DC, MC, V. Jkt. *Specialties:* poached salmon w. dill, filet mignon capella, rack of lamb w. herbs, game (in season), duck à l'orange, crêpes Suzette. Wholly remarkable wine list. *Note:* Formal classic French-inspired cuisine, executed w. great success. Very handsome hi-tech setting and fabulous panoramic view of Phoenix and the Valley of the Sun at sunset (ask for a table nr. the picture window). Svce of a high order. Free shuttle (a Cadillac) from the hotel's parking lot at the foot of the hill. One of the best rests. in Phoenix. Resv. a must. Valet parking. *French/Continental.* **E**

Christopher's (vic.), 2398 E. Camelback Rd., Phoenix (957-3214). A/C. Dinner only, nightly; closed hols. AE, CB, DC, MC, V. Jkt. *Specialties:* Sea-bean soup w. scallops and zucchini blossoms, confit of duck w. turnips and lavender honey, gratin of veal w. walnut sauce, chocolate tower. Excellent wine list. *Note:* Former chef de cuisine of Phoenix's illustrious Vincent Guerithault Restaurant, Cris Gross was recently named one of the ten best chefs in the U.S.; his cuisine is a miracle of contemporary delicacy and imagination. Small but elegent setting, rich w. brocade and Limoges china. Ultra-polished svce; formal atmosphere. Resv. essential. *French/American.* **E-VE**

8700 at the Citadel (vic.), 8700 E. Pinnacle Peak Rd., Scottsdale (994-8700). A/C. Dinner only, daily; closed hols. and Sun–Mon June–Aug. AE, CB, DC, MC, V. Jkt. *Specialties:* pumpkin soup, smoked duck w. jalapeño pasta, pheasant sausage w. corn cake, linguine w. green-chile pesto and sea scallops, rack of lamb w. Mendocino mustard and roasted pistachios, filet of salmon w. grilled poblano peppers, mesquite-grilled cabrito (baby goat) w. adobo and smoked-chile chipotle, sumptuous homemade desserts. Large list of European and American wines. *Note:* The area's finest southwestern rest., where the standbys are green chile, blue corn, pine nuts, and dishes broiled over mesquite wood. Charming Santa Fe–rustic decor and a wonderful view out over the valley at sunset from the second-floor bar. Open-air dining in a pleasant patio. Courteous, efficient svce. Resv. highly advisable. Well worth the 25-min. drive from dwntwn. Valet parking. *American.* **M-E**

La Chaumière (vic.), 6910 Main St., Scottsdale (946-5115). A/C. Dinner only, Mon–Sat; closed hols. and mid-July to mid-Aug. AE, DC, MC, V. Jkt. *Specialties:* poached salmon, chicken Cynthia, veal normande, bouillabaisse, duck in green-peppercorn sauce, rack of lamb, chocolate mousse. Good wine list. *Note:* Hidden in an orange grove, this charming country inn w. its big fireplace and vaulted ceiling serves serious French food, impeccably prepared. Stylish glass-enclosed patio. Very attentive svce; relaxed atmosphere. Resv. a must. Valet parking. *French.* **M**

Mancuso's (vic.), in the Borgata, 6166 N. Scottsdale Rd., Scottsdale (948-9988). A/C. Dinner only, nightly; closed Thanksgiving, Dec 25. AE, CB, DC, MC, V. Jkt. *Specialties:* fresh homemade pasta, cannelloni Alfredo, chicken Agnesi, sautéed frogs' legs, duck à l'orange, sole Oscar, tournedos béarnaise. Good list of European and domestic wines. *Note:* Slightly theatrical decor in the style of a Renaissance château, but the mostly

French and Italian food is of great quality. Exemplary svce. In the heart of the Borgata shopping center; heavily patronized by locals. Resv. advised; valet parking. *Italian/Continental.* **M**

☀☏♈ **El Chorro Lodge** (vic.), 5550 E. Lincoln Dr., Scottsdale (948-5170). A/C. Breakfast/lunch/dinner daily; closed June-Sept. AE, CB, DC, MC, V. Jkt. *Specialties:* chicken livers, chateaubriand, rack of lamb, deep-fried lobster, good desserts (cinnamon "sticky buns"). *Note:* One of the handsomest western settings in Arizona, w. an enchanting patio for open-air dining. The cuisine is particularly polished, the svce impeccable, and the decor countrified elegant w. wood beams and fireplaces. A Phoenix landmark since 1937. Resv. a must; valet parking evenings. *Continental/American.* **M**

♈♈ **Tomaso's** (nr. dwntwn), 3225 E. Camelback Rd., Phoenix (956-0836). A/C. Lunch Mon–Fri, dinner nightly; closed hols. AE, CB, DC, MC, V. *Specialties:* pasta w. beans, caponata (marinated eggplant w. capers), insalata caprese, seafood pasta, chicken cacciatore, veal scaloppine milanese, braciolone (Sicilian rolled beef), bouillabaisse, apple-and-walnut cheesecake. Good list of Italian wines. *Note:* Tomaso Maggiore, energetic proprietor of the rests. Chianti and When in Naples, opened Tomaso's in 1981, and since then it has established itself as one of the best places in Phoenix for lovers of true Italian food. There is no praise too high for the fresh homemade pasta. Warm Mediterranean setting; friendly, attentive svce. Resv. strongly advised. Other location: 610 E. Bell Rd., Phoenix (866-1906). *Italian.* **I–M**

☀☏ **Golden Belle** (vic.), in Rawhide, 23023 N. Scottsdale Rd., Scottsdale (563-5111). A/C. Dinner nightly, brunch Sat–Sun. AE, MC, V. *Specialties:* broiled steak and chicken, roast beef, barbecued meats, fried rattlesnake. *Note:* Re-creation of a 19th-century saloon w. superb walnut bar. The meats are choice, and the cowboy atmosphere as real as can be. An entertaining place, and ideal for a quick dinner between two mock bandit attacks on a stagecoach at the picturesque western village of Rawhide (see "Theme Parks," above). Live country and western, just as it should be. 30 min. from dwntwn. *American/Steak.* **I**

☀☏ **Monti's La Casa Vieja** (vic.), 3 W. 1st St. at Mill Ave., Tempe (967-7594). A/C. Lunch/dinner daily; closed Jan 1, Dec 25. AE, CB, DC, MC, V. *Specialties:* steak, T-bone, fried half chicken, Maine lobster. *Note:* A real local landmark which prides itself on being the oldest rest. in town (1871). If you like good steak, it's also one of the best values in town. Pretty Spanish Colonial decor; good svce; no resv. Locally very popular. *Steak.* **I**

☀☏ **Depot Cantina** (vic.), 300 S. Ash Ave., Tempe (966-6677). A/C. Lunch/dinner daily. AE, MC, V. *Specialties:* fajitas, carnitas, pollo mole negro (chicken in black-chocolate sauce), menudo (tripe), tamales, chile relleño, steak ranchero. *Note:* This colorful establishment in Tempe's historic Old Town train depot offers generous helpings of all the standard Mexican dishes, flawlessly prepared. Considerate svce in a kitsch setting. Resv. advised. An excellent place, 15 min. from dwntwn and almost on the Arizona State U. campus. *Mexican.* **I**

☀☏ **Pinnacle's Peak Patio** (vic.), 10426 Pinnacle Peak Rd., Scottsdale (563-5133). A/C. Dinner nightly, brunch Sun; closed Thanksgiving, Dec 24–25. AE, MC, V. *Specialties:* charcoal-broiled T-bone steak (1 lb./450g) and porterhouse steak (2 lb./900g), chateaubriand, hamburger, broiled chicken. *Note:* Enormous (seats 2,000) western-style steakhouse w. the McDowell Mountains in the background. The view of the valley at sunset is worth the trip all by itself, but so are the enormous servings of prime beef. Relaxed svce; country music and dancing. Mock gunfights. Very touristic atmosphere; no resv.; don't wear a tie! *Steak.* **B–I**

♈ **The Quilted Bear** (vic.), 6316 N. Scottsdale Rd., Scottsdale (948-7760). A/C. Breakfast/lunch/dinner daily; closed Dec 25. AE, CB, DC, MC, V. *Specialties:* homemade soups, gazpacho, salads, sandwiches, steak, roast beef, catch of the day, fried chicken. *Note:* Rest.-cafeteria w.

comfortable, picturesque atmosphere. Colorful decor w. stained glass and a profusion of greenery. Excellent family-style cuisine and the best salad bar in the valley. Locally popular. *American.* **B–I**

Cafeterias/Fast Food
Lunt Avenue Marble Club (vic.), 2207 W. Peoria Ave., Phoenix (863-9791). Quiches, sandwiches, pizza, crêpes at moderate prices, and the best hamburgers in town. Inviting decor. Open daily. Other locations: 2 E. Camelback Rd., Phoenix (265-8997); 6202 N. Scottsdale Rd., Scottsdale (998-3505).
Miracle Mile Deli (dwntwn), Park Central Mall, 3121 N. Third Ave., Phoenix (277-4783). Breakfast/lunch/dinner daily. Outstanding New York–style deli: overstuffed sandwiches, homemade soups and desserts, and an impressive salad bar. The best corned beef in town. Other locations: 70th and Camelback Rd., Scottsdale (945-9966).

BARS & NIGHTCLUBS
Like other major cities, Phoenix has a magic phone number, the **Jazz Hotline** (254-4545), giving programs for all the jazz clubs.
Chuy's (vic.), 410 S. Mill Ave., Tempe (968-5568). The best modern-jazz club in town (but also blues and reggae); college crowd. Open nightly.
Oscar Taylor (nr. dwntwn), 2420 E. Camelback Rd., Phoenix (956-5705). Singles bar got up like a Chicago speakeasy during Prohibition. Lots of action. Also an acceptable rest. Open nightly.
The Other Place (vic.), 7101 E. Lincoln Dr., Paradise Valley (948-7910). Live jazz; also a very good rest. (see above). Open nightly.
Rustler's Rooste (nr. dwntwn), The Pointe at South Mountain, 7777 S. Pointe Pkwy., Phoenix (231-9111). Very good live country music; dancing. Also an acceptable western rest. with a wonderful view of the city. Open nightly.
Seeker's Comedy Nite Club (vic.), 4519 N. Scottsdale Rd., Scottsdale (949-1100). Locally popular comedy club; the biggest names. Open nightly.
Timothy's (nr. dwntwn), 6335 N. 16th St., Phoenix (277-7634). Excellent live modern jazz; also praiseworthy seafood rest. Locally popular. Open daily.
Toolie's Country (nr. dwntwn), 43rd Ave. and Thomas Rd., Phoenix (272-3100). Western saloon and dance hall featuring live country music 7 nights a week, with an array of top-name entertainers. Voted the "Friendliest Club in Arizona."
What's Your Beef (vic.), 8111 E. McDonald Dr., Scottsdale (998-1987). Popular nightspot attracting a youngish crowd. Contemporary live music and Top-40 hits nightly.
Zazoo (nr. dwntwn), 909 E. Camelback Rd., Phoenix (241-0999). The favorite disco of the local yuppies; jacket required. Open nightly.

NEARBY EXCURSIONS

ARCOSANTI (65 mi./104km north on I-17 to the Cordes Junction exit) (632-7135): A prototype of the city of the future, under construction since 1970; this first attempt at a synthesis of architecture and ecology has been dubbed "arcology." It's the work of visionary Italian architect Paolo Soleri, with the help of many students and young volunteers; the desert megalopolis, still largely in embryo, displays strange, rounded shapes which are worth going out to see. Workshop open to visitors daily. See also the Cosanti Foundation, below.

CASA GRANDE RUINS NATIONAL MONUMENT (52 mi./84km SE via U.S. 60E and Ariz. 87S) (723-3172): One of the most amazing monuments of Native American civilization in the U.S. Built around 1350 by the Hohokam peoples (the word means "those who have disappeared"), the imposing structure, four stories high and with walls 4 ft.

11in. (1.5m) thick at the base, bears obvious resemblances to the ruins at Zacatecas in Mexico; it still constitutes a riddle for archeologists. Was it an official residence, a temple, an astronomical observatory, or a watchtower looking out over the valley? No one knows. The Hohokam, a race of remarkable builders and near relatives of the Anasazi and Pueblo peoples, left their mark on the valleys of the Gila River and Salt River from 300 B.C. to A.D. 1400, when they mysteriously disappeared; in particular, they built dozens of miles of irrigation canals, 6 ft. 6 in. (2m) wide and 3 ft. 3 in. (1m) deep, to water their crops of beans, corn, squash, and cotton. The **Casa Grande** ("Big House," in Spanish) was so named by Fr. Eusebio Kino, the Jesuit missionary who explored southern Arizona in the 1690s. Built of caliche, a composition of clay gravel and calcium carbonate, Casa Grande has been protected since 1932 by a metal roof, not aesthetically appropriate but essential because caliche crumbles easily. Archeological museum. Open daily.

COSANTI FOUNDATION (6433 Doubletree Rd., Scottsdale) (948-6145): Workshop of the famous Italian architect Paolo Soleri, a pupil of Frank Lloyd Wright and the creator of Arcosanti (see above), the "city of the future" rising north of Phoenix. Exhibition of futurist urban projects, including a model of Arcosanti, and windbells by Paolo Soleri. Fascinating. Open daily.

FOUNTAIN HILLS (26 mi./42km NE via Scottsdale Rd. and E. Shea Blvd.) (837-1654): The world's largest fountain, leaping 560 ft. (170m) from the middle of a little lake. The column of water weighs 8 tons.

GILA RIVER INDIAN ARTS & CRAFTS CENTER (30 mi./48km south along I-10 to Exit 175 at Casablanca Rd.) (963-3981): Replicas of Native American villages tracing the history of the Hohokam, Pima, Maricopa, and Apache tribes. Museum; handcrafts center. Should be combined with the trip to Casa Grande Ruins National Monument (see above).

SUN CITY (14 mi./22km NW on Grand Ave., U.S. 60): Model community for well-to-do retirees, opened in the early '60s. **Sun City West,** another equally luxurious residential development, is under construction 2½ mi. (4km) west.

TALIESIN WEST (108th St. north of E. Shea Blvd., Scottsdale) (860-2700): Winter home and studio of the most famous American architect of the 20th century, Frank Lloyd Wright. The stone, glass, and steel buildings, modern and austere, contrast vividly with the surrounding desert; they house Wright's school of architecture, operated since his death in 1959 by the Taliesin Foundation. The buildings are a designated historic monument. Open daily except holidays and when it rains.

FARTHER AFIELD

APACHE TRAIL (168 mi./268km r.t. via Ariz. 88E and U.S. 60W): The old trail of Cochise and Geronimo, through wonderful desert-mountain scenery in violently contrasting colors. Your first stop is at **Tortilla Flat,** an old gold-prospectors' camp (population: 6) in the heart of the **Superstition Mountains,** complete with saloon, hotel, restaurant, and post office; open daily year round (984-1776). Then drive along picturesque **Apache Lake,** a perch-fisherman's paradise, as far as the imposing **Roosevelt Lake,** formed by the construction in 1910 of **Roosevelt Dam,** one of the largest dams in the world made entirely of hand-cut stone. Fishing, boat rentals. Very close is ☀⚐ **Tonto National Monument,** in the midst of a 1,100-acre (450ha) park covered in giant cactus. Clinging to the rock vault above the visitor center (467-2241; open daily) are two very fine Native American cave dwellings, each with a score of rooms, which can be reached with relative ease; dating from the 14th century, they are the work of the Salado people, cousins of the famous Anasazi.

Then on to ☀⚐ **Globe,** once famous for its silver and copper mines. See the ☀ **Besh-Ba-Gowah Indian Ruins** on Jesse Hayes Rd., site of a huge cave dwelling inhabited by the Salado peoples between A.D. 1225 and 1400, with more than 200 rooms. Archeological excavations under way.

At **Inspiration,** 3 mi. (5km) west of Globe on U.S. 60, see also the immense open-pit copper mine of the **Consolidated Copper Co.,** open Mon–Fri.

At **Superior,** 17 mi. (27km) farther west, don't fail to visit the ☀⚐ **Boyce Thompson Southwestern Arboretum** on U.S. 60 (689-2811), open daily, a beautiful 39-acre (16ha) botanic grdn with more than 10,000 species of desert plants from around the world, meticulously labeled; a must-see.

On the return trip, make a small detour between Florence Junction and Apache Junction, turning left off U.S. 60 to ⚐ **Kings Ranch,** an authentic 19th-century Far Western village where movies are often made.

In **Mesa,** is our last stop: ⚐ **Champlin Fighter Museum,** Falcon Field, 4636 Fighter Aces Dr., Mesa (830-4540), open daily. Here you'll find some 30 pursuit planes from World Wars I and II, splendidly restored, as well as souvenirs of U.S. fighter aces. A must for aviation buffs.

The trip is ideal for nature lovers, but take note that part of the road from Tortilla Flat to Roosevelt Lake is unsurfaced, and treacherous in wet weather. Allow 1–2 days.

Where to Stay En Route

NEAR GLOBE   The **Best Western Copper Hills Inn,** U.S. 60, Miami, AZ 85539 (602/425-7151). 68 rms. Conventional but very well run motel. **I–M**

☀⚐⚐⚐⚐ **GRAND CANYON NATIONAL PARK** (218 mi./350km NW via I-17 and U.S. 180): One of the seven wonders of the world; see Chapter 41 on the Grand Canyon. 4½-hr. drive from Phoenix.

⚐⚐ **MOGOLLON RIM** (239 mi./382km r.t. via Ariz. 87N, Ariz. 260E, Old Rim Rd. West, and Ariz. 87S): Leave Phoenix by McDowell Rd. and Ariz. 87N. Wonderful scenery of wooded mountains, stretches of desert, lakes, and wild canyons as you cross ☀ **Tonto National Forest.**

Your first stop will be at ☀⚐ **Payson,** an old gold-prospectors' town now known for its rustic cowtown heritage and its many festivals: the Festival of Country Music at the end of June; the Sawdust Festival, a national lumbermen's contest, at the end of July; a giant rodeo in mid-Aug; and the Old-Time Fiddlers' Festival of folk music at the end of Sept. For schedules, call 602/474-4515. Local color guaranteed.

Near the little tourist resort of Kohl's Ranch, 17 mi. (27km) east on Ariz. 260, visit ☀⚐ **Zane Grey's Cabin** (602/478-4243), open daily year round, a little mountain lodge where the famous author of westerns wrote some of his bestsellers, including *To the Last Man.*

After another 10 miles on Ariz. 260, turn left on Old Rim Rd. toward the enchanting ☀ **Woods Canyon Lake, Bear Canyon Lake,** and **Knoll Lake.** This picturesque little mountain road (to be avoided in winter or bad weather) snakes along the ridges of Tonto National Forest before rejoining Ariz. 87 a little north of **Strawberry,** a hill resort much appreciated by inhabitants of Phoenix seeking relief from the city's midsummer heat. Following Ariz. 87 about 5 mi. (8km) south of the Mormon village of **Pine,** take a look at the ☀ **Tonto Natural Bridge,** the world's largest natural arch of travertine limestone; 400 ft. (121m) across, it rises 183 ft. (55m) above the waters of Pine Creek, a tributary of the Verde River.

Return to Phoenix, 100 mi. (163km) south, on Ariz. 87. This 2- or 3-day trip is particularly recommended for lovers of wide-open spaces and woodland hikes.

Where to Stay En Route

IN PAYSON   The **Best Western Paysonglo Lodge,** 1005 S. Beeline Hwy., Payson, AZ 85541 (602/474-2382). 28 rms. Small, very comfortable motel, the ideal base for a number of excursions into Tonto National Forest. **I–M**

NAVAJOLAND (Canyon de Chelly, Monument Valley, etc.; about 250 mi./400km NE via I-17, U.S. 89, and U.S. 160): The land of the Hopi and Navajo; see Chapter 40 on Navajoland.

OAK CREEK CANYON (322 mi./515km r.t. via I-17N, Ariz. 69N, U.S. Alt. 89N, Ariz. 179S, and I-17S): First stop is **Arcosanti,** the futurist city of architect Paolo Soleri (see "Nearby Excursions," above). Then follow Ariz. 69 to ※🔭 **Prescott,** founded in 1864 and once capital of the Arizona Territory, which to this day retains something of a frontier-town flavor. Witness the interesting Native American material in the **Smoki Museum,** 143 N. Arizona Ave. (602/445-7615), open Tues–Sun June–Sept (by appointment the rest of the year); also the group of buildings from 1860–80 which constitutes the **Sharlot Hall Museum,** 415 W. Gurley St. (602/445-3122), open Tues–Sun, including the **Governor's Mansion, Old Fort Misery,** and the **John C. Frémont House.** Don't miss it. Prescott is also the scene every July 4 of a rodeo famous throughout the West. Lovely pinewoods around the town.

Some 30 mi. (48km) farther north, you'll come to the remarkable little mining town of ※🔭 **Jerome,** now a kind of ghost town, with little wooden houses clinging to the mountainside; its population has fallen from 15,000 in 1929 to fewer than 500 today. Many craft shops, art galleries, and restaurants; mining museum on Main St., open daily. **Jerome State Historic Park** on U.S. 89A (602/634-5381), open daily, traces the history of Jimmy "Rawhide" Douglas, the picturesque founder of the United Verde Mine. You shouldn't miss Jerome.

Continue north on U.S. Alt. 89 to **Cottonwood,** a tourist resort in the Verde Valley, where you'll be very near ※ **Tuzigoot National Monument,** the ruins of a 12th-century Native American pueblo with no fewer than 92 enormous rooms. Archeological museum, on Broadway (602/634-5564). Open daily. Worth the side trip.

Your next stop, the charming ※🔭 **Sedona,** once a pioneer town, is now a renowned resort with a flourishing artists' colony; painter Max Ernst lived here from 1945 to 1953. Stroll through the streets of **Tlaquepaque,** the business district with its original Mexican houses.

From Sedona you can conveniently visit ※🔭 **Oak Creek Canyon,** just north of the town: a splendid rocky gorge 16 mi. (26km) long, whose walls display a range of ocher, yellow, and white hues; it's almost as spectacular as the Grand Canyon of the Colorado, and many westerns have been shot here. It's scenery you mustn't miss.

Leaving Sedona along Ariz. 179 and I-17S, you'll come to ※🔭 **Montezuma Castle National Monument,** an extraordinary cave dwelling five floors high, perched 70 ft. (21m) above the ground in a cleft of the cliff's rock. Built by the Sinagua peoples, it dates from the 13th century, and is so remarkably preserved that it is one of the finest monuments of primitive culture in the U.S. Although you're not allowed inside, you shouldn't miss it. Visitor center open daily; for information, call 602/567-3322.

On the way back to Phoenix, stop at the ※🔭 **Fort Verde State Historic Park,** 2 mi. (3km) east of Camp Verde. This 1870s cavalry fort on U.S. 279 (602/567-

3275), open daily, was the U.S. Army's principal base for its many operations against the Apache tribe; it has now been splendidly restored, and is worth the side trip.

This very full 3- to 4-day journey would be worth the trip to Arizona all by itself, but you can combine it conveniently with a visit to the Grand Canyon (see Chapter 41) or to Navajoland (see Chapter 40).

Where to Stay En Route

IN PRESCOTT The ☀ ▥ **Hassayampa Inn,** 122 E. Gurley St., Prescott, AZ 86301 (602/778-9434). 67 rms. Charming old hotel going back to the 1920s; pleasant and comfortable. Highly thought-of rest. **M–E**

    Sierra Inn, 809 White Spar Rd., Prescott, AZ 86301 (602/445-1250). 49 rms. Inviting, comfortable motel, open year round. **I–M**

    Motel 6, 1111 E. Sheldon St., Prescott, AZ 86301 (602/776-0160). Small, well-run low-priced motel; this place is ideal for budget travelers. **B**

IN SEDONA ☀ ▥ **Los Abrigados,** 160 Portal Lane, Sedona, AZ 86336 (602/282-1777). 183 suites. Luxurious Spanish Colonial–style tourist complex; lovely grdns. **E–VE**

    Poco Diablo Resort, Ariz. 179, Sedona, AZ 86336 (602/282-7333). 144 rms. Charming little vacation hotel w. very comfortable individual villas standing in a grdn. **M–E**

    Sky Ranch Lodge, Airport Rd., Sedona, AZ 86336 (602/282-6400). 78 rms. Conventional but inviting motel overlooking Oak Creek Canyon. Good value. **I–M**

Where to Eat En Route

IN JEROME The �be **Jerome Palace,** 410 Clark St. (634-5262). Lunch/dinner Fri–Sun only. Picturesque little Victorian-style rest. **B–I**

IN SEDONA ☟☟ **L'Auberge de Sedona,** 301 Little Lane (602/282-7131). Breakfast/lunch/dinner daily. Elegant, imaginative French cuisine in a romantic setting. **I–M**

    Shugrue's, 2250 W. Ariz. 89A (602/282-2943). Breakfast/lunch/dinner daily. Attractive, contemporary decor and cuisine. **B–I**

☀▨ **PETRIFIED FOREST NATIONAL PARK** (225 mi./360km NE via Ariz. 87 and I-40): The world's largest petrified forest, with innumerable animal and vegetable fossils. At the southern entry to the park, on U.S. 180, you can visit an interesting museum explaining the process of fossilization. The nearby **Painted Desert** displays canyons, mesas, and pillars of stratified rock in a striking palette of colors. See Chapter 40 on Navajoland.

TUCSON & SOUTHERN ARIZONA (370 mi./592 km r.t. via Ariz. 87, I-10S, U.S. 80S, Ariz. 82W, Ariz. 83N, I-10N, and U.S. 89N): This spectacular tour, requiring 4 or 5 days, begins with a visit to ☀▨ **Casa Grande Ruins National Monument** (see "Nearby Excursions," above). Continuing south on I-10 you'll come to ☀▨ **Saguaro National Monument** (602/883-6366), open daily year round, a fine wildland park full of giant cactus (saguaro) growing to 50 ft. (15m), such as you might find in the Sonora Desert. Spectacular flowering in May and June.

Next stop, ☀ **Tucson.** Rearing up like a mirage from its mountains and deserts, this former capital of Arizona has experienced, since its foundation in 1775, some of the most exciting times recorded in the Far West. Belonging in turn to the Apache, the Spaniards, the Mexicans, and finally the Americans, Tucson (which the locals pronounce *"Too*-sahn") was described by 19th-century travelers as "the kingdom of crime, vice, and debauchery," or in short, "the worst hell-hole in the West." Today a favorite stopping place for tourists as well as a vigorous commercial metropolis, Tucson has an interesting museum of Native American culture, the ❋ ☖ **Arizona State Museum,** Park Ave. and University Blvd. (602/621-6302), open daily; the splendid ❋ ☖☖ **Mission San Xavier del Bac,** San Xavier Rd. (602/294-2624), open Mon–Sat, a masterpiece of Spanish Colonial baroque; one of the most beautiful zoological/botanical grdns in the country, the ☖☖ **Arizona-Sonora Desert Museum,** Kinney Rd. (602/883-1380), open daily; a remarkable museum of aviation displaying more than 130 aircraft of all periods, the ☖☖ **Pima Air Museum,** 6000 E. Valencia Rd. (602/574-9658); and ☖ **Old Tucson,** an engaging mock–Far West village built in 1939 for making western movies, at 201 S. Kinney Rd. (602/883-6457), open daily.

Between Tucson and Tombstone, 70 mi. (113km) south, make a detour to ☖ **Colossal Cave,** Colossal Cave Rd. (602/791-7677), open daily, a spectacular cavern with many marine fossils, proving that in a prehistoric era the Arizona desert was covered by the ocean.

Last stop, ❋ ☖☖ **Tombstone,** the Far West's most famous ghost town, scene of the bloody "Gunfight at the O.K. Corral." Immortalized in many westerns, Tombstone still has many buildings dating from its glory days; if you're nostalgic about the Winning of the West, here's the place to daydream. Don't miss it.

Back to Phoenix via U.S. 89, which runs from the Mexican to the Canadian border; also known as the ☖☖ **Pinal Pioneer Trail,** it's one of the most spectacular highways in the West.

For more details on the places, towns, and monuments mentioned in this itinerary, as well as for recommended accommodations and dining, see Chapter 43 on Tucson.

TUCSON 🌵🌵

□ □ □

And Southern Arizona

Rearing up like a mirage from the surrounding mountains and desert, this former capital (1867–1877) of the Arizona Territory has lived through more exciting times in its two–century life span than almost any other city in the far West. First Native American then Spanish (who built the first fort in 1776 to fend off the Apaches), then Mexican, and finally American, Tucson (pronounced "*Too*-sahn") was described in the 19th century as "the kingdom of crime, vice, and debauchery." With its dozens of dangerous saloons, dubious gaming houses, and ill-famed brothels, it was dubbed by contemporary newspapers "The Worst Hellhole in the West."

As in too many cities where the bulldozer has been allowed to run riot, Tucson has in the last three decades razed to the ground its old residential downtown, replacing it with graceless air-conditioned office buildings. But there are still interesting fragments of the city's heritage, such as the enchanting **Mission San Xavier del Bac,** called "the white dove of the desert," or **Frémont House.** And there are always wonderful things to see in southern Arizona: the giant cactus of **Saguaro National Park;** the wild landscapes of the **Chiricahua National Monument,** once the stronghold of the tribal chiefs Cochise and Geronimo; the Spanish mission at **Tumacacori;** the living museum of the **Arizona-Sonora Desert;** and the epic town of **Tombstone,** made notorious by the famous "Gunfight at the O.K. Corral."

A favorite stopping place for tourists, Tucson is also a lively business metropolis, ranking fifth among major American cities in its economic growth rate. Because of its exceptionally low humidity, it performed an odd service for the airline industry during the great world oil crisis of 1973–74; many American and European airlines lacking fuel to fly their jets parked them at Tucson airport, where they could be left without fear of rust.

Singer Linda Rondstadt was born in Tucson.

BASIC FACTS: State of Arizona. Area code: 602. Time zone: mountain. ZIP Code: 85702. Founded: 1775. Approximate population: city, 370,000; metropolitan area, 700,000.

CLIMATE: Tucson averages 318 days of clear skies every year, one of the highest figures in the U.S. The persistent sunshine results in oppressive temperatures in summer (July average, 89°F/32°C), and scarcely less so in spring and fall. However, the exceptionally dry air and the cool of the desert evening make the heat bearable. With a Dec–Jan average of 53°F (12°C), winter is a joy if you like your days brisk and sunny.

DISTANCES: Albuquerque, 441 mi. (705km); Mexican border, 65 mi. (104km); Los Angeles, 512 mi. (819km); Phoenix, 118 mi. (189km); San Antonio, 883 mi. (1,412km); San Diego, 415 mi. (664km).

ARRIVAL & TRANSIT INFORMATION

AIRPORT: Tucson International Airport (TUS), 7 mi. (11km) south (573-8000). First municipal airport opened in U.S. (1919).

AIRLINES: American (623-7571), America West (623-8917), Continental (623-3700), Northwest (622-2014), TWA (624-2771), United (622-1214), and USAir (623-3428).

CITY LINK: The **cab** fare from the airport to downtown is about $18–$22; time, 20 min. Bus: **Arizona Stagecoach** (889-9681), serves principal dwntwn hotels; fare, $8–$14; time, 25–35 min., depending on destination. Municipal bus: Sun Tran Line No. 8, until 10pm; fare, 60¢.

The rudimentary public-transportation (bus) system provided by **Sun Tran** (792-9222), the very high cab fares given the size of the city, and the many fascinating excursions into the surrounding country combine to suggest the wisdom of renting a car with unlimited mileage.

CAR RENTALS (at Tucson International Airport unless otherwise noted): Avis (294-1494); Budget (294-3436); Dollar (573-1100); Hertz (294-7616); National (294-1451); Practical Rent-a-Car, 5756 E. Speedway Blvd. (571-0099), a local renter with favorable rates; and Thrifty, 7051 S. Tucson Blvd. (889-5761). For downtown locations, consult the local telephone directory.

LIMOUSINES: Carey Limousine (toll free 800/336-4646) and Dav El Limousines (toll free 800/922-0343).

TAXIS: Cabs may not be hailed on the street, but may be summoned by phone: **ABC Cab** (623-7979), **Checker Cab** (623-1133), and **Yellow Cab** (624-6611).

TRAIN: Amtrak station, 400 E. Toole St. (toll free 800/872-7245).

INTERCITY BUSES: Greyhound, 2 S. Fourth Ave. (792-0972).

INFORMATION & TOURS

TOURIST INFORMATION: The **Tucson Convention and Visitors Bureau,** 130 S. Scott Ave., AZ 85701 (602/624-1889).

GUIDED TOURS: Gray Line Tours (bus) (622-8811): Guided bus tours of the city and surroundings; serves principal hotels.

Tucson Tour Company (bus), 180 E. Tangerine Rd. (297-2911): Guided van tours of Tucson, the Arizona-Sonora Desert Museum, and Old Tucson. Operates daily.

SIGHTS, ATTRACTIONS & ACTIVITIES

ADVENTURES: Balloon America (balloon), in the Westin La Paloma Resort, 3800 E. Sunrise (299-7744): Hot-air balloon trips over Tucson and the surrounding desert; spectacular. Free bus shuttle. Daily Oct–June.

Saguaro Whitewater (boat), 3223 E. Lee St. (326-6206). Rafting down the Salt River Canyon; 1-day trip. Spectacular. Daily Feb–Sept.

Southern Arizona Balloon Excursion (balloon), 530 W. Sahuaro (624-

3599): Hot-air-balloon trips over Tucson and the surrounding desert; spectacular. Daily year round.

Sunshine Jeep Tours (Jeep), 641 E. Windward Circle (742-1943): Half-day or longer Jeep trips into the desert around Tucson.

ARCHITECTURAL HIGHLIGHTS: ⚲ **Pima County Courthouse,** 155 N. Church Ave. (792-8011): An old baroque building whose dome is covered with colored tiles in geometric patterns. A mixture of Spanish Colonial style, with columns, arches, and carved facade, and typical southwestern architecture. Pretty interior courtyard with fountain. Open Mon–Sat.

☀ **University of Arizona,** Park Ave. and University Blvd. (621-5130): Founded in 1885, this is now one of the most important universities in the Southwest, with 37,000 students. The huge campus, covering 345 acres (140ha), is embellished with lovely gardens and flowerbeds and several remarkable buildings: the **McKale Memorial Center,** the **College of Law,** the **Library,** and the **College of Medicine,** as well as several interesting museums described below.

CHURCHES/SYNAGOGUES: ☀⚲ **Mission San Xavier del Bac,** San Xavier Rd., 9 mi. (14km) SW of Tucson on I-19 (294-2624): Nicknamed "the white dove of the desert" on account of its elegant silhouette and immaculate white walls, the mission was originally founded in 1700 by Jesuit Fr. Eusebio Kino in his attempt to convert the Pima tribespeople to Christianity. The present buildings were erected by the Franciscans between 1783 and 1797; with asymmetrical bell towers and ocher-colored facade, it is the finest surviving example of Spanish Colonial architecture in the U.S. Splendid baroque interior with Native American wall paintings. Open daily.

St. Augustine Cathedral, 192 S. Stone Ave. (623-6351): Another perfect example of Spanish religious architecture, this one dating from 1896. Wonderful carved sandstone facade, modeled after the cathedral at Querétaro in Mexico, surmounted by a statue of St. Augustine and three symbols of the desert: the yucca, the saguaro, and the horned toad. Open daily. (Don't miss the vibrant and colorful mariachi mass, Sun at 8am.)

HISTORIC BUILDINGS: John C. Frémont House, 151 S. Granada Ave. (622-0956): Dating from the 1880s and furnished in period, this modest adobe house of typically Mexican appearance was the home of the explorer Gen. John C. Frémont, then governor of the Arizona Territory. Interesting temporary exhibitions. Open Wed–Sat.

MUSEUMS OF ART: Center for Creative Photography, 843 E. University Blvd. (621-7968): One of the country's finest photography museums. A remarkable collection, with more than 100 of the most famous photographers represented; also changing exhibits. A must for camera buffs. Open Tues–Fri.

Tucson Museum of Art, 140 N. Main Ave. (624-2333): Housed in six meticulously restored 19th-century adobe buildings that were once part of the Tucson Presidio, this museum offers a very impressive selection of pre-Columbian and Mexican art, as well as Spanish Colonial and contemporary art in the southwestern U.S. Open Tues–Sun.

University Museum of Art, Olive Rd. and Speedway Blvd. (621-7567): Splendid art museum on the university campus, whose contents include a part of the famous Kress collection of Renaissance paintings, and an impressive group of modern paintings and sculptures from the Leonard Pfeiffer and E. J. Gallagher collections: Picasso, Rodin, Moore, Andrew Wyeth, etc. A must-see. Open Sun–Fri.

MUSEUMS OF SCIENCE & HISTORY: Arizona Historical Society, 949 E. 2nd St. at Park Ave. (628-5774): History of Arizona from the Spanish settlers to the present day; geological specimens; costume museum; well-stocked library on the history of the West. Should be seen; open daily.

Arizona State Museum, Park Ave. and University Blvd. (621-6302): Fascinating panorama of prehistoric (as far as 10,000 years back) and contemporary Native American culture; one of the best archeological collections in the Southwest. Open daily.

Grace H. Flandrau Planetarium, Cherry Ave. and University Blvd. (621-7827): Very modern space museum and planetarium of innovative spherical design. Observations through the telescope every evening. For budding astronomers; open Tues–Sun.

Fort Lowell Museum, 2900 N. Craycroft Rd. (885-3832): Partly rebuilt military post, which was important in the Indian Wars at the end of the 19th century. Interesting Apache Wars Museum. Open Wed–Sat.

Mineralogical Museum, E. North Campus Dr., Geology Bldg. (621-4227): 10,000 different mineral specimens; large collection of precious stones from around the world and Arizona fossils. Open Mon–Fri.

Pima Air Museum, 6000 E. Valencia Rd., 9 mi. (14km) east to Exit 269 on I-10 (574-9658): More than 200 civil and military aircraft, from the end of the '30s to the present day, collected in one place. One of the country's finest private aircraft collections; a spectacular history of American aviation from the venerable *Liberator* to the gigantic B-52 *Stratofortress*. More than a million visitors have passed through its gates since the museum opened in 1976. Open daily.

PANORAMAS: ☼⚲ **Mount Lemmon,** 35 mi. (56km) NE on the Catalina Hwy.: Fine view over Tucson Valley and the surrounding mountains; reached over a lovely scenic highway.

⚲ **Sentinel Peak Park,** Sentinel Peak Rd. at Congress St.: Spectacular view of the city, particularly at nightfall when the lights of Tucson are twinkling at your feet. The giant "A" on the mountainside is the brand of the University of Arizona. Open daily 7am–10pm.

PARKS & GARDENS: ⚲ **Randolph City Park,** Broadway and Alvernon Way (325-2811): Huge, shady park in the center of town; two public golf courses, pool, 24 tennis courts, rose garden, and mini-zoo. Open daily.

⚲ **Reid Park,** 22nd St. and Country Club Rd. (791-4873): Pleasant oasis of greenery in the heart of Tucson. Pretty rose garden; small but well-designed zoo; picnic area; sizable lake (fishing permitted). Open daily.

☼⚲ **Tohono Chul Park,** 7366 N. Paseo del Norte (742-6455): Glorious 35-acre (14ha) garden displaying more than 400 species of arid-zone and desert plants, grouped by genus. Paths for strolling. Also a bird sanctuary: from roadrunners to hummingbirds and from cactus wrens to woodpeckers. A must for nature lovers. Open daily.

☼⚲⚲ **Tucson Mountain Park,** 12 mi. (19km) west via Ariz. 86 and Kinney Rd. (883-4200): The "green lung" of Tucson; 16,000 acres (6,500ha) of sun-scorched ocher rocks, succulents, and giant cactus. This is the park most visited by tourists; the western part of the Saguaro National Monument (see "Nearby Excursions," below), including Old Tucson (see "Theme Parks," below) and the extraordinary zoological/botanic garden of the Arizona-Sonora Desert Museum (see "Zoos," below). Open daily.

PERFORMING ARTS: For daily listings of all shows and cultural events, consult the entertainment pages of the daily papers *Arizona Daily Star* (morning) and *Tucson Citizen* (evening).

Centennial Hall, University of Arizona Campus, University Blvd. (621-3364): Classical and jazz concerts, Broadway hits, ballet, top-performer recitals.

Convention Center Music Hall, 260 S. Church Ave.: Concerts, recitals, opera. Home of the Arizona Opera (293-4336) and the Arizona Light Opera Company (Oct–Mar), and of the Tucson Symphony (principal conductor: Robert Bernhardt) (882-8585) (Oct–May).

Convention Center Theater, 260 S. Church Ave. (622-2823): Contemporary and classic theater. Home of the Arizona Theater Company (Oct–Apr).

Gaslight Theatre, 7000 E. Tanque Verde Rd. (886-9428): Musical comedies, melodrama, family shows. Year round.

Invisible Theater, 1400 N. First Ave. (882-9721): Experimental and Off Broadway theater (Sept–June).

Reid Park Bandshell, 22nd St. and Country Club Rd. (791-4873): Open-air classical concerts by the Tucson Pops Orchestra (May–July).

SHOPPING: **Old Town Artisans,** 186 N. Meyer Ave. (623-6024): Some 150 local artists and craftspeople exhibit their work in a picturesque 19th-century adobe building in the heart of old Tucson. Lovers of authentic Native American crafts will go to **Desert Son,** 2900 E. Broadway; **Indian Territory,** 4719 E. Sunrise Dr.; and **Kaibab Shop,** 2841 N. Campbell Ave. Anywhere else, you may often find that your prized Native American artifact is stamped "Made in Hong Kong."

SPECIAL EVENTS: For the exact schedule of events below, consult the **Tucson Convention and Visitors Bureau** (see "Tourist Information," above).

Festival in the Sun (Feb–Mar): Tucson's newest winter arts festival by the University of Arizona. Features classical, folk, and jazz concerts, art exhibitions, dance performances, etc.

Fiesta de los Vaqueros (Feb): Tucson's big annual event since 1928. History parade, concerts, dances, rodeos.

Tucson Festival (Apr): Mexican fiesta, Native American dances, shows, opera, parades through town, craft exhibitions. A month-long festival that blends Native American, Spanish, Mexican, and Anglo-pioneer traditions.

Yaqui Indian Easter Celebration (Easter): Very colorful Native American festival.

Pima County Fair (Apr): Big agricultural fair; horse show, Native American art exhibition. Guaranteed local color.

San Xavier Fiesta (Apr): Religious procession, Native American dances, fireworks commemorating the founding of the San Xavier del Bac Mission.

SPORTS: Tucson is home to one professional major-league baseball team for spring training, and a minor-league team:

Baseball: Cleveland Indians, Hi Corbett Field (791-4266): spring-training camp, Feb–Mar; Tucson Toros, Hi Corbett Field (325-2621), Apr–Aug.

THEME PARKS: ※♨ **Old Tucson,** 201 S. Kinney Rd. in Tucson Mountain Park (883-6457): Built in 1939 as a setting for the movie *Arizona,* this replica of Tucson in the 1860s has 100 houses and saloons, a prison, a gold mine, and a steam railroad. Has been and still is used from time to time for movies and TV series (*Rio Bravo, Gunfight at the OK Corral, High Chaparral,* and so on). Mock gunfights, stunt shows, stagecoach rides. Entertaining; open daily.

WINTER SPORTS RESORTS: ※♨ **Mount Lemmon Ski Valley,** 35 mi. (56km) on Lemmon Hwy. (576-1400): 3 lifts; open late Dec to mid-Apr. The southernmost ski resort in the U.S.

ZOOS: ※♨♨ **Arizona-Sonora Desert Museum,** Tucson Mountain Park, 14 mi. (22km) west via Ariz. 86 and N. Kinney Rd. (883-1380): One of the country's most interesting zoological/botanical gardens, devoted to plants and animals of the southwestern deserts. Hundreds of desert animals, from mountain lions and jaguars to prairie dogs, from tarantulas to rattlesnakes, living in their natural habitat. An underground gallery allows you to watch the behavior of creatures that live below the surface. Splendid wild scenery. Open daily.

ACCOMMODATIONS

A Note on Accommodations: Room rates in Tucson are coded as follows: **VE,** Very Expensive ($140 and up); **E,** Expensive ($90–$140); **M,** Moderate ($60–$90); **I,** Inexpensive ($30–$60); **B,** Budget (up to $30). A listing of toll free numbers is in the Appendix.

Personal Favorites (in order of preference)

※ 🏨🏨🏨🏨 **Westin La Paloma** (vic.), 3800 E. Sunrise Dr., AZ 85718 (602/742-6000; toll free, see Westin). 486 rms, A/C, color TV, in-rm movies. AE, CB, DC, MC, V. Free valet parking, pool, 12 tennis courts, two golf courses, sauna, health club, three rests. (including La Villa), four bars, 24-hr. rm svce, disco, boutiques, concierge, free crib. *Note:* Ultramodern luxury vacation and convention hotel a 15-min. drive from dwntwn, at the foot of the Santa Catalina Mountains on 650 acres (263ha) of beautiful untamed scenery. Very successful Spanish-mission architecture, w. pastel-washed arcades and flower-filled grdns. Spacious, well-designed rms w. minibars; excellent svce; comprehensive sports facilities. Caters to upscale business clients and well-heeled tourists. The golf courses were designed by former U.S. champion Jack Nicklaus. Free airport shuttle. Lots of quality and style. **VE,** but lower rates off-season.

Sheraton El Conquistador (vic.), 10000 N. Oracle Rd., AZ 85737 (602/742-7000; toll free, see Sheraton). 440 rms, A/C, color TV, in-rm movies. AE, CB, DC, MC, V. Free parking, two pools, 16 tennis courts, three golf courses, putting green, health club, sauna, horseback riding, three rests. (including the White Dove), coffee shop, bars, 24-hr. rm svce, nightclub, boutiques, concierge, free crib. *Note:* One of the most modern and luxurious resort hotels in the Southwest; a sort of oasis in the desert a 30-min. drive north of Tucson. Intimate, inviting little three-story buildings surrounded by grdns and palm trees in the shadow of the Santa Catalina Mountains. Elegant, comfortable rms w. minibars and private balconies or patios, the best overlooking the huge pool in the middle of the grdns. Exemplary reception and svce; very comprehensive sports facilities. If you want a complete change of scene, this is it. **E–VE,** but lower rates off-season.

Doubletree Hotel (nr. dwntwn), 445 S. Alvernon Way, AZ 85711 (602/881-4200; toll free 800/528-0444). 296 rms, A/C, color TV, in-rm movies. AE, CB, DC, MC, V. Free parking, pool, health club, three tennis courts, putting green, rest. (Cactus Rose), coffee shop, bar, rm svce, disco, free crib. *Note:* Right opposite Randolph Park, this large, modern nine-story hotel is a favorite w. business travelers. Spacious rms w. refrigerators and private patios. Efficient, attentive svce; free airport limo. Group clientele; interesting wknd discounts. **E–VE,** but lower rates off-season.

Holiday Inn Broadway (dwntwn), 181 W. Broadway, AZ 85701 (602/624-8711; toll free, see Holiday Inns). 310 rms, A/C, color TV, in-rm movies. AE, CB, DC, MC, V. Free gar., pool, rest., bar, rm svce, nightclub, free crib. *Note:* Typical modern hotel a stone's throw from La Placita and its shopping. Serviceable comfort and facilities; so-so rest. Group and business clientele. A Holiday Inn at its best; very central location adjacent to the Convention Center; good value on balance. **M–E,** but lower rates off-season.

Motel 6 Central (nr. dwntwn), 960 S. Freeway, AZ 85745 (602/628-1339). 112 rms, A/C, color TV, free in-rm movies. AE, DC, MC, V. Free parking, pool, adj. 24-hr. coffee shop. *Note:* The best buy in Tucson if you're driving through; functional comfort at unbeatable prices. 5 min. from dwntwn. **B**

Other Accommodations (from top bracket to budget)

Loews Ventana Canyon Resort (vic.), 7000 N. Resort Dr., AZ 85715 (602/299-2020; toll free, see Loews). 398 rms, A/C, color TV, in-rm movies. AE, CB, DC, MC, V. Free parking, two pools, 10 tennis courts, golf, putting green, health club, sauna, three rests. (including the Ventana Rm), bars, 24-hr. rm svce, disco, boutiques, concierge, free crib. *Note:* On a mesa w. a splendid view of Tucson Valley 3,000 ft. (900m) below and the surrounding mountains, this luxury hotel boasts a superb wild setting. The typically southwestern building overlooks an 80-ft. (24m) waterfall which feeds a little lake lying below the hotel. Spacious, inviting rms w. balconies and refrigerators; attentive svce; quality rest. Wonderful golf course in the open desert. A very good place to stay, 20 min. from dwntwn. **VE,** but lower rates off-season.

Westward Look (vic.), 245 E. Ina Rd., AZ 85704 (602/297-1151; toll free 800/722-2500). 245 rms, A/C, color TV, in-rm movies. AE, CB, DC, MC, V. Free parking, three pools, eight tennis courts, health club, horseback riding, rest. (Gold Rm), bar, rm svce, disco, free crib. *Note:*

Luxury hotel in 78 acres (31ha) of grdn and woodland in the foothills of the Santa Catalina Mountains, w. spectacular view over Tucson and the valley. Pretty one- or two-floor cottages around the pool, w. very comfortable rms (minibars and private patios). Worthwhile AP and MAP packages; the rest. is highly regarded. Cheerful, friendly svce. A Tucson landmark for 40 years. **E–VE,** but lower rates off-season.

Radisson Suite (nr. dwntwn), 6555 E. Speedway Blvd., AZ 85710 (602/721-7100; toll free, see Radisson). 304 rms, A/C, color TV, in-rm movies. AE, CB, DC, MC, V. Free parking, pool, health club, 17 tennis courts and golf course adjoining, putting green, rest. (Café Dorado), bar, rm svce, free breakfast and cocktails, free crib. *Note:* Modern, inviting hotel w. suites only, spacious, w. balcony, refrigerator, and microwave; the best look out on the pool-patio. Efficient svce; Business and convention clientele. 12 min. from dwntwn. **M–E,** but lower rates off-season.

Best Western Aztec Inn (nr. dwntwn), 102 N. Alvernon Way, AZ 85711 (602/795-0330; toll free, see Best Western). 156 rms, A/C, color TV. AE, CB, DC, MC, V. Free parking, pool, adj. rest., rm svce, hrdrsr, free crib. *Note:* Very engaging Spanish Colonial architecture and interior; comfortable rms w. refrigerators, the best overlooking the charming patio w. pool. Rms w. kitchenettes and no-smoking rms available. Efficient reception and svce; good value. 10 min. from dwntwn. **M,** but lower rates off-season.

La Quinta Inn (nr. dwntwn), 665 N. Freeway, AZ 85705 (602/622-6491; toll free, see La Quinta Motor Inns). 132 rms, A/C, color TV, in-rm movies. AE, CB, DC, MC, V. Free parking, pool, adj. 24-hr. coffee shop, valet svce. *Note:* Elegant Mexican-style building; huge, intelligently designed rms w. separate sleeping alcoves. Friendly reception; very good value. **I–M**

Park Inn International (formerly the Skytel Motor Inn; vic.), 2803 E. Valencia Rd., AZ 85706 (602/294-2500; toll free 800/437-7275). 95 rms, A/C, in-rm movies. AE, CB, DC, MC, V. Free parking, pool, rest., bar, rm svce, free crib. *Note:* Very good value 5 min. from the airport (free shuttle) and 15 min. from dwntwn. Entirely redecorated and re-equipped. Comfortable rms; reception and svce w. a smile. **I**

GUEST RANCHES: Guest ranches, commonly known as "dude ranches," are the ideal solution if you like open-air vacations and horseback riding; they offer luxury comforts and svce while you play cowboy.

Tanque Verde Guest Ranch (vic.), 14301 E. Speedway Blvd., AZ 85710 (602/296-6275). 58 rms, A/C, color TV available. AE, MC, V. Free parking, two pools, five tennis courts, putting green, horseback riding, outdoor sports, rest., bar, valet svce, disco, crib $15. *Note:* Old stock ranch and stagecoach station dating from 1868; picturesque rustic decor. Spacious rms w. refrigerators and private patios, some w. fireplaces. Open-air barbecues; excursions in the area. Informal but elegant atmosphere; a very good place. Free airport limo. Open year round. **VE** (American Plan), but lower rates off-season.

Hacienda del Sol (vic.), 5601 N. Hacienda del Sol Rd., AZ 85718 (602/299-1501). 45 rms, A/C, color TV. AE, CB, DC, MC, V. Free parking, pool, tennis court, horseback riding, outdoor sports, rest., bar, rm svce, library, crib $10. *Note:* Hacienda-style guest ranch nestled in the foothills of the Catalina Mountains. Traditional adobe buildings (*casitas*); very inviting rms w. views of nearby mountains, some w. private patios or balconies. Friendly svce. Open year round. 20 min. from dwntwn. **E–VE** (American Plan).

White Stallion Ranch (vic.), 9251 Twin Peaks Rd., AZ 85743 (602/297-0252). 30 rms; no A/C. No credit cards. Free parking, pool, two tennis courts, horseback riding, outdoor sports, rest., bar, free crib. *Note:* Authentic ranch, straight out of a western movie, w. herds and real cowboys, on 4,000 acres (1,600ha) of untamed land. Comforts of rather a rustic nature, but engaging family atmosphere. Open-air barbecues, rodeos, horse-and-cart rides. Free airport limo. Open Oct–May only. **E–VE** (American Plan).

Airport Accommodations

Best Western Inn at the Airport (vic.), 7060 S. Tucson Blvd., AZ 85706 (602/746-0271; toll free, see Best Western). 147 rms, A/C, color TV, in-rm movies. AE, CB, DC, MC, V. Free valet parking, pool, health club, whirlpool, putting green, rest. (The Inn Place), bar, rm svce, free breakfast, free crib. *Note:* Typical airport motel, inviting and comfortable. Spacious, well-soundproofed rms w. balconies or patios, some w. refrigerators. Exceptionally friendly, cheerful svce. Free airport limo. Business clientele. Excellent value. 20 min. from dwntwn. **M**

RESTAURANTS

A Note on Restaurant Prices: Tucson restaurant prices, per person, excluding drinks and service charges, are coded as follows: **VE,** Very Expensive ($60 and up); **E,** Expensive ($40–$60); **M,** Moderate ($25–$40); **I,** Inexpensive ($15–$25); **B,** Budget (up to $15).

Personal Favorites (in order of preference)

Janos (dwntwn), 150 N. Main Ave. (884-9426). A/C. Dinner only, Mon–Sat; closed hols. and Mon mid-May to Sept. AE, MC, V. Jkt. *Specialties:* calzone w. goat cheese and spinach; roast duckling w. purée of red peppers and broiled shrimp; roast loin of lamb w. wild-rice pancakes and pineapple chutney; grilled Norwegian salmon w. red butter, asparagus custard, and wild mushrooms. Menu changes regularly. Skimpy wine list. *Note:* The young chef Janos Wilder broke new ground when (in 1985) he opened the first rest. serving American nouvelle cuisine in Tucson, a city not overburdened w. good rests. Since then his success has never faltered. The rest. occupies a picturesque 19th-century adobe building w. exposed beams, a designated historic monument. Open-air dining on fine days. Excellent svce. Tucson's most inspired and imaginative food; resv. are a must. *American.* **M–E**

Café Terra Cotta (nr. dwntwn), 4310 N. Campbell Ave. (577-8100). A/C. Lunch/dinner daily; closed hols. AE, DC, MC, V. *Specialties:* pizzas nouvelle cuisine, garlic custard w. warm salsa vinaigrette and herbed hazelnuts, roast chili pepper stuffed w. chicken and corn, prawns stuffed w. goat cheese, black-bean and beef chili. Engaging homemade desserts. Menu changes regularly. *Note:* Another talented newcomer on the local gastronomic scene. Inventive, praiseworthy contemporary southwestern cuisine; airy and comfortable decor; cheerful svce. Resv. requested. Excellent value. *American.* **I–M**

Scordato's (nr. dwntwn), 4405 Speedway Blvd. (624-8946). A/C. Dinner only, nightly; closed July 4, Thanksgiving, Dec 25. AE, CB, DC, MC, V. Jkt. *Specialties:* classic Italian food: veal Stresa, fresh homemade pasta, catch of the day, broiled prime cuts. Good wine list. *Note:* On a height overlooking the city, this charming little house w. its tile roof has been for 20 years one of Tucson's best Italian rests., and one of the most popular. Elegant, romantic atmosphere. The veal, represented by no fewer than 13 different recipes on the menu, is the choicest reared in Wisconsin. Attentive svce; resv. requested. Other location: 6335 E. Tanque Verde (721-0333). *Italian/Continental.* **I–M**

El Adobe (dwntwn), 40 W. Broadway between Church St. and Stone Ave. (791-7458). A/C. Lunch/dinner daily; closed hols. AE, MC, V. *Specialties:* flautas, tamales, enchiladas, carne seca (sun-dried beef), Sonoran-style dishes. Excellent homemade margaritas. *Note:* In this pretty adobe hacienda dating from 1868 the food is authentically Mexican; there's also a romantic shady patio-grdn. Prompt, efficient svce. Locally very popular; right in the historic district. *Mexican.* **B–I**

Pinnacle Peak (vic.), 6541 Tanque Verde Rd. (296-0911). A/C. Dinner only, nightly; closed Thanksgiving, Dec 25. MC,

V. *Specialties:* choice steak, ribs, and other meats; barbecued chicken; broiled fish. *Note:* Same successful formula as its sister spot in Phoenix: excellent beef cuts broiled over a mesquite fire. Pleasant western decor; locally popular. Well worth the 20-min. drive from dwntwn. No resv. *Steak.* I

☼♀ **Samaniego House** (dwntwn), 222 S. Church Ave. (622-
❖♀ 7790). A/C. Lunch/dinner daily; closed hols. AE, CB, DC, MC, V. *Specialties:* sandwiches, ranch chow (steak w. spicy sauce), carne seca (sun-dried beef), barbecued chicken, Mexican dishes, catch of the day, sopaipillas. *Note:* Original 1881 colonial-style building w. adobe walls and exposed beams. Typical local cuisine; nice atmosphere. In the heart of dwntwn Tucson. *American/Mexican.* B–I

Other Restaurants (from top bracket to budget)

☼♀♀♀ **Charles** (vic.), 6400 E. El Dorado Circle (296-7173). A/C.
Lunch Mon–Fri, dinner nightly; closed Memorial Day, July 4, and Sun June–Sept. AE, DC, MC, V. Jkt. *Specialties:* stuffed quail, lamb cutlets bouquetière, veal Charles béarnaise, game (in season), shrimp à l'orange, baked salmon. Menu changes regularly. Fine wine list. *Note:* In an elegant freestone manor house which once belonged to the Pond cosmetics family, this luxury rest. serves some of the most refined traditional cuisine in Tucson. Very polished reception and svce; distinguished background music; prices to match. A lovely cypress avenue leads up to the rest. 20 min. from dwntwn; valet parking; resv. strongly advised. *Continental.* I–M

♀♀♀ **Daniel's** (nr. dwntwn), Plaza Palomino, 2300 N. Swan Rd.
❖❖ (742-3200). A/C. Lunch Mon–Sat, dinner nightly; closed hols. AE, CB, DC, MC, V. Jkt. *Specialties:* zuppa di pesce, spinach and smoked salmon pasta, seafood vermicelli, veal cutlet stuffed w. ham and cheese, lamb cutlet Provençal, filet of beef w. green peppercorns. Fine list of American wines. *Note:* The rest., opened in 1986 by Daniel Scordato, heir of a dynasty of local restaurateurs, is attempting to produce a contemporary version of classic French and Italian cuisine. Elegant modern decor in pastel tones of peach. Somewhat ceremonious svce. A fashionable place; resv. advised. *Italian/French.* I–M

♀♀ **Jerome's** (vic.), 6958 E. Tanque Verde Rd. (721-0311). A/C.
Lunch Tues–Fri, dinner Tues–Sun, brunch Sun; closed Dec 25. AE, MC, V. Jkt. *Specialties:* Cajun calzone (w. spiced Louisiana sausage), sweetwater barbecued duck, blackened redfish, Créole and Cajun dishes, broiled fish. *Note:* With its paneled walls, exposed beams, and big brick fireplace, the decor is more Boston than Louisiana, but Jerome's food is authentic New Orleans. Swift, efficient svce; successful, so resv. advised. 25 min. from dwntwn. *Créole.* I–M

♀♀ **Le Rendez Vous** (nr. dwntwn), 3844 E. Fort Lowell Rd. (323-
❖❖ 7373). A/C. Dinner only, Tues–Sun; closed Jan 1, Dec 25. AE, CB, DC, MC, V. *Specialties:* scallops au gratin, salmon coulibiac, bouillabaisse, pepper steak, sweetbreads w. mushrooms and Dijon-mustard sauce, rack of lamb provençal, soufflé Grand Marnier. Good wine list. *Note:* Inviting, intimate little bistro w. lots of charm serving the first-rate classical cuisine of chef Jean-Claude Berger. Elegant enclosed patio. Flawless svce. For those who value real French food at reasonable prices, this is the best place to eat in Tucson. Resv. advisable. *French.* I–M

♀ **Olive Tree** (nr. dwntwn), 7000 E. Tanque Verde Rd. (298-
❖ 1845). A/C. Lunch Mon–Sat, dinner nightly; closed hols. AE, MC, V. *Specialties:* lamb chops, Greek dishes, broiled fish. *Note:* Enormously popular rest. 20 min. from dwntwn. Mainly Greek food, straightforward and tasty. Open patio w. fountain for open-air meals, or more intimate dining rm. Efficient svce; very good value; an excellent place. *Greek/Continental.* I

☼♀ **El Charro** (dwntwn), 311 N. Court Ave. (622-5465). A/C.
❖ Lunch/dinner daily, brunch Sun; closed hols. AE, CB, DC,

MC, V. *Specialties:* tostada con carne seca, stuffed chile, chimichangas, topopo salad (chicken and avocado), burritos, pastelito de fruta, almendrado. *Note:* Typical Mexican rest., serving authentic food since 1922. In an 1887 building in the heart of old Tucson. Inviting patio for outdoor dining; diligent, friendly svce. Locally popular; excellent value. *Mexican.* **B–I**

Cafeterias/Fast Food
Piccadilly (nr. dwntwn), 6767 Broadway Blvd. (886-0529). Open daily (till 8:30pm). No credit cards. Roast beef, fried chicken, homemade soups and desserts. Good cafeteria food at modest prices.
Sanchez Burrito Co., 2530 N. First Ave. (622-2092). Lunch/dinner daily. Highly acceptable Mexican food at delightfully low prices. Try the giant burritos and the red-chile tamales. Check the phone book for five other branches in Tucson.

BARS & NIGHTCLUBS
The Baron's (nr. dwntwn), 2401 S. Wilmot Rd. (747-3503). Trendy disco; locally popular. Open nightly. Also rest.
Hidden Valley Inn (vic.), 4825 N. Sabino Canyon Rd. (299-4941). Western disco with live music; warm atmosphere. Also a good steakhouse. Open nightly; 25 min. from dwntwn.
Javelina Cantina (nr. dwntwn), in the Doubletree Inn (see "Accommodations," above) (881-4200). Singles bar-disco much favored by the young professional crowd and the students of the nearby university. Noisy live rock. Open nightly.
Laffs Comedy Café (nr. dwntwn), 2900 E. Broadway (323-8669). The best comedy club in town. Open Tues–Sun.
The Maverick (nr. dwntwn), 4700 22nd St. (748-0456). Country-and-western music; very cowboy atmosphere. Open nightly.
Terry & Zeke's (nr. dwntwn), 4376 E. Speedway Blvd. (325-3555). Hole-in-the-wall spot turned out a local institution. Live Texas blues and R&B nightly. Great beer selection.

NEARBY EXCURSIONS

BIOSPHERE 2 (30 mi./48km north via U.S. 89 and Ariz. 77 in Oracle) (602/896-2920): The world's most ambitious ecological project, in the Santa Catalina Mountains north of Tucson a giant greenhouse (7.2-million-cu.-ft, 204,000m^3) is sealed under 4 acres (1.6ha) of glass. It contains some 3,800 species of plants, insects, and animals that feed each other as in nature. The Biosphere is arrayed in seven different climatic zones or "biomes," and is designed to be totally independent of the outside world except for electricity—making its own oxygen, processing its own carbon dioxide, and recycling its own wastes. The experiment is expected to be applicable to colonies in outer space. Tours are conducted daily. Call toll free resv. 800/828-2462.

CASA GRANDE RUINS NATIONAL MONUMENT (69 mi./110km NW via I-10 and Ariz. 87) (602/723-3172): See Chapter 42 on Phoenix.

COLOSSAL CAVE (25 mi./40km SE via I-10 and Colossal Cave Rd.) (602/791-7677): Unique natural caves, only partially explored, with astonishing crystal formations. Many marine fossils bear witness that Arizona was once the bed of a prehistoric sea. The temperature in the caves stays at 72°F (22°C) year round. Open daily.

CORONADO NATIONAL FOREST: 1,790,000 acres (720,000ha) of forest and desert around Tucson, Nogales, Patagonia, Benson, and Wilcox. Scenic drives, camping, fishing, horseback riding, skiing in winter, etc. For information, contact the Supervisor, Federal Bldg., 300 W. Congress St., Tucson, AZ 85701 (629-6483). There's a **visitor center** at Sabino Canyon (see below).

DAVIS-MONTHAN AIR FORCE BASE (Craycroft Rd. at Golf Links Rd., 7 mi./11km SE) (602/750-3204): More than 20,000 warplanes, from World War II relics to Vietnam War jets, parked in endless rows. You can view the 2-mi.-long (3km) graveyard through the airfield fence when you travel west on Irvington Rd. to Wilmot Rd. Visit by resv. An absolute must for aviation buffs.

KITT PEAK NATIONAL OBSERVATORY (56 mi./90km SW via Ariz. 86 and Ariz. 386) (602/325-9200): Considered by scholars one of the world's greatest astronomical observatories. At an elevation of 6,882 ft. (2,098m) up in the Sonora desert, it boasts the largest solar telescope in the world and the third-largest optical telescope in the U.S., 158 in. (4m) in diameter and weighing 375 tons, housed in a 19-story building. Open daily; fascinating. Splendid surrounding scenery.

SABINO CANYON (16 mi./25km east via Tanque Verde Rd. and Sabino Canyon Rd.) (602/749-2327): A kind of green oasis in the desert of the Santa Catalina Mountains; forms part of the immense Coronado National Forest. No private cars are permitted in Sabino Canyon, but there are guided bus tours every hour. A must for nature lovers.

SAGUARO NATIONAL MONUMENT (17 mi./27km east via Broadway and Old Spanish Trail; or 16 mi./25km west via W. Speedway Blvd. and Saguaro Rd.): America's most spectacular giant-cactus forest; some saguaros grow 52 ft. (16m) tall and live for two centuries. Wide variety of flora and fauna, including coyote, peccary, and various kinds of deer. The park is divided into two sections: the **Rincon Mountain Unit** (east of Tucson), the more spectacular, and the **Tucson Mountain Unit** (west of Tucson). Try to go in May and June, when the saguaros are in flower. Visitor centers open year round; hiking trails, camping permitted. For information, contact the Superintendent, 3693 Old Spanish Trail, Tucson, AZ 85730 (602/296-8576).

Where to Eat

Saguaro Corners, 3750 S. Old Spanish Trail (886-5424). Opposite Saguaro National Monument East. Open for lunch/dinner Tues–Sun; closed Aug. I

TITAN MISSILE MUSEUM (Duval Mine Rd. in Green Valley, 26 mi./41km south on I-19 to Exit 69) (602/791-2929): World's only ballistic-missile museum. Guided tour (exhausting) of the silo containing the huge nuclear missile, 110 ft. (33m) high, deactivated in 1983 after standing on 24-hr. alert for 19 years. Impressive. Open daily Oct–May, Wed–Sun the rest of the year.

GHOST TOWNS: There are a good 20 ghost towns dating from the gold rush days in the area around Tombstone, Nogales, and Chiricahua National Monument. Some, such as Ruby (near Nogales), are closed to the public; others, such as

TUCSON
AND ENVIRONS

Apache San Carlos
Indian Reservation

Douglas
Bisbee
Sierra Vista
Nogales

Mt. Lemmon
Saguaro
Tucson

Tumacacori

MEXICO

Mesa
Scottsdale
Phoenix
Tempe
Casa Grande

Casa Grande
Gila R.
Indian Reservation

Organ Pipe Cactus

Gila Bend

CALIFORNIA

Yuma

▲ Ski Area
□ National Monument

Hilltop or Paradise (near Chiricahua National Monument) are quite hard to reach. In addition to Tombstone—the liveliest, least ghostly ghost town in the West—(see "Tombstone," below), two others are well worth seeing: Gleeson (16 mi./26km east of Tombstone) and Pearce (28 mi./45km NE of Tombstone).

FARTHER AFIELD

CHIRICAHUA NATIONAL MONUMENT (121 mi./ 194km SE via I-10E and Ariz. 186E): Picturesque rock formations of volcanic origin in a former Apache hunting ground (see "Tombstone," below).

NOGALES (145 mi./232 km r.t. via I-19S, Ariz. 82, Ariz. 83N, and I-10W): Picturesque excursion toward the Mexican border, beginning with a visit to the ☀️🏛 **Mission San Xavier del Bac** (see "Churches/Synagogues," above). Drive on to ⚜ **Tubac Presidio State Historic Park,** on U.S. 89 (602/398-2252), open daily, the first Spanish settlement in Arizona. The remains of the fort, now a museum, date from 1752.

Then 5 mi. (8km) south, at ☀️⚜ **Tumacacori National Monument,** see the Franciscan mission of San José, built around 1800, with a lovely courtyard garden. The Native American village of Tumacacori (602/398-2341) was first visited in 1691 by Jesuit Fr. Eusebio Kino, the great Spanish missionary to Arizona. Open daily.

At the end of I-19, **Nogales,** a very touristy border town bisected by high fences, is worth a look. No documents are required for U.S. citizens if you're just going to cross the border for a few hours of shopping (pottery, leather goods, baskets, glass, and tin items) or sightseeing. Some shops worth visiting are El Changarro (93 Calle Elías), El Continental (98 Obregón Ave.), and El Zarape (161 Obregón Ave.).

Continue east along the 200-acre (80ha) **Patagonia Lake,** complete with beach, marina, etc., and the picturesque little town of ⚜ **Patagonia.** Don't miss the unusual **Stradling Museum of the Horse** at 350 McKeown Ave. (602/394-2264), open daily, containing everything that has to do with "man's noblest conquest," from classical Greece to the age of the cowboy. Not far from Patagonia, on Ariz. 82, is the wonderful ⚜ **Patagonia-Sonoita Creek Sanctuary,** where willows, ash, and sycamores along the banks of the Sonoita brook shelter more than 250 different species of birds. Many western movies were shot in the neighboring **Empire Valley** (around **Sonoita** and **Elgin**) in the late 1940s and 1950s: *Duel in the Sun, Red River,* and *Winchester 73* among others.

On the way back, visit the ⚜ **Colossal Cave** (see "Nearby Excursions," above) and the ☀️🏛 **Pima Air Museum** (see "Museums of Science and History," above). A wonderful expedition for nature lovers.

Where to Eat in Nogales

La Rocca, 91 Calle Elías, is a typical restaurant on the Mexican side. Open daily 11am–midnight (706/20-760).

ORGAN PIPE CACTUS NATIONAL MONUMENT (139 mi./222km west via Ariz. 86W and Ariz. 85S): One of the country's wildest and loveliest desert-land parks, on the Mexican border. The cactuses for which the park is named reach 20 ft. (6m) in height, with as many as 30 vertical arms stacked like organ pipes; they flower in May and June. Two scenic highways traverse this seldom-visited park, which is well worth the side trip. Visitor center open year round; camping permitted. For information, contact the Superintendent, Rte. 1, Ajo, AZ 85321 (602/387-6849).

TOMBSTONE (355 mi./568km r.t. via I-10E, U.S. 80E, an unsurfaced road between Rodeo–Portal and Chiricahua National Monument in summer only or U.S. 666N and Ariz. 181E in winter, Ariz. 186W, Apache Pass Rd., and I-10W): This spectacular trip, full of sights for the lover of frontier history, begins with a visit to ☼☖☖ **Tombstone,** "The Town Too Tough to Die," so called both because of its innumerable shoot-outs (such as the famous "Gunfight at the O.K. Corral" between the Earp brothers and the Clanton brothers, and for the series of catastrophes that overtook its gold and silver mines). Today it's a museum town, with many picturesque buildings from the 1880s: the **Boothill Graveyard,** on U.S. 80 (602/457-3348), with its unusual epitaphs; a **courthouse** dating from 1882 with many remembrances of the town's eventful past, at Toughnut St. and 3rd St. (602/457-3311), open daily; the **Bird Cage Theater,** Allen St. and 6th St. (602/457-3421), open daily, which was once dubbed "the wildest and wickedest spot between Basin St. and the Barbary Coast," and numbered the beautiful Lola Montez among its attractions; the **Crystal Palace Saloon,** 5th St. and Allen St., open daily, another house of ill-repute famous in the 1880s; the office of the *Tombstone Epitaph,* 5th St. and Allen St. (457-2211), the local daily paper founded in 1880 and published continuously since then; the **O.K. Corral** on Allen between 3rd St. and 4th St. (602/457-3456), scene of the famous gunfight; and more. No horse-opera buff can afford to miss Tombstone. For information, contact the **Tombstone Tourism Association,** 9 S. 5th St. (602/457-2211).

Next stop is ☼ **Bisbee,** a real pioneer town sprawled along the sides of Mule Pass Gulch with turn-of-the-century houses. Luckier than Tombstone, it remained prosperous for a full century, its last open-pit copper mines closing only in 1975. Visit the underground ☖ **Queen Mine** copper mine, where the temperature in the bowels of the earth never rises above 49°F (9°C)—but take a sweater or a jacket even in summer—and its open-pit neighbor the **Lavender Pit,** on U.S. 80 (602/432-2071 for both mines), open daily. At the ☖ **Bisbee Mining Historical Museum,** 5 Copper Queen Plaza (602/432-7071), open daily, are interesting souvenirs from Bisbee's mining days.

Continue south on U.S. 80 to **Douglas,** an engaging stagecoach-stop town on the Mexican border; don't fail to take a look at the extravagant ☖☖ **Gadsden Hotel,** originally built in 1907 and rebuilt after a fire in 1929; the sumptuously rococo interior has been used as a set for many westerns.

Your next stop is at ☖ **Chiricahua National Monument,** whose spectacular landscape of volcanic rocks and deep gorges once gave sanctuary to the Apache chiefs Cochise and Geronimo. Wonderful scenic drive (Bonita Canyon Rd.) and dozens of miles of trails. Camping permitted. Visitor center at the park entrance on U.S. 181 (602/824-3560). Not far away, at ☖ **Fort Bowie National Historic Site** (602/847-2500), you'll see the ruins of two military posts built to protect the coaches of the legendary Butterfield Stage Coach line from Native American attacks. The site can only be reached by walking 1 mi. (2km) on a foot trail; beware of flash floods and rattlesnakes. Open daily.

Drive back to Tucson along the Texas Canyon, by way of ☖ **Willcox;** see the **Cochise Visitor Center** on Fort Grant Rd. (602/384-2272), open daily, the best museum of the Apache days.

For this itinerary you should set aside 2 or 3 days. If you're a western-history buff, this is the trip for you.

Where to Stay En Route

IN BISBEE The ☼ ☖ **Copper Queen Hotel,** 11 Howell Ave., Bisbee, AZ 85603 (602/432-2216). 43 rms. Charming turn-of-the-century hotel, now elegantly restored. **I–M**

IN DOUGLAS   The ☼ 🏨 **Gadsden Hotel,** 1046 G. Ave., Douglas, AZ 85607 (602/364-4481). 145 rms. Beautiful rococo 1920s hotel, a designated historic monument. **I–M**

IN TOMBSTONE   The 🍸 **Best Western Lookout Lodge,** on U.S. 80, Tombstone, AZ 85638 (602/457-2223). 40 rms. Inviting motel w. a view of the Dragoon Mountains. **I–M**

IN WILLCOX   The 🍸 **Best Western Plaza Inn,** 1100 W. Rex Allen Dr., Willcox, AZ 85643 (602/384-3556). 93 rms. Comfortable motel of the usual type. **I–M**

OTHER FROMMER TRAVEL GUIDES: Readers may be interested in Frommer guides that treat the Southwest and mountain areas in greater detail: *Frommer's Southwest* and *Frommer's New Mexico* (June, 1991). There are three city guides to this area: *Frommer's Denver, Boulder, and Colorado Springs; Frommer's Salt Lake City,* and *Frommer's Santa Fe, Taos, and Alberquerque.*

   Frommer travel guides are available in most bookstores, or can be ordered by mail from Frommer Books, Prentice Hall Press, 15 Columbus Circle, New York, N. Y. 10023. Turn to the last pages of the book to learn about Frommer's **Dollarwise Travel Club,** and for ordering information.

PART SIX

THE NORTHWEST

CHAPTER 44

PORTLAND

□ □ □

Dominated by the imposing, snow-crowned **Mount Hood** (11,235 ft./ 3,424m) in the distance, Portland figures consistently at the head of America's 243 major cities in various surveys having to do with the "quality of life." Downtown, where high-rises are few and all vehicular traffic is forbidden with the exception of (free) buses and cabs, the pedestrian zone of the **Mall,** with its stores, restaurants, fountains, and statues, is proof of the concern of Portland's inhabitants for their environment. By way of setting a good example, the mayor commutes to his office every day on a bicycle.

If you want to gather an overall impression of the "City of Roses," the best way is to drive around the 50-mi. (80km) **Scenic Drive,** which encircles the city, from the heights above it through its innumerable parks and its botanic garden. Famous for its rose gardens (whence its nickname), its humidity, and its mountain scenery, Oregon's largest city is a vigorous commercial and industrial metropolis, important in lumber, electronics, food, clothing, and aluminum. Stern legislation has banished smog and pollution; salmon are once again being taken from the **Willamette River,** which divides the city in two, and the drinking water drawn from it is rated among the purest in the western U.S.

Although 112 mi. (180km) from the ocean, Portland is one of the most active seaports on the Pacific coast, handling more than 26 million tons of cargo annually. It boasts the largest floating drydock in the western U.S.

Many excursions can be made, using Portland as a base, into the mountains of the **Cascade Range** and the **Coast Range,** or up the splendid **Columbia River Gorge.** The region is famous for its seafood: salmon and sturgeon from the **Columbia River,** trout and crayfish from the **Sun River,** oysters and crabs from the Pacific. So make a point of visiting some of the multitude of (excellent) seafood restaurants in town.

Among Portland's famous native sons are Linus Pauling, the Nobel Laureate in chemistry, and food critic James Beard.

BASIC FACTS: State of Oregon. Area code: 503. Time zone: Pacific. ZIP Code: 97208. Founded: 1842. Approximate population: city, 390,000; metropolitan area, 1,430,000. 25th-largest metropolitan area in the U.S.

CLIMATE: With more than 150 days of rainfall a year, Portland is one of the wettest cities in the country, but it is precisely this fine, persistent, London-style drizzle that has made it a garden city. Winter (Jan mean, 40°F/4°C) is relatively mild, with little snow; spring is cool, but it rains, on average, every other day from Oct to May. The best time to visit the city is between June and Sept, when the thermometer hovers around 68°F (20°C) and it sometimes doesn't rain for 2 weeks on end (whereupon the locals become anxious and talk about drought).

DISTANCES: Reno, 574 mi. (918km); Salt Lake City, 768 mi. (1,230km), San Francisco, 634 mi. (1,015km); Seattle, 175 mi. (280km).

ARRIVAL & TRANSIT INFORMATION

AIRPORT: Portland International Airport (PDX), 9 mi. (14km) NE. For information, call 234-8422.

AIRLINES: Alaska (224-2547), America West (228-0737), American (241-9145), Continental (224-4560), Delta (225-0830), Eastern (224-7550), Northwest (toll free 800/225-2525), TWA (282-1111), United (226-7211), and USAir (284-5193).

CITY LINK: The **cab** fare from the airport to dwntwn is about $20; time, about 25 min. Bus: **Raz Trans Airporter** (246-4676) leaves every 30 min., serving principal dwntwn hotels and the Greyhound terminal; fare, $5; time, 30 min. (60 min. during rush hour).
   Tri-Met Max, 701 SW Sixth Ave. (233-3511), provides remarkable public transportation by bus (free in the dwntwn area) and streetcar. However, since the metropolitan area is extensive and the number of (recommended) excursions into the surrounding country considerable, it's advisable to rent a car with unlimited mileage.

CAR RENTAL (at the airport unless otherwise indicated): Avis (249-4950); Budget (249-4550); Dollar (249-4792); Hertz (249-8216); National (249-4900); Thrifty, 10800 NE Holman St. (254-6563). For dwntwn locations, consult the local telephone directory.

LIMOUSINE SERVICES: Dav-El Limousines (toll free 800/922-0343) and Oregon Limo Service (283-2275).

TAXIS: Taxis are comparatively few and dear; they may not be hailed on the street, but can be taken from the waiting lines outside the major hotels, or summoned by phone: **Broadway Cab** (227-1234) or **Radio Cab** (227-1212).

TRAIN: Amtrak station, 800 NW Sixth Ave. (241-4290).

INTERCITY BUSES: Greyhound, 550 NW Sixth Ave. (243-2323).

INFORMATION & TOURS

TOURIST INFORMATION: The **Portland Convention and Visitors Association,** 26 SW Salmon St., OR 97204 (503/222-2223 or 275-9750).
   For a **recorded message** giving a list of all current cultural events and shows, call 233-3333.

GUIDED TOURS: Eagle Flight Center (airplane), Portland-Hillsboro Airport, Hillsboro (648-7151): Flights over Mount St. Helens, the Columbia Gorge, or the Pacific coast (during the whale migrations). Spectacular. Year round, weather permitting.
   Gray Line Tours (bus), 400 SW Broadway (226-6755): Guided bus tours of Portland and surroundings (Mount Hood, Columbia River, Mount St. Helens, etc.). Daily mid-May through Oct.
   Oregon Vineyard Tours (bus), 2701 NW Vaughan (Suite 700), Montgomery Park (247-7709): Guided tours of Oregon's principal wine growers; includes lunch and wine-tasting. Resv. required.
   Sternwheeler M/V Columbia Gorge (boat), N. Waterfront, 606 NW Front Ave. (223-3928): Sternwheeler trips on the Willamette River and Columbia River, Fri–Sun Oct 1–June 15. The rest of the year the *Columbia Gorge* makes daily excursion trips through the Columbia Gorge, leaving from Cascade Locks.

SIGHTS, ATTRACTIONS & ACTIVITIES

ADVENTURES: **Go-for-it Adventures** (boat), 15745 NW Norwich St., Beaverton (645-4337): Rafting down the Columbia River, Clackamas River, and Willamette River; June–Sept.

River Drifters Whitewater Tours (boat), 13570 NW Lakeview Dr. (645-6264): Rafting down different rivers in the area; June–Sept.

ARCHITECTURAL HIGHLIGHTS ☀️ ⛪ **Arlene Schnitzer Concert Hall,** 1057 SW Broadway (248-4496): Formerly the Paramount, this is a magnificent, flamboyantly rococo movie palace from the 1920s converted at a cost of $9 million into an auditorium, the Arlene Schnitzer Concert Hall (known locally as "The Schnitz"), where you can hear concerts of classical music as well as jazz and pop. Home of the Oregon Symphony Orchestra. With three other contiguous performance facilities, it constitutes the **Portland Center for the Performing Arts.** An absolute must.

⛪ **Civic Auditorium,** 222 SW Clay St. (248-4496): Ultramodern concert hall, acoustically one of the finest in the U.S. Home of the Portland Opera Association and the Portland Ballet. In front of the building lies Ira's Fountain (see "Monuments," below) with its spectacular array of terraces, basins, and waterfalls.

⛪ **Portland Building,** 1120 SW Fifth Ave.: The most defiantly ultramodern building in the U.S.; a sort of gigantic concrete birthday cake (others think that "jukebox" is more appropriate), in pastel tones of blue, beige, and brown, housing federal government offices, shops, and a restaurant. It's a 1982 work of architect Michael Graves, and you should see it, if only out of curiosity.

⛪ **Portland Center for the Performing Arts (PCPA),** SW Broadway and Main St. (248-4496): Opened in 1987, this elegant architectural exercise in red brick and smoked glass comprises two adjoining auditoriums: the 900-seat **Intermediate Theater** and the 370-seat **Dolores Winningstad Theater;** the **Arlene Schnitzer Concert Hall** (see above) is across the street, and the **Civic Auditorium** (see above) is five blocks south. In this cultural heart of Portland you'll find the Civic Theater, the New Rose Theater, and the Oregon Shakespeare Festival.

⛪ **U.S. Bancorp Tower,** 111 SW Fifth Ave. (275-6111): An unexpected kind of skyscraper: beautiful pink granite and mirror glass, dubbed "Big Pink" by its admirers. One of the major features of the Portland skyline.

CHURCHES/SYNAGOGUES: ⛪ **First Congregational Church,** 1126 SW Park Ave. (228-7219): A fine example of Venetian Gothic from around 1900. Its helical spire and downstairs gallery of contrasting beige and black stone are well worth seeing. Open daily.

☀️⛪ **The Grotto (Sanctuary of Our Sorrowful Mother),** Sandy Blvd. and NE 85th Ave. (254-7371): Open-air cathedral carved out of the foot of a great rock face 10 stories high. At the top of the cliff is a monastery surrounded by beautiful gardens, overlooking the Columbia River. Opened in 1924, this Marian sanctuary is visited each year by half a million of the faithful. Open daily.

HISTORIC BUILDINGS: The ⛪ **Bybee-Howell House,** Howell Park Rd., Sauvie Island, 14 mi. (22km) north via U.S. 30 (621-3344): A typical 19th-century farmhouse, originally built in 1856 and scrupulously restored. Illustrates the life-style of the first Oregon settlers; interesting little museum of agriculture. Open Wed–Sun June to early Sept.

DOWNTOWN PORTLAND

N

30

FREMONT BRIDGE

N.W. THURMAN ST.

N.W. FRONT AVE.

Willamette River

To Portland Int'l Airport, Fort Vancouver

N.W. QUIMBY ST.

N.W. PETTYGROVE ST.

N.W. OVERTON ST.

N.W. NORTHRUP ST.

N.W. MARSHALL ST.

BROADWAY BRIDGE

405

N.W. LOVEJOY ST.

N.W. KEARNEY ST.

N.W. JOHNSON ST.

N.W. IRVING ST.

Union Station

N.W. FRONT AVE.

STEEL BRIDGE

N.W. HOYT ST.

Bus Terminal

N.W. GLISAN ST.

N.W. 20 AVE.
N.W. 19 AVE.
N.W. 18 AVE.
N.W. 17 AVE.
N.W. 16 AVE.
N.W. 15 AVE.

N.W. FLANDERS ST.

N.W. EVERETT ST.

N.W. DAVIS ST.

North Park Blocks

American Advertising Museum

N.W. COUCH ST.

W. BURNSIDE ST.

30

OLD TOWN

BURNSIDE BRIDGE

To Washington Park, Pittock Mansion, Int'l Rose Test Garden

S.W. ALDER ST.

S.W. ASH ST.

S.W. OAK ST.

S.W. PINE ST.

S.W. STARK ST.

Saturday Market and Sunday Too

Fountain Plaza

S.W. MORRISON ST.

Civic Stadium

S.W. 11 AVE.
S.W. 10 AVE.
S.W. 9 AVE.
S.W. PARK AVE.
S.W. BROADWAY
S.W. 6 AVE.

S.W. WASHINGTON ST.

CHINATOWN/YAMHILL MARKET

Waterfront Park

To Lewis & Clark Memorial

S.W. YAMHILL ST.

S.W. TAYLOR ST.

S.W. 5 AVE.
S.W. 4 AVE.
S.W. 3 AVE.
S.W. 2 AVE.
S.W. 1 AVE.

To Forest Park

S.W. JEFFERSON ST.

S.W. SALMON ST.

S.W. MAIN ST.

Pioneer Post Office

Central Bus Depot

MORRISON BRIDGE

To Museum of Science, Portland Zoo

26

Oregon Art Institute

S.W. COLUMBIA ST.

South Park Blocks

Oregon Historical Center

Court House

Portlandia Statue

City Hall

Plaza Blocks

S.W. MADISON ST.

S.W. CLAY ST.

Portland Building

S.W. MARKET ST.

26

26

Ira's Fountain

HAWTHORNE BRIDGE

Portland State University

Tinted area is Fareless Square

       ▲ **City Hall,** 1220 SW Fifth Ave. (226-3161): Designed by architect William Whidden to look like an Italian palazzo, this unusual building is rich in rococo ornament and decoration in true 19th-century style (1895).

       ▲ **Pioneer Courthouse,** Fifth Ave. and Morrison St. (221-3800): This elegant Victorian courthouse, the first federal building in the Northwest (1875), has recovered its original luster after long and careful restoration. Its architecture is one of the charms of Pioneer Courthouse Sq., a complex of gardens with fountain, waterfall, and stepped terraces which appeals greatly to strollers.

       ☼▲ **Pittock Mansion,** 3229 NW Pittock Dr. (248-4469): Built between 1909 and 1914 by the founder of *The Oregonian,* the most important daily paper in the city, this enormous manor house in French Renaissance style still has an abundance of antique furniture as well as 46 acres (19ha) of beautiful gardens. Wonderful view of the city and the distant mountains. Open daily; closed hols. and the first 2 weeks in Jan.

INDUSTRIAL TOURS: The **Blitz-Weinhard Brewery,** 1133 W. Burnside St. (222-4351): The largest of the local micro-breweries (Portland boasts the most breweries of any U.S. city: seven in total). Visit to the plant where beers have been brewed for over 100 years. Free tasting. Open Mon–Fri.

    The **Pendleton Woolen Mills,** 10505 SE 17th Ave., Milwaukie (654-0444), 6 mi. (10km) south on Ore. 99E: Some of the finest sweaters and woolens in the U.S. come from the famous Pendleton plant. You can watch every stage in the manufacturing process, from the sorting of raw wool to washing and weaving. Interesting. Visits Mon–Fri by appointment; closed the first 2 weeks in July.

MARKETS: ▲ **Saturday Market and Sundays Too,** 108 W. Burnside St., under the Burnside Bridge (222-6072): Every Sat and Sun 10am–5pm more than 300 artists, craftspeople, and farmers display their wares in this picturesque open-air market. Very popular with the locals since 1973. Open from Easter to Christmas.

MONUMENTS: ☼▲ **Ira's Fountain,** Third Ave. and SW Clay St.: A spectacular futurist design by Lawrence Halprin comprising basins, waterfalls, and fountains down which flows 13,000 gal. (49,500 liters) of water a minute. In the heart of downtown; lots of splashing around in summer.

       ☼▲ **Portlandia,** 1120 SW Fifth Ave.: This gigantic figure by Raymond Kaskey, 35 ft. (10m) high, represents a kind of marine Venus, on her knees with a trident in one hand. Its size never fails to surprise visitors. Standing in front of the Portland Building (see "Architectural Highlights," above), this comically pompous work in beaten copper turns out to be nothing but a giant reproduction of the city's official seal.

       ☼▲ **Weather Machine,** Pioneer Courthouse Sq.: Built by the Omen Design Group, the whimsical *Weather Machine,* dating from 1988, is one of the city's most bizarre public artworks. The 25-ft. (7.6m) column gauges the changing environmental conditions with an eccentric collection of lights, figurines, and symbols. The best time to visit the mechanical sculpture is during the daily forecast at noon, a 2-min. festival complete with fanfares, plumes of steam, and flashing lights.

MUSEUMS OF ART: ☼▲ **American Advertising Museum,** 9 NW Second Ave. at Couch St. (226-0000): The world's first museum entirely devoted to commercial publicity in all its forms, from 18th-century shop signs and sandwich-man's boards to modern radio and TV spot commercials. More than 7,000 ads, some of which are genuine works of art. Unusual and fascinating. Open Wed–Sun.

Lawrence Gallery, 842 SW First Ave. (224-9442): Temporary exhibitions of painting, ceramics, sculpture, modern jewelry, etc., with more than 150 different artists represented. Open Mon–Sat.

Oregon Art Institute, 1219 SW Park Ave. (226-2811): One of the best art museums in the Northwest, with fine collections of pre-Columbian, Far Eastern, African, and Pacific Northwest Native American material. The museum also features the very productive contemporary art community in the area. The main building, by Pietro Belluschi, dates from 1932. The open-air Sculpture Mall with its fountains is worth a visit all to itself. Open Tues–Sun.

MUSEUMS OF SCIENCE & HISTORY: Oregon Historical Center, 1230 SW Park Ave. (222-1741): A comprehensive panorama of the Native American civilizations of the Pacific Northwest, both before and after the coming of the white man. The history of the Oregon Trail and its pioneers is illustrated by collections of miniature covered wagons and boat models. Well-stocked library on the settlement of the Northwest. Interesting; open Mon–Sat.

Oregon Museum of Science and Industry/OMSI, 4015 SW Canyon Rd. (222-2828): A remarkable museum of science, instructive and up-to-date, covering the whole span from prehistory to outer space. Among its principal attractions are a robot with 3-D vision and a model of the space station of the future. Also the home of the Kendall Planetarium. Open daily.

World Forestry Center, 4033 SW Canyon Rd. (228-1367): Across from Washington Park Zoo, this group of modern all-wood buildings has an information center on one of Oregon's principal natural resources: its forests. Exhibits relating to the forest-products industry; 70-ft. (21m) "talking tree"; very realistic re-creation of a forest fire; model of a paper mill, etc. Interesting; open daily.

PANORAMAS: Atwater's: See "Restaurants," below.

Council Crest Park, SW Greenway Ave. (796-5193): This little public park not far from downtown rises to a maximum elevation of 1,073 ft. (327m), the highest point in the city. Belvedere with unobstructed view of the Willamette River, Mount Hood, Mount St. Helens, and the Portland skyline below.

Pittock Mansion: See "Historic Buildings," above.

PARKS & GARDENS: Crystal Springs Rhododendron Garden, SE 28th Ave. near SE Woodstock Blvd. (771-8386): A must for every visitor; more than 2,500 rhododendron bushes, as well as azaleas, flower here in Apr–May, and a superb sight they are. Open daily.

Hoyt Arboretum, 4000 SW Fairview Blvd. (228-8732): Established in 1928, this 180-acre (73ha) garden, part of Washington Park (see below) contains the largest collection of conifers in the country: 650 varieties. 10 miles of gentle trails wind past such special features as the Vietnam Veterans' Memorial and the Winter Garden, while offering spectacular views of the city and Mount Hood. Open daily.

Mount Tabor Park, SE 60th Ave. between Yamhill St. and Division St. (796-5193): The only municipal park in the country that occupies the crater of an extinct volcano. Fine view of the city and the mountains; public concerts in summer. Open daily.

Sauvie Island, 14 mi. (22km) NW on U.S. 30: This island in the Columbia River is very popular in summer, the ideal place for picnics, fishing, walking, bicycling, or just doing nothing. Among its main attractions is the Bybee-Howell House (see "Historic Buildings," above).

Tom McCall Waterfront Park, SW Front Ave. between Steel Bridge and River Place: This pretty, tree-shaded 23-acre (9ha) park, the pride of Portland, occupies land originally intended for a riverfront highway. With its many shops and restaurants along the edge of the park, it's an agreeable place for a walk, a stone's throw from downtown.

☀🔭 **Washington Park,** reached by West Burnside St. or Canyon Rd. (796-5193): This 145-acre (60ha) park overlooks Portland from its hilltop emplacement; it features the very beautiful **Japanese Garden** and the magnificent **International Rose Test Garden,** with more than 400 different varieties of roses. The best times for a visit are June and Sept. Splendid view of the city.

PERFORMING ARTS: For daily listings of all shows and cultural events, consult the entertainment pages of the daily paper *The Oregonian* (morning and evening) as well as the weekly *Willamette Week.*

Arlene Schnitzer Concert Hall, 1057 SW Broadway (248-4496): Very fine 1920s building, magnificently restored. Classical concerts and recitals. Home of the Oregon Symphony Orchestra (principal conductor: James De Preist).

Memorial Coliseum, 1401 N. Wheeler Ave. (239-4422): Pop and rock concerts; big-name shows.

New Rose Theater, 904 S.W. Main St. (222-2487): Contemporary theater; Off Broadway shows.

Portland Center for the Performing Arts, 1111 SW Broadway (248-4496): Very up-to-date entertainment complex offering contemporary and classical theater, ballet, and concerts. The West Coast Chamber Orchestra, the Pacific Ballet Theater, and the Oregon Shakespeare Festival/Portland make their home here.

Portland Civic Auditorium, 222 SW Clay St. (248-4496): Concerts, Broadway hits, musicals. Home of the Portland Opera Association (performances Sept–May) and the well-known Portland Ballet.

Portland Civic Theater, 1530 SW Yamhill St. (226-3048): Contemporary theater, drama, comedy.

Portland Repertory Theater, 25 SW Salmon St. (224-4491): Contemporary theater; wide-ranging program. The best local repertory company.

Storefront Actors' Theater, 6 SW Third Ave. (224-4001): Contemporary theater, Off Broadway shows.

Washington Park Amphitheater, Washington Park (226-1561): Open-air public concerts and free recitals (late July to Aug).

SHOPPING: Lloyd Center, NE Ninth Ave. and NE Multnomah St. (282-2511): One of the oldest and largest shopping centers in the country, with more than 100 shops and department stores. Flower-planted walkways. Skating rink in winter. Spectacular. Open daily.

Powell's Books, 1005 W. Burnside St. (228-4651): A Portland institution. With about a million books, this is one of the largest new- and used-book stores in the country. The very pleasant Anne Hughes Coffee Shop is part of the store. Pick up a map of the cavernous one-block-long building as you enter, or you risk getting lost. Open daily.

Water Tower at John's Landing, 5331 SW Macadam Ave. (228-9431): Picturesque shopping center in a renovated turn-of-the-century furniture factory. Congenial shops, pubs, and restaurants around a delightful cobbled courtyard. Open daily.

Yamhill Marketplace, SW First Ave. and Yamhill St. (224-6705): Dozens of food shops, stores, and stalls of all kinds, around a glassed-in lobby four stories high. Lively and colorful, in the heart of downtown Portland.

SPECIAL EVENTS: For the exact schedule of events below, consult the **Portland Convention and Visitors Association** (see "Tourist Information," above).

Rhododendron Show (second wknd in May): Beautiful flower show at the Crystal Springs Rhododendron Garden.

Portland Rose Festival (15 days in June): Procession of flowered carnival parades, flower show, auto races, dirigible-balloon rally, etc. Very popular since 1907.

Chamber Music Northwest (mid-June to mid-July): A well-known chamber-music festival of 25 recitals; for information, call 223-3202.

Mount Hood Festival of Jazz (early Aug): 2 days of open-air jazz concerts, with leading performers, at Gresham, 15 mi. (24km) east on I-84 (666-3810).

Artquake Festival (early Sept): Concerts, ballets, art shows on the Mall and in Old Town; very popular.

Pacific International Livestock Show (Oct): The biggest stock fair in the Northwest; rodeos, horse shows. Colorful.

SPORTS: Portland has teams in three professional sports:

Baseball (Apr–Oct): Beavers, Civic Stadium (223-2837).

Basketball (Oct–Apr): Trail Blazers, Memorial Coliseum (239-4422).

Ice Hockey (Oct–Apr): Winter Hawks, Memorial Coliseum (238-6366).

Horse Racing

Portland Meadows, 1001 N. Schmeer Rd. (285-9144), with thoroughbred and quarter horse racing Oct–Apr.

STROLLS: ☼ ⌂ **The Mall,** SW Fifth Ave. and SW Sixth Ave. around SW Alder St.: A huge pedestrians-only zone with brick sidewalks and cobbled streets lined with shops and restaurants, and embellished with gardens, fountains, and statues. The only wheeled vehicles allowed are the (free) buses and cabs. Very lively.

☼ ⌂ **Old Town,** SW 1st St. to SW Fifth Ave. on either side of W. Burnside St.: The historic heart of Portland along the Williamette River, with one of the country's finest remaining groups of 19th-century cast-iron building fronts. Antique dealers, amusing shops, restaurants, cafés. A likable place.

WINERIES: Located just west and south of Portland, are more than 35 wineries that make up Oregon's prime wine Country. The climate in this area is similar to that of northern Europe and many of Oregon's wineries have won just acclaim. Tasting rooms are open to the public year round. Among the best known:

Amity Vineyards, 18150 Amity Vineyards Rd. in Amity, 48 mi. (77km) SW via Ore. 18 and Ore. 99W (835-2362): A small family operation specializing in pinot noir. Tasting room open daily June–Oct; wkends only Nov–May.

Chateau Benoit Winery, 6850 NE Mineral Springs Rd. in Carlton, 36 mi. (57km) SW via Ore. 18 (864-3666): Located on a scenic hillside near Lafayette, this winery established in 1972 features premium varietal and sparkling wines. Tasting room open daily. Visitors are welcomed to picnic and enjoy the view.

Rex Hill Vineyards, 23 mi. (36km) SW at 30835 N. Ore. 99W, in Newberg (538-0666): Specializes in pinot noir and chardonnay. Tasting room open daily Apr–Dec, Fri–Sun Feb–Mar; closed Jan.

Sokol Blosser Winery, 5000 Sokol Blosser Lane, in Dundee, 26 mi. (42km) SW on Ore. 99W (864-2282): The vineyards have a very fine view over the Willamette Valley and the mountains. Tasting room open daily year round.

Tualatin Vineyards, Clapshaw Hill Rd., in Forest Grove, 30 mi. (48km) west via U.S. 26 and Ore. 8 (357-5005): One of Oregon's largest wine cellars, which you may visit. Tasting room open daily Feb–Dec.

WINTER SPORTS RESORTS: ☼ ⌂⌂ **Mount Bachelor Ski Area,** 180 mi. (288km) SE via I-5, Ore. 22, U.S. 20, and Century Dr. (382-2442): The best resort in Oregon, with 12 lifts; open Nov–June.

🔔🔔 **Mount Hood Meadows,** 68 mi. (108km) east via I-84, U.S. 26, and Ore. 35 (337-2222): 9 lifts; open Nov–May.

🔔 **Summit Ski Area,** 57 mi. (91km) east via I-84 and U.S. 26 (272-3351): 3 lifts; open Nov–Mar.

🔔🔔 **Timberline Lodge Ski Area,** 60 mi. (96km) east via I-84 and U.S. 26 (272-3311): 7 lifts; open Nov–May.

ACCOMMODATIONS

A Note on Accommodations: Room rates in Portland are coded as follows: **VE,** Very Expensive ($140 and up); **E,** Expensive ($90–$140); **M,** Moderate ($60–$90); **I,** Inexpensive ($30–$60); **B,** Budget (up to $30). A listing of toll free numbers is in the Appendix.

Personal Favorites (in order of preference)

☼ 🏠🏠🏠🏠 **The Heathman** (dwntwn), 1009 SW Broadway at Salmon, OR 97205 (503/241-4100; toll free, see Preferred). 152 rms, A/C, color TV, in-rm movies. AE, CB, DC, MC, V. Valet gar. $8, rest. (Heathman Restaurant), bar, 24-hr. rm svce, nightclub, concierge, free crib. *Note:* After rejuvenation at a cost of $16 million, this time-honored 1920s palace, rife w. wood paneling, Italian marble, and white Spanish granite, has recovered all its old luster. Many works of art, including a collection of Andy Warhols, add something new to its plush elegance. Very spacious, comfortable rms; exemplary svce. Its rest. is the best in town. A stone's throw from the Center for the Performing Arts. By far the best place to stay in Portland. **E–VE**

🏠🏠🏠 **Marriott** (dwntwn), 1401 SW Front Ave., OR 97201 (503/226-7600; toll free, see Marriott). 506 rms, A/C, color TV, in-rm movies. AE, CB, DC, MC, V. Valet gar. $8, pool, health club, sauna, two rests. (including King's Wharf), two bars, rm svce, disco, hrdrsr, concierge, free crib. *Note:* Big, rather bulky convention hotel pleasantly located on the Willamette River. Ultramodern comforts; spacious rms, some w. balconies and refrigerators, the best w. a view of the river and Mount Hood. Efficient svce; so-so rests. w. a beautiful view. Pretty Japanese garden. Group and business clientele; in the heart of dwntwn. VIP floor. **E–VE**

🏠🏠🏠 **Hilton Portland** (dwntwn), 921 SW Sixth Ave., OR 97204 (503/226-1611; toll free, see Hilton). 455 rms, A/C, color TV, in-rm movies. AE, CB, DC, MC, V. Gar. $8, pool, health club, sauna, rest. (Alexander's), coffee shop, bar, rm svce, nightclub, hrdrsr, free crib. *Note:* Huge, relatively modern 23-story tower in the heart of the financial district. Completely redecorated. Inviting, comfortable rms; good svce. The rest. doesn't deserve its reputation but has a fine view of distant Mount Hood. Group and convention clientele. **E**

🏠🏠 **Imperial Hotel** (dwntwn), 400 SW Broadway (at Stark), OR 97205 (503/228-7221; toll free 800/547-8282). 168 rms, A/C, in-rm movies. AE, CB, DC, MC, V. Free parking, rest., bar, rm svce, free crib. *Note:* Older, very well-run hotel in the center of Portland. The decor may be a little tired, but there's nothing at all wrong w. the comfort. Friendly reception and svce. Excellent value; regular and business clientele. **I–M**

🏠 **Red Lion Coliseum** (formerly the Thunderbird Inn; nr. dwntwn), 1225 N. Thunderbird Way, OR 97227 (503/235-8311; toll free, see Red Lion Inns). 214 rms, A/C, color TV, in-rm movies. AE, CB, DC, MC, V. Free parking, pool, rest., coffee shop, bar, valet svce, nightclub, free crib. *Note:* Large, conventional motel on the Willamette River, opposite the Memorial Coliseum. Spacious, well-designed rms; cheerful reception and svce; free airport limo. Excellent value; group clientele. **I–M**

🏠 **Mallory Hotel** (nr. dwntwn), 729 SW 15th Ave. (at Yamhill St.), OR 97205 (503/223-6311; toll free 800/228-8657). 144 rms, A/C, color TV, in-rm movies. AE, CB, DC, MC, V. Free parking, rest., bar, rm svce, free crib. *Note:* Aging but inviting hotel, recently modernized, a stone's throw from dwntwn and across from the Portland Civic Theater. Quiet location. Agreeable, pleasantly furnished rms, some w. refrigerators. Perfect for budget travelers; good value. **I–M**

Other Accommodations (from top bracket to budget)

Alexis Hotel at Riverplace (dwntwn), 1510 SW Harbor Way, OR 97201 (503/228-3233; toll free 800/345-3457). 84 rms, A/C, color TV, in-rm movies. AE, CB, DC, MC, V. Valet gar. $8, whirlpool, sauna, rest. (The Esplanade), bar, 24-hr. rm svce, nightclub, boutiques, free breakfast, concierge, free crib. *Note:* A newcomer on the local scene, this small luxury hotel is part of an ultramodern real-estate development w. a marina, residential buildings, restaurants, etc., on the Willamette River. The interior decoration and furnishing are of unusual elegance. Spacious, comfortable rms in delicate pastel shades of pale yellow and lime green, w. balconies, the best overlooking the river. Reception and svce of a high order. Well-regarded rest. serving American cuisine. VIP and upscale business clientele; a very fine place to stay. **E–VE**

The Benson (dwntwn), 309 S. Broadway, OR 97205 (503/228-2000; toll free 800/426-0670). 320 rms, A/C, color TV, in-rm movies. AE, CB, DC, MC, V. Valet parking $11, two rests. (including the London Grill), bar, 24-hr. rm svce, nightclub, concierge, free crib. *Note:* Massive grand hotel in the heart of dwntwn, built around 1910 and long regarded as the *grande dame* on the Portland scene. Comfortable, not to say plush, but the furniture of the rms is a touch outdated. Exemplary svce. The more famous of the two rests., the London Grill, isn't what it used to be. Business and convention clientele. Interesting wknd packages. **E–VE**

Red Lion Inn Columbia River (vic.), 1401 N. Hayden Island Dr., OR 97217 (503/283-2111; toll free, see Red Lion Inns). 350 rms, A/C, color TV, in-rm movies. AE, CB, DC, MC, V. Free parking, pool, two tennis courts, putting green, sauna, rest. (Misty's), coffee shop, two bars, rm svce, disco, hrdrsr, boutiques, free crib. *Note:* Luxury motel on the Columbia River. Inviting, well-designed rms w. private patios and balconies. Good physical-fitness facilities; agreeable grdn and setting. Very good svce. Group and convention clientele; 15 min. from dwntwn, 10 min. from the airport (free shuttle). Interesting wknd packages. A good place for the exhausted executive. **E**

Red Lion Inn Lloyd Center (formerly the Sheraton; nr. dwntwn), 1000 NE Multnomah St., OR 97232 (503/281-6111; toll free, see Red Lion Inns). 520 rms, A/C, color TV, in-rm movies. AE, CB, DC, MC, V. Free parking, pool, health club, two rests. (including Maxi's), coffee shop, bars, rm svce, disco, free crib. *Note:* Large, comfortable, modern 15-story hotel, recently renovated, adj. the enormous Lloyd Center shopping mall. Inviting, spacious rms w. views of the city, the river, or the mountains, many w. private balconies or patios and refrigerators. Efficient svce; acceptable rest. Group and business clientele. 5 min. from dwntwn; free airport limo. **E**

Portland Inn (dwntwn), 1414 SW Sixth Ave., OR 97201 (503/221-1611; toll free 800/648-6440). 172 rms, A/C, cable color TV. AE, CB, DC, MC, V. Free parking, pool, rest., bar, rm svce, free crib. *Note:* Older but completely renovated motel halfway between the Civic Auditorium and the university campus. Comfortable, inviting rms; efficient svce. Business and group clientele. Good value on balance. **M**

Travelodge Viscount Hotel (nr. dwntwn), 1441 NE Second Ave., OR 97232 (503/233-2401; toll free, see Travelodge). 240 rms, A/C, color TV, in-rm movies. AE, CB, DC, MC, V. Free parking, pool, rest., bar, rm svce, free crib. *Note:* Typical 10-story motel nr. the Memorial Coliseum and Lloyd Center shopping mall. Comfortable and well run; efficient svce; free coffee in rms; free airport shuttle. Business clientele. Good value. Part of the British Trusthouse-Forte hotel chain. **M**

☕ **Caravan** (nr. dwntwn), 2401 SW Fourth Ave., OR 97201
🛏 (503/226-1121). 40 rms, A/C, color TV, in-rm movies. AE,
CB, DC, MC, V. Free parking, pool, coffee shop, bar, valet svce, crib $4. *Note:*
Modest but well-run small motel 8 min. from dwntwn. Spacious, serviceable
rms w. free coffee; friendly reception and svce. Good value; ideal if you're driving
since it offers direct access to the highway system. **I**

☕ **Motel 6** (nr. dwntwn), 3104 SE Powell Blvd., OR 97202
🛏 (503/238-0600). 70 rms, A/C, color TV, free in-rm movies.
AE, DC, MC, V. *Note:* Small, unpretentious economy motel 10 min. from
dwntwn across the Ross Island Bridge. Very acceptable level of comfort; one of
the best buys in Portland. Ideal for the budget traveler. **B–I**

Airport Accommodations

☕☕ **Sheraton Inn Airport** (vic.), 8235 NE Airport Way, OR 97220
🛏 (503/281-2500; toll free, see Sheraton). 216 rms, A/C, color
TV, in-rm movies. AE, CB, DC, MC, V. Free parking, pool, health club, sauna,
rest. (Première), coffee shop, bar, 24-hr. rm svce, disco, crib $5. *Note:* Classic air-
port hotel 3 min. from the terminal (free shuttle). Comfortable and serviceable.
Acceptable rest.; good svce; interesting wknd packages. Business clientele. **E**

YMCA/Youth Hostels

Portland International Hostel (nr. dwntwn), 3031 SE Hawthorne Blvd.,
OR 97214 (503/236-3380). 50 beds. Well-run youth hostel; open year round.

RESTAURANTS

A Note on Restaurant Prices: Portland restaurant prices, per person, excluding drinks and service charges, are coded as follows: **VE,** Very Expensive
($60 and up); **E,** Expensive ($40–$60); **M,** Moderate ($25–$40); **I,** Inexpensive
($15–$25); **B,** Budget (up to $15).

Personal Favorites (in order of preference)

🍷🍷🍷 **Heathman Restaurant** (dwntwn), in the Heathman (see "Accommodations," above) (241-4100). A/C. Breakfast/
lunch/dinner daily. AE, CB, DC, MC, V. Jkt. *Specialties:* Spanish-style tapas,
Chinook salmon w. capers and horseradish sauce, Umpqua oysters w. mignonette of jalapeño pepper, Thai pork on a skewer w. apricots and mandarin sauce.
Menu changes regularly. Fine, reasonably priced wine list. *Note:* The cuisine of
this elegant, intimate luxury rest. emphasizes local produce, particularly seafood;
it's prepared in ways that are often innovative and delicate. Beautiful old-world
setting and atmosphere (the hotel dates from 1928). Very polished svce. The
preferred dwntwn location for business meals; successful enough that resv. are
strongly advised. *American/Seafood.* **I–M**

🍷🍷🍷 **Couch Street Fish House** (dwntwn), 103 NW Third Ave.
(223-6173). A/C, Dinner only, nightly; closed July 4,
Thanksgiving, Dec 24–25. AE, CB, DC, MC, V. Jkt. *Specialties:* anything that
swims, served broiled, poached, or in a sauce—Dungeness crab, Chinook salmon, Oregon sturgeon, excellent mahi-mahi (dolphin Hawaiian style). Good list
of Northwest wines. *Note:* The best known of Portland's many seafood rests., in
the heart of Old Town. Everything is absolutely fresh and impeccably cooked.
Pretty Victorian decor on a background of exposed-brick and white walls. Svce a
touch pompous. Valet parking. Resv. strongly advised. *Seafood.* **I–M**

🍷🍷 **Sweet Tibbie Dunbar** (nr. dwntwn), 718 NE 12th Ave. (232-
1801). A/C. Lunch Mon–Fri, dinner nightly, brunch Sun;
closed Dec 25. AE, MC, V. Jkt. *Specialties:* roast duck, prime rib, leg of lamb,
catch of the day, seafood. *Note:* Fashionable rest. charmingly got up as an old
English inn. Very polished cuisine at reasonable prices; the delightful adj. pub
allows you a pleasant wait until your table is free. Smooth svce; resv. advised.
American/Seafood. **I**

Ringside West (nr. dwntwn), 2165 W. Burnside St. (223-1513). A/C. Dinner only, nightly; closed hols. AE, MC, V. Jkt. *Specialties:* steak, prime rib, superb onion rings, fresh seafood. Mediocre wine list. *Note:* Long-established steakhouse, three blocks west of the Civic Stadium. Dimly lit roadhouse atmosphere, w. sports decor and prizefight pictures (as the name implies). Excellent beef cuts moderately priced. New York strip is a favorite. Efficient tuxedo-clad waiters. Locally popular. Resv. essential. Other location: The Ringside East, 14021 NE Glisan (255-0750); lunch Mon–Fri, dinner nightly. *Steak/Seafood.* **I**

Henry Thiele's (nr. dwntwn), 2305 W. Burnside St. (223-2060). A/C. Breakfast/lunch/dinner daily; closed Jan 1, July 4, Dec 25. AE, CB, DC, MC, V. *Specialties:* German pancakes, wienerschnitzel, sesame chicken, frikadellen. Good desserts (notably Princess Charlotte pudding). *Note:* An honorable part of the local gastronomic scene since 1908; the food, predominantly German, is as solid and serious as the setting. Locally popular. Svce on the abrupt side, but very reasonable prices. *German/American.* **B–I**

Other Restaurants (from top bracket to budget)

Atwater's (dwntwn), U.S. Bancorp Tower, 111 SW Fifth Ave. (220-3600). A/C. Dinner nightly, brunch Sun. AE, CB, DC, MC, V. Jkt. *Specialties:* grilled razor clams w. soy-sesame butter; poached salmon in a wine-and-cream sauce; sturgeon sautéed w. fennel, Pernod, and grapefruit; roast chicken breast filled w. basil pesto and black-walnut cream sauce. Remarkable wine list, especially for northwestern vineyards. *Note:* Not many of the country's skyscraper rests. deserve three glasses; this one does. On the 30th floor of the U.S. Bancorp Tower in the heart of dwntwn Portland, Atwater's will entice you not only w. its contemporary regional cuisine featuring local seafood, but also w. a panoramic view of city and mountains. Elegant setting; faultless svce; big business clientele. Resv. strongly advised. *American/Seafood.* **M–E**

Alessandro's (dwntwn), 301 SW Morrison St. (222-3900). A/C. Lunch Mon–Fri, dinner Mon–Sat; closed hols. AE, CB, DC, MC, V. Jkt. *Specialties:* ravioli w. ricotta filling, Alessandro's bucatini, fritto misto, saltimbocca, risotto w. mushrooms. Good list of Italian wines. *Note:* By offering a Roman-inspired cuisine and featuring the finest raw materials, chef Alessandro Fasani has acquired a devoted following. His baby veal Provimi, porcini mushrooms, De Cecco pastas, and Pacific seafood are outstanding. Sumptuous setting w. antiques and works of art. Very good svce. Reserve ahead. *Italian.* **I–M**

John's Fish and Meat Market (nr. dwntwn), 115 NW 22nd Ave. (223-2119). A/C. Lunch Mon–Fri, dinner nightly; closed hols. AE, CB, DC, MC, V. Jkt. *Specialties:* steak, stuffed breast of chicken, fish of the day, roast beef, fresh salmon in season. Very good homemade pastry. *Note:* The waiters wear big butchers' aprons, the decor is pleasantly kitsch, and the food, particularly the meat, is faultless. A classic of its kind. *Steak/Seafood.* **I**

Rheinlander (nr. dwntwn), 5035 NE Sandy Blvd. (288-5503). A/C. Dinner nightly; brunch Sun; closed Thanksgiving, Dec 24–25. AE, MC, V. *Specialties:* wienerschnitzel, sauerbraten, hassenpfeffer (jugged hare in cream sauce), apfelstrudel. *Note:* Generous portions of authentic German food in an appropriate Bavarian-inn setting. Noisy but cheerful music. Locally popular; very good value. *German.* **I**

Dan and Louis Oyster Bar (dwntwn), 208 SW Ankeny St. (227-5906). A/C. Lunch/dinner daily; closed hols. AE, MC, V. *Specialties:* oysters on the half shell, oyster soup, shellfish, crabs, fisherman's stew. No wine, beer, or liquor. *Note:* A true local institution, this venerable seafood rest. has its own oyster beds on the Pacific coast. Since 1907, four generations of fishermen and restaurant-keepers of the Wachsmuth family have succeeded to this establishment; photos, ship models, and personal souvenirs adorn the walls. Often crowded and noisy. A place you shouldn't miss. *Seafood.* **B–I**

🍷 **Uncle Chen** (dwntwn), 529 SW Third Ave. (248-1199). A/C.
🍸 Lunch Mon–Sat, dinner nightly. AE, MC, V. *Specialties:* Szechuan shrimp, General Tso's chicken, typical Hunan and Szechuan dishes. *Note:* The place is modest but the food is serious. Spacious, airy Far Eastern decor. The best Chinese food in the area; locally popular. *Chinese.* **B–I**

🍷 **Rose's West** (nr. dwntwn), 315 NW 23rd Ave. (227-5181).
🍸 A/C. Breakfast/lunch/dinner daily; closed hols. DC, MC, V. *Specialties:* kosher dishes, stuffed cabbage, corned beef, blintzes, overstuffed sandwiches, Viennese pastry. *Note:* A deli in the grand old New York tradition; the desserts are absolutely superb. Open late; locally popular. Other location: NE 122nd Ave. at Glisan St. (254-6545). *American.* **B**

Cafeterias/Fast Food

☼ **Original Pancake House** (vic.), 8600 SW Barbur Blvd. at 24th Ave. (246-9007). Breakfast/lunch only, Wed–Sun. No credit cards. Has reigned unchallenged for more than a quarter of a century—pancakes w. apple, w. orange, w. cointreau, w. cream, w. cherries, and on and on. A local landmark, overrun on wknds. Pleasant colonial-style decor. Well worth the 15-min. drive from dwntwn on I-5S to Exit 296B.

BARS & NIGHTCLUBS

Be Bop USA (vic.), 11753 Beaverton Hillsdale Hwy. at Beaverton (644-4433). Rock 'n' roll of the '50s and '60s nightly. Attracts a very young crowd. The biggest weekend party in town. A 20-min. drive from dwntwn on U.S. 26 W and Beaverton-Tigard Hwy. (Ore. 217S).

Brasserie Montmartre (dwntwn), 626 SW Park Ave. (224-5552). Classy nightspot featuring live jazz 7 nights a week. Also appealing rest.

Bridgeport Brewpub (nr. dwntwn), 1313 NW Marshall St. (241-7179). Brewery and pub offering outstanding pizzas and some of the best homemade beers brewed in the Pacific Northwest. Rustic and warm atmosphere. Open Tues–Sun.

Goose Hollow Inn (dwntwn), 1927 SW Jefferson St. (228-7010). Friendly, congenial pub belonging to Portland's mayor. Locally popular with aspiring progressive politicos.

☼ **Jake's Famous Crawfish** (dwntwn), 401 SW 12th Ave. (226-1419). Fashionable bar, famous for more than a century. Crowded and noisy. Also an acceptable but overpriced rest. Open nightly.

Key Largo (dwntwn), 31 NW First Ave. (223-9919). Blues, jazz, or rock at its best. Tropical atmosphere with open patio (weather permitting). Open nightly.

The Last Laugh (dwntwn), 426 NW Sixth Ave. (295-2844). The oldest and best local comedy club; the most famous comics appear here. Also a reputable rest. Open nightly.

Starry Night (dwntwn), 8 NW Sixth Ave. (227-0071). Trendy disco; New Wave music.

Warehouse (nr. dwntwn), 320 SE 2nd St. (232-9645). Hot top-40 dance club with an under-21 crowd.

NEARBY EXCURSIONS

☼ **COLUMBIA RIVER GORGE** (65 mi./104km east as far as the Hood River via U.S. 30 or I-84): Some of the grandest scenery in the Northwest. The Columbia River, marking the northern border of the state of Oregon, cuts its channel between the steep rock faces of the mountains of the **Cascade Range.** Two fine roads parallel it: I-84, which follows the river at the foot of the gorges, and the scenic U.S. 30, which zigzags along the heights between forest and precipice, passing 11 great waterfalls from **Troutdale** to Bonneville Dam. Unforgettable view from **Crown Point State Park,** rising 1,968 ft. (600m) above the romantic landscape of fjords delineated by the Columbia River.

About 23 mi. (38km) from Portland you'll come upon **Multnomah Falls,** fourth highest (620 ft./189m in two stages) in the U.S., spanning the basalt cliff like the **Latourell Falls,** a little farther on, where the river suddenly drops 246 ft. (75m). And 9 mi. (14km) east of Multnomah Falls, stop at **Bonneville Dam** to watch the salmon (in springtime) and other kinds of fish (Mar–Nov) ascending the Columbia River; spectacular. An excursion well worth taking is the 2-hr. cruise aboard the 600-passenger sternwheeler *Columbia Gorge* from **Cascade Locks,** daily mid-June to Sept; for resv. call 374-8427 or 223-3928.

FORT VANCOUVER NATIONAL HISTORIC SITE (10 mi./16km north across the Columbia River in neighboring Vancouver, Wash.) (206/696-7655): One of the oldest white settlements in the Northwest. Between 1825 and 1849 this was the center of operations for the legendary Hudson's Bay Company and its fur-trading empire; in 1848 the U.S. Army built its first military post here. The fort and the stockaded pioneer village have been reconstructed by the National Park Service as a facsimile of the original. A must for history buffs. Open daily.

WARM SPRINGS RESERVATION (119 mi./190km SE on U.S. 26): Established by a treaty of 1885, this reserve, inhabited by the Paiute and Wasco tribes, is visited every year by thousands of Americans and foreigners, attracted by the hot springs, authentic Native American dances (every Sun May–Sept), many open-air activities (horseback riding, rafting, golf, fishing, etc.), very comfortable hotel run by the Inter-tribal Council, and the excellence of its food. Resv. must be made as far ahead as possible.

Where to Stay

Kah-Nee-Ta Lodge and Village, P.O. Box K, Warm Springs, OR 97761 (503/553-1112; toll free 800/831-0100). Besides the hotel's 140 rms, there are a score of rustic cottages and even tepees for lovers of local color. *Hotels and cottages,* **M–E;** *tepees,* **I**—but lower rates off-season.

FARTHER AFIELD

COLUMBIA RIVER GORGE & MOUNT HOOD (190 mi./360km r.t. via U.S. 30E, Wash. 14E, I-84W, Ore. 35S, and U.S. 26W): As far as Bonneville Dam, follow the route described above for a visit to the **Columbia Gorge** (see "Nearby Excursions," above). From Bonneville Dam, take the Wash. 14 scenic route along the north bank of the Columbia River as far as ⚓ **The Dalles,** the western end of the famous Oregon Trail. It was at this once-active little river port that the pioneers from far-off Missouri left their heavy covered wagons for boats, in which they traveled to the mouth of the Columbia River on the last stage of their long odyssey. See mementos of the period at the **Fort Dalles Museum,** 15th St. and Garrison St. (296-4547), open Tues–Sun May–Sept, Wed–Sun the rest of the year; and at the **Wasco County Courthouse,** 406 W. 2nd St. (296-4798), open Tues–Sat Apr–Oct.

After a look at the dam and enormous lock on the Columbia River at the **Dalles Dam and Reservoir,** 3 mi. (4.8km) east on I-84, open daily in summer, Mon–Fri the rest of the year, return to the Hood River on the Interstate which follows it. The very scenic Ore. 35S will then take you through the wooded mountains of the **Cascade Range** to the winter-sports resort of ⚒ **Mount Hood**

Meadows, halfway up 11,235-ft. (3,424m) **Mount Hood,** highest peak in Oregon. Wonderful view of the surrounding crests; however, novices are not advised to try climbing Mount Hood.

Return to Portland on U.S. 26. This trip is a nature lover's delight.

Where to Stay En Route

☼⛤♺♺♺ **Columbia Gorge,** 4000 Westcliff Dr., Hood River, OR 97031 (503/386-5566; toll free 800/345-1921). 46 rms. Handsome 1920s hotel overlooking the gorges. Excellent rest. **E–VE**

☼⛤♺♺ **Timberline Lodge,** 6 mi. (10km) NE on U.S. 26 in the Timberline Ski Area, OR 97028 (503/272-3311). 59 rms. Picturesque resort hotel at the foot of Mount Hood. **I–M**

☼⛤🔭 **MOUNT ST. HELENS NATIONAL VOLCANIC MONUMENT** (210 mi./336km r.t. via I-5N, Wash. 504E, and the reverse on the way back): This national monument, with an area of about 110,000 acres (44,517ha), was created as recently as 1982; it encompasses Mount St. Helens itself and the whole area devastated by the volcano's sudden eruption on May 18, 1980, after a century of deceptive slumber. The gigantic explosion threw ashes and burning gas 12 mi. (19km) up into the atmosphere, and caused the death of 58 people. Five subsequent eruptions reduced the surrounding countryside to ashes and created some startling lunar landscapes. Having lost 1,300 ft. (396m) of its height in the course of the first eruption, Mount St. Helens now reaches an elevation of only 8,377 ft. (2,554m).

Two scenic roads are open year round: Wash. 503 to **Yale Lake,** south of the volcano, or Wash. 504 to the visitor center on **Silver Lake,** west of Mount St. Helens. The **visitor center** (206/274-6644), open daily, has much movie and still-photo documentation of the 1980 eruption, as well as a giant model of the volcano. The forest roads to the east of Mount St. Helens (FR 25, FR 81, FR 83, and FR 90 in particular), from which you can get the most spectacular views, are generally impassable in bad weather, and closed by snow Oct–May. For highway information in the volcano area, call 206/696-7500. In summer, 100 climbers a day are allowed to climb as far as the crater under the supervision of guides from the U.S. Forest Service. Visitors can also fly over Mount St. Helens in a small plane or helicopter; call Pacific West Aviation (206/748-0035) or Bluebird Helicopters (206/238-5326).

For **general information,** contact Mount St. Helens National Volcanic Monument, Rte. 1, Box 369, Amboy, WA 98601 (206/247-5473). It's well worth going out of your way to visit Mount St. Helens and the surrounding countryside.

☼⛤🔭 **PACIFIC COAST, SALEM & OREGON CITY** (380 mi./608km r.t. via U.S. 30W, U.S. 101S, U.S. 20E, and I-5N): Wonderful seascapes and picturesque fishing villages along the Pacific coast between **Astoria** (particularly fine view from the **Astoria Column** at the mouth of the Columbia River) and **Newport,** 135 mi. (216km) to the south. Take the trip if only for the beauty of the scenery. For a detailed description of this part of the itinerary, see Chapter 46 on the Pacific Coast.

You return to Portland via U.S. 20E and I-5N, stopping at ⚑ **Salem,** capital of the state of Oregon. Visit the **State Capitol,** a handsome marble building in Greek Revival style, at Court St. and Summer St. (378-4423), open daily; also ⚑ **Mission Mill Village,** 1313 Mill St. SE (585-7012), open Tues–Sat, an interesting group of carefully restored old houses.

Your last stop will be at ⚑ **Oregon City,** at the foot of the falls on the Williamette River; the **McLoughlin House National Historic Site** at 713 Center St. (656-5146), open Tues–Sun, is a perfect example of an 1845 colonial residence. This splendidly restored museum-home was built by the former administrator of the Hudson's Bay Company and of the British territories in the Northwest from 1824 to 1846.

Where to Stay En Route

☼♛♛♛♛ **Salishan Lodge,** on U.S. 101, Gleneden Beach, OR 97388 (503/764-2371). 200 rms. One of the best hotels in the U.S. Contemporary urbanity on Siletz Bay. **E–VE**

♛♛♛ **Embarcadero Resort,** 1000 SE Bay Blvd., Newport, OR 97365 (503/265-8521). 110 rms. Luxurious hotel-marina on the Yaquina River. **M–E**

♛♛ **Tolovana Inn,** 3400 S. Hemlock St., Tolovana Park, OR 97145 (503/436-2211). 180 rms. Comfortable vacation motel w. views of the ocean and Haystack Rock. **I–M**

CHAPTER 45

SEATTLE

□ □ □

Hidden away at the head of the fjord called **Puget Sound,** almost surrounded by water, crowned from afar by the snowy pyramid of **Mount Rainier,** 14,140 ft. (4,392m) high, and the crests of the **Cascade Mountains,** the "San Francisco of the North" rejoices in some of the country's most magnificent scenery. Like its California equivalent, Seattle is fortunate in having a setting and a climate that are an inseparable part of its identity.

Named after the Native American chief Noah Sealth, who in 1851 gave a friendly reception to the first white settlers, five families from the Midwest, Seattle was originally no more than a village of trappers and loggers. Its prosperity came first with the Klondike gold rush of 1897, and subsequently with its two natural resources, lumber and fish. The millions of ties that went into the construction of the first western railroads came mostly from around Seattle and from the state of Washington. Though the famous 605-ft. (184m) **Space Needle,** left over from the 1962 "Century 21 Exposition," and its attendant downtown high-rises have supplanted what was once a forest of Douglas pines, lumber still accounts for a good deal of the local wealth, as does the sea (one out of every six inhabitants owns a boat) and its products. The leading fishing port in the U.S., Seattle is also the capital of the aerospace industry. Almost one out of every two airliners now in service in the Western world first took off from **King County International Airport,** headquarters of Boeing Corporation. A downtown building boom with many skyscrapers in the 60-story range and the tallest building on the West Coast, the 76-story **Columbia Center,** led in 1989 to a drastic measure sharply limiting the size and quantity of downtown towers.

The largest city in the state of Washington has grown from the ashes of a disastrous fire in 1889 that spared only the picturesque **Pioneer Square** enclave, once the heart of the ill-famed Skid Row district. The soggy climate of the "Emerald City," as Seattle is sometimes called, has made it one of the greenest places in the U.S. Moreover, within easy reach the tourist will find the magnificent forests of **Olympic National Park,** while the superb snowfields of **Snoqualmie National Forest** await the skiing enthusiast. If you enjoy the pleasures of the table, you'll find in the city's restaurants the whole gamut of local seafood which is the gastronomic glory of the Pacific Northwest: oysters from Olympia and Quilcene, Chinook salmon from the Copper River, Columbia River sturgeon, squid from Puget Sound, and Dungeness crabs, to name only the most enticing. The people of Seattle are among the most friendly and hospitable in the U.S.

Author Mary McCarthy, the late choreographer Robert Joffrey, and guitarist Jimi Hendrix were all born in Seattle.

BASIC FACTS: State of Washington. Area code: 206. Time zone: Pacific. ZIP Code: 98101. Founded: 1851. Approximate population: city, 500,000; metropolitan area, 2,360,000. 15th-largest metropolitan area in the U.S.

CLIMATE: Slickers and umbrellas are appropriate in Seattle at all times of year. With an annual average of 160 days of rainfall, the better part of it between Oct and Apr, it's one of the dampest cities in the country. Warmed on one side by the Japan Current in the Pacific, and protected on the other by the Cascade range, Seattle enjoys a temperate climate even in winter (Jan average, 41°F/5°C), while in summer the mercury rarely rises above 78°F (25°C); the average for July is 66°F (19°C).

DISTANCES: Portland, 175 mi. (280km); Salt Lake City, 834 mi. (1,335km); San Francisco, 810 mi. (1,295km); Vancouver, 144 mi. (230km); Yellowstone, 762 mi. (1,219km).

ARRIVAL & TRANSIT INFORMATION

AIRPORT: Sea-Tac International Airport (SEA), 14 mi. (23km) south. For information, call 433-5217.

U.S. AIRLINES: Alaska (433-3100), America West (763-0737), American (241-0920), Continental (624-1740), Delta (433-4711), Eastern (622-1881), Hawaiian (toll free 800/367-5320), Northwest (433-3500), Pan Am (toll free 800/221-1111), TWA (477-9400), United (447-3700), and USAir (587-6229).

FOREIGN CARRIERS: Air Canada (622-5509), British Airways (toll free 800/247-9297), Japan Airlines (toll free 800/525-3663), and SAS (toll free 800/221-2350).

CITY LINK: The **cab** fare from the airport to downtown is about $22–$24; time, 25 min. Bus: **Gray Line Airport Express** (626-6088); leaves approx. every 20 min., serving principal dwntwn hotels; fare, $6; time, about 25 min. The **Metro Transit System** (bus nos. 174 and 194) also provides service from Sea-Tac International Airport to dwntwn Seattle every 20–30 min.; fare, $1.

Excellent **public transportation** by bus, trolley car, and streetcar (free in dwntwn). Spectacular **monorail** link between Seattle Center and Westlake Mall at Fourth Ave. and Pine St., leaving every 15 min. 10am–midnight; fare, 50¢; time, 95 sec. Don't miss it. For information on public transportation, call Metro Transit System (447-4800).

Cabs are expensive and their drivers not always honest.

You won't need to rent a car unless you're planning excursions (recommended) around Puget Sound or into the surrounding mountains.

CAR RENTALS: (at Sea-Tac International Airport unless otherwise noted): Avis (433-5231); Budget (243-2400); Dollar (433-5825); Hertz (433-5264); National (433-5501); Thrifty, 18836 Pacific Hwy. S. (246-7565). For dwntwn locations, consult the local telephone directory.

LIMOUSINE SERVICES: Carey Limousine (285-5505), Park Place Limousine (363-9902), and Star Limo Service (824-1124).

TAXIS: May be hailed on the street, taken from the waiting lines outside major hotels, or summoned by phone. Recommended companies are **Farwest Cabs** (292-0569) and **Yellow Cab** (622-6500).

TRAIN: Amtrak, King St. Station, Third Ave. and Jackson St. (464-1930).

INTERCITY BUSES: Greyhound, Eighth Ave. and Stewart St. (628-5530).

FERRIES: B.C. Stena Line, Pier 48, 101 Alaskan Way S. (206/624-6986; toll free 800/962-5984). Car-ferry between Seattle and Victoria, B.C.; the *Princess Marguerite* and the newer *Vancouver Island Princess* carry vehicles and passengers daily year round. Time: 4½ hr. each way.
    Clipper Navigation, Pier 69, 2701 Alaskan Way (206/448-5000; toll free 800/888-2535). Service between Seattle and Victoria aboard the catamaran *Victoria Clipper*. Daily year round. Time: 2½ hr. each way.
    Washington State Ferry System, Pier 52 (Colman Dock), Alaskan Way S. at Marion St. (206/464-6400; toll free 800/542-7052). Passenger and vehicle service to Bremerton and Winslow daily throughout the year. Splendid views; low fares.

INFORMATION & TOURS

TOURIST INFORMATION: The **Seattle Convention and Visitors Bureau,** 520 Pike St., Suite 1300, WA 98101 (206/461-5800).

GUIDED TOURS: ※ **Bill Speidel Underground Tours** (walking tours), 610 First Ave. (682-4646): Guided tours of the original houses and shops on Pioneer Sq. spared by the great fire of 1889 and now 10 ft. (3m) below the surface. Unusual and entertaining. Resv. a must; tours daily.
    Chinatown Tours (on foot), 628 S. Washington St. (624-8801): Tour the International District, Seattle's bustling Asian quarter, on your own (detailed map provided). There's an introductory 45-min. audiovisual show at the Nippon Kan Theater. Resv. required.
    Gray Line Tours (bus or boat), 720 S. Forest St. (624-5077): Conducted tours of the city and surroundings, serving principal hotels.
    Seattle Harbor Tours (boat), Pier 55, Waterfront (623-1445): Boat trips in the harbor and on Elliott Bay; daily May–Oct.

SIGHTS, ATTRACTIONS & ACTIVITIES

ADVENTURES: Downstream River Runners, Inc., 12112 NE 195th St., Bothell (206/483-0335): Rafting down the rivers of the Pacific Northwest, Apr–Oct.
    Orion River Expeditions, 1516 11th Ave. NW (322-9130): Air-rafting down the rivers of Washington State, of the Cascade Range, or of British Columbia; trips last 1–5 days. Apr–Oct.

ARCHITECTURAL HIGHLIGHTS: ※♨ **Boeing Field–King County International Airport,** 5 mi. (8km) SE on Fourth Ave. (344-7380): The testing ground for Boeing Corp.; from an observation deck, you can watch the evolutions of 737s, 747s, 757s, and 767s as they come off the production line. Superb Museum of Flight (see "Museums of Science and History," below). For aviation buffs. Open daily.

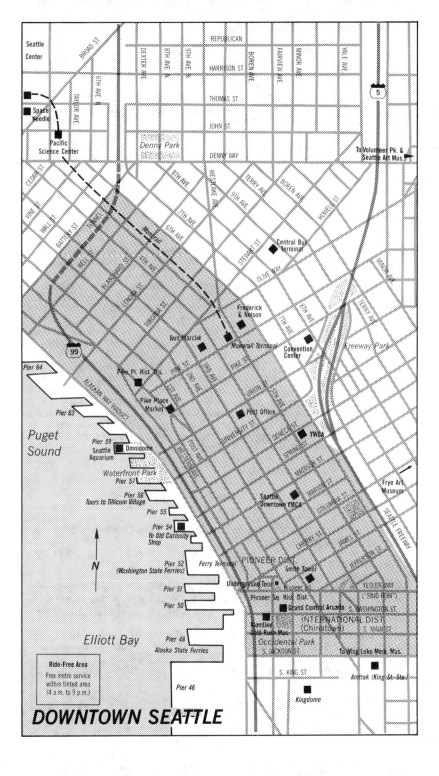

DOWNTOWN SEATTLE

Evergreen Point Floating Bridge, on Wash. 520E between Seattle and the suburb of Bellevue: The longest (7,514-ft./ 2,291m) floating bridge in the world, with 33 pontoons. Very fine view of Lake Washington.

The Kingdome, 201 S. King St. (340-2100): Impressive 60,000-seat covered stadium in the heart of downtown. The Seattle Mariners and Seattle Seahawks play their home games here; also rock concerts and trade shows. Adjoining is the **Royal Brougham Sports Museum.** Guided tours Mon–Sat mid-Apr through Nov, Mon–Fri the rest of the year.

Lake Washington Canal, linking Puget Sound to Lake Union: After those of the Panama Canal, the largest locks in the Western Hemisphere. An impressive sight. An unobstructed view of the seagoing traffic moving through the **Hiram M. Chittenden Locks** may be had from Seaview Ave. NW or 54th St. NW. Visitor center (783-7059) open daily mid-June to mid-Sept, Thurs–Mon the rest of the year.

Pier 59, Alaskan Way at the foot of Pike St.: The jewel of Seattle's waterfront rejuvenation program, with two of the city's most popular tourist attractions: the **Omnidome Theater** (622-1868), open daily, with its giant circular screen for 70-mm movies; and the remarkable **Seattle Aquarium** (see "Museums of Science and History," below).

Seattle Center, Fifth Ave. and Harrison St. (684-7200): A 73-acre (30ha) tourist and arts complex on the site of the 1962 World's Fair. Comprises several museums, an opera house, theater, convention hall, covered stadium, dozens of shops and restaurants, and the Space Needle, a spectacular 605-ft. (184m) tower (see "Panoramas," below). A monorail takes you from Westlake Mall, at Fourth Ave. and Pine St., to the Seattle Center in 95 sec. Open daily.

University of Washington, 17th Ave. NE and NE 45th St. (543-9198): Founded in 1861, this is one of the oldest universities in the western U.S., as well as one of the largest, with 35,000 students. Noteworthy buildings on the enormous campus are the **Henry Art Gallery** with 19th- and 20th-century material, the **Burke Museum** (see "Museums of Science and History," below), and the enchanting **Henry Suzzallo Library,** based on an Italian Renaissance model. On Red Sq. is *Broken Obelisk,* an interesting sculpture by Barnett Newman. On University Way, known to the student body as "The Ave.," are bars, boutiques, bookstores, taverns, and record stores. Visitor center at 4014 University Way, open Mon–Fri.

DEEP-SEA FISHING: If you dream of catching salmon (chum, Coho, or blackmouth), Seattle is where your dream can come true. Many charter boats go daily into Puget Sound from Piers 54 and 56. Some recommended operators are **Ballard Salmon Charters** (789-6202), **Ledger Marine Charters** (283-6160), and **Major Charters** (783-8873).

Also recommended, at Edmonds, just north of Seattle, is **Captain Coley's Charters** (778-4110).

INDUSTRIAL TOURS: **Boeing 747 Plant,** on Wash. 526 in Everett, 29 mi. (47km) north on I-5 to Exit 189 (342-4801): The assembly plant for the jumbo jets and the 767s; largest covered space in the world. Bus tours (90 min.) Mon–Fri year round. Impressive. Resv. required.

Château Sainte Michelle, 14111 NE 145th St. in Woodinville, 15 mi. (24km) NE via I-90 and Wash. 405 (488-1133): Fine 87-acre (35ha) estate of vineyards with a pretty château modeled on those in the bordeaux country of France. Tour of the cellars and tasting daily in summer, Mon–Fri the rest of the year.

MARKETS: **Pike Place Public Market,** First Ave. and Pike St. (682-7453): Since 1907 this colorful covered market has been displaying its stalls of fish, fruit, or vegetables side by side with jewelers' booths, fabric shops, junk dealers, little restaurants, etc. Picturesque, noisy, and enjoyable. Well worth seeing; open daily in summer, Mon–Sat the rest of the year.

MUSEUMS OF ART: ⚓ **Frye Art Museum,** 704 Terry Ave. (622-9250): Very rich private collection of European paintings, emphasizing the Munich and Vienna Schools, as well as 19th- and 20th-century American works; also interesting temporary exhibitions. A new wing houses a collection of Alaskan art. Open daily.

☀⚓⚓ **Seattle Art Museum,** 14th Ave. and E. Prospect St., Volunteer Park (625-8901): The beautiful Fuller Collection of Far Eastern (Chinese jade, Haniwa pottery figures) and Inuit art, the White Collection of African art, and the Kress Collection of works from the Italian Renaissance and the golden age of Dutch painting; also interesting temporary shows, particularly of Native American art from the Pacific Northwest. Open Tues–Sun.

MUSEUMS OF SCIENCE & HISTORY: ☀⚓ **Burke Museum,** University of Washington campus, NE 45th St. at 17th Ave. NE (543-5590): Fine museum devoted to the natural history and ethnology of the Pacific Rim; one of the finest U.S. collections of Native American art (particularly some superb masks) from the Pacific Northwest. Open Tues–Sun.

⚓ **Klondike Gold Rush National Historical Park,** 117 S. Main St. (442-7220): Recapitulates the epic of the gold rush to Alaska in 1897–98; many photographs from the period, as well as original tools and possessions of the Klondike miners. Picturesque and instructive; open daily.

☀⚓ **Museum of Flight,** 9404 E. Marginal Way S., King County International Airport (764-5720): Long tucked away into the historic "Red Barn," a turn-of-the-century structure in which the first Boeing aircraft were assembled in 1916, this very fine aeronautical museum has since 1987 had a new and worthier setting, adjoining Boeing Corp.'s test field. The $15-million glass-and-steel building houses some 30 aircraft from the heroic age, beginning with the 1916 B&W hydroplane and ending with the B-17 bomber. Also a gallery devoted to space exploration: "Twenty-Five Years of Manned Space Flight." An absolute must for aviation buffs. Open daily; 10 min. from dwntwn.

⚓ **Museum of History and Industry,** 2700 24th Ave. E. (324-1125): Remarkable panorama of the history of Boeing Corp., and of the city since its foundation in 1851. Objects salvaged from the great fire of 1889, mementoes of the gold rush, maritime exhibition, etc. Open daily.

⚓ **Nordic Heritage Museum,** 3014 NW 67th St. (789-5707): Devoted to the enormous human and cultural contribution of the Scandinavian peoples to the Pacific Northwest, from the 18th century to the present day. Also temporary exhibitions of modern Scandinavian art and folk art. Interesting. Open Tues–Sun.

☀⚓⚓ **Pacific Science Center,** 200 Second Ave., Seattle Center (443-2001): Ultramodern museum, nicknamed the "Cathedral of Science." Spectacular design by Minoru Yamasaki (creator of New York's World Trade Center), with decorative arches, pools, and fountains. From volcanology to astronomy and the exploration of space; particularly interesting are an enormous fiberglass model of the moon, a NASA space module, a planetarium, a scale model of Puget Sound complete with miniature waves and tides, and a reconstruction of a Pacific Northwest Native American longhouse. Fascinating; open daily.

☀⚓⚓ **Seattle Aquarium,** Pier 59, at the foot of Union St. (386-4320): One of the finest aquariums on the West Coast. Through the underwater viewing dome you can watch while, all around you, the sharks, octopuses, fish, and all kinds of sea creatures strut their stuff in the 400,000-gal. (1.5-million-liter) pool. Truly spectacular. Open daily.

⚓ **Wing Luke Asian Museum,** 407 Seventh Ave. S. (623-5124): Illustrates Chinese immigration into the northwestern U.S.

from the 1860s to the present day. Galleries devoted to Far Eastern art and folk-lore. Exhibitions of photography and Chinese calligraphy. A must for history buffs; open Tues–Sun.

PANORAMAS: ☼ 🏔 **Ballard Bridge,** reached via 15th Ave. NW: Spectacular view of Lake Union and the Fishermen's Terminal looking from south to north; turn around and look south and you'll see the city with Mount Rainier in the distance.

Columbia Center Building, Columbia St. and Fourth Ave. (386-5151): The tallest high-rise in Seattle: 954 ft. (290m) and 76 stories. The Observation Platform on the 73rd floor offers a breathtaking view of the downtown buildings, Puget Sound, and Mount Rainier. Open Mon–Fri 9:30am–5pm.

Space Needle, Seattle Center, 203 Sixth Ave. N. (443-2100): Giant tower on three legs, 605 ft. (184m) high, with glass-walled elevators, revolving restaurant, and observation platform 520 ft. (160m) up. The most beautiful view of Seattle, with an unmatched panorama of the bay, the city, and the mountains. Since it was opened in 1962 it has become Seattle's emblem. Open daily till midnight (till 1:30am in summer).

PARKS & GARDENS: 🏔 **Arboretum,** Lake Washington Blvd. between E. Madison and Montlake (543-8800): More than 5,000 species of trees and plants from around the world, with a particularly fine display of azaleas and rhododen-drons. Lovely Japanese garden, gift of Seattle's twin Japanese city, Kobe. Fine view of Lake Washington. A must; open daily.

Carkeek Park (NW 110th St.) and **Golden Garden Park** (Seaview Ave. NW): Two big parks on the shore of Puget Sound; splendid view of the fjord and the distant mountains. Great for picnics; swimming, too, for the foolhardy (water temperature in summer, 54°F/12°C).

Discovery Park, 3801 W. Government Way (386-4236): On a headland overlooking the entrance to the Washington Ship Ca-nal, this large (more than 500 acres/200ha) public park, with its undulating meadows and woodlands, gives you a superb view over Puget Sound from Mag-nolia Bluff. 2-mi. (3.2km) beach, but no swimming. Picnic areas, hiking trails. The **Daybreak Star Indian Cultural Center** (285-4425), with its exhibitions of Native American arts and crafts, is open Mon–Fri; the park itself is open daily dawn–11pm.

Freeway Park, in the heart of downtown Seattle: Represents a successful attempt by the city government to "cover the ditch" created by sunken motorways in the center city. Part of it sits atop I-5 and part above an underground municipal parking garage. It boasts an engaging artificial stream and cascade (with a window behind it through which you can watch the traffic passing below), trails for urban hill-climbers, and pleasingly varied plant-ings. An elegant, urbane oasis above the traffic.

Gas Works Park, N. Northlake Way and Meridian Ave. (625-4671): Pretty 20-acre (8ha) park around an old gas works, deft-ly converted into a modern sculpture; fine view of the city, Union Lake, and the passing ships. Open daily.

Seward Park, Lake Washington Blvd. and S. Juneau St.: Popu-lar park and beach, with swimming from June to early Sept, on Lake Washington, with the snowy peak of Mount Rainier as a backdrop. Won-derful view. Open daily.

Volunteer Park, 15th Ave. E. and E. Prospect St. (684-4743): At the top of Capitol Hill, this beautiful public park around the Seattle Art Museum offers a clear view of the Olympic Mountains, the Space Nee-dle, and Puget Sound. Observation platform on a Gothic Revival water tower, 520 ft. (159m) high (no elevator).

Waterfront Park, Alaskan Way: Picturesque walk along the dockside. At Pier 59 there's the last word in great aquariums (see the Seattle Aquarium, under "Museums of Science and History," above); there are gardens at the water's edge from Pier 57 to Pier 61 and Pier 71 to Pier 89. Wonderful view of Puget Sound and its shipping.

    Woodland Park, 50th St. and Phinney Ave. N. (789-7919): Huge park on Green Lake, whose western section is a zoo of very modern design with more than 1,000 animals. Splendid rose garden. Open daily.

PERFORMING ARTS: For daily listings of all shows and cultural events, consult the entertainment pages of the daily papers *Post Intelligencer* (morning) and *Seattle Times* (evening).

    Bagley Wright Theater, 225 W. Mercer St., Seattle Center (443-2222): Interesting postmodern design crossed with art nouveau. Classic and contemporary theater. Home of the famous Seattle Repertory Theater (director: Daniel Sullivan) (Oct–Apr).

    Bathhouse Theatre, 7312 W. Green Lake Dr. N. (524-9108): Experimental theater.

    Coliseum, Seattle Center (684-7200): Rock concerts, big-name shows.

    A Contemporary Theatre/ACT, 100 W. Roy St. (285-5110): Modern theater, comedy, drama. One of the major resident theaters in the country.

    Empty Space Theater, 95 S. Jackson St. (587-3737): Experimental theater.

    5th Avenue Theater, 1308 Fifth Ave. (625-1418). Broadway shows, pop concerts.

    Opera House, Seattle Center (443-4711): Concerts, ballet. Home of the Seattle Opera Association (Sept–May; director: Speight Jenkins), the Pacific Northwest Ballet, and the Seattle Symphony (Sept–Apr; principal conductor: Gerard Schwarz).

    Paramount Theater, 907 Pine St. (682-1414): Elegantly restored old theater; big-name shows.

    Pioneer Square Theater, 512 Second Ave. (622-2016): Modern and Off Broadway theater.

    Seattle Center Playhouse, 155 W. Mercer St., Seattle Center (626-0782): Modern and experimental theater; home of the Intiman Theatre Co.

SHOPPING: Food Circus Court, Center House, 305 Harrison St., Seattle Center (684-7200): Cooking and food products from around the world (26 shops), set in an indoor garden with fountains. Perfect for a meal on the run.

    Nordstrom, 1501 Fifth Ave. (628-2111): The flagship of the well-known clothing-store chain.

    Pier 70, 2815 Alaskan Way (448-0708): Souvenir and clothing shops, exotic boutiques, and restaurants in a huge warehouse building by the old harbor. Amusing and picturesque. Open daily.

    Uwajimaya, Sixth Ave. S. and King St. (624-6248): The largest Asian supermarket in the U.S.; foods and gifts. Open Mon–Sat.

    Westlake Center, 400 Pine St. (467-1600): Shopping center of ultramodern design in the heart of downtown, with 65 luxury boutiques, shops, cafés, and restaurants around a four-story glass atrium. Handsome plaza paved in contrasting colors of granite. The terminus of the monorail line between the Seattle Center and downtown is here.

    Ye Olde Curiosity Shop, Pier 51, 601 Alaskan Way, Waterfront (682-5844): Wonderfully kitschy bazaar, almost a century old—museum and souvenir shop at the same time. Many Far Eastern goods. Not to be missed; open daily.

SPECIAL EVENTS: For the exact schedule of events below, consult the **Seattle Visitors and Convention Bureau** (see "Tourist Information," above).

    International Film Festival (late Apr to mid-May): A flourishing tradition since 1974.

Asian Week (early May): Colorful parades; shows. The big celebration for Seattle's Oriental communities.

Pacific Northwest Arts and Crafts Fair (end of July): Very popular arts-and-crafts show, held at Bellevue, 4 mi. (6.5km) east on I-90.

Wagner Festival (end of July to Aug): Complete "Ring" cycle, alternately in German and English.

Seattle Seafair (late July to early Aug): Processions, regattas, marathon, ship review.

SPORTS: Seattle has three professional teams:
Baseball (Apr–Oct): Mariners, Kingdome (628-3555).
Basketball (Oct–Apr): Supersonics, Coliseum (281-5800).
Football (Aug–Dec): Seahawks, Kingdome (827-9777).

Horse Racing
Longacres Racetrack, 1621 SW 16th St., at Renton (226-3131), 11 mi. (17km) SE on I-5 and I-405: Racing Fri–Mon Apr to mid-Oct.

STROLLS: ☼⚓ **Fishermen's Terminal,** W. Emerson St. at 15th Ave. W.: The largest fishing harbor in the U.S., and winter quarters of the Alaska fishing fleet. Hundreds of boats of all sizes are moored along the Washington Ship Canal. Many seafood restaurants. Fine view from Ballard Bridge.

⚓ **International District,** bounded by Fifth Ave. S., Eighth Ave. S., S. Yesler Way, and S. Lane St.: Seattle's Chinatown and Japantown. Many Far Eastern shops and restaurants, Japanese theater, Chinese opera house, Buddhist temple. At the intersection of King St. and Maynard St. is a fine gateway presented by the city of Taipeh. Lively and picturesque.

☼⚓ **Pioneer Square District,** bounded by First Ave., James St., and Yesler Way: This is where Seattle was founded in 1851. Yesler Way, called "Skid Row" in the days of the 19th-century gold rush, was the "hottest" street in this pleasure district. The street was named "Skid Row" because in the earliest days of Seattle logs were "skidded" (dragged by teams of horses) down here from the surrounding hills for the construction of the first houses. These once built, the street was almost abandoned and became the preferred resort of drunks and bums. Today it's lined with shops, art galleries, and congenial restaurants. On Pioneer Sq. itself there's a 59-ft. (18m) totem pole carved by the Tlingit peoples. Very lively, especially after dark.

☼⚓ **Waterfront Drive,** Alaskan Way along Elliott Bay: Souvenir shops, Native American Inuit, and Far Eastern craft shops, bars, and seafood restaurants are arrayed in dozens along the piers. The elevated highway (Alaskan Way Viaduct) offers a fine view of harbor and bay.

THEME PARKS: ⚓ **Enchanted Village,** 36201 Enchanted Pkwy., Federal Way (836-1700), 27 mi./47km south along I-5 to Exit 142b and Enchanted Pkwy.: A sort of miniature Disneyland. Enchanted Village itself is a family amusement park with carousels, roller coasters, children's museums, musical shows, etc. Adjoining it is **Wild Waves Water Park,** with giant water slides, artificial surf, heated lagoon-pool, and rafting down the rapids. Locally very popular. Both parks are open daily Memorial Day–Labor Day; Enchanted Village is also open wknds Apr–Memorial Day and in Sept.

☼⚓ **North West Trek,** 11610 Trek Dr. E., Eatonville (832-6116 or 847-1901), 55 mi./88km south along I-5 and Wash. 161: Very handsome safari-zoo covering 600 acres (240ha) where a comprehensive selection of animals of the Northwest—elk, caribou, bison, various kinds of deer, eagles, lynx, cougar, mountain goat, and bighorn sheep—roams a romantic mountain-and-moorland landscape. You can choose between a 1-hr. guided tour by mini-train or an independent visit on foot. Well worth going out of your way for. Open daily mid-Feb through Oct, Fri–Sun the rest of the year.

WINTER SPORTS RESORTS: ☀️⛷️ **Alpental,** 54 mi. (86km) SE on I-90 and Alpental Rd. (236-1600): 8 lifts. Open mid-Nov to Apr.

☀️⛷️ **Crystal Mountain,** 80 mi. (128km) SE via I-5, Wash. 169, Wash. 410, and Crystal Mountain Rd. (663-2265): 10 lifts; lovely resort on the slopes of Mount Rainier. Open Nov–Apr.

⛷️ **Ski Acres,** 58 mi. (92km) SE on I-90 (236-1600): 13 lifts. Open mid-Nov to Apr.

⛷️ **Snoqualmie Summit,** 56 mi. (89km) SE on I-90 (236-1600): 12 lifts. Open mid-Nov to Apr.

ACCOMMODATIONS

A Note on Accommodations: Room rates in Seattle are coded as follows: **VE,** Very Expensive ($140 and up); **E,** Expensive ($90–$140); **M,** Moderate ($60–$90); **I,** Inexpensive ($30–$60); **B,** Budget (up to $30). A listing of toll free numbers is in the Appendix.

Personal Favorites (in order of preference)

🛎️🛎️🛎️ **The Westin** (dwntwn), 1900 Fifth Ave. (at Westlake), WA 98101 (206/728-1000; toll free, see Westin). 865 rms, A/C, color TV, in-rm movies. AE, CB, DC, MC, V. Valet gar. $10, pool, health club, sauna, two rests. (including the Palm Court), coffee shop, three bars, 24-hr. rm svce, disco, hrdrsr, boutiques, concierge, free crib. *Note:* Flagship of the admirable Westin hotel chain. Two circular towers, 40 and 45 stories high, in the dwntwn business district. The rms, huge and comfortable, w. minibars, all have a spectacular panoramic view of city, mountains, or Puget Sound. Elegantly redecorated interior; efficient svce; good luxury rest. (Palm Court). Big business and group clientele. Seattle's most glittering hotel. Interesting wknd packages. **E–VE**

☀️🛎️🛎️🛎️ **The Sorrento** (dwntwn), 900 Madison St., WA 98101 (206/622-6400; toll free, see Preferred). 76 rms, A/C, color TV, in-rm movies. AE, MC, V. Valet parking $7, rest. (Hunt Club), bar, rm svce, concierge, free crib. *Note:* Luxurious small palace hotel in the European style, three-quarters of a century old and now restored to its pristine glory. Period furniture; spacious, comfortable rms w. minibars; personalized svce. The Hunt Club is a highly regarded rest. The VIP's favorite; a good place to stay. **E–VE**

🛎️🛎️🛎️ **Stouffer Madison** (dwntwn), 515 Madison St., WA 98104 (206/583-0300; toll free, see Stouffer). 554 rms, A/C, color TV, in-rm movies. AE, CB, DC, MC, V. Garage $8, pool, health club, rest. (Prego), coffee shop, 24-hr. rm svce, nightclub, hrdrsr, concierge, free crib. *Note:* Modern 28-story tower in the heart of the business district. Exceptionally comfortable, well-designed rms w. minibar, most w. a fine view of Puget Sound or the mountains. Acceptable panoramic rest. Highly professional svce. Business clientele; two VIP floors. **E–VE**

☀️🛎️🛎️ **Edgewater Inn** (nr. dwntwn), 2411 Alaskan Way, Pier 67, WA 98121 (206/728-7000; toll free 800/624-0670). 240 rms, A/C, color TV, in-rm movies. AE, CB, DC, MC, V. Free valet parking, rest. (Ernie's), bar, rm svce, nightclub, hrdrsr, drugstore, free crib. *Note:* Modern, comfortable hotel right on the water. If your room overlooks the bay, you can rent a rod at the desk, fish from your balcony, and take your catch down to the rest. to be cooked (but if you want such a rm, you must reserve it well ahead!). Decor and facilities totally renovated. Good value; 5 min. from dwntwn. **M**

🛎️🛎️ **Mayflower Park Hotel** (dwntwn), 405 Olive Way, WA 98101 (206/623-8700; toll free 800/426-5100). 190 rms, A/C, color TV, in-rm movies. AE, CB, DC, MC, V. Valet parking $4, rest., bar, rm svce, free crib. *Note:* Elderly hotel, completely renovated, in the heart of town a stone's throw from the waterfront. Comfortable and well run; spacious rms w. slightly faded charm; friendly svce. Good value; clientele of regulars. **M–E**

♀♀ **Days Inn Towne Center** (dwntwn), 2205 Seventh Ave., WA 98121 (206/448-3434; toll free, see Days Inns). 92 rms, A/C, cable color TV. AE, CB, DC, MC, V. Free parking, rest., bar, rm svce, free crib. *Note:* Excellent value right in the business district. Rms adequately large and comfortable; reception and svce with a smile. Group and business clientele. 5 min. from the Seattle Center. I

Other Accommodations (from top bracket to budget)

♀♀♀ **Four Seasons Olympic** (dwntwn), 411 University St., WA 98101 (206/621-1700; toll free, see Four Seasons). 450 rms, A/C, in-rm movies. AE, CB, DC, MC, V. Valet gar. $10, pool, health club, sauna, two rests. (including the Georgian Rm), coffee shop, bars, 24-hr. rm svce, disco, hrdrsr, boutiques, concierge, free crib. *Note:* For decades regarded as the great lady of the Seattle hotel scene, the Olympic has recaptured its former grandeur after a complete remodeling in 1982. The Italian Renaissance–style structure, in the heart of Seattle, is a designated historic monument. Very spacious, comfortable rms w. minibars; urbanely elegant interior. Well-regarded rest.; exemplary svce. Big business and VIP clientele. A very fine place to stay. **VE**

☼ ♀♀♀♀ **Alexis Hotel** (dwntwn), 1007 First Ave., WA 98104 (206/624-4844; toll free 800/345-3457). 52 rms, A/C, color TV, in-rm movies. AE, CB, DC, MC, V. Valet parking $8, two tennis courts, sauna, rest. (Café Alexis), bar, 24-hr. rm svce, concierge, free breakfast, free crib. *Note:* All the charm and elegance of a magnificently restored luxurious private home from around 1900. Elegant, tastefully decorated interior; spacious rms w. period furniture and minibars, some w. balconies and fireplaces. Beautiful view. Personalized svce of a high order; excellent rest. Very conveniently located an easy walk from the business district and the Pike Place Public Market. The favorite of those in-the-know. **E–VE**

♀♀♀ **Sheraton Hotel and Towers** (dwntwn), 1400 6th St., WA 98101 (206/621-9000; toll free, see Sheraton). 880 rms, A/C, color TV, in-rm movies. AE, CB, DC, MC, V. Valet parking $10, pool, health club, sauna, rest. (Fuller's), coffee shop, bars, 24-hr. rm svce, disco, hrdrsr, drugstore, concierge, free crib. *Note:* Big, modern 35-story tower, right in the business district, whose ineffably insipid exterior is belied by a carefully thought-out, imaginative scheme of interior decoration involving some 2,000 art objects, paintings, and sculptures by local artists. Spacious, ultra-comfortable rms, most looking out on Puget Sound or the mountains. Three VIP floors. Fuller's is the city's best rest. Flawless reception and svce. Group and upscale business clientele. **E–VE**

♀♀ **Meany Tower Hotel** (formerly the University Hotel; nr. dwntwn), 45th St. and NE Brooklyn Ave., WA 98105 (206/634-2000; toll free 800/648-6440). 155 rms, A/C, cable color TV. AE, CB, DC, MC, V. Free parking, rest., bar, rm svce, free crib. *Note:* Modern 16-story tower nr. the university, 10 min. from dwntwn. Excellent reception; comfortable rms, most w. panoramic view of Lake Washington and the mountains. Good value. Group clientele. **M–E**

♀♀ **Best Western Continental Plaza** (nr. dwntwn), 2500 Aurora Ave. N., WA 98109 (206/284-1900; toll free, see Best Western). 94 rms, A/C, cable color TV. AE, CB, DC, MC, V. Free parking, pool, coffee shop (breakfast and lunch only), rm svce, free crib. *Note:* Very comfortable motel 15 min. from dwntwn. The rms, most w. balconies, some w. kitchenettes, look out on Lake Union and the mountains. Good value; appeals to motorists, since it's 5 min. from the entrance to I-5. **I–M,** but lower rates off-season.

♀ **Travelodge University** (nr. dwntwn), 4725 25th Ave. NW, WA 98105 (206/525-4612; toll free, see Travelodge). 75 rms, A/C, color TV. AE, CB, DC, MC, V. Free parking, pool, nearby rest. *Note:* Well-managed small motel nr. the university; recently renovated. The rms are serviceably comfortable; some have kitchenette. Good value; 15 min. from dwntwn. I

☕ **Vance Hotel** (dwntwn), 620 Stewart St., WA 98101 (206/
441-4200; toll free 800/426-0670). 164 rms; no A/C; color
TV. AE, CB, DC, MC, V. Free gar., coffee shop (The Gas Lamp), bar, valet svce,
free crib. *Note:* Aging hotel, rather outmoded as to comfort, in the very center of
Seattle; principal attractions are the excellent location and the low rates. Friendly
reception and svce. **I**

Airport Accommodations

☕☕☕ **Red Lion Inn Sea-Tac** (vic.), 18740 Pacific Hwy. S., WA 98188
(206/246-8600; toll free, see Red Lion Inns). 850 rms, A/C,
color TV, in-rm movies. AE, CB, DC, MC, V. Free parking, pool, health club,
two rests. (including Maxi's), coffee shop, bars, rm svce, disco, hrdrsr, concierge,
crib $5. *Note:* Huge, ultramodern luxury motel in a 28-acre (11ha) grdn, capped
by a 14-story tower w. glass-walled elevators. Spacious rms w. balconies and superb views of Lake Washington and the mountains. Comprehensive facilities. Efficient reception and svce; group and business clientele. Opposite the airport
(free limo), 20 min. from dwntwn. **E**

☕ **Motel 6** (vic.), 18900 47th Ave. S., WA 98188 (206/241-
1648). 147 rms, A/C, color TV, in-rm movies. AE, DC, MC,
V. Free parking, pool. *Note:* Spacious, engaging rms, but rather noisy surroundings; unequalled value 3 min. from the airport, 20 min. from dwntwn. Ideal if
you're driving. **B**

YMCA / Youth Hostels

AYH International Hostel (dwntwn), 84 Union St., WA 98122 (206/622-
5443). 125 beds. Typical youth hostel, impeccably run.
YMCA (dwntwn), 909 Fourth Ave., WA 98104 (206/382-5000). 212 rms.
Men, women, families. Health club, pool.

RESTAURANTS

A Note on Restaurant Prices: Seattle restaurant prices, per person, excluding drinks and service charges, are coded as follows: **VE,** Very Expensive ($60
and up); **E,** Expensive ($40–$60); **M,** Moderate ($25–$40); **I,** Inexpensive
($15–$25); **B,** Budget (up to $15).

Personal Favorites (in order of preference)

🍸🍸🍸 **Fuller's** (dwntwn), in the Sheraton Hotel and Towers (see "Accommodations," above) (447-5544). A/C. Lunch Mon–Fri,
dinner Mon–Sat. AE, CB, DC, MC, V. Jkt (J&T at dinner). *Specialties:* gravlax of
salmon and ahi tuna; spinach salad w. smoked duck; seafood chowder Puget
Sound; roast sweetbreads w. caviar; grilled halibut w. pistachio butter; pork tenderloin w. fennel-peach purée; and cream of port wine. Menu changes daily.
Superb list of French and American wines, emphasizing the finest vintages
of the Northwest. *Note:* By far the most elegant rest., serving the most sophisticated food, in Seattle. The light, imaginative recipes of the young chef,
Caprial Pence, feature local seafood. Many works by such northwestern artists
as Morris Graves and Mark Tobey and a remarkable collection of glass from
the local Pilchuck School embellish the decor by happy coincidence, the rest.
bears the name of the late founder of the Seattle Art Museum, Richard Fuller.
Svce a touch pretentious. Resv. strongly advised; big business clientele. *American.* **M–E**

☕☕☕ **Hunt Club** (dwntwn), in the Sorrento (see "Accommodations," above) (622-6400). A/C. Breakfast/lunch/dinner
daily, brunch Sun. AE, CB, DC, MC, V. Jkt. *Specialties:* venison sausage w.
forestière sauce, timbale of wild mushrooms w. alder-smoked duck breast,
fennel-marinated king salmon w. pinot noir–butter sauce, crab Louis Sorrento
(w. pink mayonnaise), rabbit in port-wine sauce flavored w. rhubarb and orange,
white-chocolate ganache w. Chehalis goat cheese and raspberries. Splendid wine
list. *Note:* Chef Barbara Figueroa, formerly with Los Angeles's famous Spago
rest., is a virtuoso of the airy sauce and unexpected blend of flavors; results are

usually very praiseworthy. Sumptuous English-club decor. Open-air terrace for fine days. Efficient, polished svce. Be sure to reserve ahead. Excellent value; one of the finest rests. in the Northwest. *American.* **I–M**

    ♟♟ **Settebello** (dwntwn), 1525 E. Olive Way, at Denny Way (323-7772). A/C. Lunch Mon–Fri, dinner Mon–Sat; closed hols. AE, CB, DC, MC, V. *Specialties:* panzotti alla genovese w. walnut sauce, wafer-thin lasagne noodles w. clams, tuna carpaccio w. red cabbage, salmon w. tomatoes and polenta, tiramisú, sherbet. Very good homemade desserts. Menu changes regularly. *Note:* With its rustic red-tiled floor and its happy, rather noisy atmosphere, the setting is authentically Italian. Very popular locally; resv. advised; valet parking. *Italian.* **M**

    ♟♟ **Nikko** (nr. dwntwn), 1306 King St. (322-4905). A/C. Dinner only, Mon–Sat; closed hols. AE, MC, V. *Specialties:* sushi, sashimi, sautéed geoduck (a local variety of clam), w. fried Rex sole filets, sake kasu black cod. *Note:* Experts say that this is the most imaginative, and the best, of Seattle's many Japanese rests. The prodigious culinary and aesthetic skills of chef Shiro Kashiba are particularly well displayed in the preparation of sushi. The setting is truly Japanese. A worthwhile experience; be sure to reserve ahead. *Japanese.* **I–M**

    ☼♟♟ **Jake O'Shaughnessey's** (nr. dwntwn), 100 Mercer St. (285-1897). A/C. Dinner only, nightly; closed hols. AE, CB, DC, MC, V. *Specialties:* Puget Sound sea stew, roast saloon beef in salt crust, barbecued salmon, blackberry ice cream. *Note:* Despite its Irish name this local landmark, decorated in the manner of a 19th-century saloon, serves 100% American food such as the barbecued salmon, which attracts devotees throughout Seattle. Well-stocked bar with more than 20 brands of scotch. Unfortunately no resv. *American.* **I**

    ☼♟ **Emmett Watson's Oyster Bar** (dwntwn), 1916 Pike Pl. (448-7721). Lunch only, Mon–Sat (11am–5pm); closed hols. No credit cards. *Specialties:* oysters (Quilcenes, Canterburies, Olympias, Middlebrooks, etc.) on the half shell, chowder, clams, ceviche. More than 50 brands of beer on draft or in bottle. *Note:* The best-known eating place in Pike Place Public Market, offering one of the widest selections of oysters on the West Coast, all of exemplary freshness and quality. No interior decoration to speak of: just a dozen bar stools and a few outside tables in fine weather. Quick, efficient svce. Local color guaranteed. *Seafood.* **B**

Other Restaurants (from top bracket to budget)

    ♟♟♟ **Canlis** (nr. dwntwn), 2576 Aurora Ave. N. (283-3313). A/C. Dinner only, Mon–Sat; closed hols. AE, CB, DC, MC, V. Jkt. *Specialties:* pan-fried oysters, shrimp Capri, lamb chops, steak, poached salmon w. sauce hollandaise, mahi-mahi (Hawaiian-style dolphin fish), salade Canlis. *Note:* Flagship of a chain long famous throughout the West Coast and Hawaii, this rest. has been serving excellent broiled meats and uncommonly fresh seafood for more than 30 years, w. a slight aura of the exotic thrown in. Plushy atmosphere; excellent svce (in kimono); very fine view over Lake Union and the city. Locally popular; resv. recommended. *Steak/Seafood.* **M**

    ♟♟ **Rover's** (nr. dwntwn), 2808 E. Madison St. (325-7442). No A/C. Lunch Mon–Fri, dinner Mon–Sat; closed hols. AE, MC, V. Jkt. *Specialties:* warm-duck salad w. walnut and raspberry-vinegar dressing, seared cod w. purée of basil and sautéed mushrooms, grilled king salmon w. oyster-and-ginger sauce, Alaskan red snapper w. mango butter, grilled chicken breasts w. black beans and goat-cheese sauce. Good homemade desserts. *Note:* This recently opened rest., under the master hand of the accomplished French chef Thierry Ratureau, has quickly established itself as one of the city's best. The food is a happy blend of French and Pacific northwestern traditions; gracious countrified decor; w. an inviting grdn for open-air dining on fine days. Friendly svce. Resv. suggested. 20 min. from dwntwn. *French.* **I–M**

🍸🍸 **Green Lake Grill** (nr. dwntwn), 7850 Green Lake Dr. N. (522-
3490). A/C. Lunch daily May–Sept, dinner nightly; closed
hols. AE, CB, DC, MC, V. *Specialties:* oyster and salmon-caviar pancakes, Alaska
king salmon broiled w. thyme and horseradish butter, baked rabbit w. sweet peppers, rockers iko (spiced seafood stew), tuna w. mussels and chanterelle mushrooms. Very good homemade pies. *Note:* Since he opened his first rest. in 1979,
Karl Beckley has been recognized as one of the best younger chefs in the area, and
this new rest. confirms his reputation. Light, imaginative cuisine in an elegant
setting w. modern-art pieces, north of Green Lake; courteous, diligent svce. Locally popular; resv. advised. 25 min. from dwntwn. *American.* **I–M**

🍸🍸 **McCormick's Fish House** (dwntwn), 722 Fourth Ave. (682-
3900). A/C. Lunch Mon–Fri, dinner nightly; closed hols.
AE, DC, MC, V. Jkt. *Specialties:* oysters on the half shell; Dungeness crab; bouillabaisse; more than 40 kinds of fish (salmon, white sturgeon, yellowfin tuna,
swordfish, mahi-mahi, scorpion fish, etc.) broiled, poached, or sautéed; steak.
Good wine list at reasonable prices. *Note:* On the street level of the Columbia
Center Building, this locally popular rest. offers a huge variety of the freshest possible fish and shellfish. The decor is that of an old-time Irish pub. At both lunch
and dinner the two oyster bars are overrun by businesspeople. Highly professional svce; resv. advisable. A true local landmark in the heart of the business district.
Seafood. **I–M**

🍸🍸 **Metropolitan Grill** (dwntwn), 818 Second Ave. (624-3287).
A/C. Lunch Mon–Fri, dinner nightly; closed hols. AE, DC,
MC, V. Jkt. *Specialties:* oysters on the half shell, broiled salmon, filet mignon,
roast beef. Wine list featuring local vineyards. *Note:* A typical steakhouse, cozy
and comfortable. Excellent beef and good broiled fish. Inviting bar; thoughtful,
efficient svce. Resv. advisable. A business district landmark. *Steak.* **I–M**

🍸🍸 **Le Provençal** (vic.), 212 Central Way, in Kirkland, 30 min.
from dwntwn via the Evergreen Point Floating Bridge (827-
3300). A/C. Lunch Mon–Fri, dinner nightly; closed hols. AE, CB, DC, MC, V.
Specialties: frogs' legs provençale, salmon in pastry shell, filet Casanova, cassolette
of seafood, roast rack of lamb w. garlic and herbs, fish of the day, dessert cart.
Menu changes regularly. Good wine list. *Note:* Charming little country inn, typically French. The very Mediterranean cuisine of owner-chef Philippe Gayte justifies the rest.'s name. Cheerful, friendly svce. Business clientele; resv. advised. An
excellent place to eat. *French.* **I–M**

☀🍸🍸 **Ray's Boat House** (nr. dwntwn), 6049 Seaview Ave. NW
(789-3770). A/C. Lunch/dinner daily; closed Jan 1, Easter,
Dec 24–25. AE, CB, DC, MC, V. *Specialties:* chowder, broiled salmon w. sorrel,
crab, oysters, scallops, smoked black cod, calamari in black-bean sauce. Good list
of northwestern wines. *Note:* Burned to the ground in 1987, the rest. has risen
from its ashes like a phoenix. As with other Seattle seafood rests., fresh salmon is a
house specialty at Ray's. Pretty, countrified decor w. lots of paneling and greenery; splendid view of Shilshole Bay and the mountains. Engagingly romantic atmosphere in the evenings. Popular, so resv. advised. 20 min. from dwntwn.
Seafood. **I–M**

🍸🍸 **Mikado** (dwntwn), 514 S. Jackson St. (622-5206). A/C. Dinner only, Mon–Sat. AE, DC, MC, V. *Specialties:* sushi bar,
crabmeat batayaki, tempura, teriyaki, sukiyaki. *Note:* One of the best Japanese
rests. in Seattle (which has a significant Japanese community), a stone's throw
from the Kingdome. You can choose between a Western setting and the traditional tatami mats. All the fish dishes are admirable. Swift, efficient kimono-clad
svce. *Japanese.* **I**

🍸 **Four Seas** (dwntwn), 714 S. King St. (682-4900). A/C.
Lunch/dinner daily (until 2 am); closed Jan. 1, Thanksgiving,
Dec 25. AE, MC, V. *Specialties:* sweet-and-sour pork, Cantonese beef, moo goo
gai pan, garlic spareribs, hot-and-spicy chicken. *Note:* The best rest. in Chinatown, and one of the most elegant. Modern Far Eastern decor; rather sophisticated Cantonese food; inefficient svce. Locally popular. *Chinese.* **B–I**

☀☿ **Ivar's Acres of Clams** (dwntwn), Pier 54, at the foot of Madison St. (624-6852). A/C. Lunch/dinner daily; brunch Sun; closed Thanksgiving, Dec 25. AE, MC, V. *Specialties:* fish soup, clam chowder, shellfish, smoked black cod, curried poached halibut, broiled or barbecued fish. *Note:* The most popular of Seattle's innumerable seafood rests., directly on the waterfront near the ferry terminal. Oyster bar open till 2am; open-air terrace in summer. Generally packed at lunch. Resv. only for groups of six or more. Fine view of Elliott Bay. A local institution since 1938. *Seafood.* **B–I**

Cafeterias/Fast Food/Specialty Spots

☿ **Café Sport** (dwntwn), 2020 Western Ave. (443-6000). Breakfast/lunch/dinner daily. AE, DC, MC, V. *Specialties:* Black-bean soup, Dungeness crabcakes, pan-fried oysters w. cucumber-and-sprout salad, steamed mussels in lemony broth, broiled or braised catch of the day. *Note:* An engaging art deco bistro; the light menu emphasizes local fish and shellfish at remarkably low prices. Excellent value; a splendid place very nr. Pike Place Public Market.

BARS & NIGHTCLUBS

Celebrity Bar & Grill (dwntwn), 315 Second Ave. S. (467-1111). This congenial, lively singles bar on Pioneer Sq. is a favorite with local yuppies. Open nightly.

F. X. McRory's (nr. dwntwn), Occidental Ave. and King St. (623-4800). Oyster bar, very popular with the locals. Huge selection of beer and bourbon. On the noisy side, but entertaining; also an acceptable rest. Open nightly until 2am.

Jake O'Shaughnessey's (nr. dwntwn), 100 Mercer St. (285-1897). Lively, noisy Irish pub (see "Restaurants," above). Open nightly till 2am.

Jazz Alley (dwntwn), Sixth Ave. at Lenora St. (441-9729). The best jazz club in town; intimate and engaging.

Swannies Comedy Underground (dwntwn), 222 S. Main St. (628-0303). Typical comedy club, presenting the biggest names in the genre.

The University Bistro (nr. dwntwn), 4315 University Way NE (547-8010). Bar-disco near the university; all kinds of live music from blues to reggae. Youthful, relaxed crowd. Open Tues–Sat.

NEARBY EXCURSIONS

☀⚗♨ **MOUNT RAINIER NATIONAL PARK** (95 mi./153km SE via I-5, Wash. 7, and Wash. 706): Mountain scenery in all its grandeur; many glaciers and fields of eternal snow. Wash. 706, open year round, takes you as far as **Paradise Visitor Center,** 5,398 ft. (1,646m) up. The northern part of the park is generally not accessible in winter. If you intend to climb the rest of the way to the 14,410-ft. (4,392m) summit of this great volcano, now 2,000 years dormant, you'll need wiry legs and some mountaineering experience even in the company of your officially licensed guides.

The most popular of the 300 mi. (483km) of hiking trails in the park is the **Wonderland Trail,** which winds around the slopes of the mountain, crossing in succession deep forests, wildflower-covered alpine meadows, and glaciers. The 140 mi. (224km) of surfaced road that encircles the highest peak in the Cascades will afford you fabulous views of Mount Rainier's three crests and some of its 26 glaciers; Wash. 410 and Wash. 123 are particularly rewarding.

Don't miss this trip. For information, contact the Superintendent, Mount Rainier National Park, Tahoma Woods, Star Rte., Ashford, WA 98304 (206/569-2211).

Where to Stay

☀♨♨ **Paradise Inn,** on Wash. 706 (20 mi./32km east of the Nisqually entrance to the park), Ashford, WA 98304 (206/

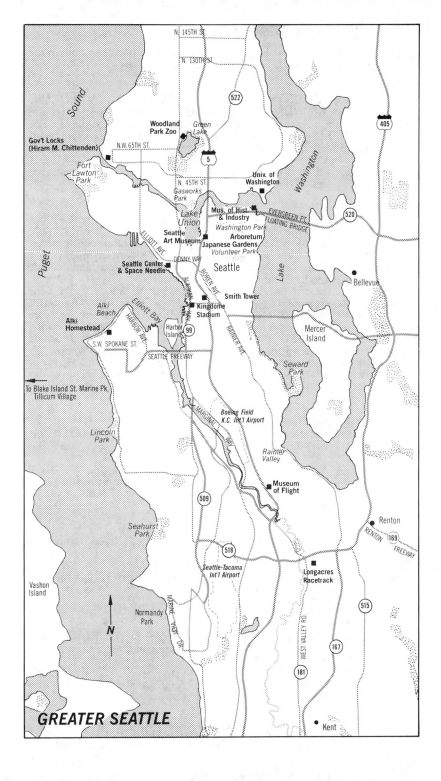

N. 145TH ST.

N. 130TH ST.

522

405

Woodland
Park Zoo

Green
Lake

Sound

Gov't Locks
(Hiram M. Chittenden)

N.W. 65TH ST.

5

Fort
Lawton
Park

N. 45TH ST.

Univ. of
Washington

Gasworks
Park

Lake
Union

Mus. of Hist.
& Industry

EVERGREEN PT.
FLOATING BRIDGE

520

Washington Park

Puget

ELLIOTT AVE.

Seattle
Art Museum

Japanese Gardens

Arboretum

Volunteer Park

Lake
Washington

Seattle Center
& Space Needle

DENNY WAY

Seattle

BOREN AVE.

ALASKAN WAY

Bellevue

Smith Tower

Alki
Beach

Elliott Bay

HARBOR AVE.

Kingdome
Stadium

99

Mercer
Island

Alki
Homestead

Harbor
Island

S.W. SPOKANE ST.

SEATTLE FREEWAY

RAINIER AVE.

Seward
Park

To Blake Island St. Marine Pk.,
Tillicum Village

E. MARGINAL WAY

Boeing Field
K.C. Int'l Airport

Rainier
Valley

Lincoln
Park

Museum
of Flight

509

Renton

Seahurst
Park

RENTON
FREEWAY

169

518

515

Vashon
Island

Seattle-Tacoma
Int'l Airport

Longacres
Racetrack

MARINE VIEW DR.

WEST VALLEY RD.

167

N

Normandy
Park

181

GREATER SEATTLE

Kent

569-2275). 127 rms (95 w. bath). *Note:* Very pretty rustic chalet built in the 1920s in an outstandingly beautiful location. Open mid-May–Sept. **I–M**

MOUNT ST. HELENS NATIONAL VOLCANIC MONUMENT (153 mi./245km south via I-5S and Wash.

504E): One of the most recently active of American volcanoes, recording a major eruption on May 18, 1980. Breathtaking lunar landscapes. Highways are closed for a 20-mi. (32km) radius around the crater, but many hiking trails open to the public. There's a **visitor center** with a giant model of the volcano on Wash. 504 at Silver Lake, 5 mi. (8km) east of I-5 (206/274-4038); open year round. (For details, see excursion section in Chapter 44.)

OLYMPIC NATIONAL PARK (reached by ferry to Wins-

low, then 89 mi./142km NW via Wash. 305, Wash. 3, Wash. 104, and U.S. 101): More than 1,430 sq. mi. (3,700km²) of unspoiled wilderness, with astonishing contrasts between the glaciers of **Mount Olympus** (7,965 ft./2,428m), the luxuriant forests of the slopes facing the ocean, and the little desert islands along the Pacific. Rains of tropical violence fall daily Oct–Apr on the west face of the park (average annual rainfall, 140 in./356cm), so that the thickly wooded slopes of the region are referred to as "rain forests." Abundant wildlife: black bear, eagles, elk, deer, mountain lion, seal, and sea elephant. More than 600 mi. (966km) of hiking trails crisscross the park, and around it runs a magnificent 330-mi. (531km) circular highway, the **Olympic Peninsula Scenic Drive** (U.S. 101). For **information,** contact the Superintendent, Olympic National Park, 600 E. Park Ave., Port Angeles, WA 98362 (206/452-4501, ext. 230). Park open year round (winter skiing at the **Hurricane Ridge Ski Area,** with 3 lifts); don't miss it. You can combine it with a trip to Port Townsend (see below).

Where to Stay in the Park

Kalaloch Lodge, U.S. 101, Kalaloch Beach, WA 98331 (206/ 962-2271). 58 rms and bungalows. Rustic motel on a cliff overlooking the ocean. Spectacular views; open year round. **I–M**

Lake Crescent Lodge, U.S. 101, Port Angeles, WA 98362 (206/928-3211). 49 rms and cottages. The main chalet dates from 1916 while the cottages are newer; they stand beside a wonderful mountain lake. Praiseworthy rest. Open May–Oct. **I–M**

PORT TOWNSEND (reached by ferry to Winslow, then 49

mi./78km NW via Wash. 305, Wash. 3, Wash. 104, and Wash 20): Charming little port town on Puget Sound, with fine San Francisco–style pastel-washed Victorian houses and splendid seascapes, and two delightful 19th-century inns. Port Townsend is well worth visiting; you can do so along with Olympic National Park (see above).

Where to Stay

Manresa Castle, 7th St. and Sheridan St., Port Townsend, WA 98368 (206/385-5750). 42 Victorian-style rms, most overlooking the bay. AE, MC, V. **I–M**

James House, 1238 Washington St., Port Townsend, WA 98368 (206/385-1238). 12 comfortable rms w. period furniture and pretty views. MC, V. **I–M**

SNOQUALMIE NATIONAL FOREST (about 50 mi./

80km east on I-90): 1,220,000 acres (490,000ha) of deep forests, lakes, mountains, waterfalls, superb scenery, and well-equipped winter sports resorts, all less than an hour's drive from Seattle. Many excursions. Don't miss this trip.

Where to Eat

🍷🍴 **Salish Lodge,** on Wash. 202 at North Bend (206/888-2556). Breakfast/lunch/dinner daily. AE, CB, DC, MC, V. *Note:* Very popular locally. Overlooks the famous Snoqualmie Falls. Also a hotel w. 90 comfortable rms. *American.* **I–M**

TILLICUM VILLAGE (on Blake Island, reached by boat from Pier 56) (206/ 329-5700): Although a longtime favorite with visitors, I was not impressed with this re-creation of life in a 19th-century Native American village, the price of the tribal-style salmon dinner ($30), or the folk-dance exhibition.

FARTHER AFIELD

☀️🏔️ NORTH CASCADES & GLACIER NATIONAL PARKS (1,548 mi./2,476km r.t. via I-5N, Wash. 20E, Wash. 155S, Wash. 174E, U.S. 2E, Wash. 25N, Wash. 20E, U.S. 2E, U.S. 89N, Going-to-the-Sun Rd. W., U.S. 2W, U.S. 93S, and I-90W): An ideal 1-week to 10-day trip for lovers of the wide-open spaces, taking in two of the Northwest's loveliest national parks, North Cascades National Park and Glacier National Park, on the Canadian frontier.

☀️🏔️ North Cascades National Park

You come first to North Cascades National Park, 132 mi. (211km) from Seattle, its 504,000 acres (204,000ha) of magnificent mountain scenery—glaciers (318 of them), innumerable lakes, and majestic crests covered with bristling forests—sitting astride the Canadian border. Many hiking trails crisscross this expanse of unspoiled wilderness north of the Cascades. It took 15 million years of glacial erosion to carve the granite into narrow valleys and abrupt crests like **Goode Mountain** (9,220 ft./2,810m) and **Mount Shuskan** (9,127 ft./ 2,782m). Watered by the moist breezes from the Pacific, the western slope of the park is luxuriantly wooded and abounds in wild animals (grizzly, black bear, elk, wolves, eagles), whereas its eastern counterscarp is characterized by sparser growths of conifers and brush. Camping, fishing, rock climbing, hiking in summer; cross-country skiing in winter. Well worth going out of your way for.

Information centers are open in summer at Marblemount, Sedro Wooley, and Colonial Creek (206/856-5700).

☀️🏔️ Grand Coulee Dam and Roosevelt Lake

Continue on scenic Wash. 20, one of the most spectacular highways in the state of Washington, to **Grand Coulee Dam.** At 5,223 ft. (1,592m) wide and 550 ft. (168m) high, this impressive piece of engineering and the generating station that it houses make up one of the largest reinforced-concrete structures in the world (total weight used, 20 million tons). Open daily; for information, call 509/633-9265.

Penned back by the dam is the 151-mi. (243km) **Franklin D. Roosevelt Lake,** a popular vacation and water-sports area. Following the shore of Roosevelt Lake and continuing to the east, you pick up the scenic Wash. 20 again at Kettle Falls. From here, crossing the northern part of Idaho, you come upon the fish-filled **Lake Pend Oreille** and the **Kaniksu National Forest,** before reaching the incomparably lovely wilderness of Glacier National Park.

☀️🏔️ Glacier National Park

This and Yellowstone are America's two most beautiful national parks. Lying in the northern part of Montana, 611 mi. (978km) northeast of Seattle on the Canadian border (it is the U.S. section of the **Waterton-Glacier Internation-**

al Peace Park, of which the adjoining Canadian section is the Waterton Lakes National Park in Alberta, Canada), this huge expanse of mountainous territory covers 1,583 sq. mi. (4,100km²) and is bisected from north to south by the Continental Divide. There is a particularly striking contrast between its two faces: the western face is humid, with pines, aspens, and red cedars flourishing below the meadows on the precipitous crests; while the eastern face is drier, windy, and often rendered dangerous by the Chinook. With its 60 glaciers (some of them accessible), its 650 azure lakes of all sizes, its waterfalls, and forests, the park is definitely alpine in character. It shelters a wealth of wildlife: grizzly, black bear, elk, bighorn sheep, and mountain goat, to name only a few.

The **Going-to-the-Sun Road,** 50 mi. (80km) of unbelievable hairpin bends blasted out of the side of a very steep mountain, crosses the park from side to side, crossing the Continental Divide at **Logan Pass** (closed by snowfalls from mid-Oct to mid-June), 6,664 ft. (2,031m) above sea level, before beginning the long and gripping descent to Lake McDonald, affording you some unforgettable views of the scenery.

It's worth coming to the Northwest just to see this park. There are many campsites (62) and motels inside the park, often full in July and Aug (more than two million people come here every year). The park is open year round, but watch out for avalanches in winter. For **information,** contact the Superintendent, Glacier National Park, West Glacier, MT 59936 (406/888-5441).

Leaving the park via U.S. 2W and U.S. 93S, you follow the shore of the enormous **Flathead Lake** for some 20 mi. (32km) to I-90W, on which you return to Seattle, 472 mi. (755km) west.

☖ Spokane

On the way you should stop at Spokane, Washington's second-largest city. The very fine **falls** on the Spokane River are illuminated at night. See also the magnificent Gothic **Cathedral of St. John the Evangelist,** 1125 S. Grand Blvd. (509/838-4277), open daily, and **Riverfront Park,** on Spokane Falls Blvd., site of the 1974 World's Fair, for the first international exhibition for the protection of the environment.

Then it's back to Seattle on I-90W. If you're a nature lover, the glorious scenery you'll encounter on this trip will thrill you.

Where to Stay En Route

COEUR D'ALENE, IDAHO 🛏🛏 **Coeur d'Alene Resort,** 702 Apple Way, Coeur d'Alene, ID 83814 (208/664-2300). 340 rms. AE, MC, V. *Note:* Large, modern 18-story hotel on Cocur d'Alene Lake. Spectacular. **M–E**

GLACIER NATIONAL PARK ☼ 🛏 **Glacier Park Lodge,** on Mont. 49 (near the intersection with U.S. 2), East Glacier Park, MT 59434 (406/226-5551). 155 rms. MC, V. *Note:* Large, picturesque hotel dating from 1912 w. splendid views, open mid-June to mid-Sept. **I–M**

☼🛏 **Lake McDonald Lodge,** Going-to-the-Sun Rd., West Glacier, MT 59936 (406/226-5551). 102 rms. MC, V. *Note:* Rustic hotel and bungalows on Lake McDonald; lovely views. Open June to mid-Sept. **I–M**

☼🛏 **Many Glacier Hotel,** U.S. 89, East Glacier Park, MT 59434 (406/226-5551). 210 rms. MC, V. *Note:* A four-story structure built of local timber in 1917. Superbly located on Swiftcurrent Lake; open June to mid-Sept. **I–M**

🛏 **Izaak Walton Inn,** U.S. 2, Essex, MT 59916 (406/888-5700). 30 rms. MC, V. *Note:* Older, historic hotel south of the park; open year round. **I–M**

🛏 **St. Mary Lodge,** junction of U.S. 89 and Going-to-the-Sun Rd., St. Mary, MT 59434 (406/732-4431). 105 rms. AE, MC, V. *Note:* Very inviting motel on the river. Open mid-May to Oct. **I–M**

GRAND COULEE DAM, WASHINGTON ⚑ **Coulee House,** 110 Roosevelt Way at Birch St., Coulee Dam, WA 99116 (509/633-1101). 61 rms. AE, CB, DC, MC, V. *Note:* Comfortable little motel w. a view of the dam. **I–M**

SPOKANE, WASHINGTON 🏨 **Cavanaugh's Inn at the Park,** W. 303 North River Dr., Spokane, WA 99201 (509/326-8000). 266 rms. AE, CB, DC, MC, V. *Note:* Ultra-comfortable motel across from Riverfront Park. **M–E**

🏨 **Westcoast Ridpath Hotel,** 515 W. Sprague at First Ave., Spokane, WA 99210 (509/838-2711). 350 rms. *Note:* Inviting hotel in the heart of dwntwn. **M**

🛡 THE PACIFIC COAST, FROM NEAH BAY TO HOQUIAM-ABERDEEN (408 mi./653km r.t. by ferry to

Winslow, then Wash. 305N, Wash. 3N, Wash. 104N, U.S. 101N, Wash. 112W, Wash. 112E, U.S. 101S, U.S. 12E, Wash. 8E, U.S. 101S, and I-5N): Magnificent coastal route requiring 3–4 days, and taking in **Port Townsend** (see "Nearby Excursions," above), the ☀ **Makah Reservation, Olympic National Park** (see "Nearby Excursions," above), and the twin towns of **Hoquiam-Aberdeen,** with numerous stretches of scenic highway along the **Straits of San Juan de Fuca** and the Pacific coast.

On the way back, stop at ☀🛡 **Olympia,** the capital of Washington State, an old, delightful, flower-planted city at the head of Puget Sound. While there, be sure to see the imposing Doric **Legislative Building** on Capitol Way (586-8687), open Mon–Fri, with its 287-ft.-high (88m) dome; also the **State Capitol Museum,** 211 W. 21st Ave. (753-2580), open Tues–Sun, with interesting works of art and historical material displayed in a gracious Spanish-style building dating from 1920.

Drive back to Seattle on I-5N by way of **Tacoma,** birthplace of Bing Crosby.

🛡 VICTORIA & VANCOUVER, BRITISH COLUMBIA (by

car-ferry or catamaran in summer to Victoria; 144 mi./230km north on I-5 to Vancouver): Two captivating Canadian cities which attract many tourists. There's a complete contrast between the English Tudor of Victoria and the 20th-century modernism of Vancouver. The Seattle–Victoria ferry is operated by BC Stena Line, Pier 48, 101 Alaskan Way, Seattle (624-6986); the crossing takes 4½ hr., and there are two daily. The catamaran, operated by Clipper Navigation, Pier 69, 2701 Alaskan Way, Seattle (448-5000), takes only 2½ hr., and there are daily trips year round.

For tourist information, contact the **Vancouver Travel Info Center,** 562 Burrard St., Vancouver, BC V6C 2J6 (604/683-2000); or **Victoria Tourism,** 812 Wharf St., Victoria, BC V8W 1T3 (604/382-2127). Both cities amply justify the side trip.

Note: U.S. citizens need no passports to cross into Canada, but are advised to be in possession of proof of citizenship (birth certificate, voter's registration, or the like). Non-U.S. nationals should carry their passports, with a valid U.S. visa, to be sure of being readmitted to the U.S.

CHAPTER 46

THE PACIFIC COAST🌵🌵

□ □ □

From the Olympic Mountains to San Francisco Bay

Favored by a springlike climate for 8 months of the year, the Pacific coast extends for hundreds of miles, its long, sandy beaches often almost deserted— perhaps because the icy currents sweeping down from the Arctic make bathing hazardous as well as uncomfortable. Nature is usually benign here—with some catastrophic exceptions, such as the eruption of **Mount St. Helens** in 1980, after 123 years of slumber, which killed 58 people and did millions of dollars of damage.

While the winters in northern California are relatively dry, the Oregon coast, and even more the Washington coast, can expect regular heavy showers Nov–Mar; the Olympic Mountains, in the extreme northwest, hold the U.S. record for rainfall with an average 142 in. (3,556mm) annually. As a result, the vegetation is often lush; not for nothing is Washington called "The Evergreen State."

For the 1,060 mi. (1,700km) between the Canadian border and San Francisco Bay, the Pacific coast alternates rocky shores, immense forests of giant conifers, swift-running rivers down which you can raft, and long stretches of white-sand beach punctuated by dozens of picturesque little fishing ports. Between the ocean and the coastal mountains of the **Coast Ranges** and the **Cascade Range** lie several national parks, among the most beautiful in the West and well worth seeing. Outstanding among them are the extraordinary **Olympic National Park** with its impenetrable rain forests; **Redwood National Park** with its thousand-year-old sequoias; **Crater Lake Park,** where one of the world's loveliest lakes (also, at 1,932 ft./589m, the deepest in the U.S.) lies in the crater of an extinct volcano; and **Oregon Caves National Monument** with its superb caverns of marble.

In short, a bounteous landscape, still largely unspoiled, which contrasts with the "civilized," built-up coast of southern California several hundred miles farther south.

BASIC FACTS: States of Washington, Oregon, and California. Area codes: 206 (Washington), 503 (Oregon), 707 (California). Distance from Cape Flattery (Washington) to San Francisco: about 1,060 mi. (1,700km).

CLIMATE: Two parallel mountain ranges running a little inland, the Coast Ranges and the Cascade Range, shelter the Pacific coast against the chill winds from the northeast, so that its climate from the Canadian border to San Francisco is uniformly temperate. In winter the thermometer seldom goes below 42° – 46° F (6° – 8° C), while in summer temperatures hover around 68° F (20° C), ideal for a visit. Spring is measurably warmer and dryer than fall; the (very wet) rainy season lasts from Oct to Mar.

ARRIVAL & TRANSIT INFORMATION

AIRLINES: At the **Eureka-Arcata** airport: American (toll free 800/433-7300) and United (toll free 800/241-6522).
　　At the Portland, Seattle, and San Francisco airports: see Chapters 44, 45, and 50 respectively.

AIRPORTS: The **Eureka-Arcata Airport** (ACV), 16 mi. (25km) north.
　　Portland International Airport (PDX): See Chapter 44 on Portland.
　　San Francisco International Airport (SFO): See Chapter 50 on San Francisco.
　　Sea-Tac International Airport (SEA): See Chapter 45 on Seattle.

BUS OR CAR RENTAL? The Greyhound Bus Co. has excellent service along the whole Pacific coast. However, the distances are so great, and the attractions so many, that it makes a lot of sense to rent a car or a mobile home with unlimited mileage. Rates are usually lowest in California.

CAR RENTAL: See Chapters 44 on Portland, 45 on Seattle, and 50 on San Francisco.

TRAIN: For the Amtrak stations in Portland, Seattle, and San Francisco, see Chapters 44, 45, and 50 respectively.

INTERCITY BUSES: Greyhound has terminals along the Pacific coast at 956 SW 10th St., Newport, Ore. (503/265-2253), and 1603 4th St., Eureka, Calif. (707/442-0370).
　　For terminals in Portland, Seattle, and San Francisco, see Chapters 44, 45, and 50 respectively.

INFORMATION, TOURS, ADVENTURES & SPECIAL EVENTS

TOURIST INFORMATION: Information on the Pacific coast is available from both state government and local sources.

State Government Sources
　　California Office of Tourism, 1121 L St., Suite 103, Sacramento, CA 95814 (916/322-1397); toll free 800/862-2543, ext. 99.
　　Oregon Economic Development Dept.–Tourism Division, 775 Summer St. NE, Salem, OR 97310 (503/373-1270; toll free 800/547-7842).
　　Washington Tourism Development Division, 101 General Administration Bldg., Olympia, WA 98504 (206/786-2088; toll free 800/544-1800).

Local Sources

Astoria Chamber of Commerce, Port of Astoria Bldg. (P.O. Box 176), Astoria, OR 97103 (503/325-6311).

Coos Bay Chamber of Commerce, 50 E. Central Ave., Coos Bay, OR 97420 (503/269-0215; toll free 800/824-8486).

Eureka Chamber of Commerce, 2112 Broadway, Eureka, CA 95501 (707/442-3738; toll free 800/346-3482).

Newport Chamber of Commerce, 555 SW Coast Hwy., Newport, OR 97365 (503/265-8801; toll free 800/262-7844).

For **Portland, Seattle,** and **San Francisco,** see Chapters 44, 45, and 50 respectively.

GUIDED TOURS: For **Portland, Seattle,** and **San Francisco,** see Chapters 44, 45, and 50 respectively.

For **other localities,** consult the local *Yellow Pages* under "Sightseeing."

ADVENTURES: 6- to 8-hr. trips down the Rogue River by raft or motorboat:

From Gold Beach, Ore.

Court's White Water Trips, Rogue River Bridge (503/247-6504), Apr–Nov; **Jerry's Rogue Jet Boat Trips,** Rogue River Bridge (503/247-4571), mid-May to Oct; and **Mail Boat Whitewater Trips,** Mail Boat Dock (503/247-7033), mid-May to Oct.

From Grants Pass, Ore.

Hellgate Excursions, 971 S. 6th St. (503/479-7204), mid-May to Sept; and **Orange Torpedo Trips** (503/479-5061), May–Aug.

SPECIAL EVENTS: For exact dates of the events listed below, check with the chambers of commerce listed under "Tourist Information" (above) as well as with those below.

Crescent City Chamber of Commerce, Cultural Center, 1001 Front St. (P.O. Box 246), Crescent City, CA 95531 (707/464-3174).

Depoe Bay Chamber of Commerce, P.O. Box 21, Depoe Bay, OR 97341 (503/765-2889).

Port Orford Chamber of Commerce, Battle Rock Park, U.S. 101S (P.O. Box 637), Port Orford, OR 97465 (503/332-8055).

Astoria, Ore.

Great Astoria Crab Feed & Seafood Festival (early Apr): Celebration of Astoria's maritime heritage; food, wine, arts and crafts.

Scandinavian Midsummer Festival (mid-June): Parades, folk dancing, craft shows.

Crescent City, Calif.

World Championship Crab Races (end of Feb).

July 4th Celebration (July 4): Parades, marathon, fireworks.

Depoe Bay, Ore.

Fleet of Flowers Ceremony (Memorial Day): Commemoration of victims of the sea, with religious service and chaplets of flowers thrown into the water.

Eureka, Calif.

Rhododendron Festival (late Apr to early May): Parades, races, art shows, etc.

Newport, Ore.
Loyalty Days and Sea Fair Festival (late Apr to early May): Regattas, boat review, art shows, etc.

Port Orford, Ore.
Port Orford Jubilee Celebration (July 4): Commemoration of the Battle of Battle Rock against the Native Americans; giant barbecue, parade, fireworks.

A NORTH TO SOUTH ITINERARY

The section of this guide devoted to the Pacific coast has been organized as an itinerary, starting at Neah Bay and ending at San Francisco, a distance of about 1,060 mi. (1,700km). You may choose not to drive the whole distance; Seattle, Portland, and San Francisco, as well as many points in between, are linked by air, bus, and train. Car rentals are not hard to find; bear in mind, however, that rates are often lower in California than in Washington and Oregon, and that there may be a significant charge if you rent a car in one state and drop it off in another. In any case, it shouldn't be difficult to select from the following travel plan the parts that appeal to you most!

Distances Down the Pacific Coast

From	*To*	*Distance*
Neah Bay	Quinault	113 mi. (182km)
Quinault	Hoquiam-Aberdeen	40 mi. (64km)
Hoquiam-Aberdeen	Westport	20 mi. (32km)
Westport	Long Beach	75 mi. (120km)
Long Beach	Astoria	23 mi. (36km)
Astoria	Fort Clatsop Nat'l. Memorial	6 mi. (10km)
Fort Clatsop	Seaside	10 mi. (18km)
Seaside	Cannon Beach	8 mi. (13km)
Cannon Beach	Tillamook	39 mi. (62km)
Tillamook	Pacific City	27 mi. (43km)
Pacific City	Lincoln City	15 mi. (24km)
Lincoln City	Depoe Bay	12 mi. (19km)
Depoe Bay	Devil's Punchbowl State Park	5 mi. (9km)
Devil's Punchbowl	Newport	8 mi. (12km)
Newport	Yachats	24 mi. (39km)
Yachats	Sea Lion Caves	15 mi. (24km)
Sea Lion Caves	Florence	12 mi. (19km)
Florence	Reedsport	32 mi. (51km)
Reedsport	Coos Bay	27 mi. (44km)
Coos Bay	Bandon	24 mi. (38km)
Bandon	Port Orford	27 mi. (43km)
Port Orford	Gold Beach	53 mi. (84km)
Gold Beach	Crescent City	59 mi. (95km)
Crescent City	McKinleyville	70 mi. (112km)
McKinleyville	Eureka	10 mi. (16km)
Eureka	Avenue of the Giants	41 mi. (65km)
Avenue of the Giants	Fort Bragg	86 mi. (138km)
Fort Bragg	Noyo	2 mi. (4km)
Noyo	Mendocino	5 mi. (8km)
Mendocino	Point Arena	35 mi. (56km)
Point Arena	Fort Ross	48 mi. (76km)
Fort Ross	Bodega Bay	22 mi. (36km)
Bodega Bay	Point Reyes Nat'l. Seashore	32 mi. (50km)
Point Reyes	San Francisco	35 mi. (56km)

A Note on Accommodations: Room rates along the Pacific Coast are coded as follows: **VE,** Very Expensive ($140 and up); **E,** Expensive ($90–$140); **M,** Moderate ($60–$90); **I,** Inexpensive ($30–$60); **B,** Budget (up to $30). A listing of toll free numbers is in the Appendix.

A Note on Restaurant Prices: Pacific Coast restaurant prices, per person, excluding drinks and service charges, are coded as follows: **VE,** Very Expensive ($60 and up); **E,** Expensive ($40–$60); **M,** Moderate ($25–$40); **I,** Inexpensive ($15–$25); **B,** Budget (up to $15).

NEAH BAY: At the western tip of the **Olympic Peninsula** the little ports of **Neah Bay** and **Sekiu,** about 12 mi. (19km) apart, are very popular sportfishing resorts (boat rentals). Drive to **Cape Flattery,** the northwesternmost point in the contiguous United States, with a land's end of cliffs, caves, pounding sea, and isolated **Tatoosh Island.** At Neah Bay is the interesting archeological museum of the **Makah Reservation,** on B/A Hwy. 1 (206/645-2711), open daily in summer, Wed–Sun the rest of the year; it houses more than 55,000 works of art or handcrafts, some of them more than 500 years old.

QUINAULT: Starting point for a visit to **Olympic National Park,** a superb and inviolate nature reserve covering 1,430 sq. mi. (3,700km^2), whose treasures include the glaciers of **Mount Olympus,** rain forests, desert isles along the Pacific shore, and a unique population of wildlife. Deep-blue **Lake Quinault** and glacier-fed streams offer some of the finest steelhead trout fishing in the Northwest. Views of wonderful scenery. Be sure to see the rain forest and the Enchanted Valley. Open year round. For details, see Chapter 45 on Seattle.

Where to Stay

Lake Quinault Lodge, South Shore Rd., Quinault, WA 98575 (206/288-2571; toll free 800/562-6672). 54 rms; no A/C. AE, MC, V. Free parking, pool, sauna, boating, beach, rest., bar. *Note:* Comfortable historic little country inn on Lake Quinault dating back to the 1920s. Rms w. balconies, some w. fireplaces. Friendly reception; very acceptable rest. For nature lovers. Open year round. **M–E**

Where to Eat

Lake Quinault Lodge, South Shore Rd. (206/288-2571). No A/C. Breakfast/lunch/dinner daily. AE, DC, MC, V. *Specialties:* fresh salmon, fish of the day, shellfish, steak, prime rib. *Note:* Pretty, rustic decor w. a clear view of Lake Quinault and the mountains. Admirable hotel food; cheerful svce. Resv. advised; a good place to eat. *Steak/Seafood.* **B–I**

HOQUIAM-ABERDEEN: Picturesque harbor town on Grays Harbor Gulf, comprising the twin cities of **Hoquiam,** the commercial and fishing port, and **Aberdeen,** with its woodworking plants and fish canneries.

Where to Stay

Nordic Inn, 1700 S. Boone St., Aberdeen, WA 98520 (206/533-0100). 66 rms; no A/C; cable color TV. AE, CB, DC, MC, V. Free parking, rest., bar, nightclub, free crib. *Note:* Typical but inviting motel; spacious rms, some w. refrigerator; acceptable rest. Good value. **I**

Red Lion, 521 W. Wishkah St., Aberdeen, WA 98520 (206/532-5210; toll free, see Red Lion Inns). 67 rms; no A/C; color TV, in-rm movies. AE, CB, DC, MC, V. Free parking, crib $5. *Note:* Modern motel not far from dwntwn Aberdeen. Adj. rest. Spacious, serviceable rms; free morning coffee. **I–M**

Westwood Lodge, 910 Simpson Ave., Hoquiam, WA 98550 (206/532-8161). 65 rms; no A/C; color TV, in-rm movies.

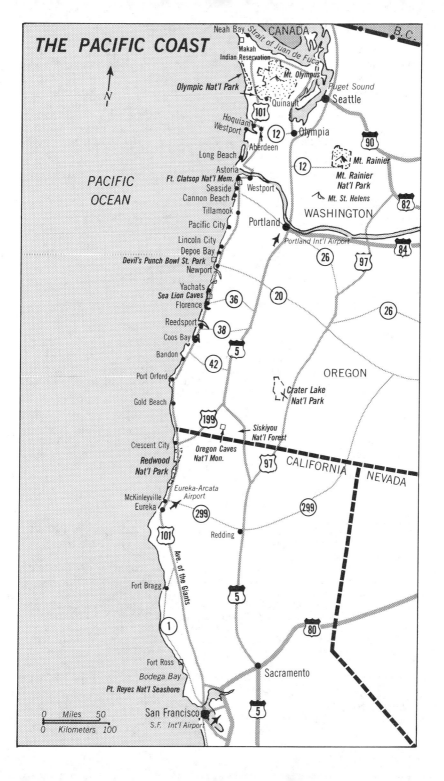

THE PACIFIC COAST

N

PACIFIC OCEAN

CANADA
B.C.

Neah Bay
Strait of Juan de Fuca
Makah Indian Reservation
Mt. Olympus
Puget Sound
Seattle
Olympic Nat'l Park
101
Quinault
Hoquiam
Westport
12
Olympia
90
Aberdeen
Long Beach
Astoria
12
Mt. Rainier
Ft. Clatsop Nat'l Mem.
Seaside
Westport
Mt. Rainier Nat'l Park
82
Cannon Beach
Mt. St. Helens
Tillamook
WASHINGTON
Pacific City
Portland
Lincoln City
Portland Int'l Airport
84
Depoe Bay
Devil's Punch Bowl St. Park
26
97
Newport
Yachats
Sea Lion Caves
36
20
Florence
26
Reedsport
38
Coos Bay
5
Bandon
42
OREGON
Port Orford
Crater Lake Nat'l Park
Gold Beach
199
← Siskiyou Nat'l Forest
Crescent City
Oregon Caves Nat'l Mon.
Redwood Nat'l Park
97
CALIFORNIA
NEVADA
Eureka-Arcata Airport
McKinleyville
Eureka
299
299
101
Redding
Ave. of the Giants
Fort Bragg
5
1
80
Fort Ross
Bodega Bay
Sacramento
Pt. Reyes Nat'l Seashore

0 Miles 50
0 Kilometers 100

San Francisco
S.F. Int'l Airport
5

AE, MC, V. Free parking, nearby coffee shop, crib $5. *Note:* Conventional, unpretentious motel; comfortable rms, some w. kitchenette. Free morning coffee; good value. **I**

Where to Eat

Bridge's, 112 N. G St. (206/532-6563). A/C. Breakfast/lunch/dinner daily; closed hols. AE, DC, MC, V. *Specialties:* seafood, fish, prime rib, prime cuts, oysters. *Note:* Praiseworthy seafood rest. nr. the harbor; everything is absolutely fresh. Attractive modern decor; good svce; no-smoking area. Resv. advised. *Steak/Seafood.* **B–I**

WESTPORT: This little port, with its fleet of 150 charter boats, is a favorite summer resort for sportfishing (salmon, bass, halibut, etc.). Its **Westport Aquarium,** 321 Harbor St. (206/268-0471), open daily Feb–Dec, is justly renowned. The nearby **Twin Harbors State Park** has beautiful beaches, but swimming is hazardous.

Where to Stay

Château Westport (formerly the Canterbury), on Wash. 105, Westport, WA 98595 (206/268-9101). 110 rms; no A/C; cable color TV. AE, CB, DC, MC, V. Free parking, pool, crib $3. *Note:* Inviting motel on the beach. Spacious rms w. balconies and refrigerators, some w. kitchenettes and fireplaces. Pleasant reception and svce; free breakfast; nearby rest. **I–M**

Where to Eat

Sourdough Lil's, 202 Dock St. (206/268-9700). No A/C. Lunch/dinner daily; closed Oct 15–Jan. MC, V. *Specialties:* fish of the day, shellfish, prime rib, steak. *Note:* Like a 1900s saloon, w. ragtime piano and banjo, and songs w. the diners joining in the chorus. Good fish and meat. Entertaining atmosphere. *Steak/Seafood.* **B–I**

LONG BEACH: Sweeping 28 mi. (45km) in a single stretch, this is one of the world's longest sand beaches. **Wash. 103,** the coast road from Long Beach to **Oysterville,** is a scenic highway; it will take you to **Fort Canby** (206/642-3078), open daily mid-May to Oct, wknds only the rest of the year. On Wash. 101 you'll find **Fort Columbia** (206/777-8221), open daily mid-Apr to Sept, Wed–Sun the rest of the year. From either one of these meticulously restored military posts dating from pioneer days, there's a wonderful view of the mouth of the Columbia River.

Where to Stay

Chautauqua Lodge, 304 14th St. NW, Long Beach, WA 98631 (206/642-4401). 180 rms; no A/C; cable color TV. AE, MC, V. Free parking, pool, sauna, adj. rest., bar, disco, crib $2. *Note:* Large, modern motel w. direct beach access; huge, well-designed rms w. balconies and refrigerators, some w. kitchenettes. Good svce; a fine place to stay. **I–M,** but lower rates off-season.

O'Connor's Shaman, 115 3rd St. S., Long Beach, WA 98631 (206/642-3714). 40 rms; no A/C; color TV, in-rm movies. AE, MC, V. Free parking, pool, adj. coffee shop, free crib. *Note:* Typical motel nr. the beach; huge inviting rms, some w. kitchenette and fireplace. **I,** but lower rates Oct–May.

IN NEARBY CHINOOK **Youth Hostel,** Fort Columbia State Park, Chinook, WA 98614 (206/777-8755). 23 beds. Open year round.

Where to Eat

Surfside, in the Surfside Inn, 31512 J Pl. (206/665-5211). No A/C. Dinner only, nightly; closed Dec 25. MC, V. *Special-

ties: seafood, steak, Japanese dishes. *Note:* This rest., specializing in dependably fresh seafood, also offers a pretty ocean view. Dancing Fri–Sat. evening. *American/Japanese.* **B–I**

☼🛆 **ASTORIA:** Dating from 1811, this is one of the oldest American settlement points west of Mississippi. It was originally a trading post for furs, belonging to the wealthy John Jacob Astor, owner of the American Fur Co. Today it's a charming little fishing port with a strong flavor of the 19th century. If you climb the 128 steps of the **Astoria Column** you'll be rewarded with a wonderful view. There's also the interesting **Columbia River Maritime Museum** at 17th St. and Marine Dr. (503/325-2323), open daily Apr–Oct, Tues–Sun the rest of the year. You should certainly see Astoria.

Where to Stay

♀ **Crest Motel,** 5366 Leif Erickson Dr., Astoria, OR 97103 (503/325-3141). 34 rms; no A/C; color TV, in-rm movies. AE, CB, DC, MC, V. Free parking, whirlpool bath; no bar or rest. *Note:* Engaging motel on a cliff overlooking the Columbia River. Spacious, very comfortable rms, some w. balcony and refrigerator. Inviting grdn; friendly reception and svce. Free morning coffee. **I–M,** but lower rates off-season.

♀♀ **Red Lion Inn,** 400 Industry St., Astoria, OR 97103 (503/325-7373; toll free, see Red Lion Inns). 124 rms; no A/C; color TV, in-rm movies. AE, CB, DC, MC, V. Free parking, rest., coffee shop, bar, disco, free crib. *Note:* Wonderfully located facing the harbor and the Columbia River. Spacious, comfortable rms w. balconies and fine view; acceptable rest.; free airport limo. A fine place to stay. **I–M,** but lower rates off-season.

Where to Eat

♀♀ **Pier 11 Feed Store,** 77 11th St. (503/325-0279). A/C. Breakfast/lunch/dinner daily; closed Thanksgiving, Dec 25. MC, V. *Specialties:* catch of the day, shellfish, prime cuts, grilled salmon, Dungeness crab. Interesting wine list. *Note:* As its name tells you, the rest. occupies a 19th-century grain and feed warehouse on the docks, w. a good view of the Columbia River. Faultless food and svce. Resv. advised. *Steak/Seafood.* **B–I**

☼🛆🛆 **FORT CLATSOP NATIONAL MEMORIAL:** A major landmark in the Winning of the West, marking the limit of the territory explored by the famous expedition of Lewis and Clark. Leaving St. Louis, Mo., in May 1804 on the orders of Pres. Thomas Jefferson, the two officers and their 27 companions crossed the northwestern U.S. in search of the quickest way to the Pacific Ocean. They reached the mouth of the Columbia River in Nov 1805 and returned to a hero's welcome in St. Louis in Sept 1806. It was thanks to Lewis and Clark that Americans began to recognize the enormous dimensions of their nation, or rather of the continent with which it was co-extensive. Fort Clatsop, completely reconstructed using original documents, now houses an interesting museum on the odyssey of Lewis and Clark; you'll find it on U.S. 101A (503/861-2471), open daily.

🛆 **SEASIDE:** A well-known oceanside resort for more than a century, with a fine 2-mi. (3km) beach. At 200 N. Promenade St. there's an interesting aquarium (503/738-6211), open daily Mar–Nov, Wed–Sun the rest of the year.

Where to Stay

♀ **Best Western Ocean View,** 414 N. Promenade St., Seaside, OR 97138 (503/738-3334; toll free, see Best Western). 75 rms; no A/C; cable color TV. AE, CB, DC, MC, V. Free parking, pool, sauna, adj. coffee shop. *Note:* Modern, very well maintained motel on the beach; comfortable rms w. sun deck and ocean view; family packages. **I–M**

City Center, 250 First Ave. at Columbia St., Seaside, OR 97138 (503/738-6377). 34 rms; no A/C; color TV, in-rm movies. MC, V. Free parking, pool, sauna, crib $5. *Note:* Small, well-run conventional motel; nearby coffee shop, free morning coffee; some rms w. kitchenettes. **I,** but lower rates Oct–May.

Where to Eat

The Crab Broiler, intersection of U.S. 26 and U.S. 101 (503/738-5313). No A/C. Lunch/dinner daily; closed Thanksgiving, Dec 24–25, early Jan. AE, CB, DC, MC, V. *Specialties:* catch of the day, seafood, lobster. *Note:* Agreeable rustic atmosphere (four fireplaces, grdn view) and excellent seafood impeccably broiled or otherwise prepared. Very good svce; resv. advised. *Seafood.* **B–I**

CANNON BEACH: Very popular resort, with a beach 6.8 mi. (11km) long; another bird and aquatic refuge, its principal feature is a huge solitary rock, 235 ft. (72m) high just offshore from the beach, known as **Haystack Rock.** Flourishing artists' community. From here you have your choice of two interesting excursions: to the 3,820-ft. (1,000m) **Saddle Mountain,** for its views of the coast and the ocean; or to **Ecola Park** on the shoreline, with its seabird and sea lion rookeries on offshore rocks.

Where to Stay

IN NEARBY TOLOVANA PARK The **Tolovana Inn,** 3400 S. Hemlock St., Tolovana Park, OR 97145 (503/436-2211; toll free 800/333-8890). 180 rms; no A/C; color TV, in-rm movies. AE, MC, V. Free parking, pool, sauna, rest., bar, disco, free crib. *Note:* Large vacation motel w. direct access to beach. Spacious, comfortable rms w. private patios or balconies and refrigerators, some w. kitchenettes. Ask for a rm looking out on the ocean and Haystack Rock. Interesting family discounts. 2-day minimum stay on wknds and in July–Aug. **I–M**

TILLAMOOK: Nicknamed "Little Holland" because of its dikes and dairy farms. **Loop Rd.** is a very beautiful scenic highway 19 mi. (31km) long around **Cape Meares** and the Pacific shore.

Where to Stay

Best Western Mar-Clair, 11 Main Ave., Tillamook, OR 97141 (503/842-7571; toll free, see Best Western). 47 rms; no A/C; cable color TV. AE, CB, DC, MC, V. Free parking, pool, sauna, coffee shop, crib $5. *Note:* Modern motel in the center of town; comfortable rms, some w. kitchenettes. Solarium. **I,** but lower rates off-season.

PACIFIC CITY: Famous for its fishermen and their wooden dories which can ride the long Pacific swells (for a small fee you can come along). On your way, stop to look at the ocean from **Cape Lookout,** 18 mi. (30km) north.

LINCOLN CITY: A popular town for summer homes, with five communities grouped around a beach 3.7 mi. (6km) long. Many art galleries and crafts shops.

Where to Stay

The Inn at Spanish Head, 4009 S. U.S. 101, Lincoln City, OR 97367 (503/996-2161; toll free 800/547-5235). 120 rms, cable color TV. AE, CB, DC, MC, V. Free valet parking, pool, sauna, rest., bar, nightclub, free crib. *Note:* A 10-story hotel facing the ocean. Vast, comfortable rms, most w. private balconies or patios and an outstanding ocean view; all w. kitchenettes. Adj. beach. Good svce; a fine place to stay. **M–E,** but lower rates off-season.

 Shilo Inn, 1501 NW 40th St., Lincoln City, OR 97367 (503/ 994-3655; toll free 800/222-2244). 186 rms; no A/C; color TV, in-rm movies. AE, CB, DC, MC, V. Free parking, pool, sauna, rest., bar, rm svce, nightclub, crib $10. *Note:* Three-story motel (no elevator) overlooking the ocean; spacious, comfortable rms w. fireplaces, the best w. a fine view. Free airport limo. Very commendable rest. Good value. **I–M**

 Lincoln Shores (formerly Nidden Hof), 136 NE U.S. 101, Lincoln City, OR 97367 (503/994-8155; toll free 800/423-6240). 29 rms; no A/C; cable color TV. AE, DC, MC, V. Free parking, nearby coffee shop, crib $5. *Note:* Engaging little motel across from D River Park. Inviting rms w. balconies. Beach nearby. **I,** but lower rates Nov–May.

IN NEARBY GLENEDEN BEACH The ☀ **Salishan Lodge,** U.S. 101, Gleneden Beach, OR 97388 (503/764-2371; toll free, see Preferred). 200 rms; no A/C; color TV, in-rm movies. AE, MC, V. Free covered parking, pool, four tennis courts, golf course, sauna, health club, rest. (Dining Rm), coffee shop, bar, rm svce, disco, hrdrsr, art gallery, boutiques, concierge, crib $10. *Note:* One of the best hotels in the country; up-to-date elegance in the middle of 700 acres (283ha) of woods and grdns. Wonderful setting between the forest and Siletz Bay. Inviting, comfortable two-story buildings overlooking the golf course; spacious rms w. fireplaces, private balconies and patios, the best w. ocean view. Rest. of a high order; excellent svce. A memorable place to stay. 2-day minimum stay wknds and July–Sept. **E–VE,** but lower rates Nov–Apr.

Where to Eat

 Shilo Inn (formerly Henry Thiele's), in the Shilo Inn (see "Where to Stay," above) (503/994-5255). A/C. Breakfast/ lunch/dinner daily. AE, CB, DC, MC, V. *Specialties:* potato pancakes, prime rib, catch of the day. *Note:* Laudable German-inspired dishes, but also good seafood. Lovely ocean view; dancing Tues–Sat. Resv. advised. *German/Seafood.* **B–I**

IN NEARBY GLENEDEN BEACH **The Dining Room,** in the Salishan Lodge (see "Where to Stay," above) (503/764-2371). A/C. Dinner only, nightly (two seatings, at 6 and 10pm), brunch Sun. AE, CB, DC, MC, V. Jkt. *Specialties:* Dungeness crab, Chinook salmon, filet of sole, chateaubriand, Oregon lamb chops. Very good wine list, with more than 1,000 labels. *Note:* One of the best rests. on the Pacific coast. Three-level dining rm, recently renovated, elegantly paneled and w. a pretty view over the bay. Carefully worked-out cuisine, based on remarkably fine local produce—seafood, lamb, game, wild mushrooms, etc. Exemplary svce. Resv. a must, especially on wknds. *Continental/Seafood.* **M–E**

 Chez Jeannette, 7150 Old U.S. 101 (503/764-3434). No A/C. Dinner only, Tues–Sat; closed Oct–Jun. AE, MC, V. *Specialties:* catch of the day and seafood, rack of lamb, game (in season). *Note:* Elegant, meticulously prepared cuisine of French inspiration, in a charming 1920s country cottage. Friendly, efficient svce. Resv. advisable. Locally popular. *French/American.* **I–M**

 DEPOE BAY: Tiny, picturesque fishing port; you must stop in the center of town to look at the **Spouting Horns,** natural rock tubes that spout like geysers under the violent assault of the waves; don't miss them. Depoe Bay is a good base for deep-sea fishing.

Where to Stay

Best Western Surfrider, U.S. 101, Depoe Bay, OR 97341 (503/764-2311; toll free, see Best Western). 40 rms; no A/C; color TV, in-rm movies. AE, CB, DC, MC, V. Free parking, pool, sauna, rest., bar, disco, crib $2. *Note:* Small, likable, serviceable motel at the water's edge; comfortable rms w. balconies overlooking the Pacific (some w. kitchenettes and fireplaces). Excellent reception. **I–M,** but lower rates Oct–May.

IN NEARBY OTTER ROCK **The Inn at Otter Crest,** Otter Rock, OR 97369 (503/765-2111; toll free 800/547-2181), a quarter mi. west of U.S. 101. 150 rms and studios; no A/C; color TV, in-rm movies. AE, DC, MC, V. Free parking, pool, sauna, four tennis courts, miniature golf, beach, rest. (Flying Dutchman), bar, disco, crib $5. *Note:* Comfortable, inviting motel on a wooded headland overlooking the Pacific. Pretty woodland decor. Spacious rms w. private balcony and refrigerator (some w. kitchenette and fireplace). Studios have two bedrooms. Very acceptable rest.; efficient, smiling svce. Wonderful view of the ocean. A fine place. **M–E**

DEVIL'S PUNCH BOWL STATE PARK: Giant bowl-shaped rock formation which fills at each high tide. Beach; aquatic garden. From **Cape Foulweather,** so named by British navigator Capt. James Cook in 1778, you'll have a fine view of the ocean.

NEWPORT: One of the busiest fishing ports on the Pacific coast, with fine Victorian houses and colorful docks. **Hatfield Marine Science Center,** Marine Science Dr. (503/867-3011), open daily, is an excellent museum of oceanography affiliated with Oregon State University. There's also a renowned saltwater aquarium, **Undersea Gardens,** at 267 SW Bay Blvd. (503/265-2206), open daily, which offers views of marine plants and native sealife, including Armstrong the giant octopus, through large underwater windows.

Where to Stay

Embarcadero Resort, 1000 SE Bay Blvd.; Newport, OR 97365 (503/265-8521; toll free 800/547-4779). 110 rms; no A/C; color TV, in-rm movies. AE, CB, DC, MC, V. Free parking, pool, sauna, marina, boating, rest. (Embarcadero), bar, rm svce, nightclub, free crib. *Note:* Luxurious vacation hotel on the Yaquina River, w. marina and boat dock. Elegant, comfortable rms, all w. private balconies or patios, some w. kitchenettes. Flawless reception and svce; excellent rest.; beautiful views of the bay. **M–E,** but lower rates Nov–Apr.

Sylvia Beach, 267 NW Cliff St., Newport, OR 97365 (503/265-5428). 20 rms; no A/C. AE, MC, V. Free parking, rest. (Tables of Content), library. *Note:* A booklover's paradise. Every bedroom in the whole, huge 1912 wooden structure overlooking the ocean is dedicated to a different writer and decorated accordingly. The most original are the Edgar Allan Poe Rm, Colette Rm, and Agatha Christie Rm. Almost all have a fine ocean view. Four floors, no elevator. Commendable rest.; free breakfast. You should reserve a long way ahead, especially in summer. **M–E**

Budget Host Jolly Knight, 606 SW Coast Hwy., Newport, OR 97365 (503/265-7723). 43 rms, cable color TV. AE, MC,

V. Free parking, adj. 24-hr. rest., free crib. *Note:* Small, unpretentious oceanfront motel; spacious, serviceable rms, the best with a fine view. **I**, but lower rates Oct–May.

Youth Hostel, 212 NW Brook St., Newport, OR 97365 (503/265-9816). 24 beds. Open year round.

Where to Eat

⚇⚇ **Embarcadero,** in the Embarcadero Resort (see "Where to Stay," above) (503/265-8521). A/C. Breakfast/lunch/dinner daily, brunch Sun. AE, CB, DC, MC, V. *Specialties:* catch of the day, shellfish, steak.

Note: All-purpose seafaring decor but pretty view of the harbor. First-class food; absolutely fresh seafood. *Steak/Seafood.* **B–I**

⚇ **Mo's,** 622 SW Bay Blvd. (503/265-2979). No A/C. Lunch/dinner daily. MC, V. *Specialties:* clam chowder, oysters on the half shell or barbecued, crab salad, broiled fish, peanut-butter cake, apple cobbler. *Note:* One of the Oregon coast's long-standing beacons. The parent establishment, as well as the annex across the road and the half dozen other Mo's rests. scattered along the coast from Lincoln City to Coos Bay, serve the best clam chowder in the state as well as impeccably fresh seafood at reasonable prices. Amusing seafaring decor. Noisy but not disagreeable; a fine place to eat. *Seafood.* **B–I**

YACHATS: Fashionable seaside resort with a beautiful fine-sand beach and a very craggy shoreline. (**Cape Perpetua,** just south of town, is the highest point on the Oregon coast: 800 ft./243m.) The coastal highway here is beautiful beyond description. Good sea fishing.

Where to Stay

Adobe Motel, U.S. 101 (P.O. Box 219), Yachats, OR 97498 (503/547-3141; toll free 800/522-3623). 58 rms; no A/C; cable color TV. AE, CB, DC, MC, V. Free parking, whirlpool, sauna, rest., bar, crib $4. *Note:* Appealing little motel right on the ocean; huge, inviting rms w. refrigerators (most w. balconies and fireplaces), the best overlooking the Pacific. Cheerful reception and svce; free morning coffee. An excellent place to stay. **I–M,** but lower rates off-season.

Where to Eat

⚇ **La Serre,** 2nd St. and Beach St. (503/547-3141). A/C. Lunch daily late May to Sept, dinner Wed–Mon, brunch Sat–Sun; closed Feb. AE, DC, MC, V. *Specialties:* catch of the day, seafood, steak, homemade desserts. *Note:* A nice, attractive rest. serving honest, tasty (but not very imaginative) food in a family atmosphere. Locally popular. *American.* **B–I**

SEA LION CAVES (U.S. 101) (503/547-3111): A basalt grotto 1,500 ft. (450m) long, 208 ft. (63m) below the surface, inhabited by wild sea lions (elevator). The animals can easily be observed in their natural surroundings outside the cave in spring and summer, or inside the cave in fall and winter. Open daily; touristy, but spectacular nonetheless.

FLORENCE: A charming little town with an interesting "Old Town" area and a wealth of flowers on the Siuslaw River, very near a chain of 17 lakes well stocked with fish and the **Siuslaw National Forest.** It marks the northern boundary of the **Oregon Dunes National Recreation Area,**

a huge sandspit 50 mi. (80km) long, whose dunes rise as high as 524 ft. (160m). Dunebuggy rides available (503/271-3611). Shouldn't be missed.

Where to Stay

Le Château, 1084 Coast Hwy., Florence, OR 97439 (503/997-3481). 48 rms; no A/C; cable color TV. AE, DC, MC, V. Free parking, pool, sauna, nearby coffee shop, crib $4. *Note:* Typical vacation motel w. direct beach access. Functionally comfortable rms; cheerful reception; free morning coffee. **I**

Where to Eat

Windward Inn, 3757 U.S. 101 (503/997-8243). A/C. Breakfast/lunch/dinner daily; closed Mon mid-Oct to May, Thanksgiving, Dec 24–25. AE, CB, DC, MC, V. *Specialties:* fish and shellfish of the day, very fine prime cuts, fresh fruit and vegetables. *Note:* The two major achievements of this excellent rest., much appreciated by those in-the-know, are the low prices it charges for materials of the highest quality, and its well-stocked wine list. *Steak/Seafood.* **B–I**

REEDSPORT: Both saltwater and freshwater fishing enthusiasts can enjoy themselves here at the head of **Winchester Bay.** The headquarters of the **Oregon Dunes National Recreation Area** (see above) is here, at 855 Highway Ave. (503/271-3611).

COOS BAY: The world's biggest lumber port; also a busy fishing port. At **North Bend,** on the same bay, there's an interesting museum devoted to the settlement of Oregon, the **Coos County Historical Museum,** Simpson Park on U.S. 101 (503/756-6320), open Tues–Sun June–Sept, Tues–Sat the rest of the year.

Crater Lake National Park

Some 182 mi. (292km) SE of Coos Bay via Ore. 42 and Ore. 38 is one of the loveliest mountain lakes in the U.S., or indeed in the world, in the caldera of the extinct volcano **Mount Mazama.** A violent eruption some 6,600 years ago created this steep-sided, circular basin, 7 mi. (11km) across and, at 1,932 ft. (589m), the deepest lake in the country. The reflection of the surrounding peaks and craters in its clear dark-blue waters delineates a surprisingly beautiful volcanic landscape. **Rim Drive,** a 33-mi. (53km) scenic highway, follows the shoreline; there are many **hiking trails,** including a steep path leading up to Watchman's Peak (8,022 ft./2,457m) with its unparalleled view. There are **observation platforms,** which can be reached by car, at the top of Cloudcap (8,060 ft./2,457m) and Pinnacles (5,585 ft./1,672m), strange needles of tufa and pumice carved out by erosion. Many wild animals live around Crater Lake: black bear, elk, red fox, coyote, wildcat, and others; fish, on the other hand, are few and fishing is strictly regulated. Boat rides may be taken on the lake, but be careful if you go swimming: the water is ice-cold even in summer.

Given the status of a national park in 1902, Crater Lake is open year round (except for the northern entrance, which is closed mid-Oct to mid-June because of snowslides). At any time of year take warm clothing—it snows 10 months out of the 12. Campsites and a rustic motel are inside the park.

For **information,** contact the Superintendent, Crater Lake National Park, P.O. Box 7, Crater Lake, OR 97604 (503/594-2211). A trip not to be missed.

Where to Stay

Red Lion Inn, 1313 N. Bayshore Dr., Coos Bay, OR 97420 (503/267-4141; toll free, see Red Lion Inns). 145 rms, A/C, cable color TV. AE, CB, DC, MC, V. Free parking, pool, rest., bar, rm svce, disco, free crib. *Note:* In a lovely situation w. a view of the bay. Vast, inviting rms; up-to-date, comfortable facilities, good svce; free airport limo. **I–M**

Youth Hostel, 438 Elrod, Coos Bay, OR 97420 (503/267-6114). 20 beds. Open late May to Sept.

BANDON: Little harbor, very popular with tourists, at the mouth of the Coquille River. Lovely beaches famed for the agates and other semiprecious stones you can pick up here.

Where to Stay

Bandon Beach Motel, 1110 W. 11th St., Bandon, OR 97411 (503/347-4430). 28 rms; no A/C; color TV, in-rm movies. AE, MC, V. Free parking, adj. coffee shop, crib $4. *Note:* Tiny motel on a cliff overlooking the beach; decent standard of comfort; some rms w. balconies and kitchenettes. **I–M,** but lower rates Oct–May.

Youth Hostel, 375 2nd St., Bandon, OR 97411 (503/347-9632). 35 beds. Open year round.

Where to Eat

Bandon Boatworks, 275 Lincoln Ave. SW (503/347-2111). No A/C. Lunch/dinner Tues–Sun; closed Jan and hols. MC, V. *Specialties:* fish of the day, steak, milk-fed veal, Mexican dishes. *Note:* Excellent fish, as well as some good Mexican dishes on wknds. Nice view of the jetty and lighthouse. Congenial atmosphere; good svce. *American/Mexican.* **B–I**

PORT ORFORD: Some of the loveliest seascapes on the Oregon coast. In 1851 the little port, which was then the westernmost city in the contiguous U.S., was the scene of a bloody battle between native tribes and white settlers. At **Cape Blanco,** 7½ mi. (12km) NW on U.S. 101, there's a strange black-sand beach.

Where to Stay

Sea Crest, U.S. 101, Port Orford, OR 97465 (503/332-3040). 18 rms, cable color TV. MC, V. Free parking, nearby coffee shop, crib $3. *Note:* Mini-motel w. ocean and mountain views. Rms no better than serviceable, but inviting grdn and cheerful reception. **I,** but lower rates off-season.

GOLD BEACH: Owes its name to the gold nuggets that used to be found at the mouth of the **Rogue River** until, in 1861, a disastrous flood swept them all out to sea. Fine excursions into the nearby **Siskiyou National Forest;** also rafting down the Rogue River (see "Adventures," above).

Where to Stay

Tu Tu Tun Lodge, 96550 N. Bank Rogue, Gold Beach, OR 97444 (503/247-6664). 18 rms; no A/C. MC, V. Free parking, pool, boating, fishing, putting green, rest., bar, free crib. *Note:* Charming country cottage on the Rogue River; boat trips available. Spacious, inviting rms w. balconies; well-stocked library for inveterate idlers. An agreeable, relaxing stopover. Closed Nov–Apr. **E**

Ireland's Rustic Lodges, 1120 S. Ellensburg, Gold Beach, OR 97444 (503/247-7718). 32 rms and cottages; no A/C; cable color TV. No credit cards. Free parking, private beach, nearby coffee shop, crib

$5. *Note:* Pretty little bungalows in a grdn overlooking the ocean; the best have ocean views. Spacious rms w. balconies, some w. kitchenettes and fireplaces. Good value on balance. **I–M,** but lower rates Oct–May.

 CRESCENT CITY: The first important town across the northern border of California, deriving its name from its crescent-shaped coastline. Interesting saltwater aquarium, **Undersea World,** 304 U.S. 101S (707/464-3522), open daily. From here you can easily venture into Redwood National Park with its amazing redwood forests.

※ Redwood National Park
Just 4 mi. (6km) east of Crescent City, this forest of giant sequoias (redwoods), 46 mi. (75km) long by 6 mi. (10km) wide, stands on the shore. Some redwoods, more than 10 centuries old, have grown to 295 ft. (90m); the present record is held by the prosaically nicknamed **Tall Tree,** 368 ft. (112m) high, with a diameter of 14 ft. (4.20m). This is the largest-known living creature in the world. Abundant wildlife: elk, deer, mountain lion, bald eagle, brown pelican, and peregrine falcons. The park is traversed by a splendid scenic highway, U.S. 101. Many hiking trails, campsites, and picnic areas.

There are three other redwood forests nearby: **Jedediah Smith State Park, Del Norte Coast State Park,** and **Prairie Creek State Park;** along with Redwood National Park they make up the **Redwood Empire,** a vast tract of woodlands extending from the northern border of California to the outskirts of San Francisco.

For **information,** contact the Superintendent, Redwood National Park, 1111 2nd St., Crescent City, CA 95531 (707/464-6101).

※ ꙮ Oregon Caves National Monument
These marble caverns, 85 mi. (136km) NE of Crescent City via U.S. 199 and Ore. 46, comprising a number of evocatively named chambers—Paradise Lost, Ghost Chamber, Joaquin Miller's Chapel—were discovered in 1874 by a hunter in pursuit of a bear; they are among the most unusual and beautiful in the U.S. Their air temperature is a constant 42°F (6°C). Tours (exhausting) daily year round. For **information,** contact Oregon Caves National Monument, P.O. Box 128, Cave Junction, OR 97523 (503/592-3400).

Around the caves is ꙮ **Siskiyou National Forest,** whose cedars—200- to 300-year-old pine trees growing as tall as 130 ft. (40m)—conifers, orchids, and rare plants make it a botanist's paradise.

Where to Stay
 Budget Host Royal Inn, 102 L St. (at Front St.), Crescent City, CA 95531 (707/464-4113). 35 rms; no A/C; cable color TV. AE, MC, V. Free covered parking, nearby rest., free crib. *Note:* A fine ocean view is the main attraction of this typical small motel. Comfortable rms; free morning coffee. **I,** but lower rates off-season.

IN NEARBY SMITH RIVER The **Best Western Ship Ashore,** U.S. 101, Smith River, CA 95567 (707/487-3141; toll free, see Best Western). 50 rms; no A/C; cable color TV. AE, CB, DC, MC, V. Free parking, whirlpool, boating, fishing, coffee shop, bar, disco, crib $6. *Note:* Small, modern motel overlooking the ocean; comfortable rms w. balconies and Pacific or river views. Boat rentals for sportfishing. Free morning coffee. Parking for motor homes. **I–M,** but lower rates off-season.

Where to Eat
 Harbor View Grotto, 155 Citizen's Dock (707/464-3815). A/C. Lunch/dinner daily; closed Jan 1, Thanksgiving, Dec 25. No credit cards. *Specialties:* clam chowder, seafood, prime rib, steak, catch of

the day. *Note:* Classic fish rest. on the docks; absolutely fresh seafood nicely prepared. From the upstairs rm you have a harbor view. *Steak/Seafood.* **B–I**

McKINLEYVILLE: Look over the world's largest totem pole, 162 ft. (50m) high and weighing 26 tons. It was carved from the trunk of a single tree, more than 500 years old.

EUREKA: This very busy port town has a sheltered harbor at the head of **Humboldt Bay,** but is often foggy even in summer. Many beautiful frame houses (wood is the principal local resource). Picturesque **Old Town District** (bounded by 1st St., 3rd St., C St., and G St.) with original buildings of early Eureka, plus antiques and specialty shops. See the splendid 1885 **Carson Mansion** at 143 M St., a perfect specimen of Victorian architecture, unfortunately not open to visitors.

A dozen miles to the south, the little town of **Ferndale** is a living museum of the Victorian style.

Where to Stay

Eureka Inn, 7th St. and F St., Eureka, CA 99501 (707/442-6441; toll free 800/862-4906). 108 rms; no A/C; cable color TV. AE, CB, DC, MC, V. Free parking, pool, sauna, rest. (Rib Rm), coffee shop, rm svce, nightclub, free crib. *Note:* Elegant, comfortable Tudor-style inn dating from 1922; huge, inviting rms w. balconies and minibars. Exemplary svce; very commendable rest.; free airport limo. An excellent place to stay. **M–E**

Royal Pacific, 1304 4th St., Eureka, CA 99501 (707/443-3193; toll free 800/235-3232). 50 rms, color TV, in-rm movies. AE, CB, DC, MC, V. Free parking, pool, sauna, adj. coffee shop, bar, crib $5. *Note:* Well-kept conventional motel; inviting rms w. balconies; free morning coffee. **I–M**

IN NEARBY ARCATA **Motel 6,** 4755 Valley West Blvd., Arcata, CA 95521 (707/822-7061). 81 rms, A/C, color TV, free in-rm movies. AE, DC, MC, V. Free parking, pool; no bar or rest.; free crib. *Note:* Unbeatable value 10 min. from dwntwn Eureka. Serviceable comfort; friendly reception. Ideal for the budget traveler. **B–I**

IN NEARBY FERNDALE The **Gingerbread Mansion,** 400 Berding St., Ferndale, CA 95536 (707/786-4000). 8 rms; no A/C. MC, V. Free parking, bicycles, rest., free breakfast. *Note:* Delightful turn-of-the-century Victorian house in a very pretty English-style grdn in the heart of Ferndale's historic district. Elegant rms w. period furniture, some without baths. Impeccable reception and svce. Resv. essential, well ahead. Totally nonsmoking. **M–E**

Where to Eat

Lazio's Seafood, 327 2nd St. (707/443-9717). A/C. Lunch/dinner daily; closed hols. AE, CB, DC, MC, V. *Specialties:* crab, fresh seafood, sourdough bread. *Note:* Opened in 1946 in an old fish cannery, this rest. is the proud possession of the Lazio family, fishermen from father to son for more than a century. The seafood is superb, as you'd expect. New decor w. trilevel dining; attentive svce. *Seafood.* **B–I**

Samoa Cookhouse, Samoa Blvd. (707/442-1659). No A/C. Breakfast/lunch/dinner daily; closed Thanksgiving, Dec 25. AE, CB, DC, MC, V. *Specialties:* barbecued meats, western-style food. *Note:* This locally popular place is more like a museum than a rest., w. its many mementoes of pioneer days. Dates from 1885. Specializes in lumber camp–style cooking; excellent value. *American.* **B**

☼ ♟♟ **AVENUE OF THE GIANTS:** An extraordinary slash through the middle of the redwoods of **Humboldt National Forest,** the Avenue of the Giants runs parallel to U.S. 101 for 33 mi. (52km), beginning south of Pepperwood, like a sort of giant green tunnel lined with 300-ft.-tall (92m) redwoods; it's a sight you should try to see.

Where to Stay

IN GARBERVILLE   The ☼ ♟♟ **Benbow Inn,** 445 Lake Benbow Dr., Garberville, CA 95440 (707/923-2124). 55 rms, A/C, cable color TV (in half the rms). AE, MC, V. Free parking, private beach, golf course, putting green, boating, rest., bar, nightclub, classic vintage movie nightly. *Note:* An old English manor house on the shore of a wooded lake, for a perfect picture-postcard vacation. Charming decor and reception. Avoid the third and fourth floors—no elevators. Closed in early Dec and Jan 2 to mid-Apr. **M–E**

IN PIERCY   The ♟♟ **Hartsook Country Inn,** 900 U.S. 101, Piercy, CA 95467 (707/247-3305). 62 rms; no A/C; color TV (in lounge). AE, MC, V. Free parking, private beach, rest., crib $3. *Note:* Spacious, comfortable rms in little bungalows along the Eel River in a 30-acre (12ha) park. Very acceptable rest.; friendly reception and svce. Closed Oct to mid-Apr. Good overall value. **I–M**

Where to Eat

IN GARBERVILLE   The ♟♟ **Benbow Inn,** in the Benbow Inn (see "Where to Stay," above) (707/923-2125). Breakfast/lunch/dinner daily; closed Jan to mid-Mar and 3 weeks in Dec. AE, MC, V. *Specialties:* fresh salmon in season, filet mignon, fish of the day, sweetbreads Marnie, rack of lamb. *Note:* Praiseworthy hotel rest. in a pretty waterside park w. open-air dining in summer. Faultless food; agreeable background music. Totally nonsmoking. *Continental/Seafood.* **B–I**

☼ ♟ **FORT BRAGG:** This charming little harbor town, originally founded in 1857 and standing in the center of a superb stretch of rocky coast, was rebuilt after the 1906 earthquake that also destroyed San Francisco. The scenery is lovely. Take a ride on the **California Western Railroad** (affectionately known as "The Skunk"), a Far West–style line which follows the Noyo River through some magnificent redwood (sequoia) forests as far as Willits, a 40-mi. (64km) scenic trip; it leaves from Laurel St.(707/964-6371). The round-trip takes 7 hr. and operates daily year round.

Where to Stay

♟ **Harbor Lite Lodge,** 120 N. Harbor Dr., Fort Bragg, CA 95437 (707/964-0221). 70 rms; no A/C; color TV, in-rm movies. AE, CB, DC, MC, V. Free parking, beach, sauna, nearby coffee shop, crib $6. *Note:* Vacation motel a stone's throw from the beach. Inviting rms w. balconies, the best overlooking Noyo harbor. Direct beach access; good value. **I–M,** but lower rates off-season.

Where to Eat

♟♟ **The Restaurant,** 418 N. Main St. (707/964-9800). Lunch/dinner Thur–Tues; closed 3 weeks in Mar, Thanksgiving, Dec

25. MC, V. *Specialties:* fresh salmon in season, pork schnitzel, trout stuffed w. crabmeat, saltimbocca of chicken. *Note:* This little rest. in the heart of dwntwn serves some rather unusual fare at a very reasonable price. Resv. advised. Totally nonsmoking. *Continental.* **I**

NOYO: Picturesque little fishing village at the mouth of the Noyo River. The **Mendocino Coast Botanical Gardens,** on Calif. 1 (707/964-4352), open daily, is a magnificent 17-acre (6.8ha) flower garden overlooking the ocean.

MENDOCINO: Very pretty little harbor town perched on a rock, which has retained a carefully cultivated 19th-century flavor with its Victorian houses, artists' colony, art galleries, antique dealers, and tourist restaurants.

Another 3.7 mi. (6km) south, **Van Damme State Park** on Calif. 1 is a very unusual pigmy forest. The poverty of the soil has stunted the trees so that some of them, as much as 20 years old, are only 3 ft. (1m) tall and 2 in. (6cm) through the trunk.

Where to Stay

Mendocino Hotel, 45080 Main St., Mendocino, CA 95460 (707/937-0511; toll free 800/548-0513). 51 rms, 6 cottages, A/C, cable color TV (in most rms). AE, MC, V. Free parking, rest., bar, rm svce, free breakfast. *Note:* Picturesque hotel from the 1870s, beautifully preserved. The rms (some without bath) and cottages are inviting and tastefully decorated; a certain number have balconies and fireplaces. Three stories (no elevator). Laudable rest.; magnificent grdn. Lovely views of the harbor and ocean; attentive reception and svce; free airport limo. A fine place to stay, but you must reserve well ahead of time. **E–VE,** but lower rates off-season.

IN NEARBY LITTLERIVER The **Heritage House,** 5200 Calif. 1, Littleriver, CA 95456 (707/937-5885). 10 rms and 5 cottages; no A/C. No credit cards. Free parking, rest., bar. *Note:* Delightfully romantic little cottages on a cliff overlooking the ocean. The main building dates from 1877. Elegant old furniture; spacious, attractive rms w. private balconies or patios, the best overlooking the Pacific. Renowned rest. w. an outstanding wine list. In spite of the high rates, this is a very good place to stay; you have to reserve well in advance. Was the setting for the movie *Same Time Next Year.* Closed Dec–Jan. **E–VE**

Where to Eat

Café Beaujolais, 961 E. Ukiah St. (707/937-5614). No A/C. Breakfast/lunch daily, dinner Thurs–Sun; closed Jan–Feb, Thanksgiving, Dec 25. No credit cards. *Specialties:* white-bean and tomato soup, polenta, fresh salmon (in season), waffles, coffee cake. *Note:* Delightful bistro; decor a faithful Victorian re-creation w. an outdoor patio for fine days. Traditional but pleasing food. Resv. advisable. Totally nonsmoking. *Continental/Seafood.* **B–I**

Mendocino Hotel (see "Where to Stay," above) (707/937-0511). A/C. Breakfast/lunch/dinner daily. AE, MC, V. *Specialties:* fish of the day, steak, tartare, prime rib, homemade cakes. *Note:* The dining rm of that magnificent designated landmark, the 1878 Mendocino Hotel, w. crystalware, beveled mirrors, and Oriental rugs. Charming and picturesque; the setting deserves better in the way of food. Resv. advised. *Steak/Seafood.* **B–I**

IN NEARBY LITTLERIVER The **Ledford House,** Calif. 1 (707/937-0282). No A/C. Dinner nightly, brunch Sun; closed Thanksgiving, early Dec, Dec 25. No credit cards. Jkt. *Specialties:* shrimp cannelloni, fish of the day, baked lamb. *Note:* Beautiful, inviting century-old house looking out on the ocean; inspired cuisine

and some fine California wines. Attentive svce; resv. a must. *Continental/Seafood.*
I–M

IN NEARBY ALBION   The ✲☟☟ **Albion River Inn,** 3790 Calif. 1 (707/937-1919).
No A/C. Dinner only, nightly. MC, V. Jkt. *Specialties:* pasta primavera, linguine
w. clams, bouillabaisse, fish of the day. *Note:* Delightful little inn perched on a
cliff overlooking Albion Cove. Simple but careful cuisine; many works by local
artists adorn the walls. Romantic atmosphere; resv. advised. A fine place.
Continental/Seafood. **I**

🔔 **POINT ARENA:** Beautiful ocean view from Point Arena,
with its famous lighthouse; **Manchester Beach** is nearby.

Where to Stay

IN NEARBY GUALALA   The ✲ 🏚 **St. Orres,** Calif. 1, Gualala, CA 95445 (707/884-
3303). 8 rms and 11 cottages; no A/C. MC, V. Free parking, whirlpool, sauna,
rest., free breakfast. *Note:* Charming tiny inn, w. architecture reminiscent of a
Russian *dacha* and its onion-domed towers, facing the ocean; inviting rms w. balconies (some without bath), or little individual redwood cottages. Unusual interiors w. lovely old paneling. Top-quality rest.; direct beach access. One of the best
places to stay on the coast. **M**(rooms), **E–VE**(cottages).
　　　✲☟☟ **Gualala Inn,** on Calif. 1, Gualala, CA 95445 (707/884-3441).
19 rms, A/C, color TV in lounge. AE, MC, V. Free parking,
rest. (Gualala), bar, wine shop w. tastings. *Note:* Picturesque little turn-of-the-
century hotel across from the beach. Small but tastefully decorated rms, of which
two-thirds have no private bath. Antique furniture, library, interesting rest. Very
good value; you should reserve well ahead. **I**

Where to Eat

IN NEARBY GUALALA   The ✲☟☟ **St. Orres,** in the St. Orres Hotel (see "Where to
Stay," above) (707/884-3335). No A/C. Dinner nightly, brunch Sun in summer; closed Jan and Wed Oct–May. No credit cards. Jkt. *Specialties:* rack of lamb
dijonnaise, roast quail, New York steak, catch of the day. *Note:* Pretty stained-
glass window and old paneling; very successful French-inspired cuisine. Charming, romantic atmosphere; resv. a must. Totally nonsmoking. *Continental.*
M(prix fixe).

☀🔔🔔 **FORT ROSS:** The main Russian outpost in America, this
trading post was founded in 1812 by the Russian-American
Co. as a base for seal hunting. It was sold in 1841 to the Swiss John Sutter, founder of Sacramento and an important figure in the early development of California.
There remain only the fine Russian Orthodox chapel, dating from about 1820,
and a few other buildings from the fort. It's on Calif. 1 (707/865-2391), open
daily.

🔔 **BODEGA BAY:** Attractive little harbor at the head of a very
deep bay. Bodega Bay was the setting for Alfred Hitchcock's
movie *The Birds.*

Where to Stay

🏔 **Best Western Bodega Bay Lodge,** Calif. 1, Bodega Bay, CA
94923 (707/874-3525; toll free, see Best Western). 78 rms;
no A/C; color TV, in-rm movies. AE, CB, DC, MC, V. Free parking, pool, sauna. *Note:* Functional motel overlooking Bodega Bay and Doran Park beach. Spacious rms w. balconies, and refrigerators, some w. fireplaces. Nearby rest.; adj.
golf course; free morning coffee. Rates on the high side for an ordinary motel.
E–VE

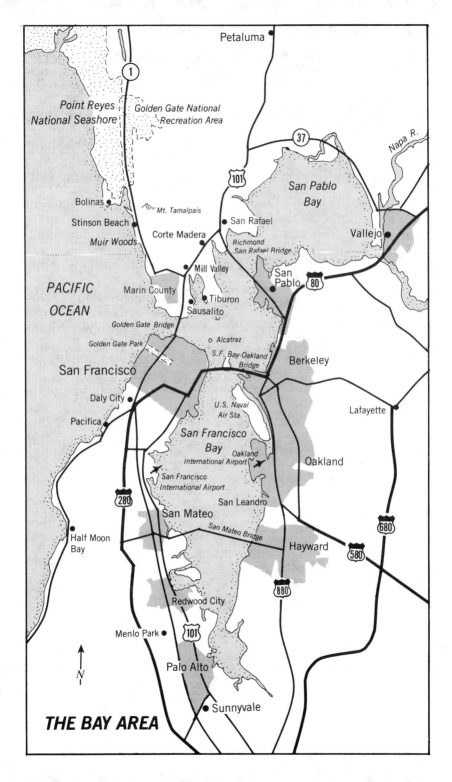

THE BAY AREA

POINT REYES NATIONAL SEASHORE (35 mi./56km NW of San Francisco): 74,000-acre (29,960ha) wildlife reserve on the Pacific; see Chapter 50 on San Francisco.

Where to Stay

Youth Hostel, Point Reyes Station, CA 94956 (415/663-8811). 44 beds. Open wknds only.

PART SEVEN

THE WEST

CHAPTER 47

LAS VEGAS

□ □ □

"The Gambling Capital of the World" bears no relation to any ordinary city. It is a huge, enthralling slot machine that functions around the clock. This brilliant, showy outburst of neon and glass plumb in the middle of the Mojave Desert is well worth going out of your way to see. Arriving by air at night is a whole show in itself.

Las Vegas (a name which in Spanish means "valley of fertile farmland") was founded in the mid-19th century by Mormons on the colonial trail from Santa Fe to California. Thereafter it went into a long decline until the construction of the Union Pacific's first line of track in 1905. The adoption of new gambling laws by the State of Nevada in 1931 made the fortune of Las Vegas, which writer Tom Wolfe has called "the most American of American cities." The population has grown from barely 8,000 in 1940 to 620,000 today. This figure does not include the 17–18 million tourists who come, year after year, to try their luck at the casino tables, sports and race betting, or the famous slot machines. Las Vegas has some 33,000 slot machines and 1,300 blackjack tables. In this city everything revolves around gambling, an industry with annual revenues of almost $3 billion —there are slot machines even in rest rooms. Nevada's largest city cannot show a single monument or museum worthy of its standing; its only gesture in the direction of culture is the big floor show, presenting the brightest stars in the entertainment firmament, from Jerry Lewis or Frank Sinatra to Liza Minnelli, or Donna Summer to Julio Iglesias.

The glittering palaces along the "Strip," Las Vegas's main drag, offer their rooms at bargain-basement prices. Food at the city's 725 restaurants, cafeterias, and snack bars costs half what it would anywhere else in the country. But don't mistake this for philanthropy or hospitality—it reflects a (justified) expectation that visitors or conventioneers, bitten by the gambling fever, will rush to unload precious dollars on the green baize tables or in the slots of the "one-armed bandits" before plane or bus comes to take them away.

If gambling, show business, and conventions are Las Vegas's principal industries, the dozens of "wedding chapels," open until midnight on weekdays and around the clock on weekends, represent the brighter side of the local economy. Las Vegas has more churches, chapels, and other places of worship per thousand inhabitants than any other city in the country. Every year, under the accommodating laws of Nevada, more than 60,000 "marriages on the wing" are performed in Las Vegas by an army of ministers familiarly known as "Marryin' Sams"—between games of poker, blackjack, or baccarat.

Thanks to its low car-rental rates Las Vegas is also a good base for excursions nearby (**Lake Mead, Valley of Fire, Hoover Dam, Red Rock Canyon, Mount Charleston**) or farther afield (the **Grand Canyon** of the Colorado, **Death Valley,** the **Utah national parks**).

BASIC FACTS: State of Nevada. Area code: 702. Time zone: Pacific. (3 hr. behind New York City). ZIP Code: 89114. Founded: 1855. Approximate population: city, 200,000; metropolitan area, 620,000.

CLIMATE: Dry heat and a cloudless sky are the rule here. Summer is a scorcher (as high as 104°F/40°C or even higher in July–Aug). Spring and fall are more temperate (68°–77°F/20°–25°C on the average), but as always, in the desert the nights can be chilly. In winter, although the sun still shines (as it is guaranteed to do for 320 days a year), temperatures vary around a mean of 50°F (10°C).

DISTANCES: Denver, 780 mi. (1,248km); Furnace Creek (Death Valley), 142 mi. (227km); Los Angeles, 282 mi. (451km); Phoenix, 285 mi. (456km); Salt Lake City, 439 mi. (702km); San Francisco, 568 mi. (908km).

ARRIVAL & TRANSIT INFORMATION

AIRPORT: McCarran International Airport (LAS), 10 mi. (6km) south, handles more charter traffic than any other airport in the world. Spectacular futuristic decor. For information call 798-5410.

AIRLINES: Air Nevada (736-8900), America West (736-1737), American (385-3781), Continental (383-8291), Delta (731-3111), Northwest (385-2400), Scenic Air Lines (739-1900), Southwest (382-1221), TWA (385-1000), and United (385-3222).

CITY LINK: Your cab fare to the Strip will run about $10 (to dwntwn, $15); time, about 15–20 min. Bus: **Gray Line Airport Express** (384-1234; toll free 800/634-6570) leaves every 10 min. for the Strip, every 45 min. for dwntwn. Serves principal hotels; fare, $4; time, about 25–35 min.

Cabs are expensive; **public transportation** (bus, Las Vegas Transit System) is low priced and relatively efficient (but should be avoided at night); for information, call 384-3540. Bus no. 6 runs the whole length of the Strip around the clock. The **Trolley Shuttle** runs along Las Vegas Blvd. to the Casino Center dwntwn. Walking can be exhausting, particularly in summer; the city's avenues are unending, straight as a die, and without the least patch of shade or the smallest tree; remember that summer temperatures are in the range of 95°–104°F (35°–40°C). Air-conditioned cars can be rented anywhere at attractive prices.

CAR RENTAL (at McCarran International Airport unless otherwise noted): Abbey, 3745 Las Vegas Blvd. (736-4988), a local company with attractive rates; Avis (739-5595); Budget, 4744 Paradise Rd. (736-1212); Dollar (739-8400); Hertz (736-4900); National (739-5391); Thrifty, 5468 Paradise Rd. (736-4706). (All except Abbey and Avis offer free pickup/delivery at place of residence.) For dwntwn locations, consult the local telephone directory.

LIMOUSINE SERVICES: Bell Limousine (736-4428) and Dav El Limos (toll free 800/922-0343).

TAXIS: Cabs may be hailed on the street or taken from the lines outside the big hotels, but it's more convenient to use the phone. Recommended companies: **Checker** (873-2227), **Desert Cab** (736-1702), **Whittlesea Blue Cab** (384-6111), or **Yellow Cab** (873-2227).

TRAIN: Amtrak Station, Union Plaza, 1 Main St. (386-6896; toll free 800/872-7245).

INTERCITY BUSES: Greyhound, 200 S. Main St. (382-2640).

INFORMATION & TOURS

TOURIST INFORMATION: The **Las Vegas Chamber of Commerce,** 2301 E. Sahara Ave., NV 89104 (702/457-4664).
   Las Vegas Convention and Visitors Authority, Convention Center, 3150 Paradise Rd., NV 89109 (702/733-2323; toll free 800/332-5333).

GUIDED TOURS: American Sightseeing LTR (384-1230), and **Gray Line Tours,** 1550 Industrial Rd. (384-1234): Guided (bus) tours of the city, serving the principal hotels.
   Lake Mead Yacht Tour (boat), Nev. 41, Boulder Harbor (293-6180): 1½-hr. excursions on Lake Mead as far as Hoover Dam; daily year round.

SIGHTS, ATTRACTIONS & ACTIVITIES

ADVENTURES: Black Canyon, Inc. (boat), P.O. Box 96, Boulder City, NV 89005 (293-3776): Rafting down the Colorado River from Boulder City; summer only.
   National Nuclear Test Site Tours (bus), in Mercury: 10½-hr., 260-mi. (420km) bus tour offered three to four times every week to the Nevada Test Site, the proving ground at which the nation's nuclear weapons are tested. Tours arranged by the Nevada Operations Office of the U.S. Department of Energy, 2753 S. Highland Dr., Las Vegas, NV 89193 (702/295-1000). American citizens must provide their name, address, birth date, and Social Security number at least 4 weeks in advance. Foreign nationals must give 45 days' notice. ID's with photo (such as a driver's license) must be presented at the time of the tour. Visitors must be at least 18 years old. Pregnant women are discouraged from visiting, "because of long bus rides and rough terrain." Highly unusual tour.
   Scenic Airlines (air), 241 E. Reno Ave. (739-1900): Air trips over the Grand Canyon. **Air Nevada,** (air), 6005 S. Las Vegas Blvd. (736-8900): 1-day excursion, including lunch, $180; daily year round.

ARCHITECTURAL HIGHLIGHTS: ☀️🏛 **Circus Circus,** 2880 Las Vegas Blvd. (734-0410): Looking like the Big Top of some gigantic circus, this is the most originally designed hotel-casino in Vegas. While the gamblers are trying their luck at the casino tables, trapeze artists, tightrope walkers, and acrobats are strutting their stuff overhead. Children are permitted in the gallery but not on the casino floor.
   🏛 **Convention Center,** 3150 Paradise Rd. (733-2244): One million square feet (100,000m²) of covered exhibition space make this modern steel-and-concrete structure the country's largest one-level convention hall. It has room for more than 7,000 participants at meetings or banquets. Las Vegas has developed the convention business (the city averages one a day) into a source of revenue second only to gambling.

CHURCHES/SYNAGOGUES: The **Wedding Chapels:** With some 30 of these institutions at last count, Las Vegas can style itself the country's wedding capital as well as its gaming capital. There is only one requirement under Nevada law: that both prospective spouses be over 18 (or over 16 with parental consent). No blood test is asked for; no time-consuming banns need be read. All you need is a $25 license—obtainable at Clark County Court House, 3rd St. and Carson

St. (455-3156), open daily—and the wedding chapel will do the rest! They are open 8am–midnight Mon–Fri, and around the clock on weekends. The cost of solemnizing a marriage, including the minister's fee and the hired witnesses, generally runs $60–$100. An astounding 60,000 people are married each year in churches or chapels here.

HISTORIC BUILDINGS: ⚐ **Old Las Vegas Fort,** 908 Las Vegas Blvd. N. (entrance only from Cashman Field Parking Lot B) (382-7198): Built in 1855 by a group of 30 Mormon pioneers from Utah, this adobe construction, originally designed to protect the settlers from attack by local Native American tribes, is the oldest building in the entire state. Fine example of architectural restoration. Open Sat–Mon. For lovers of the Old West.

MUSEUM OF ART: ⚐ **Art Museum,** 3333 W. Washington Ave. (647-4300): Works by local and other American artists; interesting temporary exhibitions. Open Tues–Sun.

MUSEUMS OF SCIENCE & HISTORY: ⚐ **Clark County Heritage Museum,** 1830 S. Boulder Hwy., Henderson (455-7955): Interesting history museum. Depicts southern Nevada historical heritage from dinosaur fossils to the first European settlements. Re-created ghost town and turn-of-the-century railroad. Open daily.

⚐ **Imperial Palace Auto Collection,** 3535 Las Vegas Blvd. (794-3174): This collection of more than 200 valuable antique cars is to be found on the fifth floor of the Imperial Palace Hotel parking garage. It includes the King of Siam's 1928 Delage, Howard Hughes's 1954 Chrysler, an armored Mercedes that once belonged to Hitler, and other cars formerly the property of Al Capone, Eleanor Roosevelt, etc. A must for antique-car enthusiasts. Open daily.

⚐ **Las Vegas Museum of Natural History,** 3700 Las Vegas Blvd. S. (798-7757): This spectacular new natural-history museum displays one of the country's largest collections of prehistoric animals; life-size animated models of dinosaurs, triceratops, etc. Open daily.

☼⚐ **Liberace Museum,** 1775 E. Tropicana Ave. (798-5595): An entire museum devoted to the self-glorification of the late pianist and showman Liberace: from his collection of antique cars and pianos to his glittering million-dollar wardrobe. The triumph of unrestrained Hollywood kitsch. Open daily.

NIGHTTIME ENTERTAINMENT: ☼⚐⚐ **Casino Center,** around Fremont St. and Casino Center Blvd.: The heart of the city's gaming kingdom; the country's (and perhaps the world's) largest concentration of casinos and gambling houses. Particularly spectacular after dark, when Fremont St., better-known to locals as "Glitter Gulch," is illuminated to daytime levels by an extravagance of lights and multicolored neon signs.

☼⚐⚐ **"The Strip,"** Las Vegas Blvd. between Tropicana Rd. and Sahara Ave.: The name is a pun, with references both to striptease and to neon strip-lighting; it describes the city's 3-mi. (5km) multicolored light show offered by its principal hotels, casinos, and nightclubs. The sight of "the Broadway of Las Vegas" after dark is fascinating indeed.

PANORAMAS: ⚐ **Skye Room,** 128 E. Fremont St. (382-1600): A bar-restaurant-dance hall on the 23rd floor of the Binion's Horseshoe Hotel, in the heart of downtown. Offers the most spectacular after-dark view of the city (admission charge). Glass-walled outside elevator. Open daily.

PERFORMING ARTS: For current listings of shows and cultural events, consult the entertainment pages of the daily papers, *Las Vegas Review-Journal* (morning and evening) and *Las Vegas Sun* (morning), as well as the monthly *Nevada* magazine.

Artemus W. Ham Concert Hall, U. of Nevada campus, 4505 Maryland Pkwy. (739-3801): Opera, ballet, jazz, and concerts; home of the Nevada Dance Theater.

Judy Bayley Theater, U. of Nevada campus, 4505 Maryland Pkwy. (739-3801): In the little plaza adjoining the theater, be sure to take a look at Claes Oldenburg's colossal (39-ft./13m) sculpture *Flashlight.* Modern and classical theater; big-star shows.

Theater Under the Skies, Spring Mountain Ranch (see "Nearby Excursions," below) (875-4141): Open-air shows; modern and experimental theater. June–July.

Thomas and Mack Center, U. of Nevada campus, 4505 Maryland Pkwy. (739-3900): Pop and rock concerts.

SPECIAL EVENTS: For exact dates, consult the **Las Vegas Convention and Visitors Authority** (see "Tourist Information," above).

Panasonic Invitational PGA Golf Tournament (late Apr to early May).

Helldorado Festival (end of May or early June): Rodeos, street parades, beauty contest.

Jaycee State Fair (late July to early Aug): Carnival, big-star shows, livestock shows.

Senior Classic PGA Golf Tournament (Nov).

National Finals Rodeo (Dec): The "Superbowl" of professional rodeos, the richest rodeo in the country. Attracts top cowboys in every event.

SPORTS: Baseball (Apr–Aug): Stars (Triple-A farm club of the San Diego Padres), Cashman Field (386-7200).

THEME PARKS: ⚲ **Bonnie Springs Ranch/Old Nevada,** 20 mi. (32km) west on W. Charleston Blvd. (875-4191): Pioneer village of 1843, with nicely restored saloons and stores. Far Western railroad; shows; mock gun battles between sheriff and outlaws. Western buffs will enjoy it. Open daily.

⚲ **Wet 'n Wild,** 2600 Las Vegas Blvd. S. (737-7873): Huge aquatic amusement park; the artificial surf has 4-ft. (1.2m) waves. The giant slide is 75 ft. (23m) high; also waterfalls, shooting the rapids, etc. Locally popular. Open daily Apr to mid-Sept.

WINTER SPORTS RESORTS: ⚲ **Mount Charleston Park** and **Lee Canyon,** 34 mi. (54km) NW on U.S. 95 and Nev. 157: Beautiful pine forest rising to 11,918 ft. (3,623m) on Mount Charleston, and winter-sports resort at Lee Canyon, both very popular at all times of year. For a report on snow conditions during the skiing season, call 385-0181. Three ski lifts.

The ☼ ☾ **Mount Charleston Inn,** 2 Kyle Canyon Rd., Mount Charleston, NV 89124 (872-5500), is a likable chalet with a rest. serving very acceptable meat and game dishes. Open daily; 63 rms. **I–M**

ACCOMMODATIONS

A Note on Accommodations: Room rates in Las Vegas are coded as follows: **VE,** Very Expensive ($140 and up); **E,** Expensive ($90–$140); **M,** Moderate ($60–$90); **I,** Inexpensive ($30–$60); **B,** Budget (up to $30). A listing of toll free numbers is in the Appendix.

A Further Note on Accommodations: Over and above the gamblers and the entertainment fans (some of the top shows in the country are given in Las Vegas), there is a year-round crush of groups and conventions filling the 75,000 available hotel rooms, so reservations are essential. If you call 702/736-1666, or toll free 800/873-5577, you'll be told what rooms are available at any given mo-

LAS VEGAS
AT A GLANCE

ment, and you can make your reservation for free on the spot. Note that at certain times of the year some hotels require a minimum stay of 3 nights.

Personal Favorites (in order of preference)

☀ 🏨🏨🏨🏨 **The Mirage** (nr. dwntwn), 3400 Las Vegas Blvd., NV 89109 (702/791-7111; toll free 800/627-6667; reservations for shows, 702/792-7777 for show resv.). 3049 rms, A/C, color TV. AE, CB, DC, MC, V. Free valet parking, two pools, tennis court, health club, sauna, six rests., coffee shop, 24-hr. bars, rm svce, nightclub, shows, casino, boutiques, free crib. *Note:* Vegas's most elaborate hotel extravaganza, opened in Nov 1989. The more than 3,000 rms in the triple 30-floor towers boast their own amusement park, complete with artificial volcano erupting every 15 min., tropical jungle under glass, giant aquarium complete w. sharks and a clutch of white tigers roaming around in semi-freedom. The whole megillah cost $630 million. Spacious, extremely comfortable rms, acceptable rests., lovely indoor grdns bright w. orchids and bougainvilleas among the 80-ft. (25m) palm trees. The casino has a private rm for high rollers, where the lowest stake is $1,000. Part of the Golden Nugget hotel chain. **E–VE**

🏨🏨🏨 **Desert Inn and Country Club** (nr. dwntwn), 3145 Las Vegas Blvd. S., NV 89109 (702/733-4444; toll free, see Preferred, 800/634-6906 for show resv.). 819 rms, A/C, color TV, in-rm movies. AE, CB, DC, MC, V. Free valet parking, two pools, golf course, 10 tennis courts, health club, sauna, putting green, four rests. (including Portofino), coffee shop, 24-hr. bars, rm svce, shows, hrdrsr, boutiques, free crib. *Note:* The quietest of the local palaces; even the decor has a degree of self-control. Very comfortable rms w. private balconies or patios and refrigerators. Remarkable rm svce. Good rests. This was where the late billionaire Howard Hughes liked to come for a rest. The best location on the Strip, set in 160 acres (62ha) of lawns and grdns. Highly regarded golf course. **M–E**

🏨🏨🏨 **Alexis Park** (nr. dwntwn), 375 E. Harmon Ave., NV 89109 (702/796-3300; toll free 800/223-0888). 500 suites, A/C, color TV, in-rm movies. AE, CB, DC, MC, V. Free parking, three pools, two tennis courts, health club, sauna, putting green, two rests. (including Pegasus), coffee shop, 24-hr. bars, 24-hr. rm svce, nightclub, hrdrsr, concierge, free crib. *Note:* One of the newest, finest flowers in the local bouquet of deluxe hotels and one of the few Las Vegas hotels without a casino. Has only spacious suites, splendidly fitted out, with minibars and refrigerators. Exemplary reception and svce. 10 acres (4ha) of lovely grdns w. waterfalls and fountains, only a few steps away from the Strip. Admirable luxury hotel rest. Caters to VIPs. Quiet and relaxed atmosphere. **E–VE**

🏨🏨 **Imperial Palace** (nr. dwntwn), 3535 Las Vegas Blvd. S., NV 89109 (702/731-3311; toll free 800/634-6441). 2,700 rms, A/C, color TV. AE, CB, DC, MC, V. Free valet parking, pool, six rests. (including the Ming Terrace), six 24-hr. bars, rm svce, entertainment, casino, hrdrsr, boutiques, antique-car museum, crib $8. *Note:* This vast 19-story barracks is decorated in would-be Far Eastern style, but the rms are comfortable, w. refrigerators and private balconies. Group clientele. Good overall value, w. rate reductions for stays of 2 or more nights. Right on the Strip. **I–M** (single rms), **M** (double rms).

🏨🏨 **Hacienda** (nr. dwntwn), 3950 Las Vegas Blvd. S. NV 89119 (702/739-8911; toll free 800/634-6713). 840 rms, A/C, color TV. AE, CB, DC, MC, V. Free valet parking, pool, six tennis courts, rest. (Charcoal Rm), 24-hr. coffee shop, 24-hr. bar, rm svce, nightlife, casino, boutiques, free crib. *Note:* Modern, comfortable hotel-casino right on the Strip; spacious, welcoming rms, some w. refrigerators. Nicely landscaped grounds. Friendly svce. Parking for motor homes. Very good value. **I–M**

☀ 🏨🏨 **Circus Circus Hotel** (nr. dwntwn), 2880 Las Vegas Blvd. S., NV 89109 (702/734-0410; toll free 800/634-3450). 2,793 rms, A/C, color TV. AE, CB, DC, MC, V. Free valet parking, three pools, two rests., two 24-hr. coffee shops, 24-hr. bars, casino, circus, hrdrsr, boutiques, crib $4. *Note:* Right on the Strip, w. a newly constructed 29-story tower adj. the original building. The interior is the most enterprising in all of Las Vegas, w. trapeze artists and tightrope walkers cavorting above the heads of the casino gamblers beneath a pink-and-white make-believe circus marquee. The favorite hotel of parents w. children. Huge, inviting rms; acceptable buffet meals at modest prices. Very good value. Worthwhile discounts on wknds. Enormous parking lot for RVs. **I,** but lower rates off-season.

Motel 6 (nr. dwntwn), 195 E. Tropicana Ave., NV 89109 (702/798-0728). 880 rms, A/C, color TV, in-rm movies. AE, DC, MC, V. Free parking, pool, nearby rest., free breakfast, free crib. *Note:* Vegas's best bargain, offering functional but inviting rms at unbeatable prices. A few steps away from the Strip and the airport. **B–I**

Other Accommodations (from top bracket to budget)

Caesars Palace (nr. dwntwn), 3570 Las Vegas Blvd. S., NV 89109 (702/731-7110; toll free 800/634-6001 for rm resv., 800/634-6661 for show resv.). 1,608 rms, A/C, color TV, in-rm movies. AE, CB, DC, MC, V. Free valet parking, two pools, four tennis courts, squash, health club, sauna, four rests. (including the Bacchanal Rm), coffee shop, 24-hr. bars, rm svce, disco, shows, casino, hrdrsr, boutiques, cinema, concierge, crib $10. *Note:* Long the Las Vegas favorite hotel in the heart of the Strip: 22 floors of marble, stucco, crystal, and red velvet. The style—a Hollywood version of ancient Rome—is rather eccentric; the waitresses are dressed straight out of the movie *Ben Hur.* Huge, luxurious, comfortable rms; sumptuous suites. Svce diligent to the point of excess. Several highly acceptable rests. The Las Vegas style at its highest pitch; this place alone is worth the trip. Resv. long in advance. Undergoing a complete remodeling and renovation. **E–VE**

Bally's–Las Vegas (formerly the MGM Grand; nr. dwntwn), 3645 Las Vegas Blvd. S., NV 89109 (702/739-4111; toll free 800/634-3434). 2,830 rms, A/C, cable color TV. AE, CB, DC, MC, V. Free valet parking, pool, 10 tennis courts, health club, sauna, four rests. (including Gigi), three coffee shops, six 24-hr. bars, rm svce, nightlife, shows, casino, cinema, hrdrsr, boutiques, free crib. *Note:* Gigantic hotel-casino comprising two modern 26-story towers. Completely renovated since a fire which caused 84 deaths in 1980, and now the masterpiece of Las Vegas kitsch. Spacious, comfortable rms w. balconies, good sports facilities, good svce, but so-so rests. Intrusive group and convention clientele. Puts on some of the best shows in Vegas. Right on the Strip. **M–E**

Golden Nugget (dwntwn), 129 E. Fremont St., NV 89125 (702/385-7111; toll free 800/634-3454). 1,965 rms, color TV, in-rm movies. AE, CB, DC, MC, V. Free parking, pool, health club, sauna, three rests. (including Lilly Langtry's), 24-hr. coffee shop, bars, rm svce, entertainment, casino, hrdrsr, free crib. *Note:* An unlikely marriage between a marble-fronted Victorian house abundantly paneled in mahogany, and an ultramodern 22-story tower (Town House Tower) w. sumptuous duplex suites. The opulent interior in the style of the Roaring '20s is sufficient justification for a visit. Huge, ultra-comfortable rms; excellent svce. Boasts one of Las Vegas's two most expensive ($1,500-a-night) suites. Recently rejuvenated at a cost of $75 million. Along with the Mirage, this is the most spectacular hotel, and the most enjoyable casino, in Las Vegas. Right in the middle of Casino Center with its bustling nightlife. **M–E**

Hilton Las Vegas (nr. dwntwn), 3000 Paradise Rd., NV 89109 (702/732-5111; toll free, see Hilton 800/732-7117 for show resv.). 3,174 rms, A/C, cable color TV. AE, CB, DC, MC, V. Free valet parking, pool, health club, sauna, six tennis courts, putting green, 12 rests. (including Le Montrachet), coffee shop, four 24-hr. bars, rm svce, disco, shows, hrdrsr, boutiques, free crib. *Note:* With 30 floors of glass and concrete, this is one of the largest hotels in Vegas. It's taken by assault year round by the throngs of package tourists and conventioneers. Spacious rms w. balconies; lively ambience. In spite of the hotel's size the svce is good. Inside, a "children's hotel" offers childcare for parents trying their luck at the tables. Renovated after a fire in 1981. Very near the Strip and the Convention Center. **M–E**

Sands (nr. dwntwn), 3355 Las Vegas Blvd. S., NV 89109 (702/733-5000; toll free 800/634-6901). 1,000 rms, A/C, color TV, in-rm movies. AE, CB, DC, MC, V. Free valet parking, two pools, six tennis courts, health club, putting green, two rests. (including the Regency Rm), 24-hr. coffee shop, 24-hr. bars, rm svce, shows, casino, hrdrsr, boutiques, free crib. *Note:* With its 18-story round white tower and semicircular balconies the Sands looks like a huge lighthouse set down in the middle of the Strip. Spacious, well-laid-out rms w. private balconies or patios, the nicest overlooking the grdn. First-class reception and svce; well-regarded luxury-hotel rest. One of the best hotels in Vegas. Extensive expansion under way. **M–E**

Tropicana Resort (nr. dwntwn), 3801 Las Vegas Blvd. S., NV 89109 (702/739-2222; toll free (800/462-8767). 1,900 rms, A/C, cable color TV. AE, CB, DC, MC, V. Free valet parking, pool, health club, sauna, golf course, putting green, four tennis courts, six rests. (including Rhapsody), two 24-hr. coffee shops, six 24-hr. bars, rm svce, nightclub, shows, casino, hrdrsr, boutiques, concierge, free crib. *Note:* One of Vegas's crowning glories since 1957. Opulent, flamboyant decor. Sophisticated sports facilities including air-conditioned indoor tennis courts. Home of the "Folies Bergères" show. Huge, comfortable rms w. private balconies; beautiful tropical (hence the name) grdn w. waterfalls and lagoons. Three VIP floors. On the Strip, very nr. the airport. **M–E**

Holiday Inn–Hotel Casino (nr. dwntwn), 3475 Las Vegas Blvd. S., NV 89109 (702/369-5000; toll free, see Holiday Inns). 1,725 rms, A/C, color TV, in-rm movies. AE, CB, DC, MC, V. Free valet parking, pool, health club, sauna, four rests. (including Claudine's), two 24-hr. coffee shops, 24-hr. bars, rm svce, entertainment, casino, hrdrsr, boutiques, free crib. *Note:* The world's largest Holiday Inn, in size and in number of rms. Built to resemble a giant Mississippi paddlewheeler and topped by an ultramodern 23-story tower, it is unusual enough to surprise even those well acquainted w. the Las Vegas style of architectural extravagance. Comfort and facilities are above the Holiday Inn standard, but the svce doesn't measure up. Group and convention clientele. In the heart of the Strip. Recently renovated and expanded. **M–E**

Fitzgeralds (formerly the Sundance Hotel; dwntwn), 301 E. Fremont St., NV 89101 (702/388-2400; toll free 800/634-6519). 650 rms, A/C, cable color TV. AE, CB, DC, MC, V. Free parking, health club, sauna, two rests., 24-hr. coffee shop, 24-hr. bar, rm svce, nightclub, casino, crib $4. *Note:* Modern, comfortable hotel in Vegas's tallest high-rise (34 stories). Large, inviting rms, friendly reception and svce. Well located in the heart of dwntwn's Casino Center. Good value on balance; useful wknd packages. **I–M**

La Quinta (nr. dwntwn), 3782 Las Vegas Blvd. S., NV 89109 (702/739-7457; toll free, see La Quinta). 114 rms, A/C, color TV, in-rm movies. AE, CB, DC, MC, V. Free parking, pool, coffee shop, valet svce, free airport limo, free crib. *Note:* Modern, comfortable motel right on the Strip, pleasantly decorated in the style of a Spanish hacienda. Commodious, well-laid-out rms. **I–M**

Union Plaza Hotel (dwntwn), 1 Main St., NV 89125 (702/386-2110; toll free 800/634-6575). 1,036 rms, A/C, color TV, in-rm movies. AE, CB, DC, MC, V. Free valet parking, pool, four tennis courts, two rests. (including Center Stage), coffee shop, 24-hr. bar, rm svce, shows, casino, boutiques, crib $8. *Note:* Modern comfort and facilities housed in a 22- and a 25-story tower in the heart of dwntwn Vegas, adjoining the Greyhound bus terminal and the Amtrak train station. Inviting rms w. balconies and refrigerators. From the rest. There's a spectacular view of the dwntwn casino-hotels. Very good overall value. Free parking for RVs. **I**

♀ **Vegas World** (nr. dwntwn), 2000 Las Vegas Blvd. S., NV ℔ 89104 (702/382-2000; toll free 800/634-6277). 891 rms, A/C, cable color TV. AE, CB, DC, MC, V. Free valet parking, pool, rest., coffee shop, two 24-hr. bars, casino, entertainment. *Note:* Huge 23-floor motel right on the Strip, decorated in the style of *2001: A Space Odyssey.* Functional and comfortable; recently renovated and expanded; good value. **I**

♀ **Vagabond Inn** (nr. dwntwn), 4155 Koval Lane, NV 89109 ℔ (702/731-2111; toll free 800/522-1555). 360 rms, A/C, color TV. AE, CB, DC, MC, V. Free parking, two pools, 24-hr. rest., bar, nightclub, crib $5. *Note:* Modest but very acceptable motel right nr. the Strip and the huge Bally's–Las Vegas. Functional comfort. Worthwhile wknd discounts. Wonderful for slender budgets. **I**

YMCA/Youth Hostel

AYH Hostel (nr. dwntwn), 1236 Las Vegas Blvd. S., NV 89104 (702/382-8119). 50 beds. Youth hostel.

RESTAURANTS

A Note on Restaurant Prices: Las Vegas restaurant prices, per person, excluding drinks and service charges, are coded as follows: **VE,** Very Expensive ($60 and up); **E,** Expensive ($40–$60); **M,** Moderate ($25–$40); **I,** Inexpensive ($15–$25); **B,** Budget (up to $15).

Personal Favorites (in order of preference)

♙♙♙ **Pegasus,** in the Alexis Park (see "Accommodations," above) (796-3300). A/C. Dinner only, nightly; bar open around the clock. AE, CB, DC, MC, V. Jkt. *Specialties:* pheasant-and-avocado pâté, médaillon of veal Lucullus, lobster Imperial, flambéed roast duck, bass w. fennel, chicken w. kiwi fruit and shrimp. Handsome wine list. *Note:* Grand-rest. French derived cuisine flawlessly prepared and served. Opened in 1984, Pegasus is one of the few rests. in Las Vegas that can be described as both luxurious and discreet. Perfection in every detail—which must, of course, be paid for. Open-air dining on fine days. Resv. required. *French/Continental.* **E–VE**

♙♙♙ **Le Montrachet** (nr. dwntwn), in the Hilton Las Vegas Hotel (see "Accommodations," above) (732-5111). A/C. Dinner only, nightly. AE, CB, DC, MC, V. Jkt. *Specialties:* warm foie gras w. apples, scallops provençal, lobster w. basil butter, Dover sole meunière, médaillon of veal w. morels sautéed in Noilly. Big wine list w. 400 varieties. *Note:* This relative newcomer was quickly recognized as one of the best rests. in Las Vegas. Imaginative and delicate cuisine. The interior—marble floors, leather chairs, and damask-clad walls—is a little overdone. Very good svce; resv. strongly advised. *French.* **M–E**

♙♙♙ **Bacchanal Room** (nr. dwntwn), in Caesars Palace (see "Accommodations," above) (734-7110). A/C. Dinner only, Tues–Sun. AE, CB, DC, MC, V. Jkt. *Specialties:* The prix-fixe menus (seven courses from hors d'oeuvres to dessert, accompanied by three different wines) change regularly. French-inspired Continental food. *Note:* Local taste apparently requires that every waitress wear a *peplos* while the waiters are tricked out as Roman centurions—but the food generally meets high standards. Prices match the opulent "Pompeian" scheme of decoration. Resv. required. Two seatings nightly, beginning at 6pm. *Continental.* **E** (prix fixe).

♙♙ **Port Tack** (nr. dwntwn), 3190 W. Sahara Ave. (873-3345). A/C. Lunch/dinner daily (until 3am); closed hols. AE, CB, DC, MC, V. *Specialties:* lamb chops, catch of the day, salmon steak, broiled prime cuts, roast beef, Maine lobster, Alaska king crab. *Note:* Along w. its sister establishment (**Starboard Tack,** 2601 Atlantic Ave.; 457-8794), this is one of the rests. most favored by the locals. The catch of the day is excellent. Charming rustic-seafaring decor; likable relaxed atmosphere and some of the best seafood in town. *Steak/Seafood.* **I–M**

🍸🍸 **André's** (dwntwn), 401 S. 6th St. (385-5016). A/C. Dinner only, nightly; closed hols. and 3 weeks in July. AE, DC, MC, V. Jkt. *Specialties:* endive salad w. smoked breast of chicken, poached salmon w. celery, sole Véronique, chicken in cream and mushrooms. Dessert cart. More than 300 varieties on the wine list. *Note:* Charming French-style inn away from noisy dwntwn Las Vegas. Chef André Rochat produces attractive meals in generous portions at relatively low prices. Excellent place, locally popular; resv. required long in advance. Valet parking. *French.* **I–M**

🍸🍸 **Chin's** (nr. dwntwn), 3200 Las Vegas Blvd. S. (733-8899). A/C. Lunch/dinner daily; closed hols. AE, MC, V. *Specialties:* shark's-fin soup, spring rolls, shrimp puffs, chicken w. strawberries, beef à la Chin's, crystal shrimp, crispy pudding. *Note:* In the unanimous view of the purists this is the best Far Eastern rest. on the Strip. Authentic (if slightly Americanized) Chinese food; for instance, the chicken w. strawberries is a local variant on the classic Chinese lemon chicken. The result is almost always delicious, and the decor is elegant; accordingly the place has been very successful, and resv. are strongly advised. Valet parking. *Chinese.* **I–M**

🍸🍸 **Vineyard** (nr. dwntwn), 3630 Maryland Pkwy. (731-1606). A/C. Lunch/dinner daily; closed hols. AE, MC, V. Jkt. *Specialties:* fresh homemade pasta (fettuccine Alfredo, lasagne, cannelloni), pizza, veal parmigiana, scampi sauté. *Note:* Straightforward Italian-inspired food in a Neapolitan-operetta setting (including an accordionist). Friendly, smiling svce. Attracts crowds from the community. No. resv. *Italian.* **I**

🍸 **Garcia's** (nr. dwntwn), 1030 E. Flamingo Rd. (731-0628). A/C. Lunch/dinner daily; closed Thanksgiving, Dec. 25. AE, CB, DC, MC, V. *Specialties:* chimichangas, fajitas, tacos, enchiladas, fried ice cream. *Note:* Authentic Mexican food and excellent margaritas in a brightly colored hacienda setting. In the hottest days, the profusion of plants creates the pleasant illusion that you're in a green, growing grdn. Attentive svce. Locally popular. *Mexican.* **B**

Other Restaurants (from top bracket to budget)

🍸🍸🍸 **Regency Room** (nr. dwntwn), in the Sands Hotel (see "Accommodations," above). A/C. Dinner only, nightly. AE, CB, DC, MC, V. *Specialties:* scampi provençal, stone crabs w. mustard sauce, roast beef and Yorkshire pudding, rack of lamb bouquetière. *Note:* The decor is a little intense (red velvet and crystal). The food lives up to the hotel's high reputation; there are some conventional palace-rest. dishes, but also lighter and more imaginative creations. Polished svce. Resv. advisable. *Continental.* **M–E**

🍸🍸🍸 **Ah-So Japanese Steak Garden** (nr. dwntwn), in Caesars Palace (see "Accommodations," above) (731-7110). A/C. Dinner only, nightly. AE, CB, DC, MC, V. Jkt. *Specialties:* sushi, sashimi, teppanyaki (broiled steak, lobster, and vegetables). *Note:* The chefs wield their knives w. devilish dexterity under the eyes of the diners, in a charming plastic reproduction of a Japanese tea house, complete w. grdns, streams, and miniature bridges. Friendly, efficient svce. Resv. advised. *Japanese.* **M** (prix fixe)

🍸🍸 **Golden Steer Steak House** (nr. dwntwn), 308 W. Sahara Ave. (384-4470). A/C. Dinner only, nightly (till midnight); closed Thanksgiving, Dec 25. AE, CB, DC, MC, V. *Specialties:* giant (1½-lb.) steaks, prime rib, steak au poivre, rack of lamb, fresh pasta (first-rate ravioli and linguine with clams), game, roast suckling pig. Good wine list. *Note:* Remarkable steakhouse, but often crowded and noisy; a local favorite for almost 25 years. Western-1900s decor; exemplary svce; resv. advised. Valet parking. *Steak/American.* **I–M**

🍸🍸 **Tillerman** (nr. dwntwn), 2245 E. Flamingo Rd. (731-4036). A/C. Dinner only, nightly; closed hols. AE, CB, DC, MC, V. Jkt. *Specialties:* broiled steak, scallops in cream sauce, sole meunière, catch of the day. *Note:* In this light-filled space w. its green plants, its giant ficus trees, and its enormous skylights, you have the agreeable feeling that you're dining under the stars. First-quality meat and fish impeccably prepared. Excellent svce; one of Vegas's most highly recommended rests. *Steak/Seafood.* **I–M**

    Alpine Village Inn (nr. dwntwn), 3003 Paradise Rd. (734-6888). A/C. Dinner only, nightly; closed Thanksgiving, Dec 25. AE, CB, DC, MC, V. *Specialties:* sauerbraten, wienerschnitzel, frikadellen, kohlrouladen, apfelstrudel. German beers. *Note:* Decorated as a Swiss-Bavarian chalet, somewhat incongruous where the mercury goes up to 95° F (35°C) in the shade! Plentiful, decent food; efficient svce (in Tyrolean costume). There's a noisy piano bar/tavern in the cellar. A Las Vegas landmark since 1950, opposite the Las Vegas Hilton. Valet parking. *German/Continental.* **I**

    Battista's Hole in the Wall (nr. dwntwn), 4041 Audrie St. (732-1424). A/C. Dinner only, nightly; closed Thanksgiving and the last 2 weeks in Dec. AE, CB, DC, MC, V. Jkt. *Specialties:* fresh homemade pasta (spaghetti cacciatore, lasagne, etc.), scampi, eggplant parmigiana. *Note:* The most Italian of Vegas's Italian rests.; the decor and the agreeable atmosphere suggest an old trattoria, and the resemblance is enhanced when the owner, Battista Locatelli, belts out a few operatic arias. Unlimited free house wine. Locally popular; resv. advised. *Italian.* **I**

    Santa Fe (nr. dwntwn), 1213 Las Vegas Blvd. (384-4444). A/C. Lunch/dinner daily. AE, MC, V. *Specialties:* fajitas, chimichangas, ceviche, fried squid, Aztec tortilla soup, Taos salad, steak picado, pizza Pueblo. *Note:* Quite recently opened, this typical southwestern rest. serves tasty food enlivened by traces of Mexican, American, Spanish, and Native American influences. Tiled floors, fountains, regional handcrafts, and other Santa Fe details. Friendly, smiling svce. Very popular locally; a fine place to eat. *American/Mexican.* **B–I**

    Silver Dragon (nr. dwntwn), 1510 E. Flamingo Rd. (737-1234). A/C. Lunch/Dinner daily (till 5am). AE, MC, V. *Specialties:* lemon shrimp, Silver Dragon crab claws, Lover's Delight, Szechuan lobster, other characteristic Cantonese and Szechuan dishes. *Note:* One of the best, and most frequented, Chinese rests. in Vegas. Even if the decor is the usual cliché, the food is really Chinese. Svce on the abrupt side, but hard-working. *Chinese.* **B–I**

    El Burrito Café (nr. dwntwn), 1919 E. Fremont St. (387-9246). A/C. Lunch/dinner daily. No credit cards. *Specialties:* enchiladas, chicharrones, chile relleño, menudo (tripe), tamales, steak ranchero. *Note:* Very acceptable small Mexican rest. offering guaranteed local color; tiny and often overcrowded. Resv. advised. A Las Vegas classic for 25 years. *Mexican.* **B**

    Golden Nugget Buffet (dwntwn), in the Golden Nugget (see "Accommodations," above) (385-7111). A/C. Lunch/dinner daily. *Specialties:* barbecued spareribs, roast beef, Chinese dishes, hamhock w. sauerkraut, salads, good desserts (including bread pudding). Unbeatable value in the heart of dwntwn; you can fill your plate as often as you choose. Locally popular. *American/Continental.* **B** (prix fixe).

Cafeterias / Specialty Spots

New York Deli (nr. dwntwn), 2565 E. Flamingo Rd. (733-9594). Lunch Mon–Fri, dinner Mon–Sat. MC, V. By far the best-stocked deli in town. Giant sandwiches, pastrami, corned beef, chopped liver. Don't miss the matzoh-ball soup.

BARS & NIGHTCLUBS

HOTEL SHOWS: No city in the world boasts more bars, casinos, discos, shows, or strip joints to the square mile than Las Vegas. All the major hotels offer, besides several bars and discos apiece, very high-quality shows, of which the most popular are those at **Bally's–Las Vegas, Caesars Palace,** the **Desert Inn,** the **Dunes Hotel,** the **Hilton Las Vegas** (Moulin Rouge Revue), the **Mirage, Sahara, Sands, Stardust** (Lido de Paris Revue), and **Tropicana** (Folies Bergère Revue).

OTHER CHOICES: Botany's (nr. dwntwn), 1700 E. Flamingo Rd. (737-6662). Trendy disco; also a good Créole rest. Open daily around the clock.

Gipsy (nr. dwntwn), 4605 Paradise Rd. (731-1919). Disco with a big local following; late at night the life-forms can be very varied. Open daily.

Silver Dollar Saloon (nr. dwntwn), 2501 E. Charleston Blvd. (382-6921). Live country music; certified cowboy music. Open nightly.

State Street (nr. dwntwn), 2570 State St. (733-0225). Bar-rest. favored by show-business stars (Frank Sinatra, Eddie Murphy, Don Rickles, and Engelbert Humperdinck in particular). Very acceptable Italian food; excellent live jazz. The owner is actor Gianni Russo, who played Carlo in *The Godfather.* Open nightly till 5am.

For lovers of the female form divine and of (relatively) daring floor shows:

Crazy Horse Saloon (nr. dwntwn), 4034 Paradise Rd. (732-1116).

Palomino Club (nr. dwntwn), 1848 Las Vegas Blvd. N. (642-2984).

NEARBY EXCURSIONS

LAKE MEAD & HOOVER DAM (27 mi./43km SE on U.S. 93): This beautiful artificial lake, one of the largest in the world, is 116 mi. (180km) long; it was formed by the construction of the Hoover Dam, which holds back the waters of the Colorado River after it passes through the Grand Canyon. The azure waters are as deep as 590 ft. (180m). Fishing, waterskiing, and sailing are on offer along the 550 mi. (880km) of shoreline, and each year more than seven million visitors come here. The 726-ft. (221m) dam and the impressive generating plant date from 1935, and are ranked among the country's greatest architectural achievements. Visitor center open daily (702/293-8367); don't miss it.

OVERTON (65 mi./104km NE on I-15 and Nev. 169): Just 5 mi. (8km) south of this former 19th-century Mormon colony lies a huge Native American settlement, along the banks of the Muddy River, which 1,200 years ago was peopled by the ancestors of the Hopi. Interesting museum at the dig (**Lost City Museum**), with a rich archeological collection (397-2193): pottery, wickerwork, primitive tools. Open daily.

You can advantageously combine this excursion with a visit to the **Valley of Fire** (see below); it's worth the side trip.

RED ROCK CANYON (15 mi./24km west along W. Charleston Blvd.): Wonderful rocky gorges of white and reddish sandstone, with spectacular views. Gorgeous 13-mi. (21km) panoramic drive. Visitor center (363-1921). Well worth the side trip.

SPRING MOUNTAIN RANCH (18 mi./29km west along W. Charleston Blvd.) (875-4141): This fine 528-acre (214ha) ranch, very near Red Rock Canyon, dates back to the 1870s, and has been the property of Vera Krupp, heiress of the German steel tycoons and then of Howard Hughes. It now belongs to the State of Nevada. Interesting. Self-guided tours daily. Guided tours available on wknds and hols.

VALLEY OF FIRE STATE PARK (58 mi./93km NE on I-15): Very beautiful rock-strewn desert of reddish hue (whence the name), overlooking Lake Mead, formed 150 million years ago. A spectacular sight at sundown, and offers some astonishing landscape panoramas at any time. Many petroglyphs (Native American rock drawings). Camping permitted. Visitor center open daily year round. A must-see. For information, call 875-4191.

☀ **GHOST TOWNS:** 🔔 **Calico,** 143 mi. (230km) SW on I-15: The most picturesque and best preserved of California's ghost towns. There were rich silver mines here in the 1880s, and the place had as many as 3,000 inhabitants; today there are a dozen. After the restoration undertaken in 1950, Main Street looks as though it has been taken bodily from a John Ford western. It's on the main highway to Los Angeles; don't miss it. For information, call 619/254-2122.

🔔 **Goldsprings,** 38 mi. (60km) SW by I-15 and Nev. 161: At its height around a century ago this little gold-rush town boasted as many as 2,000 inhabitants; today there are about 100. The **Pioneer Saloon** is a magnificent period piece. Worth the detour.

NATIONAL PARKS NEARBY

☀🔔🔔🔔 **DEATH VALLEY** (142 mi./228km NW on U.S. 95, Nev. 373, and Cal. 190): America's most beautiful desert; see Chapter 48 on Death Valley.

☀🔔🔔🔔 **GRAND CANYON OF THE COLORADO** (291 mi./ 465km SE on U.S. 93, I-40, and Ariz. 64): One of the seven natural wonders of the world. See Chapter 41 on the Grand Canyon.

☀🔔🔔 **ZION NATIONAL PARK** (162 mi./260km NE on I-15 and Utah 9) and **Bryce Canyon** (243 mi./389km east on I-15 and Utah 20, U.S. 89, and Utah 12): Two of the country's best-known national parks. See Chapter 32 on Utah's national parks.

CHAPTER 48

DEATH VALLEY NATIONAL MONUMENT▮▮▮

□ □ □

Long the unchallenged domain of the Panamint tribe, an offshoot of the Shoshone, Death Valley is one of the two or three most enthralling natural wonders in the United States. If you are fortunate enough to set eyes on it for the first time from atop the rocky platform symbolically named **Dante's View,** you may well feel that you are present at the Creation. At the foot of the dizzying sheer drop of 5,120 ft. (1,600m) there sprawls in blinding clarity the vast expanse of the salt flats and the lowest point on the continent, 282 ft. (86m) below sea level. On the other side of **Devil's Golf Course** and its weird salt formations, the eternal snows of distant Mount Whitney rise in striking contrast with dun-colored rocks and sun-blasted dunes. This two-billion-year-old valley, once the bed of an Ice Age sea, is home to a surprisingly diverse animal life. Among its denizens are no fewer than 36 species of mammals, including coyote, porcupine, and kangaroo rat; dozens of insect and reptile species, including the formidable rattlesnake; and birds, notably crows and vultures. Certain kinds of small fish such as the pupfish can be found nowhere on earth except in the scanty waters of this splendid but terrifying blast furnace: **Salt Creek** or the palm groves of **Furnace Creek** in the center of the valley. The region was named when a group of California-bound pioneers died of thirst and fatigue while attempting to cross the valley on Christmas Day 1849. The area experienced short-lived activity in the 1880s when borax was discovered; with its many industrial uses, borax became known as "the white gold of the desert."

Two excellent paved highways span the valley north to south and east to west. This living desert museum is today one of the most popular tourist spots in California. The extraordinary landscapes, veiled during the heat of the day by a soft-hued, ever-changing haze, draw thousands of visitors to the three motels in Death Valley each winter and spring (two stay open in summer). It goes without saying that reservations are recommended, except in summer, when Death Valley is virtually abandoned by tourists because of scorching heat.

HINTS TO MOTORISTS: When visiting Death Valley by car, drive at a moderate speed, especially during the summer, to avoid overheating the engine. Before you set out, make sure that you have a full tank of gas, check your oil, and deflate the tires by a couple of pounds below normal pressure. If you break down between Death Valley Junction and Furnace Creek, or between Stove Pipe Wells and Scotty's Castle, there won't be a living soul within 30 miles! Main roads, however, are regularly patrolled. When driving on unpaved roads, *always* have with you a few gallons of reserve water; in summer, an untrained person will die of dehydration in 3 hr. under the Death Valley sun.

BASIC FACTS: State of California (extending into Nevada). Area code: 619. Time zone: Pacific. Zip Code: 92328. A National Monument since 1933. Area: 3,123 sq. mi. (8,090km²), one-fifth of it below sea level. Approximate dimensions: 140 mi. (225km) long, 4–16 mi. (6–26km) wide. Recommended time for visiting: Oct to late Apr.

CLIMATE: As you might expect from its name, Death Valley is one of the most inhospitable areas on the planet. In summer, temperatures frequently reach 113°F (45°C) in the shade (the record, set in July 1913, is 134°F/56.7°C). From late Oct to Apr, on the other hand, the mercury rarely goes above 86°F (30°C) in the daytime, with very cool nights, especially during the winter months (record low: 15°F/−9°C). Rainfall is practically nonexistent—less than 2 in. (5cm) per year.

DISTANCES: Las Vegas, 142 mi. (228km); Los Angeles, 305 mi. (490km); Reno, 285 mi. (456km); San Francisco, 531 mi. (851km).

ARRIVAL & TRANSIT INFORMATION

NEAREST AIRPORTS: The **Death Valley Municipal Airport** (DTH): 1 mi. (2km) west.
    Las Vegas McCarran International Airport (LAS): 142 mi. (228km) SE.
    Los Angeles International Airport (LAX): 305 mi. (490km) SW.

AIRLINES: Air Nevada (toll free 800/634-6377) offers charter flights from Las Vegas to Death Valley Municipal Airport. For other airlines, see Chapter 47 on Las Vegas and Chapter 54 on Los Angeles.

CAR RENTAL: See Chapter 47 on Las Vegas and Chapter 54 on Los Angeles.

TRAIN: For the closest Amtrak station, see Chapter 47 on Las Vegas.

INTERCITY BUSES: For the closest bus stations, see Chapter 47 on Las Vegas.
    Greyhound does not serve Death Valley, but the Las Vegas–Tonopah–Reno Stage Line company (LTR), 200 S. Main St., Las Vegas (384-1230), makes daily runs between Beatty (north entrance of Death Valley) and Las Vegas. Given the long distances involved, however, renting a car with unlimited mileage (preferably in California where the rates are lowest) is the best plan.

INFORMATION

TOURIST INFORMATION: Superintendent, Death Valley National Monument, Death Valley, CA 92328 (619/786-2331).
    Visitor center at Furnace Creek, open daily; also a desert museum.

SIGHTS, ATTRACTIONS & ACTIVITIES

ARCHITECTURAL HIGHLIGHTS: ☼🏠 **Scotty's Castle,** 52 mi. (84km) NW of Furnace Creek on Calif. 190 and Grapevine Rd.): The valley's only monument worthy of the title, a mirage in the middle of the desert. Wealthy Chicago businessman Albert Johnson and his friend, Walter Scotty, a professional cowboy from the Buffalo Bill troupe, built this sumptuously decorated and improbable castle in Hollywood Hispano-Moorish style between 1922 and 1931. Don't miss it—you may never see anything else like it! Guided tours promptly on the hour. Open daily.

PANORAMAS & EXCURSIONS (all distances measured from Furnace Creek): ☀️🏛 **Aguereberry Point,** 48 mi. (77km) west. A wonderful view of the valley, especially in the afternoon, from an altitude of 6,275 ft. (1,961m). The last 5 mi. (8km) of the ascent are unpaved. Worth the trip.

🏛 **Artists Drive,** 11 mi (18km) south: Narrow, one-way road amid splendid gorges and multicolored landscapes. A treat for color photographers. An absolute must-see.

☀️🏛🏛 **Badwater,** 16 mi. (26km) south: This spring is the source of undrinkable water, which never dries up even in the middle of summer. Next to the lowest point on the American continent (282 ft./86m below sea level), it's also the hottest place in the valley.

🏛 **Charcoal Kilns,** 61 mi. (98km) SW: Beehive-shaped charcoal kilns from pioneer days. Picturesque. The last 2 mi. (3km) of the road are unpaved.

☀️🏛🏛🏛 **Dante's View,** 23 mi. (38km) SE: One of the most breathtaking landscapes in creation, this panoramic platform 5,475 ft. (1,669m) high offers an unforgettable view of the valley. The road up is very steep and quite hard on the transmission.

☀️🏛🏛 **Devil's Golf Course,** 8 mi. (12km) south: A vast salt flat studded with 20-in.-high (50cm) salt rocks that really lives up to its name.

🏛 **Golden Canyon,** 4 mi. (6km) south: This 0.6-mi. (1km) footpath cuts through splendid rock formations of gold, bright red, ochre, and bronze. A photographer's dream.

🏛 **The Racetrack,** 83 mi. (134km) NW: This long clay valley, the scene of strange geological displacements, is one of the valley's biggest mysteries. Unpaved road for the last 27 mi. (44km). For lovers of legends.

☀️🏛🏛 **Sand Dunes,** 21 mi. (35km) NW: Enormous sand dunes perpetually reshaped by the wind. A miniature Sahara in the middle of California. An absolute must-see.

☀️🏛🏛 **Telescope Peak,** 65 mi. (104km) SW: The highest point in the valley, at 11,049 ft. (3,368m). From **Mahogany Flat** (the last 2 mi./4km unpaved), a 6.8-mi. (11km) steep and arduous footpath leads to the summit, where you may enjoy an exceptional view of Death Valley and the neighboring mountains. Do not undertake this trip in summer. In any case, consult the ranger station in neighboring **Wildrose.**

🏛 **Titus Canyon,** 33 mi. (54km) north: The 26 mi. (42km) of the one-way track through this steep gorge are accessible only to four-wheel-drive vehicles. Superb landscapes.

🏛 **Twenty-Mule-Team Canyon,** 6 mi. (10km) SE: A tortuous, unpaved, one-way route zigzags through this splendid rocky setting. Not to be missed.

🏛 **Ubehebe Crater,** 55 mi. (88km) NW: The only volcanic crater in the area is 2,560 ft. (800m) across and 390 ft. (122m) deep. Worth a look.

☀️🏛🏛 **Zabriskie Point,** 6 mi. (10km) SE: Strange, rocky "dunes" in tawny shades offering a superb view of the valley, Telescope Peak, and the Panamint Mountains, especially at sunrise and sunset. The setting for the Antonioni film of the same name.

ENTERTAINMENT: ☀️🏛 **Amargosa Opera House,** intersection of Calif. 127 and Calif. 190, Death Valley Junction (31 mi./50km SE of Furnace Creek on Calif. 190) (619/852-4316): The smallest opera house in the world. Martha

DEATH VALLEY
NATIONAL MONUMENT

Becket plays and dances solo to Offenbach's *La Vie Parisienne, Swan Lake,* and other classics. Surprising show and decor. Open Mon, Fri, and Sat evenings Oct–May.

GHOST TOWNS (all distances measured from Furnace Creek): 🏛 **Harmony Borax Works,** 1 mi. (2km) north: Remains of an old borax mine. From here borax was transported to the Mojave railway, 162 mi. (260km) farther south, on heavy carts which, even in the hottest weather, were drawn by the unbelievably enduring "20-mule teams."

🔔 **Panamint City,** 77 mi. (124km) SW: Remains of a 19th-century mining town. On the way, visit another ghost town, **Ballarat.** Difficult access road.

🌞🏛 **Rhyolite,** 36 mi. (59km) NE: Vestiges of one of the most famous 1904 gold-rush towns, which had as many as 16,000 inhabitants around 1910. See the unusual house made of 50,000 bottles. You can also discover the history of the Stone City at Rhyolite's Desert Museum.

🔔 **Skidoo,** 46 mi. (74km) west: Former miners' camp that has been periodically revitalized over the course of a century. The last stretch of the access road is difficult. Had as many as 500 inhabitants in its day, circa 1906.

NATIONAL PARKS NEARBY: 🌞🏛 **Sequoia National Park,** 362 mi. (580km) west on Calif. 190, 178, 65, and 198. This kingdom of the forest giants is barely 87 mi. (140km) away as the crow flies, but almost 375 mi. (600km) by road, a spectacular route through Panamint Valley and Sequoia National Forest. Not to be missed. For the park itself, see Chapter 52.

SUGGESTED TOURING ITINERARIES IN THE VALLEY

🌞🏛 **NORTH CIRCUIT** (150 mi./241km r.t. from Furnace Creek): Visit **Rhyolite** (see "Ghost Towns," above), **Titus Canyon** (four-wheel-drive vehicles only), **Scotty's Castle** (see "Architectural Highlights," above), and **Ubehebe Crater** (see "Panoramas and Excursions," above). Optional excursion to **Racetrack** for four-wheel-drive vehicles only.

🌞🔔🔔 **WEST CIRCUIT** (126 mi./202km r.t. from Furnace Creek): Visit **Sand Dunes, Aguereberry Point, Charcoal Kilns,** and optional excursions to **Telescope Peak** (for all of which, see "Panoramas and Excursions," above).

🌞🔔🔔 **SOUTH CIRCUIT** (88 mi./142km r.t. from Furnace Creek): Visit **Zabriskie Point, Twenty-Mule-Team Canyon, Dante's View, Golden Canyon, Artists Drive, Devil's Golf Course,** and **Badwater** (for all of which, see "Panoramas and Excursions," above). The most spectacular circuit through the valley.

ACCOMMODATIONS & RESTAURANTS

A Note on Accommodations and Restaurants: Room rates in Death Valley are coded as follows: **VE,** Very Expensive ($140 and up); **E,** Expensive ($90–$140); **M,** Moderate ($60–$90); **I,** Inexpensive ($30–$60); **B,** Budget (up to $30). A listing of toll free numbers is in the Appendix.

Death Valley restaurant prices, per person, excluding drinks and service charges, are coded as follows: **VE,** Very Expensive ($60 and up); **E,** Expensive ($40–$60); **M,** Moderate ($25–$40); **I,** Inexpensive ($15–$25); **B,** Budget (up to $15).

Personal Favorites (in order of preference)

🍴 **Furnace Creek Inn,** Calif. 190, Furnace Creek, CA 92328 (619/786-2361; toll free 800/528-6367). 68 rms, A/C, color TV. AE, CB, DC, MC, V. Free parking, pool, four tennis courts, sauna, horseback riding, two rests. (including the Oasis Supper Club), bar, rm svce, disco, library, service station, free breakfast. *Note:* Very busy luxury motel built in 1927 in a vaguely Spanish, massive, and ungraceful idiom. Vast rms that are functional at the expense of elegance; the best open onto a lovely tropical grdn w. palm trees. Antiquated plumbing and other facilities, unprofessional personnel. The pretentious rest. (jacket required, servers in long dresses) offers mediocre and expensive food. An ideal point of departure for a number of valley excursions (Dante's View, Badwater, and Zabriskie Point are less than 30 min. away by car). Motel is open mid-Oct to mid-May only. Free aiport shuttle. **VE** (American Plan on request).

Stove Pipe Wells, Calif. 190, Stove Pipe Wells Village, CA 92328 (619/786-2387). 82 rms, A/C. MC, V. Free parking, pool, coffee shop, bar, disco, grocery store, service station, crib $5. *Note:* This small motel offering functional comfort appears to rise out of the desert like a mirage amid a dramatic dune landscape. Mediocre cafeteria but a pleasant bar. Svce less than friendly. Motel open year round. **I–M,** but lower rates off-season.

Furnace Creek Resort, Calif. 190, Furnace Creek, CA 92328 (619/786-2345; toll free 800/528-6367). 224 rms, A/C, color TV, in-rm movies. AE, CB, DC, MC, V. Free parking, pool, golf, two tennis courts, horseback riding, coffee shop, rest. (winter), bar, grocery stores, service station. *Note:* Classic motel built in a sort of oasis shaded by palm, date, and other trees. Inviting rms (some w. balconies) plus an adequate cafeteria. Ideal place from which to explore the whole valley. Adjacent motor-home parking. Motel open year round. Organizes guided tours of Death Valley. **M–E,** but lower rates off-season.

Scotty's Castle, Grapevine Rd., Grapevine Canyon, CA 92328. Cafeteria open 9am–6pm year round. Service station. Across from the astonishing Scotty's Castle. A green oasis in the heart of the desert.

CHAPTER 49

RENO

□ □ □

And Lake Tahoe

"The biggest little city in the world," coyly announces an enormous arch spanning the main street of this former gold prospectors' town, 120 years old. Long known as the world capital of divorce, Reno today has also become the capital of love at first sight, to judge from the innumerable "Wedding Chapels" where, for the modest sum of $60–$80—credit cards accepted—those aged 18 and over who wish to be married can be lawfully wedded instantly, day or night, 7 days a week. This is possible because Nevada law is particularly liberal in matters of marriage and divorce. In the case of divorce, the law requires the petitioner to be a resident of Nevada for 6 weeks before the granting of the decree; marriage, however, requires but one formality: the purchase of a $25 license from the Marriage Bureau at the Washoe County Courthouse, S. Virginia St. and Court St., Reno, NV 89520 (702/328-3275), open daily 8am–midnight. The ceremony at the Wedding Chapel, which lasts no more than 10 min., requires two witnesses (provided by the chapel if necessary). Flowers (plastic), rice, and the obligatory "Wedding March" cost extra. More than 30,000 such instant weddings are performed annually in Reno.

Though honeymooners constitute a significant part of the local hotel trade (the number of honeymoon suites in the great hotels and even in motels is beyond number), the bulk of business is provided by lovers of roulette, baccarat, and slot machines (total annual earnings: $800 million). Though less flashy and ostentatious, Reno is a sort of replica of Las Vegas, about 400 mi. (700km) away across the desert. As at Las Vegas, slot machines greet the visitor right at the airport, overflow from the casinos onto the sidewalks of **Virginia St.**—the local Broadway or Wilshire Blvd.—in the local supermarkets, and clatter away day and night in the gaming room of one of the largest casino-hotels in the world, **Bally's Reno.**

You should not, however, allow the lure of gambling to distract you altogether from the splendid scenery in the nearby **Sierra Nevada,** beginning with **Lake Tahoe** and **Pyramid Lake,** two of the most beautiful mountain lakes in the U.S. Not far from Lake Tahoe, the ghost town of **Virginia City,** one of the great gold-rush towns of the 19th century, preserves its old houses and saloons almost intact, like something right out of a western.

BASIC FACTS: State of Nevada. Area code: 702 (or 916 in South Lake Tahoe, Tahoe Vista, and Kings Beach, California). Time zone: Pacific. ZIP Code: 89501. Founded: 1868. Approximate population: city, 102,000; metropolitan area, 240,000.

CLIMATE: Reno, in the heart of the desert, enjoys a dry climate, sunny and invigorating. Summers are dazzlingly bright, but only moderately hot (July average, 68°C/20°F). Spring and fall are usually chilly; at night the temperature falls rapidly. Because of the altitude (4,498 ft./1,370m), winter offers a standing invitation to skiers in the area's resorts (Jan average, 34°F/1°C). With more than 300 days of sunshine a year and beautiful surroundings, the Reno–Lake Tahoe area is a nature lover's paradise.

DISTANCES: Las Vegas, 447 mi. (715km); Los Angeles, 470 mi. (752km); Portland, 574 mi. (918km); Salt Lake City, 523 mi. (837km); San Francisco, 229 mi. (366km).

RENO

ARRIVAL & TRANSIT INFORMATION

AIRPORT: Reno-Cannon International Airport (RNO), 4 mi. (6km) SE. For further information, call 785-2575.

AIRLINES: America West (348-2777), American (329-9217), Continental (322-9075), Delta (323-1661), Northwest (toll free 800/225-2525), United (329-1020), and USAir (329-9365).

CITY LINK: The **cab** fare from the airport to dwntwn is about $6; time, about 10 min.

Bus: **Airport Limousine** (702/323-3727), serves major dwntwn hotels; fare, $3; time, about 15 min.

LTR Stage Lines (702/323-3088), serves the Lake Tahoe area.

Except for nearby excursions (recommended), the small size of the town makes renting a car unnecessary. Public transportation (bus) is not very efficient (**Reno Citifare:** 323-2800).

CAR RENTAL (all at the airport unless otherwise indicated): Avis (785-2727); Budget (785-2545); Dollar (348-2800); Hertz (785-2554); National (785-2756); and Thrifty, 2697 Mill St. (329-0096). For dwntwn locations, consult the local telephone directory.

LIMOUSINE SERVICES: Bell Limousine (786-3700), Dav-El Limousines (toll free 800/922-0343), and Executive Limousine (826-7776).

TAXIS: Taxis are relatively affordable, but few in number. They can be called by telephone or taken from the waiting lines outside the major hotels. Recommended companies: **Reno-Sparks Cab** (333-3333), **Whittlesea Checker Taxi** (323-3111), and **Yellow Cab** (331-7171).

TRAIN: Amtrak Station, E. Commercial Row and Lake St. (329-8638; toll free 800/872-7245).

INTERCITY BUSES: Greyhound, 155 Stevenson St. (322-2970).

INFORMATION & TOURS

TOURIST INFORMATION: The **Greater Reno Chamber of Commerce,** 405 Marsh Ave., NV 89505 (702/786-3030).

Reno-Sparks Convention and Visitors Authority, 4590 S. Virginia St. (P.O. Box 837), NV 89504 (702/827-7600; toll free 800/367-7366).

Reno-Tahoe Visitors Center, 135 N. Sierra St., NV 89505 (702/348-7788).

GUIDED TOURS: Gray Line Tours (bus), 2570 Tacchino St. (329-1147): Guided tours of the city and surrounding area.

Reno-Tahoe Tour Co. (bus), 1325 Airmotive Way (322-9044): Guided tour of Lake Tahoe, Virginia City, Carson City, etc.

Zephyr Balloons (balloon), 120 Mary St. (329-1700): Balloon tours over the Reno and Lake Tahoe region. Truly spectacular.

SIGHTS, ATTRACTIONS & ACTIVITIES

ADVENTURES: Ram River Expeditions (boat), 4050 Falling Water Dr. (746-1400): Air-rafting down the Truckee River (May–Sept).

ARCHITECTURAL HIGHLIGHTS: ※ ⚓ **Reno Arch,** Virginia St. at Commercial Row: Reno's arch, spanning Virginia Street with its renowned slogan— "The Biggest Little City in the World"—is one of the most recognized city symbols in America. The new art deco arch with its 1,600 lightbulbs and 800 ft. (245m) of neon is actually the fourth arch since the original was built in 1927 and is dedicated to the millions of tourists who visit Reno each year.

MUSEUMS OF ART: ⚓ **Sierra Nevada Museum of Art,** 549 Court St. (329-3333): Located in the Neo-Georgian Hawkins House, a designated historic monument, this museum displays an interesting collection of works by contemporary artists of the American West, including paintings, sculpture, prints, decorative arts, and Native American art. Also temporary exhibitions. The **E. L. Wiegand Museum** is in the annex at 160 W. Liberty St. Open Tues–Sun.

MUSEUMS OF SCIENCE & HISTORY: ⚓ **Fleischmann Planetarium,** 1650 N. Virginia St. (784-4811): Very modern in conception, this planetarium is located on the University of Nevada–Reno campus. Laser shows, museum of astronomy, telescopes available for stargazing. A treat for lovers of astronomy. Open daily.

⚓ **Harold's Club Gun Collection and Museum,** 250 N. Virginia St. (329-0881): Very fine collection of old firearms, from 16th-century Chinese cannon to the Remingtons, Colts, and Winchesters of the Old West. More than 500 different items, some of them very interesting. On the second floor of Harold's Club, one of the oldest casinos in Nevada (1935). Open daily.

※⚓⚓ **William F. Harrah Foundation Automobile Museum,** 10 S. Lake St. at Mill St. (333-9300): Billing itself as "one of the great national treasures of America," this automobile museum has a fine collection of hundreds of old vehicles. Many are extremely rare or one of a kind, splendidly restored, such as the 1890 Philion, one of the oldest existing American-built automobiles, or the 1907 Thomas Flyer that won a 25,000-mi. (40,250km) race from New York to Paris through Alaska and Siberia. The museum's new home is a state-of-the-art building conceived as a piece of sculpture. Open daily.

⚓ **Liberty Belle's Slot Machine Collection,** 4250 S. Virginia St. (826-2607): An amusing collection of old player pianos and slot machines (the oldest dating from 1898), maintained by the Liberty Belle Saloon. Open daily.

⚓ **MacKay Mining Museum,** 9th St. and N. Virginia St. (784-6988): Extensive geological collection (minerals, precious stones, fossils, etc.). Displays on the history of the gold rush. A facility of the MacKay School of Mines, one of the oldest (1874) and most highly regarded mining schools in the U.S. Interesting. Open Mon–Fri.

⚓ **Nevada Historical Society Museum,** 1650 N. Virginia St. (789-0190): Displays on the prehistory and modern history of

Nevada. Beautiful collection of Native American artifacts. Mementoes of the Winning of the West. Open Tues–Sat.

☼🔔 **Wilbur D. May Museum,** 1502 Washington St., in Rancho San Rafael Park (785-5961): This new museum has hundreds of fascinating items collected by the late Wilbur D. May, department-store magnate, pilot, adventurer, world traveler, and big-game hunter during the 1920s and '30s. The relics of May's Indiana Jones–style life include his re-created trophy room with mounted heads of more than 80 animals as well as rare horse sculptures from the T'ang Dynasty. Beautiful adjoining arboretum. One of the most interesting small museums in the West. Open Tues–Sun in summer, Wed–Sun the rest of the year.

NIGHTLIFE: As in Las Vegas, the most important aspect of nightlife in Reno, Sparks, and South Lake Tahoe is to be found in the gaming rooms of the casinos. Most of the big hotels—**Bally's, Harrah's,** the **Hilton, John Ascuaga's Nugget** —also offer frequent floor shows, big-name performers, discos, bars, etc. (see "Accommodations," below).

PERFORMING ARTS: For daily listings of all shows and cultural events, consult the entertainment pages of the daily morning paper *Reno Gazette Journal* and the monthly *Nevada* magazine.

Church Fine Arts Theater, on the University of Nevada–Reno campus, 9th St. and N. Virginia St. (784-6505): Classical and contemporary plays, and musicals. Home of the Nevada Repertory Company.

Little Theater, 690 N. Sierra St. (329-0661): Modern theater. Drama and comedy (Sept–June). Also offers children's theater.

Pioneer Theater Auditorium, 100 S. Virginia St. at State St. (786-5105): Classical music concerts, opera, ballet, recitals. Home of the Nevada Festival Ballet (Sept–Jan), the Nevada Opera (Oct–Apr), and the Reno Philharmonic (Oct–Apr), under Ron Daniels, principal conductor.

Reno-Sparks Convention Center, 4590 S. Virginia St. (827-7366): Pop concerts. Hosts an International Jazz Festival annually (Mar).

Trinity Episcopal Church, Rainbow Island Ave. (329-4279): Concerts by the Reno Chamber Orchestra (Oct–Apr).

Wingfield Riverside Park, S. Arlington Ave. at Island St. (851-0759): Free outdoor concerts in this park on the banks of the Truckee River. Mon–Fri at noon, June–Aug.

SPECIAL EVENTS: For the exact schedule of events below, consult the **Reno-Sparks Convention and Visitors Authority** (see "Tourist Information," above), the **Carson City Chamber of Commerce,** 1900 S. Carson St., Carson City, NV 89701 (702/882-1565), or the **Lake Tahoe Visitors Authority,** P.O. Box 16299 South Lake Tahoe, CA 95706 (916/544-5057).

Silver State Square Dance Festival (Reno; Apr–May): One of the most important square-dance festivals in the U.S. More than 7,000 dancers come from all over the U.S. and Canada to take part. A great spectacle, and a tradition for more than 40 years.

Reno Rodeo (Reno; 5 days in mid-June): A rodeo festival famous throughout the West. Those not wearing western dress are fined. Exciting atmosphere.

Lake Tahoe Summer Music Festival (Lake Tahoe, various lake sites; July–Sept): Weekend outdoor classical concerts and midweek chamber-music performances. Also musicals and Broadway revues.

Shakespeare Festival (Lake Tahoe; Aug): *The* place to be for theater lovers in summer. Shakespearean plays performed outdoors in the lovely natural setting of Sand Harbor State Park. For information, call 916/583-9048.

Great Reno Balloon Race (Reno; Sept): A hot-air-balloon race, usually with more than 100 entrants. In Rancho San Rafael Park.

☼ **National Championship Air Races** (Reno; 4 days in mid-Sept): Prop-plane races since 1963, the most famous such competition in the world. Also an aerobatics display. Truly spectacular. At Stead Air Field. For information, call 826-7500.

Nevada Day Celebration (Carson City; 4 days in late Oct): Parades, "pow-wow," grand costume ball. Commemorates Nevada's joining the Union in 1864.

SPORTS: Baseball (Apr–Sept): Silver Socks (Triple-A farm club of the San Diego Padres), Moana Stadium (702/825-0678).

THEME PARKS: ☼▲▲ **Ponderosa Ranch,** at Incline Village, 35 mi. (56km) SW via U.S. 395, Nev. 431, and Nev. 28 (831-0691): This legendary ranch above Lake Tahoe was owned by the Cartwright family in the television series "Bonanza." Reconstructed western frontier town with a general store, a saloon, a firehouse, and a little church. Tours on horseback or by stagecoach. Entertaining. Open daily.

WINTER SPORTS RESORTS: ▲▲ **Alpine Meadows,** 48 mi. (76km) SW via I-80 and Calif. 89 (916/583-4232): 13 lifts; open mid-Nov to June.

▲ **Donner Ski Ranch,** 43 mi. (68km) SW on I-80 (916/426-3635): 7 lifts; open Dec–Apr.

☼▲▲ **Heavenly Valley,** 59 mi. (94km) south via U.S. 395 and U.S. 50 (702/541-1330): 24 lifts; open mid-Nov to mid-May.

▲ **Mt. Rose Ski Resort,** 24 mi. (38km) SW via U.S. 395 and Nev. 431 (702/849-0704): 5 lifts; open mid-Nov. to Apr.

▲▲ **Northstar,** 39 mi. (62km) SW via I-80 and Calif. 267 (916/562-1010): 14 lifts; open Nov–Apr.

▲ **Ski Incline,** 35 mi. (56km) SW via U.S. 395, Nev. 431, and Nev. 28 (702/832-1177): 7 lifts; open mid-Nov to mid-Apr.

☼▲▲▲ **Squaw Valley,** 44 mi. (70km) SW via I-80 and Calif. 89 (916/583-6985; toll free 800/545-1010): 27 lifts; open mid-Nov to Apr. A famous resort, scene of the Winter Olympics in 1960.

ACCOMMODATIONS

A Note on Accommodations: Room rates in Reno are coded as follows: **VE,** Very Expensive ($140 and up); **E,** Expensive ($90–$140); **M,** Moderate ($60–$90); **I,** Inexpensive ($30–$60); **B,** Budget (up to $30). A listing of toll free numbers is in the Appendix.

Personal Favorites (in order of preference)

☼ ♀♀♀♀ **Bally's Reno** (nr. dwntwn), 2500 E. 2nd St., NV 89595 ☼ 🏩🏩🏩🏩 (702/789-2000; toll free 800/648-5080). 2,000 rms, A/C, color TV. AE, CB, DC, MC, V. Free valet parking, pool, two health clubs, sauna, eight tennis courts, bowling (50 lanes), six rests. (including the Café Gigi), 24-hr. bars, rm svce, floor shows, casino, hrdrsr, boutiques, two movie theaters, free airport shuttle, free crib. *Note:* One of the greatest of the American casino-hotels. On the ground floor, 163,000 sq. ft. (1.5ha) in area, this 26-story high-rise houses a gigantic casino, with 2,000 slot machines and more than 120 roulette, blackjack, and baccarat tables. The hotel's theater boasts the world's largest stage. Interior decoration is in a nouveau-riche Hollywood style, but rms (w. refrigerators) are vast and comfortable. Extensive sports facilities. Efficient svce, despite the hotel's size; decent rests. Usually overcrowded and noisy. Worth a trip all by itself. Very good value. Attractive wknd packages. Parking for campers. **M–E**

♀♀♀ **Harrah's Reno** (dwntwn), 219 N. Center St., NV 89504 🏩🏩🏩 (702/786-3232; toll free 800/648-3773). 565 rms, A/C, color TV, in-rm movies. AE, CB, DC, MC, V. Free valet parking, pool, health club, sauna, three rests. (including the Steak House), 24-hr. coffee shop, bars, rm svce, floor shows, casino, hrdrsr, boutiques, free airport shuttle, free crib. *Note:* A casino-hotel in the great Las Vegas tradition, luxurious and flashy, in a noisy area of dwntwn Reno. The best floor shows in Reno. Modern and comfortable rms (the best are in the new tower). Caters to groups. Good rest. (Steak House). **M–E,** but lower rates off-season.

    Eldorado Hotel (dwntwn), 4th St. and Virginia St., NV 89505 (702/786-5700; toll free 800/648-5966). 800 rms, A/C, cable color TV. AE, CB, DC, MC, V. Free valet parking, pool, six rests. (including the Vintage), 24-hr. coffee shop, bars, rm svce, floor shows, casino, free crib. *Note:* Big casino-hotel in the middle of dwntwn Reno topped by a new 25-story tower inaugurated in 1989. Spacious, comfortable rms w. refrigerators. Good svce. Rather noisy neighborhood. Caters to groups and conventions. Acceptable rests. Good value. **I–M**

    Riverboat (dwntwn), 34 W. 2nd St. (at Sierra St.), NV 89501 (702/323-8877; toll free 800/888-5525). 120 rms, A/C, color TV. AE, CB, DC, MC, V. Free valet parking, rest., bar, rm svce, nightclub, casino, free crib. *Note:* Relatively new casino-hotel styled after an old-time Mississippi paddlewheeler. Extremely comfortable; efficient svce; rest. acceptable but no more. Very centrally located. Good value. **I–M**

    Motel 6 Central (nr. dwntwn), 866 N. Wells Ave., NV 89512 (702/786-9852). 142 rms, A/C, color TV, free in-rm movies. AE, DC, MC, V. Free parking, pool. *Note:* One of the best hotel values in Reno. Comfortable modern rms. 8 min. from dwntwn. **B–I**

Other Accommodations (from top bracket to budget)

    Hilton Flamingo Reno (formerly the Sahara; dwntwn), 225 N. Sierra St., NV 89501 (702/322-1111; toll free, see Hilton). 599 rms, A/C, color TV. AE, CB, DC, MC, V. Free valet gar. four rests., 24-hr. coffee shop, 24-hr. bars, rm svce, casino, floor shows, hrdrsr, free crib. *Note:* Big Las Vegas–style casino-hotel. Pleasant, spacious rms (ask for one w. a view of the Sierra). Vast gaming rms at street level. Rather noisy area. Acceptable rest. (Top of the Hilton). Svce somewhat overburdened. Caters to groups and package tours. In the heart of dwntwn Reno. **M–E**

    John Ascuaga's Nugget Casino Resort (nr. dwntwn), 1100 Nugget Ave., Sparks, NV 89431 (702/356-3300; toll free 800/648-1177). 1,000 rms, A/C, cable color TV. AE, CB, DC, MC, V. Free valet parking, pool, five rests. (including Trader Dick's), 24-hr. coffee shop, 24-hr. bars, rm svce, floor shows, disco, casino, free crib. *Note:* Ultramodern 28-story casino-hotel. Comfortable, spacious rms w. balconies. Efficient reception and svce. Obtrusive group clientele. Recently enlarged. 15 min. from dwntwn. **M–E**

    Peppermill (nr. dwntwn), 2707 S. Virginia St., NV 89502 (702/826-2121; toll free 800/282-2444). 629 rms, A/C, color TV. AE, CB, DC, MC, V. Free valet parking, pool, health club, sauna, two rests. (including Le Moulin), coffee shop, 24-hr. bars, rm svce, casino, nightclub, hrdrsr, free crib. *Note:* A 15-story casino-hotel recently modernized and enlarged. Comfortable rms (especially the new wing). Efficient svce. Caters to groups and conventions. Good value. Situated 5 min. from the airport (free shuttle) and 8 min. from dwntwn (free shuttle). **I–M**

    Circus Circus (dwntwn), 500 N. Sierra St., NV 89503 (702/329-0711; toll free 800/648-5010). 1,625 rms, A/C, color TV. AE, CB, DC, MC, V. Free valet parking, two rests., 24-hr. coffee shop, bars, casino, crib $4. *Note:* Clever decor, like a gigantic, multicolored circus tent. Circus shows and gambling all over the place; worth a look. Servicably comfortable; attractive rates. A good choice in the center of Reno, much frequented by families. **B–I,** but lower rates off-season.

    Motel 6 West (nr. dwntwn), 1400 Stardust St., NV 89503 (702/747-7390). 122 rms, A/C, color TV, free in-rm movies.

AE, DC, MC, V. Free parking, pool. *Note:* One of the best values in Reno. Comfortable, modern rms. 5 min. from dwntwn. **B–I**

RESTAURANTS

A Note on Restaurant Prices: Reno restaurant prices, per person, excluding drinks and service charges, are coded as follows: **VE,** Very Expensive ($60 and up); **E,** Expensive ($40–$60); **M,** Moderate ($25–$40); **I,** Inexpensive ($15–$25); **B,** Budget (up to $15).

Personal Favorites (in order of preference)

    🍷🍷🍷 **La Table Française** (nr. dwntwn), 3065 W. 4th St. (323-3200). A/C. Dinner only, Tues–Sun; closed hols. AE, CB, DC, MC, V. Jkt. *Specialties:* snails w. Roquefort, confit of duck, quail w. fresh fruit, scallops w. leeks and ginger, spiced duck w. honey, game (in season), hazelnut chocolate mousse cake. Menu changes regularly. Good wine list. *Note:* The retirement in 1984 of Yves Pimparel, head chef and source of inspiration for this excellent French rest., made many fear the worst. But his daughter, Muriel, who succeeded him, has a master's touch, and this remains the best rest. in Reno. The cooking is a perfect blend of French and Californian nouvelle cuisine. Charmingly got up as both inn and windmill. Well-trained staff; romantic atmosphere. Resv. essential. 8 min. from dwntwn. *French/Continental.* **M**

    🍷🍷🍷 **Steak House** (dwntwn), in Harrah's Reno (see "Accommodations," above) (786-3232). A/C. Lunch Mon–Fri, dinner nightly (until midnight). AE, CB, DC, MC, V. Jkt. *Specialties:* frogs' legs provençal, steak Diane, sea bass in puff pastry, médaillons of beef w. shallot-truffle sauce, roast rack of lamb. Very good desserts. *Note:* Despite its name, the specialty of this rest. is not its good, big steaks—which are, nonetheless, excellent—but subtler dishes such as sautéed mahi-mahi (Hawaiian dolphin, a fish) and excellent curries. Elegant decor; good svce. On the ground floor of Harrah's. Valet parking. *Continental.* **I–M**

    🍷🍷 **Leonardo's** (nr. dwntwn), 2450 S. Virginia St. (827-6200). A/C. Dinner only, nightly; closed Thanksgiving, Dec 25. AE, CB, DC, MC, V. Jkt. *Specialties:* fettuccine Alfredo, lasagne, eggplant parmigiana, scampi alla ventuno, spaghetti alla Pavarotti (w. garlic, green peppers, and chicken livers), saltimbocca, crêpes Da Vinci (filled w. strawberries). Very nice wine list (the best in Reno). *Note:* The favorite rest. of the show-biz crowd, as witness the numerous signed photos of stars on the walls. Excellent Italian cuisine, impeccably prepared and served. Popular locally; resv. strongly advised. *Italian.* **I–M**

    🍷🍷 **Ichiban** (dwntwn), 635 N. Sierra St. (323-5550). A/C. Lunch Mon–Fri, dinner nightly; closed Dec 25. AE, CB, DC, MC, V. *Specialties:* sushi, tempura, teppanyaki, chicken teriyaki. *Note:* The best Japanese food in Reno. Rather banal Far Eastern decor. Attentive svce. Popular locally; resv. advised. Tatami-style seating for purists. *Japanese.* **I**

    🍷 **Club Cal-Neva** (dwntwn), 2nd St. and Virginia St. (323-1046). A/C. Breakfast/lunch/dinner daily around the clock. No credit cards. *Specialties:* steak, roast beef, salads, catch of the day, good desserts. *Note:* A godsend to Reno's hungry visitors any hour of the day or night, 7 days a week. This dwntwn casino has three rests.: The Top Deck, The Copper Ledge, and The Hofbrau, which offer an around-the-clock 99¢ breakfast and a $4.95 prime rib dinner. These generous portions of well-prepared food are an excellent value. *Steak/American.* **B**

Other Restaurants (from top bracket to budget)

    🍷🍷🍷 **Top of the Hilton** (dwntwn), in the Hilton Flamingo Reno (see "Accommodations," above) (322-1111). A/C. Dinner nightly, brunch Sun. AE, CB, DC, MC, V. Jkt. *Specialties:* salmon w. three sauces, roast duck w. raspberry sauce, bouillabaisse, rack of lamb. *Note:* From the 21st floor of the Hilton Flamingo Reno, this deluxe rest. offers a spectacular view of the city and surrounding mountains. Flawless traditional hotel cuisine; elegant decor and svce; very high prices by local standards. Resv. advised. Dancing nightly; valet parking. *Continental.* **M**

    Rapscallion (nr. dwntwn), 1555 S. Wells Ave. (323-1211). A/C. Lunch/dinner daily, brunch Sun; closed Thanksgiving, Dec 25. AE, MC, V. *Specialties:* oysters on the half shell; shellfish; Maine lobster; catch of the day broiled, baked, or prepared w. sauce; bouillabaisse. Adequate wine list. *Note:* The best seafood rest. in Reno. Everything is delivered daily, by air, for absolute freshness, and more than 20 kinds of fish figure on the menu. Nice 1900 setting with old gaslights and Tiffany-style stained glass. Competent, friendly svce. Resv. advisable. *Seafood.* **I–M**

    Presidential Car at Harolds Club (dwntwn), 250 N. Virginia St. (329-0881). A/C. Dinner only, nightly. AE, CB, DC, MC, V. *Specialties:* prime rib, catch of the day, cheesecake. *Note:* Clever 19th-century railroad setting; good though unimaginative food; efficient svce. Very good value. *Steak/Seafood.* **I**

    Louis' Basque Corner (dwntwn), 301 E. 4th St. (323-7203). A/C. Lunch Mon–Sat, dinner nightly. AE, CB, MC, V. *Specialties:* tripe, chicken basquaise, paella, tongue à la basquaise, braised calves' sweetbreads, mutton stew, oxtail. *Note:* This rest., w. its family atmosphere and walls decorated w. earthenware and pictures from the Pyrenees, features Basque cooking, both French and Spanish (there are many shepherds of Basque origin in Nevada). Chef Louis Erreguible's robust delicious food treats your wallet gently, served in the generous portions you'd expect. Congenial atmosphere; a great place to eat. Very popular locally. No resv. *French/Spanish.* **B–I**

    El Borracho (nr. dwntwn), 1601 Virginia St. (322-0313). A/C. Lunch/dinner daily; closed Thanksgiving, Dec 25. AE, CB, DC, MC, V. *Specialties:* chiles relleños, tacos, enchilada verde, flauta encantada. *Note:* A little Mexican place, popular locally. Authentic, unpretentious food. Good value. Pretty hacienda decor. *Mexican.* **B**

LAKE TAHOE

ACCOMMODATIONS

    A Note on Accommodations: Room rates in Lake Tahoe are coded as follows: **VE,** Very Expensive ($140 and up); **E,** Expensive ($90–$140); **M,** Moderate ($60–$90); **I,** Inexpensive ($30–$60); **B,** Budget (up to $30). A listing of toll free numbers is in the Appendix.

Personal Favorites (in order of preference)

    Harrah's Lake Tahoe, U.S. 50 and Stateline Ave., Stateline, NV 89449 (702/588-6611; toll free 800/648-3773). 540 rms, A/C, color TV, in-rm movies. AE, CB, DC, MC, V. Free valet parking, pool, health club, sauna, five rests. (including The Summit), 24-hr. coffee shop, 24-hr. bars, rm svce, floor shows, casino, disco, hrdrsr, boutiques, concierge, free airport shuttle, free crib. *Note:* Prestigious casino-hotel with a 393-ft.-long (120m) gaming rm. Its floor shows and amenities rival the best in Las Vegas. Spacious rms, modern and elegant (the best have a view of Lake Tahoe), w. minibars; outstanding svce; good rests. Excellent location between the lake and the mountain. A very fine hotel; you pay accordingly. **E–VE,** lower rates off-season.

    Lakeland Village, 3535 Lake Tahoe Blvd., South Lake Tahoe, CA 95705 (916/541-1685; toll free 800/542-4253). 212 suites and studios, A/C, color TV, in-rm movies. AE, DC, MC, V. Free parking, two pools, two tennis courts, sauna, boating, fishing, private beach, adj. rest., snack bar, free crib. *Note:* Attractive resort facility right on the beach; comfortable suites and studios w. refrigerator, kitchenette, fireplace, and private balcony, the best w. lake view. Also two-story town houses w. one to four bedrooms. At the water's edge w. 19 acres (7ha) of lawns and grdns. Friendly reception and svce. 5 min. from casinos and ski slopes. Good overall value. **M–E** (town houses E–VE), but lower rates off-season.

Tahoe West Motor Lodge, 4082 Pine Blvd., South Lake Tahoe, CA 95729 (916/544-6455; toll free 800/522-1021). 59 rms; no A/C; cable color TV. AE, CB, DC, MC, V. Free parking, pool, sauna, coffee shop nearby, free crib. *Note:* Pleasant little motel a stone's throw from Lake Tahoe and the casinos. Comfortable rms w. private balconies or patios. Private beach privileges. Very good value. Friendly reception and svce. **I–M,** but lower rates off-season.

Cedar Glen Lodge, 6589 N. Lake Blvd., Tahoe Vista, CA 95732 (916/546-4281; toll free 800/341-8000). 31 rms; no A/C; cable color TV. AE, CB, DC, MC, V. Free parking, pool, sauna, adj. beach, coffee shop nearby, free crib. *Note:* Charming little motel beside Lake Tahoe, surrounded by pretty grdns. Cozy rms w. private patios (half w. kitchenettes). Calm, countrified atmosphere. Friendly svce. Very good value overall. **I–M,** but lower rates off-season.

Other Accommodations (from top bracket to budget)

Hyatt Regency Lake Tahoe, Lakeshore Blvd. and Country Club Dr., Incline Village, NV 89450 (702/831-1111; toll free, see Hyatt). 460 rms, A/C, color TV, in-rm movies. AE, CB, DC, MC, V. Free valet parking, pool, health club, sauna, two tennis courts, private beach, bicycles, three rests. (including Hugo's Rôtisserie), 24-hr. coffee shop, 24-hr. bar, rm svce, casino, hrdrsr, boutiques, concierge, free crib. *Note:* Luxurious casino-hotel in a lovely wooded setting on the shores of Lake Tahoe. Spacious, ultra-comfortable rms w. balconies (some w. refrigerators and fireplaces), the best overlooking the lake. Efficient svce; very acceptable rest. Ideal for a long vacation stay. Two VIP floors. Recently underwent a $20-million renovation. **E–VE,** but lower rates off-season.

Lake Tahoe Horizon, U.S. 50, Stateline, NV 89449 (702/588-6211; toll free 800/648-3322). 536 rms, A/C, color TV, in-rm movies. AE, CB, DC, MC, V. Free valet parking, pool, sauna, two rests. (including Stetson's), 24-hr. coffee shop, 24-hr. bars, 24-hr. rm svce, nightclub, casino, hrdrsr, boutiques, free crib. *Note:* Classic Las Vegas–style casino-hotel, w. 1,200 slot machines and dozens of gaming tables. Recently renovated. Pleasant, large rms (some w. balconies and lake views). Good svce. Attractive vacation packages. Caters to groups. **E,** but lower rates off-season.

Cal-Neva Lodge, 2 Stateline Dr., Crystal Bay, NV 89402 (702/832-4000; toll free 800/225-6382). 220 rms, A/C, cable color TV. AE, CB, DC, MC, V. Free parking, pool, health club, sauna, tennis court, bicycles, two rests. (including Sir Charles), 24-hr. coffee shop, bars, rm svce, nightclub, casino, hrdrsr, boutiques, crib $15. *Note:* Modern grand hotel on a headland overlooking the lake that marks the border between California and Nevada (whence the name). Comfortable rms w. mountain and lake views, some w. private balcony. Efficient svce in an agreeable setting. A Lake Tahoe landmark. **M–E,** but lower rates off-season.

Royal Valhalla, 4104 Lakeshore Blvd., South Lake Tahoe, CA 95729 (916/544-2233). 80 rms, no A/C, cable color TV. AE, CB, DC, MC, V. Free parking, pool, private beach, valet svce. *Note:* Comfortable little motel w. direct access to the beach. Inviting rms w. lake or mountain views (most w. private patios or balconies; one-third w. kitchenettes). Good svce. Free morning coffee. Just minutes from the casinos of Stateline. Good overall value. **I–M,** but lower rates off-season.

Motel 6, 2375 Lake Tahoe Blvd., South Lake Tahoe, CA 95731 (916/542-1400). 140 rms. A/C, color TV, free in-rm movies. AE, DC, MC, V. Free parking, pool. *Note:* Unbeatable value two steps from the lake. Modern and comfortable. Midway between the ski slopes and the casinos. **B–I**

RESTAURANTS

A Note on Restaurant Prices: Lake Tahoe restaurant prices, per person, excluding drinks and service charges, are coded as follows: **VE,** Very Expensive ($60 and up); **E,** Expensive ($40–$60); **M,** Moderate ($25–$40); **I,** Inexpensive ($15–$25); **B,** Budget (up to $15).

Personal Favorites (in order of preference)

Le Petit Pier, 7250 N. Lake Tahoe Blvd., Tahoe Vista (916/546-4464). A/C. Dinner only, Wed–Mon. AE, CB, DC, MC, V. Jkt. *Specialties:* country pâté, braised pheasant forestière, tournedos w. marrow in marchand de vin sauce, quail w. green peppercorns. Good wine list. *Note:* Some of the best fare in Lake Tahoe, w. a lovely view of the mountains thrown in. Fine French dining, elaborate and elegant. Preppie atmosphere. Excellent svce. Resv. advised. *French.* **I–M**

Captain Jon's, 7220 N. Lake Blvd., Tahoe Vista (916/546-5819). A/C. Lunch Tues–Sun in summer, dinner Tues–Sun; closed the first 3 weeks in Dec. AE, CB, DC, MC, V. *Specialties:* roast duck w. oyster sauce, sautéed scallops w. shiitake mushrooms and snow peas, rack of lamb, catch of the day. Very good desserts. *Note:* This inviting inn rises straight from the water; the European-style food is elegantly prepared and served. Agreeable seafaring decor and summer open-air terrace w. a view out over Lake Tahoe. Efficient svce; good value; resv. a must. Two dinner sittings only: 6 and 9pm. *Continental.* **I–M**

Swiss Chalet, Lake Tahoe Blvd. at Sierra Blvd., South Lake Tahoe (916/544-3304). A/C. Dinner only, Tues–Sun; closed Easter, Thanksgiving, Dec 25. AE, MC, V. *Specialties:* schnitzel St. Moritz, sauerbraten, steak, veal Cordon Bleu, daily catch. *Note:* Decor and atmosphere of an alpine chalet. French- and German-inspired cooking. Warm and cozy. A landmark since 1957. Resv. recommended. *Continental.* **I–M**

Other Restaurants (from top bracket to budget)

The Summit, in Harrah's Lake Tahoe (see "Accommodations," above) (702/588-6611). A/C. Dinner only, nightly. AE, CB, DC, MC, V. Jkt. *Specialties:* lobster bisque, red snapper Rockefeller, filet mignon béarnaise, saddle of veal Black Forest, tournedos Alaska, pheasant w. sauerkraut in champagne sauce, bananas Foster, soufflé Grand Marnier. Good wine list. *Note:* Superb view of lake and mountains from the 18th floor of Harrah's. The decor is exceedingly elegant. Rather pompous luxury-hotel cuisine, but impeccably prepared and served. Stylish and classy. Very high prices by local standards. Resv. strongly advised. *Continental.* **M–E**

Chart House, Kingsbury Grade (1.5 mi./2.5km off U.S. 50), Stateline (702/588-6276). A/C. Dinner only, nightly; closed Dec 26. AE, MC, V. *Specialties:* filet of beef teriyaki, prime rib, catch of the day. *Note:* Congenial little rest. w. a fine panoramic view of Lake Tahoe from the heights of Stateline. Good food w. no fuss. Friendly svce. A good spot, away from the hustle and bustle of the big casino-hotels along the lake. *American.* **I–M**

La Playa, 7046 N. Lake Blvd., Tahoe Vista (916/546-5903). No A/C. Lunch/dinner nightly, brunch Sun. AE, DC, MC, V. Jkt. *Specialties:* roast quail, rack of lamb, tournedos, swordfish steak, catch of the day. Skimpy wine list. *Note:* Charming inn on the shores of Lake Tahoe. Conventional cooking, but very well done. Open-air patio for fine-weather dining, w. views of the lake and the mountains. Friendly reception and svce. A fine place to eat. Resv. recommended. *Continental.* **I–M**

Sierra Restaurant, in Harrah's Lake Tahoe (see "Accommodations," above) (702/588-6611). A/C. Breakfast/lunch/

dinner (around the clock). AE, CB, DC, MC, V. *Note:* Americanized Chinese food, but also sandwiches, steaks, and hamburger, 24 hr. a day. A few dishes are very acceptable. Often packed. All-purpose modern decor. *Chinese/American.* **B–I**

NEARBY EXCURSIONS

BERLIN-ICHTHYOSAUR STATE PARK (175 mi./ 280km SE via I-80, U.S. 50, Nev. 361, and Nev. 844): Unknown to most tourists, this park, lying east of Gabbs in Union Canyon, is nonetheless fascinating for two reasons. First, it includes the ghost town of **Berlin,** a former miners' community which had several hundred inhabitants at the turn of the century, but has been completely abandoned for more than 75 years. The second and more important of the park's attractions is its large number of fossilized ichthyosaur remains. These enormous prehistoric reptiles, up to 65 ft. (20m) long, with characteristics of both fish and lizard, made their appearance on the planet some 225 million years ago and became extinct 155 million years later. A total of 34 fossilized ichthyosaurs has been discovered so far in the Shoshone Mountains, all uncovered by water erosion during the last glacial period. Guided tours (867-3001) of the park and Berlin are offered Sat–Sun at 11am Mar–Sept. The park is open daily mid-June to Labor Day, Fri–Mon the rest of the year, but is always closed during bad weather. Well worth a visit.

CARSON CITY (30 mi./48km south on U.S. 395): Founded in 1858, Carson City—named after the famous scout Kit Carson, who undertook the first explorations of Nevada, in 1843–45 —is one of the smallest state capitals in the U.S. Nonetheless, the city has a beautiful group of Victorian mansions. The **State Capitol** on N. Carson St., opened in 1871, with its typical silver dome symbolic of Nevada's principal mineral resource, is worth a look; open Mon–Fri. The **Nevada State Museum** deserves a visit, with interesting displays of relics from the days of the pioneers and prospectors; you'll find it on N. Carson St. and Robinson St. (885-4810), open daily. Also see its annex, the **Nevada State Railroad Museum,** S. Carson St. and Fairview Dr. (885-5168), open Fri–Sun and hols. June–Oct., featuring old steam engines, freight cars, and passenger cars.

DONNER PASS MEMORIAL STATE PARK (43 mi./ 68km SW on I-80): This mountain pass was the scene of a famous episode in the history of the westward expansion. In Oct 1846, 89 pioneers attempting to cross the Sierra Nevada found their way blocked by the snows of an unusually early winter. With no food left, and unable to go on through the blizzards, 42 of them died from hunger and exhaustion. The other 47 survived only by resorting to cannibalism. The **Emigrant Trail Museum,** on the old U.S. 40 (916/587-3841), open daily, traces the story of the Donner party. Well worth going out of your way for.

FORT CHURCHILL HISTORIC STATE MONUMENT (85 mi./136km SE via Nev. 341, U.S. 395, U.S. 50, and Nev. 28): Remains of a small fort used by the U.S. Army in the 1860s in the war against the Paiute tribe. The fort also served as a staging post for the riders of the Pony Express. Visitor center open daily (702/577-2345).
On the way, visit **Virginia City** (see below). Worth a side trip.

LAKE TAHOE (34 mi./54km SW via U.S. 395 and Nev. 431, or U.S. 395 and U.S. 50): Lying in the heart of the Sierra

Nevada at an altitude of 6,230 ft. (1,900m), this superb mountain lake, its azure depths reaching down to 1,600 ft. (490m), is among the country's greatest tourist attractions. The clarity of the lake dazzles visitors who gaze through many fathoms of water at objects far below on the sandy bottom. In fact, Lake Tahoe is reputed to be the purest body of water in the world. Surrounded by granite peaks and coniferous forests, this immense stretch of water (200 sq. mi./520km²) is bordered by a very beautiful scenic road about 72 mi. (116km) long. At the southwestern end of the lake, be sure to see the enchanting **Emerald Bay** and **Eagle Falls,** which plunges 1,508 ft. (460m) down the mountainside.

There are many hotels and restaurants in South Lake Tahoe, Incline Village, Crystal Bay, Stateline, and other towns on the lake (see Lake Tahoe "Accommodations" and "Restaurants," above).

Ideal for lovers of water sports, the lake has no fewer than 12 public beaches. Paddlewheel-boat trips aboard the M.S. *Dixie* depart from the Zephyr Cove Marina, 4 mi. (6.5km) north of Stateline on U.S. 50 (702/588-3508), open daily May–Oct; or the *Tahoe Queen* departs from the Ski Run Marina, at the foot of Ski Run Blvd., South Lake Tahoe (916/541-3364), open daily year round. Lake Tahoe alone is worth the trip to Reno.

LASSEN VOLCANIC NATIONAL PARK (150 mi./ 240km NW via U.S. 395, Calif. 36, and Calif. 89): The southernmost outpost of a long chain of volcanic mountains in the Cascade Range, which stretches from Mount Baker, Mount Rainier, and Mount St. Helens (Washington) in the north, by way of Mount Hood and Crater Lake (Oregon) in the middle, to Mount Shasta (California) in the south, Lassen Peak is one of the only two active volcanos in the continental U.S. (the other being Mount St. Helens).

Lassen Peak, named after the Danish explorer Peter Lassen, has not erupted since 1921, but it could happen at any time. The landscape is strange and awe-inspiring, with desolate fields of lava, black ash, plumes of smoke and sulfurous vapors, little lakes teeming with fish, thick forests, and muddy hot springs. The 10,457-ft. (3,187m) summit of Lassen Peak, with a superb panoramic view of the area, can be reached by a 2- to 3-hr. walk up a marked trail. There is also a fine scenic drive 30 mi. (48km) long between the park's southern entrance and Manzanita Lake (Lassen Park Rd.).

The park is open year round, but heavy snowslides prevent access to Lassen Park Rd. and certain areas of the park from late Oct through early June. Seven fully equipped campgrounds. Well worth a detour. For **information,** contact the Superintendent, Lassen Volcanic National Park, Mineral, CA 96063 (916/595-4444). **Visitor center** open in summer on Manzanita Lake.

Where to Stay

Childs Meadow Resort, on Calif. 89 (P.O. Box 3000), Mill Creek, CA 96061 (916/595-3383), 9 mi. (14km) south from the SW entrance of the park. 47 rustic but comfortable motel rms. I

PYRAMID LAKE (36 mi./58km NE via I-80 and Nev. 447; return by Nev. 445): Last vestige of the prehistoric inland sea known as Lake Lahontan, Pyramid Lake, 30 mi. (48km) long by 9 mi. (14km) wide, is strangely, captivatingly beautiful, surrounded by bald and barren mountains whose tawny red hues are reflected in its crystalline blue waters. Gen. John C. Frémont, the first European to explore the region, in 1844 christened it Pyramid Lake on account of the conical shape of several islands of porous volcanic rock that rise from its center. The largest of these, Anahoe Island, serves as a sanctuary for a colony of 10,000 white pelicans. Pyramid Lake is also famous for its rainbow and cutthroat trout, which weigh up to 50 lbs. (23kg), as well as for the curious qui-ui fish, a prehistoric survival. Fishing permits are issued at the offices of the Native American reservation at Sutcliffe, Pyramid Lake Indian Tribal Enterprises, Star Rte. (702/673-6335). The northern part of the lake, with its strange lunar landscapes, is sacred ground to the Paiute people, and off-limits to tourists. Not to be missed.

VIRGINIA CITY (25 mi./40km SE on U.S. 395 and Nev. 341): This, the most famous mining town of the Old West, is not, properly speaking, a ghost town—about 700 people still live here today. Founded in 1859 on the site of the richest vein of gold and silver in Nevada, the legendary Comstock Lode—which alone produced more than $1 billion worth of precious metals—Virginia City in its heyday during the 1870s boasted up to 30,000 inhabitants. As evidence of its unabashed wealth at the time, the town could show off four banks, six churches, a luxurious opera house in which the great Caruso once sang, six theaters, and the only elevator between Chicago and San Francisco, not to mention 110 saloons, by official count.

Clinging to the slopes of Mount Davidson, Virginia City has been in large part restored as it was in its golden age in the 19th century, its principal street (C St.) lined with covered galleries and wooden sidewalks, many small museums (**The Way It Was Museum, The Wild West Museum, Nevada State Fire Museum,** etc.), the offices of the *Territorial Enterprise,* where Mark Twain worked as a reporter, and many saloons with picturesque names (the Bucket of Blood Saloon, the Delta Saloon with its famed Suicide Table, etc.). Also not to be missed are **Piper's Opera House,** B St. and Union St. (702/847-0433), open daily mid-May through Sept. (by appointment the rest of the year), and **The Castle,** a luxurious Norman-style manor built in 1868 by the superintendent of the Empire Mine, at 70 B St. (702/847-0275), open daily.

An entertaining little steam train, the **Virginia and Truckee Railroad** (702/847-0380), operating daily May–Oct, links Virginia City with Gold Hill. Truly spectacular **camel and ostrich races** take place on Labor Day weekend. Visitor center, on C St. between Taylor St. and Union St. (702/847-0177), open daily.

A visit to Virginia City is truly not to be missed.

Where to Stay En Route

The Gold Hill Hotel, on Nev. 341 (P.O. Box 304), Virginia City, NV 89440 (702/847-0111). 14 rms. Nevada's oldest hotel (1859). Rooms furnished w. period antiques (some w. fireplaces). Charming and colorful. Very acceptable rest. (Crown Point). **I–M**

YOSEMITE NATIONAL PARK (177 mi./283km south on U.S. 395 and Calif. 120): Breathtaking waterfalls and superb granite peaks. One of the two or three most beautiful national parks in the U.S. A must-see. Note that Calif. 120 is closed in winter, necessitating a detour on Calif. 108. For more information, see Chapter 53 on Yosemite National Park.

FARTHER AFIELD

LAKE TAHOE & VIRGINIA CITY (145 mi./232km r.t. via U.S. 395S, Nev. 431S, Calif. 28S, Calif. 89S, U.S. 50E, Nev. 341N, and U.S. 395N): Your first stop will be at **Mount Rose Ski Resort,** a very popular winter sports resort in a lovely natural setting. Make a detour to see **Ponderosa Ranch** at Incline Village, which served as the setting for the television series "Bonanza" (see "Theme Parks," above).

Then take the successive scenic highways along **Lake Tahoe,** with its splendid scenery (Calif. 28, Calif. 89, and U.S. 50; see "Nearby Excursions," above). Along the way, don't miss **Squaw Valley,** the famous resort where the 1960 Winter Olympics were held. At the southern end of the lake, stop off at beautiful **Emerald Bay State Park,** where the water is as clear as crystal. At **Stateline,** on the California-Nevada border, there are many luxury hotels and casinos.

Now on to ⌂ **Carson City,** the state capital and a city of Victorian charm (see "Nearby Excursions," above).

Your last stop on this 2- or 3-day journey should be at ※⌘ **Virginia City,** the most famous gold-rush town in the West, which looks like something out of a John Ford or Sam Peckinpah movie. Then back to Reno on U.S. 395N.

A very full itinerary, worth the trip to Reno for its own sake.

CHAPTER 50

SAN FRANCISCO 👢👢👢

□ □ □

And the California Wine Country

They say that "If you live in San Francisco, you never have to take a vacation." Where else would you find a more beautiful sight than its bay? Or a more enjoyable climate than the 59°F (15°C) average, winter and summer alike, which makes San Francisco the world's first naturally air-conditioned city? Tourists—about eight million of them every year—and longtime residents alike share a love at first sight for this charming, colorful city. Generating about $3.4 billion in revenue annually, tourism is the city's No. 1 industry.

Luxurious mansions jostling little pastel-colored cottages on steep hillsides; the old **cable cars** struggling up, or hurtling down, the precipitous streets; the cutting edge of the **Transamerica Pyramid** towering above the exotic pagodas of Chinatown, one of the largest Far Eastern communities outside Asia; the huge, flamboyant silhouette of the **Golden Gate Bridge** framed against the Pacific; the splendid backdrop of **San Francisco Bay,** with the dark island of Alcatraz anchored amid its icy blue waves, especially at sunset—all these are the details of an amazing urban composition. San Francisco, "the Pearl of the West Coast," tops the list of cities "where every American dreams of going to live."

Although today's San Francisco, standing at the crossroads of East and West, is one of the world's great financial clearinghouses, the city came on the scene comparatively late. The first men to explore the Pacific coast, Portuguese Juan Rodríguez Cabrillo and English Sir Francis Drake, both missed the narrow passage into the bay. It was not until 1776 that the great Franciscan missionary to California, Fray Junípero Serra, built the **Mission Dolores,** dedicated to St. Francis of Assisi, a little south of the site of the present imposing City Hall. At the same time, there arose on what is now **Portsmouth Square,** at the edge of Chinatown, a hamlet which the Spaniards called Yerba Buena ("Good Herbs"). Some 70 years later, on July 19, 1846, when Capt. John B. Montgomery of the U.S.S. *Portsmouth* took possession of the town in the name of the people of the United States, it was still no more than a little settlement of trappers and whalers.

The discovery in 1848 of the first veins of gold in California's rocks touched off the famous "gold rush" in the following year, and the population of the town exploded in the space of 2 years from 900 inhabitants to 50,000. Since then nothing—not even the terrible earthquake of 1906, which registered 8.2 on the Richter Scale, or the conflagration that followed it—has impaired the magnetic attraction of "Baghdad by the Bay" for generations of immigrants. Chinese, Mexicans, Japanese, Italians, White Russians, South Americans, French Basques, Filipinos, Germans, and Irish have all been drawn hither, and have all contributed to the city's cosmopolitan character. Even now, 43% of its inhabitants are first- or second-generation Americans, and newspapers are published here in 13 languages including English. The beneficent effects of the melting pot have made of this polyglot place the most amusing, the most tolerant, and one of the most sophisticated cities in the U.S. In spite of the AIDS epidemic (9,000 cases registered so far, and 6,000 deaths), San Francisco has more gay people (110,000) of both sexes in relation to its population (barely 730,000 inhabitants) than any other American city; there are even gay deputy mayors on the city council of America's "spiritual capital" of homosexuality. This same respect for minority rights, reinforced by a tradition of nonconformity, has allowed a number of contemporary ideologies to flourish in San Francisco: the beatniks in the '50s, student protest at **Berkeley** and the hippies in the '60s, the psychedelic movement at the beginning of the '70s, and so on. The flip side of the coin is a disquieting multiplication of sects, "religions," and small extremist groups like the Black Panthers, the Symbionese Liberation Army, or the fundamentalist sect whose members committed mass suicide at Jonestown.

Another cloud on the horizon is the proximity of the **San Andreas Fault,** which runs 560 mi. (900km) along the California coast, and keeps San Francisco permanently at risk of another earthquake like that of 1906, or the one of Oct 1989, more vivid in everyone's memory (66 people dead, more than $7 billion in property damage); there is even a telephone number (329-4025) which San Franciscans can call for current information on shocks registered by local seismographs.

Continuing a century-old tradition, three renowned universities, the Roman Catholic **University of San Francisco,** founded in 1855, with 7,000 students; the **University of California at Berkeley,** founded in 1868, with 32,000 students; and **Stanford University** at **Palo Alto,** founded in 1891, with 13,000 students, make San Francisco one of the most important centers of higher education and research in the country.

No trip to California can be called complete without an attentive visit to this joyful, flamboyant city which has inspired so many poets, movie directors, novelists, and songwriters, and which has served as a photogenic backdrop to dozens of movies and television shows from *Bullitt* to *Vertigo* and from *The Maltese Falcon* to *Presidio.* From the gaudy frontages of Chinatown to the sublime panorama of the bay seen from the Golden Gate, by way of the roller-coaster contours of **Telegraph Hill,** the arrogant high-rises of the **Financial District,** where such great corporations as Chevron, Bank of America, Bechtel, Wells Fargo, and Levi Strauss make their headquarters, or the sea scent of **Fisherman's Wharf,** San Francisco is unique. Its immediate, and more distant, surroundings are in themselves worth the visit, beginning with the charming little ports of **Sausalito** and **Tiburon** across the bay, and moving on to the renowned vineyards of the **Napa Valley,** the magnificent **Seventeen-Mile Drive** between Monterey and Carmel —one of the most spectacular highways in the U.S.—and the legendary **Silicon Valley,** headquarters of electronics research and development for the entire country, with one of the heaviest concentrations of high-tech industries in the world. As for longer trips, the motorist's hardest problem is to choose among **Sequoia** and **Yosemite National Parks** (see Chapters 52 and 53), the mountain grandeur of **Lake Tahoe** (see Chapter 49 on Reno), or Calif. 1, the wonderful coast road from San Francisco to Los Angeles, better known as the **Cabrillo Hwy.** (see Chapter 51 on the California Coast).

Food is not the least of San Francisco's attractions. With New York, Los Angeles, and New Orleans, the Golden Gate City is one of the four gastronomic capitals of the U.S. Its Chinese and Japanese restaurants are among the best in the world, and its French and Italian restaurants are as good, not to mention its renowned restaurants serving seafood and a gamut of exotic cuisines: Korean, Filipino, Mexican, Indian, Javanese, Armenian, Caribbean, Vietnamese, and many more. In spite of their boast that their city has more restaurants per capita (more than 4,300) than any other in the country, the favorite sport of San Franciscans seems to be discovering new ones. Note also that although the city claims more international-class hotels for its size than any city in the U.S., they're often completely booked; reservations should be made far in advance.

There is no end to the list of the city's famous children. They include writers Jack London and Irving Stone, poet Robert Frost, movie director Mervin LeRoy, newspaper magnate William Randolph Hearst, dancer Isadora Duncan, banker and statesman Robert S. McNamara, actor Clint Eastwood, musician Carlos Santana, and singer Johnny Mathis.

Warning: Never use the abbreviation "Frisco" for "San Francisco"; the inhabitants consider it insulting.

BASIC FACTS: State of California. Area code: 415 and (starting 1991) 510 (for the East Bay). Time zone: Pacific. ZIP Code: 94101. Founded: 1776. Approximate population: city, 760,000; metropolitan area, 5,960,000. Fourth-largest metropolitan area in the U.S.

CLIMATE: "Disconcerting" is the mildest word that can be applied to San Francisco's climate; Mark Twain wrote, "The coldest winter I ever spent was a summer in San Francisco." There are so many micro-climates that meteorologists run out of technical terms for them. In broad terms, late spring, summer, and a good part of the fall are sunny but cool; temperatures average 61°F (16°C) June–Oct. Winter is gloomier, though the mercury rarely drops below 58°F (10°C) in Dec–Jan. Showers are frequent Nov–Mar, as is morning fog over the bay in summer and fall.

DISTANCES: Denver, 1,234 mi. (1,975km); Las Vegas, 568 mi. (908km); Los Angeles, 381 mi. (608km); Portland, 634 mi. (1,015km); Reno, 229 mi. (366km); Salt Lake City, 750 mi. (1,200km).

ARRIVAL & TRANSIT INFORMATION

AIRPORTS: The **Oakland International Airport** (OAK), 18 mi. (28km) SE (577-4000).

San Francisco International Airport (SFO), 16 mi. (26km) south (761-0800), one of the most up-to-date in the country, ranking sixth in volume of traffic among U.S. airports (31 million passengers per year), but ranks at the bottom among major airports in terms of on-time arrival of planes.

U.S. AIRLINES: Alaska (931-8888), American (398-4434), America West (839-1292), Continental (397-8818), Delta (552-5700), Eastern (474-5858), Hawaiian (toll free 800/367-5320), Northwest (392-2163), Pan Am (toll free 800/221-1111), Southwest (885-1221), TWA (864-5731), United (397-2100), and USAir (956-8636).

FOREIGN CARRIERS: Air Canada (toll free 800/422-6232), Air France (toll free 800/237-2747), British Airways (toll free 800/247-9297), Canadian Airlines International (toll free 800/426-7000), Lufthansa (toll free 800/645-3880), and UTA (toll free 800/237-2623).

CITY LINK: The **cab** fare from the San Francisco airport to dwntwn is about $26–$28; time, about 35 min. (45 min. during rush hr.). Cab fare from the Oakland airport to dwntwn, about $30; time, about 35 min. Bus: **Airporter** (495-

8404), leaving the San Francisco airport every 15 min.; serves principal hotels dwntwn, in the financial district, and around Fisherman's Wharf, and the Airlines Terminal at Taylor St. and Ellis St.; fare, $6; time, about 40 min. The **Bay Area Airporter** (632-5506) also links the Oakland airport and the Airlines Terminal; fare, $7; time, 50 min. Van: **Bay Area SuperShuttle** (558-8500) serves all the dwntwn hotels; fare, $8. **Municipal bus** lines 7b and 7f connect dwntwn San Francisco and the two airports; fare, $1.25; time, about 50 min.

The **public transportation system,** both surface by bus and streetcar, MUNI (673-6864), and by express subway, BART (788-2278), is excellent throughout the Bay Area. Cabs are numerous but very expensive.

Given the attractive rates offered in California and the large number of enticing excursions around San Francisco, it's highly advisable to rent a car with unlimited mileage. *Warning:* When parking on a hill in San Francisco, it's mandatory to turn your front wheels inward toward the curb to prevent the vehicle from slipping.

CAR RENTALS (at the San Francisco International Airport unless otherwise indicated): Avis (877-6780); Budget (875-6850); Dollar (952-6200); Hertz (877-1600); National (877-4745); Bob Leech's Auto Rental, 435 S. Airport Blvd., South San Francisco (583-2727), a local agency with attractive rates; Thrifty, 309 E. Millbrae Ave., Millbrae (692-0660). For dwntwn locations, consult the local telephone directory.

LIMOUSINE SERVICES: Carey Limousine (468-7550), Dav El Limousines (toll free 800/922-0343), and Four Star Limousine (386-9220).

TAXIS: Cabs may rarely be hailed on the street, but can be found on the waiting lines outside major hotels, or better still, summoned by phone. Fares are very high. Try **Allied Taxi** (826-9494), **Luxor Cab** (282-4141), **Veteran's Cab** (552-1300), or **Yellow Cab** (626-2345).

TRAIN: Amtrak, Transbay Terminal, 425 Mission St., at 1st St. (982-8512); avoid this neighborhood after dark. There is a regular shuttle-bus link with the station at Oakland, terminus for the major routes to the east and along the Pacific coast.

INTERCITY BUSES: Greyhound, 50 7th St. (558-6789).

FERRIES: Golden Gate Ferries, Ferry Bldg., Market St. (332-6600): Service to Sausalito.
Red & White Fleet, Pier 41, Fisherman's Wharf (546-2896): Service to Tiburon.

INFORMATION & TOURS

TOURIST INFORMATION: The **San Francisco Convention and Visitors Bureau,** 201 Third St., CA 94101 (415/974-6900).
Visitor Information Center, Hallidie Plaza, Powell St. and Market St. (415/391-2000).
International Visitors Center, 312 Sutter St., Suite 402 (415/986-1388): Reception facilities for foreign visitors.

San Francisco Chamber of Commerce, 465 California St., CA 94104 (415/392-4511).

For a **telephone recording** with an up-to-date listing of cultural events and shows, call 415/391-2001.

GUIDED TOURS: Alcatraz Tours (boat), Pier 41, The Embarcadero (546-2896): Guided tours of the penitentiary; it's advisable to make resv., one or more days in advance in summer, through Ticketron (392-7469). Not to be missed.

Bay cruises (boat), Blue & Gold Fleet, Pier 39, The Embarcadero (781-7877), and Red & White Fleet, Pier 41, The Embarcadero (546-2896): Boat trips on the bay; wonderful views. Daily year round; not to be missed.

Commodore Helicopters (helicopter), Pier 43, The Embarcadero (332-4482): Helicopter flights over the bay; unforgettable. Daily.

Express Tours (bus), serving the principal hotels (621-7738): 1-day excursions to Yosemite National Park, Lake Tahoe, Hearst Castle, etc.

Gray Line Tours (bus), 350 8th St. (558-9400): Many tours in the city and surroundings.

Star Lane Tours (minibus), 416 Francisco St. (982-2223): Visits to the wine cellars of Napa Valley; also 1-day trips to Carmel, Monterey, Yosemite National Park, and Muir Woods.

Wine Adventures, Inc. (bus), P.O. Box 3273, Yountville, CA 94599 (707/944-8468): 1- or several-day visits to Wine Country cellars; limo transfer from San Francisco.

SIGHTS, ATTRACTIONS & ACTIVITIES

ARCHITECTURAL HIGHLIGHTS: ☀🏛 Alcatraz Island, a rocky island in the bay, reached by boat from Pier 41 (556-0560): Nicknamed "The Rock," this former fort, converted in 1934 to a high-security prison, numbered among its famous inmates Al Capone, Alvin Karpis, Robert Stroud (alias "The Birdman of Alcatraz"), "Doc" Barker, and "Machine Gun" Kelly. Owes its name to the innumerable pelicans (*alcatraces* in Spanish) that used to roost there. Reputed to be "the prison from which no one escapes," the penitentiary was closed in 1963 by order of then–Attorney General Robert Kennedy because of its excessive operating costs; it has been converted into a museum visited by 800,000 people a year. It was occupied by a group of Native Americans from 1969 to 1971, by way of a symbolic protest. The visit is worthwhile, because the experience is unique and the island affords you an otherwise-unobtainable view of the bay, but it's a tiring excursion. Open daily (see "Guided Tours," above).

🏛 **Castro Theater,** Castro St. and Market St. (621-6120): Extravagant 1930s-style movie house in the heart of the gay district. Shows American and foreign classics, complete with an organist and enthusiastic audiences.

🏛 **City Hall,** Civic Center Plaza (554-4000): Imposing 1915 building in the French classical revival idiom, capped by a dome higher than the Capitol's in Washington.

☀🏛 **Embarcadero Center,** Clay St. and Sacramento St. between Drumm St. and Battery St.: The new business district, with a group of high-rises by well-known architect John Portman. Pedestrian walkways at several levels, fountains, modern sculpture, open-air concerts on fine days. A must-see.

🏛 **Ferry Building,** Embarcadero and Market St. (332-6600): Once the terminal for the ferries that crisscrossed the bay in all directions before the construction of the Golden Gate and Bay Bridges. Its 236-

ft. (72m) tower, erected in 1903, is a copy of the Moorish La Giralda tower in Seville. Today it houses the Port Authority; ferries leave for Sausalito from the southern end of the building. Should be seen.

Golden Gate Bridge, linking San Francisco to Sausalito, to the north of the bay: Designed by Joseph Strauss, the world's most famous (and most beautiful) bridge was built between 1933 and 1937 at a cost of $35 million. Its construction was a technological masterpiece, involving 200,000 tons of steel, 523,000 cu. yds. (400,000m³) of concrete, and 80 mi. (128km) of high-tension steel cable. It's also the world's most "deadly" bridge; 11 people were killed during construction, and another 700 have committed suicide from it since it was opened on May 28, 1937. The shining Golden Gate Bridge towers 220 ft. (67m) above the waters of the bay, and is used every day by almost 120,000 vehicles. Maintenance for the two 746-ft. (227m) towers and the 8,856-ft. (2.7km) span is provided by a team of 25 painters, who use 2 tons of red lead every week. Unforgettable view of San Francisco and the bay (overlook parking at the north end of the bridge). There's a toll, for southbound vehicles only. Worth the trip to San Francisco all by itself.

Levi Strauss Factory, 250 Valencia St. (565-9153): This is where, around the middle of the 19th century, Levi Strauss created history's first pair of blue jeans—and it's still operating. Adopted first by the miners of the gold rush, then by cowboys, blue jeans still serve as an emblem of American life. Tours Wed. Resv. requested.

Louise M. Davies Symphony Hall, Van Ness Ave. and Grove St. (431-5400): Home of the San Francisco Symphony Orchestra. Opened in 1980, this ultramodern 3,000-seat concert hall by Skidmore, Owings and Merrill has extremely sophisticated acoustics.

Marriott Hotel, 777 Market St. (896-1600): Nicknamed "The Wurlitzer," this 40-floor tower looking like a jukebox or a giant thermometer is San Francisco's most controversial building. Designed by California architect Tony Lumsden and opened in Nov 1989, the 1,500-room hotel is part of Yerba Buena Gardens, a 22-acre (8ha) real-estate development still under construction. Its two-colored mirror-glass frontage has a certain shock value—at least worth taking a look at.

Transamerica Pyramid, 600 Montgomery St. (983-4000): Designed by architect William L. Pereira, this 48-floor pyramid capped by a knife-edged point cost $34 million to build, and is considered by many to be the most spectacular and original high-rise in the U.S. Since the 853-ft. (260m) building was completed in 1972, it has become one of the emblems of San Francisco. A sight not to be missed.

War Memorial Opera House, Van Ness Ave. and Grove St. (864-3330): Home of the San Francisco Opera since its inauguration (1932). In 1945 the United Nations came into existence in this auditorium, and in 1951 it witnessed the signing of the American-Japanese peace treaty. Worth seeing.

BEACHES: **Baker Beach,** Lincoln Blvd., Presidio: Wonderful for sunbathing, but no swimming allowed.

China Beach, Sea Cliff Ave. and 29th Ave.: Small fine-sand, wind-protected beach near Lincoln Park; swimming permitted in summer.

Ocean Beach, Great Highway: 4 mi. (6km) of beaches and dunes, much frequented by hang-glider enthusiasts. Swimming here is unsafe.

Stinson Beach, 16 mi. (25km) NW on Calif. 1: Pretty beach at the foot of a mountain; swimming permitted in summer.

CABLE CARS: San Francisco's open-air **cable cars**—drawn by cables as the name implies—the city's most famous tourist attraction since 1873, were suspended from service from Sept 1982 to the spring of 1984 for an overhaul of their traction system. Since this involuntary interruption, the city's engaging streetcars, with standing passengers clustering on the steps like bunches of grapes, are once again scaling the steep streets of Nob Hill and Russian Hill, whose gradient in places reaches 21%. Of the 19th century's eight lines and 112 mi. (180km) of area reached, only three lines remain today, covering 11 mi. (17km): No. 59 (Powell-Mason), No. 60 (Hyde-Powell), and No. 61 (California–Van Ness). There is a flat $2 fare; the most scenic line is No. 60, from Hyde St. to Powell St.

CHURCHES/SYNAGOGUES: ☀ St. Mary's Cathedral, Geary St. and
Gough St. (567-2020): San Francisco's new (1970) cathedral, a spectacular modern building designed by Italian architect Pier Luigi Nervi on the site of the old basilica, which burned down in 1962. It comprises four soaring vaults of concrete clad in white Italian travertine, which meet at a height of 196 ft. (60m) in the shape of a cross. Don't miss the futuristic sculpture above the altar. Open daily.

HISTORIC BUILDINGS: ☀🏛 Haas-Lilienthal House, 2007 Franklin St. (441-
3004): Dating from 1886, this magnificent example of Queen Anne–style Victorian is one of the few private houses that survived the 1906 earthquake. Very fine furniture of the period. Open Wed and Sun afternoons.

    ☀🏛🏛 **Mission Dolores** (sometimes called **Mission San Francisco de Asis**), 16th St. and Dolores St. (621-8203): Sixth of the 21 missions built in California by the Franciscan Fr. Junípero Serra, this is the historic birthplace of San Francisco (1776). A fine Spanish Colonial building of whitewashed adobe brick that survived four major earthquakes. In the little cemetery adjoining are the graves of the first settlers and of the Native Americans who built the mission. Beside it, and in startling contrast to the primitive humility of the mission itself, is the huge Basilica of Mission Dolores (1916), a pompous piece of Spanish-Mexican baroque. Open daily.

    ☀🏛 **Whittier Mansion,** 2090 Jackson St. (567-1848): Built in 1896 by a wealthy businessman named William Whittier, this imposing Romanesque mansion with its red sandstone facing and stout anchoring towers is also a survivor of the 1906 earthquake. It's now the home of the California Historical Society. Sumptuous rococo interior; be sure to see the Turkish Smoking Room. Open Wed, Sat, and Sun afternoons; library open Tues–Sat.

MUSEUMS OF ART: ☀🏛🏛 Asian Art Museum, Golden Gate Park (668-
8921): The collection of Avery Brundage, once president of the International Olympic Committee, includes more than 10,000 works of art from Japan, China, Korea, etc., some more than 3,000 years old; their value, particularly that of the T'ang ceramics and the Khmer sculptures, is impossible to estimate. Because of the size and importance of the collection, it is exhibited in rotation. One of the most beautiful Far Eastern museums in the world, housed in the west wing of the M. H. De Young Museum (see below). An absolute must; open Wed–Sun.

    ☀🏛🏛 **California Palace of the Legion of Honor,** Lincoln Park (750-3600): The only museum in the U.S. entirely devoted to the art of France. Master paintings from the 16th to the 20th century: Fragonard, Georges de la Tour, Corot, Monet, Cézanne, etc. Fine Gobelins tapestries and an exceptional graphic-arts collection with more than 100,000 drawings, engravings, and illustrated books. Sculptures by Rodin. The Beaux Arts building, dating from 1924, is an exact replica of the Palace of the Legion of Honor in Paris. Fine surrounding park and splendid view of the Golden Gate. Open Wed–Sun.

    🏛 **Mexican Museum,** Fort Mason Center, Bldg. D, Laguna St. and Marina Blvd. S. (441-0404): Temporary exhibitions and

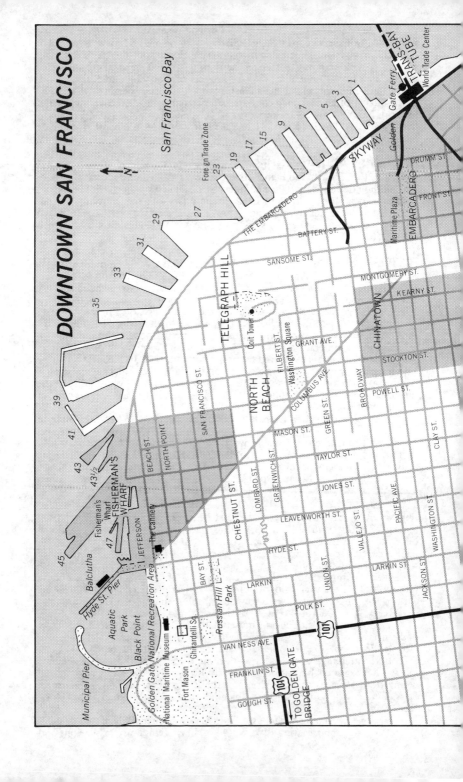

DOWNTOWN SAN FRANCISCO

San Francisco Bay

N

Foreign Trade Zone

TRANS-BAY TUBE

World Trade Center

Golden Gate Ferry

SKYWAY

DRUMM ST.

FRONT ST.

THE EMBARCADERO

Maritime Plaza

EMBARCADERO

BATTERY ST.

SANSOME ST.

MONTGOMERY ST.

KEARNY ST.

TELEGRAPH HILL

Coit Tower

Gilbert ST.

GRANT AVE.

CHINATOWN

STOCKTON ST.

Washington Square

NORTH BEACH

COLUMBUS AVE.

GREEN ST.

BROADWAY

POWELL ST.

SAN FRANCISCO ST.

MASON ST.

BEACH ST.

NORTH POINT

GREENWICH ST.

TAYLOR ST.

CLAY ST.

CHESTNUT ST.

JONES ST.

PACIFIC AVE.

FISHERMAN'S WHARF

Fisherman's Wharf

LEAVENWORTH ST.

VALLEJO ST

WASHINGTON ST.

JACKSON ST.

The Cannery

JEFFERSON

LOMBARD ST.

HYDE ST.

LARKIN ST.

Balclutha

Hyde St. Pier

Aquatic Park

Black Point

Golden Gate National Recreation Area

National Maritime Museum

Ghirardelli Sq.

Fort Mason

Russian Hill Park

BAY ST.

LARKIN

UNION ST.

POLK ST.

101

Municipal Pier

VAN NESS AVE.

FRANKLIN ST.

GOUGH ST.

101

TO GOLDEN GATE BRIDGE

29

27

31

33

35

39

41

43

43½

45

47

permanent collection of Mexican art from the pre-Columbian and colonial periods to the present day. Also works by modern Mexican-American artists. Open Wed–Sun.

☀️♨️♨️ **M. H. De Young Museum,** Golden Gate Park (750-3600): One of the best art collections in the U.S., with superb representation in Asian art (see the Asian Art Museum, above), but no less so in African, Egyptian, European, Polynesian, and other sectors—all housed in an 1894 building which was once part of the California Midwinter International Exposition. Among the best-known works on display are a *Madonna and Child* by Tintoretto, El Greco's *St. John the Baptist,* Frans Hals's *Cavalier in White,* and Bellini's *Portrait of the Doge Leonardo Loredano.* Note also the very fine John D. Rockefeller Collection of American art, with such major works as Charles Willson Peale's *Self-Portrait* and Charles Demuth's *Blue Plums.* Open Wed–Sun.

♨️ **Museum of Modern Art,** 401 Van Ness Ave. at McAllister St. (863-8800): The best of contemporary art; hundreds of remarkable paintings and sculptures from Matisse and Mark Rothko to Jackson Pollock and Clyfford Still. Occupies the third and fourth floors of the War Memorial Veterans Building. Open Tues–Sun.

MUSEUMS OF SCIENCE & HISTORY: ♨️ Balclutha, Hyde St. Pier, Aquatic Park (556-6435): A maritime museum, in an authentic British Cape Horner, built in 1886, which rounded the Horn 17 times. It's part of the National Maritime Museum (see below). Open daily.

☀️♨️ **Cable Car Barn Museum,** Washington St. and Mason Sts. (474-1887): Picturesque museum of San Francisco's own streetcars, including the first to be put into service in 1873. Movies, old photos, etc. See the strange traction system of the cable cars. Open daily.

☀️♨️ **California Academy of Sciences,** Golden Gate Park (750-7145): Comprehensive museum of natural history, including the **Morrison Planetarium** and the renowned **Steinhart Aquarium,** with more than 14,000 sea creatures. Fine collection of fossils and of North American birds. The **Earth and Space Hall** features a very realistic reproduction of an earthquake. Open daily.

♨️ **Chinese Historical Society of America,** 17 Jack Kerouac St. at Grant Ave. (391-1188): Illustrates the important part played by Chinese immigrants in the founding of San Francisco and the settlement of the American West. Unusual mementoes; fine collection of photographs. A must for history buffs; Open Wed–Sun.

☀️♨️ **Exploratorium,** 3601 Lyon St. (563-3200): This remarkably well-conceived and instructive museum of science and technology was opened in 1969, in a sort of imitation Greco-Roman temple originally built as the Palace of Fine Arts for the 1915 Panama-Pacific International Exposition. It offers more than 600 participatory exhibits in the fields of science, art, and human perception. Fascinating. Open Wed–Sun.

♨️ **National Maritime Museum,** Polk St. and Beach St. (556-8177): Interesting maritime museum in an Edwardian casino. Ship models and objects illustrating the history of navigation on the Pacific coast. The "floating" section of the museum is moored at the adjoining Hyde St. Pier: it comprises half a dozen carefully restored old ships, including the three-master *C. A. Thayer* (1895), the paddlewheel ferryboat *Eureka* (1890), the schooner *Alma* (1891), and the tug *Hercules* (1907). Open daily.

♨️ **Old U.S. Mint,** 5th St. and Mission St. (974-0788): Along with those in Denver and Philadelphia, one of the country's three mints. A fine 19th-century classical revival building. Note the impressive heap of gold ingots in the circular vault. Numismatic museum. Open Mon–Fri.

♨️ **U.S.S. *Pampanito*,** Pier 45, Fisherman's Wharf (929-0202): World War II submarine which took part in the Pacific campaigns. Visiting the interior of the vessel requires a certain aptitude for gymnastics! Open daily.

    Wells Fargo Bank History Museum, 420 Montgomery St. (396-2619): "History Room" with a Far Western stagecoach (Wells Fargo began life as a stagecoach company). Mementoes of the 1848 gold rush and the 1906 earthquake. Picturesque. Open Mon–Fri.

NIGHTTIME ENTERTAINMENT: Ever since the 19th century, when the legendary Barbary Coast was an irresistible attraction to sailors, adventurers, settlers, and gold prospectors, San Francisco has always been broad-minded about its nightlife. Witness today the porno dives and risqué nightclubs of Broadway and Columbus Ave., the domain of the topless, of dancing nude couples, and of mud-wrestling women. The biggest concentration of nightlife is in the **North Beach** neighborhood, particularly around Washington Sq., but jazz joints, bars, nightclubs, comedy clubs, and discos flourish all over town. As a general rule, nightclubs are not permitted to serve alcoholic beverages after 2am (see "Bars and Nightclubs," below).

OUTDOOR ART & PLAZAS: **Embarcadero Center,** Clay St. and Sacramento St. between Drumm St. and Battery St.: The sidewalk galleries and plazas of this ultramodern complex are embellished with monumental sculptures by Willi Gutmann, Louise Nevelson, and Nicholas Schöffer, as well as with many paintings and tapestries. At the eastern end of the center is an astonishing futuristic fountain by Armand Vaillancourt; should not be missed.

    St. Mary's Square, California St. and Quincy St.: Resplendent stainless-steel statue by Benjamino Bufano of Sun Yat-sen, founder and first president (1911–12) of the Republic of China, who lived in San Francisco for a while.

PANORAMAS: **Bank of America,** 555 California St. (433-7500): In the heart of the financial district, the West Coast's answer to Wall Street. Bar-restaurant (so-so), the Carnelian Room, on the 52nd floor (admission charge); one of the finest views of the city. Open daily.

    Coit Tower, Telegraph Hill Blvd. (362-8037): This 210-ft. (64m) tower, erected in 1933 on the top of Telegraph Hill as a memorial to the city's volunteer firemen, offers as beautiful a panorama of the bay as you're likely to find, especially at dawn or sunset. Beautiful mural frescoes. Open daily (elevator).

    Golden Gate Bridge, north of Presidio Park via U.S. 101: Wonderful panorama of the city and bay, looking south; overlook parking at the northern end of the bridge. Worth the trip all by itself (see "Architectural Highlights," above).

    San Francisco–Oakland Bay Bridge, between San Francisco and Oakland via I-80: Opened 6 months before the Golden Gate, on November 12, 1936, this enormous two-deck bridge has a particularly spectacular view of the city and bay, looking west (its upper deck was severely damaged by the earthquake of October 17, 1989); a sight not to be missed.

    Sausalito and Tiburon: See "Nearby Excursions," below.

    Twin Peaks, Twin Peaks Blvd.: Nicknamed "los pechos de la Chola" (the Indian woman's breasts) by the first Spanish settlers, these twin peaks, 910 ft. (277m) high, are famous for their clear view of San Francisco and the bay, especially along Market St., particularly at twilight.

PARKS & GARDENS: **Acres of Orchids,** 1450 El Camino Real at Calif. 82, South San Francisco (871-5655): The world's largest display of orchids and gardenias. Splendid tropical gardens. Guided tour of the laboratory where orchids are cloned. Fascinating. Open daily.

Angel Island, in the bay, reached by boat from Pier 43½: Small garden-island reserved for pedestrians, cyclists, and picnickers, with dozens of free-roaming stags and does. Frequent boat service daily in summer; weekends only the rest of the year. Fine view of the town.

Golden Gate Park, bounded by Lincoln Way, Great Hwy., Fulton St., and Stanyan St. (558-4268): Lying on the ocean to the west, this magnificent 1,017-acre (412ha) park, one of the most beautiful in the U.S., was reclaimed beginning in 1868 from a tract of bare sand dunes. Contains more than 6,000 different species of trees and plants, including acacia, spruce, and eucalyptus. Several museums (see above). Splendid Japanese garden and tropical hot houses. An absolute must.

Golden Gate Promenade, Marine Dr. between Fort Point and Fort Mason: Landscaped park along the shore of the bay; from Fort Point you have a clear view of the bridge and the city skyline.

Harding Park, Lake Merced Blvd. and Sloat Blvd.: Huge oceanfront park taking in Lake Merced (canoeing, fishing), a modern zoo, and a public golf course. Very popular with San Franciscans in summer.

Lincoln Park, 34th Ave. and Clement St.: On the ocean at the NW extremity of the city; very fine view of the Golden Gate Bridge, the city, and the Pacific.

The Presidio, bounded by Lincoln Blvd., Mason St., W. Pacific Ave., and Lyon St. (561-3870): The headquarters of the U.S. Sixth Army is on the site occupied by the original Spanish garrison fort in 1776, and lies in 1,450 acres (588ha) of park and shady garden. Military museum open Tues–Sun. Enter from Lombard St. and Lyon St. to the east, or 25th Ave. and El Camino del Mar to the west; there's a lovely scenic drive between these two points.

Seal Rocks, Point Lobos Ave.: Reefs thronged with elephant seals, sea lions, marine birds, and other ocean life; fine view.

Sigmund Stern Memorial Grove, along Sloat Blvd. nr. 19th Ave. (398-6551): Natural amphitheater sheltered by eucalyptus, redwoods and fir trees. On summer Sun afternoons hosts free outdoor concerts, Broadway musicals, operas, and ballets. This 63-acre (25.5ha) grove is also the perfect place for barbecues and picnics.

PERFORMING ARTS: For daily listings of all shows and cultural events, consult the entertainment pages of the daily papers *San Francisco Chronicle* (morning) and *San Francisco Examiner* (evening), especially their joint Sunday edition, as well as the monthly *San Francisco* magazine.

Note that **STBS,** a kiosk on Stockton St. at Union Sq. (433-7827), provides half-price, in-person sales of unsold tickets for day-of-performance events. Cash only, Tues–Sat.

Civic Auditorium, Civic Center (431-5400): Recitals; concerts by the San Francisco Pops Orchestra.

Club Fugazzi, 678 Green St. (421-4222): An old North Beach standby; cabaret-style shows.

Curran Theater, 445 Geary St. (474-3800): Musicals, Broadway hits.

Geary Theater, 415 Geary St. (673-6440): Home of the American Conservatory Theater; classical and contemporary theater (Oct–June).

Golden Gate Theatre, Taylor St., Golden Gate St., and Market St. (474-3800): Contemporary theater, Broadway hits.

Herbst Theatre, Civic Center, 401 Van Ness Ave. (626-6596): Ballet, opera, concerts, children's shows.

Louise M. Davies Symphony Hall, Civic Center, 201 Van Ness Ave. (431-5400): Home of the San Francisco Symphony, under principal conductor Herbert Blomstedt (Sept–May); recitals, concerts.

Magic Theater, Fort Mason Center, Bldg. D, Laguna St. and Marina Blvd. (441-8822): Modern and avant-garde theater.

Mason Street Theater, 340 Mason St. at Geary (981-3535): Off Broadway theater, comedy.

Masonic Auditorium, 1111 California St. (776-4917): Classical concerts, recitals, ballet.

Orpheum Theatre, 1192 Market St. (474-3800): Drama, comedy, touring companies. Home of the Civic Light Opera (May–Dec).

Palace of Fine Arts Theatre, 3601 Lyon St. (567-6642): Opera, concerts. The International Film Festival is held here annually.

Sigmund Stern Memorial Grove, Sloat Blvd. and 19th Ave. (398-6551): A 25,000-seat open-air auditorium; symphony concerts, opera, jazz, ballet. Free shows every Sun at 2pm June to mid-Aug, a tradition more than 50 years old.

Theatre on the Square, 450 Post St. (433-9500): Contemporary theater, drama, comedy.

Theater Rhinoceros, 2926 16th St. (861-5079): Modern and avant-garde theater of interest to the gay community.

War Memorial Opera House, Civic Center, 301 Van Ness Ave. (864-3330): Home of the San Francisco Ballet (artistic director: Helgi Tomasson), oldest company in the U.S. and, along with American Ballet Theater and New York City Ballet, one of the most highly regarded; also home of the San Francisco Opera Company (musical director: Terence McEwen). Sept–Dec.

SHOPPING: The Cannery, 2801 Leavenworth St. at Jefferson (771-3112): The 19th-century Del Monte fruit-processing factory, now a deluxe shopping center, with 50 boutiques, stores, and restaurants, a stone's throw from Fisherman's Wharf. Open daily.

Cost Plus Imports, 2552 Taylor St. (928-6200): Gadgets and objects from around the world at rock-bottom prices, a stone's throw from Fisherman's Wharf. Open daily.

Cow Hollow, Union St. between Van Ness Ave. and Steiner St.: The district for antique dealers and smart stores, with many bars and restaurants. Used as a setting for the movie *The Conversation.* Picturesque old houses.

Crocker Galleria, 50 Post St. (392-5522): Opened in 1982, this innovative shopping arcade is arranged on three levels under a spectacular glass canopy 70 ft. (21m) high and 275 ft. (83m) long; it resembles the well-known Galleria Vittorio Emmanuele in Milan. More than 50 shops, stores, and restaurants.

Ghirardelli Square, 900 North Point St. (775-5500): Incorporated into a former chocolate factory near Fisherman's Wharf, this picturesque shopping complex, embellished with patios and fountains, is a textbook example of urban renewal. A round 100 shops and restaurants. Very popular with tourists. Open daily.

Japan Center, bounded by Post St., Geary St., Laguna St., and Fillmore St. (922-6776): Designed by famous architect Minoru Yamasaki, this huge commercial development dates from 1986; it houses dozens of boutiques, shops, and art galleries as well as many restaurants, sushi bars, and Japanese baths. Exotic. Open daily.

Pier 39, The Embarcadero (981-7437): Yet another example of the city's talent for converting old industrial buildings (in this instance, a commercial dock not far from Fisherman's Wharf) into lively modern shopping centers. More than 140 different shops and restaurants. Open-air shows. Open daily.

San Francisco Center, 865 Market St. (495-5656): The city's newest shopping mall—in a city already legendary for its shopping centers—opened in 1989. Nine-level atrium with a circular escalator designed by Mitsubishi, the first in the country. Four floors are devoted to small shops, while Nordstrom's occupies the top five, earning the title of "store in the sky."

SPECIAL EVENTS: For the exact schedule of events below, consult the **San Francisco Convention and Visitors Bureau** (see "Tourist Information," above).

Chinese New Year (late Jan to Feb): Colorful dragon procession and fireworks through Chinatown's streets.

International Film Festival (late Mar to Apr): The oldest film festival in the U.S., and one of the most distinguished, held at the Palace of Fine Arts.

Cherry Blossom Festival (Apr): Festival of the Japanese community, timed to coincide with the flowering of the cherry trees in Japantown. Flower show, Japanese art festival.

Bay to Breakers Race (mid-May): World's biggest footrace: 7.5 mi. (12km) through the streets of San Francisco. Almost 100,000 contestants every year, some in the most bizarre costumes—a mixture of marathon and Mardi Gras.

Gay Freedom Day Parade (end of June): Tumultuous parade of the San Francisco gay community; colorful. Some 200,000 participants.

Midsummer Music Festival (June–Aug): Open-air classical-music festival in the Sigmund Stern Memorial Grove.

San Francisco Marathon (mid-July): Third in importance (after Boston and New York) in the U.S.; attracts more than 10,000 participants.

San Francisco Fair & Exhibition (Sept): Annual event.

Columbus Day Parade (Oct): Parades, drum majorettes, and oom-pah-pah oom-pah-pah; the Italian community festival at North Beach and Fisherman's Wharf.

Fleet Week (Oct): U.S. Navy regatta in the bay, with the Blue Angels doing their stuff overhead. The great sailors' festival.

Grand National Rodeo and Livestock Exposition (late Oct to early Nov): Horse show, cattle fair, rodeos. Cowboy atmosphere. At the Cow Palace.

SPORTS: San Francisco has four professional teams:

Baseball (Apr–Oct): Oakland A's, Oakland Stadium (638-4900); Giants, Candlestick Park (467-8000).

Basketball (Oct–Mar): Golden State Warriors, Oakland Coliseum (638-6000).

Football (Aug–Dec): 49ers, Candlestick Park (468-2249).

Horse Racing

Bay Meadows Racecourse, Bayshore Fwy. (U.S. 101) and Hillsdale Blvd., San Mateo, 20 mi. (35km) south (574-7223): Thoroughbred racing, Wed–Sun early Sept through Jan.

Golden Gate Fields, 1100 Eastshore Hwy., Albany, across the San Francisco–Oakland Bay Bridge (526-3020): Thoroughbred racing Feb–June and harness racing mid-June to mid-Aug, Tues–Sat.

Deep-Sea Fishing

Sport-fishing enthusiasts will find a charter fleet based year round at Fisherman's Wharf, with boats going out every day at dawn, particularly during salmon season (mid-Feb to mid-Nov). Average cost is $40 per person. Some recommended operators include **Captain Ron's Pacific Charters** (285-2000), **Ketchikan Sport Fishing Boat** (981-6269), **Lucky Lady Charter Boat** (826-6815), and **Wacky Jacky Sportfishing** (586-9800).

STROLLS: ⚱ **Castro Street,** around Market St.: The heart of San Francisco's most important gay neighborhood. Bars, restaurants, movie houses, and stores all—or almost all—bear the impress of one of the largest and most organized homosexual communities in the U.S., 110,000 strong. Straights are welcome; gawking is not.

☀☌ **Chinatown,** bounded by Broadway, Bush St., Kearny St., and Stockton St.: With 80,000 inhabitants, one of the largest Chinese cities outside Asia. Pagoda roofs, tea houses, dragon-shaped lamps, and gaudy shopfronts make this the most picturesque neighborhood in the city; its restaurants are among the best in the country, and its foodstalls are justly renowned. You should see the Chinatown Gateway Arch at Grant Ave. and Bush St., the monumental entry to Chinatown, erected in 1970; Old St. Mary's Church, the former cathedral built in 1854, at Grant Ave. and California St.; the Buddha Universal Church on Washington St. across from Portsmouth Sq., the largest Buddhist temple in the U.S.; and the surprising statue of Sun Yat-sen, founder and first president of the Republic of China, on St. Mary's Sq. Tours organized by the Chinese Cultural Center, 750 Kearny St. (986-1822).

    Cow Hollow (see "Shopping," above).

    Filbert Street, between Hyde St. and Leavenworth St.: The steepest street in San Francisco, at an angle of 31.5°. Spectacular; has to be seen.

    Fisherman's Wharf, the Embarcaderos, between Taylor St. and Powell St.: Once the city's fishing port, with more than 400 boats; today excessively commercialized. Cafés, bars, restaurants (mostly mediocre) in a fairground atmosphere. The most popular tourist attraction in the U.S. after Walt Disney World, drawing 13 million visitors a year.

    49 Mile Drive: A 49-mi. (78km) circular drive, marked by signs showing a blue-and-white seagull. The trip can be made by car inside a day, and will take you to most of the city's tourist attractions: Chinatown, Nob Hill, Fisherman's Wharf, Golden Gate Park, Mission Dolores, the Civic Center, Golden Gate Bridge, Telegraph Hill, etc. A free map of the route may be obtained from the Visitor Information Center, Hallidie Plaza (lower level), Powell St. and Market St. You should plan to make the trip.

    Japantown/Nihonmachi, Geary St. and Post St. between Fillmore St. and Laguna St.: A Japanese enclave in the heart of San Francisco. Japan Center, with dozens of stores, tea houses, and Japanese restaurants (see "Shopping," above); kabuki theater; Cultural Center, with interesting temporary exhibitions. Note the handsome Peace Plaza with its monumental gate, Japanese gardens, and Peace Pagoda. Martial-arts demonstrations; Japanese music and dance.

    Lombard Street, between Hyde St. and Leavenworth St.: The crookedest (and most blooming) street in San Francisco, with 10 hairpin bends in less than 500 ft. (150m). One of the chase sequences in the movie *Bullitt* was shot here.

    Nob Hill, around California St. and Powell St.: "Millionaires' Hill," rising to a height of 376 ft. (115m). Once home to California gold-mining and railroad tycoons ("Nob" is a contraction of "Nabob"); now a neighborhood of luxury hotels and smart apartment buildings. Remains a bastion of the city's old money. Note the Gothic Revival Grace Cathedral at 1051 Taylor St. and the Masonic Temple at California St. and Taylor St. Elegant.

    North Beach, around Washington Sq.: The city's Little Italy and Greenwich Village, both. In spite of its name, it has no beach; it's more like a neighborhood in Genoa or Bologna. A multitude of food shops, *trattorie*, cafés, strip joints, nightclubs (this is where the "topless" phenomenon first saw the light, to say nothing of beatniks and hippies). A colorful neighborhood, where at least a third of San Francisco's 150,000 Italians make their homes, as well as Basque and Chinese descendants. You should visit the **City Lights bookstore** at 261 Columbus Ave. (362-8193), a shrine of modern American poetry made famous by Lawrence Ferlinghetti; also the nearby literary bars, **Vesuvio's Cafe,** 255 Columbus Ave. (362-3370), and **Tosca Café,** 242 Columbus Ave. (391-1244). An absolute must.

    Russian Hill, around Green St. and Leavenworth St.: In the 19th century this was the artists' and writers' quarter; now it's one of the city's smartest residential neighborhoods. Dozens of interesting homes and buildings along Green St.

SoMa (South of Market St.), bounded by Mission St., 1st St., Townsend St., and Division St.: San Francisco's version of New York's SoHo. Once the rough, threatening preserve of butcher-supply houses, winos, struggling artists, and gay men dressed in black-leather motorcycle outfits, SoMa has suddenly become fashionable. Now the streets are lined with hit restaurants, art galleries, nightclubs, and trendy fashion outlets.

Telegraph Hill, around Lombard St. and Kearny St.: The steepest of San Francisco's hills, rising up to the Coit Tower and its famous view. A tangle of steep lanes, flights of steps, tiny gardens, and enchanting old frame houses on Montgomery St., Filbert Steps St., Greenwich Steps, Calhoun Terrace, Alta St., and so on. A demanding walk, but you mustn't miss it.

Union Square, bounded by Powell St., Stockton St., Post St., and Geary St.: The heart of the city's shopping district, with shops, department stores, hotels, restaurants, and fashionable bars. Very lively. On the east side of the square, with its gardens and fountain by Ruth Azawa, is the elegant little Maiden Lane, lined with luxury shops. In the 19th century it was the most ill-famed street on the Barbary Coast, the old red-light district destroyed by the 1906 earthquake.

THEME PARKS: Marine World Africa USA, Marine World Pkwy., in Vallejo, 30 mi. (48km) NE on I-80 (707/643-6722): Huge theme park and zoo with over 1,000 animals, from killer whale and dolphin to elephant and tiger. Also such water sports as boating and waterskiing; animal acts. Open Wed–Sun year round; 40 min. from dwntwn. Ferry service from Fisherman's Wharf (50 min.) by Red and White Shuttle Line (546-2896).

Great America Theme Park, in Santa Clara, 45 mi. (72km) SE on U.S. 101 (408/988-1800): A 100-acre (40ha) amusement park with more than 100 attractions including four giant roller coasters and The Edge, a real terrorizer, free-fall ride. Variety shows. Reconstructions of pioneer villages. Open daily in summer, wknds only in spring and fall; closed in winter. 45 min. from dwntwn.

ZOOS: San Francisco Zoo, Sloat Blvd. at 45th Ave. (661-2023): Zoo of very modern design on the ocean. More than 1,000 animals from around the world, including such rarities as a white tiger, dwarf hippopotamus, okapis, and koalas. Fine collection of apes and exotic monkeys. Mini-train for visitors. You should see it, if only for the beauty of the setting. Open daily.

ACCOMMODATIONS

A Note on Accommodations: Room rates in San Francisco are coded as follows: **VE,** Very Expensive ($140 and up); **E,** Expensive ($90–$140); **M,** Moderate ($60–$90); **I,** Inexpensive ($30–$60); **B,** Budget (up to $30). A listing of toll free numbers is in the Appendix.

Personal Favorites (in order of preference)

Stanford Court Stouffer (dwntwn), 905 California St., CA 94108 (415/989-3500; toll free, see Stouffer). 402 rms, A/C, cable color TV. AE, CB, DC, MC, V. Valet gar. $18, two rests. (including Fournou's Ovens), bars, rm svce, hrdrsr, boutiques, concierge, free crib. *Note:* The European-style grand hotel at its best. From the Tiffany-style stained-glass dome in the lobby to the four-poster beds in the rms or the miniature TV sets in the marble bathrooms, you'll find a happy combination of luxury and elegance in an atmosphere exuding the charm of a gentleman's club. Svce is exemplary, and the rest. one of the most popular in San Francisco. In the heart of the fashionable Nob Hill district. This is one of the 12 best hotels in the U.S. Big business clientele; no groups, no conventions. A San Francisco landmark since 1912. **VE**

Mandarin Oriental (dwntwn), 222 Sansome St., CA 94104 (415/885-0999; toll free 800/526-6566). 160 rms, A/C, color TV, in-rm movies. AE, CB, DC, MC, V. Parking $18, health club, rest. (Silks), bar, 24-hr. rm svce, nightclub, boutiques, concierge, free crib. *Note:* A grand hotel in the sky, on the top 11 floors of the First Interstate Center, two twin 48-story towers, linked by "skybridges" w. an unparalleled view of the city and the bay. On each floor there are no more than seven very spacious rms or suites w. private balconies, minibars, and wonderful views. Ultra-luxurious pastel-toned decor and furnishings. Exemplary svce; fine quality rest.; well-equipped business center. Belongs to Hong Kong's Mandarin chain of luxury hotels. **VE**

Sherman House (nr. dwntwn), 2160 Green St., CA 94123 (415/563-3600; toll free 800/345-3457). 15 rms, A/C, cable color TV. AE, MC, V. Gar. $10, rest., bar, 24-hr. rm svce. *Note:* Enchanting four-story Victorian house (no elevator), regarded as the "in" place to stay in San Francisco. Perfection in every detail, from the luxurious Second Empire decor of its rms (w. fireplaces and four-poster beds) to the inspired cuisine of Swiss chef Paul Grutter and the faultless svce; you'll have a memorable stay here. Frequented by show-biz personalities (Bill Cosby and Johnny Carson among them) who appreciate its intimacy and elegance. You'll have to reserve a long time in advance.**VE**

Mansion Hotel (nr. dwntwn), 2220 Sacramento St., CA 94115 (415/929-9444). 19 rms, no A/C. AE, CB, DC, MC, V. Limited parking, rest. (reserved for hotel guests), 24-hr. rm svce, concierge, free breakfast. *Note:* Elegant Queen Anne–style home in the heart of Pacific Heights, a designated historic landmark, w. a score of comfortable period-furnished rms. Interesting, unusual ambience and decor; note the sculptures by Benjamino Bufano. Highly recommended rest. Winning reception and svce; concerts every evening; nice little private grdn—in a word, everything you could want if you hate mass tourism. **E–VE**

Beresford (dwntwn), 635 Sutter St., CA 94102 (415/673-9900; toll free 800/227-4048). 114 rms; no A/C; color TV. AE, CB, DC, MC, V. Gar. $11, coffee shop, bar, valet svce, free crib. *Note:* Charming old British hotel atmosphere, a stone's throw from Union Sq. Rms a little small but comfortable, some w. refrigerators; private grdn; courteous, efficient svce. Very good value; clientele of regulars. **M**

Cartwright (dwntwn), 524 Sutter St., CA 94102 (415/421-2865; toll free 800/227-3844). 114 rms, A/C (in a third of the rms), color TV. AE, DC, MC, V. Parking $10, coffee shop (breakfast and lunch only), valet svce, free crib. *Note:* Small hotel nr. Union Sq., aging but remarkably well run. Rms relatively small but comfortable and prettily decorated (antiques and fresh flowers in every rm), w. views over the city, most of them w. refrigerators. Rather noisy neighborhood. Good value; clientele of regulars. **M**

Essex (dwntwn), 684 Ellis St. (at Larkin), CA 94109 (415/474-4664; toll free 800/453-7739). 100 rms; no A/C; color TV. AE, MC, V. No private parking; coffee shop adj., free crib. *Note:* Elderly but very well kept small hotel near the Civic Center. Serviceably comfortable, meticulously clean rms, some w. balconies but some sharing a bath. Reception w. a smile. An excellent buy for the budget traveler. **I**

Other Accommodations (from top bracket to budget)

Four Seasons Clift (dwntwn), 495 Geary St., CA 94102 (415/775-4700; toll free, see Four Seasons). 329 rms, A/C, color TV, in-rm movies. AE, CB, DC, MC, V. Valet parking $18, two rests. (including the French Rm), bar, piano bar, 24-hr. rm svce, concierge, free crib. *Note:* Distinguished old grand hotel, elegantly and tastefully decorated; spacious rms w. minibars. The personalized svce is quite remarkable. Renowned rest. and wine cellar; superb art deco bar (Redwood Rm). Upscale business clientele. One of the best places to stay in San Francisco since 1915. Interesting wknd discounts. **VE**

🍴🍴🍴🍴 **The Mark Hopkins Inter-Continental** (dwntwn), 1 Nob Hill, CA 94108 (415/392-3434; toll free, see Inter-Continental). 392 rms, A/C, color TV. AE, CB, DS, MC, V. Valet gar. $18, two rests. (including Nob Hill), coffee shop, two bars (including the famous Top of the Mark, with 360° panoramic views of the city), 24-hr. rm svce, nightclub, hrdrsr, boutiques, concierge, free crib. *Note:* All the great have patronized this local institution, from Frank Sinatra to the late Emperor of Ethiopia, Haile Selassie. From "Millionaires' Hill"—Nob Hill—this elegant caravanserai overlooks Chinatown and the financial district; the rms on the upper floors (some w. balconies) have a superb view of the bay. Polished, efficient svce; one of the best-known bars in San Francisco. Has recently opened its doors to groups. Interesting wknd packages. **VE**

☀🍴🍴🍴 **Campton Place** (formerly the Drake Wiltshire Hotel; dwntwn), 340 Stockton St., CA 94108 (415/781-5555; toll free, see Preferred). 120 rms, A/C, color TV. AE, CB, DC, MC, V. Valet parking $20, rest. (Campton Place), bar, rm svce, concierge, free crib. *Note:* Small luxury hotel just off Union Sq., entirely renovated at a cost of $18 million. All the comfort, elegance, and refinement of a European grand hotel. Soundproofed rms w. period furniture and marble bathrooms. Polished, attentive svce; butlers available as needed! Rest. of a very high order; roof grdn. The favorite of those in-the-know. **VE**

🍴🍴🍴 **The Donatello** (formerly the Pacific Plaza; dwntwn), 501 Post St., CA 94102 (415/441-7100; toll free 800/227-3184). 95 rms, A/C, color TV. AE, CB, DC, MC, V. Valet gar. $16, health club, sauna, rest. (Donatello), bar, rm svce, concierge, free crib. *Note:* One of the new stars of the local luxury-hotel scene, just off Union Sq. Elegant Italian Renaissance decor; spacious, elegant rms w. balconies, minibars, and a profusion of houseplants. Personalized svce; serene, intimate ambience. Very good Italian rest. Clientele of VIPs and wealthy Europeans. Member of the prestigious Relais et Châteaux hotel chain. **VE**

☀🍴🍴🍴 **Fairmont Hotel and Tower** (dwntwn), 950 Mason St., CA 94106 (415/772-5000; toll free, see Fairmont). 595 rms, A/C, color TV, in-rm movies. AE, CB, DC, MC, V. Valet gar. $16, health club, five rests. (including Squire), eight bars, 24-hr. rm svce, disco, hrdrsr, boutiques, concierge, crib $30. *Note:* A venerable, reputable grand hotel now topped by a rather brutally modern tower. The older (and better) part of the hotel, destroyed in the 1906 earthquake, was rebuilt in the following year. Still has style in spite of the throng of conventioneers, but sometimes crowded and noisy. Flawless comfort and svce. Wonderful view of the whole city from the Crown Rm rest. at the top (reached by an outside, glass-walled elevator). Roof grdn. Boasts one of the most expensive suites in the U.S., at $5,000 a night plus tax. VIP and upscale business clientele. Was the model for the St. Gregory in ABC's "Hotel" TV series. **VE**

🍴🍴🍴 **Hyatt Regency San Francisco** (dwntwn), 5 Embarcadero Center, CA 94111 (415/788-1234; toll free, see Hyatt). 803 rms, A/C, color TV, in-rm movies. AE, CB, DC, MC, V. Valet gar. $18, three rests. (including the Equinox), coffee shop, revolving bar at the top, 24-hr. rm svce, disco, hrdrsr, boutiques, concierge, free crib. *Note:* Building of interesting futuristic structure, inspired by the Aztec pyramids, in the Embarcadero Center, within easy reach of the business district; dramatic 17-story lobby w. indoor grdns, fountains, and sculpture. Modern, comfortable rms, but mediocre svce. Group and business clientele; very lively. Two VIP floors. Wknd discounts. **VE**

🍴🍴🍴 **Nikko** (dwntwn), 222 Mason St. (at O'Farrell St.), CA 94102 (415/394-1111; toll free 800/645-5687). 525 rms, A/C, color TV, in-rm movies. AE, CB, DC, MC, V. Valet parking $16, pool, health club, sauna, two rests. (including Les Célébrités), coffee shop, bars, 24-hr. rm svce, nightclub, hrdrsr, drugstore, concierge, free crib. *Note:* Ultramodern and impressive 25-floor tower; huge elegant rms w. marble bath, minibar, and remote-control TV. Rest. of quality; fully equipped business center; thoughtful, polished svce. Both Japanese and American big business favor this hotel, which has free shuttle svce with the financial district. Interesting wknd packages; very central location. **VE**

Holiday Inn Financial District (dwntwn), 750 Kearny St., CA 94108 (415/433-6600; toll free, see Holiday Inns). 566 rms, A/C, color TV, in-rm movies. AE, CB, DC, MC, V. Free gar., coffee shop, bar, rm svce, nightclub, boutiques. *Note:* Enormous 27-floor tourist barracks nr. Chinatown. All rms have balconies; many overlook the bay. The essence of Holiday Inns. Group and business clientele; rates are too high for what it is. **E–VE**

Miyako (nr. dwntwn), 1625 Post St., CA 94115 (415/922-3200; toll free 800/533-4567). 208 rms, A/C, color TV, in-rm movies. AE, CB, DC, MC, V. Gar. $15, rest. (The Restaurant), bar, rm svce, boutiques, concierge, free crib. *Note:* Modern, comfortable tower in the Japan Center; spacious lobby overlooking pretty Japanese grdns. Choice of Western or tatami rms. Efficient bilingual svce; acceptable rest. but no more. Clientele of Japanese tourists and American business travelers. Recently underwent a $10-million renovation. **E–VE**

Queen Anne (nr. dwntwn), 1590 Sutter St., CA 94109 (415/441-2828; toll free 800/227-3970). 49 rms; no A/C; color TV. AE, CB, DC, MC, V. Valet gar. $4; no bar or rest.; valet svce, concierge, free breakfast, free crib. *Note:* Beautiful century-old Victorian building, a designated historic landmark, now elegantly restored. Each rm or suite (some w. fireplace) is decorated in a different style. Much period furniture; fine carved staircase. Romantic atmosphere; attentive reception and svce. Excellent place to stay, 10 min. from dwntwn. **E–VE**

Raphael Hotel (dwntwn), 386 Geary St. at Mason, CA 94102 (415/986-2000; toll free 800/821-5343). 152 rms, A/C, color TV, in-rm movies. AE, CB, DC, MC, V. Valet gar. $13, rest., bar, rm svce, free crib. *Note:* Charming, cozy, comfortable hotel nr. Union Sq. Elegantly decorated rms, some on the skimpy side. Personalized svce. Very centrally located. Good value overall; a fine place to stay. **E**

Villa Florence (dwntwn), 225 Powell St., CA 94102 (415/397-7700; toll free 800/553-4411). 177 rms, A/C, color TV, in-rm movies. AE, CB, DC, MC, V. Valet gar. $14, rest. (Kuleto's), bar, rm svce, concierge, free crib. *Note:* Older European-style hotel, friendly and inviting. The decor of the lobby is a little faded, but rms are comfortable and pleasant, w. refrigerator. Very good rest. serving (as it should) Italian food. Friendly svce. Conveniently located a block from Union Sq. but in a spot with lots of noise, particularly from streetcars. Package-tour and convention clientele. **E**

Canterbury–Whitehall Inn (dwntwn), 750 Sutter St., CA 94109 (415/474-6464; toll free, see Best Western). 267 rms, A/C, color TV, free in-rm movies. AE, CB, DC, MC, V. Gar. $8, rest., bar, valet svce. *Note:* Charming older hotel in the heart of dwntwn. Much antique furniture. Intimate atmosphere, comfortable rms. The rest., Lehr's Greenhouse, is indeed a sort of tropical greenhouse, and worth seeing. Friendly, cheerful svce; rather noisy environment; recently renovated. **M–E**

Chancellor (dwntwn), 433 Powell St., CA 94102 (415/362-2004; toll free 800/428-4748). 140 rms; no A/C; color TV, in-rm movies. AE, CB, DC, MC, V. Adj. parking $14, rest. (By the Square), bar, valet svce, free crib. *Note:* Modernized old hotel centrally located in the heart of San Francisco. Original Edwardian decor w. marble lobby, orchids, and potted palms. Rather skimpy rms. Comfort and svce above average; acceptable rest. Good value. Family owned since 1914. **M–E**

Seal Rock Inn (nr. dwntwn), 545 Point Lobos Ave., CA 94121 (415/752-8000). 27 rms, A/C, cable color TV. AE, CB, DC, MC, V. Free parking, pool, rest. (breakfast and lunch only), valet svce, crib $2. *Note:* Charming little rococo hotel right on the ocean. Fine view of the Pacific and the reefs populated w. sea creatures. Spacious, inviting rms w. refrigerators, some

w. kitchenettes and fireplaces. Private grdn and patio. An excellent place to stay if you like to be away from it all; 25 min. from dwntwn. **M–E,** but lower rates mid-Sept to mid-May.

♀♂ **Grant Plaza** (dwntwn), 465 Grant St., CA 94108 (415/434-3883; toll free 800/472-6899). 72 rms, A/C, color TV. AE, MC, V. Parking $8, adj. 24-hr. coffee shop, valet service, crib $7. *Note:* Small hotel, economy-class but acceptable, on the edge of Chinatown. Recently redecorated and refurnished. Functionally comfortable rms. Book at least 2 weeks ahead. Good value. **I–M**

♀♂ **San Remo** (dwntwn), 2237 Mason St., CA 94133 (415/776-8688). 62 rms, A/C. MC, V. No private parking; bar. *Note:* Nice elderly hotel of Victorian appearance, halfway between Fisherman's Wharf and North Beach. Antique furniture and original works of art. Inviting rms, all w. shared bath. Friendly svce; good value overall. **I–M**

♀♂ **Sheehan Hotel** (dwntwn), 620 Sutter St., CA 94102 (415/775-6500; toll free 800/848-1529). 56 rms, A/C, color TV. AE, DC, MC, V. Parking $6, pool, health club, valet svce, free breakfast. *Note:* Clean, comfortable old hotel close to Union Sq. and across the street from trendy art galleries. Elegant lobby. Friendly management. A very good value. **I–M**

Airport Accommodations

♀♂♀ **Amfac Hotel** (formerly the Airport Marina; vic.), 1380 Bayshore Hwy., Burlingame, CA 94010 (415/347-5444; toll free, see Amfac). 329 rms, A/C, color TV, in-rm movies. AE, CB, DC, MC, V. Free parking, pool, rest., coffee shop, bars, rm svce, nightclub, hrdrsr, boutiques, concierge, free crib. *Note:* Large, modern, functional 10-story hotel. Rather overburdened svce; comfortable, well-soundproofed rms, some w. refrigerators, many overlooking the bay. 5 min. from the airport; free limo. Ideal for a stopover between flights. 25 min. from dwntwn. **E**

Accommodations in the Vicinity

☼♀♀♀ **Claremont Resort Hotel** (vic.), Domingo Ave. and Ashby Ave., Oakland, CA 94623 (415/843-3000; toll free, see Preferred). 239 rms, A/C, color TV, in-rm movies. AE, CB, DC, MC, V. Valet parking $10, pool, health club, 10 tennis courts, sauna, massage, rest. (Pavilion Rm), coffee shop, bar, rm svce, disco, hrdrsr, free crib. *Note:* Splendid turn-of-the-century castle on 20 acres (8ha) of park and grdn. Elegant Victorian decor w. period furniture, Oriental rugs, and a fine collection of artwork. The guestbook bears the signatures of innumerable celebrities, from former Pres. Harry S Truman to actor Clint Eastwood. Spacious, inviting rms, the best overlooking San Francisco Bay; excellent rest.; comprehensive health spa w. exercise rms and saunas; unusually polished svce. A tranquil green oasis 35 min. from dwntwn San Francisco. Free shuttle to/from the Oakland airport. **E–VE**

☼♀♀ **Alta Mira Hotel** (vic.), 125 Bulkley Ave., Sausalito, CA 94965 (415/332-1350). 36 rms and 14 cottages; no A/C. AE, CB, DC, MC, V. Valet parking $6, rest., bar, rm svce. *Note:* Enchanting little hotel on the heights of Sausalito, looking out over the bay and the splendid panorama of San Francisco. Elegantly decorated rms, some w. views of the city and the Golden Gate. Individual cottages w. fireplaces. Attentive, personalized svce; acceptable rest. An elegant, comfortable haven of peace 25 min. from dwntwn across the Golden Gate Bridge. Resv. advised, well ahead of time. **M–E** (rms), **E–VE** (cottages).

☼♀♀ **Casa Madrona** (vic.), 801 Bridgeway, Sausalito, CA 94965 (415/332-0502). 32 rms and 5 cottages; no A/C. AE, MC, V. Free parking, boating, rest., bar, rm svce, free breakfast. *Note:* Italianate mansion dating from 1885. Period furniture in the rms, most of which have refrigerators, fireplaces, and balconies; those in the new wing are particularly comfortable. Courteous reception and svce; romantic atmosphere; pretty, country-style

decor. Very praiseworthy rest. serving French-Californian food. You should reserve far in advance. **E–VE** (hotel), **VE** (cottages).

YMCA / Youth Hostels

Golden Gate Hostel (vic.), 941 Fort Barry Rd., Sausalito, CA 94965
(415/331-2777). 60 beds; resv. a must in summer. Rustic youth hostel set
among trees and grdns. 30 min. from dwntwn, across the Golden Gate Bridge.

San Francisco International Hostel (nr. dwntwn), Bldg. 240, Fort Mason,
San Francisco, CA 94123 (415/771-7277). 165 beds. Clean youth hostel offering limited comfort. Resv. advised. 20 min. from dwntwn.

YMCA (dwntwn), 166 Embarcadero, San Francisco, CA 94111 (415/392-
2191). 270 rms. Men and women. Very centrally located. Pool, health facilities,
rest.

YMCA (nr. dwntwn), 220 Golden Gate Ave., San Francisco, CA 94102
(415/885-0460). 100 rms. Men and women. Health club, pool. 5 min. from
dwntwn.

RESTAURANTS

A Note on Restaurant Prices: San Francisco restaurant prices, per person,
excluding drinks and service charges, are coded as follows: **VE,** Very Expensive
($60 and up); **E,** Expensive ($40–$60); **M,** Moderate ($25–$40); **I,** Inexpensive
($15–$25); **B,** Budget (up to $15).

Personal Favorites (in order of preference)

Campton Place Restaurant (dwntwn), in the Campton Place
(see "Accommodations," above) (781-5155). A/C.
Breakfast/lunch/dinner daily, brunch Sun. AE, CB, DC, MC, V. Jkt. *Specialties:*
cedar-smoked sea scallops, lamb chops w. wild-onion cakes, sautéed veal steak w.
white truffles, rock lobster w. blue-corn cakes, banana sour-cream pancakes w.
black-walnut butter. Very good list of California wines; menu changes regularly.
Note: Long directed by Barry Ogden, one of the most talented exponents of
American nouvelle cuisine (see the Lark Creek Inn, below), Campton Place
makes it a point of honor to use only the finest regional ingredients, drawn from
all over the U.S. The result is an imaginative, sophisticated bill of fare deserving
all manner of high praise. Plush, intimate decorative scheme in tones of taupe
and salmon-pink w. some exotic Oriental touches. Flawless svce; resv. several
days ahead. One of the best rests. in California. Valet parking. *American.* **E–VE**

Lark Creek Inn (vic.), 234 Magnolia Ave., Larkspur (924-
7766). Lunch Mon–Fri, dinner daily; closed Dec 25. AE, CB,
DC, MC, V. *Specialties:* clambake; braised oxtail w. scalloped turnips; roast quail
w. homemade egg noodles and wild mushrooms; braised pork shoulder w. white
beans, kale, and smoked hamhock; grilled salmon w. shrimp and scallion fritters;
Yankee pot roast; butterscotch pudding. Menu changes daily. Magnificent wine
list at enticing prices. *Note:* Bradley Odgen, who created a golden age at
Campton Place (see above) took over the reins in Apr 1989 at this delightful
country house in the heart of the woods. Inspired country cooking: highest quality fresh-grown produce at very reasonable prices served in an elegant Victorian
setting. Outdoor dining on fine days. Svce w. a smile. Well worth the 25-min.
drive from San Francisco over the Golden gate Bridge and along U.S. 101N to
the Tamalpais-Paradise exit. The newest great rest. in San Francisco. *American.*
I–M

Tommy Toy's Haute Cuisine Chinoise (dwntwn), 655 Montgomery St. (397-4888). A/C. Lunch Mon–Fri, dinner daily;
closed hols. AE, CB, DC, MC, V. Jkt. *Specialties:* snails à la chinoise, minced
squab Imperial, lamb Szechuan w. spinach, lobster in black-bean sauce, veal tenderloin w. ginger sauce, chicken chrysanthemum, mango mousse w. raspberry
coulis, green-tea ice cream. *Note:* Tommy Toy, also owner of the flashy, popular
Imperial Palace, is the unchallenged king of "Asian nouvelle cuisine," a refined,
delicate blending of French and Chinese traditions. Opulent decor inspired by

the Empress Dowager's reading rm. High caliber reception and svce. Resv. a must. *Chinese.* **M**

☕☕ **Square One** (dwntwn), 190 Pacific Ave. at Front St. (788-1110). A/C. Lunch Mon–Fri, dinner daily; closed hols. AE, DC, MC, V. Jkt. *Specialties:* mixed salads, veal chop w. pappardelle pasta, paella, baked sturgeon w. grilled eggplant, couscous w. coriander vinaigrette, feijoada (Brazilian national dish), strawberries w. moscato-amaretto mousse. Superb wine list at restrained prices. *Note:* The contemporary decor w. a view of the open kitchen is no great added attraction, but the Mediterranean-inspired cooking of Joyce Goldstein is worth a visit for its own sake. Emphasis is on quality ingredients; the menu changes daily according to season. Exemplary svce; many regular patrons. Resv. strongly advised. *American.* **I–M**

☀☕☕ **Tadich Grill** (dwntwn), 240 California St. (391-2373). A/C. Lunch/dinner Mon–Fri (until 9pm); closed hols. No credit cards. Jkt. *Specialties:* clam chowder, tortellini Alfredo, sole Rex, hangtown fry, cioppino (California seafood stew), broiled sea bass, shrimp Diablo, steak, lamb chops, catch of the day. Excellent cheesecake. *Note:* The oldest rest. in San Francisco, dating from the gold-rush year 1849, keeps delighting lovers of steak and seafood generation after generation. Choice ingredients; the old-pub decor is original. Ultra-professional svce. Packed at lunch, mostly w. bankers and businesspeople; no resv., but you can have an agreeable wait at the bar nr. the entrance where regulars prefer to have their lunch. *Steak/Seafood.* **I–M**

☕☕ **China Moon Café** (dwntwn), 639 Post St. (775-4789). A/C. Lunch Mon–Sat, dinner daily; closed hols. MC, V. *Specialties:* dim sum, 10-spice pork, pot-browned noodle pillows, spicy lamb w. sweet red peppers and onions, steamed salmon w. mustard sauce. Interesting selection of California wines. *Note:* This nontraditional Chinese food reflects the originality of the excellent American chef, Barbara Tropp. The Californian and Chinese blend results in some new and often admirable taste sensations. Cafeteria decor and atmosphere in vaguely art deco style. No smoking; resv. ahead. *Chinese/American.* **I–M**

☕ **Cadillac Bar** (dwntwn), 1 Holland Court off Howard (543-8226). A/C. Lunch/dinner dinner; closed hols. AE, CB, DC, MC, V. *Specialties:* tacos, carnitas, broiled fish Veracruzana, crabmeat enchiladas, Botana platter (half chicken, steak, carnitas, queso flameado). Excellent house margaritas. *Note:* In a huge converted warehouse w. ceiling fans, very nr. the Moscone Convention Center, Cadillac attracts a host of devotees of real Mexican food and mesquite-grilled specialties. The chefs perform before your eyes, behind great walls of glass. Congenial but noisy atmosphere, w. the inevitable mariachi band. Prompt, cheerful svce. Locally popular, especially at lunch. *Mexican.* **I**

Other Restaurants (from top bracket to budget)

☕☕☕ **Masa's** (dwntwn), in the Vintage Court Hotel, 648 Bush St. (989-7154). A/C. Dinner only, Tues–Sat; closed July 4 and Dec 25 to early Jan. AE, MC, V. Jkt. *Specialties:* filet of lamb w. green peppercorn and Zinfandel sauce, foie gras sautéed w. truffles, mussel soup w. saffron, boudin of lobster, pheasant w. morel mushrooms. Very good desserts, particularly the frozen praline soufflé. Remarkable wine list. *Note:* The most innovative rest. serving French nouvelle cuisine in San Francisco. After the founder, Masataka Kobayashi, died lamented by all in 1985, he was succeeded by the talented Bill Galloway, then more recently by the young Julian Serrano, whose cuisine is both delicate and inspired; the appearance of his dishes is in itself a feast for the eye. Modern paneled decor w. superb flower arrangements, but a tiny space w. only 14 tables. Flawless svce. Resv. indispensable, several days or weeks ahead. A very good place indeed, but the prices are stiff. Valet parking ($5). *French.* **E–VE**

☕☕☕ **Fleur de Lys** (nr. dwntwn), 777 Sutter St. (673-7779). A/C. Dinner only, Mon–Sat; closed hols. and the first 2 weeks in June. AE, CB, DC, MC, V. J&T. *Specialties:* foie gras w. braised endives in ginger sauce, consommé of snails, médaillon of veal w. red-pepper mousse, marinated squab in juniper-berry sauce, lamb cutlets roasted w. thyme sauce, scallops and salmon in orange butter, lobster w. olives and fennel, filet of venison w. sautéed raisins and spätzle, tropical sherbets. Large wine list. *Note:* High-flown decor in a sort of campy *Thousand and One Nights* style, but the cuisine of Hubert Keller, a disciple of the famous French chef Roger Vergé, is a miracle of lightness and delicacy. Reception and svce flawless in all respects. The favorite rest. of San Francisco society. Resv. a must; a very fine place to eat. Valet parking ($4). *French.* **E–VE**

♆♆♆ **Donatello** (dwntwn), in the Donatello (see "Accommodations," above) (441-7182). A/C. Breakfast/lunch/dinner daily. AE, CB, DC, MC, V. J&T. *Specialties:* fresh homemade pasta, lobster and scallop ravioli, wild-mushroom risotto, médaillon of lamb w. herbs and juniper berries, stuffed quail w. sausage, bacon and broiled polenta, filet of pork w. apples and grappa, roast veal w. bacon and vodka; excellent desserts. Very fine list of Italian wines. *Note:* The best, and most expensive, of San Francisco's innumerable Italian rests., on the ground floor of the luxurious Donatello Hotel. Northern Italian food which avoids the beaten path. Decorated in a classic, tasteful combination of tapestries, Italian marble, and pastel colors. Attentive, polished svce. Upscale business clientele. Resv. necessary; valet parking. *Italian.* **E–VE**

♆♆♆ **Ernie's** (dwntwn), 847 Montgomery St. (397-5969). A/C. Dinner only, nightly; closed hols. and the first 2 weeks in Jan. AE, CB, DC, MC, V. J&T. *Specialties:* cream of clams, smoked salmon w. fennel, poached oysters w. leeks, gingered duck, fresh pasta w. seafood ragoût and capers, saddle of lamb en rognonnade, chicken w. cream of pears and endives, orange soufflé. Very fine wine list. *Note:* A haunt of celebrities, local or passing through, this San Francisco landmark has recently updated its menu w. some very nouvelle cuisine dishes. Victorian ambience w. elegant champagne-colored silk walls and crystal chandeliers (served as a backdrop for the Hitchcock movie *Vertigo*). Exemplary svce; resv. essential; valet parking ($4). *Continental.* **M–E**

☼♆♆♆ **Stars** (nr. dwntwn), 150 Redwood Alley (861-7827). A/C. Lunch Tues–Fri, dinner nightly. AE, DC, MC, V. Jkt. *Specialties:* chilled avocado soup w. chili, smoked duck w. turnips and aioli, oysters w. spiced lamb sausage, tuna steak w. ginger-and-coriander vinaigrette, James Beard's apple pie. Enormous list of California wines in all price ranges. *Note:* Jeremiah Tower, who forsook architecture for the stove, is one of the gurus of contemporary American cuisine; he works wonders w. light sauces, unexpected taste combinations, and a mesquite grill. Engaging old-fashioned brasserie setting, w. retro posters for decoration and noisy ambience. Relaxed but efficient svce. Heavily patronized by lawyers and politicians (the Civic Center is in easy reach); resv. strongly advised. *American.* **M–E**

☼♆♆ **Bix** (dwntwn), 56 Gold St. (433-6300). A/C. Lunch Mon–Fri, dinner daily. AE, MC, V. Jkt. *Specialties:* asparagus w. walnut gratin, sweet-corn custard w. sauce of shallots and shiitake mushrooms, salmon w. mushrooms in truffle oil, lamb chops w. minted onions, swordfish w. vegetable ragoût, gratin of chocolate. *Note:* This monument to art deco, which looks like a luxury liner from the '30s, has been very successful since it opened in 1988. The kitchen is supervised by the brilliant Cindy Pawlcyn, justly renowned as the former presiding genius at San Francisco's Fog City Diner and of the Mustards Grill in the Wine Country (see below). Magnificent two-level dining rm w. elegant mezzanine and inviting bar decorated with frescos in Cotton Club style. Prices quite moderate for such cooking. Svce still a little uncertain. Live jazz at dinner. Resv. a must. *American.* **M**

♆♆ **Enoteca Lanzone** (dwntwn), 601 Van Ness Ave. (928-0400). A/C. Lunch Mon–Fri, dinner Mon–Sat (till midnight); closed hols. and 2 weeks in Sept. AE, CB, DC, MC, V. Jkt. *Specialties:* fresh homemade pasta, ravioli w. walnut sauce, roast rabbit w. endive, lobster sautéed w. brandy, sherry, and tomatoes. Good wine list (but rather steep prices). *Note:* It's generally agreed that San Francisco, w. its very important Italian community, counts a dozen or so excellent Italian rests. Among the best is Enoteca Lanzone. The house-made pastas would be enough to rate it an honorable mention. Elegant, comfortable atmosphere; generally packed; resv. advised. *Italian.* **M**

    ☺☺ **Monsoon** (dwntwn), 601 Van Ness Ave. (441-3232). A/C. Lunch Tues–Fri, dinner Tues–Sun; closed hols. MC, V. Jkt. *Specialties:* Thai chicken salad, siu mai (little steamed dumplings w. shrimp and pork) in hot vinegar sauce, shellfish in coconut-milk soup, venison saté, steamed catfish, wok-fried Dungeness crab in ginger sauce, blood-orange crème caramel. Great Asian beer selection. *Note:* East meets West in this new San Francisco favorite. The delicate and imaginative cuisine of chef-owner Bruce Cost is a mix of Asian and Californian nouvelle. Elegant, spacious, and comfortable Asian decor. Excellent svce. Locally popular; resv. strongly advised. *Asian.* **M**

    ☺☺☺ **The Mandarin** (nr. dwntwn), Ghirardelli Sq., 900 North Point St. (673-8812). A/C. Lunch/dinner daily; closed Thanksgiving, Dec 25. AE, CB, DC, MC, V. Jkt. *Specialties:* shark's-fin soup, ginger crab, prawns Szechuan style, beggar's chicken, diced squab, duck smoked over tea leaves, Mandarin glazed bananas. *Note:* The delightful decor of this rest. (in Ghirardelli Sq., a charmingly remodeled old chocolate factory) blends a Chinese and contemporary European aesthetic w. exposed beams and carved paneling. Fine view of the bay (ask for a table nr. the window). Delicate, innovative cuisine; some dishes such as Peking duck and beggar's chicken must be ordered 24 hr. in advance. Confused, perfunctory svce. Resv. advised. *Chinese.* **I–M**

    ☺☺ **Eddie Jack's** (dwntwn), 1151 Folsom St. (626-2388). No A/C. Lunch Mon–Fri, dinner Mon–Sat; closed hols. AE, MC, V. *Specialties:* Fried polenta sticks w. Gorgonzola sauce; Chinese chicken salad; fried-cod sandwich w. warm mayonnaise sauce; Angus steak w. sesame-ginger-soy sauce; open-face grilled-lamb sandwich w. melted feta, onions, and calamata olives; ice-cream sandwich. Skimpy wine list. *Note:* Trendy rest. w. an outlandish decor of massive papier-mâché beer cans and cigarette packs. Young chef Thom Fox's California cuisine is original. Don't miss the house apértif, Essensia Royale. Resv. a must. *American.* **I–M**

    ☺☺ **Gaylord India** (nr. dwntwn), Ghirardelli Sq., 900 North Point St. (771-8822). A/C. Lunch/dinner daily, brunch Sun; closed Thanksgiving, Dec 25. AE, CB, DC, MC, V. Jkt. *Specialties:* mulligatawny soup, samosas, chicken tikka masala, chicken tandoori, lamb w. cream and walnuts, curries. *Note:* All the subtle flavors of true Indian cuisine; luxurious decor and splendid views of the bay from every table. Attentive svce; agreeable background music. Resv. advised. Other location: 1 Embarcadero Center (397-7775). *Indian.* **I–M**

    ☺☺ **Greens** (nr. dwntwn), Bldg. A, Fort Mason (771-6222). A/C. Lunch/dinner Tues–Sat, brunch Sun. MC, V. *Specialties:* fresh pasta w. vegetables, homemade soups, mixed salads, pizza provençal, vegetable soufflés, quiches, vegetable hotpot, good homemade desserts. List of French and California wines at reasonable prices. *Note:* Purists look on this as the crowning glory of California vegetarian cuisine; the excellent chef, Deborah Madison, devises light, sophisticated, innovative dishes. The floor-to-ceiling windows of this former military barracks give you a superb view of the bay and the Golden Gate Bridge. Very popular w. the business community at lunch; 10-min. drive from dwntwn. Resv. a must. *American.* **I–M**

    ☺☺ **Scott's Seafood** (nr. dwntwn), 2400 Lombard St. (563-8988). Lunch/dinner daily; closed Thanksgiving, Dec 25–26. AE, CB, DC, MC, V. *Specialties:* fisherman's stew, grilled sole petrale, fried calamari, sautéed seafood, catch of the day, shellfish. Good desserts. *Note:* In a small, two-story rowhouse typical of San Francisco, this rest. has achieved great local popularity by serving simple food without fuss, and the freshest fish you could ask for. Cheerful svce; often crowded. No dinner resv. are taken, so waits can be very long. Other location: 3 Embarcadero Center (981-0622); both are excellent places to eat. *Seafood.* **I–M**

※☼♈ **Yamato** (dwntwn), 717 California St. (397-3456). A/C. Lunch Tues–Fri, dinner Tues–Sun; closed hols. AE, CB, DC, MC, V. Jkt. *Specialties:* beef teriyaki, sukiyaki, tempura, shabu shabu, sushi. *Note:* With its miniature waterfalls, grdns, and indoor pools, the oldest Japanese rest. on the West Coast is a masterpiece of architectural elegance. The same elegance is evident in its cuisine. Discreet, efficient svce (in kimono). You can choose between Western-style dining and a tatami rm. Locally popular; resv. highly advisable. *Japanese.* **I–M**

♈ **Zuni Cafe** (dwntwn), 1658 Market St. (552-2522). A/C. Breakfast/lunch/dinner Tues–Sun; closed hols. AE, MC, V. *Specialties:* pumpkin soup w. chili and escarole, crab-and-shrimp rémoulade w. aioli, squab salad, roast chicken w. bread salad, baked polenta w. shiitake mushrooms, caramel "pot de crème." Very fine wine list at very reasonable prices. *Note:* In 2 or 3 years Zuni has succeeded in becoming a local landmark; it has been enlarged and spruced up (but avoid the little rms on the second floor). The talented Judy Rogers dishes up a California cuisine which never fails in originality and flavor. The setting is Santa Fe style. Erratic svce. Wildly popular, so resv. a must. *American.* **I–M**

♈ **Corona Bar & Grill** (dwntwn), 88 Cyril Magnin St. (392-5500). A/C. Lunch/dinner Mon–Sat. AE, CB, DC, MC, V. *Specialties:* clam-and-corn chowder w. cream and cilantro pesto, grilled prawns w. black-bean cake and tomato salsa, empanada of chorizo (spicy sausage) and chili poblano, quesadillas w. shiitake mushrooms and Roquefort and Jack cheese, papaya sorbet, coconut custard. Short but well-thought-out wine list. *Note:* Shimmering blue-and-pink setting w. Mexican masks, and a riot of plants and cactus. Friendly but noisy. Excellent svce. Resv. advised. A very good place. *American/ Mexican.* **I**

♈ **Little Joe's** (dwntwn), 523 Broadway (982-7639). A/C. Lunch/dinner Mon–Sat; closed hols. No credit cards. *Specialties:* minestrone, spaghetti al pesto, calamari in red wine sauce, roast chicken w. rosemary, beef tongue w. green sauce, saltimbocca, cacciucco alla livornese (fish soup). *Note:* A landmark of the Italian district of North Beach, in a huge, virtually undecorated old warehouse. Tasty, reasonably priced Italian food prepared by an army of cooks who bustle around their stoves under the admiring eyes of the patrons. Congenial atmosphere. Huge portions. Unfortunately no resv., and a wait is very likely. Very good value. *Italian.* **I**

♈ **Pacific Heights** (nr. dwntwn), 2001 Fillmore St. (567-3337). A/C. Lunch Mon–Fri, dinner nightly, brunch Sun. AE, MC, V. *Specialties:* oysters on the half shell, crabcakes, shrimp in beer w. rémoulade, grilled tuna w. coriander batter, sesame salmon. Good list of California wines at reasonable prices. *Note:* San Francisco's best oyster bar; on any given day it serves at least 10 different varieties of the succulent bivalve from both Pacific and Atlantic. The other seafood offered is also impeccably fresh. Charming Victorian decor. A very fine place; excellent value. Resv. advised; valet parking at dinner. *Seafood.* **I**

♈ **Yuet Lee Seafood** (dwntwn), 1300 Stockton St. (982-6020). A/C. Lunch/dinner Wed–Mon. No credit cards. *Specialties:* clams in black-bean sauce, congee (rice w. fish, chicken, and vegetables), fried calamari and oysters, lobster sautéed w. garlic, fried shrimp w. chile. *Note:* Hong Kong–style seafood rest., very popular w. those in-the-know. The Formica decor, appropriate to the combined retail-fish-store-and-rest. operation, is no asset, but the seafood is absolutely fresh and cooked to perfection. No wine or beer (you may bring your own). Other location: 3601 26th St. (550-8989). *Chinese/ Seafood.* **B–I**

♈ **Bistro Clovis** (dwntwn), 1596 Market St. (864-0231). A/C. Lunch/dinner Mon–Sat (until 11pm). MC, V. *Specialties:* pâtés, cheeses, cold cuts, salads, daily specials. Very good selection of French and California wines by the bottle or the glass. *Note:* Engaging little wine bar usually crowded at lunchtime; the "Parisian" setting owes more to myth than reality. Friendly, smiling svce; a great place for pre- or post-theater dining. *French.* **B**

☀☌ **Obrero Hotel** (dwntwn), 1208 Stockton St. (989-3960). No A/C. Dinner only, nightly. No credit cards. *Specialties:* home-made soup, cassoulet, pasta w. clams, oxtail ragoût, roast lamb, roast beef, sole Rex. Wine or beer. *Note:* The last of San Francisco's legendary Basque hotels, serving traditional boardinghouse meals at long, family-style tables. Hearty din-ner in a friendly atmosphere. Only one sitting, at 6:30pm every evening. Guaran-teed local color. Resv. advised. Unbeatable value. *French.* **B**

Restaurants in the Vicinity

♟♟♟♟ **Lark Creek Inn** (see "Personal Favorites," above).

♟♟ **Chez Panisse** (vic.), 1517 Shattuck Ave., Berkeley (548-♟♟ 5525). A/C. Lunch/dinner Mon–Sat (café), dinner Tues–Sat (rest.) AE, DC, MC, V. *Specialties:* pizza gourmet, herbed roast lamb, catch of the day. Good wine list, outrageously priced. *Note:* Chef Paul Bertolli's contem-porary Californian cuisine is interesting if unsophisticated. But Chez Panisse is only a shadow of what it was under the guiding hand of its founders Jeremiah Tower and Alice Walters. Prices, especially on the wine list, continue to go up. If food-lovers still come here, it's in reverent pilgrimage to the historic shrine of California cuisine. *American.* **I–M** (café), **E** (rest.).

Cafeterias / Fast Food

Mama's (dwntwn), 398 Geary St. (788-1004). Breakfast/lunch/dinner daily (till 1am). AE, DC, MC, V. *Specialties:* roast chicken, sandwiches, daily spe-cials, good homemade desserts. Beer and wine. *Note:* Excellent cafeteria food; inviting atmosphere. Locally popular.

Salmagundi (dwntwn), 442 Geary St. (441-0894). Open daily (till mid-night). No credit cards. *Specialties:* homemade soup, quiche, salad, homemade desserts. Beer and wine. *Note:* Praiseworthy, well-prepared food; very popular at lunchtime. Other locations: 2 Embarcadero Center (982-5603), open till 9pm; 1236 Market St. (431-7337), open till 9pm.

Where to Eat What

American: Bix (p. 969), Campton Place (p. 967), Chez Panisse (p. 972), Eddie Jack's (p. 970), Greens (p. 970), Lark Creek Inn (p. 967), Square One (p. 968), Stars (p. 969), Zuni Café (p. 971).

Chinese: China Moon Café (p. 968), The Mandarin (p. 970), Tommy Toy's Haute Cuisine Chinoise (p. 967), Yuet Lee Seafood (p. 971).

Continental (European): Ernie's (p. 969).

Cafeterias/Fast Food: Mama's (p. 972), Salmagundi (p. 972).

French: Bistro Clovis (p. 971), Fleur de Lys (p. 968), Masa's (p. 968), Obrero Hotel (p. 972).

Indian: Gaylord India (p. 970).

Italian: Donatello (p. 969), Enoteca Lanzone (p. 969), Little Joe's (p. 971).

Japanese: Yamato (p. 971).

Mexican: Cadillac Bar (p. 968), Corona Bar & Grill (p. 971).

Seafood: Pacific Heights (p. 971), Scott's Seafood (p. 970), Yuet Lee Sea-food (p. 971).

Steak: Tadich Grill (p. 968).

BARS & NIGHTCLUBS

☀ **Buena Vista Café** (dwntwn), 2765 Hyde St. (474-5044). One of San Francisco's most renowned cafés, credited with launch-ing the fashion of Irish coffee in the U.S. Fine view of the bay and Alcatraz. Also a commendable rest. Very popular with tourists. Open nightly.

☀ **Caffè Trieste** (dwntwn), 609 Vallejo St. (392-6739). The city's best-known literary café; since it opened in 1956, this longtime haunt of the Beat poets has played host to every prominent literary figure in town. Francis Ford Coppola wrote the script of *The Godfather* here. Italian-bohemian atmosphere. Open daily.

Caesar's Latin Palace (nr. dwntwn), 3140 Mission St. (648-6611). California's biggest Latino nightclub. The huge room can hold 1,000 people. Here merengue and salsa are king. Open nightly.

Club DV8 (dwntwn), 540 Howard St. (777-1419). One of the city's hottest nightspots in the famous SoMa (south of Market) district. Live entertainment and nightly disco. Punk, chic crowds.

☼ **Eli's Mile High Club** (vic.), 3629 Martin Luther King Way, Oakland (655-6661). The best blues joint on the West Coast; worth the trip across the bay. The patrons are a very Berkeley crowd.

El Rio (nr. dwntwn), 3158 Mission St. (282-3325). Another Latin nightclub, very popular locally. The rhythms you'll meet here—samba, merengue, rock, Afro-Cuban, and Caribbean—are almost as varied as the clientele of artists, yuppies, gays, and Latinos. Open nightly.

Finocchio's (dwntwn), 506 Broadway (982-9388). The best-known nightspot featuring female impersonators in the U.S. Open Tues and Thurs–Sun.

Great American Music Hall (dwntwn), 859 O'Farrell St. (885-0750). Live big-name rock and jazz concerts. Open nightly.

Hard Rock Café (dwntwn), 1699 Van Ness Ave. (885-1699). Facsimile of the famous London nightclub of the same name. Hard rock; youthful patrons. Good hamburgers; locally very popular. Open nightly.

Harry's Bar and Grill (dwntwn), 500 Van Ness Ave. (864-2779). Inviting bar across from City Hall, a hangout for local politicians. Relaxed, congenial atmosphere. Also an Italian rest. serving broiled dishes and good tiramisù. Open nightly.

I-Beam (nr. dwntwn), 1748 Haight St. (668-6806). The favorite of San Francisco's younger set for rock and new wave. Live music and disk jockeys turn and turn about. Very noisy, with laser lights and giant video screens. Mostly students and well-brought-up yuppies. Open nightly.

Kimball's (dwntwn), 300 Grove St. at Franklin St. (861-5555). Highly regarded jazz club featuring the biggest names in the business (Wed–Sat). Also a very acceptable rest., open nightly.

Milestones (nr. dwntwn), 376 5th St. (777-9997). One of the newest, and best, of San Francisco's jazz clubs; locally popular. Open nightly.

Oasis (nr. dwntwn), 11th St. and Folsom St. (621-8119). Fashionable disco in what used to be a public swimming pool; outlandish hi-tech decor. Youthful, trendy clientele. Open nightly.

☼ **Perry's** (dwntwn), 1944 Union St. (922-9022). Singles bar in the New York tradition; youthful, relaxed atmosphere. Also an unassuming rest. Recommended as a premier pickup spot; open nightly till midnight.

Punch Line (dwntwn), 444 Battery St. (397-7573). The best and best known of the city's comedy clubs; showcases beginners as well as established stars. Very popular locally. Open nightly.

☼ **Top of the Mark** (dwntwn), in the Mark Hopkins Inter-Continental (see "Accommodations," above) (392-3434). Elegant panoramic bar in a superb art deco setting. Dancing; fine view of the bay. Open nightly till 1:30am.

Tosca Café (dwntwn), 242 Columbus Ave. (986-9651). A popular hangout in the old Italian neighborhood of North Beach. The jukebox plays only opera records.

☼ **Washington Square Bar and Grill** (dwntwn), 1707 Powell St. (982-8123). Lively bar-saloon; also an acceptable Italian rest., but the food is only an excuse to talk, celebrate, and rub elbows w. those in-the-know. Agreeable jazz piano. Open nightly.

Wolfgang's (dwntwn), 901 Columbus Ave. (441-4334). Live rock, reggae, and jazz; youthful, very with-it atmosphere. The trendy place. Open nightly.

Yoshi's (vic.), 60300 Claremont Ave., Oakland (652-9200): One of the best jazz spots on the coast; the biggest names perform here. Very good Japanese rest. adj. 25 min. from dwntwn over the Bay Bridge. Open nightly.

NEARBY EXCURSIONS

☀️🅰️ **BERKELEY** (12 mi./20km east via the San Francisco–Oakland Bay Bridge and I-80): A cosmopolitan place filled with museums, libraries, theaters, bookstores, and other cultural sites, this city of 120,000 on the east side of San Francisco Bay became a symbol for a generation. The Free Speech Movement—the first campus revolt of the 1960s—began here, capturing the attention of the nation. The University of California's largest campus (32,000 students), Berkeley is one of the oldest (1868) and most famous schools in the country. Among its 1,600 faculty members are no fewer than 12 Nobel Prize winners and 76 members of the prestigious National Academy of Sciences. From its 307-ft. (93m) campanile, a copy of that on the piazza San Marco in Venice, you'll have a wonderful view (there's an elevator). The imposing **Bancroft Library** on University Dr. is one of the nation's richest, with six million volumes. The **visitor center** in the Student Union Building, Bancroft Way and Telegraph Ave. (642-5215), organizes guided tours of the campus Mon–Fri. You should also see the university's very beautiful **Art Museum** at 2626 Bancroft Way (642-1207), open Wed–Sun. Don't miss Berkeley.

☀️🅰️ **MUIR WOODS NATIONAL MONUMENT** (16 mi./25km north via the Golden Gate Bridge, U.S. 101, and Calif. 1): Splendid redwood forest, with some trees, more than 2,000 years old, growing 230 ft. (70m) or more and 12 ft. (3.6m) in diameter. From the top of nearby Mount Tamalpais (2,604 ft./794m) there's a magnificent view over San Francisco Bay and the Pacific. Access is along a panoramic road from Mill Valley. You should make this trip. No camping or picnicking permitted. For more information, contact the Site Manager, Mill Valley, CA 94941 (415/388-2595).

☀️🅰️ **OAKLAND** (10 mi./16km east across the San Francisco–Oakland Bay Bridge): This busy port and industrial city, founded in 1850, has a large African American community (the Black Panthers originated here), and one of the most beautiful, and original, museums to be found on the West Coast. The 🅰️🅰️ **Oakland Museum,** at 1000 Oak St. (273-3401), open Wed–Sun, is the work of architect Kevin Roche; its tiered design, with terraced gardens, is quite outstanding. It houses rich material on California art and history, as well as paintings by Hans Hofmann and a splendid film library. Worth a visit.

Note also the picturesque 🅰️ **Jack London Square** around the Inner Harbor, bounded by Broadway, Webster St., and the Embarcadero (444-3188), with restaurants, bars, and shops got up in the turn-of-the-century spirit of Jack London's life and writings. The novelist lived in the vicinity, and wrote a number of his books at Heinold's First and Last Chance Saloon, 56 Jack London Sq. Don't fail to make this visit. Open daily.

☀️🅰️ **POINT REYES NATIONAL SEASHORE** (35 mi./56km north via the Golden Gate Bridge, U.S. 101, and Calif. 1): A 70,000-acre (28,000ha) wildlife reserve on a peninsula jutting out into the Pacific, harboring more than 350 species of birds and mammals. The landscape is beautifully flower-bedecked Feb–July. Beaches; camping; swimming permitted in summer. For lovers of authentic nature. **Visitor centers** at Bear Valley, open daily, and at Drakes Beach, open Sat–Sun and holidays (663-1092).

🅰️ **SAN RAFAEL** (19 mi./30km north via the Golden Gate Bridge and U.S. 101): The **Mission San Rafael Arcángel,**

20th and next-to-last of those founded by the Franciscans in California, was built in 1817 and rebuilt in 1949 on the original site at 1104 Fifth Ave. at A St. (456-3016), open daily. Worth the detour.

See also the very fine **Marin County Civic Center,** one of the last major works of the great Frank Lloyd Wright, who died in 1959 before it was completed; it's 2 mi. (3.2km) north on San Pedro Rd. (499-7407). Guided tours by appointment Mon–Fri.

☼🔔🔔 **SAUSALITO** (8 mi./12km north via the Golden Gate Bridge and U.S. 101): The California equivalent of a fashionable European resort like Juan-les-Pins or Portofino, equally attractive to millionaires, artists, and hippies. This gracious pleasure harbor lies across the Golden Gate Bridge from San Francisco, with a wonderful view of the bay. Many shops and art galleries, congenial bars and restaurants. You should see the **San Francisco Bay and Delta Model,** 2100 Bridgeway (332-3870), open Tues–Sat, an enormous (2-acre/0.8ha) hydraulic model which faithfully reproduces the tidal action and marine currents of San Francisco Bay. Sausalito definitely deserves a visit.

SILICON VALLEY: See "South of the Bay and Silicon Valley," under "Farther Afield," below.

🔔 **TIBURON** (18 mi./28km north via the Golden Gate Bridge, U.S. 101, and Calif. 131): Another charming little pleasure harbor near Sausalito, north of the bay. Wonderful view of San Francisco. Many bars, fashionable shops, and fish and seafood restaurants with fine views of the bay. A place that contrives to be both elegant and relaxing; you should see it.

THE CALIFORNIA WINE COUNTRY

California, which produces more than 70% of all U.S. wines, boasts more than 250 wineries grouped in three main regions. The Central Valley around Fresno produces mass-market table wines. Santa Clara and Monterey, south of San Francisco Bay, produce light, likable wines, particularly whites. Finally, the Napa Valley and Sonoma Valley areas, north of San Francisco Bay, indisputably produce the state's finest wines, beginning with the renowned Cabernet Sauvignon.

☼🍷 **VISITING THE WINERIES:** Napa Valley and Sonoma Valley, about 50 mi. (80km) NE of San Francisco, are known as "Wine Country." You can arrange for visits and tastings at many of its wineries; for information, contact the **Napa Valley Chamber of Commerce,** 1900 Jefferson St., Napa, CA 94559 (707/226-7455), and the **Sonoma Valley Visitors Bureau,** 453 E. 1st St., Sonoma, CA 95476 (707/996-1090). Among the most interesting wineries are:

Calistoga
Calistoga is 29 mi. (46km) NW of Napa on Calif. 29.
Château Montelena Winery, 1429 Tubbs Lane (707/942-5105), open daily, is a century-old stone castle with a Chinese garden alongside.
Sterling Vineyards, at 1111 Dunaweal Lane (707/942-5151), a lovely estate with the look of an Italian monastery which perches atop a knoll reached by a 300-ft. (92m) aerial tramway, is open for (tiring) visits daily.
On the way, see 🔔 **Old Faithful Geyser,** 1299 Tubbs Lane (707/942-6463), which spouts a steamy 60-ft. (18m) plume about every 40 min.

Napa
Napa, 44 mi. (70km) north of San Francisco via I-80 and Calif. 29, is one of the centers of wine making in California.
Clos du Val, 5330 Silverado Trail (707/252-6711), is open daily.

Oakville

Oakville is 13 mi. (20km) NW of Napa on Calif. 29.

Robert Mondavi, 7801 St. Helena Hwy. (707/963-9611), is open daily. Arts exhibits and concerts are frequently presented in the graceful building modeled on a Franciscan mission.

Rutherford

Rutherford is 15 mi. (24km) NW of Napa on Calif. 29.

Beaulieu Vineyard, 1960 St. Helena Hwy. (707/963-2411), has cellars dating from the turn of the century; open daily.

Inglenook Vineyards, on Calif. 29 (707/967-3300), is in a fine 1883 Gothic Revival cellar house with a half-mile approach avenue leading to the ivy-covered main building, and has an interesting museum of viticulture; open daily.

St. Helena

St. Helena is 19 mi. (30km) NW of Napa on Calif. 29.

Beringer Vineyard, 2000 Main St. (707/963-7115), features the Rhine House built by the founders in 1883 to emulate their ancestral home in Germany; open daily.

Christian Brothers, 2555 Main St. (707/967-3112), has one of the largest cellars in the world, belonging, as its name indicates, to a religious order; visits daily.

Heitz Wine Cellars, 436 St. Helena Hwy. (707/963-3542), is open daily.

Charles Krug, 2800 Main St. (707/963-2761), whose handsome decor dates from 1861, is open daily.

Louis Martini Winery, 254 St. Helena Hwy. S. (707/963-2736); open daily.

Finally, **Spring Mountain Vineyard** is headquartered in the manor house from the TV series "Falcon Crest," 2805 Spring Mountain Rd. (707/963-5233); open daily.

Sonoma

Sonoma, 16 mi. (25km) west of Napa on Calif. 12, along with Napa is the center of the California wine industry. These vineyards, of which Europe is now envious, were started in the 1820s by Spanish Franciscan missionaries, and have been tended since then by German, French, Hungarian, and Italian growers. The vintage is harvested from Sept to early Nov. Some of the more interesting wineries are:

Buena Vista Winery, 18000 Old Winery Rd. (707/938-1266), open daily, is the oldest wine-making estate in California, founded in 1857 by the Hungarian Agoston Haraszthy. Classical concerts in summer.

Sebastiani Vineyards, 389 4th St. E. (707/938-5532), has an interesting museum of viticulture and collection of antique carved vats; open daily.

On the way, take a look at ※▲ **Jack London State Historic Park,** on Calif. 12 at **Glen Ellen** (707/938-5216), where the famous author of *Call of the Wild* killed himself in 1916; he's buried here. Beautiful scenery; museum open daily. Also, be sure to see the ▲ **Mission San Francisco Solano** with its pretty plaza, 21st and last of the missions founded in California by the Spanish Franciscans, in 1823. It's on E. Spain St. and 1st St. E. (707/938-1519); open daily.

Kenwood

Kenwood is 13 mi. (20km) NW of Sonoma.

Château St. Jean, Calif. 12 (707/833-4134), is a very handsome winery in Bavarian peasant style.

Yountville

Yountville is 10 mi. (16km) NW of Napa on Calif. 29.

Domaine Chandon, 1 California Dr. (707/944-2280), is the U.S. property of the great French champagne house of Moët et Chandon. Cellars open to visitors daily. You'll learn about all the different stages in the manufacture of champagne.

BALLOON EXCURSIONS: For an unforgettable overview of the Napa Valley take a hot-air-balloon ride. Offered by **Balloon Aviation of Napa Valley,** 2299 3rd St., Napa (707/252-7067), and **Once in a Lifetime Balloon Co.,** P.O. Box 795, Calistoga, CA 94515 (707/942-6541). Cost is $150 per person, including brunch.

FOOD & LODGING IN WINE COUNTRY: As you might imagine, where there is wine, there are restaurants—and places to bed down for the night as well.

Rutherford

Auberge du Soleil, 180 Rutherford Hill Rd., Rutherford, CA 94573 (707/963-1211). 48 rms. The most chic and best-known place to stay in the Wine Country. A very luxurious European-style inn with a remarkable rest. (see below). Member of the prestigious Relais et Châteaux hotel chain. **VE**

Auberge du Soleil (see above). Lunch/dinner daily. Quite remarkable French-Californian nouvelle cuisine and a superb setting, with a view clear across the Napa Valley. A wonderful place to eat, but the prices are very high (especially the wine list). **E**

Sonoma

Sonoma Hotel, 110 W. Spain St., Sonoma, CA 95476 (707/996-2996). 17 rms. Lovely old (1872) hotel, tastefully renovated. **M–E**

Sonoma Mission Inn, 18140 Sonoma Hwy., Boyes Hot Springs, CA 95476 (707/983-9000; toll free 800/358-9022). 170 rms. Wonderful, and wonderfully renovated, Spanish-mission-style hotel from the '20s. Unsurpassed svce and facilities; prices to match. **E–VE**

St. Helena

Meadowood Resort, 900 Meadowood Lane, St. Helena, CA 94574 (707/963-3646; toll free 800/345-3457). 14 rms and 64 suites. Everything that a first-class modern luxury hotel should be: a blend of country elegance and sophistication. Enormous rms or individual cottages surrounded by a great forested park. First-rate rest. **E–VE**

Wine Country Inn, 1152 Lodi Lane, St. Helena, CA 94574 (707/963-7077). 25 rms. Charming old country inn. **E–VE**

Knickerbocker's, 3010 St. Helena Hwy., North St. Helena (707/967-9300). Lunch Tues–Sat, dinner Wed–Sun. Imaginative California cuisine in a country chalet w. a grdn for open-air dining. **I–M**

Tra Vigne, 1050 Charter Oak Ave. (707/963-4444). Lunch/dinner daily. Refined Italian-Californian cuisine in a stunning setting. **I–M**

Yountville

Burgundy House, 6711 Washington St., Yountville, CA 94599 (707/944-2855). Tiny inn w. only 6 rms; elegantly countrified. Rms recently remodeled. **M–E**

Mustards Grill, 7399 St. Helena Hwy. (707/944-2424). Lunch/dinner daily. Excellent entrées grilled over a wood fire; locally popular. **I–M**

The Diner, 6476 Washington Ave. (707/944-2626). Breakfast/lunch/dinner Tues–Sun. Mexican-American food.

B–I

FARTHER AFIELD

☼🔭 **CALIF. 1, THE COASTAL HIGHWAY** (398 mi./639km r.t. via I-280S, Calif. 17S, and Calif. 1S and 1N): One of the most beautiful drives in the U.S. For a good way it follows the old Camino Real, the 200-year-old highway of the Spanish Franciscan missions. You'll see **Monterey, 17-Mile Drive, Carmel, Big Sur,** and the **Hearst Castle** (see Chapter 51 on the California Coast); then back to San Francisco by the coastal road. Can readily be combined with a visit to areas south of the bay and Silicon Valley (see below). You shouldn't miss this 2- to 3-day trip.

☼🔔 **LASSEN NATIONAL PARK** (246 mi./394km NE via I-5, Calif. 36, and Calif. 89): One of the only two active volcanoes on the U.S. mainland (the other is Mount St. Helens). Rugged scenery. For details, see Chapter 49 on Reno.

☼🔭 **REDWOOD EMPIRE** (345 mi./552km r.t. via U.S. 101N, Calif. 20W, and Calif. 1S): Magnificent redwood forests inland, and wonderful seascapes along the Pacific coast; can easily be combined with a visit to the vineyards of the **Wine Country** (see above). You'll pass through **Clear Lake,** a huge mountain lake with fishing and sailing; the picturesque fishing ports of **Fort Bragg** and **Mendocino; Noyo,** with its superb 17-acre (6.8ha) botanic garden overlooking the Pacific; and **Fort Ross,** a Russian trading post founded in 1812. It still has many of its original buildings, including its Russian Orthodox chapel; for details, see Chapter 51 on the California Coast. Your last stop might be **Point Reyes National Seashore** (see "Nearby Excursions," above). A 2- to 3-day trip you shouldn't miss.

Where to Stay En Route

☼🏨 **Heritage House,** 5200 Calif. 1, Littleriver, CA 95456 (707/ 937-5885), south of Fort Bragg. 69 rms. Delightful little cottages on the ocean. Good rest. Closed Dec–Jan. **E–VE**

☼🏨 **St. Orres,** on Calif. 1, Gualala, CA 95445 (707/884-3303), between Mendocino and Fort Ross. Charming tiny (17 rms) inn; excellent rest. **M–E**

☼🔭 **SACRAMENTO & LAKE TAHOE** (448 mi./716km r.t. via I-80E, Calif. 89S, U.S. 50W, and I-80W): Lake Tahoe is one of the loveliest mountain lakes in the U.S. (see Chapter 49 on Reno), in an area which offers all kinds of recreational sports in summer and many ski resorts in winter.

On the way you pass through 🔔 **Sacramento,** capital of the state of California, with a history as interesting as any city in the West. Now nicknamed the "Camellia Capital of the World," it first rose to prominence as a center of the 1848–49 gold rush. You should certainly see the 🔔 **State Capitol,** more than a century old and now sumptuously restored, on 10th St. at Capitol Mall (916/324-0333), open daily. Take in **Sutter's Fort State Historic Park,** an adobe fort built in 1839 by the Swiss John Sutter, founder of Sacramento, at 2701 L St. (916/445-4209), open daily. Finally, visit the **Old Sacramento Historic District,** a picturesque old neighborhood along the Sacramento River, restored to the way it looked in the period 1850–80. Some buildings you shouldn't overlook: the **Old Eagle Theater,** oldest in California (1849), at Front St. and J St., open Tues–Sun; the **California State Railroad Museum,** as fine as any in the country, 111 I St., open daily; and the **Hastings Building,** once the western terminus of the legendary Pony Express, whose hundred dauntless horsemen (one of them the great Buffalo Bill) used to cover in 10 days, at full gallop, the 1,965 mi. (3,145km) between St. Joseph, Missouri (see Chapter 28 on Kansas City), and Sacramento. It was only the coming of the telegraph, in the 1860s, that put an end to their feats. The Hastings Building also at one time housed the California Supreme Court. It's at 2nd St. and J St.; open daily.

Near Sacramento are many ※ **mining towns** from the gold-rush days; among the most picturesque are **Coloma** (where gold was first discovered in 1848), **Placerville, Fair Play, Rough and Ready, Grass Valley,** and **Nevada City.**

This spectacular trip will take you 3–4 days; it shouldn't be missed.

Where to Stay in Sacramento

♀♀♀ **Hyatt Regency,** 1209 L St., Sacramento, CA 95814 (916/ 443-1234). Brand-new palace hotel across from the State Capitol, w. all the usual Hyatt comforts. **E–VE**

♀♀♀ **Clarion,** 700 16th St., Sacramento, CA 95814 (916/444-8000). 239 rms. Elegantly renovated old hotel standing in a lovely grdn across from the Governor's Mansion. Commendable rest. **E**

♀♀ **Radisson** (formerly the Woodlake Inn), 500 Leisure Lane, Sacramento, CA 95815 (916/922-2020). 314 rms. Luxurious convention hotel located on a private lake. **M–E**

♀ **Motel 6,** 1415 30th St., Sacramento, CA 95816 (916/457-0777). 94 rms. Motel, no-frills but acceptable, nr. Sutter's Fort and the State Capitol. **B**

Where to Eat in Sacramento

♀♀♀ **Chanterelle,** in the Sterling Hotel, 1300 H St. (916/442-0451). Breakfast/lunch/dinner daily. One of the city's best culinary offerings. *American.* **I–M**

♀♀ **Biba,** 2801 Capitol Ave. (916/455-2422). Lunch/dinner daily. All the mainstays of Italian cuisine, impeccably prepared and served. *Italian.* **I–M**

※♀♀ **Firehouse,** 1112 2nd St. (916/442-4772). Lunch Mon–Fri, dinner Mon–Sat. A handsome antique setting in an 1853 firehouse. *Continental/American.* **I–M**

♀♀ **Crawdad's River Cantina,** 1375 Garden Hwy. (916/929-2268). Fashionable rest. on the banks of the Sacramento River serving inventive, flavorful Tex-Mex food. **I**

※※ **SEQUOIA NATIONAL PARK** (270 mi./432km SE via I-580, I-5, and Calif. 198): The kingdom of the forest giants. See Chapter 52 on Sequoia National Park.

※※ **SOUTH OF THE BAY & SILICON VALLEY** (155 mi./248km r.t. via U.S. 280, U.S. 101S, and I-280N): Leaving San Francisco along U.S. 280, you should first visit ▲ **Filoli** on Cañada Rd., Woodside (415/364-2880). This imposing Georgian-style manor house, built in 1919, was the set for the Carrington mansion in the TV series "Dynasty." Also open to the public are the 16 acres (6ha) of splendid landscaped gardens around the property. Open Tues–Sat. Continuing along U.S. 280 you will come to **Palo Alto,** home of ※ **Stanford University,** on Camino Real and Calif. 82, with no fewer than 10 Nobel laureates on the faculty. With 13,000 students, it's one of the most highly regarded of U.S. universities, particularly in the fields of technology, medicine, and high-tech electronics. Elegant red-tiled Romanesque buildings; you get a good view of the campus from the 285-ft. (87m) Hoover Tower. Campus open daily; for information on times, check with the Information Center at Tresidder Union (415/723-2560). Don't miss it.

Heading south, you will come to **Mountain View,** the gateway to Silicon

Valley, where space buffs will certainly visit the **Ames Research Center** at the Moffett Field exit from U.S. 101 (415/694-6497). NASA's research laboratory here boasts one of the largest wind-tunnels in the world, powered by six giant turbines. The laboratory can be seen (a 2½-mi./4km trip on foot) by appointment only; you must reserve well ahead. Open Mon–Fri.

Stop off at ☀ **Great America,** the huge theme park at **Santa Clara** (see "Theme Parks," above).

Though ☀ **Silicon Valley** (named after the silicon chips on which electronic circuits are based) may not be found on most maps, for two decades a surprising number of very bright people have been working here. For a radius of 30 mi. (50km) around **Sunnyvale, Los Altos, Mountain View,** and **Santa Clara,** yesterday's almond and orange groves have given way to the world's leading hothouse for innovation. Some 3,000 corporations in all, from giants like National Semiconductor and Intel to workshops employing half a dozen people, make Silicon Valley the world capital of electronics. As a living illustration of "neocapitalism," not only are the technicians and researchers employed in Silicon Valley among the best-paid employees in the U.S., but also many participate in the management, and in the profits, of their firms.

Drive 3 mi. (5km) south of Santa Clara to ☀ **San Jose,** the former state capital, to see the ▲ **Egyptian Museum** and its important collection of antiquities at 1342 Naglee Ave. (408/287-2807), open daily; ▲ **Alum Rock Park,** 16240 Alum Rock Ave. (408/259-5477), and the curious rock formations that have earned it the name of "Little Yosemite"; the ▲ **Lick Observatory,** with its 36-in. (91cm) telescope, 25 mi. (40km) SE on Mount Hamilton (408/274-5061), with visits by appointment daily, for astronomy buffs; the **Mirassou** wine cellars, 3000 Aborn Rd. (408/274-4000), open daily; and above all the unbelievable ☀▲▲ **Winchester Mystery House,** 525 S. Winchester Blvd. (408/247-2101), open daily, with its 160 bedrooms, 13 baths, 2,000 doors, 10,000 windows, 47 fireplaces, secret corridors, blank walls, trap doors, and false staircases. This was the last home of Sarah Winchester, widow of the famous gunmaker, and during the last 38 years of her life (1884–1922) she never stopped adding to the house—a clairvoyant had told her that she would not die as long as she went on building! It cost her $6 million—a much huger sum then than now.

Your last stop will be in **Saratoga,** where you should visit the elegant ▲ **Villa Montalvo,** with its art galleries and beautiful gardens, at 15400 Villa Montalvo Rd. (408/741-3421); gardens open daily, galleries open Thurs–Sun. Also the **Paul Masson** winery, 14831 Pierce Rd. (408/741-5181), open daily; there are classical and jazz concerts June–Sept.

This trip can be made inside a day, but it's best combined with the itinerary along Calif. 1, the Coastal Highway (see above).

Where to Eat in Silicon Valley

🍷🍷🍷 **Lion and Compass,** 1023 N. Fair Oaks Ave., Sunnyvale (408/745-1260). Lunch Mon–Fri, dinner Mon–Sat. AE, CB, DC, MC, V. The valley's best-known rest. Rather sophisticated Continental cuisine. *Continental.* **I–M**

☼🍷 **MacArthur Park,** 27 University Ave., Palo Alto (415/321-9990). Lunch Sun–Fri, dinner nightly. Noisy but congenial rest. in a converted railroad station. Classic American food. *American.* **I**

☼▲▲▲ **YOSEMITE NATIONAL PARK** (210 mi./336km east via I-580, I-205, and Calif. 120): Nature in the raw; don't miss it. See Chapter 53 on Yosemite.

CHAPTER 51

THE CALIFORNIA COAST

□ □ □

San Francisco to San Diego

From the extraordinary panorama of **San Francisco,** 604 mi. (974km) to the north to lovely San Diego on the Mexican border, the California coast offers the visitor some of the country's most spectacular landscapes. It is an unexpected patchwork of fertile valleys, great cities, and unspoiled forests of pine or sequoia, of rocky headlands and wonderful beaches (though the currents sweeping in from the north can often chill the water). The California coast, however, is more than a colorful tract of American geography; it embodies a typically Californian way of life compounded of sun, relaxation, and communion with nature.

From the steep cliffs of **Big Sur,** a favorite meeting place for America's literary bohemia, to the fine sand beaches of **Santa Barbara** or **Huntington Beach,** the surfer's paradise, this great "Pacific Riviera" is a standing invitation to travelers, and to lovers of beauty. Thus the motorist who takes the celebrated coastal Hwy. 1 (Calif. 1), the "Cabrillo Highway," will encounter the period charm of the old Spanish colonial settlements like **Monterey,** so beloved by John Steinbeck; the trendy elegance of **Carmel;** the fabled castle of billionaire William Randolph Hearst at **San Simeon;** the rosary of Franciscan missions that runs the length of the coast from **San Juan Bautista** to **San Juan Capistrano;** or the mighty silhouette of **Morro Rock,** the Gibraltar of the West Coast, whose massive 563-ft. (172m) bulk looms over the Pacific. And let's not overlook the untold wealth of the late J. Paul Getty's Roman villa at **Malibu,** or the luxury of **La Jolla,** with its Riviera-like beauty. Along the incredible **"Seventeen-Mile Drive"** (27km) between Carmel and Monterey, are centuries-old cypresses and tidal rocks covered with sea anemones and peopled with sea lions and elephant seals, where every winter and spring you may watch the passing migration of the gray whales. The California coast, goal of any east-west trip across the U.S., will never cease to enchant the visitor.

For detailed information on the larger cities along the California coast, see the chapters on **Los Angeles, San Diego,** and **San Francisco.**

Note: The name "California," used by the first Spanish conquistadors, comes from a tale of medieval chivalry, and denotes a legendary isle lying to the east of Paradise, inhabited by dusky Amazons and by gryphons, with eagles' heads and lions' bodies.

BASIC FACTS: State of California. Area codes: 619 (San Diego), 714 (San Bernardino), 213 (Los Angeles), 805 (Santa Barbara), 408 (Monterey), 415 (San Francisco), 818 (Burbank). Time zone: Pacific. Founded: 1769 (San Diego);

1770 (Monterey); 1776 (San Francisco). Approximate distance from San Francisco to San Diego: 604 mi. (974 km).

CLIMATE: The California coast is no less fortunate in its climate than in its scenery. In winter (though this is no name by which to call such a season), the mercury never dips below 46°–50°F (8°–10°C), though there can be heavy rains at times in the northern and central parts of the state. Summer is very hot but dry; spring and autumn are wonderful to behold, and filled with unbelievably vibrant light, especially in the south. Aside from a few short weeks of bad weather in winter, this is a year-round paradise.

ARRIVAL & TRANSIT INFORMATION

AIRPORTS: There are five major airports on the California coast:
    Los Angeles International Airport (LAX) (see Chapter 54 on Los Angeles).
    Monterey Peninsula Airport (MRY), 4 mi. (6.5km) SE; for information, call 408/373-1704.
    San Diego Lindbergh International Airport (SAN) (see Chapter 55 on San Diego).
    San Francisco International Airport (SFO) (see Chapter 50 on San Francisco).
    Santa Barbara Municipal Airport (SBA), 10 mi. (16km) west; for information, call 805/683-4011.

AIRLINES: See the Los Angeles, San Diego, and San Francisco chapters for listings of domestic and international airlines.

CAR RENTAL: See the Los Angeles, San Diego, and San Francisco chapters.

BUS OR CAR RENTAL? Greyhound buses provide frequent, convenient service for the entire coastal region of California. On the other hand, car-rental rates in the state are very low—and the possibilities for interesting side trips are almost unlimited—so it's a very good idea to rent a car, or mobile home, with unlimited mileage.

TRAIN: The Amtrak stations are: in **Oxnard,** 200 E. 4th St. (toll free 800/872-7245); in **Salinas (Monterey),** 40 Railroad Ave. (toll free 800/872-7245); in **San Luis Obispo,** 1011 Railroad Ave. at Santa Rosa St. (805/541-5028); in **Santa Barbara,** 209 State St. (805/687-6848); see the Los Angeles, San Diego, and San Francisco chapters for offices in these cities.

INTERCITY BUSES: In addition to the Greyhound offices in San Francisco, Los Angeles, and San Diego (see these chapters for details), there are California coastal offices at 351 del Monte Ave., **Monterey** (408/372-1419); 150 South St., **San Luis Obispo** (805/543-2123); 34 W. Carrillo St., **Santa Barbara** (805/965-3971); and 425 Front St., Santa Cruz (408/423-1800).

INFORMATION & TOURS

TOURIST INFORMATION: For general information on the region, write or call the **California Office of Tourism,** 1121 L St., Sacramento, CA 95814 (916/322-1397; toll free 800/862-2543, ext. 99). For more specific information, contact the following:
    Los Angeles Visitors & Convention Bureau (see Chapter 54 on Los Angeles).

Monterey Chamber of Commerce, 380 Alvarado St., CA 93940 (408/649-1770).
San Francisco Visitors Bureau (see Chapter 50 on San Francisco).
San Luis Obispo Chamber of Commerce, 1039 Chorro St., CA 93401 (805/543-1323).
Santa Barbara Conference and Visitors Bureau, 1 Santa Barbara St., CA 93101 (805/965-3021).

GUIDED TOURS: See the chapters on San Francisco, Los Angeles, and San Diego; for other cities, look under "Sightseeing" in the local *Yellow Pages*.

SPECIAL EVENTS: For exact dates on the events listed below, consult the local chambers of commerce listed under "Tourist Information" (above), as well as the **Carmel Business Association,** Vandervort Court, on San Carlos, CA 93921 (408/624-2522); the **Oxnard Convention & Visitors Bureau,** 400 Esplanade Dr., CA 93030 (805/485-8833); the **San Clemente Chamber of Commerce,** 1100 N. El Camino Real, CA 92672 (714/492-1131); the **Santa Cruz Convention and Visitors Bureau,** 105 Cooper St., CA 95061 (408/423-1111); the **Solvang Chamber of Commerce,** 433 Alisal Rd., CA 93463 (805/688-0701); and the **Ventura Visitor and Convention Bureau,** 89-C California St., CA 93001 (805/648-2075).

Carmel
Carmel Bach Festival (last 2 weeks in July, beginning of Aug): Concerts, opera, poetry recitations, theater.
Gilroy
Garlic Festival (July): Features a giant open-air kitchen, a Garlic Queen pageant, garlic braiding, arts and crafts. Last full wknd of July.
Monterey
Monterey Jazz Festival (end of Sept): Attracts the biggest names in jazz today. The oldest continuous jazz festival in the nation.
Oceanside
San Luís Rey Fiesta (July): Reenactment of the Padres, an elaborate pageant that takes place the third wknd in July. Dances, entertainment. Spanish-style pit barbecue.
Oxnard
Channel Islands Harbor Parade (early Dec): Spectacular naval parade with decorated and illuminated boats.
Pebble Beach
Classic Cars Elegance Contest (end of Aug): Almost 200 classic cars, from the Bugatti Royale to the Cord L-29. One of the world's largest rallies of luxury cars.
San Clemente
La Cristianita Pageant (end of July): Commemorates the first baptisms by the Spanish missionaries.
San Luis Obispo
Mozart Festival (end of July to early Aug): Concerts, choirs, recitals.
Santa Barbara
Music Academy of the West Festival (July–Aug): Chamber and orchestral concerts, opera.
Old Spanish Days Festival (early Aug): Parades, historic pageants.
Santa Cruz
Cabrillo Music Festival (end of July to early Aug): Classical and contemporary music; one of California's most celebrated festivals.

Solvang
Danish Days Festival (3rd wknd in Sept): Costume festival celebrating the Danish national holiday.
Theaterfest (July to the end of Sept): Open-air theatricals.

Ventura
County Fair (Oct): Parades, carnival, rodeo, cattle show. Very colorful.

A NORTH-TO-SOUTH ITINERARY

Down the California Coast from San Francisco

To:	Distance	To:	Distance
Santa Cruz	81 mi. (131km)	Ventura	413 mi. (666km)
Gilroy	104 mi. (166km)	Oxnard	421 mi. (679km)
San Juan Bautista	115 mi. (185km)	Malibu	455 mi. (734km)
Castroville	132 mi. (213km)	Pacific Palisades	463 mi. (747km)
Monterey	143 mi. (231km)	Santa Monica	472 mi. (761km)
17-Mile Drive	145 mi. (234km)	Los Angeles	490 mi. (790km)
Carmel	157 mi. (253km)	Huntington Beach	520 mi. (839km)
Big Sur	184 mi. (297km)	Newport Beach	526 mi. (848km)
San Simeon	248 mi. (400km)	Laguna Beach	535 mi. (863km)
Morro Rock	276 mi. (445km)	San Juan Capistrano	547 mi. (882km)
San Luis Obispo	290 mi. (468km)	San Clemente	554 mi. (894km)
Lompoc	327 mi. (527km)	Oceanside-Carlsbad	580 mi. (935km)
Solvang	339 mi. (547km)	La Jolla	589 mi. (950km)
Santa Barbara	386 mi. (623km)	San Diego	604 mi. (974km)

A Note on Accommodations: Room rates along the California Coast are coded as follows: **VE**, Very Expensive ($140 and up); **E**, Expensive ($90–$140); **M**, Moderate ($60–$90); **I**, Inexpensive ($30–$60); **B**, Budget (up to $30). A listing of toll free numbers is in the Appendix.
A Note on Restaurant Prices: California Coast restaurant prices, per person, excluding drinks and service charges, are coded as follows: **VE**, Very Expensive ($60 and up); **E**, Expensive ($40–$60); **M**, Moderate ($25–$40); **I**, Inexpensive ($15–$25); **B**, Budget (up to $15).

SANTA CRUZ (81 mi./131km): Busy fishing port with a long pier and 28 mi. (45km) of public beaches much frequented by swimmers. Last refuge of the hippies. Reproduction, one-half original size, of the Santa Cruz Mission, destroyed by an earthquake in the 19th century and now undergoing restoration. At **Año Nuevo State Reserve** (21 mi./ 34km north on Calif. 1), the unusual spectacle of hundreds of sea lions, elephant seals, and other marine animals lazily sunning themselves on the rocks. At **Felton** (7 mi./11km north on Calif. 9) is the Roaring Camp and Big Trees Railroad (408/335-4400), where a picturesque little train from the early West will take you through the sequoia forests (daily May–Sept.). Worth the side trip.

Where to Stay
Dream Inn, 175 W. Cliff Dr., Santa Cruz, CA 95060 (408/ 426-4330). 164 rms, A/C, cable color TV. AE, CB, DC, MC, V. Free parking, pool, rest., bar, rm svce, disco, free crib. *Note:* Modern 10-floor motel, comfortable and attractive; the best rms (w. balconies) overlook the beach. Good svce. Direct access to beach. **E–VE**

Where to Eat

♀ **Crow's Nest,** 2218 E. Cliff Dr. (408/476-4560). A/C.
Lunch/dinner daily (till 2am), brunch Sun; closed Thanksgiving, Dec 24–25. AE, MC, V. *Specialties:* fresh salmon (in season), fish of the day, steak. *Note:* Likable fish rest. standing on the jetty of the yacht basin; beautifully fresh fish prepared without any imagination. Svce w. a smile. Terrace for fine days, w. a view of the harbor. Dancing. Resv. advised. *Steak/Seafood.* **B–I**

♀ **Taco Moreno,** 1053 Watcher (408/429-6095). A/C.
Lunch/dinner daily. No credit cards. *Specialties:* tacos, burritos (w. barbecued pork, carnitas, beef asado, beans, tongue, and green chile), quesadillas. *Note:* This hole-in-the-wall joint run by Esteban Moreno and his family offers the best burritos in town. The four tables are squeezed between cases of natural sodas or boxes of tortillas and its jukebox occupies about a quarter of the dining rm. A favorite of the students at University of California Santa Cruz. No resv. *Mexican.* **B**

IN NEARBY CAPITOLA ☆☆ **Shadowbrook,** 1750 Wharf Rd. (408/475-1511). No A/C. Dinner nightly, brunch Sat–Sun. *Specialties:* fresh salmon (in season), abalone, excellent meat. *Note:* One of the coast's most popular rests., reached by a little funicular from the highway, below which it stands on the edge of a pretty inlet, surrounded by greenery. Good svce; resv. advised; dancing nightly in summer. *Steak/Seafood.* **I**

Ⓐ **GILROY** (104 mi./166km): Will Rogers called this self-proclaimed "garlic capital of the world" "the only town in America where you can marinate a steak by hanging it on the clothesline." Gilroy is famous for its Garlic Festival, an annual extravaganza held the last full wknd of July, complete with garlic-recipe cook-off, garlic braiding, and Gourmet Alley's alfresco kitchen with more than 85 food booths. Worth the side trip.

☀Ⓐ **SAN JUAN BAUTISTA** (115 mi./185km): The **Mission of San Juan Bautista,** 2nd St. and Mariposa St. (408/623-4528), open daily. California's largest Franciscan mission (1797), and one of the best preserved. Fine **plaza** with many buildings from the 1850s, including the splendid Plaza Hotel on 2nd St. (408/623-4881), open daily. Shouldn't be missed.

Where to Eat

☀♀ **Cademartori's,** 1st St. and San José St. (408/623-4511). No A/C. Lunch/dinner Tues–Sun; closed July 4 and 3 weeks in Dec. AE, DC, MC, V. *Specialties:* veal parmigiana, saltimbocca, abalone, homemade pasta. *Note:* This Italian-American rest. occupies a former outbuilding of the San Juan Bautista Mission, standing in a beautiful grdn. It offers honorable, meticulous cuisine and a wonderful view over the San Juan Valley. Open-air patio in summer; a good place. *Italian/American.* **B–I**

Ⓐ **CASTROVILLE** (132 mi./213km): In this town, modestly styling itself the "artichoke capital of the world," you may try this delicious vegetable prepared in every conceivable way—fried, boiled, as a cream soup, sautéed, or even in a cake—at the Giant Artichoke Restaurant, 11241 Merritt St. (408/633-3204). Entertaining festival every Sept, with election of an "artichoke queen."

Where to Stay

IN NEARBY SALINAS ▯ **Motel 6,** 1010 Fairview Ave., Salinas, CA 93901 (408/758-2122). 78 rms, color TV, free in-rm movies. AE, DC, MC, V. Free parking, pool, free crib. *Note:* A small, reasonably priced motel offering serviceable comfort on a shoestring. An unbeatable value. **B–I**

☼⚹ ᗩᗩ **MONTEREY** (143 mi./231km): Lively and colorful, Monterey is the most Spanish of Californian towns, still evidencing many traces of its colonial days: the **Presidio** (1846), seat of the Spanish government, on Pacific St. (408/647-5414), open Mon–Fri; the old **Custom House** (1827), 1 Custom House Plaza; the **Royal Presidio Chapel,** at 550 Church St., founded by Spanish settlers in 1770; **California's First Theater,** the oldest theater in the state, at Pacific St. and Scott St. (408/375-4916), where performances have been given without interruption since 1847; the **Colton Hall Museum,** formerly the City Hall, at 522 Pacific St., whose cellar was used as a prison during the Mexican War. There are some charming **old houses,** one of which, at 530 Houston St., belonged to Robert Louis Stevenson, the author of *Treasure Island*.

You should also see the harbor district and **Cannery Row,** made famous by John Steinbeck; at 886 Cannery Row (408/648-4888) is the splendid, ultramodern **Monterey Bay Aquarium,** inaugurated in 1984, open daily, with more than 5,000 specimens including many sharks and giant octopi; it was used as a setting for the movie *Star Trek IV*.

Where to Stay

🍷🍷🍷 **Hyatt Regency,** 1 Old Golf Course, Monterey, CA 93940 🛏🛏🛏 (408/372-1234; toll free, see Hyatt). 579 rms, color TV, in-rm movies. AE, CB, DC, MC, V. Free parking, two pools, six tennis courts, golf course, health club, sauna, two rests. (including the Peninsula); rm svce, bars, disco, beauty parlor, concierge, free crib. *Note:* One of the best hotels along the California coast; modern and elegant, w. almost 15 acres (6ha) of grdns facing the Del Monte golf course. Excellent svce; favored by groups and wealthy sportslovers. Recently modernized and enlarged. Two VIP floors. **VE**

☼⚹🍷🍷🍷 **Monterey Plaza,** 400 Cannery Row, Monterey, CA 93940 🛏🛏🛏 (408/646-1700; toll free 800/631-1339). 290 rms, A/C, cable color TV. AE, CB, DC, MC, V. Valet gar. $8, health club, private beach, rest. (Delfino), coffee shop, bar, rm svce, boutiques, concierge. *Note:* The most recent of Monterey's palaces; three elegant four-story Spanish Colonial buildings on Cannery Row halfway between Fisherman's Wharf and the Aquarium. The interior decoration, featuring Oriental rugs, teak panels, a profusion of marble, objets d'art, and period furniture, comes together in a magnificent triumph of luxury and sophistication. Huge, comfortable rms, most w. ocean view; impeccable svce. Honorable Italian rest. One of the best places on the Pacific Coast. **E–VE**

🍷 **Cypress Tree Inn,** 2227 Fremont Rd., Monterey, CA 93940 🛏 (408/372-7586). 55 rms, cable color TV. AE, MC, V. Free parking, rest., crib $6. *Note:* Typical small motel, modest but well run. Spacious rms w. balconies and mini-refrigerators (some w. kitchenettes). Free morning coffee. Located 5 min. from dwntwn and from Monterey State Beach. **I–M,** but lower rates off-season.

🍷 **Motel 6,** 2124 N. Fremont St., Monterey, CA 93940 (408/ 🛏 646-8585). 51 rms, color TV, free in-rm movies. AE, DC, MC, V. Free parking, pool, free crib. *Note:* Small budget hotel nr. dwntwn, adequately comfortable. Unbeatable value. **I**

Where to Eat

☼⚹🍸🍸🍸 **The Old House in Old Monterey** (formerly Gallatin's), 500 🛏🛏🛏 Hartnell St. (408/373-3737). A/C. Dinner only, nightly. AE, CB, DC, MC, V. Jkt. *Specialties:* confit of duck, shrimp à la dijonnaise, grilled salmon. Menu changes regularly; very good wine list. *Note:* This distinguished French rest., in a splendid 19th-century dwelling house, is run w. a master's hand by Léonce Picot, owner of several celebrated rests. in Florida (including Casa Vecchia and Down Under). Sumptuous setting w. antique furniture, rich rugs, and dazzling flower arrangements. Classic French cuisine impeccably prepared and served; stylishly elegant. Resv. recommended. *French.* **M**

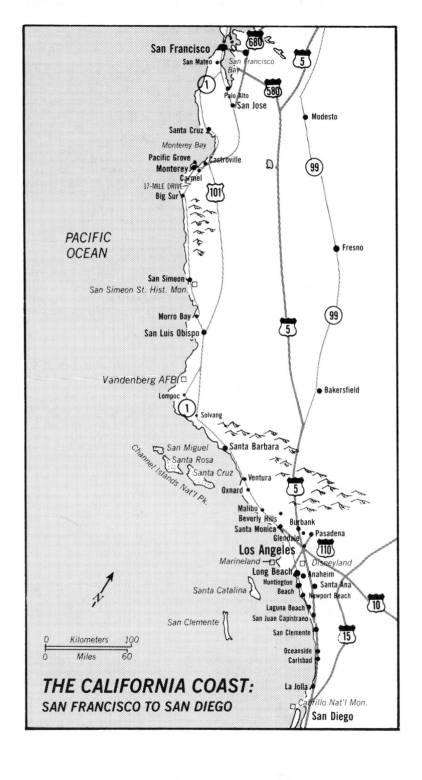

THE CALIFORNIA COAST:
SAN FRANCISCO TO SAN DIEGO

�W�W **Sardine Factory,** 701 Wave St. (408/373-3775). A/C. Din-
ⲎⲎ ner nightly, brunch Sun; closed for 1 week at Christmas. AE,
CB, DC, MC, V. J&T. *Specialties:* abalone bisque, fish of the day, shellfish,
broiled shrimp w. shallots, tournedos Cannery Row. Fine list of reasonably
priced wines. *Note:* This famous rest., though its former glory has perhaps faded a
trifle, still overlooks the beautiful bay. Exemplary meat and fish prepared in a
rather outdated fashion. Engagingly got up as a tropical greenhouse. Svce so-so.
Comfortable, welcoming bar. Resv. advisable. Valet parking. *Continental/
Seafood.* I–M

�W **The Fishery,** 21 Soledad Dr. (408/373-6200). A/C. Dinner
Ⲏ only, Tues–Sat; closed Dec–Jan. MC, V. *Specialties:*
fishburgers, broiled filet of Coho salmon, catfish Louisiana style, Thai-style seafood platter, squid. *Note:* The community's favorite fish rest., serving the freshest
possible food prepared w. some exotic touches (Malaysian and Thai recipes in
particular) and at very acceptable prices. Rather elaborate Oriental decor. Fast,
deft svce. In view of its popularity, resv. advised. *Seafood.* I

☀☖☖ **"SEVENTEEN-MILE DRIVE"** (between **Monterey** and
Carmel, 145 mi./234km): One of the country's most scenic
roads, it circles the Monterey Peninsula along the shore. **Cypress Point** features a
superb cypress grove at the edge of the ocean. At **Seal Rock** there are large numbers of marine animals as well as dream houses and the world-famous **Pebble
Beach golf course.** If you saw nothing else in California, this would still make
the trip worthwhile, as attested by the 1½ million visitors every year.

☀☖☖ **CARMEL** (157 mi./253km): This charming little artists'
community, spruce and covered in flowers, has become a fash-
ionable tourist attraction and a Shangri-La for lucky retirees and personalities (including actor Clint Eastwood, former mayor of Carmel). Along Ocean Ave. and
the nearby streets are many open-air restaurants, art galleries, and boutiques. See
the beautiful **San Carlos Borromeo Mission** (1770), and the tomb of Fray
Junípero Serra, founder of the California missions, at 3080 Rio Rd. (408/624-
3600), open daily. The **Biblical Garden** at Lincoln St. and Seventh Ave. (408/
624-3550) has a complete collection of the trees, plants, and flowers mentioned
in the Bible or originating in the Holy Land.
   Point Lobos State Reserve (3 mi./5km south along Calif. 1), with its
rocks thronged with sea lions and sea birds, and its centuries-old cypress trees, is a
must for nature-lovers. There is a popular Bach Festival at the end of July. Make a
point of coming here, but try to avoid the crowds on summer weekends.

Where to Stay
   ☀ＬＬＬ **Quail Lodge,** 8205 Valley Green Dr., Carmel, CA 93923
(408/624-1581; toll free, see Preferred). 96 rms (cottages),
A/C, cable color TV. AE, CB, DC, MC, V. Free parking, two pools, tennis
court, putting green, sauna, bicycles, rest. (The Covey), two bars, rm svce, nightclub, hrdrsr, library, concierge. *Note:* Delightful country inn set in beautiful
grdns w. duck ponds, adj. the Carmel Valley golf course. Luxuriously decorated
rms w. fireplaces, minibars, patios, and private balconies. Polished, attentive svce;
elegantly romantic atmosphere. Interesting golf and tennis packages. **VE**

ＬＬ **La Playa,** Camino Real at 8th St., Carmel, CA 93921 (408/
624-6476; toll free 800/582-8900). 75 rms, A/C, cable color
TV. AE, DC, MC, V. Free valet parking, pool, rest. (Spyglass), bar, rm svce, free
crib. *Note:* Attractive Spanish Colonial hotel dating from the early 20th century,
w. an entirely renovated interior. Large, comfortable rms w. mini-refrigerators
and private patios, the best offering a view of the ocean and the Point Lobos wildlife reserve. Inviting grdns; efficient svce. **E–VE**

Ⲏ **Pine Inn,** Ocean Ave. at Monte Verde St., Carmel, CA 93921
(408/624-3851). 49 rms, cable color TV. AE, MC, V. Free

parking, rest., bar, rm svce, crib $5. *Note:* Small hotel almost on the beach; comfortable rms w. brass beds and fine views, each decorated in a different style. Fine Victorian decor w. stained glass and old floor lamps. Svce and reception both leave something to be desired. **M–E**

♀ **Jade Tree Inn,** Junipero St. and Sixth Ave, Carmel, CA 93921
🛏 (408/624-1831). 55 rms, cable color TV. AE, MC, V. Free parking, pool, nearby coffee shop, crib $5. *Note:* Inviting small motel nr. the San Carlos Borromeo Mission; large, comfortable rms w. fireplaces and shaded patios, some w. ocean view. You are made welcome w. a smile here. **M**

IN NEARBY PEBBLE BEACH 🛏🛏🛏🛏 **The Lodge,** 17-Mile Dr., Pebble Beach, CA 93953 (408/624-3811), 3 mi. (5km) north of Carmel. 163 rms, A/C, cable color TV. AE, CB, DC, MC, V. Free valet parking, private beach, pool, 12 tennis courts, four golf courses, sauna, riding, sailing, three rests. (including Club XIX), coffee shop, bar, 24-hr. rm svce, hrdrsr, boutiques, concierge, free crib. *Note:* Pure luxury on the ocean. Exceptional comfort and svce; tasteful decor w. period furniture and many artworks. Spacious rms w. fireplaces and minibars, and balconies or patios w. a view of the ocean (in the better ones) or the golf course. Excellent rest. (Club XIX). Remarkable sports facilities. Airport limo. Interesting golf and wknd packages. Resv. should be made well in advance. One of the 12 best hotels in the country. **VE**

Where to Eat

🍸🍸 **Crème Carmel,** San Carlos St. and Seventh Ave. (408/624-
🍸 0444). A/C. Dinner only, nightly; closed Jan 1, Thanksgiving, Dec 25. MC, V. *Specialties:* lamb w. chutney, apple, and mint; bass stuffed w. crabmeat; red snapper Hawaiian; filet of beef au cabernet; roast duck; soufflés; goat-cheese pie. The menu changes regularly. *Note:* Small (35-seat) rest. w. a warm, vital ambience. Modern Californian cuisine, elegant and imaginative, but feebly supported by the wine list. Svce is the best; an excellent place to eat. Resv. a must. *American/Continental.* **I–M**

🍸🍸 **Rio Grill,** Calif. 1 at Rio Rd. (408/625-5436). A/C. Lunch/
🍸 dinner daily, brunch Sun; closed Thanksgiving, Dec 25. MC, V. *Specialties:* "Firecracker", catfish Créole; oakwood-grilled chicken, fish, and meat; quesadillas; excellent homemade desserts. Menu changes daily. *Note:* Under the same management as the Fog City Diner in San Francisco and Mustards Grill in Napa Valley, this fashionable rest. offers inventive and elegant California cuisine. Decor recalls the Native American pueblos of New Mexico: adobe walls, heavy exposed beams, and cactus. Svce on the relaxed side, but a very congenial atmosphere. A discovery. *American.* **I**

🍸🍸 **Rocky Point,** Calif. 1 at Rocky Point, 12 mi. (19km) south of
🍸 Carmel (408/624-2933). A/C. Lunch/dinner daily; closed Thanksgiving, Dec 25. AE, MC, V. *Specialties:* meat from the broiler, swordfish, barbecued chicken. *Note:* Perched on a cliff, this popular rest. looks right out over the ocean and its wildlife (the rocks below are floodlit at night). Satisfying steaks and irreproachably fresh fish of the day. Resv. advised. *Steak/Seafood.* **I**

🍸 **Hog's Breath Inn,** San Carlos St. and Fifth Ave. (408/625-
🍸 1044). A/C. Lunch/dinner daily. AE, MC, V. *Specialties:* sandwiches, variety of salads, catch of the day, good homemade desserts. *Note:* Country inn w. appealing shady patio – perfect for a pleasant meal on the wing. Honest, unpretentious food; the owner is none other than the famous actor (and former mayor of Carmel) Clint Eastwood. *American.* **B–I**

🍸 **Shabu Shabu,** Carmel Plaza, Mission St. between Ocean Ave.
🍸 and 7th (408/625-2828). Lunch Mon–Sat, dinner nightly. MC, V. *Specialties:* tempura, teriyaki, shabu shabu (steak, tofu, and vegetables). *Note:* Tasteful, traditional Japanese country-style rest. w. three selections cooked at your table. Named for its specialty. *Japanese.* **B–I**

IN NEARBY PEBBLE BEACH ♔♔♔ **Club XIX,** at the Lodge (see "Where to Stay," above) (408/625-1880). A/C. Lunch/dinner daily. AE, CB, DC, MC, V. Jkt. *Specialties:* abalone, filet of beef en croûte, fresh salmon (in season), grilled pheasant, rack of lamb bouquetière, soufflé Grand Marnier. Good wine list. *Note:* Elegant, sumptuous rest. appropriate to a palatial hotel. Classic but delicate French cooking. Magnificent view of Pebble Beach golf club and the ocean. Exemplary svce. Dining by candlelight. One of the best on the coast. Resv. advised. *French.* **M–E**

☀️🛏️ **BIG SUR** (184 mi./297km): In the 1950s this was the haunt of America's literary bohemians. Its splendid rocky cliffs and its pine and redwood forest have served as a backdrop for innumerable movies, TV series, and novels. Henry Miller, who passed his last years here, devoted one of his most famous passages to the place. Very beautiful beach, deserted more often than not. Well worth visiting.

Where to Stay
☀️🏨 **Ventana Inn,** Calif. 1 at Ventana Village, CA 93920 (408/667-2331; toll free 800/628-6500). 60 rms, A/C, color TV, in-rm movies. AE, CB, DC, MC, V. Free parking, two pools, sauna, solarium, rest., bar, free breakfast. *Note:* Romantic country inn nestled in a mountain meadow 1,000 ft. (305m) above the Pacific. One of the most widely known hotels on the California coast, w. a spectacular ocean view. Very comfortable rms w. fireplaces, balconies, and minibars, but even so, rates are high for the quality of the svce and facilities. **VE**

🔑 **Big Sur Lodge,** Calif. 1, Big Sur, CA 93920 (408/667-2171). 61 cottages; no TV or telephones in rms. MC, V. Free parking, pool, sauna, coffee shop, grocery store. *Note:* Comfortable bungalows (some w. fireplaces and kitchenettes) in the midst of a grove of redwoods, which is part of Pfeiffer–Big Sur State Park. Very rustic atmosphere; ideal for family parties. **M**

Where to Eat
☀️🍷 **Ventana,** at the Ventana Inn (see "Where to Stay," above) (408/667-2331). A/C. Lunch/dinner daily. AE, DC, MC, V. *Specialties:* veal w. tomato and artichoke hearts, fish and meat from the wood-fire grill, rack of lamb, very good homemade desserts. Fine list of California wines. *Note:* Beautiful greenhouse of a dining rm looking out over the ocean (*ventana* is the Spanish word for window); cedar paneling, warm colors. Overhanging the water is a terrace where you can enjoy your meal in the open air. Modern California-style cuisine; friendly, relaxed svce. One of the best-known establishments on the coast. Resv. required for dinner. *American.* **I–M**

☀️🍷 **Nepenthe,** Calif. 1, 3 mi. (5km) south of the entrance to the state park (408/667-2345). No A/C. Lunch/dinner daily. AE, MC, V. *Specialties:* ambrosia burger, quiche, broiled fish, roast chicken. *Note:* From its clifftop, this well-known country inn gives you a splendid view of the sea. Limited menu of food straightforwardly prepared, at reasonable prices. Enjoyable if slightly touristy atmosphere; good svce. *American.* **B–I**

☀️🏰🏰🏰 **HEARST–SAN SIMEON STATE HISTORICAL MONUMENT** (248 mi./400km): The imposing Spanish-Moorish castle that crowns the hill of **Cuesta Encantada** was designed and built by newspaper magnate William Randolph Hearst, and is without a doubt America's most extravagant and insanely baroque edifice. Hearst's larger-than-life-size eccentricities were the inspiration of Orson Welles's masterpiece, *Citizen Kane.* From 1919 until Hearst's death in 1951, armies of workers labored on the enormous mansion standing in its splendid Italianate gardens—but it is still unfinished in spite of the $30 million (in comparatively uninflated money!) spent on it. The interior, a mixture of Etruscan, Roman, Greek, Gothic, and Renaissance styles, holds hundreds of works of art which Hearst's unbridled passion for collecting, and his wealth, led him to acquire in Europe for immense sums. Don't miss the enormous banquet hall, Neptune's swimming pool, the great salon with its priceless tapestries, and the owner's lavish private quarters. Several guided tours daily, of which tour no. 1, leaving hourly on the half hour, is the most interesting. Resv. advisable through California MISTIX agencies (check for addresses in local telephone books). For information on timetables and prices, call 805/927-2020; for resv., call toll free 800/444-7275. A visit to Hearst Castle is worth the trip all by itself.

Where to Stay

San Simeon Pines Resort, 7200 Moonstone Beach Dr., San Simeon, CA 93452 (805/927-4648), 1½ mi. (2.5km) south of the Hearst Castle. 60 rms, color TV, in-rm movies. AE, MC, V. Free parking, pool, golf, beach, nearby coffee shop, crib $5. *Note:* Comfortable little motel in a wood environment nr. the ocean; some rms w. terraces and extensive views. Ideal for visiting the castle. Free morning coffee. Agreeable svce and reception. Good value. **I–M**

Best Western Cavalier Inn, 9415 Hearst Dr., San Simeon, CA 93452 (805/927-4688; toll free, see Best Western), 3 mi. (5km) south of the Hearst Castle. 90 rms, color TV, in-rm movies. AE, CB, DC, MC, V. Free parking, two pools, coffee shop, rm svce, hrdrsr, boutiques, free crib. *Note:* Modern, functional beachfront motel; comfortable rms w. private balconies and mini-refrigerators (most w. fireplaces), the best w. ocean view. Good svce; good value. **I–M**

Where to Eat

IN NEARBY CAMBRIA **Brambles Dinner House,** 4005 Burton Dr., Cambria (805/927-4716), 9 mi. (15km) south of the Hearst Castle. No A/C. Dinner only, nightly; closed Dec 25. AE, MC, V. *Specialties:* broiled fresh salmon (in season), steak broiled over wood, roast beef w. Yorkshire pudding, roast rack of lamb. *Note:* Fine Victorian house, tastefully decorated. First-rate broiled meat and fish. Thoughtful svce; romantic atmosphere. Resv. advisable in summer. *Steak/Seafood.* **I–M**

Grey Fox Inn, 4095 Burton Dr. at Center St. (805/927-3305). No A/C. Lunch/dinner Thurs–Tues, brunch Sun; closed Dec 25. AE, MC, V. *Specialties:* chicken Kiev, roast beef, fish of the day, fresh vegetables. *Note:* Charming little rest. (seats barely 40) w. slightly old-fashioned decor. Open-air dining in good weather. Meticulous cuisine and svce; very good value. *American/Continental.* **B–I**

MORRO ROCK (276 mi./445km): Called the "Gibraltar of the Pacific," this 563-ft. (172m) monolith of volcanic rock dominates the approach to the pretty fishing port of **Morro Bay.** Beautiful nearby beaches include **Cayucos Beach, Atascadero Beach,** and **Morro Strand Beach.** Very near here, in the marshes at the mouth of **Los Oros Creek,** the largest wetlands on the California coast, live no fewer than 250 varieties of birds.

Where to Stay

Inn at Morro Bay (formerly the Best Western Golden Tee), 19 Country Club Dr., Morro Bay, CA 93442 (805/772-5651; toll free 800/321-9566). 97 rms, color TV, in-rm movies. AE, CB, DC, MC, V. Free parking, pool, golf course, bicycling, fishing, rest. (Bay Rm), bar, rm svce, disco, crib $10. *Note:* Pleasant motel almost in the ocean, exactly halfway between San Francisco and Los Angeles. Private marina. Comfortable rms w. balconies; view over the bay and Morro Rock. Amiable, competent svce; very acceptable rest. All in all, good value; recommended. **M–E**

Bay View, 225 Harbor St., Morro Bay, CA 93442 (805/772-2771; toll free 800/742-8439). 22 rms, color TV, in-rm movies. AE, CB, DC, MC, V. Free parking, whirlpool bath, nearby coffee shop, crib

$4. *Note:* Small, rustic motel nr. the water. Large, comfortable rms w. fireplaces and mini-refrigerators, the best w. ocean view. Free morning coffee. Price a little steep for what's on offer. **I–M,** but lower rates off-season.

☕ **Motel 6,** 298 Atascadero Rd., Morro Bay, CA 93442 (805/772-5641). 72 rms, color TV, free in-rm movies. AE, DC, MC, V. Free parking, pool, free crib. *Note:* Small budget hotel, adequately comfortable. Unbeatable value. **B–I**

Where to Eat

🍷🍷 **Dutch's Fine Dining,** 2738 N. Main St. (805/772-8645). No A/C. Lunch Mon–Fri, dinner daily, brunch Sun. AE, CB, DC, MC, V. *Specialties:* sole à la cardinal, broiled lobster, crab Quo Vadis. *Note:* An outstanding place for seafood-lovers: absolutely fresh produce prepared with real talent. The old stone house is massive but comfortable and inviting. Open-air terrace in summer. *Seafood/Continental.* **B–I**

☼🏛 **SAN LUIS OBISPO** (290 mi./468km): Founded in 1772 by the Spanish Franciscan Fray Junípero Serra, this commercial town, overlooked by four cone-shaped volcanic peaks, is the site of the magnificent **San Luis Obispo de Tolosa Mission,** now a parish church and museum, at Monterey St. and Broad St. (805/543-6850), open daily. Very near the mission is the interesting **San Luis Obispo County Historical Museum,** 696 Monterey St. (805/543-0638), open Wed–Sun, devoted to the history of the Spanish colonial era. Some 19th-century commercial buildings should not be overlooked: Sinsheimer Bros. at 849 Monterey St. and Ah Louis Store at 800 Palm St. A must-see.

Where to Stay

☼🏨 **Madonna Inn,** 100 Madonna Rd., San Luis Obispo, CA 93401 (805/543-3000). 109 rms, cable color TV. No credit cards. Free parking, rest., bar, rm svce, disco, free crib. *Note:* The craziest hotel in the entire West—a rococo four-story building w. no elevators, where every rm is decorated in a different style or period, from tropical jungle to fake Louis XVI—not to mention the rm w. artificial moonlight or the celestial suite full of cherubs. A triumph of Hollywood kitsch and bad taste. Some of the rms (the Cloud Nine Suite, w. angels, or the Elegance Room, in lavender, blue, and pink) are booked 3–6 months ahead. Well worth a visit. Rest. (Gold Rush Rm) acceptable but no more. Svce doesn't measure up. **M–E**

☕ **Motel 6,** 1433 Calle Joaquin, San Luis Obispo, CA 93401 (805/549-9595). 87 rms, color TV, free in-rm movies. AE, DC, MC, V. Free parking, pool, free crib. *Note:* Small budget hotel, adequately comfortable. Unbeatable value. **B–I**

IN NEARBY AVILA BEACH The 🏨 **San Luis Bay Inn,** Avila Rd., Avila Beach, CA 93424 (805/595-2333; toll free 800/592-5928). 75 rms, A/C, cable color TV. AE, MC, V. Free parking, pool, tennis court, golf, rest. (Cove), bar, rm svce, disco, free airport limo, crib $10. *Note:* Beautiful resort hotel a few feet from the beach. The best rms (w. balconies) look out over Avila Beach and the charming little port of San Luis. Excellent svce; one of the best hotels on the Pacific coast. Resv., several weeks ahead, are a must. Lovely grdns. Deep-sea fishing. **E–VE**

IN NEARBY LOS OLIVOS The ☼ 🏨 **Los Olivos Grand Hotel,** 2860 Grand Ave., Los Olivos, CA 93441 (805/688-7788; toll free 800/626-7249). 21 suites, A/C, cable color TV. AE, MC, V. Free parking, pool, rest., bar, rm svce. *Note:* In the heart of the Santa Ynez Valley, this delightful turn-of-the-century inn boasts some 20 luxurious suites, each decorated in the style of a famous European impressionist painter. Magnificent grdns; svce and reception very polished; rest. offers truly remarkable French cooking. A peaceful, sophisticated retreat a little more than 2 hrs. by road from Los Angeles. Children under 16 not admitted. **VE**

Where to Eat

☼☽🍷 **Gold Rush Room,** at the Madonna Inn (see "Where to Stay," above) (805/543-3000). A/C. Dinner only, nightly. No credit cards. *Specialties:* abalone, filet mignon, seafood. *Note:* Decorated, as is the rest of the hotel, in dubious taste; the rest rms in the basement alone are worth the visit all by themselves. Cuisine and svce are unwarrantably pretentious. Dancing. May interest novelty-hunters. *Seafood/American.* **I–M**

🔥 **LOMPOC** (327 mi./527km): Near **Vandenberg Air Force Base** and its missile launchers, this little town of 20,000 people, known as "Valley of the Flowers," accounts for more than half of all the flower seeds sold throughout the world. North 3 mi. (5km) along Calif. 246 is **La Purísima Concepción Mission,** founded in 1787 and rebuilt in 1812, at Purisima Rd. and Mission Gate Rd. (805/733-3713), open daily. It is one of the finest, and best restored, in California, with beautiful gardens. A must-see.

☼☽🏛 **SOLVANG** (339 mi./547km): A little corner of Scandinavia in the heart of California. Founded by Danish settlers in 1911, this unexpected glimpse of old Europe, with its windmills, bakeries, and dovecotes, attracts many tourists. You'll like the stores and restaurants. The attractive **Santa Inés Mission,** at 1760 Mission Dr. (805/688-4815), is open daily. A must-see.

Where to Stay

☼☽🍷🍷🍷 **Alisal Guest Ranch,** 1054 Alisal Rd., Solvang, CA 93463 (805/688-6411), 3 mi. (5km) south of Solvang. 66 rms and 3 bungalows, cable color TV in main lounge. AE, MC, V. Free parking, pool, tennis court, golf, riding, boating, rest., bars, rm svce, disco. *Note:* A real stock ranch carrying more than 2,000 head of cattle on almost 9,900 acres (4,000ha) of rolling land with a large private lake. For lovers of the Far Western way of life there are horseback riding and open-air barbecues. Very comfortable; relaxed svce and reception. Excellent value. **VE** (Modified American Plan).

☼☽🍷🍷 **Petersen Village Inn,** 1576 Mission Dr., Solvang, CA 93463 (805/688-3121; toll free 800/321-8985 in California). 42 rms, A/C, cable color TV. AE, CB, DC, MC, V. Free parking, whirlpool, rests., bar, rm svce. *Note:* Gracious old-world-style country inn, part of a re-created Danish village w. shops, galleries, bakery, and sidewalk cafés. Spacious, beautifully decorated rms w. canopy beds (some w. private patios or balconies). Charming atmosphere. Very good svce. A very fine place to stay. **E–VE**

🍷 **Best Western King Frederik,** 1617 Copenhagen Dr., Solvang, CA 93463 (805/688-5515; toll free, see Best Western). 46 rms, A/C, cable color TV. AE, CB, DC, MC, V. Free parking, pool, nearby coffee shop, free breakfast, crib $4. *Note:* Charming little Scandinavian-style motel; comfortable rms w. balconies; in the heart of town. Good value. **I**

Where to Eat

☼☽🍷🍷 **Danish Inn,** 1547 Mission Dr. (805/688-4813). A/C. Breakfast/lunch/dinner daily. AE, MC, V. *Specialties:* smörgåsbord, beef Lindström, veal Oscar, fresh salmon, rack of lamb, Danish pastries. *Note:* This spruce, comfortable rest. w. its Scandinavian contemporary decor (try to sit in the Windmill Rm) is deservedly a favorite w. visitors to Solvang. *Scandinavian/Continental.* **B–I**

☼☽🏛🏛 **SANTA BARBARA** (386 mi./623km): Enchanting seaside resort at the foot of the Santa Ynez Mountains which has become a favorite home for movie stars and the California rich. Many Spanish-style adobe houses. The **Santa Barbara Mission** (1786), E. Los Olivos St. and Upper Laguna St. (805/682-4713), with its twin pink-and-white towers, is one of the state's most popular tourist attractions. Nicknamed "the queen of the missions" because of its architectural splendor, it has a wonderful view over the town and the ocean. Open daily.

Other remarkable specimens of the colonial style include the Spanish-Moorish palace of the **County Courthouse,** 1100 Anacapa St., with spacious lawns and panoramic views from the tower, and the **Presidio** (1782), 123 E. Cañon Perdido (805/966-9719), one of the four fortresses built by the Spanish in California. Buildings include a chapel, barracks, residence, and padres' quarters. And don't forget the very beautiful **Museum of Art** at 1130 State St. (805/963-4364), open Tues–Sun, renowned for its collection of Greek and Roman art; or the picturesque **De la Guerra Plaza** and **El Paseo,** a group of courtyards, plazas, and alleys dating from 1827 and now boasting art galleries, boutiques, and sidewalk cafés.

See also the unusual giant fig tree, the **Moreton Bay Fig Tree,** at Chapala St. and Montecito St., more than 110 years old, whose branch spread—160 ft. (49m)—can shade 10,000 people from the sun; and the **Stearns Wharf,** at the foot of State St., a three-block-long wharf built in 1872, featuring restaurants, shops, and marine-life exhibits.

Where to Stay

Four Seasons Biltmore, 1260 Channel Dr., Santa Barbara, CA 93108 (805/969-2261; toll free, see Four Seasons). 229 rms and 11 cottages (holding two to eight people each), color TV, in-rm movies. AE, CB, DC, MC, V. Free valet parking, two pools, sauna, tennis court, putting green, beach, rest., coffee shop, bar, rm svce, disco, drugstore, concierge. *Note:* One of the oldest palace hotels on the California coast, housed in a beautiful Spanish-Moorish building at the edge of the ocean surrounded by 19 acres (7.7ha) of superb tropical grdns. Luxurious rms w. private balconies and an unobstructed view of either the Santa Ynez Mountains or the Pacific. Efficient svce. Has ranked as one of the country's finest hotels since it opened in 1927. **VE**

El Encanto Hotel & Garden Villas, 1900 Lasuen Rd., Santa Barbara, CA 93103 (805/687-5000). 100 cottages, color TV, in-rm movies. AE, CB, DC, MC, V. Free valet parking, pool, tennis court, rest. (El Encanto), bar, rm svce, disco, concierge, free airport limo, free crib. *Note:* Captivating adobe cottages nestling in a glorious exotic grdn, thick w. eucalyptus trees, which looks clear over the Pacific and the Santa Barbara heights. Luxurious, comfortable suites w. private balconies or patios. Exemplary svce (the beds are turned down every day). Rest. highly recommended. This place has the style and atmosphere of a European resort hotel. **E–VE**

Miramar Hotel-Resort, 1555 S. Jameson Lane, Santa Barbara, CA 93108 (805/969-2203; toll free 800/322-6983). 200 rms, color TV. AE, CB, DC, MC, V. Free parking, two pools, four tennis courts, saunas, health club, private beach, rest., coffee shop, rm svce, hrdrsr, crib $8. *Note:* With its unusual blue roof, this old (and somewhat dated) palace right on the ocean is the connoisseurs' favorite. Commodious, comfortable rms or individual cottages w. kitchenettes. Caters to groups and conventions. Direct beach access. Svce inconsistent. The ideal place for railroad buffs (there's a miniature train running across the grdn!). On balance, good value. **M–E**

Motel 6 Beach, 443 Corona del Mar, Santa Barbara, CA 93103 (805/564-1392). 52 rms, color TV, free in-rm movies. AE, DC, MC, V. Free parking, pool, free crib. *Note:* Small, reasonably priced motel, nr. the beach as its name suggests, and a few steps from the zoo. Unsurpassable value. **I**

Motel 6 State Street, 3505 State St., Santa Barbara, CA 93105 (805/687-5400). 60 rms, color TV, free in-rm movies. AE, DC, MC, V. Free parking, pool, free crib. *Note:* Another small, reasonably priced motel 8 min. from dwntwn. Serviceable comfort on a shoestring; another unbeatable value. **I**

IN NEARBY MONTECITO The ☼ 🏛 **San Ysidro Ranch,** 900 San Ysidro Lane, Montecito, CA 93108 (805/969-5046). 43 cottages, cable color TV. MC, V. Free parking, pool, tennis court, riding, rest., bar, rm svce, nightclub, crib $15. *Note:* The small hotel of your dreams, in a 494-acre (200ha) grdn surrounded by mountains. For nearly a century the little white cottages have been home to some of the greatest names in art and politics, including Sir Winston Churchill, Somerset Maugham, and Sir Laurence Olivier. President and Mrs. Kennedy spent their honeymoon here. Huge, sumptuous rms, some w. fireplaces. Exemplary svce. Excellent rest. (Stonehouse). Resv. essential—and well in advance. Very highly recommended. **VE**

IN NEARBY REFUGIO PASS The ☼🏛 **Circle Bar B Guest Ranch,** 1800 Refugio Rd., Goleta, CA 93017 (805/968-1113), 1¼ mi. (2km) south of Refugio Pass. 12 rms. AE, MC, V. Free parking, pool, riding, rest., bar, shows (June–Oct). *Note:* This rustic ranch on 988 unspoiled acres (400ha) some 20 mi. (32km) north of Santa Barbara is a big attraction: its next-door neighbor is Rancho del Cielo, the country home of former Pres. Ronald Reagan. Simple but comfortable rms, agreeable atmosphere. Heavily attended theatrical shows in summer. Resv. advised a number of weeks ahead. Well worth a stay. Very fine view of the ocean and the Channel Islands. **M–E** (Modified American Plan).

Where to Eat

🍷🍷🍷 **Michael's Waterside Inn,** 50 Los Patos Way (805/969-0307). A/C. Dinner nightly, brunch Sun; closed the first week in Jan. AE, DC, MC, V. Jkt. *Specialties:* soufflé suissess, baked salmon persillade, pigeon w. shallot sauce, duck w. olives, tournedos w. red wine and mushrooms. Remarkable desserts, particularly the roulé marquis. *Note:* Elegant Victorian house which quickly earned itself a reputation for some of the finest food on the coast. The talented chef, Michael Hutchings, a graduate of London's famous La Gavroche, presides over a light, inventive cuisine, much sought after by celebrities and movie stars. A fine establishment w. attentive svce; resv. a must. *French/ Continental.* **M–E**

🍷🍷🍷 **El Encanto Dining Room,** at El Encanto Hotel & Garden Villas (see "Where to Stay," above) (805/687-5000). Lunch/ dinner daily, brunch Sun. AE, DC, MC, V. Jkt. *Specialties:* vol-au-vent of snails w. peppers, médaillon of veal Baumanière, pheasant w. almonds and amaretto, marzipan tart. Fine wine list. *Note:* Imposing, palatial, 1930s-style dining rm, whose enormous bay window gives a clear view of the city and its lights. Open-air terrace in summer. Urbane, up-to-date French-inspired cuisine; svce exemplary in all respects; romantic atmosphere. Resv. a must. Highly recommended. *French/ Continental.* **I–M**

🍷 **Pescados,** 422 N. Milpas St. (805/965-3805). Lunch/ dinner daily. MC, V. *Specialties:* burritos and seafood fajitas, broiled fish of the day, tacos, frijoles negros. *Note:* Outstandingly fresh fish and shellfish, imaginatively prepared Mexican fashion. Charming rustic-modern decor. A successful rest., popular in the community, where on some days you may have a long wait for a table. Friendly, efficient svce; one of the best little rests. on the coast. *Seafood/Mexican.* **B–I**

🍷 **La Super-Rica,** 622 N. Milpas St. (805/963-4940). Lunch/ dinner daily. AE, MC, V. *Specialties:* tacos, frijoles and chorizos, chiles relleños, tamales, broiled chicken. *Note:* The tireless Mama Gonzalez, bustling behind her stoves, keeps a sharp eye on the preparation of her sauces, marinated meats, and spiced frijoles to ensure that they will be to the taste of her regular customers. Absolutely authentic cooking; the decor is insignificant —but so are the prices. Inviting covered patio for lunch or dinner al fresco. Has a large local following. *Mexican.* **B**

IN NEARBY MONTECITO ♈ **Piatti,** 516 San Ysidro Rd. at Calif. 192 (805/969-7520). A/C. Lunch/dinner daily; closed Dec 25. AE, MC, V. *Specialties:* pizza from a wood-burning oven, homemade pasta, fritto misto, excellent mesquite-grilled fish and meat, authentic regional Italian dishes. *Note:* Pleasant Californian decor, brightened w. large mural paintings; gracious, congenial svce. A good spot. *American/Italian.* **I**

IN NEARBY OJAI The ☀☈☈☈ **Ranch House,** 102 Besant Rd. (805/646-2360). A/C. Lunch/dinner Wed–Sun; closed hols. AE, DC, MC, V. *Specialties:* crab voisin, beef Bali Hai, pork au Cointreau, fish of the day, excellent desserts. Choice wine list. *Note:* One of the most innovative rests. In California; chef Alan Hooker's cuisine is refined and inventive. Herbs and vegetables fresh from the grdn; excellent home-baked bread and pastry. You'll enjoy the grdn; background music is classical and agreeable. Two sittings a night, at 6 and 8pm. A local institution for more than 30 years. *American/Continental.* **I–M**

🏛 **VENTURA** (413 mi./666km): The **San Buenaventura Mission,** 211 E. Main St. (805/643-4318), was the last (1782) to be founded by the great Franciscan missionary, Fray Junípero Serra. It still has its original wooden bells. Open daily. Interesting **County Museum** at 100 E. Main St. (805/653-0323), open Tues–Sun, and fascinating **archeological excavations** in progress at 113 E. Main St. Worth the detour.

An Offshore Side Trip

☀🏊♨🏖 **Channel Islands National Park** (about 10 mi./16km offshore): Group of five small uninhabited islands stretching for some 150 mi. (242km) parallel to the coast. The five islands—**Anacapa, San Miguel, Santa Barbara, Santa Cruz,** and **Santa Rosa**—are now marine-life sanctuaries; their flora and fauna are different from those of the mainland, and include 830 species not found anywhere else in California. But it is the animal and marine life that constitutes their principal attraction: sea anemones, sea urchins, abalone, crayfish, dolphins, sponges, foxes, seabirds, and half a dozen varieties of sea lions, for a start.

Camping is allowed, by previous arrangement, on Anacapa and Santa Barbara. For **park information,** contact the Superintendent, Channel Islands National Park, 1901 Spinnaker Dr., Ventura, CA 93001 (805/644-8262).

The islands can be reached only by boat from Oxnard or Ventura on the mainland. The recommended carrier is **Island Packer Company,** 1867 Spinnaker Dr., Ventura (805/642-1393). You shouldn't miss this trip.

Where to Stay

🏨 **Pierpoint Inn,** 550 San Jon Rd., Ventura, CA 93001 (805/643-6144). 80 rms, color TV. AE, CB, DC, MC, V. Free parking, pool, tennis court, rest., bar, rm svce, disco, free crib. *Note:* Small, charming English-style inn; rms (w. balconies or terraces) are pleasing and almost all offer a fine view of Pierpoint Bay. Good rest.; interesting wknd packages. Good value. **I–M**

🏨 **Motel 6,** 2145 E. Harbor Blvd., Ventura, CA 93003 (805/643-5100). 200 rms, color TV, free in-rm movies. AE, DC, MC, V. Free parking, pool, free crib. *Note:* Small, reasonably priced motel; serviceable comfort. Unsurpassable value. **B–I**

Where to Eat

♈ **Sportsman,** 53 S. California St. (805/643-2851). A/C. Lunch/dinner daily, brunch Sun; closed hols. MC, V. *Specialties:* broiled meat and fish, roast beef, sandwiches. *Note:* The simple, unpretentious cuisine rates a big hand. Lovers of hunting and fishing will enjoy the decor. Popular in the community. *Steak/Seafood.* **B–I**

OXNARD (421 mi./679km): Like Ventura, a departure point for trips to the **Channel Islands,** 10 mi. (16km) offshore, where tens of thousands of birds, sea lions, and other marine animals can be seen in their natural environment. (See "An Offshore Side Trip" under Ventura, above.)

Where to Stay

Casa Sirena Marina, 3605 Peninsula Rd., Oxnard, CA 93030 (805/985-6311; toll free 800/228-6026). 274 rms, color TV. AE, CB, DC, MC, V. Free parking, two pools, three tennis courts, putting green, health club, saunas, bicycles, marina, rest. (Lobster Trap), two bars, rm svce, free airport limo, free crib. *Note:* Vast, well-equipped resort hotel. Rms w. balconies and harbor view. Ideal for visits to the Channel Islands. A little boisterous and overcrowded. Good rest.; worthwhile discount packages. **M**

Where to Eat

Lobster Trap, at Casa Sirena Marina (see "Where to Stay," above) (805/985-6361). A/C. Breakfast/lunch/dinner daily, brunch Sun. AE, CB, DC, MC, V. *Specialties:* abalone, fish of the day, shellfish, prime cuts. *Note:* Good hotel cuisine, well prepared w. few surprises. Fine view over the yacht basin and beyond. Slowish svce. Agreeable oyster bar. *Steak/Seafood.* **B–I**

MALIBU (455 mi./734km): Immense fine-sand beach. Home of such movie celebrities as Sylvester Stallone, Barbra Streisand, Larry Hagman, Julie Andrews, Robert Redford, and Steven Spielberg. Don't miss the **J. Paul Getty Museum,** one of the two or three wealthiest in the world. There is an exact replica of the 1st-century A.D. "Villa of the Papyrus" from Herculancum near Naples. (See "Museums" in Chapter 54 on Los Angeles.)

PACIFIC PALISADES (463 mi./747km): Resort town and, like Malibu, home to many movie and television stars. **Will Rogers State Park,** on Sunset Blvd. between Amalfi Dr. and Brooktree Rd., former ranch home of the famous movie cowboy and humorist, is worth a visit (see Chapter 54 on Los Angeles).

Where to Eat

Gladstones 4 Fish, 17300 W. Pacific Coast Hwy., Pacific Palisades (454-3474). A/C. Breakfast/lunch/dinner daily (until midnight). *Specialties:* All kinds of fish and shellfish. Valet parking. *Seafood.* **I**

SANTA MONICA (472 mi./761km): Enormous, busy beach. Picturesque pier with amusements.

Where to Eat

See Chapter 54 on Los Angeles for the following restaurant recommendations: **Camelions, DC3, Knoll's Black Forest Inn, Michael's,** and **Valentino.**

LOS ANGELES (490 mi./790km): See Chapter 54 on Los Angeles for information on the city and its surroundings.

HUNTINGTON BEACH (520 mi./839km): Another vast beach popular with surfers and skin-divers (beware of sharks!).

NEWPORT BEACH (526 mi./848km): One of California's smartest and most fashionable beaches, with splendid homes and luxury boutiques and restaurants—but also a very busy fishing port (**New-**

port Pier) for more than a century. The beauty of its coastal scenery has earned it the nickname "The American Riviera." The **Harbor Art Museum** at 850 San Clemente Dr. (714/759-1122), open Tues–Sun, makes this a mecca for lovers of the avant-garde and of American experimental art. Well worth the detour.

Where to Eat

IN NEARBY NEWPORT ♛♛♛ **John Domini's,** 2901 W. Coast Hwy. (714/650-5112). A/C. Lunch/dinner daily. AE, DC, MC, V. *Specialties:* clam chowder; sashimi; cioppino; Chinese chicken salad; opakapaka; lobster and fish, broiled, baked, or sautéed; excellent desserts. Good wine list at very full prices. *Note:* An affiliate of the famous John Domini's in Honolulu (see Chapter 56), this luxurious beachside establishment serves the same remarkable selection of fish and seafood in the same extravagant setting, complete w. huge picture windows, fountains, and indoor waterfalls, as the Hawaiian original. The proceedings close w. the same exorbitant bill. Absolutely fresh seafood, sometimes overcooked; relaxed, efficient svce. Resv. highly advisable. *Seafood.* **M–E**

🔔 **LAGUNA BEACH** (535 mi./863km): Very beautiful, fashionable beach lying at the foot of steep hills. Many boutiques and open-air restaurants.

Where to Stay

♛♛ **Casa Laguna Inn,** 2510 S. Coast Hwy., Laguna Beach, CA 92651 (714/494-2996; toll free 800/233-0449). 20 rms, A/C, cable color TV. AE, CB, DC, MC, V. Free parking, pool; no bar or rest.; free breakfast. *Note:* Enticing little Spanish Colonial–style inn w. panoramic view of the Pacific. As far as you can get from production-line tourism. Elegantly decorated rms, each in a different style. Private, luxuriant patios and grdns. Polished svce and welcome. Interesting vacation packages. **E–VE**

☼♛♛ **Ben Brown's Aliso Creek Inn,** 31106 Coast Hwy., South Laguna, CA 92677 (714/499-2271). 61 rms w. kitchenettes, cable color TV. AE, MC, V. Covered parking, pool, golf, sauna, rest., bar, rm svce, disco, crib $3. *Note:* Likable little hotel hidden in a peaceful inlet beside the ocean. Huge, comfortable rms w. balconies. Very acceptable rest. Hard-working, congenial svce. A nice place, 1 hr. by car from Los Angeles. **M–E**

♛♛ **Hotel Laguna,** 425 S. Coast Hwy., Laguna Beach, CA 92651 (714/494-1151). 70 rms, color TV, in-rm movies. AE, CB, DC, MC, V. Free parking, private beach, rest. (Claes), bar, rm svce, disco, hrdrsr. *Note:* For more than 50 years the Hotel Laguna has been the delight of summer vacationers, captivated by the convenience of its private beach in the center of town. The best rms look over the ocean. Good svce and adequate rest. **M,** but lower rates off-season.

IN NEARBY LAGUNA NIGUEL The ♛♛♛ **Ritz Carlton,** 33533 Ritz Carlton Dr., Laguna Niguel, CA 92677 (714/240-2000; toll free 800/241-3333). 393 rms, A/C, color TV, in-rm movies. AE, CB, DC, MC, V. Free valet parking, two pools, four tennis courts, golf, health club, sauna, two rests. (including the Dining Rm), coffee shop, bars, 24-hr. rm svce, nightclub, hrdrsr, boutiques, concierge, free crib. *Note:* On its clifftop overlooking the Pacific, this four-story palace opened in 1984 as one of the latest blossoms of American luxury hotelkeeping. Mediterranean-style architecture surrounded by magnificent grdns w. fountains and covered patios. Splendid view of the ocean and Catalina Island. No visiting VIP can afford to miss it, which is why resv. must be made many days, or weeks, ahead. Sumptuous rms w. private balconies, minibars, and period furniture; antiques and works of art in the public rms and foyer. Ultrapolished svce and reception. The Dining Rm is one of the best rests. on the West Coast. VIP floor. Free bus to the beach. **VE**

IN NEARBY EL TORO **Coto de Caza,** 22000 Plano Trabuco Rd., Trabuco Canyon, CA 92678 (714/858-1500); take the El Toro Rd. E. exit off I-5. 100 rms, cable color TV. AE, MC, V. Free parking, two pools, 10 tennis courts, bowling, riding, shooting, hunting, sauna, health club, bicycles, rest. (Silverado Dining Rm), bar, cinema, disco, crib $10. *Note:* Enormous game reserve—as its name suggests—w. more than 4,940 acres (2,000ha) at the foot of the Santa Ana Mountains, and just 20 min. from the ocean. Paradise for hunters (pheasant, quail, woodpigeon) and sports enthusiasts (the hotel has a computer-equipped medical center that offers personalized diet and exercise programs). Friendly svce, pleasant rms. Attractive half-board packages. **E**

Where to Eat

Las Brisas, 361 Cliff Dr. (714/497-5434). A/C. Lunch/ dinner daily, brunch Sat–Sun; closed Thanksgiving, Dec 24. AE, CB, DC, MC, V. *Specialties:* fish Mexican style, sopa de frijoles, carne asada, enchiladas, squid. *Note:* Inviting terrace overlooking the ocean, or a comfortable dining rm w. indoor waterfall. Good Mexican cuisine tailored to North American tastebuds. Has had a large following in the community for more than 10 years. Resv. a must. Valet parking. *Mexican/Seafood.* **I**

Beach House, 619 Sleepy Hollow Lane (714/494-9707). Breakfast/lunch/dinner daily; closed Thanksgiving, Dec 25. AE, MC, V. *Specialties:* oyster on the half shell, fish kebab, abalone amandine, good desserts. *Note:* Likable fish rest. w. ocean view. Open-air terrace in good weather. A relaxed place. *Seafood.* **B–I**

IN NEARBY LAGUNA NIGUEL The Dining Room, at the Ritz Carlton Laguna Niguel (see "Where to Stay," above) (714/240-2000). A/C. Dinner only, nightly. AE, CB, DC, MC, V. J&T. *Specialties:* ragoût of snails w. chanterelles, sweetbreads in flaky pastry w. morels, sautéed duck foie gras w. peaches, rabbit w. mustard, paupiettes of sole w. sauce caviar, medallions of veal w. cream of truffles, broiled filet of beef w. shallots, roast duckling w. cherries and port wine, vacherin w. white chocolate, fresh fruit sherbet. Very fine wine list. *Note:* While it lacks the unobstructed view of the Pacific and Catalina Island enjoyed by most of the rms in the Ritz Carlton, this palatial rest., w. its old master paintings and crystal chandeliers, is redolent of luxury and good taste. Quite remarkable classic French cuisine (but prices to match). Svce polished to a high gloss. Distinguished background music. Resv., several days ahead, a must unless you're staying at the hotel. Some of the finest food in southern California. *French/Continental.* **E–VE**

SAN JUAN CAPISTRANO (547 mi./882km): Perched between mountain and sea, the **San Juan Capistrano Mission** is the most famous, and probably the most beautiful, in California; take I-5, leave it at the Ortega Hwy. exit (714/493-1424), open daily. Founded in 1776 by Fray Junípero Serra, this lovely mission, laid out in the shape of a Latin cross, was almost entirely destroyed by an earthquake in 1812. There survive the Serra Chapel, the ruins of the cloister, and a little museum surrounded by superb tropical gardens where, every year, the swallows come to nest about Mar 20.

Don't overlook the **Regional Library & Cultural Center,** at 31495 El Camino Real (714/493-1752), open Mon–Sat, whose elegant postmodern architecture bears the name, and the stamp, of Michael Graves.

Where to Stay

Best Western Capistrano Inn, 27174 Ortega Hwy., San Juan Capistrano, CA 92675 (714/493-5661; toll free, see Best Western). 108 rms, A/C, color TV, in-rm movies. AE, CB, DC, MC, V. Free parking, pool, 24-hr. rest. adj. bar, valet svce, crib $4. *Note:* Comfortable motel very nr. the famous San Juan Capistrano Mission. Agreeable rms, some w. balconies; a perfect stopover for visiting the mission. Free morning coffee. **I–M**

IN NEARBY CAPISTRANO BEACH The ♗ **Best Western Marina Inn,** 24800 Dana Point Harbor Dr., Dana Point, CA 92629 (714/496-1203; toll free, see Best Western). 135 rms (one-third w. kitchenettes), A/C, color TV, in-rm movies. AE, CB, DC, MC, V. Free parking, pool, sauna, rest. adj., free crib. *Note:* Modern, functional motel overlooking the pleasure-boat harbor of Dana Point, where boats may be rented. Commodious rms w. balconies, the best overlooking the Pacific. Free morning coffee. **M**

Where to Eat

☼♗♗ **El Adobe,** 31891 Camino Capistrano (714/493-1163). A/C. Lunch/dinner daily, brunch Sun; closed Labor Day, Dec 25. AE, MC, V. *Specialties:* prime rib, steak, Mexican dishes. *Note:* Old (1766) courthouse, a designated historical monument, converted into a handsome rest. Menu limited, but first-class meats. Enjoyable atmosphere, w. a roof that opens in summer. Resv. advised. *Steak/American.* **B–I**

♗ **SAN CLEMENTE** (554 mi./894km): Beach resort made fashionable by former Pres. Richard Nixon, who made his summer home there (Casa Pacifica) during his term of office.

♗♗ **OCEANSIDE-CARLSBAD** (580 mi./935km): Miles of beach, almost deserted except for surfers and surf fishers. 4 mi. (6.5km) east along Calif. 76 stands the imposing **San Luis Rey de Francia Mission** (619/757-3651), one of the few in California that was *not* founded by the tireless Fray Junípero Serra, but rather by one of his assistants, Father Lasuén, in 1798. Dedicated to the canonized King Louis IX of France, it once housed 3,000 Native Americans, and still displays many mementoes of Spanish colonial days in its remarkable museum. It continues to serve its original purpose as a parish church and school for the surrounding tribal reservations. Open daily.

A further 48 mi. (77km) east along Calif. 76 is the famous ♗♗ **Mount Palomar Observatory** with its 200-inch (5.1m) reflector telescope, one of the world's largest. The dome may be visited daily; for information, call 619/742-3476. (See Chapter 55 on San Diego).

Where to Stay

☼♗♗♗ **La Costa Hotel & Spa,** Costa del Mar Rd., Carlsbad, CA 92008 (619/438-9111; toll free 800/854-6564). 485 rms and individual cottages, A/C, cable color TV. AE, CB, DC, MC, V. Free parking, five pools, 25 tennis courts, two golf courses, health club, sauna, hot spring, riding, seven rests. (including the Champagne Rm) and bars, coffee shop, rm svce, hrdrsr, boutiques, free crib. *Note:* Resting on almost 5,000 wooded acres (2,025ha) nr. the ocean, this is one of the finest vacation complexes on the West Coast. Comfortable, luxuriously decorated rms or suites. Impeccable svce; excellent facilities. A paradise for sports-lovers or those taking a cure, but priced accordingly (some suites run $900 a day). Wknd and American Plan packages are interesting. For those who love going on a (costly) diet. **VE**

♗ **Best Western Beach View,** 3180 Carlsbad Blvd., Carlsbad, CA 92008 (619/729-1151; toll free, see Best Western). 41 rms, A/C, color TV, in-rm movies. AE, CB, DC, MC, V. Free parking, pool, sauna, beach, nearby coffee shop, crib $6. *Note:* Friendly small motel facing the beach; comfortable rms w. mini-refrigerators, some also w. balconies or fireplaces, the best overlooking the ocean. Reception w. a smile. **M**

♗ **Motel 6,** 1403 Mission Ave., Oceanside, CA 92054 (619/721-6662). 79 rms, color TV, free in-rm movies. AE, DC, MC, V. Free parking, free crib. *Note:* Small, reasonably priced motel; serviceable comfort. Unsurpassable value. **B**

IN NEARBY RANCHO SANTA FE The ☼ ♗♗ **Inn at Rancho Santa Fe,** Linea del Cielo, Rancho Santa Fe, CA 92067 (619/756-1131; toll free 800/654-2928). 79 rms,

A/C, color TV. AE, CB, DC, MC, V. Free parking, pool, three tennis courts, golf, riding, rest., bar, rm svce, crib $10. *Note:* Deluxe motel and pleasing bungalows set in 19 acres (7.7ha) of beautiful grdns; ideal for lovers of sports and fresh air. Very satisfactory rest. Spacious rms w. private patios, some w. kitchenettes. Good svce, good value. **E–VE**

Where to Eat

IN NEARBY LAKE SAN MARCOS The 𝕏𝕏 **Quails Inn,** 1025 La Bonita Dr. (619/744-0120). A/C. Lunch/dinner daily, brunch Sun. AE, MC, V. *Specialties:* seafood salad bar, prime rib, lobster, barbecued chicken. *Note:* The rest. of this beautiful Lake San Marcos resort is festooned in colors of peach, coral, and light blue-green, w. a view of the lake from almost every seat. Good basic American menu and Sun buffet brunch. Friendly svce. Resv. advised. *American.* **I–M**

IN NEARBY RANCHO SANTA FE 𝕏𝕏 **Mille Fleurs** (see Chapter 55 on San Diego).

IN NEARBY DEL MAR 𝕏𝕏 **When in Rome,** 828 N. U.S. 101 (619/944-1771). No A/C. Dinner only, Tues–Sun; closed hols. AE, MC, V. *Specialties:* fresh home-made pasta, filet of beef w. peppers, scaloppine w. lemon, broiled fish, chicken cacciatore. *Note:* One of southern California's best Italian rests., serving light, delicate food. The colonnaded rm is full of light; the svce comes w. a smile; this is a first-rate place. *Italian.* **I**

LA JOLLA (589 mi./950km): California's most sought-after summer resort, a sort of West Coast equivalent of Europe's Amalfi or Juan-les-Pins. Beautiful beaches hidden by little inlets, luxurious oceanfront homes, open-air stores, and restaurants. Important museums, particularly the **Museum of Contemporary Art.** (See "Nearby Excursions" in Chapter 55 on San Diego.)

Where to Eat

See Chapter 55 on San Diego for the following restaurant recommendations: **Cindy Black's, Su Casa,** and **Top o' the Cove.**

IN NEARBY PACIFIC BEACH See Chapter 55 on San Diego for my restaurant recommendation of **El Chalan.**

IN NEARBY CORONADO See Chapter 55 on San Diego for the following restaurant recommendations: **Chez Loma, Marius,** and the **Prince of Wales Grill.**

SAN DIEGO (604 mi./974km): See Chapter 55 on San Diego for information on the city and its surroundings.

CHAPTER 52

SEQUOIA NATIONAL PARK

□ □ □

And Kings Canyon

Domain of the giant trees, Sequoia National Park is, after Yellowstone, the oldest national park in the U.S. Set up in 1890 to safeguard the redwood (sequoia) forests on the slopes of the **Sierra Nevada,** the park's magnificent scenery embraces granite mountain-crests, canyons, mountain lakes, and dense forests. Around Sequoia and the adjoining **Kings Canyon National Park,** inaugurated in 1940, lie giant mountain peaks including **Mount Whitney,** highest in the "lower 48" (14,495 ft./4,418m), **Split Mountain** (14,054 ft./4,285m), and **Mount Goethe** (13,274 ft./4,047m). But though the natural setting is incomparable, the main interest of the two parks is their forests of giant conifers.

The redwood, or sequoia, owes its name to the famous Native American leader Sequoyah, inventor of the alphabet in which the Cherokee language is written. The tree has been known to grow as high as 295 ft. (90m), with a circumference at the base of 98 ft. (30m) or more. Its bark, 2 ft. (60cm) thick, is resistant to both fire and insects. The largest redwood now standing in the park, the **General Sherman Tree,** stands more than 275 ft. (84m) tall, and its estimated age of 2,500 years makes it the oldest living creature on earth.

In spite of the huge area they cover, Sequoia and Kings Canyon National Parks have only 75 mi. (120km) of surfaced roads between them; points off these highways can be reached only on horseback or on foot. There are, however, 900 mi. (1,450km) of walking trails. Sequoia National Park, while it remains open year round, can be negotiated only with chains or snowtires Oct–May; Kings Canyon is closed all winter.

The motels in the two parks have a limited capacity of 300 rooms; reservations should therefore be made far in advance.

BASIC FACTS: State of California. Area code: 209. Time zone: Pacific. ZIP Code: 93262. Approximate Area: 1,300 sq. mi. (3,370km²). Founded: 1890 (Sequoia); 1940 (Kings Canyon).

CLIMATE: Icy and snowy in winter (the snowfall can reach 13 ft./4m, and the thermometer sometimes drops to $-4°$ F/$-20°$ C), the climate of Sequoia National Park is brisk and invigorating at all times of the year. Even in midsummer, bring warm clothes for the evenings.

DISTANCES: Las Vegas, 506 mi. (810km); Los Angeles, 220 mi. (354km); Sacramento, 257 mi. (411km); San Francisco, 270 mi. (432km).

ARRIVAL & TRANSIT INFORMATION

AIRPORTS NEARBY: The **Fresno Municipal Airport** (FAT), 70 mi. (112km) west.
Visalia Municipal Airport (VIS), 45 mi. (72km) NE.

AIRLINES (at the Fresno Municipal Airport unless otherwise noted): American Eagle (toll free 800/433-7300), American Eagle (at the Visalia Airport: toll free 800/433-7300), Delta (toll free 800/221-1212), and United (252-5711).

BUS OR CAR RENTAL? Given the distances and the attractive rates offered in California, the sensible solution is to rent a car with unlimited mileage.

CAR RENTALS (all at the Fresno Municipal Airport): Avis (251-5001), Budget (251-5515), Dollar (252-4000), Hertz (251-5055), and National (251-5577).

TRAIN: The nearest Amtrak station is at 2650 Tulare St., Fresno (toll free 800/872-7245).

INTERCITY BUSES: There is no regular service to Sequoia or Kings Canyon National Park. (A daily **shuttle bus** links Fresno to Sequoia National Park, but in summer only; for information, call GSI at 561-3314.)
The nearest regular-service bus stations, both **Greyhound,** are at 1033 Broadway, Fresno (268-1829), and 211 S. Court St., Visalia (734-3507).

INFORMATION & SIGHTSEEING

INFORMATION: Contact the **Superintendent, Sequoia and Kings Canyon National Parks,** Ash Mountain, Three Rivers, CA 93271 (209/565-3341).
Visitor centers are located at Lodgepole (565-3341, ext. 631), Ash Mountain (565-3456), and Kings Canyon Grant Cove (335-2315).
For information on **road and weather conditions** (and snow conditions in winter), call 565-3351.

MOUNTAINEERING: ☀⚠ **Mount Whitney,** reached by the High Sierra Trail, east of the Kern Canyon Ranger Station: Mount Whitney, at 14,495 ft. (4,418m), is the highest peak in the contiguous United States. The top can be reached by a number of routes, some requiring technical climbing skills. The easiest and most popular, the 10.7-mi. (17km) **Whitney Trail,** can be followed by hikers. The round-trip can be made in 12–14 hr. by the very fit. **Camping** is by permit only, and only 50 campers may stay on the mountain each night May 20–Oct 15. Requests should come to the Mount Whitney Ranger District, P.O. Box 8, Lone Pine, CA 93545. A ranger (call 619/876-5542) will answer questions about the choice of trails.

SCENERY & SIGHTS: ☀⚠ **Cedar Grove,** reached on Calif. 180: The village at the dead end of Kings Canyon River South Fork. The surrounding peaks look down on the riverbed from a height of more than a mile (1,600m). Road closed in winter. A wonderful sight.

    ⚠ **Crystal Cave,** 6 mi. (9km) east of Giant Forest Village: Splendid limestone cavern with astonishing mineral growths; the temperature inside holds steady near 50°F (10°C). Vehicle road, then foot trail; mid-June to mid-Sept, daily.

    ☀⚠ **Giant Forest,** around Giant Forest Village on Calif. 198: Here you'll find the biggest redwoods in the park, including the **General Sherman Tree,** 275 ft. (84m) high and 103 ft. (32m) around the base;

estimated weight is 2,000 tons. There's enough wood in the tree to build 40 five-room cabins. At about 2,500 years, this is the world's oldest living thing.

    Grant Grove, intersection of Calif. 180 and Calif. 198: Stand of giant redwood including the second-tallest in the park, the **General Grant Tree,** 267 ft. (81m) high and 107 ft. (33m) around.

    High Sierra Trail: 40-mi. (64km) hiking trail linking Giant Forest Village to the western tip of the park and the John Muir Trail. Splendid scenery. For walkers in good physical shape.

    John Muir Trail: A hiking trail about 80 mi. (128km) long, running north-south along the eastern edge of the park. Spectacular landscapes. For seasoned walkers with some mountain experience. Horses and mules may be rented at Wolverton Stables, Grant Grove, and Cedar Grove.

    Kings Canyon, reached by Calif. 180: The gorges of the Kings River South Fork display some of the most breathtaking scenery in the park: steep granite cliffs and dizzying drops of up to 8,216 ft. (2,505m), frozen lakes, and giant redwoods. Their beauty is reminiscent of the Yosemite Valley (see Chapter 53). The 36-mi. (58km) route east into the national park (Calif. 180) hangs on the edge of a cliff, 3,000 ft. (915m) above crashing white water before descending to river level inside the park. Road closed in winter.

    Moro Rock, 4 mi. (6km) south of Giant Forest Village: One of the most impressive granite monoliths in the Sierra Nevada range, rising 2,080 ft. (1,300m) above the banks of the Kaweah River Middle Fork. There's a path to the top, from which you'll have a fine all-around view of the mountains and the surrounding forest.

    Muir Grove, reached by footpath from Lost Grove on Calif. 198: Very fine redwood stand. A must-see.

    Zumwalt Meadow, reached by footpath from Cedar Grove: Huge alpine meadow, particularly beautiful when the summer wildflowers are in bloom.

WINTER SPORTS RESORTS: Giant Forest Village and Lodgepole: 35 mi. (56km) of cross-country skiing; no lifts.

    Wolverton Ski Bowl (565-3381): 3 lifts: open mid-Nov to mid-Apr.

ACCOMMODATIONS

A Note on Accommodations: Room rates in the National Park Area are coded as follows: **VE,** Very Expensive ($140 and up); **E,** Expensive ($90–$140); **M,** Moderate ($60–$90); **I,** Inexpensive ($30–$60); **B,** Budget (up to $30). A listing of toll free numbers is in the Appendix.

Personal Favorites Inside the Parks (in order of preference)

For reservations inside Sequoia and Kings Canyon National Parks, contact the **Reservations Manager,** Sequoia and Kings Canyon Hospitality Service, Sequoia National Park, CA 93262 (209/561-3314).

    Giant Forest Lodge, on Calif. 198, Giant Forest Village, CA 93262 (209/565-3381). 245 rms (half w. baths); No A/C. MC, V. Free parking, bicycles for rent, skiing, horseback riding, coffee shop, bar, crib $4. *Note:* Rustic motel in the heart of the redwood forest; cottages w. basic comforts. So-so cafeteria. Some bungalows have open-air barbecues. Open year round. **I–M**

    Cedar Grove Lodge, at the end of Calif. 180, King's Canyon National Park, CA 93633 (209/561-3314). 18 rms, A/C. MC, V. Free parking, fishing, coffee shop, crib $4. *Note:* The most inviting motel in the park, well located on the Kings River itself. Serviceably comfortable; rms w. balcony. Open mid-May to mid-Sept only. **M**

Ⓟ **Stony Creek Lodge,** Generals Hwy., Sequoia National Park,
CA 93262 (209/561-3650). 11 rms; no A/C. MC, V. Free
parking, coffee shop (open till 9pm). *Note:* Small, rustic but relatively comfortable hotel deep in the forest. Acceptable cafeteria. Open from the end of May to mid-Sept only. **M**

Ⓟ **Grant Grove Lodge,** Calif. 180, King's Canyon National Park,
CA 93633 (209/335-2314). 51 rms (9 w. bath); no A/C.
MC, V. Free parking, coffee shop (open till 9pm), bar, groceries, crib $4. *Note:* Cottages and bungalows w. primitive comforts (most have fabric roofs and no electricity). Only for open-air enthusiasts. Open year round but fewer facilities in winter. **I**

Personal Favorites Outside the Parks (in order of preference)

Ⓟ **Best Western Holiday Lodge,** on Calif. 198, Three Rivers, CA
93271 (209/561-4119; toll free, see Best Western). 47 rms,
A/C, cable color TV. AE, CB, DC, MC, V. Free parking, pool, free coffee in rms, fishing, rest. half mi. away, crib $4. *Note:* Smart little motel looking out on the Kaweah River. Spacious rms w. balconies, some w. fireplaces and refrigerators. Inviting tree-shaded pool. Serviceable facilities; good value. 10 min. by car from the western entrance to the park. **I–M**

Ⓟ **The River Inn,** 45176 Sierra Dr. (Calif. 198), Three Rivers, CA
93271 (209/561-4367). 12 rms, A/C, cable color TV. MC,
V. Free parking, adj. cafeteria and grocery store. *Note:* Tiny motel overlooking the Kaweah River in a pretty, natural setting. Comfortable rms w. balconies and refrigerators. 15-min. drive from the western entrance to the park. **I**

Ⓟ **Lazy J Ranch,** 39625 Sierra Dr., Three Rivers, CA 93271
(209/561-4449). 18 rms, A/C, color TV, in-rm movies. AE,
MC, V. Free parking, pool, fishing, free coffee in rms, adj. cafeteria, free crib. *Note:* Small rustic cottages, some w. kitchenettes and refrigerators, on the Kaweah River. Only moderately comfortable, but well situated. Pretty tree-shaded grdns. 15-min. drive from the western entrance to the park. **I–M**

NEARBY EXCURSIONS

HANFORD (63 mi./100km SW on Calif. 198): Founded in
1882 to house the immigrant Chinese working on the Southern Pacific Railroad, this was one of the country's largest Chinatowns in the 19th century. From its pioneer past there remain today only a few buildings around China Alley, scrupulously restored, including a Taoist temple and one of the most remarkable restaurants in the U.S.

Where to Eat

Imperial Dynasty, 2 China Alley, 7th St. and Green St. (209/
582-0196). Dinner only, Tues–Sun. AE, MC, V. Run by the
Wing family since 1883, this rest., whose food is a strange but wholly successful blend of French and Chinese traditions, is well worth going out of your way for. Be sure to call 1 week ahead for the spectacular $50 nine-course gourmet dinner. **I–M**

GHOST TOWNS: Mineral King and **Silver City,** on Mineral
King Rd., reached by driving 3 mi. (4km) north of Three Rivers on Calif. 198: The remains of two towns from gold-rush days; a stretch of the road is unsurfaced. Closed in winter.

FARTHER AFIELD

DEATH VALLEY NATIONAL PARK (362 mi./580km
east via Calif. 198, Calif. 65, Calif. 178, and Calif. 190): The
distance is barely 87 mi. (140km) as the crow flies, but almost 375 mi. (600km)

SEQUOIA AND KINGS CANYON NATIONAL PARKS

Lone Pine

Mt. Langley

John Muir Wilderness

FORESTER PASS

Mt. Whitney

Junction Meadow

NAT'L SCENIC TRAIL

Inyo National Forest

Kern Hot Springs

KERN CANYON

KERN RIDGE

HIGH SIERRA TRAIL

Golden Trout Wilderness

Needham Mtn.

GREAT WESTERN DIVIDE

GLACIER RIDGE

DEADMAN CANYON

Bearpaw Meadow

Mineral King

Silver City

Alta Peak

SEQUOIA NATIONAL PARK

Wolverton Ski Bowl

PARADISE RIDGE

Hockett Meadows

Visitor Center

Giant Forest Village

General Sherman Tree

Sequoia National Forest

Moro Rock

Ash Mtn. Park Hdqts.

Garfield Grove Giant Forest

Muir Grove

Crystal Cave

PINE RIDGE

ASH PEAKS RIDGE

Hammond

Three Rivers

Kaweah River

Kaweah

Lake Kaweah

Kaweah River

Pinehurst

Badger

245

J21

198

J30

miles 5
kms 5
0

along the often spectacular roads through Sequoia National Forest and the Panamint Valley. Loveliest of American deserts. (See also Chapter 48 on Death Valley.)

☀☖☖☖ **YOSEMITE NATIONAL PARK** (178 mi./284km NW via Calif. 198, Calif. 180, and Calif. 41): One of the country's most beautiful national parks (see Chapter 53).

YOSEMITE NATIONAL PARK 🕯🕯🕯

□ □ □

The surpassing beauty of Yosemite National Park should be seen for the first time in May or June, when the waterfalls, swollen by snowmelt, plunge dizzily out of the sky for hundreds of feet to the rocks below. Some, like **Yosemite Falls,** the world's second largest after Angel Falls in Venezuela, are as much as 2,425 ft. (739m) from lip to basin—13 times as high as Niagara! In summer and fall the falls dry up, but you can still contemplate the grandeur of the million-year-old glacial **Yosemite Valley,** walled in by steep granite cliffs 5,000 ft. (1,500m) high. On the uplands, stands of giant redwoods and plateaus covered in flowery meadows contribute to a landscape of unspoiled splendor.

This huge (as large as Rhode Island) wildlife reserve deep in the **Sierra Nevada** (naturalists have counted no fewer than 220 species of birds and 75 of mammals—including deer, wild goat, black bear, and coyote) draws about 3½ million visitors each summer. Because it's within relatively easy reach of San Francisco and Los Angeles, it has become one of California's most popular tourist attractions; in July and August traffic jams paralyze its two main access roads. Yet until as late as 1851, when the Yosemite Gap was first discovered by the soldiers of the Mariposa Battalion, this had been for 4½ millennia the secret kingdom of the Miwok people and their forebears. They called it Ahwahnee, "the deep grassy valley."

When you set eyes on Yosemite Valley and the peaks of the **High Sierras** from the lookout at **Glacier Point,** or when you see **El Capitan,** a monolith 2½ times as high as the Rock of Gibraltar, whose lowering granitic mass forms a kind of natural fortress in a bend of the valley, you'll feel that scenery of this magnificence is enough to make the trip worthwhile in spite of the summer crowds.

Yosemite National Park (the name is a corruption of *U-zu-mate,* the Native American word for grizzly bear) is open year round.

BASIC FACTS: State of California. Area code: 209. Time zone: Pacific. Zip Code: 95389. Founded: 1890. Area: 1,190 sq. mi. (3,082km²).

CLIMATE: As in most of the western national parks, spring and fall, both sunny but cool, are the best times for seeing Yosemite. Runoff from the snowmelt swells the waterfalls to their heaviest rate of flow in spring. Fall paints the forests in a splendor of glowing bronze. Summer is dry and reasonably warm, averaging 71°F (22°C). In winter the snow can lie more than 13 ft. (4m) deep, and daytime temperatures average 34°F (1°C). Cross-country skiers take note: information on snow conditions can be obtained by calling 209/372-1338.

DISTANCES: Las Vegas, 465 mi. (745km); Los Angeles, 315 mi. (504km); Reno, 177 mi. (283km); San Francisco, 210 mi. (336km).

ARRIVAL & TRANSIT INFORMATION

NEAREST AIRPORTS: The largest nearby is **Fresno Municipal Airport** (FAT), 97 mi. (156km) SW. McCoy's Charter Service, 1819 Olive St. (268-2237), provides bus service from the Fresno airport.

Other local airports include the **Merced Municipal Airport** (MCE), 82 mi. (131km) west; and the **Modesto Municipal Airport** (MOD), 103 mi. (165km) west.

AIRLINES (all at the Fresno airport): American (toll free 800/433-7300), Delta (toll free 800/221-1212), United (252-5711), and USAir (252-2821).

BUS OR CAR RENTAL? Given the distances to be covered, and the attractive rates offered in California, the best solution is to rent a car with unlimited mileage.

CAR RENTAL (at the Fresno airport unless otherwise indicated): Avis (251-5001); Budget (251-5515); Dollar (252-4000); Hertz (251-5055), and at Merced Municipal Airport (384-1627); and National (251-5577).

TRAIN: The nearest Amtrak station is at 324 W. 24th St., Merced (toll free 800/872-7245).

INTERCITY BUSES: There is no regular bus service to Yosemite National Park. There are daily shuttle buses between Fresno, Merced, and Yosemite; for information and/or a timetable, contact **Yosemite Via Bus Lines,** 300 Grogan Ave., Merced, CA 95340 (209/722-0366); or **Yosemite Gray Line,** P.O. Box 2188, Merced, CA 95344 (209/383-1563).

The nearest **Greyhound bus stations** are at 1033 Broadway in Fresno (268-1829) and at 725 W. Main St. in Merced (722-2121).

INFORMATION & TOURS

TOURIST INFORMATION: Superintendent, **Yosemite National Park,** P.O. Box 577, CA 95389 (209/372-0264).

There are **visitor centers** at Tuolumne Meadows (summer only) and Yosemite Village (year round).

For information on 1- to 7-day trips on foot or on horseback, and for reservations, call 209/252-4848. For **information** on activities in the park, call 209/372-0298. For **weather and highway conditions,** call 209/372-4605.

GUIDED TOURS: Golden Eagle Tours (airplane), Fresno Municipal Airport (255-8900): Flights over Yosemite National Park and the peaks of the High Sierras. Spectacular.

Shuttle Bus: There is free shuttle-bus service in the valley, leaving from the visitors center at Yosemite Village (summer only).

Yosemite Mountain–Sugar Pine Railroad (steam train), on Calif. 41 in Fish Camp, 4 mi. (6km) south of the southern entrance to the park (209/683-7273): Beautiful ride across the Sierras on a little narrow-gauge railroad; amusing. Open daily mid-Apr to mid-Oct; closed the rest of the year (see The Narrow Gauge Inn under "Accommodations," below).

Yosemite Transportation System (bus): Trips around the park, starting from The Ahwahnee in Yosemite Village (252-4848).

SIGHTS & ATTRACTIONS

ADVENTURES: Outdoor Adventure River Specialists (OARS) (boat), P.O. Box 67, Angels Camp, CA 95222 (209/736-4677): 1- or 2-day raft trips down the Kern River, American River, Tuolumne River, and Merced River. Daily Apr–Oct. Angels Camp is a 2-hr. drive from Yosemite Village along Calif. 120W and Calif. 49N. Spectacular.

SCENERY & SIGHTS: ☼⚏ **Waterfalls:** Most of these are in Yosemite Valley; they reach their most impressive proportions in the spring, dry up in the summer heat from mid-July to Aug, and revive with the first storms of autumn. The most spectacular are **Yosemite Falls,** with a total height of 2,425 ft. (739m) in three stages; **Ribbon Fall,** 1,612 ft. (491m); **Bridal Veil Fall,** 620 ft. (189m); and **Nevada Fall,** 594 ft. (181m). One of the great beauties of nature.

☼ **Giant Sequoias Stands:** The finest is **Mariposa Grove,** near the southern entrance. It includes the 2,700-year-old Sequoia **Grizzly Giant,** 209 ft. (64m) high and 34 ft. (11m) in diameter. A must-see.

☼⚏ **Glacier Point,** 5 mi. (8km) SE of Yosemite Village by (difficult) footpath, or 36 mi. (57km) by road: Splendid panoramic view of the valley 3,254 ft. (992m) below, the waterfalls, and the peaks of the Sierra Nevada: **North Dome, Basket Dome, Mount Watkins, Half Dome,** and others. Hiking trail or vehicle road (open in summer only). The finest view in the park.

☼⚏ **Tuolumne Meadows,** 55 mi. (89km) NE of Yosemite Village: Wonderful unspoiled grassland in a lovely mountain setting; a paradise for campers and hikers. Abundant wildlife including black bear and deer. Access road closed in winter. Well-known rock-climbing school (372-1335 June–Aug or 372-1244 Sept–May). Must definitely be seen.

☼⚏⚏ **Yosemite Valley,** west of Yosemite Village: Enclosed valley such as you might find in the Alps, about 8 mi. (13km) long, coming to a dead end. Walled in by vertical granite cliffs 3,300 ft. (1,000m) high, over which, when the snow melts, tumble dizzying waterfalls. Most impressive is **El Capitan,** a 3,591-ft. (1,095m) monolith, the dream (or nightmare) of every rock climber. Its southern wall is overlooked by the huge **Sentinel Rock,** 7,035 ft. (2,145m) high, the most characteristic rock of this mountain setting. It's worth coming to the park just to see this spectacular valley.

WINTER SPORTS RESORTS: ⚐ **Badger Pass Ski Area,** 21 mi. (33km) south of Yosemite Village via Calif. 41 and Glacier Point Rd. (372-1330): 6 lifts; cross-country skiing; open late Nov to mid-Apr.

⚐ **Yosemite Valley:** Cross-country skiing only; late Nov to mid-Apr. For a recording giving snow conditions, call 372-1338.

ACCOMMODATIONS

A Note on Accommodations: Room rates in the Yosemite area are coded as follows: **VE,** Very Expensive ($140 and up); **E,** Expensive ($90–$140); **M,** Moderate ($60–$90); **I,** Inexpensive ($30–$60); **B,** Budget (up to $30). A listing of toll free numbers is in the Appendix.

Personal Favorites Inside the Park (in order of preference)

To make reservations at the four following hotels, contact the **Yosemite Park and Curry Co.,** Yosemite National Park, CA 95389 (209/252-4848).

Unless the contrary is specifically indicated, none of the following hotels is air-conditioned.

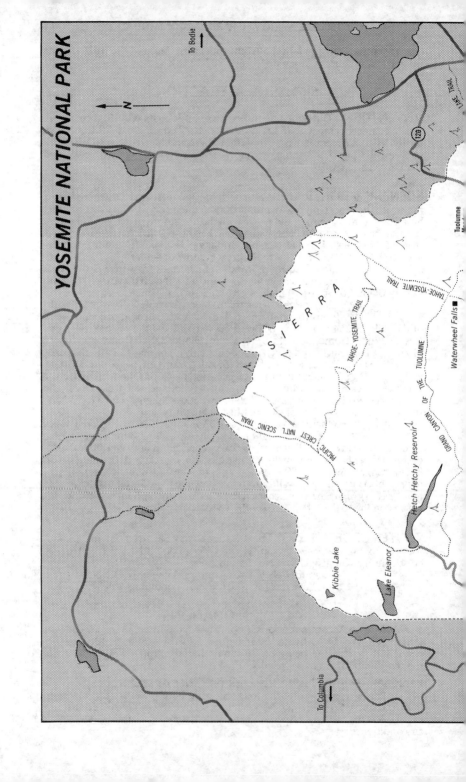

YOSEMITE NATIONAL PARK

N →

To Bodie ↑

To Columbia ↓

S I E R R A

Kibbie Lake

Lake Eleanor

Hetch Hetchy Reservoir

GRAND CANYON OF THE TUOLUMNE

Waterwheel Falls

Tuolumne

PACIFIC CREST NAT'L SCENIC TRAIL

TAHOE-YOSEMITE TRAIL

TAHOE-YOSEMITE TRAIL

LAKE TRAIL

120

☀️♀♀ **The Ahwahnee,** on Calif. 140 in Yosemite Village, Yosemite
🏂 🛏️ National Park, CA 95389 (209/252-4848). 121 rms, some w.
A/C, some w. color TV. AE, CB, DC, MC, V. Free parking, pool, two tennis
courts, horseback riding, bicycling, rest. (resv. required), bar, rm svce, nightclub,
crib $5. *Note:* Luxurious 1920s hotel built like a fortress, w. stone walls and ex-
posed beams. Opened in 1927, the Ahwahnee was conceived to enhance the material grandeur of the towering cliffs of Yosemite; craftspeople incorporated
Native American motifs, boulders, and entire logs into the design. Huge, comfortable rms, some w. fireplaces and balconies; also 24 rms in adj. cottages. The
interior is rustic but elegant. Rest. so-so (jkt. required at dinner) w. wonderful
views of the surrounding peaks. Offhand svce. Noisy and crowded in summer.
Open year round. Celebrities who have stayed here over the years include Herbert Hoover, John F. Kennedy, Walt Disney, Queen Elizabeth II and the Duke of
Edinburgh, Sir Winston Churchill, and Gertrude Stein. Fall and winter are less
busy times at the Ahwahnee (in summer, resv. are a must, a year in advance). **VE**

☀️♀♀ **Wawona Hotel,** on Calif. 41, Yosemite National Park, CA
🏂 🛏️ 95389 (209/252-4848). 105 rms (a third w. bath), color TV
in bar. AE, CB, DC, MC, V. Free parking, pool, golf course, tennis court, horseback riding, rest. (resv. indispensable), bar. *Note:* Charming old hotel in the Victorian style dating from 1856 in a beautiful country setting. Deer roam freely
across the lawn. The rms provide only rather primitive comforts; cheerful reception and svce; good rest. Stagecoach rides around the countryside. The favorite
hotel of those in-the-know. Open Mar–Nov; a 40-min. drive from Yosemite Village. **I–M**

♀ **Yosemite Lodge,** at the intersection of Calif. 140 and Calif.
🛏️ 41, Yosemite National Park, CA 95389 (209/252-4848). 484
rms (75% w. bath), 179 bungalows (half w. bath). AE, CB, DC, MC, V. Free
parking, pool, bicycling, rest., coffee shop, bar, crib $5. *Note:* Relatively modern
motel surrounded by very rustic bungalows; comforts are rudimentary but
there's a fine view out over the valley. Overrun in summer. Nonexistent svce.
Open year round. **M** (in lodge), **I** (in bungalows).

♀ **Curry Village Motel,** at the intersection of Calif. 140 and
🛏️ Calif. 41, Yosemite National Park, CA 95389 (209/252-
4848). 190 rms and bungalows (only half w. bath), and 420 tents. AE, CB, DC,
MC, V. Free parking, pool, skating (in winter), bicycling, horseback riding, coffee shop, bar, camping facilities, crib $5. *Note:* Motel and bungalows are
functionally comfortable but no more than that. The Yosemite climbing school is
located here. Rafting trips organized in summer. Nonexistent svce. For open-air
enthusiasts; open Mar–Oct. **I–M** (in motel or bungalows), **B** (in tents).

Personal Favorites Outside the Park (in order of preference)

☀️♀♀ **The Narrow Gauge Inn,** on Calif. 41, Fish Camp, CA 93623
🏂 🛏️ (209/683-7720). 27 rms, color TV. AE, CB, DC, MC, V.
Free parking, pool, rest., bar, rm svce, crib $6. *Note:* Picturesque little alpine cha-
let 4 mi. (6km) from the southern entrance to the park; rms w. private balconies
or patios and fine mountain view. Very acceptable rest.; friendly reception and
svce. Excursions in a little steam train (for information, call 209/683-7273).
Closed Nov to mid-Mar. **M–E**

♀♀ **Shilo Inn Oakhurst,** 40644 Calif. 41, Oakhurst, CA 93644
🛏️🛏️ (209/683-3555). 80 mini-suites, color TV, in-rm movies. AE,
CB, DC, MC, V. Free parking, pool, health club, sauna, adj. rest., free Continental breakfast, crib $6. *Note:* Modern (1988) four-story all-suites motel, 25 mi.
(40km) from the southern entrance to the park. Very comfortable mini-suites w.
microwaves, refrigerators, and wet bars; some w. private patios or balconies. Reception w. a smile. Good value on balance for families. **M–E,** but lower rates
off-season.

♀♀ **Boulder Lodge,** on Calif. 158, June Lake, CA 93529 (619/
🛏️🛏️ 648-7533). 60 rms, cable color TV. AE, MC, V. Free parking,

pool, sauna, tennis court, fishing, skiing in winter, nearby coffee shop. *Note:* Comfortable motel, w. less comfortable bungalows, on June Lake, 22 mi. (35km) SE of the eastern entrance to the park via U.S. 395 and Calif. 120 (the latter closed in winter). Friendly reception. A good base for a visit to Devils Postpile National Monument. Open year round. Very good value. **I–M,** but lower rates off-season.

☼♀♀ **Pines Resort,** North Shore Rd., Bass Lake, CA 93604 (209/ 🏄 ᛒᛒ 642-3121). 84 bungalows w. kitchenettes, cable color TV. AE, MC, V. Free parking, beach, health club, tennis court, boating, waterskiing, rest., bar, disco. *Note:* Engaging frame bungalows w. private patios, some w. fireplaces, an easy walk from the lake. It's 18 mi. (28km) from the southern entrance to the park via Calif. 222 and Calif. 41, far from the hurly-burly of Yosemite's vacationers; ideal for families. Open year round. **E,** but lower rates off-season.

♀ **Best Western Yosemite Gateway Inn,** 40530 Calif. 41, Oak- 🏄 hurst, CA 93644 (209/683-2378; toll free, see Best Western). 92 rms, A/C, color TV, in-rm movies. AE, CB, DC, MC, V. Free parking, pool, adj. rest., bar. *Note:* Small, appealing motel deep in the woods, 15 mi. (24km) from the southern entrance to the park on Calif. 41. Very comfortable rms, some w. kitchenettes and refrigerators, most w. mountain views. Cheerful reception and svce; good value. **I–M,** but lower rates off-season.

♀ **Yosemite View Lodge,** on Calif. 140, El Portal, CA 95318 🏄 (209/379-2681). 65 rms, cable color TV. MC, V. Free parking, nearby coffee shop. *Note:* Small rustic motel overlooking the rapids of the Merced River (ask for a rm w. river view), 2 mi. (3km) from the western entrance to the park. Acceptable comforts; some rms w. balconies and refrigerators. **I–M**

♀ **Best Western Lake View,** 30 Main St., Lee Vinning, CA 🏄 93541 (619/647-6543; toll free, see Best Western). 45 rms (half w. A/C), color TV, in-rm movies. AE, CB, DC, MC, V. Free parking, putting green, nearby coffee shop, crib $5. *Note:* Typical small motel very nr. Mono Lake, 14 mi. (22km) from the eastern entrance to the park on Calif. 120 (closed in winter), and 21 mi. (33km) south of the ghost town of Bodie on U.S. 395. Functionally comfortable; attractive landscaping; free coffee in rms. **I**

♀ **Ducey's Bass Lake Lodge,** North Shore Rd., Bass Lake, CA 🏄 93604 (209/642-3131). 40 rms and bungalows (two-thirds without bath). MC, V. Free parking, private beach, boating, waterskiing, rest., bar, disco (in season). *Note:* Modest, unpretentious motel 18 mi. (28km) from the southern entrance to the park via Calif. 222 and Calif. 41. Attractively situated on a lake; very acceptable rest. **M**

RESTAURANTS

A Note on Restaurant Prices: The Yosemite area restaurant prices, per person, excluding drinks and service charges, are coded as follows: **VE,** Very Expensive ($60 and up); **E,** Expensive ($40–$60); **M,** Moderate ($25–$40); **I,** Inexpensive ($15–$25); **B,** Budget (up to $15).

Personal Favorites (in order of preference)

☼♀♀♀ **Erna's Elderberry House,** Victoria Lane at Calif. 41, Oakhurst ☼ ᛒᛒᛒ (683-6800). A/C. Lunch Wed–Fri, dinner Wed–Mon, brunch Sun. MC, V. Jkt. *Specialties:* Brie-and-artichoke quiche, curried lamb w. celeriac, broiled salmon w. basil butter and tomato purée; remarkable desserts; menu changes regularly. Very good wine list but no hard liquor. *Note:* Some of the best food in California is to be found in this remote little village, nestling in the foothills of the Sierra Nevada some 15 mi. (24km) from the southern entrance to Yosemite National Park. Chefs Erna Kubin and Fernando Madrigal serve up a wonderful, light, creative cuisine at very attractive prices. Their six-course dinners are a feast for the eye as well as the palate. Elegant Provençal decor; open-air terrace in good weather. Flawless svce. A very fine place—definitely reserve ahead. *French/Continental.* **I–M**

⚐⚐ **The Narrow Gauge Inn,** in the Narrow Gauge Inn (see "Accommodations," above) (683-6446). A/C. Breakfast/dinner daily; closed Nov to mid-Mar. AE, CB, DC, MC, V. *Specialties:* broiled steak and fresh seafood, homemade desserts. *Note:* Chalet-style rest. w. good mountain views. Acceptable but unimaginative food. Rustic decor w. open-air terrace in summer and inviting fireplace in winter. Friendly reception and svce. Good value; resv. advised in summer. *Seafood/American.* **B–I**

⚐ **Charles Street Dinner House,** Calif. 140 at 7th St., Mariposa (966-2366). A/C. Dinner only, Wed–Sun; closed Dec 25. MC, V. *Specialties:* beef en brochette, steak, catch of the day. *Note:* Nice little rest. 30 mi. (48km) from the main park entrance; good flavorful food, good svce, good value. *Steak/Seafood.* **B–I**

NEARBY EXCURSIONS

☀🏛 **BODIE** (96 mi./153km east of Yosemite Village via Calif. 140W, Calif. 120E, U.S. 395N, and Calif. 270E): This old gold prospectors' town had 10,000 inhabitants in 1880 and enjoyed an unhappy celebrity for its violence—seven shoot-outs a week on average. It was destroyed by two great fires, in 1892 and 1932. There remain some several dozen buildings more or less well preserved, including the church, the school, and the prison; there's also a little museum. Spectacular. *Note:* The last 3 mi. (5km), by unsurfaced road, are impassable in winter.

On the way, glance at the large saltwater **Mono Lake** on Calif. 120 (closed in winter), now a refuge for waterfowl; worth seeing.

☀🏛 **COLUMBIA** (80 mi./128km NW of Yosemite Village via Calif. 140W, Calif. 120W, and Calif. 49N (209/532-4301): One of the best-preserved ghost towns in California. Museums, workshops, and many restored buildings including the picturesque **State Driver's Retreat Saloon,** the **What Cheer Saloon,** and the **City Hotel.** It's certifiably in period, just the way it was in the palmy days of the gold rush.

On the way, take a side trip to look at **Sonora,** a place of importance in the westward expansion.

Where to Stay

☀ **City Hotel,** Main St., Columbia, CA 95310 (209/532-1479). 9 rms. AE, MC, V. An Old West period hotel. Rest. open daily for lunch/dinner. **M**

NATIONAL PARKS IN THE VICINITY

☀🏛 **DEVIL'S POSTPILE NATIONAL MONUMENT** (98 mi./156km SE of Yosemite Village via Calif. 140W, Calif. 120E, U.S. 395S, and Calif. 203W): An unusual sight—hundreds of bluish basalt shafts, 50–60 ft. (16–18m) high and perhaps 100,000 years old, which look like the torn-up pages of a book. All this is set against a luxuriant backdrop of forests, mountain streams, hot springs, and lava flows. Spectacular. Park open mid-June through Oct; well worth the side trip. *Note:* Calif. 120 is closed in winter.

For **information,** contact the Ranger Station, P.O. Box 501, Mammoth Lakes, CA 93546 (619/934-2289 mid-June through Oct, 209/565-3341 the rest of the year).

☀🏛 **SEQUOIA & KINGS CANYON NATIONAL PARKS** (178 mi./284km SE of Yosemite Village via Calif. 41 and Calif. 180): Forests of giant sequoias and majestic granite crests; not to be missed. See Chapter 52 on Sequoia National Park.

CHAPTER 54

LOS ANGELES♔♔

□ □ □

With Hollywood, Disneyland, and Palm Springs

The first great U.S. city designed and built in the Automobile Age, Los Angeles has become a prototype of the modern American metropolis. It consists of a group of distinct urban areas, often a long way apart, which lie like the rim of a wheel around the center city hub, here reduced to its lowest common denominator. The scale of Los Angeles—90 mi. (145km) long by 50 mi. (80km) wide—defies belief. Around it lie the suburbs, each of which amounts to a miniature city, from **Glendale, Van Nuys,** and the foothills of the **San Gabriel Mountains** on the north to **Anaheim, Costa Mesa,** and **Long Beach** on the south; from **Ontario** and **Pasadena** on the east to **Santa Monica, Redondo Beach,** and the shores of the Pacific on the west. This vibrant, sprawling city is surpassed only by New York in population, and only by Jacksonville, Florida, in area; at 464 sq. mi. (1,202km²) it's about half the size of the state of Rhode Island.

A sign of the times: the TV giants, ABC, CBS, and NBC, have ousted the movie studios from Hollywood. The run-down slum areas of **Watts** lie a short distance from the daring office skyscrapers of **Bunker Hill** and the twin 52-story towers of **Atlantic Richfield/ARCO Plaza.** The huge arena of the **Memorial Coliseum,** where the Olympic Games were held in 1932 and 1984, sits cheek-by-jowl with the fairy kingdom of **Disneyland.** The fashionable restaurants of **Sunset Boulevard**—a name dear to all movie addicts—and the plush homes of **Bel Air,** with their azure-blue pools and manicured lawns, coexist with futurist factory buildings or the famous **Stack,** a giant four-level traffic interchange not far from the **Music Center.** Bohemian **Venice,** with its colorful population of roller-skaters, and **South-Central L.A.,** where cocaine wars rage, are hardly a half hour's drive from the millionaires' boutiques of **Beverly Hills** or the new business district of **Century City.**

The ever-choked freeways—L.A. is linked by more than 687 mi. (1,100km) of urban highways—and the oilwells in the heart of the city are parts of its urban landscape, as are the surf on the beaches, the interminable tracts of small suburban houses, the intrusive areas of wasteland, and the purple-colored smog, the city's tribute to the internal-combustion engine. Because of the city's sheer size, its residents ("Angelenos") spend twice as much time every day in their cars as anyone else on the face of the earth. As a result, there are by now innumerable drive-in banks, drive-in restaurants, drive-in movie theaters, and even drive-in churches.

El Pueblo de Nuestra Señora la Reina de Los Angeles de Porciúncula (The Town of Our Lady of Porciúncula, Queen of the Angels)—Los Angeles for short—was founded in 1781 by Don Felipe de Neve, governor of Spanish California; the site had been explored as early as 1542 by the Portuguese-born navigator,

Juan Rodriguez Cabrillo. The California gold rush of 1849 inaugurated a period of rapid growth, further accelerated by the completion of the Southern Pacific's railroad in 1876 and the first oil discoveries in 1892. In half a century the city's population grew 2,600%, from 50,000 in 1890 to 320,000 in 1910 and 1,500,000 in 1940. Today this huge urban nebula numbers, with its outlying communities, more than 13 million inhabitants, including at least 2.5 million "Chicanos" of Mexican origin, and is oriented toward the cutting edge of industry—electronics, aviation, petrochemicals, printing, publishing, tourism (more than 40 million visitors a year), television, movies (more than three-quarters of those made in the U.S.)—but also banking and insurance, to the point where Los Angeles has superseded San Francisco, its older sibling to the north, as New York's economic counterpart on the West Coast.

The city, first of all and most of all, is a patchwork of exotic races and nationalities: the Far Eastern neighborhoods of **Chinatown, Little Tokyo,** and **Koreatown,** the Mexican stretch along **Olvera Street,** the African American slums of **Watts** and the "Latino" ghettos of **East Los Angeles** and **Boyle Heights.** With its hundreds of thousands of Chinese, Japanese, Koreans, Filipinos, Vietnamese, Formosans, Thais, and Laotian immigrants, Los Angeles has already become the most Asian of U.S. metropolises. At the same time, after New York and Tel Aviv, Los Angeles has the world's third-largest Jewish population.

Angelenos, more relaxed and approachable than the people of the great eastern seaboard cities, emphatically affirm that Los Angeles is principally a state of mind, the so-called mellow way of life, which is special in being "cooler" and more harmonious. True, one humorist has defined the place as "a bunch of suburbs in search of a city," but in spite of its size Los Angeles is truly a whole, and a unique one. **Sepulveda Boulevard,** for example, stretches unbroken for 45 mi. (72km). In the absence of decent public transportation this city's traffic assumes nightmare proportions every rush hour on the urban highways so misleadingly referred to as "freeways." The interchange between the Harbor Fwy. and Santa Monica Fwy. (I-10 and Cal. 110), in the heart of Los Angeles, holds the world record for traffic density, with peaks of 480,000 vehicles a day. Another, even less enviable record: the country's highest concentration of carbon monoxide pollutants from internal-combustion engines.

After nurturing for many years a cultural inferiority complex toward New York, the U.S. capital of movies and TV has for more than a decade been living through an intellectual boom—artistic (music, ballet, cinema, architecture, graphic arts), scientific, and cultural. Witness its 35 museums, including the new and spectacular **MOCA (Museum of Contemporary Art),** its dozens of art galleries (Los Angeles is the premier American market for contemporary art, after New York), its hundred or so theaters, 29 symphony and chamber orchestras, 17 theater and opera companies, and 36 ballet companies, some of world class. On the scientific side, thanks to its famous universities and research institutes such as **UCLA, Loyola University, CalTech,** and the **Jet Propulsion Laboratory,** Los Angeles can pride itself on the world's highest concentration of Nobel laureates.

The economic and cultural capital of the West Coast has been called (not without reason) "dynamic," "fascinating," "inhuman"; it may seduce you or shock you, according to your taste. Only one thing is for sure: the visitor who encounters this enormous and sometimes disturbing city for the first time will not soon forget it. In spite of its TV and film portraits, it's relatively safe: FBI statistics rank it 15th among American cities for crime (but first for rape).

Among the city's famous children are Pres. Richard M. Nixon (born in the nearby suburb of Yorba Linda); Democratic presidential candidate Adlai Stevenson; the late sculptor Isamu Noguchi; Chief Justice (former California governor) Earl Warren; actresses Marilyn Monroe, Liza Minnelli, Candice Bergen, and Mia Farrow; and actors Robert Redford, Dustin Hoffman, and Ryan O'Neal.

BASIC FACTS: State of California. Area codes: 213 (Los Angeles), 818 (San Fernando Valley, Burbank, and Glendale), 714 (Anaheim). Time zone: Pacific.

ZIP Code: 90053. Founded: 1781. Approximate population: city, 3,450,000 (second largest in the U.S.); metropolitan area, 13,900,000 (also second largest), including 150,000 Chinese, 160,000 Japanese, 200,000 Koreans, 2,460,000 Chicanos of Mexican origin, 350,000 Salvadorans, 200,000 Nicaraguans, and 60,000 Guatemalans.

CLIMATE: Before the coming of the automobile, Los Angeles had one of the most pleasant climates on the West Coast, dry and sunny, with a mild and rainy winter (lows of 50°F/10°C), a very tolerable summer averaging 75°F (24°C), in spite of 95°F (35°C) peaks when the hot Santa Ana wind blows out of the desert, and a glorious spring and fall. The smog has ruined everything. Given windless weather and auto pollution, when smog clamps down on the center city and the San Fernando Valley basin, whole districts disappear in the thick, corrosive murk, which sometimes lingers for a full week, especially in summer.

DISTANCES: Denver, 1,059 mi. (1,695km); Las Vegas, 282 mi. (451km); Phoenix, 390 mi. (625km); San Diego, 125 mi. (200km); San Francisco, 381 mi. (610km).

ARRIVAL & TRANSIT INFORMATION

Note: Given the sheer size of Los Angeles, the concepts of "downtown" and "suburb" lose all meaning. The places, museums, and monuments referred to below are classified by *districts:* downtown, Hollywood, Beverly Hills, Santa Monica. Establishments not found in any particular district are listed under Los Angeles. Unless otherwise indicated, all phone numbers in this chapter are in area code 213.

AIRPORTS: Los Angeles International Airport (LAX), 17 mi. (27km) SW. Fourth-largest airport in the world by volume of traffic, handling 45 million passengers a year, and the country's third-largest international gateway. For information, call 646-5252.

Regional airports include: **Hollywood-Burbank Airport** (BUR), 15 mi. (24km) NW (for information, call 818/840-8847); **Long Beach Municipal Airport** (LGB), 21 mi. (33km) SE; **Ontario International Airport** (ONT), 50 mi. (80km) east; and **Orange County–John Wayne Airport** (SNA), 30 mi. (48km) SE.

U.S. AIRLINES: Alaska (toll free 800/426-0333), American (935-6045), America West (980-0150), Continental (772-6000), Delta (386-5510), Hawaiian Air (toll free 800/367-5320), MGM Grand Air (414-0163), Northwest (380-1511), Pan Am (toll free 800/221-1111), Southwest (485-1221), TWA (484-2244), United (772-2121), and USAir (935-5005).

FOREIGN CARRIERS: Air Canada (toll free 800/422-6232), Air France (614-0999), British Airways (toll free 800/247-9297), Japan Air Lines (620-9580), KLM (toll free 800/777-5553), and Lufthansa (toll free 800/645-3880).

CITY LINK: The **cab** fare from Los Angeles International to dwntwn is about $28; to Beverly Hills, $24; to Hollywood, $30; to Santa Monica, about $15. Time, depending on destination and time of day, 50–75 min.

Airport bus: Several shuttle van companies can be summoned through courtesy phones in the baggage claim area or by calling 417-8988. There is no need to make a reservation. The best one, **Super Shuttle** (213/338-1111; toll free 800/554-6458) provides door-to-door service to any address in Los Angeles; fare varies according to destination, $12 (dwntn) to $35 (Orange County).

Cabs are very expensive, and often impossible to find away from the big hotels. Public transportation is sadly lacking—a **light-rail system** covering a 22-mi. (35km), 22-station route between dwntn and Long Beach, the "Blue Line," began operation in July 1990; one-way fare, $1.10. A subway line from dwntn to San Fernando Valley, **Metro Rail**, should be completed by 1998—but no promises. For information on the **public bus and rail (RTD) service** or the **downtown shuttle** (DASH), call 213/626-4455.

The only solution that makes sense is to rent a car; rates with unlimited mileage in California are among the best in the country.

CAR RENTAL (at Los Angeles International Airport unless otherwise indicated): Avis (646-5600); Budget (645-4500); Dollar (645-9333); Hertz (646-4861); National (670-4950); Rent-A-Car-Cheep, 4760 W. Century Blvd. in Inglewood, just east of the airport (678-9146), a local renter with very attractive rates; Thrifty, W. Century Blvd. (645-1880). For dwntn locations, consult the local telephone directories.

LIMOUSINE SERVICES: Carey Limousine (275-4153), Royal Coach Livery (872-3510), Scripps Edward Limousine (toll free 800/223-6710), and VIP Limo Service (273-1505).

TAXIS: Cabs may be hailed on the street, taken from the stands outside the major hotels, or summoned by phone. This is one of the more expensive cities in the country for cab rides. Recommended companies include: **Bell** (221-1112), **Independent** (385-8294), **Los Angeles Taxi** (627-7000), or **United** (653-5050).

TRAIN: Amtrak, Union Terminal, 800 N. Alameda St., dwntn (624-0171). An ill-reputed district, dangerous at night.

INTERCITY BUSES: Greyhound has terminals at 208 E. 6th St., dwntwn (620-1200 or 629-8400), a rough neighborhood at night, and at 1409 N. Vine St., Hollywood (466-6381).

INFORMATION & TOURS

TOURIST INFORMATION: The **Automobile Club of Southern California,** dwntwn at 2601 S. Figueroa St., CA 90007 (213/741-3111): Practical information for motorists, maps. Fine Colonial building.

Greater Los Angeles Visitors and Convention Bureau, 515 S. Figueroa St., 11th floor, CA 90071 (213/624-7300): Accepts only written requests for information.

Los Angeles Chamber of Commerce, 404 S. Bixel St., CA 90054 (213/629-0602).

Visitors Information Center, dwntwn at 695 S. Figueroa St., CA 90071 (213/689-8822): Information on Los Angeles and the metropolitan area; multilingual hostesses. Other location: 6541 Hollywood Blvd., Hollywood (213/461-4213).

GUIDED TOURS: Grave Line Tours (bus), East Wall of Mann's Chinese Theater, on Hollywood Blvd. at Orchid Ave., Hollywood (876-0920): The name, with overtones of macabre humor, perfectly describes the purpose of the tour—to show you the places where celebrities and movie stars (Rudolf Valentino,

Marilyn Monroe, Sharon Tate, and the like) drew their last breath, or now lie awaiting eternity. It lasts 2 hr. and you ride in an old Cadillac hearse. For lovers of the spooky and the unusual. Reserve ahead (876-4286).

Gray Line Tours (bus), 1207 W. 3rd St., dwntwn (213/481-2121): Guided tours of the city; pickup at all major hotels.

Hollywood Fantasy Tours (bus), 1651 N. Highland Ave., Hollywood (213/469-8184): Guided tour of the neighborhoods where the movie stars live and other attractions; pickup at all major hotels.

Hollywood on Location, 8644 Wilshire Blvd., Beverly Hills (213/659-9165): For movie addicts; maintains an up-to-date schedule of movies currently in production, with practical advice on how to watch. Operates daily.

Mardigras/Buccaneer Cruises (boat), Ports O'Call Village, Harbor Blvd., San Pedro (213/547-2833): 1-hr. mini-cruises around the Port of Los Angeles and Long Beach. Also dinner cruises. Year round.

Starline Tours (bus), 6541 Hollywood Blvd., Hollywood (463-3131): Guided tour of city and surroundings; pickup at all major hotels. Operates daily.

SIGHTS, ATTRACTIONS & ACTIVITIES

ARCHITECTURAL HIGHLIGHTS: ⌂ **Capitol Records,** 1750 Vine St., Hollywood: Amusing structure, shaped like a stack of records, concept of composer Johnny Mercer and his associate Nat King Cole. No visits.

⌂ **Civic Center,** bounded by Sunset Blvd., Grand Ave., 1st St., and San Pedro St., dwntwn: The administrative center of Los Angeles, comprising **City Hall** (1928), the **Music Center** (see below), the **Police Building,** and the **County Courthouse** and **Law Library.** Fountains, gardens, interesting modern architecture.

⌂ **Coca-Cola Bottling Co.,** 1334 S. Central Ave., dwntwn: 1935 bottling plant disguised as an art deco steamboat; a triumph of California kitsch by architect Robert Derrah. No visits.

⌂ **Fox Plaza,** 2121 Ave. of the Stars, Century City (213/282-0047): Two triangular buildings designed by Minoru Yamasaki, also architect of New York's World Trade Center. These spectacular twin towers are among the city's most-photographed, and were the backdrop for introductory footage for episodes of the series "Remington Steele." Former President Reagan maintains his office on the 34th floor.

☼ **Hollywood Sign,** Durand Dr., North Hollywood: As famous as the Eiffel Tower or the Statue of Liberty, these nine great white letters, each 45 ft. (12m) high, since 1923 have been the trademark of Los Angeles. Reached via Beechwood Dr.

⌂ **Los Angeles Memorial Coliseum,** 3911 S. Figueroa St., dwntwn (747-7111): Built for the 1932 Olympics, this magnificent art deco stadium, with a capacity of 102,000, was completely renovated for the 1984 Olympics. Between times, it houses the home football games of the L.A. Raiders, rodeos, pop concerts, motocross races, etc. Open daily.

☼⌂ **Music Center,** 135 N. Grand Ave., dwntwn (972-7438): Built in 1964 at the considerable cost of $34 million, this is the Los Angeles equivalent of New York's Lincoln Center or Washington's Kennedy Center. Three futuristic-looking concert halls—the **Dorothy Chandler Pavilion,** the **Ahmanson Theater,** and the **Mark Taper Forum**—frame a marble plaza with a vast pool and an impressive sculpture by Jacques Lipchitz entitled *Peace on Earth.* Every year the Oscar award ceremony is held here. Open Mon–Tues and Thurs–Sat. For information on shows, call 972-7211.

⌂ **Pacific Design Center,** 8687 Melrose Ave., West Hollywood (657-0800): Nicknamed "The Blue Wheel," this amazing 1975 tinted-glass building designed by Cesar Pelli houses showrooms of home-furnishings manufacturers. Two adjoining cubic red buildings, also designed by Cesar Pelli, were opened in 1988.

 Tail o' the Pup, 329 N. San Vicente Blvd., West Hollywood (213/652-4517): Bar shaped like a giant hot dog, one of the few surviving relics of California pop architecture. Amusing.

 Union Station, 800 N. Alameda St., dwntwn (624-0171): The city's central station is a magnificent 1939 example of the Hollywood-Spanish style; more than 65 movies have been shot here. Worth seeing, but avoid the neighborhood after dark.

 University of California–Los Angeles (UCLA), 405 Hilgard Ave., Westwood (206-8147): Founded in 1919, the local campus of the University of California moved to its present site in 1929. With 34,000 students it's the state's largest. Among the many points of interest on the huge 410-acre (166ha) campus are: a very lovely **botanic garden** with modern sculpture, including works of Matisse and Noguchi; **Schoenberg Hall,** named in memory of the Austrian composer who taught here in the '30s and '40s; and above all the **Wight Art Gallery** (see "Museums of Art," below). Campus open daily.

BEACHES: **Corona del Mar State Beach,** 42 mi. (67km) SE: One of the most beautiful beaches around Los Angeles, perfect for swimmers.

 Huntington Beach, 36 mi. (58km) SE: The surfers' paradise; the sport began here in 1907, and the U.S. Championships are held here every year. On the beach is a monument to the Unknown Surfer.

 Laguna Beach, 48 mi. (76km) SE: The favorite beach for artists and yuppies, reached by a magnificent coastal road from Newport Beach.

 Long Beach, 22 mi. (35km) south: One of the most popular beaches in the Los Angeles area.

 Malibu, 19 mi. (30km) West: One of the region's most beautiful, particularly **Malibu Surfrider State Beach,** but with big waves. For experienced surfers.

 Manhattan Beach, 18 mi. (29km) SW: Agreeable, relatively uncrowded beach, popular with teenagers.

 Santa Monica, 15 mi. (24km) west: This popular beach and promenade has been virtually taken over by hundreds of homeless. Picturesque pier and amusement park.

 Sunset Beach, 33 mi. (54km) SE: The favorite beach of seasoned surfers.

 Venice, 16 mi. (26km) SW: The kingdom of the roller-skaters. "Pop" and amusing by day; riskier after dark. Also popular with bodybuilders ("**Muscle Beach,**" 1800 Ocean Front Walk).

 Zuma Beach, 25 mi. (40km) west: The nudists' beach, with great surf.

BROADCASTING & MOVIE STUDIOS: ABC, 4151 Prospect Ave., Hollywood (557-4396): Tapings of TV shows, open to the public. Tickets must be applied for 1 or 2 days in advance. Open daily.

CBS, 7800 Beverly Blvd., Los Angeles (852-2455): Tapings of TV shows, open to the public. Tickets must be applied for 1 or 2 days in advance. Open daily.

NBC, 3000 W. Alameda Blvd., Burbank (818/840-3657): The country's largest TV studio. Taping of TV shows, open to the public. Tickets must be applied for 1 or 2 days in advance. Also, guided tour of the studios. Open daily.

Burbank Studios VIP Tours, 4000 Warner Blvd., Burbank (818/954-1744): Tour on foot and by minibus through the movie and TV studios of Warner Bros. and Columbia Pictures. You can watch the shooting of a movie or a TV show being taped. Resv. must be made well ahead. Highly recommended to movie buffs, but exhausting. No movie or still cameras or tape recorders allowed. Price, $20; open Mon–Fri.

Paramount, Bronson Ave. and Melrose Ave., Hollywood: The wrought-iron entrance gates were made famous by the movie *Sunset Boulevard.* No admission to the studio.
Paramount Film and TV Studios, 5555 Melrose Ave., Hollywood (213/468-5575): Offers a 2-hr. walking tour of the studios twice daily, and tapings of sitcoms and talk shows.
Universal Studios Tour, 3900 Lankershim Blvd., Universal City (818/508-9600): A kind of theme park dedicated to the Seventh Art; offers 2-hr. conducted mini-train tours behind the scenes of Hollywood's largest movie studio. From the *Star Wars* style of attack from outer space through the collapsing railroad bridge, the *Ten Commandments* passage of the Red Sea, the devouring Great White shark from *Jaws,* or the exploits of *King Kong* on the streets of New York to the duel between *Conan the Barbarian* and the giant dragon, nothing, or almost nothing, is spared the sensation-seeking visitor. Kitsch and crowded, but amusing; it draws three million people a year. Open daily except Thanksgiving and Dec 25. Admission: $22 (adults), $16.50 (children).

CHURCHES/SYNAGOGUES: **Crystal Cathedral,** 12141 Lewis St., Garden Grove, 28 mi. (45km) SE on I-5 (714/971-4013): Philip Johnson's star-shaped, beveled-glass, 3,000-seat church-auditorium, the most modern in the U.S. A spectacular sight, 10 min. by car from Disneyland. Open daily.
Los Angeles Mormon Temple, 10777 Santa Monica Blvd., Los Angeles (474-1549): One of the largest Mormon temples in the world standing in 20 acres (8ha) of beautiful landscaped garden. The temple's principal tower, 257 ft. (78m) high, is crowned by a 15-ft. (4m) statue of the Angel Moroni. Non-Mormons are not admitted to the Temple itself, but the interesting visitor center is open daily. Worth seeing.
St. Vincent de Paul Church, 612 W. Adams Blvd. at Figueroa St., Los Angeles (749-8950): Generally admired as one of the city's handsomest churches; the Spanish baroque architecture and Mexican mosaic ornamental tiling make a stunning impact. Worth going out of your way. Across the intersection at 514 W. Adams is **St. John's Church,** a modern replica of the great 11th-century church at Toscanello in Italy; don't miss it.
Wayfarer's Chapel, 5755 W. Palos Verdes Dr., Rancho Palos Verdes (377-1650): Designed by Lloyd Wright, architect son of the great Frank Lloyd Wright, this splendid 1949 glass-and-sequoia-wood chapel overlooks the Pacific. Open to all denominations. An absolute must-see. Open daily.

HISTORIC BUILDINGS: **Bradbury Building,** 3rd St. at Broadway, dwntwn (489-1893): One of the country's few office buildings designated as a historic monument (1893). Marble staircases and Victorian wrought-iron balconies. Wonderful interior lobby under an elegant skylight. An absolute must-see. Open Mon–Sat.
Bullocks Wilshire, 3050 Wilshire Blvd., dwntwn (382-6161): With its unusual greenish tower and beacon light, this curious 1929 building is one of the most perfect examples of California art deco. Designated a historic monument. Open daily.
Casa de Adobe, 4605 N. Figueroa St., Highland Park (221-2163): An exact replica of an 1850s Mexican hacienda, the building dates from 1918 and is used as an annex to the Southwest Museum (see below). Interesting period decoration and furniture. Worth a visit. Open Tues–Sun.
El Pueblo de Los Angeles State Historic Park (see "Strolls, Downtown," below).
Hollyhock House, 4800 Hollywood Blvd., Hollywood (662-7272): Built in 1919 as the home of oil heiress Aline Barnsdall, Frank Lloyd Wright's first Los Angeles building was inspired by pre-Columbian

themes, and is considered one of his greatest achievements. An absolute must-see. Open Tues–Thurs and Sat–Sun.

    Lummis Home, 200 E. Ave. 43, Lincoln Heights (222-0546): Picturesque turn-of-the-century home of rustic character (rough-hewn stones and exposed beams), once the property of the distinguished historian and archeologist Charles Lummis. Now the headquarters of the Historical Society of Southern California. It can conveniently form part of a combined expedition to the Casa de Adobe (see above) and the Southwest Museum (see "Museums of Science and History," below). Open Wed–Sun.

    Mann's Chinese Theater, 6925 Hollywood Blvd., Hollywood (464-8111): Opened in 1927 and originally known as Grauman's Chinese Theater, this is probably the world's most famous movie house. Cast in cement on the sidewalk in front of it are the footprints of 160 stars of the silver screen. The architecture is Hollywood Chinese, and the interior is the finest kitsch.

    Mission San Fernando Rey de España, 15151 San Fernando Mission Blvd., Mission Hills (818/361-0186): Spanish mission founded in 1797 by the indefatigable Fr. Junípero Serra (the 17th of 21 missions built by Spanish religious between 1769 and 1823). Original adobe architecture with walls 4 ft. (1.20m) thick, and a very lovely arcade. Superbly restored, and surrounded by beautiful gardens. Museum. Open daily.

    Mission San Gabriel Arcangel, 537 W. Mission Dr., San Gabriel (818/282-5191): The oldest (1771) stone building in California, the work of Fr. Junípero Serra, and one of the most beautiful of the Spanish missions in the U.S. Renowned for its vineyards; interesting museum.

    Pico House (see El Pueblo de Los Angeles Historic Monument in "Strolls, Downtown," below).

    Queen Mary, Pier J, Long Beach (435-3511): The largest (81,000 tons) and longest ocean liner still afloat. Launched in 1934, this one-time pride of the British merchant marine is now a convention hotel and floating museum. Open daily.

    Simon Rodia Towers, 1765 E. 107th St., Watts (569-8181): Eight surrealist metal towers, built single-handed over 33 years with the most incongruous of salvaged material (70,000 shells, bottles, tin cans, tiles, etc.) by an Italian immigrant, Simon Rodia, who died in 1956. An astonishing achievement of naïve art. An absolute must-see.

    Spruce Goose, Pier J, Long Beach (435-3511): The world's largest commercial transport plane: wing span, 320 ft. (100m), the length of a football field; takeoff weight, 180 tons; intended capacity, 700 passengers. This all-wooden monster, brainchild of billionaire Howard Hughes, made a single hop of 1 mi. (1,600m) in Los Angeles harbor on November 2, 1947; this was the one and only flight of Hughes's H-2 Hercules, better known ever since by its nickname, "Spruce Goose." It now sits under a 128-ft. (40m) dome next to the *Queen Mary* (see above). Open daily.

INDUSTRIAL TOURS: Lawry's California Center, 570 W. Ave. 26, Los Angeles (225-2491): If you like Lawry's seasonings and food products, you won't want to miss the 45-min. guided tour (Mon–Fri), which takes in the kitchens where new recipes are tested, and the manufacturing plant. There are food stores and pleasant restaurants; open daily year round for lunch, and nightly May–Oct for dinner. All this stands among very lovely gardens.

MARKETS: **Farmers Market,** 6333 W. 3rd St. at Fairfax Ave., Los Angeles (933-9211): Picturesque covered market with more than 160 food stalls; also vendors of clothing and handcrafts from around the world. An ideal place to eat on the run, but somewhat touristy. Open daily.

    Grand Central Market, 315 S. Broadway, dwntwn (624-2378): A little less touristy, but no less colorful, than Farmers

Market (see above). You can find anything here, from sheep's heads, fresh chilis, tripe, and fish to costume jewelry, bargains in clothing, and bottles of vitamins. A sight to be seen. Open Mon–Sat.

⚱ **Olvera Street,** between Alameda St. and Main St., dwntwn: Lively, colorful Mexican market of **El Pueblo de Los Angeles** (see "Strolls, Downtown," below). Stalls, handcrafts, restaurants. Very touristy.

MUSEUMS OF ART: ☼🏛 **J. Paul Getty Museum,** 17985 Pacific Coast Hwy., Malibu (458-2003): Housed in the replica of a Roman villa of the 1st century A.D. (the "Papyrus Villa" at Herculaneum near Naples), the museum displays a fabulous collection of Greek and Roman material, and of European furniture, bronzes, painting, and sculpture from antiquity through the 18th century, as well as such remarkable contemporary masterpieces as *The Entry of Christ into Brussels in 1889* by James Ensor or *Irises* by Vincent van Gogh acquired in Mar 1990. Splendid gardens and fountains. Parking space must be reserved at least 24 hr. in advance. Excellent museum cafeteria. Worth the trip all by itself. Open Tues–Sun.

☼🏛 **Henry Huntington Library,** 1151 Oxford Rd., San Marino (818/405-2100): The very rich collection includes almost five million old manuscripts and 500,000 rare books, as well as English 18th- and 19th-century paintings, housed in an elegant Greek Revival building dating from 1911 and recently renovated after a fire. Splendid 200-acre (81ha) botanic garden. Among the well-known works on exhibit: Gainsborough's *Blue Boy, Pinkie* by Sir Thomas Lawrence, Turner's *The Grand Canal, Venice,* Constable's *View of the Tower,* the Ellesmere Manuscript of Chaucer's *Canterbury Tales,* a 1455 Gutenberg Bible, and a manuscript autobiography of Benjamin Franklin. Open Tues–Sun.

☼🏛 **Los Angeles County Museum of Art (LACMA),** 5905 Wilshire Blvd., Los Angeles (857-6111): One of the country's most remarkable museums of art, notwithstanding the controversial modern design by architects William Pereira and Norman Pfeiffer, of which the only successful component is the covered-patio entryway. Splendid collection of impressionists and of contemporary painting and sculpture. Among the well-known exhibits: a supposed portrait of Nicolò Barberini by Lorenzo Lotto, Rembrandt's *Raising of Lazarus,* Georges de la Tour's *The Magdalene with the Candle,* Veronese's *Allegory of Navigation,* Copley's *Portrait of Hugh Montgomerie,* Cézanne's *Still Life with Cherries,* van Gogh's *St. Paul's Hospital,* Picasso's portrait of Sebastian Juñer Vidal, and the famous *Codex Hammer,* Leonardo da Vinci's notebook. In front of the museum is a very fine modern sculpture, *Phoenix,* by Alexander Liberman. Open Tues–Sun.

☼🏛 **Museum of Contemporary Art (MOCA),** 250 S. Grand Ave., dwntwn (626-6222): Five buildings of red sandstone and glass in pure geometric shapes—a cube, a pyramid, the arc of a circle—a masterpiece by Japanese architect Arata Isozaki, opened in Dec 1986 at a cost of $23 million. Houses a sumptuous collection of modern painting and sculpture by Mark Rothko, Claes Oldenburg, Franz Kline, Robert Rauschenberg, Roy Lichtenstein, Willem de Kooning, Edward Ruscha, Jackson Pollock, Frank Stella, Ellsworth Kelly, Louise Nevelson, Richard Serra, etc. The temporary exhibitions are often quite enthralling. Open Tues–Sun.

⚱ **Museum of Neon Art (MONA),** 704 Traction Ave., dwntwn (617-0274): Here you will learn that even neon can be a means of artistic expression. Surprising and entertaining; worth a visit. Open Tues–Sat.

☼🏛 **Norton Simon Museum,** 411 W. Colorado Blvd., Pasadena (818/449-6840): Cultural showcase of the University of California at Los Angeles (UCLA), art in all its forms in a rather disconcerting futurist building. Many modern paintings (Paul Klee, Kandinsky) and sculptures (Rodin's *Burghers of Calais*), but also Far Eastern art (note particularly a group of 10th-century Chola bronzes) and European masters, including Raphael's *Virgin* *and Child with a Book,* Dierick Bouts' *Resurrection,* Bassano's *The Flight into Egypt, Exotic Landscape* by the douanier Rousseau, Cézanne's *Tulips in a Vase,* Braque's *Still Life with Pipe,* and 88 bronze figurines by Degas. Open Thurs–Sun.

Pacific Asia Museum, 46 N. Los Robles Ave., Pasadena (818/449-3730): A Chinese-style imperial palace built around a "meditation garden," housing interesting temporary exhibitions of Asian and Pacific art. It is best visited in conjunction with the Huntington Library and Norton Simon Museum (see above). Open Wed–Sun.

Temporary Contemporary Museum, 152 N. Central Ave., dwntwn (626-6222): This old warehouse in Little Tokyo was used as a temporary shelter for the museum's collection while the new building was under construction; now it serves as an annex, and attracts sizable crowds. Works by Rothko, Rauschenberg, Claes Oldenburg, Roy Lichtenstein, and Jasper Johns, along with many avant-garde American artists. Trendy cultural events in an unexpected setting. Open Tues–Sun.

Wight Art Gallery, 405 Hilgard Ave., on the north UCLA campus, Westwood (825-9345): An art museum built to house (often very interesting) temporary exhibitions. Also collections of African and Asian art. Adjoining it is a lovely modern-sculpture garden. Open Tues–Sun.

MUSEUMS OF SCIENCE & HISTORY: Amateur Athletic Foundation, 2141 W. Adams Blvd., Los Angeles, 5 mi. (8km) SW via the Santa Monica Fwy. (730-9600): A must for all sports fans; the collection contains more than 50,000 items drawn from all kinds of sports, from Jack Dempsey's boxing gloves through the track shoes of sprinter Jesse Owens to the baseball uniforms of Babe Ruth, Lou Gehrig, Stan Musial, and so on. Replicas of medals from the Olympics and other competitions. Also an extensive sports library. Open daily.

Cabrillo Marine Museum, 3720 Stephen White Dr., San Pedro (548-7562): Fine oceanographic museum, with no fewer than 34 aquariums containing specimens of more than 100 forms of Pacific marine life. Fascinating. In winter, boat trips are organized for closeup observation of whale migrations. Don't miss visiting here. Open Tues–Sun.

California Museum of Science and Industry, 700 State Dr., Exposition Park, Los Angeles (744-7400): Nicknamed "the museum that loves to be touched," it contains dozens of robots and hands-on displays that involve viewer participation. New IMAX theater with a six-story-high screen. One of the country's best teaching museums; don't miss it. Open daily.

Gene Autry Western Heritage Museum, 4700 Zoo Dr., Los Angeles (667-2000): This handsome museum in Griffith Park celebrates the tradition of the Far West with more than 16,000 exhibits, ranging from tools, weapons, and clothing of cowboys, Native Americans, and pioneers to old western movies and relics of the Spanish Colonial era. Among its proudest possessions are Buffalo Bill's saddle, Teddy Roosevelt's Winchester, and many works of art by Frederic Remington, Charles Russell, and others. Open Tues–Sun.

George C. Page La Brea Discoveries Museum, 5801 Wilshire Blvd., Los Angeles (936-2230): More than a million prehistoric fossils (including 9,000 mammals) of creatures engulfed 9,000–40,000 years ago in the nearby "tar pits," dug up and now on exhibit as fragments or reconstructed skeletons, including a 10-ton mammoth and the "La Brea Woman," 9,000 years old. Many stone tools. Dozens of excavations still under way. Fascinating. Open Tues–Sun.

Hollywood Studio Museum, 2100 N. Highland Ave., Hollywood (874-2276): The old barn where in 1913 Cecil B. deMille shot the industry's first full-length feature, *The Squaw Man,* now a museum with displays and screenings from the heroic days of silent film. Fascinating. Open Tues–Sun.

ᚼ **Hollywood Wax Museum,** 6767 Hollywood Blvd., Hollywood (462-8860): More than 170 movie stars in "flesh and wax" (so to speak), from Marilyn Monroe to Raquel Welch and from Gary Cooper to Paul Newman. The movie industry's answer to Madame Tussaud's. Open daily.

ᚼ **Natural History Museum,** 900 Exposition Blvd., Exposition Park, Los Angeles (744-3414): Interesting museum of natural history and ethnology with important collections of archeology (pre-Columbian art), mineralogy (one of the largest in the world), dioramas of animals in their native habitats, and marine ecology. Open Tues–Sun.

ᚼ **Southwest Museum,** 234 Museum Dr., Highland Park (221-2163): Museum of Native American civilization, designed by historian Charles F. Lummis around an exceptional collection of tribal art and handcrafts. Will delight devotees of the history of the Old West. Open Tues–Sun; closed mid-Aug to mid-Sept.

ᚼ **Wells Fargo History Museum,** 333 S. Grand Ave., dwntwn (253-7166): It's like being there in the days of the westward expansion: stagecoaches, a collection of gold nuggets, 19th-century post office, posters, photographs, etc. Amusing. Open Mon–Fri.

OUTDOOR ART & PLAZAS: Boyle Heights and East Los Angeles: These Chicano neighborhoods have some of the finest street murals in the city—on Grand Vista Ave., Alcazar St., Olympic Blvd., Lorena St., Ramona Gardens, Estrada Courts, etc. Dangerous after dark, even in a car.

The Mall, Main St. and Los Angeles Sts., nr. City Hall, dwntwn: Gardens, fountains, statuary, and the extraordinary glass **Triforium Tower,** which in the evenings offers a computer-generated symphony of sound and color. Fascinating.

Venice (see "Strolls, West and North Los Angeles," below): Wonderful pop-art murals in trompe l'oeil on the fronts of several buildings near the Arcades in the center of Venice and on Windward Ave. on the ocean. Visit not recommended on foot after dark.

PANORAMAS: ᚼ **City Hall,** 200 N. Spring St., dwntwn (485-2121): Was the home of the *Daily Planet* on TV's "Superman" show. Splendid view of the dwntwn high-rises and—on a clear day—of the mountains and the Pacific, from the 22nd floor. Open Mon–Fri.

☼ᚼᚼ **Mullholland Drive,** North Beverly Hills: A twisting road which winds across the crest of the Santa Monica Mountains, offering a wonderful view of the city and the ocean in clear weather (best after dark). Very popular with lovers at night. Reached by Laurel Canyon Blvd. in Hollywood or by Coldwater Canyon Dr. in Beverly Hills.

ᚼ **Griffith Park** (see "Parks and Gardens," below).

PARKS & GARDENS: ᚼ **Descanso Gardens,** 1418 Descanso Dr., La Cañada (818/790-5571): Some 100,000 camellias bloom here Nov–Mar in the middle of a lovely oak grove. Rosebeds; Japanese garden.

ᚼ **Elysian Park,** Academy Rd., Los Angeles: Beautiful 552-acre (225ha) crescent-shaped landscaped park very near the Dodger stadium. Its hilly terrain offers some fine views of the dwntwn skyline.

☼ᚼᚼ **Forest Lawn Memorial Park,** 1712 S. Glendale Ave., Glendale (241-4151): This splendid landscaped cemetery is a sort of funerary theme park, unique in the U.S. Many marble and bronze replicas of famous classical sculptures, and a gigantic (192- by 44-ft./60- by 14m) *Crucifixion* by Jan Styka, the largest devotional painting in the world. Inspired Evelyn

Waugh's novel *The Loved One.* Tombs of Clark Gable, Errol Flynn, Humphrey Bogart, Sammy Davis, Jr., and Jean Harlow among others. Open daily.

      Griffith Park, Los Feliz Blvd. at Vermont Ave., Los Angeles (665-5188): The country's largest city park (4,107 acres/ 1,663ha), with a planetarium-observatory from which in fine weather there's a wonderful view of the city, especially at night. Also an ultramodern zoo (see "Zoos," below) and **Travel Town,** a transportation museum with an interesting collection of old locomotives, plus lovely rural landscapes, three golf courses, horseback riding, picnic grounds, and 50 mi. (80km) of footpaths.

      Hollywood Bowl, 2301 N. Highland Ave., Hollywood (850-2000): A 17,000-seat open-air amphitheater with perfect acoustics; every year since 1922 classical jazz and rock concerts as well as variety shows have been given here. Built on a former Native American campsite.

      Hollywood Memorial Park, 6000 Santa Monica Blvd., Hollywood (469-1181): The cemetery of the stars: tombs of Rudolph Valentino, Cecil B. deMille, Douglas Fairbanks, Tyrone Power, and dozens of others. Sumptuously kitsch. Open daily. (One great name not to be found here is Marilyn Monroe. Admirers take note: she's buried in a small, bucolic graveyard, **Westwood Memorial Park,** 1218 Glendon Ave., Westwood.)

      Palisades Park, Ocean Ave. between Colorado Ave. and San Vicente Blvd., Santa Monica (393-7593): This beautiful park has been called "California's French Riviera." Bordered with palm trees, it snakes along a cliff overlooking, and offering a fine view of, the Pacific, from the Palos Verdes peninsula on the south as far as Malibu to the north.

      Will Rogers State Park, 14253 Sunset Blvd., Pacific Palisades (454-8212): This big public park used to be the ranch of the legendary cowboy-humorist Will Rogers; his personal memorabilia are on display, along with collections of Native American artifacts. Footpaths for strollers, polo matches Sat–Sun, picnics, horseback riding. Open daily.

PERFORMING ARTS: For current listings of shows and cultural events, consult the entertainment pages of the two daily morning papers, *Los Angeles Times* and *Los Angeles Daily News,* as well as the monthlies *Los Angeles* and *California.* After New York, Los Angeles has more theaters and concert halls (some 200 in all) than any other city in the country.

    Ahmanson Theater, 135 N. Grand Ave., in the Music Center, dwntwn (972-7211): Home of the Center Theater Group. Comedy, drama, modern and classical theater; musical comedies and operettas.

    Doolittle Theater, 1615 Vine St., Hollywood (462-6666): Musicals, shows, touring companies.

    Dorothy Chandler Pavilion, 135 N. Grand Ave., in the Music Center, dwntwn (972-7211): Home of the Los Angeles Philharmonic under principal conductor Esa-Pekka Salonon (Oct–May), the Los Angeles Civic Light Opera, Los Angeles Master Chorale, and the Joffrey Ballet.

    Embassy Theater, 851 S. Grand Ave., dwntwn (622-3200): Beautiful Beaux Arts building: home of the Los Angeles Chamber Orchestra.

    Greek Theater, 2700 N. Vermont Ave., Griffith Park, Los Angeles (410-1062): Open-air concerts with major pop or rock stars (May–Oct).

    Henry Fonda Theater, 6126 Hollywood Blvd., Hollywood (634-1300): Broadway hits.

    Hollywood Bowl, 2301 N. Highland Ave., Hollywood (850-2000): Vast 17,000-seat natural amphitheater. Classical concerts with the Los Angeles Philharmonic; also jazz, rock, and variety shows (June–Sept).

    Los Angeles Theater Center, 514 S. Spring St., dwntwn (627-5599): Ultramodern four-hall complex opened in 1985; home of the Los Angeles Actors' Theater (contemporary and avant-garde theater); also jazz, classical concerts, and ballet. Has a superb skylight and a very fine marble interior.

    Mark Taper Forum, 135 N. Grand Ave., in the Music Center, dwntwn

(972-7211): Circular theater for chamber-music concerts; the Center Theater Group performs here in its repertory of contemporary plays.

Orange County Performing Arts Center, 600 Town Center Dr., Costa Mesa (714/556-2787): This ultramodern 3,000-seat auditorium was opened in 1986 at a cost of more than $70 million. Now it offers year-round prestige programs: opera, symphony concerts, ballet, etc.

Pantages Theater, 6233 Hollywood Blvd., Hollywood (642-4242): A 1930s art deco movie house, magnificently restored. Musical comedies, Broadway hits, modern plays with famous actors. The Oscar awards were given here from 1949 to 1959.

Pasadena Playhouse, 39 S. El Molino Ave., Pasadena (818/356-7529): Opened in 1925, it is regarded as one of the finest repertory houses for modern and contemporary theater.

Shrine Auditorium, Jefferson Blvd. and Royal St., Los Angeles (749-5123): This enormous (6,300-seat) 1926 hall offers remarkably fine acoustics for its concerts, operas, and ballets. On occasion, hosts the Oscar awards ceremony.

Shubert Theater, 2020 Ave. of the Stars, ABC Entertainment Center, Century City (553-9000): Musical comedies, star vehicles.

Terrace Theater, 300 E. Ocean Blvd., Long Beach (432-7926): Home of the Long Beach Symphony Orchestra, and the Long Beach Civic Light Opera and Long Beach Ballet companies. Musicals, musical comedies, etc.

Universal Amphitheatre, 3900 Lankershim Blvd., Universal City (777-4464): In the Universal Studios complex. Big-name recitals, musicals. Year round.

Westwood Playhouse, 10886 Le Conte Ave., Westwood (208-5454): Near the UCLA campus; contemporary and avant-garde theater.

Wilshire Theater, Wilshire Blvd. and La Cienega Blvd., West Hollywood (467-1199): Comedy, drama, modern theater.

Wiltern Theater, 3790 Wilshire Blvd. at Western Ave., Los Angeles (216-6666): Handsome art deco theater, home of the Los Angeles Opera. Also classical concerts.

SHOPPING: Atlantic Richfield/ARCO Plaza, 505 S. Flower St., dwntwn: The country's largest underground shopping center: dozens of stores, boutiques, art galleries, and restaurants occupying several levels under the giant ARCO/Bank of America Towers. If you suffer from claustrophobia, forget it.

Beverly Center, Beverly Blvd. and La Cienega Blvd., West Hollywood: Elegant, ultramodern shopping center whose hi-tech architecture seems to be modeled on the Musée Beaubourg in Paris. More than 200 boutiques and stores, 13 restaurants, 15 cinemas and theaters; even a disco. Worth seeing. Open daily.

Garment District, Los Angeles St. between 7th St. and Washington Blvd., dwntwn: Clothing of all kinds at unbeatable prices for more than half a century, particularly in the **California Mart** or the **Cooper Building.**

Larry Edmund's Bookstore, 6658 Hollywood Blvd., Hollywood (463-3273): The best specialist bookstore in the country for the movie industry; a kind of living history of the silver screen. Open Mon–Sat.

Melrose Avenue between La Cienega Blvd. and La Brea Ave., Los Angeles: Trendy fashion boutiques; the California "in" style.

Miracle Mile, Wilshire Blvd. between Highland Ave. and Fairfax Ave., Los Angeles: Elegant boutiques and shops w. the last word from America and Europe.

Rodeo Drive, between Santa Monica Blvd. and Wilshire Blvd., Beverly Hills: The country's, and possibly the world's, smartest street, equivalent to Madison Ave. in New York, Bond St. in London, or the rue Faubourg St-Honoré in Paris. From Giorgio to Hermès, from Tiffany to Gucci, not to mention the unbelievable Bijan, the most outrageous of luxury boutiques are to be found here. The brand new **Two Rodeo Drive,** at Rodeo Drive and Wilshire Blvd., is even more upscale.

Seventh Market Place, 735 S. Figueroa St., dwntwn: Extraordinary mixture of an underground shopping center, a Japanese garden, and a tropical conservatory, designed by Jon Jerde. Absolutely must be seen. Open daily.

Tower Records, 8801 Sunset Blvd., West Hollywood (657-7300): One of the country's largest record stores. Open daily until midnight.

SPECIAL EVENTS: For exact dates, consult the **Anaheim Visitor and Convention Bureau,** 800 W. Katella Ave., Anaheim, CA 92803 (714/999-8999); the **Laguna Beach Chamber of Commerce,** 357 Glenneyre St. (P.O. Box 396), Laguna Beach, CA 92652 (714/494-1018); the **Long Beach Convention and Visitors Council,** 1 World Trade Center, Long Beach, CA 90802 (213/436-3645); the **Los Angeles Visitors and Convention Bureau,** 515 S. Figueroa St., Los Angeles, CA 90071 (213/624-7300); or the **Pasadena Convention and Visitors Bureau,** 171 S. Los Robles Ave., Pasadena, CA 91105 (818/795-9311).

Anaheim
Holloween Festival (end of Oct): Parades; giant masked ball.

Chinatown
Chinese New Year (mid-Jan or early Feb): Dragon Parade and costumed processions in honor of the Chinese New Year. Picturesque.

Downtown Los Angeles
L.A. Marathon (Mar): Third-largest marathon in the country after New York and Boston.

Academy Awards Ceremony (late Mar or early Apr): The world-famous ceremony at which moviedom's prized Oscars are conferred.

El Pueblo de Los Angeles
Cinco de Mayo Procession (May 5): The great annual festival of the Mexican-American community.

Las Posadas (end of Dec): Christmas festivities Mexican style; colorful.

Hollywood
Hollywood Bowl Summer Festival (July–Aug): The Los Angeles Philharmonic offers more than 40 concerts at its summer home. Wknd fireworks spectaculars. Also jazz and pop concerts.

Laguna Beach
Winter Festival (Feb): Art exhibitions, shows, handcrafts fair.

Little Tokyo
Hanamatsuri (Apr): Festival in honor of Buddha's birth.

Nisei Week (Aug): Annual Japanese cultural festival, very popular locally.

Long Beach
Long Beach Toyota Grand Prix (late Mar or early Apr): Formula I Grand Prix along the streets of dwntwn Long Beach; spectacular, drawing more than 200,000 spectators every year. Spectacular.

California Sea Festival (Aug): Very lively, with boat races, regattas, processions, competitions.

Pasadena
Tournament of Roses (Jan 1): Flower-covered floats, two dozen bands, and 300 equestrians parade along Orange Grove Blvd. and Colorado Blvd.; a million spectators on the streets and 100 million more watching on television. Timed for a few hours before the Rose Bowl football game. Celebrated its 100th birthday in 1988.

Pomona
Los Angeles County Fair (end of Sept): The country's biggest fair-exhibition; 28 mi. (45km) SE of dwntwn.

SPORTS: Los Angeles is blessed with a multitude of professional teams, as well as three racetracks:

Baseball (Apr–Sept): California Angels, Anaheim Stadium (714/937-6700); Dodgers, Dodgers Stadium (224-1400).

Basketball (Oct to late Apr): Clippers, L.A. Sports Arena (748-0500); Lakers, The Forum, Inglewood (674-6000).

Football (Sept–Dec.): Raiders, L.A. Coliseum (322-5901); Rams, Anaheim Stadium (714/937-6767).

Ice Hockey (Sept to late Apr): Kings, The Forum, Inglewood (673-1300).

Horse Racing

Del Mar Thoroughbred Club, Jimmy Durante Dr., Del Mar (619/755-1141): Directly on the beach; open late July to mid-Sept.

Hollywood Park, Century Blvd. and Prairie Ave., Inglewood (419-1500). Racing from mid-Apr to late July and mid-Nov to the end of Dec.

Santa Anita Park, Huntington Dr. and Baldwin Ave., Arcadia (818/574-7223): Racing from early Oct to early Nov and late Dec to late Apr.

STROLLS: Los Angeles is so big, with so many delightful areas for strolling, that this section is divided into two parts: Downtown, and West and North L.A.

Downtown

Chinatown, bounded by Alpine St., Spring St., Yale St., and Bambas Lane, dwntwn: Stalls, restaurants, pagoda-shaped buildings; a pungent, gimcrack, lively Chinese district.

El Pueblo de Los Angeles Historic Monument, bounded by Macy St., Alameda St., Spring St., and Arcadia St., dwntwn: The historic heart of Los Angeles since its foundation in 1781. From the **Avila Adobe,** the city's oldest (1818) house, now a museum of California history, to the **Old Plaza Firehouse** (1884), and from the **Church of Nuestra Señora Reina de los Angeles** (1822) to the **Merced Theater** (1870) or the **Pico House,** once the city's most luxurious hotel (1870), El Pueblo can show you a dozen or more 19th-century buildings, carefully restored, along **Main Street, Olvera St.,** and **Old Plaza,** a delightful, shady little square in the purest Spanish-Mexican style, with a wrought-iron bandstand. A living picture of the past, not to be missed. The **visitor center** is at 620 N. Main St. (628-1274). Also see, on the south wall of the Italian Hall, the superb giant (16- by 80-ft./5- by 24.5m) **fresco** created in 1932 by the famous Mexican artist David Alfaro Siqueiros. Rather touristy but pleasant atmosphere. Open daily. Guided tours Tues–Sat.

Financial District, bounded by 1st St., 6th St., Olive St., and Figueroa St., dwntwn: "The Wall Street of the West Coast." Scarcely 15 years old (until 1957 there was a 13-floor limit on construction because of the earthquake hazard), this new financial district now collects skyscrapers. Among the most striking are the First Interstate Tower, with 62 stories the city's tallest building; the five 35-floor glass cylinders of the Westin Bonaventure Hotel, the 48-story Wells Fargo Building, the Security Pacific Bank (55 stories), and the twin 52-story towers of the ARCO/Bank of America building.

Little Tokyo, bounded by 1st St., Alameda St., 3rd St., and San Pedro St., dwntwn: Los Angeles, with 160,000 inhabitants who are Japanese or of Japanese descent, is the largest Japanese city outside Asia. Many stores, Buddhist temples, art galleries, restaurants. Exquisite Japanese garden and very active cultural center.

West and North Los Angeles

Bel Air and Beverly Hills, north of Sunset Blvd.: The two smart neighborhoods of Los Angeles; mansions of millionaires and movie stars hidden behind trees and locked iron gates, including that of former

president, Ronald Reagan, at 668 St. Cloud Rd., Bel Air. Super-deluxe boutiques on Beverly Hills' Rodeo Dr. Even the local post office at 312 S. Beverly Dr. offers valet parking to its customers—which says it all. For a little daydreaming.

Hollywood, around Hollywood Blvd. and Vine St.: Once "the movie Mecca," and known as Tinseltown—but the industry, which was officially born in 1910 when the first studio was built, has now only its former glories to live on. The legendary Hollywood is a community of undistinguished stores, gloomy motels, tattered palm trees, sex shops on Hollywood Blvd., and an intimidating local populace after dark (walking at night is definitely not recommended). Among its attractions are Mann's Chinese Theater (see "Historic Buildings," above), the Hollywood Studio Museum (see "Museums of Science and History," above), and the celebrated Walk of Fame (see below). A laudable attempt to clean up the community has recently been set in motion.

Marina del Rey, Admiralty Way: Superb marina on the Pacific, where more than 6,000 boats are moored; a favorite place with prosperous bohemia and trendy night-owls. A bogus but picturesque New England fishing village (Fisherman's Village). An absolute must.

Pasadena, via the Pasadena Fwy.: One of the country's scientific strongholds; CalTech (California Institute of Technology), 1201 E. California Blvd., is a veritable hotbed of Nobel laureates in physics and chemistry. Its visitor center is at 315 S. Hill Ave. (818/356-6328). The jewel in CalTech's crown is NASA's Jet Propulsion Laboratory, where the *Voyager* space vehicles were assembled, "permitting more astronomical discoveries in two decades than in the preceding two millennia." JPL is open to visitors, by advance resv., twice a month; call 818/354-0287. See also the entries on the Norton Simon Museum and the Pacific Asia Museum (see "Museums of Art," above).

Ports O'Call Village, Berths 76–79, Harbor Blvd., in San Pedro, 36 mi. (51km) south along the Harbor Fwy. (831-0287): Recaptures the atmosphere of a Spanish-colonial port of the 1850s, with its gas-lit cobbled streets, its dozens of stalls and restaurants. Boat trips around the harbor.

Santa Monica Pier, Ocean Ave. at the foot of Colorado Ave., Santa Monica (458-8900): The granddaddy of California's amusement parks, built on the pier in 1909. The giant carousel figured in the setting of the movie *The Sting.* Well-mannered kitsch.

Sunset Boulevard, from Doheny Dr. to Vine St., Beverly Hills/Hollywood: This legendary "main drag of the movies," blazing at night from all its billboards, is a good part of Los Angeles's nightlife. Restaurants, rock clubs, hotels—but also agents, recording and movie studios. The central section of Sunset Blvd., "The Strip," is the stronghold of show business. Not to be missed (best time, at night).

Venice, around Ocean Front Walk and Venice Blvd., Venice: This beach resort was founded in 1904 by Abbot Kinney, an eccentric millionaire who sought to reproduce the city of the doges, canals and all, on the Pacific coast; he even imported genuine gondolas with singing gondoliers. With its eclectic mix of body-builders, roller-skaters, gays, artists, gigantic pop murals ("murales"), and drug dealers, it is today the most bohemian—and the most entertaining—beach in California.

"Walk of Fame," along Hollywood Blvd. and Vine St., Hollywood: "The promenade of the stars," where nearly 2,000 bronze stars set in the sidewalk evoke the greats of the silver screen, radio, and television; new names are added to the list every month. Worth a snapshot, but don't walk it after dark.

Westwood Village, around Westwood Plaza, Westwood: Los Angeles's "Latin Quarter" or "Greenwich Village"; stroll on the vast UCLA campus (see "Architectural Highlights," above). Dozens of bookstores, record shops, movie houses, restaurants, etc. Very lively, especially after dark.

THEME PARKS: ☼🔔 **Disneyland,** 1313 Harbor Blvd., in Anaheim, 24 mi. (38km) SE on I-5 (714/999-4565): Opened by Walt Disney himself in 1955, this is the archetype of the great American amusement parks. Much smaller than its two Florida siblings, Walt Disney World (opened in 1971) and EPCOT (1982), Disneyland is still one of the country's most popular tourist attractions, visited so far by more than 300 million people, big and little. From "Sleeping Beauty's Castle" to "Fantasyland" and on to "Pirates of the Caribbean" by way of the Far West train which takes you to "Frontierland," not to mention the mysterious jungle of "Adventureland" or "Carnival in New Orleans," 60 different attractions await the visitor. The latest of these is an outer-space Disneyland, in tune with the times, entitled "Star Tours" and created under the supervision of the famous movie director George Lucas. 45 min. by car from dwntwn. Open daily year round. Set aside at least one whole day for your visit. Crowded at weekends. Admission: $26 (adults), $21 (children).

☼🔔 **Knott's Berry Farm,** 8039 Beach Blvd., in Buena Park, 20 mi. (32km) SE on I-5 and Calif. 39 (714/220-5200): 10 min. by car from Disneyland you'll find a reconstruction of the Far West: attacks on stagecoaches, ghost town, etc.; also an amusement park with 135 attractions and impressive roller coasters, including Montezuma's Revenge. Big-name shows. This ranks as the country's fourth most popular amusement park, next after the Disney trio. Admission: $21 (adults), $16 (children). Open daily.

🔔 **Movieland Wax Museum,** 771 Beach Blvd., Buena Park, 20 mi. (32km) SE via I-5 and Calif. 39 (714/522-1154): What the Grévin Museum is to Paris or Mme Tussaud's to London, this is to the movie industry. More than 200 waxwork stars in scenes or settings from the movies that made them famous. Costumes, memorabilia, and old posters recapitulate the history of the "Seventh Art." You can combine the museum with a visit to the nearby Knott's Berry Farm (see above). Open daily.

🔔 **Raging Waters Park,** 111 Raging Waters Dr., San Dimas (714/592-6453): Huge water-sports amusement park with more than 40 attractions including giant slides with artificial surf and riding-the-rapids. Worth a visit. Open daily mid-June to mid-Sept, wknds only May to mid-June and mid-Sept to mid-Oct.

☼🔔 **Six Flags Magic Mountain,** 26101 Magic Mountain Pkwy., in Valencia, 32 mi. (52km) NW on I-5 (805/255-4100): A 260-acre (105ha) theme park with 100 attractions including the world's largest roller coaster (1.8 mi./3km long with dizzy drops of 92 ft./30m); if your heart is weak, don't ride it. Less touristy but no less entertaining than Disneyland. Open daily June–Sept, wknds and school breaks only the rest of the year.

WINTER SPORTS RESORTS: 🔔 **Angeles National Forest,** about 62 mi. (100km) NE via I-5 and Calif. 2: Mount Waterman, with 3 ski lifts (818/440-1041); Ski Sunrise, with 5 lifts (619/249-6150).

🔔🔔 **Big Bear Lake,** 112 mi. (180km) east via I-10 and Calif. 18: Bear Mountain, 8 lifts (714/585-2519); Snow Summit, 12 lifts (714/866-5766); open mid-Nov to mid-Apr.

🔔 **Mount Baldy,** 51 mi. (82km) east on I-10 and Calif. 83 (714/981-3344): 4 lifts.

☼🔔🔔 **Snow Valley,** 76 mi. (122km) NE along I-10 and Calif. 30, Calif. 330, and Calif. 18 (714/867-2751): 13 lifts; this most popular of local ski resorts is crowded on wknds. Open mid-Nov to mid-Apr.

ZOOS: ☼Los Angeles Zoo, Griffith Park, 5333 Zoo Dr. (666-4090): One of the top 10 zoos in the country, with 2,500 animals from all around the world distributed over 113 acres (46ha) of rolling hills. Among the biggest draws is the Ahmanson Koala House and its collection of these engaging Australian mammals. Open daily.

ACCOMMODATIONS

A Note on Accommodations: Room rates in Los Angeles are coded as follows: **VE,** Very Expensive ($140 and up); **E,** Expensive ($90–$140); **M,** Moderate ($60–$90); **I,** Inexpensive ($30–$60); **B,** Budget (up to $30). A listing of toll free numbers is in the Appendix.

Note: In a city this big, concepts such as "dwntwn" or "vic." don't apply; Wilshire Blvd., the main east-west artery, is 16 mi. (27km) long. The hotels (and restaurants) mentioned below are designated by districts (such as dwntwn, Beverly Hills, Hollywood, and so on; Los Angeles for those not in any particular district).

Personal Favorites (in order of preference)

Regent Beverly Wilshire, 9500 Wilshire Blvd. (at Rodeo Dr.), Beverly Hills, CA 90212 (213/275-5200; toll free 800/545-4000). 381 rms, A/C, cable color TV. AE, CB, DC, MC, V. Valet gar. $12, pool, health club, sauna, two rests. (including The Dining Rm), coffee shop, two bars, 24-hr. rm svce, hrdrsr, florist, concierge, free crib. *Note:* Now part of the Regent luxury-hotel chain of Hong Kong, this aging (1928) palace underwent a complete renovation in 1988 at a cost of $65 million. The Beverly Hills landmark, a stone's throw from the boutiques of Rodeo Dr., is again the symbol of refinement and elegance that it was for more than half a century. Huge, comfortable rms w. period furniture and minibars. Polished, discreet svce; rest. of the highest order. One of the dozen best hotels in the country. **VE**

Four Seasons, 300 S. Doheny Dr. (at Burton Way), Los Angeles, CA 90048 (213/273-2222; toll free, see the Four Seasons). 285 rms, A/C, color TV, in-rm movies. AE, CB, DC, MC, V. Valet parking $8, pool, health club, two rests. (including Gardens), bar, 24-hr. rm svce, 24-hr. concierge. *Note:* Opened in 1988, this palace hotel (smallish for its kind), is one of the smartest and most luxurious in California. The handsome postmodern 16-story building, in a splendid tropical grdn w. waterfalls and fountains, stands in a quiet residential area on the border of Los Angeles and Beverly Hills. The interior is gracious and in excellent taste: huge, superbly comfortable rms w. private balcony, minibar, and all-around view. Considerate, personalized svce. Free limousine to Rodeo Dr.'s fashionable boutiques. Excellent rest. serving excellent contemporary food. **VE**

Hotel Bel Air, 701 Stone Canyon Dr., Bel Air, CA 90077 (213/472-1211; toll free, see Preferred). 92 rms, A/C, color TV, in-rm movies. AE, CB, DC, MC, V. Free valet gar., pool, rest., bar, 24-hr. rm svce, nightclub, florist, concierge. *Note:* This charming small hotel, in the Spanish mission style, stands among bougainvilleas on a little lake w. swans, breathing a serene intimacy. Elegant rms w. private patios, some w. fireplaces. Honeymooners reserve here months in advance. Fussy rest. (Bel Air Dining Rm). A favorite w. the Establishment. **VE**

Disneyland Hotel, 1150 W. Cerritos Ave., Anaheim, CA 92802 (714/778-6600; toll free 800/647-7900). 1,174 rms, A/C, cable color TV. AE, CB, DC, MC, V. Parking $8, three pools, 10 tennis courts, private beach, marina, four rests. (including Granville's), coffee shop, bars, rm svce, disco, boutiques, free crib. *Note:* Both a resort and a convention hotel, this enormous complex is linked directly to Disneyland by monorail. Its three 14-story towers rise around an enormous lagoon/swimming pool. Very comfortable rms w. private balconies or patios and refrigerators. Efficient svce. Beautiful tropical grdn w. waterfalls and little lakes stocked w. goldfish. Somewhat obtrusive package tourists and conventioneers predominate here. 5 min. from the Anaheim Convention Center. **E–VE**

☀☐ **Roosevelt Hotel,** 7000 Hollywood Blvd., Hollywood, CA
90028 (213/466-7000; toll free 800/950-7667). 310 rms,
A/C, cable color TV. AE, CB, DC, MC, V. Valet parking $7, pool, rest.
(Theodore's), bar, rm svce, disco, boutiques, concierge, free crib. *Note:* A hallowed spot in the history of the cinema. The first Oscars were awarded here in
1929; it was here also that Clark Gable and Carole Lombard concealed their love
affair from the public eye. All the great stars, from Errol Flynn to Douglas Fairbanks and Maureen O'Hara, came here in its heyday. It reopened its doors in
1986 after a $40-million restoration program, and has now recaptured all its former magnificence. The splendid interior is Neo-Castilian crossed with art deco.
The rms, w. minibars, are comfortable and inviting; the Cinegrill bar is famous.
Friendly, smiling svce. The Celebrity Floor is reserved for VIPs. Opposite the
renowned Mann's Chinese Theater, in the middle of the "Walk of Fame." **E–VE**

☐☐ **Sportsmen's Lodge,** 12825 Ventura Blvd., Studio City, CA
91604 (818/769-4700; toll free 800/821-8511). 196 rms,
A/C, color TV. AE, CB, DC, MC, V. Free parking, pool, health club, bicycling,
rest., coffee shop, bars, rm svce, free crib. *Note:* Luxuriously comfortable motel in
a beautiful grdn w. falls, lagoons, and swans. Inviting rms w. private balconies or
patios. Attentive svce. Group clientele. Good value. Near Hollywood, Beverly
Hills, and Universal Studios; 20 min. from dwntwn. Limo svce to Burbank Airport. **E**

☐ **Comfort Inn–Wilshire,** 3400 W. 3rd St., Los Angeles, CA
90020 (213/385-0061; toll free 800/228-5150). 130 rms,
A/C, color TV, in-rm movies. AE, CB, DC, MC, V. Free parking, pool, coffee
shop, rm svce, free crib. *Note:* Typical utilitarian motel a 5-min. drive from the
financial district. Comfortable rms, some w. kitchenette and refrigerator. Efficient svce. Very good value. **I–M**

☐ **Best Western Executive Motor Inn,** 603 S. New Hampshire
Ave., Los Angeles, CA 90005 (213/385-4444; toll free, see
Best Western). 89 rms, A/C, cable color TV. AE, CB, DC, MC, V. Free parking,
pool, health club, sauna, adj. rest. and bar, free crib. *Note:* Comfortable little
Spanish-style motel nr. the financial district; attentive reception and svce; spacious, well-designed rms w. refrigerators. Good value. 10 min. from dwntwn.
I–M

☐ **Oasis Motel,** 2200 W. Olympic Blvd., Los Angeles, CA 90006
(213/385-4191). 69 rms, A/C, color TV. AE, CB, DC, MC,
V. Free parking, pool, adj. coffee shop. *Note:* Modest but comfortable small motel 5 min. from the Convention Center and dwntwn Los Angeles. Agreeable reception and svce. Functional rms w. refrigerators; some have kitchenettes. Very
good value. **I**

Other Accommodations (from top bracket to budget)

☐☐☐☐ **Beverly Hilton,** 9876 Wilshire Blvd., Beverly Hills, CA 90210
(213/274-7777; toll free, see Hilton). 592 rms, A/C, color
TV, in-rm movies. AE, CB, DC, MC, V. Valet gar. $12, two pools, health club,
four rests. (including L'Escoffier), two coffee shops, bars, 24-hr. rm svce, hrdrsr,
boutiques, concierge, free crib. *Note:* The crown jewel of the Hilton chain, remarkably elegant and polished for a hotel of its size. Comfortable rms w. refrigerators and balconies. Efficient, hard-working svce. Very honorable rests. Favored
by the jet set and show business. A little away from dwntwn Beverly Hills. Very
well-equipped business center. Recently completed a $35-million renovation. **VE**

☐☐☐☐ **J. W. Marriott,** 2151 Ave. of the Stars, Century City, CA
90067 (213/277-2777; toll free, see Marriott). 375 rms,
A/C, color TV, in-rm movies. AE, CB, DC, MC, V. Valet gar. $12, two pools,
health club, sauna, two rests. (including J.W.), bars, 24-hr. rm svce, hrdrsr, boutiques, concierge. *Note:* Brand-new hotel, entertainingly designed to resemble a
Hollywood palace of the '30s. Flawless comforts and facilities. Spacious rms w.
minibar, private patio or balcony, and all-around view. Efficient svce. Rests. at the

usual undistinguished Marriott level. Free limo to Rodeo Dr. in Beverly Hills. Business clientele; interesting wknd packages. **VE**

🏰🏰🏰🏰 **L'Ermitage,** 9291 Burton Way, Beverly Hills, CA 90210 (213/278-3344; toll free 800/345-3457). 112 suites (each w. one or two bedrooms), A/C, color TV, in-rm movies. AE, CB, DC, MC, V. Free valet gar., pool, private rest. (Café Russe), bar, roof grdn, 24-hr. rm svce, concierge. *Note:* Very luxurious residential hotel in the European manner, in the smartest neighborhood of Beverly Hills. Sumptuously decorated suites w. balconies and minibars, some w. kitchenettes. Elegant, intimate setting w. period furniture and numerous works of art by Chagall, Renoir, van Gogh, and Miró. The svce is of a distinction seldom encountered. The hotel has a presidential supersuite at $1,300 (plus taxes) a night. Setting aside considerations of expense, one of the best addresses in Beverly Hills. **VE**

🏰🏰🏰🏰 **Westwood Marquis,** 930 Hilgard Ave., Westwood Village, CA 90024 (213/208-8765; toll free, see Preferred). 256 suites, A/C, color TV, in-rm movies. AE, CB, DC, MC, V. Valet gar. $8, two pools, health club, sauna, two rests. (including the Garden Restaurant), two bars, rm svce, hrdrsr, florist, concierge, crib $6. *Note:* Modern 17-story luxury hotel originally built as a student residence for nearby UCLA. Has only suites, elegantly decorated and luxuriously equipped. Personalized svce. Clientele drawn from the upper echelons of business and the movies. The neighborhood is lively both day and night. Very good rest. Free limo to Beverly Hills. **VE**

🏰🏰🏰 **Ma Maison Sofitel,** 8555 Beverly Blvd., West Hollywood, CA 90048 (213/278-5444; toll free, see Resinter). 311 rms, A/C, color TV, in-rm movies. AE, CB, DC, MC, V. Valet parking $10, pool, health club, two rests. (including La Cajole), two bars, nightclub, 24-hr. rm svce, hrdrsr, boutiques, concierge, free crib. *Note:* A newcomer to the city's luxury-hotel scenc; an imaginative modern building w. an interior in the Mediterranean (and an atmosphere in the French) manner. Comfortable, well-designed rms; beautiful flower arrangements. Diligent, efficient svce. La Cajole is an engaging brasserie, but the rest. (Ma Maison) is affected and overpriced. Very well located in the heart of "Restaurant Row" and across from the Beverly Center. Business and European clientele. **VE**

🏰🏰🏰 **Westin Century Plaza,** 2025 Ave. of the Stars, Century City, CA 90067 (213/277-2000; toll free, see Westin). 1,072 rms, A/C, color TV, in-rm movies. AE, CB, DC, MC, V. Valet parking $10, two pools, health club, adj. health club and tennis courts, four rests. (including Yamato), coffee shop, five bars, 24-hr. rm svce, entertainment, hrdrsr, boutiques, concierge, free crib. *Note:* The first modern luxury hotel in the new business district of Century City. Enormous pie-wedge-shaped tourist barracks surmounted by a massive 30-story tower; the interior is, fortunately, more gracious. Vast, comfortable rms w. balconies (the best are in the new tower). Excellent svce. Former president Reagan occasionally alights in the $3,000-a-night suite here. Caters to package tours and conventions. Inviting grdn. Faces the ABC Entertainment Center. **VE**

🏰🏰🏰 **New Otani Hotel and Garden,** 120 S. Los Angeles St. (dwntwn), Los Angeles, CA 90012 (213/629-1200; toll free 800/421-8795). 448 rms, A/C, color TV, in-rm movies. AE, CB, DC, MC, V. Parking $8, health club, sauna, three rests. (including Commodore Perry's), coffee shop, two bars, 24-hr. rm svce, hrdrsr, boutiques, free crib. *Note:* Japanese style, geared to American taste; modern and well designed. Rms w. tatami mats or Western style, w. refrigerators. Very pretty Japanese grdn. Courteous, efficient svce. Business clientele. Very nr. the Little Tokyo business district. Recently renovated at a cost of $2 million. **E–VE**

🏰🏰 **Radisson Bel Air Summit,** 11461 Sunset Blvd., Bel Air, CA 90049 (213/476-6571; toll free, see Radisson). 162 rms, A/C, color TV, in-rm movies. AE, CB, DC, MC, V. Free valet parking, pool, tennis court, rest. (Echo), bar, 24-hr. rm svce, free breakfast, free crib. *Note:*

Small, gracious, comfortable hotel set in a lovely grdn and recently renovated. Spacious, elegant rms w. refrigerators and private balconies or patios. Good svce; very commendable rest. **E–VE**

Beverly Pavilion Hotel, 9360 Wilshire Blvd., Beverly Hills, CA 90212 (213/273-1400; toll free 800/421-0545). 110 rms, A/C, color TV, AE, CB, DC, MC, V. Valet gar. $6, roof pool, rest. (Colette), bar, rm svce, free crib. *Note:* Small, inviting up-to-date hotel a few minutes' walk from the smart shopping of Rodeo Dr. The pool and solarium on the eighth floor have an all-around view of the city. Spacious, pleasant rms w. refrigerator; friendly, smiling svce. Praiseworthy French rest. **E–VE**

Château Marmont, 8221 Sunset Blvd., Hollywood, CA 90046 (213/656-1010; toll free 800/826-0015). 62 rms and cottages, A/C, color TV, in-rm movies. AE, CB, DC, MC, V. Valet gar. $6, pool, rest., bar, rm svce. *Note:* A movie monument, in which innumerable stars (Greta Garbo, Boris Karloff, John Lennon, Robert de Niro, Richard Gere, Sidney Poitier, John Belushi) once lived, or still live, it looks like a fake château rendered in Hollywood kitsch. Spacious rms w. private balconies and refrigerators, or pleasant bungalows around the pool. Small tropical grdn. An oasis of rest and peace in the heart of the "Strip." Inconsistent svce. Good value on balance. **E–VE**

Portofino Inn, 260 Portofino Way, Redondo Beach, CA 90277 (213/379-8481; toll free 800/338-2993). 192 rms, A/C, cable color TV. AE, CB, DC, MC, V. Free parking, pool, fishing, marina, bicycling, rest. (Sea Bucket), bars, rm svce, crib $10. *Note:* Most likable hotel-marina in Los Angeles, overlooking the Redondo Beach yacht basin. Comfortable rms w. private patio or balcony and minibar. Friendly, smiling svce. Entirely redecorated and refurnished after a destructive tidal wave. Free airport shuttle. **E–VE**

Ramada Inn, 12500 E. Firestone Blvd., Norwalk, CA 90650 (213/868-0401; toll free, see Ramada Inns). 253 rms, A/C, cable color TV. AE, CB, DC, MC, V. Free parking, two pools, rest., bar, rm svce, disco, free crib. *Note:* Comfortable motel in a grdn; spacious, well-designed rms w. private patios. Courteous reception and svce. 10 min. from Disneyland and Knotts Berry Farm. Interesting family packages. Halfway between Disneyland and dwntwn. **M–E**

Sheraton Anaheim, 1015 W. Ball Rd., Anaheim, CA 92802 (714/778-1700; toll free, see Sheraton). 500 rms, A/C, color TV, in-rm movies. AE, CB, DC, MC, V. Free parking, pool, rest., coffee shop, bar, rm svce, free crib. *Note:* A motel in a Tudor idiom as reviewed and corrected by Hollywood. Comfortable, spacious rms w. minibars. Family clientele; ideal for visiting Disneyland (free bus) and Knotts Berry Farm. Good svce. Very good value. **M–E**

Holiday Inn Downtown, 750 Garland Ave. (dwntwn), Los Angeles, CA 90017 (213/628-5242; toll free, see Holiday Inns). 204 rms, A/C, color TV, in-rm movies. AE, CB, DC, MC, V. Free gar., pool, rest. (Gardens), coffee shop, bar, rm svce, free crib. *Note:* Conventional six-story motel very nr. the Convention Center; functionally comfortable. Business clientele. Good value. Newly renovated. **M–E**

Best Western Mikado, 12600 Riverside Dr., North Hollywood, CA 91607 (818/763-9141; toll free, see Best Western). 58 rms, A/C, color TV. AE, CB, DC, MC, V. Free parking, pool, rest., bar, rm svce, free breakfast, crib $10. *Note:* Friendly motel in the hills overlooking Hollywood; vaguely exotic decor. Comfortable rms; friendly reception and svce. Very acceptable Japanese rest. Good value. **M**

Hotel Hollywood, 5825 Sunset Blvd., Hollywood, CA 90028 (213/462-5400; toll free 800/445-0021). 90 rms, A/C, color TV. AE, CB, DC, MC, V. Gar. $5, rest., bar, rm svce, disco, free crib. *Note:* Modern hotel w. a rest. on the top floor offering a fine view of Hollywood and its hills. Spectacular outside elevator. Art deco–style interior. Inviting rms; ideal for visiting Hollywood and Universal Studios. **M**

Hallmark Hotel, 7023 Sunset Blvd., Hollywood, CA 90028 (213/464-8344). 72 rms, A/C, color TV, in-rm movies. AE, CB, DC, MC, V. Free parking, pool; no bar or rest., but breakfast served every morning. *Note:* Amiable reception; utilitarian rms, some w. kitchenette and Jacuzzi, most w. balcony overlooking the pool and picnic tables. Good overall value 5 min. from "the Strip" and the sights of Hollywood. **I–M**

Vagabond Inn, 1904 W. Olympic Blvd., Los Angeles, CA 90006 (213/380-9393; toll free, see Vagabond Inns). 54 rms, A/C, color TV. AE, DC, MC, V. Free parking, pool, adj. coffee shop, free breakfast, free crib. *Note:* Small, standard, but well-run motel, centrally located 5 min. from the Convention Center. Functional rms; friendly reception. Good value. **I–M**

Vagabond Inn, 3101 S. Figueroa St., Los Angeles, CA 90007 (213/746-1531; toll free, see Vagabond Inns). 72 rms, A/C, color TV. AE, DC, MC, V. Free parking, pool, 24-hr. coffee shop, free breakfast, free crib. *Note:* Great value very close to Exposition Park and the Memorial Coliseum. Serviceably comfortable rms; reception and svce w. a smile. 8 min. from dwntwn. **I–M**

Westward Ho 7 Seas, 415 W. Katella Ave., Anaheim, CA 92802 (714/778-6900; toll free 800/777-7123). 175 rms, A/C, color TV. AE, MC, V. Free parking, pool, free breakfast, crib $5. *Note:* Ordinary motel, 3 min. from Disneyland by car. Modest but well run. Good value. **I,** but lower rates off-season.

Motel 6, 1001 S. San Gabriel Blvd., Rosemead, CA 91770 (818/572-6076). 130 rms, A/C, color TV, free in-rm movies. AE, DC, MC, V. Free parking, pool, café adj. open 24 hrs. *Note:* Modern, functional motel at ultra-reasonable prices, 20 min. from dwntwn along Calif. 60 and U.S. 101. Ideal if you're driving; excellent value. **B–I**

Motel 6, 7450 Katella Ave., Stanton, CA 90680 (714/891-0717). 207 rms, A/C, color TV, free in-rm movies. AE, DC, MC, V. Free parking, pool. *Note:* Typical motel at ultra-reasonable prices; ideal as a base for visiting Disneyland and Knott's Berry Farm (10 min. by car). Excellent value. **B–I**

Airport Accommodations

Sheraton Plaza La Reina, 6101 W. Century Blvd., Los Angeles, CA 90045 (213/642-1111; toll free, see Sheraton). 807 rms, A/C, color TV, in-rm movies. AE, CB, DC, MC, V. Valet parking $6, pool, health club, two rests. (including Landry's), three bars, 24-hr. rm svce, nightclub, hrdrsr, concierge, crib $10. *Note:* Luxury airport motel of ponderous and rather depressing appearance. Rms comfortable rather than elegant, w. minibar. Efficient but impersonal svce. Landry's is a very acceptable rest. The guests, mostly conventioneers, are not quiet and retiring. Free shuttle-bus connection w. airport (3 min.) and beach. **E–VE**

Nendels Airport Century Inn, 5547 W. Century Blvd., Los Angeles, CA 90045 (213/649-4000; toll free 800/547-0106). 150 rms, A/C, color TV, in-rm movies. AE, CB, DC, MC, V. Free parking, pool, rest., 24-hr. coffee shop, bar, rm svce, free airport limo, crib $4. *Note:* Recently renovated airport motel. Spacious, comfortable rms, the best overlooking the pool. Very efficient svce. A good value, 5 min. from the terminal. **I–M**

YMCA/Youth Hostel

YMCA, 1553 N. Hudson Ave., Hollywood, CA 90028 (213/467-4161). 29 beds, pool, health club, coffee shop. For men and women; also a youth hostel.

AYH–Santa Monica International Hostel, 1436 2nd St., Santa Monica, CA 90401 (213/393-9913). 200 beds. Opened in late 1989. Near the Santa Monica Pier and the beach.

RESTAURANTS

A Note on Restaurant Prices: Los Angeles restaurant prices, per person, excluding drinks and service charges, are coded as follows: **VE**, Very Expensive ($60 and up); **E**, Expensive ($40–$60); **M,** Moderate ($25–$40); **I,** Inexpensive ($15–$25); **B,** Budget (up to $15).

Personal Favorites (in order of preference)

Citrus, 6703 Melrose Ave., Los Angeles (857-0034). A/C. Lunch/dinner Mon–Sat. AE, CB, DC, MC, V. Jkt. *Specialties:* cabbage salad w. crabmeat, sautéed salmon w. leek purée, oyster flan w. spinach and basil, lobster timbale w. morels and fresh pasta, sautéed veal loin w. zests of lime, hot soufflé Grand Marnier w. walnuts. Remarkable desserts and pastries. *Note:* The truculent but genial Michel Richard, one of the most original young French chefs working in this country, is a virtuoso at combining French and Californian nouvelle cuisine. Immaculate modern decor w. inviting open grdn-patio (but noisy w. uncomfortable chairs). Courteous, efficient svce. A favorite of movie stars and celebrities. Resv. essential—this is an "in" place. Valet parking. One of the country's finest rests. *French/American.* **M–E**

L'Ermitage, 730 N. La Cienega Blvd., Los Angeles (652-5840). A/C. Dinner only, Mon–Sat; closed hols. AE, CB, DC, MC, V. J&T. *Specialties:* mousse of duck liver w. juniper berries, shredded duck w. cabernet, roast pigeon w. cassis, filet de St. Pierre (dory) w. morels, lobster salad w. zucchini and truffles, sautéed filet of striped bass w. red beet coulis, saddle of lamb en croûte, chocolate soufflé. Big wine list but rather indecent prices. *Note:* Until the death of its chef and owner, Jean Bertranou, this could reasonably have claimed to be the best rest. in the country. Michel Blanchet has succeeded brilliantly in safeguarding his culinary legacy. Food and svce of the highest order, equal to the finest three-star rests. in France. Elegant, recently remodeled pastel decor enhanced by Miró and Chagall paintings. Pretty covered patio. Valet parking. *French.* **VE**

Saint Estephe, 2640 Sepulveda Blvd., Manhattan Beach (545-1334). A/C. Lunch Tues–Fri, dinner Tues–Sat; closed hols. AE, CB, DC, MC, V. Jkt. *Specialties:* carne adobada, ravioli w. cream and goat-cheese sauce, blue corn tortillas w. caviar, millefeuille of lobster w. coriander and calabacita, veal sweetbreads, "chile con queso," steamed salmon "Painted Dessert," warm lamb salad (w. jicama, radishes, and oranges). Menu changes regularly. Wine list at outrageous prices. *Note:* John Sedlar, in a subtle marriage of French and southwestern U.S. strains, has created an original cuisine which might be dubbed "nouvelle cuisine Santa Fe style." The chili, blue corn, and coriander make up a symphony of unfamiliar flavors which will delight the gourmet. Sober, austere pueblo-style interior w. green plants and Peruvian tapestries. Resv. advised. 40 min. from dwntwn. *American.* **M**

Campanile, 624 La Brea Ave., Los Angeles (938-1447). A/C. Dinner only, Mon–Sat. AE, MC, V. Jkt. *Specialties:* penne w. black-olive purée, ravioli w. potatoes and truffles, lamb carpaccio, grilled prime rib w. white beans and sautéed bitter greens, fabulous desserts. The menu changes from time to time. *Note:* Charlie Chaplin built this imitation Italian *palazzo* in the '20s; Campanile opened here in June 1989 and has been a roaring success. If you want to try Mark Peel's and Nancy Silverton's "country *haute cuisine*" you had better reserve days, or even weeks, ahead. The trip is worthwhile just for the breads—onion and anchovy, olive, fig, chocolate and cherry, etc.—turned out at their adj. La Brea Bakery. The setting is half Moorish, half medieval; svce is efficient and cheerful. *Italian/American.* **M**

Rebecca's, 2025 Pacific Ave., Venice (306-6266). A/C. Dinner only, nightly. AE, CB, DC, MC, V. *Specialties:* broiled tunafish tostadas w. black beans, ceviche, tamales w. red-chile sauce, duck-stuffed chiles rellenos, grilled whitefish w. lime butter, broiled lobster w. pink-grapefruit salsa, leg of lamb adobado, quesadillas, flan, espresso ice cream. *Note:* Decor by

Frank Gehry, the farthest-out in all Los Angeles, w. a giant mural fresco and croc-odiles in Plexiglas or Formica hanging from the ceiling. But the main reason for a visit to Rebecca's is its remarkable Mexican food, as updated by proprietor Bruce Marder (who also owns the fashionable West Beach Café and DC 3; see below). Add generously conceived drinks, an interesting wine list at reasonable prices, smiling, helpful svce, and a fashionable clientele which comes more to eat than to see and be seen, and you have the sure-fire formula for Rebecca's overwhelming success. Resv. a must. Valet parking. *Mexican.* **I–M**

    Katsu, 1972 Hillhurst Ave., Los Angeles (665-1891). A/C. Lunch Mon–Fri, dinner Mon–Sat. AE, MC, V. *Specialties:* sushi, tempura, kaiseki dinner (Japanese ceremonial banquet). *Note:* A place of pilgrimage for sushi lovers, very nr. Griffith Park, because of the exceptional freshness of the seafood and the refinement w. which it is prepared and pre-sented. The decor is a rather chilly modern, relieved by a collection of Mineo Mizuno's beautiful ceramics. The sushi is excellent value, but beware of the bill for the kaiseki dinner, which in any case may disappoint you. This is a small rest., so resv. are recommended. *Japanese.* **I–M** (for kaiseki dinner).

    Pacific Dining Car, 1310 W. 6th St., Los Angeles (438-6000). A/C. Breakfast/lunch/dinner daily (open around the clock). AE, MC, V. Jkt. *Specialties:* chili, french-fried zucchini, spareribs, excellent steaks broiled to perfection, fish of the day, Caesar salad, cheesecake. Fine wine list (300 labels). *Note:* Since 1921 this authentic railroad diner and its annex have brought joy to Angeleno meat-lovers around the clock. The beef and lamb are of the high-est quality, and the wine list includes some remarkable labels at appropriate prices. When you order, make it quite clear how you like your meat cooked. Good svce. Resv. advised. Valet parking at dinner. *Steak.* **M**

    Korean Gardens, 950 S. Vermont Ave., Los Angeles (388-3042). A/C. Lunch/dinner daily. AE, MC, V. *Specialties:* juk (rice w. abalone), kunjol pan (vegetable pancake), mandu-kuk (beef bouillon w. dumplings), bul-kogi (marinated beef), tabletop barbecue of beef, pork, and chicken. *Note:* With some 200,000 Koreans living in Los Angeles, the food here has to be authentic. Many delicate flavors, but spicy-hot dishes as well, thanks to the redoubtable Korean kim chee (pickled shredded cabbage w. fermented shell-fish). Vaguely exotic decor, diligent svce. For lovers of the unusual. *Korean.* **B–I**

    R.J.'s. The Rib Joint, 252 N. Beverly Dr., Beverly Hills (274-7427). A/C. Lunch/dinner Mon–Sat, brunch Sun. AE, CB, DC, MC, V. *Specialties:* barbecued spareribs, short ribs, chili, broiled chicken, steak, fresh fish of the day, chocolate cake. *Note:* A real local institution, w. saw-dust on the floor and ceiling fans. Straightforward, tasty food in generous por-tions, w. more than 55 dishes on the menu. Gigantic salad bar. Very popular locally, so resv. advisable. One of the best buys in Los Angeles. Valet parking (evenings). *American.* **I**

Other Restaurants (from top bracket to budget)

    Michael's, 1147 3rd St., Santa Monica (451-0843). A/C. Lunch/dinner, brunch Sat–Sun; closed hols. and 10 days at the end of Dec. AE, CB, DC, MC, V. Jkt. *Specialties:* broiled lobster w. basil and fresh pepper pasta, scallops w. watercress purée, sautéed chicken w. duck foie gras, Oregon salmon w. beurre blanc, pigeon w. leeks and raspberry vinegar, caramelized veal w. lemon. Remarkable desserts (chocolate caramel pie). Fine wine list. *Note:* A shrine of California gastronomy. The cuisine of the tal-ented chef Michael McCarty, though French-inspired, is authentically American, as are the materials he uses. His delicate, imaginative touch is highlighted by his talent for presentation. Elegant neo-modern dining room in the Bauhaus style, w. contemporary works of art worthy of a museum. Charming patio w. umbrella tables for fine days. Friendly, diligent svce. Resv. a must. *American.* **E–VE**

    L'Orangerie, 903 N. La Cienega Blvd., Los Angeles (652-9770). A/C. Dinner only, nightly; closed hols. AE, CB, DC,

MC, V. *Specialties:* fish soup w. rouille, médaillons of veal w. three mustards, filet of lamb w. parsley sauce, steamed chicken w. vegetables, sea bass w. tarragon and crayfish-cream sauce. Unusually good desserts. The wine list is admirable, the prices less so. *Note:* Classical French cooking, contemporary style, in an elegant greenhouse setting. Ultra-polished svce. Favored by local society; a very distinguished environment. Resv. a must. Valet parking. *French.* **E–VE**

Valentino, 3115 Pico Blvd., Santa Monica (829-4313). A/C. Lunch Fri only, dinner Mon–Sat (until midnight); closed hols. AE, CB, DC, MC, V. Jkt. *Specialties:* gnocchi w. seafood, vegetable risotto, carpaccio of tuna, baby lamb w. broccoli and mousse of lima beans, roulade of swordfish w. shrimp and lime juice, ragoût of kidneys, venison w. polenta. One of California's finest cellars (50,000 bottles) w. the best wines from California, France, and Italy. *Note:* Unlike the legendary Rudolf Valentino, whose name the rest. has borrowed, the proprietor, Piero Selvaggio, is Sicilian not Apulian. His brilliant, inventive cooking, his elegantly renovated decor, and his polished svce combine to make this one of the best rests. in the country. Very fashionable clientele; resv. a necessity. Valet parking. *Italian.* **M–E**

Camelions, 246 26th St., Santa Monica (395-0746). A/C. Lunch Tues–Sat, dinner Tues–Sun, brunch Sun. *Specialties:* poached oysters and scallops in basil dressing, sautéed whitefish w. ginger sauce, cold eggplant soup w. roast pepper, Peking duck salad w. cucumber, sautéed king salmon in truffle butter, roast squab w. thyme and wild rice, lemon pie, banana cream pie. Rather abbreviated wine list. *Note:* The chef's whim, and availability of ingredients, determine daily changes in the menu, but the outcome is invariably a success. Mediterranean-villa setting w. pretty patio, wrought ironwork, lots of greenery, pastel-washed walls. Very good svce. Resv. strongly advised. *American.* **M–E**

La Toque, 8171 Sunset Blvd., West Hollywood (656-7515). A/C. Lunch Mon–Fri, dinner Mon–Sat; closed hols. AE, CB, DC, MC, V. Jkt. *Specialties:* eggs en croûte w. aroma of truffles, fresh tuna tartare, gratin of St. Pierre (dory) w. sea urchins, roast squab w. blackcurrant sauce, saddle of lamb w. tarragon. Menu changes regularly. The wine list falls short of brilliance. *Note:* Ken Frank, one of the most gifted American chefs of his generation, has risen in a comparatively few years to the top of the profession on the wings of his innovative talent, his airy sauces, and the delicacy w. which his dishes are presented. Romantic old-French-inn setting; attentive svce. Resv. necessary, given the rest.'s size. Valet parking. *French.* **M–E**

DC 3, 2800 Donald Douglas Loop N., Santa Monica Airport, Santa Monica (399-2323). A/C. Lunch/dinner daily, brunch Sat–Sun. AE, MC, V. *Specialties:* oysters on the half shell, grilled swordfish w. basil butter, lamb saddle roasted w. pancetta, lemon pie, hot-fudge sundae. *Note:* The only airport rest. in the entire U.S. to rate three stars. The new fashionable place for Los Angeles's trendsetters to eat, a collaboration among three recognized masters: the innovative architecture is Frank Gehry's, the elegant modern decor Chuck Arnoldi's, while the general manager is Bruce Marder, owner of two other renowned rests., West Beach Café and Rebecca's. The huge, bright, light-filled dining rm offers you a view of aircraft entering and leaving Santa Monica Airport. The simple, light, straightforward food is much to the yuppie taste. The svce, always w. a smile, is not always efficient. Resv. advised. Valet parking. *American.* **M**

The Ivy, 113 W. Robertson Blvd., West Hollywood (274-8303). A/C. Lunch/dinner Mon–Sat. AE, CB, DC, MC, V. *Specialties:* corn chowder, Louisiana crabcakes, Cajun pizza, homemade fresh pasta, mesquite-grilled catch of the day, chicken in chardonnay sauce, lemon and white-chocolate pie. *Note:* This engaging artists' bistro attracts stars of stage and screen for its eclectic California cuisine. The decor is pleasing, the atmosphere noisy but relaxed, svce generally efficient. Resv. strongly advised. An "in" place. Valet parking. *American.* **M**

♈♈ **The Palm,** 9001 Santa Monica Blvd., West Hollywood (550-
☆☆ 8811). A/C. Lunch Mon–Fri, dinner nightly; closed hols.
AE, CB, DC, MC, V. Jkt. *Specialties:* prime beef, lamb chops, broiled fish, Maine
lobster, homemade cheesecake. *Note:* A subsidiary of New York's well-known
Palm. Same wonderful steaks, same caricatures on the wall, same enormous helpings (lobsters of 4½ lb./2kg and up). Noisy, relaxed atmosphere; very good svce
(unlike its New York counterpart). *Steak/Seafood.* **M**

♈♈ **Patout's,** 2260 Westwood Blvd., Los Angeles (475-7100).
☆☆ A/C. Lunch Wed–Fri., dinner nightly, brunch Sat–Sun. AE,
CB, DC, MC, V. Jkt. *Specialties:* spaghetti w. shrimp, gumbo, redfish filet and
crabmeat in lemon butter, Cajun-style fish, crayfish à l'étouffée (in season),
tournedos Patout. *Note:* A sister establishment of the renowned Patout's in New
Orleans, this authentic Cajun rest. is a genial goodwill ambassador for bayou
country. Fish and shellfish are flown in daily from New Orleans. First-class svce.
This place can be highly recommended. Resv. advisable. Valet parking (evening).
Créole. **M**

♈♈ **Knoll's Black Forest Inn,** 2454 Wilshire Blvd., Santa Monica
☆☆ (395-2212). A/C. Lunch Tues–Fri, dinner Tues–Sun. AE,
MC, V. Jkt. *Specialties:* sauerbraten w. potato pancakes, maultaschen (German
ravioli), wild boar w. wild rice, roast goose, veal cutlet w. sour cherries, médaillon
of venison w. chanterelle mushrooms, Black Forest cake. *Note:* Since 1960 this
has been the best place in Los Angeles for lovers of good German food. As well as
the classics of German cooking it offers lighter dishes, and some that are una-
shamedly innovative. Pleasantly renovated and enlarged, w. a charming grdn for
open-air meals. Very good svce. Resv. advised, valet parking. *German.* **I–M**

♈♈ **Langan's Brasserie,** Century City Marketplace, 10250 Santa
☆☆ Monica Blvd., Century City (785-0961). A/C. Breakfast Mon–
Fri, lunch/dinner daily, brunch Sun. AE, MC, V. *Specialties:* Pheasant sausage w.
chestnut sauce, roast quail w. bubble-and-squeak patties, fritto misto, spinach
soufflé, grilled swordfish, fish and chips, chocolate pudding w. fresh raspberries.
Note: California branch of London's famous Langan's Rest., w. the same noisy,
cheerful atmosphere, same amusing engravings, paintings, and posters. Enormous, eclectic menu w. emphasis on first-rate seafood at reasonable prices. The
svce is youthful and likable, if not of the highest efficiency. Trendy clientele. Resv.
advisable. Valet parking. *Continental.* **I–M**

♈♈ **Le Dome,** 8720 Sunset Blvd., Los Angeles (659-6919). A/C.
☆☆ Lunch Mon–Fri, dinner Mon–Sat. (until midnight). AE, CB,
DC, MC, V. Jkt. *Specialties:* ragoût of veal w. mustard and fresh thyme, cassoulet,
rabbit chasseur, osso buco, choucroute garnie, catch of the day. Tempting desserts; good wine list. *Note:* A few really earthy dishes make this luxurious, trendy
brasserie one of the most likable of Los Angeles's fashionable eating places. Elegant modernist decor. Broad, inviting circular bar. Resv. advised. Valet parking.
French. **I–M**

♈♈♈ **The Mandarin,** 430 N. Camden Dr., Beverly Hills (272-
☆☆☆ 0267). A/C. Lunch Mon–Fri, dinner nightly; closed hols.
AE, CB, DC, MC, V. Jkt. *Specialties:* shark's-fin soup, hot-and-sour shrimp,
chopped squab in lettuce, Mongolian lamb, Peking duck, beggar-man's chicken.
Fine wine list. *Note:* Same quality and same elaborate decor, w. numerous Far
Eastern art objects, as the parent establishment in San Francisco. The majority of
the 125 dishes on the menu can be ordered in small sizes so that Mandarin patrons can experience as many different tastes as possible. Impeccable svce. Resv.
advisable. Valet parking at dinner. *Chinese.* **I–M**

♈♈ **Pazzia,** 755 N. La Cienega Blvd., Los Angeles (657-9271).
☆☆ A/C. Lunch Mon–Fri, dinner daily; closed hols. AE, CB, DC,
MC, V. *Specialties:* soufflé, caponata, tomato aspic, ravioli stuffed w. zucchini,
fresh homemade pasta, risotto of the day, roast rabbit, veal w. clams, broiled bass
w. white-bean purée, homemade gelati. Short but seductive wine list. *Note:* A recent venture of Mauro Vitelli, who also owns the super-snob, ultra-expensive Rex

Ristorante, this modern, elegant *trattoria* serves a light, sunlit cuisine worthy of any fine rest. in Italy. Its ever-growing reputation is sufficiently justified by the fresh pasta and risottos. Hi-tech setting w. a giant mural depicting a bicycle race and open patio in fine weather. Friendly, casual svce. Resv. advisable. Valet parking. *Italian.* **I–M**

☆☆ **West Beach Café**, 60 N. Venice Blvd., Venice (823-5396). A/C. Breakfast/lunch Tues–Sun, dinner nightly (until 1:30am). AE, CB, DC, MC, V. Jkt. *Specialties:* steak tartare, braised lamb w. baked garlic cloves and roasted potatoes, seafood sausage w. herbs, asparagus risotto, sabayon w. fruit. *Note:* Highly imaginative California-style cuisine and avant-garde setting w. frequently changing modern paintings are the two principal attractions at this stylish rest. just one block from the ocean, while the spectacular bar and fine svce also contribute to its success. The menu changes regularly, and there is a wide selection of wines by the glass or the bottle. Caters to local artists and trendy Angelenos. Resv. highly recommended. Valet parking. *American.* **I–M**

☆☆ **Antonio's,** 7472 Melrose Ave., Los Angeles (655-0480). A/C. Lunch Tues–Fri, dinner Tues–Sun; closed July 4 and Labor Day. AE, MC, V. Jkt. *Specialties:* green pepper stuffed w. coriander, chicken pipián, steak w. green sauce, ropa vieja, beef in mole Oaxaca style, jicama salad, fruit flan. *Note:* Antonio Gutierrez offers delicious and inventive Mexican fare, keeping well off the beaten track of Mexican rest. clichés. Despite a rather loud color scheme, the decor is much less original than the food. Good wine list. Friendly svce. Mariachi bands at dinner. Popular locally. Resv. recommended. Valet parking at dinner. Other location: 1323 Montana Ave., Santa Monica (395-2815). *Mexican.* **I**

☆☆ **Musso & Frank Grill,** 6667 Hollywood Blvd., Hollywood (467-7788). A/C. Lunch/dinner Mon–Sat; closed hols. AE, CB, DC, MC, V. Jkt. *Specialties:* calves' liver w. onions, bouillabaisse, chicken pot pie, lamb chops, sauerbraten, corned beef and cabbage, creamed spinach, fish of the day, flan. *Note:* Of roughly the same age as the movie industry (1919), Musso & Frank is a Hollywood monument. The food is uneven, but generally pleasing and substantial; the svce is surly. Comfortable interior w. dark-wood paneling and red leather. Much frequented by press and movie people. *Continental/American.* **I**

☆☆ **Siamese Princess,** 8048 W. 3rd St., West Hollywood (653-2643). A/C. Lunch Wed–Fri, dinner nightly. AE, CB, DC, MC, V. *Specialties:* nam chim salad, mu wan (calamari w. coriander), duck w. ginger, sea bass and mussel mousse, lamb saté, ma haw (spiced pork), chicken wing kai. *Note:* The best of the multitude of Thai rests. that have grown and flourished in California over the past decade. Tasty but delicate food, and (what's uncommon in a Far Eastern rest.) a very good wine list. Slightly kitsch Victorian interior w. portraits of the Thai royal family and other dignitaries on the walls. Very good svce. Resv. advised. *Thai.* **I**

☆☆ **Sofi,** 8030 3/4 W. 3rd St., Los Angeles (651-0346). A/C. Lunch Mon–Sat, dinner daily; closed Jan 1, Dec 25. AE, MC, V. *Specialties:* dolmades, moussaka, keftedes, (meatballs), kreatopita, souvlaki, swordfish kebabs, arni bouti (marinated leg of lamb), baklava, galaktoboureko (cream-filled pastry). Good selection of Greek wines. *Note:* One of Los Angeles's few Greek rests. to emphasize food rather than decor or atmosphere. Talented chef Sofi Lazaridis, a former doctor who traded his stethoscope for a skillet when he left his native Greece, prepares fine examples of all the classic Greek dishes, particularly moussaka. Enticing patio-grdn on fine days. Very good svce. A splendid place. Resv. advised; valet parking. *Greek.* **I**

☆☆ **Yamato,** in the Westin Century Plaza (see "Accommodations," above), Century City (277-1840). A/C. Lunch Mon–Fri, dinner nightly; closed Labor Day, Thanksgiving, Dec 25. AE, CB, DC, MC, V. Jkt. *Specialties:* beef sukiyaki, shrimp tempura, teppanyaki, shabu shabu, sushi bar, steak teriyaki. *Note:* Traditional Japanese decor w. meditation grdn, but also a conventional Western dining rm. The food is perfectly prepared and served (kimono-clad). Same management as the well-known rest. of the same name in San Francisco. Locally popular; resv. advised. *Japanese.* **I**

    Yang Chow, 819 N. Broadway, dwntwn (625-0811). A/C. Lunch–dinner Mon–Sat. AE, MC, V. *Specialties:* wonton soup, moo shu pork, Yang Chow lamb, Szechuan beef, shrimp in garlic sauce, Kung Pao chicken. Chinese beer. *Note:* This is one of the places where the dwellers in Chinatown like to eat. Always crowded and noisy. The cuisine is inspired and delectable; the decor is general-purpose Far Eastern. Efficient svce—a point worth stressing at a Chinese rest. Full of regulars; a very good place to eat. *Chinese.* **I**

    Alouette, 7279 Santa Monica Blvd., West Hollywood (650-6772). A/C. Dinner only, Wed–Sun. MC, V. *Specialties:* frogs' legs provençal, coq au vin, pepper steak, roast chicken w. tarragon, sweetbreads chasseur, crème caramel. *Note:* Los Angeles's best buy for devotees of French *cuisine bourgeoise,* straightforward and unpretentious, at very alluring prices. Country decor and relaxed atmosphere. Svce w. a smile. Resv. advised; very good value. *French.* **B–I**

    Chin Chin, 8618 Sunset Blvd., West Hollywood (652-1818). A/C. Lunch/dinner daily. AE, MC, V. *Specialties:* dim sum, chicken salad, spring rolls, moo shu pork, ginger duck, barbecued spareribs. *Note:* The rest. that introduced dim sum (tasty hot or cold hors d'oeuvres Cantonese style) to Los Angeles, and started a fashion. The other specialties of the house are just as good. Usually crowded and noisy; hard-working svce; regular customers; very good value. Other locations: 11740 San Vincente Blvd., Brentwood (826-2525), and 12215 Ventura Blvd., Studio City (818/985-9090). *Chinese.* **B–I**

    El Cholo, 1121 S. Western Ave., Los Angeles (734-2773). A/C. Lunch/dinner daily; closed Thanksgiving, Dec 25. AE, MC, V. *Specialties:* enchiladas, tacos, burritos dorados, chiles relleños, tamales verdes, tostadas. *Note:* Of the innumerable Mexican rests. in Los Angeles, purists think this is the best overall value, w. its absolutely authentic food and setting. Comfortable dining rms and patios. A classic of its kind since 1927; resv. advised. *Mexican.* **B**

    Nate 'n Al's, 414 N. Beverly Dr., Beverly Hills (274-0101). A/C. Breakfast/lunch/dinner daily (until 8:30pm). CB, DC, MC, V. *Specialties:* giant sandwiches, herring in sour cream, roast turkey, pastrami, stuffed cabbage, corned beef, homemade cheesecake. *Note:* A Beverly Hills classic since 1945, an authentic New York deli serving generous portions at very modest prices. Unpretentious decor; efficient, smiling svce. Very popular locally, especially at lunchtime. No resv. *American.* **B**

CAFETERIAS/SPECIALTY SPOTS: ✳ **Cassell's,** 3300 W. 6th St., Los Angeles (480-8668). Lunch only, Mon–Sat. No credit cards. The best hamburgers in all Los Angeles; excellent sandwiches.

    Gorky's Café and Russian Brewery, 536 E. 8th St., dwntwn (627-4060). Open daily around the clock. No credit cards. Engaging dwntwn bistro serving solid, flavorful Slavic food as well as excellent home-brewed beer. Amusing bohemian atmosphere; entertainment nightly; locally very popular. Other location: 1716 N. Cahuenga Blvd., Hollywood (463-4060).

    Jody Maroni's The Sausage Kingdom, 2011 Ocean Front Walk at Venice Blvd., Venice (821-1950). Lunch/dinner daily (until 8pm). No credit cards. This modest stall fronting the beach serves no fewer than 22 varieties of delicious homemade sausage, from "Yucatan" (chicken, duck, coriander, and chile serrano) to "Bombay Bangers" (lamb curry and raisins) and Cajun boudín.

    Original Pantry, 877 S. Figueroa St., Los Angeles (972-9279). Open daily around the clock. No credit cards. Excellent cafeteria food and commendable steaks at very reasonable prices; popular for half a century.

Philippe's The Original, 1001 N. Alameda St., dwntwn (628-3781). Breakfast/lunch/dinner daily. No credit cards. A local landmark since 1908. Overstuffed "French dip sandwiches" (choice of ham, beef, pork, or lamb) for $3. You'll see truck drivers here alongside bank directors and tourists shoulder-to-shoulder w. bums. Right next to Union Station.

☼ **Pink's,** 711 N. La Brea Blvd., dwntwn (931-4223). Open daily (until 3am). No credit cards. By general consent the best hot dogs in the city (and a dynamite chile sauce); also good hamburgers. Very popular locally.

Where to Eat What in Los Angeles
American: Camelions (p. 1043), Citrus (p. 1041), DC 3 (p. 1043), The Ivy (p. 1043), Michael's (p. 1042), Musso & Frank Grill (p. 1045), Nate 'n Al's (p. 1046), The Rib Joint (p. 1042), Saint Estephe (p. 1041), West Beach Café (p. 1045).

Chinese: Chin Chin (p. 1046), The Mandarin (p. 1044), Yang Chow (p. 1046).

Continental: Langan's Brasserie (p. 1044), Musso & Frank Grill (p. 1045).

Créole: Patout's (p. 1044).

Cafeterias/Fast Food: Cassell's (p. 1046), Gorky's Café and Russian Brewery (p. 1046), Jody Maroni's The Sausage Kingdom (p. 1046), Original Pantry (p. 1046), Philippe's The Original (p. 1047), Pink's (p. 1047), R.J.'s The Rib Joint (p. 1042).

French: Alouette (p. 1046), Citrus (p. 1041), Le Dome (p. 1044), L'Ermitage (p. 1041), L'Orangerie (p. 1042), La Toque (p. 1043).

German: Knoll's Black Forest Inn (p. 1044).

Greek: Sofi (p. 1045).

Italian: Campanile (p. 1041), Pazzia (p. 1044), Valentino (p. 1043).

Japanese: Katsu (p. 1042), Yamato (p. 1045).

Korean: Korean Gardens (p. 1042).

Mexican: Antonio's (p. 1045), El Cholo (p. 1046), Rebecca's (p. 1041).

Seafood: The Palm (p. 1044).

Steaks: Pacific Dining Car (p. 1042), The Palm (p. 1044).

Thai: Siamese Princess (p. 1045).

Late-night Service: Le Dome (Mon–Sat until midnight), Gorky's Café and Russian Brewery (daily 24 hr.), Original Pantry (daily 24 hr.), Pacific Dining Car (daily 24 hr.), Pink's (daily until 3am), Valentino (Mon–Sat until midnight), West Beach Café (daily until 1:30am).

BARS & NIGHTCLUBS
The insistent rhythm of Los Angeles by night makes it hard to draw up a list of "in" places; discos, bars, and nightclubs grow, wither, and die here with the leaves on the trees. However, here are some more durable bets.

Baxter's Underground, 1050 Gayley Ave., Westwood (208-3716). Fashionable disco near the UCLA campus. Student/yuppie mix. Open nightly.

Carlos 'n' Charlie's, 8240 Sunset Blvd., Hollywood (656-8830). Very popular singles bar; noisy and absolutely relaxed. Disco-rock music. Respectable Mexican food. Open nightly.

Carroll O'Connor's Place, 369 N. Bedford Dr., Beverly Hills (273-7587). Likable bar with commendable rest., where local celebrities come. Owned by actors Patrick O'Neal and Carroll O'Connor. Open Mon–Sat till 2am.

Casey's, 613 S. Grand Ave., dwntwn (629-2353). Favored by yuppies from the dwntwn financial district. Warm paneled interior with sporting posters. Trendy.

The Comedy Store, 8433 W. Sunset Blvd., West Hollywood (656-6225).

One of the West Coast's best-known and most popular comedy clubs, where the biggest names in the business appear regularly. Trendy people in a trendy place.

Hard Rock Café, 8600 Beverly Blvd., Los Angeles (276-7605). Los Angeles version of the well-known London nightclub of the same name. Rock 'n' roll theme-park decor complete with a green Cadillac plunging through the roof. Perpetually crowded and noisy, good hamburgers, hard rock, young customers. Open nightly until 12:30am.

Harry's Bar, 2020 Ave. of the Stars, Century City (277-2333). California branch of the famous bar/rest. in Venice of which Hemingway wrote. Also acceptable Italian rest. Open nightly.

☼ **The Improv.,** 8162 Melrose Ave., West Hollywood (651-2583). Granddaddy of the local comedy clubs; shows generally of high quality, sometimes with big-name stars. The rest., despite its name (Hell's Kitchen), is acceptable.

Mondrian Lounge, in the Mondrian Hotel, 8440 Sunset Blvd., West Hollywood (650-8999). This lounge-terrace with a glittering view of Los Angeles is a good place to watch the sun set over the smog and listen to the jazz nightly. The dress mixes high fashion w. jeans and black leather jackets.

The Palace, 1735 N. Vine St., Hollywood (462-3000). 1930s dance hall, wonderfully restored. Thunderous PA system. Laser machines, TV clips, good live music. Open nightly.

Palomino, 6907 Lankershim Blvd., North Hollywood (818/764-4010). The fashionable country and western place; come in boots and cowboy hat. Open nightly.

☼ **Polo Lounge,** in the Beverly Hills Hotel, 9641 Sunset Blvd., Beverly Hills (276-2251). This bar has been famous for half a century; all the big names of the cinema came here, come here, or will come here. Ideal for a working breakfast. Open nightly.

Redwoods 2nd Street Saloon, 316 W. 2nd St., dwntwn (617-2867). Most of the customers here work at the *Los Angeles Times*. Setting and atmosphere are comfortable.

Roxy, 9009 Sunset Blvd., West Hollywood (276-2222). The mecca of California rock; music live. Dates vary. Decor in the style of the Roaring '20s.

The Troubadour, 9081 Santa Monica Blvd., West Hollywood (276-1159). Live rock; many pop-rock stars performed here early in their careers, including Joan Baez, Bob Dylan, and Rod Stewart. Open Tues–Sun.

Vertigo, 1024 S. Grand Ave., dwntwn (747-4849). Really "in" disco where the elite of Los Angeles hang out. You must be smart but informal. The bouncers are inexorable. Open Thurs–Sat.

Vine Street Bar & Grill, 1610 N. Vine St., Hollywood (463-4375). Jazz, blues, and swing nightly in an intimate art deco setting.

NEARBY EXCURSIONS

☼ 🔔🔔 **MISSION SAN JUAN CAPISTRANO** (49 mi./78km along I-5 to the Ortega Hwy. exit) (714/493-1424): Perched between the mountains and the sea, this was the most famous, and probably the loveliest, of California's missions. Founded in 1776 by the Spanish Franciscan Fr. Junípero Serra, it was badly damaged by an earthquake in 1812, but retains part of its cloister, Serra's chapel, ruins of the church with arches and pillars, and the priests' dormitory. In its enchanting gardens thousands of swallows nest Mar–Oct; there's also an interesting little archeological museum. Open daily; don't miss it.

See also the **Regional Library and Cultural Center** at 31495 El Camino Real (714/493-1752), an elegant postmodern building by Michael Graves with temporary art exhibits. Well worth the side trip. Open daily.

⛪ MOUNT WILSON OBSERVATORY (25 mi./40km NE
on Calif. 2) (818/713-3100): This small astronomy museum and observatory boasts a 100-in. (2.54m) telescope; it is reached by a beautiful access road with a magnificent view of the entire Los Angeles region. Open daily.

☀⛪ RICHARD NIXON LIBRARY & BIRTHPLACE (18001
Yorba Linda Blvd. at Eureka St., Yorba Linda, 30 mi./48km SE via I-5 and Calif. 91E) (714/993-3393): Inaugurated in July 1990, this 9-acre (3.6ha) museum features Nixon's small wooden birth house (the 37th president was born here in 1913), a pink limestone Spanish-style library and museum, and four gardens. Included in the museum are a 292-seat theater, a biographical gallery, a re-creation of the Lincoln Sitting Room from the White House, and a Watergate area where visitors can hear excerpts from the sadly famous White House tapes. Open daily.

☀⛪ SANTA CATALINA ISLAND (or CATALINA IS-
LAND) (22 mi./35km offshore from San Pedro): A paradise for bicyclists and big-game fishermen, this 22-mi.-long (35km) island, purchased in 1919 by chewing-gum king William Wrigley, Jr., who had dreams of making it into a second Capri, is now entirely given over to tourism. There's a casino, some decorously rococo hotels, and boat trips.

Two good rests. in the port of Avalon are the **Ristorante Villa Portofino,** 111 Crescent Ave. (510-0508), open for lunch Thurs–Sun and for dinner nightly, with an Italian menu, and **Armstrong's,** 306 Crescent Ave. (510-0113), open for lunch/dinner daily, with very good grilled fish.

The island can be reached in 20 min. by the **Helitrans** helicopter service, Berth 95, Harbor Blvd., San Pedro (548-1314 for resv., required); or in 2 hr. by boat, **Catalina Island Cruises,** Berths 95 and 96, Harbor Blvd., San Pedro (514-3888), and **Catalina Express** (519-1212).

⛪ WHITTIER (12 mi./19km SE via Whittier Blvd. and Calif.
72): Visit **Pio Pico State Historic Park,** 6003 Pioneer Blvd. (695-1217). Partially destroyed by flood in 1883, the former residence of Pio Pico, last Mexican governor of California (1852), was seriously damaged by a recent earthquake. This fine example of 19th-century Spanish Colonial architecture is temporarily closed to the public during the renovation process; but you can still visit the beautiful park that surrounds the residence. Open Wed–Sun.

GHOST TOWNS: Rosamond, 75 mi. (120km) north on I-5 and Calif. 14, is the site of the 19th-century **Tropico Gold Mine** (805/256-2644), which may be visited Thurs–Sun. The little town from the days of the westward expansion has been scrupulously restored.

Nearby ⛪ **Edwards Air Force Base,** where the space shuttle regularly touches down, has an interesting little space museum, part of NASA's **Ames-Dryden Flight Research Center.** Though Edwards AFB is usually off-limits to civilians, visitors are allowed in to watch each shuttle touch-down. For information on dates, timetables, etc., call 808/258-3520.

NATIONAL PARKS NEARBY: ☀⛰ **Death Valley,** 305 mi. (490km) NE on I-15, Calif. 127, and Calif. 190: One of the natural wonders of the world (see Chapter 48 on Death Valley). On the way, stop at ⛰ **Calico,** 10 mi. (16km) northeast of **Barstow,** a wonderful ghost town from the days of the gold rush (see "Ghost Towns" in Chapter 47 on Las Vegas).

☀⛪ **Sequoia National Park,** 220 mi. (354km) north along I-5 and Calif. 198: The home of the giant trees (see Chapter 52). On the way, see ⛪ **Kern County Pioneer Village,** 3801 Chester Ave. (3 mi./5km east of Calif. 99), in Bakersfield (805/861-2132), open daily. Largest and best-preserved pioneer village in the entire state; see the Far West in its natural grandeur.

FARTHER AFIELD

☼☪ **JOSHUA TREE NATIONAL MONUMENT** (304 mi./
486km r.t. via the Pomona Fwy./Calif. 60, I-10, and Calif.
60E, I-10E, and return): Cactus desert in flower Mar–May: a place of wild beauty. The yuccas, or Joshua trees, which have given the park its name, can grow to 64 ft. (20m). From **Salton View** (altitude 4,972 ft./1,554m), you can see as far as the Mexican frontier, 93 mi. (150km) to the south. Splendid rocky landscapes, but watch for the temperature, especially in summer; it can rise high enough to cause engine overheating—and there are only three places in the whole park where you can get water. The **visitor center** at Twentynine Palms Oasis (619/367-7511) is open daily.

On the road, go a little out of your way through ☪ **Riverside,** capital of the "Orange Empire," for a look at two of the most unusual buildings on the West Coast: **Heritage House,** 8193 Magnolia Ave., dating from 1891, an incredible mixture of Spanish, Victorian, and Tudor styles; and the **Mission Inn,** 3649 7th St. at Orange (714/784-0300), a charming Spanish-Moorish hotel, now almost a century old, where many well-known personalities (including Humphrey Bogart and Richard Nixon) have been married in the adjoining wedding chapel.

Also visit **Palm Springs** (see below) and **Perris,** the home of hot-air ballooning.

☼☪☪ **PALM SPRINGS** (216 mi./344km r.t. by I-10E, Calif.
111S, and return): A millionaires' city built in the middle of a desert at the foot of 8,516-ft. (2,596m) **Mount San Jacinto.** Don't miss the trip to the top by cable car on the **Palm Springs Aerial Tramway,** Tramway Rd. (619/325-1391); at 2.5 mi. (4km) it's the world's longest single-span aerial tramway.

Once no more than a stagecoach stop, Palm Springs has become, in less than a century, one of the snootiest resorts in the country; dozens of celebrities from Bob Hope to Frank Sinatra, from President Ford to Dean Martin, have favored it. Palm Springs and neighboring **Rancho Mirage** boast no fewer than 7,000 pools (one for every five inhabitants), 400 tennis courts, and 70 golf courses. The dry climate and continual (350 days a year) sunshine attract almost two million tourists a year. Hotels offer attractive rates in summer. There's a very fine **Desert Museum,** 101 Museum Dr. (619/325-7186), open Tues–Sun Oct–June.

Where to Stay in the Palm Springs Area

☼ ♛♛♛♛ **Hyatt Grand Champions Resort,** 44-600 Indian Wells Lane,
Indian Wells, CA 92210 (619/341-1000; toll free, see Hyatt). Splendid new palace hotel w. 321 very comfortable rms and suites as well as 20 individual villas, standing in 35 acres (14ha) of landscaped grdn. Two golf courses. The acme of luxury. **VE**

♛♛♛ **Marquis Hotel,** 150 S. Indian Ave., Palm Springs, CA 92262
(619/322-2121). 267 rms. Luxurious resort hotel looking clear out across the San Jacinto Mountains. Unsurpassed comfort. **VE**

☼ ♛♛ **Shadow Mountain Resort,** 45-750 San Luis Rey, Palm Desert, CA 92260 (619/346-6123; toll free 800/472-3713).
125 elegant, comfortable suites. Tennis heaven (16 courts). **M–E**

♛ **Motel 6,** 595 E. Palm Canyon Dr., Palm Springs, CA 92262
(619/325-6129). 124 rms. Strictly functional motel at unbeatable prices. **I**

Where to Eat in the Palm Springs Area

♈♈♈ **Le Vallauris,** 385 W. Tahquitz-McCallum Way, Palm Springs (619/325-5059). Lunch/dinner daily; closed Aug. AE, CB, DC, MC, V. *French.* **M–E**

♈♈ **Dominick's,** 70-030 Calif. 111, Rancho Mirage (619/324-1711). Dinner only, Wed–Mon; closed Aug. AE, MC, V. Bob Hope's favorite steakhouse. *Steak/Seafood.* **M**

☼♈♈ **Las Casuelas Nuevas,** 70-050 Calif. 111, Rancho Mirage (619/328-8844). Lunch/dinner daily; closed Thanksgiving, Dec 25. *Mexican.* **I–M**

♈ **Billy Reed's,** 1800 N. Palm Canyon Dr., Palm Springs (619/325-1946). Three meals daily. MC, V. *American.* **B–I**

☼ **COASTAL ROAD CALIF. 1 TO SAN FRANCISCO OR SAN DIEGO:** One of the country's most spectacular panoramic highways; see Chapter 51 on the California Coast.

CHAPTER 55

SAN DIEGO⛾⛾

☐ ☐ ☐

Discovered in 1542 by Juan Rodríguez Cabrillo, a Portuguese explorer in the Spanish service, San Diego Bay is one of the most spectacular natural settings on the West Coast. Don Gaspar de Portolá established the first garrison (Presidio) here in 1769 on the site of the present-day **Presidio Park,** thus making San Diego the point of departure for Spanish settlement in California. At the same time, the celebrated Franciscan Fr. Junípero Serra built here the first of his missions. From this storied colonial past, California's second-largest city (after Los Angeles) has retained vestiges of Spanish and Mexican as well as American influence.

San Diego is not only an important market for the produce of the fertile lands around it (for example, two-thirds of the avocados consumed in the U.S. are grown here), but a vigorous port and industrial city with its face turned resolutely toward the future, with its centers of electronics, aerospace (General Dynamics), missile technology, medicine (the Salk Institute), and oceanography (Scripps Institution of Oceanography). This southernmost city in California has the 13th-fastest economic growth rate among U.S. metropolitan areas, and its population is keeping pace, rising 44% between 1970 and 1985. Finally, it's the largest naval base in the country after Norfolk, Virginia; in fact, the navy is the largest employer in the San Diego area with 140,000 people on active duty. The movie *Top Gun* was shot at the **Miramar Naval Air Station** north of San Diego.

For a number of years a huge urban-renewal project has been in progress in downtown San Diego, testimony to the city's economic vigor; its symbol is the astonishing **Horton Plaza** commercial complex. At the same time, its gentle climate, its relaxed life-style, its exotic overtones (the Mexican city of **Tijuana** is half an hour's drive across the border), and its setting among green hills rising from the turquoise waters of its bay, combine to make it a vacation and convention city overrun by visitors summer and winter alike. Tourism ranks third among San Diego's industries, bringing in $3 billion a year. The crime rate, among the lowest in the country, is not the least of its attractions.

Over and above the vestiges of the Spanish Colonial era—including **Old Town** and **San Diego de Alcala,** the oldest Franciscan mission in California (1769)—San Diego offers dozens of miles of superb beaches, a paradise for surfers and scuba-divers; the tropical luxuriance of **Balboa Park** and its world-famous zoo; **Coronado** island and its legendary 19th-century Hotel del Coronado; and the unequalled view of the Pacific from **Point Loma.** The adjoining community of **La Jolla** (a corruption of the Spanish "La Joya," the jewel) is a charming little beach resort which is establishing itself more and more firmly as the chic, trendy place for a vacation home in southern California.

Famous people born in San Diego and La Jolla include actors Gregory Peck (La Jolla), Robert Duvall, and Cliff Robertson.

BASIC FACTS: State of California. Area code: 619. Time zone: Pacific. ZIP Code: 92101. Founded: 1769. Approximate population: city, 1,100,000; metropolitan area, 2,370,000. Sixth-largest city and 18th-largest metropolitan area in the U.S.

CLIMATE: Sheltered at the head of its bay, San Diego lives in a perpetual spring-time; the yearly average temperature is 64°F (18°C). Mild in winter though with occasional storms (Jan. average: 55°F/13°C), deliciously temperate in spring and fall, quite warm during the summer days (up to 86°F/30°C) but cool at night the year round, San Diego's climate approaches perfection. You'll need a swimsuit and sunglasses no matter when you come.

DISTANCES: Las Vegas, 331 mi. (550km); Los Angeles, 125 mi. (200km); Mexican border, 18 mi. (28km); Phoenix, 355 mi. (568km); San Francisco, 540 mi. (865km); Tucson, 414 mi. (662km).

ARRIVAL & TRANSIT INFORMATION

AIRPORT: Lindbergh International Airport (SAN), 3 mi. (5km) NW. Charles Lindbergh's immortal *The Spirit of St. Louis* was built in San Diego, whence the airport's name. For information, call 231-7361.

U.S. AIRLINES: America West (560-0727), American (232-4051), Continental (232-9155), Delta (233-8040), Northwest (239-0488), Southwest (232-1221), TWA (295-7009), United (234-7171), and USAir (574-1234).

FOREIGN CARRIERS: British Airways (toll free 800/217-9297).

CITY LINK: The **cab** fare to city center is about $7–$9; time, about 10 min. Bus: **Super Shuttle** (278-8877) and **Rainbow Ride** Shuttle (695-3830), serving principal dwntwn hotels; fare, $3. Municipal bus: **San Diego Transit** line 2 stops on Broadway; fare, $1.
   The city bus system, the SDTS, is extensive, but slow (for information, call 233-3004). There is also a modern express trolley system, still at an early stage of development: **San Diego Trolley** (for information, call 231-8549).
   Taxis are reasonably inexpensive, but renting a car with unlimited mileage is advisable, given the large number of attractions outside the city. California has very favorable car-rental rates.

CAR RENTAL (at the airport unless otherwise indicated): Avis (231-7171); Budget (297-3851); Dollar (234-3388); Hertz (231-7000); Ladki (local renter with very competitive rates), 929 W. Laurel St. (233-9333); National (231-7100); and Thrifty, 2100 Kettner Blvd. (239-2281).

LIMOUSINE SERVICES: Carey Limousine (225-9551), Coronado Livery Service (435-6310), and VIP Limousine Service (299-7000).

TAXIS: Cabs may be summoned by phone or taken from the waiting lines outside the major hotels. Recommended companies: **Checker Cab** (234-4477), **Orange Cab** (291-3333), and **Yellow Cab** (234-6161).

TRAIN: Amtrak station, 1050 Kettner Blvd. at C St. (239-9021).

INTERCITY BUS: Greyhound, 120 W. Broadway at First Ave. (239-9171).

INFORMATION & TOURS

TOURIST INFORMATION: The **San Diego Convention and Visitors Bureau,** 1200 Third Ave., Suite 824, CA 92101 (619/232-3101).
   Visitor Information Center, 11 Horton Plaza (619/236-1212).

GUIDED TOURS: Gray Line Tours (bus), 1670 Kettner Blvd. (231-9922): Guided tours of the city and surroundings; serves major hotels.

Molly Trolley (bus) (233-9177): Guided tours of the major tourist attractions in and around San Diego on a bus got up to look like an old-timie trolley car. Board and get off as many times as you like along the route. Daily year round. Pickups at leading hotels.

San Diego Harbor Excursion (boat), Broadway at Harbor Dr. (619/234-4111): Boat trips around the harbor and bay, daily year round.

Skydance Helicopters (helicopter), 1935 N. Marshall, El Cajon (562-1887). 15- or 30-min. chopper trips over San Diego Bay leaving from Lindbergh Airport. A fine spectacle. Resv. required; daily year round.

Tijuana Trolley (231-8549): Fast, ultramodern light railway connecting the Amtrak station in the center of San Diego (Kettner Blvd. at C St.) to the suburb of San Ysidro on the Mexican border across from Tijuana. Leaves every 15 min. 5am – 1am; takes about 40 min; fare, $2.

SIGHTS, ATTRACTIONS & ACTIVITIES

ADVENTURES: Sky Surfer Balloon Co. (balloon), 1221 Camino del Mar, Del Mar (481-6800): Dirigible-balloon trips over San Diego and the Pacific coast. Spectacular. Daily year round.

Whale-Watching Trips: The **Natural History Museum,** Park Blvd., Balboa Park (232-3821), arranges boat trips to watch whale migrations between mid-Dec and mid-Feb. At least 200 whales are encountered daily off San Diego during this period. Also at **Fisherman's Landing,** 2838 Garrison St. (221-8500), and **H. & M. Landing,** 2803 Emerson St. (222-1144).

ARCHITECTURAL HIGHLIGHTS: ☀️🏛 **Horton Plaza,** bounded by First Ave., Fourth Ave., Broadway, and G St. (239-8180): The farthest-out shopping center in the U.S. is to be found in the heart of downtown San Diego, featuring the daring postmodern design and pastel mauve, green, orange, and pink decor of architect Jon Jerde. It's an extravagant hodgepodge of facades, colonnades, and porticos which might remind you of a Venetian palace, an art deco theater, or a Spanish mission, but for the unusual modern sculptures. In the midst of all this you'll find mimes, magicians, jugglers, and strolling musicians doing their thing. Construction cost $140 million, and the finished product boasts four department stores, more than 150 retail outlets, restaurants, movie houses, etc. Open daily.

☀️🏛 **San Diego Convention Center,** 111 W. Harbor Dr. at Fifth Ave. (239-1989): The most imaginative, and the handsomest, convention center in the country. Opened in Nov 1989, the spectacular building, which takes the form of a huge concrete sailboat anchored beside San Diego Bay, is by architect Arthur Erickson. The main Exhibition Hall, covering 250,000 sq. ft. (24,000m²) can accommodate 6,000 people at meetings or banquets.

🏛 **University of California at San Diego/USSD,** La Jolla Village Dr., I-5, and N. Torrey Pines Rd., La Jolla (534-4831): Founded in 1912 and now numbering more than 17,000 students, this campus specializes in biological and medical research. Its Cray X-MP 48 computer, one of only six in the world, cost $14 million and is one of the most powerful in existence, operating at a speed of 1.86 billion computations a second. On the lawns of the campus is a fine collection of modern sculpture. Each of the four colleges is built in a different architectural style.

BEACHES: ⚑ **Black's Beach,** 15 mi. (25km) north along I-5, Genesee Rd., and Torrey Pines Scenic Dr.: Since you must first go down a 300-ft. (92m) cliff (and, of course, eventually go back up again), this beach south of Torrey Pines State Park is not easy of access; perhaps for that reason, it draws many nudists.

    ⚑ **Border Field Beach,** 20 mi. (32km) south via I-5 and Monument Rd.: Right at the Mexican border. Horseback riding authorized on the beach; surfing.

    ⚑ **Coronado Municipal Beach,** 5 mi. (8km) west on Calif. 75: A family beach, with huge white-sand stretches.

    ☀⚑⚑ **La Jolla Cove,** 12 mi. (19km) NW via I-5 and Ardafer Rd.: The prettiest beach, and the most chic. Protected by cliffs on three sides; wonderful scuba-diving and hang-gliding.

    ⚑ **Mission Beach,** 8 mi. (12km) NW on W. Mission Bay Dr.: Favorite of the local younger set; usually overcrowded in summer.

    ⚑ **Ocean Beach,** 6 mi. (9km) west on U.S. 8: Dangerous marine streams, so relatively uncrowded.

    ☀⚑⚑ **Torrey Pines State Beach,** 20 mi. (32km) north via I-5 and County Rd. 21: Huge unspoiled beach with overhanging cliffs and pine woods. Lovely seascapes.

    ☀⚑⚑ **Windansea Beach,** 10 mi. (16km) north along Mission Blvd. and La Jolla Blvd.: One of San Diego's most picturesque beaches. Here the surfboard reigns unchallenged.

HISTORIC BUILDINGS: ☀⚑ **Hotel del Coronado,** 1500 Orange Ave., Coronado (435-6611): One of the most historic hotels in the U.S. Opened in 1888, the "Del," as San Diegans affectionately call it, was the first hotel in the world to be equipped with electric power (the installation was done under the personal supervision of Thomas Edison) and elevators. The imposing Victorian frame building, with its bright-red pointed roofs, was a setting for the movie *Some Like It Hot.* Legend has it that it was here, in 1920, that the future King Edward VIII of England first met the woman for whom he later gave up the throne, Wallis Simpson, who was to become Duchess of Windsor. Guided tours Sat afternoons.

    ☀⚑⚑ **Mission San Diego de Alcala,** 10818 San Diego Mission Rd. (283-7319): Known as "The Mother of Missions," this oldest mission in California was originally built on the site of the present-day **Presidio Park** in 1769 by the Spanish Franciscan Fr. Junípero Serra (beatified in 1988 by papal decree). Destroyed by earthquakes in 1803 and 1812, it was rebuilt following the original plans on the banks of the San Diego River in 1813, and is one of the most beautiful religious edifices on the West Coast. San Diego de Alcala was the first of the 21 missions built by the Franciscans between the Mexican border and Sonoma 540 mi. (860km) to the north, beyond San Francisco Bay, along what later became known as El Camino Real (the Royal Way). Each of the missions was built one day's journey on horseback from its neighbors. Open daily.

    ☀⚑⚑ **Old Town San Diego State Historic Park,** bounded by Congress St., Wallace St., Twigg St., and Juan St.: The historic center of San Diego, with its Spanish Colonial adobe houses. Many interesting buildings from the years 1820–70, lining a huge plaza where cockfights and bullfights were once held. Note the **Casa de Estudillo** (1820), residence of the governor of San Diego when it was part of Mexico. The **Casa de Lopez** (1834) houses a quaint candle museum. The **San Diego Union Building** is the office of a newspaper first published in 1868. The **Seeley Stables** (1869) was long the depot for the stagecoaches of the U.S. Mail. Collection of horse-drawn vehicles. The **Old California Museum,** besides a collection of horse-drawn vehicles, has a model of

19th-century San Diego. At the north corner of the plaza, where the **Casa de Pico,** residence of the first governor of California, once stood, is now the **Bazaar del Mundo,** a replica of a typical Spanish-Mexican marketplace, with craft shops, souvenir shops, art galleries, and restaurants set in courtyards and gardens. There is a signposted walk through Old Town for the benefit of visitors. Shouldn't be missed, despite its touristy atmosphere; **visitor center** at 2645 San Diego Ave. (237-6770). Open daily.

☼🔔⚱ **Villa Montezuma,** 1925 K St. (239-2211): Magnificent piece of Victorian architecture contemporary with the Hotel del Coronado (1887). Colorful exterior decoration; very fine rococo interior with superb stained-glass windows. Temporary art exhibitions. Open Tues–Fri and Sun.

🔔 **Whaley House,** 2482 San Diego Ave. (298-2482): The oldest (1856) brick building in southern California; until 1871 it housed the local law courts. Believed to be haunted by the ghost of a man who was hanged here in 1852. Original furnishings and decoration. An easy walk from Old Town Plaza.

MONUMENTS: ☼⚱ **Cabrillo National Monument,** Cabrillo Memorial Dr. at Point Loma, 10 mi. (16km) west on Calif. 209 (557-5450): Dedicated to Juan Rodríguez Cabrillo, discoverer of California, the monument with its lighthouse, dating from 1855, gives you a fine view of San Diego Bay and the Pacific Ocean. It shares with the Statue of Liberty in New York the distinction of being the most-visited monument in the U.S. From here you can watch the offshore migration of the gray whales mid-Dec to mid-Feb. Museum. Open daily. The monument closes at sunset.

MUSEUMS OF ART: ☼⚱ **La Jolla Museum of Contemporary Art,** 700 Prospect St., La Jolla (454-3541): If it were only for its site, in a garden overlooking the ocean, this superb museum of modern art would be worth visiting—but among 3,000 works on display there are also some signed by Roy Lichtenstein, Andy Warhol, Frank Stella, Ellsworth Kelly, Richard Serra, and many others. Temporary exhibitions of painting, sculpture, photography, design, and architecture. Open Tues–Sun.

☼🔔⚱ **Museum of Art,** Plaza de Panama, Balboa Park (232-7931): A vast panorama of the history of art—European, American, and Far Eastern—in a typical Spanish Colonial building. From Rembrandt and Rubens to Salvador Dalí and the richly wrought frescoes of Mexican artist Diego Rivera. Among the most famous works on display: Zurbarán's *Agnus Dei,* Canaletto's *View of the Mole at Venice,* Frans Hals's *Portrait of Isaac Massa,* and *Still Life* by Juan Sanchez-Cotán. One of the best art museums on the West Coast; open Tues–Sun.

🔔 **Museum of Photographic Arts,** Casa de Balboa, Balboa Park (239-5262): Display of photographs old and new by photographers foreign and American; a must for shutterbugs. Open daily.

☼🔔⚱ **Timken Art Gallery,** Plaza de Panama, Balboa Park (239-5548): In a building which is not among the great successes of modern architecture you'll find a fine collection of Russian icons, 19th-century American painting, and European masters—Brueghel, Rembrandt, Cézanne, and others. Among the best-known paintings here: *Death of the Virgin* by Petrus Christus, *The Parable of the Sower* by Brueghel the Elder, El Greco's *The Penitent St. Peter,* Martin Heade's *Magnolia Grandiflora,* and John Singleton Copley's portrait of *Mrs. Thomas Gage.* Open Tues–Sun; closed the month of Sept. A must-see.

MUSEUMS OF SCIENCE & HISTORY: ⚱ **Aerospace Museum,** 2001 Pan American Plaza, Balboa Park (234-8291): History of aviation and space flight from 1880 to the present day. Many models of old aircraft and gliders; also a life-size replica of Lindbergh's legendary *The Spirit of St. Louis,* the original of

N

Torrey Pines
University City

Miramar College

Miramar
15

163

Univ. of California, San Diego
La Jolla Bay

ESCONDIDO FRWY.

CABRILLO FRWY.

5

La Jolla

52

Clairemont

INLAND FRWY.

San Diego River

Santee

805

Pacific Beach

SAN DIEGO FRWY.

San Diego Stadium

ALVARADO FRWY.

125

Mission Beach

Mission Bay

OCEAN BEACH FRWY.

CAMINO DEL RIO

Mission San Diego

La Mesa

B.R. 8

Old Town

163

San Diego Int'l Airport

Balboa Park Zoo

HELIX FRWY.

Lemon Grove

Point Loma

209

La Presa

California Western Univ.

Coronado

Coronado Bridge

Encanto

Cabrillo Nat'l Monument

75

San Diego Bay

National City

Bonita

SILVER STRAND HWY.

Southwestern College

Chula Vista

PACIFIC OCEAN

Palm City

MONTGOMERY FRWY.

Imperial Beach

San Ysidro

UNITED STATES

MEXICO

Tijuana Int'l Airport

kms. 0 — 8
miles 0 — 5

SAN DIEGO AND ENVIRONS

which was built in San Diego in 1927, and a space capsule. Hall devoted to the heroes and heroines of the story of aeronautics. Well-stocked aviation library. Open daily.

Mormon Battalion Memorial, 2510 Juan St. (298-3317): Military museum dedicated to the memory of 500 soldiers of a Mormon battalion which, during the Mexican War of 1846–47, made the longest march in the history of the U.S. Army: more than 2,000 miles from Illinois to San Diego. Only 350 of them reached their goal. Also an exhibition on the history of the Mormons. Open daily.

Museum of Man, 1350 El Prado, Balboa Park (239-2001): Superb natural-history museum in an elegant Spanish Colonial building, one of whose notable possessions is the skeleton of Del Mar Man, the oldest humanoid ever found in the U.S. (about 48,000 years old). Giant model of the human body. Fine collection of Hopi and Mayan art. Open daily.

Natural History Museum, 1788 El Prado, Balboa Park (232-3821): Fauna and flora of southern California; the whale skulls are impressive. A seismograph registers all earth tremors, no matter how slight. Open daily.

Reuben H. Fleet Space Theater, 1875 El Prado, Balboa Park (238-1168): The largest planetarium in the U.S., with a wholly remarkable audiovisual program. Giant OMNIMAX hemispheric screen for 70mm projection. Exhibitions on space technology. Hands-on science center. A must for amateur astronomers; open daily.

Scripps Aquarium-Museum, 8602 La Jolla Shores Dr., La Jolla (534-6933): On the campus of the University of California at San Diego, this handsome museum of oceanography, one of the best known in the country, displays a comprehensive selection of Californian and Mexican marine life. Beach open to the public, with picnic areas. Open daily.

Serra Museum, 2727 Presidio Dr., Presidio Park (297-3258): The history of California and its missions, with a valuable antiquarian library, in a charming Spanish Colonial–style building dedicated to the Franciscan missionary Junípero Serra and built on the site of the first Presidio erected by the Spaniards in 1769. Fine view of Mission Bay. Open Tues–Sun.

Star of India, 1492 N. Harbor Dr., Embarcadero (234-9153): Launched in Britain in 1863 and taken out of service in 1923, this is one of the last great 19th-century sailing ships still afloat. She sailed around the world 21 times. Belongs to the Maritime Museum. Open daily.

PANORAMAS: **Cabrillo National Monument,** Cabrillo Memorial Dr. at Point Loma, 10 mi. (16km) west on Calif. 209 (557-5450): On a promontory overlooking San Diego Bay, the lighthouse and adjoining monument command an unequalled view of the Pacific Ocean to the west, La Jolla to the north, Mexico to the south, and the city to the east. Dec–Feb you can watch from here the migration of the gray whales offshore in the bay. A sight not to be missed. Open daily. The monument closes at sunset.

PARKS & GARDENS: **Balboa Park,** reached by way of El Prado or Park Blvd. (239-0512): This superb 1,158-acre (468ha) tropical park of woods, lawns, and lakes in the heart of San Diego shelters half a dozen museums (see above); a world-famous zoo (see below); the **Spreckels Outdoor Organ,** world's largest open-air organ, with 5,000 pipes; and the **Old Globe Theatre,** a replica of William Shakespeare's theater in London, home to the very popular National Shakespeare Festival (see "Special Events," below); two golf courses; a well-known botanical garden; etc. It was the site of the Panama-California International Exposition in 1915.

Mission Bay Aquatic Park, West Mission Bay Dr., Sea World Dr., and E. Mission Bay Dr.: 4,600 acres (1,860ha) of parkland around the great body of water that is Mission Bay; fishing, waterskiing, surfing, beaches, etc. Beautiful scenery. The famous **Sea World** marine zoo is here. Visitor center at 2688 E. Mission Bay Dr. (276-8200).

🔔 **Presidio Park,** Presidio Dr.: This wooded hill overlooking the **Serra Museum** (see above) marks the original site of the first Spanish fortifications, built in 1769 (the Presidio). Pretty view of Mission Bay.

PERFORMING ARTS: For daily listings of all shows and cultural events, consult the entertainment pages of the daily papers *Evening Tribune* (evening) and *San Diego Union* (morning), as well as the weekly *Del Mar News-Press* and free San Diego *Reader,* and the monthly *San Diego* magazine.

Arts Tix, a kiosk in Horton Plaza, 121 Broadway at First Ave. (238-3810), sells tickets for all shows at reduced prices on the day of performance. Cash only; open Tues–Sat.

California Theatre, 1122 Fourth Ave. (233-0392): Theater tours, Broadway hits.

Cassius Carter Centre Stage, Balboa Park (239-2255): Drama, musicals, modern theater (Sept–May); adjoins the Old Globe Theatre.

Civic Theatre, 202 C St. (236-6510): Home of the San Diego Opera, Ian Campbell, director; also of the California Ballet Company.

Gaslamp Quarter Theatre, 547 47th Ave. (234-9583): Contemporary theater.

Golden Hall, 202 C St. (236-6500): Rock concerts, shows by top performers. With the Civic Theatre, part of the huge San Diego Convention and Performing Arts Center.

La Jolla Playhouse, on the UCSD Campus, 2910 La Jolla Village Dr. and Torrey Pines Rd., La Jolla (9534-3960): Classical and contemporary plays; musicals.

Lyceum Theatre, 79 Horton Plaza (235-8025): Home of the San Diego Repertory Theatre; drama, comedy.

Marquis Public Theater, 3717 India St. (295-5654): Traditional, contemporary, and experimental theater.

Old Globe Theatre, Balboa Park (239-2255): Replica of Shakespeare's Globe Playhouse in London; destroyed by fire in 1978, it was rebuilt by public subscription. Every summer the National Shakespeare Festival is held here.

Symphony Hall (Fox Theater), 1245 Seventh Ave. (699-4205): Classical concerts and recitals; home of the San Diego Symphony under principal conductor Yoav Talmi.

Theatre in Old Town, 4040 Twiggs (298-0082): Contemporary theater; musicals.

SHOPPING: **Bazaar del Mundo,** Juan St., Old Town (296-3161): Picturesque Mexican-style market with restaurants and shops selling clothing, gifts, jewelry, etc. Very aesthetically pleasing decor even through the touristy atmosphere. Open daily.

☀ **Horton Plaza,** bounded by First Ave., Fourth Ave., Broadway, and G St. (239-8180): The country's most spectacular shopping center, in the downtown Gaslamp district. Rather disconcerting postmodern architecture, embellished with original sculpture and galleries at several levels. Four department stores, more than 150 stores, restaurants, movie houses. Definitely deserves a visit. Open daily.

La Jolla, around Girard Ave. and Prospect St.: The two shopping streets of this elegant beach resort. Fashionable shops, chic stores, and art galleries. The luxury shopping center at **Coast Walk,** 1298 Prospect St. (454-3031), designed by architect Robert A. M. Stern, is one of the handsomest in the U.S.—with prices to match.

Seaport Village, Pacific Hwy. and W. Harbor Dr. (235-4013): Unusual shopping center on the ocean, which reconstructs the atmosphere of a 19th-century Victorian village in California: 15 restaurants; 70 stores, shops, and art galleries. Wonderful turn-of-the-century-style carousel. Open daily.

Tijuana: See "Nearby Excursions," below.

SPECIAL EVENTS: For the exact schedule of events below, consult the **San Diego Convention and Visitors Bureau** (see "Tourist Information," above).

New Year's Day Yacht Regatta (Jan 1): Sailboat race in San Diego Bay.

Andy Williams Open (early Feb): Golf tournament at Torrey Pines Golf Course in La Jolla.

Fiesta de la Primavera (4 days in mid-May): Mariachi concerts, art shows, banjo competition, buffalo barbecue. In Old Town.

Corpus Christi Fiesta (late May to early June), at the Mission San Antonio de Pala, 50 mi. (80km) north via I-15 and Calif. 76: Open-air mass, folk dancing. A typical Spanish fiesta celebrated every year since 1816; colorful.

Del Mar Fair (late June to early July): Flower and horse show on the Del Mar Fairgrounds, 9 mi. (14km) north; very popular locally.

National Shakespeare Festival (mid-June to mid-Sept): Shakespeare plays in series throughout the summer, at the Old Globe Theatre, Balboa Park. A very well-attended festival.

Festival of the Bells (wknd in mid-July): Festival of bells commemorating the foundation of the Mission of San Diego de Alcala on July 17, 1769.

Admission Day (early Sept): Commemorates California's admission to the Union in 1850. Mariachi concerts, folk dancing, food festival.

Cabrillo Festival (late Sept): Celebrates the discovery of California. Dancing, folklore displays, parades; very lively.

Mother Goose Parade (Nov): Amusing parade with costumes based on the Mother Goose tales, at El Cajon, 6 mi. (10km) NE.

Christmas–Light Boat Parade (third Sun in Dec): Procession of illuminated boats in Shelter Yacht Basin, San Diego Harbor.

SPORTS: San Diego has two professional teams:

Baseball (Apr–Oct): Padres, Jack Murphy Stadium (283-4494).

Football (Aug–Dec): Chargers, Jack Murphy Stadium (280-2121).

Horse Racing

Del Mar Racetrack, County Fairgrounds (755-1161). Thoroughbred racing Wed–Mon late July to mid-Sept.

Deep-Sea Fishing

Every year tens of thousands of rod-and-reel enthusiasts go deep-sea fishing in the waters of southern California, to the Mexican border and beyond: their destined prey include barracuda, sea bass, yellowtail, bonito, and blue marlin. The charter rates for a fully equipped deep-sea-fishing boat are about $400 for a half day of 6 hr. and $500 for a full day of 10 hr. Some recommended charterers: **Fisherman's Landing,** 2838 Garrison St. (221-8500); **H. & M. Landing,** 2803 Emerson St. (222-1144); **Lee Palm Sportfishing,** 2801 Emerson St. (224-3857); and **Point Loma Sportfishing,** 1403 Scott St. (223-1627).

STROLLS: ☼⚓ **Embarcadero,** Harbor Dr. between Market St. and Grape St.: San Diego's fishing and commercial harbor; fine view of bay and shipping. The World War II vessels of the U.S. Navy moored at Broadway Pier may be visited Sat–Sun 1–4pm; for information, call 235-3534.

⚓ **Gaslamp Quarter,** Fifth Ave. between Broadway and Market St.: The 16-block historic district downtown. A lot of work has gone into restoring the old buildings, many of which date to the 1880s. The Gaslamp Quarter Foundation, 410 Island Ave. (233-5227), offers guided tours of the historic buildings and neighborhoods every Sat.

    🏦 **Harbor and Shelter Islands,** reached via North Harbor Dr. and Rosecrans St.: Two big artificial islands built at the north of the bay on millions of tons of material dredged from the bay itself. A wonderful place for fishing, or loafing, surrounded by marinas, yachts, restaurants, and luxury hotels.

    ☀️👓🏦 **Old Town,** around Wallace St., Congress St., and Juan St.: The historic heart of San Diego, with many shops, restaurants, old houses (see "Historic Buildings," above). Lively and colorful.

    ☀️👓🏦 **Scenic Drive:** A 52-mi. (84km) loop posted with signs in the form of a blue-and-yellow seagull. In about 3 hr. driving you'll see most of the tourist attractions described above: the Embarcadero, Shelter Island, Cabrillo National Monument, Old Town, Balboa Park, etc. The drive begins at Broadway Pier.

THEME PARKS: ☀️👓🏦 **Sea World,** 1720 S. Shores Rd., Mission Bay Park (226-3901): In a 135-acre (55ha) parkland setting, this huge marine-life theme park boasts more than 5,500 sea creatures, including seals, sea elephants, dolphins, and three killer whales. Giant 26,400-gal. (100,000-liter) aquarium just for the sharks. Japanese fishing village; Skytower, a 321-ft. (98m) observation tower. A must-see for visitors since 1964; open daily.

    ☀️👓🏦 **Wild Animal Park,** 15500 San Pasqual Valley Rd., Escondido (480-0100), 30 mi. (48km) NE via I-15 and Calif. 78: A 1,800-acre (730ha) wildlife park with more than 2,200 free-ranging animals: lions, zebras, giraffes, rhinoceroses, etc. African village. One of the finest safari zoos in the U.S.; you see it by monorail. Not to be missed. Open daily.

ZOOS: ☀️👓🏦 **San Diego Zoo,** Zoo Dr., Balboa Park (234-3153): The richest and most beautiful zoo in the U.S., visited each year by almost four million people, with more than 3,500 wild animals and 3,000 exotic birds drawn from 800 animal species, in 100 acres (40ha) of superb undulating tropical gardens with luxuriant vegetation. Among the rarest creatures are Australian koala bears, Komodo dragons (giant lizards from Indonesia), and the only New Zealand kiwis acclimatized to life in the U.S. Your visit can be made by bus, on a moving sidewalk, or by the Skyfari cable car. Not to be missed; open daily.

ACCOMMODATIONS

    A Note on Accommodations: Room rates in San Diego are coded as follows: **VE,** Very Expensive ($140 and up); **E,** Expensive ($90–$140); **M,** Moderate ($60–$90); **I,** Inexpensive ($30–$60); **B,** Budget (up to $30). A listing of toll free numbers is in the Appendix.

Personal Favorites (in order of preference)

    🏨🏨🏨🏨 **Marriott Hotel & Marina** (formerly the Inter-Continental; dwntwn), 333 W. Harbor Dr., CA 92101 (619/234-1500; toll free, see Marriott). 1,355 rms, A/C, color TV, in-rm movies. AE, CB, DC, MC, V. Valet parking $8, two pools, four tennis courts, health club, sauna, water sports, private marina w. 450 berths, four rests. (including the Marina Sea Grill), three bars, 24-hr. rm svce, nightclub, hrdrsr, boutiques, concierge, free crib. *Note:* San Diego's most spectacular hotel, two splendid modern towers w. mirrored elliptical facades, whose 26 stories overlook Seaport Village and the bay. Ultracomfortable rms w. private balconies and minibars; very complete facilities; very good svce. Lobby richly adorned w. Oriental ceramics and works of art; interior patios embellished w. grdns and waterfalls. Business and group clientele; adjacent 6,000-seat convention hall. **E–VE**

    ☀️🏨🏨🏨 **U. S. Grant** (dwntwn), 326 Broadway, CA 92101 (619/232-3121; toll free, see Preferred). 280 rms, A/C, color TV, in-rm movies. AE, CB, DC, MC, V. Valet gar. $10, health club, two rests. (including the Grant Grill), bar, 24-hr. rm svce, nightclub, concierge, crib $15. *Note:* Built around 1910 by Ulysses S. Grant, Jr., son of the 18th president of the U.S., this luxurious grand hotel has been sumptuously restored to its original elegance. Works of art, antique furniture, marble floors, and crystal chandeliers adorn the lobby and public rms. Rms are huge, agreeably furnished in Queen Anne style w. travertine bathrooms. Excellent business rest.; ultra-polished svce; intimacy and distinction. In the heart of dwntwn across from the Horton Plaza Mall. Upscale business clientele. A designated historic monument, reopened in Dec 1985. **VE**

☼ ᒪᒪᒪ **Humphrey's Half Moon Inn** (nr. dwntwn), 2303 Shelter Island Dr., CA 92106 (619/224-3411; toll free 800/345-9995). 141 rms, A/C, color TV, in-rm movies. AE, CB, DC, MC, V. Free parking, pool, bicycling, putting green, boating, marina, rest. (Humphrey's), bar, rm svce, nightclub, free crib. *Note:* A charming little hotel in a beautiful grdn, looking out over glorious San Diego Bay. Pretty South Seas decor; comfortable rms w. balconies and views over the bay or the marina (some w. refrigerators and kitchenettes); friendly reception and svce. Agreeable rest.; free airport limo. Good value; an excellent place to stay. **E**

ᒪᒪᒪ **Town and Country Hotel** (nr. dwntwn), 500 Hotel Circle N., CA 92108 (619/291-7131; toll free 800/854-2608). 960 rms, A/C, color TV, in-rm movies. AE, CB, DC, MC, V. Free parking, three pools, health club, two rests. (including Le Pavillon), two coffee shops, five bars, rm svce, disco, hrdrsr, boutiques, free crib. *Note:* Big convention hotel in 32 acres (12ha) of nicely landscaped grdns, in Mission Valley, 10 min. from dwntwn and the same from the airport. Its dimensions make it a favorite of groups and conventioneers. Huge rms and very comfortable facilities; efficient svce; good value. **M–E**

ᒪᒪᒪ **Catamaran Resort** (nr. dwntwn), 3999 Mission Blvd., Pacific Beach, CA 92109 (619/488-1081; toll free, see Loews). 315 rms, A/C, cable color TV. AE, CB, DC, MC, V. Free parking, pool, health club, sauna, boating, beach, rest., bar, rm svce, disco, crib $15. *Note:* Luxury convention hotel on the ocean. Elegant Polynesian decor; spectacular lobby w. tropical grdns and waterfalls. Supremely comfortable rms w. balcony overlooking Mission Bay or the Pacific, most w. refrigerator. Efficient, considerate svce. Group/convention clientele. 20 min. from dwntwn. A very fine place to stay. Recently completed a $25-million renovation. **E–VE**

ᒪᒪ **Seapoint Hotel** (nr. dwntwn), 4875 N. Harbor Dr., CA 92106 (619/224-3621; toll free 800/345-9995). 244 rms, A/C, color TV, in-rm movies. AE, CB, DC, MC, V. Free parking, pool, health club, sauna, coffee shop, rm svce, free crib. *Note:* Large, modern, comfortable hotel across from San Diego's municipal sportfishing pier. Spacious, inviting rms looking out over the bay or marina, some w. private balcony or patio and refrigerator. Efficient, amiable svce. 5 min. from the airport (free shuttle); 10 min. from dwntwn. Good value on balance. **M–E**, but lower rates off-season.

ᒪ **Sands of La Jolla** (vic.), 5417 La Jolla Blvd., La Jolla, CA 92037 (619/459-3336). 38 rms, cable color TV. AE, CB, DC, MC, V. Free parking, pool, rm svce, free breakfast. *Note:* Small, inviting motel a stone's throw from the beach, 5 min. from La Jolla's shopping district, and 25 min. from dwntwn San Diego. Comfortable rms w. refrigerators (some w. balconies and views over the ocean). Friendly reception and svce. Good value off-season. Interesting holiday packages. **M,** but lower rates off-season.

ᒪ **Friendship Inn Town House Lodge** (nr. dwntwn), 810 Ash St., CA 92101 (619/233-8826; toll free, see Friendship Inns). 55 rms, A/C, color TV. AE, CB, DC, MC, V. Free parking, pool, 24-hr. coffee shop. *Note:* Modest but very well run motel very nr. dwntwn, a stone's throw from Balboa Park and the business district. Serviceable, completely renovated rms; free coffee in rms; good value. **I**

Other Accommodations (from top bracket to budget)

ᒪᒪᒪᒪ **The Westgate** (dwntwn), 1055 Second Ave., CA 92101 (619/238-1818; toll free 800/453-9450). 223 rms, A/C, color TV, in-rm movies. AE, CB, DC, MC, V. Valet gar. $9, two rests. (including the Fontainebleau Rm), bar, rm svce, nightclub, boutiques, concierge, free crib. *Note:* The refined luxury of a great European hotel, w. an authentic Velázquez presiding over the lobby, but lackluster modern architecture. Spacious rms, elegantly decorated in Louis XV or English Regency style, with Italian marble bathrooms and minibars. Ultra-polished svce; excellent grand-hotel rest. One of the best hotels on the West Coast, very centrally located; free airport limo. A favorite of those in-the-know. **E–VE**

Hyatt Regency La Jolla (vic.), 3777 La Jolla Village Dr., La Jolla, CA 92122 (619/552-1234; toll free, see Hyatt). 432 rms, A/C, color TV, in-rm movies. AE, CB, DC, MC, V. Valet gar. $8, pool, health club, tennis court, three rests. (including Barcino), two bars, 24-hr. rm svce, nightclub, concierge, crib available. *Note:* A newcomer on the local luxury-hotel scene. The spectacular neo-modernist structure by Michael Graves is worth seeing for its own sake. Spacious, extremely comfortable rms w. minibar. Flawless svce. Two VIP floors. Direct access to the ultramodern Aventine complex of rests., boutiques, and stores. Convention and business clientele. **E–VE**

Hotel del Coronado (nr. dwntwn), 1500 Orange Ave., Coronado, CA 92118 (619/435-6611; toll free 800/356-8392). 689 rms (half w. A/C), cable color TV. AE, CB, DC, MC, V. Valet parking $9, two pools, health club, sauna, six tennis courts, private beach, boating, bicycling, two rests. (including the Prince of Wales), 24-hr. coffee shop, bars, 24-hr. rm svce, disco, hrdrsr, boutiques, concierge, free crib. *Note:* The Victorian grande dame of local hotels, a 5-min. drive from dwntwn by the San Diego Coronado Bay Bridge; almost every president of the U.S. in the past century, as well as many visiting VIPs, has stayed here. Built in 1888, this was the first hotel in the world to be equipped w. electricity and elevators. Elegant period atmosphere. Direct beach access. Relatively spacious rms w. refrigerators and private patios or balconies, the best w. ocean view. Some shortcomings in comfort and facilities; polished svce; lovely grdns. Part of the movie *Some Like It Hot* was made here. If you cultivate golden moments from the past, this is for you. **E–VE**

Horton Grand Hotel (dwntwn), 311 Island Ave., CA 92101 (619/544-1886; toll free 800/533-4667). 110 rms, A/C, cable color TV. AE, CB, DC, MC, V. Valet parking $6, rest. (Ida Bailey rest.), bar, rm svce, nightclub, concierge, free crib. *Note:* Charming 19th-century hotel which has retained its Victorian elegance, centrally located in the heart of the Gaslamp district. Superb carved exterior; interior decoration and fittings opulently renovated; impressive grand staircase and picturesque skylight in the lobby. Spacious rms w. fireplaces, some w. balconies and period furniture. Very agreeable Tea Rm. Intimate atmosphere; faultless svce. Upscale business clientele; free airport limo. **E–VE**

Best Western Shelter Island Marina Inn (nr. dwntwn), 2051 Shelter Island Dr., CA 92106 (619/222-0561; toll free, see Best Western). 97 rms, A/C, color TV, in-rm movies. AE, CB, DC, MC, V. Free parking, pool, marina, boating, rest., bar, rm svce, nightclub, free airport limo, free breakfast, free crib. *Note:* Modern, comfortable motel w. magnificent views of the bay and yacht basin. Spacious rms w. view, some w. patios. Pleasant tropical decor. Good reception. Moorings available for boats. Good overall value. **M–E**

Clarion Balboa Park (formerly the Lafayette; nr. dwntwn), 2223 El Cajon Blvd., CA 92104 (619/296-2101; toll free, see Clarion). 142 rms, A/C, color TV, in-rm movies. AE, CB, DC, MC, V. Free gar., pool, rest., bar, rm svce, concierge, free airport shuttle, free breakfast, free crib. *Note:* Quiet, elegant '30s hotel a long way from the dwntwn frenzy. Agreeably restored colonial architecture w. impressive colonnade, and Greek Revival pediment. Comfortable, inviting rms, some w. fireplace and private balcony. Highly professional svce. 5 min. from Balboa Park, 10 min. from dwntwn. Very good overall value. **M–E**

🍴🍴 **Stardust Handlery Hotel and Country Club** (nr. dwntwn),
🛏🛏 950 Hotel Circle N., CA 92108 (619/298-0511; toll free
800/223-0888). 216 rms, A/C, color TV, in-rm movies. AE, CB, DC, MC, V.
Free parking, pool, eight tennis courts, two golf courses, health club, putting
green, 24-hr. rest. (Crane Rm), 24-hr. coffee shop, bars, rm svce, nightclub,
hrdrsr, free crib. *Note:* Comfortable, inviting motel 15 min. from dwntwn. Surrounded by pretty grdns. Spacious rms, some w. private balconies or patios.
Comprehensive sports facilities. Cheerful svce. Group and convention clientele.
Good value off-season. **M–E**, but lower rates off-season.

🍴 **7 + 1 Motel** (dwntwn), 1919 Pacific Hwy., CA 92101 (619/
🛏 232-1077; toll free 800/822-2820). 67 rms, A/C, color TV,
in-rm movies. AE, CB, DC, MC, V. Free parking, pool, adj. coffee shop. *Note:*
Congenial, very well run motel well located nr. the Embarcadero. Comfortable
rms w. refrigerators, some w. balconies. Friendly reception and svce; free coffee
in rms. Totally renovated. **I–M**, but lower rates off-season.

🍴 **Travelodge Mission Bay** (nr. dwntwn), 4610 De Soto St., CA
🛏 42109 (619/483-9800; toll free, see Travelodge). 85 rms,
A/C, color TV, in-rm movies. AE, CB, DC, MC, V. Free parking, pool, coffee
shop and bar nearby. Breakfast served daily. *Note:* Very new small motel next to
the Mission Bay golf course. Comfortable, serviceable rms, some w. view.
Friendly reception; efficient svce. 15 min. from dwntwn on I-5. Ideal if you're
driving. **I**

🍴 **Motel 6** (nr. dwntwn), 2424 Hotel Circle N., CA 92108
🛏 (619/296-1612). 92 rms, A/C, color TV, free in-rm movies.
AE, DC, MC, V. Free parking, pool, adj. rest. *Note:* Unbeatable value a stone's
throw from Mission Bay Park and Old Town. Serviceably comfortable. 8 min.
from the airport, 10 min. from dwntwn. **I**

Accommodations in the Vicinity

☀🍴🍴🍴 **Rancho Bernardo Inn** (vic.), 17550 Bernardo Oaks Dr., Ran-
🛏🛏🛏 cho Bernardo, CA 92128 (619/487-1611; toll free 800/854-
1065). 287 rms, A/C, color TV, in-rm movies. AE, CB, DC, MC, V. Free parking, two pools, health club, sauna, massage, two golf courses, 12 tennis courts,
putting green, horseback riding, bicycling, two rests. (including El Bizcocho),
bars, 24-hr. rm svce, disco, hrdrsr, drugstore, concierge. *Note:* Luxurious sports-
lover's paradise w. two golf courses and 12 tennis courts, nr. Wild Animal Park
and 30 min. from dwntwn. Charming Spanish Mission decor; spacious, elegant
rms w. balconies or private patios. Lovely grdns; excellent svce; young, upscale
crowd. Well-known tennis school; interesting golf and tennis packages. The ideal
vacation hotel. **VE**

Airport Accommodations

🍴🍴🍴 **Sheraton Harbor Island** (nr. dwntwn), 1380 Harbor Island
🛏🛏🛏 Dr., CA 92101 (619/291-2900; toll free, see Sheraton). 712
rms, A/C, color TV, in-rm movies. AE, CB, DC, MC, V. Valet parking $6, two
pools, health club, sauna, four tennis courts, marina, boating, two rests. (including Merlano's), two bars, 24-hr. rm svce, nightclub, boutiques, concierge, free
crib. *Note:* Large, luxurious, modern airport hotel w. very comprehensive facilities. Comfortable rms w. balconies, the best overlooking the bay or the marina.
Efficient svce. VIP suites on the top three floors; beautiful grdns. Business clientele; 2 min. from the airport (free limo). One of the best places to stay in San
Diego. **E–VE**

🍴 **Travelodge Airport** (nr. dwntwn), 2353 Pacific Hwy., CA
🛏 92101 (619/232-8931; toll free, see Travelodge). 74 rms,
A/C, cable color TV. AE, CB, DC, MC, V. Free parking, pool and rest. nearby,
free breakfast. *Note:* Conventional but well-run small motel 3 min. from the airport (free shuttle) and 5 min. from dwntwn. Functional comfort; friendly svce.
Very good value. **I**

YMCA/Youth Hostels
Point Loma Hostel (nr. dwntwn), 3790 Udall St., CA 92107 (619/223-4778). 80 beds. Youth hostel near Mission Bay Park.
YMCA (dwntwn), 500 W. Broadway, CA 92101 (619/232-1133). 265 rms. Pool, health club, rest. Men and women; also youth-hostel members. Very central.

RESTAURANTS

A Note on Restaurant Prices: San Diego restaurant prices, per person, excluding drinks and service charges, are coded as follows: **VE,** Very Expensive ($60 and up); **E,** Expensive ($40–$60); **M,** Moderate ($25–$40); **I,** Inexpensive ($15–$25); **B,** Budget (up to $15).

Personal Favorites (in order of preference)

Mille Fleurs (vic.), 6009 Paseo Delicias (Country Sq. Courtyard), Rancho Santa Fe (756-3085). A/C. Lunch Mon–Fri, dinner daily; closed Thanksgiving, Dec 25. AE, CB, DC, MC, V. Jkt. *Specialties:* mixed salads, salmon in honey-mustard sauce, fresh homemade foie gras w. redcabbage salad in sherry vinaigrette, rack of Sonoma baby lamb w. garden vegetables, filet of turbot encrusted w. fresh herbs, rib-eye steak of Angus beef w. Roquefort-and-tarragon sauce, veal chop w. morel mushrooms, excellent desserts (try the Bavarian cream w. chocolate mousse). Menu changes regularly. Large wine list. *Note:* Chef Martin Woesle, a creator of outstanding sauces, was trained at Munich's famous L'Aubergine French rest., which boasts three stars in Michelin. French-inspired nouvelle cuisine, imaginative and light-handed. Charming, cool Hispano-Moorish decor w. old mosaics, and pretty patio—as romantic a setting as anyone could wish. Resv. a must. 25 min. from dwntwn. One of the finest rests. in the country. *French.* **E–VE**

Anthony's Star of the Sea Room (dwntwn), 1360 Harbor Dr. (232-7408). A/C. Dinner only, nightly; closed hols. AE, MC, V. J&T. *Specialties:* clams genovese, broiled filet of swordfish, sole à l'Admiral, abalone gourmet, salmon in pastry shell, shellfish, strawberries San Diego. Good wine list at high prices. *Note:* One of the best seafood rests. in the country. Enormous choice of absolutely fresh seafood, perfectly cooked. The Ghio family, which directs this luxury establishment, has its own fishing fleet. Fine view of harbor and bay through huge picture windows. Flawless svce; upscale business clientele. Valet parking. *Seafood.* **E**

Marius (nr. dwntwn), in the Meridien Hotel, 2000 2nd St., Coronado (435-3000). A/C. Dinner only, Tues–Sun. AE, CB, DC, MC, V. J&T. *Specialties:* lobster consommé, scallop mousse w. horseradish, salmon w. wild mushrooms and champagne sauce, fresh goose liver w. pepper sauce and poached pears, sautéed fresh tuna w. tapenade, lamb medallions w. thyme sauce and tian provençal, white-chocolate and dark-chocolate mousse. Opulent wine list. *Note:* The palace rest. in all its majesty. The Provençal-inspired cooking contrives to be sophisticated and simple at once. Sober, elegant decor w. wonderful flower arrangements adding a touch of color. Attentive svce in the French manner. Resv. highly advisable. 15 min. from dwntwn; valet parking. A favorite place w. those in-the-know. *French.* **E**

Dobson's (dwntwn), 956 Broadway Circle (231-6771). A/C. Lunch Mon–Fri, dinner Mon–Sat. AE, MC, V. Jkt. *Specialties:* mussel bisque, oysters w. white butter and caviar, rack of lamb in bordelaise sauce, broiled salmon w. three kinds of peppercorns, sautéed scallops provençal, medaillon of veal w. morel mushrooms, gâteau St. Honoré. *Note:* Historic old pub, now a hangout for politicians, yuppies, and local businesspeople, particularly at lunch. Nice turn-of-the-century decor agreeably restored. Ask for a table upstairs w. a view of the bar. Usually a lively place; very good food in the heart of dwntwn. Resv. a must. *Continental.* **I–M**

 Nino's (nr. dwntwn), 4501 Mission Bay Dr. (284-9266). A/C. Lunch Tues–Fri, dinner Tues–Sat; closed hols. AE, MC, V. Jkt. *Specialties:* fresh homemade pasta, sautéed scampi, fried eggplant and zucchini, veal marsala or Florentine, catch of the day. Good desserts. *Note:* Charming Italian rest.; discreet, romantic atmosphere and authentic northern Italian food. Good svce; locally popular—and not large, so resv. essential. 10 min. from dwntwn. *Italian.* **I–M**

 Casa de Bandini (nr. dwntwn), 2574 Calhoun St., Old Town (297-8211). A/C. Lunch/dinner daily; closed hols. AE, CB, DC, MC, V. *Specialties:* crabmeat enchiladas, chimichangas, burritos, fish Veracruz style. Giant margaritas. *Note:* Surrounded by grdns, flowers, and fountains, and adjoining Old Town State Historic Park, this enchanting house built in 1829 by a rich Mexican businessman, Juan Bandini, belongs in a museum of Spanish Colonial architecture. The food draws on traditional Mexican and California recipes; the fish is unusually good. Svce and atmosphere as colorful as the setting; mariachi bands. A must for every visitor. Reserve ahead. *Mexican.* **B–I**

 Point Loma Seafoods (nr. dwntwn), 2805 Emerson St. (223-1109). A/C. Lunch/dinner daily (till 8pm); closed hols. No credit cards. *Specialties:* crabmeat sandwiches, seafood salad, fish taquitos, fried shellfish, broiled or hickory-smoked fish. Wine and beer but no hard liquor. *Note:* Local seafood-lovers have been coming here for more than 30 years. Point Loma Seafoods, both fishmarket and café, lays claim to "the freshest fish in town"—and you can see them being offloaded from the nearby boats! Inviting patio overlooking harbor and bay. Relaxed setting and svce. No resv.; excellent value. *Seafood.* **B**

Other Restaurants (from top bracket to budget)

 Le Fontainebleau (dwntwn), in the Westgate (see "Accommodations," above) (238-1818). A/C. Lunch Mon–Fri, dinner nightly, brunch Sun. AE, CB, DC, MC, V. J&T. *Specialties:* rack of lamb, steak Diane, médaillons of veal Vieux Carré, flaming desserts. Large wine list. *Note:* The lavish Louis XV setting and the tuxedo-clad, white-gloved svce combine to make this the most elegant, and formal, rest. in San Diego. Classic and sophisticated grand-hotel food; background music of distinction. The upscale business favorite, especially at lunch; resv. a must. *French/Continental.* **M–E**

 Top O' the Cove (vic.), 1216 Prospect St., La Jolla (454-7779). A/C. Lunch/dinner daily, brunch Sun; closed hols. AE, MC, V. Jkt. *Specialties:* linguine w. baby vegetables, langosta (lobster) w. guacamole, brochette of sweetbreads, squab w. fresh-peach garnish, filet of venison w. blueberry sauce. Huge wine list w. more than 900 selections. *Note:* Chef Julius Semon's dishes are delicate and inventive; the English country-cottage setting is acceptably luxurious, the ocean view magnificent, and the crowd well-heeled, including many stars of both large and small screen. The check is also gilt-edged. Resv. required. 25 min. from dwntwn. Valet parking. *Seafood/Continental.* **M–E**

 Cindy Black's (vic.), 5721 La Jolla Blvd., La Jolla (456-6299). A/C. Dinner only, Tues–Sun. MC, V. Jkt. *Specialties:* grilled eggplant salad w. Belgian endive, shellfish soup w. sherried whipped cream, veal breast rolled w. chopped vegetables, leg of lamb w. creamed-garlic sauce, pan-fried Norwegian salmon, grilled duck w. fried ginger shreds on a bed of leeks. Limited but reasonably priced wine list. *Note:* Talented Cindy Black, who rose to fame as chef at the renowned (but now closed) Sheppard's Restaurant a few years back, has now decided to fly solo. Her new rest., opened early in 1990, has consistently drawn crowds. Attractive flower-adorned setting. Excellent svce; resv. a must. A very fine place. *American.* **M**

 Pacifica Grill (dwntwn), 1202 Kettner Blvd. (696-9226). A/C. Lunch Mon–Fri, dinner daily; closed hols. AE, CB, DC,

MC, V. *Specialties:* grilled lobster tacos, Mexican ravioli, seafood mixed grill, curried lamb empanadas w. papaya and mango salsa, canarditas (duck carnitas), jumbo sea scallops w. jalapeño cream, sautéed Hawaiian ahi w. wild mushrooms, crème brûlée. Menu changes regularly. *Note:* This elegant rest., occupying a shrewdly restored old warehouse, specializes in original and eclectic, southwestern cuisine. Excellent svce; resv. a must. Next to the Amtrak station in the heart of dwntn. Valet parking $2. *American.* **I–M**

☕🍸 **Chez Loma** (nr. dwntwn), 1132 Loma Ave., Coronado (435-0661). A/C. Lunch Tues–Fri, dinner Tues–Sun, brunch Sun. *Specialties:* shrimp provençal, snails à la niçoise, braised chicken w. madeira sauce, grilled duck w. green peppercorn sauce, scallop brochette w. saffron dressing. Uninspired desserts. *Note:* The most charming of the local French bistros, w. pleasant antique decor and congenial patio. The building, dating from 1898, is a designated historic monument. Light, tasty food; svce w. a smile. Very popular locally; resv. strongly advised. Very nr. the Del Coronado Hotel. *French.* **I–M**

☕🍸 **Papagayo** (dwntwn), Seaport Village, 861 W. Harbor Dr. (232-7581). A/C. Lunch/dinner daily. AE, CB, MC, V. Jkt. *Specialties:* shrimp fried w. coconut, brochette of seafood, sea bass Cabo San Lucas style, fish and shellfish marinated in fruit juice and grilled over a mesquite fire. Good wine list. *Note:* This engaging rest. in picturesque Seaport Village serves what could be described as "Latino seafood." Since it opened it has drawn consistent crowds. Exotic decor and pretty bay view; deft, cheerful svce. A very good place; resv. advised. *Seafood.* **I–M**

☕🍸 **Prince of Wales** (nr. dwntwn), in the Hotel del Coronado (see "Accommodations," above) (435-7240). A/C. Dinner only, Mon–Sat; closed hols. AE, CB, DC, MC, V. Jkt. *Specialties:* rack of lamb crown roast, broiled beef cuts, catch of the day. *Note:* Legend has it that it was in this grand-hotel rest. that the Prince of Wales, the future Edward VIII, first met Mrs. Simpson, the future Duchess of Windsor, for whom he later gave up his throne. The decor is very plush and—as it should be—very British. Excellent broiled foods; flawless svce; resv. a must. *Continental.* **I–M**

☕🍸 **La Gran Tapa** (dwntwn), 611 B St. (234-8272). A/C. Lunch Mon–Fri, dinner Mon–Sat; closed hols. AE, MC, V. *Specialties:* black-bean soup, spiced lamb skewers, gambas al ajillo (shrimp w. pepper and garlic), deep-fried calamari, Catalan-style snails, empanadas w. ground-beef or wild-mushroom filling, eggs baked w. artichoke hearts and chorizo sausage, so-so desserts. Good selection of sherries and Spanish wines. *Note:* You could easily believe you were in a real Madrid *tasca* when you visit this congenial bar serving tapas (hot and cold Spanish hors d'oeuvres), which has drawn crowds since it opened in 1988. Warm, inviting wood-paneled decor; diligent svce. A theater-district rest., crowded before and after the show. Same management as Dobson's (see above). Resv. advised. *Spanish.* **I**

🔆☕🍸 **Su Casa** (vic.), 6738 La Jolla Blvd., La Jolla (454-0369). A/C. Lunch/dinner daily, brunch Sun; closed Thanksgiving, Dec 25. AE, CB, DC, MC, V. Jkt. *Specialties:* crabmeat enchiladas, abalone, Mexican dishes, excellent broiled fish. *Note:* Modeled on an 18th-century hacienda, this engaging rest. offers some unusual dishes based on old local recipes. Agreeable background music. One of the best Mexican rests. on the California coast. 25 min. from dwntwn. *Mexican.* **I**

🔆☕🍸 **Tom Ham's Lighthouse** (nr. dwntwn), 2150 Harbor Island Dr. (291-9110). A/C. Lunch Mon–Fri, dinner nightly, brunch Sun; closed Dec 25. AE, CB, DC, MC, V. *Specialties:* scallops, carne asada, broiled sea bass, steak. *Note:* In a genuine 19th-century lighthouse, this popular tourist rest. has a fine view of the bay and the city. Classical marine decor; very decent if not terribly imaginative food. Good svce; resv. advised. Very good value. *Steak/Seafood.* **I**

🔆☕🍸 **Alfonso's Hideaway** (vic.), 1251 Prospect St., La Jolla (454-2232). A/C. Lunch/dinner daily. AE, MC, V. *Specialties:*

carne asada, steak ranchero, burritos, chile colorado, tacos. *Note:* With the Mexican border only 18 mi. (26km) away, the Mexican food at Alfonso's cannot but be authentic. Some sauces are very spicy, but the steak ranchero is tasty. Charming shady patio. Often crowded and noisy; an excellent, colorful place, 25 min. from dwntn. Other location: 135 Broadway, dwntn (234-7300). *Mexican.* **B–I**

    El Chalan (nr. dwntn), 1050 Garnet Ave., Pacific Beach (459-7707). A/C. Lunch/dinner daily; closed hols. AE, MC, V. *Specialties:* ceviche (marinated raw fish), papas rellenãs (potatoes stuffed w. meat), pescado Huancaína (fish w. rice), steak Chorrillana (w. garlic and tomatoes). *Note:* As distinct from San Diego's innumberable Mexican rests., El Chalan serves Peruvian food, a touch less highly seasoned but just as tasty. Friendly, congenial atmosphere; resv. advised. Pleasant open patio; guitar background music. 20 min. from dwntn. *Latin American.* **B–I**

    Corvette Diner, Bar & Grill (nr. dwntn), 3946 Fifth Ave. (542-1001). A/C. Lunch/dinner daily (until midnight); closed hols. MC, V. *Specialties:* burgers, meatloaf, chicken-fried steak, blue-plate specials, milkshakes. *Note:* Amusing 1950s-style diner complete w. old-fashioned soda fountain, assorted memorabilia, and a shiny red Corvette displayed nr. the bar. Very good mid-American diner fare. Lively (but noisy) atmosphere. Voted San Diego's favorite informal dining spot. No resv. *American.* **B–I**

    Golden Lion Tavern (dwntn), 801 Fourth Ave. (233-1131). A/C. Lunch Mon–Fri, dinner Mon–Sat. AE, MC, V. *Specialties:* sandwiches, daily specials, broiled fish; oyster bar. *Note:* Successor to the famous Golden Lion Pub, founded in 1907, this agreeably nostalgic tavern serves commendable food, especially fish. Very popular 49-ft.-long (15m) bar. Generally crowded. In dwntn San Diego. *American.* **B–I**

Cafeterias/Fast Food

Hob Nob Hill (dwntn), 2271 First Ave. (239-8176). Breakfast/lunch/dinner Sun–Fri. AE, CB, DC, MC, V. *Specialties:* superb family cooking at very considerate prices: corned beef and cabbage, turkey croquettes, ham and yams, chicken-fried steak, roast pork w. apple sauce, very good homemade desserts. *Note:* A local landmark since 1946. The service is commendable but you may have a long wait; resv. advised.

BARS AND NIGHTCLUBS

Bacchanal (vic.), 8022 Clairemont Mesa Blvd. (560-8022). Rock, disco. Locally popular. Open Wed–Sat.

Cannibal Bar (nr. dwntn), in the Catamaran Resort (see "Accommodations," above) (488-1081). Excellent live jazz and disco. Pleasant outdoor patio. Open Tues–Sat.

Chuck's Steak House (vic.), 1250 Prospect St., La Jolla (454-5325). One of the oldest local jazz clubs; top performers. Open Wed–Sun. Good rest.

Club Diego's (nr. dwntn), 860 Garnet Ave., Pacific Beach (272-1241). Fashionable rock disco with giant video screens; also a commendable Mexican rest. Open nightly.

The Comedy Store (vic.), 916 Pearl St., La Jolla (454-9176). Comedy 7 nights a week, stand-up Wed–Sat. Amateur nights Mon–Tues.

Confetti's (vic.), 5373 Mission Center Rd., Mission Valley (291-8635). Very hot nightspot. Deejays play Top-40 hits Mon–Sat; Sun nights are reserved for underground music.

Marine Room (vic.), 2000 Spindrift Dr., La Jolla (459-7222). This classy oceanfront lounge on the shore has a splendid view of the Pacific. Likable reception; ditto music. Good rest. adjoining. Open nightly.

Old Pacific Beach Café (nr. dwntn), 4287 Mission Blvd., Pacific Beach (270-7522). Fashionable rock joint with live "muscle" music. Open nightly.

Pal Joey's (nr. dwntn), 5147 Waring Rd., Allied Gardens (286-7873). A rather kitschy big dance hall, 1930s style. Live Dixieland weekends. Near San Diego State University.

Rio's (dwntwn), 4258 W. Point Loma Blvd. (225-9559). Live rock; very popular with the locals. Open nightly.

Whaling Bar (vic.), in the La Valencia Hotel in La Jolla (454-0771). Yuppie bar; also a decent rest.; well-heeled, trendy patrons. Open nightly.

NEARBY EXCURSIONS

ANZA BORREGO DESERT STATE PARK (90 mi./ 144km NE via I-8, Calif. 79, and Calif. 78): 600,000 acres (240,000ha) of largely unexplored desert wilderness adjoining the **Salton Sea,** largest lake in California, 278 ft. (85m) below sea level in the **Colorado Desert** (sailing, water sports, abundant fishing). The contrast between the lake, dotted with holidaymakers, and the nearby desert is particularly striking. Two surfaced roads cross the park from side to side. Among its most remarkable sights are **Font's Point, Borrego Palm Canyon, Split Mountain,** and **Seventeen Palms Oasis.** When the desert plants and shrubs are in flower, late Jan to Apr, they are a sight to be seen. *Note:* Temperatures run very high in summer; be sure to carry drinking water. **Visitor center** open daily year round at Borrego Springs (619/ 767-5311). On the way, visit the mining town of Julian (see below).

Where to Stay

La Casa del Zorro, Yaqui Pass and Borrego Springs Rd., Borrego Springs, CA 92004 (619/767-5323; toll free 800/ 325-8275). 77 rms. AE, CB, DC, MC, V. Luxurious 1930s oasis hotel in the middle of the desert. Three pools, adj. golf course, highly regarded rest. **E–VE**

LA JOLLA (pronounced "La Hoya"; 12 mi./19km NW via I-5, Ardath Rd., and Torrey Pines Rd.): The fashionable place for a summer home, the California equivalent of Palm Beach or Saint Tropez. Lovely beaches, luxurious oceanfront homes, trendy shops, and restaurants. You ought to visit the **Museum of Contemporary Art** with its very fine modern-art collection; and the **Scripps Aquarium-Museum,** one of the most famous museums of oceanography in the world (see "Museums of Art" and "Museums of Science and History," above). La Jolla shouldn't be missed.

MINING TOWNS: **Julian,** 64 mi. (102km) NE via I-8 and Calif. 79: This picturesque prospectors' town, which had several thousand inhabitants in 1885 and barely 1,300 today, still boasts many buildings preserved from its adventurous past, including the very fine **Julian Hotel,** where Ulysses S. signed the register when it was a stop on the Butterfield Stagecoach route. Visit the legendary **Eagle Mine,** a gold mine dating from 1870, on C St. (765-9921); open daily.

Where to Stay

Julian Hotel, Julian, CA 92036 (619/765-0201). 16 rms. No credit cards. **M–E**

Julian Lodge, 2720 C St. (Calif. 78), Julian, CA 92036 (619/ 765-1420). 23 rms. AE, MC, V. **M**

Where to Eat

Bailey Barbecue, 2307 Main St. (765-9957). Open daily. MC, V. **B**

MOUNT PALOMAR OBSERVATORY (65 mi./104km NE via I-15 and County Rd. S.6) (742-3476): One of the most famous astronomical observatories in the world; for two decades its 200-in. (508cm) telescope, with a 13-ton lens, was the largest in the world (until 1976, when the Russians surpassed it). An impressive sight. Visitors' gallery open daily; well worth the detour. The surrounding mountains are very beautiful.

TIJUANA (18 mi./28km south on I-5): Mexican border town, fake but colorful, full of pleasure spots intended for the tourist. Bullfights Sun May–Sept, dog track, horse races, casino, jai-alai Fri–Wed. Many tax-free craft shops and bazaars, including **Sara,** 635 calle Revolución; **Mercado Artesanía,** avenida Negrete and calle 1; **Dorian's Niños,** avenida Heroes and Calle 2; **Tolan,** calle Revolución 1111, opposite the jai-alai fronton; **Maxim,** 717 calle Revolución; and **Bazar Las Palomas,** calle 6 between Revolución and Madero. Open daily.

Calle Revolución, near the main border-crossing point with the United States, is still dotted with noisy honky-tonks, cabarets, tattoo parlors, and strip joints catering, as in decades past, to young American men looking for female company.

Note: Foreign drivers must obtain temporary Mexican insurance, for sale at the border. Tourists may be unpleasantly surprised by Tijuana cab fares (see Tijuana Trolley under "Guided Tours," above). No visa is necessary for U.S. citizens visiting Mexico for less than 72 hr., or not traveling more than 75 mi. (120km) from the border. Tourists of other nationalities should consult the Mexican Consulate in San Diego, 1333 Front St. (231-8414).

Where to Eat

Pedrin's, calle 7 at Revolución (85-40-62). Lunch/dinner daily. Excellent fish/seafood rest. across from the jai-alai fronton. **I**

Reno, calle 8 and Revolución (706/685-8775). Lunch/ dinner daily. Mexican and American food. **I**

PART EIGHT

HAWAII AND ALASKA

CHAPTER 56

HONOLULU AND THE HAWAIIAN ISLANDS⚑

□ □ □

This mecca for honeymooners and vacationers, the "navel of the Pacific," or as it is also known, the "Aloha State" (*aloha* means "welcome" in Hawaiian), has only three industries: tourism, agriculture—and the armed services! The enormous base at **Pearl Harbor** is America's nerve center for Pacific defense. **Waikiki Beach** in Honolulu boasts the world's greatest concentration of hotels, far ahead of Florida, the Balearics, or Hong Kong: 220 hotels to the square mile (80 to the square kilometer), with a total of 40,000 rooms.

Discovered in 1778 by the famous British explorer Capt. James Cook (who was killed the following year by the Hawaiians), the islands have been endowed by nature with some of the planet's lushest landscapes. With its ideal climate and legendary natural beauty, the Aloha State attracts more than six million visitors every year, and some $7 billion of tourist money. Most of these visitors are Americans, but there are a growing number of Japanese, Canadians, and Australians. The usual array of leis and pareos (wrap-around skirts) awaits the battalions of tourists who land every day on charter flights or in tour groups at Honolulu, capital of the island of **Oahu** and principal city of the Hawaiian archipelago.

Besides swimming and surfing on **Waikiki** and **Makaha Beaches,** the visitor will no doubt want to discover all the other local places of pilgrimage: **Pearl Harbor** (where the sunken U.S.S. *Arizona* impressively commemorates Japan's surprise attack on December 7, 1941, and attracts a million visitors a year); **Diamond Head,** a well-mannered volcano overlooking magnificent Honolulu Bay (*honolulu* means "placid bay" in Hawaiian); the splendid **State Capitol,** whose architecture contrives to be at once elegant and daring; **Punchbowl Crater,** a great military cemetery with an unforgettable view of the Waikiki skyscrapers and the ocean beyond; or the famous **Iolani Palace,** the only royal palace ever built on (what later became) American soil.

As with other cities that are financially and otherwise dependent on the tourist industry, Honolulu's Shangri-La image has its flip side: real-estate speculation is out of control, architecture is flashy, atmospheric pollution is bad and getting worse, and local growth industries include prostitution and pickpocketing. If the present rate of construction continues, the island of Oahu just might sink under the weight of concrete. Another drawback for the tourist are the skyrocketing prices of everything from hotel rooms to T-shirts and snack foods.

Alone among the 50 states, Hawaii has a minority (28%) of Caucasian inhabitants. The five main islands of the chain have a population 48% Asian (28% Japanese, 12% Filipino, 5% Chinese), and 20% indigenous (more or less, reflecting many generations of intermarriage), that speaks Hawaiian, a Polynesian-derived language which has only five vowels and seven consonants.

Food is held in high honor in the islands, and some delectable surprises await you, such as pupu (Hawaiian appetizers), opakapaka (steamed fish), lomi-

lomi (raw fish marinated with vegetables), laulau (pork and fish wrapped in taro leaves and cooked), mahi-mahi (slices of Pacific dolphin—the fish, not the mammal—fried or broiled), kalua (roast pork), or poi (a gruel made from taro).

The airlines flying between California and Hawaii offer very attractive excursion fares and discount packages for the various islands: **Hawaii,** the largest, with its two active volcanoes (Mauna Loa and Kilauea) and its black sand beaches; **Maui,** with its famous Haleakala nature reserve; **Kauai,** the lush garden island; and **Molokai,** famous for its Polynesian temples and for the former leper colony founded by Father Damien.

The Hawaiian Islands were settled comparatively late: it was not until the fifth century of our era that the first inhabitants arrived from the Marquesas, followed four or five centuries later by Tahitians. For a long time the archipelago was wholly isolated from the rest of the world, developing a culture which, despite its Polynesian roots, was all its own. The first white missionaries and traders came in the 1820s; not far behind were the Chinese and Japanese fieldworkers destined for the pineapple and sugarcane plantations (Hawaii is today the largest sugar-growing state in the Union, and the world's largest producer of pineapples). Meanwhile, the indigenous population was decimated by imported diseases to which it had little natural resistance. Those of pure Hawaiian stock now account for only 1.3% of the population of the islands.

BASIC FACTS: Honolulu is the state capital of Hawaii (a word of Polynesian origin meaning "native country"). Area code: 808. Time zone: Hawaiian (five hours behind New York). ZIP Code: 96815. First European contact: 1778. U.S. possession since: 1898. Became the 50th state of the Union in 1959. Approximate population: city of Honolulu, 430,000; island of Oahu, 860,000; total for the state, 1,100,000.

CLIMATE: The subtropical climate of the Hawaiian Islands can best be described in a single word: delightful. The mean temperature in winter is 68°F (20°C) and in summer 77°F (28°C); from year's end to year's end it doesn't move far from these levels. Even in mid-Aug the nights are cool and pleasant, thanks to the trade winds. Hours of sunshine at all seasons reach levels unknown in less fortunate regions. Between Apr and Oct a south wind known as the "kona" often brings with it brief local downpours. The highest temperature recorded in downtown Honolulu was 88°F (31°C); the lowest was 57°F (14°C).

ARRIVAL & TRANSIT INFORMATION

AIRPORT: Honolulu International Airport (HNL), 5 mi. (8km) NW. For information, call 836-6413. The nation's fourth-largest international gateway.

U.S. AIRLINES: Aloha (836-1111), American (526-0044), America West (toll free 800/247-5692), Continental (523-0000), Hawaiian (537-5100), Northwest (955-2255), TWA (toll free 800/221-2000), and United (547-2211).

FOREIGN CARRIERS: Air New Zealand (toll free 800/521-4059), Canadian International (922-0533), Japan Airlines (521-1441), Qantas (toll free 800/227-4500), Singapore Airlines (524-6063), and UTA (947-1222).

CITY LINK: The **cab** fare to Waikiki is about $16–$18 (to dwntwn, $12); time, 20–25 min. Bus: **Gray Line Hawaii** (834-1033) leaves approximately every 20 min., serving the principal Waikiki hotels; fare, $8; time, about 40 min. Cab fares are high, but the **public transportation (bus)** network is excellent and cheap. The many excursions around Honolulu, and the attractive car-rental rates available in Hawaii, make it advisable to rent a car with unlimited mileage.

CAR RENTAL (all at the Honolulu International Airport): Avis (834-5564); Budget (836-1700); Dollar (831-2330); Hertz (836-2691); National (831-3800); Thrifty (836-2388); Tropical Rent-a-Car (836-1041), a local organization with good rates. For dwntwn locations, consult the telephone directory.

LIMOUSINE SERVICES: Carey Limousine (836-1422), Dav El Limousines (toll free 800/922-0343), and Silver Cloud Limo (524-7999).

TAXIS: In theory cabs can't be hailed on the street, though in practice they often stop. You can phone for a cab from **Aloha State Cab** (847-3566), **Charley's** (955-2211), or **Sida** (836-0011).

CITY BUSES: Both in and outside Honolulu, the best and cheapest (60¢) way of getting around is usually the bus service of the **Municipal Transit Lines,** informally called **"TheBUS."** Information is available in all hotels or from HDT, Mass Transit Division, 725 Kapiolani Blvd. (531-1611).

INFORMATION & TOURS

TOURIST INFORMATION: Statewide, try the **Hawaii Visitors Bureau (HVB),** with headquarters in Honolulu at 2270 Kalakaua Ave., Suite 801, HI 96815 (808/923-1811).

GUIDED TOURS: Ani Ani Glass Bottom Boat, Kewalo Basin (923-2061): On this mini-cruise off Waikiki you may admire the coral gardens and the brightly colored tropical fish through the transparent bottom of your boat.
    Atlantis Submarine, 500 N. Nimitz Hwy. (536-2694): Explore the seabed of Honolulu Bay off Diamond Head in a 46-seat submarine with big portholes. The 45-min. trip takes place at a mean depth of 100 ft. (30m) so that you have a fine view of the underwater fauna and flora. Fascinating. Daily, year round. Leaves from the Hilton Hawaiian dock; fare, $68.
    Enoa Tours (bus), 1110 University Ave. (941-6608): Guided minibus tour of the island.
    Gray Line Tours (bus) (834-1033): Guided bus tours of city and island; pickup at principal hotels.
    Pearl Harbor Cruises (boat), Kewalo Basin (536-3641): 3-hr. boat tour of Pearl Harbor Bay and the U.S.S. *Arizona* Memorial; two departures daily, at 9:30am and 1:30pm.
    Royal Helicopters, Waikiki Helipad, 216 Lagoon Dr. (941-4683): Spectacular helicopter trip over the bay and the island; $25–$150, depending on duration.
    Waikiki Trolley (526-0112): Guided tour of Waikiki, Chinatown, and dwntwn Honolulu in a mock-up of an old-time streetcar. Board and leave as often as you like along the route. Highly recommended for a quick overview. Daily 9am–6:30pm; fare, $10.
    Windjammer Dinner Sail, Pier 7, Honolulu Harbor (922-1200): Entrancing sunset trip and dinner aboard a sailboat. Leaves at 5:15pm and 7:45pm every evening; resv. essential.

CRUISES: American Hawaii Cruises, 550 Kearny St., San Francisco, CA 94108 (415/392-9400; toll free 800/227-3666): 7-night inter-island cruise departing Sat from Honolulu aboard the S.S. *Independence* and S.S. *Constitution,* each of 30,000 tons and a passenger capacity of 790. Year round. Cost, $1,050–$3,700 including transfers.

SIGHTS, ATTRACTIONS & ACTIVITIES

ARCHITECTURAL HIGHLIGHTS: ※🏛 **State Capitol,** 400 S. Beretania St. (548-2211): This futuristic building, elegantly designed in the form of an open crater (a reference to the volcanic origins of the islands) and surrounded by tall columns symbolizing palm trees, houses the State Legislature. Built in 1969. Open Mon–Fri. In front of it, note the very fine statue of Queen Liliuokalani, who while a prisoner for 9 months in 1894, after the demise of the monarchy, wrote the words of the famous song "Aloha O'e."

BEACHES: ※🏛 **Hanauma Beach,** 10 mi. (16km) east via Hi. 72: In its conspicuously beautiful setting, this beach is very popular with residents of the area; scuba-diving. The beach where Burt Lancaster and Deborah Kerr had their romantic encounter in the movie *From Here to Eternity.*

🏛 **Kahana Bay Beach Park,** 32 mi. (51km) north along Hi. 61 and Hi. 83: Deserted and peaceful, far away from the throngs of Waikiki.

🏛 **Kailua Beach Park,** 25 mi. (40km) north along Hi. 61: All kinds of sailing; a quiet family beach.

※🏛 **Lanikai Beach,** 27 mi. (43km) NE on Hi. 61 and Kalaheo Dr.: A gem of white sand and azure water. Mokulua Island and the offshore reefs shelter the beach from strong currents. Crowded on weekends but often empty during the week.

🏛 **Makaha Beach,** 38 mi. (60km) west by H-1 and Hi. 93: The champion surfers' beach; only for the seasoned athlete.

🏛🏛 **Sunset Beach,** 46 mi. (73km) NW on H-1, H-2, Hi. 99, and Hi. 83: The most famous surfing beach in all the Hawaiian islands; safe in summer but dangerous in winter.

※🏛🏛 **Waikiki Beach,** Kalakaua Ave.: One of the best-known beaches in the world, with 2½ mi. (4km) of sand overlooked by a forest of huge hotels. Often crowded. Good for novice surfers.

🏛 **Waimanalo Beach Park,** 19 mi. (30km) east along Hi. 72: For hang-gliding enthusiasts. Spectacular views of the Koolau Mountains.

※🏛🏛 **Waimea Beach Park,** 42 mi. (67km) NW by H-1, H-2, Hi. 99, and Hi. 83: Very popular in summer; only for experienced surfers in winter. In a magnificent setting.

※🏛 **Yokohama Bay Beach,** 43 mi. (69km) NW along H-1 and Hi. 93: Huge sandy beach; the water is sometimes rough but the sunsets are magnificent.

CHURCHES/SYNAGOGUES: ※🏛 **Kawaiahao Church,** 957 Punchbowl St. (538-6267): Nicknamed "The Westminster Abbey of the Pacific," this was the church of the kings of Hawaii from 1842 on. The classic ecclesiastical architecture makes use of an unconventional material: 14,000 blocks of coral cut from the local reefs! The tomb of King Lunalilo is in the garden. Services in Hawaiian and English every Sun, open daily.

🏛 **Royal Mausoleum,** 2261 Nuuanu Ave. (537-1716): Contains the tombs of the former Hawaiian monarchs of the Kameha Dynasty; an unexpected cross-shaped Neo-Gothic chapel under skies. Open Mon–Fri.

HISTORIC BUILDINGS: 🏛 **Iolani Palace,** Ki 1471): The only royal palace ever built on

David Kalakaua in 1822 and served as a prison for the last monarch, Queen Liliu-okalani, in 1894. In the Florentine style; notice the throne room and the grand dining room. A historical curiosity set in beautiful gardens. Very popular public concerts on Fri. Guided tours Wed–Sat; resv. advised (522-0832).

🛏 **Judiciary Building,** 417 South St.: Built in 1874, this neoclas-sical palace, which once housed the Hawaiian parliament, will look familiar to fans of the TV series "Hawaii Five-O," several episodes of which were filmed here. Worth seeing; open Mon–Fri. Enthroned in front of the build-ing is an imposing copy in gilded bronze of a statue of King Kamehameha I, called "The Napoleon of the Pacific" (the original is on the island of Hawaii). The king wears the *malo,* the great royal cape of feathers, and the traditional Hawaiian headdress. For his feast (Kamehameha Day, June 11), the statue is bedecked with a mass of leis, or necklaces of flowers.

🛏 **Queen Emma's Summer Palace,** 2913 Pali Hwy. (Hi. 61) (595-3167): This elegant Victorian (1843) house standing above the luxuriant Nuunau Valley was the summer residence of Queen Emma; after her husband King Kamehameha IV died in 1863, she retired here. Original furniture and decoration; many memorabilia of the Hawaiian monarchy. Hand-some tropical gardens. Open daily.

🛏 **Washington Place,** Beretania St. and Miller St.: Washington Place, across from the state capitol, was built in 1846 by John Dominis, a wealthy sea captain and merchant who later became governor of Oahu. Since 1922 it has been the official residence of the governors of Hawaii. Fine Federal design with a colonnaded gallery encircling the building. No visitors.

MARKETS: ※🛏 **Tamashiro Market,** 802 N. King St. (841-8047): Colorful Japanese market very close to the Bishop Museum; piles of fish and shellfish; lots of bustle; nice little Japanese restaurants. Open daily.

MONUMENTS: ※🛏 **U.S.S. *Arizona* Memorial,** Halawa Gate Boat Landing, Pearl Harbor (422-0561): Impressive memorial erected in the center of Pearl Harbor Bay over the wreck of the battleship *Arizona,* which was sunk with 1,102 of the crew during the Japanese surprise attack on December 7, 1941. The muse-um, open Tues–Sun, attracts nearly 1.5 million visitors a year. U.S. Navy boats leave the visitor center for the memorial every 30 min.

MUSEUMS OF ART: 🛏 **Contemporary Museum,** 2411 Makiki Heights Dr. (526-0232): Housed since 1988 in its new quarters here, this interesting muse-um of modern art displays works by 500 contemporaries from Andy Warhol to David Hockney (his remarkable stage set for *L'enfant et les sortilèges* is well worth seei⟋ Hawaiian artists such as Isami Doi, Madge Tennet, and Satoru Abe are pr⟋ ly featured. Traveling exhibitions. Also offers a fine view of the city. A ⟋n Wed–Mon.

Honolulu Academy of Arts, 900 S. Beretania St. (538-1006): ⟋raceful modern building with fine collections of Far Eastern ⟋orean) as well as European art, including such well-known ⟋gh, Matisse, and Picasso. Among the best-known works ⟋naventura's *Madonna and Child* and John Singleton ⟋l Allen. Open Tues–Sun.

HISTORY: ※🛏 **Bishop Museum,** 1525 ⟋m, founded in 1898, houses not only the ⟋art, but also a center for anthropological ⟋l as remarkable exhibits of historic ob-⟋nces of Hawaiian music and dance.

HONOLULU

Punahou School

National Memorial Cemetery of the Pacific

Punchbowl

Foster Botanic Garden

Chinatown

State Capitol
Archives Building
Iolani Palace
Mission Houses
Kamehameha Statue
Kawaiaho Church
Federal Building

Aloha Tower

Honolulu Harbor

to Honolulu International Airport

Civic Center

Neal S. Blaisdell Memorial Center

Ala Wai Field and Park

Ala Moana Park

Banyan Garden

Magic Island

Kewalo Basin

Fort Armstrong Channel

N. KING ST
N. BERETANIA ST
SMITH ST
NUUANU AVE
KUKUI ST
S. VINEYARD BLVD
H-1
61
BISHOP ST
RICHARDS ST
S. HOTEL ST
ALAKEA ST
PUNCHBOWL ST
SOUTH ST
HALEKAUWILA ST
QUEEN ST
KOULA ST
KEAWE ST
COOKE ST
CORAL ST
KAMAKEE ST
AHUI ST
ILALO ST
EMERSON ST
SPENCER ST
PROSPECT ST
IOLANI ST
QUEEN EMMA ST
PENSACOLA ST
PIIKOI ST
LILIHA ST
KEWALO ST
KINAU ST
VICTORIA ST
YOUNG ST
WAIMANU ST
KAPIOLANI BLVD
WARD AVE
ELM ST
RYCROFT ST
HAMAILE ST
KONA ST
KEEAUMOKU ST
KAHEKA ST
KALAKAUA AVE
MAKALOA ST
S. KING ST
S. BERETANIA ST
PUNAHOU ST
WILDER AVE
METCALF ST
NEHOA ST
MANOA ST
MAKIKI ST
CITRON ST
FERN ST
WILIWILI ST
MCCULLY ST
HANOLI ST
PUMEHANA ST
KANUNU ST
ALA MOANA
ATKINSON DR
ALA WAI BLVD
MAMAKE ST
H-1
92
92

Falls of Clyde, Pier 7, Honolulu Harbor (536-6373): Moored at the foot of the Aloha Tower (see "Panoramas," below), this huge sailing ship, built in Scotland in 1878, is one of the last four-masters afloat. For long the principal means of transport among the Hawaiian Islands, it is now a floating museum. Fascinating. Open daily.

Fort de Russy Army Museum, Kalia Rd. (438-2821): A comprehensive museum of arms, from the primitive weapons used by the natives of Hawaii to those of World War II and Vietnam. For military-history buffs. Open Tues–Sun.

Mission House Museum, 553 King St. (531-0481): The three missionaries' houses here are the oldest on the islands, dating from 1821, and have their original furnishings and fittings. An interesting glimpse of Hawaiian history. Open daily.

Pacific Submarine Museum, Bowfin Park, Kamehameha Bay (423-1341): Brand-new museum devoted to the age of the submarine from World War I to the present day. Many historical documents, photographs, and various objects culminating in an authentic U.S. Navy sub which survived World War II, the U.S.S. *Bowfin,* which may be inspected in detail. Next to the *Arizona* Memorial Visitor Center. Open daily.

PANORAMAS: Aloha Tower, Fort St. Mall (537-9260): Built in 1925, this

was long the tallest building on the island. Fine view of the old city and its harbor from the 10th floor (reached by elevator). Once the symbol of the city. Open daily.

National Memorial Cemetery of the Pacific, 2177 Puowaina Dr. (541-1430): From this enormous military cemetery, lying in the crater of an extinct volcano (also known as Punchbowl Crater) above the city, you'll have a wonderful view of Waikiki and Honolulu harbor. More than 34,000 G.I.s who died in battle are buried here. Open daily.

Round Top Park, Tantalus Dr. and Round Top Drs.: The most spectacular prospect of Honolulu, from a beautiful mountainside tropical park.

PARKS & GARDENS: Ala Moana Park, Ala Moana Blvd.: This lovely

76-acre (30ha) park fringes Honolulu's favorite beach, and also draws numerous joggers. Many picnic areas; unobstructed view of the bay and the Waikiki skyline.

Diamond Head State Monument, Diamond Rd.: A 400,000-year-old extinct volcano, rearing its 760 ft. (232m) over Waikiki Bay. The interior of the crater may be visited (the path begins at Makalei Place). The volcano owes its name to 19th-century European sailors who mistook shiny volcanic glass for diamonds. A Hawaiian legend has it that the volcano was the dwel place of Pele, the goddess of fire. Allow 90 min. to reach the top of the cr turn; for information, call 548-7455. Open daily.

Foster Botanic Garden, 180 N. Vineyard Blvd. (533-3214): All the flora of the Pacific can be seen at this one spot in the spectacular orchid house. Open daily.

olani Park, Kalakaua Ave. and Montserrat Aves.: Hawaii's ublic park, dating from 1877, boasts a very lovely rose o, splendid aquarium, public concerts, Hawaiian Tues–Fri at 10am; for information, call 833- ir snapshots of their vacations. Open daily.

3737 Manoa Rd. (988-6686): Very lovely xuriant orchid garden, bamboo grove, wa-, all in their natural state. 15 min. from

shows and cultural events, con-s, *Honolulu Advertiser* (morning) and *Honolulu Star Bulletin* (evening), as well as the weekly *Sun Press* and the monthly *Honolulu.*

Blaisdell Center Arena, Ward Ave. and King St. (527-5400): Rock concerts; star-studded shows.

Blaisdell Concert Hall, Ward Ave. and King St. (537-6191): Home of the Honolulu Symphony Orchestra (principal conductor: Donald Johanos) Oct–May; also operatic performances Jan–Feb, recitals, etc.

John F. Kennedy Theater, University of Hawaii, 1770 East-West Rd. (948-7655): Classical and modern theater, ballet.

Manoa Valley Theater, 2833 E. Manoa Rd. (988-6131): Home of the Hawaii Performing Arts Company. From Shakespeare to avant-garde theater in a delightfully rustic setting.

Ruger Theater, 520 Makapuu Ave. (734-0274): Home of the Honolulu Community Theater, the islands' best stock company. Drama, comedy, and Broadway hits.

Waikiki Shell, Kapiolani Park (521-2911): Open-air concerts in summer, including a number by the Honolulu Symphony Orchestra.

SHOPPING: Ala Moana Center, Ala Moana Blvd. at Atkinson Dr.: One of the country's largest and newest shopping centers, with more than 200 stores and exotic restaurants. Open daily.

International Market Place, 2330 Kalakaua Ave.: For quarter of a century this Polynesian version of a Middle Eastern open-air bazaar, with its lantern-decorated giant banyan tree, has been drawing strollers and shoppers in droves. You should certainly take a look. Open daily.

Royal Hawaiian Shopping Center, 2201 Kalakaua Ave.: Largest in the islands, laid out on three levels along Kalakaua Ave. From luxury fashion boutiques (Vuitton, Cartier, Chanel, etc.) to Hawaiian handcraft stores. Many cafés and restaurants. Street performers (mimes, jugglers, musicians, etc.) and open-air concerts. A must-see. Open daily. Don't miss either the fragrant lei-stringing shops lining Maunakea St. and Beretania St. Maile or orchid leis cost about $12–$15. **Cindy's,** 1034 Maunakea St., probably has the best prices, selection, and staff.

SPECIAL EVENTS: For exact dates, consult the **Hawaii Visitors Bureau (HVB)** (see "Tourist Information," above).

Hula Bowl (mid-Jan): Annual college all-star game at Aloha Stadium.

Hawaiian Open International Golf Tournament (Feb): $500,000 PGA golf tournament featuring top professional golfers. Waialae Golf and Country Club.

Chinese New Year (mid-Jan to Feb): Parades, costumed processions. Chinatown in Honolulu, and on the other islands.

King Kamehameha Celebration (June 11): Public holiday in honor of King Kamehameha I (c.1738–1819), the first to establish his rule over the entire island chain. His statue in Honolulu is draped with many leis. Processions, floats—a very colorful occasion.

Japan Festival (July): The island's Japanese heritage is commemorated in Honolulu and Waikiki. Music, food, arts, etc.

Hula Festival (Aug): Hawaiian dancing (Honolulu).

Aloha Week (Sept–Oct): Parades, concerts, dances, boat races in Honolulu and the other islands. The archipelago's biggest festival.

Ironman World Triathlon Championship (Oct): The most grueling spo event in the world: a 2.4-mi. (3.8km) swim, a 112-mi. (180km) bike ri 26.2-mi. (42km) run at a stretch. For super-athletes only. Kailua Island.

Surfing Championships (Nov–Dec): Profess Makaha Beach and the beaches on the North Sh beaches, for example).

SPORTS: Deep-Sea Fishing: Thousands of deep-sea fishermen flock to Hawaii every year in (usually successful) pursuit of the local mahi-mahi (dolphin), ono (wahoo), ahi (yellowfin tuna), aku (skipjack tuna) or even, for the most venturesome, the renowned a'u (marlin). Reckon $450 for a full-day charter of 8 hr., $250 for a half-day (4-hr.) charter. Among the most reliable charter boats:
  Honolulu: Island Charters (536-1555), *Coreene C* Charters (536-6577), and Tradewinds Sailing Charters (533-0220).
  Hawaii: Glen Hodson, Kailua Kona (329-6303), Larry Pries, Kailua Kona (325-6374), and Don Cruz, Kohala Coast (885-7883).
  Kauai: Sea Fever Sport Fishing, Hanalei (826-6815), and Sport Fishing Kauai, Koloa (742-7013).
  Kaui: Ken Takashima, Lahaina (661-0480), and Ben Hall, Makawao (877-3333).

STROLLS: ⚓ **Chinatown,** around King St. and Smith St.: Honolulu's picturesque Chinese quarter. Buddhist temple, open-air market, and restaurants by day; rather sleazy nightclubs and sex shops after dark.
  Waikiki, along Kalakaua Ave.: The heart of the tourist's Honolulu, with dozens of skyscrapers, luxury hotels, restaurants, boutiques, and the world-renowned (and partly artificial) **Waikiki Beach,** nirvana of surfing and other water sports.

ACCOMMODATIONS
  A Note on Accommodations: Room rates in Hawaii are coded as follows: **VE,** Very Expensive ($140 and up); **E,** Expensive ($90–$140); **M,** Moderate ($60–$90); **I,** Inexpensive ($30–$60); **B,** Budget (up to $30). A listing of toll free numbers is in the Appendix.

Personal Favorites (in order of preference)
  Halekulani Hotel (nr. dwntwn), 2199 Kalia Rd., HI 96815 (808/923-2311; toll free, see Preferred). 456 rms, A/C, color TV, in-rm movies. AE, CB, DC, MC, V. Valet parking $8, pool, private beach, health club, three rests. (including La Mer), two bars and a piano bar, 24-hr. rm svce, nightclub, boutiques, hrdrsr, concierge. *Note:* Waikiki Beach's super-luxury hotel, set amid 5 acres (2ha) of flower grdns. This urbane ultramodern structure occupies the site of a 1920s predecessor, and retains a few vestiges of its distinguished past, notably the bar and two of the three rests. Luxuriously comfortable, spacious rms w. private verandas, minibars, and very complete facilities; most have an ocean view. The swimming pool, w. its enormous blue mosaic of an orchid   orth a look all by itself. Svce and reception of the highest order make this   best hotels in the country. Its name (*halekulani* means in Hawaiian "a   of paradise") is well deserved. **VE**
          Hawaii Prince Hotel (nr. dwntwn), 1677 Ala Moana Blvd. (at   omoana St.), Honolulu, HI 96815 (808/956-1111; toll   21 rms, A/C, color TV, in-rm movies. AE, CB, DC,   pool, health club, five rests. (including the Prince   club, boutiques, concierge. *Note:* On an episode of   und the world watched the dynamiting of the   n this site; it was replaced by twin 32-story   d early in 1990. The innovative design is by   comfortable rms, each overlooking the   nibar, VCR, and Italian-marble bath-   from the turmoil of Waikiki. Con-

          la Ave., HI 96816 (808/734-   rms, A/C, color TV, in-rm movies. AE, CB, DC, MC, V. Valet-parking $8, two pools, sauna, health club, six tennis courts, beach, boats, three rests. (including Maile), bars, 24-hr. rm svce, disco, hrdrsr, boutiques. *Note:* Plushy 12-story building and a group of charming bungalows, clustered around a tropical lagoon (w. dolphins), far from Waikiki's crowds. Lavish, comfortable rms w. refrigerators and private balconies; commanding views of the ocean or Diamond Head. Exemplary svce, and one of the city's finest rests. A jewel among local hotels since 1964; its guestbook has been signed by former President Reagan and Prince Charles of England, among others. 20 min. from dwntwn. **VE**

☀☺☺ **Colony Surf** (nr. dwntwn), 2895 Kalakaua Ave., HI 96815 (808/923-5751; toll free 800/367-6046). 108 suites, A/C, cable color TV. AE, CB, DC, MC, V. Free parking, beach, two rests. (including Michel's), bar, rm svce, disco. *Note:* Charming small hotel opposite Kapiolani Park in the shadow of Diamond Head, offering remarkably spacious and comfortable studios and mini-suites w. kitchenettes, the best w. a splendid view of the ocean. Highly polished reception and svce. Michel's rest. does not wholly deserve its high reputation. The favorite hotel of those in-the-know. **E–VE**

☺☺ **New Otani** (nr. dwntwn), 2863 Kalakaua Ave., HI 96815 (808/923-1555; toll free 800/421-8795). 138 rms, A/C, color TV. AE, CB, DC, MC, V. Free parking, beach, two rests. (including Hau Tree Lanai), bar, rm svce. *Note:* Of modest size compared to the giants of Waikiki Beach, this intimate, comfortable hotel across from Kapiolani Park is the favorite of Japanese businessmen. Friendly rms, a little on the skimpy side; rms and suites newly redone. Excellent svce; very commendable (but very expensive) Japanese rest. Direct access to the beach. A good place to stay. **M–E**

☺ **Outrigger Waikiki Surf** (nr. dwntwn), 2200 Kuhio Ave., HI 96815 (808/923-7671; toll free 800/367-5170). 303 rms, A/C, color TV. AE, CB, DC, MC, V. Free parking, pool, rest., bar, rm svce, free crib. *Note:* Honolulu's big bargain—modern, large, and well maintained, 5 min. from Waikiki Beach. Friendly reception. Attractive rms w. balconies, some w. kitchenettes. One of the best values in the city. Family clientele. Entirely renovated in 1988. **I–M**

☺ **Pleasant Holiday Isle** (nr. dwntwn), 270 Lewers St. (at Kalakana Ave.), Honolulu, HI 96815 (808/923-0777). 264 rms, A/C, cable color TV. AE, CB, DC, MC, V. Gar. $4, pool, bar, boutiques. *Note:* Relatively new tower right in the center of Waikiki and one block from the beach. Serviceably comfortable rms w. balcony. On the noisy side. Friendly reception and svce. Good value on balance. **I–M**

Other Accommodations (from top bracket to budget)

☀☺☺☺ **Sheraton Moana Surfrider** (nr. dwntwn), 2365 Kalakaua Ave., HI 96815 (808/922-3111; toll free, see Sheraton). 803 rms, A/C, color TV, in-rm movies. AE, CB, DC, MC, V. Valet gar. $6, pool, private beach, boating, three rests. (including Banyan Court), coffee shop, bar, 24-hr. rm svce, nightclub. *Note:* The oldest (1901) palace hotel on the island, known as "the first lady of Waikiki." The Victorian decor was magnificently restored in 1989, and the building is a designated historic monument. Rms completely done over in pastel shades w. exotic furnishings and minibars. Lovely roof grdn. Direct beach access. Amelia Earhart and the Prince of Wales are among the celebrities who have stayed here. **VE**

☺☺☺ **Hilton Hawaiian Village** (nr. dwntwn), 2005 Kalia Rd., HI 96815 (808/949-4321; toll free, see Hilton). 2,524 rms, A/C, color TV, in-rm movies. AE, CB, DC, MC, V. Valet gar. $6, three pools, boating, private beach, putting green, grdns, six rests. (including Golden Dragon, Bali by the Sea), two coffee shops, five bars, rm svce (24-hr. on VIP floor), disco, nightclub, show, more than 100 boutiques (in the Rainbow Bazaar), drugstore, free parking, free crib. *Note:* The largest hotel in the Pacific, 38 floors above Waikiki Beach in the midst of tropical gardens.

Wonderful lagoon-style pool surrounded by palm trees. The rms in the Rainbow and the Tapa towers have a fine ocean view. Commendable comfort; efficient svce. Caters mostly to groups and conventions. Offers sailing trips in a catamaran. Recently underwent a $100-million rejuvenation. **VE**

Hyatt Regency Waikiki (nr. dwntwn), 2424 Kalakaua Ave., HI 96815 (808/923-1234; toll free, see Hyatt). 1,234 rms, A/C, color TV, in-rm movies. AE, CB, DC, MC, V. Valet parking $6, pool, private beach, boats, five rests. (including Bagwell's 2424), coffee shop, three bars, rm svce, disco, hrdrsr, 70 boutiques. *Note:* Twin 40-story towers dominating all of Waikiki Bay and constituting a sort of miniature city within the city. The 10-story lobby comes complete w. tropical forest, lagoon, and waterfalls; sumptuous and spectacular. Spacious, elegantly decorated rms w. private lanais, the best overlooking the beach, others the city. Impeccable comfort; exemplary svce. Bagwell's 2424 is a very good rest. Interesting vacation and wknd packages. Two floors reserved for VIPs. **VE**

Sheraton Royal Hawaiian Hotel (nr. dwntwn), 2259 Kalakaua Ave., HI 96815 (808/923-7311; toll free, see Sheraton). 525 rms, A/C, color TV, in-rm movies. AE, CB, DC, MC, V. Parking $5, pool, private beach, two rests. (including the Monarch Rm), coffee shop, bars, 24-hr. rm svce, nightclub, Polynesian show. *Note:* "The hotel of kings and presidents," a 1920s palace known as "the pink lady" because of its pastel-colored Spanish-Moorish facade. Loads of rococo charm. Most rms are huge and comfortable but some are a little cramped (avoid those in the new wings). Efficient svce. Luau on Sun. Beautiful tropical grdns. Caters mostly to vacationers. **VE**

Waikiki Parc Hotel (nr. dwntwn), 2233 Helumoa St., HI 96815 (808/921-7272; toll free 800/422-0450). 298 rms, A/C, cable color TV. AE, CB, DC, MC, V. Valet gar. $6, pool, two rests., bar, rm svce. *Note:* The plainer, cheaper younger brother of the renowned Halekulani Hotel next door. Brand new and comfortable; elegant decor and furnishing. Polished Japanese-style svce. A fine place almost on the beach. **E–VE**

Holiday Inn Waikiki Beach (nr. dwntwn), 2570 Kalakaua Ave., HI 96815 (808/922-2511; toll free, see Holiday Inns). 640 rms, A/C, color TV, in-rm movies. AE, CB, DC, MC, V. Parking $3, pool, private beach, rest., coffee shop, bar, rm svce, nightclub, crib $10. *Note:* A typical Holiday Inn right on Waikiki Beach, most w. a splendid view of the ocean and Diamond Head. Modern and functional; group clientele. Captain's Table is a very decent rest. Good value out of season. Very close to the zoo and Kapiolani Park. **E,** but lower rates off-season.

Imperial Hawaii Resort (nr. dwntwn), 205 Lewers St., HI 96815 (808/923-1827; toll free 800/367-8047, ext. 225). 270 st⸻os, A/C, color TV. AE, CB, DC, MC, V. Free parking, pool, sauna, coff⸻ *Note:* Resort hotel, recently renovated. Consists of studio units w. o⸻ ⸻drooms, all w. private terraces and an ocean view. Modern and ⸻ good value off-season. A good place to stay, one block off the ⸻ ⸻er rates off-season.

⸻n the Park (nr. dwntwn), 1920 Ala Moana Blvd., HI ⸻ (808/946-8355; toll free 800/922-7866). 230 rms, ⸻ MC, V. Free parking, pool, rest., two bars, rm svce. ⸻otel. Rms w. terraces and refrigerators, some over⸻ ⸻verall. **M–E,** but lower rates off-season.

⸻iki (nr. dwntwn), 175 Paoakalani Ave. (808/ ⸻ see Quality Inns). 451 rms, A/C, color ⸻ Gar. $5, two pools, rest., bar, valet svce. ⸻e. Inviting, comfortable rms (ask for ⸻ Efficient reception and svce. One ⸻r families. **M–E**

⸻), 444 Kanekapolei St., HI ⸻ 800/367-5205). 197 rms,

A/C, color TV. AE, CB, DC, MC, V. Free parking, rest., bar. *Note:* Modest but pleasant, well-run hotel, recently modernized, away from the hurly-burly of Waikiki. Good value 5 min. from the beach. **M**

Outrigger Edgewater (nr. dwntwn), 2168 Kalia Rd., HI 96815 (808/922-6424; toll free 800/367-5170). 184 rms, A/C, color TV, in-rm movies. AE, CB, DC, MC, V. Free parking, pool, rest. (Trattoria), bar, rm svce, shops, free crib. *Note:* Serviceable comfort and smiling svce. Enticing Italian rest.; some rms w. kitchenettes. Very good value, a few steps from the beach. **I–M**

Outrigger Royal Islander (nr. dwntwn), 2164 Kalia Rd., HI 96815 (808/922-1961; toll free 800/367-5170). 98 rms, A/C, color TV. AE, CB, DC, MC, V. Free parking, rest. *Note:* Contemporary comfort; somewhat cramped rms w. terraces and a view of Waikiki Beach. Overall good value. **I–M**

Royal Grove Hotel (nr. dwntwn), 151 Uluniu Ave., HI 96815 (808/923-7691). 90 studios and mini-apts, A/C, color TV. AE, MC, V. On-street parking, pool, grdns, valet svce. *Note:* Charming rose-colored residential hotel w. only comfortable studios or mini-suites; each has a private balcony and kitchenette. Congenial family atmosphere. No bar or rest. Two blocks from Waikiki Beach. Very good value. **I–M**

Waikiki Marina Hotel (nr. dwntwn), 1956 Ala Moana Blvd., HI 96815 (808/955-0714). 323 rms, A/C, color TV. AE, CB, DC, MC, V. Free parking, pool, nearby rest., bar. *Note:* Modest but acceptable hotel nr. the Ala Wai Canal. Functional comfort; good value. **I–M**

Airport Accommodations

Best Western Plaza Hotel (formerly the Ramada; vic.), 3253 N. Nimitz Hwy., HI 96819 (808/836-3636; toll free, see Best Western). 268 rms, A/C, color TV, in-rm movies. AE, CB, DC, MC, V. Free parking, pool, rest., bar, rm svce, nightclub. *Note:* Modern, friendly eight-story motel 3 min. from the airport and 25 min. from Waikiki. Comfortable rms w. refrigerators; cordial reception and svce. The best place to stay for a stopover between flights, w. free 24-hr. airport limousine svce. 5 min. from Aloha Stadium, 10 min. from Pearl Harbor. **E,** but lower rates off-season.

Accommodations Around the Island of Oahu

Hilton Turtle Bay (formerly the Kuilima Hyatt), Kamehameha Hwy., Kahuku, HI 96731 (808/293-8811; toll free, see Hilton). 487 rms and cottages, A/C, color TV, in-rm movies. AE, CB, DC, MC, V. Parking $5, two pools, golf course, 10 tennis courts, horseback riding, water sports, private beach, two rests. (including Cove), coffee shop, two bars, rm svce, disco, hrdrsr, boutiques. *Note:* Luxury hotel in the middle of a 5-mi. (8km) beach on the north shore of the island, 1½ hr. by car from Honolulu. Luxury in peace. The huge, comfortable rms overlook the ocean. Excellent svce; very good sports facilities, w. golf course designed by Arnold Palmer. For lovers of tranquility and of nature. **E–VE**

YMCA/Youth Hostel

Hale Aloha Youth Hostel (nr. dwntwn), 2417 Prince Edward St., HI 96815 (808/926-8313). 50 beds. Two blocks off Waikiki Beach. Resv. required.

Manoa Hostel (nr. dwntwn), 2323A Seaview Ave., HI 96822 (808/946-0591). 40 beds. Clean, well-run youth hostel nr. the university. Very busy year round.

RESTAURANTS

A Note on Restaurant Prices: Hawaii restaurant prices, per person, excluding drinks and service charges, are coded as follows: **VE,** Very Expensive ($60 and up); **E,** Expensive ($40–$60); **M,** Moderate ($25–$40); **I,** Inexpensive ($15–$25); **B,** Budget (up to $15).

A Note on Hawaiian Food: Hawaiian cuisine, a blend of Polynesian and Asian (Philippine, Chinese, Japanese, and Korean) strains, draws extensively on local produce simply prepared: pork, fish, taro leaves, sweet potatoes, Maui onions, avocado, pineapple, guava, etc. Typical dishes include the following:

haupia: coconut pudding.

laulau: pork, taro, and fish wrapped in the fresh leaves of the local ti plant, and steamed.

lilikoi: passion fruit, pastry filled with fruit.

lomi-lomi: strips of raw salmon with tomatoes and green onions.

mahi mahi: Pacific dolphin (fish) roast, broiled or fried.

malasadas: sugared doughnuts eaten hot.

manapua: dumplings stuffed with roast sucking pig (a kind of Hawaiian dim sum).

poi: paste of boiled taro flour, the Hawaiian substitute for potatoes.

Personal Favorites (in order of preference)

☀ ♟♟♟♟ **La Mer** (nr. dwntwn), in the Halekulani Hotel (see "Accommodations," above) (923-2311). A/C. Dinner only, nightly. AE, CB, DC, MC, V. Jkt. *Specialties:* tartare of Hawaiian fish, broiled opaka paka (sea bass) stuffed w. black olives, warm duck salad w. papaya and truffles, lobster w. spinach custard, filet of beef w. sweet peppers, sautéed curried moana, gratin of strawberries; excellent desserts. Menu changes regularly. *Note:* Occupying the original 1920s building of the old Halekulani Hotel, this magnificent rest. looking out to sea is the most elegant, the most polished, and the most costly in Honolulu. Superb, inspired French-Polynesian nouvelle cuisine from chef George Mavrothalassitis; first-class svce. The sound of the surf on the nearby beach underlines the elegance of the decor. One of the best rests. in the country w. prices to match. Resv. a must. Valet parking. *French/Seafood.* **E–VE**

♟♟♟ **Maile Restaurant** (nr. dwntwn), in the Kahala Hilton (see "Accommodations," above) (734-2211). A/C. Dinner nightly, brunch Sun. AE, CB, DC, MC, V. Jkt. *Specialties:* snails w. black-bean sauce, potpourri of seafood, roast duckling Waialae, ragoût of wild mushrooms, uhu (parrot fish) steamed in ti leaves. Here nouvelle cuisine scores a triumph under tropic skies, w. superb salads and minimally cooked fish (moist yet not rare). Fine wine list. *Note:* A rather dark, cavelike setting complete w. fountains, flowers, and abundant greenery; smiling, gracious svce in Far Eastern style. One of the best rests. in the islands. Resv. a must. Valet parking. *French/Polynesian.* **E–VE**

♟♟♟ **Nick's Fish Market** (nr. dwntwn), in the Waikiki Gateway Hotel, 2070 Kalakaua Ave. (955-6333). A/C. Dinner only, nightly (until 2am). AE, CB, DC, MC, V. Jkt. *Specialties:* Every imaginable kind of seafood is cooked and served here: Maine lobster, Florida stone crab, and Louisiana soft-shell crab (delivered by air daily) appear cheek by jowl w. Pacific dolphin (mahi-mahi), swordfish, and bass (opaka paka). Excellent bouillabaisse and linguine w. clam sauce; also top sirloin steaks. Very good wine list. *Note:* One of the country's outstanding fish rests.; elegant maritime decor; exemplary svce. Resv. a must. Valet parking. *Seafood.* **M–E**

♟♟ **Roy's** (vic.), 6600 Kalaniaole Hwy., Hawaii Kai (396-7697). A/C. Lunch/dinner daily. AE, MC, V. *Specialties:* pork meatballs w. soy vinaigrette, California-style pizzas, fried seafood dumplings w. sesame butter, broiled shrimp in curry-chutney sauce, scallops w. ginger-and-basil sauce. Menu changes regularly. *Note:* The young and talented chef Roy Yamaguchi opened this very up-to-date establishment in 1989 in the residential suburb of Hawaii Kai. His cuisine is a happy blend of Oriental ingredients and California style. The second-floor dining rm has a fine view of Maunalua Bay and the mountains. Warm, attentive svce. Well worth the 15-min. drive from Waikiki along Hi. 1E and Hi. 72. Resv. suggested. *American/Japanese.* **I–M**

♟♟ **Miyako** (nr. dwntwn), in the New Otani Hotel (see "Accommodations," above) (923-1555). A/C. dinner only, nightly.

AE, CB, DC, MC, V. *Specialties:* sukiyaki, tempura, shabu-shabu, sushi, kaiseki dinner. *Note:* Elegant hotel dining rm from whose enormous picture windows you can see straight down to the beach and the ocean. If you're a purist you may eat sitting on the floor in a tatami rm. Splendid, refined Japanese food. The kaiseki menu offers a formal gourmet dinner of seven, eight, or nine dishes, and must be ordered at least 24 hr. ahead. Flawless svce; resv. highly advisable. **I–M**

☀☆♈♈ **The Willows** (nr. dwntwn), 901 Hausten St. (946-4808). A/C. Lunch/dinner daily; closed hols. AE, CB, DC, MC, V. *Specialties:* the whole gamut of Polynesian dishes—laulau, limu kohu, lomi-lomi, haupia—as well as scallops Royale and some very good curries. Excellent desserts, such as "Sky High" lemon meringue pie. *Note:* Picture-postcard perfect w. its luxuriant, leafy setting complete w. waterfalls and fishpools; for more than 40 years it has been a "must" for tourists. Good svce; resv. essential. Valet parking. 10 min. from dwntwn. *Polynesian.* **I–M**

☀☆♈ **Fisherman's Wharf** (nr. dwntwn), 1009 Ala Moana Blvd. (538-3808). A/C. Lunch/dinner daily. AE, CB, DC, MC, V. *Specialties:* every variety of Pacific seafood, absolutely fresh and at prices easy on your wallet; shrimp Louie salad, clam chowder, cioppino, scampi sautéed in garlic butter. *Note:* Honolulu's most popular fish rest. for three decades; often crowded and noisy, in spite of which the waitresses contrive to work miracles. Pleasant nautical decor and pretty view of Kewalo yacht basin. Resv. recommended. *Seafood.* **I–M**

♈ **Kim Chee Two** (nr. dwntwn), 3569 Waialae Ave. (737-0006). A/C. Lunch/dinner daily. MC, V. *Specialties:* seaweed soup, bi bim kook soo (noodles w. meat and vegetables), man doo (fried dumplings stuffed w. pork, cabbage, and tofu), barbecued chicken and meat dishes, fried yellowfish w. rice and vegetables. *Note:* The readers of *Honolulu* magazine have picked this as Honolulu's best Korean rest. for 3 years in a row—a noteworthy decision in a city where Korean food has long been respected. Some dynamite condiments, but overall the flavors are subdued, the servings generous, and the prices low. The decor adds nothing, and the place is often noisy. Very popular locally. Other location: 1040 S. King St. (536-1426). *Korean.* **B**

Other Restaurants (from top bracket to budget)

☀☆♈♈♈ **John Dominis** (dwntwn), 43 Ahui St. (523-0955). A/C. Dinner only, nightly. AE, CB, DC, MC, V. Jkt. *Specialties:* every kind of Pacific seafood oven-broiled or cooked in its broth, clam chowder, cioppino (a Californian seafood stew), macadamia-nut cream pie. Good wine list. *Note:* One of the best, and handsomest, rests. in all the islands. Absolutely fresh-caught fish and shellfish. Splendid glass-walled dining rm, from which you can see the sea creatures swimming in their saltwater holding pools carved out of living rock. Splendid view of the harbor, w. Diamond Head in the distance. Cordial, smiling svce; friendly bar; the favorite of the local smart set. Resv. advised. *Seafood/Polynesian.* **E–VE**

☀☆♈♈♈ **Golden Dragon** (nr. dwntwn), in the Hilton Hawaiian Village (see "Accommodations," above) (946-5336). A/C. Dinner only, nightly. AE, CB, DC, MC, V. *Specialties:* crisp lemon chicken, stir-fried lobster in curry sauce, Peking duck, ginger ice cream, haupia (coconut pudding), delicious homemade desserts. A large wine list, not commonly found in Asian rests. *Note:* The most luxurious and expensive Chinese rest. in Honolulu, featuring impeccably prepared and served Cantonese haute cuisine from the skilled hand of chef Dai Hoy Chang. Some extremely sophisticated dishes such as the Imperial Beggar's Chicken (wrapped in lotus leaves and braised for 6 hr. in a hermetically sealed clay pot) must be ordered 24 hr. ahead. Sumptuous setting w. a view over a dream lagoon. Faultless svce. Resv. strongly advised. *Chinese.* **M–E**

♈♈ **Hy's Steak House** (nr. dwntwn), 2440 Kuhio Ave. (922-5555). A/C. Dinner only, nightly. AE, CB, DC, MC, V. Jkt. *Specialties:* oysters Rockefeller, Delmonico steak, filet mignon, glazed New York peppercorn steak, barbecued pork chops, beef burgundy, roast rack of lamb, cherries Jubilee. *Note:* If you enjoy filling food, this is your place. Excellent beef broiled to perfection over an open flame at the end of the rm. Elegant clubhouse setting; super-professional tuxedoed waiters. Resv. recommended. Valet parking. *Steak.* **M**

Bon Appetit (nr. dwntwn), 1778 Ala Moana Blvd. (942-3837). A/C. Lunch Mon–Fri, dinner Mon–Sat. AE, CB, DC, MC, V. *Specialties:* mousse of scallops w. caviar, fish soup w. saffron, snails in puff pastry, sliced breast of duck w. four-peppercorn sauce, tarte tatin. Menu changes regularly. *Note:* Guy Banal, rules w. dexterity and finesse over the stove of this charming French-style bistro located unexpectedly in the middle of the Discovery Bay Shopping Center. Walls decorated w. bamboo; pastel-colored tablecloths. Very friendly reception and svce. If you like authentic French cooking and affordable prices, this is one of the best places on the island for you. Resv. advised. *French.* **I–M**

Keo's Thai Cuisine (nr. dwntwn), 625 Kapahulu Ave. (737-8240). A/C. Lunch Mon–Sat, dinner nightly. AE, MC, V. *Specialties:* spicy chicken soup, minted spring rolls, beef w. coconut milk, Penang duck, beef-saté w. hot peanut sauce, mango sherbet. *Note:* Given the enormous menu w. its more than 200 dishes ranging from the mildest through the moderately spicy to the volcanic, the lover of exotic foods should not fail to visit this friendly, elegant temple of Thai cooking. Charming tropical-grdn decor w. hanging orchids; attentive, efficient svce; an "in" place to eat. Resv. an absolute must. Other location: 1200 Ala Moana Blvd., Ward Center (533-0533). *Thai.* **I–M**

Suntory (nr. dwntwn), 2233 Kalakaua Ave. (922-5511). A/C. Lunch Mon–Fri, dinner nightly. AE, MC, V. *Specialties:* miso soup, chawan mushi, teppanyaki, shabu shabu, sashimi, sushi. *Note:* In the opinion of connoisseurs, the island's best Japanese rest. Refined, elegant Japanese setting, thoughtful svce. On the 30th floor of the Royal Hawaiian Center. Western-style seating or tatami available. Uptight atmosphere. An excellent place. *Japanese.* **I–M**

Hard Rock Café (nr. dwntwn), 1837 Kalakaua Ave. at Kapiolani Blvd. (955-7383). A/C. Lunch/dinner daily (until midnight). AE, MC, V. *Specialties:* hamburger, barbecued beef, ice-cream sundaes. *Note:* Like its namesakes in London, New York, and other cities it is both a fashionable rest. serving honorable, typically American food—and a rock-and-roll museum. Fans can see the aloha shirt worn by Tom Selleck in the TV series "Magnum P.I." The music is ear-splitting. No resv.; valet parking. *American.* **B–I**

King Tsin (nr. dwntwn), 1110 McCully St. at Young St. (946-3273). A/C. Lunch/dinner daily. AE, CB, DC, MC, V. *Specialties:* Hunan shrimp, Shanghai fried noodles, moo shu pork, pot stickers, Szechuan duck, Mongolian beef, "Beggar's Chicken," Hunan pork w. broccoli. *Note:* The decor of this little rest. is nothing to write home about, but the Szechuan-style food is 100% authentic, and some of the best Chinese cooking to be found on the island. Some dishes are highly spiced. Repeat customers. A fine place to eat; resv. advised. *Chinese.* **B–I**

Ono Hawaiian Food (nr. dwntwn), 726 Kapahula Ave. (737-2275). A/C. Lunch/dinner Mon–Sat (until 7:30pm). No credit cards. *Specialties:* rice soup w. chicken, Kalúa pig (roast sucking pig), lomi-lomi, laulau, curried beef, pipíkaula (spiced sun-dried beef), haupia. *Note:* In spite of some major flaws (no alcoholic beverages, no resv., no credit cards accepted) Ono Hawaiian food has always drawn crowds. Every afternoon from 4:30 on patrons line up outside the entrance for one of the rare available tables. The reason is the excellent, authentic Hawaiian food. *Ono* means "delicious" in Hawaiian. An absolute must for every visitor to the islands. *Polynesian.* **B**

Wo Fat (dwntwn), 115 N. Hotel St. (537-6260). A/C. Lunch/dinner daily. AE, CB, DC, MC, V. *Specialties:* crisp gau gee, bird's-nest soup, sweet-and-sour pork, ginger duck, fried noodles w. beef in oyster sauce. *Note:* Honolulu's oldest (1882) and largest Chinese rest., complete

w. a pagoda roof. Typical Cantonese fare. Svce a little abrupt. Outrageously touristy but funny atmosphere. *Chinese.* **B–I**

Cafeteria/Fast Food

Garden Café (dwntwn), in the Honolulu Academy of Arts, 900 S. Beretania St. (538-3693). Lunch only, Tues–Fri. No credit cards. In the museum's modern setting, excellent sandwiches, salads, and daily specials. Closed June–Sept.

The Patisserie (nr. dwntwn), Kahaka Mall Shopping Center, 4211 Waialae Ave. (735-4402). Breakfast/lunch/dinner daily. MC, V. Good cafeteria food at extremely attractive prices: homemade soups, salads, sandwiches, daily specials, excellent pastry. A good place to eat on the wing. For other locations, see the phone book.

BARS & NIGHTCLUBS

Annabelle's (nr. dwntwn), in the Ilikai Hotel (949-3811). Fashionable disco with a fine view over the bay.

Bagwell's Lounge (nr. dwntwn), in the Hyatt Regency (see "Accommodations," above) (922-9292). Trendy bar adjoining the rest. of the same name. Open nightly.

Beach Bar (nr. dwntwn), in the Sheraton Moana Surfrider (see "Accommodations," above) (922-3111). For 80 years this has been Honolulu's most famous bar; the perfect spot for your before-dinner drink. Open nightly.

Bobby McGee's Conglomeration (nr. dwntwn), in the Colony Surf (see "Accommodations," above) (922-1282). Favorite yuppie bar/disco. Also a tasty rest. Open nightly.

Hilton Dome (nr. dwntwn), in the Hilton Hawaiian Village (see "Accommodations," above) (949-4321). This is where you come to see well-known Hawaiian singer and showman Don Ho; a real local institution.

Masquerades (nr. dwntwn), 224 McCully St. (949-6337). Lively bar-disco with a mixed bag of patrons from local punk to tourists in gaudy aloha shirts. Open nightly.

Monarch Room (nr. dwntwn), in the Sheraton Royal Hawaiian Hotel (see "Accommodations," above) (923-7311). Very popular Polynesian show by the brothers Cazimero.

Trapper's (nr. dwntwn), in the Hyatt Regency (see "Accommodations," above) (922-9292). Piano bar, jazz; intimate and relaxing atmosphere. Open nightly.

The Wave (nr. dwntwn), 1877 Kalakaua Ave. (941-0424). Locally popular nightclub with live music; you'll find the best local rock groups like Sonia and Revolución. Open Wed–Sat.

LUAUS (BUFFET & POLYNESIAN SHOW)

Paradise Cove Luau (vic.), a 40-min. drive from Honolulu (free buses from principal Waikiki hotels) (973-5828). Resv. required. Excellent buffet dinner and Polynesian show in a lovely natural setting. Slanted to tourists and crowded, but recommended nonetheless. Open nightly.

Polynesian Cultural Center (vic.), 1½ hr. from Honolulu by car via Hi. 61 and Hi. 83; transportation (for a fee) available from Waikiki hotels (call 293-3333 for resv.). Open Mon–Sat. The biggest and best Polynesian show in the Pacific. Since the center is run by the Mormons, no alcoholic beverages.

Also at the **Sheraton Royal Hawaiian Hotel** (Sun) and the **Sheraton Waikiki** (Tues).

NEARBY EXCURSIONS

HAIKU GARDENS (46-336 Haiku Rd., Kaneohe, 15 mi./ 24km north on Hi. 61) (247-6671): Tropical jungle with bamboo thickets and giant waterlilies at the foot of the **Koolau Mountains**. An exotic picture-postcard sight.

☼🔔 **Valley of the Temples Memorial Park,** at 47-200 Kahekili Hwy., Kaneohe (239-8111), adjoining Haiku Gardens, is an exact replica of the famous Byodoin temple near Kyoto in a wonderful natural setting of Japanese gardens, fountains, and statues. Open daily.

Stop at **Nuuanu Pali Lookout,** offering one of the best views on the island. In 1795 this was the scene of a bloody battle, after which hundreds of the defeated warriors were hurled over the cliff by the soldiers of King Kamehameha.

☼🔔🔔 **POLYNESIAN CULTURAL CENTER** (at Laie, 38 mi./ 60km north along Hi. 61 and Hi. 83) (293-3333; toll free 800/367-7060): The most popular attraction of the Hawaiian Islands. Seven carefully reconstructed Polynesian villages, representing the whole gamut of Pacific cultures (Hawaii, Tahiti, Samoa, Fiji, Tonga, etc.), standing in 42 acres (17ha) of beautiful gardens. Excellent displays of folk-dancing (resv. recommended for the evening buffet dinner shows). Not far away is a spectacular Mormon temple (the Mormons manage the Polynesian Cultural Center). Open Mon–Sat. Bus svce from Honolulu; 1½ hr.

🔔 **SEA LIFE PARK** (on Makapuu Point at Waimanalo, 16 mi./ 26km east on Hi. 72) (259-7933): Outstanding marine zoo opposite the very beautiful Makapuu Beach; offers a complete selection of Pacific marine life from sea anemones to sharks and from dolphins to sea lions. Whaling museum. 30 min. from dwntwn. Open daily.

☼🔔 **WAIMEA FALLS PARK** (42 mi./67km NW on H-1, H-2, and Hi. 83) (638-8511): 1,730 acres (700ha) of jungle, tropical gardens, trails, and rock terraces with some very lovely waterfalls in which swimming is permitted. Open daily.

THE ISLANDS: HIGHLIGHTS

GETTING THERE: You can get from island to island by recreational tour boats and luxury cruisers (consult your travel agent), or by air. **Aloha Airlines** (808/836-1111) and **Hawaiian Airlines** (808/537-5100) offer inter-island transportation. Passengers holding full-fare round-trip tickets from the mainland may travel to other islands for an additional charge of about $40–$50 per stopover.

THE ISLAND OF HAWAII: "The Volcano Isle," 40 min. from Honolulu by air (also known as "The Big Island" or "Orchid Island"). At 4,038 sq. mi. (10,460km²)—almost the size of Connecticut—Hawaii is the largest island in the chain. Its sources of revenue are tropical produce (particularly orchids), cattle rearing, and tourism. The island's largest city (and capital), **Hilo,** acts as food, lodging, and transportation hub (flights to/from the mainland and other islands) for visitors. Hawaii is a microcosm of the physical geography of the islands, with its luxuriant vegetation, its white, green, and black sand beaches, and its two active volcanoes: **Kilauea,** in perpetual eruption since Jan. 1983, and the stately **Mauna Loa,** whose 13,000-ft. (4,000m) crest is crowned with snow in winter—an unusual sight in these tropical latitudes. The **Keck Telescope** with its giant 396-in. (10m) lens stands atop the extinct volcano Mauna Kea, highest point in the islands at 13,796 ft. (4,206m); it's the world's most powerful, twice as large as the instrument at Mount Palomar in California. It is expected to begin operations toward the end of 1991.

It was from this island that the great Kamehameha, seeking to end the internecine quarrels of the archipelago, set out to conquer the neighboring islands and unite their people under his rule. Hawaii's southern extremity, **Ka Lae** or **South Cape,** is the southernmost point of U.S. territory.

The Sights

Among the island's most interesting tourist attractions are:

Akaka Falls State Park, north of Hilo along the beautiful Hamakua coast road: Lovely park with giant 432-ft. (135m) waterfalls.

Atlantis Submarine, Hotel King Kamehameha, 75-5660 Palani Rd., Kailua Kona (329-3175): A 45-min. trip to the ocean floor off Kailua Kona on a 46-seat submarine with big portholes. Spectacular sights; fare, $68.

Captain Cook Monument, at Kealakekua Bay, where the British explorer was killed by the Hawaiians in 1779. Splendid ocean view. Daily boat trips from Kailua Kona.

Kalapana Beach: Black sand (powdered-lava) beach at the eastern end of the island. A lava flow from Kilauea Volcano about 500 yards (460m) wide has engulfed half the beach, in times past one of the island's best surfing spots. Visitors are no longer allowed.

Lapakahi Historical State Park, near Mahukona: Site of a 600-year-old fishing village. Ongoing archeological excavations. Don't miss the view.

Mauna Kea Observatories, reached via Hi. 200 and Mauna Kea Rd., 40 mi. (64km west of Hilo: Group of nine astronomical observatories built since 1968 atop the Mauna Kea volcano (13,796 ft./4,206m). This is the largest scientific facility of its kind in the world. Access highway, with unforgettable views, open to the public—but you need a four-wheel-drive vehicle.

Orchid Farms around Hilo: Several of these may be visited, particularly **Nani Maui Gardens,** 421 Makalika St. (959-3541), and **Orchids of Hawaii,** 2801 Kilauea Ave. (959-3581). This is the world's largest orchid-exporting center. Open daily.

Rainbow Falls, Waianuenue Ave., Hilo: Beautiful waterfalls on the Wailuku River, with guaranteed rainbows on sunny mornings. Splendid trails for walkers.

Volcanoes National Park, 29 mi. (47km) SW of Hilo on Hi. 11: The only U.S. nature reserve with two active volcanoes— Mauna Loa, the more impressive (13,680 ft./4,275m), and Kilauea (4,077 ft./1,274m), the world's most active volcano, which has been erupting almost continuously since 1983. A panoramic ring road, **Crater Rim Drive,** goes around Kilauea (when it isn't rendered impassable by magma!), and offers a fine view of molten lava flows, forests of giant ferns, and land laid waste by earlier eruptions. If you call 967-7977, a recorded message will advise you of the current level of volcanic activity. You can stay at Volcano House (see below). Interesting museum of volcanology at the park headquarters, open daily. For information, contact the Superintendent, Hawaii Volcanoes National Park, Hawaii, HI 96785 (808/967-7311). Don't fail to visit it.

The Island's Best Beaches

Hapuna Beach State Park, on Hi. 19, 30 mi. (48km) north of Kailua Kona: Fine long sandy beach edged with palm-planted lawns. Swimming here in rough weather is imprudent.

Kaunaoa Beach, reached by footpath along the shore, 1 mi. (1.6km) north of Hapuna Beach (see above): A huge, beautiful crescent of white sand. For the very lovely access footpath, wear shoes or sandals. Largely overlooked by tourists.

Where to Stay

☀ ☖☖☖☖☖ **Hyatt Regency Waikoloa,** 1 Waikoloa Beach Resort, Waikoloa, HI 96743 (808/885-1234; toll free, see Hyatt). 1,244 rms, A/C, color TV, in-rm movies. AE, CB, DC, MC, V. Valet parking $6, six pools, artificial lagoon, beach, eight tennis courts, three golf courses, health club, sauna, Turkish bath, massage, horseback riding, boating, water sports, fishing, hunting, auto race track, seven rests., bars, rm svce, luau nightly, nightclub. *Note:* Billed as the world's most costly ($360-million) resort complex, this exuberant luxury palace hotel with its 1,244 rms—half Walt Disney World, half hotel—stands in 62 acres (25ha) of magnificent tropical grdns on Waiulua Bay. Among its numberless attractions: six freshwater pools, including one enormous basin w. Jacuzzis, waterfalls, and artificial sea caves; a monorail and fake Venetian canals linking the three principal buildings; an auto racetrack; wild-boar hunts in the nearby mountains; etc. The rms in the three towers are unusually spacious and comfortable; 75% of them overlook the ocean. Ultra-comprehensive physical-fitness facilities. Large as the place is, the svce is efficient. One of the best hotels in the country. **VE**

☀ ☖☖☖☖ **Mauna Lani Bay Hotel,** Hi. 19, Kohala Coast, Kawaihae, HI 96743 (808/885-6622; toll free 800/367-2323). 351 rms, A/C, color TV, in-rm movies. AE, CB, DC, MC, V. Free valet parking, pool, golf course, putting green, 10 tennis courts, sauna, private beach, fishing, boating, horseback riding, four rests. (including the Gallery Restaurant), coffee shop, three bars, rm svce, disco, boutiques. *Note:* One of the most luxurious hotels in the Pacific basin; a modern building designed like a ship's prow and standing in its own lovely tropical grdns. Splendid lobby w. indoor pool and palm trees. Elegant, richly furnished rms w. ocean or mountain view. Attentive, personalized svce. Caters mostly to groups and a monied clientele. **VE**

☀ ☖☖☖ **Hilton Kona Beach & Tennis Resort,** Alii Dr. (P.O. Box 1179), Kailua Kona, HI 96740 (808/329-3111; toll free, see Hilton). 452 rms, A/C, color TV, in-rm movies. AE, CB, DC, MC, V. Free parking, pool, private beach, golf course, four tennis courts, water sports, horseback riding, four rests. and bars, coffee shop, piano bar, rm svce, disco. *Note:* Futuristic building right on the ocean; beautiful rms w. private patios and spectacular view of the Pacific. Tropical grdns. Comprehensive sports facilities. Good svce. One of the best hotels in the Islands. Group clientele. **E–VE**

☖☖☖ **Kona Surf Hotel,** 78-128 Ehukai St., Keauhou Kona, HI 96740 (808/322-3411; toll free 800/367-2603). 532 rms, A/C, color TV, in-rm movies. AE, CB, DC, MC, V. Free parking, two pools, golf course, three tennis courts, sauna, fishing, rest., bars, rm svce, nightclub, hrdrsr, boutiques. *Note:* Very lovely modern hotel on the ocean. Comfortable rms w. refrigerators and private balconies. Excellent svce. Magnificent tropical gardens. Very good value; the favorite of those in-the-know. **E–VE,** but lower rates off-season.

☖☖ **Kanaloa at Kona,** 78-261 Manukai St., Kailua Kona, HI 96740 (808/322-9625; toll free 800/777-1700). 118 suites and villas; no A/C; cable color TV. AE, CB, DC, MC, V. Free parking, three pools, two tennis courts, beach, golf, rest., bar. *Note:* Luxurious resort complex on magnificent Keauhu Bay, in 13 acres (5ha) of tropical grdns. Comfortable, spacious suites and villas, all w. kitchenette and private terrace. Elegant layout and decor. Interesting vacation packages. A good place. **E–VE**

☖☖ **Keauhou Beach,** 78-6740 Alii Dr., Keauhou Kona, HI 96740 (808/322-3441). 317 rms, A/C, color TV, in-rm movies. AE, CB, DC, MC, V. Free parking, pool, six tennis courts, sauna, health club, private beach, rest. (Ocean Terrace), bar, rm svce. *Note:* Modern, comfortable hotel partly overhanging the water. Huge, well-laid-out rms w. private balconies

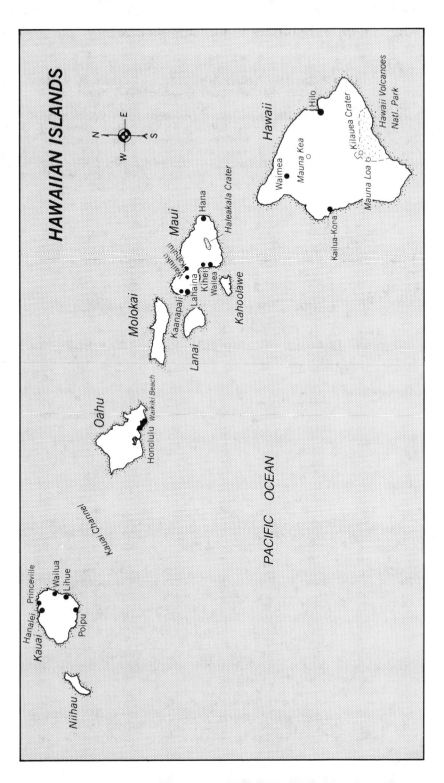

HAWAIIAN ISLANDS

Niihau

Kauai
Hanalei
Princeville
Wailua
Lihue
Poipu

Kauai Channel

Oahu
Honolulu
Waikiki Beach

Molokai

Lanai

Maui
Kaanapali
Lahaina
Kihei
Wailea
Kahoolawe
Kaeleku
Wailuku
Kahului
Hana
Haleakala Crater

N
E
W
S

Hawaii
Waimea
Mauna Kea
Mauna Loa
Kailua-Kona
Hilo
Kilauea Crater
Hawaii Volcanoes Natl. Park

PACIFIC OCEAN

and panoramic views. Good value, but svce a little undependable. **M–E,** but lower rates off-season.

Hilo Bay Hotel (Uncle Billy's), 87 Banyan Dr., Hilo, HI 96740 (808/935-0861; toll free 800/367-5102). 150 rms, A/C, color TV. AE, CB, DC, MC, V. Free parking, pool, rest., valet svce, nightclub. *Note:* Engaging little countrified family hotel standing in pleasant tropical grdns w. a goldfish pool. Serviceably comfortable rms w. terrace, the best overlooking the grdn; some w. kitchenette and refrigerator. Friendly reception and svce. Good value. **M**

Parker Ranch Lodge, on Hi. 19 (P.O. Box 458), Kamuela, HI 96743 (808/885-4100). 20 rms; no A/C; cable color TV. AE, MC, V. Free parking, rest. and bar adjoining. *Note:* Small, sound, unpretentious motel. Huge, comfortable rms, half w. kitchenette. Good value on balance. **M**

Volcano House, Hi. 11, in Volcanoes National Park, HI 96718 (808/967-7321). 37 rms; no A/C. AE, CB, DC, MC, V. Free parking, sauna, rest., bar. *Note:* One of the loveliest sites in the islands, in the heart of Volcanoes National Park. Cordial country-inn-style comfort; very acceptable rest. (but mobbed by visitors at lunch). You should reserve as far ahead as possible. Some rms have a fine view of the crater. Open year round. Excellent value. **I–M**

Country Club Hotel, 121 Banyan Dr., Hilo, HI 96720 (808/935-7171). 149 rms, A/C, color TV. AE, CB, DC, MC, V. Free parking, pool, rest., bar, disco. *Note:* Small, relatively modern hotel on the ocean, in tropical grdns surrounded by palm trees. Homelike rms w. private balconies, most w. refrigerators. Svce w. a smile. Interesting vacation packages. Near the airport. Good value. **I**

Where to Eat

Merriman's, on Hi. 19 at Opelo Plaza, Waimea (885-6822). A/C. Dinner nightly, brunch Sun. AE, MC, V. *Specialties:* sea-urchin consommé, fresh pasta w. basil and macadamia nuts, fern shoots w. Maui onions, sautéed mahi mahi w. shiitake-mushroom sauce, papaya chicken w. lime-and-pepper sauce, remarkable desserts. *Note:* The young chef Peter Merriman, formerly at the renowned Mauna Lami Bay Hotel, is one of the most original and imaginative in the islands. His cuisine features local produce and local techniques. Since his rest. opened in Dec 1988 it has gained acceptance as one of the finest in Hawaii. Interesting, slightly exotic contemporary decor. Reception and svce w. a smile. Resv. a must. A very good place. *American/Polynesian.* **M**

Edelweiss, Kawaii Hae Rd. at Hi. 19, Kamuela (885-6800). A/C. Lunch/dinner Tues–Sun; closed Sept. MC, V. *Specialties:* papaya Edelweiss (stuffed w. scallops and baked), médaillons of wild boar, pasta al fresco, roast pork w. sauerkraut, roast duck Bigarade, Black Velvet cake. *Note:* A misplaced Bavarian chalet under tropical skies, Edelweiss is the brainchild of another refugee from the Mauna Lani Bay Hotel, the accomplished German chef Peter Hager. His cooking, though predominantly Continental, admits the occasional exotic touch. First-class svce; a local favorite since 1983. Unfortunately no resv., so expect a wait. *Continental.* **I–M**

S.S. James Makee, in the Kona Surf Hotel (see "Where to Stay," above) (322-3411). A/C. Dinner only, nightly. AE, CB, DC, MC, V. *Specialties:* European-inspired food w. a touch of the exotic, tempting homemade desserts. *Note:* Some interesting dishes, such as médaillon of beef Diablo and shrimp Polynesian, in an attractive nautical setting. Resv. advised. *Continental/Polynesian.* **I–M**

Parker Ranch Broiler, Hi. 19 and Hi. 190, Kamuela (885-7366). A/C. Lunch/dinner daily; closed Dec 25. AE, DC, MC, V. *Specialties:* grilled red meats and fish, panlolo stew. *Note:* The excellent beef is home-reared on the ranch; so are the vegetables, grown without chemical fertilizer. The chef is one of the best on the island; attractive Victorian bar and lobby. Resv. advised. *Steak/Seafood.* I

☻ **K. K. Tei,** 1550 Kamehameha Ave., Hilo (961-3791). Lunch Mon–Sat, dinner nightly. AE, DC, MC, V. *Specialties:* teppanyaki, tempura. *Note:* Japanese cuisine tailored to the American taste: acceptable on the whole. Pleasant grdn decor. Locally popular since 1947. *Japanese/American.* I

☻ **Kona Inn,** Kona Inn Shopping Village, 75-5744 Alii Dr., Kailua Kona (329-4455). A/C. Lunch/dinner daily, brunch Sun. AE, MC, V. *Specialties:* fried oysters, broiled scampi and calamari, catch of the day, steak, roast beef, guava sherbet. *Note:* Congenial rest. on Kailua Bay w. a fine view of the ocean and its magnificent sunsets. Inviting wood-paneled setting. The freshest of local produce prepared honorably but without much imagination. Hard-working svce. Very popular locally; resv. advised. *American.* I

☻ **Volcano House–Ka Ohelo Dining Room,** in the Volcano House (see "Where to Stay," above) (967-7321). A/C. Lunch/dinner daily. AE, CB, DC, MC, V. *Specialties:* teriyaki (broiled marinated meat), mahi-mahi (broiled dolphin), steak, prime rib. *Note:* A superb setting inside Volcanoes National Park itself. Very decent food. Buffet at lunchtime. Friendly svce. Resv. a must. *Japanese/Polynesian.* I

☻ **Ocean View Inn,** 75-5683 Alii Dr., Kailua (329-9988). Breakfast/lunch/dinner Tues–Sun. No credit cards. *Specialties:* broiled catch of the day; hamburgers; Japanese, Chinese, and Polynesian dishes. The huge menu boasts some 200 different dishes and combinations. *Note:* One of the most popular rests. on the Big Island, right across from the harbor. The food is a strange medley from around the Pacific Rim: Hawaiian, Japanese, Chinese, Philippine, and American. Sturdy helpings; low prices. Usually noisy and crowded, but full of local color; a local landmark for more than half a century. Resv. accepted. *American/Polynesian.* B–I

MAUI: "The Valley Isle," 25 min. from Honolulu by air. Maui is the second largest of the islands in area: 729 sq. mi. (1,890km²). It's called the "Valley Isle" because of the long, low-lying fertile isthmus that joins the island's two craggy extremities. On the southeast coast stands the astonishing extinct volcano Haleakala, whose enormous arid crater could hold Manhattan Island. In 1802 King Kamehameha I chose Maui as the site of his capital, Lahaina. Now it's a favorite vacation spot for lovers of big-game fishing and scuba-diving.

The Sights

Haleakala National Park, 26 mi. (42km) SE of Kahului on Hi. 37 and Hi. 378: Big nature reserve, over which looms the Haleakala volcano (known as "The House of the Sun"), which has been dormant for 200 years; the huge crater is 6 mi. (10km) long, 3 mi. (5km) wide, and about 2,900 ft. (900m) deep. According to Hawaiian legend it was the home of the god Maui, who was able to make the sun stand still in its course. If you want to visit the crater you should be in good shape, and wear stout shoes and warm clothing. Spectacular view of much of the island chain. Visitor center open daily; for information, call 572-9306, or 572-7749 for recorded information on the weather.

Hana Highway, Hi. 36, Hi. 360, and Hi. 31 from Lower Paia to Obeo Gulch: In its 50-mi. (80km) length this scenic highway clinging to a mountainside overlooking the ocean has 600 turns and some 50 one-way bridges. All this in a setting of tropical jungles, waterfalls, and precipitous ravines. Tourists, unfortunately, flock here. Try the drive late in the afternoon or early in the morning to avoid the rush.

Iao Valley State Park, near Wailuku: Wonderful green valley, over which towers a spectacular rock needle 1,197 ft. (365m) high, overgrown with verdure. A must-see.

    Kaanapali Beach, near Lahaina: One of the finest beaches in the entire state—but also the most crowded—on the island's northwest shore.

    Lahaina: Picturesque little harbor that was a favorite port of call for whalers in the 19th century. An amusing little train drawn by a steam engine runs a connecting service to Kaanapali (661-0080). Japanese cultural center, the Lahaina Joda Mission on Ala Moana St., with a giant statue of Buddha; open daily. Worth going out of your way for.

The Island's Best Beaches

    D. T. Fleming Beach County Park, on Hi. 30, 5 mi. (8km) north of Kanapali (take the turnoff to the ocean): Lying between two rocky, wave-beaten headlands is a lovely sand beach, uncrowded on weekdays.

    Hamoa Beach, on Hi. 31, 1 mi. (2.5km) south of Hana: One of the loveliest in the islands; a wonderful semicircle of sand beach fringed with palm trees. Glorious swimming.

    Maluaka Beach, reached via Hi. 31 and Makena Rd., 1 mi. (1.6km) south of Makena, beyond Keawalai Church): Huge wide beach protected by dunes and plantations of kiawe trees. Ample public parking near the Maui Prince Hotel.

Where to Stay

    Hyatt Regency Maui, 200 Nohea Kai Dr., Kaanapali Beach, HI 96761 (808/661-1234; toll free, see Hyatt). 815 rms, A/C, color TV, in-rm movies. AE, CB, DC, MC, V. Valet parking $6, two pools, two golf courses, five tennis courts, health club, sauna, boats, four rests. (including the Swan Court), coffee shop, seven bars, rm svce, disco, hrdrsr, boutiques. *Note:* Three ultramodern buildings on the beach w. splendid tropical grdns, indoor waterfalls, and a giant swimming pool. Spacious, comfortable rms. The interior decoration includes many Asian and Polynesian works of art. Excellent svce; comprehensive sports facilities; beautiful setting. Private heliport. Interesting vacation packages. One of Hawaii's best hotels. VIP suites on the top three floors of the main building, including one of the islands' most expensive—$1,400 a night. **VE,** but lower rates off-season.

    Inter-Continental Maui Hotel, 3700 Ala Nui St., Wailea, HI 96753 (808/879-1922; toll free, see Inter-continental). 540 rms, A/C, cable color TV. AE, CB, DC, MC, V. Valet parking $5, three pools, two golf courses, 14 tennis courts, private beach, water sports, fishing, three rests. (including La Pérouse), four bars, rm svce, nightclub, hrdrsr, boutiques. *Note:* Luxury hotel on the ocean w. 1,450 acres (587ha) of tropical grdns and woodlands. Spacious, completely refurbished rms w. views of the ocean or Mount Haleakala. Comfort and facilities above reproach; very good svce; very commendable rests. This is a hotel of quality—one of the finest in the islands. **VE**

    Kaanapali Beach Hotel, 2525 Kaanapali Pkwy., Kaanapali, HI 96761 (808/661-0011; toll free 800/367-5170). 431 rms, A/C, color TV, in-rm movies. AE, CB, DC, MC, V. Free parking, pool, tennis court, golf course, private beach, rest. (Tiki Terrace), coffee shop, bar, nightclub. *Note:* Modern deluxe resort hotel, standing almost in the ocean. Relaxed atmosphere; comfortable rms w. private balconies and refrigerators. Agreeable svce; mediocre rest. Good overall value. **E–VE**

    Maui Lu Resort, 575 S. Kihei Rd., Kihei, HI 96753 (808/879-5881; toll free 800/922-7866). 170 rms, A/C, cable color TV. AE, CB, DC, MC, V. Free parking, pool, two tennis courts, rest. (Longhouse), bar. *Note:* Hotel decorated in tropical style w. direct beach access; 19 acres (7.7ha) of grdns and palm groves. Comfortable rms w. refrigerators, some w. kitchenettes. Less-than-ideal svce, but good overall value. Luaus. **M–E,** but lower rates off-season.

    Coconut Inn, 181 Hui Rd., Napili Bay, HI 96761 (808/669-5712; toll free 800/367-8006). 41 apts and studios, color TV.

AE, MC, V. Free parking; no bar or rest.; free breakfast (the homemade banana bread is justly famed). *Note:* Nice little residential hotel just off the beach. Huge, comfortable apts or studios w. fully equipped kitchenette. Friendly reception and svce. Good value on balance. **M–E**

Where to Eat

Gerard's, in the Plantation Inn, 174 Lahainaluna Rd., Lahaina (661-8939) A/C. Breakfast/lunch/dinner daily. AE, MC, V. *Specialties:* raw fish à la tahitienne, frogs' legs, squid w. lime and ginger, bouillabaisse, confit of duck fricassée, partridge à l'étouffée. Desserts are irresistible. The menu changes daily. *Note:* One of the best—if not *the* best—French rest. in the islands. The cuisine of master chef Gerard Reversade is a delicate blend of French ideas with Maui-grown ingredients and produce such enchantments as ahi (tuna) w. béarnaise sauce and bean sprouts. Very good wines to complement the food. Brightly lit decor w. period oak and stained glass. Smooth and informal svce. Resv. essential. **M–E**

La Pérouse, in the Inter-Continental Maui Hotel (see "Where to Stay," above) (879-1922). A/C. Dinner only, nightly. AE, CB, DC, MC, V. Jkt. *Specialties:* callaloo-crab soup, bouillabaisse, Pacific snapper w. crab and dill, sautéed scallops w. black beans and cucumber, veal loin w. ginger and chives. Excellent desserts. *Note:* Elegant luxury hotel dining rm in a beautiful Polynesian setting. Cuisine innovative and delicate. Attentive svce. One of the best places on the island. Resv. advised. *French/Polynesian.* **M–E**

Chez Paul, Hwy. 820C, Olowalu Village, Lahaina (611-3843). A/C. Dinner only, nightly. AE, CB, DC, MC, V. *Specialties:* frogs' legs, duck La Pérouse, scampi Olowalu, sauté of veal w. apples and Calvados, mahi-mahi in buerre blanc, tournedos Madagascar. *Note:* Very good French-inspired food, w. prices to match. Pleasant setting and atmosphere; very popular locally. Resv. advised. *French/Polynesian.* **I–M**

Mama's Fish House, 799 Poho Pl., Paia (579-9672). A/C. Lunch/dinner daily. AE, DC, MC, V. *Specialties:* fried calamari, cold papaya-and-coconut soup, crab cooked in beer, oven-baked fish w. tarragon, ahi (tuna) teriyaki w. ginger, fried sweet potatoes, Hookipa sundae. *Note:* As the name suggests, the house specialty is fish of all kinds; the menu also features chicken and meat. Beautiful location on the beach w. wrap-around ocean view through huge picture windows. Efficient svce. A fine place for seafood enthusiasts. Resv. advisable. *Seafood.* **I–M**

Ming Yuen Chinese Restaurant, 162 Alamaha St., Kahului (871-7787). A/C. Lunch Mon–Sat, dinner nightly. AE, CB, DC, MC, V. *Specialties:* hot-and-sour soup, sweet-and-sour shrimp, broccoli beef, eggplant Szechuan style. *Note:* Informed opinion rates this Maui's best Chinese rest.; what's more, the prices are very reasonable. Real Chinese food, mostly Cantonese or Szechuan; one-scheme-fits-all Far Eastern decor. Small, successful, and noisy; resv. advised. *Chinese.* **B–I**

KAUAI: "The Garden Isle," 25 min. from Honolulu by air. **Mount Waialeale,** a huge (5,208-ft./1,587m high) extinct volcano, holds the world's wet-weather record, with 350 rainy days and 460 in. (11.45m) of rainfall yearly! Nicknamed "The Garden Isle" for the luxuriance of its vegetation, Kauai was the first Hawaiian island visited by Captain Cook (1778). It was also the last independent kingdom in the archipelago. Its tortuous contours make for difficult traveling. The capital of the island is **Lihue.**

The Sights

Among the more interesting places to visit are:

Hanalei: A fashionable spa nestling at the head of a sweeping bay.

Na Pali Coast: This rocky shoreline at the NW end of the island can be reached only by a difficult footpath leading from the end of Hi. 56. This road from Princeville to Kee Beach has a spectacular 10-min. (16km) drive among idyllic, rarely crowded beaches and impressive ridges of rock covered with lush vegetation; this sight alone is worth the trip to Kauai.

⛛🜄 **Wailua Falls,** north of Lihue: Beautiful twin falls, and the spectacular **Fern Grotto** carpeted with tropical ferns. This popular attraction can be reached only by boat from Wailua River Marina. Don't miss it.

⛛🜄🜄 **Waimea Canyon State Park,** near Waimea: Magnificent gorges with walls of multicolored rock, reminiscent of Colorado's Grand Canyon. The last section of the road to **Kalalau Lookout** offers some fine views. There are two beautiful panoramic roads: **Waimea Canyon Drive** (Hi. 550), from Waimea to Puu Ka Pele Forest Reserve; and **Kokee Road** (Hi. 55), between Kekaha and Waimea Canyon State Park.

The Island's Best Beaches

🜄 **Kauapea Beach,** reached by a steep footpath from Kauapea Rd. near Kilauea Lighthouse: Deserted coral-sand beach.

🜄 **Kee Beach,** at western end of Hi. 56, 2 mi. (3km) west of Haena: Fine-sand beach several miles long. The surf here is dangerous in winter.

⛛🜄 **Polihale State Park,** reached via a 5-mi. (8km) unsurfaced but usable road at the western end of Hi. 50: Huge sandy beach overlooked by the magnificent inaccessible cliffs of Na Pali.

Where to Stay

🜏🜏🜏🜏 **Westin Kauai,** Hi. 51 at Kalapaki Beach, Lihue, HI 96766 (808/245-5050; toll free, see Westin). 850 rms, A/C, color TV, in-rm movies. AE, CB, DC, MC, V. Free valet parking, two pools, five Jacuzzis, private beach, hot spring, Turkish bath, health club, sauna, massage, nine tennis courts, two golf courses, boating, fishing, water sports, bicycling, horseback riding, six rests. (including The Masters), coffee shop, five bars, 24-hr. rm svce, nightclub, disco, Polynesian show, 70 boutiques. *Note:* The island's super-palace, an 800-acre (323ha) tropical oasis on a half-mile (1km) private beach east of Kauai. The modern architecture surrounded by idyllic grdns is a little overwhelming. Luxurious if slightly flashy interior. Largish rms in pastel colors w. private patio and refrigerator. Remarkable sports facilities (the two golf courses were designed by Jack Nicklaus). Good hotel rests. Efficient, good-natured svce. Package-tour and convention clientele. **VE**

⛛🜏🜏🜏 **Sheraton Mirage Princeville,** 5520 Kahaku Rd., Princeville, HI 96746 (808/826-9644; toll free, see Sheraton). 300 rms, A/C, color TV, in-rm movies. AE, CB, DC, MC, V. Free valet parking, pool, 21 tennis courts, two golf courses, boating, water sports, horseback riding, three rests. (including Nobles), two bars, rm svce, disco, concierge. *Note:* One of the newer grand luxury hotels in the islands, built in an original terraced style on a cliff rising from the magnificent Hanalei Bay. Spacious, ultra-comfortable rms w. refrigerators and private patios, the best overlooking the ocean. Rest. of great distinction. Very complete sports facilities; can be warmly recommended in spite of its very high rates. **VE**

⛛🜏🜏 **Coco Palms Resort Hotel,** Hi. 56 and Hi. 580, Wailua Beach, HI 96766 (808/822-4921; toll free 800/542-2626). 390 rms and private cottages, A/C, cable color TV. AE, CB, DC, MC, V. Free parking, three pools, nine tennis courts, sauna, private beach, three rests. (including the Sea Shell Rm), bars, rm svce, nightclub, boutiques, mini-zoo. *Note:* Very handsome Polynesian-style hotel in a palm grove; a favorite w. honeymooners. Has been the scene of numerous movies, *Blue Hawaii* among them. The palm grove, 45 acres (18ha) of splendid tropical grdns, and the lagoons were once part of a royal property. Spacious rms w. refrigerators (the cottages by the lovely lagoons are preferable). Irreproachable standards of comfort and svce. Rest. highly recommended. Polynesian shows. Good value. For those who love the out-and-out exotic. **E–VE**

🍷🍷 **Outrigger Plantation Hale,** 484 Kuhio Hwy., Kapaa, HI
96746 (808/822-4941; toll free 800/367-5170). 160 suites, A/C, cable color TV. AE, CB, DC, MC, V. Free parking, pools, putting green, adj. rest. *Note:* Near the Wailua River and almost on the beach, this inviting, well-run residential hotel has congenial suites w. kitchenette and private terrace. Friendly reception. Lovely exotic grdns. Recently renovated. The adj. Coconut Plantation Market Place has numerous rests. and stores. **E**

🍷🍷 **Stouffer Poipu Beach Hotel,** 2251 Poipu Rd. (Hi. 520),
Poipu, HI 96756 (808/742-1681; toll free, see Stouffer's). 139 rms, A/C, color TV, in-rm movies. AE, CB, DC, MC, V. Free parking, pool, six tennis courts, beach, rest., bar, rm svce, nightclub. *Note:* Welcoming modern motel on one of the island's most beautiful beaches. Comfortable, spacious rms all w. kitchenettes and refrigerators. Svce w. a smile. A fine place in a very beautiful setting. **E**

🍷🍷 **New Kauai Beach Boy,** 484 Kuhio Hwy., Waipouli Beach, HI
96746 (808/777-1700; toll free 800/367-5205). 243 rms, A/C, cable color TV. AE, CB, DC, MC, V. Free parking, pool, tennis court, private beach, rest., bar. *Note:* Comfortable modern hotel on the site of an old coconut plantation. Large, friendly rms w. refrigerators and private verandas overlooking the ocean. Good svce. Ideal if you love the beach. **E**

Where to Eat

🍸🍸 **The Beach House,** Lawai Rd., Poipu Beach (742-7575).
Lunch/dinner daily; closed Thanksgiving. MC, V. *Specialties:* every kind of seafood, as well as excellent grilled meats. *Note:* One of the best rests. on Kauai, according to those who live there, w. absolutely fresh local produce. Rebuilt after being swept off by Hurricane Iwa. Beautiful multilevel dining rm w. an ocean view; don't miss the sunset at dinnertime. *Seafood/Polynesian.*
I–M

🌞🍸🍸 **Coco Palms–Sea Shell Room,** in the Coco Palms Resort Hotel (see "Where to Stay," above) (822-4921). A/C. Dinner only, nightly. AE, CB, DC, MC, V. Jkt. *Specialties:* coconut chicken, Cantonese food, creative Polynesian and European dishes, catch of the day. Good wine list. *Note:* Open-air pavilion w. spectacular Polynesian decor. Attentive svce. Locally popular; resv. required. *American/Polynesian.* **I–M**

🍸🍸 **Plantation Gardens,** in the Kiahuna Plantation Resort, Poipu
Rd., Koloa (742-1695). Dinner only, nightly. AE, MC, V. Jkt. *Specialties:* crab-stuffed mushrooms, sashimi, poached oysters, opakapaka w. citrus butter, fresh catch of the day. *Note:* A lovely old house overlooking tropical grdns. Good svce. Highly regarded locally, so resv. advised. *French/Polynesian.*
I–M

🍸 **Barbecue Inn,** 2982 Kress St., Lihue (245-2921). A/C.
Breakfast/lunch/dinner Mon–Sat. AE, MC, V. *Specialties:* steak teriyaki, shrimp tempura, baked salmon steak, seafood platter, T-bone steak, corned beef and cabbage. *Note:* Decent, flavorful Japanese-American food at delightfully low prices. Decor on the gloomy side, but a likable place, and very popular locally. Excellent value; resv. unnecessary. *Japanese/American.* **B–I**

🍸 **Rosita's Mexican Restaurant,** Kukui Grove Center, 3-2600
Kaumualii Hwy. (245-8561). A/C. Lunch/dinner daily. AE, DC, MC, V. *Specialties:* tacos, enchiladas, burritos, chile relleño. *Note:* Praiseworthy small, unpretentious Mexican rest. w. congenial decor and food. A local favorite. Generously poured margaritas. Resv. advisable wknds. *Mexican.* **B–I**

MOLOKAI: "The Friendly Isle," 25 min. from Honolulu by air. This rectangular island, 38 mi. (61km) long by 10 mi. (16km) wide, was long a religious sanctuary guarded by the Kahuna priesthood from profane intrusion. In the 19th century a Belgian missionary, Joseph de Veuster, known as Father Damien, established a leper colony here. Even today the island is relatively ignored by tourists, yet the Kalaupapa Peninsula is—without exaggeration—the most spectacular view in Hawaii. Mossy volcanic cliffs rise up at extraordinary angles from a lurid ultramarine sea set with dramatic little islands.

The Sights

Halawa Valley, at the NE of the island on Hi. 450: A succession of tidal waves has sharply reduced the once-large population of this fertile valley. Spectacular waterfalls and numerous Polynesian temples (*heiaus*), once the scene of human sacrifices.

Father Damien's Leprosarium, at Kalaupapa: Site of the old leprosarium founded in 1873 by the famous Belgian missionary; he himself contracted, and died of, the dread disease in 1889 at the age of 49, and his tomb is here. Impressive. More than 100 former sufferers of Hansen's disease, as leprosy is now known, remain at Kalaupapa. Open daily (but only to visitors over 16 years old). For the mule ride (7 hr. round-trip) to get there, resv. required at least 5 days in advance; contact Damien Tours (567-6171 or 567-6675).

Molokai Ranch Wildlife Park Safari, Hi. 460 at Maunaloa (552-2767): Safari zoo on 1,000 acres (400ha) of scrubby, semi-desert savanna, scarcely at all reminiscent of the natural habitat of the African and Asian animals kept here: giraffe, zebra, antelope, nandu, oryx, etc. Four 1½-hr. minibus tours daily, leaving from the Kaluakoi Hotel.

Umilehi Point: From near here rears the world's highest cliff, towering dizzily 3,296 ft. (1,005m) above the sea.

The Island's Best Beaches

Kepuhi Beach, reached via Hi. 460 and Kepuhi Rd., 5 mi. (8km) NW of Maunaloa: Fine white-sand beach much frequented by surfers.

Papohaku Beach Park, adjoining Kepuhi Beach, above: Largest and loveliest on the island. Magnificent white sand, but dangerous for swimming in winter and sometimes even in summer.

Other uncrowded beaches are **Halava Beach, Moonomi Beach,** and **Kahaiawa Beach.**

Where to Stay

Kaluakoi Hotel & Golf Club, Kepuhi Beach, HI 96770 (808/552-2555; toll free 800/777-1700). 288 rms, A/C, color TV. AE, CB, DC, MC, V. Free parking, pool, golf course, four tennis courts, private beach, two rests. (including Ohia Lodge), two bars, nightclub, boutiques. *Note:* The 32 charmingly pretty Polynesian cottages stand at the water's edge. Tranquil, elegant setting. Spacious, comfortable rms w. refrigerators. Good svce. A great place to stay to live in isolation. **M–E**

Wavecrest Resort, Star Rte. 155, Kaunakakai, HI 96748 (808/558-8101). 126 mini-apts, color TV. MC, V. Free parking, pool, two tennis courts, putting green. *Note:* Modern building, right on the beach, w. mini-apts and studios (w. maid service) for one to six persons, all w. kitchenette and private terrace. Good value for family parties. Minimum stay of 3 nights. No bar, no rest. **I–M**

LANAI: "The Pineapple Isle," 30 min. from Honolulu by air. This small island, only 17 mi. (27km) long, is the most authentic—and the least visited—in the Hawaiian chain. It belongs to the food conglomerate, Dole Pineapple Company, and boasts the world's largest pineapple plantation. Tourism is still in its infancy here, so there are superb beaches standing almost empty.

The Best Beach on the Island

Hulo Poe Beach, at the southern end of Manele Rd.: Wonderful white-sand beach shaded by palm trees; its usually calm water makes it very attractive for swimming and diving.

THE ISLANDS OF NIIHAU & KAHOOLAWE: These two islands, alone in the chain, have escaped (but for how long?) the tidal wave of tourism. The former is privately owned by the Robinson family; its 250 or so inhabitants speak only Hawaiian. The latter is an arid military reservation, closed to visitors and used as an artillery and bombing range.

OTHER FROMMER TRAVEL GUIDES: Readers may be interested in Frommer guides that treat Hawaii and Alaska in greater detail: *Frommer's Alaska* and *Frommer's Hawaii on $60 a Day.*

Frommer travel guides are available in most bookstores, or can be ordered by mail from Frommer Books, Prentice Hall Press, 15 Columbus Circle, New York, N.Y. 10023. Turn to the last pages of this book to learn about Frommer's Dollarwise Travel Club, and for ordering information.

CHAPTER 57

ANCHORAGE AND ALASKA 🔥🔥

□ □ □

With its skyscrapers rising against the mountain backdrop, its bustle and its cosmopolitan crowds, Anchorage may at first sight look like the Manhattan of the Far North, but it turns out to have some rustic ways as well. The 20-story hotels and modern office buildings rub shoulders with old frame houses standing in their own little gardens. The new glass-and-steel **William A. Egan Convention Center** faces the **Visitors Information Center,** housed in a log cabin that would have been at home in the gold rush. It's not uncommon for Alaskans to fly 500 mi. (800km) or more out of the bush to Anchorage to see the latest movie or hear a special concert; parked outside a deluxe French restaurant you may well see a four-wheel-drive wagon that would be more at home on a backcountry trail. This pioneer atmosphere is not the least of Alaska's charms.

The city, founded in 1915 as a work camp on the Alaska Railroad, has grown up slowly around the excellent harbor provided by Cook Inlet (the "anchorage" from which it derives its name). In 1940 the future economic capital of Alaska had barely 3,500 inhabitants; its strategic importance only became apparent during World War II. The first oil discoveries in the Kenai Peninsula in 1957, and those at Prudhoe Bay 11 years later, made the city's fortune. Its population rose from 48,000 in 1970 to the present 250,000—almost half the population of the entire state.

Anchorage nestles at the foot of Cook Inlet, the great arm of the sea discovered two centuries ago by British explorer James Cook. Today it is the largest city in the state and its economic capital, as well as an important way-station for transpolar air flights, with more than three million passengers passing through its air terminal every year. Even the severe earthquake of 1964, which destroyed part of the city, scarcely checked its growth-oriented civic spirit. Nevertheless, the local economy has had difficulty getting over the substantial drop in raw oil prices during the past 10 years, the real-estate stagnation, and the negative fallouts on tourism of the *Exxon Valdez* oil spill in the area close to Valdez and Prince William Sound (see "Alaska's Highlights," below). Having only just celebrated its 75th birthday, Anchorage is short on historic buildings, but it offers the visitor its incomparable site, two remarkable museums of Native American and Inuit art, the **Museum of History & Art,** the **Heritage Library & Museum,** and the country's most northerly rose garden. Its location, on the sea and behind the natural barrier of the **Chugach Mountains** to the north and east, gives Anchorage a surprisingly temperate climate. Winter is only a little colder than in Denver or Chicago, and summer is often warmer than in San Francisco.

Anchorage is also an ideal base for exploring the whole of northern Alaska, from **Nome** and **Kotzebue,** in the land of the Midnight Sun and the dogsled, to the **Pribilof Islands** and **Katmai National Park** with their unusual wildlife. Then there are the eternal snows of **Mount McKinley,** at 20,320 ft. (6,193m) the highest mountain in North America (see "Alaska's Highlights," below).

BASIC FACTS: State of Alaska. Area code: 907. Time zone: Alaska (4 hr. behind New York) and Aleutian/Hawaiian (5 hr. behind New York). ZIP Code: 99502. Founded: 1915. Approximate population: 250,000.

CLIMATE: With its relatively mild winters (averaging 13°F/−9°C in Jan), agreeable summers (57°F/15°C in July), and sunlit autumns (though snow can often fall heavily after mid-Oct), the climate of Anchorage is far from being the stereotype of Far Northern severity.

The rest of Alaska, on the other hand, does offer wider swings in temperature, differing from one part of the state to another. The south coast is windy and rainy; average temperatures at **Sitka** are 32°F (0°C) in Jan and 66°F (19°C) in July. The uplands of the interior have a dry, continental climate, with temperatures at **Fairbanks** sometimes rising above 86°F (30°C) in the summer, and falling to −42°F (−40°C) in the winter. The **Arctic North,** or Far North (a quarter of the state's area lies above the Arctic Circle), is very windy and dry, with truly polar winter readings as low as −79°F ([-]62°C) and more temperate summers averaging 64°F (18°C); the short summer is followed by a mild fall. At **Barrow,** the northernmost city in the country, the harbor is ice-bound Oct–Aug—but the sun never sets from May 10 to Aug 2. Equally, it never rises from mid-Nov to the end of Jan. Unless you're a winter-sports enthusiast, Alaska is best visited between early June and late Sept, when average temperatures should run from 35°F (2°C) at the low end to 86°F (30°C) at the highest.

DISTANCES: Denali National Park, 239 mi. (382km); Fairbanks, 364 mi. (582km); Haines, 775 mi. (1,240km); Seward, 127 mi. (203km); Skagway, 890 mi. (1,424km); Valdez, 317 mi. (507km); Whitehorse (Canada), 715 mi. (1,145km).

ARRIVAL & TRANSIT INFORMATION

AIRPORT: Anchorage International Airport (ANC), 5 mi. (8km) SW.

Other major airports in Alaska are **Fairbanks International Airport** (FAI), 4 mi. (6.5km) SE of Fairbanks; and **Juneau Municipal Airport** (JNU), 8 mi. (13km) north of Juneau.

U.S. AIRLINES: Alaska (243-3300), American (toll free 800/433-7300), Delta (toll free 800/221-1212), Markair (243-6275), Northwest (toll free 800/225-2525), Reeve Aleutian (243-4700), Ryan Air Service (248-0695), United (toll free 800/241-6522), and Wilburs (243-7878).

FOREIGN CARRIERS: Air France (243-3400), British Airways (toll free 800/247-9297), Japan Airlines (274-3551), KLM (277-1414), Korean Airlines (243-3329), Lufthansa (243-3142), Sabena (toll free 800/645-3790), SAS (243-4106), and Swissair (243-7771).

CITY LINK: The **cab** fare from the airport to dwntwn is about $14; time, 15 min. Bus: **Dynair Svces** (243-3403) leaves every 30 min. serving principal hotels; fare, $6; time, 20 min. The local bus line, the **People Mover** (343-6543), provides good service to major dwntwn hotels Mon–Sat. Given the climate, renting a car for excursions is advisable only Apr–Sept.

CAR RENTAL (at Anchorage International Airport unless otherwise indicated): Avis (243-2377); Budget (243-0150); Hertz (243-3308); National (243-3406); and Thrifty, 3730 Spennard Rd. (276-2855). In other cities, check the local telephone book.

LIMOUSINE SERVICES: Dav El Limousines (toll free 800/922-0343).

TAXIS: Few and costly; may not be hailed on the street but must be called by phone: **Alaska Cab** (563-5353), **Checker Cab** (276-1234), and **Yellow Cab** (272-2422).

TRAIN: Alaska Railroad, 411 W. 1st Ave. (P.O. Box 107500), Anchorage, AK 99510 (907/265-2623; toll free 800/544-0552): Serves Anchorage–Fairbanks via Denali National Park and Anchorage–Seward–Whittier. Runs year round, with reduced service Sept–May. Resv. a must—at least 2 weeks ahead. Spectacular. Call or write for information.

INTERCITY BUSES: Alaska Sightseeing Co., 543 W. Fourth Ave. (276-1305): Serves Haines and Skagway, with dependable connections to the Alaska Marine Hwy. (see "Ferry," below). **White Pass & Yukon Motorcoaches,** P.O. Box 100479, AK 99150 (907/279-0761): Two weekly trips to Whitehorse, Yukon, with ongoing connection to Haines.

FERRY: The **Alaska Marine Highway,** 333 W. Fourth Ave. (907/272-4482), is a kind of seagoing bus, carrying cars and passengers on comfortable, modern ships; it gives the ports of southeastern Alaska on the Inside Passage route (Haines, Juneau, Ketchikan, Petersburg, Sitka, Skagway, Wrangell) a year-round connection to Seattle and to Prince Rupert in Canada. Spectacular landscapes. Another year-round service leaves Whittier, Valdez, and Cordova for Kodiak Island and the Kenai Peninsula. For timetables, write P.O. Box R, Juneau, AK 99811; or call: in Anchorage (907/272-4482), Haines (907/766-2111), Juneau (907/465-3941), Prince Rupert, B.C. (604/627-1744), Seattle (206/623-1970), Skagway (907/983-2941), or toll free 800/642-0066.

INFORMATION & TOURS

TOURIST INFORMATION: Contact the **Alaska Division of Tourism, Information Office,** P.O. Box E-001, Juneau, AK 99811 (907/465-2010), for information on Alaska in general.
　　Alaska State Division of Parks, P.O. Box 7-001, Anchorage, AK 99510 (907/561-2020): Information on Alaska's national parks and wildlife reserves.
　　Anchorage Convention & Visitors Bureau, 1600 A St., Anchorage, AK 99501 (907/276-4118); also a **Visitors Information Center,** Log Cabin, 546 Fourth Ave. (at F St.), Anchorage, AK 99509 (907/274-3591).
　　A **recorded message** gives information on current cultural and sporting events at 907/276-3200.

GUIDED TOURS: Alaska Sightseeing Tours (bus), 543 W. Fourth Ave., Anchorage, AK 99501 (907/276-1305; toll free 800/637-3334): Guided tours of the principal cities and regions of Alaska, serving Anchorage, Fairbanks, Haines, Juneau, Ketchikan, and Skagway (for local numbers in these cities, consult the telephone book for the appropriate city).
　　Era Helicopters, 6160-T S. Airpark Dr., Anchorage, AK 99502 (907/248-4422; toll free 800/843-1947): Helicopter flights over the mountains and glaciers around Anchorage, Fairbanks, Juneau, Prudhoe Bay, or Valdez (for local numbers in these cities, consult the phone book for the appropriate city).
　　Gray Line Tours of Alaska (bus), 547 W. Fourth Ave., Anchorage, AK 99510 (907/277-5581; toll free 800/544-2206): Guided tours of the principal cities and regions of Alaska, serving Anchorage, Fairbanks, Juneau, Ketchikan,

Skagway, and Valdez (for local numbers in these cities, consult the phone book for the appropriate city).

SIGHTS, ATTRACTIONS & ACTIVITIES

ADVENTURES: Advanced Balloon Adventures, 8701-T Solar Dr., Anchorage, AK 99507 (907/346-3495). Balloon trips over Anchorage and surrounding country; year round.

Alaska Whitewater (raft) (338-0471): Rafting down the Eagle River in the Chugach Mountains; transportation from Anchorage provided. June 1–Sept 10.

Chugach Express Dog Sled Rides, P.O. Box 261-T, Girdwood, AK 99587 (907/783-3266): 1-hr. dogsled rides on the slopes around Anchorage. Nov 15–Apr 15.

CRUISES: The popular Inside Passage cruises visit such ports as Juneau, Ketchikan, Skagway, Sitka, and Glacier Bay. The newer Gulf of Alaska sailings visit ports between Vancouver and Anchorage, including Inside Passage ports. These two cruising areas are not affected by the 1989 *Exxon Valdez* oil spill.

Among the principal tour operators are:

Clipper Cruise Line (toll free 800/325-0010): Sails on 7- and 14-day Inside Passage cruises from late May through Sept.

Cunard (toll free 800/528-6273): Sails on 11-day Gulf of Alaska itineraries between Vancouver and Anchorage from June to late Aug.

Holland America Line–Westours (toll free 800/426-0327): Sails on 7-day Inside Passage cruises from Vancouver and 14-day Gulf of Alaska cruises between Vancouver and Seward. Late May to late Sept.

Princess Cruises (toll free 800/421-0522): Sails on 7-day Inside Passage cruises from Vancouver and 10-day round-trip sailings from San Francisco. Late May to Sept.

Regency Cruises (toll free 800/457-5566): Offers 7-day Gulf of Alaska sailings from mid-May to mid-Sept.

CHURCHES/SYNAGOGUES: ⚓ **St. Innocent's Church,** 6724 E. 4th St. (333-9723): Typical Russian Orthodox church; interesting view; can be seen by appointment only.

HISTORIC BUILDINGS: ⚓ **Oscar Anderson House,** 420 M St. (274-2336). Built by a Swedish immigrant in 1915, this modest frame house is one of the oldest in the city. Carefully restored, the Anderson House with its great cast-iron stove and its period furniture is a living vestige of the past, with a fine view over Cook Inlet. Open Wed–Sun in summer and in Dec.

MUSEUMS: ⚓ **Heritage Library & Museum,** Northern Lights Blvd. at C St. (276-1132): Native American and Inuit handcrafts and mementos of the gold rush. Large collection of works on the history of Alaska. Open Mon–Fri.

⚓ **Museum of History and Art,** 121 W. Seventh Ave. (343-4326): Prehistoric tools, art from the Aleutian, Inuit, and Athapascan cultures, works of contemporary local artists, works from the 19th century onward inspired by Alaska. Interesting temporary exhibitions. Open Tues–Sun.

⚓ **Wildlife Museum,** at Fort Richardson, Bldg. 600 (5 mi./8km NE via Glenn Hwy.) (863-8113): Stuffed fish, mammals, and birds, more than 200 specimens covering the whole range of Alaskan wildlife—a must for those interested in zoology. Open Mon–Fri.

PANORAMAS: ⚓ **Earthquake Park,** at the western end of Northern Lights Blvd.: Overlooking Cook Inlet and its seascapes, this beautiful 135-acre (54ha) park bears eloquent witness to the violence of the 1964 earthquake. Splendid view of **Talkeetna Mountains** to the NE and **Chugach Mountains** to the east.

👓 **Resolution Park,** Third Ave. and L St.: This downtown park offers you not only a statue of Captain Cook (who visited these parts in 1778 in his famous ship *Resolution*), but also a very fine view over Cook Inlet and the legendary **Mt. Susitna,** whose shape suggests a sleeping woman. On a fine day you can see as far as **Mt. McKinley,** 140 mi. (225km) away as the crow flies.

PERFORMING ARTS: For daily listings of all shows and cultural events, consult the entertainment section of the two daily newspapers, the *Anchorage Daily News* (morning) and the *Anchorage Times* (morning and evening), or call 276-ARTS (276-2787) for a recorded list of current cultural events.

Alaska Repertory Theater, 705 W. Sixth Ave. (276-2327): Stages classical, modern, and avant-garde theater Nov–Apr.

Egan Convention Center, 555 W. Fifth Ave. (333-2582): Presents comedian Larry Beck in his *Alaska Show,* in which the poems of Robert Service are used to evoke the days of the pioneers and the gold rush. Daily June–Sept.

Performing Arts Center, Fifth Ave. and G St. (343-1948): Building of very forward-looking design opened in 1988 and comprising three separate auditoriums. Concerts, big-name recitals, modern theater, Broadway shows.

Sydney Laurence Auditorium, Sixth Ave. and F St. (276-8688): The home of the Anchorage Civic Opera (Sept–Mar) and the Anchorage Symphony Orchestra (Nov–Apr).

University of Alaska–Anchorage Theater, 3211-T Providence Dr. (786-1800): Classical and contemporary theater Nov–Mar.

SHOPPING: A few addresses for those interested in authentic Native American and Inuit artifacts in horn, leather, or wood, jewelry, etc.: **Alaska Heritage Arts,** 211 E. Fifth Ave.; **Alaska Native Arts and Crafts Showroom,** 333 W. Fourth Ave.; **Arctic Cache,** 429 W. 5th St.; and the **Rusty Harpoon,** 411 W. Fourth Ave.

SPECIAL EVENTS: For a current schedule, inquire at the **Anchorage Visitors & Convention Bureau** (see "Tourist Information," above).

Fur Rendez-Vous (Feb): Dogsled races, shows, costume ball, sports events, etc., held at the time of the great annual fur auction.

Iditarod Trail Sled Dog Race (Mar): World-famous annual dogsled race from Anchorage to Nome, with more than 50 entries for these 2 weeks of racing. A classic for more than 50 years. Record time for the race: 11 days, 1 hr., 53 min., and 23 sec. (by Susan Butcher, in 1990).

Midnight Sun Baseball: A popular local event held every year at 10pm on June 21.

Midnight Sun Hot Air Balloon Classic: Also on the evening of June 21, attracts dozens of entries.

SPORTS: The **Sled Dog Race Track** on Tudor Rd. pits local against "foreign" champions, Sat–Sun only during the winter months. For a timetable, call 562-2235.

WINTER SPORTS RESORTS: The popular 🎿**Alyeska Resort,** 40 mi. (64km) SE via Ak. 1 (783-2222), has four ski lifts and a hotel. Season: Nov–Apr; also summer skiing.

ZOOS: The relatively new 🦌**Alaska Zoo,** 9 mi. (14km) out via Ak. 1 and O'Malley Rd. (346-3242), offers full range of native Alaskan animals: polar bears, brown and black bears, foxes, reindeer, moose, etc. Open daily year round.

ACCOMMODATIONS

A Note on Accommodations: Room rates in Anchorage are coded as follows: **VE,** Very Expensive ($140 and up); **E,** Expensive ($90–$140); **M,** Moderate ($60–$90); **I,** Inexpensive ($30–$60); **B,** Budget (up to $30). A listing of toll free numbers is in the Appendix.

Personal Favorites (from top bracket to budget)

Captain Cook Hotel (dwntwn), Fifth Ave. and K St., AK 99150 (907/276-6000; toll free, see Preferred). 560 rms, color TV, in-rm movies. AE, CB, DC, MC, V. Indoor parking $6, pool, health club, sauna, four rests. (including the Crow's Nest), 24-hr. coffee shop, four bars, rm svce, disco, boutiques, hrdrsr. *Note:* A palace of luxury comprising three modern towers, one of which is crowned by a panoramic rest. (the Crow's Nest) on the 20th floor. Tropical sea-style decor. Most of the large, comfortable rms offer a fine view of the bay or the mountains. Very good svce; business clientele; in the heart of dwntwn; open year round. **E–VE**

Hilton (dwntwn), Third Ave. and E St., AK 99501 (907/272-7411; toll free, see Hilton). 591 rms, A/C, color TV, in-rm movies. AE, CB, DC, MC, V. Free gar., pool, sauna, health club, two rests. (including Top of the World), bars, rm svce, disco, boutiques. *Note:* Two modern towers with all-around view of Cook Inlet and the mountains from the Top of the World rest. on the top floor. Very comfortable rms; efficient svce; decor and facilities entirely renovated. In the heart of dwntwn; open year round. **E–VE**

Sheraton (dwntwn), 401 E. Sixth Ave., AK 99501 (907/276-8700; toll free, see Sheraton). 375 rms, A/C, color TV, in-rm movies. AE, CB, DC, MC, V. Free gar., health club, sauna, two rests. (including Josephine's), coffee shop, bars, 24-hr. rm svce, disco. *Note:* The most luxurious of Anchorage's large modern hotels. Beautiful foyer w. transparent roof and grand staircase in jade; spacious, elegantly decorated rms, excellent svce. The hotel preferred by those in-the-know. In the heart of dwntwn; open year round. **E–VE**

Westmark Hotel (dwntwn), 720 W. Fifth Ave., AK 99501 (907/276-7676; toll free 800/544-0970). 200 rms, color TV, in-rm movies. AE, CB, DC, MC, V. Free parking, rest. (House of Lords), coffee shop, bar, 24-hr. rm svce. *Note:* Modern, comfortable 14-story hotel very nr. the Convention Center. Large, comfortable rms w. private balconies, some w. refrigerators. On the top floor the panoramic bar offers an unimpeded view of city, mountains, and ocean. Good svce; business clientele; open year round. **E**

Holiday Inn (dwntwn), 239 W. Fourth Ave., AK 99501 (907/279-8671; toll free, see Holiday Inns). 252 rms, A/C, color TV. AE, CB, DC, MC, V. Free parking, pool, sauna, rest. (The Greenery), coffee shop, bar, rm svce, crib $8. *Note:* Classic, comfortable three-story Holiday Inn w. a good dwntwn location—but the rms on the Fourth Ave. side are a little noisy at night. Caters mostly to groups; open year round. **M–E**

Anchorage Hotel (dwntwn), 330 E St., AK 99501 (907/272-4553; toll free 800/544-0988). 60 rms, A/C, cable color TV. AE, CB, DC, MC, V. Parking adj.; no bar or rest.; valet svce. *Note:* Small, delightful hotel dating from 1916, reopened after long disuse in 1988. The remodeling has preserved the Victorian flavor. Attentive reception and svce. Dwntwn, very nr. the Convention Center w. its rests. and stores. Elegance and character. **M–E,** but lower rates off-season.

Voyager Hotel (dwntwn), 501 K St., AK 99501 (907/277-9501). 38 mini-suites, A/C, color TV, in-rm movies. AE, DC, MC, V. Parking $6, rest. (dinner only), bar, valet svce. *Note:* Small hotel for the business traveler offering only comfortable mini-suites w. fully equipped kitchenette. Tasteful decor and layout; efficient svce; convenient dwntwn location. Excellent value. **M**

Northern Lights Inn (nr. dwntwn), 598 W. Northern Lights Blvd., AK 99503 (907/561-5200). 137 rms, color TV. AE,

DC, MC, V. Free parking, rest., bar, rm svce, hrdrsr, free airport limo. *Note:* Comfortable modern hotel halfway between dwntwn and the airport. Good svce; caters mostly to business travelers and groups. Good overall value; open year round. **I–M**

Super 8 Motel (nr. dwntwn), 3501 Minnesota Dr., AK 99503 (907/276-8884; toll free 800/843-1991). 84 rms, color TV, in-rm movies. AE, CB, DC, MC, V. Free parking, adj. rest., free airport limo. *Note:* Modern, functional hotel halfway between dwntwn and the airport. Comfortable rms, free morning coffee; overall good value; open year round. **I–M**

YMCAs/Youth Hostels

AYH, Minnesota Dr. and 32nd Ave., AK 99503 (907/276-3635). Youth hostel open year round.

Airport Accommodations

Best Western–Barratt Inn (nr. dwntwn), 4616 Spenard Rd., AK 99517 (907/243-3131; toll free, see Best Western). 217 rms, color TV, in-rm movies. AE, CB, DC, MC, V. Free parking, rest. (Safari), bar, free 24-hr. airport limo svce. *Note:* Welcoming country-style motel nr. the seaplane base at Spenard Lake, and 3 min. from the international airport. Very comfortable rms, some w. kitchenettes. Acceptable rest.; efficient svce; open year round. Ideal for a stopover between flights. **M**

RESTAURANTS

A Note on Restaurant Prices: Anchorage restaurant prices, per person, excluding drinks and service charges, are coded as follows: **VE,** Very Expensive ($60 and up); **E,** Expensive ($40–$60); **M,** Moderate ($25–$40); **I,** Inexpensive ($15–$25); **B,** Budget (up to $15).

Personal Favorites (from top bracket to budget)

Crow's Nest (dwntwn), in the Captain Cook Hotel (see "Accommodations," above) (276-6000). A/C. Dinner Tues–Sun, brunch Sun. AE, CB, DC, MC, V. Jkt. *Specialties:* lobster bisque in pastry shell, salmon stuffed w. shrimp, halibut à la Berval, game and venison (in season), choice meats. Good wine list. *Note:* From the 20th floor of the Captain Cook Hotel, this distinguished rest. offers a fine panorama of the mountains and Cook Inlet. Grand-hotel cuisine supervised by chef Jens Hansen, making full use of local resources in game and seafood. The stylish svce anticipates your needs. Best rest. in all of Alaska; resv. highly advisable. *Continental/Seafood.* **M–E**

House of Lords (dwntwn), in the Westmark Hotel (see "Accommodations," above) (907/276-5404). A/C. Lunch Tues–Fri, dinner Tues–Sat., AE, MC, V. Jkt. *Specialties:* filet of halibut Olympia, sole Louis XIV (w. shallots and white wine), bouillabaisse, rack of lamb bouquetière, piccata of veal marsala. Good wine list. *Note:* Another well-regarded, grand-hotel rest. on the ground floor of the Westmark Hotel. Opulent interior w. crystal, pewter, and ancestral portraits. Impeccable cuisine of European inspiration. Very good svce; resv. advisable. *Continental/Seafood.* **M**

Marx Bros. Café (dwntwn), 627 W. Third Ave. (907/278-2133). Dinner only, Mon–Sat; closed hols. AE, MC, V. *Specialties:* crab Imperial, catch of the day, seafood mousse napolitano, venison dishes (in season), halibut macadamia, roast duck w. raspberries, rack of lamb. Fine wine list. *Note:* Located in a picturesque little house built in 1916, this American-style rest. is very popular locally. Some original dishes; good svce; resv. advised. *American/Seafood.* **M**

Black Angus Meat Market (nr. dwntwn), 1101 W. Firewood Lane (279-3122). A/C. Lunch Mon–Fri, dinner daily; closed hols. MC, V. *Specialties:* Alaska crab, shrimp tempura, broiled halibut, steak, prime rib. *Note:* This rest., halfway between dwntwn and the airport, boasts an ordinary red-and-white frontage and an unmemorable decor, but its beef and seafood are of the highest quality and broiled to a turn. Efficient svce; resv. advised. *Steak/Seafood.* **I–M**

🍷 **Simon & Seafort's** (dwntwn), 420 L St. (907/274-3502). A/C. Lunch Mon–Sat, dinner nightly; closed hols. AE, MC, V. *Specialties:* steak, prime rib, fresh homemade pasta, grilled halibut w. lime butter and ginger, catch of the day, Alaska fish and shellfish (in season), fried zucchini hollandaise, brandy ice cream. Very good wine list. *Note:* Pleasantly decorated as a saloon from the days of the gold rush. Good, tasty food at very reasonable prices for Alaska. Remarkably fresh fish, cooked as you wish—grilled, fried, or poached. Relaxed setting and fine view of the mountains and Cook Inlet. Try it. Resv. suggested. *Steak/Seafood.* **I**

🍷 **Kumagoro** (dwntwn), 533 W. Fourth Ave. (272-9905). A/C. Breakfast (from 9am)/lunch/dinner daily. AE, MC, V. *Specialties:* sushi, miso soup, teriyaki, shabu shabu. *Note:* The preferred rest. of Japan Airlines crews stopping over at Anchorage—a good reference. All-purpose Oriental decor. Diligent svce; excellent value. *Japanese.* **B–I**

🍷 **Downtown Deli** (dwntwn), 525 W. 4th St. (907/274-0027). Breakfast/lunch/dinner daily. MC. *Specialties:* homemade soups, sandwiches, corned beef, kosher specialties, fish, daily specials, homemade desserts. *Note:* An Anchorage institution, much patronized by businessmen and local dignitaries. Usually crowded at breakfast and lunch. Friendly, smiling svce. Well-located, very nr. the Captain Cook and Hilton hotels. *American.* **B**

NEARBY EXCURSIONS

EKLUTNA (26 mi./42km NE via Ak. 1): A picturesque Athapascan village whose Russian Orthodox church. **St. Nicholas Church** (built in 1870), has an interesting collection of icons. The grave-markers in the cemetery are topped, Native American fashion, with a little house for the departed spirit to live in. Here, you can also visit beautiful **Lake Eklutna** and its waterfalls.

PORTAGE GLACIER (50 mi./80km SE via Ak. 1): Offers an impressive spectacle as it "calves," shedding great pieces of itself which tumble into Portage Lake below. Visitor center open daily in summer; not-to-be-missed boat trip along the glacier on the *Ptarmigan* (277-3714).

AN ALASKA OVERVIEW

At once the largest and the least populous state in the Union, Alaska runs to extremes in everything: climate, geography, natural resources, and, above all, distances. The south shore of **Misty Fjords National Monument** in the southern part of the state is 1,435 mi. (2,300km) away from **Barrow,** the northernmost town in the U.S. From the western tip of the great **Aleutian Islands,** pointed toward Siberia like the tusk of an elephant at bay, to the frontier with Canada's Yukon and British Columbia, Alaska (from a Native American word meaning "great land") sprawls across two time zones. Its area of 586,400 sq. mi. (1,520,000km²) is 2½ times that of Texas, but is home to barely half a million inhabitants, 70,000 of whom are Native Americans, Inuit (Eskimos), and Aleuts.

INTRODUCING ALASKA

The history of Alaska is inseparable from that of *Homo sapiens* in North America. The settlement of the continent was begun in 35,000–25,000 B.C. by invaders from Asia who at that time were able to cross what is now the Bering Strait on foot. And it was from Alaska that the "Amerindians" leapfrogged down the Pacific coast, reaching Tierra del Fuego, the southernmost point of South America, a few thousand years later. The history of the state in modern times goes back no further than 1728, when Vitus Bering, a Danish explorer in the service of Tsar Peter the Great of Russia, discovered the 57-mi. (92km) passage between Siberia and North America that still bears his name. In 1867 Secretary of State William H. Seward purchased Alaska, which had become a Russian colony, for $7.2 million, or around 2¢ per acre—a deal that his political opponents, who knew nothing of the fabulous wealth below Alaska's surface, nicknamed "Seward's Folly," or "Seward's Icebox." But Seward's vision was corroborated by the gold discoveries of 1896 and the large-scale oil discoveries, the first of which was made in 1957.

Today, Alaska (which became the 49th state in 1959) spends considerably more a year on publicity than the $7.2 million that more than a century ago was the purchase price paid to the Russians for their American colony—because, along with crude oil, fisheries, and forest products, tourism (700,000 visitors a year) is one of the mainstays of the local economy. A visit to the "Frontier State," as it is sometimes called, will give you a deeper insight into Alaska's attraction for lovers of nature, solitude, and wide-open spaces. There are no grander landscapes than the snowy peaks of **Mt. McKinley,** highest in North America, or **Denali National Park;** the mysterious depths of **Tongass National Forest** (twice the size of Ireland) and of **Wrangell–St. Elias National Park;** the blue-shadowed expanse of **Glacier Bay National Park;** the picturesque necklace of islands along the **Inside Passage** with its history-laden little harbors at **Sitka, Petersburg, Ketchikan,** and **Wrangell;** the fissured shores of **Kenai Fjords National Park** or **Prince William Sound** (damaged by the Mar 1989 oil spill); the desolate tundra of **Gates of the Arctic National Park;** the scalding mineral springs of **Circle Hot Springs,** or the "Valley of 10,000 Smokes," in **Katmai National Park.** All of these are unforgettable sights, especially at dawn, or when the summer evenings draw out forever in sunsets of glowing bronze. The state is also heaven on earth for fishermen, hunters (who must have permits), or just plain nature photographers, who won't know where to point their lenses in such a wealth of wildlife: black and brown bear, grizzlies, wolves, mountain goats, Sitka deer, elk, lynx, eagles, caribou, beavers, otters, wolverines, seals, walruses, sea lions—and, unfortunately, mosquitos, plague of the Alaskan summer.

ALASKA'S HIGHLIGHTS

ADMIRALTY ISLAND NATIONAL MONUMENT
(reachable by seaplane from Juneau and Sitka, or by Alaska Marine Hwy. ferry): Lying at the heart of the Inland Passage, this wild and beautiful island, 100 mi. (160km) long by 25 mi. (40km) wide, is inhabited by more brown bears and Sitka deer than humans. Its rain forests, mountain peaks, dozens of lakes and rushing streams, and rocky coasts make it a small-scale replica of Alaska. Admiralty Island is also home to the largest eagle colony in North America.

Shelter: Log cabins and camping sites only. For lovers of nature in the raw. For **information,** contact the U.S. Forest Service, 101 Egan Dr., Juneau, AK 99801 (907/586-8751).

ALEUTIAN ISLANDS (reachable by plane from Anchorage): This island chain stretches more than 1,500 mi. (2,400km) southwestward from Alaska toward the shores of Asia. Almost uninhabited, these magnificent windswept islands with their numerous wildlife reserves are a very beautiful destination for the tourist (direct flights between

SOVIET
UNION

Chukchi Sea

International Date Line

Colville River

Noatak River

Noatak Nat'l Preserve

Kobuk Valley Nat'l Park

Kotzebue

Kobuk River

Gates of the

Arctic Circle

Bering Land Bridge Nat'l Preserve

Nome

St. Lawrence I.

● Galena

Yukon River

● McGrath

Bethel

Kuskokwim River

BERING SEA

Pribilof Is.

N

Lake Clark Nat'l Park

Homer ●

Dillingham ●

King Salmon ●

Katmai Nat'l Park

Bristol Bay

Kodiak ●
Kodiak I.

0 km 80
0 miles 50

Cold Bay ●

Alaska Peninsula

Aniakchak Nat'l Mon.

Aleutian Is.

Dutch Harbor ●

ALASKA

Highways ————
Ferry routes ------------
National parks – – – –

Barrow ●

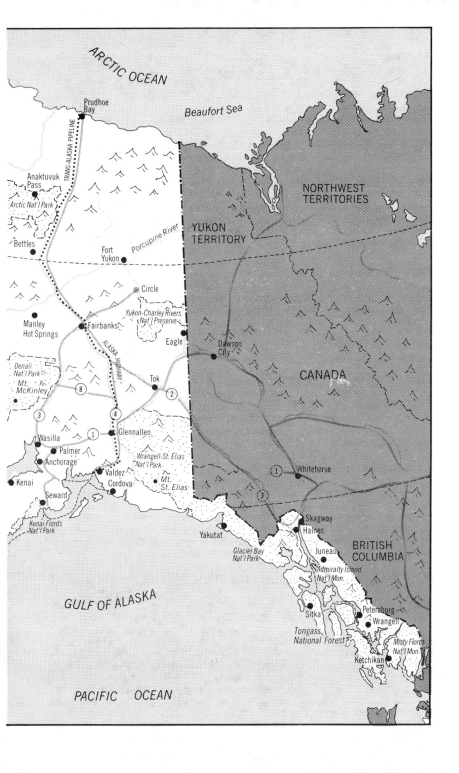

Anchorage and Dutch Harbor/Unalaska). The Aleutians were the scene of a 19-day battle in May 1943 between U.S. and Japanese forces, the only mainland U.S. territory to see combat during World War II. The island of **Attu,** westernmost in the chain, is nearer to Moscow or Tokyo than to Washington, D.C.

Where to Stay

Unisea Inn, Pouch 503-T, Dutch Harbor, AK 99692 (907/581-1325). 46 rms, cable color TV. MC, V. Rest., bar, boutiques. *Note:* Serviceable, pleasant, welcoming small motel facing the Mall. Open year round. The ideal place to stay for a visit to the Aleutians. **M**

BARROW (reachable by air from Fairbanks or Anchorage): A picturesque Inuit village whose 2,200 people make their living from fishing and handcrafts, particularly bone carving. Lying 340 mi. (544km) north of the Arctic Circle, this is the northernmost town in the U.S. At the airport there is a memorial to cowboy-movie star and humorist Will Rogers and his pilot, Wiley Post, who were killed in an air crash nearby in 1935. The midnight sun shines here for 82 successive days every summer.

Where to Stay

Top of the World, P.O. Box 189-T, Barrow, AK 99723 (907/852-3900). 40 rms, color TV, in-rm movies. AE, MC, V. Adj. rest. (Pepe's). *Note:* The farthest-north hotel in the Americas; rustic, even though comfortable. Stuffed polar bears to welcome you in the lobby. Friendly, refrigerator-equipped rms. Unobstructed view of the Arctic Ocean. Highly recommended Mexican rest.; entirely redecorated in 1986. About as complete a change of scenery as you can get! Free airport shuttle; open year round. **E**

CIRCLE HOT SPRINGS (136 mi./218km NE of Fairbanks along Ak. 2 and Ak. 6): Around these hot (139°F/59°C) springs, discovered in 1897 by a gold prospector, has grown up a spa very popular with Alaskans in winter and with tourists the rest of the year. Thanks to a network of hot-water canals, market gardeners of the region produce the finest fresh vegetables in Alaska.

COLUMBIA GLACIER: See Valdez.

CORDOVA (reachable by air from Anchorage and Juneau, or by Alaska Marine Hwy. ferry from Whittier and Valdez): This old copper-mining town, which flourished from 1908 to 1938, has taken a renewed lease on life as a busy fishing port. Beautiful site to the east of Prince William Sound. There is an interesting historical museum, the **Cordova Historical Museum,** Centennial Bldg. (907/424-6665); open year round.

DENALI NATIONAL PARK (125 mi./201km south of Fairbanks and 240 mi./386km north of Anchorage on Ak. 3; also reachable by train from Anchorage on the Alaska Railroad, a 7-hr. 45-min. trip): This second-largest (9,375 sq. mi./24,280km², 2½ times the size of Yellowstone) of our national parks was established in 1917; it is also one of the wildest and most majestic. Almost at the center of the park, and often hidden in summer by clouds, **Mt. McKinley,** the highest peak in North America, stands 20,320 ft. (6,205m) tall. An 87-mi. (140km) road in the northern part of the park, as well as many trails, allow the visitor to reach the heart of Denali National Park (its name is from a Native American word meaning "the high one"), and to observe its exceptionally rich wildlife—grizzlies, wolves, caribou, elk, and more than 155 species of birds. From both the **Polychrome Overlook** and the **Eielson Visitor Center** (sled-dog demonstrations every day in summer) there are unobstructed views over mountain, forest, and glacier. You'll need warm clothes, a raincoat, and stout shoes. There's a daily guided visit by bus year round from the **Riley Creek Visitor Center** (907/638-2686).

For **information,** contact the Superintendent, Denali National Park, P.O. Box 9, Denali Park, AK 99755 (907/638-2238). This park alone is worth the trip to Alaska.

Where to Stay

Denali National Park Hotel, Park Rd., Milepost 240, Denali Park, AK 99755 (907/276-7234). 100 rms. AE, MC, V. Free parking, rest., coffee shop, bar. *Note:* Adjacent to the Alaska Railroad train station and the visitor center, this is the only hotel in the park itself, offering you friendly rms w. bath. The hotel can arrange excursions in the park, rafting on the river, or flights in light aircraft. Open end of May through Sept. Resv., far in advance, are a must. **E**

Harper Lodge at Denali, Parks Hwy., Milepost 238.5, Denali Park, AK 99755 (907/683-2282). 192 rms. AE, MC, V. Free parking, open-air Jacuzzis, two rests., bar. *Note:* The newest hotel in the park, on the Nana River w. spectacular mountain views. Very comfortable rms decorated Alaskan style; acceptable rests. Free airport and railroad-station shuttles. A fine place. Open late May to mid-Sept. **E,** but lower rates off-season.

McKinley Chalets, Park Hwy. (Ak. 3, Milepost 238), Denali Park, AK 99755 (907/276-7234). 216 mini-suites. AE, MC, V. *Note:* Rustic but very comfortable chalets, on the bank of the Nenana River, w. a fine view. Excellent rest. Can arrange park excursions, rafting, or light-aircraft trips. Very nr. park entrance; caters mostly to groups and conventions. Open mid-May through Sept; resv. must be made well in advance. **M–E**

FAIRBANKS (365 mi./588km north of Anchorage by Ak. 3; direct flights from most cities in Alaska; train from Anchorage on the Alaska Railroad, an 11-hr. trip): Alaska's second city (pop. 22,600), almost at the geographical center of the state, is first and foremost a supply base for the towns north of the Arctic Circle and for the oilfields of Prudhoe Bay, and thus a busy commercial hub. The most notable of its attractions include:

Alaskaland, Airport Way and Peger Rd. (907/452-4529): This amusement park (open daily) has a replica of a gold-rush town, open-air museum, restaurant aboard an old paddlewheel steamer, etc. Entertaining.

Ester (8 mi./12km SW on Ak. 3): An authentic turn-of-the-century gold-prospectors' town. The old Cripple Creek District and the Malemute Saloon are worth going out of your way to see.

University Museum, University Campus, College Rd. (907/474-7505), open daily, has an interesting natural-history collection including a 36,000-year-old buffalo, and Native American and Inuit art and handcrafts. A visit to the **campus** is recommended.

Four-hr. **cruises** on the Chena River and Tanana River aboard picturesque paddlewheel steamers: *Riverboat Discovery,* Discovery Rd. (907/479-6673), mid-May to mid-Sept. Unusual. For more information, check with the **Fairbanks Convention & Visitors Bureau,** 550 First Ave., Fairbanks, AK 99701 (907/456-5774).

Where to Stay

Westmark Fairbanks, 820 Noble St., Fairbanks, AK 99701 (907/456-7722; toll free 800/544-0970). 240 rms, A/C, color TV, in-rm movies. AE, DC, MC, V. Free parking, rest. (Bear 'N Seal), coffee shop, bar, rm svce, nightclub. *Note:* Typical dwntwn business hotel. Comfortable rms; very acceptable rest.; efficient svce. Free airport shuttle. **E–VE**

Captain Bartlett Inn, 1411-T Airport Way, Fairbanks, AK 99701 (907/452-1888; toll free 800/544-7528). 200 rms, color TV. AE, DC, MC, V. Free parking, sauna, health club, rest. (The Captain's Table), bar, rm svce, free airport limo. *Note:* Comfortable hotel decorated in a picturesque "Far North" style (the reception area is floored w. spruce logs), and boasting "the biggest fireplace in Alaska." Comfortable rms; rest. deserving of respect; winning atmosphere; good svce. Nr. the Alaskaland theme park and the airport; 8 min. from dwntwn. Open year round. **M–E**

    Great Land Hotel (formerly the Chena View Hotel), 723 First Ave., Fairbanks, AK 99701 (907/452-6661). 90 rms, cable color TV. AE, DC, MC, V. Free parking, rest., bar, rm svce. *Note:* Dwntwn motel w. unimpeded view of the Chena River. Spacious, comfortable rms; friendly welcome and svce; overall good value. Open year round. **I–M**

    Super 8 Motel, 1909 Airport Way, Fairbanks, AK 99701 (907/451-8888; toll free 800/843-1991). 77 rms, color TV, in-rm movies. AE, CB, DC, MC, V. Free parking, adj. rest., free morning coffee, free airport limo. *Note:* Typical motel featuring functional comfort. 8 min. from dwntwn. Open year round. **I–M**

Where to Eat

    Clinkerdagger, Bickerstaff & Petts (nr. dwntwn), 24 College Rd. (452-2756). A/C. Lunch Mon–Fri, dinner nightly; closed hols. AE, DC, MC, V. *Specialties:* steak, catch of the day, homemade desserts. *Note:* A local favorite got up like a fake-Tudor English pub. Decent food, generous helpings. Live music at dinner. Resv. advisable. *Steak/Seafood.* **I**

    The Pump House (nr. dwntwn), 1.3 mile Chena Pump Rd. (479-8452). A/C. Lunch/dinner daily, brunch Sun. AE, DC, MC, V. *Specialties:* choice meat and fish from the broiler; lavish buffet at Sun brunch. *Note:* A real pump-house (and designated historic monument) on the Chena River, handsomely transformed into a rest. w. magnificent terrace for open-air meals in summer. A local favorite. No resv. needed. *American.* **I**

    Tiki Cove, in the Polaris Hotel, 427 First Ave. (452-1484). Lunch/dinner daily. MC, V. *Specialties:* Cantonese and Hunan cooking, steak, seafood. *Note:* Worthy (but no more) Chinese food and much-admired Polynesian cocktails in a congenial exotic setting w. a fine view of the distant mountains across the Chena River. Locally popular so resv. advisable. *Chinese/American.* **B–I**

    Alaska Salmon Bake, in the Alaskaland theme park, Airport Way and Peger Rd. (452-7274). Lunch/dinner daily mid-May to mid-Sept. No credit cards. *Specialties:* fresh salmon, halibut, king crab, barbecued meats. *Note:* A must for every tourist: the Alaska equivalent of a New England clam bake—delicious open-air cooking at a very reasonable price. A colorful, entertaining experience which you shouldn't miss. Free transportation from dwntwn. *Seafood.* **B**

    FORT YUKON (reachable by air from Fairbanks): Former Hudson's Bay Co. trading post dating from 1847 and situated astride the Arctic Circle. Attracts many tourists for its authentic Native American handcrafts and its furs. Temperatures as high as 107°F (42°C) in summer and as low as −78°F (−61°C) in winter have been recorded here.

    GATES OF THE ARCTIC NATIONAL PARK (reachable only by charter plane from Fairbanks): Established in 1980, this enormous park lies wholly north of the Arctic Circle. With the adjoining **Kobuk Valley National Park** (weird sand dunes and traces of glacial deposits) and **Noatak National Preserve** (on the trail of caribou, black bears, and wolves), it is one of the last wholly wild reservations in North America. Wonderful mountain and tundra landscapes, with the Noatak River slashing a 62-mi. (100km) canyon across this wilderness untouched by human hands. Unfortunately, it's difficult of access for the general run of tourists.

Information: Superintendent, Gates of the Arctic National Park, 201 First Ave., Fairbanks, AK 99707 (907/456-0281).

GLACIER BAY NATIONAL PARK (reachable by air or boat from Juneau): One of Alaska's noblest and most impressive natural beauties, this glorious bay, 50 mi. (80km) long by 2.5–10 mi. (4–16km) broad and reminiscent of the Norwegian fjords, is cradled between two mountainous peninsulas whose many glaciers (including the superb **Muir Glacier**) throw off dazzling blue-white reflections. Rearing above the whole is the majestic outline of 15,320-ft. (4,663m) **Mt. Fairweather.** Great chunks of the glaciers are continually falling into the bay with a deafening roar which enhances the fascinating spectacle. Rich wildlife and marine life.

You can take a 1-day boat trip across Glacier Bay—not to be missed—on **Catamaran Cruise Lines,** Juneau (907/586-6835; toll free 800/622-2042). Operates from late May to mid-Sept. Also glacier overflights on a seaplane from **Channel Flying Service,** Merchant's Wharf, Juneau (907/789-3331). These two excursions are worth the trip all by themselves.

Park access is limited during tourist season.

Where to Stay

Glacier Bay Lodge, Bartlett Cove (P.O. Box 108), Gustavus, AK 99826 (907/697-2225; toll free 800/426-0600). 55 rms. MC, V. Marina, boating, fishing, riding, rest., bar. *Note:* The only hotel in Glacier Bay National Park; the ideal starting-point for trips by boat, by plane, or on foot in Glacier Bay. Elegant rustic architecture in the heart of a forest. Comfortable rms; rest. w. a panoramic view. A place that nature-lovers won't forget—but you should book far ahead. Open from the end of May through mid-Sept. Campsite adj. **E–VE**

Where to Eat

Glacier Bay Lodge Dining Room, in Glacier Bay Lodge (see "Where to Stay," above) (697-2225). Breakfast/lunch/dinner daily; closed from the end of Sept through the end of May. MC, V. *Specialties:* salmon, trout, halibut, king crab, shellfish, meats from the broiler. *Note:* Wonderful hotel dining rm w. a view of Glacier Bay and the mountains that is one of Alaska's finest. Excellent cooking, relying heavily on local seafood. Attentive service; resv. a must. *American/Seafood.* **I–M**

HAINES (775 mi./1,240km SE of Anchorage by the Alaska Hwy. and Haines Hwy.; reachable by air from Juneau, or by the Alaska Marine Hwy. ferry): This little fishing port, tucked between the sea, the Chilkat River, and Mt. Kipinsky at the northern end of the Inside Passage, offers a number of attractions:

Sheldon Museum, Main St. at the Boat Harbor (907/766-2366): Devoted to the history of the Alaska pioneers and collections of Native American objects; open daily in summer, on Mon and Wed the rest of the year.

Fort William H. Seward, Mud Bay Rd. (907/766-2540): A turn-of-the-century army post with a replica of a small Native American village (Totem Village). Not to be missed are the demonstrations of tribal dancing on Mon, Wed, and Sat in summer. Open Mon–Fri.

Chilkat Bald Eagle Preserve, adjoining the town: Home from late Oct to Dec of every year of 4,000 eagles, the world's largest colony of this species. **Chilkat Guides,** P.O. Box 170, Haines, AK 99827 (907/766-2049), offers 4-hr. guided trips by boat during the migration period.

Where to Stay

Hotel Hälsingland, 13 Fort Seward Dr., Haines, AK 99827 (907/766-2000; toll free 800/542-6363). 60 rms (50 w. bath). AE, CB, DC, MC, V. Free parking, rest. (Commander's Rm), bar. *Note:* This picturesque Victorian-style hotel occupies what used to be the officers' quarters of Fort Seward, offering a fine view of the Lynn Canal and the surrounding mountains. Friendly rms w. functional comfort (most w. private bath). Very creditable rest.; welcome w. a smile. Facing Totem Village and adj. a campsite. Very good value. Open Mar–Nov. **I–M**

Where to Eat

         🍸 **Commander's Room** in the Hotel Hälsingland (see "Where to Stay," above) (766-2000). Breakfast/lunch/dinner daily; closed from the end of Nov to early Mar. AE, CB, DC, MC, V. *Specialties:* fresh salmon, halibut, scallops, sautéed prawns, steak. *Note:* Very creditable hotel cuisine served in the former officers' mess of Fort Seward. Fine view of the Lynn Canal and the mountains. Cheerful, friendly svce; very good value. *American/ Seafood.* **B–I**

HOMER (225 mi./360km SW of Anchorage by Ak. 1; reachable by air from Anchorage; Alaska Marine Hwy. ferry connection to Kodiak): A deep-water, ice-free port. Boat trips to the beautiful 🏛 **Kachermark Bay,** rimmed by the Kenai Mountains. A small, well-laid-out natural-history museum is the 🏛 **Pratt Museum,** 3779 Bartlett St. (907/235-8635); open daily May–Sept, Tues–Sun the rest of the year. Lovely city and bay views from **Skyline Drive,** reached via E. Hill Rd.

     For information, go to the **Homer Visitor Center,** Small Boat Ramp, Homer Spit (907/235-7740).

Where to Stay

        🏨 **Best Western Bidarka Inn,** 575 Sterling Hwy., Homer, AK 99603 (907/235-8148; toll free, see Best Western). 74 rms, color TV, in-rm movies. AE, DC, MC, V. Free parking, health club, rest., bar, free airport shuttle. *Note:* Comfortable, inviting motel on Kachermak Bay in an agreeable rustic setting. Spacious rms, some w. kitchenette. Friendly reception. Open year round. **M**

        🍴 **Driftwood Inn,** 135 W. Bunnell Ave., Homer, AK 99603 (907/235-8019). 20 rms, color TV. AE, MC, V. Free parking; no bar or rest., but free coffee. *Note:* Charming old hotel of family type, one block from the water and nr. dwntwn. Rustic but comfortable. Good-humored svce. Sea-fishing parties organized. Good value; open year round. **I–M**

JUNEAU (reachable by direct flights from Anchorage or Seattle, or by Alaska Marine Hwy. ferry): Nestling at the feet of the snowcapped **Mt. Juneau** and **Mt. Roberts,** Alaska's picturesque capital is nicknamed "Little San Francisco" because of its narrow streets and the flights of wooden steps hugging the hillsides on which its multicolored houses are built. Besides the ultramodern **State Capitol,** Main St. and 4th St. (admission Mon–Fri in summer only), and the elegant **Governor's Mansion,** Calhoun Ave. at 9th St., with its colonial pillars, you should see the unusual Russian Orthodox 🏛 **St. Nicholas Church,** at 5th St. and Gold St., a wooden octagon dating from 1894 (open daily). The 🏛 **House of Wickersham,** 213 7th St. (907/586-9001), open Sun–Fri mid-May through Sept, offers you a fine sweeping view, as well as collections of historical memorabilia from the days of the pioneers and the Russian colonists.

     The very fine 🏛 **Alaska State Museum,** Whittier St. at Egan Dr. (907/465-2901), open daily, displays an instructive panorama of the history of Alaska's Inuit and Native Americans (Aleuts, Athapascans, Tlingits), as well as mastodon tusks more than 50,000 years old, totem poles, etc.

     The 🏛 **Juneau-Douglas City Museum,** 4th St. and Main St. (586-3572), open daily, concentrates on Alaska's 19th-century mining boom. Many memorabilia, photos, tools, and everyday articles from the pioneer period.

     For information, contact the **Juneau Visitors Information Center,** Seward St. and 3rd St. (907/586-2284).

A short trip (35 mi./56km NW via Glacier Hwy.) to 🔺🔺 **Mendenhall Glacier** should be given high priority. This great river of ice, 12 mi. (19km) long by 1.5 mi. (2.5km) wide, is retreating at about 67 ft. (21m) a year; it has taken more than 10,000 years to move 4.3 mi. (7km) back from the sea, giving birth to a lake at the foot of the dizzying crevasses that fall sheer to the floor of the valley it has carved out. Visitor center with observatory at the foot of the glacier. Bus service to the glacier through **MGT** (907/789-5460).

On **Douglas Island,** offshore from Juneau, is the **Eagle Crest** winter sports resort (907/586-5284), open Dec–Apr.

Juneau is also a base for boat trips to the 🔺 **Tracy Arm–Ford's Terror Wilderness,** where the glaciers tumble into fjords 960 ft. (300m) and more deep.

Where to Stay

🔆🍸🍸 **Baranof Westmark Hotel,** 127 N. Franklin St., Juneau, AK 🔺 🛏 99801 (907/586-2660; toll free 800/544-0970). 226 rms, color TV, in-rm movies. AE, DC, MC, V. Free parking, rest. (Gold Rm), coffee shop, bar, rm svce. *Note:* The grande dame of local hostelries, right on Franklin St., the historic main street of dwntwn. Opulent decor; comfortable rms (some w. kitchenettes); good rest.; attentive svce. Caters mostly to groups; open year round. **M–E**

🍸 **Breakwater Inn,** 1711 Glacier Ave., Juneau, AK (907/586-🛏 6303). 49 rms, color TV, in-rm movies. AE, CB, DC, MC, V. Free parking, rest., bar. *Note:* Very comfortable motel w. a spectacular view of the harbor and the mountains. Pleasant rms w. private balconies (some w. kitchenettes). Smiling svce; good value; open year round. **M**

🍸 **Driftwood Lodge,** 435 Willoughby Ave. W., Juneau, AK 🛏 99801 (907/586-2280; toll free 800/544-2239). 62 rms, color TV, in-rm movies. AE, MC, V. *Note:* Inviting dwntwn motel not far from the ferry terminal. Modern and comfortable; some rms w. kitchenette. Friendly reception and svce. Free shuttles to the airport and the ferry terminal. Open year round. **I–M**

Where to Eat

🍸🍸 **The Diggins,** in the Prospector Hotel, 340 Whittier Ave. (586-🍴🍴 3737). Breakfast/lunch/dinner daily; also dancing. AE, DC, MC, V. Jkt. *Specialties:* fish of the day and all kinds of seafood; prime cuts from the broiler. *Note:* Elegant little hotel dining rm very close to the harbor. Cuisine mostly seafood, as fresh as you could wish. Very good svce; very popular locally; resv. advised. *American/Seafood.* **I–M**

🔆🍸🍸 **Silverbow Inn** (in hotel of the same name), 120 2nd St. (586-🍴🍴 4146). Lunch/dinner daily; closed hols. AE, DC, MC, V. *Specialties:* regional French dishes, catch of the day; menu changes regularly. *Note:* Charming old (1914) building, pleasingly restored. Ultra-romantic setting (dinner by candlelight) and rather high-flying French-derived cooking. Attentive svce; resv. advisable. *French/American.* **I**

🔆🍸 **Mike's Fine Food and Spirits,** 1102 2nd St., in nearby, Douglas (364-3271). Lunch/dinner daily. AE, DC, MC, V. *Specialties:* king crab, fresh salmon, catch of the day, steak. *Note:* A local landmark across the Juneau-Douglas Bridge, Mike's claims to be one of Alaska's oldest rests. Excellent fish and seafood; spectacular view of Gastineau Channel and the harbor. A very good place; resv. advised. *American/Seafood.* **I**

🍸 **Armadillo Tex-Mex Café,** 431 S. Franklin St. (586-1880). 🍴 Lunch/dinner daily. MC, V. *Specialties:* chili, fajitas, enchiladas, tacos. *Note:* Spicy, flavorful Tex-Mex food at modest prices. A local favorite. Across from the Old Ferry Terminal. *American/Mexican.* **B–I**

🔆 **KATMAI NATIONAL PARK** (reachable by air from An-🍴 chorage, or from Kodiak as far as King Salmon): A beautiful nature preserve of 4.1 million acres (16,600km²) in the NE of the Alaska Peninsula. Deep forests shelter brown bears, which are clever salmon-fishers (don't overlook a visit to the ♨ **McNeil River Sanctuary** at the east end of the park). Many lakes and active volcanoes. The unusually violent eruption of **Mt. Katmai** in 1912 created the lunar landscape of the ♨ **Valley of Ten Thousand Smokes,** as well as striking cliffs of white ash 90–300 ft. (30–100m) high.

For **information,** contact the Superintendent, Katmai National Park, P.O. Box 7, King Salmon, AK 99613 (907/246-3305); open early June to Sept.

KENAI (158 mi./252km SW of Anchorage along Ak. 1; or reachable by air from Anchorage): This is the second-oldest city in the state (founded by Russians in 1791) and, thanks to an active offshore drilling program, one of the oil capitals of Alaska. The old **Fort Kenay,** Mission Ave. and Overland Ave. (907/283-7294), open daily from June through mid-Sept, was originally built by the U.S. Army in 1869 and rebuilt for the Alaska Centennial in 1967. It faces a fine Russian Orthodox church of 1896, the ♨ **Assumption of the Virgin Mary Church,** which is well worth a look; visit by appointment (907/283-4122). For local information, contact the **Kenai Visitors Center,** Main St. and Kenai Spur Hwy. (907/283-7989).

Where to Stay

🏮 **King Oscar's Motel,** 10352 Spur Hwy., Kenai, AK 99611 (907/283-6060). 50 rms, color TV, in-rm movies. AE, CB, DC, MC, V. Free parking, rest., bar, nightclub. *Note:* Classic motel 1 mi. (1.6km) east of town on the Kenai Spur Hwy. Modern comforts; great if you're driving through. Good value; open year round. **I–M**

KENAI FJORDS NATIONAL PARK: See Seward.

KETCHIKAN (reachable by air from Seattle, Juneau, or Sitka; or by Alaska Marine Hwy. ferry): Alaska's southernmost city holds the U.S. record for rainfall—160 in. (4m) a year! Nicknamed "the world's salmon capital," this important fishing port is also home to the world's largest collection of Native American totem poles in ♨♨ **Saxman Totem Park,** 3 mi. (5km) south on S. Tongass Hwy. (open daily); the **Totem Heritage Center,** 601 Deermount St. (907/225-5900), open daily in summer, Tues–Fri the rest of the year; and the **Totem Bight Historical Site,** 10 mi. (16km) north on N. Tongass Hwy., open daily. There are more than 60 totem poles in these three locations, and they're worth the trip all by themselves. But while you're here, take a look at the charming little frame houses on Creek St., and visit the interesting **Tongass Historical Museum,** 629 Dock St. (907/225-5600), open daily in summer, Wed–Sat the rest of the year, with Native American and gold-rush exhibits. For information, contact the **Ketchikan Visitors Bureau,** 131 Front St. (907/225-6166).

Where to Stay

☀🏮 **Ingersoll Hotel,** 303 Mission St., Ketchikan, AK 99901 (907/225-2124; toll free 800/544-0970). 60 rms, color TV. AE, DC, MC, V. Free parking, rest. (Charley's), coffee shop, bar, rm svce. *Note:* This charming older hotel, at the center of "The Block," the heart of historic Ketchikan, and looming over the harbor, has recently undergone some renovation. Pleasant rms, locally popular rest, and likable atmosphere. Open year round. **M**

First United Methodist Church, Grant St. and Main St., Ketchikan, AK 99901 (907/225-3319). Youth hostel open from the end of May to the end of Aug.

Where to Eat

🍸 **Kay's Kitchen,** 2813 Tongass Ave. (225-5860). Breakfast/lunch only, daily (Tues–Sat in summer). MC, V. *Specialties:* soup, crab and shrimp Louie, catch of the day, homemade pie. *Note:* Likable little restaurant with a view of busy Bar Harbor. Honest, tasty *cuisine bourgeoise;* good-natured welcome and svce; excellent value. *American/Seafood.* **B–I**

KODIAK (reachable by air from Anchorage or by Alaska Marine Hwy. ferry from Homer and Seward): Capital of Russian America (1784–99) and now the home port of the state's most important fishing fleet. For an insight into Alaska's Russian heritage, don't fail to visit the ⚓ **Baranof Museum,** 101 Marine Way (907/486-5920), open daily, Alaska's oldest building (1793), a frame structure which the colony's governor, Alexander Baranof, used for fur storage; or the ⚓ **Holy Resurrection Church** (1794), again the state's oldest, with its typical bulbous domes and some very fine icons and old paintings; visits by appointment (907/486-3854). The **Kodiak Information Center** is at Center St. and Marine Way (907/486-4782).

The western half of Kodiak Island is a ⚓ **nature reserve,** rich in wildlife—particularly the giant brown Kodiak bear, which can grow up to 1,500 lb. (600kg); a total of 2,400 Kodiak bears live on the island. The reserve can be reached by boat or plane from Kodiak. For information, contact Kodiak Wildlife Refuge, 1390 Buskin River Rd., Kodiak, AK 99615 (907/487-2600).

Where to Stay

🏩 **Westmark Kodiak** (formerly the Sheffield), 236 Rezanof W., Kodiak, AK 99615 (907/486-5712; toll free 800/544-0970). 90 rms, color TV, in-rm movies. AE, DC, MC, V. Free parking, rest., bar, rm svce. *Note:* Typical contemporary motel. Serviceably comfortable rms, some very small. Well located across from the fishing-boat harbor. A giant Kodiak bear (stuffed) presides over the lobby. Good value on balance. Open year round. **M–E**

🏩 **Shelikof Lodge,** 211 Thorsheim Ave., **Kodiak,** AK 99615 (907/486-4141). 39 rms, color TV. MC, V. Free parking, rest. (Fox Inn), bar. *Note:* Overlooking the harbor and the city, this modern, comfortable two-story motel is not far from the ferry terminal. Rms recently renovated; acceptable rest.; overall good value. Open year round. **I–M**

Where to Eat

🍷 **Chartroom Restaurant,** in the Westmark Kodiak (see "Where to Stay," above) (486-5712). A/C. Breakfast/lunch/dinner daily. AE, DC, MC, V. *Specialties:* Alaska crab, grilled salmon, steak, catch of the day. *Note:* Faultless but unimaginative hotel food. The rest. has a fine view of the harbor. Good svce. *American.* **I**

KOTZEBUE (reachable only by air, from Anchorage, Fairbanks, and Nome): Just north of the Arctic Circle, this little (pop. 2,000) town is home to one of the oldest Inuit communities in Alaska, which has lived there at least 300–400 years. It owes its name to the Baltic baron Otto von Kotzebue, who explored these parts around 1840. The ice covering its bay melts in spectacular fashion around the beginning of June. The very modern and interesting ⚓ **Nana Museum of the Arctic,** near the airport (907/442-3304), open daily, will show you scenes of everyday Inuit life (dances, songs, the blanket game, dogsled races, handcraft demonstrations) and well-designed dioramas of the Arctic environment, particularly the region's wildlife. A must.

Another interesting museum half a mile north of the airport on Second Ave. (907/442-3401), open Mon–Fri in summer and by appointment the rest of the year, is the **Ootukahkuktuvik** ("Place full of Old Things" in Inuit), displaying Native American masks, clothing, whale-catching tackle, and ivory ornaments lent to the museum by local residents.

Where to Stay

☼🏩 **Nullagvik Hotel,** P.O. Box 336-T, Kotzebue, AK 99752 (907/442-3331). 80 rms. AE, MC, V. Rest., bar, hrdrsr. *Note:* In spite of its tongue-twisting name, this comfortable motel is a favorite w. visitors to the Far North; in summer, you can sit at your ease and admire the midnight sun as well as the view of the Arctic Ocean and Kotzebue Sound. Unusual decor; excellent buffet; very good svce. Open year round. **M–E**

MALASPINA GLACIER: See Yakutat.

MENDENHALL GLACIER: See Juneau.

MISTY FJORDS NATIONAL MONUMENT (reachable by boat or seaplane from Ketchikan): Lying between two narrow bays, this lovely natural park, encompassing glaciers, granite cliffs falling sheer into the ocean, and many crystal-clear lakes, marks the southern frontier between Alaska and Canada. Rich wildlife, comprising particularly seals, whales (in the **Behm Canal**), and innumerable waterfowl.

For **information,** contact the U.S. Forest Service, Federal Bldg., P.O. Box 6137, Ketchikan, AK 99901 (907/225-2148).

MOUNT McKINLEY: See Denali National Park.

☀ **NOME** (reachable only by air, from Anchorage or Fairbanks): Standing on the Bering Sea only an hour's flying time from the Soviet Union, this busy port city reached its apogee in 1898 with the first gold rush, which attracted 40,000 prospectors; today it has 2,900 inhabitants. The commercial and economic capital of northwestern Alaska, Nome (a contraction of "No Name") has since 1979 witnessed a sharp upturn in exploration for crude oil, and has also become a tourist center for lovers of fishing, hunting, Inuit dances, and Native American handcrafts. An interesting museum of Inuit art, the **Carrie McClain Memorial Museum** on Front St. (907/443-5133), open Mon–Fri, also has displays on the history of the gold rush on the shores of the Bering Sea. Nome is also the scene of the celebrated annual ⚑ **Iditarod Trail Race,** the dogsled marathon that is run every Mar over the 1,049 mi. (1,680km) of virgin country between Nome and Anchorage.

Where to Stay

☀ ⚑ **Nugget Inn,** Front St. (P.O. Box 430-T), Nome, AK 99762 (907/443-2323). 47 rms (25% w. color TV). AE, DC, MC, V. Rest., bar. *Note:* With its wooden exterior and "Gold Rush" decor, the Nugget Inn might be a set for an adventure movie. Very comfortable rms (the best looking out over the Bering Strait). Likable bar (Gold Dust Saloon). Svce comes w. a smile. Caters mostly to groups and organized tours. Open year round. **M–E**

Community United Methodist Church, W. 2nd St. and D St., Nome, AK 99762 (907/433-2865). Youth hostel, open year round.

PETERSBURG (reachable by air from Juneau or Sitka, or by Alaska Marine Hwy. ferry): Nicknamed "Little Norway" because of its many Scandinavian settlers, this charming little fishing port situated at the center of the Inside Passage is a point of departure for boat or seaplane excursions to the spectacular ⚑ **Le Conte Glacier,** 25 mi. (40km) away; for information, contact Viking Travel, Main St., Petersburg, AK 99833 (907/772-3818). The town's ⚑ **Clausen Memorial Museum,** 2nd St. and Fram St. (907/772-3598), open daily in summer, Wed–Thurs and Sun the rest of the year, offers a real lure for fishing enthusiasts: the biggest salmon ever caught (126.5 lb./57kg!). For general information, contact the **Petersburg Visitors Center,** 221 Harbor Way (P.O. Box 649-TD), Petersburg, AK 99833 (907/772-3646).

PORTAGE GLACIER: See Anchorage.

☀ 👓 **PRIBILOF ISLANDS** (reachable only by air from Anchorage and Cold Bay): Lost in the Bering Sea, 750 mi. (1,200km) from Anchorage as the crow flies, this chaplet of green islands shrouded in fog and mist is heaven on earth for naturalists, with more than 200 species of animals and the world's largest seal colony (over a million between May and Sept); it's the Far North's answer to the Galapagos.

St. Paul, the archipelago's largest island, boasts a picturesque Aleut village with a pretty Russian Orthodox church. A side trip you shouldn't pass up. Season: early June to late Aug.

For **information,** contact Reeve Aleutian Airways, 4700-T International Airport Rd., Anchorage, AK 99502 (907/234-4700).

PRUDHOE BAY (reachable by air from Anchorage and Fairbanks or by car from Fairbanks via Dalton Hwy., 450 mi./ 720km): With crude-oil and natural-gas reserves equivalent to 2½ times those of Texas, Alaska's black-gold capital stands amid a flat and desolate landscape on the shores of the Arctic Sea. The terminal of an enormous (800-mi./1,280km) pipeline, which since 1977 has linked it to the harbor of Valdez on the Pacific, Prudhoe is a living museum of technology. You will be able to see for yourself the technology involved in tapping a reservoir which lies under the permafrost, with wells that sometimes go to a depth of 1.5 mi. (3,000m)—and you will see it in a town which in summer is surrounded by herds of wandering caribou and flocks of migrant birds. Visits from late May to Sept.

For **information,** contact the Arctic Caribou Lodge (907/659-2368).

Note: The James W. Dalton Hwy. is open to regular automobile traffic only as far as Disaster Creek, 211 mi. (338km) north of Fairbanks. You'll need a special permit for your car (they're granted very sparingly) for the section of Dalton Hwy. between Disaster Creek and Prudhoe Bay; check with the local authorities at Fairbanks. If you have a breakdown, the Dalton Hwy. has only two gas/ service stations along its entire length: at the Yukon River crossing (Mile 56) and at Coldfoot (Mile 175). For lovers of the great unspoiled outdoors, **Gray Line Tours,** 1980 S. Cushman St., Fairbanks (907/456-7742; toll free 800/544-2206), has regular bus service along Dalton Hwy. as far as Prudhoe Bay, returning by air to Fairbanks.

Where to Stay

Prudhoe Bay Hotel, Pouch 34004, Prudhoe Bay, AK 99734 (907/659-2449). 207 rms. AE, MC, V. Sauna, rest. (no alcoholic beverages since Prudhoe Bay is a "dry" town), TV lounge. *Note:* Large modern hotel adjacent to the airport. Comfortable rms; clientele mostly groups and those w. business in the oilfields. Open year round. A boon to the traveler; the nearest town (Barrow) and hotel are 240 mi. (386km) away as the crow flies. **M–E**

SEWARD (127 mi./203km south of Anchorage via Ak. 1 and Ak. 9; or reachable by air or the Alaska Railroad from Anchorage): Ringed by mountains at the southern tip of the Kenai Peninsula, this little fishing port was badly damaged by the 1964 earthquake. Terminus of the Alaska Railroad, which links it to Fairbanks, the town takes its name from Secretary of State William H. Seward, who negotiated the Alaska Purchase in the 19th century. The tourist office, **Visitor Information Cache,** Third Ave. and Jefferson St. (907/224-3094), is housed in the old sleeping car that Pres. Warren G. Harding used on his visit to Alaska in 1923. Be sure, too, to visit ⚓ **St. Peter's Episcopal Church,** Second Ave. and Adams St., for the beautiful painting of the Resurrection, done in 1925 by the Dutch artist Jan van Emple, using Alaskans as models and Resurrection Bay as a background.

Aside from its lovely natural setting, Seward is also the starting-point for excursions, by boat, seaplane, or automobile, to ☀⚓ **Kenai Fjords National Park.** Embracing several vast icefields on the eastern slope of the Kenai Mountains (one of which is the **Exit Glacier**), this park, set up in 1980, is a tangled network of fjords and jagged shores, where whales, porpoises, seals, and sea birds hold undisputed sway. The southern shore of the park was significantly damaged by the "black tide" resulting from the *Exxon Valdez* episode in Mar 1989, but the accident had only a slight impact on tourist activities: boat excursions leaving from Seward are confined to nearer and unpolluted coastal zones.

For **information,** contact the Superintendent, Kenai Fjords National Park, P.O. Box 1727, Seward, AK 99664 (907/224-3874).

Where to Stay

Breeze Inn Motel, Small Boat Harbor, Seward, AK 99664 (907/224-5237). 50 rms, cable color TV. AE, MC, V. Free parking, rest., bar. *Note:* Modern, comfortable motel w. splendid view of Resurrection Bay, the Kenai mountains, and the Small Boat Harbor. Very acceptable rest. A fine place; open year round. **I–M**

Marina Motel, Mile 1 on Ak. 9, AK 99664 (907/224-5518). 11 rms, color TV, in-rm movies. AE, CB, DC, MC, V. Free parking. *Note:* Friendly little motel w. a splendid view of bay and harbor. Comfortable rms, inviting grdns w. a picnic area. Free morning coffee; free airport and ferry limo. Open year round. **I–M**

Where to Eat

Fairweather Café, 106 Fourth Ave. (907/224-3907). Lunch/dinner daily. AE, MC, V. *Specialties:* homemade soups, quiches, wienerschnitzel w. mushrooms, catch of the day, chicken Cordon Bleu. *Note:* Straightforward, unassuming rest. serving very decent food. Friendly svce. Very good value. *American.* **B–I**

SITKA (reachable by plane from Juneau, Ketchikan, or Seattle; or by Alaska Marine Hwy. ferry): The splendid site was discovered in 1741 by the explorer Vitus Bering, and the town, once nicknamed "the Paris of the Pacific," was picked in 1804 as Alaska's capital by Alexander Baranof, first governor of Russian America; it remained so until 1906, when Juneau was chosen to replace it.

Proud of its history, Sitka offers the visitor many evidences of its Russo-American heritage: **St. Michael's Cathedral,** Lincoln St. (907/747-8120), open daily June–Sept (by appointment the rest of the year), with its valuable icons, is an exact replica of the original Russian Orthodox church of 1844, which was destroyed by fire in 1966. The **Russian Bishop's House,** Lincoln St. (907/747-6241), open daily in summer, is Bishop Ivan Veniaminor's log cabin dating from 1842, a designated historic monument.

Among other noteworthy attractions are the **Sheldon Jackson State Museum,** Sheldon Jackson College Campus, 104 College Dr. (907/747-8981), open daily in summer (Sun and Tues–Fri the rest of the year), which has memorabilia of the Russian period, as well as Native American and Inuit masks; and the **Sitka National Historic Park,** at the end of Lincoln St. (907/747-6281), open daily year round, site of the "battle for Alaska" between Russians and Tlingit tribe in 1804, the last stand of the original inhabitants against white domination. Fine collection of 18 Native American totem poles.

For information, contact the **Sitka Visitors Center,** 330 Harbor Dr. (907/747-5940). Every Alaska itinerary should include Sitka.

Where to Stay

Westmark Shee Atika Lodge, 330 Seward St., Sitka, AK 99835 (907/747-6241; toll-free, 800/544-0970). 98 rms, cable color TV. AE, CB, DC, MC, V. Free parking, fishing, rest., bar, rm svce.

Note: Modern hotel opposite the Convention Center, of unusual design which draws heavily on local materials, particularly wood. Comfortable, spacious rms looking out either over the harbor or toward the mountains. Good svce. Open year round. **M–E**

Potlatch House, 709 Katlian St., Sitka AK 99835 (907/747-8611). 30 rms, cable color TV. AE, DC, MC, V. Free parking, rest., bar. *Note:* Comfortable motel 5 min. by car from dwntwn (free shuttle). Comfortable rms overlooking the harbor or Mt. Edgecumbe. You'll be a welcome, well-looked-after guest. Good value; open year round. **I–M**

Where to Eat

Channel Club, 2908 Halibut Point Rd., 3½ mi. (6km) north of town (907/747-9916). Dinner only, nightly; closed hols. AE, DC, MC, V. Jkt. *Specialties:* steak, fresh salmon, king crab, fish of the day. *Note:* Highly regarded locally for its excellent food and its magnificent view of the Western Channel and the impressive Mt. Edgecumbe. Choice seafood and prime cuts. Resv. highly advisable. *Steak/Seafood.* **I–M**

SKAGWAY (reachable by air from Haines or Juneau, or by Alaska Marine Hwy. ferry): Formerly the port of entry for the Klondike, Skagway has preserved the appearance and atmosphere of the 1898 gold rush better than any other town in Alaska. At that time it boasted 20,000 inhabitants; today, only about 800. **Broadway,** Skagway's main drag, and the **Trail of '98 Museum,** City Hall, Seventh Ave. and Spring St. (907/983-2420), open daily in summer (by appointment in winter), perfectly reconstruct the age of the 19th-century gold prospectors. Recommended: *In the Days of '98,* tragi-comic melodrama about the gold rush, staged in Eagles Hall, 6th St. and Broadway (907/983-2545), presented daily May to mid-Sept.

On the outskirts, be sure to see the "ghost town" of **Dyea** (11 mi./18km NE on the Klondike Hwy.) or **Bennett Lake** (65 mi./106km NE on the Klondike Hwy.), on the edge of which stands the picturesque Canadian village of Carcross.

Reopened in 1988 after an interval of several years, the narrow-gauge railroad of the **White Pass & Yukon Route** takes tourists from Skagway to Fraser in the footsteps of the Klondike gold-rush pioneers. The 30mi. (48km) trip crosses some of the most spectacular country in Alaska, including the famous White Pass (2,900 ft./885m) straddling the Canadian frontier. The White Pass & Yukon Route railway, First Ave. at Broadway (907/983-2214; toll free 800/343-7373), operates from the end of May to mid-Sept, depending on the incidence of snowslides.

Hardier visitors will brave the rigors of the **Chilkoot Trail,** a scenic mountain trail once used by the prospectors (a 3- to 4-day hike to Lake Bennett).

Skagway is one of the most popular tourist attractions of Alaska; you shouldn't fail to see it.

Where to Stay

Golden North Hotel, 3rd St. and Broadway, Skagway, AK 99840 (907/983-2451). 34 rms. AE, DC, MC, V. Free parking, rest., bar. *Note:* With its singular gilded dome, this agreeable little hotel, a survivor from the gold rush, is one of Skagway's most interesting buildings, as well as being the oldest still-functioning hotel in Alaska (since 1897). Comfortable rms w. period furnishings, each decorated in a different style. Guaranteed local color. Open year round. **I–M**

Westmark Inn, (formerly the Klondike Hotel), 3rd St. and Spring St., Skagway, AK 99840 (907/983-2291; toll free 800/544-0970). 220 rms AE, MC, V. Free parking, rest. (Chilkoot Rm), coffee shop, bar. *Note:* Enormous, ungraceful modern motel, whose interior decoration is intended to evoke the great days of the Klondike. Comfortable and functional; favored by rather intrusive tour groups. Free airport and ferry limo. Rates excessive for a motel. Open mid-May to the end of Sept. **E**

Where to Eat

Northern Lights Café, Broadway at 4th St. (907/983-2225). Lunch/dinner daily. MC, V. *Specialties:* fresh salmon, halibut, steak. *Note:* A longtime Skagway classic; decent, unpretentious cooking at very reasonable prices. A boon to the tourist. *American/Seafood.* **B–I**

TONGASS NATIONAL FOREST (reached by boat or seaplane from Juneau, Ketchikan, Petersburg, Sitka, etc.): Largest national forest in the U.S.: 17 million acres (69,000km²). Covers most of the Alaska panhandle from Juneau to Ketchikan. Notable features are **Misty Island National Monument** and **Misty Fjords National Monument** (see above). A verdant paradise of deep fjords, unspoiled islands, rocky mountains more than 10,000 ft. (3,000m) high in places, and trackless rain forests. Camping permits available; also rustic bungalows.

For **information,** contact the U.S. Forest & National Park Service, 101 Egan Dr., Juneau, AK 99801 (907/586-8751), or 3031 TP Tongass Ave., Ketchikan, AK 99901 (907/225-2148).

VALDEZ (317 mi./507km NE of Anchorage via Ak. 1 and Ak. 4; also reachable by air from Anchorage or Fairbanks, and by Alaska Marine Hwy. ferry from Whittier or Seward): Standing north of the Arctic Circle in a grandly mountainous setting at the foot of Prince William Sound, Valdez, once dubbed "the Switzerland of Alaska," is the terminal of the Prudhoe Bay crude-oil pipeline — and the third-busiest port in the U.S. in terms of tonnage. You can arrange a fascinating visit to the ⚓ **Trans-Alaska Pipeline.**

Valdez is also the starting point for an expedition to the great 3.7-mi.-wide (6km) ⚓⚓ **Columbia Glacier** where it falls sheer into the sea. For information, contact Columbia Glacier Cruises (907/276-8866), Era Helicopters (907/835-2595), or Gray Line Tours (907/835-2357).

It was some 50 nautical miles south of Valdez that on March 24, 1989, the tanker *Exxon Valdez* ran aground, causing the largest "black tide" in U.S. history: 260,000 barrels (34,000 tons) of crude oil spilled into the majestic waters of Prince William Sound, wreaking havoc on marine, bird, and terrestrial wildlife. Some 34,000 birds, more than a thousand seals and sea otters, and dozens of bears and other large mammals were killed, according to the official count, without reckoning the thousands of tons of fish polluted by the deadly seepage. However, in spite of an oil slick that affected 1,100 mi. (1,760km) of shoreline, less than 1% of the Alaska coast was touched by the black tide—a fleabite on the continent's skin. After two cleanup campaigns involving 11,000 people and 1,400 boats, 80% of the surface of Prince William Sound was restored, more or less, to its original condition. With the help of nature and the ocean currents, the work of recovery should be completed in the next year or two—a fact which should reassure the 700,000 visitors who come to Alaska on vacation every year.

For information, contact the **Valdez Visitors Center,** 245 N. Harbor Dr. (907/835-2330).

Where to Stay

Westmark Valdez, 100 Fidalgo Dr., Valdez, AK 99686 (907/835-4391; toll free 800/544-0970). 100 rms, cable color TV. AE, MC, V. Free parking, marina, boat, fishing, rest. (Captain's Table), bar, rm svce. *Note:* Comfortable motel on the yacht basin. Spacious, comfortable rms (the best overlooking the harbor). Satisfactory rest. Nr. the Ferry Terminal. Guided tours of Columbia Glacier daily in summer. Open year round. **E**

Village Inn, Meals Ave. and Richardson Hwy., Valdez, AK 99686 (907/835-4445). 100 rms, color TV. AE, MC, V. Free parking, health club, sauna, rest. (Gay Nineties), bar. *Note:* Modest but well-run motel nr. the Ferry Terminal offering your choice of functionally comfortable rms (some w. private bath) or individual cottages w. kitchenettes. Guided tours of Columbia Glacier daily in summer. Open March to the end of Sept. **M–E**

WRANGELL (reachable by air from Ketchikan or Juneau, or by Alaska Marine Hwy. ferry): The only city in Alaska to have flown, in succession, the Russian, British, and U.S. flags, Wrangell has also lived through no fewer than three gold rushes, in 1863, 1873, and 1898. Be sure to see the ⚓ **Bear Tribal House,** Chief Shakes Island (907/874-3505), open varying days and times, for its fine carved totem poles, and the mysterious ⚓ **Native American rock carvings** that may be seen at low tide on the beach near the Ferry Dock.

For information, contact the **Wrangell Visitors Bureau,** Front St. and Outer Dr. (907/874-3901), open May–Sept (call 907/874-3770 the rest of the year).

WRANGELL–ST. ELIAS NATIONAL PARK (reachable by the Glenn Hwy. and Richardson Hwy. to the north of the park, or by boat from Yakutat to the south of the park): With an area of 12,730 sq. mi. (39,270km²), and created in 1981, this is our largest national park—3½ times the size of Yellowstone. The peaks of **Mt. Blackburn** (16,523 ft./4,995m) in the Wrangell Mountains and **Mt. Steller** (10,360 ft./3,238m) in the St. Elias Mountains rear above this great stretch of wildland, which, with the adjoining **Kluane National Park,** to the south across the Canadian border, makes up the world's largest assembly of glaciers, other than those of the polar icecaps. Among them is the enormous **Malaspina Glacier,** the biggest icefield in North America. There are only two roads for vehicles into the park interior: the Nabesha Rd., open year round, and McCarthy Rd., open May–Oct.

For **information,** contact the Superintendent, Wrangell–St. Elias National Park and Preserve, P.O. Box 29-T, Glenallen, AK 99588 (907/822-5235), and at the ranger stations at Chitina, Copper Center, and Slana. For lovers of unspoiled nature-in-the-raw.

YAKUTAT (reachable by air from Anchorage or Juneau): A former Tlingit village, on the sea halfway between Cordova and the Inside Passage, Yakutat is the ideal jumping-off point for a boat or kayak trip along **Russel Fjord** and the **Hubbard Glacier,** or for a flight over the majestic **Malaspina Glacier,** bigger than the state of Rhode Island.

For **information,** contact Gulf Air Taxi, Yakutat, AK 99689 (907/784-3240).

SPECIAL EVENTS AROUND ALASKA

For exact dates on the following special events, check with the following sources of travel information:

Cordova Chamber of Commerce, P.O. Box 99-T, Cordova, AK 99574 (907/424-7260).

Fairbanks Convention & Visitors Bureau, 550 First Ave., Fairbanks, AK 99701 (907/456-5774).

Haines Chamber of Commerce, P.O. Box 518-T, Haines, AK 99827 (907/766-2202).

Juneau Convention & Visitors Bureau, 76-T Egan Dr., Suite 140, Juneau, AK 99801 (907/586-1737).

Kodiak Area Chamber of Commerce, P.O. Box 1485-T, Kodiak, AK 99615 (907/486-5557).

Nome Convention and Visitors Bureau, P.O. Box 251-T, Nome, AK 99762 (907/443-5535).

Seward Chamber of Commerce, P.O. Box 756-T, Seward, AK 99664 (907/224-3094 in summer, 907/224-8051 in winter).

Sitka Convention & Visitors Bureau, 330-T Harbor Dr., Sitka, AK 99835 (907/747-5940).

Skagway Convention & Visitors Bureau, P.O. Box 415-T, Skagway, AK 99840 (907/983-2854).

Valdez Convention & Visitors Bureau, P.O. Box 1603-T, Valdez, AK 99686 (907/835-2984).

Whittier Chamber of Commerce, P.O. Box 608-T, Whittier, AK 99693 (907/472-2337).

CORDOVA: Ice Worm Festival (early Feb): Colorful parade through the town's streets led by a 100-ft.-long (30m) "ice worm" supposed to be emerging from hibernation.

FAIRBANKS: North American Championship Sled Dog Races (end of Mar): Hotly contested dogsled championship.

Yukon 800 River Boat Race (mid-June): Outboard-motor boats race 800 mi. (1,280km) along the Yukon River.

Midnight Sun Baseball: A popular local match played between 10pm and midnight every June 20.

World Eskimo Indian Olympics (end of July): Sporting and cultural events bringing together representatives of the main Native American, Inuit, and Aleut tribes.

HAINES: Chilkat Dancers (June–Sept): Twice-a-week displays of Native American dance at Fort William H. Seward.

JUNEAU: Alaska Folk Festival (early Apr): Shows, dance, music, arts and crafts exhibits.

Golden North Salmon Derby (Aug): Salmon-fishing championship.

KODIAK: King Crab Festival (end of May): Annual festival in honor of the region's most famous crustacean.

Cry of the Wild Ram (wknds in Aug): Historical evocation of the life of Alexander Baranof, first Russian governor of Alaska. In the Frank Brink Amphitheater (907/486-5291), the only open-air theater in Alaska; wear warm clothes.

Rodeo & State Fair (mid-Aug): Heavily attended fair-exhibition-rodeo.

SEWARD: Mount Marathon Race (July 4): With 200 runners from all over the world.

SITKA: Summer Music Festival (June): Chamber-music recitals.

New Archangel Dancers (June–Sept): Displays of Russian folk dancing; in the Centennial Bldg.

Alaska Day (Oct 18): Annual reenactment of the transfer of authority from Russia to the U.S. on October 18, 1867; on Castle Hill.

SKAGWAY: *In the Days of '98* (mid-May to mid-Sept): Tragi-comic melodrama about the 1898 gold rush; staged in Eagles Hall, nightly.

VALDEZ: Winter Carnival (mid-Mar): Dogsled races, dance displays, concerts, festival of food.

Gold Rush Days (early Aug): Can-can dancing, street parades, games, and big free buffet.

WHITTIER: Alaska Crab Festival (mid-Apr): Fishing competition for the largest crab caught.

APPENDIX

□ □ □

STATE TOURIST OFFICES

Alabama: Bureau of Tourism & Travel, 532 S. Perry St., Montgomery, AL 36104 (205/242-4169; toll free 800/252-2262).

Alaska: Division of Tourism, Information Office, P.O. Box E, Juneau, AK 99811 (907/465-2010).

Arizona: Office of Tourism, 1100 W. Washington St., Phoenix, AZ 85007 (602/542-8687).

Arkansas: Department of Parks & Tourism, 1 Capitol Mall, Little Rock, AR 72201 (501/682-7777; toll free 800/628-8725).

California: Office of Tourism, 1121 L St., Suite 103, Sacramento, CA 95814 (916/322-1397; toll free 800/862-2543).

Colorado: Tourism Board, 1625 Broadway, Suite 1700, Denver, CO 80202 (303/592-5410; toll free 800/433-2656).

Connecticut: Department of Economic Development, 865 Brook St., Rocky Hill, CT 06106 (203/258-4289).

Delaware: Travel Service, 99 Kings Hwy. (P.O. Box 1401), Dover, DE 19903 (302/736-4271; toll free 800/441-8846).

District of Columbia: Washington Area Convention & Visitors Association, 1212 New York Ave. NW, Washington, DC 20005 (202/789-7000).

Florida: Division of Tourism, 126 Van Buren St., Tallahassee, FL 32301 (904/487-1462).

Georgia: Tourist Division, P.O. Box 1776, Atlanta, GA 30301 (404/656-3590).

Hawaii: Visitors Bureau, 2270 Kalakaua Ave., Suite 801, Honolulu, HI 96815 (808/923-1811).

Idaho: Travel Council, 700 W. State St., Boise, ID 83720 (208/334-2470; toll free 800/635-7820).

Illinois: Office of Tourism, 620 E. Adams St., Springfield, IL 62701 (217/782-7139; toll free 800/223-0121).

Indiana: Tourism Division, 1 N. Capitol St., Indianapolis, IN 46204 (317/232-8860; toll free 800/289-6646).

Iowa: Department of Economic Development, Tourism and Film Office, 200 E. Grand Ave., Des Moines, IA 50309 (515/281-3100; toll free 800/345-4692).

Kansas: Travel & Tourist Division, 400 W. 8th St., 5th Floor, Topeka, KS 66603 (913/296-2009).

Kentucky: Department of Travel Development, Capitol Plaza Tower, Frankfort, KY 40601 (502/564-4930; toll free 800/225-8747).

Louisiana: Office of Tourism, P.O. Box 94291, Capitol Station, Baton Rouge, LA 70804 (504/342-8119; toll free 800/334-8626).

Maine: Publicity Bureau, 97 Winthrop St., Hallowell, ME 04347 (207/289-2423).

Maryland: Office of Tourism Development, 217 E. Redwood St., Baltimore, MD 21202 (301/333-6611).

Massachusetts: Division of Tourism, 100 Cambridge St., Leverett Saltonstall Bldg., 13th Floor, Boston, MA 02202 (617/727-3201).

.avel Bureau, Department of Commerce, P.O. Box 30226, Law
., Lansing, MI 48909 (517/373-0670; toll free 800/543-2937).

.a: Tourism Division, 375 Jackson St., St. Paul, MN 55101 (612/296-
29; toll free 800/657-3700).

sippi: Department of Tourism Development, P.O. Box 849, Jackson, MS
39205 (601/359-3297; toll free 800/647-2290).

souri: Division of Tourism, 308 E. High St. (P.O. Box 1055), Jefferson City,
MO 65102 (314/751-4133).

Montana: Travel Promotion Bureau, 1424 Ninth Ave., Helena, MT 59620
(406/444-2654; toll free 800/541-1447).

Nevada: Tourism Travel Division, Capitol Complex, Carson City, NV 89710
(702/687-4322; toll free 800/638-2328).

New Hampshire: Office of Vacation Travel, 105 Loudon Rd. (P.O. Box 856),
Concord, NH 03301 (603/271-2666).

New Jersey: Division of Travel & Tourism, CN 826, Trenton, NJ 08625 (609/
292-6335; toll free 800/537-7397).

New Mexico: Travel Division, 1100 St. Francis Dr., Santa Fe, NM 87503 (505/
827-0291; toll free 800/545-2040).

New York: Division of Tourism, State Dept. of Commerce, 1 Commerce Plaza,
Albany, NY 12245 (518/474-4116; toll free 800/225-5697).

North Carolina: Travel & Tourism Division, 430 N. Salisbury St., Raleigh, NC
27611 (919/733-4171; toll free 800/847-4862).

North Dakota: North Dakota Tourism Promotion, Liberty Memorial Bldg.,
600 East Blvd., Bismarck, ND 58505 (701/224-2525; toll free 800/
437-2077).

Ohio: Office of Travel & Tourism, P.O. Box 1001, Columbus, OH 43216 (614/
466-8844; toll free 800/282-5393).

Oklahoma: Tourism Promotion Division, 505 Will Rogers Bldg., Oklahoma
City, OK 73105 (405/521-2409; toll free 800/652-6552).

Oregon: Tourism Division, 775 Summer St. NE, Salem, OR 97310 (503/373-
1270; toll free 800/547-7842).

Pennsylvania: Bureau of Travel Development, 453 Forum Bldg., Harrisburg,
PA 17120 (717/787-5453; toll free 800/847-4872).

Puerto Rico: Tourism Development Cy., 301 San Justo St., San Juan, PR 00901
(809/721-2400).

Rhode Island: Tourist Promotion Division, 7 Jackson Walkway, Providence, RI
02903 (401/277-2601).

South Carolina: Division of Tourism, P.O. Box 71, Columbia, SC 29202 (803/
734-0235).

South Dakota: Division of Tourism, 711 Wells Ave., Pierre, SD 57501 (605/
773-3301; toll free 800/843-1930).

Tennessee: Department of Tourist Development, 601 Broadway (P.O. Box
23170), Nashville, TN 37202 (615/741-2158).

Texas: Travel & Information Division, P.O. Box 5064, Austin, TX 78763
(512/467-3719).

Utah: Travel Council, Council Hall, Capitol Hill, Salt Lake City, UT 84114
(801/538-1030).

Vermont: Travel Division, 134 State St., Montpelier, VT 05602 (802/828-
3236).

Virginia: Division of Tourism, 202 N. 9th St., Richmond, VA 23219 (804/786-
4484).

Washington: Tourism Development Division, 101 General Administration
Bldg., Olympia, WA 98504 (206/786-2088; toll free 800/544-1800).

West Virginia: Department of Commerce, Tourism Information Office, Capitol
Complex, Charleston, WV 25305 (304/348-2286; toll free 800/225-
5982).

Wisconsin: Division of Tourism, P.O. Box 7606, Madison, WI 53707 (608/
266-2161; toll free 800/432-8747).

Wyoming: Travel Commission, I-25 at College Dr., Cheyenne, WY 8200☐ (307/777-7777; toll free 800/225-5996).

PRINCIPAL HOTEL/MOTEL CHAINS

For reservations, see "Toll-Free Numbers," below.

Best Western, Best Western Way (P.O. Box 10203), Phoenix, AZ 85604 (602/957-4200).

Four Seasons, 1165 Leslie St., Toronto, ON M3C 2K8, Canada (416/449-1750).

Friendship Inns, 2627 Paterson Plank Rd., North Bergen, NJ 07047 (201/863-3443).

Hilton, 9336 Civic Center Dr., Beverly Hills, CA 90210 (213/278-4321).

Holiday Inns, 3796 Lamar Ave., Memphis, TN 38195 (901/362-4001).

Howard Johnson, Inc., 145 Rte. 46W Wayne, 07470 NJ 07007 (201/256-9030).

Hyatt, Madison Plaza, 200 W. Madison St., Chicago, IL 60606 (312/750-1234).

La Quinta Motor Inns, 10010 San Pedro (P.O. Box 790064), San Antonio, TX 78279 (512/366-6000).

Marriott, 1 Marriott Dr., Washington, DC 20058 (301/380-9000).

Motel 6, 14651 Dallas Pkwy., Dallas, TX 75240 (214/386-6161).

Quality Inns, 10750 Columbia Pike, Silver Spring, MD 20901 (301/593-5600).

Radisson, Carlson Pkwy. (P.O. Box 59159), Minneapolis, MN 55441 (612/540-5526).

Ramada Inns, 3838 E. Van Buren St., Phoenix, AZ 85008 (602/273-4000).

Rodeway Inns, 3838 E. Van Buren St., Phoenix, AZ 85008 (602/273-4550).

Sheraton, 60 State St., Boston, MA 02109 (617/367-3600).

Travelodge, 1973 Friendship Dr., El Cajon, CA 92090 (619/448-1884).

Westin, Westin Bldg., Seattle, WA 98121 (206/443-5000).

TOLL-FREE NUMBERS

Toll-free numbers, recognizable by their "800" area code, are available for your convenience from many airlines, car-rental companies, hotel chains, etc. When you call "1-800" plus a normal seven-digit number, your call is paid for by the subscriber, no matter how far away you may be. Here follows a list of useful toll-free numbers (if you need one not listed here, call 800/555-1212 to reach "information" for all 800 numbers):

AIRLINES: See the individual city chapters for local airline phone numbers.

BUS: Greyhound (800/528-6055); see the individual city chapters for local Greyhound phone numbers.

HOTELS/MOTELS: The following are the national toll-free reservations numbers for the major hotel chains:

Best Western (800/528-1234)
Clarion (800/252-7466)
Days Inns (800/325-2525)
Fairmont (800/527-4727)
Four Seasons (800/332-3442)
Friendship Inns (800/453-4511)
Hilton (800/445-8667)
Holiday Inns (800/465-4329)
Howard Johnson's (800/446-4656)
Hyatt (800/233-1234)
Inter-Continental Hotels (800/332-4246)

Omni (800/843-6664)
Preferred (800/323-7500)
Quality Inns (800/228-5151)
Radisson (800/333-3333)
Ramada Inns (800/228-2828)
Red Lion Inns (800/547-8010)
Resinter (800/221-4542)
Rodeway Inns (800/228-2000)
Sheraton (800/325-3535)
Stouffer (800/468-3571)
Travelodge (800/255-3050)

tor Inns (800/531-5900)   **Treadway Inns** (800/873-2392)
/223-0888)   **Vagabond Hotels** (800/522-1555)
300/228-9290)   **Westin** (800/228-3000)
(800/543-4300)

-RENTAL AGENCIES: The following are the national toll-free reserva-
.s numbers for the major car-rental chains:

Agency Rent-A-Car (800/321-1972)   **Hertz** (800/654-3131)
Alamo (800/327-9633)   **National** (800/227-7368)
Avis (800/331-1212)   **Rent-A-Wreck** (800/535-1391)
Budget (800/527-0700)   **Sears Rent-A-Car** (800/527-0770)
Dollar Rent-A-Car (800/421-6868)   **Thrifty** (800/367-2277)
General Rent-A-Car (800/327-7607)

The local numbers for many car-rental agencies will be found in the individual city chapters.

TRAINS: Amtrak's 800 numbers vary from state to state; consult local telephone directories. The national toll-free number is 800/872-7245 (800/USA-
RAIL).

FOR THE FOREIGN VISITOR: MEASUREMENTS & CONVERSIONS

THE AMERICAN SYSTEM OF MEASURES

Length

1 inch (in.)	=	2.54cm				
1 foot (ft.)	=	12 in.	=	30.48cm	=	.305m
1 yard	=	3 ft.	=	.915m		
1 mile (mi.)	=	5,280 ft.	=	1.609km		

To convert miles to kilometers, multiply the number of miles by 1.61 (for example, 50 mi. × 1.61 = 80.5km). Note that this conversion can be used to
convert speeds from miles per hour (m.p.h.) to kilometers per hour (km/h).
To convert kilometers to miles, multiply the number of kilometers by .62 (example, 25km × .62 = 15.5 mi.). Note that this same conversion can be used to
convert speeds from kilometers per hour to miles per hour.

Capacity

1 fluid ounce (fl. oz.)	=	.03 liter				
1 pint	=	16 fl. oz.	=	.47 liter		
1 quart	=	2 pints	=	.94 liter		
1 gallon (gal.)	=	4 quarts	=	3.79 liter	=	.83 Imperial gal.

To convert U.S. gallons to liters, multiply the number of gallons by 3.79 (example, 12 gal. × 3.79 = 45.48 liters).
To convert U.S. gallons to Imperial gallons, multiply the number of U.S. gallons by .83 (example, 12 U.S. gal. × 83 = 9.95 Imperial gal.).
To convert liters to U.S. gallons, multiply the number of liters by .26 (for example, 50 liters × .26 = 13 U.S. gal.).
To convert Imperial gallons to U.S. gallons, multiply the number of Imperial
gallons by 1.2 (example, 8 Imperial gal. × 1.2 = 9.6 U.S. gal.).

Weight

1 ounce (oz.) = 28.35 grams
1 pound (lb.) = 16 oz. = 453.6 grams = .45 kilograms
1 ton = 2,000 lb. = 907 kilograms = .91 metric ton

To convert pounds to kilograms, multiply the number of pounds by .45 (example, 90 lb. × .45 = 40.5kg).
To convert kilograms to pounds, multiply the number of kilos by 2.2 (example, 75kg × 2.2 = 165 lb.).

Area

1 acre = .41 hectare
1 square mile (sq. mi.) = 640 acres = 2.59 hectares = 2.6km

To convert acres to hectares, multiply the number of acres by .41 (example, 40 acres × .41 = 16.4ha).
To convert square miles to square kilometers, multiply the number of square miles by 2.6 (example, 80 sq. mi. × 2.6 = 208km).
To convert hectares to acres, multiply the number of hectares by 2.47 (example, 20ha × 2.47 = 49.4 acres).
To convert square kilometers to square miles, multiply the number of square kilometers by .39 (example, 150km × .39 = 58.5 sq. mi.).

Temperature

°C −18° −10   0   10   20   30   40

°F 0° 10 20 32 40 50 60 70 80 90 100

To convert degrees Fahrenheit to degrees Celsius, subtract 32 from °F, multiply then divide by 9 (example, 85°F − 32 × 5/9 = 29.4°C).
To convert degrees Celsius to degrees Fahrenheit, multiply °C by 9, divide by 5, and add 32 (example, 20°C × 9/5 + 32 = 68°F).

CLOTHING SIZES

Women's Dresses, Coats, and Skirts

American	3	5	7	9	11	12	13	14	15	16	18
Continental	36	38	38	40	40	42	42	44	44	46	48
British	8	10	11	12	13	14	15	16	17	18	20

Women's Blouses and Sweaters

American	10	12	14	16	18	20
Continental	38	40	42	44	46	48
British	32	34	36	38	40	42

Women's Stockings

American	8	8½	9	9½	10	10½
Continental	1	2	3	4	5	6
British	8	8½	9	9½	10	10½

Women's Shoes

American	5	6	7	8	9	10
Continental	36	37	38	39	40	41
British	3½	4½	5½	6½	7½	8½

Note: Foot width should also be taken into account.

...lothing

	3	4	5	6	6X
...al	98	104	110	116	122
	18	20	22	24	26

...en's Shoes

...rican	8	9	10	11	12	13	1	2	3
...ntinental	24	25	27	28	29	30	32	33	34
British	7	8	9	10	11	12	13	1	2

Men's Suits

American	34	36	38	40	42	44	46	48
Continental	44	46	48	50	52	54	56	58
British	34	36	38	40	42	44	46	48

Men's Shirts

American	$14\frac{1}{2}$	15	$15\frac{1}{2}$	16	$16\frac{1}{2}$	17	$17\frac{1}{2}$	18
Continental	37	38	39	41	42	43	44	45
British	$14\frac{1}{2}$	15	$15\frac{1}{2}$	16	$16\frac{1}{2}$	17	$17\frac{1}{2}$	18

Note: Shirts are sized on a combination of collar and sleeve length.

Men's Shoes

American	7	8	9	10	11	12	13
Continental	$39\frac{1}{2}$	41	42	43	$44\frac{1}{2}$	46	47
British	6	7	8	9	10	11	12

Note: Foot width should also be taken into account.

Men's Hats

American	$6\frac{7}{8}$	$7\frac{1}{8}$	$7\frac{1}{4}$	$7\frac{3}{8}$	$7\frac{1}{2}$	$7\frac{5}{8}$
Continental	55	56	58	59	60	61
British	$6\frac{1}{4}$	$6\frac{7}{8}$	$7\frac{1}{8}$	$7\frac{1}{4}$	$7\frac{3}{8}$	$7\frac{1}{2}$

INDEX

GENERAL INFORMATION

DESTINATIONS

1144 □ INDEX

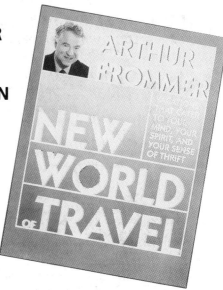

NOW, SAVE MONEY ON ALL YOUR TRAVELS!
Join Frommer's™ Dollarwise® Travel Club

Saving money while traveling is never a simple matter, which is why the **Dollarwise Travel Club** was formed 31 years ago. Developed in response to requests from Frommer's Travel Guide readers, the Club provides cost-cutting travel strategies, up-to-date travel information, and a sense of community for value-conscious travelers from all over the world.

In keeping with the money-saving concept, the annual membership fee is low —$20 for U.S. residents or $25 for residents of Canada, Mexico, and other countries—and is immediately exceeded by the value of your benefits, which include:

1. Any TWO books listed on the following pages.
2. Plus any ONE Frommer's City Guide.
3. A subscription to our quarterly newspaper, *The Dollarwise Traveler*.
4. A membership card that entitles you to purchase through the Club all Frommer's publications for 33% to 40% off their retail price.

The eight-page **Dollarwise Traveler** tells you about the latest developments in good-value travel worldwide and includes the following columns: **Hospitality Exchange** (for those offering and seeking hospitality in cities all over the world); **Share-a-Trip** (for those looking for travel companions to share costs); and **Readers Ask . . . Readers Reply** (for those with travel questions that other members can answer).

Aside from the Frommer's Guides and the Gault Millau Guides, you can also choose from our Special Editions. These include such titles as **California with Kids** (a compendium of the best of California's accommodations, restaurants, and sightseeing attractions appropriate for those traveling with toddlers through teens); **Candy Apple: New York with Kids** (a spirited guide to the Big Apple by a savvy New York grandmother that's perfect for both visitors and residents); **Caribbean Hideaways** (the 100 most romantic places to stay in the Islands, all rated on ambience, food, sports opportunities, and price); **Honeymoon Destinations** (a guide to planning and choosing just the right destination from hundreds of possibilities in the U.S., Mexico, and the Caribbean); **Marilyn Wood's Wonderful Weekends** (a selection of the best mini-vacations within a 200-mile radius of New York City, including descriptions of country inns and other accommodations, restaurants, picnic spots, sights, and activities); and **Paris Rendez-Vous** (a delightful guide to the best places to meet in Paris whether for power breakfasts or dancing till dawn).

To join this Club, simply send the appropriate membership fee with your name and address to: Frommer's Dollarwise Travel Club, 15 Columbus Circle, New York, NY 10023. Remember to specify which single city guide and which two other guides you wish to receive in your initial package of member's benefits. Or tear out the next page, check off your choices, and send the page to us with your membership fee.

FROMMER BOOKS
PRENTICE HALL PRESS
15 COLUMBUS CIRCLE
NEW YORK, NY 10023
212/373-8125

Date_____

Friends: Please send me the books checked below.

FROMMER'S™ GUIDES

(Guides to sightseeing and tourist accommodations and facilities from budget to deluxe, with emphasis on the medium-priced.)

☐ Alaska $14.95	☐ Germany $14.95
☐ Australia $14.95	☐ Italy. $14.95
☐ Austria & Hungary $14.95	☐ Japan & Hong Kong $14.95
☐ Belgium, Holland & Luxembourg $14.95	☐ Mid-Atlantic States $14.95
☐ Bermuda & The Bahamas. $14.95	☐ New England. $14.95
☐ Brazil $14.95	☐ New Mexico (avail. June '91) $12.95
☐ Canada $14.95	☐ New York State $14.95
☐ Caribbean. $14.95	☐ Northwest $15.95
☐ Cruises (incl. Alaska, Carib, Mex, Hawaii,	☐ Portugal, Madeira & the Azores $14.95
Panama, Canada & US) $14.95	☐ Scandinavia (avail. May '91). $15.95
☐ California & Las Vegas $14.95	☐ South Pacific $14.95
☐ Egypt. $14.95	☐ Southeast Asia $14.95
☐ England & Scotland $14.95	☐ Southern Atlantic States $14.95
☐ Florida $14.95	☐ Southwest $14.95
☐ France $14.95	☐ Switzerland & Liechtenstein $14.95

☐ USA $16.95

FROMMER'S $-A-DAY® GUIDES

(In-depth guides to sightseeing and low-cost tourist accommodations and facilities.)

☐ Europe on $40 a Day $15.95	☐ Israel on $40 a Day. $13.95
☐ Australia on $40 a Day $13.95	☐ Mexico on $35 a Day $14.95
☐ Costa Rica; Guatemala & Belize	☐ New York on $60 a Day. $13.95
on $35 a day (avail. Mar. '91). $15.95	☐ New Zealand on $45 a Day $13.95
☐ Eastern Europe on $25 a Day $15.95	☐ Scotland & Wales on $40 a Day $13.95
☐ England on $50 a Day. $13.95	☐ South America on $40 a Day $15.95
☐ Greece on $35 a Day $13.95	☐ Spain on $50 a Day $15.95
☐ Hawaii on $60 a Day. $14.95	☐ Turkey on $30 a Day. $13.95
☐ India on $25 a Day $12.95	☐ Washington, D.C. & Historic Va. on
☐ Ireland on $40 a Day. $14.95	$40 a Day. $13.95

FROMMER'S TOURING GUIDES

(Color illustrated guides that include walking tours, cultural and historic sites, and other vital travel information.)

☐ Amsterdam. $10.95	☐ New York $10.95
☐ Australia $10.95	☐ Paris $8.95
☐ Brazil $10.95	☐ Rome. $10.95
☐ Egypt. $8.95	☐ Scotland. $9.95
☐ Florence. $8.95	☐ Thailand. $10.95
☐ Hong Kong $10.95	☐ Turkey $10.95
☐ London $10.95	☐ Venice $8.95

(TURN PAGE FOR ADDITONAL BOOKS AND ORDER FORM)

1290

FROMMER'S CITY GUIDES

(Pocket-size guides to sightseeing and tourist accommodations and facilities in all price ranges.)

☐ Amsterdam/Holland	$8.95	☐ Minneapolis/St. Paul	$8.95
☐ Athens	$8.95	☐ Montréal/Québec City	$8.95
☐ Atlanta	$8.95	☐ New Orleans	$8.95
☐ Atlantic City/Cape May	$8.95	☐ New York	$8.95
☐ Barcelona	$7.95	☐ Orlando	$8.95
☐ Belgium	$7.95	☐ Paris	$8.95
☐ Berlin (avail. Mar '91)	$8.95	☐ Philadelphia	$8.95
☐ Boston	$8.95	☐ Rio	$8.95
☐ Cancún/Cozumel/Yucatán	$8.95	☐ Rome	$8.95
☐ Chicago	$8.95	☐ Salt Lake City	$8.95
☐ Denver/Boulder/Colorado Springs	$7.95	☐ San Diego	$8.95
☐ Dublin/Ireland	$8.95	☐ San Francisco	$8.95
☐ Hawaii	$8.95	☐ Santa Fe/Taos/Albuquerque	$8.95
☐ Hong Kong	$7.95	☐ Seattle/Portland	$7.95
☐ Las Vegas	$8.95	☐ St. Louis/Kansas City (avail. May '91)	$8.95
☐ Lisbon/Madrid/Costa del Sol	$8.95	☐ Sydney	$8.95
☐ London	$8.95	☐ Tampa/St. Petersburg	$8.95
☐ Los Angeles	$8.95	☐ Tokyo	$7.95
☐ Mexico City/Acapulco	$8.95	☐ Toronto	$8.95
☐ Miami	$8.95	☐ Vancouver/Victoria	$7.95

☐ Washington, D.C. $8.95

SPECIAL EDITIONS

☐ Beat the High Cost of Travel	$6.95	☐ Motorist's Phrase Book (Fr/Ger/Sp)	$4.95
☐ Bed & Breakfast—N. America	$14.95	☐ Paris Rendez-Vous	$10.95
☐ California with Kids	$15.95	☐ Swap and Go (Home Exchanging)	$10.95
☐ Caribbean Hideaways	$14.95	☐ The Candy Apple (NY with Kids)	$12.95
☐ Honeymoon Destinations (US, Mex &		☐ Travel Diary and Record Book	$5.95
Carib)	$14.95	☐ Where to Stay USA (From $3 to $30 a	
☐ Manhattan's Outdoor Sculpture	$15.95	night)	$13.95

☐ Marilyn Wood's Wonderful Weekends (CT, DE, MA, NH, NJ, NY, PA, RI, VT) $11.95

☐ The New World of Travel (Annual sourcebook by Arthur Frommer for savvy travelers) $16.95

GAULT MILLAU

(The only guides that distinguish the truly superlative from the merely overrated.)

☐ The Best of Chicago	$15.95	☐ The Best of Los Angeles	$16.95
☐ The Best of France	$16.95	☐ The Best of New England	$15.95
☐ The Best of Hawaii	$16.95	☐ The Best of New Orleans	$16.95
☐ The Best of Hong Kong	$16.95	☐ The Best of New York	$16.95
☐ The Best of Italy	$16.95	☐ The Best of Paris	$16.95
☐ The Best of London	$16.95	☐ The Best of San Francisco	$16.95

☐ The Best of Washington, D.C. $16.95

ORDER NOW!

In U.S. include $2 shipping UPS for 1st book; $1 ea. add'l book. Outside U.S. $3 and $1, respectively.
Allow four to six weeks for delivery in U.S., longer outside U.S.
Enclosed is my check or money order for $_____

NAME _____

ADDRESS _____

CITY _____ STATE _____ ZIP _____

1290